A Dictionary of 20th-Century Communism

A Dictionary of

20th-Century Communism

EDITED BY

Silvio Pons and
Robert Service

TRANSLATED BY

Mark Epstein and
Charles Townsend

PRINCETON UNIVERSITY PRESS

PRINCETON AND OXFORD

English translation copyright © 2010 by Princeton University Press

This is a translation of *Dizionario del comunismo nel xx secolo,* A cura di Silvio Pons e Robert Service, © 2006 Giulio Einaudi editore s.p.a., Torino

Requests for permission to reproduce material from this work should be sent to Permissions, Princeton University Press

Published by Princeton University Press, 41 William Street, Princeton, New Jersey 08540 In the United Kingdom: Princeton University Press, 6 Oxford Street, Woodstock, Oxfordshire OX20 1TW press.princeton.edu

Library of Congress Cataloging-in-Publication Data

Dizionario del comunismo nel xx secolo. English
    A dictionary of 20th-century communism / edited by Silvio Pons and Robert Service; translated by Mark Epstein and Charles Townsend.
        p. cm.
    Includes bibliographical references and index.
    ISBN 978-0-691-13585-4 (hardcover : alk. paper)   1. Communism—History—20th century—Dictionaries—English.   I. Pons, Silvio.   II. Service, Robert, 1947-   III. Epstein, Mark.   IV. Townsend, Charles.   V. Title.
    HX40.D5913 2010
    335.409'0403—dc22   2009052374

British Library Cataloging-in-Publication Data is available

This book has been composed in Garamond Pro

Printed on acid-free paper. ∞

Printed in the United States of America

10 9 8 7 6 5 4 3 2 1

Contents

Introduction   vii

Acknowledgments   xiii

List of Entries   xv

List of Contributors   xxvii

Acronyms and Abbreviations   xxxiii

Entries   1

Index   895

Introduction

The time has come to make an assessment of communism in the 20th century. Twenty years ago this would have been a much more complicated task, at a time when Communist states covered a third of the world's surface and their influence could be felt well beyond their borders. The great change occurred in 1989 with the fall of the Berlin Wall. In Central and Eastern Europe, Communist regimes collapsed one after the other in a period of less than two months, under the pressure of mass protests and without any intervention by the Soviet Union. Statues of Lenin were toppled; the legacy of the October Revolution was rejected. In resignation they acknowledged their unpopularity, and most of the parties in power moved aside, either dissolving or changing their name and doctrine. New non-Communist governments came to power, and so did multiparty political systems and market economies. In 1991 it was the Soviet Union's turn. Mikhail Gorbachev's reforms had allowed the peaceful changes of 1989 and the end of the Cold War to take place, but they also unleashed economic collapse and political and social chaos in the country. After the failure of the coup attempted by orthodox Communists in August 1991, the leaders of the opposition forced Gorbachev's resignation and the abolition of the Soviet federal government. Communist power was abolished in its own place of origin.

Today only a few countries still adhere faithfully to Communist ideology: China, Vietnam, Cuba, and North Korea. Notwithstanding their proclamations of Marxist orthodoxy, China's evolution points to a different reality: unrestrained capitalist development. Vietnam has taken the same path. Even Cuba has opened its economy to a restricted number of foreign enterprises. North Korea remains as the lone, irreducible custodian of the Communist past. In those countries where Communist parties were never in power, a rush to abandon Leninism and embrace the Social Democratic tradition has occurred. Not all Communists have agreed to scrap their identity, and in Asia and Latin America especially, small splinter parties have kept it. But Communist parties mostly have been shaken by the events of 1989–91. Those parties that remained politically loyal to Moscow lost the financial support that had kept them going for decades. The few that were more independent still had to change their identity. They have all lost the supranational dimension that existed into the 1980s, even if it was a much paler and weaker version than the original.

The collapse of most Communist governments has led to the accumulation of an enormous amount of information, thanks to the opening of the archives. Reform-oriented Communists themselves disclosed a significant quantity of secret documents before losing power. After the regimes' dissolution, the opening has begun to look more like a flood of new knowledge. Conferences, articles, books, and editions of documents—in large numbers—are changing the foundation for historical work. This "archival revolution" could not be contained within the experts' world, even though its echo has mostly reached the wider public in a distorted fashion. Public opinion's interest in Europe and elsewhere has mostly been drawn to revelations that were more alleged than real, and in any case not always well documented and presented. This interest still appears to be very much alive and does not cease to cause controversies in formerly Communist countries, or in others, like Italy and France, where the Communist presence was substantial. It is difficult to establish whether there is a widespread awareness that the political and intellectual life of the present cannot be deprived of a historical understanding of the past, including the Communist past. Not to mention the fact that although today's world is quite different from the one that gave rise to the October Revolution, the circumstances that led the Communists to increase their influence—poverty, inequalities, unemployment, social immobility, national conflicts, and poor education—have not disappeared. Certainly one of this volume's main goals is to aid in the diffusion of more specialized forms of knowledge, especially those that have accumulated in recent years, among a broader spectrum of educated public opinion. Communism's "presence" in public discourse, and even in people's political psyche and outlook, is still significant in Europe, but less so historical knowledge of the phenomenon.

The October Revolution changed world politics. Initially it appeared improbable that the Bolsheviks would hold on to power for a long time. But they solidified their position during the ensuing civil war, and in March 1919 founded the Third International (Comintern) in Moscow. In the space of a few years almost every country in the world had a Communist Party affiliated with the Comintern, the veritable headquarters of the world revolution. Each one of these parties, whether legal or clandestine, accepted the rules and doctrine that the Bolsheviks imposed, and in this manner a break developed in their relations with Socialists who remained tied to their own traditions. Having conceived of themselves as the answer to the Socialist parties' and Second International's inadequacy in confronting nationalism and imperialism, the Communists became an element and a contributing factor to the radicalization of European politics after the war—one destined to witness the birth of a Fascist radical Right. The world between the wars was basically the scene of a struggle between communism, fascism, and parliamentary democracy.

This struggle modified the plans for world revolution that the Bolsheviks had entertained in 1917. Europe passed through the postwar crises unscathed, and its political order did not collapse due to pressure from a proletarian revolution. Revolutionary Russia was isolated. The Communist movement had its ups and downs, but was deprived of an immediate revolutionary perspective, especially after the last illusion of a German revolution was dispelled, in October 1923. The Communist revolution seemed to inescapably become a long-term goal, the outcome of an entire era of future social and political struggles. As a result, the original connection between the Soviet state and the Communist movement was strengthened, following the agenda of "socialism in one country." Stalin was both the architect of the Soviet state and system, on foundations laid by Lenin, and a leader bent on centralizing the Communist movement.

He eliminated other Bolshevik factions; in many respects he reinforced the Leninist tradition, and in others he deformed it. But he certainly elevated the USSR to the level of European and Asian power in the 1930s, creating a "model" to follow for all those Communists who might come to power. This model was based on dictatorship as well as the social and political violence that Bolshevism had experimented with, taking the use of terror as a tool of government to extremes.

This did not affect the blind devotion to the cause, messianism, and identification with the Soviet state that were characteristic of most Communists. Self-denial, sacrifice, and discipline had been distinctive traits of the Communist ethos since Lenin's times. The consequences for militants were often serious, both in and out of Russia: persecutions, prison, and concentration camps. Numerous European and U.S. Communists volunteered for the republican cause in Spain. Most Chinese Communists who participated in the Long March did not live to see its conclusion. Communists of all nationalities lost their life to Stalin's web of terror in the USSR without abandoning their faith.

The ten-year period between the mid-1930s and mid-1940s saw communism reach its highest level of consolidation, even if in pursuit of different and frequently contradictory political choices. Antifascism substituted for anti–Social Democratic sectarianism around the mid-1930s, but was then discarded in favor of the imperatives of a Hitler-Stalin alliance in 1939. Only after the invasion of the USSR by Nazi Germany in 1941 did antifascism once again return to center stage. Communists led movements for the liberation from fascism and Nazism in Europe in several instances. The Communist movement seemed to develop new momentum with the combination of anti-Fascist legitimation and the USSR's defeat of the Third Reich.

In the aftermath of World War II the USSR had become a great power, apparently able to defy the most important force emerging in the West—the United States. The Soviet Union was no longer an isolated state but instead surrounded by a belt of countries subjected to its influence; in a few years, between 1945 and 1948, these countries, too, became Communist. In 1949, the "Socialist camp" witnessed a second formidable expansion with the victory of the Chinese Communists in the civil war and the birth of the People's Republic of China. Mao Zedong's emphasis on the revolutionary potential of the countryside seemed to open new paths to communism outside of Europe. In the adversaries' camp Communist parties increased their influence. The division of Europe blocked German communism from reestablishing itself in the Federal Republic of Germany, while the Greek Communist Party was swept away after having precipitated a civil war. But in France and Italy mass Communist parties managed to take root, and had an important social and political role. In the third world the Communist presence would be significant in countries like Korea, Vietnam, and later Indonesia.

The Communist world, however, was monolithic in appearance only. In the 1920s the Communists were divided into factions, and had fought one another both in and out of Russia. This tradition was suppressed by Stalinism's triumph, with the exception of the Trotskyist heresy, which was lively but reduced to a few followers who ambitiously founded the Fourth International outside the USSR. Trotsky's assassination at the hands of a killer hired by Stalin in 1940 symbolically laid the last brick in the foundation of the monolith. But the emergence of a system of Communist states after World War II did not contribute to this building's strength; in fact it actually weakened it.

The West's anti-Communist reaction had essential long-term consequences. After World War I, a parliamentary and democratic reaction had gradually given way to an authoritarian and Fascist one, which contained or destroyed some of the main European Communist parties (in the 1930s the German and Czech parties), but it also offered the Communists renewed forms of legitimation in the anti-Fascist resistance. The definitive emergence of the United States to the world stage after 1945 saw a renewed democratic anticommunism. The beginnings of U.S. containment initially led to greater restrictions in the Soviet sphere of influence, but over time its effects on the stability and endurance of the system of USSR satellite states could be felt, and this contributed to undermining the system's credibility. At the same time the Cold War permanently excluded Western Communists from the government.

The sources endangering the cohesion and expansion of communism were above all internal, though. The dissolution of the Comintern in 1943 was mostly a tactical move by Stalin, who felt secure in his control of "national" Communist leadership groups and conducted bilateral relations with each party by means of the Communist Party of the Sovet Union's International Department. In 1947 he once again adopted centralist criteria: the Cominform's founding was meant to close the ranks of the main Communist parties faced with the Cold War

in Europe. And yet this postwar reorganization of the Communist movement immediately revealed significant limits and cracks. The break between the USSR and Yugoslavia in 1948 was a blow to Soviet hegemony in Eastern Europe and cut the Cominform's role down to size. Not long after the outbreak of the Korean War, Stalin planned a renewed push for the Cominform, but nothing really happened. The Cominform was dissolved by Stalin's successors, who did not pursue the restoration of a Communist organization and replaced it with periodic international conferences.

With Stalin's disappearance, unity and compactness soon became a memory, especially after Khrushchev had denounced his crimes. Eastern Europe was immediately shaken by rebellions, whose climax was the 1956 revolution in Hungary. Moscow's violent reaction and the invasion of the country exposed the ferocity of Soviet domination. But centrifugal tendencies appeared once more during the Prague Spring in 1968. The Soviets again intervened using force, but in the long term it did not increase their authority or the stability of the satellite countries, as Poland's experience ten years later was to prove. The Eastern European Communist regimes' dependence on Moscow fundamentally compromised their legitimacy. From Moscow's point of view Eastern Europe was a geopolitical area distinguished by the servility of the Communists in power and the widespread hostility of the respective populations.

In the meantime the split between Moscow and Beijing had ended international communism's unity. While they had already surfaced during Stalin's era, the ideological and governmental tensions between the two main Communist states exploded after 1956, became public in the 1960s, and reached the point of armed conflict in 1969. Unlike the Yugoslavs who had attempted to adopt a revised Soviet model after breaking with Moscow, the Chinese acted as defenders of Stalinist orthodoxy and accused the Soviets of "revisionism." But even after Mao's death and the advent to power of the "revisionist" Deng Xiaoping, the wound between the two states did not heal and in fact worsened. Communists divided into followers of the USSR and followers of China, even if the latter remained a minority, and only counted Albania as the other country in which a sympathetic regime was in power. The numerous attempts made by the Soviets to excommunicate the Chinese from the movement's world pulpit were unsuccessful because of the opposition of a fairly significant number of parties, including the Romanian and Italian. Communism could claim two especially important successes, Cuba and Vietnam—two countries that for a while would give new life to its symbolic resurgence. The national liberation movements in the third world were still an area in which the movement's influence, in an anti-imperialist vein, could be felt. But from the 1960s on, no one could seriously argue that the Communist movement was monolithic or expanding according to a unitary design.

In the 1970s this monolithic appearance was given a final blow by the emergence of Eurocommunism. The two main Western Communist parties, the Italian Communist Party and the French Communist Party, together with the Spanish Communists, formed an alliance, while arguing for "socialism with a human face" along with respect for democratic principles and human rights—positions that for Soviet orthodoxy were akin to heresy. The Eurocommunists had silent sympathizers in the more moderate Communist establishments, especially in Hungary and Poland. They influenced other parties, even outside Europe, as in the case of Japan. They started a dialogue with the Chinese. In actuality, however, theirs was a temporary and somewhat incoherent alliance, politically divided and subject to the USSR's influence, especially in the case of France. Yet it was the first time that the destiny of some Communist parties was entrusted explicitly to policies based on not only an increased distance from the USSR as a "leading state" but also the social and political model it represented, which had been exported, or in any case adopted in its fundamental outlines by all Communist states. The idea of a reformed communism was viewed with hostility by the Soviets, even though the USSR certainly did not intend to renounce Leninist or Marxist legacies. Even though Eurocommunism fizzled out before the decade's end, the strongest Western party, the Italian Communist Party, continued to represent a thorn in Moscow's side. In many respects, the banner of reform communism was to be picked up by Gorbachev and carried to its extreme. On the eve of his exit he had virtually emptied communism of its Leninist components.

The fragmentation of communism as a supranational movement is inseparable from its decline. In the last twenty years of its life Soviet communism lost whatever residual attraction it still had after Stalin's myth had been demolished. The protest movements of 1968 gave rise to a minority neo-Leninist and neo-Marxist Left, but one that was hostile to the old Communist parties. At a deeper level, sociocultural changes in the West marginalized communism's ideological appeal, while the eco-

nomic and technological changes in capitalist systems were destined to outperform the stagnant systems of a Soviet type. The USSR and its Eastern European satellites followed the path of inertia and conservatism up to Gorbachev's failed attempt at reform. China soon ceased to represent an alternative source of legitimacy, once it was clear that Mao had been Stalin's equivalent in the 20th-century gallery of horrors, and that Pol Pot, Cambodian and pro-Chinese, had actually outdone both of them. The romantic mythologies built around the figures of Ho Chi Minh, Fidel Castro Ruz, and Ernesto "Che" Guevara did not last long.

It was nationalism instead that was to play an ever-increasing role. Stalin had been the first to resort to patriotism and nationalism, especially during World War II. The instrumental use of nationalism was characteristic of other Communist leaders like Gomułka and Ceaușescu. Western Communists always cultivated the idea of their own "national path." Outside of Europe Communists used nationalism for anti-imperialist purposes. All this produced continuous tensions with the internationalist and universalist tradition—a symptom of the Communist movement's fragmentation. In the early 1980s communism's crisis was proclaimed starting from its Achilles' heel, Eastern Europe. Only a few Communist leaders were actually aware of it. But Communist political culture was revealed as incapable of renewing itself without self-destructing. In any case, remedies arrived too late.

Notwithstanding fragmentation, crisis, and decline, the Communists' sense of belonging to a common history and reality never weakened. Differences and distances, controversies and disputes, did not stop the overwhelming majority from feeling part of the same "world movement" that had originated in the October Revolution, and believing in its Leninist virtues. Among simple militants, even those belonging to different generations, the tendency to review one's past, even after the shock of 1956, was limited. But it was never significantly encouraged by Communist leadership groups either. Those parties that abandoned the idea of being part of an "international Communist movement" were forced to by circumstances or did so very late. Even those Communists in power who had been excommunicated by the Soviet pulpit, like the Yugoslavs, renewed relationships with orthodox parties, even though only partially and without renouncing their experience; or like the Chinese, they tried to establish a rival system of relationships, but without much success. Even the most successful Communists in the West, those most able to distinguish themselves on the level of intellectual legacy and political culture, like the Italians, feared a break with the Soviet Union would represent an irreparable loss of roots and identity. Before Gorbachev's ascent to power, no important Communist Party, with the exception of the Italian Communist Party and the League of Yugoslav Communists, seriously questioned their belonging to an organized movement, while the Chinese and parties close to them disputed Soviet hegemony more than the notion of a Communist movement itself. Not even the few who were fairly aware of the crisis (Gorbachev himself and the heirs of "reform communism" in the East and West), following in the steps of ideas and human beings born seventy years earlier, conceived of the possibility that communism did not have a future.

In other words, during their entire history, the Communists thought of themselves subjectively as the protagonists of a unified movement, whatever the forms and variations it might assume. *A Dictionary of 20th-Century Communism*'s editors believe that this can and should be taken as a criterion for its historiographical orientation. Until now published studies have alternately stressed monolithic or pluralist aspects, international or national elements. An entire tradition of "Sovietological" studies separated knowledge of Communist societies and regimes from communism as a worldwide phenomenon. Ever-burning passions have had a determining influence on interpretation, following polarizations that started within the history of the Communist movement itself, or arising from the ideological opposition of pro- and anti-Communist. Even during the time that has passed since the fall of the Soviet Union and Communist regimes in Europe, the renewal made possible by the archives' opening has still not produced a noticeable change in outlook. Sometimes archival documentation has simply been used to confirm or deny preestablished lines of reasoning. And it has not necessarily helped broaden historians' perspective to include more general issues.

When the Italian edition of this dictionary first appeared, in 2006, we wrote that "we still do not have a true history of world communism at our disposal." New histories of 20th-century communism have been written by Robert Service (*Comrades: A World History of Communism*, 2007), Archie Brown (*The Rise and Fall of Communism*, 2009), and David Priestland (*The Red Flag: A History of Communism*, 2009). So our dictionary is now part of a growing literature, while maintaining its own distinctiveness. The task of completing an encyclopedic work like this dictionary has been particularly arduous. The difficulty is due to several factors: historiography based on archival material is still fairly recent; both comparative and national approaches in ex-Communist countries are weak; and strong tensions exist between two requirements that cannot be renounced—a moral condemnation of the mass crimes that are scattered through the history of communism and a historical understanding of communism itself. At the same time, we believe that precisely this difficulty may provide a justification for this enterprise and underscore its usefulness.

This volume contains more than four hundred entries on 20th-century communism, written by a sizable group of authors chosen among major experts from Europe, Russia, the United States, and other countries on the basis of their past contributions and most recent significant studies. The entries include figures, historical events, organizations, institutions, societies, and numerous keywords. The authors present a plurality of approaches and interpretations that cannot in any way be reduced to a single perspective. *A Dictionary of 20th-Century Communism* does not claim to give its readers an interpretation but rather a historical and historiographical overview. It does not claim to be based on single-cause or one-dimensional views; in fact it tries to avoid them. It does, however, offer an accurate system of references. The entries overlap each other, and crossreferencing allows the dictionary to present communism as a global historical phenomenon, which affected the principal social and political, state and supranational, military and international, mythological and ideological aspects of the past century at its most important moments. Communism is treated here as a fundamentally homogeneous phenomenon during the period from 1917 to 1989–91, from its roots in the experience of the Soviet Union to its most significant developments, especially in Europe and Asia.

Communists followed the most diverse paths during the history of the 20th century. When they were not in power, they contributed to struggles for liberation and social emancipation. When they were in power, they established oppressive and tyrannical regimes. But communism has come to the end of its road, losing the fundamental challenges it launched with the October Revolution. The revolutionary threat it posed may have forced capitalism to undertake some reforms, but that was not its goal. Its universalism has not left any substantial cultural or institutional legacy. Its capacity for global expansion has been matched by the speed of its decline. Communism's experiment on social structures has been revealed to be as disastrous as it was gigantic. Its ambition to build an alternate model of society, economy, and modernity has not survived reality's tests. At the state level the original dream of a liberating palingenesis was transformed into a totalitarian nightmare. At the global level it ended up affecting imperial policies more significantly than the urgent problems of the world we live in. Its memory cannot be separated from some of the worst tragedies and most infamous crimes against humanity perpetrated in contemporary history. In some countries, communism's survival seems to be proportional to its capacity to embrace the lessons learned from its long-standing enemies: nationalism and capitalism.

It was not a phenomenon that was extraneous to the 20th century, though; it was an integral part of it. We will only be able to understand our recent past and immediate future with difficulty, if we do not take the place of communism in this history into account.

SILVIO PONS AND ROBERT SERVICE

Acknowledgments

The completion of *A Dictionary of 20th-Century Communism* would not have been possible without essential contributions by several people, most especially Luigi Tomba. He put his considerable expertise to work for us, and his help in the area of Asian communism was invaluable. We would also like to thank Alberto Filippi, an indispensable and generous collaborator in the area of Latin American communism. Michele Luzzatto followed the project from its planning phases to its completion, and was always available to share in the resolution of problems and difficulties with great lucidity. Gianluca Fiocco performed the important task of reading and editing the contributions in a critical spirit. Anna Farcito contributed her competence and experience to the entries' final editing. Marco Del Bufalo corrected various errors. Rosalba Provantini and Paola Rodinò also provided timely and invaluable assistance. The editors wish to thank them all sincerely, while taking full responsibility for the work's perspectives, choices, and characteristics.

SILVIO PONS AND ROBERT SERVICE

Entries

Afghan War
Elena Dundovich

Agrarian Question
Alessandro Stanziani

Amendola, Giorgio
Roberto Gualtieri

Americanism
Federico Romero

Andropov, Yuri
Vladislav M. Zubok

Anti-Americanism
Alessandro Brogi

Anticommunism
Abbott Gleason

Antifascism
Silvio Pons

Anti-Fascist Resistance
Lutz Klinkhammer

Anti-imperialism
Rana Mitter

Anti-Semitism
Laurent Rucker

Aragon, Louis
Nicole Racine

Architecture and Urban Planning
Alessandro de Magistris

Arendt, Hannah
Abbott Gleason

Atheism, Soviet
Arto Luukkanen

Atomic Bomb
David Holloway

Avant-garde
Gian Piero Piretto

Bauer, Otto
Leonardo Rapone

Beijing Spring
Luigi Tomba

Beria, Lavrenty
Oleg V. Chlevnjuk

Berlin Crisis of 1948–49
Michail M. Narinskij

Berlin Wall
Norman M. Naimark

Berlinguer, Enrico
Silvio Pons

Bierut, Bolesław
Andrzej Paczkowski

Bipolarity
Mark Kramer

Bolshevism
Robert Service

Bolshevization
Kevin F. McDermott

Bonapartism
Ian D. Thatcher

Borders
Sabine Dullin

Brecht, Bertolt
Paolo Chiarini

Entries

Brest-Litovsk, Treaty of
Jon S. Jacobson

Brezhnev, Leonid
Vladislav M. Zubok

Brezhnev Doctrine
Mark Kramer

Browder, Earl
Fraser Ottanelli

Bukharin, Nikolay
Anna di Biagio

Bureaucracy
E. Arfon Rees

Cadres
Oleg V. Chlevnjuk

Camps
Pierre Rigoulot

Castro, Fidel
Loris Zanatta

Catholic Church
Agostino Giovagnoli

Ceausescu, Nicolae
Florin Constantiniu

Censorship
Matthew Lenoe

Charter 77
Francesco M. Cataluccio

Chernobyl, Catastrophe of
Andrea Romano

Chicherin, Georgy
Anna di Biagio

China-Vietnam War
Luigi Tomba

China's Armed Forces
You Ji

Chinese Agrarian Policies
Thomas P. Bernstein

Chinese Revolution
Anthony Saich

Cinema, Soviet
Peter Kenez

Citizenship
Carlo Spagnolo

Classes
Igal Halfin

Clientelism
Graeme Gill

Cold War
Odd Arne Westad

Collapse of Capitalism
Anna di Biagio

Collectivization of the Countryside
Lynne Viola

Comecon
Michael C. Kaser

Cominform
Leonid Ja. Gibjanskij

Comintern
Kevin F. McDermott

Command Economy, The
Robert W. Davies

Communist Autobiography
Igal Halfin

Communist Party in Albania
Ana Lalaj

Communist Party in Australia and New Zealand
Rick Kuhn

Communist Party in Austria
Aleksandr I. Vatlin

Communist Party in Belgium
José Gotovitch

Communist Party in Bulgaria
Vitka Toshkova

Communist Party in Central Asia
Catherine Poujol

Communist Party in China
Luigi Tomba

Communist Party in Cuba
Loris Zanatta

Communist Party in Czechoslovakia
Karel Kaplan

Communist Party in East Germany
Wilfried Loth

Communist Party in Finland
Kimmo Rentola

Communist Party in France
Marc Lazar

Communist Party in Germany
Aleksandr I. Vatlin

Communist Party in Great Britain
Andrew J. Thorpe

Communist Party in Greece
John O. Iatrides

Communist Party in Hungary
Gyorgy Foldes

Communist Party in the Indian Subcontinent
Olle Tornquist

Communist Party in Indonesia
Olle Tornquist

Communist Party in Iran
Jamshid Arman and Biancamaria Scarcia Amoretti

Communist Party in Israel
David Bidussa

Communist Party in Italy
Aldo Agosti

Communist Party in Japan
Arthur Stockwin

Communist Party in Kampuchea
David P. Chandler

Communist Party in Korea
Andrei N. Lankov

Communist Party in Latin America
Alberto Filippi

Communist Party in the Middle East and the Maghreb
Antonello F. Biagini and Daniel Pommier Vincelli

Communist Party in Mongolia
Luigi Tomba

Communist Party in the Netherlands
José Gotovitch

**Communist Party in the Nordic Countries
and the Baltics**
Ragnheiður Kristjánsdóttir

Communist Party in Poland
Andrzej Paczkowski

Communist Party in Portugal
João Arsénio Nunes

Communist Party in Romania
Florin Constantiniu

Communist Party in Southeast Asia
Luigi Tomba

Communist Party in the Soviet Union
Graeme Gill

Communist Party in Spain
Antonio Elorza

Communist Party in Sub-Saharan Africa
Giampaolo Calchi Novati

Communist Party in Switzerland
Brigitte Studer

Communist Party in the United States
Fraser Ottanelli

Communist Party in Vietnam
Sophie Quinn-Judge

Communist Party in Yemen
Frederick Halliday

Communist Party in Yugoslavia
Leonid Ja. Gibjanskij

Conference on Security and Cooperation in Europe
Vojtech Mastny

Constitutions
Graeme Gill

Containment
Melvyn P. Leffler

Coup in the USSR (1991)
Archie Brown

Cuban Missile Crisis
Alberto Filippi

Cuban Revolution
Loris Zanatta

Cuban-Soviet Intervention in Africa
Piero Gleijeses

Cult of Personality
E. Arfon Rees

Entries

Cultural Policies
Gian Piero Piretto

Cultural Revolution in China
Maurizio Marinelli

Decolonization
Giampaolo Calchi Novati

Democratic Centralism
Francesco Benvenuti

Demographic Policies
Alain Blum

Deng Xiaoping
Luigi Tomba

Deportation of Nationalities in the USSR
Norman M. Naimark

Despotism
Fabio Bettanin

De-Stalinization
Elena U. Zubkova

Détente
Wilfried Loth

Dictatorship of the Proletariat
Robert Service

Dimitrov, Georgi
Leonid Ja. Gibjanskij

Diplomats
Sabine Dullin

Dissent in the USSR
Elena Dundovich

Dissolution of the USSR
Mark Kramer

Djilas, Milovan
Leonid Ja. Gibjanskij

Dubček, Alexander
Karel Kaplan

Dzerzhinskii, Feliks
Iain Lauchlan

Economic Reforms
Sergio Bertolissi

Eisenstein, Sergei
Richard Taylor

Elections
Graeme Gill

Enemies of the People
Oleg V. Chlevnjuk

Ethnic Cleansing
Norman M. Naimark

Eurocommunism
Silvio Pons

European Integration
Donald Sassoon

Family
Anna di Biagio

Famine under Communism
Stephen G. Wheatcroft

Fascism
Marco Palla

Fellow Travelers
Abbott Gleason

Festivals
Richard Stites

Five-Year Plans
Robert W. Davies

Foibe Massacres
Giampaolo Valdevit

Gagarin, Yury
Andrea Romano

Gheorghiu-Dej, Gheorghe
Florin Constantiniu

Gierek, Edward
Andrzej Paczkowski

Gomułka, Władysław
Andrzej Paczkowski

Gorbachev, Mikhail
Archie Brown

Gosplan
Mark Harrison

Gottwald, Klement
Karel Kaplan

Gramsci, Antonio
Giuseppe Vacca

Grand Alliance, The
Geoffrey K. Roberts

Great Leap Forward
Maurizio Marinelli

Great Patriotic War, Rhetoric of
Andrea Romano

Great Terror
Oleg V. Chlevnjuk

Greek Civil War
John O. Iatrides

Gromyko, Andrei
Vladislav M. Zubok

Guerrilla Warfare in Latin America
Alberto Filippi

Guevara de la Serna, Ernesto Rafael
Alberto Filippi

Gulag
Nicolas Werth

Havel, Václav
Francesco M. Cataluccio

Hilferding, Rudolf
Leonardo Rapone

History and Memory
Maria Ferretti

Hitler, Adolf
Richard J. Overy

Ho Chi Minh
Sophie Quinn-Judge

Holodomor
Andrea Graziosi

Honecker, Erich
Wilfried Loth

Hoxha, Enver
Ana Lalaj

Hundred Flowers Movement
Luigi Tomba

Hungarian Republic of Councils
Stefano Bottoni

Hungarian Revolution
Attila Szakolczai

Husák, Gustav
Karel Kaplan

Hu Yaobang
Luigi Tomba

Iconography
Gian Piero Piretto

Immigration to the USSR
Elena Dundovich and Francesca Gori

Imperialism
R. Craig Nation

Insurrection in Germany
Aleksandr I. Vatlin

Intelligentsia
E. Arfon Rees

International Brigades
Gabriele Ranzato

International Conferences after Stalin
Leonid Ja. Gibjanskij

International Trade Union Organizations
Vsevolod Možaev

Internationalism
R. Craig Nation

Islam
Renzo Guolo

Jacobinism
E. Arfon Rees

Jaruzelski, Wojciech
Andrzej Paczkowski

Jiang Zemin
Luigi Tomba

Kádár, János
Stefano Bottoni

Kaganovich, Lazar
E. Arfon Rees

Kamenev, Lev
Aleksandr I. Vatlin

Kardelj, Edvard
Leonid Ja. Gibjanskij

Katyn Massacre
Natalja S. Lebedeva

Entries

Kautsky, Karl
Leonardo Rapone

Kennan, George Frost
Anders Stephanson

KGB
Marta Craveri

Khmer Rouge
David P. Chandler

Khrushchev, Nikita
William Taubman

Killing Fields
David P. Chandler

Kim Il Sung
Andrei N. Lankov

Kirov, Sergey
Francesco Benvenuti

Koestler, Arthur
Tom Villis

Kolkhoz
Lynne Viola

Kollontay, Aleksandra
Anna di Biagio

Korean War
Kathryn Weathersby

Kronstadt Revolt
Robert Service

Kulak
Andrea Romano

Kun, Béla
Kevin F. McDermott

Kurón, Jacek
Francesco M. Cataluccio

Kuusinen, Otto Wilhelm
Kevin F. McDermott

Labor
Donald A. Filtzer and Luigi Tomba

Legal Marxism
Vittorio Strada

Lenin, Vladimir
Robert Service

Leningrad, Siege of
John D. Barber

Lenin's Testament
Robert Service

Liebknecht, Karl
Ottokar Luban

Lin Biao
Luigi Tomba

Literacy, Soviet Union Campaign for Adult
Charles E. Clark

Literature in Soviet Russia
Stefano Garzonio

Litvinov, Maksim
Sabine Dullin

Liu Shaoqi
Luigi Tomba

Long March
Maurizio Marinelli

Lukács, Georg
Nicolas Tertulian

Lunacharsky, Anatoly
Christopher Read

Luxemburg, Rosa
Ottokar Luban

Malenkov, Georgy
Vladislav M. Zubok

Malraux, André
Nicole Racine

Manuilskii, Dmitrii
Kevin F. McDermott

Mao Zedong
Timothy Cheek

Maoism
Robert J. Alexander

Marchais, Georges
Sandro Guerrieri

Mariátegui, José Carlos
Alberto Filippi

Markets, Legal and Illegal
Mark Harrison

Marshall Plan
Carlo Spagnolo

Martial Law in Poland
Mark Kramer

Marxism, Western
Leonardo Paggi

Marxism-Leninism
Vittorio Strada

Mayakovski, Vladimir
Stefano Garzonio

McCarthyism
Ellen Schrecker

Messianism
Igal Halfin

Michnik, Adam
Francesco M. Cataluccio

Militancy
Marc Lazar

Militarization
Francesco Benvenuti

Military-Industrial Complex
Irina V. Bystrova

Modernization
Fabio Bettanin

Molotov, Vyacheslav
E. Arfon Rees

Molotov-Ribbentrop Pact
Silvio Pons

Münzenberg, Willi
Aleksandr I. Vatlin

Mussolini, Benito
Marco Palla

Nagy, Imre
Vjacheslav Sereda and Aleksandr S. Stykalin

National Question, The
Jeremy R. Smith

National Roads to Socialism
Marc Lazar

Nationalism
Francesco Benvenuti

Nationality Policies
Jeremy R. Smith

Nations and Empire in the USSR
Victor Zaslavsky

Neruda, Pablo
Alberto Filippi

New Economic Policy
Nicolas Werth

New Left
Ermanno Taviani

New Man
Brigitte Studer

New Thinking
Archie Brown

Nomenklatura
Oleg V. Chlevnjuk

Nonalignment
Giampaolo Calchi Novati

North Atlantic Treaty Organization
Vojtech Mastny

Novotný, Antonín
Karel Kaplan

Ordzhonikidze, Grigoriy (Sergo)
Francesco Benvenuti

Orthodox Church, Russian
Michael Bourdeaux

Orwell, George
Tom Villis

Ostpolitik
Wilfried Loth

Partisans of Peace
Philippe Buton

Peaceful Coexistence
Anna di Biagio

Peasants in the USSR
Lynne Viola

People's Democracy
Norman M. Naimark

Perestroika
Archie Brown

Entries

Péri, Gabriel
  Sergio Luzzatto

Piatnitskii, Osip
  Kevin F. McDermott

Pieck, Wilhelm
  Wilfried Loth

Planning
  Sergio Bertolissi

Plekhanov, Georgy
  Vittorio Strada

Pol Pot
  David P. Chandler

Polish-Soviet War
  Norman Davies

Politburo
  Oleg V. Chlevnjuk

Political Pilgrims
  Paul Hollander

Pollitt, Harry
  Andrew J. Thorpe

Polycentrism
  Aldo Agosti

Popular Front
  Kevin F. McDermott

Portugal's Carnation Revolution
  João Arsénio Nunes

Post-Soviet Communism
  Stephen White

Power Politics
  Mark Kramer

Prague Coup
  Leonid Ja. Gibjanskij

Prague Spring
  Mark Kramer

Preobrazhensky, Evgeny
  Donald A. Filtzer

Press
  Matthew Lenoe

Proletkult
  Gian Piero Piretto

Propaganda, Communist
  Peter Kenez

Public Opinion
  Jurij Levada

Purges
  E. Arfon Rees

Radek, Karl
  Kevin F. McDermott

Rajk, László
  Vjacheslav Sereda and Aleksandr S. Stykalin

Rákosi, Mátyás
  Vjacheslav Sereda and Aleksandr S. Stykalin

Rapallo Treaty
  Jon S. Jacobson

Real Socialism
  Archie Brown

Red Army
  Francesco Benvenuti

Red Guard
  You Ji

Red Terror
  Fabio Bettanin

Reunification of Germany
  Norman M. Naimark

Revisionism
  R. Craig Nation

Revolution, Myths of the
  Antonello Venturi

Revolution from Above
  E. Arfon Rees

Revolutions in East-Central Europe
  Mark Kramer

Russian Revolution and Civil War
  Robert Service

Rykov, Alexei
  Francesco Benvenuti

Sakharov, Andrey
  Elena Dundovich

Sandinista Revolution
  Alberto Filippi

Sartre, Jean-Paul
Nicole Racine

Science
Alexei Kojevnikov

Second Cold War
Frederick Halliday

Secret Speech
Fabio Bettanin

Self-Criticism
Robert Service

Shalamov, Varlam
Stefano Garzonio

Shevardnadze, Eduard
Archie Brown

***Short Course,* The**
David Brandenberger

Shostakovich, Dmitry
Francesco Salvi

Single-Party System
Graeme Gill

Sino-Soviet Split
Luigi Tomba

Slánský, Rudolf
Karel Kaplan

Social Democracy
Donald Sassoon

Social Fascism
Kevin F. McDermott

Social Policy
Robert Johnson

Socialism in One Country
Jon S. Jacobson

Socialist Camp
Leonid Ja. Gibjanskij

Socialist Consumer Society
Elena A. Osokina

Socialist Emulation
Francesco Benvenuti

Socialist International
Leonardo Rapone

Socialist Market Economy
Luigi Tomba

Socialist Realism
Vittorio Strada

Solidarity
Francesco M. Cataluccio

Solzhenitsyn, Aleksandr
Stefano Garzonio

Soviet Bloc
Mark Kramer

Soviet Industrialization
Robert W. Davies

Soviet Occupation of Germany
Norman M. Naimark

Soviet Patriotism
David Brandenberger

Soviet-Yugoslavia Break
Leonid Ja. Gibjanskij

Sovietization
Leonid Ja. Gibjanskij

Soviets
Robert Service

Spanish Civil War
Antonio Elorza

Spies
John Earl Haynes

Sports
Mario Alessandro-Curletto

Stakhanovism
Francesco Benvenuti

Stalin, Joseph
Silvio Pons

Stalin, Myth of
Marc Lazar

Stalingrad, Battle of
Silvio Pons

Stalinism
E. Arfon Rees

State, The
E. Arfon Rees

Entries

Suslov, Mikhail
Archie Brown

Television in the Soviet Era
Ellen Mickiewicz

Terrorism
Ermanno Taviani

Thälmann, Ernst
Aleksandr I. Vatlin

Third Worldism
Giampaolo Calchi Novati

Thorez, Maurice
Serge Wolikow

Tito, Josip Broz
Leonid Ja. Gibjanskij

Togliatti, Palmiro
Silvio Pons

Tomsky, Mikhail
Francesco Benvenuti

Totalitarianism
Abbott Gleason

Trade Unions
Stephen F. Crowley

Transportation
E. Arfon Rees

Trotsky, Leon
Robert Service

Trotskyism
Ian D. Thatcher

Tukhachevskii, Mikhail
Lennart Samuelson

Ulbricht, Walter
Wilfried Loth

Unidad Popular
Alberto Filippi

United Nations
Vojtech Mastny

Urbanization
Robert Johnson

Utopia
Richard Stites

Varga, Eugen
Anna di Biagio

Vietnam War
Ilja V. Gajduk

Vietnam-Cambodia War
Sophie Quinn-Judge

Voroshilov, Kliment
Francesco Benvenuti

Vyshinsky, Andrey
Michail M. Narinskij

Walesa, Lech
Francesco M. Cataluccio

War, Inevitability of
Anna di Biagio

War Communism
Nicolas Werth

Warfare
R. Craig Nation

Warsaw Pact
Vojtech Mastny

Welfare State
Donald Sassoon

Winter War
Kimmo Rentola

Women, Emancipation of
Anna di Biagio

Workers
Donald A. Filtzer

World Revolution
Aldo Agosti

World War II
Michail M. Narinskij

Yakovlev, Aleksandr
Archie Brown

Yalta Conference
Geoffrey K. Roberts

Yeltsin, Boris
Adriano Guerra

Yezhov, Nikolay
Oleg V. Chlevnjuk

Youth
Juliane Fuerst

Zetkin, Clara
Aleksandr I. Vatlin

Zhdanov, Andrey
Vladislav M. Zubok

Zhdanovism
Elena U. Zubkova

Zhivkov, Todor
Vitka Toshkova

Zhou Enlai
Luigi Tomba

Zhukov, Georgii
Lennart Samuelson

Zimmerwald Conference
R. Craig Nation

Zinovyev, Grigory
Aleksandr I. Vatlin

Zionism
Laurent Rucker

Contributors

Agosti, Aldo
University of Turin, Italy

Alessandro-Curletto, Mario
University of Genoa, Italy

Alexander, Robert J.
Rutgers University (emeritus)

Arman, Jamshid

Barber, John D.
University of Cambridge, UK

Benvenuti, Francesco
University of Bologna, Italy

Bernstein, Thomas P.
Columbia University

Bertolissi, Sergio
University of Naples-L'Oriental, Italy

Bettanin, Fabio
University of Naples-L'Oriental, Italy

Biagini, Antonello F.
Sapienza University of Rome, Italy

Bidussa, David
Feltrinelli Foundation, Milan, Italy

Blum, Alain
École des hautes études en sciences sociales, Paris, France

Bottoni, Stefano
University of Bologna, Italy

Bourdeaux, Michael
Oxford University, UK

Brandenberger, David
University of Richmond

Brogi, Alessandro
University of Arkansas

Brown, Archie
Oxford University, UK

Buton, Philippe
University of Reims, France

Bystrova, Irina V.
Institut Rossijskoj Istorii RAN, Moscow, Russia

Calchi Novati, Giampaolo
University of Pavia, Italy

Cataluccio, Francesco M.
Milan, Italy

Chandler, David P.
Monash University, Melbourne, Australia

Cheek, Timothy
University of British Columbia, Vancouver, Canada

Chiarini, Paolo
Sapienza University of Rome, Italy

Chlevnjuk, Oleg V.
Gosudarstvennyj Archiv Rossijskoj Federacii, Moscow, Russia

Clark, Charles E.
University of Wisconsin, Stevens Point

Constantiniu, Florin
Institutul de Istorie "N. Iorga," Bucharest, Romania

Craveri, Marta
École des hautes études en sciences sociales, Paris, France

Crowley, Stephen F.
Oberlin College

Contributors

Davies, Norman
Oxford University, UK

Davies, Robert W.
Birmingham University, UK

de Magistris, Alessandro
Milan Polytechnic, Italy

di Biagio, Anna
University of Florence, Italy

Dullin, Sabine
Université de Paris I Panthéon Sorbonne, France

Dundovich, Elena
University of Florence, Italy

Elorza, Antonio
Universidad Complutense de Madrid, Madrid, Spain

Ferretti, Maria
Tuscia University, Viterbo, Italy

Filippi, Alberto
University of Camerino, Italy

Filtzer, Donald A.
University of London, UK

Foldes, Gyorgy
Institute of Political History, Budapest, Hungary

Fuerst, Juliane
Oxford University, UK

Gajduk, Ilja V.
Institut Rossijskoj Istorii RAN, Moscow, Russia

Garzonio, Stefano
University of Pisa, Italy

Gibjanskij, Leonid Ja.
Institut Slavjanovedenija RAN, Moscow, Russia

Gill, Graeme
University of Sydney, Australia

Giovagnoli, Agostino
Catholic University of the Sacred Heart, Milan, Italy

Gleason, Abbott
Brown University

Gleijeses, Piero
Johns Hopkins University

Gori, Francesca
Unidea Foundation, Milan, Italy

Gotovitch, José
Université Libre de Bruxelles, Belgium

Graziosi, Andrea
Frederick II University, Naples, Italy

Gualtieri, Roberto
La Sapienza University, Rome, Italy

Guerra, Adriano
Rome, Italy

Guerrieri, Sandro
La Sapienza University, Rome, Italy

Guolo, Renzo
University of Padua, Italy

Halfin, Igal
Tel Aviv University, Israel

Halliday, Frederick
London School of Economics and Political Sciences, UK

Harrison, Mark
University of Warwick, UK

Haynes, John Earl
Library of Congress, Washington, DC

Hollander, Paul
Harvard University

Holloway, David
Stanford University

Iatrides, John O.
Southern Connecticut State University

Jacobson, Jon S.
University of California, Irvine

Johnson, Robert
University of Toronto, Canada

Kaplan, Karel
Institute of Contemporary History, Prague, Czech Republic

Kaser, Michael C.
Oxford University, UK

Kenez, Peter
University of California, Santa Cruz

Klinkhammer, Lutz
German Historical Institute, Rome, Italy

Kojevnikov, Alexei
University of Georgia

Kramer, Mark
Harvard University

Kristjánsdóttir, Ragnheiður
University of Iceland, Reykjavik, Iceland

Kuhn, Rick
Australian National University, Canberra, Australia

Lalaj, Ana
Instituti i Historise, Tirana, Albania

Lankov, Andrei N.
Kookmin University, Seoul, South Korea

Lauchlan, Iain
Oxford University, UK

Lazar, Marc
Sciences Po, Paris, France

Lebedeva, Natalja S.
Institut Vseobshchej Istorii RAN, Moscow, Russia

Leffler, Melvyn P.
University of Virginia

Lenoe, Matthew
University of Rochester

Levada, Jurij
Analiticheskij Centr Jurija Levady, Moscow, Russia

Loth, Wilfried
University of Duisburg-Essen, Germany

Luban, Ottokar
Berlin, Germany

Luukkanen, Arto
University of Joensuu, Finland

Luzzatto, Sergio
University of Turin, Italy

Marinelli, Maurizio
University of Bristol, UK

Mastny, Vojtech
Woodrow Wilson International Center for Scholars, Washington, DC

McDermott, Kevin F.
Sheffield Hallam University, UK

Mickiewicz, Ellen
Duke University

Mitter, Rana
Oxford University, UK

Možaev, Vsevolod
Vseobshchaja Konfederacija Profsojuzov, Moscow, Russia

Naimark, Norman M.
Stanford University

Narinskij, Michail M.
Moskovskij Gosudarstvennyj Institut Mezhdunarodnych Otnoshenij, Moscow, Russia

Nation, R. Craig
U.S. Army War College

Nunes, João Arsénio
Higher Institute of Business and Labor Sciences, Lisbon, Portugal

Osokina, Elena A.
University of South Carolina

Ottanelli, Fraser
University of South Florida

Overy, Richard J.
University of Exeter, UK

Paczkowski, Andrzej
Instytut Studiow Politycznych, Warsaw, Poland

Paggi, Leonardo
Modena University, Italy

Palla, Marco
University of Florence, Italy

Piretto, Gian Piero
Milan University, Italy

Pons, Silvio
Tor Vergata University, Rome, Italy

Poujol, Catherine
Inalco, Paris, France

Quinn-Judge, Sophie
Temple University

Contributors

Racine, Nicole
Sciences Po, Paris, France

Ranzato, Gabriele
University of Pisa, Italy

Rapone, Leonardo
Tuscia University, Viterbo, Italy

Read, Christopher
University of Warwick, UK

Rees, E. Arfon
European University Institute, Florence, Italy

Rentola, Kimmo
University of Helsinki, Finland

Rigoulot, Pierre
Institute of Social History, Nanterre, France

Roberts, Geoffrey K.
University College Cork, Ireland

Romano, Andrea
Tor Vergata University, Rome, Italy

Romero, Federico
University of Florence, Italy

Rucker, Laurent
Paris, France

Saich, Anthony
Harvard University

Salvi, Francesco
Rome, Italy

Samuelson, Lennart
Stockholm School of Economics, Sweden

Sassoon, Donald
Queen Mary University of London, UK

Scarcia Amoretti, Biancamaria
La Sapienza University, Rome, Italy

Schrecker, Ellen
Yeshiva University

Sereda, Vjacheslav
Institut Slavjanovedenija RAN, Moscow, Russia

Service, Robert
Oxford University, UK

Smith, Jeremy R.
University of Birmingham, UK

Spagnolo, Carlo
Bari University, Italy

Stanziani, Alessandro
IDHE-Cachan, Paris, France

Stephanson, Anders
Columbia University

Stites, Richard
Georgetown University

Stockwin, Arthur
Oxford University, UK

Strada, Vittorio
Ca' Foscari University, Venice, Italy

Studer, Brigitte
Bern University, Switzerland

Stykalin, Aleksandr S.
Institut Slavjanovedenija RAN, Moscow, Russia

Szakolczai, Attila
Institute for History of 1956, Budapest, Hungary

Taubman, William
Amherst College

Taviani, Ermanno
University of Catania, Italy

Taylor, Richard
Swansea University, UK

Tertulian, Nicolas
École Des Hautes Études En Sciences sociales, Paris, France

Thatcher, Ian D.
Brunel University, UK

Thorpe, Andrew J.
University of Exeter, UK

Tomba, Luigi
Australian National University, Canberra, Australia

Tornquist, Olle
University of Oslo, Norway

Toshkova, Vitka
Bulgarian Academy of Sciences, Sofia, Bulgaria

Vacca, Giuseppe
Istituto Gramsci Foundation, Rome, Italy

Valdevit, Giampaolo
Trieste University, Italy

Vatlin, Aleksandr I.
Moskovskij Gosudarstvennyj Universitet, Moscow, Russia

Venturi, Antonello
Pisa University, Italy

Villis, Tom
University of Sussex, UK

Vincelli, Daniel Pommier

Viola, Lynne
University of Toronto, Canada

Weathersby, Kathryn
Woodrow Wilson International Center for Scholars, Washington, DC

Werth, Nicolas
Institut d'histoire du temps présent, CNRS, Paris, France

Westad, Odd Arne
London School of Economics and Political Science, UK

Wheatcroft, Stephen G.
University of Melbourne, Australia

White, Stephen
University of Glasgow, UK

Wolikow, Serge
Bourgogne University, Dijon, France

You Ji
National University of Singapore

Zanatta, Loris
Bologna University, Italy

Zaslavsky, Victor
Luiss-Guido Carli University, Rome, Italy

Zubkova, Elena U.
Institut Rossijskoj Istorii RAN, Moscow, Russia

Zubok, Vladislav M.
Temple University

Acronyms and Abbreviations

ANC	African National Congress
APRA	Alianza popular revolucionaria americana
ASEAN	Association of South-East Asian Nations
ÁVH	Allamvedelmi hatosag ([Hungarian] State Defense Authority)
AWS	Akcja Wyborcz Solidarnosc (Solidarity Electoral Action)
BAM	Bajkalo-Amurskaya Magistral' (Baikal-Amur Railway)
BCF	Balkan Communist Federation
BKP	Bulgarska kommunisticheska partia (Bulgarian Communist Party / BCP)
CC	Central Committee
CCP	Chinese Communist Party
CDU	Christlich Demokratische Union (Christian Democratic Union [Germany])
Cektran	Centralnyj komitet sojuza transportnch rabochich (Central Committee of the Transport Workers Union)
CGIL	Confederazione generale italiana del lavoro (General Italian Labor Confederation)
CGT	Confederation general du travail (General Confederation of Labor)
CGTU	Confederacion general del trabajo unitaria (United General Confederation of Labor)
Cheka	Chrezvychajnaja komissija (Extraordinary Commission). Cf. VChK
CIA	Central Intelligence Agency
CNRS	Centre national de la recherche scientifique (National Center for Scientific Research)
CNT	Confederación Nacional del Trabajo (National Confederation of Labor)
Comecon	Council for Mutual Economic Assistance. Cf. SEV
Cominform	Communist Information Bureau
Comintern	Kommunisticheskij internacional (Communist International)
COW	Correlates of War
CPA	Communist Party of Australia, Communist Party of Austria; Communist Political Association
CPA-ML	Communist Party of Australia (Marxist-Leninist)
CPB	Communist Party of Belgium; Communist Party of Britain
CPCz	Constituent Assembly of the Communist Party of Czechoslovakia
CPG	Communist Party of Germany
CPGB	Communist Party of Great Britain
CPH	Communistische Partij Holland (Communist Party of Holland); Communist Party of Hungary
CPI	Communist Party of India
CPIM	Communist Party of India (Marxist)
CPIML	Communist Party of India (Marxist-Leninist)
CPK	Communist Party of Kampuchea
CPN	Communistische partij in Nederland (Communist Party of the Netherlands)
CPNZ	Communist Party of New Zealand
CPP	Communist Party of Poland
CPS	Communist Party of Slovakia
CPSU	Communist Party of the Soviet Union
CPT	Communist Party of Thailand
CPUSA	Communist Party of the United States of America
CPYu	Communist Party of Yugoslavia
CSCE	Conference on Security and Cooperation in Europe
DC	Democrazia cristiana (Christian Democratic Party [Italy])

Acronyms and Abbreviations

DKP Danmarks Kommunistiske Parti (Communist Party of Denmark)

DWK Deutsche Wirtschaftskommission (German Economic Commission)

EAM Ethnikon apeleftherotikon metopon (National Liberation Front)

ECC Executive Committee of the Comintern

EEC European Economic Community

ELAS Ethnikos laikos apeleftherotikos stratos (People's National Liberation Army)

ETA Euskadi Ta Askatasuna (Basque Homeland and Freedom)

FBI Federal Bureau of Investigation

FDN Fuerza democrática nicaraguense

FGCI Federazione giovanile comunisti italiani (Italian Communist Youth Federation)

FLN Frente de liberación nacional (National Liberation Front)

FRG Federal Republic of Germany

FSLN Frente Sandinista de liberación nacional (Sandinista National Liberation Front)

GDR German Democratic Republic

GKO Gosudarstvennyj komitet oborony (State Defense Committee)

Glavlit Glavnoe upravlenie po delam literatury i izdatel'stv (Main Directorate for Literary and Publishing Affairs)

Glavpolitprosvet Glavnyj politiko-prosvetitel'nyj komitet Narkomprosa RSFSR (Chief Committee for Political Education of the Narkompros of the Russian Soviet Federative Socialist Republic [RSFSR])

Glavpolitput Glavnoe politicheskoe upravlenie putei (Main Political Directorate of the Commissariat for Transport)

GMD Guomindang (Nationalist Party)

Gosplan Gosudarstvennaja planovaja komissija (State Planning Commission)

GRU Glavnoe razvedyvatel'noe upravlenie (Main Intelligence Directorate)

gulag Glavnoe upravlenie lagerej (Main Camps Administration)

HUAC House Un-American Activities Committee

ICBM Intercontinental Ballistic Missiles

ICFTU International Confederation of Free Trade Unions

IFTU International Federation of Trade Unions

Ikki Ispol'nitel'nyj komitet kommunisticheskogo internacionala (Executive Committee of the Communist International)

IMF International Monetary Fund

INAIL Istituto nazionale per l'assicurazione contro gli infortuni sul lavoro (National Insurance against Work-Related Injuries)

INAM Istituto nazionale assistenza malattia (National Health Insurance Board)

INF Intermediate Nuclear Force

INPS Istituto nazionale della previdenza sociale (National Social Security Institute)

ITT International Telephone and Telegraph Corporation

IU Izquierda unida (United Left)

IWA International Workers' Aid

JCP Japanese Communist Party

KGB Komitet gosudarstvennoj bezopasnosti (Committee for State Security)

KKE Kommunistiko komma Ellados (Communist Party of Greece)

Komsomol Kommunisticheskij sojuz molodezhi (Communist Youth Union). Cf. VLKSM

KOR Komitet obrony robotnikow (Workers' Defense Committee)

KPD Kommunistische Partei Deutschlands (Communist Party of Germany)

KPDÖ Kommunistische Partei Deutschlands Österreichs (Communist Party of Germany and Austria)

KPÖ Kommunistische Partei Österreichs (Communist Party of Austria)

KPRP Komunistyczna partia robotnicza polski (Communist Party of Polish Workers); Khmer People's Revolutionary Party

KPSS Kommunisticheskaja partija sovetskogo sojuza (Communist Party of the Soviet Union)

KWP Kampuchea's Workers' Party; Korean Workers' Party

LEF Left Front for the Arts

Maki Mifleghet Komunistit eretsisraelit (Communist Party of the Land of Israel)

MDP Magyar dolgozok partja (Hungarian Workers' Party)

Mezhrabpom (MRP)	Mezhdunarodnaja rabochaja pomoshch (Workers' International Relief)
MGB	Ministerstvo gosudarstvennoj bezopasnosti (Ministry for State Security)
Mid	Ministerstvo inostrannych del (Ministry for Foreign Affairs)
MOPR	Mezhdunarodnaja organizacija pomoshchi borcam revoljucii (International Organization for Assistance to Revolutionary Fighters)
MPR	Mouvement republicain populaire (People's Republican Movement)
MPRP	Mongolian People's Revolutionary Party
MSZMP	Magyar szocialista munkaspart (Hungarian Socialist Workers' Party)
MTS	Mashino-traktornaja stancija (Machine and Tractor Station)
MVD	Ministerstvo vnutrennych del (Ministry of the Interior)
Narkomindel	See NKID
Narkompros	Narodnyj komissariat prosveschchenija (People's Commissariat for Education)
NASA	National Aeronautic and Space Administration
NATO	North Atlantic Treaty Organization
NEP	Novaja ekonomicheskaja politika (New Economic Policy)
NKGB	Narodnyj komissariat gosudarstvennoj bezopasnosti (People's Commissariat for State Security)
NKID	Narodnyj komissariat inostrannych del (People's Commissariat for Foreign Affairs)
NKPut	Narodnyj komissariat putej soobshchenija (People's Commissariat for Transport Communications)
NKTP	Narodnyj komissariat tjazheloj promishlennosti (People's Commissariat for Heavy Industry)
NKVD	Narodnyj komissariat vnutrennich del (People's Commissariat for Internal Affairs)
OATUU	Organization of African Trade Union Unity
Obkom	Oblastnoj Komitet (Regional Committee)
Osoaviachim	Obshchestvo sodejstvija oborone, aviacii i chimii (Union of Societies of Assistance to Defense and Aviation-Chemical Construction of the USSR)
OSS	Office of Strategic Services

PASOK	Panellinio sosialistiko kinima (Panhellenic Socialist Movement)
Pce	Partido comunista de España (Communist Party of Spain)
Pcf	Parti communiste français (French Communist Party)
Pci	Partito comunista italiano (Italian Communist Party)
Pcp	Partido comunista de Perú (Communist Party of Peru); Partido comunista portugues (Portuguese Communist Party)
PDFLP	Popular Democratic Front for the Liberation of Palestine
PDRY	People's Democratic Republic of Yemen
Pds	Partei des demokratischen Sozialismus (Party of Democratic Socialism)
PKI	Partai Komunis Indonesia (Communist Party of Indonesia)
PKSh	Partia Komuniste e Shqiperise (Communist Party of Albania)
PKWN	Polski komitet wyzwolenia narodowego (Polish National Liberation Committee)
PLP	Progressive Labor Party
Pob	Parti ouvrier belge (Belgian Labour Party)
Politbjuro	Politicheskoe bjuro (Political Office; politburo)
Poum	Partido obrero de unificacion marxista (Marxist Unification Workers' Party)
PPR	Polska partia rabotnica (Polish Workers' Party)
Pps	Polska partia socjalistyczna (Polish Socialist Party)
PPSh	Partia e Punes e Shqiperise (Albanian Workers' Party)
PRC	People's Republic of China
Profintern	Krasnyj Internacional profsojuzov (Labor Unions' Red International)
Proletkult	Proletarskaja kul'tura (Proletarian Culture)
Psi	Partito socialista italiano (Italian Socialist Party)
Psoe	Partido socialista obrero espanol (Spanish Socialist Workers' Party)
Psp	Partido socialista del Perú (Socialist Party of Peru)
PSUC	Partit socialista unificat de Catalunya (Unified Socialist Party of Catalonia)
PUR	Politicheskoe upravlenie revvoensoveta (Political Directorate of the Red Army)

Acronyms and Abbreviations

PZPR	Polska zjednoczona partia robotnicza (Unified Polish Workers' Party)
Rabkrin (Rab)	Narodnyj komissariat raboche-krest'janskoj inspekcii (People's Commissariat of Workers' and Peasants' Inspection)
RAF	Rote Armee Fraktion (Red Army Faction)
RAPM	Rossijskaja associacija proletarskich muzykantov (Russian Association of Proletarian Musicians)
RCP	Russian Communist Party; Revolutionary Communist Party; Romanian Communist Party
RKP(b)	Rossijskaja kommunisticheskaja partija (bol'shevikov) (Russian Communist Party [Bolshevik])
RSDLP	Russian Socialist Democratic Labor Party
RSDRP	Rossijskaja socialdemokraticheskaja rabochaja partija (Russian Social-Democratic Workers' Party)
RSDRP(b)	Rossijskaja socialdemokraticheskaja rabochaja partija (bol'shevikov) (Russian Social-Democratic Workers' Party [Bolshevik])
RSFSR	Rossijskaja Sovetskaja Federativnaja Socialisticheskaja Respublika (Russian Soviet Federative Socialist Republic)
SALT	Strategic Arms Limitation Treaty
SBZ	Sowjetische Besatzungszone (Soviet Occupation Zone)
SCP	Swiss Communist Party
SED	Sozialistische Einheitspartei Deutschlands (Socialist Unity Party of Germany)
SEV	Sovet ekonomicheskoj vzaimopomoshchi (Council for Mutual Economic Assistance). Cf. Comecon.
Sfio	Section francaise de l'Internationale ouvriere (French Section of the Workers' International)
SKDL	Suomen Kansan demokraattinen liitto (Finnish People's Democratic League)
SNK-Sovnarkom	Sovet narodnych komissarov (Council of Peoples Commissars)
SPD	Sozial-Demokratische Partei Deutschlands (Social Democratic Party of Germany)
START	Strategic Armaments Reduction Treaty
Stasi	Ministerium fuer Staatsicherheit (Ministry for State Security); Secret Police of East Germany
SUP	Socialist Unity Party
SVAG	Sovetskaja voennaja administracija v Germanii (Soviet Military Administration in Germany)
TKP	Turkiye komunist partisi (Communist Party of Turkey)
UAR	United Arab Republic
UCYu	Union of Communists of Yugoslavia
UPWP	United Polish Workers Party
USPD	Unabhängige Sozial-Demokratische Partei Deutschlands (Independent Social Democratic Party of Germany)
USPG	United Socialist Party of Germany
VChK	Vserossijskaja chrezvychajnaja komissija po bor'be s kontrrevoljuciej i sabotazhem (Special All-Russian Commission for the Struggle against the Counterrevolution and Sabotage). Cf. Cheka
VKP(b)	Vsesojuznaja kommunisticheskaja partija (bol'shevikov) (Communist Party of the Union [Bolshevik])
VLKSM	Vsesojuznyj leninskij kommunisticheskij sojuz molodezhi (USSR Communist-Leninist Youth Union)
VRT	Hungarian Workers' Party
WFTU	World Federation of Trade Unions
YSP	Yemen Socialist Party
Zhenotdel	Otdel po rabote sredi zhenshchin pri komite-tach VKP(b) (Section for Work among Women at the VKP(b)'s Committees)

A Dictionary of 20th-Century Communism

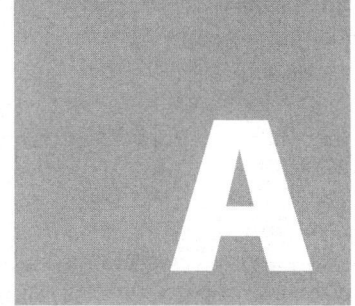

A

Afghan War

On December 27, 1979, at dawn the Soviet armed forces invaded Afghanistan, starting a war of attrition that was to last almost ten years. The Afghan fighters, known since the 18th century for the tenacity with which they had fought first the czarist empire and, in the following century, the British Empire, strenuously fought against the invader with the support of Pakistan and the United States, which welcomed the opportunity to take an active role in the matter.

Until Stalin's death, Afghanistan had been outside the circuits of major international politics. With Khrushchev's rise to power, a new approach to foreign policy toward developing countries took shape, and the Kremlin began to engage in third world aid and assistance initiatives, soon to be joined by the United States. In the 1960s, the Americans did not seem interested in Kabul's fate, while Soviet interest grew: Afghanistan, a rival of Pakistan's for the control of the region's Pashtun majority (and an ally of the United States), was from a diplomatic point of view a convenient bridgehead toward India, another rival of Pakistan over Kashmir. In the Soviet empire's view of the balance of power, Afghanistan represented an important cushion on its southern border. Soviet influence was called into question, however, when in 1963 the Afghan royal family removed Prime Minister Mohammed Daoud Khan, a cousin of the king, for his excessive friendliness toward Moscow. This affront led Moscow to support the establishment of the People's Democratic Party of Afghanistan, founded by Mohammad Taraki in 1965, which immediately split into two internal factions: the more moderate Parcham tendency, and the more Marxist Khalq tendency. Daoud returned to power in a coup d'etat that transformed the monarchy into a republic in 1973. Yet even after these develop-

ments, the Soviets did not manage to regain the terrain they had lost. On the contrary, persuaded in no small measure by significant financial aid from Iran, which was doing Washington's bidding, Daoud started leaning more heavily toward the United States. In April 1978 Daoud was assassinated, and Taraki, Babrak Karmal, and Hafizullah Amin swept into power in the name of the People's Democratic Party of Afghanistan.

The Soviets were extraneous to what became known as the "Great April Revolution" and its obvious Communist orientation, but they were late in trying to take advantage of the situation and soon found themselves boxed into a corner. The radical reforms that Taraki and Amin intended to undertake provoked revolts not only in the population but also in the military, and the Soviet attempt to control the situation by using Babrak Karmal, the most moderate of the three, failed miserably when the attempted coup d'etat he had planned was discovered and he was forced into exile. Beginning in March 1979, incapable of controlling the events, Taraki and Amin began insistently asking for Soviet military assistance. The situation worsened drastically in the following months because of regional instability that followed the shah of Iran's removal in 1979 and the ensuing proclamation of the Islamic Republic of Iran by Ruhollah Khomeini in April. Chaos finally overtook Afghanistan when, in circumstances that are still not entirely clear, Taraki died during a mysterious clash with Amin, who for months the Soviets had suspected was a U.S. spy. The Soviet leadership hesitated a long time before engaging in military operations: their consequences, especially at the international level, were carefully examined. Ultimately the leadership's decision to intervene in Afghanistan in December 1979 was based not on detailed expansionist plans but rather on the fear of another diplomatic failure in an area considered of vital importance. According to Soviet global defense strategy, its "security zone" included Finland and Afghanistan as well as the countries of Eastern Europe, Mongolia, and Korea.

In this regard Afghanistan occupied an atypical position. It was not part of the first of the three sets of countries that had originally constituted the Soviet security zone, the countries occupied by the Red Army at the end of World War II. It did not share the experience of countries like Yugoslavia, China, Vietnam, Chile, Cuba, Somalia, Ethiopia, Angola, and Nicaragua—nations that had autonomously created Marxist-Leninist regimes that, at least initially, were in accord with the Kremlin's evaluations and desires. Afghanistan did not fit the more extensive military, political, or economic interpretation of the Soviet bloc that had come to be accepted from the 1960s on. Yet in the eyes of the Soviet leadership, it was necessary to add Afghanistan and Finland to these two groups of countries: in an altogether different interpretation, they were also part of Moscow's sphere of influence due to their geographic proximity to the USSR's borders. Leonid Brezhnev was the first leader who, in 1966, compared the cases of Afghanistan and Finland, two countries in which "good neighbor" policies were yielding excellent results. This bloc's special characteristics led Moscow to carefully consider a broad spectrum of strategies to maintain its stability. At first, the goal with Afghanistan and Finland, however, was not to intervene with the same measures that were regarded as options in the other two sets of countries: supplying weapons, sending political or military instructors, or sending in the Red Army. The "Finlandization" of Afghanistan remained a valid option until the civil war opened up unknown scenarios in the central Asian region and simultaneously revealed the failure of the USSR's third world policies. The innovative instruments of international policy that the USSR had adopted for twenty years had proven ineffective, and the Soviets still considered the Red Army thirty-five years after the end of the war the best weapon in their foreign policy arsenal. Since the integrity of the Soviet bloc, even in its most peripheral or least typical areas, could not be put into question without risking a diminution of its superpower status, the choice to invade was not easy, but ultimately inevitable.

Once the invasion began, President Amin was assassinated. He was replaced with Babrak Karmal, up to that point an exile in Czechoslovakia, who would stay in power until May 4, 1986. But the attack provoked a negative reaction from the Islamic populations of the Caucasus and central Asia which had been looking hopefully at events in Iran for some time. This is how Iran and Pakistan became the logistical bases for supplying and training the Afghan mujahideen, foot soldiers of faith who took up arms against the Soviets and quickly grew to ninety thousand men. Pakistan immediately obtained unconditional support from the United States, which was anxious to see Moscow bogged down in its own Vietnam. Once the Red Army had occupied the country's principal centers, it moved toward the Khyber Pass and the other passes that connected Afghanistan to Peshawar and Rawalpindi, where Pakistan had helped the mujahideen establish logistical bases. Still, the goal of blocking the frontier failed because many Soviet soldiers were Muslim and refused to engage an enemy of the same faith. In order to subdue the rebels, the Soviets unleashed a chemical war whose targets included the population supporting the mujahideen: they used toxic gases, nerve gases, mycotoxins, and "yellow rain." But nothing stopped the Afghan resistance, and the war soon became a long drawn out bloodletting for the Soviet forces.

In 1983 Yuri Andropov, aware of the high economic costs of the war, made the first move to reach a peace agreement and simultaneously divide the enemy front, composed of seven political parties ranging from traditionalist to fundamentalist, by offering an armistice to the forces of Ahmed Shah Massoud, the most able and famous of the mujahideen leaders. The United States, since it wanted to take advantage of the predicament the Soviets found themselves in, had reservations about seriously engaging in the peace process, and the other combatant groups' pressure on Massoud led to the plan's failure. During the next two years the Soviets went from defeat to defeat, with little help from the local government, so the occupiers substituted Karmal with Mohammed Najibullah. In the course of these years the Soviet invasion was transformed into a war of "resistance" focused, to the greatest extent possible, on avoiding losses to an enemy—the mujahideen—that was always on the attack and controlled 80 percent of the territory.

The losses, the enormously high costs of the war, and the discontent among the population—fanned by demonstrations of the mothers of young Soviet soldiers who had died in Afghanistan—led Mikhail Gorbachev to try to disengage immediately after he came to power. This was not only the result of the politics of containment, the military pressure and deterrence the Americans had adopted, or the new leader's reformist course. The invasion had been one of the last gasps of the dying Stalinist old guard; the beginning of withdrawal marked the emergence of a new generation of politicians, aware that for decades the rapid industrialization and urbanization of the USSR had led to epochal economic and social changes, which Brezhnev had intentionally ignored, and whose culmination was perestroika. Low-key disengagement began in 1986, but the peace negotiations held by the United States, Pakistan, the Soviet Union, and Afghanistan, with UN mediation, were long and complex. Neither the United States nor the USSR collaborated with the United Nations in establishing a coalition regime for the postwar period: this facilitated the emergence of fundamentalist forces in a society that had traditionally been hostile to religious fundamentalism. The negotiations concluded with the Geneva Accords signed on April 14, 1988. On February 15, 1989, the last Russian soldier closed the door to a Tupolev military plane ready to take off from the Kabul airport.

The costs of the war were extremely high: at least five hundred thousand dead among the rebels, more than thirteen thousand dead and thirty-five thousand wounded on the Soviet side, countless amputees and other wounded among the civilian population, and four million inhabitants (out of a total of nine million) who were forced to leave their lands and settle in Pakistan or Iran.

See also Borders; Cold War; Islam; Nations and Empire in the USSR; Power Politics; Second Cold War; Socialist Camp; Soviet Bloc.

FURTHER READING

Bleaney, H., and M. A. Gallego. *Afghanistan: A Bibliography.* Leiden: Brill, 2006.

Cordovez, D., and H. Selig. *Out of Afghanistan: The Inside Story of the Soviet Withdrawal.* New York: Oxford University Press, 1995.

Dundovich, E. *Dalla Finlandia all'Afghanistan. L'URSS in Afghanistan: la lunga storia di David e Golia.* Florence: Centro Stampa 2P, 2000.

Kakar, H. *Afghanistan: The Soviet Invasion and the Afghan Response, 1979–1982.* Berkeley: University of California Press, 1995.

Magnus, R. H. *Afghanistan: Mullah, Marx, and Mujahid.* Boulder, CO: Westview, 1998.

O'Ballance, E. *Afghan Wars, 1839–1992: What Britain Gave Up and the Soviet Union Lost.* New York: Brassey's, 1993.

ELENA DUNDOVICH

Agrarian Question

Debates on the commune and the agrarian question were expressions of what, starting in the 1840s, the Russian intelligentsia thought about the peculiarities of its own country as compared to Europe (England especially), on both the cultural and economic level; they were also, secondarily, debates about the peasant question. After the failure of the first "going to the people" movement in the 1870s, a new generation of economists and intellectuals, mostly based in Moscow, pointed to the agrarian question's solution not so much in terms of inciting the peasants to revolution and expropriating the lands of the aristocracy but rather supporting generalized but especially technical and professional education for the entire rural population. The number of statistical surveys on the quality of life, economic organization, demographic dynamics, and so on, in the countryside mushroomed. Most of these studies reflected the statisticians' socialist and radical ideologies, and seemed to confirm the importance of the agrarian question: the amount of land given to the peasants, in terms of both quantity and quality, together with the taxes and debts they had incurred to redeem the land, prevented any form of investment and economic growth. The peasants' living conditions even seemed comparatively worse than during serfdom. These conclusions were not particularly appreciated by the reformist nobles who headed the zemstvo (the form of local government instituted during the liberal reforms in imperial Russia). The conflicts with radical statisticians multiplied from the mid-1880s to the revolution of 1905.

At least during the 1890s, the difference between populists and Marxists (who both shared a Marxist background) centered on what was to be done after the aristocracy's and state's land had been expropriated. The Marxists favored the development of small-scale peasant agriculture, so as to start a class-differentiation process, analogous to the one that had occurred in England; the populists instead insisted on the need to preserve the peasant commune and thus avoid the peasants' proletarianization. The parameters of the debate were changed when Struve and Bulgakov devised the first forms of Russian revisionist Marxism (predating their German equivalents). Some Marxists also began to highlight both the commune's positive effect overall and the peasants' professional education as solutions to the agrarian question. This led to the birth of the *Ovsobozhdenie* (liberation) movement, which united a good portion of the reformist intelligentsia (liberal, Marxist, and populist) in the 1900–1905 period, with the sole exception of the Marxists who defined themselves as "orthodox" (Vladimir Lenin, Georgy Plekhanov, and Julius Martov), in opposition to the revisionists. Given their different backgrounds, however, it is not surprising that the movement fell apart precisely on the agrarian question. All sorts of solutions were advanced, including expropriation (in different versions), redemption, and agrarian innovation, but no clear-cut position emerged. The movement broke up after the revolution of 1905.

These same divisions reoccurred between 1905 and 1914, when the Duma (representative assembly) was being established. The Social Democrats supported an expropriation of state and aristocratic lands in favor of the peasants, even though Lenin's positions moved further away from Martov's (the future leader of the Menshevik wing) after 1905, and did so precisely on the issue of what to do after expropriation. Martov held to the orthodox social democratic stance of the privatization of peasant lands in order to favor capitalism's development in Russia, whereas Lenin began to take an interest in the revolutionary potential of the peasant commune.

The conservative parties were instead in favor of a strictly technical solution to the problem: peasant agriculture needed to be rationalized, and to this end it was necessary to privatize the peasant commune and consolidate all the scattered landholdings that belonged to the same family. This position was the foundation of Peter Stolypin's reforms, which between 1906 and 1914 (the assassination of Stolypin himself in 1911 notwithstanding) massively restructured the communes. Between these positions—the ultraliberal, on the one hand, and the socialist and revolutionary, on the other—the "Liberal" Party, otherwise known as the Cadet Party, was uncertain which side to take. The choice of a more radical orientation led a whole new generation of agrarian specialists (Chayanov, Bruckus, and Chelincev) to distance themselves from the Cadet Party. They often held socialist, but not Marxist, beliefs, were in favor of transferring

aristocratic lands to the peasants, critical of Stolypin's reforms, and nonetheless underscored the need to improve the rational organization of peasants' enterprises. On the eve of World War I, the Russian intelligentsia appeared to be irredeemably divided on the agrarian question, with those favoring technical progress at odds with those supporting expropriation.

Recent studies question the traditional historiographical thesis according to which the period between 1861 and 1914 witnessed the progressive impoverishment of the mass of Russian peasants. According to these studies the traditional approach was based on statistics compiled by politically committed intellectuals and provided by local organs, which tended to fabricate data so as to confirm the impoverishment thesis. A more detailed analysis reveals how demographic growth must have been a reflection of increased per capita income in the countryside. The constant increase in the number of conscripts and the reduction in the winter mortality rates (which was due to insufficient caloric intake), rather than in the summer rates (due to hygiene), confirm this hypothesis. Other sources of confirmation have come from fiscal analysis, urban and industrial purchases made by peasants, and the massive purchases of state and aristocratic lands by peasants.

Yet this growth also contained the seeds of the crisis: the head of the family had a crucial position in the peasant family, but access to the land, combined with time spent in the city, encouraged a yearning for independence among its younger members. The ancient patriarchal family and the large family units split up, giving rise to smaller agricultural concerns with insufficient land and little capital. This was one of the principal causes of the peasants' difficulties, a growth in productivity notwithstanding. As far as Stolypin's reforms are concerned, recent analyses underscore how one cannot, strictly speaking, talk of privatization. Most of the measures requested and realized by the local agrarian committees consisted of the consolidation of each family's landholdings within the commune's confines. The result was therefore neither privatization nor a traditional commune but an intermediate solution.

World War I broke out in the midst of this fluid situation, interrupting such consolidations. In spring 1917 and especially 1918, this led to protests by young peasants returning from the war who also wanted to enjoy independence from the heads of the family. The elites' position remained ambiguous. Most of the agrarian specialists tied to the cooperatives, independent socialists, liberals, Marxists, and some Social Revolutionaries founded the League for Agrarian Reform in the spring of 1917. The league's program demanded first and foremost a coordinated redistribution of state and aristocratic lands to the peasants, but redistribution was supposed to be accompanied by the restructuring of properties (the consolidation of landholdings) and above all the introduction of new agrarian methods. This position was disputed by the Bolsheviks and Social Revolutionaries. The latter insisted on a generalized expropriation of all state and aristocratic lands, and their socialization in the context of the traditional commune. The former, and especially Lenin, rapidly changed their earlier position, gradually adopting the Social Revolutionaries' stance. This stance was spontaneously put into action by the peasants between October 1917 and March 1918, and was approved after the fact by the Bolsheviks.

Despite protests by Chayanov and the other non-Bolshevik agrarian experts, these decisions were initially not accompanied by any additional measures in the area of agrarian policy. Lenin and the Bolsheviks only recognized the necessity of additional measures in the course of the civil war (with serious hesitations) and to an even greater extent during the 1920s, when the agrarian question became synonymous with low productivity tied to the small size of family holdings within the commune's framework. At the time, the solution was thought to be an increase in the average size of the agricultural concerns. The means to achieve this goal was first thought to be (by Nikolay Bukharin and Lenin in his last period) the establishment of cooperatives, but later (by the dominant wing in the Bolshevik Party from 1927 on) collectivization. The latter became the solution to the atavistic agrarian question, which although presented in an economic context (how to develop an efficient agricultural system capable of supporting industrial production) was in reality mostly political (how to eliminate peasant resistance and the danger of a green counterrevolution).

See also Bolshevism; Collectivization of the Countryside; Legal Marxism; New Economic Policy; Peasants in the USSR.

FURTHER READING

Bartlett R. P., ed. *Land Commune and Peasant Community in Russia*. London: Macmillan, 1991.

Danilov V. P. *Rural Russia under the New Regime*. Bloomington: Indiana University Press, 1988.

Pallot J. *Land Reforms in Russia, 1906–1917*. Oxford: Clarendon, 1999.

Robinson G. T. *Rural Russia under the Old Regime*. New York: Longman, 1932.

Stanziani A. *L'économie en révolution: le cas russe, 1870–1930*. Paris: Albin Michel, 1998.

Volin L. *A Century of Russian Agriculture*. Cambridge, MA: Harvard University Press, 1970.

ALESSANDRO STANZIANI

Amendola, Giorgio

Giorgio Amendola (1907–80) can be regarded as an emblematic figure in Palmiro Togliatti's "new party": he embodied some of the Italian Communist Party's most distinctive characteristics and some of its greatest contradictions. The main representative of the party's "right wing," sensitive to issues of alliances and government, he favored dialogue and exchanges with social democracy, and consistently opposed a break with the Soviet Union. Culturally and politically he had been influenced by the thought of Antonio Gramsci and Togliatti; he favored a historicist reinterpretation of Marxism, recognizing its ties to Antonio Labriola and Benedetto Croce.

His perspective was informed by an awareness of the limits to Italy's process of unification and the fragility of the Italian bourgeoisie. These had contributed to the establishment of fascism, and their influence was particularly evident in the straitened circumstances of the internal market, and the economic, social, and civic backwardness of the South (which in turn had a negative impact on national unification and the strength of the bourgeoisie). This view led to his belief in a "national function" of the working class, which in his opinion should have helped complete the business that the ruling classes of the Risorgimento (a historical period and movement in the 19th century that led to the national unification of Italy) had left unfinished. In this interpretation it was precisely the failures of these ruling classes, as evidenced by the advent of fascism, that made the task of integrating the masses into the state a revolutionary one. According to Amendola, only the Communist Party was up to this task, and by following its own "national path," this course of action would eventually lead to a socialist society.

Amendola was born to Giovanni and Eva Kühn in Rome in 1907. His father, a liberal with democratic inclinations, was a leader of the constitutional opposition to Benito Mussolini and the "Aventine secession" (the withdrawal of the Italian Socialist Party from the Chamber of Deputies after the assassination of Giacomo Matteotti) and died in exile in 1926 of the aftereffects of an assault by a Fascist action squad. Amendola joined the Italian Communist Party (Pci) in 1929 and was arrested in 1932, sent to forced residence in Ponza until 1937, and then exiled to France. He returned to Italy in 1943 and was a member of the reconstituted Roman "center" of the party, which he also represented in the National Liberation Committee. After Togliatti's return to Italy, Amendola was one of the most enthusiastic supporters of the "Salerno Turn" (*svolta di Salerno*, a change of course in Pci policy); he then transferred to the occupied North, where he was an organizer of the April 1945 insurrection. After the liberation he was undersecretary to the prime minister in both the Ferruccio Parri government and the first Alcide de Gasperi government, and a member of the Pci's national party leadership.

Between 1947 and 1954 he was one of the protagonists in the construction and consolidation of the new party in the South, helping to organize a broad coalition of political, social, and intellectual forces around the agrarian struggles of the time. Partly because of these efforts, his policies represented a counterweight to the class-based activities of Pietro Secchia on the Central Organizing Commission, thus helping to push the Christian Democratic Party (DC) in a reformist direction: these developments allowed the Pci to double its vote in the South during the elections of 1953. After Stalin's death, Togliatti made him one of the protagonists of the "reconquest" of the party; Amendola helped him by once again promoting the Salerno Turn line, and Togliatti placed him at the head of the Central Organizing Commission, replacing Secchia. From this position Amendola started a process of radical renewal of the party's leadership, which culminated at the party's Eighth Congress at the end of 1956. His trusting support of the de-Stalinization process started by Khrushchev led to his first disagreements with Togliatti (who did not share an approach based on the condemnation of the "cult of personality"); but they still agreed on the fundamental objective of the Pci's renewal. Amendola pursued this objective under the guise of fighting sectarianism and by pushing for the "generation of the Eighth Congress" to establish itself in leadership positions. This group's antifascism had fundamentally Italian roots, and it would constitute the backbone of the Pci's leadership until the 1980s.

In the 1960s, Amendola contributed to the creation of a platform based on the notion of "democratic planning" aimed at enlarging the domestic market and achieving structural reforms, which the Pci hoped would appeal to the experimental center-left coalition. In 1965, after Togliatti's death, in the pages of the newspaper *Rinascita*, Amendola made his famous proposal for reunification with the Socialist Party of Italy (Psi), in which he admitted the dual defeat of communism and social democracy in the West. Notwithstanding the foreseeable failure of the proposal, during the Eleventh Congress (1966), he played a major role in the party's internal majority center-right faction, which gathered around Secretary Luigi Longo. Amendola placed his own interpretation of events against Pietro Ingrao's analysis of "neo-capitalism" (which emphasized the risks that an integration of the working class into the capitalist system posed): he repeated his skepticism about the Italian bourgeoisie's ability to lead the country's modernization process.

After having been nominated to the position of Enrico Berlinguer's assistant secretary (1969), Amendola repeatedly distanced himself from Berlinguer by once again emphasizing the need for dialogue with the other parties, with the goal of forming a new majority that would include the Pci, and he criticized the relative "opening" to the 1968 movement by the Pci. Simultaneously, he repeatedly defended the Soviet Union from criticisms within the leadership group, underscoring its decisive role as a pillar of the international order and a protagonist in the process of détente. Amendola was not much persuaded by Berlinguer's strategy of the "historic compromise" (*compromesso storico*, a policy based on compromises with existing parliamentary forces aimed at allowing the Pci to participate in the government), which he interpreted as an attempt to attenuate differences with the DC, or by Eurocommunism, to which he preferred the path of closer relationships with European social democracies. In the 1970s he devoted himself increasingly to European questions, thus contributing to the Pci's "European" outlook, which was to become one of its distinctive characteristics; he would later become the president of the Communist group at the European Parliament in Strasbourg. He endorsed the reasons for ending the national solidarity experience (an emergency alliance of the parliamentary opposition and majority meant to aid in the fight against domestic terrorism), and in 1980 opposed the Pci's condemnation of the Soviet intervention in Afghanistan. Amendola died in Rome on June 5 of the same year.

See also Antifascism; Eurocommunism; European Integration; National Roads to Socialism; Togliatti, Palmiro.

FURTHER READING

Cerchia, G. *Giorgio Amendola. Un comunista nazionale. Dall'infanzia alla guerra partigiana, 1907–1945.* Soveria Mannelli: Rubbettino, 2004.

Gualtieri, R. "Giorgio Amendola dirigente del PCI." *Passato e presente* 67 (2006): 27–41.

Matteoli, G., ed. *Giorgio Amendola, comunista riformista.* Soveria Mannelli: Rubbettino, 2001.

ROBERTO GUALTIERI

Americanism

Marxists have always reserved a special, if small, place in their historical imagination for the United States, for two good reasons. As a society devoid of feudal and premodern traditions, the United States, more than others, represented the transformative powers of capitalism and seemed to embody capitalism's future in the purest form. As a site of advanced technological and organizational experiments as the 20th century progressed, the United States also constituted the principal measure of modernization—of every project aimed at growth and the rationalization of production, including the Soviet one. It is for this reason that a Communist, and more generally a European Marxist, Americanism has existed. It shared several features with the Americanism of many non-Marxist European observers, especially the choice of the United States as a metaphor for capitalism and the future, as a space in which to see one's prophecies confirmed or denied, instead of as a place of real historical transformations that could be analyzed and interpreted.

Lenin and the Bolsheviks saw a threat to their socialist prophecy in the U.S. social model: the triumph of a fully bourgeois civilization, with democratic freedoms and greater material prosperity, could attract significant sectors of the working class (the "worker aristocracy") to adopt its values and customs, thus affecting socialism's "necessary" appeal. In Russia, however, where leaders were occupied with the requirements of building socialism, a different perspective on the United States emerged. In the 1920s the United States was a financial power that represented the "center of world imperialism," and therefore the enemy, but it also shined as the

site of the most advanced capitalist modernity and the culturally modernist nation par excellence.

On a theoretical level, this led a Communist intellectual like Antonio Gramsci to innovative reflections on the sociocultural characteristics of Americanism and the problems of cultural hegemony in modern society. In the Soviet context of building socialism—and most particularly of industrialization—the interest in the United States was more immediately pragmatic. As Trotsky would say (and other Soviet leaders, including Stalin, would echo): "American technology joined with the Soviet organization of society will produce communism." U.S. pragmatism and technical efficiency attracted the interest of a regime that desperately wanted to develop large-scale industrialization quickly, starting from almost nothing, with a workforce of peasant origin. So in the 1920s Soviet leaders looked to the rationalization and productive standardization procedures that were Fordism's distinctive features, with great interest. The Soviets not only imitated these procedures but in several cases also imported them directly to the USSR. Soviet leaders and technicians saw Fordism, from their productivist perspective, as pure engineering rationality organized from above, a useful tool in the context of central planning, while they obviously ignored the consumerist expansion of the market that was also an intrinsic component of the model. Soviet leaders therefore understood U.S. capitalism imperfectly: for them it represented a political enemy, a social antithesis, and an example of technical and modernist development to emulate.

This process of technical and organizational imitation peaked between 1928 and 1932, in the context of the First Five-Year Plan, when the Soviets commissioned U.S. businesses, Ford among them, to design some of the largest and most emblematic industrial construction projects (the large tractor factories, the steelworks at Magnitogorsk, and the auto plants), and got U.S. engineers and technicians to oversee their completion. At that juncture, when for some years the United States was the leading exporter to the USSR, the only limit to this imitative process seemed to be the Soviet lack of foreign currency, which became significant as the economic depression in the West deepened.

In the 1930s the successes of Soviet industrialization, especially when compared to the economic stagnation in the West, increased Soviet national-Communist engineering pride and diminished the fascination with U.S. technology. The United States, however, still remained the main yardstick with which to measure and exalt the advances of the Soviet economy. The same phenomenon would occur a generation later, in the competitive context of the Cold War, when Khrushchev explicitly (and as it would turn out, unsuccessfully) committed the USSR to reaching and overtaking the U.S. economic standard of well-being in the following twenty years.

Soviet Americanism did not influence only technical and productive areas. A powerful, almost superstitious idealization of U.S. prosperity was at work in the Russian population, partly as a result of hearsay from the great emigration that had occurred at the beginning of the century. In urban areas, moreover, the products of the new mass culture taking hold across the Atlantic were beginning to circulate widely: U.S. films constituted almost half of the Soviet market between 1923 and 1928, and in slightly more exclusive circles the rhythms of jazz and the foxtrot were all the rage. Futurist artists and intellectuals were greatly attracted to the urban and "machinist" energy emanating from U.S. metropolises, and they often associated the Soviet effort to construct a new society with the modernist vigor with which the United States was transcending tradition. This collective fascination went hand in hand with a growing criticism of the United States as a place not only of exploitation and racism but also of cultural leveling and materialist individualism. Toward the end of the decade this criticism—which echoed some criticisms from conservative European elites—became intellectually dominant and, above all, part of an official campaign by the Soviet regime against the decadent corruption of U.S. cultural events, which were rapidly removed from the scene. From that point on, up until the collapse of the USSR, attraction to the United States was reduced to a limited and basically clandestine phenomenon. The official image of the United States was that of a political adversary, and with the onset of the Cold War, a fundamental and irreducible opponent.

Communists in Europe, particularly in Italy, had a brief Americanist period in the 1940s. Within the political framework of the anti-Nazi alliance—which elevated the United States to the role of not only an indispensable strategic partner but also a democracy that was experimenting with socially progressive solutions during the New Deal—one could legitimately look at the country with renewed cultural interest. Intellectuals close to the Italian Communist Party promoted a rediscovery of U.S. culture, particularly literature, and this phenomenon in turn contributed to the explosion of the postwar collective myth of America in an Italy (and Europe) in which the United States was by now a daily and far-reaching presence. Fed once again by curiosity about a democratic mass culture that combined prosperity, innovation, and individual freedom, this attraction did not last long in Communist circles. The rise of bipolar antagonism trickled down from politics to all other aspects of Communist culture, and from 1947 onward the United States became the emblem of the highest form of imperialism to be fought everywhere.

The increasingly difficult and ultimately insoluble problem for Western Communists became how to reconcile an ideological and strategic antagonism toward the United States with the influence and popular consumption of U.S. mass culture on their socioelectoral base, and the anthropological changes it was producing. Those same popular classes, especially the working classes, that supported the Communist parties in France and Italy were both deep believers in the USSR and avid consumers of U.S. mass culture products. If their identities as producers tied them to Communist political and labor unions, their transformation into consumers accelerated their assimilation to the cultural norms and styles of the affluent society. During the Cold War these tensions remained open and unresolved, but starting roughly in the mid-1960s, the decline of Communist culture and complementary triumph of consumer individualism became unstoppable.

See also Anti-Americanism; Antifascism; Cold War; Gramsci, Antonio; Marshall Plan; Modernization; Planning.

FURTHER READING

Ball, A. M. *Imagining America: Influence and Images in Twentieth-Century Russia.* Lanham, MD: Rowman and Littlefield, 2003.

D'Attorre, P. P., ed. *Nemici per la pelle: sogno americano e mito sovietico nell'Italia contemporanea.* Milan: Angeli, 1991.

Gramsci A. "Notes on Americanism and Fordism." In *Notes on Macchiavelli: Prison Notebooks.* New York: Columbia University Press, 1992.

Gundle, S. *Between Hollywood and Moscow: The Italian Communists and the Challenge of Mass Culture, 1943–1991.* Durham, NC: Duke University Press, 2000.

FEDERICO ROMERO

Andropov, Yuri

Yuri Vladimirovich Andropov was born on June 15, 1914, at Nagutskaia Station, Stavropol region. His father was a railroad worker and his mother taught music. Both parents died early, leaving Yuri an orphan at the age of thirteen. Andropov finished seven years of school in Mozdok. As a teenager he worked as a loader, a telegraph clerk, and a sailor for the Volga steamship line and from 1932 to 1936 studied at the technical school of water transportation in Rybinsk, Yaroslavl district. After graduation he worked as secretary of the Young Communist (VLKSM) organization at this school, and then at the Rybinsk shipyards.

The void in the Soviet nomenklatura created by the Great Purge opened the doors to a political career for Andropov. In 1937 he became secretary, and in 1938 first secretary, of the Yaroslavl Regional Committee of the VLKSM. In 1939 he joined the Communist Party. In 1940, after the Soviet-Finnish war, Stalin organized the newly annexed Finnish territories as the Karelia-Finnish Republic. Andropov became the first secretary of the Central Committee of VLKSM of this republic. After Germany attacked, the Finns reoccupied these territories as well as parts of Soviet Karelia; Andropov coordinated guerilla movement in Karelia. In 1944 he was transferred to the party committee of Petrozavodsk and in 1947 became the second secretary of this committee. In 1944–51 he took classes at the Petrozavodsk state university, and then at the Supreme Party School of the CC CPSU in Moscow.

During the final years of his "Karelian period," Andropov escaped the dragnet of the Leningrad Affair, the purge that cost the lives and careers of hundreds of party and state officials in the region. At the same time he became a protégé of the party leader of the Karelia-Finnish Republic, O. Kuusinen, a relic of the Comintern cadres who combined a sophisticated Marxist education with an internationalist background. Under his tutelage, Andropov became interested in Marxist theory and developed extensive contacts on the more "intellectual" flank of the party elite. He grew to like music, theater, and art; he composed verses. Gorbachev remembers him as "a brilliant and large personality, generously endowed with gifts by nature, and a true intellectual."

Education helped his career: from 1951 to 1953 Andropov worked for the CC CPSU apparatus; from 1953 to 1957 he worked at the Ministry of Foreign Affairs, first as a head of the Fourth European division (which dealt with Poland and Czechoslovakia), and then, from 1954 to 1957 as ambassador to Hungary. Andropov took an extremely hard line against the Hungarian revolution in October–November 1956. The Soviet embassy was under siege; many Hungarian communists beseeched armed assistance; Andropov's wife suffered a breakdown, and his own health deteriorated and was compromised ever after. His cables and memoranda to Moscow persuaded the wavering politburo (presidium) that "counterrevolution" and "Fascist revolt" in Hungary must be crushed by armed force. Andropov developed "Hungarian syndrome," a fear of spontaneous radical violence, that later shaped his highly negative attitude toward cultural liberalization, Soviet dissidents, and Western campaigns for "human rights."

From 1957 to 1967 Andropov headed the CC CPSU's department for liaisons with the Communist and workers' parties of the Soviet bloc countries. He also became member of the Central Committee (1961) and CC secretary (1962). He organized the first group of CC CPSU "consultants," which consisted of journalists and scholars who supported de-Stalinization and the concept of communism "with human face." Andropov supported détente with West Germany and coordinated the ideological and propaganda struggle against Maoism in China after the Sino-Soviet split. In 1968 Andropov took a hard line against the "Prague Spring" and was one of those who persuaded Brezhnev that there was no alternative to a Soviet military invasion.

In 1967 Andropov became chairman of the KGB, and he remained in that post until 1982. During his tenure, KGB methods were "refined." Dissent was severely repressed, and dissidents frequently confined to psychiatric hospitals. Andropov became a politburo member in 1973. From 1970 to 1974 he was a co-architect of Brezhnev's policy of simultaneous détente with the West and suppression of dissident movements in the USSR. He supported Jewish emigration as a means of letting off the steam of discontent. While he personally realized that reforms were inevitable, at the politburo he cleaved to the hard line, fearing that any liberalization might doom his political ascendancy. During the last years of Brezhnev, Andropov was a leading member of the ruling "troika" (with A. Gromyko and D. Ustinov). He supported Soviet military and political expansion in the third world and drew dark scenarios of strategic Sino-American plots against the USSR.

In December 1979 his reports to Brezhnev contributed decisively to the decision to intervene in Afghanistan.

From 1980 to 1982 Andropov was increasingly disconcerted by the demise of détente, the deadlock in Afghanistan, the endemic instability in Eastern Europe, and above all by the corruption and stagnation in the Soviet economy and political system. He opposed plans to occupy Poland after the emergence of the Solidarity movement and promoted younger, reform-minded, and noncorrupt party cadres, including M. Gorbachev, Y. Ligachev, and N. Ryzhkov.

After Brezhnev's death in November 1982, Andropov became general secretary of the party. He immediately initiated an anti-corruption campaign and persecuted and arrested many of Brezhnev's cronies. At the same time, he moved to impose strict discipline on all state employees and on state industries. Andropov's tactic in foreign affairs was to use the peace movement and KGB contacts to dissuade Western Europeans from accepting U.S. cruise missiles and Pershings. In September 1983 a Soviet fighter accidentally shot down a Korean airliner, killing all aboard; Andropov authorized public denial of this act. By the end of that year, U.S. missiles moved to Western Europe, and Andropov publicly denounced the Reagan administration. Many Russians and some scholars still debate whether Andropov might have proved a real reformer had he lived longer. But when he assumed power he was already terminally ill. He died on February 9, 1984, of acute kidney failure.

See also Brezhnev, Leonid; Gorbachev, Mikhail; Hungarian Revolution; KGB; Socialist Realism.

FURTHER READING

Arbatov, G. *The System: An Insider's Life in Soviet Politics*. New York: Random House, 1992.
Gorbachev, M. *Memoirs*. New York: Doubleday, 1996.
Medvedev, Z. A. *Andropov*. New York: Penguin, 1984.
Volkogonov, D. *Autopsy of an Empire: The Seven Leaders Who Built the Soviet Regime*. New York: Free Press, 1998.

VLADISLAV M. ZUBOK

Anti-Americanism

The most comprehensive definition of anti-Americanism is a systematic hostility toward the government, culture, history, and people of the United States. As is the case with any such generic category, one almost elevated to the level of ideology, the term reflects a fairly fictitious essentialization of the opposite concept—namely, Americanism, or being American. The dimensions, range, and virulence of anti-American sentiments have therefore often been directly proportional to the definition of Americanism as a set of beliefs. In this sense anti-Americanism is the specular opposite of the claim to superiority, universality, and the subsequent expansion abroad of the experience, politics, and customs of the United States.

There is no universally accepted origin or definition of anti-Americanism. Various theories emphasize jealousy and envy of U.S. success, and thus a feeling based in irrational prejudice or fanaticism. Others concentrate on the elitism of intellectuals that for two centuries have despised the mediocrity of U.S. culture without understanding its complexity and emancipatory qualities. Still others, above all on the Left, cite anti-Americanism as a justified opposition—both on the part of intellectuals and on the part of the masses—to certain expansionist, arrogant, and superficial aspects of U.S. power and culture. Almost all agree that in many ways, anti-Americanism also reflects fears within each country. The United States offers a constant point of reference—frequently as a scapegoat—for debates on economic, political, and cultural transformations that are only partially due to U.S. influence. If the United States is perceived as the social model of the future, fear or hostility toward the United States has coincided with a fear of modernization. While in the 19th century this modernity was above all political (the Enlightenment republic founded on individual rights and democracy), in the next century the term came to include the entrepreneurial spirit and a set of social practices (a society devoid of precapitalist traditions, and founded on constant technological innovation, consumption, and mass culture). Both forms of modernization have provoked fear that established social hierarchies and national identities in their respective countries will be lost.

This recognition of the United States as a symbol of modernity has stimulated further reflections on an imaginary that had been constructed since the first European explorations of the American continent had occurred. Fears and delusions arose almost naturally from the hopes and expectations that the new land had evoked. The metaphor of America as a tabula rasa where Europeans might reinvent themselves and become, as individuals, masters of their own destiny was easily redefined as a civic and cultural desert, in which the traditions of the old continent were lost in a void. For the entire 19th century anti-Americanism remained an elite phenomenon among Europeans, which in part reflected the tension between European romanticism and the ideas of the Enlightenment that the United States represented. Envy, aristocratic disdain, and an examination of the average American's defects were also clearly visible in the work of such writers as Joseph de Maistre, Charles Baudelaire, Anthony Trollope, and Charles Dickens. From the beginning of the 20th century, when the challenge of U.S. power first materialized for Europe, fears about the star-spangled republic become more widespread. These feelings were remarkable for their variety: anti-Americanism targeted the government in its social or foreign policy, or the nation, its customs, its way of life, and even certain values, especially pragmatism, identified as especially American. Various elements of anti-Americanism rarely coexist in a coherent whole, however. Pro- and anti-American feelings have coexisted in the same group, and even in the same person: an individual can feel resentment toward U.S. policies and admire its culture, or vice versa. Among the different ideologies, communism has exhibited the greatest coherence in combining the various political, sociological, and cultural components of anti-Americanism. But even in this extreme case there were ambiguities, which left room for feelings of fascination, admiration, and even emulation of the United States as the main locus of rationalization as well as modern technological and social experimentation.

Ideology was the foundation of Communist opposition to liberalism and capitalism, best represented by the U.S. experience. The origins of Communist anti-Americanism as a system of thought and strategy should be sought in the contrast between the alternative global solutions that the United States and Bolshevik Russia respectively offered a Europe devastated by World War I: the liberalism and capitalism of President Woodrow Wilson and the revolutionary socialism of Vladimir Lenin. During the Cold War, messianism and proselytism on both sides (later extended to China) permeated this ideological struggle. Elaborating on Karl Marx's theories about the consolidation of monopolies, Lenin argued that state monopoly capitalism was the key to understanding the United States. The U.S. government intervened at the beginning of the 20th century, he argued, not against but rather in alliance with other monopolies in order to preserve the capitalist system. But the global conflict between monopolies was also the principal cause of imperialist conflicts

that would sooner or later cause the collapse of capitalism. From the Soviet point of view, the Marshall Plan in 1947 was necessary for the continued expansion of capitalist monopolies; survival was the essential goal of every U.S. reform, even Lyndon Johnson's welfare-oriented Great Society program. Concessions to the working and peasant classes or ethnic minorities were used above all to prevent their unionization or other more radical choices. This palliative notwithstanding, so the Communist theorists contended, monopolies still managed to influence politics by means of direct participation—especially in the Dwight Eisenhower administration—and by means of "hired goons" from the petty bourgeoisie, like Johnson or Richard Nixon.

Character profiles aided ideological anti-Americanism. Joseph Stalin, for instance, portrayed the United States as a formidable power, but one that was governed by short-sighted Wall Street billionaires—a power that could not combine its economic weight with an equivalent valor on the battlefield. Finally, ideological anti-Americanism was sustained by nationalist sentiments, which in their turn were strengthened by a siege mentality in Russia and a victim's attitude in China. A contradictory mix of emulation and confrontation marked the two nations subject to comparison with the West—a West from which they also desired recognition as equivalent superpowers. At the peak of this emulation, Nikita Khrushchev launched a campaign to "overtake" the United States so that an industrial, technological, and scientific Russia would prevail in industry, technology, science, and prosperity by the end of the 1950s.

The ideological expression of Communist anti-Americanism was an essential corollary for another series of nationalist battles. Since Marxism derived from a mostly European matrix, many Latin American intellectuals, and later the Fidel Castro regime, used it during the Cold War to both assert the emancipation of the subcontinent from U.S. hegemony and better express already-widespread anti-American sentiments. Similarly, in the Middle East, Syria and Egypt were among the non-Communist countries that made common cause with Soviet communism against the United States for nationalist reasons.

While ideological confrontation largely explains Western anti-Sovietism, the reason for the overlap of anti-Americanism and anticapitalism is much less clear. Communist anti-Americanism was fed by many non-Marxist sources, including a European tradition replete with metaphors and stereotypes of the United States as a source of hope that turned bad, a promised land that negated and contradicted its own promises, a country often described as a cultural desert, spiritually empty, mechanized and afflicted by a consumerist, conformist, racist, militarist materialism. Communism above all developed an image of the United States as a variant of modernity bent on reducing the individual to pure mechanism, in a society devoid of both a sense of community and cultural authenticity. Communist intellectuals and leaders in many ways simply amplified what others thought and feared about the United States. At the same time, they looked to the Soviet Union as an alternative model of experimentation and modernization, an alternative to capitalist rationalization, a place in which technology was at the service of humankind, not against it, and the "machine" was a vector of progress, instead of being parasitical and alienating. The Soviet Union harshly criticized the hedonism and corruption of U.S. society, and the childishness of its mass culture. Generally speaking, to identify the United States with a more or less fictitious civilization, created in part by the most exported U.S. industry, Hollywood, was a way to diminish its seriousness and reliability as a world power, and extend criticism of its foreign policy so as to encompass the entire social structure. But within Western European Communist circles anti-Americanism depended on long-standing traditions of criticism that often included polemics used for internal political reasons. For Italian and French Communists, after their brief government experience in the aftermath of World War II and the ensuing glorification of the anti-Nazi front, mounting tensions led to their exclusion, and sparked a struggle against the massive and all-pervasive influence of the United States in Europe. Palmiro Togliatti best exemplified the complex combination of politicocultural motifs in European Communist anti-Americanism when, in an article published in *L'Unità* in May of 1947, he announced a policy of independence not only from the United States as a world power but also "against the tide of coarse stupidity" coming from the United States, a country incapable of guiding the world because it was "devoid of historical preparation and mental acumen." The political element—the defense of sovereignty—therefore went hand in hand with the cultural element—the defense of intelligence. This appeal had strength in the eyes of a Europe that was counting on compensating for its decline as a major power with a proclaimed cultural superiority and hence a greater diplomatic influence. Under the complementary line of reasoning, America's military and economic strength was matched by a corresponding cultural vacuity and superficiality.

By placing themselves in the vanguard of this cultural confrontation, French and Italian Communists managed to enroll many of the most prominent intellectuals. While the Italian Communist Party could boast a Gramscian tradition that already extolled the role of culture, the French Communist Party also defined itself as the *parti de l'intelligence*. Initiatives such as the "Alliance for Culture," promoted by Emilio Sereni in 1948, proposed to defend the natural cultural heritage against the "cosmopolitan" culture of U.S. imperialism. American capitalism was therefore seen as a threat to national initiatives in both the economic and cultural spheres. The major characteristic of this cultural cosmopolitanism, however, was its corrupting and narcotic effect on the masses. According to this view, U.S. mass culture was clearly manipulated, and more specifically it reduced citizens to mere conformist spectators, incapable of genuine social and political participation. In addition to the distinction between culture as "opium" for or "elevation" of the masses, the battle against U.S. civilization also involved the debate about modernism and the related issue of affluence. The economic miracles and the arrival of a consumer society that co-opted even the working classes by the 1960s, placed that subject at the head of the list of threats that U.S. policies represented.

By deciding to fight the risk that affluence (previously identified with Fordism) would also function as an opiate for the working classes, introducing elements of prosperity (consumerism), European Communists insisted that materialism and modernism were not equivalent to a better standard of living or human emancipation, and that consumerism generated an endless growth of desires that could not be satisfied. The Communists also deplored the ethics of success and the "comfort civilization" as essentially asocial and antihuman. In Italy, the glorification of social commitment and a spirit of sacrifice vaguely echoed the Fascist condemnation of the United States as plutocratic, unrealistic, and incapable of "living dangerously." Without any relationship to the "tragic," the United States both refused to confront the difficulties of existence and, basically, engage with history. In this sense material affluence prevented the search for ideals and resulted in the greatest possible forms of oppression. It was a case of "soft despotism," as Jean-Paul Sartre defined it. For the French philosopher, in a pervasive consumerist culture in which every myth of optimism and happiness represented an escape from reality, even dreams were engineered. The result was the greatest possible degree of conformism. As Jean-Marie Domenach observed in 1960, although in the United States the state was liberal, its society was "probably the most totalitarian in the world," a mass of what Alain de Benoist would later call "happy robots," in which rebellion became virtually impossible.

The repeated reference to the United States as a totalitarian and homogenizing society was often a response to the American condemnation of the Soviet Union as a place where totalitarianism had been achieved. With a community only vaguely defined by ethnic roots or a cohesive cultural heritage, U.S. identity had been founded on a set of values and the reiteration of those values. Equating or even unfavorably comparing the United States with oppression in the East (and frequently, with Nazism) was diametrically opposed to the assertion that Americanism was the only path to individual emancipation.

The Cold War provided the circumstances to search for the greatest consensus on the values of liberal-capitalist democracy. U.S. leaders identified challenges to such a view, above all from the Left, as "un-American." American anti-Communist fanaticism, especially immediately following World War II, led many European intellectuals to fully identify with the Communist parties and condemn episodes such as the "lynching" of the Rosenbergs.

The United States fed anti-Americanism in other ways as well. First, it did so in a spontaneous and inadvertent fashion, since in Europe the image of the powerful overseas hegemon crystallized precisely at the moment in which the United States itself offered the greatest possible stereotype of its own society: that of the placid, consumerist, and conformist 1950s. Second, the inspiration for many European Communist intellectuals often came from American authors such as C. Wright Mills, David Riesman, William H. Whyte, and Paul Goodman, and their condemnation of a homogenizing society based on mass consumption and culture.

But the greatest paradox of anti-Americanism in a domestic vein was its development during the 1960s into a culture of dissent that made possible an identification between the U.S. "rebels" and the European Left (European philosophers such as Herbert Marcuse and Jacques Derrida were to provide the main intellectual connections). With the emphasis on existential problems and those of individual emancipation (the student movement, feminism, the rights of homosexuals, and the environment), the U.S. New Left fed the economic

and political dialectics of European Marxism, and established a dialogue between the new generations across the Atlantic. This activism restored a certain intellectual and political respect for aspects of U.S. culture and society that now appeared decidedly pluralist, even if still permeated with hedonism, among many European Communists. This corresponded to a diminution of the Soviet myth after the repression of the Hungarian (1956) and Czech (1968) uprisings. Not even the reaffirmation of an exclusive form of Americanism during the Ronald Reagan years modified the image of a superpower that after the Vietnam War, the economic crisis of the 1970s, and the continuous expression of dissent, took on a more humane, varied, and once more experimental appearance for the European Left. Only in the aftermath of the Cold War, with the eclipse of the Soviet Union, did fears about an arrogant and expansionist America resurface.

The defects of Marxist anti-Americanism soon became obvious. As is the case with any exaggerated form of propaganda, that emanating from the Kremlin left the public rather skeptical, and even attracted it to U.S. culture. The other handicap of this type of propaganda in the Soviet Union and elsewhere was its predication on two contradictory notions. Originally anti-Americanism centered on the idea of a proletariat that would transcend all forms of nationalism as a bourgeois product; but under the pressure of the Cominform in 1947, and in the campaigns for the defense of national traditions (on the part of all Communist parties, in power or not) against U.S. power and mass culture, patriotic impulses prevailed. In the 1970s in particular, the notion of an international proletariat allowed Communist rhetoric to distinguish the government and the governed in the United States, and therefore to depict the American people more as victims of rather than participants in capitalist exploitation. But this added an extra degree of fascination, especially among Western Communists, with rebel America and the political pluralism it reflected.

The gravest error, however, that revealed itself as fatal especially in relation to Communist appeal for the younger generations, was underestimating the influence of mass culture and consumerism. Since both of these developments were identified with the United States, Communists generally made little effort to understand their reach and incorporate them into their modernization project. As Enzo Forcella put it, a Marxist theory about the mass media had never been formulated. A fundamental form of anti-Americanism developed into a dogmatism that condemned the principal means for the diffusion of individualist consumerism, the mass media, a priori, thus permitting their advance.

See also Americanism; Anti-imperialism; Cold War; Messianism; Modernization; Nationalism.

FURTHER READING

Aga-Rossi, E., and G. Quagliarello, eds. *L'altra faccia della luna. I rapporti tra PCI, PCF e Unione Sovietica.* Bologna: Il Mulino, 1977.

D'Attorre, P. P., ed. *Nemici per la pelle: sogno americano e mito sovietico nell'Italia contemporanea.* Milan: Angeli, 1991.

Fehrenbach, H., and U. G. Poiger, eds. *Transactions, Transgressions, Transformations: American Culture in Western Europe and Japan.* New York: Berghahn Books, 1999.

Lipset, S. M. *American Exceptionalism: A Double-Edged Sword.* New York: Norton, 1996.

Roger, P. *L'ennemi américain: généalogie de l'antiaméricanisme français.* Paris: Seuil, 2002.

Ross, A., and K. Ross, eds. *Anti-Americanism.* New York: New York University Press, 2004.

Shiraev, E., and V. Zubok. *Anti-Americanism in Russia: From Stalin to Putin.* New York: Palgrave, 2000.

Zhang Hong. *America Perceived: The Making of Chinese Images of the United States, 1945–1953.* Westport, CT: Greenwood Press, 2002.

ALESSANDRO BROGI

Anticommunism

Does anticommunism constitute a coherent movement, of which the history can be written? Or is it merely a shadowy epiphenomenon of the history of communism, whose story is inseparable from the grander tale of radicalism, from the big bang of the French Revolution to the ideologically conservative present? Most commentators would agree that the story of anticommunism has, after some two hundred years of history (and prehistory), separated itself sufficiently from the history of the extreme Left to merit a separate accounting. But even if this is so, the contours of anticommunism are not easy to define. It has at times appeared as merely a visceral hostility to the far Left, hard to distinguish from the garden-variety conservatism of those with a lot to lose. It has at times been connected to a strong belief in free market econom-

ics. It has occurred within a socialist frame of reference and among those known in the late 1940s as "Cold War liberals." It even bubbled up from beneath the surface of Soviet life. At other times anticommunism took on many of the characteristics of a right-wing movement, obsessed with spies and hostile toward even moderate liberalism. But with the virtual destruction of the radical Left worldwide in the 21st century, a few preliminary observations can be made.

First of all, anticommunism is a bigger and more important story in the United States than elsewhere in the world. This is only partly because the United States dominated the Western side during the Cold War. Europe had a long history of ideological politics, even before the French Revolution, and in a way even before the Enlightenment. A specific European hostility toward communism came on top of more than a century of disagreements between monarchists, nationalists, liberals, and moderate socialists about political issues and social policy, on top of religious wars and divisive rival nationalisms. But in the United States, anticommunism had far fewer ideological precursors. One of them, however, was nativism. By the time of the Russian Revolution of 1917, predominantly Protestant Americans were already suspicious of recent immigrants from eastern and southern Europe and from East Asia. Hostility to Irish immigrants was well established before the 19th century was far advanced in the United States, and anti-Semitism followed. By the 1880s, bomb-throwing anarchists and radical labor unions like the syndicalist International Workers of the World had already begun to serve as political targets for a nervous U.S. elite.

The end of the First World War brought the Russian Revolution in its train. Now there was a Communist state, which brought with it a wave of radicalism all over Europe and even in the United States. Shaky governments responded to the challenge, both at home and abroad, as coercively as they felt it necessary or dared. In the United States, an antiradical crackdown began with the U.S. entry into the war in 1917, but escalated dramatically two years later. Many Americans initially saw the "Reds" as agents of the "Huns." The small U.S. Left, on the other hand, was heartened by the Russian Revolution, in which radicals like John Reed took a minor part.

The year 1919 produced the first of several "Red Scares" in the United States. It began with a "general strike" in Seattle in late January; the mayor claimed a workers' soviet was about to be established. May Day brought riots in many U.S. cities. There were bombings and thousands of arrests in New York, and in the so-called Palmer Raids in Chicago, hundreds of alleged Reds were arrested and in many cases deported. The governor of Massachusetts, Calvin Coolidge, rode the breaking of the Boston police strike to the White House. There were some thirty-six thousand strikes in the United States during 1919.

The situation was far more serious among the defeated powers in Europe, especially in Germany, which appeared for a time to be on the brink of a proletarian revolution similar to what had taken place in Russia. With the abdication of the kaiser in November 1918, power in Berlin was transferred to a socialist coalition government; there was a massive antiwar uprising of German sailors in Kiel a few days earlier. Munich fell under anarchist control for a short time and then was briefly the site of a Soviet Republic in 1919, as was Budapest. The Left was strong in the polarized political climate of 1920s Germany, and the Communist Party of Germany was a powerful force in German politics until it was suppressed by Hitler in 1933.

The victorious European powers fared better in the short run. In Britain and France the parties of the Right were victorious in the postwar elections, but their triumphs proved increasingly hollow over the course of the following decade. The Left recovered, despite its division into deeply opposed socialist and Communist camps, and antiwar sentiment remained extremely powerful in both countries. There was considerable industrial unrest in postwar Britain, and the Labor Party soon eclipsed the Liberal Party as the principal opposition to the reigning conservatives. French and British Communist parties appeared in 1920, a year after the American Communist Party was born.

The initial chapters of the anticommunism story in both Europe and the United States were dominated by the strong opposition of the Roman Catholic Church to proletarian dictatorship and antireligious violence, in countries as diverse as France, Italy, Germany, and the United States. Catholic opinion was particularly outraged by the suppression of the Russian Church and the murder of Polish and Russian priests. Mussolini's seizure of power in 1922 ensured that anticommunism in Italy would have a Fascist as well as Catholic dimension. Right-wing nationalism in Germany also overtook Catholicism as the most militant force opposed to communism. In most European countries the labor movement tended variously to the Left, but in the United States conservative labor leaders helped stave off U.S. recognition of the Soviet Union until 1933. The nonrecognition of the Soviet Union was about the only issue on which the American Federation

of Labor, the Roman Catholic Church, and the National Association of Manufacturers agreed.

The collapse of the stock market in 1929 and the ensuing Great Depression increased the appeal of the Soviet sociopolitical model to intellectuals in both Europe and the United States, especially after the Soviets adopted a Popular Front with the non-Communist Left against fascism in 1935. On the other hand, the escalation of purging in the Soviet Union increased the feeling among many Americans that communism and fascism were more similar than different, both part of a new phenomenon called "totalitarianism." Still, as the 1930s drew to a close and Hitler's aggressive intentions became increasingly unmistakable, anticommunism had to take a backseat to the necessary war against fascism, which meant an alliance between the Soviet Union, Britain, and the United States.

For obvious reasons, the Second World War produced a hiatus in the anticommunism of the United States and the non-Fascist countries of Europe. But the eruption of the Cold War in 1946 reanimated the struggles over the Communist issue across Europe and the United States. In those nations under Soviet control, anticommunism was of course suppressed. In Italy, France, and West Germany, "Christian Democracy" reestablished Catholic parties and voters as a principal source of political opposition not only to communism but also to Socialist parties more or less sympathetic to Moscow and skeptical of Washington, DC. The political Left was strong in both France and Italy; from the early 1960s on, its strength grew in West Germany as well. In England, the Labor Party surged to power in summer 1945 with an elaborate plan for the democratization of the country, but its leadership remained resolutely pro-American on international issues in the opening years of the Cold War, despite its dislike of Senator Eugene McCarthy's witch hunt for subversives in Washington.

Anticommunism was so powerful and pervasive in the United States partly due to the country's leading role in the Cold War, and partly due to the lack of any strong left-wing tradition there. President Franklin D. Roosevelt set limited store by anticommunism and had always been confident of his ability to manage relations with Stalin's Soviet Union. But the situation changed with Harry S. Truman in the White House, Eastern Europe falling under Soviet control, and the Soviet Union attempting a forward policy in Iran and Turkey. In the U.S. congressional elections of 1946, the Republican Party defined the fundamental issue as a fight between communism (in a number of cases tied to radicals in the U.S. labor movement) and "Americanism." This campaign brought it control of both houses of Congress for the first time since 1928. Anticommunism was clearly going to be a major political weapon in U.S. domestic politics, of which the Democratic Party had to take notice. With Britain drawing back from commitments in the eastern Mediterranean, Truman moved to a more unequivocally anti-Soviet foreign policy. The announcement of the "Truman Doctrine" in March 1947 was designed to help beleaguered democracies worldwide maintain their independence in the face of "totalitarian" (read Soviet) aggression. The Marshall Plan, announced by the secretary of state at the Harvard University commencement in June, committed to a major program under the European Recovery Act, financed by the United States.

These developments split the U.S. Left. The majority ultimately embraced the anticommunism of the administration and founded such organizations as the Americans for Democratic Action. The "containment" policy advocated by George Frost Kennan became the official policy of the Truman administration. A substantial minority, however, refused to take a strongly anti-Communist position and ultimately supported Henry Wallace for president of the United States in 1948. Among them were a small number of Communist Party members and former Communists, a few of whom—in both Britain and the United States—had been involved in espionage activities on behalf of the Soviet Union. U.S. conservatives, with the sometimes uneasy support of the Cold War liberals, began a hunt for Communists and former Communists in government, journalism, and academia. Some individuals from the "Old Left" were strikingly unwilling to give up a benign view of the Soviet Union. Some of their conservative attackers slid into demagogy, supporting the wild claims of Senator McCarthy about large numbers of Communists in the U.S. government.

The "McCarthy period" constituted a second Red Scare in the United States. Hollywood writers and directors were blackballed. Some college and university professors who took the Fifth Amendment, which protected them from self-incrimination when they were asked about their Communist activities or associations, lost their jobs. Some schoolteachers faced the same challenge. Others called to testify before Congress "named names," for which they often faced opprobrium from liberals. Investigations of subversive individuals were supplemented by legislation. Spurred on by the outbreak of the Korean War, the Internal Security Act of 1950 (also known as the McCarran Act) passed both houses of Congress. It provided for the registration of the Communist Party and all groups described by the U.S. attorney general as "Communist front organizations."

There were a number of former Communists in public life and a few actual spies. Apparently the well-schooled and well-connected diplomat Alger Hiss was a Soviet agent, and so was the Jewish leftist Julius Rosenberg. Hiss served several years in prison for perjury, but Rosenberg, together with his wife Ethel, was executed in 1953 for "conspiracy to commit espionage." Both the execution of the Rosenbergs and the Hiss case provoked passionate arguments for more than half a century, not only between liberals and conservatives, but also among people regarding themselves as "on the left." As the United States became more conservative after 1980, the volume of literature attacking the Old Left and especially those regarded as Soviet agents grew, and sometimes grew more strident, as ideological polarization increased. Many intellectuals who had begun as Cold War liberals moved into quite conservative positions. McCarthy, on the other hand, has been almost universally condemned, as have the activities of the House Un-American Activities Committee, led by Senator Pat McCarran, the principal center for the investigations of Communist infiltration into the U.S. government.

The situation in Western Europe was rather different. Hostility to the Soviet Union there tended to be more measured, except for the immediate postwar period in West Germany. French intellectual culture in the 1950s and 1960s was hostile to U.S. capitalism, and with the philosopher Jean-Paul Sartre setting the tone, tortuously pro-Communist. The most significant anti-Communists in France were the conservative-liberal sociologist Raymond Aron and the writer Albert Camus, but the anti-Americanism of Sartre really held sway until the appearance in the 1970s of Aleksandr Solzhenitsyn's *The Gulag Archipelago*, which demonstrated incontrovertibly the depth and breadth of the concentration camp system in the Soviet Union. Solzhenitsyn's three volumes were probably the most influential anti-Communist polemic ever.

In Italy, as in France and West Germany, Catholic politicians and parties continued in the vanguard of the struggle against communism. In the United States, the isolationism and hostility to the activist state that had long characterized the Republican Party gradually gave way to a zeal for prosecuting the Cold War that entailed acceptance of the "national security state," large military budgets, and global intervention against Soviet and pro-Soviet forces. The face of U.S. conservatism changed considerably over the course of the Cold War.

All of this was complicated by the youthful radicalism of the so-called 1960s, which in the United States actually developed after 1965 and was largely over by the middle of the following decade. The year 1968 may have been the high-water mark of student radicalism in France, Germany, and elsewhere in Europe as well as in the United States. As the student Left flourished, anticommunism and the Cold War itself became more controversial than ever before. Was the Cold War really a prudent and stalwart attempt to "contain" communism, as conservatives and Cold War liberals maintained? Or was it an attempt to protect corporate U.S. economic interests in the developing world? If the Soviet Union tyrannized over Eastern Europe, surely the United States did the same in Latin America. However different from the "Old Left" of the 1930s, the "New Left" of the 1960s repudiated the chastened pragmatism of the Cold War liberals, and recovered the visionary and utopian reforming impulse of the earlier generation, and in some instances its Marxism. The young (and not-so-young) radicals soon produced a conservative and neoconservative backlash, though, which was a powerful force in U.S. anticommunism until the end of the Cold War.

Eastern Europe also became an important locus for anticommunism after 1968. Direct expressions of it were still forbidden, of course, but intellectuals in Poland, Czechoslovakia, and Hungary turned increasingly and openly against Marxism and Soviet occupation. There was still a small Marxist Left in Western Europe in the late 1970s and 1980s, whereas intellectual Marxism was completely extinct in the East European countries forced to live under what was called "really existing socialism" by the Soviet occupiers. In retrospect, opposition movements like Solidarity in Poland and Charter 77 in Czechoslovakia were among the most significant signs of the waning of both the power and will to power of the Soviet elite.

Finally, the so-called dissident movement inside the Soviet Union and out played an important role in stimulating and maintaining anti-Communist politics in Western Europe and especially the United States. Soviet Jews who wanted to emigrate to Israel or the United States but were prevented from doing so by Soviet authorities were especially crucial in the United States, where influential Jewish writers and publicists rallied to their defense, and added an important component to conservative anticommunism. But not all Soviet citizens with reservations about the regime embraced openly critical attitudes. Some young

reformers of the Khrushchev period resurfaced to complete their work under Gorbachev, after lying low during the long winter of Brezhnev's leadership. Many of them were particularly critical of the repression of the "Prague Spring" in 1968, which helped convince them of the hollow character of Soviet liberationist claims.

In conclusion, it bears repetition that anticommunism was not a unified movement, nor was it centered in any one place, not even Washington, DC. Everywhere, varying degrees of hostility to the Soviet Union and its policies, domestic and foreign, interacted with local and regional traditions, with political and religious viewpoints. Nor was anticommunism wholly conservative, although it played a predominant role in defining conservatism in the Cold War West. At least for now, one may conclude that the composite forces and influences we sum up as anticommunism largely turned back the challenge of coercive social radicalism of an extreme sort, although the Euro-American world is a profoundly different place than it was before it confronted the social movement called communism.

See also: Anti-Fascist Resistance; Catholic Church; Charter 77; Cold War; Containment; Dissent in the USSR; Fascism; Kennan, George Frost; McCarthyism; Orthodox Church, Russian; Solidarity; Solzhenitsyn, Aleksandr; Totalitarianism.

FURTHER READING

Engerman, D. *Know Your Enemy : American Sovietology and the Making of the Cold War.* New York: Oxford University Press, 2009.

Furet, F. *Passé d'une illusion.* Paris: Éditions Robert Laffont, 1995.

Gaddis, J. L. *We Now Know: Rethinking Cold War History.* Oxford: Clarendon Press, 1997.

Powers, R. G. *Not without Honor.* New Haven, CT: Yale University Press, 1998.

Schrecker, E. *Many Are the Crimes.* Princeton, NJ: Princeton University Press, 1999.

Solzhenitsyn, A. I. *The Gulag Archipelago.* 3 vols. New York: Harper and Row, 1973–78.

ABBOTT GLEASON

Antifascism

With the victory of the anti-Fascists in World War II, the European Communists enjoyed a consensus and prestige not since equaled. The Communist parties acquired a national legitimacy and, in many cases, also a place in the government for the first time under the aegis of anti-fascism. With the advent of the Cold War, anti-Fascist rhetoric remained a strategic resource for the Western Communist parties in the opposition and became a state ideology for the Eastern Communist parties in power. The relation between communism and antifascism thus has become one of the most debated and controversial issues of 20th-century political history.

Some historians view antifascism as a Communist invention and an instrument of Communist propaganda, aimed at achieving an otherwise impossible legitimacy, and therefore a mostly artificial phenomenon, compromised by its association with communism. Other historians see antifascism as a significant, albeit parenthetical, phase of 20th-century history, and the Communists as the most cogent anti-Fascists, capable of exercising a hegemonic role, and harmoniously combining the concepts of class and nation. Both of these interpretations are widespread, and both analyze the relation between antifascism and communism almost as if the two phenomena were homogenous, complementary and inseparable. The question is whether the link between antifascism and communism corresponds to historical perspectives that are sufficiently removed from the times and phenomena they describe.

From the perspective of the international Communist movement (one shared by other political movements of the period), antifascism became important some time after Adolf Hitler's ascent to power. Before 1933, international communism had paid some attention to the analysis of fascism in Italy, but the more widespread generalizations typical of Marxist and Bolshevik culture interpreted it as a reactionary regression of postwar capitalism. This analysis concluded that the opponents of Benito Mussolini's regime were anti-Fascists, but did not seem to provide greater detail. Italian Communists had, since the 1920s, attempted to develop a more sustained analysis of the specific characteristics of the authoritarian mass regime in Italy; this work could have been the basis for further analysis beyond Italy's borders, but was basically ignored in Moscow. Even after Hitler's rise to power, the realignment of the Comintern's perspective and line was slow and clumsy. As late as December 1933, the Thirteenth Plenum adopted the classic definition of fascism as the "dictatorship of the most reactionary and chauvinist elements of the capitalist bourgeoisie," a doctrinaire and stereotypical definition incapable of providing the conceptual tools necessary to understand the nature of Nazism and grasp the qualitative leap that its hold on power in Europe implied.

This definition was the foundation of Communist conceptions on the eve of two events that occurred in February 1934, and that changed the perception of international fascism: the resistance by and repression of "Red Vienna," and the strike in Paris by a united opposition against the threat of a coup d'état from the Right. So the birth of an anti-Fascist spirit in Europe did not follow but instead predated the orientation of international communism. In this respect antifascism was not a product of the Communist movement. The Communists seized the political opportunity presented by this spontaneous mass mobilization, saw its potential for expansion, and adapted to it. The Comintern made the challenge of antifascism its own under Georgi Dimitrov's guidance, until the official "turn" of the Seventh Congress (July–August 1935). International fascism became the "principal enemy" of the Communist movement and the USSR. Having set aside their traditional undifferentiated vision of the capitalist world, the Communists now pointed to fascism as the real agent of war, and made a distinction between Fascist and democratic states. Revolutionary social transformations were no longer on the agenda; now the Communists designated themselves as defenders of democracy. Where once they had been responsible for many of the divisions on the Left that had contributed to Hitler's ascent, the Communists now promoted a policy of unity—the Popular Fronts. The real test of the Communist attempt to lead an anti-Fascist mobilization was the Spanish civil war. The impact of the civil war on both European public opinion and European politics proved decisive in giving antifascism an international resonance. At that point the strength of the bonds between communism and antifascism was such that they almost seemed to merge into a new identity: one could certainly be an anti-Fascist without being a Communist, but it was difficult to conceive of the opposite.

Antifascism therefore had important implications for the Communist movement. On the level of analysis, it required a certain degree of distinction between fascism and capitalism, which put many economicist and determinist certainties up for debate: if fascism represented the principal enemy, then democracy was not a simple ruse of the ruling classes; if fascism was the determining factor causing war, then not all imperialist states would conduct themselves in the same fashion or have the same responsibilities; if fascism could be beaten, then war was not inevitable. On the level of political action, opting for antifascism required one to pursue a strategy of unity with the forces of the workers' movement and even with those of "bourgeois democracy." This option risked blurring the original distinctive characteristics of the Communist movement: its elitist and sectarian nature, tempered by the Russian Revolution and the European counterrevolution, was no longer adequate to the times, and could be seen as exhausted. The idea that peace, not war, was the authentic condition for revolutionary change, and that the defense of democracy would produce new transitional regimes that would be more egalitarian and democratic, seemed to allow for the development of new political possibilities. But this development proved partial and limited in nature—a consequence of the limits of antifascism as a political movement. Antifascism was a "negative principle" that left the door open to diverse interpretations, allowed for the participation of multiple and heterogeneous subjects, and obstructed the birth of a true anti-Fascist political culture. The emotional energy and activism it generated were not sufficient to either fuse differing traditions, values, and experiences, or suppress stronger preexisting allegiances. The French Popular Front soon exhausted its élan. The Spanish civil war provided a formidable incentive to coalesce anti-Fascist forces, but it did not erase their divisions, which instead contributed to the Republicans' defeat. The international repercussions of the Great Terror in the USSR fed these divisions and weakened the Communists' credibility.

The principal weakness of the anti-Fascist movement, however, appears to have been the Communists' inability to substantially modify their founding characteristics. The centrality of the USSR to the identity, culture, and politics of the Communists played a decisive role in this regard. With the turn to antifascism, the Comintern adopted the foreign policy line Moscow had promoted since the end of 1933 as a response to Hitler's foreign policy, under the banner of "collective security." The security interests of the Soviet state coincided with the new orientation of international communism. Recasting its universalistic mission, the USSR presented itself as a bulwark of peace and essential Enlightenment freedoms, now threatened by fascism and a bourgeois, liberal civilization. But this position would soon be revealed as fragile and fictitious. In the atmosphere of suspicion, violence, and xenophobia of the Great Purges, militant antifascism was increasingly seen more as a sin than a virtue, or even as an insidious agent of democratic contamination incompatible with the Bolshevik regime. The final turn of the screw of the Soviet police state corresponded to the increasing duplicity of Joseph Stalin's foreign policy. Stalin gradually loosened the ties that bound the goal of the USSR's safety to the defense of peace in Europe. In the initial Soviet intervention on the side of the republic in the Spanish civil war, Stalin perceived the dangers of an anti-Fascist orientation and a possible confrontation with Nazi Germany more vividly than the advantages. Western appeasement provided an essential factor reinforcing this interpretation, but the interpretation had had its own autonomous roots, based on internal developments in the USSR, that were there for all to see.

Antifascism had in fact helped legitimize international communism, but ultimately the Soviet leadership could not support it. The tradition of Bolshevism in which the Soviet leadership was steeped held that capitalist states constituted an undifferentiated whole, imperialism inevitably led to war, and peace was an unrealizable objective without some palingenetic upheaval. The voices that opposed such a perspective, such as those of Maxim Litvinov and Georgi Dimitrov, were weak and marginal. Stalin defined the fundamental interests of the USSR on the basis of this tradition, and the political result of following a course that combined hyper realism with ideology was the pact between the USSR and Nazi Germany (August 23, 1939). Subjected to the crushing priorities of the USSR's interests, the Communist movement was forced to renege on the anti-Fascist commitments of the preceding five years. Once again it launched into the most stereotypical anti-imperialist tirades, shattering the identification of communism with antifascism. This was the result of not only hierarchical impositions and an unconditional discipline to Moscow's directives but also a stronger and preexisting loyalty that linked the reasons for being a Communist to the existence of the Soviet state. The guiding light and ultimate goal of the Communists remained the Soviet model, not anti-Fascist democracy.

Having failed in times of peace, Communist antifascism was once again launched in times of war. After Hitler's attack on the USSR, the Communist movement once again muted its anti-imperialist rhetoric to denounce the aggression of international fascism. Starting in June 1941, the Communist parties promoted a new policy of national unity aimed at aiding the USSR's war effort, supporting its alliance with Western powers, and rebuilding credibility after the damage caused by the Molotov-Ribbentrop Pact, above all in France. The Comintern was dissolved in June 1943 with the explicit intent of providing the Communist parties with some credibility as national forces. Moscow imparted directives that encouraged an orientation toward "national front" policies; these policies were pursued with particular vigor in the last phase of the war, and national fronts were adopted on the entire continent, without distinction between Western and Eastern Europe. To a large degree, these policies were successful for two reasons. The first was the political faith and militant self-denial of the Communists in resisting Nazi fascism. The anti-Fascist identity had not dissolved and was in fact an expression of some Communists' most deeply held passions; their practice remained true to this identity. The second reason was the change in the nature of antifascism itself. In the war years, antifascism was no longer simply a political movement but also represented the states allied against Hitler, apparently overcoming the international isolation of the USSR. Even in countries where the Red Army had not arrived, such as Italy and France, the Communists achieved positions of strength, becoming part of coalition governments that reflected the composition of the international coalition, and were destined to remake the state and democracy after the war. Antifascism's legitimation of communism thus took another qualitative leap because of the lessons learned from the war.

But soon after the end of the war, the divisions among the anti-Fascists prevailed over their bonds. As in the previous decade, the anti-Fascist movement once again proved incapable of developing as an autonomous political entity with its own culture. In fact, the emergence of deeper interests among the allied states along with the end of the cohesion provided by the fight against Hitler weakened the political impact of antifascism and left it an essential but not decisive component of European political culture. On the one hand, antifascism continued to play an important role in European domestic politics. In countries such as Germany and Italy, where the legacy of Nazism and fascism was especially important, antifascism left a lasting impression on the cultures, identities, and languages of existing political forces. One could even say that its impact led Europe to reject the idea of a war of aggression. But on the other hand, antifascism lost the transnational and universalistic nature that had been its principal impulse in the 1930s. As the divisions of the Cold War were reproduced within individual countries and the mutual interdependencies within each bloc became of paramount significance to all political subjects, the states' actions consigned the anti-Fascist experience to the past. Ultimately, though, antifascism's fate was decided by its own incongruities. The impact of the Cold

War revived dormant ideals and political divisions. Antifascism became a model for Europe's new foundations on the ashes of Hitler's "new order": a component of national identities, a leitmotif of political discourse on the Left, and an important link to the past for collective memory. But it was not a force to be reckoned with in the realization of future projects or the struggle for government leadership.

The conduct of the USSR and international communism was as critical as that of the United States in determining this outcome. From Stalin's point of view, the fascism versus antifascism opposition did not represent a conceptual or political compass. He had demonstrated this initially in his alliance with Hitler, and to an even greater degree once nazism was buried. For some time, Stalin stuck to the idea that it was in the Soviets' interest to prolong the collaboration with Western powers and push the Communist parties to collaborate with other anti-Fascist forces. But his strategic perspective was different, as we learn from Dimitrov's *Diary*. Starting with the Yalta Conference, Stalin based his strategy on what he foresaw as a future conflict between capitalism and communism, which related to his experience of the prewar period and the core of his political culture. The antifascism of the war period, therefore, like that of the 1930s, was simply a means to an end that could have no genuine future for him. This point of view was reflected in the actions of the Soviet state and the Communist movement, especially in Central and Eastern Europe. It soon became evident that the moderation Moscow was recommending to Communists at a national level as a basis for alliances and social transformations could not become the foundation of a trustworthy plan. The same was true for antifascism as a paradigm of the "people's democracies." In the Soviet sphere of influence, since the war had ended, the logic of power and control from the center went hand in glove with attempts to establish a basis for the totalitarian exercise of power throughout Eastern Europe. This could not be reconciled with either a "nationalization" of the Communist parties or the maintenance of anti-Fascist coalitions, starting with Poland. The anti-Fascist discourse became an appendix to anticapitalism, in the service of Sovietization, which in turn was presented as the only means capable of uprooting the Fascist legacy. Antifascism was no longer seen as a real-life experience but rather as rhetoric, as a justification for the Soviet Cold War and an instrument of propaganda aimed at Western anticommunism. Communism not only had ended its identification with antifascism but also had emptied antifascism of its original antitotalitarian meaning.

Western Communists agreed unconditionally with the Soviet transfiguration of antifascism in the Cold War. The dual symbols of an anti-Fascist identity and the myth of the Soviet Union, founded on a victory in war and the overwhelming sense of power emanating from the USSR, were an indivisible source of legitimation for the Communists. The irresolvable contradiction between the totalitarian nature of the USSR and the democratic nature of the anti-Fascist paradigm therefore remained hidden. The appropriation of antifascism by the Western Communists was more complex and articulated, however, because this was the task they had set themselves in order to achieve legitimacy. Anti-Fascist moderation held up better over time, at the very least as a legal safeguard for the Communist parties in the adversaries' camp. Anti-Fascist discourse was present across the political spectrum in the cultures of Western Europe, setting the stage for competition and rift but not for violent suppression. Communist claims to represent "authentic" antifascism, as opposed to the anti-Communist variety, could not but avail themselves of the notions of democracy and nation. In Italy, the Communists added the appeal to the Constitution to the previous two concepts—a product of anti-Fascist unity before the definite onset of the Cold War. To a large extent antifascism became a mythical figure, yet unlike in the East, it also became a point of cultural and intellectual consensus, as both a shared value and a deterrent against a return to the Fascist past. Still, antifascism no longer represented the foundation of a policy or a political project. Antifascism proved it no longer possessed any contemporary appeal when the Italian Communist Party attempted to resurrect it in the 1970s.

The encounter between antifascism and communism was much more contradictory and less organic than it has been made to appear. The Communists did not invent antifascism, but more than others they attempted to develop its political potential. Antifascism was a fundamental vehicle for the legitimation of the Communist movement. It was not a mask or a fiction but rather an identity that was superimposed on an original revolutionary vocation. Yet antifascism was neither communism's sole nor principal identity. Antifascism never truly breached Soviet political culture—in other words, the heart of the Communist movement. Antifascism's existence was always subject to the primacy of Soviet statism, the fundamental and therefore decisive factor for all Communists. As a consequence, antifascism was reduced to an instrument of Communist policy. At the end of World War II its legitimizing function and fusion with the sense of Communist belonging could neither be ignored nor removed. But its significance was twisted to serve the logic of the Soviet Cold War, and the stronger and epochal rivalry between communism and capitalism.

See also Anti-Fascist Resistance; Anti-imperialism; Cold War; Fascism; Molotov-Ribbentrop Pact; Popular Front; Revolution, Myths of the; Second Cold War; Spanish Civil War.

FURTHER READING

De Bernardi, A., and P. Ferrari, eds. *Antifascismo e identità europea.* Rome: Carocci, 2004.

De Felice, F., ed. *Antifascismi e resistenze.* Rome: La Nuova Italia Scientifica, 1997.

Furet, F. *The Passing of an Illusion: The Idea of Communism in the Twentieth Century.* Chicago: University of Chicago Press, 1999.

Hobsbawm, E. J. *Gli intellettuali e l'antifascismo.* In: *Storia del marxismo.* III/2. Turin: Einaudi, 1981.

———. *Age of Extremes: The Short Twentieth Century, 1914–1991.* London: Michael Joseph, 1994.

Maier, C. S. *I fondamenti politici del dopoguerra.* In *Storia d'Europa.* Vol. 1. Turin: Einaudi, 1993.

Müller, J.-W., ed. *Memory and Power in Post-War Europe Studies in the Presence of the Past.* Cambridge: Cambridge University Press, 2002.

Paggi, L., ed. *La memoria del nazismo nell'Europa di oggi.* Florence: La Nuova Italia, 1997.

Pons, S. *L'impossibile egemonia: l'URSS, il PCI e le origini della guerra fredda (1943–1948).* Rome: Carocci, 1999.

SILVIO PONS

Anti-Fascist Resistance

From the postwar point of view of the USSR and other states that successfully fought fascism, anti-Fascist resistance started after the German attack on the Soviet Union on June 22, 1941. Anti-Fascist resistance, however, did not begin during World War II, despite our focus here. In a strict sense, the term includes resistance against the Italian Fascist regime as well as regimes in countries that used the Italian Fascist dictatorship as a model and then succeeded in transforming a Fascist movement into a dictatorship. It therefore also includes the fight against Nazism in Germany after the collapse of the Weimar Republic, the struggle against Fascist regimes and their collaborators by émigré groups, or the struggle against Fascist combatants active in other European countries—for instance, during the Spanish civil war. Given the policy of military aggression pursued by Fascist countries and their allies, especially after the outbreak of World War II (the date at which individual countries became involved varies, leading to different periodizations and interpretations), the idea of anti-Fascist resistance as a public or clandestine struggle against an internal enemy shifted to a military confrontations against an external enemy (Nazi, Fascist, or Nazi Fascist) and its collaborators. This fight became known as *Résistance*, or anti-Nazi and anticollaborationist resistance—in other words, anti-Fascist in a broad sense, fighting a form of domination that was not homogeneous but instead specific to individual national realities.

Phases of the Anti-Fascist Resistance

Between 1938 and 1944 Nazi Germany—allied with Fascist Italy until the summer of 1943—created occupation regimes in Czechoslovakia, Poland, Norway, Denmark, Luxemburg, Belgium, Holland, France, Greece, Yugoslavia, the Baltic countries, Belorussia, Ukraine, Russia, and finally Italy, Albania, and Hungary. In all these countries, a portion of the population decided to voluntarily and clandestinely oppose the occupation forces during the war—by means of both political agitation and propaganda as well as obstructionism, sabotage, or the refusal to cooperate. Some took up arms in the course of clandestine struggle or organized themselves into partisan groups. The geographic features of specific areas were fundamental to the development of military resistance. The importance of political resistance notwithstanding (it was key for postwar political arrangements in many countries), partisan warfare became the dominant form both during the war and in the public's perception afterward. If the resistance appeared isolated and limited in terms of both size and support in the first years of the war, as the conflict expanded and its repercussions became more significant (the forced recruitment of labor, treatment of prisoners of war, and pursuit of a war of extermination), the resistance became much better organized, ultimately affecting even allied countries such as Italy. The motivation of individual resisters varied, but by 1944 1.5 million individuals had been mobilized

militarily to aid the resistance. The percentages of people involved fluctuated from country to country. In most Western European countries, resisters were well below 5 percent of the population (and perhaps closer to 1 percent), as in France, Belgium, and Denmark, while the numbers reached 25 percent in Poland.

There are at least three phases of anti-Fascist resistance: one lasting until June 1941, a second tied to the German attack on the Soviet Union, and a third tied to German military defeats and losses, which increased at a rapid pace after the summer of 1943. It was only during this last phase that resistance movements turned into mass movements all over Europe.

The first phase was influenced by Joseph Stalin's decision to ally himself with Adolf Hitler in August 1939. This decision had a devastating effect on the forms taken by anti-Fascist resistance, since Communist parties in Western Europe supported the USSR's policies. The Communist parties' rigid subordination to Moscow, and the Soviet insistence on the thesis that Great Britain's and France's war against Hitler's Germany was an imperialist enterprise, limited the Communists' freedom of maneuver. The underground Communist Party of Germany (the KPD, which had already been violently repressed by the Nazis and had lost about twenty thousand militants) would continue its struggle against nazism, ignoring the pact, but it could not question the Soviet decision. This situation precipitated a political dilemma that, not coincidentally, led various underground groups in Germany to distance themselves from the KPD's leadership abroad during the war and also to establish contact with resisters from different political backgrounds. Instead, in German-occupied Serbia during the spring of 1941, the Communist Party rapidly organized a resistance of considerable size. The partisan war in Yugoslavia (both on the Communist side and that of the nationalist Chetniks) was above all the result of a process of radicalization caused by the occupying institutions—a process that was to be repeated later in other occupied countries. The occupying forces' repression immediately targeted the entire population—even without taking the Ustasha (a Croatian right-wing terrorist group aligned with the Nazis) terror in the "Independent State of Croatia" into account. The massacres in Kraljevo, where the Wehrmacht killed more than four thousand civilians in the course of a week in October 1941, and Kragujevac, which resulted in about twenty-three hundred deaths, but also the killings of Serbian Jews by means of trucks' exhaust fumes, all acquired symbolic significance.

The German attack on the Soviet Union gave the resistance a decisive impulse. Once the obstacle of the Molotov-Ribbentrop Pact had been removed, both an armed and a political resistance developed quickly in all those countries occupied by the National Socialists and their allies. The resistance relied on a mass base that ultimately proved stronger than that of the nationalist movements; the populations joined or supported various partisan groups in response to the methods and reprisals used by the occupying forces. While in Belorussia the German occupation troops were initially welcomed in 1941 as a means of liberating the country from the Communist yoke, with the implementation of extermination and the *Generalplan Ost*, including plans to intentionally massacre millions of Slavs, the population was forced to resist. The Communist Party of the Soviet Union was able to form the first partisan groups very rapidly, reacting much faster than occupied Western Europe had previously. In the Soviet Union the partisans often destroyed the resupply bases for German troops, thus also depriving the population of their means of sustenance. The rural population, as in other parts of Europe, was generally reluctant to give the partisans any food supplies, even if in the postwar period this fact was obscured by the myth of a popular resistance. While the German "struggle against the partisans" in the West increasingly was synonymous with homicidal rampages against the civilian population, in the East this practice actually obscured the implementation of a war of extermination.

In Western Europe the resistance took the form of partisan warfare and reached massive dimensions only after the summer of 1943. In 1943–44, Germany's pragmatic and opportunistic policies developed along two opposite tracks: on the one hand, Germany attempted to increase the size of its collaborationist forces; on the other hand, it imposed forced labor and engaged in repression without limits, which in turn only helped to lastingly strengthen the resistance. The collaborationist model began collapsing in 1943 with the requisition of human resources—in other words, with the employment of forced labor and the rounding-up of a labor force to be sent to Germany: these policies marked the beginning of mass opposition to German occupation. The radicalization of the partisan struggle started in France after the Normandy landing in June 1944, while in Italy it began with the German loss of Rome and central Italy in June–July 1944.

If one compares German losses on the front with those from partisan warfare, the latter were quite limited: in the Soviet Union, approximately eighteen thousand German soldiers were killed, and most of them were victims of assaults against trains, mines, and derailments.

The Contested and Monopolized Resistance

Due in large part to its political nature, there are few topics as deeply permeated by myths and legends as that of European partisan movements. The subsequent historical reconstruction was also shaped by political interests.

Victorious partisan movements created legends about the overwhelming military force and political cohesion of the "people's war." In Soviet bloc countries, the Communist movement was presented as the only active liberation force, with praise going to the "proletarian internationalism" of the struggle, whereas nationalist resistance movements were condemned as traitors or even repressed. Everywhere there was a recognition, however, that the partisans had played a considerable role in the Germans' defeat. In the course of the armed struggle itself (and for reasons of psychological warfare) partisan groups' numbers were inflated. Often the number of fighters given was one that had only been reached at the war's end—which saw the largest resistance—and frequently even this number was exaggerated. In order to bolster the rhetoric of victory, the dimensions and cohesion of the partisan movement were greatly inflated on the one side, as were the German losses on the other. According to Soviet estimates, for instance, partisan warfare had led to 1.5 million Germans and collaborationists either being killed or incapacitated (as against the 50,000 deaths that Alfred Jodl testified tox at Nuremberg).

In Western European countries national debates about the German occupation took place after the end of the war (with the support given by Fascist Italy all but forgotten), and they were mostly premised on the opposition between resistance and collaborationism. A terminological debate about the ties between resistance, antifascism, and totalitarianism developed—for example, during the international congresses of the resistance movements that took place in Lieges (1958) and Florence (1959)—in order to agree on who should be included in the set of those actively resisting. The definition given by Henri Michel included bourgeois or military groups that were not inspired by antifascism: "The resistance movement is a patriotic struggle for the liberation of the Fatherland. It is additionally a fight against totalitarianism for the dignity and freedom of human beings." Each country attempted to arrive at a definition that reflected its experiences of the resistance, taking its own specific situation during the war into account: one part of France wanted General Charles de Gaulle to be seen as the center of the resistance; in Italy there was a tendency to merge the anti-Fascist resistance that had occurred under the Fascist regime with the resistance of 1943–45; and where there had not been militarily significant forms of resistance, as in the Scandinavian countries, attempts were made to separate antifascism from the resistance or to define the resistance not exclusively in terms of military actions but also as "the refusal of a country to accept foreign occupation."

In the countries of the Soviet bloc the considerable differences between patriotic-nationalist resistance and Communist resistance, and between Communist Party and local populations, were not acknowledged by the victorious Communist Party, which managed to monopolize the relevant historiography and official commemorations by claiming that only in the case of Soviet Russia could one speak of a "Great Patriotic War" that was also anti-Fascist. Especially after 1991, those suppressed and divided memories reemerged not only in Poland but also in various parts of the former Soviet Union (leading to preoccupying forms of reevaluation of the collaborationists and indigenous SS groupings seen as anti-Communist "liberators").

The ethical and political value of the resistance cannot be measured by its military effectiveness. The military importance of the resistance consisted in its ability to immobilize significant numbers of German (and Italian) troops, but except for Yugoslavia, where Tito's partisans liberated most of the country before Soviet troops entered by way of Romania and Bulgaria, the resistance did not succeed in liberating their countries with their own forces. Rather, the regular armies, of both the Western Allies and the Soviet Union, finally managed to liquidate the Nazi occupation. The political and moral dimension as well as the military one, however, cannot be totally separated either. The resistance's impact was demonstrated by clandestine operations, as in the case of the attempt on Reinhard Heydrich's life in May 1942, which was followed by the Lidice massacre, the sabotage of the nuclear reactor in Vermork, Norway, in February 1943, and the attempt on Hitler's life by Claus von Stauffenberg on July 20 1944 followed by the attempted coup by the German resistance. It was also demonstrated by uprisings or visible protests with great symbolic value, like the Warsaw Ghetto uprising in April–May 1943, the insurrection of the Armia Krajowa (Polish resistance movement) in Warsaw in August 1944, and the general strike in occupied Italy in March 1944.

See also Antifascism; Grand Alliance, The; Great Patriotic War, Rhetoric of; Totalitarianism; World War II.

FURTHER READING

Burgwyn, H. J. *Empire on the Adriatic: Mussolini's Conquest of Yugoslavia, 1941–1943*. New York: Enigma, 2005.

Chiari, B., and J. Kochanowski, eds. *Die polnische Heimatarmee. Geschichte und Mythos der Armia Krajowa seit dem Zweiten Weltkrieg*. Munich: Oldenbourg, 2003.

Hill, A. *The War behind the Eastern Front: The Soviet Partisan Movement in North-West Russia, 1941–1944*. London: Cass, 2005.

Kühnrich, H. *Der Partisanenkrieg in Europa, 1939–1945*. Berlin: Dietz, 1965.

Meyer. A. *Die deutsche Besatzung in Frankreich 1940–1944. Widerstandsbekämpfung und Judenverfolgung*. Darmstadt: Wissenschaftliche Buchgesellschaft, 2000.

Peli, S. *La Resistenza in Italia. Storia e critica*. Turin: Einaudi, 2004.

Schmider. K. *Partisanenkrieg in Jugoslawien, 1941–1944*. Hamburg: Mittler, 2002.

Schulz, D., ed. *Partisanen und Volkskrieg: zur Revolutionierung des Krieges im 20. Jahrhundert*. Göttingen: Vandenhoeck und Ruprecht, 1985.

LUTZ KLINKHAMMER

Anti-Imperialism

Anti-imperialism was, in the early 20th century, the form through which much of the nationalism in colonized, non-Western societies was expressed. The Leninist definition of imperialism also became influential during this period: namely, imperialism as a form of exploitation, primarily economic exploitation, that derived from the inevitable failure of capitalism to find adequate domestic markets. However, this definition proved insufficient on its own to explain the dynamic between anti-imperialism and non-European nationalism during this period. The term "anti-imperialism" remained powerful even after the ending of the era of territorial empires, and it has been revived in the post–Cold War global environment as an expression of distrust for a perceived hegemonic social and political order.

Imperialism as an ideological phenomenon emerged as a clear province of discussion in the late 19th century, and anti-imperialism was to be one of the most powerful strains of thought in the non-Western world into the early 20th century. Much of the language and terminology with which it was discussed emerged from political discussions in the metropole. Marxist thinkers, most notably Lenin, became dominant spokesmen in the field, but there were influential non-Marxist anti-imperialists as well, such as J. L. Hobson, who argued in 1902 that imperialism was largely a product of the need for private capital to find markets outside the home country, and as such, was a means of increasing capitalist exploitation. While the circumstances of the early 20th century made anti-imperialism an obvious tool for criticism of the establishment and the exploitation of formal territorial colonies by the European powers, this was not the only channel for anti-imperialist sentiment.

Some of the earliest critics of British imperialism came from within the metropole. For instance, Hobson's argument was not so much a condemnation of imperialism per se, but rather an argument against its inefficiency as he saw it employed in practice. The emergence of the British Labour Party in the early 20th century brought opposition to empire yet more fully into the mainstream of metropolitan politics, but it still fell short of an outright, fully theorized position of opposition to the structures of empire. Radicalization of the idea of anti-imperialism moved further with the Bolshevik Revolution of 1917 and the establishment of a Soviet state. The desire to harness anti-imperialism as a driving force for the new Soviet Union shaped the development of the Comintern, the foreign policy instrument of the USSR which aimed to foment revolution outside the USSR's borders. Initially, the rulers of the new state hoped that this would be a relatively swift process. They were disappointed in that hope, but the Comintern nevertheless played a significant role as a sponsor of anti-imperialist feeling in the non-European world.

Unsurprisingly, the notion of anti-imperialism had particular significance in the colonial world of the early 20th century. One of the societies in which the Marxist-Leninist interpretation of anti-imperialism was particularly influential was China. The Chinese Communist Party (CCP) was founded in 1921, and it drew heavily on the atmosphere of the largely anti-traditional May Fourth Movement, and the closely associated New Culture Movement which shaped much radical thinking in China in the early years of the Republic (1912–49). The

Communist Party was by no means unique in seeking to use opposition to the imperialist presence in China as part of its political message. From the Opium Wars of the mid-19th century onward, China's political elites had considered foreign encroachment in the form of extraterritoriality, lack of tariff autonomy, and outright colonial occupation, to be a grave political crisis, and sought means to oppose it. At the grassroots level, the incursion of traders, soldiers, and missionaries into the interior of China allowed antiforeign feeling to thrive. The introduction of Western thought provided a new means for those elites to conceptualize China's place in the world in the early 20th century, and a nationalism explicitly shaped around the idea of opposition to imperialism emerged at around that same time. The arrival of the Republic after the 1911 Revolution paved the way for a nationalist politics based on opposition to "warlordism without, imperialism within." This formulation expressed what nationalists of all persuasions felt were the two major problems facing China: political division that made a mockery of the "republic," and imperialist aggression that prevented unity. The Chinese Nationalist party (Guomindang) led by Sun Yatsen until his death in 1925 was one of the primary vehicles for anti-imperialist sentiment in China, and the Nationalist government established by Chiang Kaishek in 1928 made the recovery of Chinese sovereignty a key part of its platform. However, the Nationalists regarded imperialism as a threat because of the dominant world order which accorded unequal status to different states, rather than because imperialism was the inevitable product of the move toward capitalism. While not denying the economic significance of imperialism, the Nationalists did not theorize the term in great detail.

Anti-imperialism was given a much more explicitly Marxist economic definition by the CCP, formally founded in 1921. This definition was heavily influenced by the Comintern advisers to the party, who encouraged a definition of imperialism that stressed the ways in which national capitalist elites sought to exploit colonies and other smaller nations. Anti-imperialism, in the CCP definition, demanded the overthrow of these exploitative structures so that China could achieve self-determination. The works of Bukharin, Stalin, and Lenin were translated and propagated by CCP members as a means of promoting the anti-imperialist strategy as part of a Communist program, and an understanding of imperialism, defined in Leninist terms, was an essential part of the training for membership of the party after 1925. After the split with the Nationalists in 1927, the CCP's need to compromise its definition of anti-imperialism was significantly lessened, and it became a vigorously argued part of its agenda, along with class warfare.

The Nationalist movement in French Indochina was also significantly influenced by a Marxist definition of anti-imperialism. By the mid-1940s, the leading independence movement, the Viet Minh, led by Ho Chi Minh, was dominant in the struggle against French, and later Japanese, colonialism in the region. Elsewhere in the colonial world, the establishment of Communist parties promoted the spread of anti-imperialist sympathies; as, for instance after the establishment of the South African Communist Party in 1921, which from the 1940s was allied with the African National Congress.

Marxist influence was widely felt in anti-colonial struggles around the world in the early 20th century. However, the specifically Marxist-Leninist definition of anti-imperialism as a key stage in the class struggle was not shared by all such movements of the era. For instance, the Indian struggle for independence against the British was marked by various ideological strands, including secular socialism (exemplified by Nehru and the Congress Party), countermodern pacifism (Gandhi), and from the 1940s, a drive for a separate Muslim state, as well as radical and moderate communalism. While an Indian Communist Party existed from 1921, and in fact had significant influence, particularly among intellectuals, it was not the dominant shaper of anti-imperialism during the period, although its position was aided by radicalization caused by the Bengal famine of 1943. While Gandhi, for instance, regarded economic exploitation as a crucial element for the rallying of anti-imperialist feeling, his response was not Leninist, but rather anti-industrial (championing a return to localized production) and based on moral suasion (for instance, civil disobedience expressed through the breaking of laws on salt production). Gandhi's program for the Congress Party in India, while enjoying immense moral authority, was never wholly accepted by nationalists throughout India; but even among those who turned to other forms of anti-British opposition, only a relative minority held with a strictly Marxist definition of anti-imperialism.

The contrast between developments in India and China, ostensibly both agrarian countries suffering from the effects of imperialism (albeit in different forms), suggests one reason for the inadequacy of a purely Marxist/ Bolshevik definition of anti-imperialism. Perhaps the Marxist definition's greatest shortcoming was its emphasis on economic exploitation over issues of culture. Naturally, the distortions in social development that are caused by the economic exploitation of imperialist powers was a significant argument in support of anti-imperialism, as the boycotts of western goods in India and China in the interwar period demonstrate. Yet the issues of nationhood and racism, treated by many Marxists as relatively incidental to the wider issues of economic exploitation, in fact loomed rather larger in the minds of many of the most potent anti-imperialist movements. Essentially, therefore, the classic Marxist analysis fell short because it sought to define anti-imperialism as being in some way forced to deviate to take account of nationalism, rather than accepting nationalism as a primary product of anti-imperialism in its own right.

The Japanese empire in Asia during the early 20th century perhaps best shows how the language of anti-imperialist nationalism could be used in the service of exploitative imperialism, rather than in resistance to it. Japan's imperialism, from the late 19th century onward, was fuelled by a mutually contradictory pair of ideologies: one declaring that Japan was uniquely fitted through racial destiny to rule in Asia; the other, that Japan had a duty to liberate its colonized neighbors (China and the countries of Southeast Asia) from Western imperialist rule. The recipe that the Japanese military offered for the latter, namely the replacement of Western imperialism with Japanese, was hypocritical in the extreme. Nonetheless, the willingness of pan-Asian thinkers, starting with Okakura Tenshin, to develop the idea that "Asia is one" sparked interest among many Eastern Nationalist intellectuals, notably Tagore in India and Sun Yat-sen in China. Pan-Asian thought, a variant of anti-imperialist nationalism based on the idea of an "Asian" identity that transcended borders and cultures, was a prime example of a powerful anti-imperialist stream that owed little to the economic determinants of the Marxist version, not least since one of its primary exponents, Japan, was an economic exploiter in the most classic sense.

Also worth noting is the disparity between the language and behavior of the two major anti-imperialist powers of the prewar era. Accusations of being an imperialist power were always particularly hurtful to the United States, which viewed its own liberation from empire (the British empire of the 18th century) and its assistance to other nations seeking self-determination as central to its identity. For the United States, anti-imperialism was a moral and cultural issue more than an economic one. Yet the radicalization of politics in one of its immediate neighbors, Mexico, was shaped by a Marxism at least in part defined by opposition to the perceived economic imperialism of the United States, and which allowed the government of Lazaro Cardenas (1934–40) to institute a radical policy of land redistribution. In general, Latin American revolutions (such as that in Cuba in 1959) have used opposition to U.S. imperialism as a means of gaining support. The USSR has frequently been in support of such movements. Yet the latter's own explicit anti-imperialism was belied by its retention of czarist territorial acquisitions, and by its further incursions—into Ukraine, Central Asia, and the Baltic states—as well as by the maintenance of a ring of satellite states during the Cold War, whose economic relationship to the USSR certainly fitted the classic Leninist definition of exploitation.

The postwar world was marked by the process of decolonization, and by the 1970s, there were very few formal colonies left in the world. Nonetheless, the Cold War saw the great Communist powers, the USSR and China, continuing to use anti-imperialist rhetoric in defense of their legitimacy. Mao Zedong's model of anti-imperialist struggle took on particular vigor during the 1950s and 1960s as China sought to portray the USSR as a once-revolutionary state now backsliding into revisionism and stagnation. The two Communist superpowers found themselves in direct competition for the adherence of global Communist parties and states, and while the USSR succeeded for the most part in retaining the support of the European parties, the Chinese model made greater inroads into the third world. While there was evidence of Chinese involvement in particular conflicts, notably in Korea (1950–53), the reality in large part failed to match the rhetoric. However, the willingness of China to portray itself as a third world mentor to newly liberated states meant that it played a particularly powerful role in areas outside its traditional sphere of influence, such as Africa, where it helped develop health care and railway infrastructure, and India, where the Naxalite peasant movement took its inspiration from Mao.

One of the longest lasting anti-imperialist conflicts of the Cold War era, the war in Vietnam, provided a prominent opportunity for both the Soviets and the Chinese to exercise their rhetoric of third world liberation. However, the war also showed up the unbridgeable contradictions in the ways in which the two states used the term. After the defeat of the French in 1954 and the subsequent division of Vietnam into a Communist north and non-Communist south, the government of the north under Ho Chi Minh began to undermine the southern regime as part of the former's project of national reunification. The fact that the southern government was a dictatorship with relatively little public support enabled the USSR and China to portray the struggle for reunification as not only a Nationalist movement, but also one symbolic of a wider anti-imperialism aimed at the United States. However, the North Vietnamese government never fully trusted the Chinese, and from the late 1960s, broke off their alliance with the Chinese partly out of fear that Mao's state was seeking to establish a version of a more traditional East Asian order in which Vietnam would become a secondary state within China's orbit. China's anti-imperialist credentials were further wrecked during its unsuccessful 1979 incursion into Vietnamese territory, which was quickly repulsed. The USSR's own credibility as an anti-imperialist power had been damaged earlier in the Cold War by its invasions of Hungary (1956) and Czechoslovakia (1968), and became yet more untenable in 1979 when the Soviet Union invaded Afghanistan because it perceived the country as a destabilizing influence on its borders.

The end of the classic territorial empires did not render the anti-imperialist model obsolete. After the Cold War concern turned to the ways in which seemingly rational and neutral international bodies might in fact embody norms that entrenched the hegemonic power of one country, in particular that of the United States, limiting the autonomy of states to defend their borders, set up trade barriers, or define human rights in their own terms. Ironically, the collapse of the Soviet Union allowed the circumstances for anti-imperialism, used primarily but not exclusively in an economic sense, to re-emerge as a term of critique. After the breakdown of the bipolarity of the Cold War world, an effectively unipolar world arose, in which increasingly globalized economic and geopolitical structures (such as the World Bank, the World Trade Organization, and the International Monetary Fund) now threatened to dominate. Anti-globalization movements and sentiments frequently use the language of anti-imperialist struggle to express themselves in the present day.

See also Antifascism; Cold War, Collapse of Capitalism; Comintern; Decolonization; Imperialism; Nationalism; Third Worldism; Vietnam War; War, Inevitability of.

FURTHER READING

Hardt, M., and A. Negri. *Empire*. Cambridge, MA: Harvard University Press, 2000.
Hobson, J. A. *Imperialism: A Study*. London: Archibald Constable, 1905.

Hunt, M. H. *The Genesis of Chinese Communist Foreign Policy.* New York: Columbia University Press, 1996.

Lenin, V. I. *Imperialism: The Highest Stage of Capitalism.* London: Archibald Constable, [1916] 1934.

McDermott, K., and J. Agnew. *The Comintern: A History of International Communism from Lenin to Stalin.* Basingstoke: Macmillan, 1996.

Van Ness, P. *Revolution and Foreign Policy: Peking's Support for Wars of National Liberation.* Berkeley: University of California Press, 1970.

RANA MITTER

Anti-Semitism

Neither Marxism's founders nor Communist leaders have been able to capture the nature of modern anti-Semitism. This failure starts with Karl Marx himself, who totally neglected this aspect of the "Jewish question," an issue to which he devoted a youthful work in which he reiterated numerous stereotypes about Jews and money. Although Friedrich Engels and Vladimir Lenin recognized that Jews were the victims of anti-Semitism, they did not analyze anti-Semitism as a product of social and political modernity but instead as a "reaction of backward, medieval, social strata to a modern society essentially composed of capitalists and wage-laborers," or "as a ruling class weapon to divert the anti-capitalism of the working masses of the petty bourgeoisie towards a false objective." For Marxist theorists, anti-Semitism— like Judaism—was destined to disappear in socialist and industrial society. This "class analysis" prevented them from understanding the specificity of modern anti-Semitism and therefore from imagining the instruments with which to confront it. Since Marxists' only interpretative framework was the assimilation of the Jews, they were not able to comprehend either the persistence of anti-Semitism in Western Europe, as confirmed by the Dreyfus affair, nor the conditions of oppression in which the Jews of Eastern Europe lived.

This incapacity considerably limited the influence of social democracy within European Judaism up to 1917, especially in the czarist empire; this benefited Jewish social democracy (the Bund) and above all the Zionist movement. After 1917 the facts on the ground changed. Although discrimination against Jews as subjects of the czarist empire was abolished during the February and not the October Revolution, the Bolshevik revolution attracted the sympathies of Russian and European Jews to the Communist movement.

The struggle against anti-Semitism became part of the official policies of the Bolshevik government. For the first time in Russian history Jews had access to political and administrative positions, even in the security organs. Far from disappearing, however, anti-Semitism was fueled by these changes. In the eyes of many Russians, the October Revolution was a "Jewish-Bolshevik" plot against Russia and hence illegitimate. The presence of Jews in the party and state remained limited overall, but in the organs of power the percentage of Jewish members was higher than it was in the general population. In part due to this more visible presence, anti-Semitism appeared even at the highest party levels in the 1930s, intertwined as it was with Joseph Stalin's elimination of Jewish leaders—from Grigory Zinovyev and Lev Kamenev, to Genrich Jagoda and Leon Trotsky. During the occupation of the USSR in the years 1941–44, the Nazis unleashed their persecution of Judaism and Bolshevism, and found some support in the population, especially in Ukraine and Belorussia.

After World War II, with the establishment of what could be called a true form of state anti-Semitism, repressive policies targeted certain Jews as the new "enemies of the people," first in the Soviet Union, and then in the other people's democracies. These were not openly anti-Semitic policies. The victims were accused of participating in a "Zionist plot in the service of imperialism," of promoting a "rootless cosmopolitanism" and a "bourgeois Jewish nationalism." The Jewish Anti-Fascist Committee, created in 1941 to mobilize Soviet and Western Jews to support the USSR's war effort, was liquidated. Its president, the actor Solomon Mickoels, was assassinated on Stalin's orders in January 1948, and the other leaders were put to death in 1952, after a preliminary inquiry and an in camera trial whose proceedings Stalin followed and approved step by step. Under the guise of the "struggle against cosmopolitanism," the purges targeted Jews who were active in the fields of science, literature, and journalism. This state anti-Semitism reached a climax in 1953, in the "doctors' case" against Jewish physicians accused of having attempted to kill Soviet leaders, including Stalin himself (some have argued that this was meant to be the prelude to a mass deportation of Jews, although no documents attesting to such a plan have been found in the Soviet archives). Eastern Europe was also the scene of anti-Semitic episodes and purges. In Budapest (the Rajk case), Prague (the Slansky case), Bucharest (the Paulker case), and East Berlin (the Merker case), Jewish party cadres were targeted and accused of participating in a Zionist plot.

Why did the Jews become the principal target of Stalinist repression after 1945? Stalin's decision to single out the Jews as the new enemies of the people was a function not so much of an anti-Semitic obsession but rather of political choices. The explanation of this anti-Semitic campaign must therefore be sought in a complex series of factors: first, the presence of anti-Semitism in the USSR and Eastern Europe. In part Stalin decided to utilize popular anti-Semitism instrumentally in order to erase the preconception that power in party institutions was in Jewish hands. This political decision needs to be seen in the context of the "second Stalinism," which was characterized by a return to Great Russian nationalism, the Russification of the party-state apparatus, and the elimination of cadres belonging to minorities, Jews in particular.

The second factor was tied to the manner in which Stalin's totalitarian system of power functioned. It was a system fed by an atmosphere of crisis and tension that could be used to justify widespread repression after the "discovery" of plots on which the system's malfunctions could be blamed. After the war, there were no more "kulaks," "deviationists," or "Trotskyists" to be eliminated. The Jews were the new hatchers of plots. In addition, the power of the Stalinist system was based on a clan logic, which forbade any type of loyalty beyond that owed to the chief. Consequently no social, religious, local, or professional group could exhibit any form of autonomy, and thus any other form of loyalty.

From Stalin's point of view Jews had broken this tacit principle in at least two ways. On the one hand, during World War II the leaders of the Jewish Anti-Fascist Committee gradually had become autonomous spokespeople for Soviet Judaism, to the extent that they had proposed the creation of a Jewish republic in Crimea to Stalin and Vyacheslav Molotov in 1944. On the other hand, the USSR's support for the creation of Israel in 1947 made Soviet Jews think they could openly show their enthusiasm toward the Jewish state. Stalin deemed this attitude—which was particularly evident in the warm welcome given to Golda Meir, the first Israeli ambassador to the USSR, by the Moscow synagogue—combined with the "representative" autonomy of the leaders of the Jewish Anti-Fascist Committee, an intolerable violation of his power.

The third factor was the war between the clans. The Jews were the principal target of repression in 1946 because they were also instrumental in the power struggle within Stalin's close circle of associates. The campaign against the Jews also fulfilled Stalin's (primary?) goal of eliminating leaders that he suspected of acquiring excessive power or autonomy, specifically his old associate Molotov and the all-powerful Lavrenty Beria, who was in charge of the organs of repression. The denunciation of these "Zionist plots" targeted these two leaders among others, and Stalin intended to get rid of them in the context of a new Great Purge, which would have allowed him to promote new cadres that were absolutely faithful to him. Stalin died before being able to carry out his plans.

Communism in power never resorted to openly anti-Semitic discourse. Anti-Semitism within the movement, however, allowed for the development of a rhetoric that although devoid of the usual anti-Semitic references, functioned as a coded language perfectly understood by those it addressed. Marxist anti-Zionism, which initially was simply a theoretical and political negation of the Jewish national plan, was transformed into an instrument with which to denigrate a people destined to be proscribed. The topic of the "Jewish plot" was associated with other anti-Semitic commonplaces like that of the ritual homicide; in the doctors' case, for example, the Communist movement and the Soviet leaders intentionally fed this confusion, using anti-Zionism to both criticize Israeli policy and justify repression of the Jews.

See also Deportation of Nationalities in the USSR; Nationalism; Stalinism; Zhdanovism; Zionism.

FURTHER READING

Klier, J. D., and S. Lambroza. *Pogroms: Anti-Jewish Violence in Modern Russian History.* Cambridge: Cambridge University Press, 1992.

Kostyrchenko, G. V. *V plenu u krasnogo faraona. Politicheskie presledovanija evreev v SSSR v posledenee stalinskoe desatiletie.* Moscow: Mezhdunarodnye otnoshenija, 1994.

Rapoport, L. *Stalin's War against the Jews: The Doctors' Plot and the Soviet Solution.* New York: Free Press, 1990.

Rucker, L. *Staline, Israel et les Juifs.* Paris: Presses Universitaires De France, 2001. Traverso, E. *The Marxists and the Jewish Question: The History of a Debate (1843–1943).* Atlantic Highlands, NJ: Humanities Press, 1993.

LAURENT RUCKER

Aragon, Louis

Louis Aragon (1897–1982) had very close ties to communism that lasted over half a century. Born in France, he abandoned the study of medicine in 1924, and identified with André Breton's *Surrealist Manifesto*. He followed Breton on the path to political and social engagement taken by the surrealist group, and moved closer to the Communist Party. In January 1927, Aragon was the first of five surrealists to join the Communist Party (the others were Breton, Paul Eluard, Benjamin Péret, and Pierre Unik). Aragon's life changed after making Elsa Triolet's acquaintance in 1928, marrying her and traveling to the USSR in 1930. In November 1930 he took part, with Georges Sadoul, in the Revolutionary Writers Conference in Charkov, without prior approval from either the surrealist group or the Communist Party to which they belonged. After his return to France he published the poem *Front rouge*, inspired by agitprop principles, which led to his indictment in 1932: he was charged with instigating homicide. Breton defended him in the name of freedom of expression, but Aragon distanced himself from Breton because of the latter's criticisms of the Communist Party. This led to Aragon's break with the surrealist group.

A second trip to Russia between the spring of 1932 and the spring of 1933 put him in touch with the world of the Comintern. Having returned to Paris in April 1933, Aragon played an active role in the cultural policies of the Communist Party toward intellectuals. He was a very important figure for the anti-Fascist movement in the field of culture and a supporter, at the time of the Popular Front, of welcoming fellow travelers. Aragon was among the most active organizers of the World Congress of Writers in Defense of Culture held in Paris in June 1935, and he later played an important role in the International Association of Writers for the Defense of Culture, on whose behalf he organized many activities, some of the most significant being events in support of republican Spain. He praised the Soviet experience and Stalinist policies in many of his works. Maurice Thorez entrusted him with the coeditorship, shared with Jean-Richard Bloch, of an important evening daily, *Ce soir*, which started publication in March 1937. The periodical supported republican Spain, criticized the Munich Accords, and defended the German-Soviet pact, before it was shut down together with the rest of the Communist press by the Daladier government.

Drafted into the army medical corps on September 3, 1939, Aragon was captured during the German offensive of May 1940. He escaped and settled in Nice with Elsa Triolet in December 1940, without having reestablished contact with the party. In July 1941 he returned clandestinely to Paris at the party leaders' request and argued for an inclusive writers' association, in line with the National Front policies. Having returned to the south of France at the party's request, he organized the resistance on the cultural front. Aragon and Triolet returned to Paris in September 1944, where he renewed his editorship of *Ce soir*. His reputation as the nation's poet and activities within intellectual organizations that developed during the resistance allowed him to exercise a form of Communist hegemony, particularly in the National Committee of Writers. For Aragon the Cold War meant years of strict orthodoxy and also, as an artist, profound isolation. He defended the Communist Party's positions in the political and scientific debate involving the geneticist Trofim Denisovich Lysenko in 1948, supported Stalinist trials in the people's democracies, and participated in propaganda activities supporting socialist realism in the field of painting. But he still had to perform an act of self-criticism after having published a controversial portrait of Stalin by Pablo Picasso in an issue of *Lettres françaises* (March 12, 1953) devoted to the dictator's death. Pierre Daix dates Aragon's devastating coming to terms with Soviet reality to the winter of 1952, when he and Triolet went to Moscow to participate in the Nineteenth Congress of the Communist Party of the Soviet Union, and where Aragon physically perceived the atmosphere of terror.

During the 1960s he dedicated himself to the party's liberalization (he was a substitute member of the Central Committee starting in 1950 and a full member from 1961 on). Thanks to his efforts and influence, the party passed a resolution against Yuli Daniel's and Andrei Sinyavsky's sentencing in Moscow. Aragon supported the Prague Spring and published a protest on behalf of the National Writers Committee against the Warsaw Pact troops' entry into Czechoslovakia in August 1968. He took a stand against "normalization," which the French Communist Party instead supported, and he wrote the preface to the French edition of *Žert* (*The Joke*) by Milan Kundera. Aragon never questioned his loyalty to the party, but his literary works suggest that this loyalty was not without its intimate struggles, as shown by the poems of *Roman inachevé* (1956), published the same year as the Communist Party of the Soviet Union's Twentieth Congress, and the prefaces and commentary to his *Oeuvre poétique* (1974–81).

See also Antifascism; Fellow Travelers; Socialist Realism.

FURTHER READING

Aragon, L. *Oeuvre poétique, 1917–1979.* Paris: Livre-Club Diderot, 1989–90.

———. *Oeuvres romanesques completes.* Paris: Gallimard, 1997–2003.

NICOLE RACINE

Architecture and Urban Planning

In their conceptual origins and theoretical developments, the idea of the city and the Socialist/Communist settlement share some views and theories about urban and territorial planning; the latter also contributed to some fundamental transitions in the historical evolution of urban studies between the modern and contemporary periods. Those images and conceptions that constitute the figures and horizon of modernity, such as continuity, the critique of concentration (the condition that produces inequality, exploitation, violence, and social differences), equilibrium, and rationality, were all outlined between the 16th and 19th centuries (but were already present in antiquity to some degree). They led, through a process of radicalization to which the founders of scientific socialism also contributed, to the Socialist/Communist ideas of city and settlement. These ideas, in turn, led to two fundamental tendencies in both the ideology and the construction practices of the "Communist" habitat: to reorganize the urban settlement according to more egalitarian criteria, and to overcome the opposition of town and country.

In the 20th century these tendencies would inspire programs and plans as well as urban and territorial transformations, in the context of the experiences of "real socialism." Experts in economic and urban geography have shown how these developments differ from those that are typical of urban models tied to the development of industrialized cities in a capitalist environment. An examination of the Soviet experience provides a paradigmatic model of the socialist city as it emerged from the broader context of experiments in architecture and urban planning realized during the development of communism in the 20th century. This model city established itself internationally in the middle decades of the 20th century, before the crisis of the Communist bloc led to an increasing convergence with those forms of contemporary urban development that have come to dominate the capitalist world—a convergence that became obvious, starting in the 1990s, in all countries that were part of the ex-USSR or Eastern Europe, but especially in China. The basic source for the contemporary idea of the Communist city and its implementation, and more generally for modern thought about urban studies, must be sought in the tradition of utopian thought, which was prefigured in the modern period by Thomas More and Tommaso Campanella, and developed significantly in the 18th and 19th centuries (by Robert Owen, Charles Fourier, and Henri de Saint-Simon).

This tradition became a catalyst for a view of urban space that in terms of social organization and its physical projection, was tied to a harmonious, rational, and just order. This utopian thought, developed while the first explorations of the New World were taking place, was dominated by perspective and the rediscovery of the architectural language of the classical period (due to quattrocento authors such as L. B. Alberti, Filarete, and Francesco di Giorgio) as well as the idea of the closed city, which it associated with the idea of perfect form. In the 16th century, progress in the technologies and strategies of warfare along with other political and historical developments contributed concretely to this concept of perfection, which is reflected in the genre of military treatises. The 17th and 18th centuries, characterized by a powerful drive to colonize new territories, also marked a crucial period for the development of a more detailed image of the ideal city and its harmonious social and living arrangements, inspired by the ideas of rationality, hygiene, and salubriousness, and of a formal order guaranteed by the rules of classical composition and control over production (Claude-Nicolas Ledoux).

This also was the century in which the outlines of the contemporary conception of urban planning took shape. They would be extended to urban space as a whole, and not limited to a formal domination of some of its parts; from this conception the theme of public buildings and spaces would emerge and, starting with the French Revolution, triumph. This was a culture that liked to plan, particularly influenced by medical and engineering concerns, and that had been shaped by the polytechnic's view of the world; these plans guided the urban modernization that accompanied the dramatic growth of the capitalist industrial city in the 19th century. Alternate conceptions of development, centered on the more or less radical critique of the large city and the denunciation of its living conditions, also emerged during this period—a result of technical and professional approaches whose principal goals included management and reform.

Friedrich Engels's contribution (one of the fundamental contributions to the ideology and revolutionary legacy of the 20th century, starting of course with the Soviet experience) belongs to a tradition whose historic origins included 19th-century "utopias" and utopians, who were engaged in the elaboration of ideal models of habitation (Fourier) as an alternative to then-current forms of development. From Engels's point of view, the problem of the living conditions of the proletariat excluded partial technical remedies, and had to be addressed on the basis of the social question—in other words, by overturning the capitalist mode of production; once this had been accomplished, the housing crisis could be addressed by resorting to radical redistribution operations. The end of the 19th century would witness a decisive contribution to proposals for large-scale alternative forms of human habitation: the development of the idea of the garden city. In its original formulation in the work of Ebenezer Howard (*Tomorrow: the Peaceful Path to Real Reform* [London, 1898]), the garden city was based on a multiplicity of references (Marshall, Edward Bellamy's utopia, and Pyotr Kropotkin's thought): its goal was to provide a definitive answer, albeit a reformist one, to the evils of modern urban development; and it was inspired by a sort of "philanthropic" capitalism, organized on a cooperative basis. In addition to inspiring some fundamental concepts of international 20th-century urban planning, including some on an institutional level (Peter Hall), especially those tied to the socialist movement and actions undertaken by social democratic municipalities in the Weimar Republic, this model constituted a fundamental point of reference for the Soviet revolution's prewar plans, whose principal legislative foundation, from the point of view of urban and territorial planning, were the measures adopted in 1917 on the public control of land.

One can find different possible models for the idea of a Communist city at different points in Soviet history. Ideas of radical territorial reorganization and urban decentralization dominated the first postrevolutionary phase, which was marked by "spontaneous" urban decline during the years of War Communism (1918–21). Urban policies during this phase included the socializa-tion of land and existing urban housing stock (with the decree of August 20, 1918), accompanied by significant redistribution in large cities; the institutionalization of cohabitation became the means for confronting the serious housing crisis in late imperial Russia's principal cities.

If the state's control of land and the housing stock, imposed during this first revolutionary period, was a given in the urban economy of the Soviet Union and socialist experiences inspired by this model—with the exception of the New Economic Policy, during which the possibility of a resurgence of the mixed urban economy, and the return of large segments of this economy to private ownership, seemed to take hold—a variety of architectural and urban planning conceptions existed during different phases of Soviet history. The form of the Soviet city and the theories inspiring its construction were influenced by ideas coming from the Western tradition of planning, especially the modern movement, which was particularly influential during the 1920s. The idea of a "spread-out" city, in the form of either agroindustrial cities or the radical disurbanism theorized by Mikhail Okhitovic and other representatives of the period's avant-garde inspired by the severe architectonic style of the modern movement, and by the radically egalitarian ethos manifested in experiments with communal housing (the commune houses) dominated the first years of the first *pjatiletka* (First Five-Year Plan).

Starting in the early 1930s, however, a more traditional idea of urban form emerged, drawing from the greatest examples of 19th-century urban planning proposed by the modernization of great "bourgeois" capitals, like Paris and Vienna. This more traditional idea emphasized celebratory and collective spaces, extensive green areas, and the central compositional role of large residential and monumental administrative complexes (featuring perimetral development, or *kvartaly*); it embodied the dictates of socialist realism as outlined in those years. The more traditional idea of urban form dominated the period's great experiments in urban reconstruction, especially in Moscow, and served as a model for the Communist city until the late 1950s. The types of development that occurred in the Soviet capital in the postwar period culminated in the construction of postwar Stalinist "skyscrapers," which symbolized socialism's technological achievements, capable of competing with the U.S. vertical city—an unchallenged though ambiguous expression of 20th-century modernity—and its social superiority, since its development is planned.

The principal skyscrapers, built and arranged in Moscow between the end of the 1940s and the mid-1950s—officially called "tall buildings" (in place of the literal Russian translation of skyscrapers, a way of distancing them, even at the level of terminology, from the U.S. phenomenon)—were designed to valorize the urban landscape and the skyline. They were arranged on the city plan to form a star, a pattern that recalled one of the regime's fundamental icons. The explicit goal of this vision was to use the constructed urban form, seen as a single integrated work of art (by Boris Groys), as an example of realized utopia. The different styles were meant to signify a superior synthesis of the greatest expressions in architectural history, realized during the era of communism's triumph.

The traditional model, which following the dictates of socialist realism was declared "socialist in content and national in form," was exported to other countries in the Communist bloc and adapted to different historical and contextual conditions. Its diffusion was exemplified by the Stalinallee in East Berlin or the original plans for new industrialized cities in Eastern Europe, like Nowa Huta, near Kraków, Poland. It was shelved rapidly, however, as a consequence of Khrushchev's radical turn: he placed housing issues among his top priorities in an attempted reform of the post-Stalinist regime, and this required moving beyond the cohabitation that had dominated the country until the 1950s. These attempted reforms therefore also led to a denunciation of the wastefulness characteristic of the monumental style and, more generally, of compact models of urban planning. Khrushchev favored a model inspired by the "rational" city, characterized by large mass housing complexes and heavy prefabricated construction similar, at least at the planning stage, to the expansion of public housing projects, such as the *grands ensembles* located in suburban districts and promoted by public policies in Western cities during the second half of the 20th century.

Among the most important urban and architectural developments influenced by the radical goals of the workers' movement in the prewar period was the "ethical tradition of Austro-Marxism and its economic policies," in social democratic Vienna between 1930 and 1933 ("*das Rote Wien*"), which resulted in rent control and the construction of monumental worker housing (such as the Karl Marx Hof) with social services that guaranteed the residents' quality of life. These complexes became legendary because of the worker residents' resistance to Hitler's brownshirts.

The Situationist International movement, founded in 1957 after the fusion of the International Movement for an Imaginist Bauhaus (1954–57) with the Lettrist International (1952–57, the result of a radical split within the Lettrist group, founded in 1946), and the London Psychogeographical Committee, reflected on and experimented with plans and artistic form; its activities contributed to theories about the organization of living spaces, offering radical alternatives to what could be found in the capitalist order. These theories were partly inspired by a heterodox interpretation of the Marxism developed by the Soviet avant-garde in the 1920s, and destined to profoundly influence both the views and actions of some strains of the radical protest movement of the 1960s and 1970s in postwar Western Europe. Moving in the space between the political and aesthetic avant-garde, starting with the critique of alienation in the neocapitalist city and an optimistic vision of economic development in advanced societies, which were destined, according to the movement's theoreticians (Asger Jorn, Guy Debord, and Constant Nieuwenhuys), to free time from the constraints of work and favor social creativity, as its point of departure, situationism then focused on what can only be called a real vision of urban planning. Its objectives were antifunctionalist and playful, theoretically focused on the idea of "situation" as an element capable of generating revolutionary transformations both in one's way of life and the urban environment. This vision would lead to a direct involvement in the events of May 1968 in France: Situationism was one of its fundamental sources of inspiration.

Situationist views of urban planning found their highest expression in a cycle of research projects by the Dutch artist and architect Constant; developed between 1956 and 1974, the cycle was inspired by the idea of a New Babylon. It dealt with a suspended collective residential megastructure, separated from vehicular traffic located below it and extended by means of connections between the various residential units to the entire urban settlement. This megastructure was endowed with a wealth of environments and stimuli, destined to be periodically renewed by "teams of specialized creators, which will therefore be professional *situationists*."

See also Five-Year Plans; Modernization; New Economic Policy; Planning; Socialist Realism; Urbanization; Utopia.

FURTHER READING

Aman, A. *Architecture and Ideology during the Stalin Era: An Aspect of Cold War History*. Cambridge, MA: MIT Press, 1992.

Colton, T. J. *Moscow: Governing the Socialist Metropolis.* Cambridge, MA: Belknap Press, 1995.

De Magistris, A. *La costruzione della città totalitaria: il piano di Mosca e il dibattito sulla città sovietica tra gli anni venti e cinquanta.* Milan: Città Studi, 1995.

French, R. A., and F. E. I. Hamilton, eds. *The Socialist City: Spatial Structure and Urban Policy.* New York: Wiley, 1979.

Stadler, S. *The Situationist City.* Cambridge, MA: MIT Press, 1998.

Stites, R. *Revolutionary Dreams: Utopian Vision and Experimental Life in the Russian Revolution.* New York: Oxford University Press, 1989.

Tafuri, M. *Vienna rossa: la politica residenziale nella Vienna socialista, 1919–1933.* Milan: Electa, 1980.

ALESSANDRO DE MAGISTRIS

Arendt, Hannah

Among the major philosophical and political writers dealing with communism, Hannah Arendt occupies an unusual and important place. In the English-language literature of the Cold War, many of the influential writings critical of the Soviet Union in theory and practice emerged, methodologically speaking, from straightforward comparisons between "dictatorship and democracy," as they were perceived in the West before and after the Second World War, initially by journalists, in a more or less positivist vein. Some of the most significant of these comparisons eventually took on academic form, like Carl J. Friedrich and Zbigniew K. Brzezinski's *Totalitarian Dictatorship and Autocracy* (1956). Other critiques derived from some form of Left Marxism, either via Trotsky or the Frankfurt school. Isaac Deutscher's three-volume biography of Trotsky (1954–63) and Herbert Marcuse's *Soviet Marxism* (1958) are representative early examples.

Arendt's *Origins of Totalitarianism* (1951) came out of an entirely different tradition: that of phenomenology, and particularly the work of Martin Heidegger, of whom Arendt had been a student and with whom she had had an intimate relationship in the 1920s. It should be said immediately that the initial focus of Arendt's remarkable book was not communism but German National Socialism. Indeed it is apparent even at a first reading that the author knew far more about Germany than

the Soviet Union. Nevertheless, her use of the nascent term "totalitarianism" made it inevitable that her massive study would influence those studying the Soviet and East European experience of dictatorship as well as the German one. Communism and nazism, she belatedly came to think, were "two sides of the same coin," to cite Julia Kristeva's words. Neither of them was opposed to evolving European modernity, as other theorists opined; both of them represented its most dreadful depths.

A major aspect of the *Origins of Totalitarianism* is Arendt's account of breakdown and its consequences in Europe, centering on the collapse of public space, in the century after the French Revolution. Arendt saw the emergence of the totalitarian state amid the wreckage of the relatively stable world of the 19th century. European racism and imperialism were central to European self-destruction. As the century drew to a close, Arendt saw the citizen, the person concerned with public affairs, increasingly replaced by the bourgeois: private economic interest replaced the citizen's commitment to thinking and judging in a political arena. She believed that the loneliness, uprootedness, and superfluousness that increasingly afflicted Europe at the turn of the 20th century amounted to the loss of civilization itself. And according to Margaret Canovan, it was that "widespread experience of 'superfluousness' [greatly magnified by the First World War] that prepared the way for the concerted eradication of human individuality" so instrumental in giving birth to both communism and fascism.

Arendt's stress on the "loneliness" and "homelessness" of large numbers of 20th-century Europeans clearly shows her debt to Heidegger, as does her belief that modern industry was deeply connected to the functioning of the concentration and death camps in both Germany and the Soviet Union. And like Heidegger, she made classical antiquity a central part of her story of civilization followed by decline, though she configured her narrative quite differently than he did. Her vision of the public realm, the "solid, durable common world" as Canovan put it, derived ultimately from the Greek polis, key elements of which were sequentially recovered and lost over the centuries.

Toward the end of her life, Arendt focused increasingly on reading and thinking about Karl Marx, as evidenced by *The Human Condition*. She was no democrat. In dramatic opposition to Marxist utopianism, she believed that "the political value of equality has been realized in the fact of sameness," noted Sheldon Wolin. As Marx privileged the social, Arendt privileged the political: the public space, the forum, the agora, where human beings could prove themselves by political deeds. She was never particularly interested in the characters and personalities of the leaders, Hitler and Stalin. It was the triumph of the systems that brought them to power that interested her.

As her work on the *Origins* drew toward a conclusion, Arendt came to believe that the ultimate aspiration of both the Soviet Union and National Socialism in Germany was to remake human nature according to an ideology, largely through the terror and coercion of the concentration camp. All nontotalitarian reality had to be eliminated for consistency's sake.

Arendt's influence on the anti-Communist literature of the following decades was subtle and indirect. Her criticism of the unrestrained workings of the capitalist system made her difficult for many European and U.S. cold warriors to adapt to their purposes. But her work made it possible to see "totalizing behaviors" and "practices" as premonitory of political extremism, and in an attenuated form that critique has endured to this day.

See also: Anticommunism; Cold War; Fascism; Totalitarianism.

FURTHER READING

Canovan, M. "Arendt's Theory of Totalitarianism: A Reassessment." In *The Cambridge Companion to Hannah Arendt*, ed. D. Villa. Cambridge, UK: Cambridge University Press, 2000.

Hinchman, L. P., and S. K. Hinchman. *Hannah Arendt: Critical Essays*. Albany: State University of New York Press, 2000.

Kristeva, J. *Hannah Arendt*. New York: Columbia University Press, 2001.

Young-Bruehl, E. *Hannah Arendt: For Love of the World*. New Haven, CT: Yale University Press, 1982.

ABBOTT GLEASON

Atheism, Soviet

As the position that affirms the nonexistence of god or deities, or denies the metaphysical beliefs in god/gods or spiritual entities, Soviet atheism was historically based on the experience of the Russian "generation of freedom" of the 1860s. The background and philosophy of this generation derives from the Left Hegelian concepts of rationality and the need for change. Another source of the materialist *weltschaaung* was the tradition of the French Enlightenment. Nevertheless, the Russian materialist generation of the 1860s developed its own special wordview, which adored and worshipped science and was especially directed against the existing imperial system in which the Russian Orthodox Church was fused already in 1721.

The generation of "nihilists" loathed the union between the czar's throne and altar with the moral condemnation of Socialist-Revolutionary fervor. The government and its reaction turned the representatives of this generation, particularly Nikolay Chernyshevsky (1828–89), into martyrs. During his fourteen years of imprisonment Chernyshevsky wrote a "key novel," *What Is to Be Done?* [*Chto delat?*], which became the catechesis of the Russian radical intelligentsia. This book worshipped the role models of the new active people and professional revolutionaries, who would sacrifice themselves for the good of people and a new "rational" society.

The Russian Marxist movement adopted easily the spiritual legacy of the nihilists. "The father of the Russian Marxist movement," G. V. Plekhanov (1856–1918), and the founder of Bolshevik Party, Lenin (1870–1924), were especially inspired by the aggressive atheist outlook of the 1860s' generation.

Lenin's atheism and opinions on religion were later studied as the source of Soviet atheism. For Lenin, religion was a philosophically incompatible notion. Morally he considered atheism a sign of proper mental hygiene, but as a politician he was willing to take into consideration religion as a political force. In the early period (1900–1905) he was willing to accept persecuted Russian sectarians as political allies, but later (1905–17) he rejected all possibilities that religion could work as a progressive political force. During the revolution of 1905, orthodox priest G. A. Gapon had been leading the demonstrators, and the imperial secret police, Okhrana, tried to utilize religion as a source of a progovernment, Christian socialist movement. This movement was organized by police officer S. V. Zubatov, who had also established relations with Gapon.

In his writing "Socialism and Religion," Lenin defined his atheist position and declared that together with Marx's famous phrase that religion was "opium," it was also a "moonshine," which the exploiting classes were willingly serving to the masses in order to keep them in the dark. This rather indifferent stand of Lenin was sharpened during the reaction, which followed the 1905 revolution, especially when part of the Russian intelligentsia started to "flirt" with religion and some of Lenin's ardent followers began to create their own "semi-religious" heresies. For example, former Marxists S. N. Bulgakov (1871–1944) and N. A. Berdyayev (1874–1948) strayed to religious contemplations, and Lenin's former chief of staff A. A. Bogdanov (1873–1928) along with political allies such as A. V. Lunatsarsky (1875–1933) and benefactors such as the writer Maksim Gorky willingly forgot the hard atheism of Lenin.

The Bolshevik revolution of 1917 separated the paths of the Russian Orthodox Church and the new Communist state. Still, against the wisdom declared by the "Cold War warriors," the atheist society was not created once and for all after the revolution. During the revolution and Russian civil war (1917–21), the Bolshevik Party was more interested in its political survival than in conducting atheist campaigns. The legacy of education was given to the new Commissariat of education, which indeed formally practiced nonreligious versus antireligious education.

The Communist Party itself started to organize antireligious work only after the civil war. In this sense the party had ambiguous goals: the idea of the New Economic Policy was not to upset the peasants, and therefore the fervor of the antireligious campaigns of young Communists were seen by "culturalists" of the party as "counterproductive." Many "interventionist" Communists, however, were not happy about this more conciliatory approach, and saw religion as similar to matters such as "cocaine, booze and syphilis." The interventionist grouping in the party favored a massive and violent attack on religion, whereas the culturalists preferred education and wished to allow religion to die a natural death.

The official atheism was then conducted by a special organization, which active representatives of the Moscow party organization created around the publishing house Ateist in 1922. The Moscow party committee published a series of essays such as "Communism and Religion" and "Science and Religion," but the real official atheist activities started in December 1922 when the newspaper *Bezbozhnik* (Godless) was established by Emil'ian Mikhailovich Yaroslavskii (1878–1943)

This newspaper acted as a flag bearer of official atheism, and was surrounded by other newspapers and circulars such as *Ateist*, *Bezbozhnik u stanka* (Godless on the Bench) for workers, and *Derevensky Bozbozhnik* for peasants. These publications had official assisting societies such as the Moscow Society of the Godless and, later, the all-union League of the Militant Godless.

The highlight of official atheism in the Soviet Union was in the early 1930s, when the Communist Party under the leadership of Stalin (1879–1953) conducted its "cultural revolution" against the old world. At that time, the membership of the League of the Militant Godless was nearly identical with the party's membership. The outcome of the league's activities was disappointing, however; as U.S. scholar Daniel Peris put it, the League of the Militant Godless was "a nationwide Potemkin village of atheism" suffering from bureaucracy and lack of involvement from its members. The same could be said about the success of the official atheist celebrations such as Red weddings, funerals, baptisms, and so on. It seemed that the church and its festivals could compete more effectively in the fields of rituals.

During World War II the league continued its activities, but was it more on the margins of Soviet society. Only after the rise of N. S. Hrustsev in 1964 did atheism receive new stimulus due to the third party program, created in 1961. During this era, between 1959 and 1964, the Soviet Union restarted the closures of churches.

Yet the main emphasis of this antichurch campaign was in the official new ideology. The Soviet Union was heading to the final goal of a Communist society, and in order to get there it was time to get rid of the remnants (*perezhitki*) of the past. The younger generation together with the intelligentsia were, in particular, supposed to eradicate religion.

Together with the intensified purge against believers, the party created a new "semi" academic field of study, scientific atheism, which became an integral part of official academic Soviet life. Everybody trying to get a higher education was supposed to receive some credits from this new discipline.

The official position of atheism was derived from the Soviet constitution, which recognized the fundamental right of each citizen to conduct antireligious propaganda and at the same time practice their religious beliefs, but not the right to conduct religious propaganda (article 50 of the USSR Constitution of 1977 and the 1978 Constitution of the Ukrainian Soviet Socialist Republic).

Scientific atheism did not have a particular theoretical base other than in the writings of Marx, Engels, and Lenin along with some party-based philosophical writings, which were all then nominated as a basis for dialectical materialism. Nevertheless, scientific atheism was part of the core studies of the university curricula, and the official emphasis was "preemptive" or "clinical"—studying scientific atheism on the origins and social role of religion was supposed to make students "overcome" religion. The role of official atheism continued until 1991, when the new law concerning religious organizations was published. This law ended the official status of scientific atheism in the Soviet Union, just before the collapse of the Soviet system itself.

See also Catholic Church; Islam; New Man; Orthodox Church, Russian; Propaganda, Communist.

FURTHER READING

Husband, W. B. *Godless Communists: Atheism and Society in Soviet Russia, 1917–1932.* DeKalb: Northern Illinois University Press, 2000.

Luukkanen, A. *The Party of Unbelief: The Religious Policy of the Bolshevik Party, 1917–1929.* Helsinki: Studia Historica, 1994.

———. *The Religious Policy of the Stalinist State: A Case Study: The Central Standing Commission on Religious Questions, 1929–1938.* Helsinki: Studia Historica, 1997.

Peris, D. *Storming the Heavens: The Soviet League of the Militant Godless.* Ithaca, NY: Cornell University Press, 1998.

Shevzov, V. *Russian Orthodoxy on the Eve of Revolution.* Oxford: Oxford University Press, 2004.

Wynot, J. J. *Keeping the Faith: Russian Orthodox Monasticism in the Soviet Union, 1917–1939.* College Station: Texas A&M University Press, 2004.

Young, G. *Power and the Sacred in Revolutionary Russia: Religious Activists in the Village.* University Park: Pennsylvania State University Press, 1997.

ARTO LUUKKANEN

Atomic Bomb

1939–45

The discovery of nuclear fission in Berlin at the end of 1938 aroused great excitement among physicists in the Soviet Union when the news reached them at the end of February 1939. Like their colleagues in other countries, they saw that it might now be possible to harness atomic energy for practical purposes. They understood that if a nuclear fission chain reaction could be achieved, atomic energy might be used for electric power generation and nuclear bombs. They pursued the same lines of research as physicists in other countries, and made important progress in establishing the conditions under which nuclear chain reactions, both controlled and explosive,

could take place. The Academy of Sciences set up a Uranium Commission in June 1940 to coordinate nuclear research, but no bomb project was established in this period. Nuclear research was still seen by most scientists and the authorities as far from practical application.

This research was brought to a stop by the German invasion of June 22, 1941. The atomic bomb was still a remote prospect, and the Soviet Union had to mobilize all its resources to prevent a Nazi victory. Soon after the German invasion, however, the Soviet intelligence services began to obtain information about nuclear research abroad, especially in Britain. In 1941 British physicists understood better than anyone else how a bomb might be built. The British government had set up the Maud Committee in 1940 to investigate the feasibility of an atomic bomb, and this committee concluded in July 1941 that a bomb containing 11 kilograms of uranium-235 could be made before the end of 1943. This was one of the documents passed to Moscow by Soviet agents in the British government, but the Soviet authorities took no immediate action.

On September 28, 1942, Stalin signed a decree setting up a small project to investigate whether the atomic bomb was feasible. It seems to have been the prompting of scientists who feared that Germany was developing the atomic bomb, rather than the intelligence from Britain and the United States, that led Stalin to this decision. The physicist Igor Kurchatov was put in charge of the atomic project. In late 1942, he was shown the intelligence reports (including the Maud Report) about foreign research and quickly became convinced that the bomb was indeed feasible.

It took time to set up the atomic project under the difficult wartime conditions. Kurchatov gradually assembled a small group of scientists in the newly created Laboratory No. 2 in Moscow. Before the middle of 1945, this group devoted itself to the analysis of the extensive intelligence information that the Soviet Union was receiving about the Manhattan Project. Kurchatov's laboratory was able to do theoretical calculations, but experimental research was much more difficult to organize. Uranium was in short supply, and it was not until September 1944 that Kurchatov managed to reconstitute a cyclotron that had been built in Leningrad before the war. He was frustrated by the lack of progress and a lack of support from the authorities. He understood, thanks to the intelligence about U.S. progress, just how great the gap was between the Manhattan Project and the Soviet one. Kurchatov wrote to Beria in September 1944 to urge that serious measures be taken to speed up Soviet work.

As the war with Germany drew to an end, the atomic project expanded. Steps were taken to organize uranium exploration and plans were drawn up to move the project on to an industrial footing. A team of scientists was sent to Germany in May 1945 to learn what the German atomic project had achieved. The most important discovery they made was 100 tons of uranium oxide, which speeded up the construction of the first Soviet experimental reactor by one year. In spite of these measures, though, the project did not yet have the overriding priority it was to acquire in August 1945. This lack of priority suggests that the Soviet leadership did not grasp before Hiroshima the enormous strategic significance of the atomic bomb.

In July 1945, before the opening of the Potsdam Conference on July 17, Stalin received information that the U.S. atomic test at Alamogordo, New Mexico, was about to or had already taken place. He of course knew about the Soviet project and surely understood what Harry S. Truman had in mind when the U.S. president told him on July 24 that the United States now possessed a new weapon of "unusual destructive force." Yet he did not seem to have grasped that the bomb would be used soon against Japan to devastating effect. On August 7, the day after the bombing of Hiroshima, he advanced by two days the date of Soviet entry into the war against Japan, apparently fearing that Japan would surrender quickly as a result of the use of the atomic bomb.

Soviet forces entered the war against Japan on August 8, and Stalin managed to secure the Far Eastern gains promised to him under the Yalta Agreement. There is little doubt, however, that he regarded the use of the bomb by the United States as an anti-Soviet move designed to thwart the Soviet Union of strategic gains in the Far East. He feared that the United States would try to use its atomic monopoly to shape the postwar world in its favor, and was determined not to let that happen.

1945–49

On August 20, 1945—two weeks to the day after Hiroshima—Stalin signed a decree setting up the Special Committee of the State Defense Committee (later of the Council of Ministers) to direct the atomic project. Chaired by Beria, the committee included among its nine members party leaders, industrial managers, and scientists. It was given extraordinary powers to build the atomic bomb as quickly as possible: that was now "Problem No. 1" for the Soviet state. Attached to the Special Committee was a Technical Council, which was to consider scientific and technical questions. Ten days later the First Chief Directorate of the State Defense Committee was established, with B. L. Vannikov as its head, to provide day-to-day direction of the research institutes, design bureaus, and industrial plants involved in the atomic project.

A whole new industry had to be created to mine, process, and enrich uranium, build reactors for plutonium production, and design and fabricate the bomb. The number of people involved in the whole project, including mining and construction, was probably in the hundreds of thousands. This was an enormous undertaking for the Soviet Union, which had lost twenty-six to twenty-seven million citizens in the war, and saw thousands of towns and villages destroyed. It required an act of intense political will to give overriding priority to the atomic project under such circumstances.

There was no dissent in the party leadership about the decision to build the bomb as quickly as possible. The Soviet Union was a great power, which had grown even greater as a result of World War II, and it was therefore right and proper for it to have the bomb. It was also the first socialist state with the mission of leading the world to communism, and it therefore needed to counterbalance the atomic might of the leading imperialist countries. It was important to deprive the United States of any political advantage from its atomic monopoly and show that the Soviet Union would not be intimidated. Stalin said little in public about the bomb, and what he said was designed to belittle its significance, but the priority he gave the atomic project shows that he took it seriously indeed.

The atomic project was another example of Stalin's policy of "catching up and overtaking" the West. Stalin rejected the argument that the Soviet Union should try to find its own, cheaper path to the bomb. The technical choices made by the Soviet project were greatly influenced by the Manhattan Project. A plutonium production complex, with reactors as well as reprocessing and metallurgical plants, was built near the town of Kyshtym in the Urals, a gaseous diffusion enrichment plant was built in the central Urals, and a small electromagnetic enrichment plant was constructed in the northern Urals. A bureau (KB-11) for the design and development of the bomb was established at Sarov, 400 kilometers to the east of Moscow. This bureau, the Soviet equivalent of Los Alamos, was instructed to produce two bombs— one with plutonium and the other with highly enriched uranium—for ground tests in 1948; the designs were to be as close as possible to those of the first two U.S. bombs, since it was thought that copying existing designs would shorten the development time and provide the best guarantee of success.

The Soviet project encountered many difficulties. Uranium supply was a critical problem; in August 1945 it was not clear where the uranium would come from. The most important source of supply in the early postwar years was Eastern Europe, and especially from the Soviet zone of Germany. (In 1950, 460 tons of uranium were mined in the Soviet Union and 1,808 tons were mined in Eastern Europe.) On December 25, 1946, the first Soviet experimental reactor went critical. Serious problems arose, though, with the plutonium production reactors and gaseous diffusion enrichment plant, and the dates for the first tests had to be deferred as a result. Plutonium became available before highly enriched uranium, and the first test explosion took place on August 29, 1949, on the steppes of Kazakhstan. The device detonated was a plutonium bomb modeled on the one tested at Alamogordo on July 16, 1945, and it produced about the same explosive yield (20 kilotons). In 1951 two further tests followed, of more efficient designs that used highly enriched uranium as well as plutonium.

The Soviet atomic project received considerable help from abroad. More than two hundred German specialists, including thirty-three scientists and seventy engineers, worked on the project. Most of the German specialists worked on uranium enrichment, which did not affect the time it took to produce the first Soviet bomb. Still, a small group headed by Nikolaus Riehl did play a key role in the production of uranium metal. Information about the Manhattan Project also had a significant impact on the Soviet project, helping to get it started and influencing key technical choices. It enabled the Soviet Union to break the U.S. atomic monopoly sooner than it could otherwise have done—perhaps by a year or two, though how much more quickly is difficult to say. Even with the help from abroad, the Soviet project was still a major undertaking. Soviet scientists and engineers had to test all the information for themselves, and it is only because they were competent that they were able to make good use of the assistance they received.

The Soviet stockpile of atomic bombs grew slowly. The Soviet Union did not accumulate enough plutonium for a second bomb until December 1, 1949, three months after the first test, and the first three series of production bombs were produced only in December 1951. In 1949 and 1950, the Soviet government took the decision to expand greatly its capacity to produce plutonium by building new reactors at Chelyabinsk-40, where the first production reactor had been built, and Tomsk-7 and Krasnoyarsk-26.

Stalin did not believe, in the early postwar years, that a new world war was imminent. Yet he did regard war as inevitable in the longer term, after an interval of perhaps twenty or thirty years—similar to the gap between World War I and World War II. Stalin's postwar decisions reflected that perspective. He cut back the Red Army, but invested heavily in military technologies that would have a long-term impact on Soviet strength—jet propulsion, radar, missiles, and the atomic bomb. By 1949, however, the Cold War had grown more intense, and the prospect of war was looming larger. The Soviet Union ended the postwar demobilization and began to increase Soviet forces in Eastern Europe.

Apart from setting up the Soviet atomic project, Stalin made other adjustments in his defense policy to deal with the nuclear threat. He invested heavily in air defense and the Long-Range Air Force. Nevertheless, he did not believe that the atomic bomb marked a fundamental transformation of war or international politics. He continued to assert that a new world war was inevitable and therefore had to be prepared for. In 1949 and again in 1952 Georgy Malenkov, in major speeches expressing the party line, claimed that World War I had led to the October Revolution and World War II had led to the creation of a socialist camp. World War III, he asserted, would end in the defeat of imperialism.

The Hydrogen Bomb

At the end of World War II, Soviet intelligence learned that Los Alamos was investigating the possibility of a hydrogen bomb in which a fission weapon would detonate a thermonuclear explosion that was much more powerful than an atomic bomb. Soviet physicists looked at that possibility in 1945, but the atomic fission bomb—which was in any case necessary for a thermonuclear weapon—was their main priority. In June 1948, after receiving new information from Klaus Fuchs about U.S. work, the Special Committee organized two research groups. One of these, which included Andrey Sakharov, worked in Moscow without access to intelligence and came up with an original design, which proved to be workable but less powerful than a true thermonuclear weapon could be. It was tested in August 1953, with a yield of 400 kilotons.

The second group worked at KB-11 with intelligence information about the U.S. "Classical Super" design.

U.S. scientists proved unable to make that design work, and the Soviet scientists fared no better. In 1951 the Americans made a breakthrough, coming up with a new design that made it possible to build a hydrogen bomb with almost infinite explosive power. In 1952 and again in 1954, they conducted tests that showed that they had mastered this new design. In 1954 Soviet physicists, apparently independently, came up with the same idea. In November 1955 the Soviet Union tested the new design with a yield of 1.6 megatons; what was important, though, was not the yield but rather the fact that the Soviet Union was now capable of producing thermonuclear weapons with enormous yields. By this time the United States had already tested several thermonuclear bombs, one of which had a yield of 15 megatons—that is, more than a thousand times more powerful than the bomb that destroyed Hiroshima. In 1961, the Soviet Union tested a bomb with a yield of 50 megatons.

U.S. thermonuclear tests in the Pacific in spring 1954 helped to trigger a debate in Moscow about the relationship between war and revolution. Malenkov, who had asserted that World War III would lead to the defeat of imperialism, took a different position in March 1954 when he stated that a new world war would mean the end of world civilization. Scientists in the nuclear weapons program supported this position, writing shortly afterward to Khrushchev, Malenkov, and Molotov that a nuclear war could lead to the end of all life on earth.

Malenkov's new position was politically untenable. Khrushchev and Molotov criticized him roundly for what they regarded as a serious political error, taking a position that caused confusion at home and abroad and giving greater priority to peace than to the struggle against imperialism. The Twentieth Party Congress in 1956 reaffirmed the older position that a new world war would lead to the defeat of imperialism, but it also proclaimed that Lenin's thesis of the inevitability of war was no longer operative because the Soviet Union had the means—that is, nuclear weapons—to rebuff an aggressor. Khrushchev and the other party leaders were well aware of the destruction that a nuclear war would bring and were determined to avoid it. Peaceful coexistence was now presented as the alternative to nuclear war, as a strategy for the long term.

The position taken by the Twentieth Party Congress remained essentially unchanged for the next thirty years: a new world war was not inevitable but it might happen nonetheless; the policy of the Soviet Union was to prevent such a war, but at the same time to prepare for it in case it should take place; if there were a new world war, it would end in the defeat of imperialism. This had important consequences for military policy because it meant that the armed forces had to prepare to defeat the imperialist powers in a world war. This precluded the adoption of a strategy of minimal deterrence and committed the Soviet Union to all-out military competition with the United States. It was only after Mikhail Gorbachev came to power that this position was abandoned and replaced by the "New Thinking."

The Chinese Bomb

In the early 1950s, the Chinese party leadership became interested in acquiring its own atomic bomb. Khrushchev was reluctant to get involved, but in 1955 the Soviet Union concluded the first of a series of agreements with China to help it develop its nuclear science and nuclear industry. The assistance provided by the Soviet Union under these arrangements was considerable. Soviet specialists helped with uranium exploration and processing, the design and assembly of the first experimental reactor, and the design of the first plutonium production reactor and gaseous diffusion enrichment plant. They also supplied detailed information about the nuclear weapon design that the Soviet Union had tested in 1951. Hundreds of young Chinese scientists received training in the Soviet Union. In October 1957 the Soviet Union agreed to deliver to China a mock-up of an atomic bomb, with a full set of technical documentation, but in 1958 it had second thoughts and canceled the delivery of the bomb. In 1959, the Communist Party of the Soviet Union's Central Committee wrote to its Chinese counterpart to advise it not to develop nuclear weapons and inform it that all Soviet aid for strategic weapons development would be suspended for two years. China proceeded to develop the bomb without further Soviet help and conducted its first test on October 16, 1964.

By the time of the Chinese nuclear test, the two parties were already engaged in bitter open polemics in which nuclear war occupied a prominent place. The Chinese were opposed to the Limited Test Ban Treaty of 1963 and Soviet efforts to restrain the spread of nuclear weapons. They also accused the Soviet leaders of betraying the cause of revolution in the vain hope of avoiding war. The Soviet leaders, for their part, criticized the Chinese leaders for having an irresponsible attitude to nuclear weapons and taking actions that would intensify the nuclear arms race and increase the risk of nuclear war. These arguments, which echoed those put forward in the Soviet debate about nuclear weapons after Stalin's death, show what critical implications nuclear weapons had for Marxist-Leninist strategies of revolution. Sino-Soviet relations continued to deteriorate in the 1960s, and in 1969, when relations reached a point of crisis, the Soviet Union dropped veiled but unmistakable hints that it was contemplating nuclear strikes against China. That threat helped to bring about the rapprochement between China and the United States.

See also Cold War; Military-Industrial Complex; Peaceful Coexistence; War, Inevitability of.

FURTHER READING

Andrjušin, A., A. K. Černyševeju, and J. A. Judin. *Ukroščenie jadra: stranicy istorii jadernogo oružija i jadernoj infrastruktury SSSR.* Sarov, 2003.

Cochran, T. B., R. S. Norris, and O. Bukharin. *Making the Russian Bomb: From Stalin to Yeltsin.* Boulder, CO: Westview Press, 1995.

Holloway, D. *Stalin and the Bomb: The Soviet Union and Atomic Energy, 1939–1956.* New Haven, CT: Yale University Press, 1994.

Lewis, J. W., and Xue Litai. *China Builds the Bomb.* Stanford, CA: Stanford University Press, 1988.

DAVID HOLLOWAY

Avant-garde

The collaboration that started in the early 1920s between Soviet power and preexisting avant-garde groups mostly focused on the attempt to create a new public. Representatives of the most varied "isms," of the many schools and splinter groups that starting in the 1910s had mobilized the European cultural scene, transferred their efforts to Russia. In addition to developing appealing cultural products that were also didactically appropriate, the avant-garde focused, or claimed it focused, on the complex concept of "procedure," exposing mechanisms of influence, propaganda, and manipulation that remained hidden in traditional art. The old way of representing the world had to be put aside in an attempt to transfigure it. The only way to combat the arrogant effects of technical rationalism and overcome the old ways of doing things and the devastating consequences of progress was to rise above them, to eradicate all that was old and obsolete

in order to build the new, purified of the nefarious influences of the past. The October Revolution provided, on the political front, the conviction that the moment to unleash the attack had come: an extraordinary occasion for avant-garde artists and intellectuals to translate their theoretical constructs into practice. The Russian formalists defined procedures as artifices, elevating them to the rank of artistic procedures, convinced that they would contribute to the creation of a new public capable of looking at the new world with eyes that were just as new, thus focusing more on a utopian modification of humankind than on art. The order of the day could have been: do not produce unknown cultural texts for an old public but instead shape an innovative public that will be capable of using its gaze in unforeseen ways.

Avant-garde artists did not set themselves any boundaries, they looked to the future as an infinite space yet to be created, and they believed they should therefore have equally unlimited means at their disposal. Their collaboration with political power was dictated not only by contingent forms of opportunism but also, and above all, by the absolute necessity to which their plan aspired: organize the artistic program in such a manner that it would be transformed into a social and political one. Constructivism informed every aspect of existence: aesthetic, artistic, and productive. This monopolistic control of the cultural terrain worried the Bolsheviks, who saw a dangerous exclusion of other currents in this dictatorship of the avant-garde. With the advent of the New Economic Policy in the country, a new artistic market was born. The reborn bourgeoisie demanded different artistic forms, forms that might be dangerously seductive for the new and still precariously ideologized proletarians. The avant-garde reacted by radicalizing its positions even further. The Left Front of the Arts, the most active and determined current, evolved from constructivism to productivism, theorizing yet another artistic dictatorship: both production and everyday life were supposed to be organized according to artistic methods. Any independent artistic activity needed to be condemned and fought.

These creative ferments, and the notion of chaotic frenzy interpreted as creation and experimentation, were silenced in 1932 when the party's Central Committee dissolved literary-artistic currents it deemed "sectarian" and subjected cultural practices to its own administrative rule. Stalin's First Five-Year Plan proceeded to establish a concept of art that would be accessible, problem free, and immediately understood by the masses, thus matching massive industrialization and the collectivization of land on the cultural front. The experimentations of the avant-garde were deemed too complex and elitist for a mass public: this public was supposed to find an answer to its demands in socialist realism, in which reality became indistinguishable from dreams, and the natural coincided with the artificial.

Socialist realism not only manifested itself as a return to mimetic imagery but also made wide use of the imagery that had been created and circulated by new media. Images that were broadcast and circulated by means of movie theaters, manifestos, paintings, and their reproductions in the thousands shared a particular "logic": the facts were not supposed to be represented as they actually were but rather as ideological desire conceived them. The work of art needed to contain the experiences and emotions that one intended to convey, in addition to the inevitable narration. Empathy and kitsch became the basis for this operation. Effects dominated procedures, but the image's falsehood was accepted on the basis of its claims to the ideal. Falsehood created a truth that was ideal. The rhetoric of the socialist realist artistic text was concerned not with truth and falsehood but efficacy and functionality instead. Boris Groys has theorized this procedure not as an a priori refusal of the avant-garde but as its radicalization, aimed at unmasking the strategies of the avant-garde so as to utilize them differently.

These reflections, and the debate on the Soviet avant-garde, would once more become topical at the end of the period of the great socialist realist narratives, when in the 1970s a movement called Sots-art would deconstruct Stalinist rhetoric, unveiling its procedures and revealing the void beneath. This tendency, whose promoters were the artists Vitaly Komar and Alex Melamid, is today interpreted as a phase of transition to Russian postmodernism, when communism was in its final stages and becoming aware of a postmodern future. Postmodernism is the heir of Soviet communism. Both share a hyper-real nature and a cold passion for ideological allegories as well as the clichés of popular consciousness. More than being merely a chronological point of transition, Sots-art exists at the intersection of two phenomena. In the visual perception of the end of communism, Sots-art deconstructs the cult of the sign, the symbol, the empty image devoid of any consistency or transparency, the slogan, the superabundance of redundant and ever-present messages, the only wealth of Soviet discourse. In this regard it can be compared to U.S. pop art, which had displayed the superabundance of products and the repetitiveness of the rituals of consumption as the most glaring side of U.S. consumerism.

This movement's aesthetics, which embody the population's passivity in the face of the official and monumental nature of Soviet propaganda, would eventually be designated *stiob*. The avant-garde of the 1970s elaborated ironic forms to handle the symbols of power in original and unpredictable ways: hyperidentification with the symbols of power itself, and the combination of symbols belonging to different areas to obtain a result that would ridicule Soviet ideological strategies. Relatively significant movements, like Muscovite conceptualism or Leningrad's rock music, would develop from these principles. The only goal of this avant-garde consisted in demonstrating the absurdity of so-called Soviet reality and it certainly did not aim to undermine the political system's foundations.

When the Soviet Union ceased to exist, and the effort to diffuse its ideology disappeared, the aesthetics of stiob lost its relevance. Mikhail Gorbachev's glasnost first and the realities of postcommunism later, however, stimulated an interesting inversion of direction, defined as reverse stiob. Those methods and artifices that had originally been used to mock the government's messages were exploited to subject any message that was addressed too aggressively to the socialist past—such as the explicit mockery of Soviet sacredness, Western feminism, savage anticommunism—to ridicule. Soviet symbols were given a new life in order to mock perestroika or positively redefine those signs, now freed from the pathos of Soviet excess, which the young generations of the 1990s rehabilitated, without becoming part of the much-acclaimed phenomenon of nostalgia, in a casual and provocative manner. The places and manifestations of this subculture were inspired by Soviet vocabulary and history: propaganda circle, Gagarin rave party, Gorky Café. Today this phenomenon no longer has any avant-garde quality and has slid to a low commercial touristy level, while the debate about the continuity of the avant-garde's trajectory from the 1920s, through Stalinism and postcommunism, is only beginning.

See also Cinema, Soviet; Cultural Policies; Literature in Soviet Russia; Mayakovski, Vladimir; Proletkult; Socialist Realism; Utopia.

FURTHER READING

Balina, M., N. Condee, and E. Dobrenko, eds. *End-quote: Sots-art Literature and Soviet Grand Style*. Evanston, IL: Northwestern University Press, 1999.

Gray, C. *The Russian Experiment in Art, 1863–1922*. London: Thames and Hudson, 1962.

Groys, B. *The Total Art of Stalinism: Avant-Garde, Aesthetic Dictatorship, and Beyond*. Princeton, NJ: Princeton University Press, 1992.

Stites, R. *Revolutionary Dreams: Utopian Vision and Experimental Life in the Russian Revolution*. New York: Oxford University Press, 1989.

GIAN PIERO PIRETTO

Bauer, Otto

One of the most remarkable representatives of Austrian social democracy and "Austro-Marxism," and one of the founders of the prestigious journal *Der Kampf*, Otto Bauer (1881–1938) was already recognized at the beginning of the new century for his theoretical inclinations. After the end of the World War I and the collapse of the Habsburg Empire he became a prominent figure in Austrian political life (in 1918–19 he was foreign minister for a few months) and the international socialist debate. Reflections on the Russian Revolution and the construction of socialism in the USSR were at the center of his intellectual and political preoccupations. He distinguished himself because his intent was to unite what were, in his judgment, two separate aspects of current events. On the one hand, he affirmed an incontrovertible relationship between Soviet-Russian events and the social and historical peculiarities of prerevolutionary Russia, and from this he derived the impossibility of using Bolshevism as a model for socialist action in the West; on the other hand, he saw an indissoluble link between the Soviet experiment and the cause of world socialism. This led both to the necessity of defending the revolution, given the objectively progressive nature of its historical role internally as well as internationally, and the hope that it would develop in a manner that would avoid a stiffening of its authoritarian forms, which were due to the backwardness of the Russian socioeconomic framework and, within it, the isolation of its industrial proletariat.

Convinced that different paths to socialism, each best suited to specific national conditions, might exist, Bauer did not agree with the attitude of those socialists who highlighted the contrasts between the principles of democratic socialism and the nature of Soviet communism; but at the same time, and for the same reason, he maintained that the democratic path should remain the main road to socialism in Central and Western Europe. He believed that the workers' movement, in the context of political democracy and by developing social struggles and constructing a majoritarian social bloc, should prepare the terrain for a reversal of power relations. Thus Bauer contemplated the possibility that the adversary's forces, in order to forestall the realization of such a possibility, would resort to reactionary means, following the example of Italian fascism. In such an event socialists would be forced to resort to revolutionary measures. The theory of the "defensive" resort to violence was one of the distinctive aspects of the contributions of Austrian social democracy (the Linz program in 1926), although in the face of the progressively deteriorating political situation in Austria, Bauer himself, starting in the late 1920s and anticipating the unfavorable balance of power, hesitated to put them into practice. Instead he continued to place his trust in a pacific evolution of the crisis, even after the sharp authoritarian turn in early 1933 imparted by the government headed by Chancellor Engelbert Dollfuss.

Forced into exile in Czechoslovakia and then in France after the Social Democratic Party's in extremis attempt in February 1934 to suppress the insurrection, Bauer warmed to the idea of the dictatorship of the proletariat, conceived as a transitional phase between the anti-Fascist revolution and an original version of socialist democracy that, unlike the USSR, would see equality and freedom conjoined. He simultaneously and forcefully urged a political collaboration between the Socialist and Communist Internationals against fascism, well before the era of Popular Front policies, and an alliance between the Western democracies and the USSR to face the emergent threat of war from Germany. Convinced of the success and the intrinsically positive nature of Soviet planning as a tangible demonstration of the possibilities for realizing a socialist economic order, Bauer hoped that the Stalinist dictatorship, strengthened by its achievements in the socioeconomic modernization of the country, might evolve in the direction of a "workers' democracy." Consequently he outlined the picture of an "integral socialism," in which both the reformist and revolutionary hypotheses, social democracy and communism, would be integrated in a superior synthesis. This process of adjustment might be helped by taking advantage of the new world war, which Bauer estimated was both close and inevitable, using it as an occasion to relaunch the struggle for socialism on a European level.

See also Antifascism; Bolshevism; Dictatorship of the Proletariat; Hilferding, Rudolf; Kautsky, Karl; National Question; Planning; Popular Front; Socialist International.

FURTHER READING

Leichter, O. *Otto Bauer. Tragodie oder Triumph.* Vienna: Europa Verlag, 1970.

Löw, R. *Otto Bauer und die russische Revolution.* Vienna: Europaverlag, 1980.

Natoli, C. "Otto Bauer: un profilo politico e intellettuale." In *Il Ponte* 60, no. 2–3 (2004): 117–43.

LEONARDO RAPONE

Beijing Spring

In the spring of 1989, a movement characterized by public demonstrations on the part of university students and other segments of civil society demanded the rehabilitation of the former secretary of the Chinese Communist Party, Hu Yaobang, and the establishment of a dialogue with the government and party on reforming the political system. Although the movement is generally associated with Tiananmen Square (Gate of Heavenly Peace), in the center of Beijing, during the seven-week period in which these events took place, demonstrations occurred in almost all of the country's major cities and most of the universities. The movement developed because the political climate was generally favorable, and some groups within the party along with the intellectuals tied to them believed that after a decade of economic reforms, times were ripe to address the prickly issue of reforming the political system. For other groups, however, like the teams from autonomous workers' unions that occupied the square during the second half of May, their dissatisfaction was tied to worsening work and livelihood condi-

tions, the continued decrease in state assistance, and an economic crisis that had affected traditional segments of the working class as a result of the economic reforms.

Hu's death on April 15 triggered the first demonstrations in Beijing and Shanghai. He served as party secretary during the early 1980s, but was removed in early 1987 because he had refused to put an end to another wave of student demonstrations in the winter of 1986. His death, due to natural causes, gave the students a legitimate motive to take to the streets. Initially the demonstrations were limited to expressing emotions, shared by many intellectuals, for a leader who was deemed closer to the students' aspirations for modernity and democracy—topics discussed in dozens of "democracy salons" in Chinese universities during these months. At the state funeral on April 22, the students loudly demanded Hu's rehabilitation. After being sharply criticized in a *People's Daily* editorial on April 26, the students returned peacefully to the square on April 27 and May 4, so as to coincide with the date of demonstrations for "science and democracy" in 1919. At this point the students were requesting a "dialogue among equals" and the recognition of the patriotic nature of the protests.

After the successful May 4 demonstration and conciliatory statements from a segment of the party leadership, two different tendencies emerged among the students: one thought it had reached its goals and wanted students to return to their institutions; another more radical one wanted to continue the demonstrations. The latter tendency became dominant when it began a hunger strike on Tiananmen Square on May 13. With the party and government apparently not able to arrive at unanimous decisions on the protests, the number of youths camping out on the square increased immensely, and the national and international media coverage underscored the dramatic and symbolic nature of the events. On May 15, the historic visit by Mikhail Gorbachev—the first Soviet leader to visit China since the break in diplomatic relations in 1960—had to start at the airport, far from the square.

On May 20, the internal party struggle that had paralyzed the decision-making process was resolved by declaring martial law in Beijing. The outcome was a defeat for the general secretary, Zhao Ziyang, who personally went to the square that evening and asked the students to return to their institutions in order to avoid a bloodbath. It was to be the last act of his political career. During the final two weeks the square was occupied by the most inflexible groups, supported by large segments of the population and groups of workers. On the night of June 3–4, the military intervened to end the demonstrations. An unknown number of demonstrators and civilians lost their lives during the clashes.

See also Deng Xiaoping; Perestroika; Post-Soviet Communism; Socialist Market Economy.

FURTHER READING

The Gate of Heavenly Peace. Produced and directed by Richard Gordon and Carma Hinton, 1995. Documentary. Boston: Long Bow Group.

Liang Zhang. *The Tian'an Men Papers.* New York: Public Affairs, 2001.

Minzhu Han, ed. *Cries for Democracy: Writings and Speeches from the 1989 Democracy Movement.* Princeton, NJ: Princeton University Press, 1990.

Saich, T., ed. *The Chinese People's Movement: Perspectives on Spring 1989.* Armonk, NY: Sharpe, 1990.

LUIGI TOMBA

Beria, Lavrenty

One of Stalin's closest comrades in arms, Lavrenty Beria (1899–1953), occupied key posts in the Soviet party-state system and had control of the party's penal system. Beria was born in Abkhazia to a family of peasants. From 1906 to 1915 he attended an elementary school in Sukhumi, and then went to a mechanics and construction school in Baku, graduating in 1919. During his studies Beria took part in the work of a Marxist circle. In March 1917 he joined the Bolshevik Party. Beria worked in the Bolshevik underground in Azerbaijan from 1918 to the beginning of 1920, and then was sent to do underground work in Georgia. He was arrested by Georgian authorities but was released due to pressure from the Soviet Russian government. After the establishment of Soviet power in Trans-Caucasia, Beria occupied various leading posts in Cheka organs in Azerbaijan, Georgia, and the Trans-Caucasian Federation up until 1931, earning his way to an appointment as chair of the Trans-Caucasian State Political Management Office.

Stalin's patronage was an important factor in Beria's subsequent political career. The leaders of the Trans-Caucasian Federation had been fighting with each other for several years, and Stalin was looking for a Trans-Caucasian leader who could put an end to these political squabbles. Ultimately he decided on Beria. In a letter to Lazar Kaganovich in August 1932, Stalin characterized Beria as a "good organizer, a business-like and capable worker." In 1932 Beria was named the first secretary of the Georgian Regional Committee, also filling the post of the first secretary of the Georgian Communist Party. After the abolition of the Trans-Caucasian Federation in 1936, Beria remained as the ruler of Georgia.

In 1938, when Stalin began preparations for ending the Great Terror, he chose Beria as the new people's commissar for Internal Affairs of the Soviet Union, to replace Nikolai Yezhov, who had fallen out of favor. Named to this post in November 1938, Beria purged the Cheka apparatus of Yezhov's protégés and, on the basis of Stalin's directives, halted mass repressive operations. In so doing, however, he managed to strengthen the apparatus of the People's Commissariat for Internal Affairs. In 1939–41, under Beria's leadership, repressive measures continued, but not on as massive a scale as under Yezhov. In February 1941, in addition to his post as people's commissar, Beria was named vice chair of the Council of Peoples' Commissars of the USSR. During the war Beria not only occupied these posts but also became a member of the State Defense Committee and entered the informal, close-knit leading group of the Soviet government, the so-called top five.

During the last years of Stalin's life Beria was one of the most influential figures in the politburo. As vice chair of the Council of Ministers of the USSR, Beria supervised the whole gulag system. Stalin's faith in him grew, especially after the Soviet atomic project, which Beria directed, was successfully realized in 1949. Yet Beria, like other members of the Soviet ruling elite, was periodically subjected to attacks from Stalin. Historians believe that Beria, in particular, was blamed for the so-called Mingrel affair, the mass arrest of leading workers carried out in Georgia in 1951–52. One opinion suggests that fears for his own life caused Beria to try to organize Stalin's murder. This view, however, is not supported by any documented data.

After Stalin's death on March 5, 1953, Beria achieved the pinnacle of his career: leading the Ministry of Internal Affairs of the USSR, which now was united with the Ministry of State Security. As one of the main members of the post-Stalin leadership, Beria used his extraordinary energy to introduce many important reforms. He initiated a massive amnesty, and brought about reconsideration of some of the most odious political matters fabricated under Stalin (for example, the so-called doctors' plot). He handed over to the economics ministries many structures and enterprises that had been directed by the Ministry of the Interior, an action that was a beginning of the dismantling of the gulag. Judging by all available evidence, Beria supported a more flexible policy with respect to both the national republics of the USSR and the Eastern European satellites. Specifically, Beria was against imposing Soviet-style socialist transformations on East Germany. All of Beria's initiatives have attracted attention and caused debate among historians. Yet the consistency of Beria's intentions and his ultimate goals remain open questions. Alarmed by Beria's growing influence, the members of the Soviet ruling elite arrested Beria on June 26, 1953, and he was executed by a firing squad on December 26, 1953.

See also Atomic Bomb; De-Stalinization; Great Terror; Gulag; KGB; Stalin, Joseph.

FURTHER READING

Gorlizki, Y., and O. Khlevniuk. *Cold Peace: Stalin and the Soviet Ruling Circle, 1945–1953.* Oxford: Oxford University Press, 2004.

Knight, A. *Beria: Stalin's First Lieutenant.* Princeton, NJ: Princeton University Press, 1993.

Naumov, V., and I. Sigachev, eds. *Lavrentij Berija, 1953.* Moscow: Mezhdunarodnyi fond Demokratija, 1999.

OLEG V. CHLEVNJUK

Berlin Crisis of 1948–49

Germany was fundamental to Soviet efforts to create and maintain a strong Soviet presence in postwar Europe. In the first year or so (1945–46) Stalin employed a cautious strategy. Thus, in June 1945, he advised the German Communists to declare themselves in favor of an anti-Fascist, democratic parliamentary regime but not in favor of directly installing a Soviet system. In 1947, however, the world situation led to increasing discord on the German question between the Soviet Union, on the one hand, and the United States, Great Britain, and France, on the other.

The Soviet leadership sought to maintain control over the Soviet (East) occupation zone and to influence the general question of Germany through a mechanism involving the four "allies." Moscow was attempting to conclude a peace treaty with Germany with the goal of restoring a "united, democratic Germany." This envisaged the creation of a "democratic national German government."

By 1948, it was clear that the four victorious powers could not achieve agreement on matters concerning Germany. The Western powers organized a separate London Conference on the German question, with the participation of the United States, Britain, France, Belgium, the Netherlands, and Luxembourg. The conference plotted a course of action to be taken by the West to create a West German state that would be included in the Western bloc.

The USSR wanted to forestall the breakup of Germany and its inclusion in the Western bloc under the auspices of the United States. The decisions taken at the London Conference certainly upset the Soviet leadership, which began to seek ways of countering Western policy on Germany. On March 20, the Soviet representative, Marshal Sokolovsky, conspicuously walked out of a session of the Allied Control Council, so that the activity of this organ, for practical purposes, was halted. In the beginning of March 1948, Moscow elaborated a plan to limit lines of communications between Berlin and the Western occupation zones. This plan went into effect on April 1.

At the same time, in the spring of 1948, preparations were going forward toward separate financial reforms in West and East Germany, since efforts to achieve a coordinated reform had failed. Berlin, which was in the Soviet occupation zone, was governed by a joint Allied command and was divided into four sectors. The financial reform in the three Western zones was carried out on June 20 and was extended to the Western sectors on June 23. On June 22, the Soviet commander in chief announced the establishment of financial reforms in the Soviet occupation zone and the area of Greater Berlin as well. The Soviet authorities demanded that all of Berlin be included in the financial system of the Soviet occupation zone. On June 24, they completely cut off land communications between the Western occupation zones and the Western sectors of Berlin, citing "technical reasons." Thus began the "Berlin Blockade." The United States responded by organizing an "airlift" linking the Western occupation zones with West Berlin. All essential cargo, such as food and fuel, was transported by air.

Berlin was now the center of an international crisis. The Western powers were intent on consolidating their policy of "separation" on the German question. The Soviet leadership was trying, at a maximum, to force the West to give up its plan for a separate West German state or, at a minimum, to squeeze the Allies out of West Berlin. At a discussion between leaders of the Socialist Unity Party (SUP) of Germany and Stalin on March 26, 1948, Wilhelm Pieck noted that the results of the elections scheduled for October of that year would hardly be better for the SUP than they were in 1946 (19.8 percent of the votes). Pieck went on to say that they "would be glad to get the Allies out of West Berlin." Stalin remarked, "Let's make a common effort and perhaps we'll succeed in getting them out."

The demand for inclusion of all of Berlin into the financial-economic system of the Soviet occupation zone (which assumed a complete ouster of the Western powers from Berlin) was set forth by Stalin and Vyacheslav Molotov during their negotiations with representatives of the Western powers in Moscow in August 1948. This was part of what the Soviet leadership saw as its main task: to force the Western powers to abandon their decisions on the German question taken at the London Conference, including their decision to create a West German state.

The leaders of the United States, Britain, and France, though, had no intention of making any concessions on this question. On September 1, 1948, a Parliamentary Council was summoned to work out a constitution for West Germany. In response, Moscow hardened its position on the question of introducing a common currency in Berlin. Attempts at a compromise did not succeed.

Proceeding simultaneously were preparations for the creation in the Soviet occupation zone of an East German state of a people's democracy type, with German Communists playing an active part. In 1948–49, the German People's Congress finished work on a proposal for a constitution for the German Democratic Republic. The constitution was approved on May 28–29, 1949. Its preparation was personally supervised by Stalin.

During all this both sides practiced restraint in order to avoid any broad-scale military conflict. The Western powers were afraid to try to break the Soviet blockade of Berlin by armed force. The Soviet leadership, for its part, took no measures against U.S. aircraft carrying out the airlift. All diplomatic maneuvers on the Berlin question in fall and winter 1948–49—discussions by the UN Security Council, attempts by the chair of the Security Council, Juan Bramuglia, to be a mediator, and the work of a committee of special experts from six neutral countries—achieved no results.

By February 1949 the defeat of the Soviet policy of the Berlin Blockade was obvious, and Soviet-U.S. negotiations to settle the crisis began. An agreement was reached on May 4 to rescind all limitations on communications, transportation, and trade between Berlin and the Western zones of Germany, and also between the Eastern and Western sectors of the city. For their part, the Western powers agreed to summon one more session of the Council of Ministers for External Affairs to examine the German question. But the Paris Session of the council (May–June 1949) also had no positive result.

The Berlin Crisis of 1948–49 ended as a political defeat for the Soviet leadership. The march toward splitting up Germany culminated in the establishment of the Federal Republic of Germany and the German Democratic Republic in September–October 1949. For the Soviet leadership, the Berlin Blockade was part of its struggle to consolidate and expand its sphere of influence in Europe as much as possible. For the West, especially the United States, opposition to the actions of the USSR in Germany was part of its "containment of communism" policy. Both sides strove to prevent the breakout of any major armed conflict.

See also Cold War; Containment; North Atlantic Treaty Organization; Red Army; Soviet Occupation of Germany.

FURTHER READING

Naimark, N. M. *The Russians in Germany: A History of the Soviet Zone of Occupation, 1945–1949.* Cambridge, MA: Harvard University Press, 1995.

Narinskij, M. M. "The Soviet Union and the Berlin Crisis, 1948–49." In *The Soviet Union and Europe in the Cold War, 1943–53,* ed. F. Gori and S. Pons. London: Macmillan, 1996.

MICHAIL M. NARINSKIJ

Berlin Wall

The Berlin Wall was a symbol of the Cold War in Europe in the post-Stalin period. Its initial construction on the night of August 12–13, 1961, inaugurated an era of stabilization of Cold War tensions in Europe. Its dramatic opening on November 9–10, 1989, when thousands of East Berliners poured into the streets of West Berlin, in many ways marked the end of the Cold War.

The symbolism of the wall was enhanced by the notable speeches that were delivered on its western side: John F. Kennedy's famous "I am a Berliner" pronouncement on June 26, 1963, and Ronald Reagan's dramatic invocation to the Soviets: "Mr. Gorbachev, tear down this Wall!" on June 12, 1987.

The Berlin Wall also was a significant factor in relations between the two Germanys, the Federal Republic of Germany (FRG) and the German Democratic Republic (GDR). It halted the annual exit from the GDR of hundreds of thousands of East Germans and made the division of Germany a more permanent aspect of European political reality. This made possible new diplomatic negotiations between the FRG and GDR in the early 1970s, which in turn eased restrictions on mutual visits, facilitated trade, and encouraged bilateral relations. In the West, West German foreign minister and then chancellor Willy Brandt's initiatives of *Ostpolitik* would have been inconceivable without the building of the wall. Socialist Unity Party (SED) chief Walter Ulbricht's policies of building up the GDR as an independent and sovereign state, a "normal" member of the world community, also depended on the sharp differentiation between the FRG and the GDR that the Berlin Wall facilitated. The development of the identities of two separate Germanys, one "capitalist" and belonging to NATO and the West, the other "Socialist" and belonging to the Warsaw Pact and the East, was solidified by the building of the wall.

But it is also important to point out the hardships that the Berlin Wall brought the East German population. Initially, the "wall" was a haphazard patchwork of barbed wire and roadblocks. Eventually it became a four- to four-and-a-half-meter-high barrier encircling West Berlin and separating it from GDR territory that was both imposing and frightening to common East Germans. It was some 144 kilometers long with a cleared 100-meter strip on the GDR side and was guarded by 295 watchtowers, in addition to dogs, mines, trip wires, and automatic firing devices. As many as 260 people were killed trying to cross the wall. Probably twice as many were killed trying to escape the GDR at its other borders. Many thousands of others risked imprisonment and were often caught trying to escape in truck beds, through underground tunnels, concealed in automobiles, or using falsified documents. "Flight from the Republic" (or attempted flight) became a familiar political crime in the GDR. During the 1980s, as many as 30,000 persons convicted of this charge were bought out of prison by the West German government in the so-called *Menschenhandel* (trade in humans). The

East German government also earned hard currency by providing for "family reunifications" of East Germans seeking to move to the West. This unsavory business aside, countless citizens in the East felt trapped by the wall and lived their lives in its ominous shadow. The official culture of the GDR was shaped in interesting and contorted ways by its attempts to look away from the wall. It is hardly surprising that many former East German citizens continue to suffer from what is commonly called "the Wall in the Mind."

The decision to build the wall evolved out of the series of crises that beset Berlin and the GDR following Khrushchev's November 1958 ultimatum. The Soviets insisted that the Western Allies sign a peace treaty and agree to transform West Berlin into a demilitarized "free city." Khrushchev threatened that if there was no such agreement, the Soviets would turn over to the GDR full control of East Berlin and of Allied access routes to Berlin. The West refused to accede to Khrushchev's demands, but East German citizens, unsure how long they would still be able to move to the West, started leaving the GDR in even larger numbers than previously. (Some three-and-a-half million Germans left the East between 1945 and 1961.) During the first six months of 1961, approximately 50,000 to 65,000 East Germans left for the West; 20,000 left in June; 30,000 in July. Both Khrushchev and Ulbricht realized that something had to be done to stem the tide. Ulbricht suggested setting up a barrier to prevent people from leaving from Berlin, as well as closing the exit routes from Berlin to West Germany so that West Berlin could be "neutralized." Khrushchev hoped that some solution to the Berlin problem and to the German question as a whole could be reached together with the West. Ulbricht was insistent that immediate measures had to be taken to maintain the integrity of the GDR. In the end Khrushchev acceded to the idea of the wall, but he rejected the plan to cut off the access routes as too dangerous and a potential threat to peace. From Khrushchev's point of view, the primary goal in building the wall was to maintain the status quo, while continuing to work for an all-German solution. Thus he gave the go-ahead to build the barrier, but only in stages, all the time fearing that the West might take aggressive actions in Berlin as a consequence.

A major crisis in the building of the wall took place in late October 1961, when the East German authorities attempted to check the papers of official American personnel entering East Berlin. This violation of Four-Power rights to Berlin as a whole was seen by the United States as an East German move toward taking exclusive control over East Berlin. General Lucius Clay threatened military force to back Allied rights and sent American tanks to Checkpoint Charlie, the Allied crossing point. The Soviets also brought tanks to the border, so that on October 27, ten American tanks faced off against ten Soviet. Some of the American tanks were outfitted with bulldozer equipment, intended, if necessary, to bring down the wall. At this point, American president John F. Kennedy initiated secret communications with Khrushchev, who in turn assured Kennedy that Allied rights would be respected. In a choreographed withdrawal, both sides gradually withdrew their tanks from Checkpoint Charlie. The wall, however, remained. It was a permanent fixture of Berlin's geography and of the Cold War until November 9, 1989, when East Germans poured through the checkpoints into West Berlin.

See also Cold War; Kruschev, Nikita; Reunification of Germany; Soviet Occupation of Germany; Ulbricht, Walter.

FURTHER READING

Gati, C. *The Bloc That Failed: Soviet-East European Relations in Transition.* Bloomingon: Indiana University Press, 1990.

Harrison, H. *Driving the Soviets Up the Wall: Soviet-East German Relations, 1953–1961.* Princeton, NJ: Princeton University Press, 2003.

Hertle, H., K. Jarausch, and C. Klessmann. *Mauerbau und Mauerfall: Ursachen, Verlauf, Auswirkungen.* Berlin: Christoph Links Verlag, 2002.

Hildebrandt, A. *Die Mauer: Zahlen, Daten.* Berlin: Verlag Haus am Checkpoint Charlie, 2001.

Timmermann, H., ed. *1961–Mauerbau und Aussenpolitik.* Muenster: Lit, 2002.

NORMAN M. NAIMARK

Berlinguer, Enrico

Enrico Berlinguer (1922–84) was born in Sassari, Italy, to a middle-class family with anti-Fascist and liberal-democratic values. He became a member of the Italian Communist Party (Pci) in August 1943 and a year later he was a young party functionary in Rome. In 1946 he joined the Central Committee and in 1947 the Pci leadership. From 1949 to 1956 he was secretary of the Italian Communist Youth Federation (FGCI, the Pci's youth federation). In 1958 he became a member of the party's National Secretariat and starting in 1960 he was responsible for party organization. In this role he also gathered some international experience, and in 1964 he was part of the delegation that went to Moscow after Palmiro Togliatti's death and Nikita Khrushchev's destitution. Having remained in the shadows for several years, he was elected to parliament in 1968. Berlinguer distinguished himself from other Pci leaders for his role in the aftermath of the Soviet invasion of Czechoslovakia, leading a mission to Moscow in November 1968 to express the Italian Communists' reasons for dissenting from the repression of the Prague Spring. Once he became undersecretary, he went to Moscow again for the World Conference of Communist Parties in June 1969; once again he supported the principles of autonomy and the "national paths" (to communism), thus distancing the Pci further from the idea of the "leader state" (the USSR). From this point on he assumed a major role in the national and international policies of the Pci, and increasingly also fulfilled the role of party secretary, held by Luigi Longo, who had fallen seriously ill in 1970. In 1972 Berlinguer was elected general secretary at the Thirteenth Congress of the Pci.

In September and October of 1973, Berlinguer wrote three articles in the party's weekly, *Rinascita*, in which he outlined the strategy of the "historic compromise" (with the Christian Democratic Party of Italy). Citing the dramatic events of the military coup d'état against the Unidad Popular government in Chile, he argued that in Italy, only a collaboration between Catholics and Communists would allow Italy to overcome its crisis, avoid dangerous splits, and avert a reaction similar to what had occurred in Chile. On the political level this meant proposing the Pci as a viable candidate for Italy's government, and a national unity government over the more traditional policy of Left front opposition. This national strategy was developed in unison with a clear international political line. Alone among Western European Communist parties, the Pci supported the European community and sent its own delegation to the Strasbourg Parliament in 1969. The Pci simultaneously fully supported the *Ostpolitik* of the Social Democratic Party of Germany. These orientations toward Europe and détente, the defense of "socialism with a human face," anchored Italian communism to the Western system and the existing coordinates of Italian foreign policy to a greater degree. Berlinguer made this orientation even clearer when he adopted a "for a Europe neither anti-Soviet nor anti-American" slogan (February 1973), and later renounced a call for Italy's withdrawal from the North Atlantic Treaty Organization (NATO) that the Pci Central Committee had adopted in December 1974 and the Fourteenth Congress had supported in March 1975. In June 1976, in an interview with the *Corriere della Sera*, he declared that he thought the Pci's autonomy was better served within NATO than in the Warsaw Pact.

Berlinguer intended to unite the Communist parties of Western Europe around the international policies of the Pci. He cultivated relationships with the French and Spanish Communists based on the principle of a democratic and pluralist socialism more than a true political platform. "Eurocommunism" soon acquired an international resonance, causing alarm bells to go off in both Washington and Moscow. Yet Berlinguer's interpretation of communism did not involve a break with the USSR. On the contrary, he intended to maintain an understanding with the Soviets and their East European allies, in the hope that détente would open the door to change after the Helsinki Accords, and that the Pci would have the opportunity to influence other Communist parties. This was the gist of his address to the Twenty-fifth Congress of the Communist Party of the Soviet Union (February 1976) in which he defended the pluralist ideas of the Italian Communists. On June 29–30, 1976, he traveled to the Conference of European Communist Parties in Berlin, a gesture that allowed him once again to support the Eurocommunist perspective and simultaneously maintain diplomatic relations with the Soviets.

The success of the Pci in the national elections of June 20, 1976, raised the issue of Communist participation in an Italian government in a real way. The Communists' abstention allowed for the formation of a new government led by the Christian Democrats, thus giving life to the "national solidarity" formula. At this time Berlinguer had to face the decisive test of his national strategy, attempting to attain full Communist participation in the government. In January 1977 he coined the "austerity" formula, which alluded to not only the policies of strictness he advocated to overcome the economic crisis but also the idea of modifying the capitalist model of consumer society. Berlinguer thus gave the Pci a strong ethical imprint, destined to reinforce the image of a party whose goal was a socialist transformation of Italian society. The agreement on a program with other parties in June 1977 and the joint parliamentary vote on foreign policy of November 1977 seemed to sanction the national legitimacy of the Italian Communists. But this phase of national solidarity also contributed to the decline of the

Pci, whose social support eroded because of the anticrisis measures it had supported. Its entry into the government majority occurred in March 1978, during the dramatic period of the abduction of Aldo Moro by the Red Brigades. Moro's assassination deprived Berlinguer of his main interlocutor inside the Christian Democratic Party. The Pci's firm line against terrorism and in defense of the democratic state was not sufficient to secure a place for the party in the government. In January 1979 Berlinguer decided to return to the opposition, thus ending the national solidarity phase.

The Eurocommunist strategy also fell victim to crisis. The relationship between the Pci and the French Communist Party had never amounted to a significant alliance, given the political differences between the two parties. The Madrid meeting between Berlinguer, Georges Marchais, and Santiago Carrillo, held in March 1977, was the climax of Eurocommunism but also the beginning of its decline. The USSR's harsh reaction, alarmed above all by the Eurocommunist contagion in Eastern Europe and its destabilizing effects, started a then-secret confrontation with the Western parties. Berlinguer traveled to Moscow in November 1977, where he publicly defended his heterodox positions, celebrating the "universal value" of democracy. At this point his disagreement with Leonid Brezhnev no longer only regarded dissent in Czechoslovakia and "Europeanism"; it extended to the full spectrum of the Pci's foreign policy in the Western world, its national unity policy, and the issue of human rights in the East. The harshest moments of the confrontation occurred during the meeting that Brezhnev and Berlinguer had in October 1978. But on this occasion Berlinguer once again avoided any break, remaining faithful to his principle that the Pci should not return to orthodoxy but also not give rise to new heresies. He held on to Eurocommunism's rudder, which by that point mostly represented a message that the Italian Communists had propagated, but not a true political movement.

The end of national solidarity and the crisis of Eurocommunism constituted a dual signal of defeat for Berlinguer's Pci. His attempt to modify the outlines of a divided Europe, allowing a Communist Party to enter the government of a Western European country, had met with fatal opposition both within and outside Italy. The U.S. veto that Henry Kissinger had imposed played an essential role and was eventually basically also reaffirmed during the Jimmy Carter presidency, thereby favoring the Pci's domestic adversaries. The principal governments of Western Europe also upheld this "external veto." The Soviet's opposition had the effect of reinforcing it, as a matter of fact if not intent. The disappearance of détente deprived the Pci of a fundamental space between the two blocks and a penetrating influence within the underground reformist tendencies in Eastern Europe. And yet the defeat was also a fruit of the limits of Berlinguer's strategy. Entrusting national legitimation to the historic compromise, the Europeanist option, and the acceptance of NATO was not sustained by an adequate effort at international legitimation. The idea that this problem could be resolved by the development of détente and the weakening of U.S. leadership after the Vietnam War was revealed as illusory. The Eurocommunist strategy presupposed a change in the Communist world that did not take place, and it simultaneously prevented the Pci from cutting the umbilical cord that still tied it to that world. The Pci's capacity to establish significant alliances with social democracy in the West was revealed as weak, since the party continued to invest its principal political resources in the East.

In the last years of his life, Berlinguer consolidated the innovations and peculiarities that distinguished the Pci from all the other Communist parties, yet without outlining a new political strategy. The historic compromise was dashed when in November 1980 Berlinguer launched the "democratic alternative" strategy. This did not entail a choice in favor of alternating government majorities, however, and therefore a government of the Left. It was at this point that Berlinguer raised the "moral issue." He thus demonstrated an acute ethical sense, which led him to criticize the corruption and degradation of national life. But he also substituted moral judgment for politics. In actuality the Pci excluded itself from Italy's political maneuverings.

Lacking allies on the domestic front, Berlinguer developed his relationships on the international front, without abandoning his Eurocommunist perspective. He refused to follow the "bloc" logic that had been triggered by the Second Cold War. Berlinguer supported the Pci's opposition to the West's choice of Euromissiles, but he didn't align himself with Moscow and condemned the Soviet invasion of Afghanistan, triggering a new polemic and the end of the Soviet funding that had still been forthcoming into the late 1970s. Elected to the European Parliament in 1979, he established a relationship with Willy Brandt. He followed the same philosophy as Brandt and Olof Palme on the issue of North-South relations as well as the topic of European security. Berlinguer

did not propose to build a true political alliance with the social democracies, though. The idea of reforming communism continued to be his guiding light. He favored a dialogue between government and labor unions during the Polish crisis, and strongly condemned the coup d'état by General Wojciech Jaruzelski in December 1981. When Berlinguer declared that the "forward progress" of Soviet communism had been "exhausted," this earned him a public rebuke in Moscow, the so-called tear (*strappo*). But even at this juncture he did not contemplate breaking with the Soviets. His pacifist struggle in the last years was informed by the notion that the Pci should not renounce its role in building a bridge between the East and West, above all because of its own identity. Under his leadership, the Pci gradually abandoned the organic relation with Moscow that dated back to Togliatti's times, but he did not separate its destinies from Moscow's.

Berlinguer's sudden death from a stroke in June 1984 caused a wave of emotion throughout Italy. His funerals were followed by a million people. His nonrhetorical but charismatic personality along with his ethical aspirations had made him one of the most popular and respected figures in the history of the Italian republic. He had given the Pci a role and resonance on the international stage that it had never previously had, and that will likely never again be reached. The Eurocommunist message was to become one of Mikhail Gorbachev's inspirations, and he was present at the funeral and was personally moved by the occasion.

Berlinguer's heritage, however, was contradictory and controversial. He transformed the political culture of Italian communism, detaching it from the class-based and doctrinaire axioms that instead held sway for longer periods of time in all the other Communist parties. His political agenda was closer to the moderate forces of nonalignment and those of the European social democratic Left. His Europeanism was the foundation for a shift toward a system of values that differed from the one that was characteristic of the Communist tradition. But his idea of a "third way" between social democracy and "real socialism," appeal to the Italian Communists' "different" identity, and obstinate vocation as a Communist reformer were all elements that made the Pci into a self-referential entity. Berlinguer did not manage either to detach Italian communism from Soviet communism or integrate it into the European Left. He always saw the transformation of the Pci into a variant of social democracy as a danger to be avoided. Berlinguer instead believed that Soviet communism, although it was not a model to be followed, still had a global role as both a counterweight to the United States and an anticapitalist example. He was therefore not fully aware of the deep crisis that communism was undergoing at the end of the 1980s, nor of its repercussions on the Pci itself. Its vitality and national peculiarities notwithstanding, Italian communism was not to pass unscathed through the collapse of the Berlin Wall in 1989.

See also Détente; Eurocommunism; European Integration; Prague Spring; Real Socialism; Second Cold War; Social Democracy.

FURTHER READING

Barbagallo, F. *Enrico Berlinguer*. Rome: Carocci, 2006.

Fiori, G. *Vita di Enrico Berlinguer*. 2 vols. Rome: l'Unità-Laterza, 1992.

Gualtieri, R., ed. *Il PCI nell'Italia repubblicana, 1943–1991*. Rome: Carocci (Fondazione Istituto Gramsci, Annale XI), 2001.

Pons, S. *Berlinguer e la fine del comunismo*. Turin: Einaudi, 2006.

SILVIO PONS

Bierut, Bolesław

Born on April 18, 1892 (died March 12, 1956), on the outskirts of Lublin, then in Russian Poland, to the poor, devout family of a worker, Bolesław Bierut had not yet finished public school when, in 1906, he was called to participate in a student strike demanding the right to use the Polish language in school. He was apprenticed to a printing house and completed evening business courses, which enabled him to find a job as a minor clerk in a consumer's cooperative. Bierut began his political activity by joining the Polish Socialist Party of the Left (Pps-Left). In December 1918, he found himself, together with the Pps-Left, in the illegal Communist Workers' Party of Poland. He moved up in the cooperative and party hierarchy, and in 1925 became a party official.

His activity in the Communist Workers' Party was punctuated by various arrests and trips to the Soviet Union, where (in 1925, 1926, and from 1928 to 1930) he took courses at the Lenin School of International Studies. For short periods he was a Comintern emissary to Austria, Czechoslovakia, and Poland. After returning to

Poland he spent the years 1933–38 in prison. He was by that time already an experienced operative, but his lack of a strong personality and intellectual inclinations kept him out of the party elite. Following the outbreak of World War II, Bierut managed to reach the territory annexed by the Soviet Union, but in summer 1941, he was unable to escape the advancing German troops and was forced to settle in Mińsk Białoruski, where his knowledge of German allowed him to find work in the municipal administration. He was discovered there by Soviet intelligence and, in summer 1943, was sent to Warsaw.

Bierut's path to a great career began: he became a member of the "central managerial troika" of the reactivated (under the name "PPR") party and then, on January 1, 1944, became chair of the National People's Council, the Communist alternative to the Polish Underground State. At the time he had conflicts—caused by his politics and ambitions—with Władysław Gomułka, the party's secretary general, but this did not affect his position. On the contrary, in July 1944 Bierut became the number-one person in the state, with the title of president of the republic.

It is difficult to say whether he displayed any exceptional servility toward Moscow, but when in 1948 Stalin recommended that the Communist-ruled lands begin to search for an "internal enemy," Bierut became the most zealous bloodhound on the trail of "deviations" and also an important promoter of the Sovietization of Poland. Like many leaders of totalitarian states, he played the role of a just pater familias. He surrounded himself with writers and people of science, while tens of thousands of people languished in prison, the Primate of Poland was arrested, and Bierut rejected, one after another, pleas for those sentenced to death. He studied the transcripts of confessions of arrested "renegades" (including Gomułka's) with special ardor.

Bierut made never-ending speeches to thunderous applause, and the celebration of his sixtieth birthday became a national holiday. He agreed with the acquiescence of Poland to "Big Brother" with absolute conviction and even sent Poland's proposed constitution to Stalin for his comments (and then personally translated the corrections that Stalin sent back). When the first hints of the "thaw" appeared after Stalin's death, Bierut succeeded in controlling the situation by, among other things, unloading all responsibility onto the security apparatus and hushing up the nation's economic calamities. He died on March 12, 1956, in Moscow, where he had gone to participate in the deliberations of the Twentieth Congress of the Communist Party of the Soviet Union. It is true that he was already sick when he left Warsaw, yet reading Khrushchev's famous speech was not the best medicine for Bierut. His death initiated the skirmish over who would succeed him and contributed to the political destabilization in Poland, opening the way for his old rival, Gomułka, to assume power.

See also Gomułka, Władysław; Socialist Camp; Sovietization.

FURTHER READING

Fejto, F. *A History of the People's Democracies*. New York: Praeger, 1971.

Kozłowski, C. *Namiestnik Stalina*. Warsaw: BGW, 1993.

Lipiński, P. *Bolesław Niejasny: Opowieść o Bolesławie Bieruci, Forescie Gumpie polskiego komunizmu*. Warsaw: Prószyński i S-ka, 2001.

ANDRZEJ PACZKOWSKI

Bipolarity

One of the most distinctive features of the Cold War was the bipolar distribution of power (especially military power) in the international system. In a bipolar system, two countries are far more powerful than all others and are widely perceived as such—a status enjoyed by the United States and the Soviet Union during the Cold War. The term "superpower," which was reserved only for those two countries, was indicative of their special role in the world. Although other important actors after 1945—notably the People's Republic of China after it split with the Soviet Union at the end of the 1950s, the nonaligned movement of third world countries and Yugoslavia, the European Community (in its various incarnations), and Japan—complicated the picture, the international system remained bipolar from the mid-1940s through the beginning of the 1990s. Not until the Cold War ended and the Soviet Union collapsed did the international system's bipolar configuration give way to a mostly unipolar structure.

Conceptualizing Polarity

Modern theories of international relations use the notion of polarity to characterize the distribution of power in the international system. A unipolar system is one in which a single state (or statelike entity) is dominant over all others, as Rome was during the height of its empire and France was during the brief reign of Napoléon. A multipolar system is one in which three or more states are the strongest powers, as in Europe during several periods (for example, in the late 15th and early 16th centuries, and the 19th century under the Concert of Europe). Bipolarity in the international system is relatively uncommon, but some rough historical precedents exist for the structure of the Cold War era, including the relationship between Carthage and Rome before the Punic Wars, between the Habsburg and Ottoman empires in 1521–59, and between Great Britain and France during most of the 18th century.

The task of determining how many great powers exist in the international system at any given time is not as straightforward as it may seem, in part because of the difficulty of defining and measuring "power." One of the most widely used techniques was originally developed by the Correlates of War (COW) project, a systematic effort that began at the University of Michigan in the early 1960s to compile historical data about key features of the international system. The COW Capability Data Set enables scholars to calculate each state's power using a composite metric of military capabilities, demographic capabilities, and industrial capabilities. The data for individual countries can then be aggregated to indicate the total amount of power in the system. With the help of a relatively simple formula to find the "concentration of power" (a coefficient based on the number of states in the system and the share that each state possesses of the total power in the system), scholars can track how power is distributed around the world over time. The closer the concentration is to 0 (on a continuum from 0 to 1), the more evenly distributed power is. A concentration of 0.5 or higher (meaning that one state possesses half or more of the total power in the system) is clearly indicative of unipolarity, and even a concentration as low as 0.4 may suggest a unipolar system (i.e., a system in which no other state is at least half as strong as the most powerful state). A concentration of 0.2 to 0.4 is usually associated with a bipolar or multipolar system.

A number of modifications to the COW methodology have been proposed. Bruce Buena de Mesquita has argued that it makes more sense to determine polarity by looking at the combined power of clusters of states rather than the power of individual states. To illustrate the point, Buena de Mesquita maintains that if four great powers of roughly equal strength pair off and form two opposing alliances, the result will be a bipolar rather than multipolar system. This assertion has been rejected by Randall Schweller, who avers that Buena de Mesquita is "conflating the distinct concepts of polarity (the number of poles) and polarization (the number of alignments in the system)." Schweller contends that polarity should be used only in "a purely structural sense" to denote the "number of Great Powers in the system." He distinguishes two types of great powers: those that are genuine "poles," and those that should be regarded as "lesser great powers" (LGPs). Schweller defines an LGP as a great power that possesses less than 50 percent of the military strength of the most powerful state. LGPs can play important roles as stabilizers and spoilers, but they are unable to sustain themselves on their own against full-fledged great powers (i.e., poles). Only the "polar" states—that is, the first tier of great powers—can withstand challenges from other poles. This two-tiered gradation of great powers is useful in understanding the Cold War system.

Bipolarity versus Other Configurations

An often-debated question in the international relations literature is whether bipolar systems are more stable (i.e., less prone to war between great powers) than are unipolar or multipolar systems. The "classical realists" such as Hans Morgenthau claimed that a multipolar distribution of power with fluid alliances is the system most conducive to international stability, whereas the proponents of "neorealism," notably Kenneth Waltz, have long insisted that a bipolar distribution of power is inherently more stable than a multipolar or unipolar system. (Before the collapse of the Soviet Union, Waltz described bipolar systems as intrinsically more stable than multipolar systems, but after 1991 he averred that he should have portrayed them as "less war-prone.") Other scholars such as Jack S. Levy have sharply disputed Waltz's claim, arguing that Waltz provides "very little supporting evidence" for his assertions about the supposed stability of bipolar systems. Levy contends that Waltz is merely drawing unwarranted generalizations from the Cold War, a period in which "the existence of nuclear weapons and other key variables"—rather than bipolarity—accounted for the lack of great-power war. Levy avers that "bipolarity is no less war-prone than multipolarity" and that "polarity is not a primary causal factor in the outbreak of war." He and other analysts such as Ted Hopf maintain that the incidence of great-power war is determined not by polarity but rather by the "offense-defense balance" (a

term encompassing the relative performance of military technologies, the availability of power resources, and the strategic beliefs held by national leaders).

Although most of the debate has focused on bipolar versus multipolar systems, a considerable amount of discussion since 1991 has also dealt with unipolar and tripolar systems. On these matters, too, scholars have often expressed sharply conflicting assessments. Structural realists such as Waltz, John Mearsheimer, and Christopher Layne have asserted that unipolarity is inherently unstable because other states will inevitably seek to gang up against the dominant state, eventually offsetting its preponderance. Waltz describes unipolarity as "the least durable of international configurations." By contrast, scholars such as Emerson Niou, Peter Ordeshook, and Gregory Rose allege that a "highly asymmetric resource distribution," which permits a single state to maintain a dominant position in the world, is apt to be the "most peaceful" and stable—not the most war-prone—arrangement. Echoing this view, William Wohlforth holds that the unipolar system that emerged after 1989–91 can endure "for many decades" or even longer because the distribution of material power—military, economic, technological, and geographic—is so heavily in favor of the United States. According to Wohlforth, the overwhelming "concentration of material power in the United States" will frustrate any attempt by a hostile coalition to undercut U.S. hegemony.

On the question of tripolarity, the extent of disagreement has been less. Although a few scholars, such as Charles Ostrom, John Aldrich, and David Garnham, have claimed that "the likelihood of war is lowest for a tripolar system," most analysts have taken strong exception to this view. Robert Gilpin, for example, has characterized tripolarity as the "most unstable configuration," and Waltz has emphasized that tripolar systems have a "distinctive and unfortunate" tendency to "revert to bipolarity" because "two of the powers can easily gang up on the third [and] divide the spoils." Schweller's study of tripolarity during the interwar period (1930–39) is not always convincing in its historical detail, but his nuanced theoretical discussion bears out the notion that tripolar systems are likely to be highly unstable. Schweller argues that in a tripolar system, each pole "must ensure that a hostile coalition does not form against it" and is therefore strongly tempted to forge "a coalition [of its own] with one of the other poles." But any coalition that forms between two poles is bound to "throw the system wildly out of balance, gravely endangering the isolated third" pole. Schweller's conceptual framework for analyzing tripolar interactions can be adapted to shed light on U.S.-Sino-Soviet relations during the Cold War.

The Bipolar Cold War Structure

The theoretical literature on international politics highlights crucial features of the bipolar Cold War system. The composite index for the post-1945 period in the COW Capability Data Set suggests that the Cold War began with a unipolar structure headed by the United States, and then shifted to bipolarity in the early 1950s and later tripolarity in the early 1960s. But this depiction is misleading because it understates the enormously disproportionate military strength of the United States and the Soviet Union compared to the rest of the world. (It also overstates the significance of China's huge population.) Using only the data for military capabilities, we find that the Cold War was indeed bipolar from start to finish. The United States in overall power was always ahead of the Soviet Union, but in sheer military strength the Soviet Union more than held its own.

In terms of what Schweller calls "polarization" (the number of alignments in the system), the structure was also predominantly bipolar. The United States was militarily allied with Canada and most of the West European countries via the North Atlantic Treaty Organization (NATO) from 1949 on. The United States also established allied defense pacts with Japan, South Korea, Australia, New Zealand, and some third world countries, and pursued more informal arrangements with other countries. The Soviet Union, for its part, established a bloc in Eastern Europe (eventually codified in the Warsaw Treaty Organization, which was set up in 1955), and maintained important military links with East Asia countries (Mongolia, North Korea, North Vietnam, and China from 1950 until 1959) as well as Cuba (after 1959) and some other third world countries. By any measure, the U.S.-led coalition was larger and more powerful than the Soviet-led grouping, especially after a bitter dispute emerged between the Soviet Union and China.

Each bloc experienced some erosion over the years, but the defections were generally more costly on the Soviet side, particularly the rift with China. Yugoslavia and Albania broke away from the Soviet orbit in Eastern Europe (in 1948 and 1961, respectively), and a few third world countries, such as Egypt, shifted their alignments from the Soviet Union to the United States. The United

States did not lose any of its European allies (even France remained a member of NATO's political councils after pulling out of the integrated military commands in 1966), but it did experience some significant losses in the third world after regimes changed in Iraq (1958), Cuba (1959), South Vietnam (1975), Ethiopia (1977), Iran (1979), and Nicaragua (1979). Despite these defections, the two blocs overall remained largely intact throughout the Cold War.

Some groupings of states existed outside the orbits of the two superpowers. The nonaligned movement was originally proposed at the Bandung Conference in 1955 and then formally set up in 1961, originally with twenty-five countries, including Yugoslavia. Over time, the membership increased to more than a hundred countries. The declared goal of the member states was to avoid "becoming pawns in the struggles between the major powers." Most of the members did remain nonaligned during the Cold War, but some (e.g., Cuba, Afghanistan, Ghana, and Indonesia prior to 1965) were in fact closely aligned with the Soviet Union, and others (e.g., the Philippines and Pakistan) maintained extensive defense ties with the United States. The nonaligned movement added an element of complexity to the Cold War international structure, but the nonaligned movement's impact was far too limited to alter the underlying configuration of bipolarity.

A greater degree of complexity was introduced when China left the Soviet bloc. Because of the political, military, and demographic importance of China, it carried a degree of influence in the third world that threatened the Soviet Union's (and United States') positions there, and even Soviet positions in Eastern Europe. By the early 1960s, China was actively competing with the Soviet Union for influence among radical anti-Western movements and governments in the third world. The People's Republic of China also sought to tempt some of the East European countries to follow its example in breaking away from the Soviet bloc. This effort succeeded with Albania, which aligned itself with China, and partly with Romania, which refused to endorse Soviet polemics and actions directed against China. Nonetheless, the group of states that followed China's lead was never particularly large, and never a genuine competitor with the Soviet- and U.S.-led blocs.

Nor was bipolarity altered by the increasing diversity within the world Communist movement from the late 1960s on. For many years, Communist parties throughout the world had been rigidly beholden to the Soviet Union. This pattern was eroded by the split with Yugoslavia and—far more significantly—the rift with China, but an equally significant change in the complexion of the world Communist movement was precipitated by the Soviet-led invasion of Czechoslovakia in 1968. As the Prague Spring unfolded in Czechoslovakia in 1968, the Communist parties in Western Europe, especially those in Italy and Spain, had watched with great sympathy and hope. The violent suppression of the reforms aroused vehement opposition to the Soviet Union within these parties and stimulated the rise of what became known as Eurocommunism. The defection of most of the major West European Communist parties from the Soviet orbit mitigated potential Soviet influence in Western Europe and created new openings in West European politics. But none of this engendered any appreciable change in the bipolar East-West structure.

Although China was never a full-fledged pole during the Cold War, its status was somewhere between a pole and an LGP. In that respect, the role of China illustrates the potential for instability in a nascent tripolar structure. During the 1950s the Soviet Union and China were closely aligned, but after the Sino-Soviet split emerged, China acted for more than a decade on its own, displaying hostility toward both of the superpowers. But in the 1970s, as Schweller's analysis would lead one to expect, the triangular relationship shifted more toward a U.S.-China alignment against the Soviet Union. The Sino-U.S. rapprochement that followed President Richard Nixon's surprise visit to China in February 1972 (after a secret trip by his national security adviser, Henry Kissinger, the previous year) ushered in nearly two decades of increasingly close security cooperation between the United States and China. By the mid- to late 1970s, Chinese leaders were openly talking about the need for a "united front" against the Soviet Union—a front that would include not only China and the United States but also Japan. Although the U.S. government did not move as far in this direction as some Chinese officials would have liked, Soviet leaders were dismayed by what they regarded as the "formation of a hostile [Sino-U.S.] military bloc." The degree of hostility between the Soviet Union and China gradually diminished after the early 1980s, but the U.S.-Sino-Soviet relationship illustrated the precariousness of triangular great-power ties.

The emergence and consolidation of the European Economic Community (later known as the European Community) did not erode the bipolar structure of the Cold War. On the contrary, bipolarity was reinforced by European economic and political integration. Except for Ireland, all the European Economic Community/European Community countries were member states of NATO, and the economic progress they achieved contributed not only to political stability in Western Europe but also to the military capabilities of NATO. It was precisely because of the bipolar Cold War standoff that the United States vigorously promoted European integration via the Marshall Plan and maintained strong support for it afterward. Had the Cold War not arisen, U.S. officials might not have been as enthusiastic as they were about the prospect of an integrated Europe.

U.S. support for European integration as part of the broader Cold War struggle against the Soviet Union underscores one of the most important aspects of the bipolar system that emerged after World War II. The reason the system endured for more than four decades is not that it was inherently stable (as Waltz argued) but rather that the conflicting ideologies of the two leading powers drove them apart and kept them apart after their wartime alliance against a common enemy dissolved. Bipolarity was underwritten as much by ideological antagonism as by military power. When the fundamental clash of ideologies waned and disappeared in the late 1980s, the bipolar structure quickly eroded. The breakup of the Soviet Union at the end of 1991 carried this trend to its logical conclusion, paving the way for an era of U.S. hegemony.

See also Cold War; Containment; Dissolution of the USSR; Eurocommunism; Peaceful Coexistence; Soviet Bloc; Warsaw Pact.

FURTHER READING

Lynn-Jones, S., and S. Miller, eds. *The Cold War and After.* Cambridge, MA: MIT Press, 1993.

Mearsheimer, J. J. *The Tragedy of Great Power Politics.* New York: Norton, 2001.

Paul, T. V., J. J. Wirtz, and M. Fortmann, eds. *Balance of Power: Theory and Practice in the Twenty-First Century.* Stanford, CA: Stanford University Press, 2004.

Sabrosky, A. N., ed. *Polarity and War: The Changing Structure of International Conflict.* Boulder, CO: Westview Press, 1985.

Segal, G. *The Great Power Triangle.* New York: St. Martin's Press, 1982.

Thompson, W. R., ed. *Systemic Transitions: Past, Present, and Future.* New York: Palgrave Macmillan, 2009.

MARK KRAMER

Bolshevism

Bolshevism had one inventor in Lenin, but Lenin had the collaboration of many Bolsheviks in developing his invention; and indeed some Bolsheviks claimed to have patented a more adequate version of the basic ideas than Lenin's. There was constant struggle over the ownership and contents of the movement.

The origins of the Bolshevik tendency in the Russian Social-Democratic Workers' Party were almost accidental. At the Second Party Congress in July–August 1903, the ascendant group—the editors of *Iskra*—fell out. The majority in the group called themselves *bol'sheviki* (Majoritarians) and the others, with a misplaced sense of irony, accepted being designated as *men'sheviki* (Minoritarians). The immediate cause of the split was a disagreement over the qualifications for party membership. Both sides concurred on the need for a centralized, disciplined, and clandestine party, but the Bolsheviks stipulated that members should be highly active, while the Mensheviks were less insistent on this point. The dispute veiled unease among Mensheviks about what kind of party it was that Lenin really wished to lead. His bullying style as well as his admitted softness for the agrarian-socialist terrorists of the 1870s and 1880s called into question whether he and his followers were fit to organize a respectable Marxist party. The Bolsheviks replied that the Mensheviks were merely proving they lacked a fundamental commitment to the practical requirements of making revolution in autocratic Russia.

Thus the Bolshevik-Menshevik split right from the start had implications for Marxism as a theory. Pushed to explain himself, Lenin reverted to what he had written in his booklet *What Is to Be Done?* (1902). There he had maintained that the working class would never develop revolutionary ideas without the intervention of the socialist intelligentsia. Leadership and indoctrination were key to preventing workers from falling for peaceful methods of improving their conditions, and Lenin castigated all the contemporary forms of watered-down Marxism known as revisionism. With a well-organized and correctly informed party, he proposed, the proletariat would be able to become the vanguard of the revolutionary struggle. Workers would assemble support from every oppressed and exploited social group across the empire.

As yet Bolshevism had not become a fully separate faction in the Russian Social-Democratic Workers' Party. Not all Marxists in Russia approved of the émigrés plunging them into internal wrangles. But both the Bolshevik and Menshevik leaderships abroad tried to coordinate their followers in the Russian Empire, and separate organizations sprouted up in several principal cities. It was under these circumstances that the explosion of revolutionary activity caught the nascent factions unaware at the beginning of 1905. The Bolshevik response, headed by Lenin, involved a fundamental reconsideration of the tasks of revolution in Russia. His articles specified the need for a "revolutionary democratic dictatorship of the proletariat and the peasantry." His intuition was that middle-class liberals could not be trusted to stay the course in trying to overthrow the Romanov monarchy. Instead the Marxists should repose confidence in the peasantry. A "bourgeois-democratic" revolution would take place, which would foster a surge of capitalist development in a political frame of unprecedented civic freedoms.

This perspective was approved at the congress of Bolsheviks in London in April of 1905. (The Bolsheviks, despite meeting alone, called it the Third Party Congress.) It caused much indignation in the rest of the Russian Social-Democratic Workers' Party. The stress upon dictatorship, terror and peasant participation was criticized by Mensheviks as a derivative of Russian agrarian socialism. Lenin was accused of being not merely an unorthodox Marxist but no Marxist at all. He in turn charged the Mensheviks with abandoning Marxism in their quest for an alliance with the parties of the middle class; and he noted with asperity their growing willingness to subordinate their purposes to those parties. Quietly the Mensheviks seemed to be ditching the idea of the working class as the "vanguard of the revolution."

Inside Bolshevism, too, conflicting tendencies were coming to the fore. In 1905–6 Lenin found that some in his faction had ideas different from his own. Many Bolsheviks in Russia, imbibing Lenin's idea that workers by themselves would attain only "trade union consciousness," refused to join trade unions. Or they would join them only if they ran them. They rejected the soviets for the same sort of reason. Election of each soviet by workers seemed to make them little better than trade unions and therefore suspect. Bolshevik skepticism was also directed at the State Duma, which a reluctant Emperor Nicholas II convoked in 1906. Lenin saw the revolutionary tide was ebbing; he wanted Bolsheviks to take part in the elections to the Duma in order to secure a platform for party propaganda. Most Bolshevik leaders disagreed on the grounds that participation would merely encourage parliamentary illusions among the working class. They wanted nothing less than insurrection. Had not Lenin himself ridiculed the anti-Bolsheviks in the Russian Social-Democratic Workers for being chary of organizing armed uprising against czarism?

Lenin succeeded in reversing these policies in his faction only gradually, and he could not do it alone. He had to enlist the support of the Mensheviks—of all people—at the Fourth Party Congress in Stockholm for the party's participation in future elections to the Duma. Bolshevism continued, however, to be internally divided. On the agrarian question, Lenin was an extremist. He urged that when the revolutionary dictatorship took power, it should expropriate the land into the hands of the state. Most Bolshevik delegates to the Fourth Party Congress dissented, arguing that the peasants should simply be permitted to parcel out the land among themselves as they wanted. They maintained that Lenin's policy would alienate the peasantry. In fact the Mensheviks held a majority and secured endorsement for "land municipalization of land." Disagreement among Bolsheviks on the agrarian question meanwhile rumbled on.

So too did the question about parliamentary engagement. Lenin's fellow Bolshevik leader Alexander Bogdanov was never reconciled to his defeat over the State Duma. There were three types of opponents of the Duma among Bolsheviks. One group wanted to boycott the Duma elections, a second—when the first failed—wanted to recall Bolshevik deputies elected to the Duma; a third wanted to present them with an ultimatum on party behavior. Bogdanov and Lenin became a thorn in each other's flesh. They even battled over philosophy. Bogdanov and his supporters wanted to adapt some of the latest ideas about epistemology and cultural development to Marxism. In *Empiriomonism*, a vast trilogy, Bogdanov asserted that there was no such thing as "absolute truth," that operational versions of "reality" had to be developed through experimentation and that the doctrines of Marx and Engels were only an initial guide toward sound revolutionary strategy. He also contended that cultural change was as important in history as economic and political change. He called for the fostering of a "proletarian culture" independent of the prescriptions of middle-class revolutionary intellectuals.

This time it was Lenin who stood out as the inflexible figure. Bogdanov's work was an implicit attack on everything he stood for, and Lenin in *Materialism and Empiriocriticism*—written in London in 1908 and published in the following year—suggested that Bogdanov

had finally lapsed from a Marxist standpoint. Lenin argued that Marx's *Capital* was an irremovable cornerstone of human knowledge. It could never be surpassed, only added to. He scoffed at the supposition that an entirely new culture needed to be created. Lenin believed that "bourgeois culture" already supplied valuable elements of the socialist culture of the future. Bogdanov retorted that Lenin was an unreformed individualist, even an egoist and misanthrope, who could not assimilate himself to collectivist aspirations.

There were indeed some eccentric ideas current among the supporters of Bogdanov. Anatoli Lunacharski, for example, proposed a program of "god-building" whereby the working class would be treated as a new secular divinity. The intention was to harness existing religious beliefs to the practical requirements of the labor movement in the early 20th century. Nothing very much came of this (except perhaps for the subsequent attention given by Bolsheviks to ceremonies, rituals, parades, and imagery). Lenin, however, had had enough. In 1909 he secured a decision by the Bolshevik leadership to declare that Bogdanov and his followers had placed themselves outside the faction. Bogdanov went on proclaiming himself a Bolshevik. Indeed there were several strands in organized Bolshevism before the First World War. Lenin was determined to secure acceptance as the factional leader even if this meant a reduction of the number of Bolsheviks under his aegis. He also continued to operate inside a united Russian Social-Democratic Workers' Party. While he had disputes with others in his faction it was in his interest to maintain contact with the other factions. And by allying on several questions with various "national" sections of the party in Poland and Lithuania he often secured successes in policy making.

The price he paid was that he had to compromise with those sections. He was also badgered to release the money he held from bank robberies organized by Bolsheviks in recent years. Mensheviks pestered him too for a share of finances acquired by the Bolshevik faction in the form of a (dubiously engineered) legacy. But Lenin kept hold of his treasury and so was to be able to continue subsidizing factional activity of his own. Bolshevik newspapers, journals, and books were printed. Bolshevik groups in Russia received assistance. Bolshevik agents moved between Western Europe and Russia. The Bolsheviks—or at least Lenin's Bolsheviks—were a party inside a party.

Exasperation with the other factions came to a head in 1911–1912 and Lenin opted to hold a factional conference which would declare itself the legitimate conference of the entire party. As a fig leaf of due procedure he invited a tiny minority of Mensheviks. The conference met in Prague in January 1917. A Central Committee was elected which was to function in competition with the Organizational Committee of the Mensheviks. This drastic step allowed Lenin to coordinate the Bolsheviks with fewer external constraints. But he did not entirely dominate Bolshevik politics. The main conference organizer, Sergo Ordzhonikidze, represented a large body of opinion in Russian Bolshevism that Lenin was excessively drawn to bookish polemics and organizational divisiveness at the expense of the tasks of making revolution. This opinion was shared in St. Petersburg, where the Duma deputies from the Bolshevik faction announced their intention of establishing a popular daily newspaper, *Pravda*. The fulcrum of Bolshevik activity was scheduled to pass from the emigration to the Russian Empire.

Lenin moved to Kraków in Austrian-ruled Poland to regain authority, and from there he conducted an ill-tempered but generally effective relationship with both the *Pravda* editorial board and the Bolshevik deputies to the State Duma. To his delight the Bolsheviks across the Russian Empire got stuck in the business of leading strikes against employers and the government. At last Bolshevism as a doctrine and an organized force had recovered from the debacle of 1905–7.

The outbreak of the First World War set back the faction's cause. Many Bolsheviks supported the Russian war effort despite their previous commitment to oppose any military budget for Nicholas II. Among those who stood fast by the commitment, moreover, most were aghast at Lenin's insistence that the best outcome would be Russia's defeat. He also caused annoyance by issuing a demand for "European civil war." At a time when one of the faction's main appeals lay in campaigning for peace in Europe, he seemed intent on highly theoretical posturing. And he did so on a European scale at conferences of far-left political grouplets in the Swiss Alpine villages of Zimmerwald and Kienthal in 1915–16. The number of his supporters in the Russian Empire fell off drastically. His contact with Russian cities became minimal, and he buried himself in writing and studying in Swiss libraries. It seemed that Bolshevism was more fractured and further from power than ever.

When Nicholas II was unexpectedly overthrown in the February Revolution of 1917, it was the Mensheviks and Socialist-Revolutionaries who were the beneficiaries. They tendered conditional support to the liberal-led provisional government. Many Bolsheviks, including Central Committee members Lev Kamenev and Joseph Stalin, took a not dissimilar approach. The nub of the problem for them was that "old Bolshevism" had predicted that without a revolutionary dictatorship there would be no politically secure system of civic freedom and market economy. The provisional government proved otherwise. Plainly a rethinking of Bolshevik strategy was necessary. Already many Bolsheviks were expressing fury that the Russian Bureau of the Central Committee was only weakly opposing the provisional government.

Lenin in Switzerland shared this antagonism, and on his return to Petrograd in April 1917 he called on Bolsheviks to campaign unequivocally for a second revolution. His standpoint triumphed at the Bolshevik conference held at the end of the month. The result was the final, irreversible separation of Menshevism and Bolshevism into two separate parties. There was much crossover from one faction—or rather party—to another. Bolshevism also attracted an entire mini-faction, the Interdistricters, in summer; and the renowned anti-Bolshevik Lev Trotsky was wooed to the Bolshevik side.

Such a situation might have made the Bolsheviks retreat back into internal polemics; and indeed the party was affected by divisions over questions old and new, and organizational control exerted by the Central Committee was minimal: lower party committees said and did whatever they liked during the year. Far from being a tightly disciplined and organized party, the Bolsheviks were as fissiparous as all the other mass parties of 1917. About two things, however, they were at one. First, they wanted a socialist revolution and the removal of the provisional government; second, they wished for an end to the "imperialist war." These two goals kept them together. Tactical implementation was another matter. The Soviets' support for the provisional government against the Bolsheviks after the July Days induced Lenin to call for a withdrawal of "all power to the Soviets" as a slogan. The rest of the party leadership disagreed: the party had too closely identified itself with the slogan for it to be politic to abandon it. But all Bolsheviks agreed that power ought to be seized from the provisional government. The Bolshevik Party was not going to disintegrate over tactics.

More serious in the long term was the uncertainty about what kind of government was going to exist under the Bolsheviks. The Central Committee did not resolve this at its meetings on October 10 and 16; it confined itself to deciding that the time had come to eject the provisional government. But when Kerensky was overthrown on October 25, the issue could no longer be avoided. (It was a tribute to Lenin's deviousness that he had kept it off the agenda until that moment.) Lenin and Trotsky were delighted that most Socialist-Revolutionaries and nearly all Mensheviks walked out of the Second Congress of Soviets when power was presented to it. They wanted a government of the extreme political Left and were willing to entertain only the Left Socialist-Revolutionaries as coalition partners. But the majority of the Central Committee was eager to negotiate with all socialist parties. Probably most Bolsheviks had agreed to a seizure of power on the assumption that a broad socialist coalition ministry would be formed. Unfortunately for them, the Mensheviks and Socialist-Revolutionaries refused to submit themselves to a government dominated by Lenin and Trotsky.

This was not the only question on which, after the October Revolution, Bolshevism had to define its standpoint amid controversy. Many Bolsheviks wanted a unitary state without administrative-territorial concessions to "nationalism." There was also a widespread aspiration toward to the total nationalization of industry. On the party's Left, what is more, Bukharin and others espoused arguments for the rapid collectivization of agriculture. And the vast majority of Bolshevik militants thought that if revolution failed to break out elsewhere in Europe, the duty of the Bolshevik Party was to start a "revolutionary war" on the eastern front to carry the revolution westward.

Lenin, however, was more cautious. He and Stalin throughout 1917 had asserted that the party had to make concessions to the non-Russian peoples of the former Russian Empire or else face insuperable hostility. Lenin in particular argued for economic nationalization to be limited to those sectors that had attained a high level of capitalist development: large-scale industry, banking, transport, and foreign trade. He warned that land nationalization would turn the peasantry into enemies of the party. Above all, in the winter of 1917–18 he came to the conclusion that the Soviet state could not hold out against the demands of the Central Powers for a separate peace. Lenin was accused of betraying Bolshevism and the "European socialist revolution," By March 1918 he had succeeded in winning a majority of the Central Committee to his way of seeing, and the treaty of Brest-Litovsk was signed. His other policies too were officially accepted. He seemed at last to have conquered his party without paying the price of splitting it into fragments.

Yet Bolshevism, born of schism and grown with internal divisions, was still not monolithic. Factionalism continued to affect the party over the next decade: the Military Opposition (1918–19), the Democratic Centralists (from 1919), the Workers' Opposition (from 1920), the Left Opposition (from 1923), the Leningrad Opposition (1925–26), the United Opposition (1926–28), and the Right Deviation (1928–29). Once in power, however, the central party leadership treated disunity as an unaffordable luxury. Doctrine and judgment were brought to bear, a process that quickened as unexpectedly difficult circumstances arose at home and abroad. The party was centralized and disciplined from the winter of 1918–19 onward. Each subsequent year the screw was tightened. At the same time the scope of official debate inside Bolshevism was narrowed. Steadily the oppositionist factions were defeated and eliminated. The implicit ruling principle was that the party could never make a mistake. Lenin's personal authority, despite never becoming unchallengeable, was greater than any other leader's. Even Trotsky was a lesser figure.

When Lenin died in January 1924 he was turned into an object of supreme cultic devotion. Marxism itself was renamed Marxism-Leninism; the purpose was both to honor Lenin and to distinguish his version of Marxism from other versions that were condemned as inauthentic. The leading members of the Central Committee sought to summarize the contents of Marxism-Leninism. Stalin's booklets were to the fore in the codifying process. Debate continued about the rival offerings, and the oppositionist groups in particular subjected them to blistering criticism. But the process of turning Bolshevism into a catechism of tenets learned by rote was already far advanced. It reached its ultimate stage under Stalin's despotism in the 1930s when the *Short Course* of the party's history was published. Was it Bolshevism any longer? Opinions differ. For Stalin and his supporters—as well as for some of his political critics and a few historians—the book was the ultimate logical summary of Lenin's ideas and practice. For others, including Marxist critics of Stalin as well as many historians—"Stalinism" dug the grave of Bolshevism.

See also Agrarian Question; Dictatorship of the Proletariat; Legal Marxism; Lenin, Vladimir; Marxism-Leninism; Russian Revolution and Civil War; Socialist International; Stalin, Joseph; Zimmerwald Conference.

FURTHER READING

Daniels, R. V. *The Conscience of the Revolution.* Cambridge, MA: Harvard University Press, 1960.

Getzler, I. *Martov: A Political Biography of a Russian Social-Democrat.* Cambridge: Cambridge University Press, 1967.

Keep, J.H.L. *The Rise of Social-Democracy in Russia.* Oxford: Oxford University Press, 1963.

Schapiro, L. *The Communist Party of the Soviet Union.* 2nd ed. London: Eyre and Spottiswoode, 1970.

Service, R. *Lenin: A Political Life*, vols 1–3. London: Macmillan, 1985–1995.

ROBERT SERVICE

Bolshevization

In Western historiography, the term "Bolshevization" refers to the process, begun in the mid-1920s, by which the hitherto relatively pluralistic Comintern and its constituent Communist parties were increasingly subject to Bolshevik hegemony. This trend was reflected in the Russification of the ideological discourses and organizational structures of the international Communist movement, and the canonization of the Leninist principles of democratic centralism, iron party unity, and conspiratorial discipline. More specifically, Bolshevization is defined as the concentration of Comintern decision-making power in the hands of the Russian Communist Party (RCP) leaders and their appointed delegates. The longer-term significance of Bolshevization is that almost imperceptibly Soviet state interests took precedence over the Comintern's original mission of world revolution, with the Communist International gradually becoming a mere appendage of Stalin's foreign diplomacy, which favored stabilization and trade with capitalist governments rather than their immediate overthrow. In this sense, Bolshevization has generally been perceived by Western historians as the logical precursor of the Stalinization of the Communist International—a view that also gained currency among late Soviet and post-Soviet experts.

For many years, scholars regarded this accretion of Bolshevik dominance as inherent in the highly centralized, undemocratic structure of the Comintern and its "Twenty-one Conditions on Entry" (1920), which emphasized the guiding role of the Russian Communists and the binding nature of all central decisions on member parties. Bolshevization, it is commonly argued, was imposed "from above" by the Soviet leaders in Moscow, resulting in bureaucratic ossification, ideological monolithism, and a concomitant lack of political independence for both Comintern and national Communist

party leaders. Furthermore, with the failure of revolution abroad, the USSR was left isolated and largely defenseless. In this situation, the argument continues, the ruling Stalinists decreed in the late 1920s that the overriding task of the Comintern was to protect the Soviet bastion against imperialist attack. This could only be guaranteed if Communist parties operated on Bolshevik lines, strictly subordinate to the RCP majority and its current policies, and purged of any oppositional factions. Hence, Bolshevization included the expulsion of those recalcitrant foreign Communists—Trotskyites, later Zinovyevites, and finally Bukharinites—who refused to bow to the dictates of the emergent Stalinists in the RCP.

Given the highly contentious nature of the term Bolshevization, it is perhaps surprising that at the time, the Russian leaders were quite explicit about its usage. Indeed, the Fifth Comintern Congress in summer 1924 and the Fifth Plenum of its Executive Committee in April 1925 adopted mammoth resolutions on Bolshevization. The theses stated that the essential attributes of a Bolshevized party were: it "must be a real mass party," organically linked to the industrial proletariat by "factory cells"; "its tactics should not be sectarian or dogmatic"; "it must be revolutionary Marxist in nature"; and "it must be a centralized party, permitting no factions, tendencies, or groups," with the ultimate goal being a totally united "homogeneous Bolshevik world party permeated with the ideas of Leninism." As such, all "social democratic," "federalist," and "autonomous" remnants had to be expunged. This last injunction was particularly ominous, because vital to an understanding of Bolshevization is the context in which it was originally framed by its Soviet architects, notably Zinovyev and Stalin.

This context was the sharp internecine power struggles in the RCP following Lenin's incapacitation and eventual death in January 1924. It was inevitable that these battles, which initially pitted the Zinoviev-Kamenev-Stalin triumvirate against Trotsky and his supporters, would enter the Comintern, and from the troika's point of view Bolshevization represented the perfect ruse for eliminating Trotskyism from the ranks of international communism. Hence, in the course of the mid-1920s many leading European Trotskyists were expelled from Communist parties and replaced by loyal Bolshevized (i.e., Stalinist) officials. The message emanating from Moscow was crystal clear: adopt the Bolshevik model, "purify" your parties, and align them with the "correct" policies of the RCP majority, or face demotion, expulsion, and marginalization.

This "from above" interpretation holds real explanatory potency, and certainly archival discoveries demonstrate, inter alia, Stalin's penchant for *otsechenie* (the "chopping off" of troublesome comrades). But in recent years more nuanced arguments have suggested that there were moods, attitudes, and circumstances "from below," within the Communist parties themselves, that were conducive to the Bolshevization of the international Communist movement, or more accurately, specific aspects of it. To a limited extent, Bolshevization was, in this view, an interactive process with exogenous and indigenous pressures commingling to produce subtle variations from country to country. In addition, the implications of Bolshevization were dimly apparent to the more critically minded foreign Communists, and thus there was always a subterranean tension between the strivings of the Bolsheviks to "control" the Comintern, and the tendency of national Communist parties to carve out a measure of tactical and organizational autonomy vis-à-vis the centralizing impulses of the Russians.

Several components of Bolshevization struck a chord with many foreign Communists: the stress on organizational and ideological unity appeared to bolster those parties that were faced with neo-Fascist repression; the strident antisocial democratic rhetoric appealed to "leftist" Communists who decried the authoritarian nature of Social Democratic administrations, notably in the Weimar Republic; conversely, the renewed emphasis on united front tactics found a favorable response among those "rightist" Communists who sought more meaningful relations with Social Democratic organizations; and even the overt Russifying elements chimed with the undoubted deference displayed toward the Bolsheviks by many foreign comrades. Less auspicious were those aspects of Bolshevization that threatened traditional working-class practices: party organization according to a factory cell rather than a territorial branch; and the creation of Communist factions in reformist trade unions, which seemed to many Red unionists to be illogical, self-defeating, and overly clandestine.

Bolshevization "from below," then, presents a contradictory picture. The Soviet leaders' aim of creating strictly centralized mass Leninist parties met with differing responses from foreign Communists: willing acceptance and sincere enthusiasm, resigned acquiescence and passive resistance, veiled dissent and overt opposition. Conditions and attitudes conducive to Bolshevization *did* exist, but it must be concluded that the prime stimulus came from Moscow, not from the leaders of the national Communist parties. They could endeavor to influence the Comintern's decision making and even delay the introduction of unwelcome measures, but increasingly their principal function was to fulfill directives rather than initiate them. The Comintern's Russian-dominated Executive Committee determined the goals of Bolshevization and the vituperative inner-party struggles revealed its unspoken essence: foreign Communists were to display total loyalty to the RCP majority, and defend the interests of the USSR against internal and external "enemies."

See also Bolshevism; Comintern; Democratic Centralism; Stalin, Joseph; Trotskyism; Zinovyev, Grigory.

FURTHER READING

Degras, J., ed. *The Communist International, 1919–1943: Documents*. Vol. 2. London: Frank Cass, 1971.

Saarela, T., and K. Rentola, eds. *Communism: National and International*. Helsinki: Finnish Literature Society, 1998.

Vatlin, A. I. *Komintern: idei, resheniia, sud'by*. Moscow: ROSSPEN, 2009.

KEVIN F. McDERMOTT

Bonapartism

In several historical essays, most famously "The Class Struggles in France: 1848 to 1850" (1850) and "The Eighteenth Brumaire of Louis Bonaparte" (1852), Karl Marx interpreted the triumph of Napoleon III in December 1851 as representing the defeat of the revolution of 1848. Marx understood the rise of this "mediocre and grotesque individual" as the consequence of a peculiar stage in the class struggle in France. Louis Bonaparte (1808–73) headed a military dictatorship, seemingly enjoying the unlimited power of an independent executive ruling over society. No single class had been able to establish its hegemony during the revolution. Napoleon III ruled over classes "equally mute and equally impotent, before the rifle butt."

In fact, Napoleon III's regime did represent a form of class rule, albeit contradictory and unstable. Napoleon III was most obviously the champion of the most numerous class in France, the conservative small peasant proprietors who wished to preserve their smallholdings. For Marx, this class was scattered and isolated. It had to rely on a dictator to pursue its interests on the national stage. At the same time, Bonaparte also sought to maintain "bourgeois order." He had common interests with the French bourgeoisie to the extent that they both wished to repulse the proletariat and would issue decrees in the economic interests of the bourgeoisie while at the same time suppressing its political rights. Finally, Bonaparte thought of himself as a populist monarch enjoying broad social support, evident in voting and plebiscites. He liked to act as a "patriarchal benefactor of all classes." For Marx, however, Bonaparte's regime would not be long lasting. This was partly because it could not satisfy the competing demands of the various classes that supported it. To favor one class meant to disadvantage another. An early fall from power would also be a consequence of Bonaparte representing the most reactionary and historically unviable elements of French society. As these elements decayed further, so the government of Bonaparte would crumble.

Although Marx and Engels did not employ the term "Bonapartism," it has enjoyed wide currency among Marxists to describe a reactionary regime that seizes power when a revolutionary upsurge has crested. When progressive forces cannot seize power and the old order is unable to reassert its domination, a "Bonapartist" dictator thus seizes power as a "neutral" arbitrator over equally exhausted classes. In the summer of 1917, Lenin and Trotsky noted the potential for a Russian Bonaparte in the figures of Kerensky and Kornilov. In the 1930s Trotsky contrasted Fascist Bonapartism (Hitler), an extreme attempt by the bourgeoisie to save itself from a proletarian revolution, with Soviet Bonapartism (Stalin), in which a privileged bureaucracy preserved social forms of ownership while suppressing the legitimate demands of the proletariat. A concern with Bonapartism survived into late Soviet communism. In 1964, for example, the charge sheet against Khrushchev included the claim that he had become "Bonapartist," surrounding himself with "sycophants" and relying on "crude threats" to get his way.

See also Dictatorship of the Proletariat; Jacobinism; Stalin, Joseph; Trotskyism.

FURTHER READING

Fernbach, D., ed. *Karl Marx Surveys from Exile*. London: Allan Lane, 1973.
Lenin, V. I. *Collected Works*. 25 vols. Moscow: Progress Publishers, 1964.
Trotsky, L. *Writings 1934–35*. New York: Pathfinder, 1974.

IAN D. THATCHER

![] Borders

Borders

The *Communist Manifesto* saw the future from the perspective of proletarian internationalism: the "course of history" entailed the progressive disappearance of borders. This was not to be. On the contrary, in Communist countries borders play a pivotal role: they hark back to ancient customs for the delimitation and appropriation of territory, but above all the regime's borders outline a space symbolic and sacred even in its closure. This entry discusses the concept of Communist border mostly in relation to the Union of Soviet Socialist Republics, whose name, having eliminated all national references, invited future soviet socialist republics to join the already-existing entity.

The revolutionary dynamism that was characteristic of pan-Soviet Bolshevik plans did not harmonize particularly well with the territorial status quo. The founders' political speeches and work by jurists tended in fact to diminish the borders' role. Revolutionary legitimacy was based first of all on the denunciation of the czarist empire as the "people's prison," and on a critique of previously established international borders, the fruit of deals between great imperialist powers. The borders imposed by enemies during World War I and later the civil war (the Treaty of Brest-Litovsk in March 1918 and the Treaty of Riga in March 1921) appeared to be temporary concessions, following Vladimir Lenin's famous motto: yield ground in order to gain time.

The Decree on Nationalities in November 1917 recognized the independence of "foreign" republics, leading to a proliferation of borders; but Bolshevik actions in the course of the civil war did not match these declarations. The new frontiers were interpreted as limits to national sovereignty internal to an expanding revolutionary space even prior to the creation of the USSR in 1922. The revolution needed to be extended gradually by means of the establishment of friendly Soviet republics whose only acceptable form of sovereignty was to be exercised by the working classes. Territory remained undefined in the first constitutions of the Russian Soviet Republic and later the Ukrainian (1918–19), since sovereignty belonged to all workers and peasants, whatever their nationality. Even prisoners of war could become citizens. These new ideological motherlands were symbolized by their emblems and flags: a red background lit by the sun's rays, or a hammer and sickle framed by a crown of ears of grain. Proletarian solidarity justified conquest. It was frequently intervention by the Red Army, arriving to support local minority worker governments (such as the Red Army's entry into Tiflis in February 1921), which led to the republics joining Soviet space. The establishment of the USSR did not end this process. When Stalin intervened during the second session of the Congress of Soviets, on January 26, 1924, he stated: "The USSR, open to all national republics, even if constituted by means of armed uprising, does not have an established territory, and is susceptible of indefinite enlargement and its goal is the suppression of all classic borders." And this was precisely the motive for the fear at its borders, the fear of states jealous of their independence—states that after the wave of peace treaties during the years 1920–21 were pressing, like the Finns, for a prompt demarcation of the border and garnering the self-interested support of the great powers, which were concerned with the establishment of a cordon sanitaire. These states sought to define their new national identity within the wider landscape, thus containing Bolshevik pressure.

For their part, the Bolsheviks worked to make this "symbolic differential" between the old and new world visible. They developed an architecture for border crossings. The arches bore the inscription "Proletarians of the world unite!" with the intent of showing the traveler the transition not from one country to another but rather from the present to the future. The USSR's advantage was also economic, social, and cultural. Highlighting this sense of passage from the present to the future was part of the purpose for the creation in 1925 of a commission charged with the development of the western border areas in Ukraine, Belorussia, and around Leningrad; it was given the impossible task of developing these desolate peripheral areas and transforming them into showcases for the building of socialism. In addition to ideological demonstrations of socialism's superiority in the 1920s and then again immediately after World War II, the regime also exploited nationalist aspirations. The autonomous republics of Moldavia (1924) and eastern Karelia (1923) sought to become the "Piedmonts" of the 20th century for the Moldavian and Karelian causes, targeting the populations of Romania and Finland. Similarly, Azerbaijan and Kazakhstan adopted policies supporting the abortive experiences of the republic of northern Iran and eastern Turkestan after the end of World War II. The Soviet regime then, since its inception, utilized both class and nationality to change its internal and external bor-

ders. Linguistic and ethnographic criteria took on a political dimension during repeated border demarcations (the incorporation on June 29, 1945, of sub-Carpathian Ruthenia as the last "bit of Ukraine" into the Soviet Socialist Republic of Ukraine; or the integration, based on linguistic criteria, of the border districts of the Soviet Socialist Republic of Latvia into the Russian Soviet Socialist Republic in 1947 and 1953). These unifications were repeatedly portrayed as democratic, a realization of the people's wishes (votes by the Supreme Soviets, plebiscites) and based on the desire to live together in the Soviet fatherland, thereby obscuring the real nature of these Soviet territorial annexations.

The October Revolution also created new frontiers: a pioneering ideological front, on the one hand, and internal borders demarcating national boundaries within the federation, on the other; and this led to a multiplication of borders, with Russia finding itself contained within a sequence of "shells." The logic of a pioneering front, whose revolutionary content is attenuated without jeopardizing its founding principle, presupposes territorial contiguity. In justifying the timidity of its support for revolutionary causes, Soviet discourse pointed to the absence of common borders (Lazar Kaganovich in October 1936 while discussing republican Spain, or Mikhail Suslov in October 1959 talking about the Algerian National Liberation Front).

The dynamic character of the USSR's external shell, which became more rigid in 1948 after a series of annexations at the expense of bordering countries, coexisted with a sacralization of Soviet space, which the border guards symbolized quite well. The Bolsheviks endowed the institution of the border guards—reestablished in 1918 and placed, after November 1920, under the Cheka's (and its successors') supervision—with a political function: protecting the security and economic well-being of Soviet territory, which was supposed to remain both inviolate and impenetrable to capitalist infiltration. With a monopoly on foreign trade, smuggling (whose growth was stimulated, up to the USSR's disintegration, by the scarcity of consumer goods) became a crime against socialist property. After the civil war, with the adoption of the concept of capitalist encirclement, political categories were superimposed by the relevant Soviet institutions on forms of behavior that were not political, especially starting at the end of the 1920s: to cross the border without the proper authorization was almost espionage; an act of pillage carried out by bandits could be transformed into a capitalist provocation.

In this context, entry into the territory could seem even more suspicious than exit. In the first case the socialist community was in danger; in the latter it was specific individuals who were excluding themselves from the community. External interference was thus combined with a form of defensive protectionism and gave rise to diverse, though not contradictory, ways of reasoning. Starting in 1922 a border zone several miles deep was created; it was later declared a special zone with the introduction of internal passports (1934), then designated a "prohibited area" (decree of 1946) before being partially reopened under Khrushchev. A siege mentality became fully developed during the Stalin era and contradicted the original objective of an attractive showcase in the peripheral areas of the socialist motherland. The deportation of ethnic minorities suspected of cross-border ties (from the mid-1930s to the late 1940s) illustrates Stalin's choices during this period: a hermetically sealed border, to the detriment of real influence beyond one's borders. In reality this closure was extremely difficult to implement, given the length of the borders to be watched, the persistence of traditional customs among local populations not aware of the dangers of unauthorized border crossings, and the low level of cultural and ideological education of corruptible border guards—all problems that were the object of recriminations and self-criticism by the relevant administrations and party organizations.

Border guards, though, became cult objects beginning in the 1930s and indeed during the entire existence of the Soviet Union. A coin with the effigy of a border guard was minted in the 1940s; in 1949 a medal was created for the "best border guard"; and a successful series of eight films titled *National Borders* (*Gosudarstvennaâ Granica*) was produced in 1980–88. The borders' landscapes at the end of the Stalin era symbolized the hermetic condition it claimed to have realized: barbed wire, electronic barriers (Turkish-Soviet border), trenches, no-man's-land, the technique of the control strip that was raked over to check for signs of footsteps (on the Soviet border as well as the border between Angola and Namibia), and patrols by border guards under the command of officers trained in the USSR. These surveillance measures, whose degree of implementation and success across Soviet territory differed greatly as a function of their location along the border, could be found in the various bloc countries to which the Soviet Union had exported its techniques starting in the 1950s. The external borders of the socialist community expressed this closure in a particularly emblematic fashion (the Berlin Wall) as did measures that seemed to recall the front in a time of war (the border between the two Koreas).

The broadening of communism's territorial demarcation to the entire Eurasian continent, from Maoist China to the German Democratic Republic, did not entail the extension of the USSR's federal experience and its mobile border apparatus (internal/external). Under de-Stalinization, the mobility rules became less rigid. Bordering socialist countries implemented some forms of cross-border cooperation. National borders were preserved, however, even though the countries of Eastern Europe had become Soviet satellites, and at Moscow's request, ideological as well as, later, political and military communities that limited the individual countries' sovereignty (by means of the Cominform, Comecon, and Warsaw Pact) were also created.

During this period borders were legitimized through public statements. In 1949 on the occasion of the thirty-second anniversary of the October Revolution and after a series of treaties had been signed with the bloc's countries during the previous two years, Georgy Malenkov declared, "Never in the entire course of our history has our Motherland had such well-defined and legitimate national borders." In the Eastern bloc countries, the tensions that had been inherited from the war led to an extensive process of "ethnicization" of the borders, leading to the forced transfer of populations. In the early 1950s, under Soviet tutelage, these new borders were recognized via a declaration by East Germany and Czechoslovakia that no territorial disputes existed, and that the Sudeten Germans had been irrevocably transferred on June 25, 1950; through the Treaty of Görlitz signed by the German Democratic Republic and Poland to confirm the common border in August 1950; and via changes to the Soviet-Polish border with the territorial exchanges of February 15, 1951. Starting at this time, Soviet diplomacy worked for the international recognition of both the USSR's European frontiers and that of its Eastern European satellites, invoking the sacrifices made during the war, but also as far as its own territory was concerned, the historical rights inherited from the Russian Empire. This occurred in 1975 with the so-called Helsinki Final Act. But since then, Soviet military interventions, like the one in Afghanistan in 1979, have not led to border modifications, contrary to what had occurred in Finland in 1939.

In the new Communist China, the denunciation of the unequal treaties imposed in the 19th century did not principally aim to overturn previous borders but rather to relegitimize them by means of bilateral negotiations that without substantially modifying the borders themselves, would lead to their once again being endowed with the desired status and national dignity. Treaties concerning China's borders were signed with thirteen of its fourteen terrestrial neighbors, despite ongoing disputes with nine maritime neighbors. Mao Zedong's China could thus act as the spokesperson for anti-imperialism and support neighboring countries (Korea and Cambodia), but its objective remained the "liberation" of all those territories that were historically considered Chinese, Tibet included. Ho Chi Minh's Vietnam did not dispute the legal validity of the demarcations that France had made. But Enver Hoxha denounced the Allies' interference during the Paris Conference in 1946 and affirmed the indisputable nature of Albanian borders, which, he added tautologically, "do not include a single millimeter of foreign soil." In Romania, legitimation included arguments about the natural circular frontier traced by rivers and the unifying territorial function of the Carpathian Mountains. The establishment of both state and national frontiers did not in actuality prevent military interference (Hungary in 1956 and Prague in 1968); belonging to the same ideological community did not prevent conflicts between some of these powers (the China-USSR border conflict in 1969, and the China-Vietnam conflict in 1979).

The regimes' borders are undoubtedly still inscribed in the respective landscapes, demarcating asymmetries in development (between the two Koreas, or within reunified Germany), while the once-forbidden zones, ecologically preserved, have often become natural parks in a post-Communist Europe. The borders' spiritual influence has undoubtedly left its mark, as the stories and memoirs of those who "escaped" communism attest to (from Eastern European dissidents to the exodus of the Cuban *balseros* in 1994) or museums document (such as the Checkpoint Charlie museum in Berlin and the Smugglers' Museum in Joensuu in eastern Finland). Territorial demarcation, however, has not left behind the sense of belonging to an ideological and supranational community. On the contrary, the Communist experience seems to have further solidified feelings of national or regional identity, even creating new ones, as the relative solidity of the USSR's republican borders, now nation-state borders, bears witness to.

See also Berlin Wall; Conference on Security and Cooperation in Europe; Deportation of Nationalities in the USSR; National Question, The; Nationality Policies; Socialist Camp; Soviet Bloc.

FURTHER READING

Calvez, J.-Y. "Doctrine de la frontière en URSS." In *Les frontières européennes de l'U. R. S. S., 1917–194*, ed. J. B. Duroselle. Paris: Fondation Nationale des Sciences Politiques, 1958.

Chandler, A. *Institutions of Isolation: Border Controls in the Soviet Union and Its Successor States, 1917–1993*. Montreal: McGill Queen's University Press, 1998.

Coeuré, S., and S. Dullin, eds. *Frontières du communisme. Mythologies et réalités de la division de l'Europe de la révolution d'Octobre au mur de Berlin*. Paris: La Decouverte, 2007.

Dullin, S. "L'emergence d'une frontière de guerre froide à l'Ouest de l'Union Soviétique, 1945–1949." In *Une Europe malgré tout: échanges culturels, intellectuels, et scientifiques dans la guerre froide, 1945–1990*, ed. A. Fleury and L. Jilek. Brussels: Peter Lang–PIE, 2006.

Foucher, M. *Fronts et frontieres. Un tour du monde géopolitique*. Paris: Fayard, 1994.

Martin, T. D. *The Affirmative Action Empire: Nations and Nationalism in the Soviet Union, 1923–1939*. Ithaca, NY: Cornell University Press, 2001.

Nguyen-Roualt, F. "La politique juridique extérieure de la République populaire de Chine. Territoire et souveraineté." PhD diss., Université de Pantheon–Assas, Paris, 2003.

Nordman, D. "La Frontière." In *Dictionnaire critique de la République*, ed. V. Duclert and C. Prochasson. Paris: Flammarion, 2002.

SABINE DULLIN

Brecht, Bertolt

Bertolt Brecht (1898–1956)—poet, dramatist, and theatrical man of the 20th century—in many respects embodied the meeting of art and ideology. His path as an author initially began amid the European avant-garde from 1918 to 1926, the years between the collapse of the Wilhelmine Empire and the troubled birth of the Weimar Republic. These were complex historical developments, contradictory and filled with dramatic tension; a young Brecht reacted to them by gradually combining his anarchist subjectivism with a curiosity that we might already call sociological. The writer looked with a fearless, provocative, and (apparently) neutral gaze on this simmering reality. The critic Herbert Jhering stated at the time that Brecht "is neither bourgeois nor antibourgeois, he does not affirm or negate, he does not fight for or against. He does not exalt technology, he does not refuse today's mechanization." Brecht's works of the period deal with a variety of themes. In *Baal* (1918–22), he insists on the natural and biologic dimension of human behavior, but does not separate it from the awareness of a "second" nature—that of the new metropolitan reality, superimposed on the first. In *Trommeln der Nacht* (1919–22), he examines the protagonist's withdrawal into a private realm, set against the shifting background of the Spartacist uprising in Berlin. In other theatrical texts we find the capitalist microcosm, governed by the rules of profit, such as in *Lux in tenebris* (1919); the individual's solitude and struggle for existence in mass society, as in *Im Dickicht der Städte* (1921–24); and his anonymous interchangeability in *Mann ist Mann* (1924–26). As Brecht himself notes, he observed these phenomena with a detached and impartially "sporting" attitude, a cynical and clinical coldness. The same desecrating tone can be heard in his first and most celebrated collection of poems, *Hauspostille* (1927).

Brecht's disenchanted inquiry into the contemporary German situation soon becomes much more clear-cut: on the Brechtian stage the struggle for existence acquired class characteristics and gradually revealed its economic roots. He began a new project in 1924, *Joe Fleischhacker in Chikago*, a new play whose plot centered on the grain exchange in the U.S. city and for which he needed to document the techniques used for financial speculation in the capitalist system—a need that led to his encounter with the Marxian magnum opus. Brecht started this project several times, before finally abandoning it; but it led him to read Karl Marx's *Capital*, in which in his own words, he was "immersed up to his neck" in October 1926. Looking back at his dramatic production, a little later he wrote: "Reading Marx's *Capital* I understood my own works, works for which he was the only possible spectator." From then on the dynamics of capitalism provided the framework for many of his stage productions, starting with the *Dreigroschenoper* (1928), which made use of Pierre-Joseph Proudhon's thesis "property is theft." Brecht continued in this vein in the play *Heilige Johanna der Schlachthöfe* (1929–30), which can be considered a reworking of the previously abandoned project of 1924, but incorporating the ideological and superstructural phenomena that accompany the unfolding of capitalism's economic laws.

At the end of the 1920s Brecht's path took another turn: 1929 was, in fact, not only the year of the great crash (whose repercussions are clearly visible in *Heilige Johanna*) but also the moment in which Brecht moved closer to the German Communist Party and started attending the Marxistische Arbeiterschule (MASCH/Marxist Worker School) in Berlin. There he took courses in historical and dialectical materialism taught by the philosopher and sociologist Hermann Duncker (with whom he stayed in contact until 1956); Albert Einstein, Walter Gropius, and Bruno Taut also lectured at MASCH. Brecht had established ties with another important sociologist, Fritz Sternberg, whose active role in the world of Brechtian ideas has yet to be fully examined. A direct reflection of this increased commitment, on the political and ideological level, but also from the point of view of experimentation with new dramatic forms, were the "didactic dramas." A representative example is *Die Maßnahme* (spring–fall 1930), which contains the Leninist theme of the party as collective consciousness, and also assigns to the new theater the function of contributing, in Marxian fashion, to the "transformation of the world."

By 1928 Brecht had met Karl Korsch, and most probably already in 1926 had read his essay "Marxismus und Philosophie." Korsch, a Communist intellectual (later expelled from the party for ideological reasons), had been an interlocutor for the Augsburg dramatist since the times when, at MASCH, he had heard Korsch's lessons on "What Is Alive and What Is Dead in Marxism." In the course of an intense dialogue that continued until Brecht's death, the writer always saw Korsch as an ideal "teacher," motivator, and maieutician in the strictest sense of the word. As Brecht wrote in a brief essay of 1934 titled, appropriately enough, "Ueber meinen Lehrer" (About My Teacher), "His help is invaluable to my works. He discovers all the weak points. And immediately suggests counter-proposals." Their partnership grew stronger during Brecht's fourteen years of exile, particularly in Svendborg (Denmark), where Korsch passed the summer months between 1934 and 1936 at Brecht's house. In the course of an intensive dialogue with Brecht, Korsch concluded his monograph on *Karl Marx* (1938), which Korsch himself later called "the Svendborg Marx." Such close exchanges (in which Walter Benjamin also participated during those years) can function as a litmus test for the different phases of Brecht's reflection: his confronting, in a constant interplay, Marxist doctrine, on the one hand, and the Soviet Union's domestic and international political practices, on the other.

While Brecht agreed with Korsch in considering Marxism a historically determined theory, he also wondered if the fundamental presuppositions of capitalism, property relations, and forms of production had not remained essentially the same for the working class—if, in other words, the critique of 19th-century liberal capitalism that Marx had developed did not actually contain a method that was also applicable "to our age," the age of monopoly capitalism (as he wrote in a letter of June–July 1934). Both Korsch and Brecht were critical of a mechanical interpretation of reflection theory, according to which the transition to socialism occurs almost automatically; they also invoked the *Eleventh Thesis on Feuerbach* (1845) as a principle that considers praxis as the criterion of its own objective truth. Yet Brecht did not share Korsch's radical and voluntaristic subjectivism. Quite the opposite: in the previously cited letter of 1934 Brecht warned of the dangers of intellectual "shortcuts," of a sort of "revolutionary impatience."

Their disagreements were even more explicit on the Soviet model of the state, whose Stalinist bureaucratic involution Korsch had denounced in a timely fashion. This long-standing dispute between the two was renewed in February–March 1939 when Brecht argued, "Why not treat the Soviet Union from the point of view of the Marxian theses? The regime, the state apparatus, the Party, its leadership (if you will) develops the productive forces. The national form, in which it will have to prepare for the decisive battle, also develops these forces. And finally let us not forget the class character of international politics—the global civil war." Two years later, in November 1941, Brecht stated, "Naturally I continue to be unhappy about your attitude towards the first workers' State in history, an attitude which is evident in practically every article of yours. It is in fact not only a workers' *State*, but also a *workers'* State! It seems to me that this specific state form (the Stalinist) was developed with very close links to the socialization of the economy (five-year plans), and to the collectivization and industrialization of the economy and defense." Still, he concluded that he was interested in a historical analysis of the relations between the structure of the soviets and the "Party-form," which was in actual fact destined to prevail.

Brecht had already manifested this interest when confronting the events that characterized the global civil war, starting with the German-Soviet Nonaggression Pact (1939), with its secret protocol (which remained secret until 1946) about the division of Poland. In his *Arbeitsjournal* (Work Diary), starting in 1938, but above all during the years of World War II, Brecht formulated

his positions on the themes that were also at the center of his correspondence with Korsch; in these diary entries he did so more dialectically, however, often pointing in the direction of a stronger consensus. In July 1938, while working on the novel *Die Geschäfte des Herrn Julius Caesar*, Brecht observed that "even the proletarian revolution (in the country in which, after the revolution, only two classes have been struggling, the workers and the peasants) has made the dictatorship of a single individual possible," underscoring a "Bonapartist" drift that was present in both domestic and international Soviet politics. There is no doubt that "it is proceeding in the construction of socialist elements," he wrote, but the Nonaggression Pact with Adolf Hitler's Germany carried with it "the mark of having aided fascism, before the eyes of the whole world's proletariat" (September 9, 1939); therefore the Soviet Union was not engaged in "a socialist foreign policy" (January 1, 1940). Several months before he had noted that "the Russians' entry into Poland has occurred in a strangely Napoleonic fashion. It was not preceded by any kind of war propaganda, 'public opinion' was not at all prepared, no Soviet deliberated or ratified anything. The government decreed" (September 19, 1939). Two days later, these reflections concluded with a severe judgment about the decision-making mechanisms employed within the political apparatus, and denounced a considerable deficit of "democracy from below": "The gossip one hears everywhere, in other words that the Bolshevik Party has completely changed, is certainly not accurate. After having been in power two decades, for the Party the people continues to constitute the all-purpose 'lever.'" The topic is then pursued in an entry on July 19, 1943, in which the Russian proletariat's efforts to build socialism in one country had really concluded with the "transformation of the professional revolutionary into a bureaucrat, of an entire revolutionary party into a group of functionaries," following an interpretation that Korsch had already been outlining in the 1920s. On the same page, Brecht—reading the "depressing" book by Boris Souvarine on Joseph Stalin (published in Paris in 1935)—performs a sort of inverted comparison between fascism and Bolshevism (as he did elsewhere in the *Arbeitsjournal*): "In fascism socialism sees its own image distorted in the mirror: with none of its virtues, but with all its vices."

The "work in progress" Brecht was observing was "the easy thing it is difficult to accomplish," to quote the words he had already used in 1932 while writing *Die Mutter* (from Maksim Gorky's novel with the same title).

And it remained just as difficult when in 1948, after his return to Europe from the United States, Brecht took up residence in Berlin, in the German Democratic Republic. Here, in the context of a state that claimed to be building socialism while repeating the more negative experiences of the Soviet model—namely, the bureaucratic and authoritarian dirigisme from on high—Brecht could not help but sit, dialectically, on the narrow ridge between two fronts. On the one hand, the Berlin workers' revolt of June 17, 1953, against the increase in working hours led him to enter the following in his *Work Diary*: "Notwithstanding the absence of a goal and the pitiful ineptitude, the workers' demonstrations still prove that the rising class is here. It is not the petit bourgeois who are acting, it is the workers. Their mottoes are confused and lack conviction, stuffed into their heads by their class enemy; they are absolutely incapable of organizing, no Council has arisen, no plan is taking place." On the other hand, such remarks, combining his innate and pragmatic "spirit of contradiction" with a historical horizon marked by a difficult question, found poetic expression in some of the *Bukower Elegien*, which were written immediately after witnessing some of the events just described: "After the revolt of June 17 / the secretary of the Writers' Union / had some flyers distributed in the Stalinallee / on which one could read that the people / had betrayed the government's trust / and could only regain it / by working twice as hard. Would it not / be simpler, then, for the government / to disband the people and / elect another one?" And again: "On the side of the road. / The driver changes the tire. / I don't like where I am coming from. / I don't like where I am going. / Why do I watch the changing of the tire / with impatience?" On the historical level, the question about the feasibility of the work-in-progress has gone unanswered. Brecht died on August 14, 1956, but the Hungarian uprising in October of that same year posed the question again, only much more dramatically.

See also Avant-garde; Bonapartism; Dictatorship of the Proletariat; Marxism, Western; Revolution, Myths of the; Stalinism.

FURTHER READING

Brüggemann, H. "Bert Brecht und Karl Korsch. Fragen nach Lebendingen und Totem im Marxismus. In *Arbeiterbewegung. Theorie und Geschichte*. Vol. I. Frankfurt am Main: Fischer, 1973.

Chiarini, P. *Krieg und Literatur in Brechts "Arbeitsjournal."* In *Schuld und Sühne. Kriegserlebnis und Kriegserdeutung in*

deutschen Medien der Nachkriegszeit, 1945–1961, 1:371–85. Amsterdam: Rodopi, 2001.

Schlenstedt S. "Auf der Suche nach Spuren: Brecht und die MASCH." In *Brecht und Marxismus. Dokumentation*, 18–28. Berlin: Henschelverlag, 1983.

Schölzel, A. *Korsch, Brecht und die Negation der Philosophie*. In *Schuld und Sühne. Kriegserlebnis und Kriegserdeutung in deutschen Medien der Nachkriegszeit, 1945–1961*, 1:32–44. Amsterdam: Rodopi, 2001.

Sternberg, F. *Der Dichter und die Ratio; Erinnerungen an Bertolt Brecht*. Göttingen: Sachse und Pohl, 1963.

Wizisla, E. *Benjamin und Brecht. Geschichte einer Freundschaft*. Frankfurt am Main: Suhrkamp, 2004.

Brecht's correspondence with Korsch can be found in the Brechtian *Werke* (*Große kommentierte Berliner und FrankfurterAusgabe*, vols. 28, 29, or *Briefe 1* (1913–36) and *Briefe 2* (1937–40) (Frankfurt am Main: Suhrkamp, 1998). The so-called Marxist studies, including *Über meinen Lehrer*, can be found in *Werke*, vol. 20, *Schriften 2* (1993).On the Berlin uprising of June 17, 1953, see the letter to Walter Ulbricht on that same date, and especially the one to Peter Suhrkamp, written July 1, in *Briefe 3* (1950–56), in addition to the notes in *Journale 2* (1941–55), *Werke*, vol. 27 (1995). For the *Bukower Elegien*, cf. *Werke*, vol. 12, *Gedichte 2* (1988).

PAOLO CHIARINI

Brest-Litovsk, Treaty of

The new Bolshevik government of Russia concluded a separate armistice with the Central Powers (the German Empire, the Austro-Hungarian Empire, the Ottoman Empire, and the kingdom of Bulgaria) on December 5, 1917. Peace negotiations opened in Brest-Litovsk—now Brest, Belarus—on December 22. Adolf Joffe led the Soviet delegation. He was assisted initially by Lev Kamenev, Grigori Sokolnikov, and Lev Karakhan. Subsequently Trotsky, the commissar for foreign affairs, became the leading delegate. The German delegation was headed by Foreign Secretary Richard von Kühlmann and included General Max Hoffman, chief of staff to the commander in chief of the army on the eastern front. Count Ottokar Czernin, the minister of foreign affairs, led the delegation from Austria-Hungary. In the first stage of the conference, the Russians presented Lenin's peace program—no annexations, no indemnities, and self-determination for all peoples. The latter, if adopted and implemented, would have resulted in an east-central Europe of dozens of competing claims for sovereign nationhood put forth by various ethnicities that probably would have resulted in chaotic conditions and social unrest. The German delegation presented the Russians with a demand that Russia renounce those areas of the former czarist empire occupied by the German army: Poland, Lithuania, and Kurland.

On February 10—after weeks of playing for time, hoping that revolution would break out in Central Europe—Trotsky refused to sign a peace treaty, withdrew the Russian delegation from the negotiations, declared that Russia was leaving the war and demobilizing its troops opposing the Central Powers, and left immediately for Petrograd. He calculated that imperial Germany would be exposed as plundering the Russian Empire and trampling on the rights of self-determination while popular unrest in Germany and Austria-Hungary would compel them to accept the "no war, no peace" solution. He prevailed temporarily over Lenin, who wanted to conclude an immediate peace with Germany, and over a slight majority of the Bolsheviks, who wanted to defy the Germans outright and launch a revolutionary war against the Central Powers.

The Central Powers responded on February 18 by repudiating the armistice and resuming military operations. In the next two weeks they seized most of Ukraine and the Baltic provinces, and a German fleet approached the Gulf of Finland threatening Petrograd. At Lenin's assistance, the Bolshevik delegation accepted the ultimatum of the Central Powers and agreed to the terms they dictated. A peace treaty was signed on March by a delegation headed by Sokolnikov.

The terms were harsher than those rejected by the Bolsheviks in December. Poland, Lithuania, and Kurland, over which Russia had lost military control, were separated from Russian sovereignty. Russian troops were to withdraw immediately from Estonia, Livonia, Finland, and the Åland Islands. Red Guards were to leave Ukraine. In the Caucasia, the Armenian districts of Ardahan and Kars as well as the Georgian district of Batum were ceded to Turkey. What had been the Russian Empire was reduced by 780,000 kilometers and 56,000,000 people. That territory contained one-third of its rail network, 73 percent of its iron production, and 89 percent of its coal supply. The treaty also required the Bolsheviks to stop conducting revolutionary agitation (propaganda) in Germany. A follow-up treaty, signed in

Berlin on August 27, required Russia to pay substantial war reparations.

The treaty had an effective life of eight months. The terms of the November 11 armistice with the Western Allies forced Germany to renounce the treaty, and Russia also declared it null and void. Subsequently, Finland, Estonia, Latvia, Lithuania, and Poland became independent sovereign states. Ukraine became a member of the Soviet Union.

See also Diplomats; Lenin, Vladimir; Russian Revolution and Civil War.

FURTHER READING

Debo, R. *Revolution and Survival: The Foreign Policy of Soviet Russia, 1917–18*. Toronto: University of Toronto Press, 1979.

Wheeler-Bennett, J. W. *The Forgotten Peace: Brest-Litovsk, March 1918*. New York: Norton, 1939.

JON S. JACOBSON

Brezhnev, Leonid

Leonid Brezhnev (1906–1982) was born on June 12, in Kamenskoye, Yekaterenislav region of Ukraine. He grew up in a worker family and went to work himself at the age of fifteen. His mother managed to get Brezhnev into the local gymnasium, where he studied seven years. In 1921 he began to work at the metallurgical plant that employed his father. From 1923 to 1927 he was a student at the Land and Melioration Technical School in Kursk. He later continued his higher technical education at the Metallurgical Institute in Dneprodzerzhinsk. As a young man, Brezhnev acted in a workers' theater, recited poetry, and had an active social life. From 1927 to 1930 he worked as an agronomist, then as a local land official in the Urals, and married Viktoria Denisova. Brezhnev participated in the forced collectivization in the Urals. In 1931 he returned to Dneprodzerzhinsk, Ukraine, where he worked as an engineer at a large metal plant and joined the party. In 1935 he was a political commissar of the tank company in the Far East. In 1936 he returned to the Dneprodzerzhinsk plant, where he worked until the turmoil of the Great Purge opened new doors for him. He worked on the Dneprodzerzhinsk city council, then was transferred to party work. Brezhnev became the head of the defense industry department of the Dnepropetrovsk regional party committee in May of 1937, and 1939 became secretary of that committee. He developed expertise as an economic administrator.

In 1941, after the German invasion, Brezhnev volunteered for the army; during the war he served as deputy head of the Political Directorate of the Southern Front, head of the Political Department of the 18th Army, and head of the Political Directorate of the Fourth Ukrainian Front. Brezhnev's war record was not spectacular, but he took part in combat actions during the defense of the Caucasus, the liberation of Ukraine, and operations in the Carpathian Mountains. The war with the Nazis forever remained a pivotal episode in Brezhnev's life, shaping his attitudes toward the issues of war and peace. He ended the war as a major general and the head of the Political Directorate of the Cis-Carpathian military district; in June 1945, he participated in the victory parade in Moscow and attended a state banquet that Stalin hosted for parade participants. Brezhnev retained respect for Stalin as commander in chief for the rest of his life.

In August 1946, Brezhnev joined the high echelon of the party nomenklatura as first secretary of the Zaporozhie regional party committee; the following year he assumed the same post in the Dnepropetrovsk region. In July 1950, he became party leader of Moldavia. Stalin took notice of Brezhnev around that time and in October 1952 promoted him, along with a group of younger apparatchiks, to the CC Secretariat and the enlarged politburo (presidium) as a candidate member. After Stalin's death, however, Brezhnev lost these positions; he was demoted to first deputy head of the Chief Political Directorate of the Soviet Army and Navy (Glavpur). From 1954 to 1955 he was first secretary in Kazakhstan where he coordinated the monumental campaign to cultivate "virgin lands." It was during his Kazakhstan tenure that he won the attention and trust of Khrushchev. At the Twentieth Party Congress in February of 1956, Brezhnev became, for the second time, a candidate member of the politburo and a member of the CC Secretariat. In June 1957 Brezhnev and a group of CC secretaries and Central Committee members rescued Khrushchev after he was deposed by the politburo majority. After that Brezhnev became a full member of the politburo.

In 1956–60 Brezhnev assisted Khrushchev in implementing his numerous agricultural initiatives (Sovnarkhoz, etc.). He also supervised the military-industrial complex, including atomic and missile projects; and together with Khrushchev he received the first cosmonauts. Handsome, photogenic, gregarious, and always smiling,

Brezhnev was an ideal host for official state occasions and from 1960 to 1964 occupied the largely ceremonial post of chairman of the Supreme Soviet. During 1964 he became one of leaders of the plot to overthrow Khrushchev, and at the October plenum became first secretary of the CC CPSU. Other ambitious politburo and secretariat members underestimated Brezhnev's political abilities and regarded him as a transitional figure.

Initially, Brezhnev kept a low profile at the politburo, allowing others (A. Kosygin, N. Podgorny, A. Shelepin, etc.) to dominate foreign and domestic political agendas, while he and his supporters skillfully used the levers of the party apparatus to win the support of regional party secretaries. His praise of Stalin's wartime role and generous allocations to the army and the navy won him military support. Brezhnev also became popular among the peasantry as the state allocations and credits to agriculture skyrocketed, greatly exceeding state taxes. As for party intellectuals, some considered him a lesser evil than others. By 1968 Brezhnev's protégés had assumed positions in the KGB and the army. In 1968–69 Brezhnev faced severe challenges in Czechoslovakia after the "Prague Spring" and in the Far East during the Sino-Soviet border clashes. His decision to invade Czechoslovakia alienated reform-minded party intellectuals and split the Western Communist movement, but at the same time reaffirmed Brezhnev's credentials as a Cold War statesman.

From 1969 to 1974, Brezhnev was the main force behind the Soviet policy of détente with Western countries. Before a reluctant and skeptical politburo he defended diplomatic rapprochement with West Germany, and in 1971 he met with Willy Brandt in the Crimea. In the spring of 1972, despite strong politburo resentment of U.S. military actions in Vietnam, Brezhnev and his supporters achieved a political consensus that enabled him to hold a May summit with Richard Nixon in Moscow. Brezhnev believed that his personal "friendship" with Nixon would initiate a new period of arms control and economic cooperation between the two superpowers. In 1973 he met with Nixon again in the United States; and after Nixon's resignation, with Gerald Ford in Vladivostok in 1974. In August 1975 he signed the Helsinki Act that gave international legitimacy to the post–World War II borders in Europe. Brezhnev enjoyed his international stature; he entertained foreign dignitaries at sumptuous banquets and hunting lodges, and took to collecting foreign cars. After Vladivostok, Brezhnev's health (problematic since 1969) drastically deteriorated, and he became habituated to powerful barbiturates that he took to control his shaky nervous system. He spent most of his time at dachas and at a hunting lodge near Moscow. The decline of détente in the years 1975 to 1977 caused Brezhnev to withdraw from active statesmanship. He delegated foreign affairs to the troika of Andropov, Gromyko, and Ustinov. At the same time, in 1977, he assumed a second position as the head of the Supreme Soviet, nominally the post of the head of state. Brezhnev's summit in Vienna with Jimmy Carter was his last contribution to détente.

Brezhnev presided over the Soviet Union at the height of its power and international prestige. He became a major architect of international détente and of arms control agreements (SALT and the ABM treaties); he was an energetic, affable, and flexible negotiator. The policies he authorized and supported allowed the Soviet Union to reach strategic parity with the United States; the Soviet army and navy could project its power to every corner of the world. Domestically, Brezhnev's philosophy was "live and let live": large groups within the citizenry improved their living standards, moved to new housing, and gained access to a wider assortment of consumer goods.

At the same the general secretary lacked many leadership qualities: his education and cultural horizons were not broad, and he had no knack for systematic and analytical work. A born administrator, he knew little about ideological and cultural affairs and let others (e.g., M. Suslov) coordinate them. Brezhnev's physical decline came to symbolize stagnation and a worsening crisis in the Soviet political and economic systems. Toward the late 1970s, the black market and under-the-counter distribution of goods proliferated; cities outside Moscow experienced shortages of meat, fats, and produce. Numerous cronies of the general secretary, as well as regional party secretaries, benefited from Brezhnev's policy of "cadres' stability." Brezhnev's daughter was married to the minister of interior; both were implicated in scandals and dubious schemes. Widespread corruption, incompetence, and a shameless cult of the senile leader delivered the final blows to popular belief in the Communist "dream." In December 1979, Brezhnev, incensed by the assassination of his protégé, First Secretary M. Taraki of the Peoples Democratic Party of Afghanistan, authorized a Soviet military invasion. Unexpectedly, this led to the eight-year war in Afghanistan.

The last two years of Brezhnev's life were slow agony: his détente project lay in ruins and the relative stability in the Soviet bloc was shattered by the rise of Solidar-ity in Poland. Even the long-awaited Moscow Summer Olympics of 1980 were marred by a U.S. boycott. Brezhnev died of a heart attack on November 11, 1982, in the arms of his bodyguards at his dacha. He was buried with full regalia in the Kremlin wall. By the time of his death he was Marshal and four-times hero of the Soviet Union and possessed the Order of Victory as well as two hundred Soviet and foreign decorations.

See also Brezhnev Doctrine; Dissent in the USSR; Stalinism.

FURTHER READING

Alexandrov-Agentov, A. M. *From Kollontai to Gorbachev.* Moscow: International Affairs, 1994.

Arbatov, G. *The System: An Insider's Life in Soviet Politics.* New York: Random House, 1992.

Brezhnev, L. *Memoirs.* Moscow: Progress Publishers, 1983.

Volkogonov, D. *Autopsy of an Empire: The Seven Leaders Who Built the Soviet Regime.* New York: Free Press, 1998.

VLADISLAV M. ZUBOK

Brezhnev Doctrine

The term "Brezhnev Doctrine" was coined in the West in September 1968 to refer to the collection of authoritative statements issued by the Soviet Union as justifications for the August 1968 invasion of Czechoslovakia. Until 1989, Soviet leaders denied that any such doctrine existed, and the term until then was used only in the West, not in the USSR. The doctrine was named after Leonid Brezhnev, who served as general secretary of the Soviet Communist Party (CPSU) from October 1964 until November 1982. In that capacity, Brezhnev headed the CPSU politburo during its deliberations in 1968. Although the Brezhnev Doctrine did not go beyond the principles enunciated earlier by Stalin and Khrushchev, it was important in reaffirming the acceptable norms for Soviet–East European relations.

The most elaborate presentation of the Brezhnev Doctrine appeared in *Pravda* on September 26, 1968, under the title "Sovereignty and the Internationalist Obligations of Socialist Countries," by Sergei Kovalev, a commentator who frequently published articles on behalf of the CPSU politburo. Kovalev linked the fate of each socialist country with that of all others, stipulated that every socialist country must abide by the norms of

Marxism-Leninism as interpreted in Moscow, and firmly rejected "abstract sovereignty" in favor of the "laws of class struggle." His article thus laid out strict "rules of the game" for the socialist commonwealth:

> Without question, the peoples of the socialist countries and the Communist parties have and must have freedom to determine their country's path of development. Any decision they make, however, must not be inimical either to socialism in their own country or to the fundamental interests of the other socialist countries. . . . A socialist state that is in a system of other states composing the socialist commonwealth cannot be free of the common interests of that commonwealth. The sovereignty of individual socialist countries cannot be set against the interests of world socialism and the world revolutionary movement. . . . Each Communist party is free to apply the principles of Marxism-Leninism and socialism in its own country, but it is not free to deviate from these principles if it is to remain a Communist party.

Brezhnev himself reaffirmed the eponymous doctrine three months after the invasion in a lengthy speech before the Fifth Congress of the Polish United Workers' Party. During the speech, Brezhnev acknowledged that the intervention in Czechoslovakia had been "an extraordinary step, dictated by necessity," but he warned that "when internal and external forces hostile to socialism are threatening to turn a socialist country back to capitalism, this becomes a common problem and a concern of all socialist countries." Subsequently, that theme was enshrined as a "basic principle" of relations among socialist states, giving the Soviet Union not only a right but also a "sacred duty" to preserve the "socialist essence" of all socialist states.

The enunciation of the Brezhnev Doctrine restored a firmer tone to Soviet–East European relations and demarcated the limits of permissible deviations from the Soviet model of communism. By redefining the norms of international law within "the general context of class struggle," and rendering paramount the interests of the "socialist commonwealth," the Brezhnev Doctrine in effect transformed the Warsaw Pact into a more formally ideological alliance than it had been in the past. When the Warsaw Treaty Organization was set up in May 1955, the founding document indicated that all states were free to join the alliance "irrespective of their social and state systems." The Brezhnev Doctrine essentially annulled this provision and thereby narrowed the prospects for individual alliance members to deviate from Soviet policy.

See also Brezhnev, Leonid; Prague Spring; Soviet Bloc; Warsaw Pact.

FURTHER READING

Dawisha, K. "The 1968 Invasion of Czechoslovakia: Causes, Consequences, and Lessons for the Future." In *Soviet-East European Dilemmas: Coercion, Competition, and Consent*, ed. K. Dawisha and P. Hanson, pp. 9–25. London: Heinemann, 1981.

Kramer, M. "The Czechoslovak Crisis and the Brezhnev Doctrine." In *1968: The World Transformed*, ed. C. Fink, P. Gassert, and D. Junker, pp. 111–74. New York: Cambridge University Press, 1998.

MARK KRAMER

Browder, Earl

Earl Browder (1891–1973) was secretary of the Communist Party of the United States of America (CPUSA) from the early 1930s to the end of World War II, the period of greatest Communist influence and prestige in U.S. society. He wanted the party to adopt a program, a language, and an organizational structure suited to the complex realities of the United States at the time, and his policies reflected these priorities. His efforts remained well within the bounds of an undeniably subordinate relationship with Moscow.

The Communists became indispensable to the rebirth and expansion of the workers' movement in the United States during the New Deal by implementing the policy of "Americanization." They established themselves as the principal force on the U.S. Left, and for a while at least, were even recognized as a component of the broad progressive coalition backing Franklin Delano Roosevelt.

Born in Wichita, Kansas, Browder was a descendant of North America's first colonists. He joined the Socialist Party in 1907, and was imprisoned with his two brothers for pacifist activities during World War I. In 1920, soon after his release from jail, he joined the Communist Party and became involved in union matters. In 1922 the Comintern summoned him to Moscow. He undertook many missions abroad on its behalf, including one to China that kept him away from the United States until

1929. On returning home, he became a member of the party's collective secretariat and eventually, in 1932, its leadership.

Starting in 1934, in the context of the Communists' relations with Roosevelt, Adolf Hitler's ascent to power, and the political evolution of the Comintern, Browder promoted a policy of alliances. Three years later this new tendency culminated in Communist support of "the party of the New Deal," as Browder defined it. In his estimation it was composed of the left wings of the Democratic and Republican parties, the union movement, and progressive political parties. This coalition of forces, united in support of Roosevelt's domestic policies, would be all the more effective since it corresponded to the traditional U.S. two-party system, or so Browder thought. The conclusions he reached at this stage, reflecting on the appropriate political line for the party, led him to propose the dissolution of the CPUSA in 1944.

The success of Communist policies at the end of the 1930s led to an increase in party memberships. But above all it increased the party's influence both in the union movement and the world of politics. In the union movement, the Communists succeeded in leading organizations that collectively represented about one-third of the membership of the Committee of Industrial Organizations. In the political arena, the Communists became a recognized component of the broad progressive coalition that also included significant segments of the Democratic Party.

The period of "imperialist war" (September 1939–June 1941) exposed the CPUSA to a campaign of repression that culminated in Browder's arrest; he was sentenced to four years in prison. The repression devastated the alliances that the Communists had cultivated with care. Once this brief but traumatic period concluded with the Nazi invasion of the USSR, Browder, who had been released from prison thanks to Roosevelt's direct intervention, tenaciously devoted himself to bringing the Communists back into the broad progressive coalition from which they had been excluded. This political calculation is what moved Browder to propose the dissolution of the CPUSA, an organization with an autonomous electoral policy, and substitute it with the Communist Political Association, which would act as a lobbying group within the U.S. two-party system. The most remarkable achievement for Browder and the policies that he had promoted for at least ten years (with the exception of the period of imperialist war) was the dissolution of the CPUSA in 1944. These policies stemmed from

the realization that within a two-party system in which both the Democratic and Republican parties represented coalitions of heterogeneous forces and ideologies, to remain a third party would have signified "isolating ourselves from the country's political life."

Almost a year after the party's dissolution, in April 1945, an article by Jacques Duclos denouncing the dissolution of the CPUSA in harsh terms appeared in *Les Cahiers du Communisme*, the theoretical journal of the French Communist Party. The CPUSA's leadership correctly interpreted this as Moscow's condemnation of Browder's policies. Browder's removal from the position of party secretary and the reestablishment of the CPUSA marked the end of the long and complex experiences of U.S. communism in the 1930s. This shift of 1945 had disastrous consequences for the CPUSA. The abandonment of Browder's attempt at promoting a policy of alliances and the return to a rigid form of dogmatism determined the Communists' isolation at the outset of the postwar anti-Communist campaign, and led to the rapid disappearance of the CPUSA from the U.S. political scene. Expelled from the party in 1946, Browder unsuccessfully attempted to join it again after the Twentieth Congress of the CPSU. After retreating to private life, he died in Princeton, New Jersey, in 1973.

See also Americanism; Antifascism; Grand Alliance, The; McCarthyism.

FURTHER READING

Buhle, M. J., P. Buhle, and D. Georgakas, eds. *Encyclopedia of the American Left*. New York: Oxford University Press, 1998.

Ottanelli, F. *The Communist Party of the United States: From the Depression to World War II*. New Brunswick, NJ: Rutgers University Press, 1991.

FRASER OTTANELLI

Bukharin, Nikolay

Nikolay Bukharin (1888–1938) was born in Moscow to parents who were both teachers. After completing high school, he enrolled in a university and took economics courses at a law school. His political life began when he was sixteen years old, as an activist in the revolutionary student circles that participated in the agitations of 1905.

He joined the Bolshevik wing of the Russian Workers' Social Democratic Party in 1906, and worked for two years as an organizer and propagandist. In 1908, at the age of twenty, Bukharin became a member of the party's committee in Moscow. Arrested by the Okhrana, he was deported to Archangelsk in 1911, but soon managed to escape and flee abroad. He met Vladimir Lenin in Kraków in 1912. The following year he moved to Vienna, where he met Leon Trotsky, helped Joseph Stalin in his research for the essay on the national question, and continued his own studies, developing some interest for non-Marxist economic theories or at least ones that were heterodox when compared to Bolshevik positions. At the onset of the war he first stayed in Switzerland, where in 1915 he participated in the Bolshevik conference in Bern and opposed Lenin on the national question; he then moved to Sweden and Norway. In November 1916 he left for New York, where he stayed until his return to Russia, collaborating with Trotsky on the Russian daily *Novy Mir*.

During his exile, Bukharin wrote many of the works that earned him a reputation as an eminent Marxist theoretician. The essay "Imperialism and World Economy" (1915) was particularly important; in it he formulated a theory of imperialism that although influenced by Rudolf Hilferding, displayed some original features when compared to the works of other Marxists and Lenin himself. According to Bukharin, the distinctive feature of capitalism in highly industrialized countries of the period was the state's new interventionist role, which allowed it to control the anarchic tendencies of free trade and to remedy the disorganization of the individual national economies. Since the state was endowed with the ability to plan and eliminate imbalances in the domains it controlled, it would become an omnipotent "modern Leviathan," reducing workers to the status of "white slaves." But "organized capitalism" would only be able to overcome its own internal contradictions, while the struggle with other national states for control of the international market would be exacerbated. Capitalism's collapse would therefore not be due to the internal contradictions of capitalism itself but rather to wars between competing states, whose root cause Bukharin isolated in the inevitable conflict of interests between the industrial system of developed countries and the agrarian system of colonial areas. In the age of imperialism, in his view, the opposition of "world city" to "world country" would reach international dimensions, and become the cause of new world wars.

Once he returned to Russia in May 1917, Bukharin became one of the most notable Bolshevik leaders in Moscow. He was elected to the party's Central Committee in August, and as a member of the Revolutionary Military Committee, he participated in the assumption of power in October. In February 1918, he headed the group of Left Communists who opposed Lenin's proposal to conclude the Brest-Litovsk peace treaty, proposing that the Bolsheviks should have instead conducted a revolutionary war to promote the disintegration of the world order. Bukharin was already editor in chief of *Pravda* in 1918, and in 1919 he was elected candidate member of the Political Office and member of the Executive Committee of the Comintern. In his essay "The Economics of the Transition Period" (1920) he proposed "war communism," and specifically the method of "extra-economic coercion," as the fundamental principle for the construction of a future socialist society, thus endowing it with theoretical legitimacy. In 1921, he joined Trotsky in the conflict that split the Bolshevik leadership on the role of labor unions in the Soviet state. The defeat he suffered at the Tenth Congress (March 1921) spurred him to rethink some of his radical positions and brought him closer to Lenin, who in his testament remembered Bukharin as the party's "favorite son," but castigated him for not having ever fully understood Marxism or dialectics.

His political ascent started after Lenin's death, when he became a member of the politburo (May 1924) and the most stalwart supporter of the New Economic Policy, which he defended from the attacks of the Left opposition that had allied itself with Stalin. But he agreed with Stalin on the choice of building "socialism in one country," even though in his version the new theory was not tinted with nationalist accents and left open the possibility the final result might lead to some form of backward socialism. Convinced that he was building on Lenin's reflections from the last period of his life, starting in 1924 Bukharin began to elaborate a strategy for development that was unmistakably moderate. His thoughts centered on the issue of expanding the consensus for the Soviet regime, especially in the countryside. Once the illusions of war communism had fallen by the wayside, the party should have kept and strengthened its support among the peasants, following an approach whose goal was not to force the time frame for the transformation of the agrarian order, so as to avoid resorting to violence and risk unleashing a "third revolution." This is the reason why Bukharin engaged in a bitter struggle with Evgeny Preobrazhensky, a onetime friend and an important economist of the Left, who supported the "law of social-ist primitive accumulation," according to which, in stark contrast to Bukharin's views, the industrialization of So-viet Russia could only be financed by resorting to peas-ant income without an equivalent reciprocation of value on the part of industry. Even though he passionately fought the Left's arguments, maintaining that Soviet Russia would only proceed on the road to socialism by way of a market economy, Bukharin was extremely vague about the manner in which plan and market would co-exist during the transition period, and he never pushed his ideas to the point of theorizing the permanence of some market relations even in a fully developed socialist economy.

Starting in 1926 he welcomed the principle of inten-sified accumulation at the peasants' expense to favor industrialization, but he objected to an excessive orienta-tion toward heavy industry, which he felt would have provoked stronger social tensions and had serious politi-cal repercussions on the relationship between state and society. He argued this position in "Notes of an Econo-mist," published in September 1928 in *Pravda*, where in place of the previous cautious "snail's pace" approach, he stated that he was favorable to a fast-paced and intense development. He warned about the destructive conse-quences of a course of action that pursued unsustain-able rhythms and unlimited goals, instead advocating a curtailment of overly ambitious projects that caused the population to endure excessive sacrifices, with the ensu-ing risk of a mass repressive action by the state.

From the perspective of the party's "Right," Bukharin did not provide a coherent theoretical program. His idea that one ought to proceed without further revolution-ary upheavals or leaps forward only related to Russia's development, not that of countries where Communist parties were still waiting to come to power. By revising many aspects of his own 1918 internationalism, Bukharin ultimately envisioned the world revolution as a longer, more complicated process, but not any less subversive or radical in its goals. In 1926, when he took over the Comintern's leadership and attempted its reorganiza-tion, his goals were to reduce the Russians' role in its apparatus, and restructure its leadership organs so as to make them more federative. This proposal for a new course of action originated in Bukharin's understanding that different European Communist parties had to op-erate in markedly different situations from the Russian one; for other parties, it would be impossible to adopt a moderate course before installing the dictatorship of the proletariat. He also attempted to resolve the dichotomy between the interests of Communist internationalism and the national interests of the Soviet state, which had been provoked by Moscow's decision to build socialism in one country. Bukharin favored a revolutionary re-newal of the Comintern's mission, toward wide-ranging initiatives for the subversion of the international order, understood as an important instrument in the defense of the USSR's security—one that would discourage for-eign powers from unleashing an anti-Soviet crusade. He was the first to formulate the "class against class" line, intended to reinforce the autonomous identity of the Communist parties as entities antagonistic to social de-mocracy by means of enforcing a Manichaean vision of the social conflict inspired by an increasingly radical and sectarian line. He reproposed the essential points of the theory of imperialism that he had prepared in the years of exile, thus endowing these old analytic instruments with renewed validity to interpret the new international conditions, recognizing the tendencies toward a stabi-lization of capitalism, but denying that the imperialist powers had the opportunity to avoid a new world war. This reiteration of the ideas that he had upheld in 1916 exposed his position to the critique that his revolution-ary perspectives were entirely dependent on a future im-perialist war as well as the even more serious charge of having been influenced by Hilferding.

During 1927, conditions developed that would lead to Bukharin's removal from political life. When the Cen-tral Committee's majority decided to resort to coercive measures to extort grain from the peasants, Bukharin went from spokesperson of the official line to forcefully opposing Stalin, highlighting the danger that the use of mass coercion against the majority of the peasant popu-lation would once again land the country in a civil war. Even though he had the support of two other impor-tant members of the Political Office, Aleksey Rykov and Mikhail Tomsky, Bukharin's opposition ended in defeat. His battle was conducted at the upper leadership levels, but he did not make his break with Stalin public, nor did he engage in it with full energy and conviction. In April 1929, he was denounced by the majority of the Central Committee as the inspiration for a "right-wing devia-tion" in internal and Comintern policy. At the end of the year, after having been expelled by the politburo and relieved of all his duties, Bukharin retracted his positions and admitted the correctness of Stalin's line. He was thus allowed to fulfill administrative and scientific duties in his role as director of the Institute for the History of Science and Technology as well as the Academy of Sciences, but was excluded from active politics.

In the spirit of reconciliation with former opponents that seemed to have been inaugurated at the beginning of 1934, Bukharin was invited to speak at the Seventeenth Party Congress, once again filling a public position of some note. Yet even though he was named editor in chief of *Izvestia* and a member of the commission in charge of drafting a new USSR constitution, he did not regain the power and influence he had previously enjoyed. In the spring of 1936 he was sent abroad to negotiate the purchase of Marx's archives on behalf of the Soviet government with the German social democrats. During his stay he met one of the negotiators, the Menshevik Boris Nikolaevsky, with whom he had some confidential conversations, during which he seems to have harshly criticized Stalin and his policies. Having returned to Moscow in May 1936, Bukharin at first did not appear to notice the many signals of the impending storm. In August those accused in the trial against the "unified trotskyist centre" claimed that Bukharin had plotted against Stalin. An inquiry against him was immediately started. Bukharin naively saw Stalin as his only hope to prove that he was extraneous to the crimes of which he was charged. In order to convince Stalin of his innocence, he continued to write him even after his expulsion from the party and arrest in February 1937. In his last letter, written on December 10, 1937, on the eve of the trial where he was to be condemned to death, and with full knowledge of his fate, he once more attempted to convince Stalin of his innocence and asked him to send some poison so he might avoid the firing squad. His request was not granted. The last act in this drama was the trial in March 1938 against the so-called right-wing Trotskyist bloc. The defendants were accused of the most absurd crimes. Bukharin, who had confessed his guilt, rejected the most slanderous accusation against him until the end: that he had plotted with the Social Revolutionaries in 1918 to assassinate Lenin. On March 13, he was condemned to be executed by firing squad.

Before being arrested he had asked his young wife to memorize the text of a dramatic letter, addressed to "the future generation of party leaders," in which he reiterated his faith in Communist ideals and asked to be posthumously readmitted to the party. His widow preserved this letter during the over twenty years of her own imprisonment in the Tomsk concentration camp reserved for "family members of traitors to their country" and her confinement to Novosibirsk. In 1961, she transmitted the text of the letter with a request for her husband's rehabilitation and readmission to full membership to the party's Central Committee. Her request was rejected in 1977. In March 1978, Bukharin's son asked Enrico Berlinguer to participate in a campaign for his father's rehabilitation, since his innocence was still denied in the USSR. Numerous members of European Socialist and Communist parties joined the campaign. These appeals fell on deaf ears until, in February 1988, the Supreme Court of the USSR declared Bukharin's sentence null and void. This was not only a question of recognizing a serious judicial error. Bukharin's rehabilitation was part of a larger political process—organized by Mikhail Gorbachev—that presented him as a precursor of reforms that were intended to make a planned economy and the market coexist in a socialist economy. Boris Yeltsin's rise to power marked the end of Bukharin's fortunes. Breaking with Communist ideology, the new leader no longer needed to resort to the theoretical legitimation that Bukharin could provide for the attempt to push the Russian economy toward "market socialism," without surrendering to capitalism.

See also Bolshevism; Comintern; Hilferding, Rudolf; Imperialism; Lenin, Vladimir; New Economic Policy; Peasants in the USSR; Preobrazhensky, Evgeny; Socialism in One Country; Stalin, Joseph; War Communism; World Revolution.

FURTHER READING

Bertolissi, S. *Bukharin tra rivoluzione e riforme.* Rome: Editori Riuniti, 1982.

Cohen, S. F. *Bukharin and the Bolshevik Revolution: A Political Biography, 1888–1938.* New York: Oxford University Press, 1980.

Larina, A. *This I Cannot Forget: The Memoirs of Nikolai Bukharin's Widow.* New York: Norton, 1993.

ANNA DI BIAGIO

Bureaucracy

The Soviet leadership viewed bureaucracy as a perennial problem with which they had to grapple, but whose causes they found difficult to fathom, and for which solutions proved to be extremely elusive. Critics of the Soviet system, saw bureaucracy as one of the system's defining characteristics. For anti-Marxists such as

L. von Mises (*Socialism*, 1936) and F. A. Hayek (*The Road to Serfdom,* 1940), the one-party state and the centralized planned economy were forces that themselves nurtured bureaucracy. For Marxist critics, such as Trotsky (*Revolution Betrayed,* 1936), the Soviet system was seen as the embodiment of the rule of a new vested interest, namely the "Bureaucracy," which comprised the leading personnel (those who were part of the *nomenklatura*) in all party, government, economic, military and security institutions that controlled the state. Members of this Bureaucracy used their position to dominate society. For Milovan Djilas (*The New Class,* 1957) office holders in the party and state institutions constituted a "new class," whose members treated state property as though it were personal property, exploited those subject to their control, and passed on their privileges to their offspring. Tony Cliff (*Russia: A Marxist Analysis,* 1964) went further. The Soviet system was characterized not only by the rule of a "new class" but constituted a form of "state capitalism."

For Lenin, a strong critic of the bureaucracy of the czarist regime, the problem of bureaucracy as it manifested itself in the Soviet area was especially perplexing. The bureaucratic nature of the czarist state was seen as intrinsically linked to the nature of czarist absolutism with its highly centralized, highly institutionalized structures and the low level of competence of its officialdom. Czarist bureaucracy was seen as both a product and a symptom of the cultural backwardness of the country. It was associated with the ethos and culture of state institutions: their stress on hierarchy, their inability to delegate authority, their distrust of subordinates, and the requirement to refer even relatively minor matters for approval to central authorities. The administrative system was thus characterized by inertia, inflexibility, the slow processing of requests, slavish adherence to rules and precedence, the generation of prodigious paperwork even for trivial matters, the lack of a clear demarcation of responsibilities between different institutions and tiers of administration, and the lack of any mechanisms for complaint or for bringing officials to account. It was marked by official high-handedness, irresponsibility, favoritism, nepotism, corruption, graft, and bribe taking.

It is indeed easy to paint a very bleak picture of bureaucratic institutions in Russia in the late czarist period. But this picture can be overdrawn. Attention needs also to be paid to developments in administration that point in other directions. The local *zemstvo* councils, from the 1870s onward, developed quite new techniques of ad-

ministering local affairs and drew into their work many educated and technically proficient individuals. In the 1890s, the Ministry of Finance, under Count Witte, became a driving force behind the state-sponsored push for industrialization, drawing on the experience of other countries, notably Bismarck's Germany.

For Russian Marxists the problem of creating a modern, efficient system of administration in Russia after the October Revolution was heavily colored by ideological considerations. The desire to purge the state administration of hostile officials and the new Red Army of die-hard pro-czarist officers was balanced by the need to employ competent personnel from the old regime—civil servants, military officers, engineers, technicians, and specialists of all kinds—whose know-how and experience made them indispensable. In the early years of the Soviet regime a system of surveillance of these potentially disloyal elements was instituted.

The system of state administration that was created in the years of the civil war (War Communism) was highly centralized and saw an enormous expansion in the ranks of officialdom, as control over the economy, trade, distribution, and grain requisition tightened, while the ranks of the Red Army and the Cheka also swelled. A shortage of qualified Communist Party cadres made controlling these institutions difficult. And the problem was further compounded by a lack of clarity in the administrative structure, a lack of clear procedures, and by the general problem of maintaining control over multiple tiers of administrations in the vast territorial expanse of the USSR. Moreover, as in many poor countries, access to state employment was viewed as an important resource that was to be exploited for personal gain.

Controlling the state bureaucracy—making it accountable, imposing on it standards of efficiency, and curtailing waste—was a dominant concern of Lenin in his final years. He spoke of the Soviet state as the czarist state slightly repainted, as a state that had its own momentum, that was not fully under the control of the party, but was rather like a car, in which the steering wheel and the wheels were disconnected. In "Better Fewer but Better" and his article "How We Should Reorganize Rabkrin," he advanced a series of proposals to deal with the problem. The most important of these was the creation of a specialist body to oversee the state bureaucracy, to institute reform in structure and procedures, to train new qualified cadres, to draw on Western experience, and to assist in policy formation; but also, in line with Marxist theory, to draw ordinary workers into the task of overseeing the work and operation of institutions, enterprises, shops, schools, and other bodies.

At the time Lenin's proposal drew the jibe that the Soviet answer to bureaucracy was to create another bureaucratic structure to deal with it. Indeed, during the whole Soviet period this was the solution that was adopted. A plethora of organizations existed whose function it was to check, investigate, and report on the work of other institutions. Soviet works referred to three types of control—party control, state control, and popular or mass control. The administrative system as it developed, especially from the late 1920s onward, was essentially a control-centered, if not a control-obsessed system, in which subordinates were under constant surveillance and required to give account of their actions. Together the closed, monopolistic political system, with its suppression of pluralistic political structures, and the removal of economic competition based on the market, created an environment in which bureaucracy thrived. In the literature of the period we encountered endless references to the problem of bureaucratism, red-tape, departmentalism, and the formation of family circles of mutual protection by officials

At the very highest level of the party state, the central party apparatus of the Orgburo and Secretariat employed instructors and inspectors whose task it was to visit party, state, and economic institutions to check on the way policies were being implemented, and to issue guidance and timetables as to when decisions should be put into effect. This system was duplicated at all levels of the administrative hierarchy. There were also specialist agencies of party and state control—the Central Control Commission and the Workers' and Peasants' Inspectorate, replaced in 1934 by the Commission of Party Control and the Commission of State Control. In addition the party, trade unions, the local soviets, and the press played a role in highlighting shortcomings in the administrative system. For more serious offences, such as corruption, administrative malpractice, wrecking, and sabotage, the Procuracy and the Secret Police could be called in. Frequent resort was made to the courts, and penalties and fines for failures were common.

Not surprisingly, these methods of control proved quite ineffective. They demonstrated a naive faith in the power of central control that took little account of the response of lower level officials, who dealt with the problems of control and surveillance by resorting to subterfuge, collusion, concealment, and the subversion of the controlling agencies. The center responded to this situation by further intensifying control, which, predictably, produced the same counterresponse. Small wonder that in the 1930s there was a dramatic escalation in the use of repression in controlling the party-state apparatus.

The Soviet political leadership showed a very poor understanding of the roots of bureaucracy within their own state, so much so that their responses often were not only misguided but actually made the problem worse. This is hardly surprising as the one-party state and the state-owned, centrally planned economy themselves helped to nurture the problem. The state apparatus involved such a concentration and centralization of power that information flows between decision makers and administrative officials were complex in the extreme. The system of economic decision making—with the pursuit of often highly unrealistic targets for growth—fostered a system that inevitably lead to the concealment and distortion of information. This had very serious implications for planning, as there was no secure basis on which rational decisions could be made. It was a system calculated to reinforce the pursuit of bureaucratic, departmental interests and to encourage the formation of cliques intent on preserving their own position.

The Communist one-party state encouraged the growth of bureaucracy in other ways as well. The party was extremely wary of the threat to its hegemony that departmental or specialist interests might pose. Party officials particularly feared the challenge to their power and position that might come from particular groups: managers, military officers, and scientists. This encouraged a system that inhibited and contacts between such specialists that were not under strict party control. The result was a striking failure to develop a modern, professional civil service with its own career structures, systems of recruitment, and training and professional advancement. Insofar as some professionalization of administration took place this was achieved through specialist party schools.

Also striking is the fact that there was no serious scholarly examination of the problem of administration in a modern industrial society. Some attempts to do this were undertaken in the 1920s, but were halted because of what was seen as the pernicious influence of non-Marxist ideas in the field of administration. This examination of Western administrative ideas was also cut off because of the priorities associated with the revolution from above: the need to force the pace, and to require state and administrative bodies to cleave to the dictates of party policy. In such an atmosphere control took precedence over innovation. In the USSR there was some limited interest in the examination of Western administrative theory from the 1960s onward, but this was still circumscribed by the requirements of the one-party state and the centrally planned economy.

The centralized economy generated its own problems of bureaucracy. Planning and resource allocation posed an enormous burden on central authorities whose responsibility it was to determine what should be produced, and in what quantities, and how this output was to be allocated between other economic units. A situation of information overload developed, which denied lower administrative units discretion in decision making. This system generated concealment of information, and with that produced its own economic irrationalities, as attempts were made to cope with the failure of the overcentralized decision-making system through local initiatives and improvizations that ran counter to set rules and procedures. This had far-reaching implications in inhibiting innovation and in the diffusion of new technology. The system that was created established a producer monopoly, at the expense of the interests of the consumer.

In the Stalin era the problem of bureaucracy was treated in a crude manner. The failings of the system were seen as either the failings of individual officials exhibiting incompetence, irresponsibility, or malice, or as the deliberate actions of saboteurs. No doubt there was incompetence, irresponsibility, and corruption aplenty. But the focus on individual failures overlooked the causes of bureaucracy that were self-generated or systemic features of the system of Communist political and economic administration. Some efforts were made to improve the system of administration from the center outward and to raise the caliber of the officials, but the structural problems remained.

After Stalin's death in 1953 some attempts were made to address these problems. To deal with the problems of inefficiency in economic management, Khrushchev in 1956 sought to delegate decision making through the creation of regional economic councils (*sovnarkhoz*). Kosygin's 1965 economic reforms granted greater decision-making power to individual enterprises. The *sovnarkhoz* reform only created the new problem of a lack of coordination between regional councils. The Kosygin-period reform was undone by relentless pressure from central planners to raise output target, with planners and central ministries clawing back power from the enterprises.

By the 1980s the problems of the inefficiency of the economy and the growing technological lag behind the West forced the Soviet political leadership to seriously confront the systemic problems associated with the planned economy and the system of state administration. Economic and political development required a more open, pluralistic, competitive system. In an era of rapid technological change, economic management based on predictable, risk-averse thinking could not meet the need for innovation, which required rapid decision making and a willingness to take risks. The ill-considered economic reforms instituted by Mikhail Gorbachev from 1995 onward failed to address this central problem, and had the effect of destroying the centrally planned economy without putting anything in its place.

See also Command Economy; Planning; Single-Party System; State, The.

FURTHER READING

Cohen, Y. "Administration, politique et techniques. Réflexions sur la matérialité des pratiques administratives dans la Russe stalinienne, 1922–1940." *Cahiers du monde russe* 2003, 44/2–3.

Kornai, J. *The Socialist System: The Political Economy of Communism.* Princeton, NJ: Princeton University Press, 1992.

Rees, E. A. "Politics, Administration and Decision-Making in the Soviet Union, 1917–1953." In *The Yearbook of Administrative History 2004.* Vol. 16, ed. E. Volkmar Heyen, 259–90. Baden-Baden: Nomos, 2004.

Rowney, D. K. *Transition to Technocracy: The Structural Origins of the Soviet Administrative State.* Ithaca, NY: Cornell University Press, 1989.

Shearer, D. R. *Industry, State and Society in Stalin's Russia, 1926–1934.* Ithaca, NY: Cornell University Press, 1996.

Spécialistes, Bureaucratie et Administration dans l'Empire russe et en URSS, 1880–1945. Special edition of *Cahiers du monde russe et soviétique*, vol. 32 (4), October–December, 1991.

E. ARFON REES

Cadres

The term "cadres" (in Russian, *kadry*, plural only) in the USSR most often designated the leading workers at various levels. The shortage of reasonably well-qualified cadres, devoted to the regime, was one of the basic problems faced by the Bolsheviks immediately after they came to power. The problem was aggravated by the expulsion of several thousand oppositionists during intraparty strife, and hence their departure from leading posts in the party. During the years of the New Economic Policy, many of the prominent positions in the economics sphere were filled by so-called bourgeois specialists, who had received their training and made their careers in the prerevolutionary period. By the end of the 1920s, however, this policy was declared a mistake. In the course of the purges unleashed by the Shakhtin Case (1928), a court trial of the Prompartiya (Industrial Party), many bourgeois specialists were arrested or dismissed.

During the same period, the policy of preparing the party's own "proletarian" cadres was one of the key elements of the Cultural Revolution. In the first half of the 1930s, due to the massive promotion of cadres and the development of a network of persons with university or at least secondary school educations, the country witnessed the emergence of a huge number of new young leaders. Many historians believe that the presence of this layer of new officials and specialists was one of the main reasons for the comprehensive purge of cadres, carried out in 1936–38. This purge eliminated the old generation of worker leaders and replaced it with a newly promoted group of workers who, in the normal course of personnel rotation, would have had to wait their turn for many years.

These two generations of leaders, which exchanged positions during the second half of the 1930s, had many traits in common, and yet differed essentially from each other. The leaders "promoted by the terror" were younger than their predecessors. The two groups differed not only in age but also in political experience. The older cadres formed during the prerevolutionary or early postrevolutionary years followed the many traditions of the Bolshevik Party of the Lenin period, while the younger cadres received their power directly from Stalin and adhered to the norms of political life established in the 1930s. In terms of their training and practical experience in the field, the new leaders were more technocratic than their older counterparts had been, although they were certainly technocrats of the Soviet type, for whom political considerations absolutely prevailed over more practical economic goals. These individuals promoted by the terror would make up the core of the generation of Soviet leaders who would control the party until the early 1980s (Leonid Brezhnev, Mikhail Suslov, Dmitry Ustinov, and many others).

Since mass purges similar to those of the 1930s had been discontinued, the 1940s and 1950s under Stalin were marked by a stabilization of the corps of leading cadres, and the political situation became even more stable during the post-Stalin years. By May 1959, for example, out of 730 secretaries of regional committees, district committees, and central committees of the Communist parties of the individual republics, only 100 persons (14 percent) were under forty, and 144 persons (20 percent) were over fifty, whereas in 1940, 57 percent of these leaders had been under thirty-five. Despite numerous shake-ups of the cadres during and after the Khrushchev period, the political leadership became even more stable and the cadres kept getting older. The situation reached its apogee in the 1970s and the beginning of the 1980s. The lack of mobility within the corps of leading cadres, the increasingly poor quality of the cadres, and their inability to cope with the upcoming transformations were the most important reasons that the Communist

Party of the Soviet Union lost power. The new leaders who took power in the 1990s were a mixture of Soviet bureaucrats at various levels, and a new generation of officials from the periods of perestroika and democratic reforms.

See also Bureaucracy; Great Terror; Intelligentsia; Single-Party System.

FURTHER READING

Fitzpatrick, S. "Stalin and the Making of a New Elite, 1928–1939." In *The Cultural Front: Power and Culture in Revolutionary Russia.* Ithaca, NY: Cornell University Press, 1992.

Mawdsley, E., and S. White. *The Soviet Elite from Lenin to Gorbachev: The Central Committee and Its Members, 1917–1991.* Oxford: Oxford University Press, 2000.

OLEG V. CHLEVNJUK

Camps

For a long time, Communists denied the existence of detention camps in the countries where they held power. *The Great Soviet Encyclopedia* (1935) defined the camps as "special detention facilities created by Fascist states in Germany, Poland, Austria. . . . A barbarous regime, that oppresses its peoples, fascism continuously increases the number of its detainees: normal prisons no longer suffice. A system complementary to the prison system is created, that of the concentration camps." In the course of trials that created a stir in France, such as those of the deserter Viktor Kravchenko in 1949 or David Rousset in 1950, the Communists accused their adversaries of having "invented" the Soviet camps, arguing that only "re-education centers" existed, "worthy of admiration" and constituting "one of the achievements the Soviet Union should be most proud of."

Communist systems were certainly not the only political systems to develop camps. Camps existed under the Fascist regime in Italy (in Ferramonti, Calabria, for instance), under the Francoist regime in Spain (in Miranda de Ebro, in Burgos Province, for example), but also in democratic societies like France in 1939 (the Vernet camps in the Pyrenees or Milles in Provence) or the United States in 1942, where Japanese residents and even Americans of Japanese descent were interned in nine camps in the West. The Communists could not

even claim to have created them first. In fact, this institution was devised to deal with hostile masses in an era of democracies, nation-states, and colonies. The camps circumscribed a space reserved for potential enemies, an indirect consequence of mass conscription into the army. As Jean-Claude Farcy has written, "The camps demonstrate that, at the beginning of the twentieth century war becomes total and involves civilians to the same degree as the military."

In 18th-century prerevolutionary France, the frequent harassment of the civilian population notwithstanding, there was a clear distinction between civilians and soldiers. The subjects of foreign kingdoms with which France was at war traveled without restrictions on French soil. It was Gracchus Babeuf who, taking an opposing point of view, hypothesized the possibility of "confining foreigners outside of their usual place of residence" in "correctional facilities." During the colonial wars at the beginning of the 20th century the transition from hypotheses to facts occurred: foreign civilians, or those deemed to be, and therefore considered enemies or potential accomplices of the enemy, were detained in camps. Similar measures were taken by both the Spaniards against the Cuban rebels in 1896–98 and the British in South Africa against the Boers in 1900–1902 (more than a hundred thousand people were interned in camps in Natal, Transvaal, and Orange Free State). At the time, internment was limited to the duration of the conflict, but all the ingredients of the camps were already emerging: groups and categories were targeted more than individuals; internment was based on decisions by the state administration as a preventive measure; and life conditions were precarious.

After World War I and the "brutalization of behavior," to borrow George Mosse's expression, that it engendered, a new conception of politics was established when the Bolsheviks detained their "internal enemies." They were convinced it would be a good idea to preventively confine counterrevolutionaries, who were suspect by definition. Starting in August 1918, Vladimir Lenin requested that "ambiguous elements" be quarantined in a concentration camp. A decree by the Soviet of the People's Commissars dated September 5, 1918, was concerned with "protecting the Soviet republic against class enemies, by isolating them in concentration camps." The Soviet experience extended the concept of war to social and political struggles. The "total" character of the war now allowed the forces of repression to intern "fellow nationals" in concentration camps.

The USSR and, following its example, other Communist states did not create simple internment camps whose purpose was to temporarily isolate individuals seen as suspicious or dangerous—for instance, "enemy fellow nationals" on the eve of a conflict, political militants who were guilty in the eyes of the law (like the Portuguese anti-Fascists interned in the Tarrafal camp on the Cape Verde Islands in 1936), or refugees considered dangerous (such as the Spanish Republicans interned in the Djelfa camp in Algeria in 1939). The war between classes was not a temporary phenomenon, and therefore Communist camps were managed on the basis of systematic and long-term plans. These were concentration camps in the full sense of the word, similar to those found in all totalitarian regimes: the existence of the Soviet gulag, the Chinese *laogai* (an abbreviation of *laodong gaizao*, "reeducation through labor"), and the North Korean *Kwan Il So*, often officially defined as a "special dictatorship zone," were not limited to periods of serious crisis or war. The purpose of these camps was the continuous humiliation of the regime's presumed enemies, their reeducation (fictitious, of course), the utilization of their labor (not profitable), and sooner or later, their annihilation (a matter of fact more than intention).

One function of the concentration camp, an essential component of the totalitarian system, was to filter out those elements it regarded as pollutants and prefigure the new society. These camps differed from the extermination or immediate elimination camps, found exclusively under the Nazi regime (there were four—Belzec, Chelmno, Sobibor, and Treblinka—in addition to two mixed institutions, that is, concentration and extermination camps—Auschwitz-Birkenau and Majdanek). Camps such as the one in Lovec in Bulgaria or Hoeryong in North Korea were in no way less awful than the Nazi camps in Mauthausen or Dora; but they were not comparable to the extermination camps just cited. Planned extermination, an integral part of a more extensive genocidal plan and therefore intentional, was at work in Sobibor and Treblinka. It was the deplorable hygienic, work, and food conditions along with the surveillance personnel's indifference to the loss of human life that led to high mortality rates, as in Spač in Albania or Elgue in eastern Siberia. Yevgenia Ginzburg, who was detained there, wrote, "Our hell . . . was marked by the peculiarity that on its entrance one could not read the motto 'Abandon all hope ye who enter here.' We had hope. They did not send us to the gas chambers or the guillotine. Together with work that was basically a death sentence, there were other jobs that allowed one to survive." Not even the "special points"—places where Soviet detainees were executed on an almost industrial scale, like Butovo near Moscow or Bikin between Chabarovsk and Vladivostok—were part of a systematic plan designed to erase a people from the face of the earth. This distinction also means that one cannot proceed from the undeniable chronological priority of the gulag over the Nazi camps to define the latter, as Ernst Nolte does, as an extension of the Communist experience or a reaction to it. Strictly speaking, the Shoah is not part of the concentration camp experience.

On the other hand, Nazi and Communist camps do share some features. They were both permanent institutions. They basically appeared with the creation of the new state and disappeared with it. Dachau opened in 1933. The Czech forced labor camps were established in October 1948. The first Cuban labor camp was established in Guanajay in 1960. Often camps were instituted as soon as a country or territory became Communist. This is the case with China and Vietnam. The Greek Communists created a camp at Bulkes, on the border with Yugoslavia. During the civil war, the Spanish Communists set up *campos del pueblo* in 1938 for Trotskyists, priests, and homosexuals in Catalonia.

In the case of democracies and authoritarian regimes, the camps only appeared at a specific time and were a temporary measure. Under totalitarian regimes, by contrast, the camps are part of the permanent plan to eliminate anyone who can become an obstacle to history's development: the triumph of the proletariat in the Communist view or the dominion of a superior race from the Nazi perspective. The unity of the people or race must be realized by liquidating those elements that bar the path to a new society while often forcing them to first work for its realization. Camps therefore also have an economic function, but the ideological one is the most important. In addition to repressing any form of opposition, the camp was a "pedagogical" place in which the detainees were supposed to correct their faults and discover the new regime's virtues. Work, frequently nonproductive and humiliating, was justified by this reeducational context. The goal of making the camp economically productive by using labor that was almost free of cost and could be exploited at will did not establish itself immediately.

Ideology explains the hierarchical rankings in Communist camps much better than economic goals. In the USSR there were camps that were designated as "normal," while others were called "special." Analogously in North Korea one must distinguish between forced labor camps with local characteristics, camps for the families of political prisoners, camps or parts thereof for "redeemable prisoners," and those for "irredeemable prisoners." China established *laogai, laojiao* ("education through labor") camps, and *jiuye* ("assignment to a profession") camps. The distinguishing characteristics of Communist camps compared to those of other totalitarian camps consisted in the fact that detention was justified on the basis of a historicist philosophy: the detainees were confined to a concentration camp in the name of the people, the working class fighting for socialism, or the person who symbolized this power. Forced labor was presented as a means for redemption. The camp's economy conformed to the planned and centralized nature of the entire Communist system, including the resort to wise doses of ideological and materialistic stimuli in order to attain normalization. The camp, however, had a more important economic function under Communist regimes than under the Nazi regime. Initially Dachau was not a labor camp. It was the difficulties encountered by the German army and increasing labor scarcity that led the Nazis to make the detainees, including Jewish ones, work while they were waiting to die, or be killed because of the particularly harsh conditions in which they had to work and live.

The significance of certain national or cultural characteristics must also be pointed out. Propaganda spread by means of readings, films, or theatrical representations was found in Soviet or Eastern European camps. In Asian Communist camps ideological education, which was complementary to forced labor, was especially critical. The practice of introspection, criticism and self-criticism, and overcoming one's "reactionary" or "bourgeois" past seems to have had a more important role in Asia. In Yodok's Camp 15, in North Korea, meetings were held twice a week, and they concluded with a reading of the *Rodong Shinmun*, the repetition or memorization of Kim Il Sung's works, his life, the history of the revolution, and the party line. In some cases, gratuitous violence or barbarous practices could be observed—for example, in Titoist camps, especially on the island of Goti Otok. Detainees were often also struck in Bulgarian camps, at least according to available testimony. Some camps in Laos and North Korea organized the ritual stoning of the corpses of detainees killed in failed escape attempts. Differences can be

observed in the attitude toward families as well. In the Stalinist or Chinese camps, families were separated; in the North Korean camps, families might be kept together. These "family" internments were connected to a specific concept of responsibility, though. The idea of personal responsibility was replaced by that of social prophylaxis. Since the family members had been ideologically contaminated by the political criminal (who had been arrested and detained separately), they could spread counterrevolutionary germs, so they also had to be interned in appropriate camps.

In analyzing concentration camps as a central element of the totalitarian state, the experience of Eastern European countries is of special interest. There is no doubt that the terrible "special camps" that the Soviets set up in East Germany immediately after the war's end—sometimes reutilizing Nazi camps like Buchenwald and Sachsenhausen—were closed in 1950. Elsewhere the camps closed between 1954 and 1964, but the regimes in power continued to declare themselves Communists for another quarter of a century. During these twenty-five years the sociopolitical structures didn't change, but they did not function as efficiently as in the past. Repression was relaxed to a certain degree. In countries such as Hungary and Poland, tacit compromises between the government and what remained of civil society were reached; after 1956 free spaces were tentatively opened. This post-totalitarianism was not synonymous with the triumph of liberty, but the camps' disappearance was an indication that communism had evolved. By contrast, not long before the collapse of communism, Albania still had fourteen camps in 1990. Statements about moves toward openness, in North Korea and even China, must be valued carefully, at least as long as the camps are still in existence. Generally speaking, however, one can say that concentration camps are an intrinsic characteristic of totalitarianism.

See also Gulag; History and Memory; Shalamov, Varlam; Solzhenitsyn, Aleksandr; Totalitarianism.

FURTHER READING

Chol-Hwan Kang, and P. Rigoulot. *The Aquariums of Pyongyang: Ten Years in a North Korean Gulag*. New York: Basic Books, 2001.

Farcy, J.-C. *Les camps de concentration français de la Première Guerre mondiale, 1914–1920*. Paris: Anthropos, 1995.

Ginzburg, E. S. *Le ciel de la Kolyma*. Paris: Seuil, 1980.

Kotek, J., and P. Rigoulot. *Le siècle des camps*. Paris: Lattès, 2000.

Pasqualini, J. *Prisonnier de Mao*. Paris: Gallimard, 1975.
Wu, H. H. *Bitter Winds*. New York: Wiley, 1994.

PIERRE RIGOULOT

Castro, Fidel

Fidel Castro Ruz, born in Birán, Cuba, on August 13, 1926, was raised in a well-to-do family of Galician immigrants, allowing him to study at prestigious Jesuit schools in Havana and, starting in 1945, a law school, where he took his first steps into the political life of the island. During the violent confrontations between groups that made Cuba a hotbed of political activity in the restless democratic decade following World War II, the young Castro attracted attention for two key personality traits: an innate charisma that predisposed him to command and a radical nationalism, which he soon manifested in the anti-imperialist milieu he helped organize. He was accused of Communist sympathies, mistakenly but prophetically, for the first time in 1948, when he became involved in the unrest in Colombia following the assassination of Eliécer Gaitán. Uninterested in Marxism, Castro moved in the circles around Eddy Chibás and the radical wing of the nationalist and populist Ortodoxo Party, whose leader Chibás was, and he was a candidate on this party's list when Fulgencio Batista's coup d'état in March 1952 put an end to Cuba's precarious democracy.

This is when Castro's path as revolutionary caudillo started: he distanced himself from the party, which he considered too moderate, and started a newspaper, *El Acusador*, recruited followers called *fidelistas*, and continued on the road toward armed struggle against the dictatorship. On the political front he favored a return to the constitution of 1940; on the military one, he advocated the conquest of some strategic objective from which to proceed, once the population had arisen, to the liberation of the entire country. This was a strategy that the Cuban Communists of the Partido Socialista Popular interpreted as a typical case of petty bourgeois adventurism. The result was a disastrous assault on the Moncada barracks in Santiago de Cuba on July 26, 1953, a century after the birth of José Martí, the icon of Cuban nationalism; Castro always portrayed himself as Martí's natural heir, to the point that years later, he would claim Martí,

with some distortions, as the forerunner of his own revolution. Luck and Santiago's archbishop saved Castro's life and that of his brother Raúl; they did not, however, spare Fidel a sentence of fifteen years in prison. But prison did not stop him: he then founded the Movimiento 26 de julio and used the trial to publicize his political manifesto, known to Cubans as *La historia me absolverá* (History Will Absolve Me).

Starting at that time Castro revealed his extraordinary gifts as an orator, which would later lead him to address huge crowds in his long and fiery rallies, key moments in the ritual encounters between the people and its leader that pepper the history of his regime. His ideology, however, was somewhat vague, although later many people, whether to denigrate him or prove the purity of his past, would look for signs of future Marxist beliefs in his words. Devoted to the revolution, Castro appealed to democracy and social justice in terms that were then popular among many Latin American populist leaders, and supported economic measures that were certainly radical but could be traced more to a nationalist than a Communist set of beliefs. Still, in 1955, with the complicity of the United States, which was worried that the brutal path Batista had been following would transform a faithful ally into a burden, Castro and his group were granted amnesty as long as they left the island. They went to Mexico, where Castro picked up his revolutionary path, and where it crossed that of Ernesto "Che" Guevara, culminating on November 24, 1956, in the *Granma*'s (the by now famous vessel with which Castro and other revolutionaries landed in Cuba) expedition toward Cuba's shores. Batista's troops forced Castro to take refuge in the Sierra Maestra together with the few remaining survivors from the landing. From then to January 1, 1959, when the *barbudos* (Spanish term to refer to the revolutionaries, meaning "bearded ones") entered Havana in triumph, the rural guerrillas guided by Castro won over urban allies with their ideas and methods, prefiguring the future revolutionary order and favoring the concentration of power in Castro's hands. Whether Castro had a Communist "conversion" in the Sierra depends on whose version of events one relies on; what is certain is that even if he did absorb Che's Communist ideas, he was careful not to express them. In fact, his frame of reference remained that of a rural nationalist and anti-imperialist insurrectionary. Whether Castro was already convinced that he wanted to turn Cuba into a Communist laboratory or instead the United States forced him to that conclusion with its opposition is impossible to say with certainty. In any case, the implacable logic of the Cold War slowly pushed him, in order to be able to defend Cuban independence and in the name of a radical egalitarianism, closer to the Soviet Union and its model. Castro's road to Moscow was tortuous and restless, and he never fully lost the prestige and autonomy that the undoubted national roots of his revolution assured him.

For Castro and the revolution, the first years in power were the most epic and heterodox. While he initially avoided the limelight, he kept the leadership of the armed forces for himself, and then gradually accumulated, in person or by proxy, a series of posts and powers; he purged adversaries and ex-friends, until under the iron grip of the single party that he led he reunited the different revolutionary factions, occupied all the vital nerve centers of the state, and founded a personalistic regime on top of which he emerged as the *líder máximo*. The democracy that from this time on was his point of reference was no longer of the representative variety he had invoked when keeping the anti-Batista front united, but a social democracy where people and nation were understood as communities threatened by internal and external enemies, by empire and capitalists; Castro's ambition was to embody with his charisma the univocal will and identity of that community, more than a specific class.

The United States was complicit in the outcome of this situation, since it was bent on overthrowing Castro, to the point of plotting the failed Bay of Pigs invasion against him in April 1961. Hence, given the opportunity to protect himself with the aid of the Soviet umbrella, Castro's nationalist populism found a natural outlet in a one-party regime with a state ideology, which over time took on characteristics analogous to those of the Soviet regime, although its origin and mettle had been different. Instead of becoming one more pearl in the already-long necklace of Soviet satellites, Castro raised notable and unusual expectations, making friends and gaining esteem well outside the Communist fort among nationalists, radicals, and the nonaligned from all over the world. These developments led to his rather sweet and sour relationship with the Soviets: on the one hand, he afforded them an outpost in the Americas, but on the other hand, his revolutionary ardor raised the level of confrontation with the United States and sometimes seemed to move Castro closer to the Chinese shores of the then quite-frazzled Communist family, thereby exposing Moscow to adventures it wanted to avoid. The manner and outcome

of the Cuban missile crisis in October 1962 engendered a good dose of rage and realism in Castro—both because Khrushchev had decided for him, and because the defeat had shown him limits that it was impossible to move beyond. From then on, Castro the revolutionary gradually metamorphosed into Castro the statesman, and his path diverged from that of his friend Che.

Challenged by unrelenting U.S. hostility, Castro had proclaimed his regime to be socialist and had officially adhered to Marxism-Leninism. But by 1968, with the dream of exporting the revolution dashed, Castro cooled off in the ranks of Muscovite orthodoxy and even espoused its most intransigent aspects when he zealously approved the suppression of the Prague Spring. With the failure of industrialization starting in 1970 (moral incentives to increase production had proven inefficient and the great sugar cane *zafra* had not succeeded), even the proud economic independence he had cultivated bowed to reality. Cuba carved out its little niche as an agricultural producer within the Council for Mutual Economic Assistance, which Cuba joined in 1972, adjusting to dependence on massive Soviet subsidies.

Put on the defensive, isolated in Latin America, and tied up in the nets of pacific coexistence, domestically Castro was concerned with solidifying his regime's structures and coating the tropical features of his socialism with a thick layer of normalization. This was how, after having received the Lenin prize from Leonid Brezhnev in 1972, he arranged for the First Congress of the Communist Party to be held in 1975, and in 1976 he organized a plebiscite in which well over 99 percent of Cubans approved a new socialist constitution. At that point Castro was head of the single party, the state, the army, and the government. His nationalist vein, however, which had by now turned Castroism into a special type of socialism, did not dry up: from 1979 to 1983 he headed the Non-Aligned Movement, which he tried to move closer to Soviet positions, and he gave political and military support to African liberation movements in the 1970s—sometimes also in support of Soviet interests, but more frequently in accord with an ideology of solidarity with the third world. Together with détente, these activities allowed Castro to reopen embassies that had been closed for years, especially in Latin America, and even ease tensions in his relationship with the United States when Jimmy Carter entered the White House.

Everything changed in the 1980s, however: the Sandinista triumph in Nicaragua, whose origins Castro was so close to, and the escalation of the Cold War under the

Ronald Reagan presidency, rekindled his hope and gave new vigor to his never-fading nationalism. He perceived menace and abandonment in the reforms that Mikhail Gorbachev had proposed, and which Castro opposed firmly. Having unfurled the old banners, Castro then rode the Latin American crusade against foreign debt, with little success. Once the Soviet Union had collapsed, and the revolutions in Central America and southern Africa had been contained, he found himself alone in a hostile world, without protectors or economic aid. The United States was waiting to give him a final shove, and the Cuban economy was on the brink of collapse, casting a shadow on the social services that the revolution had created.

In light of this, Castro introduced the long and extremely harsh "special period" in 1991 with the slogan of *socialismo o muerte* (socialism or death). The regime closed in on itself, waiting for better times, at the cost of painful measures: the opening to foreign capital, some concessions to private production, a rigid rationing of consumption (which expanded the black market), and tighter suppression of internal dissent. Castro finally set aside state atheism, allowed believers back into the party, and gave greater freedom to the Catholic Church, thus laying the groundwork for John Paul II's historic visit to Cuba in 1998. With this visit, the crisis of the "Washington consensus," worldwide reactions to globalization, and a general neopopulist wave that hit Latin American shores at the beginning of the millennium, a new phase in Castro's long political life began. This period partially lifted Cuba's isolation, strengthened nationalist anti-imperialism, guaranteed Castro new and useful economic partners, and led him back to the place of his political birth, before the Cold War brought him to Moscow's court: the diverse family of Latin American populism.

See also Anti-imperialism; Cuban Missile Crisis; Cuban Revolution; Cuban-Soviet Intervention in Africa; Guevara de la Serna, Ernesto Rafae; Nonalignment; Third Worldism.

FURTHER READING

Coltman, L. *The Real Fidel Castro*. New Haven, CT: Yale University Press, 2003.

Franqui, C. *Vida, aventuras y desastres de un hombre llamado Castro*. Mexico City: Planeta, 1988.

Latell, B. *After Fidel: The Inside Story of Castro's Regime and Cuba's Next Leader*. London: Palgrave Macmillan, 2005.

Quirk, R. E. *Fidel Castro*. London: Norton, 1993.

Skierka, V. *Fidel Castro: A Biography*. Cambridge, MA: Polity Press, 2004.

Szulc, T. *Fidel: A Critical Portrait*. New York: Morrow, 1986.

Among the numerous volumes that contain Castro's speeches and writings, see *Pensiamento marxista*, 2 vols. (1971); *Politica cultural de la Revolución Cubana: Documentos* (1973); *La Revolución de Octubre y la Revolucion Cubana; discursos, 1959–1977* (1977); *Discursos*, 3 vols. (1979); *José Marti, el autor intelectual* (1983); *Fidel y la religion: conversaciones con Frei-Betto* (1985); *Ideología, conciencia y trabajo político 1959–1989* (1991).

LORIS ZANATTA

Catholic Church

In his *Syllabus of Current Errors* (1864), Pius IX dedicated a few lines to communism, which he grouped with socialism, secret societies, biblical societies, and clerical-liberal societies as among the century's "pestilences." In the eyes of that pope, the condemnation of communism required few words, but the relationship between the church and communism is complex, going back to the origins of communism itself—those pages in the Acts of the Apostles that describe the primitive community have repeatedly been interpreted as a sort of communist manifesto much older than Karl Marx's. If we understand communism to mean the usage in common of the earth's bounty along with the abolition or stringent limitation of private property, it is possible to find its elements in many pages written by the church fathers and medieval theologians. Even if we restrict the period to the contemporary and the definition to a narrower one, with communism understood as the politicoideological movement that recognized itself in Marx and Engels's ideas, and that found its historically most notable expression in the Soviet Union, this background cannot be ignored.

The Catholic attitude toward communism has been shaped by the church's encounter with earlier socialist movements and ideology. In the 19th and 20th centuries, Catholic reactions to the "Red menace" ranged from opposition to competition. Later, the consequences of the Russian Revolution became the determining factor in the Catholic attitude toward communism. When the czarist empire fell, Rome did not mourn; on the contrary, the Vatican tried to establish diplomatic relations with the state entity that was emerging from this fall, but the antireligious policies adopted by the Soviets and Moscow's lack of interest soon extinguished this hope. A difficult period for Catholics followed in the USSR, during which Rome tried to infiltrate and establish a clandestine presence with priests who had studied communism at centers created by the church. In 1937 the church solemnly condemned communism with Pius XI's encyclical *Divini Redemptoris*.

During World War II, the Holy See did not oppose U.S. Catholics who supported an alliance with the USSR against Germany and it did not entertain Nazi appeals to support the anti-Bolshevik crusade. The improving relations between Stalin and the Russian Orthodox Church in the meantime introduced a new element into Soviet religious policy, also as far as Catholics were concerned. Soviet leaders used the long-standing Orthodox hostility toward the Vatican to remove the most important Catholic presence in the USSR: that of the Greek Catholic Ukrainians, who were forced to return to orthodoxy in 1946. Not all accepted, and some were forced to lead a difficult existence between jail and the underground. Once the war ended, U.S. attempts to encourage diplomatic relations between the Vatican and Moscow clashed with the Holy See's position—a possible accord was conditional on the establishment of true freedom of religion in the USSR—and Moscow's lack of interest.

In the following years, the main battle between communism and Catholicism took place in the countries of Eastern Europe that had become part of the Soviet sphere of influence. Where, on the one hand, there was the initially nonhostile attitude of the Czech Catholics led by Cardinal Josef Beran, on the other hand there was the prejudicial hostility of Hungarian cardinal József Mindszenty, but the outcome was not particularly different. Communist regimes ended up adopting a persecutory attitude, imprisoning or isolating bishops so as to deprive churches of their leadership, favoring the collaboration of elements in the clergy who dissented with the bishops and encouraging lay interlocutors whom they valued as an authentic expression of the "Catholic base." Rome interpreted all of this as the coherent and inevitable result of an antireligious ideology, whose most dramatic result was the trial against Mindszenty, during which he recognized his guilt and confessed to having practiced currency contraband.

The situation in Eastern Europe inspired the decree by the Holy Office of July 1, 1949, that excommunicated Communist supporters. Personally brought about by the Pope, arousing some perplexities among his collabora-

tors, excommunication has appeared as the most important act, symbolically at least, that the Catholic Church has undertaken in its relationship with communism. It is difficult to measure its actual impact, however. In the following years, while anti-Catholic persecution continued in Communist countries, Pius XII excluded recourse to war as a way of fighting communism; the Catholic side instead encouraged strong vigilance so such "slippages" would not occur in countries like Italy. The line of absolute intransigence that excommunication represented was partially contradicted with the accord that Polish primate Stefan Wyszinski negotiated with authorities in his country, arousing Rome's doubts. In Poland in 1956 this openness to negotiations produced some concrete results for the church, while the short-lived liberation of Mindszenty during the Hungarian uprising marked the beginning of his long "reclusion" in the U.S. legation.

Starting in 1956 the Soviet attitude toward the Holy See showed signs of change, but the Vatican did not alter its overall relationship with the Soviet bloc. Even after the election of John XXIII, the influence of Domenico Tardini and Alfredo Ottaviani actually grew, and they strongly believed that communism's goal—the destruction of the church—left no room for mediation. The new pope did not change this line, but he did use sorrowful tones when alluding to the painful situation of Catholics in Communist countries. Rather than giving voice to judgments and condemnations, he instead expressed a strong desire for peace, an indirect but decisive premise to new possibilities for dialogue. John XXIII and Khrushchev established contact, and although it was distant and devoid of immediate diplomatic or political implications, the Soviet leadership allowed two orthodox representatives to be sent to the council, and eventually liberated Cardinal Josyf Slipyj, a Ukrainian. In a climate of cautious thaw, diplomatic relations between the Holy See and the USSR seemed possible, and Alexei Adzhubei, Khrushchev's son-in-law, was granted an audience with John XXIII, over the objections of some of the Pope's collaborators. The *Pacem in Terris* encyclical only increased the Soviet's esteem of the Pope. His death, however, interrupted this dialogue at a distance immediately following the first act of this future *Ostpolitik*: Cardinal Agostino Casaroli's trip to Prague. The Second Vatican Council, in the meantime, avoided reiterating a condemnation of communism, while the ecumenical thrust that emerged from this council favored a series of interdenominational contacts that went against the grain of the bipolar tensions of the period.

In the following decades the Ostpolitik line was developed, which in a certain sense reached its peak with the Holy See's participation in the Helsinki Conference of 1975. Multiple diplomatic initiatives were developed in different Eastern European countries, where in any case the situation for Catholics varied. Some have credited Pope Paul VI with faith in the instruments of diplomacy, as shown in his relations with Communist countries; others believe John Paul II rejected this line in favor of total opposition. Neither thesis is entirely accurate. As Casaroli has written, Paul VI was doubtful about the appropriateness of developing diplomatic relations with Communist countries, and supported them mostly in the hope of avoiding worse. Elsewhere, in the years following the council, initiatives for dialogue between Communists and Catholics became more widespread, while in Latin America and other areas of the world there was a push for collaboration between believers and Marxists who shared a revolutionary perspective. But Paul VI continued to reject any accommodation with communism and expressed his disappointment with the lack of change in the Soviet bloc.

Many things shifted with the election in 1978 of a pope from a Communist country, the Pole Karol Wojtyla. John Paul II did not interrupt the network of relationships developed by Ostpolitik, even though he supplemented it with a personal line of intervention tied to his direct knowledge of situations, and not only in Poland. In his country he not only promoted a direct opposition but also favored increasing the influence of the church in Polish society, thus gradually removing the society from the regime's influence, and emptying the regime of its power. The Russian world was an important interlocutor for him, and he granted Mikhail Gorbachev an audience at the Vatican. John Paul II was adamantly opposed, however, to the mixture of Catholicism and Marxism present in some forms of liberation theology, and in his *Centesimus Annus* he denounced the fundamental anthropological error present in Marxism. Even after the collapse of the Soviet bloc, communism has continued to present a problem for the Catholic Church in some countries, above all in China.

See also Atheism, Soviet; Dissent in the USSR; Orthodox Church, Russian; Ostpolitik; Solidarity.

FURTHER READING

Barberini, G. *L'Ostpolitik della S. Sede. Un dialogo lungo e faticoso.* Bologna: Il Mulino, 2007.

Barberini, G., ed. *La politica del dialogo. Le carte Casaroli sull'Ostpolitik vaticana.* Bologna: Il Mulino, 2008.

Carrère d'Encausse, H. "Paul VI et l'Ostpolitik," In AA. VV, *Paul VI et la modernité dans l'Eglise,* pp. 547–57. Actes du colloque organisé par l'Ecole Francaise de Rome, Rome 2–4 juin 1983. Roma : Ecole Francaise de Rome, 1984.

Casaroli, A. *Il martirio della pazienza. La Santa Sede e i paesi comunisti (1963–89).* Torino: Einaudi, 2000.

Chenaux, Ph. "Pie XI et le communisme (1930–1939) d'après les archives du Vatican." In *Le paupeté contemporaine (XIX–XX siècles),* ed. J. P. Delville and M. Jakov, pp. 471–82. Louvain la Neuve-Leuven-Città del Vaticano: Revue d'Histoire ecclésiastique e Collectanea Archivi Vaticani, 2009.

Giovagnoli, A. "Ostpolitik. Per un bilancio storiografico." In *L'Ostpolitik di Agostino Casaroli 1963–1989,* ed. A. Silvestrini, pp. 101–31. Bologna: Edizione Dehoniane, 2009.

Melloni, A., ed. *Il filo sottile. L'Ostpolitik vaticana di Agostino Casaroli.* Bologna: Il Mulino, 2007.

Morozzo della Rocca, R. *Le nazioni non muoiono. Russia rivoluzionaria, Polonia indipendente e Santa Sede.* Bologna: Il Mulino, 1992.

Petracchi, G. "I gesuiti e il comunismo tra le due guerre." In *La Chiesa cattolica e il totalitarismo,* ed. V. Ferrone, pp. 123–53. Firenze: Loescher, 2004.

Riccardi, A. *Il Vaticano e Mosca (1940–1990).* Roma-Bari: Laterza, 1992.

———. "Le religioni dei due imperi." In *Un ponte sull'Atlantico. L'alleanza occidentale 1949–1999,* ed. A. Giovagnoli e L. Tosi, pp. 79–91. Milano: Guerini, 2003.

———. "La chiesa cattolica, il comunismo e l'Unione sovietica." In *La Chiesa cattolica e il totalitarismo,* ed. V. Ferrone, pp. 79–92. Firenze: Loescher, 2004.

Roccucci, A. "Russian Observers at Vatican II. The 'Council for Russian Orthodox Church Affairs' and the Moscow Patriarchate between Antireligious Policy and International strategy." In *Vatican II in Moscow (1959–1965),* ed. A. Melloni, pp. 45–69. Leuven: Bibliotheek van de Facultet Godgeleerdheid, 1997.

———. "Unione Sovietica e Santa Sede tra coesistenza pacifica e politica antireligiosa." In *Pacem in terris tra azione diplomatica e guerra globale,* ed. A. Giovagnoli. Milano: Guerini, 2003.

Stehle, H. *Die Ostpolitik des Vatikans 1917–1975.* Munchen-Zurich: Piper, 1975.

Wenger, A. *Rome et Moscou 1900–1950.* Paris: Desclée de Brouwer, 1987.

———. *Le card Villot (1905–1979). Segretaire d'Etat de troi papes.* Paris: Desclée de Brouwer, 1989.

AGOSTINO GIOVAGNOLI

Ceausescu, Nicolae

Nicolae Ceausescu (1918–89) was born to a peasant family in Romania and, at the age of fifteen, became a militant in the Union of Communist Youth. At eighteen he joined the Romanian Communist Party (RCP) and received his first sentence of two years in prison because of his Communist beliefs. During 1940–44 he was interned in a concentration camp and developed close ties to the future general secretary of the RCP, Gheorghe Gheorghiu-Dej, a fierce opponent of then-secretary Ștefan Foriș. After the coup on August 23, 1944, and the country's occupation by the Red Army, Ceausescu held numerous positions in both the party and state government. During the RCP's National Conference in October 1945, he was elected to its Central Committee, and was part of it until his death. In 1950 he became head of the army's Political Directorate, whose purpose was to indoctrinate the armed forces, despite an ideological preparation apparently limited to his having read Joseph Stalin's *Problems of Leninism*. Thanks to Gheorghiu-Dej's help and faith in him, Ceausescu became a substitute member of the Political Office in 1954 and a regular member the following year. He also held the positions of secretary of both the Central Committee and the extremely important "cadre section." He became general secretary of the RCP after Gheorghiu-Dej's death, excluding Gheorghe Apostol, one of the deceased's faithful comrades, from the succession, thanks also to the help of Prime Minister Ion Gheorghe Maurer.

"Nicolae Ceausescu's era," as the regime's flatterers would later call it, began in 1965 with the regime's liberalization. In foreign policy Ceausescu continued and expanded the policies promoted by Gheorghiu-Dej, whose goal had been to establish greater autonomy for the country in its relations with the Warsaw Pact. The firmness with which Ceausescu declared his support for the principles of independence and nonintervention in the internal affairs of other countries earned him the sympathy of many Western governments, and was reiterated by his firm condemnation of the 1968 intervention in Czechoslovakia.

This period of liberalization ended in 1971 with the launch of a campaign that aimed to increase the party's control over all areas of social life. There was talk of a "mini Cultural Revolution," a reference to the Chinese model. Ceausescu concentrated all power in his own hands, adding the role of head of government to his other positions in 1967; his personality became the object of a cult that as time passed, grew to truly grotesque proportions. Soon the cult was also extended to his wife, Helena, who rapidly climbed the party's and state's hierarchies. Ceausescu portrayed himself as heir to the medieval tradition of the Romanian *voivodes* (Slavic word for various types of aristocratic administrative positions), and convinced himself he was an important international statesman; he wanted to put the stamp of his personality on both Romania's present and its future.

To this end, he involved the country in significant efforts to develop its heavy industry, modernize its villages, and realize great works, but the economic difficulties generated by these efforts, combined with the decision to pay off foreign debts, led to draconian measures to save food, heating fuel, electricity, and other resources. Poverty and the surveillance methods of the secret police (Securitate) caused extreme discontent among the Romanian people. An opponent of Mikhail Gorbachev's reform policies, Ceausescu became increasingly isolated on the international front and was perceived as a conservative dictator, incapable of dropping the old Stalinist shackles. Hated and discredited, his regime collapsed almost instantly after a popular revolt exploded in Bucharest on December 22, 1989. He was arrested and executed with his wife after summary proceedings.

See also Cult of Personality; Despotism; Stalinism; Warsaw Pact.

FURTHER READING

Câmpeanu, P. *Ceaușescu: Anii numărătorii inverse*. Iași: Polirom, 2002.

Fischer M. E., *Nicolae Ceaușescu: A Study in Political Leadership*. Boulder, CO: Rienner, 1989.

Kunze, T. *Nicolae Ceaușescu. Eine Biographie*. Berlin: Links, 2000.

FLORIN CONSTANTINIU

Censorship

Government agents have sought to control the public expressions of citizens/subjects for as long as large-scale states have existed. Even modern liberal states such as Great Britain, the United States, and France have engaged in overt and informal censorship in recent history, particularly in wartime. There are myriad forms of censorship in modern states, including government licensing of publications, police shutdown of publications, fines and/or jail terms for editors, prepublication vetting of manuscripts and galley proofs, postpublication confiscation of offending works, "consultations" between state officers and journalists, the cutting off of newsprint supplies, subsidies, or other forms of government support, and more.

Yet in spite of the ubiquity of censorship in modern states, it is fair to say that Communist regimes established some of the tightest censorship regimes in world history.

The world's first Communist state, the Soviet Union, rose from the ashes of the Russian Empire, an authoritarian state with a tradition of tight state control of publications going back to the introduction of the printing press. Although the czars loosened state censorship of the press after the emancipation of the serfs in 1861 and again after the abortive revolution of 1905, many Russian bureaucrats and intellectuals continued to believe in the necessity of keeping the supposedly dangerous, amoral production of commercial publishers out of the hands of "the masses." This belief made Russian society fertile ground for a speedy recrudescence of censorship after the October Revolution of 1917.

The Bolshevik Party, along with other Russian socialists, regularly attacked czarist censorship before 1917. Still, the Bolsheviks were quite clear (as was the young Karl Marx) that a dictatorship of the proletariat was required to overthrow the capitalist world order. Such a dictatorship would seem to imply censorship, especially given the Marxists' analysis of cultural production (newspapers, books, plays, paintings, etc.) as a tool of ruling-class domination. It was logically consistent that the proletarian dictatorship should exercise control of the press and other cultural products in its own class interests. Given that the Bolsheviks seized power in wartime, and that their hold on power was initially precarious, it is not surprising that they immediately resorted to censorship. They began by closing down all "bourgeois" daily newspapers and then moved on to other measures.

During the period 1917–22, when civil war and chaos reigned throughout the former Russian Empire, Communist censorship was disorganized and covered mostly the periodical press. This was not due to a disinclination to censor; in fact, there were *too many* institutions claiming the right to censor. These included party organizations at all levels, regional and central governments, and the Commissariat of Enlightenment, responsible for supervising education, scholarship, and cultural production in the new Soviet republic.

The confusion of censorship responsibility was nominally cleared up on June 6, 1922, with the creation of the Central Directorate of Literature and Art (known by the acronym Glavlit) within the Russian Republic Commissariat of Enlightenment. Glavlit was to screen newspapers, books, plays, posters, and other cultural products for military secrets, "bourgeois" ideas, and anything else deemed harmful to the party/state. It generally censored works before publication or presentation. Each republic in the Soviet Union had its own Glavlit section, but the Russian Republic Glavlit was the leading censorship organ (no all-Soviet Glavlit was set up). Under various names Glavlit would exist to the end of the Soviet era.

The rapid expansion of Glavlit's powers, at least on paper, was extraordinary. By the middle of the 1930s Glavlit had the authority to censor paintings on exhibition, stamps, buttons with images on them, and labels on wine bottles, not to mention the obvious newspapers, books, plays, and radio scripts. According to regulations, all of these products required a "visa" from a Glavlit censor before mass production. It is doubtful that all of the regulations were enforced, but it is clear that the people who wrote them aspired to control every aspect of cultural production outside the home.

From the date of its institution, Glavlit was supposed to have a representative in every publishing house and every county (*raion*) in the Soviet republics. Early in its history, however, the organization suffered from a severe lack of qualified personnel. Many Glavlit representatives had only an elementary school education, and the party even appealed for Communist print workers to volunteer as censors as part of their "civic" duty to the party. Another solution from the 1920s to the 1940s was to appoint local newspaper editors as the censor for their area.

There were substantial privileges to being a censor, such as exemption from military service. Censors were also paid well compared to factory workers, at least in the 1930s. As a result, the state was eventually able to recruit thousands of censors with higher education. The censorship apparatus expanded rapidly. In 1939, Glavlit had just over six thousand paid full-time employees; in the late 1980s, it had around seventy thousand.

Direct prepublication censorship, though, was just one part of the total system of control over culture in the Soviet Union and other Communist states. A. V. Blium enumerates five categories of Soviet censorship. In "self-censorship," authors and artists sought to create material fitting the regime's guidelines. In "editorial censorship," editors cut dubious passages from writers' work or advised them to rewrite. Then there was the Glavlit censor (sometimes the same as the editorial censor, mentioned above). Blium's "police censor" refers to censorship by the secret police (Cheka, OGPU, NKVD, and MGB), which monitored artists and writers through a network of informers, and prepared lists of forbidden literature to be removed from libraries. Finally, upper-level party officials exercised "ideological censorship" with circular letters, personnel decisions, and interventions in favor of or against one particular work or another. Party leaders also penalized publications by cutting newsprint allocations, reducing cash subsidies, and encouraging criticism by lower-level activists.

The image of the freedom-loving artist or writer battling the repressive Communist censor is an oversimplification. Multitudes of journalists, writers, and artists contributed to the maintenance of Communist regimes by producing ideologically acceptable products. Most informed experts and many of the producers themselves agree that in Communist regimes, self-censorship and editorial censorship have been more important in sustaining the boundary between acceptable and unacceptable culture than the official state censors. This is parallel to the situation in liberal democracies, where self-censorship and editorial restraint also seem to be important in defining the limits of acceptable discourse (even though the limits are different than in Communist states).

The range of acceptable discourse has varied greatly in different Communist states and different eras. During the "Hundred Flowers" campaign in the People's Republic of China (1956) the *Guangming Daily*, a semi-independent newspaper permitted to publish by party authorities, openly challenged the party's monopoly on political power, as did *Wenhui Bao*, another paper. Yet the party soon fired the editors and journalists involved, and tightened control over both organs. The Soviet Union during perestroika (the late 1980s), and the Communist states in Poland and Yugoslavia, also permitted a relatively wide range of policy discussion and entertainment-oriented visual and print production. The Romanian Communist regime had one of the strictest censorship regimes in the Leninist world.

Censorship considerations have strongly influenced the development of mass media technologies in Communist societies. Soviet authorities preferred cable radio to wireless because the former allowed greater state control over the audience's listening choices. Live television

broadcasts in the Soviet Union were extremely rare in the USSR before the perestroika era, because censors wished to screen scripts before broadcast. Chinese propaganda officials welcomed television because it allowed them to reach right into people's homes with their messages. On the other hand, the spread of Internet use in China (accelerating after 1994) has created tremendous headaches for censors. State strategies for control have included purchasing of software that censors Web searches from international corporations and routing all applications for Internet accounts through the central Ministry of Information Industries.

It is crucial not to exaggerate the power of censorship as a tool of cultural control. In Communist societies, as in other modern societies, the ability of government officials to shape the agenda of the mass media is the most important state tool of influence over mass culture. Direct censorship really plays only an auxiliary role. Even in liberal democracies, state bureaucracies have substantial power to define what qualifies as news, what problems need to be addressed, and what events are significant. In Communist societies where the government owns nearly all of the mass media, party/state apparatchiks have even greater power to set agendas. They do so not just by consultation or direct instructions but also simply by producing "flagship" organs such as the newspaper *Pravda* in the USSR or the official Chinese news service Xinhua. Journalists and many writers follow the example of these organs closely. But presumably the threat of direct censorship helps to keep most artists' and writers' minds focused on the party/state's official line.

See also Cultural Policies; Dictatorship of the Proletariat; KGB; Press; Propaganda, Communist; Television in the Soviet Era.

FURTHER READING

Blium, A. V. *Sovetskaia tsenzura v epokhu totalnogo terrora, 1929–1953*. Saint Petersburg: Akademicheskii proekt, 2000.

Lynch, D. C. *After the Propaganda State: Media, Politics, and "Thought Work" in Reformed China*. Stanford, CA: Stanford University Press, 1999.

Mickiewicz, E. *Split Signals: Television and Politics in the Soviet Union*. Oxford: Oxford University Press, 1988.

O'Neil, P. H., ed. *Communicating Democracy: The Media and Political Transitions*. London: Lynne Rienner Publishers, 1998.

Yuezhi Zhao. *Media, Market, and Democracy in China: Between the Party Line and the Bottom Line*. Urbana: University of Illinois Press, 1998.

MATTHEW LENOE

Charter 77

Charter 77, a Czech opposition organization, was founded by dramatist Václav Havel as a committee for the respect of human rights based on the Helsinki Accords. It had a unique structure: "It doesn't have 'members' because it is not an organization. This not only constitutes a prudent tactical move as regards Czech law, but derives from its internal meaning. Charter cares about the universal not the particular, in the sense of the affirmation of the interests of this or that particular group, component, part of society or social stratum. It is a free society of citizens who have affirmed their civic responsibilities with their signature."

The public opinion movement that gave rise to Charter 77 resulted from the persecution of the rock group the Plastics and their leader, Ivan Jirous, a friend of Havel's. An open letter against the musicians being brought to trial (signed by the future Nobel laureate Jaroslav Seifert, the literary critic Vaclav Cerny, the philosopher Karel Kosik, and about seventy other people) was sent to author Heinrich Böll. This episode rippled through the stagnant post-1968 waters; it showed that some courageous representatives from civil society, and quite a few former members of the Communist Party, did not mind going public or facing subsequent risks to defend human and democratic rights. The first foundational meeting of Charter 77 took place on December 10, 1976, with Havel, Zdenek Mlynar, Pavel Kohout (who came up with the name), Jiří Némec, and Vendelín Komeda in attendance. It was agreed that there would be three spokespeople for Charter 77. The first were historian Jiří Hájek, Catholic philosopher Jan Patočka, and Havel. Signatures for Charter 77 were gathered between Christmas and New Year's Day. Two hundred forty-three people signed the document. In November 1989, arrests and intimidation notwithstanding, the signatories had grown to two thousand.

The first signatory and spokesperson for Charter 77 was Patočka (1907–77), a pupil of Edmund Husserl who had been dismissed from Prague's Charles University in 1948. In order to survive he became a librarian. In 1968 Patočka was rehired to a teaching position, but he was then definitively fired in 1972. Up to that time, he had always avoided a direct confrontation with Communist authorities, bearing witness to his opposition with a proud and tenacious affirmation of his freedom of thought. He immediately lent a strong moral grounding to Charter 77's initiative, especially since he died almost immediately during one of the heavy-handed interrogations to which the police subjected all the signatories. Among the signatories representing Charter 77's varied social, political, and religious membership were Hájek, a former member of the Communist Party's Central Committee and a foreign minister in 1968; the Catholic mathematician and philosopher Václav Benda, who was its spokesperson in 1978 and 1984; the evangelical philosopher Ladislav Hejdánek; the journalist and writer Eva Konturkova; the actor and dramatist Pavel Landovsky; the literary critic Jan Lopatka; the Communist politician Mlynar, who emigrated to Vienna in 1978; the Catholic philosopher and psychologist Némec; the psychologist Jaroslav Sabata, ex-secretary of the Communist Party of Brno, imprisoned from 1971 to 1976; the writer and literary critic Jan Trefulka; the ex-student leader and mechanical engineer Peter Uhl; and the writer and translator Zdenek Urbanek.

Charter 77 symbolized a Czech moral reawakening, and it was of great importance in making the West (and also the USSR) understand that Gustáv Husák's "normalization" had not swept away the experiences and values of the Prague Spring. Its members understood that their salvation lay in their close ties to Europe, in the search for a tight-knit network of political contacts (for example, in Italy with the Psi and the Pci, thanks to the indefatigable efforts of the ex-director of Czech television, Jiri Pelikan, who had taken refuge in Rome). But they also sought closer relations with other Eastern European "dissidents." The meeting of Havel, Jacek Kuron, and Adam Michnik in the Sudeten mountains in the summer of 1978 was well publicized. To a greater extent even than the Prague Spring, the Charter 77 spirit was revealed as a dangerous threat and a hope for all of Eastern Europe.

See also Conference on Security and Cooperation in Europe; Dissent in the USSR; Havel, Václav; Kurón, Jacek; Michnik, Adam; Prague Spring.

FURTHER READING

Patochka, J. *Il senso dell'oggi in Cecoslovacchia*. Milan: Lampugnani Nigri, 1970.

Various authors. *Charta 77. Cinque anni di non consenso*. Bologna: Cseo, 1982.

FRANCESCO M. CATALUCCIO

Chernobyl, Catastrophe of

On April 26, 1986, at 1:23 a.m., a test of the cooling system began in nuclear reactor number 4 at the Chernobyl nuclear power station. The power station had been completed in 1978 near the Ukrainian town of Pripyat, about seventy miles north of Kiev and about ten miles from what was then the Soviet Republic of Belorussia. At the time the plant was composed of four different reactors (two others were in the construction phase), with the dual purpose of producing electricity for civilian use and plutonium for military use. Unlike Western nuclear reactors, the Chernobyl plant had been built without an external containment structure (capable of containing radioactive leaks in case of accidents), it was moderated by graphite (in order to facilitate the production of plutonium), and was equipped with a water-cooling system that lacked intermediate circuits in the piping system (so as to directly produce steam to be sent to the turbines). These were all characteristics that would be revealed as critical in the chain of events that led to the catastrophe.

In the course of the test that day, certain emergency systems were deactivated and the reactor's power level dropped excessively. As a consequence of other mistaken operations, this led to a rapid and uncontrolled power surge. In the space of a few seconds the thermal energy generated by the reactor increased more than one hundred times as compared to the nominal value, causing a gigantic steam explosion, with the ensuing breach of the reactor, and the graphite, exposed to air and water, caught fire. The result was the traumatic dispersal into the atmosphere of a quantity of radioactive material that was four hundred times times greater than that produced by the atomic bomb in Hiroshima. This material started to disperse over a wide area, also as a consequence of the meteorologic conditions in the region.

For well over thirty-six hours afterward, Soviet authorities kept the events a secret, limiting themselves to sending emergency and cleanup squads to the site of the disaster and evacuating the civilian population from settlements in the immediate vicinity of the plant. The first indications about what had happened arrived on the evening of April 27 from Sweden, where personnel at the local Forsmark nuclear power station registered an abnormal level of radioactivity in the air. At that point an area equivalent to about sixty thousand square miles

of the Soviet Union had been contaminated, 60 percent of it in nearby Belorussia and the rest of it in Ukraine and the nearby Russian province of Brjansk, while radioactive particles spread by the winds reached the Baltic Sea and Scandinavian countries.

The immediate victims of the explosion and fire were about thirty, all either personnel at the plant or in charge of emergency and cleanup operations at the disaster site. Those affected by the medium and long-term consequences of radioactive dispersal were much more numerous: almost two thousand Soviet children were killed by thyroid cancer, many others were born with serious deformities, and adults developed forms of tumors induced by contact with radioactive substances. For the top levels of the Soviet leadership, one year after Mikhail Gorbachev became the leader of the Communist Party of the Soviet Union and in the early days of perestroika, this was a harsh blow to the USSR and its international image. The overall fragility of the USSR's productive apparatus, whose inefficiency escaped the authorities' control, suddenly emerged, with consequences that went well beyond the USSR's borders, and that generated concern in the world's public opinion. This was one of the reasons the Chernobyl catastrophe would be remembered as symptomatic of the rapid political and economic decline of the Soviet Union.

See also Atomic Bomb; Dissolution of the USSR; Military-Industrial Complex; Perestroika; Science.

FURTHER READING

Baranovskaya, N. P. *Chernobyl'skaja katastrofa v publikacijach.* Kiev: Institut Istorii Ukrainy, 2004.
Chernushenko, V. M. *Chernobyl: Insight from the Inside.* New York: Springer, 1991.

ANDREA ROMANO

Chicherin, Georgy

Georgy Chicherin (1872–1936) was born to aristocratic parents from a family with ancient roots that had given many prestigious diplomats to the czarist government. Having obtained his degree in history and philology at the University of Saint Petersburg, Chicherin entered the imperial diplomatic service as an archivist. He emigrated to Berlin in 1904, and developed numerous ties to the most notable representatives of the Social Democratic Party of Germany. After having joined Julius Martov's Menshevik internationalist splinter group, from 1907 to 1914 he was secretary of the Foreign Central Bureau of the Russian Workers' Social Democratic Party. At the onset of the war Chicherin transferred to London, where he collaborated with the internationalist wing of the Labour Party. Arrested in August 1917 for his opposition to the war, he was exchanged for British ambassador George Buchanan.

Chicherin joined the Bolshevik Party on his reentry to Russia in January 1918, and participated in the final phases of the Brest-Litovsk negotiations. In May 1918 he was appointed commissar for foreign affairs, a post he occupied until July 1930. His nomination was helped by Lenin, who appreciated Chicherin's valuable skills and talents as a tireless worker. Nevertheless, his aristocratic origins and Menshevik past were the source of widespread distrust, excluding him from the decision-making centers of the Bolshevik Party; he was only elected to the Central Committee in December 1925.

Already at the outset of his commission, Chicherin understood the need for Soviet diplomacy to adapt to the rules and practices of traditional diplomacy, with an eye toward the normalization of relations with the outside world and Russia's return to its role in the assembly of nations. To this end he repeatedly asked that the role and functions of his ministry, in charge of the defense of Soviet security, be clearly outlined and distinguished from those of the Comintern, which operated in the interests of international communism. Thanks to his education, which combined an in-depth knowledge of traditional diplomacy and the ability to formulate the needs of realpolitik in a Marxist idiom, he elaborated his own view of Soviet Russia's global policies, which he synthesized in the following formula: politics toward the East, and economics toward the West. This fundamental distinction entailed a dual line of action: seeking alliances with the "exploited peoples" of the Asian Orient to encourage their revolt against the imperialist powers, on the one hand; looking for "peaceful coexistence" with governments on the Western front, on the other hand, aimed at reestablishing and developing commercial exchanges. In 1922, having been named head of the Soviet delegation to the Geneva Conference, he devised the Treaty of Rapallo, which laid the foundation for political collaboration with Germany, the other power that at the time was looking to be readmitted into the community of European nations.

Chicherin's fortunes started to decline at the beginning of 1927. In addition to the long-standing friction with his second in command, Maksim Litvinov, Nikolay Bukharin led a series of attacks against Chicherin and the German government. Having returned to Moscow from Wiesbaden in June, Chicherin realized that Litvinov had for all intents and purposes taken over as head of the Ministry of Foreign Affairs. He tried to block his rival's rapid ascent, repeatedly threatening to resign and demanding that Litvinov be removed from all assignments in the People's Commissariat for Foreign Affairs. But it did not stop his fall. In 1928 he requested to go to Germany for health reasons. He returned in 1930 to the USSR, where in July, in accordance with his requests, he was removed from all assignments that had now de facto been performed by Litvinov for the previous three years.

See also Diplomats; Litvinov, Maksim; Peaceful Coexistence; Rapallo Treaty.

FURTHER READING

Gorochov, I. M., L. M. Zamjatin, and I. N. Zemskov. *G. V. Chicherin, diplomat leninskoj shkoly.* Moscow: Politizdat, 1973.
Sokolov, V. V. "Neizvestnyj G. V. Chicherin. Iz rassekrecennych archivov MID RF." *Novaja i novejshaja istoria*, no. 1 (1994).

ANNA DI BIAGIO

China-Vietnam War

The war between China and Vietnam lasted a little less than a month, from February 17 to March 16, 1979, but its significance can only be understood in the context of the readjustment of power relations in Southeast Asia at the end of the Vietnam War and the withdrawal of U.S. troops in 1975. In the course of twenty-five years of conflicts (1950–75, first with the French and then with the Americans), China had been Vietnam's principal ally. During this period the Chinese government had given Vietnam financial assistance valued at between fifteen and twenty billion dollars, and most important, sent over three hundred thousand technicians and military advisers. In the early 1970s, Soviet and Chinese interests clashed on several occasions in Asia, and this was one of the reasons that led China to seek closer relations with

Washington—a phase marked by Richard Nixon's visit in 1972 and the reestablishment of diplomatic relations in 1979. This, in turn, inevitably cooled Sino-Vietnamese relations and led Vietnam, especially after reunification, to entertain closer relations with Moscow. The Soviet Union seemed to be an ally that was better disposed to finance the huge needs of postwar reconstruction. In 1978, two years after the creation of the Socialist Republic of Vietnam, Hanoi signed a twenty-five-year friendship and collaboration agreement with the Soviet Union, thus increasing fear of Soviet "encirclement" in the Chinese leadership.

In order to break this encirclement and counterbalance increased Soviet influence, Beijing supported and assisted Pol Pot's bloody regime in bordering Cambodia. Pol Pot had come to power in April 1975, and his ferociously repressive policies, which included violence directed at the Vietnamese ethnic minority, created open hostility in Hanoi. After border skirmishes in 1977 and the first part of 1978, the Vietnamese invasion of Cambodia in December 1978 put an end to the Khmer Rouge regime, but also provoked a Chinese reaction. On February 17 of the following year Chinese troops invaded Vietnam, in what is still today called a "punitive expedition"; it was destined to last only a few weeks and shared similarities with the brief skirmish with India in 1962. The Vietnamese, however, avoiding open conflict and adopting the guerrilla tactics they had experimented with for two decades while fighting occupying troops, succeeded in inflicting heavy losses on the People's Liberation Army's troops (it is estimated that forty-six thousand Chinese soldiers died in this war). On March 16 the Chinese troops, whose purpose was not a large-scale invasion and who were exhausted by the fighting, completed their withdrawal.

Even though the official version of the conflict describes it as a "lesson" imparted to the ungrateful Vietnamese, in actuality the most important lesson was learned by the Chinese military leadership. The conflict revealed inadequacies in the Chinese military apparatus and the need to include the People's Liberation Army in the planned "four modernizations" (agriculture, industry, technology, and precisely, defense) that the new post–Mao Zedong Chinese leadership was promoting. Moreover, closer ties with the United States and the "open-door policy" notwithstanding, the conflict damaged the new China's image with its Southeast Asian neighbors, who interpreted it as another proof of the "danger" that increased Chinese influence in the area posed.

See also Pol Pot; Vietnam War; Vietnam-Cambodia War.

FURTHER READING

Gilks A. *The Breakdown of the Sino-Vietnamese Alliance, 1970–1979.* Berkeley, CA: Institute of East Asian Studies, 1992.

Hood, S. J. *Dragons Entangled: Indochina and the China-Vietnam War.* Armonk, NY: M. E. Sharpe, 1992.

LUIGI TOMBA

China's Armed Forces

China's armed forces are made up of three components: the People's Liberation Army (PLA), the PLA reserve force, and the militia. The PLA constitutes the primary force and plays the decisive role in the country's national defense. Given its special relations with the ruling Chinese Communist Party (CCP), it is also a key interest group in China's domestic politics.

History and Ideology

The PLA was created by the CCP on August 1, 1927, in the name of the Red Army. In the next twenty-two years it experienced two rounds of civil war with the Nationalist Party (1927–36 and 1946–49) and, under the name of the Eighth Route Army, fought ferociously the invading Japanese (1937–45). In 1947 it was renamed the Chinese Liberation Army. Immediately after the founding of the People's Republic of China (PRC), it entered the Korean War (1950) and achieved a stalemate with U.S. forces. Subsequently, until the late 1980s, it was involved in eight limited wars, mainly territorial disputes with its neighbors. The last decade and a half has been a rare period in which the PLA has not engaged in any action. Historically, a few useful points are worth mentioning.

First, the PLA was an army of revolution. After the failure of late Qing reform and in the face of worsening warlordism in the early days of the Republic of China, Chinese intellectuals saw the salvation of China only in light of revolutionary change through armed struggle. The creation of the PLA symbolized political radicalization in the country.

Second, the PLA is an army dedicated to nationalist goals. Its founders' primary motivation was expelling the colonial powers from China. This goal was given fresh impetus by the war against the Japanese invasion, which actually helped the PLA to develop into a powerful force.

Third, the PLA is an army built on Communist ideology. It was designed as an instrument of the class struggle of the poor against the rich, and its ultimate purpose was seizing national power. After 1949 it served as an instrument for exporting the Maoist revolution. Although the PLA's ideological color has faded in the aftermath of post-Mao reform, its influence has remained strong, more now as a force for nationalism than communism.

The Organization, Doctrine and the Supreme Command

The PLA is composed of four services: the ground force, the air force, the navy, and the strategic missile force. The army is the largest of these and dominates the PLA, largely because the other special services were created from within the ground force. At this writing the PLA numbered 2.5 million, with the army making up about 70 percent of the total. The percentage of the other services is respectively: the navy, about 10; the air force, about 16; and the missile force, about 5 percent.

The Army

The army is structured according to seven military regions, each responsible for the military affairs of a number of provinces. In these military regions twenty-one group armies are stationed with the mission of conducting strategic campaigns not only in the region but nationally. Each MR also commands a number of provincial military districts that are responsible for local security, recruitment, and the training of the reserve force and militia. In recent years there has been a clear trend toward a reduction in the size of the army. After two rounds of streamlining (cutting half a million troops in 1998 and 200,000 in 2002), the army is presently at its smallest since the founding of the PRC.

The Nuclear Force

The SMF is the smallest service in the PLA. It nevertheless assumes a disproportionate share of responsibility for strategic deterrence against the major powers. The Chinese nuclear strategy was one of minimum deterrence, defined as non–first use of nuclear weapons against any nation. In recent years the PLA has reviewed this strategy and concluded that placing too much reliance on the success of a second strike is an excessive stance. The idea is emerging that the SMF should develop first strike and tactical capabilities. Western analysts use the term "limited deterrence" to characterize this new evolution. Although Beijing insists that its policy of minimum deterrence remains intact, the PLA has continuously modernized its nuclear force in the direction of achieving creditable first strike capability. To this end new generations of nuclear missiles and submarines will enter service in the years to come.

The Navy

The PLA navy is in a phase of major transformation from a coastal force to a force capable of operations in the deep oceans of the West Pacific. This is being accomplished step by step through a blue-water maritime strategy that the PLA put forward in 1987. Under this strategy the navy should by 2000 have acquired sea-control power within its coastal waters. During the decade between 2010 and 2020, it should have a kind of sea-denial capability within the first island chain in the West Pacific. Then, by 2050 it should have global reach with deep ocean fleets. Since 2000, the rate of transformation has visibly accelerated. The number of major surface combatants and submarines has more than doubled that of the 1990s. If this fast growth track continues, China may attain its second and third phase naval objectives according to the plan schedule.

The navy's main combat force is its three fleets: the North Sea Fleet, the East Sea Fleet, and the South Sea Fleet. Each has over three dozen major warships: destroyers, frigates, and submarines. They are assisted by a naval air force and other special units. Currently the navy is addressing the two primary weak links in realizing its blue-water strategy: antisubmarine warfare and area air defense in deep oceans. To cater for the war scenario in the Taiwan Strait, capabilities for sea blockade and amphibious operations have been accorded a priority status in force development. These will guide the PLA navy's preparation for war in the 21st century.

The Supreme Command

China's top military command is the Central Military Commission (CMC) of the CCP. Its chair is concurrently party general secretary and state president. Therefore, this body is the most influential political institution in the country. It is responsible for formulating national defense strategy, for troop deployment, and for the preparation of war plans. It plays the decisive role in the national security policy process and has an important say in key foreign and domestic policy deliberations.

The Transformation Strategy

The PLA is effecting two fundamental changes: change from a quantitative military to a qualitative military;

and change from a manpower-intensive military to a knowledge-intensive military. In 2002 China substantially revised its 1992 national defense strategy, which was officially titled "winning a regional limited war under high-tech conditions." The new strategy resets the direction of the PLA's modernization: from seeking superiority through mechanization (enhancing high-tech hardware) to realizing dual transformation through mechanization and informatization (IT integration). In PLA terminology this is called "a revolution of double construction."

The PLA is using the Revolution in Military Affairs (RMA) as the central link to integrate new military theories into PLA reforms. Most importantly, information technology is seen as the engine of global military change and the key to the success of PLA transformation. This new strategy will have profound impact on the PLA, as it sets a new direction of for PLA modernization. Until recently the PLA has focused on upgrading hardware and platforms. How to match this mechanization-centered force development with measures of network warfare is a new and difficult challenge. U.S.-led IT-centered military transformation has created new types of warfare, forcing China to adjust its military doctrine, structure, and war preparations accordingly. The PLA is now making substantial investments in the areas of informational warfare and has established digital units in order to be able to fight a 21st-century war.

The Civil-Military Relationship

As in all Communist countries, the ruling party and the military are partnered in an intimate relationship. In China this relationship had been for a long time defined as a symbiosis: one's demise would trigger the death of the other. Indeed, the military is not slow to intervene in domestic politics, often in the name of protecting the leadership of the party. It has in fact saved the party on a number of occasions, the most recent being the Tiananmen Square uprising of 1989. This role gives the PLA a prominent place in the country's political system and has earned it the right to get involved in inner party politics. The intervention either takes the form of following the call of one paramount leader, or serves the purpose of protecting the PLA's own vested interests. The special party-army relationship also provides the PLA easy access to influence government processes. It exercises leadership in setting the national security agenda and plays an active role in other policy areas, such as budget allocation, foreign affairs, and domestic development.

The profound political and social changes that have taken place in post-Mao China have also altered the country's civil-military interaction. Increasingly, "symbiosis" can no longer adequately describe the relations between the CCP and the PLA. In the longer term and in times short of crisis the CCP's survival is more dependent on economic development, effective administration of state affairs, and forceful campaigns against corruption than on the suppression of dissenting views through the gun. The military can sustain the CCP leadership but not the legitimacy upon which the party's ultimate fate is decided.

Increasingly the CCP/PLA relationship is centered on the sharing of interests. Each benefits from the CCP's monopoly of national power. Additionally, shared vested interests are supplemented by their shared national goal of making China socially stable, economically prosperous, and militarily powerful. So far the CCP is the PLA's best partner, granting it what it wants as no other political force can. This bond of interdependence will not only help the army and party to stay together in the years ahead, but will also help them to work together efficiently under the new and more clearly defined rules of the game. For instance, military modernization is linked to the CCP's effort to raise China's international profile, which in turn enhances the party's popularity with the people. Inevitably, building a more capable fighting force entails continued increases in military spending. This has resulted in the provision in the National Defense Law that the PLA's budget should rise in keeping with the growth rate of the GDP. At the same time, the PLA accepts the party's priority of developing the national economy because it agrees with the CCP argument that military strength ultimately lies in the country's comprehensive strength. PLA generals have repeatedly voiced support for Hu Jintao's New Deal, which establishes economic development as his top priority.

The post-symbiotic ties reflect the fact that the PLA is no longer the only dominant interest group in China's political system. Other groups of powerholders now exist parallel to the PLA, such as the state administration. Certainly in this diversified power structure, the PLA is still the first among the equals in terms of its political weight. Indeed conflicts of interest do take place between the PLA and other power groups. The military's pursuits are even sometimes at odds with the party's. In fact the changing nature of civil-military relations in post-Mao China revolve around attempts to manage these differences in interests. We have witnessed the different ways of interaction between CCP and PLA leaders: from crude domination by Mao and Deng to Jiang and Hu's efforts of institutionalizing party/army ties.

Post-Mao military modernization has strongly promoted professionalism in the PLA. The embrace of the revolution in military affairs (RMA) and the changing composition of PLA personnel (a technocrats-centered force in the making) have contributed to the change of civil-military relations in China. Moreover a new trend of depoliticization and deideologization has strongly emerged among the population from which the conscripts are drawn. Technocrats have begun to permeate the rank and file of the PLA. This makes it almost impossible for the CCP to extract absolute obedience from the soldiers. Gradually, another theoretical model of civil-military relations, namely objective control, has begun to affect the PRC. This model enshrines professionalism as a primary value in the armed forces and inhibits soldiers' nonmilitary ambitions. It also promotes an institutionalized process of civilian supremacy over the generals. This makes the military more a client of the state than the tool of a political leader.

In the next few decades the CCP/PLA relationship will become more complicated. The two ultimate interests of the PLA are the improvement of its combat capabilities and the improvement of its corporate identity. The CCP naturally shares the former goal. A strong PLA best serves the interests of the CCP, as it can give party leaders enhanced say in both international and domestic affairs. The latter interest elicits a more complex reaction from the CCP. The military's efforts to perfect professionalism differentiate it from other political organizations. Obviously a professional military helps the CCP leadership. At the same time if the army has an independent corporate identity, this could shake the party's "absolute control" over the gun when party and military disagree over key issues. Smooth relations depend on a delicate balance. On the other hand, a more professional and less politically oriented military could also be less interventionist. In other words, the CCP might have greater success in maintaining its control over the gun by promoting professionalism than by political indoctrination. If the party and the PLA continue to share strategic interests, a united PLA would be a guarantee for the continued CCP monopoly of national power. However, if the PLA acquires a strong corporate identity, it could mount pressure on the party over fundamental political differences. Furthermore, a united PLA could also ren-der it difficult for party leaders to resort to the Maoist divide-and-rule method of control.

See also Chinese Revolution; Red Army; Red Guard; Warfare.

FURTHER READING

Mulvenon, J. C., and A.N.D. Yang, eds. *The PLA as Organization*. Santa Monica, CA: National Security Research Division, RAND, 2002.

Shambaugh, D. L. *Modernizing China's Military: Progress, Problems and Prospects*. Berkeley: University of California Press, 2004.

You Ji. *The Armed Forces of China*. Sydney: Allen & Unwin, 1999.

———. "China's New National Defense Strategy, Naval Transformation and the Taiwan Conflict." *Stockholm Journal of East Asian Studies* 15 (2005), 75–88.

YOU JI

Chinese Agrarian Policies

The relations between the Chinese Communist Party (CCP) and the peasantry during the history of the People's Republic of China represent something of a puzzle. Most elsewhere in the Communist world, Communist parties were composed of urban intellectuals and the urban proletariat. Marxists widely regarded the petite bourgeoisie peasantry as striving to preserve and enlarge its smallholdings, and as difficult to mobilize as a "sack of potatoes," in Karl Marx's famous phrase. As urbanites, Communists shared the widespread disdain for the backward rustics. When they came to power, the urban-based parties were isolated from the countryside. When they started socialist transformation, state-peasant relations became highly conflictual. Collectivization required a great deal of coercion and pressure—a major cause being that the collectives were used to extract agricultural resources for the benefit of the urban-industrial sector.

China should have been an exception. The establishment of the People's Republic of China in 1949 was the culmination of a twenty-year revolutionary process in the countryside, during which the CCP acquired extensive experience in mobilizing various social forces and winning support from poor peasants. This experience was successfully applied in the newly occupied areas of central, southern, and western China. By the end of 1952, the old social and political elites had been overthrown. Under CCP auspices, redistribution created a large group of rural beneficiaries. Most important, villages were for the first time in Chinese history tied organizationally into the national political system—an unprecedented achievement. Conditions for socialist transformation were thus far more propitious than in most other Communist countries.

During the era of Mao Zedong's China (1949–76), the reality proved very different. After entering the cities, the CCP privileged the urban sector, especially industrial workers. In the mid-1950s, peasants became second-class citizens bound to the land. State-peasant relations, though for the most part not as bad as under Stalin, were fraught with major conflicts. First, China established a Soviet-style economy in which rural resources were extracted for the benefit of industrialization. Already in 1953, a state monopoly over grain and other commodities was imposed. The delivery quotas in principle respected peasant incentives to grow surpluses. In practice, especially when, as often happened, harvests fell short of the plan, the state encroached on peasant subsistence, with extraction reaching a peak during the Great Leap Forward (1958–60). State prices were usually below those obtained on free markets, while the state also maintained price scissors between agricultural and industrial commodities to the disadvantage of the peasants. This was one major cause of rural discontent, expressed in sporadic rioting and other acts of resistance. Under these conditions, the extraction of resources was a cause for the stagnation of peasant incomes between 1957 and 1978.

Second, there was the socialist transformation. In 1949, Mao recognized that the "serious problem is the education of the peasantry"—that is, peasants needed to be convinced that collective farming was superior to smallholder family farming. In order to maximize the chances for peasant consent, the regime initially adopted moderate and long-term goals. Collectivization would begin with small mutual aid teams, which built on pre-Communist practices. Over time, as experience in cooperation increased, managerial skills rose, and peasant incomes from collective undertakings was gained, the collective units would gradually be increased, while sideline production and peasant markets would continue to make an essential contribution to household incomes. Only in the distant future, when industry would be able to supply machinery, perhaps in ten to fifteen years, would full-scale collective farms be established similar to those in the Soviet Union. For a brief period in the early 1950s this moderate approach was practiced, and it succeeded in appealing to a good many peasants.

The moderate approach was undercut by the state's procurement program and crucially by Chairman Mao's deep yearnings for the rapid transformation of China. While many of his subordinates doubted the appropriateness of accelerating the speed of collectivization, Mao's power, authority, and prestige carried the day. A series of intensive mobilization campaigns succeeded in enrolling virtually the entire peasantry in advanced forms of collective farming by the end of 1956, years ahead of schedule.

Many or perhaps most peasants were not prepared for this acceleration. In securing compliance, the reliance on normative and material incentives necessarily shifted toward coercion. This applied to middle and especially "upper-middle peasants" who were able to farm on their own, and on whom harsh pressures were unleashed. In contrast, still poor peasants, many short of labor, could be expected to support the changes since they would benefit from the pooled productive assets of their richer neighbors. Cadres who had been recruited from among the poor owed their upward mobility to the party. A subset of these beneficiaries became unquestioningly loyal to Chairman Mao to the point implementing policies grossly disadvantageous to the village. More generally, villagers were well aware of the CCP's willingness to use force against designated enemies, many having participated in the early campaigns against landlords and "counterrevolutionaries." In each village a pariah group of class enemies reminded everyone else of the consequences of falling afoul of regime preferences.

After collectivization, incomes did not increase and inputs contributed by middle peasants were not paid for. Disaffection among collectivized farmers led to disturbances and an exodus in 1956–57, but one that paled in size to the Soviet exodus in the spring of 1930. Despite the discontent, Mao came to believe that he had correctly estimated the willingness of "poor and lower-middle peasants" to embrace socialism, and that therefore new campaigns of mass mobilization could be launched and collectives could be raised to an even more extreme level. Instead of rationalizing the new collectives to make them more acceptable to its members, the regime in 1957 embarked on a high-pressure "socialist education campaign" designed to make it clear to peasants that socialism was superior. This campaign stilled dissent and paved the way for the Great Leap Forward, which sought to achieve a developmental breakthrough using utopian means, as in the form of highly egalitarian people's communes. The Great Leap collapsed amid a disastrous famine.

The retreat from the extremes of the Great Leap entailed a return to family farming in parts of the country, sanctioned for a brief period as an emergency measure even by Mao. But despite his vaunted "mass line," Mao insisted that peasant preferences for family farming were not acceptable. In the summer of 1962 he called for renewed socialist advances under the slogan "Never forget class struggle." Still, the communes emerged from the retreat in a downsized form and with a small private sector. The lowest and smallest subdivision of the communes became the unit of distribution, which to a limited extent accommodated peasants' demand for small units in which individual effort could be measured and rewarded.

During the remaining years of the Mao era this relatively moderate level of collectivism stayed largely in place, despite periodic campaigns to revitalize socialist commitments among cadres and peasants. The ultra-radicalism of the Cultural Revolution spilled over into the countryside, resulting in a great deal of factional violence and drives to "cut off capitalist tails"—that is, to socialize private plots and small privately held livestock, and raise the unit of distribution to a higher level in the name of egalitarianism.

Next came the reform era. During their "postmobilization" stages, Communist countries moderated their rural policies, especially by providing meaningful incentives. China was no exception. The dramatic turn against Maoist extremism that began in 1978 affected agriculture immediately. Central leaders recognized that perhaps a 150 to 200 million peasants had neither adequate food nor clothing. Fearing rebellion, reform leaders immediately took remedial steps within the framework of maintaining the collective system. They raised state procurement prices, allowed the reopening of rural markets, and strengthened the private sector. These measures were soon eclipsed by a dramatic turnabout—namely, the return to family farming similar to the practices that Mao had condemned as capitalist in 1962. "Household contracting" tied family incomes to output, so that families reaped the fruits of their labor. This extraordinary retreat was achieved as a result of peasant pressure from below and ever more supportive officials from above. Family farming swept across the country. Striking successes in raising output and incomes were attained by 1984. Socialist features persisted, however. Land remained under collective ownership, and state procurement quotas were

maintained for another twenty years or so, thereby ensuring adequate grain supplies for the cities. The implementation of the Marxist goal of establishing large, mechanized farms run along industrial lines was indefinitely postponed.

The return to family farming unleashed the entrepreneurial energies of the Chinese family, which the communes had fettered. In the eastern provinces, where favorable conditions obtained—markets, sources of investment, and transportation—the result was an explosion of small-scale rural industry, which within a few years successfully competed with state industry and became a major source of growth. Contrary to expectations widely held in Europe that party bureaucrats would resist reform, it was village and township party secretaries who often took the lead in building enterprises. Profits and taxes generated from local industry and commerce enabled the local leaders to support education, infrastructure construction, and the provision of welfare.

Nevertheless, in the central and western regions conditions for local industrialization were less propitious. These regions depended primarily on agriculture for income. From 1985 on, living off agriculture became increasingly difficult because of disadvantageous price scissors and the growing impact of disadvantageous market forces. Dependency on agriculture caused severe conflicts in the central and western areas between villagers and local officials—conflicts that defined much of the 1990s. Local officials were under severe pressure from their superiors to engage in developmental activities, road and school building, electrification, and so on. Yet the superiors did not provide the necessary funds, counting on local growth to generate the needed revenues. Funding for rural education, for instance, was largely delegated to the localities. This worked in the eastern provinces, but not nearly as well as in the agriculture-dependent regions. There, local officials had to extract funds, often forcibly, from villagers to pay for various projects—a situation that fostered widespread corruption. Tensions over brutal collection methods led to riots, demonstrations, and visits to higher levels to plead for relief. Peasant discontent, it is important to note, did not threaten the regime as such. Villagers protested in the name of the central authorities, whom they believed to be on their side. This was indeed the case, but at the same time policies emanating from Beijing were also responsible for the peasants' plight.

Early in the 21st century the central leaders changed course and decided to give significantly more financial support for rural development. Growing urban-rural disparities—in "socialist" China, income distribution is about as unequal as in India—as well as growing rural unrest motivated this departure from the long-standing policies of disadvantaging the countryside in favor of the cities. Still, new conflicts, especially over the requisitioning of farmland for development, strain state-peasant relations.

China still has a long way to go to eliminate the second-class status of villagers. Since the mid-1980s, restrictions on migration have been loosened but not fully eliminated. The social benefits open to urbanites have only recently begun to be extended to migrants. Competitive village elections provide a modest form of democracy at the grass roots, fostering a sense of citizenship, but villagers continue to be grossly underrepresented in the decision-making organs of the party and state.

See also Collectivization of the Countryside; Great Leap Forward.

FURTHER READING

Bernstein, Thomas P., and Xiaobo Lu. *Taxation without Representation in Contemporary Rural China.* New York: Cambridge University Press, 2003.

Bianco, Lucien. *Peasants without the Party: Grassroots Movements in Twentieth Century China.* Armonk, NY: M. E. Sharpe, 2001.

Friedman, Edward, Paul G. Pickowicz, and Mark Selden. *Chinese Village, Socialist State.* New Haven, CT: Yale University Press, 1991.

Oi, Jean C. *Rural China Takes Off: Institutional Foundations of Economic Reform.* Berkeley: University of California Press, 1999.

THOMAS P. BERNSTEIN

Chinese Revolution

The Chinese revolution of the 20th century (1911–49) comprised in effect a series of revolutions that on occasion overlapped, clashed, or complimented one another. The revolutions occurred as a response to the internal collapse of the Qing dynasty in 1911, and each sought to find a suitable state form by which to modernize Chinese society. The search did not end in 1949 with the Communist victory. In fact its ramifications reverberate to the present day. The revolutions include an uprising against rule through the "mandate of heaven," an abortive attempt to introduce a liberal political order, a failed nationalist movement, and a series of local Communist uprisings that were knitted together by the organization of the Chinese Communist Party (CCP) to achieve national power.

Collapse of the Old and Aborted Attempts to Give Birth to the New (1911–27)

The CCP was a direct product of the intellectual ferment that accompanied the anti-imperialist demonstrations commonly referred to as the May Fourth Movement (1919). Its longer-term origins lay in the collapse of the imperial system and the social and political vacuum that followed its fall. Disillusioned with the imperial system, disaffected intellectuals challenged the premises of state power and began to discuss what sort of system might bring China into the "modern world." With no obvious successor to dynastic rule, the logic of the situation demanded a republic. However, initial attempts failed to establish a predictable and effective system of parliamentary rule. At the same time, the authority of the center fragmented and warlordism increased.

The nominal government in Beijing continued to rule and was accorded the respect of foreign governments, but it was influenced by the shifting fortunes of a number of powerful political cliques. Its frail legitimacy was further eroded by the May Fourth Movement, which began as a series of anti-Japanese demonstrations but unfolded into a period of intellectual ferment and discussion. The movement embraced a wide-ranging cultural and nationalist renaissance and opened up a Pandora's box of solutions to China's problems. Yet no answer was offered on the crucial question of political power. Pragmatic liberalism, anarchism, and the various forms of socialist thought that were popular in these years did not seem to offer the quick and total solution to China's problems that many saw as necessary. Intellectuals like Hu Shi, the liberal reformer who proposed reform by "inches and drops," seemed increasingly irrelevant.

The Bolshevik revolution of 1917, by contrast, seemed to demonstrate possibilities for radical change within a context of underdevelopment, and it attracted a small number of urban intellectuals. Slowly they began to discover the latent power of China's growing working class, and through the 1920s they attempted build an increasingly radical, urban-based proletarian movement. While the Chinese Communist Party had its own historical roots, the Comintern took a strong interest in its development and forced it into an alliance with China's Nationalists that lasted from 1923 to 1927.

Lacking a strong grass-roots presence, the CCP tried to control the labor and rural movements from above. The apparent success of this strategy lulled the party leadership into a false sense of security. A CCP-led revolution on the back of a swelling nationalist, anti-imperialist revolution seemed to be a possibility. However, reality on the ground was different. In the 1920s, the CCP did not develop the necessary support base in urban China; nor was it able to build up solid support in the southern countryside. This meant that once the Nationalists became concerned about the CCP and turned their military power against it, the CCP had very little with which to defend itself. In 1927 Communist supporters were driven out of the major cities and the remnants of the movement withdrew to the countryside.

Despite thise defeat, the 1920s did bring certain benefits to the CCP. Cooperation with the GMD had allowed the CCP to develop its organization on a much wider scale, especially in the south, than would otherwise have been the case. Further, it had been a valuable learning experience for the CCP. With expanded membership, the party had begun to pay serious attention to its organizational structure. Despite all the problems, it had gained influence in the southern labor movements and more significantly in the southern peasant movements, and it had a trained body of cadres. The CCP had no army of its own, but among its members were a number of military officers who had been trained in the Whampoa Military Academy. These officers would play an important role in the next phase of the revolution.

Surviving in the Countryside and Building Political Power (1927–49)

Even though CCP ideology stressed the preeminence of working-class leadership, political reality forced it to form an eclectic set of alliances with local rural power-holders, warlords, and peasants. The party became much more pragmatic and was successful when local cadres adapted to local conditions, set down roots, and developed policies to build strong coalitions that could overthrow local elites and sustain Communist rule in the face of backlash.

Two main explanations have been put forward for the CCP's success. Chalmers Johnson argued that the Communist revolution was essentially propelled by nationalism. It fed off the Japanese invasion (1937), building its credentials as a patriotic party that was more willing to engage the Japanese and defend the nation than were Chiang Kai-shek's Nationalists. This attracted many young urban intellectuals to the Communist base areas who were disgusted with the greed and corruption of the nationalist government. By contrast, Mark Selden maintained that it was the Communist's program of socioeconomic transformation that paved the way for their ultimate success. These explanations both contain kernels of truth, but there was an infinitely more complex relationship between the party's policies and its relationship to different social forces in the Chinese countryside.

In reality, the CCP had enormous difficulty in mobilizing support within society. Establishing effective contact with workers and peasants continued to be a problem. Mobilization was so difficult on occasion that the question is not why the Communists were so successful but rather how did they ever manage to gain state power against such odds. The answer is that local party leaders compromised on party ideological principles. The CCP was successful in putting down local roots when it showed flexibility in adapting policy to local circumstances, where it was good at micropolitics. By contrast, attempts to transform local environments to conform to predetermined ideological predispositions were unsuccessful. But by bypassing ideology, local leaders were left open to attacks by the party center or its commissioners for various forms of "capitulation" or "corruption."

The CCP's defining experiences took place in the countryside from 1927 onward, first in the base areas in south China, the best known of which was the Jiangxi Soviet (where Mao and the party leadership resided), and later in the central and northern base areas with Yan'an (Shaan-Gan-Ning) as the core. In these bases, the CCP developed its skill at governing, built a tight organization that brooked no dissent and an armed force that was able to survive the Japanese (1937–45) and then to take on and defeat the much larger and better-equipped Nationalist armies in the civil war (1945–49).

The power of the peasantry that Mao Zedong saw in the 1920s impressed him, and he subsequently combined rural organization with military power. Although Mao never formally renounced proletarian leadership he concentrated on the role and strength of the poor peasantry and on the sanctuary that the countryside could provide. Rural support, however, proved to be no easier to achieve than support in the urban areas. Also, once peasants were mobilized, the party found it difficult to maintain the momentum and keep things under control.

The sine qua non for CCP success was sustained control over a particular locality based on military force. This provided the party with the time and space to devise policies relevant to the particular region. Moreover, continuous CCP presence backed by armed force caused the local elite either to cooperate or at least to acquiesce to CCP rule. For the peasantry it offered a continuity of rule to which they could respond. Simple military control and rule through repression, however, would have made the CCP no different from the warlords. As a result, the CCP had to devise policies to suit localities without compromising its general principles, while simultaneously avoiding driving potentially hostile groups into outright opposition.

In the Jiangxi Soviet (1931–34) Mao and his supporters first put together the strategy of the "holy trinity" of CCP organization, territorial control, and military power. These were the necessary building blocks for taking national power. Initially, this approach went hand-in-hand with a harsh policy of land reform that alienated the middle and rich peasants who were crucial to CCP success. While moderate land policies were adopted to correct this, the Communist base areas came under increasing pressure from Nationalist forces, and in 1934 the CCP was forced to abandon the Soviets and embark on the Long March that eventually brought them to the remote northwestern area of Shaanxi Province.

Yan'an was a remote area allowing the CCP respite from both Nationalist harassment and the Japanese invaders. The chance to recuperate and rebuild was enhanced by the conclusion of the second United Front with the Nationalists (1937–45), which brought an uneasy peace between the two warring giants. From 1937 on, Mao put together policies that would help bring the Communists to power in 1949. Social and economic policy was moderate while innerparty policy toughened to instill orthodoxy. By 1945 Mao stood as the unchallenged head of a unified party that enjoyed domestic prestige and that oversaw not only a well-disciplined party machine but also a trained, experienced fighting force.

Policy moderation was dictated by prior experience and the need to put forward a friendlier face in the United Front. This helped the party build a broad range of alliances. Contrary to conventional wisdom, in the period after 1937 the rural elite was more readily attracted to the CCP program of resistance than was the local peasantry. Indeed, the threat posed by the Japanese forces bonded the CCP and the local elite together in an uneasy marriage of convenience. Further positive support came

from rural students and teachers. In fact, based on experiences from another major base area (Jin-Cha-Ji), the CCP devised policies to neutralize any possible threat from the local elites to their power by co-opting them into the new power structure.

In addition, economic policy was moderated to give local elites a stake in the base area's development. The goal was to meet the needs of the people and the military, and thus agriculture, industry, and commerce would be privately managed by smallholding peasants, artisans, and merchants. State-owned industry, with the exception of the armaments industry, would play only a residual role. One leader dismissed the idea of developing a huge number of state-owned industries as trying to build a "skyscraper on shifting sands" or "painting a picture of a cake to prevent hunger." However, there was to be a strong role for cooperatives to prevent private capital gaining too much control.

Co-optation was accompanied by promises of social reform to gain the support of the local peasantry. In the process, the CCP attempted to define political and economic relations in the villages in terms of class rather than by the traditional forms of patronage and familial relationships. The introduction of class as a defining characteristic in village life was new, however, and the party had problems in precisely defining classes in the countryside and in working out policies for land redistribution or interest- and rent-reduction based on these suppositions.

Despite CCP emphasis on the support of poor peasants, that support was never firm, and when the rural dispossessed did act, they tended to take matters into their own hands, often advancing to a radicalization that went beyond party wishes. Lucien Bianco has written that the CCP was in the difficult position of trying to initiate a peasant movement without peasants. In fact, support was always conditional and this moderated CCP policy in important ways. It might be argued, however, that widespread and deep-seated support was not necessary for CCP success. What was most important was that key and potentially hostile groups should acquiesce to party control. The lack of any viable alternatives assisted the CCP: the Japanese invasion had broken down traditional power structures, and the Nationalists appeared morally bankrupt and economically incompetent.

In contrast to this moderate economic policy, the atmosphere within the party toughened with the solidification of Mao's power. Potential alternatives to his rule were eliminated, but success brought its own new problems. The need to tighten up organization and to produce ideological conformity was increased by the influx of new members who had been recruited through rapid membership drives and by the numbers of urban intellectuals who had come to Yan'an as patriots to resist the Japanese rather than as good Communists dedicated to social revolution. Mao defined the new organizational and ideological orthodoxy that was sought in such a way as to position himself in the central role of the CCP's revolutionary history, thus providing himself with the legitimacy necessary to secure an unchallengeable leadership position.

This orthodoxy was achieved through the Rectification Campaign (1941–44), which ensured that most party members would behave in a predictable way most of the time despite the enormously varied environments in which they operated. This left the security apparatus merely the task of cleaning up the mess where such a system broke down.

With the collapse of the imperial system, intellectuals as a group had been detached from the function of public service that they had fulfilled in the Confucian order. The new orthodoxy provided the basis for the "reattachment" of those disaffected intellectuals who had moved to the base areas. For those who wavered, the linking of the Rectification Campaign with harsher attempts to investigate cadres and purge dissident intellectuals served as a warning. In Yan'an, Mao made it quite clear that the independent critical role of the intellectual as it had developed in the May Fourth Movement would no longer be tolerated within his republic.

Legacies of Revolution

The experiences in Yan'an forged a unified leadership that helped the CCP win the civil war (1945–49), but this new system created a number of problems that the ruling party has grappled with to this day. First, independent intellectual criticism is distrusted and has been associated with a lack of loyalty. Policy differences have regularly been interpreted as antiparty activity. Second, the emphasis on ideological correctness has led to recurrent campaigns to ensure orthodoxy. The style of personal criticism developed in Yan'an would return in even more violent form in the antirightist campaigns of the 1950s and the Cultural Revolution of the 1960s.

Third, mass mobilization has been used to achieve policy objectives. It is not enough to accept a policy passively. It is necessary to show positive, active support. This has been a continual feature of post-1949 policy im-

plementation, and it has reduced the method to a ritual. Especially since the Cultural Revolution this has resulted in the devaluation of the effectiveness of mass mobilization through overuse or through the direction of the movement toward spurious targets.

Fourth, the CCP had been successful where cadres understood the local environment and where they were good at micropolitics. On assuming power, the CCP's policy-making center moved away from the countryside, and leaders soon forgot that survival and expansion had depended on detailed negotiation and brokerage. With state power in their hands, senior party leaders no longer felt the need to negotiate with other social forces. When party members thought about the lessons of the revolution, it was increasingly in terms of the myth that had been created; namely, that the CCP had been swept into power on a massive wave of popular peasant support. The party leadership became increasingly divorced from the everyday realities of politics and policymaking began to suffer.

Fifth, this tendency was enhanced by the fact that the CCP on coming to power was independent of all social forces. While it took power in the name of the proletariat, the CCP had had no effective contact with that proletariat for over twenty years. Thus, it abrogated to itself the right to speak on behalf of a class that was not fully developed and that had no real influence in the higher reaches of the party.

Sixth, the stress on organizational stability and ideological orthodoxy went, somewhat paradoxically, hand in hand with the accretion of power in Mao's hands. The Mao cult, which reached its zenith in the Cultural Revolution, lowered the valuation of collective leadership and loyalty to the CCP as an organization. This helps account for the casualness with which Mao treated organizational norms after 1949, a laxity that the post-Mao leadership has struggled to rebuild.

See also Anti-imperialism; Comintern; Long March; Mao Zedong; Maoism; Marxism-Leninism; Nationalism.

FURTHER READING

Apter, D. E., and T. Saich. *Revolutionary Discourse in Mao's China.* Cambridge, MA: Harvard University Press, 1994.

Bianco, L. *The Origins of the Chinese Revolution, 1915–1949.* Trans. Muriel Bell. Stanford: Stanford University Press, 1971.

Fairbank, J. K. *The Cambridge History of China, Republican China 1912–1949,* vol. 13, part 1. Cambridge, UK: Cambridge University Press, 1983.

Fairbank, J. K., and A. Feuerwerker, eds. *The Cambridge History of Republican China, 1912–1949*, vol. 13, part 2. Cambridge, UK: Cambridge University Press, 1986.

Johnson, C. *Peasant Nationalism and Communist Power: The Emergence of Revolutionary China, 1937–1945*. Stanford, CA: Stanford University Press, 1962.

Saich, T. *The Rise to Power of the Chinese Communist Party: Documents and Analysis*. Armonk, NY: M. E. Sharpe, 1996.

Saich, T., and H. van de Ven, eds. *New Perspectives on the Chinese Communist Revolution*. Armonk, NY: M. E. Sharpe, 1995.

Selden, M. *China in Revolution: The Yenan Way Revisited*. Armonk, NY: M. E. Sharpe, 1995.

ANTHONY SAICH

Cinema, Soviet

The Bolsheviks were always convinced that cinema was a powerful tool for political "education," and therefore from the beginning of their rule attempted to use it. To the question of how successful they were, there is no clear-cut answer.

The Soviet regime between 1917 and 1991 went through enormous changes. As the political context changed, so did the propaganda themes, methods, and expectations of the activists. During the civil war, for example, the most significant Bolshevik venture in this field was sending trains and ships into the countryside, equipped with projectors and hastily, poorly made short agitational films. The revolutionaries correctly expected the peasant audience to be attracted by what must have seemed to them a miracle: a moving picture. Once the peasants assembled and were exposed to the primitive message of the films—the wickedness of the White enemy and the bright future that awaited workers and peasants—they were addressed by trained agitators, who conveyed the important and more complex propaganda themes. At this point, cinema was hardly more than a fairground attraction.

After the conclusion of the devastating civil war, Soviet studios were not in a position to produce feature films in sufficient numbers to be a significant component of the overall propaganda effort; Soviet theaters almost exclusively showed foreign and prerevolutionary films. It is clear from a letter written by Lenin in 1922 that the Bolshevik leader still thought of films primarily as a means of attracting an audience, and expected that the propaganda message would be delivered by newsreels and agitators. He did not realize that the feature film itself could become the most valuable instrument.

Only in the second half of the 1920s was the Soviet film industry sufficiently well developed to be able to become a significant component of the political education system. It was a golden age. Studios in Moscow and Leningrad as well as the capitals of the national republics turned out about 120 films a year. It was a time when Sergey Eisenstein, Lev Kuleshov, Vsevolod Pudovkin, and other talented directors acquired worldwide reputations and influenced filmmakers everywhere. The Bolsheviks insisted ever more strongly that every Soviet-made film should instruct in the spirit of socialism. Although Soviet cinema was widely admired, the Stalinist leadership was dissatisfied. The Bolsheviks considered film to be an excellent instrument for bringing their message to the people, and they intended to use it, more than any other medium of art, for creating the "new socialist man." The excessively high expectations were bound to lead to disappointment: films that were artistically successful and made in a Communist spirit did not attract a large enough audience. The Bolsheviks wanted artistically worthwhile, commercially successful, and politically correct films. It turned out that these requirements pointed in different directions, and no director could possibly satisfy them all.

The task was new, the demands unclear and contradictory, and it is not surprising that the situation occasioned passionate debates. The activists were disappointed with the performance of the Soviet film industry in its most glorious age. If we accept the self-evaluation of activists, film propaganda was a failure. Audiences preferred to see German and U.S. films rather than revolutionary spectacles.

The greatest change in the character of Soviet film occurred, as in all other aspects of Soviet life, with the introduction of collectivization, industrialization, urbanization, and the Cultural Revolution. From this time on, until the end of the Stalin era, the main task of Soviet cinema was—though it was never articulated as such—to create an "alternate reality"—that is, to show people not how life was but rather how life should have been. This was as much a negative as a positive role: the task of art was to deny reality, to cover up how people really lived, what really concerned them, and what they really thought. Because of the camera's ability to create an appearance of reality, cinema was especially powerful. The overall effect of Soviet films on the viewer was confusion; people, in some recesses of their minds, started to doubt their own perceptions. The variety available to the audiences greatly diminished: foreign films altogether disappeared from Soviet screens, and because of heavy censorship domestic industry was able to produce only about thirty to thirty-five films a year. At the same time cinema became widely available to Soviet audiences, and moviegoing, given the lack of other forms of entertainment, became extremely popular.

It is difficult to measure the success of Soviet film propaganda, partly because at different times it had different tasks, and partly because its ambition and nature varied greatly between films. Some films were made to persuade people to buy lottery tickets, wash their hands, or participate in sports; other, more ambitious movies aimed to increase patriotism, encourage people to work harder, and turn people into new socialist human beings. Propagandists were more likely to succeed when people had no direct ways to check the truthfulness of the message. The industry produced many films, for example, that showed the desperate plight of the unemployed in the West, and many Soviet people came to believe that the workers in capitalist countries lived in constant uncertainty. On the other hand, it was hardly possible to convince collective farm peasants that their life was gay and easy, and food abundant. Furthermore, it is obviously easier to sell ideas that are consistent with beliefs and values that people already hold than those that are not. During World War II, for instance, cinema made a great contribution to raising the morale of the Soviet peoples. The seventy-eight films that were made in the course of the war were all propaganda films in the sense that they depicted a brutal enemy and a heroic Soviet people. Conversely, today it is clear that the attempts to create a new humanity with the help of propaganda, or to persuade people to work harder for the benefit of community and the "glory of work," obviously failed. Socialist humanity was never born.

The precondition of genuine change was the removal of the tyrant by death, in March 1953. This was followed by profound changes in the political order. The revival of Soviet film came remarkably quickly; it was a part of the thaw that benefited every component of Soviet culture. In the mid-1950s, many of the old restrictions were lifted. Directors who had done interesting work in the distant past once again took advantage of the opportunity and returned to experimentation. New and talented directors had a chance to show what they could do. Artists turned to genuine issues and expressed themselves with passion. Cinema became heterogeneous. The output of the industry grew impressively. In the early 1970s, when cinema was most popular, thirty-nine Soviet studios made approximately 130 films yearly. Later, as television became widely available, the popularity of cinema declined. Although Soviet cinema never again achieved the worldwide acclaim it had enjoyed in the late 1920s, films once again became worth watching.

In the era of Khrushchev and Brezhnev, the freedom allowed to filmmakers varied not only from year to year but also from month to month. On occasion films appeared in theaters that more or less explicitly contradicted some of the claims of the propagandists, or even attacked the underlying principles of the regime. But at the same time first-rate films for no obvious reason were kept "in the can" for years—for example, *Andrei Rublev*, the work of the great director Andrei Tarkovskii. At least one director, Alexander Askoldov, the director of *Commissar*, was punished for his daring by complete exclusion from the film industry.

Because the Soviet system politicized all aspects of life and claimed credit for all achievements, a film that depicted the world more or less realistically, and thus pointed to problems, was inherently subversive. Directors depicted the gap in between generations and the loss of idealism among the young. Others showed the utter hypocrisy of Soviet political speech. Rolan Bykov's *Scarecrow* portrayed the dreariness of Soviet life, the triumph of materialist values, and took the side of the courageous individual against the corrupt collective. At the end of the Soviet era, Tengiz Abuladze's *Repentance* with its harsh denunciation of the Stalinist terror was practically a call to arms.

One wonders why the Soviet leaders who continued to censor political speech allowed a greater freedom of expression to filmmakers. Perhaps their liberalism was an expression of their own increasing self-doubts. The great irony of Soviet cinema is that it came into being largely as a propaganda instrument in the struggle for creating a new, socialist human being, but it ended up, decades later, as a subversive force further undermining the decrepit Soviet regime.

See also Avant-garde; Censorship; Cultural Policies; Eisenstein, Sergei; New Man; Propaganda, Communist; Socialist Realism; Television in the Soviet Era.

FURTHER READING

Christie, I., and R. Taylor. *Inside the Film Factory: New Approaches to Russian and Soviet Cinema*. London: Routledge, 1991.

Kenez, P. *Cinema and Soviet Society from the Revolution to the Death of Stalin.* Rev. ed. London: I. B. Tauris, 2001.

Leyda, J. *Kino: A History of the Russian and Soviet Film.* New York: Macmillan, 1960.

Taylor, R. *Film Propaganda: Soviet Russia and Nazi Germany.* 2nd ed. London: I. B. Tauris, 1998.

Woll, J. *Real Images: Soviet Cinema and the Thaw.* London: I. B. Tauris, 2000.

Youngblood, D. J. *Soviet Cinema in the Silent Era.* Ann Arbor, MI: UMI Research Press, 1985.

———. *Movies for the Masses: Popular Cinema and Soviet Society in the 1920s.* Cambridge, UK: Cambridge University Press, 1992.

PETER KENEZ

Citizenship

Theoretical Profile

Here, "citizenship" means both belonging to a state, and the rights and obligations that derive from this condition. The first part of the definition deals with an ascriptive category that establishes the criteria for national affiliation, and the second with a prescriptive category of civil and political rights along with the eventual social standards that the state guarantees its members. As a political theory, communism does not admit any distinction between these two aspects of citizenship; they have, however, triggered a contradictory dynamic in the history of socialist states.

On a theoretical level, communism aims to integrate all human civilization into a single political community of equals within which all members would enjoy the same status and rights. For Marx and Engels, communism aspired to emancipate human beings from nature's bonds, from exploitation and alienation, and to establish a free and equitable social order in which the rule "from each according to their ability, to each according to their need" would be realized. In this sense we can say that communism seeks to eliminate citizenship as a legal category, by making it superfluous. Marx and Engels criticized the formal equality of rights characteristic of the liberal tradition as a false consciousness that masked real class relationships in bourgeois society—hence the demand, during the Second International, for the implementation of rights that would counteract the

inequalities determined by the market. While in capitalist countries this would give rise to special protections on a category-by-category basis, one from whose generalization the so-called social rights would be derived (T. H. Marshall), in the countries of "real socialism" the overcoming of "bourgeois law" as well as the establishment of a political system based on work and collective property would provide the appropriate guarantees, or so it was thought.

The socialist state's goals, modeled on the Soviet experience, were progressively identified with the scientific version of historical materialism elaborated by Lenin and Stalin (Marxism-Leninism). The Soviet concept of democracy was of a positivist, holistic, and organicist origin. Socialism would create the *good* citizen. This transformed the law into ethics and the Leninist party into the ultimate arbiter of the people's will. It also postulated an identity of interests between individuals and society, and between society and the socialist state. Alienation and exploitation were explained as the results of private property and profit, which socialism remedied by means of collective property and a rational, planned development of resources. Rights were conceived as social positive rights given by the state, without a metapolitical natural law or theological foundation. Freedom was considered an attribute of socialist societies, arising from the recognition of its historical necessity. Individual freedom was stigmatized as lawless, and no rights that contrasted with the state were admitted.

In this view, democracy came to be reduced to the social standards promised to all workers and their families: full employment, the right to a home, health care, education, and coverage for disability, illness, and old age. The construction of socialism was translated into material terms: the creation of a surplus from production sufficient to satisfy collective needs. At the end of this palingenetic perspective one finds a contractualist concept of citizenship (state-people).

In Soviet legal theory (Pashukanis, Stucka) citizenship was thus reduced to affiliation. Individual rights were grounded in socialist democracy and the fulfillment of one's duties toward it. Up to the 1930s the law was considered a bourgeois remnant that survived in Soviet society during the transition to communism, but it did not apply to the sphere of the socialist state. In the Labor Code of November 1918, work became an obligation people owed to the state, and a failure to perform it well exposed the worker to charges of sabotage or betrayal. The exercise of political rights was geared toward the defense of the revolution. This entailed an enormous margin of bureaucratic discretion, because of both the dependence of the magistracy on political power and the absence of an administrative jurisdiction.

Leninist orthodoxy was the vehicle for this conception of absolute power. Considering the state exclusively as an instrument of class domination and law as a fetish, Leninism was not able to provide justifications for the state's existence except through force. In a classless socialist society, and one that is therefore devoid of antagonisms, the reasons for domination and exploitation should have in fact disappeared, and nothing should have been able to justify the survival of the state, legislation, and coercion. Aspiring to suicide—the "extinction" of the state mentioned by Engels (in *Antidühring*)—the revolutionary state represented its own worst threat. Class conflict within the country and the imperialist conflict(s) outside it were thus essential to the perpetuation of the state, and they were consistently invoked—starting with Lenin—to consolidate the Bolshevik Party. Civil rights were first subordinated to the achievement of social equality and the nationalization of the means of production, and then to forced industrialization. The failure to achieve socialist economic objectives could only be attributed to the enemy, sabotage, or adverse conditions. Attributing internal contradictions to objective causes justified the limitation of rights.

The construction of "socialism in one country" turned the original objective of the state's extinction on its head, redefining its purposes in terms of security. Under Stalin, socialism stabilized and became a transitional stage in which it was not possible to fully enjoy the rights of citizenship until the state had been strengthened. With the advent of planning, the notion of "socialist legality" also became established: it saw the law no longer as a fiction but rather as a legitimate coercive power of the ruling class. This view fed the ascriptive side of the concept of citizenship, and aimed at the complete nationalization of the economy, thus abandoning Marx's aspirations to the autonomy of producers and cultural pluralism.

Even though in varied forms, the aforementioned dualism of the concept of citizenship can be found once more in the experiences of those socialist states that came about after World War II, Marxism-Leninism was the point of reference for anti-imperialist and revolutionary liberation movements, which in turn entailed a clear predominance of national or ethnic affiliation in Asia and Africa. In China with the socialist modernization undertaken in 1978, the principal theoretical justification that was invoked was that the "fundamental contradiction," was no longer between labor and capital but instead between the growing needs of the population and the country's technical backwardness.

Although postulated by socialist states as already having been resolved and as such neglected in their legal theory, citizenship has constituted *the* problem for these states' legitimation.

Historical Profile
Affiliation

The *Declaration of Rights of Russia's Peoples* (1917), one of the Soviet state's first acts, proclaimed the equality, sovereignty, and self-determination of Russia's peoples, including their right to secede; the abolition of all privileges based on ethnicity and religion; and the freedom of national minorities. The civil war made this program less current, but it did indelibly mark the way Soviet power represented itself.

With its Constitution of 1924, the USSR established a single federal citizenship for all its republics, and a latent dualism between citizenship in the union and the individual republics, whose resolution was entrusted to the "Chamber of Nationalities."

The USSR distinction between republican and federal citizenship was valid as regards civil effects and family law, whereas in criminal law it was not recognized. Characteristic of Soviet citizenship was its originally universalistic character, deriving from proletarian internationalism, and for this reason any foreign worker could obtain it by submitting a request to the Supreme Soviet of the USSR or one of its republics. Citizenship in the union was presumed to be freely chosen: it could be acquired not only by bloodline (at least one of the citizen's parents) or by being born in its territory (naturalization) but also merely due to residence. It was an obligatory attribute of all people present in the territory of the ex-czarist empire in November 1917, unless they could prove a different citizenship. Attribution of citizenship was a sovereign act: it required exclusive loyalty to the state, and dual citizenship was not admitted. Equality of the sexes made mixed marriage (forbidden from February 1947 to November 1953) an accidental attribute and insufficient to affect citizenship. One could not renounce it, but one could lose it due to prolonged absence from the territory, identified with opposition to the revolution or because of crimes against the state.

This pseudoelective connotation disappeared with the resolutions on citizenship by the presidium of the Supreme Soviet of the USSR in November 1930 and April 1931, which led to ethnic affiliation (*ius sanguinis*) prevailing. The law on citizenship of August 19, 1938, which enacted article 21 of the Constitution of 1936, and remained in effect for over forty years, completed the work of the prior resolutions. It was nationalist in character and further enhanced the discretionary power of federal authorities. Even though the article sanctioned the equality of rights of nations and ethnic groups, it distinguished between federal and autonomous republics and allowed the demographic, economic, and political weight of Russia even greater freedom to assert itself. Article 21 restricted the possible paths to naturalization, retroactively created a large group of stateless people who were exposed to persecutions, distinguished between the position of minors and that of parents, allowed for the renunciation of citizenship only with the authorization of the Supreme Soviet, and marked the definitive supremacy of federal over republican citizenship, reflecting a general limitation in the sovereignty of the republics. In those territories acquired after 1939, this ethnic conception of citizenship was instrumental in forced assimilation and massive population transfers.

After 1945 in multiethnic socialist states, ascriptive citizenship masked the gap between the legal nation, internationalist and geared to the working class, and the real nation, still partly peasant in nature and often composed of ethnic groups hostile to the dominant group, and it thus impeded reciprocal cooperation.

Rights and Obligations

The Soviet revolution introduced an integral and organic concept of citizenship founded on labor. The *Declaration of the Rights of the Exploited and Working People* (January 1919)—incorporated into the constitutions that followed—proclaimed Russia to be the republic of the soviets of workers, soldiers, and peasants. The source of power lay exclusively in the working population, with the soviets as their organ. The declaration stated that the purpose of the Soviet state was the abolition of exploitation, elimination of classes, establishment of a socialist society, and victory of socialism around the world. Private property in land was abolished, and natural resources, forests, and banks were nationalized. At the same time, obligatory conscriptions to work and join Red Army were also established in the declaration.

The Bolshevik Constitution promised labor unions that they would control companies (socialization) and that factories would be self-managed. Assurances were given to the working class that it would be given the means to realize its new rights of citizenship: freedom of speech would be accompanied by access to print shops, the right of assembly guaranteed by the availability of suitable meeting places, and the right to education by free instruction. For the first time in history the right to work, free health care, pensions, and paid vacations were guaranteed to all workers. The abolition of inequalities entailed the absolute parity of the sexes and a politically active role for women insofar as they were workers. These innovations would be supported by an innovative Code of Family Rights (1918), and protections for maternity and childhood (family checks, paid vacations before and after childbirth, kindergartens at places of work, and so on).

In 1918, the dissolution of the Constituent Assembly restricted political freedoms. The "dictatorship of the proletariat," which Marx (*Critique of the Gotha Programme*) pointed to as the last stage of capitalist development before the establishment of communism, was understood from the inception of the First Constitution of the Russian Soviet Federative Socialist Republic in July 1918 as the concentration of powers in a central organ, the Pan-Russian Congress of Soviets, and its executive organ, the Council of People's Commissars. The dictatorship of the proletariat had to create the new society. The door was therefore opened to a dual form of democracy: repressive toward the old ruling classes, and pedagogical toward the peasants and the petty bourgeoisie. Electoral law reflected this pedagogical mission by overrepresenting urban areas. The 1918 Constitution also contemplated the exclusion from political rights of whoever impeded the interests of the socialist revolution (article 23), most especially the exploiting classes (article 65)—in other words, capitalists and landowners, whose civil rights were also limited. Since one could not do without their technical skills, however, the exploiting classes represented a constant counterrevolutionary danger that was to be held in check by the people's tribunals. Looking for "parasitic" minorities who deprived citizens of their right to equality, the war dictatorship created a repressive apparatus, centered in the political police, which could be employed against the entire population.

Within the Soviet leadership, a disagreement about citizenship emerged, centered on the choice between the New Economic Policy and planning. While Lenin and Nikolay Bukharin saw the dictatorship of the proletariat as a provisional phase leading to the liberation *of the workers*, Stalin (*Principles of Leninism*, 1924) theorized socialism as the *national* liberation of the less-developed countries, oppressed by imperialism. Internationalism no longer consisted in class solidarity but rather in aiding the national movements of oppressed countries with the goal of unifying the various nationalities in a single federal state. Nationalization replaced socialization. Having been progressively alienated in favor of the party, citizenship rights were emptied due to the progressive weakening of the local soviets. The party statutes (1917, 1926, 1934, 1939, 1952, and 1961) reflected the material makeup of the political dimension of citizenship.

The Constitution of 1936 substituted the people for the local soviets as the basis of power and introduced direct universal suffrage by secret ballot in place of an indirect suffrage for election to the Supreme Soviet. Electoral rights were handed back to ex-capitalists. A single electoral list was created whose only trick was an excess number of candidacies equal to half the available positions. The candidacies had to be screened by the party or collateral organizations (labor unions, cooperatives, and so on). The guiding role of the party thus became part of the Constitution. The socialist property of the soil, forests, factories, workshops, and instruments of production was sanctioned. Unemployment, misery, and exploitation were declared to have been suppressed; social rights like that to work (a right and an obligation), rest, and education were confirmed. Private property of one's home and consumer goods were allowed, and so was their hereditary transmission, which had been abolished between 1918 and 1922.

The principle "from each according to their ability, to each according to their need" was applied, thereby justifying differentials in salary, status, and the enjoyment of rights; only in a later phase would such inequalities be reduced. A differentiated system was created for the distribution of wealth that penalized the countryside and rewarded the intellectual and technological elite as well as the highest ranks of the military and bureaucracy. At the same time the nationalization of the means of production, complete in industry and only partial in agriculture, entailed broadening the category of worker, and therefore also that of fundamental rights, so as to include all citizens and not only the "working class," as in the Constitution of 1918. Mothers and housewives became workers too. The right to work was made more inclusive: this was not just a generic right to some form of employment, as in some Fascist states, but to a job that suited one's capabilities and education as well.

Many rights were only to be enjoyed on paper; the freedom of movement, for example, was abolished by the bond that tied workers to their company, and by the separation of country and city imposed by the notorious registration of one's residence (*propiska*), established in czarist times and abolished in 1917, but reintroduced in December 1932.

After the defeat of fascism in many Western countries, socialist citizenship became a reference point for the introduction of the welfare state and limits on private property. The Universal Declaration of Human Rights in 1948 along with the two international conventions on civil and political rights as well as economic, social, and cultural rights in 1966 embodied some of its principles. The Soviet model of citizenship of 1936 was reused by the "people's democracies" in central Eastern Europe after 1945. Starting in 1956, the end of "capitalist encirclement" and the state's full control of the economy undermined the justifications that had been invoked for the limitation of rights. Yet the revolts that occurred in Poland and Hungary in 1956, the Prague Spring of 1968, and the requests by Georg Lukàcs, Aleksandr Solzhenitsyn, and Václav Havel for a "socialism with a human face" were all attributed to capitalist influence.

The USSR most especially did not succeed in conceiving of the possibility of abandoning the priorities accorded to security and instead focusing on the enactment of citizenship rights, without falling back on the dilemma of the state's extinction. Attempts at reform were undermined by the implications of ascriptive citizenship and its guarantor, the party. The international accords in Helsinki in 1975 introduced protections for individual freedom of thought that although embodied in the Soviet Constitution of 1977—in which the list of fundamental civil, social, and cultural rights was extended—were not respected given the repressive measures undertaken against dissent. The Danzig Accords of August 31, 1980, included the freedom to strike and freedom of choice in union representation, but they were suspended by the Polish government on December 13, 1981, and enacted slowly starting in 1984. Mikhail Gorbachev's perestroika introduced freedom of thought, the free market, and pluralism in representation in the 1980s, without eliminating the Communist Party of the Soviet

Union's monopoly on power. With the dissolution of the USSR and its allies between 1989 and 1991, the extinction of the socialist state came to fruition instead.

In China, with the absorption of Hong Kong and Macao as well as the opening to the outside world, Deng Xiaoping partially renewed Stalin's and Mao Zedong's ideas: the two systems could coexist on the same territory without negatively affecting one another. In the Chinese Constitution of 1982, citizens' rights for the first time preceded the section on the organization of the state. Yet their enjoyment was limited by "the interests of the State, society and the collectivity," the rights of other citizens (article 51), and "sabotage of the socialist system" (article 1).

See also Constitutions; Marxism-Leninism; Nationality Policies; Single-Party System; Social Policy; State, The.

FURTHER READING

Blackburn, R., and J. Polakiewicz, eds. *Fundamental Rights in Europe: The European Convention on Human Rights and Its Member States, 1950–2000.* Oxford: Oxford University Press, 2001.

Ginsburgs, G. *Soviet Citizenship Law.* Leyden: Sijthoff, 1968.

Procacci, G. *Il partito nell'Unione sovietica, 1917–1945.* Rome: Laterza, 1975.

Schlesinger, R. *Soviet Legal Theory: Its Social Background and Development.* London: K. Paul, Trench, Trubner, 1946.

Triska, J. F., ed. *Constitutions of the Communist Party-States.* Stanford, CA: Stanford University Press, 1968.

CARLO SPAGNOLO

Classes

Classes were the most fundamental concept in the Communist theoretical and political thinking. The Communist class analysis was predicated on Marx's understanding of capitalism, its cruelty, promise, and historical role. Paradoxical as it may sound, Communists saw capitalism as salvational. The capitalist stage of history could not be skipped because it was capitalism that pulled people out of their state of ignorance and pushed them, now conscious, into the world. The suffering inflicted on humanity was accepted for the sake of the accompanying enlightenment. The effects of capitalism, Communists argued, were "dialectical": tearing people from the immediacy of their vocations and dehumanizing them, capitalism gave people a chance to transgress their specific, limited predicament and rise to universalism.

The immediate impact of capitalism was negative. Emancipated from the bonds of instinct, humanity was hurried into the new bondage of capital—an abstract, impersonal force that urges the human subject to produce and consume at an ever faster rate, imprisoning people in a circle of meaningless activity. Fortunately, this situation, identified with the rule of the class of the bourgeois proprietors, the sole owners of the means of production, was destined to be reversed. While perfecting itself, capitalism inadvertently but inexorably produced the social forces that brought on its own demise. Marx declared that "the development of modern history cuts from under the bourgeoisie's feet its own foundation." Not only would capitalism have "forged the weapons that bring death to itself; it would call into existence the men who are to wield those weapons, its own gravediggers." With the help of the messianic agents that capitalism itself brought into being, capitalism was to be dismantled, the genie of constantly expanding production was to be tamed, and labor was to become a vehicle of human self-expression.

But once Marx had come to the conclusion that narrow, interest-driven consciousness—the great hindrance to salvation—was derived from a material source (private property), he realized that reason alone could not destroy particularity and ensure the triumph of salvational universalism. In recognizing that emancipation required not only an idea but also a material force to embody it, Marx confronted the problem of power. As he put it in his famous phrase, "Ideas cannot carry out anything at all. In order to carry out ideas men are needed who can exert practical force." Emancipation could be brought about only if the Marxist salvational message "gripped the masses." Universalist philosophy needed a lever, an agent who would convey reason and universalist consciousness to the living world.

The task of serving as the lever of human emancipation, the material force that was to implement Marx's teaching, was to fall to the proletariat—the class messiah in the Marxist mythology. The struggle of the proletariat against the bourgeoisie was declared to be the motor of the historical process. Placed in the center of production, in the center of society, the proletariat was said to bear the tasks of human emancipation on its shoulders. The switch to a proletarian perspective produced stupendous results because, as the Communists explained, only the class that exploits no one, the class that strives to abolish all exploitation in society, was capable of discovering the true, steady links between the various facets of social relations. Propertyless, the proletariat alone was endowed with undistorted epistemology, alone able to perceive reality objectively though the Marxist lens.

It is the Marxist notion of history as a specifically redemptive process that explains what made the proletariat unique in Marx's eyes. In the manuscripts of the 1840s, Marx described the proletariat as "not the naturally arising poor but the artificially impoverished, not the human masses mechanically oppressed by the gravity of society, but the masses resulting from the drastic dissolution of society." The proletarians were those excluded from the true community of human beings and thus deprived of their human nature. Marx believed that the disastrous isolation from this essential nature is incomparably more universal, more intolerable, more dreadful, and more contradictory than mere isolation from the political community. Hence, too, the abolition of this isolation—even a partial reaction to it, an uprising against it—is just as much more infinite.

The Marxists were adamant that the industrial proletariat was the only possible candidate for the role of messiah. To be sure, by splitting humans in two, the industrial machine degraded the worker. Yet without it, the future producer qua integrated human was impossible. Tearing human faculties asunder, separating between manual and mental labor, and causing immeasurable pain in the process, capitalism had to be endured because it opened up the possibility of a later conscious reintegration of human faculties in the face of the true proletarian and the socialized labor process.

Though the Bolsheviks took power in Russia in 1917 in the name of the proletariat, it was unclear who the true proletarians were and how they could be identified. Those who did not fit the bill were easier to identify. These were first and foremost those who belonged to the ruling classes of the old regime—the nobility, the bourgeoisie, and the clergy—as well as the new, New Economic Policy bourgeoisie and the remnants of the old intelligentsia. But it was much harder to describe the ideal proletarian that the Soviet regime sought to promote. The simplest definition equated proletarian with the propertyless manual laborer. Yet the Bolsheviks were aware that such a definition would render the country in which they carried out the first proletarian revolution insufficiently proletarian, since manual laborers were scarce. The majority of the population of

the Soviet Union of the 1920s was described as peasants, so there was a discussion about whether or not peasants were proletarians of sorts. Some Bolshevik social scientists believed that the claim could be made for at least a part of the rural population. Little, they claimed, distinguished workers who sold their labor in the cities from landless agricultural laborers who did the same in the countryside. Eventually, official sociologists worked out a compound definition—some peasants, and not only industrial workers, deserved the honorable title of proletarian.

What could be said about the other classes present in Lenin's and Stalin's Soviet Union, the peasantry and the intelligentsia? Examined in its own right, the peasantry turned out also to be a complex entity that included poor peasants, the middling peasants, and the peasant exploiters, the notorious kulaks. The last category was made up of those who took advantage of agricultural laborers in the villages and those who were clearly not proletarians. The poor and the middle peasants were perceived as proletarian to the extent that they lived off their own work. The intelligentsia proved an even more difficult category to define in class terms. Before 1917, the intelligentsia, at least its revolutionary wing, was well regarded by the Marxists. But the revolution stripped the term of its positive meaning as the bearer of proletarian class consciousness and left the intelligentsia only with the negative meaning of a selfish intellectual caste. Now the intelligentsia was a questionable ally of the working class at best and a dangerous fifth column at worst. Still, the intelligentsia retained a tinge of its former messianic sense in the 1920s and the early 1930s. Insofar as the revolution was yet incomplete, the nation's working class shrunken and dispersed, the Bolsheviks had to set about to create a new proletarian vanguard, a "new intelligentsia" (*novaia intelligentsiia*) coming from its own ranks, an intelligentsia that was unquestioningly loyal to the party. If the party held the old intelligentsia in contempt, it regarded the new intelligentsia as a healthy outgrowth of the proletarian dictatorship.

A watershed in Soviet history, Stalin's Constitution of 1936 pronounced that a nearly classless society had been laid and a second phase of development of the Soviet state had begun. The exploitation of man by man was a matter of the past, and classes were declared basically liquidated. The proletariat was not abolished but transcended—the Soviet worker metamorphosed into the Stalinist New Man, a creature with improved emotional and cognitive capacities. A full classless society, however, was still around the corner. This, according to party propagandists, was because some vestiges of capitalism in the economy and consciousness persisted. Stalin's Constitution divided Soviet society into two main classes—workers and peasants—and an intelligentsia layer. While there were no more "contradictions" (*protivorechiia*) between classes, "differences" (*razlichiia*) between classes remained. The extinction of the separation between agricultural and industrial labor, and between manual and mental labor, had to await the complete victory of communism.

Among the most conspicuous omissions in the late 1930s' political discussion was the subject of class, now largely irrelevant to the appraisal of individual identities. On the one hand, the politburo allowed the children of kulaks to obtain passports and granted class aliens equal opportunities in education and employment; on the other hand, it characterized those who insisted on resisting the triumphal march of communism not as "class aliens" but rather as "enemies of the people." Thanks to the end of class struggle and the now evident individual response to the Communist calling—some chose the side of good (Stalin) and others the side of evil (Trotsky), class analysis, the alpha and omega of Marxism, became basically irrelevant. Class position, the starting point of the voyage toward the light, turned out to be little more than an index of the individual's subjective moral properties; it no longer predicted moral choice, only registered it after the fact.

In order to expose his or her moral core, each and every individual had to be brought into the spotlight. Yet no amount of enlightenment could reform the one who chose evil. Was communism, then, a universalist or particularist creed? Scholars who see it as universalist point to its general appeal: official theoreticians posited that offspring of all classes could assume the proletarian perspective and be redeemed. Scholars who believe otherwise prefer to highlight the identification of the Communist gospel with a single class: the proletariat. Ultimately, the issue hinges on the relation between class and ethics. Marxist class theory may be seen as an attempt to recast as a scientific challenge a key moral question that Christianity had left unresolved: How would one respond to the salvational call? Marxism, argue those who stress Communist particularism, prided itself on the discovery of a key regularity: workers tend to embrace communism; bourgeoisie tend to reject it. Their universalist opponents respond that this presentation is misleading: communism never maintained in such a sweeping fashion that class affiliation and ethical disposition always went hand in hand. The party believed it was quite possible that a particular worker will be a carrier of a petit bourgeois ideology. Party historians marshaled a long list of workers who had turned out to be hopelessly wicked: worker Mensheviks, worker oppositionists, and in the most extreme cases, agent provocateurs. Inversely, an offspring of a nonproletarian class could adopt a proletarian outlook—with Marx and Lenin being the obvious cases in point.

Stalin himself can be cited to the effect that "all classes can potentially be integrated into Communist society." The general secretary urged members of the military council in June 1937 to judge individuals by their deeds and not their class:

> General criteria, wholly accurate when describing classes, are totally inapplicable to individuals. When we speak of nobles' hostility to the laboring people, we mean the nobility as a class. . . . But that does not mean that certain individuals who are from the nobility, like Lenin, cannot serve the working class. . . . Engels was the son of a factory owner—also a non-proletarian element, if you will. Marxism is not a biological science, but a sociological one.

At first glance, it is surprising to find Stalin, then in the midst of a frantic search for the internal enemy, stressing that class could be transcended. But this universalism melted into thin air as soon as Stalin came to deal not with unconscious human conglomerates—classes—but with discrete individuals who had elected to support the enemy. Universal conversion, so went his core assumption, was impossible because conversion to communism was constantly competing with and taking place parallel to conversion to counterrevolution.

See also Dictatorship of the Proletariat; Enemies of the People; Intelligentsia; Internationalism; Kulak; Marxism-Leninism; New Man; Workers.

FURTHER READING

Balibar, E. *Masses, Classes, Ideas: Studies on Politics and Philosophy before and after Marx.* London: Routledge, 1994.

Bussard, R. L. *The "Dangerous Class" of Marx and Engels: The Rise of the Idea of the Lumpenproletariat.* Oxford: Pergamon, 1987.

Fitzpatrick, S. *Education and Social Mobility in the Soviet Union, 1921–1934.* Cambridge, UK: Cambridge University Press, 1975.

Lovell, D. W. *Marx's Proletariat: The Making of a Myth.* London: Routledge, 1988.

Marx, K. *Class Struggles in France, 1848–1850.* New York: International Publishers, 1964.

———. *Capital: A Critique of Political Economy.* 3 vols. London: Penguin, 1992–93.

———. *Grundrisse: Foundations of the Critique of Political Economy.* London: Penguin, 1993.

Marx, K., and F. Engels. *The Economic and Philosophic Manuscripts of 1844 and the Communist Manifesto.* Amherst, NY: Prometheus Books, 1988.

Shanin, T. *The Awkward Class: Political Sociology of Peasantry in a Developing Society: Russia, 1910–1925.* Oxford: Oxford University Press, 1972.

Siegelbaum, L. H., and R. G. Suny, ed. *Making Workers Soviet: Power, Class, and Identity.* Ithaca, NY: Cornell University Press, 1995.

Solomon, S. G. *Controversy in Social Science: Soviet Rural Studies in the 1920s.* London: Minerva, 1973.

Wessell, L. P. *Karl Marx, Romantic Irony, and the Proletariat: The Mythopoetic Origins of Marxism.* Baton Rouge: Louisiana State University Press, 1979.

IGAL HALFIN

Clientelism

One of the principal means of analyzing Communist societies has been through notions of clientelism, or patron-client relations. Clientelism refers to a relationship between at least two actors in which the glue of the relationship is the exchange of mutual favors. The relationship rests on a personal basis, although this does not necessarily mean that each party knows the other personally; rather, they support one another and provide the other with particular resources of value that in theory, they may not otherwise be able to obtain. Clientelism has been identified in all societies and a wide range of organizational structures, but it has been seen to be particularly important in Communist societies, and not only in the political realm.

Politically, the sources of clientelism lie in the lack of normative authority of the rules that purport to govern political life and the consequent lack of security enjoyed by officeholders throughout much of the lives of these regimes. Also important is the lack of transparency with which positions of responsibility were filled. The principal form of political clientelism was the vertical symbi-

otic relationship between patron and clients in which the higher-level patron provided promotion (and thereby access to increased material goods) and protection in exchange for support for the patron and their policies in party forums. The patron would use the powers of office and in particular the capacity to make appointments (see below) to ensure as much as possible that party bodies contained a significant number of the patron's supporters. In those bodies, the patron's clients supported the patron both in any political conflicts in which the patron was involved and in terms of the policy lines with which the patron was associated. This sort of dyadic relationship could spread right up the political hierarchy, with a patron at one level being the client of a patron at a higher level. It was this mechanism that many have seen as crucial in the rise to power of Stalin.

The main organizational mechanism which made this possible was the *nomenklatura* system. Formally, this was the principal personnel regime within the party. It comprised two lists held by party organs at all levels of the structure: one was a list of positions that it was within the competence of that particular party organ to fill, and the other was a list of the people who were qualified to fill those positions. The higher up the political structure one went, the more important the positions a particular party organ was able to fill. Control over the power to appoint to positions was thus a major weapon of personal power, and it was routinely used to promote supporters into positions of influence throughout the structure under one's control. With appointment from above the main way of filling positions, even those formally subject to election, this opened the way for its use as a means of ensuring the consolidation of support at lower levels.

In some instances, patron-client relations could have their sources in common attitudes toward particular policy issues. Such relations, however, usually were rooted in more personal factors, and especially personal ambition. Given that positions were not filled through elections but by appointment from above, anyone who wanted political advancement needed the support and patronage of someone in a position to bring about the appointment or promotion. This might come about through the personal knowledge of the patron, perhaps acquired through earlier working relationships with the client or because both came from the same geographic area, or it may arise through the recommendation of an existing client. The latter route reflects the complexity that could characterize a long set of patron-client relations, with many people being both patron and client simultaneously.

The prominence of patron-client links undercut the formal structures of power and responsibility. As personal loyalty to a patron became a prime consideration for lower-level officials, the formal structures and processes of the political system were subverted. What became critical was the satisfaction of the demands of one's patron rather than the formal principles whereby the system was meant to function. But this created an uncertain existence: a client's position was dependent on the continuing power of the patron and the continuing satisfaction of their wishes. The formal structures did not have the institutional authority or integrity to defend a client against either a change in attitude on the part of the patron or the wrath of the patron's successful enemies. This absence of institutional certainty, added to the principles of clientelism, opened the way for the development throughout all of the Communist parties of small groups whose autonomy was seen as a threat by the party leadership. Such groups and their activities went by various names in different parts of the Communist world and at different times: family groups, factions, localists, and cliques were some of the epithets used to describe them. These were essentially self-protective and self-advancement mechanisms, resting on the personal basis of clientelism, which were formed by subordinate officials to both consolidate their hold on a specific region and defend themselves against attack from without and above. By controlling all of the avenues of information into and out of their particular region and through the projection of often falsified information about their performance, clients hoped to keep their patrons happy and give their enemies no reason for attack. Such groups became at various times in different states the real powers in the local regions, and what kept them hooked into the center was their part in the long chains of patrons and clients that spanned the party structure.

Many have claimed that this sort of clientelism was a form of corruption, because it subverted the formal institutional channels and replaced them with a form of politics based on personal loyalty and association. But the way the Communist system was established from the outset meant that this mode of operating was the norm. The appeal to personal loyalty, development of personal followings, and use of the personnel mechanism as a weapon were characteristic of Communist parties even before they got to power, and this quality was merely strengthened once power had been achieved. The reliance on personal support and the promotion of followers into positions from which they could proffer such support was therefore not alien to the regimes' operating principles but was embedded in those principles from the start. Clientelism was thus not a corruption of the way the system operated but rather its essence. In this sense, what would have been alien would have been a drive to make the formal institutional norms the actual rules of the game whereby Communist politics functioned.

Clientelism was also evident outside the political system. Leading figures in all walks of life acted as patrons of others, facilitating their access to the resources of the Communist state and assisting them to go about their lives. This was especially noteworthy in the arts. Sometimes leading political figures acted as the patrons of cultural figures, giving them political protection when necessary and perhaps facilitating their pursuit of their craft. In a nonmarket system where administrative controls were omnipresent, a powerful political patron could make life much easier for an artist and thereby contribute to the cultural development of the state. In return, such client artists could burnish the public image of their patrons, as manifested most clearly in the cults of personality that blossomed in many of the Communist states, including Stalin's USSR, Mao's China, Ceaușescu's Romania, and Ho's Vietnam.

Clientelism was therefore a major element in Communist societies. Even at the day-to-day level of ordinary citizens, these sorts of contacts were necessary for the pursuit of their lives. Possessing contacts who could provide benefits, usually in exchange for other benefits, was essential to get by in a satisfactory fashion in the consumer goods–deficit economies of most Communist states. Personal relationships—the development of patron-client arrangements—were thus central to the functioning of the Communist system. Rather than being an abuse of that system, they lay at its very heart.

See also Bureaucracy; Cult of Personality; Nomenklatura; Single-Party System.

FURTHER READING

"Clientelism." *Studies in Comparative Communism* 12, nos. 2–3 (1979): 159–211.

Gill, G., and R. Pitty. *Power in the Party: The Organization of Power and Central-Republican Relations in the CPSU*. Basingstoke, UK: Macmillan, 1997.

Holmes, L. *The End of Communist Power: Anti-Corruption Campaigns and Legitimation Crisis*. Melbourne: Melbourne University Press, 1993.

Rigby, T. H., and B. Harasymiw. *Leadership Selection and Patron-Client Relations in the USSR and Yugoslavia.* London: Allen and Unwin, 1983.

GRAEME GILL

Cold War

The term "Cold War" is most generally used to describe the period of confrontation between the United States and the Soviet Union—often referred to as the "superpowers"—between the end of World War II and the Eastern and Central European revolutions of 1989. It is also used more broadly as a term for the conflict between capitalist and socialist ideologies worldwide and for European and American attempts at containing the Soviet Union after the Bolshevik revolution of 1917. During the Cold War era, the term was typically used to describe what were seen as consistently confrontational actions by the other side. Neither the Americans nor the Soviets acknowledged that *they themselves* were engaged in waging Cold War against their opponents. Today the term is increasingly becoming the name of an era or an époque, thus freeing itself from the opprobrium it at first conveyed.

Revolution and Cold War

After the 1917 Russian revolutions, the governments of the main capitalist states in Western Europe, America, and East Asia feared the spread of Bolshevism to their own countries and to the areas they controlled. Their interventions in the Russian civil war were intended to discourage the involvement of the Soviet government in social movements outside its own borders, rather than to effect the overthrow of the Bolshevik regime per se. In the wake of World War I, as left-wing parties mobilized for change all over Europe and anticolonial parties began organizing in Asia, the established regimes believed that with assistance from the Soviet Union the revolutionaries in their own countries and empires would have a good chance at succeeding. If such revolutions were to be avoided, Lenin's party would have to be contained and the Soviet state isolated.

The Soviet government, for its part, also believed in the international imperative of the Bolshevik revolution. Without support from revolutionary socialist governments that would come into power elsewhere in Europe, Lenin believed, the Soviet regime would not be able to survive. The 1920/21 Soviet intervention in Poland was an attempt at pushing the necessary historical developments in the right direction. The Comintern, formed in 1919, had as its mission assisting other Communist parties, which were coming into existence inspired by the Russian Bolsheviks, to develop their organization and policies following the Russian model. The Soviet government also set aside considerable amounts of money to help revolutionaries in other countries. Lenin never tired of underlining the *internationalism* of the Russian Revolution. The Bolsheviks did not differentiate, he claimed, between workers of different nationalities, countries, or empires.

The struggle between the Bolshevik Revolution and its opponents was therefore international from its very beginning in 1917. The Cold War was based on a clash between opposing visions of how the world should be organized; one revolutionary, proletarian, and egalitarian; the other ensconced, capitalist, and market-oriented. In the early 20th century, these two broad ideological camps formed themselves in deliberate contrast to one another and within a belief system that allowed for the future survival of only *one* of them.

Stalinism and Cold War

With Stalin's coming to power within the Soviet Communist Party in the mid- to late 1920s, Moscow increasingly gave up on the expectation that revolutions would soon take place in the main capitalist countries and began curtailing its internationalist ambitions, at least for the short term. Stalin believed that the international Communist movement's primary task was to help protect the Soviet Union. He also hoped that divisions within the capitalist world—which he had scouted for eagerly since the early 1920s—would prevent an all-out attempt at crushing the Soviet Union. Stalin saw the advent of Italian fascism and German national-socialism in exactly such a light, and his alliance policies of the mid- and late 1930s were intended to play one group of capitalist states against another, thereby increasing Soviet security.

Stalin not only failed in his alliance policies, but also missed the key change in the global political and economic system of the late interwar period: the rise of the United States as the dominant capitalist power. Even as late as 1945, when his belated alliance with the democratic capitalist states had helped him save the Soviet revolution from the German onslaught, Stalin still believed that the postwar world would be dominated by competition between the Western powers, first and foremost the United States and Great Britain. The Soviet strategy was therefore to secure a buffer zone of control in Eastern Europe in the postwar carve-up of the world by Washington and London, a zone that Stalin believed his Western allies would not object to, given the methods their own rivalries would lead them to use in securing their possessions against each other.

With the advent of the United States as the hegemonic capitalist power of the postwar period, Stalin's attempts at controlling Eastern Europe came to be seen primarily through the lens of the most ideologized of the capitalist powers. In Washington, the Truman administration interpreted the Eastern European Communist parties' crushing of their oppositions as a clear sign that Soviet foreign policy was aggressive and intent on eventually controlling all of Europe. The right-wing and social-democratic governments of Western Europe did their best to further these perspectives vis-à-vis the Americans, who were, they believed, the only power that could help them retain their postions if they were challenged both by their domestic left-wings and by the Soviet Union. The U.S. responses to Stalin's domination of Eastern Europe—the Marshall Plan and NATO—made it clear that Washington would not allow any government outside the Soviet zone of control to be influenced by left-wingers or Communists.

By late 1947 Stalin had realized that what opposed him in Europe—and increasingly in the rest of the world—was not another system of capitalist rivalries, but an increasingly unified capitalist world system with the United States as the hegemonic power, economically as well as ideologically. The dangers to a Soviet state confronted by such a system were great, Stalin believed, and much of the increased domestic repression, rearmament, and international threats and aggression that characterized his last years in power have to be understood against this background. The Korean War, which began in 1950 after Stalin had given his support to the North Korean Communists' plans to reunify their country by force, was one consequence of this thinking.

The U.S. mobilization against Stalin's policies gave rise to an unprecedented arms race, especially in nuclear weapons. Together, the terror Stalin launched in Eastern Europe and the U.S. consolidation of capitalist power in Western Europe made people-to-people contacts across the division lines increasingly difficult. As the prime ex-ample: the policies of the Superpowers led to the long-term division of Germany, based on the existence of one capitalist and one Communist state. Meanwhile, most Western European Communist parties, which were hindered by covert U.S. interventions and defeated by their failure to condemn Stalinist terror in Eastern Europe, ceased being a serious threat to stability inside the capitalist countries themselves.

The Post-Stalin Era

Military confrontation between the superpowers reached its high point during the Korean War, when forces from the new Communist government in China, aided by Soviet pilots and supplies, fought directly against U.S. forces. After Stalin died in March 1953, all sides hurried to get a ceasefire in place. The post-Stalin Soviet leadership understood that some of Stalin's actions had helped unite other powers against Moscow in the Cold War. The new Soviet leader, Nikita Khrushchev, believed that the Soviet Union and the world's Communists would be better off if the competition were ideological rather than military, at least until the economic and technological balance had tilted more in the direction of the Communist countries. Khrushchev also hoped to appeal to neutralist and left-wing opinion in Western Europe, especially in Italy, France, and West Germany. The new Soviet emphasis on "peaceful coexistence" transformed the Cold War and reduced tensions in Europe, in spite of the Soviet intervention against the Hungarian uprising in 1956.

Although the Korean War had contributed to a witch hunt against left-wingers in the United States in the early 1950s, the Eisenhower administration retained the political and military posture of the Truman years, which was based on containing communism rather than going to war directly against the Soviet Union. Even though Eisenhower was unwilling to respond to Khrushchev's repeated call for large-scale negotiations between East and West, his administration was also opposed to further militarization of the United States and preferred to rely on U.S. nuclear weapons' superiority and an expanding system of alliances to achieve effective containment. In Western Europe, the 1950s saw expanding cooperation in NATO and increased U.S. influence on European economies, social life, and culture. By the early 1960s one could speak of a U.S.-led transformation of most countries in Western Europe, which had become more egalitarian, more consumerist, more integrated, and more capitalist under American tutelage.

The Cold War and the Third World

In 1961, the year John F. Kennedy replaced Eisenhower as U.S. president, Cold War hostilities seemed to be yielding to stability in Europe. The situation was very different in Asia, Africa, and Latin America. The Cuban Revolution had created the first dedicated socialist regime in the Western Hemisphere, with strong links to the Soviet Union. In Vietnam, the Communist government in Hanoi had given its support to an uprising against the U.S.-linked regime in the southern half of the country. And in Africa the second generation of liberation leaders, people like Patrice Lumumba in Congo, were pointing the way to much more radical politics for its newly independent states. By the mid-1960s, thanks in great part to the interventionist policies of Kennedy and his successor Lyndon Johnson, the third world had become the new arena for Cold War competition.

The intersection between decolonization and the Cold War also played a significant role in bringing about superpower confrontation. With more than thirty new states being set up between 1958 and 1962, the search for new patterns of development became intense. In many cases liberation leaders borrowed aims and ideals from the Cold War contest in order to secure rapid political, social, or economic development for their countries, and thereby established patterns of alliances that internationalized the competition for power within their own countries. The Cold War in the third world therefore had many dimensions: Seen from one angle, it was a social and political conflict within the newly constructed countries themselves over the direction that their states should take. From another angle, it was a series of conflicts between local elites over power and influence. And, seen from yet a third angle, it was about the antirevolutionary interventionism of the United States, the hegemonic capitalist power, and—to a lesser extent—about Soviet interventions in support of revolutionary socialist change.

By the late 1960s and 1970s the Cold War in the third world had come to overshadow the conflict in Europe. The Cuban missile crisis of 1962 had shown how intense the rivalry over superpower influence in the third world could become. In the years that followed, the war in Vietnam became the focus of confrontation between the two social systems, and a core element of U.S. foreign policy. Marxist movements lost out in the competition for power in most third world countries, but in Africa and Asia a number of states that claimed to be building socialism came into being, supported by the Soviet Union and its allies.

Challenges to the Cold War

At the same time as the Cold War seemed to be spreading to all corners of the globe, it also began to be challenged from below, from divergent and heretical opinions within the power blocs themselves and from new social movements that built on other values than those of either side in the Cold War. Since both U.S. and Soviet policies were to a large extent designed as much to discipline their own populations as to fight the Cold War abroad, the renewed disorder of the mid-1960s and 1970s was a challenge that both systems found it difficult to overcome.

In the United States and Western Europe large segments of the youth began rebelling against what they saw as an oppressive and stagnant form of capitalism and against U.S. wars of intervention in the third world. The long-term political effects of this opposition were negligible on the domestic scene, but it signaled to the Western political elites that some form of settlement of the Cold War might be necessary in order to undertake limited reform at home. Disaffection with Cold War dynamics also told Western European leaders that they would need to stake out more of their own policies on East-West relations in the future and rely less on direct U.S. guidance. This latter trend was reinforced by Western Europe's economic recovery, which made it less dependent on the United States than in the past. With West Germany's new *Ostpolitik* as the centerpiece, Western Europe began to build its own détente with Eastern Europe, while keeping its military alliance with the United States.

On the Soviet side, multiform challenges were in the making. Moscow's international position had been weakened by China's defection from the Soviet camp in the early 1960s and, especially, by the launch of the Cultural Revolution in 1966, which seemed aimed at undermining the bureaucratic stability that Soviet leaders so cherished at home. The more aggressive anti-U.S. policies of their allies in Hanoi and Havana also at times rattled the Soviet Communists and made them seek some limited accommodation with the West. Last, young people in Eastern Europe and in the Soviet Union itself were influenced by the music, the tastes, and the slogans of young people in other parts of Europe and in America, and the Moscow elite saw a need to call them back to order by stressing the successes of socialism at home and abroad.

Outside Europe and North America, the world was also changing in the 1970s. Regimes of all kinds—nativist, capitalist, and socialist—were coming under increasing pressure because of their inability to deliver improvements on people's daily lot. By the late 1970s the most potent challengers to the established regimes were no longer Marxists, but groups inspired by ethnic or religious identity. Even though, as in Afghanistan, such groups were often happy to ally themselves temporarily with the superpower enemy of the power they were fighting, their ideologies and their long-term aims were very different from any that could be recognized in a Cold War context.

The End of the Cold War

By the 1980s the Cold War as a world order was crumbling at its edges. Both superpowers had been weakened in terms of political influence within their own alliances. The conflicts in the third world were changing character. No longer concerned with finding alternatives to colonialism, they now focused on resistance to the global "West." The international economy—and especially its financial sector—had helped to integrate markets on a global scale, pitting those who benefited from the market development against those who did not. And, within Europe—East and West—the great majority of people were turning away from socialist alternatives and toward welcoming a consumer society, organized along the lines of American capitalism.

The intensification of the Cold War confrontation in the early 1980s, during the first part of Ronald Reagan's presidency, was a response to this crumbling of the system. During the latter half of the 1970s the Soviets had attempted to improve their positions in the third world as a demonstration of renewed dedication to socialist principles, and in response to what they saw as a weakened United States. By the early 1980s, most of these interventions had already gone badly wrong. Then, when Reagan launched a renewed economic, political, and military offensive against the Left on a global scale, not only did it become clear that the tide was turning against socialism in the third world, but also that the Soviet Union was increasingly lagging behind the United States in capabilities in all fields. With the room to maneuver for both superpowers gradually diminishing, the military tension between them brought them to the edge of confrontation.

The Cold War ended when the new Soviet leadership under Mikhail Gorbachev in the late 1980s dramatically reversed Moscow's policies of armament and third world interventions. Gorbachev believed that the Cold War with the United States and Western Europe had to be ended if the Soviet Union was to become a democratic and prosperous socialist state. By 1989 the Soviet Union had signed the epochal Intermediate-Range Nuclear Forces Treaty with Washington, eliminating both sides' stocks of intermediate- and medium-range land-based nuclear missiles. It had also withdrawn its forces from Afghanistan, where they had participated in a bloody civil war since 1979, and its support from other left-wing third world regimes.

The Eastern and Central European revolutions of 1989, which replaced Communist regimes through elections in a belt from Poland to Bulgaria, were possible because Gorbachev refused to prop up his Warsaw Pact allies. On the contrary, he had concluded that the dictatorships that had existed in the eastern half of Europe since the late 1940s were obstacles to reform and opening in the Soviet Union itself. But while these countries were transitioning from planned to capitalist economies in 1990/91—and the Soviet's former ally, East Germany, reunifying with the Federal Republic of Germany in the process—the Soviet economy proved much harder to change. By mid-1991, with the economy in crisis and many constituent republics asserting their sovereignty, Soviet power collapsed after an unsuccessful coup d'etat against Gorbachev by disgruntled Communists in Moscow. In December of 1991 Gorbachev resigned and the Soviet Union ceased to exist.

The fall of the USSR signified the end of the Cold War as an international system on a global scale. But for most people, in most parts of the world, the conflict had already by then been replaced as the focus of their daily attentions by other concerns, such as religious or ethnic strife, or economic competition. It could therefore be said that the Cold War did not so much collapse as dwindle gradually in the 1970s and 1980s. Since for both sides the purpose of the conflict was as much about the extension of their ideologies as about strategic or military power, the moment when other alternatives began replacing the Soviet and American models of social systems marked the end of the Cold War world order.

See also Bipolarity; Decolonization; New Thinking; Peaceful Coexistence; Second Cold War; Socialist Camp; Soviet Bloc; Warsaw Pact.

FURTHER READING

Gaddis, J. L. *We Now Know: Rethinking Cold War History*. Oxford: Clarendon Press, 1997.

Hanhimaki, J. M., and O. A. Westad. *The Cold War: A History in Documents and Eyewitness Accounts*. New York: Oxford University Press, 2003.

Jian, Chen. *Mao's China and the Cold War*. Chapel Hill: University of North Carolina Press, 2001.

Judt, T. *Postwar: A History of Europe since 1945*. New York: Penguin, 2005.

Mastny, V. *The Cold War and Soviet Insecurity: The Stalin Years*. New York: Oxford University Press, 1996.

Reynolds, D. *One World Divisible: A Global History Since 1945*. New York: Norton, 2000.

Westad, O. A. *The Global Cold War: Third World Interventions and the Making of Our Times*. New York: Cambridge University Press, 2005.

ODD ARNE WESTAD

Collapse of Capitalism

The idea that capitalism's crisis could intensify to the point of becoming an economically and politically destructive process became widespread during the course of World War I. If in 1915 Nikolay Bukharin had recognized the possibility of controlling those internal contradictions, which according to Marx's analysis were destined to cause capitalism's collapse, by resorting to the state's new interventionist role in the economy, Lenin had defined imperialism as a parasitic and decomposing form of capitalism, in order to highlight the catastrophic side of these crises and their irreversibility. There were some utopian elements in these expectations of a collapse of the capitalist system. The unprecedented catastrophe of the Great War, however, generated such explosive social tensions that it made plausible the hypothesis Rosa Luxemburg had advanced in 1913: that the destabilizing tendencies of imperialism characterized "the final phase of capitalism as a period of catastrophes." The revolutionary internationalism that the Bolsheviks had transformed into a dominant paradigm therefore required an unconditional effort to radically transform an international order that was thought to be on the brink of collapse. The world revolution would develop in the shape of an answer to a disintegrating imperialism.

As such, the strategic perspective at the basis of the Comintern's founding (March 1919) was predicated on two tightly connected and ultimately unfounded prognoses: on the one hand extremely optimistic evaluations of the revolutionary potential in capitalist countries, and on the other hand, an uncritical endorsement of a

Leninist theory of imperialism led the Communists to believe that bourgeois structures could no longer endure or recover. The theory of collapse thus became part of the Communist identity, an element that distinguished Communists from their reformist and social democratic adversaries. Yet the connection established between a "general crisis" of capitalism and its revolutionary outcome was destined to meet a series of crushing denials. In 1923, notwithstanding the devastating economic crisis in Germany that worsened with the occupation of the Ruhr, the Communist Party of Germany's (KPD) attempt to organize an insurrection was a total failure, and in its turn this deflated the illusion that the Russian Revolution could expand to other countries in the near future. Even so, the Communists were late in recognizing the changes the world economy had undergone as a consequence of the war of 1914, which made the desired collapse of capitalism neither as close nor as inevitable as the resolutions of Comintern congresses would have led one to believe. The "relative stabilization" that the Bolshevik leadership began to acknowledge in 1925–26 was mostly considered a hiatus, a pause, which was to precede the onset of a new and even more serious general crisis of capitalism. The analysis of capitalism's basic tendencies remained substantially the same, notwithstanding Evgenij Varga's and Bukharin's attempts to correct those who maintained that the destabilization of capitalism was so advanced as to render collapse inevitable.

Intolerance toward any form of revision of Leninist orthodoxy became stronger with the Communist parties' Bolshevization, which the Comintern started at its Fifth Congress (1924). Conceived as a way of achieving a monolithic unity of the Communist movement, it was particularly incisive and cut deep on the ideological terrain: it imposed a closed doctrine, codified according to increasingly rigid forms, that proclaimed to be the true and authentic "Marxism of the imperialist era," opposed to all other tendencies within the international Left. The elevation to the status of dogma of the analyses on capitalism's state of health coincided with Bukharin's defeat and Stalin's victory. Already in December 1927 Stalin had advanced his thesis that the period of relative stabilization would end, giving way to a new revolutionary cycle. During work for the Comintern's Sixth Congress (1928) there were several attempts to resist this simplification. Bukharin in particular tried to overcome the narrow interpretations of the general crisis, criticizing the excesses in the overvaluation of capitalism's degenerative tendency while calling attention to the constant technical developments, the development of the capitalist economy beyond the prewar levels, and the increase in productive forces in the most important countries in the West. His effort at reaching a compromise between Stalinist dogmatism and the restlessness of those who were attempting to analyze the transformations in the world economy met with failure. The Comintern's Sixth Congress adopted the position of Stalin and his new allies, which tended to liquidate those processes Bukharin had pointed to as desperate attempts by capitalism to avoid an unstoppable and uncontrollable crisis. The Great Crash of 1929 was therefore seen as a confirmation of the thesis according to which the period of stabilization was only to be considered a hiatus and a proof of Stalin's infallibility. In fact, the only Communist who had foreseen the course of events in 1929 was Varga, who for some time had tried to reconcile the favorable data of some indexes he had obtained from his empirical analyses of economic trends with the thesis of the unstoppable crisis and the ensuing exacerbation of the class struggle.

During the Tenth Plenum of the Ikki (1929) he proposed some correctives to the catastrophic view of the capitalist world, noting how the technological progress in the West had brought about undeniable improvements in the living conditions of the working class. This statement earned him the accusation of representing, with Bukharin, the "right deviation" and attempting to revise the Leninist theory of imperialism by resorting to Rudolf Hilferding's theory of "organized capitalism." Varga's condemnation prepared the terrain for the Stalinization of the analyses of capitalism's state of health, which led to a far-reaching shift in all fields of scientific research in the USSR, and hinged on an axiom regarding capitalism's collapse: the existence of the USSR and the strengthening of its economy became both an expression of and a catalyst in capitalism's crisis. Soviet planning became the only alternative solution to the anarchy produced by the market economy. To support organized capitalism meant to openly challenge this theorem, insofar as it meant admitting that a market economy would have had the capabilities and means to control its own crises, and an even more serious matter, to call into question the superiority of the Soviet system as compared to the capitalist one. Starting at this time the opposition between a capitalism on the brink of collapse, devoid of the capability to regenerate itself, and a socialism in the process of being built became a fundamental and enduring component in the Communists' mental outlook, so strong in fact as to resist history's denials for a long time. The recognition that instead capitalism had

found some exit strategies from the crisis of 1929 occurred late and with obvious uncertainties in the analyses, given the risks that any open attempt to revise Leninism would have entailed for its authors' well-being.

The delay the Communists had incurred in adapting to the profound economic and social transformations of the West emerged in its full breadth and depth only after World War II. Varga's timid attempts in 1947 to overcome the now dominant dogmatic approach in analyses of capitalism's state of well-being encountered the same reactions as in 1929. His call to reconsider the catastrophic view of a capitalist world, which for some time had been depicted as the reign of chaos, would have tarnished the claimed superiority of the Soviet system. So when, starting in the 1950s, one observed an extraordinary phase of capitalist growth, exhibiting a combination of economic boom, full employment, and a mass consumer society, the Communists continued to talk about the system's "putrefaction," denying or minimizing the extent and effects of these socioeconomic developments. Only well into the 1960s did some Communist parties start to define the nature of capitalism more realistically and see its potential for development as well as its contradictions.

But these analyses did not lead to a strategic review, capable of confronting the challenges posed by the changes that were affecting the economies and social structures of Western countries. The economic crisis at the beginning of the 1970s intervened not only to put an end to the "Golden Age of capitalism" but also to prepare the terrain for the implosion of the economic system of the Soviet bloc countries, whose superiority Communists had never doubted or openly challenged. Even when some parties started theorizing a "third way," which would differ from both the experiences of Eastern Europe and those of the social democracies, they still maintained that their inspiration was a model of socialism not substantially different from the Soviet one. This can help one to understand the delay with which the Communists, under the heavy pressure of the economic disaster that was emerging ever more clearly even in the USSR itself, finally surrendered to the idea that they had lost their challenge with capitalism.

See also Imperialism; Internationalism; Marxism-Leninism; Messianism; Planning; Revolution, Myths of the; Social Democracy; War, Inevitability of; World Revolution; Varga, Eugen.

FURTHER READING

Agosti, A. *Bandiere rosse. Un profile storico dei comunismi europei*. Rome: Editori Riuniti, 1999.

di Biagio, A. "L'URSS e l'Occidente nell'analisi di E. S. Varga." In *Il pensiero sociale russo. Modelli stranieri e contesto nazionale*, ed. Alberto Masoero and Antonello Venturi. Milan: Angeli, 2000.

ANNA DI BIAGIO

Collectivization of the Countryside

The collectivization of agriculture was a central feature of 20th century (mainly) Marxist regimes in countries ranging from Eastern Europe to Africa, Asia, and Latin America. Although Marx never fully or explicitly envisioned collectivization, Marxist regimes deemed collectivized agriculture to be an essential condition of socialism following the example set by the Soviet Union in its collectivization drive of the First Five-Year Plan (1928–32). Collectivization proved to be a transformative experience for many regimes and their people, resulting in violence, repression, population dislocation, and food shortages, while simultaneously increasing the political rigidity of administrative controls in the countryside.

The aim of collectivization was to create a large-scale socialized agricultural economy, based on modern techniques of agronomy and animal husbandry and organized into state and collective farms. While state farms were to replicate the conditions of nationalized industry with state ownership and the employment of a salaried rural workforce, collective farms were to be profit-sharing organizations, in which farmers tilled the land collectively and governed and managed the farm through a collective farm assembly and elected officers. Collectivization was meant to transform the rural sector, replacing communal forms of peasant land tenure and/or small, private farms, as well as ridding the countryside of a rural bourgeoisie, capitalism, and the market.

The idea of collectivization was founded upon ideological, economic, and political principles. The tenets of Marxism-Leninism judged collectivization to be not only a more just and rational economic system than capitalist modes of farming based on market forces, but presumed collectivization to be the logical outcome of the progressive dynamics of class forces in the countryside. Marxist-Leninists grafted urban concepts of class and class struggle onto the peasantry in what was, at best, an awkward fit. They divided the peasantry into poor peasants and rural proletarians (the natural allies of the working class), middle peasants (a large and politically wavering intermediate stratum sharing features common to both the proletariat and the bourgeoisie), and the kulak (a rural bourgeoisie with social and economic power disproportionate to its relatively small numbers). They assumed that poor peasants and agricultural laborers would rally to the side of the collective farm for motives of class interests, swaying the middle peasant to their side and defeating the kulak in the process. In practice, peasants rarely performed according to class principles, instead uniting together in defense of common goals and values—subsistence, ways of life, and beliefs—threatened by the theory and practice of collectivization. The poor peasant in most cases failed to come to the aid of the working class (in the concrete form of the urban Communists and factory workers who were mobilized to implement collectivization), and the regime's inability to provide a clear and consistent definition of the "kulak" most often meant that politics rather than social or economic status determined who was so classified.

Collectivization was viewed as an essential ingredient in the "construction" of socialism. In the Soviet Union and elsewhere, socialist construction meant not only the eradication of rural capitalism, but also the industrialization and modernization of the country. The collectivization of agriculture would facilitate the control and transfer of economic resources from the rural to the heavy industrial sector in a process that Soviet Communist theorist E. A. Preobrazhensky labeled "primitive socialist accumulation." By increasing grain production and mechanizing agriculture, collectivization was expected to free up capital and labor for industry and food resources for a growing urban industrial workforce. And although most historians agree that collectivization did not pay for industrialization, at least in the short term, it is clear that this expectation was an important motivation behind collectivization, particularly in conditions of economic isolation.

Finally, collectivization was a central aspect of state building, as regimes sought to expand political and administrative controls to the countryside, where in the Soviet Union and most of Eastern Europe (with the exception of the former Czechoslovakia) the majority of the population lived. The peasant commune and scattered small, private farms represented semiautonomous loci of power. Through the mobilization of urban forces, an expansion in rural party membership, and the creation of new, Soviet organs of power (the state farm, collective farm, machine-tractor stations, etc.), the Communist Party endeavored to offset its relatively weak base of power in the countryside. Auxiliary policies aimed against religion and the kulak sought to eliminate the alternative power centers of the church and local authority figures.

In reality, the Soviet Union and the countries of Eastern Europe after World War II faced a largely resistant peasantry and smallholding farming population, uninterested in collectivized agriculture and generally impervious to Marxist class principles. Collectivization consequently was a top-down, state-initiated transformation implemented by coercion and the mobilization of outside forces and animated by a fiercely urban bias and antipeasant prejudice. While collectivization in Eastern Europe generally occurred with less violence, and in some cases, more in the breach, collectivization in the Soviet Union was an upheaval of cataclysmic proportions.

Collectivization in the Soviet Union

In November 1929, Stalin proclaimed that the middle peasant had begun to flock to the collective farms. In fact, collectivization had increased dramatically by this time, surpassing the relatively modest rates projected for the socialized sector of agriculture after the Fifteenth Party Congress of December 1927 placed collectivization on the immediate agenda. At the Sixteenth Party Conference in April 1929, in its First Five-Year Plan on agriculture, the Central Committee of the Communist Party had projected the collectivization of 9.6 percent of the peasant population in the 1932–33 economic year, and 13.6 percent (or approximately 3.7 million households) in 1933–34. These projections were revised upward in the late summer and fall of 1929, when first *Gosplan* (the state planning commission) called for the collectivization of 2.5 million peasant households in the course of 1929–30, and then *Kolkhoztsentr* (the central agency leading collective farm administration) resolved that 3.1 million peasant households would be incorporated into collective farms by the end of 1929–30.

In actuality, by June 1, 1928, 1.7 percent of peasant households were in collective farms; and between June 1 and October 1, 1929, alone, percentages rose from 3.9 to 7.5. The increase was especially marked in major grain-producing regions. The Lower Volga and North Caucasus surpassed all other regions with percentages of

collectivized peasant households reaching 18.1 and 19.1, respectively, in October. The high rates achieved in the regional collectivization campaigns lay behind Stalin's statement that the middle peasantry was entering collective farms. By arguing that the middle peasant was turning voluntarily to socialized agriculture, Stalin was claiming that the *majority* of the peasantry was *ready* for collectivization. In reality, it was mainly poor peasants who were joining collectives. And, although there was apparently some genuine enthusiasm "from below," the regional campaigns had already begun to resort to coercion to achieve their high percentages.

Even at this stage, collectivization was largely imposed "from above." Orchestrated and led by the regional party organizations, with implicit or explicit sanction from Moscow, district-level officials and urban Communists and workers brought collectivization to the countryside. A volatile antipeasant mood prevailed in the cities, especially among rank-and-file Communists and industrial workers. It was founded on bread shortages, continuing news of "kulak sabotage," and long-simmering urban-rural antipathies, and it infected the cadres and other, newer recruits sent to the country from urban centers. A combination of official endorsement, regional initiative and direction, and unrestrained action on the part of lower-level cadres produced a radical and ever-accelerating momentum of collectivization. The "success" of the regional campaigns then provided the necessary impetus for Moscow to speed collectivization even further in what became a deadly and continual tug-of-war between center and periphery to keep pace with one another as reality exceeded plan and plans were continually revised to register, keep pace with, and push forward collectivization tempos.

The November 1929 Communist Party plenum formally ratified the policy of wholesale collectivization, leaving the specifics of the policy's implementation to a politburo commission that would meet the next month. The commission called for the completion of collectivization in major grain-producing regions in one to two years; in other grain-producing regions in two to three years; and in the most important grain-deficit regions in three to four years. The commission also resolved that an intermediate form of collective farm, the artel, which featured the socialization of land, labor, draft animals, and basic inventory, would be the standard, and that private ownership of domestic livestock needed for consumption would be maintained. Any movement to extend socialization of peasant properties beyond the artel would depend on the peasantry's experience and "the growth of its confidence in the stability, benefits, and advantages" of collective farming. The kulak faced expropriation of his means of production (which would then be transferred to the collective farms) and resettlement or exile. The subcommittee on the kulak recommended a differentiated approach to the elimination of the kulak as a class. Finally, the commission warned against any attempt either to restrain collectivization or to collectivize "by decree."

The politburo commission published its legislation on January 5, 1930. The legislation stipulated that the Lower Volga, Middle Volga, and North Caucasus were to complete collectivization by fall 1930, spring 1931 at the latest; and that all remaining grain-producing regions were to complete collectivization by fall 1931, spring 1932 at the latest, thus accelerating yet again the pace of the campaign. No mention was made of the remaining areas. The legislation also specified that the artel would be the main form of collective farm, leaving out any particulars from the commission's work. Stalin had personally intervened on this issue, ordering the editing out of "details" on the artel, which should, he argued, more appropriately be left to the jurisdiction of the Commissariat of Agriculture. The kulak would be "eliminated as a class," as Stalin had already noted in his December 27, 1929, speech at the Conference of Marxist Agronomists, and excluded from entry into the collective farms. Stalin and other maximalists in the leadership were responsible for radicalizing further an already radical set of guidelines by revising the work of the December commission, keeping the legislation vague, and including only very weak warnings against violence.

By the time this legislation was published, collectivization percentages in the Soviet Union had leaped from 7.5 in October to 18.1 on January 1, 1930, with even higher rates in major grain-producing regions (Lower Volga, 56–70 percent; Middle Volga, 41.7 percent; North Caucasus, 48.1 percent). Through the month of January, reality continued to outpace planning. By February 1, 1930, 31.7 percent of all households were on collective farms, with rates still higher in individual regions (Moscow, 37.1 percent; Central Black Earth Region, 51 percent; the Urals, 52.1 percent; Middle Volga, 51.8 percent; Lower Volga, 61.1 percent; North Caucasus, 62.7 percent).

The elimination of the kulak as a class, dekulakization for short, had also spread far and wide through the country as regional party organizations enacted their own legislation and issued their own directives in advance and in anticipation of Moscow. A politburo commission led by V. M. Molotov, politburo member and Stalin's right-hand man, met from January 15–26 in an effort to draw up central legislation on dekulakization. Following the policy recommendations of December, the commission divided kulaks into three categories. The most dangerous category, some 60,000 heads of households, faced execution or internment in concentration camps, while their families were expropriated of their properties and all but the most essential items and sent into exile in remote parts of the country. An additional 150,000 families deemed to be somewhat less dangerous but still a threat, also faced expropriation and exile to remote regions. The main places of exile for these two categories were the northern region (scheduled to receive 70,000 families), Siberia (50,000 families), the Urals (20–25,000 families), and Kazakhstan (20–25,000 families). The final category of well over one-half million families was to be subjected to partial expropriation of properties and resettlement within their native districts. The term "kulak" was defined broadly to include not only kulaks (an ambiguous term to begin with) but (using the parlance of the day) active White guards, former bandits, former White officers, repatriated peasants, active members of church councils and sects, priests, and anyone "currently manifesting c[ounter]-r[evolutionary] activities."

Collectivization and dekulakization had long since jumped the rails of central control. Brigades of collectivizers with plenipotentiary powers, toured the countryside, stopping briefly in villages where, often with gun in hand, they forced peasants, under threat of dekulakization, to sign up to join the collective farm. Collectivization rates continued to rise through February, reaching 57.2 percent by March 1, and the unreal regional percentages of 74.2 in the Moscow region, 83.3 in the Central Black Earth region, 75.6 in the Urals, 60.3 in Middle Volga, 70.1 in Lower Volga, and 79.4 in North Caucasus. The high percentages belied the fact that most collective farms at this time were "paper collectives" with artificial membership figures attained in a "race for percentages" by regional and district party organizations. Collectivization often amounted to little more than a collective farm charter and chairman, the socialization of livestock, and the terror of dekulakization.

Collectivization came to an abrupt halt on March 2, 1930, when Stalin published "Dizziness from Success," blaming the outrages on the lower-level cadres who were indeed dizzy from success, but failing to admit central responsibility. Soon collectivization percentages began to tumble drastically as peasants invoked Stalin's name in their struggle against the cadres of collectivization and quit the collective farms in droves.

Collectivization resumed the following fall at a slightly less breakneck speed. The major grain-producing regions attained wholesale collectivization by the end of the First Five-Year Plan in 1932; other regions climbed more gradually to that goal, generally reaching it by the end of the 1930s. In the meantime, over one million peasant families (five to six million people) were subjected to some form of dekulakization during the years of wholesale collectivization. Of these, some 381,026 families (with a total population of 1,803,392) were exiled in 1930 and 1931, the two years of heaviest deportation. The deportations were perhaps one of the most horrendous episodes in a decade marked by horror, and, through the vast expansion of the use of internal exile, the concentration camp system, and the political police, helped to establish the foundations for the Stalinist police state.

Collectivization in Eastern Europe

Collectivization in the Communist countries of Eastern Europe (defined here as the former German Democratic Republic, Czechoslovakia, Hungary, Poland, Bulgaria, Romania, Yugoslavia, and Albania) followed patterns similar to Soviet collectivization. Following occupation by Soviet military forces, these countries were subject to a process of Sovietization, which, in the years before the death of Stalin in 1953, was tantamount to Stalinization. Political repression, the nationalization of industry, and the beginnings of agricultural collectivization were carried out in the years between 1948 and 1953. As in the Soviet Union, collectivization was a state-directed policy and met with little or no support from the peasantry. Collectivization in Eastern Europe also entailed the elimination of a rural bourgeoisie, leading to national policies of dekulakization. By 1953, collectivization in most of Eastern Europe had been only partially implemented. The brief "thaw" in policy following the death of Stalin meant in most cases a respite for the peasantry and a temporary halt to collectivization. The second stage of collectivization came in the late 1950s, with the result that collectivization was completed throughout Eastern Europe by 1962, with the notable exceptions of Poland and Yugoslavia, which did not experience a second collectivization drive and had largely abandoned collectivization after the initial drive of the late Stalin period.

Eastern European collectivization patterns exhibited some national variation. While the initial collectiviza-tion drive in Poland was relatively moderate, collectivization in Bulgaria, for example, was brutal and much closer in style to the Soviet drive of 1930. And in spite of initial collectivization campaigns, private agriculture continued to dominate the rural economies of Poland and Yugoslavia. In Hungary, the policies of the New Economic Mechanism after 1968 gradually introduced market forces into the socialized agricultural economy, diminishing the intensity of collectivization. And, as in the case of the Soviet Union, a private sector based on the household economies of collective farmers played an important role in both collective farmers' income and the nation's consumer needs throughout Eastern Europe.

See also Agrarian Question; Famine under Communism; Five-Year Plans; Gulag; Holodomor; Kolkhoz; Kulak; Modernization; New Economic Policy; Revolution from Above; Sovietization.

FURTHER READING

Davies, R. W. *The Industrialisation of Soviet Russia 1: The Socialist Offensive, 1929–1930.* Cambridge, MA: Harvard University Press, 1980.

Lewin, M. *Russian Peasants and Soviet Power: A Study of Collectivization.* Trans. Irene Nove. New York: Norton, 1975.

Pryor, F. L. *The Red and the Green: The Rise and Fall of Collectivized Agriculture in Marxist Regimes.* Princeton, NJ: Princeton University Press, 1992.

Viola, L. *Peasant Rebels Under Stalin: Collectivization and the Culture of Peasant Resistance.* New York: Oxford University Press, 1996.

Viola, L., V. P. Danilov, N. A. Ivnitskii, and D. Kozlov, eds. *The Tragedy of the Soviet Countryside: The War Against the Peasantry.* Trans. Steven Shabad. New Haven, CT: Yale University Press, 2005.

LYNNE VIOLA

Comecon

The Council for Mutual Economic Assistance (abbreviated to Comecon for Anglophones and SEV for Russophones) was both founded (in January 1949) and abolished (in September 1991) when its operation was contrary to the economic interests of its members, the USSR, and states under the Soviet political wing (initially Bulgaria, Czechoslovakia, Hungary, Poland, and Romania). Sole Soviet sponsorship was evident from the convocation of East European heads of planning offices to Moscow by the Communist Party's Central Committee secretary in charge of relations with foreign Communist parties, Mikhail Suslov, without advance information to invitees on an agenda. Suslov had two objectives. The first, ostensible aim, as reflected in the session's communiqué, was that "these countries did not consider it appropriate that they should submit themselves to the dictatorship of the Marshall Plan." U.S. grants, credits, and technical assistance would have been valuable as much for the war-damaged Soviet Union as for its bloc, tempted by the U.S. aid offer of 1947; Czechoslovakia accepted, but was compelled to withdraw. Because the Marshall Plan participants had formed the Organization for European Economic Cooperation (later the Organization for Economic Cooperation and Development), Comecon would serve as an organizational rival and was intended to counter its success in coordinating West European recovery within market frameworks. The second, implicit aim was in the context of the just-achieved expulsion from the East European leaderships of "national deviationists" in favor of Soviet nominees, which was accompanied in economic planning by Suslov's advocacy of targets in physical units rather than in values influenced by a price mechanism. He led the attack on Nikolai Voznesensky, chair of the USSR Gosplan until he was dismissed in March 1949, who sought to render more cost-effective the Soviet practice of "balancing" material inputs and outputs. Suslov and his faction (victors in the "Leningrad Affair") saw a function for Comecon in implementing such balancing for exchanges among the East European economies and with the USSR. Another rationale was the imposition by the opposing military grouping, the North Atlantic Treaty Organization, of trade controls in physical terms—by 1950, the U.S. Combatant Commands embargoed export to the Soviet bloc and China to 50 percent of the international nomenclature of tradable items.

A first session of the council was convened in Moscow (April 1949), but substantive discussions began at the second session in Sofia (Bulgaria being the first member state in alphabetical order), on scientific and technological cooperation as well as the coordination of long-term plans, and continued at a third session (November 1950), publicly in Moscow and informally in Hollohaza (Hungary). Stalin then put the organization into hibernation. A small staff and a council of representatives of member countries (by then joined by Albania and the German Democratic Republic [GDR]) of some forty persons oc-

cupied an elegant 19th-century villa just off the Sadovoye kol'tso in Moscow, but conducted no practical business, with the chair concluding brief monthly sessions with "Let us carry on as hitherto."

Khrushchev's leadership after Stalin's death revivified Comecon, as he sought for the Soviet economy generally: the fourth session (Moscow, March 1954) sketched intermember trade targets for 1956–60 plans and bilateral agreements for production specialization. A follow-up (Moscow, June 1954) considered the investment implications of those plans and initiated the first joint project: the unification of national electricity grids. The council (of senior ministers of member states) then resumed meeting in their countries by Russian alphabetical order—in Budapest (December 1955) and East Berlin (May 1956). The latter set up the organizational form, which would remain in place for the rest of Comecon's existence. Twelve standing commissions were established to which member countries nominated staff from the relevant ministry. These were soon expanded into fifteen, several covering all branches of production, plus six concerned with functional policies—macroeconomy, statistics, foreign trade, scientific research, monetary and financial policy, and standardization. The Comecon secretariat servicing commissions was divided into corresponding departments, as also for information and water resources (to service conferences of water-resources agencies). The twelfth session of the council (Sofia, December 1959) agreed on a charter and the Convention on Immunities, and the thirteenth session (Budapest, July 1960) formulated rules of procedure for the council, the council of representatives, and standing commissions. Comecon thereby became formally an international agency and participated in UN meetings with which it had functional relations, notably the Economic Commission for Europe. Whereas in Comecon's early days national civil servants performed most of the staffing functions, just as within the parallel Organization for European Economic Cooperation, the enlargement of Comecon's responsibilities required servicing by a career staff and larger office premises. Because all members were one-party states (Mongolia joined in 1962), the secretariat was "intergovernmental" rather than "international" like that of the United Nations. The uniform political inspiration of Comecon's work was made evident by the importance attached to occasional meetings of representatives of national Communist parties, each determining significant policies. The first (May 1958) accepted world market prices for trade among members;

the second (February 1960) responded to the deficiencies in the region's farming due to collectivization by agreeing on programs for feed grains and agricultural engineering; the third (June 1962) ratified *Basic Principles of the International Socialist Division of Labor* on the specialization of production and narrowing of the "substantial differences in the level of development" of member states, but rejected Khrushchev's call for a supranational planning agency; and the fourth (July 1963) learned of acceptance of participation by the USSR in joint investment projects, from which since their initiation in 1959 it had held aloof. All four sessions were held in Moscow, but a fifth was convened in Bucharest (July 1966) to agree on broad lines of specialization until 1970.

The Soviet-led invasion of Czechoslovakia in August 1968 brought the substitution of a general movement to liberalize economic systems, begun in the GDR in 1964, by imperative "socialist economic integration"—a response to the European Economic Community, founded in 1957. Comecon integration, however, was inhibited by its members' exchange of "hard" goods only against hard goods, and "soft" goods only against soft goods—the criterion being the salability for convertible currency. Convertibility among Comecon currencies should have been fostered by the creation of the International Bank of Economic Cooperation in 1963 (with an office in Moscow), but persistent bilateralism kept the share of trade settled by a mutual clearing around 5 percent. The quintupling of the world price of oil in 1973 changed the terms of trade within Comecon sharply in favor of the USSR and Romania, both suppliers of hard products, oil and gas, against the GDR, Czechoslovakia, Hungary, and Poland, increasingly dependent on the USSR because of their biases toward heavy industry as well as a network of oil and gas pipelines from Siberian deposits. Cuba (brought in as member in 1972) was salved from the U.S. trade and credit embargo by support from all Comecon members. A potentially disastrous balance-of-trade crisis was averted throughout the rest of the 1970s by Soviet subsidization and Western credits made possible by quiescence in the Cold War. The aggregate of the subsidies that Comecon members in East Europe received from the USSR (the difference it paid for not importing/exporting from/to the West the goods traded with East Europe) during the 1970s coincided with the amount of credits they took from the West. The further doubling of the world oil price in 1979 exacerbated their situation, and a debt crisis in 1980 compelled a change of course, within a new geopolitical configuration as two

polarized Cold War leaders left the scene (the end of President Ronald Reagan's term of office and the death of Leonid Brezhnev) and authoritarian Communist governments were shaken by the Solidarity upsurge in Poland. Successive summit meetings of party and government heads, the Warsaw Treaty Organization (January 1983), and Comecon (June 1984, December 1985, and November 1986) charted policies expectant of East/West détente, while consolidating their own military and economic security. Comecon hopes, as expressed at the 1984 summit, of agreement with the European communities were soon dashed, but the accession of Mikhail Gorbachev to the Soviet leadership in 1985 began a widespread devolution of domestic economic management that demanded a corresponding decentralization of external relations. Delegations from Comecon and the European Economic Community met for the first time in Geneva in September 1986, when four Comecon members—Hungary, Poland, Romania, and Vietnam (a member since 1978)—were in the International Monetary Fund and World Bank, and hence obliged to aim at liberalizing exchange control. The intermember impact of Gorbachev's perestroika was explicitly acknowledged at the Comecon council session of October 1987, together with a cutting back of the organization's functions as market mechanisms were strengthened among members; by the end of that year all European members save for the GDR and the USSR were at stages of negotiation with the European Commission, with the two others being brought in during 1988.

The recognition that the accession of non-Communist governments was putting Comecon "in a state of crisis" was acknowledged at an executive committee meeting in October 1989 and a conference with the European Community with the pledge that Comecon members "will become more open to the West." By the year's end, all East European states had embraced democracy and the market system, with Mongolia doing likewise the following year. A council session of January 1990 recognized that these required the organization to abandon its main functions of multilateral economic cooperation and plan coordination, and proposed, in vain as it soon proved, a replacement agency along the lines of the Organization for Economic Cooperation and Development. Comecon's Standing Commission on the Defense Industry was abolished in December 1990 in view of the impending closure of the Warsaw Treaty Organization (the only formal statement that it had ever made since its secret creation in 1957). Following the Soviet government change of April 1991, the Supreme Soviet called in June for the abolition of Comecon, validated two days later by Comecon's final council session (Budapest, June 28–29). After a delay occasioned by the Moscow coup attempt of August, Comecon's liquidation committee effected termination on September 9, 1991.

See also Command Economy; Economic Reforms; Gosplan; Planning; Socialist Camp; Soviet Bloc; Warsaw Pact.

FURTHER READING

Kaser, M. C. *Comecon: Integration Problems of the Planned Economies.* New York: Oxford University Press, 1965.

Lascelles, D. *Comecon to 1980.* London: Financial Times, 1976.

Schaefer, H. W. *Comecon and the Politics of Integration.* New York: Praeger, 1972.

Wiles, P. J. de la Fosse. *Communist International Economics.* Oxford: Basil Blackwell, 1968.

MICHAEL C. KASER

Cominform

A term first coined in the West, "Cominform" later became the worldwide abbreviation for the Information Bureau of Communist Parties, the international organ of a number of European Communist parties. The Cominform operated under Soviet direction from 1947 to 1956. From 1949 on, it was also referred to in some of its documents as the Information Bureau of Communist and Workers' Parties.

The Cominform was created at a congress of Communist parties that took place in Szklarska Poręmba in Poland on September 22–28, 1947, as a result of a decision made by the Kremlin. Long before this, the idea of creating the Cominform had been discussed in meetings between Stalin and various Eastern European Communist leaders, such as Matyas Rakosi of Hungary and Josip Broz Tito of Yugoslavia. Yet Stalin kept waiting for a suitable moment to establish the new organization. Then, on June 4, 1947, he proposed to Władisław Gomułka, the head of the Polish Workers' Party (PWP), as the Polish Communist Party of that time was called, that he take the initiative in calling a meeting of Communist parties. In the middle of August, Gomułka, in the name of the PWP's Central Committee, sent out a secret invitation, agreed on in advance with Stalin, to selected party leaders. In addition to the Communist Party of the Soviet Union (CPSU, or literally the All-Union Communist Party of the Bolsheviks) and the PWP, these were the heads of the parties of Yugoslavia, Bulgaria, Czechoslovakia, Romania, Hungary, France, and Italy. (Stalin considered and rejected the idea of including Belgium and Finland.) As he had agreed to with Gomułka, Stalin made no mention of creating an information bureau, but stated as the goal of the meeting an exchange of information and opinions among the delegates about the situations in their respective countries and the problems confronting Europe's Communist parties. Still another goal was the creation of an international press organ. All these points were included in the invitation dispatched by Gomułka. The Kremlin, though, kept it secret from the leaders of the PWP and the other parties that Stalin was planning to propose an information bureau, one that would have not only informational but also coordinating functions.

At the meeting, after opening statements and the delegation reports about the activity of their parties, the CPSU representatives introduced a proposal that although unexpected, was unanimously approved, to discuss two main questions: the international situation and the coordination of the activities of the Communist parties.

The first report, prepared in advance in Moscow, was given by Andrey Zhdanov, a close associate of Stalin. The central point of the report suggested that the world was now forming into two opposed camps. One camp, the people's democracies with the USSR playing the leading role, was designated the "anti-imperialist and democratic camp." The other one, consisting of the Western countries with the United States playing the leading role, was characterized as the "imperialist and anti-democratic" camp. According to this dichotomy, international relations would center on the confrontation between the aggressive policies of the second camp and the first camp, which was trying to resist the confrontation and was conducting a policy of peace, reining in the "instigators of war," as well as supporting the struggles of the world's peoples for freedom and independence. For practical purposes, this doctrine proclaimed the forced confrontation of the Soviet bloc with the "capitalist world," first and foremost with the countries of the West. The notion of the two camps was inserted into Zhdanov's report by Vyacheslav Molotov, who at the time was in the Caucasus together with Stalin. Thus, the proposal likely had been initiated by Stalin, who was controlling and determining all the activities of the Soviet delegation in the preparation and conduct of the conference.

The doctrine of the confrontation of the two camps imposed on the Soviet bloc and its Communist parties was the absolute need to mobilize internally and accelerate the conversion of people's democracies into a Communist monopoly of power, and strengthen the discipline and subordination of these regimes in carrying out the policy lines set by Moscow. One after another, the Eastern European participants at the conference declared these policies to be both opportune and rightful. From the Communist parties outside the Soviet bloc, especially those in the countries of the West, the doctrine of confrontation of the two camps demanded organized resistance to the "imperialist policies" of these countries, particularly those of the United States, and the implementation of the Marshall Plan in those states. It focused on the struggle against the "right-wing socialists," whom it declared to be "accomplices of the imperialists." Zhdanov accused the French and Italian Communist parties of indecisiveness and surrendering their positions, and demanded their return to the orientation outlined in his report. The Eastern European delegates supported this. The representatives of both the criticized parties confessed their "mistakes" and promised that their parties would comply with the directions delineated in Zhdanov's report.

After the conference, its constituents wrote up and published the Declaration on the International Situation, based on Zhdanov's report. But for tactical reasons, neither the declaration nor the variant of Zhdanov's report that was also published after the conference directly criticized the French and Italian parties (and everything that was said in the discussions at the meetings was held in strict secrecy).

Members of the PWP delegation, who had been assigned by the CPSU the task of presenting the report on coordinating the activities of the Communist parties, which itself implied the creation of the Cominform, had actually been lobbying behind the scenes against the Kremlin's plan. Stalin had named Warsaw as the future site of an information bureau, but the Poles objected that this would interfere with their purchase from the West of goods essential to Poland and the proposed fusion of the Polish Socialist Party with the PWP. And Gomułka had come out definitively against the formation of any such organ as an information bureau. After a few days, however, the Poles expressed their readiness to cooperate with the Soviet plan; by that time all the other participating parties had consented in behind-the-scenes lobbying with the CPSU. As a result, Gomułka yielded and gave a report in his own name proposing the creation along Kremlin lines of a Cominform with the functions of exchange of opinions and coordination of the activities of all the Communist parties. The creation of the Cominform was ratified by all the parties present at the meeting in Szklarska Poręba. Nevertheless, the location of the Cominform and its publishing organ was changed at the request of Yugoslavia, and approved by Stalin, from Warsaw to Belgrade.

The Cominform was made public a week after the congress. Still, during its first nine months, its activity was restricted to the publication of its newspaper, *For Lasting Peace and People's Democracy!* The editorial board was at that time the only organized part of the Cominform. The paper was created at a meeting of representatives of the Central Committees of Communist Party participants at a meeting in Belgrade on October 30–31, 1947, specifically called for this purpose, first as a temporary organ and then, at a similar meeting on January 18, 1948, also held in Belgrade, as a permanent organ. Only the second meeting was announced publicly, and after the fact at that. All decisions regarding the publication and the makeup of its editorial staff were first made in Moscow and then rubber-stamped at the meetings. The newspaper initially came out twice a week, in Russian, French, and English. Then it was published weekly, and over time, editions were added in Italian, German, Spanish, Chinese, Swedish, and the languages of the people's democracies. The positions taken by the paper and its editorial staff were those of CPSU officials; the editor in chief until spring 1950 was a Stalinist ideologue named Pavel Yudin, and after that came a similar ideologue named Mark Mitin. The newspaper's financial backing was first 40 percent and then 50 percent Soviet, with the remainder of the costs distributed in various proportions among the other participating parties.

In addition to publishing its newspaper, the Cominform now began to assume three more basic organizational functions. The first was conducting meetings of party representatives, similar to the 1947 gathering, to examine major political questions. There were two such meetings, held on June 19–23, 1948, in Romania and on November 16–19, 1949, in Hungary. The second organizational function involved meetings of the Secretariat of the Cominform. In line with a decision made at the 1948 meeting, the Secretariat was to be made up of all the participant parties. The Secretariat meetings considered mostly practical organizational questions. There were four of these meetings in all: July 5, 1948; June 14–15, 1949; April 20–22, 1950; and November 22–24, 1950. At the Cominform conferences and meetings of the Secretariat, decisions about policy, agenda, and results to be achieved were always made by the Soviet leadership first, and then the other parties rendered their consent. The third organizational function involved the work of the Office of the Secretariat. This office was a constantly functioning apparatus. It was created and began its activity at the end of August 1948 by a decision made in Moscow, although officially its existence, structure, and functions were established at a meeting of the Secretariat only in 1949. The office's work was invariably under the control of the Central Committee of the CPSU. The latter determined the personnel involved as well. The heads of the office and all four of its sections were always Soviet. All political workers ("referents") and even the majority of the technical workers of the apparatus were also Soviet. Aside from preparation of Cominform congresses and Secretariat meetings, the basic functions of the office were the collection and analysis of information about various aspects of the current situation, and the activities of the Communist parties, in particular those that were members of the Cominform, about the execution by the parties of congress decisions made from 1947 to 1949 and decisions made at Secretariat meetings, and finally, about the foreign and domestic policies of the people's democracies. The office established a system in which it would constantly receive information and reports from the leading organs of the parties, and Soviet officials from the office were periodically dispatched to Eastern European countries of the Soviet bloc for purposes of reconnoitering and inspection. On this basis, the office put together its informational and analytic materials, which were then sent to the CPSU's Central Committee. Certain materials received from the Communist parties were also sent there. The office also controlled the work of the editors of *For Lasting Peace and People's Democracy!* and its publishing houses, and from 1949 on, directed the radio center that broadcast to Greece and Yugoslavia, by now enemies.

The Cominform's activities were cloaked in secrecy. Its conferences, including the one in 1947, were reported on only after they had ended, without precise information about the places and dates they took place. This was followed by announcements about general political decisions taken at the meetings, and also, although usually in a much changed form, the public release of reports and speeches made at the 1947 and 1949 conferences. But a good part of the decisions and reports (particularly from the 1948 meeting) remained secret, as did all of the discussions at the conferences. The very existence and all the activities of the Secretariat and the Office of the Secretariat remained hidden from view, as did the Charter of the Cominform, which was approved at a meeting of the Secretariat in June 1949 and then confirmed by a Cominform congress in November of the same year.

After the Yugoslav-Soviet conflict broke out in 1948, an important task of the Cominform lay in directing its efforts against the Communist regime of Yugoslavia. The leaders of the other parties of the Cominform, now familiar with Soviet accusations against the Yugoslav leadership, united in solidarity with the Kremlin and supported its proposal to call a Cominform congress to discuss the situation of the Communist Party of Yugoslavia (CPYu). On June 12, 1948, members of the *For Lasting Peace and People's Democracy!* editorial board, on behalf of all parties except the CPYu itself, condemned the policy of the CPYu's Central Committee. Several days later at a congress of the Cominform, not attended by the Yugoslavs, a resolution prepared in Moscow and based on a report by Zhdanov was approved, expelling the CPYu from the Cominform and the Communist movement in general. The location of the Cominform and its editorial office was transferred from Belgrade to Bucharest. A Cominform conference in 1949 declared the Yugoslav leaders to be a "clique of murderers and spies," which had "deserted to the camp of capitalism and reactionaryism," and carried out a "transition to fascism." Secretariat meetings in July 1948 and April 1950 questioned whether decisions linked to the breakup with Yugoslavia had been properly carried out. Led by Moscow, the Office of the Secretariat coordinated and checked the anti-Tito propaganda of the Communist parties of the Cominform and the people's democracies on a daily basis, including the illegal dispatch of propaganda materials to Yugoslavia as well as the organization of anti-Tito Yugoslav emigrations into European countries of the Soviet bloc.

Other functions of the most intensive Cominform activity involved questions of the organization and propaganda of the so-called movement of peace campaigners, the struggle against Western European social democracy, and measures taken by the people's democracies against "hostile ideology." Much attention was paid to the effect of propaganda on Western Europe; in particular, a meeting of the Secretariat in April 1950 raised the idea of intensifying radio propaganda aimed at France, Italy, and Belgium.

Except for the expulsion of the CPYu, the roster of Cominform parties stayed the same. Desires on the part of the Communist parties of Greece, Albania, and Finland to join the Cominform were, in the case of the first two, considered by the Soviet side to be inexpedient—a position that was confirmed at the congress in June 1948. By a Soviet recommendation at the same conference, the Finnish request was postponed to a later time, but the matter did not come up again.

In the fall of 1950, the Kremlin considered expanding the functions of the Cominform. The intent was to convert the Secretariat to a permanently functioning organ, which would exert stronger and more systematic control over the activities of the parties and how well they carried out Cominform decisions. Where absolutely necessary the Secretariat would issue directives straight to the member parties. A proposal to implement this, at Moscow's instructions, was submitted as his own by a French Communist Party functionary named Étienne Fajon at a Secretariat meeting in November 1950, where it was unanimously approved, and a new Cominform congress was called to confirm the indicated changes. But in early 1951, the Italian Communist Party leader, Palmiro Togliatti, whom Stalin now wanted to make the general secretary of the Cominform, not only began to try to convince Stalin of the impracticality of his own assignment but even expressed doubts about the usefulness of the Cominform in the future. As a result, neither the scheduled congress nor the planned reorganization of the Cominform took place. From that time on no more Cominform conferences or Secretariat meetings were held. Decisions in the name of the Cominform were no longer approved. This meant a serious decline in its political significance.

Still, the work of the Office of the Secretariat and the newspaper continued. The Cominform finally ceased operating after Stalin's death, as Kremlin policy changed. A particularly important role was played here by the turnaround in Soviet policy that ended the conflict with Yugoslavia. The curtailment and then absolute cessation of anti-Tito propaganda, which included the discontinuance in September 1954 of Cominform broadcasts aimed at Yugoslavia and also the beginning of the liquidation of Yugoslav emigrant organizations in Soviet bloc countries, deprived the Cominform of one of its main functions. With this new policy—leading to the unprecedented visit, on May 26 to June 2, 1955, of the most eminent Soviet leaders to Yugoslavia, where they actually expressed regret for Stalin's anti-Yugoslav campaign—the further usefulness of the Cominform, now enormously compromised as the instrument of this campaign, became extremely awkward for the Kremlin. Finally, the existence of the Cominform emerged as completely inimical to positions declared at the Twentieth Congress of the CPSU. A month and a half after the congress, in the middle of 1956, the member parties announced a decision to cease the activities of the Cominform, inasmuch as it had now "exhausted its functions," and "in terms of both its makeup and the content of its work" no longer was in service of the "new conditions" that had come into being.

See also Cold War; Comintern; Internationalism; Marshall Plan; Partisans of Peace; Socialist Camp; Soviet Bloc; Soviet-Yugoslavia Break.

FURTHER READING

Adibekov, G. M. *Kominform i poslevoennaja Evropa, 1947–1956 gg.* Moscow: Rossija molodaja, 1994.

Adibekov, G. M., et al., eds. *The Cominform: Minutes of the Three Conferences, 1947/ 1948/1949.* Annali della Fondazione Giangiacomo Feltrinelli, XXX. Milan: Feltrinelli, 1994.

Gori, F., and S. Pons, eds. *Dagli Archivi di Mosca: L'URSS, il Cominform e il PCI (1943–1951).* Fondazione Istituto Gramsci: Annale VII (1995). Rome: Carocci, 1998.

Pons, S. *L'impossibile egemonia: L'URSS, il PCI e le origini della guerra fredda (1943–1948).* Rome: Carocci editore, 1999.

LEONID JA. GIBJANSKIJ

Comintern

The Comintern, or Communist (Third) International, was a Bolshevik-inspired organization created in Moscow in March 1919 and disbanded in June 1943. Its original goal was to foster world socialist revolution on the Russian model by founding mass Communist parties dedicated to the armed overthrow of capitalism and imperialism. Although in the 1920s the Comintern successfully established Communist parties on a global scale, these parties proved incapable of leading the workers to revolution, despite several abortive attempts. Indeed, rather than becoming a vibrant fomenter and organizer of world revolution, the Comintern under Stalin turned into a compliant Bolshevized instrument of the Soviet state and its changing diplomatic requirements. The reasons for this unintended outcome have occupied scholars for many decades. Yet it is only since the partial opening of the Comintern's voluminous archives in the early 1990s that experts have been able to address these and many other contentious issues on the basis of solid empirical research.

The Comintern was very much the brainchild of Lenin, the charismatic leader of the Russian Bolsheviks and the driving force behind their seizure of power in October 1917. Lenin believed that the socialists' vote for war credits in August 1914 represented the death knell of social democracy. From then on, he insisted on a fundamental rupture with the socialist Second International, with his rallying cry: "Long Live the Third International." This dream came to fruition in March 1919, when a gathering of Bolsheviks and a handful of their European supporters created the Comintern, confidently predicting that rotten "bourgeois democracy" would imminently be superseded by superior "Soviet democracy." Lenin and the Bolsheviks were utterly convinced of the historical inevitability of world revolution, but despite the German "November Revolution" of 1918, the declaration of short-lived Soviet republics in Hungary, Bavaria, and Slovakia in 1919, and ill-conceived uprisings in Germany in March 1921 and October 1923, the Comintern was unable to unfurl the red flag over the European heartlands. At its Second Congress in summer 1920, the Comintern adopted the infamous "Twenty-one Conditions on Entry" with the intention of turning the Communist International into a highly centralized "world party," ruthlessly purged of "reformist dross," and its organizational structures closely resembling those of the Bolshevik Party. This embryonic Bolshevization of the Comintern was epitomized by the dominant position of the Russian Communists in its Executive Committee. Zinovyev, the first president of the Comintern, Bukharin, who replaced Zinovyev in 1926 as de facto head of the Comintern as a result of the post-Lenin power struggles, Radek, Trotsky, Lenin, and subsequently Stalin all played key roles in determining the Communist International's strategy and tactics.

By 1921 it was becoming clear to the despondent Bolsheviks that a longer-term consolidation and organization of the international Communist movement, not an outright frontal assault on the bastions of capitalism, was the order of the day. Hence, the united front tactics were ratified as a means of undermining social democratic influence among the working class and attracting the proletariat to Communist principles. This represented a more circuitous route to revolution, and as such reflected the shift to the moderate New Economic Policy introduced in Soviet Russia in the same year. The idea of the united front was to rally the workers behind a Communist-led defense of achievements gained since 1918 (the eight-hour working day, the legalization of trade unions, etc.), which, it was believed, were under threat by a "capitalist backlash." By exposing the social democrats as collaborators with the bosses, it was confidently expected that the mass of workers would transfer their loyalty to the Communists, thus creating mass parties for the eventual overthrow of capitalism. If this was the intention, the reality was sadly different. The united front tactics failed to attract the mass of workers, humiliating defeats (the British general strike in May 1926 and the Chinese Revolution in 1925–27) were suffered, important initiatives (national and international trade union unity) ended dismally, and by the late 1920s the Social Democrats, notably in Germany, were beginning to go on the offensive against Communist "infiltration."

Consequently, in 1928–29 Comintern leaders oversaw a dramatic transformation in orientation: "class against class" tactics, and the theory of "social fascism." A new revolutionary "Third Period" was prognosticated based on the emerging economic crisis of capitalism and the radicalization of the working masses. The Social Democrats were declared a bulwark of the capitalist state and the main enemy of communism. The prime task was thus to smash their restraining influence over the working class and make the Communists the sole party of the proletariat. This bitterly divisive policy proved largely disastrous, particularly in the Weimar Republic, where the existing gulf between the Communist Party of Germany and the Social Democratic Party of Germany was exacerbated, thereby facilitating Hitler's rise to power. Moreover, many "rightist" and "centrist" Communists were expelled from their parties as a result of the Stalinists' attack on Bukharinism in the USSR; not a few parties and Red trade unions were split asunder. Independence of thought and action in the Comintern, already in short supply, became a luxury as the process of Stalinization took hold—a process closely linked with Stalin's domestic "revolution from above" launched in 1928–29. Only in the course of 1934 was the "social Fascist" line belatedly reevaluated following the Nazis' destruction of the German labor movement, the gradual realignment of Soviet foreign policy toward "collective security" with the "bourgeois" powers, and indigenous strivings "from below" for working-class anti-Fascist solidarity.

Georgi Dimitrov, the new Bulgarian general secretary of the Comintern, played an important role in this shift to more realistic tactics. By all accounts, he persuaded Stalin to mollify the attacks on social democracy and seek broader cooperation with those forces prepared to struggle against the spread of fascism. The outcome was the announcement at the Comintern's Seventh World Congress in summer 1935 of the Popular Front, a policy designed to create anti-Fascist collaboration among Communists, socialists, liberals, and even the Catholic Church. The Popular Front was at some levels a remarkable success. The membership of many Communist parties mushroomed, and their influence in working-class organizations grew proportionately. In France and Spain, Popular Front governments were elected in 1936 on a platform of social and political reform. The Popular Front era, though, was marked by a deep unresolved tension between inherited Leninist ideological and organizational structures, and the initiatives of Communist parties to reengage with democratic national political cultures: how to prepare Soviet-style revolution while simultaneously defending parliamentary rule and so-called bourgeois civil rights?

Arguably the greatest paradox was that at precisely the time the Communist International had embraced a more flexible policy of cross-class alliances against fascism, Stalin unleashed his violent assault on the Comintern and foreign Communists. The bloodbath of the Great Terror (1936–38) elicited a profoundly negative response from the Communists' erstwhile partners in the Popular Front. Liberals and socialists recoiled from the barbarity of the repressions, jeopardizing any realistic chances of cooperation. In Spain, where a vicious civil war between ultraright nationalists and a coalition of Republican left-ists had been raging since July 1936, Stalin's personal war against Trotskyism seriously undermined the unity of the Republican camp, contributing in no small way to Francisco Franco's victory. Large numbers of loyal Comintern functionaries and rank-and-file foreign Communists, especially Central and East European émigrés resident in the Soviet Union, found their way into the Stalinist meat grinder accused of spying and wrecking. The Polish party was totally disbanded on Stalin's orders, and over a hundred thousand ethnic Poles living in the USSR were shot. In these circumstances, it appears that Comintern headquarters in Moscow ceased to operate in any meaningful manner, its officials driven half mad with fear. Historians do not agree on the causes of this mass repression, but most argue that the Stalinists were deeply worried about the threat of a potential fifth column in the event of war and thus sought to eliminate physically all those who may have formed an anti-Soviet, pro-Fascist front in the USSR.

The period August 1939 to June 1943 is universally regarded as marking the apogee of the Comintern's subordination to the dictates of Stalin's changing foreign policy. The dramatic about-face of September 1939, the volte-face of June 1941 after the Nazi invasion of the USSR, and the dissolution of the Communist International in May–June 1943 are eloquent testimony to this view, supported by much archival evidence. The Popular Front policy came to an inglorious end with the signing of the Nazi-Soviet Non-Aggression Pact in August 1939. In early September, Stalin informed Dimitrov that there was now no distinction between democratic and Fascist states; both were equally responsible for the outbreak of the "imperialist war." The Comintern immediately stopped all anti-Fascist propaganda, and insisted that Communists should oppose the war and their belligerent governments. The pact and its aftermath sowed deep confusion among many foreign Communists, notably in Britain and France, but with true Stalinist discipline nearly all approved it as an astute diplomatic ruse designed to gain the Soviet Union time to remilitarize.

The Comintern's position of neutrality toward the war persisted, with few exceptions, until Operation Barbarossa in June 1941. Overnight, Communist indifference to the war gave way to a life-and-death struggle against the Nazi forces of darkness. Everything was to be sacrificed to aid the war-ravaged Soviet Union. Communists were once again enjoined to form broad national fronts against Hitlerism. But already by spring 1941 Stalin had concluded that the Comintern was more a hindrance than a help for Soviet diplomacy, and in May 1943, after the momentous Battle of Stalingrad, the generalissimo decided to disband the Communist International largely as a sop to his Western allies. The irony was that even though the Comintern had been dissolved, a more rigid and hierarchical relationship between Moscow and the Communist parties was the postwar result. The road to polycentrism in the international Communist movement was to be long and hard.

Given this historical trajectory from an idealistic and relatively pluralistic world party of the revolution to a stiflingly bureaucratized Stalinist mouthpiece, it is hardly surprising that most historians have emphasized the abject failure of the Comintern, in particular the fact that no country, with the possible exception of Mongolia, experienced a Bolshevik-style revolution in the entire 1919–43 period. Scholars have also found precious little glory in other Comintern actions: legitimating the absurdities of social fascism; justifying the unjustifiable mass repression of loyal Communists under Stalin's tyranny; supporting the ideologically reprehensible Nazi-Soviet Non-Aggression Pact; and offering no resistance to Stalin's dissolution of the organization.

One way of assessing the Comintern's legacy is to outline the major controversies that have divided experts ever since the 1930s. They can be summarized as follows:

1. Continuities and discontinuities between the Leninist and Stalinist regimes in the Communist International: Was the latter the logical outcome of the former?

2. Relations between the central Comintern bodies in Moscow and the nominally independent national Communist parties: Was the highly centralist Bolshevik model universalized, or did the parties retain a measure of autonomy?

3. The relationship between the Comintern and official Soviet foreign policy: Was the Communist International merely a tool of Soviet realpolitik, or did its leaders maintain an ideological commitment to worldwide revolution?

4. The crucial issue of the attitudes adopted by Communists toward the Social Democrats: How to win over a majority of the organized working class for revolutionary perspectives in an essentially nonrevolutionary era?

5. More recently, the construction of Stalinist mentalities and identities: By what cultural and intellectual processes were critically minded non-Russian Communists forged into obedient Stalinists?

There are, of course, no definitive answers to these intriguing dilemmas. Suffice it to say that mulitiple and complex explanations are required. Stalin's triumph in the power struggles of the 1920s is clearly of enormous significance. It is hard to imagine that Trotsky, Zinovyev, or even Bukharin would have been quite as assiduous as Stalin in imposing Soviet state interests on the Comintern, reducing it to near total dependence on the Russian party. Yet Stalin could scarcely control the entire international Communist movement from his Kremlin office. Indeed, although the Soviet politburo constantly supervised the work of the Comintern Executive, its ability to elaborate effective policies for each national party was to a certain extent dependent on the level of accurate information from the parties themselves. Hence, even in the formidably centralized Comintern of the 1930s there was a dynamic interplay between the center and periphery, between the Russified executive in Moscow and the national parties operating in diverse political and socioeconomic conditions. Comintern directives had to be interpreted and implemented on the ground, and foreign Communists could exert some influence over central decision-making processes, as in the transition to the Popular Front in 1934.

Furthermore, the failure to spread revolution cannot be understood solely in terms of Stalin's "betrayal" of Leninist principles. Two external circumstances must be remembered. First, just about everywhere in the interwar years Communist parties remained weak minority organizations incapable of seriously challenging the established order (the Spanish party during the civil war and the Chinese under Japanese occupation are the main exceptions). Second, from the early 1920s bourgeois Europe was being recast, and capitalist stabilization in the industrially advanced countries rendered the situation essentially nonrevolutionary. The Great Depression did not fundamentally change this state of affairs, and whoever donned Lenin's mantle would have had to contend with this totally unforeseen outcome. It seems fanciful to conclude that, say, Trotsky would have translated this defensive scenario into a worldwide proletarian revolution under the auspices of the Comintern.

Finally, evaluating the Third International should not be reduced to the single issue of world revolution. Such categorical imperatives as total success or outright failure are not the stuff of historical analysis. The Comintern's legacy is surely deeply ambiguous. There *are* positive features among the many negative phenomena. In the 1920s, the Communist International nurtured an impressive range of theoretical responses to the problems of the day: the threat of fascism, the transition to socialism, the relationship of the state to society, and the attitudes to be adopted toward the Social Democrats, lower middle class, and peasantry. Trotsky, Bukharin, and Gramsci, to name but three, offered diverse solutions to these problems, and inspired various sections of the Left well into the 1970s and 1980s. In short, the Communist movement's theoretical arsenal is far richer than the Stalinist straitjacket would suggest.

From the Soviet perspective, the Comintern helped lay the foundations of postwar Communist expansion in Central and Eastern Europe by consolidating disciplined parties led by an efficient, highly trained, and fiercely loyal band of Stalinist cadres capable of administering the new "people's democracies." In those countries where Communist parties were legal, they strove to defend the daily interests of working-class people in local communities—the "Little Moscows" of Wales and Scotland, for example—and encouraged indigenous radical cultural trends. It is also likely that the threat of communism was a not inconsiderable factor in persuading capitalist governments to undertake social reform in the hope of assimilating labor movements. In concrete terms, during the Popular Front era and the years 1941–45, Communists were among the most active anti-Fascists, fighting in Spain and organizing the resistance to nazism in many occupied territories. The unprincipled zigzags of Stalinist policy should not blind us to these accomplishments.

In the final analysis, however, the Comintern and more broadly the international Communist movement became increasingly subject to an undifferentiated Stalinist general line applicable to all parties, regardless of local contexts. What is more, that line was determined by the Soviet leadership with Soviet state interests in mind, not the interests of foreign Communists.

See also Bolshevization; Bukharin, Nikolay; Dimitrov, Georgi; International Brigades; Internationalism; Lenin, Vladimir; Molotov-Ribbentrop Pact; Popular Front; Radek, Karl; Social Fascism; Stalin, Joseph; Zinovyev, Grigory.

FURTHER READING

Adibekov, G. M., et al., eds. *Politbiuro TsK RKP(b)-VKP(b) i Komintern, 1919–1943: Dokumenty.* Moscow: ROSSPEN, 2004.

Borkenau, F. *World Communism. A History of the Communist International.* Rev. Ed. Ann Arbor: University of Michigan Press, 1971.

Broué, P. *Histoire de l'Internationale communiste, 1919–1943.* Paris: Fayard, 1997.

Claudin, F. *The Communist Movement: From Comintern to Cominform.* Harmondsworth, UK: Penguin, 1975.

Degras, J., ed. *The Communist International, 1919–1943. Documents.* 3 vols. London: Frank Cass, 1971.

LaPorte, N., K. Morgan, and M. Worley, eds. *Bolshevism, Stalinism and the Comintern: Perspectives on Stalinization, 1917–53.* Basingstoke, UK: Palgrave Macmillan, 2008.

McDermott, K., and J. Agnew. *The Comintern: A History of International Communism from Lenin to Stalin.* Basingstoke, UK: Palgrave Macmillan, 1996.

Panteleev, M. *Agenty Kominterna: Soldaty mirovoi revoliutsii.* Moscow: 2005.

Rees, T., and A. Thorpe, eds. *International Communism and the Communist International, 1919–43.* Manchester: Manchester University Press, 1998.

Studer, B., and B. Unfried, "At the Beginning of a History: Visions of the Comintern after the Opening of the Archives." *International Review of Social History* 42, part 3 (1997): 419–46.

Vatlin, A. I. *Komintern: Idei, resheniia, sud'by.* Moscow: ROSSPEN, 2009.

KEVIN F. McDERMOTT

Command Economy, The

Until 1989, a Soviet-type economic system prevailed in the Soviet Union, Eastern Europe, China, Vietnam, North Korea, and Cuba, embracing about one-third of the world's population. By 2000, it remained only in North Korea and Cuba. In Soviet-type economies, most capital and land were owned by the state, and the state sought to direct the economy to achieve definite economic goals. Traditionally, they were known as "planned economies," on the grounds that purposive planning had replaced the market and the price mechanism as the guiding principle of economic activity.

Long-term plans, sometimes known as "general plans," covering ten to twenty years, set out the major economic and social goals. Five-year plans stipulated in more detail the investment projects and production targets that would achieve the next stage in the long-term goals. These were broken down into annual plans, which were put into practice by "operational plans," covering three months or even shorter periods. Subdivisions of the plans dealt with particular industries and regions, and with investment, production, trade and supplies, labor, finance, and foreign trade. "Balances" (budgets in physical and financial terms) coordinated the various aspects of the economy.

Many students of these systems concluded, however, that they were not adequately characterized as "planned economies" for at least three somewhat incompatible reasons. First, the term covers a wider range of economies than the Soviet-type system. During the Second World War and the decades that followed, several major economies outside the Soviet bloc, including Britain, France, and India, could be categorized as partially planned economies, in which a substantial part of national capital was owned and directed by the state. The most informative book on the behavior of this aspect of the British economic system during the Second World War was called *Planning in Practice*. And economic planning was often seen as a characteristic of even more market-oriented economies, because they were regulated by fiscal and monetary policy. This was sometimes termed "indirect planning" in contrast to Soviet "direct planning."

Second, Soviet-type planning in practice fell far short of its ideal type. Long-term plans rarely acquired official status and had little practical significance. The annual and operational plans were poorly coordinated; improvised investment and production decisions replaced coherent plans; and different aspects of the economy were rarely in balance. The principal Western authority on Soviet planning, Eugène Zaleski, while retaining the word "planning" in the titles of his books, argued that the plans were merely instruments to enforce the aims of the central political authority, and were "changing and often ephemeral"—the economy was "centrally managed" rather than planned.

A third school of criticism pointed out that planning as envisaged by Marx, Engels, and other socialists assumed that plans would not be imposed centrally by the state but instead would emerge as a result of democratic discussion and bargaining between producers and consumers. In Soviet Russia, all forms of workers' management, syndicalism, or guild socialism were rejected as early as 1918; attempts to combine workers' management were made only in Yugoslavia after the break with the Soviet Union and briefly in the Soviet Union under Gorbachev.

In recent years the Soviet-type system has usually been described as a "command" or "administrative-command" economy. Commands enforced by the state administration replace the profit motive that purportedly controls economic behavior in capitalist economies.

In practice, there is no economy in which the major economic decisions are taken entirely by state command or market forces. In modern capitalist economies, competition is imperfect and prices are distorted. The large health, education, defense, and transport sectors of the economy are owned by the state, and the state's huge purchasing power influences economic behavior. Macroeconomic equilibrium is not achieved spontaneously by the market but instead is brought about by government intervention. Large firms and multinational corporations are ultimately subject to the market, but the internal decisions within each firm are imposed by administrative command and/or reached by a bargaining process.

In the Soviet Union, at least three types of economic system existed, in which the command and market systems were combined in different proportions. The predominant system during the civil war of 1918–20 became known as "War Communism." Industry was nationalized, industrial output was allocated physically, consumer goods were rationed, and labor was directly controlled. Owing to inflation, the economy was virtually moneyless. In principle this was the closest approach in Soviet history to the ideal form of the command economy. But peasants—over 80 percent of the population—continued to work their own land, and no serious attempt was made to socialize agriculture. And in practice commands from central government were often ineffective, and illegal barter and local quasimarkets occupied a large place in economic life. What was the real economic system?

In 1921–29, the period of the New Economic Policy, the state ownership of large-scale industry was combined with private agriculture through a regulated market. Within and between the key state industries, a command system existed, and central goals were to some extent enforced, but the influence of the command system was constrained by the market.

From 1930, the command economy became predominant. One group of historians (including, for example, E. H. Carr) argues that the triumph of the command system was due to the inherent instability of the mixed economy of the 1920s. A second group (for instance, including Paul Gregory) claims that it was an inevitable consequence of the domination of the Bolshevik (Communist) Party and its monopoly of political power. A third group (including, for example, Stephen Cohen) insists that the overwhelming dominance of the command system was due to the political victory of Stalin or his wing of the party, and that a combination of command and market—a modified form of the New Economic Policy—could have enabled successful long-term economic development. A fourth group (including the present author) suggests that the command system primarily emerged as a consequence of the decision to embark on rapid industrialization, and that this decision, while controversial, was not arbitrary, but deeply rooted in the Bolshevik assessment of the dangers facing the weak Soviet economy in a hostile capitalist world. Probably all would agree that the command economy took an extreme form because, in Carr's words, "Stalin's personality combined with the primitive and cruel traditions of Russian bureaucracy, imparted to the revolution from above a particularly brutal quality."

The establishment of the command system involved and resulted from the doubling of the proportion of investment in the national income in the course of three or four years. This was accomplished by inflationary policies that switched labor and production from consumption to investment. The market relation between the town and countryside was disrupted, and in order to feed the growing urban population, private peasant agriculture was reorganized into a sector of collective farms, which were nominally cooperatives, and a smaller state farm sector. This "revolution from above" enabled the state to impose "compulsory deliveries" of agricultural products. Agriculture as well as industry was now subject to the command system.

Within the rapidly expanding industrial sector, the system of physical controls was greatly extended. Prices were fixed, and materials and equipment were distributed to existing factories and new building sites through a system of priorities, which enabled new factories to be built and bottlenecks in existing industries to be widened. The plans set targets for the output of major intermediate and final products; the physical allocation system was designed to see that these could be achieved.

In their quest for maximum output, the authorities adopted taut plans (commands), which the enterprises responsible for carrying them out sought to minimize. These planning methods resembled both War Communism and the wartime planning controls used in capitalist economies to shift resources to the war effort.

The imposition of the priorities of the state through an economic hierarchy was supplemented by horizontal relations between state enterprises. These horizontal interconnections, involving unplanned and even illegal exchanges and agreements, complemented the rather crude controls of the central plan, and made them workable. While the central authorities could always have the final say, a process of bargaining between all levels in the hierarchy, from the politburo to the factory department, was crucial to the effectiveness of the plans.

The command economy was an economy of scarcity. To overcome shortages, purchase agents, known as "pushers" (*tolkachi*), were sent from the consuming to the supplying enterprises in search of materials, replacing the sales' representatives characteristic of a market system. Each industrial ministry or subministry sought to become a self-contained "Empire," carrying out waste-

ful backward integration in order to control its supplies. Factories sought to build up stocks of materials while the central authorities sought to minimize them.

For a brief period in the early 1930s the authorities attempted to design a command system on War Communism lines. But this proved to be unworkable without the incorporation of important market or quasi-market elements, which became permanent though auxiliary features of the predominantly command system:

1. Each collective farm and state farm household was permitted to work a personal plot, and possess its own cow and poultry. This private or household sector was responsible for a substantial part of food production. After the compulsory deliveries to the state had been completed, each collective farm household, and each collective farm as a unit, was permitted to sell its produce on a free market ("collective farm market") at prices reached by supply and demand. Their large income from these sales on the free market partly compensated the peasants for the low prices they received from the state. Collective farmers were remunerated for their work for the collective partly in-kind and partly in money.

2. Manual and office workers in the state sector were paid a money wage, differentiated according to skill and the intensity of work, and most employees were free to change their jobs. The existence of a labor market (albeit imperfect) meant that wage levels were modified in response to supply and demand. There were major exceptions. The labor of some employees was subject to direct allocation from the center, especially of course the growing forced labor sector, which involved some three million people by 1939. About two million of these were working as forced labor, out of a total state-employed labor force (excluding collective farmers and individual peasants) of thirty-eight million.

3. Consumer goods were rationed only during 1930–35 and the war years of 1941–47. Otherwise, consumers were free to spend their income, in the state shops or on the free market, on whatever goods were available. In state-owned retail trade, prices were fixed, but the authorities endeavored—with indifferent success—to balance supply and demand through the use of fiscal measures, particularly the "turnover tax" (a purchase tax sharply differentiated according to the product).

4. All state enterprises were subject to financial controls through so-called economic accounting (*khozraschet*). Cost reduction targets, set for every ministry and enterprise, were an auxiliary but significant part of the annual plans.

This was then a money economy as well as a physically planned one. The money flows corresponded to all the physical flows, and the government sought to achieve financial equilibrium by means of a plethora of taxes, credit and cash controls, and currency plans. Most plans were approved as both physical commands and allocations or targets expressed in financial terms. In production planning, targets in physical terms usually predominated, but investment plans were discussed and approved by the politburo in financial terms, and were supplemented by the physical allocation of building materials and capital equipment. Some money transactions (for example, wage payments and sales on the free market) were not normally accompanied by physical controls.

The command economy (and its auxiliary quasi-market elements) prevailed in every country in which the Communist Party took power. It has sometimes been described not as a "command-administrative" but rather as a "command-repressive" system because of the role played by political repression. The term is most apposite for the Stalin period, when extreme coercion and the gulag were major instruments of control. During the purges of 1937–38, most of the heads of the economic departments of state, and most senior members of their staff, were executed. But even after Stalin's death the secret police continued to play an important role in every Communist country. Censorship greatly restricted economic debate. Permission to travel abroad, read foreign publications, and meet citizens of foreign countries was always greatly restricted.

How far was the Soviet command system economically effective? It achieved several of its major aims. First, unemployment was abolished and the Soviet Union established a boom economy during the years of world capitalist crisis. The economy was transformed into a socialist economy, in the sense that agriculture and trade as well as industry were nationalized or closely controlled by the state. Yet whether Soviet society, with its privileged ruling elite and its centralized state system, could properly be described as having achieved "socialism" remains a matter of controversy.

The command system successfully enforced the allocation of a high proportion of the national income to investment in general and to investment in the capital goods and defense industries in particular. Central control of investment enabled advanced technology to be diffused rapidly throughout the USSR in certain priority sectors. Important economies of scale were achieved through the standardization of products. The production drive induced managers and workers to exert great efforts to fulfill the plans. The priority system enabled the Soviet Union to develop a powerful armaments industry that in crucial respects outperformed the economically more advanced Nazi-German economy. After the Second World War, it enabled the Soviet Union to become one of the world's two superpowers, armed with nuclear weapons, and a serious contender in space travel and research.

The system also had great failures and weaknesses. In agriculture, output declined drastically; by 1940, the food output per head of population had not recovered to the 1928 level. Consumers suffered generally; the increase in the urban housing stock, for example, was far smaller in the Stalin period than the increase in the urban population. Millions of people died prematurely as a result of the 1933 famine and the harsh repressions that were endemic in the Stalin period.

The centralized system proved inherently clumsy in its effects at the point of production. The control of quality through centrally determined indicators proved difficult. And the central planning indicators greatly restricted initiative throughout the system. By the end of the 1930s it was already becoming apparent that the system that had managed to bring about technological revolution and economic growth from above was incapable, without drastic reform, of encouraging technological innovation from below.

As the Soviet economy and those of Eastern Europe matured, numerous largely unsuccessful attempts were made to modify the system by reducing the role of central command and increasing the importance of initiative from below. The political system played a significant part in the failure to reform the economic system. More radical attempts to establish some form of "market socialism" were outlawed by the party leaders. Whether market socialism or a successfully modified command system could have successfully replaced the Soviet-type system continues to be disputed.

See also Bureaucracy; Economic Reforms; Five-Year Plans; Gulag; Markets; Modernization; Planning; Revolution from Above; Socialist Market Economy; Soviet Industrialization; State; War Communism.

FURTHER READING

Berliner, J. *Factory and Manager in the USSR*. Cambridge, MA: Harvard University Press, 1957.

Devons, E. *Planning in Practice: Essays in Aircraft Production in Wartime*. Cambridge, UK: Cambridge University Press, 1950.

Granick, D. *The Management of the Industrial Firm in the USSR*. New York: Columbia University Press, 1954.

Gregory, P. R. *The Political Economy of Stalinism*. Cambridge, UK: Cambridge University Press, 2004.

Kornai, J. *Economics of Shortage*. Amsterdam: Elsevier, 1980.

Nove, A. *The Soviet Economy*. London: Allen and Unwin, 1977.

Rees, E. A., ed. *Decision Making in the Stalinist Command Economy, 1932–1937*. Basingstoke, UK: Macmillan, 1997.

ROBERT W. DAVIES

Communist Autobiography

Only worthy comrades, those who contributed body and soul to the victory of revolution, deserved membership in the Bolshevik Party. Participatory rights in the brotherhood of the elect depended not on age, status, or geography but rather on dedication and will. Communist autobiographies were one of the main standards by which entrance into the brotherhood of the elect was determined. By spotlighting the poetical structure of these documents, we must consider how party applicants told the story of who they were, how their stories varied according to the identities of their narrators and audiences, and how the rules for the construction of the Communist life story interacted with wider Bolshevik practices. Because applicants modeled their narratives on descriptions of spiritual growth, telling their lives up to the moment of "rebirth," the Communist autobiography de-individualized lives. Details could be pruned, embellished, or ignored in order to fit the author into the Communist literary conventions and write them into the Soviet order.

Every individual who wanted to become a party member had to submit an autobiography. In addition to cover letters and questionnaires, the personnel files kept by the primary party cells that have become accessible to historians after the breakup of the Soviet regime contain a considerable number of handwritten autobiographies, one to ten pages in length. Autobiographies allowed ap-

plicants to rewrite their selves, Communist style. Suitability for party membership was largely determined by the applicant's ability to present a cogent autobiographical claim to having reached the light of communism.

Explicit directives were not always given as to how the party applicant was supposed to write the autobiography. But party gatherings, evenings of reminiscences, and the reading of revolutionary hagiographies (in the 1920s, mostly endless versions of Lenin's life) gave individuals hints about what sort of text was acceptable. In constructing their autobiographies, authors were enjoined to consider the social status of their parents, the modes of thought and opinions of the elder members of their family, and the atmosphere typical of their childhood, education, and so on. Yet Communist autobiography was much more than a random collection of statements about the applicant's past. Rather than telling a detailed individual chronicle, the Bolshevik autobiographer carefully selected and ordered a set of events from his or her life, typically presenting a complex narrative with spiritual development as its crux. Events mentioned by party applicants were significant not in themselves but as indicators of the presence or absence of consciousness. Thus the autobiographical scheme usually continued with consideration of the especially important moments in the author's life, the formation of his worldview, the influence of his close friends, books, and crucial signposts in finding the Communist truth. Hurdles on the way had also to be examined, sometimes in considerable detail. Many autobiographies dwelled on the protagonist extricating themselves from religious superstitions, family feuds induced by his atheism, other differences in convictions, and so forth.

The brief, hand-scribbled autobiographies mimicked eschatological themes characteristic of the Bolshevik discourse. The party applicant/autobiographer claimed that he or she had reached a mature Communist consciousness (which had motivated the application for party membership) and narrated his or her life up to this current moment of "rebirth" as a process of spiritual growth and illumination. Indeed, the Communist autobiography was structurally analogous to Christian confession. The achievement of Communist perfection required an imperfect starting point: an unconscious, ideologically naive state. At the decisive moment, when the author claimed to have seen the light of communism, an individual's consciousness and the party line (which embodied the suprapersonal proletarian consciousness) were supposed to be merged. From the moment of conversion, the Communist's consciousness became permanent and perfect, and the author was now expected to devote himself or herself to the conversion of others.

Before conversion, the author claimed to have been passive and sinful; immediately thereafter he became active and pure. It was a crucial feature of the poetics of the Communist autobiography that the description of conversion involved a shift from the realist to the romantic literary style. The realist self is a self that is controlled by its social and physical environment, a self shaped by historical, economic, and social conditions, by the author's milieu with regard to his thoughts, volition, and morality. Such approach was taken by the autobiographer when he treated the "formative influence of his milieu." The narrative was informed by the Marxist materialistic determinism—the autobiographer described the unpleasant but necessary starting point of his story as an unfortunate state of mind resulting from an adverse environment. Floating, carried by the stream, the author's self renounced at this stage responsibility for the actions that were attributed to it.

When consciousness and action were emphasized, the Communist autobiography demonstrated it has a romantic side as well. In the romantic framework, people are able to change the world. Human beings are not mere products of their past, and the future is something they themselves shape. The romantic individual has the power to improve and even perfect humanity through an act of will. When the writer converted to communism and entered the land of freedom, the romantic side of his individuality supposedly became prominent. The author extricated himself from bourgeois influences and asserted his revolutionary will. The understanding that his environment was a social construct and not a natural given released the autobiographer from what had been the reality of that environment, and the author thereby became capable of changing it.

The autobiography was a central piece, read, reread, and cross-examined, in party admissions and party purges. Thus, autobiography intersects with related documents such as the minutes of the purge commissions, questionnaires, letters of recommendation, denunciations, and appeals composed by the victims of the purges. Success or failure was largely determined not by any objective biographical detail but instead by the author's ability to defend, in a set of closely monitored procedures, their claim to possess true Communist consciousness. A well-executed autobiography coupled with the ability to successfully uphold its claims in the face of possible counternarratives contributed greatly toward convincing authorities that the author was worthy of induction. The politics and poetics of these rituals must be distinguished. If politics refers to individuals' struggles to defend their Communist credentials when facing representatives of the central party apparatus as well as their local denouncers, poetics refers to the construction of their autobiography on the basis of rules prescribed by the official paradigm that demanded the author be constantly moving toward the light.

By the mid- to late 1930s, the autobiographical genre underwent important transformations pointing to the essentialization of moral features in the Stalinist era. If in the 1920s the autobiography had been a complex genre that dwelled on the phenomenological evolution of the individual's worldview and their arduous work of self-correction and self-discovery, in the 1930s the autobiography had become an extremely monotonous literary form that presented an unchanging, unalterable picture of the autobiographer's soul. If in the past autobiographers had drawn on a range of model selves, now there were two basic types: the good soul, and the wicked soul. The wonderful stories of self-transformation had been replaced by compendiums of the actions most illustrative of a moral ontology. The focus of the autobiographies had no longer anything to do with following the soul through its metamorphosis; all the Stalinist inquisitors wanted was to find previous illustrations of the individual's moral kernel. Those who wrote their autobiographies during the years of terror did not speak of becoming Communists; they simply insisted that they had never been anything else.

The flattening of subjectivity so visible in the autobiographies of the late 1930s resulted directly from the messianic assumption prevailing during mature Stalinism that the gap between the signifier and the signified had been completely erased. One was what one appeared, without residue or supplement. The mature Stalinist autobiographer had ceased to function as an individual and had completely internalized the perspective of the collective. The autobiography had come to resemble a completed questionnaire: they were not "composed" but "filled out."

The following questions established the framework for Communist autobiographies under Stalin: (1) What are my date of birth and social origins? (2) What is the social standing of my parents, and what is their relation to Soviet power? (3) Who are my brothers and sisters, and how do they relate to Soviet power? (a) Have any of my family members been disenfranchised? (b) Does anybody from my family live abroad? (4) When and where did I begin working? (5) Was I a wage laborer? (6) What party work or social work do I do? (7) What is the record of my education from childhood to the present? Communists were now invited to discuss their present before turning to their past. One's contribution to Soviet economic construction was usually examined prior to one's political development. Note that the issue of education, which appeared sixth in the scheme, was the first that demanded any chronological presentation at all. Items arranged around the theme "me and the party" came next: Who accepted me to the party and when? Was I in the opposition? For what have I been censured by the party? Have the censures been removed? Was I ever elected to any public post? Insofar as one's party record had to be discussed before one got to the circumstances of one's admission, there was no possibility of a conversion narrative.

A typical autobiography of the late 1930s will state when the author was born, what high school he or she attended, when he or she were conscripted, demobilized, or returned to the study bench, and so on. Next will come a list dispatched by the various party committees, political departments, and economic agencies. Extremely monotonous, the autobiography of this period is structured after a chronicle—something steadfastly avoided earlier. Since spiritual transformation did not figure in the story, the narrator's use of the passive voice was more or less consistent; one remained what one had always been—a loyal proletarian dedicated to party duties. The Central Committee had moved one from place to place like a pawn, and that person loved it, just as he embraced the opportunity to strip himself of all agency. At no point in the presentation of his party record did the autobiographer offer any sort of experiential observation about himself.

There was no talk of personal commitment to the victory of the movement, no excitement about the classless society looming ahead—not so much as a hint of these rattled the format of a digest. The autobiography was now no more than a compendium of good (or wicked) deeds spread around the calendar. This was a text that could likely have turned up in a juridical setting; it is informative and careful, not enlightening and sensational. This autobiography was most suitable to stand up in court, and indeed, many of the purges and show trials from the time of Ezhovshchina took the form of autobiographical interrogation.

See also Messianism; Militancy; Purges; Self-Criticism; Stalinism.

FURTHER READING

Fitzpatrick, S. "Lives under Fire: Autobiographical Narratives and Their Challenges in Stalin's Russia." *Die Russia et d'alleurs. Melanges Marc Ferro.* Paris, 1995.

Fitzpatrick, S., and Y. Slezkine, eds. *In the Shadow of Revolution.* Princeton, NJ: Princeton University Press, 2000.

Halfin, I. *Terror in My Soul: Communist Autobiographies on Trial.* Cambridge, MA: Harvard University Press, 2003.

Hellbeck, J. "Fashioning the Stalinist Soul: The Diary of Stepan Podlubnyi, 1831–1838." *Jahrbucher fur Geschichte Osteuropas,* no. 3 (1996).

Holquist, P. "State Violence as Technique: The Logic of Violence in Soviet Totalitarianism." In *Landscaping the Human Garden: 20th Century Population Management in a Comparative Framework,* ed. A. Weiner. Stanford, CA: Stanford University Press, 2003.

Pennetier, C., and B. Pudal, ed. *Autobiographies, autocritiques, aevux dans le monde communiste.* Paris: Belin, 2002.

Studer, B., et al. *Parler de soi sous Stalin. La construction identitare dans le communisme des annees trente.* Édition de la Maison des sciences de l'homme: Paris, 2002.

IGAL HALFIN

Communist Party in Albania

The Communist Party of Albania (PKSh) was founded clandestinely in Tirana on November 8–10, 1941, during a meeting of representatives from the major Communist groups. The representatives decided to merge existing Communist groups in the country and create a single Communist Party—in an agreement mediated by two representatives from the Communist Party of Yugoslavia, Miladin Popovic and Dushan Mugosha. The meeting also approved a provisional Central Committee composed of seven members: Enver Hoxha, Qemal Stafa, Tonin Jakova, Koçi Xoxe, Ramadan Citaku, Kristo Themelko, and Gjin Marku. Finally, this gathering approved a resolution and appeal to the Albanian people, calling on them to join the armed uprising against the Fascist occupier. The PKSh's organizational principle was democratic centralism, while its ideological basis was Marxism-Leninism. The Communists wanted a leading role in the war, and they succeeded because of their personal example: courage in battle, self-denial toward comrades, iron discipline, and propaganda about social equality.

After the war, the PKSh seized power in Albania, but the party's legitimacy was questioned in light of its violent and deceitful techniques. In 1948 the PKSh changed its name to Albanian Workers' Party (PPSh), emerged from the underground (from among the ranks of the Anti-Fascist National Liberation Front), and announced it was the only force ready to lead the country. The PPSh's operational mainstays were centralized government and secret decisions. Officially the party's leadership was collective, but in reality it was only exercised by the Communist hierarchy. All state apparatuses were controlled by Enver Hoxha and the PPSh Central Committee's politburo, and the party's decisions were law. The PPSh's plenums took place behind closed doors, and the population was informed about the proceedings by means of standard communiqués. Hoxha conducted a harsh battle within the party against the so-called antiparty groups for the duration of the PPSh's existence. Dissident anti-Communist groups, critical of the PPSh's political line, were never allowed to hold high-ranking positions in the party.

The PPSh tried to overcome the country's economic and cultural backwardness, and establish a political and social base, composed of the so-called working class, peasants inclined to cooperativism, and intellectuals with roots among the people. The party established schools and educational courses in cities as well as the remotest corners of Albania; created hospitals and medical centers throughout the country; and built factories, workshops, power plants, roads, and railroads to connect the country's rural and urban centers. The PPSh's attention to infrastructure extended to laying electrical grids and drinking water pipelines throughout Albania. The participation of women, both de jure and de facto, in the economic, political, and social life of the country was guaranteed, and old customs were banned. The party declared that Albania was the only atheist country in the world.

These efforts went hand in hand with rigged trials in which capital sentences were meted out, and families of anti-Communist opponents or antiparty groups were imprisoned or deported; freedom of speech and expression were denied, the country was militarized, and propaganda helped ensure the continuation of a psychological state of revisionist-imperialist encirclement. All of this kept Albanians in a permanent state of anxiety. The PPSh Central Committee had its own daily, *Zëri i Popullit* (Voice of the People)—but in actuality, the voice of the party—and its editor in chief was also a member of the Central Committee.

As far as foreign policy was concerned, after World War II the PPsh oriented itself toward the USSR and Yugoslavia up to 1948. From 1960 to 1978 it was principally allied with China. Albania was isolated from both the West and East after 1978. Police and state violence increased, as did poverty, and survival became difficult for most Albanians. The democratic changes in 1991 rectified this situation.

See also Cult of Personality; Despotism; Marxism-Leninism.

FURTHER READING

Pearson, O. *Albania as Dictatorship and Democracy.* London: Centre for Albanian Studies in association with I. B. Tauris, 2006.

PPSh. Dokumente kryesore. 8 vols. Tirana: Institute of Marxist-Leninist Studies–Albanian Communist Party Central Committee, 1971–86.

ANA LALAJ

Communist Party in Australia and New Zealand

In October 1920, the Communist Party of Australia (CPA) was set up in Sydney. The founding conference included representatives from the Australian Socialist Party, based in Sydney, and other small Communist groups and several New South Wales union officials. The party, with fewer than 250 members, was recognized by the Communist International in August 1922.

The Communist Party of New Zealand (CPNZ) was established at a conference in Wellington, over Easter 1921. Its initial members were drawn from the Wellington Socialist Party, several Marxist study groups, and former adherents of the Industrial Workers of the World.

In 1924, the CPNZ had only fifty-eight members and decided to become a component of the CPA. Visits by party organizers from Australia helped the New Zealand Communists consolidate their organization and establish their press. The CPNZ had a membership of less than one hundred, but a base in the seamen's and especially the miners' unions in 1928, when it was recognized as an independent affiliate of the Communist International.

At the end of 1928, the CPA had around three hundred members. The depression in Australia coincided with the Bolshevization of the party. Under the supervision of a plenipotentiary of the Communist International, a new leadership of unswerving loyalty to Moscow was installed over an organization in which the scope for debate was now restricted. General Secretary J. B. Miles along with his lieutenant and successor, Lance Sharkey, dominated the party from 1931 through the 1960s.

While the Australian Labor Party was in office federally and in several states during the depression, following the Comintern's current sectarian line did not prevent the CPA from growing, although most members were unemployed. The activities of the Communist-led Unemployed Workers' Movement attracted new members to the party. As the economy recovered, the rank-and-file groups that made up the Communist-led Minority Movement won control in several trade unions, influence in others, and control within the Left of the Australian Labor Party.

Another area of successful Communist work was the Movement against War and Fascism, particularly as the party, following the line of the Communist International, turned away from "Third Period" to nationalist "Popular Front" tactics. The transition to the new line in the NZCP was not smooth and involved intervention by CPA leaders.

For several years before the Hitler-Stalin Pact, the CPA had over four thousand members. The party was banned in May 1940 and operated underground, where necessary, until Germany invaded the Soviet Union. At that point the CPA reemerged, justifying support for the Australian war effort on nationalist lines. For this reason, Communist union officials preached harmony between workers and employers, and even broke workers' picket lines in industrial disputes.

Australian nationalism and the USSR's military efforts against Nazi Germany led to growth; by the end of the war, the CPA had sixteen thousand members, a representative in the Queensland Parliament, and control of a couple of municipal governments, and was a major force in the union movement. The CPNZ's maximum membership, in 1943, was fifteen hundred members.

The Cold War miscalculations in the conduct of the 1949 miners strike derived from the Moscow-initiated left turn of the late 1940s, and the Soviet invasion of Hungary in 1956 undermined Communist influence in Australia. Party members remained, however, in the leadership of important trade unions up through the 1980s.

Most of the CPA's leadership lined up with Moscow in the Sino-Soviet split in the international Communist movement. Dissenters, led by Ted Hill, set up the Communist Party of Australia (Marxist-Leninist, or CPAML) in 1964. It was largely confined to Victoria, where it retained control of some unions. Both the CPA and CPAML attracted a new layer of members from the students' and workers' struggles during the late 1960s and early 1970s, but with rapprochement between the United States and China, the CPAL rapidly waned.

In New Zealand the pro-Beijing current was in the majority. The minority, which included most of the party's trade union leaders, established the Socialist Unity Party in 1966.

The CPA's evolution along Eurocommunist lines and its condemnation of the Soviet invasion of Czechoslovakia precipitated a further split by Moscow-liners to form the Socialist Party of Australia in 1971.

Having facilitated the Prices and Incomes Accord between the Hawke Labor government and the union movement in 1981, which cut real wages, the CPA went into a terminal decline during the 1980s, finally dissolving in 1991. The Socialist Unity Party did likewise, while the CPNZ moved through a pro-Albanian position to Trotskyism. The Socialist Party of Australia, despite its small, aging, and mainly inactive membership, held on and reclaimed the name Communist Party of Australia in 1996.

See also Cold war; Eurocommunism; Nationalism; Popular Front.

FURTHER READING

Macintyre, S. *The Reds: The Communist Party of Australia from Origins to Illegality*. St. Leonards: Allen and Unwin, 1998.

O'Lincoln, T. *Into the Mainstream: The Decline of Australian Communism*. Sydney: Stained Wattle Press, 1985.

Trapeznik, A., and A. Fox, eds. *Lenin's Legacy Down Under: New Zealand's Cold War*. Dunedin: University of Otago Press, 2004.

RICK KUHN

Communist Party in Austria

The Communist Party of German Austria (as the party was called up to 1920) was created on November 3, 1918, by the union of several groups of left-wing socialists.

A few days later, the Austro-Hungarian Empire collapsed. When the Austrian Republic was proclaimed, the Communists argued for an immediate socialist transformation on the Soviet Russian model, but they did not find support among the masses. In spring and summer 1919, the more radically oriented leaders of the Communist Party of Austria (CPA), influenced by the example of the Hungarian Soviet Republic, made several efforts to seize power in Vienna, but their demonstrations were dispersed by the police. The Communists exercised a certain influence in the workers' soviets during the first years of the Austrian Republic, yet they proved unable to compete with the Social Democrats. Lenin wrote about the Austrian Communists in 1920 that they had not yet parted with the illusion that "apparently, just by declaring themselves Communists, the group can become a force without any struggle to gain influence among the masses."

As the Austrian Republic was stabilizing itself, the CPA concentrated its efforts on penetrating the labor union movement, and participated in carrying out a number of mass strikes. Vienna became one of the loci of the bond between the Executive Committee of the Comintern and various individual Communist parties, and many Austrian Communists worked in Germany and the Balkan countries. In 1922, a struggle for the CPA's leadership broke out between Josef Frei and Karl Toman, thereby undermining the efficiency of the party in the fight against "Austrofascism," which was beginning to gain strength. The election of Johann Koplenig as general secretary of the CPA in fall 1924 stabilized the internal party politics. The CPA abandoned the notion of a reunification with Germany and the plans for creating a Danube Federation in 1925, instead turning its attention to working within the institutions of the Austrian Republic proper.

When, on July 15, 1927, a spontaneous workers' demonstration protesting the exoneration of a number of Fascist murderers was fired on by the police, the end of an era of internal political stability was at hand. The CPA called for a general strike and summoned the workers to arms, but it failed to gain the support of the socialists. In the aftermath, varying appraisals of the events of July provoked a new wave of ideological discussions in the party leadership; for example, the question was raised as to whether it was necessary to issue slogans calling for the formation of workers' soviets.

By the 1930s, the CPA had more than five thousand members and received about twenty thousand votes in the parliamentary elections. The consolidation of the authoritarian regime of Chancellor Engelbert Dollfuss was accompanied by increased repressions against the Communists, and in 1933 the party was banned. During the clashes in 1934, the Communists played an active role among the Schutzbundists; in Vienna alone some 350 party members were arrested. After its defeat, the CPA brought forward the slogan of unity of action with the "revolutionary socialists" and the creation of illegal labor unions.

The CPA concentrated its efforts during the later 1930s on propaganda for maintaining the national sovereignty of Austria against the "Anschluss" (annexation) with Hitler's Germany. In 1937 the party theoretician Alfred Klahr issued a statement in support of the integrity of the Austrian nation. A hundred thousand Austrian citizens signed an open letter to the government of Kurt Schussnigg proposing the creation of a national front against Hitler.

After the annexation of Austria by the Third Reich, the Communists took an active part in the resistance, thereby subjecting themselves to harsh reprisals from the Gestapo. From its emigration base in Moscow, the CPA continued to conduct its radio propaganda, publish its newspaper, the *Rote Fahne* (Red Flag), select personnel to be dispatched to Austrian territory, and organize partisan and diversionary activities. The liberation of Austria from Nazism led to the legalization of the CPA, which then issued a program for an "authentic people's democracy." The Communists took advantage of the support of the Soviet occupation administration in Austria. Koplenig became vice chancellor in the provisional government of Karl Renner. With the CPA's participation, this government adopted laws relating to denazification and nationalization. In the parliamentary elections of November 1945, the CPA received 175,000 votes and won four deputy mandates.

With the beginning of the Cold War, the CPA, which unconditionally supported the foreign policy line of the USSR, was shunted to the political sidelines, and by the end of the 1940s its only representatives were in regional and municipal power organs. When Austrian neutrality was declared, the Communists maintained their course and came out against the integration of Austria into the common market. They supported the broadening of contacts with the USSR and neighboring Eastern European countries. In 1958, an extraordinary CPA congress adopted the "Austrian Path to Socialism" program. From 1959 on the party was no longer represented in the

Austrian parliament. In subsequent decades the CPA, though it criticized the direction of the Austrian government, played no noticeable role at all in the political life of the country.

See also Antifascism; Comintern.

FURTHER READING

Hautmann, H. *Die verlorene Räterepublik. Am Beispiel der KPDÖ* [The Lost Soviet Republic: The Example of the CPDÖ (Communist Party of Democratic Austria)]. Vienna: Europa, 1971.

Historische Kommission beim zk der KPÖ. *Die Kommunistische Partei Österreichs. Beiträge zu ihrer Geschichte und Politik* [The Communist Party of Austria: Papers on Its History and Politics]. Vienna: Globus, 1987.

Koplenig, J. *Reden und Aufsätze, 1924–1950* [Speeches and Essays, 1924–50]. Vienna: Stern, 1951.

ALEKSANDR I. VATLIN

Communist Party in Belgium

The Communist Party of Belgium (CPB) was born in September 1921 from the Comintern-imposed merger of a small antimilitarist, antiparliamentary group (with approximately two hundred militants), which itself had emerged from Jeunesses socialistes, with a minority (about seven hundred members) that had been expelled from the Socialist Party (Parti ouvrier belge, Pob). Up to 1927 the party never had more than about one thousand militants. It had a weak presence in Flanders, but took root in working-class circles and among unionized employees in Brussels as well as the industrial areas of Wallonia, in the heart of areas dominated by social democracy. Following the July 1932 strikes in Wallonia, the CPB attracted more working-class members, tripling its membership and electing three representatives that same year. The Pob regained the initiative, though, by adopting Henri de Man's economic plan.

In 1935 the CPB adopted the Comintern's Popular Front line. The party's previous leadership group was replaced, and the revolutionary labor union groups were dissolved. The rise of powerful Fascist movements in Flanders and Wallonia favored the anti-Fascist strategy. Socialist and Communist youth merged into a single organization. In 1936, the CPB again expanded and achieved electoral success, this time due to the failure of de Man's plan and a revived social movement. The party went from twenty-five hundred members in 1935 to eighty-five hundred in 1936; nine representatives were elected, with almost 12 percent of the vote in Brussels and 6 percent on the national level. The general strike of May–June 1936 and solidarity with republican Spain consolidated party support. On the eve of the war, the CPB had a solid electoral presence at all levels and about ten thousand members. Following the national policies adopted by the Comintern's Seventh Congress, and to confront the development of Flemish nationalism with Fascist tendencies, the party created a Flemish Communist Party within its ranks and organized conferences in Wallonia.

Like all other Western Communist parties, the CPB had to adapt to the shift from anti-Fascist defense to the struggle against two imperialisms after the 1939 Molotov-Ribbentrop Pact. It launched the Front de l'Indépendence, which became the most important popular movement of the anti-Nazi resistance. During the war, the party extended its alliances and, for the first time in its history, became a serious contender to the Socialist Party. It had wide-ranging contacts within the masses, both in labor unions and in patriotic circles, and hoped to translate this into political support. With one hundred thousand registered members, the CPB took part in the national unity government of September 1944. But despite its best electoral showing ever (12 percent of the vote), the party was disappointed by the 1946 elections in the face of higher expectations. It held several ministerial positions (in Supply, Public Works, and Health), and adopted a productivist approach, opposed strikes, and placed all its energies at its ministers' disposal. It sacrificed its union organizations, which had developed during the war, on the altar of unity, while the Front de l'Indépendence refused to play the social and political role that the party had hoped it would. As had been the case before the war, the party found itself without "transmission belts"—in other words, deprived of those "mass organizations" that constituted the strength of the other Belgian parties, especially socialist and Catholic groups. The CPB voluntarily left the government in March 1947 over the issue of the price of coal; caught between the need for a policy of austerity and workers' dissatisfaction, its position had become untenable. The Cold War led the party back to its previous outlook: a fortress under siege. It paid dearly for its isolation during the 1949 elections, after which it would undergo a long and continuous "descent to the depths" on the electoral front, leading to its total disappearance in terms of parliamentary representation in 1985.

The CPB exhibited all the characteristics of Communist parties in the Cold War period—sectarianism, cult of personality, expulsions from labor unions, and antisocialist aggression—set against a generalized anti-American backdrop. Under the guidance of the French Communisty Party, the CPB expressed its loyalty to the Soviet troops that freed the country. The Vilvorde Congress of 1954, the "tutelage" of French and Italian comrades notwithstanding, witnessed a radical shift in the CPB's policies, getting rid of a party leadership that had been in charge since the end of the war. The CPB attempted to reinsert itself into Belgian society, without renouncing its unconditional support for the Soviet Union. The party now aimed for concerted action with socialist militants, and the Communists joined the socialist labor union. The cadre of this fundamentally worker-based party was only mildly influenced by the Budapest events in 1956, thereby dashing any electoral hopes: in 1958 the CPB received about 1.8 percent of the vote and only two representatives. Between 1961 and 1965 the party experienced a brief revival (the number of representatives climbed first to five and then to six), mostly due to a general strike that mobilized almost one million workers. The CPB's influence could be felt in the large Walloon factories, the public sector, and the universities. Once the party leadership condemned the invasion of Czechoslovakia, however, it lost the support of workers' federations in the country's south, as they came to grips with the collapse of the traditional bastions of the Walloon economy—coal mining and the steel industry.

From that moment on the CPB had to strike an impossible balance between, on the one side, the working-class strongholds tied to past forms of struggle and pro-Soviet orthodoxy, and on the other side, new groups of workers and intellectuals attempting to construct tangible alternatives and even new alliances, especially with Christians. The party was too weak and marginal at this point to make any headway under Mikhail Gorbachev's reforms. It completed its federalization in 1989 (as had the other Belgian parties), and this not only exposed the weakness of its three autonomous components (Brussels, Flanders, and Wallonia) but also the cultural and political differences dividing them. The fall of the Berlin Wall and the Soviet Union's disappearance caused the party to fragment into several local nuclei, without cohesion or consistency.

See also Anti-Fascist Resistance; National Roads to Socialism.

FURTHER READING

Gotovitch, J. *Du rouge au tricolore. Les communistes belges de 1939 à 1944*. Brussels: Labor, 1992.

JOSÉ GOTOVITCH

▬▬

Communist Party in Bulgaria

The Bulgarian Social Democratic Party (BSDP) came into being in 1891, thirteen years after the liberation of 1878 marked the end of five centuries of Ottoman domination and rule. The establishment of the party was officially noted the first issue of *Rabotnik* (Worker), a BSDP publication. The party mimicked the existing socialist parties in Europe. Its ideological platform was not critical of Marxist socialism's theoretical views, and it underestimated national problems.

After the unification of the BSDP with the Bulgarian Social Democratic Union (BSDU) in 1894, the Bulgarian Workers Social Democratic Party (BWSDP) was created. During the next twenty years the BSWDP had limited public potential and became a peripheral but ever-present political force. The BSWDP split in 1903. The fraction led by D. Blagoev formed the BWSDP (Narrow Socialists), with twelve hundred members. The Narrow Socialists defended the Marxist orientation of the Bulgarian socialist movement and encouraged Bolshevism's influence.

At the start of the First World War, the BSWDP (N.S.) declared its opposition to Bulgaria's participation in the war, criticizing its "aggressive and imperialistic nature." The party adopted the Bolshevik slogan regarding the defeat of the Bulgarian government and the transformation of the imperialistic war into a "civil" war.

Bulgaria's national catastrophe as Germany's ally during World War I, with territorial losses and approximately 150,000 dead, facilitated the recovery and expansion of the organizational structure of the BSWDP (N.S.), and the number of its members grew to twenty-five thousand. The party's reputation with the public was influenced favorably by events in Russia in 1917.

A sharp change in the strategies and tactics of the BSWDP (N.S.) came about in 1919, when the party became a member of the Comintern. It adopted the Bolshevik principles of revolutionary class struggle. In May of 1919, during its First Congress, BSWDP changed its name to the Bulgarian Communist Party (Narrow Socialists), BCP (N.S.). With the consent of its full leadship and without any break in the party's unity, the BCP (N.S.) became a member of the Comintern in 1919, a move that transformed the BCP (N.S.) into one of the most stable components within the Comintern's structure and an undiscriminating follower of its strategies and tactics. The period 1919–23 saw the culmination of the process of strengthening the BCP (N.S.) poistion within Bulgaria. The party won a large number of votes (approximately 175,000) in the 1919 parliamentary elections.

V. Kolarov's election as general secretary of the Comintern's General Secretariat on December 6, 1922, eased the way for implementing the Comintern's line, which called for taking power and creating a workers-and-peasants government in Bulgaria. The Comintern's leadership condemned the neutrality of BCP (N.S.) in the events following the coup on June 9, 1923, that toppled A. Stamboliiski's government. A Comintern directive (September 14, 1923) called on the BCP (N.S.) "to immediately commence an open struggle." V. Kolarov's instructions called for an uprising and set the date for September 22–23. The uprising was crushed, and its main leaders, V. Kolarov and G. Dimitrov, fled to Yugoslavia and Austria.

The Law of Defense of the State (LDS, 1924) approved the government's repressions against the attempt to legalize the BCP (N.S.). The Comintern countermanded the course toward an armed uprising in March of 1925. The new instructions called for the party's "digging in" among the masses and performing actions in defense of their economic interests.

The argument that the BCP (N.S.) was insufficiently Bolshevized was used to justify the party's failure in its struggle against the government. This "weakness'" was overcome by training most party functionaries in the USSR. This became standard practice in the relations between the Comintern and the BCP (N.S.) and predetermined the BCP's pro-Soviet orientation, transforming it into a main conductor of Soviet influence in Bulgaria. The Bolshevized BCP approved the party leadership's authoritarian style. The Fifth Congress of the BCP (N.S.), held in 1922, was the last during the organization's existence as an opposition party within Bulgaria. After 1925, for a period of several years, the party leadership functioned outside Bulgaria, and some of its leading functionaries, such as G. Dimitrov and V. Kolarov, remained in exile in the USSR until 1944–45.

The Comintern maintained a low profile during the factional conflict, refusing to demonstrate clear preferences, but it disallowed the removal from leadership positions of Dimitrov and Kolarov. Dimitrov's faction reevaluated the party's policies. Dimitrov directed attention toward the need for a broad, unified anti-Fascist front, outlining this task clearly in his speech before the Seventh Congress of the Comintern (1935). He was nominated as secretary general of the Comintern and was recognized as a "leader" of the BCP.

In 1938 a resolution for the unification of the WP with the BCP (N.S.) was adopted. The unification process was completed in 1940 and the new party assumed the name BWP. The nonaggression pact concluded between Germany and the USSR on August 23, 1939, was a serious blow to BWP's efforts to create a united anti-Fascist front. It registered almost no reaction to Bulgaria's accession to the Tripartite Pact (March 1, 1941).

The Nazi aggression against the USSR brought clarity at last to BWP's strategies and tactics. The Comintern's instructions (issued on June 22, 1941) for the organizing of an armed resistance in support of the USSR and for a tactical reorientation to prepare for assuming political power after the expected victory of the anti-Nazi coalition were accepted. The armed anti-Fascist resistance was organized under unfavorable political conditions in Bulgaria. With Berlin's assistance, there had been a partial territorial revision in Bulgaria's favor, and after March 1, 1941, there was in effect no occupation in the classic sense. The resistance destabilized the political order and justified the Bulgarian government's reluctance to break off diplomatic relations with the USSR and to send troops to the Eastern front.

Under the Comintern's instructions, a program was announced in Bulgaria on July 17, 1942, that called for the creation of the Fatherland Front (FF). This national anti-Fascist front's implementation was the work of the BWP, which secured the participation of the Left and anti-German political faction. In 1943 partisan detachments began to form, made up of Communists, nonparty members, and leftist members of the agrarian union. Via the adopted tactics of active resistance against Bulgaria's participation in Hitler's union and the unification of part of the opposition under the platform of FF, the BWP won public support and secured a strategic advantage for itself. On September 8 and 9, 1944, it took power through a coup in the capital and partisan actions in the countryside. The success of the action was ensured by timing: the antigovernment military and political strike coincided with the Red Army's entry into Bulgaria on September 8, 1944, which paralyzed any potential resistance to the coup. The FF coalition gained its victory with the indirect assistance of the Soviet forces.

The government organized on September 9 by FF, BWP (which by the end of September assumed the name BWP Communists) included four ministries, among them the Ministry of the Interior. The leadership of the BWP did not allow itself to assume power and rule independently ahead of time, but limited the capitalist system's influence by implementing various measures, eliminating political opposition, and removing the monarchy via a nationwide referendum (September 8, 1946). It won election to the NA in November of 1945 and to the the GNA in 1946, adopting the new constitution of the People's Republic of Bulgaria (December 4, 1947). In the end of 1946, BWP (C) elected the prime ministers. G. Dimitrov was the first Communist prime minister after September 9, 1944. The BWP (C) radically reconstructed the economic system in 1947–48, nationalizing private industrial and commercial enterprises, banks, and mines.

At its Fifth Congress, held December 18–25, 1948, the BCP proclaimed its itself the principal political power and announced a transition from capitalism to socialism. The party leadership followed Moscow's instructions without totally neglecting national peculiarities—for example, it did not nationalize the land property and preserved the "peoples democratic" regime—but confirmed Bulgaria's pro-Soviet orientation.

The BCP's coalition partners (with the exception of the BAPU) gradually lost their political influence and eventually their existence as independent political parties. The Kremlin's intervention assisted the conducting of inner party purges. Traycho Kostov, one of the BCP's leaders, was sentenced and executed in 1949. The BCP was a cofounder of the Cominformburo (September 1947) and backed the resolution against the YCP (1948), but reluctantly declared the breakup with Yugoslavia, because in 1947 the conditions for a Bulgarian-Yugoslavian federation were coordinated.

Centralized economic leadership overcame the crisis, increased the rate of development, and improved living conditions, though without attaining the maximalist forecasts for the performance of the first economic plans. The BCP lowered its industrialization rates after Stalin's death. Social discontent, as in other Eastern European states, forced BCP's leadership to increase the production of consumer goods (Sixth Congress, 1954).

The April Plenum (April 2–6, 1956) marked the start of large-scale de-Stalinization. The deposition of the cult toward personality degraded V. Chervenkov, party leader at the time, and uplifted Todor Zhivkov, who remained at the top for more than thirty-three years. Although his political talents did not distinguish him from fellow party members and he had played no significant role in the anti-Fascist resistant, Zhivkov was nonetheless elected to lead the BCP. He was at first considered as a "temporary, compromise figure," but proved adept at keeping Bulgaria on a moderate course of post-Stalinist ideological, political, and economic development. As first secretary of the CC of the BCP, Zhivkov pragmatically and skillfully adapted to changes in Soviet policies. He managed to avoid the tensions that erupted into turmoil in Poland and Hungary (1956) and in Czechoslovakia (1968). With his measured self-criticism and balanced approach to the removal of the "old guard" Zhivkov won the right to determine the direction of the People's Republic of Bulgaria. At the Seventh Congress (1958), Zhivkov rendered an exaggerated account of accomplishments and proclaimed the complete victory of socialism in Bulgaria.

The permanent removal of leadership cadres from the past, identified as culprits responsible for the personality cult and for "inflicted heavy damages" to the BCP and the PRB (V. Chervenkov, among others) took place at the Eighth Congress (1962). Zhivkov forbade deviations like the "Chinese," "Albanian," or "Yugoslavian" models and eliminated from power those who attempted his removal during the middle of the 1960s. At the Ninth Congress, the twenty-year prospects for the construction of socialism and the transition to communism's construction were copied from Moscow. Zhivkov secured the Soviets' aid against proposals (rejected by the Kremlin on July 31 and December 4, 1963) for "convergence" and the subsequent "amalgamation" of the PRB with the USSR (as the 16th Soviet Republic). Zhivkov created a higher ruling elite and party nomenclature and with its loyal assistance maintained "the ideological and political unity" of BCP members (who numbered approximately nine hundred thousand by 1985). The loyal cultural functionaries, nonparty members, represented a privileged caste.

Unrealistic plans for the socialist society's construction by 1980 were corrected at the Tenth Congress (1971) by adopting a program that called for the construction of "a developed socialist society." This aim remained in BCP's designs, presented at the Eleventh (1976), Twelfth (1981), and Thirteenth (1986) congresses.

Zhivkov interpreted Gorbachev's call for speedy restructuring as summons to perfect socialism. Soviet perestroika radicalized relations between the BCP and the CPSU. Zhivkov tried to reform Bulgarian socialism without either yielding his personal power or declining to cooperate closely with the USSR. His "July concept," dated 1987, was an effort to find a way out of economic crisis. The document proposed a "new model" of economic activities and the reorganization of banking and commercial activities. Zhivkov's "independent course," with its gradual distancing from Moscow at last convinced Gorbachev and the Bulgarian reformers (longtime associates of Zhivkov, who included P. Mladenov and A. Lukanov) that he should be removed from party and state authority. The Plenum of the CC (November 10, 1989) accepted Zhivkov's "resignation."

The Soviet scenario for Bulgaria did not play out according to schedule. It was expected that the first democratic elections, held in June 1990, would result in the party's voluntary retreat from power. But the BCP, regardless of the expectations of some influential figures from the state and party leadership, obtained public support and remained a paramount factor in government.

The beginning of 1990 saw the Extraordinary Fourteenth Congress of the BCP. Events of 1989 had disrupted the BCP's political homogeneity. Factions came into being, which, in 1990–91 formed themselves into several Communist parties and alternative socialist formations, which with their "elected leaders" reproduced and "saved" the former BCP nomenclature, cast out as compromised (or left in "reserve") of the reforming BCP. On April 3, 1990, the BCP adopted the name "Bulgarian Socialist Party" (BSP) via a referendum. The BSP leadership did not wish to focus on tactics against the increasingly confrontational behavior of the political opposition. The BSP underwent an ideological evolution, freeing itself from the Bolshevik, Stalinist, and neo-Stalinist model of socialism. After November 10, 1989, it proclaimed the unclarified formula of "democratic socialism," a concept that allowed the party leadership to criticize and propose a cardinal restructuring of the existing system.

At the Fourteenth Congress the old designations of the party leadership organs were brought back into use: higher party council (Central Committee), presiding body (politburo); the Congress elected Alexander Lilov as chairman; the newspaper *Rabotnichesko delo* was renamed *Duma*. New bylaws and a political declaration, the "Manifesto for Democratic Socialism," were adopted. A new numbering of the congresses was put in place: the Fourteenth Congress became the Thirty-ninth Congress of the BSP. Ideologically, the BSP adopted socialist and social democratic values, distancing itself from Marxism with the intention of transforming itself into a "modern left party" and redirecting Bulgaria's political and economic system toward market capitalism. The unconvincing application of these values did not increase the party's or its leadership's public authority, but turned instead into a source of "tension and instability." The opposition's integration into the government (a coalition government with BSP's participation was created in April of 1991) did not provide the BSP with a successful formula for interaction during the transition to democracy and for overcoming an economic crisis. Just before the Fortieth Congress (December 1991)—conducted for the first time in opposition (Zhan Videnov was elected as chairman)—the party lost the parliamentary elections (October 1991) and more than half its members.

At the Forty-first Congress (June 1994), the BSP took a course toward pre-term parliamentary elections, which it won in December with an absolute majority. Videnov formed a government, which functioned in conditions of a deepening economic crisis and insurmountable contradictions among BSP's leadership. These conditions led to Videnov's resignation from both positions, declared before the Forty-second Extraordinary Congress of the BSP in December 1996. G. Parvanov was elected as party chairman and returned the mandate for the forming of a new government to President Zh. Zhelev (February 4, 1997). The BSP lost the pre-term parliamentary elections for the Thirty-eighth NA (April 19, 1997).

BSP's government secured associate membership for Bulgaria in the European Union on February 1, 1995 and filed an application for EU membership on December 16 that year, commenced individual dialogue with NATO on February 2, 1996, and became a member of the Central European Initiative (CEI). The United States gave Bulgaria permanent most favored nation status on July 17, 1996, and Bulgaria became a member of the World Trade Organization (WTO) on October 2, 1996.

At the Forty-third Congress (May 1998), G. Parvanov was reelected as BSP chairman. At the Forty-fourth Congress (May 2000), BSP's orientation toward NATO was officially noted, but the party leadership did not conduct an internal referendum regarding the resolution. "Coalition for Bulgaria" was created at BSP's initiative on January 28, 2001. Parvanov was nominated for president on September 29, 2001, and won the November 8 election.

As a result, Sergey Stanishev was elected BSP chairman at the Forty-fourth Congress. The BCP was accepted as a regular member of the Socialist International on October 28, 2003.

The first session of the Forty-fifth Congress convened on June 8–9, 2002. At the beginning of 2005, a decision was made to hold the congress during the autumn of 2005, after the parliamentary elections for the Fortieth NA (June 25), at which it was expected that the BSP, in coalition with several other parties, would win full majority.

See also Dimitrov, Georgi; Zhivkov, Todor.

FURTHER READING

Banac, I., ed. *The Diary of George Dimitrov, 1933–1949.* New Haven: Yale University Press, 2003.

Bell, J. D. *The Bulgarian Communist Party from Blagoev to Zhivkov.* Stanford, CA: Hoover Institution Press, 1986.

Brown, J. F. *Bulgaria Under Communist Rule.* London: Pall Mall Press, 1970.

Oren, N. *Bulgarian Communism: The Road to Power, 1934–1944.* New York: Columbia University Press, 1971.

Rothschild, J. *The Communist Party of Bulgaria: Origins and Development, 1883–1936.* New York: Columbia University Press, 1959.

VITKA TOSHKOVA

Communist Party in Central Asia

Communism appeared in Central Asia, in Turkistan and in the steppe region, at the very end of the 19th century. It was the consequence of a decade of political activism on the part of czarist political deportees, centered on the colonial railways and mines. In 1894–97, the Social Democrat A. S. Kotcharovskaja was deported to Verny. According to the state archives of Uzbekistan, czarist police in the main cities of Turkistan were concerned about Marxist and socialist circles operating in their territory. The most important of these was the Pushkin Society, created in Tashkent in the early 20th century, which became increasingly politicized after the student rebellions in Petersburg, Moscow, and Kiev were crushed in 1902 and during the 1905 revolution. Others seen as dangerous were the V. D. Kornijushin circle in Tashkent; the railway workers' Circle "Vperëd," created by K. D.

Litvishko; the Tashkent General Revolutionary Group directed by Ilia Shendrikov; and the Marxist typograph N. I. Koptsov who was distributing Lenin's "Iskra." There were problems in Samarkand as well, where the Bolshevik Social Democrat M. V. Morozov was publishing the newspaper "Samarkand," in which he expressed Marxist, Menshevik, Bolshevik, and even Anarchist and Zionist ideas. In December of 1904, the Group of Social Democrats of Ashkhabad was created in Turkmenistan; it had close connections with the Bakou and Tiflis social democratic organizations, besides other groups in Krasnovodsk, Kyzyl-Arvat, and Bayram-Ali, all railway stations on the Transcaspian line.

A definitive split between social democratic and Socialist Revolutionary groups took place after 1906 and led to the meeting in Tashkent of the first Regional Conference of the Social Democratic Organizations in Turkistan, which brought to light a lack of indigenous involvement and the need for agitation among the Muslim population. Numerous groups were formed in Margelan, Skobolev, Kokand, and Kazalinsk, with Tashkent, the home of fifteen soldiers' and workers' organizations, playing a prominent role as the political and economic center, while Ashkhabad played a secondary role.

There was also some Marxist influence, in the steppe region, especially among the Russian intelligentsia, a few years before the October Revolution. The first Russian revolutionary organizations were set up in Omsk in 1904 (the Siberian Socio-Democrate Union), and the first Marxist groups were created in Akmolinsk, Petropavlovsk, Uralsk, Verny, and Semipalatinsk, where they operated among the Ural miners and the Russian and indigenous railway workers of the Transaralian Line.

The First Stage of Organization

The first stage of Communist organization in Central Asia (1917–24) shows a twofold tendency: the recruitment of new members into the Russian CP (including the entire CP of the Tajik Autonomous Republic) and the setting of a single CP of Turkistan. The first mention of the creation of a genuine Communist Party was in Kyrgyzstan, where on the April 2, 1918, the Bolshevik Soviet of Bishkek elected A. I. Ivanitsyn as its head, charged with organizing other soviets in all the main cities of the country.

The number of the party's members reached 3,200 in 1925. Its primary function was to organize the First Congress of the Communist Party of Turkistan, which took place on June 17, 1918. This event was important at the regional level because the Turkistan CP was supposed to gradually gather together all of the Bolshevik organizations in Turkistan, as well as in North Tajikistan and Pamir. It operated until its dissolution on June 12, 1924, at the time of the "Great Territorial Demarcation."

At about the same time, in November of 1918, the CP of Bukhara was founded by Communist activists from Bukhara and members of the pro-Bolshevik Young Bukharian Reformist Party. Under its patronage, and with the help of General V. V. Kuibichev and General M. V. Frunze, the Emir Alim Khan was overthrown on September 1, 1920, and the Popular Republic of Bukhara was proclaimed. After its suppression in 1924, the Bukharan Party was purged, 14,000 members were expelled, as well as reformists and nationalists. Only 1,500 remained, all Russians.

The first Communist organization in the steppe region appeared in 1919–20. It consisted of five hundred different groups spread over the entire region, and was set up by Russian activists in the Aral and Petropavlovsk districts, aided militarily by Kuibichev, Frunze, and V. I. Tchapaev (who finally at the end of 1919 defeated the White Army of Admiral Koltchak). After its First Conference in Orenbourg (October 4–12, 1920), S. Mendeshev was elected as the chief of the Central Executive Committee of the Kirghiz (Kazakh) Autonomous Soviet Socialist Republic. It numbered 8,000 members in 1924. Among them was a large group of liberal intellectuals who, deceived by the failure of the February Revolution, had set up the Alach Party (under the influence of A. Bukheykhanov) and been granted amnesty and integrated to the CP in April of 1919. In the Turkmen region after 1917, a group of Social Democrats created a Communist structure in Kyzyl-Arvat and convened its first congress in February of 1925.

After the First Genuine Congresses: Purges and Long-Lasting Secretaries

After the death of Lenin in 1924 came the Stalinist repressions, massive purges of so-called nationalist and opportunist party members, as well as the establishment of the official Communist parties of the Republics and their progressive *korenizacija* (adhesion of non-Russian members).

The Uzbek Communist Party was founded on September 23, 1924, and at first included ex-Djadids, ex-Social Democrats, and Bolsheviks such as Akmal Ikramov and Fayzullah Khodjaev. After a period of intense repression, they were replaced by officials of provincial origin, such

as Usman Yusupov, Niyazov, and Sharaf Rashidov. In the 1950s, a few Uzbek CP members were able to join the Central Committee of the CPUS: Nurridin Muhiddinov was a member of the politburo and secretary of the Central Committee of the CPUS; Y. S. Nasredinova was the chief of the Soviet of Nationalities in the Soviet Parliament from 1970 to 1974. Small wonder that the Uzbek CP became in the 1970s one of the most important Communist regional organizations in the USSR, Sharaf Rashidov being the first general secretary of the Uzbek Party from 1959 until his death in 1983 and a member-candidate of the politburo.

The Turkmen Communist Party held its first congress on February 14, 1925, then suffered mightily from purges in 1936–37 (20,000 members were arrested, and N. Aitakog, president of Supreme Soviet of Turkmenistan, received the death penalty for the crime of "nationalism") A long period of stability began in 1969 with the election of M. N. Gapurov as first secretary, which lasted until his replacement in 1986 by Saparmurad Niyazov.

The Tajik Communist Party was founded on June 1, 1930, after the establishment of the Socialist Federative Republic of Tajikistan in 1929. After World War II, five general secretaries were elected, among them the famous historian Babajan Gafurov (1946–56), D. Rasulov (1962–82), and Rahmon Nabiev (1982–85).

In Kazakhstan, the First Congress of the Kazakh Communist Party took place in June of 1937, after a few years of purges. A series of first secretaries would replace one another (Brezhnev, Ponomarenko), all ethnic Russians, until Din-Muhammed Kunaev was elected in 1964. Kunaev served until 1986.

The First Congress of the Kirghiz Communist Party was held from July 5–16, 1937. M. K. Amosov was elected for one year, followed by A. V. Vagoc (1938–45), N. S. Bogoluibov (1945–50), and I. P. Razzakov (1950–61). As in many of the other republics, the Khrushchev era was characterized by a first secretary of long tenure: Turdakul Usubaliev, who held the post from 1961 to 1985. It was also the time of maximum involvement of the Muslim citizenry in the party's structure.

A period of comparative stagnation ended with the death of Brezhnev in 1983. Before the election of Mikhail Gorbachev in 1985, two first secretaries, Yuri Andropov, and then Konstantin Chernenko, tried to introduce reforms in the regional Communist structures. In Kazakhstan, the nomination of the Russian Genadii Kolbin to replace the Kazakh Kunaev was followed by the first mass political outburst in Almaty, on December 16,

1986. Nursultan Nazarbaev then came to power and ruled from 1989 to August 22, 1991, when he voluntarily resigned from the Central Committee, before being elected president of the Kazakh Republic on December 1, 1991. In the meantime, on September 7, 1991, the Kazakh CP voted its own dissolution and created a new Socialist Party. A few months later, a Communist Party was refounded. In 1996, Serykbolsin Abdil'din, a retired agricultural engineer and former speaker of the Parliament, became its first general secretary. He received just over 12 percent of the votes in the second presidential elections January 9, 1999.

In Kyrgyzstan, T. Usubaliev was replaced in 1985 by Absamat Masaliev, a prominent politician from Osh, who was first secretary of Central Committee, then president of the Supreme Soviet of the Kirghiz Republic in 1990. He was defeated during the presidential election of 1991 by Askar Akaev. The Kirghiz CP was banned for six months in 1991, then regained its access to political life to the point that it formally won the legislative elections of February 22, 2000. Newly reconstituted as the Party of the Communists of Kyrgyzstan it is today the country's main political structure.

In Uzbekistan, the situation was tense after the disruptions created by Andropov in 1983 and the beginning of purges in relation with the Coton Affair. The leaders after the suicide of Sharaf Rashidov were Usman Khodjaev, Rafiq Nishanov, and then Islam Karimov, the current president of the Uzbek Republic. After the collapse of the USSR, on September 14, 1991, the Uzbek CP was replaced by the Popular Democratic Party of Uzbekistan. Clandestine Communist parties were formed: one created by Bektash Azimov, former first secretary of the Andijan "Obkom" (Regional Committee); another, by Sarvar Azimov, previous minister of foreign affairs. They eventually split into five factions, all of which were banned.

In Tajikistan, after Rahmon Nabiev was dismissed in December 1985—officially for health reasons, but in fact for "irresponsibility in the treatment of apartment repartition in buildings built at Party expense,"—he was replaced by K. Makhkamov, who remained in office until September of 1991. In November 1991 Rahmon Nabiev was elected president, and he held the post until September 9, 1992. During these transitionnal years, the party's activities were halted and its name was changed to the Socialist Party. The old name was restored on January 20, 1991, when the conservative Communist block took power in Dushanbe, during the civil war (1992–96).

In Turkmenistan, after the dismissal of M. N. Gapurov in January of 1986 for pro-Brezhnev leanings, Saparmurad Niyazov, the current president, was elected as chief of the supreme Soviet on October 26, 1990. On December 16, 1991, three months after the proclamation of independence, the Turkmen CP was transformed into the Democratic Party of Turkmenistan. In 1996 A. Kuliev, who was then minister of foreign affairs, attempted unsuccessfully to create a Communist faction. He migrated to Russia, and then to Norway.

In most of the Central Asian republics today there is an active political scene. New Communist parties continue, supported by the nostalgia of former activists and by furor against the current post-Soviet governments.

See also Islam; Nationality Policies; Nations and Empire in the USSR.

FURTHER READING

Allworth, E. *Central Asia: 129 Years of Russian Rule.* Durham, NC: Duke University Press, 1989.

Ershov, V. V. *Revoliutsiia 1905–1907 gg. v Uzbekistan: Sbornik statej i vospominanii.* Tashkent, Izdatel'stvo Akademii Nauk Uzbekskoi SSR, 1955.

Kommunisticheskaya Partiya Uzbekistana, t. 2, 1938–1959, Tashkent, Uzbekistan, 1998.

Piaskovskii, A. V. *Revoliutsia 1915–1907 godov v Turkestane.* Moscow: AANS.S.S.R. 1958.

Poujol, C. Le Kazakhstan, Que-sais-je. Paris: PUF, 2000.

———. *Dictionnaire de l'Asie centrale.* Paris: Ellipses, 2001.

CATHERINE POUJOL

Communist Party in China

The Chinese Communist Party (CCP, or Zhongguo gongchandang) was founded July 1, 1921, in Shanghai, and started with fifty-seven members. Eighty years later, in 2002, the CCP was the largest national Communist organization in existence, with over sixty-six million members.

The CCP has governed the People's Republic of China from the republic's founding in 1949 until today, undergoing leadership changes and significant shifts in its fundamental economic policies as well as its strategies for economic and social development. The party's ideological foundation is Marxism-Leninism, but as its leadership has shifted over the years, the names of the most significant Chinese leaders have been added to those of Marx and Lenin, and their theoretical formulations have been recognized in the party's constitution. In the most recent version of the party's statute, "Mao Zedong Thought," "Deng Xiaoping Theory," and the "Important Thought of the Three Represents" (Jiang Zemin) are all part of the CCP's fundamental doctrine, "socialism with Chinese characteristics." The 1982 statute, last modified in 2002, once more describes the CCP as a traditional Leninist party, modeled after the Communist Party of the Soviet Union. The CCP's principal organizational principle is democratic centralism, and is administered by a hierarchical structure. Previous statutes, in 1969, 1973, and 1977, had instead placed Mao's thought, image, and ideal of the "permanent revolution" at their ideological core; among other things, this entailed limiting the recruitment of new party members to revolutionary classes only (workers, poor and fairly poor peasants, and soldiers). These statutes were brief and devoid of formal obligations to observe democratic procedures internally, resulting in the party's transformation into a flexible instrument, exposed to the arbitrary decisions of the central leadership—a fact that was reflected in the party's behavior during the years of Maoist radicalism.

The CCP represents itself as the vanguard of the Chinese working class, people, and nation, and therefore believes it is entitled to exercise the dictatorship of the proletariat on which the People's Republic of China is based. The CCP's ultimate goal is the creation of a Communist society, but today communism is formally defined as an ideal "that will only be achievable when socialist society will be fully developed and advanced." The development of the socialist system remains a "long historical process."

History, 1921–49

Marxism was introduced to China by young intellectuals active in the nationalist movement, which reached its culmination in the demonstrations of May 4, 1919. The most immediate cause for the movement was a provision in the Treaty of Versailles that granted Japan sovereignty over part of the Chinese province of Shandong, but it became a means to diffuse the ideas of science and democracy as fundamental motors for the transformation of old China into a modern, powerful nation following the fall of the last imperial dynasty (1911). The first Chinese socialists were inspired more by Pierre-Joseph Proudhon's and Mikhail Bakunin's anarchism and the utopian socialism of Charles Fourier than by Marxism. This was

a consequence of the places that these young Chinese individuals chose to study or live in exile—Japan, but most especially France, where many of the leading cadre of the future Communist Party were educated, including Zhou Enlai (who would become prime minister) and Deng Xiaoping (who would become general secretary). The First Congress in 1921 was the result of preparatory work by Comintern envoys in a Communist movement that was still extremely fragmented and immature.

During the CCP's first years of existence, the Comintern's main goal was the creation of a republican China. It therefore focused especially on a strategic relationship with the Nationalist Party (GMD, or Guomindang), a revolutionary party much larger than the CCP with a structure that its historic leader, Sun Yat-Sen (Sun Zhongshan), had transformed into one similar to that of the Soviet party. Under the Comintern's guidance, the Communists' actions were oriented toward mobilizing a tiny and fragmented urban working class. The CCP and the GMD formed an alliance with Moscow's support in 1924 known as the First United Front. The strategic collaboration between the two movements became more complex after Sun's death and Chiang Kaishek's (Jiang Jieshi) rise to power as head of the GMD in 1925. The attempts by the new nationalist leader to reunite the country and Chiang's intolerance of an alliance with the Communists soon led to a confrontation with the CCP, and severe repression that decimated the Communist ranks and put an end to the United Front. Between 1927 and 1936 the two parties fought a civil war, until the Japanese invaders' advance (they had occupied Manchuria in 1931) and the military success of the Communist guerrillas in the countryside convinced the two parties to form a new alliance (the Second United Front). It lasted into the early 1940s, when hostilities broke out once more, and only concluded with the definitive seizure of power by the Communists in 1949, and the nationalists' escape to Taiwan.

In the 1920s, the party's failure to organize the working class in the cities led to a peculiar analysis of the class situation in the Chinese Socialist Revolution. The party's organizing and propaganda efforts were supposed to start in the country—where there was resentment toward not so much the local political powers but rather the "feudal" landowners—and not in the factories. This was the principle, together with the "need to understand the needs of the masses" (the "mass line"), that, based on organizational intuition, would allow the CCP to withstand numerous defeats, reunify the country, and finally take its place in the Forbidden City, replacing the Qing emperors. This interpretation led to a split in the CCP between the "Bolshevik" and Maoist lines. Mao, who endorsed a rural strategy, successfully began to create Red bases in the mountains between the provinces of Jianxi and Hunan, where the first "Soviet Chinese Republic" was established in 1931. The Jianxi Soviet, which in the early 1930s had a population of about ten million, became a thorn in the side of the nationalist government, leading the government to intensify military actions. In 1934, the GMD's military pressure was such that it convinced the Communist army, which was in bad shape, to abandon the soviet and march for a year and over eight thousand miles in order to escape encirclement. It was during this disastrous strategic retreat that Mao emerged as the supreme leader of the Communist movement. The political struggle between Mao and the group of young leaders who were faithful to Moscow, known as the "Twenty-eight Bolsheviks," was resolved in favor of the former during the Zunyi political conference, held in the midst of the Long March in 1935.

Between 1937 and 1945, the party's headquarters was located near the city of Yan'an, in northwestern Shaanxi Province. There, the CCP experimented with many developments that would later become characteristic of CCP government culture after 1949, from land redistribution to agrarian reform, from a leadership style based on the mass line and mobilization, to a strategy of guerrilla warfare and popular militias (which contributed to the success of the war of resistance against the Japanese and remained part of fundamental military doctrine after the liberation), to cultural policies and revolutionary art.

History, 1949–2004

From 1949 on, the history of the CCP and the political history of Communist China coincided to a large degree. From the creation of the People's Republic of China until 1954, the country was governed without a constitution. The first party congress in the new era took place in 1956, when the process of nationalization of the economy was already in its final stages. The local leadership groups were often made up of the same soldiers who had freed the various areas of the country, and several years passed before the party was able to create a ruling class that was able to govern and a civil administration was installed. During those years, known as the period of "new democracy," the CCP tried to gather all political and economic forces that were not hostile to the revolu-

tion around the reconstruction effort. On the basis of the errors of the Soviet collectivization effort, the economic reform policies were initially more gradual, both in the country and in the industrial sector.

In the country, for instance, the forced requisitions at first targeted only the lands of absentee landlords and rich farmers, while land belonging to small landholders (the "middle" farmers) was exempted. The land was redistributed to benefit the poorer strata, while maintaining the small landholders' store of experience relatively intact, therefore helping to maintain a good level of productivity in the countryside. Starting in the mid-1950s, the process of collectivization continued with the creation of cooperatives and later people's communes in 1958.

The influence of the USSR's experience (and its substantial economic aid) on China's first steps toward the construction of socialism was evident in the First Five-Year Development Plan—started in 1953, and inspired by the idea of accumulation and the priority of heavy industry—as well as the country's first Constitution (1954), based largely on the Soviet one. (The Five-Year Development Plan concluded with the nationalization of all the remaining industrial firms in 1956.) The idyll between the two largest Communist parties of "real socialism" started to lose its luster in 1956 with the process of de-Stalinization, begun during the Communist Party of the Soviet Union's Twentieth Congress, and the gradual shifts in Chinese economic policies, which had become more radical and productivist under Mao's leadership. The split concluded with the withdrawal of Soviet technicians in 1960, and had lasting consequences for the CCP's economic strategies, since China was now isolated by both blocs and forced to rely on its own resources. Only in 1989, with Mikhail Gorbachev's visit to Beijing, would the normalization of political relations between the two countries be complete. Mao's distrust of Nikita Khrushchev's new course was the flip side of Mao's admiration for the USSR's economic success, and the fundamental role Soviet experts and capital had played in the construction of China's basic industry.

The Great Leap Forward's failure (1958–61) upset political stability. Mao performed a rare act of self-criticism in front of the party. The "gradualists," led by Liu Shaoqi, went back to balancing policies of moderate industrial growth with slowing down the collectivization process in the countryside (during brief periods there was even a return to family-based forms of agriculture). But the radicals' leadership soon gathered strength, and between

1962 and 1966, by means of a series of political education campaigns, Mao's supporters regained lost ground. Supported by a group of young radicals and using the population's dissatisfaction with an unbalanced process of development, in 1966 Mao launched the Great Proletarian Cultural Revolution, whose principal aim was to eliminate those in the bureaucracy who were "taking the capitalist road." The party leadership at all levels was decimated as a result, and during years of confrontations in the squares, universities, and factories, the CCP became more radicalized. The presence of soldiers in the party increased greatly (about 45 percent of elected members as against 19 percent in 1956), to the detriment of representatives of mass organizations and civil institutions. The Ninth Congress of 1969 brought about a split between the two main components of the radical wing that had dominated the most violent years of the Cultural Revolution: the army led by Lin Biao, and the so-called Group for the Cultural Revolution led by Mao's wife, Jiang Qing.

Following the death in 1971 of Lin Biao, who had been at Mao's side during the harshest phases of the Cultural Revolution, the party was prey to the clash between the radical Maoists and a bureaucratic apparatus that was being reborn. It was Premier Zhou Enlai's task to once again provide the CCP with credible leadership that would be able to stabilize the political and economic situation, in part by recalling Deng Xiaoping to lead the government after years of political exile. Only Mao's death in 1976 finally enabled Deng's faction to settle accounts with the radical faction, which from that moment on was known as the Gang of Four (in addition to Mao's last wife, Jiang Qing, Zhang Chunqiao, Yao Wenyuan, and Wang Hongwen). The four, arrested only weeks after the death of their protector, became scapegoats for all the errors and violence of the preceding period, while a new leadership, with Deng at the rudder, rebuilt the party's institutions.

The Third Plenum of the Eleventh Congress in October 1978 marked the Maoists' final defeat and the beginning of a series of economic reforms partially inspired by those of the early 1960s. This line, which pursued reforms and was more welcoming to the outside world, resulted in the reopening of the Chinese market to foreign investments and the progressive introduction of market mechanisms in the economy's management. Deng became the incarnation of the new course, but his pragmatic style led to the emergence of collegial management in party matters, replacing the cult of personality that

had been so damaging under Mao. The party opened its doors to contributions from groups that had previously been victims of radical ostracism, like intellectuals, and Marxist doctrine began to adapt to the "material conditions" of contemporary China. In the 1980s the party was led by Hu Yaobang, a reformer and a follower of Deng's, who several times attempted to introduce programs for the reform of the political system. In 1986, Hu became a victim of his efforts to reform a party in which a conservative gerontocracy still had the ability to tip the scale in factional disputes. Student demonstrations favoring deeper political reforms during the last months of that year ended with Hu's removal from office. His successor, Zhao Ziyang, a member of the same faction, was subjected to the same fate in 1989. That year the demonstrations for democracy (which had begun precisely in order to commemorate Hu's death) led to clashes between demonstrators and the party's hawks, which finally convinced Deng that military repression was inevitable. Zhao and many of the men who had guided the era of reforms in the 1980s were removed from power. The rapid economic development that had characterized the 1980s was halted during a time of uncertainty about which faction would prevail during Zhao's succession. Jiang Zemin filled the position of general secretary, but it was another symbolic gesture by Deng that once more set the party on the reform path. In 1992, an aging Deng traveled to the special economic zones in the South and pointed to them as models for the future development of China.

The process of economic opening continued under Jiang's leadership. After 1989, and with Deng's death in 1997, however, the party maintained a clear distinction between economic liberalization and political power, still based in forms of democratic centralism. Even though Jiang was the secretary with the longest tenure in the CCP's history, his personal power never was comparable to Mao's or Deng's. While in the economic arena the party accepted a liberal framework for its policies, in which both the market and private property were granted more room as well as economic and legal protection, in the political arena the single-party structure remained unaltered as well as unwilling to undertake substantial political reforms. With the introduction of the "Important Thought of the Three Represents" (the party represents the advanced forces of production, advanced culture, and the interests of the majority of the population), Jiang also enlarged the party's potential base, thus recognizing that the economic transformations require the party itself to adapt to a society whose interests have become more complex and contradictory.

In 2002 the Jiang cycle concluded with the selection of Hu Jintao as party secretary, a so-called Fourth Generation leader.

Organization

The party's structure remained basically stable during its long history. It reproduced itself, moving from the center to the periphery, and was able to penetrate social and economic activities throughout the country. Party cells existed in each institution, company, residential neighborhood, and people's commune. Each one of them was a tool for popular mobilization that could be used by the higher levels (central, provincial, municipal, and district).

At the center, the party congress is the formally sovereign organ within the organization: composed of a variable number of representatives from around the country, its power is limited to the ratification of policies developed by the leadership and the selection of a restricted organ called the Central Committee. The CCP held its first six congresses between 1921 and 1928 (the last was the only one to be held outside China, in Moscow, after the bloody repression of 1927), the seventh in 1945, and the eighth, the first after the seizure of power, in 1956. The congress has met only eight times since then, but only recently with a certain regularity—about every five years. The Central Committee—formed by a number of members that grew from the initial 100 of the first period (1949–66) to 198 in 2002—meets more frequently (up to two or three times a year, as necessary) in what are known as plenums, or plenary sessions. Ordinary activities between two plenums are managed by the Permanent Committee of the Central Commitee. The Central Committee has the powerful Central Committee for Discipline at its side. The executive organ is the politburo, with a variable number of members (the least numerous had 11 members, and the one selected in 2002 had 24).

Starting in 1956 the highest level of party leadership was restricted even further, with the creation of a politburo Standing Committee that at the time had five members and subsequently has always had an uneven number of members (between five and nine). Directly below this Standing Committee is the Secretariat, generally led by a member from the same body; this member receives the title of general secretary and is in charge of the party's policies. The position of general secretary, which is currently held by the person at the top of the political hierarchy, Hu Jintao, never really was Mao's, who preferred to assign it to Deng starting with the Cultural Revolution in 1966, while he kept the position of president for himself. The position of general secretary was abolished during the years of the Cultural Revolution (1966–76), and it was Deng who wanted to reestablish it in the 1980s, when it was first held by Hu Yaobang (until 1986), then by Zhao Ziyang (until 1989), Jiang Zemin (until 2002), and then Hu Jintao. The party also selects a Central Military Commission, in command of the People's Liberation Army. As a revolutionary army, it swears allegiance to the revolution and its guardian, the CCP, not to organs of state power. Control of the Central Military Commission is usually a sign of who controls power in the party and the country.

The party's base has continued to grow (from 60.4 million members in 1997, to 66.3 million in 2002). This growth in party membership notwithstanding, the party's ability to manage, control, and determine social change has decreased with the gradual privatization of both the labor market and the education, social services, and housing markets. Chinese Communists are prevalently men (women constitute 16.6 percent) and older (only 23.1 percent are less than thirty-five years old), with an above average educational level (about 47 percent have at least a high school diploma). Even though party affiliation does not have any practical benefits, the prestige associated with the party often guarantees special treatment. Belonging to the party is an advantage, especially for professionals who work for state organizations. A situation quite frequently occurs where in order to be guaranteed a promotion to higher levels of responsibility, employees will be explicitly required to join the party. Membership is not automatic and requires one to have no criminal record, a relatively long educational history, and to take an exam to test one's knowledge of the party's fundamental principles and history. During some periods, access to the party was reserved only for members of "good" classes, workers and peasants. Later, due to the more complex set of interests represented, the party allowed even elements considered bourgeois (especially private businesspeople) to become full-fledged members.

See also Chinese Revolution; Cultural Revolution in China; Deng Xiaoping; Great Leap Forward; Long March; Mao Zedong; Marxism-Leninism; Single-Party System; State, The.

FURTHER READING

Lieberthal, K. *Governing China: From Revolution through Reform*. New York: Norton, 1995.

MacFarquhar, R., ed. *The Politics of China: The Eras of Mao and Deng.* Cambridge: Cambridge University Press, 1997.

Saich, T., and T. Cheek, ed. *New Perspectives on State Socialism in China.* Armonk, NY: M. E. Sharpe, 1997.

Saich, T., and B. Yang. *The Rise to Power of the Chinese Communist Party: Documents and Analysis.* Armonk, NY: M. E. Sharpe, 1996.

LUIGI TOMBA

Communist Party in Cuba

The Partido comunista de Cuba was formed on October 3, 1965, as the end result of a process of institutionalizing the revolution that had come to power on January 1, 1959. Fidel Castro Ruz was elected as its secretary. The roots of Cuban communism were deeper, however, and the party led by the Castro brothers, with Fidel as secretary (Raúl also had an important role)—as only partly connected to that earlier history. The revolution was thus a watershed event.

The first Communist Party was born underground on August 16, 1925, influenced to some degree by the October Revolution, from a radical wing of Cuban nationalism; with a Marxist-Leninist outlook, it joined the Comintern. Julio Antonio Mella (1903–29) was its young and brilliant ideologist, whose reflections on the connections between nation and revolution resembled those of his contemporaries, Antonio Gramsci and José Carlos Mariátegui. His death at the hands of dictator Gerardo Machado's hired assassins prevented the same sort of dissensions within the Comintern that had developed in the other two cases. The party was at first little more than a small urban sect, perpetually fighting against those who opposed its guiding role in the labor unions. Yet it soon attracted students and militants critical of Moscow's orthodoxy, as they searched for a "national road" to socialism that was attentive to the revolutionary potential of peasants and petty bourgeoisie.

The party grew stronger as the consequences of the Great Depression hit Cuba, and it contributed to the mostly spontaneous general strike in 1933, which overthrew the dictatorship. Faithful to the struggle against the social fascism line, the party opposed the short-lived reformist government led by Ramón Grau San Martín, even though many workers were more supportive. Following a shift by the Comintern and led by Blas Roca Calderío, the Cuban Communists also pursued Popular Front policies starting in 1935. Cuba, it seems, was not ready for a socialist revolution; it was better to create an alliance with the national bourgeoisie and progressive forces instead, thus detaching them from the oligarchy, which as in Spain was attracted by fascism. But because the Cuban Communists were not well regarded by either reformists or the middle classes, and because they had been burned by Communist sectarianism in the past, they moved closer to the person who had recently persecuted them, Fulgencio Batista, now comfortable in his new clothes as a populist leader. In 1938, Batista allowed the Communists to operate openly and lead the Confederación de Trabajadores de Cuba. Communist support for Batista, in the midst of serious crises and purges within the party, also continued during the war when, following the principles embraced by U.S. Communist leader Earl Browder, the party changed its name to Partido socialista popular in 1948.

The Partido auténtico's election victory and the beginning of the Cold War, however, changed the course of Cuban communism, which had just posted its best electoral result, 197,000 votes, in the 1946 elections. On the ideological front, Cuban Communists rejected Browderism, and instead advocated class struggle and anti-imperialism. On the political and social fronts, Communists were violently attacked by the auténticos government, which wrested control of the labor union movement from them. Electoral defeat in 1948 and repression in 1950 led to the weakening of Cuban communism in the following decade, except within some labor union circles and Afro-Cuban communities. Prior to Batista's coup in 1952, the Partido socialista popular did not engage in political violence, and when Castro assaulted the Moncada Barracks in 1953, the party denounced his adventurism; starting in 1958, though, the Partido socialista popular established workers' committees to oppose the dictatorship and supported the armed struggle to overthrow Batista.

When the revolution triumphed, everything changed for the Partido socialista popular: it had experience, organization, and international ties—all indispensable resources for the revolution—even though it did not have any power. A fitful phase followed, leading to the party's integration into the Organizaciónes revolucionarias integradas in 1961. In 1963, this in turn became the Partido unido de la revolución socialista, and in 1965 the Partido comunista de Cuba was born, now the revolution's only party, under Castro's strict control. The *líder maximo* was in fact the one who had pushed the Communists and Movimento 26 de julio to unite, after they had become embroiled in a struggle within the Confederación de trabajadores; Castro increasingly relied on Communist experience to prop up his regime, which was under U.S. attack, and provide direction for a socialist path. The tacit understanding was that the older Communists would remain quiet in the new structure that Castro now controlled. For example, when the older Communists took control of the Organizaciónes revolucionarias integradas, thus increasing their influence, Castro accused them of sectarianism. Only a few of them were allowed to sit on the party's Central Committee, Blas Roca and Carlos Rafael Rodríguez among them, but none made it into the politburo. The key positions went to the "new Communists," men who had fought with Castro on the Sierra, emblems of a party, refusing dogmas and denying the Soviet Union's primacy, to the extent that it preferred alliances with revolutionary or national liberation movements to ties with old parties aligned with Moscow. Internally, though, the party was the pivot around which Castro structured his regime, the forge for individuals who were given positions at all levels of the administration, to perform for the new regime, keep the revolutionary spirit high, and cultivate popular participation in the construction of socialism.

From that point on, the party's history was intertwined with the evolution of the revolutionary regime. Toward the end of the 1960s, following the revolution's many political and economic failures, the party's radical and romantic phase came to an end, leaving the door open to the rigid institutionalization of the 1970s. The party held its first congress in 1975, although Castro had announced it for 1967. The new Constitution was approved at the congress, and endorsed the following year by 97.7 percent of all Cubans. In it, the party was described as the "organized vanguard of the Cuban nation and a superior entity in the leadership of society and the state." The Castro brothers were confirmed as, respectively, first and second secretary, as they were during later congresses, sanctioning the union of party and state. In theory the party's vanguard role was balanced by the institutions of popular power, elected by citizens at the local level; yet in practice, the party controlled any autonomous trends, performing a similar role within the

revolution's institutional system to that of its fraternal parties in the people's democracies of the Communist bloc. Its distinctive character was derived from Castro's charismatic leadership and the daily clashes with the United States, an inexhaustible source of revolutionary regeneration. In the 1970s and 1980s the party, the regime's backbone, grew in size and importance. On the one hand, it underwent a process of bureaucratization; on the other hand, it reflected transformations in Cuban society. The military influence in its leadership organs diminished, and that of the cadre and white-collar sectors grew, while the membership's schooling went through the roof.

During 1986, when Castro started the "rectification" in order to confront economic difficulties, and in 1991, when the Fourth Congress inaugurated the "special period" to face the dramatic consequences of the Soviet collapse, the party was forcefully reminded of its revolutionary roots. It was also called on to "lead" instead of "administer," and to refurbish the ties between the revolution and the masses. Its doors were once again opened to Catholics, and a radical renewal of its leadership organs took place, both in terms of individuals and generations as well as an increase in membership. Once the emergency had passed, with its Fifth Congress of 1997, the party returned to its old ways and halted liberalization; the military, the political cadre, and the state functionaries regained the positions they had previously lost, and a defense of the revolutionary status quo once again became the party's essential function. When in 2006 health concerns led Castro to delegate power to his brother, Raúl, the latter pointed to the party as the guarantor of order and the continuity of the socialist regime.

See also Anti-imperialism; Castro, Fidel; Nationalism; People's Democracies.

FURTHER READING

Eckstein, S. E. *Back from the Future: Cuba under Castro*. Princeton, NJ: Princeton University Press, 1994.

García Montes, J., and Alonso Ávila A. *Historia del Partido Comunista de Cuba*. Miami: Editorial Universal, 1970.

Leogrande, W. M. *The Cuban Communist Party and Electoral Politics: Adaptation, Succession, and Transition*. Miami: Institute for Cuban and Cuban-American Studies, University of Miami, 2002.

Rojas Blaquier, A. *El primer Partido Comunista de Cuba, sus tácticas y estrategia, 1925–1935*. Vol. 1. Santiago de Cuba: Editorial Oriente, 2005.

Tutino, S. *L'ottobre cubano. Lineamenti di una storia della rivoluzione castrista*. Turin: Einaudi, 1978.

LORIS ZANATTA

Communist Party in Czechoslovakia

The Constituent Assembly of the Communist Party of Czechoslovakia (CPCz) was held in May 1921. It was preceded by two years of struggle among the Social Democrats over the political orientation of the strongest party. The left-wing faction won out and chose to join the Communist International.

The CPCz came into being as a party of the masses— it had more than 150,000 members, and its mass character held firm through many later twists and turns. The postwar revolutionary period and overall political atmosphere were propitious for radical political moods as well as for maintaining the CPCz's public influence. This influence was reflected in the parliamentary elections in 1925. The CPCz emerged as the second-strongest party; it received 934,000, or 13.2 percent, of the votes. In 1925, urged on by the Comintern, it went through its first phase of Bolshevization. The departure of a number of the party's leading functionaries did not result in any substantial drop in membership and voters.

The CPCz went through its second phase of Bolshevization in 1928–29, during which it experienced an internal crisis. The Comintern played a role in this crisis, supporting the critics of the party leadership. A group of young functionaries, led by Klement Gottwald, demanded that the leadership be replaced, but more importantly, labored to bring about a change in the work and politics of the party—something it expressed in a document titled *From Opportunistic Passivity to Bolshevik Activity*. The Comintern suspended the CPCz's leadership and, at the Fifth Party Congress, turned its reins over to Gottwald. A new leadership was chosen, which included many of his supporters, and Gottwald was named general secretary.

From its emergence, the CPCz stood in opposition to the government. Its policy turnabout after the Fifth Congress resulted in the implementation of the secretary of the Comintern's political line. The CPCz led the struggle against "social fascism" (social democracy) and the "Fascist character" of the Czechoslovak government, and during the presidential election, issued slogans like "Not Masaryk, but Lenin" and "For government by Soviets." The consequences of Bolshevization were soon at hand. Party membership was reduced by a third, and in the parliamentary elections of 1929, the CPCz gained 753,400 votes—now only 10.2 percent of the total. During the economic crisis of 1929–32, the party concentrated on organizing social clashes, strikes, demonstrations, and marches by unemployed workers, and it radicalized its oppositional activities inside and outside Parliament. Yet it achieved successes only intermittently. For one thing, it failed to implement the line of the secretary of the Comintern, particularly as it regarded the Socialist parties, labor unions, and workers. The CPCz's social battles and particularly the miners' strike in 1932 were carried on directly by Comintern organs. Still, the party's activities during the economic crisis strengthened its influence in the poorer regions of the country. In the 1935 elections, it received 849,000 votes, or 10.3 percent, and was the only Czech party that did not to lose voters.

The Comintern's shift to the tactics of the Popular Front brought about a change in the policies of the CPCz. At the congress in 1936, the CPCz proclaimed that its main tasks were the fight against fascism as well as the defense of democracy and the republic. These goals brought it closer to the Socialist parties, but it still differed in being critical of the regime and its efforts to control the Popular Front. These "corrections" in CPCz policy provoked conflicts within the party and also criticism from the Comintern, which reproached the Communist Party leadership for its incorrect implementation of its policy toward the Popular Front. A change in the CPCz leadership followed (Rudolf Slánský, Jan Sverma, and others) along with a self-critical acknowledgment of errors. The party's commitment to the anti-Fascist struggle and defense of the republic contributed to the growth of its authority.

The CPCz's influence and recognition in society rose considerably, particularly during the Munich crisis in 1938. It was a determined opponent of the Munich Accords, fought for their rejection, for armed defense of the state, and against capitulation. It felt assured of the military support of the USSR and the world public. The party's positions in 1938 were aligned with those of most Czechoslovak people at the time; they were identical to the views of many representatives of political parties and were supported in public demonstrations. In 1938, the Communist Party of Czechoslovakia was officially dissolved, but it was simply banned. Some of its leading functionaries went into exile. A foreign CPCz leadership was formed in Moscow, with Gottwald as its head, though some functionaries went to London instead. At home, an illegal leadership was in operation. During the war there were four different ones. With the creation of the Slovak state, the independent Communist Party of Slovakia (CPS) was formed. It was headed by five successive central administrations, all subordinate to the foreign CPCz leadership in Moscow. In Bohemia and Moravia, the Communists led a national struggle for liberation from the Nazi occupation; in Slovakia, the emphasis was on ousting the clerical-Fascist puppet regime there. All these efforts, and particularly attempts to unify the resistance units, were hampered by the Comintern's policies. These same policies also instilled in the CPCz leadership a hostile stance toward Eduard Beneš and his government in exile.

The situation changed after the Soviet Union entered the war in 1941. The Soviet government recognized Czechoslovakia with President Beneš as its head, and two years later the two governments signed an agreement that made them allies. The CPCz leadership adapted its policies to this change, recognized the president and his government, and announced as its goal the restoration of a united Czechoslovakia. The activities of both the illegal party and the party in exile focused on the organization of an armed resistance at home and the creation of a Czechoslovak military component in the USSR. The domestic leaderships of the CSCz and the CPS both played decisive roles as the main organs of national uprisings in both Slovakia, and in Bohemia and Moravia. With the arrival of the Soviet army, the Communists' position in the resistance and their influence on the government in exile solidified. The decision-making center regarding the future disposition of the republic shifted to the CPCz leadership in Moscow. This leadership negotiated with President Beneš about the first steps after the liberation of Czechoslovakia. It adopted the notion, approved by the Soviets, which later evolved into the concept of a national state of Czechs and Slovaks, without national minorities. The two currents of the foreign resistance came together, and at the instigation of the CPCz, their representatives created the National Front, in which the four Czech and two Slovak parties affiliated with each other.

In March 1945, the Communists approved a new program and a proposal to form a postwar government. The Communists would occupy three key ministries—Interior, Agriculture, and Information—and also the post of vice chair of the government, to be occupied by Gottwald. In the newly freed republic, the CPCz would be a respected political party. Its strong position in Czech political life would be recognized. Its leading functionaries returned from Moscow equipped with ideas about their future policies; most important was that the party had to act as a representative of the whole nation. It had to capitalize on the postwar wave of patriotism and place this at the head of its own policy. It would be the initiator of social transformations, building a people's democracy that would be different from traditional democratic regimes. The party would take advantage of the public's great interest in public affairs and exploit this interest to create a party of the masses. The CPCz's leadership proposed nationalizing the economy and reforming agriculture, and it supported the dominance of the National Front. It would remove a large part of the bourgeoisie from the organs of power.

Within ten months, the CPCz membership had increased to over a million. The party won the May 1946 parliamentary elections convincingly, with some two million votes, or 38 percent. The government, headed by Gottwald, approved a plan called the "Comprehensive Program of Consolidation," which had been proposed by the Communists. The leading Communists had returned from their exile with a comprehensive idea of how they would accomplish their political ends. The first goal was to achieve a monopoly of power, a prerequisite of their second goal, which was to build a socialist system. The coalition parties were happy to accept the proclamation by the CPCz's Central Committee, in September 1946, concerning the Czechoslovak path to socialism. In reality, of course, this path followed the Soviet model.

In the meantime, efforts to create a robust bloc of three Socialist parties and a party of left-wing Social Democrats failed utterly. In January 1947, the Central Committee of the CPCz declared its aim: to gain a majority of the national vote in the next elections, thereby achieving a monopoly of power. The already tense relations among the parties only became more strained, particularly over the Marshall Plan and a constituent assembly of the Information Bureau (of Communist and Workers' Parties). The Communist leadership decided to push through its power program, regardless of the means. By now, though, it was confronting stronger and stronger resistance, and all the parties concentrated their energies on gaining a monopoly of power. The Communists intensified their offensive, leading to a political crisis that affected the activity of the government and Parliament. The National

Front was paralyzed, and under these circumstances any conflict could result in a clash. And this is just what happened in February 1945, during a governmental crisis provoked by the resignation of the ministerial representatives of the non-Communist parties. The CPCz's leadership took advantage of the crisis to stage a successful coup and take over the state.

The 1948 coup installed Communist power in Prague and put Czechoslovakia firmly within the Soviet bloc. The emergence of a Communist regime placed the triumphant CPCz in a new situation. Its roles and tasks changed. It had now become not only the builder of a new regime but also its pillar of support. The party had once been a participant in the struggle for power; now it had to wield and execute it. Its institutions became so identical with those of a state that any significant decision it made would be like an act of state, and any resistance to the decision would be an act against the state. The party also had to cope with a flood of new members, who had joined either out of true conviction or under pressure. Over the course of four months, the CPCz's membership increased by almost 800,000, and by the end of 1948 the party had more than 2,330,000 members. By 1951, though, two vetting operations had reduced this number to 1,740,000, and the decline increased; by the end of 1951 membership was down to 1,400,000.

The CPCz began curtailing intraparty democracy and strengthening its already rigorous party discipline. Moscow's goals and the way that the Communist Party of the Soviet Union (CPSU) exploited its leading position in the bloc, were the two factors most influencing CPCz policies and thus Czech society. The ideological and political linkage of the leading Communists, first with the Comintern and then with the CPSU, was one of dependence. This bond was achieved in various ways, including through conviction, fear, direct orders, requirements, or a network of advisers. The CPCz leadership supported and served the great-power goals of the USSR, and subordinated the needs and interests of its own country to them.

The party's general line was proclaimed by the Ninth Congress of the CPCz in 1949. The party would establish the foundations of socialism under the influence and according the model of the USSR. It would restructure the social system, and introduce a new mode of governing and a new economic direction. During 1948–53, it created a political power mechanism capable of both dominating and supervising society, stifling all sources of its spontaneous activity, and imposing its own intentions.

In addition to the party, the organs of State Security, whose power increased until it became uncontrollable, were pillars of the system. The CPCz's policies led to the structural transformation of the economy. This industrial country was now isolated from other countries with advanced economies, and forced to subordinate itself to the interests and needs of the USSR and other bloc countries. This erratic development limited the opportunities and potential of the Czechoslovak economy, which soon lost the ability to satisfy the demands of its citizens and create resources that might have enhanced the evolution of a modern industrial society. The system of political power constructed by the mid-1950s underwent various modifications, but the basic underpinning for the Communist monopoly of power, as enshrined in the Constitution of 1960, was always the "leading role of the party." Economic policies might change, but the general principle of central management was never challenged. The ever-present domination of heavy industry over light industry guaranteed a constantly feeble economy.

The foundations of the Communist regime had been laid by 1953, but that year both the political and economic areas underwent a crisis. The Communist leadership first reacted to it with a financial reform, which caused a noticeable drop in the standard of living. At Moscow's instigation, certain changes in policy followed. The Central Committee approved them in September 1953, and the Tenth Congress of the CPCz followed suit in June 1954. The general policy line adhered to up to then was declared to be the correct one, and so only cosmetic adjustments were permitted in the economy.

The regime that the CPCz had forced on Czechoslovak society was maintained by repression, persecutions, political trials, and other kinds of restraint and coercion. No fewer than 250,000 to 280,000 citizens were subjected directly to various forms of repression and persecution, and the number of those affected indirectly was many times greater. Nevertheless, the supports propping up the regime were crumbling.

Four events during the period from 1948 to 1956 were of strategic importance for the CPCz. The chair and symbol of the party, Gottwald, died in 1953. Three other shocks weakened people's faith in the party's policies and leadership: the trial, in 1952, of Rudolf Slánský and some of his associates; massive public protests six months later centering on financial reforms; and the events of 1956, following the revelation of Stalin's crimes at the Twentieth Congress of the CPSU. The year 1956 was less dramatic in Czechoslovakia than it was in some neighboring countries. The country was like a Soviet wedge in the Central European chunk of the Soviet bloc. The CPCz leadership showed unconditional support for Soviet policy; it even offered to send troops to aid the Soviets in putting down the Hungarian revolt. At home, it was able to thwart criticism and calls for changing its policies. It squelched any discussion of ticklish questions (i.e., rehabilitation of the victims of the trials) and focused instead on the economy. After the Hungarian uprising, the party was even able to strengthen its position, which had become somewhat shaky. Similarly, the leadership proved able to handle the ensuing struggle against revisionism in the party and punish those who had been critical of it in 1956. In a CPCz Central Committee decree, issued in 1960, parliament approved the constitution and a change of the country's name to the Czechoslovak Socialist Republic. The foundations of socialism had indeed been successfully laid.

With the beginning of the 1960s, though, the CPCz began to face different problems. Its leaders were becoming powerless in the face of economic concerns and looked for solutions in vain. Both the public and party were increasingly aware of the need for political reforms. In the years from 1963 to 1967, the reform movement became crucial in the country's political life. Supporters of the reforms were now active in both the CPCz and the government as well as in other, primarily cultural institutions. The party veered toward a crisis, as did society in general. By 1965, supporters of the changes had put through an economic reform, and in Slovakia a demand arose for organizing a federal state. The result was a reappraisal of the highest party and state functions, and then the dismissal of Antonín Novotný from his position as first secretary of the CPCz's Central Committee. In January 1968 he was replaced by Alexander Dubček.

The eight-month period of Czechoslovakia's efforts at reform became known as the Prague Spring. In April, the new CPCz leadership announced the so-called Action Program for reforms, to be implemented as soon as possible. It either brought about the reforms itself, or refused to stand in the way of measures leading to the democratization of the Communist regime. The leadership gained so much trust and authority, particularly Dubček, that no force in the country was capable of halting the developments. From the beginning, the leading functionaries in the USSR government and the rest of the bloc countries took a negative stance toward the reforms. They feared that the reforms would reverberate in their own countries and lead to undesirable consequences.

Thus, on August 21, 1968, they intervened militarily. The Prague Spring became an important event in postwar European history. Its reforms had been thwarted by outside forces, but in the end it would contribute heavily to the breakup of the Communist regime and Soviet bloc.

The destruction of the reform movement and ensuing Soviet occupation left its mark on Czechoslovak society, and also caused some changes in the CPCz. Mistrust of the USSR reached huge dimensions among the populace, turning into outright hostility toward the occupiers. The CPCz itself split into two factions. One faction continued to work for the reforms, even if limited in scope. The other, supported by Moscow, pressed toward halting the reform program and purging the party of reformists. Between these two factions stood advocates of granting gradual concessions to reformists; these people had only been partial participants in the reforms. The struggle ended in a victory for this "middle" group, which gave ground to the radicals on both sides. One result of the "victory" was the replacement, at the behest of the Soviets, of Dubček by Gustav Husák in April 1969.

Dubček's fall and the collapse of his leadership hastened the departure of many Communists and functionaries from the Czech Communist Party. Some half a million Communists, almost a third of the party's members, were expelled. Most suffered some kind of demotion in social or employment status, as did tens of thousands of non-Communists. The foremost task of the party was to return to its prereform status so that it could remain at the center of power in the now-occupied country. The Communist leaders' utter subordination to Moscow was underscored by the presence of the Soviet army, and this increased their own self-confidence. The CPCz's goal during the next twenty years was political "normalization," to make sure that society would remain quiescent, and also increasing the standard of living and stabilizing "real socialism."

Between 1969 and 1989, though, dissatisfaction with the status quo continued to grow, and there were a number of outbursts and "actions." Influenced by international events, citizens' opposition groups emerged, the most famous of which was Charter 77. The CPCz was unable to solve the problems it still faced, not least because it was afraid to introduce any reforms substantial enough to make a difference. The replacement of Husák by Milos Jakeš, in 1987, did not improve matters. Then, toward the end of the 1980s, the Soviet bloc began to fall apart. This process resulted in a social crisis in Czechoslovakia and the gradual collapse of the CPCz. Fatally weakened, the party was unable to avert the fall of the Czechoslovak regime. The CPCz itself survived only in the Czech Lands—as the Communist Party of Bohemia and Moravia.

See also Charter 77; Dubček, Alexander; Gottwald, Klement; Havel, Václav; Husák, Gustav; Prague Coup; Prague Spring; Slánský, Rudolf; Socialist Camp; Soviet Bloc.

FURTHER READING

Fejto, F. *La fin de démocraties populaires*. Paris: Seuil, 1992.

Hájek, J. *Praga 1968*. Rome: Editori Riuniti, 1978.

Havel, V. "The Power of the Powerless." In *Open Letters: Selected Writings, 1965–1990*. New York: Knopf, 1991.

Kaplan, K. *Nekrvavá revoluce*. Prague: Mladá fronta, 1993.

———. *Pět kapitol o únoru*. Brno: Doplnek, 1997.

Kural, V., V. Mencl et al. *Ceskoslovensko roku 1968*. 2 vols. Prague: Parta, 1993.

Madry, J. *Sovětska okupace Českolovenska*. Prague: USD, 1994.

Otáhal, M. *Normalizace 1969–1989*. Prague: USD, 2002.

Rupnik, J. *Histoire du Parti Communiste Tchéchoslovaque*. Paris: Presses de la Fondation Nationale des Sciences Politiques, 1981.

Skilling, G. H. *Czechoslovakia's Interrupted Revolution*. Princeton, NJ: Princeton University Press, 1976.

KAREL KAPLAN

Communist Party in East Germany

The Socialist Unity Party of Germany (SED, or Sozialistische Einheitspartei Deutschlands) was the German Democratic Republic's (GDR) Communist Party. Its "guiding role," founded on serving as the "vanguard of the working class and the working people," was established in the Constitution. The SED was the product of a plan developed by the leadership of the Communist Party of Germany (KPD) during its World War II exile in Moscow. The leadership wanted to create "a vast mass party of the working people," which in addition to being based on class, was meant to mobilize the anti-Fascist forces within the population, among whom there were also numerous Social Democrats. With the help of this party, the German Communists were supposed to take the lead in constructing a democratic Germany. Many Social Democrats endorsed the idea of unifying the two workers' parties after experiencing the National Social-

ists' seizure of power. But in May–June 1945, the KPD's leadership rejected the Social Democratic Party of Germany's (SPD) merger proposal, fearing that SPD president Otto Grotewohl wanted too much power within the new German party. A unified party was supposed to prevent the SPD from assuming a dominant role and preserve the Communists' influence.

With the help of the Soviet occupation forces, the unification of the two workers' parties was completed in winter 1945–46. The SPD's Central Committee approved the merger on February 11, 1946—after much internal debate and intimidation—and the proposal was then modified during a joint congress of the KPD and the SPD on April 21–22 in Berlin. The KPD's Wilhelm Pieck and the SPD's Grotewohl would share the presidency of the new Sozialistische Einheitspartei Deutschlands. The merger would be limited to Germany's Soviet occupation zone, since a majority of SPD members in Berlin's western sector opposed immediate unification. Appeals by SED leaders to proceed with unification also in the western occupied zones went nowhere. Consequently, the unification of the workers' parties in the East was a step toward the division of Germany.

In the eastern part of Germany, Communist leaders worked within the SED to attain their objective of leading the party and country, in addition to disciplining and homogenizing the base. Walter Ulbricht was especially zealous during this phase, and he was already trusted by the Soviet military administration as a competent organizer. In June 1948, Ulbricht transformed the SED into a "party of a new type" (in a decision adopted at the twelfth meeting of the party leadership, on June 28–29, 1948), which was based on the model of the Communist Party of the Soviet Union (CPSU), and took the lead in shaping the political, economic, and cultural life of East Germany. Anton Ackermann was forced to revise his thesis of a "specific German way toward socialism." A "party central control commission," led by Hermann Matern, was given the task of monitoring the party membership, and its leadership shifted to the politburo (during deliberations at the First Party Conference, on January 25–28, 1949). Ulbricht became the head of the politburo's "restricted secretariat."

Following the establishment of the GDR, the SED's Third Congress in July 1950 elected a Central Committee for the first time. On July 25, 1950, the committee nominated Ulbricht as the party's general secretary. Ulbricht's dominant position was put in doubt when, after Joseph Stalin's death in March 1953, the Soviet leadership criticized the "accelerated construction of socialism" in the GDR. On June 26, 1953, the politburo's Organizing Committee decided to abolish the position of general secretary. Ulbricht was only saved thanks to Vyacheslav Molotov's intervention and Lavrenty Beria's fall. Ulbricht proceeded by excluding his principal detractors, Rudolf Herrnstadt and Wilhelm Zaisser, from all leadership roles, as alleged followers of Beria, and on June 26, 1953, the Central Committee elected him as their "first secretary."

Ulbricht's leadership was questioned once again in February 1956 during the CPSU's Twentieth Congress when Nikita Khrushchev's accounting with Stalinism provoked a debate about reforms within the SED's ranks. High-ranking party and state functionaries like Karl Schirdewan and Ernst Wollweber argued for the adoption of more pragmatic policies, and a group of intellectuals around Wolfgang Harich even asked that the Communists renounce their claim of exercising a guiding role. Yet Ulbricht managed to neutralize this opposition. The writers who had opposed him were condemned to severe prison sentences, and his opponents within the party lost their seats in the politburo and Central Committee in February 1958. Having thus regained control of the party, in 1960 Ulbricht adopted the position of those economists who wanted to increase the autonomy and responsibility of individual enterprises, and labor's productivity, thanks to "a new system of economic planning and management." These suggestions did not please the functionaries in the party apparatus. An opposition to Ulbricht's leadership formed around Erich Honecker, and in February 1971, it convinced Leonid Brezhnev to replace Ulbricht. On May 5, 1971, Ulbricht was forced to resign "due to old age," and the Central Committee elected Honecker as its new first secretary.

Honecker initially succeeded in gaining support from both the party's base and the population. Under his leadership, Günter Mittag became influential in guiding the economy; Kurt Hager was responsible for ideological issues; Joachim Herrmann was in charge of propaganda; and Erich Mielke was given an increasingly important position as head of State Security. Issues of defense, foreign policy, and transportation, in addition to the selection of cadre, remained in Honecker's hands. In May 1976, the role of first secretary was once more replaced with that of "general secretary," and in October 1976 as the head of the State Council, Honecker also became the GDR's head of state. Under Honecker's leadership, the SED became the largest party within the Eastern bloc

relative to population size. At its founding the SED had approximately 1.3 million members, and grew to 2 million by June 1948. This number fell to 1.2 million by June 1951 due to purges, but starting in 1952, there was a continuous increase in membership: from 1.6 million members in December 1961, to 1.9 million in June 1971, up to 2.3 million in May 1989. At that time, out of every 100 GDR citizens over eighteen years of age, 19 were members of the SED or were waiting to join. Party members were organized at the workplace by means of "base organizations," and those who were not employed belonged to "residential party organizations." People's lives were thus determined by centrally guided campaigns and constant party controls.

For a long time the SED's leadership avoided the appeals to perestroika issued by Mikhail Gorbachev starting in 1985. Only on October 17, 1989, did a group of politburo dissidents, led by Egon Krenz, manage to get Honecker to resign. The new general secretary, Krenz, attempted to prevent the collapse of the SED regime by means of political liberalization. This top-down movement to reform the GDR, which began in September 1989 in Leipzig with demonstrations, extended to the SED's base. Different party "platforms," which had emerged after the fall of the Berlin Wall, led to an extraordinary congress. On December 3, 1989, the Central Committee and politburo resigned as a group. While many members left the party, another congress convened on December 8, 1989, in Berlin, where a majority of those in attendance opposed the party's dissolution and elected Gregor Gysi, a young lawyer, as its new president. On December 16–17, during a second session, the congress decided to rename the movement: Sozialistische Einheitspartei–Partei des demokratischen Sozialismus (SED-PDS, or Socialist Unity Party–Party of Democratic Socialism). The new leadership later decided, on February 4, 1990, to rename the political organization yet again, as the Party of Democratic Socialism (Pds). The party claimed a membership of three hundred thousand at the time; in comparison, more than 2 million members had contributed to the collapse of the GDR with their resignation.

See also Berlin Wall; Honecker, Erich; Pieck, Wilhelm; Reunification of Germany; Soviet Occupation of Germany; Ulbricht, Walter.

FURTHER READING

Herbst, A., G.-R. Stephan, and J. Winkler, eds. *Die SED. Geschichte—Organisation—Politik. Ein Handbuch.* Berlin: Dietz, 1997.

Loth, W. *Stalin's Unwanted Child: The Soviet Union, the German Question, and the Founding of the GDR.* New York: St. Martin's Press, 1998.

Malycha, A. *Die SED. Geschichte ihrer Stalinisierung, 1946–1953.* Paderborn: Schöning, 2000.

WILFRIED LOTH

Communist Party in Finland

With the collapse of the Russian Empire in 1917, Finland gained independence, but in January 1918 a civil war broke out between the Whites and the Reds. After three months of fighting and a German intervention, the Reds were defeated and many guardists, as well as most of their leaders, escaped to the Soviet Russia.

On August 29, 1918, the Finnish Communist Party was formed in Moscow by the exiled leaders, including O. V. Kuusinen, Yrjö Sirola, and Kullervo Manner, the former speaker of the Finnish parliament. They (in particular Kuusinen) rose to important positions in the Comintern, both because they were there from the beginning and because they were well versed in the Western labor movement. The Finns also played a prominent role in Soviet domestic politics in the northwestern regions, in particular in Soviet Carelia, where Edvard Gylling headed the government.

In Finland, the Social Democratic Party was revived. It was controlled by its right wing led by Väinö Tanner, but left-wing currents were strong as well, and in May 1920 a separate left-wing Socialist Party was founded, which developed close contacts with the exiled Communists. The CP remained prohibited in Finland, but legal left-wing socialist parties participated in the elections (gaining on average 15 percent of the votes), published newspapers, and controlled the trade unions. From 1928 the Comintern ultra-left line inflicted severe strains on this structure as factional differences threatened to split the leftists.

In 1929–30 a strong extreme right-wing movement developed, and all legal activities of the Left were banned. However, a right-wing dictatorship was not established, and parliamentarism prevailed.

With the Popular Front line of the Comintern in the mid-1930s and the growth of a student left wing in the SDP (Mauri Ryömä among others), Communists were again able to participate in Finnish political life. The strength of the trade unions increased, and in 1937 a left-center government of Social Democrats and the agrarians came into power and introduced many social reforms.

At the same time in the Soviet Union, exile Finnish Communist activities were suppressed during the Stalinist Terror. All traditional CPF leaders except Kuusinen were arrested, most of them were shot, and others sent to the camps. It is estimated that about twenty thousand Finnish Communists perished in the Stalinist terror, outnumbering the victims of the 1918 White Terror. From September 1937 on, the CPF party organs were no longer able to function, although the party was not formally abolished, as was Polish party. The safest place for a Finnish Communist at that time was in a Finnish prison.

After securing his sphere of influence during the first stage of the Winter War, on November 30, 1939, Stalin attacked Finland. A puppet government was set up, headed by Kuusinen, but it did not receive any significant support in Finland, not even among the Communists, mainly because of developments in the two countries during the past few years. Party General Secretary Arvo Tuominen, exiled in Stockholm, gradually defected from the Comintern. Many rank-and-file Communists had fought in the Finnish Army against the Soviet Union. Stalin was forced to abandon the puppet government and to make peace with the government of Finland, which he did on March 13, 1940.

After the Winter War, a new and vigorous left-wing movement was born in Finland, under the aegis of a Finnish-Soviet friendship society founded by Mauri Ryömä. Many hoped for swift changes. Events in Europe seemed to be moving quickly, with even strong states like France collapsing. However, the authorities suppressed this movement, and Finland joined the German attack on the Soviet Union in 1941. This time, the Communists were firmly against the war, but support for the government was so widespread that they were not able to produce any significant resistance.

In 1944, Finland made a separate peace agreement, and its domestic political system underwent some changes. Extreme right-wing activities were prohibited, while the Communist Party was legalized. Together with left-wing socialists expelled from the SDP, the Communists founded a broader party, the Democratic League of the Finnish People (SKDL), which developed into one of the strongest in the country, regularly receiving over

20 percent of the vote. Its most popular leader was Hertta Kuusinen, the daughter of O. V. Kuusinen.

The Communist Party entered into the government, where it took a moderate stance, promoting cooperation with agrarians and Social Democrats. One of the new leaders of the party, Yrjö Leino, was appointed minister of the interior, and Communists controlled the security police for three years.

In 1947, the Communists' relations with the allied parties soured, and during the spring of 1948 rumors circulated about a Communist seizure of power. By agreeing to a military pact with the Soviets in 1948, however, President J. K. Paasikivi satisfied the Soviet basic need for security, and that was enough for Stalin. After heavy losses in the elections of 1948, Communists were ousted from the government.

The Communists remained a strong party, especially in Finland's industrial cities, but also in the poorer northern parts of the country. There were, in fact, two different communisms, quite distinct both socially and culturally. Fear of communism was a main factor influencing the Finnish government to create a modern welfare state.

In the mid-1960s, a reform movement developed in the CPF, and in 1966 a moderate and nationalist leadership was elected, headed by Aarne Saarinen. The party returned to government. However, Stalinists organized a vigorous opposition, and when the CPF condemned the invasion of Czechoslovakia, the opposition began to receive Soviet support. An open split ensued in 1969, but the following year the Soviets forced the two sides together.

During the 1970s, there were in effect two parties under one roof. The situation was further complicated by the fact that most members of the radical youth movement of the late 1960s became supporters of the minority CPF wing, so that Stalinism did not die a natural death. Locked in a perpetual internal schism, the Communists began to lose influence and voter support, a process that accelerated in the 1980s. In 1990, both the CPF and the SKDL ceased their political activities and a new party, the Left-Wing Alliance (Vasemmistoliitto) was founded as a "red-green" coalition. It has the support of about 10 percent of voters and participates in the government.

See also Winter War.

FURTHER READING

Lebedeva, N. S., K. Rentola, and T. Saarela. *"Kallis toveri Stalin!" Komintern ja Suomi.* Helsinki: Edita, 2002.

Saarela T., and K. Rentola. *Communism: National and International.* Helsinki: Finnish Literature Society, 1998.

KIMMO RENTOLA

Communist Party in France

The French Communist Party (Pcf), one of the most important in Western Europe, is something of an enigma. The reasons for this are many: its organization, propensity for secretiveness, sociological characteristics, international ties, deep social roots, successes and failures, and capacity to change its policies from one day to the next. The party's originality is best explored through the principal stages of its history, highlighting two dimensions—on the one hand, the French dimension, and on the other hand, the international one, which is connected to a privileged relationship with the USSR.

The Pcf was born at the Tours Congress, in December 1920, from a split in the French Section of the Workers' International (Sfio). This historic split of the French Left in turn affected the labor union movement: in 1921 the majority of the General Confederation of Labor (CGT) isolated the revolutionary minority, which founded the United General Confederation of Labor (CGTU). Soon dominated by the Communists, the latter would have a decisive role in recruiting workers for the party. The Pcf's beginnings were difficult. The new group was divided, most especially on the application of the twenty-one conditions given by the Communist International and regarding the "United Front" strategy. Its virulent campaigns against the French occupation of the Ruhr isolated the new Communist Party and subjected it to government repression. In the elections of spring 1924, the Pcf received less than nine hundred thousand votes and got twenty-six representatives. It lost many members, but also recruited young workers faithful to the revolutionary cause.

Bolshevization, first agreed to at the Comintern's Fifth Congress, and later Stalinization, radically modified the Pcf's organization, strategy, and cadre. Starting at the end of 1927, and in conformity with Moscow's orders, the Pcf adopted the "class against class" line, which led it to fight the bourgeoisie, imperialism, but also and above all the socialists. Finally, in 1931, as a result of the International's initiative, a working-class cadre emerged that was destined to dominate the party for over thirty years, causing it to easily fall into workerism. The young militants who made up the leadership had been educated by the Comintern, and they owed it everything—starting with the politburo's secretary, Maurice Thorez, who led the party until his death, in 1964. The establishment of this Stalinist apparatus, strictly monitored and advised by *missi dominici* from the Comintern, initially led to a drop in the Pcf's influence. The party became a sect that in 1932 barely had twenty-five thousand members, and that same year it only received 8.4 percent of the vote—in other words, 3 percent less than in 1928. Still, the Pcf had a reliable apparatus by this time, made of disciplined militants and selected cadre; thanks to the CGTU and various associations, the party could influence worker wards and managed to mobilize famous intellectuals like Romain Rolland on issues such as peace.

Three new factors changed the picture in the 1930s. In 1931 the economic crisis hit France, greatly increasing unemployment: the Pcf and the CGTU immediately deployed significant resources for help and solidarity. The events of February 6, 1934, (anti-parliamentary demonstrations organized by far-right leagues) provoked a mobilization of the Left in support of unity against the perceived Fascist threat. Finally, as a result of Adolf Hitler's victory in Germany, the USSR changed its foreign policy and worked to build an international anti-Fascist alliance. In May 1934, the Comintern expressed its intent to move closer to the Social Democrats after having earlier rejected this approach and removed one of the Pcf members, Jacques Doriot, who had been its spokesperson.

France was one of the best places in which to experiment with the Popular Front policy, which Thorez applied and perfected. So after the unity pact with the Sfio, signed on July 27, 1934, in autumn the party moved to broaden the accord to include the Radical Party and constitute a "Popular Front of labor, freedom and peace," which resulted in a program and an electoral agreement. The Pcf called for a vast alliance against the "two hundred families" who had all the power and extended a hand to the Catholics. In 1935 after the Franco-Soviet mutual assistance pact, the party supported national defense. While continuing to present itself as the vanguard of the working class, it also wanted to be seen as the best representative of the nation. The mixture of antifascism and defense of worker interests both Soviet and national produced excellent results. The Pcf grew numerically—in September 1937, it had 328,000 members—and in electoral terms—in the 1935 municipal elections, especially in the Paris region, where the "Red suburbs" would deliver consistently for a long time, and then in 1936, when it doubled its votes and gained seventy-two representatives. After the Popular Front's victory, the Comintern forbade the Pcf from participating in the Léon Blum government. The Pcf was active in the strikes of May–June 1936, preventing them from degenerating, and active in organizing support for the Spanish republic. The Communists especially benefited from the labor union reunification of March 1936; they consolidated their base, especially among specialized workers but also among anti-Fascist intellectuals. The defeats and divisions of the Popular Front weakened it, and yet its roots in France's social and political reality still held strong. From then on, membership in the Pcf or a vote in its favor did not simply reflect a political or ideological option but rather an existential choice, not to say a religious belief.

The German-Soviet pact of August 1939 placed the Pcf in an extremely difficult position and made it the target of an intense anti-Communist campaign. After having long denounced Hitlerian warmongering and having voted for military funding in Parliament on September 2, the Pcf stood with Stalin. The party therefore defined the war as imperialist, and attacked the French and British bourgeoisie above all. On September 26 the government dissolved the Pcf. The militants' disorientation, the disorganization of the party's activities, and the repression caused a severe drop in membership, from 270,000 before the declaration of war to less than 10,000 during the *drôle de guerre*. Defections grew among the representatives, but the apparatus and the cadre proved their unshakable loyalty. Following the German attack of May 1940 the Pcf blamed the imperialists for the defeat. The party campaigned for Thorez as prime minister, even though he had already deserted and secretly gone to the USSR, and it contacted the German authorities in Paris to be allowed to continue to publish *l'Humanité*.

If the first exhortations to struggle against the occupier were the result of personal initiatives, the party's entry into the resistance really occurred once the USSR had been invaded by German troops. The Pcf again indulged in one of its great shifts, and resumed relations with the anti-Fascist and patriotic forces. Its organizational abilities, the discipline and courage of its militants, and its willingness to engage in armed struggle made it the most powerful and dynamic element in the resistance. Since it had not managed to create its own direct hegemony in the domestic resistance and make it autonomous from Charles de Gaulle, in 1943 the party recognized de Gaulle's preeminence, and the following year it received some ministerial positions.

Subsequently, the party developed a dual-power strategy. Thorez, having returned to France in November 1944, inaugurated another shift that had been developed personally by Stalin. The Pcf participated in the government and engaged in "the battle of production"; at the same time that it moved its pawns, it pushed de Gaulle to resign, infiltrated the state, and mainly because of the power it exercised over the CGT, controlled entire sectors of society. The Pcf was France's first party: in 1946 it had 814,000 members, and it reached its peak in the November elections with over 28 percent of the vote. But the international and national situations became tense when on May 4, 1947, the socialist Paul Ramadier removed the Communist ministers. After having said for several months that it wanted to return to the government, the Pcf also entered the Cold War.

This change in orientation once again came from the international Communist movement. In September 1947 the Cominform replaced the Comintern, which Stalin had dissolved in 1943, forcing the Pcf and the Italian Communist Party to perform self-criticisms, and redefine the new organization's objectives. It was now a question of defending the peace, threatened by the United States, fighting the U.S. imperialists and "their lackeys," especially the socialists, and exalting the Communist countries and their leader, Stalin. The Pcf, the eldest child in the Communist church, devoted itself fully to pursuing these aims. Capitalizing on the serious social malaise, the party provoked some huge strikes in 1947–48. It denounced the threats that it thought were a menace to national independence—for instance by preventing, with an objective convergence with the Gaullists, the formation of the European Defense Community in 1954. It also conducted campaigns for peace, sometimes inclusive, with the participation of prestigious intellectuals, Catholic or from other backgrounds, and at other times more violent and confrontational, as on the occasion of General Matthew Ridgway's visit to Paris in May 1952.

In reality the Pcf had undertaken a sectarian retreat that resulted in a strong decrease in its membership and a Stalinist glaciation. Facing repression, the militants closed ranks around the party, the USSR, Stalin, and Thorez, the objects of a well-orchestrated cult. Periodically, following a rhythm dictated by Moscow, cases exploded internally that would allow for the elimination of certain leaders (for example André Marty, Charles Tillon,

or Auguste Lecoeur) who were deemed to be opponents. Yet the Pcf remained France's top party. It represented a vigorous "countersociety," and for the entire duration of the fourth republic it got almost a quarter of the votes. Stalin's death in 1953, and de-Stalinization starting in 1956, which the leadership opposed, caused defections among the intellectuals, but that did not affect the bulk of the party.

The Pcf instead took a hard hit when de Gaulle returned to power. The party's share of the vote had fallen to 18.6 percent in the fall 1958 elections. For the next fifteen years, its electorate stabilized at a somewhat higher level. The Pcf seemed incapable of grasping Gaullism's original features; it had to come to terms with it on international political issues, but was unable to discern the profound social transformations that were taking place. It also disappointed the youths, who regarded it as too timid on the issue of the war in Algeria. Since they were still part of the strongest party on the Left, however, the Communists made agreements with the socialists, and in 1965 and 1967 this took the form of an electoral agreement. Waldeck Rochet, who had replaced Thorez in 1964, worked prudently for a greater opening to other social classes, accepting political pluralism in a future socialist society, recognizing cultural freedom, and condemning the invasion of Czechoslovakia by troops from the Warsaw Pact in 1968.

During the great French crisis in that same year the Pcf remained isolated. It fought the *gauchiste* demonstrations and proved its perfect control over its working-class strongholds. Once Georges Marchais replaced Rochet, who was ill, a strategy to reunite the Left was relaunched on the basis of a common program signed in 1972 with François Mitterand's new Socialist Party. At first the agreement was advantageous. The Pcf regained some ground, its membership increased, and in 1977 it took control of numerous municipalities. At the same time it tried to deepen its connections to current developments, moved closer to the Italian Community Party within the framework of Eurocommunism, and formulated its own critiques of the USSR. But it soon became obvious that the Socialist Party was growing at the Pcf's expense, and that the policy of greater openness was creating upheavals within the party itself. Given these developments, Marchais preferred to leave the Union of the Left in 1977, which led to its defeat during the following year's political elections. The Pcf attacked its former ally and began to side with the USSR once again, approving of its evolution overall as well as its intervention in Afghanistan, and expelling from its ranks all those who disapproved of this new orientation. The party fought alone against everyone.

This splendid isolation cost it dearly in political terms, and the party seemed as if it were divorcing itself from French society. Its membership declined, and Marchais was humiliated by gathering only 15 percent of the vote during the 1981 presidential elections, which Mitterand won. This failure marked the beginning of a constant and rapid decline, which brought the Pcf below the 10 percent mark. Forced to participate in the government in 1981, it really didn't know how to manage its four ministers, who in their turn found themselves in a marginal position. In 1984 it ended this experiment. Internal dissent grew, weakening a party that was now destabilized by Mikhail Gorbachev's policies and later by the USSR's collapse. The Pcf withdrew to its rural and working-class strongholds, which were however under siege.

Marchais's replacement with Robert Hue, in January 1994, opened another cycle. The Pcf started going down a road of tentative transformation. It partly recognized past errors, opened up to the outside, tolerated the expression of internal differences, rethought its positions regarding several political and social topics, and redefined its strategy. A minority party, it participated in the "Plural Left" government around socialist Lionel Jospin between 1997 and 2002. But its electoral results were disappointing (during the presidential elections of 2002 Hue received only 3.4 percent of the ballot), the membership diminished (in 2003, there were 130,000 members), and its funds declined. Its lengthy participation in the government only sharpened its crisis. In 2003 Hue left the party presidency, which he had taken in 2001, and Marie-George Buffet, who had already been general secretary for two years, became number one.

From that moment on the Pcf attempted to regain its strength; it did so without breaking with the Socialist Party, but making distinctions between the two parties clearer, and by allying itself with left-wing movements, but without falling into the dynamics of mere protest. This was a risky course: the Pcf was trying to combine a revolutionary identity, full-court protest actions, and support for "responsible" positions. Even though it joined others in opposing a European constitutional treaty, in 2005 the party remained weak. The Pcf stayed on the political sidelines, but communism as an ideal, however degraded, and a social attitude, as a magical place of memory, endured and continued to influence the French Left.

See also Antifascism; Eurocommunism; Marchais, Georges; National Roads to Socialism; Popular Front; Post-Soviet Communism; Revolution, Myths of the; Thorez, Maurice.

FURTHER READING

Buton, P. *Communisme une utopie en sursis?* Paris: Larousse, 2001.

Courtois, S., and M. Lazar. *Histoire du Parti communiste français.* Paris: Presses Universitaires de France, 2000.

Kriegel, A. *Les communists frannçais, 1920–1970.* Paris: Seuil, 1985.

Lavabre, M. C., and F. Platone. *Que reste-t-il du PCF?* Paris: Autrement, 2003.

Lazar, M. *Maisons rouges. Les Partis communistes français et italien de la Libération à nos jours.* Paris: Aubier, 1992.

Pudal, B. *Prendre parti. Pour une sociologie historique du PCF.* Paris: Presses de la FNSP, 1991.

MARC LAZAR

Communist Party in Germany

The Communist Party of Germany (CPG) was founded at a Constituent Assembly held from December 30, 1918, to January 1, 1919, in Berlin. This event was preceded by the organization of a left-wing component in the Socialist Workers' movement in Germany during World War I. Its adherents came out against the policy line of the Social Democratic Party of Germany (SDPG), which was supporting the government and civil peace that reigned in the country at the time, and instead declared themselves in favor of ending the war quickly without demanding any annexations or war indemnities. In April 1917, the Independent Social Democratic Party of Germany split off from the main body of the SDPG. This faction included the most radical workers' movement leaders, who formed the Spartacus Union. The union carried on antiwar activities in both the armed forces and on the home front, and the kaiser's government responded with harsh reprisals.

The end of World War I and the fall of the monarchy led to the release from prison of the two leaders of the Spartacus Union, Karl Liebknecht and Rosa Luxemburg, who took command of the radical wing of the German revolutionary movement in 1918–19. In their newspaper, *Die Rote Fahne* (The Red Flag), they criticized the inconsistencies in the socialist coalition government, and called for the transfer of all power to the Councils of Workers' and Soldiers' Deputies. The Spartacus Union leaders hewed to the Russian model and worked with the Bolshevik Party leadership, up to early November 1918 through the Soviet Embassy in Berlin and, later, various Moscow emissaries there, such as Karl Radek.

The CPG's program, as approved at a Constituent Assembly, oriented Communists toward socialist transformations within the framework of a dictatorship of the proletariat and demanded that they work actively among the working masses and support Soviet Russia in every way. Contravening Luxemburg, the majority of the delegates supported a boycott of elections to the Constituent Assembly, sharing as they did radical feelings about a decisive encounter between the proletariat and bourgeoisie for preeminence in the government. The CPG refrained from political terrorism, but also emphasized its readiness to resort to military intervention to help resolve this class conflict. The unsuccessful attempt at an armed uprising in Berlin in early January 1919 under the slogan "All Power to the Soviets" led to a civil war within the revolutionary camp itself. Liebknecht and Luxemburg were murdered, and CPG functionaries now had to operate illegally. Similar events in Bavaria, where a Soviet republic had been declared in the spring, also ended with the failure of the left-wing radicals.

After uniting with the left wing of the Independent Social Democratic Party of Germany in December 1920, the CPG became a major political force, with more than four hundred thousand members. The CPG regarded itself as a national faction of the universal party of the proletariat—the Communist International, which had been formed in March 1919. Comintern funds largely financed CPG periodicals as well as the maintenance and training of party functionaries in the middle and higher echelons. The development of CPG strategies and tactics, and the selection of the party's leading personnel, were also carried out under the watchful eye of the Comintern's Executive Committee, often leading to conflicts between the party leadership (Zentrale) and Moscow.

In March 1921, under pressure from Bela Kun and August Kleine, two Comintern representatives who had recently arrived in Berlin, the CPG incited workers in central Germany to an armed revolt, which was put down quite cruelly. The head of the CPG, Paul Levi, who did not agree with resorting to such putsches, made his disagreement public through the press and appealed to the Executive Committee of the Comintern for its support. This conflict was discussed at the Third Congress of the Comintern in 1921. The Comintern decided to condemn the leftist "attack theory," which did not take into account the real dangers of a resulting political struggle. At the same time, Levi was accused of opportunism, removed from his posts, and later expelled from the CPG.

As the revolutionary period faded in Europe, the German Communists were forced to pay greater attention to parliamentary activity and the struggle to raise the workers' standard of living. The CPG intensified its efforts in the large workers' organizations and took part in defending the democratic institutions of the Weimar Republic from reactionary attacks, without concealing its ultimate goal: the establishment in Germany of a proletarian dictatorship based on soviets. The CPG was compelled by the logic of the political struggle to admit the necessity of forming a "united workers' front"—that is, cooperating with the Social Democrats and trade unions to defend the essential interests of the working masses. In December 1921, the tactics of the united workers' front were approved by the Comintern and became obligatory for all Communist parties.

The domestic political crisis of 1923 in Germany once again raised the Communists' hopes that decisive battles were near. With the help of the Comintern and the USSR, the CPG began preparing for an armed uprising. The party leaders entered the coalition governments of two German states, Saxony and Thuringia, and started to form and arm insurgent detachments—the "proletarian companies." This time, however, the government was able to forestall the Communists, and the Reichswehr forces carried out so-called imperial execution. An attempt to launch an armed conflict in Hamburg (on October 25, 1923) was quashed by the police, and the CPG was once again declared illegal.

The Comintern's Executive Committee interpreted the defeat of the German Communists in fall 1923 as a consequence of the indecisiveness and "right-wing errors" of their leadership. The CPG chiefs, Heinrich Brandler and August Thalheimer, were relieved of their duties and sent into honorary exile in Moscow. They were replaced by new people from the Berlin organization of the CPG, Ruth Fischer and Arkady Maslow, who were distinguished by their radical left-wing positions and efforts to gain greater independence from Moscow for the party. Nevertheless, they enjoyed the special patronage of the chair of the Executive Committee of the Communist International, Grigory Zinovyev. In spite of the CPG's success in the parliamentary elections of May 1924, the

Fischer-Maslow group refused to operate within the structures of the Weimar Republic; it called on Communists to withdraw from the trade unions, and for practical purposes, boycotted the policies of the United Front. The party apparatus purged itself of its new members from the Social Democratic movement, whom it now labeled "Luxemburgians." After many admonishments, the Executive Committee of the Comintern managed to dismiss the representatives of the Fischer-Maslow group from their posts in 1925.

By the mid-1920s, the CPG leader was Ernst Tellman, who had been active in the Hamburg uprising. He followed a policy of trying to attract individuals from various party factions to high-level work in the CPG. This "policy of concentration of forces" was officially approved at a CPG congress in Essen in March 1927. Tellman was twice a candidate for the presidency of Germany, in 1925 and 1932, and received 6 and 13 percent of the vote, respectively.

The years of stability did not bring the CPG any significant successes, and the party remained on the fringes of German political life. This was largely due to the leadership's inability to adjust its program to the changed situation in the country and world. The fact that the public viewed the party as "the hand of Moscow" also played a role. In September 1928, opponents of Tellmann in the Central Committee of the CPG attempted to remove him from his post as party chair. This caused a storm of protest in Moscow, where Stalin saw this initiative as an intrigue on the part of his opponent, Nikolay Bukharin, who was in charge of Comintern matters within the Soviet Communist Party. The salvation and rehabilitation of Tellman turned into a regular purge of the CPG apparatus, from which both "right-wingers" and their "accomplices" were now removed. Any nonconformism within the party was seen as criminal, and among Communist functionaries there emerged a new Stalinist type of hero: the "soldier of the party," ready to die for the Communist cause, but incapable of any critical reasoning about it.

The economic crisis of 1929–33 raised doubts about the viability of capitalism and gave a second wind to the German Communists, who supported a revolutionary socialist perspective. The CPG's ranks were augmented by unemployed workers who had lost faith in the ability of the trade unions to defend their interests. This gave the party radicals a boost, but also weakened their position in the organized workers' movement. The CPG doubled its representation in the Reichstag, though it was still excluded from making legislative decisions. The political struggle moved increasingly into the streets of the large cities, where adherents of the CPG emerged as the most determined adversaries of the Nazi storm troopers.

At the same time, the chief ideological opponents of the CPG were still the Social Democrats, whom the Communists now called "social Fascists." When the Berlin police, within which the SDPG wielded considerable influence, fired on the May Day demonstration of 1929, the mutual hatred between the two parties grew. The Communists' appeal for a "united front from the bottom" could not compensate for the energy they expended on exposing the SDPG. The Comintern leadership certainly bore its share of responsibility for imposing an ultraleft, sectarian policy on the CPG, with the slogan "After Hitler, It's Us." The inability of party workers to join in the struggle against the radicals of the Right was one of the factors contributing to the establishment of the Nazi dictatorship in Germany.

The first wave of repressions struck the CPG soon after Hitler came to power. Using the burning of the Reichstag as an excuse for state terror against the Communists, the Nazis crushed the party's underground apparatus in spring 1933 and arrested its leaders, including Tellman. During the Nazi years, about half of the three hundred thousand members of the CPG ran afoul of the Gestapo and were either killed or thrown into concentration camps. The Communists nevertheless took their place in the ranks of the resistance, and many informed the outside world about the crimes of the Nazi regime. The CPG headquarters was transferred to Moscow. After the Seventh Congress of the Comintern, the party renounced its attacks on the Social Democrats, and after the Brussels Conference (which took place on October 3–15, 1935, outside Moscow), it worked out a strategy for its struggle against the anti-Fascist Popular Front, adapting it to conditions in Germany. The new party chair was Wilhelm Pieck, and his right-hand man for many years was Walter Ulbricht.

Pieck and Ulbricht were confirmed as leaders of the émigré center of the CPG after a period of tense struggle, in which Stalin's circle directly intervened. The losers were soon subjected to the Soviet repressions of 1936–38, which were carried out against a significant number of German political émigrés and members of their families. After the signing of the Molotov-Ribbentrop Pact, the Moscow leadership of the CPG was forced to refrain from active anti-Fascist propaganda, instead concentrating its attention on establishing links with the Communist underground in Germany proper. Germany's invasion of the Soviet Union brought the party back into the anti-Fascist ranks, and its representatives played a leading role in the resistance during the closing years of World War II. The Communists disseminated propaganda among German prisoners of war and also began to groom likely subjects for a political role in postwar Germany.

As early as April 1945, the first groups of CPG functionaries arrived from Moscow on German territory, already freed by the Red Army, to take over the process of the postwar regeneration of the country. Communists who had survived the Nazi period in Germany itself also took an active part in the creation of organs of democratic self-government (the so-called anti-Fascist committees), which were not recognized by the occupation authorities. On June 11, 1945, the CPG was the first German party to declare its revival. In the CPG manifesto published that same day, the party announced its plans for the anti-Fascist democratic transformations to come, though at the time warning against any blind imitation of the Soviet experience. In April 1946, in order to assure that the Communists would receive leading positions in the postwar democracy, CPG organizations joined forces with the social democratic groups in the Soviet occupation zone. The resulting new party, the United Socialist Party of Germany (USPG), in close cooperation with the zone's military administration, aimed to achieve sociopolitical transformations based on the Soviet model in East Germany.

As the Cold War progressed in the Western occupation zones, the CPG gradually became weaker, although it did send fifteen deputies to the first Bundestag. In 1956, the West German Constitution banned the CPG as a party that advocated changing the political system of the Federal Republic of Germany by force. The West German Communists did not acquire legal status again until 1968, when the party was reorganized and renamed the German Communist Party (GCP). The GCP's weak support among the masses in West Germany's postindustrial society and the constant splintering off of various radical ideological groups (Trotskyites, Maoists, Stalinists, and the like) prevented the GCP from regaining its previous influence. Its adherents, though, maintained a certain representation in the trade unions and were active in the pacifist movement in the early 1980s.

By the late 1940s, the USPG, after undergoing a series of interparty purges and crises at the top level, had become a typical "people's republic" party, ruled by a Stalinist *nomenklatura*. Until its virtual collapse in 1989,

the USPG remained the ruling political force in the German Democratic Republic, devoting itself to building a "developed socialist society" and fostering a strong unity within the Eastern European bloc. After the East German surrender to democracy and the reunification of Germany, the Party of Democratic Socialism, which had grown out of the USPG and united itself with West German left-wing organizations, declared itself heir to the best traditions of the German socialist movement, which embraced the history of the German Communists as well.

See also Antifascism; Comintern; Insurrection in Germany; Liebknecht, Karl; Luxemburg, Rosa; People's Democracy; Pieck, Wilhelm; Social Fascism; Soviet Occupation of Germany; Ulbricht, Walter.

FURTHER READING

Angress, W. T. *Stillborn Revolution: The Communist Bid for Power in Germany, 1921–1923*. Princeton, NJ: Princeton University Press, 1963.

Flechtheim, O. K. *Die KPD in der Weimarer Republik* [The CPG in the Weimar Republic]. Frankfurt am Main: Europäische Verlagsanstalt, 1969.

Weber, H. *Die Wandlung des deutschen Kommunismus; Die Stalinisierung der KPD in der Weimarer Republik* [The Transformation of German Communism; The Stalinization of the CPG in the Weimar Republic]. 2 vols. Frankfurt am Main: Europäische Verlagsanstalt, 1969.

ALEKSANDR I. VATLIN

Communist Party in Great Britain

The Communist Party of Great Britain was formed in August 1920 as an amalgamation of small groups, most notably the British Socialist Party. Disputes over a number of issues, such as affiliation to the Labour Party, had delayed the party's formation, but Lenin's condemnation of the ultra-left facilitated matters. The new party was well financed by the Comintern, but it struggled, and reorganization followed the report of a party commission in 1922. Two Communists were elected to parliament in 1922 (one as a Labour MP), but both lost their seats in 1923, and although there was one Communist MP during the periods 1924–29 and 1935–45, and two between 1945 and 1950, the party was never able to develop a significant parliamentary nucleus. There was some progress in the trade unions, via the National Minority Movement; and the general strike and mining lockout of 1926 occasioned a doubling of party membership. However, the peak was less than 13,000, and most memberships were short-lived. This failure of the party to grow meant that the leadership was ultimately unable to resist pressure from within the party and from Moscow for a change of line in 1927–29. But the new line, strongly critical of the Labour Party, brought little success. Membership continued to fall, to little more than 2,000 in mid-1930. Even the collapse of the second Labour government in 1931, while "proving" Communist arguments about Labour betraying the workers, brought no tangible political benefits to the Communists, other than a brief rise in membership.

In December 1931, the Comintern and the party leadership agreed that Harry Pollitt (party general secretary since 1929) should be regarded as leader of the party, and that the largely unsuccessful attempt to form separate "Red" unions would be abandoned in favor of working through the established trade union movement. This, and the fight against fascism from 1933 onward, helped the party to develop. The logical conclusion of this process was the abandonment of class against class in late 1934; between then and 1939 the party campaigned hard for a Popular Front against fascism, and also pursued its union work with increasing success, not least among skilled workers like engineers. By 1939 the party had a larger membership—around 18,500—and a higher profile than ever before.

But a crisis followed the British declaration of war on Germany in September 1939. Moscow deemed that it was not a war against fascism, but a clash of rival imperialisms with which Communists should have nothing to do. Pollitt opposed the change, and as a result was ousted from the leadership. A new secretariat comprising Rajani Palme Dutt, William Rust, and D. F. Springhall took over. However, the day-to-day work of Communists changed less than one might think, and Pollitt soon reentered the higher echelons of the party. The new line, while alienating some, appealed to others; if anything, party membership rose in the months of the "phony war." After the fall of France in the summer of 1940, the party concentrated largely on exploiting popular discontent with wartime conditions. In January 1941 the resulting People's Convention and the ban on the party's newspaper, the *Daily Worker*, showed that the party was not irrelevant. Ultimately, the German invasion of the Soviet

Union in June 1941 marked a significant shift, with the party supporting the British war effort in alliance with the USSR. Pollitt was reinstated as secretary and pursued an ultrapatriotic line of support for the Churchill coalition. This, and Red Army heroism, led party membership to surge to 56,000 in 1942. However, this proved to be a peak; and hopes of an electoral breakthrough in 1945 were dashed when only two of the party's twenty-one candidates were elected at the postwar election; neither held his seat in 1950.

By 1947, the party had moved strongly to the left, because of a reaction against wartime super-patriotism, increasing hostility toward the policies of the Labour government, and the onset of the Cold War. Its association with the USSR did little to help the party after 1945: the Soviet split with Tito in 1948, the increasingly naked Soviet anti-Semitism of the later Stalin years, and most especially the events of 1956—with Khrushchev's secret speech and the Soviet invasion of Hungary—all harmed the party. In 1956 about a third of the party's members, including many high-profile intellectuals, left in protest. The same year also saw the departure of Pollitt from the party secretaryship; his successors as general secretary—John Gollan (1956–75), Gordon McLennan (1975–90), and Nina Temple (1990–91)—were nowhere near being Pollitt's political equals. Although party membership remained above prewar levels until the 1980s, the party was never able to regain its wartime numbers.

Although party membership recovered later in the 1950s and into the 1960s, the party was damaged by a scandal surrounding Communist ballot rigging in the Electrical Trades Union in the early 1960s. The Soviet suppression of the Prague Spring in 1968, although criticized by the party, dealt yet another heavy blow to its image. The 1960s were a difficult decade for the Labour Party, but the CPGB was not the sole beneficiary: many found alternatives like Trotskyism and Maoism more attractive. Increasingly influenced by the ideas of Antonio Gramsci and by "Eurocommunism," some Communists began to campaign for changes. While the party had formally rejected revolution in its program *The British Road to Socialism* (1951), there was still a feeling that some members were too much committed to "old-fashioned" communism. The stage was set for a struggle between "modernizers," who favored a more Gramscian approach and hard-line "tankies." This struggle continued to the end of the party's life. The party as a whole moved toward the modernizers, but its paper, the *Morning Star*, remained under the control of more traditional Communists. The CPGB was finally dissolved following the collapse of the Soviet Union in 1991. Most of its members joined a short-lived successor body, the Democratic Left; hard-liners went into a new Communist Party of Britain (CPB, formed in 1988), which claimed the hammer and sickle as its emblem. But the historic CPGB was no more.

See also Eurocommunism; Grand Alliance.

FURTHER READING

Callaghan, J. *Cold War, Crisis and Conflict: The CPGB 1951–68.* London: Lawrence and Wishart, 2003.
Eaden, J., and D. Renton. *The Communist Party of Great Britain since 1920.* Basingstoke: Palgrave, 2002.
Thorpe, A. J. *The British Communist Party and Moscow, 1920–1943.* Manchester: Manchester University Press, 2000.

ANDREW J. THORPE

Communist Party in Greece

In 1922, inspired by the Bolsheviks' victory, a faction of Greek socialists joined the Comintern as the Greek Communist Party (KKE) and adopted its revolutionary doctrine. Ignored by a nation steeped in nationalistic lore, the KKE attracted few followers and was viewed as the instrument of the Comintern whose advocacy of an independent Macedonia threatened to truncate Greece. In 1936, the Communists emerged briefly as the linchpin in parliament while fomenting violent strikes. The Ioannis Metaxas dictatorship (1936–41) banned parties and imprisoned prominent Communists, however; others were coerced into denouncing their party. Nevertheless, a clandestine Communist network survived, and during the Axis occupation (1941–44) mobilized the country's largest resistance army, ELAS.

The Communists employed ELAS to disperse rival resistance bands, and failing to enter the cabinet in exile (August 1943), sponsored their own shadow government. In May 1944, perhaps on Moscow's advice, the KKE joined the newly formed national government, but broke with it when, following liberation, the authorities ordered ELAS to disband. Unprepared to seize power, the KKE called for demonstrations that led to serious fighting in Athens (December 1944). British troops drove ELAS out of the capital and forced it to disarm.

The December 1944 crisis frightened the nation and tarnished the KKE's image. Communists suffered right-wing persecution, and some fled to the mountains. Led by Moscow-appointed Nikos Zahariadis, the KKE challenged the traditional parties to dialogue but was rebuffed. The Communists boycotted the March 1946 elections and stepped up violence. The party ordered its newly formed "Democratic Army" to seize Greece's northern provinces, and hoping for foreign recognition, announced a provisional government (December 1947)—this despite Stalin's ambivalence regarding the insurgency, meager foreign assistance, and the KKE's shunning by the Cominform. If the KKE hoped to pressure its opponents to negotiate, it blundered into full-scale revolution. The party was outlawed (October 1947), and its leaders charged with sedition. Backed by Britain and the United States, the government forces defeated the insurgency (August 1949). Many Communists fled to the Soviet bloc countries; others were imprisoned or forced underground.

With Stalin's support, Zahariadis remained in control and dealt harshly with his detractors. In 1956, Moscow instructed the KKE Central Committee to unseat Zahariadis and elect a new politburo. The change split cadres in exile, and Greece into pro- and anti-Zahariadis factions. In 1968, ordered to resolve internal dissension, the politburo broke up, ostensibly over the failure to resist the military dictatorship in Greece (1967–74); the deeper cause was the party's disastrous policies under Zahariadis. Remaining loyal to Moscow, the politburo's inner core seized control and expelled the others as "revisionists." Supported by cadres in Greece the dissidents formed the "KKE-Interior," a new socialist party that repudiated the policies that produced civil war and rejected Moscow's tutelage.

Since democracy's restoration (1974) the two parties have retained separate identities, occasionally collaborating with other leftists to gain votes. Under the old guard the KKE upholds its revolutionary dogma, is staunchly anti–United States and anti–North Atlantic Treaty Organization, opposes entry into the European Community, and attacks all other domestic parties. Through its bolder message, better organization, and more resources, it has consistently attracted a small but loyal following, especially in urban centers (about 10 percent of the voters), and is a minor fixture of the political landscape. The KKE-Interior, renamed the Greek Left (EA), has adopted a reformist, Eurocommunist program. Although its followers include prominent intellectuals, it receives less than 2 percent of the vote.

Both parties have suffered from the stigma of civil war and the collapse of communism. But their greatest handicap has been the emergence of the new socialist party (PASOK), which has attracted most leftists, and governed during 1981–89 and 1993–2004. In 1989, the KKE joined the conservatives in a coalition government of limited duration to cleanse the state of PASOK's corruption, with Communists serving as ministers of the interior and justice. Otherwise, its outmoded ideology and authoritarian character appear to relegate the KKE to a marginal role, at least as long as PASOK survives. The EA's failure to attract a larger following renders its future uncertain.

See also Eurocommunism; Greek Civil War.

FURTHER READING

Katsoulis, G. *Istoria tou Kommounistikou Kommatos Elladas.* Athens: Nea Synora, 1976–78.

Kousoulas, D. G. *Revolution and Defeat: The Story of the Greek Communist Party.* Oxford: Oxford University Press, 1965.

Solaro, Antonio. *Storia del Partito Comunista Greco.* Milano, Teti, 1973.

JOHN O. IATRIDES

Communist Party in Hungary

The Communist Party in Hungary was founded by workers and the intelligentsia in November 1918, and it went by the name of the Party of the Communists in Hungary. The founders were, on the one hand, either earlier Social Democrats who became Bolsheviks in the Soviet Union and returned to Hungary from there—as, for example, Béla Kun or Károly Vántus—or on the other hand, they came from the Left of the Social Democratic Party—as, for instance, Béla Vágó and László Rudas. The revolutionary socialists joined them later on, as did the subsequently executed Ottó Korvin.

History knows of few modern parties that came into power only three months after their foundation. Yet this is precisely what happened to this party in Hungary. In March 1919, the Hungarian Communists and Social Democrats succeeded in taking over power peacefully in Hungary, proclaimed the Hungarian Soviet Republic, and after having gathered into one party, they put the dictatorship of the proletariat into operation.

How could this have happened? Ever since the beginning of the 20th century, many have believed that the only way Hungary could and should be delivered from its accumulated social problems and backwardness was by revolution. Among them was Endre Ady, the greatest Hungarian poet of the era, and Ervin Szabó, the leftist theoretician with excellent international relationships. Add to this the defeat of World War I. Subsequently, due to the goals of the Allies and the intentions of gaining ground in the new states that formed after the breaking up of Austria-Hungary, the Hungarian nation suffered a major blow: it lost such territories as well as population, which was primarily or completely Hungarian. Bearing the responsibility of the lost war and the forfeiture of territorial integrity on its shoulders, the conservative Right was unable to act, whereas the liberal bourgeois movement lacked the strength after the bourgeois democratic revolution of October 1918. The Social Democrats believed in an evolutionary solution: democracy first, followed by the elimination of feudal relics, then economic development, structural transformation, and finally socialism. As a ruling party, the democratic Left had to face the extortion of the Allies and ensure the defense of the nation. Social democracy found an ally in resistance in the Communists, already possessing a significant power to sway the masses and cherishing a hope in a world revolution and the Soviet Army.

The question inevitably arose among Communist theoreticians as to whether it was right to seize power when the requirements were not present for the establishment of a new society, nor were the indispensable outer and inner conditions set for the keeping of power. Georg Lukacs, the great Hungarian Marxist sociologist thinker who joined the Communist movement, answered his own question with another: Is it right not to seize power when the possibility presents itself, and rather leave the realization of ideas to the unforeseen future? Is it not more sensible to flow with history and the mood of the masses, thusly effectuating all that is possible at a given time and place for the building up of a more equal and just society? All of the aforementioned, due to the international pressure imposed on the country, combined with a patriotic temper as well.

The Hungarian Soviet Republic was short-lived, yet it was supported not only by the workers and the poor of the villages but also by part of the intelligentsia, as they could identify with its social and cultural goals. The Communist ideas were, however, curtailed by the excessive socialization and the Red Terror. Finally, the military defeat brought with it the collapse of the Béla Kun–led Commune. In the successive counterrevolutionary regime the Communist Party was forced into undercover activity, and its members were persecuted. The majority of its leaders were left with no other option but exile. They fought for supremacy within the party according to the rules of existence in their emigration, yet still played a significant role in the Comintern. Many of the Communist Hungarian emigrants later became the victims of the Stalinist cleansing.

Few results, and almost no influence on the internal and foreign affairs of the country—these were the characteristics of the activities of a party that often got to the state of total collapse and yet always managed to rebuild itself. With the Commune behind them and the Soviet Union nearby, the Horthy governments, allies of the German fascism, always paid close attention to the outlawed Communist movement. In the Hungary of the interwar period, the defining Christian nationalistic, conservative right-wing ideology had anticommunism as a determinant factor. For the counterrevolution, liberalism was the antechamber of communism.

The members of the illegal party were primarily industrial workers, miners, and agrarian proletarians. Utilizing conspiratorial methods, its members had an arguable influence in certain Social Democratic organizations and trade unions. The strategy of the party centered around sparking a proletarian revolution, for which there was absolutely no real chance at the time. The party existed in the isolated state of a sect under the Comintern's control and was incapable of making alterations. These changes were brought about only after the German Fascists came to power, as the Communist Party gained influence among the forces organized against the open fascism and the German occupation with the idea of establishing a Popular Front, coordinating the fight for independence, and later attempting armed resistance.

The advance of the Soviet Army and the liberation of Hungary created an immense advantage for the reappearance of the Hungarian Communist Party. The former people's commissar, Mátyás Rákosi, who had been incarcerated and later returned to Hungary from the Soviet Union, became the party's leader. The party played a pivotal role in the national renewal, establishment of the democratic order, reconstruction of economic and social life, and agrarian reform, and its ministers held key positions in the coalition government. In just a few months, the association became a party with popular support—with the backing of some hundred thousand people—and although falling short of expectations, it gained 17 percent of the votes in the 1945 elections.

From the beginning of 1947 onward, the Hungarian Communist Party—taking advantage of the decisive Soviet influence, and not boggling at having to use judiciary or illegal means—changed from the road marked by the notions of a people's democracy and mixed economy, to the one leading to the establishment of a totalitarian Socialist political system. Georg Lukacs and Imre Nagy stood up against this volte-face without any success whatsoever. Within a year, the Communists eliminated the multiparty system and absorbed the Social Democratic Party. The Hungarian Workers' Party was formed, and from 1948 onward it declared a large-scale modernization program focusing on industrialization and cultural revolution. It also started to implement collectivization and the irrational development of a national defense. The Sovietization of the country was accompanied by the cult of personality, the setting aside of any kind of possibility for control, the subordination of the party and the trade unions, and a series of intimidating show trials. Due to the harsh dictatorship the social unrest did not openly unfold. Rectification took place solely after the death of Stalin and the Berlin uprising, characteristically due to the influence of direct Soviet intervention.

This "new phase" brought with it the suspension of the terror, an increase in the standard of living, more balanced economic development, and the termination of forced collectivization. The battle between the followers of the old and new regimes was once again decided by the Soviets at the end of 1954 for the former—that is, to the benefit of Rákosi's group. The dismissed Nagy set about outlining the idea of a "national Communism" based on national independence, patriotic feelings, and realistic social expectations.

The Twentieth Congress of the Communist Party of the Soviet Union initiated a grave moral and political crisis in the Hungarian Communist Party. This proved to be a pivotal antecedent of the 1956 October uprising in which Nagy as well as the ideology of democratic socialism, self-government, and the equal status of nations played significant parts. The Communist Party collapsed entirely and then reformed itself as the Hungarian Socialist Workers' Party. Its leader, János Kádár, lent his name to the Soviet intervention.

Following the suppression of the national resistance, the reorganized Communist Party employed harsh retaliation to stabilize the position of the country and itself.

Kádár restored the Soviet regime, but he first tried to make corrections, later endeavored to implement reforms, and then attempted to improve the former Soviet model. After 1956, the complete interweaving of the Communist Party and the state, the intervening into the private lives of the inhabitants, and the industrialization at the expense of the living standard all ceased. The way the Communist Party realized the reorganization of large-scale farming differed greatly from the "classic" method. During the 1960s, it made an attempt to integrate the market and the plan by establishing a new economic mechanism.

At the end of 1961 Kádár declared the policy of "Who is not against us, is with us," from which a sort of reconciliation, amnesty, and an opening up of the borders for the Hungarian population inevitably arose. When Khrushchev announced the slogan of "to catch up and leave behind," and the switch to building communism, Kádár claimed that Marxism and Leninism should not be employed to experiment on the people but rather to help the people live better. This emphasis on the present, precaution, and a demand to uphold stability became the characteristics of the policy of the Hungarian Socialist Workers' Party for decades. What was sufficient, however, when the conditions were set for economic growth, or to maintain workability, was not enough for dynamism and the establishment of competitiveness. The social and economic policy of the Communist Party leveling to the benefit of the workers failed by the 1980s, as it kept back the performance of the social groups interested in modernization. The insufferable extent of external indebtedness and the alteration in the power relations of world power shattered the Hungarian model. The interaction between these two factors—that is, the exhaustion of domestic reserves and the change in external circumstances—became the most intense precisely when Kádár was overthrown by a group of party members who intended to support adding political reforms to the newer market reforms to solve the crisis. In 1988, the Communist Party decided to loosen its monopolistic exercise of power. Yet it was too late; the society affected by the atmosphere of the crisis saw the solution in the multiparty system and political transformation. The Communist Party played a major role in the peaceful transition, and elimination of the demarcation line between the East and West. It later gave way to a new party set up according to social democratic principles—the Hungarian Socialist Party.

See also Hungarian Republic of Councils; Hungarian Revolution; Kádár, János; Kun, Béla; Nagy, Imre; Rákoski, Mátyás; Socialist Camp; Soviet Bloc.

FURTHER READING

Mevius, M. *Agents of Moscow: The Hungarian Communist Party and the Origins of Socialist Patriotism, 1941–1953.* New York: Oxford University Press, 2005.

Romsics, I. *Hungary in the Twentieth Century.* Budapest: Corvina, 1999.

GYORGY FOLDES

Communist Party in the Indian Subcontinent

The Communist Party of India (CPI) was initiated in exile in late 1920 by M. N. Roy, the legendary Comintern emissary. It remained insignificant, however, until the mid-1930s when the new anti-Fascist Popular Front doctrine enabled activists to link up with the left wing of the Congress Party. Communists were thus able to take over the popular mass movement in what is now Kerala and to strengthen their influence within the all-India trade union movement. They also constituted the major revolutionary nationalist force among the peasants in present Andhra Pradesh and among the tenants, workers, and, occasionally, ex-terrorist radical aristocrats in undivided Bengal.

Further advances were halted in 1942 when the CPI had problems combining its commitment to the international anti-Fascist movement with Gandhi's nationalist "Quit India" policy, and in 1948, when the party adjusted to Moscow's new Cold War hard line and opted for sustaining its revolutionary activity even though the British had left. It was also at this time that a separate Communist Party of Pakistan was founded, within which the East Pakistan section was the most active, thus forming a separate party already in 1968, before the independence of Bangladesh. Meanwhile, the Communist Party of Nepal was also formed from India (1949), and during the period of harsh British repression in Sri Lanka, several of its primarily anti-Stalinist Communists worked there as well.

By the early 1950s, Moscow approved the plan of the CPI members who wanted to return to a more cautious strategy of cooperating with the Congress Party (deemed to represent the "national bourgeoisie") on issues related to anti-imperialism, the building of an independent national economy, and anti-feudal land reforms. Meanwhile, the CPI would retain its independence and organizations.

On the one hand, the new strategy enabled the central leadership to influence the "tall national leaders" in New Delhi and to advance its own importance in Kerala, West Bengal, and later in Tripura. Similarly, the Communists in Sri Lanka (most of whom were Trotskyites organized as the Lanka Sama Samaja Party) were also able to retain their leading role in the struggle against the British.

On the other hand, while the Sri Lankan activists lost out in the 1960s to their new populist coalition partner (the Sri Lanka Freedom Party), the Indian Communists did not regain their dominant position in Andhra Pradesh after the brief policies of insurrection in the late 1940s, lost much of their influence within the trade union movement (most dramatically in Bombay/Mumbai), and still largely remain confined to their other old strongholds.

Four major issues have been subject to intense debate within the Communist movement in the subcontinent. The first is cooperation with nationalist parties like the Indian Congress or the Awami League in Bangladesh and the related question of what parties represent the "national" or "big-bourgeois and landlord" interests. In conjunction with the Sino-Soviet conflict in the 1960s, the disputes ended in schism. The majority of the CPI members formed the CPI-Marxist party, especially in West Bengal and Kerala under widely respected leaders such as Jyoti Basu, Harekrishna Konar, A. K. Gopalan, and E.M.S. Namboodiripad. While the CPI retained its allegiance to Moscow, intensified its cooperation with the Congress, and supported state-led "noncapitalist development" by even defending Mrs. Gandhi's infamous state of emergency between 1975 and 1977, the CPI-M leaned toward Beijing, denounced the Congress as siding with big business and the landlords, and talked more of class struggle. Remarkably, however, the CPI-M also defended democracy, launching a broad front against the centralist Delhi rule in general and the emergency regulations in particular. This fit well with the party's strategy at that time of expanding into strongholds like Kerala and West Bengal, turning them into showcases, and thus gaining more influence in other states as well as finally in New Delhi.

While the protection of India's democracy was vital for the country as well as to CPI-M's reputation, the strategy of advancing from strongholds in a few states did not prove successful, and debates over the character of the bourgeoisie and related parties became less relevant. Deterministic class analysis was simply not very helpful in understanding the increasing importance of corruption and the general abuse of state and politics in India's combination of primitive and advanced accumulation of capital as well as the expansion of neoliberalism and caste- and religion-based identity politics.

The second major subject of debate is over the use of peaceful and democratic means versus armed struggle. The latter tendency lost out after the aborted insurgencies in the late 1940s but gained prominence again with Beijing's critique of Moscow. The brief Maoist-led revolt in the small Darjeeling village of Naxalbari in 1967 was the symbolic starting point, and a significant number of CPI-M activists formed a new Marxist-Leninist party. Rather than widespread uprisings, however, this was followed mainly by new schisms, the multiplication of rival groups and parties, limited campaigns in some particularly harshly exploited tribal areas of Bengal, Bihar, and Andhra Pradesh, and a much less heroic urban terror campaign in Calcutta/Kolkata. There were similar developments in neighboring countries. The major Maoist arguments about the primacy of "semi-feudalism" and the importance of a "bureaucratic" version of the old colonial comprador bourgeoisie that rests with imperialism rather than on a basis of its own, rarely made sense on a general scale, neither in India nor in the other countries on the subcontinent. In spite of Nepal's being much more feudal and having a more conservative Congress Party, this may partially be relevant there as well. An impressively broad and effective people's movement succeeded in using peaceful means to introduce multiparty democracy in 1990 and to build a broad Communist Party ("Unified-Marxist-Leninist"), which continues the struggle along similar lines against the restored royal dictatorship and on that basis builds bridges to the Maoist insurgents as well.

Meanwhile, however, there has been little improvement in backward areas and among severely oppressed sections of the population, in India, Nepal, and elsewhere. It has not always been possible for the downtrodden to make use of democratic reforms. The mainstream Left has often been unable to address complicated forms of subordination and exploitation, including the importance of caste. Hence, revolutionary Maoist perspectives subsist on the sidelines. In India, for instance, those who prefer working within legal bounds include the Marxist-Leninist Liberation Group, while the major factions that prioritize armed struggle recently came together under a Communist Party-Maoist banner similar to that of their insurgent counterparts in Nepal.

The third major issue involves working within the broader movement of workers and peasants and within other social movements. The major tendency is still to "provide leadership," that is, party politicization. This has generated immense problems of cooperation among various activists, as well as the granting of clientlike favors to various party followers, especially after the schisms in the 1960s. Hence, the mainstream Left has also been accused of "dirty politics" and of indirectly contributing to the negation of politics by civic organizations and "new social movements."

Moreover, while the broad support for Communists in West Bengal (where the Left Front has been in power since 1977) and in Kerala (where the Communists have participated in several governments since 1957) is largely due to land reforms intended to promote human development, it has proved difficult to follow up the reforms to fulfill this aim. The most downtrodden sections of the populations were never fully included, and the outcomes are debatable. In post–land reform West Bengal, agricultural production has increased with modern inputs, new investments and coordination thanks to impressive political and administrative decentralization, but vital problems remain with regard to equality, democracy, and the character of growth. In Kerala, the reforms were more consistent but neither accompanied by improvements of the productive forces nor related to decentralization to promote cooperation and thus improve production on scattered pieces of land. At times, the new owners of land even developed unproductive divisive interests. This adds to the previously mentioned combination of old party–politicization and new dissident negation of politics in making the current impressive attempts in Kerala at democratic decentralization and peoples' planning very difficult. Similarly, Communists in the subcontinent at large have the additional challenge of addressing a range of secondary social dilemmas (in addition to class conflicts over land, labor, and capital) with regard to such matters as caste, ethnicity, religion, gender, environment, transparency, corruption, and further democratization.

The fourth and final Communist dilemma is more conventional. It is about reconciling the immediate need to contribute to the widest possible democratic unity against ethnic and religious chauvinism with the long-term goal of fighting exploitation and inequalities by advancing socialism. And it is about doing so on both the national level, where Communists tend to be weak, and in local contexts, where they are strong. While much of old-style communism is likely to disappear in this process, the mainstream parties and activists with this background are still among the actors who might make a difference on the subcontinent.

See also Anti-imperialism; Marxism-Leninism; Nationalism.

FURTHER READING

Banerjee, S. *India's Simmering Revolution: The Naxalite Uprising.* London: Zed Books, 1984.

Brass, P. R., and M. F. Franda, eds. *Radical Politics in South Asia.* Cambridge, MA: MIT Press, 1973.

Harriss-White, B., S. Bose, and B. Rogaly, eds. *Sonar Bangla: Agricultural Growth and Agrarian Change in West Bengal and Bangladesh.* New Delhi: Sage, 1999.

Hutt, Michael, ed. *Himalayan People's War: Nepal's Maoist Rebellion.* London: Hurst and Co., 2004.

Mallick, Ross. *Indian Communism: Opposition, Collaboration and Institutionalization.* New Delhi: Oxford University Press, 1994.

Nossiter, T. J. *Communism in Kerala: A Study in Political Adaptation.* New Delhi: Oxford University Press, 1982.

Omvedt, Gail, *Reinventing Revolution: New Social Movements and the Socialist Tradition in India.* New York: M. E. Sharpe, 1993.

Ranjith Amarasinghe, Y. *Revolutionary Idealism and Parliamentary Politics: A Study of Trotskyism in Sri Lanka.* Colombo: Social Scientists' Association, 1998.

Roy, A. K. *The Spring Thunder and After: A Survey of the Maoist and Ultra Leftist Movements in India 1962–75.* Calcutta: Minerva Associates, 1975.

Sen Gupta, B. *CPI-M: Promises, Prospects, Problems.* New Delhi: Young Asia Publications, 1979.

Sharma, T. R. *Communism in India: The Politics of Fragmentation.* New Delhi: Sterling Publishers, 1984.

Törnquist, O. *What's Wrong with Marxism? On Capitalist, State, Peasants and Workers in Indonesia and India,* vols. 1–2. New Delhi: Manhoar, 1989 and 1991.

Törnquist, O., with P.K.M. Tharakan. *The Next Left? Democratisation and Attempts to Renew the Radical Political Development Project: The Case of Kerala.* Copenhagen: NIAS Books, 1995.

OLLE TORNQUIST

Communist Party in Indonesia

Asia's first Communist Party was Indonesia's Partai Komunis Indonesia (PKI). It was formed in 1920 by Social Democrats who also worked within Indonesia's first modern mass-based Nationalist movement, Sarekat Islam, to thus broaden their social base beyond trade unions and to unite as many as possible against "semi-feudalism" and colonialism. Their foremost leader, Sneevliet (Maring), brought the strategy to Comintern's Second Congress, where it was adopted and spread to the new Chinese party as well. Subsequently, however, the Chinese applied instead Stalin's idea of close cooperation with the Kuomintang and were massacred in Shanghai; the Indonesians failed to take over the mass movement and became mired in schisms and abortive revolts in western Java (1925–26) and Sumatra (1927).

The PKI did not regain significance until the 1940s, when leftist youth groups took part in fighting the Japanese, in forming the new Republic, and in resisting the return of the Dutch. While non-Stalinist Communists (under Tan Malaka) made common cause with radical Nationalists, the mainstream allied with Moscow's anti-Fascist Popular Front and managed to get a few followers into government. This cabinet lost out to conservative coalition in 1948, and the Cold War began. The Communists (led by Musso) opted for a hard line with the party at the helm. Subsequently the PKI was threatened in its stronghold in Solo (Central Java), and the members in nearby Madiun staged a revolt that gave the government an excuse to crack down on communism in general.

Two years later four young leaders—Aidit (chairman), Lukman, Njoto, and Sudisman—gained control of the run-down party. Having failed in the politics of confrontation and been forced underground, the leaders reappraised the situation and decided on a more careful strategy that preceded the international recommendations.

The PKI cleaved to the hard line of leading Popular Fronts "from below" but also paid heed to Lenin's critique of left-wing communism by adding a united front "from above" in alliance with progressive bourgeois Nationalists. These were identified based on their position with regard to anti-imperialism and antifeudalism, and included the Nationalists behind President Sukarno, their friends in the armed forces, and pragmatic Muslim groups—as against pro-Western Socialists, Muslims, and their allies within the army.

The PKI's new strategy began to bear fruit quite soon. The Nationalists accepted the PKI as an ally and provided basic protection. The party's front organizations grew quickly. Nationalist governments supported by the PKI gained the upper hand. Indonesia played a significant role in the third world (later non-aligned) movement initiated at the Bandung conference. The pro-Western anti-Communists began to be politically isolated and

did not live up to expectations in the 1955 elections. The PKI, on the other hand, became the fourth largest party and made dramatic additional gains in the partial 1957 local elections. These advances were primarily in Java-Bali with favorable cultural identities, but the PKI also had strongholds on the "outer islands," and it was Indonesia's only modern party with a genuine program and class base.

Theoretically, however, there were two problems. First, the relevance of "anti-imperialism and anti-feudalism" were never analyzed critically in the Indonesian context but were taken for granted. Second, the politically selected allies were automatically upgraded to the so-called national bourgeoisie, the members of which, in accordance with Stalin's and Mao's determinism, simply must favor land reform and an independent economy.

These problems became critical in the mid-1950s. The attempts to build a national economy through import substitution were undermined by rent seeking; and Java was pitted against the outer islands, which relied more on the export of colonial products. The regional opposition turned into a rebellion that related to the Cold War as well as Sukarno's vision of the third world movement.

Sukarno countered this by calling for national unity and the nationalization of foreign companies in the face of Dutch refusal to give up the last part of its colony, West New Guinea, and American support for the regional rebels.

The PKI was enthusiastic. The new trend even fitted into Moscow's latest ideas of national democracies and "non-capitalism." But Sukarno did not rely only on the PKI and his usual allies among nationalists and pragmatic Muslims. He also forged links with the central military command to curb the regional rebellion. In return, the military took over most of the nationalized companies, gained influence within the bureaucracy, and contained the PKI. Liberal parliamentary democracy was replaced with so-called guided democracy.

The PKI's support of these measures seems to have been a turning point. On the one hand, the PKI gained sustained protection and more followers and influence, including, in principle, gains for land reform in principle, and real progress toward anti-imperialist goals. By the early 1960s the party was the largest outside the Soviet Union and China with between two and three million members and fifteen to twenty million organized sympathizers, almost a sixth of Indonesia's entire population at the time. On the other hand, it lost the support of most intellectuals, it lost the democracy that had served its expansion so well, and it lost the chance to launch class-based struggle among workers and peasants. For instance, an attempt in 1960 at a union-based protest against the poor standard of living of Indonesia's workers and the increasing corruption in the country had to be called back in the face of outright repression by the police and the armed forces.

There was no organized opposition in the party, but the innovative way in which the leadership tried to solve problems was clearly inspired by Beijing: to launch class struggle from within the framework of Sukarno's anti-imperialism.

First, the increasingly powerful military and associates within state and business were categorized (with Mao) as "bureaucratic capitalists" in league with world capitalism and Western imperialism. Logically, it would be possible to disclose their true character and undermine their powers by radicalizing Sukarno's programs through, among other measures, nationalizing more companies, by demanding good patriotic management, and by confronting the British and Americans. However, while it was possible to implement these strategies, they neither threatened the fundamental positions and interests of the enemies nor did they allow the workers to unleash their capacity. Rather, the "bureaucratic capitalists" were able to use the state and nationalism to boost their primitive accumulation of capital.

Second, the poor implementation of antifeudal policies was explained in terms of unchallenged landlords whom it would be possible to fight by launching popular campaigns among the peasants and rural poor for the consistent implementation of Sukarno's land reforms. Again, these campaigns proved feasible, but the outcome was disappointing. Serious infighting among the peasants and an inability to isolate big landlords forced the PKI to call off the offensive. The ownership of land was not as concentrated or straightforward nor the mechanisms of its control as easy to understand and untangle as those who drafted the land reform legislation had supposed.

In brief, while the PKI seemed to be quite powerful, it was in reality dependent on the protection of Sukarno and unable to make use of its popular mass base. Hence, it must have been rational for the leadership to resort to elitist maneuverings when rumors spread by mid-1965 that Sukarno had fallen ill and that generals were planning a coup while lower-ranking officers were preparing countermeasures.

On September 30, the dissident officers tried to arrest the generals. Some PKI-related activists were also involved and a few top leaders knew about the plans—but otherwise the Communist movement was in the dark. As the actions failed, General Suharto (who had not been targeted but possibly was informed) sidetracked his superiors and gained control of the situation. The details are still disputed. Many actors with different scenarios were involved.

Suharto restored unity within the armed forces by putting the blame on the Communists. A massive propaganda campaign with fabricated lies portrayed the Communists as a major threat against law and order and peace and security. The message was that Indonesia had to be cleansed of such evil elements. The West supported the campaign while the Soviet Union was passive and China did little. Suharto formed a special command for "the restoration of security and order" and used his own strategic reserve as a spearhead for persecuting perceived and real Communists. Quite frequently the troops functioned as catalysts instigating, authorizing, and directing various local militias, vigilantes, and militant activists in political and religious youth organizations to do the job for them. Nobody knows how many people were arrested, tortured, and killed. The usual estimate of the dead is between 0.5 and 1 million. The PKI was unable to put up any significant resistance. The movement was eliminated, repression was sustained for decades, and Indonesia has yet to come to terms with its history of political violence.

Competing factions of surviving middle-ranked leaders have tried to preserve the PKI, at least in name, initially for instance with the support of the Chinese. But they have been able to neither produce intellectually convincing analyses of the experiences and challenges, nor initiate significant activity on the ground. Other perspectives, movements, and groups are in the forefront of the reinvention of radical popular action and political representation in Indonesia.

See also Anti-imperialism; Marxism-Leninism; Nationalism.

FURTHER READING
Cribb, R., ed. *The Indonesian Killings 1965–1966: Studies from Java and Bali.* Clayton, Victoria, AU: Centre of Southeast Asian Studies, 1990.

Hindley, D. *The Communist Party of Indonesia 1951–1963,* Berkeley: University of California Press, 1964.

McVey, R. *The Rise of Indonesian Communism.* Ithaca, NY: Cornell University Press, 1965.

Mortimer, R. *Indonesian Communism under Sukarno: Ideology and Politics 1959–1965*. Ithaca, NY: Cornell University Press, 1974.

Tornquist, O. *Dilemmas of Third World Communism: The Destruction of the PKI in Indonesia*. London: Zed Books, 1984.

OLLE TORNQUIST

Communist Party in Iran

The Communist Party of Iran (Hezb-e Komunist-e Irān) was formed on June 20, 1920, in Azerbaijan. The presence of locally active Social Democratic groups, which were in touch with their counterparts in the Russian and later Soviet part of the region, along with the establishment in Rasht, in the adjacent area of Gīlān, of a short-lived (1920–21) republic supported by the Red Army (and bloodily suppressed by then colonel Ridā Khān), also aided its birth. At its First Congress, the party's analysis focused on the international landscape after the victory of the October Revolution and the plausible anti-imperialist role that Iran could perform, since, given the country's institutional weaknesses, it should have been possible to at least partially disrupt Soviet encirclement.

History took a different course. Repression began when the first Shāh Pahlavī, Ridā Khān, seized power in 1924, and by the end of the 1920s, this led to the almost total disappearance of the party's leading cadre and offices. Starting in 1925, however, the party helped form a solid workers' rights movement in the oil industry, in the country's South; the first strike in the sector occurred in May 1929. In 1931, the shah prohibited any organization with a Communist orientation, making any form of activity in the country impossible, at least until 1934; political activity therefore moved abroad. Unfortunately the party's most important base, in Berlin, then experienced another major blow because of the rise of Nazism. The party's history during the early decades can be divided into three phases: 1920–27 (the Second Congress), 1927–34, and 1934–41. The third phase saw the establishment of structures suited to an underground existence, and thus the party was reconstituted in 1941 under a different name—Hezb-e Tude-ye Irān, later simply Tudeh (mass)—by a group of Communists who had long been imprisoned in Iran.

The Tudeh definitely gravitated toward the USSR: it did not aim at revolutionary uprisings in the short term but rather supported a progressive and democratic program, following, among other models, the path of the traditional Persian constitutionalist opposition, which had experienced its highest point during the Constitutional Revolution in 1906–11. The moving spirit of the new party was Taqī Erāni. Party recruitment was focused on the nascent working class; the working class, though, continued to be more sensitive to the labor unions connected to the party (the Central Council of the Trade Unions of Iran), which had a much higher number of members than did the party itself. The bourgeois upper-middle class continued to provide the leadership cadre. Muhammad Ridā succeeded his father, who had been forced to abdicate because of the pro-German positions he had taken during World War II, in 1941, but his outlook did not change, and in 1949 the party was banned once more, although it did not disband and in fact remained relatively active.

In the meantime the region registered yet another political failure. In Iranian Azerbaijan, in an area inhabited by Sunni Kurds, the Autonomous Kurdish Republic of Mahabad was established, initially with Soviet backing, between January and December 1946; it also enjoyed the armed protection of Mullā Mustafā Bārzani, the founder of the Democratic Party of Kurdistan (1946). The republic ended because of a massacre perpetrated by Iranian troops, and Bārzani took refuge in the USSR, where he would remain until 1958. The outcome was also a result of the withdrawal of Soviet troops from Azerbaijan in May 1946, but Kurdish sources, and not only them, accused the Tudeh of insufficient support for the Republic of Mahabad's survival.

The 1950s in Iran witnessed policies favoring the Iranian National Front (Jabhe-ye Melli-ye Irān), which had been established in 1949 as a coalition of different forces, all of which were both secular and anticolonialist. The undisputed leader of the front was Mohammed Mossadegh. Elected prime minister in 1951, he promoted a certain political liberalization, but launched an operation that would lead to the nationalization of foreign oil companies active on Iranian soil. The operation failed because of the 1955 U.S.-organized coup, which reinstalled the shah on the throne. This was the Tudeh's first major challenge. Facing the shah and the forces backing him, some leaders left the country, a move that not everyone understood or approved. Yet the Tudeh still managed to establish a cell within the army, and increase its credibility among students and intellectuals.

In 1963, the Tudeh's organizational networks were once again destroyed, due to the shah's clampdown, which had been provoked on the one hand by Ayatollah Ruholla Mussaui Khomeini's first attacks on the new political course—the so-called White Revolution that while promoting a deceitful agrarian reform, did affect some of the "religious men's" privileges—and on the other by the shah's attempt to reach a better understanding with a new version of the National Front. The Tudeh followed the same path as other Communist parties in the Near and Middle East: it needed Soviet help, and thus supported the Soviet policy of selecting petty bourgeois nationalist movements as its favored interlocutors. This policy, as was the case with the Western European Communist parties, favored alliances with the middle classes during the process of social transformation—alliances that would be elaborated theoretically starting in 1976 by Nureddin Kyànuri, the party leader at the time and destined to perish in the prisons of the Islamic Republic.

In 1978, the first large demonstrations that would result in the Islamist Khomeinist Revolution occurred. When the masses took to the streets, the Communist militants—following the watchwords of anti-imperialism, freedom, and independence—took their side and supported the establishment of the Islamic Republic of Iran. This did not really signify a change of position with regard to the USSR, and the protests about the Soviet invasion of Afghanistan (1979) were rather bland. The support for the new regime continued even in the absence of constitutional guarantees on the formal level, even when involutionary tendencies became obvious—for instance, when the new power reneged on its promise to grant autonomy to the Kurds. In 1982, apparently quite suddenly, the party leaders were imprisoned and brought to trial, and this time, unlike in 1955, they were not able to choose exile. The hunt for militants began. There were ten thousand executions, according to one estimate; a certain number of cadre and militants escaped abroad, but many remained underground. The Tudeh's ideological position can be summed up in the demands for democracy and social justice, for the separation of religious and political spheres, and therefore the refusal of the *velàyat-e faqih*—in other words, the assumption according to which in order to have a correct Islamic government, a "guarantor" is necessary, one who is endowed with the powers and role that were once Khomeini's and later 'Ali Khamene'i's.

See also Anti-imperialism; Islam; Nationalism.

FURTHER READING

Javànshir, F. M. *Tajrobe-ye Mordàd*. Teheran: 1980.

Khàteràt-e Kyànuri. Teheran: 1991.

Mehrabàn, R. *Gushehà-ye az Tarikh—mu'aser-e Iràn*. Teheran: 1981.

Scarcia Amoretti, B. "A proposito del fenomeno Iran: questione nazionale, movimento islamico, marxismo." *Oriente Moderno* 62, nos. 1–12 (January–December 1982).

JAMSHID ARMAN AND BIANCAMARIA SCARCIA AMORETTI

Communist Party in Israel

The Palestinian Communist Party, later called the Israeli Communist Party (after the proclamation of the state of Israel in May 1948), has maintained the same profile. It has always represented the unity of Jewish and Arab revolutionaries and been founded on the principle of binationalism. Since the party's inception, this principle has been the foundation of its ideological history, political experience, and militant practice. In actuality this principle presents itself simultaneously as a principle and a goal, since all the splits and new foundations in the party have been the result of the ethnic divisions between Arab and Jewish militants.

The Palestinian Communist Party was founded as the Communist Party of Palestine (or in Yiddish, the Palestinische Kommunistische Partei) in January 1922, following a split in the Jewish socialist Left. Over the next twelve months, two political lines confronted one another in the party: the first line was in the majority, whose objective was to engage in the political struggle within the Jewish settler group; and the second, in the minority, wanted to focus instead on building a party to unite Arabs and Jews, and developing an anticolonial policy similar to the one approved at the Baku Congress of Peoples of the East (September 1–8, 1920). The resultant split, in July 1923, led to the creation of a new party, the Communist Party of Palestine (Kommunistische Partei fun Palestine).

That same year, the party reunited by following the political line advocated by the secessionists and formally joined the Third International. Between 1924 and 1929, the party's leadership group developed a political line opposed to Jewish immigration and in support of the Arab peasants' struggle. Consisting exclusively of Russian Jews, the party leadership was removed as a consequence of the 1929 uprisings, when Palestine became the setting for attacks against and killings of Jewish colonists by Arab peasants. Most of the leadership moved to Moscow, and the principal leaders (Wolf Averbuch, Yosef Berger-Barzilay, and Nahun Leshinsky) disappeared during Stalin's purges in the 1930s. The new political leadership emphasized its anti-Zionist nature and supported the anti-Jewish revolt of 1936–39. This resulted in a new split and the birth of an autonomous Jewish wing, which during World War II favored military cooperation with the Allies, and later supported the struggle for partition and the birth of two autonomous states. This position was endorsed and supported by the Soviet Union's choices in the war's aftermath as well as during discussions at the United Nations, which led to the approval of resolution 181 on November 21, 1947, in favor of partition. The Communist Party of Palestine changed its name to Maki (Mifleghet Komunistit eretsisraelit, or the Communist Party of the Land of Israel), reflecting the decision to become part of the new state's political system and reiterating the binationalist line in the party's political program.

A new shift occurred starting with the Korean War and the first signs of anti-Semitic persecutions in the USSR in 1950. Zionism went from becoming an accredited liberation movement as it had been in 1947–48 to a political expression of imperialism, and therefore a movement to be fought. The Maki emphasized the anti-Zionist and pro-Palestinian political line. The choice corresponded to the party's support of a position favorable to the Non-Aligned Movement and contrary to Israel's international politics. The party backed the nationalist Arab policies that Gamal Nasser was beginning to implement, even though this decision did not avoid internal party conflicts due to the repressive anti-Communist policies pursued by the nationalist, Moscow-supported Arab countries. The conflict that emerged between the USSR and Egypt in 1959 reopened this issue. Within Maki, the political decisions led to a situation in which the party was simultaneously opposed to the nationalist policies of the Israeli government and the anti-Israeli policies of the Arab governments, which in their programs still subscribed to the nonrecognition and destruction of the state of Israel.

This dual platform experienced a crisis in the early 1960s, and once again the dividing line was a consequence of the leadership groups' and party militants' national affiliations. The result was a split, sanctioned by the convocation of two separate congresses (August 3,

1965): a meeting of the Jewish group, and another for the Arab Palestinian one. The split was mostly ethnic, with Maki (mostly composed of the Jewish group) on one side, and the new group (Reshimaà komunistit hadashà, or the New Communist List) largely made up of the Arab Palestinian component on the other side. The elections in November 1965 only gave Maki a minimal vote (1.1 percent), while Rakah's support was slightly better (2.3 percent and three representatives). Maki slowly disbanded: part of the group joined the Zionist socialist Left, and a smaller group joined Rakah. Starting with the Six-Day War, Rakah emphasized its Palestinian character, in both the party's composition and the political line, until finally a neonationalist stance prevailed. In the 1990s this led to the creation of a nationalist group, which received a large portion of the Israeli Arab vote, but also served as confirmation of the end of the Communist political experience.

See also Anti-Semitism; Nationalism; Zionism.

FURTHER READING

Greilsammer, A. *Les communistes israeliens*. Paris: Presses de la Fondation Nationale des Sciences Politiques, 1978.

———. "La disparition du communisme juif en Israël." *Communisme* 3, no. 6 (1984): 27–46.

Laqueur, W. Z. *Communism and Nationalism in the Middle East*. London: Routledge and Kegan Paul, 1956.

DAVID BIDUSSA

Communist Party in Italy

For more than forty years the Italian Communist Party (Pci) was the strongest of the nongoverning Communist parties in the world—in terms of membership, electoral success and political influence, intellectual dynamism, and the ability to affirm itself on the international scene. The anomaly represented by the Pci's history after 1944 has led to piles of publications by historians, sociologists, and political scientists, foreign as well as Italian. One way of rereading and interpreting a history that lasted over seventy years in a short entry is to focus on the original characteristics that shaped the party's experience, and the manner in which it interacted with Italian history.

The Pci was the last of the Communist International's sections to be formed, in January 1921. Its creation followed the logic of "revolution around the corner"; in other words, its goal was separating the vanguard of an organized proletariat from the swamp of reformism and "centrism," and then establishing a regime of soviets. Paradoxically, however, Italy witnessed an increase in violence against the workers' movement, and this highlighted the anachronistic nature of the party's goals. The Pci therefore shared in the destiny of all European Communist parties: it was conceived and formed as the instrument for a revolution that was deemed imminent, while it had to survive and consolidate in a situation that if it ever had been revolutionary, was so no longer. It also had to act in a country that was the cradle and laboratory for an unprecedented form of reaction, a political experiment that was initially deemed peculiar to Italy, but was destined to shape the history of the first half of the 20th century: fascism. One consequence was a second original characteristic: since it had to deal with fascism from its inception, the Pci was subjected to an imprinting that would long shape its history and would make it more susceptible than other parties to a process of grafting antifascism onto its original political culture.

Like most other European Communist parties, the Pci arose as a combative but relatively small minority from a split. It managed to establish itself throughout the country, mostly reproducing the geographic distribution of the Socialist Party, but elections in May 1921 demonstrated it was not able to translate its numbers in the (socialist) sections into proletarian voters. Still, within a relatively brief period, the party made up for its initial disadvantage. It did so even as the workers' movement's forces were being defeated, and accomplished this feat thanks to its organizational strength and the dedication of its militants, who managed to contain the flood of adversity. This capacity attracted a small but representative group from other anti-Fascist forces, and it was the foundation of the Pci's unexpected influence after fascism's defeat. Adding to this was the belief among Pci militants that they were only one unit in an international army, with faith in the ultimate victory of socialism—an especially important sense of identity for what would soon become a small, persecuted, underground force. This also explains the depth of the "ironclad relationship" with the Soviet Union—a tie that was made more binding by the fact that for twenty years, the party's survival depended logistically and financially on the Communist International.

The Pci's leadership group, marked by an above-average political and intellectual stature when compared to other Communist parties, was thus forged under these difficult circumstances. After Antonio Gramsci's change of course in 1923–24, this leadership group fully accepted its role as a cog in the larger mechanism of the global party of revolution, and realistically assessed its narrow margin of autonomy; yet it continued to reflect, at least until 1928, on the specific characteristics of the Italian situation. It certainly did not emerge unscathed from the damage caused by the Comintern's "leftward" shift in 1929, which it translated into an unlikely scenario of imminent "revolutionary radicalization" in Italy, and into an even more absurd equation of the forces of democratic and socialist antifascism with "social fascism." Even the identity of its leadership group was affected, and internal debate was severely affected as a consequence. And yet even during these years, especially after 1931, a deeper analysis of the characteristics of Fascist dictatorship as a reactionary mass regime, one capable of organizing the masses' passive consensus, was not completely lost. This analysis would be given its most mature expression in the "Lectures on Fascism" given to Communist cadre by Palmiro Togliatti in Moscow in January 1935.

Italian Communists were increasingly aware of the need to penetrate fascism's mass organizations, exploiting all legal spaces to undermine the consensus on which the new regime rested. But it was not always easy for them to reconcile this need with the Comintern's shifting tactics; after 1934, Italian Communists concentrated on creating alliances against the aggressive policies of international fascism. The party searched for a shared political line that would correspond to the needs of anti-Fascist unity among émigrés, but also connect with the discontent (often overestimated) in the ranks of fascism's mass organizations. This, in turn, led to tactical swings that were not always suited to the task. The onset of the civil war in Spain was the starting point for a new strategic evaluation, and Togliatti emphasized it even at the international level. The Comintern's goal in Spain was to establish a "democracy of a new type," defended by the working class and founded on eliminating the social and political roots of fascism, and it also became the goal of anti-Fascist struggle in Italy, leading to a new united action pact endorsed by the Pci and the Italian Socialist Party (Psi) on July 26, 1937. The Popular Front era introduced new elements into the Pci's political culture, and provided a more complex understanding of the relation between capitalism and fascism. The poisons of the Great Terror and, later, the Molotov-Ribbentrop Pact, however, corroded the ties that had slowly been reestablished with other anti-Fascist forces and almost seemed to nullify this revision process. Yet German aggression against the USSR once more opened the door to discussions about the transition from dictatorship to democracy, and gave new life to policies favoring wide-ranging alliances.

The speed with which the Pci reorganized after fascism's fall was due to several factors: the presence of a Communist nucleus in nonelite Italian society, which had already developed in the 1920s, even though with great difficulty; and disciplined and experienced cadres, returning from prison and forced residence, ready to prove their mettle in direct confrontations with the Germans and Fascists. The Pci did not limit its effort to the armed struggle but also supported the organization of social and economic protests, especially in occupied areas. Togliatti's return to a liberated Italy, and the decision to focus on national unity amid debates about future institutional arrangements, gave the Pci legitimacy as a governmental force in the rising new democracy, while its appeal was increased by the USSR's prestige and sharing in the victory over Nazism.

Italian Communists successfully established themselves in Italy after liberation, and indeed demonstrated such an extraordinary capacity for growth that no other party with a popular base in the country had ever matched it. One of the foundations of this strength was an "endogenous" factor, peculiar to the Italian situation: the historical weakness of reformism, in both its democratic bourgeois and socialist manifestations. One of Togliatti's great accomplishments was to perceive this, and since Italy's international position precluded it from taking a revolutionary path, decide to occupy the void or partial void. Following liberation, the Pci took the place of a nonexistent social democracy, one that had never managed to develop. This "replacement" function was not guaranteed, though, and the Cold War seriously endangered it, putting the Pci on the defensive against a state that most of its militants deemed foreign and hostile. These dangers notwithstanding the party stayed the course. When the Pci came under pressure in 1947, as a consequence of the Cold War's glaciation, it took an unavoidable international position, but also chose to defend the republic's Constitution. The Italian Communists' work for the Constituent Assembly and tenacious efforts to jointly define a "state plan" with the other anti-Fascist forces in Italy would become significant. The defense and implementation of the Constitution was central to Italian political life for many years, and the social struggles led by the Communists had the Con-

stitution's programmatic norms as their reference point. The traditional idea of the Italian state, in which the aspirations of the lower classes were necessarily linked to subversion, their only option for redress being a revolution, was thus turned upside down, and the Pci gained a democratic legitimacy that allowed it to counter the repeated attempts to outlaw the party.

By virtue of this role reversal, the Pci contributed to a form of civic education and "nationalization" similar to the one performed by the Socialist Party from the end of the previous century to World War I, only on a much grander scale. It defended and ensured the development of parliamentary democracy in Italy—a process that was threatened more "from the Right" than the Left, at least from 1948 on. The party's militants were educated to respect those forms of democratic participation that represented a significant step in establishing a civil society, transforming millions of "subjects" or "rebels" into citizens. The Pci thus filled a dual role: guaranteeing Parliament's prerogatives within the complex institutional balance of power in the country, and integrating the world of labor into the new democratic state. This path partially followed the "negative integration" of German social democracy in the Wilhelmine era, while uniting the different forces and subcultures of the Italian Left, disciplining its heritage of subversiveness.

Such developments were possible because the party had already adopted a mass organization structure in 1944—one that was open to the outside world. Of course, Togliatti's "new party" should not be idealized. It faced the rigid constraints of "democratic centralism," hindering internal debate. But the party's prior experiences in the struggle against the "reactionary mass regime" had left organizational traces throughout the country, including deeply rooted connections to civil society, and this later supported the creation of a network of unions and cooperatives, professional and social organizations, and educational and sport groups. Thus, the Pci was able to establish itself as a vital organism because it effectively represented the demands for innovation expressed by an evolving society over an extended period. It was better equipped than socialists or Social Democrats to serve as a shock absorber in an extremely rapid process of modernization—one that entailed significant social costs.

Italian communism flourished under the first center-left government, despite persistent ideological simplifications and a belated awareness by the party of the profound changes affecting Italy between the late 1950s and late

1960s. Since it did not hold to opposition at all costs but rather acted as a critic of reformist developments, the Pci took advantage of an increased space for democracy, and succeeded in being the main interlocutor and primary beneficiary of a series of social struggles—by students and workers—that in terms of both amplitude and intensity had few precedents in advanced capitalist countries.

A negative factor for the Pci during this process of legitimation was the ironclad relationship as Togliatti himself defined it—with the USSR and other Communist states. This was not only an issue of uncritically endorsing the choices made by the "socialist camp" in international politics (starting with the position taken during the Soviet repression of the people's uprising in Hungary in 1956). The ties, including those of an organizational nature, with the international Communist movement continued well past the dissolution of the Cominform, and could be felt, for instance, in the ideological preparation of several generations of cadres educated at party schools in Moscow or Prague, or in the level of financial dependence that although it diminished over time, continued into the early 1980s. Above all, the Pci's political culture was permeated by the reaffirmation of the "superiority" of the Soviet socialist system, constantly repeated, in which the echo of the polar capitalism-socialism opposition that had crystallized in the 1930s continued to reverberate. This inevitably also led to a skewed analysis of both political and class relations within the country itself. So insisting on the need for an understanding between the parties fighting for real social transformation in Italy—a request by the party addressed especially to the socialists, but also the reformist currents within the Christian Democrats and other minor secular parties—was ultimately undermined by a more basic "choice of civilization" on an international scale—one that made it difficult to decide how much credence to give these openings at the policy level, thereby rendering them ineffective. The Pci's path toward an international position autonomous from the USSR, timidly pursued after 1956, was accelerated in 1968 with the "disapproval" of the Soviet intervention in Czechoslovakia, even if it did not lead to any dissociation from the international Communist movement. For this reason, too, the era of great social struggles ended without any appreciable movement of the Italian political scale to the Left.

The need to move beyond such immobility coupled with concerns about the stability of the democratic system in Italy led the Pci under Enrico Berlinguer to propose the "historic compromise," uniting the solidaristic traditions of the Catholic movement with the Communist and socialist ones of collective struggle, under the aegis of a gradual supersession of capitalism. The Pci benefited not so much from the success of this line, which met with socialist diffidence and the exhausting obstructionism of the majority of the Christian Democrats, but starting in 1974, from more dynamic forms of collective mobilization, and an increased demand, both quantitatively and qualitatively, from Italian society for democracy. It became the most important Italian party in all the large cities during the 1975 administrative elections, and was catapulted into the government of six regions and many of Italy's major municipalities. In the course of the 1976 elections its results improved even further.

On the organizational level, the Pci was faced with a new and complex series of problems. Italian Communists had to manage one of the most diverse electorates that had ever endorsed a Communist party in the course of free elections and respond to a varied list of demands. On the political level, the historic compromise proved inadequate to the task of dismantling the Christian Democrats' system of power, especially in a transitional phase rendered more unstable by terrorism and inflation. The loss of 4 percent of the vote in the elections in June 1979 signaled the end of a favorable period for the Pci. The diversification of Italian society penetrated to the party's core in terms of social background, cultural experiences, and militants' personal expectations. The 1980s was thus marked by a profound crisis. Berlinguer made courageous choices in the international arena (explicitly recognizing the dwindling "propulsive energy" of the October Revolution and the constellation of socialist states). On the other hand, he understood the implications of integrating the Pci into the European Parliament: the Pci would have to concern itself more seriously with the European Economic Community, pushing for its transformation from a pure common market into an institution that was also responsible for activist policies in the areas of peace and reforms. References to the "Euro Left" gradually supplanted Eurocommunism within the space of a couple of years, in both the party's language and its policies.

These developments, however, did not halt the Pci's progressive marginalization from the Italian political scene, dominated by the alliance between Christian Democrats and the Psi. Beyond electoral losses and a decrease in membership, starting in the late 1970s, it was the party's identity crisis that got significantly worse, especially after Berlinguer's death. The many steps on the Pci's difficult journey included a definitive break with the international Communist movement, its placement within the European Left, the acceptance of the market, a profound revision of its class postulates, "secularization," and renunciation of democratic centralism. More generally, the Pci's last ten years were impacted by the increasingly evident crisis in the Communist world and the repercussions of the first signs of crisis of social democracy. An erosion of the social, political, and cultural foundations of the workers' movement along with its political expressions was also taking place, and the decreasing faith in the resources of collective action even affected the labor union movement. The Pci bore the brunt of the neoliberal challenge that forced social democracy into a disorderly retreat, and it additionally had to face the psychological impact of the collapse of a symbolic universe—one that for many of its militants had been part of their entire lives.

The Pci's peculiarity and "diversity" affected how Italian communism faced the final crisis of world communism, with the courageous, if not painless, choice to renew itself; this led to the breakup of the party's different components, all of which claimed to be its heirs; and five years later, the largest of these components participated in the country's government. The difficulties the party has faced while attempting to transform and reconstitute itself have, however, been exacerbated by the institutional, political, and moral crisis of the very republican democracy of which the Pci was a constitutive and founding element.

See also Antifascism; Berlinguer, Enrico; Eurocommunism; Gramsci, Antonio; National Roads to Socialism; Post-Soviet Communism; Revolution, Myths of the; Socialist Camp; Togliatti, Palmiro.

FURTHER READING

Agosti, A. *Palmiro Togliatti: A Biography*. London: IB Tauris, 2008.

Flores, M., and N. Gallerano. *Sul PCI. Un'interpretazione storica*. Bologna: Il Mulino, 1992.

Gozzini, G., and R. Martinelli. *Storia del Partito comunista italiano. Dall'attentato a Togliatti all'VIII Congresso*. Turin: Einaudi, 1998.

Gualtieri, R., ed. *Il PCI nell'Italia repubblicana, 1943–1991*. Rome: Carocci, 2001.

Martinelli, R. *Storia del partito comunista italiano. Il "Partito nuovo" dalla Liberazione al 18 aprile*. Turin: Einaudi, 1995.

Spriano, P. *Storia del partito comunista italiano*. 5 vols. Turin: Einaudi, 1967–75.

Vittoria, A. *Storia del PCI 1921–1991*. Rome: Carocci, 2006.

ALDO AGOSTI

Communist Party in Japan

The Japan Communist Party (*Nihon Kyōsantō*) was first founded in 1922, refounded in 1926, almost destroyed by police arrests in 1928, and remained illegal until after the defeat of Japan in 1945. The government authorities were implacably hostile to what was virtually the only political organization in Japan advocating abolition of the Emperor system. In its weak and persecuted state, the JCP was guided by directives from Comintern operatives in Moscow, who knew little of Japanese conditions.

The party's fortunes were transformed from 1945 by the Allied Occupation of Japan, which lifted bans on left-wing political activity and released Communist leaders from prison. The JCP enjoyed prestige after the war for its resistance to Japanese militarism, and it gained influence in the newly resurgent labor union movement. But its popularity was blunted by its support for the Soviet Union, which had "stabbed Japan in the back" near the end of the war and by its harsh criticism of Socialists and other groups on the Left.

Many Communist leaders had recanted their beliefs in prison and henceforth worked alongside the government. Those who held out and remained incarcerated emerged after the war as hardened and dedicated leaders. Most prominent among them was the firebrand Kyūichi Tokuda, one of Japan's most colorful politicians of the time.

A leader who had trodden a different path was Sanzo Nosaka, an intellectual and graduate of the London School of Economics, who had escaped from prison in 1930 and spent the next decade in Moscow, where he became a member of the Comintern presidium. In 1940 he joined Mao Zedong in the caves of Yenan and gained insight into the Chinese Communist approach to revolution. With Japan defeated, Nosaka managed to return home, and made a dramatic reappearance at a JCP rally in January 1946.

For the next four years the party was under the joint leadership of Tokuda and Nosaka, with the influence of Nosaka (full of the latest ideas from the Chinese Communists and from Moscow) dominant in policymaking. Recognizing that the democratizing reforms of the Allied Occupation in its early stages were not entirely alien to his party's aspirations, Nosaka softened the JCP's message under the slogan "a lovable Communist Party." Doctrinally, this stemmed from the idea that revolution should be in two stages, first targeting "feudal elements," which he associated with Japanese militarism, and only later, after some considerable time, proceeding to a proletarian-Socialist revolution.

In early general elections following Japan's defeat, very few JCP candidates were elected. In contrast, the Japan Socialist Party became part of a coalition government for eighteen months in 1947 and 1948, and Communist attempts to form a united front with that party foundered. On the other hand, the JCP made substantial inroads into the labor union movement, though ultimately the Socialists wrested control of the main unions from them. The general elections of January 1949, however, provided an unexpected bonanza for the JCP. The Socialists had been badly discredited by the failure of the coalition governments, and the Communists won thirty-five seats in the Lower House with 9.7 percent of the total vote. For a short while, it seemed as if the JCP could look forward to a bright future in Japanese politics.

This view was to change a year later, when Moscow attacked the "lovable Communist Party" idea and ordered the JCP to concentrate its attacks on "American imperialism in Japan." The resultant hardening of the party's line lost it most of its electoral support, and led to factional conflict between those wishing to preserve aspects of moderation (Tokuda and Nosaka) and those wanting full implementation of Moscow's new prescriptions (Kenji Miyamoto and Yoshio Shiga). At a critical stage of the Cold War (with revolution having recently occurred in China and the Korean War approaching) the American occupiers cracked down on the JCP with a "Red purge" that drove the party underground, though it was not banned outright.

Thus began a bleak period for the JCP, from which it took over a decade to recover. The year 1955 marked a coming together of the competing factions, with Nosaka and Miyamoto taking over the leadership (Tokuda had died in Beijing in 1953). A group influenced by the Italian Communists was expelled from the party in 1961, and in 1964 Miyamoto (now the dominant leader) broke with the USSR by opposing the nuclear test ban treaty. This led to the pro-Soviet Shiga's exit from the JCP. A period of pro-China policies followed, but ended in 1966 with an acrimonious quarrel with Mao Zedong over pursuit of the Vietnam War.

At last the JCP was largely free of both Soviet and Chinese influence and free to pursue an independent line tailored to Japanese conditions. The party made substantial electoral gains, and by the 1970s appeared to be an up-and-coming political force. The government responded with a disinformation campaign, and to some electoral effect revealed that Miyamoto had been personally involved in the murder of a police spy in 1933.

During the 1980s and 1990s the JCP was a stable, if minor, force in Japanese politics, deriving some of its support from the perception that it would stick to its principles and avoid compromises with the ruling Liberal Democrats, unlike other opposition parties. Power gravitated to Tetsuzo Fuwa, who became party chairman on Miyamoto's retirement in 1997. The youthful Kazuo Shii became his deputy. In the unstable national politics of the late 1990s, the JCP made significant electoral gains, but a new Lower House electoral system worked to its disadvantage, and in the general elections of September 2005 it won a mere 9 seats out of 480.

There is a curious footnote about Nosaka. In 1992 he admitted to having in 1939 denounced a comrade to the Comintern as a spy, leading to his execution on Stalin's orders. The JCP expelled this most famous of Communists from the party and stripped him of his honors. He was 100 years old at the time. Nosaka died in 1994 at the age of 101.

See also Marxism-Leninism; Nationalism.

FURTHER READING

Beckmann, G. M., and O. Genji. *The Japanese Communist Party 1922–1945*. Stanford, CA: Stanford University Press, 1969.

Berton, P. "The Japan Communist Party: The 'Lovable Party.'" In *The Japanese Party System,* ed. R. J. Hrebenar. Boulder, CO: Westview Press, 1992.

Scalapino, R. A. *The Japanese Communist Movement, 1920–1966*. Berkeley: University of California Press, 1966.

ARTHUR STOCKWIN

Communist Party in Kampuchea

The Cambodian Communist movement came into being in 1951 during the first Indochina War, when the Vietnamese Communists, or Viet Minh, sponsored the creation of the Khmer Peoples' Revolutionary Party

(KPRP). The party's statutes were first written in Vietnamese and then translated into Khmer. Its leaders were Cambodians from southern Vietnam who were fluent in Vietnamese. Most party members were poor peasants, attracted by the movement's anti-French rhetoric and its vague socialist platform. The role given to party members was to assist the Vietnamese struggle against the French. At the Geneva Conference in 1954, the KPRP (unlike its counterpart in Laos) was not given a regroupment zone inside Cambodia, and over a thousand sympathizers and party members sought asylum in Hanoi.

In the meantime, several middle-class Khmer studying in France had joined the French Communist Party. These included Saloth Sar (1925–98; he later used the alias Pol Pot), Son Sen (1930–97), Ieng Sary (1928–), and Khieu Samphan (1931–). Sar returned to Cambodia in 1953 and briefly joined the Viet Minh–led resistance. Later in the 1950s, he worked with other former KPRP cadre led by Tou Samouth, who was assassinated in 1962 by the Cambodian police. The movement had little formal structure in this period. It made little headway in the 1950s and 1960s, when it was hampered by police harassment, Prince Norodom Sihanouk's popularity, and the movement's ambiguous links with Hanoi as well as its leaders' policy of keeping their activities and programs a secret from outsiders. In September 1960, perhaps with Vietnamese encouragement, twenty-one members of the movement convened a three-day meeting in Phnom Penh. The movement took on the characteristics of a full-scale party and renamed itself the Workers' Party of Kampuchea (WPK).

In 1963, Sar, by then the secretary of the Central Committee of the WPK, went into hiding at a Vietnamese Communist base on the Vietnam-Cambodia border. He visited North Vietnam and China in 1965–66, where he presented the revolutionary program of the WPK as developed at the September 1960 meeting. Sar's counterpart in Vietnam, Le Duan, criticized the document severely for its failure to mention the Vietnam War or take international factors into consideration. Sar came away from his visit angered by Vietnamese efforts to control the WPK and the Cambodian revolution. When he visited China in early 1966, however, he was greatly impressed by the radical fervor and autonomy of the Chinese Cultural Revolution.

When he returned home, Sar renamed the WPK the Communist Party of Kampuchea (CPK), putting it semantically on a level with the Chinese Party and above the level of the Vietnamese Workers' Party. Membership remained restricted. The name change and the party's existence were kept secret from outsiders. Several of the CPK's leaders including Nuon Chea (1927–), Sary, Sen, and Ta Mok (1930?–) remained in place for many years. Others were purged after the CPK came to power in 1975.

The party inaugurated armed resistance against Sihanouk's government in 1968, but government forces easily contained its poorly armed guerrillas. Two years later, though, when Sihanouk fell from power in a right-wing coup, the CPK joined the Vietnamese Communists in an alliance that aimed ostensibly to return Sihanouk to office but in reality sought to gain power for the CPK. In the ensuing civil war, the party remained hidden, and in 1973 its leaders launched a harsh policy of collectivization in some of the territories under their control. By then, Vietnamese forces had largely withdrawn from Cambodia, and the war pitted Khmers against Khmers.

The CPK was victorious in April 1975 when its forces occupied Phnom Penh. Calling itself Angkar Loeu (the Higher Organization), it swiftly set in motion a radical socialist program. Within a week, the CPK's hidden leaders abolished money, markets, schools, monasteries, laws, freedom of movement, and private property. Inhabitants of towns and cities were forced into the countryside en masse to become agricultural workers. When the new regime formally established itself in January 1976, it took the name of Democratic Kampuchea (DK) and occupied Cambodia's seat at the United Nations. The party's leaders, however, did not reveal their Communist affiliations (or their international alliances with China, North Korea, and Vietnam) for another year. Instead, they preferred to suggest that the revolution was sui generis, and owed nothing to other revolutions or other socialist states.

In mid-1976, the CK leadership drafted a utopian four-year plan that aimed to double Cambodia's rice production within a year and sought to use the revenue derived from sales of rice to purchase mechanical farm equipment. Heavy burdens were placed on the northwestern part of the country, which in prerevolutionary times had been Cambodia's rice basket. This region was now densely populated with evacuees from Cambodia's towns. These people had no agricultural experience and were cruelly treated by CPK cadre. Tens of thousands of these "new people" died over the next two years of malnutrition and overwork. Thousands more were executed summarily as enemies of the state.

By 1977, tensions had begun to develop between the DK and Vietnam. Some of the tension derived from ideological differences between the two regimes; others stemmed from Cambodian cross-border raids, which inflicted heavy civilian casualties. Full-scale combat broke out between the two states at the end of 1977, shortly after Pol Pot returned from a triumphal state visit to China, which offered limited support for his confrontation with Vietnam. Whatever went wrong in the DK was blamed, in a Stalinist fashion, on sabotage conducted by alleged enemies of the state, and the CPK ended up by executing thousands of party members, often on trumped-up charges. Before the DK was driven from power by a Vietnamese invasion in January 1979, over 1.7 million Cambodians, or one in five, had died of malnutrition, overwork, misdiagnosed diseases, and executions, making the Cambodian revolution, on a per capita basis, the most destructive in world history. The CPK announced its dissolution in 1981, but its leaders remained unpunished and in place. The movement collapsed in the late 1990s, following internal factionalism and massive defections to the Phnom Penh government.

See also Killing Fields; Marxism-Leninism; Pol Pot; Vietnam War.

FURTHER READING

Chandler, D. *Brother Number One: A Political Biography of Pol Pot*. Rev. ed. Boulder, CO: Westview Press, 1999.

Chandler, D., B. Kiernan, and C. Boua, eds. and trans. *Pol Pot Plans the Future*. New Haven, CT: Yale University Press, 1988.

Jackson, K., ed. *Cambodia 1975–1978: Rendezvous with Death*. Princeton, NJ: Princeton University Press, 1989.

Ponchaud, F. *Cambodia Year Zero*. New York: Henry Holt, 1978.

DAVID P. CHANDLER

Communist Party in Korea

The Korean Communist movement began to develop in the late 1910s under the impact of the Russian Revolution of 1917. By that time Russia had a large ethnic Korean community (about a hundred thousand), from which the first Korean Communists were largely recruited. Some Russian Koreans joined the party before the October Revolution—Alexandra Stankevich (née Kim) being the most famous. But the spread of Communist ideas began in earnest during the Russian civil war of 1918–22, when the numerous ethnic Korean communities in the Russian far east generally sided with the Reds.

In 1918, Yi Tong-hui, a prominent Korean nationalist leader then residing in Russia, established the Korean Socialist Party, which united Left-leaning Korean exiles. Soon afterward, Communist groups appeared among Korean exiles in China and Korean students in Japan. The relations between groups were uneasy due to frequent clashes of personal ambitions and intense competition for official recognition by the Comintern.

In 1925, representatives of the assorted Communist groups secretly met in Seoul to create the Communist Party of Korea, which received the Comintern's approval. Yet the party had to operate amid constant police harassment, with all its prominent leaders soon imprisoned. The factional rivalry also continued. In such a situation, in 1928 the Comintern resorted to an unusual measure: formally disbanding the Communist Party in Korea.

Until 1945, there was no central Communist Party inside Korea, even though Communist and leftist groups continued their activity. Ethnic Koreans were also present among prominent members of the Communist parties in China and the Soviet Union. Many Koreans were involved in the guerrilla resistance in Manchuria (including Kim Il Sung, the future North Korean leader who joined the Chinese party around 1932). A large group of leftist Korean exiles lived in Yanan, the wartime headquarters of the Chinese Communists, where they established the Korean Independence League.

On August 15, 1945, Korea regained its independence. A few days later, the Communist Party was restored in Seoul. It was headed by Pak Hon-yong, a lifelong underground Communist activist who had spent the 1930s in Korea.

Immediately after liberation, the country was divided into the U.S.-occupied South and the Soviet-occupied North. This created vastly different environments in two parts of Korea. The Soviet military authorities were suspicious of the Seoul Party, which operated outside their direct control. On October 13, 1945, the North Korean Bureau of the Communist Party of Korea was established in Pyongyang with Soviet endorsement (later, official North Korean sources claimed that the correct date was October 10, which is still considered the "KWP Foundation Day" in North Korea). The North Korean Bureau was initially subordinate to Pak Hon-yong's Central Committee in Seoul. The North Korean Bureau was chaired by Kim Yong-bom, who in December 1945 was replaced by Kim Il Sung. Throughout spring 1945, under

Soviet pressure, the North Korean Bureau was upgraded to an independent party, officially known as the Communist Party of North Korea. It continued to cooperate with the Communists of the South who technically established a separate party. In late 1946, the Communist Party of South Korea was banned by the U.S. military authorities, and the party leadership moved to the North.

From the beginning, a prominent role in the Communist Party of North Korea was played by the ethnic Korean cadres from the USSR who were sent to North Korea by the Soviet authorities. They were instrumental in introducing the Stalinist bureaucratic traditions to the North. Some ethnic Korean activists from China also joined the Communist Party of North Korea, but others created their own New People's Party (established on February 16, 1946). The program of the New People's Party was close to that of the Communists.

In summer 1946 Kim Il Sung, Pak Hon-yong, and other Korean Communist leaders were secretly flown to Moscow, where they met Stalin. Following Stalin's instructions, it was decided that the Communists and the New People's Party should merge. On August 28–30, 1946, the First Congress of the united party took place. It was called the North Korean Workers' Party. Its first chair was Kim Tu-bong, the former leader of the New People's Party and a prominent scholar, but for all practical purposes the leadership was dominated by Kim Il Sung. After the official inauguration of the Democratic People's Republic of Korea in September 1948, the North Korea Workers' Party became the ruling Leninist party of the new North Korean state.

In late 1946, the underground leftist parties of the South merged as well, creating the South Korean Workers' Party, which was immediately banned, with all its major leaders running its clandestine operations from exile in North Korea. Pak Hon-yong remained the head of the South Korean Workers' Party.

The South and North Korean Workers' parties finally merged in 1949, creating the Korean Workers' Party (KWP), which claimed the right to operate both in the South and North. Kim Il Sung was named the chair of the united KWP, with Pak Hon-yong appointed as his first deputy. For a while, the KWP had significant support among South Korean intellectuals and workers. During the Korean War of 1950–53, however, the KWP clandestine cells in the South were destroyed. The guerrilla movement in South Korea also was wiped out by 1955, and since that time the KWP operated exclusively in North Korea.

Initially, the KWP leadership included four distinct factions whose rivalry determined its history until the late 1950s. These were the domestic group (former underground activists who prior to 1945 operated in Korea), the Yanan group (ethnic Koreans who spent the war years in the Chinese Communist forces), the Soviet group (Soviet officials of Korean origin who were dispatched to Pyongyang in 1945–50), and the guerrilla group (ethnic Koreans who in the 1930s took part in the guerrilla campaign in Manchuria together with Kim Il Sung).

The 1950s was a time of intense struggle between those factions. In 1953–55 the domestic faction was purged, with Pak Hon-yong and other leaders accused of spying and subversion, subjected to show trials, and executed or imprisoned. In August 1956, the Yanan faction and a part of the Soviet faction undertook a joint attack on Kim Il Sung's supremacy. They subjected him to sharp critique during a plenary meeting of the KWP Central Committee. They hoped to replace Kim Il Sung with a more liberal leader, and make Korea follow the de-Stalinization drive. But the opposition could not win majority support, and a large purge of the opposition and its supporters ensued. The Soviet Union and China intervened, demanding to stop the purges, but this interference had only a temporary impact on the situation.

By 1960, Kim Il Sung and his faction of former guerrillas emerged from the purges as complete masters of the situation in the KWP, with nearly all prominent leaders from other factions being purged or demoted. This was followed by a buildup of Kim Il Sung's personality cult, which from the late 1960s reached unprecedented heights, surpassing Stalin's cult in the USSR and Mao Zedong's cult in China. Throughout the 1970s Kim Il Sung began to arrange the transition of power to his son, Kim Jong Il (1942–). This scheme was officially confirmed at the sixth conference of the KWP in 1980.

Throughout the late 1960s and early 1970s, the KWP undertook some attempts to instigate a revolutionary movement in South Korea and reestablish underground party cells there, but these attempts were generally unsuccessful.

Throughout the Sino-Soviet split, the KWP remained neutral, with Kim Il Sung skillfully maneuvering between Moscow and Beijing, and receiving aid from both. In the KWP official ideology there was a gradual shift from Marxism-Leninism to Kim Il Sung's Juche ideas. The latter were characterized by intense Korean nationalism and an emphasis on economic self-reliance.

In terms of organization and inner structure the KWP has followed the Soviet prototypes, becoming a typical Leninist state-party. Compared to other Leninist regimes, the KWP bureaucracy was more closely involved with the management of the economy. From the early 1960s, under a new system of industrial management, the party secretaries formally became the chief executives of their respective work units, with directors and professional managers being relegated to auxiliary positions.

The KWP remained a secretive institution; even the precise number of its members was considered a state secret. It is estimated that in 2000, some four million people (out of a total population of some twenty-two million) were KWP members. KWP membership was a necessary prerequisite for any successful career in North Korean society, and was much coveted by more ambitious North Koreans.

Kim Il Sung's death in 1994 was followed by the first dynastic transition in Communist history. In 1997, after three years of mourning, his son Kim Jong Il became the chair of the National Defense Committee and the general secretary of the KPW, combining the highest positions in both the state and society. Nonetheless, under Kim Jong Il the role of the KWP and its bureaucracy diminished. No party congresses have taken place since 1980, and the official propaganda increasingly emphasizes the significance of the army rather than the party.

See also Cult of Personality; Kim Il Sung; Korean War; Marxism-Leninism; Single-Party System.

FURTHER READING

Chong-Sik, L., and R. A. Scalapino. *Communism in Korea.* Berkeley: University of California Press, 1972.
Kong, D. O., and R. C. Hassig. *North Korea through the Looking Glass.* Washington, DC: Brookings Institution, 2000.
Suh, D.-S. *Kim Il Sung: The North Korean Leader.* New York: Columbia University Press, 1988.

ANDREI N. LANKOV

Communist Party in Latin America

Socialism's various tendencies, which sometimes differed even in their ideas about the relation of reform to revolution, had established a significant presence in Latin America since the times of the First International. Between 1864 and 1881, various "sections" of revolutionaries who identified with Marxism and socialism were formed in various countries. In Montevideo, in 1875, the number of members who belonged to the local section of the First International was higher than the combined total for Austria-Hungary, Russia, Scandinavia, and Turkey. Prior to 1914, a number of parties that followed the different orientations of the Second International, and especially Austro-Marxism and German social democracy, Karl Kautsky and Eduard Bernstein, but also British, French, Italian, and Spanish socialism, had formed. A key factor was the presence of many immigrants who had connections with European socialist parties, and who brought these new ideas with them to their new places of residence: Buenos Aires, Porto Alegre, Rosario, Sao Paulo, Montevideo, Havana, and Rio de Janeiro.

Many of these "internationalists" had already been militants in Europe. One of the most significant examples is Vittorio Codovilla, who became one of the historic leaders of Latin American communism. Born in February 1894 in the province of Pavia and a member of the Italian Socialist Party's youth section, when he was eighteen he emigrated to Argentina, where together with Orestes Ghioldi he contributed to the newspaper *Palabra Socialista* and not long afterward collaborated with the group Adelante. In 1903 Argentina was already participating in the Bureau socialiste internationale (at the International Conference in Brussels), and the following year at the International Socialist Congress in Amsterdam it was represented by the young author Manuel Ugarte and a Milanese socialist, Dino Rondani. At the Stuttgart Congress (1907), Argentina, which was considered the most "European" country in Latin America, was confirmed as the only member of the Second International from this continent. One of the founders of the Partido socialista obrero internacional (which later became simply Argentino) in 1894, Juan Bautista Justo (Giusto), born in Buenos Aires in 1865, was also of remote Italian descent, a follower of Bernstein, and one of the first to translate Karl Marx into Spanish.

The Eurocentric view of socialism was unexpectedly and violently disturbed by the "revolution against *Capital,*" the Russian Revolution of October 1917, which led to a rethinking of the Marxian understanding of the Americas, and to extraordinary political expectations for the workers' movement and socialism generally throughout the continent. If even a backward capitalist country with a significant peasant presence could raise the issue of the seizure of power, the revolution became a possibility in non-European societies and "peripheral countries" like Argentina, Brazil, Peru, or Mexico as well. The Comintern from its inception, however, had a noticeable Euro-Asian orientation, and direct participation by Latin American members was limited. In 1921, the Hungarian Máthyás Rákosi was made responsible for relations with the Communist parties of Latin America. Up to the Third Congress, Latin American representatives on the International's Executive Council consisted of Russians, Swiss, Indians, or North Americans. At the Fourth Congress in 1922, the members elected to represent Latin America were the Swiss Edgar Woog and the Indian Manabendra Nath Roy. Of the eight heads of the Comintern's Secretariat between 1921 and 1941 none came from Latin America. Between 1924 and 1928 the secretaries representing the "Romance" countries of Europe were also responsible for Latin America: Palmiro Togliatti (1925–27) and Henri Barbé (1928). There were four Latin American Comintern sections in the South (Argentina, Brazil, Chile, and Uruguay) and two in the North (Mexico and Cuba). The most unusual case of export "of the first communist party outside Soviet Russia" was the Mexican one, where the group that would later form the Communist Party in 1919 was composed of Roy (who would soon become the party's first secretary), the Soviet emissary Mikhail Borodin, and U.S. citizen Richard Francis Phillips, who participated the following year in the Comintern's Second Congress, "representing" Mexico. Mexico was also the first country in Latin America to recognize the USSR, in 1924. Prior to World War II Uruguay, Colombia, and Argentina also established diplomatic relations with the USSR. In 1924, the Fifth Congress of the International decided to create a South American Secretariat, installed the following year in Buenos Aires with delegates from the Argentinean, Uruguayan, Chilean, and Brazilian parties as well as the International itself. Codovilla was second in command to the Swiss Jules Humbert-Droz, who headed the Comintern's Latin American Secretariat, and José Fernando Penelón, secretary of the Argentinean Communist Party, was elected member of the Comintern's Executive Committee and its representative in South America. The South American Secretariat operated in Buenos Aires from 1925 to 1930, and Montevideo from 1930 to 1935, publishing the journal *La Correspondencia Sudamericana*.

A new chapter in the Communist movement's history in Latin America began with the Comintern's Sixth Congress, held in Moscow in 1928. For the first time delegates from Argentina, Chile, Brazil, Colombia, Cuba, Ecuador, Mexico, Uruguay, and Paraguay participated.

In May 1929, the Congreso sindical latinoamericano in Montevideo decided to create the Confederación sindical latinoamericana. The First Latin American Communist Conference (Buenos Aires, 1929), attended by many leaders from the International and thirty-eight Latin American delegates from fourteen parties, not only confirmed the great organizational effort that went into the event but also the predominance of the Soviet perspective globally. The interpretation of the political and economic situation in Latin America was one-sided, and in many respects mistaken, and the watchwords of "class against class" and struggle against "social fascism" revealed the limits of their ideological origins. The Executive Committee's representative at the conference at the time was a Bukharin follower, Humbert-Droz (Luis). Few of the issues addressed the real ongoing struggles in Latin America—such as whether to support the fight led by General Augusto César Sandino (who was later killed in 1934 by the Guardia nacional) against North American troops in Nicaragua. José Carlos Mariátegui defended the Andean and *indio* specificity of the peasant question, the relative uniqueness of socialism in Peru, and the need to strengthen the anti-imperialist fight against the United States; these positions were all criticized. In 1930, the Third Latin American Labor Union Conference and the Second Latin American Communist Conference gathered in Moscow, and in October 1934, once again in the Soviet capital, the last reunion of the Comintern's Latin American section was held.

The new policies launched by Georgi Dimitrov at the Comintern's Seventh Congress inaugurated the complex era of popular fronts, also schematically applied to Latin America, and once again subordinated the "national" and continental policies of the Latin American Communist parties to the defense of the USSR. Before the Congress, on May 20, 1935, the Comintern's theoretical journal *L'Internationale Communiste*, published a long article on the situation of the Latin American Communist movement—written by the functionary responsible for Latin America, Chinese leader Chen Shaoyu (Wang Ming), who would hold this position until 1937—analyzing the dynamics of the global situation between the Sixth and Seventh Congresses. While recognizing the diversity and specificities of the individual continental realities, the common anti-imperialist front was supposed to be an absolute priority; the way it was applied could vary, but the tactic had to remain the same. On the other hand, by confusing the nature of European imperialism in Asia (and especially British imperialism in

India) with that of the United States in Latin America, an opportunity to understand and fight U.S. strategy in Latin America, which had by then replaced British imperialism as the dominant influence on the continent, was missed. The Reunion of Communist Parties of the Western Hemisphere, organized in July 1939, thus ended with a declaration—signed by Earl Browder (United States), Tim Buck (Canada), Carlos Contreras Labarca (Chile), Blas Roca (Cuba), Hernán Laborde (Mexico), and Juan Bautista Fuenmayor (Venezuela)—that the principal enemy was not imperialism but rather the Fascist powers. In order to defeat this enemy, the declaration continued, it was necessary to seek "the unity of the peoples of Latin America and North America, and cooperation with Roosevelt's government by consistently following a democratic 'good neighbor' policy."

This line was suddenly interrupted in August 1939, when the Hitler-Stalin Pact threw Latin American communism into utter confusion. But after Hitler's aggression against the USSR in June 1941 the theme of alliances was once again the order of the day in the United States. This stance became known as "Browderism" (named for the secretary of the Communist Party of the United States, Earl Browder): an interpretation of U.S. imperialism in light of the struggle against Nazi fascism in Europe. Browder's moderate theses were accepted by the majority of Latin American Communist parties. The Cuban and Argentinean parties pushed Browderism to its limits, though. Once Browder fell into disgrace in 1945, his Latin American followers were also forced to recognize that they had incurred a "Right deviation."

In Brazil, the Communist Party was formed thanks to the organizational efforts of some anarchist groups (and Masons), which then sent a representative to the Comintern's Fourth Congress; he had been chosen by nine delegates, who in turn were elected by seventy-five cells scattered throughout the country. A major development in this party's history was Luís Carlos Prestes's request to join; he was the legendary "knight of hope," having traveled nineteen thousand miles in twenty-seven months near the frontier with Bolivia between 1925 and 1927 at the head of the so-called *colonna invincible*. The first coup by soldiers who would later become Communists was an event that echoed loudly in Latin American nationalist and left-wing circles until about the midcentury mark. For the first time, the Communists actually considered the political issue of an alliance with the fighters in Prestes's column, or seen in a broader context, an alliance between the revolutionary proletariat under the Com-

munist Party's leadership and the popular masses, especially peasants, under the column's leadership. In 1929 the leadership of the Brazilian Communist Party listed Prestes as its candidate for the presidency of the republic. Prestes participated in the Third Conference of the Communist Parties of South America and the Caribbean in 1934, and joined the party. Immediately afterward he became the leader of another insurrection, which was repressed by the government of Getúlio Vargas. He was arrested in Rio de Janeiro in 1936 and condemned to sixteen years in prison. After having declared his support for the president to defend Brazil from the Nazi Fascist threat, Prestes was freed in April 1945, and from then on was repeatedly elected as the party's general secretary (1945, 1954, 1960, and 1967). After the 1964 military coup the Communist Party was outlawed, and Prestes went underground and later traveled to the USSR in 1971. He returned to Brazil after the 1979 amnesty, opposing the new party line that aimed to "broaden, deepen and strengthen political democracy as an indispensable step on the road to socialism." Prestes was removed from his position as general secretary in 1980.

Criticism of the orthodoxy and policies of the USSR began to emerge in Latin America only after Khrushchev's denunciation of Stalin at the Twentieth Congress. But the Cuban Revolution had the greatest influence on the Latin American Communist parties. As the years passed—and the Cuban Revolution went through different phases—the parties moved from initial surprise to a position of relative support and later one of increasing criticism of the "exporting the armed struggle" line— criticism softened by the reliable pro-Soviet stance that always tied orthodox Communists to Castroism. The most important moments in the relation between the Communists and Cuba were the Cuban missile crisis of 1962, Ernesto "Che" Guevara's criticisms of the USSR, and the guerrilla movements of the 1960s. On all these issues the USSR's dual role as state and party on the American continent was decisive, and often contradictory.

Latin American Communists—disciplined militants, experienced at underground resistance, and frequently heroic when accused of being "traitors of the people"— produced a vast array of small parties or small groups due to divisions and expulsions within their own ranks. In doing so, they kept the idea of communism itself distant from the *masas obreras y campesinas* (the masses of peasants and workers) that they so often invoked as essential to making the revolution (but this is also the case with Trotskyism and the many variants of the guerrilla parties in the 1960s). The Argentine Communist Party is the most representative instance of this ongoing nominal "refoundation" of orthodoxy. A series of ideological purges began in 1928, with the expulsion of the party's general secretary, José Fernando Penelón, who was accused of being a "social-democrat, secessionist and renegade," and then went on to found the Partido comunista de la region argentina (later Partido comunista de la república argentina, and Partido de la concentración obrera). Protected by his loyalty to the Soviets' changing needs, Gerónimo Arnedo Alvarez served as the party's general secretary from 1938 to 1982, except for a brief interruption. The Partido comunista—Comité nacional de recuperación revolucionaria was formed in 1967, only to become the Partido comunista revolucionario the following year. In 1976, the Partido comunista marxista leninista was born, only to split off that same year to become the Partido comunista marxista leninista maoista. This was followed by the Comunistas democráticos and the Comunistas auténticos in 1986, the Comunistas disidentes and the Comunistas terceristas in 1990, and in 1994, the Partido comunista—Corriente nacional marxista leninista.

A majority of Venezuelan Communists, who had opposed the invasion of Czechoslovakia in 1968, led the most significant experiment in detaching themselves from the Soviet model (and the relations that the Communist Party of the Soviet Union entertained with the other Latin American parties). Led by Pompeyo Márquez and Teodoro Petkoff, the Movimiento al socialismo (MAS) arose in 1970; it refused to follow the "guiding party" line, instead searching for a "Venezuelan road" to socialism through freedom and democracy. The MAS identified with the positions expressed in Togliatti's "Yalta Memorial" and the theses advocated by the Italian Communists, according to which "unity in diversity" would favor a greater articulation of forces in the fight against imperialism. The MAS founders embraced these positions starting in June 1969, encouraged by Enrico Berlinguer's defense of the autonomy of "national roads to socialism" at the World Conference of Communist Parties in Moscow.

With the exception of Mariátegui and a few others, the Latin American Communists' theoretical contributions to a renewal of Marxism were not original, nor were they helpful in addressing the difficulties that the Marxist vulgate encountered in understanding the continent's political realities. One of these exceptions is the case of two intellectuals who were expelled from the

Argentine Communist Party in the 1960s, and who decisively contributed to the knowledge and diffusion of Antonio Gramsci's work in Latin America: José Aricó and Juan Carlos Portaniero. They founded the journals *Pasado y Presente* and, in the 1980s, *La Ciudad Futura*, in addition to the Club de cultura socialista; drawing on Gramsci, they developed some essential reflections on Argentina's specific characteristics (but to a large extent these could be extended to Latin America as a whole), most especially on the contradiction between "passive revolution" and "active revolution" as key to analyzing the relationship between the "national question" and the "globalization of the economy." Their view on the role of intellectuals offered a critical understanding of the distance between Communist Party leaders and the popular masses. They also developed notions relevant to Latin America on the creation of a "national popular will" and a "civilian hegemony," which following lived experiences with the various dictatorships, was radicalized to express the definite refusal of any form of dictatorship and "authoritarian fanaticism." Moreover, they proposed a path toward socialism that stressed freedom and justice as shared values, and political and juridical conditions as equally important in establishing democracy.

After the collapse of the military regimes and the end of the neoliberal experiments of the 1990s, a series of governments built around center-left alliances with reformist and progressive agendas—in some cases, even forms of neopopulism that defined themselves as socialist—began to affirm themselves; they were given relative and temporary support by the existing, albeit small, Communist parties, even though the latter remained just as divided as they had been in the past century, especially over the question of reformism or revolution.

See also Anti-imperialism; Browder, Earl; Comintern; Cuban Revolution; Gramsci, Antonio; Guerrilla Warfare in Latin America; Mariátegui, José Carlos; Nationalism; National Roads to Socialism.

FURTHER READING

Aricó, J. *La cola del diablo. Itinerario de Gramsci en América Latina* (1988). Buenos Aires: Siglo XXI, 2005.

Caballero, M. *Latin America and the Comintern, 1919–1943*. Cambridge: Cambridge University Press, 1986.

Carr, B., and S. Ellner. *The Latin American Left: From the Fall of Allende to Perestroika*. Boulder, CO: Westview Press, 1993.

Chilcote, R. H. *The Brazilian Communist Party: Conflict and Integration, 1922–1972*. New York: Oxford University Press, 1974.

Filippi, A. *Las Americás para Marx* (1983). In *Instituciones e Ideologías en la Indipendencia Hispanoamericana*, intro. J. Aricó. Buenos Aires: Alianza editorial, 1988.

Jeifets, L., V. Jeifets, and P. Huber. *La internacional comunista y América Latina, 1919–1943. Diccionario biográfico*. Moscow: Institut pour l'histoire du communisme, 2004.

Miller, N. *Soviet Relations with Latin America, 1959–1987*. Cambridge: Cambridge University Press, 1989.

Petkoff, T. *Checoslovaquia: el socialismo como problema* (1969). Caracas: Monte Avila, 1990.

Rees, T., and A. J. Thorpe, eds. *International Communism and the Communist International, 1919–1943*. Manchester: Manchester University Press, 1998.

Sodré, N. W. *A Coluna Prestes: análise e depoimentos*. Rio de Janeiro: Civilizaçao Brazileira, 1980.

ALBERTO FILIPPI

Communist Party in the Middle East and the Maghreb

The history of Communist parties and movements in North Africa and the Middle East can only be understood in the context of the post–World War I national liberation and anticolonial struggles. The link between nationalism and communism is thus also essential in understanding the strength and role of Communist forces in the Middle East and the Maghreb. This link has been defined as "difficult" by historians, with moments of both convergence and divergence; it is a link that has always placed the Communists in a subaltern position with respect to the nationalists' forces and regimes, often leading to harsh repression. The type of party that these Communists built, however, exercised an influence far beyond its real political strength, and from the 1950s on, was first translated into the organizational structure of the nationalist parties themselves and then into the bureaucratic, top-down party-state model that these regimes built. Such are the paradoxes of this complex relationship. On the one hand, communism was rejected as an extraneous body and a model imposed from the outside; on the other hand, the Communists' organizational model and the ways it took root in society, as in the case of the relationship between labor union and political party, were reproduced within nationalist regimes in countries like Tunisia, Egypt, Algeria, Syria, and Iraq.

The end of World War I, outbreak of the October Revolution, and beginning of the Soviet experience, the dissolution of the Ottoman Empire and the birth of new states in its territories, often subject to the hegemony or direct colonial control of Western countries—all these events led to profound changes in the social and political arrangements in the prevalently Arab and Islamic area of the Maghreb and Mashrek. Communist parties arose and operated in Algeria, Egypt, Syria, Lebanon, Palestine, and Iraq between the wars. They were mostly marginal, but endowed with outstanding organizational and recruiting skills. In the countries of the Maghreb, their membership mainly included immigrants of European origin and sectors of the Arab working class, creating an organic link with the labor union organizations; in the Middle East, by contrast, the membership consisted of different ethnic and religious minorities, who engaged in revolutionary activities in a nationalist and anticolonialist context. The Comintern's Second Congress in 1920 established the first substantial alliance between Communist forces and nationalist movements in the name of an anti-imperialist struggle. During the 1920s, the Communists supported the anticolonial struggles of the nationalist movements, such as the Moroccan Rif Republic in 1925. But the Communists distanced themselves from nationalist forces by placing a greater emphasis on the Popular Front and anti-Fascist strategies of 1935–36 than on the anti-imperialist struggle.

The "Algerian section," born as an appendix to the French Communist Party, was initially composed of *petits blancs*; the number of native Muslims in its ranks increased, and in 1936 it became the Communist Party of Algeria. This movement's position on the issue of independence followed the French and Soviet ones and went through three phases: strong support for independence (1920–mid-1930s); a more nuanced position that saw Algeria as a "developing nation" (mid-1930s–mid-1940s); and support for Algerian nationalism, yet without advocating separation from France (mid-1940s until at least 1955). The Communist Party was the only force in Algeria that brought Europeans and Arabs together, but their agreement was limited by ambiguities on the issue of independence. The Communists therefore had weaker social roots when compared to nationalist or populist Islamist forces, like the Party of the Algerian People, founded by Messali Hadji in 1937, a predecessor of the National Liberation Front that led to the war of independence in the 1950s.

The first Egyptian Communist Party, the Socialist Workers' Party of Alexandria, was established in 1920, thanks to the initiative of Egyptian intellectuals and European immigrants such as the Jew Jakob Rosenthal and the Egyptian Mahmud Husni al-'Urabi, who became the party's secretary. In 1922 the party joined the Comintern and changed its name to Egyptian Communist Party. It was repressed and banished by Anglo-Egyptian authorities in March 1924 because of its participation in a series of strikes in Alexandria. The Syrian Communist Party's history is part and parcel of its Lebanese analogue, at least until 1944. Even though the party was founded in Beirut in 1924, it was later dominated by its Syrian component following the election of the Syrian Khalid Bakdash as its secretary in 1932. The history of the Lebanese party in the 1920s was influenced by the country's complex ethnic and religious composition—most party members were Armenian Christians. Bakdash only began work on an Arabization of the party and on recruiting in the countryside in the 1930s. He also undertook the first translation of Karl Marx's and Vladimir Lenin's works into Arabic. The Communist Party of Palestine was founded in 1919 by Eastern European Jewish immigrants, but from its inception it had Arab participation. It took a strongly anti-Zionist position, thereby isolating it from the rest of the Jewish Left. Founded in 1934, the Communist Party of Iraq was led by the charismatic Chaldean Christian Yusuf Salman, known as "comrade Fahd" (panther). The party's base was among non-Muslims, Shiites, and the country's intellectual bourgeoisie.

Another profound difference between nationalism and communism related to the proximity and attraction that the nationalists developed toward one another as well as Nazi Germany and Fascist Italy in the 1930s and World War II. The most active nationalist sectors, such as young army officers, were impressed by Nazi fascism's nationalist message, and its opposition to England and France. In contrast, the North African and Middle Eastern Communists' anti-Fascist stance did not have much of a following among the Arab masses, especially in Egypt. The Communists were able to maintain a solid relationship with the nationalist movements in Algeria, though, because of the anti-Arab repression during the Vichy regime.

In Turkey, during the confusing period that goes from its military defeat at the side of the Central Powers in 1918 to the proclamation of the republic led by Mustafa Kemal in 1923, various radical organizations inspired by Bolshevism were born, like the People's Communist Party and the Communist Party of Turkey (TKP), both founded in 1920. The latter, founded by Mustafa Subhi, later took part in the Baku Congress of Peoples of the East, rapidly becoming a force in Anatolia and officially recognized by Moscow. Fearing the TKP's revolutionary perspective and the possibility that it could turn the relation with Bolshevik Russia against him, Kemal created an official "Kemalist" Communist Party. Subhi and the TKP's leadership were killed in 1921 in the so-called Black Sea incident, which appears to have been orchestrated by Kemal himself. From that moment on, the Communist movement ceased to be a significant force on the Turkish political scene at least until the 1960s, when the Workers' Party of Turkey enjoyed a brief moment of glory, only to be banished after the 1980 coup. Starting in the 1960s, the various Turkish Communist organizations were the first to pay attention to the Kurdish issue.

The Communist parties and movements of the Middle East and North Africa entered a complicated phase with the end of World War II, the creation of the state of Israel, and the explosion of the Arab-Israeli conflict as well as the processes of decolonization and affirmation of "Arab socialism" and "pan-Arabism." If on the one hand they were still subjected to all the forms of repression imposed by pro-Western authoritarian monarchies and regimes, on the other hand they developed interrelationships with Arab socialism, which starting in the 1950s took root in Algeria, Egypt, Libya, Syria, Iraq, and Sudan. The Communist parties were alternately used by the hegemonic forces of Arab socialism in the construction of authoritarian regimes and then more or less severely repressed when this form of cooperation (which often took the form of national fronts) was unnecessary.

The Soviet Union, toward whom almost all these parties demonstrated very strict loyalty, remained neutral and placed its strategic interests in the area above the living conditions of its "fraternal parties." This dynamic was obvious in Gamel Nasser's Egypt. Nasser first repressed the Communist Party, and then in 1962, integrated it into the Arab Socialist Union. The Communist Party in Syria was also ferociously repressed in 1958, when Syria joined Egypt in the United Arab Republic (UAR). The party's leaders escaped to Eastern Europe just as the Soviet Union was building a relationship with the UAR. In Iraq, the Communist Party was first utilized as a principal ally and then repressed by the nationalist and pro-Soviet general Qasem, who ousted the Hashemite monarchy in 1958. With the establishment of Ba'thist regimes in Iraq and Syria (in 1963 and 1968, respectively), the Communist parties in these two countries were absorbed into the various national fronts. The Iraqi history was even more problematic: the accord between the Communists and Saddam Hussein's Ba'th party lasted until 1975, but then the deterioration of the Kurdish issue and relations with the USSR followed. After 1979, the Iraqi Communists were subjected to an extremely harsh repression.

In 1954, the Algerian Communist Party started supporting the anti-French armed struggle. It was once again banished in November 1962, however, with independence and the establishment of Ben Bella's single-party system. From this moment on, especially after the coup by Houari Boumedienne (an important member of Bella's government) in 1965, the outlawed Communist Party continued its activities and even supported the Marxist-Leninist shift in the very same regime that had banned it. Although still officially outlawed, the party changed its name to the Socialist Vanguard Party in 1966. Its tacit understanding with the regime lasted until the late 1970s.

The history of the Lebanese Communist Party is more complex, given its involvement in a dramatic civil war and with Israel. In 1975 the party joined the National Lebanese Movement, an inclusive progressive and left-wing grouping led by the Druse Kamal Jumblat, who supported the armed Palestinian struggle, and the right of the Organization for the Liberation of Palestine to maintain its armed bases in Lebanon and engage in actions against Israel. Once civil war broke out between the pro-Palestinian faction and the Phalangist Party, representing the Christian Maronites and the Jamayyil family, the Communist Party, like other Lebanese forces, created its own armed militia, which was active in the Muslim camp led by Jumblat.

In the Maghreb, the Moroccan, Tunisian, and Algerian Communist parties progressively freed themselves from dependence on the French Communist Party and its ambiguous stance regarding the national aspirations of the Arab world. The North African Communists attempted to build autonomous political platforms joining an anti-imperialist and nationalist perspective with a socioeconomic program. Unlike in the Maghreb, where the French Community Party was influential, in the Middle East the inclination toward national independence was strongest within the Syrian, Iraqi, and Lebanese Communist parties, even if it was the result of many political and ideological shifts. In some cases the Communists proposed a multicultural national process—such as in Iraq, defined as a nation of Arab-Kurdish culture in contrast to the strict Arabism of the Ba'th party-regime. Parties in this area had strong ties with unions and a variety of social sectors, and thus provided a model for the various nationalist frontist experiences, like the National Liberation Front in Algeria or Egypt after 1958. While they were secularist by inclination, the Communist parties of the Middle East and the Maghreb engaged in religious dialogue and even accepted religious support. According to Algerian Communist leader Bachir Hadj Alí, one could act "with the Koran in one hand and Capital in the other." But the Communists parties were hindered in their competition with nationalism by their connection to the Soviet Union, which constrained their actions and, in the minds of the local population, made them appear untrustworthy during the course of national liberation struggles.

With the dissolution of the Soviet Union and "real socialism," many of these parties were reduced to mere witnesses. Still, there is a new vitality in the post–Cold War era, embodied in organizations such as the New Communist List or Rakah, born in 1965 from an Arab split from the Israeli Communist Party or Maki. Even today, Arab Israelis most often vote for these forces, which are represented in the Knesset by the Hadash parliamentary group. Within the Palestinian National Authority, the Popular Party, an heir to the Communist Party, obtained two seats during the 2006 elections to the Legislative Council. The Communist Party in Iraq reemerged following the end of Saddam's regime, and it is currently the oldest Iraqi political force. It took part in the provisional government (2004), and won two seats (or about seventy thousand votes) in the January 30, 2005, elections for the National Assembly.

See also Anti-imperialism; Decolonization; Islam; Nationalism.

FURTHER READING

el-Rayyes, Riad N., and Dunia Nahas, eds. *The Dragon and the Bear: A Study of the Communist Involvement in the Arab World.* Beirut: An-Nahar Press Services S.A.R.L., 1973.

Galissot, R. *Libération nationale et communisme dans le monde arabe.* In *Le siècle des communismes*, ed. M. Dreyfus, 259–72. Paris: Éditions de l'Atelier, 2000.

Gökay, B. *A Clash of Empires: Turkey between Russian Bolshevism and British Imperialism, 1918–1923.* London: Tauris Academic Studies, 1997.

Ismael, T. Y. *The Communist Movement in the Arab World.* New York: RoutledgeCurzon, 2005.

Rodinson, M. *Marxism and the Muslim World.* New York: Monthly Review Press, 1982.

Tachau, F. *Political Parties of the Middle East and North Africa*. London: Mansell, 1994.

ANTONELLO F. BIAGINI AND DANIEL POMMIER VINCELLI

Communist Party in Mongolia

The Mongolian People's Revolutionary Party (MPRP, or MAXH in Mongolian) was founded in 1921 by a group of Mongolian intellectuals. From its beginning up to the collapse of the Communist regimes in Eastern Europe and the Soviet Union in 1989–91, the MPRP's path was parallel to that of Soviet communism, and the People's Republic of Mongolia was long considered to be the "sixteenth republic" of the Soviet Union. The MPRP is also one of the few national Communist parties that continued in power even after the liberalization of the political system and the end of single-party rule in the 1990s.

In 1921, with the Red Army's help, the newly founded MPRP seized power and founded the People's Republic of Mongolia. From the start, the party presented itself as the guardian of a national Mongolian identity and the savior of this autonomy from long-standing Chinese interference, in a country of peasants and nomad herders that up to that point had been governed by a religious monarchy with Lamaist traditions. The organization of the party, the pursuit of forced collectivization, and the repression of Buddhist monasteries followed Stalinist policies, to the extent that Khorloogiin Choibalsan, who led the party and the country from 1928 to 1952, was given the nickname of "Mongolian Stalin." The violence that accompanied collectivization in Mongolia notwithstanding, the MPRP's effects on agricultural and pastoral practices were not as substantial as in the USSR or China after 1949.

The country's development was dependent on its Soviet neighbor (as late as 1980, 95 percent of Mongolia's foreign trade was with the USSR), and after the break between Moscow and Beijing in 1960 the Soviets increasingly used Mongolia as a cushion, keeping a significant military presence there. The MPRP, which was led between 1952 and 1984 by Yumjaagiin Tsedenbal, continued to be modeled in both structure and policies on the Soviet exemplar. The reform of the party and

the country's political system, in the mid-1980s, corresponded to the first signs of change in Moscow. In 1984 the party elected a new leader, Jambyn Batmonh, whose policies of renewal were similar to those of Russian perestroika and were focused on revitalizing the socialist economy. The year 1989 marked a crucial stage in the transition. As had been the case in other socialist countries, the events of 1989 caused the split between conservatives and reformists to widen, and led to the birth of alternative political organizations to the MPRP. Unlike what happened in Beijing, in Mongolia it was the reformist faction that gained the upper hand, and the entire Central Committee guided by Batmonh resigned in 1990. The new leader, Punsalmaagiyn Ochirbat, promoted a gradual transition to new constitutional arrangements and the creation of other political parties. The MPRP, however, survived the impact of political reforms, and during the first free parliamentary elections (with a transitional bicameral system, composed of a Great Khural and a Small Khural) in 1990 it was rewarded with resounding success, principally the result of the greater visibility and experience of its candidates in the provinces as well as a less compromised reputation compared to that of other Communist parties in Eastern Europe. The 1992 Constitution established a unicameral presidential system (the Great Khural), but also led to the first victory by the opposition (which had chosen a candidate whom the MPRP had originally rejected, then-president Ochirbat) in the 1993 presidential elections, though it did not weaken the MPRP as the principal political force in the country. Only between 1996 and 2000 did the Mongolian Democratic Union obtain a parliamentary majority, but the MPRP seized it once more in 2000 under the leadership of the current president, Nambaryn Enkhbayar. Currently, the MPRP presents itself as a socialist-inspired reformist party, and it has been a member of the Socialist International since 2003.

See also Perestroika; Post-Soviet Communism; Single-Party System.

FURTHER READING

Fish, M. S. "The Inner Asian Anomaly: Mongolia's Democratization in Comparative Perspective." *Communist and Post-Communist Studies* 34 (2001): 323–38.

Ginsburg, T. "Political Reform in Mongolia: Between Russia and China." *Asian Survey* 35, no. 5 (May 1995): 459–71.

LUIGI TOMBA

Communist Party in the Netherlands

Its small size notwithstanding, the Communist Party of the Netherlands (CPN) has occupied a special position in the Western Communist family. Its history began before the October Revolution and came to an end in 1990 with a precocious transformation into a party of the ecologist Left. The party's unique ties to the Comintern, the international profile of some of its leaders, and its pioneering engagement in anticolonial actions all underscore its specific path.

In 1907 a left-wing opposition within social democracy formed around the journal *De Tribune*, and in 1909 it formed the Social Democratic Party and chose a revolutionary stance. The "tribunists," who had prestigious intellectuals in their ranks, established ties with the Bolsheviks. The party elected two representatives during the first universal suffrage elections in July 1918. It actively participated in the violent demonstrations of July 1917 and November 1918, in a country that had, moreover, been spared by the war. In 1918 the party changed its name to the Communist Party of Holland (CPH), and in 1935 changed it once more to the CPN. It joined the Comintern immediately, in March 1919.

The CPH participated in various town and provincial counsels; it was well represented especially in Amsterdam, Rotterdam, and the industrial areas of northern Holland. Already in 1920 it contributed to the formation of the Communist Party of Indonesia, the first Communist Party in Southeast Asia, and began a struggle against Dutch colonialism. It was the only party to call for the independence of the colonies. In 1933 two of its four deputies were Indonesian, one of whom had a seat in Parliament until 1946.

From the CPH's inception the party was the scene of various splits, caused in many cases by its most prestigious founders—in 1920 by the supporters of "Council communism"; in 1925 by the party's president, expelled due to his rightist positions after pressure from the Comintern, but in actuality because of a lack of discipline toward Moscow; and finally in 1927 because of supporters of the Russian opposition. The Bolshevization of the party could therefore only be completed once there was no longer a single 1909 founder left in its ranks. Another peculiarity in the party's history was that for many years, the Comintern supported the official existence of a minority and a majority within the party.

As far as membership is concerned, the CPN reached roughly two thousand members during the party's first years of existence, only to later stagnate with around one thousand in the early 1930s. The party's newspapers acquired a certain importance, though, with the number of subscribers rising from five thousand in 1924 to twenty thousand in 1933, until it reached thirty thousand in 1939. The shift that occurred with the Comintern's Seventh Congress, which led to changes in the party's name and its newspaper, did not allow the CPN to end the isolation caused by the anti-Communist attitude of the Socialist Party and the labor union connected to it, both in the forefront of anticommunism in Western Europe. Facing the advances of the General Dutch Fascist League, the CPN did gain some support in the capital's intellectual circles, and its actions in favor of republican Spain also found some support outside its ranks. The CPN also distinguished itself for its actions, both political and material, in favor of Jewish refugees from Germany, who were especially numerous in the Netherlands.

The Communists were able to garner further support during the war by organizing the opposition against the German occupiers. Their most glorious moment—real but also magnified to mythical proportions in the memory of Dutch Communists—was the February 1941 strike, which broke out in Amsterdam as a reaction against the anti-Jewish raids. It was the only public demonstration of solidarity with the Jews in Nazi-occupied Europe, and the CPN led it. The party reached its greatest influence in 1946 with 10.6 percent of the vote and ten representatives, fifty thousand members, and a three hundred thousand print run for its daily newspaper. It emerged from the war at the head of a labor union, the Eenheidsvakcentrale (Unified Trade Union Federation), which was especially active in the two port cities. But unlike the other Communist parties of Western Europe, the CPN was not invited to participate in the liberation governments. Starting in 1947 it became the object of both political and police persecution.

In addition to supporting the orthodox positions of the International Communist movement during the Cold War years, the CPN defended the cause of Indonesian independence, and this isolated it even further. Notwithstanding these drawbacks it always had four to five representatives, and in the early 1970s that number rose to seven. The 1977 elections, however, led to a difficult defeat (only two representatives), provoking a reexamination of both the Communist line and its practice. The CPN tried to adapt to changes in society and adopted a feminist line, relegating Marxism to the role of a "source of inspiration."

During the 1989 elections a coalition by the name of Groen Links (Green Left) was formed, which included the CPN, the Pacifist Socialist Party (many of whose members were former Communists), a progressive Christian group, and another radical Christian group. This ecological, progressive, and socialist configuration immediately got six representatives, and increased that to eleven in 1998. The Green Left held on to eight representatives in the 2003 elections. Once the coalition became a party in 1990, the CPN officially ended its existence during a congress held on June 15, 1991.

See also Anti-Fascist Resistance; Decolonization.

FURTHER READING

McVey, R. T. *The Rise of Indonesian Communism.* Ithaca NY: Cornell University Press, 1965.

JOSÉ GOTOVITCH

Communist Party in the Nordic Countries and the Baltics

The collapse of the Russian and German empires in the First World War led to the establishment of the three independent Baltic republics: Estonia, Latvia, and Lithuania. Communists were prominent in the region during and immediately following the Russian Revolution. In the years of independence (ca. 1920–40), however, their radical and pro-Soviet stance secured their exclusion from official participation in politics. In Latvia and Lithuania the Communist parties were proscribed throughout this period, and the same happened in Estonia following a failed Communist coup in December 1924. By the mid-1930s all three countries had developed authoritarian systems, which lasted more or less until 1940, when they were annexed by the Soviet Union as Soviet Socialist Republics.

The history of communism in the Nordic countries was of a different nature. The geopolitical conditions in Denmark, Sweden, Norway, and Iceland as well as the political culture of these countries resulted in a more peaceful relationship between Communists and other political forces. With the exception of the Norwegian and Danish parties during the German occupation in the Second

World War, the Communist parties of these countries all worked in legality throughout their lifetimes.

As regards the development of the Communist movement in the Nordic countries, we can discern two main patterns. On the one hand, there were the Scandinavian Communist parties (in Denmark, Norway, and Sweden). Except for a brief period around 1945, these parties had little popular support, never managing to threaten the strong and well-established Scandinavian Social Democratic parties. On the other hand, there was the development in Iceland, where Communists were a part of a broad-based radical socialist movement with considerable popular support, especially in the years during and following the Second World War. (In this respect, a resemblance can be seen between Iceland and Finland.)

The first Nordic party to join the Comintern was the Swedish Social Democratic Left Party (Sveriges Social-demokratiska Vänsterparti), which joined in 1919. The following year the newly formed Danish Left Socialist Party (Venstresocialistisk Parti) joined the Comintern, changing its name in the process to the Communist Party of Denmark (Danmarks Kommunistiske Parti). The Danish party was weak in the first years, suffering from factional strife and never receiving more than 0.5 percent of the vote in parliamentary elections. Even though it made some progress in the 1930s, when support for the party rose above 1 percent, it remained small.

The Communist Party of Sweden (Sveriges Kommunistiska Parti), which was formed in 1921 following a split in the Swedish Social Democratic Left Party, dealt with factional struggles similar to those in Denmark. Nevertheless it fared better, receiving as much as 6.4 percent of the vote in the parliamentary elections of 1929. But in the 1930s, as a result of disputes over the ultraleftist line of the Comintern, Swedish Communists divided into two parties. The core of the Communist Party of Sweden parted with the Comintern, and the Comintern part of the movement was severely affected (receiving around 3 percent of the parliamentary votes throughout the decade).

In Norway, on the other hand, radicals had gained control in 1918 of the well-established Norwegian Labour Party (Det norske Arbeiderparti) and the following year the party joined the Communist International. But the Labour Party's allegiance with international communism turned out to be problematic, and in November 1923 Norwegian Communists formed their own party (Norges Kommunistiske Parti). Despite repeated attempts at broadening the base of the party in the 1920s and 1930s it failed to pose a real threat to the Labour Party. As the latter grew stronger, the Norwegian Communist Party became weaker, with its electoral support going from 6.1 percent in the parliamentary elections of 1926 to under 2 percent (compared with the Labour Party's 40 percent) in 1933.

In the 1920s in Iceland, communism developed as a small oppositional group within the Social Democratic Party (Alþýðuflokkurinn). While some Communists were eager to found their own party, others were more hesitant. The same was true of the Comintern, which did not give definite instructions for the founding of a party until 1928. The Communist Party of Iceland (Kommúnistaflokkur Íslands) was founded in November 1930, and its life span was short. In 1938, unity talks between the Communist Party of Iceland and the Social Democratic Party ended with a split in the Social Democratic Party. A Left faction broke away and joined the Communist Party in forming a new People's Unity Party–Socialist Party (Sameiningarflokkur Alþýðu–Sósíalistaflokkur). During its short life span, the Communist Party of Iceland managed to establish a relatively strong base, receiving as much as 8.5 percent of the votes in the parliamentary elections of 1937. While the pro-Soviet stance of the Socialist Party's leading members complicated matters for the party (particularly during its first couple of years), the base established by the Communist Party of Iceland in the 1930s undoubtedly helped in securing the Socialist Party an important place in the political arena. In its first parliamentary elections of 1942, the support of the party (16.2 percent) had surpassed that of the Social Democratic Party (15.4 percent), and it maintained this position more or less throughout its lifetime. From 1956 onward the Socialist Party was a part of an electoral organization, the People's Alliance (Alþýðubandalagið), which in 1968 became a political party. At the same time the Socialist Party was dissolved.

The political development during the latter half of the Second World War (most important, the German occupation of Denmark and Norway) reinforced the Communist movement in Scandinavia. In the last years of the war the Communist parties of Norway, Denmark, and Sweden were all stronger than before. This success was, however, short-lived. The position of the Communist movement in Scandinavia, unlike Iceland, declined with resumed skepticism toward communism in the late 1940s. The strong position of the Social Democratic parties as well as the social, political, and economic stability of Scandinavia throughout the 20th century made it difficult for the Communist parties to gain momentum. Communists did at certain points become prominent in the political struggle—for example, in the campaign against European Economic Community membership in the 1970s—but gradually lost their initiative on the far Left to the Left socialist parties that emerged in the 1960s and 1970s.

See also Antifascism; Social Democracy.

FURTHER READING

Arbeiderbevegelsens historie i Norge. Vols. 2–6. Oslo: Tiden, 1987–90.

Arens, O., and A. Ezergailis. "The Revolution in the Baltics." In *Critical Companion to the Russian Revolution, 1914–1921.* Indiana: Indiana University Press, 1997.

Bolin, J. *Parti av ny typ? Skapandet av ett svenskt kommunistiskt parti, 1917–1933.* Stockholm: Almqvist and Wiksell International, 2004.

Lippe, J., ed. *NKPs historie.* Oslo, 1966.

Ólafsson, J. *Kæru félagar. Íslenskir sósíalistar og Sovétríkin, 1920–1960.* Reykjavík, 1999.

Rauch, G. von. *Geschichte der baltischen Staaten.* Munich: Kohlhammer, 1977.

Schmidt, Werner. *Kommunismens rötter i första världskrigets historiska rum.* Stockholm: Stehag, 1996.

———. *C-H Hermannsson: en politisk biografi.* Stockholm: Leopard, 2005.

Thing, M. *Kommunismens kultur. DKP og de intellektuelle, 1918–1960.* Vols. 1–2. Copenhagen, 1993.

Thing, M., and J. Bloch-Poulsen. *Danmarks Kommunistiske Parti, 1918–1941.* Copenhagen, 1979.

RAGNHEIÐUR KRISTJÁNSDÓTTIR

Communist Party in Poland

Unlike its counterparts elsewhere, the Communist Party of Poland (CPP) arose not from a split but from a union of the already-existing Social Democracy of the Kingdom of Poland and Lithuania (SDKPiL), founded in 1894, and the Polish Socialist Party—The Left (PPS-Lewica)—itself the result of a split, in 1906, in the Polish Socialist Party (PPS). The Bolshevik revolution played a decisive role by bringing the two Polish parties together. The Communist Party of Polish Workers (KPRP), after 1923 the Communist Party of Poland (CPP), was founded on December 16, 1918, in Warsaw. Later, the CPP was joined by members from the PPS, the Bund and the Poalej Syjon (Zion), the Jewish Democratic Workers Party. The CPP was one of the founding parties of the Communist International, but its members did not play an eminent role in Comintern structures.

The party took a stand against the uprising whose purpose was to create a free Polish state and, instead, formed Workers' Councils (Soviets), which planned to take power; however, this caused the party to be declared illegal. The isolation of the party increased when, in July 1920, the Red Army moved into the Polish lands, and Polish Communists (among others, Feliks Dzierżyński) formed a Temporary Polish Revolutionary Committee in Białystok, which existed for only three weeks. The party changed its policy in 1922, adopting a negative stance toward the "bourgeois" Polish state and declaring itself in favor of surrendering the eastern Polish lands to the Soviet Union, and Upper Silesia to the Germans; nevertheless, it did take part in the Polish parliamentary elections.

The CPP was completely dependent on the Comintern and the factional struggles in the Russian party, and thus its own policies underwent violent changes. For example, in 1924, its leadership was seized, with Stalin's support, by a group of ultraradicals, who recognized that individual terror could "galvanize the masses" and launch a revolution. A year later, the Comintern censured them and their leadership was changed. Internal friction also arose from divergences of opinion between supporters of an alliance with the left-wing parties, and between advocates of recognition the Polish state and Parliament (these were the majority, who included Adolf Warski and Wera Kostrzewa) and those who regarded other parties as "social traitors" and believed that only strikes resulting in a revolution would bring victory (these were the minority, who included Julian Lenski and Jan Paszyn). In 1929, Stalin supported the latter group, and thus quite a large part of the former party elite were deprived of their ability to inluence the CPP.

From approximately 1925, the majority of the CPP leadership and a large part of the membership of the party could be found in the Soviet Union, Germany, France, or Czechoslovakia. In the Soviet Union alone there were between three and five thousand, and in Poland itself there were only around ten thousand. The CPP was thus, to a considerable extent, a party in exile. Party congresses and Central Committee meetings were held outside of Poland. In 1923, the presence of Polish nationalities

outside of Poland led to the creation of the Communist Party of the Western Ukraine and the Communist Party of Belorussia. A large number of party members were Jews, who were particularly well represented in the leadership's elite (for example, in the Central Committees of the CPP and the Western Ukraine and Belorussian parties; in 1936, there were seventeen Poles and twenty-one Jews in leadership roles). The Communists saw no problem in this, but public opinion in Poland felt that this circumstance made the party dependent on a people that were hostile to Poland and were foreign in national identity. All in all, it reinforced in people's minds the stereotype of the "Jewish commune."

In spite of the resolute struggle that the Polish government carried on against the CPP (there were numerous arrests and trials), the party was able to expand its share of the vote in elections—from 190,000 (2 percent) in 1922, to 600,000 (5 percent) in 1928, to around 700,000 (6 percent) in 1930. It remained, nonetheless, a marginal party. Unable to operate openly, the CPP created legal "party annexes," but none of them lasted longer than three or four years. The CPP exerted its greatest influence in the years from 1935 to 1937, when, thanks to the idea of a Popular Front and its anti-Fascist slogans, it succeeded in attracting a considerable part of the left-wing intelligentsia. The civil war in Spain also played a role in mobilizing left-wing opinion.

During this period, however, a breakdown occurred that was not a result of repressions from the Polish government, but rather was a consequence of the slaughter, during the Great Purge, of almost the entire CPP elite. Another result was the dissolution of the party by the Comintern (made official in June 1938) under the excuse that it had been "corroded by internal provocations." This decision was a shock to the Polish Communists, although generally speaking, they submitted to it without objection. In May 1939, the Comintern appointed a Temporary Steering Committee to reactivate the party, but the breakout of the war halted these operations. The majority of the active Communists were in the lands annexed by the Soviet Union in 1939. There, they were distrusted, and it was not until 1941 that they began to be accepted into the Communist Party of the Soviet Union (CPSU).

The situation changed after the Germans invaded the Soviet Union. Party activists were brought together into the Comintern School, and an "Initiative Group" was selected to be parachuted into Polish territory. On January 5, 1942, these new arrivals formed the Polish

Workers' Party (PWP). The Comintern gave the new party its name and program. In conformity with Stalin's new tactics, the PWP initiated a program called the National Front and immediately undertook partisan actions. These actions proved to be incompatible with the strategies of the Polish Underground State, which was preparing its own general revolt, and carrying out on the spot intelligence, defensive and diversionary activities, and building a civilian resistance. The PWP was thus treated as a party dependent on Moscow and which acted against the interests of the state. In spite of a crisis caused by the failure to form a partisan army, as well as by the deaths, resulting from internal conflicts, of two consecutive general secretaries (Marcel Nowotka and Edward Molojec), the German defeat at Stalingrad turned the war around, and the PWP slowly began to grow. At the end of 1943, it took the initiative in creating an alternative to the Polish government called the National Council of State. This was a repeat of the tactics of the Popular Front; that is, it brought together operatives from the various left-wing parties. The leading figures of the PWP at the time were Władysław Gomułka (the secretary general) and Boleslaw Bierut (the head of the KRN [NCN]). As the front moved west into Poland, the PWP Communists, supported by Soviet diversionary groups, began armed activity. At that time, the PWP and its partisan units numbered, together, some eight to ten thousand persons. The Communists who had been in the Soviet Union in 1941 and 1942 (Wanda Wasilewska and Jakub Berman, among others) took a hostile stance toward the army of resistance in Poland proper and the Polish government. And when, after the revelation of the Katyn crime, Stalin broke off relations with Poland, the PWP Communists, at his recommendation, formed a new Union of Polish Patriots (UPP) and a new army (the Kosciuszko Division). The beginning of 1944 saw the creation of the Central Bureau of Polish Communists (CBPC), which was not, however, a new party, but more of a coordinating body.

After the Red Army began moving into lands that Moscow recognized as Polish, a temporary authority was created, which on July 22, 1944, issued a manifesto containing patriotic rather than revolutionary slogans. This authority, though many of its official positions came from pro-Communist operatives from other parties (for example, the PPS) as well as from Polish army units that had fought alongside the Red Army, was dominated by the PWP. Communists gradually arriving from Moscow joined the party, and the new leadership took on operatives who had participated in the resistance (Bierut, Gomulka) and from the CBPC (Berman, Hilary Mine, Aleksander Zawadzki). Land allotments (free of redemption payments) of large farms began as early as September, and this greatly increased PPR influence in the countryside. By December 1944, the party already had some twenty thousand members. Settlements reached at the Yalta Conference produced the Provisional Government of National Unity, bringing together several thousand anti-Communist politicians (among them, Stanislaw Mikolajczyk), but the PWP retained control over the army as well as over a fast-growing security apparatus, and in the minds of the public the party held de facto power. The PWP ranks grew quickly (in December 1945 there were 230,000 members, and by 1948 the number had grown to 950,000), due both to the influx of peasants grateful for their land allotments, of workers encouraged by a new opportunity to improve their position in society, and of course of careerists. The party leadership was composed of members of the Communist Party of Poland (CPP), and the party leader was Gomułka. Bierut acted as a "nonparty" president. However, the bottom layers of the party found it difficult to identify with a Communist past that they did not know, and they had to be subjected to ideological indoctrination. The most important elements of this indoctrination involved not the vision of a world revolution, but the rebuilding and modernization of the country, the management of the lands taken over from Germany, a revolution in education, the elimination of unemployment, and the alliance with the Soviet Union as a guarantee of their new western frontier. The party made good use of the instruments of power at its disposal and, during the initial period, the help of the Red Army and the NKVD. Through terror, aggressive propaganda, and the party's internal discipline, the Communists succeeded, over the period from 1945 to 1947, in defeating their opponents, one after the other, and in reducing the other parties to the status of vassals.

By 1948, though, Gomułka had been designated as an "internal enemy" and a "vehicle of right-wing-nationalist deviationism," and a process of accelerated Sovietization began. On December 15, 1948, the PWP was absorbed into a United Polish Workers' Party (UPWP), in which an overwhelming number of posts were occupied by Communists, and of which Bierut became the sole leader. Planning and management of the economy were centralized, collectivization of farms was launched, a system of nomenclature was instituted, and heavy industry emphasizing raw materials and arms was forcibly expanded.

Workers were promoted to managerial positions, farm and factory youths were admitted to advanced institutions of learning, and workers' vacations, cafeterias, and day care centers were organized. Meanwhile, almost all of society was overseen by the security apparatus (in 1950, there were some thirty thousand political prisoners), Gomułka and a core of party activists were jailed, the Catholic Church lay under attack, compulsory instruction in the Russian language was introduced, and textbooks were crammed with a simplified Marxism. A significant number of key decisions, including personal ones, had to be first cleared with Moscow, which would also "recommend" concrete steps to be taken. And even as late as November 1949, the Polish minister of defense was the Soviet marshal Konstantin Rokossowski.

The UPWP had approximately 1.4 million members and over fifty thousand party cells in the workplace. The party apparatus itself numbered some thirteen thousand. Those in leadership roles were required to belong to the party; for example, 80 to 90 percent of the officer corps, the security apparatus, and the public prosecutor offices were filled with party members. In addition, the majority of Poles belonged to organizations subordinate to the party ("transmission belts" to it), such as labor unions and women's, veterans', and youth groups. Thanks to this, not only members of the UPWP, but the entire society could be maintained in a constant state of mobilization by rallies, demonstrations, or mass votes in "elections" to the Parliament, signings of appeals for peace, celebrations of Stalin's seventieth birthday or Bierut's sixtieth, and so forth.

The system became more relaxed after Stalin's death, and notably more relaxed after the Twentieth Congress of the CPSU and Bierut's death in March 1956. There now emerged divergent views among UPWP leaders; some supported liberalization and reforms in management of the economy; others gave voice to populist battle cries, such as agitation for a rise in salaries, but there were anti-intellectual and anti-Semitic slogans as well. All this was accompanied by manifestations of public dissatisfaction—the workers' revolt of June 28 in Poznan, which was bloodily suppressed, and the participation of over a half million persons in a pilgrimage to Jasna Gora on August 15. The growing tension, however, abated after the Eighth Plenum of the Central Committee of the UPWP (on October 19–21), which decided to bring back Gomułka as party leader. Never before and never after did a party leader enjoy such spontaneous support, which was now the stronger because Gomułka's nomination was opposed by Moscow.

This "October turnaround" brought great changes. Some were similar to those that had taken place in other Communist states, such as the renunciation of mass terror. Others were unique to Poland, such as the discontinuance of collectivization, recognition of the independence of the Church, and greater freedom of speech. The basic element of the system, however, was preserved: the Communist monopoly of power in the state and in all areas of economic, social, and cultural life. The suppression of the popular revolt in Hungary strengthened the conviction that the socialist system was the only possible (realistic) one. The party saw another mass influx (in 1970, there were approximately two million members), and once again people entered the party to advance their careers rather than for ideological reasons.

Generational changes were now also taking place. Young activists turned in the direction of "national communism" and now tended to reject the "old Communists." A conflict arose during 1967 and 1968 against a background of protests by intellectuals (among other incidents were the student strikes in March 1968) against limitations of freedom of speech and the abandonment of reforms ("going back on October"). Since a certain sector of the "old people" were persons of Jewish origin, the conflict took on characteristics of an anti-Semitic campaign. Gomułka held out for the time being. But in December 1970, a new crisis, caused by strikes put down by the army with considerable bloodshed, forced the removal of Gomułka and other figures from the government. These ousters marked the departure of the last ranks of the "Comintern generation." For its successors, ideology was now mere regalia and a way of keeping ties to Moscow, rather than a real profession of faith.

On December 20, 1970, Edward Gierek became the head of the party. He adopted a new course for the economy (now based on credits from the West). Gierek liberalized the system somewhat and ended the open struggle with the Church, but the party continued to function according to the old rules and retained its accustomed place in the state. The party now had more people working in intelligence than it had ordinary workers. In effect, the UPWP constituted a major power bloc (in 1980, it had 3.2 million members), but one that was out of touch with ordinary people's lives. Slogans about the "moral and political unity of the people," or the "building of a mature socialism," were designed to cover up existing social conflicts and an inefficient economy.

After a period of prosperity from 1971 to 1975, the economy weakened and dissatisfaction grew. At the same time, an illegal democratic opposition came into being, and the Church experienced a great triumph: the election of a Pole to the papacy. The UPWP was already losing its ability to mobilize support, something which became obvious in the summer of 1980, when a wave of strikes broke out, and the Solidarity movement emerged. About one million party members defected to Lech Walesa and Solidarity. Gierek, like Gomułka before him, became the scapegoat. This time, things did not stabilize, because this time there was a political alternative in Solidarity.

The UPWP leadership now had a choice: either seek to weaken its opponents and force them into the existing system, or smash and liquidate them. An advocate of the first solution was the new (named on September 6, 1980) First Secretary Stanislaw Kania, and also the party reformers, but this first alternative found no support in the party apparatus or key segments of the government. The second solution, since the UPWP was by now hardly viable, was to resort to the army. However, despite pressure from Moscow, Prague, and Berlin, as well as from the hardheads (the so-called concrete of the party), preparations for use of the military took a long time. In the meantime, the legitimacy of the UPWP was weakening by every moment, and the party base was eroding.

Finally, in October 1981, the military preparations were complete and the post of first secretary was given to an army general, Wojciech Jaruzelski, which was supposed to guarantee the successful outcome of the operation. The introduction of martial law, on December 13, 1981, brought the military to the fore, and the government was now administered by Jaruzelski, together with several secretaries of the Central Committee, and two generals, who had also once been members of it. In the "strength departments" of the party apparatus, as well as among some of the retired party workers, there was a desire to use martial law to re-Stalinize the system and return it to ideological orthodoxy. There were even suggestions that the PZPR be dissolved with a new revolutionary, avant-garde party to take its place. However, if one discounts the mass arrests in the early period (some ten thousand people), Jaruzelski's team actually adopted quite moderate policies, which included a flirtation with the Church and some attempts at economic reform.

This did not stabilize matters, though, nor did it revitalize the party. Having been brought to power by Mikhail Gorbachev, Jaruzelski had more room to maneuver than any of his predecessors, but his attempts to co-opt representatives of the opposition and potential allies from the Church bore no fruit. After much hesitation, Jaruzelski

ceased his attempts to implement his "Chinese model" of economic reforms without political reforms. It was now clear that the existence of the underground Solidarity movement had rendered this model unworkable, and that Jaruzelski would have to enter into negotiations with his opponents. Despite strong opposition, he was able, in the middle of January 1989, to force his plan through the plenum of the Central Committee. The UPWP, however, proved to be utterly unprepared for a political confrontation and was completely defeated in partially democratic elections that took place on June 4, 1989. Jaruzelski assumed the newly created post of president of the state and formally suspended his party membership, but the UPWP could no longer hold on to its monopoly of power or even retain its dominant position in the state. In the fall of 1989, with the party now lacking any real power, its members saw no more reason for its existence, and it began to break apart. On January 28, 1990, the Eleventh Congress of the UPWP decided to dissolve the party. And so, overnight, the Communists became non-Communists, even though the majority of them were still loyal and felt nostalgic for the "good old times."

See also Bierut, Bolesław; Gierek, Edward; Gomułka, Władysław; Martial Law in Poland; People's Democracy; Revolutions in East-Central Europe; Socialist Realism.

FURTHER READING

de Weydenthal, J. B. *The Communists of Poland: An Historical Outline.* Stanford, CA: Hoover Institution Press, 1986.

Dudek, A. *Reglamentowana rewolucja: Rozklad dyktatury komunistycznej w Polsce 1988–1990.* Kraków: Arcana, 2004.

Dziewanowski, M. K. *The Communist Party of Poland.* Cambridge, MA: Harvard University Press, 1959.

Simoncini, G. *The Communist Party of Poland.* New York: Edwin Mellen Press, 1993.

Zaremba, M. *Komunizm, legitymizacja, nacjonalizm: Natcjonalistyczna legitymizacja władzy komunistycznej w Polsce.* Warsaw: Trio i Instytut Studiów Politycznych, 2001.

ANDRZEJ PACZKOWSKI

Communist Party in Portugal

The Portuguese Communist Party (Pcp) was founded in 1921, thanks to the initiative of the revolutionary syndicalists. At the time of the First Parliamentary Republic the party could count on about two thousand members, and its influence was limited to groups of industrial and service workers in the country's two major cities along with workers on the estates in the southern part of Portugal. The party's first general secretary, Carlos Rates, attempted to establish contacts with sectors of the republic's Left, with the aim of increasing unity among the anti-Fascist forces, but these attempts did not prevent the establishment of a dictatorial regime in 1926. Starting in 1929 the party was reorganized on the initiative of a worker from the Lisbon arsenal, Bento Gonçalves, following the "class against class" line, and it became active in the labor unions and was prepared to go underground. Leading party figures at this time were the Czech Bernard Freund, known as "René," and his wife, Wilma, both of whom were executed in the USSR, and the Comintern delegate Francisco de Paula Oliveira, known as "Pavel," who would later become the Mexican art critic Antonio Rodriguez. In 1935 the Pcp had about four hundred militants. The transition to the Popular Front policy occurred while Gonçalves was still general secretary. Yet Gonçalves, along with a part of the leadership group, died in the Tarrafal (Cape Verde) concentration camp in 1942. In the late 1930s the party's organization was dismantled by harsh political repression, but this period also marks the beginning of a lasting Communist influence among intellectuals.

One of these intellectuals, Álvaro Cunhal, took part in the party's reorganization in 1940–41, and became the party's most influential figure until the end of the century. The Pcp created an organization that would be able to stand up to repression, and helped organize important strikes, becoming a permanent feature in the country. At the war's end, the party boasted about seven thousand militants, and together with other forces, was the main impetus behind the Movement of Democratic Unity. Stalinism was only a marginal presence in the Pcp during the Cold War, but it contributed to the party's relative isolation in the early 1950s. Cunhal was also imprisoned starting in 1949. He managed to escape in January 1960, together with nine other members from the leadership group. New space opened up for the Pcp's organization and activities in the 1960s, as transformations in Portuguese society, especially the outbreak of the colonial wars in 1961, shook the foundations of the Antonio de Oliveira Salazar dictatorship. The Pcp's strategy of a democratic and national revolution, outlined in 1964–65, aimed to unite the anti-Fascist opposition in order to achieve political freedom and organize elections, while at the same time attempting to grant the colonies' independence, realize agrarian reform, and nationalize private monopolies.

As a consequence of the military uprising of April 25, 1974, and the popular movement that followed, it appeared as if this strategy could be implemented. The armed forces' movement agreed to a "socialist option" and several measures that were also part of the Communists' program. In one year the Pcp grew from the two to three thousand members it had in the underground to about a hundred thousand, and it became the most important force in the labor unions among southern rural workers, who led the agrarian reform movement. The party's electoral results (12.5 percent in 1975, and 14.4 percent in 1976) revealed limitations in how the party was structured as well as within the Portuguese workers' movement, which was weak in most of the country north of the river Tagus. Socialist Party policies, and the loss of influence of the most radical factions in the armed forces once the issue of the colonies' independence had been resolved, put an end to the revolutionary process (November 25, 1975).

The Pcp's organization and its electoral influence grew in the following years (18.8 percent in the 1979 legislative elections; two hundred thousand members in 1983). The Communists continued to identify the social objectives of the 1976 Constitution as partial realizations of their "democratic revolution" program. Starting in the mid-1980s, though, the party saw both its membership numbers and electoral percentages decline. The collapse of the Socialist bloc caused various types of ideological dissent within the party. It reacted to this situation by renewing its leadership (Cunhal himself resigned from the post of general secretary in 1992 and was replaced by the economist Carlos Carvalhas), adopting a new program of "advanced democracy," and embracing new statutes (that reaffirmed "Marxism-Leninism" and "democratic centralism," but in a more flexible guise). Subsequently some leaders who were influential in the intellectual sectors of the party attempted to push for closer relations with the governing Socialist Party, emphasizing "the Left" to the detriment of a specifically Communist identity. This attempt failed and provoked a reaction in defense of the party's identity, which was also impacted by the worsening social circumstances at the beginning of the new century. The 2004 party congress elected the former metalworker and labor organizer Jerónimo de Sousa as its general secretary. At that time the party had about seventy-five thousand members, about half of whom were workers. In the 2005 parliamentary elections the PCP got 7.6 percent of the vote.

See also Antifascism; Portugal's Carnation Revolution.

FURTHER READING

Cunhal, Á. *Duas Intervenções numa Reunião de Quadros.* Lisbon: Ed. Avante, 1996.

Partido Comunista Português. *60 Anos de Luta ao Serviço do Povo e da Pátria.* Lisbon: Ed. Avante, 1982.

Raby, D. L. *Fascism and Resistance in Portugal (1941–74).* Manchester: Manchester University Press, 1988.

JOÃO ARSÉNIO NUNES

Communist Party in Romania

The Social Democratic Workers' Party of Romania was formed in 1893, with the decisive contribution of Solomon Katz, a Russian Marxist theorist known in Romania by the name of Constantin Dobrogeanu-Gherea. This party led an ephemeral existence since it had no mass base; it disappeared because of a so-called betrayal by its leaders, who joined the National Liberal Party. Reorganized as the Social Democratic Party of Romania, one of its members was the Bulgarian revolutionary Christian (Hristo) Rakovsky, a naturalized Romanian. The development of the workers' movement was noticeably influenced by Romania's annexation of some provinces in 1918, at the war's end. Transylvania and the Banat were important industrial centers with large concentrations of workers; Bessarabia was home to a Bolshevik-oriented Communist movement; and there was a well-organized Social Democratic movement in Bucovina and Transylvania.

The Bolshevik victory in Russia in 1917 radicalized the workers' movement throughout Romania and led to the first repressions, like the one targeting a peaceful solidarity demonstration in support of striking Bucharest typographers (December 13, 1918). King Ferdinand's promise of agrarian reform isolated the workers' movement, which explains why the general strike organized by the Socialist Party and the labor unions in October 1920 failed. The Socialist Party, gathered in Bucharest in May 1921, voted by a large majority to join the Comintern on the basis of the twenty-one conditions set by Moscow, and announced the formation of the Socialist-

Communist Party. The Second Congress, held in October 1922, voted on the party's statutes and renamed it the Communist Party of Romania (CPR), elected the Central Committee, and nominated Gheorghe Christescu to the position of general secretary.

The CPR's creation caused a split within the workers' movement and weakened the socialist movement, which had made some gains after the end of the World War I. Strictly subject to the Comintern, and servile executor of its orders, the CPR never became a mass party. The Comintern imposed its definition of Romania as a multinational state after the war, and in its resolutions introduced the principle of self-determination, including separation from the state. Since Soviet Russia (and later the USSR) had never recognized the union of Bessarabia and Romania, the CPR was perceived as the spokesperson for Soviet interests in Romania, an enemy of the unity and stability of the Romanian state. This explains both the limited number of Romanians who joined the party, and also the large number of members of ethnic minorities (Jews, Hungarians, Bulgarians, Russians, etc.) who filled out its ranks and leadership. In order to guarantee against any nationalist deviation, the Comintern nominated individuals who belonged to ethnic minorities, and in some cases even foreigners, to be CPR secretaries between 1924 and 1940: Elek Köblös (Hungarian), Vitali Holostenko (Ukrainian), Alexander Danieluk-Ştefanski (Polish), Boris Stefanov (Bulgarian), and Ştefan Foriş (Hungarian). Perceived as a menace by the Romanian state, the CPR was banned by the liberal government and went underground in 1924. The party congresses were held abroad—the Third Congress in Vienna (1924), the Fourth Congress in Harkov (1928), and the Fifth Congress near Moscow (1931). The party was torn by factional struggles, since it had basically remained a sect. An energetic intervention by the Comintern put an end to these internal conflicts. The Fifth Congress, deemed the most important, laid out the party's strategy and tactics. After the Comintern's Seventh Congress (1935), the CPR attempted to establish an anti-Fascist Popular Front to confront the "Iron Guard" on the extreme Right, but without much success.

Following the signing of the Molotov-Ribbentrop Pact and the outbreak of World War II, the CPR accepted all of Moscow's directives, even approving of the annexation of Bessarabia and Northern Bucovina by the Soviet Union (June 1940). And after Romania entered the war on Germany's side (June 22, 1941), the CPR launched an appeal for the creation of a unified National Front, whose sole condition for participation was attitude toward Germany and the pro-German regime of Marshal Ion Antonescu. Given the current state of documentation it is difficult to tell if the CPR maintained relations with Moscow during the period 1941–44. Repression by authorities, and the conflict between the CPR's general secretary Ştefan Foriş, who remained free even though underground, and the group of Communists who were imprisoned, led by Gheorghe Gheorghiu-Dej, paralyzed the party. In what could be defined as a "party coup," Emile Bodnaraş sidelined Foriş, and a troika composed of Bodnaraş, Constantin Pârvulescu, and Iosif Rangheţ took over the party leadership with Gheorghiu-Dej's support. The overthrowing of Antonescu's regime (August 23, 1944) and the occupation of the country by the Red Army drastically altered the CPR's position: a skeleton party with no more than a thousand members became the governing party in a coalition that included the country's historically significant parties.

On March 6, 1945, Moscow imposed a government formally led by Petru Groza, but basically controlled by the Communists. At the beginning of the year Stalin had personally designated Gheorghiu-Dej as the party's secretary general, disapproving of Ana Pauker's candidacy, which Vyacheslav Molotov had supported. The "father of peoples" had decided that the party should be led by a worker and not by a bourgeoisie. The CPR's national conference in October 1945 changed the party name—from the Communist Party of Romania to the Romanian Communist Party—and elected Gheorghiu-Dej to the post of general secretary. In February 1948, with the so-called unification of the Communist and Social Democratic parties (in actuality the first took over the latter), the Romanian Workers' Party was created, with Gheorghiu-Dej as its general secretary. Gheorghiu-Dej revealed himself to be an excellent Romanian disciple of Niccolò Machiavelli, eliminating his rivals and adversaries one at a time: L. Patraşcanu in 1948, subsequently killed in 1954; Pauker, Vasile Luca, and Teohari Georgescu in 1952; and Miron Constantinescu and Iosif Chişinevschi in 1957. If one disregards the various labels that were used on each occasion to denigrate his victims (bourgeois nationalist, right-wing deviationists, and so on), it was nothing more than a classic power struggle. "Too many crimes for such a small party," one of the party's leaders is supposed to have said during the 1980s during a confidential conversation. After having applied Moscow's worst orders (such as police terror, and forced industrialization and collectivization), Gheorghiu-Dej

"discovered" national communism when he saw his position threatened by Nikita Khrushchev's policies of de-Stalinization. Gheorghiu-Dej intended to oppose Soviet hegemony with his "April Declaration" of 1964 (known in Romania as the "Declaration of Independence") as a means to save his own power.

This orientation was maintained and even strengthened by Nicolae Ceausescu, who succeeded Gheorghiu-Dej in 1965. The Ninth Party Congress (1965) decided to once more change the party's name to the Romanian Communist Party. Having achieved popularity thanks to his policy of independence, Ceausescu became a dictator who, in the early 1970s, basically reduced the party to nothing. Unable to modify his conservative orientation, hated by the population, and isolated internationally, he was overthrown by a popular uprising and executed with his wife, Elena, on December 25, 1989. With his death, the CPR exited the scene, and the Communist regime collapsed.

See also Ceausescu, Nicolae; Gheorghiu-Dej, Gheorghe; People's Democracy.

FURTHER READING

Frunzaž, V. *Istoria stalinismului in România*. Bucharest: Humanitas, 1990.

King, R. R. *History of the Romanian Communist Party*. Stanford, CA: Hoover Institution Press, 1980.

Tismăneanu, V. *Stalinism for all Seasons*. Berkeley: University of California Press, 2003.

FLORIN CONSTANTINIU

Communist Party in Southeast Asia

In addition to the numerous revolutionary experiences that brought Communist parties to power in the Asian region of the Pacific (China, Korea, and Vietnam), other Communist parties have been active in the countries of Southeast Asia in the 20th century. They were inspired at different times by either the Comintern or the Maoist revolutionary experience.

The Communist Party of the Philippines was founded in 1930 and accepted as a Comintern member in 1935. In 1932 the party was declared illegal, and it went underground until 1937. Another Marxist party was legally active during that period, the Socialist Party, and was later absorbed by the Communist Party in 1938. During World War II, the party supported and organized resistance against the Japanese, thus considerably strengthening its support among peasants and workers. The party participated in the presidential elections of 1946 with limited success, but was violently repressed immediately afterward; as a result, it started an armed guerrilla movement against the U.S.-backed government. The military actions of the Popular Liberation Army, which at some points had ten thousand soldiers, lasted until 1954, since the party's entire leadership had been arrested in 1950. In 1968 the New Popular Army was formed, as an armed element of the Maoist faction of the party. After the split with the Communist Party, and especially during the years of Ferdinand Marcos's dictatorship (from 1972 to 1981), both the Maoist party and its armed element were militarily active against the government of the Philippines. In 2002, the U.S. government listed the New Popular Army as a terrorist organization.

The Communist Party of Thailand (CPT) was founded after the other Communist parties in the region, in 1941. Mostly urban, and inspired more by the Chinese experience than by the Soviet one, it recruited members mostly among Chinese and Vietnamese immigrants as well as urban intellectuals. When in 1947, after the end of World War II and free elections (in which the Communists had only one delegate elected), the military gained control of the country with the support of the United States, the CPT was declared illegal—and remains so to this day. In the 1960s during the Vietnam War and the expansion of the U.S. presence in Thailand, the CPT received active support from both China and Vietnam, and in a shift in strategy, reestablished its influence in rural areas. After three years of relative liberalization of political life, the military regained control of the country in 1976, and many members of the progressive intelligentsia as well as students who were victims of repression took refuge in the countryside under the CPT's protection. The armed wing of the party, the People's Liberation Army of Thailand, had about fifteen thousand soldiers at the time. The Communist victory in Vietnam in 1975 seemed to indicate that Thailand would soon be added to the Communist expansion in Asia. Instead the war between China and Vietnam, which exploded in 1978, was fatal for the CPT. The party's pro-Chinese position ended the essential aid it was receiving from Vietnam, which in turn led to the isolation of the Communist bases on the border between the two countries, followed by the rapid military and political decline of the CPT. The rees-

tablishment of diplomatic relations between China and Thailand, and the amnesty that the country's military leadership issued for CPT members in 1982, further reduced the party's appeal. Those who did not surrender were vanquished militarily.

The Communist movement did not have the same following in Malaysia. Founded in 1930 in Singapore, the party was involved in the guerrilla activities of the resistance after the Japanese invasion of 1941; during this period it received military support from the British. The involvement of Chinese and Indian ethnic groups in the development of Communist ideology in Southeast Asia made the movement unpalatable to the Malaysian urban elites, who feared these minorities should a Communist revolution succeed. After the defeat of the Japanese the party reorganized, especially with the support of the over three million Malaysians of Chinese origin, who were not satisfied since they had not been granted the same political rights as other ethnic groups in the Malaysian Federation, created in 1948. The Malayan Races Liberation Army, founded after the war, started a form of total guerrilla warfare against British and Malaysian troops that lasted from 1948 to 1960. During the conflict's thirteen years about ten thousand people lost their lives on both sides. The movement never managed to obtain the support of the Malaysian population, its nationalist and anticolonialist tone notwithstanding. The anticolonial justification disappeared when Malaysia gained its independence in 1957. The last gasps of military resistance by the Malayan Races Liberation Army came to an end between 1958 and 1960.

See also Anti-imperialism; Maoism; Marxism-Leninism; Vietnam War.

FURTHER READING

Tarling, N., ed. *The Cambridge History of Southeast Asia.* 4 vols. Cambridge: Cambridge University Press, 2000.

LUIGI TOMBA

Communist Party in the Soviet Union

The Communist Party of the Soviet Union (CPSU) was the ruling party in the Soviet Union from the revolution in October 1917 until the party was banned in Russia in November 1991. From the party's inception in

1898, it experienced a series of name changes: the Russian Social Democratic Labour Party (RSDLP) (March 1898–March 1918), the Russian Communist Party (March 1918–December 1925), the All-Union Communist Party (Bolsheviks) (December 1925–October 1952), and the Communist Party of the Soviet Union (October 1952–91).

The party began its life as an illegal revolutionary organization with a founding congress in Minsk in March 1898, although its thin ranks were immediately decimated by the arrest of most of the delegates to that founding conference. The party did not take a stable institutional form until the so-called second congress in Brussels and London in July–August 1903. Right from the beginning the party was fragmented, with the leadership divided by differences over theory, strategy, and personal ambition. Claiming to be guided by the writings of Marx, the party was continually subject during its years out of power to doctrinal disputes about both what Marx's writings meant for the contemporary situation and what was a legitimate development of his thought under new conditions. The leading group was soon violently at odds over these sorts of questions, culminating in an effective split of the party into two factions: the Bolsheviks and the Mensheviks. The former were gathered around Vladimir Lenin, while the latter looked to Yulii Martov for leadership. The split between these two factions was maintained at the elite level until after the revolution when the Mensheviks were banned. At the lower levels of the party, the lines between these factions were much less clearly established or maintained as many rank-and-file members had little understanding of the differences between their leaders, and little concern with their implications. But this does not mean that the party was a united body below its leadership.

Like most Russian revolutionary movements at that time, the RSDLP was split between its leadership, which was found in exile abroad, and most of its members, who worked in the underground in Russia. The latter sought to establish party cells, mainly in the urban working-class areas of the country since it was as the representative of that class that the party gained its sense of ideological legitimacy and raison d'être. The aim of such cells was to consolidate their support within the working class and work for the development of a revolutionary situation in Russia. When this came about, as they were sure it would, they would then be well placed to lead that revolution to the victory of socialism.

There was little to distinguish the RSDLP from many other revolutionary parties and movements seeking the overthrow of the czarist power structure at this time. What ultimately was to distinguish the RSDLP and contribute significantly to its victory in 1917 was the single-mindedness and drive of the Bolshevik leader, Lenin. When czarism collapsed in February 1917, Lenin set about radicalizing the party. Initially party leaders had believed that a revolution bringing the proletariat to power was not imminent. Yet through the force of his arguments, personality, and persistence, Lenin was able to transform the party's outlook and, by September 1917, persuade the party leadership actively to seek to seize power. This the party did in October in the capital, with local party organizations following suit throughout the country in succeeding months. Party rule was not to be secure for some years, however, and the divisions that the drive to seize power laid bare within the party elite were not to be eliminated for more than a decade.

The Party in Power

In the early years in power, the party set about consolidating its position of rule. Other parties were banned, the independent press crushed, private ownership in the economy abolished (although this was in part reinstituted with the introduction of the New Economic Policy in 1921), and principally through the civil war, central control expanded across the country. A new political system comprising a range of new legislative and administrative organs was constructed in which the party was the central, controlling body. At this time, too, efforts were made to increase discipline in the party, and regularize and centralize its functioning. These processes went together.

For the first thirteen years of the party's rule, politics at the apex was vigorous and disputatious. While Lenin lived, virtually all aspects of policy were subject to open and often bitter debate, with the decision finally being made in Lenin's favor in various party forums. From 1922 on, the policy debate was overlaid by the struggle to succeed Lenin, with Stalin and his supporters successively defeating Trotsky, the Left Opposition, the United Opposition, and the Right Opposition, leading to the emergence by 1930 of Stalin as the predominant leader. This conflict was fought out partly in policy terms, culminating in the policies of agricultural collectivization and forced pace industrialization, and partly in terms of the structuring of internal party life. In this latter sphere, the 1920s saw a process of the centralization of control as increasingly the party's central organs asserted their power over lower-level party bodies, and the Central

Committee secretariat and Organization Bureau controlled by Stalin used their power over personnel placement in the party to strengthen Stalin's position. Stalin had been made general secretary of the party in April 1922—a position that gave him formal responsibility for the party's administrative machinery and the practical capacity to manipulate this in order to achieve his ends. He was able to use this power to build up support within the ranks of the party and fill party organs with his supporters. As a result, when issues came before the leading organs of the party, especially from the middle of the 1920s, they were resolved in Stalin's favor. He was also able to use this position to consolidate his personal control of the party.

Under Lenin, major decisions had been made in the leading party bodies. Such decisions had certainly usually been preceded by much personal maneuvering and manipulation, but the issues had still ultimately been resolved in the party forums, mainly the politburo, but also the Central Committee and party congress. This changed with Stalin's consolidation of his personal power. From the early 1930s, but especially following the Terror of 1936–38, Stalin was the unquestioned leader, or *vozhd*, whose authority in the party was unchallenged. Increasingly, open debate within the party was stifled as the public discourse turned into a turgid expression of policy interlaced with extravagant praise of the leader. For the party organs, this meant that they largely ceased to be the scene of vigorous debate and lost any sense of institutional integrity. The leading party organs met when the leadership decided they should, rather than according to a set timetable, and they exercised little independent initiative. Much of the decision making seems to have occurred in more informal meetings between Stalin and some of his colleagues. During the war, to the extent that there was an institutional focus of supreme power and decision making, it was the State Defense Committee rather than party bodies. In the initial seven years after the war, national policymaking was dominated by informal groups of leaders around Stalin, with leading party bodies in danger of atrophying completely.

When Stalin died, an attempt was made to revive the leading party organs and regularize their functioning. From this time on, party bodies generally met when they were required to, and most of the important decisions emanated from their meetings. At no time during the initial three decades between Stalin's death and the party's demise were these leading organs the site of public contestation, but from 1985, they were often the

arena within which a vigorous exchange of views did occur. Throughout this period, but especially following Khrushchev's removal in 1964, it was also clear that the party bodies were the most important political institutions in the political system; to the extent that key decisions were made in formal political institutions, it was in the institutions of the party.

Under Brezhnev, although party organs met regularly, their proceedings were highly ritualized and drained of life. This changed dramatically under Gorbachev when, in one sense, the party came full circle: 1985–91 was a period in which the elite was badly split and such conflict was played out in leading party forums, just as it had been under Lenin. As Gorbachev's attempts to reform the system became increasingly radical and slipped out of his control, opposition mounted in party organs. As a result, the discussion in leading party bodies became more and more fractious and public. The established doctrine of party unity and discipline was eroded, as at the same time the party's dominant position and traditional modus operandi were called into question. As successive measures sought to remove the party from its dominant position in the economy, replace its institutional dominance in the political sphere by new state organs, and change its internal operating regime through the introduction of competitive elections and the reconfiguring of various party organs, the internal party consensus over its role and raison d'être collapsed. Unable to act decisively and discredited by the August 1991 coup, the party was sidelined, eventually to be dispatched by Yeltsin's ban in November 1991.

Party Structure and Functioning

The key principle whereby the party was meant to function was democratic centralism. This was a formula that was meant to combine democratic decision making with disciplined adherence by lower party bodies and members to the decisions emanating from higher organs. In practice in party life, it was the centralist, disciplinary aspects of this formula that prevailed. All decisions of higher-ranking bodies were held to be binding on those below them, and there was to be no questioning of those decisions once taken. This principle of centralist control was also evident in the way in which the electoral principle, which was built into democratic centralism, operated. In theory, leading positions in the party were filled by election. In practice, such positions were filled by appointment and ratified by election. Control over such appointments was vested in various levels of the party, with the central organs having the power to appoint to all of the most important posts, while lower-level bodies were able to fill significant positions within their geographic areas of responsibility. This system, known as the *nomenklatura*, was meant to ensure that only reliable people gained leading party office, and was a key factor in Stalin's rise. It was also a major factor tying the party together into a disciplined machine, even if it did make a mockery of the principles of democracy and elections.

Fundamental to democratic centralism was the notion of party discipline. The party demanded absolute obedience on the part of its members to all party rules and decisions. Disobedience was met by a range of punishments extending from reprimand to expulsion. The exercise of disciplinary powers was vested in special organs, the control commissions, until 1961, when the responsibility was shifted to primary party organizations (PPO).

The party was structured on a hierarchical and mainly geographic basis. The lowest level was the PPO, called before 1934 a cell. This was to be found in every institution in the country where there were at least three party members. It was therefore a feature of every workplace in the USSR and also many apartment blocks (to cater to the unemployed, mainly pensioners). Every party member had to belong to a PPO. These organizations were the main tentacles of the party extending into the depths of Soviet society. The structure of the PPOs differed depending on size, but they were all to meet regularly, and involve party members in party and public life. As well as being the eyes and ears of the party in the society at large, they had major responsibilities for the ideological education and training of individual party members. In 1986, before the party began to shrink, there were 440,363 PPOs in the country.

Between the PPO and the national-level party organs, the party structure shadowed the administrative structure of the country. With the exception of the Russian Republic, all of the republics of the union had a republican party organization; below this there was a party organization at each of the major administrative levels (for example, the region, city, or district) into which the country was divided. At most levels there was a conference (a congress at the republican level), formally elected by the lower-level party organizations, and this conference would elect a committee, which in turn would elect a bureau. This structure was also to be found at the national, Soviet level.

At the national level, the congress was held annually until the mid-1920s, when the frequency and regularity decreased. From the Twenty-second Congress in 1961, congresses met every five years. The congress was formally the sovereign body of the party. It adopted binding party decisions, formally elected the Central Committee to run the party between congresses, and until 1939 exercised some disciplinary functions. But from the mid-1920s on, the congress was too large to be an effective decision-making organ; in practice, it was more significant as a symbolic and legitimizing body. Only at the Twenty-eighth Congress in 1990 did the ritualized nature of congress deliberations give way to a more unstructured and fractious process. The executive organ of the congress, the Central Committee, was more important. In the 1920s this had been a real venue of debate and disagreement, but with Stalin's dominance it was reduced to a more ritualistic and symbolic role. Throughout most of the regime's life, the Central Committee met twice a year, with each session devoted to a different topic. There was little debate, with speeches stylized and decisions reached outside the meeting, although under Gorbachev when the elite was badly split, this became the scene for the airing of differences and disagreements. The Central Committee formed a series of executive organs: the politburo, secretariat, and until 1952, the Organizational Bureau; from 1939 on, it also formed the central control (or disciplinary) apparatus, and beginning in 1966 it elected the general secretary. There were two sorts of members: full members, who had voting rights, and candidate members, who did not.

The most important bodies formed by the Central Committee were the politburo (1952–66 presidium) and the secretariat. Respectively, these were the effective political decision-making center of the party, and the organization with the responsibility for ensuring that those decisions were carried out. The politburo was a small body, and had both full and candidate members. It generally had up to twenty members, although its meetings were often attended by many nonmembers who had responsibility for particular items under discussion. The politburo met weekly, although under Stalin starting in the 1930s this schedule was varied and meetings were frequently more irregular, and all major decisions were meant to be made here. The secretariat comprised Central Committee secretaries elected by the Central Committee. They each had particular spheres of responsibility and headed departments designed to provide administrative support for the fulfillment of those responsibilities. The departments were organized so that they could both administer the party's internal affairs (for instance, departments for personnel and ideology) and shadow the Soviet government (for example, there were departments dealing with foreign affairs, industry, and agriculture). The personnel within those departments comprised the central administrative machinery of the party. Some secretaries were full members of the politburo, while the leading secretary, the general secretary (1953–66 first secretary) was recognized as the leader of the party.

The party's internal structure and functioning formally were governed by the party's rules. These were amended periodically by the congress, and while in a descriptive sense they gave an accurate picture of the formal party structure and some aspects of party life, generally their significance was formal and legitimizing rather than normative. The party's ideology, called for most of its life Marxism-Leninism, was not embodied in a particular book or set of writings, except perhaps the collected writings of Lenin, Marx, and Engels. At times there were efforts to promote particular publications as having central doctrinal significance, especially during Stalin's lifetime, but there was no single handbook of ideology to which people could refer. There was a party program (1919, 1961, and 1986), which was meant to set the longer-term goals of the party and be based on the ideology. Yet the program should be seen as a set of ideals rather than a specific guide to policy, because it never contained a clear indication of the policy lines that the party would pursue.

The Party's Role

According to the 1977 state constitution, the party was the "leading and guiding force" in Soviet society. In essence, this meant that the party was the institution in which all major decisions about all aspects of life were made. This is why party bodies, in theory, existed in all collectives in Soviet society and why the party shadowed the state structure at all levels; if an issue came up in a nonparty body, the corresponding party organ could meet and make a decision that its members, who were subject to party discipline, would carry into that nonparty body. In practice, because throughout the system all leading figures were party members, separate meetings usually were not needed. Party members were the dominant figures, and through them the party dominated the decision-making process, not just at the national level, but throughout the system.

The omnipresence of party organizations throughout the country gave the party the capacity to exercise significant supervisory and control functions. With members

subject to party discipline and occupying responsible posts throughout society, one of their main responsibilities was ensuring that central decisions were carried out. In this way, the lower levels of the party structure were in a position to be able to act to ensure that policy was carried out—a crucial function in a society in which there were no independent sources for the center to verify what was happening at lower levels. The reverse side of this positive role of facilitating implementation was that party organizations were able to maintain a watching brief on what was going on in society. One of the most important roles of party members, especially in the early years, was to act as the party's eyes and ears against the development of opposition, or the decline in popular enthusiasm and support. As part of this, they also had an educative function. Party members were meant to proselytize the party's ideology, policy, and message, to act as role models for their nonparty colleagues, and as the means of spreading the party's values into society at large. This role in particular relied on continuing a fervent commitment by party members to the party and its aims—a commitment that was noticeably waning in the late 1980s.

The party was also the chief staffing agency in the USSR. The nomenklatura extended not only to party posts but also to the most important positions in the political structure more generally. The occupation of all responsible posts in the society was subject to party control. In this way, the party was both the primary agent of political recruitment in the USSR and the decisive influence on the course of an individual's career.

Party Membership

In 1986, there were 18,309,693 full and 728,253 candidate members of the party, constituting 9.7 percent of the adult population; only 28.8 percent of these members were women. Entry to the party was never open; people had to be nominated, have their backgrounds checked, and serve a candidate stage where their performance was monitored before being admitted to full membership. Prior to 1939, people of a working-class background were given priority in entry. Members were subject to party discipline, and had to attend regular party meetings, obey party instructions, pay membership dues, and always conduct themselves according to the party's rules and the principles of what it meant to be a good Communist. Membership was essential for anyone with aspirations to rise into a responsible position in any sphere of Soviet society. Party members gained few advantages over nonparty citizens, although officeholders were more fortunate in this regard. Officeholders enjoyed a graduated scale of access to privileges and goods not widely available in Soviet society. In a deficit economy like the Soviet Union's, such access made a crucial difference to individuals' lifestyles, and because the occupation of leading positions was determined by the party, such access was determined by the party. The party and membership of it was thus the key to access to privilege in the USSR.

Party Funding

In official terms, the party was funded through the membership dues paid by its members and the revenues generated by the sale of the party's publications. In practice, however, such sources of income were from the outset substantially supplemented by funds from the state budget. It is not clear how much money was siphoned from the state into the party, but given the large expenditures made by the party as well as the amount it would have taken in from membership and sales, this must have been a significant amount. As the Soviet Union disintegrated in the late 1980s, large amounts of this money were transferred abroad to locations that have not been tracked.

The CPSU's dependence on the state in this way emphasizes the interconnectedness of the party with all other aspects of life in the Soviet Union. It was clearly the most important force in the society, structurally embedded in a dominating position and exercising its power to consolidate its control. That such a political organization could disintegrate as it did at the end of the 1980s was due to many factors, including the organization's resistance to change. But crucial was the erosion of commitment of many of its members. Built on ideology and sustained by that ideology, when belief in it wavered among a sufficiently large number of its members, the party could not survive the challenge posed by new forms of politics and new (for the USSR) ideas. But the party's failure should not blind us to the fact that it was the first, and up until now most successful, of a new type of political structure: the single-party system.

See also Command Economy; Democratic Centralism; Nomenklatura; Politburo; Propaganda; Single-Party System; State, The.

FURTHER READING

Gill, G. *The Collapse of a Single-Party System: The Disintegration of the Communist Party of the Soviet Union.* Cambridge, UK: Cambridge University Press, 1994.

Millar, J. R., ed. *Cracks in the Monolith: Party Power in the Brezhnev Era.* Armonk, NY: M. E. Sharpe, 1992.

Schapiro, L. *The Communist Party of the Soviet Union.* London: Methuen, 1970.

White, S. *Soviet Communism: Programme and Rules.* London: Routledge, 1989.

GRAEME GILL

Communist Party in Spain

The first Communist organization was established in Spain on April 15, 1920, as a result of emissaries from the Comintern moving to transform the Federación de juventudes socialistas into the Partido comunista de España (Pce). A short while later, on April 13, 1921, the Partido comunista obrero español was born from the maximalist wing of the Socialist Party (Psoe). On November 14, 1921, in an atmosphere of constant clashes, due more to personal than political issues, the two parties merged following the Comintern's instructions.

The new party's rapid decline was accelerated by the consolidation of General Primo Rivera's dictatorship in September 1923. Catalonia was the scene of an analogous failure to build on the initial anarchosyndicalist enthusiasm for the Russian Revolution. The two secretaries of the Confederación nacional del trabajo, Andrés Nin and Joaquín Maurín, were those most involved in this failure, the second having attempted to follow the French model of the Revolutionary Syndicalist Committees.

In April 1931 when the Second Republic was formed, the Pce was only a small radical group, with several hundred members concentrated in a few areas; it endorsed the "class against class" line and supported the establishment of soviets, a concept that most people were not aware of. Following the lead of Dmitrij Zacharovic Manuil'skij, who did not know much about the Spanish circumstances, the Comintern contributed to the general disorientation, while laying the blame on the Spanish leadership. At the Fourth Party Congress held in Seville in March 1932 the leadership was confirmed by the 11,750 members, and so at this point Moscow decided to intervene, sending the Italo-Argentinean Vittorio Codovilla to do the job. Codovilla schemed to oust the leadership group led by José Bullejos, and imposed a leadership that included only those members who were most faithful to Moscow, including José Díaz as general secretary, but also Dolores Ibarruri (the "Pasionaria") and other younger members like Vicente Uribe, who would remain at the party's highest levels into the 1950s. Until 1937, though, Codovilla was the party's real leader.

The party's political line, which insisted on denouncing the "social Fascists" in the government, didn't change until the November 1933 elections brought the center-Right to power; the party also refused to recognize the Alianzas obreras, groupings of many other revolutionary organizations, until just before the insurrection of October 1934.

The party's subsequent growth is due to its last-minute participation in this insurrection as well as the Soviet Union's prestige—the workers' great hope since they were confronted by both an economic crisis and nazism's rise to power. Intellectuals began to join the party at this time, with Rafael Alberti being the most emblematic figure.

Another significant increase in the party's recognition followed the introduction of the Popular Front strategy, which in Spain mostly went by the name *bloques populares*. The Pce signed the Popular Front Pact (January 15, 1936), not without some hesitation, with the support of the socialist Left, and a month later, for the first time in its history, seventeen of its representatives were elected. The Confederación general del trabajo unitaria, a small Communist labor union, merged with the larger Unión general de trabajadores, but the Socialist Youth, merging with the much smaller Communist Youth, became the Juventudes socialistas unificadas and gravitated toward the Comintern under the leadership of Santiago Carrillo. The "unified party" never became a reality in all of Spain, but it did in Catalonia, where the minuscule Catalan Communist Party, together with three other minor organizations, became the Partit socialista unificat de Catalunya immediately after the outbreak of the civil war.

During the civil war the Pce became the center of republican resistance, following Comintern tactics, which in 1936 had begun to treat the defense of democracy against the threat of fascism as an absolute priority. Socialist decline, one of whose signs was Psoe members transferring into the ranks of the Pce, helped elevate the Communist Party to the position of main protagonist in a conflict that it defined as a "war of independence" against Fascist invaders. Figures like the Pasionaria acquired worldwide notoriety, and the arrival of the International Brigades, organized by the Comintern, in November 1936 as well as aid from the USSR contributed to the party's central role. The downside to this newfound importance was the party's decreasing popularity among those who were critical of its proselytism as well as those who held more lukewarm opinions of the

resistance. In November 1936 the Pce entered the Largo Caballero government with two ministers, and starting in May 1937 became the principal supporter of the resistance at any cost line, put forward by the government of the centrist socialist Juan Negrín. The Pce became the "party of war," "Ercoli's" (Palmiro Togliatti) efforts notwithstanding; as a Comintern emissary, from August 1937 to March 1939, Togliatti attempted to pursue a true Popular Front unity line. The Communists increasingly fell into disrepute with their allies starting in June 1937, as there were attempts to import the type of terror that characterized the Moscow trials to Spain. The assassination of Andrés Nin, the leader of the Partido obrero de unificacion marxista—a party that was considered "Trotskyist" and that supported a Bolshevik-style insurrection against the democratic republic—was emblematic of the type of demonization that the Pce engaged in, all in the name of a military victory.

The fate awaiting most Spanish Communists after the republic's defeat was jail, exile, or the firing squad. Between 1942 and 1944 Spanish Communists actively participated in the French resistance, and once liberation arrived they thought it was time to proceed to the liberation of Spain, mistakenly convinced that the people were ready to rebel against Francisco Franco. The war of independence myth lasted until the 1950s, giving legitimacy to a costly underground movement, which was inspired by the French maquis and 19th-century Spanish guerrillas; the underground continued its activities until 1951–52, at which point it lost all hope. In the meantime, after briefly taking part in the republican government in exile, the party returned to its isolation, and its subsequent history was a reflection of the repressive policies of international Stalinism. The most sensational case was the condemnation of Joan Comorera, general secretary of the Partit socialista unificat de Catalunya since its establishment in 1936, who was accused of Titoism in 1949. This case provided the opportunity to suppress the Catalan party's independence. These were leaden years, with Carrillo leading the organization in France, while the party secretary position went to Dolores Ibarruri in 1942, after José Díaz's suicide due to severe illness.

Twenty-two years after its previous congress in Seville, the Pce held its Fifth Congress in Prague in 1954. The Pce still aimed to overthrow the dictatorship, but the only positive element in Dolores Ibarruri's report was socialism's worldwide advance. The postwar strategy was leading nowhere, even though there was continued talk of a national front to defeat fascism. The only sign of change was the rise of the Juventudes socialistas unificadas generation: Carrillo, Fernando Claudín, Gregorio López Raimundo, and Jorge Semprún ("Federico Sánchez"). The generations clashed in 1956 over Spain's entry into the United Nations, which was defended by the younger members from the attacks of the "number two," Vicente Uribe. This led to a changing of the guard, which saw Carrillo emerge as party leader, proposing a "national reconciliation" platform—in other words, an alliance of all those forces committed to regime change by means of a "peaceful and democratic" transition, thus moving beyond the past represented by the civil war. Although he had undertaken this realist change of course, Carrillo continued to believe that Franco's regime was weak and that it would collapse if the people were mobilized against dictatorship. The idea was to oppose "the country to the regime." This was to become an impossible dream, given the Pce's political isolation. The Pce continued to take hold among intellectuals, professionals, and workers—in the case of the latter, thanks to the Comisiones obreras. Modernization also affected areas of foreign policy, leading to the condemnation of the invasion of Czechoslovakia by the Warsaw Pact in August 1968.

After Franco's death in 1975 the Pce thought the moment had come for it to earn the reward for its commitment, almost alone in this regard, to the struggle against the regime, as opposed to the Psoe's absence. It put forward the "socialism in freedom" platform, and its international prestige grew when that same year, Enrico Berlinguer's Italian Communist Party started promoting a line later known as Eurocommunism. After its legalization in 1977, and just before free elections were held, the number of party members was about two hundred thousand. During the June elections, however, it only received 20 representatives out of a total of 350—gaining almost 20 percent of the vote in Catalonia, but just a little over 7 percent in the rest of Spain. Having just reappeared after a long absence, the Psoe became the first party of the Left, and it would remain in that position. The party's spectacular disavowal of Leninism did not serve any purpose. A process of rapid self-destruction followed: after expelling the "innovators" in 1981–82, Carrillo left the post of general secretary, with the party reduced to four representatives and 4 percent of the vote. Gerardo Iglesias, his successor, attempted to regroup and reach some form of understanding with the Psoe, but Carrillo fought him at the party's Eleventh Congress (December 1983) and founded a new party. In 1984 the pro-Soviet wing of the party split off, founding the Partido comu-nista de los pueblos de España, which by the end of the decade merged with the Pce once again.

The attempt to gather various left-wing organizations around the party, using the Izquierda unida (IU) name, did not produce significant gains in the 1986 elections, but during the following decade the results improved, until it once more garnered over 10 percent of the vote and about twenty representatives in 1996. The IU mask allowed the Pce to survive, but in the meantime it also underwent an irreversible aging process and progressively lost militants. In 1991 it still had fifty-five thousand members, but by the late 1990s this figure had dropped to twenty-six thousand. It had only a residual presence throughout the country, in its historic strongholds: Andalusia, Madrid, and the Asturias. Starting in 2000 the party's most dynamic segments joined the IU leadership, and the Pce was reduced to a party whose ideology was inspired by old forms of orthodoxy, without an electoral presence and tied to the IU's role in the opposition, which sank once again to historic lows, with five parliamentary representatives. The Pce's overall position was one of opposition to the system, and it focused on a critique of globalization.

See also Eurocommunism; International Brigades; Popular Front; Spanish Civil War.

FURTHER READING

Cebrián, C. *Estimat PSUC*. Barcelona: Empúries, 1997.

Cruz, R. *El Partido Comunista de España en la Segunda República*. Madrid: Alianza, 1987.

Elorza, A., and M. Bizcarrondo. *Queridos camaradas: la Internacional Comunista y España, 1919–1939*. Barcelona: Planeta, 1999.

Moran, G. *Miseria y grandeza del Partido Comunista de España, 1939–1985*. Barcelona: Planeta, 1986.

Ramiro Fernandez, L. *Cambio y adaptación en la izquierda: la evolución del Partido Comunista de España y de Izquierda Unida (1986–2000)*. Madrid: Centro de Investigaciones Sociológicas, 2004.

ANTONIO ELORZA

Communist Party in Sub-Saharan Africa

Unlike Asia, Africa never witnessed a revolution led by a Communist Party. Nationalist African thought never regarded the class struggle as relevant to the continent's historical dynamics. In part because of the absence of private property in the form of land (real estate), traditional society's principal means of production, class differences were slight, and differences based on gender, age, or ethnic group were more important. "Orthodox" historical analysis in a Marxist sense long held that before the advent of colonialism, and therefore the export of capitalism, it was not appropriate to speak of classes in Africa. Yet studies prepared by the Africa Institute of the Soviet Academy of Sciences primarily focused on societies that were on the road toward emancipation. Anticolonialism's goal was the acquisition of sovereignty, and social divisions appeared to be secondary. No African nationalist party has ever defined itself as Communist or explicitly professed communism. Equating liberation movements and communism was an interpretative bias that could be found, mirrorlike, at the two extremes of the political spectrum: on the one hand, in "militant" and "third world" literature, which was induced by a form of self-deception to exaggerate the revolutionary nature of those struggles; and on the other hand, in a literature that cannot resign itself to the "loss" of these colonies by Europe and the West, seeing the threat of communism everywhere.

In actuality decolonization in Africa, at least in the 1950s and 1960s, was the work of a moderate leadership, interested in leaving colonialism behind, but doing so in a manner that would not throw the countries into confusion or disturb relationships with the ex-metropolis. Some Marxist-inspired insurrections, as in the case of the Union des populations camerounaises, were quashed before independence. Even movements with a socialist orientation (in Ghana, Guinea, Mali, and Tanzania) were qualified ("African socialism" or "African road to socialism") so as to distance them from Marxism and European socialism. Detachment from historical materialism was never completely overcome, because of the attachment of African culture to a spiritual conception of life, individuals, and community. Generally speaking, the influence of Marxism has been stronger in areas that were colonized by "Romance" countries, because of the collaboration and exchange of ideas with the Communist parties of France, Portugal, and Italy with various political forces in the colonies, especially in those cases where decolonization was denied or slowed down by the choices of the colonial power. The most extreme case is the ultracolonialism of Portugal, which led to a progressive unification of the exiled anti-Fascist parties, and the wars of liberation in Angola, Mozambique, and Guinea-Bissau.

Because of the meager results obtained by a process of gaining independence that could not see beyond a purely nationalist perspective, gradually those policies that had been introduced to struggle against colonialism and neo-colonialism grew more radical in all parts of Africa south of the Sahara. The nature of African society was subjected to a critical revision, and there was a growing recognition that because of the changes introduced by colonialism and capitalism, antagonistic social blocs had also formed in Africa. Eminent leaders of African socialism like Kwame Nkrumah (the ex-president of Ghana) and Julius Nyerere (president of Tanzania) adapted their ideology and programs in order to highlight their "class" aspects. The liberation movements in the Portuguese colonies definitely moved in a Marxist direction, opening up the possibility of aid from the USSR (or sometimes China, because of the Sino-Soviet split). Quite a few military regimes moved conceptually closer to Marxism (in Dahomey, Congo-Brazzaville, Madagascar, and Somalia), implementing a top-down choice, which left the problem of identifying the class to whom the role of revolutionary agent could be assigned still undecided. The results were not promising. The most exposed countries fell into a counterproductive isolation. The alliance with the USSR was not sufficient to counteract the weight of the Western powers' obvious superiority in terms of the economy and international trade. Only in Ethiopia did the "revolution," which in 1974 led to the fall of the feudal monarchy, prove that it could be inspired by the Russian example.

During the first phase of decolonization, the USSR's policies in Africa were limited to supporting anticolonialism from outside. The Cold War only landed there at a later stage. Africa was never divided rigidly between East and West, and it did not witness the creation of military blocs, as had happened in the Middle East or in Southeast Asia. As could be observed in the Congo crisis of 1960, Moscow's ability to intervene was limited, and notwithstanding the harsh exchanges in the United Nations, which Nikita Khrushchev personally participated in, the USSR had to powerlessly witness the end of the Patrice Lumumba government and his murder at the hands of secessionists from Katanga. The presence of so many newly independent African countries had changed the numbers, but not the substance of the balance of power at the international level.

It was only with the struggles in Angola and Mozambique that the USSR's role in Africa became decisive, and it was better able to protect its allies. The military intervention by the USSR and Cuba in Angola and Ethiopia between 1975 and 1978 marked a shift in Africa and the world. The U.S. government reacted by wanting to renegotiate the structure of a relationship that in addition to the main agreements on armaments control and the prevention of nuclear war, was supposed to imply self-restraint on the periphery. The overturning of the alliances of Somalia and Ethiopia that changed sides in 1977 (Somalia went from the USSR to the U.S. side, while Ethiopia did the opposite) was a crucial transition of the so-called Second Cold War. The impression was also confirmed that in the case of many African crises, it was the local actors who promoted and were not subject to the action of the superpowers, using a bipolar world to their own advantage. Referring to the informal bloc formed by the ex-Portuguese colonies and left-wing military regimes, some scholars used the term "Afrocommunism." Mozambique requested membership in Comecon and obtained observer status.

The history of the Communist Party of South Africa is instead quite unique in sub-Saharan Africa. Founded in 1921, its first struggles—during a phase of accelerated industrialization, and in the presence of the black masses streaming into the cities and mines from the countryside—were mostly aimed at defending the rights and interests of the white working class. During World War II, the party abandoned all forms of racial prejudice and fully embraced the cause of emancipation for the African population. Its own organization dissolved into the antiracist movement, above all the African National Congress (ANC), allowing the practice of dual membership. Communist members were also to be found as leaders of parties that represented Asians, "coloreds," and whites who were engaged in the struggle against racism, and who elaborated the Freedom Charter in Kliptown in 1955 together with the ANC. There is a good reason that one of apartheid's pillars was the Suppression of Communism Act, passed in 1950, and widely utilized by the white repressive apparatus, accusing of or categorizing as Communist any form of opposition to the racist system.

No Communist or quasi-Communist experience has survived the crisis of "real socialism" of the late 1980s, or the dissolution of the Soviet bloc.

See also Anti-imperialism; Cuban-Soviet Intervention in Africa; Nationalism; Second Cold War.

FURTHER READING

Morison, D. L. *The U.S.S.R. and Africa.* London: Oxford University Press, 1964.

Ottaway, D., and M. Ottaway. *Afrocommunism.* New York: Africana Publishing Company, 1986.

Potekhin, I. I. *L'Afrique regard vers l'avenir.* Moscow: Academie des Sciences de l'URSS, 1962.

———. *African Problems: Analysis of Eminent Soviet Scientist.* Moscow: "Nauka" Publishing House, 1968.

Sik, E. *The History of Black Africa.* 4 vols. Budapest: Akadémiai Kiadó, 1966.

GIAMPAOLO CALCHI NOVATI

Communist Party in Switzerland

On the national level, the Swiss Communist Party (SCP) was formed in March 1921 after a split within the Swiss Socialist Party; it received less than 2 percent of the vote in the elections held between the wars. Its diminutive size notwithstanding, the SCP occupied a relatively important position within the Communist International, for both historical and geopolitical reasons. The SCP from the beginning enjoyed a certain prestige among Bolshevik leaders, because some key international conferences had taken place in Switzerland, especially the Zimmerwald conference in 1915 and the Kienthal conference in 1916. The party also could count on skilled militants who personally knew the Russian leaders and worked in the central apparatus in Moscow. Later, with the Nazis' seizure of power, the position that the country occupied in the center of Europe meant that the SCP was a good base for carrying out international operations. Its tasks included welcoming German Communist militants and their material possessions, editing the journal *Inprekor*, and serving as a transfer center for volunteers in the Spanish civil war.

Until the late 1920s, the SCP had relatively good relations with the International, even though it had barely acknowledged "Bolshevization." But in 1928 a struggle ensued between the Comintern and the SCP, lasting until 1930 and then flaring up again in 1932. The struggle started with the SCP's protest against the International's intervention in the German party during the Wittorf-Thälmann affair (a corruption scandal involving Ernst Thälmann and his protégé, John Wittorf). After a series of escalating disagreements, the SCP declared its opposition. A dozen emissaries and instructors were sent to Switzerland between 1929 and 1932 in order to impose the Comintern's line. Among them were Eugen Fried, Julian Lenski (Leszczynski), Walter Ulbricht, Arthur Dombrowski, the Swiss Siegfried Bamatter, and Georgi Dimitrov, who was responsible for the Westeuropeische Büro in Berlin. Between May 1929 and December 1931 the party's leadership was reorganized five times. The effects of this "normalization" were catastrophic on all levels. The party lost Schaffhausen, one of its most important cantonal sections, its third daily newspaper, and one of its two seats on the National Council (a loss it barely could compensate for by regaining a seat in the canton of Zurich). The party militants remained demoralized, membership decreased, and the leadership was paralyzed. Given the extent of the crisis, Jules Humbert-Droz, excluded from the Comintern's secretariat, was sent to Switzerland in 1931 to put the party on the right track. But since he was opposed to the "social fascism" line and tied to the group of "conciliators," Humbert-Droz was removed during the Twelfth Extended Plenum in summer 1932. The Comintern imposed new changes in the SCP's leadership, but the situation did not stabilize, and new emissaries succeeded one another until 1935.

The shift to the Popular Front strategy gave the party some breathing room, but starting in late 1936 membership started to decline again. The SCP increasingly became marginalized, even though it moved closer to Léon Nicole's socialists in Geneva. In 1937 and 1938, it was banned in many Swiss cantons of French Switzerland and, at the end of 1940, throughout the country. According to some sources at that time the party did not have more than 350 members. After having survived underground for the rest of the war, the SCP was reconstituted in 1944 with the name Swiss Party of Labor, and for several years it was electorally successful, especially in the cantons of Geneva, Vaud, and Basel. But the Cold War and the Hungarian insurrection once again caused the party to lose most of the consensus it had gained.

See also Popular Front; Social Fascism.

FURTHER READING

Rauber, A. *Histoire du mouvement communiste suisse*. Vol. 1, *Du XIX siècle à 1943*. Vol. 2, *De 1944 à 1991*. Geneva: Slatkine, 1997–2000.

Stettler, P. *Die Kommunistische Partei der Schweiz, 1921–1931: ein Beitrag zur schweizerischen Parteiforschung und zur Geschichte der schweizerischen Arbeiterbewegung im Rahmen der Kommunistischen Internationale*. Bern: Francke, 1980.

Studer, B. *Un parti sous influence. Le Parti communiste suisse, une section du Komintern, 1931 à 1939*. Lausanne: Editions L'Age d'Homme, 1994.

BRIGITTE STUDER

Communist Party in the United States

In September 1919 two Communist parties formed in the United States. Reflecting the complex nature of the country's Left, as it had emerged in the early 20th century, the Communist Party of America was mostly composed of political organizations formed by Eastern European immigrants, while the Communist Labor Party was a gathering of the English-speaking socialist Left. The Communist movement in the United States at this time had about twenty to forty thousand members, and only about 10 percent spoke English. On the Comintern's orders the two organizations merged in 1921, as the Communist Party of the United States of America (CPUSA).

The party's history in the 1920s was marked, on the one hand, by intense government repression, and on the other hand, by a series of policies and tactics that had little to do with the country's reality, and instead reflected struggles within the Soviet leadership. This period of internal strife came to an end with the expulsion of Leon Trotsky's and Nikolay Bukharin's followers in 1928, including the party leader at the time, Jay Lovestone, the following year.

The Communist Party's influence and prestige in the United States reached its acme in the 1930s. Although in 1930, exhausted by the travails of the preceding years, the CPUSA had only about seventy-five hundred members, as the economic crisis deepened, the Communists organized and led struggles by workers, the unemployed, and African Americans. A new generation of militants emerged during the years from the Great Depression to the end of World War II. Although they were mainly immigrants' children, this new generation of Communists had been formed politically and culturally in the United States. Earl Browder, the party's secretary, thus attempted to create a revolutionary organization that reflected the country's complex social, cultural, and political reality—a process described as the "Americanization" of the CPUSA. The success of the CPUSA's policies in these years could be seen in its membership, which reached one hundred thousand, but also the increased prestige with which Communists were regarded in the workers' movement. Thanks to their organizational abilities, party cadres at the end of World War II led labor unions that represented about one-third of all the members of the Congress of Industrial Organizations.

A key element of the CPUSA's policy during this period was its support for Franklin Delano Roosevelt. The party considered the New Deal policies as indispensable to mitigate the consequences of the economic crisis on workers, guarantee the extension of labor legislation, and defend democratic institutions. This course reached its climax in 1944 with the decision by then-secretary Browder to support the Communists' participation in the two-party system in the United States, and his disbanding of the CPUSA as an independent electoral structure, replacing it with the Communist Political Association.

The reconstitution of the CPUSA on Moscow's orders in 1945 (followed by Browder's expulsion), under the leadership of William Foster, had disastrous results for the party. The abandonment of policies based on alliances with progressive forces and the return to a policy of rigid dogmatism led to a break with the left wing of the Democratic Party, and also the Communists' isolation within the labor union and liberal movements, right at the outset of the postwar anti-Communist campaigns. Between the late 1940s and mid-1950s, the U.S. government's campaign of arrests and persecutions of both leaders and simple militants weakened the party. The exodus from the CPUSA, however, took on significant dimensions after the failure—by many who had joined the party in the 1930s—to reform the party after the Hungarian events and the revelations of the Twentieth Congress of the CPSU. The events of 1956 and their consequences marked the definitive marginalization of the CPUSA from the U.S. political scene.

See also Browder, Earl; Grand Alliance, The; McCarthyism.

FURTHER READING

Buhle, M. J., P. Buhle, and D. Georgakas, ed. *Encyclopedia of the American Left*. New York: Oxford University Press, 1998.

Ottanelli, F. *The Communist Party of the United States: From the Depression to World War II*. New Brunswick, NJ: Rutgers University Press, 1991.

FRASER OTTANELLI

Communist Party in Vietnam

The Vietnamese Communist Party (VCP) has, like most other parties, created a standard history for itself, which is periodically revised. But it has never completely succumbed to the imposed truths of one paramount leader, as the Soviet party did to Stalin's version of history in 1938, or the Chinese did with Mao Zedong's views in 1945 with their *Resolution on Certain Questions of Party History*. The history of the VCP is a compromise among the views of different party factions, which often disagreed on policy. This makes it a vague and confusing narrative at different points, and leaves many lacunae in the record. The party marked its 75th birthday in 2005, but these gaps in its history still exist for periods of particular discord, such as the years from 1929 to 1938, when the Comintern's Sixth Congress policies on class war had a strong influence in Vietnam. Other periods for which our knowledge of VCP history is thin are the years 1947–51 and 1967–68. The VCP still has a monopoly on power and can use the accusation of "divulging party secrets" to imprison members without trial. The party's laws still take precedence over the SRV's constitution when it comes to the legal rights of the citizen. Thus it is not surprising that so few revelations come out of Hanoi or Ho Chi Minh City regarding the workings of the VCP and its past.

The official history of the VCP links its origins to the early career of Ho Chi Minh, from his adherence to the French Communist Party in 1920 in Paris, to his first contacts with the Comintern in Moscow, to his early training courses for patriotic émigrés in Guangzhou during the years of the United Front in southern China. His role in unifying competing Communist factions in February 1930 caused some friction at the time, as he had no specific instructions from the Comintern to act upon. But in 1964, when the party needed to emphasize unity as it prepared to do battle with the United States, his 1930 fence mending took on symbolic significance. Over the years Ho's image became the public face of the VCP—his ardent nationalism, his simple lifestyle, and his years as a worker on shipboard and in hotel kitchens. In the West most analysts assumed that Ho was the dominant leader, even though he was known to rule collegially. His demonizing by right wing commentators over the years is the result of this portrayal of Ho as the paramount leader of the party.

It should be noted that the Vietnamese Party has made several name changes over the years. From February to October 1930 it was known as the Vietnamese Communist Party; from October 1930 to 1951, on Comintern instructions, it was renamed the Indochinese Communist Party. In 1951 at the Second Party Congress it became the Workers' Party (Dang Lao Dong), and finally in 1976 when Vietnam was reunified it once again became the Vietnam Communist Party.

With new archival sources available in France, Russia, and Eastern Europe, our knowledge of the VCP has expanded to the point where it is possible to say that the history of the VCP is not coterminous with the biography of Ho Chi Minh. We can now see that although the VCP maintained a facade of unity over the years, Ho's power was often contested and overtaken by competing factions in the leadership. One of the major gaps in the party's history has been the failure to take account of the role of early Chinese Communist organizations within Vietnam. The whole idea of Chinese influence on the Vietnamese revolution became a taboo topic in the late 1970s, when Vietnam and China were in conflict. This influence has been a long-term factor in Vietnamese politics, however, and was at times at odds with Ho's desire to maintain his party's freedom of action.

French archives show that by 1927 the French Foreign Ministry was receiving reports about an Indochinese branch of the CCP's Nanyang or Southseas Committee, referred to as the Cochinchine-Cambodge branch. It was composed of Chinese resident in South Vietnamese ports and in Phnom Penh. That year overseas Chinese in southern Vietnam were involved in sending young Vietnamese to Canton for training, under the sponsorship of the GMD and Ho Chi Minh's Association of Revolutionary Youth, usually known as Thanh Nien. By 1928–29, after Ho had left China, the Chinese Left's influence seems to have become a more important factor. In those years when the Comintern presence in China was greatly reduced, Communist policy was more likely to filter to Vietnam via different CCP organizations connected to the Nanyang Committee or the Pan-Pacific Trade Union Congress than from Moscow or Paris. In fact, when the Comintern's Far Eastern Bureau (FEB) in Shanghai was instructed in 1929 to recruit young Southeast Asians for an anti-imperialist congress in Berlin, the European personnel said that they had no contacts with indigenous revolutionary youth organizations in Indochina or other countries of the region. The only possibility, they told Berlin, was to work through Chinese organizations in the region.

The issue of Chinese influence would become important in 1929, when an open split developed in the Thanh Nien association. One group, led by members in Tonkin, began a "proletarianization" campaign by sending its members to work in mines, plantations, and workshops. When one of their leaders, Ngo Gia Tu, came to Saigon in mid-1929, he concentrated on organizing the proletariat there. The hostility between this radical faction and the Thanh Nien central committee in Hong Kong was apparently not a passing phenomenon. Even after the two groups were unified by Ho Chi Minh in February 1930 and Chinese Communists in Vietnam were instructed by the Comintern to join the new VCP, tensions continued. From the events of the "Revolutionary High Tide" of 1930–31, when soviets were created in a number of villages in Vietnam's two north-central provinces of Nghe An and Ha Tinh, it appears that Li Lisan's policies for China had influenced some members of the new VCP. According to Comintern documents, the northern party committee, which controlled the lower-level committees in Nghe-Tinh, had demonstrated separatist tendencies and had refused to accept the Comintern's instructions. Although it has long been speculated that Ho Chi Minh was behind the soviet movement, he had been working to diminish Li Lisan's influence in Southeast Asia in the middle part of 1930, by forming a national CP in Malaya on the FEB's instructions. (He characterized many of the actions of the previous, CCP-linked party in Malaya as putchist and narrowly focused on the Chinese community.) He was clear about his preference for affiliating the new Vietnamese Party directly with Moscow, instead of making his party answerable to the Chinese CP's Central Committee. This was less a demonstration of pro-Soviet leanings than an expression of Ho's wish to retain some distance between his movement and the CCP.

The issue of Chinese residents in Vietnam joining the Vietnamese Party was a problem that did not go away in 1930. The CCP maintained a separate existence in southern Vietnam into the late 1940s, and in some areas its membership was significant. As late as 1949, French military intelligence captured a document in the Mytho Sector, which said that the central committees of the two parties, the CCP and the ICP, had agreed to make Chinese Party sections in Vietnam answerable to the ICP. If the Chinese and Vietnamese members of a section were equal in number, the section could be divided into two cells, under the command of the province committee. We can see, then, that there may have been an issue of divided allegiance among Communists in Vietnam.

It is useful to examine the leadership of the early radical faction in Vietnam, as there is a large degree of continuity between this group and the core of leftist leaders who controlled the party in North Vietnam from 1951 to 1956. This was a group that was strongly influenced by CCP policies on land reform and party rectification. Among these leaders were Le Van Luong and Hoang Quoc Viet, who lived together in Saigon in late 1929, along with Ngo Gia Tu, who died in an escape attempt from Con Son prison island. Truong Chinh (Dang Xuan Khu), party leader from 1941 to 1956 and briefly again in 1986, had worked with one of his schoolmates from Nam Dinh in 1929 to produce the labor union newspaper of the radical faction. This schoolmate was Nguyen Duc Canh, one of the instigators of the split in 1929 and one of the main leaders of the soviet movement in Nghe-Tinh.

When the party line from Moscow was supported by the CCP leadership, the Chinese influence within the Vietnamese Party was not necessarily divisive. From 1932 to the Seventh Comintern Congress and during the wartime anti-Fascist alliance of Chinese Nationalists and Communists, the mainstream of the Vietnamese Communist movement followed policies emanating from Moscow and endorsed in Beijing. (At times, of course, Trotskyism was a strong force in Vietnam's left-wing politics, and in southern Vietnam the Communist movement was splintered by a variety of factions.) The United Front politics of the Second World War led to the birth of the Viet Minh alliance, which saw Ho Chi Minh return to a position of influence in his party in 1941. Although not all Communists within Vietnam agreed with his policy that the national revolution should take precedence over the class revolution, the Viet Minh emerged from the war strengthened by their ties to the Allies. (Paradoxically, the August Revolution of 1945 was also facilitated by the initial noninterference of the defeated, but heavily armed, Japanese.) The Viet Minh came to stand for Vietnamese communism in the West, and the subsequent twists and turns of Vietnamese politics were often viewed by Western analysts as stage-managed political ploys.

But the fact is that the group of Communists who were Ho's closest collaborators in the Viet Minh, in particular Vo Nguyen Giap and Pham Van Dong, saw their power bases limited to the executive branch of government, while the more radical proponents of class struggle developed a strong base within the Communist Party, particularly after the party resurfaced in 1951 as the Workers' Party. After the failure of Ho's negotiations at Fontainbleau in 1946, and the French attack on Haiphong and Hanoi at the end of that year, Ho's conciliatory policies were subjected to strong criticism. As early as September 1946 Truong Chinh criticized a "lack of firmness in the repression of counterrevolutionary elements" as one of the weaknesses of the August seizure of power. He also called for rapid progress in carrying out the anti-feudal tasks of agrarian reform and moving to the construction of socialism. In 1949 the Viet Minh's former representative in Paris wrote to Moscow to complain about Ho's dissolution of the Communist Party in 1945 (albeit a temporary stratagem) and followed this up with a letter decrying the "Nationalist, petty-bourgeois element" which dominated his party. He blamed this on the "personality of Ho Chi Minh." Ho traveled to Moscow in 1950 after the CCP's victory, to seek aid and recognition from Stalin. As Khrushchev's memoirs reveal, Stalin treated Ho coldly and according to Chinese sources, it was only after Mao Zedong defended Ho's policies that Stalin was willing to endorse Ho's leadership. At this juncture, however, the Chinese were given responsibility for guiding Vietnam's revolution and they promised to send advisers to help the Vietnamese correct their "ideological shortcomings." The price of Mao's support was his domination of Vietnamese policy in the coming years.

In 1951 when the rebaptized party surfaced at the Second Party Congress, the party endorsed Ho's role as "the soul of the Vietnamese revolution" but awarded to Truong Chinh, the first secretary, the place of "builder and commander of the revolution." Around this time a number of intellectuals deserted the resistance, as the class policies of the party began to make them feel unwanted. The party rectification movement headed by Le Van Luong began in 1952 as a movement to educate the 90 percent of party members who came from petty bourgeois or peasant origins. But it developed into a witch hunt that attacked even old resistance cadres on the basis of their class origins. Recently one veteran party leader, Hoang Tung, has said that this campaign would have destroyed the party, had it not been halted in 1956, after the Soviet Twentieth Party Congress. The land reform had also got out of hand, with increasing violence being shown to those classified as landlords. Vo Nguyen Giap's apology for the excesses of the land reform in October 1956 restored some faith in the party and was a moral victory for him personally. But it did not win him friends in leftist party circles. After Truong Chinh's demotion, in 1957 a cadre with long experience in the south, Le Duan, as a compromise was named first secretary. This assignment was confirmed at the Third Party Congress in 1960.

The Vietnamese Communist leadership retained its facade of unity by adhering to the Bolshevik discipline instilled in the Soviet party under Lenin and Stalin. The beginning of the U.S. escalation in 1964 made political cohesion all the more important, and the call for "Dai Doan Ket" (Greater Solidarity) became an important wartime slogan. But it appears that at different periods from 1956 onward, this unity was maintained by fear. At two different periods during the American war, in 1963–64 and then again in 1967–68, heavy pressure was brought to bear on party members associated with the revisionist policies of Khrushchev. A number were removed from positions of power at the time of the Ninth Plenum in December 1963; in the late summer and autumn of 1967 another wave of "anti-revisionism," stoked by fears of a Soviet coup plot, swept through the party. This time around three hundred mainly mid-level cadres were arrested, in what became known as the Anti-Party Affair. At least two of those arrested had served on General Giap's staff at Dien Bien Phu, and those who lived to tell the story of their interrogations report that they were closely questioned about Giap's activities. Giap himself departed for Hungary for medical treatment, the Hungarian archives reveal. Once the Tet offensive had forced the United States to announce a suspension of bombing in the north, negotiations did begin in Paris and the tensions of the Anti-Party affair abated. But those arrested remained in prison until 1972–73 and then were kept under house arrest until 1978.

Today these ideological struggles of the 1950s and 1960s are still barely discussed in Hanoi. The VCP went through a period of alliance with the USSR against China in 1978–89 and is now once again a fairly close ideological ally of the CCP. But the inner workings of the party have mainly been made known via the memoirs and open letters of disaffected cadres, especially those who were imprisoned in 1967. Even though communism is no longer a guiding force in Vietnam's daily life, the old factions continue to exist, transmuted into regional power blocs and groups with differing views on the nature of economic and political reform. These reforms began in 1986 under the leadership of Nguyen Van Linh and are known as *Doi Moi* (Change for the New). A period of intellectual glasnost also occurred during Linh's tenure, but it came to a sudden end in 1989 with the death of communism in Eastern Europe. When in 1991 veteran northern leader Do Muoi became party chief, the VCP moved closer to the policies of the CCP: political conservatism and economic liberalization. Since then the government technocrats and economists associated with the southerners Vo Van Kiet and Phan Van Khai, a former and current prime minister, have come to represent the forces more open to the West and reform. The two most recent VCP general secretaries, Le Kha Phieu and Nong Duc Manh, have not been thought to wield much power. Certain branches of the military are now seen as the defenders of class interests and the state-run economy. There are numerous calls for reform and democratization coming from within the party, however, and it seems only a matter of time before the anachronism that the VCP has become will be transformed. In the meantime, it has erected a new ideology for itself, extracted from the writings and life of Ho Chi Minh: Ho Chi Minh Thought.

See also Ho Chi Minh; Marxism-Leninism; Vietnam War.

FURTHER READING

Boudarel, G. "L'idéocratie importée au Vietnam avec le maoisme." In *La Bureaucratie au Vietnam,* 31–106. Paris: L'Harmattan, 1983.

Duiker, W. *The Communist Road to Power in Vietnam*. Boulder, CO: Westview Press, 1996.

Moise, E. E. *Land Reform in China and North Vietnam*. Chapel Hill: University of North Carolina Press, 1983.

Quinn-Judge, S. "Rethinking the History of the Vietnamese Communist Party." In *Rethinking Vietnam*, ed. D. McCargo, 27–39. London: Routledge Curzon, 2004.

Turley, W. S., ed. *Vietnamese Communism in Comparative Perspective*. Boulder, CO: Westview Press, 1980.

Vasavakul, T. "Vietnam: The Changing Models of Legitimation." In *Political Legitimacy in Southeast Asia: The Quest for Moral Authority*, ed. M. Alagappa, 257–89. Stanford, CA: Stanford University Press, 1995.

SOPHIE QUINN-JUDGE

Communist Party in Yemen

Yemen, in 2004 a country with a population of close to 20 million at the southwest corner of the Arabian Peninsula, was the site of one of the most profound social and political upheavals of the 1960s and 1970s in the Middle East. Its then separate southern region, known as South Yemen or in colonial times as Aden or South Arabia, was the scene for the only example of a Marxist regime in the Arab world, the People's Democratic Republic of Yemen. The PDRY lasted from the British withdrawal from Aden in November 1967 until the merger of the PDRY with its former Cold War rival in the north into a single Republic of Yemen in May 1990.

The area known as Yemen was in modern times divided into a more populous, independent, and traditionally autocratic North Yemen, with its capital at Sanaa, and the more developed British-ruled area of South Yemen, with its capital at Aden. The modern revolutionary politics of Yemen begin with a radical Nationalist, anticlerical, and "anti-feudalist" revolution against the ruling imams, on September 26, 1962. This was followed by eight years of civil war in which Nasserite Egypt, backed by the Soviet Union, fought a rebel republican force supported by Saudi Arabia and Britain. Within this context, the republican forces included many intellectuals, civil servants, and members of the popular militias, who were influenced by radical anti-imperialism and Marxism, as much Chinese as Soviet. Their influence was only contained with the defeat of Left forces in 1968, a process that led to end of the civil war, with the peace agreement of 1970 between republicans and royalists. For twelve years thereafter, however, radical social forces and Marxist intellectuals, grouped first in the Revolutionary Democratic Party and then in the Yemeni Socialist Movement, continued guerrilla warfare, with the backing of the South Yemeni state, against successive governments in Sanaa.

The radicalization of South Yemen followed, between 1963 and 1967, in what has been termed the "Cuban Path." A small pro-Soviet Marxist group had existed in Aden since the 1950s. The Popular Democratic Union led by Abdullah Badhib, the stronger left-wing force that emerged in the guerrilla war of the 1960s came, as it had done in North Yemen, from the radicalization of hitherto pro-Egyptian Arab nationalism. This initiallly had less to do with the influence of the Soviet Union and more to with the ideological crisis of pan-Arabism of the mid-1960s, a rejection of what these radicals saw as the "capitulationist" conduct of Egypt vis-à-vis the royalists in North Yemen and in the Palestine context. Out of this ideological turmoil and the war in North Yemen, the National Liberation Front, originally set up with Egyptian support, came to adopt more radical positions. When it took power with the British withdrawal in November 1967 its more radical wing, initially on the defensive, proclaimed itself "Marxist-Leninist," as did its cognate groups among the Palestinians, the PFL and PDFLP. A process of Sovi-

etization then occurred with the emergence in 1978 of an orthodox "ruling party of the new type." But factionalism continued within the party and regime, and in 1986 a bloody outbreak of violence among party members and the armed forces seriously weakened the regime. By the late 1980s, ideologically exahusted, and with the USSR no longer able to sustain it, the PDRY, which had always espoused the popular slogan of "Yemeni Unity," sought a phased merger with North Yemen. Little now remains of the Socialist and Communist period in Yemen. The YSP failed to maintain its influence within the united Yemen and in 1994 the north launched an invasion of the south that effectively ended YSP control of the administration there. While the YSP remains one of the three legitimate parties in Yemen, it is confined in influence to some urban areas and to regions of the former PDRY to the north of Aden. The policy of the ruling elements within Yemen is to blot out the history of socialism and reform in the south and to cast the YSP as agents of a foreign power, alternatively the USSR or Britain.

Within the broader context of Communist and "Socialist-oriented" states of the period, the PDRY was marked by four striking characteristics. One was its extreme factionalism, a trend that, despite the best efforts of the Soviets, continued to erupt. Second was its revolutionary internationalism, as evident in the commitment to exporting revolution to North Yemen (up to 1982), to Saudi Arabia (to 1975), and, in a ten-year guerrilla war in the neighboring province of Dhofar, to Oman (1965–75). Third was the attempt to introduce radical, Soviet-influenced social and economic reforms into a very poor and underresourced economy. Finally, and despite all the importing and sometimes imposition of ideological models derived from the Marxist-Leninist trend in the Palestinian resistance movement, the USSR or China, South Yemeni politics exhibited a vivacious, indigenous radicalism that reasserted itself. Whatever else, the experiment in the PDRY produced two slogans unique in the annals of modern communism and revolutions: "Arm the Women!" and "Long Live the Alliance of Workers, Peasants, Fishermen, Beduin and Nomads!"

See also Anti-imperialism; Islam; Marxism-Leninism; Nationalism.

FURTHER READING

Halliday, F. *Arabia without Sultans*. Reprint. London: Saqi, 2000 [1974].
Lackner, Helen. *PDR Yemen: Socialist Outpost in Arabia*. London: Ithaca Press, 1980.

Naumkin, Vitali. *Red Wolves of Arabia*. Reading: Garnett, 2004.

FREDERICK HALLIDAY

Communist Party in Yugoslavia

The Communist Party of Yugoslavia (CPYu) was created in April 1919 by combining a number of other parties and organizations. Most of the latter belonged to the left wing of the Social Democratic movement and were based in the various national territories brought together on December 1, 1918, to form Yugoslavia, which until 1929 was officially called the Kingdom of the Serbs, Croats, and Slovenes, and then was renamed the Kingdom of Yugoslavia. The party was composed of separate Communist groups that had come into being through the influence of revolutionary events in Russia and Hungary. This new party, first called the Socialist Workers' Party of Yugoslavia (Communists), and then in June 1920 renamed the CPYu, joined the Comintern.

In the ferment of left-wing protests and currents that emerged after World War I among a large segment of the lower classes, particularly in the cities, the CPYu soon gained a predominant influence in the Yugoslav workers' movement. In the elections to the Constituent Assembly in November 1920 it came in third among parties in its number of deputies. The government authorities, frightened by the CPYu's success on the ballot, its revolutionary declarations, and particularly the major strikes it helped organize, prohibited Communist activities in 1920, albeit at first only temporarily—a ban that caught the party completely unaware. Then, in 1921, attempts by certain activists against the lives of highly placed figures in the ruling circles led to the even harsher Law for the Provision of Public Security and Order in the State, driving the CPYu underground. The Independent Workers' Party of Yugoslavia, which was formed in January 1923 as a legal cover for CPYu activity, was also banned after a year and a half. Many members of the CPYu were imprisoned; others were subjected to repression and forced to emigrate.

Now illegal, the CPYu continually decreased in size and its influence fell sharply. For a long time it was largely absent from the Yugoslav political scene, although it did demonstrate some activity, mostly in left-wing trade unions, which would be banned off and on by the authorities. The CPYu's central leadership was forced to emigrate, and its makeup was changed frequently by orders from the Executive Committee of the Comintern International. The CPYu personnel that did remain were rent by the internal struggle of its groups ("factions"), which kept accusing each other of "right-wing" or "left-wing" opportunism. Each of these factions tried to enlist the Executive Committee's support, which would then provide them with directives that always followed any changes in Soviet policies. Specifically, the Executive Committee pressured the CPYu, first in the mid-1920s to support a partition of the multinational Yugoslav state, which Moscow regarded as a link in the "anti-Soviet cordon sanitaire," and then later as the threat from Hitler increased to support a united Yugoslavia, though one that would respect the rights of the separate nationalities.

During the second half of the 1930s, most of the leading figures of the CPYu in the USSR (Filip Filipovic, Sima Markovic, Vladimir Copic, and others) perished in the Stalinist purges, as did the party chief at that time, Milan Gorkic, who had been specially summoned from Paris to Moscow. The new party leadership, finalized in November 1940, was assumed by Josip Broz Tito, who became the general secretary. The creation of the new leadership, now no longer in emigration but in Yugoslavia itself, coincided with the rise of general left-wing inclinations in the country, enabling the underground CPYu to become more active, and grow in size and influence.

This surge proved important when Yugoslavia was occupied by the Fascists in April 1941. The CPYu succeeded in organizing a large-scale partisan movement for the country's liberation and emerged as the victor in the Yugoslav civil strife that broke out during the last years of the war. As a result, when the country was liberated in 1944–45, a Communist regime was established, and the Federal Republic of Yugoslavia was proclaimed (to be renamed the Socialist Federal Republic of Yugoslavia in 1963). The CPYu—now with a monopoly of power, many times larger, and with stern internal discipline—was transformed from a mere party to the principal political and administrative structure of the regime.

Right after World War II, the Communist leadership of Yugoslavia, led by Tito, followed Soviet policies within both the party and the international arena. Its territorial ambitions and desire for hegemony in the Balkans soon brought it into conflict with the Kremlin's interests. This resulted in the Soviet-Yugoslav quarrel of 1948, and the expulsion of the CPYu from the world Communist movement and Yugoslavia from the Soviet bloc. In the face of Stalin's attack against the Yugoslav leadership, the CPYu managed to stand fast. It kept control of the party-state apparatus, and retained the support of most of the party and its supporters. The party's reprisals enabled it to suppress the discernible but small segment of the population that held out for pro-Moscow positions.

The circumstances resulting from the conflict with the Kremlin had, by the first half of the 1950s, brought about significant changes in the political direction of the Yugoslav Communist regime. These changes, in turn, facilitated the gradual development of a Yugoslav model of socialist evolution that was to last almost to the end of Communist rule there.

The earliest and most important changes were in Yugoslavia's foreign policy. Finding itself not only outside of but under severe pressure from the Soviet bloc, which included an economic blockade and the danger of military attack, the Yugoslav regime was forced to pursue a partial rapprochement with the Western powers. The West provided Yugoslavia with the economic and military aid necessary for its survival, including against the Stalinist threat. At the same time, the Yugoslav leadership strove to maintain a certain distance in its relations with the West. It tried to sustain a neutral stance in its defense of small nations as well as its disagreement with the confrontation between the Soviet and Western blocs.

When, after Stalin's death, the Kremlin moved toward a rapprochement with Yugoslavia, Tito began to maneuver between the two blocs, following a policy of partial cooperation when it benefited the Yugoslav regime, yet aloofness or even opposition when this better suited Belgrade's interests. This maneuvering, in spite of occasional twists and turns depending on the international situation, remained unchanged until Tito's death in 1980, and during the post-Tito decade of Communist power as well. An integral part of this strategy was the so-called nonalignment (no bloc) policy, begun in the mid-1950s by Yugoslavia, India, and Egypt, leading in the early 1960s to the Non-Aligned Movement of what was then a large number of states. As one of the main leaders of this movement, Yugoslavia became an influential political player in the international area, far out of proportion to its actual economic and military might.

The nonaligned orientation of the Communist leadership of Yugoslavia was combined, however, with its active support of a number of radical nationalist and left-wing regimes and movements in the third world, including some that resorted to military action or terrorist acts against the countries of the West and Israel. In certain cases, the Yugoslavs even rendered secret assistance to terrorist groups all too prepared to take advantage of aid proferred by the nonaligned regimes and movements.

In the area of domestic affairs, the Yugoslav leaders, starting in the early 1950s, embarked on a policy of maintaining the totalitarian basis of their power, yet with significant steps toward reform, which in many cases were imposed on them by internal circumstances. For one thing, the regime halted the forced collectivization of the peasantry—a practice borrowed from Soviets, and one that caused political and economic complications in the country. As a result, alongside the partially established collectives of the so-called social sector, private farms continued to exist and indeed remained preeminent in the agricultural sphere throughout Communist rule.

Another step toward reform was the introduction of "self-governing labor collectives" in state-run enterprises (even during the first years of Communist power these collectives were formed in almost all industrial enterprises, transportation, and a large part of the trade structure) and "public self-government" in local territorial administrative units. At first this measure, officially regarded as a move toward "authentic socialism" and an alternative to the Stalinist "bureaucratic distortion of Marxism-Leninism," was more for effect than anything else, and its practical significance lay in the fact that it offered an ideological counterweight within Communist doctrine to the Soviet conception of socialism. But its stake in a maximal industrial growth, which would satisfy the country's needs and thereby strengthen the regime, impelled the Yugoslav leadership to make realistic departures from the model it had inherited from the Soviet Union: ineffective, centrally administered state control of the economic sector. By the end of the 1950s, and particularly into the 1960s, these departures led to a serious dismantling of the Soviet model and its gradual replacement by another one, in which enterprises would receive greater independence in their economic activities, and there would even be certain market relationships established between them. Furthermore, even those functions of administrative economic control and regulation that remained in the state system would be increasingly transferred from central government organs to regional and local authorities.

These transformations, which signaled economic liberalization, had previously been carried out under the banner of increasing the self-government of the workers and public. But with the absence of political democracy and the impossibility of any public self-organization independent of the authorities, the result of the reforms was not so much the acquisition of any real rights by "labor collectives" or citizens in local territorial units, as it was the strengthening of the role and power of the regional or local party and state authorities and the upper echelons in the separate enterprises.

The reform of the political structure began formally in the early 1950s, and until the end of Communist power it remained a work in progress. Even Yugoslavia's Constitution was changed three times during that period: in 1953, when the so-called Constitutional Law replaced the 1946 Constitution; and then in 1963 and 1974, when new constitutions were approved. The reforms in the political sphere, however, except for purely propagandistic gestures, amounted only to changes in the structure and organization of state organs at various levels, and a mere redistribution of functions among them. They never involved the fundamental bases of the existing one-party regime and what was effectively the monopoly of power of the party-state bureaucracy.

In November 1952, at the height of the confrontation with Stalin, at the Sixth Congress of the CPYu, the Yugoslav leadership denounced the Soviet system as a departure from the socialism perpetrated by the ruling bureaucracy of the USSR. It rejected the notion that the CPYu was an unmediated operational leader that issued direct orders for governance of the state administration and public life. It publicly declared that the party would implement its policies regarding the development of state and society through its own political and ideological activity—hence, through persuasion—and that it was therefore the party's educational role that was of paramount importance. In accordance with this new role, the party was even renamed the Union of Communists of Yugoslavia (UCYu). Yet the ruling circles of the UCYu moved almost immediately to make sure that the implied reforms would not actually take place. And Milovan Djilas's attempt to not only realize the policies adopted at the Sixth Congress but also achieve an increasing democratization of the UCYu resulted in his removal from the leadership in January 1954. The subsequent history of the Communist regime was marked by periods of repression within the UCYu itself and against the populace, alternating with more liberal periods, although under the regime's strict control. These fluctuations were accompanied by internal, mostly covert struggles atop the pyramid of power between adherents of the opposing tendencies. These struggles were often entwined with personal or group rivalries for power. The most notable event, and with the greatest impact on the public, was the removal from the party-state leadership in mid-1966 of Aleksandar Ranković, who had been one of Tito's closest associates, and the subsequent purges in state security organs and the police, which had long been under Ranković's control.

From the mid-1960s, the Yugoslav political stage began to be occupied by the problem of relations between the national republics. Up to that period, the Communist regime had tried to assure equal rights among the nationalities and keep potential conflicts among them from coming to a head. The federative system, officially introduced when Communist power was established and the country divided into six republics (with two autonomous republics in the largest of them, Serbia), long remained mostly a formality, though. The government was in fact rigidly centralized, with actual power in the hands of Tito and his top deputies. Manifestations of specifically national or ethnic-regional aspirations, particularly those of a political nature, were contradictory to the ideas and interests of the Communist leadership, the stability of the country in general, or worse, the existence of the regime—and all such displays were regarded by the regime as nationalistic and were categorically suppressed, sometimes, if seen as particularly hostile, with harsh methods. During approximately the first two postwar decades, nationalist aspirations mostly came from those who were opposed or hostile to Communist rule. But by the mid-1960s and the period that followed, the ruling Communist elites in the various Yugoslav republics began to emerge as standard-bearers of their regional or ethnic interests. This changed the situation fundamentally, because it threatened to weaken and undermine the existing system from within. As long as Tito remained in power, his charismatic authority enabled him to counteract this "communist nationalism." When, for example, in 1971 mass demonstrations broke out in Croatia, with the partial support and participation of the Croatian leadership, and the goal of gaining semi-independent status for the republic, Tito replaced the leadership altogether. Still, even under Tito, during the second half of the 1960s and the 1970s the regional Communist elites were able to bring about an expansion of the powers of the republics and autonomous regions. Yugoslavia's federative system was now not strictly formal but real. The approval of the Constitution of 1974 gave the two autonomous republics in Serbia (Kosovo and Vojvodina), though they still remained a part of Serbia, a status near that of the regular republics. The same federalization took place in the UCYu: It transformed itself into an association of six republican and two regional organizations, thereby acquiring greater independence and parity in the central organs of the party.

This federalization became obvious in the 1980s when, after Tito's death, the government of Yugoslavia lost its center of gravity; before then, Yugoslavia had stood above the republics and autonomous regions, and was largely independent of them. But with the beginning of the post-Tito period, serious conflicts arose, both among the component parts of the federation (notably in the areas of economics and finance) and among the nationalities within the various republics, which were themselves largely multinational. With the worsening economic position of the country overall, largely due to a huge external debt that had to be paid off, the interregional and interethnic conflicts assumed an increasingly political character. The most important catalyst in the emerging strife was the crisis in the autonomous republic of Kosovo where, although the overwhelming majority of people were Albanians, the small Serbian minority remained dominant. A nationalist movement quickly developed among the Albanians, who now lobbied for complete separation from Serbia, and acceptance of their own Yugoslav republic with full and equal rights. Mass demonstrations in 1968 and 1981 in support of these goals were put down by force. As the 1980s progressed, however, an increasing number of Serbs were driven out of Kosovo by physical and psychological pressure from the Albanian population and its officials. The Albanian majority in the party-state leadership of the region supported this process or even actively promoted it. Slobodan Milošević, who had taken over the leadership of Serbia in 1986, responded to this by placing the two semi-independent autonomous regions of Serbia (Vojvodina as well as Kosovo) under his strict control. In order to compel the Yugoslav government to make the decisions necessary for this radical restructuring, the Serbian leadership resorted to various power plays. In the case of both Kosovo and Vojvodina, and the Republic of Montenegro as well, these moves succeeded, but they provoked strong opposition in most of the other Yugoslav republics. Intense fighting over mutual relationships within the federation necessitated a fundamental restructuring, and this inevitability led to the dissolution of the UCYu. In early 1990, the party organizations of the republics of Slovenia and Croatia reconstituted themselves as independent parties, and the parties of the other republics soon did likewise. The UCYu's collapse brought about the fall of the Communist regime. Yugoslavia broke up in 1992, setting the stage for the ensuing wars among the various nationalities.

See also Djilas, Milovan; Kardelj, Edvard; Nationalism; Nonalignment; People's Democracy; Soviet-Yugoslavia Break; Tito, Josip Broz.

FURTHER READING

Lampe, J. *Yugoslavia as History: Twice There Was a Country.* Cambridge, UK: Cambridge University Press, 2002.

Pirjevec, J. *Il giorno di San Vito: Jugoslavia 1918–1992, Storia di una tragedia.* Turin: Nuova Eri, 1993.

LEONID JA. GIBJANSKIJ

Conference on Security and Cooperation in Europe

Rooted in the Soviet advocacy of "collective security" during the 1930s, the idea of a European security conference was first raised in 1954 by Soviet foreign minister Vyacheslav Molotov in an effort to disrupt the U.S.-sponsored European Defense Community project. After the project's failure had deprived the idea of topical interest, Moscow renewed the call for the conference in 1966, when a crisis within the Western alliance opened up the prospect of excluding the United States from Europe while isolating West Germany. But the resolution of the crisis along with the onset of one within the Soviet Union's own alliance delayed active pursuit of the conference project until after the 1968 Soviet intervention in Czechoslovakia.

The advent of East-West détente, the weakening of the United States by the Vietnam War, and the threat of a Soviet-Chinese war provided the background of the March 1969 Budapest appeal by Soviet bloc leaders to convene what subsequently became known as the Conference on Security and Cooperation in Europe (CSCE). Conceived as a forum from which discussion of troops and armaments would be excluded, the conference was designed to obtain international recognition of Europe's post–World War II territorial and political status quo and create conditions for the mergence there of a new security system that the Soviet Union could dominate.

Unlike the previous initiatives, the Budapest appeal envisaged convening a conference of all European states, without preconditions, and keeping the door open for U.S. and Canadian participation as well. Moscow initially sought an early meeting at the highest level, which would endorse general principles of interstate relations, and a system of follow-up conferences suitable to shape the discussion of security and cooperation in accordance with Soviet hegemonic aspirations. The United States under the Richard Nixon administration regarded the project as a trap, and made the acceptance of it contingent on progress in arms control. But most of Washington's Western European allies as well as the Soviet allies perceived the CSCE as an opportunity to demilitarize the East-West rivalry while asserting their particular interests through multilateral negotiations that would reduce the influence of the superpowers.

During the preparatory talks, which lasted until 1975, the countries of the European Economic Community acted for the first time as a group in international negotiations. They engaged the Soviet side in a protracted debate, which resulted in precise agreements on a whole range of nonmilitary issues pertinent to security. These were spelled out in the Helsinki Final Act of August 1, 1975, which balanced general principles and specific provisions, particularly on human rights. Known as "Basket Three," the provisions included such rights as the freedom of movement of people and ideas, the denial of which was a mainstay of the repressive Soviet system.

The Final Act thus embodied the revolutionary principle that the way sovereign states treat their own citizens is a legitimate concern of other states because of its bearing on international security. Although not legally binding, the document carried weight as a voluntary declaration of intentions, which affected political credibility. The Basket Three provisions, regarded by Moscow as paper provisions that no one would expect it to honor, assumed political substance once they were effectively invoked by dissidents challenging the Soviet-style regimes.

The ensuing "Helsinki process" enabled the participating states to review each other's performance. The U.S. government turned into an active promoter of the CSCE under pressure from public opinion and Congress, which demanded holding the Soviet Union to its commitments. The Congressional Commission on Security and Cooperation in Europe and a variety of human rights advocacy groups provided unprecedented input into foreign policies that had thus far been an exclusive domain of officials. During the first follow-up conference in Belgrade, in 1977–78, the United States took the lead in exposing human right abuses by the Soviet Union, which resisted by invoking the Helsinki principle of noninterference in internal affairs.

The expansion and redefinition of security by including its nonmilitary aspects was the CSCE's novel contribution to the conduct of international relations, which assumed particular significance once détente began to falter in the late 1970s. During the lengthy follow-up conference in Madrid in 1980–83, Soviet representatives in effect accepted the Western security agenda by challenging the West's own record on human rights rather than taking shelter behind the noninterference clause. At the same time, it sought to divert attention from the Western notions of human rights, with their emphasis on individual freedoms, toward material rights, which were supposedly well provided for by Communist states, and even the "right" to survival in the face of the threat of war. Critics charged the Soviet Union with holding its citizens' human rights hostage to détente, as if this were the sole alternative to nuclear annihilation.

Moscow's advocacy of "military détente" served to refocus the CSCE from nonmilitary security to the arms race. In Madrid, the Warsaw Pact countries proposed a conference that would supplement the unproductive Mutual and Balanced Force Reduction talks between the two alliances with a multinational forum that could exploit widespread Western European opposition to the North Atlantic Treaty Organization's modernization program to reverse the program without jeopardizing the Warsaw Pact's own military buildup. But once the conference met in Stockholm in 1984, it concentrated on the Western agenda of "confidence-building measures" that would make a resort to force more difficult, such as the advance notification of troop movements and the presence of observers at military exercises.

The success in Stockholm presaged new Soviet thinking on security, subsequently implemented by the Mikhail Gorbachev leadership. The changes underscored the importance of reassuring the West about Soviet intentions for the sake of the country's own security as well as improving its human rights record to better qualify for admission into the "common European house." Those had been two key issues pioneered and promoted by the CSCE.

Following the adoption by the Warsaw Pact of a defensive military doctrine in 1987, the merging of the confidence-building measures and the Mutual and Balanced Force Reduction talks into the CSCE review conference in Vienna resulted finally in a radical reduction of troops and armaments on the continent as well as the end of military confrontation there. The agreements on the limitation of conventional forces laid the foundations of Europe's remarkably successful "security architecture" in the aftermath of the Cold War.

Another turning point was reached in 1989, when the government of Hungary, pleading the primacy of its CSCE commitments over its commitments to the Warsaw Pact, opened its western borders to the outflow of East German defectors. The decision precipitated the crisis leading to the collapse of the Berlin Wall, Communist rule in Eastern Europe, and Soviet domination of the area.

Within the unique setting of the Cold War, the CSCE demonstrated the growing importance of "soft power" at the expense of military power, the potential of multilateral diplomacy in limiting the excesses of power politics, and the relevance of individual citizens and their groups in shaping the security policies of states. These accomplishments, however, remained largely limited to Europe. Once institutionalized, the Organization for Security and Cooperation in Europe declined in importance as one of many international organizations. The CSCE ideas and experience in the promotion of security and human rights were nevertheless absorbed by many of these organizations—the European Union, the Council of Europe, and the North Atlantic Treaty Organization—and helped to inspire grassroots political movements, such as the "colored revolutions" in Georgia or Ukraine in the early 21st century.

See also Dissent in the USSR; Ostopolitik; Socialist Camp; Soviet Bloc; Warsaw Pact.

FURTHER READING

Andréani, J. *Le Piège: Helsinki et la chute du communisme.* Paris: Jacob, 1995.

Ghebali, V.-Y. *La diplomatie de la détente: la CSCE, 1973–1989.* Brussels: Bruylant, 1989.

Lehne, S. *The Vienna Meeting of the Conference on Security and Cooperation in Europe, 1986–1989: A Turning Point in East-West Relations.* Boulder, CO: Westview, 1991.

Maresca, J. J. *To Helsinki: The Conference on Security and Cooperation in Europe, 1973–1975.* Durham, NC: Duke University Press, 1985.

Mastny, V. *Helsinki, Human Rights, and European Security, 1975–1985: Analysis and Documentation.* Durham, NC: Duke University Press, 1986.

———. *The Helsinki Process and the Reintegration of Europe, 1986–1991: Analysis and Documentation.* New York: New York University Press, 1992.

Meneguzzi Rostagni, C., ed. *The Helsinki Process: A Historical Reappraisal.* Padua: Cedam, 2005.

Thomas, D. C. *The Helsinki Effect: International Norms, Human Rights, and the Demise of Communism.* Princeton, NJ: Princeton University Press, 2001.

Wenger, A., V. Mastny, and C. Nünlist, eds. *Origins of the European Security System: The Helsinki Process Revisited, 1965–75.* London: Routledge, 2008.

VOJTECH MASTNY

Constitutions

Like most modern states, the Communist states were formally all governed by written constitutions. These documents, like their non-Communist counterparts, outlined the formal structure of the state institutions—legislative, executive, and judicial—that together comprised the institutional structure through which the state was governed. Formal lines of accountability and descriptions of the power of the various institutions were spelled out in these documents, giving an appearance of the primacy of law in these countries. The constitutions also often spelled out a series of rights, including rights to a variety of welfare provisions that reflected the regime's formal commitment to the construction of a socialist society and distinguished these constitutions from those of their non-Communist counterparts. These were therefore ideological rather than strictly legal documents.

This is reflected in the way in which each constitution described its particular state. The commitment to a Marxist teleology meant that the description of the state changed as it developed along that teleological line. Thus, the Soviet Union was described as a "socialist state of workers and peasants" in the 1936 constitution and a "socialist state of the whole people" in the constitution of 1977, while many of the newly founded postwar states of Eastern Europe were initially depicted "people's democracies"; Albania, China, and Vietnam called themselves "dictatorships of the proletariat." The inclusion of these ideological labels in the constitutions meant that when the country was perceived to have developed out of that stage, either amendment of the constitution or the introduction of a new constitution was necessary.

Amendment of the constitution generally was, in formal terms, at the discretion of the legislature, although the introduction of a new constitution often required a popular referendum. Constitutions were usually easy to change, requiring only majority support in the relevant legislature, and given that the legislature was controlled by the Communist Party, this was never a problem. This reflects the way in which the constitutions had little normative authority and were not accurate representations of the distribution of power in the society. Real power in the Communist state rested with the Communist Party, which used the political institutions of the state in an instrumental fashion. No state constitution clearly spelled out the party's role, although it could be hinted at, as in the 1977 Soviet Constitution, which referred to its "leading and guiding" role in the society.

Although the constitution was instrumental and used by the ruling party elite as a means of consolidating its control, it was important symbolically. For the Communist rulers, it was important to be recognized as the rulers of a modern state the equal of those capitalist states that opposed it, and the constitution bolstered such a claim. It also enabled them to maintain that the rule of law actually applied in these societies—a crucial assertion in the context of the cold war competition that prevailed throughout the postwar period when most of the Communist states came into existence. It also gave a formal anchoring to law and legislation within the country, and thereby provided a source of formal legitimacy. In these ways, the constitution was much more important in a symbolic sense than in a practical one. In most cases when Communist regimes fell, these constitutions were replaced rather than simply amended.

See also Citizenship; Dictatorship of the Proletariat; Elections; Single-Party System; State.

FURTHER READING

Brunner, G. "The Functions of Communist Constitutions: An Analysis of Recent Constitutional Developments." *Review of Socialist Law* 3 (1977): 121–53.

Triska, Jan F. *Constitutions of the Communist Party States.* Stanford, CA: Hoover Institution Press, 1968.

Unger, Aryeh L. *Constitutional Development in the USSR: A Guide to the Soviet Constitutions.* London: Methuen and Co., 1981.

GRAEME GILL

Containment

Containment was the strategy by which the United States waged the Cold War. It had a variety of meanings at its inception, and evolved over the forty-five years of its existence. The key goals of containment were to limit the spread of Soviet power and Communist ideology. Yet containment was never a defensive strategy; it was conceived as an instrument to achieve victory in the Cold War.

At the end of World War II, President Harry S. Truman and his advisers possessed no clear strategic vision. Truman said that he wanted to get along with the Soviet Union, but he also acknowledged that cooperation meant that the United States should get its way 85 percent of the time. Truman sometimes denounced Soviet perfidy, yet he said that he yearned for peace as well and could negotiate deals with Stalin, the Soviet dictator.

In early 1946, the diplomat George F. Kennan helped to clarify the situation. Kennan was a career foreign service official, one of America's first Russian experts. Toward the end of the war, he returned to the U.S. embassy in Moscow as a chargé d'affaires. He admired Russian culture and loved Russian literature, but he abhorred Stalin and detested communism. Communism, Kennan thought, had corrupted all that was good in the Russian past. Communists simply wanted to aggrandize their power and impose their will wherever they could. When asked for his interpretation of Soviet policy in February 1946, Kennan sent an eight-thousand-word telegram to Washington, DC. Known as the "long" telegram, Kennan wrote that Soviet leaders exploited the idea of capitalist encirclement in order to justify their totalitarian rule at home. The Soviets would seek to expand everywhere. They would not negotiate in good faith. They understood only the logic of force.

Kennan's telegram was greeted with enthusiasm in Washington. His hard-line attitudes resonated with many influential career diplomats at the U.S. Department of State and many leading officials in the Pentagon. When General George F. Marshall became secretary of state in early 1947, he asked Kennan to head a new Policy Planning Staff in the Department of State.

Kennan was encouraged to disseminate his views widely. In July 1947, he wrote an article in *Foreign Affairs,* the most prestigious journal of international relations in the United States. Titled "The Sources of Soviet Conduct," Kennan's piece argued that "the political personality of Soviet power as we know it today is the product of ideology and circumstances." Soviet leaders were dedicated Marxists. They yearned for power and hoped to expand wherever they could. The political action of the Kremlin, wrote Kennan, "is a fluid stream which moves constantly wherever it is permitted to move, toward a given goal. Its main concern is to make sure that it has filled every nook and cranny available to it in the basin of world power. But if it finds unassailable barriers in its path, it accepts these philosophically and accommodates itself to them."

The appropriate strategy, therefore, was containment. "It is clear that the main element of any United States policy toward the Soviet Union must be that of a long-term, patient but firm and vigilant containment of Russian expansive tendencies." The Soviet assault on the free institutions of the Western world, Kennan emphasized, could "be contained by the adroit and vigilant application of counter-force at a series of constantly shifting geographical and political points, corresponding to the shifts and maneuvers of Soviet policy, but which cannot be charmed or talked out of existence."

But Kennan had in mind more than the containment of Soviet expansion. He believed that the Soviet Union was fundamentally weak, its inhabitants were "physically and spiritually tired," and its economy vulnerable. The problems afflicting the country were endemic to the system; they could not be overcome. If the "unity and efficacy" of the party were disrupted, Kennan prophesied, "Soviet Russia might be changed overnight from one of the strongest to one of the weakest and most pitiable of national societies."

While this article appeared anonymously under the authorship of "X," Kennan's thinking shaped the nation's strategy. In November 1948, the newly formed National Security Council approved a policy enumerating U.S. objectives with regard to the USSR. In times of peace as well as times of war, U.S. goals were:

a. To reduce the power and influence of the USSR to limits which no longer constitute a threat to the peace, national independence and stability of the world family of nations.

b. To bring about a basic change in the conduct of international relations by the governments in power in Russia, to conform with the purposes and principles set forth in the UN charter.

But U.S. officials in 1947 and 1948 did not have precise ideas about how to implement containment. Should

containment be applied everywhere? Should it be applied militarily? Should the United States focus on economic aid to nations seeking to reconstruct their economies? Should the United States assign priority to occupation policies, especially in Germany and Japan?

Initially, in what became known as the Truman Doctrine, the U.S. president proposed military aid to Greece and Turkey, and declared that the United States would contest totalitarian expansion everywhere. But his subordinates quickly recognized that they had to calculate priorities carefully. They decided that they should focus on economic reconstruction in Western Europe rather than military rearmament; that they should seek to erode support for Communist parties in France, Italy, and Greece; and that they should manage the revitalization of western Germany and Japan, and co-opt their future power. Containment meant that Soviet influence and Communist ideology should be contained within the areas occupied by the forces of the Soviet Union at the end of World War II.

In June 1947, the United States announced the Marshall Plan to help rebuild Europe. The governments of most Western European nations were happy to receive U.S. money and participate in a reconstruction program. But they possessed deep fears about the revival of German power. In order to get the French to cooperate, the United States promised to retain its occupation forces inside Germany, and to collaborate militarily should efforts to revive Germany provoke Soviet aggression or rekindle German revanchism. In reality, the North Atlantic Treaty was signed as part of a duel containment policy against Soviet Russia and a future Germany, whose political direction and future alignment was far from certain.

The initial focus of containment was on Western Europe, western Germany, and Japan. But very quickly U.S. officials began to think that their efforts in the industrial core of Eurasia depended on containing Communist influence and Soviet power in the periphery of Southeast Asia, the Middle East, and North Africa. Japan, for example, could not be reconstructed without preserving markets and raw materials in Southeast Asia and South Korea; the United Kingdom and Western Europe needed oil and the repatriation of investment earnings from the Middle East. Yet many of these areas were threatened by insurrectionary forces led by revolutionary nationalists subject to varying degrees of Communist influence.

Containment thus demanded tough choices about where to extend U.S. commitments. Truman administration officials realized that they did not have the resources to contain communism and revolutionary nationalism everywhere. They did not intervene to stop the Communist takeover of China. But after the Soviet Union exploded its first atomic device in August 1949, U.S. officials worried that Soviet leaders would be emboldened and that Communist partisans would be heartened. Truman encouraged his subordinates to rethink the nature of containment. Kennan's influence waned as most of his colleagues now favored rearmament, military alliances, and containment on the periphery. Secretary of State Dean Acheson eased Kennan out of his job and placed Paul Nitze as the head of the Policy Planning Staff.

In early 1950, Nitze composed a new strategy document, known as NSC 68. The overall objective of U.S. policy was to "foster a world environment in which the American system can survive and flourish." To achieve this goal, the United States had to practice containment. Containment meant blocking the expansion of Soviet power, exposing the falsities of Soviet pretensions, inducing a retraction of Soviet control, and nurturing the seeds of destruction within the Soviet system. In order to achieve these goals, military rearmament was indispensable. Military capabilities, Nitze stressed, constitute the "indispensable backdrop." Containment, after all, was a "policy of calculated and gradual coercion." Without superior military power, it was no more than "a policy of bluff."

President Truman endorsed the strategy of NSC 68, but hesitated to allocate the financial resources to support it. Only after the Korean War erupted in June 1950 did he ask Congress for the money to finance the military buildup envisioned in NSC 68. Over the next three years, U.S. military spending almost tripled, reaching about $40 to $50 billion per year. Believing that North Korean aggression was inspired by Stalin, Truman deployed U.S. troops to Korea. At the same time, he committed the United States to contain the expansion of Chinese Communist influence.

Thereafter, containment assumed global dimensions. But debates about it became shrill. Truman's critics called for the rollback of Soviet power. They did not realize that containment envisioned rollback. They did not know that the Truman administration's version of containment already included covert action and psychological warfare throughout the world, including Communist China and Eastern Europe. These critics did not have access to NSC 68, which said that "the cold war was in fact a real war." Still, the real war envisioned in the containment strategy of the Truman administration prudently sought to avoid direct fighting with the Soviet Union lest it trigger the full-scale Soviet invasion of Western Europe and a nuclear war.

When Dwight D. Eisenhower was elected president in November 1952, he decided that the United States could not sustain the military posture envisioned by NSC 68. Eisenhower wanted to practice containment without overtaxing the economy and bankrupting the U.S. treasury. He and John Foster Dulles, his secretary of state, talked of brinksmanship and massive retaliation. Air-atomic capabilities, they knew, were cheaper than conventional forces. So were covert actions and psychological warfare. Eisenhower supported the overthrow of Mohammed Mossadegh in Iran and Jacobo Guzman Arbenz in Guatemala. He believed charismatic nationalists and populist leftists would be outmaneuvered by Communist parties tied to the Kremlin. Around the world he embraced right-wing dictators, not because he liked them, but because he deemed them instrumental to containing the spread of Communist influence and Soviet power. Should any single nation fall to communism, he feared, it would have a "domino" effect on its neighbors. He believed that the United States had to continue to follow the policy of containment, but to do so shrewdly, cheaply, covertly, so that the nation did not become a garrison state.

When John F. Kennedy was elected president in 1960, he felt that the containment as practiced by Eisenhower was faltering. Kennedy thought Eisenhower was too conservative, too cautious. The Soviet Union, Kennedy and his advisers maintained, was gaining in power and influence. Moreover, the appeal of communism seemed greater than ever. Colonial peoples were throwing off the shackles of European rule, seeking rapid modernization, experimenting with command economies, and looking to the Soviet Union as a model of state building and rapid economic advancement.

Kennedy called on the U.S. people to practice containment with renewed vigor. Possessing a different conception of the role of government than did Eisenhower, Kennedy believed that through fiscal and monetary policy, the U.S. government could invigorate economic growth and support a bolder foreign policy. He called for an arms buildup, more flexible conventional forces, and more imaginative counterinsurgency techniques. He called for more economic aid to the emerging nations in Africa and Asia. Kennedy launched the Alliance for Progress in Latin America, hoping for social and land reform as well as industrial modernization. Everywhere, around the globe, Kennedy sought to contain the march of communism, and contain or co-opt the appeal of revolutionary nationalists. When Kennedy was assassinated, Lyndon B. Johnson intensified these efforts. To contain communism, Johnson deployed over five hundred thousand troops to Indochina and expanded the bombing of North Vietnam. Should Vietnam be "lost," U.S. credibility would be shattered and Johnson's domestic political enemies would be emboldened. His "Great Society" at home, Johnson thought, depended on the success of containment abroad.

Johnson's efforts to succeed in Vietnam backfired militarily, diplomatically, and politically. Richard Nixon, a Republican, won the presidency in 1968. Nixon and Henry Kissinger, his national security adviser, felt that U.S. strength was waning. They hoped that through détente with Russia and rapprochement with China they could manage the withdrawal of U.S. troops from Vietnam and maneuver the two Communist rivals to balance one another. By holding out the promise of trade and investment, Nixon and Kissinger hoped to encourage the Soviet Union to exercise self-restraint in Asia and Africa. Should self-restraint not work, Nixon and Kissinger also wanted to give military aid to reliable, strong allies in the third world, like Iran. With Congress less willing to support military action, and with skyrocketing oil prices weakening U.S. economic strength, Nixon and Kissinger maneuvered to keep containment alive through a sophisticated mix of détente, rapprochement, and military assistance.

These policies provoked much controversy in the United States. They were discredited when the president was impeached and forced to resign as a result of a domestic scandal and the attempted cover-up. For the first time since the beginning of the Cold War, Americans were deeply divided about containment. Some experts doubted whether the Soviet Union still sought world domination. Much of Africa, Asia, and the Middle East seethed with unrest, they said, not because of Soviet machinations and ambitions but because of poverty, indigenous unrest, and regional strife. When the Democrat Jimmy Carter won the presidential election in 1976, he and his secretary of state, Cyrus Vance, talked about reconfiguring U.S. strategy. They dwelled more on North-South and less on East-West relations. Improving ties with Soviet Russia and Communist China seemed more important than containing them.

But such thinking ended abruptly in December 1979 when the Soviet Union sent troops into Afghanistan to put down an insurrection against a newly formed Communist government. The Soviets again seemed to be on the march. Neoconservative critics of Carter and Vance had argued all through the mid-1970s that the administration was being duped by the Kremlin. These neoconservatives insisted that the Soviet Union was surpassing the United States in strategic weapons as well as conventional capabilities. They claimed that the Soviet Union was using Cuban troops as proxies to gain influence in Angola and the Horn of Africa. They charged that the United States was abandoning the strategy of containment and allowing the Soviet Union to gain preponderant power in the international system.

In 1980, Ronald Reagan used these themes to win the presidency. He condemned Carter for a policy of weakness. The Soviet Union, he declared, was an "evil empire." The United States would have to rebuild its military power and conduct negotiations from a position of strength. Reagan deployed a new generation of intermediate range missiles to Europe. Secretly, and sometimes not so secretly, he supported anti-Communist factions in the third world, in such places as Angola and Nicaragua. Reagan quite openly supported military aid to the mujahideen fighting Soviet forces in Afghanistan. More discreetly, he assisted Solidarity in Poland.

When a new Soviet leader, Mikhail Gorbachev, consolidated power and sought to reform communism through the policies of glasnost and perestroika, Reagan entered into arms control talks. Gorbachev wanted to limit arms expenditures, and instead focus more attention on revitalizing the Soviet economy and improving living conditions. He was shaken by the explosion of a nuclear reactor at a power plant in Chernobyl. Cognizant of the interdependent nature of the modern world as well as the advances in technology and communications, Gorbachev emphasized that common problems united humanity more than class conflict divided it. Such statements in 1987, 1988, and 1989 signified an entirely new orientation of the Soviet Union toward international relations. Intuiting that he was dealing with a new type of Soviet leader, Reagan dared Gorbachev to lift the iron curtain and tear down the Berlin Wall. The world was stunned when popular movements in Poland, Czechoslovakia, and Hungary overthrew Communist governments, and Gorbachev did not intervene. Nor did he intervene when East Germans demolished the wall and demanded unification with the Federal Republic. And nor did he use force to stymie the independence movements of the Baltic republics inside the Soviet Union.

Containment worked. In 1947, Kennan predicted that vigilant, determined efforts to contain the expansion of

Soviet power would eventually expose the inherent weaknesses of totalitarian communism. From the outset, U.S. officials debated how to apply containment. Their first priority was to rebuild Western Europe, Germany, and Japan, and prevent the Kremlin from fomenting Communist subversion in these countries or luring them into a Soviet orbit. Their second priority was to contain the spread of Communist influence and Soviet power into key areas of Southeast Asia and the Middle East—areas deemed essential to the health of the industrial core of Eurasia. But while debating how best to achieve these objectives, U.S. officials also hoped to find the means of luring Soviet satellites away from the Kremlin and promoting democratic change inside them. What they often disregarded was the appeal of European social democracy along with the resonance of U.S. popular culture and consumer capitalism. What they had not expected was a Soviet leader who was so intent on change, so intent on revitalizing communism inside Russia, that he would essentially abet the success of America's containment strategy. Gorbachev's reforms and his failures, along with the vibrancy of democratic consumer capitalism, allowed containment to succeed, much as Kennan had predicted it would.

See also Americanism; Anticommunism; Bipolarity; Cold War; Gorbachev, Mikhail; Kennan, George Frost; Power Politics; Second Cold War; Totalitarianism.

FURTHER READING

Barrass, G. S. *The Great Cold War: a Journey Through the Hall of Mirrors.* Stanford, CA: Stanford University Press, 2009.

Etzold, T. E., and J. L. Gaddis, eds. *Containment: Documents on American Policy and Strategy, 1945–1950.* New York: Columbia University Press, 1978.

Gaddis, J. L. *Strategies of Containment: A Critical Appraisal of Postwar American National Security Policy.* Rev. ed. New York: Oxford University Press, 2005.

Garthoff, R. *Detente and Confrontation: American-Soviet Relations from Nixon to Reagan.* Rev. ed. Washington DC: Brookings Institution, 1994.

———. *The Great Transition: American-Soviet Relations and the End of the Cold War.* Washington, D.C.: Brookings Institution, 1994.

Kennan, G. F. *Memoirs.* Boston: Little, Brown 1967.

Layne, C. *The Peace of Illusions: American Grand Strategy from 1940 to the Present.* Ithaca, NY: Cornell University Press, 2006.

Leffler, M. P. *A Preponderance of Power: National Security, the Truman Administration, and the Cold War.* Stanford, CA: Stanford University Press, 1992.

———. *For the Soul of Mankind: the United States, the Soviet Union, and the Cold War.* New York: Hill and Wang, 2007.

Lippmann, W. *The Cold War: A Study in U.S. Foreign Policy.* New York: Harper, 1947.

Mayers, D. *George Kennan and the Dilemmas of US Foreign Policy.* New York: Oxford University Press, 1988.

McMahon, R. *The Cold War: a Very Short Introduction.* New York: Oxford University Press, 2003.

Mitrovich, G. *Undermining the Kremlin: America's Strategy to Subvert the Soviet Bloc, 1947–1956.* Ithaca, NY: Cornell University Press, 2000.

Njolstad, O., ed. *The Last Decade of the Cold War: From Conflict Escalation to Conflict Transformation.* London: Routledge, 2004.

MELVYN P. LEFFLER

Coup in the USSR (1991)

Many of the changes in the Soviet Union during the perestroika years were anathema to leading officials within the Communist Party and state apparatus, the military-industrial complex, and substantial sections of the KGB and Ministry of Internal Affairs. The last straw for many of them was the draft Union Treaty agreement, which was to be signed in a Kremlin ceremony on August 20, 1991.

The document—which was the fourth draft of such a treaty to be produced—had been agreed on by the leaders of nine of the Soviet Union's fifteen republics and by the federal authorities, led by the President Mikhail Gorbachev. It was the result of difficult and lengthy negotiations conducted at the Novo-Ogarevo dacha outside Moscow, known accordingly as the Novo-Ogarevo process. In the final agreement, substantial powers were devolved to the republics—so much so that those who led the coup were convinced these powers would lead to the disintegration of the union. In the draft treaty, the letters "USSR" were no longer to stand for the Union of Soviet Socialist Republics but for the Union of Soviet Sovereign Republics. The powers that had been accorded the executive presidency of the USSR in March 1990 were much diminished—many of them were devolved to the republics—but the fact that the holder of the all-union presidency would be chosen by direct election throughout all the republics stood to give the president a countrywide legitimacy and substantial authority.

For Gorbachev and his family, and their immediate entourage, the coup began on August 18, 1991, although it was the following day that the rest of the country and the outside world learned about it. Gorbachev was on holiday at Foros on the Crimean coast. In the late afternoon of August 18 all his communications with Moscow and the outside world were cut off, and at ten minutes to five the head of his bodyguard, KGB general Vladimir Medvedev (who had not been part of the plot), informed Gorbachev that a delegation was waiting to see him. The delegation was headed by the chief of the Soviet military industry, Oleg Baklanov, and included politburo member Oleg Sheynin and Gorbachev's Kremlin chief of staff, Valeriy Boldin. They demanded that Gorbachev hand over his powers—on a temporary basis, it was disingenuously added—to the Committee for the State of Emergency. That self-appointed committee consisted of eight people: Baklanov; Vladimir Kryuchkov, the head of the KGB; Dmitriy Yazov, the minister of defense; Gennadiy Yanaev, the vice president (who was to be the acting president); Valentin Pavlov, the prime minister; Boris Pugo, the minister of the interior; Vasiliy Starodubtsev, the head of the Peasants' Union, a pressure group opposed to private farming; and Aleksandr Tizyakov, a leading representative of defense-related state industry.

Gorbachev flatly refused to go along with the demands made of him, and so the remainder of the drama was played out in Moscow. In the early morning of August 19, Russian citizens were informed that the president (Gorbachev) was too ill to carry out his duties and that Yanaev would be the acting president. That this was a putsch was made sufficiently clear, however, by the attacks that were simultaneously made by members of the "committee" and their allies on Gorbachev's policies. The chairman of the Supreme Soviet, Anatoliy Lykyanov, had been involved in discussions with the putschists prior to their coup, and once the state of emergency had been declared, he took the opportunity to attack the Union Treaty that the coup had been mounted to avert.

Boris Yeltsin, who had been elected president of Russia in June 1991 (and thus enjoyed a high degree of popular support and political legitimacy), made his way on the morning of August 19 to the Moscow White House, which was at that time the home of the Russian parliament. Yeltsin and the White House became the focal points of the resistance to the coup. The plotters had failed to cut off their means of communication with the outside world, and foreign leaders were able to send their messages of support to Yeltsin. Although tanks had been brought into central Moscow by the putschists, a substantial number of Muscovites—some two hundred thousand over the several days and nights the coup lasted—stood guard outside the White House. They could easily have been overcome by a determined military assault, but their presence raised the political costs of storming the White House. Ironically, the putschists, who had berated Gorbachev for, among other things, "indecisiveness," were notably indecisive themselves. They did not use the kind of force that would have been required to secure the status quo ante they wished to achieve. While most republican and regional leaders accepted the supposed new regime from the outset, their confidence in its staying power quickly drained as the stalemate in Moscow continued. The coup had crumbled by August 21, and on the night of August 21–22, Gorbachev flew back to Moscow.

The putschists' action produced three major unintended consequences. First and most crucially, it speeded up the disintegration of the Soviet Union that the coup had been intended to reverse. One republic after another now declared its independent statehood, and by the end of the year the Soviet Union was no more. Second, it enormously strengthened Yeltsin's political position, not least vis-à-vis Gorbachev, whom Yeltsin went out of his way to humiliate, and who was open to the criticism that while he had been a victim of the putsch, he was nevertheless responsible for having made the bad appointments that gave the coup plotters their high state offices. The third unintended consequence for the putschists was that instead of continuing to hold such office, they found themselves in jail. Yet even the leading coup plotters, such as Kryuchkov, served a maximum of two and a half years in prison. They were amnestied by the Russian parliament early in 1994. One of the eight members of the Committee for the State of Emergency had already inflicted a worse fate on himself. Pugo committed suicide when the coup failed, as did the former chief of the defense, Staff Marshal Akkhromeyev, and a senior Central Committee official, Nikolai Kruchina. By the early 21st century, however, the surviving putschists were being feted by many Russians as people who had tried to preserve a Soviet Union whose demise a majority of the population regretted. But the way they pursued that aim (and others) combined illegality, lies, and incompetence.

See also Dissolution of the USSR; Gorbachev, Mikhail; Perestroika; Yeltsin, Boris.

FURTHER READING

Chernyaev, A. *My Six Years with Gorbachev*. University Park: University of Pennsylvania Press, 2000.

Gorbachev, M. *The August Coup: The Truth and the Lessons*. London: HarperCollins, 1991.

Hahn, G. M. *Russia's Revolution from Above: Reform, Transition, and Revolution in the Fall of the Soviet Communist Regime*. New Brunswick, NJ: Transaction Publishers, 2002.

Stepankov, V., and E. Lisov. *Kremlevskiy zagovor*. Moscow: Ogonek, 1992.

Yeltsin, B. *The View from the Kremlin*. London: HarperCollins, 1994.

ARCHIE BROWN

Cuban Missile Crisis

Arthur Schlesinger defined the Cuban missile crisis as "the most dangerous moment of the Cold War and of all human history." It occurred after the invasion of the Bay of Pigs, April 17–18, 1961, which proved to be both a military and political failure. The John F. Kennedy administration, which as a consequence had been accused of incompetence, and the Cuban exiles, beaten but not defeated, decided to undertake a clandestine operation code-named Mongoose. The operation's purpose was the elimination of the Castro regime and possibly the assassination of Fidel himself. The Soviet and Cuban secret services knew about the increase in sabotage activities directed by the Central Intelligence Agency on the island of Cuba. The frequency of military exercises in the Caribbean in summer 1962 also increased. The world Communist movement decided to side with Castro, partly because of his great popularity and partly to defend the surprisingly successful revolution that the young Cubans had started. The Communists made this commitment even though all guarantees of protection on the part of the USSR (and the Warsaw Pact) would have been of little use in case of war, since the island could not be defended with conventional weapons. Khrushchev hoped that a display of Soviet power would be effective on two different fronts. On the one hand, it would show the various left-wing movements in Latin America that it was possible to directly challenge the imperialism of the United States in

Central America and the Caribbean. On the other hand, it would establish a visible political and military superiority over Communist China in the Americas.

Cuban leaders urgently requested enough military aid to confront the threat of invasion. Khrushchev responded with a deliberately risky move, and proposed a lot more: "to install our missiles in Cuba, in order not only to protect it, but also to re-establish that which the West likes to call a balance of power," he wrote many years afterward in the first volume of his memoirs. Between 1957 and 1959, the United States had concluded agreements with the British, Turkish, and Italian governments for the installation of medium-range Thor and Jupiter nuclear missiles on their soil. The Kremlin's calculations therefore had two objectives: to defend Cuba, but also to modify the relative balance of power between the two great rivals. This resulted in indirectly destabilizing the situation in Germany (Kennedy had emphatically declared to the world that the defense of Berlin was one of his priorities) and other North Atlantic Treaty Organization countries. In an interview with Jean Daniel (December 21, 1963), Castro explained that Khrushchev's offer "surprised us at first and made us hesitate for a long time. In the end we accepted the Soviet proposal because on the one hand the Russians convinced us that the United States would not have been intimidated by conventional weapons, while on the other it was unthinkable that we on the island not share the risks the Soviet Union was incurring in order to save us." Whatever the intent, by deploying several dozen missiles in Cuba, the Soviets could not overcome the significant gap that separated their nuclear arsenal from that of the United States.

Discussions about the "Military Pact" and entire Anadyr operation (in other words, the shipping of troops and nuclear warheads for the SS4 and SS5 missiles, which in reality never reached the island) were restricted to a few members of the Communist Party of the Soviet Union's presidium and the Cuban leadership group, and concluded in August 1962. The text for the "Treatise of Military Cooperation for the Defense of the National Territory of Cuba in Case of Aggression" was composed during Raúl Castro's visit to Moscow and was finalized in Khrushchev's dacha in Crimea during Ernesto "Che" Guevara and Emilio Aragones's follow-up mission. Aragones was one of the six members of the Cuban Party's Secretariat. Fidel insisted on immediately making the "Treatise" public. His request was rejected by the Soviets, who did not want to risk making the existence of the bases public before their installation was complete. The

Soviets knew the capabilities of U.S. air surveillance all too well; the first U2 had been shot down over Soviet airspace in 1961.

The formal beginning of the crisis came when Major Richard Heyser, aboard a U2 on October 14, 1962, spotted the military fortifications built to install the forty-two missiles (which were on their way to Cuba). The photos he took were quickly sent to the National Photographic Interpretation Center, where they were compared with the information given to the Central Intelligence Agency earlier by a Soviet spy, Oleg Penkovsky (a colonel in the Information Services of the Soviet General Staff), who had started passing the United States firsthand information on the military capabilities of the USSR in 1961. Kennedy summoned his advisers to a meeting on October 16 of what would later be called the Executive Committee (ExComm) of the National Security Council. For the next two weeks the committee conducted harsh exchanges about how to confront the Soviets. On one side were those who advocated a strong and decisive military response, which would include an initial aerial attack to eliminate the bases, followed by an invasion of the island. On the other were those who suggested opening negotiations with the Soviet Union.

While these exchanges were taking place, Kennedy asked Congress to approve the recall of 150,000 reservists. He also authorized a previously planned military exercise in which about 7,500 marines would land on the island of Vieques near Puerto Rico. Subsequently disclosed documentation reveals that Kennedy, partly on the advice of his brother Robert and Theodore Sorensen, thought the most reasonable solution was a naval blockade of the island, which would therefore also force the withdrawal of the missiles. This solution would allow for confrontation with the Soviets, but without provoking an uncontrollable nuclear escalation. The day after this operational consensus on the blockade was reached, on October 21, the Soviets, in the person of Aleksander Fomin (Soviet embassy counselor in Washington, but also the local KGB head), let it be known that a solution would only be possible if two conditions were met. Once the missiles were withdrawn, the United States would have to formally commit both to not invade Cuba and not overthrow the Castro regime. On October 22 Kennedy gave a tough speech, consisting of seven points, and concluded by asking for the implementation of a "quarantine" (this term seemed less bellicose than "blockade") to prevent the shipment of further military matériel, and demanding that Khrushchev withdraw the missiles

and bombers that had reached the island. Kennedy intentionally avoided mentioning Castro in his speech, taking for granted that his real counterpart in the negotiations, if not the only one, was the USSR, and he did not even threaten to invade the island or overthrow the new regime.

From the perspective of international law, as applicable at the time, the enactment of this quarantine was based not so much on the UN charter as on that of the Organization of American States, which authorized its member states to "take collective measures to ensure the safety of the Americas." The approval of the Organization of American States was sought and obtained on October 23. The United States also presented a resolution to the UN Security Council, in which it demanded the dismantling of the missile ramps along with the removal of the missiles and bombers, in addition to the creation of a UN Observer Group that would inspect Cuba to verify the removal. Castro, in a brief speech that same day, stated that anyone who wanted to enter Cuban territory would have to be prepared for a fight: "We refuse any inspection: Cuba is not the Congo . . . our arms are not offensive." U Thant, secretary general of the United Nations, tried to mediate: he proposed that the Soviets suspend the arms transport, and that the United States wait before imposing its quarantine. Playing his own move in this chess game, Kennedy refused the proposal, saying that before suspending the blockade, the missiles that were already in Cuba would have to be removed. Now it was Khrushchev's turn. In his reply to U Thant, and notwithstanding the blockade, he showed that he was open to negotiations, giving another signal he was reversing course. It was a response similar to the one he had given Bertrand Russell, who in an open letter had attempted to intervene in order to avert nuclear catastrophe.

On October 27, Khrushchev sent Kennedy a letter stating that he was open to negotiations on the removal of the missiles. On the same day a U2 was shot down over Cuba (killing the pilot, Major Rudolf Anderson, the sole victim of the missile crisis) and noticeable panic ensued. This was partly because Castro claimed responsibility for shooting down the U2, thus hinting that not all missiles in Cuba were under Moscow's control. Within ExComm, some asked for immediate reprisal against Cuba and the destruction of the antiaircraft batteries. Kennedy ordered all nuclear and conventional U.S. forces around the world to be put on alert. In a move that further complicated the situation, Khrushchev sent Kennedy a second message, this time proposing the withdrawal of missiles from Cuba in exchange for the withdrawal of fifteen Jupiter missiles from Turkey. Disconcerted by such substantially different proposals from the Soviet first secretary, Kennedy decided to respond only to the first letter and ignore the second. He made the noninvasion of Cuba conditional on the withdrawal of Soviet missiles. Secretary of State Dean Rusk intervened at the same time with U Thant, asking him to support Kennedy's request.

On the night of October 27, probably with Frol Kozlov and Leonid Brezhnev's opposition, Khrushchev confirmed that his "first letter" was an expression of his real intentions. As a proof of good faith he gave immediate orders to stop the construction of the missile ramps, which were then to be dismantled and returned to Russia. The Cuban leaders were not consulted about the conclusion of the crisis. Fidel, on hearing this news in the presence of Che, expressed his anger and disdain toward the Soviet leader, who had in fact trampled on what had been the most important principle of the Movimiento 26 de Julio in its fight against Fulgencio Batista: Cuba's independence and the defense of its sovereignty against all foreign powers.

The direct negotiations between the United States and the USSR, and the unexpected resolution that was its outcome, had all the appearances of "a betrayal" to the Cubans, as Che told Anastas Mikoyan during a lengthy meeting, after the Soviet statesman had arrived on the island to justify and explain the USSR position. The initial violent reaction of the *líder máximo,* Castro, eventually softened during his long trip to the Soviet Union six months later, when Khrushchev welcomed him as a hero, "protagonist of socialist unity," and defender of Moscow's policy of pacific coexistence. In actuality the Kennedy-Khrushchev agreement brought Cuba's foreign policy (most especially that toward Latin America) within the confines of the bipolar administration of limited sovereignties. The results produced by this kind of administration, imposed and enforced by the two superpowers, after Kennedy and Khrushchev had rapidly exited the scene, can be seen as late as the Soviet invasion of Czechoslovakia and the military coup supported by the Richard Nixon administration against the Unidad Popular government of Salvador Allende Gossens (to which the Soviet Union reacted with passivity). The Cuban Revolution had been conceived by its young protagonists on the ship *Granma* as following in the steps of of José Martí's anti-imperialism. The revolution's increasing Sovietization was one of the contributing causes

that made it impossible for a Latin American–style communism to come to power and stay there. For well over thirty years, up to the dissolution of the USSR, conditions abroad and in Latin America would continue to make this impossible.

See also Castro, Fidel; Cold War; Cuban Revolution; Khrushchev, Nikita; Power Politics; Socialist Camp; Soviet Bloc.

FURTHER READING

Blight, J. G., B. J. Allyn, and D. A. Welch. *Cuba on the Brink: Fidel Castro, the Missile Crisis, and the Collapse of Communism.* New York: Pantheon Books, 1993.

Chang, L., and P. Kornbluh, eds. *The Cuban Missile Crisis.* New York: New Press, 1992.

Fursenko, A. A., and T. J. Naftali. *One Hell of a Gamble: Khrushchev, Castro, and Kennedy, 1958–1963.* New York: Norton, 1998.

Jones, H. *The Bay of Pigs.* Oxford: Oxford University Press, 2008.

Matthews, H. L. *Fidel Castro.* New York: Simon and Schuster, 1970.

Nuti, L., ed. *I missili di ottobre. La storiografia americana e la crisi cubana dell'ottobre 1962.* Milan: LED, 1994.

Schlesinger, A. M. *A Thousand Days: John F. Kennedy in the White House.* New York: Fawcett, 1965.

ALBERTO FILIPPI

Cuban Revolution

The revolution that took place in Cuba under Fidel Castro Ruz's leadership, and that seized power on January 1, 1959, had a variety of causes. One was the "national question," the unresolved issue of Cuban independence and its relation to the United States. The island had acquired independence from Spain in 1898 only to be subjected to a type of political, economic, and military protectorate imposed by the United States. In addition there was a serious "social question": even though Cuba enjoyed relatively decent living standards compared to the Latin American average, the increased cultivation of sugar cane and expansion of capitalist production in the countryside had transformed many farmers into farm laborers who were unemployed for large portions of the year, when work on the plantations stopped. The revolution was therefore helped less by backwardness and misery than by the profound transformations that had occurred in the Cuban social structure. The importance of U.S. capital to the island's economy also made it appear as if the national and social questions were two sides of the same coin.

Starting in 1952 a "political cause" emerged: Fulgencio Batista's coup destroyed the already-fragile structures of representative democracy and pushed the generation of young nationalists that was making its first appearance on the national stage toward insurrection. Since in the following years Batista proved to be among the most reliable allies of the Eisenhower administration, the political question tended to be viewed together with the national question, thus anticipating the clashes that were to occur later between the revolutionary regime and the United States.

Another cause, which ultimately proved decisive, was the charismatic figure of the young Castro. The famous main stages of the triumphal revolution were, from this time until 1959, tied to his name: from the failed assault on the Moncada Barracks in 1953 to the subsequent founding of the Movimiento 26 de julio, from the *Granma*'s expedition in November 1956 to the creation of a guerrilla *foco* on the Sierra Maestra, where together with other *barbudos*, including the most important, like the commanders Raúl Castro, Ernesto "Che" Guevara, and Camilo Cienfuegos, he laid the foundations for military success and the new revolutionary order.

Many other forces and factors contributed to the revolution's success, especially the polarization caused by Batista's authoritarian government and its brutal violence. With time this allowed the guerrillas on the Sierra Maestra, who demonstrated their skill in formulating a political program, and by invoking generically nationalist and idealistic democratic forms of inspiration, to gather these disparate forces around them—and persuade them to follow an insurrectionary path organized around a rural guerrilla movement, rather than engage in a mass struggle in the cities. These forces included the students of the Directorio revolucionario and Catholic lay organizations, leaders from the traditional political parties and the Communists from the Partido socialista popular, who were initially hostile to Castro's methods, along with U.S. liberals and Latin American democrats. The former were hostile to the White House's alliance with Latin American dictators, while the latter, especially the Venezuelan Rómulo Betancourt, were bent on cleansing the region from the military caudillos who still infested it.

Many of these people, however, either abandoned the revolution or were marginalized by it when Castro—after a first phase in which he agreed to a provisional government led by the liberal José Miró Cardona—later took the path of social revolution and militant anti-imperialism, both at home and abroad, setting aside his commitment to restore parliamentary democracy. To what extent this outcome was inscribed in the ideals of the revolutionary leaders and the island's structural conditions, and to what degree it was a reaction to the U.S. obsession of renewing its protectorate over Cuba's destiny, has been a subject of endless political and historical controversy. What is certain is that the revolution adopted economic, social, and political reforms that brought it ever closer to the socialist model over time, and these were finally enshrined by the adoption of the principles of Marxism-Leninism and the choice of the Soviet side in the Cold War, following the United States' attempted Bay of Pigs invasion in April 1961.

In the economic area, the government nationalized industries and services, and implemented a radical agrarian reform. The state effectively gained control of the means of production within a few years. The plan to industrialize the island and diversify the economy, though, did not achieve its intended objectives. Due to the U.S. embargo, Cuba also did not have many other options besides becoming part of the Comecon and relying on generous Soviet subsidies. On the social level, the revolution was motivated by a strong egalitarian impulse, both in terms of salary and employment policies, and its largely successful goal of improving and universalizing access to public education and health services. On the political terrain, the Cuban revolutionaries imagined they could realize either a people's or a direct democracy, which would be fed by the moral energies of the "new man" born from revolutionary catharsis. To this end they created a system of political participation that was an alternative to the "bourgeois democracy" they abhorred, and established numerous mass organizations, from the Committees to Defend the Revolution to the Cuban Women's Federation, from the Union of Pioneers to the Student Federation, and so forth.

Fairly soon, however, as revolutionary fervor began to weaken, and facing the need to make the machinery of both the state and economy work, the institutions of so-called popular power lost both prestige and spontaneity. They instead became organs by means of which the Communist Party of Cuba exercised its power. As this institutionalization unfolded, the Cuban Revolution's political regime took on the characteristics of single-party socialist regimes with a state ideology. The state's Constitution of 1976 and later the constitutional reform of 2002 sanctioned this turn of events, and defined the socialist path taken by Cuba as "irreversible." To a large extent the result of a national question that turned gangrenous, the revolution never totally lost its nationalist origins beneath the socialist regime's skin. It survived the end of the Cold War, and continued to hold some residual legitimacy in the eyes of many Cubans and Latin Americans.

See also Anti-imperialism; Castro, Fidel; Cuban Missile Crisis; Guevara de la Serna, Ernesto Rafael; Nationalism.

FURTHER READING

Fernandez, D. J. *Cuba and the Politics of Passion*. Austin: University Press of Texas, 2000.

Franqui, C. *Family Portrait with Fidel: A Memoir*. New York: Random House, 1984.

Lievesley, G. *The Cuban Revolution: Past, Present, and Future Perspectives*. New York: Palgrave Macmillan, 2003.

Paterson, T. J. *Contesting Castro: The United States and the Triumph of the Cuban Revolution*. New York: Oxford University Press, 1994.

Pérez-Stable, M. *The Cuban Revolution: Origins, Course, and Legacy*. New York: Oxford University Press, 1999.

LORIS ZANATTA

Cuban-Soviet Intervention in Africa

By the early 1970s, the Soviet Union had stumbled from one failure to another in Africa, leading CIA director William Colby to write that "Africa in the 1973 edition of the Key Intelligence Questions hardly rated a mention." The Soviet threat had been defanged. Why worry?

Three years later, however, thirty-six thousand Cuban soldiers landed in Angola, the former Portuguese colony that had descended into civil war in 1975. Suddenly the Soviet threat to Africa had never loomed larger. Until then, armed interventions in Africa had been the preserve of the United States and its allies, with one exception, which had been duly noted in U.S. intelligence reports but had escaped the attention of policymakers: prior to 1975, small numbers of Cuban military forces, totaling little more than one thousand people, had been sent to Algeria, Congo Leopoldville (later called Zaire), Congo Brazzaville, and Guinea-Bissau.

The arrival of the Cuban troops in Angola stunned the world. Shock waves reverberated through Washington, DC, which responded with fierce cries: the Cubans were Soviet proxies, mercenaries doing Moscow's bidding. But it is now beyond question that as a Soviet official stated in his memoirs, the Cubans sent their troops "on their own initiative and without consulting us." Indeed even Secretary of State Henry Kissinger, who had dismissed the Cubans as Soviet proxies, has reconsidered. "At the time we thought he [Castro] was operating as a Soviet surrogate," he wrote in the final volume of his memoirs. "We could not imagine that he would act so provocatively so far from home unless he was pressured by Moscow to repay the Soviet Union for its military and economic support. Evidence now available suggests that the opposite was the case."

Castro had sent his troops across the Atlantic to stop the South African army, which with Washington's encouragement, had invaded Angola to prevent Agostinho Neto's Left-leaning Popular Movement for the Liberation of Angola (MPLA) from defeating two rival movements supported by Pretoria and Washington.

By deciding to send troops, Castro challenged Moscow, for he knew that Leonid Brezhnev opposed it. Brezhnev distrusted Neto, and he did not want to do anything that might jeopardize the ongoing SALT II negotiations with the United States. Castro also knew that his troops could face a serious military risk: Pretoria, urged on by Washington, might have escalated its involvement, and the Cuban soldiers might have faced the full fury of the South African army without any guarantee of Soviet assistance. (Indeed, it took two months for Moscow to begin to provide essential logistical support to the airlift of Cuban troops to Angola.) Furthermore, the dispatch of Cuban troops jeopardized relations with the West precisely at a moment when they were improving markedly: the United States was probing a modus vivendi, the Organization of American States had just lifted its sanctions, and West European governments were offering Havana low-interest loans and development aid. Realpolitik would have demanded that Cuba refuse Luanda's appeals. Had he been a client of the Soviet Union, Castro would have rebuffed Neto.

What motivated the decision to send troops was idealism. The victory of the Pretoria-Washington axis would have meant the victory of apartheid, the tightening of the grip of white domination over the people of southern Africa. It was a defining moment. Castro sent his soldiers. As Kissinger himself now says, Castro "was probably the most genuine revolutionary leader then in power."

The Cubans halted the South African advance and then pushed it back until, on March 27, 1976, the last South African troops withdrew from Angola. Cuba's victory prevented the establishment of a government in Luanda beholden to the apartheid regime. The tidal wave unleashed by the Cuban victory washed over southern Africa. Its psychological impact, the hope it aroused, is aptly illustrated by an editorial in the *World*, South Africa's major black newspaper. "Black Africa is tasting the heady wine of the possibility of realizing the dream of total liberation," it announced in February 1976. "Black Africa is riding the crest of a wave generated by the Cuban success in Angola." There would have been no heady dream, but rather the pain of crushing defeat, had the Cubans not intervened.

The impact was more than moral. It had clear, tangible consequences throughout southern Africa. It forced Kissinger to turn against the racist white regime in Rhodesia and kept Jimmy Carter on the narrow good path until Zimbabwe was finally born in 1980. And it marked the real beginning of Namibia's war of independence against South African rule. The South West Africa People's Organization (SWAPO) had begun armed struggle in 1966, but its efforts did not gain momentum until after the MPLA victory in Angola. As South African General Jannie Geldenhuys writes, "For the first time they [SWAPO] obtained what is more or less a prerequisite for successful insurgent campaigning, namely a border that provided safe refuge."

Having pushed the South African army out of Angola, the Cubans wanted to withdraw their troops gradually over a three-year period, giving the MPLA time to strengthen its armed forces. But by 1978 it had become clear that these troops were the only shield that could protect Angola from further South African aggression. The Cuban soldiers were instrumental in finally forcing South Africa to agree to Namibian independence in December 1988. It was only then that the Cuban troops began their phased withdrawal from Angola. The last Cuban soldiers left in 1991.

Whatever tensions had existed between Moscow and Havana over Angola in 1975 had dissipated by February 1976, both because the Cuban operation had been successful and because it had become clear that the SALT II negotiations had stalled. Havana and Moscow would clash again over Angola—indirectly—during an attempted coup against Neto in May 1977. The plotters

enjoyed the sympathy, if not the active support, of the Soviet embassy, while the Cubans played a decisive role in defeating the revolt. But the Soviets were graceful in defeat; they did not complain about Cuba's actions, and Havana did not press the point. With this one exception, the Soviets were loyal supporters of the Angolan regime, and it was Soviet economic and military aid that made it possible for Havana to maintain its troops in Angola.

It was on November 25, 1977, that Castro, responding to the urgent appeals of the government in Addis Ababa, decided to send troops to Ethiopia to help defend that country from Somalia, which had invaded to annex the Ogaden, a large region in eastern Ethiopia inhabited by ethnic Somalis. This time there had been close consultation between Moscow and Havana, and the Cuban decision was warmly welcomed by Brezhnev, who wrote to Castro expressing "our complete agreement with your policy. We are pleased that our assessment of events in Ethiopia coincides with yours, and we sincerely thank you for your timely decision to extend internationalist assistance to Socialist Ethiopia." Consultation, however, did not mean subservience. The evidence in the U.S. and Cuban archives indicates that Castro's decision to send the troops, eventually numbering sixteen thousand, was due to his belief that "a real revolution is taking place in Ethiopia" that deserved to be defended. In a two-month offensive in early 1978, Cuban and Ethiopian troops, supported by Soviet planes, threw the Somalis out of Ethiopia. Yet the Cubans refused to join in the fight against the Eritrea secessionists. Castro had stressed on the day he decided to send troops that "these soldiers are to fight exclusively on the Eastern Front against Somalia's foreign aggression," and the Cubans were true to their word. They not only refused to fight in Eritrea but they also tried to mediate a resolution to that conflict.

By the end of the 1970s, the Soviet bloc seemed on the ascent in sub-Saharan Africa. In addition to the presence of forty thousand soldiers in Angola and Ethiopia, the Cubans maintained military missions in several African countries, as did the Soviets. Cuban and Soviet military instructors were training insurgents from South Africa, Namibia, and Rhodesia in Angola, and several countries in the region—notably Angola, Mozambique, and Ethiopia—had chosen the path to socialism. But if Cuba was unique in the world for the number of its troops in Africa, it was equally unique for the scope and generosity of its nonmilitary aid: almost ten thousand Cuban aid workers—mainly in the fields of health, education, and construction—worked in a score of African countries at little or no cost to the host governments, while thousands of young Africans studied in Cuba, all expenses paid by the Cuban government. Marrack Goulding, the British ambassador to Angola, would note in his memoirs that the Cubans "had done wonders for Angola's education and health services," while Nelson Mandela asked in 1991, "What other country can point to a record of greater selflessness than Cuba has displayed in its relations to Africa?"

See also Anti-imperialism; Decolonization; Internationalism; Power Politics; Third Worldism.

FURTHER READING

This entry is based on documents from the closed Cuban archives, and U.S. and European archives. To my knowledge, only Vladimir Shubin (see below) has been able to use a significant number of relevant Soviet documents.

Brezhnev, L. I. Letter to Fidel Castro, Moscow, November 27, 1977. Centro de Información de las Fuerzas Armadas Revolucionarias, Havana.

Castro, F. In "Niederschrift über das Gespräch zwischen Genossen Erich Honecker und Genossen Fidel Castro am Sonntag, dem 3. April 1977, von 11.00 bis 13.30 Uhr und von 15.45 bis 18.00 Uhr, im Hause des ZK." Berlin, April 3, 1977, 20–21, 23, DY30 JIV 2/201/1292. Stiftung Archiv der Parteien und Massenorganisationen der DDR im Bundesarchiv, Berlin.

———. In "Respuesta de Fidel a Senén, 14–15.00 hrs—25. 11.77—via telf. Secreto." Centro de Información de las Fuerzas Armadas Revolucionarias, Havana.

Colby, W., with P. Forbath. *Honorable Men: My Life in the CIA.* New York: Simon and Schuster, 1978.

Dobrynin, A. *In Confidence: Moscow's Ambassador to America's Six Cold War Presidents.* New York: Crown, 1995.

Geldenhuys, J. *A General's Story: From an Era of War and Peace.* Johannesburg: Jonathan Ball Publishers, 1995.

Gleijeses, P. "Truth or Credibility: Castro, Carter, and the Invasions of Shaba." *International History Review* (February 1996): 70–103.

———. *Conflicting Missions: Havana, Washington, and Africa, 1959–1976.* Chapel Hill: University of North Carolina Press, 2002.

———. "Moscow's Proxy? Cuba and Africa, 1975–88." *Journal of Cold War Studies* 8, no. 2 (Spring 2006): 3–51.

Goulding, M. *Peacemonger.* Baltimore: Johns Hopkins University Press, 2002.

Kissinger, H. *Years of Renewal.* New York: Simon and Schuster, 1999.

LeoGrande, W. *Cuba's Policy in Africa, 1959–1980.* Berkeley: University of California Press, 1980.

Mandela, N. *Granma* (Havana), July 27, 1991, 3.

Patman, R. *The Soviet Union in the Horn of Africa: The Diplomacy of Intervention and Disengagement.* New York: Cambridge University Press, 1990.

Risquet, J. "Angola: El camino hacia la victoria." *Temas* (Havana), April 2004, 159–67.

Shubin, V. *ANC: A View from Moscow.* Bellville, South Africa: Mayibuye Books, 1999.

Westad, O. A. "Moscow and the Angolan Crisis, 1974–1976: A New Pattern of Intervention." *Cold War International History Project Bulletin,* nos. 8–9 (Winter 1996–97): 21–37.

World (Johannesburg), February 24, 1976, 4.

PIERO GLEIJESES

Cult of Personality

At the Twentieth Congress of the Soviet Communist Party in February 1956, Khrushchev criticized Stalin's criminal abuse of power. He used the term *kult' lichnosti,* translated "cult of the individual" or "cult of personality," to explain the changes that took place in the Soviet leadership system after 1934. Khrushchev criticized "the accumulation of immense and limitless powers in the hands of one person" and the abandonment of the principle of "collegiality." Stalin, with his "despotic character," could not tolerate any opposition to himself or to his concepts. In place of persuasion he relied on "administrative violence, mass repression and terror." In time the cult turned Stalin into a kind of god, an omniscient and infallible being.

Khrushchev's speech initiated the process of de-Stalinization, which had implications that reached beyond the ways in which Stalin as a leader was to be remembered. It affected the organization of the institutions of power, which now would aim at maintaining collective leadership and ensuring a degree of accountability of the leadership before the party. It also initiated a relaxation of repression and changes in policy designed to secure popular consent and ease relations with the West. At the Twenty-second Party Congress in October 1961, Khrushchev renewed his attack on Stalin, and Stalin's body was removed from the mausoleum.

Khrushchev's attempt to blame the criminal excesses of the Stalin period on a "cult of personality" were criticized as inadequate by the Italian Communist leader Palmiro Togliatti, who argued for a more thoroughgoing Marxist examination of the Stalin era that would take into account the traditions of Russia, the circumstances of the time, and the nature of Marxist-Leninist ideology. Khrushchev's analysis, by focusing on Stalin's personal role, was intended to absolve other leaders and the Communist Party in general from criticism and to limit the nature of the criticism of Stalin himself. His 1920s achievements in defeating opposition groups, carrying through the First Five-Year Plan, collectivizing agriculture, and destroying the kulaks as a social class were to be respected.

The concept of a cult of personality was not Khrushchev's invention. The term has a long past, and can be traced back to the writings of Marx and Engels on the role of great men in history. Stalin himself often used the term to disparage, as a deviation from Marxism, the adulation heaped on individual leaders.

Modern political leader cults share certain characteristics with the cults of leaders from classical antiquity, the cults of monarchs, and the cults of saints. It is with the French Revolution and the Napoleonic period, however, that we date the rise of modern dictatorial systems and their leader cults. These need to be viewed alongside the cults of other political figures—the Führer and leader cults of the Nazi and Fascist states, the lesser cults of nationalist leaders, and those of politicians in democratic states.

The Soviet leader cult must also be set in a wider context of the ideas and cultic behaviors that accrued to venerated individuals, institutions, symbols of the state, foundation dates of the state, and other important dates in its history. The Soviet regime could not base its legitimacy, pace Max Weber, on tradition, on rational legal authority, or on charismatic authority. Instead it sought to persuade the population of its right to rule. It sought to construct legitimacy by evoking symbolic or affective attachments based on popular identification with the regime, its ideology, institutions and leaders, and by these same means to sanctify the state and the regime.

Leader cults, like religious cults, attempt to make one man a point of reference for an entire belief system, a human embodiment of doctrine. The Soviet Communist regime from its inception displayed a strong proclivity toward cultic practices, in which the leader assumed a central role. The construction of the mausoleum in 1924 marked a key stage in the development of Lenin's posthumous cult, which was used by Stalin in his struggle for the succession. The celebration of Stalin's 50th birthday in December 1929 was the first large public manifestation of his cult, which was consolidated with the rise of his personal dictatorship, the growing authoritarianism of the regime, and the militarization of aspects of political and social life.

The Stalin cult became one of the central bases for legitimating the Soviet regime. The leader was the interpreter of the ruling ideology, Marxism-Leninism, presented as a rarefied science and the embodiment of truth, and he was projected as someone possessing almost superhuman powers—keen intuition, exceptional powers to formulate solutions to problems, and an uncommon ability to inspire and mobilize those around him to work for his ends. Alongside the veneration of the leader there were lesser cults around subordinate leaders, extending out to leaders in the republics and localities.

The leader cult was thus deliberately constructed and managed to provide the state some semblance of legitimacy. It was disseminated through the mass media and the educational system, with cultic propaganda tailored to different target populations: ethnic groups, children, youth, men, women, the various professions, the armed forces, and the security services. Literature, art, song, poetry, sculpture were commandeered to serve the cult. Festivals, celebrations, and the granting of honors and awards to outstanding citizens were used to reinforce the bonds of allegiance between the people and the state.

The cult depicted the dictator as idealized leader, teacher, and friend, creating a strongly paternal image. The leader was the father of his people, the father of the nations. Stalin was venerated as *tsar batyushka*, the czar as the little father. The cult was related to a conception of politics that was millenarian and heroic, which celebrated service, sacrifice, and martyrdom for the cause. In the 1930s the cult was associated with a growing nationalist/patriotic theme in official discourse. This attained its height during the Second World War, when the war was used to legitimize the leader and the regime. His 70th birthday celebrations in 1949 projected Stalin as a world statesman and head of the international Communist movement.

The cult of the leader had its own icons—the official biography, the official history of the movement, and Stalin's collected works were accorded canonic status. Relics of the leader were preserved in museums, and museums were constructed around the place where he lived. The birthday of the leader was always a high point of cultic celebration, an opportunity for the expression of public gratitude. Finally with the death of the leader, the embalming of his body, and its preservation in a mausoleum, Stalin's deification was complete. His name was bestowed on state awards, prizes, state constitutions on towns, factories, and institutions. His modesty and asceticism were highlighted, as was his attentiveness to the views and opinions of ordinary workers and party members. By modulating its expression Stalin could, during his lifetime, check the dangers of the cult degenerating into excess, and thus further reinforce his own position. The leader cult always tended toward an impersonal depiction of the leader, with his persona projected as the physical and spiritual embodiment of the state.

In the postwar years the Soviet leader cult was exported to the new people's democracies of Eastern Europe and even to nonruling Communist parties. In China the cult of Mao Zedong during the Cultural Revolution of 1966 attained heights of extravagance that exceeded the cult of Stalin in the USSR. Leader cults flourished also in North Korea and North Vietnam. The leader cults in China and North Korea influenced cults in Romania and Albania. The cults surrounding Nikolai Ceausescu, Josip Bros Tito, Enver Hoxha, and the posthumous cult of Georgi Dimitrov were particularly powerful. In some cases—with Tito, Hoxha, and later Ceausescu—the leader's cult came to play a role in movements for national independence.

The Communist regimes of the USSR, Yugoslavia, Albania, China, North Korea, North Vietnam, and Cuba all developed out of relatively small vanguards of highly ideologized, militant revolutionaries. All were tempered by their experiences of the underground, of revolution, civil war, partisan warfare, or a national liberation struggle. The leaders of these movements commanded an authority that in most cases lasted several decades. Figures such as Lenin, Stalin, Tito, Hoxha, Mao, Ho Chi Minh, Kim Il Sung, and Fidel Castro were outstanding historical actors, invested with the aura of successful military leaders and state builders, around whom its was easy to weave myths and legends. The activists of the underground and the commissars and commanders of the civil war periods would dominate the new governing structures of the party-state.

The leader cult served to regulate these leaders' relations with their immediate subordinates, with the governing stratum of the state, and with the wider society. It could be used to reinforce hierarchical control, but it could also be part of a strategy of mass mobilization as part of antibureaucratic campaigns. The reception of

the cult by the wider society is more difficult to predict. However, the dismantling of leader cults met in some instances with quite strong resistance, evidence that they had a strong popular base.

See also Despotism; Great Patriotic War; Iconography; Nationalism; Propaganda; Stalin, Myth of; Stalinism.

FURTHER READING

Apor, B., J. C. Behrends, P. Jones, and E. A. Rees, eds. *The Leader Cult in Communist Dictatorships: Stalin and the Eastern Bloc.* Basingstoke: Palgrave, 2004.

van Ree, E. *The Political Thought of Joseph Stalin: A Study in Twentieth-century Revolutionary Patriotism.* London: Routledge-Curzon, 2002.

E. ARFON REES

Cultural Policies

While the Soviet state was concerned with recognizing both the importance of and need for culture, it did so by distancing itself from the past, the bourgeoisie, and the old intelligentsia, and emphasizing the creation of an innovative and authentically revolutionary system. After a period of heated and violent iconoclasm, the USSR realized the significance of cultural heritage, and resources were invested to save what was strategically defined not as antiquated tradition but rather the affirmative past. The avant-garde at first supported the Soviet state, since they were engaged in the creation of original and experimental models, even if these were extraneous to the direct "consumers" of culture: the newborn proletarians.

Agitprop (agitators and propagandists), *proletkul't, narkompros,* and various associations and institutions sometimes disagreed and sometimes cooperated. But all these new forces tended to be involved in political discourse, pursuing the task of uprooting mentalities, habits, and tastes that centuries of backwardness and serfdom had made endemic to the Russian people. Workers' circles were created as an alternative to the bar and church. The cultural space of the factory was promoted as an ideal (no longer forced) place of work, socialization, awareness, and responsible productivity. Especially during the New Economic Policy, an attempt was made to fight the temptations that the neocapitalism of the nouveaux riches brought into play, distracting the young Bolsheviks from the construction of the state, and a conduct that was in line with the principles of sobriety and discipline that the revolution had launched—distractions that artistic-behavioral currents like constructivism repeatedly stigmatized. One campaign targeted much-beloved domestic junk, the philistine concept of family intimacy, and communism understood as theatrical representation, aestheticizing and superficial. Artists like Vladimir Mayakovski hurled their poetic bolts against those who indulged in vulgar pastimes, perpetuating the tradition of the *pošlost'*—a form of self-satisfied Russian triviality with an ancient and execrable past. In an attempt to combine past tastes with present needs, literary genres, characters, and cultural realities that survived Bolshevik attacks were tinted Red; in this fashion, with a dash of Sovietization, they became popular once more. These forms of adaptation were supposed to make them politically correct, using their captivating origins in a didactic effort to involve the masses. This is how Red detective stories, Red comic strips, and Red cabarets were born. The results were not promising; consumers resisted reading between the lines, and tended to perceive only what they already knew and found reassuring, omitting the innovative and educational aspects.

Cultural discourse also shifted under the First Five-Year Plan and subsequent transition to Stalinism. Stalin began a campaign inspired by the concept of *kul'turnost'*—a Russian abstract noun that can be translated as "good manners education"—while he was also intervening in the economy, pursuing massive industrialization and the collectivization of the land. The most cutting phase of revolutionary agitation was over. The New Economic Policy signaled a transition period, "normalizing" the frenzied pace of life. The image of the rough yet severe and rigorous proletarian from 1917 was supplanted with that of the refined Soviet citizen. No more simple clothing, no more awkward houses with unadorned furniture—at least not for everyone. Stalinist cultural policy attempted to both organize and hierarchize the country. Images of exemplary citizen-workers, a model for the rest of the nation, and deserving of the privileges they flaunted, filled newspaper pages and set the tone for a series of cultural mythologies.

"Socialist realism," launched in 1934, identified rules meant to program behavior in both public and private settings, with the goal of harmonizing reality. Since the actual reality did not lend itself easily to be so harmoniously transformed, the focus shifted to marvelous superficial appearances that would, by aesthetic means, create the illusion of harmonious uniformity. Reality was made into theater. The entire country became a stage on which to choreograph demonstrations, parades, and other activities to arouse empathetic emotions and involve the population. All forms of culture, from the most articulated and complex to the most banal, contributed to this model world, which was supposed to provide inspiration and which people were meant to invest in, while waiting for an imminent radiant future. Of course, it was supposedly understood that the old distinctions between high and low culture had ceased to exist, in the name of leveling values and taste. This is not to say that the quality of the literary or cultural texts did not suffer, though. It was generally dismal and contemptible, even though in all its perversity, the strategy that underlay their construction was based on refined creative techniques, and the products featured a subtle mosaic of subtexts, even if their overall appearance might have been coarse. For Stalinist culture it remained essential that the synthesis of the arts, illustration par excellence, was adequate to the task and would transmit the ideological spirit of the era according to the principles of the verbal text, thus guaranteeing its correct interpretation by the masses, the only one power could allow and which it tended toward.

After Stalin's death in 1953 a radical transformation took place, during Khrushchev's so-called thaw. Culture came out in the open; the socialist realist canon and its asphyxiating conventions were abandoned, thus deluding a whole generation into thinking that censorship and terror were things of the past. If the party's youth organization, the Komsomol, called, thousands of youths left their homes and families to cultivate virgin lands, experimenting with the excitement of adventure, with the unprecedented physical nature of existence, while rediscovering poetic and cultural texts that had been removed as "not recommended" during previous decades. Communication flourished once more, following forgotten styles and forms. The public's appetite for debate, discussion, and doubt reemerged after years of unquestionable certainties. Such freedoms were not to last long. During the Leonid Brezhnev years, the culture of Moscow evenings, reading poems beneath the monument to Mayakovksy, performing songs by singer-songwriters, and spending nights in the taiga under the stars with a guitar, vodka, and an Ernest Hemingway novel in one's pocket would all once more be enclosed in the narrow confines of urban kitchens. The Soviet kitchen had been turned into a space for private culture, an alternative to the official and public one; it could expand in space and time, welcoming an improbable number of people for what history would later mythologize as "the nocturnal conversations of the Russians." These were nights in which each topic of discussion was faced with an Aesopian detachment from reality, reaffirming one's position of a-Sovietism, more than anti-Sovietism, even as official culture again proposed socialist realist models, which an artistic current called Soc-art deconstructed to reveal its emptiness.

As public dissent grew, and the indifference and tacit resignation espoused by much of the intelligentsia seemed to lose its hold, Soviet culture was transformed by perestroika. Mikhail Gorbachev's cultural policies, as was the case on the economic and political fronts, promoted effective forms of activism that previous times and positions had led people to forget.

See also Avant-Garde; De-Stalinization; Intelligentsia; Socialist Realism; Soviet Patriotism; Stalinism; Utopia.

FURTHER READING

Fitzpatrick, S. *The Cultural Front: Power and Culture in Revolutionary Russia*. Ithaca, NY: Cornell University Press, 1992.

Gleason, A., P. Kenez et al., eds. *Bolshevik Culture: Experiment and Order in the Russian Revolution*. Bloomington: Indiana University Press, 1985.

Lahusen, T., and E. Dobrenko, eds. *Socialist Realism without Shores*. Durham, NC: Duke University Press, 1997.

Paperny, V. *Architecture in the Age of Stalin: Culture Two*. Cambridge: Cambridge University Press, 2002.

GIAN PIERO PIRETTO

Cultural Revolution in China

The Cultural Revolution (*wenge*)—or in its extended version, the Great Proletarian Cultural Revolution (*wuchanjieji wenhua dageming*)—represents one of the most magmatic and controversial episodes in contemporary Chinese history. Some of the most common definitions of the Cultural Revolution include: uninterrupted class struggle and attacks against the party's bureaucratization, the climax of Mao Zedong's personality cult, a mass movement of urban youths, an economic and social disaster, or the apotheosis of political fanaticism with the ensuing purges of intellectuals and political functionaries.

The vast literature on the subject suggests two different temporal subdivisions. The first, which goes from 1966 to 1969, places its beginning at the time the *May 16 Circular* was published and its end during the Ninth Party Congress, when Mao declared the Cultural Revolution a success. The second subdivision comprises the entire 1966–76 decade—the so-called ten years of catastrophe—and identifies the end of the Cultural Revolution with the death of the Great Helmsman on September 9, 1976, and the subsequent arrest, on October 6, of the "Shanghai Group," better known as the "Gang of Four" (Mao's wife, Jiang Qing, along with Wang Hongwen, Yao Wenyuan, and Zhang Chunqiao). Anita Chan defines the period 1966–69 as the "universally recognized" interval of the Cultural Revolution until "the politicians who seized power after Mao's death decided, for their own political reasons, to designate the period 1966–1976 as 'the ten years of the Cultural Revolution' and in this manner they attempted to strategically merge, in the public's opinion, the period 1966–1969 with the seven years of repression that followed."

The Cultural Revolution's origin can be tied to the complex power dynamics relating to the launch and failure of the Great Leap Forward, which forced Mao to step aside in order to concentrate on "Marxist-Leninist theoretical work," and allow the more moderate political line supported by Liu Shaoqi, Zhou Enlai, and Deng Xiaoping to guide the country, while Mao prepared to return to battle. As early as 1965 a Maoist-inspired document for the first time attacked "some Party members who have power, but who have taken the capitalist road." Another possible origin of the Cultural Revolution lies in the debate about the historical drama *Hai Rui's Destitution* (1960), a work by the deputy mayor of Beijing, Wu Han, which tells the tale of a virtuous functionary who is removed by a corrupt emperor. In 1965, Jiang Qing and Yao Wenyuan criticized the work as a "poisonous weed," which following the allegory, pointed to Mao as the corrupt emperor and Peng Dehuai as the virtuous functionary who had been removed. But Peng Zhen, Beijing's mayor, created a committee (the "Group of Five") that on February 12, 1966, published the *Outline Report on the Current Academic Discussion*, which basically said that the Central Propaganda Department and the Party Committee of the Borough of Beijing intended to defend Wu Han, and keep the discussion within academic boundaries. The counterattack by Mao's followers was launched both during the conference on literary and artistic work in the armed forces, held in Shanghai on February 2–20, 1966, and by means of various articles, in May 1966, that denounced Peng Zhen and Wu Han. The Cultural Revolution began in this climate, and can be subdivided into three phases.

The first phase, May 1966–April 1969, was distinguished by four elements: the close collaboration between Mao, Lin Biao and Jiang Qing, progressive mass mobilization, cultural iconoclasm, and an escalation of violence. A "circular" issued on May 16 served as the programmatic document of the Cultural Revolution: it identified Liu Shaoqi as the "Chinese Khrushchev," and issued a universal appeal to fight against the "representatives of the bourgeoisie who have infiltrated the party, the government, the army and all areas of culture, and who constitute a band of revisionist counterrevolutionaries." A new organ was also created: the "central Group" of the Cultural Revolution, with Chen Boda as leader, Jiang Qing deputy director, and Kang Sheng counselor, replacing the Group of Five led by Peng Zhen. The most powerful visual and emotional symbol, however, was the image of Mao, who on July 16, 1966, then sixty-four years old, swam in the Changjiang (Yangtze); the media event was a clear signal that Mao, after years of retirement, had returned to the battlefield, full of energy and determined to seize power once more.

On August 8, 1966, the Eleventh Plenum of the Eighth Party Central Committee approved the "Sixteen Articles," a document reiterating that the Cultural Revolution's principal target was the "people with a position of power in the Party" who had "taken the capitalist road." This document sanctioned the resort to violence: responding to the appeal "rebellion is justified," thousands of Red Guards were encouraged to "bombard the bourgeoisie's headquarters." On August 18, Mao appeared in public on the Tiananmen Square for a Red Guard gathering, organized by Lin Biao, to fight the "Four Olds" (Old Customs, Old Culture, Old Habits, and Old Ideas) that were attributed to the bourgeoisie and the exploiting classes. The Red Guards were groups of youths coming from "Red families of five types" (workers, poor and lower-middle farmers, revolutionary cadres, revolutionary soldiers, and/or tied to revolutionary martyrs) and they became the protagonists of this period of "Red terror." Responding to Mao's appeal to "sweep away all the monsters and demons"—the class enemies—the Red Guards engaged in "revolutionary" actions whose aim was to destroy the Four Olds, cultivate the "Four News" (New Customs,

New Culture, New Habits, and New Ideas) of the proletariat, and fight the "capitalists" at the various levels of the party-state's structure. In summer 1966 the schools were closed and the revolution overwhelmed the whole society; the Red Guards sacked the houses of the representatives of the "Black Seven Categories" (landowners, rich farmers, counterrevolutionaries, evil elements, right-wing elements, capitalists, and reactionary intellectuals) looking for proof of counterrevolutionary activity, and confiscated their property. "Class enemies" were unmasked and publicly criticized, dragged along the streets and humiliated, beaten and tortured, forced to "reform through labor" (manual), and sent to the countryside or remote mountainous regions. There were many dead.

During the 1967 "January Revolution" (instigated by Jiang Qing and Lin Biao), workers were organized in over seven hundred associations, and held positions of power in the media and the administrative organs. On February 5 the Shanghai's People Commune was created, later to be renamed the Shanghai Municipal Revolutionary Committee, and subsequently the "proletarian revolutionary rebels" were engaged throughout the country in reclaiming power from "those who had taken the capitalist road." The Cultural Revolution thus entered a new phase of "widespread civil war," but various Red Guard and "rebel" factions did not join the struggle for power as Mao had expected. During 1967–68 armed struggle between various rival groups ensued, and the situation became so critical that the army had to intervene. Moreover, it seems that Mao deemed the Shanghai Commune experiment to be inappropriate, risky, and that it might possibly lead to the country's breaking up. It was for this reason that by September 5, 1968, revolutionary committees were established throughout the country: small groups under the command of local urban governments, rural people's communes, universities, and other institutions. Each group included representatives from the masses, the People's Liberation Army, and select revolutionary cadres. The revolutionary committees became the main form of organization in an attempt to restore order and slow the destructive and anarchic impulse of the Cultural Revolution.

The second phase began with the Party's Ninth Congress, on April 1–24, 1969, which approved the abolition of the Cultural Revolution group, and elected Jiang Qing, Zhang Chunqiao, and Yao Wenyuan to the politburo. On this occasion Lin Biao, Mao's potential successor, saluted the "great victory" of Maoist theory regarding "the continuation of the revolution under the proletariat's guidance." It was to be Lin Biao's climactic moment, before his inexorable fall. Lin Biao and Chen Boda in fact became the "new enemies": a possible obstacle to the party's being cast in a new mold. Chen was arrested in summer 1970, after all the radical intellectuals with ties to him, who contributed to the journal *Hongqi* (Red Banner), had been purged. In February 1971 Lin Biao had apparently begun to plan a military coup. Having failed, he tried to escape to the Soviet Union, but was killed in a mysterious plane crash on September 13, 1971. After this so-called accident, Wang Hongwen seemed to be Mao's next possible successor, and in August 1973 he was elected to the post of party vice president. In the meantime with Zhou Enlai's help, a certain number of functionaries returned to power, including Deng Xiaoping.

The third phase of the Cultural Revolution was the scene of a clash between the party veterans and the Gang of Four, who attempted to use the campaign Mao had launched in March 1973 "against Lin Biao and Confucius" in order to remove prime minister Chou from power. After Chou's death, on January 8, 1976, and the ensuing public commemoration on April 5, 1976, which coincided with the festival for the dead, the Gang of Four unleashed a campaign to criticize Deng Xiaoping and "the right-wing deviationist faction." After Mao's death, however, his successor Hua Guofeng allied himself with Ye Jianying, Wang Dongxing, and Li Xiannian, and succeeded in having the Gang of Four arrested. During the Communist Party of China's Eleventh National Congress, on August 12–18, 1977, Hua declared the Cultural Revolution to be over, while actually referring to its third phase.

The Resolution on Certain Questions in the History of Our Party since the Founding of the People's Republic of China, adopted on June 27, 1981, repudiated the Cultural Revolution, attributing it to Mao's "erroneous leadership" as well as the manipulations of the "counterrevolutionaries Lin Biao and Jiang Qing," and condemned it for "having caused serious disasters and brought disorder to the Party and the Chinese people." A large portion of the historiography tends to see the Cultural Revolution as a political struggle within the ruling elite, and an attempt by Mao to reclaim power. Following this interpretation, it would therefore be more a case of ideological struggle than a real revolutionary movement bent on creating an egalitarian society. Yet the Cultural Revolution can also be interpreted as a mass mobilization of urban youths,

responding to Mao's appeal to continue the revolution, in an attempt to prevent the creation of a bureaucratized Communist state on the Soviet model. The Cultural Revolution also provoked a serious economic crisis: industrial production decreased by 12 percent between 1966 and 1968. Historian Anne Thurston defines the Cultural Revolution as "an extreme situation" and underscores how, from the many interviews she collected, a profound sense of loss "of everything that gives life meaning" emerges. It was a period of unprecedented violence, and excesses that caused numerous purges and deaths.

One of the most controversial questions concerns the nature of the Cultural Revolution. Different theories have been proposed: the "struggle between two lines," the "struggle for power," the theory of the "externalization of Maoist idealism," the theory of the "inevitable final result of the deteriorating (Maoist) extreme left-wing line," and the theory of the "two cultural revolutions." The different theses are often associated with the analysis of the "cult of personality" established by Mao with Lin Biao's help. It seems that the key to motivating thousands of people to participate in these political campaigns was their devotion to the Great Helmsman, which took on almost godlike proportions. Some experts argue that the historiography published in the West about the Cultural Revolution is frequently theoretical and written with the benefit of distance from the events, while Chinese historiography is "inspired by official policies" and discourages research on this topic since it is considered dangerous to party unity. The attempt to overcome these differences, though, runs the risk of focusing on Mao and changes at the top of the party hierarchy exclusively. A historical study of the documents from the period 1966–69 allows an analysis of what Mao would have wanted to occur, compared with what actually did happen, by means of a general retrospective that examines the purges along with the difficult social, cultural, and economic issues. Other studies, for instance by historian Liu Guokai, look at the thoughts and actions of common people: individuals, even though gathered in groups, who were involved in and overcome by national political events. Liu Guokai also attributes a moral motivation to some groups that attacked party leaders and government functionaries, and grants the short-lived liberties that common folk enjoyed, while criticizing those in a position of power and making life-and-death decisions with impunity, recognition as a form of social and political capital.

The Cultural Revolution has also been visually narrated by fifth-generation directors (Zhang Yimou, Chen Kaige, and Tian Zhuangzhuang) who combined personal or family microcosms with history's macrocosms in films like *To Live*, *Farewell My Concubine*, and *The Blue Kite*. Historical documentaries on the Cultural Revolution (such as *It's Right to Rebel!* and *The Morning Sun*—and their respective Web sites) offer a unique combination of historical narration, short features from the period, and individual interviews, and examine not only the chronological sequence and causal chain of events but also, in a panoptic perspective, the hypertextual qualities of cultural production and criticism that emerged from the Cultural Revolution.

See also Camps; Classes; Cult of Personality; Great Leap Forward; Lin Biao; Mao Zedong; Red Guard.

FURTHER READING

Barnouin, B., and Changgen Yu. *Ten Years of Turbulence: The Chinese Cultural Revolution.* New York: Kegan Paul International, 1993.

Chan, A. *Children of Mao: Personality Development and Political Activism in the Red Guard Generation.* Seattle: Washington University Press, 1985.

Chan, A., and Guokai Liu, eds. *A Brief Analysis of the Cultural Revolution.* Armonk, NY: M. E. Sharpe, 1987.

Dongping Han. *The Unknown Cultural Revolution: Educational Reforms and Their Impact on China's Rural Development, 1966–1976.* New York: Routledge, 2000.

Jiaqi Yan and Gao Gao. *Turbulent Decade: A History of the Cultural Revolution.* Ed. D. W. Y. Kwok. Honolulu: University Press of Hawaii, 1996.

Law Kam-Yee. *The Chinese Cultural Revolution Reconsidered: Beyond Purge and Holocaust.* New York: Palgrave Macmillan, 2003.

MacFarquhar, R. *The Origins of the Cultural Revolution.* Vol. 3, *The Coming of the Cataclysm, 1961–1966.* Oxford: Oxford University Press, 1997.

Schoenhals, M., ed. *China's Cultural Revolution, 1966–1969: Not a Dinner Party.* Armonk, NY: M. E. Sharpe, 1996.

White, L. T. *Politics of Chaos: The Organizational Causes of Violence in China's Cultural Revolution.* Princeton, NJ: Princeton University Press, 1989.

Woei Lien Chong, ed. *China's Great Proletarian Cultural Revolution: Master Narratives and Post-Mao Counternarratives.* Lanham, MD: Rowman and Littlefield, 2002.

MAURIZIO MARINELLI

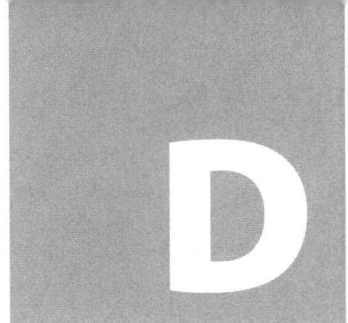

Decolonization

The term "decolonization" was coined intentionally to describe the liberation—meaning more than just the granting of sovereignty—of the European powers' territorial possessions in Asia and Africa. It represented the political, cultural, and idealistic reaction of colonized peoples to the entrenched colonial domination of the second half of the 19th century. Just as colonial imperialism was a well-defined and chronologically circumscribed reality connected to European overseas expansion, to the transplantation of its institutions and the capitalist mode of production to "external" areas, spurred by competition between rival powers, so also did decolonization follow its own path. A definition of decolonization that focuses on "detachment" from the colonizers' world—though important, since the result was deliverance from the colonial system—is limited to the colonial experience itself, and thus not welcomed in the nationalist thought of Arabs, Africans, and Asians. They view the entire phenomenon more like a "Renaissance," with the restoration or achievement of independence, recovery of their history, and reappropriation of their national resources.

Because of its geopolitical location and historical dynamics, decolonization essentially concerned the West's colonial hinterland. The historiography that is best disposed toward colonialism attributes decolonization to the European powers' initiative. And anticolonialism derived, in the first instance, from the application of conceptual categories of European origin, such as nationalism, fatherland, and freedom. The movement's leadership usually came from an elite that had been educated in and shared interests with the Western world—that is, something like a national bourgeoisie. Some authors deplore the choice of the nation as the space in which self-determination was wrested from colonialism because it

led the newly independent states to follow the logic of liberalism and capitalism.

On the other hand, decolonization rightfully became part of communism's history, given the "national question's" significance in Marxist thought about imperialism, and later in the policies of the USSR, China, and Cuba after Castro's revolution. In some cases the anticolonial struggle was led by Communist parties or movements inspired by Marxism in different ways. The revolution that ended with the People's Republic of China in 1949 can be considered part of this movement, even though China was never strictly speaking a colony, because of the value that this experience assumed in the eyes of colonized peoples and the influence it exerted on liberation movements, especially in Asia.

Decolonization was implicitly part of the modernizing and progressive agenda of colonial powers, who initially thought of granting self-government rather than independence. In India, the origins of anticolonial nationalism date from the formation of the Congress Party in 1885. Elsewhere nationalist organizations developed in the period between the two world wars. Some symptoms of what would become decolonization were visible in the outcomes of World War I and events like the Bolshevik Revolution, or declarations such as U.S. president Woodrow Wilson's fourteen points, which were followed by the establishment of the League of Nations, with its (at least virtual) functions as a global government.

Egypt's independence in 1922 signaled a reversal of this trend. Since World War II was seen as a struggle between freedom and fascism on a worldwide scale, the push toward decolonization acquired new strength. The emancipation of the territorial possessions of the European powers resulted from political, constitutional, and military struggles by individual nations, but it was encouraged and aided, in a context in which the repudiation of colonialism was gaining the upper hand, by the political and economic changes taking place worldwide.

The 1939–45 conflict favored the ascent of two powers like the United States and Soviet Union, which supported the liberal-democratic and socialist currents of anticolonialism, respectively, overturned the previous balance of power, and sanctioned the end of imperialism, or at least imperialism in its colonial form. One of the war's first consequences was that following its defeat, Italy lost its colonies in Africa, as Germany had after its defeat in World War I. During World War II, the major colonial powers had not always successfully defended their possessions. In the conferences between the Allies, France's and Great Britain's right to regain possession of Asian territories that had passed into the hands of a Japanese administration was openly questioned.

The more general implications of decolonization increasingly favored a movement toward the independence of all colonized peoples, but it was still subject to the calculations of stronger powers. The implementation in both Asian and African countries of the principle of self-determination, which was inserted in the UN Charter and the Universal Declaration of Human Rights adopted by the UN General Assembly in 1948, faced various obstacles due to the Cold War. What had been the colonial world was now a sort of no-man's-land—referred to as the third world—and it became the preferred site for a confrontation between two ideologies and systems of power that both had universal pretensions. The confrontation between East and West repeated previous East-West antagonisms, even though the East in question was a very different one, Soviet Russia and its bloc, which played the role of "other" to a West that included Europe but was dominated by the United States. The USSR supported anticolonialism even when it was not led by Communist or Marxist forces, both because it believed in it, and because of the benefits it would gain from the erosion of control by capitalism and rival powers. The United States soon abandoned the idealism that President Franklin Delano Roosevelt had exhibited. While it was interested in removing the barriers to the internationalization of the economy in the entire "free world," in actual fact it intervened in defense of the colonial policies of its European allies each time that decolonization seemed as if it might lead to revolution, or to an advance by the USSR or China into the "power vacuum" left by the retreat of the colonial powers. Still, during an event that was emblematic of decolonization such as the Suez crisis in 1956, the United States opposed France's and Great Britain's colonial revanchism, and ended up on the same side as the USSR.

Decolonization was characterized by its contradictory nature: on the one hand, it was a far-reaching process for the emancipation and liberation of colonized peoples; on the other hand, it was a power redistribution from the top down on the basis of the balance of power inherited from World War II. Viewed from the perspective of center-periphery dynamics, it did not mark the end of asymmetrical interdependence but instead seemed to make it more permanent. The end of the colonial empires did not exclude the continuation of a system of control, exercised by Western Europe and the United States, by means of the less formalized instruments of the economy, aid, cultural influence, or the presence of military forces and bases as signs of a neocolonial or big-power policy. Decolonization was a product of the postwar balance of power, but those states that had most recently gained their sovereignty—in a century marked by the rise of the United States to the rank of an absolute power—were obviously not in a position to shape the modern world of exchanges, capital, and technology. Many of the objectives of decolonization were to prove unrealistic, both because of intrinsic limitations and external constraints. The USSR and the forces of international communism participated in this struggle with different strategies as well as varying results in the hope that the scale would tip their way. They especially helped national liberation struggles, but they paid the price for both not having well-developed relations with the world of the ex-colonies and their obvious inferiority to the capitalist West when it came to the global economy.

The dissolution of the colonial empires that belonged to the European powers, and the ensuing independence of the territories that had been part of them, was one of the great events of 20th-century history and put an end to the exclusive nature of a Eurocentric worldview. As the English historian Geoffrey Barraclough writes, "Such a revolutionary event in such a brief period of time had never previously occurred in the course of the entire history of humanity. This change in the position of Asian and African peoples with respect to Europe was the most distinctive symptom of the rise of a new era." The outcome of decolonization went well beyond all the plans for the autonomy and development of colonized peoples that had ever been entertained by the various colonial powers. Europe had ceased to be the center of a world that held the extra-European continents in its grasp, and the world's surface was now being occupied by a multitude of states with the formal prerogatives of sovereignty. If colonialism had concentrated political power in the hands of a small group of European states, denying the countries of Asia, Africa, and the Arab world their identities and rights as nations, with the achievement of independence the number of actors on the international scene had greatly increased. Sooner or later all these states were admitted to the United Nations.

Decolonization roughly followed a geographic itinerary. It started in the Middle East in 1945, leaving an open wound with the creation of the state of Israel, which immediately became the object of Arab opposition. It continued in the Indian subcontinent and Southeast Asia, where a war of liberation was fought in Vietnam and the rest of Indochina that lasted from 1946 to 1954. Decolonization reached North Africa in the 1950s, with another long war in Algeria (1954–62), and reached deeper into Africa in 1960, which entered the history books as "Africa's year." The independence of the British Raj in 1947, with its division into two states, India and Pakistan, so as to give Muslim Indians representation, came to have epochal significance. The defeat of the French army in the battle of Dien Bien Phu (May 1954) demonstrated the vulnerability of great European powers facing wars of liberation. The nationalization of the Suez Canal undertaken by Gamal Nasser on July 26, 1956, also had a great impact. Although Egypt had not been a colony for quite some time, this act became the symbolic counterpart of the construction of the canal during imperialism's rise.

Decolonization did not stop with the achievement of independence: it was a process that by dismantling conceptions as well as political, economic, and psychological practices that accompanied conquest, "liberated" peoples and resources in the entire non-European world. Neutralism—in its different formulations, from the Afro-Asianism launched by the Bandung Conference (April 1955) to nonalignment, elaborated with the fundamental contribution of Tito's Yugoslavia between 1956 and 1961—would guarantee those states that had recently acquired independence a certain degree of autonomy from both the powers and dynamics involved in the Cold War, which was an expression of the "center's" policies. China participated as a full member in the Bandung Conference. The "second Bandung," which had been planned for 1965, but was postponed because of the crises in Algeria and Indochina, was never held, also because of the increasing tensions between the USSR and China.

A first shift in the policies of the USSR, and therefore also international communism, toward the world that was emerging from decolonization occurred in 1955 with Nikolay Bulganin's and Nikita Khrushchev's trip to India,

Burma, and Afghanistan. Another country that the USSR accorded great importance to was Egypt, which in 1955 signed an agreement with Czechoslovakia for the provision of military equipment. In 1956 the USSR firmly supported Nasser during the entire course of the Suez crisis, and threatened to retaliate against France and Great Britain after their joint military intervention in Egypt on Israel's side. Those countries that had recently acquired independence—even when they were seen as led by "national bourgeoisies"—were credited by emphasizing the adjective "national," interpreted as the expression of a tendency or will to cut colonial or neocolonial ties. They were also included by a post-Stalin USSR in the anti-imperialist, anticapitalist, and peace "camp," together with socialist countries and the Communist parties of the Western world. Moscow's reservations toward non-Communist solutions in the ex-colonies had disappeared. It did not matter much that Communists were marginalized or even persecuted in many "friendly" countries. The basic idea was that statism or dirigisme, or even industrial plants or great projects such as the Assuan dam, limited the forces tied to capitalism and opened the road toward socialism. In colonized countries, the proletariat was weak and could not aspire to lead an anticolonial revolution.

The Communist parties were decisive only in special situations. The most significant example is still Vietnam, where a Communist Party that had belonged to the Third International was active in both the cities of the North and the countryside, among the peasants of the plantations. Generally speaking, even those wars of liberation that had a substantial impact, as in Algeria, were headed by middle-class elements with a reformist rather than a revolutionary program. Amilcar Cabral, whose ideological constructs resembled Marxism in many ways, assigned the revolution's leadership in Guinea-Bissau and other Portuguese colonies to the petty bourgeoisie of the cities in alliance with the peasants. The issue of anticolonialism became one of the crucial points of contention in Sino-Soviet relations. China rightly considered itself part of the Afro-Asian movement and accused the USSR of not using all its resources in favor of a global revolution. It is a fact that the USSR did not succeed in adequately defending its allies in the Middle East and Africa, at least until the 1970s, when a military apparatus took shape that was also capable of intervening at great distance. The USSR also tolerated the U.S. war in Vietnam without making it a central issue in its relations with Washington. As a matter of principle, recently decolonized countries attempted to keep their distance from the two blocs on the policy level, and refused close alliances with all the great powers. Moscow was a reference point for many national liberation struggles, providing weapons, logistical support, and political cover, but its opportunities to exert influence diminished once a national liberation movement became a state and interactions at the economic level became paramount. In this area the West enjoyed more advantages than the USSR.

See also Anti-imperialism; Chinese Revolution; Cold War; Cuban Revolution; Imperialism; Nationalism; Nonalignment; Socialist Camp; Third Worldism; United Nations; Vietnam War.

FURTHER READING

Betts, R. F. *Decolonization.* New York: Routledge, 1998.
Calchi Novati, G. *Decolonizzazione e Terzo mondo.* Rome: Laterza, 1979.
————. *La decolonizzazione.* Turin: Loescher, 1983.
Ferro, M. *Histoire des colonisations: des conquétes aux indépendances, XIIIe–XXe siècle.* Paris: Seuil, 1994.
Fieldhouse, D. K. *Economics and Empire, 1830–1914.* London: Weidenfeld and Nicholson, 1973.
Owen, R. *State, Power, and Politics in the Making of the Modern Middle East.* New York: Routledge, 2000.
Westad, O. A. *The Global Cold War: Third World Intervention and the Making of Our Times.* New York: Cambridge University Press, 2005.

GIAMPAOLO CALCHI NOVATI

Democratic Centralism

"Democratic centralism" refers to a set of strict rules about organization and disciplinary ethos that directed the internal life of Communist parties almost until their disappearance. Originally, however, its meaning was significantly different. The term first appeared in the statutes of the Russian Social Democrat Workers' Party that were approved during the Fifth Congress (London, May–June 1907; both the Bolshevik and the Menshevik wings participated). It referred to a party structure in which the organizations of the party's base were established or recognized by a regional committee, which in its turn was elected during conferences or congresses in which the base's organizations participated. The base organizations enjoyed autonomy in their internal activities and the right to publish their own newspapers.

From the Eighth Congress (December 1919) on, though, democratic centralism related to a politico-organizational hierarchy in the party's structure modeled on the new state's territorial-administrative hierarchy. The party organization within a specific territorial district was politically ranked below that of a larger district—one encompassing the smaller district. The entire hierarchy was subject to the Central Committee, elected by the party congress of the whole USSR. This congress consisted of delegates sent by congresses from the federated republics. The latter congresses were composed of delegates elected by the congresses of organizations ranked one level below that of republic (regions, administrative districts, and districts), following an ascending rank order that originated in the congresses of the administratively lowest-ranking organizations (the villages) and in the "cells" at one's workplace. At each level, the local party congress elected both its own leadership committee and the delegates to the congress at the higher territorial level. It was a system in which the democratic investiture of the party's leading organs went from lowest to highest, from organized groups of members on up to the Central Committee, following a process of pyramidal representation. From there authority and political leadership were redirected downward, from the Central Committee down through the hierarchy of the territorial leadership committees elected by the congresses.

The two complementary notions within the concept of democratic centralism—centralism and democracy—were treated with equivalent emphasis at the end of the civil war. At the Ninth Congress (April 1919), a group of delegates opposed the increased militarization and centralization of the party, adopting the name "democratic centralism." Their adversaries sometimes identified them as "party constitutionalists," because of the defense they mounted for the prerogatives of the elective territorial committees of lesser rank, the autonomy of the party organizations in the Red Army from the military command, and finally, the embryonic power divisions that had existed up to that time between the different central party institutions.

The balance between centralism and democracy shifted during the Tenth Congress (March 1921), the same congress that adopted the New Economic Policy and established the single-party system. Following Lenin's proposal, the congress also approved the On Unity Resolution, whose seventh paragraph (which was kept secret) forbade general political discussions and groupings ("deviations," or "splinter tendencies") on the basis of competing political platforms for a brief, but indefinite period of time. This was a drastic politico-organizational innovation, since political groupings had existed within the Bolshevik Party since its inception, and had continued even after the conquest of power at the Sixth, Seventh, Eighth, and Ninth congresses.

The first step toward including these antisplinter measures in the system of democratic centralism was their actual publication, decided by the Thirteenth Party Conference (January 1924). The conference also recognized that these single-party conditions made the election of leaders to the territorial organizations inopportune and legitimized the then-established practice of their being nominated from the top, by the Central Committee's Secretariat. From that point on, the concept of democratic centralism was brandished by the Central Committee's majority as a means to intimidate and get rid of the opposition, by expelling their representatives from the Central Committee and the party. Stalin fought splinter groups on the basis that their real goal was to threaten party unity and its monopoly of power within the state. Already at the Fifth Congress (June–July 1924), this reinterpretation of democratic centralism started to extend to the parties of the Communist International, thereby inaugurating the Bolshevization process within the Communist parties' organizational praxis and political line. The seventh paragraph of the On Unity Resolution was finally included in the statutes of the Soviet party at its Seventeenth Congress (January–February 1934). This norm was maintained in the Communist Party of the Soviet Union until its Eighteenth Congress (July 1990), when on Mikhail Gorbachev's initiative, three different political platforms faced one another.

See also Bolshevism; Bolshevization; Bureaucracy; Single-Party System; State, The.

FURTHER READING

Dan. F. I., and J. O. Martov. *Storia della Socialdemocrazia russa*. Milan: Feltrinelli, 1973.

Di Biagio, A., ed. *Democrazia e centralismo. Il dibattito nel PCUS, 1923–1924*. Milan: Il Saggiatore, 1978.

Lenin, V. I. *What Is to Be Done?* Oxford: Clarendon, 1963.

Procacci, G. *Il partito nell'Unione Sovietica, 1917–1945*. Rome: Laterza, 1974.

Schapiro, L. *The Communist Party of the Soviet Union*. London: Eyre and Spottiswoode, 1970.

Service, R. *The Bolshevik Party in Revolution*. London: Macmillan, 1977.

FRANCESCO BENVENUTI

Demographic Policies

After the revolution, the Bolsheviks entertained grandiose theoretical ambitions in the area of the family. Starting in 1918, a set of laws and decrees, rooted in Friedrich Engels's theories on the bourgeois family but also in numerous misunderstandings, attempted to modify family law. The new government needed to create a model that would clearly distinguish the Communist and bourgeois families. A true model was never realized; instead a series of provisions (mostly decrees) was adopted, whose intent was to review the most repressive family laws. Already in 1917 divorce was granted simply at the request of one of the two spouses. This decree broke most radically with the past, approving a union between spouses that was the outcome of both parties' free choice. The change would be formalized in the 1926 family code. Abortion was decriminalized in 1920, and was granted simply on a woman's request. Offspring born within or outside the confines of marriage were granted identical rights. Religious marriage was discredited, and it was exclusively civil marriage that made a union legal.

These changes were not accompanied by demographic policy measures. The debates that took place during the preparation of the 1926 code show some tension between those who supported revolutionizing family customs, supporting the more equal sharing of numerous activities, the development of unions based on simple agreement, and freedom of choice in giving birth; and those, more numerous and dominant at the leadership level, who favored a more gradual approach that would create a less profound break with the past. A proactive set of health policies was instead developed rapidly, and it attempted to confront worries relating to the elevated mortality rate (by European standards)—worries that had grown since the late 19th century; these policies were also inspired by the goal of improving the human race, and sometimes included strands of a eugenic tradition, although it never took root in the Soviet Union. The political spin amounted to pointing to the high mortality rate as a problem from the past that had now disappeared. "Social" diseases (tuberculosis for instance, but more generally all infectious diseases) were the object of particular attention. The successes achieved in decreasing the mortality rate were certainly helped by both budgetary allocations and the creation of a centralized structure for medical care. The centralized structure was especially effective in an era in which infectious diseases were the main cause of death. Several decades later, though, starting in the early 1960s, this centralized structure would become an obstacle to such efforts due to its size and rigidity.

The provisions and initiatives of the first postrevolutionary period, however, did not get far, because moral reactions during the 1930s caused a noticeable regress—a phenomenon that can be explained by both the repressive and conservative model introduced by Stalinism, and a preoccupation, expressed in various ways, with achieving rapid demographic growth. This preoccupation had two principal causes. First, the USSR was obsessed with using international comparisons to prove socialism's success. Data obviously became fundamentally important, and the utilization of demographic growth as evidence of the superiority of one camp over the other was key. Second, in line with the then-widespread European tradition, demographic growth was considered necessary for a nation's power.

Stalinism's conservative nature impacted how the family was portrayed. Abortion began to be perceived as an expression of decadence, a practice inherited from the previous regime's privileged classes, and in 1936, freely chosen abortions were outlawed. Divorce started to be viewed as endangering the family order. This is how conservative measures intended to boost the birthrate were intertwined, especially after 1936, with the abolition of freely chosen abortions. It is true that the demographic catastrophes of the early 1930s, and especially the famine in 1933, caused a serious decline in the population, which Stalin did not want to recognize. In any case measures to improve the birthrate were an indirect response to this catastrophe. The basic goal toward which policies of the Stalin era tended was therefore dictated by an obsession with demographic growth and support for a higher birthrate.

Starting in 1936, the state increased reimbursements for maternity expenses and necessary care for small children. Mothers of large families (with more than seven children) received even greater subsidies, and so did women who were raising children alone. A subsidy for the birth of a third child was introduced in 1944, and

medals for mothers (with at least five children) and heroic mothers (at least ten children) were also coined. Maternity leave was extended from nine to eleven weeks. In 1944, registered civil marriages once again became the only recognized forms of union, and divorce was made more difficult and costly, and hence out of reach for most couples. The importance that these initiatives were given appears almost ridiculous when compared to the enormous losses caused by Stalinist policies in the late 1920s and the 1930s, including the famine in 1933, as well as the gigantic losses incurred during World War II. Most of the incentive measures were, in fact, repressive and limited to the birthrate alone, ignoring health problems and excluding international migrations as a source of population growth. Thus, the Soviet population numbers actually declined in this period, even if Stalin did not want to admit it.

The years following Stalin's death did not substantially change these demographic policies. The most repressive measures were abolished: in 1955 abortion once more became available on request; and in 1964–65 divorce became much easier and its cost was noticeably reduced. In addition, efforts were made to improve access to family homes, and the capacity and quality of kindergartens and schools, although the subsidies for them were not increased. Demographic issues slowly returned to the fore, however, almost exclusively in the guise of birthrate queries—a rate that was decreasing, as it was in other European countries. Discussions about demographic policy were once again seen as important, especially in 1976 at the Communist Party of the Soviet Union's Twenty-fifth Congress.

In the early 1980s, a series of measures was adopted that increased financial aid and support to child care institutions, and helped to reduce conflicts between women's ability to work and the care of children. These decisions led to a temporary extension in the maternity leave, and provisions for the protection of pregnant mothers and mothers of small children. Other fiscal measures were also adopted, aimed at penalizing individuals who were not married and, to a lesser extent, families with few children—a sort of inverse fiscal proportionality. The state imposed a special tax on men between the ages of twenty and fifty, and women between twenty and forty-five, who were not married or were married with fewer than three children. The revenue from this tax went toward monthly subsidies for mothers raising children by themselves or those with numerous offspring. These measures were not effective, though; they led to earlier pregnancies in women who intended to have children, but without increasing the overall number of offspring. Nor did the mortality situation, whose consequences can still be seen today, or migration policies, which were almost nonexistent, become the object of serious debate. The discussions were dominated by partial analyses, which led to the adoption of similarly partial and ineffective measures.

The Eastern European countries experienced the same problems and limitations. The most symbolic aspects of family policy were adopted in these countries after World War II to mark the difference with the past: legalization of divorce and abortion, along with policies supporting motherhood. Such actions were often more declarations than serious policies, and in the following decades often contradictory paths evolved in the different countries. The common denominator in these countries was a birthrate-oriented family policy, whose realization took unforeseen paths—and differed from the ways that social issues were addressed. In these countries, in-depth analyses of demographics and the family were limited in number, and thus policies were improvised and frequently at odds with social dynamics. For example, the first measures liberalizing abortion were introduced between 1956 and 1957 in Bulgaria, Poland, Hungary, Romania, and later Czechoslovakia; they greatly resembled one another, and had undoubtedly been suggested by the USSR. As worries about the birthrate came to the fore, many of these countries abruptly reversed course. This was especially the case in Romania, which made abortion illegal in October 1966, leading to the subsequent explosion in the birthrate. Bulgaria imposed limits on abortion in 1967, while some restrictions had already been introduced in Czechoslovakia in 1962. When these measures affected delicate aspects of family life, such as divorce, individual national cultures once more took the upper hand. This explains why legislation on matters of divorce was so heterogeneous and exhibited such continuity with the past. Poland was more conservative than Czechoslovakia, for instance. Rather than a coherent model, these differences revealed common legislative and governing practices that were not well suited to social transformation. As was the case in the USSR, the degree of stagnation, if not the actual increase, in the adult mortality rate, was largely ignored—further proof that the attempts at boosting the birthrate lacked credibility, and were masking difficult social and health conditions.

See also Family; Social Policy; Women, Emancipation of.

FURTHER READING

Barbagli, M., and D. I. Kertzer, eds. *Family Life in the Twentieth Century.* New Haven, CT: Yale University Press, 2003.

Blum, A. *Naître, vivre et mourir en URSS.* Paris: Plon, 2004.

Goldman, W. Z. *The State and Revolution, Soviet Family Policy, and Social Life, 1917–1936.* Cambridge: Cambridge University Press, 1993.

ALAIN BLUM

Deng Xiaoping

Deng Xiaoping's (1904–97) international fame is a result of his role in the Chinese Communist Party (CCP) after the end of the Cultural Revolution and the death of Mao Zedong (1976), when he became its dominant political figure, and sponsored a series of economic reforms that accelerated the country's modernization and its transition toward a "socialist market economy." The mark that Deng left on contemporary Chinese history, however, extends over a much longer period, from the 1920s to the Communist takeover in 1949, and long periods in the second half of the 20th century.

Born in the southwestern province of Sichuan, Deng first came in contact with Marxism and revolutionary thought during his stay in Paris as a student in the early 1920s. After a subsequent preparatory period as a Communist activist in Moscow, he returned to China in 1926. In 1930 he joined the Jiangxi Soviet founded by Mao and he offered Mao's faction his support, at a time when the party was still strongly influenced by the Comintern's Bolshevik line. From that point on, his party career was closely connected, for better or worse, to Mao. In the 1930s he also held organizational positions in the Red Army. Deng's lack of military experience notwithstanding, he headed numerous campaigns with the Second Army Group of the People's Liberation Army during the war of resistance against the Japanese and the civil war, leading to the liberation of Southwest China in 1949.

After the civil war's end, in 1949, Deng first held important posts in his province of origin, Sichuan, and was later called to Beijing to fill government positions, assured of protection by Premier Zhou Enlai (1898–1976), someone Deng had worked with in Shanghai in the 1920s. He became vice premier in 1952, and finance minister the following year. In 1954 Deng left governmental hierarchies to become party general secretary, a position he kept until his fall from grace during the Cultural Revolution (1966–76). In those years, his name was associated with that of another political victim of the Cultural Revolution: the republic's president, Liu Shaoqui (1898–1969). Accused of revisionism because of their support for moderate economic policies, Liu and Deng became, in the jargon of the radical Left, elements number one and two of the faction that had "taken the capitalist road." Liu died in 1969, while Deng survived the difficulties of the Cultural Revolution, during which he worked in a tractor factory for several years. After the end of the radical phase of the Cultural Revolution, and Mao's continuing suspicions notwithstanding, Deng was asked by Chou to fill the position of vice prime minister in 1973. With the decline in Chou's and Mao's health (both would die in 1976), Deng found himself at the center of the struggle for succession. The radical wing, called the "Gang of Four," attempted to exploit the power vacuum during Mao's last months to criticize Deng and have him sent away. Only Mao's death in September, immediately followed by the arrest of Mao's wife, Jiang Qing, and the other members of the Gang of Four, led to the de-Maoization process along with the beginning of modernization and economic reforms. Deng's political triumph led to the shift represented by the Third Plenum of the Eleventh Central Committee of the CCP. This plenum initiated the progressive abandonment of the previously dominant practice known as "politics in charge"; it constituted a first step in the process of critiquing radical Maoist policies; and it opened the door to the return of those pragmatic economic policies that had already characterized Deng's and Zhou's work in the early 1960s. These reforms also represented a gradual but irreversible reopening of China to the outside world (which had started with President Richard Nixon's visit in 1972) and a transition to a more collegial form of government.

Deng never again served as secretary general (the position was filled by Hu Yaobang and Zhao Ziyang in the 1980s, and Jiang Zemin in the 1990s), but he remained in charge of the powerful party Central Military Commission. He made crucial decisions during moments of acute leadership disagreement in the 1980s, such as the removal of Hu Yaobang from the party Secretariat in 1987, violent repression of the Tiananmen Square demonstra-

tions in 1989, and selection of a new party leadership at the end of the same year. Deng was always aware that his political work's legacy was having once again placed China on the map of international relations, and having reenergized its economy with concessions to the market and openings to international capitalism. When these results were put in doubt by the political and confidence crisis that followed the Tiananmen Square massacre, Deng undertook his last political and symbolic act. In 1992, at age eighty-eight, he went on a "trip to the South" during which he visited the sites of the so-called special economic zones (Zes), and imparted his blessings on the results they had obtained during the reform years. The Zes, something like capitalist oases designed to attract foreign investment, represented the most advanced form of Deng's strategy. They embodied the idea of a country that was developing at two different paces: an accelerated economic development on the eastern seaboard, which in turn was designed to stimulate the economic development of areas in the interior. This trip silenced his party critics, and gave renewed confidence to investors who had long remained on the sidelines to see how these internal conflicts would develop. Deng died in 1997, only a few months before China regained sovereignty over the ex-British colony of Hong Kong—a goal he had been pursuing for two decades.

Deng will be remembered not so much as the long-lived leader of the largest Communist Party in the world but rather as the person who first unlocked, then left ajar, and finally opened the door to capitalism and globalization. Just as it would be a mistake to credit him alone for China's economic, social, and political development in the last three decades, however, it would be just as mistaken to forget that his influence spreads over eighty years of Chinese political history, during which only Mao had a comparable impact on the country. Deng and his generation share the responsibility for having allowed Maoist radicalism to make foul decisions on the Chinese people's behalf, like the Great Leap Forward campaign (1959–61) and its developmental policies, which led the country to the worst famine in its modern history, and during which Deng was the party's general secretary.

In the early 1960s, Deng pushed for a correction of these hypercollectivist policies: he scaled back the role of popular communes, partially returned land cultivation to peasant families, and attempted to reevaluate the excessive egalitarianism in the distribution of industry salaries. The fact that he championed these moderate policies was what led to his being accused of revisionism during the Cultural Revolution. Yet at the same time, his past earned him a leading position after Mao's death. He reintroduced forms of economic organization directly inspired by the so-called revisionism that repudiated the collectivization and excessive egalitarianism of the 1960s and 1970s, and this became a central part of Chinese economic policy in the early 1980s. For instance in terms of the distribution of social wealth the popular communes were replaced by a system of family responsibility, and the principle "to each according to their needs" was replaced by that of "to each according to their work." Deng's return to the country's leadership in 1978 also marked the return of an organic relation between the intellectuals and the party. Persecuted during the Cultural Revolution, intellectuals, technicians, and scientists became one of the foundations of Chinese reconstruction after 1978.

Deng's political activities were principally marked by pragmatism. Phrases are attributed to Deng that are meant to prove how the end is more important than the means: "it doesn't matter if the cat is black or white, as long as it catches the mouse" is perhaps the best known. Deng's person did not possess that aura of infallibility that had surrounded Mao's until 1978, because Deng made a conscious choice to oppose the cult of personality whose consequences he had personally experienced. Deng understood that he was not, like Mao, a "rising sun," that he would not be able to exercise the same type of influence on a population that was disenchanted by ten years of violence and the domain of the political. Instead, the transformation and modernization of the country required the ability to coalesce a broad alliance of political, social, and economic forces guaranteeing the country's stability and once again giving legitimacy to the party's leadership in a situation that had become much more complex. Deng governed the country with the help of those who were able to maintain this collegiality and the legitimacy of the party's power, getting rid of them once they became a source of divisiveness. He encouraged the emergence of an "affluent society," accepting the fact that some would "become wealthy before others," co-opting segments of the, especially urban, population that had emerged victorious from the reform process.

Another one of Deng's slogans, "cross the river stepping on the stones," revealed the need for Chinese politics under Deng to place political and economic objectives ahead of ideology, adopt a flexible and nondogmatic attitude in order to achieve the goals of economic and social policies, and accept the fact that political decisions were the outcome of successive approximations in the form of experiments and not infallible campaigns. In order to achieve this, Deng limited his ideological constructs to vague formulas (the socialist market economy, socialism with Chinese characteristics, and the initial phase of socialism) that could be adapted to the circumstances of the country's development and the CCP's rule. This led to China developing a fairly contorted and unorthodox version of socialist ideology, which left the field open to the development of neoliberal economic doctrines, while retaining Leninist democratic centralism as the principle behind the party's power.

Deng's writings were never raised to the level of "thought" (*sixiang*) as had occurred with "Mao Zedong's thought," and they are today inserted in the party statutes as "Deng Xiaoping's theory" (*deng xiaoping lilun*). His theoretical contribution to the development of Marxism-Leninism was limited, but the impact of his style of government on the political stability of the largest still-extant Communist Party was enormous. The difference in the leadership style exhibited by Mao and Deng is summed up concisely in the form of the funeral rites with which the two leaders were honored: Mao lies in an imposing mausoleum constructed in record time at the center of Tiananmen Square, while Deng's ashes were scattered from an airplane.

See also Beijing Spring; Chinese Revolution; Cult of Personality; Cultural Revolution in China; Great Leap Forward; Mao Zedong; Socialist Market Economy.

FURTHER READING

Baum, R. *Burying Mao: Chinese Politics in the Age of Deng Xiaoping.* Princeton, NJ: Princeton University Press, 1996.

Goodman, D. S. G. *Deng Xiaoping and the Chinese Revolution: A Political Biography.* London: Routledge, 1994.

Shambaugh, D., ed. *Deng Xiaoping, Portrait of a Chinese Statesman.* New York: Oxford University Press, 1995.

LUIGI TOMBA

Deportation of Nationalities in the USSR

The Bolsheviks' "Declaration on the Nationalities" of November 1917 guaranteed to the people of the newly established Soviet polity the right to establish control over their own destinies. In reality, the nationalities of the former czarist empire, Karl Marx's "prison-house of nations," could not secede from the newly formed Union of Soviet Socialist Republics, nor could they exercise political independence from Moscow. Instead, the Soviet state encouraged them to develop forms of national and cultural identity that would serve as the basis for the eventual transformation of "bourgeois" national characteristics into proletarian international ones. They were allowed to engage in the process of "indigenization," that is, to develop policies for the linguistic, folkloric, and cultural development of their designated republics, regions, and even collective farms. Especially during the first decade of Soviet rule, local indigenous cultures flourished as the multinational Soviet Union made real efforts to allow for national differences. But there were also dangers inherent in this program that threatened minority nationalities. The Soviet state arrogated to itself the right to control national elites through the workings of the Communist Party and, when it felt necessary, to deport national groups from their home territories. Thus, while in some senses helping to create nations and their national territories, the Soviet state could also destroy them and remove them from their lands.

From the time of the civil war, 1918–21, through the early 1950s, the Soviet government engaged in policies of the forced deportation of nationalities. (During World War I, the Russian imperial government also pursued policies of forced deportation, especially of Jews, Poles, and Germans in its western territories.) It is difficult to distinguish those deportations of the 1920s and 1930s that were primarily class-based from those that were focused on nationality. For example, as a consequence of Cossack opposition during the civil war, the Soviets engaged in repressions and deportations of the Terek Cossacks (1920) and of so-called "kulak" Cossacks from the region of Semirechye (1921). Kulaks were supposedly well-to-do farmers, but they were often simply opponents of the Communist regime. Similarly, the collectivization and "dekulakization" campaigns of the late 1920s and early 1930s often meant the deportation of political opponents in the Soviet countryside to Siberia and the Far North. These campaigns were aimed at supposed class enemies, but they also had a strong national component, especially in Ukraine. The famine of 1932–33 in Ukraine and in the Kuban region, which was also heavily populated by Ukrainians, assumed genocidal proportions. The combination of deportations, shootings, and starvation reduced the Ukrainian population by six to seven million people; the repercussions continue to affect Russian-Ukrainian relations to this day. In another combined social and national attack, the collectivization and "de-nomadization" campaign against the Kazakh

people wreaked demographic havoc in Kazakhstan. Not only did one to two million Kazakhs die in the process of being forcibly settled on the land, many hundreds of thousands migrated out of their traditional lands either into the Soviet Union or into China, Mongolia, and beyond. This form of forced deportation may have involved as many as two million people.

There was less ambiguity about what motivated the forced deportations of nationalities during the 1930s from the Soviet borderlands, especially those nationalities whose populations straddled the border. According to Pavel Polian's data, in the western borderlands, these deportations included some 30,000 Ingermanland Finns in 1935 and 450,000 Poles and Germans, in 1935–36. In the south, in 1937, some 2,000 Kurds and others were deported from the borderlands to Central Asia. And in the east, approximately 172,000 Koreans were deported, most to northern Kazakhstan and to Uzbekistan. In some ways, these deportations may be seen as part of Stalin's preparations for potential war at the end of the 1930s, both on the European and on the East Asian fronts.

As a consequence of the Nazi-Soviet Pact in August 1939 and the subsequent invasions of Poland by the Nazis on September 1 and the Soviets on September 17, Stalin obtained a new western border. In the newly absorbed territories of the Baltic states and in western Ukraine and western Belarus (which together were called eastern Poland), the Soviets again engaged in massive forced deportations of alleged counterrevolutionaries and Nationalists. These deportations were less about securing territory in case of war with the Nazis than they were about forcing the Sovietization of these lands and removing potential opponents. The number of ethnic Poles deported in four large waves in 1940–41 from the newly acquired Soviet Ukrainian and Belarusan territories has been variously estimated as anywhere from 275,000 to 1.3 million. Recently, the lower number, which comes from declassified NKVD documents, has been the most widely used. Included in these numbers were the Ukrainians, Jews, and Belarusans, who were deported from these same areas. Most of the deportees of the 1939–41 period ended up in Kazakhstan, Uzbekistan, Siberia, and the Far North.

Stalin did not cease to use forced deportation as an instrument of state policy during the war itself. The single largest national group subjected to deportation was the Germans, close to half a million of whom were Volga Germans who had lived in the middle Volga region since the late 18th century. During a major NKVD and

Red Army operation in early September 1941, roughly 370,000 Volga Germans were deported to Kazakhstan and Siberia. In total, close to a million Germans scattered all over European Russia and the Caucasus were forcibly moved from their homes. The justification for this mass deportation was the presence of Nazi spies and saboteurs among the Germans, and the allegation that the German population protected them from exposure. There was no doubt some truth, and these deportations consequently can be seen as, in some measure, "preventative." But there was no effort to differentiate the masses of innocent Volga Germans from real or even suspected Nazi sympathizers. At the same time, some 89,000 Finns from the Leningrad region faced the same fate, also with no attempt made at differentiating innocent members of the national group from the supposed potential enemies in their midst.

The deportations of the peoples of the Northern Caucasus in 1943–44 were punitive in nature. The so-called punished peoples of the Northern Caucasus—Chechens, Ingush, Karachaevtsy, and Balkars—were accused of having sympathized with and aided the Third Reich in its advances into the region. The Kalmyks, too, were added to this list. NKVD chief Lavrenti Beria oversaw the operations, which Stalin specifically ordered. ("According to your orders . . . ," as Beria often put it in his summary reports about the operations.) Red Army and NKVD troops carried out the quick and violent deportation of whole nations: men, women, old folks, and children. No one was to be left behind. Resisters, passive protesters, and those unable to be moved were often simply shot. Using the data of Nikolai Bugai, who pioneered Russian archival studies of the deportations, and Pavel Polian, who has continued them, the numbers of those deported were approximately 393,000 Chechens; 91,000 Ingush; 123,000 Kalmyks; 71,000 Karachaevtsy; and 40,000 Balkars. Members of these national groups were not only deported from their homeland, but also from the other locations in the USSR where they resided. They were even demobilized from the armed forces and sent into exile with their respective peoples.

The Crimean Tatars, some 189,000 altogether, were also deported from their traditional homelands in the Crimean peninsula. Their case is complicated by the fact that a large number of Crimean Tatars, unlike most of the peoples from the Northern Caucasus cited above, did indeed cooperate with the Nazis during the Nazi occupation of the Crimea from the fall of 1941 to the early spring of 1944. Many openly collaborated and joined Nazi-organized local police forces. But this was as true of Ukrainians in Ukraine, as it was of Tatars in Crimea. Stalin and Beria's reasons for deporting the Crimean Tatars had little to do with the actual level of Tatar collaboration. Rather, they sought to turn the Crimea, a strategic peninsula in the Black Sea and a traditional object of Russian expansionism and colonization, into a fully Slavic and Sovietized domain. In fact large numbers of non-Tatars were also deported from the Crimea—Greeks, Armenians, Bulgarians, Turks, and others—some 45,000 people altogether.

The appellation "punished peoples" is apt not only because of the forced deportations of these nationalities for alleged crimes during the war, but also on account of the horrendous treatment they received both during the transports and after they had arrived at their destinations. They were told of the deportation order only at the last minute, given a matter of hours to pack a few belongings, and then were marched or trucked to local train stations. They were herded like cattle into freight cars. Even NKVD reports noted that there was little food, poor sanitation, and virtually no medical care for the long journeys to Kazakhstan and other Central Asian and Siberian destinations. The freight cars were opened only to remove and bury corpses. The NKVD also reported that when these peoples arrived at their remote destinations wood for shelter and heating and food for sustenance were often missing altogether. The local populations, already suffering themselves under wartime conditions, were not interested in helping the new and alien "special settlers." As a consequence, the deportees searched where they could for food, housing, and work. Tens of thousands died of hunger, exposure, and disease before the bulk of the newcomers found a way to survive and sometimes even to prosper in exile. The "punished peoples," with the exception of the Crimean Tatars, were allowed to return to their homelands only after Khrushchev's "secret speech" in 1956.

Before the war ended, other nationalities were deported as well. The largest groups included the Meskhetian Turks, Kurds, and Khemshins from the Caucasus, some 92,000 people altogether, who were transported to Central Asia in late 1944. Even after the war was over, forced deportation continued to be used as an instrument of Soviet nationality policy. This was especially the case in the Baltic region and western Ukraine and western Belarus (eastern Poland), which Stalin incorporated into the Soviet Union with the consent of his Western allies, as a consequence of the victory over Nazi Germany.

While in 1939–41 the Poles were the major victims of Soviet deportation orders, now in the post-war period, Ukrainians, especially those who allegedly belonged to OUN (the Organization of Ukrainian Nationalists), their families and supporters, some 175,000 people altogether, were deported to the east. Similarly, in 1948 and 1949, alleged "bandits" in Estonia, Latvia, and Lithuania, along with their families and supporters, were deported, mostly to the Siberian gulag. Polian uses the figures of 49,000 Lithuanians, 42,000 Latvians, and 20,000 Estonians deported in this period, in addition to the 36,000 Moldovans who were also deported for alleged banditry during the Soviet takeover of Moldova after the war.

A second wave of deportations in 1951 and early 1952 accompanied alleged and real resistance to collectivization in these newly incorporated regions. Some 35,000 supposed "kulaks" were deported in this period from the Baltic republics, Western Ukraine and Western Belarus, as well as Moldova. There is inconclusive evidence that Stalin may have intended to deport the European Jewish population to Siberia in response to growing anti-Semitic agitation over the so-called Doctors' Plot in late 1952 and early 1953. But the history of Soviet forced deportations of nations essentially ended with the death of Stalin in March 1953.

Some scholars argue that the deportation of nations served the rational ends of the state, by clearing borderlands of potentially traitorous minorities and providing cheap labor and increased economic potential to underdeveloped regions of the Soviet Union. Most, however, question the utility of deportations, especially when so many suffered and died in the process of transfer and settlement. Moreover, the Soviet Union and the Russians earned the deep enmity of the deported peoples. When the deported Estonians, Western Ukrainians, or Lithuanians returned from exile to their homelands, they tended to intensify the Nationalist ferment against Moscow. Deported and resettled Poles and Germans often sought to leave the Soviet Union as soon as possible. Chechen insurgents fight to this day with memories of the harsh deportation of their people in mind.

See also Collectivization of the Countryside; Ethnic Cleansing; Great Terror; Gulag; Holodomor; Katyn Massacre; Kulak; Molotov-Ribbentrop Pact; Nationality Policies; Nations and Empire in the USSR; Sovietization.

FURTHER READING

Bugai, N. F. *L. Beria—I. Stalinu: "Soglasno vashemu ukazaniiu."* Moscow: AIRO XX, 1995.

Conquest, R. *Soviet Deportation of Nationalities.* New York: St. Martin's Press, 1960.

Martin, T. *The Affirmative Action Empire: Nations and Nationalism under the Soviet Union, 1923–1939.* Ithaca, NY: Cornell University Press, 2001.

Naimark, N. M. *Fires of Hatred: Ethnic Cleansing in 20th Century Europe.* Cambridge, MA: Harvard University Press, 2001.

Nekrich, A. *The Punished Peoples: The Deportation and Fate of Soviet Minorities at the End of the Second World War.* New York: Norton, 1978.

Pohl, O. J. *Ethnic Cleansing in the USSR, 1937–1949.* Westport, CT: Greenwood, 1999.

Polian, P. *Against Their Will: The History and Geography of Forced Migrations in the USSR.* Budapest: Central European University Press, 2004.

NORMAN M. NAIMARK

Despotism

Despotism as a political category has a long history. In its best-known versions, it offers a useful instrument for the analysis of events involving Communist regimes in the 20th century, yet it can only be applied to specific moments and aspects of this history. Any attempt to endow it with a universal validity, whether spatial or temporal, is exposed to the danger of simplifying, if not deforming, the social and historical context being examined. Since Aristotle, despotism has been understood as a form of the relationship between those who govern and those who are governed, which develops where there are peoples who are predisposed to being enslaved (in Asia for Aristotle, in the Ottoman Empire for Niccolò Machiavelli, and in Russia for Jean-Jacques Rousseau and Edmund Burke). Despotism in this interpretation is distinguished not so much by excessive violence when compared to authoritarian or dictatorial regimes but rather by the objective nature of the relationships that exist between the top and bottom of society—relationships that have solidified during long-term historical processes. It can therefore only be applied to immobile regimes or ones that transform extremely slowly. And this is not the case with either the Soviet Union or China, the two most significant examples of Communist regimes in the 20th century.

Russia was still a backward country at the time of the 1917 revolutions, but one that had undergone an important industrialization process. During the civil war, the Bolsheviks had to struggle against both the defenders of an "old regime" whose distinctive characteristic—according to Richard Pipes's analysis—was the duration over time of its wealth, and those sectors of Russian society (the representatives of a small Russian bourgeoisie, many intellectuals and artists, and the majority of peasants) bent on defending the achievements of the revolution, but opposed to the goals of the new regime. The Chinese Communists took power in October 1949, in a country deeply torn by a century of peasant struggles and long without a centralized state, whose role in the organization of public works, especially in the area of waterworks, had been vital, at least according to Karl Wittfogel's study, in giving Oriental societies a despotic character.

The actions of an exogenous factor, the USSR's presence, with its military and bureaucratic apparatuses, was decisive in the rapid formation of socialist regimes in the countries of central Eastern Europe—countries with different histories and social structures. The absence of a trustworthy state tradition made the conquest of power by the socialist regimes that formed in the 1960s and 1970s in Africa and Latin America that much easier. The "despotic" traits some of these regimes developed were not inherited from the past but instead were mostly the product of the need to control the formative mechanisms of the new society. These regimes' history is distinguished by alternating relations of social mobilization and repression, rather than by a rigid and unchanging relationship between those governing and the governed.

The common trait shared by various forms of socialism in the 20th century is the constant effort to promote modernization. The internal consensus and international popularity that they enjoyed appear to be tied to this trait, and the different strategies for overcoming backwardness offer a succinct index that can be used to define the differences between these socialist regimes. Is it possible to speak of an "enlightened despotism" that used force to push immobile societies on the road to progress? The human costs of the "great shifts" and "great leaps" were enormous. The attempts to interpret the principle of social equality literally were transformed into tragic dystopias, and were almost everywhere abandoned before the collapse of the socialist regimes. The rates of economic growth of the vanguard country, the Soviet Union, if considered over the entire socialist period, were modest. Those of socialist China and the countries of the socialist bloc in central Eastern Europe were greatly inferior to those reached by the "Asian tigers" and European countries that had taken the road to capitalism. The Cultural Revolution in China, the repression of the Prague Spring, the worker uprisings in Poland in 1970 and later during the time of Solidarity, and the systematic persecution of dissidents in the USSR were products of the need to resolve the social and political problems created by the development of a socialist economy by resorting to repression, and not problems inherited from the past. The anticolonial and anti-imperialist revolutions in Cuba and other countries of the third world that declared themselves socialist only partially reached the objective of guaranteeing development and independence from outside help (and they have often missed them completely).

For those who observe these processes using the category of enlightened despotism, one would think that since many practical failures were typical of these regimes, their inability to debate these failures' causes would be central. The theories about imperialism and the contradictions of capitalism were a screen that prevented the protagonists from seeing the processes of globalization that were taking place. The myth of economic planning prevented an in-depth discussion of the reasons for the failed reform of the socialist economies. The process of decolonization found the theorists of Marxism-Leninism unprepared to grasp its different aspects and perspectives. The preeminence of economics on "metaphysics," proclaimed during the "four modernizations" undertaken in China in 1975, was the first sign of a general renunciation to undertake modernization following the dogmas of Marxism-Leninism. It is perhaps not a coincidence that the only great socialist regime that survived the 1989 revolution was the Chinese one.

Another essential component in the experience of these socialist regimes was the enormous power invested in the general secretaries of the party-state—so extensive as to generate forms of cult and justify the use in Western countries of the suffix "-ism" to designate entire periods by referring to the figure of its principal protagonist. The pathological aspects that this phenomenon often assumed correspond perfectly to the definition that Montesquieu gave of despotic regimes as "arbitrary, absolute governments by a single person." The greatest numbers of works were published about this aspect of despotism after the collapse of real socialism. Helped by the documentation that was made accessible after the archives in formerly socialist countries opened, numerous biographies have described and analyzed the pathological personality traits of the major exponents of the 20th-century world Communist movement, and sometimes also of the secondary ones. The contribution these works have made to a better understanding of personal as well as ideological factors involved in the mechanisms of power in Communist states is noteworthy. Taken together, however, they have described a sort of "subterranean world," where for decades the negative selection of the worst elements of society was practiced, leaving many questions unanswered. Why were leaders who did not have this predisposition to despotism defeated in the struggle for power? How can the international popularity that despotic leaders such as Vladimir Lenin, Joseph Stalin, Mao Zedong and Fidel Castro Ruz enjoyed be explained? Is it possible to consider despotism as a phenomenon that was limited to the 20th-century Communist movement?

The results have been more convincing when historical analysis has considered only one aspect, which by itself is sufficient to define the uniqueness of the socialist countries during a century marked by the disappearance of various monarchies, or their reduction to an ornamental role. The principal Communist leaders (Stalin, Leonid Brezhnev, Mao, Castro, Kim Il Sung, and János Kàdàr) held uncontested power for decades. Attempts at forming a collective leadership that would have represented the sort of bureaucratic pluralism characteristic of more well-established socialist regimes, were short-lived. Perhaps only in China, after Mao, did an open struggle between Communist leaders take place—one that ended with the removal of party secretary Hu Yaobang. Elsewhere the absence of formal mechanisms for the resolution of political conflicts resulted in the impossibility of removing leaders incapable of properly performing their functions, if for no other reason because of their physical condition. The manner in which Mátyás Ràkosi, Antonin Novotný, Władysław Gomułka, and Edward Gierek, "little Stalins" that had become unpopular, stayed in power was the source of the Hungarian Revolution in 1956, the Prague Spring, the worker uprisings in Poland in 1970, and the birth of Solidarity in Poland. Among major Communist leaders, only Khrushchev left the scene due to decisions by the party's leadership; the accusations of "subjectivism" made against him are perfectly compatible with the interpretation of despotism as arbitrary government.

Even given the differences in national context and historical circumstances, the results of this process exhibit common characteristics that can be traced back to a sense of omnipotence and increasing estrangement from social reality, a lack of interest in the consequences of political decisions, and the attention that was primarily paid to the conservation of power. One of the ironies of history was that after Stalin's death, the despotic traits of his personality were utilized by his successors to absolve the system: faults, crimes, and errors could be laid at the door of a single individual, and not traced to socialism and the institutions that represented it. The impact of ignoring the deeper causes of the problems affecting Communist regimes are well known, and they demonstrate that the category of despotism can only be applied with difficulty in politics as well as historical analysis.

See also Cult of Personality; Marxism-Leninism; Modernization; Planning; Red Terror; Revolution from Above; Secret Speech; Single-Party System; Stalinism; Totalitarianism.

FURTHER READING

Lewin, M. *Storia sociale dello stalinismo.* Turin: Einaudi, 1988.

Pipes, R. *The Formation of the Soviet Union: Communism and Nationalism, 1917–23.* Cambridge, MA: Harvard University Press, 1997.

Sofri, G. *Il modo di produzione asiatico. Storia di una controversia marxista.* Turin: Einaudi, 1969.

Volkogonov, D. A. *The Rise and Fall of the Soviet Empire: Political Leaders from Lenin to Gorbachev.* London: HarperCollins, 1998.

Wittfogel, K. A. *Oriental Despotism: A Comparative Study of Total Power.* New Haven, CT: Yale University Press, 1957.

Zhisui, Li. *The Private Life of Chairman Mao.* New York: Random House, 1994.

FABIO BETTANIN

De-Stalinization

The concept of "de-Stalinization" has several interpretations. Most widespread is the understanding of de-Stalinization as the campaign of criticism against Stalin and the revelation of Stalinist crimes. Sometimes the term is used too broadly, to characterize all the reforms undertaken in the Soviet Union after Stalin's death, during the period of the so-called thaw. Just as controversial is the question of the chronological boundaries of de-Stalinization; sometimes it envisages the prewar period (this usage is then based on the presence of anti-Stalinist mind-sets in the party and society), and sometimes it infers the whole period up to the present ("incomplete de-Stalinization").

All these different readings of the term result from the fact that de-Stalinization in the Soviet Union developed as a multifaceted and contradictory phenomenon. The content of the term can be defined as an effort to modernize the Soviet system by renouncing the most odious manifestations of Stalinism: terror, the cult of the leader, a cruel centralization of management, dictatorship in the cultural sphere, and the policy of confrontation in international affairs. De-Stalinization was supposed to create a more attractive picture of actual socialism—within the party and outside its limits. It was a process managed from above and expected to develop in spontaneous forms below—hence, "managed" and "spontaneous" de-Stalinization. The latter was more radical, and was essentially an attempt to amend and enhance the de-Stalinization managed from above. To a certain extent, spontaneity was also possessed by those who had inspired the process in the first place: the Soviet leadership. There was no "de-Stalinization plan"; it was an idea to be incarnated into life, often by a method of trial and error.

If we keep in mind the political aspects of de-Stalinization and look at de-Stalinization *as a policy*, then this phenomenon must be consigned to the period from 1953 to 1964. De-Stalinization was the main component of the new political course adopted by the Soviet leadership, although the term was not used officially. The phrase "criticism of the cult of personality and its consequences" was used instead.

The expression "cult of personality," was first uttered by Georgy Malenkov, the new Soviet premier, the day after Stalin's funeral, on March 10, 1953. Expressing his dissatisfaction with the way the funeral ceremonies had been handled by the press, which had actually raised him to the status of the new "supreme leader," Malenkov stated: "I consider it absolutely necessary to halt the politics of the 'cult of personality.'" In this way, the criticism of the cult of personality was originally tied publicly to a propaganda retuning, a certain abstention from the bestowal of external attributes in the celebration of leaders.

In actual policy, de-Stalinization began with an effort to restructure the organization of power by replacing the model of supreme leadership with one of "collective" leadership. This plan was basically utopian, since it reflected the particular situation (the absence of a single leader) rather than the actual intentions of the rulers at the top, among whom conflicts and power struggles were already commencing. The new Soviet rulers decided against criticizing Stalin openly right away, since the immediate situation was ambiguous; the "cult of personality" and Stalin himself were still separate concepts. (The cult of personality was condemned, but Stalin's name was not yet linked to it publicly.) The first official criticism of the cult of personality was in an article titled "The Communist Party: The Guiding and Governing Force of the Soviet People," published in *Pravda* on June 10, 1953. Among certain Marxist theoreticians inveighing against the cult of personality, however, Stalin's name did come up as well.

The caution and inconsistency surrounding the first steps in criticizing Stalin, cloaked by the euphemism "cult of personality," can be explained by the differing views on this question among the top leaders. Even Malenkov, one of the main initiators of the campaign against the cult, could not find an adequate expression to denote it. At a Plenum of the Central Committee of the Communist Party of the Soviet Union (CPSU), he used the awkward but also noteworthy formulation "cult of personality of *Comrade* Stalin."

For ordinary citizens, the doubts and shifting plans of the leaders with regard to Stalin long remained secret, and for them de-Stalinization began not with criticism of the cult of personality but instead with more tangible and noticeable things. Life in the country was gradually returning to a more normal state. In September, the "night" schedule of work at Soviet government organizations was repealed. (Until then workers at the various ministries and offices had been forced to remain at work until late, in imitation of Stalin, who liked to work at night.) Journals and publishing houses began to publish "seditious" authors like Anna Akhmatova, Boris Pasternak, and various foreign writers. The journal *Novy Mir* was becoming popular and gradually turning into a rather special club for the liberal intelligentsia. Jazz, which had hitherto been considered "bourgeois" music, emerged from the "underground," and foreign variety shows began to be heard over Soviet radio. In February 1954 the Museum of Gifts to Stalin was transformed into the Pushkin Museum of Fine Arts, and an exhibition of Impressionist artists, who had until recently been forbidden, also opened. All these occurrences were perceived by the public as steps toward an open Soviet society, and a signal of hope that the times of dictatorship and isolationism would recede into the past.

The year 1953 marked the beginning of the *rehabilitation of victims of political repressions*. The first decision of the rehabilitation program to become public knowledge, taken in April 1953, concerned the Kremlin doctors who had been accused of plotting against Stalin. The "Doctors' Plot" (in the newspaper terminology of the time they were "doctor saboteurs") was now officially acknowledged to have been a falsification. The rehabilitation of the doctors was followed by that of figures condemned for other major postwar transgressions, including those connected with the so-called Leningrad Affair. All these measures were carried out under the slogan of the resurrection of "socialist legality."

In September 1953, the Special Conference of the Ministry of Foreign Affairs of the USSR—an organ of extralegal reprisals that had become a unique symbol of the repression era—ceased its existence. A reform of the gulag system began. By an amnesty declared in March 1953, more than one million persons—almost half the population of the gulag at the time of Stalin's death—were released from camps and prisons. Nevertheless, the amnesty included practically no political prisoners. The mass liberation of these prisoners began only in 1954, when a special decision was made requiring an audit of sentences issued for political misdeeds.

Political rehabilitation was handled by a Central Commission headed by the general prosecutor of the USSR and similar commissions in the provinces (so-called prosecutor's commissions). During its work from May 1954 to January 1956, these commissions examined some 237,000 cases of persons condemned for political crimes, but almost half were rejected under review (and only 3 percent of the prisoners were actually rehabilitated). Khrushchev, on familiarizing himself with the activity of the rehabilitation commissions, was dissatisfied with both the tempo and results of their work. After this, in January 1956, not long before the Twentieth Congress of the CPSU, new commissions were created, called "party" commissions, because they were usually headed by a party secretary. It fell to these commissions, though they functioned for only six months, to handle the basic work of the rehabilitation of political prisoners.

The rehabilitation commissions were to decide the fate of living prisoners, but at the same time another commission studied materials concerning the victims of the 1930s' terrors. The work of this commission, created by a special decree of the Presidium of the Central Committee of the CPSU on December 31, 1955, was led by a secretary of the Central Committee, Petr Pospelov. He was charged with presenting data, based on secret sources, on repressions that had been carried out against delegates of the Seventeenth Congress of the CPSU. And indeed, the content of the final document issued by the commission on February 8, 1956, went beyond the parameters originally assigned to it. It was basically the first document citing data, albeit in a general form, about the scale of the Stalinist terror. The material from Pospelov's commission became the basis of the famous report, "On the Cult of Personality and Its Consequences," that Khrushchev delivered at the Twentieth Party Congress. Thus, up until its culminating point—this congress—the process of de-Stalinization in the Soviet Union had already achieved certain things, but there were obvious errors as well. The main error lay in the effort to pass over Stalin in silence, to move ahead without looking back. This "conspiracy of silence" about Stalin's name was broken by Khrushchev on February 25, 1956.

The decision about the special "secret" speech was made on the eve of the Congress, on February 13, 1956, at a session of the Presidium of the Central Committee of the CPSU, and hence was a collective decision. Yet the idea of raising the question of Stalin before the delegates at the congress was largely Khrushchev's. Furthermore, it was because of the personal participation of the Soviet leader that the "Pospelov material" became "Khrushchev's speech," and acquired the shape and resonance that made it a "historical" document.

The criticism of Stalin and Stalinism that appeared in Khrushchev's report was emotional, and its evaluations were contradictory. First Stalin was put on a pedestal, where he was given credit for his successful struggle against opposition within the party, for collectivization of farms, and for industrialization. Then he was transformed into the main culprit, and here the list of his mistakes and crimes was much longer than the list of his accomplishments. Khrushchev accused Stalin of organizing mass repressions against Communists (there was no mention, though, of the ordinary Soviet citizens who were also victims of the terror), of mistakes in military strategy during World War II, of the execution of an ineffective economic policy, especially in agriculture, and of complicating international situations as a result of his confrontation with his Western partners and his dictatorship of policy toward his allies in the socialist camp. Khrushchev kept far away from including discussion of any shortcomings of the Communist system itself. He characterized the Communist system as "correct" from its very beginnings, and therefore the system's vices could be laid directly at the door of Stalin. The reluctance of the Soviet leadership to acknowledge the real compatibility of the Communist system with Stalin's personality and of Stalinism itself severely circumscribed the ways in which future de-Stalinization could be fostered.

Khrushchev's report about the cult of personality was given at a closed session of the conference to which even representatives of foreign Communist parties were not admitted, and it is known everywhere in the world as the "secret" speech. Keeping it secret was indeed a successful public relations move, which teased the public's interest. Two days after Khrushchev's speech, on February 27, 1956, a "secret" text of it was distributed by special manuscript to the leaders of foreign Communist parties. On March 5, the third anniversary of Stalin's death, the Presidium of the Central Committee of the CPSU made the decision to share the contents of the report with Soviet party and Komsomol activists. And that meant that the whole country would learn of them as well.

Khrushchev's report had a huge resonance in the Soviet Union. Society was split in its reception of the speech. Some thought that Khrushchev's revelations did not go far enough and demanded that the authorities "go all the way"; others argued for "not raking up the past." In certain regions there were cases of vandalism against monuments to Stalin, and at some meetings there were proposals to remove Stalin's body from the Mausoleum. Some called for the "regeneration" of the Soviet system, pointing to its lack of democracy, and there were appeals to "go back, to return to Lenin." Utterances like this were evaluated by the authorities as "hostile sorties" that should result in expulsion from the party.

The most dramatic events occurred in Georgia, where from March 5 to 9, 1956, mass demonstrations took place in support of Stalin. These demonstrations were crushed by force of arms—the first instance in which the new authorities had resorted to open violence against peaceful citizens (before then, weapons had been used only to put down disturbances in prison camps).

The unmasking of Stalinist crimes caused a crisis in Communist ideology and raised doubts about the practical results of communism, particularly in the Soviet Union. Orthodox Communists lost their bearings, and anti-Communist-inclined intellectuals received a weighty argument in their favor. The results of the crisis

touched not only the Soviet Union. To no lesser a degree they affected the Communist parties of other countries as well.

In the consciousness of foreign Communists, Stalin embodied not only the Soviet Union but also the whole Communist idea. After the criticism of Stalin the Soviet experience could no longer be considered a model to imitate and because of this, the Soviet Union forfeited its exclusive right to world leadership in the Communist movement. Other leaders, such as Tito in Europe and Mao Zedong in Asia, could now vie for Stalin's place in the hierarchy of world communism. The Chinese Communist Party was the only party in the socialist camp to criticize Khrushchev's "secret" speech.

Khrushchev's anti-Stalinist report exposed the leaders of the Eastern bloc countries to some danger, since many of them could have been accused of the same things as Stalin was. The leaders of the Western Communist parties were also vulnerable, and the popularity of Communists in these countries began to drop sharply. Massive desertions from the party began and the Communists lost the support of the left-wing intellectuals. All these issues became more dynamic after June 5, 1956, when the *New York Times* published the text of Khrushchev's "secret" speech, which then rapidly spread around the world.

After the publication of the text of the speech, criticism of communism in general and the Soviet system in particular got a second wind. The overall radicalization of moods was noticeable in the Communist environment as well. One of the most authoritative leaders of the Communist movement, Palmiro Togliatti, averred that the "cult of Stalin could have been born only in the Soviet system." The Moscow leadership continued to stand firm, denying that there was any mutual connection between Stalin's dictatorship and the Soviet political system. (On June 30, 1956, a decree by the CPSU's Central Committee titled "On Overcoming the Cult of Personality and Its Consequences" gave this denial special emphasis.)

De-Stalinization was the cause and simultaneously one of the results of the political crises in the countries of Eastern Europe, which assumed their most radical forms in Poland and Hungary in the fall of 1956. The popular uprising in Hungary, which the controlled Communist press designated as nothing other than a "counterrevolutionary mutiny," was crushed by the armed intervention of the USSR.

Fearing a repetition of such events in the other countries of the socialist camp, including in its own country, the Soviet leadership decided to call a halt to the anti-Stalinist campaign. De-Stalinization was suspended; new treatments of the role and position of Stalin in Soviet history appeared (not particularly acclaiming him but also not subjecting him to critical attacks), and those that continued to reason in the spirit of the Twentieth Congress were subjected to a wave of repressions, which became particularly noticeable in 1957. Khrushchev did not renew his criticism of Stalin until five years later, in October 1961, at the Twenty-second Party Congress. This time, the content of the criticism was better thought through and argued. Still, without the original sensationalism, the new revelations lacked the resonance that they had in 1956.

The criticism of Stalin became most conspicuous, both in its content and consequences, through the implementations of de-Stalinization. And ideology was not the only sphere in which, during the years of the "Thaw," changes took place that involved some of the most essential aspects of the Soviet system. These changes were in the system of government (decentralization), in culture (the "new wave" in literature, the cinema, and painting), in the economy (an attempt to resurrect market forces), and in other areas of life. The reforms of the Khrushchev era were notable for their spasmodic nature and inconsistency, and, in any case, never went as far as equating Stalinism with socialism. De-Stalinization was conceived of and carried out as a process of "purging" socialism from "layers" of Stalinism. These efforts were doomed to failure, yet it was precisely this failure that permitted the Communist reformers of the 1980s to avoid repeating the mistakes of the past.

See also Cult of Personality; Gulag; Khrushchev, Nikita; Peaceful Coexistence; Secret Speech; Socialist Camp; Soviet Bloc; Stalin, Myth of; Stalinism.

FURTHER READING

Burlackij, M. *Khrushchev and the First Russian Spring.* London: Weidenfeld and Nicolson, 1991.

Filtzer, D. A. *The Khrushchev Era: Destalinization and the Limits of Reform in the USSR, 1953–1964.* Basingstoke, UK: Macmillan, 1993.

Krushchev, N. *Report of the Central Committee to the 20th Congress of the Communist Party.* Moscow: Foreign Languages Publishing House, 1956.

———. *The Secret Speech: Delivered to the Closed Session of the 20th Congress of the Communist Party of the Soviet Union.* Nottingham, UK: Spokesman Books, 1976.

Zubkova, E. U. *Russia After the War: Hopes, Illusions, and Disappointments, 1945–1957.* Armonk, NY: M. E. Sharpe, 1998.

ELENA U. ZUBKOVA

Détente

A policy of détente existed for the entire duration of Cold War. On both sides of the iron curtain, doubts emerged about whether the other side was as aggressive and powerful as argued by those who denounced Soviet aggression or, conversely, Western imperialism. Voices were continuously raised to underscore the costs of the East-West confrontation: the need to invest significant resources in armaments without any assurance they were really intimidating the opponent; but also the development of authoritarian tendencies within both sides' societies, and the danger of atomic catastrophe. And those who were particularly harmed by the blocs' antagonism also tirelessly rose in protest: the Germans who were forced to endure their country's division; European nations that felt diminished by their dependence on world powers; and those groupings that the confrontation reduced to perennial losers within their respective domestic political arenas.

The goal of suppressing the East-West conflict was always difficult, however. One needed to get rid of exaggerated fears that had become solid ideological certainties. One needed to overcome the vast coalition of forces that profited from the confrontation and therefore—consciously or not—were "secondary causes" of the Cold War. Finally, one needed to be willing to take some risks to engage with one's opponent. Since these conditions were not being realized sufficiently fast, efforts to contain the East-West conflict alternated with renewed drives toward escalation. Phases of détente and Cold War have often existed together within the protagonists themselves. Only rarely has one form of the confrontation between East and West managed to openly and completely dominate the other, making it impossible to neatly divide the periods of détente from those of the Cold War.

The first climactic moment in the policy of détente occurred after Stalin's death, on March 5, 1953. Stalin's successors spoke of the "possibility of a lasting coexistence" and came out in favor of a "peaceful competition between the two different systems." The Korean War was interrupted by an armistice, and the Soviet government reestablished diplomatic relations with Yugoslavia, Greece, and Israel. Georgy Malenkov, the head of the Soviet government, and Interior Minister Lavrenty Beria simultaneously exerted pressure so that an agreement with Western powers might be reached by neutralizing Germany. To achieve this, they would have been willing to give up the predominance of the Socialist Unity Party of Germany in East Germany. British prime minister Winston Churchill also worked to reach a similar agreement; after the West had strengthened its position, the time had come in his opinion to end the Cold War.

Yet Beria's and Churchill's initiatives did not lead far. After the repression of the June 17, 1953, revolt in East Germany, and Beria's subsequent arrest, Walter Ulbricht was able to preserve his power in the German Democratic Republic (GDR). Konrad Adenauer for his part committed Western powers to stick to negotiations that would have resulted in the integration of a unified Germany into the Western bloc. This led to the failure of the meeting of foreign ministers that took place in Paris during the months of January and February 1954. The Soviet government, now led by Khrushchev, in order to show it was still available for an agreement, accepted the neutralization of Austria in spring 1955; after signing the State Treaty on May 15, 1955, Soviet troops withdrew from the country.

Discussions during the following years dealt with Soviet proposals for establishing a collective system of European security (February 1954), and controlling disarmament, whose goal was to gradually arrive at a mutually agreeable upper limit, identical for all sides (May 1955). During the course of the first "Four Powers" summit, in July 1955 in Geneva, U.S. president Dwight Eisenhower agreed to start disarmament talks and begin a noticeable reduction of U.S. troops in Europe. In early 1957, it was the head of the British opposition, Hugh Gaitskell, and Polish foreign minister Adam Rapacki who enlivened discussion with proposals for controlled disarmament in Central Europe. According to Gaitskell, all foreign troops could be withdrawn from the two Germanies, Poland, Czechoslovakia, and Hungary; Rapacki proposed that these states be declared nuclear-free zones. Adenauer, contradicting this reasoning, instead managed to have the North Atlantic Treaty Organization (NATO) forces in Europe supplied with atomic weapons in December 1957. The fear of a reduced U.S. presence was therefore compensated by an increase in the nuclear deterrent.

Faced with this new push toward rearmament, Khrushchev threatened in November 1958 to grant the GDR control over the access routes to West Berlin (the "Berlin Ultimatum"). His aim was to force the West to recognize the GDR and renounce supplying the Federal Republic of Germany (FRG) with nuclear weapons. Khrushchev's maximum goal was the integration of West Berlin into the GDR. The tensions generated by the ultimatum only dissolved with Khrushchev's decision in July 1961 to make do with the blockade of West Berlin. The building of the Berlin Wall that emerged as a result—starting in August 13, 1961—was opposed by U.S. president John F. Kennedy, who nonetheless avoided claiming the Allies had rights to all of Berlin. He instead started negotiations with Khrushchev; his goals were the de facto recognition of both German states along with the signing of both a nuclear nonproliferation treaty and another to halt nuclear testing. After a further exacerbation of the confrontation between the USSR and the United States because of the Cuban crisis in October 1962, Khrushchev and Kennedy agreed in June 1963 to have a hotline installed between the two centers of government in order to prevent the escalation of new crises in the future. A first accord to ban nuclear testing in August 1963 (Partial Test Ban Treaty) forbade atomic explosions in the atmosphere.

In the course of new negotiations, Kennedy's and Khrushchev's successors agreed on the basic outlines of a treaty on the nonproliferation of nuclear weapons, which was later signed on July 1, 1968, after long and complex negotiations with countries that did not yet possess these kinds of weapons. In March 1966, the Soviet leadership agreed to a U.S. request to start negotiations aimed at banning missile defense systems, but only on the condition that negotiations for the limitation of "strategic" weapons—intercontinental ballistic missiles and submarine-launched nuclear missiles—be started at the same time. In June 1969, the Richard Nixon administration agreed to this dual proposal, and on November 17, 1969, the Strategic Arms Limitation Talks (SALT) started in Helsinki.

In the meantime, French president Charles de Gaulle had committed himself to achieving European cooperation "from the Atlantic to the Urals," and in the FRG a majority had been reached, even if initially a slim one, to engage in a policy of "change through rapprochement," in Egon Bahr's formulation: the FRG was ready to recognize the loss of East German territories and negotiate agreements with the GDR. Willy Brandt's and Walter Scheel's government accepted the principle of the "inviolability" of existing European borders, including those between the FRG and the GDR, at the Moscow Accords on August 12, 1970. The Soviet government in return agreed to receive a letter in which the FRG government declared it would continue to work for "a state of peace in Europe in which the German people regains its unity in free self-determination." Similar agreements were reached between the FRG and Poland (December 1970), and the FRG and Czechoslovakia (December 1973), in addition to the Four-Power Agreement that regulated access routes to West Berlin: it was to be represented at the international level by the FRG (September 1971). In November 1972 the two German governments signed the "Basic Treaty," after which the GDR paid for international recognition with a further increase in circulation between the two Germanys.

President Nixon, during a summit with the Communist Party of the Soviet Union's general secretary, Leonid Brezhnev, and concurrently with German *Ostpolitik*, signed a first batch of treaties for the limitation of strategic armaments (SALT I) on May 26, 1972, in Moscow. One of the agreements limited missile defense systems to two per side; the number of launchpads for intercontinental ballistic missiles would be frozen at the then-current level for five years, and the upper limit for submarine-based systems was also fixed. In addition, agreements for the peaceful use of space, technological and medical collaboration, the prevention of maritime incidents, and ecological collaboration were signed. The two great world powers also stated in a declaration of principles that they would each recognize their respective spheres of influence in the interests of security, and renounce claims on their counterpart at the global political level. Nixon, acceding to Brezhnev's wishes, agreed to convene the Conference on Security and Cooperation in Europe (CSCE) during the following summer. In another meeting of both NATO and Warsaw Pact members convened for that purpose, the reduction of conventional forces in Europe was supposed to be discussed (Mutual and Balanced Force Reductions).

The CSCE opened on July 1973 in Helsinki. Representatives from thirty-five states—all the countries in Europe with the exception of Albania, along with Canada and the United States—discussed European security, collaboration in economic, scientific, and technical areas, and cooperation on humanitarian and ecological issues. The conference concluded on August 1, 1975, with the signing of a document in which an increase in economic relations (favored by the Soviet Union) was matched with a declaration recognizing human rights and fundamental freedoms. Measures to ensure the "free exchange of people, information, and opinion" as well as the creation of a climate of trust on the military level were also agreed to.

If these accords encouraged the development of movements for freedom in the Soviet bloc, the negotiations for troop reductions in Europe instead only proceeded painfully. After difficult preliminary discussions, negotiations between the FRG, the Benelux states, Great Britain, the United States, and Canada on one side, and the GDR, Poland, Czechoslovakia, and the Soviet Union on the other, started in Vienna. The remaining countries from NATO and the Warsaw Pact only took part as observers, while France did not participate. While the West was focused on reaching a balance in conventional forces in Europe, representatives from the Warsaw Pact insisted on reaching a percentage-based reduction in armed forces.

Negotiations for further reductions in strategic armaments and reductions in conventional armaments in Europe came to a halt because of reciprocal mistrust. The second group of accords relating to strategic armaments (SALT II), signed by Brezhnev and U.S. president Jimmy Carter after complex negotiations during the Vienna summit on June 18, 1979, was immediately criticized in the United States. The Soviets began modernizing their medium-range missiles (a topic that the United States initially did not want to discuss), leading NATO to adopt a "dual resolution" on December 12, 1979, with which it announced the deployment of new medium-range and cruise missiles in Europe in case it were not possible to obtain an—unspecified—reduction in the Soviet missile arsenal.

The Soviet intervention in Afghanistan began a few days later, and the dialogue between Russia and the United States broke down. Carter suspended the ratification of the SALT II accords, and his successor, Ronald Reagan, elected in November on a wave of criticisms of détente, concentrated at first on public attacks on the Soviet Union and strengthening the U.S. arsenal. The European allies, and especially French president Valéry Giscard d'Estaing and German chancellor Helmut Schmidt, convinced Reagan to resume negotiations on medium-range missiles only with difficulty. During the negotiations, the Reagan administration insisted in pursuing its objective of increasing U.S. superiority. In March 1983 Reagan announced the Strategic Defense Initiative, with the aim of installing a missile defense system in space, which ran the risk of becoming a unilateral withdrawal from the existing balance of nuclear deterrents.

These weapons' increasing dangerousness and the Reagan administration's aggressive attitude provoked the growth of a peace movement in both Western Europe and the United States. This movement did not manage, however, to prevent the November 1983 decision to install new medium-range missiles in Europe, after a complex series of negotiations had been completed. Still, the constructive strengthening of relations within Europe and between German states continued, even after Poland declared a state of emergency in December 1981. The FRG government, led by Chancellor Helmut Kohl of the Christian Democratic Union, who had come to power in October 1982, continued the policy of détente begun by the German Social Democratic Party.

A more comprehensive détente in East-West relations was only reached once Mikhail Gorbachev decided to make radical proposals on disarmament. Initially he proposed a 50 percent reduction in offensive strategic weapons, then a "zero solution" for medium-range missiles—in other words, their complete removal—and additionally a program for the complete elimination of nuclear weapons by the year 2000. Finally, he declared he was also available to discuss a substantial reduction in conventional weapons "from the Atlantic to the Urals," with mutually agreed-to mechanisms for local verification. Reagan could not attempt to avoid these offers nor—convinced he had in the meantime reestablished U.S. supremacy—did he continue to; therefore, in the course of a meeting with Gorbachev in Reykjavik on October 11–12, 1986, he informally agreed with the Soviet offer. During a subsequent summit held in Washington on December 8, 1987, a treaty for the total elimination of medium-range missiles, which also contained provisions for local verification inspections, and an accord on the principle of reducing offensive strategic weapons by 50 percent were both signed.

The actual conclusion of the accord to halve each side's nuclear arsenal would have to wait awhile. U.S. experts refused to include sea-launched cruise missiles in the agreement because they wanted to keep them as a strategic reserve. They also opposed a reduction in arma-

ments based on limiting the number of nuclear warheads per missile because it would have been easy to circumvent. It was not until July 31, 1991, that Gorbachev and George H. Bush signed the Strategic Armaments Reduction Treaty, which limited the number of nuclear warheads to six thousand for each side (a reduction of about 20 to 35 percent) and also included specific verification procedures.

The issue of the limitation of conventional armaments was instead resolved more rapidly. In the course of negotiations on conventional armed forces in Europe, which had begun in Stockholm in March 1989, Soviet representatives agreed to both a more than proportional reduction in the armed forces of the Warsaw Pact and the verification of the accords with a detailed system of inspections. During a CSCE summit that took place in Paris on November 19–21, 1990, a treaty was signed that set a low upper limit for both sides' weapons systems. The participants also agreed to increase the exchange of information on their armed forces and military activities as well as transform the CSCE into the Organization for Security and Cooperation in Europe, with a secretariat, bodies to observe elections and prevent conflicts, and a parliamentary assembly.

The Warsaw Pact was dissolving in the meantime, the Communist Party's monopoly on power in the Soviet Union had been broken, and Germans in the GDR had voted in favor of joining the FRG. The liaisons between military representatives of the East and West, which had been established during efforts at détente, accompanied the dissolution of the Soviet empire and strengthened relations of cooperation during this phase. While negotiations for the unification of the GDR and the FRG, which began in April 1990 and ended with the signing of treaties on September 12–13, were continuing, German chancellor Kohl agreed to a reduction in the Bundeswehr (the FRG's armed forces), renounced the presence of Allied forces and nuclear weapons on the territory of the ex-GDR, and made significant financial contributions to help with the withdrawal of Soviet troops. A unified Germany supported further reforms in the Soviet Union and the development of collective security structures.

See also Atomic Bomb; Bipolarity; Cold War; Conference on Security and Cooperation in Europe; North Atlantic Treaty Organization; Ostpolitik; Peaceful Coexistence; Perestroika; Second Cold War; Warsaw Pact.

FURTHER READING

Garthoff, R. L. *Détente and Confrontation: American-Soviet Relations from Nixon to Reagan.* Washington, DC: Brookings Institution, 1994.

———. *The Great Transition: American-Soviet Relations and the End of the Cold War.* Washington, DC: Brookings Institution, 1994.

Loth, W. *Overcoming the Cold War: A History of Détente, 1950–1991.* New York: Palgrave, 2002.

WILFRIED LOTH

Dictatorship of the Proletariat

The "dictatorship of the proletariat" was said by Lenin to lie at the core of orthodox Marxism, and when writing *The State and Revolution* he found several uses of the term by Karl Marx. The October Revolution promoted the Bolsheviks to the leadership of far-left politics in Europe and to the formation of the Communist International. Among the results was the acceptance of Leninist doctrines as the sole legitimate expression of the Marxist tradition in the 20th century.

In fact, Marx in his long career had deployed the term—either as the dictatorship of the proletariat or in some other variant—little more than a dozen times. It was scarcely a frequent slogan, far less a fundamental aspect of his historical thinking. Furthermore, Lenin's contemporary critics cast doubt on whether Marx's references to dictatorship could necessarily be interpreted as approving the installation of a formal class dictatorship that denied political and civil rights to the nonproletarians in any future revolutionary society. Karl Kautsky and Yuli Martov, for example, insisted that socialism in power was uncongenial for Marx unless associated with universal rights. Marx, according to their analysis, had seen capitalism as a form of bourgeois dictatorship. They contended that when socialists took power, the authority of the working class should become dominant but should not involve—and, because of the popularity of socialist policies, would not need to involve—constitutional restrictions on the middle and upper classes.

Lenin had introduced the dictatorship of the proletariat to the program of the Russian Social-Democratic Workers' Party at its Second Congress in 1903. Martov and Plekhanov, his allies at the time, had not demurred since they did not yet appreciate Lenin's fanatical literalism. As Lenin's doctrinal zest for police-state methods, including terror, became clearer, they criticized the whole basis of Leninism. In 1917 they warned that Bolshevik policies would bring the country to ruin and Marxism into discredit.

Lenin himself was in a bit of a quandary as a theoretician since he recognized that the "proletariat" was far from constituting the majority of the population of the former Russian Empire. Ever ready to adapt the works of Marx and Engels to current political purposes, he modified his guiding slogan and started talking about the need for a "dictatorship of the proletariat and the poor peasantry"—and sometimes even a "dictatorship of the proletariat and the peasantry." Once his party held power, he reverted more often to his conventional preference: the dictatorship of the proletariat. The richer peasants by then were being treated as enemies of the Soviet system. Until the October Revolution, furthermore, he had moderated his discourse of terror, civil war, and antidemocratic procedures. This tactical restraint fell away as the Bolshevik leadership established their dictatorial rule. Lenin was not alone in "theorizing" what needed to be done. Bukharin and Trotsky were to the fore in arguing that socialism could not be introduced without dictatorship, and Trotsky proposed in his *Terrorism and Communism* that extensive state terror was unavoidable.

The first Soviet constitution of June 1918 incorporated this way of thinking as "the former people" were disenfranchised; and the Red Terror from September 1918 brought class dictatorship into brutal realization as aristocrats, industrialists, landowners, and priests were routinely persecuted. Imprisonment and execution became the norm in the civil war.

Leninists by then took it for granted that a violent seizure of power and a systematic dictatorship were the prerequisites of the successful consolidation of a socialist state. This was accepted by all the parties belonging to the Communist International; and when Trotsky founded his own (Fourth) International in 1938 he had no quarrel with the desirability of dictatorship and terror. The argument was that the possibility for a peaceful transition to socialism had been disabled by the transformation of world capitalism by the early 20th century. Imperialism and militarism supposedly made such a transition a utopian dream. What Communists were asked to overlook was the fact that workers in the USSR did not exercise collective self-rule. *The State and Revolution* had promised that the proletariat would enjoy the freedom to take charge of political and economic affairs. Bolshevik oppositionist groups contended that instead a dictatorship of the party had been constructed. The vision of proletarian liberation had in practice been abandoned. The official leadership admitted that workers were not running everything; but they put this down to the cultural backwardness of the working class and its exhaustion in the civil war.

Stalin in 1936 decided that the Soviet Union needed to gain a reputation for universal political and civil rights even though he was currently conducting a terror campaign of the greatest ferocity. The new USSR constitution therefore omitted mention of dictatorship. Allegedly the need for such an order has passed. There could hardly have been a more misleading presentation of contemporary reality. Stalin engaged in a similar obfuscation when overseeing the construction of Communist states in Eastern Europe after 1945. They were called "people's democracies" rather than dictatorships. The doctrinal rationale was that the USSR's military victory and occupation of the countries in the region meant that anti-Communist forces could not effectively resist communization; and this in turn did away with the necessity of dictatorship. Mao Zedong in China also avoided defining his new state as a proletarian dictatorship. He favored the term "people's democratic dictatorship." Both in Eastern Europe and the People's Republic of China the facts of the situation were different from the official theories: the Communist states really were dictatorships.

Not proletarian dictatorships, of course; for in none of them did the working class exert class power over the rest of society. The Communist apparatus ruled. The nature of the apparatus differed from country to country depending on the balance of power among party, government, police, and army. Lenin's dream in *The State and Revolution* endured only as a primordial myth of the Communist order. Only when the Euro-Communists asserted themselves in the 1970s did any large group of Communists reject the entire justification for the dictatorship of the proletariat.

See also Citizenship; Constitutions; Eurocommunism; Marxism-Leninism; Red Terror.

FURTHER READING

Lenin, V. *The State and Revolution.* Ed R. Service. London: Penguin, 1992.

Service, R. *Lenin: A Political Life*, vols. 1 and 2. London: Macmillan, 1985 and 1991.

ROBERT SERVICE

Dimitrov, Georgi

Georgi Dimitrov (1982–49), one of the most well-known leaders of the Comintern and the Bulgarian Communist Party, headed the Communist regime in Bulgaria during the second half of the 1940s.

Dimitrov was born to a modest village family of refugees from Macedonia, which moved soon after his birth in search of work and settled in Sofia. There his father sewed and sold fur hats. Dimitrov received only an elementary school education, and as the oldest son in a family with many children, went to work in a printing office when he was twelve. The young worker actively educated himself and read a great deal. He soon began to take part in the labor union movement, and rose to be an activist in the printers' union and then in the Bulgarian Social Democratic Workers' Party, becoming a member in 1902. At that time the party was racked by a struggle between its left-leaning radical movement, the so-called narrow socialists (or *tesniaks*, from the Bulgarian word *tesen*, meaning narrow) and the more moderate movement, the so-called broad socialists. Dimitrov took the side of the tesniaks, and later, when due to a split in the Bulgarian Social Democratic Workers' Party in 1903 the two movements became separate parties, quickly became a prominent functionary and then one of the leaders of the Tesniak Party and the labor unions under the influence of that party. He became known not only for his organizational activity, which included leading strikes, but also as a propagandist and party publicist.

In 1913 Dimitrov was elected as a deputy to the Bulgarian Parliament, representing the tesniaks. When his party, one of the closest to the Russian Bolsheviks in the Second International, took an antiwar position during World War I and came out against Bulgaria's participation, Dimitrov, who was actively promoting this line, was accused of inciting servicemen to disrespect rank and discipline, and was sentenced in 1918 to three years of imprisonment. But after serving only four months the authorities were forced to release him through an amnesty following the defeat of Bulgaria, which been an ally of Germany, and because of mass antigovernment demonstrations.

Like everyone in the Tesniak Party, Dimitrov welcomed the revolution in Russia in 1917 and the establishment of Soviet power there. He was one of the members of the party leadership who protested when, in 1919, his party joined the Comintern and its name was changed to the Bulgarian Communist Party (BCP). From that time forward the activity of the BCP and Dimitrov himself, who had quickly mastered the basic ideological-political and organizational directives of Bolshevism, began to align party policies with those of the Comintern; as time passed, these policies came to be increasingly determined by the course chosen by the Soviet Union.

Toward the end of World War I and afterward, as people throughout Europe became radicalized, the Comintern and the new Communist parties directed their efforts toward fanning the "flames of the proletarian revolution," in hopes of spreading the Bolshevik Revolution. During these years, the activity of the BCP also developed largely along these lines, and included organized strikes, demonstrations, and other mass actions, in which Dimitrov played a leading role. As happened with Communist parties in most countries, the Bulgarian Communists, though then the second most influential party in the country, did not succeed in sparking revolution. Still, a special situation developed in Bulgaria: a semiauthoritarian regime advanced by the Agricultural Union established itself in March 1920. This Left-oriented party aspired to reorganize the state and society in the interests of defending the working peasants' property as the basis of an economic and political system. The BCP and the Agricultural Union were ideological-political rivals, and, in essence, mutual opponents on the Left.

On June 9, 1923, the Agricultural Union regime was deposed by a military coup organized by right-wing groups, and a government led by Aleksandr Tsankov came to power. The BCP's leadership, postulating that this was a struggle between the urban and rural bourgeois, declared itself neutral. Dimitrov, with other BCP leaders, was active in developing this position. Moscow, however, disagreed with this stance, holding instead that Europe was on the threshold of a "second revolutionary war," and the Balkans would be its next home. Accordingly, the Executive Committee of the Comintern (ECC) demanded that the Bulgarian organization rise up to overthrow the Tsankov regime and seize power themselves. The BCP leadership was forced to change

its neutral position, and Dimitrov was the most vocal advocate of this shift, appealing to the public to join the forthcoming power struggle. When the peasantry staged armed antigovernment rallies in a number of Bulgarian regions in the second half of September 1923, Dimitrov emerged as one of the most prominent Communist leaders who helped convert these protests into a full revolt. But at the end of September, after government troops had quashed the demonstrations, Dimitrov and a group of his party comrades were forced to flee to Yugoslavia, and a few days later Austria.

Thus began a twenty-two-year exile for Dimitrov. During the first nine and a half years, before his arrest by the Nazi authorities in March 1933, he fulfilled various important functions in the foreign organs of the BCP and the organizational structure of the Comintern.

Until spring 1925 Dimitrov was in charge of the BCP's Foreign Committee, formed in Vienna, which was reorganized in March 1924 into the Foreign Legation of the Party, which by now was underground. At the same time he became secretary of the Vienna-based Presidium of the Balkan Communist Federation (BCF), a regional organ under the supervision of the ECC that coordinated the activities of the Balkan Communist parties. Dimitrov participated as both a BCP and BCF representative in the Fifth Comintern Congress, on June 1924, where he was selected as a candidate for membership to the ECC; he was again selected at the Sixth Comintern Congress in 1928 (he had previously participated in the Third Comintern Congress in 1920, and the first two Profintern congresses, and in December 1922 had served as a member of the Executive Bureau of the Profintern). In spring 1925 he was transferred to Moscow to work in ECC personnel, and in March 1926, in a restructuring of the leading organs and ECC personnel, Dimitrov was selected as a candidate for membership in the Presidium and Secretariat, and also in the ECC Orgbiuro (Organizational Bureau). He was also appointed executive secretary of the so-called Sectional Secretariat (later the Ländersekretariat) for Polish and Baltic States Affairs, and made a member of the same Secretariat. By the end of 1926, however, the ECC was reorganized again, and Dimitrov lost his positions.

Dimitrov turned his attention to working with the BCP and BCF leadership in Vienna again. In January 1929 the BCP's Foreign Bureau and newly constituted Executive Bureau of the BCF (Dimitrov now held the post of political secretary in the latter) moved to Berlin, and thus Dimitrov moved there too. He was appointed head of the ECC's Western European Bureau, also located in Berlin, in April 1929. This bureau, created in 1928, coordinated and controlled the operational activities of the majority of the Communist parties in Europe, and Dimitrov continued his work there until being arrested by the Nazis in March 1933. In all these posts he fell in line with every shift in Comintern policy, which in turn followed all Kremlin decisions. He gained a reputation as a midlevel Comintern functionary who displayed good capabilities in carrying out these policies.

After Dimitrov's arrest in Germany, he and several other defendants—mostly Communists from Bulgaria and Germany—were subjected to a trial lasting from September 21 to December 23, 1933, partly in Leipzig and partly in Berlin (though it is known as the "Leipzig trial"), that unexpectedly thrust Dimitrov onto the world stage. The Nazis, who had come to power not long before, charged Dimitrov and the other defendants with taking part in a "Communist plot" to set fire to the Reichstag on the evening of February 27, 1933. To advance their anti-Communist views, the Hitlerites made this trial as public as possible. And Dimitrov, charged with being the main organizer of the arson, used the trial as well. His courageous behavior in the face of threats and pressure, and skillful refutation of the fabricated "proof," gained him great popularity, but also aided the Communist movement. The international campaign organized on his behalf only increased his popularity. The court was forced to exonerate Dimitrov and the other Communist defendants, and in the process, Dimitrov became a symbol of the fight against Nazism.

Dimitrov remained in prison a full two months after the trial, and then, on February 27, 1934, the Germans banished him to the Soviet Union, where he was received as a hero. Stalin took advantage of Dimitrov's newly acquired international popularity to make him the head of the Comintern in order to improve the latter's image. At the same time, Stalin calculated that Dimitrov could ensure changes in Comintern policy, thereby broadening the Communist influence beyond the borders of the USSR, and creating conditions for successful Soviet influence on the political situation at home and in Europe. In April 1934, Dimitrov became a member of the Political Secretariat of the ECC and the Political Commission, the operative organ of the Political Secretariat. He became a member of the Presidium of the ECC in May, and was picked to be the main speaker at the upcoming Seventh Comintern Congress. From that time on, encouraged by Stalin, Dimitrov occupied a key posi-

tion in the ECC leadership and played a leading role in preparations for the Seventh Congress.

At the Congress itself, from July 25 to August 21, 1935, Dimitrov was the main spokesperson for changes in the Comintern's political line, which departed substantially from the positions in the Communist movement up to then. The Comintern and its Communist Party sections in foreign countries had always stressed the "proletarian revolution" and "dictatorship of the proletariat." This time, though, the emphasis was on the struggle against fascism as the major new danger, and thus the need to defend the democracies in the developed countries—still known in the Bolshevik lexicon as "bourgeois democracies"—against the possible establishment of Fascist dictatorships. Accordingly, the Comintern proposed the creation of an anti-Fascist front, later called the Popular Front. Whereas the previous line had focused on the struggle against the Social Democrats, or "social Fascists," the task now was to cooperate with the Social Democratic parties and other democratically oriented segments of the workers' movement. In preparation for the Congress, Dimitrov had emerged as the initiator of these new positions, which were met with various degrees of support by some ECC functionaries, but with palpable resistance on the part of others. Stalin had also once pressed similar initiatives, but had doubts, particularly when Dimitrov first presented his ideas, about some of the proposals, viewing them as excessive. (From the currently available documentation, it is still unclear how the ultimate policy-shift decision was arrived at during the behind-the-scenes congress preparations.) Finally, though, Stalin approved the positions that Dimitrov set forth at the congress. Many researchers believe that Stalin did this because of the need to create an effective movement within the Communist Party to counteract, particularly in Europe, the rising danger of fascism, which might also threaten the Soviet Union.

On August 21, 1935, Dimitrov was promoted to head the Comintern as general Secretary of the ECC. The restructuring of the ECC and its apparatus carried out at the congress gave the general secretary much greater power in shaping the Comintern and defining the tasks of the Communist parties. In his post Dimitrov combined the ability to rule firmly, make crucial decisions, and display initiative in the areas within his competence, but he also remained subordinate to the Kremlin and Stalin, able to grasp the essence of their positions and apply them in concrete situations. Stalin valued Dimitrov as a trusted colleague who could cope with any task assigned him.

Dimitrov soon entered the circle of the top Soviet leaders headed by Stalin himself. He became his own person there, but also mastered the reigning customs, style of behavior, and way to conduct relationships. Under his leadership, the Comintern ensured that the international Communist structure adhered to Soviet foreign policy, from the work of the Popular Front, especially in Europe and during the Spanish civil war, to the resistance against the Japanese in China, and the problem of relations between the Communist Party there and the Kuomintang, to other matters. He adjusted the Comintern's policy to fall in line with Stalin's every twist and turn in both the international and domestic arenas, whether it was the "Stalinist purges," which included Comintern personnel, or the Nazi-Soviet alliance in 1939, which required the whole Communist movement to disown its previous anti-Fascist views.

When Hitler invaded the Soviet Union on June 22, 1941, Dimitrov's activity as head of the ECC changed to suit the interests of the Soviet war effort. The Comintern's energies were now focused on developing resistance movements in both countries occupied by the Axis and the Axis states themselves. Politically speaking, this meant reviving a policy, approved by Stalin and carried out by Dimitrov, of uniting all anti-Fascists prepared to fight. These combined forces would now be called "National (National-Liberation) Fronts." These resistance movements aimed not only to provide support for the Soviet armed forces and render aid to the other two powers in the anti-Hitler coalition, Great Britain and the United States, but also help to liberate the Axis-occupied countries. In so doing the Kremlin, Dimitrov, and Communists in the countries mounting the resistance movements strove to expand Communist influence and achieve military-political positions from which, when the correct circumstances arose, the Communists could grasp power in the liberated states.

Dimitrov, with Stalin's approval, orchestrated the management of similarly ambiguous policies within the Communist parties. He would see to it that the parties camouflaged their revolutionary goals in anti-Fascist liberationist garb, and that they did not strike too soon. He reined in those parties that were too radical, urging patience in the creation of a broad anti-Fascist front in their own countries, so as to maintain crucial relationships between the USSR and its Western allies.

In May 1943, as part of this camouflage tactic, Stalin formally dissolved the Comintern—a maneuver executed in a disciplined fashion by the ECC leadership, led by Dimitrov. The ECC announced the move in special public resolutions, issued in May–June 1943. The resolutions pointed out that the Communist parties were entirely independent entities in their countries. In actual fact, of course, only the leading organs of the Comintern, including the ECC, were officially abolished; the greater part of the central apparatus was reorganized and placed under the newly created International Information Section (OMI) of the Central Committee of the Bolshevik Communist Party. The OMI continued to fulfill the basic functions previously belonging to the ECC. When the OMI was formed in mid-June 1943, Dimitrov was named one of two deputies to head this section, but in reality he led the work of the OMI, and six and a half months later was formally appointed as leader. He played an active role in the Soviets' control of the foreign Communist parties during the concluding phase of World War II. In particular, he focused on the parties of Eastern Europe, in whose countries "people's democracies" were installed after the war, either with the cooperation or through the direct intervention of the USSR.

On November 2, 1945, with Stalin's approval, Dimitrov returned to Bulgaria from his long exile, where in September 1944, a people's democracy had also been established. As the leader of the BCP (its chair and then general secretary) he became the practical head of the regime, although for tactical reasons, during his first year he held no government positions, except for that of leader of the parliamentary faction of the Communist party. In November 1946, though, Dimitrov officially became the Bulgarian prime minister and held this post as well as his position as BCP head up until his death on July 2, 1949.

In Bulgaria he played the role of the charismatic Communist "supreme leader," a sort of mini-Stalin. His rule differed little from that of the other Communist heads governing the other people's democracies in the first years of these regimes. Dimitrov's policy consisted of establishing and consolidating the Communist monopoly of power under the guise of democracy. One of the most important aspects of his policy was the suppression of the opposition through the use of fear and mass repressions, which included death sentences for opponents in show trials, as happened, for example, to the opposition leader Nikola Petkov, who was executed on falsified accusations of plotting against the government. Dimitrov's role in the purges of Communist functionaries that began in 1949 is not entirely clear. In the beginning he tried to rescue his old comrade in arms, Traiko Kostov, who Stalin had accused of hostility toward the Soviet Union at the end of 1948. But Dimitrov allegedly later joined in the accusations against Kostov, who was executed in December 1949, after being sentenced to death during a show trial—after Dimitrov himself had died. In both his domestic and foreign policy, Dimitrov unerringly followed Moscow's lead and frequently solicited instructions from the Kremlin himself. Even so, in both 1947 and 1948, he was bitterly criticized by Stalin for having engaged in actions and statements, without Kremlin guidance, related to Bulgarian-Yugoslav cooperation and planning a federative association of Eastern European people's democracies. Dimitrov responded with a confession of his "mistakes." When the Soviet-Yugoslav conflicts began in 1948, Dimitrov did not want a break with Yugoslavia, yet he also did not want to risk opposing Stalin, and in the end also took part in the Kremlin's campaign against Tito.

See also Antifascism; Comintern; People's Democracy; Popular Front; Soviet-Yugoslavia Break; Stalin, Joseph.

FURTHER READING

Adibekov, G. M., K. M. Anderson, and K. K. Shirinia, eds. *Politbiuro CK RKP(b)–VKP(b) i Komintern: 1919–1943 gg. Dokumenty*. Moscow: Rosspen, 2004.

Adibekov, G. M., E. N. Shakhnazarova, and K. K. Shirin. *Organizational Structure of the Comintern, 1919–1943*. Moscow: Rosspen, 1997.

Dallin, A., and F. I. Firsov, eds. *Dimitrov and Stalin, 1934–1943: Letters from the Soviet Archives*. New Haven, CT: Yale University Press, 2000.

Damie, V. V., et al. *The Comintern against Fascism: Documents*. Moscow: Science, 1999.

Dimitrov, G. *Works*. Vols. 1–16. Bulgarian Communist Party Press, 1951–59.

———. *Journal (March 9, 1933 to February 6, 1949)*. Ed. D. Sirkov, P. Boev, N. Avreiski, and E. Kabakchieva. Sofia: University Publishing House "St. Kliment Oxridski," 1997.

———. *Diary: The Moscow Years, 1934–1945*. Ed. S. Pons with L. Gibianskij. Turin: Einaudi, 2002.

———. *The Diary of Georgi Dimitrov, 1933–1949*. Ed. I. Banac. New Haven, CT: Yale University Press, 2003.

Lebedeva, M., M. Narinskij, K. M. Anderson, and A. O. Čubar´jan, eds. *Komintern i Vtoraja mirovaja vojna* [The Comintern and World War II]. Moscow: Pamjatniki istoričeskoj mysli, 1994–98.

LEONID JA. GIBJANSKIJ

Diplomats

Could the revolution do without diplomats? Leon Trotsky thought so during the elation of the October Revolution. In actuality all Communist regimes rapidly reorganized a Ministry for Foreign Affairs. The nature of this foreign policy is controversial to this day, though. Was one supposed to take the revolutionary and anti-imperialist messianism of leaders like Vladimir Lenin, Mao Zedong, or Fidel Castro Ruz literally, reveal the subterranean activities of Communist secret services abroad, and conclude that there was indeed a long-term strategy of destabilizing the capitalist world at work? Or was one supposed to believe that a normalization of diplomatic relations would occur with those Communist countries trapped in an interplay between national and geopolitical legacies, and simply interpret this state of affairs as another variant of realpolitik?

The revolution produced a break that initially left the diplomatic services of these new regimes in a state of crisis. The subversive speeches by each country's leaders put its diplomats on the defensive. When the new Bolshevik government rejected the czarist legacy by publishing secret treaties, refused to honor the debts incurred before the war, and conducted a separate peace, it chose a confrontational strategy in its relations with the European powers. The denunciation of "unequal treaties" by Maoist China was also part of this disruptive strategy. The new classes' diplomats were perceived in the West as troublemakers precisely because their atypical characteristics were a reminder of the revolution's tabula rasa.

The first generation of these new diplomats was composed of revolutionaries whose background was worlds apart from the often-aristocratic traits of a diplomatic environment that had, since the Congress of Vienna, conformed to a "common code of conduct." Bolshevik Russia's People's Commissariat for Foreign Affairs resorted to a pool of ex-revolutionary émigrés, Bolsheviks but also Mensheviks and Social Revolutionaries who had sided with the new regime. Maoist China's first diplomats were mostly men who had participated in the Long March or the war against Japan. Preference was given to those among them who had been educated abroad or had experienced exile. In order to become a passable diplomat it was sufficient to know a foreign language. Georgy Chicherin and Maksim Litvinov, who succeeded one another in leading Soviet diplomacy between the wars, had spent long years of exile in London. Chou En-lai, who took charge of foreign affairs for Communist China, had studied first in Japan and then in France.

The struggle for recognition was the first goal of all Communist diplomatic missions, and therefore the opening of each new embassy was greeted as a revolutionary victory. This was not an easy task: the Soviet Union spent seven years before being recognized by France and Great Britain, and sixteen before establishing official relations with the United States. Fear and hostility toward communism were quite real, and being a Communist diplomat could be quite risky: Vatslav Vorovsky, Soviet Russia's representative to Italy, was assassinated in May 1923. The USSR's obvious diplomatic vulnerability in the 1920s resulted in an obsession: prevent the establishment of a hostile capitalist bloc, a danger that had proven all too real when foreign powers had intervened during the civil war, at all costs. The tactic to be employed, devised earlier by Lenin, was thus to exploit interimperialist rivalries in order to carve out a spot on the international scene. A symbol of these policies was the treaty signed by Germany and Soviet Russia at Rapallo in 1922. The situation changed after World War II because the number of Communist countries had increased. No other Communist state was subjected to the kind of isolation experienced by revolutionary Russia at this later date. In October 1950 China had eleven foreign embassies, and eight were accredited in the countries of the Soviet bloc. Intra-Communist diplomacy was to constitute the first step in the development of international relations by these countries during this period.

While Communist rhetoric was arguing for isolationism, and proving hostile to international law and its procedures for international arbitration as well as conciliation (accused of being bourgeois), diplomats from Communist countries were working hard to be accepted by international organizations. The Soviet Union led the way when in September 1934 it joined the League of Nations, which up to that point it had vehemently criticized. The Conference for Security and Cooperation in Europe that Vyacheslav Molotov had argued for already in 1954—and that in the framework of détente, resulted in the Helsinki Accords in 1975—was considered the highest form of legitimation by the Soviets, since it sanctioned both the Soviet bloc's existence and its borders just as they had emerged from the war.

States that considered themselves Communist also had to win a competition against other entities competing for legitimacy. The exiled Russian, Armenian, and Georgian representatives after World War I, or those of the Baltic states whose annexation by the USSR had not been recognized after World War II, were given less consideration in determining European policies toward the USSR than Cuban refugees in Miami were in determining U.S. policy. Maoist China, North Korea, and the German Democratic Republic found themselves in a particularly sensitive situation, since their legitimacy was contested by rival states: Taiwan, South Korea, and the Federal Republic of Germany. It was within the framework of détente in the 1970s that these three states obtained true diplomatic recognition, thanks to Willy Brandt's Ostpolitik and Sino-American détente. In October 1971 Beijing was given China's seat on the UN Security Council, which had been Taiwan's until then, while in 1973 the United Nations' Thirtieth Assembly voted in favor of Pyongyang and against Seoul, thus ending the activities of the Commission for the Unification and Rehabilitation of Korea.

Most Communist countries were gradually integrated into the international system during the 1970s; it was what these regimes had sought, but simultaneously, what they were still suspicious of. Diplomacy did take place within a peculiar political context, dominated by anticapitalist and anti-imperialist analytic and explanatory frameworks. What was the place of diplomacy in the Communist political system? Decided at the highest levels of the Communist Party, the foreign policy of Communist regimes was under the purview of different organs, which sometimes competed and sometimes cooperated. The state-party dualism was particularly visible in foreign policy since its tasks were shared by the Ministries for Foreign Affairs, which answered to the government, on the one hand, and the Central Committee's international departments, charged with maintaining and financing relations with foreign Communist parties, on the other. These organs (the International Department led by Boris Ponomarëv in the USSR and the International Liaison Department of the Chinese Communist Party led by Hu Jintao, for instance) survived all the forms of international Communist organization (Comintern and Cominform). If during a phase of initial revolutionary romanticism a certain confusion between the diplomatic and professional roles of communism might have persisted (as the part diplomatic and part revolutionary actions of Karl Radek toward Germany and Poland in the aftermath of World War I attests), subsequently, driven by the obvious goal of normalizing diplomatic relations, one witnessed a separation and division of tasks. Embassies functioned as points of arrival and departure for both intelligence services and the Communist parties themselves, but each organization had its own objectives and sources of funding.

Diplomats—whose reason for existence consisted in the best possible management of coexistence with a milieu that, from a Marxist perspective, was intrinsically hostile since it was capitalist—provoked suspicions among Communist leaders at regular intervals. Diplomacy, even Communist diplomacy, still continued to have a certain whiff of the ancien régime about it, and the image of a diplomat wearing a tuxedo conversing at mundane cocktail parties contrasted with that of the Communist as a revolutionary militant or a builder of socialism. In order to follow the agenda of pacific coexistence, diplomats were supposed to develop adaptive skills, which automatically engendered suspicions of complicity with foreign capitalists and their lifestyle.

In the Soviet case, these suspicions were reinforced by the presence in their ranks of opponents who had been moved aside during the 1920s and given an appointment abroad (a practice that should basically be considered standard in all diplomatic corps), and some notorious cases of defection. In the context of Joseph Stalin's Great Terror, diplomats were to prove one of the most visible targets. Accused of having foreign ties (notice the irony) at a time when political loyalty trumped professional competence, 62 percent of them were victims of the purges, and their places were taken by new men, causing serious problems for diplomatic activity right before the war's outbreak. Similar accusations against diplomats, accused of wallowing in bourgeois luxury, were made during the Cultural Revolution in China (even if the old guard was not removed), and they were the reason for various diplomatic purges in the Cuban diplomatic service. One of the methods subsequently adopted by all Communist regimes to ensure against the risk of diplomats defecting because of their prolonged contact with the enemy was to recall ambassadors frequently and rotate functionaries.

Over time a political homogenization of these functionaries occurred. By the end of the 1930s the Soviet diplomatic corps was made up of young men, with a lower-class background, educated in the Soviet system, and faithful to the party and Stalin. The number of diplomats who had positions of responsibility in the Communist Party also increased in China and Cuba. Gradually diplomacy became one of the ways to excel within the Communist state apparatus. Molotov created

a specific recruitment mechanism for diplomats when he founded the Moscow State Institute of International Relations, and its first students graduated in 1948. This was the beginning of the professionalization of the diplomatic corps. In the Leonid Brezhnev era, the Institute for International Relations became one of the symbols of the regime's new elitism. In Cuba, the Institute for Diplomatic Service saw its first students graduate in 1974.

Although they were subject to the party system and fed an ideological literature about the outside world, not all Communist diplomats developed the same strategies. They had to first establish compromises with a series of legacies. Both in the Soviet Union and China, one continued to look at the national interest through great power lenses, whether this status was calculated in traditional terms of territories and spheres of influence, or more in terms internal to the Communist bloc. It is not possible to understand the Sino-Soviet confrontation without this backdrop. Relatively little is known about the diplomatic activities of the people's democracies. Even though they were still dependent on big brother, Eastern European countries like Romania, Poland, and Yugoslavia were able to emphasize some national perspectives in their respective diplomatic activities, and in some cases, by connecting to previously existing regional strategies, were accorded a certain amount of prestige within or even outside their bloc.

Personalities also had their role in creating this diversity. Several diplomats from Communist countries made their influence felt on the evolution of international relations. In some cases an important factor was their relative longevity compared to their capitalist counterparts. The extended residence abroad of some ambassadors, like Ivan Maisky, who was in London from 1932 to 1943, or Anatoly Dobrynin, who was nominated by Nikita Khrushchev in March 1962 and stayed in Washington until 1986, made them their country's top experts in bilateral relations. This gave diplomacy the means to maintain a continuity that could have been jeopardized by abrupt changes of course decided at the highest levels, like the German-Soviet pact of 1939, or the deployment of the SS20s and the Soviet intervention in Afghanistan. Two individuals emerge as particularly emblematic of this diplomatic longevity: Zhou Enlai and Andrey Gromyko. The former, who was foreign minister from 1949 to February 1958, and prime minister from 1949 until his death, on January 8, 1976, was the key to Communist China's foreign policy and a master in the "war of words," as he defined diplomacy. The latter was the

USSR's foreign minister from 1957 to 1985, and when he became a member of the politburo in 1972, some in the West started speaking about the establishment of a real "diplocracy" in the Soviet Union.

The diplomats' impact was never as important as during periods of détente, openness, or change. It was particularly important in the 1930s, with the policies of collective security promoted by Litvinov, and during the Khrushchev era, when peaceful competition with the United States led Soviet diplomacy to intervene in the third world. In both cases, relying on a multitude of Communist or crypto-Communist organizations in cultural, technical, and humanitarian fields, Communist diplomats proved their usefulness in the context of international propaganda, playing the role of leaders of the most noble causes: antifascism and the defense of peace, anti-imperialism, and the Non-Aligned Movement. This served to stimulate or even amplify the successes of Communist diplomacy, which compared to other diplomatic services, seemed to exhibit "greater caring." Already during the 1960s and to an even greater extent in the 1970s, however, the disintegration of the Communist bloc revealed the priority of national objectives over ideological ones, while the decline of the USSR's influence in the world underscored the extent to which Soviet diplomacy was missing a fundamental weapon: an efficient economy.

See also Chicherin, Georgy; Détente; Gromyko, Andrei; Litvinov, Maksim; Marxism-Leninism; Peaceful Coexistence; Power Politics; Zhou Enlai.

FURTHER READING

Craig, G. A., and F. Gilbert, eds. *The Diplomats, 1919–1939.* Princeton, NJ: Princeton University Press, 1953.

Craig, A. G., and F. L. Loewenheim, eds. *The Diplomats, 1939–1979.* Princeton, NJ: Princeton University Press, 1994.

Daesook Suh. *The Organization and Administration of North Korean Foreign Policy.* In *North Korea in a Regional and Global Context,* ed. R. A. Scalapino and Lee Hongkoo. Berkeley: University of California Press, 1986.

Domínguez, J. J. *To Make a World Safe for Revolution: Cuba's Foreign Policy.* Cambridge, MA: Harvard University Press, 1986.

Dullin, S. "Les ambassades soviétiques en Europe dans les années 1930." *Communisme* 49–50 (1997): 17–28.

———. "Une diplomatie plébeienne? Profils et competences des diplomats soviétiques, 1936–1945." *Cahiers du monde russe* 44, nos. 2–3 (April–September 2003): 437–64.

———. *Men of Influence: Stalin's Diplomats in Europe, 1930–1939.* Edinburgh: Edinburgh University Press, 2008.

Jan, G. P. "The Ministry of Foreign Affairs in China since the Cultural Revolution." *Asian Survey* 17, no. 6 (June 1977): 513–29.

Klein, D. W. "Peking's Evolving Ministry of Foreign Affairs." *China Quarterly* 4 (1960): 28–39.

———. "Les politiques étrangères des Etats satellites de l'URSS, 1945–1989." *Cahiers du CERES* 25 (May 2001).

———. "La politique internationale de l'URSS: nouvelles approches." *Communisme* 74–75 (Winter 2003).

Rey, M.-P. "Diplomatie et diplomates soviétiques à l'ère du dégel." *Cahiers du monde russe* 44, nos. 2–3 (April–September 2003): 309–22.

SABINE DULLIN

Dissent in the USSR

In the years following the October Revolution and especially after Stalin's rise to power in 1929, the Russian intelligentsia was forced to become subservient to the regime's dictates. Everything became "political"; from morality to the economy, from leisure time to personal relationships, from the arts to sport, everything became an area of interest to the state. It was only during the "thaw" years after Stalin's death, in March 1953, that feelings of opposition toward this reality began to animate Soviet intellectuals. Writers in particular became convinced of the genuineness of the shift represented by the Communist Party's Twentieth Congress in February 1956 and the ensuing de-Stalinization, and this awareness was manifested especially on the political level, as the invasion of Hungary would prove.

The first manifestation of "dissent" that was not limited to individual consciousnesses occurred between 1958 and 1960, when a small group of students in their twenties, including Yuri Galanskov, Vladimir Bukovsky, and Aleksandr Ginzburg, periodically met in front of the Vladimir Mayakovski monument in Moscow. This initiative drew a certain following among youths and became the first act of group civil disobedience. Ginzburg edited and duplicated *Syntaksis,* a typescript collection of poems by authors who had often been censored, and it soon was widely circulated thanks to samizdat, which had already been around for several years: the hand copying of works forbidden by the regime into notebooks, and their subsequent circulation from acquaintance to acquaintance.

The regime could not remain passive in the face of these activities. In July 1960, Ginzburg was arrested and condemned to two years in a camp for anti-Soviet propaganda. It would be the first in a long series of arrests and detentions. The diffusion of a nonconformist culture found its greatest impulse in literary circles, but it also developed in other fields. In the late 1950s, for example, a school was formed in the house of painters Evgeny and Lev Kropivnicky, father and son, in Liazonovo near Moscow; each Sunday painters, poets, and intellectuals discussed art and culture. Another popular form of communication was the music of singer-songwriters, which was recorded on audiocassette and then duplicated following the same criteria used for written texts, only this time they were called *magnitizdat*. This was how the songs of Aleksandr Galich, Vladimir Vysocky, Bulat Okudzhava, and many others were circulated.

In this climate of relative renewal an ex-prisoner of the Soviet camps, Aleksandr Solzhenitsyn, wrote a story titled *One Day in the Life of Ivan Denisovich*, which appeared in the November 1962 issue of the journal *Novy Mir*. The story described a single day in the life of a prisoner in a Soviet forced labor camp in a detached manner. Its publication had a significant impact, because nearly everyone felt called on to remember and testify personally. More than a literary event, it marked a moral and social event in Soviet life, and one that produced a movement in public opinion. At the same time that Solzhenitsyn was publishing *Ivan Denisovich* and was beginning to think about his next work, *The Gulag Archipelago*, Varlam Shalamov was writing his *Tales of Kolyma*, Yevgenia Ginzburg was drafting her *Journey into the Whirlwind*, Nadezhda Mandel'stam was circulating her memoirs, *The Times and the Wolves*, via samizdat, and Andrej Tarkovsky was writing the script for his film *Rublëv*. The regime could tolerate this no longer; starting in 1964, open venues in the official press were closed one after the other.

After Khrushchev's removal, Leonid Brezhnev and Aleksey Kosygin tried to regain control of a civil society bubbling with the ferments of protest. In the press, attempts at Stalin's rehabilitation became more frequent, and so did censorship. In order to reestablish order, several articles were added to the penal code in 1966 (a code that had replaced Stalin's in 1960); articles 190 and 191 allowed the authorities to legally pursue individuals for matters of minor importance, crimes of opinion, and the dissemination of information. The following year the new KGB head, Yuri Andropov, created Directorate V, which became infamous in the repression of dissent. Notwithstanding these effects, dissent continued to find sources of inspiration and support. The powerful KGB, although it was the institution most aware of the life and thoughts of its citizens, was vigilant, cynical, and omnipresent, but because of its ideological orientation also blind, fideist, and inefficient as well as incapable of grasping the truth of these developing cultural phenomena.

With this new leadership in power, trials against dissidents were held in Moscow and Leningrad. The purpose of the trials was to intimidate intellectuals, yet they instead became one of the initial setbacks for the regime. It was not the first time that the regime incriminated writers for their works, but it was the first time that defendants publicly rejected accusations of anti-Sovietism and defended themselves during trials, thus breaking the tradition of repentances and mutual denunciations.

Among the most famous trials of those years were those against the young poet and the favorite pupil of the great poetess Anna Akhmatova, Josef Brodsky, whom Andrey Zhdanov had banned, and whose verses had been circulating in samizdat form since 1958. Or that against two young writers from Moscow, Andrei Sinyavsky and Yuli Daniel, who were guilty of having published their works abroad for years, using pseudonyms. Theirs was the first arrest broadcast by Western Russian-language radio stations, which many listened to surreptitiously in the USSR. Even though the trial concluded with the most severe sentencing possible for Sinyavsky (seven years) and Daniel (five years), overall their trial was perceived as a victory because it gave a defining impulse to the movement in defense of human rights, and would lead to the second phase of dissent in the country.

In 1967–68, Galanskov, Aleksei Dobrovol'sky, Vera Lashkova, and Aleksander Ginzburg were involved in a new trial because they had prepared a white paper on the Sinyavsky-Daniel case. The most important demonstration of support ever seen in the Soviet Union was organized on their behalf. Ginzburg was sentenced to five years. Galanskov was sentenced to seven years, but didn't survive the camp, dying at the age thirty-three in 1972. The trial heralded a new era, marked by defense campaigns and collective "open letters"—a step that consolidated the dissident movement.

The journal *Chronicle of Current Events* was also first published during this time—the first and most significant samizdat periodical. Between 1968 and 1983, sixty-five issues appeared regularly, and with it the history of independent information in the USSR also began. The *Chronicle* was an improvement over the previous journals published between 1959 and 1965, which had only given expression to cultural positions, but had not disseminated information with the intent of creating an independent public opinion. Initially the regime attempted to avoid any false moves while it repressed what on cursory inspection appeared to be an information bulletin, but the KGB soon became alarmed and began to persecute the *Chronicle*'s contributors. The poetess Natalya Gorbanevskaya was arrested and interned in a mental asylum for criminals. Then Vladimir Bukovsky was arrested, and sentenced to five years in a camp and seven years of forced residence. Such persecutions notwithstanding, the *Chronicle* continued to be distributed, and the movement surrounding it grew geographically (Ukraine, Baltic countries, Caucasus, and Siberia), in content (religion, justice, culture, nationality, work, emigration, and art), and in terms of the social milieus involved.

The Soviet invasion of Czechoslovakia in 1968 marked a turning point in the evolution of dissent. The invasion, as Andrey Sakharov was later to recall, was the event that pushed many dissidents to explicitly oppose the regime. The events in Prague led to reflection on two issues. On the one hand, the movement needed to find an international point of reference, and one that could diffuse its requests. In the late 1950s the first Muscovite dissidents, later followed by some Ukrainians, had tried to organize street demonstrations; even later, with the beginning of the trials, there had been attempts to form pickets in support of the accused outside the tribunals, followed by petition campaigns. Although the samizdat had catalyzed public opinion in the USSR, the influence of protests on the regime was limited. Only by drawing the attention of the international community to the repression of human rights in the USSR and the countries of the Socialist bloc would it actually be possible to exercise some sort of real pressure on the Soviet government. Andrei Amalrik, at the time in his thirties, became an expert at developing relations with the outside world, and thanks to his skills documents, appeals, novels, and essays crossed the border.

On the other hand, the invasion made dissidents more aware of the need to formulate precise political objectives, while sticking to the principle of nonviolence and making respect for the "law," understood as the only instrument for the defense of the moral and physical integrity of human beings, the basic tenet of their agenda. These premises shaped the movement in defense of human rights. Numerous groups formed during those years: the Initiative Group for the Defense of Human Rights (1969), which addressed several appeals to the United Nations and resisted a series of arrests until 1979; the Committee for Human Rights (1970), which deluded itself into thinking it was aiding the government by consulting on human rights; a Soviet section of Amnesty International (1973), which lasted until 1983 when its last representative, the author Georgy Vladimov, was forced into exile; the Study Commission on the Use of Psychiatry for Political Ends (1977); and the Group for the Right to Emigration (1979).

The most renowned of these organizations was the Group to Aid in the Application of the Helsinki Accords in the USSR (1976), later called simply the Helsinki Group, and it included notable individuals like Yuri Orlov, Aleksandr Ginzburg, and Anatoly Sharansky; it appealed to that part of the accords in which the USSR explicitly committed itself to the respect of human rights. In August 1975, after two years of work in Helsinki, the Conference on Security and Cooperation in Europe had concluded; the final document committed the signatory states to respect basic freedoms, borders, and the noninterference in the internal affairs of other states (Moscow was particularly interested in these last two points). After the accords were signed in August 1975, Soviet newspapers published the entire text of the Helsinki Final Act, thus giving dissidents new fuel for their demands, now based not only on the observance of Soviet law but also international accords. The Helsinki Group was active for over six years, despite persecution, and during this time managed to distribute ninety-five dossiers with detailed complaints. Some of the group's greatest successes occurred during two international conferences that were held to verify the accords, in Belgrade in 1977 and Madrid in 1978, where on the basis of materials submitted by the Helsinki Group, the Soviets were accused of a series of human rights violations. Moreover, as a result of initiatives undertaken by the Moscow group, Ukrainian and Lithuanian Helsinki Groups were also created (1976), followed by Georgian (1977) and Armenian (1977) groups, while in Poland the Committee in Defense of Workers and in Czechoslovakia Charter 77 were founded in September 1976.

Inspired by these groups, an extensive debate opposing Solzhenitsyn and Sakharov took place on the clandestine pages of the samizdat in the 1970s. The former held Christian and conservative views, the latter scientific, lay, and progressive ones. Sakharov was initially convinced that it would be possible to reform the Soviet system; later, disillusioned, he became a supporter of the thesis that there was a fundamental link between the internal situation in the Soviet Union and the USSR's position internationally. The struggle for human rights in the USSR could not be detached from the international situation, especially after the Helsinki Conference. Solzhenitsyn instead became the interpreter of a Slavophile dissent, whose centerpiece was the spiritual rebirth of a new Russia and its national values. He was arrested, deprived of Soviet citizenship, and expelled in February 1974 because of the trauma caused by the publication in France the previous year of his masterpiece, *The Gulag Archipelago*, which exposed the world to the reality of the Soviet camps. Once abroad, the author created the Fund to Aid Political Prisoners and Their Families with royalties from his book; it was headed by Aleksandr Ginzburg in the USSR.

In order to control both dissent and the human rights movement, the KGB began to resort to psychiatry against dissidents with increasing frequency. Many were locked in insane asylums, and although completely sane, were subjected to "cures" that involved the use of electroshock and psychotropic drugs. Some of these asylums became notorious, including Kazan', Dnepropetrovsk, and Blagovshchensk. Repression became even more severe at the end of the decade, when the Soviet invasion of Afghanistan in December 1979, the U.S. boycott of the Moscow Olympics the following year, and finally the Polish crisis of 1981 led to the end of détente. The question of human rights, which had been recognized as an important part of the international scene, now became purely a question of the regime's internal politics. In November 1979, the most visible personalities in the world of dissent were arrested; Sakharov and his wife, Elena Bonner, were put under house arrest. It was a simultaneous attack against all groups and currents, including the media—in other words the samizdat. It was clear that there had been another shift in the regime's policies, and that its intent was now to suppress dissent in all its forms. Groups disappeared one after another, the publication of almost all journals was suspended, and in 1983 the *Chronicle of Current Events* ceased publication. The sentences became much more severe, prisoners were often rearrested as soon as their term had expired, and there were many suspicious deaths in the prisons.

If the resumption of persecution was aided by changes in the international situation, by the end of détente, it was also caused by the regime's internal weakness—a weakness confirmed by the continuous leadership changes that occurred up to Mikhail Gorbachev's rise to power in 1985. Gorbachev tried to reform the Soviet Union, to save it from the then-current economic and political crises. In order to demonstrate his goodwill to international public opinion and particularly the United States, in a surprise move Gorbachev freed the Sakharovs from their exile in Gor'kij on December 1, 1986—the first of many releases. Gorbachev's move was not a defense of freedom of opinion but rather an attempt to convince the world of the genuineness of his glasnost and perestroika policies. The freeing of political prisoners did not prevent episodes of repression from occurring during the perestroika years. There was the case of Anatoly Marchenko, for instance. Tried in 1981 for the sixth time, he was sentenced to ten years in the camps and five years of house arrest (after having already served fifteen years in prison), but he died in the Chistopol prison in December 1986 under murky circumstances. In 1986, 209 dissidents were interned in asylums, and 189 dissidents were arrested for crimes related to freedom of opinion in 1988.

By the end of the 1980s dissent brought its historic mission in the Soviet Union to a conclusion. A true public and civic opinion formed, which inherited the experiences of dissent. Those who had been involved in dissent and were now contributing to civic discussion divided according to the types of more or less radical reform they thought the country awaited.

See also Charter 77; De-Stalinization; Détente; History and Memory; Perestroika; Prague Spring; Public Opinion; Real Socialism; Sakharov, Andrey; Solzhenitsyn, Aleksandr.

FURTHER READING
Dell'Asta, M. *Una via per incominciare. Il dissenso in URSS dal 1917 al 1990*. Milan: La Casa di Matriona, 2003.
Piretto, G. P. *Il radioso avvenire. Mitologie culturali sovietiche.* Turin: Einaudi, 2001.
Sinatti, P., ed. *Chronika Tekushchich Sobytij. Il dissenso in URSS nell'epoca di Brezhnev: antologia della "Cronaca degli avvenimenti correnti."* Florence: Vallecchi, 1978.
Vaissié, C. *Pour votre liberté et pour la notre. Le combat des dissidents de Russie*. Paris: Laffont, 1999.

ELENA DUNDOVICH

Dissolution of the USSR

On December 31, 1991—some seventy-four years after the Bolsheviks, led by Lenin, had taken power in Russia—the Soviet regime and the Soviet state itself formally ceased to exist. This momentous event occurred less than seven years after Mikhail Gorbachev became the general secretary of the Communist Party of the Soviet Union (CPSU). Soon after taking office in March 1985, Gorbachev had launched a series of drastic changes that he hoped would improve and strengthen the Communist system. But these changes, far from strengthening Communism, led inadvertently to the unraveling of the Soviet state.

The Unexpected Nature of the Collapse
Until the late 1980s, the prospect that the Soviet Union would disintegrate seemed almost entirely fanciful. The leaders of the CPSU maintained a firm grip on power in Moscow, supported by millions of troops in the Soviet armed forces and the State Security Committee (KGB). The dissident movement had been crushed during Leonid Brezhnev's long reign (1964–82), and ethnic tensions were largely dormant. Slower economic growth rates in the 1980s were a problem for the leadership, but not a fatal one.

To be sure, a few observers prior to the late 1980s had speculated that the Soviet Union might one day break apart. As far back as 1969, the exiled Soviet dissident Andrei Amalrik wrote an essay claiming that the Soviet Union would not survive until 1984. The sociologist Randall Collins wrote an essay in 1980 predicting the gradual decline (though not the collapse) of the Soviet Union. Neither Amalrik nor Collins, however, provided useful guidance for what actually happened. Amalrik posited that the Soviet Union would go to war with China and that the ensuing chaos would enable national groups in the USSR to break away from Soviet control. Collins speculated that Soviet power would gradually decline in a mechanistic way, and his analysis therefore left out all the highly contingent events and unexpected twists that were actually responsible for the demise of the USSR. Although most scholars by the early 1980s were well aware that the Soviet government faced substantial economic and social challenges, no one at the time expected that the Communist regime and the Soviet state would self-destruct less than a decade later.

The downfall of the Soviet Union at the end of 1991 was astonishing in its own right, but what was even more striking was the way it occurred: with only minimal violence. As late as mid-August 1991 (just before an attempted coup d'état in Moscow), few observers, if any, anticipated that the Soviet Union would peacefully break apart. Whenever large, multiethnic empires disintegrated in the past, their demise usually came after extensive warfare and loss of life, in some cases stretching over decades. A similar fate seemed likely to befall the Soviet Union, a country whose leaders had used horrific violence in the past to consolidate and maintain their power.

Contrary to expectations, though, the collapse of the Soviet state was largely free of bloodshed. Although some violence did occur under Gorbachev—riots in Kazakhstan in 1986, battles between Armenia and Azerbaijan from 1988 on, a crackdown in Georgia in April 1989, clashes in the Ferghana Valley in June 1989 and 1990, a large-scale incursion by the Soviet Army into Azerbaijan in January 1990, and a more limited crackdown in the Baltic states in January 1991—these tragic incidents were surprisingly infrequent at a time of such rapid and disorienting political change, and they were certainly not enough, in and of themselves, to precipitate the breakup of the Soviet state. Moreover, the events in December 1991 that culminated in the final dissolution of the Soviet Union occurred with no violence at all.

The generally peaceful end of the USSR is often taken for granted nowadays and is sometimes depicted as inevitable, but in the late 1980s and early 1990s (not to mention in the pre-Gorbachev era) this outcome seemed almost wholly implausible. Those who depict the breakup of the Soviet Union as inevitable are wont to assume—implicitly or explicitly—that the choices made by Soviet policymakers from 1985 on and the unforeseen circumstances that arose at key points ultimately made no difference. In reality, the peaceful dissolution of the Soviet Union, far from having been preordained, was an intricate and highly contingent process, and was frequently spurred on by chance occurrences and twists of fate. Choices did exist. Dramatic events often seem inevitable in retrospect, but the reality almost always is more complex, as it was in this case.

The Implications of Gorbachev's Reforms
In the first half of the 1980s the Soviet Union experienced three changes of leadership: the first after the death of Brezhnev in November 1982, the second after the death of Yuri Andropov in February 1984, and the

third after the death of Konstantin Chernenko in March 1985. The rapid sequence of three elderly and ailing leaders plunged the country into a period of stasis. If the orthodox chief of the Moscow party committee, Viktor Grishin, had emerged as the successor to Chernenko in March 1985—as he very nearly did—the Brezhnev era system would have been preserved. Gorbachev's ability to outmaneuver Grishin and another rival, Grigorii Romanov, was crucial in setting the USSR on a different course.

Gorbachev's initial program of *uskorenie* (acceleration) was intended to boost the Soviet economy through traditional means (e.g., investment in heavy industry), but it soon gave way to a much broader and bolder program of perestroika (restructuring) and glasnost (official openness). Having failed to achieve an immediate turnaround in the economy, Gorbachev concluded that far-reaching political liberalization would be a prerequisite for economic advancement. Nor did he stop there. From mid-1988 on, he combined perestroika and glasnost with *demokratizatsiya*, including the first free elections that the Soviet Union had ever held. As the CPSU gradually relinquished its grip over political and social life, unrest emerged in many parts of the Soviet Union, particularly the Baltic republics, the Caucasia, and Moldova. The emergence of destabilizing unrest in a society that previously had been tightly controlled from above was reminiscent of the pattern described by Alexis de Tocqueville in *L'Ancien Régime et la Révolution*: "When people who have long endured an oppressive regime without complaint suddenly find it relaxing its pressure, they rise up violently against it. . . . Experience reveals that the most dangerous moment for a bad government usually comes when it begins to reform itself. . . . A grievance is patiently endured so long as it seems permanent, but it comes to appear intolerable once the thought of removing it arises."

The freer flow of information under glasnost contributed to the decline of central control. Soviet citizens became aware of the full magnitude of Stalin era crimes, the wide range of social problems afflicting the Soviet Union—alcoholism, juvenile delinquency, declining health indexes, homelessness, spiritual malaise, crime, poverty, and the disaffection of young people—and the destruction caused by natural disasters, accidents, and environmental pollution. The stream of disclosures about the Soviet past and deficiencies of Soviet society did not spark mass unrest but did have the cumulative impact of delegitimizing the Soviet regime in the eyes of many Russians as well as non-Russians.

Glasnost also had a profound impact on Soviet elites, who were suddenly free to talk about the regime's past iniquities and the Soviet Union's "failure to measure up to the civilized world" (as Soviet foreign minister Eduard Shevardnadze put it). The exposure of Stalinist crimes and the outpouring of criticism about the continued shortcomings of Soviet life eroded the morale of elites who had previously been loyal to the Communist system. The historian Crane Brinton suggested in his influential *Anatomy of Revolution* that "a ruling class jeopardizes its rule when many of its members begin to believe that they hold power unjustly, that beliefs they took for granted were false or silly, and that they should help those who are challenging the status quo." This is precisely what unfolded in the Soviet Union in the late 1980s and early 1990s.

The vastly greater leeway for political protest and mobilization in the late 1980s came at the same time that economic conditions had begun deteriorating rapidly. Ironically, in the two years prior to Gorbachev's emergence as leader of the CPSU, the Soviet economy had actually been improving. Although economic growth rates had been lagging since the early 1970s, the economy was not in crisis in 1985 and could probably have continued functioning indefinitely. Gorbachev's own economic policies, which led to macroeconomic imbalances, soaring inflation, rampant shortages, the stripping of assets of large firms, and a rapid buildup of foreign debt, destabilized the economy and produced a genuine crisis by 1990 and 1991, but these problems could have been avoided through the adoption of sounder policies. The hardships that resulted from Gorbachev's failure to pursue an effective economic program generated widespread discontent.

The confluence of these trends by the end of the 1980s produced a highly volatile mix that was made even more combustible by the increasing polarization of key elites. On one end were hard-line officials in the CPSU and KGB who wanted to roll back the reforms and reassert centralized control. On the other end were radical reformers (including former dissidents) who were disappointed that Gorbachev was not moving faster and were intent on creating new political parties to supplant the CPSU. The more moderate reformers led by Gorbachev were increasingly isolated in a tenuous middle position.

Many of the radical reformers coalesced around Boris Yeltsin, who had staged a remarkable political comeback in 1989 after being demoted and humiliated by Gorbachev in October 1987. Although Yeltsin remained a

CPSU member until July 1990, he increasingly presented himself as an antiestablishment and populist figure who would confront the party hierarchy. Voters in Moscow overwhelmingly elected Yeltsin to the new Soviet legislature, known as the USSR Congress of People's Deputies, in March 1989, despite strong opposition from senior CPSU officials. Yeltsin used this new platform to call repeatedly on Gorbachev and the CPSU to move much faster with political and economic reforms.

Yeltsin's position was strengthened still further in June 1990 when he gained the chair of the newly created Russian parliament, and a few weeks later, demonstratively walked out of the CPSU's Twenty-eighth Congress and renounced his party membership. Over the next year, he kept up his pressure on Gorbachev and continued to demand much bolder reforms. When Yeltsin was elected by a wide margin to the new Russian presidency in July 1991, he had an even stronger vantage point from which to challenge Gorbachev and the Soviet regime.

The Failed Coup and the Dissolution of the USSR

Despite Yeltsin's increasing assertiveness, Gorbachev tried to hold the Soviet Union together by forging a new relationship between the center and the union republics. Prolonged negotiations toward this end in 1990–91 were plagued by difficulties, but the talks might eventually have paid off had it not been for hard-liners in the KGB, army, military-industrial complex, and CPSU who launched a coup d'état on August 19, 1991, the day before the scheduled signing of a Union Treaty that would have reconfigured center-republic ties. The coup did not come entirely out of the blue. It was preceded by the abrupt resignation of Shevardnadze in December 1990 (as he warned of an impending hard-line backlash), a violent crackdown in Lithuania and Latvia in January 1991, an attempt to stage a "constitutional coup" in June 1991, and the publication of an ultra-hard-line "Word to the People" [*Slovo k narodu*] manifesto in July.

Several months prior to the coup, Gorbachev had authorized planning for a general crackdown, and he therefore knew at least in broad terms that a coup was in the offing. But the evidence suggests that Gorbachev did *not* condone the specific attempt that occurred on August 19, and that his refusal to back the conspirators proved decisive in the coup's failure on August 21. By all indications, the leaders of the putsch—who set up a State Committee on the State of Emergency (GKChP) to oversee matters—were hoping that Gorbachev would reluctantly join them if they forced his hand. Although it is impossible to know what Gorbachev might have done if the coup had lasted longer and the conspirators had been more resolute in cracking down, his refusal to lend his imprimatur to the putsch during the critical early days was crucial in depriving the GKChP of any legitimacy it might have attained and ensuring the coup's failure.

The coup failed not because the plotters lacked enough force to carry it out—they in fact had immense numbers of well-armed troops at their disposal—but because they were averse to taking responsibility for large-scale bloodshed unless they received explicit authorization from the country's highest command authority (namely, Gorbachev). This dynamic underscores the enormous importance of the top leader's role in the Soviet political system. Even though the heads of the key institutions of power in the Soviet Union—the army, KGB, Internal Affairs Ministry, military-industrial complex, and CPSU apparatus—were all complicit in the coup, their backing was insufficient without direct authorization from the top. If the CPSU general secretary was unwilling to resort to mass repression, other high-ranking officials did not want to accept responsibility for causing widespread loss of life.

The failure of the putsch prefigured the collapse of the Soviet Union itself four months later. Three broad consequences of the aborted coup were especially significant.

First, the failure of the coup gave unstoppable momentum to several of the union republics—the Baltic states, Georgia, Moldova, and others—in their drives for independence. Of particular importance was Ukraine. In the absence of the failed coup attempt, the independence movement in Ukraine probably would not have gained the momentum that it did by December 1991. As recently as March 1991, when a countrywide referendum was held on the future of the Soviet Union, nearly three-quarters of voters in Ukraine had been in favor of preserving the union. But the aborted coup profoundly altered public sentiment in Ukraine. The Ukrainian parliament reflected the new mood by adopting an independence declaration on August 24, 1991. When a republic-wide referendum was held in Ukraine on December 1, more than 90 percent voted in favor of full independence—a result that led a week later to the signing of the Belovezhskaya Pushcha accords that codified the end of the Soviet Union.

Second, Yeltsin's highly visible role in the resistance to the putsch—symbolized most vividly by his standing on top of a tank—enabled him to gain clear ascendance over Gorbachev once the coup was rebuffed. The Russian leader promptly recognized the independence of the Baltic states, Georgia, and Moldova. Although Yeltsin initially wanted to preserve the rest of the union as a Russian-led federation, he was intent on reducing the Soviet regime to a mere figurehead status. His efforts in this regard in the last few months of 1991 accelerated trends that ultimately forced him to accept the outright disintegration of the union.

Third, the failed coup undermined the CPSU and severely weakened the KGB, army, and Soviet government. None of these institutions was in any position after August 21 to rely on violence as a last-ditch means of holding the Soviet Union together. Yeltsin promptly suspended and then banned the CPSU, bringing a de facto end to Communist rule. The KGB and army were temporarily immobilized, and thus were incapable of resisting the breakup of the Soviet state. The failed coup was decisive in eliminating any further willingness on the part of top elites to resort to large-scale repression. Although Gorbachev raised the possibility of a military crackdown in a private conversation with the Soviet defense minister as late as mid-November 1991, he undoubtedly realized that it was too late for such a step even as he proposed it.

With Gorbachev relegated to a subordinate position in the aftermath of the coup, Yeltsin worked sedulously in fall 1991 to ensure that the Soviet regime would play no more than a ceremonial role in a new political structure. No longer did Yeltsin seek to cooperate with Gorbachev in any sustained way. Although both men hoped to preserve a union after August 21, their conceptions of the entity that should emerge were incompatible. The resounding shift of public opinion in Ukraine in support of outright independence, as reflected in the voting results on December 1, is what ultimately forced Yeltsin to change his goals and precipitate the demise of the Soviet Union through the Belovezhskaya Pushcha agreements. But even if the situation in Ukraine had not changed so dramatically, it is questionable whether a viable union structure could have been devised that would have satisfied both Yeltsin and Gorbachev.

When ordinary Russians suddenly learned on December 8, 1991, that the Soviet Union was going to be dissolved at the end of the year, they did not take to the streets in protest. On the contrary, Russian society reacted to the Belovezhskaya Pushcha accords with evident relief and even, in some cases, indifference. Gorbachev had desperately wanted to preserve the Soviet Union, but his effort to do so was greatly complicated by the public mood in Russia during the final few months of 1991. The dissolution of the Soviet Union seemed inconceivable before Gorbachev came to power, but one of the consequences of his policies—obviously an unintended consequence—was the growing public perception in Russia that the demise of the Soviet state was bound to occur and therefore not worth resisting. Although Russians were not inclined to rise up in armed revolt against Soviet rule, the important thing by the end of 1991 was that all the major social groups in Russia no longer had a stake in the future existence of the USSR.

See also Cold War; Command Economy; Coup in the USSR; Gorbachev, Mikhail; Nations and Empire in the USSR; Perestroika; Second Cold War; Single-Party System; State, The; Yeltsin, Boris.

FURTHER READING

Beissinger, M. R. *Nationalist Mobilization and the Collapse of the Soviet State.* New York: Cambridge University Press, 2002.

Dawisha, K., and B. Parrott, eds. *The End of Empire? The Transformation of the USSR in Comparative Perspective.* Armonk, NY: M. E. Sharpe, 1997.

Hough, J. F. *Democratization and Revolution in the USSR, 1985–1991.* Washington, DC: Brookings Institution, 1997.

Kramer, M. "The Collapse of East European Communism and the Repercussions within the Soviet Union (Part 1)." *Journal of Cold War Studies* 5, no. 4 (Fall 2003): 178–256.

———. "The Collapse of East European Communism and the Repercussions within the Soviet Union (Part 2)." *Journal of Cold War Studies* 6, no. 4 (Fall 2004): 3–64.

———. "The Reform of the Soviet System and the Demise of the Soviet State." *Slavic Review* 63, no. 3 (Fall 2004): 505–13.

———. "The Collapse of East European Communism and the Repercussions within the Soviet Union (Part 3)." *Journal of Cold War Studies* 7, no. 1 (Winter 2004–5): 3–96.

Remnick, D. *Lenin's Tomb: The Last Days of the Soviet Empire.* New York: Vintage Books, 1994.

MARK KRAMER

Djilas, Milovan

Milovan Djilas (1911–95), a prominent Communist leader, broke with communism, and then became well known as the author of works containing critical analyses of the foundations of Communist theory and practice. A native of Montenegro who showed literary abilities early on, Djilas enrolled in Belgrade University in 1929. There he started to take part in the Communist movement, was arrested a number of times, and spent three years in prison. After his release in 1936, he began his career as a functionary of the Communist Party of Yugoslavia (CPYu), which was then illegal. When the CPYu's leadership was reconstituted at the end of 1930s with Josip Broz Tito at its head, Djilas was not only included among the top leaders but together with Edvard Kardelj and Alexander Ranković formed a troika of Tito's closest associates. He held this position during both the armed struggle, organized by the CPYu during 1941–45 against the Axis occupation of Yugoslavia, and the first years of Communist power, which was established when the country's independence was restored.

Still high in the CPYu ruling circle, Djilas had the crucial task of managing the spheres of propaganda, culture, and the mass media. Together with Kardelj, he was essentially the party's leading ideologue. His views, public political speeches, writings on current affairs, and activity within the party up to the Soviet-Yugoslav rift, like all the ideology and policies of the CPYu at the time, conformed to Bolshevik canons in their Stalinist interpretation, which were still regarded as the bases of Marxism-Leninism. After the Soviet-Yugoslav break, when the Yugoslav leadership started to criticize Stalin and Soviet policies, and by the early 1950s, had gradually evolved into a model of so-called self-governing socialism, Djilas proclaimed this model to be an authentic socialist alternative to the "Stalinist deformations." He was among the most active initiators and prosecutors of this new path. Nevertheless, his ideas about how to move along this path began to go further than was acceptable for the rest of the leadership, including Tito.

Djilas expressed these ideas in a series of articles published through fall 1953 and up to January 1954 in the newspaper *Borba* (Struggle), the central organ of the Union of Communists of Yugoslavia (UCYu), as the CPYu began to be called in 1952, and the journal *Nova Misao* (New Thought). One of the ideas in his articles that attracted broad public attention was that in Yugoslavia, along with the contradictions and struggles between socialist and bourgeois forces typical of the revolutionary period, there was now a conflict within the newly triumphant socialist ranks. It was a conflict between the more conservative faction embodied in the party and state bureaucracy that was hampering the democratic process, and a progressive faction in favor of increasing democratization. The bureaucracy was criticized for being essentially an elite class striving to dictate the country's politics with its own interests, habits, and morals. Also being advanced, though, was the notion of free expression of opinion and open discussion among the various sectors of socialism. For practical purposes, this was a call for a certain tolerance of pluralism in the UCYu and the organizations it controlled. And this implied, in turn, a real movement toward democratization.

In early January 1954, a directive from above forbade further publication of these articles. At a plenum of the UCYu's Central Committee held in mid-January, with Tito and Kardelj setting the tone, Djilas's ideas were condemned as "Bernsteinism" and "anarchic liberalism," and he was removed from all his leadership positions. Djilas, who had not yet freed himself from his own party consciousness, preferred the ritual self-criticism at the plenum. Nevertheless, a few months later, he left the UCYu. He quickly evolved into a dissident, and began to write memoirs and theoretical works. In the memoirs he realistically and unapologetically depicted the history of the CPYu/UCYu, the policies and development of the party's elite class (including his own role in it). In his theoretical works he developed his criticism of Communist ideology and policies—a criticism that gradually became more radical and finally turned into an outright rejection of them.

Djilas's writings were smuggled out to the West and published there. In Yugoslavia itself his works were banned by the Communist authorities (they were also banned in other countries with Communist regimes), and only when the regime fell did they to come to light in Yugoslavia. For the publication of his writings in the West and also for interviews he gave Western journalists, Djilas was tried three times and twice went to prison, for a total of perhaps nine years, over the course of twelve years (1955–66). Each time he was released only because of the need to take into account world opinion. Of the theoretical works he wrote as a dissident, the best known are his two books: *The New Class* (1957) and *The Imperfect Society* (1969), which analyzed the society and state under Communist rule. His best-known memoir is *Conversations with Stalin* (1962).

See also Bureaucracy; Communist Party in Yugoslavia; Soviet-Yugoslavia Break; Stalinism; Tito, Josip Broz.

FURTHER READING

Djilas, Milovan. *The New Class: An Analysis of the Communist System.* New York: Praeger, 1957.

———. *Land without Justice.* New York: Harcourt Brace, 1958.

———. *Conversations with Stalin.* New York: Harcourt Brace, 1962.

———. *The Unperfect Society: Beyond the New Class.* New York: Harcourt Brace, 1969.

———. *Memoir of a Revolutionary.* New York: Harcourt Brace, 1973.

———. *Wartime.* New York: Harcourt Brace, 1977.

———. *Tito: The Story from Inside.* Harcourt Brace, 1980.

———. *Of Prisons and Ideas.* San Diego: Harcourt Brace, 1985.

———. *Rise and Fall.* San Diego: Harcourt Brace, 1985.

LEONID JA. GIBJANSKIJ

Dubček, Alexander

The changing political path taken by Alexander Dubček (1921–92) reflects the difficulty of the break this important political figure made with Communist ideology and the party, and the way he came to terms with his own political past. Dubček's Communist convictions had their roots in his family and his fourteen years of residence in the Soviet Union, where his family had moved when he was four. He returned to Czechoslovakia in 1938. Dubček joined the Communist Party of Czechoslovakia (CPCz) at eighteen, engaged in illegal work (during the Nazi period), and took part in the Slovak National Uprising. Before that he had studied to be a machine fitter and had been a manual laborer up to 1949.

In 1949, Dubček began a twenty-year stint as a worker in the party's political apparatus. He worked in the regional and central apparatus of the Slovak Communist Party (CPSl). In January 1953, he was elected chief secretary of the CSPl for the Bratislava region, and two years later a member of the CPSl. Following that he studied at the Political Training College in Moscow, and then in 1958, again filled a leading position in the Bratislava region, after which he became a member of the Central Committee of the CPCz. After two more years he was named a secretary of the CPCz's Central Committee and was again elected as a deputy to Parliament (his

first term was from 1951 to 1955). His arrival in Prague would not have been possible without the instigation of the first secretary of the CPCz's Central Committee, Antonín Novotný, who counted Dubček as one of his favorites. Still, Dubček did not remain long at the CPCz. He was transferred back to Slovakia, perhaps at his own wish or perhaps also because of Novotný's own desire to buttress the Slovak party leadership by adding younger functionaries.

Dubček's return to Slovakia was a consequential event in his political development and life. In November 1962, he was named secretary and a member of the Presidium of the Central Committee of the CPSl. Five months later he became the highest party functionary in Slovakia—the first secretary—who was also a member of the Presidium of the Central Committee of the CPCz. Novotný had been considering another candidate for this post, Michal Chudík, who, he correctly assumed, would continue the line of the hitherto party chief of Slovakia, K. Bacilek, who had recently been recalled. At the time of Dubček's return, both the party and country were facing difficult circumstances. The political waters had been stirred up by a reexamination of the political trials involving leading Communists in the mid-1950s. The results of the economic crisis were also becoming evident. Popular discontent had forced a political relaxation, which in turn was affecting the political situation in Slovakia. The issue of rehabilitations (Dubček was a member of the commission of the CPCz's Central Committee that had recommended them) was causing repercussions in Slovakia and rapidly becoming the nucleus of a national political movement. Its then-representatives, led by Gustav Husák, were announcing further demands. Foremost were the issues of Slovakia's position in the country, the possible creation of a federative Slovak state, and changes in the political system and relations within the CPCz. Dubček was under pressure from two sides: on the one hand, the dissatisfied elements in the party, primarily the intelligentsia; and on the other hand, their opponents, who were resisting the changes being demanded. Yet he managed to cope with this onerous situation.

Dubček's position was made more difficult by two other circumstances. In 1963 he was either not known at all, or not well known in the party or by the public. And the CPCz leadership was using power politics within the system to banish all speeches by critics and dissatisfied individuals. Dubček refused to resort to such machinations. He did not consider these people enemies, even if he did condemn their actions and some of their demands. He believed that negotiations and discussions with them would prove successful. Soon after his accession to the leading position in Slovakia, his disparate views began to become obvious. Some of these concerned the methods in the political work of the party. During the next three years (1965–67), these differences broadened and, more seriously, started to involve broader political issues. They formed an important component of his efforts to bring about reforms, where he faced struggles with his opponents, in particular Novotný. The national political movement in Slovakia, which Dubček and the Slovak leadership were already in control of, was one of the main currents of the reform movement, and one of the main elements of the growing crisis within the party and among the people. Contributing to this upsurge was the insensitivity of Novotný and his supporters to the national feelings of the Slovaks as well as the conflicts evoked by the president's visits to Slovakia.

The most consequential Dubček versus Novotný conflict came at a meeting of the CPCz's Central Committee on October 30, 1967. Dubček proposed a party program, based on an analysis of the state of society, that would answer to the needs of the country, and reform the relationship between the party and the people on the principle "that the party does not rule the people, but leads it." He went on to demand improvements in the internal life of the party and its democratization. Among his demands was the elimination of the "accumulation of functions," something aimed indirectly at Novotný, who exercised the two highest functions in the country. Novotný reacted sharply. He condemned Dubček's speech and accused the whole CPSl leadership of nationalism. This was not the first time Dubček had been criticized by Novotný. Already before that Novotný had tried to steer his supporters in the CPSl's Central Committee and the Presidium against Dubček. The latter found out that State Security was interested in him and was compiling a dossier about his past activities, a suspicion confirmed by an investigative commission. Novotný had already attempted to replace Dubček with Chudík in 1966. He tried to prove that the CPSl leadership was not following the decrees or party line of the CPCz, and that Dubček was not up to leading the party. But Novotný's views did not hold sway. A second attempt on his part to discredit Dubček failed in December 1967. At a special session of chosen leaders and functionaries, Novotný repeated these same accusations of nationalism and weak leadership in Slovakia. Dubček brought this to the attention of

the CPSl leadership, which decisively rejected the claim of deviations from the party line.

During his four-year leadership, Dubček had acquired great authority in the party and with the Slovak people. And the internal political situation was now also different. There were calls for changes both in policies and practice as well as the leadership. The October fracas with Novotný had caused Dubček and his closest colleagues to change their position toward the former. Up to then Dubček had believed in the possibility of coming to an agreement with Novotný. But after October and December 1967, he realized that Novotný would have to give up his function as first secretary of the CPCz's Central Committee. Other members of the CPCz reached the same conclusion, and on January 5, 1968, under pressure from the Central Committee, Novotný resigned his post. Then, after some lengthy negotiations, Dubček was chosen to succeed Novotný. His selection was a compromise between adherents and opponents of the changes.

In January 1968 Dubček entered a terrain almost unknown to him in politics. He had no clear idea of the consequences that the change of party heads might provoke in Czechoslovak society. He was aware of the need for reforms, but there was no focused plan for them even for the immediate future. Dubček was still adjusting to the situation in April 1968 when he was ratified as president. In the meantime, the activities of various strata of the population and groups of citizens were going on unchecked; these forces were coming forward with demands, breaking the rules of the power structure that had been in force up to then (for instance, censorship), and were themselves expanding the sector of freedom. Democratization of the regime was proceeding without restraint, and from above. The "anti-Novotný front" of January was breaking up. It was being replaced both by representatives of a genuine reform movement and by some who were against thoroughgoing social changes. At the head of the reform movement stood Dubček, whose authority had grown and who had become a symbol of social mobility. His authority had the effect of isolating the opponents of reform, so that they were unable to use their power to halt the democratic process and bring off a political reversal. The reformers, who by now were determining internal political developments, were themselves somewhat divided. Yet those demanding an acceleration and expansion of the reforms were getting stronger, and exerting pressure on the supporters of gradual changes more commensurate with the political realities. Dubček was a leading advocate of this second direction.

Negotiations with representatives of the Soviet Union and the other bloc states (in Dresden, Moscow, Warsaw, Cíerna nad Tisou, and Bratislava) along with reports from various other sources made Dubček realize that the Czechoslovak reforms were under threat from the outside. The Warsaw Pact ratcheted up their pressure, and tried to prevail on Dubček and his adherents to crush the reforms themselves ("strangle the reforms with their own hands"). He tried to find a middle road between internal development and external pressure, and believed that he could convince the increasingly dissatisfied allies of the correctness of the reforms. Dubček did not believe in the possibility of armed intervention by the USSR. The assault on Czechoslovakia on August 21, 1968, by the Warsaw Pact armies shocked him. Still, he realized that his "evaluation of Soviet intentions had turned out to be wrong. . . . That night I understood how deeply mistaken I was."

On August 21 Dubček was arrested by agents of the Soviet and Czechoslovak secret police, and spirited away to be interned in the USSR. He was informed that he would be placed before a revolutionary tribunal. But the political, international, and internal failure of the invasion forced the Soviet side to negotiate with Dubček, who insisted on the participation of the entire CPCz leadership. At first he refused to sign the so-called Moscow Protocol handed him by the Soviet leaders, but then he changed his mind at the urging of reform supporters. He gave a speech in which he defended the reform policies and declared the armed invasion a tragic mistake. The Soviets broke off negotiations, but returned after Czech president Ludvík Svoboda pleaded the Czechoslovaks' case. Dubček justified his decision to sign the protocol as the lesser evil and an expression of hope that the reforms would continue, even if limited in scope, and that he would at least succeed in salvaging the results so far and preventing the mass persecution of the reforms' active supporters. After August 1968, it became apparent that Dubček's hopes for continuing the reform program were ill founded. The situation went in the opposite direction, changing under the pressure and according to the wishes of the occupying power. This pressure reawakened the activity of the reforms' opponents, which Dubček and his supporters were powerless to hinder. They feared that all was lost, although they proceeded on the principle of not voluntarily yielding the whole field to their opponents, but all they succeeded in doing was diminishing Dubček's authority and his popularity among the people.

Pressured by the Soviet leadership and its Czechoslovak allies, Dubček resigned as first secretary of the Central Committee and recommended Husák as his replacement. Dubček's departure was not met with any significant response from the public. He was named chair of the National Assembly. In this capacity he signed a legal provision against the activities of "antisocialistic forces," refuting his own reform policies and curbing citizens' rights. He later acknowledged that this was a political mistake. The provision was used to quell demonstrators against the occupation, who were calling out Dubček's name—as a symbol of reform. From December 1969 to June 1970 Dubček served as ambassador to Turkey. Then he was expelled from the CPCz and began work on a forestry team. From here he went into retirement in 1981. State Security kept a constant watch on him.

His isolation in Bratislava and the incessant surveillance restricted his activity in the opposition movements in the 1970s and 1980s. He also held different views from the opposition on the methods and goals of its activity. Dubček did not sign Charter 77, although he agreed with it and condemned the persecution of opposition groups. He employed his own means of opposition activity, in line with his view that the starting point for any reforms should be an overhaul of the Communist Party. The protests and complaints that he sent to party leaders and government organizations were passed along to citizens as well. He joined the revolution in 1989 immediately, and his participation was welcomed by the public. Dubček became a prominent though by no means leading figure in the new movement. He assumed that he would be chosen president of the republic, but after some negotiations withdrew his candidacy. In December he was made chair of the National Assembly and refused to join the CPCz. He finished his political career as a Social Democrat, and was named as chair of the Social Democratic Party in Slovakia in 1992. He died in November of the same year as a result of an auto accident.

Dubček's political life went through a number of phases. His path from an aware Communist believing in the correctness of the party's ideas and politics, to an utter break with Communism was long and problematic. The public revelation of Joseph Stalin's crimes shook Dubček's faith and conviction. His work with the Rehabilitation Commission of the Central Committee of the CPCz brought more concerns to his attention. "I believe that by the end of my work with the commission I was no longer the same person," Dubček said. He was convinced, though, that it was simply a matter of mistakes made in carrying out correct ideas and policies. He made attempts at reform, only to run up against the lack of understanding and resistance of leading Communists in the party. Dubček's conversion into a reform Communist began during the mid-1960s, especially after his October 1967 conflict with Novotný and his supporters. He remained a Communist even after August 1968, all the way to the mid-1980s. Dubček kept believing in the possibility and necessity of a reform of the party and regime, and hoped that Mikhail Gorbachev's leadership would create favorable conditions for this. Only after the collapse of the Communist system in the USSR and the Soviet bloc states did Dubček break with reform Communism and join the Social Democratic Party.

Dubček's performance in the highest posts in Slovakia and particularly his national (Czechoslovak) positions mostly involved his efforts to democratize the regime. His political approach to his work revealed democratic elements that differed from official practice and were marked by a tolerance of other people's opinions.

Dubček was and still is a symbol of the Czechoslovak reform movement of 1968, known the world over as the Prague Spring. The Prague Spring was a significant event in the postwar history of Europe and contributed to the disintegration of the Soviet bloc. In 1968 Dubček found himself in a difficult, complex, and dramatic situation, full of taxing contradictions for the skilled politician he matured into "during the march." He kept searching for solutions under pressure from two sides. He did not believe that Moscow would take the drastic step it ultimately did, and employed a strategy to thwart this possibility. Dubček countered the external pressure by trying to hide "with his back" the possibility that the reform movement at home might hold up. August 1968 showed that Moscow would not allow the process to develop. Yet Dubček did not choke off the reforms with his own hands, as the Soviet leadership wanted; he never sank into self-criticism, and always proudly adhered to the Prague Spring and its tradition.

See also Brezhnev Doctrine; Charter 77; Communist Party in Czechoslovakia; De-Stalinization; Dissent in the USSR; Husák, Gustav; Novotný, Antonín; Prague Spring; Revolutions in East-Central Europe.

FURTHER READING

Bencik, A. *Utajovaná Pravda o Dubčekovi*. Prague: Ostrov, 2001.

Dubček, A. *Il nuovo corso in Cecoslovacchia*. Rome: Editori Riuniti, 1968.

————. *Le ventimila parole di Dubcek, per un'autentica democrazia socialista (30 ottobre 1967–4 agosto 1968)*. Milan: Il Saggiatore, 1969.

————. *Hope Dies Last: The Autobiography of Alexander Dubcek*. Ed. and trans. J. Hochman. New York: Kodansha America, 1993.

Maxa, H. *Alexander Dubček*. Bratislava-Brno: Kalligram-Doplněk, 1998.

KAREL KAPLAN

Dzerzhinskii, Feliks

Born September 11, 1877, the fourth child of eight, Feliks Edmundovich Dzerzhinskii (Dzierzynski) was raised in rural isolation on his family's estate, Dzierzynowo, near Minsk in the Vil'no Province of the Russian Empire. His parents were both pedagogical nationalistic Polish Catholics, descended from landed gentry. Dzerzhinskii's father, Edmund-Rufin, worked as a math teacher in Taganrog. Tuberculosis led to Edmund's retirement and premature death on the ancestral estate in 1883, at age forty-nine—the same life span as both Dzerzhinskii and his only child, Janek (1911–60).

In 1887 Dzerzhinskii moved to Vil'no to study at a classical gymnasium. He excelled in canon law and contemplated entering the Catholic priesthood, but then lost his Christian faith. This was probably due to a number of factors: his increasing involvement in revolutionary circles from 1894 on, and by 1896, the dual shock of the deaths of both his younger sister Wanda (possibly accidentally shot by Dzerzhinskii) and his mother (née Helena Januszewska). From hereon Dzerzhinskii devoted himself body and soul to the Social Democratic movement in the Polish-Lithuanian borderlands of the Russian Empire. Yet in spite of claiming a complete conversion to atheism, he did not entirely shake off his Catholic education. His sparse early written works—autobiographical, political, and poetical—seem to be the sentimental cogitations of a lapsed Jesuit missionary, seduced by a revolutionary career because it offered a more practical direction in which to pursue spiritual meaning, justice, martyrdom, and salvation.

In 1899, Dzerzhinskii founded the Social Democratic Party of the Kingdom of Poland and Lithuania. During the upheavals of 1905 to 1907, he imposed a strict conspiratorial ethos and rigid central discipline on the organization, akin to Lenin's model party. Dzerzhinskii was made a member of the Russian Social Democratic Party's Central Committee in 1906, and was an occasional ally—but not a devoted follower—of Lenin. After 1911 Dzerzhinskii sided with Rosa Luxemburg's Berlin-based Social Democratic Main Directorate (the Zarzadowcy) against Józef Unszlicht's Warsaw faction (the "Splitters," or Rozlamowcy).

He survived an underground career more grueling than that of any other Soviet leader, having spent eleven of twenty years in prison and exile between 1897 and 1917: 1897–99, 1900–1902, July–October 1905, December 1906–June 1907, April–November 1909, and 1912–17. He escaped from prison and exile three times (in 1899, 1902, and 1909). When at liberty, he chose to live mostly inside the Russian Empire on the run from the czarist secret police. Dzerzhinskii was subjected to vicious beatings while in prison. The effects on his health and temperament were profound: he was forced to take rest cures in Switzerland, Zakopane, Capri, Switzerland again, and the Caucasia in 1902, 1903, 1910, 1918, and 1925, respectively. Dzerzhinskii's ordeals intensified his anxious flight from melancholy, his suspicious nature, fierce temper, and self-flagellation. He often slipped close to nervous breakdown, such as in March 1917, summer 1918, the New Year's celebration of 1918–19 (when having had too much to drink, Dzerzhinskii begged to be executed), and September 1920. His declining health was accelerated by an ascetic and restless disposition: he ate poorly, smoked a lot, worked long hours, and slept little. Dzerzhinskii developed tuberculosis in prison in his twenties and was coughing blood by his forties.

When the revolution came in 1917, it liberated Dzerzhinskii from Moscow's infamous Butyrki prison. Dzerzhinskii backed Lenin in 1917; both were eager to force the pace of revolution. Though they clashed in 1917 and 1922 on the national question, Lenin found Dzerzhinskii useful in practical matters: his experience in prison, exile, and the underground constituted a master class in the art of social control and political repression. Dzerzhinskii was instrumental in the creation, expansion, and survival of the Soviet security police (as head of the Cheka from December 1917 and the State Political Directorate [GPU] from 1922). He also involved the *chekisty* in his ever-widening portfolio of duties: Dzerzhinskii led the fight against typhus in 1918; chaired the Commissariat for Internal Affairs from 1919 to 1923; was lined up as Marshal Pilsudksi's replacement in the failed Bolshevik invasion of Poland in 1920; led a vast orphanage construction program in 1921; chaired the Transport Commissariat from 1921 on; organized the embalming and display of Lenin's corpse in 1924; was a candidate member of the politburo, the chair of VSNKh, the Supreme Council of the National Economy (directing Soviet economic policy), and even more ambitiously, a member of the Society for the Study of Interplanetary Travel starting in 1924. Always involved in propaganda, he also chaired the Society of Friends of Soviet Cinema from 1925. Dzerzhinskii sided with Stalin and Bukharin in the party feuds of 1923–26. He was due to replace Zinovyev as a full member of the politburo on Stalin's recommendation in July 1926. At a Kremlin Central Committee plenary session on July 20 that year, Dzerzhinskii delivered a rambling and wrathful speech attacking the nascent united opposition. Directly after this, apparently unwell, he retired to an adjoining room, suffered a heart attack, and died.

See also KGB; Red Terror; Russian Revolution and Civil War; War Communism.

FURTHER READING

Blobaum, R. *Feliks Dzierzynski and the SDKPiL: A Study of the Origins of Polish Communism.* New York: Columbia University Press, 1984.

Leggett, G. *The Cheka: Lenin's Political Police.* New York: Oxford University Press, 1981.

Rayfield, D. *Stalin e i suoi boia: una analisi del regime e della psicologia stalinisti.* Milan: Garzanti, 2005.

Valachanovich, A. I. *Feliks Edmundovich Dzerzhinskii: Kratkii ocherk zhizni i dejatel'nosti.* Minsk: Natako, 1997.

IAIN LAUCHLAN

Economic Reforms

The Soviet economy's "new course," already significant in the early 1950s, was really inaugurated after Stalin's death (1953), and produced a brief but intense period in which attempts to reform the economic system as well as the relevant research were undertaken. It developed on both a theoretical level, with debates between economists, and on a practical level (and this was what really distinguished it from a similar period in the 1920s), with the introduction of a series of laws that starting in the mid-1960s, attempted to modify the delicate relationship between the plan's decisional center and its peripheral elements, the individual enterprises, whose role was decisive for the plan's realization. The first phase of the new course for the post-Stalinist economy was uncertain and visibly marked by the ongoing political struggle. The struggle for power ended with Khrushchev's victory, which eliminated the Stalinist "old guard" in the space of two years, and gave birth to a brief period of hope in a country that was now removed from "terror"—a period prudently named the "thaw."

The economic situation, determined by the political conditions, followed its own peculiar path, a result of both the war's terrible past, but also the choices that had been made previously and were now being confirmed. From 1959 to 1964, agriculture only averaged a 1.5 percent annual growth rate, compared with the 7.6 percent of the 1955–59 period, and for the entire period, early grain production per inhabitant was barely superior to that of 1913. Khrushchev launched the "virgin lands" campaign in 1954, several years after the war had ended, hoping to resolve this sector's historical crisis, but it failed, reducing the harvest on monoculture lands by 65 percent, and in 1956 the government was forced to import more than twelve million tons of grain for about one billion U.S. dollars. Productivity also decreased during this same period, stabilizing at 3 percent as compared to the 9 percent of the 1953–58 period. Industrial production was also lower than expected (10.2 percent per year during the 1957–61 period), and it led to the interruption, in 1958, of the Sixth Five-Year Plan (1956–60) in order to launch a Seven-Year Plan (1959–65), which was meant to account for the discovery of new natural resources. This plan was intended to lead to progressive growth throughout the period—85 percent in heavy industry, 62 percent in light industry, 70 percent in agriculture, 65 percent in the national income, and 40 percent in real salaries—so as to allow the USSR to "reach and overtake the USA" in 1965, as Khrushchev was to peremptorily declare during the Twenty-first Party Congress (1959), where the "USSR's passage from socialism to communism" was also announced.

The data pertaining to Soviet economic reality during de-Stalinization give the lie to official declarations, and once more confirmed the system's structural crisis, at least the system as it had been conceived in the 1930s and then repeatedly reaffirmed, including in the postwar period. The persistent disconnect between the plan's goals and its actual results became a peculiarity, in this case permanent, of the Soviet planning system, made even worse during Khrushchev's tenure because of the pronounced voluntarism in decision making, and the approximate nature of its realizations. It is at this time that the most significant attempt in Soviet history to reform the economic system began—one that intended to at least partially modify the relationships between sectors, while preserving the guiding principles of the command economy, and the plan's function in society and the political system overall. It was inevitable that the political arena should provide the impulse for the economy's normalization, given the way it was constantly subjected to Khrushchev's abrupt changes of plan: his removal on October 15, 1964, concluded the heroic phase of de-Stalinization, which had done more to create new hopes than to bring about real changes in society. The Leonid Brezhnev era began with a more pragmatic orientation in the economic sector, and a more collegial one in the area of political leadership, but rapidly became the longest period of "stagnation" in Soviet history, decisively contributing to the end of the Soviet Union as a political entity.

Brezhnev, the Communist Party's first secretary, and Aleksey Kosygin, president of the Council of Ministers, immediately implemented the normalization of the political administration, and moved toward some cautious liberalization in the economy. The first and most important move in the economic sector was the so-called Kosygin reform, which was started in September 1965. The text of the related resolution naturally did not mention reform, but instead used the term "improvement," referred to planning as well as reinforcing the economic independence of individual enterprises and improving the organization of industrial management. These decisions were made in keeping with opinions of Vasily Nemchinov, one of the best economists of the period, who had lucidly highlighted "the gap that exists between the plan's production goals and those for the supply of materials, between the quantitative goals and the efficiency (profitability) indices, between the use of productive capacities and the introduction of new technologies." These remarks were the inspiration for the 1965 resolution, which nevertheless restricted itself to granting enterprises a greater degree of autonomy, reducing obligatory production quotas and allowing them to establish direct relationships among themselves, by way of the enterprise associations (*obedinenya*, whose bylaws were only approved in 1973), and replacing the goal of global production with that of sales volume, thus recognizing the importance of the enterprise's profitability. The principle of "commercial accounting" (*khozraschet*), which allowed each economic unit to have its own "profits and losses account," and was supposed to be managed according to commercial, efficient criteria, was also introduced. This first set of measures was then complemented in October 1965 by the adoption of a constitution for enterprises, and in 1967, the reform of wholesale prices. Faith in the positive outcome of these initiatives that had been introduced in 1965, in order to correct the economic system, was such that in the course of that same year, the three most significant economists of the period, who had also been the main protagonists of the ongoing debate on the fate of the Soviet system—Leonid Kantorovich, Viktor Novozhilov, and Nemchinov—were awarded the Lenin prize.

By the end of 1966, only 1.5 percent of all enterprises had been affected by the new regulations, and in 1970, when the "reform" was already stagnating, the overall quota was 72 percent, representing 81 percent of all labor employed in industry. Replacing the goal of overall production, as had been observed in the 1965 resolution, "does not really orient enterprises to produce goods that are necessary to the economy and the population," with "the goal of marketable production, in other words sales volume," became a merely verbal operation, since the "gross" remained the standard for measuring labor's productivity, salaries, and ultimately even incentives. Efforts to improve innovation and labor productivity were rendered useless from the start because of calculation criteria that were normally applied to the entire economic system, in order to measure the overall impact of any changes. The enterprise's autonomy, even though it was affirmed as a principle, faced a fundamental obstacle in the system of calculations adopted for the national economy as a whole, which privileged the criterion of the ruble "level attained," and even led to increasing the consumption of material used per unit, thus sacrificing the use of efficient and less costly tools and machinery. Another example of the actual problems raised by the 1965 "reform" was the famous experiment in personnel reduction undertaken by the management of the Schekino factory which, in 1967, while reducing its labor force by 15 percent, managed to simultaneously increase its production by 34.2 percent and productivity by 2.3 percent The experiment was later extended to other enterprises, but by mid-1973 only seven hundred enterprises, equivalent to 1 percent of the gross national product, had adopted the new measures. The slow pace with which the reform was adopted, in addition to its internal contradictions, and above all the simultaneous existence of two different levels of calculation, at the national and local level, only underscored how deadlocked the initiative, once supported by Kosygin, now was.

The political circumstances certainly also favored increased rigidity after the Soviet invasion of Czechoslovakia in 1968—a situation that contrasted with the diffusion of much more decisive and consistent (when compared to the USSR) forms of economic experimentation in Poland and Hungary. It was the real economy's situation, however, that led to pessimistic prognoses. The goals of the Eighth Five-Year Plan were adjusted twice, while in 1969 no data regarding those enterprises that had adopted the reform were provided. That same year data showed there was a general deceleration of economic growth, while at the end of the Ninth Five-Year Plan (1975), industrial production had increased by 43 percent compared to a planned 47 percent, the production of consumer goods had increased by 37 percent instead of the planned 48.6 percent, agricultural production by 13 percent instead of the planned 21 percent, and 18 percent of industrial enterprises had failed to meet the plan's objectives.

In order to confront this situation political authorities intervened with two distinct provisions, which were supposed to correct the reform's negative results. In 1971 an obligatory index that measured increases in labor productivity was introduced, and it was calculated on a yearly basis for the plan's duration, from 1971 to 1975 (1970 was adopted as the base year for calculations); it was supposed to result in qualitatively appropriate production. The following year another obligatory index was added, and it was supposed to measure "the realization of new products, whose characteristics should correspond to the best indices of national and foreign technologies"; the result was that the enterprises' autonomy, the centerpiece of the 1965 reform, was now increasingly hampered by the restrictions imposed by the State Planning Commission.

The second provision adopted by political authorities in 1973 was the regulation of "industrial unions," which were supposed to facilitate greater coordination between the ministry and individual enterprises, by both unifying them into a single management structure and providing a connection between different enterprises operating in the same sector. These unions had adopted the khozraschet system and decided the allocation of resources to individual enterprises, but they still had to face the insurmountable limit of the central distribution mechanisms between industries and subsectors. At the end of 1976 all industrial unions produced less than one-fourth of all industrial production, and in 1978, during the Tenth Five-Year Plan (1976–80), they still only accounted for 50 percent of the total, to the extent that in 1979, authorities declared that another two to three years would be needed to complete their realization. In 1979, the growth rate was 2 percent, but in order to meet the plan's objectives it would have had to be 5.5 percent, and in many sectors not only were the objectives not achieved but the results were negative—especially in agriculture, where the harvest of 179 million tons of grains, 59 million less than the 1978 harvest, was far from the 220 million tons the plan was aiming for, notwithstanding the massive investments on its behalf.

It was within this foreboding context, in terms of both the real economy's data and the efforts to correct the planning system that had been undertaken to date, that political authorities undertook the last attempt to slow the economy's decline, and with it the fate of the country as a whole. This was the third effort after the 1965 reform and the 1973 provisions on industrial unions. In 1979 a provision was introduced based on two fundamental points. From that moment on the Five-Year Plan was given an "imperative" interpretation, replacing those yearly management "directives" that could be adjusted according to the plan's actual implementation. This point was supposed to lead to the utilization of each single year in the plan, and not just the last two (as normally occurred), to achieve the planned quotas; severe sanctions were the penalty for noncompliance. The second point also entailed the adoption of a "net normative product" criterion (a sort of "value added" measure) instead of the two criteria introduced in 1965 (the sales volume and profitability), so that the notorious "gross" measure of production would be replaced by a net index, which was calculated on the basis of the labor force cost per product unit. The idea of strictly controlling the creation of the product and its cost basis, at all levels, which was motivated by the need to regulate the flow of information that went from the lower to the higher levels of the plan, meant that because of these information requirements, it would be necessary to undertake calculations for more than two hundred thousand types of product. This was an impossible task, or rather, a measure that created more uncertainty and chaos than real benefits. In addition, the plan continued to be calculated on the basis of the "level reached" the previous year, thus adding a specific increased growth percentage after the fact, which did not take the changes that had actually occurred in the productive processes into account. This, in turn, frustrated the intended objectives of increased systemic efficiency and productivity. At this point, the tangled morass of norms and the levels of their application were already out of control.

Brezhnev himself, during the Communist Party's Twenty-sixth Congress in 1981, had to admit that "compared to the best world indices, we use more raw materials and energy per national income unit than they do." The challenge of implementing possible corrections to the planned economic system had now run out of steam, according to the testimony of the country's leaders themselves, who from then on would abstain from proposing overarching or demanding measures. They instead limited themselves to supporting the course of planned production with various types of incentives or privileges, or resorting to forms of discipline imposed on the labor force (sanctions, firings, and transfers). The wish that Oskar Lange had formulated after the party's Twentieth Congress—that "economic reform concern the separation of the management of the national economy from the state's extra-economic activities, in other words the exercise of political power"—had been disregarded by the Soviet Union's leadership group while implementing its economic policy, thereby leading to the creation of a black hole with foreseeable results.

The issues of economic reform in the countries of Eastern Europe had both a different origin and a different history when compared to those in the Soviet Union, both because of the adoptive nature that the Soviet-type plan originally had, which meant, for example, that it did not affect agriculture and was not subjected to collectivization, and because of the periodic social objections to its application.

See also Command Economy, The; Five-Year Plans; Planning.

FURTHER READING

Antonov, O. K. *La pianificazione sovietica*. Florence: Vallecchi, 1968.

Bernocchi, P., ed. *Le riforme in URSS*. Milan: La Salamandra, 1977.

Bertolissi, S. *Alla ricerca dell'economia sovietica*. Naples: Istituto universitario orientale, 1994.

Chachaturov, T. S. *L'economia sovietica nella fase attuale di sviluppo*. Milan: Feltrinelli, 1977.

Delamotte, J. *Shchekino, entreprise soviétique pilote*. Paris: Les Éditions ouvrières, 1973.

Ellman, M. *Planning Problems in the USSR: The Contribution of Mathematical Economics to Their Solution, 1960–1971*. Cambridge: Cambridge University Press, 1973.

Katz, A. *The Politics of Economic Reform in the Soviet Union*. New York: Praeger, 1972.

Lewin, M. *Economia e politica nella società sovietica: il dibattito economico nell'URSS da Bucharin alle riforme delgi anni sessanta*. Rome: Editori Riuniti, 1977.

Lieberman, E. G., V. S. Nemchinov, and V. Trapeznikov. *Piano e profitto nella economia sovietica*. Rome: Editori Riuniti, 1965.

Nove, A. *An Economic History of the U.S.S.R.* New York: Penguin, 1982.

Skilling, H. G., ed. *Interest Groups in Soviet Politics*. Princeton, NJ: Princeton University Press, 1971.

Zaleski, E. *Planning Reforms in the Soviet Union, 1962–1966*. Chapel Hill: University of North Carolina Press, 1967.

SERGIO BERTOLISSI

Eisenstein, Sergei

Sergei Eisenstein (1898–1948) was arguably the leading director and theorist of Soviet cinema in his lifetime, but he was also a theater and opera director, scriptwriter, graphic artist, teacher and critic, and a major proponent of the ideology of revolutionary culture.

Eisenstein was born in Riga, then part of the Russian Empire, of German Jewish descent on his father's side and Russian on his mother's. His parents divorced when he was twelve, and his relationship with his father, a civil engineer responsible for many of the finest art nouveau buildings in the city, remained complex, even after the latter's premature death in exile in Berlin in the early 1920s. Educated in Riga's German-language Gymnasium, Eisenstein was groomed for his father's occupation, but rebelled against both his father and authority in general after the October 1917 Revolution. When he was almost twenty years old he abandoned his studies and joined the Red Army. Assigned to an army theater troupe, Eisenstein began making set designs and, on the strength of this experience, later joined the Proletkult Theatre, one of the most radical groups in Moscow. His first stage production as a director, an updated revolutionary version of Alexander Ostrovsky's *Enough Simplicity for Every Wise Man* (1923), included his first venture into filmmaking, a short comedy film, *Glumov's Diary*. His next theatrical production—of Sergei Tretiakov's *Gas Masks* (1924), staged on location in the Moscow gas works—was an attempt to bridge the gap between the artificiality of the stage and the reality of everyday life. The attempt failed: the reality of the gas works merely showed up the artifice of the drama, and so, as he himself put it, Eisenstein "fell into cinema."

Eisenstein had already worked with Esfir Shub on re-editing Fritz Lang's *Doctor Mabuse* for Soviet audiences in 1923, but his first full-length film was *The Strike* (1925), set in 1905, in which he applied to cinema his theory of the "montage of attractions," outlined in a 1923 article with that title. Eisenstein thought that montage—the way in which individual shots were juxtaposed—depended on a *conflict* between contrasting elements from which a new synthesis would arise, rather than on the smooth *continuity* that characterized the classical Hollywood film and the work of other early Soviet filmmakers. This notion developed partly from Eisenstein's study of Japanese and Chinese ideograms and partly from his understanding of the Marxist dialectic: thesis plus antithesis equals synthesis. It followed from the primacy accorded to montage in Eisenstein's theory of filmmaking that the actor's role was diminished, while the director's significance was, not perhaps surprisingly, enhanced. In his silent films Eisenstein more often than not used amateur actors who were the right physical types for the part and he called this "typage." Hence all the parts in *The Battleship Potemkin* (1925) were played by unknowns and an unknown worker, Nikandrov, played the role of Lenin in *October* (1927).

It was *The Battleship Potemkin* that secured Eisenstein's reputation both at home and abroad, especially in Germany, where it was a spectacular success and attracted far greater audiences than within the USSR itself. This reception was partly due to the strength of the German Communist Party and its affiliated organizations and partly to the film's reputation as something innovative and exotic. Like *The Strike*, *Potemkin* was set in 1905 and used the mutiny on the battleship as *pars pro toto* for the revolutionary events of that year. The six-minute scene of the massacre on the Odessa Steps, a fictional invention, is one of the most powerful and influential sequences in the history of cinema. After *Potemkin* Eisenstein started work on a film about collectivization, *The General Line*, but broke off to make *October* for the 10th anniversary of the October Revolution. In *October* Eisenstein further developed his idea of intellectual montage, in which an ideological argument was to be developed by visual means, the audience provoked into a predetermined reaction by the juxtaposition of individual frames. Eisenstein cited the "Gods sequence" as the paradigm of this method.

By the time that he returned to *The General Line* and completed it in 1929, the party's general line on agriculture had changed and Trotsky had fallen from grace. The film therefore had to be re-edited, and it was finally released under the title *The Old and the New* (1929). The problems that Eisenstein encountered in this film were to recur in his subsequent work. In 1929 he went abroad, even before the premiere of *The Old and the New*, with his assistants Eduard Tisse and Grigori Alexandrov, to study the new medium of sound film. The three toured Western Europe and then traveled to Hollywood to work for Paramount. Eisenstein's projects for the studio (*Sutter's Gold* and *An American Tragedy* among them) were rejected as too complex and difficult and therefore insufficiently commercial, and in 1930 he went south to Mexico to start filming *Que Viva Mexico!* with funds provided by American writer Upton Sinclair.

This project collapsed in acrimonious exchanges, and Eisenstein returned to the USSR in 1932, just as socialist realism was emerging as the dominant cultural doctrine. After several aborted projects, including *Moscow*, a history of the Russian capital, *The Black Consul*, which would have starred Paul Robeson, and a film version of Karl Marx's *Das Kapital*, he began making his first sound film, *Bezhin Meadow* in 1935. This venture too was dogged with problems and was eventually dropped on the orders of the head of Soviet cinema, Boris Shumiatsky, in March 1937. Eisenstein was forced into a public confession of his alleged errors and this, together with the dismissal and arrest of Shumiatsky in January 1938, enabled him to start filming *Alexander Nevsky* (1938), an allegorical warning of the consequences of a German invasion, as he explained in his article "My Subject Is Patriotism." This was Eisenstein's most accessible and popular film and rehabilitated him in the eyes of Stalin.

When not filming, Eisenstein was nonetheless busy, teaching at the State Institute of Cinema (VGIK) where he had been head of the directing department since his return from abroad in 1932 and a professor since 1935. He also devoted an increasing amount of time to his theoretical writings, but his magnum opus *Direction*, like his other work, *Mise-en-scène*, remained unfinished. *Alexander Nevsky* was a great success, however, and led to Eisenstein being entrusted with another historical film project on a grand scale: *Ivan the Terrible*, originally conceived in three parts. This last film was also unfinished: the filming of Part One of *Ivan the Terrible* was begun in 1943 in Alma-Ata, where the Moscow studios had been evacuated because of the war, and released in 1945, when it became an instant success and earned Eisenstein the Stalin Prize. In Part Two, however, the historical parallels between Ivan and Stalin became too obvious and uncomplimentary and, although completed, the film was not shown until 1958, after the deaths of Stalin, Eisenstein, and the film score's composer, Sergei Prokofiev. Part Three was never finished, but Eisenstein incorporated the color sequences into Part Two. He died of a heart attack in January 1948, his ill health exacerbated by the stress caused by the problems he had encountered with *Ivan*.

Eisenstein died under a cloud in his own country, but he has since been universally acknowledged as one of cinema's greatest creative geniuses and a towering figure in the culture of the 20th century. Although he never joined the Communist Party of the Soviet Union, he remained committed to the ideology of revolutionary culture until his untimely death.

See also Cinema, Soviet; Proletkult; Socialist Realism.

FURTHER READING

Ejzenstejn, S. M. *The Eisenstein Reader*. Ed. R. Taylor. Berkeley: University of California Press, 1998.

Taylor, R., and D. W. Spring, eds. *Stalinism and Soviet Cinema*. London: Routledge, 1993.

RICHARD TAYLOR

Elections

All of the Communist regimes were characterized by elections, ostensibly to fill leading positions within the political system. In theory, all posts within the legislative structure, from town councils to national legislatures and presidencies, were filled by election. In most Communist states, the usual form of election was direct, with the citizens directly electing representatives to fill positions, but in some states (including China, Cuba, Hungary, and Yugoslavia) the system also included some indirect elements with some deputies elected by the deputies at the next lower level. The elections invariably were reported to have a high turnout and high levels of support for official candidates—typically more than 90 percent support on a more than 90 percent turnout. Suffrage was generally universal, although during the early years of the various regimes, it was often restricted in class terms. In formal terms, voting was not compulsory, but there was significant social pressure to bring people to the polls.

Elections in the Communist states, at least until the final years when the systems were undergoing reform, were generally not competitive, with voters having no choice or only a strictly limited choice. Most elections had only one candidate standing for each position, with electors able to vote either for or against that candidate. Where there was more than one candidate, all candidates were officially vetted before they were able to stand, and the system was frequently structured in such a way as to advantage official candidates over others. Until the final stages of Communist rule, even when alternative candidates were allowed to stand, they were not permitted to articulate significantly different political programs. This reflected the fact that it was claimed that the society was united around common interests that were fully represented through the Communist Party and the other institutions of the socialist state; only in Yugoslavia was there an acceptance that the society comprised different interests that could gain electoral representation, but even here "antisocialist" interests were not accepted.

Until the erosion of its control toward the end of the regimes' lives, the Communist Party exercised close control over the electoral process. At each stage of that process—nominating, campaigning, and voting—the party's organs played the principal role in shaping its course. Party organs identified potential candidates and got them nominated, ran the election campaign leading up to the day when voting was to occur, and supervised the voting, the counting of the ballots, and the announcing of the result. It is clear that the election was not an exercise in which the citizens freely elected their governors.

Nevertheless, elections performed a number of functions in the Communist states:

1. The election constituted a ritualized affirmation of regime legitimacy. With such a high percentage of the populace reported to be participating and the overwhelming majority of those participants supporting official candidates, it was claimed that this represented popular affirmation of the regime and its right to rule. This was crucial to the regimes' claims to democratic legitimacy.

2. The election was an educational and propaganda exercise. The campaign in particular provided an opportunity for the regime to seek to both reaffirm the values for which it stood and emphasize its successes. It was thus an opportunity to further its aims of socialization of the populace.

3. The election was a means of bringing about a crushing display of popular unanimity, designed in part to strengthen the sense of isolation among potential nonconformists.

4. The election did provide one avenue for the populace to register preferences with the authorities. This occurred less through the voting than through popular interaction with functionaries trying to ensure that the electors actually took part in the election. People could use the leverage this gave them to both seek local concessions and pass complaints on to the authorities. This means that the elections could also be useful to the regime as a means of identifying potential problems.

5. The election was a means of publicly honoring model citizens.

Thus, although the elections were not the means of choosing the real governors in Communist states, they did perform useful functions in helping to consolidate Communist rule.

See also Citizenship; Constitutions; Propaganda, Communist; Single-Party System; State, The.

FURTHER READING

Friedgut, T. H. *Political Participation in the USSR.* Princeton, NJ: Princeton University Press, 1979.

Hernet, G., R. Rose, and A. Rouquie, eds. *Elections without Choice.* London: Macmillan, 1978.

Holmes, L. *Politics in the Communist World.* Oxford: Oxford University Press, 1986.

Pravda, A. "Elections in Communist Party States." In *Communist Politics: A Reader*, ed. S. White and D. Nelson. Houndmills, UK: Macmillan, 1986.

White, S. "Non-competitive Elections and National Politics: The USSR Supreme Soviet Elections of 1984." *Electoral Studies* 4, no. 3 (1985).

GRAEME GILL

Enemies of the People

"Enemies of the People" is a phrase that was used in the USSR to designate real or imagined opponents of the regime, who could then be subjected to repression. The concepts enemies of the people and "those under suspicion," borrowed from the terminology of the French Revolution, entered the Bolsheviks' vocabulary immediately after their leaders came to power in fall 1917. Mass repressions (arrests, executions, and imprisonment in concentration camps) against members of the formerly privileged classes ("enemies of the working people") were a result of both the doctrinal notions of the Bolsheviks, a class struggle that would culminate in the total annihilation of the exploiting classes, and the realities of the civil war.

The moving force behind the suppression and destruction of class enemies was the Stalinist revolution from above—the forced collectivization and industrialization that began at the end of the 1920s. During this period, the new images of the enemies of the people were now the kulaks, the "saboteurs," who belonged to the prerevolutionary so-called engineering intelligentsia, and other groups. The term enemy of the people and other

similar expressions were widely used during the mass repressions of the second half of the 1930s. The term was applied not only to previous oppositionists (Trotskyites, Zinovyevites, and right-wingers) as well as party-state leaders and officials who had already been liquidated but also to hundreds of thousands of regular citizens, who were often divided into the categories of enemy classes and those under suspicion. In the postwar years, enemies of the people were also subdivided into "cosmopolitans," "spies," and "doctor-murderers," all closely linked to the hostile Western world. Beginning with Khrushchev's de-Stalinization, though, the notion of enemy of the people became politically compromised. The emphasis was now on exposing the external enemy, imperialism, which threatened a new world war.

The constant resurrection of the image of the enemy of the people was one method of maintaining the stability of the Soviet regime and manipulating the consciousness of the public. The failures and crimes of the regime along with the hardships of everyday life for people were laid at the door of real (and often mythical) enemies. In addition, the use of such widely used and legally ill-defined terms as enemy of the people were an important component of the Soviet penal system, which was focused, at least up until the beginning of the 1950s, on discrimination against and isolation or physical destruction of whole layers of the population, without any regard to individual guilt. Millions of people during the 1920s and 1930s were deprived of their right to vote as well as other rights on the basis of their social origin ("the disenfranchised").

During the end of the 1920s and the beginning of the 1930s, several million peasants were arrested, deported, or deprived of their property, based on criteria of ownership (the kulaks). The mass operations during the Great Terror of 1937–38 were carried out against whole groups of the population, who were formally singled out as a potential hazard to the regime; the best examples of this were the special operations against the wives and children of "traitors to the fatherland," and against representatives of individual nationalities, which were declared to be infected by espionage. The Soviet penal codes permitted repression against persons who even though acquitted of charges of committing actual crimes, were nevertheless declared enemies of the working class or "socially dangerous elements."

See also Citizenship; Classes; Great Terror; Gulag; Kulak; Red Terror.

FURTHER READING

Alexopoulos, G. *Stalin's Outcasts: Aliens, Citizens, and the Soviet States, 1926–1936*. Ithaca, NY: Cornell University Press, 2003.

OLEG V. CHLEVNJUK

Ethnic Cleansing

The term "ethnic cleansing" was originally used by Serbs in the 1980s to denounce their alleged treatment at the hands of Kosovar Albanians. In 1992–93, during the war in the former Yugoslavia, journalists, human rights advocates, and Western politicians, among others, picked up the term to describe attacks by Serbs on Bosnian Muslims for the purposes of driving the Muslims out of areas of Bosnian territory targeted by the Serbs. Eventually, "ethnic cleansing" was also applied to similar attacks by Croats on Bosnian Muslims, as well as, retroactively, the attacks of Serbs and Croats on each other during the fighting of the summer and fall of 1991. In 1999, the concept of ethnic cleansing was similarly evoked to describe the attacks of Serbs against Kosovar Albanians, which prompted an enormous refugee crisis, and, subsequently, allied military intervention. In 2005 Kosovar Albanians were accused of the ethnic cleansing of Serbs living in Kosovo. Beyond the Balkans, ethnic cleansing has also been used to analyze attacks on native minority populations. In Sudan, for example, the deadly fate of the mostly Muslim Fur people at the hands of Janjaweed Arab militias has been characterized as a case of ethnic cleansing.

From the outset of the war in Yugoslavia, some analysts challenged (and some continue to challenge) the validity of the term ethnic cleansing, alleging that it is a euphemism for genocide. But the term continues to be used precisely to distinguish this form of crime against humanity and war crime from genocide. The definition of genocide, codified in the *UN Convention on the Prevention and Punishment of the Crime of Genocide* of December 9, 1948, and upheld in the International Courts formed for the purposes of trying those accused of war crimes in the Yugoslav and Rwandan conflicts, focuses on the intentional murder of part or all of a particular ethnic, religious, or national group. (In 1948, the Soviet Union successfully lobbied to keep "social" or "political" groups out of the definition.) The purpose of ethnic cleansing is the forced removal of a population from a designated piece of territory. Although campaigns of ethnic cleansing can lead to genocide or have genocidal effects, ethnic cleansing is a fundamentally different kind of criminal action against an ethnic, religious, or national group. The transcripts of the International Criminal Tribunal for Former Yugoslavia frequently mention ethnic cleansing, but subsume it under the category of "forced deportation," a crime against humanity that was widespread particularly in Bosnia. Genocide, on the other hand, has been much more difficult to establish, since it involves the intentional murder of a part or all of a population. However, the mass murder of roughly 7,000 Bosnian Muslim men and boys in Srebrenica in July 1995 has been designated by the court as genocide.

Genocide and ethnic cleansing occupy adjacent positions on a spectrum of aggression against ethnic and national groups. At one extreme, ethnic cleansing is closer to forced deportation or what has been called "population transfer," which is defined as impelling people to move by means that are legal or semilegal. At the other extreme ethnic cleansing and genocide are distinguishable only by their ultimate intent. Here, both figuratively and literally, ethnic cleansing bleeds into genocide, as mass murder is committed in order to rid the land of a people. Further complicating the distinctions between ethnic cleansing and genocide is the fact that forced deportation often takes place in the violent context of war, civil war, or other forms of aggression. People do not leave their homes willingly. The result is that forced deportation, even in times of peace, quickly turns to violence, as peoples are violently ripped from their native towns and villages and killed if they try to stay.

The linkages between ethnic cleansing and the history of communism in power are manifold. Communist governments, wherever they arose, sought to increase the purview of their states by homogenizing, categorizing, and making more transparent their populations. These were classic "gardening states," to use Zygmunt Baumann's terminology. The state would weed out the weak and ungovernable (the "bourgeoisie," the nobility, and the independent peasantry); fertilize the healthy and valued (the "proletariat"), and eliminate those ethnicities or nationalities that proved able to perpetuate their cultural, political, and economic distinctiveness. Communist governments took censuses, issued internal passports, and regularized the distinctions between citizenship and nationality. They both reified the concept of nationality and deprived it of serious meaning by undermining genuine efforts toward political and cultural autonomy. The slogan "Nationalist in form and Socialist in content" took hold everywhere the Communists seized power. Applying the precepts of Marxist-Leninist ideology, they also centralized state power and assumed control of the infrastructure of the polity. This gave them powerful weapons to control, intimidate, and, when deemed necessary, move large numbers of peoples, including subject nationalities. For ethnic cleansing can only take place when a state is strong enough to fund, arm, and direct its campaigns, identify its objects, organize transports, and manage the movements of populations. Communist states were particularly well fitted to these tasks. From the time of the Bolshevik revolution and Russian Civil War, the willingness of Communist leaders to use extreme force against their own populations to accomplish their goals made ethnic cleansing an acceptable option for dealing with recalcitrant nationalities.

From the outset of the Soviet regime, Lenin and the Bolsheviks attacked their opponents in the civil war in what can be labeled campaigns of ethnic cleansing. In these military attacks, followed by Cheka (Special Police) actions, Polish communities in Ukraine were eliminated, Cossack lands were seized, and many Ukrainian districts that supported the insurgency of Semyon Petlyura were cleansed of their inhabitants. But at least for the first decade of Bolshevik rule, the main objects of attack were class and not ethnic groups, though the two sometimes overlapped. Even in the largest attack on a class opponent in Soviet history, the "dekulakization" campaigns of the early 1930s, there was often a confluence of communities identified as class enemies and national groups, in this case especially Ukrainians, Poles, and Germans. With the approach of World War II and the promulgation of the 1936 "Stalin" constitution, which proclaimed the defeat of the class enemy and the victory of socialism, violent campaigns of forced deportation increasingly targeted national groups. The most complete deportation, which in some ways established the operational basis for those to follow during the war, took place in 1937, when the Soviets removed the Korean population of the far eastern region, some 172,000 people altogether, to Central Asia. Soviet ethnic cleansing, unlike other variants, focused on the removal of an ostensibly dangerous and offensive people. It did not seek to supplant the Koreans with a necessarily homogeneous nationality, nor did it do them the favor, in this case or others, of deporting them beyond the Soviet boundaries. Instead, it sought

to use this human material to build up isolated, harsh, and otherwise sparsely populated areas of Central Asia and Siberia.

In apparent preparation for the coming of war, Stalin also order the forcible deportations of tens of thousands of Germans, Poles, and Finns from the border areas in the west to Central Asia and Siberia. Forced deportation continued when the Soviet Union occupied the eastern territories of Poland and the Baltics in 1939–41 as a consequence of the Nazi-Soviet Pact. One could certainly talk about a Soviet campaign of ethnic cleansing against Poles in which thousands were murdered and another 230,000 or so deported, primarily to Soviet Central Asia. Baltic peoples, Ukrainians, Jews, and Belarusans were also deported to the Soviet interior in these years.

Despite the fearsome demands of the struggle against the Nazis, Stalin found the resources to engage in large-scale campaigns of ethnic cleansing during World War II. Lavrenty Beria, chief of the NKVD, was put in charge of these operations, which claimed the lives of many hundreds of thousands of Soviet citizens. In addition to the Volga Germans, who were moved wholesale from their homelands in the middle Volga region to Central Asia, Stalin deported the peoples of the Northern Caucasus (Balkars, Karachaevtsy, Chechens, and Ingush), the Kalmyks, and the Crimean Tatars for ostensible collaboration with the Nazis. Characteristic of other cases of 20th-century ethnic cleansing were the Soviet actions against the related Chechens and Ingush people. Beria coordinated the NKVD-Red Army operations of February 1944, which saw the entire Chechen and Ingush nations, some 496,000 men, women, and children, brutally rounded up in their homelands, packed into crowded freight cars, and deported to Kazakhstan and Kirghizia. Tens of thousands died as a result of the horrid conditions of transport. Due to shortages of food, housing, and medical care, roughly another 100,000 perished in the first three years of exile. The designated territorial entity of the Chechens and Ingush, like that of the Crimean Tatars, was erased from the map; the monuments of these peoples were destroyed, and their role in history was obliterated. Unlike the Crimean Tatars, the Chechens and Ingush, together with the other "punished peoples," were eventually allowed to return to their homelands after Khrushchev's "secret speech" of 1956. But the experience of deportation and exile has not been forgotten.

World War II did not end the history of Soviet ethnic cleansing. During the incorporation of the western borderlands, Soviet authorities arrested and deported hundreds of thousands of Estonians, Latvians, and Lithuanians. Large numbers of Western Ukrainians and Poles were also deported to the gulag. In these cases, ethnic Russians were often brought into the newly acquired territories to replace the indigenous populations, defuse local Nationalist movements, and help the cause of Sovietization. The history of ethnic cleansing in the Soviet Union ended with the death of Stalin in March 1953. Yet before he died, the unveiling of the so-called Doctor's Plot in January 1953 and the unleashing of a virulent public anti-Semitic campaign indicated that the Soviet authorities might well have been preparing the ground for the forced deportation of the Jews from European Russia. The evidence for this is not unambiguous, and in any event Stalin's death ended such potential plans as there may have been.

Ethnic cleansing and communism are linked not only in the history of the Soviet Union and Stalin. The Khmer Rouge in Cambodia, for example, forcibly deported the Muslim Cham people before, under the leadership of Pol Pot, engaging in a policy of genocide against them. In Eastern Europe at the end of World War II and the beginning of the peace, Communist and Communist-influenced governments, most notably in Poland and Czechoslovakia, engaged in the ethnic cleansing of their German populations. Approximately twelve million Germans were forcibly deported from their home territories in East Central Europe where their families had resided for centuries. Despite the orders of the Allies at Potsdam (July–August 1945) that the "transfer" be as humane and orderly as possible, the ethnic cleansing of Germans involved great brutality: killing, rape, and severe deprivation. As many as two million may have died in the process. There were other examples of ethnic cleansing in Eastern Europe, as well. Communist governments saw it in their interests to establish ethnically homogeneous states and territories, sometimes even claiming that "national" expulsions constituted a "social" revolution, since those expelled were the bourgeois or aristocratic "oppressors" of the native peoples. Slovaks forcibly deported Hungarians until the process was brought to a halt by Soviet authorities in Hungary. Poles removed Ukrainians and Belarusans. Poles were deported from Ukraine to Poland. Ethnic cleansing in this period remains a source of considerable controversy, as post-Communist historians have the opportunity to investigate a previously hidden history.

See also Deportation of Nationalities in the USSR; Holodomor; Nationality Policies; Nations and Empire in the USSR; Pol Pot.

FURTHER READING

Conquest, R. *The Nation Killers*. Glasgow: Macmillan, 1970.

Naimark, N. M. *Fires of Hatred: Ethnic Cleansing in 20th Century Europe*. Cambridge, MA: Harvard University Press, 2001.

Nekrich, A. *The Punished Peoples: The Deportation and Fate of Soviet Minorities at the End of the Second World War*. New York: Norton, 1978.

Pohl, A. J. *Ethnic Cleansing in the USSR, 1937–1949*. Westport: Greenwood, 1999.

Polian, P. *Against Their Will: The History and Geography of Forced Migrations in the USSR*. Budapest: Central European University Press, 2004.

Rieber, A., ed. *Forced Migration in Central and Eastern Europe, 1939–1950*. London: Frank Cass, 2000.

Ther, P., and A. Siljak, eds. *Redrawing Nations: Ethnic Cleansing in East-Central Europe, 1944–48*. Lanham MD: Rowman and Littlefield, 2001.

NORMAN M. NAIMARK

Eurocommunism

The term "Eurocommunism" was coined by the Italian press in 1975. It referred to the preferential relationship that Italian Communists seemed to want to establish with their French and Spanish counterparts, based on ideas of detachment from the Soviet model and autonomy from the USSR as well as a Western model of socialism founded on democratic principles. Since the Soviet invasion of Czechoslovakia in 1968, the Italian Communist Party's (Pci) leadership had discussed creating a Western Communist entity, expanding on Palmiro Togliatti's idea of "polycentrism."

The first practical step, however, was not taken until January 1974, when Enrico Berlinguer proposed the first conference of Western Communists, which gathered in Brussels. The conference was not successful: the attempt to bring the positions of the other Communist parties closer to those of the Pci, which favored European integration and détente, did not end on a promising note. The only significant allies were the French Communists, who like the Italians were searching for greater political legitimation, but had a negative opinion of the European Economic Community. Yet Berlinguer pursued his plan with determination. He met with Spanish leader Santiago Carrillo (July 1975) and French leader Georges Marchais (November 1975), drawing public attention because the two represented the largest Communist parties in the West, and the smaller Spanish party was still engaged in the transition from Francisco Franco's regime to democracy. Berlinguer himself used the term Eurocommunism during a rally with Marchais in Paris on June 3, 1976. Immediately afterward, at the Berlin Conference, the Pci's secretary again used the term positively in front of an international Communist audience. The most significant moment in the partnership of the three parties, and also the one with the greatest impact on international public opinion, was the meeting between Berlinguer, Carrillo, and Marchais in Madrid on March 3, 1977.

For Berlinguer, Eurocommunism was not a means of establishing a new organizational center for Communist parties, rivaling Moscow. The idea of a Western Communist "pole" was qualified, in order to avoid recalling past divisions in the Communist movement. Berlinguer focused on creating a list of principles and a specific agenda for Western Communists, given their unique historical experiences and geopolitical location. Some of the proposed principles were an acceptance of the values of democracy; a moderate criticism of "real socialism" in light of "socialism with a human face"; following the example of the Prague Spring, the idea of "overcoming the division into blocs," but based on their recognition, following the example of German *Ostpolitik*; and a choice favoring Europe as a political entity, a new international subject, if not quite as a "third force." This plan would have been understood, if not agreed to, by the Communists in the East and the Soviets in order to continue interacting with them at the level of international politics, especially in order to promote détente after the Helsinki Accords. These principles were the core of Berlinguer's speech at the Berlin Conference, they created quite a stir since they proposed a "pluralist" scenario within the international Communist movement.

The French Communists never really favored Berlinguer's plan. Although in the mid-1970s their public image seemed close to that of the Pci, their areas of disagreement were much more significant. The French Communist Party (Pcf), after having first expressed the same "disapproval" as the Pci toward the Soviet invasion of Czechoslovakia, then proceeded to back down. Its leadership exhibited a much higher degree of pro-Sovietism, which made the Pcf's conversion to socialism with a human face and human rights critiques of the USSR, briefly following the lead of its Italian counterpart, not

altogether credible. The French Communists' positions differed greatly from those of the Italians on essential issues. Although it had sent a delegation to the European Parliament in 1973, the Pcf was contrary to ceding national sovereignty and to European elections (based on universal suffrage), and viewed détente as a form of submissiveness that might weaken the principle of anti-imperialism.

Faced with the Carnation Revolution in Portugal, the two parties took opposite sides, revealing different attitudes toward democracy: the French supported the line taken by the Portuguese Communist leader Alvaro Cunhal, who wanted to follow the people's democracies model; the Italians, together with the Spaniards, publicly condemned his authoritarian tendencies. In reality, the Pcf was not a protagonist of international politics on a par with the Pci. The tactical calculations in terms of internal politics, also dictated by contrasting electoral successes (the Pcf was in decline, while the Pci was at its height), made it an unreliable political partner, as was to soon become apparent. Unlike Marchais, Carrillo adopted positions close to Berlinguer's and was even more cutting in his criticism of real socialism—a fact that earned him a public rebuke by the Soviets in 1977, after he published a pamphlet titled *Eurocommunism and the State*. But the Spanish party was not as large as the other two, nor did it have national responsibilities comparable to those of the Pci.

Eurocommunism's fragility as a political movement was not fully understood at the time. Both superpowers were seriously concerned about the movement for different reasons, but they sometimes expressed themselves in a similar fashion. Moscow's attack on Carrillo was also a direct warning to Marchais and Berlinguer. The Soviets had tolerated the rise of Eurocommunism in the climate of bipolar détente, although they did not trust its centrifugal implications and the underlying political message, which was not in harmony with their objective of exercising leadership over European communism. The Berlin Conference had been dedicated to containing, if not reabsorbing, this phenomenon, in the formal and highly ideological context of a tribunal of European communism. But Berlinguer's speech left its mark. After Berlin the Soviet's attitude became more inflexible. Eurocommunism created some not overly veiled forms of consensus in some Eastern European parties, such as the Hungarian and Polish ones. Some dissidents even saw the Western parties as guarantors in the Communist world of the Helsinki agreements on human rights.

The first signs of a crisis in détente, a concept tied to U.S. president Jimmy Carter's human rights campaign, made the situation even less reassuring in Moscow's eyes. The entry of the Pci, the largest Communist Party in the Western world, into the government (its participation in the "national solidarity" government began in August 1976) seemed to signal that an autonomous, hard-to-control, alternate pole of attraction was taking shape. The Soviets started to view Eurocommunism as not only a "revisionist" phenomenon in the light of Marxist-Leninist axioms but also a phenomenon that might destabilize the bipolar order in Europe, beginning with their sphere of influence in Central and Eastern Europe. This shift revealed analogies between the Soviet perspective and that of Henry Kissinger, the architect of U.S. policies toward Europe, especially between 1974 and 1976. Kissinger did not deny the Western Communist parties' autonomy from Moscow, particularly in the Pci's case. But he thought that as part of the government, the Pci would undermine the North Atlantic Treaty Organization's (NATO) premises, still serve the USSR's interests, and introduce a destabilizing element in bipolar détente. The Carter administration initially believed that Eurocommunism needed to be given greater credit and that it posed more of a problem for the USSR than for the United States. Faced with a crisis of détente, though, Washington feared that Eurocommunism would create a dangerous situation for NATO.

Eurocommunism never took off as a political movement, and entered a period of crisis due more to its protagonists than to the two superpowers. The French Communists soon returned to orthodoxy and realigned themselves with Moscow, even justifying the invasion of Afghanistan. Their electoral strength was noticeably reduced, and this was the only reason they were able to join the government in a subordinate position after François Mitterrand's victory in the elections (June 1981). After a significant pro-Soviet faction split-off, the Spanish Communist Party decreased even further in size, which in turn led to further divisions among Eurocommunists and Carrillo's being sidelined (1982). In many ways the Soviet reaction against Eurocommunism was successful: with the beginning of the Second Cold War, centripetal tendencies in European communism prevailed once more, within both the parties belonging to the Soviet bloc and the Western parties. Eurocommunism had, in truth, always been more of a political message, launched by the Italian Communists, than a movement based on a political platform.

Indeed, the Italian Communists were the only exception to this realignment process, even after their return to the opposition (January 1979). The danger of a split encouraged by Moscow notwithstanding (the actual degree of danger was never determined), they condemned the Soviet invasion of Afghanistan, refused to take part in the pro-Soviet Paris conference on Euromissiles (May 1980), came out against the repression of the opposition during the Polish crisis, and condemned Wojciech Jaruzelski's coup (September 1980–December 1981). Berlinguer thus remained the solitary proponent of Eurocommunism. By now this term had come to represent merely a distinctive trait of the Italian Communists' identity, a synonym of the third way between real socialism and social democracy.

At the height of détente, Eurocommunism represented a significant challenge to the Cold War system. With the end of détente, for some time it maintained its value as a critique of the logic of opposed political blocs and bipolarism, seen as an order that was now in crisis. Eurocommunism, however, never enjoyed a broad enough consensus either among the Communist parties or in the eyes of international public opinion. The implicit hegemonic aims of Eurocommunism, cultivated by Berlinguer—shifting the leadership of the Communist movement that had once belonged to the USSR toward Western communism, and thus contributing to a new type of socialism in the West and the reformation of its Eastern counterpart—had been exposed as overly ambitious. Eurocommunism was ambiguous: it brought Italian communism closer to the European Left, but also represented an obstacle to the Left's integration, since Eurocommunism itself continued to have a strong identity. Although Eurocommunist ideas would come to represent a valuable heritage for the reformers who were about to come to power in the USSR, their importance in Europe in the early 1980s was destined to rapidly diminish. Already toward the end of Berlinguer's life, and especially after his death, the term fell into disuse.

See also Berlinguer, Enrico; Bipolarity; Cold War; Détente; European Integration; Marchais, Georges; National Roads to Socialism; Ostpolitik; Polycentrism; Real Socialism; Social Democracy.

FURTHER READING

Pons, S. *Berlinguer e la fine del comunismo*. Turin: Einaudi, 2006.
Rubbi, A. *Il mondo di Berlinguer*. Rome: Napoleone, 1994.

Timmerman, H. *The Decline of the World Communist Movement: Moscow, Beijing, and Communist Parties in the West.* Boulder, CO: Westview, 1987.

Urban, J. B. *Moscow and the Italian Communist Party: From Togliatti to Berlinguer.* London: Tauris, 1986.

SILVIO PONS

European Integration

In the climate of the Cold War it was not surprising if the USSR viewed with suspicion any plan aimed at integrating, even partially, the countries of Western Europe. All Western Communist parties and most of the Socialist parties were equally alarmed at the prospect. The Left's anti-Europeanism had multiple motivations. For the Communist parties it was imperative to follow the Soviet lead in a major international policy matter. For the Socialist parties in neutral countries, such as Sweden and Austria, it was essential to uphold their neutrality. More generally, European integration went against the strategic model both Socialists and Communists shared: the concept of a national road to socialism. For both it was essential that, once they had captured power they should be as free as possible from external constraints, free to expand the public sector, free to control their own resources, their own exchange rates and, more generally, their own economy.

Not only the Communists but also many Socialists had rejected such early moves toward integration as the aborted proposal to create a European Defence Community (EDC) or the Schuman Plan to establish a European Coal and Steel Community (ECSC). The construction of the European Economic Community (or Common Market, as it was often called)—sponsored mainly by conservative forces—encountered the opposition of most Socialists and the hostility of all Communists. The EEC started life bearing the unmistakable marks of the free market. Its avowed objective was the removal of barriers to competition. Its ideology was one of liberalism. Its rationale was the creation of a powerful zone of free exchange that would provide the basis for a large market. This was openly backed by the United States, which believed that an economically prosperous Europe would be a bulwark against communism. This made it even more difficult to conceive of the EEC as anything other than an obstacle to Socialist policies.

The EEC was then, as well as later, criticized for being a narrow-minded organization of inward-looking prosperous countries. Though there is some truth in this, a less severe assessment would also point out that the EEC was a European answer to the growing internationalization of the world economy, to the rise of two multinational world powers, and to the development of a nonaligned movement. All of these phenomena underlined how reduced had become the prospects for the traditional nation-state and how necessary it had become to share sovereignty with other countries. This was happening precisely at a time when the European Socialist movement had made its peace with the nation-state, and when West European Communists were constructing a "national" road to socialism grounded in the appropriation of patriotic sentiments. These and other political circumstances surrounding the birth of the EEC—the Cold War, the weakness of social democracy, the successes of capitalism, and the developing consumer society—account for the singular absence of a significant "social space" (as it would later be called) in the EEC.

The French Communist Party's (Pcf) opposition to any supranational organization was total. This was expressed in its habitually immoderate language: Jean Monnet was accused of being an American agent; the Schuman Plan was described as the continuation of Hitlerism; and the Adenauer government was referred to as "the Neo-Nazi in Bonn," while the Mollet government was seen as similar to the Vichy regime. Georges Cogniot, Thorez's main adviser on European matters, had no qualms: the EEC entailed "a very serious abdication of national sovereignty"; it would deprive the French Parliament of all powers over tariffs, prices, taxes, and investments. French wages would collapse because the free movement of labor would lead to massive immigration from Italy and would keep down the wages of French workers. Furthermore, modernization would lead to the closure of low-productivity small farms and a consequent exodus from the countryside, which proved to be an accurate prediction. The Pcf was not just a working-class party. It had acquired a sizeable following among the peasantry, especially in the south, and it wished to expand further.

The Pcf's defense of national sovereignty was directed against both the Americans and the supranationalism of the EEC. As this reflected the enduring popularity of nationalist discourse in France, it is understandable that the Pcf did not relinquish it. A few months after the EEC Treaty became operational (January 1, 1958), Charles de Gaulle was called back to the helm of the country and developed further a peculiarly national conception of European integration. As often happened, the pessimistic predictions of the Pcf were not fulfilled. German capital went on growing but did not destroy France or the prosperity of the French working class. French agriculture did undergo a massive transformation, but the EEC's agricultural policy cushioned French farmers more than adequately. The purpose of the Pcf, however, was not to make accurate forecasts. The regular predictions of doom and gloom were part and parcel of its electoral appeal: the Pcf was the sole opposition to "the system," to change, to technological progress. It rallied the discontented, achieving the remarkable objective of being at once a deeply conservative party and a revolutionary one. All changes were for the worse, yet the future belonged to socialism. Thus the Pcf's ideological parameters were always contradictory: it was a nationalist party subservient to a foreign power (the USSR) and a revolutionary party continuously suspicious of novelty.

Eventually the Pcf adopted a more flexible attitude, less hostile toward the European community, but it never embraced European integration. It accepted the EEC as a fact of life and no longer wished France to withdraw from it, but remained committed to national sovereignty and convinced that any further integration would strengthen the powers of multinational companies. This corresponded, by and large, to the position of the USSR until the advent of Gorbachev.

The Italian Communist Party (Pci) was, at first, aligned with the French in its opposition to the EEC, but it used softer language. On March 24, 1957, its Executive Committee, while calling for a revision of the Treaty of Rome (whose contents had not yet been revealed), stressed that it was "understandable and correct" that narrow national markets should be enlarged and that new forms of international cooperation should be sought. In principle the working class should not be against this. Nevertheless, like the Pcf, the Pci opposed the treaty on the grounds that it would spell the ruin of Italian agriculture, that the EEC would be dominated by "monopoly capital," and that the division of Europe would become further entrenched. Its ideological constraints, however, were quite different. The Pci, though always careful to stress its patriotic credentials, could not play the national card in as truculent a manner as its transalpine counterpart. The failure of fascism had made nationalism suspect (as it did in Germany). Furthermore European integration was seen as a further step toward the modernization of the country. In Italy to oppose

modernity would have been political suicide, for to be antimodern is a luxury available only in modern countries. Two further elements led the Pci to adopt a less intransigent posture toward the EEC. The first was the desire to avoid antagonizing the Italian Socialist Party (Psi), which had adopted a positive view of the EEC as it was preparing to enter government with the Christian Democrats in the early 1960s. The second was the pressure it was under from the main trade union, the Confederazione Generale Italiana del Lavoro (CGIL), whose leader, Communist Giuseppe Di Vittorio, was keen to preserve trade union unity with the Socialists.

The Pci's opposition to the EEC increased rather than decreased in the following few years, but it was motivated by their catastrophic forecast of the consequences of the EEC for the Italian economy rather than by any principled animosity to supranationalism. The forecast was, of course, altogether mistaken: in that period (1958–63) Italy experienced an export-led boom of massive proportions, with the fastest growth rate in its entire history. The Pci's pessimistic view of Italy's potential for capitalist development had, once again, turned out to be wrong. By the 1960s the party began to adopt a Europeanist approach that would lead it to embrace, in the 1980s, an outspoken federalism.

Most European Socialist parties shared anti-European feelings, in one way or the other. In Britain the majority of the Labour Party, though not its leadership, remained opposed, in one way or other, to European integration until the 1980s, as did the Socialist and Social Democratic parties of Sweden, Norway, Denmark, and Greece. The German SPD became pro-European only in the early 1960s, as did the Italian Socialist Party.

The Left's gradual change of attitude was due in part to the evident successes of the European Union, but increasingly also to the recognition that it was unrealistic to believe that any country could buck international trends and go it alone. The U-turn forced upon the Socialist-Communist government in France in 1983 was further evidence that the era of the national road was over. A further factor in the growing enthusiasm for the European Union by some of the Communist parties (in particular those of Italy and Spain) was that Europe was becoming more and more "social" with greater rights been given to workers and unions at a time (the 1980s and 1990s) when it had become increasingly difficult to defend those rights as beneficial to the nation-state. The EEC, which soon would transform itself into the European Union, might still be a capitalist club, but it was one in which Social

Democrats and moderate Communists could participate wholeheartedly.

See also Cold War; Eurocommunism; National Roads to Socialism; Social Democracy; Welfare State.

FURTHER READING

Dewit, P., and J.-M. De Waele, eds. *La Gauche face aux mutations en Europe.* Brussels: Éditions de l'Université de Bruxelles, 1993.

Eley, G. *Forging Democracy: The History of the Left in Europe, 1850–2000.* Oxford: Oxford University Press, 2002.

Featherstone, K. *Socialist Parties and European Integration.* Manchester: Manchester University Press, 1988.

Newman, M. *Socialism and European Unity: The Dilemma of the Left in Britain and France.* London: Junction Books, 1983.

Sassoon, Donald. *One Hundred Years of Socialism.* New York: New Press, 1997.

Scharpf, F. *Crisis and Choice in European Social Democracy.* Ithaca, NY: Cornell University Press, 1991.

DONALD SASSOON

Family

References to the family in the writings of the most popular and prestigious Bolshevik theorists are rare and limited to brief mentions, mostly concerned with the condition of women and their need to be freed from the chains of domestic work. Lenin agreed it was necessary to cut this traditional tie between women's oppression and domestic work. Yet for him detachment from the traditional family did not lead to either the creation of a new one or a freedom without rules but rather party membership. His was a politicized idea of the family that had been influenced by the utopian tradition of the proponents of social engineering, who advocated the abolition of all intermediate institutions that could become semiautonomous units, detached from the state. The family was one of these units, because it encouraged egotistical leanings in individuals, with disruptive effects on the state, which was charged with protecting the general interests of the collectivity.

The Bolsheviks did not want to initiate a legal reform of the family's status, as the Russian liberals had advocated in the early 20th century, but instead preferred to use the law to conduct a simultaneous battle on two fronts: against the "bourgeois" family, understood in Marxian fashion as a superstructure in an economic system based on private property and therefore destined to disappear; and against the patriarchal peasant family, in order to accelerate the destruction of all forms of "relic" from the past, which the family helped perpetuate because of the strong influence the church still exercised within it. Czarist legislation had in fact transferred all matters relating to marriage and divorce to ecclesiastical courts. The need to arrogate all responsibilities relating to family law to themselves explains some of the decrees that the Bolsheviks issued after coming to power—

collected in the Code on Marriage and the Family of 1918. Marriage was secularized, but not abolished. Civil marriage was introduced, and it simply required registration at the General Register Office. Divorce proceedings were also made much simpler. Adoption was forbidden because it was considered a camouflaged form of exploitation of childhood labor, while the legalization of abortion, introduced in November 1920, was motivated by the scarcity of resources available to ensure an extensive child care network. In order to cut the family's ties with laws regarding property and inheritance, inheritance was abolished, and so was the concept of the legitimate child; both had been traditionally associated with the power structures and economic interests of the bourgeois family. The concept of matrimony as the transfer of a woman's legal and economic dependence from her family of origin to her husband's was also abolished. Once private property had been abolished, women would be in a position of complete equality with men, free to choose whether to keep their last name and a place of residence that differed from their husband's. In addition, marriage was defined as a "free and voluntary union" of two individuals enjoying equal rights.

Even though family legislation did not abolish the family as an institution, it did attest to the enormous gap that existed between Bolshevik theories and Russia's social reality at the time. The family structure under attack had either never existed in Russia, like the bourgeois family, or underwent significant changes starting in the second half of the 19th century—due to migrations from the countryside toward the new industrial centers—that had affected many of the traditional functions of the patriarchal peasant family. The new government had too much faith in political and legislative intervention from above, and was not bothered by the population's reluctance to welcome these provisions into their everyday lives. In any case, the disintegration of millions of families depended more on the chaos and destruction into which the country fell during the civil war than on political interventions from the center.

The disastrous conditions in which peace was reestablished led the government to rethink many of the ideas that had matured in the course of "war communism" and adopt a more realistic approach to the country's problems. In a context marked by a scarcity of financial resources, one therefore witnessed a rediscovery of many traditional functions of the family, which had prematurely been declared obsolete in 1918. The reconquest of the Asian provinces of the ex-empire also led to the realization of just how enormous and complex the geographic dimensions of Russian backwardness were, and further heightened an awareness of how difficult it would be to overcome it, not only from the economic, but also the cultural point of view.

The general tendency to a return to more traditional views about the role of the family was caused by, more than any other form of social pressure, the phenomenon of the *besprizorniki*, children abandoned by their families, mostly during the famines of 1921–22: they poured into the cities forming bands of minors devoted to begging, theft, alcoholism, and prostitution, and thus created a world of their own, hostile to all forms of authority. The government discovered that in order to fight the phenomenon, it would be more efficient to help the families, rather than sending the children to institutions that would not have been able to accommodate all those in need. With this goal in mind, a government decree in April 1926 reintroduced adoption and promoted a series of economic incentives to encourage peasant families especially to take care of abandoned children. But the phenomenon risked turning into a chronic problem, if those portions of the 1918 code that favored, instead of contrasting, the disintegration of families were not modified.

In the mid-1920s, the USSR had the highest divorce rate in Europe. And yet the reform of the family code, approved at the end of 1926, introduced changes that were a prelude to the abolition of marriage. Marriage could now be recognized as legally valid if oral testimony proved cohabitation. Divorce could be granted at the request of one party—a proof that conjugal relations had ended. The new norms were adopted even though a vast opposition had emerged, composed in large part of peasants. Legislators defended these norms on the grounds they were protecting the weaker and more vulnerable partners in de facto unions (women and children), while simultaneously freeing marriage from all types of con-

straint. The main Asian republics of the union were excluded from this provision, however, because it would have frustrated attempts to fight polygamy as well as "tribal and patriarchal relics," which had been ongoing in those regions since 1924.

Stalin's decision to undertake modernization from above using administrative and coercive methods landed the country in a condition of permanent mobilization, almost as if in a war. The most destructive effects for the social order were caused by the forced collectivization of the countryside. In the course of a few years tens of millions of peasant families were destroyed, while the regime encouraged the young to rebel against the old, the children against the parents, the new generations against bureaucrats and privileged elites. Conferring the title of martyr on Pavlik Morozov, who was killed by his relatives because he had denounced his father to the authorities for his connivance with the kulaks, introduced children to a new duty: putting the interests of the state before those of the family. Stalin's new order intended to destroy all previous forms of solidarity, because they were considered potential focal points of rebellion, and a place in which local and particular interests were reproduced. Networks of solidarity needed to be forbidden in the name of the superior interests of the state, by disaggregating the family as a unit composed of individuals of different ages, and with different social and productive functions.

But these pressures from above did not affect all families. In fact, a clear difference was established between families composed of rejects, those who were deprived of all rights and who were to be repressed by any means, and those composed of individuals who had been accepted, to be integrated and regimented. This fundamental distinction helps to explain the ambivalence that characterized the attitude of the Stalin regime toward the family. In relation to the families of the "enemies of the people," the regime assumed destructive intentions, passing a series of laws that also targeted the relatives of those who were found guilty of "crimes against the state." In relation to accepted families, the regime instead adopted the position that it should attempt to regulate the daily life of its members, above all by means of the party's organizational networks, so that it would become the place in which symbolic activities mostly aimed at increasing social cohesion were performed.

Starting in 1935, official propaganda directed its attention to more traditional goals. The party was caught up in a moralizing campaign that began by condemning all forms of sexual promiscuity, easy marriages and divorces, bigamy, and adultery. A series of more restrictive measures in the areas of divorce and the banning of abortion followed in 1936. These new norms were introduced in the context of the regime promoting a general return to order, after the chaos that the revolution from above had caused. This conservative shift affected different areas, most particularly cultural life and the world of education, but it was not pursued in a coherent fashion. Divorce was not abolished but was instead made more difficult. The recognition of de facto unions and the legal equivalence of legitimate children and children born outside of wedlock would only be abolished in 1944, with a series of decrees inspired by the need to reverse the trend toward a fall in the birthrate and to counteract the demographic imbalance between men and women that the war was then aggravating. With this goal in mind, an edict of July 8, 1944, increased financial aid to mothers with more than six children, even if single; they were actually helped more than married women when subsidies were assigned. In this way the government, while opting for a reevaluation of the family's role, at the same time legitimized single motherhood.

The modifications of the family code introduced by Stalin's regime were therefore not indicative of a complete change in the state's attitude toward family stability. The most important work on the Soviet family, *A Book for Parents* (1937) by the pedagogue Anton Makarenko, which would be published in the aftermath of World War II in all Communist countries, China and Cuba included, was permeated by an obvious dualism: the many responsibilities of parents and the family were underscored, as was the right of the state to interfere in their behavior; yet the book stated that authority needed to be vested in the parents themselves, so as to mold the character of the future citizens based on the parents' exemplary behavior. In other words, the Soviet family was supposed to become an instrument in strengthening the state's influence and control on society, and a means to diffuse values that conformed to the dominant ideology.

The Communist regimes that developed after World War II in Eastern and Central Europe and Asia formally emulated the Soviet legislation on the family, and embodied its main goals: the elimination of the political power of the bourgeoisie, the abolition of private property, and the education of citizens according to a lifestyle both disciplined and regulated by rigid moral norms—a model the Communists thought was the prerequisite for realizing the new social order. In China the law on

marriage adopted on April 13, 1950, after all the codes of the preceding government had been abolished, included divorce without restrictions as it had been formulated in the Soviet legislation of 1926. In Eastern Europe, by contrast, there was an attempt to defend the conjugal family. The formula adopted did not list precise motives for granting divorce, but only authorized it in the case of complete and permanent breakdown of conjugal relations. All the Communist regimes adopted Soviet legislation in regard to both the equal rights granted to legitimate children and those born out of wedlock, and property rights in marriage, which included the concept of the common ownership of goods acquired during marriage.

After Stalin's death and the "thaw" that followed, there was a rediscovery of the family not so much in terms of its social functions but rather its individual ones. In the new atmosphere characterized by a general reevaluation of private life and its autonomy with respect to public life, the Soviet government acceded to requests to abolish the restrictive norms it had introduced in 1936 and 1944. The other Communist regimes also took note of the new atmosphere that had developed in Moscow and attempted to weaken the influence of the Soviet model, giving family policy a more national character. The Polish Communists asked for a greater respect of individual rights, and introduced restrictions on both abortion and divorce. The Chinese Communists instead abandoned their policy of imitating the Soviet model after 1957, and in the realm of the family also elaborated a system that was partly inspired by Chinese traditions and partly by Soviet practice during the period of war communism.

The many variants introduced by the various Communist regimes notwithstanding, some traits they shared with the Soviet regime remained unchanged. The most remarkable was the principle according to which there were no limits to interference in the private lives of individuals by the state, which was a guardian of the superior interests of the collectivity. In all Communist countries the ample discretionary power of judges remained, which tended to transform family courts into ethical tribunals in which prejudices and ideological conformism frequently prevailed on legal consistency and respect for the law. The state's interest in interfering in private life was founded on a view of the family that saw it as a center of resistance to the new models of behavior and social living that were being proposed; it was the locus for the conservation of memory, the space in which the cultural traditions of individuals were perpetuated. Mikhail

Gorbachev appeared to take notice of the resistance to change when, in 1987, he invited women to return to the family and once again fill their role, traditional and "purely feminine," of taking care of and working for the benefit of all family members. It was an implicit admission of the failure to orient individuals' behavior from above, by means of legislative interventions that only led to formal adaptations to a law that was perceived as extraneous and incomprehensible by citizens who had continued to live their daily routine according to traditional patterns.

See also Citizenship; Demographic Policies; Modernization; New Man; Social Policy; Women, Emancipation of; Youth.

FURTHER READING

de Biagio, A. "I bolscevichi e la famiglia eurasiatica." *Passato e presente* 20, no. 57 (September–December 2002).

Geiger, H. K. *The Family in Soviet Russia*. Cambridge: Cambridge University Press, 1968.

Goldman, W. Z. *Women, the State, and Revolution: Soviet Family Policy and Social Life, 1917–1936*. Cambridge: Cambridge University Press, 1993.

ANNA DI BIAGIO

Famine under Communism

According to Marxist theory, communism is a social structure that makes possible an abundance whereby food and other forms of wealth are provided from some according to their ability to others according to their needs. Historically societies that found communism to be attractive were not the most wealthy, but rather some of poorest, desperately keen to escape the poverty trap and famine. Two kinds of famine have affected Communist societies: (1) external famines, whose causes often predate the introduction of the Communist system, and in fact often contributed to the circumstances of social breakdown out of which the Communist system emerged; and (2) internal famines resulting in part from extreme development policies applied by the Communist state at a later stage once the initial crisis had passed.

Russian and Soviet Famines

Russia had experienced numerous famines and food crises in the 19th century. Its population grew very rapidly and the Black-Earth and the Volga Regions could no longer provide the surpluses needed by the great northern cities. When droughts struck in 1871, 1880, and 1891 these regions experienced harvest failures that resulted in famine. However in the newer regions of the South (Ukraine and the North Caucasus), the East (the Kazakh Steppe), and Western Siberia, the population was less dense and a large export industry developed. There were food shortages in 1916 because of the poor harvest of that year, coupled with difficulties in transporting the southern and eastern surpluses to the North given the military's use of the railways. Essentially these were food crises caused by distribution problems. Supplies in the South were ample, especially as no grain was being exported.

Between 1917 and 1920 the northern cities, especially St. Petersburg and Moscow, experienced intense food shortages that result in starvation, epidemic diseases, and massive depopulation. The cause of the famine was the failure of grain to reach the northern cities as a result of Ukraine, Siberia, and other parts of Russia being occupied by enemy forces—the German occupation of Ukraine in 1918, and then the civil war. Rationing was introduced in the northern cities, but food supplies were still far from adequate. Mortality rose sharply and hundreds of thousands fled the cities. Armed requisition squads were sent to the countryside where they used force to extract grain from the peasants. However, supplies remained insufficient to halt starvation in the cities. Eventually, in late 1920, the situation in Moscow and Petrograd began to stabilize.

In March 1921 the New Economic Policy was introduced, which promised to replace the requisitioning policy with a tax in-kind that would leave the peasants with a surplus of grain that could be sold to the towns in the restored markets. The objective was to give the peasants an incentive to increase their sowings and to build a link (*smytchka*) with the towns. But before such a policy had any effect, the country was engulfed in one of the periodic droughts that had regularly caused problems. The grain harvest of 1921 was disastrously low, not because of the peasants' reducing their sown acreage, but because of the extremely low yields caused by the drought. The government was aware that it had extremely low levels of stocks as a result of the previous northern famines and it immediately appealed for international assistance. Assistance came from both the International Red Cross headed by Nansen, and from the American Relief Administration headed by Hoover. By the spring of 1922 over twelve million people, mainly children, were being fed by these international organizations. Nevertheless the famine was intense, and in combination with massive pandemics of infectious diseases caused the death of at least three million people. Livestock levels also fell precipitously, partly as a result of the drought.

A good harvest in 1922 dramatically improved the situation. There was a minor drought in 1924, but the food supply situation was generally good until the crisis of the winter of 1927. Suddenly state grain collections were well below target and the levels of the previous years. It became clear not only that there would be no grain to export, but that there was a risk that the army and the growing population in the cities would face shortages. Despite the government's resort to extraordinary measures and forced procurements, there was a great strain on urban supplies. Market prices increased and rationing was reintroduced. Rural areas also faced grain shortages, but here the shortages resulted more in cutbacks in livestock feed and thus a reduction in livestock numbers, rather than in shortfalls for direct human consumption. After two more years of rising food problems, the government introduced a policy of mass collectivization and dekulakization in early 1930. Fearing that rebellions against these policies would adversely affect production, there was a slight moderation in policy in March 1930. As it turned out the weather was extremely favorable that year, and the 1930 harvest was surprisingly good. But the government, instead of building up its stocks or leaving more grain in the countryside, pressed ahead with high procurement targets and exported about six million tons of grain. There is evidence that the government was greatly misled about the scale of production and surpluses. Reductions in livestock numbers were repeatedly ascribed to kulak sabotage, rather than to logical peasant responses to reduced supplies of grain.

The year 1931 was a drought year with a very low harvest. Food shortages increased throughout the country, and the government, fearing starvation in the towns, enforced heavy grain procurements on all regions, including Ukraine and North Caucasus, which had earlier been treated relatively favorably. As in 1921, the center of gravity of the famine switched from the urban areas to the rural ones. The state responded to reports of famine deaths by secretly releasing supplies. The famine was more or less contained in 1931–32. Livestock levels had fallen greatly, but mercifully there had not been the pandemics of infectious diseases that had contributed so much to the high mortality of 1921–22.

But unlike 1921, the 1931 drought year was not followed by a good harvest. Instead, 1932 produced yet another poor harvest, in which excessive dampness probably played a role. In addition there were a number of worsening agrotechnological problems, many of which were related to the low livestock levels. There may also have been some problems resulting from overcropping of the land. The state denied that the harvest was as poor as it was. It made some adjustments to its procurement targets, which were clearly insufficient, and it continued to squeeze as much grain as it could out of the peasants, who were now starving and had very few reserves. The result was that famine was avoided in the major northern cities but was very severe in the rural areas, especially in the South. It is estimated that about four million people died, making this the largest recorded famine of the time.

The USSR also experienced famine during World War II. The German war plans clearly indicated that they envisaged mass starvation in the northern cities would result from their occupation of the southern food surplus areas. Beseiged Leningrad suffered a million famine deaths, and there were signs of famine among the population of the occupied areas and in the Urals, where much of the evacuated population was located. More surprisingly there was also a recurrence of famine in 1946–47 following another severe drought that damaged the 1946 harvest, at a time when reserves were still low. But all of these, unlike the famine of 1931–33, were clearly externally imposed famines.

Chinese Famines

Pre-Communist China was often referred to as "the land of famine." Famines had been frequent throughout China's long history, and China had developed a very elaborate granary system in an attempt to minimize the effects of the recurring severe shortages. The granary system was most highly developed in the 18th century, but began to decline in the 19th century with the decline of the state, the destruction caused by peasant rebels and foreign intruders. As in Russia, the main problem was to supply a northern capital in a grain-deficit region with supplies from the South. This problem became particularly severe when the British cut connections on the Grand Union Canal during the Opium Wars. This led to the stunting of the growth of Beijing and the appearance of a secondary commercial capital in Shanghai in the South. During the late-19th and the first half of the 20th centuries the main population centers were largely fed from abroad as the domestic trading system collapsed. Japanese invasion in the 1930s led to massive destruction with the flooding of large areas, followed inevitably by famine.

The Communist victory in 1948 came after years of military destruction and waste. In the following years the internal transportation system was restored and ambitious plans made to restore the economy and to do without foreign supplies. At first it looked as though Mao would be relatively cautious in taxing the peasants. "We will not drain the pond to catch the fish." But then the "winds of exaggeration" began to blow and a scenario very similar to that of the Russian Great Leap unfolded. Ambitious industrial production targets resulted in the growth of a large urban population that needed to be fed. There was a drive to introduce more efficient larger-scale rural production units, accompanied by harsh measures to increase grain procurements.

In both the USSR and China, the state blinded itself to the real state of affairs as it attempted to force development. In both cases, after a hasty beginning there was some initial foreboding that lead to a period of temporary caution. And in both cases this time of caution coincided with favorable weather that produced totally unpredicted growth that was unrelated to the government's development policies but that nonetheless encouraged the leadership to press ahead. In both cases as the famine progressed there was censorship, a reluctance to admit what was happening, and refusal to call for outside assistance. In both cases restrictions were placed on rural mobility, and this appears to have helped reduce the level of pandemics. But in both cases the level of mortality was extremely high. In China it is now believed that there were over twenty million deaths, making this the largest of all recorded famines, far exceeding the Soviet famine of 1931–33 in absolute terms, but less severe in relative terms per capita of the population. One of the reasons why Chinese mortality was so high was the lack of livestock, which had for a few years provided some reserves and buffers in the USSR.

Indochinese Famines: Vietnam and Kampuchea

Indochina experienced a terrible famine in the late stages of the World War II as Japan forced several economies, especially the Vietnamese, to grow commercial crops instead of the rice that was needed by its own population. Again the postwar Communist states emerged out of intense wartime destruction and famine. But in addition they had to face a series of colonial wars before eventually achieving independence. There was undoubt-

edly much destruction along the way, with hunger and famine making their contribution. Most of these famines would be classified as external.

The blanket bombing of Cambodia from 1969 to 1975 is reported to have killed six hundred thousand Cambodians, many of whom would have died from famine after the attacks. These, too, were clearly externally caused famines. But later, when the Khmer Rouge seized power in Cambodia, there was a different kind of famine.

The Khmer Rouge severed Cambodia's links with all countries apart from China and North Korea and then embarked on a major social experiment based on China's Great Leap Forward twenty years earlier. Towns were depopulated, agriculture was reorganized, and there was an attempt to leap into industrialization. The result was the mass execution of "hostile elements" and massive famine, especially among the displaced urban population. This is arguably the Communist famine most obviously caused by willful state action. There was to be another famine in 1979 as the Vietnamese Army replaced the Khmer Rouge, and the West refused to acknowledge the new government.

African Famines: Ethiopia, Mozambique, and Angola

There is a long history of drought in the sub-Sahalian region, but there is no earlier record of drought and famine over so large an area as in the great drought of 1973–74.

The long-established imperial government of Haile Selassie fell in 1974 because of the perception that his response to the emergency was inadequate. As turmoil increased Ethiopia was declared a socialist state. Colonel Mengistu took power in 1977 and, with Soviet and Cuban assistance, fought a long war against Somali invaders (1978–88), and an even longer war against secessionist Eritrea. These ongoing conflicts drained the resources of this poor country, made it difficult to develop the economy, and left it totally unable to handle the ensuing droughts of the 1980s and the 1990s that once again resulted in widespread famine.

In Mozambique, Samora Machel, the leader of Frelimo, took power in 1975 following the April 1974 revolution in Portugal. The domestic situation deteriorated when 250,000 Portuguese settlers left and when the South African and Rhodesian governments supported Renamo in the ensuing civil war. In 1977 Frelimo responded to this military threat by reconstituting itself as a Marxist-Leninist party and seeking support from China and Eastern Europe. The widespread killing and devastation of the civil war led to a large-scale famine.

North Korean Famine

Unlike most of the other countries already considered, North Korea did not have a prior history of famine, and, as in Eastern Europe, communism was introduced by a successful invading Communist army. Prior to the division of the peninsula, most Korean industry had been located in the north, while the south was the main source of food supplies. The 1953 post-Korean War partition consequently created problems for the North in feeding its population. The North responded by trying to transform its local agricultural system. Applying collectivization and intense mechanization, electrification, irrigation, and chemicalization it sought to become self-reliant. North Korean agriculture became one of the world's most industrialized and input-intensive agricultural systems, with a higher use of chemical fertilizers and pesticides than Japan, and with large-scale electric-powered irrigation systems. By the late 1980s North Korean industry was highly inefficient and dependent on cheap Soviet resources and fuel. The Russian withdrawal of these resources in 1991 led to the collapse of North Korea's industry, which deprived agriculture of many of its vital inputs. Agricultural production plummeted. North Korea was already in a state of famine when it was faced with catastrophic flooding in July and August 1995. Over a million people are estimated to have died of famine in the following years, despite the arrival of large amounts of international aid. The situation was not made any better by the large amounts of funds that had been spent on militarization and on attempting to develop nuclear capability. Despite ongoing aid North Korea continues to face famine.

Conclusions

There is a close association between communism and famine, but in most instances famine was initially a direct result of external factors that cannot be attributed to communism, but may have contributed to its emergence. In the cases of the Soviet famine of 1931–33 and the Chinese famine of the Great Leap Forward (1957–59), both resulted from excessively optimistic and incautious attempts to escape from poverty that went wrong. In these circumstances the Communist authorities can be accused of criminal neglect in causing these famines, and of callousness in ensuring that the effects of the famine were felt more heavily by their opponents than their allies. However, few experts believe that these famines were deliberately engineered for political ends.

Many would see them instead as unintended consequences of the ambitious development projects undertaken by Communist states, and of the reluctance of Communists to accept the realities of their situation. Amartya Sen has argued that one of the reasons why the major famines of the 20th century occurred in Communist societies was that these were societies in which there was no free press that could publicize the existence of famine and force the government to respond. There is some truth in this argument, but on the other hand, nearly all of the Communist states that experienced famine were ones that already had a history of frequent famine, and where drastic developmental methods were required in order to escape from poverty. In many cases communism was not the cause of famine but the result of an unsuccessful attempt to escape from famine.

See also Agrarian Question; Collectivization of the Countryside; Five-Year Plans; Great Leap Forward; Holodomor; Modernization; War Communism.

FURTHER READING

Conquest, R. *The Harvest of Sorrow: Soviet Collectivization and the Terror-Famine.* Oxford: Oxford University Press, 1986.

Davies, R. W., and S. G. Wheatcroft. *The Years of Hunger: Soviet Agriculture, 1931–1933.* London: Macmillan-Palgrave, 2004.

Robbins, R. G. *Famine in Russia, 1891–1892.* New York: Columbia University Press, 1975.

Sen, A. *Poverty and Famines: An Essay on Entitlement and Deprivation.* Oxford: Oxford University Press, 1981.

Yang, D. L. *Calamity and Reform in China: State, Rural Society, and Institutional Change Since the Great Leap Famine.* Stanford, CA: Stanford University Press, 1996.

STEPHEN G. WHEATCROFT

Fascism

Many words in the vocabulary of the arts, theater, and music are of Italian origin, but only one Italian word belongs to the lexicon of 20th-century politics: fascism. This new term was either adopted, literally imported, or transliterated into every language in the world; it was also applied to contexts and phenomena ("Fascist" Germany, "Fascist" Spain) for which there were already more specific terms, such as national socialism, nazism, and Francoism. Fascism became yet another widespread

20th-century "ism," one that achieved international, although mostly European, diffusion especially in the period between the two world wars. It was also applied to historical events following 1945, as in the cases of Peronist Argentina or Greece during the colonels' regime of 1967–74. It was even extended, not always pertinently, to include dictatorial or simply despotic, tyrannical, or fundamentalist regimes in the late 20th century. The Italian origin of the term is well established, however—a sign that in the interdependent, though not yet globalized world succeeding the great divide of 1914–18, even a relatively peripheral country like Italy could blaze new trails and follow peculiar political routes during a terrible century dominated by forms of extreme polarization. The new-ism, unlike clear terms such as "conservatism" or "radicalism," or more controversial ones like "socialism" and "democracy," contained greater ambiguities, perhaps even genuine semantic obscurity: it derived from the noun *fascio*, and on its own referred to nothing more than a generic effort on behalf of, or a call to, union and federation. But the word did not point in any direction or toward any goal that its sympathizers or adherents should attempt to follow or strive toward.

Founded by Benito Mussolini in Milan in 1919, the *fasci di combattimento* (literally, fighting fasci) movement claimed to differ from all other political movements, was relatively indifferent to theoretical disputes, and was intent on establishing the primacy of action over thought, force over rhetoric, and antipolitics over politics. The transformation of the movement into a party in 1921 led to many disappointments and disagreements among the Fascists themselves, who had developed as an antiparty opposition to all other tendencies. The movement's republican orientation was abandoned in 1922 to please the king of Italy, who would reciprocate soon after by giving Mussolini greater legitimacy; republicanism, affiliation to Masonic lodges, and prior affiliation to groups across the Italian political spectrum had been common among the movement's first adherents. Like Mussolini himself, many adherents had come from the socialist movement, specifically anarchism and revolutionary syndicalism, and had rejected all their previous experiences when they converted to interventionism and a prowar stance in 1914–15.

The extreme radicalization and glorification of nationalist values was one of fascism's first ideological principles of cohesion. But fascism mostly presented itself as opposed to all purposes and ideologies, rather than proposing new values and principles. The fasci and the Fascists constituted themselves as a mass movement and a populist ideology by always opposing every adversary in a spirit of destruction and negation. They were subversive and imitated the revolutionaries, but also lacked proposals for social revolution in an Italy traumatized by the war. The fascio beckoned to all misfits and the deluded; it fanned resentments and frustrated emotions; it was a conduit for aspirations to the habitual violence that had at this point been internalized by many war veterans, who were used to deadly weapons and had been conditioned to hate the enemy. Fascism thus became synonymous with antidemocracy and antisocialism, antipacifism and antiparliamentarianism, antigradualism and antiliberalism, and even anticapitalism to the extent that it claimed to be against the rapacious "sharks" who had profited from the war while ignoring the foot soldiers' aspirations.

Mussolini and the fasci were soon serving the Italian employers' agrarian and industrial reaction in 1921–22, though, unleashing an unprecedented "social" war in the cities and countryside that targeted the institutional and political bases of socialism, and the peasants' and workers' movement. The violence was successful because of the connivance of almost every sector and apparatus of the state, but another important factor was the rhetoric with which the Fascists attempted to justify their attacks, which included proclamations that they were the defenders of the nation against the antination, the Italian fatherland against the internationalists who wanted to "do as in Russia." According to Mussolini the violence was necessary and healthy, "surgical" in fact, almost as if it alone could save Italy's ailing body. The fragile political system of liberalism did not stand up to the subversive assault by fascism, partly because it preferred worrying about safeguarding those material possessions, properties, rents, and incomes that the Fascists never showed any intention of abolishing, leveling, or redistributing.

Mussolini came to power with his March on Rome bluff in October 1922, and within a few years transformed the entire political structure into a dictatorial state with increasing tendencies to totalitarian radicalization. Even though they exhibited little respect for Parliament as an institution, the first Fascists elected to the Chamber of Deputies chose to sit on the extreme right of Montecitorio Palace's hemicycle. Fascist jargon echoed an older socialist phraseology; Fascists addressed each other as *camerata* (in English, somewhere between comrade and pal). Until the 1930s, the single-party and principal mass organizations of the regime were, especially in the inner circles, composed of middle-class cadres, with only minority components from the working and peasant classes; a large number of the aristocracy and upper middle class also became representatives of the Fascist political and administrative ruling class, whether national or local.

The Fascist state was both a police state that engaged in capillary repression of dissent, by inflicting severe sentences on its opponents for crimes of opinion or supposed conspiratorial activities, and a corporatist state that proclaimed it was opening a "third way" between socialism and liberalism, between market capitalism and the Bolshevik nationalization of production and private property. Between the mid-1920s and the 1930s, the myth of Fascist corporatism was perhaps more popular than any political or economic achievements that the regime attempted to take credit for, whether real or more often simply inventions of its propaganda. Given its competitive ambitions with regard to both the United States and the Soviet Union, Italian fascism engaged in an effort of international dimensions, way beyond the material means at its disposal, in the areas of foreign policy, diplomacy, and colonial ambition. Mussolini and Galeazzo Ciano took a decisive step toward war and imperialism in 1936 with the Rome-Berlin Axis. The Fascist International, inspired by Italian fascism and established in Montreux, Switzerland—a gesture of open defiance toward the pacifist seat of the League of Nations in Geneva and the Communist International in Moscow—had helped to lay the groundwork for the Axis. But above all, Mussolini had been preparing his aggression against Ethiopia since 1932, and had further expanded his military plans starting in 1934; the assault itself took place in 1935–36, and represented the first real attack on European peace as well as the political and diplomatic arrangements agreed to in Versailles.

In 1937 the Fascist regime withdrew Italy from the League of Nations, and joined the Anti-Comintern Pact that Germany and Japan had already signed in 1936. During 1936–39, the Fascists and Nazis together sustained Francisco Franco's nationalist secession during the Spanish civil war. Hitler annexed Austria with Mussolini's approval in 1938, and then proceeded to take the Sudeten and humiliate Czechoslovakia with the decisive "mediation" of the Italian dictator. Fascist Italy then proceeded to annex Albania and sign the Pact of Steel with Nazi Germany in 1939. The regime had transformed Italy into a racist and anti-Semitic country, imposing an apartheid-like legislation on conquered Ethiopia in 1936,

while in 1938 Italian Jews were subjected to a series of discriminatory and persecutory anti-Semitic laws. After having militarized politics from its inception and during the first phase of its government, the Fascist regime was militarizing all of Italian society, predisposing it to xenophobia, racial hatred, and the adventure of another great war. Indeed, fascism never ceased to exercise an oppressive form of social control on the entire Italian population, but only after gaining its mass participation and support.

The knot that tied regime and war, Mussolini and military adventurism, was to have fatal consequences for both the system and its leader, when increased psychological awareness in the masses began to connect the continuous series of Italian military defeats in World War II with the responsibilities of the Fascist hierarchs and the Duce. Starting in the late 1930s, more as an emulation of Nazism than of Italian fascism, Fascist parties and movements proliferated throughout Europe, growing with the development of collaborationist regimes and, in the early 1940s, subject to Hitler's New European Order. In 1932, Mussolini had proclaimed that the 20th century would be the century of fascism, but barely thirteen years later, in 1945, after having unleashed unimaginable destruction and extermination, fascism's century was at an end.

Its ambiguous nature, which had originally been compared to a sphinx's, and the fact that Italy, the country where it had first developed, was a peripheral nation, allowed fascism to long be underestimated by the international working-class movement and especially the Bolshevik leadership. During the Fourth Congress of the Comintern, Lenin, already weakened by illness and perhaps lead astray by the color of the blackshirts, compared the Fascists to the Russian counterrevolutionary sect of the Black Hundred of 1905. In the late 1920s, Stalin inspired the theory of so-called social fascism, which directed Communist parties around the world to fight Social Democrats and Fascists in equal measure as their principal adversaries. Relegated to the opposition in 1927, Trotsky was not able to influence the international Communist movement with his analyses of fascism as Bonapartism, which highlighted some of fascism's undoubted characteristics, but risked reducing it to a variant of authoritarian Caesarism. In Communist circles, an economicist and deterministic image of fascism as an agent of big capital prevailed; fascism was seen as a mere instrument of bourgeois power, an extension of a system nearing collapse and replacement by the revolution.

Only after nazism's ascent to power in 1933 did Stalin's and the Comintern's policies change. The much subtler analyses of the Italian Communists—for example, Antonio Gramsci, who highlighted the relation between fascism and its petty bourgeois social base, or Palmiro Togliatti, who also saw fascism's nature as that of a reactionary regime, but one with a mass following, with an extensive popular base, even if fraudulently and coercively obtained—were overlooked in favor of the rigid and reductive definition given by Georgi Dimitrov and Stalin. They defined fascism, in 1935, as the open dictatorship of the most reactionary, chauvinist, and imperialist sectors of finance capital. Stalin then adopted the Popular Front policy, which called on those same masses to rally against the incumbent Fascist danger. Relations between Italy and the Soviet Union had long wavered on both sides between ideology and realpolitik. At the peak of its corporatist development, Fascist militants and polymaths were authorized to attack the democracy they hated to such an extent that the new centers of ideal and political inspiration were identified as Rome and Moscow. The young intellectuals who had dared define the "proprietary corporation" as a potential expropriator of private property rights were immediately silenced. The intervention by the Fascist state in the economy and the growing dimensions of the public sector developed according to autonomous tendencies, and actually against the grain of Soviet collectivism.

But the flirtation between Italian fascism and Soviet communism was extremely brief. Fascism's "sociality" (its Labor Charter, the corporations, the social security system that was provided especially to the middle classes yet only partially to workers and peasants, like a distorted and unequal Italian form of welfare state) produced a hybrid "corporatist modernization" explicitly opposed to the egalitarian and universalistic principles of both democracy and socialism. Mussolini had granted the USSR diplomatic recognition in 1924, and had proceeded with formal policies of détente up to the Spanish civil war, when an increase in ideological radicalism and anticommunism inspired a new and more aggressive course for Italian foreign, colonial, and military policy. The Duce deluded himself for a long time that he would be able to direct Nazi expansionist ambitions toward the East and particularly against the USSR. Hitler demonstrated the cynicism of the *ultra-Realpolitiker* when he concluded a nonaggression pact with Stalin in August 1939 that allowed him to invade Poland and begin World War II. The war of aggression that Hitler and Mussolini con-ducted against the USSR in June 1941 destroyed many misunderstandings about the comparability and formal analogies between ideologies and regimes belonging to the "opposite extremes."

In the aftermath of World War II, another complex political and cultural discussion on the nature of fascism, nazism, and communism was initiated. The theory of totalitarianism highlighted commonalities more than differences, in a series of analyses, studies, and controversies that extend even to this day. On the level of philosophy and political theory, opposing totalitarianisms can tend to easily share commonalities, while on the level of historiography and the reconstruction of reality, it remains much more difficult and complicated to prove the existence of profound similarities, not merely superficial resemblances.

See also Anticommunism; Anti-Fascist Resistance; Antifascism; Anti-Semitism; Comintern; Hitler, Adolf; Imperialism; Mussolini, Benito; Popular Front; Second Cold War; Social Fascism; Totalitarianism.

FURTHER READING

Bosworth, R.J.B. *Mussolini's Italy: Life under the Fascist Dictatorship 1915–45.* New York: Penguin, 2006.

Bosworth, R.J.B., ed. *The Oxford Handboook of Fascism.* Oxford: Oxford University Press, 2009.

Cannistraro, Ph.V., ed. *Historical Dictionary of Fascist Italy.* Westport, CT: Greenwood Press, 1982.

De Grazia, V., and S. Luzzatto, eds. *Dizionario del fascismo.* 2 vols. Torino: Einaudi, 2002–3.

Gentile, E. *The Sacralization of Politics in Fascist Italy.* Boston, Harvard University Press, 1996.

Laqueur, W., ed. *Fascism: A Reader's Guide.* Harmondsworth: Penguin Books, 1979.

Larsen, S. U., B. Hagtvet, and J. P. Myklebust, eds. *Who Were the Fascists? Social Roots of European Fascism.* Bergen: Universitetsforlaget, 1980.

Lyttelton, A. *The Seizure of Power: Fascism in Italy, 1919–1929.* Princeton, NJ: Princeton University Press, 1988.

Morgan, Ph. *The Fall of Mussolini: Italy, the Italians, and the Second World War.* Oxford: Oxford University Press, 2007.

Palla, M. *Mussolini and Fascism.* Northampton, MA: Interlink Books, 2000.

Payne, S.G. *A History of Fascism, 1914–1945.* Madison: University of Wisconsin Press, 1996.

Paxton, R.O. *The Anatomy of Fascism.* New York: Knopf, 2004.

Woolf, S. J., ed. *Fascism in Europe.* London: Methuen, 1981.

MARCO PALLA

Fellow Travelers

Extreme positions of all kinds often attract adherents who for one reason or another cannot commit publicly or absolutely to "the cause." Perhaps public commitment would jeopardize their careers, their preferred style of life, their family, or even their lives. In no modern case are there more—or more vivid—instances of this mixture of militancy and discretion than among sympathizers with communism. In certain instances espionage resulted from such collisions of public and private values, as in the case of Kim Philby and the other Cambridge spies in England during the 1930s and 1940s. In others, evasion and prevarication, sometimes combined with drastic ideological evolution rightward, was the result, as times or circumstances changed. But it is common for such people, known in political cases as "fellow travelers," to live for long periods of time on the uncertain fringes of commitment.

The term fellow traveler (*poputchik, compagnon de route*, or *Mitläufer*) assumed something like its modern meaning when in *Literature and Revolution* (1923), Leon Trotsky attached it to the generation of left-wing Russian writers who were sympathetic to the Russian Revolution but not committed to Bolshevism in any deep way. Writers like Boris Pilnyak, Vsevolod Ivanov, Nikolai Kliuev, and Alexander Blok were attracted to the revolution (or the "victorious Revolution," as Trotsky wrote acidly from exile some years later) for a variety of reasons. Some, like the poet Vladimir Mayakovsky and other futurists, were acting out an aesthetic revolt; others were adherents of a peasant rebellion that accepted the proletariat as the linchpin of the revolution only faute de mieux; some were consumed by the excitement of it all; and still others simply bore witness to the most remarkable event of their time.

In Trotsky's polemic on literature and social class, written early in the Soviet period, fellow traveler was a grudgingly favorable term. The proletariat would one day produce a real working-class literature, but only after it had been properly educated and trained. Sympathetic bourgeois writers would have to do for now in the vital matter of glorifying the revolution of 1917 to the world. Many of Trotsky's more radical Soviet opponents objected to such an implicit, if partial and instrumental, acceptance of bourgeois writers.

Under Stalin, however, the meaning and import of fellow traveler underwent a major shift. Fellow traveling by Russian writers was no longer permitted; nothing but all-out enthusiasm for Soviet communism would do from the motherland's own. The fellow travelers with whom the government was concerned were foreigners. Influential foreigners could help in many ways to spread communism across the face of the globe. They could proclaim, as the American Lincoln Steffens did after returning from the Soviet Union, "I have been over to the future and it works." It was hoped in Moscow that they might prepare the way for more resolute Marxist revolutionaries who would eventually take their places. For the present, they could at least pressure their bourgeois governments to adopt more pro-Soviet policies.

Fellow traveling was far from constant or uniform over the duration of the Soviet Union. There were two major upsurges, and then, during the Cold War, an up-and-down pattern largely in the direction of decline. The first wave came in the immediate aftermath of the Russian Revolution and was dominated by intellectuals, although more ordinary socialists and trade unionists were involved as well, especially in Europe. The second and rather more important wave came after the stock market crash of 1929, which convinced many Europeans and Americans that capitalism had failed, and that socialism, along more or less Soviet lines, was the wave of the future. During the radical 1930s, large numbers of Europeans and Americans adopted positions of sympathy and support for Soviet policies as well as the system itself. Some joined the Communist Party, and some did not. Many such people, especially in the United States, eventually suffered damage to their careers for their flirtation with the party. At the dawn of the Cold War, the political center of gravity in the West moved rather quickly to the Right. Many leftists were carried toward the center by the tide; a few resisted; and an even smaller number undertook a variety of services for the Soviet Union, including espionage.

A complex mixture of blame and sympathy was the lot of the fellow traveler, depending on the politics of the critic. For conservatives, the fellow traveler was a fool and a dupe. They were wont to lay emphasis on the secrecy often displayed by supporters of communism in the capitalist world and the possibility that a fellow traveler might be—or become—a Soviet agent. As the Cold War developed, points of view that had seemed merely progressive in the 1930s began to appear "anti-American" or even treasonous in the changed world. Fellow traveler quickly became a wholly negative term in this atmosphere. This benighted individual was a fool for believing in far Left points of view and a dupe for believing that there was an idealistic dimension to communism. This person was also regarded as cowardly, insincere, or duplicitous for not embracing his or her cause openly.

Among leftists and liberals the take on fellow traveling was different. There were many sympathizers with communism in Europe, the United States, and around the world. Everyone knew that. But where was the borderline across which one stepped from sympathy into fellow traveling? Was Jean-Paul Sartre a passionate sympathizer with communism or a contemptible fellow traveler? Conservatives tended to see all sympathizers as virtual fellow travelers, while liberals and leftists were likely to separate the categories. The liberal historian David Caute saw most fellow travelers as progressives and modernizers, heirs to the (generally pre-Marxist) Enlightenment. To be sure their view of the Soviet Union was naive and utopian—deluded even, steeped in rationalism and scientism, and out of touch with ordinary life. But the imputation of evil, treachery, or the intent to do harm was largely absent. Among leftists, the fellow traveler was not generally regarded as an epicurean devotee of vicarious violence, not the person who drove Stalin's getaway car and then claimed innocence of the crimes. There could even be an element of the tragic about generous-minded progressives who had believed too long and fervently in the Soviet Union. These differing views of course expressed larger political differences between the Left and the Right in the intellectual world surrounding the Soviet Union.

It is somewhat easier to see the fellow travelers of the immediate postrevolutionary period as guilty of little more than naive enthusiasm for the new world promised by the Russian revolutionaries. Pro-Soviet sympathies carried far less baggage in the early 1920s than they had acquired a decade or two later. There was little or no explaining to be done about the gulag, although it had already begun to grow. Stalin and Stalinism lay in the future.

"Throughout the twentieth century," wrote François Furet, "communism has been like a house that each generation has gone in or out of according to circumstances." The proclamation of the so-called Popular Front policy of the Soviet Union in 1935, six years after the stock market crash, heightened pro-Soviet feelings among leftists in Europe and the United States, and brought them some reciprocity from the socialist motherland. Party membership and fellow traveling rose dramatically. In France, the romantic, antinationalist writer Romain Rolland, never actually a party member, visited Stalin in 1935, supported the purges, and was still backing the party at the time of his death in 1944. André Gide's fellow traveling at least was confined to a brief period around the middle of the 1930s. According to Furet, Gide "left France [to visit the Soviet Union] a fellow traveler [and] returned comparing Stalin to Hitler." Stephen Spender's views in England followed the same trajectory. As an Oxford undergraduate he announced his conversion to communism in the *Daily Worker* in 1936, but little more than a decade later he contributed to that classic anthology of disillusioned ex-Communists, *The God That Failed*. Despite inner doubts, Anna Seghers and Bertolt Brecht never repudiated a clear commitment to communism in Germany, but Lion Feuchtwanger and Heinrich Mann were classic fellow travelers.

The events of the early Cold War made fellow traveling more difficult. The Communist coup in Czechoslovakia (1948), the East Berlin uprising (1953), Khrushchev's Secret Speech and the Hungarian Revolt (1956), and the Prague Spring (1968) made strong pro-Soviet opinions in the West seem more and more quixotic at best, and treasonous at worst. Only the young radicals of the 1960s and their mentors, like Herbert Marcuse, changed the tone, but only briefly. And their basic position was not to rehabilitate the Soviet Union but rather merely to assert that bad as it was, it was no worse than the United States. The end of the Soviet Union made the subject of who the fellow travelers were and why they behaved as they did something largely for historians, but scholarly acrimony persists to this day.

See also Anticommunism; Antifascism; Partisans of Peace; Propaganda, Communist.

FURTHER READING

Brzezinski, Z. *The Grand Failure: The Birth and Death of Communism in the Twentieth Century.* New York: Scribners, 1989.

Caute, D. *The Fellow-Travellers: A Postscript to the Enlightenment.* New York: Macmillan, 1973.

Crossman, R. *The God That Failed.* Forward David G. Engerman. 1949. Reprint, New York: Columbia University Press, 2001.

Furet, F. *Le passé d'une illusion; essai sur l'idée communiste au XX siècle.* Paris: Laffont, 1995.

Hollander, P. *Political Pilgrims: Travels of Western Intellectuals to the Soviet Union, China, and Cuba.* New York: Harper and Row, 1981.

ABBOTT GLEASON

Festivals

Bolshevik or Russian Communist festivals, first seen on May Day 1918, had roots in various forms of European and Russian celebrations. From the fetes of the French Revolution—themselves derived in part from both classical and old French forms—came popular participation, freshly created music, mimetic performances in costume, stage settings, and revolutionary themes. From Marxist rituals—most of them in place by the founding of the Second International in 1889—were added the working-class anthem, "The Internationale," proletarian thematics, May Day, and a predominant use of red in the decor. On the territory of the Russian Empire, Polish protest rituals, largely nationalist, preceded those in Russia proper: the insurgent songs of 1830–31 and 1861–63, demonstrations, and martyrs' funerals. Russian Marxists (Social Democrats, or SDs), as well as their Socialist-Revolutionary rivals (SRs), borrowed freely from these traditions and deployed them in street demonstrations, funerals, and secret meetings, haltingly at first and then openly during the revolutions of 1905 and 1917. Like some of their European counterparts, Russian marches often employed sacred tones and solemnities redolent of Christian processions.

Unlike the revolutionaries of 1917, who publicly buried their dead and celebrated the fall of the monarchy a few weeks after that event, the Bolsheviks did not undertake a mass festival until May 1918, about six months after they took power. Winter weather and emergency circumstances inhibited an earlier date. The Bolshevik pageant master, Commissar of Enlightenment Anatoly Lunacharsky, built on the precedents of Jacques-Louis David's French revolutionary festivals. Inspired by his own interest in "proletarian culture," he aspired to make this first Bolshevik festival a celebration of the working class, the alleged victors in the October Revolution. Since this was a moment of triumph rather than illegal protest, and since the Bolsheviks now controlled the streets and squares, Lunacharsky drew on the nonradical popular custom of the *narodnoe gulyanie*, usually translated as "folk festival" or "funfair." At a funfair, all classes, though especially the lower classes, reveled among amusements and booths that offered food and entertainment. On the first Bolshevik May Day, the upper classes were conspicuously absent; and the free spontaneity of funfair rowdiness was somewhat subdued by crowd control and scripted performances with messages. Even so, in the chronicles of the Soviet festival style, May 1, 1918, stands out as the most freewheeling. Tighter scripting and greater control marked all subsequent celebratory events.

Moscow, the new Soviet capital as of March 1918, held its own festivals, as eventually did all major Soviet cities. An ancient Russian city with a clearly marked center—the Kremlin and Red Square—Moscow lent itself to a celebration style more solemn than that of Petrograd (formerly St. Petersburg) and to an image as a sacred and national center. Marchers converged up the vast square and were "reviewed" by those in power arrayed on platforms near the Kremlin (after Lenin's death, on his mausoleum, erected in the late 1920s). From 1918 to 1921, Lenin's Monumental Propaganda scheme held sway as a mode of communication with the assembled celebrants. This involved a series of monuments done in plaster or stone of figures whom the Bolsheviks claimed as forebears of the October Revolution: Spartacus, the classical avatar of revolt; various modern European revolutionaries, socialists, and martyrs; Russian peasant rebels of the early modern period; and Russian radicals from Alexander Radishchev onward. The statues "told" to viewers a narrative account of the inevitable teleological path to Bolshevism; political speakers lectured on the figures to make sure the crowds got the message. On holidays, Moscow thus became very much a "talking city," enveloped in a cloud of words.

Petrograd also featured monumental propaganda. While it lacked the deeper Russian associations of Moscow, it outshone the old/new capital in the number and variety of its public celebrations during the formative period of Soviet festival culture, roughly 1918 to 1920. An account of some of the themes chosen can give a good idea of what ideological motifs were uppermost in the minds of the city's leadership and what styles they deemed most effective for reaching the urban masses. If Moscow taught history-as-myth by means of monuments, Petrograd did so through mass indoor and outdoor theatrical spectacles reconstructing pivotal moments in revolutionary history, such as the "Fall of the Autocracy" (1919), the "Birth of the Third International (Comintern)," the "Liberation of Labor," the "Blockade of Russia," the "Worldwide Commune," and the "Storming of the Winter Palace" (all 1920). The last, a stylized recreation of the October Revolution, inspired Sergei Eisenstein's equally exaggerated film *October* (1927). Directed by professional theater people, with lavish sets, costumes, and music, these spectacles engaged several thousands in their casts (including Red Army soldiers) and played to tens of thousands of Soviet citizens in huge spaces around the city. Message-performances were supplemented by carnival-like frolics.

After 1920, the mammoth shows were abandoned and the avant-garde artistic elements of decor toned down. The parade or demonstration came to dominate proceedings, with the role of the armed forces growing each year. The new calendar replaced the old church holidays with socialist celebrations: May Day, Revolution Day, International Women's Day, Red Army Day, and so on. Though the euphoric moods and flamboyant styles of the first years did not survive into the 1920s—the era of the New Economic Policy (NEP)—some spontaneity at least could be found. With the coming of Stalin to power in 1929, the character of festivities changed. Stalin's 50th birthday in that year was turned into a national event marked by mass adulation, carefully orchestrated from the top down. Documentary footage of 1930s' parades reveal a recurring pattern: politburo leaders on Lenin's tomb reviewing a passing parade composed of the military, factory workers holding up graphs of production achievements, peasants folk-dancing on truck beds, non-Russian groups decked out in ethnic costumes, Young Pioneers, athletes, aviators, Stakhanovites (heroes of labor), and other representatives of an increasingly ascribed society. As Soviet planes overflew Red Square, the marchers cheered and held aloft icons of Stalin, Lenin, and Marx. What had started out as a festival of the revolution—and of the masses who allegedly had made it—had by the 1930s become a reverential procession by selected social and occupational "types" who glorified the supreme leader by displaying their marching ranks and the products of their labor.

The main format of the Stalinist parade persisted—with some timely updating and only occasional ruptures or disturbances—until the last years of Gorbachev. Geographically, it followed the banners of Communist revolutions or imposed regimes across Eastern Europe, parts of Asia, and Cuba, everywhere—with appropriate local colors added. The festival may have faded into routine under Communist regimes; but the practice of celebrating the overturn of an unpopular regime is still with us, as can be seen by perusing the newspaper on any given day.

See also Cult of Personality; Iconography; Lunarchsky, Anatoly; Messianism; Prolekult; Propaganda, Communist; Utopia.

FURTHER READING

Clark, K. *Petersburg, Crucible of Cultural Revolution*. Cambridge, MA: Harvard University Press, 1995.

Gleason, A., et al., eds. *Bolshevik Culture: Experiment and Order in the Russian Revolution*. Bloomington: University of Indiana Press, 1985.

Lane, C. *The Rites of Rulers*. Cambridge, UK: University of Cambridge Press, 1981.

Mally, L. *Culture of the Future: the Proletkult Movement in Revolutionary Russia*. Berkeley: University of California Press, 1990.

Mazaev, A. I. *Prazdnik kak sotsialno-khudozhestvennoe yavlenie*. Moscow, 1978.

Petrone, K. *Life Has Become More Joyous, Comrades: Celebrations in the Time of Stalin*. Bloomington: University of Indiana Press, 2000.

Stites, R. *Revolutionary Dreams: Utopian Vision and Experimental Life in the Russian Revolution*. New York: Oxford University Press, 1989.

Von Geldern, J. *Bolshevik Festivals, 1917–1920*. Berkeley: University of California Press, 1993.

RICHARD STITES

Five-Year Plans

A draft five-year plan for Soviet industry was drawn up in Gosplan, the State Planning Commission, as early as 1923, when the economy had just begun to recover from the war and civil war. This was followed in 1924 by similar plans for agriculture and transport. In March 1926, serious preparation began for a five-year plan for the economy as a whole. A bewildering series of rival drafts followed, prepared in the midst of great controversy about the future development of the Soviet economy. It was not until April–May 1929 that the Communist Party and government approved the first "Five-Year Plan of National Economic Construction," three volumes of seventeen hundred large pages covering the period October 1, 1928, to September 30, 1933.

Five years was held to be a convenient period for planning because new factories, power stations, and railway lines could be begun and completed in this time, and because a cycle of good and bad harvests would normally occur, so that an average yield could be assumed. The First Five-Year Plan covered each branch of the economy in some detail, and dealt with social and cultural as well as economic development. An entire volume was devoted to the regional breakdown of the plan. The core of the plan (as of later plans) was a list of new industrial projects, issued in 1929 as a short appendix book to the series. It formed part of a grand program to "catch up and overtake the advanced capitalist countries."

The First Five-Year Plan was at the center of the vast propaganda drive that encouraged enthusiasm for industrialization. From 1930, it was pressed ahead under the slogan "The Five-Year Plan in Four Years," or simply "5 in 4." In January 1933, the authorities triumphantly announced that the plan had been achieved in four years and three months.

This declaration was misleading in at least two important respects. First, the plan approved in spring 1929 was drastically revised upward in 1930. None of these higher targets was reached, but the fulfillment of the plan was reported in terms of the original 1929 plan. Even so, its fulfillment could be claimed only by a complex manipulation of the figures. The plan to increase consumption had in fact completely failed. The financial plan also failed. It had proposed that the value of the ruble would be improved and investment financed as a result of cost reductions in industry, but in reality costs rose considerably and the plan was financed largely by currency issues. Second, the plan proposed that most of the individual peasant farms that dominated agriculture would still remain in 1933. The forced collectivization of agriculture and the mass expulsion from the villages of the kulaks (better-off peasants, supposedly employing labor) were no part of the original plan—not to mention the decline in food production and the large-scale famine that was at its worst when the five-year plan was declared to have been completed.

Nevertheless, this was a period of substantial industrial development. Gosplan began to prepare the Second Five-Year Plan (1933–37) as early as 1931. The first drafts, like the revised First Five-Year Plan, were far too ambitious. In 1932–33 more realistic drafts were prepared with the support of impressive studies by a vast array of scientists and engineers. The plan was delayed by the economic crisis of 1933 and was adopted in 1934, over a year after it was supposed to have started. Like nearly all the Soviet five-year plans, it underestimated the resources that would be required to achieve its aims, and wrongly assumed that the ruble would be stabilized or even increase in value. Unusually, it also underestimated the output that would be obtained from the capital projects launched during the first plan, and somewhat overestimated the labor that they would require. As a result, many of its targets for heavy industry were achieved.

While the production of food and industrial consumer goods increased, as with almost all the five-year plans consumption fell far short of the plan targets.

The preparation of the Third Five-Year Plan (1938–42) began in 1936, but the decision in that year to step up the armaments drive in face of the Fascist menace, and the disruptive purges of the entire economic apparatus that started at the end of that year delayed its completion and approval until as late as March 1939. Two years later, in June 1941, the German invasion brought peacetime economic expansion to an end.

In 1943, in the midst of the Second World War, a plan for 1943–47 began to be prepared, but in August 1945, with the invaders defeated, peacetime five-year planning was resumed with the decision to compile the Fourth Five-Year Plan, covering the years 1946 to 1950. Further five-year plans followed: the Fifth Five-Year Plan (1951–55), adopted a few months before Stalin's death, and the Sixth Five-Year Plan (1956–60). In the course of 1956–58 numerous reforms were carried out by Khrushchev in industrial administration, and he also launched a series of ambitious programs. As a consequence the sixth plan was canceled and replaced by a unique seven-year plan (1959–65), which was in turn interrupted by the fall of Khrushchev in October 1964. For the next quarter of a century plans were regularly approved: the Eighth Five-Year Plan (1966–70), the Ninth Five-Year Plan (1971–75), the Tenth Five-Year Plan (1976–80), and the Eleventh Five-Year Plan (1981–85). The postwar five-year plans were much more realistic than their prewar predecessors. The Sixth Five-Year Plan, the Seventh Five-Year Plan, and the Eighth and Ninth Five-Year Plans were successful in the sense that in the 1960s and early 1970s, Soviet industry developed appreciably more rapidly than its Western rivals. From the mid-1970s, however, the rate of growth of industry gradually diminished, so that "catching up and overtaking" the advanced countries became an ever remoter prospect. Soon after Gorbachev became party general secretary he launched the Twelfth Five-Year Plan (1986–90), which proposed to accelerate growth by greater efficiency and increasing investment. This was thrown into chaos by the political, social, and economic upheavals of perestroika. In the first year of the uncompleted Thirteenth Five-Year Plan, intended for 1991–95, the Soviet Union and its five-year plans came to an end.

Nearly all the Soviet five-year plans, pre- and postwar, underestimated the growth of the state-employed labor force and the wage bill associated with it, and overestimated the possible growth of production, particularly of consumer goods. They never became operational plans. But they provided a general guide to economic priorities, an opportunity to reconsider the pattern of investment projects, and a means of demonstrating economic progress.

Five-year plans inspired by the Soviet example were a key element of economic policy in other countries. In postwar Eastern Europe, five-year plans that closely followed the Soviet pattern were universal. In China, the First Five-Year Plan (1953–57) started three years after the Communists took power; it sought to establish modern industry with strong Soviet technical support. The Second Five-Year Plan (1958–62) was disrupted by the economic crisis resulting from the Great Leap Forward, and the Third Five-Year Plan (1966–70) by the Cultural Revolution. The Fourth Five-Year Plan (1971–75) saw more steady progress in industry and agriculture, and was followed by an ambitious Ten-Year Plan (1976–85).

Outside the Communist world, in September 1936 Hitler, in his speech launching the Nazi Four-Year Plan, declared that "the German economy will either grasp the new economic tasks or else it will prove itself quite incompetent to survive in this modern age when the Soviet state is setting up a gigantic plan." The Four-Year Plan sought to manage investment, labor, and raw materials to promote economic autarky and the switch to rearmament, but left industry in private ownership. After the war, France introduced a series of four-year plans, which eschewed detailed production targets in favor of "indicative planning" covering a few major indicators. Five-year plans were fashionable everywhere in Western Europe, and British universities had their "quinquennial plans." In the 1950s and 1960s, five-year planning spread to India, Turkey, and other developing economies that sought to industrialize by modifying the Soviet experience in the light of their own circumstances. But with the rise of a global free market economy from the 1970s on, long-term plans ceased to have much influence on the mixed economies of both Europe and Asia, and were gradually abandoned as they moved further toward the capitalist model.

See also Soviet Industrialization.

FURTHER READING

Carr, E. H., and R. W. Davies. *Foundations of a Planned Economy, 1926–1929.* 1 vol. London: Penguin, 1969.

Gregory, P. R., ed. *Behind the Façade of Stalin's Command Economy.* Stanford, CA: Stanford University Press, 2001.

Nove, A. *An Economic History of the U.S.S.R.* Harmondsworth, UK: Penguin, 1990.

Zaleski, E. *Planning for Economic Growth in the Soviet Union, 1928–1932.* Chapel Hill: University of North Carolina Press, 1971.

———. *Stalinist Planning for Economic Growth, 1933–1952.* Chapel Hill: University of North Carolina Press, 1980.

ROBERT W. DAVIES

Foibe Massacres

The events of the *foibe*—natural karst cavities into which the nascent Yugoslav Communist regime presumably "disappeared" more than three thousand people—occurred in a region, the so-called Venezia-Giulia, in which for centuries the people of Italy, Slovenia, and Croatia had lived side by side. By the end of the 19th century, this territory was contested by nation-states, and its civil societies were fraught with opposing nationalisms. A succession of regional governments all exhibited a need for control, especially if they were totalitarian regimes. The foibe events could therefore be classified as episodes of state violence, and from this perspective the Communist violence shared some features with the Nazi atrocities perpetrated at the Risiera of San Sabba (whose crematorium engulfed several thousands partisans between 1944 and 1945). More specifically, the official story in both cases revolved around deportation rather than what really happened.

The foibe murders took place during two distinct periods. In September 1943 they were perpetrated on the Istrian Peninsula, while after the war had ended, during the first half of May 1945, they occurred in Trieste and the surrounding area as far away as Gorizia. In both instances the violence was triggered by what could be defined as a power vacuum (analogous to what was happening in other Eastern European contexts). In September 1943, the Italian government vanished from one day to the next, only to be replaced in about a month by the Nazi occupation regime (the so-called Operational Zone Adriatic Coast); at the end of April 1945, it was the latter regime that was undergoing its final collapse, but unlike what occurred in the rest of Italy, the troops of the Eighth Anglo-American Army arrived when the situation was already under the full control of the Yugoslav People's Liberation Army and the U.S. army stepped aside.

The two series of events have different meanings and consequences. In September 1943, about five to seven hundred people were disappeared in the Istrian foibe by Croatian partisan formations. It was a rebellious act with no greater purpose, with no political goals; it was a settling of accounts by those who, Croatians in particular, had been persecuted by the Fascist regime, and it affected those Italians who represented the social and political hierarchies that were an integral part of the Fascist regime. So in addition to political and class hatred, individual animosities and anti-institutional attitudes along with forms of violence against women (considered as war booty) came into play. At the beginning of October the power vacuum had been filled by the Nazi occupation regime, which was even more ferocious in this region than in the rest of Italy.

The second series of events has a more complex prehistory. It was based on Yugoslav political plans, in which nation building was inseparable from state building (the building of the Communist state)—the second being the dominant concern. It was basically communism in its state form, rather than as a political movement that irrupted into Venezia Giulia (and thus is not comparable to the purges that took place in Emilia in the so-called triangle of death in the war's immediate aftermath). Already in September 1944, a Slovene directive stated that liberation should take place by installing "a strong military government" in the entire territory that was to be claimed, as the only viable premise to future annexation; it was essential to have a free hand in Venezia Giulia. To further bolster this perspective, explicitly defined as a "takeover of power," another directive from the Slovenian Communist Party was issued toward the end of April 1945: the orders were to consider "the entire administrative and police apparatus . . . as an enemy army and apparatus," even though later it stated that one "should not purge on the basis of nationality" (an invitation that was ignored). It was up to the Yugoslav political police and specifically the military tribunal of the Yugoslav Fourth Army to execute these orders by means of less-than-summary proceedings followed by disappearances into the karst chasms just outside the urban area. So in the first ten days of May about seventeen thousand people were deported, and then about eight thousand of them were soon released. Investigations performed between 1945 and 1947 estimate that twenty-five hundred people were disappeared in the foibe; but further acts of disappearance were recorded up to the first months of 1946.

The foibe massacres were a conflict between nation-states—between the winner, Yugoslavia, and the loser, Italy, and the former wanted all traces of the institutional presence of the former to disappear: the police agents and personnel, civic guard (the citizen militia that had been formed under Nazi occupation), and soldiers of the Italian Social Republic (also known as Repubblica di Salò). It was also a preventive police action intended to neutralize those who in the future might act as political foes—in other words, whoever refused to recognize "the leading role of Tito's Yugoslavia," or the non-Communist representatives of the Committee of National Liberation (the Comitato di Liberazione Nazionale, the main body of the Italian resistance). Its representatives from Trieste went into hiding once again, while those in Gorizia (especially the Italian Socialist Party and Partito d'Azione representatives) were disappeared into foibe. Third, it was an act of ethnic cleansing by means of which the Slovenian national community manifested its need for liberation, acting against the policies of persecution employed by both the Fascist state and the Italian community—a community portrayed as a nonindigenous and mostly "imported" presence, and complicit with the Fascist regime, to such an extent that the equivalence between Italy and fascism would become a component of Slovenian and Croatian political discourse from that moment on. For the Slovenian national community this was an "arbitrary and uncontrolled" act of regeneration, as the Yugoslav occupation authorities were to recognize at the time, and the Anglo-American authorities who were to govern Trieste and the surrounding area (Zone A of Venezia Giulia) starting in June 1945 recognized later.

Given these characteristics, a certain terrorist component also seems to be recognizable in these events. The Italian community in Istria, which came to be under the jurisdiction of the Yugoslav military occupation authorities and, after the peace treaty of 1947, within Yugoslav borders, was forced to live with the consequences of the foibe massacres. The forced introduction of the Communist regime eliminated the preexisting social structures (with all the habits, hierarchies, and values these implied) and was accompanied by a second process of ethnic cleansing, which over a ten-year period starting in late 1946, affected about a quarter-million people. Unlike analogous cases in Eastern Europe, this was an instance of de facto expulsion, not an expulsion organized by the Yugoslav authorities; from then on, Italians from Istria referred to themselves as exiles rather than as "expelled" (*vertriebene*, as was the case with the Germans in the East).

Finally, once again keeping a comparative perspective in mind, there was a further element of differentiation from episodes of ethnic cleansing that accompanied the establishment of Communist regimes in Poland, Czechoslovakia, Ukraine, and Hungary. Ethnic cleansing in these countries also involved the use of violence against those who were forced to leave, but the sequence of events, from the state's violence with its thousands of victims prior to expulsion, to the actual expulsion, was unique to the episodes just described, as well as to the nature of Yugoslav communism, whose characteristics led to Josip Broz Tito's break with Joseph Stalin in 1948.

See also Borders; Ethnic Cleansing; Nationalism; Second Cold War; Tito, Josip Broz.

FURTHER READING

Oliva, G. *Foibe. Le stragi negate degli italiani della Venezia Giulia e dell'Istria.* Milan: Mondadori, 2002.

Siljak, A., and P. Ther, eds. *Ethnic Cleansing in East-Central Europe, 1944–1948.* Lanham, MD: Rowman and Littlefield, 2001.

Valdevit, G. *Foibe. Il peso del passato. Venezia Giulia, 1943–1945.* Venice: Marsilio, 1997.

GIAMPAOLO VALDEVIT

G

Gagarin, Yury

Yury Gagarin (1934–68), the man who would become "history's first cosmonaut," was born in Klushino near Gzhatsk, Ukraine, on March 9, in the province of Smolensk, the third of four children in a family of kolkhoz members; his father worked as a carpenter. During the Nazi occupation of the region in World War II, the two older brothers were deported to Germany and only returned at the war's end. While he finished his technical studies, and survived his family's and his own financial difficulties, Gagarin was unusually interested in airplanes and started to attend the Saratov flight school. In order to pursue this passion he enrolled in the Soviet air force in 1955, where he proved his worth as a skillful pilot, and also experimented with new techniques and tested airplanes.

In 1959, Gagarin worked hard to be included in the training programs for flights outside Earth's atmosphere—programs that the Soviet air force had started to plan in the early 1950s, and whose most significant achievements at the time had been the placement of the Sputnik satellite into orbit on October 4, 1957, and the launch of the first living creature (the dog Lajka) outside Earth's atmosphere on November 3 of the same year. After having transferred to Moscow for technical and psychophysical evaluation in early 1960, Gagarin was officially included in a group of twenty pilots, one of whom would be chosen for the first planned Soviet flight into space, to take place the following year. Gagarin was chosen for his pilot skills and technical competence. The power of his image as a model citizen of the USSR—of humble origins and raised in a family of kolkhoz members—and his political reliability—personally appreciated by the Communist Party's secretary general, Nikita Khrushchev (who was also influenced by their shared Ukrainian background)—also played their parts.

On April 12, 1961, without any prior announcements by the Soviet media, the Vostok 1 capsule, weighing 4.7 tons, lifted off from the Bajkonur cosmodrome in Kazakhstan; it entered a regular orbit, and completed the first circumnavigation of the earth in seventy-eight minutes, reaching an apogee of 213 miles and a perigee of 118 to then perform a normal reentry and land back on Earth. According to the official Soviet version, Gagarin remained in the capsule while it descended to Earth, slowed down by a parachute (the United States instead hypothesized that he had parachuted out of the capsule at about 22,000 feet).

After the success of a mission that according to the organizers themselves might well have resulted in the pilot's death, Gagarin immediately became a Soviet icon and the most powerful symbol of technical modernization achieved by the Soviet system. It was especially in this role that he was frequently used by Soviet authorities, in dozens of trips at home and abroad, during public speeches exalting the role of the Communist Party as the "organization to which all our victories are due" (a statement he made, according to Tass, while exiting the Vostok spacecraft). After a brief stint as vice president of the Supreme Soviet, Gagarin wanted to return to his air force and space work as a test pilot and designer.

On a personal level these were difficult years, marked by alcoholism and difficulties in his marriage to Valentina Gorjacheva. In October 1961 he had already been seriously injured in Crimea falling out of the window of a hotel he had been staying at with a young nurse. In his role as public ambassador of the Soviet space program, Gagarin sent party leader Leonid Brezhnev a confidential letter in October 1965 in which he complained about the poor organization of the space program in the USSR and the fact that it was falling behind, at least if measured by the advances that were being made at the time in the United States. Two years later, on March 27, 1968, he died when a military MIG-15 plane he was testing crash-landed. Despite some fantastic speculation that linked the crash to his disagreements with the Soviet leadership or the embarrassment that his lifestyle was creating, in all likelihood it was caused by the weather conditions in the area.

See also Khrushchev, Nikita; Modernization.

FURTHER READING

Doran, J., and P. Bizony. *Starman: The Truth behind the Legend of Yuri Gagarin.* London: Bloomsbury, 1998.

Gagarin, Y. A. *Road to the Stars; Notes by Soviet Cosmonaut no. 1, Yuri Gagarin.* Moscow: Foreign Languages Publishing House, 1962.

Ustinov, J. S. *Bessmertie Gagarina.* Moscow: Geroj Otechestva, 2004.

ANDREA ROMANO

Gheorghiu-Dej, Gheorghe

Gheorghe Gheorghiu-Dej (1901–65) was born on November 8 in Bârlad to a working-class family; he joined the Romanian Communist Party in 1930. During the great economic crisis of the early 1930s he led the railroad workers' strike. Sentenced to eleven years in prison, Gheorghiu-Dej remained there until 1944, informally heading up the group of imprisoned Communist prisoners that in the early 1940s, came into conflict with the party's general secretary, Ştefan Foriş. It is difficult to establish if Gheorghiu-Dej was acting on Soviet orders or not; the fact remains that on April 4, 1944, with the help of Emile Bodnaraş, who had been freed from prison a year earlier, Foriş was removed as secretary by a party coup.

After Marshal Ion Antonescu's regime was overturned, on August 23, 1944, Gheorghiu-Dej became one of the Romanian Communist Party's leaders, and on November 4 was nominated to the post of minister of communications. Stalin designated him as the party's general secretary in January 1945, but he had to confront the so-called group of Muscovites (Ana Pauker and Vasile Luca) in a battle for power. Gheorghiu-Dej's position was confirmed by the national party conference in October 1945, and he became first vice president of the Council of Ministers in 1948. His rivals had been disgraced in Moscow in the meantime: Pauker, who was Jewish, fell

victim to the anti-Zionist campaign launched by Stalin; Luca made the mistake, as finance minister, of opposing the monetary reform that Stalin desired. Gheorghiu-Dej took advantage of these circumstances to remove the two from power, together with their ally, Treasury Minister Teohari Georgescu. Khrushchev's secret report to the Twentieth Congress of the Communist Party of the Soviet Union made Gheorghiu-Dej tremble since he was responsible, with his defeated rivals, for the terrible repression of the Stalin era and had been an accomplice in Foriş's assassination in 1946. He had also had another renowned militant who had been falsely accused of treachery, Lucreţiu Pătrăşcanu, put to death in 1954. The de-Stalinization campaign launched in the Soviet Union was used by two members of the political office, Miron Constantinescu and Iosif Chişinevschi, in an attempt to remove Gheorghiu-Dej. The attempt failed, even though inspired by Moscow, and the following year the two rebels were removed from the Central Committee.

Gheorghiu-Dej was an ardent supporter of the armed intervention against the Hungarian Revolution in 1956, to the extent that he proposed the use of Romanian troops to Khrushchev. He was, however, scared by the speed with which the Kremlin changed leaders in Budapest (Matyas Rakosi, Erno Gero, Imre Nagy, and János Kádár). He therefore started to distance himself from Moscow, and taking advantage of the Sino-Soviet conflict, first proposed himself as a mediator and then proclaimed each party's right to autonomously decide its own policies in the April Declaration in 1964. Having now accumulated both the posts of secretary general and head of state (after 1961, he was also elected president of the State Council), Gheorghiu-Dej became the undisputed despot of Romania. He also opposed Soviet attempts to consolidate Moscow's control over its Comecon satellites. In order to ensure popular support he initiated a policy of liberalization (political amnesty and a return to national traditions).

Gheorghiu-Dej was stricken with cancer while attempting to gain increased autonomy within the Warsaw Pact. He died in Bucharest on March 19, 1965. Without any political culture, Gheorghiu-Dej was an able and unscrupulous political operator who knew how to take advantage of favorable circumstances. He remained a hard-line Stalinist for the entirety of his political career.

See also Comecon; Cominform; De-Stalinization; People's Democracy; Stalinism; Warsaw Pact.

FURTHER READING

Constantiniu, F. *O istorie sinceră a poporului român*. Bucharest: Univers Enciclopedic, 2002.

Tănase, S. *Elite și societate. Guvernarea Gheorghiu-Dej, 1948–1965*. Bucharest: Humanitas, 1998.

FLORIN CONSTANTINIU

Gierek, Edward

Edward Gierek (1913–2001) was born on January 6 in Porąbka, Poland, one of the largest coal-mining centers in Europe. When he was four, his father died in a mining accident, and a few years later Gierek emigrated to France with his stepfather, who was also a coal miner. There he finished grade school and, like the majority of workers' children in those days, went to work at thirteen, in a mine. He began his political activity in the French Communist Party and trade unions, but this work ended with his exile from France in 1934. Back in Poland, he did not make contact with the party.

After finishing military service, Gierek again went abroad in search of work and, in 1937, found himself in the Belgian coal-mining region of Limburg. Once he grew accustomed to his new environment, he enrolled in the Belgian Communist Party, more than a tenth of whose members were émigrés from Poland. During the German occupation, he worked in the resistance movement, mainly by supplying explosive materials, which he carried out of the mine he toiled in. After the liberation, Gierek ceased his activities in the Belgian party and signed up with a Polish émigré organization unofficially affiliated with the Polish Workers' (Communist) Party, and he quickly became its leader. In 1948, he was summoned to Poland and became a full-time party functionary. With the exception 1954–56, when he headed a section in the Central Committee, Gierek was first secretary of the Provincial Committee in Upper Silesia, a position he held until December 1970.

Any region concentrating on heavy industry and mining was appreciated by the government, and its manager was normally a member of the Political Bureau. Gierek was an efficient administrator, more valued as a manager than as an apparatchik, and Polish Katanga (Upper Silesia) set an example of regional prosperity. As a result, Gierek emerged as the best candidate to succeed a com-

promised Władysław Gomułka, and on December 20, 1970, he assumed the function of first secretary of the Central Committee of the Polish Communist Party. Gierek and his team issued the slogan "Building a New Poland," entailing a rapid modernization to be based on Western credits and licenses; they also emphasized individual consumption.

In the ensuing few years Poland actually did change for the better, which was all the more surprising since no basic reforms were undertaken in the economy's management. Liberalization took place, at least to some degree, and attempts were made to mend relations with the Church. Compared with Gomułka, Gierek was a man of the world (he knew French and Flemish); he liked to surround himself with people in the arts who were obedient to the regime, and he traveled around the country to meet "with the people." It was a period of détente, and so he could (and liked to) shine in fashionable society. All the U.S. presidents of the time visited Poland, and Gierek was a constant hunting partner of the French president.

Gierek's economic policy was based on Poland's dependence on the West, and this necessarily caused political troubles, as when the newly emerging democratic opposition found itself under the umbrella of Washington or Bonn, and economic difficulties, as when, after the collapse of the investment program in 1975–76, the burden of paying off loans proved too heavy for Poland. An economic crisis now set in, public dissatisfaction grew, and the government's legitimacy was questioned. The election of a Polish pope, John Paul II, was also added to the mix. The public was now gripped by a euphoria that struck a crushing blow to the system in general and Gierek's position in particular. When a wave of strikes began in summer 1980, Gierek found himself in a similar position to that of Gomułka ten years earlier. Recalling the experience of 1970, he was reluctant to resort to force, but his comrades in the administration then recognized that to appease the public, some guilty parties would have to be named. And thus, a few days after the signing of an agreement with the strike committees, Gierek was removed from power.

Over the next few years, Gierek and some members of his team were accused of corrupt practices and expelled from the party. All their privileges were renounced, their decorations taken from them, and when martial law was declared they were even interned. Gierek, to the end of his life, nourished hatred toward those who had removed him from power and humiliated him. He vented these feelings in his memoirs, which were published in 1989. Later on, some of the more negative effects of the restructuring of the system in Poland provoked nostalgia for the "Gierek era," so that quite a few Poles bade him farewell with heavy hearts when he died on July 29, 2001.

See also Catholic Church; Gomułka, Władysław; Socialist Camp; Soviet Bloc.

FURTHER READING

Lepak, K. J. *Prelude to Solidarity: Poland and the Politics of the Gierek Regime.* New York: Columbia University Press, 1988.

Pradetto, A. *Techno-Bureaucratic Socialism: Poland in the Gierek Era (1970–1980).* Frankfurt am Main: Lang, 1991.

Rolicki, J. *Edward Gierek: His Life and the Birth of a Legend.* Warsaw: Iskry, 2002.

ANDRZEJ PACZKOWSKI

Gomułka, Władysław

Władysław Gomułka (1905–82) was born on February 6 in the Polish village of Bialobrzegi to a working-class family. On finishing public school he worked in petroleum refineries as a metalworker. He began political work in youth organizations in 1923, and joined the Communist Party of Poland (CPP) in 1926. Gomułka was a full-time worker in pro-Communist trade unions as well as in one of the parties that were legal adjuncts of the CPP. Although he took part in Profintern congresses in Moscow (1930 and 1931), was a student of the Moscow Comintern School (1934–35), and was a member of the party's Central Trade Section, he belonged to the operatives who did the "dirty work," and wrote occasionally for the party newspapers or spoke to small groups of striking workers. Gomułka was arrested many times (he was even shot once trying to escape) and twice convicted.

At the onset of World War II Gomułka was still in prison, but he escaped and eventually succeeded in illegally crossing the Soviet-German border. Like most Polish Communists, he held a minor office job and carried on political activity in the small factory where he worked, in Lwów. In 1941 he was accepted into the Soviet Communist Party. After the outbreak of the German-Soviet war, though, he was not evacuated but returned to his original home. Ordered by the CPP to Warsaw in July 1942, he launched a political career and became a member of the CPP's Central Committee in January 1943. Following the death, under unexplained circumstances, of two general secretaries of the Central Committee superior to him, Gomułka was co-opted into the "ruling troika." Then, when the next general secretary superior to him died in November of the same year, Gomułka was given his post. He was a good conspirator and organizer and had his own political ideas, in which he combined a certain elasticity toward other left-wing groups with a firm conviction that only the Communists represented the real interests of the people. By 1944 Gomułka was, next to Boleslaw Bierut, the second most important figure in the country and the de facto leader of the party. He carried on a brutal struggle with his political opponents, but was not an enthusiast for such Soviet ideas as collectivization.

Gomułka demonstrated his independence when, in spring 1948, he offered to mediate in the Stalin–Tito conflict, and also when he pointed to the mistaken position of the CPP vis-à-vis the state. He called attention to "Luxemburgist" errors that the party had made in the populist question as well. In Moscow, Gomułka was regarded as falling into the category of "right-wing nationalist deviationist." Moreover, he found himself in a conflict with politburo comrades of Jewish origin, who—he maintained—were "cut off from the Polish nation." He informed Stalin of these objections. Then, in summer 1948, Gomułka was removed from the CPP leadership and shunted off to secondary government positions. In 1949 he was dismissed from the Central Committee, and in August 1951 was arrested, together with his wife. Yet Gomułka was never subjected to a show trial (perhaps because he refused to make any self-accusations), and in December 1954, when the "thaw" set in, he was released from prison. Until 1956, he was forbidden to engage in any political activity, but after Bierut's death (in March 1956) Gomułka began, more and more insistently, to demand his rehabilitation.

In the face of the growing social unrest in Poland, the majority of the Polish United Workers' Party recognized that the return of Gomułka, "Stalin's prisoner," to public life would allow them to calm the restless public. Gomułka agreed to return, but only if appointed leader of the party. And so, on October 19, 1956, in spite of the opposition of Khrushchev, the Central Committee elected Gomułka to the politburo, which in turn granted him the post of first secretary. Gomułka's return to power was greeted with enthusiasm by almost all of Polish society, and also favorably by the West, yet he had no intention of either expanding the freedoms of Polish citizens or reforming the economy (except for a retreat from collectivization). He succeeded in quickly stabilizing the political situation and consolidating his own power in the party. For a number of years he did not enjoy the Kremlin's full trust because of his efforts to mediate between the Soviet and Chinese leaderships. In addition to maintaining political stability in the country, Gomułka was eager to regularize Polish–West German relations—something he ultimately accomplished in 1970.

Though never a real Stalinist, Gomułka was an orthodox Communist in that he despised "bourgeois democracy" and intellectuals who were always working to achieve liberalization. But his allegiance to the preeminence of heavy industry led to economic stagnation and caused him to lose the confidence of most Polish citizens, whom he also alienated by launching a campaign against the church. Finally, things came to a political crisis, most spectacularly manifested by the student strikes of March 8–25, 1968, which he crushed by force. Another element of the crisis was the growing influence of young party workers—some of whom supported tendencies close to a "people's communism"—who were eager to eliminate the old Comintern elites and used anti-Semitism as a weapon. Gomułka did not place himself directly behind this movement, but he did permit an anti-Semitic and anti-intellectual campaign, resulting in the exodus from Poland of nearly twenty thousand persons of Jewish extraction. He was a radical opponent of the Prague Spring, and completely supported the plan for armed intervention in Czechoslovakia.

Gomułka extricated himself from these crises, but only for a short time. When workers' strikes broke out in the Baltic coast region in December 1970, and Gomułka ordered the army to suppress them (with more than forty persons killed as a result), Moscow distanced itself from him, and younger people exploited the opportunity and forced him to retreat from political life. An indignant Gomułka retired. He tried to defend his reasoning in letters to the Central Committee and extensive reminiscences, but was partially rehabilitated only shortly before his death (in Warsaw on September 1, 1982), mostly because the new leader, Wojciech Jaruzelski, was seeking various means of legitimizing his own regime.

See also De-Stalinization; People's Democracy; Socialist Camp; Soviet Bloc.

FURTHER READING
Bethell, Nicholas. *Gomulka: His Poland and His Communism.* London: Penguin Books, 1969.
Werblan, Andrzej. *Wladyslaw Gomulka: Sekretarz Generalny PPR.* Warsaw: Ksiazka i Wiedza, 1988.

ANDRZEJ PACZKOWSKI

Gorbachev, Mikhail

There is no reason to suppose that any other member of the Soviet politburo, on the eve of the death of Konstantin Chernenko in March 1985, would have pursued policies remotely similar to those of the man they chose unanimously to be Chernenko's successor: Mikhail Gorbachev. Those two statements may appear to contain a contradiction. Why vote unanimously for a person who would break with the consensus that had existed within the top echelon of the Soviet political elite?

There are three main reasons why the surviving politburo members did so. First, Gorbachev had consolidated his position as second secretary within the leadership, and there was no plausible rival who looked as if he could command a majority in the leadership. The remaining members of the politburo, all of them anxious to retain their seats at the top table, had nothing to gain and much to lose from opposing a near-certain winner. Second, Gorbachev had largely concealed his reformist intentions, coming closest to "outing" himself as a reformer with an innovative speech to a conference on ideology in December 1984, at a time when Chernenko was already in frail health and a weak position to put a stop to Gorbachev's rise. Third, Gorbachev was distinguished by an unusually open mind for a man who had spent his career in the Soviet Communist Party apparatus. He himself did not know in 1985 just how radical a departure from the past his policies would become. There were only ten members left in the ruling politburo when Chernenko died. All of the other nine subsequently opposed important elements of Gorbachev's domestic or foreign policy (or both). In some instances they voiced their criticisms within the politburo. In other cases, their condemnation became much sharper after they had been "retired" from politburo membership.

Gorbachev was born into a peasant family in the village of Privolnoe in Stavropol Krai in southern Russia on March 2, 1931. At different times in the 1930s both of his grandfathers were arrested on trumped-up political charges. Although his grandfathers survived their ordeal, Gorbachev noted years later that he knew what it was to experience the ostracism of living in the home of an "enemy of the people." Neighbors were too afraid to call on them, and other children avoided him. The war and early postwar years enabled the Gorbachev family to fully redeem themselves from their brush with the People's Commissariat of Internal Affairs, or the NKVD (which in the case of Gorbachev's maternal grandfather, had involved severe torture).

Gorbachev's father, Sergei, fought throughout the whole of the four years in which the Soviet Union was at war with Nazi Germany, and was wounded in Czechoslovakia as the end of the conflict was approaching. Returning to his work on the collective farm, he was helped by his son, who spent long summers as an assistant to his father on a combine harvester. In the summer of 1948, the Gorbachevs—father and son—brought in a record harvest. Gorbachev later recalled: "It was back-breaking labor twenty hours a day, with no more than three or four hours of sleep." The seventeen-year-old Mikhail received the Order of the Red Banner of Labor and his father received the higher Order of Lenin for their heroic efforts. While Mikhail was later to receive many other, higher Soviet awards, this was the one that always meant the most to him. (In sharp contrast with Leonid Brezhnev, he eschewed all awards after he became general secretary.)

To have established his credentials as a model manual worker was of significance for Gorbachev's subsequent career. While Moscow State University was expected to reserve some places for the children of workers and peasants, the chances of any particular child from a peasant home gaining a place in Russia's leading university were miniscule. Gorbachev's strong school record, the fact that he had been active in the Komsomol, and that he had already become a candidate member of the Communist Party all helped. What almost certainly clinched his entry to Moscow University, however, was the state award for heroic labor feats—a highly unusual acquisition for a teenager.

Moscow University, in turn, played a decisive part in Gorbachev's development. In his personal life, it was crucial, for it was there that the law faculty student, Gorbachev, met Raisa Titarenko, a student in the philosophy faculty. They were married in 1953, and their partnership remained an exceptionally close one until her death in

October 1999. Gorbachev caused a minor sensation in the early years of perestroika when he told a U.S. television interviewer that he discussed "everything" with his wife, including the most important issues of state policy.

Moscow University was critical also for Gorbachev's intellectual and cultural development. With all its limitations in the first half of the 1950s (especially during the earlier part of that period when Stalin was still alive), it nevertheless provided Gorbachev with a far better education than that achieved by other members of Brezhnev's politburo. He became the first Soviet leader since Lenin to graduate from a law faculty. His conversations with his fellow students, who in most cases had enjoyed a more privileged school education, and the full use that he and Raisa made of Moscow's cultural opportunities—within the limits of their modest means they indulged their love of the theater and cinema—also made him a much more broadly educated person than the likes of Brezhnev and Chernenko.

Gorbachev studied at Moscow University from 1950 to 1955, and graduated in the top echelon of academic achievers. He returned—with Raisa—to his native Stavropol, and began a career that saw him rise rapidly through, first, the local Komsomol and, subsequently, the regional party organization. By 1966 he was the first secretary of the Stavropol city party organization, and in 1970 he became Stavropol *kraikom* first secretary—that is to say, one of the regional party secretaries who ran the Soviet Union outside Moscow. For most of them, including Gorbachev, it carried Central Committee membership, which he attained the following year.

Gorbachev's first significant patron had been Fedor Kulakov, a first secretary of the Stavropol region during Gorbachev's earlier years back in his native territory who, by the 1970s, was a politburo member and the secretary of the Central Committee responsible for agriculture. But it was Kulakov's death in 1978 that led to Gorbachev's most significant promotion: the top leadership team in Moscow as the secretary of the Central Committee overseeing agriculture. Two other members of the politburo with Stavropol connections, Mikhail Suslov (who at one time had been the first secretary there) and Yuriy Andropov (the KGB chief, who was born in Stavropol Krai, and had been impressed by Gorbachev when he met him during the vacations he regularly took in his native region) were important supporters of Gorbachev's elevation to be the youngest member of the aging Brezhnev leadership team. At the time he took up residence in Moscow for the first time since his university student years, Gorbachev was forty-seven.

His subsequent promotion was also rapid. By 1979 he had been granted candidate membership of the politburo in addition to his secretaryship of the Central Committee. In 1980 he became a full member. When Andropov succeeded Brezhnev as general secretary on the latter's death in November 1982, he extended Gorbachev's supervisory responsibilities to embrace not just agriculture but also the economy as a whole. When Andropov's health was in terminal decline and he was no longer able to chair politburo meetings, he sent an addendum to a written report to the Central Committee, proposing that in his absence, the task of chairing the politburo and leading the secretariat should be handed to Gorbachev. This was an attempt to establish Gorbachev as heir apparent—something that was not acceptable to the old guard, who took advantage of Andropov's physical incapacity to ignore his wishes. Chernenko, in consultation with other senior colleagues, decided that Andropov's additional paragraphs referring to Gorbachev would simply not be read out to the Central Committee. Thus, with the active support of Dmitriy Ustinov and Andrey Gromyko, Chernenko was chosen as Soviet leader when Andropov died in February 1984. Both men knew that they would be able to rule supreme in their respective Ministry of Defense and Ministry of Foreign Affairs with the limited, and already physically feeble, Chernenko nominally running the country.

Andropov had, however, sufficiently advanced Gorbachev's seniority within the party hierarchy that he became the de facto second secretary to Chernenko with still wider supervisory responsibilities than hitherto. Moreover, when Chernenko was too ill to attend politburo meetings, it was Gorbachev who chaired them. Although a number of the older members of the politburo were unhappy about the prospect of a Gorbachev succession—not because they had an inkling of how radical an innovator he would become, but rather because they feared that he would be a new broom who would sweep them away—they could find no realistic alternative to him. Had Chernenko lived longer, the hard-line Leningrader Grigoriy Romanov might have become a serious rival to Gorbachev, but conveniently for those who hoped for change in the Soviet Union, Chernenko died on March 10, 1985. By the afternoon of March 11, Gorbachev was the Soviet Union's new leader.

Gorbachev began his general secretaryship as an energetic reformer and someone who believed that the Soviet system was capable of massive improvement. He sought from the outset to make the economy more efficient and to undertake a cultural and political liberalization. The word that Gorbachev used was "democratization," though in the early stages of perestroika that was a misnomer. By 1987 and still more from 1988, a serious process of democratization was under way, and the term was entirely appropriate. Among other concepts that made an appearance from the start of Gorbachev's leadership of the Soviet Communist Party, the two that had the greatest impact were glasnost, signifying openness or transparency, and perestroika itself—a suitably ambiguous notion, since those who were in favor of only minor restructuring and those who wished to reconstruct the Soviet system from its foundations upward could both subscribe to the term.

The New Political Thinking, which Gorbachev and his most reformist supporters espoused, preceded new political practice. Early in his general secretaryship Gorbachev replaced some of those who had been least enthusiastic about his elevation—notably, the senior secretary of the Central Committee, Romanov; the Moscow party first secretary, Viktor Grishin; and the chairman of the Council of Ministers, Nikolai Tikhonov. He also brought into the leadership allies, some of whom were only conditional supporters, though, and who were unwilling to continue their support as the policies that Gorbachev espoused became more radical. Notable among these newly promoted officials were Yegor Ligachev, Nikolai Ryzhkov, Alexander Yakovlev, Eduard Shevardnadze, and Vadim Medvedev.

Gorbachev's personnel changes were relatively speedy, but they did not by themselves amount to a break with Soviet political practice. Yet his espousal of serious political reform from January 1987 was a clear indication that the Soviet Union had a political leader quite different from his predecessors. In 1988 Gorbachev went much further. On his urging, the Nineteenth Party Conference in the summer of that year endorsed far-reaching reforms, of which the most notable was the proposal to have contested elections for a new legislature, the Congress of People's Deputies, which would have an inner body—the Supreme Soviet—elected by the Congress that would be in session for eight months of the year. The contrast with the single-candidate "elections" for the unreformed Supreme Soviet that was in session for only a few days each year could not have been sharper.

From the beginning of his general secretaryship, Gorbachev was also concerned with cutting military expenditure and improving the Soviet Union's relations with the outside world. He saw the Cold War both as a wasteful use of the country's resources and one of the causes of the relative backwardness of the civilian sector of the Soviet economy, as well as a source of dangerous tension that ran the risk of triggering a hot war, whether by accident or design. The catastrophe at the Chernobyl nuclear plant in 1986 underlined for Gorbachev the dangers to life on earth, many thousandfold greater, of nuclear war. As it happened, the U.S. president Ronald Reagan, for all his hard-line, anti-Communist credentials, had a horror of nuclear weapons. That, and not only a desire for U.S. military advantage over the Soviet Union, underlay his support for the so-called Strategic Defense Initiative—the (almost certainly unrealistic) attempt to construct a defensive system capable of intercepting an incoming rocket attack.

Thus, at successive summit meetings—in Geneva in 1985, Reykjavík in 1986, Washington, DC, in 1987, and Moscow in 1988—Gorbachev was able to reach agreement with Reagan on deep cuts in military arsenals. To achieve this Gorbachev was prepared to reverse the military decisions of his predecessors. Hard-liners, both in Moscow and Washington, expressed their unhappiness with parts of the new accords, but they were welcomed by the broad publics in both the West and the Soviet Union itself. Gorbachev's foreign policy was highly popular. Indeed, it is a myth, spread by Gorbachev's enemies both within Russia and the West, that Gorbachev was popular only in the West and not in the Soviet Union. On the contrary, until 1990—as the opinion poll data of the most reliable survey research center, headed by Tatiana Zaslavskaya and subsequently Yuriy Levada, testify—Gorbachev was the most popular person in Russia and the Soviet Union. It was as late as the early summer of 1990 that he was overtaken by Boris Yeltsin. In the last eighteen months of the Soviet Union's existence Gorbachev's popularity was in sharp decline, and in post-Soviet Russia he was also far from popular. He could at least take satisfaction from the fact that his nemesis, Yeltsin—according, again, to the reliable survey data of Levada's research team—had by the early years of the 21st century become substantially more unpopular than Gorbachev.

From summer 1988 onward, both the foreign and domestic policies that Gorbachev espoused went beyond mere reform. What was occurring was transformative change. Contested elections, together with the growing freedom of speech, assembly, religion, and not least, the mass media, made the political system different in kind from what it had been hitherto. In foreign policy, the withdrawal of Soviet troops from Afghanistan—another move popular with the Soviet public—was highly significant, but not as fundamental a break with the past as Gorbachev's announcement in 1988 that the people of each country had the right to decide for themselves what kind of economic and political system their state should have. When that precept was put to the test by the peoples of Eastern Europe in 1989, and the Soviet Union accepted the overt dismantling of its Communist system, the Cold War—which most Western observers would argue began with the Sovietization of Eastern Europe—was clearly over. While this outcome was in keeping with the policy goals of the United States and Western Europe, no Western leaders—whether Reagan, Margaret Thatcher, or anyone else—had expected that during their incumbency they would see the decommunization of Eastern Europe. The changes in Moscow were of a different order than anything they had imagined, except as a distant, long-term goal. And it was those changes that made possible systemic transformation in the eastern part of the European continent.

While the speed of change in Eastern Europe was politically embarrassing at home for Gorbachev, it added hugely to his already high standing in the West. There had been many skeptics, not least in the Reagan administration, who had contended that Gorbachev, with his charm and what they perceived as guile, was an even more dangerous adversary than his Soviet predecessors. They viewed him, wrongly, as a convinced Leninist who was trying to lull the West into a false sense of security.

Within the Soviet military and security establishment, and in substantial sections of the Communist Party apparatus, there was increasing concern in the course of 1989 both with the "loss" of Soviet positions abroad—even though their allies were not the peoples of Eastern Europe but instead a political stratum that relied, ultimately, on the threat of Soviet military intervention to keep their populations at bay. There was no less concern at the loss of "democratic centralism" and the "leading role of the Communist Party" at home. Democratization was a severe threat to vested interests, and Gorbachev found himself in the last years of perestroika under great pressure from conservative forces who had strong institutional bases within the party and governmental machines, and especially within the military and the KGB. It looked to him as if the big battalions, in the most literal sense, were on the side of the conservative opponents of change.

Along with concern about developments abroad, there was still greater disquiet about the rise of national aspirations and tensions within the Soviet Union itself. The liberalization and democratization of the Soviet political system had enabled the various nationalities that made up the Soviet Union to bring to the surface their accumulated grievances. The threat of the breakup of the Soviet Union began to be perceived as a real one, and no question preoccupied Gorbachev more during his last eighteen months in office than the attempt to secure agreement on a "renewed Union," a voluntary constitutional settlement or Union Treaty whereby all or, failing that, the great majority of union republics would endorse a loose federal system in place of the pseudofederation that the Soviet Union had been under Gorbachev's predecessors. He might indeed have been successful in holding within such a union a majority of the republics had not Yeltsin demanded Russian independence from the USSR. Yeltsin's ambition to remove Gorbachev took the form of asserting Russia's interests against the union as his quickest route to replacing Gorbachev in the Kremlin. The historic fact that Russia and Russians had been more than first among equals within this state—the successor state to the Russian empire and, in a sense, a greater Russia—counted for surprisingly little. The fact that the assertion of Russian independence from the union (which was a qualitatively different level of threat to it than a similar claim made by Estonia or Lithuania) might lead to the disintegration of the entire state counted for no more.

Gorbachev, from 1988 onward, was consciously engaged on a dismantling of the previously highly authoritarian political system. He strove, however, to prevent the disintegration of the Soviet state. Yet he was not prepared to do this, whatever the cost. If the price were to be massive repression—and a high cost in bloodshed would have been required, once expectations of national independence (especially in the Baltic states and Georgia) had been aroused—that was not acceptable to Gorbachev. His unwillingness to take more drastic steps to preserve the union was the prime cause of the attempted coup of August 1991 against him.

Gorbachev's role in the democratization of the political system, the introduction of a whole range of liberties, and ending the Cold War can be counted as his historic successes. His inability to resolve the nationality question was one of two major failures. Whether anyone

could have achieved a smooth transition from a unitary state with federal forms to a genuine federation, once national passions had been aroused and independence drives launched, must remain doubtful. Gorbachev's "error," in that case, was to allow such passions to emerge and such hitherto politically unthinkable claims to be asserted. Still, to have kept the lid on all forms of national dissent, while allowing greater freedom in other areas of activity, was scarcely a politically feasible or morally justifiable alternative.

His other major failure, it could be argued, was in economic reform. At the outset of perestroika, reform of the economy was high on the agenda, but it is indicative of Gorbachev's developing priorities that in 1987, the plenary session of the Central Committee on political reform preceded that on economic reform. There were many different proposals for improving the economy, and there was no consensus within the leadership on the best way forward. Gorbachev favored concessions to the market, but did not support unambiguous movement toward a capitalist system. His own political evolution took him from being a relatively orthodox Communist in his youth to a Communist reformer by the time he became general secretary, and then a socialist of a Social Democratic type by the end of the 1980s. To move the Soviet Union from a command economy to a social market economy proved to be extremely difficult, however. Gorbachev gave his blessing to a series of partial reforms, including the introduction of small-scale private enterprise and the founding of cooperatives (which in turn, were soon to become thinly disguised private enterprises), but he hesitated to free prices, knowing that this would mean huge price increases. It was left to Yeltsin in January 1992 to give the green light to Yegor Gaidar to proceed with such a policy—one that, arguably, was a painful necessity.

When it became clear that the Soviet Union could not be held together—especially following the further stimulus to disintegration provided by the failed August 1991 coup—except by using massive force, Gorbachev bowed to the inevitable and resigned from the presidency of the Soviet Union on December 25, 1991. He had become president in March 1990, and though he retained his leadership of the Communist Party, that election—by the Congress of People's Deputies of the USSR—was part of a conscious attempt on Gorbachev's part to shift power from the party to more appropriate state institutions.

Whether his political career as a whole is judged a failure or a success depends on whether the evaluation places a higher value on holding together a powerful state, even if that could be done only on an authoritarian basis, or whether leaving Russia a freer country than it had ever been, allowing the countries of Eastern and Central Europe to become independent, and removing the global threat of nuclear war between two rival superpowers should count for more. In the post-Soviet period, Gorbachev emerged still more clearly as a politician whose convictions had become those of a Social Democrat of a West European type. He headed his own foundation in Moscow, published memoirs and other volumes of reflections, and was a speaker in great demand throughout the world. In Russia, he was frequently blamed for what followed perestroika—in the Yeltsin era—and the breakup of the Soviet Union, which he had strived to avoid. Only with the passage of time is he likely to be held in the high esteem in his homeland that he was accorded during the first five of his seven years as the leader of a reformed superpower.

See also Chernobyl, Catastrophe of; Cold War; Coup in the USSR; New Thinking; Perestroika; Post-Soviet Communism.

FURTHER READING

Brown, A. *The Gorbachev Factor.* Oxford: Oxford University Press, 1996.

———. *Seven Years That Changed the World: Perestroika in Perspective.* Oxford: Oxford University Press, 2006.

Chernyaev, A. *My Six Years with Gorbachev.* University Park: Pennsylvania State University Press, 2000.

Gorbachev, M. *Memoirs.* London: Doubleday, 1996.

Gorbachev, M., and Z. Mlynář. *Conversations with Gorbachev: On Perestroika, the Prague Spring, and the Crossroads of Socialism.* New York: Columbia University Press, 2002.

Kaiser, R. *Why Gorbachev Happened: His Triumphs and His Failures.* New York: Simon and Schuster, 1991.

Ligachev, Y. *Inside Gorbachev's Kremlin.* New York: Pantheon Books, 1993.

ARCHIE BROWN

Gosplan

The Council of People's Commissars of Soviet Russia established a state planning commission, Gosplan for short, on February 22, 1921. Its functions were to institute and operate a unified state plan for the whole economy, and harmonize the plans and perspectives of other economic departments. The civil war was nearly at an end, but the tensions it had engendered were threatening to dismantle the Bolshevik regime from below. To avert this, Lenin was about to announce a sweeping curtailment of state power in the economy that soon became known as the New Economic Policy. Establishing Gosplan at this point was a signal of intentions for the distant future, not for immediate practical policy.

Some years would pass before the planned economy became a reality. In the meantime, Gosplan became a battleground between adherents of alternative approaches. Some favored planning as a means of economizing—that is, allocating scarce resources among competing private and public uses much as markets would, but more efficiently since, they believed, conscious planning would avoid the market system's unconscious tendency to temporary booms and slumps. Others were impatient with this limited notion, and preferred to think of the plan as an ambitious political mechanism to mobilize resources and enforce state priorities, leaving the residual to be rationed out among other users and consumers. In the political context of the 1920s the mobilization school of planning eventually squeezed out the economizers; this helped to give the Soviet Union's First Five-Year Plan, approved in April 1929, its character as a program to "build socialism" through sweeping state-led industrialization.

Gosplan was probably not as influential in the Stalinist state as the all-powerful "visible hand" that Western stereotypes sometimes supposed it to be, and its leaders were generally of the second rank. The role that Stalin gave it was nonetheless important. Having reorganized the economy on the strict hierarchical lines of a command system, Stalin now faced the problem of whom to trust: since he judged his other ministers and executives by economic results, all had an incentive to conceal the truth from him. Stalin needed some agents who would stand above the departmental battles for resources and rewards, and give him a truthful picture of the economy. To keep Gosplan obedient and loyal he purged it three times—in 1930, 1937, and 1949—but he also gave it the privilege of not being judged by the state of the economy or the degree of fulfillment of plans. He punished the planners only when they became advocates for other interests.

In keeping with this brief, Gosplan officials tended to stay out of detailed economic management as much as possible. In addition to the largely propagandistic five-year plans, they issued regular annual and quarterly plans that were binding on the economy as a whole and its ministerial subbranches. But these plans were too aggregated and preliminary to have much influence on what happened in particular factories and offices. The work of distributing planned tasks and resources, and linking individual suppliers and users went on within and between ministries. Thus, economic management remained more decentralized than appeared at first sight. It suited everyone to keep Gosplan out of this conflict-laden activity; the ministries retained a surprising degree of autonomy while Gosplan avoided having to take sides. This does not mean that the economy was left to manage itself, but the final responsibility for enforcing government priorities fell on political leaders in the politburo, not Gosplan technocrats.

It must be assumed that the role of Gosplan changed after Stalin as the Soviet political system shifted from harsh dictatorship to a somewhat more comfortable oligarchy, but until the more recent archives are opened we shall not know how. In total there were twelve five-year plans, with the last one finishing in 1990. Plan fulfillment appears to have improved over time, yet it seems unlikely that the reason was because Soviet producers became more obedient. Rather, they learned to manipulate plan indicators to show fulfillment. They also learned to manipulate planners' expectations, and as a result, plans became less ambitious and were increasingly likely to be fulfilled by lowering plans to match performance instead of improving performance.

In planning the mature Soviet economy, Gosplan appears to have faced three fundamental problems: how to measure the gap between potential productivity and performance in each activity, how to identify the activities where potential returns on investment and effort were rising, and how to release the necessary resources from those with declining returns. Where market mechanisms could solve these problems, Gosplan could not. Instead, it responded to all three difficulties by planning "from the achieved level"—that is, by planning in the next period to achieve the same results as in the period before, plus an increment to allow for growth. This routine proved not only conservative but also vulnerable to the manipulations described above, and contributed to the economy's increasing lag relative to the United States and Western Europe in the 1970s and 1980s.

See also Command Economy; Economic Reforms; Five-Year Plans; Planning.

FURTHER READING

Belova, E., and P. R. Gregory. "Dictator, Loyal, and Opportunistic Agents: The Soviet Archives on Creating the Soviet Economic System." *Public Choice* 113, nos. 3–4 (2002): 265–86.

Bergson, A. *The Economics of Soviet Planning*. New Haven, CT: Yale University Press, 1964.

Birman, I. "From the Achieved Level." *Soviet Studies* 30, no. 2 (1978): 153–72.

Carr, E. H., and R. W. Davies. *A History of Soviet Russia*. Vol. 3, *Foundations of a Planned Economy, 1926–1929*, part 1. London: MacMillan, 1969.

Ellman, M. *Socialist Planning*. Cambridge: Cambridge University Press, 1979.

Harrison, M. *Soviet Planning in Peace and War, 1938–1945*. Cambridge: Cambridge University Press, 1985.

Zaleski, E. *Planning for Economic Growth in the Soviet Union, 1918–1932*. Chapel Hill: University of North Carolina Press, 1971.

———. *Stalinist Planning for Economic Growth, 1933–1952*. Chapel Hill: University of North Carolina Press, 1980.

MARK HARRISON

Gottwald, Klement

Klement Gottwald (1896–1953), born out of wedlock in what is now the Czech Republic, began studying at the age of twelve to be a cabinetmaker in Vienna, where he came into contact with the workers' movement. When he returned home at the age of twenty, he was already a figure in the Social Democratic youth. A year later he was called to military service and spent the next three years on various World War I fronts. Later he worked as a laborer in a furniture factory. Gottwald became a member of the Communist Party of Czechoslovakia (CPCz) in 1921, the year of its founding.

In 1921, he worked as an administrator and later an editor for the Communist press in Slovakia. He established contacts with various officials, many of whom later formed the circle of his closest coworkers. The Bolshevization of the CPCz was an important milestone in Gottwald's political career. In the first round of this process, in 1924–25, he unfailingly adhered to the positions taken by the Comintern, which at the time was criticizing the so-called right-wing direction in the CPCz. At a CPCz congress in 1925, Gottwald was made a member of the Central Committee and the organizational secretariat, and also became a secretary of the CPCz's Central Committee. His rapid rise to the highest posts obscured two proclivities that followed him for his whole political life. First, the identity of his views with the Comintern developed into an obsequious submission to the policies of the USSR. The second was his natural penchant to connect with Moscow—something that enabled him to break away quite easily from his former political and personal friends, and sometimes to forge outright enmity with them.

In 1927 and 1928, the party's leadership began to attract increasing criticism for the slow and inconsistent pace of its Bolshevization. The CPCz was undergoing an inner-party crisis. Gottwald, who had already concentrated a group of young functionaries around him, became the chief party malcontent. As a member of the Comintern commission that was addressing the crisis, Gottwald, speaking in the name of the opposition group, mounted a stern criticism of the then-prevailing party leadership. He emerged victorious in the ensuing debate, and the Comintern made him temporary head of the party. The Fifth Congress, in 1929, which was the start of the second round of Bolshevization, named him general secretary of the party. That same year he also made his first entrance into Parliament.

Gottwald assumed the leadership of the party on the eve of an economic crisis. He concentrated on managing the societal struggles whose success was being impeded by the sectarian politics of the Comintern. At a meeting of executive leaders of the Comintern—of which he was a member, later to become a member of its Secretariat—Gottwald gave a lecture about the lessons to be drawn from the most recent and largest strike in the country, which occurred in Most in 1932. He was able to adapt the Comintern's policies, which had shifted in 1935 toward those of the people's front, to the special conditions of Czechoslovakia. The struggle that had been carried on up to then against the republic and the bourgeois democratic establishment was now converted into a defense of democracy as well as an effort to maintain it. Gottwald pressed this line actively and tried to gain the authority of even his erstwhile political opponents. His work in defending Czechoslovakia culminated in the decisive stand he took against the Munich agreement in 1938. Gottwald's subordination to the Comintern had become more pronounced in the 1930s. The positions he took reflected two models of the CPCz's relationship with the Comintern and the frequent criticism of the former by the latter. On the one hand, he took part in the political liquidation of a critic of the Comintern (J. Guttmann, though Gottwald had originally agreed with his views); on the other hand, he did not defend himself against the CPCz's criticism and accepted its condemnation of him with a show of self-criticism. In November 1938, he left for exile in the USSR. On his arrival he was obliged to defend the actions of the party during the Munich talks—something he managed successfully.

Gottwald's activity in exile first concentrated on the political management of the home (Czechoslovak) anti-Nazi resistance. With the entry of the USSR into the war, he expanded his work to include organizing armed resistance and bringing the CPCz-led Prague resistance closer together with the exiled government's resistance led from London. During the last two years of the war, he devoted himself to making plans for a liberated Czechoslovakia. He was in charge of preparations for a postwar program that included the constitution of a new government. This exile period was an important phase in Gottwald's political career. He was recognized as one of the main representatives of the resistance and the now-liberated republic. He gained new knowledge about the Soviet Union and the Comintern, thereby strengthening his connection with these two entities. The wave of big political trials in the Soviet Union, which Gottwald had unfailingly supported, was slowly coming to a halt. Still, he had become familiar with the practices of the People's Commissariat for Internal Affairs and the existence of concentration camps. He also learned about the Comintern's attempts to remove him from his party leadership and was uneasy about this fact during his entire exile in the USSR, and so he had had no contact with Stalin until January 1945.

In May 1945, Gottwald returned to Prague as a recognized and also feared political figure. It became clear during his first weeks back that he would head the strongest party, which would play a decisive role in the new state. The CPCz leadership agreed to a division of labor between the general secretary, who would answer for the activity of the party, and the chair, who would be devoted to the work of party governance. At first Gottwald occupied the post of vice chair of the party administration. After the victorious elections in May 1946 he became chair of the party administration. He formulated the political line of the party, defined its main goals, and was behind most of the important decisions of the governance and its programs. His political activities focused on one goal: gaining a monopoly of party power, a condition for installing a socialist government based on the Soviet model. Gottwald achieved this aim through the Prague Coup of February 1948, in which he played a leading role.

The February 1948 victory of the CPCz strengthened Gottwald's authority such that he was now untouchable within the party, with his views never subject to doubt. Four months after the coup he was named president of the republic. The merger of the highest functions in both the party and state assured his position as the leading figure in the Communist dictatorship. For five years he alone determined, approved, and provided the justification for the development of Czechoslovak society and the state, and the rebuilding of socialism there according to the Soviet model. He was familiar with all that attended such a socialist transformation: the unlawful acts, the political show trials, and other crimes that had to accompany it if it was to succeed. He was either directly involved in all the decisions vital to the Soviet-based restructuring or personally approved them.

Gottwald died on March 14, 1953, soon after his return from Stalin's funeral. He had been suffering from the effects of an earlier venereal disease. The cause of death officially given was a breach in his aortic wall and blood hemorrhaging into his lungs.

During his life, Gottwald had quickly become the leading functionary of the CPCz, possessed of both the experience of Comintern policies and practice as well as parliamentary democracy, in which his party moved freely. He used this experience in the party's struggle during 1945 to 1948, first for power and then for a monopoly of power. His name was in the forefront of both the party's rise to power and its establishment of a Communist regime. He became a symbol of the CPCz both quite naturally and as a result of overt propaganda. From the time he assumed the party's highest function he not only initiated but ultimately decided all policies. He had the ability to interpret the directives of the Comintern and, later, to adapt Soviet imperatives to the specific conditions in Czechoslovakia. It was part of his political skill that he was able to define a primary goal in a concise manner, and with just a few arguments, make things clear to both the party and a large part of the general public.

Gottwald was the foremost personality during the worst and most threatening times of postwar Czechoslovakia. He was the chief constructor of the foundations of the Communist regime, and the ensuing transformation of a democratic and economically advanced country into a Communist dictatorship, which brought with it all sorts of cruelties, persecutions, political trials, and murders in its struggle against its so-called enemies. Gottwald's relationship with and attitude toward the Soviet Union played a huge role in the evolution and fortunes of Czechoslovak state and society, and also his own political activity. His submissiveness to Moscow both symbolized and reinforced the dependence of Czechoslovakia on the USSR. Gottwald's policies were contrary to Czechoslovak interests and served instead the big-power goals of Moscow. But Gottwald's alliance with the Soviet Union and its Stalin-led leadership displayed one more feature.

Gottwald's return in spring 1945 from his long years of exile in Moscow and assumption of major functions in the state lifted his own confidence while also earning him the recognition of the Soviet authorities, and he strove to adhere to the Soviet line in his practical politics. But even back then, a powerful factor in Gottwald's political thinking and actions was his ideological as well as political dependence on the sovereign socialist power, the center of the Communist movement. Gottwald never really escaped this ideological dependence: his conviction that the Soviet model was the only possible socialist system. After February 1948, his decision making on important political and economic questions was not only influenced but actually determined by the desires, prompting, and outright demands of Moscow along with the views of his Soviet advisers. Yet a further trait stood out in Gottwald's relationship with the USSR, and that was his personal fear of Moscow, which grew even stronger when he discovered a listening device in his apartment. His fear caused him to decline to travel to the USSR (from September 1948 to October 1952, he never once visited the country).

Among the reasons for Gottwald's submissiveness toward Moscow were certain personal characteristics. He was afraid that Moscow would suspect him of unfriendliness, weakness, and disobedience, and his fear took many forms. Out of concern for his own fate or of being suspected of protecting enemies, he had many of his coworkers and friends imprisoned, and eleven of them executed. Not long after 1948, Gottwald began again to drink excessively. His habit became worse after the arrests of some leading Communists. In the last years of his life, he became unable to manage party organs or execute the functions of his office for several days at a time. Gottwald's political career ended with the collapse of his political personality.

See also People's Democracy; Prague Coup; Sovietization; Stalinism.

FURTHER READING

Budinsky, L. *Deset prezidentů*. Prague: Knižní klub, 2003.

Gottwald, K. *La Cecoslovacchia verso il socialismo*. Preface P. Secchia. Rome: Rinascita, 1952.

K padesátinám s. K. Gottwalda. Prague, 1946.

Matějka, J. *Klement Gottwald*. Prague: Orbis, 1973.

Nečásek, F. *O Kelentu Gottwaldovi*. Prague: SNPL, 1954.

Pernes, J. *Takoví nám vládli*. Prague: Brana, 2003.

KAREL KAPLAN

Gramsci, Antonio

Antonio Gramsci (1891–1937) was born in Ales, in the province of Cagliari, on January 22, the fourth of seven children born to Francesco, an employee at the Registry Office, and Giuseppina Marcias, a housewife. In 1911 he graduated from the Dettori high school in Cagliari, where he had previously frequented a socialist milieu and had first read Karl Marx. In October of that year he enrolled in the Department of Modern Literature and Philology at Turin University. It was in 1913, on his return from Sardinia, that he joined the Italian Socialist Party (Psi). When the war broke out he was critical of the neutralist majority in the Psi, and the following year adopted the positions of the Zimmerwald Left (headed by Lenin, it argued the proletariat ought to fight its class enemies in a civil war, rather than each other as foot soldiers in the service of imperialist wars). Between 1916 and 1918, his awareness of the epochal nature of the war and the Russian Revolution was taking shape, together with a clarification of his Marxist orientation. Having abandoned his studies, he became an editor of *Grido del Popolo* and the Turin section of *Avanti!*

Gramsci's first reflections on the Russian Revolution refer to the February Revolution, which he interpreted as a proletarian, not a Jacobin, revolution. Well before October, Gramsci shared Lenin's position that a socialist revolution in backward Russia was possible. So when the Bolsheviks came to power Gramsci wrote a famous article, "The Revolution against 'Capital'" (December 1, 1917), in which he justified the historical event, basing his argument on an interpretation of Marx that was also a preview of some of the future developments in his "philosophy of praxis." After the revolution the Bolsheviks' destinies diverged from those of European socialism, and Gramsci, by adopting their positions, not only cut his ties with the reformist wing but also started his detachment from the "intransigent" majority of the Psi.

At the same time, he immediately understood the hegemonic challenge that President Woodrow Wilson's "fourteen points" posed for the Russian Revolution. The United States was assuming the position of new hegemonic world power, and Gramsci underlined the progressive nature of the "structure of the world" that was emerging. In his opinion, Wilson's ideology was representative of the intention to build a "large supranational bourgeois state" that would create a favorable environment for the unification and integration of the world market. In a long-term perspective, therefore, the United States was "perhaps the greatest force in modern world history," but only "after Russia," because now "historical initiative" had passed into the hands of the proletariat. In actuality Gramsci's reflections exposed a contradiction that was to face the Communist movement from the outset: defining internationalism while facing the need to defend and preserve the proletarian state. As in the case of other Communists, Gramsci also thought that the USSR would be integrated into a new international order only "when the proletariat will have established its political dictatorship in the rest of the world."

Following the example of the Russian Revolution, he identified the Soviet as the organ of socialist transformation. At this point his break with Italian maximalism was outlined. It was also how his work of translating Bolshevism "into the national historical idiom" began, and it would radically transform his understanding of Marxism. In April 1919 together with Palmiro Togliatti, Angelo Tasca, and Umberto Terracini, Gramsci founded *L'Ordine Nuovo*. This weekly was published until Christmas 1920, and later was replaced, beginning January 1, 1921, by the daily *L'Ordine Nuovo*, which became the first organ of the Communist Party of Italy, founded in Leghorn on January 21. Gramsci devoted himself principally to the diffusion of the writings of Lenin and the other principal exponents of Bolshevism; this occurred during the brief period in which it really looked as if the Russian Revolution might be only the first manifestation of a world revolution. The myth of the Russian Revolution had conquered the workers and the socialist milieu in Turin, and *L'Ordine Nuovo*'s purpose became that of studying the concrete conditions for a proletarian revolution in Italy. The journal thus became the incubator for the factory council movement, an Italian variant of that council movement that between 1919 and 1920, had emerged as a revolutionary force in northern Germany, Bavaria,

Austria, and Hungary, and influenced the working-class movement in many other parts of the world. It was therefore also the crucible that transformed a group of remarkable intellectuals into revolutionary leaders with special characteristics.

During the years in which they were engaged with *L'Ordine Nuovo*, their view of the proletarian revolution became sharper, and its essential nucleus gave Gramsci's further reflections a unique character in the history of communism, socialism, and Marxism. To put it concisely, for him the "actuality of the revolution" emerged from the dramatic yet dynamic global situation that World War I had produced. With the end of the old liberal order prewar economic arrangements had been shattered, subjected to the crushing pressure of Anglo-American capitalism. Gramsci believed that only with the guidance of the proletariat would it be possible to reconstruct the global economy, naturally on a new basis that would have marked the advent of the "International." Insofar as Italy was concerned, he thought that what had been an essential element in the Russian Revolution—in other words, the ability of the working class to involve the peasant masses that the war had brought onto the historical stage in its political actions—could be replicated there as well. What was peculiar to Gramsci's perspective was his attributing to the working class the role of unifying the North and South of the country—the only social agent capable of eliminating the internal and international weakness of the Italian state.

Gramsci was editor in chief of the daily *L'Ordine Nuovo* until May 1922, when he was sent to Moscow as a party representative to the International. In August 1922, in Serebrjannyi Bor sanatorium, in the vicinity of Moscow, he met Julia Shucht, his future wife. Daughter of Apollon A. Shucht (a "penniless aristocrat," opponent of the czar, Bolshevik militant, and personal friend of Lenin's), Julia had been born in 1896 in Geneva and had studied in Rome, where in 1915 she had graduated in violin. She had joined the Bolshevik Party in 1917, and had participated in the October Revolution with her family. His relation with Julia Shucht is one of the most complex chapters in Gramsci's biography: the relations between her and Gramsci soon became an important part of the complex web of relations and disagreements with the Communist Party of Italy, the Russian party, and the Comintern, and they would leave their mark on the Italian leader's life during his long years in prison. Shucht's tasks in the Russian party, and especially her work during 1924 as a functionary of the political police, were

the source of crucial, political limitations in the emotive aspects of their relationship and private life, which up to November 1926, Gramsci and Shucht had considered strictly consensual limits. Later, prison and distance were to cast a long shadow on their relationship.

In May 1923, at a time when fascism had already been in power six months, Gramsci started to exchange letters with Palmiro Togliatti, Umberto Terracini, and Mauro Scoccimarro with the intent of forming a new party leadership group around the old core from *L'Ordine Nuovo*. This is how his engagement with political leadership started, and it led him to replace Amadeo Bordiga at the head of the party and abandon his extreme Left line in the context of the Bolshevization of Communist parties and the "socialism in one country" line that were the order of the day in the Soviet Union. Gramsci created a framework for his activities by grounding his analyses in the differences between the Russian and Italian revolutions, which in their turn were inserted in the wider framework of reflections on the morphological differences between East and West; when it came to Italy itself, he focused his attention on the so-called southern question (an important Italian debate about the impact of the unequal development of the country's northern and southern areas). In September 1923 Gramsci started a new daily, this time choosing *l'Unità* as its name (its subtitle was *Workers' and Peasants' Daily*). In the elections of April 6, 1924, Gramsci was elected deputy in the Veneto region, and in May he returned to Italy from Vienna.

In August he was elected secretary and started to prepare for the Third Congress, which would change the party's original culture. The congress was held in Lyon in January 1926. The originality of this *Lyon Theses* lay in his choosing the southern question as the central issue for the party's program. The "national function" of the working class was located in its ability to resolve Italian "dualism," giving the country a unity that the bourgeoisie had not succeeded in achieving. The keystone of the whole program was the alliance of northern workers with southern peasants. These lines of inquiry derived from Gramsci's more detailed analysis of fascism, which he considered to be on the one hand the heir of the protectionist northern bloc that had dominated Italy since unification, while on the other hand it exhibited significant innovations, and he identified the most important as the mass following it had managed to generate. The "hegemony of the proletariat," the central category of debate within the Bolshevik leadership group between 1923 and

1924, which Gramsci used to promote the party's Bolshevization, led to him to delve deeper into the "complex superstructures," which were principally responsible for the differences between East and West, and even for those between capitalist countries. The "political issue of intellectuals" emerged forcefully, and not casually, given the Italian state's characteristics. This topic was first addressed in an essay by Gramsci on the southern question (which was published in Paris only in 1930).

In the fall of 1926, alarmed by the possibility of a definite break within the Bolshevik leadership group, the Political Office of the Communist Party of Italy asked Gramsci to write a letter to the Central Committee of the Russian party informing it of the Italian party's adoption of the majority line, but also expressing its concern about the events that were unfolding and inviting all factions to avoid extreme solutions. In Moscow Togliatti deemed the letter "inopportune," and requested that the Steering Committee of the Communist Party of Italy authorize Togliatti not to submit the letter and wait for the reunion of the enlarged Executive of the Comintern in November to do so. On November 1, in the presence of Jules Humbert-Droz, who represented the International, the Italian Communist Party's (Pci) Central Committee held a clandestine meeting in a town in the Polcevera valley, near Genoa, and agreed with the resolutions adopted by the majority of the Russian party. Gramsci was unable to participate because, recognized by the police on his way to the meeting, he had to return to Rome, where on November 8, 1926, he was arrested. His letter had led the top leadership in the Russian party to suspect that the Pci might adopt Trotsky's positions, and from that moment on the letter was the pretext for recriminations and accusations of "wavering" that the Comintern repeatedly addressed to the Pci. The suspicion was principally due to the accusation of nationalism that Gramsci had directed at the behavior and platform of both the majority and oppositions. The origin of this failure was seen to lie in the Russian party's inability, after it had conquered power, to elaborate the proletariat's hegemony by forming new groups of intellectuals, and hence its inability to proceed with the construction of a new society. An extremely important topic that was to form the core of Gramsci's political reflections in prison was thus brought more sharply into focus.

After having been briefly held under house arrest in Ustica, Gramsci was tried by a special tribunal, and on June 4, 1928, was sentenced to over twenty years in prison. In July he was sent to a facility in Turi, province of Bari, where he remained until November 19, 1933, after which he was hospitalized, but still detained, in a clinic in Formia, starting on December 7. He stayed there until August 24, 1935, and from October 25 he was on probation. Gramsci was then transferred to Rome, but as soon as he had reacquired his freedom, he had a cerebral hemorrhage and died two days later.

After his arrest Gramsci's principal contacts were Tatiana Shucht, Julia's sister, for private and family matters—she was to assist him until his death and completely share his positions—and Piero Sraffa, one of his best friends from the times of *L'Ordine Nuovo*. From 1929 on, they were also his only contacts with the party and Togliatti, who personally followed the prisoner's situation. His relations with his wife, who had returned to Moscow with their two sons, and with the party soon became difficult. From 1930 on, after the failure of the first attempts to free him using a prisoner exchange agreed to by the Italian and Soviet governments, his suspicions about the party's loyalty toward him combined with his intuition about his wife's difficulties in corresponding with him—a function not so much of the illness that was consuming her but rather of the police control she was subjected to because she was tied to a foreign Communist leader who disagreed with the USSR's policies. He would only begin to openly connect the state of his relationship with his wife to the fact that he was now on the party's margins and to air his suspicions about the "double prison" he was subjected to—the Fascist prison and Stalin's—starting in February 1933. But the distance, silence, and suspicions notwithstanding, Gramsci never expressed a desire to leave Shucht. Among the papers from the last year of his life, there is a draft, written in Sraffa's handwriting, dated April 18, 1937, of a request that once free, he be allowed to leave the country to join his family in the Soviet Union; he intended to send it to the Italian authorities after his release.

In January 1929 Gramsci was given permission to write, and starting on February 8 began to compile the *Prison Notebooks*. The *Notebooks* were conceived as a continuation in the field of thought of the political struggle that Gramsci could no longer participate in directly, during the period of sectarian infighting in the Comintern, which had adopted the "class against class" slogan as well as the theory of "social fascism." In July 1929 this line was also imposed on the Pci, which reluctantly complied, abandoning the policies that Gramsci had developed in the period from 1924 to 1926. Informed of these events, Gramsci was firmly opposed, and instead proposed, during the conversations he held with comrades in Turi, to call a constitutional convention. In the prison's "collective" this led to his marginalization. It is impossible to understand the *Prison Notebooks* without taking the contemporary involution of the USSR and the Communist movement into account—an eclipse whose theoretical origins Gramsci intended to examine, and that he thought could be partially remedied by starting to elaborate new ideas and a new program, a way of also reacting to his defeat.

The *Notebooks*'s research program started from the premise that it was first of all necessary to arrive at a valid interpretation of the crisis of 1929, but also of the postwar crisis and the war itself, as the failed solutions to a previous crisis. While the international Communist movement based its policies (and its reason for existing) on the theory of the "general crisis of capitalism," in February 1933 Gramsci wrote that while studying the events that "form a catastrophic continuum from 1929 to today," "it will be necessary to fight whoever will want [to find] a single cause or origin [for it]," since one was instead dealing with a "complex process." If one were then to inquire about its origin, one could state that "the entire post-war period is one of crisis" and "for some (and perhaps they are not mistaken) the war itself is a manifestation of this crisis." In fact, "one of the fundamental contradictions" that explained the origin of these crises was that "while economic life is based on the necessary premise . . . of cosmopolitanism, the life of the state has been developing increasingly towards 'nationalism,' 'self-sufficiency,' etc. One of the most glaring characteristics of the 'current crisis' therefore, is nothing more than the exasperation of the nationalistic element in the economy." In other words, the crises were the result of the contrast between the cosmopolitanism of the economy and the nationalism of politics.

Added to the consequences of the Russian Revolution and the pressure that U.S. power was beginning to exercise on the structure of the world, the masses' new subjectivity, a by-product of the war, demanded that both the world's economy and its politics be organized in a new manner; if not, the nation-state's crisis would take on catastrophic proportions. The conclusion that Gramsci reached—that "even progressive and innovative groups" were not able to address the crisis of the state—was a way of questioning the Comintern's policies and the nature of Stalin's USSR. To Gramsci it appeared to exhibit features of "Caesarism" (even if in a progressive form), in which the hegemonic content "of the new so-cial group that has formed the new type of state" was still "prevalently of an economic nature." This critique was directed principally at the outlines of the USSR's economic planning, but Gramsci took note of the servile and scholastic conception of culture that the totalitarian state was imposing, and criticized the poverty of "Soviet Marxism." The "Russian experiment" was revealed as incapable of expansion and devoid of a hegemonic base, since it did not have (or did not yet have) universal values to propose.

These analyses implied a shift in judgment about the historical relevance of the October Revolution. In order to characterize the current phase in world politics Gramsci introduced a new paradigm, and substituted the category of "relative stabilization" with that of "passive revolution"—a valid criterion to outline an "organic" change that was, however, occurring in a "molecular" fashion, because the forces that should be representing the historical antithesis were not able to fulfill their role and so the changes occurred under the direction of the old ruling classes. The principal agent in this passive revolution at the global level was the United States. In 1934 Gramsci outlined a farsighted interpretation of "Americanism": he observed that with the "relentless growth of its economic production," America would force Europe to "change the shape of its excessively antiquated socio-economic order"; perceived that a "transformation of the material basis of European civilization" was taking place; and foresaw the "birth of a new civilization," whose protagonists would be the social groups behind the new industries. Just at the moment when Europe's destiny seemed to be a function of the dramatic choice between fascism and Bolshevism, Gramsci instead thought that by adapting "Fordist regulation" to the relation between capital and labor, and with the creation of a consumer culture, European society might be reorganized on a new democratic basis that was more inclusive and more far-reaching. Americanism and Fordism were in his estimation the really important developments, and those that pointed toward the choices of the future.

Compared with the "command economy" of Stalin's USSR—this was Gramsci's thought—the "programmed economy" of Americanism was a superior form of planned economy because it did not eliminate the market, but regulated it politically on the basis of a compromise between the most important classes. In this perspective, fascism appeared as the principal agent of the passive revolution in Europe because it expressed the need for the old ruling classes to maintain control of the passage from "economic individualism" to a "programmed economy," avoiding a compromise with the working class and destroying its autonomy so as to contain the influence of the October Revolution. But Gramsci did not conclude that in the cage of the corporatist state, the premises for an economy destined to free itself from the structures of the totalitarian state would be formed.

In Gramsci's thought, analytic categories correlate with strategic categories. The concept of passive revolution corresponds, at the political level, with that of a "war of position." On the basis of this correlation, he rethought the history of the previous fifty years. The formula of "permanent revolution," based on the "war of movement" concept, had come about "before 1848 as a scientific expression of the Jacobin experience from 1789 to the Thermidor." In Europe after 1870, it was "elaborated and overcome in political science with the formula of 'civil hegemony' " because the principal factors in the political struggle had changed (mass parties, labor unions, and the growth of the state's role), while economic interdependence had curtailed the autonomy of national economies. The passage from a "war of maneuver" to a war of position required not only a different vision of the "path to power" but also a much more sophisticated conception of the state than the one Lenin had elaborated in *State and Revolution*, because the balance of forces necessary to guarantee the stability of the state both internally and on the international level made the reaching of a "compromise" between the most important classes necessary. In sum, for Gramsci the "state is all that complex of practical and theoretical activities with which the ruling class justifies and maintains its rule; not only, but it also manages to obtain the active consent of the governed." And this conception obviously went beyond or at least radically modified the theory of the "dictatorship of the proletariat," which is not compatible with Gramsci's notion of hegemony.

See also Americanism; Bolshevism; Bolshevization; Comintern; Dictatorship of the Proletariat; Fascism; Marxism, Western; Socialism in One Country; Soviets.

FURTHER READING

Femja, J. V. *Gramsci's Political Thought: Hegemony, Consciousness and the Revolutionary Process.* Oxford: Clarendon Press, 1981.
Giasi, F., ed. *Gramsci nel suo tempo.* 2 vols. Rome: Carocci, 2008.
Paggi, L. *Antonio Gramsci e il moderno principe.* Rome: Editori Riuniti, 1970.
———. *Le strategie del potere in Gramsci: tra fascismo e socialismo in un solo paese, 1923–1926.* Rome: Editori Riuniti, 1984.
Togliatti, P. *La formazione del gruppo dirigente del Partito comunista italiano nel 1923–1924.* Preface P. Spriano. Rome: Editori Riuniti, 1984.
Vacca, G. *Appuntamenti con Gramsci: introduzione allo studio dei Quaderni del carcere.* Rome: Carocci, 1999.
———, ed. *Gramsci e il Novecento.* 2 vols. Rome: Carocci, 1999.

GRAMSCI'S WORKS

Gramsci a Roma, Togliatti a Mosca. Il carteggio del 1926. Ed. C. Daniele. Torino: Einaudi, 1999.
Lettere, 1926–1935 (with Tania Schucht). Ed. A. Natoli and C. Daniele. Torino: Einaudi, 1997.
Letters from Prison. Ed. F. Rosengarten. New York: Columbia University Press, 1994.
Prison Notebooks, I–III. Ed. and trans. J. A. Buttigieg. New York: Columbia University Press, 1992–2007.
Quaderni del carcere. Ed. Critica dell'Istituto Gramsci. Torino: Gerratana, Einaudi, 1975.
Selections from Political Writings (1910–1920). London: Lawrence and Wishart, 1977.
Selections from Political Writings (1921–1926). London: Lawrence and Wishart, 1978.
Selections from the Prison Notebooks. London: Lawrence and Wishart, 1971.

GIUSEPPE VACCA

Grand Alliance, The

The "Grand Alliance" is the most commonly used name for the World War II coalition of Britain, the Soviet Union, and the United States, an appellation popularized by Winston Churchill in his history of the Second World War. During the war the Americans usually called the coalition the "United Nations," while the British preferred "the Allies." For the Soviets the Grand Alliance was "the anti-Hitler coalition," a label that reflected their concept of the war as an anti-Nazi struggle and also the fact that the USSR did not enter the war against Japan until August 1945. Churchill's retrospective use of the term Grand Alliance harked back to his prewar campaign for a grand alliance against Hitler and was designed to emphasize his own role in the formation and promotion of the wartime coalition.

The two decisive events in the formation of the Grand Alliance were the German invasion of the Soviet Union in June 1941 and the American entry into the war in December 1941 after the Japanese attack at Pearl Harbor and Hitler's declaration of war on the United States. However, the Anglo-American component of the coalition had already emerged in 1939–40 as Roosevelt loaned more and more material aid to the British in their struggle with Nazi Germany. Even before the United States officially entered the war, Churchill and Roosevelt agreed the Atlantic Charter of August 1941, a declaration that committed the two states to a non-annexationist peace based on free trade and democracy. The Atlantic Charter was endorsed by the Soviet Union in September 1941 and reaffirmed in the Declaration of the United Nations signed by Britain, the United States, the USSR, and twenty-two other allied states in January 1942. At the Tehran conference in December 1943, Churchill, Roosevelt, and Stalin pledged to free the world of tyranny and to banish the scourge of war. At Yalta in February 1945, the Big Three issued a Declaration on Liberated Europe that envisaged a democratic Europe based on representative institutions and freely elected governments.

In addition to these general declarations of war and peace aims, the Grand Alliance partners entered into a number of bilateral agreements. In July 1941 Britain and the USSR signed an agreement on joint action against Germany. In May 1942 the same two states concluded a long-term treaty of alliance and pledged cooperation and consultation after the war. Although there was no parallel American-Soviet pact, in June 1942 the United States did sign a wide-ranging supplies agreement with the Soviet Union. Britain, Canada, and other allied states also pledged and supplied munitions, equipment, and food to the Soviet Union.

Allied supplies to the USSR entailed a high degree of economic integration within the Grand Alliance, since Soviet aid requirements had to be factored into the national economic planning and priorities of the Alliance countries. Allied aid to the USSR amounted to about 10 percent of total Soviet wartime economic requirements and played a vital role in facilitating the defeat of Germany on the Eastern front, particularly during the Red Army's triumphal advance to Berlin in 1944–45.

Alongside the development of bilateral relations between the Soviet Union and its Western allies there was extensive tripartite cooperation. In October 1943 an American-British-Soviet conference of foreign ministers was held in Moscow, at which agreement was reached on an array of wartime and postwar issues. Of particular importance was a declaration on general security that pledged to create a successor to the discredited and defunct League of Nations. This declaration led to the Dumbarton Oaks conference of August–September 1944 and then to the founding of the United Nations at the San Francisco conference of April–June 1945. The Moscow foreign ministers conference also established the European Advisory Commission (EAC), a tripartite body devoted to the formulation of armistice terms for enemy states. It was through the work of the EAC that agreement was reached on the division of Germany into American, British, and Soviet zones of military occupation. At the Tehran conference the only important specific agreement reached was that Britain and the United States would invade northern France in the early summer of 1944. But there was a frank exchange of views on a number of political issues and a significant meeting of minds among the Big Three. This spirit of trust and cooperation was carried forward to the Yalta conference where Churchill, Roosevelt, and Stalin agreed to continue their Grand Alliance after the war.

As well as meeting at summits in Tehran and Yalta, the Big Three exchanged extensive correspondence. Their letters and telegrams reveal that the Grand Alliance was beset by considerable acrimony. These disputes notwithstanding, the overwhelming impression given by the Big Three's correspondence is of a positive working relationship and a shared belief that the Grand Alliance could and should continue after the war.

Foremost among the controversies within the Grand Alliance was a clash over the opening of an Anglo-American second front in France. Stalin began demanding such an operation as early as summer 1941. In response the British and Americans indicated that they would invade continental Europe in 1942 but subsequently postponed the invasion to 1943 and then to 1944. This delay in opening the second front, which was announced at the height of the German advance to Stalingrad in summer 1942, fueled Stalin's suspicions that Britain and the United States were content to see the Soviet Union exhaust itself in war while they prepared to take advantage of Germany's defeat.

The longest running political dispute between Churchill, Roosevelt, and Stalin was over Poland. In April 1943 relations between the USSR and the Polish government in exile broke down following the Katyn affair—the discovery by the Germans of the mass graves of Polish POWs executed by the NKVD in spring 1940. Stalin's priority in relation to Poland was a postwar government friendly to the Soviet Union. Churchill and Roosevelt, on the other hand, were keen to secure a role for the pro-Western politicians of the Polish exile government. This issue was only resolved in 1945 when agreement was reached on the political broadening of the pro-Soviet government in Poland, established by Stalin following the Red Army's invasion of the country.

Stalin's attitude and policy toward the Grand Alliance went through a number of phases. Initially, his perception of the role and value of the alliance was dominated by military considerations. He desperately needed British and American supplies, and he vigorously sought an Anglo-American invasion of France that would draw German forces away from the Eastern front. But there was also an important element of political calculation in Stalin's military demands on his allies. Stalin feared the malevolent role of anti-Soviet elements in Britain and the United States and worried that Hitler might be able to split the Grand Alliance by enticing the Western states into a separate, anti-Communist peace. His demands for more supplies and for the immediate opening of a second front were politically as well as militarily motivated and were seen as a means of irrevocably committing the British and Americans to the Grand Alliance.

After the Soviet victories at Stalingrad and Kursk in 1943, Stalin's attitude toward the Grand Alliance became more positive and constructive. He began to see the Grand Alliance as a long-term partnership and as an essential ingredient in the creation of a stable and durable peace. Stalin's commitment to a peacetime Grand Alliance was articulated in numerous public and private statements in 1943–44. Central to his stated vision of the postwar world was the need to continue cooperation with Britain and the United States in order to contain a resurgent Germany. Stalin believed that a rapid revival of German power was inevitable if the country was not broken up and kept down by the Grand Alliance. Equally, the Grand Alliance was only one agency for the containment of Germany. After Yalta, Stalin came to doubt the viability of a punitive peace and began to place more hope on the creation of a self-sufficient alliance of Slavic states. Alongside this latter policy ran a strategy to construct a geoideological space in Europe that would guarantee Soviet security by political means. Stalin's conception of postwar Europe was of a zone of "new democracies"—a region of left-wing regimes, each with a strong Communist presence. He thought that his project of a people's democratic Europe was compatible with Grand Alliance aims since it was conceived as a reformist strategy for the gradual, long-term conquest of power by his Communist allies and posed no immediate threat to the continued existence of Western capitalism. However, the British and Americans increasingly saw Stalin's political and ideological maneuvers as dangerous and threatening and as overstepping the limits of an ally. This was, however, not yet obvious to Stalin in 1945. He considered his policies moderate and restrained, and his view of the landscape of the emerging postwar world was dominated not by Soviet expansionism and the spread of communism but by the rise of Anglo-American globalism.

When Roosevelt died in April 1945 and Harry Truman became U.S. president, Stalin saw no reason to abandon the Grand Alliance. Truman was viewed by Moscow as a pro-Roosevelt politician who favored continued cooperation with the Soviet Union. Molotov, Stalin's foreign minister, had a bruising first encounter with Truman at the height of the inter-allied dispute over Poland's postwar government, but the controversy was subsequently resolved to Soviet satisfaction when the pro-Communist Polish government supported by Moscow was recognized by Britain and the United States. From Stalin's point of view the Potsdam conference of July–August 1945 was almost as successful as Yalta. A detailed agreement was reached on the postwar treatment of Germany, including provision for the payment of large reparations to the Soviet Union. At Potsdam it was also agreed to establish a Council of Foreign Ministers (CFM) to negotiate the details of the peace treaties with the defeated Axis states, including Germany. Stalin and Molotov returned from Potsdam convinced that the implicit spheres of influence deal they had made with Churchill and Roosevelt at Yalta had been confirmed by Truman at Potsdam.

When the war ended, Stalin was confident that cooperation with Britain and the United States would continue in the postwar period. But there were some clouds on the horizon. At Potsdam Truman had told Stalin about the atomic bomb test and of the American intention to use the weapon against Japan. Stalin knew all about the Manhattan project from Soviet intelligence agencies, and preliminary work was already underway on a Soviet bomb, but he did not authorize a full-scale project until two weeks after the atomic bombings of

Hiroshima and Nagasaki. Stalin remained convinced that Soviet land power more than counterbalanced U.S. nuclear weapons and saw no reason why this development in military technology should disrupt the harmony of the Grand Alliance. But he was annoyed by what he saw as the Americans' use of the bomb to bring the war in the Far East to a rapid end, which preempted the Red Army's planned invasion of the Japanese home islands and led to the exclusion of the Soviet Union from the postwar occupation of Japan.

Although the Polish question had been settled, further disagreements with the British and Americans emerged over the recognition of pro-Soviet governments in Bulgaria and Rumania. The British and American refusal to recognize these governments prior to the holding of general elections seemed to indicate an emerging pattern of Western interference in the Soviet sphere of influence in Eastern Europe. More generally, there was the growing perception in Moscow that anti-Soviet forces were once again on the rise in Britain and the United States and were using their influence to deny the USSR the just desserts of victory, not only in Eastern Europe but also in the Black Sea area, in the Mediterranean basin, and in the Far East.

Stalin's concerns about relations within the Grand Alliance came to a head at the first meeting of the CFM, held in London in September 1945. The meeting went on for three weeks but ended without agreement amid procedural acrimony. The underlying causes of the collapse of the negotiations were the Western refusal to recognize the Bulgarian and Rumanian governments and Stalin's annoyance about developments in the Far East. In Moscow the diagnosis of the failure of the CFM focused on the role of reactionary political forces in the Western states.

The failure of the London CFM was a significant turning point in the history of the Grand Alliance, but much of the short-term political damage was repaired, and in the summer of 1946 a peace conference was convened in Paris to agree on peace treaties for Bulgaria, Finland, Hungary, Italy, and Rumania. The negotiations were prolonged but ultimately successful, and the scene was set for the next stage in the postwar peace settlement—CFM talks about the future of Germany. However, by 1947 Soviet-Western relations within the Grand Alliance were deteriorating rapidly. By this time Stalin had abandoned his hopes for a peacetime Grand Alliance that would continue and build upon the intensive and extensive cooperation of the war years. But he still clung to the idea of the Grand Alli-

ance as a collaborative framework for the maintenance of peaceful coexistence between the Soviet Union and the capitalist world. Even this more limited concept of the alliance was, however, undermined by the proclamation in March 1947 of the Truman Doctrine and the announcement three months later of the Marshall Plan. Truman did not explicitly name the Soviet Union as the object of his new policy of containment, but it was self-evident that the speech presaged a global struggle against communism, while the Marshall Plan seemed purposely designed to use U.S. financial resources as an instrument of Western economic interference in the Soviet sphere of influence in Eastern Europe. Stalin's response was to establish the Communist Information Buro (Cominform), an organization charged with the coordination of the anticapitalist struggle of European communist parties. At its founding conference in September 1947, Zhdanov, Stalin's ideology chief, articulated a new vision of the postwar world. Hitherto, Zhdanov and other Soviet leaders, including Stalin, had spoken of two trends in postwar world politics, one reactionary and the other progressive. With the foundation of Cominform, Soviet discourse centered instead on the concept of a world definitively divided into two camps—a camp of capitalism, imperialism, and militarism versus a camp of peace, socialism, and democracy. In effect, Zhdanov's two-camps speech at the Cominform conference was the Soviet declaration of the Cold War and a sign that Stalin's project of a peacetime Grand Alliance with Britain and the United States had finally foundered.

See also Anticommunism; Antifascism; Anti-Fascist Resistance; Cominform; Containment; Stalingrad, Battle of; Yalta Conference; World War II.

FURTHER READING

Edmonds, R. *The Big Three*. London: Penguin, 1991.

Feis, H. *Churchill-Roosevelt-Stalin*. Princeton, NJ: Princeton University Press, 1957.

Mastny, V. *Russia's Road to the Cold War: Diplomacy, Warfare and the Politics of Communism, 1941–1945*. New York: Columbia University Press, 1979.

McNeill, W. H. *America, Britain and Russia: Their Co-operation and Conflict, 1941–1946*. London: Oxford University Press, 1953.

Roberts, G. *Stalin's Wars: From World War to Cold War, 1939–1953*. New Haven, CT: Yale University Press, 2006.

Sainsbury, K. *The Turning Point*. Oxford: Oxford University Press, 1986.

Sipols, V. *The Road to Great Victory: Soviet Diplomacy 1941–1945*. Moscow: Progress Publishers, 1985.

Stalin's Correspondence with Churchill, Atlee, Roosevelt and Truman, 1941–1945. London: Lawrence and Wishart, 1958.

The Tehran, Yalta and Potsdam Conferences: Documents. Moscow: Progress Publishers, 1969.

GEOFFREY K. ROBERTS

Great Leap Forward

The expression "Great Leap Forward" (*Dayuejin*) appeared for the first time in a *People's Daily* editorial on November 13, 1957, and it referred to the economic development strategy adopted in China in the period 1958–60, which was marked by an acceleration of collectivist policies in both agriculture and industry. In the summer of 1957 the general economic situation seemed to justify optimism. The results of the first Five-Year Plan, implemented with Soviet aid, seemed positive: an industrial growth rate of 18 percent per year, a general economic growth rate of 10 percent, together with significant structural changes (such as the diffusion of agricultural cooperatives and the nationalization of industry) were attained, while incurring only moderate costs when compared to the Soviet experience. The leaders of the CCP were, however, faced with the alternative of keeping the industrial growth rate high and simultaneously stimulating agricultural production, or aiming for more modest goals. They opted for the Great Leap Forward, intended to allow the country to surpass England's industrial production in a fifteen-year period. Between December 1957 and May 1958 Mao Zedong and his supporters mobilized the entire country, promising rapid economic development and social progress: estimates of increases in steel production in the 19 percent range and in the 33 percent range for the industrial sector then seemed like reasonable goals and not absurd chimeras.

During the first three months of 1958 Mao organized three conferences of national and provincial party leaders in which he attacked bureaucratic planners, questioned the slavish imitation of the Soviet model, and exalted youth's creativity as contrasted to bookish learning and antiquated institutions. The new developmental strategy consisted in "walking on two legs": creating a modern capital-intensive industrial sector while still relying on less sophisticated technology in agriculture and on small-scale agricultural activities. At the Second Plenum of the Eighth Central Committee Meeting of the CCP (May 5 through May 22, 1958) Mao's proposal of the "general line for the construction of socialism" was approved: "give it your all, aim high in order to achieve greater, faster, better and cheaper results in the construction of socialism." Among the targets of this new revolutionary wave, the socioeconomic gap between cities and countryside and the differences between workers and peasants and intellectual and manual labor were singled out.

In this atmosphere, in which "any objective could be reached," the entire agricultural sector was reorganized, 2.5 million party cadres were transferred, 90 million people were mobilized to learn small-scale steel work, and about 20 million peasants migrated to the cities in the course of a few weeks. Forced collectivization in the countryside led to the creation, at the end of 1958, of 26,578 people's communes, representing 700 million people. Sixty million peasants were involved in off-season plans for water control, and a mass movement was launched to collect organic fertilizer, reclaim land, and improve the quality of the soil. Among the various technological innovations the substitution of shoulder-poles with carts on wheels was promoted (even though the necessary road network was not available). A campaign to exterminate the "four plagues" (flies, mosquitoes, mice, and sparrows) was also launched, but once it became clear that sparrows were a form of control on the other pests the role of fourth "plague" was shifted to bedbugs.

Communes were encouraged to create "courtyard blast furnaces" to melt steel: according to official estimates, once the 600,000 blast furnaces were all operating at full capacity they would have accounted for a total yearly steel production of 11 million tons. But this general mobilization notwithstanding, the blast furnaces' production did not reach expected levels: kitchen utensils and tractors were melted down with the sole purpose of increasing production and with negative consequences for the quality of the steel produced. The production of iron, coal, chemical compounds, wood, cement, grain, and cotton should have shown significant increases, but results were often exaggerated.

This period witnessed a massive entry of women into the labor force, both to substitute in the fields for men who were engaged in building blast furnaces and to work in the dining halls and kindergartens of the people's communes. In addition to growth in production the structural decentralization of responsibilities from central ministries to local governments was also promoted to encourage small-scale production using local financial resources and manpower. Simultaneously a movement to revolutionize industrial and management relations was launched: it targeted fawning over technicians and experts and attempted to diminish the gap between managers and workers by encouraging the participation of managerial staff in production and of workers in management.

In the spring of 1958 the results seemed satisfactory, with many waterworks completed, estimates of an abundant harvest, and great hopes placed in the flexibility and creativity of decentralized industrial activities. The meeting of the Eighth Party Congress in May 1958 was dominated by Mao and Liu Shaoqi, who managed to gather the consent of more moderate leaders. Lin Biao became a member of the Permanent Committee of the Political Office, weakening the position of Defense Minister Peng Dehuai, who was greatly opposed to the Great Leap. Policies aimed at the creation of an army on the Soviet model were also abandoned, accompanied by claims to an absolute independence in outlook, including in the development of nuclear weapons. Mass mobilization and economic adventurism were accompanied by harsh "rectification" campaigns, which were aimed at reducing the potential for dissent and creating decisional conformity among rural cadres.

Between June and November the Maoist program reached its climax, with news of results that exceeded expectations: the agricultural harvest and production of steel had doubled as compared with 1957, and this seemed to allow one to hope for similar increases in 1959. But under the shiny surface a series of problems were hidden: an excessively fast-paced and destructive acceleration in economic activity, a lack of coordination and poorly thought-out initiatives (which led to three million tons of unusable steel), excessively deep plowing, sowing at extremely short intervals, and serious environmental harm caused by the deforestation to fuel the blast furnaces. Relations with Moscow worsened during this same period; in Tibet the Khambu rebels threatened Lhasa and border skirmishes with India intensified. Between the winter of 1958 and the spring of 1959 the need to adjust production goals emerged, but the national leadership accused local cadres of not adequately implementing directives and simultaneously attempted to limit excesses. The symbolic capital that had been invested in the Great Leap was too great to admit failure.

Only in June 1959 did Mao seem to point to a slowdown, asking that revolutionary fervor be combined with a practical sense, and that realistic goals become a focus. During the meeting of the Political Office of the CCP in Lushan (July 23–August 2, 1959), Defense Minister Peng Duhai introduced a letter in which he criticized the policies of the Great Leap. Moscow simultaneously criticized the Great Leap in a *Pravda* editorial. Mao's counterattack was immediate and showed a willingness to ignore the basic underlying problems: by using patriotism and party unity as his pretexts, Peng Dehuai and the so-called antiparty clique were isolated, Peng was accused of secret conspiracy with a foreign power and had to cede his post as defense minister to Lin Biao. A campaign against "rightist deviations" was unleashed in the entire country, causing about two million cadres to be expelled from the party. Relations with Moscow continued to worsen to the point that Soviet technicians were withdrawn in 1960. In the summer of that year it seemed clear that the Great Leap had ended: the party, while not explicitly disavowing it, decided to adopt more moderate policies. But the three years from 1959 to 1961 are sadly remembered as the "three bitter years" marked by natural disasters and a ferocious famine: 14 to 30 million people died of hunger, the birthrate collapsed, agricultural production decreased (by 14 percent in 1959, by 13 percent in 1960, by 15 percent in 1961) and reached its lowest point since 1952, and industrial production, which had grown 55 percent in 1958, decreased by 38 percent in 1961 and by another 16 percent in 1962.

The revolutionary drama of the Great Leap can be considered one of the greatest human and economic disasters of the 20th century. The negative balance sheet and the estimates of 14 to 30 million dead seem to point to Mao and the political group around him as the culprits. They promoted a utopian form of industrialization on the basis of a collectivized agrarian economy created in 1954–57. A great portion of the literature emphasizes the disagreements in the party leadership between those who supported Mao's idealism and the pragmatists with a more pro-Soviet orientation, such as Liu Shaoqi and Peng Zhen; in this interpretation the Great Leap represented a radical reply to the moderate proposals for reform promoted by other political leaders in the years 1956–57.

More recent studies seem to demonstrate that, after Mao's trip to Moscow in November 1957, uncertainty about Soviet aid policies prevailed, reinforcing a spirit of self-sufficiency, thus leading to a fundamental consensus based on the resolution of economic problems by means of political mobilization, agricultural collectivization, and industrial decentralization. A reinterpretation of the origins of the Great Leap in a neoinstitutional perspective underscores the role of the bureaucracy rather than that of a single individual. Other studies, however, examine the political and economic process of decision making and, refusing an approach based on political power games and antagonisms within the party leadership, argue in favor of a political process dominated by a single agent: Mao Zedong.

A recurrent thesis is that human factors play a more decisive role than natural forces, a position also supported by Amartya Sen in his analysis of the cause of famine in various parts of the world. A detailed examination of the interrelationship between nature and human action to control it shows how Mao placed both in the service of his revolutionary dream. Some studies point to the famine of 1958–62 as China's greatest trauma, even greater than the cultural revolution, and argue that the tragedy of hunger that led to cases of cannibalism and slavery could have been avoided had Mao been placed in the minority after the first year.

See also Cultural Revolution in China; Famine under Communism; Mao Zedong; Modernization; Sino-Soviet Split; Soviet Industrialization.

FURTHER READING

Bachman, D. M. *Bureaucracy, Economy and Leadership in China: The Institutional Origins of the Great Leap Forward.* Cambridge, UK: Cambridge University Press, 1991.

Becker J. *Hungry Ghosts: China's Secret Famine.* London: J. Murray, 1996.

Chan A. L., *Mao's Crusade: Politics and Policy Implementation in China's Great Leap Forward.* New York: Oxford University Press, 2001.

Cheek T., R. MacFarquhar, and E. Wu, eds. *The Secret Speeches of Chairman Mao: From the Hundred Flowers to the Great Leap Forward Mao Zedong, 1893–1976.* Cambridge, MA: Harvard University Press, 1989.

Domenach, J.-L. *The Origins of the Great Leap Forward: The Case of One Chinese Province.* Boulder, CO: Westview Press, 1995.

MacFarquhar, R. *The Origins of the Cultural Revolution.* Vol. II, *The Great Leap Forward, 1958–1960.* New York: Columbia University Press, 1983.

Sen, K. "Democracy as a Universal Value." *Journal of Democracy* 10, no. 3 (1999): 3–17.

Shapiro, J. *Mao's War against Nature: Politics and the Environment in Revolutionary China.* New York: Cambridge University Press, 2001.

Teiwes, F. C. *China's Road to Disaster: Mao, Central Politicians, and Provincial Leaders in the Unfolding of the Great Leap Forward, 1955–1959.* Armonk, NY: M. E. Sharpe, 1998.

MAURIZIO MARINELLI

Great Patriotic War, Rhetoric of

On June 23, 1941, two days after the onset of the German attack on the USSR, *Pravda* opened with an editorial titled "The Great Patriotic War of the Soviet People." The process of sacralization of the military conflict by the Soviet leadership had thus begun, with an explicit reference to the Russo-French War fought in 1812 against Napoleon, and later referred to in Russian public parlance as the "Patriotic War" (*Otechestvennaja Vojna*). The defense against Nazi Germany was immediately named *Velikaja Otechestvennaja Vojna*, thereby establishing continuity (but with an increase in adjectival value) with this prior episode of national unity. It was also an attempt to attenuate the political impact of the effects of Operation Barbarossa: Hitler's attack had taken the Soviet leadership by surprise. In those days the entire country experienced the failure of the security strategy that Stalin and his leadership group had pursued during the previous years. The epic saga of the "construction of socialism," with the suffering it inflicted in the name of development and security, was put in question by the ease with which German troops were advancing on Soviet territory.

This was one of the urgent reasons why the government attempted to reach beyond the political sphere to guide the population's reaction to the German attack: a war that up to a couple of days earlier had been presented as a distant "clash of imperialisms," now entered the lives of Soviet citizens in the form of a war of extermination declared by Germany against the USSR's Slavic populations. The reference to Russian and pre-Soviet national history captured the motivations with which Soviet citizens lived through the first days of war, fighting for themselves rather than for Soviet power. And it allowed the party leadership to find a national mission right at the moment that its prewar strategy failure was most obvious. The first public speech held by Stalin after a long period of silence on July 13, 1941, adopted the same tone, addressing the country as "brothers and sisters, friends of mine," in addition to the more ritualistic "comrades and citizens," and appealing to the emotional side of the nation's defense. All traces of a political connection to the Bolshevik leadership of the state had disappeared. Even more explicitly, during the anniversary of the October Revolution held on November 7 of that year, while he greeted those troops that would later battle German forces engaged in the siege of Moscow (only a few miles away) from the Lenin Mausoleum on Red Square, Stalin himself would refer to a Russian pantheon of heroes with no connection to the Bolshevik tradition: "Let yourselves be guided in this just war by the heroic images of our great ancestors: Aleksandr Nevsky, Dmitry Donskoj, Koz'ma Minin, Dmitry Pozharsky, Aleksandr Suvorov, Mikhail Kutuzov."

The foundation of the myth of the Great Patriotic War, against the background of an image of national unity devoid of the symbolic dualism introduced by Bolshevism, also captured the spirit of freedom with which part of the country was participating in the epic saga of the defense against German attack. These epic deeds were for many the equivalent of a sort of collective liberation, the possibility to express their (not only military) capabilities against a real enemy and outside the traumatic impositions that Stalinism had imposed on society in the course of the 1930s. Those who were lucky enough to survive the battles of the Great Patriotic War, the so-called generation of the *frontoviki*, would remember the feeling of having regained their freedom and destiny in conditions of extreme danger. In this sense, the war had freed new energies and motivations in Soviet society as a whole, and the myth of the Great Patriotic War was able to synthesize them in a new public religious formula.

This nonpolitical, unifying, and liberating aspect of the myth would be cut down to size once the Stalin regime reacquired vigor and stability—that is, already in the final phases of World War II and above all during the first postwar years. In 1947 even Victory Day, May 9, would be demoted from a national holiday to a simple working day, a low point in the more widespread degradation of the mythology of national participation that was giving way to Stalin's new Cold War Manicheanism. This was part of the same trend that on the level of international references, would lead to the erasure from public memory of the role played in Hitler's defeat by the anti-Fascist alliance. The May 9 national holiday would be reintroduced only in the early 1960s, during the climax of the Khrushchevian rebirth of the Great Patriotic War's myth. It was a rebirth marked by the expunction of Stalin's role in the victory and focused on the role of the

people in the military confrontation—a transition made necessary by the need to counterbalance the trauma that the Communist Party's Twentieth Congress inflicted on the regime's official symbolism and promoted by the generation of *frontoviki* that was now playing a preeminent role in the country's leadership. These were the years that literally witnessed an explosion of war memoirs, in both literature and film, and that exalted that same spirit of popular tragedy and national liberation that the country had lived in 1941. This climate was not to survive the also symbolic normalization that was to occur after Khrushchev's ouster in 1964; the myth was to become increasingly stiff in its culturally defensive version, and also devoid of those participatory elements that had marked its renewed vitality.

Under Leonid Brezhnev's leadership an anti-Western dike was built around this myth, a dam against the new customs that were spreading in the West and might contaminate Soviet youths. It thus definitely lost those remaining elements of popular vivaciousness that it had acquired in the Khrushchev years and was transformed into another element in the official symbolism of the Soviet regime. As such it would survive into the late 1980s. It experienced a final partial moment of renewed vitality with perestroika and the wave of public discussions about the Soviet past, even though mostly limited to revelations about the less well-known historical aspects of the conflict. Yet it was once again lacking in the participatory dimension it had enjoyed earlier, between the 1950s and the early 1960s. At this point the myth of the Great Patriotic War was definitely stabilized as the most solid element in the historical and national legitimation of the Russo-Soviet state. And hence it would survive the end of the USSR itself, to such an extent that it could be found virtually intact in Boris Yeltsin and Vladimir Putin's Russia—even in terms of monuments and iconography, which also preserve the main symbolic elements of that myth (including the military banner and the buttons on soldiers' uniforms, which today still bear the hammer and sickle), and the proliferation of a multitude of new locations that celebrate the principal protagonists of the war (like Red Army general Georgy Zhukov).

See also Grand Alliance, The; History and Memory; Leningrad, Siege of; Red Army; Soviet Patriotism; Stalingrad, Battle of; World War II.

FURTHER READING

Ferretti, M. *La memoria mutilate. La Russia ricorda*. Milan: Corbaccio, 1993.

Gallagher, M. P. *The Soviet History of World War*, II. *Myths, Memories, and Realities*. New York: Praeger, 1963.

Tumarkin, N. *The Living and the Dead: The Rise and Fall of the Cult of World War II in Russia*. New York: Basic Books, 1994.

ANDREA ROMANO

Great Terror

The "Great Terror" is the name given to the mass repressions carried out in the USSR in 1937 and 1938, as a result of which several million ordinary citizens were shot or sent to prison camps, and a significant number of the ruling party–state elite were eliminated. For several decades prior to the opening of Soviet archives in the 1990s, the Great Terror was considered to have begun after the murder by a terrorist of the Leningrad leader and politburo member Sergey Kirov (many would accuse Stalin of having organized his murder), and increased in scale until it peaked in 1937–38. Basing their research on available sources (mostly memoirs of members of the intelligentsia who were victims of the terror, testimony of a number of People's Commissariat for Internal Affairs [NKVD] workers who escaped from the USSR, and official materials from the period of de-Stalinization during Khrushchev's reign), historians have mostly concentrated their study on repressions against the top Soviet ruling circles, military personnel under the command of Marshal Mikhail Tukhachevskii, party leaders, representatives of the artistic intelligentsia, and so forth. There have been detailed studies of the public trials in Moscow of former opposition leaders who were convicted and sentenced to be shot. Among others were Grigory Zinovyev and Lev Kamenev in August 1936, Yury Piatakov and Leonid Serebriakov in January 1937, and Nikolay Bukharin and Aleksey Rykov in March 1938. From their investigations, historians have drawn conclusions about the centralized nature of the Great Terror, whose undoubted superintendent was Stalin.

This most widely held vision of the Great Terror, however, was challenged during the 1980s by a group of historians called the "Revisionists." Pointing to contradictions—on the one hand, between the central and regional leaderships, and on the other hand, between local officials and the population at large—these historians maintained that the terror had been an elemental process on a much larger scale than had previously been assumed. They described the terror as a kind of war of everybody against everybody, provoked by regional leaders at odds with the center. They stated that Stalin did not possess the absolute power attributed to him and that the terror had simply gotten out of Moscow's control. The most radical historians of this type wrote that Stalin had played only a small part in the terror, and that his power had not only not been strengthened by the mass repressions but had, indeed, been weakened by them. There were also discussions about the accuracy of estimates of victims of the Great Terror.

The situation changed after the Soviet archives were opened at the beginning of the 1990s. Historians were now in possession of numerous documents, the most important of which were secret decrees of the politburo and NKVD orders for carrying out the mass operations of 1937–38; secret statistics about the number of arrests and persons sentenced; documents describing the mechanisms of the mass operations, of which the most important were records of investigations and various monitoring activities carried out before the cessation of mass operations was announced; and prisoner complaints and other records. The new documents showed that in 1935 and 1936, which had formerly often been included in the period of the Great Terror, repressions took place merely at a level usual for the Stalinist period. Furthermore, during this time, the regime was carrying out an inconsistent policy of "social reconciliation" with some of the previous victims of repressions—for example, a policy involving the children of exiled peasants, based on the principle that "the son is not responsible for his father." An important reason for this relatively more moderate treatment of citizens was Stalin's policy at that time of moving toward an alliance with the Western democracies against Fascist Germany and Japan.

Also during 1936 (and as has now been authenticated, at Stalin's initiative), repressions against former opposition leaders were stepped up. If in preceding years only some of the previous oppositionists had been sent to prisons or exiled, with many of them still permitted to work at secondary jobs, now the group was being almost totally liquidated. During the first half of 1937, military officers and workers in defense establishments were purged as well, and attacks began against the middle echelon of the nomenclature, especially of its regional leaders. In the ensuing months of 1937 and 1938, these attacks achieved the proportions of a mass purge of *nomenklatura* personnel. Still, measured by the norms of the Stalin period, these repressions, though quite extensive and cruel, could be considered limited in scope. If it had all been only a matter of eliminating former oppositionists, party-state functionaries, and military personnel, one could hardly justify speaking of a "great terror." Other terms, such as "major personnel purge" or "nomenklatura revolution" would be more appropriate.

The Great Terror started when massive and unbelievably cruel repressions began to envelop large segments of the population of the country. As the archives show, this mass terror was launched by a politburo decree of July 2, 1937, titled "On Anti-Soviet Elements," which ordered that telegraphed directives be sent to regional leaders. These telegrams demanded that kulaks who had fled from their places of exile and regular criminals (although the concept of "criminal" was not specified) be registered, and that it be determined how many of them should be arrested and how many shot. It also called for the organization of extrajudicial organs, called "troikas," which would make decisions about arrests and executions. On July 30, 1937, after a series of agreements, the politburo approved Operational Order NKVD USSR No. 00447, titled "On the Utilization of Repression against Former Kulaks, Criminals, and Other Anti-Soviet Elements." This order prescribed that operations be launched between August 5 and August 15, 1937 (depending on the region), and be completed within four months. Most importantly, the order specified the "contingents to be subject to repression." In practice, this meant anyone who had fought, in one way or another, against Soviet power, or who had been a victim of state terror in preceding periods, including: kulaks who had served their time in exile or had escaped from it; former members of parties that had fought against the Bolsheviks; former White Guard members; czarist officials who had survived; political prisoners who had suffered repressions in preceding years but were now free; and prisoners in camps at the time. In addition to these political categories, regular criminals were also to be subject to the purge.

According to the order, all persons subject to the repressions were divided into two categories: those to be immediately arrested and shot; and those to be sent to camps or prison for a term of eight to ten years. Each province, region, and republic was assigned a quota for each of these two categories. Altogether, 268,950 persons would be arrested, of whom 72,950 would be shot. It is important to emphasize that the order included another

mechanism for escalating the terror. Local leaders were given the right to request additional quotas from Moscow for arrests and executions. The "troikas" were chosen to sentence prisoners within the quotas approved by Moscow. As a rule, these troikas consisted of the regional NKVD leader, the secretary of the appropriate party organization, and the prosecutor.

On August 9, 1937, the politburo approved another operational order of the NKVD USSR, titled "On the Liquidation of Polish Diversionary-Espionage Groups." This order established the type of repression to be used against so-called counterrevolutionary nationality contingents. More than ten of these operations were conducted—against Poles, Germans, Romanians, Latvians, Estonians, Finns, Greeks, Afghans, Iranians, Chinese, Bulgarians, and Macedonians. A special operation was conducted against the so-called Harbinians (after the Manchurian city Harbin); these were former workers on the Chinese–Far East Railroad who had returned to the USSR after this railroad was sold in 1935. Stalin regarded all these categories of the population as breeding grounds for espionage and collaborationism. No arrest or execution quotas were assigned for these nationalities. The center controlled these operations by approving lists of sentences passed, or "albums," which were required to be sent in from the regions.

Still another category regarded by the party leadership as potentially dangerous was members of families of "enemies of the people." In accordance with NKVD Order No. 00486, of August 15, 1937, wives of "traitors to the fatherland" were subject to confinement in camps for terms of five to eight years, while children older than fifteen, who were "socially dangerous and capable of carrying out anti-Soviet actions" were subject to confinement in corrective labor colonies or special children's homes. The order also entailed the transfer of orphaned children of "enemies of the people" to children's homes or to relatives.

All these operations, which when taken together would comprise the essence of what would later be called the Great Terror, were supplemented by the ordinary activity of Soviet punitive organs. In addition to the troikas, which were instruments for carrying out mass operations, the courts were active, and in both the center and the regions show trials of "enemies" were staged. These public show trials were also approved by Moscow. Together with the regular operations, special purges in the border regions also continued to be active. The largest was the deportation of more than 170,000 Koreans from the Far East to Kazakhstan and Uzbekistan, carried out in September and October of 1937. The goal of this deportation, the government's decree stated, was to "cut off the penetration of Japanese espionage into the Far East Region."

Archival documents that have recently appeared show not only how decisions about mass operations were made in Moscow but also permit us to study the ways in which they were carried out in the regions. After arrest and execution quotas were received from Moscow, regional NKVD offices called meetings to define the tasks ahead and to assign concrete numbers to each region. At first, index cards identifying "counterrevolutionary elements" were used to make up the lists for arrests and executions, and these were kept for many years in local state security offices. After the arrests, based on these lists, an investigation would begin whose main purpose was to uncover any links between the arrested persons and "counterrevolutionary organizations." The main proof of guilt was the confession of the arrested person and the testimony of other arrested persons against him. The "testimony" needed for the investigation was obtained by various methods, most often by torture, whose use had been permitted by a special decision of the politburo. The torture, which was almost always administered by Soviet punitive organs, was especially harsh during this period. Many prisoners were killed simply by the savagery of methods used during investigations.

Evidence obtained under torture now led to new arrests, and prisoners from this "second wave" of arrests, when tortured, named still more names. Punitive operations organized in this way could, theoretically, last indefinitely and would take in a significant part of the population in the future. As they carried out the first operations established by the politburo, the local administrations, in conformity with Order No. 00447, began to ask for additional quotas for new arrests and executions, and their requests were usually granted. By the beginning of 1938, more than a half million people had been convicted under this order. These figures considerably exceeded the previous quotas specified by the order. Furthermore, though the four-month period assigned by Order No. 00447 for carrying out operations against "anti-Soviet elements" ended in December, the politburo made decisions in January and February 1938 that provided for a continuation of the mass operations. These decisions, made in Moscow, stretched the mass operations to the middle of November 1938. Numerically, the most extensive operations were undertaken against the "counterrevolutionary nationalist contingents."

The circumstances surrounding the conclusion of the Great Terror demonstrated how absolutely centralized it was. On November 15, 1938, the politburo approved a directive forbidding the investigation of cases by the troikas. On November 17, the politburo forbade all "mass operations involving arrests and evacuations of citizens." In spite of the immense scale and momentum generated by the operations, Moscow's order really did close the operations down almost simultaneously across the vast country. Individual excesses that remained were halted in a peremptory fashion, which again confirmed that the terror began and ended precisely and unambiguously on orders from Moscow.

The opening of the archives permitted certain, though not definitive, conclusions to be drawn about the total number of victims of the Great Terror. The following figures are generally accepted. In 1937 and 1938 state security organs (without the militia) arrested some 1,600,000 persons. Of these, more than 1,300,000 were convicted, and of those some 682,000 were sentenced to death (353,000 in 1937 and 329,000 in 1938). Still, a number of qualifications need to be made with regard to these figures. For example, in addition to those officially shot, an as yet unknown number of those arrested perished from torture, the terrible conditions of their confinement, and while being transported. The number of persons deported and evacuated by the government in 1937–38 needs to be made precise. Obviously, the count here can be estimated at several hundred thousand. The character and extent of the repressions carried out by the organs of the militia has not been examined at all.

Most of the arrests and executions occurred between August 1937 and November 1938, during the main period of the mass operations. Data compiled as of November 1, 1938, show that 767,000 had been sentenced under Order No. 00447 against "anti-Soviet elements" (of which almost 387,000 were shot), and 328,000 were convicted under the "nationality" operations (of which 237,000 were shot). These figures need to be amplified somewhat, since both operations continued until the middle of November.

In addition to making the scale and chronology of the Great Terror more precise, the new archival documents have made possible a definitive discussion of other disputed questions. It is obvious, for example, that the mass operations of 1937–38 had a centralized character; they were begun and ended on orders from the center and were carried out under the center's supervision. Documents have confirmed the leading role that Stalin played in both the purge of the Soviet nomenklatura and in the organization of the mass repressions of 1937–38.

Finally, new documents have substantially strengthened the point of view of historians who have ascribed the Great Terror to the growing threat of war and the effort of the Stalinist leadership, under these circumstances, to destroy any potential "fifth column." As many of the facts and documents show, the purges of the Soviet nomenklatura and the Great Terror of 1937–38 had a singular logic to them. They were an attempt by Stalin to strengthen his regime and "consolidate" Soviet society through the use of mass repressions, linked to the real danger of approaching war (the escalation of the war in Spain, the active aggression of Japan, and the growth of the military power of Germany and its allies). The goal of liquidating the "fifth column" manifested itself in operations against "anti-Soviet elements" and "counterrevolutionary nationalist contingents," along with the mass deportations of segments of the populations (for instance, the Koreans) from the border regions. The victims of these actions, which constituted the core of the Great Terror, were first and foremost those segments of the population that had fought the Bolsheviks during the Civil War: the party oppositionists, the victims of previous purges, and citizens of those nationalities linked to countries that were regarded as potential opponents in a future war.

See also Deportation of Nationalities in the USSR; Despotism; Enemies of the People; Gulag; KGB; Purges; Stalin, Joseph; Stalinism.

FURTHER READING

Chlevnjuk, O. *The History of the Gulag: From Collectivization to the Great Terror.* New Haven, CT: Yale University Press, 2004.

Conquest, R. *The Great Terror: A Reassessment.* New York: Oxford University Press, 1990.

Getty, J. A., and O. V. Naumov, eds. *The Road to Terror: Stalin and the Self-Destruction of the Bolsheviks, 1932–1939.* New Haven, CT: Yale University Press, 1999.

Gurjanov, A. E., ed. *Repressions against the Poles and Polish Citizens.* Moscow: Zveńja, 1997.

Shcherbakova, I. L. *Repressii protiv rossij skich nemcev. Nakazannyj narod.* Moscow: Zveńja, 1999.

Yunge, M., and R. Binnero. *Kak terror Stal "bolsim." Sekrentnyi prikaz n. 010477 I technologija ego ispolnenija.* Moscow: AIRO-XX, 2003.

OLEG V. CHLEVNJUK

Greek Civil War

The internecine conflict that engulfed Greece in the 1940s was rooted in the royalist-republican schism caused by World War I, polarizing the nation, politicizing the military, and leading to the Ioannis Metaxas dictatorship (1936–41) whose oppression forced the Communists underground. Its immediate setting was the power vacuum caused by defeat and foreign occupation in World War II, the collapse of the political system, widespread opposition to the return of King George, the emergence of armed resistance groups with political agendas, and the spread of communism across Eastern Europe. Beyond the great physical and human cost, the conflict exacerbated political divisions, inhibited democratic development, and caused the persecution of leftists for decades. It also led Western powers to intervene in Greek affairs and launch the Cold War strategy of containing Soviet expansionism (the Truman doctrine).

The conflict occurred in three separate but closely linked "rounds," of which only the third (1946–49) escalated to full-scale civil war; all three pitted the Communists against their adversaries and shaped the country's future. Each round had distinct characteristics and outcomes; each raised the level of violence, heightened the stakes, and set the stage for the next.

Round I

In early 1943, following Soviet victories at Stalingrad, sporadic violence among Greek resistance organizations developed into systematic attacks by the Communist-controlled ELAS, the country's largest resistance army, on its rivals. As liberation appeared imminent the attacks intensified and the Greek Communist Party (KKE), operating behind a leftist coalition front, the National Liberation Front (EAM), prepared plans to seize Athens following the Germans' withdrawal. In August, meeting with the government in exile in Cairo, the main resistance organizations demanded entry into the government and the postponement of King George's return pending a plebiscite. Opposed to both demands British officials ended the negotiations. In mid-October the KKE established liaison with Marshal Tito's headquarters, and ELAS units across the country launched coordinated attacks on its principal rival, the National Republican Greek League (EDES), in a savage, if intermittent, civil war that lasted until February. A German drive against ELAS and EDES along with strong British pressure ended the fighting between bands, and although efforts to establish a unified command failed, it was agreed that the resistance armies would participate in Allied plans to harass the Germans' withdrawal (Operation Noah's Ark). In March the KKE formed the Political Committee of National Liberation, and in June appealed to Soviet military authorities to send a liaison mission and assistance for ELAS. The request, repeated in September, went unanswered. On the eve of liberation a British-sponsored agreement (the Caserta agreement) placed ELAS and EDES under General Ronald Scobie, and ordered ELAS to remain away from Athens.

Emboldened by EAM's genuine popularity and the strength of ELAS, the KKE had prepared to impose its power on the country at the moment of liberation. Even though domestic opposition was virtually nonexistent, the KKE's plans were derailed by the British, who were determined to keep Greece out of Russia's postwar orbit.

Round II

Deterred by British intervention and receiving no encouragement from Moscow the KKE joined the national government, holding in abeyance its quest for power. Through mass demonstrations it agitated for populist programs and the punishment of wartime collaborators, many of whom remained in public service, and against the return of the monarchy. For its part, the British-backed government, whose authority did not extend much beyond the Athens region (the provinces remained under ELAS rule), could not begin to address the desperate economic conditions until it had achieved control over the country. Complicated negotiations for the disbandment of guerrilla forces broke down in late November 1944, and the Communist ministers resigned. The KKE would not accept the disarming of ELAS while the government's staunchly anti-Communist troops remained in place. On December 1, Scobie ordered the disbandment of all guerrilla groups; on the same day the KKE's chief, G. Siantos, ordered ELAS units to approach the capital. On December 3, a large antigovernment demonstration in downtown Athens was fired on by police, with many casualties. ELAS began seizing police stations and executing prisoners. Intense fighting spread across the entire city with only its center defended successfully by a small British force and Greek troops. On Christmas Eve, Prime Minister Winston Churchill and Foreign Secretary Anthony Eden flew to Athens, and at a hastily assembled conference castigated the leaders of the KKE, EAM, and ELAS for disrupting the Allies' war effort, and threatened to place Greece under international mandate. Churchill also endorsed the naming of Archbishop Damaskinos as regent, thus defusing for the moment the monarchy issue. Fighting continued but British reinforcements drove ELAS out of Athens and forced its surrender. Before capitulating ELAS took hostages, including prominent Athenians, many of whom perished. Under the Varkiza agreement ELAS was disarmed, the KKE and its allies in EAM remained legal, and plans were announced for a plebiscite and national elections.

The December crisis was the result of miscalculations, faulty communication, and suspicions for which both sides were to blame. Nevertheless, its violence revealed once more the Communists' readiness to confront the government with armed force. It reignited the passions of the 1943–44 violence, deepening the divide between the KKE and its opponents, and making reconciliation all but impossible. Round II also revealed Britain's resolve to keep Greece out of Moscow's orbit as well as America's reluctance to become involved in Greek affairs. As for Stalin, having accepted Churchill's proposal for respective spheres in the Balkans (the percentages agreement), he abandoned the Greek Communists to their fate.

Round III

Despite the Varkiza settlement, sporadic violence continued as emboldened rightist bands attacked leftists, especially ELAS veterans, with leftists responding in kind or returning to wartime hideouts. The KKE, now under Zahariadis's leadership, proposed national reconciliation based on Greek neutrality and the withdrawal of foreign troops, but was spurned by its opponents, who looked to Britain and the United States for protection. In February 1946 the KKE opted for armed "self-defense" and in March, ignoring Moscow's advice, boycotted the elections (won by the archconservatives) and launched an attack on the village of Litohoro, often cited as the start of the civil war. By a wide margin, the plebiscite, held in September with leftist participation, brought back the monarchy and solidified the conservatives' power. In December the KKE turned its armed bands into the Democratic Army of Greece (DSE), and formed a provisional government of "Free Greece," hoping for foreign recognition and support. Increasingly based on forced recruitment and large numbers of Slav-speaking Macedonians, the DSE fielded a combat force of twenty-eight to thirty thousand (May 1948), assisted by a supply system based in neighboring states, primarily Yugoslavia. Zahariadis's several visits to Moscow, where he appealed to the Soviet leaders for support, appeared to yield considerable results, but logistical problems and the Stalin-Tito split forced the DSE to remain a lightly armed guerrilla force incapable of conducting conventional modern warfare required to achieve the KKE's ambitious goals.

Initially, despite British support, the response of the weak and demoralized government was ineffective; its small poorly armed and ill-trained forces took on a defensive posture, giving the DSE the tactical advantage. By the end of 1947, however, U.S. economic and military assistance, coupled with pressures to improve the performance of state services, turned the tide against the insurgents. Under the direction of a U.S. military mission the government forces, greatly enlarged (eventually to more than two hundred thousand) and much improved in weapons and supplies of every kind, took the initiative, and during 1948–49, in a series of fierce battles in the mountains near Albania, defeated and dispersed the DSE. Soviet suggestions for a negotiated end of the civil war were ignored, and in late August 1949, Zahariadis, who had earlier sacked Markos and taken personal command of the DSE, crossed into Albania and exile, followed by several thousand of his troops. It is estimated that as a result of round III some fifty thousand died, sixty-five hundred were sentenced to death, forty thousand were sent to prison camps, and sixty thousand fled to Communist Eastern Europe.

A number of factors contributed to the insurgents' defeat. The KKE temporized and failed to launch the insurrection quickly, before government countermeasures could cut off recruitment in urban centers. The DSE remained weak in both personnel and materiel, due in part to inadequate support from abroad, but also to poor coordination and the lack of competent military commanders. The Stalin-Tito split, in which the KKE sided with Stalin, removed Yugoslavia as a staging area, supply center, and refuge for the DSE. The most decisive factor was the dramatic improvement of the strength, weapons, and effectiveness of the government's armed forces, thanks in large measure to foreign support.

In the wake of the civil war, the anti-Left solidified its hold in Greece and the KKE remained illegal until the collapse of the military junta in 1974. The conflict and its international dimensions contributed to Greece's entry into the Atlantic community and later the European Union.

See also Anti-Fascist Resistance; Cold War; Containment; Soviet-Yugoslavia Break; World War II.

FURTHER READING

Baerentzen, L., J. O. Iatrides, and O. L. Smith, eds. *Studies in the History of the Greek Civil War, 1943–1949.* Copenhagen: Museum Tusculanum Press, 1987.

Close, D. H., ed. *The Greek Civil War, 1943–1950.* London: Routledge, 1993.

Iatrides, J. O., ed. *Greece in the 1940s: A Nation in Crisis.* Hanover, NH: University Press of New England, 1981.

Woodhouse, C. M. *The Struggle for Greece, 1941–1949.* London: Ivan R. Dee, 1976.

JOHN O. IATRIDES

Gromyko, Andrei

Andrei Andreyevich Gromyko (1909–1989) was born on July 5 in the village of Old Gromyki near Mogilev, Belorussia. He joined the Communist Party in 1931 and graduated from the agricultural collage in Minsk the following year. In 1936 he worked for the Institute of Economics of the Soviet Academy of Science. His life changed when, following the Great Purges and the shift of Soviet foreign policy away from "collective security" under M. Litvinov, Stalin, and Molotov began to recruit reliable young cadres to the Commissariat of Foreign Affairs (NKID). Gromyko came to the NKID in 1939, and after a few months became head of its U.S. department and Cuban section. From 1939 to 1943 he was councilor at the Soviet embassy in the United States, after 1942 under Litvinov. Culturally cosmopolitan, ebullient, and multilingual, Litvinov characterized Gromyko as a man incapable of diplomatic work. During his first years in the United States Gromyko learned English listening to radio advertising and reading newspapers, but he never became comfortably fluent.

Stalin and Molotov trusted Gromyko and could rely on his loyal and meticulous execution of any shift of Soviet foreign policy. Their favor assured his spectacular diplomatic career. In 1943 Gromyko replaced Litvinov as Soviet ambassador. In 1944 he led the Soviet delegation at the Washington conference; he attended the Yalta conference in February 1945 and the San Francisco conference that established the United Nations. From 1945 to 1951 he was the USSR's first permanent representative at the United Nations. In 1949 he became First Deputy of Foreign Minister and in 1952 was elected a candidate member of the Central Committee. His focus was always on the United States and Great Britain and never on lesser powers. He was a participant in the diplomatic preparations for the Korean War, but in 1952 he lost Stalin's trust and became ambassador to Great Britain, where he wrote his doctoral dissertation on economics.

After Stalin's death Gromyko returned to Moscow as deputy foreign minister, and since February 1957 became minister of foreign affairs. Khrushchev used Gromyko as an obedient tool in his highly personalized foreign policy. By that time Gromyko had acquired the habit of skillfully changing his position according to the whims of the first secretary. Yet, he had a preference for realpolitik and saw the desirability of détente with the United States. He was never keen on building Soviet diplomacy on ideological principles like those, for example, that dictated the alliance with Communist China. In 1965 he and Andropov attempted to defend the policy of détente policy at the politburo, but they quickly surrendered before orthodox criticism. Between 1965 and 1970 Gromyko gained the trust of party General Secretary Leonid Brezhnev; and when Brezhnev decided to pursue the policy of détente with West Germany and the United States, Gromyko became one of the key architects of policy on such matters as the German Question and arms control (the Moscow Protocols, the agreement on West Berlin, SALT I, SALT II, and the ABM treaty). In 1973, when détente triumphed and the opposition to it inside the politburo was defeated, Gromyko became a full member of the politburo.

Gromyko's diplomatic style, shaped under the influence of Stalin and Molotov, changed little over the years. In the West he became notorious as "Mr. Nyet," an extremely tough negotiator who would doggedly and uncompromisingly insist on Soviet demands. He understood East-West détente as a balance of forces favorable to the Soviet Union and an opportunity to expand Soviet power and influence. Gromyko never acknowledged that expansionist goals, especially in the third world, undermined the policy of détente. Dissidents inside the USSR and the Western campaign for human rights evoked only his contempt. He was unflinching in his support for Soviet expansion and for the growing appetites of the Soviet military.

As Brezhnev's health deteriorated, Gromyko, together with Ustinov (Defense) and Andropov (KGB), assumed de facto decision-making prerogatives. In December 1979 they persuaded Brezhnev to sanction the Soviet invasion of Afghanistan. Gromyko clashed with U.S. sec-

retary of state George Schulz in 1983 after the Soviets shot down Korean airliner KAL007. But already by 1985 he had made efforts to reopen negotiating channels with the United States. Gromyko's influence reached its apogee in 1983–85, but he never aspired to be the national leader. In March 1985 he nominated Mikhail Gorbachev for party general secretary and soon after assumed the honorary position of Chairman of the Supreme Soviet. He supported Gorbachev's foreign policy and reforms, but in October of 1988 was forced to retire. During the period from 1987 to 1989 he privately criticized glasnost and the renunciation of force that Gorbachev proclaimed in domestic and foreign policy. He produced remarkably uninteresting memoirs. Gromyko died in Moscow on July 2, 1989.

See also Andropov, Yuri; Diplomats; Power Politics.

FURTHER READING

Zalessky, K. *Empire of Stalin: Biographical Encyclopedic Dictionary.* Moscow: Veche, 2000.

VLADISLAV M. ZUBOK

Guerrilla Warfare in Latin America

In the 1950s the Cold War led to some curious twists of its own in the Americas: anti-imperialist struggles were pursued with renewed political vigor, after a period of crisis for a political tendency that had been forcefully endorsed by Earl Browder (the secretary of the Communist Party of the United States who was in charge of guiding the policies of the Latin American Communist parties). The tendencies belonging to the various national-popular and national-revolutionary movements, which followed the tradition of José Martí and Víctor Raúl Haya de la Torre, began to prevail over those endorsed by the Latin American Communist parties of the Third International in the 1930s. It was in this context that the Movimiento 26 de Julio unfolded in 1953, led by Fidel Castro Ruz, whose purpose was to overthrow the regime of military dictator Fulgencio Batista. This movement was born from the womb of the old Partido ortodoxo, with the addition of Cubans from the urban middle classes and the "Left bourgeoisie."

Ernesto "Che" Guevara, underestimating both the original and exceptional aspects of the different phases of the developing Cuban Revolution, believed that it could and should be generalized as a theoretical model, and a "method" applicable to other countries in Latin America. He discussed his position with meticulous and didactic zeal in his essays of 1960, the manual "La guerra de guerrillas" (Guerrilla Warfare), and 1963, "La guerra de guerrillas: un metodo" (Guerrilla Warfare: A Method), which appeared in *Cuba Socialista*. Both pieces contributed to his reputation as the principal theorist of the anti-imperialist guerrilla experience. Later, Régis Debray would write an even more abstract adaptation of these positions in his essay "Revolution in the Revolution?" focusing on an ideological apologia of militarist voluntarism that was supposed to be central to the guerrilla's actions and arguing for the priority of the guerrilla *foco* over the party. In this perspective, the Cuban Revolution should not only not be considered a Latin American "exception," as Che had argued, but should instead be seen as the norm, or better, a method by the new guerrillas.

Having been taken by surprise by the Cuban Revolution, the entire Latin American Left attempted to redefine its roles and positions by choosing between reform or revolution, armed struggle or nonviolence, and a pro-Soviet, pro-Cuban, or pro-Chinese orientation. Far from the USSR and only a few miles from the United States, the Cuban Revolution became both an unpredictable and a disproportionately important terrain for confrontation between the two superpowers. They both attempted to confront the extraordinary phenomenon of the Cuban model, either by maintaining it within or attempting to move it into their own sphere of influence. After Cuba's expulsion from the Organization of American States and the precarious solution to the missile crisis, the United States undertook preventive acts of repression: sparking coups against constitutional governments, and because of the Latin American military's strategic importance, taking steps to maintain control of "hemispheric security" against the threat of Communist subversion, by applying what was later to be called the Kissinger-Nixon doctrine.

It is impossible to analyze all the different political and historical contexts in which guerrilla warfare took place in the 1960s. Some exemplary situations, however, can explain the different circumstances that prevented the application and success of Che's method.

Venezuela illustrates both the impossibility of repeating the Guevarist experience in different historical circumstances, and the complex relations that guerrilla movements would establish with Castro's Cuba. The

Venezuelan Communists were among the first to attempt to follow the example of the Cuban guerrillas. They had participated in the popular movement leading to the defeat of General Pérez Jiménez, and thus also thought it would be possible to shift the political situation further to the Left by following Castro's example. The Communists were joined by the Movimiento de izquierda revolucionaria, which had split from the Partito social reformista Acción democrática of Romulo Betancourt.

At the beginning of 1963 during a period of intense struggle in Venezuela, the Frente de liberación nacional (FLN) was born, and the Fuerzas armadas de liberación nacional (FALN) came into being as the armed component of the revolutionary struggle. At the end of 1963, during the presidential elections, the FLN used a slogan that turned out to be a disaster: *ballas si, votos no* (roughly, yes to bullets, no to votes). Most of the electorate, 90 percent, did not share the guerrillas' militarist line, yet the guerrillas returned to the cities with the Unidades tácticas de combate. They carried out spectacular operations, sometimes of an almost terrorist nature, but did not achieve important results, not even when, in order to overcome the crisis affecting both guerrilla movements—the urban and the rural—they tried to combine them in the so-called *insurección combinada*. Just as the Communists and the *miristas* were the first to begin the armed struggle, they were also the first to order a tactical retreat that would allow them to return to a policy of alliances, struggling to get dozens of leaders and militants freed from jail, and advocating respect for constitutional rights and the validity of democratic politics. This political offensive, based on implementing the democratic peace line, was launched by the Communist component of the FLN with an International Conference for Democratic Freedoms in Venezuela, held in Rome in July 1965, under the auspices of Bertrand Russell, Jean-Paul Sartre, Lelio Basso, and Alberto Moravia.

The polemics and the break with Castro were sensational, but the *líder maximo* continued to support some guerrilla groups in the mountains in the central and western areas of Venezuela, under the command of Douglas Bravo and Luben Petkoff. The guerrillas had been told by none other than Che himself that he intended to go to Venezuela to fight with them. Although politically and ideologically controversial, the high point of Cuban support for the Latin American guerrilla movement was the Conference for the Foundation of the Organización latinoamericana de solidaridad, which was held in Havana in 1966 to coordinate and expand guerrilla activities to the entire continent. Two years later, however, in 1968, Bravo himself would accuse the Cubans of being pro-Soviet, being complicit with and beholden to the policy of pacific coexistence, and having abandoned the armed struggle. In truth, even before Che's death, during Prime Minister Aleksey Kosygin's visit to Havana in July 1967, Kosygin denounced attempts to export revolution, which in his view were "playing into the hands of the imperialists and weakening the efforts of the socialist world to free Latin America and sending them off course." Castro's alignment and the decision to remain "unfailingly at the side of the USSR" were confirmed again the following year when Warsaw Pact troops invaded Czechoslovakia.

In Guatemala, the influence of a Castroist guerrilla movement was noteworthy. The first insurrectional activities, in 1960, by more than a hundred officers of the Movimiento revolucionario 13 de noviembre took place, led by Marco Antonio Yon Sosa and Luis Turcios Lima (who had graduated from the antiguerrilla training school in Fort Benning, Georgia). The two leaders would later found the Fuerzas armadas rebeldes, which the Communists of the Partido guatelmalteco de los trabajadores would then also join. During the years of repression by Julio Méndez Montenegro (1966–70), the guerrillas went through a phase of withdrawal, marked by fierce infighting, from 1966 on. That same year, in April, twenty-eight political and union leaders were thrown into the sea from an airplane. In October, Turcios Lima died in a car accident at a time when the guerrilla movement was going through a difficult crisis; Yon Sosa died in a fight in 1969. In 1970, under the presidency of Carlos Arana Osorio, the great antiguerrilla offensive came to an end.

In 1960, in Nicaragua, the Frente sandinista de liberación was formed, led by Carlos Fonseca Amador and Tómas Borge. Its symbol was the old black and red flag of General César Sandino (who had fought for Nicaraguan independence in the 1920s). The Sandinista group became the only guerrilla group that succeeded in generating a political process that eventually brought its leaders into the government, after the "revolución de julio" (1979). After free elections that they won in 1984, Daniel Ortega Saavedra governed until 1990 under tough circumstances marked by a U.S. counterrevolutionary offensive.

In Peru the two main guerrilla organizations, the Ejercito de liberación nacional (ELN) and the Movimiento de izquierda revolucionaria (MIR), while still in their early stages, latched on to an existing peasant movement in the country's south, organized by Hugo Blanco, a member of the Trotskyist Partido obrero revolucionario, while they were still in the preliminary stages of organization. Blanco was arrested in 1963 and sentenced to life in prison, but would return to politics in 1980. The most important leader of the MIR was Luis de la Puente Uceda. Just like Jorge Ricardo Masetti and many others—almost all Latin American guerrilla leaders in fact—he had stayed in Cuba for a time, getting prepared and receiving assistance. According to ELN leader Héctor Béjar, though, the scant attention given to more far-reaching political activities and the failure to organize greater peasant involvement explain why guerrilla groups had such a short life span in Peru, and were disbanded by December 1965. The guerrilla group Sendero luminoso, founded in 1970 by Abimael Guzmán, who was sentenced to life in prison in 1992, cannot be linked to Guevarist ideology but rather to a baseless "Andean" interpretation of Maoism.

In Columbia, the Fuerzas armadas revolucionarias (FARC) was formed in the mid-1970s as the armed wing of the Columbian Communist Party. The FARC's organization was based on the experience of the "self-defense zones," which had been subjected to violent army attacks during the so-called pacification campaign. The birth of the FARC inevitably led to a qualitative jump from the preceding phase of organized self-defense to a new phase of revolutionary war: the conquest of power became not only the reason for the FARC's development but also for its very existence. Other factors soon came to accelerate this process. First, there was the appearance of the Ejército de liberación nacional guerrilla movement, formed in 1965 under the leadership of Fabio Vásquez and Victor Medina, who from the start adopted the Cuban model for their struggle. The former priest Camilo Torres, after a political campaign throughout the country to create a Frente unido revolucionario, was forced to leave his religious order, and persecuted by the police, he joined the Guevarist guerrillas of the ELN in October 1965. He died in one of the first battles with the army, in February 1966. Torres's death as a guerrilla created an enormous stir in Latin America; he became one of the symbols of the Movimiento de sacerdotes para el Tercer Mundo in Argentina and the political application of "liberation theology," whose major theoretician was the Peruvian philosopher Gustavo Gutierrez, author of an essay that appeared in 1969 titled "Hacia una teologia de la liberación" (Toward a Theology of Liberation). When Vásquez fell ill, the ELN entered a lengthy period of hibernation. While the initial spark that had been provided by the ELN was fading, the FARC, led by Manuel Marulanda, continued to operate with ever-increasing autonomy, even while adopting defensive tactics: it was well organized and impossible to capture. In the meantime another guerrilla group with Maoist tendencies, the Ejército popular de liberación, founded in 1968, started operations in the mountains of the Alto Sinú. Later the FARC and the ELN formed the Coordinadora guerrillera Simón Bolivar, which during César Gaviria's presidency would start negotiations to reach a "national pacification." Yet the political, ideological, and organizational transformations that the guerrilla groups had to undergo in the following years, most especially regarding their involvement in the drug trade, make a comparison of their experience with that of other Guevarist groups impossible.

In Bolivia, after Che's death the Ejército de liberación nacional attempted to regroup, initially under Inti Peredo's command—but its network had been destroyed and its leader was killed at the end of 1969, before he could once more take to the mountains—and later, in 1970, under the command of doctor Chato Fernando Peredo, Inti and Roberto Coco's brother (the latter had died with Che). Despite the fact that General Juan José Torres's government had freed political prisoners (including Debray) and allowed some guerrillas who had been with Che to cross the border with Chile, where they were welcomed by Senate president Salvador Allende, Chato returned to fight in the mountains, in Teoponte, together with about fifty students. After three months he was alone with a few survivors; the others had either died from hardships, or had been captured and then immediately executed by the army. After Colonel Hugo Banzer's (1971–78) successful coup—financed by the Central Intelligence Agency and Brazil—and the ensuing extremely harsh repression against the guerrillas, political parties, and trade unions, the Bolivian guerrilla season started by Che also came to an end.

Pro-Cuban organizations also formed in Brazil, largely as a result of splits within the Communist Party: the Partido comunista do Brasil, which adopted a pro-Chinese position; Politica opéraria; Açao popular; the Movimiento tirandentes tied to the peasant leagues of the Northeast; in 1962 the Açao libertadora nacional of Carlos Marighela (who would be killed in São Paolo in 1969); and the Partido comunista brasileiro revolucionario of Mario Alves and Apolhonio de Carvalho. The strategic and historical military coup of April 1, 1964, against the constitutional government of Joao Goulart, inaugurated a long series of military dictatorships that gradu-

ally extended from Brazil, epicenter of the antiguerrilla policies of counterinsurgency as well as preventive and systematic repression, to Bolivia, Uruguay, Chile, and Argentina. The Movimiento 8 de octubre, descended from the Var-Palmares guerrilla group, under the leadership of Carlos Lamarca, vainly tried to move its actions from the cities to the countryside.

The Tupamaros in Uruguay were the most successful guerrilla movement in terms of creating alliances. It was also one of the most autonomous and independent—characteristics that differentiated it from the model theorized by the Castroists. The Movimiento de liberación nacional–Tupamaros was started in 1963. It was based on the farm-laborer union organizations lead by Raúl Sendic—a lawyer like Castro, who came from the old Partido socialista de Uruguay—and soon extended to many sectors of the middle classes and proletariat. For the national elections in 1971, the Tupamaros publicly declared a cease-fire and supported the new Frente amplio, which became the country's third force. But in 1973, with the help of the Central Intelligence Agency and Brazilian military, a military dictatorship was installed; it would last for twelve years.

In Argentina, with Che's backing and Cuban and Algerian support, the group Ejército guerrilliero del pueblo of Jorge Ricardo Masetti was born in 1963. Masetti's battle name was "Comandante Segundo," because the group expected the name "Comandante Primero" to be assigned to Che on his reentry to Argentina. The initial center of activity was established near Orán, in the northeast of Salta Province, almost at the Bolivian border. For various political and organizational reasons, this group's guerrilla activity got off to a poor start, and the group itself was destroyed by the army in 1964. The Ejército revolucionario del pueblo was Guevarist in character, and its military operations were urban, notwithstanding its attempt to create a guerrilla headquarters in the province of Tucumán. It was the armed wing of the Partido revolucionario de los trabajadores, affiliated with the Fourth International and founded in 1968 by Mario Roberto Santucho, who died in battle in 1973. The Cuban guerrilla experience would also exert a notable influence on the Montoneros, the movement of the Peronist revolutionary Left founded in 1969. It was led by Mario Eduardo Firmenich, who was detained and then extradited from Brazil in 1984, sentenced to thirty years in prison and then given amnesty by President Carlos Saúl Menem in 1990. With the systematic genocide carried out by the Junta Militar of Jorge Videla, Roberto

Viola, and Leopoldo Galtieri (1976–82), the Argentine guerrillas who did not succeed in escaping into exile were killed, along with thirty thousand missing.

The continuous and innovative struggle against dictatorship, for the return to democracy and the respect of human rights, made it possible to overcome and close the historical cycle started by the armed Guevarist utopia.

See also Anti-imperialism; Castro, Fidel; Cuban Revolution; Guevara de la Serna, Ernesto Rafael; Maoism; Nationalism; Sandinista Revolution.

FURTHER READING

Aldrighi, C. *La izquierda armada.* Montevideo: Ediciones Trilce, 2001.

Cannabrava Filho, P. *En el ojo de la tormenta: América Latina en los años 60/70.* México: Plaza y Valdés, 2002.

Fernández Huidobro, E. *Historia de los Tupamaros. 3 tomos.* Montevideo: Ediciones de la Banda Oriental, 1999.

Gott, R. *Guerrilla Movements in Latin America.* London: Seagull Books, 2008.

ALBERTO FILIPPI

Guevara de la Serna, Ernesto Rafael

Ernesto Rafael Guevara de la Serna (1928–67), known as "el Che" or simply "Che," grew up in an anti-Fascist and anti-Francoist family, influenced by the presence of exiled Communists and Socialists in Argentina. Politics during these years was dominated by the struggle between Juan Domingo Perón and the Unión democratica. Che would maintain his independence from political parties, however—a choice he would honor until his meeting with the brothers Raúl and Fidel Castro Ruz, in August 1955 in Mexico. He was greatly attracted to Castro's and the other young militants of the Movimiento 26 de julio's plans; many of its militants, including Castro, came from the ranks of the Partido ortodoxo and its radical-populist orientation. Che, a doctor, joined the group of eighty-two rebels, who on the night of November 24–25, 1956, left from Veracruz on the yacht *Granma* and headed to Cuba's shores. On July 21, Castro made him commander of the second column of the rebel army, and with it he would carry out operations that would prove decisive in the fall of Fulgencio Batista's dictatorship. On January 2, the columns led by Che and Camilo Cienfuegos entered Havana, which was paralyzed by an insurrectionary strike.

Performing a variety of duties, Che was influential in defining the course of the Cuban Revolution, moving many of the "Left bourgeoisie" and reformist components of the Movimiento 26 de julio toward anti-imperialist positions and closer to the Soviet Union. Che's first position, as Supervisor general de la cooperación técnica, militar y financiera, was significant: it was conceived to further anti-imperialist struggles on the continent, particularly those of the Communist parties in Venezuela, Guatemala, Columbia, and Peru, and support the national liberation fronts, such as Carlos Fonseca Amador's Sandinistas. Che also thought that the USSR's support was indispensable for consolidating the Cuban Revolution, since he was convinced of the inevitability of an armed confrontation with the United States, like the one he had observed in Guatemala where the United States had organized a coup to overthrow the constitutional government of Jacobo Arbenz.

In the revolution's aftermath, Castro's followers established privileged relations with Soviet emissaries, among them Nikolaj Leonov, who was responsible for all Committee for State Security operations in North and South America. Che underestimated the original and exceptional characteristics determining the phases of the revolution in progress; he therefore concluded that the guerrilla experience could and should be generalized as a theoretical model and "method" that could be applied to other countries in Latin America. At the same time, it was important for Cuba to be able to rely on the support of nonaligned countries and what was then beginning to be referred to as the third world. In June 1959 Guevara went on a trip to Egypt, India, Japan, Indonesia, Ceylon (Sri Lanka), Pakistan, and Yugoslavia, meeting Gamal Nasser, Jawaharlal Nehru, Sukarno, and Josip Broz Tito. Later, in October 1960, he visited the USSR for the first time, and was welcomed as the "worthy and glorious commander" by Khrushchev. Immediately afterward Che was greeted in Beijing by Mao Zedong and Zhou Enlai; they agreed to establish diplomatic relations between China and Cuba. He then returned to Cuba via Prague and Berlin.

The invasion of Cuba, directed by the John F. Kennedy administration, and the Bay of Pigs landing, on April 15–21, 1961, which was defeated by Castroist armed forces, led to a shift in relations between the Soviet

Union, Cuba, and the entire Latin American Left. For the first time, following Che's example, Castro spoke of a "socialist Cuba," and he began to think that it would be indispensable to receive not only economic aid but also significant military support from the Kremlin, significant enough to keep the United States in check. In August 1962, Che returned to Moscow to conclude an agreement with the Communist Party of the Soviet Union's leaders whose purpose was the installation of nuclear missiles on Cuban territory. The controversial solution to the "missile crisis" in October 1962, the last agreement between the Castro brothers and Che, led to a tense exchange between the Cuban leaders and Khrushchev and Anastas Mikoyan. The agreement between Kennedy and Khrushchev, establishing the reciprocal influence of U.S. and USSR policies on Latin America and Europe, de facto created the boundaries within which Cuba had some margin to maneuver in "exporting the revolution" to Latin America, subjecting it to the recognition of global spheres of influence. Relations with the Soviet Union, essential for the island's survival given the economic blockade that Washington had decreed in 1962, were to remain crucial up to the Gorbachev years. As president of the Banco Nacional (1960) and then minister for industry, Che completed some noteworthy theoretical and institutional work, whose goal was to organize the Cuban economy in an original fashion when compared to the Soviet experience. As a matter of principle Che refused "economic socialism," if it was separated from a "Communist morality." He instead defended an approach that tied political economy to ethics, believing that revolutionary consciousness was a factor in economic transformation and the creation of a "new man." Che was convinced that the edification of communism by means of an accelerated industrialization process could occur over a brief time period, skipping the socialist phase. These were positions he repeated in his speech during the Algiers Conference and they showed that he was distancing himself from a pro-Soviet position, which the Castro brothers instead still respected; at the same time he de facto accepted the break in relations between the Cuban government and China.

In 1964 he went first to Geneva and then to New York, for the annual General Assembly of the United Nations. Here he was among the few who supported Congo's cause and the desperate struggle by Patrice Lumumba's followers against Moise Chombe. After New York, Che began his last trip as a representative of the Cuban government—to China, where he met with Chou, and then to Algeria, Mali, Congo-Brazzaville (the Republic of the Congo), Guinea, Ghana, Dahomey (the Republic of Benin), Tanzania, and Egypt. Among others he met Ahmed Ben Bella of Algeria, the Ghanaian Kwame Nkrumah, Modibo Keita from Mali, Tanzania's Julius Kambarage Nyerere, Nasser, and Guinea's Ahmed Sekou Touré, who constituted the most radical group of leaders in the Organization of African Unity. On March 14, 1965, Che appeared in public in Cuba for the last time. He intended to lead the Cuban military presence in Congo personally, and undertook this difficult mission for six months; both Ben Bella and Nasser had advised against it, and Che later also considered it a "failure." During this time he was able to observe firsthand the harsh colonial heritage that undermined the oppressed insurgents' morale. On the one hand, Beijing supported Pierre Mulele's guerrilla group, which was still active in western Congo. On the other hand, in the eastern area, on the shores of Lake Tanganyika, where Che had decided to work, there was a bunch of guerrillas led by followers of Lumumba, who had survived defeat in Stanleyville; among them was Laurent Kabila, who more than thirty years later would become the president of Zaire. Supported by the Soviets and the Organization of African Unity, the guerrillas depended logistically on a base located in Burundi, on the eastern shore of the lake.

Once his strategy of guerrilla internationalism had come up short, confronted with the tough realities of Congo, Che decided to return to Latin America—not to Cuba, but to Argentina instead, where some months beforehand the experiment of the Ejército guerrilliero del pueblo guided by his friend Jorge Ricardo Masetti in Salta had failed. Dissuaded by Castro himself, Che would retreat, at least tactically, to Bolivia, which since it bordered five different Latin American countries was considered a "strategic rearguard"; the plan was to start and support guerrilla activity in Argentina and Peru. Many different causes on both the internal and international political level made it impossible for Che to realize his strategic objectives: the choice of site from which to start his guerrilla movement; a failure to establish alliances with almost any of the parties of the Left, from the Partido revolucionario de la izquierda nacional to the Trotskyist Partido obrero revolucionario to the pro-Soviet Communists of Mario Monje—with the exception of the pro-Chinese Communists led by Moisés Guevara, who died with others on August 31 in an ambush set by the Bolivian military at Vado del Yeso, because some local peasants had betrayed them; Che's underestimation of the efficiency of the Bolivian military, which had been well prepared in antiguerrilla struggles thanks to direct assistance from the United States; and above all, as he himself was later to recognize, the fact that "the peasant masses were of no help to us in any fashion." The slogan "create two, three, many Vietnams," whose purpose was to generalize the specific circumstances of the national liberation struggle led by Ho Chi Minh, highlighted the extreme prepolitical abstractness that Che's armed utopia was based on—a utopia in which militarism and voluntarism converged, indistinct and disconnected from historical reality. Effects are not causes: Congo was not Cuba; Bolivia was not Vietnam.

When, on the morning of October 9, 1967, on the orders of General René Barrientos and working together with Central Intelligence Agency agents, Che was killed in the little school of La Higuera by Sergeant Mario Terán, he was only thirty-nine years old.

See also Anti-imperialism; Castro, Fidel; Cuban Revolution; Guerrilla Warfare in Latin America.

FURTHER READING
Anderson, J. L. *Che Guevara: A Revolutionary Life*. New York: Grove/Atlantic, 1998.
Calzada Macho, I. *"Che" Guevara*. Buenos Aires: Folio, 2003.
Castañeda, J. G. *Compañero: The Life and Death of Che Guevara*. New York: Knopf, 1997.
Debray, R. *Che's Guerrilla War*. Harmondsworth, UK: Penguin, 1975.
Filippi, A. *Il mito del Che. Storia e ideologia dell'utopia guevariana*. Torino: Einaudi, 2007.
Jones, H. *The Bay of Pigs*. Oxford: Oxford University Press, 2008.
Martínez, F. *El Che, el socialismo*. Mexico: Editorial Nuestro Tiempo, 1989.
Nuñez Jimenez, A. *El Che en combate, la campaña guerrillera en Cuba central*. Havana: Instituto Cubano del libro, 1995.
O'Donnell, P. *Che. La vida por un mundo major*. Barcelona: Editorial Sudamericana, 2003.
Tutino, S. *Guevara al tempo di Guevara, 1957–1976*. Rome: Editori Riuniti, 1996.
Che's works are being published by the Centro de Estudios Che Guevara and Ocean Press in Havana (centroche@enet.cu), and Feltrinelli and Mondadori in Italy.

ALBERTO FILIPPI

Gulag

The Stalinist gulag (*Glavnoe upravlenie lagenej*, "central camp administration") was, together with the Maoist Laogai, the most extensive system of forced labor camps in the 20th century. The word "gulag" owes its notoriety to Aleksandr Solzhenitsyn's *Gulag Archipelago*, "an essay in investigative narrative," published in the West in 1974. For Solzhenitsyn the concentration camp experience was an integral part of the Soviet system from its inception, that is to say from the time of Lenin. On this fundamental issue Solzhenitsyn distanced himself from the few Western researchers who, starting in the mid 1950s, had begun to collect the scarce documentation available on the gulag. Among these pioneering works are those of the *Commission internationale contre le régime concentrationnaire*, published in 1957 under Paul Barton's direction.

The gulag's origins were one of the first elements to cause divisions among historians. Until the early 1990s the fact that Soviet archives were closed to the public prevented researchers from acquiring a deeper knowledge of the Soviet concentration camp system. The availability of the huge archives of the gulag administration, as well as of the interior and justice ministries, in recent years has allowed historians to conduct detailed research on a number of issues that had been the subject of passionate debate for decades: the number of detainees, the mortality rate in the camps, the types of sentences, the function and relevance of forced labor in the Soviet economy, and sociological information about the detainees. It has finally become possible to undertake true historical studies of the gulag.

In a pioneering study of the Nazi concentration camp system, Olga Wormser-Migot wrote: "It is difficult to deal with this topic in a static fashion, limiting it to its ideal-typical situation, and without taking the time factor into account." These reflections are even more pertinent when applied to the Soviet camp system, which lasted at least three times as long as the Nazi concentration camp system. And they will serve as a guide in the following summary of the gulag's historys.

The Gulag before the Gulag

The gulag as an administrative entity grouping all the detention facilities of the various Soviet republics together dates to 1934; the camps, however, appeared in Soviet Russia in the summer of 1918. One of the issues of debate among historians regards the origin of the 1930s camps and their possible derivation from those of 1918–22. This is a dubious derivation. During the first years of the Bolshevik regime's existence there were two types of camps: concentration camps (*kontzlageri*) and corrective labor camps. The former could be classified in the category of internment camps for migrants and refugees that had existed in many of the countries involved in World War I: with the Bolshevik twist, however, of arbitrary internment, as a precautionary measure, of specific categories of "class enemies" (kulaks, priests, bourgeois, landowners) to be used as "hostages." The Bolshevik regime simultaneously experimented with the corrective labor camp. This camp was based on two utopian principles, which, according to their intentions, ought to have inspired the novel detention policies of the new Soviet state: the self-financing of the detention facilities themselves and the reeducation of the detainees through labor. In actuality during the civil war the distinction between concentration camps and corrective labor camps was largely fictitious. Starting in 1922 the concentration camps were dismantled and the corrective labor camps were replaced by traditional prisons. Only several "special camps" supervised by the political police (OGPU) remained. In the most important of these facilities, the one located in the Solovki islands, several thousand detainees sentenced by the political police's special tribunals were gathered: political adversaries and even common criminals whose crimes had caused direct damage to the state's interests (forgers, criminals guilty of significant robberies). In the 1920s the traditional prison (in which about 98 percent of those sentenced were detained) was the norm. Starting in 1925–26, however, the idea started to spread among higher-level party functionaries that one might make the detainees work by transferring them to corrective labor camps located in inhospitable, scarcely populated areas that were rich in raw materials.

The "Great Turn": Realization and Expansion in the 1930s.

On June 27, 1929, the politburo made an important decision: all those sentenced to more than three years would from that moment on be transferred to the collective labor camps administered by the OGPU. The utopia of reeducation through labor resurfaced. The most important goal of this reorganization of the penal system was, howerver, mainly economic: in order for the First Five-Year Plan to succeed all available manpower needed to be mobilized. In the course of only a few

months there was a boom in the number of detainees. Stalin had committed himself to the Great Turn— forced collectivization of the countryside and the accompanying "dekulakization." In 1930 alone more than 300,000 kulaks were arrested: these farmers became the first great contingent of detainees to be administered by the newly instituted General Directorate of Corrective Labor Camps (GOUITL), which was supervised by the OGPU. Four years later, having absorbed all the prisons for detainees sentenced to shorter terms, which had previously been supervised by the People's Commissariat for Justice, the Central Camps Administration (GULAG, an acronym that could be more easily pronounced) made its entry into history.

The first great penal worksite, employing 120,000 detainees, involved the completion of a canal between the Baltic Sea and the White Sea. This first pharaonic project already contained all the system's flaws: inhumane living conditions (with a mortality rate on the order of 10 percent per year) and working conditions (all work was manual, done exclusively with a shovel, a pick-axe, and a wheelbarrow); uselessness or inoperability of the finished product (to finish the project on schedule the OGPU built it much shallower than specified in the engineers' plans, so the 150 miles of the canal could only be used by vessels whose draft was limited); and *tufta*, a key word in the gulag's lexicon, which simultaneously means "waste," "deceit," "false accounting," and "embezzlement."

Around the mid-1930s the gulag's geography had already been defined, in its broad outlines, for the next twenty years. From west to east, from Karelia to Sakhalin, there were eight large concentration camp complexes, each made up of dozens, if not hundreds, of mostly mobile camps that moved with the worksites. The largest of these complexes was the Dalstroy, in the immense icy and isolated territory of Kolyma. Considered strategic and top priority, the Dalstroy, which housed about 15 percent of the gulag's detainees, was tasked to mine gold. Since Kolyma did not have any land transportation routes to the rest of the country, the detainees were transported by ship to Magadan, then transferred along the only existing road to the mining areas. The living conditions there were particulary inhumane and have been masterfully described in Varlam Shalamov's *Kolyma Tales*. The second great concentration camp complex was the Pharaonic worksite at Bamlag (260,000 detainees in 1939), whose task was building the railroad: one of its main goals was to double the available tracks on the Trans-Siberian line from Lake Baikal to the Amur River. The Ozerlag was located in eastern Siberia, on the shores of the Baikal, and specialized in the production of wood. The Noril-lag was located in the extreme north, around the city of Noril'sk, which had been built by detainees: its specialty was nickel mining. The fourth large gulag complex consisted of camps at Kuzbass, which provided forced labor to the great coal *Kombinats*. Further south the great Stelag complex contained both camps for copper mining and agricultural camps that were meant to utilize the virgin soil of the Kazakh steppes. Another great complex was located in the northern Urals and it contained the Uchtpečlag camps (clear-cutting of woods, road building), the Vorkutlag camps around the city of Vorkuta (coal mining), and the Sevjeldorlag camps (whose main task was the construction of the railroad line between Kotla and Vorkuta). Finally on this side of the Urals the detention complexes in Karelia (forest exploitation) and the Dmitlag (excavation of a canal between the Moscova and Volga rivers) demonstrate that the gulag was relatively close to the most densely populated areas of European Russia.

The Prisoners' World

Contrary to a widely held belief, the gulag's detainees were not mostly political prisoners condemned by special tribunals for "counterrevolutionary activities" on the basis of one of the fourteen subsections of the sadly famous article 58 of the penal code. The so-called article 58s ranged, in fact, depending on the year, from between 20 and 25 percent of the gulag's detainees. In addition to a small minority of Stalin regime opponents (Mensheviks, Social-Revolutionaries, Trotskyists), the majority of article 58s had been sentenced either because of their "terrible" social background ("bourgeoisie" and other "people from the past") or because of professional activities tied, more or less directly, to the previous regime. Only during the Great Terror, during the years 1937–38, did the number of those arrested and sentenced for "counterrevolutionary activities" by a special tribunal become dominant. In these two years more than 800,000 people, usually sentenced to ten years in a camp, arrived in the gulag. As a result, the system registered its first "growth crisis," leading to the hurried opening of new camps and the subsequent increase in the mortality rate, which in 1938 reached about 9 percent (about triple the rate of previous years). With the exception of the years of the Great Terror, the majority of those sentenced to the gulag were not there because of supposed "counterrevolutionary activities." One cannot, however, conclude

that these were therefore only "common criminals" in the usual sense of the term either. The majority of the "nonpoliticals" was made up of normal citizens, victims of a ferociously repressive criminal law that used disproportionately severe sentencing for minor crimes, as well as for often insignificant gestures of social insubordination: an unauthorized change of occupation, a violation of the "passport laws," vandalism, "parasitism," "speculation," and above all "damaging or stealing social property." The "social property thiefs," who were often kolkhoz workers who had stolen grain in the collective fields or workers who had made off with "deficient" products, were those who made up the bulk of the gulag's principal contingents.

Contrary to another widely held belief, entry into the gulag did not mean there could be no exit. Since the average sentence was five years in a camp, each year a quarter of those detained was released, with the exception of the "politicals," who were generally sentenced to ten years (if not more, after the war), and whose sentences were mostly systematically and arbitrarily prolonged. Statistical data relative to the social and national background of the detainees point to the fact that the gulag's society, from the sociological and national point of view, was basically a faithful reflection of Soviet society in its entirety, with a noticeable predominance of detainees from the working classes and a slightly higher than average presence of intellectuals, of individuals with a high school diploma, and of those the authorities defined as "people of the past." As far as the percentages of nationalities making up "the great family of the USSR's peoples" are concerned, the national averages were respected, at least up to the second half of the 1940s. Only after World War II were these proportions subject to change. The resistance to Sovietization in the western Ukraine and in the Baltic countries accounts for the higher percentages of detainees coming from territories recently annexed by the Soviet Union.

Accounts given by former detainees (from Solzhenitsyn to Eugenia Ginzburg, from Shalamov to Jacques Rossi to Margarete Buber-Neumann, to cite only the most renowned) are unanimous in their descriptions of exhausting labor, constant hunger, a cold that penetrated to the bones (of thinned and weakened bodies) for ten out of the twelve months of the year, dirt, endemic illnesses (pellagra, scurvy, tuberculosis), epidemics (typhoid fevers), and also promiscuousness and degradation of conduct in a universe in which criminals (whom the administration would typically appoint to key positions), "politicals," illiterate kolkhoz members, and intellectuals lived cheek by jowl. These accounts, which can today be compared to numerous reports by the gulag bureaucracy, also insist on another aspect: in the gulag the worst was never certain, inevitable, or planned. Chance, disorder, sometimes even chaos were always in charge, together with corrupt guards and inconsistent discipline. The shirkers were countless: in the kitchen, in the infirmary, in those "secondary activity laboratories" whose status was uncertain, and in which the detainees sometimes managed, over the course of several days, but sometimes even of several weeks, to restore their strength. The gulag was a survival school. There were terrible camps that transformed the prisoner into a skeleton in the course of a few weeks: Kolyma, Vorkuta, and Noril'sk, for example. In Kazakhstan's agricultural colonies, however, living conditions were not nearly as tough.

How many detainees went through the gulag system? How many died? These questions have been debated at length, but the archives of the gulag administration, the prosecutor's office, the interior and justice ministries basically agree that over a period of a little more than twenty years, from the early 1930s to 1953, 20 million people experienced the gulag and about 1,800,000 died. The mortality rate varied noticeably as a function of the year and the camps affected. Before World War II, the deadliest year in the gulag was 1933, the year of the great famine in many areas of the country (Ukraine, northern Caucasus, Kazakhstan). In 1933 one out of eight prisoners would die of starvation or illness.

Survival conditions for the gulag's detainees were never as terrible as during the war. Famines, epidemics, overcrowding, inhuman exploitation: this was the fate of the prisoner who managed to survive those years. The gulag's population changed considerably: in 1941 about 600,000 prisoners who had been interned by the authorities' own admission for "insignificant crimes" were freed and immediately drafted into the Red Army. During the war, over a million detainees were freed ahead of time and went directly from the camp to the front. On the other hand, repression against the "politicals" was intensified: not one single article 58 prisoner was freed upon conclusion of sentence before the end of the war. The mortality rates were high: 20 percent in 1942, 17 percent in 1943, and 8 percent in 1944. During those three years a total of 900,000 detainees died. The most solid, and the most hardened individuals, both among the "politicals" and among the "common," were the ones who survived. In 1945 the gulag population had reached its lowest level

since the mid-1930s: 1,200,000 prisoners at the beginning of 1945 from 2,000,000 at the war's outset. The second half of the 1940s instead witnessed formidable growth, with a doubling of the population. But the gulag's climax was also marked by an unprecedented crisis in the concentration camp system.

Climax and Crisis

The gulag's population reached its highest point (about 2,700,000) during the early 1950s. This noticeable increase can be explained by the arrival of new contingents: "collaborationists," real or presumed; "nationalists," and "socially extraneous elements" from recently Sovietized countries (Baltic states, western Ukraine, Moldavia). There was, however, also a significant influx of "common citizens," the victims of extremely repressive legislation. For example, according to laws introduced on June 4, 1947, any infraction against "social property" or "state property" meant a sentence varying from five to twenty-five years in a camp. Over the course of six years, about 1,500,000 people were given harsh sentences (from six to ten years in a camp). Among those condemned for theft, working-class or kolkhoz women were numerous (these were often war widows who had stolen out of necessity or as a matter of survival). In 1949 there were more than 500,000 women detainees in the gulag. In addition to these detainees, improperly classified as "common," there was a growing number of real opponents of the Soviet system, including Baltic and Ukrainian Nationalists with guerrilla training. Starting in 1948, about 200,000 of these detainees, considered especially dangerous, were transferred to so-called special camps, which soon became hotbeds of insubordination. Between 1948 and 1953 there were about thirty hunger strikes, collective work refusals, and rebellions of various kinds in these camps. The situation was also deteriorating in the "normal" camps, however, where the administration was increasingly powerless to react to the spectacular drop in the productivity of forced labor, the multiplication of incidents involving detainees and guard personnel, the increasing power of the organized gangs (to which the administration had delegated some duties in maintenance of law and order). In an attempt to stimulate productivity, prizes and even "salaries" (truthfully quite insignificant) were introduced for individuals who went beyond the stated objectives. These "reforms" clashed with the reality of a concentration camp world run with an antiquated productive infrastructure, which had not seen new investments in recent years. The last great penal worksites of the Stalin era—the hydroelectric power plants of Kubyčev and Stalingrad, and of the Volga-Don canal—were the sites of increasing delays. From 1951 to 1952 there was a significant increase in early releases on the condition that the released detainees committed to working in the same area.

The End of the Gulag

In the days following Stalin's death, Lavrenty Beria, head of the Ministry of the Interior and Ministry for State Security complex, introduced a series of reforms that reorganized the gulag in depth. The camp system now passed to the Ministry of Justice, its economic infrastructure to the most pertinent ministries. Even more spectacular than this restructuring was the announcement on March 27, 1953, of a wide-ranging amnesty. In the course of several months, 1,200,000 detainees ("politicals" excepted) were freed. This "mass exodus" occurred in an improvised fashion and was the cause of numerous accidents, mostly due to the lack of planning. The amnesty was the source of widespread dissatisfaction among the population, the police, and those who had been excluded from the amnesty. In the confusion, complicated in the summer of 1953 by the official announcement of Beria's arrest, a wave of protests, work refusals, and disturbances hit the "special" camps: Noril'sk in May 1953, Vorkuta in July 1953, Ekibastuz and Kemguir in May 1954. The detainees created strike committees that put forward a series of demands: limiting the workday to nine hours; eliminating the detainee number on clothing; including the "politicals" in amnesty. In a sign that times were changing, negotiations were held with the prisoners and some of their requests were granted (in Noril'sk and Vorkuta). In Kemguir, however, the most important and long-lasting revolt was quashed with the use of armored cars and the "instigators" were executed. At the beginning of 1955 the long process of liberating the "politicals" accelerated after the Twentieth Congress of CPSU: in 1956–1957 about 400,000 prisoners detained on the basis of article 58 of the penal code were freed. Liberation however, did not mean rehabilitation. In those same two years fewer than 60,000 former detainees for presumed "counterrevolutionary" crimes were rehabilitated. With the liberation of the "politicals," the post-Stalin gulag initially witnessed a significant reduction in its prisoner population, then a stabilization in its numbers around the early 1960s. With the gradual exhaustion of the pioneering role of the gulag in the colonization and the exploitation of the natural resources of the Great North and the Far East of the USSR, the huge detention complexes of the Stalin era were broken up and integrated into the local economy. The gulag's geography also changed: the camps, subdivided into small "penal colonies," were once more prevalently located in the European regions of the Soviet Union. Imprisonment slowly resumed the normal regulative function of any society, although in the USSR it still retained peculiarities it acquired from belonging to a political system that was outside the norms of a constitutional state. In the wake of sociopolitical campaigns whose aim was the repression of behaviors considered deviant or intolerable, in addition to the usual criminal population, normal citizens and a tiny minority of "dissidents" (from several hundred to several thousand, depending on the year) were also imprisoned, charged in the majority of cases with "anti-Soviet agitation and propaganda."

What remains today of the gulag? Apparently, very little. Unlike the barracks in Buchenwald, Ravensbruck, or Auschwitz, the wooden barracks of the gulag have completely disappeared, swallowed up by the taiga or by the city outskirts of Komsomol'sk, Magadan, Vorkuta, Noril'sk, all built by the detainees. The gulag continues, however, to weigh on post-Soviet society. After the implosion of the USSR, the number of detainees in the penal colonies increased over time to more than a million in the Russian Federation alone, whose population was much smaller than the Soviet Union's during Stalin's era. The severity of the sentencing and the high level of social delinquency reflected the severe tensions that affected the post-Soviet regions as well as the legacy of a recent past marked by a veritable "gulagization" of the body politic, to the extent that in the space of one generation one adult in six had some experience of the camps.

See also Camps; Collectivization of the Countryside; Deportation of Nationalities in the USSR; Great Terror; KGB; Shalamov, Varlam; Solzhenitsyn, Aleksandr; Stalinism; Totalitarianism.

FURTHER READING

Applebaum, A. *Gulag: A History*. New York: Doubleday, 2003.

Chlevnjuk, O. V. *The History of the Gulag. From Collectivization to the Great Terror*. New Haven, CT: Yale University Press, 2004.

Craveri, M. *Resistenza nel Gulag. Un capitolo inedito della destalinizzazione in Unione Sovietica*. Soveria Mannelli: Rubbettino, 2003.

Dundovich, E., F. Gori, and E. Guercetti. *Reflections on the Gulag. With a Documentary Appendix on the Italian Victims of Repression in the USSR.* Milan: Feltrinelli, 2003.

Gregory, P. R., and V. A. Lazarev, eds. *The Economics of Forced Labor: The Soviet Gulag.* Stanford, CA: Hoover Institution Press, 2003.

Ivanova, G. M., *Labor Camp Socialism: The Gulag in the Soviet Totalitarian System.* Armonk, NY: M. E. Sharpe, 2000.

Solzhenitsyn, A., *Gulag Archipelago, 1918–1956: An Experiment in Literary Investigation.* New York: Harper and Row, 1985.

NICOLAS WERTH

Havel, Václav

Václav Havel (1936–) was born to a wealthy family of builders, but he did not attend high school or a university regularly. In the early 1960s he worked as a machinist, electrician, and secretary at the little Na zabradii (On the Balustrade) theater in Prague. His first pieces as a dramatist, dating from this period, were similar in character to the so-called theater of the absurd: *The Garden Party, Memorandum*, and *The Increased Difficulty of Concentration*. During the Prague Spring, Havel founded the Circle of Independent Writers. After the invasion by the Warsaw Pact and the onset of repression, Havel was not allowed to publish or stage his works (which were becoming more successful abroad), including *The Conspirators, The Beggar's Opera, Mountain Hotel*, and *Audience*.

His first open challenge to the regime came in 1967, with the publication of *Brief Intellectual Biography* by the émigré 68 Publishers, headed by Josef Skforecký in Toronto, and his open letter to the secretary of the Communist Party, Gustáv Husák, *Regarding Entropy in Politics*. Havel, an intellectual, entered politics against his will, as he confessed in *Interrogation at a Distance*: "I have never systematically concerned myself with politics. I am a writer and I have always conceived of my mission as consisting in the obligation to tell the truth about the world in which I live, to proclaim its horrors and miseries, and therefore more to warn than point towards solutions."

His next contrary act was signing the founding document of Charter 77 as its spokesperson. From that moment on, he would be repeatedly arrested and jailed (the longest period was from 1979 to 1983; he was then freed for health reasons). His political proclamations, masked as letters from prison to his wife (*Letters to Olga*), were to grant him recognition as the regime's principal inter-

nal opponent, and earn him moral and political credit with his compatriots. Given his lucid passion, Havel proved to be the theoretician of civil society's nonviolent struggle. *The Power of the Powerless* is the title of his most important political essay, which endorses a new form of politics: "apolitical" politics sustained by an obstinate search for truth against power's lies. The fact that he had never been a Communist enabled him to avoid the uncertainties and caution of some old-style politicians, who also found themselves in the opposition against their will, like Alexander Dubcek, prisoner to an idea of democratic reform of the socialist system that was to prove impractical and unpopular.

Havel's antipolitical proposals (perhaps better designated as antiparty) focused on the creation of a democracy of free individuals, in the sense that everyone could count, decide, control, and change. Therefore every organizational form must be at each individual self's service, and each institutional form must prevent the gravest dangers to democracy from being realized—the inversion of priorities between subject and function, between individuals and their instruments. Parties are necessary, but only as instruments. As parties, they should be excluded from power: "It would be better if the organized and stable forms of politics had the institutional lack of seriousness characteristic of clubs and were always inclined to defer. The choice of human beings for different positions must regard individuals whom the parties will provide with support, tools, knowledge and organizational apparatuses. Power which is transformed into a profession, a vote that becomes merchandise, leads to individuals losing themselves and the end of authentic democracy."

As author of these ideas, Havel became the leader of the so-called Velvet Revolution in November 1989. He negotiated the transition of power, in his role as head of Civic Forum, with the representatives of the outgoing regime. On December 29, 1989, he was elected president of the republic, after having been a member of the National Assembly, and was reelected at the beginning of July 1990. The Czech and Slovak republics divided under nationalist pressures that were inflaming the ex-Soviet empire. But while elsewhere ethnic divisions were transformed into violent tragedies, here, in the center of Europe, thanks to the president's indefatigable mediation and the populations' common sense, the separation occurred without drama. Havel, who was decidedly opposed to the split, and who considered the experience a personal defeat, resigned in the summer of 1992. In January 1993, however, he became the president of the newly born Czech Republic, and was reelected in 1997.

After Havel withdrew from politics, he became an even more tormented intellectual: "I believe that the causes for the crisis the world finds itself in today are based in something deeper than a specific way of organizing the economy or in a specific political system. . . . In some fashion in the background of the contemporary crisis I feel the proud anthropocentrism of modern humans, convinced they can know everything, and are able to adapt to anything."

See also Charter 77; Dissent in the USSR; Revolutions in East-Central Europe.

FURTHER READING

Havel, V. *Dell'entropia in politica*. Bologna: Centro Studi Europa Orientale, 1981.
———. *The Power of the Powerless: Citizens against the State in Central-Eastern Europe*. Armonk, NY: M. E. Sharpe, 1985.
———. *Letters to Olga: June 1979–September 1982*. New York: Knopf, 1988.
———. *Interrogatorio a distanza*. Milan: Garzanti, 1990.

FRANCESCO M. CATALUCCIO

Hilferding, Rudolf

Of Austrian origins, and therefore part of the "Austro-Marxist" political milieu, Rudolf Hilferding (1877–1941) was active mostly in Germany, becoming a German citizen in 1919. Initially engaged in political reflection, he adapted the analytic instruments and conceptual apparatus of Marxism to the study of social and economic problems that belonged to a historical period Marx himself had not experienced. This was the premise of his book *Finance Capital* (1910), the most significant contribution by a Marxist thinker after Marx to the development of economic theory. Its focus was on capitalism's most recent morphological transformations, especially the processes of concentration of capital, development of joint-stock companies, separation of ownership and management, integration of banking and industry, and export of capital. Overall Hilferding perceived a tendency toward the organization of market, financial, and productive activities within individual countries, and toward an increase in competition and conflict on the international level, in this new era of "imperialist" capitalism. This, in turn, would inevitably lead to military conflicts in his view. Hilferding's work was singled out by Lenin in his analysis of imperialism, but this was the only (minimal) area of contact between the analyses of the Austro-German social democrat and the Bolshevik Communist world.

In the postwar period Hilferding—who in 1917, dissenting from the Social Democratic Party of Germany's social patriotism, had joined the Independent Social Democratic Party of Germany—was personally involved in opposing the independent party's attempt to join the Communist International. In 1923, after the reunification of the Social Democratic Party with the Independent Social Democratic Party's non-Communist minority, Hilferding was briefly finance minister during the months that would lead to Germany's exit from its postwar inflationary spiral; he occupied the same position in 1928–29, coming into conflict with the high finance milieu right before the crisis that would engulf the German economy and the country's democratic institutions. During Weimar's Social Democratic period he established himself as new reformism's most brilliant theoretician. His notion of "realistic pacifism," which he used to distance himself from the thesis of war's inevitability, pointed to the possibility that relations between states might evolve peacefully if they took advantage of those tendencies toward understanding that were intrinsic to capitalism itself. And his concept of "organized capitalism," with which his name is still most closely associated, and which was tied to his reflections on finance capital in the prewar period, focused on the goal of "democratic control" of the economy. When in 1928–29 the struggle between Stalin and Nikolay Bukharin heated up, the former polemically compared the latter's analysis of capitalism with Hilferding's organized capitalism theories.

After the advent of Nazism, which forced Hilferding to first take refuge in Denmark, then Switzerland, and finally France, his conception of socialist politics took a radical turn. He drafted the platform for German social democracy in exile (the so-called *Prague Manifesto* of 1934), in which he broke with reformism and defined the goal as an anti-Fascist revolution that would lead to Germany's socialist transformation. His aversion in principle toward communism as well as to working relationships between social democrats and Communists remained intact. He devoted his last writings to an analysis of the totalitarian state, listing the end of the autonomy of the economic sphere and the subjection of productive functions to the goals of an all-powerful political sphere as its distinctive characteristics. Hilferding died, under ambiguous circumstances, while he was the Gestapo's prisoner in German-occupied France.

See also Bukharin, Nikolay; Imperialism; Social Democracy; Totalitarianism.

FURTHER READING

Gottschalch, W. *Strukturveranderungen der Gesellschaft und politisches Handeln in der Lehre von Rudolf Hilferdning.* Berlin: Duncker and Humblot, 1962.

Smaldone, W. *Rudolf Hilferding: The Tragedy of a German Social Democrat.* DeKalb: Northern Illinois University Press, 1998.

Wagner, F. P. *Rudolf Hilferding: Theory and Politics of Democratic Socialism.* Atlantic Highlands, NJ: Humanities, 1996.

LEONARDO RAPONE

History and Memory

In the Soviet Union, history was unusually important, because the Bolsheviks had given it such unusual significance: the interpretation of the past was the principal source of legitimation for the power that emerged from the October Revolution. This is precisely where the specific importance of history's role in the USSR lies, when compared to Western countries, since toward the end of the 19th century, the latter also produced great narrations about the past, whose purpose was forging the identity of these newly formed nation-states and legitimizing their political systems.

An unprecedented form of government, the dictatorship of the proletariat could not resort to any of the sources that had been used to legitimize power in previous centuries, whether divine right, property, or popular sovereignty. The Bolshevik dictatorship only found its legitimation in a teleological view of history of Marxian origins—one that claimed to be scientific, and according to which the ultimate and necessary goal of human civilization was communism, the reign of freedom, which would be built on capitalism's ashes by the proletariat, and whose vanguard was the Communist Party. The party, in other words, exercised its dictatorship in the working class's name in order to realize the laws, necessary and unavoidable, of historical development. It regarded itself as the sole custodian of those laws, since it alone was in possession of the correct interpretation of Marxism, raised to the status of science. The interpretation of the past justified and legitimized choices in the present, and for this reason history, after the seizure of power, was progressively subjected to more rigid forms of scrutiny by the victorious Bolsheviks. In the 1930s, this process resulted in the imposition of an official history that condemned the country, already a victim of Stalin's violence, to a mutilation of memory.

The period immediately following the revolution was characterized by a relative pluralism in the historical field and most other areas of culture. Mikhail Pokrovsky's Marxist school of historiography was established during these years. Pokrovsky, an author of pioneering studies on the economic and social history of prerevolutionary Russia, was motivated by the need to combine Marxist theory and Russian reality. The goal of his research was to demonstrate the high degree of capitalist development that the country had attained after the abolition of serfdom (1861), insisting on the similarities between European and Russian history, and minimizing their differences. He wanted to give the October Revolution the legitimacy that the Mensheviks disputed; they also appealed to Marxism and historical development's necessary laws, pointing to Russia's backwardness, but argued that the country was not ripe for a socialist revolution. While it was dominant, Pokrovsky's school was not the only one. There were different research and documentation *foyers* that, although they were controlled by the party, did enjoy a certain amount of freedom of research. The Marx-Engels Institute founded in 1921 by David Ryazanov, a fine scholar of the European workers' movement and Marxism, for example, aimed to gather all available documentation on these topics. Ideology did not have a dominant role, but then an "official history" did not exist yet either—not even a canonical version of the party's history existed at the time, and different versions were circulating.

During the later 1920s the regime's grip began to tighten, and it eventually led to the subjugation of historiography. The control exercised by Glavlit, the institution in charge of censorship, became stricter, as did the surveillance of the various collaborators to the different institutions; norms limiting access to archives and libraries were established, regulated, and refined. The turning point occurred between 1928 and 1931: the "cultural revolution" unleashed by the Stalinist leadership group in all areas of the country's artistic and cultural life, in order to regiment the intellectuals, destroyed any illusions of freedom. The establishment of the party's direct control in historiographical matters was, as in all other fields, the result of a dual process: the violent suppression of any dissenting voices, on the one hand, and the restructuring of those places where research and dissemination of information on historical matters were taking place, on the other hand, with the latter placed under strict party control. In 1930, the most prestigious representatives of the Saint Petersburg historical school (Yevgeny Tarle and Sergey Platonov), the pride of prerevolutionary Russia, were arrested and accused of plotting for the restoration of autocracy; this became a pretext for a wide-ranging purge of the Academy of Sciences. Repression did not only target historians with a liberal outlook. At the beginning of 1931 David Ryazanov was arrested and, in 1938, executed for his refusal to endorse the lies of official history; in this case as well, the accusations against Ryazanov were a pretext for a purge at the Marx-Engels Institute. Because the institute also preserved the party's historical archives, it acquired a strategic importance from the moment that Stalin decided to rewrite Bolshevism's history to make himself appear, with Lenin, the revolution's uncontested leader.

Historiography's subjugation was the premise for the affirmation of an official history that would not only justify the October Revolution but also legitimize the Stalinist dictatorship. This birth of official history, which would be written and rewritten during the 1930s under Stalin's direct supervision, was Stalin's intervention in 1931 in the disputes occurring among historians on the subject of the Second International. Stalin, as infallible party leader, proclaimed himself to be in sole possession of the interpretative truth. He decided to commission the preparation of a new party history that would supplant the plurality of existing versions. This undertaking was concluded in 1938 with the publication of the *Short Course of the History of the All-Russian Communist Party (Bolshevik)*, which consecrated Stalin's victory after the extermination of the Bolshevik Old Guard (Nikolay Bukharin, Grigory Zinovyev, Lev Kamenev, and others).

Presented as the sole depository and guarantor of Lenin's legacy, Stalin—the book's hero—was also depicted as the architect of the construction of socialism in one country, a fortress besieged by cunning enemies of the revolution, both internal and external, who thanks to his foresightedness had been vanquished, thus assuring the triumph of the Bolshevik plan. This work not only provided the canonical interpretation of the prerevolutionary past but also of the history that had occurred after the revolution. In order to justify them, Stalin's policies were presented as the enactment of the *necessary laws* for the construction of socialism as revealed by Marxism: collectivization, which caused the death of millions of peasants; forced industrialization, which had violently torn apart the country's social fabric; and mass repressions and the Great Terror. This construct condemned as "deviations" all the alternatives proposed in the 1920s by Stalin's opponents, who Stalin in turn reduced to the rank of "counterrevolutionaries" and "enemies of the people." With the *Short Course*'s publication the long gestation period of Soviet official history was concluded, and the work itself was presented as a revealed truth, normative and obligatory for all, and the party's highest ranks and especially its leader were its undisputed repository.

The affirmation of official history and the destruction of memory took place on two levels: collective and individual. Starting in 1929–30, the archives went from being places where memory was preserved, to places in which it was segregated and hidden. This process culminated in 1938 with the transfer of the state archives to the People's Commissariat for Internal Affairs. At the same time, libraries were purged: books suspected of revealing a past that differed from the official version were sent to the paper mills or locked up in special reading rooms; encyclopedias were purged, and pages were torn out of books that were dedicated to disgraced authors or individuals. Secondhand booksellers received a list—three large volumes—of forbidden books. The systematic destruction of memory even invaded the private sphere. In the course of the panic and terror that took hold of the country, people hurried to get rid of books or journals that could be considered suspicious, and destroyed letters and old photographs. This internalization of norms led to entire chunks of the past, even of the individual past, being obliterated from memory. Even within the intimacy of the family people took refuge in silence, out of fear that a child might pay a high price for a forbidden memory. Memoirs from the Stalin era have testified to the devastating nature of this erasure of memory.

Memory's destruction went hand in hand with the creation of an official memory through symbolic places (monuments and museums) and ritual commemorations, thanks to the monopoly on the means of communication and total control over literary as well as artistic production. History was rewritten, and photographs were touched up. Writers, these "engineers of the soul" of Stalinist Russia, transfigured the tragedies experienced by the inhabitants of the Soviet Union into an epic tale of the construction of socialism. One example is the hymn to forced labor in the gulag, aided by Maksim Gorky, celebrating the construction of the White Sea channel.

Only after Stalin's death (1953) was the Soviet Union able to slowly recompose the fragments of this torn memory. Memory's reawakening was a long and difficult process, which was only concluded on the eve of the USSR's dissolution. There were three principle phases. The first was the period of the thaw, between 1953 and 1964, during which Khrushchev led the country. Khrushchev's secret speech to the Twentieth Party Congress in 1956, which denounced the dictators' crimes, paved the way for a revision of the past. As harsh as it was, Khrushchev's denunciation was kept within strict boundaries, because he granted that Stalin should be credited with having built socialism; the dictator had only usurped power at a later stage, taking it from the party, the only institution that could legitimately hold it, and had turned the terror against it. If the *Short Course*, with its glorification of Stalin, was abandoned, the ideological framework on which it was based became the foundation of the new official history. The purpose of this operation was to preserve the party's legitimacy in exercising its monopolistic hold on power; memory's reawakening was only acceptable within these limits. It was literature especially that became the vehicle for this renewal, and which began to provide the first frameworks in which the past tragedies could be interpreted.

After Khrushchev's removal from power, and his replacement by Leonid Brezhnev and his conservative followers (1964), history was rewritten once again. A discreet silence enveloped the dictators' crimes; the services Stalin had rendered his country were reevaluated, especially the restoration of its imperial power status, which had been lost with the revolution, with the victory over Nazi

Germany. To the new forgetfulness the state was seeking to reimpose, memory opposed an obstinate resistance. The censors' strict surveillance notwithstanding, the Soviet Union in the Brezhnev years was a society awash in memories, in which the will to remember was jealously guarded, at least among the intellectual elite. And it was precisely that tenacious memory that nourished the desire for perestroika, giving the reforms undertaken by Mikhail Gorbachev in 1985 a radical quality that would result in the collapse of Soviet communism. With the cultural liberalization that followed Gorbachev's rise to power, memory was allowed even more space, transmitted through literature, cinema, theater, and journalism. It was precisely because of its role in legitimizing power that official history was exported from the USSR to the satellite countries of Eastern Europe; and in these countries, the reawakening of memory had an important role in the collapse of the Soviet bloc.

See also Cultural Policies; Literature in Soviet Russia; Marxism-Leninism; *Short Course*, The.

FURTHER READING

Afanas'ev, J. N., ed. *Sovetskaja istoriografija*. Moscow: RGGU, 1996.

Barber, J. *Soviet Historians in Crisis*. London: Macmillan, 1981.

Bettanin, F. *La fabbrica del mito. Storia e politica nell'URSS staliniana*. Naples: Edizioni Scientifiche Italiane, 1996.

Enteen, G. M. *The Soviet Scholar-Bureaucrat M.N. Pokrovskij and the Society of Marxist Historians*. University Park: Pennsylvania State University Press, 1980.

Ferretti, M. *La memoria mutilata: la Russia ricorda*. Milan: Corbaccio, 1993.

Heer, N. W. *Politics and History in the Soviet Union*. Cambridge, MA: MIT Press, 1971.

Markwick, R. D. *The Politics of Revisionist Historiography, 1956–1974*. New York: Palgrave, 2001.

MARIA FERRETTI

Hitler, Adolf

Adolf Hitler (1889–1945) almost succeeded in the wholesale destruction of European communism. After persecuting the Communists in Germany, where he became first chancellor in 1933, then *Führer* or "Leader" in 1934, he launched a massive invasion of the Soviet Union in

June 1941 with a handful of allied European states, with the aim of destroying utterly the Soviet state, the Soviet Communist Party, and the Communist International. From the earliest days of his political activity, Hitler regarded communism as one among a number of instruments for the Jewish enslavement of mankind. The equation of communism and Jewish conspiracy gave Hitler's anticommunism its distinctive character.

Hitler was born in the small Austrian town of Braunau am Inn on April 20, 1889, the son of a minor official. In 1906 he moved to Vienna and tried to establish a career as an artist. He painted small pictures for sale and spent a great deal of time at the opera and at the parliament building in the capital, where for the first time he watched Socialists in action. Little has survived of his views on communism from the years before 1914. He was living in Munich when the First World War broke out, and volunteered at once for the Bavarian army. He served for four years at the front, was temporarily blinded and recovering in the hospital when the armistice was signed. According to Hitler's own account in *Mein Kampf*, the book he wrote in 1924–25, it was at this late stage of the war that he came to believe that Germany's defeat was the result of the work of German Jewish Communists, who "stabbed Germany in the back" by sapping its will for war and stirring up political unrest.

In the early months after the end of the war, Hitler was employed as an army political intelligence agent in Munich, but he also had the opportunity to give occasional speeches on Marxism and the Jewish question. In September 1919 he joined the small German Workers' Party (DAP), which within a year was renamed the National Socialist Party. He dominated the party for the next twenty-five years, first as its propaganda chief, then in July 1921 as chairman, and finally in 1926 the party's *Führer*. Though on the fringes of German politics for many years, Hitler's movement became the most active and violent opponent of German communism from the moment of its foundation onward.

Hitler's obsession with communism was inextricably linked to his ideas about race. He seldom referred in his writing or speeches to the term "communism," preferring "Marxism" or, most commonly, "Bolshevism." This was a deliberate choice. Marx was emphasized not so much as the senior theoretician of European communism, but because he was Jewish. Bolshevism was used as a pejorative term, to describe the Russian brand of communism, which Hitler and many others associated with Russian Jewish intellectuals. This device allowed Hitler

to see communism as something not German, an alien fruit of Jewish conspiracy. It was for Hitler just one of the means the Jewish enemy used to subjugate nations that hosted Jewish communities. The struggle against Bolshevism was at one and the same time a struggle against world Jewry. The "object of the peace treaty," wrote Hitler in 1920 about the Versailles settlement, "is to soften up Germany for Bolshevism—or rather for Jewish dictatorship."

The correlation of Bolshevik communism and Jewish conspiracy was one of the central pillars of Hitler's worldview throughout his political career. In *Mein Kampf* he wrote that "the *real* organizer" of the German revolution of 1919 was "the international Jew" (476–77). During the Second World War in his so-called table talk Hitler returned again and again to the argument that the Jew had been responsible for Christianity and its progeny, Bolshevism, both of which were intended to weaken and subjugate pure races and strong cultures. "The religion fabricated by Paul of Tarsus," Hitler asserted in November of 1944, "is nothing but the communism of today." However, few of Hitler's comments on Marxism as a political system express clearly why he found the idea of communism so repellent. His inclinations seem generally favorable to the idea of collectivist activity and to a society no longer defined by class. He shared the Marxists' hostility toward the traditional bourgeoisie and international capitalism. Hitler's assertion that communism was by nature socially divisive and morally corrupting had only shallow intellectual roots, and it seems ultimately to have been founded in the mere conviction that Marxism represented the modern form of the race enemy.

After Hitler's appointment as German chancellor on January 30, 1933, the National Socialist movement launched a nationwide campaign against the German Communist Party. Its officials and activists were rounded up during February and March on the pretense that they constituted a revolutionary and terrorist threat. Out of 60,000 members of the Communist Party in 1933, 18,243 were prosecuted and imprisoned or killed between 1933 and 1935, thousands fled abroad, and the residual underground movement was pursued relentlessly by the state secret police (Gestapo) set up in April 1933 with the main purpose of combating Marxism. In many areas of public life Hitler led the way in condemning as Communist much of the modernist culture and ideas that had characterized the republican 1920s in Germany. The Bauhaus architectural school was accused of "building-bolshevism"; modernist artists were decried as instruments of Jewish-Bolshevik culture, their work restricted, and their pictures removed from art galleries. Any avant-garde social policies, including the right to abortion, were equally treated as the fruit of corrupt Marxist welfare policy. After 1933 "communism" became a widespread term of abuse against any policy or cultural production of which Hitler and the National Socialist movement disapproved.

In the autumn of 1936 the anticommunism of the regime reached a new pitch, encouraged by fear of Communist revolutionary victory in Spain and hostility to the French Popular Front government. In November 1936 Germany and Japan signed the Anti-Comintern Pact (Italy joined a year later), which aimed at mobilizing international opinion against the activities of the Moscow-based Communist International. In October 1936 Hitler authorized the Second Four-Year Plan for the economy, the purpose of which was to arm Germany in four years, and on the largest scale possible, in order to combat the threat from the Soviet Union. In the secret memorandum Hitler wrote before launching the plan, he outlined his belief that Germany was destined to be "the focus of the Western world against the attacks of Bolshevism." His fear of communism molded German war preparations in the 1930s, which were to produce "the premier army in the world" in order to keep in check the "menacing extent" of the Red Army. On February 20, 1938, Hitler assumed supreme command of the German armed forces and put himself directly at the head of the coming crusade against communism.

Against this background it is difficult to comprehend the decision Hitler took three years later to enter into a nonaggression pact with the Soviet Union and to revive trade relations. Other anti-Communists in Germany and abroad had assumed that the ideological gulf was too large between the two dictatorships. Hitler reached the decision only as it became clear that his intended war on Poland in 1939 might provoke the intervention of Britain and France. On August 23, 1939, a pact was signed in Moscow to ensure that the USSR would not also intervene on Poland's side and to isolate the Western powers. Only weeks after making the pact, Hitler explained to party leaders that it was a mere expedient to avoid a major two-front war; in November he told his army adjutant that he wanted to prepare "a great operation in the East against Russia." After the defeat of Britain and France in June 1940, Hitler turned to plans for the invasion of the Soviet Union. The campaign, eventually codenamed "Barbarossa," was described by Hitler in March 1941 as a "war of annihilation" (*Vernichtungskrieg*), whose central object was the utter destruction of the Jewish-Bolshevik enemy. When the invasion began on June 22, 1941, German soldiers had direct orders to identify and murder all Communist military commissars, political officers, and party officials. Over the following months thousands of Soviet Communists were killed.

Beginning in 1941, the two enemies of communism and "world Jewry" merged. The radicalization of the anti-Jewish policy went hand-in-hand with war against the Soviet Union. While non-Jewish Communists were murdered, the security forces and army killed thousands of Jews on Soviet territory as alleged partisans or bearers of the Bolshevik menace. Throughout the period from 1942 to 1945 Hitler consistently clung to the view that communism was one of the many ways in which the Jews sought to emasculate Germany and destroy European culture. In February 1945 he told Martin Bormann, head of the party chancellery, that there had never been a war "so typically and at the same time so exclusively Jewish."

It is a profound historical irony that the utter defeat of Hitler's Germany in May 1945, following Hitler's suicide in Berlin on April 30, made Soviet communism secure, and allowed communism to spread throughout eastern and central Europe, and much of eastern Asia. In 1949 the eastern regions of Germany became the Communist German Democratic Republic. In the western Federal Republic, also established in 1949, communism was again banned (as it had been under Hitler) on the grounds that it was a political movement committed to overthrowing the parliamentary state. The new West German state became part of the NATO anti-Soviet alliance. In this sense the influence of Hitler as the first "cold warrior" against communism in the 1930s lived on after the collapse of his dictatorship.

See also Anticommunism; Anti-Semitism; Bolshevism; Fascism; Grand Alliance; Molotov-Ribbentrop Pact; Stalin, Joseph; Totalitarianism; World War II.

FURTHER READING

Genoud, F., ed. *The Testament of Adolf Hitler: The Hitler-Bormann Documents.* London: Cassel, 1961.

Hitler, A. *Mein Kampf.* Ed. D. C. Watt. London: Hutchinson, 1972.

Kershaw, I. *Hitler, 1889–1936.* Milan: Bompiani, 1999.

———. *Hitler, 1936–1945: Nemesis.* London: Allen Lane, 2000.

Kershaw I., and M. Lewin, eds. *Stalinism and Nazism: Dictatorships in Comparison.* Cambridge, UK: Cambridge University Press, 1997.

Maser. W., ed. *Hitlers Briefe und Notizien: sein Weltbild in handschriftlichen Dokumenten.* Dusseldorf, Vienna: Econ, 1973.

Overy, R. J. *The Dictators: Hitler's Germany and Stalin's Russia.* New York: Norton, 2004.

Trevor-Roper, H. R., ed. *Hitler's Table Talk, 1941–1944.* London: Weidenfeld and Nicolson, 1953.

von Below, N. *At Hitler's Side: The Memoirs of Hitler's Luftwaffe Adjutant, 1937–1945.* London: Greenhill, 2001.

RICHARD J. OVERY

Ho Chi Minh

Ho Chi Minh (Ho the Most Enlightened) (1890–1969) became a world figure after the Second World War, during Vietnam's long struggle for independence from France. The first president of the Democratic Republic of Vietnam (DRV), which declared its independence in September 1945, Ho attained his greatest renown in the 1960s, during the DRV's war against the United States for control of southern Vietnam. Yet by the end of 1963 he had become a largely symbolic leader, whose role in day-to-day decision making had ended. In a world of Communist strong men and tyrants, Ho was an exception: his moral authority did not give him any more power than his single vote in the politburo. The limitations on his power have only become clear in recent years, however, as fresh archival research has revealed the extent to which his leadership was contested within his own Communist Party.

Ho's political ideas were mainly shaped in the twenty years between 1907 and 1927, the period from his adolescent years in the Nguyen dynasty's capital of Hue to his flight from China following Chiang Kai-shek's coup against the Communists in the United Front. He was born as Nguyen Sinh Cung in 1892 or 1893, according to French sources, in the rugged north-central province of Nghe An. While his years as a sailor and laborer have been strongly emphasized in official biographies, Ho was in fact the son of a successful mandarin, who by 1901 had passed the second-highest examination in the realm to become a teacher of Chinese in Hue. Ho's father did not engage openly in anticolonial activity, but the first decade of the 20th century was a time of ferment in his milieu, which could not have failed to affect him and his family. The French had removed all real power from the mandarinate in 1898, and scholars such as Phan Chu Trinh, a contemporary of Ho's father, were refusing employment in the corrupt shell of the mandarin system. These scholars started a movement to encourage Western education and indigenous manufacturing. (Young Vietnamese men, Ho Chi Minh included, had until then studied the Chinese classics alone.) Another scholar from Ho's own district in Nghe An, Phan Boi Chau, started the Dong Du (Eastern Travel) movement in 1906, which encouraged promising young men to join him in Japan to receive a modern education and military training. In 1908 when an anti-tax campaign broke out in central Vietnam, the French blamed the modernizing scholars and arrested a number of them. French troops responded to a peaceful demonstration in Hue by shooting into the crowd. Ho Chi Minh, around fifteen at the time, witnessed this violence, and it would mark him for many years.

Ho's father became a district mandarin in 1909, but an accusation of violence against a prisoner in his jurisdiction, which he contested, led to his demotion. This change in his father's fortune forced Ho to withdraw from the prestigious National Studies School in Hue, where he was continuing his education in French and *quoc ngu*, the romanized Vietnamese script. His withdrawal marked the end of his formal education, unless one counts his studies in the Comintern's institutes in Moscow. In 1911 both he and his father made their way to Saigon, from where Ho sailed for France. In view of what we now know of Ho's family connections to Phan Chu Trinh and Phan Boi Chau, we can surmise that Ho was being sent abroad to receive a Western education that would prepare him to play a role in Vietnam's struggle for independence.

After working as a shipboard cook for over a year, and having failed to gain admission to a French academy that trained the sons of "high" mandarins, Ho turned up in London in 1913 or 1914, where he worked at odd jobs and studied English. He remained in London until the end of 1916, then returned to France to consult his colleagues on the future path of the independence movement. From then until the middle of 1919, when he appeared in Paris for the Peace Conference at the close of the First World War, his movements are uncertain. But there are indications in the French and Russian archives that in 1917–18 he lived in the United States, where he heard Marcus Garvey speak in Harlem and consulted Korean independence activists. When he turned up in Paris, he began circulating a petition with the "Demands of the

Vietnamese People" for greater freedom. It was signed, "Nguyen Ai Quoc" (Nguyen the Patriot), for the Group of Vietnamese Patriots. Although Ho received help in writing this appeal from his colleague Phan Van Truong, a professional interpreter and lawyer, the idea of addressing the Peace Conference was probably his own.

Ho would be known as Nguyen Ai Quoc for the next twenty years, even though he frequently used other pseudonyms. The campaign to win concessions from the Paris Conference failed, but Ho stayed on in France to canvass support from the Socialist Party and other sympathetic organizations. When his first contacts with the radicals of the Socialist Party began is uncertain, but by 1920, when a group that affiliated itself with the Third International split from the rest of the party, he joined them and thus became a founding member of the French Communist Party. By this time he had discovered Lenin's views on imperialism, and eagerly embraced the theories of the Comintern on support to anticolonial movements. He devoted himself to political organizing from this time onward, even though he was suffering from poor health and had to earn his living. He joined the "Union Intercolonial," composed of Africans, Caribbeans, Malagasies, and a number of his Vietnamese colleagues. This union, whose newspaper *Le Paria* Ho edited, became his primary political base until he departed in secret for Moscow in June 1923. His political life in Paris had become too circumscribed by police surveillance.

Ho's arrival in Moscow is often described as the result of Dimitri Manuilski's recruitment efforts, but this explanation probably attributes too much clarity and purpose to the Comintern's dealings with Ho. (Although he would be attached to the Comintern until 1941, his status and official roles were often vaguely defined.) His trip to Moscow was organized by the Intercolonial Union, and it is uncertain that the Comintern had long-term plans to employ him when he arrived in 1923. He attended the first congress of the Peasant International (Krestintern) that October, and joined their presidium. After a number of months in Moscow he wrote a letter complaining that he had only expected to remain for three months, before moving on. He was eager to return to Southeast Asia to establish relations between the International and Indochina. But his return would not take place until November 1924, following his participation in the Fifth Comintern Congress, where he lobbied actively for more Comintern attention to the plight of colonized peoples. When the Comintern bureaucracy finally granted his

wish to travel to Canton, he was sent as a translator in the Russian news agency's bureau, without any official cover.

Ho's time in Canton was a productive and formative stage in his career. He used part of his translator's salary to fund the training of Vietnamese émigrés in Guangzhou in Leninist concepts of revolution. He and his nucleus of like-minded Vietnamese took part in the propagandizing and peasant organizing connected with the United Front. By 1926 they were able to bring a group of young Vietnamese to China for a three-month training course, followed by a second, which produced the first cell of Vietnamese Communists. They did not have their own party until 1930, so were organized into a front group known as the Thanh Nien or Youth Association. The inner core became members of the CCP. Ho was believed to have discouraged a military uprising in Vietnam in 1926, which would have coincided with the start of the Northern Campaign in China, as his network of political trainees was still too small. When in April 1927 Chiang Kai-shek's anti-Communist coup reached Canton, Ho had to depart rapidly.

He returned via Vladivostok to Moscow, then traveled to Paris, Brussels, and on to Berlin, to wait for a new assignment and funding for his return to Asia. This eventually came, but with money only to enough finance his return travel, and he was given no clear instructions beyond the suggestion that he should use his experience in China to start forming peasant unions. Ho was not invited to attend the Sixth Comintern Congress in Moscow, so made his way back to Asia, this time Siam, in the summer of 1928. He lived among the Vietnamese in northeastern Siam until mid-1929, when he was summoned to Hong Kong by the Thanh Nien leadership, to sort out the quarrels of rival Communist groups in Vietnam. He called a quick conference in Hong Kong in February 1930 for representatives of the two factions, and was able to patch together a draft party program that was in theory acceptable to both sides. Thus February 1930 became the founding date of the Vietnamese Communist Party.

This event, which has always been presented in official histories as a triumph for Ho Chi Minh, was the beginning of a stormy year for the VCP and in fact marked the start of Ho's first political eclipse. He was sent by the Far Eastern Bureau to Singapore to form a national CP for Malaya, then remained in Hong Kong to carry on liaison work. The members of the new party within Vietnam apparently came under the influence of the "revolutionary upsurge" then gaining ground in China, in the newly militant spirit of the Sixth Comintern Congress. Ho had no apparent directing role in the brief soviet movement, which broke out in his native region of central Vietnam in the autumn of 1930, and in fact his leadership was criticized in a party plenum that October. A new set of political theses in line with the Comintern's new course replaced his short program, and party leadership was handed over to a Moscow trainee named Tran Phu. Ho attempted to give advice to his comrades, under siege in the spring of 1931, but was dismissed by Tran Phu as a product of the United Front in China, whose petty bourgeois influence had been harmful to the party. The entire Central Committee and most of the provincial leaders were arrested in the spring of 1931. The British police picked up Ho Chi Minh in June.

Ho narrowly escaped deportation to Vietnam from Hong Kong, and after a long appeal process was expelled from the British colony. He hid somewhere in China until he reestablished contact with the Comintern and got passage back to Russia. There is sufficient documentation in the Comintern archives to show that Ho was in eclipse during this stay in Moscow. His arrival in mid-1934 did not merit a hero's welcome; instead he was sent to study at the Lenin School for cadres, along with Li Lisan. As preparations were underway for the Seventh Comintern Congress, two letters arrived from his party denouncing Ho's leadership as petty bourgeois and accusing him of serious lapses in security. These may have been the reason that his mandate for the Seventh Congress was revoked. He remained in Moscow afterward, and later wrote that he had been removed from any role in his party in those years. He studied at the Institute for National and Colonial Problems until the autumn of 1938, when he was finally given the green light to return to southern China to help build a united anti-Fascist front.

The undermining of Ho's authority from 1931 until 1938 set a pattern for his later career. His position was strongest when united fronts were the order of the day, as in 1924–27. On his return to China he had considerable difficulty in rebuilding contact with his party. Only in May 1941 was he able to hold a meeting, the Eighth Plenum, with members of the CC from inside Vietnam. It was then that Ho convinced them to form the Viet Minh alliance with other non-Communist parties and to concentrate on national liberation before a Socialist revolution. His other great coup was to convince the OSS to train and provide small arms to his group in the Viet Bac

in mid-1945. This alliance allowed the Viet Minh to enter Hanoi in late August 1945 as liberators sponsored by the United States, following the Japanese surrender.

Ho's Declaration of Independence on September 2, 1945, did not win his new government recognition. The disorganization and lack of cohesion of the Viet Minh front in South Vietnam, where rival Communist groups existed, made it relatively easy for the French to regain control in Saigon. Ho exhibited his skills in diplomacy and political maneuvers, but failed to secure his new state. He broadened his government, giving posts to his Nationalist rivals, and ordered the Communist party to go underground, to reassure the international community. But the French continued to press for a return to Hanoi. Ho signed a modus vivendi with France in March 1946, which arranged for the occupying Nationalist Chinese troops to be replaced by the French. He was willing to accept a place in the French Overseas Union, so long as Vietnam controlled its own government, army, and finances. But negotiations dragged on, with the French insisting that South Vietnam was an independent state. Ho returned from an extended trip to France for the Fontainebleau negotiations empty-handed. In December the French attack on the Haiphong customs post led to all-out war, and the Viet Minh retreated from Hanoi to the maquis.

Vietnamese appeals to the United States to intervene failed; by mid-1947, as the Cold War hardened attitudes in Europe, Communist movements in Southeast Asia returned to armed struggle. Ho once again came under attack within his party for negotiating with France and "disbanding" the CP. In 1950, after the Communist Chinese victory, he followed Mao Zedong to Moscow for talks, and Mao convinced Stalin to accept Ho's leadership of the DRV. But during Ho's absence, a rival leader, Truong Chinh, asserted his control over the party, and when Ho returned to the maquis, he was increasingly given the role of "soul" of the Vietnamese revolution, while Truong Chinh became its "commander." With Stalin's consent, Chinese advisers began to play a major role in the Vietnamese party's practice and ideology. The first phases of land reform got underway, and in 1952 a Party Rectification Campaign began to replace village leaders who belonged to the land-owning classes. By 1954 when the Geneva Conference brought peace to Vietnam, now divided at the 17th parallel, the political climate was quite different from that of 1945. The land reform campaign had intensified, growing more violent and often classifying middle peasants as landlords. It was probably

Khrushchev's speech to the Twentieth Congress in Moscow that made possible criticism of the land reform from within the party and led, in October 1956, to a public apology for the campaign's excesses.

Ho Chi Minh did not take the lead in the relaxation of ideological and cultural policies that occurred briefly in 1956. But he presided over them as acting general secretary after Truong Chinh was removed and the cadres associated with the excesses of land reform were demoted. He supported Khrushchev's policy of peaceful coexistence at the Communist summit of 1957, and again in 1961. However, by this time it had become clear that the Diem regime in South Vietnam would not hold elections as stipulated in the Geneva Agreements, and at the Third Party Congress in 1960 the party had already decided to reunify the country by force if necessary. A new first secretary, Le Duan, who was determined to aid the southern revolution, had been confirmed. In 1963 the Vietnamese became increasingly impatient with Khrushchev's policies and began to support Chinese attacks on his revisionism. At the end of 1963 at the Ninth Party Plenum, a resolution was passed to make Vietnam's foreign and internal policies follow those of China. Several memoirs maintain that Ho's opinions were ignored at this meeting. At a Christmas meeting with the Soviet ambassador that year, Ho announced that he would be retiring from the day-to-day running of the country. The Ninth Plenum seems to have been a personal defeat for him, although he did not disagree with the policy of making reunification a priority. He probably did disapprove the unequivocal condemnation of Soviet revisionism, however.

After 1964 the frail Ho increasingly became a symbol of the David-and-Goliath struggle between the tiny DRV and the United States. He received southern fighters and was photographed at anti-aircraft batteries. He met foreign visitors and issued inspiring messages to his people. He undertook foreign missions to win support for the DRV. But his influence on political decisions by this stage is unclear. It was sometimes hinted that he was growing senile, but American peace envoys who met him in 1967 described him as still sharp enough to converse in English and as requesting that they send their correspondence to him directly. His trips to China for medical treatment and rest grew more frequent, however, and he in fact spent most of 1967 there. He survived long enough to witness the beginning of peace negotiations in Paris in 1968, but also observed the hardships his people were enduring because of the war. In his "Last Will and Testament," part of which was suppressed, he requested tax relief for farmers and expressed a wish that the split in the Socialist camp be mended.

A Soviet embalming team was already in Vietnam when Ho died in September 1969. With considerable difficulty his body was preserved until it could be placed in its tomb on Ba Dinh Square in 1976. Thus Ho Chi Minh, against his will, became the cult figure of the Communist dynasty begun in 1945. Ironically, although he often was at odds with the policies of his party, he became the source of its legitimacy as the force of Communist ideology waned. His every writing and speech is combed for sources of Ho Chi Minh Thought, the closest thing that Vietnam now possesses to a guiding ideology. Some writers describe him as a prisoner of the system he created. He was in many respects a prisoner, but it is difficult to say that he created the system. It may be more accurate to say that he was a captive of his need for Communist support to win independence. This seriously restricted Ho's political options throughout his career.

See also Anti-imperialism; Cold War; Comintern; Decolonization; Nationalism; Vietnam War.

FURTHER READING

Brocheux, P. *Ho Chi Minh: du révolutionnaire à l'icône*. Paris: Editions Payot and Rivages, 2003.

Duiker, W. *Ho Chi Minh: A Life*. New York: Hyperion, 2000.

Goscha, C. E., and B. de Tréglodé. *Naissance d'un Etat-Parti: Le Vietnam depuis 1945*. Paris: Les Indes Savantes, 2004.

Lacouture, J. *Ho Chi Minh: A Political Biography*. Paris: Editions du Seuil, 1967.

Quinn-Judge, S. *Ho Chi Minh: The Missing Years*. London: Christopher Hurst, 2003.

SOPHIE QUINN-JUDGE

Holodomor

The famine of 1932–33, which claimed seven or eight times as many victims in half the amount time as the terror of 1937–38, was the most important event in Soviet prewar history. With an estimated six million dead, compared to the one to two million in both 1921–22 and 1946–47, it was also the most serious of the three famines to occur during the USSR's history. Tens of thousands died of hunger all over the country, but the most affected areas, outside of Kazakhstan (where hundreds of thousands had already died before autumn 1932), were Ukraine, the northern Caucasus, and regions of the Volga—in other words, the critical grain-growing regions of the country. After 1927 these were the regions where the fights over grain had been harshest, and where, already since 1918–19, the struggle between the peasants, or nomads, and the regime had become violent because of the national issues involved, or as in the Volga region, because of Russian peasant traditions and the presence of minorities, like the German minority.

With the exception of Kazakhstan, where the famine exhibited its own characteristics and had already started in 1931, the causes were similar everywhere else. They involved the devastating effects not only in terms of human cost but also to production of the campaign against the kulaks, which soon became a pogrom against the best of the countryside; forced collectivization, which made peasants destroy a good portion of their possessions; the inefficiency and misery of the new collective factories; the repeated and extreme forced requisitions, which propelled an out-of-control industrialization and urbanization, and a foreign debt that was repaid by exporting raw materials; the peasants' resistance, who resented what they called a new serfdom, and who worked less and less, both because they rejected the new system and because of the debilitation hunger was causing; and the bad weather conditions in 1932. The famine therefore appears to be the result of policies inspired by an assault on mercantile production, whose result—given what had occurred under war communism in 1919–21—should not have been difficult to predict. If one refers to the origins of the famine, and to its first symptoms on a pan-Soviet scale in 1931–32, it does not seem possible to argue that it was deliberately caused, which is the the main assertion in the theses of those who contend that hunger was intentionally provoked in order to tame the peasants' resistance or that it was part of the genocide Moscow had planned against the Ukrainians.

The intensity, progress, and consequences of the phenomenon differed greatly, as the analysis of new documents and publication of new studies confirm. Of the about six million victims of 1931–33 (demographers attribute some of the deaths, previously attributed to these years, to the deportations of 1930), 3.5–3.8 million occurred in Ukraine, 1.3–1.5 million in Kazakhstan (which was to represent the statistical peak relative to population, annihilating 8 to 9 percent of the Europeans and about 33 to 38 percent of the Kazakhs), and several

hundred thousand both in the northern Caucasus and, though somewhat fewer, the Volga region. If we consider the mortality rates per thousand inhabitants in the countryside, and we set 1926 at 100, we can observe that in 1933 they rose to 188.1 in the entire Soviet Union, 138.2 in the Russian Republic (even though it then included Kazakhstan and the northern Caucasus), and 367.7 in Ukraine, *almost three times* the amount registered there in 1926. In Ukraine, life expectancy decreased from the 42.9 years for men and 46.3 for women that had been recorded in 1926, to 7.3 and 10.9, respectively, in 1933 (and it was later to be 13.6 and 36.3, respectively, in 1941). Births in Ukraine, which on average were equivalent to 1,153,000 per year during 1926–29, were 782,000 in 1932 and 470,000 in 1933. This variation in intensity shows that famine progressed differently here, in large part because of differences in the policies pursued by Moscow.

In the spring of 1932 local functionaries, elementary school teachers, and national leaders had noticed the increase in hunger and the beginning of a rural exodus. Stalin, who also needed to respond to the Ukrainian party's request for a reduction in stockpiles, admitted in June that in the most affected areas stockpiles should be reduced, in part because of a "sense of justice." Yet he argued that this measure should only be applied in moderation, because, as Vyacheslav Molotov was later to declare, "even if today we are facing the specter of famine, especially in the grain-growing regions . . . stockpiling plans must be respected at all costs." The regime's goals appear to have been to prevent food riots in the cities, like those that had occurred in the spring, and be able to honor German bills of exchange that were about to expire. In June, however, and well before Ukrainian nationalists did, Stalin was preparing a "national interpretation" of the famine. Initially it was directed privately to the republic's leaders, whom he now burdened with the responsibility for the situation, which he claimed they had failed to address with the necessary severity. Nevertheless, between July and August, after a conference in which the Ukrainian party was explicitly polemical toward Moscow, and on the basis of police reports that accused the local Communists of being infected with nationalism, a new analysis of the situation and its causes took shape. On August 11, in a letter to Lazar Kaganovich, Stalin wrote that Ukraine was "the principal question," the party, state, and local secret police had been infiltrated by agents of Ukrainian nationalism and Polish spies, and there was a risk of "losing Ukraine."

When the stockpiles, as was foreseeable, proved unsatisfactory, Molotov, Kaganovich, and Pavel Postyshev were sent to Ukraine, the northern Caucasus, and the Volga region with the task of studying the situation, and then proposing and carrying out the necessary measures. The plan to "use the famine" can be dated to mid-November 1932, after Stalin's wife's suicide and at the peak of the crisis caused by the First Five-Year Plan. The famine was artificially and enormously worsened in this manner, as a means to punish the peasants who refused to accept the new system of servitude. The punishment was in the form of "he who doesn't work, that is, doesn't accept the kolkhoz system, doesn't eat," and similar terms were used in a letter from Stalin to Socholov. This plan then led to the decision to officially deny, even in formal replies to questions by foreign diplomats, the existence of the phenomenon itself, and to deny the areas in question any aid and instead "struggle ferociously" to meet stockpile targets.

In those areas where the peasant question was exacerbated by the national question—a tie that was explicitly affirmed in Stalin's theories on nationalism, and confirmed in the eyes of the Soviet leadership by the great social and national revolts of the Ukrainian countryside in 1919—the use of famine was more pitiless, and the lesson even harsher. On November 18, the Ukrainian Central Committee ordered the restitution of grain that had been handed out to kolkhoz members in advance as compensation for their work, while in both Ukraine and Kuban, but not in the Volga region, authorities resorted to fines in kind to sequester meat and potatoes from peasants. Vast areas of the northern Caucasus, Russian but inhabited in the Kuban especially by Ukrainians, and Ukraine itself, which had stood out for its opposition to collectivization, were punished even more severely with the requisition of all existing products, including nonagricultural ones, and in some areas with the deportation of all inhabitants. In the meantime, local leaders who had helped famished peasants—for instance, by distributing grain—were repressed by means of hundreds of executions and thousands of arrests for "populism."

The phenomenon then grew to forms and dimensions that were much more serious than could have been expected. A famine that had objectively been inferior to that of 1921–22, both in terms of areas affected and the gravity of the drought, caused four times as many victims, while in the Volga region, where the "punishment" was less severe, there were mass deaths but not extermination. In the Ukraine and Kuban, where a large part of the party apparatus and the state was suspected of connivance with the peasants, the connection that Stalin established between the peasant and national questions also had direct consequences in the area of national policies.

On December 14, 1932, the Political Office adopted a secret decree, and a similar but less serious one was adopted for Belorussia on December 19, overturning decisions taken in 1923. The decree proclaimed that the measures that had been adopted to favor the development of "backward" nationalities, as they had been applied in Ukraine, had actually strengthened nationalism instead of disarming it, thus producing enemies who now had a party badge in their pocket. The responsibility for the crisis was not only due to the peasants, as in the rest of the country, but also to the political and intellectual strata.

On December 15, a new decree abolished the policies of Ukrainianization of the Russian Republic where, because of pro-Russian choices in the drawing of borders during the mid-1920s, a million Ukrainians now lived, and up to that moment had been able to establish their own schools, newspapers, organs of self-government, and so on. The census of 1937 had established that 3 million inhabitants in the Russian Republic had declared they were Ukrainian compared to 7.8 million in 1926 (a part of this decrease, however, must be attributed to the creation of the Soviet Republic of Kazakhstan).

On January 22, 1933, soon after Postyshev, together with hundreds of Russian cadres, had been sent as a plenipotentiary to Ukraine, Stalin and Molotov ordered the secret police to halt the exodus of peasants looking for bread from the Ukraine and Kuban. In this new decree it was stated that the Central Committee and government "have no doubts that this exodus, like the one during the previous year, has been organized by enemies of Soviet power, Social Revolutionaries and Polish agents with the aim of conducting an agitation 'through the peasants' . . . against Soviet power. Last year this counter-revolutionary conspiracy escaped the notice of the organs of the party, the Soviet and the police in Ukraine. . . . This year the repetition of such a mistake will not be tolerated." Similar cordons were placed around Ukrainian cities, which were better supplied, even though still poorly, and were inhabited mostly by Russians, Jews, and Poles. Ukrainian peasants were basically told they would not be allowed to survive. In March, while in Kiev there was talk of "changes in ethnographic material" in the countryside, a report by the secretary of the Ukrainian party stated that "the famine has still not taught the kolkhoz members reason, as the sowing's disappointing results in many districts demonstrate." These measures were accompanied by a wave of anti-Ukrainian terror that showed some affinities with the "mass operations" of 1937–38. The national Communist experience born from the civil war therefore ended in this manner, with the suicide of its most important leaders, like Skrypnyk and the author Chvyl'ovyj, and the repression of thousands of its cadres.

The adoption of the term *holodomor*, which in Ukrainian means extermination by hunger and suggests the idea of intentionality, thus seems to be legitimate, also as a way of underscoring the difference with the pan-Soviet famine of 1931–33 and the Ukrainian famine that started in late 1932—two closely connected phenomena, but also profoundly different ones. The fact that the consequences of the famine were at least partially different is not due to chance. If the use of famine throughout the USSR guaranteed Stalin's victory by breaking peasant resistance, causing people to fear him in a new way, and creating a cult that was based on fear, it also opened the doors to the terror of 1937–38, and led to a qualitative jump in the level of deception that had characterized the Soviet regime since its birth. Also, by subjugating its most important republic, a fundamental step in the transformation of the Soviet state into an empire was taken. There remained a load of psychologically repressed elements and mourning that had not been worked through (three paternal uncles of Mikhail Gorbachev's also died in 1933), and in Ukraine and Kazakhstan the consequences were even deeper. In the latter case it was the traditional social structures that were affected. In the former it was both the tip and base of national society that were damaged, leading to the fact that the significance of the Ukrainian national movement during the great crisis of 1941–45, with the exception of Galitia, which was not part of the Soviet Union in 1933, was much smaller than during the 1914 crisis. The consequences of the famine and war could still be felt in 1959, when the population of the Republic of Ukraine, even including the inhabitants of the territories annexed in 1944–45, was less than forty-two million—a total that was only slightly higher than that of 1926. The number of Russians in this total had grown much more rapidly than the number of Ukrainians, and a large part of the Jewish community had been killed in the Shoah.

Given the number of victims, the famine of 1931–33 becomes a phenomenon that at least in Europe, is comparable only to the Nazi crimes that were to follow. The dynamics of the phenomenon in Ukraine and the northern Caucasus, and their connection to the interpretation that Stalin gave it and the political decisions he made as a consequence, once more raise the issue of their nature. Was it also an anti-Ukrainian genocide? The answer is no if we hypothesize a famine conceived by the regime with the intent of destroying the Ukrainian people and one adopts a rigid definition of genocide, which leads one to circumscribe the use of the term to the Shoah exclusively. But in 1948, the United Nations listed "the deliberate infliction on members of a group of life conditions such as to provoke their partial or total destruction" among possible acts of genocide. And the inventor of the term, Raphael Lemkin, had also defined it as a "plan involving the coordination of actions aimed at destroying the essential foundations of livelihood of national groups."

In this perspective, taking the differences in mortality ratios in the various republics into account and adding the millions of Ukrainians in the Russian Republic who were Russified after December 1932, along with the Ukrainian peasants who, blockades notwithstanding, managed to avoid death by escaping to other republics to the millions of dead Ukrainians, including those in the Kuban, the total number of "disappeared" is equivalent to about 30 percent of the ethnic Ukrainian population. The cause of this disappearance was the decision to utilize the famine in an anti-Ukrainian manner on the basis of the "national" interpretation Stalin had given it in the second half of 1932. And this disappearance also meant the destruction of the political and intellectual elite of the country, from the teachers in the villages to the national leaders. Given all this, the answer cannot but be positive. Between the end of 1932 and summer 1933, the Soviet regime promoted a genocide of which Ukraine still bears the traces. It was not the result of a famine provoked with this goal in mind but rather of a famine interpreted and then used in this fashion, unlike the case of Kazakhstan, where an even more terrible famine was instead the result, predictable if not desired, of "denomadization" and white disinterest toward the fate of indigenous populations.

This account modifies one's judgment of the Soviet experience and the 20th century in Europe, and it now seems impossible to understand them if one omits the Holodomor. But it is precisely these extraordinary dimensions, and their moral and intellectual consequences, that have made its interiorization difficult, especially since, due to the success of the Soviet attempt to hide the facts and due to the characteristics of 20th-century European history, it has had to occur after the fact, once the historical verdict had already been given and the "memory" of those times had already been formed without an event of this importance being part of it. To introduce it has therefore led to difficult revisions, of which the historiographical polemics, which have still not died down but at least now are at a much higher level than before, have been one of the symptoms. For a long time many historians had also ignored—if not denied—the famine of 1931–33, and even in the best cases, though partly capturing its nature of artificial famine, had not dedicated much attention to it, ignoring its national component. From this point of view, the historiography about famine and holodomor begins with Conquest's book (1986), whose conclusions were then integrated and partially surpassed by the archival as well as historiographical revolution that occurred after 1991.

Starting in 1987–88, the rediscovery and interpretation of the famine has played a fundamental role in the process of national and state construction in Ukraine, where the holodomor is at the center of political and cultural debate.

See also Collectivization of the Countryside; Famine under Communism; Gulag; Nationality Policies; National Question, The; New Economic Policy; Peasants in the USSR; Soviet Industrialization.

FURTHER READING

Conquest, R. *The Harvest of Sorrow: Soviet Collectivization and the Terror-Famine.* New York: Oxford University Press, 1986.

Danilov, V. P., et al. *Tragedija sovetskoj derevni.* Vol. 3, *1930–1933.* Moscow: Rosspen, 2001.

Davies, R. W., and S. G. Wheatcroft. *The Years of Hunger: Soviet Agriculture, 1931–33.* New York: Palgrave Macmillan, 2004.

Davies, R. W., et al. *The Stalin-Kaganovich Correspondence, 1931–1936.* New Haven, CT: Yale University Press, 2003.

Graziosi, A. *Lettere da Kharkov: la carestia in Ucraina e nel Caucaso del Nord nei rapporti dei diplomatici italiani, 1932–33.* Turin: Einaudi, 1991.

Ivnickij, N. A. *Golod 1932–1933 godov.* Moscow: Rossijskij gosudarstvennyj gumanitarnyj universitet, 1995.

Kondrashin, V., and D. Penner. *Golod: 1932–33 v sovetskoj derevne.* Samara: Samarskij gosudarstvennyj universitet, 2002.

Kul'chyc'kij, S. V. *Holodomor 1932–1933 rr v Ukraïni.* Kiev: Instytut istoriï Ukraïny NAN Ukraïny, 1993.

———. *Ukraïna mizh dvoma viynamy (1921–1939 rr).* Kiev: 1999.

Martin, T. D. *The Affirmative Action Empire: Nations and Nationalism under the Soviet Union, 1923–1939.* Ithaca, NY: Cornell University Press, 2001.

Medvedev, Z. A. *Soviet Agriculture.* New York: Norton, 1987.

Meslé, F., and J. Vallin. *Mortalité et causes de décès en Ukraine au XXᵉ siècle.* Paris: Institut national d'études démographiques, 2003.

Sapoval, J., and V. Vasil'ev. *Komandiry velykoho holodu, 1932–33 rr.* Kiev: Heneza, 2001.

ANDREA GRAZIOSI

Honecker, Erich

Erich Honecker (1912–94) was born on August 25 in Wiebelskirchen, in the Saar region. The son of a miner, he worked for a while as a roofer. In 1926 he joined the Young Communist League of Germany, the youth section of the Communist Party of Germany (KPD); in 1929 he became a member of the KPD, and starting in 1930 he was a full-time functionary. After the KPD was banned in 1933 by the Nazis, Honecker directed its clandestine activities in southern Germany. He was arrested in 1935 and sentenced two years later to ten years in prison. Honecker was detained in the Brandenburg prison until the liberation, in the spring of 1945.

After the liberation, Honecker was assigned to manage the KPD's work with youths. As the secretary for youths in the KPD's Central Committee, he started the "anti-Fascist youth committees," which gave rise in 1946 to the Freie Deutsche Jugend (Free German Youth). As president of the Freie Deutsche Jugend, he became a candidate member of the Political Office in 1950. In 1958 he became a full member and, on becoming secretary to the Central Committee for security issues, was now in a key position in the GDR's party and state apparatus. In this position he was responsible for both the preparations and then the construction of the Berlin Wall in August 1961. In the second half of the 1960s, he started assembling a majority with the intent of replacing Walter Ulbricht as head of the party and state. He was given the green light from Moscow in April 1971. On May 3, 1971, he became first secretary of the Socialist Unity Party of Germany (Sozialistische Einheitspartei Deutschlands, or

SED). In May 1976 the first secretary was promoted to secretary general, and in October 1986 Honecker became the GDR's head of state since he had also become president of the Council of State.

As the person in charge of the regime run by the SED, Honecker worked pragmatically to broaden social services and diminish ideological militancy. He simultaneously enhanced the apparatus for state security and the militarization of society. In November 1976 Honecker deprived singer-songwriter Wolf Biermann of his citizenship—an action that led to a phase of strict control on intellectuals. The order he gave to shoot at those attempting to flee along the border with the Federal Republic of Germany (FRG) and West Berlin caused numerous victims.

In his relations with the FRG, he initially accepted the "Basic Treaty" with which in 1972 the possibility of exchanges between the two countries had been established. Subsequently, however, he attempted to limit its application, and starting in November 1973 travel between the two Germanys was rendered more difficult. In 1974, references to the German nation were removed from the GDR's Constitution. Since the GDR's level of consumption was increasingly dependent on West German credit, though, inter-German relations overall were increased even further. When relations between the United States and the Soviet Union worsened at the end of 1979, Honecker was active to avoid a break in relations with the government in Bonn. A state visit to the FRG in September 1987 was the climax of his international recognition.

Honecker refused to back Mikhail Gorbachev when, already starting in 1985–86, he requested a greater opening and liberalization from the SED's regime. His opposition to perestroika did not prevent internal opposition groups, beginning in 1987, from acquiring greater recognition, and an increasing number of people escaping to West Germany. He had to powerlessly watch tens of thousands of GDR citizens demonstrate in favor of political freedom and the freedom to travel from the end of September to early October 1989. And the stiffening of his opposition to the reform movement encouraged by Gorbachev was also powerless and eventually led to his downfall. On October 17, 1989, the Political Office decided to replace him with Egon Krenz, who with a "new course" policy was given the mandate of attempting to regain the GDR citizens' faith.

In December 1989, the GDR's own authorities started legal proceedings against the former president of the Council of State. The initial accusation was abuse of power, to which the charge of instigation to homicide (along the border installations) was later added. In April 1990, stricken with cancer, Honecker entered a Soviet military hospital in Germany. In March 1991 he arrived in Moscow, and in July 1992 surrendered to German authorities. The trial against him was suspended given his worsening health conditions. Honecker was able to follow his wife to Santiago de Chile, where he died on May 29, 1994.

See also Berlin Wall; Détente; Ostpolitik; Perestroika; Real Socialism; Revolutions in East-Central Europe; Socialist Camp; Soviet Bloc.

FURTHER READING

Lorenzen, J. N. *Erich Honecker. Eine Biographie*. Hamburg: Rowohlt, 2001.
Mählert, U. *Kleine Geschichte der DDR*. Munich: Beck, 2001.

WILFRIED LOTH

Hoxha, Enver

Enver Hoxha (1908–85) was born in Gjirokastër on October 16, 1908. He graduated from high school in Korça in 1927, and thanks to a state scholarship enrolled in the biology department at the University of Montpellier in France. After a year he interrupted his studies, and went first to Paris and later to Brussels, where he began to work for the Albanian Consulate in 1934, but was fired in 1936. Hoxha returned to Albania and taught in the Korça high school; he became a member of the clandestine Communist Party and was expelled from his teaching position. Next he settled in Tirana, where he was hired by a tobacconist. The Yugoslav delegates Miladin Popoviç and Dushan Mugosha, who mediated the unification of Communist groups in Albania, appreciated Hoxha and helped him become the leader of the Albanian Communist Party. When the party was founded, on November 8, 1941, Hoxha was only one of the members of the provisional Central Committee, but during the First Party Conference in March 1943 he was elected secretary general.

At the end of the war, Hoxha was the most powerful political personality in Albania: in addition to being head of the party, he was prime minister, commander of the General Staff of the combined forces of the National Liberation Army of Albania, foreign minister, defense minister, president of the Anti-Fascist National Liberation Front, and a member of the Presidium of the People's Assembly. Energetic, and influenced by French and Albanian culture, he was a talented speaker and writer, and physically appealing; when meeting people he put his acting talents on display, smiling and easily displaying emotion, and soon became a popular figure. He masterfully tied the heritage of the anti-Fascist war with the need to establish a Communist government after the war, as well as to nationalist and Communist ideology. Hoxha implemented radical measures to eradicate the country's economic and cultural backwardness so as to bring Albania into the 20th century.

But he was also a dictator in the full sense of the term. Driven by an extreme ambition for power, he showed his intolerance for those who did not bend to his will, proving relentless against his political and personal foes, and never even contemplating responsibility for the isolation he was inflicting on the country. He organized trials against the anti-Communist opposition, which between the wars was to a large extent composed of the national elite; he ordered several capital punishments, along with deportations and incarcerations. He later adopted the same methods against his Communist adversaries as well. In foreign policy Hoxha was as doctrinaire as he was nationalistic. In his relations with the East he was pragmatic; he exploited his friendship with Yugoslavia, the Soviet Union, and China, and used their support to bolster his personal power. Toward the West, he instead exhibited forms of rejection unwarranted by the country's size and resources.

After the reunion of eighty-one Communist parties in Moscow in November 1960, Hoxha never again left Albania. Isolated by his own extended grip on power, he continued to orchestrate the cult of his own personality with the publication in 1968–90 of an edition of his works and memoirs, undertaken by the Political Office, in which manipulation of information was the rule. A subsequent edition of more works including his diaries about international politics, further memoirs, and works on special topics was also published. A whole army of historians, analysts, and activists from the Institute on Marxism-Leninism, lead by his wife, Nexhmije Hoxha, worked on collecting and editing his writings.

See also Cult of Personality; Despotism; Marxism-Leninism; Nationalism; People's Democracy; Sino-Soviet Split; Socialist Camp.

FURTHER READING

Kur u themelua Partia. Tirana: 1981.
Politika antikombëtare e Enver Hoxhës (Plenum i 2-të i KQ të PKsh, Berat 23–27 nëntor 1944). Tirana: 1995.
PPsh. Dokumente kryesore I–VIII. Tirana: 1971–86.

ANA LALAJ

Hundred Flowers Movement

The Chinese "hundred flowers" movement (1956–57) got its name from one of Mao Zedong's slogans, and was launched in April 1956. With the exhortation "Let a hundred flowers bloom; let a hundred schools of thought contend," after years of mistrust toward the most educated groups in the population, Mao invited the intellectuals to take a position, to demonstrate their support for the new Communist China and its revolutionary spirit. Mao seemed to have great confidence in the following that the new regime had among intellectuals. After the first months following Mao's appeal, however, it became clear that the mobilization's results were limited. This caution among intellectuals seemed rooted in the events of a preceding campaign of criticism that had been directed at them in 1951–52.

In February 1957, Mao intervened once more with his speech *On the Correct Handling of Contradictions among the People.* This document was aimed at transforming the hundred flowers movement into an occasion for continued improvement in adjusting the party's work methods. Mao's argument singled out the persistence of "contradictions" (*maodun*) in socialist society, and divided these into "antagonistic" contradictions and contradictions "among the people." The latter, also including the relationship of the party with intellectuals, could be resolved by means of the dialectical method, while antagonistic contradictions had to be resolved by means of the class struggle and could end only with the enemy's defeat. The speech reassured intellectuals and seemed to encourage the public expression of political opinions. But going against Mao's forecasts—and proof of the president's increasing distance from the revolution's moods—the result was not a blossoming of praise but rather a sprouting of dissent, directed at both the results of economic and social policy and the nature of the Chinese Communist Party's power itself as well as the choices of its leaders. As if this were not sufficient (and this was probably one of the main reasons for the repression that followed), the social atmosphere in the spring of 1957 became quite heated as the result of an intense protest movement in the factories. The workers' unhappiness had already regained strength in 1956, but in the first months of 1957 the strikes were constant. Between March and June, in Shanghai alone, the protest actions (interruptions of work, slowdowns in production, and boycotts) were more than two hundred, and involved the least privileged section of the working class, temporary and contract workers, excluded from the social benefits that were guaranteed to workers with a permanent job.

The apparent social instability in the country created by the controversial blooming of the hundred flowers and above all the workers' protests ended up convincing Mao that it was time to intervene. On June 8, the hundred flowers movement was brought to a halt with the publication of an editorial in the *People's Daily* (the party's official organ) that violently attacked dissenters. Those who had taken "advantage" of the party's invitation to attack the degenerations of the system created by the revolution (or if one prefers, those who had fallen into Mao's dialectical trap) were labeled as "rightist elements." In the following months at least four hundred thousand people, mostly urban residents and young "educated" people, were sent to the country to "be reeducated by contact with the masses." In the confusion and disorientation created by the repression there were also victims of personal vendettas and, once again, excessive zeal, which resulted in the removal of technicians, engineers, economists, and scientists from the urban labor market—in other words, all those who could contribute to the management of the new socialist economy.

See also Chinese Revolution; Cultural Revolution in China; Mao Zedong.

FURTHER READING

MacFarquhar, R. *The Origins of the Cultural Revolution.* Vol. 1, *Contradictions among the People, 1956–1957.* Oxford: Oxford University Press, 1974.

LUIGI TOMBA

Hungarian Republic of Councils

The Hungarian Republic of Councils (*Tanácsköztársaság*), which lasted only 133 days and was led by Béla Kun, was the only instance in which the Bolshevik model was realized in central Eastern Europe between the wars. It was founded on March 21, 1919, after a split in the country's ruling coalition, following the bourgeois-democratic revolution of October 1918. On March 20, 1919, the governments of the entente had presented the government led by Count Mihály Károlyi with conditions agreed to on February 26 by the Paris Peace Conference: the territorial cession of all of Transylvania and the acceptance of a punitive borderline, which meant that all the territories to the east of the river Tibisco, including the cities of Debrecen and Szeged, would become part of a demilitarized zone. Károlyi, counting on Soviet military support, refused the ultimatum's conditions, but was suddenly abandoned by the left-wing Social Democrats, who secretly made an agreement with the jailed Communists to seize power and create a socialist state. The state then formed a popular army, which attempted to stabilize the military situation by blocking the advance of Czech and Romanian troops, which were supported by the Western powers.

The Bolshevik dictatorship immediately created a fissure in Hungarian history, both juridically and socio-economically, because of measures such as the abolition of the separation of powers and the multiparty system, expropriation of agricultural holdings and industrial enterprises, replacement of elected county assemblies with directors appointed by the government, and creation of revolutionary tribunals (the *trojke*) made up of peasants and workers, whose sentences could not be appealed and were carried out immediately. The police and gendarmerie were replaced by workers' militias, which were aided by irregular groups (the so-called Lenin boys) that crossed the country in a sealed train with the goal of striking class enemies and large landowners. In the course of four months, these special groups carried out several hundred homicides and summary executions. The press and cultural institutions were also subject to widespread political purges, while religious denominations, especially the Catholics, saw their social role curtailed: the obligatory hour of religion was abolished in the schools. These provisions led many members of the prewar elite to openly oppose the Republic of Councils: in Szeged an "anti-Bolshevik Committee" was formed, led by future prime minister Count István Bethlen, and it soon became a countergovernment supported by the entente.

The hostility of the most mature intellectuals and politicians toward the Bolshevik experiment was countered by the enthusiastic support—of an ideologicopolitical but also a "generational" nature—of many young writers and artists (among whom were the director Béla Balázs, the writers Tibor Déry, Gyula Krúdy, and Zsigmond Móricz, and the musicians Béla Bartók and Zoltán Kodály), who saw the political crisis as a chance to renew the country's cultural environment. In addition to the support of significant sections of the literary and journalistic world, a large part of the working class—attracted by social measures such as a price freeze on lodging and basic staples, the introduction of the eight-hour workweek, and the unprecedented possibility for workers' families to move into apartments requisitioned from upper-class families—also supported the republic. The formation of a people's army, consisting of as many as two hundred thousand men, as an attempt to confront the advance of Czech and Slovak troops from the north and Romanian ones from the southeast, in the spring and summer of 1919, relied on the workers' support. After a series of initial successes, like the recapture of the city of Košice (then called Kassa) on June 7, 1919, the Hungarian army was forced to retreat, and it began to fall apart during July. On July 30, the Romanian army inflicted a serious defeat on the Hungarian army and crossed the Tibisco River near the city of Szolnok, and then continued its march toward Budapest.

Starting in June, moreover, the support of large swaths of the popular classes waned, starting with the peasants who were seriously affected by the nationalizations and the requisition campaigns conducted by the special teams, supported by revolutionary tribunals. In addition to the peasant revolts of the Transdanube region and Kalocsa (where about one hundred summary executions were performed), the republic then had to face the revolt of the cadets from the Ludovika military academy in Budapest. Aware of the change in the political climate, Kun attempted to address the difficult situation by making some concessions, such as revoking the prohibition on selling alcoholic beverages and distributing small parcels of land to poor peasants. Yet the government did not manage to regain the trust it had lost, especially among professional military personnel, who in April and May had supported the organization of the popular army

with logistical and professional aid, even though they did not share its political and ideological views.

On August 1 the executive led by Kun resigned, and was replaced by a Social Democratic government, led by the moderate Gyula Peidl, who without renouncing the republican form of government, annulled all the principal political and social provisions introduced by the Bolshevik government. The most important Communist leaders went abroad, especially to Vienna and the Soviet Union. Starting in the fall of 1919 numerous Communist and Social Democratic representatives, who had remained in Hungary and were actively involved in the experiment of the Republic of Councils, were charged and condemned. In the transition toward parliamentary authoritarianism, the political repression of 1919–20 joined forces with anti-Semitic political currents.

See also Bolshevism; Dictatorship of the Proletariat; Kun, Béla; Revolution, Myths of the.

FURTHER READING

Janos, A. C., and W. B. Slottman, eds. *Revolution in Perspective: Essays on the Hungarian Soviet Republic of 1919*. Berkeley: University of California Press, 1971.

Ormos, M. *From Padua to the Trianon, 1918–1920*. New York: Columbia University Press, 1991.

Romsics, I. *Hungary in the Twentieth Century*. Budapest: Corvina, 1999.

Tokes, R. L. *Béla Kun and the Hungarian Soviet Republic: The Origins and Role of the Communist Party of Hungary in the Revolutions of 1918–1919*. New York: Pall Mall Press (for Hoover Institution on War, Revolution and Peace, Stanford University), 1967.

STEFANO BOTTONI

Hungarian Revolution

By the summer of 1956, the policies and regime of Mátyás Rákosi had clearly failed. Rákosi had managed with Soviet support to oust the cautious reformer Imre Nagy as prime minister in the spring of 1955. But his Stalinist rule over Hungary had become unsustainable since the Twentieth Congress of the Communist Party of the Soviet Union (CPSU). Nagy still represented the cause of reform. The Hungarian Workers' Party (MDP) had become divided against itself, into camps of orthodox Communists intent on retaining the system without significant change, reformers seeking marked changes in it, and others trying to weave between the two. The situation had unnerved the army and the police, where many came to believe in reforms. And it had stretched the resolve of the political police, the ÁVH, to see victims of political show trials released from prison and some (such as János Kádár) gain senior positions again.

Several writers and journalists who had served the party hitherto became advocates of reform and wrote increasingly critical contributors to the newspapers. An intellectual debating club called the Petőfi Circle, formed under the League of Working Youth (DISZ), held ever more popular open debates in the spring and summer of 1956, exposing structural and operational faults in the system. That summer, the Soviets, keen to avoid a crisis, had Rákosi replaced as party leader by Ernő Gerő, although the two hardly differed politically. Gerő promised democratization of the system but did nothing about it.

Stalinist policies of tight central planning and forced development of heavy industry had taken the economy close to collapse. The standard of living in 1956 fell short of 1939, the last year of peace. Incomes of 40 percent of urban people left them below a breadline that was defined artificially low. General poverty, religious harassment, and insults to national awareness pride had caused nationwide disgust with the regime.

Meanwhile, those longing for change took heart from the Austrian state treaty. It seemed feasible after all for Soviet troops to withdraw from territory occupied by them. Hungary's admission to the United Nations in December 1955 implied that the organization might take serious measures on behalf of the country, as a member-state. A similar implication was read into propaganda from the Eisenhower administration: the United States would be ready to support liberation struggles by "captive nations."

By October 1956, university students demanding the withdrawal of Soviet troops as well as radical reform of the exercise of power formed a student organization independent of the MDP to pursue their program. At almost the same time came the reburial of László Rajk and his close associates, victims of an infamous show trial in 1949. The Communist Party was devastated by the official admission of their innocence.

On October 22, a student rally at Budapest Technical University listed demands under sixteen points. Their program, which became generally accepted during the revolution, included free, multiparty elections, with-drawal of Soviet troops, and higher pay, but not restoration of a capitalist social and political system. The next day, a demonstration of solidarity with the unrest in Poland was called.

On October 23, the party leaders first banned the protest, but backed down on realizing its decision could only be imposed by force, which it was loathe to resort to in the current political mood in the police and army. What began as a student protest was joined by workers and employees. By evening, 200,000 protesters had gathered before Parliament, waiting for Nagy to address them, while a crowd elsewhere in the city overturned the giant statue of Stalin, seen as a symbol of Soviet oppression. Only when called upon by the party would Nagy enter the Parliament building and address the demonstration. By then, a promise to continue his 1953 reforms failed to satisfy a crowd rapidly becoming aware of its power.

Another crowd gathered outside the radio station since morning was demanding that the sixteen points be read on the air. Instead, a speech by Gerő was broadcast, in which he called the protest unrest fomented by hostile elements. After the speech but before armed struggle broke out, the presidium of the CPSU responded to pleas from Gerő and Yuri Andropov, then Soviet ambassador in Budapest, to send Soviet forces into Budapest to end the upheaval. Before the assistance arrived, the Hungarian party leadership appointed Nagy to head a new government, but also declared martial law, a curfew, and a ban on assembly.

Sometime before midnight, state-security guards at the radio station fired on the demonstrators. The crowd responded by obtaining arms from factories, barracks, and soldiers sent to defend the radio station. The building was stormed and the armed uprising began, turning before dawn into a national liberation struggle, as the first Soviet troops arrived in the capital. Students in several other cities had held demonstrations on the 23rd too—three were killed by a volley of fire in Debrecen. But only in Budapest did armed warfare break out. Rebel units formed along the capital's main streets and junctions caused sizeable losses to the Soviets. Most units of the Hungarian army stood aside, while many officers and men went over to the freedom fighters, whose determination created a chance for a political settlement.

The party leadership was paralyzed by stalemate: advocates of a political solution and limiting military action against rebels faced hard-liners intent on crushing the revolt. Political concessions failed for lack of a clear direction. Though Nagy became prime minister and Gerő, after deadly fire had been directed on protesters outside Parliament on October 25, was replaced as party leader by Kádár, though comprehensive reform was promised on the 26th and two non-Communists included in the government on the 27th, the freedom fighters would not lay down their arms. Indeed, they swelled in number. By October 26, the strikes had become general. Mass actions pushed aside the local authorities even if ÁVH men fired on demonstrators (for example, in Miskolc and Moson-magyaróvár). Institutions of social self-government took over—revolutionary councils in communities and workers' councils in factories—each body making similar demands: an end to the fighting, withdrawal of Soviet troops, and a democratic, independent, neutral Hungary. The declared aim was to restore the pluralist system immediately preceding the Communist takeover of 1948, not the quasidemocratic system of the pre-1944 period.

By October 28, the provinces were revolutionized. It was likely that the armed resistance would become nation-wide and the Soviets would find themselves confronting units of the Hungarian army. The Soviet Union needed to withdraw its troops from the firing line, at least temporarily. It was also being pressed toward a political solution by international events. Poland (and Yugoslavia) clearly sympathized with developments in Hungary, which shed doubts about a possible joint Warsaw Pact military intervention. U.S. secretary of state John Foster Dulles, however, had stated in a speech on October 26, "We do not look upon these [Soviet satellite] nations as potential military allies." This might be taken to mean that the United States was effectively giving the Soviet Union a free hand and ruling out military intervention, so that no risk to Soviet power would be involved in a political solution. However, the Western Powers bowed on October 27 to public pressure at home and called on the UN Security Council to convene and discuss the Hungarian situation.

On the evening of October 27, Nagy and Kádár, having discussed matters with numerous delegations, made an offer to two delegates of the CPSU presidium, A. I. Mikoyan and M. A. Suslov, who had been in Budapest since October 24. A ceasefire would be declared, Soviet troops would withdraw from Budapest, and negotiations would start on their complete withdrawal from Hungary. The ÁVH would be replaced by a new security body including the revolutionaries, organizations set up during the revolution would be recognized, and the main social demands would be met. The delegates agreed, but said that Moscow would make no further concessions: order had to be restored on those terms.

The terms were announced on October 28 as success for the "vast people's movement," but failed nonetheless. The rebels were not prepared to lay down their arms or employees to return to work unless other basic demands such as a multiparty system, declaration of Hungary's neutrality, and, above all, a start to Soviet troop withdrawals were met too. Nagy then tried to restore peace at home by meeting some of these demands, trusting that Moscow would endorse his concessions later. On October 30, he announced a multiparty system, and on the following day, the fragmented Hungarian Workers' Party was replaced by a new Hungarian Socialist Workers' Party (MSZMP). A new government formed from the parties of the 1945–47 coalition. Control of the army was assumed by a revolutionary body and a high command of the national guard formed to cover the armed revolutionaries. Thereafter there were no further cases of mob law like the lynching that followed the capture of the Budapest MDP headquarters on October 30.

Nagy's tactics seemed to be vindicated by a statement from the Soviet government on October 30, promising to rectify mistakes in relation to the "people's democratic" countries. The CPSU presidium also took note of the latest developments in Hungary, but on the following day it revised its position, deciding to crush the revolution and install a new government. Khrushchev informed leaders of the fraternal parties of this decision. Gomułka took note of it and Tito offered to assist in neutralizing Nagy when the time came.

When further Soviet forces arrived on November 1, the Hungarian government withdrew from the Warsaw Pact in protest and declared Hungary's neutrality, calling on the permanent members of the UN Security Council to back its decision. In response, the revolutionary organizations announced the end of their strike, so establishing conditions for consolidation at home. But it was still unclear whether the nation would be content with democratizing the Socialist system or want to go further toward the Western model. The government was reshuffled again on November 3. Kádár was kept as a member, although he had secretly flown to Moscow on the November 1, where he agreed at a CPSU presidium meeting to head a puppet government. Another member of Nagy's team was the non-Communist political thinker István Bibó, while the defense portfolio was taken over by the Colonel Pál Maléter. That evening, the radio broadcast a speech by Cardinal József Mindszenty, head of the Catholic Church in Hungary, who had been freed from prison on October 30.

General I. A. Serov, head of the Soviet secret service (KGB) had also been in Hungary since October 24. Late on the evening of November 3, he arrested the Hungarian government delegation to the troop-withdrawal talks, and the Soviet forces attacked the following morning. The Hungarian army put up little resistance, but the freedom fighters of Budapest kept up the armed struggle for several days. Resistance was longest in Csepel, the heavy industrial center of the city, which fell only on November 11. The Soviets took about a thousand prisoners, who were sent to prison in Carpatho-Ukraine, from where they returned in December.

On November 4, Nagy and several party leaders were invited to take refuge in the Yugoslav Embassy, where they refused to resign or recognize the puppet Kádár government. The Soviet aggression was condemned by an emergency special session of the UN General Assembly, but no steps were agreed in Hungary's defense, although the question remained on the agenda until 1962.

Kádár promised an amnesty. He denied any notion of restoring the Rákosi regime and confirmed the dissolution of the ÁVH, but he broke up the revolutionary councils. The new regime arrived in Budapest on November 7 and was sworn in. The country responded to the intervention and coup with a general strike and support for the workers' councils and Nagy government. A Budapest workers' council formed on November 14 to further the aims of the revolution included delegates from provincial workers' councils. Only with Soviet military assistance could Kádár prevent a national workers' council forming on November 21. The next day Soviet help was again needed to lure Nagy and his followers out of the Yugoslav Embassy, arrest them, and deport them to Romania. Mass protests swept across the country once more.

At the end of November, Kádár yielded to pressure from the leaders of the Communist parties and the CPSU representatives by whom he was accompanied back to Hungary. He ceased his gestures of reconciliation and began to organize a party and militia based on second- and third-ranking figures from the Rákosi era. By December, the militia, helped by the Soviets, was using arms against demonstrators (in Salgótarján and Tatabánya) and mass arrests began. The Budapest workers' council called a 48-hour strike on December 11–12 in protest. Its leaders were arrested, martial law was imposed, and the internment camps were reopened.

With no hope of international help, Hungary suffered mass arrests and the first executions in the second half of December. Some 180,000 people fled the country. The Communist reprisals and terror led to 13,000 people being interned, over 20,000 imprisoned, and some 230 executed. Nagy and Maléter were executed on June 16, 1958. Bibó was sentenced to life imprisonment. Most of the prisoners were released in a 1963 amnesty, but several were held until the mid-1970s and most '56ers remained under surveillance until the change of system in 1989–90.

See also Gormułka, Władysław; Kádár, János; Nagy, Imre; Rajk, László; Rákosi, Mátyás; Socialist Camp; Soviet Bloc; Stalinism.

FURTHER READING

Békés, C., M. Byrne, and J. M. Rainer, eds. *1956: The Hungarian Revolution: A History in Documents.* Budapest: Central European University Press, 2002.

Congdon, L. W., and B. Király, eds. *The Ideas of the Hungarian Revolution, Suppressed and Victorious, 1956–1999.* Boulder, CO: Social Science Monographs–Atlantic Research and Publications, 2002.

Granville, J. C. *The First Domino: International Decision Making During the Hungarian Crisis.* College Station, TX: A&M University Press, 2004.

Györkei, J., and M. Horváth, eds. *Soviet Military Intervention in Hungary, 1956.* Trans. Emma Roper-Evans. Budapest: Central European University Press, 1999.

Litván, G., J. M. Bak, and L. H. Legters, eds. *The Hungarian Revolution of 1956: Reform, Revolt and Repression, 1953–1963.* New York: Longman, 1996.

Lomax, B. *Hungary, 1956.* London: Allison and Busby, 1976.

Orekhova, E. D., V. T. Sereda, and A. S. Stykalin, eds. *Sovietsky Soyuz i vengersky krizis 1956 goda: Dokumenty.* (The Soviet Union and the Hungarian Crisis in 1956: Documents.) Moscow: Rossiiskaya Politicheskaya Entsiklopedia, 1998.

Stykalin, A. S. *Prervannaya Revolutsiya. Vengersky krizis 1956 goda i polityka Moskvi.* (Interrupted Revolution. The Hungarian Crisis in 1956 and the Policy of Moscow.) Moscow: Novy Khronograf, 2003.

ATTILA SZAKOLCZAI

Husák, Gustav

Gustav Husák (1913–91) began his political life at age sixteen, and four years later, joined the Komsomol as a student and entered the Communist Party of

Czechoslovakia (CPCz). He studied law in Bratislava, where he also participated in the student movement called the Association of Socialist Students. After finishing law school, he worked in various law firms and other offices as well. From 1940 to 1942 he performed lower-level tasks in the various illegal resistance activities of the party, for which he spent three short periods in prison. In summer 1943, he became a member of the fifth illegal directorship of the Communist Party of Slovakia (CPS). At age twenty-nine, Husák entered the realm of higher-up Communist functionaries and launched his political career, remaining consistently within the close circle of party leaders until 1950. Significantly, he played a leading role in the preparation and conduct of the Slovak National Uprising in August and September 1944, and was a member of the Slovak National Council and its Presidium. As a member of the Slovak delegation he took part in negotiations to form the first postwar government of Czechoslovakia.

Soon after the liberation of Czechoslovakia, conflicts began to emerge between the postwar leadership in Slovakia and the nationwide leadership of the CPCz. The Slovak leadership supported a more radical approach to the monopolization of power and resisted limitations on authority. Poor relations between the leading functionaries in Slovakia and the Slovaks in the central CPCz leadership were also having their effect. The leadership of the CPCz was instigating changes in Slovakia. In August 1945, the "Slovak in Prague," Vilém Široký, and his adherents assumed the party's leadership. The position of Husák and his "insurgents" was weakened. The conflicts between these two political directions, however, were obscured by the common goal of gaining a monopoly of power for the party. This unity increased after the unsuccessful parliamentary elections in May 1946. The Slovak Communists received only 30 percent of the vote, while their rival Democrat Party received double this number. Husák assumed the chair of the Slovak Executive Committee in Slovakia, and his political position grew stronger. He became active in the struggle to reverse the balance of power in the elections. He stood in the forefront of efforts to break up and eventually liquidate the Democrat Party. Husák played a significant role in creating provocations against that party and perpetrating repression against its functionaries. His efforts were abetted by a political crisis and the so-called conspiracy in Slovakia, itself provoked by the Communists in fall 1947. Husák contributed to both initiating and carrying out these activities. Though the Communists

failed in this attempt at political liquidation of their rivals, their efforts were ultimately crowned by success in the Communist coup in 1948. Husák's key initiatives in this takeover fully reflected his political and power objectives.

Husák continued in the same vein in Slovakia from 1948 to 1950, fully participating in the lawless and repressive tactics of that period. Still, the old conflicts between the adherents of the insurgents' leadership of the CPS and the leadership of the CPCz soon came to the fore. In 1950, Husák was branded as a leading bearer of bourgeois-nationalist deviationist ideas and was removed from his functions. But he resorted to the usual self-criticism and confessed the seriousness of his errors. He later justified this step as having been necessary to prevent his expulsion from the party. In February 1951, he was arrested and, three years later, in April 1954, was given a life sentence as a traitor to his country. The trial was not public, because Husák turned out to be one of the few in those days to deny his confessions. From prison he wrote several protests and appeals for a review of his trial, but they were ignored. He was released in 1960 by presidential amnesty, and three years later, was rehabilitated both legally and politically.

On his rehabilitation, Husák ratcheted up his efforts to return to politics and make good for his past transgressions. He worked on ways of changing Slovakia's position from within the country. His influence and authority in the party rose, particularly within the intelligentsia. He became a representative of one of the currents of a national political movement in Slovakia. At the same time, he came in conflict with the CPCz leadership and turned down certain positions offered to him in Prague. The CPS leadership gained the upper hand in this national political movement, and this hampered the growth of Husák's influence. Husák welcomed the events of 1968, but did not become a leading figure in them. Through pressure exerted by his adherents on the regime he was able to enter the government as a deputy chair. He pushed for and achieved a federative organization of the country. Husák first supported Alexander Dubček's reform movement but later condemned it.

Husák took part in negotiations about the so-called Moscow Protocol and he signed it, though before then he had criticized the invasion by the Soviet troops. The Soviet leadership first had doubts about his political reliability, but soon changed its views. Already by August 1968, Husák had been chosen to head the CPS, and after some experience with him, Moscow most probably initiated and certainly welcomed Husák's replacement of Dubček in April 1969. Husák had made intense efforts to achieve his selection to this position. He succeeded, without encountering any substantial opposition, by continuing to tout himself as a man of reform. The twenty years of so-called normalization became inseparably associated with his name. He probably did not initiate all the measures of normalization—some he undertook under external and internal pressure—but he did defend the measures. He is the person most responsible for the dismantlement of the reform movement and the aftermath, which saw the restoration of the pre-Dubček Communist regime and its subsequent integration with the Soviet occupation of the country.

In May 1975, Husák achieved his goal of absolute power when he had himself named president of the republic, thereby concentrating in his own person the two highest political functions in the country. This happened during a time of relative relaxation of international tensions and when certain currents of opposition emerged inside the country. Long unsolved problems of the nation's political, economic, and cultural development evolved into something of a social crisis. Husák was unable to even understand these problems, let alone solve them. His departure as general secretary of the party became imminent and, indeed, took place in November 1987. Husák's abdication from the presidency was a natural consequence of the 1989 revolution, and he left office on December 10 of that year.

Husák entered the leading Communist circles at an early age. He belonged to those who had not gone through the Comintern school, yet his spirit and political legacy were a lasting token of his political thinking, and they determined his political activity. He was an ardent participant in bringing about the power monopoly and forging of the Communist regime. Here he demonstrated his unswerving obedience and subordination to the interests of his Soviet masters. He did not shy from the use of repression, lawlessness, persecutions, or the sacrifice of his own friends, and readily abandoned previous views and convictions. As he ascended the rungs of party politics, his youthful ideals changed into a pure craving for power. He became a man of power in a regime in which power and the way he used it were to determine his own fate.

Husák was a zealous warrior for a Communist dictatorship, collaborated in its establishment, and later was its most important representative. He experienced the delights and distresses of Communist power as an ac-tive creator of the regime. He was later its prisoner, then after that a figure in opposition to it, and then ultimately its highest functionary in the party and country. In his sometimes erratic road to the summit he endured, first and foremost, because his political thinking, formed in the struggle for power and creation of the regime, consistently determined his practical activities. Yet he never went far enough beyond the limits of this regime to grasp the nature of the new social currents and the necessity of responding to them with political changes. As a "man of the Comintern outside of the Comintern," he knew from long experience that his political fate depended on the power of the Soviet leadership and his obligation to fulfill its interests. And that is what he abided by.

Husák's political path was filled with constant struggles against his enemies outside the party and within it. He fought hard and recognized no friends in his struggle for party and personal power. He was a highly placed functionary who successfully launched a Communist regime, and then experienced its downfall, to which his own policies ultimately contributed.

See also Dubček, Alexander; Prague Coup; Prague Spring.

FURTHER READING

Husák, G. *Svědectví o Slovenském národním povstání.* Prague: Svoboda, 1970.

———. *Speeches and Writings.* London: Pergamon, 1986.

Plevza, V. *Vzostupy a pády.* Bratislava: Tatrapress, 1991.

KAREL KAPLAN

Hu Yaobang

Hu Yaobang (1915–89) held important positions in the Chinese Communist Party's (CCP) bureaucracy, especially in the new reform-oriented leadership that came to power after 1978. Under his guidance the CCP reestablished a constructive relationship with the country's intellectuals, after the years of obscurantism that had marked the Cultural Revolution, and he made moderate attempts to reform the political system. Because of his role, his being purged as party secretary in January 1987, and then his death two years later were among the causes that led to the student demonstrations in the spring of 1989.

Born in Hunan in 1915, the province that had also given birth to Mao Zedong and Liu Shaoqi, Hu Yaobang joined the party at an early age, and while still an adolescent he joined the Jiangxi Maoist Soviet. He became a leader in the Communist Youth League after having taken part in the Long March, and in 1952, during the Communist regime's first years in power, its general secretary. In Beijing Hu established good relations with Deng Xiaoping, whose own ups and downs would affect his career for better or worse. Like Deng a victim of the Cultural Revolution, he returned to Beijing in the early 1970s to serve as director of the Central Party School, where he was at the center of numerous ideological debates during those years. After Mao's death in 1976, Hu was active in promoting a critique of Maoist radicalism and became a member of the Central Committee's Political Office in 1978. As Deng's position as the country's new leader became more firmly established, Hu became the party's general secretary in 1980 and later president (the post that had been Mao's) until the position was abolished in 1982. Hu led the party until the end of 1986.

In winter 1987, student demonstrations asking for a reform of the political system occurred at different Chinese universities and in various cities, with particular intensity in Shanghai. Many of the intellectuals who had inspired the protests were to be at the center of the much more widespread movement that followed in 1989. The decision not to intervene directly to halt the demonstrations caused the conservative faction to focus its anger on Hu, costing him Deng's support and the leadership of the party, but simultaneously gaining him the intellectuals' and students' respect. Two years later, news of Hu's death, on April 15, 1989, because of a heart attack, provoked the beginning of the student and popular demonstrations that only ended on June 4, with the army's bloody intervention. Hu's possible rehabilitation is today tied to the historical evaluation of the events in Tiananmen Square (which are still considered a "counterrevolutionary" episode). Although a change in the evaluation of Hu has not yet taken shape, in 2005 the CCP held an official celebration (the first since 1989) on the occasion of the ninetieth anniversary of his birth.

Hu's leadership was extremely important in taking China out of the morass of the Cultural Revolution. It was his drive that helped build and nourish the new alliance between party and intellectuals. In 1978, he promoted the debate on "practice as the only criterion of truth," inviting people to "search for truth in the facts," a slogan that opened the doors to an open and profoundly critical evaluation of the period of Maoist radicalism and helped the process of de-Maoization. Riding that wave of enthusiasm, critiques by groups of intellectuals during that period sometimes went too far. In 1983 it was the campaign against "spiritual pollution" that led him to slow the process, while the campaign that followed the demonstrations of 1986 ("against bourgeois liberalization") cost him his position as general secretary. Hu was perhaps a leader who was ahead of his time and arrived too early for a China headed toward reforms. His line's defeat in 1986 led to a significant slowdown in the process of reforming the political system that was being discussed at different levels during the early 1980s.

See also Beijing Spring; Cultural Revolution in China; Deng Xiaoping; Mao Zedong.

FURTHER READING

Goldman, M. "Hu Yaobang's Intellectual Network and the Theory of Conference of 1979." *China Quarterly* 126 (1991): 219–42.

Schoenhals, M. "The 1978 Criterion of Truth Controversy." *China Quarterly* 126 (1991): 243–68.

LUIGI TOMBA

Iconography

The Russian term *obraz*, image, refers by definition to a sacred image, one that the rest of the world, following Greek etymology, calls an icon. Icons are so important in Russian visual culture that even during a period in which religious faith was being replaced by state atheism, forms of artistic expression and writing were influenced by their poetic value, if not their religious significance. The meaning of a sacred image that was neither a work of art nor an ornament but simply a connection between human beings and the world beyond, and whose representation (written and not painted, following the Russian lexicon) was meant to help believers see the invisible and lead them beyond a mere contemplation of figures, was transposed into and taken over by the art of poster propaganda and the mass art of the Soviet era. The icon did not narrate, it did not illustrate; instead it represented an idea or a concept in an absolute fashion. Its combination of image and words contained the essence of thought that human beings could attain by means of faith and veneration, transcending earthly experience and reaching a higher spiritual dimension.

The *lubok*, a type of popular print similar to a theatrical backdrop, developed during the 17th century and displayed at public markets and fairs, would have a different sort of impact: its narrative characteristics made it suitable for use in scenery, and encouraged viewers to consume it playfully, to the extent that it would be physically worn down. It was on this archaic basis that with infinite nuances and variations, the system of Soviet iconography was built. The culture of the 1920s, oriented toward avant-garde principles, would underscore that it was not necessary to transform or translate what was not an image into an image. Visual and verbal categories were to exist independently of one another, and not necessarily to be superimposed on or absorbed by one another. The image was not meant to illustrate or explain the word but existed autonomously; perhaps it would spark a dialogue with the viewer, but if so, quite independently.

The exact opposite occurred with the transition to Stalinist culture. With the proclamation of the socialist realist method (1934), the concept of "illustration" would become an essential principle. The word, above all the written one, acquired fundamental importance and regained the hegemonic role that the 1920s had taken from it. The word was the foundation of a thousand edicts, laws, proclamations, and slogans that the state was producing daily, and all the arts were supposed to contribute to the translation (illustration) of those principles whose conceptual or linguistic complexity caused the incomprehension of the many into appropriate and comprehensible languages, thus following in the lubok's steps. Buildings, films, propagandistic manifestoes, and paintings acquired color as well as ornamental and narrative character. The figurative arts, sculpture, music, cinema, and literature all contributed to the creation of the total work of art, an articulated and harmonious world that one could believe in, even if its appearance was in drastic contrast to what one saw every day with one's own eyes or experienced on one's own skin. To see was to believe.

According to Soviet artistic principles, the real work of art was not the original but the reproduction. The canvas or sheet on which the prototype was traced was nothing more than the point of departure for the image's multiplication. Communist art was not commercial. Since 1919, the consumer product market had vanished and artistic activity had been transformed into the distribution of aesthetic ideas. The work was not sold to an individual consumer; visual images were instead diffused on a massive scale, and in turn these became experiences and were meant to be transformed into life practices. Consequently art was meant to be accessible, nonproblematic, and immediately comprehensible by the masses.

The first real moment of crisis for this system would arrive in the 1970s, when the artists of a movement that would subsequently be named Sots-art would deconstruct Soviet socialist rhetoric precisely by using images, adding their own signatures as artists to the materials of mass propaganda, to underscore how for decades their activity had been limited to signing prefabricated products, and how Soviet culture had been overflowing with empty ideology.

See also Avant-garde; Propaganda, Communist; Socialist Realism.

FURTHER READING

Bonnell, V. E. *Iconography of Power: Soviet Political Posters under Lenin and Stalin.* Berkeley: University of California Press, 1997.

Groys, B., and M. Hollein, eds. *Traumfabrik Kommunismus. Die Visuelle Kultur der Stalinzeit/Dream Factory Communism. The Visual Culture of the Stalin Era.* Ostfildern: Hatje Cantz, 2003.

Lihachev, D. S. *Le radici dell'arte russa: dal Medioevo alle avanguardie.* Ed. E. A. Kostjukovich. Milan: Bompiani, 1995.

Tupitsyn, M. *Arte sovietica contemporanea: dal realismo socialista ad oggi.* Milan: Politi, 1990.

GIAN PIERO PIRETTO

Immigration to the USSR

When the Bolsheviks came to power in 1917 by overturning czarist autocracy, the descendants of foreign immigrants from a variety of countries, who were now for all intents and purposes Russian citizens but who had preserved the customs of their original homelands, lived in the immense Russian Empire. The most numerous descendants had, since the 18th century, belonged to German agricultural communities that had taken up residence in a region south of the Volga, or Greek communities that lived on the shores of the Black Sea and in the northern Caucasus. The Italians present were also farmers who had settled at about the same time, especially in Crimea and southern Russia. In addition to the Armenian and Jewish communities, a modest French presence was made up mostly of French preceptors who worked for aristocratic families in Moscow and Saint Petersburg, as well as artists, musicians, circus people, and traveling salespeople that came from many European countries.

In the years following the revolution and especially after the civil war's end, a new phenomenon appeared: in addition to economic migration, there was a new form of migration marked by political and ideological characteristics. On the one hand, the unstable nature of the new state, whose institutional and economic formulas had no historical precedent, led Lenin first and Stalin later to favor foreign investment. Thus engineers, technicians, and workers arrived in the Soviet Union to install new industries based on Western technology. Already in 1926, according to Soviet estimates, thirty-nine economic agreements of this type had been concluded with the Germans, twenty-two with the British, fifteen with the Americans, and four with the French. In 1929, as the New Economic Policy was abandoned and Five-Year Plans were introduced in the context of forced industrialization, the number of plants being built by foreign companies increased. The Germans built the Osram factory near Moscow; U.S., Dutch, and German capital was employed in the construction of the Scheglovsk-Kemerovo industrial center; the Italian company Riv built a ball-bearing plant in Moscow; and Umberto Nobile (Italian explorer, aviator, and engineer) was in charge of plans for the construction of the Zeppelin factory Dirizhablestroj in the capital, in which Italian personnel was also employed. During this period, attracted by the new regime's potential, many inhabitants from bordering areas decided to migrate to the Soviet Union in search of work: Romanians, Chinese (whose presence on Russian territory dated to 1898, the year in which the construction of the railroad connecting czarist Russia to the Chinese city of Harbin had begun), Iranians (who were especially attracted by employment opportunities in the Baku region, where the oil industry was flourishing), Finns, and after 1929 because of the Great Depression, Americans.

After the founding of the Third International in 1919 and to an even greater extent after the definitive victory of the Bolsheviks over the White generals' troops, the Soviet Union became a common destination for both political militants who had been summoned to Moscow to work for the Comintern or the Krestintern and anti-Fascists who were attempting to flee the growing wave of fascism that was inundating many European countries. Individuals such as Antonio Gramsci, Palmiro Togliatti, Maurice Thorez, Ernst Thälmann, Otto Kuusinen, Karl

Radek, Máthyás Rákosi, and Jules Humbert-Droz stayed in the Soviet Union for long periods of time, often in important roles in the organs of the Third International and living in close contact with key representatives of the Community Party of the Soviet Union. A large number of Communist activists also arrived from Asia, especially from China and Korea, and once they had finished their courses in party schools and returned to their countries of origin after years in the USSR, became prominent leaders in the anti-imperialist movement. They were joined at the time by simple German, Polish, Hungarian, Italian, Greek, Bulgarian, Yugoslav, Austrian, Swiss, French, Finnish, Belgian, Danish, Dutch, Latvian, Lithuanian, Estonian, Cuban, Mexican, American, Chinese, and Korean militants, hoping to find a more just society in the Soviet Union, or simply drawn there by the search for an adoptive motherland where they could find protection from the persecution of the police forces in their countries of origin.

Moscow in the 1920s thus became a hub for innumerable meetings, experiences, arrivals, and departures. Emigrants often left their countries illegally thanks to help from the International Organization for Aid to Revolutionary Fighters (MOPR), better known as International Red Aid, created at the end of 1922 during the Fourth Congress of the International in order to offer material, legal, and moral support to political prisoners, political émigrés, and their families. In 1932 Red Aid included seventy national sections with a total of about 14 million members, of which 9.7 million were affiliated with the Soviet MOPR. Once they arrived in the USSR, political émigrés needed to register with the organs of the MOPR, and if they were members of a Communist Party, seek out its representatives in the capital. These representatives lived at the Hotel Lux, while simple militants were temporarily lodged in the Emigrés' House, which the MOPR had created in 1923 and functioned until 1930. They could only stay there for a brief period of time, two months at most, with free board and lodging, while waiting for Red Aid to find them employment in the factories of Moscow or other Soviet cities. Here, bewildered by the novelty of the locale, a language they did not know, and the harsh climate, they often found that the local section of the International Clubs of Political Emigrés was a reference point to assist them in integrating into the new society they had chosen.

In the 1920s political émigrés lived an undoubtedly interesting life, if not a comfortable one. They were free

to travel, not only inside Soviet borders, but also abroad, and there were plenty of opportunities, perhaps at the end of a course they had taken in one of the many party schools, to return to their own countries on some critical mission. The debates, during the evenings they spent at the clubs or at meetings that were held at their places of work, were heated, given the tensions that existed in those years between Stalin and the various oppositions. The status of political émigré allowed one to benefit from a special food card, which granted access to stores for foreigners, and therefore also to a higher standard of living than that enjoyed by Soviet citizens.

It was in 1932 that conditions for political émigrés started to worsen, when the politburo approved a decree that obligated citizens sixteen years of age or older that resided in some of the larger cities such as Moscow, Leningrad, Char'kov, Kiev, Minsk, Rostov, and Vladivostok to obtain a passport, and then register it with the police in order to obtain a residence permit and find a job. Two years later, with the introduction of a new passport law, it was impossible to avoid the requirement of becoming a Soviet citizen, thus forcing émigrés to lose their original one and resign themselves to remaining in the USSR. The conviction that the danger of war on two fronts was imminent, after the Japanese occupation of Manchuria and Adolf Hitler's rise to power, played a role in the Soviet leadership taking these steps. From this moment on xenophobia, which in a more or less obvious manner had always characterized the regime, rose to the level of state theory: communities of foreigners that had resided in Russia for centuries (defined as "nationalities of the diaspora") and all foreigners living in Russia became "the enemy." Sergey Kirov's assassination in December 1934 only worsened the situation. This was the year that certainly not by chance, Polish, German, Finnish, Korean, and Italian "counterrevolutionary organizations" were discovered. Soon wide-reaching repression would also affect Iranian, Greek, Chinese, Korean, Swiss, French, Bulgarian, Austrian, Argentinean, Belgian, Hungarian, Dutch, Danish, Cuban, Latvian, Lithuanian, Estonian, Mexican, Romanian, Finnish, and Yugoslav émigrés—in other words, the majority of the almost ten thousand foreign citizens who, according to the data collected by the Visa and Registration Division of the Central Directorate of the People's Commissariat for Internal Affairs, lived in the USSR in the mid-1930s.

A large portion of the political émigrés of all nationalities became victims of Soviet terror in the years between 1936 and 1939: they were arrested during well-planned operations, sentenced during summary proceedings, condemned to long periods of detention in forced labor camps, and executed by firing squad. Only a few survived. The same fate awaited many Communist Party leaders, and among the more emblematic cases were those of the German and Polish Communist parties. After the German aggression, the State Committee for the Defense of the USSR passed resolution 2409ss on October 14, 1942, stating that nationals of countries at war with the Soviet Union had to be mobilized by force into labor colonies. Hundreds of Italians, Germans, and Romanians were therefore deported to Kazakhstan. At the war's end the presence of foreigners on Soviet soil was noticeably reduced, while in the years after World War II the country's borders were never reopened and the flux of émigrés ended. The only paths to entry into the USSR were the so-called political pilgrimages by intellectuals, writers, publicists, and philosophers attracted to the Soviet myth.

See also Comintern; Deportation of Nationalities in the USSR; Great Terror; Messianism; Militancy; Political Pilgrims; Revolution, Myths of the; Soviet Industrialization.

FURTHER READING

Chase, W. J. *Enemies within the Gates? The Comintern and Stalinist Repression, 1934–1939.* New Haven, CT: Yale University Press, 2001.

Coeuré, S. *La Grande Lueur à l'Est: les Français et l'Union soviétique, 1917–1939.* Paris: Seuil, 1999.

Dundovich, E., F. Gori, and E. Guercetti. *Reflections on the Gulag: With a Documentary Appendix on the Italian Victims of Repression in the USSR.* Milan: Feltrinelli, 2003.

Hollander, P. *Political Pilgrims: Travels of Western Intellectuals to the Soviet Union, China, and Cuba, 1928–1978.* New York: Oxford University Press, 1981.

Studer, B. *Un parti sous influence. Le Parti communiste suisse, une section du Komintern, 1931 à 1939.* Lausanne: Editions L'Age d'Homme, 1994.

Sutton, A. C. *Western Technology and Soviet Economic Development.* Stanford, CA: Hoover Institution Press, 1968–73.

Zhuravlëv, S. V. *"Malenkie liudi" i "bolshaia istoriia": inostrantsy moskovskogo Èlektrozavoda v sovetskom obshchestve 1920-kh–1930-kh gg.* Moscow: Rosspen, 2000.

———. *Inostrancy v Sovetskoj Rossii v 1920–1930-e gg. Istochniki i metody social'no-istoricheskogo issledovanja.* Doctoral dissertation, Institut rossijskoj istorii RAN, 2001.

ELENA DUNDOVICH AND FRANCESCA GORI

Imperialism

The decades after 1870 saw a rapid expansion of European overseas possessions, often as a result of a policy of conquest. By 1914 a majority of the world's peoples were colonial subjects of the European great powers. From the mid-1870s onward the term "imperialism" came into common usage to describe the extension of European control over the non-European world. Various explanations for the process were offered, including moral obligation, national aggrandizement, strategic rivalry, and economic self-interest. Liberal theorists and political leaders such as John Stuart Mill and Jules Ferry argued that the export of capital was essential for economic growth, and that colonies offered the most profitable field for external investment. On the Socialist Left, colonialism was viewed as a manifestation of economic exploitation. From the turn of the century onward, the Marxist tradition produced a more focused explanation, usefully characterized as the "theory of capitalist imperialism."

Karl Marx's analysis of capitalist development identified a tendency of the unconstrained market to produce a concentration of capital in fewer hands, as firms that were larger and more capital intensive devoured their less efficient rivals. In the process of overcoming feudal fragmentation, capitalism had forged the centralized state "as a weapon of the rising social order in its struggle for emancipation." Industrial capitalism, with its expanded productive potential and demands for raw materials and markets, was now bursting the bonds of the nation state as well. The result was an expanding world market and growing interdependence of nations, manifested as an increasingly sharp international division of labor and competitive struggle for economic advantage waged between the leading national centers of world capitalism. Marx never developed a systematic analysis of imperialism, and he did not argue that capitalism inexorably tended toward colonization, but his economic theory provided a foundation for such interpretations.

In his 1902 study *Imperialism: A Study*, British journalist John A. Hobson, concerned by what he perceived to be the cost involved in annexing and maintaining colonial dependencies, analyzed the phenomenon of colonialism critically from a liberal perspective. His analysis, which described imperialism as a response to domestic economic dysfunction, would provide a basis for much subsequent Marxist theory. For Hobson, the "economic tap root of imperialism" was the export of capital in search of remunerative investment no longer available domestically. His explanation grounded imperialism in the limitations of the national market, and established a linkage between capitalist production and the imperative of colonial expansion. Though Hobson did not write in a Marxist context, his argument contained the essential elements of a developed theory of capitalist imperialism.

Imperialism was a difficult theme for the Second International in both theory and practice. The logic of colonial exploitation was far removed from the trade unionist focus on improved living conditions that defined much of the movement's daily practice. Classical Marxists were often convinced that the absorption of less developed regions by the advanced centers of world capitalism was a necessary spur to modernization, and militants on the Left radical flank viewed anti-colonial struggle as a manifestation of regressive nationalism. The Second International did not formally discuss the theme of anti-colonialism until its 1900 Paris Congress, and it was only at the 1907 Stuttgart Congress that a resolution, introduced by the German Karl Kautsky, mandated Socialist parties to resist all forms of colonial exploitation. Partly inspired by this commitment, in the years immediately prior to and during the First World War (1914–18) a coherent theory of capitalist imperialism took form on the Marxist Left.

The first major work of Left radical analysis devoted to the theme of capitalist imperialism was the Austrian Rudolf Hilferding's 1910 study *Finance Capital*. Hilferding identified a process of monopolization within advanced capitalist economies, facilitated by a trend toward the merger of bank and industrial capital (finance capital), leading to rapid expansion and internationalization. The process fueled economic rivalry between the imperial powers, and tended inexorably toward great power conflict and war. In her 1913 study *The Accumulation of Capital*, the Polish Marxist Rosa Luxemburg attempted to adapt a theory of capitalist imperialism to the exigencies of struggle against reformist currents within the international labor movement. Driven by periodic overproduction crises, she argued, imperial expansion was a necessary foundation for modern capitalism. Contemporary imperialism, defined as "the political expression of the accumulation of capital in its competitive struggle for what remains still open of the non-capitalist environment," was distinguished by diminished opportunity and an increasing tendency toward crisis and confron-

tation. In 1915 the Russian Bolshevik Nikolai Bukharin reiterated the Marxist position in his *Imperialism and World Economy*. Bukharin's work echoed Hilferding in identifying imperialism as an "integral element of finance capitalism without which it would lose its capitalist meaning . . . finance capital cannot pursue any other policy." Bukharin aligned with both Hilferding and Luxemburg in describing imperialism as a predatory policy whose logical end point was war.

Cumulatively, the prewar generation of Marxist theorists succeeded in establishing the foundations of a distinctive Marxist theory of capitalist imperialism. This theory was summarized, and appropriate political conclusions drawn, in Vladimir Lenin's highly influential political tract *Imperialism the Highest Stage of Capitalism*, written in Swiss exile during the Great War and first published in 1916. The subtitle of Lenin's text, "A Popular Outline," hints at its larger purpose: to interpret the war crisis in the context of Marxist theory and to use the analysis to justify a strategy of revolutionary resistance.

The first two sections of Lenin's text, following Hilferding, document the process of monopolization and rise of finance capital, and the associated momentum of capital export and colonial conquest. For Lenin, the process contained both progressive and reactionary traits. On one hand, the concentration of capital meant enhanced planning and the rationalization of markets on a global scale. Imperialism was capitalism's "highest" phase and contained within itself new patterns of productive relations in embryo. Simultaneously, monopoly served as a brake on innovation, and in the context of private ownership encouraged a tendency toward "stagnation and decline." Most importantly, concentration proceeded unevenly, exacerbating sectoral imbalance and increasing the structural instability of the capitalist system as a whole. Concentration allowed the strong to extract "tribute" from the weak, with a widening disparity between city and country, and between imperial metropoles and colonial subjects, the result.

Lenin was anxious to address the theory of "ultra-imperialism" recently advanced by Kautsky, according to which, to the degree that monopolistic concerns shared a common interest in a stable international economic order, imperial expansion might eventually become the foundation for an era of general peace. On the contrary, Lenin insisted, cooperation between monopoly concerns could never be more than a temporary tactical maneuver given the competitive anarchy of the capitalist mode of production. Rather than establishing a foundation for peace, the struggle for control underlying imperialism was leading toward a full-scale crisis of the capitalist world system. Propelled by the demand for profitable markets and raw materials, imperialism generated a division of the world into a handful of "advanced" countries juxtaposed with a mass of brutally impoverished colonies and semicolonies. Competition for supremacy between the imperialist powers, and the widening gap between rich and poor sectors of the world economy that their policies reinforced, were creating explosive contradictions with revolutionary implications. Within the metropolitan centers of world capitalism, the profits derived from colonial exploitation permitted the creation of a relatively privileged "workers' aristocracy" that provided a foundation for revisionist tendencies within the labor movement. But the temporary advantages produced by imperialism could not be sustained. Colonialism had become essential to the survival of competing national imperialism, and with most of the world partitioned the struggle for influence would only become more intense. Herein, for Lenin, lay the underlying cause of the Great War, and a source for new wars in the future. Democratic forms would be hard pressed to survive the strains to which imperialism would give rise. Nor would colonial subjects eternally suffer the deteriorating status within the world economy to which they were condemned. Their inevitable revolt would take the form of national liberation struggles, viewed by Lenin as an integral part of the global struggle against capitalism, threatening the system's imperial lifeline and undermining its ability to maintain equilibrium.

Lenin's "popular outline" essentially summarized the theory of capitalist imperialism as it had been developed in the work of Hobson, Hilferding, Luxemburg, and Bukharin. It is the larger political vision derived from the theory that made his work so influential. The Leninist theory of imperialism defined modern capitalism as an interdependent world system whose structural contradictions provided a realistic foundation for what Lenin and his followers would soon begin to call the World Revolution. The war, by unleashing the full fury of unrestrained imperialist rivalry, had exposed the emptiness of the revisionist faith in peaceful progress. A reckoning with imperialism demanded structural transformations that could only result from "an epoch of wars and revolution."

Lenin characterized the First World War as an imperialist war. The analysis in *Imperialism the Highest Phase of Capitalism* was intended to provide a theoretical founda-

tion for revolutionary responses to the war crisis. These perceptions decisively shaped his understanding of the Russian Revolution. As Lenin opined upon his arrival at Petrograd's Finland Station in April 1917 following the fall of the czarist regime, the Russian Revolution was the first blow of "the socialist revolution on a global scale." In the wake of the Russian Revolution, the theory of capitalist imperialism in its Leninist variant would provide an ideological underpinning for the newly formed International Communist Movement.

After Lenin's death in 1924, the theory of capitalist imperialism became an article of faith for Soviet power and the Third International, closely associated with the Lenin cult and integrated into Joseph Stalin's codification of Soviet Marxism. Reduced to a dogma, the theory became the foundation for a uniform and undifferentiated view of a hostile and aggressive Western world, with significant consequences for Soviet diplomacy during the 1930s, and, eventually, for the shape of Cold War communism. Upon the outbreak of war in Europe in September 1941, Stalin briefly revived the concept as a basis for a political strategy, denouncing the conflict in progress as a "New Imperialist War" over whose outcome the Soviet Union was not concerned. Andrey Zhdanov's keynote address to the Sklarska Poreba conference in September 1947, at the outset of the Cold War, made prominent use of the concept by dividing the world into "two camps," a progressive Socialist bloc led by the USSR and a reactionary imperialist camp led by the United States, whose irresolvable contradictions were said to pose the threat of a new world war. Denunciations of imperialism became a stock in trade of Soviet propaganda, and from the mid-1950s forward the Soviet Union was an active supporter of selected national liberation struggles. Contrasting interpretations of the exigencies of anti-imperialist struggle also became a factor in the Sino-Soviet rift of the 1960s. Within the Communist world, evocations of imperialism as the basis of Communist strategy were constant, but in general lacked the intellectual force and political energy of the original Leninist formulation. Elsewhere, a critical theory of capitalist imperialism, often used to justify support for national liberation movements in the developing world, remained an important foundation for Communist political culture and was espoused by the most sophisticated proponents of a Communist vision worldwide well into the 1980s.

See also Anti-imperialism; Bukharin, Nikolay; Cold War; Collapse of Capitalism; Comintern; Decolonization; Hilferding,

Rudolf; Kautsky, Karl; Lenin, Vladimir; Luxemburg, Rosa; Third Worldism; War, Inevitability of.

FURTHER READING

Berberoglu, B. *The Internationalization of Capital: Imperialism and Capitalist Development on a World Scale.* New York: Praeger, 1987.

Fieldhouse, D. K. *The Theory of Capitalist Imperialism.* London: Longmans, 1967.

Lenin, V. I. *Imperialism, the Highest Stage of Capitalism: A Popular Outline.* Moscow: Foreign Language Publishing House, 1947.

R. CRAIG NATION

Insurrection in Germany

Because Germany had failed in its obligations regarding reparations payments, on January 11, 1923, French and Belgian troops began to occupy the Ruhr, the area of Germany that yielded 70 percent of the nation's coal and 50 percent of its steel production. The German government called on the area's inhabitants to resist by refusing to go to work. But both government officials and workers in private businesses continued to receive their wages from Berlin, and this brought about hyperinflation in the country. The number of unemployed workers reached six million. The workers who remained at work received no more than 40 percent of their prewar wages. In summer 1923, a wave of strikes spread from the Ruhr to other regions of the country and culminated in a general strike on August 11, in which up to three million workers participated. The government of Wilhelm Kuno was forced to abdicate.

The reports of Heinrich Brandler, the leader of the Communist Party of Germany (KPD), about the national crisis and growth of Communist influence raised hopes in the Comintern's Executive Committee for a new proletarian revolution. On August 15, Grigory Zinovyev formulated theses about the political situation in Germany that would enable the KPD, when the time was right, to create workers' soviets and seize governmental power. On August 23, the politburo of the Central Committee of the Communist Party of the Soviet Union (CPSU) made a series of decisions to extend material, military, and technical aid to the German proletariat. Leon Trotsky even suggested the exact date for an armed

intervention: November 9, 1923, the fifth anniversary of the founding of the "bourgeois" Weimar Republic. At the beginning of October a certain "quartet" (Karl Radek, Georgy Piatakov, Vasily Schmidt, and the Soviet plenipotentiary in Germany, Nikolai Krestinsky) was sent to Germany and charged by the politburo of the CPSU's Central Committee with coordinating preparations for a "German October."

Analogous to what had happened with the soviets in Russia, Communists were to move into the regional governments of central Germany, thus providing a legal basis for a party dictatorship. On October 10 the leaders of the KPD received the portfolios of the ministries of the governments of Saxony and, a week later, Thuringia. Immediately thereafter, "proletarian units" (*sotnias*) were formed—a prototype of the Red Army sotnias. The USSR sent special trains carrying bread to Germany in an effort to convince the German workers of the new system's advantages. By October 21, however, the plans for the German October had already misfired. After the Berlin government declared an ultimatum for the immediate disarming of the workers' detachments, Brandler, now a cabinet minister in Saxony, demanded the initiation of a general strike. He was not supported by the representatives of the industrial councils or the Social Democrats. Afraid to proceed on its own, the KPD called on its "military revolutionary councils" to retreat. The signal did not reach Hamburg, though, and the local Communists there ventured an uprising of their own and for several days even took over a number of workers' precincts. Friedrich Ebert, the president of Germany, declared martial law and removed the "Red governments" from Saxony and Thuringia. The KPD was outlawed, and those party officials who had been involved in the military and technological preparations for the uprising were arrested and placed on trial (the "Cheka Trial" of 1925).

The defeat of the German October provoked acrimonious discussions within the Bolshevik leadership. Except for Schmidt, the members of the quartet had been partisans of Trotsky, and opponents of the latter now saw a convenient chance to discredit Trotsky's policies. In January 1924, the Plenum of the CPSU's Central Committee condemned the policy line taken by Radek and Piatakov on the German question, including their debatable idea that "fascism has already defeated democracy in Germany." Events in Germany had an indirect effect on the internal evolution of Russia during its New Economic Policy. Clara Zetkin, who was in Moscow at the time, wrote to her party comrades on November 6, 1923, that "everything about the German revolution has been causing an unbelievable wave of enthusiasm here. . . . The present turn of events signifies a fall from the heights above the clouds back to the hard ground not only for the masses, but also for the leadership. I am convinced that these events are being received with much more pain in Russia than in Germany itself." The loss by the Bolsheviks of ideological legitimacy stemming from this obvious collapse of the notion of a world proletarian revolution abetted the notion of "socialism in a single country."

The reasons for the defeat of the German October were debated by the Presidium of the Executive Committee of the Communist International from January 11 to 19, 1924. Zinovyev placed blame for the failed seizure of power on the German Communist leaders, even though he himself had not long before been the most active supporter of decisive actions in Germany. Brandler and August Thalheimer were accused of indecisiveness and "right-wing deviationism," and were removed from the party leadership. After a period of interparty conflicts, one of the organizers of the Hamburg revolt, Ernst Tellman, assumed the KPD's leadership. It would take the German Communist Party a long time to recover the massive influence it had had during summer and fall 1923.

See also Comintern; Radek, Karl; Socialism in One Country; Soviets; Trotsky, Leon; World Revolution; Zinovyev, Grigory.

FURTHER READING

Bayerlein, B. H., ed. *Deutsche Oktober 1923. Ein Revolutionsplan und sein Scheitern*. Berlin: Aufbau-Verlag, 2003.
Wenzel, O. *1923. Die gescheiterte Deutsche Oktoberrevolution*. Muenster: Lit, 2003.

ALEKSANDR I. VATLIN

Intelligentsia

The term "intelligentsia" has been used in Russia to designate two rather different categories of individuals: in the late czarist period, it was used to refer to the critical element in educated society; in the Soviet period, it came to designate the stratum of the white collar/administrative workers within the labor force, as distinguished from

workers and collective farm peasants. These two meanings need to be clearly differentiated. The former is of particular importance in studies of the czarist regime, particularly of the substantial alienated element within educated society. The second refers to the sociological category developed by Soviet politicians and theorists to describe the nature of stratification under the Socialist system.

The intelligentsia in the czarist period grew with the expansion of the university system in the 1870s. Many young people from privileged background also studied in the universities in Western Europe. A striking feature of the Russian intelligentsia was its high level of learning and culture, its familiarity with Western culture, and its cosmopolitan outlook. This served to set at variance their experience of life in Western Europe with the realities of life in Russia, which gave rise to impatience with Russian backwardness and hostility toward the existing political and social order. Large numbers of educated people, graduates of the universities, found employment in government service and in the professions. The intelligentsia distinguished itself from the rest of that educated society, and from the professions, by its conception of itself as a group of politically engaged critical thinkers. The overproduction of graduates during the 1870s meant that many of these people found it difficult to make a place for themselves within the existing professions.

The pre-revolutionary intelligentsia had an ambivalent attitude toward the masses. On the one hand was a kind of idealized vision. Seeing itself as the carrier of cultured values, the intelligentsia felt a duty to assist in raising the masses to a new level of culture and to provide them with political leaders to effect a change in the existing social order. At the same time it looked on the masses as the dark people (*chernyi lyudi*), an attitude in part shaped by fear and distrust of the anarchic and violent passions of the people.

The intelligentsia provided the audience for the cultural avant-garde. It was distinguished by its preoccupation with politics and with theories of social and economic improvement drawn particularly from the works of Western writers. It became the carrier of Western ideas and attitudes in Russian society. Out of the ranks of the intelligentsia emerged the most critical theorists of Russian society, and the most prominent leaders of the new political parties and movements after 1900: Marxism, Populism, and Liberalism. To its critics, such as Nicholas Berdayev in the work *Vekhi* (*Landmarks*), published in 1909, the members of intelligentsia within the Russian revolutionary movement were characterized by a dreamy detachment from reality, a willingness to immerse themselves in theoretical fantasies, a quasireligious messianic conception of politics, and an idealization and veneration of the *narod*.

The Bolshevik regime's attitude toward those it saw as belonging to the bourgeois intelligentsia in the period after the October Revolution was mainly hostile. They were political reactionaries, carriers of bourgeois ideology. This is reflected in some of Lenin's scathing comments on the intelligentsia and its pretensions to culture. In the civil war period the intelligentsias suffered a sharp loss in status, and in 1922 on Lenin's orders a large-scale expulsion of many of the country's leading intellectuals took place.

The major turning point in the regime's relationship with the intelligentsia occurred in 1928–31, initiated by the Shakhty trial, and followed by show trials in 1930–31 of the Menshevik Bureau, the Industrial Party, and by the planned trial of the so-called Laboring Peasants Party. Although the latter trial never took place, a witch hunt against prominent intellectuals, notably Kondratiev and Chayanov, under the guise of the eradicating of the Kondratievshchina and Chayanovshchina, was undertaken in academic institutions and universities.

The attack on the intelligentsia aimed to remove so-called bourgeois specialists from positions of influence in academia and in policymaking. This was part of a general assault against "rightist" influences and part of the cultural revolution. It involved a drive to create a new Soviet intelligentsia, through an expansion of universities and technical institutions, with preferential access given, at least until 1931, to children of working-class and peasant backgrounds. From 1928 onward elite academic institutions such as the Academy of Sciences were increasingly subject to party control, and party-dominated academic institutions—the Institute of Red Professors and the Communist Academy—exerted a greater influence over the field of learning. In the Stalin era a high proportion of the pre-revolutionary intelligentsia were eliminated, although in the fields of history and the arts there was also a synthesis of Soviet and pre-revolutionary ideas.

The new Soviet intelligentsia that emerged in the 1930s was quite different from its pre-revolutionary counterpart. Significant emphasis was now placed on the development of a technological and scientific intelligentsia. Within the technological intelligentsia (ITR) the prominent place was to be occupied by engineers. The cultural intelligentsia suffered from the imposition of tighter controls over intellectual life, a system of oversight and censorship, the closing off of contacts with the outside world, the regimentation of artistic life through the unions for writers, artists, and musicians, and through the adoption of "socialist realism" as a doctrine governing their work.

The Eighteenth Congress of the CPSU in 1939 marked a significant shift in the nature of the intelligentsia. In the wake of the Great Purges, mass promotions were necessary to fill now-empty positions. The principal beneficiaries of these promotions were those in their twenties and thirties who had been educated under the Soviet regime. This new "Soviet intelligentsia" was now elevated to a position of status within Soviet society, identified as a "working intelligentsia" (*trudovaya intelligentsia*) or an "intelligentsia of a new type" (*intelligentsia novogo tipa*), recruited primarily from the working class and peasantry, trained under the Soviet regime, and serving its needs. It became the social group most strongly represented in party membership. The primacy of this group corresponded to the high priority that the regime placed on progress and the transformation of society through technological and scientific means, and to the wealth of employment opportunities provided by major projects of reconstruction.

The tremendous growth of the intelligentsia through government-sponsored training schemes was one of the most important sociological developments of the Stalin era. It was a process repeated in the union republics of the USSR, and in the people's democracies after 1945. The training was hasty, especially in the 1930s, and narrowly practical in focus, much to the detriment of the professionals it produced. Even more critical than the low caliber of the new intelligentsia was the fact that this newly elevated stratum of society, harnessed to the tasks of Socialist construction, was politically docile. The intelligentsia continued to be viewed as a *potentially* subversive element in society; however, witness the campaigns under Zhdanov in 1945 against writers.

The category of "intelligentsia" as used in Soviet discourse referred to the distinct social group of non-manual employees, as distinguished from industrial workers and the collective farm peasants. They were defined as "mental" workers, possessing education and specialized knowledge in various fields of science, technology, and culture. The category included all those engaged in white-collar professions, from routine clerical workers and secretaries, to trained professionals and those in positions of administrative or managerial responsibility. The category was extremely broad, and applied universally it concealed enormous differences of power, status, and wealth between those in highly placed positions and routine clerical workers, most of whom were more poorly paid than manual workers. The upper layers of this intelligentsia stratum were viewed by some as a new ruling bureaucracy (Trotsky), a new ruling class (Djilas), and a new bourgeoisie based on a system of state capitalism (Cliff). Others viewed it as part of a new ruling stratum of technocrats.

In the post-Stalin era the intelligentsia emerged as a more significant stratum in Soviet society, recognized as a social stratum (*prosloika*) alongside the two principal social classes: the working class and the collective-farm peasantry. Relations between these groups were defined as nonantagonistic. In this period, with the end of mass purges and more moderate levels of upward social mobility, the position of the intelligentsia became increasingly secure. This was reflected in the trend toward a kind of hereditary intelligentsia, made possible by granting access to educational institutions and positions of importance to the children of the intelligentsia.

At the same time the intelligentsia was held in check by party control and censorship and by pressures during the post-Stalin era to reduce income differentials that adversely affected those in elite positions. A further factor was the Soviet regime's policy of training a high proportion of the population for professional occupations, which yielded a superfluity of intellectuals and weakened their bargaining power as a social group. The regime's attitude toward the intelligentsia was also shaped by the fact that from the 1960s onward the most prominent figures in the dissident movement came from within the ranks of the cultural and scientific intelligentsia.

See also Bureaucracy; Science; State, The.

FURTHER READING

Bailes, K. E. *Technology and Society under Lenin and Stalin: Origins of the Soviet Technical Intelligentsia, 1917–1941.* Princeton, NJ: Princeton University Press, 1978.

Burbank, J. *Intelligentsia and Revolution: Russian Views of Bolshevism, 1917–1924.* New York: Oxford University Press, 1986.

Lampert, N. *The Technical Intelligentsia and the Soviet State: A Study of Soviet Managers and Technicians, 1928–1935.* London: Macmillan, 1979.

Read, C. *Religion, Revolution and the Russian Intelligentsia, 1900–1912: The Vekhi Debate and Its Intellectual Background.* London: Macmillan, 1978.

E. ARFON REES

International Brigades

The International Brigades were among the most important contributions that the Soviet Union made to the defense of republican Spain during the civil war (1936–39). Created by the Comintern starting in September 1936, the aim of the brigades was to reinforce the republican army, which was still being reorganized, for what appeared to be an imminent confrontation for the defense of Madrid. Recruiting was performed on a mostly voluntary basis in many countries, although since it was entrusted to a network of national Communist parties and the organizations tied to them, the flow of brigade volunteers was below expectations—a fact lamented by Palmiro Togliatti in an October 1937 letter. Spontaneous volunteerism on Spanish soil also preceded, and to a slightly lesser degree proceeded in parallel with, the organization of the brigades. In any event, the brigades were the gathering point for an imposing number of volunteers—around forty thousand from fifty countries took their turn for the cause—and also the means to organize and train these volunteers, so that they could be rapidly made available and prepared for combat.

The Communist volunteers, in addition to being the most numerically significant component, were certainly the soul of these politicomilitary formations as well. For many of them, the spirit of sacrifice with which they faced this task was informed by a revolutionary perspective, which aside from the pauses imposed by the Popular Front policies, remained the foundation of their lives. For many others, however, especially among the younger volunteers, the anti-Fascist imperative prevailed: the need to fight the menace represented by the Italian and German regimes—a need that had pushed them to join the Communist Party. In the 1930s, the Communists seemed to be the only force with the capacity and will to fight fascism. In Europe one noticed that the liberals, even thought reluctantly, were ready to come to terms with fascism. Jackson notes that "in the US the communist party almost seemed to have exclusive rights to the anti-Fascist cause and this brought it many recruits, sympathizers and friends, some of whom were probably among those who went to Spain."

Volunteers belonging to other anti-Fascist forces—anarchists, socialists, and republicans—also fought next to the Communists in the brigades, but, aside from the propaganda of the Popular Front that later made its way into much memorial literature, the fact remains that their numbers were fairly small. The number of recruits under the heading of "anti-Fascists" or "without party" was larger, even though many sources tell us that a considerable number of those joined the Communist Party during the struggle.

The International Brigades principally functioned as a Communist army. Brigade members greeted each other with the clenched fist—a salutation later extended to the entire republican army—the red star adorned caps and shirts, and the *Internationale* or other Communist songs served as the troops' chants. Political commissars were at the commanders' sides, responsible for the volunteers' political education, following the model of the Red Army in the Russian civil war. The brigades' "headquarters" were also almost entirely Communist, in terms of both the military commanders and political commissariat. Their commander in chief, André Marty, and general commissar, Luigi Longo, as well as all the commanders and commissars of the individual brigades were Communist.

Most of the brigades were in fact fairly homogeneous. The Eleventh and Twelfth International Brigade, the first to see action in November 1936, were commanded by the legendary "Emilio Kléber" and "General Lukács" (their battle names), respectively, and their commissars were Giuseppe Di Vittorio and Gustav Regler. The Thirteenth and Fourteenth International Brigade, which saw battle in December 1936, were commanded by "General Gómez" and "General Walter," and their commissars were "Suckanek" and André Hessler. The Fifteenth International Brigade, formed in January 1937, was commanded by "General Gal" and its commissar was Vladimir Copic. All these men were Communists, and during the war all those who took over their functions were also Communists. The battalions that made up the brigades, with only rare and temporary exceptions, were also commanded by Communists.

The main exception to the rule was certainly the "Garibaldi" battalion, which belonged to the Eleventh Brigade, and in which almost all the Italian volunteers served. Since these came from the country with the longest anti-Fascist tradition, the presence of non-Communists among them was greater than in other contingents. And this partially explains why the battalion was commanded until March 1937 by the republican Randolfo Pacciardi, who later left the brigades—and was replaced as commander by the Communists Agostino Casati and then Alessandro Vaia—precisely because he opposed the dominant Communist presence, reinforced by the presence of the political commissars Antonio Rosaio and later Ilio Barontini, who both represented the party. The political composition of the battalion, notwithstanding the presence of some notable non-Communist individuals (like socialist Pietro Nenni) was also dominated by Communists and "without party," many of whom then became members of the Spanish Communist Party.

The importance of the International Brigades' experience in the formation of the leadership of many Communist parties is underscored by the fact that it was a step in the cursus honorum of many of those who, especially in Eastern Europe, would come to occupy leadership positions in the party and state, with varying degrees of success. This was the case, for instance, with Walter Ulbricht and Friedrich Dichel in the German Democratic Republic, Klement Gottwald and Artur London in Czechoslovakia, Ladislav Rajk and Pal Maleter in Hungary, Karol Swierczewski (Walter) in Poland, Milovan Djilas in Yugoslavia, Enver Hoxha in Albania, and Raiko Damianov in Bulgaria.

The Communist control of the brigades also entailed some decidedly negative features. The most significant shadows were associated with Marty, who commanded the brigades until April 1937. At the base where the recruits were trained, in Albacete, Marty was pitiless when faced with indiscipline or cowardice on the part of the volunteers, many of whom had not only never fought before but frequently did not have any military experience either. He would later admit, when called before the party to explain his conduct, that he had about five hundred men executed for these failings. Yet beyond this, many volunteers—mostly anarchists and Trotskyists, or presumed to be such—were murdered, secretly or using an accusation of espionage, because they manifested their dissent with Communist policies.

The brigades' contribution to the republic's struggle, although it was controversial on the strictly military level, was nevertheless significant, at least during the first phase of the war, raising the morale of all those fighting on the republican side. One could observe this phenomenon from the brigades' first use in the battle for the defense of Madrid, where they were employed as assault forces: they strengthened the spirit of resistance among those engaged at the front and the capital's population. They later participated, almost always on the front lines, in all the most important battles of the war: the battle by the river Jarama in January–February 1937; Guadalajara in March 1937; Brunete and Belchite in summer 1937; Teruel in winter 1937–38; up to the unfortunate defense of Aragon, in March–April of 1938, and to the terrible final test of the battle of the river Ebro in July–November 1938. This last battle, during which the brigade volunteers suffered their greatest losses, was the one in which the Communists' politicoideological energy as well as motivation and encouragement of their commissars was a decisive factor in the front holding its ground for such a long time, the seriousness of their losses notwithstanding. But when, at the end of October, the brigades were let go by the republican government with a unilateral act whose goal was obtaining an armistice, they were exhausted and to a large extent destroyed. While marching down the streets of Barcelona during their farewell ceremony, the brigades were greeted by Communist leader Dolores Ibarruri with these words: "You leave with your head held high. You are history, you are legend. We shall never forget you."

For many of those volunteers, though, the struggle was not over. The Spanish civil war, and particularly having served in the brigades, became a reservoir of experience not only of a politicomilitary nature but also of organizing and motivating combatants, and it would soon reveal its worth in the resistance to nazism. This was the case in France, where many foreign ex-brigadists—several Italians among them—who had been interned in concentration camps after the fall of the Spanish republic fought for liberation; many of the French brigadists, like Henri Roi-Tanguy and Pierre Georges ("Colonel Fabien"), also held the highest leadership positions in the Communist resistance. The same was true in Italy, where Communist ex-Garibaldini from Spain participated in the resistance against fascism and the Germans, and translated the exhortation by Carlo Rosselli, "Today in Spain, tomorrow in Italy," into action. Longo, who because of the key role he played in both experiences, perhaps more than any other individual represented the continuity of the anti-Fascist–Communist struggle, successfully transmitting the sense of participating in one uninterrupted fight when in the aftermath of the Spanish defeat, he wrote that those who abandoned Spain "marched not as losers but as fighters who were shifting fronts."

See also Antifascism; Anti-Fascist Resistance; Popular Front; Spanish Civil War.

FURTHER READING

Álvarez, S. *Historia politica y military de las Brigadas Internacionales.* Madrid: Compañia Literaria, 1996.

Castells, A. *Las Brigadas Internacionales de la guerra de España.* Barcelona: Ariel, 1974.

Jackson, M. *Fallen Sparrows: The International Brigades in the Spanish Civil War.* Philadelphia: American Philosophical Society, 1994.

Richardson, R. D. *Comintern Army: The International Brigades and the Spanish Civil War.* Lexington: University Press of Kentucky, 1982.

Vidal, C. *Las Brigadas Internacionales.* Madrid: Espasa-Calpe, 1998.

GABRIELE RANZATO

International Conferences after Stalin

International conferences were an organized form of multilateral (collective) cooperation between Communist parties that began during the second half of the 1950s. Unlike the Comintern or Cominform, which was in Soviet hands, the international conferences of Communist parties, reflecting the reality of post-Stalin changes, were conducted to some degree as a true partnership of their participants, even though they were closely scrutinized by Moscow. In the beginning, while it still participated in them, Beijing also kept a close watch on the meetings, as a new entrant called on to support the worldwide Communist movement, or at least the greater part of it, along lines dictated by the Soviet and/or the Chinese leadership.

The idea for these conferences first surfaced after the suppression of the Hungarian revolt in November 1956 had complicated the relations of the USSR and those of most of the rest of the socialist states with the Communist regime in Yugoslavia, which was now outside the bloc. Although the head of this regime, Josip Broz Tito, had indeed supported the Soviet intervention in Hungary, Moscow and Belgrade were still at odds over the fate of Imre Nagy and his close colleagues in the Hungarian government, which had been removed from power by the invasion. Moscow was also irritated by the criticism of Kremlin policy, albeit somewhat muted, that the Yugoslav leadership permitted itself in an effort to demonstrate to its own public and the outside world its independence from the USSR and the rest of the socialist camp.

In January 1957 Beijing took the initiative in calling a conference of Communist Party representatives from all the socialist countries, including Yugoslavia, to discuss the new situation. Belgrade's attitude toward this proposal was guarded, but for tactical reasons it refrained from rejecting it. Instead, it advanced some preliminary conditions for the meeting that would ward off any decisions possibly unfavorable to the Yugoslavs. Informed by Beijing of the Yugoslavs' conditional consent to the conference, the Kremlin showed little enthusiasm for it. Still, in the first half of February Moscow considered it necessary to give Beijing a positive answer, though advising against any hurry and suggesting that plenty of time be taken to prepare for the conference. In the matter of organizing the conference the Soviet side yielded to the Chinese. The reserve that both Moscow and Belgrade showed toward the conference slowed the preparations to a halt. The situation changed only when, in May and June 1957, the Kremlin decided to take the initiative itself. It called for a new conference and proposed to Tito a prior Soviet-Yugoslav meeting at the highest level, to which Tito consented in early June. The meeting took place in Romania on August 1–2 with both Tito and the Soviet leader, Khrushchev, present. The accord reached at this meeting asserted a willingness to cooperate "along party lines," and seemed to clear the way for a conference of Communist parties of the socialist camp, which was to include the Union of Communists of Yugoslavia (UCYu).

The agenda announced for the upcoming conference, scheduled to take place in Moscow in November, to coincide with the fortieth anniversary of the October Revolution in 1917, was worked out by the Soviet side. Unlike previous practice, though—for example, that of the Cominform—the agenda for this conference had to be discussed and agreed upon by the other parties as well. In view of the special situation of the UCYu, the Kremlin tried to work things out with Belgrade in mid-October. But the Yugoslav leadership decided to reject participation in any conference, and to refuse to sign any declaration that would give the appearance of Yugoslavia's full political and ideological unity with the socialist camp. Soviet efforts to change the Yugoslav decision were in vain.

As a result, by agreement with leaders in Beijing and other Communist countries, the Soviet side made a tactical move: it organized a unique meeting of Communist parties in Moscow, to take place in two "acts." The first act was a conference of the socialist Communist parties on November 14–16, 1957, without the Yugoslavs. There were twelve Communist parties present, from all the parties in the socialist camp of that time and also the party from the Communist regime in North Vietnam, only recently established. The second act took place on November 16–19. This more-or-less makeshift conference was attended by representatives from sixty-four Communist parties, including the twelve parties present at the first congress and now a Yugoslav delegation as well. The participants at the first conference signed a final declaration—its most significant result—put together as a sort of program document for world Communism. The document consisted of theses describing the world situation at the time, or what it purported to be, and outlining the positions and tasks of the Communist movement. The participants at the second conference, on the other hand, signed a "Manifesto of Peace," which was more symbolic than anything else. It contained a declaration of the unacceptability of war, enjoining the participants to fight for peace and international security, and against the arms race and atomic weapons.

If China's and the USSR's original aim for the conference was to overcome, or at least mask, their contradictions with Yugoslavia, then the effect of the two-act meeting in Moscow was zero, if not outright negative. The publicly announced fact of Yugoslavia's nonparticipation in the first conference and its refusal to sign the declaration were both too blatant to be papered over by the simple maneuver of staging a second conference with the UCYu's participation. Moreover, the thesis contained in the first conference's declaration that the main danger to the Communist movement lay in revisionism was also obviously directed at the Yugoslav position, though that country was not specifically named.

With regard to the overall task of overcoming the embarrassments and disagreements that the Communist world had to contend with after the Twentieth Congress of the Communist Party of the Soviet Union (CPSU), and the political crises in Poland and especially Hungary in 1956, the results of the conferences were mixed. On the one hand, the fact that the conferences could be held at all, and that for the first time in the post-Stalin period documents could be approved jointly by the participating parties, was a kind of embodiment of Communist unity. And the declaration signed by twelve ruling Communist parties formalized a political and ideological platform which received an international Communist legitimacy and was set forth as a guiding line for the Communist movement. On the other hand, the conferences manifested certain conflicting aspirations and goals. For example, the meetings revealed a reluctance, albeit at first from only a few Communist parties, to continue the still overwhelmingly supported tradition within the socialist camp and Communist movement of a center ruled exclusively by the CPSU (the Kremlin itself, for strategic reasons, did not want this Soviet role to be mentioned in the declaration of the twelve parties, although this did occur in places). No less significant was the fact that although the final document emphasized the prevention of war as the most important goal, the Chinese leader, Mao Zedong, set forth an essentially contradictory thesis: a nuclear world war, in spite of gigantic human loss, would lead to the triumph of socialism in the world.

These contradictions did not become public then, because the 1957 conferences were conducted in strict secrecy. They were announced only after the fact, and the public was given only the final documents. In the next three years, however, the Soviet-Chinese disputes began to come to the fore, and this now moved the Kremlin to call yet another conference of Communist parties.

First, the Kremlin organized a conference of representatives from twelve Communist parties, making use of their simultaneous presence at a congress of the Romanian Workers' Party, which took place in Bucharest on June 20–25, 1960. The CPSU delegation, led by Khrushchev, presented the other participants with materials accusing the Chinese leadership of following a line contradictory to the decisions jointly taken at the 1957 conference. The Soviet charges provoked objections from the Chinese delegation, and the Albanian delegation came out against discussing the question. The result was a compromise: The communiqué about the Bucharest Conference, signed by all participating parties on June 24, did not mention the disputes. It stated that these parties confirmed the correctness of the positions agreed to at the 1957 conference.

Yet the Soviet side called a broader Communist party convocation to again consider the question of contradictions in the ideological-political platform of the world Communist movement. This conference was held in Moscow, stretched over two ten-day periods in November 1960, and was attended by delegations from eighty-one parties. Both in the interparty editorial commission, which prepared the drafts of the final conference docu-

ments, and then at the conference itself, there were sharp clashes between, on the one hand, the CPSU representatives and those speaking with them, and on the other, the Chinese and especially, the Albanian delegations. The Albanian Communist leader, Enver Hoxha, in his speech at the conference essentially reflecting the Chinese line, came down hard on the "revisionist positions" of the Twentieth Congress of the CPSU and the "anti-Marxist positions of the Khrushchev group." Nevertheless, neither side was able to force the other to change its point of view. And neither the Kremlin, which was backed by the large majority of delegations, nor the Chinese leadership yet dared to initiate an open split of the socialist camp and the Communist movement. As a result, matters again ended in a compromise: The representatives of all the parties taking part in the Moscow Conference signed a statement amounting to an expanded reiteration of the 1957 declaration, which at the same time was silent about the mutual accusations and disagreements. It was signed as an "Appeal to the Peoples of the Whole World" and was put together on the model of the "Manifesto of Peace" of 1957.

For the Kremlin this was a partial success, since the 1957 documents had been based on the Soviet position, but to a significant extent it was a failure as well, since everything remained in the same state as at Bucharest, where a direct condemnation of the Chinese position had not been accomplished. Still, the results of the Moscow Conference were even more dissatisfying for Beijing and Tirana, because the final documents did not express the deviating features of their special line, except that the statement included an open condemnation of Yugoslav policies as both revisionism and a betrayal of Marxism-Leninism (the Yugoslavs did not take part in the conference). The Moscow compromise did not last long, though. By 1961, the Kremlin and its adherents broke publicly with Tirana, and shortly after the growing Soviet-Chinese rift also became public. In the course of the 1960s the socialist camp underwent a real split, and the process of disintegration within the Communist world became evident.

Striving to counteract this, the Kremlin, both directly by itself and through the leaders of other socialist countries and Communist parties, tried to convoke a new international Communist conference. This proposal was put forward in 1962, and an effort was made to gain China's consent to participate. After Khrushchev was removed from power in October 1964, the Soviets, now led by Leonid Brezhnev, at first followed in this direction, and in particular the idea was discussed at a consultative meeting of representatives from nineteen Communist parties on March 1–5, 1965, in Moscow. Next, by an agreement reached under Soviet auspices by a number of Communist parties in November 1967, a consultative meeting of representatives from sixty-seven parties took place in Budapest from February 25 to March 5, 1968. This meeting scheduled an international conference of Communist parties for November–December 1968. Although it was announced that any party could join the preparatory committee, which began its work in April, the degree of Soviet-Chinese enmity, which by then had included some military hostilities, predetermined the anti-Beijing direction of the conference preparation initiated by the Kremlin. This provoked conflicts within the committee, only further aggravated by the invasion of Czechoslovakia, in August 1968, by the USSR and most of its Warsaw Pact partners—an action condemned by a number of Communist parties, of both a pro-Chinese and emergent Euro-Communist orientation. The conference in Moscow was thus delayed, until June 5–17, 1969.

The conference was attended by delegates from seventy-five parties. Compared with a previous conference held in November 1960, this amounted to a much lower percentage of the total number of Communist parties existing at the time. Even more striking was the situation with the Communist regimes; in addition to the usual absence of Yugoslavia, this time there were no delegations from China, Albania, North Korea, or North Vietnam, while the delegation from the now-Communist Cuba agreed to participate only as an observer. This was augmented by the position of the Romanian delegation, which took part in the conference, but immediately announced that it did not approve of Moscow and Beijing attacking each other, or of speeches with anti-Chinese accusations. Thus, the Kremlin's aspirations for the meeting were counteracted by half (seven out of fourteen) of the Communist regimes then in existence.

Certain Communist parties participating in the conference that were not in power in their own countries, including some that had previously criticized the course taken by Mao, also no longer considered it expedient to support a collective anti-Beijing declaration. Given this situation, which was apparent during the preparatory commission's work and became even more evident at the conference itself, the Soviet side was forced to agree to a final general document that did not directly condemn Chinese policy or the policy of any other Communist

Party. This document, titled "Tasks in the Struggle against Contemporary Imperialism and the Unity of Action of the Communist and Workers' Parties and of All Anti-Imperialist Forces," largely repeated the ideological clichés of the 1957 declaration and the 1960 statement. But the previous accusations of deviations from Marxism-Leninism now named no specific individuals or parties, and the notion of "right-wing revisionism" as the chief danger to the Communist movement was also removed, as were accusations against the Yugoslav leadership. The usual incantations about the necessity of internationalism in relations among the Communist parties were this time accompanied not only by an emphasis on the independence of parties and the voluntary nature of their cooperation but also by the new realization that overcoming divergences and differences in opinion would require time and patience.

Even in this form, five delegations refused to sign the final document. Four of them, including the delegation of the Italian Communist Party, agreed only with that part of the document that laid out a program of joint "struggle against imperialism" (against the danger of war, nuclear weapons, the Fascist threat, racism, and colonialism; and for peaceful coexistence, disarmament, and solidarity with the struggle of the Vietnamese people and a number of other countries against "imperialist encroachments"). The fifth delegation completely refused to support the document. And even some delegations that did sign it took stances at variance with certain Soviet positions: they expressed a negative attitude toward the invasion of Czechoslovakia; they rejected the manipulative dichotomy of the "majority" (pro-Moscow) versus "minority" (pro-Beijing) in the world Communist movement, and they declared the picture of the world given in the document to be oversimplified. The conference—which for the first time in the history of such meetings was made public—was therefore a demonstration of the contradictions among Communist parties and Communist regimes (there were only ritual statements about the hundred-year anniversary of Lenin's birth, the independence of Vietnam, the need to defend Communists in a number of countries, and the necessity of defending peace). The Kremlin could console itself only with the fact that a large majority of the participating delegations were still following its lead.

This result was largely due to the circumstance that after 1969, the Soviet leadership could no longer successfully organize international Communist party conferences aspiring to work out a common platform for the world Communist movement. The practice of holding regional party conferences, begun in the 1960s, continued, mostly in Eastern Europe, but these were devoted to concrete problems. The most significant European party congresses were held in Karlovy Vary on April 24–26, 1967, and in Berlin on June 29–30, 1976. Both focused on maintaining peace and international security in Europe. These congresses, and a number of other similar meetings, were looked on by the Kremlin as instruments of propaganda for support of Soviet foreign policy and, simultaneously, as a way of making this policy more popular among the populations of European countries.

During Gorbachev's "perestroika," almost as the curtain was coming down on the Soviet Union, the Soviet leader organized a meeting of representatives of parties and movements that had come to celebrate the seventieth anniversary of the October Revolution. But with all the changes that had taken place, this was not a typical Communist conference. At this meeting, attended by 178 delegations, some 75 were from Communist parties. There were also a good number delegations from Socialist parties, but the overall majority of those attending the conference came from a variety of Asian, African, and Latin American national-revolutionary or nationalistic parties, movements, and regimes. There were a large number of speeches made, quite diverse though primarily left wing, which were later published, but no final documents were approved. Unlike the preceding Soviet leaders, Gorbachev was no longer concerned with the ideological-political situation in the Communist movement. The meeting was much more important to him as a certain proof that his policies still enjoyed the broad support of the "progressive community of the world."

See also Anti-imperialism; Cold War; Eurocommunism; Internationalism; Peaceful Coexistence; Polycentrism; Sino-Soviet Split; Socialist Camp.

FURTHER READING

Dokumenty soveščanij predstavitelej kommunističeskix i rabočix partij, sostojavšixsja v Moskve v nojabre 1957 g., v Buchareste v ijune 1960 g., v Moskve v nojabre 1960 g. Moscow: Gospolitizdat, 1961.

Fursenko, A. A., ed. *Prezidium CK KPSS: Černovye protokol'nye zapisi zasedanij. Stenogrammy. Postanovlenija.* Vol 1. Moscow: Rosspen, 2003.

———, ed. *Prezidium TsK KPSS, 1954–1964, T. 1–3.* Moscow: Rosspen, 2004–8.

Hoxha, E. *Jetons par-dessus bord les thèses révisionnistes du XX Congres du Parti communiste de l'Union Soviétique et les positions antimarxistes du groupe de Khrouchtchev! Défendons le marxisme-léninisme!: Discours prononcé à la réunion des 81 partis communistes et ouvriers à Moscou le 16 novembre 1960.* Tirana: Editions "Naim Frashëri," 1969.

———. *The Khrushchevites (Memoirs).* Tirana: "8 Nëntori" Publishing House, 1980.

Kardelj, E. *Reminiscences: The Struggle for Recognition and Independence of the New Yugoslavia, 1944–1957.* London: Blonds and Briggs, 1982.

Khrushchev, N. S. *Vremja. Ljudi. Vlast'. Vospominanija v 4–ch kn.* Vol. 3. Moscow: Informacionno-izdatel'skaja kompanija "Moskovskie novosti," 1999.

Meždunarodnoe soveščanie kommunističeskix i rabočix partij, Moskva 1969. Prague: Izdatel'stvo "Mir i socializm," 1969.

Mićunović, Veljko. *Moskovske godine 1956/1958.* Belgrade: Jugoslovenska revija, 1984.

Ulam, A. B. *The Communists: The Story of Power and Lost Illusions, 1948–1991.* New York: Macmillan, 1992.

Vstreča predstavitelej partij i dviženij, pribyvšix na prazdnovanie 70-letija Velikogo Oktjabrja, Moskva 4–5 nojabrja 1987 goda. Moscow: Izdatel'stvo političeskoj literatury, 1988.

LEONID JA. GIBJANSKIJ

International Trade Union Organizations

The first international trade unions appeared at the end of the 19th century, when economic interactions were starting to acquire a worldwide focus and a transnational movement of capital began, which now required a coincident response from the unions.

First to be created were branches of the International Trade Secretariats, whose tasks included the exchange of information among the unions about their various actions and the demands these actions raised, and also of maintaining solidarity in their common struggle.

In 1903, the International Trade Secretariats created the International Trade Union Secretariat, which was soon joined by a number of national trade unions, mostly from Western Europe. This organ was renamed the International Federation of Trade Unions (IFTU) in 1913, and essentially became the first world trade union center. Since the staff offices of the IFTU were in Amsterdam, it was often called the Amsterdam International. The IFTU's leadership was ideologically close to the Social Democrats, the more so because the trade unions of some of the countries belonging to it (for example, Britain and Sweden) were jointly members of the Social Democratic (Laborite) parties of their countries. Like the Social Democratic movement in general, the IFTU underwent a crisis during World War I, but it resumed its activities relatively soon after the end of the war (in July 1919).

Nevertheless, the postwar wave of strikes and the radicalization of the workers' demands, largely connected with the Russian Revolution of 1917, led to the creation in 1920 of the International Council (Soviet) of Trade Unions, which a year later was renamed the Red Trade Union International (Profintern), which in turn became one of the independently organized "wings" of the Communist International (Comintern). Relations between the Comintern and Profintern were specified by a special agreement between the two organizations. The First Congress of the Profintern (in Moscow in 1921) was attended by delegates from forty-one countries representing seventeen million union members. The conditions for acceptance into the Profintern were the "recognizing and implementing in practice the principles of the revolutionary class struggle," and "breaking away from the Amsterdam International." The IFTU, for its part, issued a resolution declaring that membership in the Profintern was incompatible with membership in its own ranks.

One of the weaknesses of the Profintern was the absence of a solid system of branches: the International Propaganda Committees (later, the word "Action" was added to the word "Propaganda"), which became part of its makeup in 1923, did not carry on sustained work in the branch union movement. Still, the Profintern achieved marked success in extending aid and creating trade unions in colonial and dependent countries. Its apparatus was dissolved in 1937.

After World War I still another current of the world trade union movement came into being: the Christian trade unions. Their creation as separate organs in businesses, branch unions, and countries had begun after the publication in 1891 of an encyclical by Pope Leo XII called the *Rerum novarum*, but they became worldwide with the establishment in 1920, in The Hague, of the International Confederation of Christian Trade Unions.

During World War II, trade unions participated in the struggles of their respective peoples against nazism. As a result of the combined efforts of trade unions of the countries in the anti-Hitler coalition, a worldwide trade union conference was held in February 1945. At this congress it was resolved to summon a World Congress of Trade Unions.

This next congress was attended by leaders of all the then-extant trade union centers, with the exception of the American Federation of Labor and the Christian trade unions; the International Trade Union Secretariats were also left aside. Nevertheless, the delegates at the Congress represented some sixty-seven million trade union members. On October 3, 1945, the Congress established the Federation Syndicale Mondiale (World Federation of Trade Unions, or WFTU). Walter Citrine, head of the British Trade Union Congress, was chosen as chair; Arthur Deakin later replaced him. Louis Saillant, the representative from the Confédération Générale du Travail (French General Confederation of Labor), was named general secretary.

The WFTU was instrumental in restoring or indeed creating anew a trade union movement in former Fascist and Nazi-occupied countries. It rendered important support to the newly forming trade union movements in colonial or dependent nations: India, Indonesia, the African continent (the first All-African Trade Union Conference was held in 1947 in Dakar). The WFTU also relied on the Confederación de los Trabajadores de America Latina (Confederation of Latin American Trade Unions), led by the Mexican trade union leader and vice president of the WFTU, Vicente Lombardo Toledano.

The beginning of the Cold War had a ruinous effect on the unity of trade unions. From 1947 through 1949, a number of Western European countries as well as India witnessed the breakup of previously united trade union centers and branch unions; and in October 1948, European trade union centers, which were led by Social Democrats, left the WFTU, as did the Congress of Industrial Organizations in the United States. In December 1949, these departing organizations called their own congress, which founded the International Confederation of Free Trade Unions (ICFTU), with some forty-eight million members.

This breaking of the ranks, however, did not deal the death blow to the WFTU, which the initiators of the ICFTU had counted on. At the second World Congress of Trade Unions (in Milan in June 1949) some forty-three countries from all the continents, numbering some 71.6 million union members, were represented. The proceedings of this congress, like subsequent statutory proceedings of the WFTU, were held open to trade unions not belonging to the federation, and such union delegates later constituted a significant percentage of the participants at world congresses conducted by the WFTU. Giuseppe Di Vittorio, the prominent Italian trade union figure, was chosen as the WFTU president at this congress, while Louis Saillant remained as general secretary.

An important event now was the creation of a branch structure in the WFTU in the form of Trade Union Internationals, whereas the ICFTU had no branch organizations and had to make do with agreements for cooperation within the single, overall organization. The WFTU's nucleus was constituted by the trade union centers of the Socialist countries (which were the main source of its financing too), and also of a number of Western European (Italy, France, and a few others) and Latin American countries headed by Communists. Nevertheless, the WFTU still succeeded, thanks to its distinctly anti-imperialist positions, in rallying around itself the majority of trade unions emerging in countries that had freed themselves from colonialism, even though the countries themselves did not always officially recognize the organization.

In 1956 the International Confederation of Arab Trade Unions was formed, uniting the trade union movements of almost all the countries of the region. In 1961, the All-African Federation of Trade Unions, a left-leaning trade union center, was formed, as was, in 1973, the Organization of African Trade Union Unity (OATUU), which included unions from almost all countries on the African continent. These regional organizations established friendly relations with the WFTU.

From the beginning of the 1950s on, the WFTU and its member organizations took an active part in the antiwar struggle. In the 1980s the WFTU looked into questions of the conversion of military industry to peaceful uses, and created the International Trade Union Committee for Peace and Disarmament, which was called the Dublin Committee, after the Irish capital where it was formed.

The WFTU paid great attention to socioeconomic problems and issued some documents of considerable interest on these questions. In the 1950s, it conducted worldwide conferences of working women and youths, at which permanent committees were established to deal with the specific problems of these categories of workers. Similar organs were also established to deal with the problems of engineering, technical, and agrarian workers, and questions of labor migrations were also given thorough study. The WFTU and in particular its branch

organizations were at the forefront of creating trade union mechanisms within the framework of transnational corporations. As early as the 1970s, even before the actual concept of the transnational corporation had emerged, organizations belonging to the WFTU trade union centers, primarily the French and Italian transnational corporative structures, had begun to form coordinating committees for trade unions within the transnational corporation framework (an example was the transnational corporation Olivetti). The first international trade union conference devoted to problems of the social aspects of transnational corporation activities was held in 1973 in Santiago, Chile.

The ICFTU, led by Western European Social Democrats and labor union leaders in the United States, centered their activity on questions of trade union rights and the formation of programs of trade union activities focusing on the most important socioeconomic problems. For many years, the ICFTU determined the policy line of a group of workers from the International Organization of Labor, a worldwide tripartite organ that had joined the "family" of the United Nations after World War II.

The International Confederation of Christian Trade Unions changed its name in 1968 to the World Confederation of Labor. It removed references to its Christian dogma from its statutes ("de-Christianizing" itself), and began actively to employ anticolonial and anti-imperialist phraseology, which in turn allowed it to retain and even broaden its influence in a number of Latin American and African countries.

In 1973, the European Trade Union Confederation (ETUC) was formed. This organization at first filled the role mostly of a social partner within the "Common Market" of the European Economic Union, but later expanded its sphere of activity and drew into its framework most of the trade union centers, first of Western Europe, and then of Central and Eastern Europe as well.

The collapse of the Socialist camp and then of the Soviet Union considerably weakened the WFTU, which now began to be abandoned by the trade unions of almost all the former Socialist countries, which in turn had been under the influence of the Communists of the trade union centers of the West and a number of trade associations from the third world. At the same time, the international position of the ICFTU grew stronger.

The General Confederation of Trade Unions, which came into being on the eve of the disintegration of the

USSR as a successor to the Soviet trade unions, was now transformed into an international trade union center, embracing most of the trade union centers of the newly emerged Commonwealth of Independent States.

See also Comintern; Labor; Trade Unions.

FURTHER READING

Adibekov, G. M. *Profintern: politika kommunistov v profsojuznom dviženii*. Moscow: Profizdat, 1981.

Jurgens, I. U., and V. E. Možaev. *Profsojuzy: včera, segodnja, zavtra*. Moscow: Profizdat, 1996.

Možaev, V. E. *Novoe politiěskoe myšlenie i vsemirnoe profsojuznoe dviženie*. Moscow: Profizdat, 1990.

Tosstorff, R. *Rofintern. Die Rote Gewerkschaftsinternationale, 1920–1937*. Paderborn: Schoeningh, 2004.

VSEVOLOD MOŽAEV

Internationalism

With the creation of the International Workingmen's Association (First International) in 1864, European socialism institutionalized a commitment to international solidarity. In his keynote address at the founding of the Second International in 1889, Paul Lafargue stressed that the delegates were not assembled beneath national flags, but rather "the red flag of the international proletariat." Internationalism was considered fundamental to socialism. "The International," intoned the movement's battle hymn, "will be the human race."

Marxist theory embraced internationalism and attempted to give it an objective foundation. "The workers," proclaimed the *Communist Manifesto* in 1848, "have no fatherland." Modern capitalism had shattered national boundaries and created an international division of labor that constituted the global proletariat as a class in itself. Nonetheless, for the time being the national arena remained the primary focus of class struggle. The working class, Karl Marx asserted, must "constitute itself as the nation" as a first step toward emancipation. The apparent contradiction would only be reconciled in a future Communist society. In *Socialism: Utopian and Scientific*, Friedrich Engels summarized the process, famously remarking that "as the anarchy of social production vanishes" the modern state will "wither away."

The European Socialist movement's commitment to internationalism was found wanting at the onset of the First World War, when most parties opted to support their respective national war efforts. Following the war, internationalism was redefined within the Social Democratic and Communist branches of what had become an irrevocably divided labor movement. The Communist International (Comintern), founded in Moscow in March 1919, promulgated a doctrine of Communist internationalism inspired by Leninist analysis that perceived the Russian Revolution as the first blow of a "World Revolution" that would transform international society root and branch.

By its Third World Congress in 1921, the Comintern was forced to come to terms with the fact that the postwar wave of revolutionary assaults had run its course. Internationalism was recast to place greater emphasis upon the Soviet state, including the universal relevance of the Russian revolutionary experience and the leading role of the Russian party within the international movement. In his polemics with Leon Trotsky, Joseph Stalin introduced a doctrine of "socialism in one country," according to which the Soviet Union was capable of building socialism independently. This meant an abandonment of the early Communist movement's uncompromising internationalism on behalf of a concept of the revolutionary process grounded upon Soviet power.

In 1943, as a gesture to the wartime Allies, the Comintern was disbanded. In the postwar period, a doctrine of "proletarian internationalism" nonetheless remained useful to Communist party states, legitimizing the exercise of power and providing a rationalization for assertive international policies. In practice, the presumption that the Communist idea is inextricably linked to a project for the transformation of global society has proven robust. Mikhail Gorbachev's efforts to reform the Soviet Union after 1985 included an attempt to revive a spirit of authentic internationalism as a basis for Soviet international policy. The successors of Mao Zedong in China continue to describe their policies as a distinctly Chinese application of a doctrine with universal relevance.

See also Comintern; Nationalism; Socialism in One Country.

FURTHER READING

Holbraad, C. *Internationalism and Nationalism in European Political Thought*. Basingstoke: Palgrave Macmillan, 2003.

Light, M. *Soviet Theory of International Relations*. Brighton, UK: Wheatsheaf, 1988.

McDermott, K., and J. Agnew. *The Comintern: A History of International Communism from Lenin to Stalin.* New York: St. Martin's Press, 1997.

R. CRAIG NATION

Islam

The relationship between Islam and communism is marked by Marx's statement "religion . . . is the opium of the people" as well as actual Soviet reality. The USSR in fact had a significant Muslim population. An heir to czarist Islam, "Soviet Islam" was concentrated especially in three areas: the Volga-Ural region in its European section, the Caucasus, and Central Asia. Marxism has always looked at religion with diffidence, not granting it any form of social autonomy, and regarding it as a form of the subaltern classes' alienation. This perspective puts Marxism-Leninism and religious thought on a collision course, since religious thought resists a worldview in which a transcendent God is replaced by the secularized theology of "God of the political on earth." In our case this secularized theology takes the form of the "dictatorship of the proletariat" and the establishment of a key role for the party.

Stalin in his *Marxism and the National Question* (1913) stated that socialism would not unleash antireligious persecutions but instead would conduct "an intense propaganda against religion with the goal of preparing the triumph of the socialist world-view," since religion was "undoubtedly not in the proletariat's best interest." The concept of antireligion appeared in the Constitution of the Russian Socialist Federative Republic of 1918, which in addition to ensuring freedom of religious propaganda, also ensured freedom of antireligious propaganda. The first Constitution of the USSR, passed in 1924, reiterated this concept fully. But Soviet policy toward domestic Muslims would always oscillate between ideology and realpolitik. After the revolution the Communists, unlike the czars, guaranteed Muslims their religious freedom and did not initiate antireligious propaganda against them—although the party tended to address "Muslim workers and Islamic nations" more than Islam as such.

The new regime's policies were instead aimed at overturning those of Greater Russian imperialism had pursued toward peoples of Islamic faith. This choice was dictated by various reasons. First, the need to consolidate power: the revolution did not want enemies, especially among the peasants, a significant social group in the Muslim population. Second, there was the need to oppose anti-Russian movements whose objective was the "expulsion of the infidels" from taking hold; these had developed in the Caucasus, especially in Chechnya and Daghestan, between 1917 and 1921. Finally, there was the need to lead Oriental peoples into the anti-imperialist and anticapitalist camp, since they were deemed to be more sensitive than Western peoples to the appeal of the revolution. This thesis was also defended by Mirza Khaidargalievich Sultan-Galiev, a Muslim Bolshevik leader, later expelled from the party in 1923, who believed that the USSR needed to look toward the Orient, where the revolution could find more fertile terrain than in the West, a social environment in which the interests of capitalists and workers were closely interwoven.

Soviet politics changed after Lenin's death and Stalin's rise to power. The Kremlin's new leader addressed two sides of the question: the traditional one of religious freedom, and the new one of the socioreligious reorganization of Islam, which Stalin based on a revision of the ties between the community of faith and the nation. According to Stalin the nation was a "stable community of language, territory, economic life and psychological predisposition, formed historically and maintained by means of a common culture." The absence of any of these characteristics meant the nation did not exist. A common religious faith was therefore not sufficient to unite the Muslims who lived in Soviet territory. The absence of a common language would become the tool used to disperse them among different nations. Turkestan was divided in 1924. Four federative republics were born of this division: Uzbekistan, Turkmenistan, Kazakhstan, and Kirghiztan. New languages were codified, as previously in the case of the fifteen languages of the Caucasus, Tartar in Crimea, and Bashkir in the Volga-Ural region. The Soviet reform broke up the three great macroregional cultures and their languages: Osmanli (for Azerbaijan and Crimea), Turki (for Tartaria, Bashkiria, Astrakhan, eastern Russia, and western Siberia), and Chaghatay (in central Asia). This choice was vigorously but uselessly opposed by those who saw the Panturanic dream of the unity of peoples of Turkish culture vanish as a consequence. In the period 1925–28, the propaganda's emphasis was on the need to "free the people from superstitions." In the Soviet Constitution of 1936 freedom of religion was still guaranteed, but that of antireligious propaganda was emphasized. This measure exacerbated tensions between the party and the Muslims, which also had social and economic causes. In central Asia, subjected to agricultural collectivization and policies imposing sedentary lifestyles, both peasants and nomads were Muslim. Social and religious issues were thus inextricably fused, fueling animosities between party and peasants, between atheists and believers in Allah.

Stalin's policies also left their mark on the socioreligious organization of Islam. Already in 1924 the religious tribunals that had administered justice both in the countryside and to nomads were suppressed. The collection of the *zakat*—the ritual offering, one of the foundations or obligatory precepts of Islam, whose earthly purpose was to compensate for social inequalities—was forbidden. It was a practice that the Soviet regime considered incompatible with socialist ideology. It could not admit the existence of poverty much less a form of income redistribution that was not the result of a political decision. In 1928, religious education in schools was banned and religious schools were suppressed, including Koranic schools such as the *maktah* (at the primary school level) and the madrassa (higher education). In their place antireligious education was introduced. In the period 1928–42 more than twenty thousand mosques were closed. In 1930 properties belonging to the Waqf (religious endowment), the institution that administered Islamic property, were confiscated. In 1936 reading the Koran out loud, even in one's own home, was prohibited. This prohibition led to the renewed widespread use of the *dikhr*, or silent recitation.

The situation changed once more with World War II. In a move intended to feed patriotism, Stalin opened up to the Orthodox Church and Islam. This was a move dictated by the sometimes ambiguous behavior of Muslims during the conflict. The Tartars in Crimea (but not those in Tatarstan—that is, Kazan) collaborated with the Germans, as did some peoples of the Caucasus. In central Asia, far from the front yet an important area in terms of logistical support for the war, draft dodging was widespread. In 1943, with the enemy still at the USSR's doors, Stalin came to an agreement with Abdurrahman Rasulaev, a Tartar from the Volga region who was in charge of an old czarist institution that had survived the wavering Soviet policies on the issue of religion. Rasulaev offered Stalin Muslim support in exchange for a normalization of relations between the regime and Islam. Stalin agreed, even though he was preoccupied with containing the development of an Islam that was not under state control. This led to the creation of four *muftiat* or *nazarat*, spiritual guidance centers with a territorial base (Europe and Siberia, central Asia and Kazakhia, northern Caucasus, Shiite areas and southern Caucasus, to which a fifth center, Kazakhstan, would be added but only in 1990). Relations between Soviet power and the various nazarat came under the purview of the Religious Affairs Directorate, which answered directly to the USSR's Council of Ministers.

Between 1943 and 1944 "state Islam" was thus born, which in exchange for following basic party directives, was given a certain degree of cultural autonomy. The goal was to create an Islam that had strong ethnic and national characteristics, tied to the republics, and would therefore counter any attempt at reconstituting a Muslim community of faith within Soviet borders. The attenuation of antireligious polemics against Islam after the end of World War II resulted from the need to minimize conflict at a time when the, socially and environmentally difficult, industrialization process of central Asia was under way.

Stalin's death coincided with the restoration of "socialist legality," which included the freedom to spread antireligious propaganda. From 1954 to 1964, therefore, the second antireligious campaign was undertaken, and it weakened only after Nikita Khrushchev's fall. Leonid Brezhnev initiated a new era of tolerance, which witnessed the reopening of many mosques. This change of course was motivated by international political considerations. Good relations with Islam domestically helped the Soviet government maintain better relations with Muslim countries. The USSR supported Arab countries against Israel, the United States' partner, and presenting itself to the world as a "protector of Islam" could only serve the cause. Soviet Islam was used as a means of legitimation and penetration into the Muslim world. "The USSR, great Muslim power" was this policy's slogan in a nutshell.

Official Soviet Islam never succeeded in efficiently containing what has been dubbed "parallel Islam" or "Islam outside the mosque." Islam has traditionally been a "religion without a center," without an authority in charge of doctrine and dogma, and intolerant toward institutionalized hierarchies. In this specific case this tendency was accentuated by the fact that in the USSR, Islam was centered on Sufi Brotherhoods. Its soul was the Naqshbandiyah in central Asia and the Khadiriyah in Caucasus. During the seventy years of the USSR's existence parallel Islam allowed a religiosity outside official channels to survive. The Sufi orders also managed clandestine schools and mosques, acting as a force that was de facto opposing the system. Official Soviet Islam, however, performed a function of social integration and played a role as custodian of morality, as an institution to contain deviancy. This function became a means to transmit a traditional view of the social order, founded on religious precepts. With some remarkable ideological distortions, state Islam could thus see the Soviet state as the tool for the realization, even though in secular form, of the traditional values of Islam's religious message. It also transmitted a view of communism as a by-product of Islam, presenting it to the faithful as something imperfect but still useful.

The Iranian Revolution forced the USSR into yet another change of course. Ayatollah Ruholla Mussaui Khomeini's rise to power was a motive of pride among all Muslims, Shiite and Sunni. It was also in order to react to the possible contagion of the "green peril" that the USSR invaded Afghanistan in 1979: an act that also erased decades of Soviet Muslim policy. In this mountainous region the USSR had to confront a new phenomenon: Islamist internationalism. With the support of Pakistan and Saudi Arabia, which in their turn were being supported by the United States, and with the aid of transnational Islamist organizations, thousands of youths bent on fighting "atheism" in the name of Islam arrived in Afghanistan. The United States was bent on containing the expansion of Soviet influence in the area and creating an internal Islamic front. The operation did not succeed but the Afghan adventure cost the USSR the ability to use the Islam card in foreign policy. The withdrawal from Afghanistan in 1989 was a prelude to the USSR's rapid decline as a world superpower—a decline prophesied by Khomeini, who also invited Gorbachev to look not toward the West but toward Islam.

Gorbachev's rise to power ensured the opening to religion already sanctioned by the Soviet Constitution of 1977, which guaranteed both religious freedom and the freedom to propagate atheism, but prohibited hostility toward religious beliefs. Perestroika favored the rebirth of religious organizations. In October 1990, a law regarding religious freedom was passed, establishing the citizens' right to profess any religion and dismantling antireligious state machinery, while sanctioning the end of the state's financing of atheist propaganda. This would lead to the reconstitution of Islamic associations and mosques free of state control. With the end of the USSR, the history of Islam "with a Red star" also ended.

See also Anti-imperialism; Atheism, Soviet; Marxism-Leninism; Modernization; Nationalism; National Question, The.

FURTHER READING

Akiner, S. *Islamic Peoples of the Soviet Union*. London: Kegan Paul, 1983.

Bennigsen, A., and C. Lemercier Quelquejay. *Islam in the Soviet Union*. New York: Praeger, 1967.

———. *Le soufi et le commissaire: les confréries musulmanes en URSS*. Paris: Seuil, 1986.

Bennigsen, A., and S. E. Wimbush. *Muslim National Communism in the Soviet Union*. Chicago: University of Chicago Press, 1979.

———. *Muslims of the Soviet Empire*. Bloomington: University of Illinois Press, 1986.

Carrère d'Encausse, H., and S. R. Schram, eds. *Marxism and Asia: An Introduction with Readings*. London: Allen Lane, 1969.

Gaborieau, M., and A. Popovich, eds. *Islam et politique dans le monde (ex)communiste*. Paris: CNRS, 2001.

Gaborieau, M., A. Popovich, and T. Zarcone, eds. *Naqshbandis. Historical Developments and Present Situation of a Muslim Mystical Order: Proceedings of the Sèvres Round Table, 2–4 May 1985*. Paris: Isis, 1990.

Guolo, R. *Il fondamentalismo islamico*. Rome: Laterza, 2002.

Khomeini, R. *Lettera a Gorbaciov*. Parma: Il Veltro, 1989.

Popovich, A., and G. Veinstein, eds. *Les Voies d'Allah: les ordres mystiques dans l'Islam des origines à aujourd'hui*. Paris: Fayard, 1996.

Ro'i, Y. *Islam in the Soviet Union: From the Second World War to Gorbachev*. New York: Columbia University Press, 2000.

Roy, O. *L'Afghanistan: islam et modernité politique*. Paris: Seuil, 1985.

———. *L'Asie centrale contemporaine*. Paris: Presses Universitaires de France, 2001.

Salvi, S. *La mezzaluna con la stella rossa: origini, storia e destino dell'Islam sovietico*. Genoa: Marietti, 1993.

Saroyan, M. *Minorities, Mullahs, and Modernity: Reshaping Community in the Former Soviet Union*. Los Angeles: University of California Press, 1997.

Stalin, I. *Marxism and the National Question*. New York: International Publishers, 1942.

RENZO GUOLO

Jacobinism

Historians have long contested the relationship between Bolshevism and Jacobinism. Those anxious to stress the orthodox Marxist character of Bolshevism (Harding) tend to play down the link, while those who highlight the conspiratorial nature of Bolshevism (von Borcke, Kondratieva) tend to emphasize it. The Jacobin influence on Bolshevism had two principal sources. The first was the tradition of the Jacobins as developed by Graccus Babeuf and his "conspiracy of equals" with its vision of communism, which was further developed by Philippe Buonarotti and the conception of revolutionary coup by Louis Auguste Blanqui. The second was a specifically Russian Jacobin tradition of revolutionary thought and action that persisted late into the 19th century.

Marx and Engels were greatly influenced by the French Jacobins. They were, however, by no means uncritical admirers. The Jacobins fell, they argued, because they sought to reconcile the gulf between state and society through recourse to revolutionary terror, and through an overemphasis on the "omnipotence of the will." Moreover, Marx and Engels also tended to be highly critical of purely conspiratorial methods of political organization, which they saw as harboring the danger of new authoritarian revolutionary regimes. On this point, however, they were not always entirely consistent, and on occasions lent support to such conspiratorial groups. In *The Holy Family* (1844) they refer to Babeuf as the precursor of modern communism, and they stress the role of Buonarotti in reviving his ideas in France after 1830.

Lenin and the Bolshevik party were heirs to a particular realist tradition of revolutionary thought that had various strands, one of which was the Jacobin tradition, in its Blanquist variant. Lenin at the outset of his revolutionary career sought out contacts with those Populists

from the terrorist wing of the movement, to which his executed brother Alexander had belonged. Among his acquaintances were M. P. Yasneva, political associate of P. G. Zaichnevskii, the old Russian Jacobin and author of the 1862 manifesto *Molodaya Rossiya*. According to the accounts of contemporaries he was greatly influenced by the political ideas of P. N. Tkachev and S. G. Nechaev, both of whom had close connections with Blanquist organizations in Europe.

In Russian revolutionary thought, with its emphasis on revolutionary dictatorship, there was thus a strong Jacobin streak. The debate on party organization, which brought to the fore differences between Jacobin and anti-Jacobin thinking was prolonged and intense. S. N. Prokopovich condemned G. Plekhanov's views on party organization in the 1890s as Blanquist. In 1897 P. B. Aksel'rod warned of the danger of Russian Marxism following a Blanquist shortcut to socialism.

Lenin in *What Is to Be Done?* voiced his admiration for "the brilliant galaxy of revolutionaries of the seventies," arguing that the Social Democrats should seek to create an organization similar to the "magnificent organization" of Zemlya i Volya, the main inspiration of which had been N. P. Ogarëv. He applauded Tkachev's view that an epoch of Socialist dictatorship would be necessary to extirpate the old regime and that mass terror would also be needed. He spoke with approval of Narodnaya Volya's use of terror tactics. He mentioned with approval the terrorists P. A. Alekseev, I. N. Myshkin, S. N. Khalturin, and A. I. Zhelyabov. At the Third Congress of the Russia Social Democratic Party in 1905 Lenin cited with relish Marx's 1848 comments that in 1793–94 Robespierre's guillotine had been "the plebeian method" of eradicating the feudal order.

Lenin's views on party organization were bitterly rejected by other Marxists, most notably by Trotsky in *Our Political Tasks* (1904). Trotsky then denounced Lenin's definition of revolutionary social democracy in *One*

Step Forward, Two Steps Back: "The Jacobin indissolubly linked to the organization of the proletariat now conscious of its class interest, is precisely the social democratic revolutionary." The logic of the Jacobin's position, Trotsky argued, led to the absurdity of the guillotine. The charge of Blanquism was directed at Lenin by Rosa Luxemburg. Vladimir Akimov accused the supporters of Lenin of espousing ideas that led logically to "Nechaevism" (*Nechaevshchina*), adding, "Lenin is a Blanquist, and nothing Blanquist is alien to him." Plekhanov, too, who had initially sided with Lenin, in 1906 charged him with importing "Blanquist contraband under the flag of the strictest Marxist orthodoxy" into the party.

In 1917 Lenin repeatedly invoked the example of the Jacobins as a model of a revolutionary vanguard. On June 20, in *Pravda* he published his article "Concerning the Enemies of the People," in which he lauded the Jacobin law of 1793 that unleashed the terror. On July 7 he published the article "Can 'Jacobinism' Frighten the Working Class?," in which he dismissed attempts by the enemies of the Bolsheviks to discredit them by associating them with Jacobinism and terrorism. On July 29, in his article "The Beginning of Bonapartism" he argued that the struggle for the revolution had become a struggle between Jacobinism and Bonapartism.

Nevertheless, he repeatedly rebuffed accusations that the Bolsheviks were resorting to Blanquist methods. In "Marxism and Insurrection" (September 1917) Lenin wrote:

> To be successful, insurrection must rely not upon a conspiracy, and not upon a party, but upon the advanced revolutionary class. That is the first point. Insurrection must rely upon a *revolutionary upsurge of the people*. That is the second point. Insurrection must rely upon that *turning-point* in the history of the growing revolution when the activity of the advanced ranks of the people is at its height, and when the *vacillations* in the ranks of the enemy and *in the ranks of the weak, half-hearted and irresolute friends of the revolution* are strongest. That is the third point. And these three conditions for raising the question of insurrection distinguish *Marxism from Blanquism*.

Just a week before the Bolshevik seizure of power Lenin again took up the charge, arguing that military conspiracy was Blanquism when basic conditions were not fulfilled, when the party did not represent the interest of a definite class, when the party did not have the sympathy of the majority of the population, and so on.

In his afterword to "Can the Bolsheviks Retain State Power?" written in September–October 1917, Lenin quoted Marx's famous passage from *Revolution and Counter-revolution in Germany* on the tactics of insurrection. Here Marx speaks of insurrection as a form of war: "In the words of Danton, the greatest master of revolutionary tactics yet known: *de l'audace, de l'audace, encore de l'audace!*"

Rosa Luxemburg warned of the revolution being transformed into a dictatorship of a handful of politicians, "a dictatorship, to be sure, not the dictatorship of the proletariat, however, but only the dictatorship of a handful of politicians; that is, a dictatorship in the bourgeois sense, in the sense of the rule of the Jacobins." Yu. V. Martov, Plekhanov, Victor Serge, and Gregory P. Maximoff condemned Bolshevik tactics as Jacobin.

The Bolsheviks were entranced by the example of the Jacobins. Robespierre, Danton, Saint-Just, Marat belonged in the pantheon of revolutionary heroes for their principled defense of revolution and their uncompromising stance on terror. The struggle of the Jacobins with counterrevolution in Lyon and the Vendée were seen as having contemporary relevance for the Bolshevik state. Parallels between the French and the Russian revolutions, between the Jacobins and the Bolsheviks, run like a thread through Trotsky's celebrated *History of the Russian Revolution* with its highly favorable estimations of Robespierre, Danton, and Marat.

In the 1920s a number of figures took part in the debate on Tkachev and Zaichnevskii as forerunners of the Bolsheviks, among them M. N. Pokrovskii, B. P. Koz'min, B. I. Gorev, and S. I. Mitskevitch. N. N. Baturin, however, dismissed Jacobinism as the ideology of the petty bourgeoisie. In the early 1930s a seven-volume collection of Tkachev's works, edited by B. P. Koz'min, was published, and B. P. Koz'min edited a collection of documents on Nechaev and the Nechaevtsy. There were various attempts to rehabilitate Nechaev. This was never achieved, but the trend was significant.

Trotsky, in *Terrorism and Communism*, rejected the argument that the Bolsheviks were akin to Blanquists. Nevertheless, Blanqui enjoyed great respect in the USSR in the 1920s with several studies of his life being published. *The Great Soviet Encyclopedia* of 1927 contained a lengthy biography eulogizing him as a forerunner of Bolshevism and as a skilled practitioner of revolutionary conspiracy and insurrection. Graccus Babeuf, famous as the leader of the Conspiracy of Equals, was seen as a forerunner of communism.

In 1930 the journal *Istorik Marksist* published an article by S. Krasnyi on the development of Blanqui's political and social views. The journal at that time also published material on the history of Narodnaya Volya. Four years later, in 1934, *Istorik Marksist* published an article by N. Lukin titled, "Lenin and the Problem of Jacobin Dictatorship." Among the Soviet authorities, concern over the threat posed by terrorist attacks was growing, and the discussion on Jacobinism was closed down. The official view presented in Stalin's *Short Course* (1938) was that the Bolsheviks owed all their ideas to Marxism, as developed initially by Plekhanov and then by Lenin.

See also Bolshevism; Bonapartism; Dictatorship of the Proletariat; Lenin, Vladimir; Luxemburg, Rosa.

FURTHER READING

Harding, N. *Lenin's Political Thought. Vol. 2. Theory and Practice in the Socialist Revolution.* London: Macmillan, 1981.

Kondratieva, T. *Bolcheviks et Jacobins.* Paris: Payot, 1989.

Rees, E. A. *Political Thought from Machiavelli to Stalin: Revolutionary Machiavellianism.* Basingstoke: Palgrave, 2004.

Salvadori, M. L. "Il giacobinismo nel pensiero marxista." In *Il Modello Politico Giacobino e Le Rivoluzioni*, ed. M. L. Salvadori and N. Tranfaglia, 240–53. Florence: La Nuova Italia, 1984.

Van Ree, E. *The Political Thought of Joseph Stalin: A Study in Twentieth-century Revolutionary Patriotism.* London: Routledge-Curzon, 2002.

von Borcke, A. *Die Ursprünge des Bolschewismus: Jakobinische Tradition in Russland und die Theorie der revolutionären Diktatur.* Munich: Johannes Berchmans Verlag, 1977.

E. ARFON REES

Jaruzelski, Wojciech

In at least two respects Wojciech Jaruzelski (1923–) was an atypical communist leader: he came from a family of landed gentry, and he was a professional soldier. He was born on July 6 in an estate in Kurow, in central Poland. From 1933 to 1939, he attended the Księża Marianów Gymnasium in Warsaw, in which his education was heavily laced with devotion to both the Church and patriotism. The war interrupted his further study, and the Jaruzelski family fled to Lithuania to escape the Germans. In June 1941, in the fourth great wave of deportations, the People's Commissariat for Internal Affairs sent Jaruzelski's family to the Altai Republic, where his father died, and Jaruzelski himself worked as a common laborer.

In summer 1943, he applied for acceptance into the Polish army, then being formed under the auspices of the Communists, and was sent to a military college to become an officer. On the front line as a mounted scout, he found himself, in July 1944, on the outskirts of Warsaw and then marched with the Soviet army all the way to Berlin. When Jaruzelski entered the army, he was driven by patriotic rather than ideological motives; yet he fell under the influence of party propaganda, which in that army was particularly persistent and effective. He decided to become a professional soldier after the war ended, and for two years fought with his unit against anti-Communist partisans. In 1947, as a well-respected and intelligent lieutenant, Jaruzelski was assigned to the Central Infantry School, which trained officers for high rank in the future. There he joined the Polish Workers' (Communist) Party, where he was one of the few members from a noble family.

Because of his intellect and diligence, Jaruzelski rose quickly in the military. In 1956, he became a one-star general, the youngest in the Polish army at that time. He was assigned in 1960 to a key post, the Polish Army Office of Political Management, which was concerned with propaganda and ideological control. As a result of this, four years later, Jaruzelski became a member of the party's Central Committee. In 1965, he became chief of the General Staff, and in April 1968 was named minister of national defense, which placed him in the highest government circles. As minister, he was the commander of the Polish troops who invaded Czechoslovakia, and he also took part in the anti-Semitic "purges" in the army at that time.

After his army had been used in suppressing workers' strikes in December 1970, Jaruzelski was admitted to the Polish politburo, without then having any political ambitions. This situation changed as a result of the ensuing turmoil, the 1980 strikes, and the Solidarity revolt. Given the party's loss of face and the deeply unstable situation, a part of the party leadership, and Moscow as well, now believed that the key sector of the government and main hope of maintaining the current political system was the army. In February 1981, Jaruzelski became premier and, although he was formally still the "number two" person in the country, behind the first secretary of the Central Committee, Stanislaw Kania, in reality he soon became politically dominant, particularly as more and more officers were occupying posts in the government administration and party apparatus.

In October 1981, Jaruzelski assumed absolute power in Poland: he was simultaneously first secretary of the party, premier, and minister of national defense. On December 13, 1981, after consultations with the Kremlin, he made the decision to introduce martial law. The policy that he now conducted was a mixture of repression and brutal propaganda with concessions to the church and restraints on the party orthodoxy. If Solidarity was a "self-limiting revolution," then Jaruzelski self-limited his martial law correspondingly. It rescued the situation for the time being, but the circumstances were far from stable in the country. The government's legitimacy had been weakened, and the leadership remained in constant fear of a new outbreak. Mikhail Gorbachev's appearance and perestroika opened the way to real reforms.

Jaruzelski was one of the first Communists who perceived this and resolved to take advantage of it. In 1986, after launching some really serious reforms, he recognized that he would be unable to carry them out without a credible public partner. And so, after considerable vacillation, Jaruzelski announced that a compromise had to be made with the Solidarity underground. He did not take part in the negotiations himself but it is certain that without his knowledge and consent, no important decisions could have been made. Nevertheless, against all the intentions of Jaruzelski and the Polish Communist Party, what were supposed to be merely far-reaching reforms became a whole transformation of the system itself, in which Jaruzelski as president of Poland from July 1989 on, played the role of guarantor of the peaceful character of the changes as well as of the personal safety of his party comrades. Also, both during the time he was president (until December 1990) and later, Jaruzelski somehow became a model ex-Communist: without rejecting either his ideological principles or his old loyalties, he nonetheless accepted the democratic rules of the game.

See also Martial Law in Poland; Post-Soviet Communism; Solidarity.

Berger, M. E. *Jaruzelski*. Dusseldorf: Econ, 1990.

Berry, L. *Wojciech Jaruzelski*. New York: Chelsea House Publishers, 1990.

Kowalski, L. *General ze skazą. Biografia wojskowa gen. armii Wojciecha Jaruzelskiego*. Warsaw: Rytm, 2001.

ANDRZEJ PACZKOWSKI

Jiang Zemin

Jiang Zemin (1926–) was the first person to lead Communist China who did not possess the previous generation's political and military credentials. With a degree in engineering, experiences in the Soviet Union in the 1950s, Jiang was Deng Xiaoping's designated successor after Zhao Ziyang's fall from grace in 1989. During the 1990s Jiang was the guardian of the continued monopoly that the Communist Party held on the levers of power, and both the expansion and future of the economic reforms that Deng had started. Born too late to have accrued political capital by participating in the heroic phase of the Chinese Revolution, Jiang became a member of the Communist Party only in 1946. His political career evolved almost entirely in Shanghai, from his first positions in industrial bureaucracy in the 1950s, to his becoming first mayor and then municipal party secretary in 1985.

During the student demonstrations that occurred in Shanghai in 1989, Jiang (then municipal party secretary) and mayor Zhu Rongji managed to avoid the violence that instead marked these events in Beijing. It was perhaps because of this avoidance, but above all because of the support he gave to the uncompromising positions of the hard-liners in the national government, that Jiang was nominated to the position of general secretary that same year. Generally considered a technocrat and a compromise choice by a party shaken by the events of 1989, Jiang succeeded in rapidly moving to the center of what increasingly appeared to be a "collective" party leadership. He became the longest-lasting general secretary of the post-Mao period (1989–2002), despite all predictions, and also occupied the positions of president of the party's powerful Central Military Commission (1989) and president of the republic (1993). Jiang therefore presided over the Chinese economy's phase of most rapid transition in the 1990s, the reacquisition of sovereignty over Hong Kong's (1997) and Macao's (1999) colonial territories, and the reestablishment of the country's international position (with entry into the World Trade Organization and the selection of Beijing as the site for the 2008 Olympic Games).

Deprived at this point of ideological or historical justifications to govern the country, Jiang relied on the revival of a nationalist ideology, which was popular at the time with the intellectual and middle classes. By latching on to the aspirations of these emerging social groups, the nationalism that Jiang inspired provided the needed justification for the power of a party that could guarantee economic development and the constant improvement in the quality of life. Jiang understood the need for the party to open up to these new social agents and not only represent those classes traditionally tied to socialism (workers and peasants) but also the "advanced forces of production" (private entrepreneurs and professionals) and "advanced culture" as well as the interests of "the majority of the population." These three points make up his "Theory of the Three Represents," which are today officially part of the Chinese Communist Party's statutes, next to Marxism-Leninism, Mao Zedong Thought, and Deng Xiaoping Theory as an ideological guide to the party's actions. Under his guidance, the party was transformed from a "revolutionary party" (*geming dang*) into a "political party of government" (*zhizeng dang*), which

does not aspire to represent a class but instead the entire Chinese nation.

Jiang was also the first Chinese leader whose succession did not lead to internal struggles or crises of legitimacy. His designated successor, Hu Jintao, progressively took over the positions of general secretary in 2002, president of the republic in 2003, and president of the Military Commission in 2004.

See also Beijing Spring; Deng Xiaoping; Nationalism; Socialist Market Economy.

FURTHER READING

Gilley, B. *Tiger on the Brink: Jiang Zemin and China's New Elite.* Berkeley: University of California Press, 1999.

Lam, W.W.-L. *The Era of Jiang Zemin.* Singapore: Prentice Hall, 1999.

LUIGI TOMBA

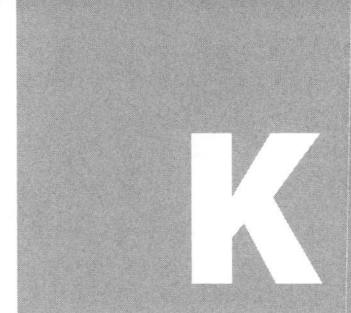

Kádár, János

János Kádár (1912–89) was the first of several children born in Fiume to a peasant family, originally from northern Hungary, and his mother, Borbála, raised him by herself; he adopted her last name, Csermanek, and used it until 1945. In 1918 the family moved to Budapest, where he survived a precarious existence during the 1920s, worsened by the social and political tensions that developed after the dissolution of the Habsburg monarchy. Once Kádár had finished his schooling, he found a job as an apprentice, but was fired in 1929, and the following year moved closer to the underground movement. In 1932 he became a member and in 1933 a secretary of the Communist Workers' Youth City Committee. Arrested in July 1932, Kádár was released from prison in 1935. He became a member of the Social Democratic Party with other members of the clandestine party that had been decimated by arrests; he remained a member until 1942, when the anti-Communist repression pursued by Miklós Kállay's government led him to interrupt his "legal" contacts in order to become a member of the Central Committee of the clandestine Communist Party until it dissolved itself in June 1943; he later became a member of the Peace Party (Békepárt), a front organization.

With the Red Army's entry into Hungary, which ended the siege of Budapest (February 13, 1945), the Hungarian Communist Party regrouped its ranks under the dual leadership of the militants who had remained in Hungary clandestinely during the war, Kádár among them, and the Moscow refugees, led by Matyas Rakosi, who had returned in the fall of 1944. During the February–April interval in 1945 Kádár was head of Budapest's municipal police; from April 1945 he was a member of the party's secretariat, and until 1947 was responsible for the Cadre Section of the party. He was elected to Parliament in the August 1947 elections, and became minister of the interior on August 5, 1948, a position he held until June 23, 1950, distinguishing himself in the preparations for the Rajk trial (1949). On April 20, 1951, he was arrested and charged with having betrayed the movement during the 1930s, and as a result of an inquiry pursued with violent means by the political police and his party comrades, Kádár was sentenced to life in prison on December 19, 1951. On July 22, 1954, he was released from prison together with other members who had fallen in disgrace during 1949–51, and he regained his political clout as the first provincial secretary for Pest (September 1955).

In the years that saw a leadership struggle between the Rakosi and Imre Nagy factions, Kádár became one of the leading representatives of the reformist faction, and in July 1956, after Rakosi's fall, he was brought into the Secretariat. During the first days of the October Revolution of 1956 he took Nagy's side, was co-opted into the two governments led by Nagy, and on October 30 participated in the founding of the new Communist Party, the Hungarian Socialist Workers' Party (Magyar Szocialista Munkaspart). On November 1 he went to the Soviet embassy with Ferenc Münnich and was taken to Moscow, where Khrushchev, having obtained Josip Broz Tito's assent to a second intervention in Hungary, put him in charge of the new regime. On November 4 Kádár announced the new "Workers-Peasants' Government's" program from the radio in Szolnok, and on November 7—since the insurrection was continuing—he made his entry into the capital with a Soviet military convoy.

After the insurrection had been quashed, the Kádár government administered the repressive phase that started with the introduction of special tribunals on December 11–13, and by 1961 had passed over 14,000 sentences, of which 229 were capital punishments. Kádár simultaneously attempted to solidify the new government using social measures: he abolished discriminatory taxation against single citizens, introduced a pension for employees of collective factories, and reintroduced the Christmas and Easter holidays. His position was strengthened politically in March 1957 when, in exchange for Nagy and his group's return from a Romanian prison and their public trial in Hungary, Moscow agreed to keep Rakosi and other followers of the Stalinist line in the USSR.

Kádár was once again head of government starting in 1961, after a three-year pause, and dedicated himself to the regime's normalization, symbolized by the motto "Those who are not against us, are with us." After releasing almost all political prisoners (1960–63), he focused on leading his country out of international isolation. The United Nations removed the Hungarian question from its permanent agenda after secret negotiations conducted with the United States in October 1962, and in 1964 a partial concordat was signed with the Vatican—a first step in the normalization of a relation that was weighed down by the Mindszenty affair. On January 1, 1968, the New Economic Mechanism, an ambitious project to reform the system of production and prices, was introduced, and by the early 1970s it had transformed Hungary into the most market-oriented Soviet satellite. Kádár's visits to the West (for example, to Italy in 1977) gave him and his regime some credit as acceptable forms of compromise between authoritarianism, paternalism, and tolerance for dissent.

The aging Kádár remained in power until May 1988, notwithstanding a phase of greater ideological rigidity in 1973–74, which ended with an attempt by the Hungarian Socialist Workers' Party's hard-liners to get rid of him, as well as the ensuing period marked by the first signs of an economic crisis (which would worsen during the 1980s); it was only then that the party's national conference elected centrist Károly Grosz to be his successor. During his last year of life, by now gravely ill, Kádár impotently witnessed the introduction of private property and a multiparty system. He died on July 6, 1989, the day that the Supreme Court pronounced in favor of Nagy's rehabilitation; his funeral was attended by tens of thousands of people.

See also De-Stalinization; Economic Reforms; Hungarian Revolution; People's Democracy; Real Socialism.

FURTHER READING

Gati, C. *Hungary and the Soviet Bloc*. Durham, NC: Duke University Press, 1986.

Huszár T. *Kádár János politikai életrajza I–II*. 2 vols. Budapest: Szabad Tér Kiadó–Kossuth Kiadó, 2001-3.

———, ed. *Kedves jó Kádár elvtárs! Válogatás Kádár János levelezéséböl 1954–1989*. Budapest: Osiris, 2002.

Varga, L., ed. *Kádár János bírái elött: egyszer fent, egyszer lent 1949–1956*. Budapest: Osiris–Budapest Fováros Levéltára, 2001.

STEFANO BOTTONI

Kaganovich, Lazar

Lazar Kaganovich (1893–1991) was one of the most important and colorful figures in the Stalinist group that ruled the Soviet Union. He was born in 1893 into a poor Jewish family in the village of Kabana, Chernobyl County, Ukraine. In 1906 he completed his formal education and went to work in Kiev as a shoemaker in a factory. In 1911 he joined the Bolshevik Party, following the lead of his older brother Mikhail, and was active in the trade union movement. He was a model of the self-educated Bolshevik worker-intellectual. He spoke Russian, Ukrainian, and some Yiddish, but never learned to write grammatically.

In 1917 he was working in Yuzovka, where he became deputy chairman of the local soviet after the February Revolution. He enlisted into the army in Kiev and in June of 1917 was elected to the All-Russian Bureau of Military Party Organizations attached to the Bolshevik Party's Central Committee, at its conference in St. Petersburg. In the autumn of 1917 he played a key role in the Bolshevik seizure of power in Gomel' and Mogilev, and thereafter was involved in organizing the new Red Army.

In May 1918 Kaganovich was sent by the Central Committee to the frontline town of Nizhny Novgorod, where he became head of the Bolshevik Party organization. In August–September 1918 he oversaw the Red Terror in Nizhny. His experience there made him a articulate advocate of centralization in party and state management, anticipating what after Lenin's death became the prevailing orthodoxy of Bolshevik party-state organization. He subsequently served in consolidating Soviet power in Voronezh, and in 1920–21 worked in Turkestan.

At the Tenth Party Congress in March 1921, Kaganovich supported Lenin's proposals on the trade unions and for the resolution outlawing the "anarcho-syndicalist deviation." Following the congress he was briefly assigned to the All-Union Central Council of Trade Unions to purge the unions of supporters of the Workers' Opposition.

In 1922 Kaganovich was appointed to work in the party secretariat in Moscow. Here he was responsible for the appointment of cadres and for organizing party instructors and inspectors, and published informative articles on these projects. He worked alongside Molotov, Kuibyshev, and Stalin, with whom he began to forge a close relationship. In 1923 he led the campaign against Trotsky in the Moscow party organization. In 1924 and 1925 he headed the campaign to revitalize the rural soviets. In 1924 Kaganovich had charge of the admission and education of the two hundred thousand industrial workers recruited into the Communist Party under the "Lenin enrollment."

In April 1925, on Stalin's initiative, Kaganovich was appointed general secretary of the Ukrainian Communist Party. As leader of the Ukrainian party he initially supported the New Economic Policy. He favored the policy of Ukrainization, which promoted the advancement of Ukrainian cadres, the recruitment of Ukrainians into the party, and the use of the Ukrainian language, but found himself caught in the middle between those who opposed the policy and those who wanted it applied more vigorously.

In June 1926 Kaganovich was elected a candidate member of the politburo. In 1926–28 he waged an implacable campaign against the United Opposition in Ukraine. By 1926 he was a convinced advocate of rapid industrialization. He ruthlessly enforced the grain procurement policy during the crisis of 1927–28. At the time of the 1927 war scare, he put the Ukrainian leadership on alert. In the spring of 1928, following the Shakhty trial of mining engineers, he headed a party commission checking on the political reliability of state employees.

In June of 1928 Stalin recalled Kaganovich from Ukraine, largely because of the hostility that his abrasive style had provoked in other Ukrainian leaders. He returned to work in the party secretariat, where he was active in the struggle with the Right opposition. He played a key part in the defeat of Uglanov in the Moscow party organization and in discrediting Tomsky in the All-Union Central Council of Trade Unions.

Kaganovich played a prominent role in the collectivization of agriculture. In 1929, following a tour of Siberia and consultations with Siberian leaders, he promoted the "Urals-Siberian method" for procuring grain. In the early months of 1930, he oversaw the implementation of collectivization in Siberia and in the Volga region. In July 1932 he attended the Ukrainian party conference in Kiev to lay down the law regarding the necessity of meeting the center's procurement targets for grain. In November 1932 he was sent to the North Caucasus to quell peasant unrest and to organize the mass deportation of Cossack villages.

From 1930 onward Kaganovich occupied the third place, after Stalin and Molotov, in the ruling triumvirate. In July 1930 he was elected a full member of the politburo. With the appointment of Molotov to head Sovnarkom in December 1930, Kaganovich took over the Orgburo and secretariat. He also managed the affairs of the politburo and worked on a plethora of politburo commissions. During Stalin's prolonged summer absences from Moscow in these years Kaganovich signed the minutes of the politburo. In 1933 he headed the party's purge commission charged with expelling disloyal and unsuitable elements. In this period he also played a key role in strengthening the system of administrative control within the state apparatus.

In April 1930 Kaganovich was appointed secretary of the Moscow party organization. Heading a team of energetic party administrators, he oversaw the reconstruction of Moscow, the building of the Metro and the Moscow-Volga Canal, and the destruction of a large part of the city's ancient architectural inheritance. In 1935 the newly opened Metro was named after Kaganovich in recognition of his contribution.

Kaganovich played a key role in promoting Stalin's cult. Contemporaries spoke of his slavish sycophancy toward Stalin. He personified the hard-driving administrator emblematic of this era. He was an accomplished speaker, and his speeches and articles are well argued and show originality, even humor. He was not a theorist but a *praktik*, a party organizer. Regarded as ambitious and ruthless, he became the party's leading troubleshooter and was dubbed by Stalin "Iron Lazar."

The years 1930 to 1934 were the apogee of Kaganovich's career, when it appeared as though he had eclipsed Molotov as Stalin's right-hand man. A veritable cult developed around him, particularly within the Moscow party organizations. However, in 1935 he lost control of the Moscow party organization, of the Commission of Party Control, and of the party secretariat and was assigned to head the Soviet railways. In 1935–36 he considerably improved the performance of the railways. In 1937 he also took over the People's Commissariat of Heavy Industry.

During the Great Terror of 1936–38 the Soviet railways and heavy industry, the two sectors for which Kaganovich was responsible, were heavily purged. Kaganovich himself signed death warrants for some thirty-six thousand individuals. He also undertook a series of visits to regional party organizations (Ivanovo, the Western Region, the Donets Basin) to accelerate the purge process in those areas. His signature appears on the order to shoot the twenty thousand Polish officers who were executed in the winter of 1939.

In April 1937 Kaganovich was included in the two five-man politburo commissions on foreign policy and economic questions, which effectively replaced the politburo. His position was weakened after 1939 by the coming to prominence of a new generation of younger Stalinist leaders, and by the upsurge of anti-Semitism in official circles that followed the Hitler-Stalin pact of 1939, which in part claimed his brother: Mikhail Kaganovich, who had played a key role in the defense industries, committed suicide in 1941.

Although he was reelected to the politburo in February 1941, Lazar Kaganovich's career underwent a dramatic decline during the war, when he was twice dismissed as head of the PC of Transport on account of the failings of the railways. As a demonstration of loyalty he volunteered as a political commissar with the Red Army and served on the North Caucasus front, where he was seriously wounded. From 1941 to 1947 he very rarely attended the meetings in Stalin's office.

In 1947 Kaganovich's political fortunes revived to some degree, and he was sent as the politburo's emissary to deal with agricultural problems in Ukraine. He survived the wave of anti-Semitism of Stalin's final years. In October 1952 he was elected to the new party presidium and its eight-member Bureau, but was excluded from Stalin's inner circle.

After Stalin's death Kaganovich occupied the role of a party elder statesman. He was hostile to Khrushchev's "de-Stalinization" policies. At the Central Committee plenum in June 1957, Kaganovich's role in the terror of the late 1930s was denounced, and he was expelled from the politburo and Central Committee as a member of the "Anti-Party Group." In 1961 he was expelled from the party. He was the last survivor of the Stalin leadership and was one of the few who wrote his memoirs. He remained until his death in 1991 an unapologetic Stalinist.

See also Great Terror; Nomenklatura; Purges; Red Terror; Stalin, Joseph; Transportation.

FURTHER READING

Chuev, F. *Tak govoril Kaganovich*. Moscow: Otechestvo, 1992.

Davies, R. W., E. A. Rees, O. V. Khlevnyuk, L. P. Kosheleva, and L. A. Rogovaya, eds. *The Stalin-Kaganovich Correspondence*. New Haven, CT: Yale University Press, 2003.

Kaganovich, L. M. *Pamyatnye zapiski rabochego, kommunista-bol'shevika, profsoyuznogo, partiinogo i sovetsko-gosudarstvennogo rabotnika*. Moscow, 1996.

Khlevnyuk, O. V., R. W. Davies, L. P. Kosheleva, E. A. Rees, and L. A., Rogovaya, eds. *Stalin i Kaganovich Perepiska, 1931–1936gg*. Moscow: ROSSPEN, 2001.

Marcucci, L. *Il Commissario Di Ferro Di Stalin*. Turin: Einaudi, 1997.

Medvedev, R. *All Stalin's Men*. Oxford: Blackwell, 1983.

E. ARFON REES

Kamenev, Lev

Lev Kamenev (1883–1936), whose real name was Rozenfeld, was born on July 6 in Moscow, the son of an engineer. He received his secondary education in Tiflis (Tbilisi) and studied law at Moscow State University, but was expelled for underground political activity. In 1901 he entered the Russian Social Democratic Workers' Party, joining the Bolshevik faction. He emigrated in fall 1902 to France, where he became acquainted with Lenin and worked in the editorial office of the newspaper *Iskra*.

Kamenev returned to Russia in fall 1903 and was active in forming party organizations and disseminating socialist publications. He was arrested by the police more than once. In Tiflis, Kamenev joined the Caucasian Committee of the Russian Social Democratic Workers' Party (RSDWP), to which Stalin also belonged, and represented this committee at the London Party Congress of 1905.

During the first Russian Revolution, he worked as a political agitator and took part in organizing the armed uprising in Moscow in December 1905. In April 1908, Kamenev was arrested again, and on his release left for Geneva, where he continued his collaboration with Lenin and Grigory Zinovyev on the editorial board of the *Proletariat*. After returning to Russia to assume the leadership of the illegal press there and coordinate the work of the Bolshevik faction in the State Duma, he was arrested and exiled to Siberia. Kamenev arrived in Petrograd with Stalin after the beginning of the second revolution in Russia and renewed his journalistic work on the editorial board of *Pravda*. In April 1917 he was elected to the RSDWP's Central Committee and represented the party on the Executive Committee of the Petrograd Soviet of Workers' and Soldiers' Deputies.

On the eve of the October uprising Kamenev, together with Zinovyev, used the press to condemn the policy of armed seizure of power, for which he incurred Lenin's wrath; however, he was able to keep his posts in the party and the Petrograd Soviet. He was chair of the Second All-Russian Congress of Soviets, which announced the transfer of power from the Provisional Government to the Soviet of People's Commissars. Kamenev supported the inclusion of all socialist parties in this body of representatives and conducted negotiations on forming a coalition with the Socialist-Revolutionaries, but his position did not gain support. He was removed from the party's Central Committee and his post as chair of the All-Russian Central Executive Committee.

Kamenev participated in the peace negotiations with Germany, and at the beginning of 1918, was sent to Great Britain and France to help in the effort to smooth over contacts with the ruling circles of these countries. He was sent back to Russia, however, and was arrested in Finland on the way. After returning to Russia in August 1918, Kamenev was elected chair of the Moscow Soviet of Workers' and Soldiers' Deputies, and in March 1919, was elected to the politburo of the Central Committee of the Communist Party of the Soviet Union (CPSU). In April 1922, it was Kamenev who had the task of submitting the proposal to appoint Stalin as general secretary of the CPSU's Central Committee.

During the Civil War years Kamenev was the plenipotentiary of the Soviet of Labor and Defense, and starting in 1922, was the vice chair of the Soviet of People's Commissars and chaired conferences of the politburo of the CPSU's Central Committee. After Lenin's retirement from political activity, Kamenev was part of a troika (consisting of Zinovyev, Stalin, and himself) that was in de facto control of the country and party. Kamenev became chair of the Soviet of Labor and Defense in February 1924. From 1923 to 1926 he served as director of the Lenin Institute and also continued his journalistic work.

When Stalin's position strengthened, Kamenev went over to his opponents, joining the so-called Leningrad Opposition. At the Fourteenth Congress of the CPSU, in December 1925, he criticized the situation in the party, declaring, "Stalin cannot fulfill the role of uniter of the Bolshevik headquarters. We are against one-man rule, we are against the creation of a supreme leader." After this opposition was defeated, Kamenev was removed from his main government posts, and became the People's Commissar for Trade and, in 1926, the USSR's plenipotentiary in Italy.

Kamenev also became one of the leaders of the "united opposition," criticizing the "right-wing deviationism" of the Stalin group on the peasant question and its evaluation of international prospects. In October 1926 Kamenev was removed from the politburo and, a year later, also from the Central Committee of the CPSU. At the Fifteenth Congress in December 1927 he gave a report for the opposition and was subsequently expelled from the party and banned from Moscow. Then, six months later, he came out with a public self-criticism, was restored to the CPSU's ranks, and was named head of the Scientific and Technical Management of the Supreme Soviet of the People's Economy. Later he worked as director of the Institute of World Literature of the Academy of Sciences. In the early 1930s, though, he was expelled several times from the party.

After the assassination of Sergei Kirov, Kamenev, along with Zinovyev, was accused of having inspired this crime and was arrested on December 16, 1934. He was condemned six months later to ten years in prison in connection with the so-called Kremlin Library Matter, where some of his close relatives had worked. A year after that, at a show trial involving a mythical "united Trotsky-Zinovyev center," Kamenev was sentenced to death and was executed by firing squad on August 25, 1936. During the repression that followed his wife, Olga, who was Trotsky's sister, and two sons also perished. Kamenev was rehabilitated in 1988.

See also Bolshevism; Russian Revolution and Civil War; Trotsky, Leon; Zinovyev, Grigory.

FURTHER READING

Adibekov, G. M., E. N. Šachnazarova, and K. K. Širnija. *Organizacionnaja struktura Kominterna, 1919–1943*. Moscow: Rosspen, 1997.
"Dejateli SSSR I revoljucionnogo dviženija Rossii." In *Enciklopedičeskij slovar'*. Moscow: Granat, 1989.

ALEKSANDR I. VATLIN

Kardelj, Edvard

Edvard Kardelj (1910–79) was one of the best-known Communist figures in Yugoslavia. A Slovene, born in Ljubljana to a working family, he finished public school and then enrolled in a pedagogical faculty. He became a professional revolutionary, joining the Union of Communist Youth in 1926 and then, the same year, the Communist Party of Yugoslavia (CPYu), both of which were then underground groups. Kardelj was arrested a number of times and spent time in prison. By the middle of the 1930s he was one of the leaders of the CPYu organization in Slovenia. At the end of 1934 he was sent to Moscow, where he studied in one of the Comintern schools. Next, having demonstrated ability in what was then considered the theory of Marxism-Leninism, he was assigned to teach in similar institutions.

Returning to Yugoslavia illegally at the beginning of 1937, Kardelj began to play a significant role in the CPYu, not only as a practical organizer of party activities, but also as an ideologue and propagandist. This proved a successful combination when he entered the new overall Yugoslav leadership of the CPYu, which formed at the end of the 1930s around Josip Broz Tito. From that time on and until the end of his life, Kardelj was one of Tito's closest associates at the highest level of Yugoslav Communists, and for an extended period, particularly in the 1940s and 1950s, was even second in rank to Tito. Kardelj played an equivalent role in leading the military-political movement organized by the CPYu during the 1941–45 struggle against the Axis occupation of Yugoslavia. Then, with the triumph of this movement, he played a similar role in the hierarchy of the new Communist government that had been established upon the liberation of the country.

Of particular significance was Kardelj's role in developing the basic forms, structure, and functional mechanisms of the political system, and also of the economic organization of Yugoslavia both at the beginning, when the Communist regime was set up, and later in the subsequent phases of its existence. Up until the USSR-Yugoslav break in 1948 Kardelj's activities followed the Soviet model, adapting it to concrete conditions in Yugoslavia. But after the Soviet-Yugoslav split, Kardelj had a central function in elaborating the model of so-called self-governing socialism, which began to take shape in Yugoslavia in the early 1950s. In both periods Kardelj was an ideologue who, in his articles, reports, and speeches, provided a theoretical basis for whatever policies were being carried out, and was the leading figure in the legislative formulation of these policies, in particular, regarding the creation of all four of the constitutions that were adopted in Yugoslavia during Communist rule: in 1946, in 1953 (the so-called constitutional law), in 1963, and in 1974.

Over the course of this period of "self-governing socialism—during which the policies of the Yugoslav leadership constantly fluctuated between a tendency toward, on the one hand, greater independence of the republics, with an autonomous federated Yugoslavia, local administrative units, and economic enterprises; and on the other hand, an opposite tendency toward centralized control, which was more traditional for a Communist regime—Kardelj, who in many ways supported the first of these tendencies, was considered a proponent of liberalism. This liberalism, however, was within the framework of an authoritarian single-party Communist system with all its limitations, though the system did soften the harshness of the regime.

Playing a key role in the foreign policy of the Yugoslav Communist leadership as well, Kardelj provided the fundamental ideological basis for the Yugoslav policy of nonalignment, propagated in the 1950s and the beginning of the 1960s, in which Yugoslavia itself had a leading position in the movement of nonaligned states.

Kardelj's many works, written before the Soviet-Yugoslav conflict, were purportedly ideological but actually more propagandistic in nature, and they did not depart from the usual Bolshevist postulates of the time. After the break with the USSR, Kardelj's works belonged to a genre that Milovan Djilas characterized as "a pragmatic mix of Leninism and Social Democracy."

See also Djilas, Milovan; Nonalignment; Soviet-Yugoslavia Break; Tito, Josip Broz.

FURTHER READING

Kardelj, E. *Put nove Jugoslavije.* Belgrade: Kultura, 1946.
———. *Problemi naše socijalističke izgradnje.* Books 1–7. Belgrade: Kultura, 1954–68.
———. *Izbor iz dela.* Vols. 1–7. Belgrade: Komunist, 1979.
———. *Reminiscences: The Struggle for Recognition and Independence of the New Yugoslavia, 1944–1957.* London: Blonds and Briggs, 1982.

LEONID JA. GIBJANSKIJ

Katyn Massacre

On September 1, 1939, Hitler's Germany invaded Poland. On September 17, by an agreement with Berlin, units of the Red Army crossed the Soviet-Polish frontier. Within a matter of days these units occupied a territory specified by a protocol in the Ribbentrop-Molotov Pact as belonging to the Soviet sphere of interest. Poland as a state ceased to exist.

In the course of the so-called liberation marches into western Belarus and western Ukraine, some 240,000 Polish servicemen were taken captive by the Soviets. There were not enough camps, food, clothing, or drinking water to support such a large number of people, however. As a result, in October of that year, by a decision of the politburo of the Central Committee of the Communist Party of the Soviet Union (CPSU), enlisted men and younger officers who were residents of the territories just annexed by the USSR were quartered in private homes, and the same two categories who were residents of the central Polish areas were handed over to Germany. About 40,000 prisoners remained in Soviet captivity. Some 8,500 Polish officers were maintained in the Kozelsky and Starobelsky camps, and about 6,500 Polish police officers were housed in the Ostashkovsky camp. About 25,000 enlisted personnel and noncommissioned officers worked on the construction of the Novograd-Volynsky-Lvov highway and in the Krivoy Rog mines. It soon became clear to the People's Commissariat for Internal Affairs (NKVD) that it had not succeeded in breaking the will of the officers and police in the these three camps to fight for the restoration of Polish sovereignty.

After the reannexation of territories assigned to Poland by the Treaty of Riga of 1921, concluded in the aftermath of the Soviet-Polish war, Cheka operational groups conducted "cleanups" of "socially alien" or "counterrevolutionary" elements. This resulted in the further incarceration of more than 10,000 Poles.

During the first days of December 1939, the politburo of the CPSU's Central Committee sanctioned the arrest of all registered Polish officers along with the massive deportation in February 1940 of "settlers" (servicemen who had been rewarded for their military exploits in the 1920 campaign with allotments of land in the eastern territories which had been attached to Poland in 1921) and their families—a total of some 138,000 people. At this time a

brigade of workers of the central apparatus of the Soviet NKVD was sent to the Ostashkovsky camp. They were given the task of formalizing accusations against the whole Ostashkovsky contingent so that they then could be handed over to the Special Conference of the NKVD. By February 1, 1940, the investigation of the Polish policemen was complete, and by the end of February the Special Conference had already decided six hundred cases. The police officers were sentenced to three to eight years of imprisonment in a camp on Kamchatka. Investigative brigades were also sent to both the Kozelsky and Starobelsky camps, but they were not given the task of preparing cases for the Special Conference. At the end of February, Lavrenty Beria suspended the Special Conference's investigation of the police officers. He had a long talk with Stalin. It was apparently precisely at that time that a cardinally different decision was made about the fate of the Polish military and police officers.

Stalin's hatred of the Poles, engendered by the Soviet defeat in the 1920 war with Poland, grew even stronger in the 1920s and 1930s, when Poland was regarded as an outpost of imperialism and as a "cordon sanitaire" against the USSR. Moscow watched Berlin's efforts to induce Warsaw toward common action against the USSR with unease. Then, when Poland linked itself closely to London and Paris, rejecting the postwar guarantees of the Soviet Union, Stalin's enmity toward its western neighbor only grew stronger. He began to regard Poland as an active participant in a western coalition attempting to obstruct the division of Soviet and German spheres of influence. The "supreme leader" was even more angered by the actions of the Polish government in exile. The cabinet of General Władysław Sikorski promoted a liberation movement for Poles in the western areas of the Belarusian and Ukrainian Socialist Republics. It proposed the removal of the USSR from the League of Nations and insisted on the active participation of the Polish military in an expeditionary force being prepared to go to Finland. It also was keen on bringing England and France into a war against the USSR.

The "Winter War," begun by Moscow against Finland on November 30, 1939, had an effect on Soviet-German relations as well. The Hitler leadership became convinced that the USSR was weakly prepared for war and began to move troops toward the Soviet frontiers. The Stalin leadership hurried to take measures to strengthen the security of the border regions. Cleansing these border areas of "unreliable elements" was also important in connection with the upcoming elections to the Supreme Soviet of the USSR, scheduled for the end of March.

On March 2, 1940, the politburo of the CPSU's Central Committee, pressed by Beria and Khrushchev, rendered a decision titled "On the Defense of Our National Borders in the Western Regions." In addition to the resettling of all residents living in an eight-hundred-meter strip along the borders, it was decided to deport 25,000 families of the captured Polish military and police officers—and also the ordinary inmates of prisons in the western areas of Ukraine and Belarus—to northern Kazakhstan for ten years. On the next day, March 3, Beria sent Stalin a note proposing that the heads of those families subject to deportation be executed by firing squad. The supreme leader signed the document and wrote on it in his own hand, "For (i.e., I'm for the proposal)." Politburo members Vyacheslav Molotov, Anastas Mikoyan, and Kliment Voroshilov countersigned the note, and Beria's proposals were also approved by Mikhail Kalinin and Lazar Kaganovich. On March 5, 1940, the politburo of the CPSU's Central Committee rendered a decision, which read as follows: "1) the files of 14,700 prisoners of war—former Polish officers, officials, landowners, police officers, intelligence officers, gendarmes, osadniks (settlers) and prison guards; and 2) the files of 11,000 ordinary prisoners arrested and now housed in prisons in the western regions of Ukraine and Belarus . . . shall be given special treatment, with the extreme punishment—death by firing squad—to be meted out."

Preparations for the execution of the imprisoned officers, police, and ordinary prisoners as well as the deportation of their families began literally on the day after the decision. The military and police officers were forced to reveal their families' addresses for the purpose of their upcoming deportation. From March 7 to March 15, meetings were held with workers of the central apparatus of the NKVD, the NKVD administrations of the Kalinin, Smolensk, and Kharkov regions, and of others as well. Information was gathered about prisoners of war whose death by firing squad was decreed by the troika of Merkulov, Kobulov, and Bashtakov.

The first lists of war prisoners to be sent to their executions were received by the camps on April 3–5 and by the prisons on April 20. These lists included 97 percent of all the military and police officers. The execution orders were drawn up not on the basis of whom to shoot but rather of whose lives should be spared. Only 395 war prisoners survived. Some were of interest to Soviet intelligence, others were bearers of important information, and still others were German nationals about whom the German embassy and Lithuanian legation had inquired. Some were not officers at all but simply operational agents or employees of ordinary penal organs.

During April and May 1940, 21,964 persons were executed: 8,348 military officers, 6,311 police officers, and 7,305 ordinary prisoners. The bodies of the officers from the Kozelsky Camp were tossed into eight graves in the Katyn Forest, about fifteen kilometers from Smolensk. The bodies of the officers from the Starobelsky Camp were interred in a forest park zone near Kharkov. The bodies of the policemen from the Ostashkovsky Camp were buried near the settlement of Mednoye in the Kalinin (now the Tver) region. Mednoye was never even occupied by German troops. The families of those shot—more than 66,000 people—were deported in the middle of April to northern Kazakhstan, where on instructions from Moscow, they were accorded neither living quarters nor work. Their mortality rate, especially among the children, was extraordinarily high.

The execution of almost 22,000 Poles was kept in the strictest secrecy. Their fate was not revealed either to their families, to the Red Cross, or to Sikorski's government in exile.

German authorities found out about the graves of the Polish officers in Katyn in 1942, but at the time had no interest in them. After the defeat of the Wehrmacht at Stalingrad, though, the Nazis attempted to use the Katyn massacre to undermine the unity of the anti-Fascist coalition. On April 13, 1943, German radio informed the world about the mass burial of Polish officers near Smolensk. Two days later Joseph Goebbels wrote in his diary: "The Katyn affair is becoming a colossal political bomb, yet one which in the present circumstances has not emitted a single blast. Even though we've been exploiting the issue with all the arts at our command."

The USSR's allies in the anti-Hitler coalition divined the goal of the Hitler leadership and did everything within their power to play down the Katyn massacre. Yet the pain felt by the Poles did not permit them to be silent. The Sikorski government appealed to the International Red Cross to investigate the slaughter of its officers. Berlin turned to this organization with the same appeal. The USSR leadership accused the Polish government in exile of plotting with the Hitlerites and immediately severed diplomatic ties.

As time went on, the Kremlin made unbelievable efforts not only to cover up the truth about the Katyn crime but, if that proved too difficult, to at least lay it at Hitler's door. At the end of September 1943, when the Soviet troops liberated Smolensk, special units of the NKVD entered the Katyn Forest and cordoned off its territory. Their operatives arrested hundreds of collaborationists and, threatening them with hanging, were able to extort false testimony from them. When the well-known neurosurgeon Nikolay Burdenko arrived in Smolensk on a mission from the Extraordinary State Commission for the Investigation of German-Fascist Crimes, he was long prohibited, on direct orders from Molotov, from investigating the Katyn affair. Only after three and a half months, by a decision of the politburo of the CPSU's Central Committee on January 13, 1944, did the Special Commission for Investigation of Hitler's Crimes in the Katyn Forest come into being, with Burdenko at its head. Molotov, with Beria's consent, proposed including in the commission the chair and another member of the Central Directorate of the Union of Polish Patriots, which had been created in Moscow. These two persons, Wanda Wasilewski and Bolesław Drobner, however, were personally deleted from the ranks of the commission by Stalin.

The members of the Special Commission arrived in Smolensk on January 18, 1944, and by January 24 had already approved a report. The document was based on an in-depth account signed by persons who had headed the Katyn massacre—the people's commissar for state security, Vsevolod Markulov, and the deputy people's commissar for foreign affairs, Sergey Kruglov. At the Nuremberg trials, the Soviet leadership attempted to obtain a confirmation of the conclusions of the Burdenko Committee by the authority of the International Military Tribunal, but the tribunal refused to accept its evidence. The Katyn execution did not figure in the tribunal's verdicts.

At the height of the Cold War the U.S. Congress formed a commission, headed by Ray J. Madden, to investigate the Katyn affair. The USSR hurried to file a note of protest. Similar notes were sent to Western countries in the 1970s and 1980s as well. And every newly elected general secretary of the CPSU's Central Committee familiarized himself with the March 5, 1940, decision of the politburo of the Central Committee and gave it top priority.

In pro-Soviet Poland, in spite of the threat of severe reprisals, the truth about Katyn was passed by word of mouth. And the Poles in emigration kept gathering fragmentary evidence about the Katyn crime. Adam Moszyński, by dint of titanic efforts, compiled a list of the executed military and police officers. In 1948, a collection of materials titled *A Documentary Basis for the Katyn Crime* was published. Various reminiscences of the few survivors of the Katyn slaughter came to life, including accounts by Józef Czapski and Stanisław Swianiewicz. Józef Mackiewicz, Janusz Zawodny, and Louise Fitz-Gibbon that contributed major studies of the Katyn massacre. It was not until 1990, though, that the first document on the subject was published from Soviet archives.

International public opinion led by Great Britain, the United States, Sweden, and other countries began demanding renewed investigations of the Katyn affair, and argued for the disclosure of documents regarding the Polish military and police officers.

Beginning in 1981, the subject of Katyn began to be actively raised in Poland by the Solidarity movement. In the second half of the 1980s the controversy hit the pages of the press, television screens, and the radio. Official Warsaw was soon forced to confront Mikhail Gorbachev with the question of finding the truth about the Katyn crime. In 1987, a bilateral party commission was formed to investigate gaps in history, and it included the extensive "expertise" of the Burdenko Commission's reports in its deliberations. Still, the Soviet representatives received no authorization to cast any doubt on the authenticity of this document.

Alexandr Yakovlev, who supervised the work of the Soviet-Polish commission, wrote: "Prolonged investigative dawdling began. The Polish side of the joint commission was putting pressure on G. Smirnov [director of the Institute of Marxism-Leninism], and he, in turn, called me and asked me to help him in the search for documents. Every time I approached Mikhail Sergeevich, his response to my repeated questions was a simple 'Well, just look for them, then!' . . . It went on like that for quite a while. But at last some of this fog was penetrated. Sergey Stankevich came up to me and told me that a historian named N. S. Lebedeva, while working on documents regarding escort trains, had unexpectedly discovered information about Katyn."

Finally, in spite of the politburo's negative stance, Yakovlev received unofficial consent to open things up, and the basic results of Natalya Lebedova's investigation were published in the weekly *Moscow News*. Then, almost three weeks later, on April 13, TASS published a statement laying responsibility for the Katyn massacre at the door of NKVD organs.

On November 3, 1990, the president of the USSR issued an order to the Soviet Union's chief public prosecutor enjoining him to investigate the criminal matter of the death of 15,000 Polish military and police officers. This investigation lasted fourteen years. In 2004 the case was finally completed, and a decision was made to transfer all the materials, once they had been declassified, to the Polish side. Even so, the Office of the Military Prosecutor, which had been handed the case, never published the results of the investigation on its own.

In 2000, cemetery complexes were set up in Katyn, Mednoye, and Kharkov to memorialize the Polish military and police officers. As of 2006, though, no churchyard cemeteries had been found in either Ukraine or Belarus, where the ashes of the ordinary prisoners, shot on Stalin's orders in April and May 1940, might be interred.

The last volume of a joint four-volume publication of the Katyn documents, to be issued by decision of the presidents of Russia and Poland, is being prepared, and a single-volume work based on the documents is being compiled at Yale University in the United States.

The Katyn massacre was a crime against the world. The Soviet attack on Poland in September 1939 was a military crime. The execution of some 22,000 military prisoners and peaceful citizens along with the deportation of more than 320,000 Poles from the territories annexed by the USSR, including the families of the executed officers, police, and ordinary prisoners, were crimes against humanity.

See also Borders; Deportation of Nationalities in the USSR; Ethnic Cleansing; Molotov-Ribbentrop Pact; Polish-Soviet War; Sovietization.

FURTHER READING

Lebedeva, N. S. *Katyn: prestuplenie protiv čelovečestva*. Moscow: Progress-Kultura, 1994–96.

———, ed. *Katyn. Mart 1940–Sentjabr 2000. Rasstril. Sud by zivych. Echo Katyni. Dokumenty*. Moscow: Izdatelstvo Ves Mir, 2001.

Materski, W., ed. *Katyn: Documents and Materials from the Soviet Archives Turned over to Poland on October 14, 1992*. Warsaw: Institute of Political Studies, Polish Academy of Sciences, 1993.

Materski, W., N. S. Lebedeva, B. Woszczyński, and N. Petrosova, eds. *Katyn: Dokumenty zbrodni*. 3 vols. Warsaw: Trio, 1995–2001.

Pichon, R. G., and A. Gejstor, eds. *Katyn. Plenniki neob javlennoj vojny. Dokumenty i materialy*. Moscow: Mezdunarodnij fond "Demokratija," 1997.

Zaslavsky, V. *Class Cleansing: The Massacre at Katyn*. New York: Telos, 2008.

NATALJA S. LEBEDEVA

Kautsky, Karl

Karl Kautsky (1854–1938), the most important socialist theorist during the years of the Second International, founded *Neue Zeit*, the most important socialist journal of the time. He stood out because he intended to select a set of principles from Marx's works that could help guide the actions of the workers' movement during the new era of mass Socialist parties. Convinced that socialism was a goal rooted in the movement of history, and that Socialist parties, utilizing the possibilities democracy offered, should tend to the organizational and political development of the proletariat within capitalist society, in view of the moment when they would be able to take power and transition to a new order, Kautsky opposed both the revisionist aims of Eduard Bernstein and the radical impulses coming from those who favored more resolute mass actions, such as Rosa Luxemburg. The outbreak of World War II and collapse of the Second International delivered a hard blow to the plausibility of his historical perspective, and the authority and prestige he still enjoyed never reached the peaks of the preceding period.

Kautsky in any case had a leading role within the European socialist milieu in refuting communism starting in 1918. Already one of Lenin's favorite targets during the war (Lenin devoted special care in attacking his "ultra-imperialism" theses, the hypothesis that capitalism, looking for more extensive economic areas to control than those available within the national state, would seek to establish forms of international collaboration), he began to take the polemical initiative himself, devoting many essays to a critique of the Bolshevik revolution. In his estimation Bolshevism's original sin consisted in forcing the laws of economic development: The reckless decision to attempt the transition to socialism in a backward country, where the conditions did not exist to ensure the revolution would obtain the consensus of the majority of the population, necessarily resulted in the despotic outcome of Lenin's experiment. With more forcefulness than before the war, when confronted with the Soviet Russian example of dictatorship of the proletariat, Kautsky argued for the indivisible nature of socialism and democracy, and rejected the hypothesis of resorting to revolutionary violence, accusing those who invoked it as an alternative to the democratic conquest of consensus—especially the parties of the Communist International—of wanting to substitute an arbitrary and artificial act to the necessarily process-bound maturing of the conditions for the passage to socialism.

In the mid-1920s, Kautsky's position became even more rigid. He contended that Socialists should not be prejudicially hostile to possible popular revolts against Communist power in the USSR; it would therefore be wrong to designate them as counterrevolutionary, since the Soviet regime—an expression of a minority that had taken control of the state apparatus—did not represent a revolutionary or proletarian power, and was not even a perhaps lamentable variant thereof, one toward whom Socialists should feel obligations of solidarity. Kautsky joined his ideal condemnation of communism with the prognostication that the Communist experiment would fail, which he repeated even after Joseph Stalin embarked on his course of accelerated industrialization, because he did not believe in the possibility of economic progress founded on terror.

Having taken up residence in Austria in 1924, he remained there until 1938; in 1935, as a precaution against the dictatorial regime that had come to power the previous year, headed by Engelbert Dollfuss, he also acquired Czech citizenship. After the *Anschluss* he spent his last days in Holland. The crisis of democratic institutions in various European countries and advance of various forms of fascism did not lead him to abandon his belief that the Socialists would only come to power by democratic means, and that they should never renounce the ideal of a democratic organization of society. On the basis of these principles, he rejected the hypothesis of a political collaboration between Communists and Socialists in the struggle against fascism. He also used his last energies to oppose the position of the left-wing segments of European socialism, whose highest theoretical expression was to be found in the work of Otto Bauer, who argued that the failure of reformist policies was a reason to reconsider the possibility of a revolutionary conquest of power and the establishment of a "new" socialist democracy, prepared by a transitional phase of revolutionary dictatorship.

See also Bauer, Otto; Dictatorship of the Proletariat; Imperialism; Social Democracy; Socialist International.

FURTHER READING

Panaccione, A. *Kautsky e l'ideologia socialista*. Milan: Angeli, 1987.

Salvadori, M. L. *Kautsky e la rivoluzione socialista, 1880–1938*. Milan: Feltrinelli, 1976.

Waldenberg, M. *Il papa rosso Karl Kautsky*. Rome: Editori Riuniti, 1980.

LEONARDO RAPONE

Kennan, George Frost

When George Frost Kennan (1904–2005) was born, Theodore Roosevelt was in the White House and still only in his first administration. A very different kind of Republican regime chose to honor the venerable Kennan on his hundredth birthday in February 2004 by linking the containment policy he is supposed to have authored with the continuing operation in Iraq. Kennan had actually criticized in print that venture as imprudent and wrongheaded. It was probably the last in a series of seemingly endless quarrels during his enormously long life as a policymaker, historian, critic of culture, writer of note, and public intellectual—one of the most prominent men of the 20th century in the United States.

Many of these controversies have indeed concerned what Kennan meant exactly by "containment" when he articulated the idea in 1947 and the extent to which the ensuing grand policy in fact followed his concept; but his views on a whole range of issues, views that have sometimes coincided with those of the Left, sometimes those of the Right, have always occasioned debate and sometimes scorn. Thus Kennan was one of the first within the U.S. mainstream in the 1950s to criticize the Cold War posture he himself was said in no small measure to have created.

Before World War II, during the early stages of his diplomatic career in Berlin, Moscow, and Prague, Kennan developed a negative view of the Soviet regime as essentially illegitimate and ineligible for international society. He found deeply discomfiting the wartime alliance with the Soviet Union and advocated privately that the Western powers cease cooperation with Moscow and retain the armistice division of Europe. For this negative policy, generated by exasperation with what Kennan took to be Rooseveltian naiveté, there was of course no support up to the end of the war. A year later, the atmosphere had changed dramatically. In February 1946, Kennan fired off an extended, blistering assessment of the Soviet position and foreign policy in the world, a document that has since become known as the "long telegram." Brilliantly and seductively composed, it had a powerful impact internally on senior officials in Washington. Developed in the pseudonymous "X article" in the July issue of *Foreign Affairs* in 1947, Kennan's thesis boiled down to four propositions: (1) that Moscow, for various historical, ideological, and geographical reasons, was a regime defined by its deep insecurity and thus in need, paradoxically, of foreign enemies to preserve its own character and power; (2) that it was an inherently expansionist regime committed "fanatically" to the destruction of all power not under its own control and so entirely opposed to every compromise with such rivals; (3) that nothing could be done from the outside for the foreseeable future to change the nature of the regime and its internal necessities; and (4) that the outward thrust of this regime and its auxiliaries could be "contained" because the West was far stronger, and if it only recognized the realities of the situation and refused to engage in any deals unless from a position where the Western position could be dictated to the Soviets, then the problem was manageable and eventually the regime would in fact change.

Kennan thought that the Soviet threat was total and that the countereffort, too, had to be total; and thus he included military means and impressive shows of potential force. Still, he believed that the conflict, if properly conducted, could be carried out by means short of war, politically and by covert action.

In essence, then, Kennan was saying that the United States and the West should cease normal diplomacy until the Soviet Union, for its part, ceased being the Soviet Union. This view was to be the over-determinant ingredient of the emerging Cold War. It had several serious shortcomings. For one thing, Kennan was conflating hostility to the outside with inherent expansionism. He was also wrong about compromises since Moscow had engaged in a whole series of such deals virtually from the inception of the Bolshevik government. He was unable, moreover, to conclude whether Moscow really was a revolutionary Marxist regime. Indeed, the very place of doctrine and ideology in its outlook was unclear to Kennan. Most important, his analysis of Soviet policy (or "conduct") was entirely derived from the domestic character of the regime: external events were meaningless or only secondary. The procedural "objectification" of the Soviet regime thus left the account without any explanation for Moscow's many actual changes of policy. It was as though the rise of fascism in the 1930s had had no real effect on Soviet foreign policy and the move toward interstate alliances. Kennan did not adhere to such absurdities; but he considered such shifts mere tactics, surface actions hiding the fundamental, unalterable realities he thought he had identified. The practical effect of his analysis was to devalue all attempts at genuine agreement with Moscow as delusional and counterproductive. Thus Kennan laid the ideological foundations for U.S. refusal to sort out the postwar issues, chiefly in Europe, that needed urgent resolution: the foundations for unilateral U.S. restoration of Western Europe and the seemingly permanent division of the continent.

This Kennan quickly realized. One reason was that Walter Lippmann, the powerful columnist, immediately took him to task in the fall 1947 precisely for forgetting about the need for traditional diplomacy and negotiation, if for nothing else then in order to get the Red Army out of Central Europe. Having grasped the validity of Lippmann's criticisms and, moreover, sensed the danger of simplistic analyses of the Soviet Union, Kennan in 1948 began gradually to develop a critical stance. He did this from one of the most powerful policymaking positions in the State Department. For in the spring of 1947, he had become head of the Policy Planning Staff instituted by the new secretary of state George Marshall. Five events in the first part of 1948 pushed Kennan to change: the beginning of a Western military alliance system, the Prague Coup, the defeat of the Left in Italy, the successful airlift against the Berlin blockade, and, finally, Tito's split with Stalin. Kennan concluded that the political stability of Western Europe and especially Germany was better than he had feared, and that, inversely, Moscow had suffered grievously across the board, not least by Tito's defection. More profoundly, he realized that a militarized version of the Marshall Plan would render the division of Europe permanent as there would be no way for Moscow safely to relax its rule over Eastern Europe. Thus he proposed a plan for disengagement and the possible neutralization of Germany. He also developed a grander strategic vision based on the premise that, in effect, there were only four regions of the world that, materially, could pose a military threat to the United States and that only one of these, the Soviet Union, was actually hostile; therefore, as long as none of the other three (the United Kingdom and its auxiliaries, continental Europe, and Japan) fell away, one might safely ignore much of the rest of the world, including the rapidly disintegrating Nationalist regime in China.

However, it was easy to see containment as essentially a negative activity, a project of holding the line while the other side had the power of initiative, the choice of where and when to attack. From here it was not a long step to argue that containment was really passive; and to be passive in the face of a limitlessly evil empire was to have fallen into the deepest moral turpitude. In 1949, the dual setbacks of Communist success in China and the Soviet atomic bomb created particular problems in this regard.

Thus was born the supposedly active counterprinciple of "rollback," the destruction of enemy power itself. Though it became a Republican slogan in the early 1950s, it was already present in veiled form in NSC 68, the global policy document that the State Department articulated in winter and spring 1950, much to Kennan's chagrin. In terms of concrete policy, there was not much difference between containment and rollback, the latter being on the whole practically impossible. As an idea and project, however, it fit much better the crusading Cold War spirit of eradicating evil. By then, Kennan had become increasingly marginalized and he would in fact leave the State Department de facto that year for secluded study at Robert Oppenheimer's new Institute for Advanced Study in Princeton. The Korean War momentarily brought him back but, apart from ambassadorial posts in Moscow in 1952 (a disaster) and Belgrade in the early 1960s, Kennan from then on was primarily to be a public intellectual and a historian.

Kennan became perhaps the sharpest critic within the establishment of Washington's Cold War policy and the "intellectual straightjacket" he thought marked it. He was profoundly troubled by the focus on all things nuclear and the escalating arms race it entailed, a position he had expressed already within the State Department in his opposition to the development of the hydrogen bomb. He also proposed mutual withdrawal from Germany and subsequent neutralization so as to allow the easing of tensions and possible easing of Soviet rule in Eastern Europe as well. As this view generated a savagely dismissive response from the orthodox establishment, Kennan once again became intensely critical of the political system and the mass culture of consumption in the United States. In denouncing McCarthyism earlier in the decade, he was especially critical of the silence and timidity of the establishment.

It is important to understand that Kennan offered these views as a conservative, a radical conservative in the U.S. context but a conservative nonetheless. His refusal, for instance, to accept hackneyed Cold War binaries and divisions of the world into good and evil, his refusal of universals in the name of particularity, meant too that he was able to denounce third world nationalism while defending, in some cases, colonial rule. In the 1960s, when he was criticizing the war in Vietnam Kennan was also an adamant supporter of Portugal's empire in Africa and opposed to any action against the white apartheid regime in South Africa. His disdainful view of the conformist culture of the 1950s, specifically among students, was replaced in the 1960s by vitriolic rebuke of the student rebellion, his desire for diversity having now become a desire for order. Throughout, however, he retained his favorable stance on rapprochement with the Soviet Union, which, by the time of Khrushchev's thaw in the late 1950s, he had begun to look upon as a regime in transition toward authoritarianism, a form of rule he considered by Western standards unremarkable. He also retained his consistently strong advocacy of nuclear disarmament, becoming in the 1980s a formidable critic of Ronald Reagan's buildup. Henceforth he was in strong sympathy with Mikhail Gorbachev's reform program.

See also Anticommunism; Cold War; Containment; Marshall Plan.

FURTHER READING

Gellman, B. *Contending with Kennan: Toward a Philosophy of American Power.* New York: Praeger, 1984.

Harper, J. L. *American Visions of Europe: Franklin D. Roosevelt, George F. Kennan, and Dean G. Acheson.* Cambridge, UK: Cambridge University Press, 1994.

Hixson, W. L. *George F. Kennan: Cold War Iconoclast.* New York, Columbia University Press, 1989.

Kennan, G. F. *American Diplomacy, 1900–1950.* Chicago: University of Chicago Press, 1951.

———. *Around the Cragged Hill: A Personal and Political Philosophy.* New York: Norton, 1993.

———. *At a Century's Ending: Reflections 1982–1995.* New York: Norton, 1996.

———. *Fateful Alliance: France, Russia and the Coming of the First World War.* New York: Pantheon, 1984.

———. *Memoirs, 1925–1950.* Boston: Little, Brown, 1967.

———. *Memoirs, 1950–1963.* Boston: Little, Brown, 1972.

———. *Nuclear Delusion: Soviet-American Relations in the Atomic Age.* New York: Pantheon Books, 1982.

———. *Realities of American Foreign Policy.* Princeton, NJ: Princeton University Press, 1954.

———. *Russia, the Atom and the West.* New York: Harper, 1958.

———. *Russia and the West Under Lenin and Stalin.* Boston: Little, Brown, 1961.

———. *Sketches from a Life.* New York: Pantheon, 1987.

———. *The Decline of Bismarck's European Order: Franco-Prussian Relations, 1875–1890.* Princeton, NJ: Princeton University Press, 1979.

Kennan, G. F., and J. Lukacs. *George F. Kennan and the Origins of Containment, 1944–1946: The Kennan-Lukacs Correspondence.* Columbia: University of Missouri Press, 1997.

Mayers, D. *George Kennan and the Dilemmas of US Foreign Policy.* New York: Oxford University Press, 1988.

Miscamble, W. D. *George F. Kennan and the Making of American Foreign Policy, 1947–1950.* Princeton, NJ: Princeton University Press, 1992.

Russell, R. L. *George F. Kennan's Strategic Thought: The Making of an American Political Realist.* Westport, CT: Westview Press, 1999.

Stephanson, A. *Kennan and the Art of Foreign Policy.* Cambridge, MA: Harvard University Press, 1989.

ANDERS STEPHANSON

KGB

The Soviet intelligence agency was also known, in the course of its history by a variety of other acronyms: VCK, GPU, OGPU, NKVD, NKGB, MGB, and finally KGB. On December 20, 1917, the Extraordinary Pan-Russian Commission, known as Cheka (Vserossijskaja crezvycajnaja komissija, or VCK), was formed as part of the Council of People's Commissars. Its principal duties were the repression of sabotage and counterrevolutionary crimes, and the incarceration of political enemies. Two other functions developed gradually and became strategically important: securing the means of transportation, and border control. Feliks Dzerzhinsky was nominated to head the Cheka. Initially the Cheka was created only as a temporary institution: once political enemies had been liquidated and the regime had consolidated its power, it was supposed to be dissolved, and for this reason its powers were never clearly and officially defined.

Absent a legal frame of reference, and with the exacerbation of the civil war, which subjected the new leadership group to severe political pressures, the Cheka widened its sphere of influence in the fight against opponents as well as the organization of repression and terror. Its role in the administration of political prisoners also gradually increased in significance because of the inability of the People's Commissariat for Justice (Narodnyj komissariat *justicii*, or NKJu) to manage its prisoners. With a decree in July of 1918 the NKJu prisons were transferred to the Cheka, which was also authorized to create a network of labor camps. At the beginning of 1922 there were about fifty thousand people detained in the Cheka's camps.

The end of the civil war, Red Army's demobilization, introduction of the New Economic Policy, and strengthening of Soviet power seemed incompatible with the continued existence of a political police that employed terroristic methods. In February 1922 the State Political Administration (Gosudarstvennoe politiceskoe upravlenie, or GPU) took the Cheka's place; it was overseen by the People's Commissariat for Internal Affairs (Narodnyj komissariat vnutrennych del, or NKVD) of the Russian Federation. The political police thus lost its temporary and extrajudicial nature along with its freedom to carry out summary proceedings, and its functions were limited to the investigative sphere. But at the same time it was an integral part of the state apparatus, and with the birth of the Union of Soviet Socialist Republics, it became a federal body, and the Unified State Political Directorate of the Council of Commissars of the USSR (Ob'edinennoe gosudarstvennoe politiceskoe upravlenie pri SNK SSSR, or OGPU), directly overseen by the Council of People's Commissars, was created in November 1923.

The OGPU, whose principal duties continued to be the repression of counterrevolutionaries, the protection of railroad and maritime transportation, and border security, was also in charge of the detention of political prisoners (members of the Socialist, Menshevik, and Social Revolutionary parties), counterrevolutionaries (czarist functionaries, members of the prerevolutionary parties, the White Army, and the clergy), and criminals. To this end the OGPU administered prisons in Moscow, Petrograd, and Suzdal', and the special-purpose camps of the North (Severnye lagerja osobogo naznacenija) in Arkhangel'sk Province. After February 1922, the government put the archipelago of the Solovki islands in the White Sea at the GPU-OGPU's disposal so that it could transfer prisoners there. The Council of People's Commissars approved a resolution in June 1929 that contemplated the transfer of all those sentenced to more than three years' detention to OGPU-administered concentration camps, which for the occasion had been renamed work and reeducation camps (Ispravitel'no–Trudovye lagerja). This allowed the OGPU to progressively extend its labor camp network during the early 1930s. Its success led the government to consider increasingly ambitious projects to be realized with forced labor—for instance, the building of a canal between the Baltic and the White Sea.

As a consequence of repressive policies targeting the peasants, the population administered in these camps by the OGPU progressively grew between 1930 and 1934, going from 179,000 to 510,300 detainees. The OGPU occupied a key position in the collectivization and dekulakization campaigns in the countryside, leading to the deportation and arrest of hundreds of thousands of peasants, and the confiscation of their property. The problems caused by these deportations—horrific life conditions, increase in mortality and invalidity rates, mass exodus, and migrations—led to the government adopting radical measures: in May 1931, the OGPU was charged with the economic and administrative organization of those kulaks who had been deported to permanent residence locations. A network of specially created bodies (*komandature*) was created in all those regions and republics to which deportees would be sent, allowing the OGPU to exercise control over immense territories where the deportees constituted the majority of the local population. Starting in 1932 the OGPU, which had by now established absolute control of the repressive apparatus, to the Commissariats for the Interior and Justice's detriment, was also given the assignment of "filtering" and "cleaning" strategic cities and locations, like border areas, removing "extraneous" and "undesirable" elements. These police operations in railway stations, markets, and various other public places led to the exile of hundreds of thousands of people. In 1934 the number of deportees was about 1.3 million.

In July 1934 the OGPU was absorbed by the USSR's new NKVD, and Genrich G. Jagoda was nominated to head it. A Special Commission (Osoboe Sovescanie) was also added to the NKVD, with the power to sentence people who were considered "socially dangerous" to deportation and forced labor; it would soon become a key tool in Stalin's purges. During the period in which Nikolai Ezhov took Jagoda's place as head of the commissariat (November 1936–November 1938), the NKVD was mostly absorbed in organizing the Great Terror and repression that extended from the party's political opponents to all levels of the state apparatus, the Komsomol, the army, and numerous other social, economic, and national categories. About 1.5 million people were arrested in the period 1937–38, 681,692 of which were executed. Although Ezhov was the main person in charge, his activity was strictly and directly controlled by Stalin, who ultimately decided to place all responsibility for the mass terror on the NKVD. Ezhov's fall, first he was removed from his posts and then condemned to death, coincided with massive purges that were conducted within the NKVD itself.

Lavrenty Beria's ascent to head of the NKVD in November 1938, followed by the war's outbreak, led to a new phase in the expansion and consolidation of the political police and Commissariat for the Interior in the political and economic life of the country. The reorganization of the system of forced labor was one of the first measures Beria undertook in order to increase the commissariat's economic influence. The dearth of labor that the Soviet Union had to face during the conflict placed the Commissariat for the Interior, which had a great labor reserve at its disposal, in an advantageous position compared to that of other economic commissariats. Unlike other commissariats, the NKVD additionally disposed of a centralized body, the Main Camps Administration (Glavnoe upravlenie lagerej, gulag), which was able to distribute and coordinate its labor force more rationally.

During the period in which the pact with Nazi Germany was in force, leading to the occupation of eastern Poland and the Baltic states, and later during the war itself, after the victory in Stalingrad and the reconquest of those territories that had been temporarily occupied by the Germans, repression and terror were conducted energetically and systematically, thousands of people were executed, and hundreds of thousands were condemned to deportation and forced labor. Special NKVD departments worked with the army to maintain control of the new territories. The political police had an important part in the deportation of the populations of Crimea and the Caucasus, and the repression of the nationalist movements in the western Ukraine and the Baltic countries. In April 1943 the NKVD was divided into two distinct commissariats: the NKVD and the NKGB (People's Commissariat for State Security). Beria remained head of the NKVD while Vsevolod Merkulov, who had been vice commissar for the interior and was one of Beria's most trusted allies, was named head of the NKGB; in this fashion Beria maintained control of the police apparatuses. The NKGB's principal tasks were espionage and counterespionage, the organization of terror and sabotage in territories occupied by the Germans, military censorship, and the protection of party leaders and members of the government. Control of the gulag remained with the NKVD, which continued to administer the camps, colonies, and places of forced residence. NKGB agents were present in all camps to disseminate propaganda and organize a network of informers among the prisoners.

A further extension of the role and structure of the security organs occurred after the war, with the expansion of Soviet influence in Eastern and Central Europe. In May 1946, Viktor Abakumov was nominated to lead the Ministry (in March all commissariats had been renamed ministries) for State Security (Ministerstvo gosudarstvennoj bezopasnosti, or MGB), which was now also in charge of military counterespionage. The MGB supervised the creation of a political police in the satellite countries. Numerous Soviet agents integrated these new security organs, and their terroristic methods were used especially during the various waves of repression that occurred in various countries after Yugoslavia's expulsion from the Cominform in 1948. Within national borders, Abakumov dedicated himself to a series of repressive campaigns, the most significant of which was the elimination of the Jewish Anti-Fascist Committee and the so-called Leningrad affair. The insufficient results obtained in the inquiry on the Jewish Committee would eventually lead to Abakumov's arrest and his being replaced by Semen Ignat'ev in summer 1951. The inquiry was then pursued by Michail Ryumin, deputy minister in the MGB and director of the department of "special" inquiries, who in addition to successfully concluding the trial against members of the Jewish Anti-Fascist Committee would take the initiative, with Stalin's full support, in the manufacture of the "doctors' plot."

On March 5, 1953, the day Stalin died, during a joint reunion of the Plenum of the Central Committee, the Council of Ministers, and the Presidium of the Supreme Soviet, a decision was made to reunite the Ministry of the Interior (the ex-NKVD) and the MGB. Beria was nominated to head the new organ, and he also held the position of council vice president. The control that Beria exercised over the political police along with the fear that he might use it to prevail over Stalin's other potential successors were among the principal reasons for his arrest and death sentence. After his execution, in July 1953, the party undertook a series of reforms of the criminal justice system and the role of the security organs in the

country, with the aim of preventing the political police from once again prevailing on the party and resorting to terror. On March 13, 1954, a decree by the Presidium of the Supreme Soviet led to the creation of the Committee for State Security (Komitet gosudarstvennoj bezopasnosti, or KGB) under the Council of Ministers' control. Ivan Serov was nominated to head it.

The main reforms that were undertaken to protect Soviet citizens from police persecution were the introduction of new laws (May 1955) and the creation of a special department for the supervision of inquiries conducted by the security organs (April 1956), which allowed the Prosecutor's Office to control and correct the KGB's work. In December 1958 the new *Fundamentals of Criminal Law* were introduced, in which the concepts of "enemy of the people" and "counterrevolutionary crimes" were abolished, criminal sentencing could only be undertaken by courts and tribunals, and only the Prosecutor's Office had investigative powers, except for crimes such as high treason, espionage, terrorism, and sabotage. But starting in 1961 the KGB's powers started to expand, the crimes under its jurisdiction became increasingly numerous and also extended to the economic sphere.

With Leonid Brezhnev's ascent to power, the KBG's prestige and role in the political and economic life of the country grew even more, and its existence became essential to the maintenance of consensus and survival of the regime itself. The control, prevention, and repression of dissent—by fabricating judicial cases against dissidents, and then detaining them in labor camps and psychiatric hospitals—became priority functions for KGB agents inside the country.

See also Borders; Great Terror; Gulag; Red Terror; Sovietization; State, The.

FURTHER READING

Albats, E. *The State within a State: The KGB and Its Hold on Russia*. New York: Farrar, Straus and Giroux, 1994.

Andrew, C., and O. Gordievsky. *KGB: The Inside Story of Its Foreign Operations from Lenin to Gorbachev*. New York: HarperCollins, 1990.

Andrew, C., and K. V. Skorkin, eds. *The Sword and the Shield: The Mitrokhin Archive and the Secret History of the KGB*. New York: Basic Books, 1999.

Chlevnjuk, O. V. *Stalin e la società sovietica negli anni del terrore*. Perugia: Guerra, 1997.

Dziak, J. J. *Chekisty: A History of the KGB*. Lexington, MA: Lexington Books, 1988.

Jansen, M., and N. V. Petrov. *Stalin's Loyal Executioner: People's Commissar Nikolai Ezhov, 1895–1940.* Stanford, CA: Hoover Institution Press, 2002.

Knight, A. *The KGB.* Winchester, MA: Allen and Unwin, 1988.

———. *Beria, Stalin's First Lieutenant.* Princeton, NJ: Princeton University Press, 1993.

Kokurin, A., and N. V. Petrov, eds. *VChK-OGPU-NKVD-NKGB-MGB-MVD-KGB, 1917–1960: spravochnik.* Moscow: Mezhdunarodnyj fond "Demokratija," 1997.

"La police politique en Union soviétique, 1918–1953." Special issue of *Cahiers du monde russe* 2–4 (2001).

Leggett, G. *The Cheka: Lenin's Political Police.* Oxford: Clarendon Press, 1981.

Levytsky, B. *The Uses of Terror: The Soviet Secret Police, 1917–1970.* New York: Coward, McCann and Geoghegan, 1972.

Parrish, M. *Soviet Security and Intelligence Organizations, 1917–1990.* New York: Greenwood Press, 1992.

———. *The Lesser Terror.* Westport, CT: Praeger, 1996.

Petrov, N. V., and K. V. Skorkin, eds. *Kto rukovodil' NKVD, 1934–1941.* Moscow: Spravochnik, 1999.

MARTA CRAVERI

Khmer Rouge

Khmer Rouge, or "Red Khmer," the dismissive name given by Cambodia's mercurial chief of state Norodom Sihanouk (1922–) in the 1960s to all left-wing opponents of his regime, ruled Cambodia between 1955 and 1970. Later on, foreign journalists used the term in particular to define the Marxist-Leninist movement that held power in Cambodia from 1975 to 1979.

During his time in power, Sihanouk was understandably unaware of the small, clandestine Communist Party of Kampuchea (CPK), whose key leaders spent much of the period in hiding. Instead, he falsely assumed that all of his left-wing opponents were either foreigners or under the supervision and control of Vietnamese Communist cadre.

When Sihanouk was overthrown by a right-wing coup in 1970, journalists used the term "Khmer Rouge" to describe the Cambodian guerrillas, allied with the Vietnamese Communists, who were trying to topple the pro-U.S. regime of General Lon Nol. The guerrillas claimed to support Sihanouk's return to power (and convinced thousands of recruits to this effect), but their leaders, who also ran the CPK, sought to seize power for themselves and install a radical socialist regime. Because these people remained hidden and kept the party's existence a secret, many observers assumed that the Khmer Rouge was a relatively amorphous, populist movement rather than a disciplined fighting force under the day-to-day control of the CPK leaders, none of whom ever used the term Khmer Rouge to describe themselves.

When Vietnam withdrew its troops from Cambodia in 1972, the guerrillas took on almost all the fighting against the Lon Nol forces. In April 1975 they occupied the Cambodian capital, Phnom Penh. Their leaders, following plans laid many years before, swiftly set in motion one of the most radical socialist programs in world history. Within a week, they abolished money, markets, schools, monasteries, and private property. People living in cities and towns were moved forcibly to the countryside to become agricultural workers. To nonmembers, the CPK called itself Angkar Loeu (the Higher Organization), and the regime styled itself as Democratic Kampuchea (DK), without admitting its socialist affiliations. In September 1976, however, after the death of the Chinese leader Mao Zedong, the CPK's leader Pol Pot (1925–98) admitted that a Marxist-Leninist party governed the DK. A year later, just before making a state visit to China, Pol Pot delivered a four-hour speech that brought the CPK into the open and gave a detailed, laudatory history of its accomplishments. Yet journalists and many other observers continued to refer to the CPK as the Khmer Rouge. At the end of 1977, Vietnamese forces invaded eastern Cambodia in retaliation for a series of brutal DK cross-border incursions. The two countries were at war throughout 1978, in an unprecedented breach of the fraternal relations that were supposed to exist between two Communist regimes. A massive Vietnamese invasion at the end of the year drove the CPK from power and ended an especially horrific period of Cambodian history, during which over 1.7 million people, or one in five, died of malnutrition, overwork, or execution.

The term Khmer Rouge remained in use in the non-Communist world throughout the 1990s, because the movement, after abandoning its Marxist-Leninist ideology, continued to resist the Phnom Penh government. Internal factionalism and defections brought the movement to an end in 1997–98 following amnesties offered by the Phnom Penh government to leaders and followers as well as the death of Pol Pot in 1998.

See also Killing Fields; Marxism-Leninism; Pol Pot; Utopia; Vietnam War.

FURTHER READING

Becker, E. *When the War Was Over: Cambodia and the Khmer Rouge Revolution.* New York: PublicAffairs, 1986.

Chandler, D. *Brother Number One: A Political Biography of Pol Pot.* Rev. ed. Boulder, CO: Westview Press, 1999.

Jackson, K., ed. *Cambodia 1975–1978: Rendezvous with Death.* Princeton, NJ: Princeton University Press, 1989.

DAVID P. CHANDLER

Khrushchev, Nikita

The monument at Nikita Khrushchev's (1894–1971) grave in Novodevichy Cemetery was designed by Ernst Neizvestny, whom Khrushchev excoriated during one of his outbursts against the artistic intelligentsia in the winter of 1962–63. It consists of intersecting slabs of white and black stone on one of which sits a bronze head of Khrushchev. The memorial captures the contradictions that were so striking in his life and career.

Born into a humble peasant family in the southern Russian village of Kalinovka, Khrushchev received no more than two or three years of formal education in a village school. Yet, he managed not only to climb into Stalin's inner circle, but also to survive the *vozhd* (*chief*) and then to succeed him.

An accomplice in Stalin's crimes, Khrushchev denounced him in a "secret speech" to the Twentieth Party Congress in February of 1956. A true believer in Marxism-Leninism, he aimed to cleanse socialism of its Stalinist stain. But his de-Stalinization campaign began the long process of unraveling the Soviet system that culminated several decades later in 1991.

Khrushchev tried to ease East-West tensions and to restrain the arms race, but he also provoked the most dangerous crises of the Cold War in Berlin and Cuba. He meant well, and he cared about his people and country, but by the time of his ouster in 1964 he was unappreciated, even despised.

Khrushchev's rise from the humblest of origins into Stalin's inner circle is a stunning success story—provided, of course, one doesn't count the cost in blood to so many whose victimization he authorized or approved, or in which he at least acquiesced—but once he reached the top, troubles crowded in on him, in agriculture, industry, culture, foreign policy, and other areas. Khrushchev's troubles were not all of his own making. Although the Stalinist system cried out for change, as even Khrushchev's most Stalinist colleagues recognized, it also stubbornly resisted reform. So did Russia itself, which Khrushchev once described to Fidel Castro as resembling "a tub full of dough. You put your hand in it, down to the bottom, and you think you're the master of the situation. When you first pull out your hand, a little hole remains, but then, before your very eyes, the dough expands into a spongy, puffy mass. That's what Russia is like!" But Khrushchev was the author of some of his troubles: He turned out to be much more successful at seizing power than at wielding it.

Khrushchev was born on April 15, 1894. In 1908, his family moved to the mining town of Yuzovka in the Donbas. Between 1917 and 1929, he rose from the periphery of the Russian revolution to a responsible position in the Ukrainian Communist Party apparatus, head of the Central Committee's organization department. That same year he enrolled in the Industrial Academy in Moscow. A mere four years later he was party boss of the capital and of Moscow province as well, and in 1938 Stalin made him party chief of Ukraine. After serving as Stalin's political commissar on several wartime fronts, and then running Ukraine again after the war, Khrushchev was called back to Moscow in 1949 to serve as a counterweight to Georgy Malenkov and Lavrenty Beria in the Kremlin. Although he seemed the least likely of Stalin's men to succeed him, Khrushchev led a conspiracy to arrest and liquidate Beria in June 1953, and then demoted Malenkov and Vyacheslav Molotov in 1955. When the two men mounted an attempted coup against him in June 1957, Khrushchev prevailed in a marathon, eleven-day showdown. So dramatic was the duel and so decisive the victory, that the main point has seemed to be the way he won. In fact, however, the real question is how he almost managed to lose. Part of the answer was the logic of power in the Kremlin: Khrushchev's rivals were bound to try to get him before he got them. Another answer is the way Khrushchev's greatest achievement, his secret speech denouncing Stalin, helped to provoke turmoil at home, unrest in Poland, and revolution in Hungary.

Khrushchev's speech at the Twentieth Party Congress, before and after which hundreds of thousands of prisoners were finally freed from the gulag, was the bravest and the most reckless act of his life. The Soviet regime never fully recovered, and neither did he. Of course, political calculations were partly behind the speech. By denouncing Stalin, Khrushchev could cleanse his own reputation while tarnishing the reputations of rivals who had been closer to Stalin than he. But the speech also reflected Khrushchev's sense of guilt and anger about his own complicity in Stalin's crimes. As early as 1940, he privately denied to a friend from childhood that he was involved in the killing of men like Leningrad party leader Sergei Kirov, Marshal Tukhachevskii, and General Iona Yakir. Asked late in life what he most regretted, Khrushchev answered, "Most of all the blood. That is the most terrible thing that lies in my soul."

The trouble was that, as in so many of his major decisions, Khrushchev did not think through the possible consequences of his action. He did not foresee the reaction to his speech, did not prepare for the process of "de-Stalinization from below," did not equip party officials and propagandists to cope with the flood of questions and criticisms that followed when his speech was read to millions of party members and others throughout the USSR. After a while, he was forced to retreat, most explicitly in a June 30, 1956, Central Committee resolution that in effect retracted much of what he had told the Twentieth Congress. But that resolution wasn't enough to calm the unrest building in Eastern Europe, and intervention to crush the Hungarian revolution sparked more protests in the USSR. In early 1957 several hundred Soviet citizens were convicted as criminals and sentenced to prison. For the rest of his time in power, Khrushchev's stance on de-Stalinization zigzagged back and forth between encouraging and discouraging it, between supporting and attempting to restrain its champions, especially in the intelligentsia.

A "thaw" in Soviet culture began before Khrushchev's secret speech but gained momentum after it. Yet, Khrushchev feared that the thaw could become a flood. His rule was marked by tirades against liberal artists and writers (in 1957, 1959, 1962, and 1963) and a vicious 1958 campaign against Boris Pasternak after the publication in the West of *Dr. Zhivago*. But Khrushchev personally authorized the publication of works like Aleksandr Tvardovsky's long poem, "Distance Beyond Distance," Yevgeny Yevtushenko's "The Heirs of Stalin," and Solzhenitsyn's *One Day in the Life of Ivan Denisovich*. The artistic and scientific intelligentsia was a natural constituency for a leader who tied his own fate to de-Stalinization, but by

the time of his ouster, they, like many others of his former supporters, had lost faith in him.

Agriculture was another area in which failures came to overshadow Khrushchev's successes. In 1953, first Malenkov and then Khrushchev suggested agrarian reforms (increased procurement prices, reduced taxes, encouragement for individual peasant plots) that gave hope to peasants beaten down by years of Stalinist exploitation. But although practical enough to see what needed doing, and bold enough to do it, Khrushchev was ideologically opposed to the very principle that underlay his own proposals; namely, that peasants should be freed from the most severe constraints of collectivism. The crash program to develop the "virgin lands," which Khrushchev forced through the presidium against Molotov's opposition, promised rapid results by ideologically pure means; instead of bribing peasants with "individual material incentives," it beckoned idealistic youths to a great socialist "adventure." But after a fast start, virgin land harvests declined. Meanwhile, Khrushchev steadily retreated from his initial encouragement of the private plots that produced so much of the nation's milk and vegetables, launched an ill-advised corn campaign that led to its being planted in far northern regions where it could not grow, and continually reorganized the party and state agencies supervising agriculture, going so far as actually to split the party apparatus itself into industrial and agricultural branches, a move that violated the party's long-standing practice of protecting its monopoly of power by centralizing its own ranks.

In foreign policy, too, Khrushchev's record boasts successes, but also devastating failures. To China he offered extensive economic and technical assistance, along with benevolent tutelage for which he assumed Mao Zedong would be grateful. At first, the Chinese were friendly, but Khrushchev's failure to consult them before denouncing Stalin, his erratic attempts to cope with Polish and Hungarian turmoil, and his request for military concessions in 1958 led to two acrimonious summit meetings with Mao (in August 1958 and September 1959), after which he precipitously withdrew thousands of Soviet technical experts from China in 1960. The result was an open and irrevocable Sino-Soviet conflict.

Khrushchev tried to bring Yugoslavia back into the Communist camp after the Moscow-Belgrade split that Stalin had provoked in 1948. Yugoslav President Tito was eager for reconciliation, but on his own terms, which Khrushchev couldn't entirely accept, so that, as with

China, Khrushchev's embrace of a would-be ally ended in new stresses.

Khrushchev's efforts to ease Cold War tensions included several East-West summits (in Geneva in 1955, an abortive session in Paris in May 1960, a meeting with U.S. President John F. Kennedy in Vienna in 1961) and innumerable trips overseas, including a tumultuous two-week tour of the United States in September 1959, and resulted in a 1963 partial nuclear test ban. But in November 1958 he sparked a crisis in Berlin (by giving the Western powers six months to either recognize the German Democratic Republic or face abrogation of rights granted to them by the postwar Potsdam accords) without being clear in his own mind as to exactly what he wanted to accomplish, how he was going to accomplish it, or about the obstacles in his way, especially West German Chancellor Konrad Adenauer and French President Charles de Gaulle. When Sergei Khrushchev asked what his father would do if the West still rejected Soviet terms when the six-month ultimatum expired, Khrushchev answered that "he intended to act in accord with circumstances and depending on our partners' reactions." He added that he hoped to get them to negotiate. What would happen if the negotiations didn't produce results, Sergei asked. "Then we'll try something else," his father answered. "Something will always turn up."

Khrushchev's decision to send missiles to Cuba wasn't thought through either. He later claimed that the decision was "worked out in the collective leadership" because he was determined that it "should not be forced down anyone's throat." In fact, he barely consulted with Foreign Minister Anatoly Gromyko, didn't consult at all with those of his aides best equipped to predict Washington's reaction (his foreign policy assistant Oleg Troyanovsky and Ambassador to Washington Anatoly Dobrynin), and he ignored a warning not to proceed from Anastas Mikoyan, who had spent more time in the United States than any other Soviet leader. When the party presidium and the Soviet Defense Council finally met, Khrushchev led off by announcing that he favored the missile deployment, with the result that no one dared express doubts about whether the missiles could really be delivered and deployed without being detected—as indeed they were on October 14, 1962. In the end, Khrushchev agreed to withdraw the missiles from Cuba in return for an American promise not to invade Cuba (and for a secret U.S. pledge to remove American rockets from Turkey), and he interpreted this result as a triumph.

In October 1964 Khrushchev was summoned back from a Black Sea vacation to face a revolt by his Kremlin colleagues. After his ouster, he lived on under what amounted to house arrest until his death on September 11, 1964. After his death, Khrushchev became a "non-person" in the USSR, his name suppressed by his successors and ignored by most Soviet citizens until his record received a new burst of attention when Mikhail Gorbachev, who considered himself a "child of the Twentieth Congress," began a new round of reform. The black and white monument at Khrushchev's grave sums up the man in whose character so many contrasts were so starkly intertwined. He was both a true believer and a cold-eyed realist, an opportunist yet principled in his own way, fearful of war while all too prone to risk it, the most unpretentious of men even as he pretended to power and glory exceeding his grasp, complicit in great evil, yet also the author of much good. Toward the very end of his life, when he was in retirement, he said, "After I die, they will place my actions on a scale—on the one side evil, on the other side good. I hope the good will outweigh the bad."

See also Cold War; Cuban Missile Crisis; Economic Reforms; Hungarian Revolution; Peaceful Coexistence; Stalinism.

FURTHER READING

Fursenko, A. A., ed. *Prezidium TsK KPSS, 1954–1964, tom 1: Chernovye protokol'nye zapisi zasedanii, stenogrammy.* Moscow: ROSSPEN, 2003.

Khrushchev, N. S. *Khrushchev Remembers.* Trans. Strobe Talbott. New York: Little, Brown, 1970.

———. *N. S. Khrushchev: Vospominaniia—vremia, liudi, vlast',* 4 vols. Moscow: Moskovskie novosti, 1999.

Khrushchev, S. N. *Khrushchev on Khrushchev: An Inside Account of the Man and His Era.* Trans. and ed. William Taubman. Boston: Little, Brown, 1990.

———. *Nikita Khrushchev and the Creation of a Superpower.* University Park, PA: Penn State Press, 2000.

———. *Nikita S. Khrushchev: Krizisy i rakety.* Moscow: Novosti, 1994.

Leonov, N. S. *Likholet'e.* Moscow: Terra, 1997.

N. S. Khrushchev (1891–1974): Materialy nauchnoi konferentsii posviashchennoi 100-letiu so dnia rozhdeniia N. S. Khrushcheva. Moscow: Rossiski gosudarstvennyi gumanitarnyi universitet, 1994.

Taubman, W. *Khrushchev: The Man and His Era.* New York: Norton, 2003.

Taubman, W., S. Khrushchev, and A. Gleason, eds. *Nikita Khrushchev.* New Haven: Yale University Press, 2000.

WILLIAM TAUBMAN

Killing Fields

"Killing fields" is a phrase used to describe the landscape and policies of Democratic Kampuchea (DK), the Communist government that ruled Cambodia from April 1975 to January 1979. Under this utopian, Chinese-inspired regime, perhaps as many as 1.7 million Cambodians, or one in five, died of overwork, executions, malnutrition and bad treatment, and misdiagnosed diseases. The deaths occurred throughout the country, but in greater numbers in the northwest, where hundreds of thousands of former urban dwellers, known to the regime as the "new people," were relocated to the countryside and forced to become agricultural workers. Mass killings also occurred in the east of the country in 1978. In this case, the victims were suspected of being pro-Vietnamese.

The phrase killing fields came into wide use in 1984 as the title of a successful and disturbing Warner Brothers film produced by David Puttnam. *The Killing Fields* was based on an eloquent memoir written by former *New York Times* correspondent Sidney Schanberg, who had worked in Cambodia in the early 1970s. The film focused on the experiences of Schanberg's Khmer assistant, Dith Pran, who endured the horrors of the DK regime after Schanberg, like other Westerners, had been sent out of the country by the new regime. Schanberg assumed that Pran was dead. The film closed with Pran and Schanberg being reunited in Thailand in 1979.

The Killing Fields graphically portrayed the hardships, ideological rigidity, and ferocity of the DK years as well as the follies of U.S. intervention in Cambodia in the early 1970s. The tough-minded Khmer American actor who portrayed Dith Pran in the film, Haing Ngor, had been a doctor in prerevolutionary Cambodia. Like Pran, he lost several members of his family, but survived the DK era. He earned a well-deserved Oscar for his passionate, compelling performance.

When the film was being shot on Thai locations, Cambodia was occupied by the Vietnamese forces that had overthrown the DK regime at the end of 1978. Accurate information about the death count inflicted in the DK era was hard for foreigners to obtain. Nonetheless, it was clear from refugee accounts and the mass graves that were being discovered throughout the country that something truly awful had happened in Cambodia under the DK, and that the Cambodian revolution, on a per capita basis, had been one of the most murder-ous events in world history. A death count estimate of 3 million put out by the regime in Phnom Penh was higher than later evidence suggested, but by the end of the 1980s, as Cambodia opened up to scholars, sufficient data accumulated to show that regime-related deaths under the DK had certainly exceeded 1.5 million and were probably higher. In the regime's secret interrogation center in Phnom Penh, known by its code name, S-21, over 14,000 suspected enemies of the state were questioned, tortured, and put to death. The meticulous interrogation and administrative records from S-21 that have survived cover more than half a million pages. They give chilling insights into the bizarre thought world and vicious practices of the DK regime. S-21 became a Museum of Genocidal Crimes in 1980, and it has been a tourist destination ever since. The execution site for most S-21 inmates, located at Choeung Ek near the capital, where over 10,000 former prisoners were buried, was dug up in 1980 and developed by the Vietnamese as a tourist site.

Whether or not the DK regime was guilty of genocide as defined by the UN convention on genocide, promulgated in 1949, has been a controversial subject among scholars, primarily since the vast majority of victims were of the same "race" as the perpetrators, but also because it is hard to demonstrate that the DK's leaders intended so many people to die. Yet the DK policies and practices clearly had genocidal effects, and the killing fields seems an appropriate description of Cambodia in the DK era.

In support of this assertion, systematic scholarly research in the 1990s revealed that hundreds of regional prisons had existed in the DK era. Tens of thousands of people were incarcerated in these facilities, which have been compared to the system of prisons that flourished under Joseph Stalin in the Society Union. In many cases, the inmates starved to death or were executed as enemies of the state. The number of people who died in the prisons is still unclear, but the fact that the prisons were all over the country adds resonance to the phrase killing fields that will haunt the Cambodian people for many years to come.

See also Khmer Rouge; Pol Pot; Vietnam-Cambodia War.

FURTHER READING

Chandler, D. *Voices from S-21: Terror and History in Pol Pot's Secret Prison*. Berkeley: University of California Press, 1999.

Locard, H. "Le goulag Khmer Rouge, 17 Avril 1975–7 Janvier 1979." *Communisme* 47–48 (1996): 127–64.

Ponchaud, F. *Cambodia Year Zero.* New York: Henry Holt, 1978.

Schanberg, S. *The Death and Life of Dith Pran.* New York: Penguin, 1980.

Sliwinski, M. *Le Génocide Khmer Rouge: une analyse démographique.* Paris: Editions L'Harmattan, 1995.

DAVID P. CHANDLER

Kim Il Sung

Kim Il Sung (1912–94) was born in Mangyŏndae, near Pyongyang. His father was a Protestant activist and schoolteacher. In 1920 the family moved to Chinese Manchuria. Kim Il Sung attended Chinese middle and high schools, where he became involved with the Communist underground. In 1932, after a short imprisonment for political activism while a high school student, he joined the Chinese Communist guerrillas in Manchuria. Around this time he also became a member of the Chinese Communist Party and assumed his nom de guerre.

Kim Il Sung had a remarkable career as a guerrilla fighter from 1932 to 1940. His most remarkable exploit was a 1937 raid on the township of Poch'onbo, on the Korean side of the Sino-Korean border. This raid made his name relatively well known, since it marked a rare case of guerrillas operating in Korea proper.

In late 1940, amid escalating Japanese pressure, Kim Il Sung fled from Manchuria to the USSR, where he became a Red Army captain and served in the Eighty-eighth Brigade, which consisted of the former Chinese and Korean guerrillas. He spent 1942–45 in an army camp near Khabarovsk, where he and his first wife, Kim Jong-suk, had their first son, Kim Jong Il, and two other children.

In September 1945, Kim Il Sung was sent to Pyongyang, where he attracted the favorable attention of the Soviet military. He was made the head of the emerging state and party bureaucracy, with Soviet backing, in late 1945–early 1946. In 1948, Kim Il Sung was appointed the prime minister of the newly established Democratic People's Republic of Korea, and he became the formal head of the Korean Workers' Party in 1949 (for all practical purposes, he dominated the party leadership from 1946). He remained the Korean Workers' Party chair and head of the North Korean state until his death. In 1972, he quit the position of prime minister, and was instead named the president of the Democratic People's Republic of Korea.

In the late 1940s, Kim Il Sung pressed Moscow for permission to attack South Korea and thus restore the unity of Korea under Communist domination. Once this permission was secured, North Korean forces invaded the South on June 25, 1950. They came close to winning the war, but the large-scale U.S. intervention changed the situation, and only Beijing's decision to send its troops to Korea saved Kim Il Sung's government from complete collapse.

The deterioration of Sino-Soviet relations in the late 1950s provided Kim Il Sung with an opportunity to distance himself from the USSR, eventually becoming one of the most politically independent leaders of the Communist bloc. He refused to follow the Soviet de-Stalinization line and launched large-scale purges of the opposition, asserting himself as the sole supreme authority in the party and state.

Throughout the 1960s and 1970s, he skillfully maneuvered between Moscow and Beijing, extracting significant aid from both sides, yet remaining beyond their control. Kim Il Sung also attempted to restart the revolutionary movement in South, but his several schemes were not successful.

Until the late 1960s, the Democratic People's Republic of Korea's economy was growing fast, but the growth slowed down around 1970, and the country began to lag behind its major rival, capitalist South Korea. The population, however, was completely cut off from all information from the outside world; even contacts with other Communist countries were strictly limited and carefully monitored.

Internally, Kim Il Sung created a system of personality cult bordering on his deification. An elaborate system of rituals in his honor was enforced, and the intensity of the cult surpassed that of Stalin and Mao Zedong. From the early 1970s on, all adult Koreans were required to wear badges with his portrait, his portraits had to be placed in all houses, and all Koreans were expected to pay tributes to his statues on national holidays. Large amounts of money were spent on building impressive monuments to Kim Il Sung and his regime as well as maintaining a 1.1 million–strong army.

Kim Il Sung began to promote his own peculiar ideology of Juche starting in the 1960s. It combined elements of Leninism with Korean nationalism and vestiges of the earlier Confucian tradition. Gradually, Juche replaced Marxism-Leninism as the official ideology. In his domestic policy, Kim Il Sung relied on former guerrilla fighters as well as his own relatives. In 1980, after years of careful preparations, his eldest son, Kim Jong Il, was officially proclaimed heir to his father.

The collapse of the Soviet bloc in 1989–91 dealt a heavy blow to North Korea. Looking for a solution, Kim Il Sung sped up the clandestine nuclear program that had been ongoing since the 1960s, and with some success used it to extract aid from the West and South Korea. Amid a deteriorating economic situation and an international crisis, Kim Il Sung died in Pyongyang in 1994. His death was followed by the only dynastic transition of power in Communist history.

See also Korean War; Marxism-Leninism; Socialist Camp; Soviet Bloc.

FURTHER READING

Martin, B. *Under the Loving Care of the Fatherly Leader: North Korea and the Kim Dynasty*. New York: St. Martin's Press, 2004.

Suh, D.-S. *Kim Il Sung: The North Korean Leader*. New York: Columbia University Press, 1988.

ANDREI N. LANKOV

Kirov, Sergey (pseudonym for Sergei Mostrikov)

Born in Urzhum, in the Vyatka gubernatorial district, to a poor family, Sergey Kirov (1886–1934) soon lost both his parents. He studied at the Kazan' and Tomsk Technical Institutes, and graduated with a degree in engineering. Kirov joined the Russian Social Democratic Labor Party at the end of 1904, participated in the revolutionary uprisings of 1905, and was sentenced to two years in prison between 1906 and 1908. After his release, in 1909 he moved to Vladikavkaz, in northern Ossetia, where he became a popular editor of the liberal-democratic newspaper *Terek*. In 1912 he married Maria Lvovna Markus; they did not have children. Between 1911 and 1912, he was once again put on trial and incarcerated for a few months. After this period of detention he adopted the pseudonym Kirov to sign his articles.

He continued to participate in the life of the Social Democratic organizations, which were distinguished by the continued ties between the Bolshevik and Menshevik wings of the party. Kirov developed significant knowledge and a caring concern for the life and political aspirations of some important ethnic groups indigenous to the Caucasus. In 1917 he was a delegate to the regional Congress of Soviets, participated in the State Conference organized in Petrograd by the president of the provisional government, Aleksandr Kerensky, as an observer, and was also one of the delegates from the Caucasus to the Second Pan-Russian Congress of Soviets. During the civil war he demonstrated resolve in the repression of the Astrakhan revolt (1919). Kirov later served in the political section of the Red Army's Eleventh Army, which was stationed there, and was co-opted into becoming one of the leaders of the Caucasus Office of the Bolshevik Party. Here, he developed a lifelong personal and political friendship with Grigorij Ordzhonikidze.

In 1920, he became the Russian Soviet Federative Soviet Republic's ambassador to the Menshevik government of Georgia, and was a member of the Soviet delegation that prepared the peace agreement with Poland in Riga. He was active in the Sovietization by military force of Azerbaijan and Georgia. Having become secretary of the Azeri party in 1921, Kirov reorganized the Baku oil industry. He left this position in 1926, when he was summoned to join the group around Stalin that was fighting Grigory Zinovyev's influence in the Leningrad party organization. Kirov soon became its secretary, and partly due to his new position was also nominated to candidate member of the Political Office. The fact that he joined Stalin's majority in the party did not prevent him from maintaining a good personal relationship with Nikolay Bukharin. In 1934 the Seventeenth Party Congress nominated Kirov to the Central Committee's Secretariat, and in the summer of that same year he was chosen, with Andrey Zhdanov, to collaborate on Stalin's plans to reform the teaching of history.

Kirov was killed on December 1, 1934, in his Leningrad office, under circumstances that are still not clear to this day. Stalin portrayed the assassination as the work of a vast conspiracy orchestrated in the party by the leaders of the old Left opposition, and based on this interpretation, he organized a sequence of trials and executions in 1935–38 known as the Great Purge.

In his "secret speech" to the Twentieth Congress of the Communist Party of the Soviet Union, Nikita Khrushchev stated that Kirov's assassination had been the work of Stalin, who had seen Kirov as a possible political rival. This revelation seemed to bolster opinions that had been circulating both inside and outside the USSR, according to which in 1934 Kirov would have been the representative of a political line, "moderate" and liberalizing—an alternative to that represented by some of Stalin's other collaborators, such as Lazar Kaganovich and Nikolai Ezhov. A consultation of Soviet archives has not allowed researchers to gather persuasive proof regarding either the identity of those responsible or the circumstances of the assassination itself, or even Kirov's political role and profile at the end of his life.

See also Great Terror; Ordzhonikidze, Grigoriy (Sergo); Secret Speech; Stalin, Joseph.

FURTHER READING

Benvenuti, F. "Kirov nella politica sovietica." *Annali dell'Istituto Italiano per gli Studi Storici* 4 (1973–75).

Conquest, R. *Stalin and the Kirov Murder.* London: Hutchinson, 1989.

Knight, A. *Who Killed Kirov?* New York: Hill and Wang, 1999.

FRANCESCO BENVENUTI

Koestler, Arthur

Arthur Koestler (1905–83) was a journalist and writer who was, at various points in his life, a Zionist, a Communist, a Social Democrat, and a conservative. He remains most famous, however, for his fictional portrayal of the Stalinist purges in *Darkness at Noon* (1940).

Koestler was born in Budapest on September 5, 1905, to Henrik Koestler, a Jewish businessman, and Adele Zeiteles, daughter of a wealthy Prague Jewish family. His family left Hungary for Austria after Admiral Horthy's right-wing coup in 1919. Koestler completed his education at the Vienna Technische Hochschule. At the university he joined the radical Zionist student organization, the "Unitas" *Burschenschaft,* and became a disciple of Vladimir Jabotinsky. In 1925 he dropped his studies and went to work on a kibbutz in Palestine. By 1927 he had become the Ullstein press correspondent in Tel Aviv.

Koestler lost faith in Zionism and gravitated toward communism from 1929 onward. He portrayed this process in *Arrow in the Blue* (1952) as the end of a boyhood infatuation. However, Cesarani has shown how this move mirrored the trajectory of many young Jewish intellectuals in the face of growing anti-Semitism and the rise of fascism. Between 1929 and 1932, Koestler worked as a journalist in Paris and Berlin, joining the Communist Party in 1931. He was paid to write about the first of the Stalinist Five-Year Plans. What he saw began a process of doubt about the Soviet experiment, but he wrote a sympathetic account his trip in *Von weissen Nächten und roten Tagen* (1933).

During the Spanish Civil War, Willi Münzenberg, a Communist deputy from the Reichstag, persuaded him to travel to Spain to obtain proof of German and Italian involvement in the nationalist cause. On a later trip to Spain in January 1937, Koestler was captured by the nationalists in Malaga and imprisoned. He lived with the daily threat of execution and was only spared because of the intervention of the British navy, which mistakenly believed him to be a British citizen. After his case became headline news in Britain, his captors became wary of causing an international incident, and he was released in May 1937. He published his experiences in *Spanish Testament* (1937). His imprisonment had a profound effect on his political ideas. It confirmed the values that imbued his later writing, the most important of which was that "man is a reality, mankind an abstraction."

According to Koestler's later account in *The God That Failed* (1950), Marx and Freud had helped liberate him "from the rusty chains with which a pre-1914 middle-class childhood had cluttered one's mind." Although "shocked" by the reality of Russia under Soviet control, he persisted with what he saw as a "necessary lie" to combat fascism. However, his imprisonment transformed this attitude and the Molotov-Ribbentrop pact ended his "addiction to the Soviet myth."

At the time, therefore, Koestler's most famous work, *Darkness at Noon* (1940), was seen as an explanation of how someone could be swept up on the revolutionary tide, even to the point of agreeing to false accusations for the sake of the cause. For the modern reader, however, the tale of Rubashov's imprisonment endures as a philosophical attack on determinism and a terrifying account of how utopianism can overcome the dignity of the individual.

During the war, Koestler endured internment in both France and Britain in 1940, and served in the Pioneer corps of the British army from 1941 to 1942. In the early 1940s he was influenced by British Social Democrats such as Michael Foot and Aneurin Bevan. Increasingly disillusioned by what he saw as the Left's opportunism and Stalinist apologias, however, he was drawn to the Right. By the late 1940s and early 1950s he became a propagandist for the Cold War, organizing the anti-Communist Congress for Cultural Freedom in Berlin in June 1950.

This rightward drift continued until his death. In the 1970s Koestler became a member of the British Conservative Party. He committed suicide in his flat in London on March 3, 1983. The second part of Koestler's life was dominated by an obsession with parascience; especially with parapsychology, extrasensory perception, and psychokinesis. Indeed, in a letter to his biographer Iain Hamilton in 1974, he wrote, "What I resent is being labelled forever as the author of *Darkness at Noon* and other political books at the expense of the second half of my work, which to my mind is the more important." Nevertheless, it is for the moving analysis of the loss of Communist faith in Koestler's earlier books that he will be most remembered.

See also Anticommunism; Antifascism; Revolution, Myths of the; Stalinism.

FURTHER READING

Cesarani, D. *Arthur Koestler: The Homeless Mind*. London: Heinemann, 1998.

Crossman, R., ed. *The God That Failed: Six Studies in Communism*. London: Hamish Hamilton, 1950.

Hamilton, I. *Koestler: A Biography*. London: Secker and Warburg, 1982.

"Koestler, Arthur," in *The Oxford Dictionary of National Biography*. Oxford: Oxford University Press, 2004.

Koestler, A. *Spanish Testament*. London: Victor Gollancz, 1937.

———. *Darkness at Noon*. London: Macmillan, 1940.

———. *Arrow in the Blue*. London: Collins/Hamish Hamilton, 1952.

———. *The Invisible Writing*. London: Collins/Hamish Hamilton, 1954.

TOM VILLIS

Kolkhoz

"Kolkhoz" is an abbreviation for *kollektivnoe khoziaistvo*, or collective farm." The kolkhoz was the basic economic unit in Soviet socialized agriculture. In the 1920s there were three types of kolkhoz: (1) the TOZ, or *tovarishchestvo po obshchestvennoi obrabotki zemli*, an association for the joint cultivation of land in which only the land and com-plex machinery were held in common; (2) the *artel'*, an intermediary form of collective in which the land, basic inventory, and draft animals were held in common; and (3) the *kommuna*, or commune, the most comprehensive form of collective in which all property was owned collectively and members lived in a communal setting. After collectivization, the artel' became the standard form of collective farm throughout the Soviet Union.

Within the kolkhoz, members lived within family units. Each family unit had a private home, plot, and domestic livestock. Kolkhoz members farmed collectively, earning their wages in work-day units known as the *trudoden'*. The kolkhoz was required to pay extremely burdensome taxes to the state in the form of grain procurements and the provision of other agricultural produce. The kolkhoz was also required to rent complex machinery from machine and tractor stations (the MTS), paying an additional portion of its annual profits for this service. Personal income levels of kolkhoz members remained extremely low through most of the Soviet era, bolstered only by earnings from the members' private plots, which formed an important part of the Soviet market in food.

Kolkhoz members had a separate legal status through most of Soviet history. When Stalin introduced internal passports in the winter of 1932–33, kolkhoz members remained outside the passport system, officially restricted in their mobility and required to seek official permission to change work or move to the city. In practice, the kolkhoz population was fluid, declining in numbers as males and young people left the countryside for work in the cities, a trend that brought the percentage of the rural population down from roughly 85 percent 1917 to under 40 percent by the mid-1970s. Kolkhoz members were also denied pensions and other kinds of social insurance available to urban workers. This would not begin to change until the second half of the 1970s, by which time kolkhoz members were deemed eligible for passports and pensions.

Soviet scholarship generally viewed the kolkhoz as the Russian peasants' path out of poverty. Given the actual situation of the overwhelming majority of kolkhoz members, however, this view is not tenable. Nor was the kolkhoz a solution to low levels of agricultural productivity, as some Soviet scholars once suggested. Western scholars have tended to highlight the low productivity of the kolkhoz and the relative profitability of the private sector within the kolkhoz system (that is, the private plots farmed by kolkhoz members and their families), emphasizing what many consider to be the complete failure of Soviet kolkhoz agriculture. It is perhaps only in the widescale exodus *out* of the kolkhoz that we may observe improvement in the lives of kolkhoz members as they left the countryside and headed for a better life in the city. Yet the resistance of kolkhoz members to privatization and de-collectivization efforts from the late 1980s should prompt scholars to reevaluate the meaning of the kolkhoz for its members.

See also Agrarian Question; Collectivization of the Countryside; Five-Year Plans; Peasants in the USSR.

FURTHER READING

Davies, R. W. *The Industrialisation of Soviet Russia,* vol. 1, *The Socialist Offensive, 1929–1930;* vol. 2, *The Soviet Collective Farm, 1929–1930.* Cambridge, MA: Harvard University Press, 1980.

Fitzpatrick, S. *Stalin's Peasants: Resistance and Survival in the Russian Village after Collectivization.* New York: Oxford University Press, 1994.

Lewin, M. *Russian Peasants and Soviet Power: A Study of Collectivization.* Trans. Irene Nove. New York: Norton, 1975.

Nove, Alec. *An Economic History of the USSR, 1917–1991.* 3rd ed. London: Penguin, 1992.

LYNNE VIOLA

Kollontay, Aleksandra

Aleksandra Kollontay (1872–1952) was born in Saint Petersburg to a family from the old aristocracy. She graduated high school at sixteen, married an engineer cousin against her parents' wishes, and bore him a child. In 1908 she abandoned both to study political economy in Zurich. When she returned to Saint Petersburg the following year, she permanently separated from her husband, but kept her child and dedicated herself to revolutionary activity. In 1905 she became popular for her oratorical skills, and in 1906 joined the Menshevik wing of the Russian Social Democratic Workers' Party.

Kollontay disagreed with the conservatism of that era's socialists on women's questions and demanded specific forms of engagement with the female proletarian masses so as to win them to the cause of socialism. A delegate to the First International Conference of Socialist Women (Stuttgart, 1907), she supported Clara Zetkin's position challenging the passive role of women in the Marxist theory of women's emancipation. In 1908 she was forced to emigrate to avoid arrest, taking refuge in Berlin, where she befriended Karl Liebknecht, Rosa Luxemburg, and Karl Kautsky, and joined the Social Democratic Party of Germany. In her role as Social Democratic propagandist and publicist she traveled throughout Europe, and also took part in the Basel Congress of the Second International (1912).

With the outbreak of World War I, Kollontay adopted an antimilitarist and internationalist position, which led her to move closer to Lenin's positions and join the Bolsheviks in 1915. Until 1917 she conducted intensive propaganda activities in Sweden, Norway, Denmark, and the United States in favor of Lenin's position on the war, and kept in close epistolary contact with him. She returned to Russia in March 1917, and was elected member of the Executive Committee of the Petrograd Soviet. Her fame and prestige as a revolutionary agitator notwithstanding, Kollontay was excluded from the upper levels of Bolshevik leadership, even though she was an enthusiastic supporter of Lenin's *April Theses* and was elected to membership in the Central Committee of the Bolshevik Party at its Sixth Congress. In August she was arrested with other Bolshevik leaders on orders from Aleksandr Kerensky's provisional government. Released in September, she once again supported Lenin's position in discussions regarding the decision to organize an armed insurrection to take power. Elected as member of the Presidium of the Second Congress of Soviets, Kollontay was nominated to the position of people's commissar for social security in the new Bolshevik government. Among the first women in history to hold a ministerial position, she resigned a few months later, in January 1918, since her position was now closer to that of the Left Communists led by Nikolay Bukharin on the controversy surrounding the Brest-Litovsk peace treaty. In 1919 she was nominated to the position of people's commissar for agitation and propaganda of the republic of Crimea and later Ukraine.

Having returned to Moscow, Kollontay was given the assignment of directing the Zhenotdel (department specifically dedicated to the issue of work among women) and she became a member of the International Women's Secretariat of the Comintern. Her radical theories about free love and a new Communist morality made her the target of much criticism, and fed suspicions that already followed her of cultivating feminist tendencies. Her fall into disgrace, however, was due to her joining the Workers' Opposition, a group that formed at the end of 1920 to demand more power for the labor unions in the management of the country's industries; along with Alexander Shlyapnikov, a close friend since her time in exile, Kollontay was one of the group's most influential spokespeople. The condemnation of the Workers' Opposition as an "anarcho-syndicalist deviation," which Lenin had the Tenth Party Congress adopt, marked the group's and Kollontay's own fate, and she was removed from all her posts.

At her request in October 1922, Stalin found her a new position as a member of the commercial delegation to Norway. In this role she started a long career in the Soviet diplomatic corps, and would become ambassador to Oslo in February 1924. This created quite a stir at the time, because it was the first time in the history of diplomacy that a woman occupied such a prestigious position. With an excellent command of foreign languages, Kollontay performed her numerous diplomatic missions efficiently: in Mexico (1925–27), again in Norway (1927–30), and Sweden, where she worked until her retirement, in 1945, for health reasons.

See also Women, Emancipation of; Zetkin, Clara.

FURTHER READING

Clements B. E., *Bolshevik Feminist: The Life of Aleksandra Kollontaj.* Bloomington–London: Indiana University Press, 1979.

Farnsworth B., *Aleksandra Kollontaj: Socialism, Feminism, and the Bolshevik Revolution.* Stanford, CA: Stanford University Press, 1980.

Kollontaj, A. M., *Molodomu pokoleniju. Vospominanja.* Moscow, 1946.

ANNA DI BIAGIO

Korean War

The Korean War of 1950–53 was a pivotal event for the Communist movement worldwide. It militarized and globalized the Cold War, shaping the larger conflict into the outline it retained until the collapse of the Soviet bloc in 1989–91. The sudden, massive assault on the American-backed South Korean state on June 25, 1950, by the armed forces of the Soviet-backed North Korean state was assumed by non-Communist leaders to be a Soviet action. It appeared to be an indication that Moscow would now use military force to expand the terri-

tories under its control beyond the limits agreed to at the end of World War II. Western leaders were united in believing that the attack on South Korea must be repelled lest the Soviets mount such attacks elsewhere and thereby bring on World War III. Consequently, led by the United States, fifteen nations entered the war on behalf of South Korea, fighting under the banner of the United Nations.

Fearing that Western Europe could be the next target of Soviet military aggression, the recently established North Atlantic Treaty Organization transformed itself from a loose political alliance to a functioning military one. In order to be prepared to meet the Soviet challenge wherever it might appear, the United States tripled its defense budget, initiating the arms race that became a central component of the Cold War. Assuming that the Communist government in China was also behind the attack on South Korea, the United States sent naval forces to neutralize the Taiwan Straits, preventing the People's Republic of China from completing its national unification. To block Communist expansion in Southeast Asia, the United States committed itself to the defense of the French position in Indochina, laying the foundation for the later war in Vietnam. As the war in Korea continued for three years following the entry of Chinese forces, the United States reached a separate peace treaty with Japan, excluding the Soviet Union, and established long-term military bases there and elsewhere. Opposition to U.S. saturation bombing of North Korea unified the Soviet bloc, and Moscow used the opportunity provided by the stalemate in Korea to re-arm its East European client states. China emerged from fighting the United States with enhanced national pride and lasting resentment of both the Soviet Union and North Korea.

Such wide-ranging consequences were far from what the leaders of the Soviet Union, China, and North Korea had intended when they planned the military campaign to reunify the peninsula under Communist Party control. Korea had been divided in half at the 38th parallel by the United States and the USSR at the end of World War II for the ostensible purpose of accepting the surrender of Japanese forces. But the two occupying powers had proved unable to agree on the composition of a government to replace Japanese colonial rule, and two separate states emerged, polarized politically along the axis created by the occupiers. The leaders of both South and North Korea were determined to end the tragic foreign-imposed division of their country, even at the cost of a military conflict. The decision to do so, however, was in the hands of the patron powers. The United States refused to countenance such a plan, but by January 1950 Soviet leader Joseph Stalin had finally acquiesced to repeated entreaties by his protégé Kim Il Sung.

Stalin's decision was part of a general strategic realignment in East Asia that he initiated in January 1950, apparently in response to a new U.S. strategic policy adopted in December 1949. In light of drastically reduced military resources and the victory of the Chinese Communist Party, the United States had committed itself to the defense of Japan and the Philippines but not to Taiwan or territory on the Asian mainland. Stalin took steps to fill the resulting power vacuum. He agreed to conclude a mutual defense treaty with the newly established People's Republic of China, recognized Ho Chi Minh's government in Vietnam, and instructed the Japanese Communist Party to shift to an aggressive policy. With China thus available to provide troop reinforcements, he acceded to Kim Il Sung's request to mount an invasion of South Korea. Experienced Soviet military officers were sent to Korea to plan the campaign together with officers of the recently established Korean People's Army (KPA), and Soviet supplies were shipped via China.

Stalin based his decision on indications that the United States would not intervene to protect South Korea. He made it clear to Kim Il Sung in April that in the event that the Americans nonetheless entered the war, North Korea would have to rely on China for reinforcements. Determined to avoid sparking a war with the United States, Stalin would not send Soviet troops to Korea. At Stalin's insistence, Kim Il Sung then secured approval and a promise of aid from Mao Zedong, who had reservations about the plan but was not in a position to reject a decision already made by Stalin. Because of Stalin's fears of information leaks, the Chinese were not further informed about the operation.

The initial plan was to disguise North Korean responsibility for starting the war by beginning with an attack on only the Ongjin peninsula. When the South Korean army counterattacked, the KPA would then move across the entire border claiming self-defense. The expectation was that with assistance from partisans in the South, the war would be won within two weeks. Three days before the June 25 launch date, however, North Korean intelligence reported that the ROK had learned of the plan and was reinforcing Ongjin. Stalin, Kim, and their military advisers all agreed to alter the plan and mount a broad offensive all along the border. This fateful choice

triggered alarm throughout the Western world. The large-scale invasion evoked memories of the Nazi aggression of the 1930s that, unchecked, had led to the recent world war.

The initial American intervention, using poorly trained occupation troops from Japan, was ineffective. The KPA, led by thousands of soldiers who had served with the People's Liberation Army during the Chinese civil war, quickly took Seoul and pushed ROK and American troops to the southernmost tip of the peninsula. However, on September 15 a daring amphibious landing by UN forces at Inchon, just west of Seoul, severed the KPA line. The North Korean army rapidly disintegrated, and UN forces easily retook Seoul and advanced into North Korea.

Facing imminent defeat, Kim Il Sung turned to Stalin for assistance, but the Soviet leader held to his prewar terms. Refusing to risk war with the United States, he instructed Kim to appeal to Beijing. Some within the Chinese leadership had second thoughts about fighting the United States just months after ending their own civil war, and without an air force, they would need Soviet air cover. After two weeks of debate, Mao sent Stalin a telegram informing him that the PRC would not, after all, send troops to Korea. Stalin then ordered Kim Il Sung to evacuate his remaining troops from Korean territory. The following day the Chinese leadership informed Moscow that the PLA would fight in Korea, disguised as "volunteers." Stalin reversed the evacuation order to Kim Il Sung, but the shock to the young Korean leader of learning that his mentor was willing to sacrifice his country was apparently profound.

Chinese troops were spectacularly successful against the far better armed Americans. With Soviet fighter jets protecting their supply routes, over the winter of 1950–51 the Chinese and North Koreans pushed the UN and ROK allies out of North Korea and retook Seoul. Impressed by American weakness, Stalin convened a meeting of the leaders of the East European client states in January 1951 to exhort them to re-arm rapidly to take advantage of what he presciently predicted would be a three-year window of opportunity.

In the spring of 1951 UN forces regrouped and halted the Chinese/North Korean offensive. The exhausted Communist allies decided to open armistice negotiations with the UN, primarily to buy time to resupply and fortify their position. Talks began in July, and by the fall of 1951 both sides had sufficiently fortified their positions in the mountainous terrain to make further advance by either side impossible. The United States increasingly turned to saturation bombing. American bombers were unable to destroy the critical bridges over the Yalu River guarded by Soviet fighter jets, but they had free reign over most North Korean territory, wreaking vast destruction. The North Koreans and Chinese moved underground or into caves, and continued fighting.

Armistice negotiations dragged on into 1953, as the Communist side rejected the U.S. demand that Chinese and North Korean prisoners of war not be repatriated against their will. Following Stalin's death on March 5, 1953, the new Soviet leadership immediately took steps to reach an armistice, which was concluded on July 27, 1953. The war left 2.5 million dead and missing, the majority from the Communist side, deep enmity between the two Korean states, and distrust between the three Communist allies who had carried out the war.

See also Cold War; Containment; Kim Il Sung; Socialist Camp; Soviet Bloc.

FURTHER READING

Chen, J. *China's Road to the Korean War: The Making of the Sino-American Confrontation.* New York: Columbia University Press, 1994.

Millett, A. R. *The War for Korea: 1945–1950: A House Burning.* Lawrence: University Press of Kansas, 2005.

Stueck, W. *Rethinking the Korean War: A New Diplomatic and Strategic History.* Princeton, NJ: Princeton University Press, 2002.

Weathersby, K. "The Soviet Role in the Korean War: The State of Historical Knowledge." In *The Korean War in World History*, ed. William Stueck, 61–92. Lexington: The University of Kentucky Press: 2004.

KATHRYN WEATHERSBY

Kronstadt Revolt

If there were two local groups of people that exemplified the Bolshevik advance to power in 1917 they were the Petrograd factory workers and the sailors of the Kronstadt naval garrison. Both gave unstinting support to the aspirations of the Bolshevik Party before the October Revolution, and both were eulogized in the pro-

paganda emitted by the Soviet state in the ensuing civil war. Kronstadt lies off the coast from Petrograd the then Russian capital. Its garrison was kept in place through the First World War as assurance against a sudden German attack. Its sailors, irked by onerous discipline and poor living conditions, yearned for an end to the war. Earlier than most conscripts in the armed forces, they turned against the provisional government and, indeed, nagged the Bolshevik Central Committee to seize power. In the anti-cabinet armed demonstration of late June 1917 they had to be restrained by speeches from Lenin himself.

The sailors of Kronstadt welcomed the October Revolution and its ending of hostilities on the Eastern front. Some among them were promoted to high rank in the new civil and military regime. But the majority of the garrison's troops were spared compulsory redeployment to the fronts of the civil war: the strategic necessity to guard the marine approaches to Petrograd remained strong.

Like the industrial working class, the Kronstadt sailors were disappointed by the Bolshevik party in power. They were not alone. Sporadic mutinies occurred in 1919–1920 in the Red Army, even in the course of the Polish-Soviet war. Most sailors came from humble urban or rural backgrounds and knew very well about the grueling conditions of life in the rear. They shared the resentment at the forcible requisitioning of food supplies. They detested the installation of the one-party dictatorship with its violent, unelected commissars. They sympathzed with the strikes by factory labor forces and kept in contact with the Petrograd strikers. They warmed to reports of peasant revolts and felt betrayed by a that which had promised to hearken to the wishes of "the toiling masses." They regarded the Bolsheviks as betrayers of their own October Revolution.

Their opinions were ignored or rejected. The Bolshevik leadership treated the sailors as traitors to their revolutionary commitment, which was not the case. The sailors had never supported the idea of a one-party dictatorship. Tense negotiations took place between the garrison commissars and the sailors in early 1921. Meanwhile a vast peasant revolt burst out in Tambov province. It was this event—and not the demands of the Kronstadt naval garrison—that induced the politburo to introduce the New Economic Policy and to scrap forcible grain requisitioning as party policy in February. Yet the Kronstadters were determined to extract further concessions from the Soviet regime. In March they too revolted. They sealed off the marine routes to the island and proclaimed the need for fundamental changes in the state order.

Their defection from the Bolshevik cause had an electric effect on Russian and international opinion. Whereas no one outside Russia had heard of the Tambov rebels, the sailors of Kronstadt were renowned for their revolutionary zeal—and if they were eager to overthrow the one-party dictatorship, then surely Lenin and the politburo were in deep trouble.

The party's Tenth Congress was happening at that time, and volunteers were sought to travel from its proceedings in Moscow to the Russian north. Red Army units under Mikhail Tukhachevski were deployed over the ice. Bloody fighting took place, but the outcome was never in doubt. Ringleaders of the mutiny were captured and either shot or dispatched to forced labor near Ukhta. Lenin and Trotsky claimed that the sailors had been duped by an international, anti-Socialist conspiracy. Allegedly agents and finances had been spirited into the garrison. It became the permanent official line that the demands of the mutineers were reactionary and unpatriotic. This was calumny. The Kronstadters had stood for reversion to the principles which had led them and others to support the Bolshevik seizure of power in October 1917.

Yet there was one aspect of the mutiny that heartened Lenin. The New Economic Policy was by no means very popular among his fellow Bolsheviks, and the mutiny distracted them from the congress debate on the matter. Lenin, although determined to suppress the mutineers, was keen to make the fiscal and commercial concessions agreed to by the politburo in February. The fact that the Kronstadters rose when they did was of benefit to his internal party purposes.

See also Dictatorship of the Proletariat; Russian Revolution and Civil War; War Communism.

FURTHER READING

Avrich, P. *Kronstadt, 1921*. Princeton, NJ: Princeton University Press 1970.

Getzler, I. *Kronstadt, 1917–1921: The Fat of a Soviet Democracy*. Cambridge, MA: Harvard University Press, 1983.

Mawdsley, E. *The Russian Civil War*. London: Allen and Unwin, 1987.

———. *The Russian Revolution and the Baltic Fleet: War and Politics, February 1917–April 1918*. London: Macmillan, 1978.

ROBERT SERVICE

Kulak

In prerevolutionary Russian the term "kulak" was normally associated with a village usurer—peasants who obtained their wealth not from agricultural activity but instead by practicing usury to the detriment of their fellow villagers. During the Soviet historical period and in Bolshevik depictions of rural society the term would become synonymous with "class enemy," referring to both an exploiter of peasant labor and one of the main enemies of Soviet power in the countryside. As such, the kulak would become the principal target of forced collectivization in the countryside, a process leading to both the abolition of independent farm enterprises and "the elimination of kulaks as a class" (which was how dekulakization was officially explained). In actuality the Bolshevik depiction of the kulak as the "farmer capitalist" bore only a scant resemblance to the actual social physiognomy of the Russian countryside at the conclusion of the great agrarian revolution that paralleled—both preceding and continuing it—the political upheaval of 1917.

After that revolution, which would abolish the aristocratic landholdings and the few capitalist farms established by a small but energetic group of agricultural entrepreneurs, the countryside had the appearance of an ocean of small family enterprises involved in a production that was mostly intended for their own consumption. In the course of the 1920s a small group of wealthier farmers, who employed labor on a seasonal basis, managed to emerge with difficulty from this socially and economically fragmented context—one also marked by the rebirth of traditional village communities. These farmers managed to sell a small part of their harvest by utilizing the opportunities that the New Economy Policy (NEP) had provided. Social and economic differentiation within villages remained limited, and was far from representing a polarization between "agrarian capitalists" and "rural proletariat," but the mobilization role that this nucleus of wealthier farmers performed was much more important. Mobilization and orientation, which gave them a cultural leadership role, if not always a directly political one, in their communities, aimed at defending the productive and commercial autonomy they had conquered during the agrarian revolution. They were therefore capable of mobilizing the villages' opposition to the delivery of grain surpluses to the state. When Soviet power decided to return to the forced stockpiling of grain, after the crisis of the NEP's agricultural transaction mechanisms had worsened between 1927 and 1928, these nuclei of the rural ruling class became the target of the new Bolshevik campaign against the countryside that culminated in forced collectivization. The official portrait of the kulak as class enemy took on increasingly vague and exaggerated outlines, until it came to coincide with rural society as a whole. The majority of this society was opposed to controls on production and social engineering, the goal of which was to resolve the issue of Soviet control of the countryside once and for all.

Between 1930 and 1931, almost two million peasants were deported to the remotest regions of the USSR, about a quarter million families abandoned the countryside and their possessions to look for refuge in the cities, and almost four hundred thousand were uprooted and forced to resettle in their own regions of residence; another four hundred thousand peasants were interned in prison camps, and some twenty-one thousand were executed. As a response to this dual decapitation and spoliation operation, an imposing wave of resistance swelled from the countryside and threatened to undermine the foundations of the Soviet regime. Thousands of collective demonstrations and acts of rebellion, which the security organs only managed to control by resorting to repressive measures, gave the emerging Stalinist system the opportunity to develop the techniques of terror that would characterize it in the following years.

See also Agrarian Question; Collectivization of the Countryside; Enemies of the People; Peasants in the USSR.

FURTHER READING

Danilov, V. P., and N. A. Ivnickij, eds. *Dokumenty svidetel'stvujut. Iz istorii derevni nakanune i v chode kollektivizacii, 1927–1932 gg.* Moscow: Izdatel'stvo Politcheskoj literatury, 1989.

Graziosi, A. *The Great Soviet Peasant War: Bolsheviks and Peasants, 1917–1933.* Cambridge, MA: Harvard University, Ukrainian Research Institute, 1996.

Lewin, M. *The Making of the Soviet System: Essays in the Social History of Interwar Russia.* New York: Pantheon, 1985.

———. *Russia–USSR–Russia: The Drive and Drift of a Superstate.* New York: New Press, 1995.

Viola, L. *Peasant Rebels under Stalin: Collectivization and the Culture of Peasant Resistance.* New York: Oxford University Press, 1996.

ANDREA ROMANO

Kun, Béla

Béla Kun (1886–1938) was born in the Transylvanian town of Szilágycseh on February 20, 1886, into a family of Hungarian Jews. In 1902, he joined the Hungarian Social Democratic Party and later studied law at the University of Kolozsvár in Cluj. Before the First World War he worked as a journalist and clerk, defending workers' interests. In 1916 Kun was taken prisoner on the Russian front, and he later joined the Bolshevik Party after the February Revolution. In November 1918 he returned to Hungary, where he was appointed leader of the newly founded Communist Party, remaining in this post until September 1936. Kun is best known for his prominent role in the short-lived Hungarian Soviet Republic (March 21 to August 1, 1919), in which he acted as the de facto head of government. In this position, he was heavily involved in formulating the military, social, and national policies of the Bolshevik-style republic. After its collapse, he was detained in Austria, but was released in mid-1920 and migrated to Soviet Russia, where he resided for the rest of his life.

In Moscow, he embarked on a long career in the hierarchies of the Communist International, as a member of its Executive Committee from 1921 to 1922, and from 1926 to 1936; a member of the Executive Committee Presidium from 1921 to 1922, and 1928 to 1935; a member of its International Control Commission for many years; and the chief of the Executive Committee's antiwar commission from 1932 to 1935. In the early 1920s, he was a strong advocate of revolutionary action, inciting, together with Grigory Zinovyev, the abortive "March Action" of 1921 and the "German October" of 1923. He was arrested in Austria in 1928, but an international protest campaign prevented the Viennese authorities from extradicting him to Hungary. From 1928 to 1929, Kun was an ardent adherent of the Comintern's "social Fascist" line and hence was a most reluctant convert to Popular Front policies in the mid-1930s.

No stranger to denouncing innocent comrades, beginning in December 1935 Kun himself became a victim of the emergent Stalinist purges. In September 1936, he was removed from the leadership of the Hungarian party, and barred from working in the Comintern as a suspected Trotskyite or Rightist. In June 1937, he was falsely accused by his erstwhile Comintern colleague, Dmitrii Manuilskii, of insulting Stalin and maintaining contacts with the Hungarian secret police since 1919. Kun was also charged with having had links to the "enemies of the people," Zinovyev, Lev Kamenev, and Osip Piatnitskii. He was arrested on June 28, 1937, and implicated in a secret police fabrication that was to be known as the "Fascist-Spy Organization of Trotskyites and Rightists in the Comintern." For whatever reason the trial of this alleged spy ring never took place, but Kun was executed nonetheless on August 29, 1938. He was rehabilitated in 1956, but details of his arrest and execution only became known during Gorbachev's glasnost.

See also Comintern; Hungarian Republic of Councils; Social Fascism.

FURTHER READING

Borsányi, G. *The Life of a Communist Revolutionary: Béla Kun.* Boulder, CO: Social Science Monographs, 1993.

Chase, W. J. *Enemies within the Gates? The Comintern and the Stalinist Repression, 1934–1939.* New Haven, CT: Yale University Press, 2001.

Lazitch, B., and M. M. Drachkovitch. *Biographical Dictionary of the Comintern.* Stanford, CA: Hoover Institution Press, 1986.

KEVIN F. McDERMOTT

Kurón, Jacek

In his youth, Jacek Kurón (1934–2004) was active in the Communist movement and, after 1956, lead the organization of the "Red scouts" (which started in opposition to the Stalinist "pioneer" movement), which by merging socialist revisionism and social Catholic values, a love of nature, and a Conradian ethos, became the hotbed from which many future dissidents would emerge.

His break with Communist power occurred in 1964 with his *Open Letter to the Party,* which he coauthored with Karol Modzelewski, a medieval historian and son of a former Communist foreign minister. In the letter they openly criticized the bureaucratic degeneration of the party in power, the exploitation of workers, and the lack of freedom of expression and research. This denunciation "from the inside," which called for a workers' revolution against the party, was taken seriously by its addressee. In the course of two in camera trials, held between 1965 and early 1966, the authors were sentenced to three years

detention. In France and Italy, Kurón and Modzelewski were considered Trotskyists. On the eve of 1968 Kurón was sentenced again and was only released in 1971. He then wrote a proclamation in which he argued for social self-organization and the rejection of violence.

In September 1976, Kurón founded the Workers' Defense Committee (KOR) in Warsaw with thirteen others: author Jerzy Andrzejewski and poet Stanislaw Barańczak, lawyers Ludwik Cohn, Antoni Pajdak, and Aniela Steinsbergowa, historians Antoni Macierewicz and Adam Szczypiorski, the great economist and old socialist Edward Lipiński; literary historian Jan Józef Lipski, classical philologist and hero of the partisan war Józef Rybicki, typographer Wojciech Ziembiński, biochemist Piotr Naimski, and priest and also a hero of the resistance, Jan Zieja. Another nine people soon joined, among whom were chemist Miroslaw Chojecki (who would be the force behind the clandestine publishing house Nowa) along with historians Wojciech Onyszkiewicz (who would be in charge of the *Robotnik* newspaper) and Adam Michnik (who, among other activities, would organize courses for the clandestine university TKN). The following year, the KOR became the Committee for Social Self-Defense KOR: it had truly become a social structure parallel to power, and would prepare the way for the independent labor union Solidarity.

Kurón was an adviser to Solidarity from the summer of 1980 up to the coup. Arrested on December 13, 1981, he was kept in prison for two and a half years without trial. In 1989, he was one of the protagonists of the Round Table between the opposition and the government. Later he was labor minister in the first non-Communist government, led by Tadeusz Mazowiecki, as well as that led by Hanna Suchocka (1992–93). He distinguished himself for his campaigns in favor of the most impoverished classes, who had been directly affected by the rapid introduction of a market economy, and this made him popular. A candidate in the 1995 presidential elections, he only garnered 9 percent of the vote and ended up withdrawing from politics, but he let his support for the antiglobalization movement be known, even while debilitated by illness.

Kurón was not an intellectual but rather a man of action. As one can gather from his autobiography, he was a dreamer, animated by a humanism with strong religious overtones. But he was also a realistic politician who looked for compromise, which he considered to be (unlike many of his fellow compatriots) something altogether different from gossip and becoming compromised. As the philosopher Leszek Kolakowski noted on Kurón's seventieth birthday, it was surprising, after all he had been subjected to, how incapable of hatred he was, how convinced he was that one could always come to an understanding with any adversary, because each human being represents a value.

See also Martial Law in Poland; Michnik, Adam; Solidarity; Walesa, Lech.

FURTHER READING

Kuron, J. *La mia Polonia*. Florence: Ponte alle Grazie, 1990.

Kuron, J., and K. Modzelewski. *Revolutionary Marxist Students in Poland Speak Out, 1964–1968*. New York: Merit, 1968.

Lipski, J. J. *KOR: A History of the Workers' Defense Committee in Poland, 1976–1981*. Berkeley: University of California Press, 1985.

FRANCESCO M. CATALUCCIO

Kuusinen, Otto Wilhelm

Otto Wilhelm Kuusinen (1881–1964) was born in Laukaa, Finland (then part of czarist Russia), on October 4, 1881. He studied aesthetics, philosophy, and art history at the University of Helsinki, graduating in 1905. In the same year he joined the Finnish Social Democratic Party, and his articles soon began to appear in the party's theoretical organ, the *Socialist Journal*. He was elected to parliament in 1908, and from 1911 to 1917 acted as party president. Kuusinen was responsible for education in the government of the Finnish Workers' Republic, from January to April 1918, escaping to Soviet Russia after its defeat. In August 1918, in Moscow, he became a founder and member of the Finnish Communist Party, which he led for many years. He returned in 1919–20 temporarily to Finland and Sweden, where he organized the left wing of the Finnish labor movement.

From 1921 to 1939 Kuusinen occupied important posts in the Communist International. Throughout these years he was the secretary of the Comintern's Executive Committee, and from 1922 a member of the presidium. He attended all seven Comintern congresses, except the second in 1920, and was involved in the drafting of numerous theses, resolutions, and directives. Lenin apparently valued Kuusinen's intellectual capabilities; "He thinks," Lenin is reported to have said. Kuusinen generally ad-

opted moderate positions in the Comintern hierarchy and was a supporter of the Popular Front from the mid-1930s on. His role in the Stalinist purges of the Comintern and foreign Communists is shadowy. His estranged second wife, Aino, was arrested in 1938, and spent fifteen years in the labor camps and prison, but, it is alleged, she received little help from her former husband. Many of his Finnish comrades were victims of the mass arrests in Soviet Karelia in 1937–38. Kuusinen himself was a loyal Stalinist who survived the Great Terror, possibly because he figured prominently in Stalin's plans for a Sovietized Finland.

In December 1939, Kuusinen indeed became head of the short-lived Finnish Democratic Republic, the so-called Terijoki government, which was created in the wake of the Red Army's invasion of Finland during the Winter War (1939–40). The Red government was still-born in the face of staunch Finnish resistance, and in 1940 Kuusinen was elected president of the presidium of the Karelo-Finnish Soviet Socialist Republic within the USSR—a post he held until 1956. He also served as the vice president of the USSR Supreme Soviet. From 1941 until his death, he was a member of the Central Committee of the Soviet Communist Party, and from 1957 to 1964 under Khrushchev, he was a member of the highest body in the Soviet Union, the presidium (politburo) of the Communist Party. In 1958, Kuusinen was elected to the Soviet Academy of Sciences, and he later coedited *Fundamental Principles of Marxism-Leninism*, which for many years was considered a standard work on dialectical materialism and Communist ideology. He died in Moscow on May 17, 1964, and his ashes were buried in the Kremlin Wall. One of the best-educated Bolsheviks, his selected works were published in 1966.

See also Comintern; Sovietization.

FURTHER READING

Hodgson, J. H. *Communism in Finland: A History and Interpretation*. Princeton, NJ: Princeton University Press, 1967.

Lazitch, B., and M. M. Drachkovitch, *Biographical Dictionary of the Comintern*. Stanford, CA: Hoover Institution Press, 1986.

Rentola, K. "Finnish Communism, O. W. Kuusinen, and Their Two Native Countries." In *Communism: National and International*, ed. T. Saarela and K. Rentola, 159–81. Helsinki: Finnish Literature Society, 1998.

KEVIN F. McDERMOTT

Labor

The Soviet Union

The Soviet system was characterized by patterns of work that differed from Western economies in several fundamental respects. Many, if not most, of these stemmed from the way in which the Stalinist leadership had industrialized the country in the 1930s.

Under Stalin, the regime attempted to control worker behavior through a mixture of incentives and coercion. The breakneck speed and bureaucratic chaos of Stalin's industrialization policies brought millions of new workers into the factories and construction sites. For most of these workers this meant exceptional hardship: low wages, serious food shortages, and appalling housing. For a small minority, economic expansion offered opportunities of upward mobility. Perhaps some 10 percent of workers during the early 1930s moved off the shop floor into positions of lower management; some achieved even more rapid advancement in the managerial hierarchy and/or Communist Party. The majority, however, did not have this chance. Because collectivization had caused a calamitous fall in the standard of living, the regime could not encourage higher productivity through economic incentives. Instead, it used a system known as "norms," or targets. The logic was simple. Each worker had to meet a production target each day or each month. Failure to reach this target meant the worker would not earn a survival wage. What is more, the regime kept increasing the targets. During the First Five-Year Plan this was done through the system of Shock Work (*udarnichestvo*). Shock Workers were those who exceeded their targets by substantial amounts, and who as a reward received scarce foods, better housing, or equally scarce consumer goods (for example, shoes, a winter overcoat, or a much-needed vacation). Managers were then instructed to take the production achievements of the Shock Workers and make these the new "norm" for all workers. The latter now had to meet the new, higher targets in order just to retain their previous wage. Meanwhile, the Shock Workers had to carry on setting new, higher records in order to continue receiving their privileges. With the end of rationing in 1935, and the monetarization of the economy, the regime adapted this system via a campaign known as Stakhanovism. The principle, however, was the same.

Ordinary workers responded to this system by quitting their jobs. Labor turnover in the early 1930s reached extremely high levels. In 1930 the average worker in industry changed jobs once every eight months; coal miners and construction workers changed jobs on average once every four months. Such high levels of turnover added to the instability afflicting industrial enterprises and jeopardized plan fulfillment. Although the regime officially tried to stem turnover by imposing ever-tighter legal restrictions on workers' freedom of movement, these proved largely ineffective until 1940, when job changing became a criminal offense punished by a prison sentence (and during World War II, by several years in a gulag labor camp). Industrial managers, therefore, had to find their own methods of persuading workers to remain on the job. Out of this arose an intricate system of informal bargaining. Managers began to grant workers various concessions in order to persuade them not to quit. In some cases this involved illegal or "semilegal" bonus payments. In other cases managers deliberately failed to raise the "norms" when the regime ordered them increased. In still other cases managers turned a blind eye to violations of discipline regulations, and even to violations of the law, including laws against quitting and absenteeism after these had both become criminal offenses.

The main legacy of this system was the duality of workers' position within the enterprise. Politically they had little freedom. They could not go on strike or organize independent trade unions. They thus had little collective power. Individually, though, because of the labor shortage and the materials shortages that perpetually plagued factory production, managers came to depend on workers to help sort out these disruptions. This in turn gave the individual worker a surprising amount of control over the speed of work and the quality with which they carried out their job. And this in turn became one of the many factors that helped lower both the productivity of Soviet industry and the quality of what it produced.

This system of informal bargaining was a specific response to the situation created in the 1930s, but it became a permanent feature of Soviet industry until the system itself collapsed in 1991.

Working conditions in Soviet factories were extremely harsh and dangerous. Only immediate production operations were relatively mechanized. Most so-called auxiliary operations (foundry work, lifting and carting parts around the shop floor, warehousing, and cleaning and repairing machinery) were done by hand. Soviet factories, given this, had a high ratio of manual auxiliary workers to production workers. The poor quality of Soviet machinery and the negligence with which many workers treated it led to frequent breakdowns. As a result, Soviet industry also had a high percentage of its workers who did nothing but repair equipment. During the 1960s it was estimated that there were more workers repairing machinery than there were manufacturing machines in engineering factories.

Safety in factories was poor. Aside from the risks of accidents due to undermechanization, few factories had adequate ventilation systems. Exposure to harmful chemicals or dust fibers was a common risk. The Soviet planning system actually made it uneconomic for managers to redress these problems by investing in safety equipment: the equipment was expensive and was not guaranteed to work properly in any case. Not surprisingly accident rates were high; so, too, was the percentage of workers with occupational illnesses. Perhaps surprisingly, workers often volunteered for dangerous jobs, because they received higher pay—the wages system thus encouraged them willingly to put themselves at risk.

This pattern of working conditions was also tied to a specific gender division of labor. Although nearly half of industrial workers were women, women became marginalized into the lowest-paid industries (textiles, garments, and food processing). Where they worked in almost equal numbers alongside men (as in engineering), they were confined to the lowest wage grades. Besides this overt discrimination in terms of pay, women—in sharp contrast to the picture in Western industry—were also marginalized into heavy, hazardous, manual jobs, such as carting, lifting, warehousing, and foundry work. If a heavy manual operation became mechanized, the pattern was for women then to be removed from this job and for it to be given to men. A further result of this gender division of labor was that women had far less power to extract concessions from their managers via informal bargaining. Sociological studies showed that women worked much more intensively, with fewer losses of work time than their male counterparts. So-called feminized industries, such as textiles and clothing, contributed disproportionately to the accumulation funds of industry as a whole—in effect, they subsidized less productive male-dominated industries.

China

For large numbers of China's urban workers, the socialist institution that dominated labor relations, the work unit (*danwei*), was also the most important administrative institution. Danweis could be factories, nonprofit organizations (like a university or hospital), or administrative units (a ministry or mass organization like the Federation of the Trade Unions). What they had in common was that they were state-owned, held administrative authority over their employees (by maintaining their personal dossiers and deciding over transfers, changes in administrative or family status, family planning, and even travel), and provided services and facilities to their members (including housing, food and dining halls, recreation activities, and schools).

For its ability to control not only the productive activities but also the consumption and socialization patterns of its members, the danwei has often been compared to a microsociety. Its members' experience of the redistributive state was mostly taking place within the walls of the danwei compound. The commercial, productive, and service network outside the walls was, in the heyday of socialism, limited, and access to items of private consumption was only possible through the work unit. Labor mobility and even independent movement were limited and controlled by the unit. The control over the lives of workers and their families was an important feature of Chinese industrial relations until the late 1980s, but work units also took over from the state the function of redistributing social services and welfare items to their workers. They provided assistance from birth to death, from schooling to old age care. The system has been described as one of organized dependence. While high degrees of dependence on the employer are found in different systems of industrial organization, what characterizes the Chinese work unit is the coexistence of physical dependence on the enterprise (as the only available provider of basic needs), political dependence on the management, the party branches, and the Leninist trade unions (which prevent forms of autonomous organization at the shop floor), and personal dependence on the supervisors, whose judgment and attitude toward individual workers are essential in determining access to resources, goods, and status in the factory.

Because socialist work units were acting as agents of the state, managers generally considered the value of labor independently from production needs. The enterprise was dependent on the state bureaucracy for the provision of production factors, including workers, raw materials, and investments. Increasing the number of workers meant the unit received more resources, while reducing the number of workers would lead to an unwelcome reduction of the resources available to run the unit. Most work units therefore hired in excess of their needs.

This became one of the reasons why, once faced with the opening up of the economy and the need to improve economic performances in the 1980s, these work units frequently found that their budget was no longer viable without the assistance received from the state.

Living and working conditions varied greatly between cities, and between different types of work units. Centrally owned and larger enterprises generally could provide better services to their workers than enterprises owned by local administrations or of a smaller size. The system was designed to maintain a certain level of egalitarianism *within* each enterprise, but could not prevent inequalities emerging *between* enterprises. Because of these inequalities and the different conditions of workers within the enterprise, during the four decades that these institutions dominated the social landscape of urban China, they experienced many more conflicts than the regime was willing to admit.

Workers' interests in socialist China have been represented by a corporatist All China Federation of Trade Unions. Despite the significant changes in labor relations that took place beginning in 1986, with individual labor contracts and later collective bargaining, the regime has, to this day, yet to allow the existence of independent trade unions. During the classical socialist era, the federation had served as a Leninist transmission belt between the party and the masses, and was a tool through which the party could mobilize workers at the grass roots. Today,

with a growing variation of types of industrial ownership and management (with private enterprises and an aggressive profit-oriented management of state-owned ones), the All China Federation of Trade Unions and its cadres are often faced with the need to adopt a much more syndicalist role. Rather than representing the interests of the socialist workers, the alleged masters of the enterprise, they face a need to defend the material interests of workers against those of public employers and private investors. Doing this within a Leninist and corporative legal framework is proving to be extremely difficult.

See also Workers.

FURTHER READING

Arnot, B. *Controlling Soviet Labour: Experimental Change from Brezhnev to Gorbachev*. London: Macmillan, 1988.

Filtzer, D. *Soviet Workers and De-Stalinization: The Consolidation of the Modern System of Soviet Production Relations, 1953–1964*. Cambridge, UK: Cambridge University Press, 1992.

———. *Soviet Workers and the Collapse of Perestroika: The Soviet Labour Process and Gorbachev's Reforms, 1985–1991*. Cambridge, UK: Cambridge University Press, 1994.

Lane, D., ed. *Labour and Employment in the USSR*. Brighton, UK: Wheatsheaf, 1986.

Perry, E. J., and L. Xiaobo, eds. *Danwei: The Changing Chinese Workplace in Historical and Comparative Perspective*. Armonk, NY: M. E. Sharpe, 1997.

Walder, A. *Communist Neo-Traditionalism: Work and Authority in Chinese Industry*. Berkeley: University of California Press, 1986.

Yanowitch, M. *Social and Economic Inequality in the Soviet Union*. White Plains, NY: M. E. Sharpe, 1977.

DONALD A. FILTZER AND LUIGI TOMBA

Legal Marxism

The expression "legal Marxism" refers to the cultural and political activities of a group of Russian intellectuals, who discussed and used Karl Marx's ideas between 1894 and 1901, and whose publications were not clandestine. The group was composed of five people: Nikolai Berdyaev (1874–1948), Sergei Bulgakov (1871–1944), Semën Frank (1877–1950), Pëtr Struve (1870–1944), and Mikhail Tugan-Baranovsky (1865–1919). They had different personalities and fields of study (from economics to philosophy), but initially they were animated by common attitudes: they endorsed Marxism in an original fashion, parallel to contemporary "revolutionary Marxism," shared a critical attitude toward populism as a premise for a new theoretical and practical interpretation of Russian reality with revolutionary Marxists, and yet unlike the "revolutionaries," the five acted as unprejudiced researchers toward Marxism itself. Theirs was truly a "critique of Marxism," similar to the one associated with Eduard Bernstein in Germany, although both distinct from it and preceding it chronologically.

One of the five, Struve, did claim priority for his revision of Marxism—a revision he had already begun during his alliance with orthodox Marxism in their shared struggle against populism, as he developed his plans for a noncapitalist development of the country. Struve's work *Critical Notes on the Economic Development of Russia*, which was published in Saint Petersburg in 1894, ended with these words: "Let us recognize our backwardness [*nekul'turnost'*] and let us take lessons from capitalism," a program aimed at populist theses, but also differing from a Marxism that postulated a revolutionary road for Russia.

The legal Marxists' further activities widened the gap between them and orthodox Marxism, taking them definitely beyond Marxism, in an idealist direction in philosophy (a collection of their essays, which Tugan-Baranovsky did not participate in, was published in Moscow in 1902 with the title *Problems of Idealism*) and a liberal direction in politics (beginning in 1902 Struve edited *Osvobozhdenie* [Liberation], the initial nucleus of the Constitutional-Democratic Party, the left wing of Russian liberalism).

While each individual legal Marxist followed his own path, a certain commonality of outlook remained, and it is not mere chance that four of them (Struve, Berdyaev, Bulgakov, and Frank) were among the authors of a collective work that had an important role in Russian cultural life in the early 20th century, and that sparked great polemics: the *Vekhi* (Milestones), published in Moscow in 1909. It expressed a profound criticism of the Russian radical intelligentsia, and its mentality and ethos, which in the authors' opinion wanted every value—philosophical, juridical, and aesthetic—to be subjected to an abstract revolutionary ideal of social justice, thus arriving at a sort of spiritual and moral nihilism.

The same names can be found among the authors of another collective work that unlike *Vekhi*, to which it was spiritually connected, went almost unremarked be-

cause it was forbidden by the censorship of the new Bolshevik state, since the book was published in Moscow in 1918. It was not reissued until 1967, in France, as *De profundis* (From the Depths), "a collection of essays on the Russian revolution," as stated in the subtitle. This work—which, like *Vekhi*, has enjoyed a second life in Russia because of its renewed relevance following the collapse of the Soviet regime—marked the beginning of the last phase for those who had been the legal Marxists. They met again in exile in Western Europe (except for Tugan-Baranovsky, who not long before his death, returned to the land of his birth, Ukraine, in 1917, where he engaged in a brief but intense bout of political activity), and became critics of Marxist communism, which had by then been transformed into a reality that they had in large part foretold. Of their works on this topic the one that is best known is Berdyaev's *The Origin of Russian Communism*, originally published in English in 1937, which was criticized by many scholars because of its tendency to locate the roots of Bolshevik communism in Russian culture. The writings that Struve, Frank, and Bulgakov devoted to communism are more interesting, but less well known in the West; Bulgakov went on to become one of the most important Russian orthodox theologians.

See also Bolshevism; Despotism; Revisionism; Totalitarianism.

FURTHER READING

Kindersley, R. *The First Russian Revisionists: A Study of Legal Marxism in Russia*. Oxford: Clarendon Press, 1962.

Strada, V., ed. *La critica al marxismo in Russia agli inizi del secolo*. Milan: Jaca Book, 1991.

VITTORIO STRADA

Lenin, Vladimir

Lenin (1870–1924) was born Vladimir Ilich Ulyanov in Simbirsk in the mid-Volga region of the Russian Empire. He was of ethnically mixed ancestry, the precise nature of which is still obscure; it certainly included a Jewish element and possibly also a Kalmyk one. This, though, had practically no effect on his upbringing. His father Ilya rose from lowly social origins to the post of province schools inspector. His mother, whose father was a doctor, was an enthusiastic musician. The children were brought up in an environment dedicated to cultural improvement and educational progress. Each of them excelled at school. The Ulyanovs seemed typical beneficiaries of the reforms introduced by Emperor Alexander II in the 1860s. They conformed to the stereotype of a family determined on high attainment for all its members.

Young Vladimir's life was shaken by two events. The first was the death of his father in 1886. This removed some of the household's rigorous constraints on behavior. The second, even more traumatic, was the arrest and hanging of the oldest son Alexander for his role in a plot to assassinate Emperor Alexander III in 1887. As a result, the Ulyanov family acquired the status of local pariahs. Yet Vladimir Ulyanov was still allowed to enter Kazan University and to take up his place in the jurisprudence faculty. Within weeks he had taken part in a protest demonstration. He was expelled from the university. He joined his mother and ineffectually tried his hand at farm management. Already, however, he had had his first experience of revolutionary politics. Like his deceased brother, he was drawn toward the groups advocating that the peasantry should somehow stand at the core of their doctrine of revolution; he also espoused terrorist activity. At the same time he studied for an external course in law at St. Petersburg University (where he achieved a first-class degree in 1891).

Many young revolutionaries of his generation were coming to the conclusion that agrarian socialism was an obsolete doctrine for a Russia undergoing rapid industrialization in the late 19th century. They had long been admirers of Marx, and under the influence of Georgi Plekhanov, they began to preach that the German variant of Marxism—with its attachment to industry, the working class, and the cities—was appropriate also for the Russian Empire. Bookish intellectuals such as Vladimir Ulyanov joined the little study groups then forming. They pored over tomes by Marx and Engels. They investigated the Russian economic transformation, especially with regard to the social differentiation occurring in the villages as the commercial economy penetrated ever deeper. Ulyanov had never been sentimental about peasants. In the famine of 1891–92 he shocked even his own family with his refusal to participate in relief work: his opinion was that palliative measures simply delayed the development of the toiling masses into revolutionaries.

By 1895 he was operating clandestinely in the Union of Struggle for the Liberation of the Working Class in St. Petersburg. Although he had contact with several workers who became its members, his priority was to establish his credential as a Marxist writer. In December he was arrested and later sent into Siberian exile. By then he had become one of the least compromising theoreticians of Marxism in Russia. He rejected any attempt to moderate revolutionary doctrine. And, with financial help from his mother's landed property as well as her pension, he resolved upon a full-time career as revolutionary. In Siberia he married Nadezhda Krupskaya. Continuing his economic studies, he finished *The Development of Capitalism in Russia*, which was legally published in 1899. Ulyanov's sentence came to an end in 1900 and he tried to resume revolutionary activity in Russia. This proved impractical. Dedicated to a revolution, he moved abroad.

His first thought was to align himself with Plekhanov and subordinate himself to his purposes. His second thought was that Plekhanov was incapable of organizing a revolutionary party capable of making a revolution. His writings called persistently for a centralized, disciplined organization of revolutionaries. Many thought this altogether too reminiscent of the terrorist conspiracies of the 1870s and 1880s. Russian Marxists tended to preferred "mass activity"; they believed that the working class as a whole should engage in revolutionary action. They disliked Ulyanov's refusal to reject unconditionally terrorist methods. Ulyanov, however, was undeterred. He badgered Plekhanov into agreeing to the setting up of an émigré newspaper. They called it *Iskra* (The Spark). The idea was to use the paper as a means to organize and coordinate a proper party. Ulyanov buffeted Plekhanov out of the way and became in essence *Iskra*'s chief editor. In 1902 he published a booklet, *What Is to Be Done?* which made a case for his own kind of party. He signed it as Lenin, and this was to become the name by which he would be known to history.

There had been a small congress of the Russian Social-Democratic Workers' Party in Minsk in 1899, but it had left no organizational legacy. Plekhanov and Lenin convoked a Second Party Congress in summer 1903 to rectify the situation. It was held first in Brussels, and then, in order to escape the Belgian police, in London. Their evident aim was not only to establish but also to control the party. Initially the Iskra group stuck together and held off its critics, including the Jewish Bund which vainly sought broad organizational autonomy for itself. The Iskraites dominated the central party apparatus elected at the congress. But several among them, notably Lenin's friend Yuli Martov, were disconcerted by Lenin's polemical extremism and conspiratorial maneuvers. The Iskra group fell apart. The majority, led by Lenin and supported for a while by Plekhanov, were unperturbed. Calling themselves the Majoritarians (*bol'sheviki* in Russian), they derided the Minoritarians (*men'sheviki*) who advocated a less strenuously disciplined party. The split between the Bolsheviks and the Mensheviks became a serious factional strife.

Bolsheviks and Mensheviks in the Russian Empire, as distinct from the émigrés, continued to collaborate with each other. The Russian Social-Democratic Workers' Party increased its recruitment among factory workers and miners. Lenin stayed abroad. By 1904 he had lost support. Even many of his Bolshevik adherents were deserting him. Plekhanov denounced him. Lenin no longer controlled the central party apparatus.

In 1905 the Russian Empire erupted into revolution. Lenin refused to return until after the October Manifesto, which appeared to offer a degree of personal security to anticzarist militants. Working out a strategy of revolution in the light of rapidly changing circumstances, Lenin urged the party to aim at setting up a "provisional revolutionary dictatorship of the proletariat and the peasantry." He argued that this was the only way to ensure that the forthcoming "bourgeois-democratic revolution" against the Romanovs would not be compromised by vacillation on the part of the middle classes. The dictatorship was to install a regime of full civic rights, which eventually would allow the working class to advance to a second revolution of its own and inaugurate socialism. The Mensheviks regarded this as a recipe for civil war and terror. But Lenin on his return was willing to work with them. His own Bolsheviks were demonstrating inflexibility in revolutionary tactics. Many refused to enter trade unions or the workers' soviets (or councils). They also declined to participate in the election to the newly announced State Duma. Lenin used the Mensheviks as a counterbalance to the Bolshevik irreconcilables.

With the suppression of the revolutionary tide Lenin returned to the emigration in late 1907. He continued to condone the retention of a united party but always ran a separate Bolshevik organization within it. His patience snapped in 1911 and he decided to call a party conference in Prague with only a nod in the direction of inviting Mensheviks. The resultant Central Committee, ignoring the rights of other factions, proclaimed itself the legitimate supreme agency of the Russian Social-Democratic Labor Party. Lenin would have nothing further to do with the Mensheviks. Pushed by Bolsheviks, he acceded to the setting up of a daily St. Petersburg newspaper to be called *Pravda* (Truth). He moved to Kraków in

Austrian-ruled Poland to keep contact with its editors. He also strengthened links with the Bolshevik deputies in the Fourth State Duma. (By then the faction was contesting the elections.) Itching for a revolution led by Bolsheviks, he refused to hand over Bolshevik funds to the common treasury of the Russian Social-Democratic Workers' Party. He wanted politics on his terms only.

The price he paid was recurrent dissent among the Bolsheviks. In 1909 Lenin had driven his rival Alexander Bogdanov from the faction. Bogdanov accused him of being an authoritarian egomaniac. The exodus from the Bolsheviks continued when Europe went to war in summer 1914. To Lenin's astonishment the admired German Social-Democratic Party voted financial credits to Kaiser Wilhelm's government. Even Karl Kautsky, the party's outstanding theoretician whom Lenin had always eulogized, refrained from outright condemnation of the German war effort. Lenin broke with the Second International. He castigated those many Bolsheviks who rebutted his call for a "European civil war." As his following dwindled, Lenin refused to be demoralized, taking comfort in the conviction that the travails of war would lead to revolution in Europe. As usual he tried to summarize developments in a treatise. In *Imperialism as the Highest Stage of Capitalism*, Lenin declared that the principal capitalist powers had been thrust into military conflict by their competition for world markets. Imperialism, to his way of thinking, was the ultimate state of capitalism. In a series of further articles he suggested that economic crises—and indeed world war—would not cease until the impoverished working classes of Europe and North America rose against their government and installed revolutionary Socialist dictatorships.

At party conferences high in the Swiss Alps—at Zimmerwald in September 1915 and Kienthal in April 1916—Lenin continued to pursue his case. Each participant was opposed to his or her national war effort. Lenin, though, wanted a firm commitment to turning the "imperialist war" into a class-based civil war across the continent. Rather than aiming at consensus, he preferred to organize a cabal of leftists at the conferences, which consisted entirely of the left wing of socialism. Although his style was unchanged, however, his perspective was undergoing alteration. In *Materialism and Empiriocriticism* (1909) he had argued that the perceptive capacity of the human mind was as accurate as a camera; absolute knowledge was attainable and Marx and Engels had supplied infallible instruments with which to achieve this end. In his wartime notebooks on philosophy he took a more flexible approach to epistemology, contending that ideas—even those of Marxism's founders—could only be considered proven when they had been tested in practice.

This theoretical adoption of experimentalism came from his readings of Hegel and Aristotle. But of course Lenin had been an experimenter in his active political career. Until the First World War, he had camouflaged this tendency by proclaiming a rigorous attachment to Marxist orthodoxy. In fact, however, his ragbag of doctrines had from the start included not only Marxism but also Jacobinism, early 19th-century Socialist extremism, Russian agrarian socialism, and even the centuries-old intellectual (and, if it dare be said, ecclesiastical) tradition that Russia had a unique and universalist destiny in the world. As theory and practice reinforced each other in Lenin's thinking, he was taken aback in his Swiss apartment by the unexpected news that revolution had broken out in the Russian Empire. In previous months he had confessed to wondering whether he would live long enough to hear of this outcome. Suddenly it was upon him. Emperor Nicholas II was overthrown, the liberal-led provisional government established. Political and civic freedom was announced. What was the best course for Marxists in this extraordinary situation?

Lenin had already been considering whether the old Bolshevik notion of a two-stage revolutionary process was valid. The February 1917 Revolution brought him to the point of decision. The provisional government, enjoying the conditional support of Mensheviks and Socialist-Revolutionaries (and indeed many Bolsheviks), had to be overthrown. He wrote frantically along these lines to the Bolshevik factional leadership in Petrograd (as St. Petersburg had been renamed). At the same time he entered into discussions with the German authorities for permission to traverse Germany and make his return to Petrograd via Scandinavia. He and other Bolsheviks were favored in Berlin because they conducted vigorous antiwar propaganda, so a deal was arranged. Lenin arrived at the Finland station in Petrograd in the early hours of April 4. In his pocket he had scribbled out what became known as his *April Theses*.

The fundamental proposal of the *Theses* was that the provisional government had to give way to a Socialist administration. Developing his ideas in articles in *Pravda* and at the Bolshevik April conference, Lenin argued that Menshevik and Socialist-Revolutionary supporters of the provisional government had betrayed their socialism. He urged that working-class organizations such as the sovi-

ets should become the core of the forthcoming Socialist regime. In subsequent weeks he stopped talking about the need for a European civil war. He attuned himself to popular opinion, which wanted peace and freedom. Lenin promised to end the war. He would give land to the peasantry, provide the industrial labor force with workers' control, and grant national self-determination to all the peoples of the former Russian Empire. He predicted that Socialist revolution in Russia would be quickly followed by revolution across the rest of Europe. A new era in the history of humankind was beginning, and Lenin heralded it with fiery aplomb. He rallied the radicals in his own faction to his banner and brought the vacillators into their camp.

Events played into his hands. The Mensheviks would have nothing to do with Lenin and, to his delight, the Bolsheviks were able to form themselves into an entirely separate mass party. The provisional government helped him too. First, foreign minister Milyukov was found to have affirmed the cabinet's commitment to expansionist war aims. This was hugely uncongenial to workers and soldiers. Then the cabinet started a June offensive. This was an unmitigated military disaster. Finally, the last premier of the provisional government, Alexander Kerensky, embroiled himself in a violent dispute with army commander Lavr Kornilov, and only the assistance of Socialist agitators—including Bolsheviks—saved him from being overthrown by his own army. Throughout these months, what is more, the economy was collapsing and the administrative and policing agencies fell into shambles. Workers and soldiers who had started by voting for Mensheviks and Socialist-Revolutionaries were by early autumn turning to the Bolsheviks, who advocated drastic reforms to stave off famine and bring about peace.

Lenin himself had gone into hiding in early July after the provisional government issued a warrant for his arrest as a German spy. He returned clandestinely to the Bolshevik Central Committee on October 10 and 16 to demand that the party exploit its rising popularity in the soviets by immediately seizing power. A majority accepted his argument. Power was seized from the provisional government on October 25, 1917, and transferred to the second congress of workers' and soldiers' deputies. Emerging from clandestinity, Lenin became head of the Council of People's Commissars (or *Sovnarkom*). He issued decrees. He propelled his comrades into revolutionary initiatives. He searched for ways toward peace that would trigger revolution in Germany. He spoke frequently at open meetings. He published, in early

1918, *The State and Revolution*, an attempt to justify the October Revolution in Marxist terms. He manipulated negotiations with the Mensheviks in November so that they would not want to form a coalition with him as a member. The only political partners he would tolerate were the Left Socialist-Revolutionaries who joined Sovnarkom in mid-November.

The problem was that Sovnarkom's writ was confined largely to the cities of Russia. The rest of the country, especially the villages, had yet to declare itself for the Bolsheviks. Elections held for the Constituent Assembly in November were a disaster for the Bolsheviks, who barely gained a quarter of the votes. Nor was Sovnarkom's foreign and security policy a success. The German high command issued an ultimatum that Sovnarkom should sign a separate peace on the Eastern front and withdraw from the war. Lenin recognized the superiority of Germany's military power and, after months of acerbic dispute in the Bolshevik Central Committee, cajoled his comrades into accepting the German terms in the treaty of Brest-Litovsk in March 1918. A "breathing space" was thus obtained for the Soviet republic.

Lenin, who had been preaching class war with intensifying eagerness, removed the constraints on the new political police known as the Cheka. He urged the creation of "committees of the village poor." Throwing aside his earlier caution, he sanctioned the total stratification of industry. (Banking, large-scale factories, and foreign trade were already in the hands of Sovnarkom.) In November the Germans surrendered to the Western Allies and Lenin, disembarrassed of the need to appease the Berlin government, called for the formation of a Communist International. By then Sovnarkom was being attacked by a succession of White armies determined to overthrow the Bolsheviks. Lenin chaired Sovnarkom and oversaw the implementation of economic and social policy. But it was the party that was truly the supreme arbiter. Power belonged to an inner subcommittee of the Central Committee, and Lenin informally headed that subcommittee. Every grand matter of war, economics, security, culture, administrative appointments, and politics came before it. Lenin insisted that the civil war had to be fought politically as well as militarily. By the end of 1919 Russia was conquered by the Reds; by March 1921 nearly all of the former Russian Empire was overrun.

The mistaken assumption of the Bolsheviks, which Lenin shared, was that wartime methods could safely be prolonged. When food supplies continued to be expropriated from the peasantry, the peasants revolted. Workers went on strike and soldiers and sailors mutinied in 1920. And yet Lenin's intuition deserted him. He threw the Red Army at the Poles in the summer of 1920 in a vain attempt to spread the revolution westward. The Reds were crushed at the battle of the Vistula. But it was the rebellious peasants who gave Lenin his most acute worries, and in February 1921 he persuaded the politburo to approve a New Economic Policy. At its core was the replacement of food requisitioning with a graduated tax in-kind set at a level that would enable peasants to trade their surplus. Simultaneously he ordered the ferocious suppression of the Tambov rural revolution and the Kronstadt naval mutiny; he also introduced, at the Tenth Party Congress, a ban on factional activity in the party.

Lenin's health was in serious decline in 1921–22, but he had to go on defending the New Economic Policy against Bolshevik critics who wanted either to abandon it or, like Trotsky, introduce more elements of state economic planning. He tried, too, to sketch a future scenario whereby the policy could be used to ease the "transition to socialism." He had not yet made a clear statement of his evolving strategy when, in the spring of 1922, he suffered a massive heart attack. On his sickbed he was angered by policies elaborated by the central party leadership. He detected a lurch into "bureaucratism." He perceived that nations such as the Georgians were being handled in a "Great Russian chauvinist" fashion by the Kremlin. He was exasperated by a proposal to relax the state monopoly on foreign trade. And in each of these matters he blamed Stalin, the party general secretary, as the main culprit. In the winter of 1922–23, fearing his imminent extinction, Lenin dictated a political testament and appended a codicil calling for Stalin's removal from his post. In March 1923, he suffered another heart attack, which ended his political career. His physical end came on January 21, 1924, after a final convulsion. He was not yet fifty-three years old.

Without Lenin the Bolshevik Party's strategy in 1917 would have been more diffuse. Without Lenin, the revolution against the provisional government might have culminated in an all-social coalition government. Without Lenin, the decisions to sign the treaty of Brest-Litovsk or to initiate the National Economic Policy probably would never have been taken. Without Lenin, there might not have been a Communist International. Without Lenin, the entire philosophical underpinning of dictatorship, terror, ideological certitude, and revolutionary optimism and amoralism would have lacked clarity and incisiveness. He was a maker of the 20th century.

See also Bolshevism; Brest-Litovsk, Treaty of; Comintern; Dictatorship of the Proletariat; Imperialism; Jacobinism; Lenin's Testament; New Economic Policy; Red Terror; Russian Revolution and Civil War; War Communism; Zimmerwald Conference.

FURTHER READING

Harding, N. *Lenin's Political Thought*, vols. 1–2. London: Macmillan, 1977–81.

Lenin, V. I. *Collected Works* (several Moscow editions).

Pipes, R., ed. *The Unknown Lenin: From the Secret Archive*. New Haven, CT: Yale University Press, 1996.

Service, R. *Lenin: A Biography*. Cambridge, MA: Harvard University Press, 2000.

———. *Lenin: A Political Life*, vols. 1–3. London: Macmillan, 1985–95.

Trotsky, L. *My Life: The Rise and Fall of a Dictator*. London: Thornton Butterworth, 1930.

ROBERT SERVICE

Leningrad, Siege of

The 872-day siege of Leningrad by German and Finnish armies in World War II was a heroic and tragic event on an unprecedented scale. Nowhere was the will of ordinary people to resist Nazi aggression more bravely manifested—and nowhere at so high a price. In the terrible winter of 1941–42, Leningrad experienced a famine on a scale unparalleled in any other city in world history. Despite the resulting demographic catastrophe, Leningrad defied all attempts by others to subdue it, and in so doing played a crucial role in the Soviet victory over Nazi Germany.

Leningrad was a key target of Operation Barbarossa, launched by Hitler on June 22, 1941, due to its industrial, scientific, and strategic importance. Within two months, Army Group North was approaching Leningrad from the south and the Finns from the north. With the fall of Mga on August 30 the last rail link between Leningrad and the rest of the USSR was cut. On September 8 the Germans captured Schlusselberg, severing the last land link and closing the ring around the city. Only by air and via the long route across Lake Ladoga to the east of Leningrad was contact with the "mainland" now possible. The *blokada* had begun.

The days that followed saw fierce fighting as German forces reached the outskirts of the city, with their ad-

vance units barely ten kilometers from the center. But Leningrad was now a highly fortified city, and its defenders under Georgii Zhukov were prepared to fight street by street. In the last days of September, Hitler saw that the attempt to take Leningrad by storm would be costly in the extreme. German artillery and infantry were diverted to join the imminent attack on Moscow. Hitler's order was to bomb, shell, and starve Leningrad into submission—and then destroy it. Even surrender would not save the city. The cradle of the Bolshevik revolution was to be wiped off the face of the earth.

This was a feasible strategy. The population of the besieged city, including many refugees, was nearly three million. There were only a few weeks' stock of food and fuel, and providing the population with adequate supplies from outside was now impossible. The destruction of the Badaev food warehouses added to the gravity of the situation. Strict rationing was introduced, but within weeks the situation was desperate. Rations were continually reduced. On November 20, with only a few days' grain left in the city, the bread ration, the only food regularly provided, was cut to 250 grams a day for workers and 125 grams for others—and this was with sawdust and other inedible ingredients added. This was starvation level. The effects were soon felt. Infants and the elderly were the first to die, but soon able-bodied adults also succumbed, and generally men sooner than women. "Alimentary dystrophy" quickly became the prime cause of death, with starving people suddenly collapsing and dying at work, in the streets, or at home. Cases of food crimes, including murder for ration cards, escalated, as did reports of cannibalism. So too did summary executions by the police to prevent the breakdown of law and order.

Leningrad was now in the grip of famine. To add to the population's plight, winter 1941–42 would be one of the coldest on record. With fuel supplies nearly exhausted, factories stopped production, and public transport, heating, lighting, electricity, and water supply ceased. The death rate rose rapidly. In peacetime it had averaged thirty-seven hundred a month; by the beginning of December it had reached one thousand a day, and by the end of December that number rose to twenty-five hundred.

The authorities' response to this situation varied. With Stalin's and the Soviet leadership's attention focused on the national war effort and the titanic battles raging outside Moscow and in the south of the country, their ability or willingness to commit resources to save Leningrad from its fate were limited. Supplies sent into the city were incapable of sustaining the lives of Leningrad's people, though no mention of their plight was allowed in the Soviet press. The Leningrad leadership, headed by Andrei Zhdanov, were largely left to their own devices. At the end of November, they succeeded in opening a route across the frozen Lake Ladoga, and the evacuation of people from the city began. After ten days, however, it was stopped on orders from the Kremlin. Priority had to be given to the transport of war material and personnel needed on the Moscow front. Attention meanwhile was focused on the offensive about to begin in the Tikhvin area that, it was believed, would end the siege.

This optimism was misplaced. The December 1941–January 1942 offensive failed to break the iron ring around Leningrad. While a rail link to Lake Ladoga was opened, the siege continued and the desperate crisis in Leningrad deepened. In January and February 1942, Leningrad was a city of death. Over 3,000 people were dying each day. On February 7 the number of deaths recorded was 4,720—and this was undoubtedly an underestimate of the actual mortality. Those registering deaths were themselves dying. People who collapsed in the street were often simply left there. The bodies of many who died at home were kept there while their starving relatives used their ration cards. The death rate in hospitals soared, while cemeteries and mortuaries were full to overflowing. At the Piskarevskoe cemetery there were 25,000 unburied corpses in February. Its mass graves would eventually be the last resting place of over half a million people.

How in these horrific conditions did anyone survive, let alone half of those who remained in the city? As in any extreme situation, some had privileged access to the necessities of life, particularly those who were party and state officials, while others obtained it through connections, crime, or selling whatever they had on the black market. Red Army soldiers stationed in or near Leningrad were also a source of food for civilians. But for most survival depended on their own powers of innovation, which enabled them to discover sources of nutrition in bark, cellulose, nettles, pine needles, plaster, and many other substances—combined with mutual support and the sheer determination not to give in. There are countless examples of Leningraders who managed to survive in defiance of all medical logic, who though starving somehow found reserves of physical and psychological strength.

The ice road across Lake Ladoga was a crucial factor in making the difference between life and death for a huge number of Leningraders between January and April 1942. Over half a million people were evacuated across the "Road of Life," which also made possible a large increase in food supplies to the besieged city. By spring, starvation was ending and Leningrad was returning to life. At the end of March, Leningrad's exhausted population was mobilized for ten days to rid the city of the filth that had accumulated over the preceding months, and by so doing it prevented the epidemics feared by the authorities. Cultural life, industrial production, and scientific work revived, though the population engaged in them by summer was only eight hundred thousand, or less than a third of the prewar level. Nothing more poignantly symbolized the city's revival than the emaciated survivors of the Leningrad Philharmonic Orchestra reuniting in August to perform Dmiytry Shostakovich's Seventh Symphony, dedicated to Leningrad, which the composer had been writing in the city as the blockade began.

But the siege went on. Leningrad was still surrounded. The Germans still occupied key points from which they bombed and shelled the city. And while the death rate declined, people continued to die from the effects of the famine during 1942. A major breach in the blockade came in January 1943 when the Red Army launched an offensive on the Leningrad and Volkhov fronts. After heavy fighting, Soviet forces on the two fronts met and opened a ten-kilometer land corridor to the besieged city. On February 7, the first train in 517 days arrived in Leningrad; over three thousand more, though shelled by German artillery, would follow it over the next year. These enabled more food, fuel, manufactured products, and raw materials to be brought into the city, and more people to be evacuated. While the enemy bombardment of Leningrad continued, conditions in the city steadily improved. By the end of 1943, the birth rate exceeded the death rate for the first time since the beginning of the siege. Yet the siege was not broken until the Red Army's offensive in January 1944, and on January 27 Leningrad was finally liberated.

How many people died during the siege of Leningrad will never be known. While the size of the population before and after is known, many refugees entered the city as the Germans approached, even though this was prohibited. Official figures of those receiving ration cards do not include people living a desperate subterranean existence. Recent research suggests that civilian deaths in Leningrad and its suburbs, including those occupied by the Germans, totaled at least 750,000. To these must be added the large number of Red Army deaths in fighting around Leningrad. The total Soviet deaths resulting from the siege were well over one million.

The immense suffering and sacrifice of Leningrad's population were recognized at the end of the war by its being the first Soviet city to be awarded the title "Hero City." This would not, however, long protect it from Stalin's suspicion that its wartime experience had created an ethos of independence that threatened Moscow's control. In the "Leningrad Affair" of 1949–50 leaders of the city were arrested and shot, and many others sentenced to imprisonment and exile.

Commemoration of Leningrad's ordeal was largely suppressed, and years would pass before the history of the siege could be properly studied. The task of writing it continues today, and it is crucial that it should—for nothing so dramatically epitomizes the triumph and tragedy of the Soviet Union and its people in World War II as the siege of Leningrad.

See also Great Patriotic War; World War II; Zhdanov, Andrey.

FURTHER READING

Barber, J., and A. R. Dzeniskevic, eds. *Life and Death in Besieged Leningrad, 1941–1944.* Basingstoke: Palgrave Macmillan, 2004.

Bidlack, R. *The Siege of Leningrad.* New Haven, CT: Yale University Press, 2006.

Salisbury, H. E. *I 900. Ggiorni: l'assedio di Leningrado.* Milan: Bompiani, 1969.

Simmons, C., and N. Perlina. *Writing the Siege of Leningrad: Women's Diaries, Memoirs, and Documentary Prose.* Preface R. Bidlack. Pittsburgh: University Press of Pittsburgh, 2002.

JOHN D. BARBER

Lenin's Testament

Lenin, dominant leader of the Soviet state in revolution and civil war, suffered serious bouts of ill health from 1921. He had had chronic physical difficulties over many years, but the latest episodes plainly suggested irreversible deterioration. Rest and recuperation were advised. Against his inclinations, Lenin took things a little easier. This was not enough. In May 1922 he suffered a heart attack and was compelled to convalesce at the Gorki sanatorium outside Moscow. His speech and movement were badly affected. Nevertheless Lenin refused to give up hope of maintaining control over policies. He received agendas and papers. He also consulted Stalin, party general secretary since the Eleventh Party Congress, about what was going on. Lenin's close watch over Stalin aimed to diminish the possibility of Trotsky turning the New Economic Policy further in the direction of state central economic planning. Lenin's judgment was that the concessions made to peasants, artisans, and traders since spring 1921 had to be maintained.

Stalin, however, began to annoy him. Three matters gave cause for concern. Lenin, like Trotsky, regarded the state monopoly of foreign trade as crucial to the economic and political security of the Soviet state. Stalin was among those Bolshevik leaders who doubted that this was practical under the NEP. It only encouraged smuggling, with a consequent of loss in fiscal revenues, across the borders. Another issue of growing worry to Lenin was his recognition of the bureaucratic degeneration of the party and government. Lenin believed that the Workers' and Peasants' Inspectorate (Rabkrin), which checked on corruption and inefficiency in public institutions, was itself a den of bureaucratism. Then there was the matter of the constitution. Stalin wished to incorporate the formally independent Soviet republics, such as Ukraine, into Russia (or the RSFSR), whereas Lenin, alert to national sensitivities, urged the formation of a federal structure with the RSFSR as one Soviet republic among several.

Lenin demonstrably did not disagree with Stalin about the primary questions of the revolution. Both endorsed the one-party state, terror, mono-ideocracy, and the treatment of society as a human resource to be mobilized. But Lenin detested being thwarted. What is more, his health aggravated his volatility of temperament; and of course his absence from Central Committee meetings increased his suspicions about what Stalin was up to.

The upshot was a tactical decision to align himself not with Stalin but with Trotsky, whom until recently he had regarded as the main threat to the success of the regime's policies. Lenin and Trotsky held not dissimilar opinions about the three matters in dispute. Nadezhda Krupskaya, Lenin's wife, illicitly kept Lenin informed about deals being done in the politburo. Stalin cursed her in filthy language, but Krupskaya kept quiet about it in Lenin's presence. Meanwhile Lenin started, with the politburo's permission, to dictate a series of articles on contemporary politics. He and Trotsky won the discussion on foreign trade in the Central Committee. Lenin also made the proposal that workers be admitted to membership of the Central Committee and Rabkrin. Most importantly, he followed up on the findings of an enquiry into Stalin's role in the imposition of strict Moscow authority over the Georgian Soviet republic, which served to confirm Lenin's conviction that Stalin, despite himself being Georgian, was acting like a "Great Russian chauvinist."

Sensing the imminence of death, Lenin in the winter of 1922–23 proceeded to dictate what became known as his political testament. He found fault with six Bolshevik leaders. He identified Trotsky and Stalin as the likeliest individuals to fight for the succession to his position— and he speculated that Trotsky might stand for the workers' interests, Stalin for those of the peasantry. Enraged by Stalin in particular, he urged his immediate removal from the general secretaryship.

It was not to be. On learning about Stalin's verbal abuse of Krupskaya, Lenin suffered a massive heart attack on March 10, 1923, and was never again able to participate in politics. He died on January 21, 1924. Stalin not only survived; he became the prime organizer of Lenin's funeral. Much was subsequently made about Lenin's perspicacity in his last writings. This is, however, hardly justified. Lenin offered no elaborated vision of a gentler form of communism than already existed in the early 1920s. Nor was he right about the ground on which Trotsky and Stalin would fight their battles after his death. Trotsky's campaign for industrialization would scarcely have eased conditions for workers, at least in the short term; Stalin's successful lunge for supremacy had nothing to do with making life more comfortable for peasants. Furthermore, Lenin's proposals for reform of the party and Rabkrin and on the national question were inadequate as solutions. But in death he was apotheosized. His cult became the unifying myth of the USSR until its demise.

See also Bureaucracy; Lenin, Vladimir; Nationality Policies; New Economic Policy; Politburo; Revolution, Myths of the; Russian Revolution and Civil War; Stalin, Joseph.

FURTHER READING

Cohen, S. F. *Bukharin and the Russian Revolution: A Political Biography, 1888–1938.* New York: Vintage Books, 1973.

Lewin, M. *Lenin's Last Struggle.* London: Collins, 1969.

Service, R. *Lenin: A Biography.* London: Basingstoke, 2000.

———. *Lenin: A Political Life*, vol. 3, *The Iron Ring.* London: Macmillan, 1995.

ROBERT SERVICE

Liebknecht, Karl

Born on August 13 in Leipzig, son of the famous founder of the German Social Democratic Party (SPD), Wilhelm Liebknecht (1826–1900), Karl Liebknecht (1871–1919) followed an altogether typical party career in the years before World War I. Starting in 1903 he was a delegate at almost all the party's congresses and meetings of the Socialist International; he was a cofounder of the International Youth Association, and from 1907 to 1910 its president; from 1902 to 1913 he was a municipal councilor in Berlin; starting in 1908 he was a deputy to Prussia's regional council; and from 1912 on he was a member of the Reichstag. In 1916, Liebknecht was stripped of the latter two political mandates since he was sentenced to prison for political reasons. His main political objectives were: the promotion and antimilitarist education of independent socialist working-class youths; the struggle against Prussia's class-based voting system, which included resorting to collective actions, especially the mass strike; and engagement against militarism and any type of warmongering activity. When, in early 1913, he discovered and denounced an episode of corruption at the Ministry of War—the Krupp armaments industry was involved—his reputation as an antimilitarist extended beyond German borders.

In August 1914 Liebknecht participated, out of loyalty to party discipline, in the vote by the SPD parliamentary group in the Reichstag in favor of war loans. Starting in December 1914, however, out of loyalty to the principles of socialist internationalism, he was the only member of his party to vote against war loans, and in Parliament he continued to reject—initially by himself, later with a second SPD deputy, and beginning in December 1915 with a minority of another nineteen Social Democratic deputies—every funding request submitted by the imperial government. His choice served the purpose of stimulating the weak opposition to the almost unlimited support given to the kaiser's government by the leadership and the majority of the SPD parliamentary group. Together with the group led by Luxemburg (later designated Internationale and then Spartakus), Liebknecht worked to coalesce the opposition within the party and promote mass actions in favor of peace. Arrested on May 1, 1916, in Berlin during an illegal demonstration against the war, and condemned for this reason to four years and one month in prison, Liebknecht was cut out of active politics for the rest of the conflict. In 1917 he was a powerless witness, behind prison bars, to the expulsion of the SPD's internal opposition and the foundation of the Independent Social Democratic Party of Germany (USPD).

Granted an early release on October 23, 1918, he pressured the representatives of the opposition in the Berlin metalworkers' union to spark an early revolutionary uprising by the workers. After the revolt's success on November 9, he proclaimed the "socialist republic" from the Berlin castle, to the applause of an enormous crowd; he fought for a continuation of the revolution and the council's ongoing existence. When the USPD, to which Liebknecht still belonged together with the Spartakus league, did not follow the radical requests of this group, Liebknecht and Luxemburg founded the Communist Party of Germany (KPD) in 1919, on New Year's Day. Liebknecht led the Berlin revolt against the Ebert-Scheidemann government, starting January 5, without having previously received the consent of the KPD's leadership. After the uprising's failure, Liebknecht was assassinated on January 15, 1919, by elements of the Freikorps.

See also Internationalism; Luxemburg, Rosa; Socialist International; Zimmerwald Conference.

FURTHER READING

Liebknecht, K. *Militarism.* New York: B. W. Huebsch, 1917.

———. *Gesammelte Reden und Schriften.* Ed. Institute for Marxism-Leninism at the SED's Central Committee. 9 vols. Berlin: Dietz Verlag, 1958.

———. *Militarisme, guerre, revolution.* Ed. C. Weill. Paris: Maspero, 1970.

Trotnow, H. *Karl Liebknecht. Eine politische Biographie.* Cologne: Kiepenhauer and Witsch, 1980.

Wohlgemuth, H. *Karl Liebknecht. Eine Biographie.* Berlin: Dietz, 1973.

OTTOKAR LUBAN

Lin Biao

Lin Biao (1907–71) was for a brief period—between 1966 and 1971—the most powerful man in China after Mao Zedong and his designated successor. After his plane and political fortunes crashed in 1971, in circumstances that remain suspicious, Lin became public enemy number one, and his image had to be erased from the numerous official photographs in which he appeared beside his mentor.

Lin's political career was primarily that of a military leader. Educated at the Whampoa military academy during the years of the First United Front, Lin entered the Red Army after the break between the Communist and Nationalist parties in 1927, and he was Mao's ally in the 1930s, both in the Jiangxi Soviet and during the Long March. Lin's entire career is tied to the organization of the People's Liberation Army as an instrument of party policy. Considered a brilliant strategist, but suffering from poor health, Lin was seriously injured in battle in 1938, and his political career was probably slowed by his poor health. A member of the Central Committee starting in 1945 and the Political Office beginning in 1955, Lin's somewhat uneventful career was catapulted toward the highest reaches of Chinese communism when Mao named him defense minister. Lin succeeded Peng Dehuai, who had criticized Mao's disastrous economic decisions during the Great Leap Forward at the Lushan Plenum in 1959.

From that moment on Lin would be Mao's liaison to the People's Liberation Army. More specifically, he was the person who promoted the idea of Mao's infallibility and the concept of "command politics" with the troops. It was Lin once more who was put in charge of editing Mao's quotations for the famous *Red Book*. The first version of the booklet, which would become the symbol of the "Red Guards," contained an introduction by Lin in which he presented absolute obedience to the president's instructions as the nation's guiding principle. In 1966, after the beginning of the Cultural Revolution and Liu Shaoqi's purge, Lin formally became the party's number two. In his hands, the army became not only an important instrument of propaganda but also the needle on the scale in the struggle between factions during the Cultural Revolution. The army was also used to reestablish order starting in 1969.

Lin's death and fall from grace in 1971 remain one of the mysteries of Chinese communism—a mystery that will perhaps never be solved. Lin died in a plane accident near the border with Mongolia while, according to official historiography, he was escaping to the Soviet Union. The explanations for the apparent escape are various: one of the most common is that Lin and his son Lin Liguo were organizing Mao's assassination. Unfortunately, the majority of the documents that would be able to prove this or other versions of the events were most probably destroyed in the years that followed. According to a different interpretation of his last days, Lin was the unconscious victim of his family's political machinations, after Mao in 1970 had given his support to a substantial softening of the radical policies of the Cultural Revolution, weakening Lin's position within the party leadership.

See also Cult of Personality; Cultural Revolution in China; Mao Zedong; Red Guard.

FURTHER READING

Qiu, Jin. *The Culture of Power: The Lin Biao Incident in the Cultural Revolution*. Stanford, CA: Stanford University Press, 1999.

Teiwes, F. C., and W. Sun. *The Tragedy of Lin Biao: Riding the Tiger during the Cultural Revolution*. Honolulu: University Press of Hawaii, 1996.

LUIGI TOMBA

Literacy, Soviet Union Campaign for Adult

On December 26, 1919, the Russian Republic's Council of People's Commissars (Sovnarkom) issued a decree "On the Liquidation of Illiteracy among the Population of the RSFSR" (O likvidatsii bezgramotnosti sredi naseleniia RSFSR), which targeted children and adults between the ages of eight and fifty. This target group numbered an estimated thirty million children and adults in Russia in 1919. While this decree spoke specifically of campaigning for literacy in the Russian Republic, the Soviet government and the Communist Party launched similar campaigns in other republics of the Soviet Union. The decree, which came to be called the "Lenin decree," arrived on the heels of earlier, postrevolution decrees addressing adult and juvenile literacy as well as prerevolution era efforts by private literacy societies scattered among major Russian cities. Sovnarkom delegated authority for this literacy effort to the People's Commissariat for Education (Narkompros), which in turn assigned the work to its Chief Committee for Political Education (Glavpolitprosvet).

Nadezhda Krupskaia, head of the Glavpolitprosvet, placed the campaign for literacy in the context of modernity, progress, and competition with Western nations. If Russia were to modernize and so compete with the bourgeoisie-controlled states of the West, Krupskaia

argued, it needed a literate workforce that understood chemistry, mechanics, and physics. In June 1920, the Narkompros created the Extraordinary Commission for the Liquidation of Illiteracy (Cheka likbez), and at the request of the commission, placed it under the control of the Glavpolitprosvet. The Cheka likbez oversaw the orchestration of the literacy effort through the use of literacy teachers and ultimately the Society for Down with Illiteracy (Obshchestvo "Doloi negramotnost," or the ODN).

The 1919 decree, coming as it did out of the era of civil war in Russia, brought to the literacy effort an attitude of militancy. Literacy schools were "illiteracy liquidation points," or likpunkty. Literacy teachers were "illiteracy liquidators" fighting on a "front" against backwardness and ignorance. With the waning of the civil war in Russia came a waning of the effort for literacy. By 1922, the war era campaign had stagnated due to strained budgets and the wartime disruption of society. If the campaign were to continue, it needed to have a renewed focus with a new theme. Thus, in 1923, the Cheka likbez and the Glavpolitprosvet inaugurated a new campaign with a terminal date of November 7, 1927, the tenth anniversary of the October Revolution.

This four-year campaign had a narrower age range for its target population, with children and adults between the ages of eleven and forty being selected as potential students. Based on an abbreviated census of 1920, the Cheka likbez estimated that seventeen million Russians between these ages were illiterate in 1923, with nearly 80 percent located in the rural areas of Russia. While there were no full census data on which to estimate the level of illiteracy in 1923, data from the 1926 census show that literacy among men between the ages of eighteen and thirty-five within Russia averaged 81 percent, and that literacy among women of the same age cohort averaged 50 percent; literacy rates for men and women in the countryside were lower at 77 and 42 percent, respectively. Census takers counted an individual as literate if he or she could read and copy out a brief passage in his or her native tongue.

With a military precision reminiscent of the war years, the Cheka likbez laid out an "offensive" for literacy that first focused on trade union members (ages eighteen to thirty-five) and teenagers of a premilitary age; union members would be addressed in the first two years of the campaign, with the rural population receiving the most attention in the second, third, and fourth years. Paid and volunteer literacy teachers carried out instruction in the likpunkty, rural reading rooms, and union club rooms. The courses were brief, ranging from three to six months of instruction and self-study. Campaign organizers and teachers admitted that the campaign courses offered only the rudiments of literacy. Graduates of these sessions were at best "semiliterate."

The 1920s' campaign for adult literacy in Russia met with mixed success. On the one hand, enrollment in literacy classes did not come close to the target set at the start of the offensive. For example, the first school year, 1923–24, saw an enrollment level of only 22 percent in literacy classes. The last year of the formal campaign, 1926–27, was the best one with an enrollment level of 56 percent. Moreover, by 1926 the Narkompros had to admit that as many children were dropping out of school before gaining literacy as there were adults being taught to read and write. In effect, there was no net gain of literacy in Russia during the years of the campaign. On the other hand, several million adults did learn to read and write during the years of the campaign; one high estimate in 1927 put the total number at between five and six million. Also in 1926, the Narkompros extended the campaign into the 1930s, with a new terminal point of 1932, which coincided with the goal of establishing compulsory education for elementary and secondary school students. Ultimately, by the post–World War II period, the Russian Republic—and the Soviet Union generally—enjoyed a high level of literacy. This was due more to compulsory public education, however, than to literacy campaigning among adults.

There was more to the Russian literacy campaign (and its sister campaigns in other Soviet republics) than simply teaching children, teenagers, and adults how to read and write. There were overtly political, social, and economic motivations. The political motivations focused on both the students and the literacy volunteers, especially those who were members of the literacy society, the ODN. Like the literacy effort itself, the ODN had its own antecedents in prerevolutionary Russia with numerous cities hosting volunteer literacy societies. The ODN was constructed much like the Communist Party, with the village- and neighborhood-level "cell" being the basic unit of organization with larger, oversight bodies at the township, county, provincial, and central levels. The ODN's titular head was politburo member Mikhail Kalinin, who stated explicitly in 1926 that the ODN served to develop the "social skills" and "social instincts" of its members. At its height in 1926, the ODN counted 1.6 million members within its ranks. For students,

the political message of the campaign was also clear. While literacy teachers were instructed not to frighten off students with aggressively political lessons, students were clearly aware of the connection between the literacy effort and the political situation in Soviet Russia. The Glavpolitprosvet orchestrated the campaign, while the readings carried such titles as "We Are not Slaves," and dramatizations promoting literacy portrayed it as a means to combat the influence of the village priest, local gypsies, and the wealthy peasantry.

Social and economic motivations worked in tandem. The 1920s' era saw a focus on alliance or *smychka* between rural and urban areas. The literacy campaign fit into this with its organizers promoting the notion that literacy in the countryside would enhance this alliance by bringing ideas of modernity and progress from the city to the village. Furthermore, a literate population was a productive population. One of the several proliteracy posters of the 1920s' campaign states that "in order to have more, one must produce more; in order to produce more, one must know more." Higher production levels would lead to higher living standards—so the logic went—in both the countryside and urban centers. Literacy campaigners as well as government and party officials also linked public health—both a social and an economic issue—with literacy.

Revolutionary movements during the 20th century with aspirations to socialism and communism looked to the Soviet Union as a model for development. In terms of spreading literacy, this is especially true of Latin American countries, such as Cuba in the 1960s and Nicaragua in the early 1980s. Each country witnessed a concerted effort to expand adult literacy, in both the countryside and urban areas.

Though politics certainly motivated leaders in Cuba and Nicaragua, just as it did in the Soviet Union, the desire to increase economic and social development was also a motivating factor. Government leaders could see the obvious link between widespread adult literacy and economic strength and social stability. India and Japan in the 1960s are examples. Whereas India had nearly three times as much land devoted to agriculture as Japan did in the 1960s, it produced eight times less per acre than Japan. The level of rural illiteracy was still high in India in the 1960s, while comparatively low in Japan.

Literacy instruction in the Russia of the 1920s focused on a potential social good that could come of Communist-motivated, revolutionary movements. While overtly politically motivated and centered on economic development, the Russian model of literacy campaigning pointed a way toward social development and inclusivity that other campaigns of the Soviet period in Russian history and the history of communism in other nations did not.

See also Cultural Policies; Modernization; Propaganda, Communist.

FURTHER READING

Arnove, R. F., and H. J. Graff, eds. *National Literacy Campaigns: Historical and Comparative Perspectives.* New York: Plenum Press, 1987.

Bogdanov, I. M. *Gramotnost' i obrazovanie v dorevoliutsionnoi Rossii i v SSSR.* Moscow: Statistika, 1964.

Brooks, J. *When Russia Learned to Read: Literacy and Popular Literature, 1861–1917.* Princeton, NJ: Princeton University Press, 1985.

Cardinal, F. S. J., and V. Miller. "Nicaragua 1980: The Battle of the ABCs." *Harvard Educational Review* 51 (February 1981): 1–26.

Chufarov, V. G. "Ural'skaia partiinaia organizatsiia v bor'be za likvidatsiiu negramotnosti sredi vzroslogo naseleniia v gody vosstanovitel'nogo perioda (1920–1925 gg.)." *Uchenye Zapiski Ural'skogo Gosudarstvennogo Universiteta* 33 (1960): 13–33.

Clark, C. E. *Uprooting Otherness: The Literacy Campaign in NEP-era Russia.* Selinsgrove, PA: Susquehanna University Press, 2000.

Eklof, B. "Peasant Sloth Reconsidered: Strategies of Education and Learning in Rural Russia before the Revolution." *Journal of Social History* 14 (Spring 1981): 355–85.

Fitzpatrick, S. *The Commissariat of Enlightenment: Soviet Organization of Education and the Arts under Lunacharsky, October 1917–1921.* Cambridge, UK: Cambridge University Press, 1970.

———. "The 'Soft' Line on Culture and Its Enemies: Soviet Cultural Policy, 1922–1927." *Slavic Review* 33 (June 1974): 267–87.

———. *Education and Social Mobility in the Soviet Union, 1921–34.* Cambridge, UK: Cambridge University Press, 1979.

Gleason, A., P. Kenez, and R. Stites, eds. *Bolshevik Culture: Experiment and Order in the Russian Revolution.* Bloomington: Indiana University Press, 1985.

Graff, H. J., ed. *Literacy and Social Development in the West: A Reader.* Cambridge: Cambridge University Press, 1981.

Guroff, G., and S. F. Starr. "A Note on Urban Literacy in Russia, 1890–1914." *Jahrbucher fur Geschichte Osteuropas* 4 (December 1971): 520–31.

Holmes, L. E. *The Kremlin and the Schoolhouse: Reforming Education in Soviet Russia, 1917–1931.* Bloomington: Indiana University Press, 1991.

Ivanova, A. M. *Chto sdelala sovetskaia vlast' po likvidatsii negramotnosti sredi vzroslykh.* Moscow: Uchpedgiz, 1949.

Kenez, P. "Liquidating Illiteracy in Revolutionary Russia." *Russian History/Histoire Russe* 9, 2–3 (1982): 173–86.

———. *The Birth of the Propaganda State: Soviet Methods of Mass Mobilization, 1917–1929.* Cambridge, UK: Cambridge University Press, 1985.

Kiseleva, T. G. *Narodnoe obrazovanie i prosveshchenie v Rossii: real'nost' i mify.* Moscow: Moskovskii Gosudarstvennyi Universitet Kul'tury i Iskusstva, 2002.

Kline, G. L., ed. *Soviet Education.* Foreword by G. S. Counts. New York: Columbia University Press, 1957.

Koval'chuk, V. M., et al., eds. *Dobrovol'nye obshchestva v Petrograde-Leningrade v 1917–1937 gg.* Leningrad: Nauka, 1989.

Krupskaia, N. K., ed. *Likvidatsiia negramotnosti. Sbornik statei, dokladov i raznykh materialov za 1920–1936 gody.* Moscow: Narkompros RSFSR, 1938.

Kumanev, V. A. *Sotsializm i vsenarodnaia gramotnost'.* Moscow: Nauka, 1967.

Mironov, B. N. "Literacy in Russia, 1797–1917: Obtaining New Historical Information through the Application of Retrospective Prediction Methods." *Soviet Studies in History* (Winter 1986–87): 89–117.

Morales, A. P. "The Literacy Campaign in Cuba." *Harvard Educational Review* 51 (February 1981): 31–39.

Odom, W. E. *The Soviet Volunteers: Modernization and Bureaucracy in a Public Mass Organization.* Princeton, NJ: Princeton University Press, 1973.

Rashin, A. G. "Gramotnost' i narodnoe obrazovanie v Rossii v XIX i nachale XX v." *Istoricheskie zapiski* 37 (1951): 28–80.

Remizova, T. A. *Kul'turno-prosvetitel'naia rabota v RSFSR (1921–1925 gg.).* Moscow: Izd-vo Akademii nauk SSSR, 1962.

Schultz, T. W. *Transforming Traditional Agriculture.* New Haven, CT: Yale University Press, 1964.

Zinoviev, M., and A. Pleshakova. *Kak byl vypolnen leninskii dekret.* Moscow: Gospolitizdat, 1961.

CHARLES E. CLARK

Literature in Soviet Russia

On a general theoretical level, the relationship between literature and communism is part of the broader relationship between art and power, and between artistic expression and society's ideological foundations. As for the relationship in Russia, one must distinguish between the prerevolutionary period and that which witnessed the coming to power and later the entrenchment of the Soviet system. Undoubtedly there is a strong connection between these different historical and artistic situations, since many of the ideological and political peculiarities that a victorious communism exhibited toward literature and its control in the new Soviet state were a function of its aesthetic, literary, and philosophical antecedents in the prerevolutionary period, or more accurately, their reception as set forth in the new official literary theory. This perspective's importance is even clearer in regard to the historicotypological rereading of Russian literature—one not limited to the immediately preceding centuries—taking Soviet historiography into account. For example, using the year in which the revolution emerged victorious as a reference point, "literature and communism" in the pre-revolutionary phase can be referred to as "literature and ideas of communism," and in the postrevolutionary phase as "literature and the realization of communism."

Pre-revolutionary Russian literature in the post-Petrist era can be schematically subdivided into classicism, sentimentalism, romanticism, realism ("critical" in the Soviet meaning of the term), and modernism in its various manifestations. Its attitude toward Communist ideas, in their developmental phase, from their Enlightenment-utopian beginnings up to the Marxist-Leninist stage, both on a philosophical and journalistic as well as creative and aesthetic level, was varied. According to Soviet historiography, landmarks in the development of this relationship to Communist ideas are the work of Aleksandr Radishchëv (author of the pamphlet-novel *Journey from St. Petersburg to Moscow* [1790], an indictment of serfdom) and his followers, based on V. Orlov's interpretation (the *radishchëvcy* poets), the Decembrist writers (but seen from Lenin's perspective and therefore "extremely distant from the people"), and the authors of "critical realism" (based on the interpretation first given by Vissarion Belinsky and later the democratic critics Nikolaj Dobrolyubov and Nikolaj Chernyshevsky), as exemplified in Alexander Herzen's work (which was somewhere between egalitarian utopianism and peasant religiosity). Further developments then led to literature with a populist and socialist orientation during the second half of the 19th century; its most important theorist was Nikolaj Michajlovsky. Obviously a large portion of Russian literature starting in the romantic period had to deal with the whole set of Communist and revolutionary ideals, thus taking an explicit position on the different currents of thought and political movements of its time.

Especially after the greater diffusion of Hegelian thought on the one hand, and French utopian thought on the other, communism as an ideal and a goal for the transformation of Russian society became key topics discussion, given Russia's social and historical specificities. This led a large number of democratically oriented intellectuals and writers to hypothesize the passage to a socialist society without an intervening capitalist phase. Questions about the national characteristics of ideologies of social and political liberation were contrasted with the great themes that characterized the social, political, and economic life of the country: the issues of serfdom and *bunt* (peasant revolt), the communistic structures of patriarchal and peasant Russia, the role of the intelligentsia, nihilism, and the backwardness of the popular masses in the Russian Empire. These issues were dealt with differently in the novels of Ivan Turgenev and Fyodor Dostoyevsky, the writings of Herzen and the *narodniki* (Nikolay Chernyshevsky's novel *What Is to Be Done?*, 1863, is a key text in this context), Nikolaj Nekrasov's poetry, the ideological and artistic confrontation between the progressive thesis novels and those of the "antinihilist" type (from Turgenev's *Fathers and Sons*, to Nikolai Leskov, Aleksey Pisemsky and on up to Dostoyevsky's *The Possessed*), and later in the grandiose and contradictory narrative and journalistic opus of Lev Tolstoy.

The revolutionary movement grew in Russia, thousands of disagreements and splits notwithstanding, and intellectuals were generally close to it. This growth led to a crescendo in these years culminating in the 1905 Revolution, in which not only Marxist and populist literature, but also works coming from the ranks of the modernists (decadents and symbolists), were involved. The new critical realism, now "revolutionary romanticism," in the work of Maksim Gorky and many other realist narrators of the period tended to transform literature into a megaphone for social struggle and revolt, and was therefore increasingly close to the theory of literature espoused by Russian Marxists from Georgy Plekhanov to Lenin. But even "niche" literature, like that of the symbolists or other poetry groups, dealt with the great topics of revolution and social justice, even if located somewhere between myth and apocalypse. This is how tendencies such as the mystical anarchism of Georgy Chulkov or the Scythianism of Ivanov-Razumnik, Aleksandr Blok, and Andrei Bely developed; during the revolutionary years, such tendencies would make masterpieces like *The Scythians* and *Twelve* by Blok and *Christ Has Risen Again* by Bely possible.

Bolshevism's victory and the birth of the Soviet Union turned the relationship between literature and communism upside down. The establishment of a proletarian literature that inherited many tendencies from pre-revolutionary socialist literature as well as popular and peasant literature (from Nikolai Nikitin to Drozzhin) led to the creation of specific literary organizations, many of which were destroyed or else forced to become part of the Russian Association of Proletarian Writers, directly under the Soviet government's control, toward the end of the 1920s. Later, in 1932, all literary and artistic organizations were closed, and in 1934, the Union of Soviet Writers was born during the First Writers' Congress. Yet initially the literary and artistic avant-garde of the 1910s, the different currents of Russian futurism, claimed to be the sole representatives of the new revolutionary and proletarian art. This tendency can be traced to Vladimir Mayakovsky and his left-wing Front of the Arts. The failure of this attempt and the reduced possibilities for free artistic expression during the 1920s—which first affected those writers who opposed communism (the many who emigrated over the decade, and the many who died, like Nikolaj Gumilëv), then the so-called *poputchiki* (fellow travelers), and then even authors with a Communist orientation—led to the creation of a monolithic system of ideological and artistic control. This system established itself during the Joseph Stalin years, leading to the Great Purges in 1937–38 and the outbreak of the war.

The 1930s witnessed an increase in repressive measures that ended in the death or silencing of most protagonists of the great literary and artistic blossoming of the pre-revolutionary period. The repression of other national literatures in the USSR was undertaken with the same intensity (for instance, the literature of Ukraine, and figures such as Mykola Chvyl'ovyj or Mykola Zerov), and its authors were often accused of harboring nationalist and antisocialist sentiments. Great authors such as Osip Mandel'stam, Isaac Babel, and Boris Pilnyak died in the gulag, while Anna Akhmatova, Michail Kuzmin, Yuri Olesha, and Michail Bulgakov were forced into silence. Many writers focused on literary translation, frequently from the literatures of other Soviet republics—for example, Boris Pasternak's invaluable translations from Georgian. Many other writers were compelled to do translations to survive economically and physically, thereby making it impossible to freely pursue their own literary work. Marina Tsvetaeva's fate was tragic: she had emigrated during the civil war years and returned to the USSR in 1940, but she soon committed suicide, just as

great poets like Sergej Esenin and Vladimir Mayakovsky had before her. During this period and especially after the war, many writers faced the real possibility of never seeing their works in print, since even the adoption of an Aesopian language, which had been traditional in the 19th century, had at this point become useless. In this fashion a tradition of literary works that were not destined for publication, at least immediately, grew alongside the regime's official literature.

This official literature brought together the revolutionary and socialist realist traditions (from Fumarov to Aleksandr Fadeev, from Fyodor Gladkov's novels about production to Mikhail Sholokhov's famous novels). Starting in the détente years, this same type of parallel literature would start to be distributed by means of the samizdat and *tamizdat*; with the "necessary" care, literary works could even be published in the USSR itself. Examples here include Michail Bulgakov's *Master and Margarita*, which would be published in Russia in 1966–67 (with numerous cuts by the censors), and Boris Pasternak's *Doctor Zhivago*, tied to a famous political and literary scandal in the late 1950s (the novel was published for the first time in Italy, causing its author to be ostracized at home), and only published in the USSR in 1988 during the perestroika years.

With de-Stalinization and détente (in Russian *ottepel'* from the novel with the same title by Ilya Ehrenburg) a new era began, foreshadowed in part by the relative slackening of state police controls during the war years—a slackening that was soon reversed with Andrey Zhdanov's famous attack against Akhmatova and Michail Zoshchenko in 1946. Up to Stalin's death, in 1953, the situation was especially difficult, particularly during the so-called campaign against cosmopolitanism (one of its victims was Vasily Grossman, whose great novels of the 1950s and 1960s were to be published abroad), and the years in which communism was supposedly triumphant and society was allegedly free of social and political conflicts (leading to the so-called literature of the *bezkonfliktnost'*). These years saw the emergence of a number of works dedicated to the war, some of the most remarkable coming from Aleksandr Tvardovskij, Viktor Nekrasov, and Konstantin Simonov, who attempted to overcome the rigid confines of Stalinist ideology by offering a truthful and varied picture of war's reality.

With the end of Stalinism and Khrushchev's rise to power, especially after the latter's celebrated denunciation of the cult of personality and the crimes of the Stalin era, the literary world could once again experience a more tolerant atmosphere. This, in turn, led to the affirmation of young poets like Yevgeny Yevtushenko and Andrey Voznesensky, the diffusion of the bard songs by Bulat Okudzhava, Aleksandr Galich, and later Vladimir Vysocky, the success of young prose writers like Vladimir Dudincev and Vasily Aksenov, and especially the publication in 1962 of Aleksandr Solzhenitsyn's *One Day in the Life of Ivan Denisovich*. The amnesties and rehabilitations that occurred during the Twentieth Congress seemed to revive Russian literature's forgotten and downtrodden heritage, but the complex bureaucratic censorship and control system never experienced a true liberalization (such as in the case of poets Gumilëv or Kuzmin, who were once again accepted in their homeland only during perestroika). Khrushchev's fall and Leonid Brezhnev's rise to power radically transformed the situation yet again, with a full restoration of ideological and censorious control.

The 1965 trial against writers Andrej Sinyavsky and Yuli Daniel, who had published works abroad critical of the Soviet regime, confirmed this return to the past. The persecution and trials of poets and writers, among whom the Nobel Prize winners Solzhenitsyn and Iosif Brodski, would follow. The tendency to publish abroad grew stronger during these years, and the distribution channels for the literature of dissent increased. Exemplary here is the case of the *Metropol'* (1979) almanac, edited by Vasilii Aksenov, Andrei Bitov, Victor Erofeev, Evgenii Popov, and others; its publication was blocked by censors in the USSR and so the work was published abroad. It unambiguously marked the difference between official and underground literature in the late Soviet era. Yet even within official Soviet literature or literature published in the USSR, some writers occasionally used their work to criticize the Soviet system, even if in a veiled manner. Here, the work of the *derevenshchiki* writers must be singled out: they linked the aspirations of the Russian countryside with national-patriotic concepts, thus coming into conflict with the official theses of proletarian internationalism. The forced exile of Solzhenitsyn, Sinyavsky, Joseph Brodsky, and other writers in the early 1970s increased writers' resistance to the Soviet regime, and simultaneously strengthened the new phase of diaspora literature (the third wave, following those after the October Revolution and World War II), which was also supported by the presence of émigré publishing houses in the United States, Germany, France, and other Western countries.

The relationship between literature and communism changed starting in 1985 with the establishment of Gor-bachev's perestroika. During the last years of Soviet power, ideological control tended to lessen and then disappear. Publishing was fully liberalized, and those works that had been banned or not republished since the October Revolution were now published once more. In the post-Soviet era, phenomena that had their roots in artistic and ideological conceptions of the Soviet era survived at the literary margins, but devoid of any references to internationalism, instead focusing on nostalgic national-Communist positions, and even forms of imperial nostalgia and orthodox echoes (the journal *Nas Sovremennik*).

In the other Communist bloc countries, the relationship between literature and communism followed routes analogous to those seen in the Soviet model, but with articulations specific to each national literature. There were tendencies that referred to the ideals of socialism or communism, and aspirations to found a proletarian literature, opposed to the official literature of the bourgeois and nationalist nations that had emerged in those territories in the aftermath of World War I, throughout Eastern Europe during the pre–World War II period, and in many Western literatures (in Bertolt Brecht's work, the many French examples from Jean-Paul Sartre to Louis Aragon, but also the Spanish literature tied to the civil war). After World War II instead the increasing ideological control exercised by the Soviet Union over the East bloc countries, the creation of analogous writers' organizations in each individual country, and the adoption of socialist realism—all led to the affirmation of literary traditions inspired by the principles of a victorious socialism and a Soviet literature with a strong propagandist and ideological component (one could mention Polish realists like Konwicki, Zalewski, or the Czech writers Sedláček, Pludek, Bernášková, and so on).

At the same time, both within these countries and in the context of the various national émigré circles, cultural and literary movements of dissent developed—sometimes tied to prewar traditions, and sometimes tied to new Western trends—and they merged in the wider current of the "other literature," but always in opposition to official literature. Polish literary examples here include Herling Grudzinski (author of *A World Apart*, first published in English in 1951 with a preface by Bertrand Russell, a book devoted to the world of the Soviet camps), Slawomir Mrozek, Czeslaw Milosz, the youthful experimentation of the group Nowa Fala (New Wave) in the 1970s, in addition to the efforts by the journal *Kultura*, published in Paris by Jerzy Giedroyc. In Czech literature, key examples include Milan Kundera, Bohumil Hrabal, Ladislav Fuks, and the new surrealism of the 1960s; in Romanian literature, the work of M. Marin Preda or Ş.A. Doina is noteworthy here. These literatures evolved in significantly different directions, especially given the varying attitudes exhibited by their respective governments toward culture: more liberal in some (Poland during détente, Czechoslovakia during the Prague Spring, but also the Yugoslav "anomaly," already starting with the positions taken by P. Şegedin and M. Krleža at the writers congresses of 1949 and 1952); more conformist and bureaucratic in others (especially in the Baltic countries annexed by the USSR).

A completely separate discussion would need to be devoted to more distant literatures, such as those of Asian communism (from the Maoist model to the many Indochinese variations), or that of Cuba, which exerted a significant influence on other Latin American literatures. In some countries the influence of a national tradition in thought and literature was strong (say, Catholicism's influence on Polish literature), and in others the spirit of emulation of Soviet models prevailed (Bulgaria before 1956, for instance). What is certain is that even with the necessary distinctions, the other literatures in Eastern Europe were also subjected to ideological and police control, and therefore repression, just as the many literatures of the peoples of the Soviet Union were (though thanks to Soviet institutions, many Asian literary traditions were able to find written expression, and thanks to translation into Russian, they were able to cross their linguistic and cultural barriers). The other literatures of the socialist bloc also followed the various stages experienced by the various Soviet literatures. The postwar years and those of late Stalinism were particularly oppressive. The Khrushchev era allowed for greater openness (even though, obviously, in countries like Hungary and the German Democratic Republic there were clear signs of restriction), followed by the sudden normalization after the events in Prague in 1968, and then the ups and downs in the Soviet Union from the years of stagnation to perestroika. Poland and Yugoslavia remained islands of relative freedom, by comparison, for most intellectuals in the Soviet bloc.

Ultimately, since the new regimes had a shorter political life, most intellectuals had been formed in the prewar years and had easier access to communication with the outside world, the experience of socialist realism and a Communist-inspired literature was much less consolidated and significant in these countries than it was in the literatures of the USSR and especially Russian literature.

See also Aragon, Louis; Avant-garde; Brecht, Bertolt; Censorship; Dissent in the USSR; Havel, Václav; History and Memory; Intelligentsia; Malraux, André; Mayakovski, Vladimir; Propaganda, Communist; Sartre, Jean-Paul; Shalamov, Varlam; Socialist Realism; Solzhenitsyn, Aleksandr; Zhdanovism.

FURTHER READING

Clark, K. *The Soviet Novel: History as Ritual.* Bloomington: Indiana University Press, 2000.

Dobrenko, E. *The Making of the State Writer: Social and Aesthetic Contexts of the Reception of Soviet Literature.* Stanford, CA: Stanford University Press, 2000.

Geller, M. J. *Il mondo dei lager e la letteratura sovietica.* Rome: Edizioni Paoline, 1977.

Jakobson, R. *Una generazione che ha dissipato i suoi poeti: il problema Majakovskij.* Turin: Einaudi, 1975.

Russkaja intelligencija. Istoria i sud'ba. Moscow: Nauka, 1999.

Strada, V. *EuroRussia: letteratura e cultura da Pietro il Grande alla rivoluzione.* Rome: Laterza, 2005.

STEFANO GARZONIO

Litvinov, Maksim

Maksim Litvinov (1876–1951) was the people's commissar for foreign affairs from July 1930 to May 1939. For Lenin, he was "the greatest crocodile among our diplomats": Litvinov was relentless in his criticism and never let go. And yet for the West in the mid-1930s, he became the emblem of the normal and respectable image that the USSR wanted to project, thanks to his public efforts for peace and collective security. A man of a thousand faces, he provoked great curiosity and perplexity among his contemporaries. There are no half measures in the numerous accounts and analyses devoted to him. Some saw the executioner of revolutionary ideals in him. For others he was an anti-Fascist puppet maneuvered by Stalin. People wondered about the sincerity of his fight against Hitler. They also asked to what degree he might have been a Stalinist.

Litvinov, whose real name was Meir Genoch Moiseevič Vallach, was born to a family of Jewish merchants in Bialystok, in eastern Poland, on the borders of the Russian Empire. After graduating from high school at seventeen, he enrolled in the Russian army and served for five years in Baku. In 1898 he joined the Russian Social Democratic Labor Party and chose a pseudonym that gave him a Russian identity. He spoke Russian with a strong Yiddish accent, however. In 1902, he met Lenin in Switzerland and was given the task of distributing the periodical *Iskra* in the Russian Empire. A delegate to the Bolshevik Central Committee from Russia's northwest, Litvinov participated in the 1905 revolution, and went into exile in 1908. After being expelled from France he settled in London, where he stayed for ten years until his return to revolutionary Russia in 1918. A secretary of the Bolsheviks' London group, at the war's outset he was also a member of the bureau of the Socialist International, provoking Rosa Luxemburg's amazement in December 1913; she considered him a "perfect idiot."

An activist, a good organizer, and resolute, Litvinov was certainly by no means a theorist. Working in London for a publisher, he slowly moved out of the ghetto of exiled revolutionaries, and assiduously frequented the milieu of the Fabian and Zionist Left, where he met Ivy Low, who became his wife in 1916. He reacted to the February Revolution with both enthusiasm and frustration since he was not in Russia. Litvinov was the unofficial representative of the soviets in London after the October Revolution; he was imprisoned on September 8, 1918, and then exchanged for British representative Bruce Lockhart, who had been arrested in Moscow. He returned to Russia in the fall of 1918, and thanks to Lenin's recommendation, became part of the People's Commissariat for Foreign Affairs (NKID) board. The revolutionary thus became a diplomat in the service of the new Bolshevik Russia.

Georgy Chicherin's vice commissar in the 1920s, Litvinov was the old Bolshevik in the NKID management. Combative, ambitious, and restless in his position as vice commissar, he worked to increase his role in the eyes of his superior, whose illness kept him further and further away from politics. Believed to be the most competent diplomat on Western European questions, during the second half of the 1920s Litvinov was invited to the reunions of the politburo with increasing frequency. Already in 1926 he was presenting the annual foreign policy report to the USSR's Central Executive Committee.

On September 27, 1928, in his new role as ad interim commissar, he had the USSR subscribe to the Briand-Kellog Pact, which committed its parties to renounce war. In his speech to the Central Executive Committee on December 10, 1928, he spoke for the first time of an "indivisible peace"—a deviation from the official isolationism of Soviet foreign policy, which made Stalin and Kliment Voroshilov grind their teeth. In fall 1929 Stalin repeatedly expressed himself in negative terms about Litvinov, who "does not see and is not interested in the revolutionary side of politics"—a judgment probably due to Litvinov's closeness to Nikolay Bukharin and Aleksey Rykov. In June 1930, however, Litvinov, already de facto in charge of the commissariat, was nominated people's commissar for foreign affairs. Once Stalin had defeated the Right opposition, Stalin was grateful to Litvinov for his skills as an orator and a diplomatic operator. But in order to test his loyalty Stalin involved him in the campaign against the "industrial party," the intent of which was to target milieus that were close to the Right opposition.

In the early 1930s Litvinov was a high-level functionary with no political clout, but recognized for his competence, thereby guaranteeing him some professional elbow room. From 1930 to 1933 he steered Soviet diplomacy toward an increasing multilateralism, which during the preparations for the Five-Year Plan, allowed the Soviet Union to reenter the community of nations and freed it from an excessively exclusive relationship with Germany. Acceding to the Western craze for pacts, in 1932 Litvinov negotiated a series of nonaggression pacts and was fairly successful at the Disarmament Conference in February 1933, proposing a universal definition of "aggressor." This was testimony to an increasingly clear-cut positioning in defense of the status quo. Faced with the Japanese threat, Litvinov came out in favor of a policy of pacification. But above all he negotiated the diplomatic recognition of the United States, which he obtained in October 1933. Having to confront the Nazi menace he pushed his policy of moving closer to France. At the end of 1933 Litvinov's choices in favor of collective security were approved by the Soviet party leadership. On December 28 Vyacheslav Molotov, as president of the Council of Peoples' Commissars, praised him publicly.

Litvinov then became the right man in the right place, the flag bearer for collective security, and Franklin D. Roosevelt's friend. In February 1934 he was elected to membership in the Central Committee. The unquestioned chief of his commissariat, Litvinov was surrounded by a group of diplomats that he had personally educated, privileging young polyglots over Russians and professional Communists. He enjoyed great prestige in the Soviet Union. In the summer of 1936, for his sixtieth birthday, he was awarded the order of Lenin. In Western capitals Litvinov cultivated the USSR's image—a policy that was to bear fruit. It relied on tools that were already well tested, especially subsidies to newspapers and journalists, but it was also based on a true public relations system. Entry into the League of Nations in September 1934, an event that Litvinov had long awaited, was an important moment for the USSR's legitimation. Litvinov was especially active and enterprising, as head of the Soviet delegation, on the occasion of a vote for sanctions against Italy (then engaged in the conquest of Ethiopia) in the autumn of 1935 and during the debates about reforming the League of Nations pact in 1936. His sharp tongue in defense of his policies and the contents of his diplomacy itself earned him deep enmities, Molotov's in particular. The party and Comintern ideologists complained that he practiced a classic type of foreign policy, maybe even a conservative one, aimed at defending the country's frontiers and creating alliances with democratic bourgeois countries.

The war in Spain left Litvinov's policies in a state of crisis in the fall of 1936. His work in support of nonintervention now faced some significant problems. Cooperation with France, even during the time of the Popular Front, was increasingly revealed to be based on deceit, and so was that with Great Britain—in fact even more so. Litvinov's personal position became proportionately precarious. His wife was moved out of Moscow, and at the end of 1936 she was forced to accept a position as a professor of English in Sverdlovsk. In the spring of 1937 the first purges started in the NKID, and they led to the decimation of the diplomatic corps. Prudent but resolute, Litvinov defended his collaborators on several occasions and attempted to prove, sometimes courageously, the absurdity of the accusations: the recurrent accusation of being in contact with foreign elements sounded ridiculous when it was directed at diplomats whose profession consisted precisely in this. Litvinov struggled in order to avoid paralysis in the work of the foreign embassies, deprived of competent personnel, and to limit the deleterious effects of the Great Terror in the eyes of the Western world. Demoralization inside the NKID worsened even more after Munich, until Great Britain rethought its position, committing itself to assist Poland and Romania in March–April 1939; this seemed to provide Litvinov's diplomacy with a new start.

But this new start was to be accomplished without him and in an opposite direction. On May 3, 1939, Litvinov was forced to resign, while all his closest collabora-

tors were arrested and interrogated. The internal reasons for his resignation appear to be obvious. They were part of the logic of the purges and tight control on the state apparatus that Stalin was implementing. Litvinov, an old Bolshevik, who had never depended on Stalin, who defended his ideas mocking the party's ideological "censors," was too strong a personality in Stalin's USSR at the end of the 1930s. In July 1939, Molotov accused him of having recruited people who were extraneous and hostile to the party. The resignation, however, can also be explained by the diplomatic situation. Already in April, Stalin and Molotov wanted to explore the possibility of negotiations with Germany, and the plan that Litvinov had devised for a triple alliance with Great Britain and France, like the personality of the people's commissar itself, made the scales tip too far on the side of the democracies.

A powerless observer of the German-Soviet pact, already in the fall of 1939 he was invited to manage one of its consequences. On October 20, he was nominated president of the Soviet delegation in the mixed German-Soviet Commission charged with organizing the transfer of the German, Ukrainian, and Belorussian populations on the two sides of the demarcation line in occupied Poland. His role acquired renewed importance after the German attack in June 1941. The reciprocal animosity between Molotov and Litvinov notwithstanding, in November he was sent as an ambassador to Washington to negotiate U.S. material aid after the agreement that had been signed in Moscow in October. He arrived a couple of days before Pearl Harbor, and therefore participated in the enactment of the Grand Alliance. In January 1942 he signed the UN declaration on the Soviet Union's behalf. Like his London analogue, Ivan Maisky, his principal task was to convince the Allies to open a second front in Europe.

Recalled to the USSR in April 1943, he was nominated vice commissar for foreign affairs, and starting on September 4 presided over the commission charged with drafting the peace treaties and overseeing European assets after the war. Litvinov and his expert notes helped prepare the great inter-Allied conferences, particularly the Moscow Conference in October 1943. Yet beginning in fall 1944 he complained that he did not have sufficient information on current diplomatic negotiations to be able to give more than general analyses. His notes still allow one to discern a personal perspective. Unlike Solomon Lozovsky or Dmitrii Manuilsky, who also participated in the preparation of this commission, Litvinov was in favor of a shared management of Europe by the USSR and Great Britain on the basis of mutually agreed spheres of influence. He was therefore contrary to a full recovery of Germany and France, and predicted that the United States would return to isolationism. Although he refused to subscribe to the prewar outlines on interimperialist contradictions and the inevitability of an anti-Soviet war, he remained insensitive to the emergence of the United States as a superpower on the European continent.

Sidelined in an interview with CBS Moscow correspondent Richard Hottelet, he criticized Stalin's territorial appetites and the new ideologization of Soviet foreign policy. He was conclusively sent into retirement on July 14, 1946, his seventieth birthday, and then shared some of his preoccupations about Cold War diplomacy with some old friends, Aleksandra Kollontay especially. Notwithstanding his strong personality, Litvinov's fate was not the same as that of many other old Bolsheviks and many other Soviet diplomats in the interwar period. In an era that indulged in the waste of human life, he had the privilege to die of natural causes, on December 31, 1951. Toward the mid-1960s his wife was able to return to England, while his nephew Pavel became one of the leaders of the dissident movement starting in 1967.

See also Antifascism; Chicherin, Georgy; Diplomats; Grand Alliance, The; Molotov-Ribbentrop Pact; Peaceful Coexistence.

FURTHER READING

Dullin, S. "Litvinov and the People's Commissariat for Foreign Affairs: The Fate of an Administration under Stalin." In *Russia in the Age of Wars, 1914–1945*, ed. S. Pons and A. Romano, 121–46. Milan: Fondazione Feltrinelli, 2000.

———. *Des hommes d'influence: les ambassadeurs de Staline en Europe, 1930–1939*. Paris: Payot, 2001.

Haslam, J. "Litvinov, Stalin, and the Road Not Taken." In *Soviet Foreign Policy, 1917–1991: A Retrospective*, ed. G. Gorodetsky, 55–61. London: Cass, 1994.

Phillips, H. "From a Bolshevik to a British Subject: The Early Years of Maksim M. Litvinov." *Slavic Review* 48, no. 3 (1989): 388–98.

Roberts, G. K. "The Fall of Litvinov: A Revisionist View." *Journal of Contemporary History* (October 1992): 642–45.

———. "Litvinov's Lost Peace, 1941–1946." *Journal of Cold War Studies* 4, no. 2 (Spring 2002): 23–53.

Shejnis, Z. *Maksim Maksimovich Litvinov, revoljucioner, diplomat, chelovek*. Moscow: Politizdat, 1989.

SABINE DULLIN

Liu Shaoqi

Liu Shaoqi (1898–1969) occupied the number two spot in the Chinese Communist Party's hierarchy from the founding of the People's Republic in 1949 until his fall from grace in 1966 with the beginning of the Cultural Revolution. If Mao Zedong was the inspiration and ideologue of the Chinese Communist Revolution, Liu was the soul and inspiration of the political and organizational machine of the party during his leadership years. In Lowell Dittmer's words, "Liu's life can be seen as the attempt to combine order with revolution, equality with economic efficiency and technocratic values." Liu is also the only Chinese Communist of the Mao era, besides Mao himself, whose writings on organization and the cultivation of self have become party doctrine. In the years of Maoist radicalism, he involuntarily became Mao's nemesis, and during the years of the "permanent revolution," he ended up representing the risks of internal party "revisionism," paying both a public and personal price for his situation.

Born in Hunan Province, not far from where Mao was born, Liu studied in Moscow in 1921–22, where he became a member of the Chinese Communist Party (CCP). Once back in China he organized Communist labor unions for a decade, as head of the party's Labor Department and later also as head of the National Federation of Labor Unions in 1931. His organizational capabilities were useful to the CCP when, in the years of the Japanese invasion, Liu became the principal architect of the party's clandestine structure in the occupied areas. This is the period in which Liu put his own imprint on the party's organizational practices and built a network of alliances, which allowed him to rise up the party hierarchy in the following years. After the end of the civil war, his strategic differences with Mao notwithstanding, and by virtue of his obedience to the party line (both preached and practiced), Liu became the most powerful man after Mao and the designated heir.

It was at the Cultural Revolution's outset, in 1966, that Mao's and Liu's differing ideas about the revolutionary party reached the point of open conflict. When Mao allowed groups of students to openly criticize those forces in the party that were "holding back" the attainment of revolutionary objectives, Liu sent "work groups" to verify the effects of the activities of these first student groups, worried about the effect this movement might have on the efficiency of both productive and party structures. This move was what triggered Mao's reaction. In the space of a few months Liu was demoted to number eight in the party hierarchy, and was soon the target of a campaign of criticism, which also involved some of his collaborators—Deng Xiaoping, for example. Liu was called the "Chinese Khrushchev," a "reactionary bourgeoisie," the first of those who had taken the "road to capitalism." The campaign against Liu continued until he was expelled from the party in 1968; he would die soon afterward, in 1969. Liu's reputation would not be rehabilitated until March 1980, in one of the first and most significant ideological turns of the new reformist leadership, now in Deng's hands, his companion in these misfortunes.

Liu's personal and political travails are useful to understand the Maoist period. Liu repeatedly backed a pragmatic analysis of the economic situation (first in the mid-1950s and later in the early 1960s), arguing for slowing the pace of a collectivization process that Mao had repeatedly accelerated, with disastrous consequences for both production and the quality of life in the countryside. Where Mao accelerated, Liu generally tried to rationalize; where Mao relied on the revolutionary spirit of the masses, Liu relied on organization, discipline, and self-discipline. Liu's writings are an example of this attitude. In "How to Be a Good Communist" (1939), his best-known essay, Liu attempted to merge the revolutionary values of Marxism-Leninism with the idea of self-discipline and taking care of oneself that is typical of the Confucian tradition, but now aimed at the "submission of all personal interests to the interests of the party." For Liu it was possible to "cultivate" a Communist morality, a candid and sincere spirit, the courage of one's actions, and self-respect and self-esteem especially by means of "revolutionary practice." The idea of taking care of oneself and the role of each party member's individual morality is combined in Liu's writings with the need for a solid party structure that is able to resolve internal contradictions.

Liu's vicissitudes also highlight some of the characteristics of Maoist thought about revisionism. The ideological errors that Mao accused Liu of included the definition of socialism as something that would unfold over "the long period" (and not the brief interlude before the advent of communism that Mao dreamed of), the attention given to developing the forces of production *before* forcing a transition to "more Communist" relations of production, and the negation of the need for class struggle in a socialist society. Even though this interpretation only

partially corresponds to Liu's ideas, the items just listed allowed Mao to find a reference point when his appeal to "never forget the class struggle" began the most radical phase of contemporary Chinese history. This dialectical divergence was transformed into a force that almost destroyed the Communist Party organization that Liu and Mao had built up to that point.

Liu's political plans were guided by a form of technocratic and scientific communism, capable of guiding a faithful and responsible society, inspired by the work of its leaders and socialist ideals. In a sort of posthumous revenge, the characteristics that were attributed to Liuist revisionism, and specifically the idea that China was still in the "initial phase of socialism," would become central aspects of the reformist rhetoric and redefinition of development's goals after Liu's rehabilitation in 1980.

See also Chinese Revolution; Cultural Revolution in China; Deng Xiaoping; Mao Zedong; Marxism-Leninism.

FURTHER READING

Dittmer, L. *Liu Shaoqi and the Chinese Cultural Revolution*. Armonk, NY: M. E. Sharpe, 1998.

Liu Shaoqi. *Collected Works*. 3 vols. Kowloon: Union Research Institute, 1969.

LUIGI TOMBA

Long March

The Long March refers to the transformation of the Red Army's strategic retreat into a heroic and semilegendary feat that, so the claims go, led the Chinese Communist Party (CCP) to safety and allowed for its rebuilding under Mao Zedong's leadership. After three years of resistance, on October 16, 1934, 130,000 soldiers, leaders, and CCP functionaries abandoned the Ruijin Soviet in Jiangzi to escape encirclement by the Guomindang's (GMD) troops, led by Chiang Kai-shek (Jiang Jieshi). One year later, on October 19, 1935, after having traveled 5,952 miles, through 11 provinces, over 18 mountain chains, and 24 rivers, the 4,000 to 8,000 survivors of the Long March, under Mao's and Zhu De's leadership, arrived in Yan'an, in Shaanxi Province. The final goal of the Long March was to find a new territorial base at the periphery of nationalist power, where the CCP could reorganize and realize its political program.

To understand the Long March, it is necessary to understand the geomorphological nature of the terrain. Southwestern China is a chessboard of basins surrounded by mountain chains; the densely inhabited plains are fed by rivers that descend from inhospitable mountains. The Red Army had to cross these rivers and mountains, avoiding the plains in order not to be annihilated by the GMD's troops. Starting from Jiangxi the Communists went west, crossed Guilin, and arrived in Yunnan, where they could have perhaps stopped if they had not been confronted by local warlords. They then went north, crossed Chengdu, and arrived in Yan'an. They often marched for days and days without either water or food. When they attempted to cross the river Xiang, in Hunan, they were attacked by GMD troops, who killed more than 40,000 people. One of the problems was the military strategy that the Communists had adopted on the advice of Comintern agent Otto Braun, who during previous encirclement campaigns by the GMD, had argued for frontal attacks across the entire battlefield, which had proved to be a failure. Braun was now advocating a march in a straight line, thereby allowing the GMD to predict the Red Army's locations. A crucial moment in the Long March was an enlarged meeting of the CCP's Political Office that took place in Zunyi, in Guizhou, on January 15–18, 1935. With the support of the Red Army's generals (Zhu, Peng Dehuai, and Lin Biao), Mao became the party's secretary and director of the Military Affairs Committee (replacing Zhou Enlai).

From that moment on, the CCP started moving away from Soviet influence, and the Red Army adopted a strategy that Mao had elaborated with Zhu's support: subdividing into smaller subunits that were difficult to identify in open spaces, Mao continued the march following a zigzagging model that made it virtually impossible for the GMD to predict their movements. In Zunyi Mao also determined the march's final goal: to reach Yan'an. On May 8 the Red Army managed to cross the Yangtze. On May 29 the Communists defeated the GMD troops in the historic battle of Luding Bridge, on the river Dadu, in Sichuan. In the official historiography, the story of the Long March often has miraculous, epic overtones. The fact that future political leaders such as Liu Shaoqi, Zhu, Lin, and Deng Xiaoping had participated in the Long March, transformed it into an important revolutionary symbol: a precursor to the 1949 victory, it has become an integral part of the myth surrounding the CCP's rebuilding.

Journalists and researchers such as Edgar Snow, Harrison Salisbury, and Dick Wilson have supported and confirmed the Communist version of events. Even though it has recently been defamed in the controversial book by Jung Chang and Jon Halliday as a fraud (the authors contend, among other things, that Chiang allowed the Red Army to pass as a "good will gesture to Russia" and that there was no battle on the river Dadu), the Long March continues to stimulate a lot of interest, as confirmed by the adventures of Ed Jocelyn and Andrew McEwen (who retraced its steps in 2003), and the recent book by Sun Shuyun. Some female researchers have paid particular attention to the women who participated in the Long March; interviews conducted by Helen Praeger Young in 1986–87, for example, cast a new light on the ties between women and revolution in Communist China.

See also Chinese Revolution; Comintern; Mao Zedong.

FURTHER READING

Jocelyn, E., and A. McEwen. *The Long March*. London: Constable and Robinson, 2006.

Lee, L. X. H., and S. Wiles. *Women of the Long March*. London: Allen and Unwin, 1999.

Praeger Young, H. *Choosing Revolution: Chinese Women Soldiers on the Long March*. Urbana: University of Illinois Press, 2001.

Salisbury, H. E. *The Long March: The Untold Story*. New York: Harper and Row, 1985.

Shuyun Sun. *The Long March*. London: HarperCollins, 2006.

Snow, E. *Red Star over China*. New York: Random House, 1968.

Wilson, D. *The Long March 1935: The Epic of Chinese Communism's Survival*. London: Penguin, 1982.

MAURIZIO MARINELLI

Lukács, Georg

Georg Lukács (1885–1971) can be viewed as communism's first metaphysician. In his last great work of philosophical synthesis, *Zur Ontologie des gesellschaftlichen Seins* (The Ontology of Social Being), he proposed the establishment of a system of categories; he intended this linked network to constitute the foundation for the transition, on the theoretical level, from the realm of necessity to the realm of freedom. The celebrated passage at the conclusion of *Capital*, in which Karl Marx laid out the conditions for the emergence of the realm of freedom, was the fulcrum of Lukács's ontological reflection.

Lukács developed and broadened Marx's intuitions by formulating the concept of the "specificity of human kind in itself" (*die Gattungsmässigkeit an-sich*, or genericalness in itself) next to the concept of the "specificity of human kind for itself" (*die Gattungsmässigkeit für-sich*, or genericalness for itself). In so doing, he provided Marxist doctrine with a rigorous speculative base.

The young intellectual, who joined the Communist Party in December 1918, had undergone a complex process of intellectual formation, and the process of assimilating Marxism took Lukács a relatively long time. The thought structure that would form the basis of his mature Marxist oeuvre only took shape in the early 1930s, after his encounter with Marx's *Economic and Philosophical Manuscripts of 1844*. In 1918, as he turned toward communism, Lukács's philosophical development was influenced by a set of heterogeneous thinkers. Reading Søren Aabye Kierkegaard had left its mark, but so had a precocious examination of Georg Wilhelm Friedrich Hegel's *Phenomenology of Spirit*. The influence of Georges Sorel and his doctrine of direct action was also worthy of note. At this time, Lukács was already aware of the conception of history developed by Hegel and Marx (his 1919 essay *Tactics and Ethics* should be consulted in this regard). His readings of Meister Eckhart and other heretical mystics (from Sebastian Franck to Saint Francis of Assisi) left sometimes deep traces. The influence of Johann Gottlieb Fichte's ethical thought along with the sociological writings of Ferdinand Tönnies, Max Weber, and Georg Simmel can also be discerned in his work of the period. Lukács's adherence to communism exhibited a strong ethical motivation, and he had to travel fairly far before being able to provide solid materialist foundations for his ethical convictions.

In the *Aesthetics* (which was published in the Federal Republic of Germany in 1963) and the *Ontology of Social Being* (three volumes, published posthumously), the two works that most fully express his Marxist thought, Lukács formulated a philosophy of immanence (*Diesseitigkeit*). It was founded on the ontological-genetic method of approaching phenomena—a method that refuses any use of transcendence, and allows one to follow the emergence of even the most subtle and complex activities of consciousness by means of the pure subject-object dialectics and its multiple mediations.

Benedetto Croce had also established himself as a promoter of the pure thought of immanence, and incessantly polemicized with theological residues and teleologism in philosophy. But apart from this impressive resemblance, Lukács's thought represented the "Anti-Croce" that Antonio Gramsci had called for, because due to its rigorous philosophical materialism, Lukács's ontology and the aesthetics that derived from it were the diametrical opposite of the Crocean "philosophy of spirit."

As an extraordinary witness to the transformations of the 20th-century Communist movement—from the advent of the Hungarian Commune of 1919, where he found himself side by side with Béla Kun (a fact that did not stop him from comparing Grigory Zinovyev's future follower to Vautrin, Honoré de Balzac's evil character)—Lukács defined himself as a special type of Communist, who had distanced himself from both the social democracy of the period and Stalinist orthodoxy, a Communist who always fought the fantasies of the Trotskyist ultra-Left. He even maintained that the political line defended by Trotsky in the 1920s would have led to the same forms of sectarianism Stalin had realized, because in his debate with Lenin on the role of the labor unions, Trotsky had given proof of an ultrasectarian and bureaucratic concept of the party. But he also categorically refused to follow the paths of the likes of Arthur Koestler and Franz Borkenau—in other words, to renege his initial commitment to communism. In his conversations with István Eörsi and Erzsébet Vezer several months before his death, Lukács had good reasons to affirm that in his long journey through communism, he had defended the democratic nature of the movement. In 1929 he had authored the *Blum Theses*, the outlines of the Hungarian Communist Party's program, in which he anticipated a transition to socialism based on an ample coalition of democratic and republican forces. He built his theoretical works on the basis of these political convictions, which were then stigmatized and rejected by Kun as "revisionist" and "rightist"; they were later also rejected by the directorate of the Communist International.

Lukács's political and philosophical itinerary illustrates the enormous difficulties faced by an authentic intellectual attempting to provide the movement to which he belonged with a complex elaboration of its doctrinal foundations. He once again took up the great Hegelian tradition and the vein of Marxian thought on history, giving particular importance to the theory of reification and alienation. The fate of his first Marxist book, *History and Class Consciousness*, which was published in 1923 and immediately subjected to public ridicule at the Comintern's Fifth Congress, was exemplary of the manner in which any attempt at autonomous Marxist reflection was ostracized—a development that would assume monstrous proportions under Stalin's rule. At a later stage in his reflections, Lukács would devote himself to a systematic formulation of his thought on questions of aesthetics and ethics, until he finally constructed a comprehensive theory of social being (his *Ontology*, with its appendix, the *Prolegomena to Social Being*), which at this point was the most mature and elaborated theory of historical materialism.

He was a minister in Communist governments twice: first as education commissar in Kun's government and military commissar of a division at the front (1919); and second as culture minister in the Imre Nagy government, which had arisen from the Hungarian popular insurrection of October–November 1956. As a consequence he became acquainted with Soviet prisons and deportation. Lukács was first incarcerated in the infamous Lubjanka, in Moscow, for two months in June–August 1941. Later, as a result of the insurrection's failure, he was transferred to Romania by the Soviets together with Nagy and other members of his government; he would remain there in forced exile for six months, until April 1957. After his return to Budapest he was attacked in most of the socialist bloc countries' publications: they denounced his so-called "revisionism" along with his participation in the "Petöfi circle," the ideological center of the Hungarian rebellion. Lukács thus experienced the history of this political movement from the inside, as both a protagonist and often a victim, for over sixty years. Mostly sidelined by the party's bureaucrats, frequently criticized and ostracized, he nevertheless became the most important philosopher of the movement.

The divorce between Stalinist communism and Lukács's philosophical and political thought was increasingly evident over the course of his life. When talking about the period of the 1930s, when he lived in exile in the Soviet Union after having fully defended Stalin against Trotsky in the controversy surrounding "socialism in one country," at the end of his life Lukács remarked that he could "peaceably state that he had by his deeds proven to have been an adversary of Stalin's methods, even while believing he was his advocate." But this divorce was most forcefully expressed after 1956, in the last fifteen years of his life, when in all his writings he began to put Stalinism, whose effects largely endured in the practice of most Communist parties, on trial at a philosophical, political, and economic level.

Lukács's most enduring contribution to the cause of communism—understood in a nondogmatic, nonsectarian, and emancipatory fashion—can be found in what he loved to designate his *Lebenswerk* (his life's work). In other words, in writings such as *The Young Hegel* (1948) or *The Destruction of Reason* (1954), *The Historical Novel* (1936) or the collection *Essays on Realism* (which constituted the fourth volume of his collected *Works* in German, eighteen of which have been published to date), *Goethe and His Time* (1946), *Balzac and French Realism* (1951), *Thomas Mann and the Tragedy of Modern Art* (1949), and the two great works of theoretical synthesis, the *Aesthetics* (1963) and the *Ontology of Social Being* (written between 1964 and 1968, and published posthumously). His principal merit was to have defended Marxism as a philosophy of universal scope, which not only entails an economic doctrine, but also a theory of political action, an ethics, and an aesthetics. Thanks to his speculative work and the ontological-genetic method he elaborated, not to mention the fundamental achievement represented by the *Aesthetics* and his numerous writings in literary history and literary criticism, Lukács made Marx's philosophy rise to the status of "great philosophy." He thus made it possible for the intellectual left to counterpoise a convincing philosophy to systems of thought like those of Martin Heidegger and Ludwig Wittgenstein; he categorically opposed neopositivism and analytical philosophy, which he designated as Marxism's principal adversaries on the scene of contemporary philosophy.

See also Marxism, Western; Marxism-Leninism; Socialist Realism; Stalinism.

FURTHER READING

Kadarkay, A. *Georg Lukacs: Life, Thought, and Politics.* Cambridge: Cambridge University Press, 1991.

Lukács, G. *Essays on Realism.* Cambridge, MA: MIT Press, 1980.

———. *History and Class Consciousness; Studies in Marxist Dialectics.* Cambridge, MA: MIT Press, 1971.

———. *Marxismus und Stalinismus.* Berlin: Rowohlt, 1970.

———. *Record of a Life: an Autobiographical Sketch.* London: Verso, 1983.

———. *The Destruction of Reason.* Atlantic Highlands, NJ: Humanities Press, 1980.

———. *The Ontology of Social Being.* London: Merlin, 1980.

———. *The Young Hegel: Studies in the Relations between Dialectics and Economics.* Cambridge, MA: MIT Press, 1975.

Tertulian, N. *Lukács. La rinascita dell'ontologia*. Rome: Editori Riuniti, 1986.

NICOLAS TERTULIAN

Lunacharsky, Anatoly

Anatoly Lunacharsky (1877–1933) has the reputation of being the "soft Bolshevik." Neither of these descriptors is entirely accurate. Though he undoubtedly possessed an artistic sensibility—he produced many collections of poetry and over seventy plays—there was in that sensibility a fashionable tough, Nietzschian, elitist streak. During the revolution he believed it was necessary to preserve the bearers of culture, as a priority over lesser mortals. As for being a Bolshevik, even in the relatively short periods of his life when he was close to Lenin and the party, he always flirted with heresy.

Lunacharsky was born in Poltava, Ukraine, and grew up in Kiev. As a student he was influenced by radical ideas and in 1894–96 found himself in Switzerland. He studied philosophy at Zurich under Richard Avenarius, who influenced him in the direction of materialism and monism. Unlike the majority of Marxists, Lunacharsky was not primarily interested in politics and economics but was driven by a passion for intellectual debate and cultural criticism. Many radical contemporaries found him rather lightweight. Exceptions to this were his first close associates, his brother-in-law A. A. Bogdanov and the novelist Maxim Gorky. In 1897 he was arrested and exiled to Kaluga, where he met Bogdanov and formed a sometimes complicated friendship that continued until Bogdanov's death in 1928. In particular, Bogdanov strengthened Lunacharsky's monistic materialism. In the period from 1904 to 1907 the two brothers-in-law and Maxim Gorky were among the most important members of Lenin's small circle of supporters. In 1907, Lunacharsky once again left Russia for Italy and France. By 1908 the Bolshevik group members were increasingly at odds with one another. A major point of contention was over the evolution of some of Lunacharsky's main ideas. In earlier exile he had also met the religious philosopher Nikolai Berdyaev, who posed religious questions that led Lunacharsky to respond with a thorough materialist critique of religion that found its fullest expression in his two-volume work *Religiia i sotsializm*

("Religion and Socialism") published in 1908 and 1911. Lenin was incensed that Lunacharsky interpreted socialism as the secular heir of religion. He contemptuously accused him of "god-building." Lunacharsky, Bogdanov, and Gorky were undeterred. They devoted their time and attention to opening a party school in Capri in 1909 as part of an ambitious plan to develop "proletarian culture." For the rest of his life Lunacharsky devoted himself mainly to the cultural aspects of revolution. In 1917 his enthusiasm and lecturing experience made him one of the leading orators of the Bolshevik Party once he, Trotsky, and other *mezhraiontsy* returned to the fold in July. Not surprisingly, he was named People's Commissar for Education in the Soviet government, even though, along with the arch-heretic Bogdanov, he had set up a separate Proletarian Cultural-Educational Association (Proletkul't) shortly before the October Revolution. Lunacharsky was influential in setting up the world's first Socialist education system. His two affiliations collided in 1921 when he, extraordinarily, disobeyed a personal directive from Lenin to force Proletkul't to submit to party instructions. Nonetheless, he survived, though Proletkul't was emasculated soon after. Through the 1920s Lunacharsky worked, with Nadezhda Krupskaya among others, to raise the cultural level of the Russian masses through literacy campaigns and worker education programs as well as through the education system. Illness began to dog him in the late 1920s. In 1929 he was relieved of his post at the Education Ministry, after which he lived largely in Western Europe, supposedly for health reasons. Lunacharsky's last posting was as Soviet ambassador to Spain, but he never reached Madrid. He died of respiratory failure in Menton, France, in 1933.

See also Bolshevism; Cultural Policies; Literacy, Soviet Union Campaign for Adult; Proletkult; Utopia.

FURTHER READING

Fitzpatrick, S. *The Commissariat of Enlightenment: Soviet Organization and the Arts Under Lunacharsky, 1917–1921*. Cambridge, UK: Cambridge University Press, 1971.

Lunacharsky, A. *On Education: Selected Articles and Speeches*. Moscow: Progress Publishers, 1981.

Lunacharsky, A., et al. *On Literature and Art*. Moscow: Progress Publishers, 1973.

O'Connor, T. E. *The Politics of Soviet Culture: Anatolii Lunacharskii*. Ann Arbor: University of Michigan Press, 1983.

Read, C. *Culture and Power in Revolutionary Russia: The Intelligentsia and the Transition from Tsarism to Communism*. Basingstoke: Macmillan, 1990.

————. *Religion, Revolution and the Russian Intelligentsia, 1900–12.* Basingstoke: Macmillan, 1979.

Tait A. L. *Lunacharsky: Poet of the Revolution, 1875–1907.* Birmingham, UK: University of Birmingham Slavonic Monographs. 1984.

CHRISTOPHER READ

Luxemburg, Rosa

Rosa Luxemburg (1870–1919) was born on March 5 in Zamość, in Russian Poland. At the end of 1893 she fled to Switzerland for political reasons, where at the University of Zurich she first studied natural sciences and later political science, receiving a doctorate in 1897. Her doctoral thesis "Industrial Development in Poland" was published in 1898. During her years in Switzerland she belonged, together with her companion Leo Jogiches, to the leadership of the Social Democratic Party of the Kingdom of Poland and Lithuania, and was the editor of its newspaper. She also published articles on Polish issues in the *Neue Zeit* (New Times), the theoretical publication of the Social Democratic Party of Germany (SPD). Luxemburg took part in the congresses of the Socialist International in 1893 and 1896 as a Polish delegate.

Having moved to Berlin in May 1898, she was directed by the SPD leadership to take part in the electoral contests in Upper Silesia. She was in Dresden for brief periods in 1898, then in Leipzig in 1901–2, and in 1905 became chief editor of *Vorwärts* (Forward), the most important newspaper of German Social Democracy. In September 1898 and April 1899, she published a defense of the party's Marxist program against revisionist attacks in *Leipziger Volkszeitung* in two series of articles, which later also appeared as a pamphlet (*Social Reform or Revolution?*); these fast led to her being more widely recognized.

Starting in 1898 Luxemburg participated in almost all the prewar SPD congresses, emerging as a force because of her contributions to discussion and often also proposals of her own. Her speeches and writing were well formulated and moving, and her incisive argumentation and resolute defense of Marxist positions made her a well-known and sought-after orator and journalist in the milieu of German and international Social Democracy. She befriended Clara Zetkin and Karl Kausky and his family in 1899. Luxemburg, despite her youth, impressed even the private circles of her comrades with her resolute manner, self-assurance, and cultural knowledge, which extended from Russian, Polish, German, and Western European authors to a mastery of German, Russian, and Polish along with a good knowledge of French and English. She participated in a series of Socialist International congresses as a delegate—in particular, in 1900 with a report to the Commission on Militarism and Colonial Policy. Subsequently she was a permanent member of the International Socialist Office, the organ responsible for coordination of the Socialist International, on behalf of the Social Democratic Party of the Kingdom of Poland and Lithuania until 1914.

On her return to Germany she published the pamphlet *Mass Strike, Party, and Trade Unions*, a political synthesis of her personal participation in the revolutionary struggles during the years 1905–6 in Russian Warsaw. In it she stated that the party needed to act more resolutely—for instance, by calling for mass strikes—in order to achieve democratic and social gains. As in all her later speeches and writings, Luxemburg argued for a basic concept of democracy: it was the proletarian masses that decided the right path toward socialism, and not the leaders, whose activities should be limited to presenting the overall picture, as well as goals in the short and medium term, to the proletariat. In such an atmosphere of freedom, the creativity and spontaneity of the masses would develop fully.

If the SPD's presidency welcomed her successful work as a publicist in contrasting revisionism, starting in 1906 Luxemburg could no longer count on the support of a party leadership—increasingly inclined to take a defensive course—when she requested it engage in a more active politics. She favored a radical and offensively oriented set of policies, but found herself increasingly isolated. Even her writing for the party press was rejected or censored, to such an extent that in 1913, together with Franz Mehring and Julian Karski (Marchlewski), she decided to start the *Sozialdemokratische Korrespondenz* (Social Democratic Correspondence) so as to have some publication venues. From 1907 to 1914, Luxemburg displayed her pedagogical talent as a professor of political economy at the SPD's central party school in Berlin. She also published studies in this field, like the much discussed and criticized volume *Accumulation of Capital: A Contribution to the Economic Explanation of Imperialism* in 1913. After having to stand trial because of her antimilitarist statements (she was sentenced to a year in prison), from the beginning of 1914 Luxemburg's popularity grew exponentially, until just before the war the respect accorded her in the party reached "an absolute climax."

At this point, she managed to push through a measure that forced the SPD's Berlin organization to adopt preparedness measures for a mass strike. The vote in favor of the war credits by the SPD's parliamentary group in the Reichstag on August 4, 1914, which went against all the discussions that had taken place in the party, shocked Luxemburg. She immediately tried to bring the forces on the Left of the SPD together. Luxemburg worked with political friends like Mehring, Zetkin, Karl Liebknecht, and Jogiches, as well as the Internationale group, which later became the Spartakus Group, in an attempt to gather a majority in the SPD favorable to both calling for mass actions and standing for peace. In 1915, she worked on the periodical *Die Internationale*, immediately forbidden, and in 1916 the periodical *Spartacus* and numerous clandestine leaflets—all illegal activities because of the state of emergency and censorship. She underscored the need to conform to the Socialist International resolutions demanding that antimilitarist and even revolutionary mass actions be undertaken, regardless of the status of the war. She distanced herself during the conspiratorial interregional reunions of her group (January 2 and March 16, 1916) from the moderate opposition gathered around Hugo Haase and Georg Ledebour. In early 1916 she vainly attempted to take the leadership of the entire internal party opposition. Defeated, Luxemburg returned to work with her moderate opponents. In April 1917, during the founding of the Independent Social Democratic Party of Germany (USPD), she also succeeded in getting the Internationale group (Spartakus) included with an autonomous program. And as a result of all these political activities, Luxemburg spent over three-quarters of World War I in prison.

It was during these years that in addition to numerous leaflets and essays, she conceived important pamphlets like *The Crisis of Social Democracy*, written in April 1915 and published illegally in 1916 under the pseudonym "Junius." This text, with its description of the war's consequences, analyzed alternative courses of action that could have been taken on the basis of the SPD's own program; this led to the conclusion that the party should have followed policies more in line with the class struggle, antimilitarism, and the fight for democracy from the war's outset. Luxemburg's most famous and most widely debated work was *The Russian Revolution*, an incomplete text, written in September 1918, and only published in 1922 by Paul Levi to support his arguments when he confronted Lenin and the Comintern's leadership. *The Russian Revolution* was critical of the Bolsheviks' governmental policies and advocated freedom of opinion as the essential condition for the creativity of the proletarian masses in the construction of a socialist society. This criticism was consistent with Luxemburg's concept of democracy at the grass roots, which she had already expressed in many of her German writings, but could be dated as far back as 1904 in her remarks (*Organizational Questions of Russian Social Democracy*) addressed to the ultracentralist party model developed by Lenin. Contrary to the opinion she had expressed in *The Russian Revolution*, after November 9, 1918, Luxemburg supported the council system as an instrument that was suited to carrying out the revolution and constructing a socialist society. She continued to reject the idea of domination by a minority combined with political repression, however, as is clear in her formulations in the Communist Party of Germany's (KPD) program, elaborated in December 1918 with the title *What Does the Spartakus League Want?*

Released from prison in Breslau and having returned to Berlin on November 10, 1918, as the editor of *Rote Fahne* (Red Flag) Luxemburg, together with Liebknecht, struggled to preserve the councils' power and lead the USPD, yet she greatly overestimated the masses' revolutionary impulse. When the USPD's presidency rejected her request to call for a national congress, she and her political group founded the KPD, on New Year's Day 1919. Here she had to contend with strong labor union forces that the efforts of the KPD's leadership notwithstanding, decided not to participate in the elections to the national assembly, thus handing her a political defeat. Initially she viewed the spontaneous uprising of Berlin workers, which had started on January 5, 1919, against the Ebert-Scheidemann government, with skepticism, and even had a motion approved by the KPD's leadership according to which Liebknecht should have withdrawn from the revolt's leadership. Nevertheless, her newspaper articles and a private letter to Zetkin left the impression that she had deluded herself about the success of the revolutionary uprising. After the revolt's failure, Luxemburg was assassinated by Freikorps' elements on January 15, 1919.

Luxemburg's ideas of socialism were banned by Stalin, who even condemned them as "semi-Menshevik" in 1931. Regardless of Stalin's remarks, Luxemburg remained one of the better-known figures of the international workers' movement, the symbol of a revolutionary and democratic socialism.

See also Imperialism; Kautsky, Karl; Liebknecht, Karl; Revolution, Myths of the; Socialist International; Soviets.

FURTHER READING

Badia, G. *Rosa Luxemburg: journaliste, polémiste, révolutionnaire*. Paris: Éditions Sociales, 1975.

Badia, G., and A. Laschitza. *Im Lebensrausch, trotz alledem. Rosa Luxemburg. Eine Biographie*. Berlin: Aufbau Verlag, 2002.

Ettinger, E. *Rosa Luxemburg: A Life*. Boston: Beacon, 1986.

Hudis, P., and K. B. Anderson, eds. *The Rosa Luxemburg Reader*. New York: Monthly Review Press, 2004.

Luxemburg, R. *Selected Political Writings*. London: Cape, 1972.

———. *Scritti scelti*. Ed. L. Amodio. Turin: Einaudi, 1976.

———. *Accumulation of Capital*. London: Routledge, 2003.

Nettl, J. P. *Rosa Luxemburg*. London: Oxford University Press, 1966.

OTTOKAR LUBAN

Malenkov, Georgy

Georgy Malenkov (1901–88) was born on January 26 in Orenburg, Russia. He grew up in the family of a railroad worker. Malenkov's son claims that the family's ancestors came from Macedonia and became ennobled through state service. Malenkov's grandfather was a colonel and the grandfather's brother was Counter Admiral. Malenkov volunteered for the Red Army in 1919, and from cavalry squadron commissar rose to the rank of political administration of the Eastern and Turkestan fronts. In 1920 he joined the Russian Communist Party (Bolsheviks). From 1921 to 1925 Malenkov was a student at the Moscow Superior Technical School; there he fought against the Trotskyite opposition among other students. Marriage to Valentina Golubtsova (1920), who worked in the CC VKP (b) apparatus brought Malenkov to the attention of Stalin's circle. In 1927 he was appointed a technical secretary of the CC politburo, where he worked under N. Yezhov. From 1930 to 1934 Malenkov headed the department for agitation and mass work at the Moscow party organization and helped Kaganovich to purge this organization of opposition members. He was head of the department of leading party agencies at the Central Committee from 1934 to 1939. Together with NKVD Commissar Yezhov, Malenkov on Stalin's instructions launched the Great Purges of the party, the military, and other segments of society. In 1937 he traveled to the Saratov and Tambov regions, as well as to Belorussia and Armenia to orchestrate the elimination of regional party, state, and cultural elites. He also took part in interrogations. Malenkov survived Yezhov's fall in 1938 and from March 1939 on he occupied positions as head of the Administration of Cadres, CC secretary, and a member of the CC Orgburo. In January of 1938 Malenkov became a member of the presidium of the Supreme Soviet, and in February of 1941 a candidate member of the politburo.

After the Nazi attack in June 1941, Malenkov joined the State Defense Committee (GKO), the wartime supreme command headed by Stalin. Several times he went to the front line. Beginning in 1942 his assignment was to supervise aircraft production. From 1943 to 1945 he headed the state committee for economic recovery in liberated areas and coordinated the extraction of resources from Germany, Austria, Hungary, and Rumania. In March of 1945 he became deputy head of the Council of Peoples Commissars (SNK). When Stalin, after many years went on vacation in October of 1945, Malenkov was part of "the four" who stayed in Moscow to run the government. After Stalin's criticism of the second senior member of his circle, V. Molotov, in November of 1945, Malenkov advanced to the position of an heir apparent to the Soviet leader. He presided over the sessions of the CC secretariat. In March 1946 Stalin promoted Malenkov to a full member of the politburo.

At the same time, however, Malenkov's career almost ended as a result of the "aircraft affair." Stalin conceived this "affair" after his son Vassily, General of the Air Force, claimed that the fighter planes he flew during the wartime had been of poor quality. After a brief inquiry a number of high officials were arrested, and on March 19, 1946, the day after his promotion, Malenkov was removed as deputy chair of the Council of Ministers. On May 4 Stalin dismissed Malenkov from the CC secretariat and Orgburo. He dictated the resolution that read, "Comrade Malenkov bears moral responsibility for the shocking things which have been exposed in these agencies (the production and acceptance of substandard planes), and for the fact that he, knowing of these outrages, did not inform the Central Committee." Malenkov spent the next two months in Central Asia and Siberia working on grain procurement.

By July–August of that year, he had already returned to the secretariat and again became deputy chair of the Council of Ministers. He also returned to the Orgburo and took active part in the launching of the campaign against Leningrad literary journals. According to new research, Stalin did not want to destroy Malenkov; rather he wanted to destroy the system of collective leadership that had emerged in wartime. Beria worked very actively to return Malenkov to Stalin's favor, and Malenkov was to play an important part in Beria's political plans after Stalin's death.

Malenkov became indispensable as an administrator of the Stalinist machinery of mobilization, terror, and surveillance. Like his new closest partner, L. Beria, he had no ideological illusions about Stalinism; rather, he sought to survive in the vortex of lethal politics that engulfed so many. He retained Stalin's trust through complete obedience, sycophancy, and permanent fear. From 1945 to 1948 Malenkov's rival for the position of Stalin's favorite was Zhdanov. After his death in August of 1948, Malenkov took over the coordination of the CC's "ideological work"; simultaneously he became a curator of agriculture. Malenkov was intimately involved, together with Beria, in preparations for the next bloody phase of Kremlin politics, which occurred in 1949 during the Leningrad and the Gosplan "affairs." Hundreds of senior officials of the Russian Federation (including N. Voznesenski, M. Rodionov, and A. Kuznetsov) were arrested, secretly tried, tortured, and, on October 1, 1950, executed. Khrushchev later blamed Malenkov for these crimes. Scholars, however, believe that he played only a secondary role, fulfilling Stalin's wishes.

Similarly, from 1944 on Malenkov carried out Stalin's attack against the Jews. In 1949–50 he coordinated the investigation and destruction of the Jewish Anti-Fascist Committee. Once again he became Stalin's heir apparent. As his health slipped, Stalin asked Malenkov to present the political report to the Nineteenth Party Congress in October of 1952. After the congress Stalin denounced Molotov and Mikoyan, but Malenkov remained in the "leading five" of the enlarged politburo (presidium).

After Stalin's death Malenkov became head of the presidium of the Council of Ministers. From March to May of 1953, together with Beria, Khrushchev, and Molotov, he introduced a "peace initiative" in Soviet foreign policy that resulted in the end of virulent anti-American campaigns, peace feelers toward Western countries, the end of the Korean war, and an opening for possible unifica-

tion talks on Germany. From the start it was apparent that Malenkov lacked the energy, charisma, and political will to compete with Beria and Khrushchev. In June of 1953 he joined in Khrushchev's plot against Beria.

After Beria's arrest on June 26, Malenkov vowed to observe the rules of the "collective leadership." Yet in August, in a public speech during a session of the Supreme Soviet, he announced sweeping agricultural reforms (a reduction of taxes, a sharp increase in state purchasing prices, the enlargement of private lots, etc.). Malenkov's popularity among the Russian peasants soared. Khrushchev and Molotov later denounced the speech as populism and as Malenkov's attempt to win a following at the expense of the rest of the leadership. Malenkov as the scion of a cultured and educated family also made a favorable impression on Western ambassadors in Moscow, among them U.S. Ambassador Charles Bohlen. Malenkov supervised Soviet atomic projects and on August 8 announced the first Soviet hydrogen test (it actually took place four days later). In March 1954, reacting to powerful U.S. thermonuclear tests, Malenkov stated publicly that "the Soviet government decisively opposes the Cold War, since that policy is the policy of preparing a new world war, which with modern weapons means the end of world civilization." His rivals, especially Khrushchev, seized this opportunity to criticize Malenkov for panic mongering, historical pessimism, and an inability to conduct negotiations against the West. By the end of 1954, the time for Malenkov's leadership was up; the apparatus of the Council of Ministers that he led became completely subordinate to Khrushchev's party apparatus. Khrushchev's other powerful tools against Malenkov were his control over the reformed security agencies (KGB) and an investigation of Stalinist crimes that revealed Malenkov's involvement. At the party plenum on January 31, 1955, Malenkov was criticized for his mistakes; he stepped down from chairmanship of the Council of Ministers without a fight. He became the minister of power plants, while remaining in the party presidium.

From 1955 to 1957, Malenkov actively supported policies of détente that continued the "peace initiative" of 1953. Some evidence indicates that he was reform-minded, unlike Molotov and Kaganovich. He was even passively supportive of the course of de-Stalinization. Khrushchev's "secret speech" against Stalin at the Twentieth Party Congress and, especially, its disastrous international consequences (revolutions in Poland and Hungary, a crisis in the world Communist movement) eroded Malenkov's support of Khrushchev. Privately he abhorred Khrushchev as culturally backward, impetuous, and lacking in prudence. In June of 1957 Malenkov joined the politburo (presidium) majority in their attempt to depose Khrushchev. Instead, Khrushchev won and ousted his opponents as the "anti-party group." Malenkov forfeited all his positions on June 26, 1957, lost his apartment and dacha as well, and was exiled to Kazakhstan. From 1957 to 1961 he worked first as the director of a waterpower plant in Ust-Kamenogorsk, then as director of a power plant in Ekibastuz. In 1961 he retired and, on instructions from the CC, was expelled from the party.

After Khrushchev's fall Malenkov was allowed to return to Moscow, but was never readmitted to the party. His wife worked as a rector of the Moscow Institute of Energy. His two sons earned PhDs in the sciences. During the last years of his life Malenkov became interested in the problem of "nuclear winter." He never produced memoirs and died on January 14, 1988, in Moscow.

See also Beria, Lavrenty; Great Terror; Peaceful Coexistence; Stalinism.

FURTHER READING

Gorlizki, Y., and O. Khlevniuk. *Cold Peace: Stalin and the Soviet Ruling Circle, 1945–1953.* New York: Oxford University Press, 2004.

Malenkov, A. *About My Father, Georgii Malenkov.* Moscow: Tekhnoekos, 1992.

Torchinov, V. A., and A. M. Leontyuk. *Stalin's Entourage: Historico-Biographical Guide.* St. Petersburg, 2000.

Zalessky, K. *Empire of Stalin: Biographical Encyclopedic Dictionary.* Moscow: Veche, 2000.

Zubok, V., and C. Pleshakov. *Inside the Kremlin's Cold War: From Stalin to Khrushchev.* Cambridge, MA: Harvard University Press, 1996.

VLADISLAV M. ZUBOK

Malraux, André

André Malraux (1901–76) abandoned his studies when he was twenty years old and began publishing in avant-garde journals. In 1923 he traveled to Cambodia with his young wife, Clara Goldschmidt. His experiences under the colonial regime pushed him to become politically active for the first time. On returning to Paris Malraux published the essay "La tentation de l'Occident" (The Temptation of the West, 1926), on the crisis of Europe and its values, and the book *D'une jeunesse européenne* (About a European Youth, 1927). He also published a series of novels: *Les conquérants* (The Conquerors, 1928), on the Canton strike of 1925; *La voie royale* (The Way of the Kings, 1930), recalling the expedition in search of the Cambodian temples; and *La condition humaine* (Man's Fate, 1933), describing the general strike in China, the Communist insurrection in Shanghai, and the repression against the Guomindang's left wing.

Although Malraux was not a Marxist, his interest in the problems of the Russian Revolution attracted Trotsky's interest, who in 1931 expressed his admiration for the novelist's work even though he criticized it ideologically. Malraux, for his part, saw Trotsky as a mythical figure of the revolution and sympathized with his theses. During Trotsky's exile in France, Malraux went to visit him in August 1933 at Saint-Palais.

With Hitler's rise to power, Malraux committed himself politically and stood at the Communists' side. Together with André Gide he took part in the campaign promoted by the Comintern to free Ernst Thälmann and other German anti-Fascists as well as the campaign for Georgi Dimitrov's liberation. He was invited to be part of the French delegation to the Congress of Soviet Writers that was held in Moscow in August 1934, along with the Communists Louis Aragon, Paul Nizan, and Vladimir Pozner, and he was the only non-Communist writer, with Jean-Richard Bloch, to participate. He met Sergey Eisenstein, Maksim Gorky, and Boris Pasternak. Increasingly sympathetic to Stalin's USSR, he refused to be associated with the campaign to free Victor Serge. Malraux was one of the most important personalities who participated in the International Writers' Congress for the Defense of Culture, which took place in Paris in June 1935.

In his novel *Le temps du mépris* (Days of Wrath, 1935), he described his commitment to the Communist side and conception of communism as a "virile brotherhood." He defended republican Spain and made a valiant effort to provide the republicans with aerial military aid, creating the España squadron, which saw combat from August to December 1936. In February 1937, he left for Canada and the United States with the intention of informing public opinion and gathering funds. Because of Malraux's favorable comments on the subject of the Moscow trials, he split with Trotsky during this trip. In July 1937 he returned to Spain, where he took part in the Second Congress for the Defense of Culture, attended by anti-Fascist intellectuals who were sympathetic to the USSR, and refused to defend Gide, the author of *Retour de l'URSS*, which Malraux had advised against publishing. The most remarkable testimony of his effort on behalf of republican Spain is the novel *L'Espoir* (Man's Hope, 1937). He directed the film *Sierra de Teruel* in Spain between July 1938 and May 1939; the film came out in France, but was immediately forbidden as "revolutionary" by the Édouard Daladier government. It would be shown in 1945 with the title *L'Espoir*.

The German-Soviet pact of August 1939 ended his activity as a Communist fellow traveler. He entered the resistance during the first months of 1944, and using the name Colonel Berger, created the Alsace-Lorraine Brigade in southwest France, which took part in the defense of Strasbourg at the end of 1944. During the January 1945 Congress of the National Liberation Movement, in which the resistance movements joined, Malraux had a leading role in preventing the movement from joining the Communist-inspired National Front. In August 1945 he met General Charles de Gaulle and saw in him a figure who embodied the myth of the nation. In 1947 Malraux was nominated as a delegate for propaganda of the Rassemblement du people français, which de Gaulle had created, and he gave violently anti-Communist speeches denouncing Stalinist totalitarianism. With the advent of the Fifth Republic de Gaulle called him into the government, first as his minister of information and later as minister of cultural affairs. He left the government in 1969, after de Gaulle had resigned.

See also Antifascism; Fellow Travelers; Spanish Civil War; Trotskyism.

FURTHER READING

Malraux, André. *The Royal Way*. New York: Harrison, 1935.
———. *The Temptation of the West*. New York: Vintage, 1961.
———. *Man's Hope*. New York: Grove, 1979.
———. *Man's Fate*. New York: Random House, 1984.
———. *The Conquerors*. Chicago: University of Chicago Press, 1992.
———. *Oeuvres complètes*. Paris: Gallimard, 1996.
———. *The Way of the Kings*. London: Hesperus, 2005.

NICOLE RACINE

Manuilskii, Dmitrii

Dmitrii Manuilskii (1883–1959) was born on September 21, 1883, in a west Ukrainian village, and was the son of an orthodox priest. In 1903, while a student at the University of Saint Petersburg, he joined the Russian Social Democratic Workers' Party and soon veered toward its Bolshevik wing. During the revolution of 1905–6, he was a party activist in Saint Petersburg, Dvinsk, and Kronstadt, and was arrested by the czarist secret police. He was deported, but soon escaped captivity and worked for the Bolshevik organization in Kiev until 1907, when he was forced into exile in western Europe, where he remained until after the February Revolution of 1917. He returned to Russia from Switzerland by train through Germany in the convoy after Lenin's. For several months in 1917, Manuilskii belonged to Trotsky's Mezhraiontsy group, which adopted an intermediate position between Lenin's Bolsheviks and the more moderate Mensheviks. The group was admitted to the former in August 1917, and at the time of the October Revolution Manuilskii was a political commissar in Krasnoe Selo. After the Bolshevik victory, he worked in the Commissariat of Food.

In 1919 he was sent on his first foreign mission, but was unable to make contact with Communist sympathizers in France and elsewhere. In 1920 he served as the commissar of agriculture in the Ukrainian government, and in that year attended the Second Congress of the Communist International as a member of the Bolshevik delegation. He became secretary of the Ukrainian Communist Party in 1921, and took part in the Third Comintern Congress as a Ukrainian representative. From 1922 on, Manuilskii began to work for the Comintern, often as its agent in foreign Communist parties. In this capacity he attended party congresses in France, Italy, and Germany. From 1924 to 1931 he made several clandestine trips to Paris as the Comintern overseer of the French Communist Party. He was also elected to the Central Committee of the Soviet party in April 1923—a post he held until 1952. At the Comintern's Fifth Congress in summer 1924, he was elected to the Executive Committee and the presidium of the Communist International, and in 1926 became a member of its political secretariat. He retained all three positions until the dissolution of the Comintern in May–June 1943. Throughout this period, he remained a committed Stalinist loyalist.

After Stalin had removed Zinovyev and Bukharin from their leading roles in the Comintern, Manuilskii was the de facto head of that organization from 1929 to 1934, acting effectively as Stalin's voice in the Comintern. He appears to have been demoted in 1934–35, however, with the appointment of Georgi Dimitrov as the general secretary of the Communist International. Together with Dimitrov and other Comintern luminaries, Manuilskii participated in the Stalinist purges in his position as secretary in charge of cadres. He denounced several former colleagues and complied with the formal dissolution of the entire Polish party in August 1938, by which time many thousands of Polish Communists had been arrested and shot.

In 1944, he was named the deputy prime minister and foreign minister of the Ukrainian government, attending the founding conference of the United Nations in San Francisco in 1945, the Paris Peace Conference in 1946, and several UN General Assembly meetings. Manuilskii was demoted again in 1950, but survived Stalin's last purges. He retired after Stalin's death, and died in Kiev on February 22, 1959.

See also Comintern; Great Terror; Stalinism.

FURTHER READING

Banac, I., ed. *The Diary of Georgi Dimitrov, 1933–1949.* New Haven, CT: Yale University Press, 2003.

Gotovitch, J., and M. Narinski, eds. *Komintern: l'histoire et les hommes. Dictionnaire biographique de l'Internationale communiste.* Paris: Éditions L'Âge d'Homme, 2001.

Lazitch, B., and M. M. Drachkovitch. *Biographical Dictionary of the Comintern.* Stanford, CA: Hoover Institution Press, 1986.

KEVIN F. McDERMOTT

Mao Zedong

Mao Zedong (1893–1976) was China's paramount Marxist-Leninist leader and theorist in the 20th century. A junior party member in the 1920s and controversial regional leader in the countryside in the late 1920s and early 1930s, by the mid-1940s Mao became the supreme leader of China's Communist movement, and in 1949, the new People's Republic of China (PRC). The personality cult around Chairman Mao culminated in outrageous popular veneration in the turbulent Cultural Revolution in the 1960s, and his memory remains vibrant in China today. His writings continued to serve as the official doctrine of the still-ruling Chinese Communist Party (CCP) in 2005, and his memory elicits strong feelings (both positive and negative) among China's diverse population as well as students of Marxism and revolution worldwide. In the international history of communism, Mao played a key role in leading the single most successful and long-enduring Communist revolution in the world outside of Russia, and in his "creative developments" or "Sinification" of Marxist-Leninist orthodoxy to suit Chinese conditions that have influenced revolutions in Asia, Latin America, and Africa.

Mao is significant as a representative of both Marxist and state socialist practice in 20th-century China, and the contributions of the Chinese experience to Communist ideology and practice worldwide. Inside China, Mao is widely viewed as filling the roles of both Lenin—generator and theorist of the revolution—and Stalin—the harsh but effective implementator of the socialist revolution in a national context. Since the late 1940s, Chinese in the PRC have been taught that the Chinese Revolution found its fruition in the life, work, and writings of Chairman Mao. Domestic histories have conflated the entire Chinese Communist revolution, from 1921, with the biography of Mao. Western studies until the 1980s predominantly followed this line. The post-Mao period has brought a diversification of the history of China's revolution and the contributions of many, many Chinese to both Marxist thought and revolutionary praxis. The story is no longer all about Mao. Names such as Li Da, key theorist in the 1920s, Liu Shaoqi, long the number two leader and primary organizational figure, Chen Boda, Mao's ideological secretary, Ai Siqi, popularizer of dialectical materialist philosophy in the 1930s and 1940s, and numerous generals who developed and implemented "people's war" have returned to history books in China and Western societies. Nonetheless, Mao remains the preeminent and representative figure of the successes and failures of Chinese revolutionary ideology and praxis.

Ideology and Practice in China

Mao was but the foremost of a host of Chinese intellectuals and activists known as the May Fourth generation (for the patriotic anti-imperialist movement centering on the demonstrations in Beijing on May 4, 1919, that protested the transfer of Chinese territory to the Japanese in the Treaty of Versailles). This generation wrestled with a confusing array of Western ideas—from anarchism to pragmatism to social Darwinism to finally, after 1917, Marxism—as a way to explain the failures of the Chinese government to resist the inroads of European and Japanese imperialism. May Fourth intellectuals were vigorously iconoclastic, crying "Down with the House of Confucius." They promoted major social reforms including free marriage (as opposed to prearranged), labor unions, and the adoption of the vernacular language in books and periodicals. It was a diverse generation that came in the 1920s to divide across the political spectrum from neoconservatives seeking a Confucian revival, to political liberals hoping for democracy, to militarists seeking order, to Communists seeking revolution.

Mao entered the May Fourth world from a rural community in central China. He was born and raised in Shaoxing, a county in Hunan Province. His father was a prosperous farmer and was able to pay to send Mao to school. Thus, Mao was not a peasant in the simple sense but was instead most emphatically a rural person who believed that the heart of China lay in the villages, not the cities. Mao soaked up the rich array of May Fourth translations from European and Japanese sources, including socialist and soon Russian Marxist writings (Mao never learned a foreign language). He chose to be a revolutionary and set off—first to Changsha (the capital of Hunan), and then to Beijing and Shanghai—to find that revolution.

Mao's career and writings can be viewed in three major stages: as a junior member of the new CCP who led the shift from an urban to a rural revolutionary strategy (the 1920s to the mid-1930s), the primary leader of the revolutionary party and army from the mid-1930s to the mid-1940s, and the undisputed charismatic supreme leader of the CCP and PRC from the mid-1940s until his death in 1976. The CCP was officially founded in Shanghai in July 1921, and Mao attended the first congress as a regional delegate from Hunan. The new party was small and under the strong influence of Comintern advisers. In accordance with Comintern policy, the CCP entered into a "block within" United Front with the stronger Nationalist Party (Guomindang, or GMD) led by Sun Yat-sen. In the mid-1920s, Mao participated in this United Front, joining the GMD (while maintaining his CCP membership) and teaching at the GMD's Peasant Training Institute at the Whampoa Military School, in the southern province of Guangdong. The GMD, with CCP members participating particularly in agitprop roles, set

out to reunify China by attacking militarist regimes in central and northern China. This Northern Expedition (1926–27) brought Mao back to Hunan, where he researched and wrote his seminal call for rural revolution, "Report on the Peasant Movement in Hunan" (1927). This text defined peasants as revolutionary and as key allies in the proletarian revolution. After the counter-revolution of April 1927, in which GMD forces under General Chiang Kai-shek (Jiang Jieshi) decimated union and Communist ranks in Shanghai and other major cities, Mao and his colleagues repaired to the countryside, setting up rural soviets in southeast China. This lasted until 1934, when GMD military forces crushed the Reds and forced them on the retreat that came to be known as the Long March.

Mao had not been a top leader during this period; he also had fallen out of favor with the Comintern-appointed Chinese leadership of Li Lisan and others. Yet the debacle of the Long March—in which urban orientation and positional warfare were shown to fail, while rural orientation and guerrilla warfare at least provided survival—catapulted Mao to some top positions. Over the next few years he skillfully built a coalition of colleagues, sensible military and social policies, and a persuasive ideological corpus that confirmed him as the leader of the Chinese Revolution.

The winning policies were built or at least expressed in terms of Mao's understanding of Marxist-Leninist ideology. Between 1936 and 1938, Mao returned to reading (translations of) Marxist-Leninist texts and produced his own writings outlining his basic philosophy. His core texts are "On Contradiction" and "On Practice" (1937)—which privilege social praxis over doctrine, and declare that the superstructure (that is, human will) can play the "leading and decisive role" in revolutionary praxis. Mao's "Introducing *The Communist*" (1939) named the "three magic weapons" for defeating the enemy in China's revolution: the United Front, armed struggle, and party building. This was the beginning of Mao's application of the Bolshevik model to China, or the Sinification of Marxism. It produced effective policies that catapulted the CCP to national leadership in a decade.

These policies were implemented in the 1940s when the CCP's capital was in the dusty Shaanxi Province market town of Yan'an in northwest China. Internally, Mao ruthlessly eliminated his rivals for leadership, and effectively streamlined and energized party rank and file. This was accomplished most clearly in the 1942–44 rectification movement. Here, Mao's writings from 1936 to 1942 became the core of the party's Sinification of Marxism: the application of general Marxist-Leninist theory (in its Stalinist form) to the realities of Chinese society and life. At the heart of Mao's approach was the "mass line" (*qunzhong luxian*): a broadly participatory mode of political administration that brought in the views, interests, and experiences of common working people in a fashion never stressed by Lenin or Stalin. This was not democracy. Indeed, Mao and the party emphasized "democratic centralism," and were ruthless in suppressing dissidents, such as the left-wing intellectuals associated with the writer Ding Ling and theorist Wang Shiwei who dared to question Mao and party practice from an independent Marxist (and feminist) stand in 1942. Mao's rejoinder to these inner-party intellectual critics included the seminal "Talks at the Yan'an Forum on Literature and Art" (May 1942) that laid down the law for arts and intellectual work under state socialism in China. Intellectuals are valuable soldiers in the revolution, declared Mao, but soldiers subject to discipline from commanding officers nonetheless. The rejoinder also included a harsh purge, replete with show trials, in the Stalinist fashion.

Yet this repression of dissent inside the party—which foreshadowed disastrously expanded versions of this tyranny in 1957 and 1966—paralleled effective organizational and public policy reforms, including simplified administration, armies that not only did not rape and pillage but also actually paid for the food they used, and a powerful ideology that mobilized a generation of cadres to "serve the people." This was based on a theoretical approach that privileged praxis over theory and stressed the marginal utility of subjective forces in history (that is, the power of human will). This revolutionary praxis—a major contribution of the Chinese experience—is summarized in the June 1, 1943, "Resolution of the Central Committee of the CCP on Methods of Leadership" written by Mao and included in his *Selected Works*. The lessons of coordinated but flexible organizing outlined in the resolution have been applied to social movements elsewhere, from the Vietcong in Vietnam to Che Guevara in Latin America, to Naxalite insurgents in Nepal. The key points are: a version of "think globally, act locally" but with a strong Leninist chain of command, a hardheaded assessment of the "masses" that one wants to mobilize (usually 10 percent activists, 80 percent average, and 10 percent backward or reactionary), a focus on nurturing that activist 10 percent to get the movement going, and the importance of coordinated propaganda to guide leadership and motivate the rank and file. This

approach's philosophical method for revolution privileges praxis in a process of "theory-practice-theory," in which an ideology (Marxism) is tested by actual efforts to do something and then modified on the bases of the practical results of one's efforts. The mechanism for this social learning is the superstructure: the human will of the "thought-reformed" cadre.

Externally, Mao led his colleagues in making the CCP and its program for China look better than the only likely alternative: the increasingly corrupt nationalist government of Chiang. By 1939, Chiang was the hero of war-torn China and the GMD began a leadership cult to establish Chiang as China's charismatic revolutionary leader. The publication of his book *China's Destiny* in 1943 brought Chiang's leadership cult to a crescendo. Thus, the 1940s' Mao cult responded to this practical challenge as well as drawing from Stalin's example. Mao adroitly cast his public utterances in moderate terms. His essay "On New Democracy" in 1940 became widely popular among urban readers, especially youth. While clearly a Marxist-Leninist document, Mao's program promised a long period of democratic transition on the road to eventual socialism and communism. Additionally, he provided a public history of China's humiliating confrontation with European and Japanese imperialism that using Lenin's ideas on imperialism as the highest form of capitalism, made sense of China's history, and more important, gave Chinese readers a sense of purpose, hope, and meaning. In the face of rampant corruption in GMD-administered areas along with the continued misery of working and rural peoples, Mao's "On New Democracy" combined with the impressive track record of the armies and administrations under CCP rule in the 1940s to create an appealing political platform and ideology of public service.

His peers certified Mao as the charismatic supreme leader at the Seventh Congress of the CCP in Yan'an in April 1945. From that time on, he was known as Chairman Mao. In the ranks of the party leadership he was, at first, restrained and practical, but all deferred to him. Externally, he was the great father of the revolution who could publicly proclaim in September 1949 that "The Chinese People Have Stood Up!" Mao's work in the new People's Republic was largely practical in the early 1950s, as this rural movement adjusted to the profound tasks of administering not only major cities but also a territory the size of Europe. The new socialist government "lent to one side"—taking on the Soviet model of a centralized command economy and joining the Soviet Union in the emerging Cold War. Russian advisers dominated the modern sector, and Stalin lent (but did not give) funds to help rebuild the war-torn nation.

By 1956 the new PRC government was feeling the pains of office. Bureaucratism, the limits of the Stalinist economic model, and restiveness among the working peoples and, of course, the intelligentsia bedeviled the CCP administration. Mao initially sought a moderate application of his dialectical approach. In 1955, he gave speeches that have been redacted as "On the Ten Great Relationships" that sought a practical and balanced mixed economy, somewhat in the Leninist New Economic Policy model. In 1957, Mao revived the rectification movement approach of self-and-mutual criticism but extended it beyond the party to the educated public, inviting intellectuals and professionals to "let a hundred flowers bloom" and criticize the ruling CCP. This was an unprecedented act for a ruling Communist Party and was vigorously opposed by Mao's senior colleagues. This was the last great public ideological effort by Mao that had some promise of success. It sought to lay the theoretical basis for limited—but real—public criticism and dissent under a ruling Communist Party. "On the Correct Handling of Contradictions among the People" (speaking text, February 1957) is a highly philosophical work that applies Marxist dialectics to distinguish between "contradictions among the people" and "contradictions with the enemy." By defining loyal opposition to party bureaucratism and abuses of power as the former, Mao went further than even the most daring of Eastern European regimes in the de-Stalinization of 1956. He was, after all, the supreme leader. This promising opening to socialism with a human face was ruined by Mao's own dictatorial style and petulance. When the invited criticisms arrived in the spring of 1957 they were not to Mao's liking, and so he turned face and declared the critics to be counterrevolutionary Rightists. The text of "Correct Handling" was significantly rewritten before its official publication in June 1957 to make Mao look good and ratchet back permissible discussion to the restricted scope familiar to other state socialist societies. It was a failed experiment.

The next decade was a grim one for China and Mao's legacy. The "Hundred Flowers" rectification of 1957 was followed by a harsh nationwide purge, the Anti-Rightist Movement. Next, Mao promoted an ambitious economic development strategy, the Great Leap Forward (1958–60), which was disastrously flawed and ruthlessly implemented. It contributed to at least twenty

million deaths by 1961. This has to be the single greatest crime of Mao's rule of China. After a thermidore in the early 1960s (administered by his number two, Liu Shaoqi) brought an end to the famine and began the economic recovery, Mao initiated a final effort at total revolution: the Cultural Revolution. It was designed to protect China from the dire threat of revisionism that Mao saw in the Soviet Union under Khrushchev. Here the practical thought-reform and rural orientation of the Yan'an period was revived, though alas not as comedy, but as a horror show. Mindless adulation of every utterance by Mao was represented in the "Little Red Book," *Quotations from Chairman Mao Zedong*. In all, some forty billion books and pamphlets of Mao material were published in the ten years between 1966 and 1976. The social results were catastrophic: Red Guard youth gangs terrorized communities in the name of "to rebel is justified" (a Mao quote), colleagues denounced each other, universities were closed to send students and faculty to the countryside "to learn from the peasants," and individuals were subject to endless "thought investigations." To the degree that the populace in China participated in this self-subjugation, the Cultural Revolution even outpaced Stalin's Russia as the closet realization of Orwellian dystopia. Mao clearly allowed this to happen and saw the suffering as a necessary cost of resisting revisionism.

Mao's final revolution was, after decades of angry confrontation with U.S. imperialism, to spring a rapprochement with Richard Nixon in 1972 in order to outmaneuver the Soviet Union. This external pragmatism softened the already faltering chiliastic rituals of the Cultural Revolution, and left China along with its ideological leaders tired and dispirited, but still standing at the time of Mao's death in September 1976. The post-Mao period saw a brief effort to deify him further, in order to secure the new leadership of Chairman Hua Guofen. This produced the controversial volume 5 of Mao's *Selected Works* in 1977 (which has since been repudiated and withdrawn from circulation). The survivors of the pragmatic thermidore leadership of the early 1960s regrouped under Deng Xiaoping, who took control from late 1978 until his death in 1997. Under this reform leadership, Mao was demoted from his godlike status, but has been maintained as the leader of the revolution and the font of ideological legitimacy. The 1981 CCP Central Committee resolution on "Some Questions in the History of Our Party" codified this assessment with the famous formula that Mao's contributions were 70 percent and his errors were 30 percent. China saw a brief "Mao craze" in the early 1990s—more an artifact of the new commercial culture in reform China and nostalgia for "simpler times" than a serious consideration of his ideology and practice—and an ongoing scholastic production of research and documentary collections of Mao writings and related materials. In 2004, it was easier to find in Shanghai bookstores the academic editions of Mao's writings or reminiscences than copies of the official *Selected Works*.

Chinese Contributions to Revolutionary Ideology and Praxis

The ideological contributions of Mao are systematized in Mao Zedong Thought (*Mao Zedong sixiang*), which is the official ideology of the CCP. Post-Mao CCP authorities have made it clear that Mao Zedong Thought is the "crystallization" of the revolutionary experience of the party *and* the contributions of numerous other Chinese Marxists. Mao Zedong Thought is Sinified Marxism, according to this official view. Hence, it is reasonable to consider the ideological contributions of Mao as the key, but not the only, representative of Chinese contributions to Marxist thought and praxis worldwide.

In terms of philosophy, Mao's approach to the Marxist analysis of society makes practice primary. It is the resolution of contradictions in material life *as experienced by individuals* that drives Maoist dialectics. By the 1960s, Mao clearly stated what had been implied in his earlier work: the law of the unity of opposites trumps either the negation of negation or the transformation of quantity into quality (both of which he saw as subsets of the first law). The mechanism for Maoist practical dialectics, however, is human will—individual and collective. Mao is thus in both the humanist and idealist wings of Marxist thought, placing the superstructure over the base as the location of the motor of history (he first articulated this in 1937 in "On Contradiction," apparently before Stalin made the same point in 1938). This can be seen in Mao's transformation of "proletarian" character from a description of a social class into a virtue that can be learned—through personality-transforming praxis and ideological education (that is, through rectification)—by any class. If Lenin thought only the Bolshevik party could push forward the wheel of history, Mao held that Bolshevization could be radically internalized in the individual (albeit under the dominating guidance of a charismatic leader).

In terms of revolutionary praxis and political policy, the experience of the CCP under Mao's leadership created a variant of the Russian model that has been influential among revolutionary movements in Asia and Latin America, and even today provides tools that may well be picked up again by those concerned with social change. First, Mao instituted the mass line, an organized form of democratic centralism that could be responsive to local needs, and included the broadest actual popular consultation and participation in any Communist movement. The dark side of the mass line was the Red Guards and the popular terror of the Cultural Revolution. Second, the CCP applied Georgi Dimitrov's call in the Comintern for party education far more thoroughly than any Communist movement, save perhaps Pol Pot's. The rectification movement of 1942–44 implemented the mass line by providing the noble goals of public service (which distinguishes the CCP's movement, then, from Pol Pot's), the means to inculcate those goals among administrators (party and government cadres), and mechanisms to test the level of success in their implementation. Used well, rectification offers one way to inform, guide, and control a revolutionary regime; used badly it leads to the excesses of the Cultural Revolution and the killing fields. Third, Mao and the CCP consistently returned to the idea of the United Front, an ideological tool that allows a Bolshevik regime to share power with other social forces. The United Front is institutionalized in the PRC government and has operated ever since the 1940s (with the exception of some years in the Cultural Revolution). As with Dimitrov's proposals on party education, the CCP's United Front takes the Soviet Popular Front idea of World War II years much further and has made it a tool that has contributed to the longevity of the CCP in power. Fourth, Mao consistently attacked bureaucratism, even though his flawed efforts (and personal faults) ultimately failed to address the issue successfully. Nonetheless, the corpus of Mao Zedong Thought provides a trenchant analysis of what Djilas called the New Class (though not with that phrase), and justifications for using the mass line and rectification to combat the abuse of political privilege. Fifth, Mao stressed rural issues and the peasantry. Integrating a primary focus on the countryside into the program of a Communist Party has, perhaps, been the single most influential contribution of Chinese revolutionary praxis worldwide. Finally, Mao was straightforward about politics and favored armed struggle. He was a violent revolutionary and a pragmatic military leader. His writings contain hundreds and hundreds of pages of practical analysis and examples of guerrilla warfare and other forms of popular violent struggle.

Those who have found themselves in intolerable social circumstances—from the Vietcong to the Naxalites—where local governments violently repress opposition have found Maoist military strategy compelling.

There are also negative contributions or negatives to each of these six developments, which are most poignantly embodied in the ideological repression of the 1957 Anti-Rightist Movement, the massive deaths of the Great Leap Forward, and the social terror of the Cultural Revolution. All were generated by the selfsame Mao Zedong Thought and the CCP. The legacy of Mao and his thought is therefore deeply mixed—having led China to "stand up" in 1949, he needlessly struck China down in over a decade of avoidable human suffering. This has led some in China and outside to a total rejection of Mao. The CCP itself has attempted selective amnesia, maintaining Mao as the font of ideological authority, but refusing to address the root causes of the disasters for which he—and the party—are responsible. Some in China today, however, from radical academics such as Cui Zhiyuan to rural activists or popular religious practitioners, seek to draw from the ideas and practices of Mao to address the problems that have emerged as China globalizes.

Stuart Schram, the doyen of Mao studies in the West, has long held that "the soberer elements in Mao's thought" from 1935 to 1965 constitute "a vehicle of Westernization" that addressed the big revolution for China: coming to terms with the new power of the West since 1850. This is true. Despite Mao's tragic errors, the CCP under his leadership has led China from a wartorn, divided, and impoverished collection of provinces to a stable nation-state and world nuclear power with a middle class in excess of a hundred million people and the ability to run its own space program. Conversely, the legacy of Mao and his thought for the rest of the world will be the contribution of the Chinese experience—both good and bad—with Marxist-Leninist praxis.

See also Chinese Agrarian Policies; Cultural Revolution in China; Great Leap Forward; Long March; Maoism; Marxism-Leninism; Stalinism.

FURTHER READING

Barmé, G. R. *Shades of Mao: The Posthumous Cult of the Great Leader.* Armonk, NY: M. E. Sharpe, 1996.

Cheek, T. *Mao Zedong and China's Revolutions: A Brief History with Documents.* Boston: Bedford Books, 2002.

Dirlik, A., P. Healy, and N. Knight. *Critical Perspectives on Mao Zedong's Thought.* Atlantic Highlands, NJ: Humanities Press, 1997.

Knight, N. *Mao Zedong on Dialectical Materialism.* Armonk, NY: M. E. Sharpe, 1990.

Li, Z., and A. Thurston. *The Private Life of Chairman Mao.* New York: Random House, 1994.

MacFarquhar, R., T. Cheek, and E. Wu, eds. *The Secret Speeches of Chairman Mao.* Cambridge, MA: Harvard Contemporary China Series, 1989.

Mao Zedong. *Selected Works of Mao Zedong.* 5 vols. Peking: Foreign Languages Press, 1975–77. Available at http://www.marx2mao.org/Mao/Index.html.

———. *The Writings of Mao Zedong, 1949–1976.* Ed. Ying-mao Kao and John Leung. 2 vols. Armonk, NY: M. E. Sharpe, 1986.

———. *Mao's Road to Power, 1912–1949.* Ed. Stuart R. Schram et al. 10 vols. Armonk, NY: M. E. Sharpe, 1992.

Saich, T. *The Rise to Power of the Chinese Communist Party: Documents and Analysis.* Armonk, NY: M. E. Sharpe, 1996.

Schram, S. R. *The Political Thought of Mao Tse-tung.* New York: Praeger, 1969.

———. *The Thought of Mao Tse-tung.* Cambridge, UK: Cambridge University Press, 1989.

Starr, J. B. *Continuing the Revolution: The Political Thought of Mao.* Princeton, NJ: Princeton University Press, 1979.

Teiwes, F. C. *Politics and Purges in China.* 2nd ed. Armonk, NY: M. E. Sharpe, 1993.

TIMOTHY CHEEK

Maoism

On October 1, 1949, Mao Zedong proclaimed the foundation of the People's Republic of China in the course of a ceremony held in Tiananmen Square in Beijing. In the following months, the Communist Party of China (CCP) established its control over all of continental China.

This was Marxism-Leninism's greatest success after November 1917. It was much more important than the victories that communism had achieved in Eastern Europe following the end of the Second World War after the Soviet army had occupied those countries, and it was a victory that owed nothing, or very little, to the Soviet Union's support.

In China, Mao's Marxist-Leninist thought had prevailed. During the republic's first years, while Joseph

Stalin was still alive in the USSR, the Chinese regime seemed to be following policies modeled on those of the Soviet regime. After Stalin's death, however, Mao had reason to think of himself as the authoritative leader of the Communist bloc. He did not hold Nikita Khrushchev's regime in high esteem, and Khrushchev in turn was not inclined to consider Mao as Stalin's successor, the "source of all wisdom" in that part of the world dominated by the Communists.

An epochal rift within the Communist world thus came into being, and the world conference of Communist parties in 1960 was not able to prevent it. As a consequence, by the late 1960s the CCP and its Soviet counterpart were addressing searing "open letters" to each other. These polemics soon led Mao and other Chinese leaders to look for the support of other Communist parties. Except for the small Communist parties of Albania and New Zealand, however, these efforts had an effect only on the parties of countries that bordered China, while elsewhere the Chinese encouraged their supporters to split from those parties that supported the Soviet line. And so a form of "international Maoism" developed.

Maoist parties not only attacked their rivals for not accepting "Mao Zedong thought" but also accused them of having abandoned Marxism-Leninism and therefore of having changed from revolutionary to reformist parties. At the same time, they followed all the political and ideological shifts that were occurring within the Chinese party, from the Great Leap Forward at the end of the 1950s to the Cultural Revolution of the following decade.

One shift in Chinese policy in particular that sparked a debate within international Maoism was the opening to the United States that Mao had begun in the early 1970s, which represented one of the greatest new elements in Chinese foreign policy. This change, however, did not stop the efforts by Mao and the Chinese party to encourage the development of "Maoist" organizations throughout the world.

One of the first Maoist parties to appear was the Progressive Labor Party (PLP) in the United States, founded by two lower-level functionaries of the Communist Party in New York State. The PLP sided decisively with the Chinese party against its Soviet counterpart, accused the latter of "restoring capitalism," and enthusiastically supported the Cultural Revolution in the late 1960s.

The PLP broke with China, though, once Mao adopted a relatively friendly stance toward the Nixon administration in 1972. The place occupied by the PLP as a Maoist party was soon taken by the Revolutionary Communist Party (RCP), whose members originally had been associated with the so-called New Left. The RCP continued to exist long after Mao's death.

Maoist parties appeared in eighteen European countries. The Communist Party of Belgium (Marxist-Leninist) was founded by dissidents who left the ranks of the pro-Soviet party. It was soon recognized by the Chinese party as its counterpart in Belgium, and for several years was one of the most important Maoist parties in Europe, until it underwent a serious split on the subject of the Great Proletarian Cultural Revolution.

The only preexisting European Communist party that declared its support for the Chinese in their struggle against the Soviet party was the Albanian one. The Communist Party of Albania gave its full support to the CCP in its struggle with the Communist Party of the Soviet Union in 1961 after a purge of the leadership undertaken by General Secretary Enver Hoxha. As a result, China replaced the Soviet Union as a provider of large-scale economic and political support to the Albanian regime. Yet after Mao's death, Hoxha denounced his successors as "revisionists" and eventually reached the point of denouncing Mao's teachings.

In Japan, where the Communist Party was significant enough to have several seats in parliament, the party initially gave the Chinese Communists' break with the Soviet party modest support, but then soon adopted a neutral stance in the dispute between them. This resulted in splits among the pro-Soviet and pro-Chinese factions. Several competing pro-Chinese parties developed, but none of these new parties ever represented a serious challenge for the Japanese Communist Party.

Maoist parties enjoyed greater success in the countries of the so-called third world. They were present in all Latin American republics as well as some overseas French territories. Maoist parties could also be found in eighteen Asian countries. Africa was the only continent with a limited number of Maoist parties, and this was mostly because in attempting to counter Soviet influence on the continent, the Chinese tended to support those governments that shared this aim.

There are many noteworthy aspects to Maoism's presence in Latin America. Some of the first Maoist parties were founded in this region. A majority were the result of a split within existing Communist parties. Latin America was one of only two global geographic areas in which a Maoist party (in Peru) led a real insurrection according to Mao's teachings on the "correct" path that a Communist

Party should follow—an attempt interrupted by the arrest of almost the entire party leadership.

Finally, Maoists in Latin America had to confront not only other traditional Communist parties but another revolutionary grouping as well—namely, Fidel Castro's followers. In fact, "Castroism" triumphed on January 1, 1959, some years before the Chinese pursued their plans for new Communist parties to rival the existing pro-Soviet ones. For many years, the efforts of Castro's followers to spark guerrilla *focos* put them in competition with Maoists, who at least in theory were dedicated to the same goal. No alliance was possible between the two groups because of the Castro regime's increasing dependence on the Soviet Union.

One of the Asian nations important to the spread of Maoism was India. In 1964 a split occurred in the traditional (pro-Soviet) Communist Party of India (CPI). Those who left the CPI declared their party, the Communist Party of India (Marxist) (CPIM), to be "Maoist." In Western Bengal, the new party joined the provincial government and soon found itself facing a peasant revolt led by dissident members of the CPIM itself. Similar uprisings followed between 1969 and 1972 in various parts of the country—some organized by the CPIM's Left, and others by local organizations.

In 1967 a party with a clearly Maoist outlook was formed, the Communist Party of India (Marxist-Leninist) (CPIML). For several years it enjoyed Chinese franchising in India, but it never managed to unite all the local and regional groups that expressed their support for the Chinese version of the revolution. The Indian government adopted heavy-handed measures against the insurrection in the cities and countryside. Thousands of members of the CPIML and other groups were arrested in the early 1970s, and the attempt to launch a peasant revolution failed.

The CPIML split several times, and yet one of its factions, the Central Committee for Reorganization, Communist Party of India (Marxist-Leninist), garnered a certain amount of attention since it belonged to the Revolutionary Internationalist Movement, the attempt in the 1980s and following years to create a "Maoist International."

One of the peculiar characteristics of international Maoism is that the CCP never attempted to organize a "Communist International" of its own. The franchising that the Chinese party extended to individual parties in other countries was limited to elaborate ritual invitations addressed to party leaders to visit China, and to greater or lesser forms of attention in Chinese publications with national or international circulation.

After Mao's death and the loss of interest for international Maoism on the part of the CCP's leadership, the Revolutionary Communist Party in the United States and Chile attempted to create a Maoist International. A meeting was organized in 1980, attended by delegates from eleven countries. The group denounced the post-Mao leadership of the CCP and prepared a lengthy document presenting the assembly's Maoist philosophy. In 1984 a second meeting of the group, attended by delegates from organizations in fourteen countries, formally instituted the Revolutionary Internationalist Movement (RIM), an organization that, to judge from its publications, had relatively generous funding but a small following.

See also Mao Zedong; Sino-Soviet Split; Third Worldism.

FURTHER READING

Alexander, R. J. *International Maoism in the Developing World*. Westport, CT: Praeger, 1999.
———. *Maoism in the Developed World*. Westport, CT: Praeger, 2001.
Lieberthal, K. *Governing China: From Revolution through Reform*. 2nd ed. New York: Norton, 2004.

ROBERT J. ALEXANDER

Marchais, Georges

Georges Marchais (1920–97) was from a working-class family and his father died before he ever knew him. After receiving his high school diploma, he moved to Paris at fifteen and became a metalworker. These were the years of the Popular Front, but he did not show much interest for politics or social struggles. After France was invaded by the German army, Marchais worked as a mechanic for an airplane motor workshop run by the occupiers. In December 1942, like many other workers, he left for Germany, where he worked in the Messerschmitt aircraft manufacturing plant. This episode would later become the focus of a bitter polemics, with legal ramifications: he maintained that he was the victim of coercion, but his protestations were not convincing.

Marchais, who likely remained in Germany until the war's end, returned to France and once again worked in the aviation industry; sometime between 1947 and

1948, he also became a member of the Confederation general du travail (CGT) and the French Communist Party (Pcf). In 1951, after engaging in labor union activism, he became a CGT functionary and, in 1955, part of the Pcf's apparatus, joining the powerful Seine-Sud Federation and serving as its secretary starting in 1956. From that moment on, he began to rise within the party, helped by Maurice Thorez, who appreciated his organizational skills. Marchais occupied increasingly important positions: in 1959 he was appointed a member of the extended Central Committee, and two years later he was secretary in charge of organizational matters and a member of the Bureau Politique.

After Thorez's death in July 1964, Marchais was well regarded by Thorez's successor, Waldeck Rochet, who entrusted him with critical tasks in the area of international relations. Marchais headed the French delegation to Moscow in October 1964, where they met with leaders from the Communist Party of the Soviet Union (CPSU) after Khrushchev's fall. Four years later, in February 1968, he led the Pcf delegation to the preparatory meetings for the Communist parties' world conference, which were supposed to take place in Moscow in June 1969. The invasion of Czechoslovakia in August 1968 initially led to a strong reaction from the French Communists, but gradually the Pcf's leaders moderated their dissent, and Marchais was among those who, during both the preparations for the Moscow conference and the event itself, actively worked to overcome these disagreements with the USSR. When Rochet took ill and the question of succession to the party leadership arose, Marchais was already in a privileged position. He had become junior general secretary in 1970, and in this role led the Pcf delegation in its negotiations with François Mitterrand's Socialist Party (which would result in the common platform, *Programme commun*, signed on June 27, 1972); in December 1972 he was elected general secretary.

Marchais not only continued but also developed the Union de la gauche (Union of the Left) policies that had been outlined by his predecessor in the mid-1960s. This alliance with the Socialists, following the signing of the joint program, obtained encouraging results during the legislative elections in March 1973; during the presidential elections of 1974, the Pcf supported Mitterrand's candidacy as sole representative of the Left. Mitterrand came close to winning in the second round with 49.2 percent of the vote. The Union de la gauche policies that Marchais embraced were part of a political and

doctrinal renewal that was supposed to underscore the distinctive characteristics of the "French road to socialism," in contrast to the Soviet example. The Pcf's new general secretary proposed socialism with "France's colors," founded on respect for parliamentary democracy, in *Le défi démocratique* (Democracy's Challenge), published in September 1973. One significant effect of this effort at renewal was Marchais's decision, approved by the party's Twenty-second Congress in February 1976, to renounce the obsolete principle of the dictatorship of the proletariat.

The French Communists' new orientation frequently conflicted with the Soviets, among other things because of French criticism of the repression of dissent. The low point in the deterioration of relations with Moscow occurred when Marchais refused to participate in the CPSU's Twenty-fifth Congress, which was held only a few weeks after the Pcf's Twenty-second Congress. This was Eurocommunism's moment, and its protagonists were the Pcf, the Italian Communist Party, and the Communist Party of Spain. This moment culminated in the Madrid meeting between Marchais, Enrico Berlinguer, and Santiago Carrillo on March 3, 1977; unfortunately, it also marked the beginning of this cooperative movement's decline.

The political and ideological opening that had started with the adoption of a shared platform between the Communists and Socialists was, in fact, soon destined to close. Worried that the electoral alliance was more advantageous to the Socialist Party led by Mitterrand, the Communist Party went on the offensive and asked that the platform be updated. The Communist Party wanted to encourage a greater nationalization of the economy—one of several major issues raised about the platform. This harder line led to the Union de la gauche's breakup in 1977. In the March 1978 elections, the Socialists and Communists reached a "peace" agreement, but the hostile climate that had already developed between the parties led to the Left's defeat, even if by a narrow margin.

Marchais intensified his attacks against the Socialist Party in the following years, and on the international front began moving closer to the CPSU. This led him to approve of the Soviet intervention in Afghanistan. The new orientation, however, did not prove beneficial on the electoral front: as a candidate for the presidential elections in 1981, Marchais obtained 15.3 percent of the vote in the first round—a mediocre result, and one that portended the party's decline over the next decade.

After Mitterrand's victory and the ensuing triumph of the Socialist Party in the legislative elections in June 1981, the Pcf's leader was forced to accept a marginal Communist participation in the Pierre Mauroy government. In July 1984, following a decline in the list of candidates he headed in the European elections, Marchais brought his party back into the opposition and had it follow an increasingly rigid ideological line, which would characterize his party leadership until his retirement in 1994, when the position passed to Robert Hue.

See also Eurocommunism; National Roads to Socialism; Thorez, Maurice.

FURTHER READING

Courtois, S., and M. Lazar. *Histoire du Parti communiste français*. Paris: Presses Universitaires de France, 2000.

Hofnung, T. *Georges Marchais. L'inconnu du Parti communiste français*. Paris: L'Archipel, 2001.

SANDRO GUERRIERI

Mariátegui, José Carlos

José Carlos Mariátegui (1895–1930) was one of the leading intellectuals and most important leaders of the socialist movement in Latin America. He knew the Europe of his time well, and lived there for almost four years, starting in 1919, especially in Italy (he married Anna Chiappe there in 1921 and participated in the Leghorn Congress as the lone representative of the Peruvian "socialist cell" in Italy). In 1926, Mariátegui would write that in the dispute between capitalism and socialism, "the problem of our epoch"—that is, the crisis of liberal societies in Europe, and the semifeudal and prebourgeois ones in Latin America—"shows that history is, and in this we agree with [Piero] Gobetti, identical to reformism, but only on condition that revolutionaries behave as such." During the same year he added: "The function of liberalism, from the historical and philosophical point of view, has now passed to socialism."

Picking up on Georges Sorel's characterization of Leninism as a factual criticism of the determinist and evolutionist degenerations of "professorial socialism," which had denied the revolutionary potential implicit in "socialist willpower's" ability to overturn the course of historical events, Mariátegui reevaluated the role of collective myth as an impulse and guide to emancipatory action. The guiding myths (like Sorel's general strike), however, needed to be reexamined in the context of the struggles and myths of the *indio* peasants, since the class composition of Andean countries differed significantly from that of European industrial societies. Latin American Socialists needed to assume, even if critically, an indigenous and mixed-blood identity (Mariátegui was the son of a mestiza) in order to lead ethnic communities toward the nation and socialism.

In 1918, he founded the journal *Nuestra Epoca* and then the newspaper *La Razón*, and organized the latter's promoters into the Grupo socialista in 1919. He reestablished contact after returning to Peru with Víctor Raúl Haya de la Torre, who during his Mexican exile in 1924 had founded the Alianza popular revolucionaria americana (American Popular Revolutionary Alliance) as a continental party, which would in turn give rise to its "national" incarnation (Partido aprista peruano). Mariátegui was a member of APRA until 1928, and promoted the three watchwords of a united anti-imperialist front, social justice, and Latin American political unity. After he broke with this party, he went on to found the Confederación general de trabajadores del Perú and the newspaper *Labor*, hoping to create alliances between the indio majority and the nascent working class. The theoretical proposals that evolved from this attempt would eventually find more complete formulation in the *Siete ensayos de interpretación de la realidad peruana* (1928).

The southern Andes would witness hundreds of uprisings and rebellions between 1919 and 1923. The tremors of this veritable "social earthquake" started in the South, almost at the border with Chile, and would reach as far as Cochabamba and Ayacucho, with their epicenter in the Peruvian highlands of Puno and Cuzco. The issues relevant to these events were summed up by Mariátegui in a lecture at the First Latin American Communist Conference (Buenos Aires, June 1929), attended by both Communist parties and others sympathetic to the cause. The conference took place just when the Comintern was about to change course by proposing the "class against class" tactic and the doctrine of "social fascism."

The previous year, Mariátegui had founded the Partido socialista del Perú (Psp); he underscored that he had not called the party "Communist" precisely to point to an openness that could be considered pre–Popular Front, thereby opposing the International's rules of admission. He also aimed to avoid the ongoing "Bolshevization."

Gravely ill, Mariátegui sent two Psp delegates to the conference with two texts to discuss: "The Racial Problem in Latin America" and "The Anti-Imperialist Point of View." In the second he stated among other things: "We are anti-imperialist because we are Marxist and in our struggle against foreign imperialisms we are performing our duty of solidarity with Europe's revolutionary masses." The debate on the first text was much more controversial. Mariátegui's representatives, Hugo Pesce and Julio Portocarrero, were alone in arguing for the particular nature of "Peruvian" as well as Latin American "reality" with regard to not only indios but also blacks; on the other hand, the recognition of separate *naciones* (nations) composed of Italian, Polish, and homeless Jewish immigrants, who were oppressed by the "dominant Argentinian nationality," was supported and passed, based on the mistaken application to South America of the Leninist-Stalinist line supporting the self-determination of peoples. The Peruvian delegates did not succeed in getting the Psp admitted to the International. Moreover, Vittorio Codovilla, who was at the time a member of the Comintern's Executive Committee, judged Mariátegui's theses to be "very dangerous," and tried to transform the Psp into a Communist Party. Codovilla succeeded with the help of Eudocio Ravines, who having arrived from Moscow in February 1930, obtained a proxy for the position of general secretary from Mariátegui. Mariátegui himself went to Buenos Aires to take care of his health; he also wanted to start the continental edition of *Amauta*. Instead he died on April 16.

Mariátegui's story thus concluded while the "third period" of the Comintern and the theory of social fascism were in full force. On May 20, 1930, the Psp changed its name to Partido comunista de Perú (Pcp), following Moscow's directions that required one to "liquidate the Socialist Party, while explaining to the masses the reasons for this measure and transforming existing organizations into Communist Party organizations." The new party disavowed the policy of alliances that Mariátegui had supported until the end and openly condemned Haya de la Torre's *apro-fascism*. On August 31, 1931, on the eve of elections called after the successful coup against Augusto Leguía's dictatorship, the Pcp published a manifesto rejecting the appeal to create a united front of the Left, and instead calling for a struggle "against reactionary right-wing forces and against Fascist aprismo." "Mariáteguismo" was fought, and *Amauta* was no longer published.

Paradoxically, Mariátegui was rehabilitated as an exemplary Marxist-Leninist at the height of Stalinism, during the years of the great alliance, when in 1943 Browderism established itself as continental Communist policy—in practice, a negation of anti-imperialism, which was the leading issue in the Latin American struggle for socialism. Years later, even guerrilla movements and Trotskyist parties invoked Mariátegui's name as an authority. The most grotesque case of ideological manipulation was that of the maoistas senderistas, whose organization was literally named Partido comunista del Perú por el sendero luminoso de José Carlos Mariátegui. Mariátegui was rediscovered in Latin America partly because of a growing awareness of Antonio Gramsci's thought, and also thanks to analogies in their methodology and intellectual biography (perceived with great clarity by José Aricó). This, in turn, enabled a critical reading of Mariátegui's work, essential to understanding socialism in a historical perspective, and not only in the Andes.

See also Anti-imperialism; Comintern; Revolution, Myths of the.

FURTHER READING

Aricó, J., ed. *Mariátegui y los orígenes del marxismo latinoamericano*. Mexico: Siglo XXI, 1978.

———, ed. "Homenaje a José Carlos Mariátegui en el 50° Aniversario de su muerte." Special issue of *Socialismo y participación* 11 (September 1980).

Filippi, A. *De Mariátegui a Bobbio. Ensayos sobre socialismo y democracia*. Lima: Editorial Minerva, 2008.

Flores Galindo, A. *La agonía de Mariátegui. La polemica con la Komintern*. Lima: Desco, 1982.

Leibner, G. *El mito del socialismo indigeno en Mariátegui*. Lima: Pontificia Universidad Católica del Perú, 1999.

Mariategui Chiappe, S., ed. *Ponencias del simposio internacional "7 Ensayos, 80 Años."* Lima: Editorial Minerva, 2009.

Vanden, H. E. *National Marxism in Latin America: José Carlos Mariátegui's Thought and Politics*. Boulder, CO: Lynne Rienner, 1986.

The various editions of Mariátegui's complete works are published by Editorial Amauta in Lima.

ALBERTO FILIPPI

Markets, Legal and Illegal

In the late 19th and early 20th centuries, when socialist ideas and practices were formed in Russia, it was widely assumed that in a socialist economy, products and labor would be exchanged directly for each other without the medium of money. The visible hand of the state would coordinate this direct exchange, and maintain equivalence by keeping count of the hours of labor carried out and embodied in different products. This mechanism would give results superior, it was thought, to the invisible hand of the market, for two reasons: first, it would strip away the veil of money behind which the employer exploited the worker under capitalism; and second, it would avoid the gluts and shortages, booms and slumps, of the market-driven macroeconomy.

Such ideas encountered reality first in the civil war period of the Russian Revolution (1918–21), and a second time under Stalin's First Five-Year Plan (1928–32). These experiences were highly disorienting. Not only did socialist economic fluctuations prove at least as violent as those under capitalism but also, despite the most intense repression, markets, rather than disappear, seemed to flourish despite conditions of illegality. Obvious markets were those for food and simple consumer goods. Behind the scenes, markets also arose within the state-owned economy as ministries and firms bargained with each other for supplies, and the phenomenon of unofficial purchasing agents sprang up. In fact, all countries that experienced socialism developed a wide range of markets, legal, illegal, and in between.

In the case of the Soviet economy Aron Katsenelinboigen classified these markets amusingly as follows. At one extreme were the legal markets, "red," where state stores sold state-produced goods to private consumers at the state price; the "pink" state stores, where secondhand goods were exchanged at prices set by the staff; and the "white" markets of collective farms where collective farmers brought their private produce to sell to urban dwellers at prices set by supply and demand. At the other extreme were "black" markets for organized trade in state goods that had been privately bought up at low state prices for resale (known as "speculation"), or stolen, and private products that were illegal by nature such as narcotics. The black market was the only one that was systematically repressed after Stalin's time. There were also "brown" markets that differed from the black ones only in that supply was disorganized; suppliers entered on an individual basis, but if they joined together the market became black. Finally, there were "gray" markets for disorganized exchanges of secondhand goods and private services that would have been legal but for the lack of authorization or registration of the transaction. The gray

markets were widespread and extremely heterogeneous. The objects traded ranged from ordinary consumer goods to apartments, personal services, materials, fuels, spare parts, and other producer goods. State-owned organizations and firms were often heavily involved in gray market trade. As a result, although gray markets were generally tolerated the transactions in them could also provide evidence of criminal behavior against almost anybody when it was required.

Such markets had important consequences. They eased the private lives of citizens, met the business needs of managers, earned fees for unofficial agents, made profits for criminals, and undermined the authority of the plan. Although private consumers were active in all markets, the gray markets also permitted a substantial flow of resources away from private consumption into the hands of organizations—a process called "siphoning" that János Kornai identified as a major factor in queues and retail shortages under socialism.

The basic problem of markets under socialism was that the plan could not meet all the requirements of the public and private activities that it defined as legitimate, and claimed to support. Moreover, most citizens and organizations had further private wants that they wished to satisfy regardless of the lack of the legal authority to do so. As time passed the temptation grew for socialist governments to accommodate to these realities by accepting a larger sphere for market relations within the socialist economy, and this gave rise to a long, ultimately fruitless process called "economic reform." The first proposals for a decentralized socialist market within the state sector, to reduce the bureaucratic overload on managers and ministers, date from the early 1930s. They would not become officially admissible, however, until the 1960s. In the meantime Stalin maintained the view that if markets persisted, it was only because the Soviet state had to trade with the collective farm peasantry and other countries on the world market.

The reasons for the failure of economic reform in the Soviet Union and Eastern Europe have been much debated, especially given its success in China. One approach to this problem stresses that investors will not commit entrepreneurial efforts or resources to markets that lack contract enforcement mechanisms, for fear that private or government thieves will steal the gains afterward. The Soviet economy and others like it could not evolve well-functioning markets as long as it was understood that their rulers or planning agents had the power to intervene at any time to correct any results of the market that they did not like. Socialist market transactions thus lacked credible enforcement, and the expected return to effort was usually higher in politics than in the market. Markets could develop in the margins of the command system only for goods and services that did not require much long-term investment. If this argument is right, the success of market-driven economic growth in China under Deng Xiaoping suggests that the Chinese market economy has developed means of enforcement that are not weakened by the central government's retention of dictatorial powers. But China watchers do not agree on how this has been achieved.

See also Command Economy; Economic Reform; Five-Year Plans; New Economic Policy; Planning; Socialist Market Economy; War Communism.

FURTHER READING

Belova, E. "Economic Crime and Punishment." In *Behind the Façade of Stalin's Command Economy: Experience from the Soviet State and Party Archives*, ed. P. R. Gregory, 131–58. Stanford, CA: Hoover Institution Press, 2001.

Grossman, G. "The Second Economy of the USSR." *Problems of Communism* 26, no. 5 (1977): 25–40.

Hayek, F. A. "The Use of Knowledge in Society." *American Economic Review* 35, no. 4 (1945): 519–30.

Hessler, J. *A Social History of Soviet Trade: Trade Policy, Retail Practices, and Consumption, 1917–1953*. Princeton, NJ: Princeton University Press, 2004.

Junker, J. *Socialism Revised and Modernized: The Case for Pragmatic Market Socialism*. New York: Praeger, 1992.

Katsenelinboigen, A. "Coloured Markets in the Soviet Union." *Soviet Studies* 29, no. 1 (1977): 62–85.

Kornai, J. *The Economics of Shortage*. 2 vols. Amsterdam: North-Holland, 1980.

MARK HARRISON

Marshall Plan

On July 2, 1947, Vyacheslav Molotov, the USSR's foreign minister, caused a sensation by abruptly leaving a trilateral conference with the French and British foreign ministers. The conference, originally announced on June 5 at Harvard University by U.S. secretary of state George C. Marshall, had begun on June 27 and was intended to discuss U.S. aid to Europe. The break was probably due to a June 30 telegram from the Soviet secret service with the news—later confirmed by U.S. diplomatic sources—that the United States and Great Britain had made a secret accord to reconstruct the West German economy and block German reparations to the USSR. In an already-deteriorating atmosphere between the United States and the USSR, the Paris conference progressed slowly. All of Europe needed assistance, but the Soviet leadership rejected the French proposal for a supranational management of U.S. aid, seeing it as a form of unwarranted intrusion in the division of labor between socialist countries. The USSR also disapproved of the English solution, which was limited to international coordination within a new organization, because it would be controlled by the United States. It therefore requested a U.S. soft loan instead of free aid, together with other German reparations. Molotov was afraid that the "people's democracies" would be attracted into the capitalist orbit and that the United States would practice forms of aid control. He thought he could persuade the French and British governments to take a common position on the basis of sovereignty. It seems that he erroneously thought—on the basis of cautious suggestions from the Soviet ambassador in Washington, Nikolay Novikov, as well as economist Evgeny Varga—that the United States was being forced to dole out the aid to support its exports and prevent an imminent cyclical crisis of overproduction.

The Marshall Plan, which had been preceded by the Harry S. Truman doctrine in February 1947, actually was meant to create a Western anti-Communist bloc led by the United States, and aid capitalism's recovery on a global scale by restoring Japan's and Germany's industrial centers. The U.S. unilateral offer of assistance freed Japan and Germany from the ties of multilateral institutions and Soviet control of the Ruhr. Given the many disagreements about the peace treaties, some form of conflict would have arisen sooner or later, even if the Soviet Union had accepted this plan. Yet the USSR fell into a clever trap prepared by the U.S. State Department, in particular William Clayton and George Kennan, who had devised the strategy of containment, and hence in the eyes of global public opinion, the Soviet Union appeared to shoulder the blame for the break with the West. The Soviet refusal sanctioned the official beginning of the Cold War and the division of Germany into two halves, which was completed in 1948. The Marshall Plan also caused the division in the World Federation of Trade Unions, with direct repercussions on left labor unions as well as Western Socialist and Communist parties, especially in France, Italy, and Belgium, because of the necessity of choosing between economic reconstruction and the defense of socialism.

The Soviet leadership's bewilderment also led to conflicts within its own area of influence. On June 24 Poland and then on July 4 Yugoslavia and Hungary all expressed their interest in the Marshall Plan. On July 5 Molotov, on behalf of the Central Committee of the Communist Party of the Union (Bolshevik), wrote to Eastern European countries asking them to join the upcoming Paris Conference, to be held on July 12, en masse in order to then sabotage it with the withdrawal of their delegations, but on July 6 and 7 he hurriedly countermanded the order. It was too late, however, to prevent Czechoslovakia from officially participating. On July 9 Poland, Bulgaria, Romania, and Yugoslavia renounced, while a Czech delegation led by Prime Minister Klement Gottwald and Foreign Minister Jan Garrigue Masaryk went to Moscow, where Stalin explained to them how the Marshall Plan was intended to isolate the USSR and that to accept would be considered a hostile act. On July 10, Prague issued a communiqué announcing its withdrawal and mentioning that such an action would have led to a Soviet reaction.

This abrupt about-face opened the Eastern European governments to the accusation of being complicit with the enemy. Moscow's next step was the creation of the Cominform, to control the region and organize international opposition to the Marshall Plan. In the fall of 1947 independent parties were disbanded in Hungary, Romania, and Poland; in March 1948, a Communist regime was established in Czechoslovakia.

See also Cold War; Containment; Kennan, George Frost.

FURTHER READING

Fejto, F. *A History of the People's Democracies: Eastern Europe since Stalin*. New York: Praeger, 1971.

Herring Jr., G. C. *Aid to Russia, 1941–1946: Strategy, Diplomacy, the Origins of the Cold War*. New York: Columbia University Press, 1973.

Narinskij, M. M. *The Soviet Union and the Marshall Plan*. Cold War International History Project, Working Paper no. 9. Washington, DC: Woodrow Wilson International Center for Scholars, March 1994.

Parrish, S. D. *The Turn toward Confrontation: The Soviet Rejection of the Marshall Plan, 1947*. Cold War International History Project, Working Paper no. 9. Washington, DC: Woodrow Wilson International Center for Scholars, March 1994.

Spagnolo, C. *La stabilizzazione incompiuta. Il piano Marshall in Italia, 1947–1952*. Rome: Carocci, 2001.

Woods Eisenberg, C. *Drawing the Line: The American Decision to Divide Germany, 1944–1949*. New York: Cambridge University Press, 1996.

CARLO SPAGNOLO

Martial Law in Poland

The imposition of martial law in Poland on December 12–13, 1981, was intended to crush a wave of unrest that had engulfed the country for the previous eighteen months. The crisis in Poland began modestly enough in early July 1980 when blue-collar workers at the PZL-Świdnik helicopter factory near Lublin embarked on a series of work stoppages to protest the government's abrupt announcement of higher meat prices. Strikes and demonstrations soon spread across the country, posing graver complications for the Polish Communist regime and for the Soviet Union than any event had since the late 1940s. Faced with crippling strikes at major shipyards and factories in August 1980, the leaders of the ruling Polish United Workers' Party (PZPR) considered resorting to a full-scale crackdown, but after deliberating they decided to eschew the use of force and—with great reluctance—to sign three landmark accords that formally recognized the establishment of Solidarity, an independent and popularly based trade union that soon rivaled the PZPR for political power. The signing of these accords in Gdansk, Szczecin, and Jastrzębie in late August and early September 1980 was followed less than a week later by the removal of Edward Gierek and the appointment of Stanisław Kania as the new leader of the PZPR—a post that he held for the next thirteen months.

Throughout the 1980–81 crisis, the pressure for change in Poland came "from below," and eventually affected every aspect of the country's political and economic system. Unlike the leaders of the Prague Spring in Czechoslovakia in 1968, who were willing to move ahead with far-reaching liberalization and a greatly relaxed form of communism, Kania and other senior officials in Poland tried to retain and restore as much of the orthodox Communist system as possible. Under growing popular pressure, Kania and his colleagues in the PZPR, notably the defense minister, General Wojciech Jaruzelski (who became prime minister in February 1981 and replaced Kania as the PZPR first secretary eight months later), made many important concessions to Solidarity and allowed greater freedom of expression. At every stage, however, the Polish authorities sought to limit and eventually reverse these concessions and thwart Solidarity's efforts.

The standoff between the regime and Solidarity was further complicated by the emergence of sharp splits within the PZPR itself. From the outset, some members of the PZPR politburo, such as Tadeusz Grabski, Stefan Olszowski, and Stanisław Kociołek, wanted to take a much more vigorous stand against Solidarity, using violent repression to crush the new trade union and restore conformity. Although the hard-line members of the Polish politburo never commanded a large following at lower levels of the party, they did enjoy enough support to pose a clear challenge to Kania and Jaruzelski. A potentially more serious problem for the PZPR leadership arose when reform-minded officials gained strength within the party. Over time, roughly 35 percent of PZPR members joined Solidarity. Although some of them merely wanted to infiltrate the new organization, many of those who joined were genuinely supportive of Solidarity's goals. The spread of reformist sentiment within the PZPR made the position of Kania and Jaruzelski all the more precarious. The rivalries and divisions throughout the party meant that almost any action taken by Kania and Jaruzelski would antagonize some key group. The lack of unity within the party greatly impeded efforts to resolve the crisis either by force or through a political compromise.

Soviet Reactions

The leaders of the Communist Party of the Soviet Union (CPSU) were alarmed by the rise of Solidarity and the growing political influence of Poland's Catholic Church, which they regarded as "one of the most dangerous forces in Polish society," and a font of "anti-socialist" and "hostile" elements. As the crisis in Poland intensified and Solidarity's strength continued to grow, Soviet condemnations of the Polish trade union became more strident, both publicly and in behind-the-scenes deliberations. The leader of the CPSU, Leonid Brezhnev, and his colleagues claimed that Solidarity and the church had joined ranks with "like-minded counterrevolutionary forces" to wage "an openly counterrevolutionary struggle for the liquidation of socialism" in Poland. Soviet officials also accused Solidarity of attempting to "seize power from the PZPR" by fomenting "economic chaos" in the country, and embarking on a wide range of other "provocative and counterrevolutionary actions." The whole course of events, they warned, was leading toward "the collapse of Polish socialism and the headlong disintegration of the PZPR," an outcome that would leave "Solidarity extremists in full control."

Throughout the crisis, Soviet leaders were concerned about not only the internal situation in Poland but also the effects the turmoil was having on Polish foreign policy and Poland's role in the Warsaw Pact. The CPSU politburo repeatedly condemned Solidarity for allegedly "inflaming malevolent nationalist passions" and spurring a "dangerous rise in anti-Sovietism in Poland." The turmoil in Poland also sparked apprehension in Moscow about the reliability of the Polish armed forces. Soviet leaders realized that the longer the crisis dragged on, the greater the likelihood that conscripts entering the Polish Army would have been exposed to Solidarity's "nefarious influence" for extended periods.

Because of Poland's location in the heart of Europe, communications and logistical links with the group of Soviet forces in Germany, projected contributions to the "first strategic echelon" of the Warsaw Pact, and numerous storage sites for Soviet tactical nuclear warheads, the prospect of having a non-Communist government coming to power in Warsaw or a drastic change in Polish foreign policy was anathema in Moscow. Soviet foreign minister Andrey Gromyko spoke for all his colleagues when he declared at a CPSU politburo meeting in October 1980 that "we simply *cannot* lose Poland" under any circumstances.

Quite apart from the situation in Poland itself, Soviet officials suspected—with good reason—that the crisis would have destabilizing repercussions in other Warsaw Pact countries. Soon after the historic Gdansk and Szczecin accords were signed in August 1980, senior commentators in Moscow began asserting that Solidarity's "strategy of permanent chaos" would inspire similar developments elsewhere in the Soviet bloc that would "threaten not just Poland but the whole of peace and stability in Europe." Of particular concern from Moscow's perspective was the growing evidence that turmoil in Poland was spilling over into the Soviet Union itself, especially into the three Baltic states, western Belorussia, and western Ukraine. From late July 1980 on, the Soviet politburo took a number of steps to propitiate Soviet workers and bolster labor discipline. These actions were motivated by an acute fear that the emergence of a free trade union in Poland would spur workers in adjoining regions of the Soviet Union to press for improved living conditions, greater freedom, and an independent trade union of their own.

Soviet leaders also tried to erect a number of barriers against Solidarity's influence. In early October 1980, at Moscow's behest, Lithuanian Communist Party officials ordered "the republic press, radio, and television to allocate more coverage to the role of [Communist-sponsored] trade unions in our country." In a separate directive, the Lithuanian authorities ordered local officials to "intensify their ideological work." This notion of tightening discipline and strengthening ideological controls was emphasized constantly during the next several months. Carefully controlled meetings were held every week, and sometimes more than once a week, at factories and other work sites throughout the Soviet Union.

As a further preventive step, the CPSU secretariat adopted a resolution on October 4, 1980, providing for "certain measures to regulate the circulation within the USSR of the Polish press." From then on, most Polish newspapers and journals were banned from circulation in the Soviet Union. In addition, the Soviet politburo sought to limit all personal contact between Soviet and Polish citizens. In August 1980 the politburo instructed the KGB and Communist Party officials in the Soviet republics bordering Poland (Lithuania, Belorussia, and Ukraine) to keep stricter control over Polish tourists and monitor the comments of Soviet tourists who visited Poland.

These measures undoubtedly limited the spillover from Poland into the USSR, but could not eliminate it altogether. Especially worrisome for the Soviet politburo was the mounting evidence that events in Poland were taking their toll on the Soviet Army. The head of the Soviet state security (KGB) organs, Yuri Andropov, reported that "mass subversive ideological actions [had been] aimed at the personnel of Soviet military units in Poland." The KGB's military counterintelligence units had to adopt extra safeguards to defeat those actions. The KGB also had to take special steps to thwart what Andropov described as "a number of attempts to form groups of servicemen around politically hostile aims." The adverse effect of the Polish crisis on Soviet troops was especially pronounced in the USSR's Baltic Military District, adjoining eastern Poland. Reports about the "grave problems" there proliferated in late 1980 and 1981.

In light of these developments, it comes as little surprise that high-ranking Soviet officials portrayed the events in Poland both publicly and privately as "counter-revolution and anarchy" that not only "threatened the destruction of the country's socialist order and alliance obligations" but also posed "a direct threat to the security of the USSR and its allies." Soviet leaders wanted to defuse the crisis as soon as possible to ensure that the incipient turmoil in the Soviet bloc could be contained and eventually reversed.

Planning for a Crackdown

By provoking Soviet anxieties about the potential loss of a key member of the Warsaw Pact and the adverse repercussions in Eastern Europe and the USSR, the Polish crisis demonstrated (as had the events of 1953, 1956, and 1968) the degree of "acceptable" change in the Soviet bloc. The crisis in Poland was more protracted than the earlier upheavals in Eastern Europe, but the leeway for genuine change was, if anything, narrower than before. From Moscow's perspective, the existence of a powerful, independent trade union in Poland could not be tolerated indefinitely. The only question was how best to get rid of Solidarity.

With Soviet backing, the Polish authorities began planning in the first few weeks of the crisis for the eventual imposition of martial law. Preparations for a violent crackdown by Polish internal security commandos led by General Bogusław Stachura were launched in mid-August 1980 under the code name Lato-80 (Summer '80). Those plans were swiftly refined, and preparations for a crackdown were initiated, but they were put on hold two weeks later amid deepening rifts within the PZPR politburo.

Much more elaborate planning for martial law was launched in October 1980 by the Polish General Staff and the Polish Internal Affairs Ministry. The combined effort was overseen by the chief of the Polish General Staff, General Florian Siwicki, who had long been a close friend of Jaruzelski. The planning was also closely supervised at every stage by high-ranking Soviet KGB and military officials, who frequently traveled to Warsaw and reported back to the Soviet politburo. The head of the Soviet KGB's foreign intelligence directorate, Vladimir Kryuchkov; the commander in chief of the Warsaw Pact's joint armed forces, Marshal Viktor Kulikov; and the Soviet ambassador in Poland, Boris Aristov, played especially important roles as envoys for the Soviet politburo and coordinators of the martial law planning in Poland.

The constant pressure exerted by Soviet political and military officials was an enormous constraint on Kania, who remained in charge of the PZPR until October 1981. Even if Kania had eventually sought to reach a genuine compromise with Solidarity and the Catholic Church, the Soviet Union would have tried to thwart it. From the Soviet politburo's perspective, any such compromise would have been at best a useless diversion, or at worst a form of outright capitulation to "hostile" forces and a "sell-out to the enemies of socialism." As Brezhnev emphasized to Kania's successor, Jaruzelski, in November 1981, the only thing that the Soviet leadership wanted was for "decisive measures" to be implemented as soon as possible against the "blatantly anti-socialist and counter-revolutionary opposition" in Poland.

The declassified transcripts of CPSU politburo meetings held in 1980–81 underscore the Soviet Union's determination to crush Solidarity via the imposition of martial law. At those sessions, Brezhnev and other senior officials repeatedly complained that Kania and Jaruzelski were proving to be "weak," "indecisive," "insufficiently bold," "untrustworthy," and "unwilling to resort to extraordinary measures despite our recommendations." The Soviet politburo castigated the Polish authorities for their "unconscionable vacillations and indecisiveness" in the face of "an open struggle for power by forces hostile to the PZPR." Soviet leaders were convinced that "the backers of Solidarity simply do not believe that the PZPR leadership will adopt harsh measures to put an end to their anti-socialist activity," and that the Polish authorities' timidity was enabling "the counterrevolutionary forces to operate with impunity in their plans to liquidate socialism in Poland."

Brezhnev and other Soviet leaders stressed these points whenever they met privately with Polish officials in bilateral or multilateral forums. Their aim was to keep up a relentless campaign of coercive diplomacy that would spur the Poles into action. Although Soviet leaders realized that the plans for martial law had to be devised and refined with care, their main concern was to ensure that either Kania or a successor would eventually implement those plans with ruthless determination. Using every available channel, Brezhnev and his colleagues demanded that Kania and Jaruzelski "put an end to the strikes and disorder once and for all," "crush the anti-socialist opposition," and "rebuff the counterrevolutionary elements with deeds, not just with words." The Soviet Union also undertook conspicuous military exercises on Polish territory and along Poland's borders, conveying the thinly veiled message that Soviet troops would step in if Polish leaders failed to act.

The pressure from Moscow throughout the crisis was extraordinary.

The Road to Martial Law

In mid-1981, PZPR hard-liners backed by the Soviet Union tried to get rid of Kania and Jaruzelski. But when this attempt failed, Soviet leaders were more inclined to allow the Polish authorities to impose martial law on their own. From then on, the Soviet politburo continued to exert fierce pressure, but made it clear that the Polish government should use "its own forces" to handle the situation. When Brezhnev met with Kania in the Crimea in August 1981, he made little effort to conceal his growing doubts about the Polish leader's willingness to act. Brezhnev emphasized that a crackdown should occur as soon as possible, but he acknowledged that the Polish authorities would have to choose the precise timing. Soon thereafter, on August 25–26, 1981, the Polish government had secretly approved the printing of thousands of leaflets announcing the "introduction of martial law." The leaflets were printed on a KGB press in Lithuania and transported to storage sites in Poland in early September, ready for distribution three months later.

Tensions escalated in early September 1981, not only because the Soviet Union launched its "Zapad-81" military exercises (some of the largest Soviet maneuvers ever conducted after World War II) along Poland's northern coast and eastern border but also because Solidarity held its first nationwide congress. The delegates at the congress adopted an "Appeal to the Working People of Eastern Europe," which pledged Solidarity's support for "workers in Eastern Europe" and "all the nations in the Soviet Union" that were seeking to form their own independent trade unions. At a Soviet politburo meeting two days after Solidarity issued this appeal, Brezhnev described the statement as a "dangerous and inflammatory document . . . aimed at sowing confusion in all the socialist countries and establishing a 'Fifth Column'" in the USSR. Three days later, a highly secretive Polish political-military organ, the Homeland Defense Committee, chaired by Jaruzelski, reached a final decision to introduce martial law. Although the Homeland Defense Committee did not set a precise date for the operation, the decision signaled a commitment to act.

The crisis reached another turning point in mid-October 1981 when, at Moscow's behest, the PZPR Central Committee removed Kania as party leader and replaced him with Jaruzelski. The ascendance of Jaruzelski gave Soviet leaders greater confidence that martial law would actually be imposed. Although they continued to worry that Jaruzelski might waver as the time for martial law approached, they believed that he, unlike Kania, would eventually make good on the Homeland Defense Committee's pledge to crack down.

In November 1981, the plans for martial law had to be hurriedly revised after a senior Polish military officer, Colonel Ryszard Kukliński, who had been one of the small group of officers on the Polish General Staff coordinating the planning, defected to the West as he was on the verge of being arrested in Poland for espionage. Soviet leaders realized, to their dismay, that Kukliński had been leaking details of the plans to the U.S. government, and they believed that U.S. officials would tip off Solidarity. In mid-November, at a plenum of the CPSU Central Committee, a senior CPSU politburo member, Mikhail Suslov, presented a detailed report about the Polish crisis outlining the final preparations for martial law and some of the steps that the Soviet Union was taking to ensure the success of the operation. In particular, Soviet officials were increasing their contacts with "healthy forces" in Poland (including Polish generals) that could, if necessary, step in and impose martial law if Jaruzelski failed to do so.

As the decisive moment approached in December 1981, Jaruzelski lost his nerve and began urging Moscow to send Soviet troops to Poland to help him introduce martial law. His initial plea for the dispatch of troops came on December 8, and he repeated this request numerous times over the next few days, with ever greater insistence. Soviet leaders by this point did not want to offer any assistance to Jaruzelski, for fear that it might give him an excuse to avoid acting as forcefully as he needed to. They were confident that the proposed martial law operation (which Soviet KGB and military officers had helped prepare) would be successful if Jaruzelski implemented it without letting up. The last thing they wanted was to give him a crutch that might cause him, if only subconsciously, to refrain from cracking down as vigorously as possible. Hence, when Jaruzelski sent cables to Moscow and placed phone calls to Soviet leaders on December 10–12 urging them to send troops to Poland, they tersely brushed aside his repeated pleas. In a climactic phone call on December 12, Suslov stressed to Jaruzelski that no Soviet troops would be forthcoming "under any circumstances" and that the Polish leader should proceed immediately.

No one can say for sure what the Soviet politburo would have done if the martial law operation had failed

and widespread violence had erupted in Poland. Under such circumstances, it seems extremely unlikely—indeed almost inconceivable—that the Soviet Union would have stayed on the sidelines and allowed the Polish Communist regime and Soviet troops in Poland to come under deadly attack. At a crucial CPSU politburo meeting on December 10, 1981, the Soviet KGB chair, Andropov, warned that the Soviet military must "take steps to ensure that the lines of communication between the Soviet Union and the German Democratic Republic that run through Poland are safeguarded." Polish leaders themselves certainly believed, as they indicated in a highly classified document of November 25, 1981, that if martial law resulted in uncontrollable violence and bloodshed, "Warsaw Pact forces would intervene."

Even though it seems highly probable that Soviet leaders would have sent troops into Poland to prevent all-out civil war and the collapse of the Communist regime, it is impossible to know for certain. Like almost any collective body, the Soviet politburo and Soviet military commanders did not want to make any final decisions about such matters unless a dire emergency forced them to. Because they were extremely confident that the martial law operation would succeed so long as Jaruzelski cracked down vigorously, they believed they could avoid deciding in advance about an unlikely and unpalatable contingency. This calculation was amply borne out. The striking success of Jaruzelski's "internal solution" on December 12–13, 1981, spared Soviet leaders from having to make any final decision about the dispatch of Soviet troops to Poland.

At 6:00 a.m. on December 13, Jaruzelski appeared on Polish television announcing the imposition of martial law "to counter a threat to the vital interests of the state and of the nation." The Polish security forces crushed Solidarity with remarkable speed and efficiency. Nearly six thousand Solidarity leaders and activists around the country, including Lech Walesa, were arrested within the first few hours. With administrative and logistical support from the Polish army, the Polish security forces eliminated all remaining pockets of resistance over the next four days. The martial law operation in Poland was a model of its kind, illustrating as it did how an authoritarian regime could quell widespread social unrest with surprisingly little bloodshed. For the next nineteen months, the Military Council of National Salvation headed by Jaruzelski was the supreme governing body in Poland. Martial law was not fully lifted until July 22, 1983.

See also Catholic Church; Jaruzelski, Wojciech; Socialist Camp; Solidarity; Soviet Bloc; Walesa, Lech; Warsaw Pact.

FURTHER READING

Kramer, M. "Colonel Kukliński and the Polish Crisis." *CWIHP Bulletin* (Winter 1998): 48–59.

———. "'In Case Military Assistance Is Provided to Poland': Soviet Preparations for Military Contingencies, August 1980." *CWIHP Bulletin* (Winter 1998): 102–9.

———. "Jaruzelski, the Soviet Union, and the Imposition of Martial Law in Poland: New Light on the Mystery of December 1981." *CWIHP Bulletin* (Winter 1998): 5–32.

———. "Poland, 1980–1981: Soviet Policy during the Polish Crisis." *Cold War International History Project Bulletin*, no. 5 (Spring 1995): 1, 116–26.

———. *Soviet Deliberations during the Polish Crisis, 1980–1981.* CWIHP Special Working Paper No. 1. Washington, DC: Cold War International History Project, April 1999.

———*The Kukliński Files and the Polish Crisis of 1980–1981: An Analysis of the Newly Released Documents on Ryszard Kukliński.* CWIHP Working Paper No. 59. Washington, DC: Cold War International History Project, March 1999.

MARK KRAMER

Marxism, Western

The story of Western Marxism is an integral part of the history of communism: it took place between the early 1920s and the end of the 1970s; its critique of capitalism was meant to point out possible paths to move beyond it. Western Marxism, on the other hand, also maintained a position that was openly critical of the organized Communist movement and the Soviet model that dominated it. When seen in historical context, its origin was marked by disagreements with Marxism-Leninism, which had been developing after Lenin's death on the basis of three assumptions: the interests of the Soviet Union were paramount; theoretical reflection was a prerogative of the party leadership; and a reliance on materialism, as it came to be defined in European culture during the second half of the 19th century by way of positivism's contributions, was key to Marxism's philosophical foundation.

Western Marxism developed in opposition to this theoretical and political structure for half a century, thanks to the contributions of individual intellectuals intent on defining the goals of communism in a manner that dif-fered from Soviet Marxism. The founding act was Georg Lukács's *History and Class Consciousness*, published in German in 1923. If the Second International had addressed the development of class consciousness in terms of propaganda and education, Lukács turned the problem upside down, and started from the worker's experience and the transformation of labor into a commodity. Lukács's analysis was built around two key concepts: *alienation*, in the original meaning that Marx had attributed to it, and *totality*, of Hegelian origin, which was understood as a way to overcome *reification* by means of an understanding of the capitalist system's functioning as a whole. While Soviet Marxism was moving toward a restoration of Georgy Plekhanov's philosophical materialism (which Lenin had never officially repudiated), the Hungarian philosopher rediscovered Hegelian dialectics as the cornerstone of a more penetrating theory of class consciousness.

With the latest defeat of the German working class in October 1923, Lukács's work was seen as related to Trotsky's attack on the new post-Leninist Soviet leadership group (together with Karl Korsch's *Marxism and Philosophy*, which dealt with similar philosophical topics, even if in a less creative fashion)—an attack that blamed the German Communist Party (KPD), but most especially the Communist International and the Bolshevik Party's leadership for the German defeat. Lukács's official condemnation was included in the report that Grigory Zinovyev used to open the Fifth Congress of the Comintern in June 1924. A tortured existence in the ranks of the Communist movement thus began for Lukács—a movement that he would never renounce, however. But the philosophical architecture of *History and Class Consciousness* continued to influence all the European Marxist research that followed, whatever the political and intellectual vicissitudes that were to affect its author.

The October events in Germany had perhaps even greater importance for Antonio Gramsci, who was not a brilliant philosopher, heir to the most advanced and sophisticated forms of German culture, but an obscure party functionary, whose starting point was the Communist movement's concrete strategic options (which had by now reached the crossroads of "world revolution" or "socialism in one country"), and who needed to address issues of political theory and science. This research led to increasing tensions with the Comintern's leadership, and resulted, right at the time Gramsci was being held in a Fascist prison, in Gramsci's excommunication and complete human and political isolation.

In Gramsci's view the insurrection that the KPD had attempted only confirmed the widespread "putschist" tendencies in the German workers' movement. The "united front" policy that had been approved during the Third and Fourth Congresses of the International under Lenin's direction was, according to Gramsci, instead meant to be pursued with a broader strategic perspective in mind. This was the political origin of Gramsci's reflections on the role of the "superstructures," which came to occupy an increasingly important position in his thought. "Politics is always behind and it is seriously behind compared to the economy," he wrote in 1926 in a report for the Italian Communist Party's Central Committee. Gramsci came to the conclusion that bourgeois society's endurance originated in subjectivity, which he had previously identified as a key factor in the acceleration of the historical process during the Bolshevik revolution (the revolution against "Capital"). The development of class consciousness was replaced by an analysis of the structures that guarantee the stability of power and the consent given to the ruling order by forms of "contradictory consciousness," which need to be investigated in their concrete historical configuration. These reflections gave birth to the notion of the intellectual as "organizer," an essential mediator between the elites and masses, but also an essential function in the construction of the working class's party. *The Prison Notebooks* are not, as some have argued, a work in which Gramsci expresses a form of self-criticism with regards to expectations of an imminent revolution. They instead reevaluate and develop the political themes of the "capitalist stabilization" that was occurring in 1924 in the increasingly complex terms of political theory.

Lukács's, Korsch's, and Gramsci's intellectual itineraries, their individual peculiarities notwithstanding, are tightly interwoven with the history of the international Communist movement. The German intellectuals who coalesced in 1933 around the Institut für Sozialforschung were instead alien to party or academic affiliations. They were isolated researchers whose solitary study focused on the fortunes of capitalist civilization, a topic that had been the focus of Max Weber's sociological research. It is perhaps also for this reason that their works essentially focused on an analysis of the forms of modernity.

This is the meaning of Walter Benjamin's wide-ranging research on the relationship between Charles-Pierre Baudelaire and Paris, a place in which the outlines of new forms of social self-representation were being drawn—outlines that would gain greater clarity and circulation during the 20th century. Benjamin's debt to the theoretical categories of *History and Class Consciousness* is obvious. The conclusions of his research are undeniably his, though, and found expression in his last dramatic text on the philosophy of history. While Adolf Hitler's armies were overrunning Europe, Benjamin accused the German working-class movement of not having understood the structural ambivalence and reversibility of progress.

In the early 1940s, Theodor W. Adorno and Max Horkheimer viewed Benjamin's *Theses* as a theoretical testament whose work needed to be continued; their *Dialectic of Enlightenment* shifted the focus of the analysis of the modern from Paris to Los Angeles, and from the *Passagen* to Hollywood. The denunciation of the crisis of the idea of progress was now extended to a theory of modernity that aimed at including Nazi totalitarianism, the manipulated mass media of U.S. capitalism, and the authoritarianism of Soviet planning as variants of the same process of involution. "We have no doubt—and this is our petitio principi—that freedom in our society is inseparable from the Enlightenment. But we also believe we have understood with the same clarity that the very idea of this form of thought, not only in its concrete historical forms, or in the social institutions to which it is tied, already contains the germ of that regression that one can today observe everywhere. If the Enlightenment cannot include a consciousness of this regressive moment within itself, it is underwriting its own failure." Published almost clandestinely in 1947, this work would only have a real impact and a proportional circulation when it was reissued in 1969, an era completely different from the one in which it had been written.

The fundamental thematic articulations of the entire subsequent history of Western Marxism had thus been fixed in the two postwar periods. And yet Western Marxism only exploded as a mass phenomenon in the early 1960s, affecting Europe, the United States, and major Latin American countries simultaneously, until it began to assume the characteristics of a cultural fashion. It circulated as the continuation of a critical analysis of mature capitalism, which had been able, thanks to U.S. hegemony, to overcome the fissures and contradictions that had fed the catastrophic tendencies of European bourgeois society. But it also represented an answer to the great questions that the demythologization of Stalin, the denunciation of his crimes, had raised about the goals and even idea of communism.

In Eastern Europe the impact of the Twentieth Congress of the Communist Party of the Soviet Union, even with its ambiguities, sparked the beginning of forms of criticism and open dissent among intellectuals toward institutional power, which unlike what would occur during the late 1970s, was still willing to express itself in the language of Marxism. Lukács's active participation in the anti-Soviet uprising of 1956, during which he occupied the post of minister of culture in the Imre Nagy government, marked the end of the long Stalinist phase that the Hungarian philosopher had embarked on since the early 1930s. In 1967 Lukács reissued his youthful works, and pointed to the lack of distinction between objectification and alienation, as could be found in the concept of work in the young Marx, the essential reason for Lukács's continuing critical detachment. This did not prevent the rich philosophical architecture of *History and Class Consciousness*—which had always, even if often in subterranean ways, remained influential—from becoming a reference point for the theoretical research of Agnes Heller in Hungary, Karel Kosik in Czechoslovakia, or the intellectuals around the journal *Praxis* (published in Zagreb), who in different ways tended to reevaluate communism's humanist component and become more insistent about the "demilitarization" of theory in the shadow of "peaceful coexistence."

In the West the developments were much more complex. Gramsci, after having been influential mostly only within Italian borders during the 1950s, where he was considered an heir to a progressive tradition of Italian thought (from Francesco De Sanctis to Benedetto Croce), rapidly became part of international culture, and did so as the theorist of the specific political forms that distinguished the "West" from the "East" (in this context the key category that garnered most of the attention was that of "passive revolution"). His most original traits gained wider currency in this way—as a Communist thinker who had opposed the philosophical and political modules of Marxism-Leninism since its inception. Gramsci's criticism of philosophical materialism contained an implicit, if not obvious, radical preoccupation with the tendency of the Soviet state to stop at a rough and repressive stage of development, thus revealing an organic incapacity to develop the complex superstructures characteristic of a new civilization.

In this same period the great collection of analyses of modernity produced by the Frankfurt school resulted in Herbert Marcuse's *One-Dimensional Man* (1964), a radical critique of consumer society as a supreme form of alienation and totalitarian oppression. Notwithstanding the intricacy of the theoretical construct, which mixed Freudian concepts and Heideggerian influences, Marcuse's book almost became a bible of the U.S. New Left;

extraneous to the logic of the mass party, it tended toward a sort of philosophy of liberation centered on the individual's revolt, and could be expressed directly in the interactions of everyday life. If knowledge of Gramsci's *Notebooks* remained compatible with and even strengthened a perspective that aimed to establish a European "workers' movement within democracy," Marcuse's work was a radical devaluation of politics in the direction of forms of thought that pushed individuals toward insubordination and rebellion. The movements of 1968 would in their turn represent the foundation for a mass expansion of Western Marxism, while internally it was becoming increasingly differentiated and complex.

The 1960s also witnessed the international recognition of the London journal *New Left Review*, which born as a product of the research and political struggles that followed 1956, by a group of Marxist historians of exceptional ability (Christopher Hill, Edward P. Thompson, Eric Hobsbawm, and Perry Anderson), soon affirmed itself as an influential center throughout the world of Anglo-Saxon culture—one marked by ongoing debate between the different positions of resurgent Marxist research. The journal expressed its political distance from the Soviet model by subscribing to Trotskyist theses.

The innovation that was perhaps most significant, as far as its effects on the list of analytic themes that came within Western Marxism's purview, was the publication of Louis Althusser's collection of essays in 1965, with the title *For Marx*, which was followed by the collective work *Reading Capital*. The guiding principle of this research, which at least partially explains its popularity, was its appeal to restoring *Marxism as science*. Althusser intended to reinstate the "epistemological break" that according to him Marx's research had introduced in the area of social thought of his age, on the basis of a theoretical model inspired by structuralism, which was dominating French culture at the time, and that counterposed the concept of *structure* to that of *subject*. This entailed a radical criticism of historicism, a tradition in which Jean-Paul Sartre, Lukács, and Gramsci were all placed, as representatives of philosophies of the subject.

Despite its theoretical vitality, Western Marxism became the object of political disputes during the late 1970s, especially in France and Italy—not coincidentally in the two countries where their respective Communist parties had a real chance to enter the government. The eschatological perspective that had underpinned the entire history of this cultural formation was on its way to becoming increasingly unsustainable, both because of a renewed comparison with the concreteness of a social democratic perspective, and because of two issues of epochal significance: the crisis of Fordism and the diffusion of new forms of "flexible accumulation," which radically altered social stratification, tarnishing the theoretical and political "aura" of foundational concepts such as working class, alienation, and class consciousness; and the Soviet system's inability to demonstrate any capacity to innovate, which would become even more serious in the following decade and lead to its final extinction. Having developed and grown as a challenge and an alternative to the Soviet model, Western Marxism ended up, paradoxically, being dragged down by the crisis of its alter ego. Its disappearance left a void that was rapidly filled by an increasingly apologetic and instrumental representation of the universal value of Western democracy, which often merely provided cover for the diffusion of neoimperial policies made possible by the end of the Cold War's equilibria.

See also Gramsci, Antonio; Lukács, Georg; Marxism-Leninism

FURTHER READING

Althusser, L. *For Marx.* New York: Vintage, 1970.

Althusser, L., and E. Balibar. *Reading Capital.* New York: Pantheon, 1971.

Anderson, P. *Considerations on Western Marxism.* London: New Left Books, 1976.

Benjamin, W. *Angelus Novus. Saggi e frammenti (1955).* Turin: Einaudi, 1962.

Gramsci, A. *Prison Notebooks.* New York: Columbia University Press, 1992.

Horkheimer, M., and T. W. Adorno. *Dialectic of Enlightenment.* New York: Continnum, 1991.

Korsch, K. *Marxism and Philosophy.* New York: Monthly Review Press, 1971.

Lukács, G. *History and Class Consciousness: Studies in Marxist Dialectics.* Cambridge, MA: MIT Press, 1971.

Marcuse, H. *One-Dimensional Man: The Ideology of Advanced Industrial Society.* Boston: Beacon, 1964.

LEONARDO PAGGI

Marxism-Leninism

Marxism-Leninism is "the scientific system of revolutionary concepts of the working class, of workers, which reflects the world's objective laws of development and the experience of the class-struggle of the popular masses against exploiters, a system that is constantly developing on the basis of the generalization of this experience and which constitutes the program, strategy and tactics of its revolutionary struggle against capitalism, for the socialist revolution and the establishment of the dictatorship of the proletariat with the goal of building communism." This definition, taken from the Soviet *Philosophical Encyclopedia* (1964), illustrates what Marxism-Leninism thought of itself, and without differing markedly from the many others in Soviet texts at different times, explains the nucleus of a doctrine that was basic to communism as a movement, party, and historically determined regime.

In the Soviet terminology of this encyclopedia entry, an organic connection was made explicit between a system of ideas that claimed to be scientific because it reflected, on the one hand, the dynamic structure of objective, natural, and historical reality (the world), and on the other, a plan for revolutionary action by the working class against capitalism and in favor of communism. Marxism-Leninism was in effect, like Marxism before it, a union of theory and praxis, a science that interpreted the world so as to transform it, not according to some abstract plan, but according to the class struggle of modern times—a specific moment in history that was close to the revolutionary transition from capitalism to communism. It is a question of establishing how this extremely condensed nucleus of Marxism evolved into Leninism, becoming by the end of the 1920s Marxism-Leninism, and how, due to Stalin and his successors, it acquired a specific form and substance. If it is true, according to the above definition, that Marxism-Leninism was a system that developed on the basis of generalizing the class struggle, there is even more truth in saying that it developed on the basis of the experiences of the power that built it, and whose instrument of ideological legitimation it became. Therefore even though its nucleus remained constant, it was Stalinist in its rising phase and anti-Stalinist in its declining one.

Marxism-Leninism reached its peak in 1938, when the *History of the Pan-Soviet Communist Party (Bolshevik): Short Course* was published. Stalin participated directly in its preparation, and the work was supposed to represent the historical and theoretical summa of the scientific system of revolutionary concepts of the working class, as this system had been conceived by the Communist Party, which according to the system itself, constituted the vanguard and guide of the working class, with no possibilities of alternatives or rivalry. It is significant that such a summa should be formulated in a historical work, as can be seen from the title, whatever one's assessment of the work's historical value. The theoretical section, devoted to dialectical and historical materialism, was part of the work's internal structure. Materialism was the general scientific horizon of the historical narration, which was dedicated to a specific topic (the Pan-Soviet Communist Party). Yet the topic was presented as the crowning achievement of world history, its point of arrival in the present and departure for humanity's future, almost as if this mirroring of narrowly focused history and materialism were an empirical confirmation of dialectical and historical materialism as a truthful conception of the universe, and an insuperable method for thought and action.

While this *History*'s intrinsic falsity became more apparent over time, the work was nevertheless significant as a central element of the Soviet and Communist ideological system. This is the reason that at the time the *Short Course* was published, a resolution of the party's Central Committee, published on November 14, 1938, for the occasion, stated that the work would mark the beginning of "a new powerful ideological and political impulse in the life of our party and of the Soviet people." These words were not just an expression of the rhetorical hyperbole that was characteristic of the regime but rather recognized the importance that the *Short Course* would have in every sector of the Soviet world as a true Communist "manual," including in all those educational institutions where Marxism-Leninism was a fundamental subject of study, or rather indoctrination. That this text was no longer published after 1954 does not alter the picture, because it was periodically replaced by other updated histories—in other words, it was gradually updated to reflect the needs of the party leadership.

The function of the *Short Course*, and the works that replaced it, was to offer a unique and definitive (even if only relatively speaking, since it had to be updated) account of the history of the first and, at the time of its original publication, only socialist country. It was a sacralized conception meant to impose a clear, simple, and secure view of the world that was being built, which had begun with the "Great socialist October revolution," and had been in the planning stages since the birth of Marxism and later Leninism. Furthermore, it was the result of a developmental process through the ages— one seen in the local, Soviet, international, and universal achievement of this world, opening onto a Communist

future. This process had evolved through five main stages: the socioeconomic formations of the primitive community, slavery, feudalism, capitalism, and finally communism (this last stage comprised a transitional stage called socialism).

It was a mythical-epical vision both simple and grandiose, whose protagonist had lately been Stalin, but only insofar as he was Lenin's heir and the person continuing his legacy. Lenin, the person who had triumphed in the proletarian revolution, was in his turn a giant standing on the shoulders of other giants, Karl Marx and Friedrich Engels, masters of revolutionary theory. The most gigantic cult of these heroes, but also the most "modest," since Stalin did not want to add an "ism" to his name, and limited himself to being honored as the guardian and executor of Marxism-Leninism—the cult of Stalin, which would later be denounced at the Twentieth Congress of the Communist Party of the Soviet Union—was not only founded on the cult of the other three doctrinal fathers but also represented an epiphenomenon when compared to the cult of the revolution and the party, or the even bigger cult, entirely directed toward the future, of communism. It was therefore a coherent and compact ideological system, meant to inspire a sense of security in those who participated in it. The fact that the *Short Course* appeared in 1938, the year in which the great and truly revolutionary processes of innovation that Stalin had implemented had reached a climax, which at least temporarily marked their realization, was also not casual. These processes had a dual meaning: as both historical processes, such as industrialization and collectivization, and juridical processes, such as those that in successive waves, had eliminated the old ruling elite and substituted it with a new one, thus confirming Marx's saying that Lenin had placed as an epigraph in his founding work *What Is to Be Done?* "A party gains strength by purging itself."

The concept of the "purge," together with the related term "purity," was essential to Marxism-Leninism. Purity was equivalent to orthodoxy. But compared to this synonym, the first term was more significant in the case of Soviet Communist ideological reality, since it extended from the doctrinal sphere to that of behavior, and above all to the image of itself that the system wanted to project in literature, cinema, painting, and so on. In this sense, socialist realism complemented Marxism-Leninism since it produced this image for internal and external use. It was the image of a new and pure world, being constantly renewed and purged (the gulag was where human impurities were discharged, eliminated, or in some cases recycled). It truly was a "permanent revolution," not in the sense that the term had in Trotsky's lexicon, but rather as an internal revolutionizing force, rigorously and rigidly guided from above by a supreme leader, enlightened by a supreme doctrine, and condensed by that leader into a book: the *Short Course*. Soviet communism, unlike fascism and National Socialism (this is only one of the differences between these phenomena), was a "totalitarianism of the Book"; unlike Mussolini and Hitler, Stalin did not exhibit similar oratorical talent and his hypnotic power of suggestion was concentrated in his writing. It was a talent on display mostly during lectures given at small conferences and not in front of seas of humanity, and this writing was in its turn based on other writings, on sacred writings that were untouchably sacred. The set of these writings, properly interpreted and organized, constituted Marxism-Leninism, a tree trunk from which national variants grew (the "national roads" to Marxism-Leninism, so to speak, with representatives of the doctrine rooted in the culture of their own country). The supreme gardener always reserved the power to prune dead branches, or even worse rotten ones, thus guaranteeing the purity of the vegetation.

How did the Marxism-Leninism of 1938 emerge (the later developments, while Stalin was still alive, were its organic development, on the basis of his latest writings, and what followed after 1954 were only increasingly arid forms accompanied by increasing fossilization)? Undoubtedly on the basis of original Marxism, that of Marx and Engels, which then witnessed developments in various directions, with the crucial development tied to Lenin's thought and actions. It was based on an intransigent opposition to any revision of Marx and Engels's doctrine that would diminish its revolutionary impulse. With Lenin, Marxism became not only an instrument crowned by revolutionary success in 1917 but especially after that date, by absolute power. On its basis party strategies and tactics were elaborated—a party that since it represented a revolutionary state and the center of an international movement, had to face tasks of an epochal nature in the context of an unforeseen global dynamic (the failed "global revolution"). Marxism was thus open to different interpretations, not so much of a theoretical as of a practical nature, and among these Stalin's was the one that historically prevailed, providing the basis of Soviet and world communism for decades to come.

This synthesis was the result of the political struggles that Stalin had waged inside the party and the Communist International, but it was prepared by work conducted in two areas less directly connected to the power struggles at the top of the system: historical research and philosophical theorizing. After October 1917 Russian culture had been purged: anything that was considered bourgeois, idealist, religious, and so on, was seen as a weed to be removed from its soil, forcing representatives of the "old" intelligentsia into exile, and leaving room only for those forces that represented Marxist tendencies. Initially, however, a margin of controlled freedom remained for artists, authors, and even historians, so long as they did not oppose the new regime. Within Marxism itself different positions clashed. The major protagonists of these clashes were Georgy Plekhanov, Mikhail Pokrovsky, and Trotsky (the first engaged in a prolonged polemic with Lenin and Bolshevik policy, but his *History of Russian Social Thought*, which interpreted Russia's specific historical development in light of the concept of "Oriental (or Asiatic) despotism" still had an impact). Pokrovsky and Trotsky instead clashed directly on the interpretation of the peculiarity of Russian history, and therefore also the nature of the Russian revolutions of the 20th century, from the 1905 revolution to that of October 1917. Pokrovsky became the official historian of the new power, while Trotsky, at the center of the struggle for Lenin's succession, was defeated not only politically but also historiographically, and his *History of the Russian Revolution* (like all his other works) was proscribed. Ultimately, though, even Pokrovsky lost his position as dictator of Soviet historiography post mortem, when during the 1930s, Stalin's historiographical "new course" was established. At the decade's end two massive volumes became his tombstone, the first titled *Against M.N. Pokrovsky's Conception of History* (1939), and the second, more catastrophically, *Against M.N. Pokrovsky's Anti-Marxist Conception* (1940).

If the polemics about the nature of Russian history and Bolshevik revolution were important in the early 1920s, at the end of the decade another discussion of more pronounced theoretical significance, although its political implications were not always clear, was sparked by the publication of Sergei Dubvrosky's book *Regarding the "Asiatic" Mode of Production, Feudalism, Serfdom, and Commercial Capitalism*, and regarded world historical development; it concluded in 1934. Even though he did not participate directly, Stalin followed the debate and summarized it in his own fashion in *Dialectical and Historical Materialism*, which became part of the *Short Course*, where socioeconomic formations or, using different terminology, the principal modes of production were established as five, without the "Asiatic mode of production," and Stalin explained the mechanisms for passage from one formation to the next. These were theoretical questions of contemporary importance for internal Soviet policy (the development from socialism to communism) as well as the policies of the Communist International (the type of revolution in "backward" countries).

Stalin's "shift" in Marxist-Leninist historiography began in the early 1930s with his direct intervention in the form of a "letter" sent to the editors of the journal *Proletarskaya Revolutsya* and published with the title "Questions Concerning the History of Bolshevism." It was an intervention not so much of a historical as of a political nature, because it was a polemic against Trotsky, now an exile, whose activities as an interpreter of the revolution's history still worried Stalin. It was a question of the "history of Bolshevism"—that is, it regarded Lenin's policies, the character of the October Revolution, which for Stalin meant, because of its interconnections with his struggle against Trotskyism, the central moment from which the Marxist-Leninist legitimation of his policies and power derived.

A later work also proved the importance that was attributed to history, but in a broader perspective than that provided by internal party history—a perspective extended to general history and especially Russian history. This was *Observations on a Plan for a Manual of the History of the USSR* (1934), and it was signed by Stalin, Andrey Zhdanov, and Sergey Kirov; its significance was pedagogical, evaluated from the point of view of school instruction, and hence its mass circulation. The observations contained criticisms of the plan because "the October revolution as a revolution that freed the peoples (of Russia) from the national yoke remains without a foundation as does also the creation of the USSR." Russia's entire past history, and more generally that of all humanity, was supposed to "found" in the Bolshevik revolution. In its turn, Stalin's revolution was supposed to derive legitimately and develop organically from the previous revolution, a faithful expression of Marxism-Leninism. History, in addition to providing these forms of legitimation, was no longer supposed to be constructed according to abstract sociological schemata, as in Pokrovsky, but needed to be told as a sequence of events, even though organized according to the five socioeconomic formations (from the primitive community to the Communist future), given meaning by the class struggle. Its center was supposed to be Russian history—the history of the czarist empire with all its peoples, lead by the Russian people as primus inter pares, since it was in Russia that the great socialist October Revolution had taken place, and it was there that the first construction of socialism was occurring, as a model to be extended to the rest of humanity.

Marxism-Leninism was not only history, it was also philosophy, and the other strand that got woven into Stalin's synthesis concerned the philosophical discussions of the 1920s. For this purpose Lenin's *Materialism and Empiriocriticism* was adopted once more, sacralized, integrated into the posthumous *Philosophical Notebooks*, and canonized together with Engels's *Antidühring* and *Dialectics of Nature*. These texts, together with all of Marx's works, formed the basis of dialectical materialism (in its union with historical materialism), an instrument of struggle against not only idealism and religion (and so-called mechanistic materialism), but also all pseudo-Marxist deviations, from those of the ex-Bolshevik Alexander Bogdanov, against whom Lenin struggled in person, to the "Menshevizing idealism of [Abram] Deborin." This theoretical moment of Marxism-Leninism was supposed to provide a secure, complete, scientific belief system, a view of the world and a method for thought and action, as well as the set of nature's and society's laws of development, a foundation from which to transform both one and the other.

For several decades Marxism-Leninism performed its ideological function, preserved even after Stalin's death and adapting to the new political situation, only finally to become an empty shell, devoid not only of its sacred qualities but its credibility, or rather, its powers of suggestion, even in the eyes of those who spread it.

See also Classes; Legal Marxism; Lenin, Vladimir; Messianism; Plekhanov, Georgy; *Short Course*; Socialist Realism; Stalin, Joseph; Stalinism; Totalitarianism; Utopia.

FURTHER READING

Kolakowski, L. *Main Currents of Marxism: Its Rise, Growth, and Dissolution*. Oxford: Clarendon, 1978.

Wetter, G. A. *Dialectical Materialism: A Historical and Systematic Survey of Philosophy in the Soviet Union*. New York: Praeger, 1958.

VITTORIO STRADA

Mayakovski, Vladimir

Vladimir Mayakovski (1893–1910) was born in Baghdati, Georgia. His father, an impoverished noble, died while he was young and the future "poet of the revolution" moved to Moscow with his family in 1906. He became a member of the Bolshevik wing of the Russian Social Democratic Party while in high school, dedicating himself to political propaganda, which led to his repeated arrest. In 1910 he was interned for six months in Moscow's Butyrka prison; once freed he enrolled in the Moscow Institute of Art, Sculpture, and Architecture. In 1911 he met David Burlyuk, who introduced the young Mayakovski to the budding futurist movement and specifically the Cubo-Futurist group. Mayakovski published his first poetry in 1912 in the group's almanac-manifesto *A Slap in the Face of Public Taste* and established himself with the tragedy *Vladimir Mayakovsky* (1913), soon becoming, with Velimir Khlebnikhov, the movement's most important and original poet.

His prerevolutionary production, seen by many critics as the poet's most genuine artistic contribution, was marked by the need to experiment and distinguish his voice from that of tradition. If in its form Mayakovski's poetry was based on accentuated rhythm, imperfect rhymes and puns, and hyperbole, and was constructed on the clash of antithetical linguistic levels, its tone was characterized by the clash between epic-rhetorical aspirations and sincere lyricism, between theatrical poses, oratorical declamation, and crude autobiographical tendencies. The choice of topics often underscored a tendency to *épater le bourgeois*, to shake the hypocrisy of the conformists, to give voice to the street, the city, the Russian proletariat, demonstrating a marked predilection for the tone, style, and ambience of urban poetry. Mayakovski also liked to deal with contemporary topics from a nonconformist point of view. His perspective on religion was particularly unusual, exhibiting a violent sacrilegious impulse and sincere sense of camaraderie. The texts' graphic layout and the author's conception of the poetry book were the features most closely tied to avant-garde experimentation, and they display aspirations to synesthesia, and toward forms of syncretism between the verbal and visual arts.

An examination of Mayakovski's poetic genealogy reveals some obvious ties to specific strands of previous Russian poetry, from Gavrila Derzhavin's odes to Nikolay Nekrasov's narrative realism, as well as Russian and French symbolist poetry (from Tristan Corbière and Émile Verhaeren to Valery Bryusov and Innokenty Annensky), regardless of the poet's statements of intent. Some of the early Mayakovski masterpieces are *A Cloud in Trousers* (1915) and the short poem *The Backbone Flute* (1916). His first lyrics included desolate urban and human landscapes, constructed according to daring graphic and rhythmic plans, which were published in *Novy Satirikon*; in them the poet took a stand against bourgeois hypocrisy, militarism, and the horrors of World War I. Mayakovski's antiwar, pacifist, and revolutionary beliefs were elaborated in his denunciation poem, *War and the World*.

He welcomed the October Revolution enthusiastically, and this made him its "drummer," the new socialist society's bard. In his *Left March! For the Red Marines: 1918*, the poet addressed the masses directly; in his satirical play *Mystery-Bouffe* (1918, second) he depicted revolutionary events allegorically. Starting in 1919 he worked for the Russian State Telegraphic Agency, writing short political pieces, including "Rosta Windows," in which he stylized popular verse. Having temporarily left topics relating to the individual in the background, Mayakovski devoted himself to poems celebrating socialism's victory (from *150 000 000* to *Vladimir Ilych Lenin* and *Good!*). The poet's work developed in thousands of verses and compositions that exhibited his technical and thematic versatility. He took part in poetic meetings all over the country and starting in 1922 also traveled abroad (including visits to Germany, France, and the United States). From 1923 to 1925 he edited the futurist movement's journal *LEF* (Left Front for the Arts). The poet's human drama, notwithstanding the provocative optimism of the propagandist, is revealed in his lyric poems of the 1920s, from *Year* (1922), which he dedicated to his beloved Lilya Brik, whom he had met in 1915, to *Of This* (1923).

The attempt to transform Russian futurism into the new art of the victorious proletariat clashed tragically with the ideological and cultural reservations of the Soviet establishment, which was not much inclined to artistic experimentation but instead oriented toward artistic forms with a traditionally realist bent (Lenin's negative assessment of futurism is well known). Mayakovski and *LEF* were attacked with increasing frequency by Soviet functionaries and the Russian Association of Proletarian Writers, and they influenced the difficult and contradictory artistic path of the late Mayakovski. The comedies *The Bedbug* (1928) and *The Bathhouse* (1929) were satirical descriptions of the survival of bourgeois values and weight of bureaucratization in the transformation of Soviet society. The text that Mayakovski devoted to Sergei Yesenin's suicide was still somewhat contradictory, but his lyric poem *At the Top of My Voice* exhibited his disappointment with the bureaucratic and centralizing involution of power, and the pathos of his opposition.

Isolated and subjected to a boycott by the country's literary and cultural organizations (the reception of his Twenty Years' Work exhibit was cool), Mayakovski shot himself in the head with a pistol in Moscow after having been denied an emigration visa. Following his death the artist's work fell into disrepute until, thanks to Brik and her husband Osip's plea directly to Stalin, the dictator declared that Mayakovski "has been and will remain the best and most talented poet of our Soviet epoch." This official endorsement of the poet's work led to the publication of new editions of Mayakovski's works and critical studies. Many of his works, especially his comedies, were ignored until after Stalin's death, despite the official recognition.

See also Avant-garde; Literature in Soviet Russia; Proletkult.

FURTHER READING

Chardzhiev, N. I., and V. V. Trenin. *Poeticheskaya kultura Majakovskogo*. Moscow: Iskusstvo, 1970.

Kacis, L. F. *Vladimiri Majakovskij*. Moscow: RGGU, 2004.

Ripellino, A. M. *Majakovskij e il teatro russo d'avanguardia*. Turin: Einaudi, 2002.

Vajskopf, M. *Vo vesgolos. Religija Majakovskogo*. Moscow: Salamandra, 1997.

STEFANO GARZONIO

McCarthyism

McCarthyism is a shorthand word that denominates the wave of anti-Communist political repression that swept through the United States during the early Cold War in the late 1940s and 1950s. Senator Joseph McCarthy, an opportunistic politician who gave that repression his name, latched on to anticommunism rather late when he burst into the headlines by telling a group of Republican women in Wheeling, West Virginia, in February 1950 that he had a list of Communist traitors in the U.S. Department of State. McCarthy's charges were not unique; for years Republican politicians had attacked the Democratic administration of Harry S. Truman as "soft" on communism, and McCarthy himself was encouraged by the party's leaders to continue his allegations, whether accurate or not. McCarthy differed from his colleagues mainly in the recklessness of his charges and his skill in publicizing them. In fact, his career might have floundered had the Korean War not broken out in the summer of 1950 and given credibility to his charges.

But the "ism" to which McCarthy lent his name had been under way for several years before he began making his notorious allegations, and it would continue even after his political demise in 1954. McCarthyism was a movement that contained many strands and performed many functions, all, however, with the goal of eliminating communism along with the individuals, groups, and ideas associated with it from any position of influence within American life. The version associated with McCarthy was a partisan one. Especially after Truman's upset victory in the 1948 presidential election, Republicans began to press charges that the Democratic administrations of Franklin D. Roosevelt and Truman harbored Communists. This was an allegation that conservatives in the Republican Party and elsewhere had been making ever since they opposed the New Deal's support for unions in the late 1930s. After World War II ended and the Cold War began, such charges focused more on foreign policy issues—the main one being the allegation that McCarthy popularized: that Communist sympathizers in the State Department had somehow "lost" China to Mao Zedong. Though these charges were widely circulated, they were essentially without foundation. There was nothing that the U.S. government could have done to prevent the Communist takeover in China.

Nonetheless, the Communists-in-government issue had become central to the anti-Communist crusade. It had considerable plausibility, especially since there had been Communists in the U.S. government during the late 1930s and 1940s, and though they had little impact on U.S. policy—as the Soviet and U.S. documents released since the end of the Cold War have definitively shown—some had been spying for the Soviet Union. Most of that espionage, including the transmission of information about the atomic bomb, took place during World War II when the United States and Soviet Union were allies, although it largely came to an end when several agents defected in the fall of 1945 and the KGB closed down its operations. Thus, by the time McCarthy announced that Washington, DC, was full of Communists, not only had the Kremlin lost its U.S. agents, but the Truman administration's own anti-Communist measures had also driven most Communists—and other left-wingers as well—from the federal payroll. By then, however, the Communists-in-government issue had taken on a life of its own.

Probably nothing, not even McCarthy's allegations, did as much to dramatize that issue as the case of Alger Hiss. Emanating from a set of hearings before the House Un-American Activities Committee (HUAC) in summer 1948, the case began with the allegation that Hiss, a former State Department official, had been a secret Communist when he worked for the New Deal in the 1930s. Although President Truman brushed off the committee's charges as a "red herring," the testimony of the ex-Communist witness Whittaker Chambers and the doggedness of HUAC member Richard Nixon ensured that the matter would not disappear. Ultimately, Chambers's production of documents showing that Hiss and a few other federal employees had spied for the Soviet Union forced the government to prosecute the former New Dealer, and gave credibility to the Republican Party's contention that the Democratic administration had been soft on communism.

Such was not the case. Not only had Truman taken a hard line against the Soviet Union after World War II but in 1947 his administration had implemented a stringently anti-Communist loyalty-security program for federal employees as well. It also put the top leaders of the Communist Party of the United States of America (CPUSA) on trial for teaching and advocating the overthrow of the country by force and violence. Prosecuting people for what they said rather than what they did ordinarily violated the First Amendment's prohibition against interfering with free speech and association. But by 1949, when the trial took place, Communists had become so vilified that even liberals tended to disregard civil liberties where the issue of communism was involved. When the U.S. Supreme Court finally ruled on the case in 1951, it recognized that freedom of speech was at stake, but claimed that the threat of communism was so dire that the government was justified in trying to suppress it.

That decision put the seal of legitimacy on—and thus intensified—the long-term campaign by FBI director J. Edgar Hoover to undermine the CPUSA. If any single individual can be identified with the anti-Communist furor of the early Cold War, it is Hoover, not McCarthy. Because of his bureaucratic skill and ideological fervor,

Hoover not only shaped and then operated the repressive machinery of the McCarthy era but also infused those operations with his own deeply conservative worldview. Bringing the Communist Party to trial, which Hoover and his aides had been trying to do for years, was just one piece of the FBI's multifaceted campaign to "educate" the public about the threat of communism to the American way of life. The FBI director also used anti-communism to expand his agency's power. Not only did the bureau perform its normal tasks of gathering evidence for the U.S. Department of Justice prosecutions, but it also took over all the investigations associated with the government's loyalty-security program and maintained surveillance over Communists and others on the Left, often by means of unauthorized methods like illegal break-ins and wiretaps. By 1960, the FBI had amassed files on more than four hundred thousand groups and individuals, and was secretly leaking information from them to selected journalists, politicians, and employers.

Central to all these activities were the criteria that were established for determining whether someone was a Communist. This was not an easy task, for the CPUSA was a secret organization. Accordingly, Hoover and his allies sought to identify people by their activities. If someone associated with Communists, supported the same causes, and belonged to organizations under the party's control, that person was probably a party member—but not always. Nonetheless, that criterion, known as "guilt by association," dominated the federal government's loyalty program; the attorney general was required to create a list of all the so-called Communist front groups, membership in which was grounds for dismissal. Within a short time, these criteria spread throughout the entire country and were utilized by local governments, patriotic organizations, private employers, and a wide variety of other public and private institutions to screen out alleged Communists. Moreover, since Hoover and his allies believed that liberals were almost as dangerous as Communists, almost anybody on the Left could come under suspicion.

Because the individuals who were identified as Communists were subjected to a variety of legal and extralegal sanctions, exposure was central to the political repression of the McCarthy era. While the FBI did this through criminal prosecutions and unauthorized leaks from its files, anti-Communist investigating committees at both the state and national level exposed suspected Communists more publicly. HUAC was the oldest and most well known of these bodies. But several other congressional committees, including Senator McCarthy's own Permanent Investigations Committee of the Senate Governmental Operations Committee, also sought to expose suspected Communists, as did investigating committees in states like Ohio, California, and Washington.

Whether they were investigating the so-called loss of China, Communist influence in the film industry, a left-wing labor union, or just calling up people in a particular city or state, these committees all operated in accordance with the same procedures. First, they would take testimony from friendly witnesses, usually FBI informers or ex-Communists who described their experiences in the CPUSA and identified their former comrades, and then call up the people who had been named to ask them, "Are you now or have you ever been a member of the Communist Party?" The witnesses, most of whom probably were Communists or former Communists, were in a bind. If they admitted their party membership, the committees would invariably ask them about other people. While many were willing to discuss their own political activities, they did not want to talk about those of others. Unfortunately for such witnesses, they risked a citation for contempt of Congress and a prison sentence if they refused to answer the committee's questions. The federal judiciary had ruled that a committee's questions about CPUSA membership did not violate the Constitution. The only way that witnesses could avoid cooperating with an investigating committee was to invoke the Fifth Amendment and refuse to testify against themselves. Furthermore, because of what came to be known as the "waiver" doctrine, witnesses could not answer questions about themselves and then refuse to name other people.

It took a few years for these legal issues to be clarified. Some earlier witnesses, like the ten screenwriters and directors who relied on the First Amendment when they defied HUAC in 1947, ended up in prison. But most of the later witnesses avoided the fate of the so-called Hollywood Ten. They took the Fifth Amendment and remained immune from legal penalties, but usually lost their jobs. After all, defying the committees looked bad, especially since the committees exploited this dilemma and asked embarrassing questions that they knew their witnesses could not answer. The publicity that ensued was particularly damaging and few indeed were the employers who risked the opprobrium of retaining a so-called Fifth Amendment Communist on their payrolls.

The Hollywood Ten were among the earliest and most well known of such victims. When they were indicted for contempt, they were fired by the film studios, which announced that they would never knowingly hire Communists. Within a few years, a secret but effective blacklist was in place throughout the entertainment industry, screening out politically controversial artists as well as people who defied congressional committees. Similar blacklists operated in other sectors of society, from public schools to steel mills to symphony orchestras. Nearly a hundred college professors were dismissed, as were nearly two thousand maritime workers screened from their jobs under a special Korean War Port Security Program. The best estimate is that somewhere between twelve thousand and fifteen thousand Americans lost their jobs because of McCarthyism. These numbers are only guesses, though, for most of these dismissals were secret, frequently the result of a quiet visit from the FBI.

There were other sanctions as well. The Internal Security Act of 1950, passed over Truman's veto at the height of the hysteria over the Korean War, not only required the CPUSA along with its front groups and members to register with the government, but also contained provisions for rounding up and incarcerating subversives during an emergency. The State Department denied passports to suspected Communists and refused visas to foreign ones. The Immigration and Naturalization Service sought to deport politically undesirable aliens. The labor movement was especially hard hit. Union leaders had to sign non-Communist affidavits, and left-wing unions were expelled from the main labor federations. States, cities, and even private companies imposed loyalty oaths on their employees. While some of these programs were trivial, like the state of Indiana's requirement that all professional wrestlers sign an anti-Communist loyalty oath, taken together they exacted a considerable personal, social, and political price.

McCarthyism ended in the mid-1950s. McCarthy's censure by his senatorial colleagues at the end of 1954 was symbolic. Liberal opinion makers who had been largely silent during the height of the furor began to speak out. The Supreme Court restored some of the rights it had refused to protect only a few years before. HUAC and the other committees continued to hound witnesses, but the story was no longer front-page news. Though it is commonly assumed that some inherent virtue in the U.S. system brought about the end of the anti-Communist witch hunt, it is just as plausible to assume that it ended because it achieved its objective. The witch hunters had run out of witches. They had helped to destroy U.S. communism, and in the process silenced many dissenting voices and narrowed U.S. political culture.

See also Anticommunism; Atomic Bomb; Cold War; Containment; Spies.

FURTHER READING

Bontecou, E. *The Federal Loyalty-Security Program*. Ithaca, NY: Cornell University Press, 1953.

Ceplair, L., and S. Englund. *The Inquisition in Hollywood: Politics in the Film Community, 1930–1960*. Garden City, NY: Doubleday, 1979.

Levenstein, H. A. *Communism, Anticommunism, and the CIO*. Westport, CT: Greenwood, 1981.

Oshinsky, D. *A Conspiracy So Immense: The World of Joe McCarthy*. New York: Free Press, 1983.

Powers, R. G. *Secrecy and Power: The Life of J. Edgar Hoover*. New York: Free Press, 1987.

Schrecker, E. *Many Are the Crimes: McCarthyism in America*. New York: Little, Brown, 1998.

Weinstein, A., and A. Vassiliev. *The Haunted Wood: Soviet Espionage in America—The Stalin Era*. New York: Random House, 1999.

ELLEN SCHRECKER

Messianism

The historical narrative that Communists upheld presented a secularized variation of a messianic plot. This narrative unfolded a moral story with a mythical beginning and a preordained end. Two philosophies of history that appear to be at loggerheads, on closer scrutiny, resemble one another insofar as they were articulated along an eschatological metaframework. The Marxist and Christian historical narratives shared interchangeable plot structures, similar agents driving these plots forward, and sometimes even the metaphors and figures used to describe them. Marx's claims to have provided scientific principles of historical analysis and broken away from the Church's mystical interpretation of history were only part of the story: underneath such goals we can find a concealed continuity of concerns with historical time and salvation.

The Marxist concept of universal history was inspired by the Judeo-Christian bracketing of historical time between the fall of Adam and the apocalypse. The original expropriation stood at the beginning of time, and represented a rupture in the timeless primitive communism that inaugurated history and set humanity on a course of self-alienation. The universal revolution, an abrupt and absolute event, was to return humanity to itself in a fiery cataclysm. Communist parties understood the series of stages in the interval between the original expropriation and the cataclysm as a great progress of history that would climax with the abolition of class society. Marxist messianic thinking described history as human moral progression from the darkness of class society to the light of communism, thereby imbuing time with a historical teleology that gave meaning to events.

Because history is seen as a redemptive process, the beginning and end of history were structured as pure, conflictless states. Having postulated an ideal past, the party projected it into the future as the telos of history. The chronological markers of the beginning and end were valorized. What has to reign in between was seen as evil. The beginning and end have been called "paradise," the time when the lion lies down with the lamb, and "communism," characterized by the fraternity of human producers. The interim was the "kingdom of sin" or "period of the exploitation of man by man." Since the agency that brings about change between the beginning and end had to be accounted for, eschatological thinking posited a messiah—"Christ" or the "proletariat"—who was able, due to some remarkable feature in its constitution, to overcome the impurities of the middle period and effect a transition from impure to pure, from evil to good.

In Marxism, catastrophic events like the original expropriation or advent of capitalism were meaningful. They drove history forward. Not by chance were human beings removed from the blissful stage of primitive communism, characterized by humans' integrated and felicitous being, and thrust into the tormented road of alienation, class struggle, and exploitation. In primitive communism, humans were aware of neither their perfection nor the world as shaped in their image. The very possibility of such awareness assumed a separation of the knower and the known, a cleavage within human beings that does not exist in the primitive producer. The original harmony of primitive humanity had to be lost at the beginning of history in order to be regained, now consciously at the end.

Messianic thinking postulates the principle of contradiction that propels the historical plot toward consummation. Christians believed that the combat between the righteous and sinful would reach its apogee in the apocalypse. Hegel translated the picturesque representation of the struggles within the biblical eschatological narrative into a rational philosophical system. In the Marxist vocabulary, the personalized contradictions of the Christian redemptive plot were called the "dialectic of the class struggle." For Marx, social contradiction was an immanent historical force that was to transform society. Positing a succession of modes of production with their own inherent contradictions, Marx did not let them stand as an endless procession. Rather, he interpreted them as stages leading to a final event that was to resolve the contradictions immanent in history.

In Marxism and Christianity alike, the story of human civilization was the story of the struggle between good and evil, and was bound to have a happy ending. Social and economic categories are not the theoretical bedrock of Marx's thinking; rather, they receive their intelligibility from the mythoreligious story they relate. This story concerned the human loss of self and regainment of self. Marx promised his disciples that the realm of freedom would be ushered in by a fundamental revolution in the mode of production that would restore the original union of humankind in a new historical form. *The Communist Manifesto*, to give the most obvious example, is the scenario for the drama of millenarian redemption. Even as it discards ancient Christian symbolism to speak in terms proper to the modern, scientific age, this canonical text advances the familiar moral view that the historical process is bound to produce the Armageddon. In *The Communist Manifesto*, the evils of industrialism were given a millenarian interpretation, as the harbingers of a final, universal judgment. The fact that they were the very worst of the evils that humanity had seen was regarded by him as proof that as in Revelation, the ultimate reversal was being prepared.

Communists see in the revolution the mythical final event destined to reverse the course of history in the Marxist narrative. It was designed to express the telos within history, its drive toward the resolution of class conflicts. The Marxist notion of revolution was reminiscent of the Christian millenarianism insofar as it suggested that history was to result in an abrupt and total transformation of the conditions of humankind into a perfect and felicitous state. The revolution, just like the apocalypse, was conceived of as inevitable, because it was compelled by iron laws of historical development, abrupt and fairly imminent. It was to be brought about through the irreconcilable clash between economic classes, in which one side (fated to prevail) embodies the historical right, and its foe, fated to be annihilated, embodies historical wrong. True to the tradition of messianic

thinking, Marx predicted that the revolution would be violent, because it was bound to be achieved by a merciless destruction of the forces of historical evil; absolute, in that instead of gradual amelioration, there was to be a dramatic transformation of the very foundation of society; and finally, universal, because it was destined to spread to the entire world.

Whereas in one sense the Communist revolution was to be a mundane historical event, the last one in a series of mundane events, in another sense it was not to be an event in history at all but an event of a metaphysical character. Communist messianic thinkers described revolution as a cataclysm that was to remove humanity from its historical conditions, and render human beings free and integrated at last. The revolution was thus not one more event with its own peculiarities (all events are peculiar in one sense or another) but rather the consummation of the entire series of events. What was to be unique about the revolution was not just that no further event was to follow it but instead that no other event need follow it, because in the revolution the whole purpose of history was to be fulfilled. Nothing more could have happened in history, because the eternal meaning that gave reality to history was to have exhausted itself.

The Communists carefully distinguished "revolutions" as events within history from "revolution" as an ultimate event that was to terminate history: "In all revolutions up to now the mode of activity always remained unscathed and it was only a question of a different distribution of this activity," Marx wrote, "whilst the Communist Revolution is directed against the preceding mode of activity, does away with labor, and abolishes the rule of classes with the classes themselves." Ultimate and irrevocable, revolution was to completely transform humanity, create a classless society, and thereby ensure that the old order could not return. In that sense, much as the apocalypse, it was to be both the end and beginning.

The vehicle of the revolution was the New Man—a creature perfect ethically and aesthetically. Marx conceived of the New Man as a subject-to-be that seeks realization. More specifically, he posited a Communist messiah as the agent mediation between the historical now and the metahistorical beyond. The New Man was the first truly free creature of history, obedient to the dictates of their own reason, not the unthinking satisfaction of desires. Marx articulated the relation between the historical man and an ideal New Man through his use of the terms "proletarians" and "Communists." As long as capitalism existed, the two sides of the same messianic coin remained distinct: while the proletariat stood for self-alienated humanity, Communists were the bearers of the proletariat's genuine spirit, the agent striving to realize the proletariat's salvational potential. The revolution could not occur without the active intervention of the Communist Party, the agent that brought about mass conversion to Marxism. Both human and divine, a real institution and an incarnated idea, the party had to be infallible. Any challenge to the validity of the laws of history it embodied was scientifically obstructive and ethically repugnant.

The Communist Party was a messianic order, not a pragmatic political organization formed to represent a concrete constituency. Whereas for liberals a party mediates between citizen and state, for Communists the party mediates between the proletarian soul, buried under false appearances (a human being as "subject to the czar," a human being as a "citizen," and so on), and its emancipation. The party could not compromise with society on the level of shared interests, nor even govern according to its own private interests because it allegedly dedicated its own private interests to the common interest of universal social justice. On its way to final victory, the party encountered many obstacles. Evil was a leading actor in the Communist historical drama. Filled with crises, history, for Communist messianic thinkers, was propelled by revolutions rather than evolutions, because counter-revolutionary machinations ensured that there could be no seamless historical development. A historical impediment, the very force that slowed emancipation down, evil made revolutionary violence morally meaningful and justified.

See also Collapse of Capitalism; Marxism-Leninism; New Man; Revolution, Myths of the; Utopia.

FURTHER READING

Abrams, M. H. "Apocalypse: Theme and Variations." In *The Apocalypse in English Renaissance Thought and Literature*, ed. C. A. Patrides and Joseph Wittreich. Ithaca, NY: Cornell University Press, 1984.

Halfin, I. *From Darkness to Light: Class, Consciousness, and Salvation in Revolutionary Russia*. Pittsburgh, PA: Pittsburgh University Press, 2000.

Klinghoffer, A. J. *Red Apocalypse: The Religious Evolution of Soviet Communism*. New York: University Press of America, 1996.

Löwith, K. *Meaning in History: The Theological Implications of the Philosophy of History*. Chicago: University of Chicago Press, 1949.

Tuveson, E. L. "The Millenarian Structure of *The Communist Manifesto*." In *The Apocalypse in English Renaissance Thought and Literature*, ed. C. A. Patrides and Joseph Wittreich. Ithaca, NY: Cornell University Press, 1984.

Wessell, L. P. *Prometheus Bound: The Mythic Structure of Karl Marx's Scientific Thinking*. Baton Rouge: Louisiana State University Press, 1984.

Zeldin, M. "The Religious Nature of Russian Marxism." *Journal for the Scientific Study of Religion* 8 (1969): 100–111.

IGAL HALFIN

Michnik, Adam

Born in Warsaw, the son of Communists, Adam Michnik (1946–) clashed with power early: he was arrested in 1965, and expelled from his university the following year, because he had founded the irreverent Hunters of Contradictions Club. He was among the protagonists of the Polish "1968," and was sentenced to two and half years in prison as a consequence. Having regained his freedom, he worked in the Rosa Luxemburg lightbulb factory in Warsaw and later as secretary for author Anton Slonimski. In 1973 he was authorized to continue studying history in Poznan, and received his degree in 1975. Michnik became convinced during these years that it was necessary to organize dissent in Poland, and attempt to move the more advanced sectors of the Catholic Church to provide political and organizational support for the Polish people's demands for freedom and democracy. As he argued in his famous book, *The Church and the Left*, "When a socialist realizes that his enemy is not religious faith, but fanaticism, lies and tyranny, he moves closer to a Church that ties its freedom to all human freedoms."

When his fraternal friend and "teacher" Jacek Kurón founded the Workers' Defense Committee in 1976, together with thirteen other intellectuals and artists, Michnik busied himself from Paris to garner the greatest amount of international support for this initiative (he had been invited by Jean-Paul Sartre). In early May 1977, before returning home, Michnik officially joined the committee and became, going in and out of prison, one of its principal moving spirits. Thanks also to the journal *Robotnik* (The Worker), he prepared the mentality and structures that led to the workers' victory in the summer of 1980. He was immediately nominated as Solidarity's counselor and, especially at first, was one of the politicians closest to Lech Walesa. Arrested on the night of December 13, 1981, Michnik was imprisoned and charged with attempting to subvert the system. Although he was released on the basis of the amnesty of July 1984, he was arrested again in February 1985 and condemned to three and a half years of prison. The fact that authorities targeted him so frequently gave him both moral and political authority. It also gave him, as he recalled ironically, a lot of time to study as well as write books and articles, translated into many languages, including *From the Histories of Honor in Poland* (1985). In this book, he found forgotten examples of courage, resistance, and sometimes martyrdom by rereading Polish history.

In the 1980s Michnik, like some other "reformist" representatives of the Unified Polish Workers' Party (such as the journalist and politician Mieczyslaw Rakowski), examined the issue of Spain's return to democracy after Francisco Franco's death as a model of bloodless transition, as an exit from a weak totalitarian regime, willed and upheld by the Soviets, without traumatic "reckonings." The "round table" in early 1989 between the government and opposition, which laid the foundations for contemporary Poland, was his greatest political success, but also the beginning of a contradictory period, replete with satisfactions (especially the founding and editorship, until 2005, of the main independent Polish daily, *Gazeta Wyborcza*) and disappointments (the dissolution of Solidarity as a political force and the clash with Walesa, the polemics due to his indulgence toward ex-Communists, and the campaign to besmirch his unquestionable moral rigor).

Michnik was one of the major representatives of the secular Left among Polish dissidents.

See also Kurón, Jacek; Martial Law in Poland; Revolutions in East-Central Europe; Solidarity; Walesa, Lech.

FURTHER READING

Michnik, A. *Letters from Prison and Other Essays*. Berkeley: University of California Press, 1985.
———. *Etica della resistenza. Scritti dalla prigione e dalla libertà*. Milan: Sugar Co., 1986.
———. *La deuxième revolution*. Paris: La Découverte, 1990.
———. *The Church and the Left*. Chicago: University of Chicago Press, 1993.
———. *Letters from Freedom: Post-Cold War Realities and Perspectives*. Berkeley: University of California Press, 1998.
———. *Wyznania nawróconego dysydenta. Szkice 1991–2001*. Warsaw: Zeszyty Literackie, 2003.

FRANCESCO M. CATALUCCIO

Militancy

From its first appearance, Communist militancy fomented polemics. On the one hand, it has been singled out as a negative example symbolizing indoctrination, dogmatism, regimentation, blindness, ignorance, lies, hypocrisy, cynicism, and fanaticism. On the other, it has been praised as an example to imitate and reflect on because of the positive qualities it seemed to represent: self-denial, courage, altruism, sincerity, efficiency, strength of faith, and power of conviction. If Communist militancy provoked this interest it is because, unlike most other groupings, the Communist parties of Western Europe did not limit themselves to enlisting members; they made serious attempts to persuade a number of those who had expressed an interest to "become Communist." The militants differed from the simple members due to their participation in the life of the organization, where they learned how to become Communists; commitment endowed their existence with meaning, to the point of assuming a religious dimension.

The organizational needs as they related to militancy were prescribed by Lenin in his *What Is to Be Done?* in which he broke with the traditions of social democracy and laid the foundations of the Bolshevik organization. According to Lenin the party was defined first of all by its plan, which presupposed a mastery of revolutionary theory and the capacity to build a solid organization governed by democratic centralism, endowed with a clandestine apparatus, composed of selected, active, and convinced militants. Since the Bolsheviks' victory in 1917 seemed to prove the relevance of these precepts, the Russian revolutionaries extended them to all sections of the Communist International by means of the twenty-one conditions for the admission of national parties, which were established at the Second Congress in 1920. These conditions were applied resolutely, especially during Bolshevization, which revolutionized the International's forms of political organization. The Stalinization that soon followed was the sign that a codified Leninism, raised to orthodoxy, was victorious, and it led to the elimination of any internal opposition and the unquestionable supremacy of the USSR's interests, thus also signaling a change in orientation compared to Leninist theory because it established worker preeminence in Communist organizations, which were called on to prove their mass character.

At Moscow's behest, to be a militant in a Communist organization from the late 1920s to the early 1960s required one to respect precise obligations, which needed to become deeply internalized thanks to constant effort, which the leadership in turn encouraged. The Communist parties imposed the assimilation of the ideology of the day (or at least its basics), an energetic defense of the organization, a total devotion to the USSR and after 1945 the "socialist camp," an absolute respect for the supreme authority (embodied in the party's, Comintern's, and Cominform's leadership), obedience to directives, respect for an almost military discipline, the hegemony of the working class, the sacralization of national and international Communist leaders, and faith in a radiant future, at the time already prefigured by the USSR. Communist party leaderships constantly kept their memberships under pressure, requiring great availability and intense activity, which often spilled over into unrestrained activism. The most eager militants worked not only in the party but also in the labor union and various associations. In this manner the parties formed a countersociety in their respective countries—sometimes closed, when small parties were involved, or more open to the rest of society in the case of powerful organizations, like the French party from the 1930s until the aftermath of World War II, or the Italian party after the end of fascism. These large parties created a language with special words and expressions, defined a sense of time organized by their internal life, invented specific rites and liturgies, celebrated their chiefs and heroes, constructed a common memory, created collective identities and cultures, established a party solidarity, and recommended a certain way of presenting oneself, if not a lifestyle and form of asceticism.

The Communist parties simultaneously behaved like enterprises that encouraged militancy and rewarded the most meritorious on the basis of an economy of retributions, even if it wasn't official. A real system was introduced, with diverse forms of distinction, preparatory schools, functionary positions, and electoral mandates. This system provided honors, prestige, social recognition, and a sense of collective and personal worth. It also offered the opportunity to become even more deeply involved in the collectivity, or part of a leadership group, sharing privileges, especially access to information and secrets, travels around the world, and the opportunity to frequent global Communist high society. The party thus formed a family to which certain members sacrificed themselves almost completely, including their private lives and sometimes even life itself. Communist parties were basically totalitarian organizations that asked their followers for the gift of themselves. This is the reason why a break, whether as the result of a lengthy process of disengagement by the militants themselves, or in the form of an exclusion or a purge, was often experienced dramatically.

The meaning and practices associated with militancy varied significantly. The political circumstances were one factor in this variation. The clandestine life experienced by Italian Communists under the Fascist regime, the French between 1939 and 1944, or the Portuguese, the Spaniards, and the Greeks for many years had important consequences for militants who were motivated by their ideals, or even their faith, more than their search for symbolic or material gratification. These moments can be clearly distinguished from the periods of legal activity, when militancy was guided by the most disparate objectives in which more noble aspirations could mix with more prosaic ones. Similarly, those periods in which the parties emphasized the quality of militants over their quantity, defining their behavior precisely—for example, in the late 1920s or during the Cold War—alternated with moments of greater relaxation of standards, during which the parties' doors were opened wide and the pressure on members lessened.

This variety also appears to be sociological. Intellectuals had high ideological and doctrinal expectations of their parties, and their militancy was subjected to recurring crises. Militants from a popular background were more difficult to choose because for them an entry into politics carried a heavy price. On the other hand, they displayed great loyalty. They were grateful to the party for having valued them, having contributed to their sense of dignity, and having been able to take advantage of a form of schooling, and sometimes having climbed the apparatus's hierarchy with a certain taste for social revanchism, but also with the sense of having remained faithful to one's class of origin. Militants' engagement also varied according to geographic parameters. To be part of the Communist minority in a hostile environment did not have much in common with militants who engaged in their activities in areas where communism was hegemonic—for example, in Emilia Romagna or

Paris's Red suburbs. The level of responsibility became an important form of demarcation between a leader and a simple member or a militant who belonged to the base. The unstable Communist militant sometimes gave up rapidly. But those who persevered, at the end of a road that was almost like an initiation, were able, according to the distinctions formulated by Max Weber, to "live from politics," something that required discipline, obedience, learning the current rules, and the ability to stand out. The obedience and conformity, finally, that sometimes crossed over to conformism, did not stop militants who had the social and cultural resources from mocking the norms, pretending to respect conventions while preserving their independence, more or less publicly ridiculing certain aspects of party policy or etiquette, and even exercising their critical judgment.

Communism, which had taken the form of a secular religion, then experienced a strong decline entailing the deterioration of party constraint and self-constraint mechanisms. The organization's power was gradually sapped by the USSR's loss of prestige, and experienced with its fall, the abandoning of democratic centralism, the renunciation of blind discipline, the difficult recognition of internal pluralism, and the slow acceptance of difference. The conflicts multiplied, and the number of militants evaporated like snow in the sun. If some remained faithful to the old models of activity, the majority experienced their engagement more individually, requiring more, reflecting more, being more circumspect—in other words, they lived it more contractually, even if the demonstrations, congresses, and festivals also succeeded in reviving collective emotions and enthusiasm.

See also Bolshevization; Communist Autobiography; Cult of Personality; Democratic Centralism; Messianism; Self-Criticism.

FURTHER READING

Cross, R., and Finn, A. "Biography Meets History: Communist Party Lives in International Perspective." *Science and Society* I (2006): 11–118.

Dreyfus, M., C. Pennetier, and N. Viet-Depaule, eds. *La part des militants: biographie et mouvement ouvrier, autour du Maitron, Dictionnaire biographiquedu mouvement ouvrier français.* Paris: Les Éditions de l'Atelier, 1996.

Gotovitch, J., and A. Morelli, eds. *Militantisme et militants.* Brussels: EVO, 2000.

Ignazi, P. *Dal PCI al PDS.* Bologna: Il Mulino, 1992.

Lazar, M. "Le parti et le don de soi." *Vingtième siècle. Revue d'histoire* 60 (October–December 1999): 35–42.

Pennetier, C., and Pudal, B., eds. *Aubtobiographies, autocritiques, aveux dans le monde communiste.* Paris: Belin, 2002.

MARC LAZAR

Militarization

"Militarization"—spreading military methods (discipline, command, hierarchy, and mass organization) and ethos (obedience, self-denial, strength of will, and heroism) to civil society—had a profound influence on the formation of Soviet policy, doctrine, and the political system during the first fifteen years of the USSR's history. It left a lasting impression on the country's organization and ideals as well as the international movement that had developed from the October Revolution. During the civil war the militarization of the economy, society, and political and administrative organizations were molded into a socioeconomic system that was to be designated "war communism."

The drive to militarization was provided by the transformation of the Red Army into a "regular" army (February–March 1918), combined with the creation of a special organizational status for members of the Bolshevik Party who had been drafted, which was finalized the following year by the Eighth Congress of the Russian Communist Party (Bolshevik). This congress's decisions extended military principles to the party itself, including the selection of organizational leaders from above (replacing an electoral procedure), "a single person's leadership" (the secretary, or a special plenipotentiary sent from the center) within each organization, and finally "iron discipline" within Communist ranks. Between the end of 1918 and early 1920 the transportation system (rail and water) was militarized, and a rigid administrative hierarchy along with severe sanctions in case of violations of the regulations, absenteeism, or other worker infractions were introduced. Joining a labor union became obligatory, and the unions' task was reduced simply to mobilization. A hierarchy of "political commissars" analogous to that in the army, and integrated with the administrative hierarchy, was integrated into the party's transport organization (Glavpolitput: Central Political Transport Administration), following the PUR (Political Directorate of the Revolutionary Military Council, basically a political administration) model of the Red

Army. The "political section" organizational module was also first introduced here, led by cadre nominated from the center. Labor union organizations in the transport sector were subjected to a military type of authority, the supreme Cektran (Central Committee of the Transport Workers Union), which included administrators, army officers, and political and labor union leaders.

In March 1920, the Ninth Party Congress decided to extend the single person's leadership and "personal responsibility" policies to the industry's leading institutions at all levels. In January 1920, Soviet citizens were subjected to obligatory "labor mobilization." Some large Red Army military units were simultaneously being employed for civilian purposes on large projects of significant social utility (for example, the provision of wood or the restoration of coal mining). The leading authorities began to theorize that after a victory in the civil war, the country's economic reconstruction could occur more rapidly and efficiently on the basis of a complete militarization of labor, and by extending the decisional and executive methods typical of the fighting army to the economy and society as a whole.

The implementation of this program clashed with the open and violent discontent of large segments of the population (the peasants in Tambov Province during winter 1920–21, workers in Petrograd, and sailors on the Kronstadt naval base in January–March of 1921) as well as the resolute dissent of Bolshevik labor union leaders. At the Tenth Party Congress (March 1921), war communism started to be replaced by the New Economic Policy, and the militarization of party and labor unions was revoked and replaced by less rigid methods of political and economic leadership. In the transport sector the political sections were disbanded. In factories the principle of the single person's leadership by the manager was abandoned, and a separation of labor union, party, and managerial functions was established. The party organ hierarchy (at least in theory) once again reflected democratic centralism's statutory norms.

Between 1927 and 1930, the term militarization appears in Soviet political language in two limited contexts: the militarization of the population, based on a program to protect and morally prepare civilians in case of war, which was in turn based on the new Osoaviachim (Society for the Promotion of the Defense of the Aeronautical and Chemical Industries) organization; and the militarization of industrial planning, which was tied to the possibility of orienting part of the industrialization effort toward the modernization and strengthening of the army. These ideas, however, did not contemplate an increase in the role of military personnel in the political and economic leadership of the society and state, as they had during war communism.

The inauguration of the collectivization of the countryside and accelerated industrialization during 1929 once again landed the country in a situation of acute social and economic crisis. As had been the case during the civil war, authorities implemented a program of militarization of the party structures (even if they did not explicitly define it as such). In early 1933, political sections in the machine and tractor stations (MTS) were added to the normal party committees at the district level, effectively supplanting them. These political sections responded directly to special sections of the Central Committee, which also selected their leadership cadre, and they also exercised authority on the party cells and leadership organs of the new collective farms (kolkhoz and sovkhoz). Soon these sorts of extraordinary bodies also reappeared in the rail and water transport sector. A new figure, the "party organizer," centrally selected, started to appear in all the country's main factories, replacing the party cell secretaries. This new wave of organizational measures—whose goal was the militarization of the party—occurred under the banner of "verification of execution." According to this view, the task of the party's territorial organs at every level was essentially to check that the directives given by the party's central organs and the state were implemented promptly and precisely by the appropriate organizations. In December 1934, the Central Committee abolished the political sections in the MTS and reinstated the political prerogatives of the party district committees in the countryside. The political sections were reintroduced at the end of 1941, several months after the German invasion. The political sections in the transport sector were preserved without interruption until 1943, when they were finally abolished along with those at the MTS. The party organizer institution was preserved until the war's end, after having been further extended on the eve of war. During the war, further militarization of the economy in support of the war effort was directed by the State Defense Committee (GKO), which was formed by members of the politburo, the principal ministries, and the army's general staff and presided over by Joseph Stalin. The State Defense Committee acted using a network of plenipotentiaries chosen among members of the Central Committee and regional party committees.

See also Cadres; Five-Year Plans; Red Army; Single-Party System; Transportation; War Communism.

FURTHER READING

Barber, B., and M. Harrison. *The Soviet Home Front, 1941–1945.* New York: Longman, 1991.

Benvenuti, F. *The Bolsheviks and the Red Army, 1918–1922.* Cambridge, UK: Cambridge University Press, 1988.

Benvenuti, F., and S. Pons. *Il sistema di potere dello stalinismo. Partito e stato in URSS, 1933–1953.* Milan: Angeli, 1988.

Procacci, G. *Il partito nell'Unione Sovietica, 1917–1945.* Rome: Laterza, 1974.

Von Hagen, M. *Soldiers in the Proletarian Dictatorship: The Red Army and the Soviet Socialist State, 1917–1930.* Ithaca, NY: Cornell University Press, 1990.

FRANCESCO BENVENUTI

Military-Industrial Complex

The 20th century was characterized by a sharp increase in military conflicts, a change in the types and methods of armed combat, and an increase in the role that economic factors played in war. Wars in the 19th century consumed an average of 8 to 14 percent of the combatants' national income, but in World War I this figure rose to almost 50 percent, and in World War II it exceeded 50 percent. From 1941 to 1945 military production in the United States reached 60.6 percent of the total national figure, while in the USSR the figure ranged from 65 to 68 percent.

There were three main features in the development of a military economy. The first involved preparation for war during the prewar period and the emergence during the war years of mass armies, along with the appearance of new branches of industry to produce new weapons of war (in World War I, tanks, airplanes, and poison gases; in World War II, rockets, atomic weapons, and radar). Another feature was the creation of an economy specifically designed to mobilize all resources needed by the military. The third feature was the development of a system of state regulation of the economy using supraeconomic methods. A warring country could now create a special link between its state apparatus and its producers of military goods—something that can be defined as a "military-industrial link." The four basic components of this system were the government officials, military commanders, managers of war industries, and scientists and builders of military technology, all involved in mobilizing the national economy for military needs.

Until World War II, war years had been marked by a total militarization of the economy, which would then give way to sharp cuts in military spending right after the war ended. After 1945, though, a different picture emerged. A number of leading countries, with the United States and the USSR at the forefront, exhibited a steady increase in military expenditures, along with a strengthening of ties between government officials, arms producers, and scientists working on war-related projects.

This increase was associated, of course, with the emergence of the Cold War, which brought about a lengthy military and ideological confrontation of two military-political blocs, which in turn brought about a race to acquire the latest arms emerging from the new scientific and technological revolution. It was precisely these conditions that led to the formation in the states participating in the Cold War (the United States, the USSR, a number of European North Atlantic Treaty Organization [NATO] states, and China) of military-industrial complexes (MICs).

The term "military-industrial complex" gained currency after its use by U.S. president Dwight Eisenhower in his farewell speech in 1961. Eisenhower defined the MIC as the "growth of an immense military establishment and a large armaments industry," which came into being during World War II and the ensuing decade and a half of the Cold War. The economic, political, and even spiritual significance of this mighty lobby was felt, in the words of the president, "in every city, in every state house, in every office of the Federal government."

In the 1960s and 1970s, a multitude of historical and political works appeared on the subject of the MIC, with reference to both the United States and the USSR, which developed its own version of a MIC during the Cold War. In the West, the MIC was generally understood as a "coincidence of military and economic interests and their pursuit of common goals, to the detriment of society as a whole." This, of course, stressed the negative aspect of the phenomenon.

Soviet official propaganda and the social sciences denied the existence of an MIC in the USSR, considering it an attribute of the reactionary and aggressive ruling circles in Western countries. The status of military construction in the USSR was kept officially secret, and source materials for investigation in this area remained sparse, not only for ideological reasons, but also due to the secretiveness of the institutes that controlled the archives where research could be undertaken.

Investigations into the Soviet "version" of the MIC began in Russia only in the 1990s, aided by the new "glasnost" and the opening of archives. The first publications were by journalists and political scientists, and many of them were sensationalist and grossly politicized. Scholarly investigations of this area in the mid-1990s, on the contrary, were mostly economics based and failed to treat the sociopolitical component of the MIC. Only at the beginning of the 21st century did comprehensive investigations of the Soviet MIC begin to appear.

The military industry of the Russian Empire in the early 20th century was largely destroyed during the revolutionary crisis in the country from 1917 to 1921. In the 1920s, a system of specialized ("cadre") military factories and plants began to be created. On the whole, though, the years of the "New Economic Policy" were characterized by a sharp reduction in military expenditures. The program of militarization of the economy, accompanied by a strengthening of the military bureaucracy's role in the political life of the country, went into effect at the beginning of the 1930s as part of the general policy of industrialization and the building of socialism in one (a single) country, which demanded the strengthening of defense capability. The defense industry as a united group of specialized military production units emerged during the second half of the 1930s. The communality of interests of the various groups of the MIC was only suggested but not specifically recognized.

The MIC of the USSR, as a steadily functioning system of ties between the economic and sociopolitical structures of Soviet society united by the need to assure the military security of the country, came definitively into being during the Cold War and was accompanied by a steady growth of military spending.

The MIC developed in roughly three stages:

1. The 1930s featured the creation of a special defense ministry (by 1939 this consisted of the people's commissariats of industry for aviation, shipbuilding, and arms and ammunition) and central management organs (Defense Committee of the Council of People's Commissars of the USSR and, attached to this, the Military-Industrial Commission), and the forced militarization of the Soviet economy (a special stage here was the prewar [and third] five-year plan).

2. The period of World War II (the Great Patriotic War) featured the total mobilization of the Soviet economy for its military. The war period saw a massive displacement of industry to the east: in all, more than thirteen hundred enterprises were evacuated, many of which had been under the management of the people's commissariats of the Ministry of Defense. Four-fifths of them were devoted to military production.

   The structure of industrial production underwent a basic change. By approximate count, military goods accounted for from 65 to 68 percent of all production during the war. The main producers were the people's commissariats of the military industry—the aviation, arms, ammunition, mortars, shipbuilding, and tank industries. At the same time, military orders were filled by still other basic branches of heavy industry, such as metallurgy, fuel and energy, and also the people's commissariats of light industry and the food industry. Clearly, the economic structure of the MIC during the war bore the stamp of a total militarization.

3. The Cold War era, from 1946 to 1991, was a key period in the history of the MIC in the USSR. The transition from war to peace was accompanied by a partial conversion of military to civilian production and a partial demobilization of the army. However, the onset of the Cold War now dictated the need for a new military-industrial mobilization. The chief focus of postwar militarization was the development of the latest weapons (nuclear, rocket, and radio-electronic).

The postwar economy underwent more than a few reorganizations (in 1946, 1948, 1953, 1957–63, and 1965), characterized at times by the fusion and at other times by the breakup of various industrial ministries.

The shift of capital and resources to peaceful goals began in spring 1945, and by June more than five hundred enterprises, among them defense-related businesses, had been switched to civilian production. To effect this change in profile, the people's commissariats (which in March 1946 on were renamed ministries) were reorganized; the tank industry was absorbed into a ministry of transportation engineering, ammunition into agricultural engineering, and mortar arms into machine and instrument engineering.

The postwar Stalinist period saw the creation, parallel to the traditional industries, of a supraministerial system of special organs attached to the Council of Ministers, which supervised new military programs of special importance—the atomic program (the Special Committee and First Primary Management), the rocket program (Committee No. 2 for jet propulsion technology), and the radar program (Committee No. 3). After Stalin's death, the management system was reorganized—the special organs were eliminated and transformed into ministries (thus, in June 1953, the Ministry of Mid-Level Engineering was created for the management of the atomic program).

At the end of the 1950s, during the period when Khrushchev decentralized the management of the national economy, the defense enterprises were divided among regional economic councils, and the overall coordination of their activity remained with the state committees overseeing the various types of defense technology. In 1965, after Khrushchev was deposed, the system of centralized management by the ministries was restored.

By the mid-1960s, the organizational structure of the Soviet MIC had been permanently established: the Ministry of Defense of the USSR (the main customer and also consumer of military production), a "set of nine" defense-industrial ministries in which military production was basically concentrated (the ministries of the aviation industry, defense industry, general engineering, radio industry, midlevel engineering, shipbuilding industry, chemical industry, electronics industry, and electrotechnical industry). It also established ten closely related ministries, producers of military and civilian goods. The political and economic leadership in this sphere was supervised by special sections of the Central Committee of the party (the Defense Industry Section and the Administrative Organs Section). Questions of security were handled by the Committee for State Security and the Ministry of Internal Affairs. Responsibility for the solution of economic, organizational, and scientific-technological questions lay with the Council of Ministers and its matching missions: the State Planning Committee, the Ministry of Finance, and the Academy of Sciences of the USSR.

The chief coordinating organ of the Soviet MIC during its heyday—from the 1960s to the 1980s—was the State Commission on Military-Industrial Questions of the Presidium of the Council of Ministers. It was headed by Dimitry Ustinov, Vasily Riabikov, Lev Smirnov, and Yury Masliukov, in that order. The State Military-Industrial Commission combined in itself the defense ministry functions of various state offices for various spheres: the Goskomstat (statistics), Gosplan (planning), Goskomcen (price policy), Goskomtrud (labor), the State Committee for Science and Technology, and the Gossnab (supply).

The most important heads of the Soviet MIC included party and political leaders (Stalin, Lavrenty Beria, Nikolay Bulganin, Khrushchev, Leonid Brezhnev, A. Epishev, and others), military commanders (M. Tukhachevskii, Georgy Zhukov, N. Kuznetsov, M. Nedelin, Rodion Malinovsky, and A. Akhromeev), chiefs of the defense industry (L. Ustinov, B. Vannikov, V. Malyshev, E. Slavsky, V. Riabikov, M. Saburov, L. Smirnov, and G. Pervukhin), leaders in science and technology (II. Kurchatov, Yu. Khariton, Andrey Sakharov, M. Keldysh, A. Aleksandrov, S. Korolev, A. Tupolev, A. Mikoian, M. Yangel, and V Chelomei), and representatives of security organs (A. Zaveniagin, A. Komarovsky, P. Sudoplatov, I. Serov, and Yuri Andropov).

In the second half of the 20th century, the MIC transformed itself into a significant and privileged part of the USSR's economic and political system. More than that, during the Cold War years the Soviet MIC came to play an essential role in world economics and international relations.

The activity of the Soviet MIC in the international arena developed in three basic directions. First, there were the relations with the capitalist bloc (military competition with the United States and NATO countries in general). The second direction was the creation and functioning of an MIC in the countries of the "socialist camp" as a unified mechanism (organs with common goals, close coordination between State Planning Committees and general staffs of both Soviet and Warsaw Pact armies along the lines of the Council of Mutual Economic Aid [and in its Permanent Committee for the Defense Industry]), and a unified system of the Anti-Aircraft Defense for the people's democracies and China. The third involved military and technological cooperation with the countries of the third world.

The Soviet MIC became the main supplier of arms for countries of the third world and the socialist camp. The state had an absolute monopoly on arms export, and the process was administered by the Ministry (State Committee) for External Economic Ties. In the early 1980s, 25 percent of Soviet arms and military technology were exported abroad. The scope of military deliveries was for many years considered especially secret information, which was made accessible to the Russian public only in the beginning of the 1990s, and then only partially.

Over the postwar period, the USSR took part in conflicts and wars in more than fifteen countries (through the dispatch of military contingents and individual specialists to these countries and also through deliveries of arms and military technology, all with the purpose of rendering "international aid"). These countries included North Korea (1950–53), Laos (from 1960 and, with short interruptions, until 1970), Egypt (1962–74), Algeria (1962–64), Yemen (1962–63), Vietnam (1965–74), Syria (1967–73), Cambodia (1970), Bangladesh (1972–73), Angola (1975–79), Mozambique (1967–69), Ethiopia (1977–79), and Afghanistan (April 1978–May 1991).

According to statistics, at the end of the 1980s the Defense-Industrial Complex enterprises produced 20 to 25 percent of the country's gross national product. The best scientific-technological projects and personnel were concentrated on "defense"; up to three-quarters of all scientific-technological and experimental work was accomplished in the Defense-Industrial Complex sphere. All this, however, led to an extraordinary inflation of "unproductive" expenditures for arms production, to the detriment of the consumption sector.

The MIC and its amalgam of sociopolitical groups occupied one of the key positions in the USSR's power system. The postwar years showed a tendency toward the "technocratization" of the process of creating arms, and accordingly, toward the strengthening of the relative role within the MIC of its scientific-technological and industrial components. Within the nucleus of the complex, there was now a contradiction between the professional "military" element (with the military managers as the customers of the production) and the "civilian" (scientific-production) element as both developer and fulfiller. The relative importance of the second element in the Soviet version of the MIC tended to grow—a proof of which was the appointment in 1976 of the head civilian administrator of the MIC, D. Ustinov, as minister of defense, and his inclusion in the narrow group of "controllers" of top-level Soviet policy.

After the breakup of the USSR, the MIC declined from a powerful superstructure to a lobby that under the present conditions, has been forced to struggle for its survival.

See also Atomic Bomb; Cold War; Command Economy, The; Five-Year Plans; Power Politics; Red Army; Soviet Bloc; Warfare; Warsaw Pact.

FURTHER READING

Almquist, P. *Red Forge: Soviet Military Industry since 1965.* New York: Columbia University Press, 1990.

Barber, J., and M. Harrison, eds. *The Soviet Defense Industry Complex from Stalin to Krushchev.* London: Macmillan, 2000.

Bystrova, I. V. *The Formation of the Soviet Military-Industrial Complex.* Stanford, CA: Stanford University, Center for International Security and Arms Control, 1996.

———. *Voenno-promyslennyi kompleks SSR v gody cholodnoj vojny: Vtoraja polovina 40-x—nacalo 60-x godov.* Moscow: IRI RAN, 2000.

Harrison, M. "The Soviet Defense Industrial Complex in World War II." In *World War II and the Transformation of Business Systems,* ed. J. Sakudo and T. Shiba. Tokyo: Tokyo University Press, 1994.

Holloway, D. *The Soviet Union and the Arms Race.* New Haven, CT: Yale University Press, 1983.

———. *Stalin and the Bomb: The Soviet Union and Atomic Energy, 1939–1956.* New Haven, CT: Yale University Press, 1994.

Kruglov, A. K. *Kak sozdavalas' atomnaja promyšlennost' v SSR.* Moscow, 1995.

Minaev, A. V., ed. *Sovetskaja voennaja mošč' ot Stalina do Gorbačeva.* Moscow: Voennyi parad, 1999.

Simonov, N. S. *Voenno-promyšlennyi kompleks SSR v 1920–1950-e gody: tempy ekonomičeskogo rosta, struktura, organizacija proizvodstva i upravlenie.* Moscow: Rosspen, 1996.

IRINA V. BYSTROVA

Modernization

"Let us march full steam ahead on the road to industrialization, towards socialism, leaving the centuries-old 'Russian' backwardness behind us. We are about to become the country of metallurgy, the automobile and the tractor. And once we have put the USSR in cars, and the *muzhik* on tractors, let the esteemed capitalists, who trumpet their 'civilization' just try and catch us. At that time we shall see which countries can be defined as backward and which as advanced." These words pronounced by Joseph Stalin in November 1929 synthesize the strategy and goals of the Soviet regime during the "Great Turn" of the 1930s, which effectively combined an imitation of and an ideological challenge to the West. Industrialization, bureaucratization, urbanization, and literacy campaigns: these processes can all be more easily comprehended within the metacategory of modernization. If modernization is defined as "the complex series of changes in the political, economic and social spheres that have marked the past two centuries," then the historical characteristic of Stalinist modernization was the absence of profound political and institutional transformations. The guiding role of the party was reinforced, and in the long term this prevented the rationalization and functional articulation of institutions. The country's industrialization took place, by choice and necessity, in conditions of absolute isolation, and this caused inefficiencies and distortions.

Today it is easy to assess their seriousness. The Soviet "command economy" was always characterized by unequal development and a rivalry between bureaucratic apparatuses—the leading cause of the Great Terror of 1937–38. The absence of individual and collective freedoms eliminated a necessary check against mistaken economic choices. Cultural autarchy sidelined the USSR, especially after World War II, preventing its access to the most dynamic sectors of international science and technology. But during the brief interlude of the Great Turn, the USSR's international image changed. A new myth formed, more malleable and solidly grounded—the planning myth—and it was now placed alongside that of the USSR as the country of revolution and Soviets. After the 1929 crisis, with the world economy in a recession and many states undergoing an authoritarian involution, there were many—even among those who did not share the ideological premises of the October Revolution—who thought that the experience the Soviet Union had embarked on, despite its repressive aspects, might be the path to overcome the stagnation that was affecting much of the world. Subsequent events only reinforced this conviction. The USSR succeeded in defeating Nazi Germany and its allies, after having to sustain the war's heaviest burden, because of its ability to reconstruct its industrial infrastructure rapidly and produce technologically advanced weaponry. Once the war ended, the imposition of the Soviet model on the countries of Eastern Europe, notwithstanding the coercive methods employed, could at first be presented as a success, because it started the transition of predominantly agricultural countries to industrial economies. The Soviet economy's capacity to sustain an economic arms race with the United States was generally interpreted as a confirmation of the success of the modernization project that the Great Turn had set in motion.

The first extensive theories formulated by scholars that interpreted Stalinist industrialization as an episode of the struggle against Russian backwardness begun by Peter I date to the late 1950s. Usually this did not imply any form of ideological endorsement, to the extent that some even described the USSR as a form of industrial despotism, while at the same time recognizing that the Bolsheviks had managed to overcome the centuries-old Russian backwardness and strengthen the power of the country they were leading. As is often the case, the USSR's image as modernization's model country started to wane right at the time of its greatest success. In 1959 the Communist Party of the Soviet Union's (CPSU) first secretary, Nikita Khrushchev, predicted that in the span of a few years, his country would pull even with the United States in the per capita production of butter, milk, and meat, and during the CPSU's Twenty-second Congress he launched a twenty-year plan for the construction of communism, which was supposed to be based on high growth rates in agricultural and industrial production. These were the initiatives of a leader who was inclined toward "subjectivism"—a fault he was accused of in 1964 when he was removed from power, but these initiatives also addressed real and urgent problems.

Contrary to what was affirmed in modernization theories that were being promoted in those years in the United States, modernization was not witnessing the convergence of different economic and political systems. The development of industrialized societies run according to different political systems did allow for comparison, however, and it was becoming less and less favorable to the USSR. In the early 1960s Soviet industrial production had increased several times compared to 1929; in terms of the number of graduates and people employed in industry, the USSR was similar to the most industrialized countries, and the Soviet consumer was beginning to benefit from the first limited fruits of the previous decades' sacrifices. But the declining growth rates, low productivity in agriculture, and imbalances in the industrial sector, which had remained stationary following 1930s' policies that assigned the steel industry a leading role, were impeding the realization of the *mot d'ordre* given during the Stalinist Great Turn and taken over by Khrushchev: to "reach and overtake the most advanced capitalist countries." The situation did not improve substantially after Khrushchev's removal—a confirmation that the difficulties could not be attributed to personal errors. Timid attempts at systemic reform that were undertaken by his successors were followed, starting in 1973, by a prolonged period of economic stagnation, and it was only thanks to the rise in the price of oil that the

USSR managed to gain the resources to maintain its superpower status. This was a paradoxical turn of events for a regime born from the condemnation of the international capitalist market.

The distance between the history of the USSR and the concept of modernization grew even further as the difficulties in applying this model to the countries of so-called real socialism in Central-Eastern Europe increased. Analogous to what had occurred in the Soviet Union, these countries first underwent a growth stage, which allowed them to become industrialized countries, but subsequently did not become economically efficient. The inevitable decline in the growth rates was exacerbated by popular protests—sparked by the deterioration in living conditions as well as opposition to the elimination of collective and individual freedoms—often violently suppressed, like in Berlin in 1953 and Hungary in 1956. The sporadic and uncertain attempts at economic reform undertaken during the following decade by countries in the area (only in Hungary's case was there an overall plan, though not a particularly successful one) were frequently a response to chronic problems that could not be resolved politically, rather than the natural choice of countries driven by a modernization impulse. These efforts did not obtain appreciable results, nor did they allow for a rational division of labor among socialist countries. The position of Soviet-type economies was rendered even more difficult by the inevitable and pitiless comparison with the better results being attained by Western European countries, comparable both historically and in terms of size. The less obvious but not inappropriate comparison with the "Asian tigers" (South Korea, Taiwan, Hong Kong, Singapore, Thailand, and Malaysia) was also not flattering. The Asian tigers were also run by authoritarian or not fully democratic regimes, had followed a capitalist model of development, and were focused on exports and international exchange—a diametrically opposite choice to that made by the countries of Central-Eastern Europe, two-thirds of whose trade was with countries in the same area.

The limited value, in time and space, of the modernization model that the USSR had followed is confirmed by the experience of so-called developing or third world countries, which at various times and with different motivations chose the path toward socialism. "The socialist economy must be planned, but it must also remain flexible. . . . In this regard the Soviet Union's lessons are of no use." This statement by Liu Shaoqi dating from summer 1957 was an omen of the imminent political split between China and the USSR, which would run its course in the early 1960s. On the basis of this claimed diversity, in 1958 China launched the Great Leap Forward, which entrusted the people's commune—a base unit that was supposed to be able to engage in agricultural, industrial, educational, commercial, and defense activities—with achieving a type of development that would avoid the phase of "primitive socialist accumulation" of a Stalinist type. The disappointing results caused divisions among the elite of the Chinese Communist Party (CCP) that were destined to be partially overcome only after Mao Zedong's death in 1976. Although negative, this experience was useful in the following decades to define an economic policy oriented toward the development of local initiative and small production units.

North Korea, and later Vietnam and Cuba, remained for the entire duration of the Cold War countries on the borders of a bipolar world. Their economies were typical of countries forced to live in conditions of real or virtual war, and were never freed from external aid. It is impossible to acquire lessons from their experience about the validity or universality of a Soviet type of modernization. The same judgment can be made about countries that proclaimed their socialist orientation after decolonization. Ethiopia, Somalia, Angola, Mozambique, southern Yemen, Afghanistan, and Nicaragua followed the Soviet example, and in some cases declared their support for the principles of Marxism-Leninism. They subjected the economy to state control to the greatest degree possible, but they were not in either the subjective or objective positions to undertake an experiment similar to Stalin's Great Turn, nor to follow, as some scholars had advocated, the path toward a mixed economy, which the USSR had followed during the New Economic Policy and later abandoned with the beginnings of the Great Turn. None of the third world countries that followed a socialist path managed to achieve growth rates remotely comparable to those of the so-called Asian tigers, nor did they achieve the same internal social and political stability.

At the end of the 20th century, interest in the topic of modernization seemed destined to remain limited to specialists who could find reasons to reflect on the sudden collapse of socialist countries, which could not only be laid at the door of their economic inferiority when compared with the capitalist world (Stalin's USSR had stood the test under much more disadvantageous conditions), but were also tied to the awareness that had grown among these countries' leaderships: that the economic choices that had allowed them to move beyond traditional societies, consolidate internal consensus, and continue the Cold War had become impractical or counterproductive. Modernization became topical once more as a moment for understanding the contemporary world because of China's experience after Mao's death. In the late 1970s China's gross national product was similar to that of France, a country with 6 percent of China's population, and its share of international trade was 1 percent. In the last thirty years China has registered a yearly economic growth rate of close to 10 percent, which has resulted in its becoming a great industrial power—according to some estimates, second only to the United States in terms of the volume of total production—and the largest export market for many Asian countries. The apparent oxymoron of the formula of an economic system based on "market socialism," officially introduced during the CCP's Fourteenth Congress in 1992, sums up the dilemmas raised by the depth and successes of Chinese modernization.

The rediscovery of the market and the contribution of capitalist entrepreneurship, both domestic and international, have contributed decisively to Chinese modernization. At the end of the 20th century the private sector contributed about two-thirds of the gross national product; the volume of international trade had increased fourfold; more than 50 percent of exports were controlled by foreign companies; and the unemployed were about thirty million according to official estimates and almost a hundred million according to some observers. There was not much of anything socialist about these data, and an attempt to compare them with Stalinist modernization would have been even more fruitless. On the other hand, the CCP had remained in control, in the course of a long, important, and deep process, in terms of institutional authority in the areas of both politics and economics, and many of its cadres had shown "the ability to adapt entrepreneurially to the conditions created by the market reforms." And if the virtual monopoly that the state maintained in energy, telecommunications, and health sectors had favored the maintenance of islands of inefficiency and patronage, it had also protected the economic system from rushed privatization in strategic sectors, which had had negative effects on the transitions of other former "command economies." It had also allowed the CCP to contain inflation and control extended corruption.

The first victim of the CCP's choice to preserve a political monopoly and the power to guide economic policy

has been democracy. But the predictions of those who after the Tiananmen Square massacre had maintained that the lack of civic and political freedoms would soon cause a slower rate of growth have proved wrong; in fact the opposite is true, and after 1989 China's rate of growth actually increased and the country survived the Asian crisis of 1997 without any problems. It is therefore not easy to establish if China is the protagonist of a much longer and more convoluted process of transition from a socialist economy to a market one. Or if instead the imperatives of economic development have favored the consolidation of an authoritarian regime, rooted in Chinese tradition (some scholars are pointing to parallels with the 18th-century Qing dynasty), based on an alliance between merchants and power. Or if market socialism is destined to last, because it cannot be taken for granted that the combination of politics and economics in regimes of a Marxist-Leninist type impedes the growth of market forces, and on the contrary, the preservation of a political monopoly by a single party might be able to provide long-term answers to general problems (most particularly energy and security) and resolve the problems posed by development (such as regional and social inequalities, reform of the educational system, and corruption).

All three hypotheses have been put forth in the debate among specialists and political experts. What is certain is that the answer to these issues will shape the 21st century, and will establish whether China's modernization in recent decades will be able to offer a model to the many areas of the world that are still in the grip of underdevelopment.

See also Command Economy, The; Great Leap Forward; Planning; Revolution from Above; Single-Party System; Socialist Market Economy; Soviet Industrialization.

FURTHER READING

Boffa, G. *The Stalin Phenomenon*. Ithaca, NY: Cornell University Press, 1992.

Dickson, B. J. *Red Capitalists in China: The Party, Private Entrepreneurs, and Prospects for Political Change*. Cambridge, UK: Cambridge University Press, 2003.

Gilman, N. *Mandarins of the Future: Modernization Theory in Cold War America*. Baltimore: Johns Hopkins University Press, 2003.

Hanson, P. *The Rise and Fall of the Soviet Economy*. London: Longman, 2003.

Maddison, A. *The World Economy: Historical Statistics*. Paris: Organization for Economic Cooperation Development, Development Center Studies, 2003.

Pasquino, G. "Modernizazzione." In *Dizionario di politica*, ed. N. Bobbio, N. Matteucci, and G. Pasquino. Turin: Unione Tipografico Editrice Torinese, 1990.

Shevchenko, A. "Bringing the Party Back: The CCP and the Trajectory of the Market Transition in China." *Communist and Post-Communist Studies* 37 (2004): 161–85.

Spulber, N. *Foundations of Soviet Strategy for Economic Growth: Selected Soviet Essays, 1924–1930*. Bloomington: Indiana University Press, 1964.

FABIO BETTANIN

Molotov, Vyacheslav

Vyacheslav Molotov (1890–1986) was second in importance only to Stalin among the architects of the Soviet regime after Lenin's death. Born in Kukarka, Vyatka guberniya, central Russia, he was, like many leading Bolsheviks of the 1920s, a man of middle-class provincial background. He attended a local gymnasium and a technical high school in Kazan. In 1905 he joined the Social Democratic Party and from 1906 sided with the Bolsheviks. In 1909 he was exiled to Vologda for his revolutionary activities. On his release in 1911 he enrolled at the St. Petersburg Polytechnic Institute. From 1912 he worked on *Pravda*. He first used the pseudonym Molotov in 1915, after a hero of the radical novelist N. G. Pomyalovskii. The name, meaning "hammer-like" reflects Molotov's unromantic, practical, uncompromising approach to revolutionary politics.

In 1915 Molotov was arrested in Moscow. He was again exiled, but escaped and returned to St. Petersburg, where he was active in the Bolshevik press. He was one of the senior Bolsheviks in the capital when the February Revolution broke out, and became senior editor of *Pravda*. His position of uncompromising opposition to the provisional government, although reversed by Stalin and Kamenev on their return from exile, was the position espoused by Lenin on his return in April.

Molotov played no prominent part in the events of October, and his record during the civil war was undistinguished. In his roles as chairman of the Northern District Economic Council in 1918, and as chairman of Nizhnii Novgorod's province soviet in 1920, he was deemed to have been a failure. Between these appointments he served as a party propagandist, working with Lenin's wife, Nadezhda Krupskaya.

Nevertheless, with Lenin's backing, at the Tenth Party Congress of March 1921, Molotov was elected to the party's secretariat, to the Orgburo, and as a candidate member of the politburo. Lenin used Molotov as a go-between in his contacts with his politburo colleagues and described him as the "best filing clerk in Russia." Through his work in the secretariat Molotov developed a close association with Stalin, supporting him against Lenin's criticisms, and became a specialist in party organizational problems and cadre appointments.

Molotov supported Stalin against Trotsky, the Joint Opposition, and the Right Opposition. He was elected a full member of the politburo in January of 1926. His report to the Fifteenth Party Congress in 1927 on work in the countryside signaled a new offensive against the kulaks, and sounded the death knell of the New Economic Policy (NEP). He accompanied Stalin to Siberia in January 1928 on his campaign of forcible grain requisitioning. At the Central Committee plenum in November of 1929, Molotov was more insistent than anyone else on the urgency of collectivization.

In the struggle with the Rightists, Molotov worked in Comintern during the years 1928 to 1930, when the policy of uncompromising opposition to the Social Democrats (branded as "Social Fascists") was expounded. He took over as secretary of the Moscow party apparatus from November 1928 to April 1929, replacing the Rightist N. A. Uglanov.

In December 1930 Molotov was appointed chairman of Sovnarkom, in place of A. I. Rykov, inheriting the post that Lenin had held from 1917 to 1923. This appointment was to ensure unity between the leading party and government agencies in decision making. He thus lost his position as the dominant figure after Stalin, within the party secretariat and Orgburo, to his keen rival Kaganovich, but as chairman of Sovnarkom he acted as chairman at meetings of the politburo. Molotov and Kaganovich constituted the two junior partners under Stalin in the ruling triumvirate, and it was they who took charge of affairs when Stalin was away from Moscow for his long summer vacations from 1930 to 1936. In the early 1930s Molotov was sent on mission to enforce collectivization policy in the regions, and in 1932 attended the Ukrainian party conference in Kiev to lay down the law regarding the necessity of meeting the center's procurement targets for grain.

Through the 1930s Molotov was absorbed in economic management in Sovnarkom, and was drawn into abrasive confrontations with the high-spending commissariats of heavy industry and transport. Under his stewardship the

Soviet economy, after the upheavals of the First Five-Year Plan, became more predictable and more rational, and Soviet industry began to grow steadily. Stalin left the complexities of economic management to Molotov, but exercised close oversight of policy relating to agriculture and the defense industries.

From 1934 onward Molotov, with Stalin's approval, sought to explore the possibility of coming to terms with Germany. In this he worked against foreign minister M. M. Litvinov's policy of "collective security," which aimed at collaboration with the Western democracies to contain the threat posed by Nazi Germany, Fascist Italy, and Japan. In 1936 Molotov fell under a cloud, possibly as a result of unguarded comments made to a foreign correspondent regarding Soviet foreign policy objectives. Significantly his name was not included in the list of potential victims of the conspirators in the trial of the "Trotskyite-Zinovievite Center" in August 1936. During the Great Terror, Molotov quickly fell into line with the policy dictated by Stalin, and oversaw the purge within Sovnarkom. In his retirement he continued to defend the purge as a means of eliminating a "fifth column" in anticipation of war. Molotov was one of those who signed the order to shoot the twenty thousand Polish officers executed in the winter of 1939.

In April 1937 Molotov was nominated as one of the five members of the politburo's commission on foreign policy matters, and as a member of the five-man politburo commission in charge of economic matters. These two commissions effectively replaced the politburo.

The Munich settlement of September 1938 administered the death blow to Litvinov's policy of collective security and brought about bitter clashes between Litvinov and Molotov. On March 3, Molotov became head of NKInDel. The NKVD purge of the commissariat reached a climax during the first years of Molotov's tenure in power.

Molotov was a novice in foreign policy matters, and his handling of foreign diplomats and statesmen tended toward the stiff and formal. He had some knowledge of German and French. He conducted for the Soviet side the unsuccessful Triple Alliance talks with British and French government representatives in 1939, which might have been the last chance to salvage the policy of collective security. The Soviet rapprochement with Nazi Germany in 1939 was a victory for the policy line advocated by Molotov. Litvinov, who had a very low opinion of Molotov's expertise in foreign policy matters, viewed the policy as a major error.

Molotov was trusted by Stalin to manage Soviet foreign policy, but Stalin himself was always very closely involved in all negotiations. It was Molotov who in the autumn of 1940 was sent to Berlin to negotiate with Hitler and the German leadership. His fiftieth birthday fell in that year and was celebrated with the granting of state awards and the renaming of towns and institutions in his honor.

In May 1941 Stalin took over the position of chairman of Sovnarkom, combining this with the post of party first secretary. Molotov remained as Sovnarkom vice-chairman and retained his post as foreign minister. It was Molotov who delivered the radio broadcast informing the people of Germany's attack on the Soviet Union. In 1942 he was sent to London and Washington to cement the wartime alliance with Britain and the United States. Throughout the war he was Stalin's deputy on the State Defense Committee (GKO). He attended the Allied conferences at Tehran, Yalta, and Potsdam, as well as the San Francisco conference that established the United Nations. He headed the Soviet delegation to the United Nations until 1949.

From 1924 to 1949 Molotov was effectively Stalin's right-hand man, as evidenced by his regular attendance at the meetings in Stalin's private study. As a deputy to Stalin he was almost indispensable. He was neither a theorist nor an orator—his speeches and writing are distinctly flat and lack originality. Molotov certainly never commanded the loyalty and admiration that Stalin enjoyed, but as minister of foreign affairs he became a world figure, his face immediately recognizable. He was a man of great self-control, impenetrable and inscrutable.

But it appears that as early as 1945 Stalin had decided that Molotov lacked the qualities to succeed him as leader. In 1949 Molotov finally fell to Stalin's paranoia, when he was sacked as minister of foreign affairs. His fall was associated with accusations directed at his wife, Paulina Zhemchuzhina, who was accused of Zionist sympathies. Molotov was elected in October 1952 to the new party presidium, but he was not one of the nine members of the bureau proposed by Stalin. In Stalin's final years Molotov was excluded from the meetings of the inner circle.

Following Stalin's death in March 1953, Molotov was reappointed minister of foreign affairs, a post he held until 1956. He opposed the easing relations with the West and Yugoslavia, and in other respects, too, became a champion of conservative Stalinist positions in opposition to Khrushchev's "de-Stalinization" policy. In June 1957 Molotov was disgraced and expelled from the politburo and Central Committee as a member of the

"Anti-Party Group." In 1961 the Twenty-second Party Congress expelled him from the party. He was appointed Soviet ambassador to Outer Mongolia for three years (1957–60) and was the Soviet representative to the International Atomic Energy Conference in Vienna from 1960 to 1962. From 1962 onward he lived modestly in retirement in Moscow. In 1984, through the influence of A. A. Gromyko, as president, Molotov was readmitted into the CPSU. He died in Moscow on November 8, 1986.

See also Collectivization of the Countryside; Five-Year Plans; Great Terror; Molotov-Ribbentrop Pact; Stalin, Joseph; Stalinism.

FURTHER READING

Chuev, F. *Sto sorok besed Molotovym: iz dnevnika F. Chueva.* Moscow: Terra, 1991.

Kosheleva, L., V. Lel'chuk, V. Naumov, et al., eds. *Pis'ma I. V. Stalina V. M. Molotovu, 1925–1936 gg.* Moscow: Sampo, 1995.

Lih, L. T., O. V. Naumov, and O. V. Khlevnyuk, eds. *Stalin's Letters to Molotov.* New Haven, CT: Yale University Press, 1995.

Medvedev, R. *All Stalin's Men.* Oxford: Blackwell, 1983.

Miner, S. M. "His Master's Voice: Viacheslav Mihailovich Molotov as Stalin's Foreign Commissar." In *The Diplomats, 1939–1979,* ed. G. A. Craig and F. Z. Lowenheim. Princeton, NJ: Princeton University Press, 1994.

Molotov, V. M. *V Bor'be za sotsializm: rechi i stat'i.* Moscow, 1935.

Watson, D. *Molotov and Soviet Government: Sovnarkom 1930–1941.* Basingstoke: Macmillan, 1996.

———. "Molotov's Apprenticeship in Foreign Policy: The Triple Alliance Negotiations, 1939." *Europe-Asia Studies* 52, no. 4 (2000), 698.

E. ARFON REES

Molotov-Ribbentrop Pact

On August 23, 1939, the foreign ministers of the Soviet Union and Germany, Vyacheslav Molotov and Joachim von Ribbentrop, signed a nonaggression pact in Moscow. News of the event was immediately announced, and it was as overwhelming to Communists as it was to Western governments and public opinion. It upset the perception of mutual political and ideological hostility between Soviet Russia and Nazi Germany, compromising the anti-Fascist orientation of the international Communist movement, and turned on their head the negotiations between Moscow, London, and Paris for the formation of a trilateral alliance, whose aim was to contain Adolf Hitler's expansionism. The pact basically gave Hitler a green light to pursue his aggressive plans, already clearly expressed toward Poland, while Joseph Stalin would no longer concern himself with the international consequences of a similar event. In actuality the pact contained a secret protocol, which agreed to a division of spheres of influence in Poland and the Baltic states. The protocol anticipated something much more serious than a nonaggression pact: the beginnings of an alliance, which would develop after the onset of World War II.

From Stalin's point of view the pact had strategic significance, even though it had been reached by means of a sudden diplomatic shift. In preceding years the "collective security" line that had distinguished Soviet foreign policy, with a pro-Western and anti-Hitler slant, developed by Foreign Affairs commissar Maksim Litvinov, was joined by a parallel line meant to leave open the possibility of an agreement with Germany, developed by the head of the Council of Peoples' Commissars', Molotov. Stalin had avoided committing himself personally to either line, basically choosing a free hands' policy. When British appeasement led to the Munich Accords of September 1938 and the dismemberment of Czechoslovakia, acceding to Hitler's demands, Stalin believed there was a clear Western intent to focus the Nazi menace toward the East. The British decision to limit its détente with Germany after the Nazis occupied Prague in March 1939, granting Poland a guarantee, reopened diplomatic maneuvering, but it did not allay Soviet suspicions. Initially, following Litvinov's lead, Moscow put forward the proposal for a triple alliance to both London and Paris. The lack of a response from Great Britain weakened Litvinov's position beyond repair, and Molotov replaced him on May 3, 1939.

From this moment on the Soviets followed "dual track" diplomacy, negotiating with the West while establishing increasingly significant contacts with the Germans. Western ambiguities, provoked by both anti-Communist ideology and mistrust of the Red Army after the Great Purges it had endured, were an important factor in the negotiations' failure. But in Stalin's eyes, Great Britain's guarantee to Poland created a new scenario: the end of the danger of a German-Polish accord and the possibility that the war could be focused on the West instead of the East. The openings with Germany simultaneously offered a second possibility: a negotiation on the creation of a Soviet sphere of influence in Eastern Europe, which the British did not want to recognize. Stalin's decision to conclude a pact with Hitler was therefore not the result of an improvised move but rather a political opportunity to obtain strategic objectives that had been previously conceived: permanently divide the capitalist camp, keep the USSR out of a new war as long as possible, acquire new space for territorial security, and increase the Soviet Union's status and strength.

After the German invasion of Poland provoked British and French declarations of war against Germany, Stalin explained his strategy in some directions he gave his aides on September 7, 1939—also reported in Georgi Dimitrov's diary. The cornerstone was the "war of attrition" among the powers participating in the conflict, which were all placed on the same level, with no distinctions between democratic and Fascist nations. The pact with Germany was presented as an instrument of medium- to long-term policies, by means of which the USSR would encourage a reciprocal weakening of the imperialist powers and extend its influence in Eastern Europe, beginning with the imminent collapse of the Polish state. On September 17, while the German war machine was overwhelming Polish defenses, the USSR invaded the Eastern section of the country (which Moscow defined as western Ukraine and western Belorussia) as had been agreed in the pact. On September 28, Germany and the USSR extended the previous month's pact further, leading to a friendship treaty, a border agreement that sanctioned the division of Poland, and a new division of spheres of influence that gave the Soviet Union Lithuania in addition to Latvia and Estonia.

Henceforth a de facto alliance existed, supported by the substantial economic and energy assistance the USSR gave the Nazi war effort. The USSR reached the point of denouncing the Western powers as those principally responsible for the war's continuation, placed the Baltic states under its own protection (and then annexed them in June–July 1940), counted on German benevolence during its war with Finland, and implemented its Sovietization policies in the occupied regions. Sovietization, in turn, led to mass deportations and massacres, such as in Katyn in April 1940. The pact was devastating for the international Communist movement. Stalin forced Dimitrov to eliminate the anti-Fascist line and embrace anti-imperialist rhetoric. The most important Western Communist Party, the French one, had to go underground and was reduced to impotence. The European Communists aligned themselves with the new policies in an orderly manner, which helped confirm their anti-imperialist identity, but did not provide them with any political line, even that of revolutionary insurrection.

The pact's ambiguity also masked an element of mutual recognition between the two regimes: the sense of mutual emulation of their abilities to enforce absolute command and affirm power. This was the most explicit moment of veiled appreciation each dictatorship gave the other in terms of the accomplishments they had realized so far: the USSR admired Nazism's capacity to organize the masses as well as the idea that in confronting the Western democracies, Hitler might pave the way for a future antibourgeois and socialist evolution of German society, in addition to continuing a conflict among capitalist states that was destined to favor the Soviet Union. And yet Stalin probably did not entertain illusions about the alliance's future stability; he was still guided by the idea he had inherited from Vladimir Lenin, concerning the inevitability of war and the antagonism between the Soviet Union and capitalist powers. Nazi Germany, however, only represented the most forward position of a hostile world. And yet it was precisely this view, centered around the imperialist motives of German policy, which prevented a focus on Nazism's radical racist ideology. This laid the groundwork for a fatal misunderstanding of Hitler's objectives and conduct.

The war of attrition strategy soon showed its limits. Estimates of a prolonged war in the West were dashed when France collapsed in June 1940. Yet Stalin did not reconsider his decisions and refused proposals for dialogue put forward by the British. He continued to maintain that the alliance with Germany was in the USSR's interests, which he believed were the end of the "old order" in Europe and the creation of a Soviet sphere of influence in Eastern Europe. Stalin even seemed disposed to discuss the USSR's inclusion in the triple alliance among Germany, Italy, and Japan of September 1940. Following a German invitation, the negotiations were led by Molotov in Berlin in November 1940. The Soviet objective was to relaunch the understanding between the two powers, in order to extend the spheres of influence to southeastern Europe, including the Turkish straits. In actuality the meeting became a dialogue of the deaf, because Hitler had no intention of making concessions in Europe and because he had already decided to attack the USSR.

The negotiations' failure was obvious to the Soviets, but they continued to entertain the illusion that a policy of détente toward Germany would lead to accords in the Balkans and prevent war. In the following months, the German invasion of Bulgaria (February 1941) and later Yugoslavia (April 1941) dashed any hopes of an accord. The USSR's reactions were limited, though, and even the Comintern's directives to renew the activities of Communist parties against Nazi occupation forces in Europe did not bring about a significant shift. In fact the idea of dissolving the Comintern, put forward by Stalin in April 1941, was probably an attempt to blandish Germany, and was only to be realized two years later in a completely different context.

Further détente efforts with Nazi Germany helped sustain the obstinacy with which Stalin deluded himself until the end, notwithstanding the mass of information that pointed to the opposite conclusion—namely, that Hitler would not open a second front and would not attack the USSR. In a secret speech given in May 1941, Stalin alluded to the possibility of a war with Germany and even a Soviet preventive strike. He was aware that the alliance was temporary. But his perspective remained that of gaining time, ignoring the fact that war was imminent. The German attack of June 22, 1941, highlighted the failure of the war of attrition as well as the territorial security and appeasement strategies toward Germany that Stalin had put forth. Nevertheless, the desire to exercise a decisive influence in Eastern Europe, which he had cultivated at the time of the alliance with Hitler, would remain at the core of the Stalinist outlook and Soviet postwar plans. From this point of view, a hidden relationship was established between Stalin's policies at the time of the pact and those pursued during the Cold War.

See also Hitler, Adolf; Power Politics; Second Cold War; Sovietization; Stalin, Joseph; War, Inevitability of.

FURTHER READING

Gorodetsky, G. *Grand Delusion: Stalin and the German Invasion of Russia*. New Haven, CT: Yale University Press, 1999.

Gross, J. T. *Revolution from Abroad: The Soviet Conquest of Poland's Western Ukraine and Western Byelorussia*. Princeton, NJ: Princeton University Press, 1988.

Haslam, J. *The Soviet Union and the Struggle for Collective Security in Europe, 1933–39*. London: Macmillan, 1984.

Pons, S. *Stalin and the Inevitable War: 1936–1941*. London: Frank Cass, 2002.

Roberts, G. K. *The Unholy Alliance: Stalin's Pact with Hitler*. Bloomington: Indiana University Press, 1989.

Vojna i politika 1939–1941. Moscow: Nauka, 1999.

SILVIO PONS

━━━

Münzenberg, Willi

Willi Münzenberg (1889–1940) was born on August 14 in Thuringia, in the German city of Erfurt. He grew up in the family of a poor innkeeper, left home early, and then worked as a shoemaker and educated himself. In 1906 he began to take part in a socialist youth movement, was forced to leave his native city, and moved to Switzerland. There he continued his political activities and became acquainted with émigrés from Russia. Münzenberg was the founder and organizer of the Socialist Youth of Switzerland, which during the war years adopted internationalist positions.

He was a participant in the Kintal (1916) and Stockholm (1917) conferences of left-wing socialists, and supported Lenin's call to transform the imperialist war into a civil war. During World War I he worked as a secretary in the International Bureau of the Socialist Youth International. In fall 1918, Münzenberg was arrested for his revolutionary activities and was banished from Switzerland. He then took an active part in the German revolution and became a member of the Communist Party of Germany (KPD). Münzenberg spent from January to November 1919 in prison.

At the Constituent Congress of the Communist Youth International, in November 1919 in Berlin, Münzenberg was chosen as the organization's secretary. In summer 1920 he went to Russia for the first time, to take part in the Second Congress of the Comintern. At the next congress Münzenberg was elected to its Executive Committee. During his work in the Communist Youth International, however, he failed to win the trust of the chairman of the Executive Committee of the Communist International, Grigory Zinovyev. Münzenberg's growing conflict with Zinovyev was a function of not only their differing views on the prospects of world revolution but also their competition to gain influence with Lenin.

At Lenin's suggestion, Münzenberg was entrusted with the organization of international aid to Russia's hungry. His efforts resulted in a permanently active "solidarity" organization, the International Workers' Aid (IWA), and Münzenberg became its secretary. By summer 1923, approximately five million dollars had been collected for various kinds of aid to the starving citizens of Soviet Russia. Münzenberg gained the sympathies of a number of leading writers and artists who had maintained their liberal convictions, but also people who were sympathetic to the social experiment going on in the Soviet Union. Even in the ensuing years the IWA was able to maintain some autonomy from the Comintern, giving material support to strikers, and plowing the funds collected by the workers into agitation and education groups as well as charitable activities. This propaganda organization emphasized the great experience and grand achievements of the USSR, and concentrated on creating an idealized image of the country in the minds of Western European workers. The various IWA institutions—publishing houses, film studios, kindergartens, and sanatoriums—were often referred to as "Münzenberg's Empire." Still another mass organization adhering to the Comintern's ideological line was the Anti-Imperialist League, created by Münzenberg at a congress in Brussels in February 1927.

Though not involving himself in the internal party struggles of the mid-1920s, Münzenberg nevertheless augmented his influence in the KPD's leadership. From 1924 to 1933 he was the KPD deputy to the Reichstag, and at a 1927 congress in Essen was elected to membership in the party's Central Committee. In 1932 Münzenberg supported the opposition Remmele-Neiman group, and after this group was removed from the party leadership, he gave up active work in the KPD, concentrating instead on international projects.

After the Nazis came to power in Germany, Münzenberg immigrated to France, where he was able to restore the scale of his "empire." His propagandistic activity dealt blows to the Fascist threat, and he managed to bring to light the provocations of Goebbels's propaganda. Münzenberg adhered to the line of the Comintern's Seventh Congress, which advocated creating an anti-Fascist Popular Front, and he tried to unite the German political émigrés in France. In October 1936, he was summoned before the International Control Commission of the Comintern and became a victim of the intrigues of the new KPD leadership, led by Wilhelm Pieck and Walter Ulbricht. Thanks to the intercession of the secretary of the Executive Committee of the Comintern, Palmiro Togliatti, Münzenberg was able to return to Paris, and in 1937 refused to obey a new summons to Moscow, since by now he knew a lot about the repression against German political emigrants in the Soviet Union.

This led to his expulsion from the KPD in October 1937 and removal from his IWA duties. On March 10, 1939, Münzenberg addressed his comrades with an open letter in which he expressed his disagreement with the Stalinist methods used by the leadership of the international Communist movement. He continued to participate in the anti-Fascist movement, and in 1939, formed the organization Friends of Socialist Unity of Germany and published a weekly newspaper called *Die Zukunft* (The Future).

After World War II broke out, Münzenberg was interned in France, but during the German invasion of France he fled from a camp at Chambarran near Lyon, in order to avoid falling into the hands of the Gestapo. In fall 1940, he was found hanged in a forest. An investigation yielded no results, and no suicide was ever confirmed. His life companion, Babetta Gross, in her biography of Münzenberg, contended that he had been murdered at the instigation of Stalin's agents.

See also Antifascism; Comintern; Propaganda, Communist.

FURTHER READING

Gross, B. *Willi Münzenberg: eine politische Biographie.* Stuttgart: Deutsche Verlags-Anstalt, 1967.

Koch, S. *Double Lives: Stalin, Willi Munzenberg, and the Seduction of the Intellectuals.* New York: Enigma Books, 1994.

Lazitch, B., and M. Drachkovitch. *Biographical Dictionary of the Comintern.* Stanford, CA: Hoover Institution Press, 1986.

McMeekin, S. *The Red Millionaire: A Political Biography of Willi Munzenberg, Moscow's Secret Propaganda Tsar in the West, 1917–1940.* New Haven, CT: Yale University Press, 2004.

ALEKSANDR I. VATLIN

Mussolini, Benito

Born in a village near Predappio in Forlì Province, the same year that Karl Marx died, Benito Mussolini (1883–1945) was thirteen years younger than Vladimir Lenin, nine younger than Winston Churchill, four younger than Joseph Stalin, one younger than Franklin D. Roosevelt, six years older than Adolf Hitler, seven years older than Charles de Gaulle, eight years older than Antonio Gramsci, nine years older than Francisco Franco, and ten years older than both Mao Zedong and Palmiro Togliatti. His mother, Rosa Maltoni, a Catholic, baptized her son, but his father had wanted to make him a revolutionary ever since he was born. His father gave him the names Benito Amilcare Andrea (a homage, respectively, to Juárez, Cipriani, and Costa, the first Italian socialist deputy).

His socialist apprenticeship was shaped by practical experiences more than any serious theoretical reflection on his readings, which were haphazard and often disorganized. The limited circulation in Italy of the classics of Marxism and international socialism prevented him from delving deeper into Marx (and the young Mussolini did not derive any theoretical suggestions on Communist utopia from Marx), while his knowledge of French allowed him to gain some familiarity with Pierre-Joseph Proudhon and the theoretician of revolutionary syndicalism, Georges Sorel. Yet it was the social scientist Gustave Le Bon and his study of crowd psychology that probably most influenced the young Mussolini.

Mussolini was intransigent and a maximalist, and he began to practice oratory, taking an interest in the ways information could be spread—an interest also developed through his journalistic activities in Liguria, the Trentino, and Romagna. He opposed Italian imperialist expansion in Libya in 1911–12, and in 1912 became national editor of the socialist daily *L'Avanti!* As in the case of other leaders of European socialism, who were overwhelmed by the national implications of war's outbreak in 1914, Mussolini was swept up in the warmongering and suddenly shifted from internationalism to nationalism, from pacifism to the invocation and cult of war. In an article that led to his expulsion from the Italian Socialist Party, he discussed the possibility of an Italian intervention in the war. This in turn led to a series of accusations and counteraccusations that marked a significant split, destined never to be mended. Mussolini's new contacts in the autumn of 1914, and the depth of his break with the socialist cause and ideals, were evident when he started a daily financed by an economic and industrial milieu that was interested in adding to the prointervention and prowar voices. The desired combination of nationalism and populism was expressed in the title of the new daily, *Il popolo d'Italia*; its subtitle, "socialist daily," was changed in 1918 to "fighters and producers daily," which

confirmed Mussolini's talent for devising slogans, and anticipated the themes of national productivity and paramilitary violence that were the basis for his *Fasci di combattimento* (fighting Fasci, a term that harks back to the triumphal processions of the Roman Empire), which he founded in 1919.

Mussolini was a critic of October 1917 and an anti-Bolshevik, even though his break with socialism had already occurred in 1914; from 1917 on he was always anti-Communist, anti-Soviet, and anti-Russian, even though he often instrumentally mentioned the 1917 revolution as the harbinger of a new age, whose opposite poles he said were Rome and Moscow ("either Rome or Moscow"), which were both alternatives—inspired by opposite goals—to an aging and despised liberal democracy. After having unleashed terrorism and subversion, especially at the local level, during 1921–22, Italian fascism grew to the point of becoming a reactionary and militarized mass party, with more than three hundred thousand members in the spring of 1922. Yet Mussolini's challenge to the liberal establishment, with his march on Rome to conquer power with weapons in hand, was pursued while simultaneously reassuring the economic and political ruling class of liberal Italy, waving the carrot of the return to order as well as the elimination of socialist political and union dominance in front of its representatives. In other words, he was selling them a sort of preventive countermove, a promise to eliminate any revolutionary risk and reassure the "strong powers," starting with the army and monarchy, both of which gave their blessing to Mussolini. King Victor Emanuel III asked him to form the government; Mussolini became its head on October 31, 1922, and was not removed until July 25, 1943.

From this moment on, Mussolini's biography and the history of fascism crossed and/or coincided, without necessarily becoming synonymous or indistinguishable. Mussolini worked in 1922–26 to lay the foundations for a full-fledged dictatorship, or what he himself called a Fascist regime, both subversive and stabilizing at the same time. He founded the Fascist Grand Council, the Voluntary Militia for National Security, the Special Tribunal for the Defense of the State, the One and Only Fascist Party, the One and Only Fascist Labor Union, the Opera nazionale Balilla and later Gioventù italiana del Littorio (both names for Fascist youth organizations), and the Opera nazionale dopolavoro (an after-work organization), thus giving birth to a new form of party-state, a dictatorial police state.

Soon this party-state started to claim all sorts of supposed Italian national "rights" abroad, to the detriment of peoples and lands in both continental Europe (especially in the Balkans and Danube), the Mediterranean, and Africa. Mussolini's diplomacy was always imperialistically attempting to enlarge Italian dominions, usually acting before negotiating. Surrounded by a vast and comprehensive propaganda apparatus that exalted the "duce" above all, promoting a cult of personality, Mussolini treated the rules of international law with contempt, distancing himself from France and England during the late 1930s, and establishing a political and military alliance with Nazi Germany. The Fascist aggression against Ethiopia in 1935–36, the joint Nazi-Fascist participation in the Spanish civil war of 1936–39 in support of the nationalist coup leaders lead by Franco, and the annexation of Albania to Italy in 1939 were the principal episodes in the Fascist demolition of the European, Mediterranean, and African balances of power, all of which helped set the stage for World War II. The party-state had assumed a racist physiognomy in the colonies, which in 1938 was extended, with the anti-Semitic laws, so as to target and discriminate against a portion of the national community on the basis of presumed "principles" of the supremacy of the Aryan race—a first in Italian history.

Mussolini was the author and promoter of all these developments, and remained the regime's most powerful individual indeed—if measured as a function of personal power perhaps more powerful than other dictators of his age. When repressing his opponents (especially Communists, anarchists, and socialists) he was vindictive, when selecting his collaborators he preferred nepotism, and in his alliance with Hitler he ended up following his ex-student deferentially. Mussolini's anticommunism, which had already manifested itself during his "crusade" in Spain, was sanctioned on the "theoretical" level by Italy's joining the anti-Comintern pact with Germany and Japan in 1937. It was confirmed when he asked to join the Nazis in their aggression against the USSR in 1941, during the creation of the Tripartite Pact, which in 1941 was intended (as an alliance of Germany, Japan, and Italy) as a challenge to most of the world.

More than confronting communism on the doctrinal level, Mussolini was attempting to push his German partner east, to focus his expansionist drive on Soviet Russia. Italy's "vital space" in the Mediterranean and Africa, but also in the Danube and Balkans as well as the southern portions of Eastern Europe, or so Mussolini hoped, would be largely safeguarded from Nazi competition the more it focused on the USSR. But the weak partner in the German-Italian alliance was overrun by the war's outcome. Part of the Italian establishment realized that Mussolini's war was lost in 1943, and the king removed Mussolini from power in July and arrested him, but the Germans then freed him. Starting in September–October, Mussolini helped set up a last incarnation of fascism by creating the Repubblica sociale italiana (Italian Social Republic, also known as repubblica di Salò). In the service of Hitler and the German occupation of Italy, an aging Mussolini collaborated in repressing the partisan movement as well as capturing Italian Jews and subsequently helping to ship them to the death camps. Captured by the partisans, he was executed on orders from the Comitato di liberazione nazionale (National Liberation Committee) on April 28, 1945.

See also Anticommunism; Fascism; Hitler, Adolf; Totalitarianism.

FURTHER READING

Bosworth, R.J.B. *Mussolini.* London: Arnold, 2002.
De Felice, R. *Mussolini.* 7 vols. Turin: Einaudi, 1965–97.
Milza, P. *Mussolini.* Paris: Fayard, 1999.

MARCO PALLA

Nagy, Imre

Imre Nagy, who was born on June 7, 1896, in Kaposvár, Hungary, and died on July 16, 1958, in Budapest, was a Hungarian Communist politician. Even before finishing high school, he began working in a factory and studied at a commercial school in Kaposvár. In May 1915 he was drafted into the army. Nagy was wounded and taken prisoner by the Russians in July 1916. In March 1918 he enrolled in the Red Army, and in May 1920 joined the Bolshevik Party in Irkutsk. Next, he went through a course of study at a special commission school. Then, in May 1921, Nagy was ordered back to Hungary to participate in the illegal Communist movement there. He worked for an insurance company. An activist and then secretary of the Kaposvár chapter of the Social Democratic Party, he voiced some criticism of the leadership at a congress and was expelled from the party, after which he established contacts with the illegal Communist Party. In 1927 he spent about two months under arrest on suspicion of illegal Communist activity. In March 1928 he emigrated to Vienna, and spent September 1928–December 1929, with one interruption, in Budapest, where he headed the Communist Party's section on work in the countryside. In 1930 Nagy took part in a Hungarian Communist Party congress outside of Moscow and was criticized there for right-wing deviationism. Remaining in the USSR, he worked at the Comintern's International Agrarian Institute. In early 1936, at the insistence of Béla Kun, Nagy was expelled from the party, but he was reinstated in 1939. In 1938 he was arrested by the People's Commissariat for Internal Affairs (NKVD) but was set free a few days later when his case was terminated. (The publication in 1993 in the Italian newspaper *La Stampa* of some sensational documents from the Committee for State Security's archives testifying to Nagy's activity as a secret informer for the NKVD in 1937 and 1938 provoked a discussion about Nagy as a person, yet did not provide grounds for any cardinal political reassessment of him in the 1950s.) Both before and during the war, he worked in radio broadcasts aimed at Hungary.

In October 1944 Nagy returned to Hungary with a number of other Communists. He was elected to the party's central leadership. On December 22, 1944, the minister of agriculture in the temporary national government presented a program of land reform aimed at dividing up large landed estates among the peasants, and Nagy worked from then until November 4, 1945, to bring this program into effect. In May 1945, he became a member of the politburo of the Central Committee of the Hungarian Communist Party (renamed in June 1948 the Communist Workers' Party). From November 1945 until March 1946, he was the minister of internal affairs and was sometimes subjected to criticism within the party for his lack of decisiveness in confronting his political opponents. In April 1946, he was named secretary of the party's Central Committee, with responsibility for agrarian policy. After the Communists' success at the polls in August 1947, he became chair of the State Assembly—a position that he held until 1949. In 1950 he became a corresponding member and then a regular member (academician) of the Hungarian Academy of Sciences. In March 1949, at a plenum of the Central Committee, he entered into a discussion with the general secretary of the Hungarian Workers' Party (VRT) for agrarian policy, Matyás Rákosi, arguing for more moderate tempos in collectivizing the peasantry. ("He's a chip off the block of our Moscow granite," Nagy later wrote, referring to the harsh positions that Rákosi took in the principal questions of building socialism in Hungary.) In September 1949, on the eve of the "Rajk matter," he was criticized at a Central Committee plenum for "right-wing deviationism" and was discharged from the politburo. Later, though, he came forward with the requisite self-criticism and was restored to the politburo in 1951.

In June 1953, Moscow recommended that Nagy be named prime minister of Hungary, and he thus inherited the arduous task of solving the rending economic and social problems brought about by Rákosi's policy of forced industrialization of Hungary. In July 1953, he came forth with an economic program aimed at improving the population's standard of living, and prioritized the development of agriculture and light industry, while also raising the possibility of freeing the peasants from collective farms. Yet Nagy's proposed reforms were not limited to economics; the first political prisoners in Hungary were released in 1954. By the beginning of 1955, however, the policies of Nagy's government were coming into conflict with Moscow's new policy of prioritizing the development of heavy industry. Rákosi now took advantage of these conditions to have Nagy removed from his post as premier. This time Nagy refused to resort to self-criticism, and was not only banished from the highest party organs but also, in December 1955, was expelled from the party itself, being accused of factional activities.

After the Twentieth Congress of the Communist Party of the Soviet Union, in a letter addressed to the VRT's Central Committee, Nagy, by now back in power, insisted on a return to the "June Program" of 1953. Especially after the fall of Rakosi in the summer of 1956, he believed that he would enjoy the support of the reform-minded faction of the party apparatus, which was looking for ways to broaden the social base of the regime, while still retaining the VRT's monopoly of power. The social structure improved by early summer 1956, and thus Nagy avoided having to participate in public actions of the opposition and distanced himself from informal social movements such as the Petofi Circle. On the other hand, Nagy made no compromises in his relations with the highest echelon leaders, rejecting their efforts to induce him to make a public avowal of his mistakes—a stance that would later enable him to return to the party unscathed by any previous challenge to the authority of its leadership. The question of Nagy held the public's attention during the whole summer and early fall of 1956. His name was associated with a more liberal domestic policy, with hopes for renewal and reforms, and with a consistent defense (following Josip Broz Tito's example) of national interests in foreign policy. The tense internal political situation at the beginning of October 1956 forced the authorities to some compromise with the demands of the masses. On October 13, Nagy was reinstated in the party and to its leadership.

Foreseeing an imminent change in leadership, Nagy and like-minded partisans began to discuss a program to lift Hungary out of its crisis. Still, on the eve of October 23, 1956, when the revolutionary uprising was about to begin in Budapest, fearing provocations, Nagy rejected a proposal by his allies to lead a student demonstration of solidarity with the events in Poland. Even on the day of the protest, Nagy's actions reflected his desire to refrain from hasty steps. When the crowd outside Parliament demanded that Nagy make a speech, he first requested permission to speak from the VRT's Central Committee. In his short talk Nagy called on the gathering to observe law and order and turn the solution of essential social problems over to whatever new government would emerge. In actual fact, his announced proposal to return to the 1953 program caused disappointment. By this time, more radical slogans had been brought forward: espousing a multiparty system and the withdrawal of Soviet troops. Nagy's speech failed to defuse the situation, and his restoration to the post of prime minister at dawn on October 24 (just as the Soviet troops were marching into Budapest) did not have the effect he and his adherents had expected. Still, the CPSu leadership, cognizant of the lack of faith the Hungarian population had in their previous leaders, realized that placing their stakes on Nagy was the best prospect. However, Nagy's radio announcement on October 25 that, after order was restored, negotiations could begin on the withdrawal of Soviet troops from Hungary, caused deep displeasure in the Kremlin.

The harsh measures taken against the participants in the popular movement (particularly the shooting of demonstrators in front of Parliament on October 25) further undermined the confidence of the Hungarian people in the leader of their government. On October 28, Nagy, having lost hope that the situation could be contained by Soviet troops, moved decisively to join hands with the insurrectionists. A cease-fire was declared, and the government recognized the insurgents' basic demands (the withdrawal of Soviet troops and the establishment of free elections). Nagy went on the radio to validate the ongoing events as part of a movement to assure national sovereignty. The Administration of State Security was abolished. At the beginning of November, the government was reorganized on a multiparty basis, which also included the parties that had comprised the ruling coalition in 1945–48. Its program aimed to reinstitute national sovereignty and guarantee democratic freedoms, but it did not provide for basic change in economic policies.

On October 31, after several days of debate, the Soviet leadership decided on a new military intervention to bring to power a government fully under Moscow's control. On November 1, citing unsanctioned Soviet troop movements on Hungarian territory, Nagy decided to withdraw Hungary from the Warsaw Pact and appealed to the United Nations for support in protecting its sovereignty.

After Soviet troops launched an attack on Budapest, on November 4, Nagy went on the radio to point out the illegality of this action, and then, with a group of his cohorts, found refuge in the Yugoslav Embassy. Despite Yugoslav pressure, Nagy refused to announce his retirement and declined to recognize the new government of János Kádár. On November 22, Nagy and his group were fraudulently removed from the embassy and transported by Soviet special service units to Romania. In diaries and unfinished memoirs written there, Nagy tried to not only justify his actions as having been dictated by revolutionary conditions but even claimed that they would "enrich Marxism-Leninism, with the events in Hungary providing a new experience in the communist battle." According to his view, in the Hungary of the 1950s, "the ideas of socialism and national independence had come to contradict each other. The basic sense of the Hungarian uprising lay in a search to find a way of removing this contradiction."

On February 26, 1956, the leadership of the Hungarian Socialist Workers' Party, having overcome the resistance of some party activists, resolved to open an investigation into the "Nagy affair." Nagy by that time had been publicly declared a "traitor," and on April 14 was returned to his homeland and imprisoned. A plan for his trial had been worked out by August; it accused him of an anti-state conspiracy. The trial, at first set for September 1956, was twice postponed at the Kremlin's insistence—the first time due to fears of complicating relations with Yugoslavia on the eve of a Communist parties' conference in Moscow, scheduled for November 1957, and the second time to avoid interfering with Soviet peace initiatives directed at the United States. On February 5, 1958, after examining the Nagy affair and his trial, Kádár called for "displaying both firmness and generosity." But the Hungarian leader did not take advantage of this opportunity for a compromise resolution. The extreme harshness he showed in the "Nagy affair" is clearly explained by the fact that Nagy personified in his very self the illegitimacy

of the Kádár regime. The trial of Nagy and his adherents took place on June 9–15, 1958. Nagy's death sentence was perceived by international public opinion as a warning to all "revisionists." The sentence was resoundingly condemned throughout the world.

The reburial of Nagy on July 16, 1989, marked by a demonstration of many thousands, symbolized the end of the Communist era in Hungary's history. On July 6, 1989, Imre Nagy was posthumously rehabilitated.

See also De-Stalinization; Hungarian Revolution; People's Democracy; Stalinism.

FURTHER READING

Dornbach, A. *The Secret Trial of Imre Nagy*. Westport, CT: Praeger, 1994.

János, R. M. *Nagy Imre. Politikai életrajz*. 2 vols. Budapest: Intezet, 1996–99.

Members of the Editorial Committee of the Congress for Cultural Freedom. *The Truth about the Nagy Affair: Facts, Documents, Comments*. Preface Albert Camus. London: Secker and Warburg, 1959.

Méray, T. *Thirteen Days That Shook the Kremlin: Imre Nagy and the Hungarian Revolution*. London: Thames and Hudson, 1958.

Nagy, I. *Egy évtized. Válogatott beszédek es irások*. 2 vols. Budapest: Szikra, 1954.

———. *On Communism: In Defense of the New Course*. Foreword Hugh Seton-Watson. New York: Praeger, 1957.

Sipos, J., et al., eds. *Nagy Imre es kora. Tanulmányok, forrásközlések*. Vol. 1. Budapest: N.I.A., 2002.

VJACHESLAV SEREDA AND ALEKSANDR S. STYKALIN

National Question, The

For Marxists, class is the primary category through which personal identity is defined and through which historical change takes place. The emergence of the nation-state across Europe in the 19th century and the fact that, by the end of that century, the Marxist movement was at its strongest in two multinational states—the Austro-Hungarian and Russian empires—meant that Marxism was forced to pay serious attention to the national question, which posed nationality as an alternative category to class for both identity and state organization. In this context "national question" refers to the problems posed by the presence of substantial national minorities in these two empires and in the Ottoman Empire, as well as the problems posed by colonized or oppressed peoples, typified in Europe by the Irish, with Switzerland and Norway providing further material for debate.

Marx's famous dictum that the workers "had no country" may suggest a dismissive attitude to the national question. Indeed, Marx and Engels considered that, while capitalism had given rise to nationalism, the eventual abolition of class exploitation would also entail the abolition of national differences. In the meantime, nationalism appeared to be a capitalist ruse designed to artificially wed workers to their own bourgeoisies and to promote divisions within the working class. But the appeal at the opening of the Communist Manifesto— "Workers of the world unite!"—showed that Marx and Engels recognized the divisive power of nationalism, and elsewhere they explicitly noted that the reality of nation-states could not be ignored. Thus, "since the proletariat must first of all acquire political supremacy, must rise to be the leading class of the nation, must constitute itself the nation, it is so far itself national, though not in the bourgeois sense of the word." In the case of oppressed nations, this might in certain circumstances make the national struggle progressive, inasmuch as it was aimed against the forces of reactionary empires.

It is apparent then that Marx and Engels recognized that while nationalism and national identity divided workers and served the interests of the bourgeoisie, there were times when national struggles might play a progressive role. One way out of this dilemma was to make a distinction between progressive and backward nations; but in practice this was often a crude distinction and seemed to later observers to rest on the sort of prejudices that most Socialists were committed to overcoming. Thus in 1848 Engels dismissed the historic claims of all the smaller Slav nations, while Marx himself has frequently been accused of anti-Semitism.

In spite of his generally disparaging attitude toward national movements, Marx's examination of the Polish national movement led him to an important positive conclusion: although the movement was dominated by, and based mostly on, the interests of the Polish aristocracy, if it was to have any chance of success against the might of the Russian Empire it would have to win the active support and participation of the Polish peasantry, and was therefore necessarily democratic and revolutionary in nature. It was this crucial observation that eventu-

ally developed into Lenin's much more consistent and less qualified support for national liberation movements. Already by the 1860s the logic of this argument had had an effect, leading Marx to reverse an earlier position and lend his support to the Irish Fenian movement and to the inclusion of a general right to national self-determination in the program of the First International in 1865.

It was left to the followers of Marx and Engels to elaborate a more sophisticated position. The vaguely defined right to national self-determination could be applied to nationalities who dominated a distinct territory, but was clearly inadequate for those groups who did not constitute a clear majority anywhere, or whose members were widely scattered across different territories and in different states. This was the case for numerous nationalities in the Austro-Hungarian Empire, as was recognized at the congresses of the Austrian Social Democratic Party in 1897 and 1899, and for Europe's Jews, whose largest Socialist organization, the Bund, adopted a position calling for "full national autonomy, regardless of the territory which it occupies" at its Fourth Congress in 1901.

It was the Austrian SDP members, or "Austro-Marxists," Otto Bauer and Karl Renner, who developed a full theoretical justification for this position. The advances in communications and education that took place under capitalism would proceed further under socialism. Far from eliminating national differences, socialism would enable even the smaller national groups to understand what differentiated them one from the other and to identify even more clearly with their own languages and culture. This represented a considerable departure from the classical Marxist position, since it implied that national differences were permanent. In other respects, however, Bauer and Renner conformed to Marxist orthodoxy in identifying a tendency for economic and state structures to become increasingly internationalized. Their solution, then, was to promote a system of personal national-cultural autonomy, under which centralized state structures could exist in parallel with a nonterritorial representative system that would administer to the educational and cultural needs of the members of a given nationality regardless of where they were living. In the short term, this meant that Socialist parties could be reorganized along national lines, as was the case with the Austrian SDP from 1897. This position had obvious appeal to members of national minorities who were radicalized by the national and economic oppression they had suffered, but were unwilling to abandon their national identities and merge into an undifferentiated revolutionary movement that might ignore their national aspirations. Outside of the Austro-Hungarian Empire, the Bund became the most powerful bearer of this message, but parties based on other minorities, in the Russian Empire and elsewhere, adopted similar positions which, consequently, had a significant bearing on the development of nationality policies after 1917.

For others, the Austro-Marxist position represented a major distortion of Marxist thinking on the national question, which threatened to divide and disrupt the revolutionary movement. The most ardent opponent of the Austro-Marxists was the Polish Socialist Rosa Luxemburg, who commanded a significant following in the Russian Social Democratic Labor Party. While allowing for a certain degree of local autonomy in cultural and linguistic matters, Luxemburg vehemently opposed any efforts to recognize the relevance of national differences to the revolutionary movement: "[The assertion of] national interests can only serve as a means of deception, of betraying the working masses of the people to their deadly enemy, imperialism." Even the notion that nations had a right to self-determination was divisive. Economic development meant that, under both capitalism and socialism, large, multinational states were more progressive than smaller, fragmented ones.

Lenin recognized to a far greater extent than his predecessors the revolutionary potential offered by the national question. The principle distinction he drew between nations, unlike Engels, was between oppressor nations like Russia and Great Britain, and oppressed nations like Poland and Ireland. By giving unqualified support to the liberation efforts of oppressed nations, Marxists could gain valuable allies in the fight against the major imperial states, and the workers of oppressor nations might rid themselves of the prejudices and national loyalties that diverted the class struggle. This included support for the right of territorially distinct nations to secede and form their own states, even where this might be perceived to work against the interests of class unity and economic progress. It might even entail forging alliances with bourgeois forces, so long as workers were organized independently and Socialist parties could criticize their Nationalist allies. Russian nationalism, on the other hand, was to be consistently opposed as chauvinistic and divisive, even while Lenin admitted and admired the superiority of Russian culture and language over those of most of the empire's minorities. At the same time, he was deeply skeptical of recognizing

national principles on any nonterritorial basis, as the Austro-Marxists and Bund did. Lenin's views on the national question became embodied in the policy of the Right of Nations to Self-Determination.

There were certainly problems with this analysis, not least the lack of clarity over the position Socialists were to take in response to specific demands for secession. Lenin's detractors have often accused him of exploiting national grievances while harboring a hidden agenda to destroy separate national identities to create a single, highly centralized state. Lenin answered this charge by drawing a parallel to support for the right to divorce, which did not entail encouraging women to actually seek divorce. Overall, the position was consistent and logical, and even principled. Although he oversaw the reincorporation of most of the territory of the Russian Empire into the new Soviet state, during his few years in power Lenin consistently supported the rights of national minorities and fought, to the very end of his active days, against any displays of what he considered to be Russian chauvinism.

With Lenin's attention diverted elsewhere after 1917, and his health eventually failing, the practical development of Soviet thinking on the national question fell to Stalin. Already in 1913, Stalin had written an article attacking the Austro-Marxist position on the national question. This included his since-famous definition of a nation as a "historically constituted, stable community of people, formed on the basis of a common language, territory, economic life, and psychological make-up manifested in a common culture." The insistence on national territory not only distinguished Stalin from the Austro-Marxists, but also informed his later efforts to promote ethnically distinct territorial units. Stalin also returned to the Marxist distinction between "backward" and "advanced" nations, although he was more concerned with their levels of economic and cultural development than with their ultimate historical role. Thus it was the duty of advanced nations to help others out of their backwardness, without disturbing the latter's national character.

Marxist discussions of the national question, starting as they did from the contradiction between class and national loyalties, could and did lead in a number of competing directions. These early debates not only informed the *nationality policies* of Communist regimes, they set much of the tone for postwar academic discussion of nationalism. For most Communist states, the national question was a problem to be solved. The reemergence of the national question across Eastern Europe in the late 1980s suggests that the problem was not solved, but this should not detract from the value of Marxist understandings of the issue.

See also Nationality Policies; Nations and Empire in the USSR.

FURTHER READING

Bottomore, T., and P. Goode, eds. *Austro-Marxism*. Oxford, UK: Clarendon Press, 1978.

Harris, N. *National Liberation*. London: Tauris, 1990.

Lenin, V. I. "La rivoluzione socialista e il diritto delle nazioni all'autodecisione." In *Opere complete*. vol. 23. Rome: Edtori Riuniti, 1966.

Luxemburg, R. *The National Question: Selected Writings*. Ed. H. B. Davis. New York: Monthly Review Press, 1976.

Stalin, I. V. *Il marxismo e la questione nazionale e coloniale*. Turin: Einaudi, 1948.

Van Ree, E. "Stalin and the National Question." *Revolutionary Russia* 7, no. 2 (December 1994): 214–38.

JEREMY R. SMITH

National Roads to Socialism

World communism, whose founding act was the Russian Revolution, exhibited a dual characteristic. On the one hand, it pursued a universalist revolutionary project, which implied a coordinated strategy, hierarchy of centralized organizations, global ideology, and one model for the creation of the apparatus and the leadership groups. On the other hand, it was distinguished by the totality of relations that each Communist Party established with the society in which it was developing. The first of these two characteristics, defined here as the teleological, was in the ideal typical case synonymous with cohesion, homogeneity, and unity, at least until 1956. The second, defined here as social, was synonymous with diversity. The relationship between the two was unequal, since the first dominated the second, but tensions between them could become manifest, as revealed in the example of the "national roads to socialism."

This concept made its appearance within the international Communist movement, and more specifically certain Western European Communist parties, in 1956, after the Communist Party of the Soviet Union's (CPSU) Twentieth Congress. The original idea related to the conditions that facilitated the pursuit of socialism, which had

to take specific national social and political conditions into account. These considerations led to a rejection of the Bolsheviks' seizure of power as a universal model—one they had attempted to impose on other Communist parties starting with the October Revolution in 1917.

The model had already been reexamined in the mid-1930s during the Communist International. At that time the debate, which had been inspired by the Spanish civil war, focused on the notions of democracy of a new type or people's democracies. The same topics reemerged in 1939–40 in the Baltic countries occupied by the Red Army, and then again between 1944 and 1947 in the European countries liberated from nazism. As a consequence, at different times, the Communist world was shaken by wide-ranging theoretical debates that raised at least two fundamental problem sets. The first set involved the relation between communism, democracy, socialism, and the dictatorship of the proletariat, which was fundamental to the Communist parties' political project and identity. The second set of problems related to the possibility of autonomy, or lack thereof, within the various Communist parties from the center—Moscow; at issue was an autonomy not only limited to reflecting the variety of different social realities, something that ultimately the Soviets might be able to tolerate, but also one that at the end of a long process freely chosen by each Communist Party, could reach a point where the element of strategy could be debated—one of the components of the teleological dimension of communism.

Already in 1934–35, the policies of the Popular Front and antifascism had interrupted those of the European Communist parties, which in spite of the various shifts by the Comintern, had consisted of preparing the revolution, the formation of the soviets, and the dictatorship of the proletariat according to the Russian example. It was in Spain, however, that for the first time high-level Communist leaders developed a more original approach. On September 18, 1936, the Comintern's secretary, Georgi Dimitrov, spoke of a "democratic republic" that entailed a "special state," "not yet a Soviet state," "but an anti-Fascist, left-wing state, in which the truly left-wing part of the bourgeoisie would take part"—in other words, "an authentic people's democracy," which he defined as a "particular form of the democratic dictatorship of the working and peasant classes in their current stage." Palmiro Togliatti also proposed some definitions of this "republic of a new type," which was anti-Fascist and adapted to the specific national situation. In a letter that Joseph Stalin, Vyacheslav Molotov, and Kliment

Voroshilov addressed to the president of the Spanish Council, Largo Caballero, at the end of the year, they explained that "the Spanish revolution opens up some roads that, in some aspects, differ from the path taken by Russia," and admitted the possibility of a parliamentary road. Historians have been divided over how to evaluate these changes: some have seen them as proof of the democratic spirit of those who proposed them; others believe it was a tactic designed to consolidate the international anti-Fascist alliance with the democracies that the USSR was attempting to sanction at the ideological level, and conversely, to organize the Communists' seizure of power in the name of antifascism. Whatever the case, Francisco Franco interrupted these reflections.

While these debates reemerged during the Sovietization of the Baltic countries in 1939–40, they arose even more forcefully in the aftermath of World War II in Central and Eastern Europe, but also in the Western countries. Togliatti, in Moscow, at the end of 1943 called for Italy to aim for a "consistent anti-Fascist democracy." When he returned to Italy in 1944, he spoke of a "progressive democracy" whose task was to destroy fascism and realize numerous reforms—a position that represented a shift from the Italian Communist Party's (Pci) previous positions. Maurice Thorez, also having returned to France from Moscow at the end of that same year, moved along a similar path. The French Communist Party (Pcf) went so far as to propose the establishment of a "new, people's, democracy"—an idea that its secretary elaborated in an interview with the *Times* on November 18, 1946, in which he underscored that it was possible to envision a transition to socialism that differed from the one taken by Russia.

The beginning of the Cold War disturbed this process, thereby provoking ongoing historical debates. Historians with a Communist sensibility generally believe these statements prove that these Communist parties were willing to pursue a democratic opening and autonomy from Moscow. Their adversaries state that the Pcf's and Pci's positions had been personally approved by Stalin, as is confirmed by newly available archival documents; that they were part of a similar plan implemented everywhere—with the fundamental difference that in the East, except for Czechoslovakia, which did not need it, the Red Army's presence allowed the Communist parties to seize power—in other words, that these same statements were not evidence of a Communist conversion to democracy. The Pcf and the Pci, however, were not actually following identical logics.

Togliatti initiated much more detailed theoretical work on an "Italian road to socialism," and attempted to make more careful distinctions between people's democracy and dictatorship of the proletariat—concepts that were instead to remain synonyms in the Pcf.

These differences came to light sensationally after 1956, when the CPSU's Twentieth Congress recognized the different roads to socialism. The Pci, initially reticent about Khrushchev's secret speech, started once more to develop the concept of an "Italian road to socialism" and alluded to the need for polycentrism, without breaking with Moscow or halting the expulsion from its ranks of those who asked for greater changes. The Belgian, Danish, Portuguese, and Spanish parties, and later the English and Swedish ones, immediately began to engage in further reflections on their own roads to socialism. Others, the Pcf among them, condemned what they defined as "revisionism" or even "national deviation." During the world conferences of Communist parties in 1957 and 1960, the French party continued to stick to traditional positions, defending the CPSU's leading role and supporting those principles that contributed to unity of action by the various Communist parties, even while admitting the possibility of some adjustments according to specific national situations. Only in the mid-1960s, especially under the leadership of the new general secretary, Waldeck Rochet, did the Pcf start to change, arguing in its turn for a "French and peaceful road to socialism," and announcing a "socialism with the colors of France" in the early 1970s. The Pcf thus moved closer to the Pci, especially during the Eurocommunist era. Both parties attempted to better define their plans and eventually changed, progressively and not without hesitations and contradictions, to the principles of democracy (recognition of pluralism, renunciation of the single party, abandonment of the dictatorship of the proletariat, respect for alternation in power, guarantee of freedom for all, and so on).

Overall the national roads to socialism resulted in a dual failure. First, the Communists' original idea that a single strategy for the seizure of power could be imposed had to be abandoned, thereby contributing to the crisis of international communism. Second, despite expending considerable energy, all the Western European Communist parties, beginning with the two most powerful ones, the French and Italian, perfected a plan that would never be implemented. Their obvious political powerlessness ultimately was one of the factors that contributed to their decline.

See also Antifascism; Eurocommunism; People's Democracy; Polycentrism; Popular Front.

FURTHER READING

Aga-Rossi, E., and G. Quagliarello, eds. *L'altra faccia della luna. I rapporti tra PCI, PCF e Unione Sovietica*. Bologna: Il Mulino, 1997.

Agosti, A. *Bandiere rosse. Un profilo storico dei comunismi europei*. Rome: Editori Riuniti, 1999.

Buton. P. *Une histoire intellectuelle de la démocratie, 1918–1949*. Paris: Seli Arslan, 2000.

Elorza, A., and M. Bizcarrondo. *Queridos camaradas: la Internacional Comunista y España, 1919–1939*. Barcelona: Planeta, 1999.

Gotovitch, J., M. M. Narinskij et al. *Komintern: l'histoire et les homes. Dictionnaire biographique de l'Internationale communiste*. Paris: Éditions de l'Atelier–Éditions ouvrières, 2001.

Machin, H., ed. *National Communism in Western Europe: A Third Way for Socialism?* London: Methuen, 1983.

Marcou, L. *Le mouvement communiste international depuis 1945*. Paris: Presses Universitaires de France, 1980.

Narinskij, M. M., and J. Rojahn. *Center and Periphery: The History of the Comintern in the Light of New Documents*. Amsterdam: International Institute of Social History, 1996.

Sassoon, D. *One Hundred Years of Socialism: The West European Left in the Twentieth Century*. London: Tauris, 1996.

Service, R. *Comrads! A History of World Communism*. Cambridge, MA: Harvard University Press, 2007.

MARC LAZAR

Nationalism

A great many of Marxism's and the Communist movement's original sources were intransigently internationalist as a matter of principle; the movement itself, however, has historically entertained an active and important relationship with various forms of nationalism. The relationship's content has been variable, both historically and geographically, and its political outcomes have been quite mixed, but it has had a crucial role in communism's ability to adapt and spread around the world.

The term "nationalism" rarely appeared in Lenin's writings prior to 1914. Yet Bolshevism's founder did approve of the republican, anti-imperialist party with a peasant base in China (the Guomindang, founded in 1909 by Sun Yat-Sen). He included it in the class of "revolutionary democracy" movements, and thought it was comparable to Russian populism, which at the beginning of the 20th century had given rise to the Socialist-Revolutionary Party. At the time Lenin considered this party a potential ally of the Marxists in toppling the czarist regime, establishing a republic, realizing agrarian reform, and introducing modern social legislation (the regime of the "democratic dictatorship of workers and peasants"). In the years immediately preceding and following World War I, during which an aggressive nationalism also started to spread among the socialist electorate in the most advanced European countries, which were ethnically relatively homogeneous, Lenin pointed to nationalism as both an enemy and a dangerous rival of socialism among the popular masses. In these countries it was a question of identifying its historically misleading and regressive nature, and fighting it head-on.

In the multinational Russian Empire, it was instead a question of neutralizing nationalism and preventing the national consciousness from conflicting or prevailing over class consciousness, distracting the working-class and popular movement from its natural revolutionary, democratic, and socialist goals. To this end, socialism could not limit itself to condemning the socially hostile and historically regressive content of nationalism; it needed to make the watchword of "national self-determination" its own. Socialists of the empire's dominant nationality, in other words, had to insist on the right of subjugated peoples to create their own separate state. The socialists who belonged to subjugated peoples were supposed to insist on remaining united to the dominant population, but in a new democratic and republican state (later to become socialist). In any case socialist parties were not supposed to organize along national lines (as had occurred with the Austrian party), to guarantee the basic unity of interests and intents of the working class they represented.

After their rise to power, the Bolsheviks attempted to qualify Lenin's prediction that the toppling of czarism would lead to a new "world revolution"—a democratic one in Russia and those parts of the world that were backward or colonial; socialist in the advanced West. They now actively worked for the creation of a new international body of Communist parties (the Bolshevik Party adopted that designation in April 1918 at its Seventh Congress) that would be capable of sparking worker-led and genuinely Marxist revolutions wherever possible. In the summer–fall of 1920, the Second Congress of the Comintern (in Moscow) and the First Congress of Peoples of the East (in Baku) focused on laying the foundations for a global movement of democratic-bourgeois forces, nationalist and socialist in backward and colonial countries, united by anti-imperialism. This orientation was only reinforced by the frequent failures that radical movements experienced in Germany, Hungary, and Italy (1919–21), the struggles that opposed the Turkish national revolution, the aspirations to complete sovereignty of the Afghan emirate and Persia from the British Empire, and the promising social and national movements that were developing in India and China. Bolshevik leaders thus hypothesized an alternative path for the world revolution: rather than immediately storming the bastions of advanced capitalism in the West, they would first focus on their colonies and fight their influence in the extra-European world.

Significant differences emerged within the Soviet party and the Comintern. Some (like Lenin) were inclined to an indiscriminate level of support for the new forces of extra-European nationalism, so long as these were oriented against the great powers. Others favored selective forms of support to those movements that were most socially aware (like the Indian Manabendra Nath Roy). Still others advocated original socialist-inspired, but also religious or ethnocultural (pan-Islamism or pan-Turkism), revolutionary hypotheses, which were potentially autonomous or even alternative to Bolshevism in numerous Asian countries, including the Soviet regions of Russia and central Asia. This was the case with the Tartar Mirza Sultan-Galiev, a member of the Russian Communist Party, who was arrested and expelled in 1923.

Even among revolutionary nationalists who engaged in dialogue with the Bolsheviks, a dualism emerged in their attitude toward the Communists. On the one hand, they appreciated the possibility of being granted the diplomatic and political help (potentially also economic and military) of the Soviet state. On the other hand, they mistrusted Communist parties and groups that were forming in their own countries (as in Kemalist Turkey, Ridā Khān's Persia, and emir Amanullah Khan's Afghanistan), and which they tended to contain and repress. Many Near Eastern and Asian nationalists were afraid that once they had come to power in their respective countries and laid the foundations for the most important national goals, the Communists would attempt to replace the institutions of the democratic-nationalist revolutions with a purely socialist revolution, as outlined in numerous authoritative programs of Russian and in-

ternational communism. In China the nationalists tried to forestall this by inviting the Communists to join their party in 1924. The Communists did indeed join, pushed by the Comintern, which had been impressed by the Indonesian Communists' collaboration with their local nationalist Islamist party (the Sarekat Islam), inspired by a syncretistic combination of socialism and nationalism that had been proposed by the Communist Tan Malaka.

The Soviet government also attempted to engage in an active relationship with European nationalism. In 1919, Karl Radek directed Moscow's attention to the anti-French and anti-English potential of German nationalism and revanchism (especially the Reichswehr's general staff, which strongly opposed the Versailles Treaty), in which the Soviets could detect a source of European political instability as well as new and more grounded revolutionary situations. The Rapallo Treaty between the USSR and Germany (April 1922) and its military clauses were proof of the two states' conviction that they had common interests, even though the German Communist Party (KPD) did not try to establish any understanding with the extreme nationalist and subversive Right, nor was it directed to do so from Moscow. In November 1923, however, the politburo changed course and pushed the KPD to start an armed insurrection, resulting in disaster. The political and diplomatic cooperation between the two governments ended after Germany's entry into the League of Nations (1926). Military cooperation instead continued until the exit of National Socialist Germany from the League of Nations in 1933.

After the failed attempts at revolution that the Comintern had promoted in Europe, Soviet hopes focused on China, where the Guomindang's left wing and the local Communists soon clashed with the party's right wing (and Chiang Kai-shek became the party's political and military leader in 1926), which wanted to postpone social transformations until after the country's reunification. The final split occurred in the spring–summer of 1927 and concluded with the nationalists' bloody victory. The previous year had also witnessed the bloody suppression of an autonomous attempt at insurrection by Indonesian Communists. Following these events, the Bolsheviks' faith in the potential for social revolution that they had originally attributed to anticolonialist and anti-imperialist nationalism was drastically reduced. The Anti-Imperialist Congress in Brussels (1927), organized by Willi Münzenberg, was the last initiative along these lines undertaken by the Communists. Two rising stars of the anticolonial movement participated in the congress: Jawaharlal Nehru, the future president of an independent India, who was interested in the Soviet sociopolitical experiment and its economic implications for backward countries; and Mohammad Hatta, the future vice president of the Republic of Indonesia (it gained independence in 1949). After 1927, though, the policies of the Comintern and the USSR's foreign policy became basically Eurocentric. Joseph Stalin had an important role in sparking the Korean War, but his aim was to lead the United States back to negotiations about the German question. Communism's international politics focused on Europe until his death.

A confirmation of this prolonged indifference for extra-European political developments was the worried state of mind with which Stalin welcomed the Chinese party's decision to initiate a civil war against the Guomindang (which was then allied with the United States) and seize power after Japan's defeat. He was afraid that this event would make U.S. negotiating positions in the context of the nascent Cold War in the European theater more intransigent. The Chinese Communists would, with the passage of time, harbor an increasing number of both political and territorial grudges of a purely nationalist character against the USSR. At the time of the political and diplomatic split between the two countries in 1962–64, the Chinese accused the Soviets of imperialism. It was also difficult to avoid seeing the Chinese move, based on a mixture of ideological and nationalist motives, as a contestation of the Soviet's lead role in the world Communist movement after that date (especially in Asia).

After the Nazi-Fascist aggression against the USSR, and above all the Comintern's dissolution in May 1943, a positive relationship with nationalism developed within European communism. Communists were exhorted to actively contribute to and even take the lead in defeating the German armies and their allies in those countries that had been overrun by them. With that goal in mind Stalin gave them an unprecedented amount of leeway, which was now deemed to be incompatible with the centralism that had dominated the old international Communist organization. The former Comintern parties were now supposed to establish wide-ranging political alliances of a patriotic and anti-Fascist nature, and build "national fronts" that could even include monarchical forces, on the basis of a national liberation, de-Fascistization, and democratization program. At the end of World War II, Moscow allowed some parties in Eastern Europe (Po-land and Czechoslovakia) and Western Europe (Italy and France) to theorize about "national roads to socialism," which were to be followed in the period after victory and liberation—roads that were meant to respect the political heterogeneity of the anti-Fascist coalitions in the liberated countries as well as their distinctive cultural, economic, and social characteristics. The national road line continued to develop in the Western Communist parties, but it disappeared in Eastern Europe with the advent of the Cold War and Sovietization of those countries, leading to one-party systems of "people's democracies."

Notwithstanding these developments, even in these countries an original mixture of nationalism and communism began to emerge. After the Soviet repression of the Hungarian national insurrection (1956), all the region's Communist dictatorships took steps to reduce their dependence on the military support and external "protection" of the USSR. In almost all cases they underwent a process of "nationalization," even though none could detach completely from their origins as regimes essentially imported thanks to the USSR's mostly military influence. The most significant cases in point are Poland (until the appearance of the social and national Solidarity movement in the 1970s), Hungary (which under János Kádár's leadership in the late 1960s autonomously experimented with the only, partially successful economic reforms in the Soviet bloc), and Romania, which starting in the 1960s witnessed the ultranationalist despotism of Nicolae Ceausescu, targeting the Hungarians in Transylvania internally and the USSR externally. A novel balance of nationalism and communism developed in Josip Broz Tito's Yugoslav Federation, which had been expelled from the "socialist camp" in 1948 by Stalin because of its aspirations for autonomy from Moscow. As a country it occupied an original position outside the international politicomilitary blocks and it attempted to implement equitable relations between the member republics (Bosnia, Croatia, Macedonia, Montenegro, Serbia, and Slovenia).

The national dimension of Communist policy was emphasized once more by Stalin during the CPSU's Nineteenth Congress (1952), when he called on the Communists of Western Europe to defend the principle of national sovereignty and their country's independence from U.S. hegemony. The national roads concept was raised once more as the official policy of international communism after the CPSU's Twentieth Congress (even if Khrushchev would have preferred the term "peaceful" or "parliamentary" roads to socialism). Palmiro Togliatti, the Italian leader, actually outlined an international Communist movement with a differentiated and "polycentric" leadership, adapted to the world's different regional contexts.

After Stalin's death, new political tendencies emerged on a global scale that, among other issues, reexamined the topicality of relations between nationalism and communism in the world's backward areas. The diverse movement of nonaligned countries, mostly Asian and African, that had emerged at the Bandung (Indonesia) Conference in April 1955, condemned colonialism and advocated its rapid destruction, called for "pacific coexistence" among states, and refused to belong to military alliances dependent on the two superpowers, in the name of "international peace and cooperation." Led by some politically significant countries (India, Egypt, Indonesia, and Kwame Nkrumah's Ghana, but also Yugoslavia), the Non-Aligned Movement found more interested interlocutors in the USSR and China than in the Western "bloc," which tended to see it as yet another Communist Trojan horse. Various backward nations sought the economic, political, and military aid of the USSR.

For its part, the Soviet Union garnered the sympathies of many countries that had embarked on a rapid decolonization process by offering cheap credit and military supplies. The countries that belonged to this group included Iran during Mohammad Mossadeq's leadership (1953) and Guatemala during the presidency of Jacobo Arbenz Guzmán, who paid for his short-lived attempt at social reform and reorientation toward the USSR by being removed from power. Crucial for the spread of this tendency in the third world was Egyptian president Gamal Abdel Nasser's rapid pro-Soviet evolution, which culminated in the brief Suez war against Anglo-French invaders (November 1956) who were challenging the Egyptian nationalization of the canal. The Egyptian example contributed to Syria's and Iraq's pro-Soviet shift during the following years, using the phrase "Arab socialism." In 1959, after their seizure of power in Cuba, Fidel Castro's young radical nationalists also converted to communism. All these leadership groups, it must be noted, started from nationalist positions with social goals, and had initially attempted to maintain a positive relationship with the United States, which turned them down because of fear they would be aiding the spread of international communism—something that the United States believed was omnipresent and insidiously polymorphic. This typical U.S. attitude toward backward

countries during the Cold War's first phase often had the effect of a self-fulfilling prophecy.

In any case, the local Communists' role during the episodes mentioned above was that of a minority, as in Iran, Syria, and Iraq, or almost nonexistent, as in Guatemala and originally Cuba. Of greater significance was the fact that some key leaders in the decolonization movement had Marxist sympathies (like Patrice Lumumba in Congo) and contacts with the international Communist movement (like Ahmed Sekou Touré in Guinea or Léopold Sédar Senghor in Senegal, via the French Communist Party). In South Africa anticolonialism was hegemonized by the Communists in Nelson Mandela's African National Congress. In other important cases, the relationship between Communists and nationalists remained tense, thus confirming the political precedents of the relationship between Communists and nationalists in Turkey and China after World War I. Nasser soon began to persecute the small group of Egyptian Communists. In Indonesia in 1965, the conservative nationalists and army under the leadership of General Suharto broke the traditional relation of collaboration between local Communists and (nationalist) President Sukarno, removing the latter and crushing the radical peasant movement influenced by the former. Vietnamese communism achieved a successful relationship with nationalism under the leadership of Ho Chi Minh, who managed to politically monopolize the forces of the local nationalists, both secular and religious (Buddhist). North Vietnam with a Communist government after the expulsion of the Japanese (1945) and the Communists of South Vietnam (organized first under the Viet Minh and later the Viet Cong) opposed the return of French colonialism to the South with an armed resistance, until they defeated the French militarily in 1954. From 1961 to 1973, the Vietnamese Communists fought a series of anti-Communist governments in the South and the U.S. troops supporting them. Ultimately the United States had to sign a peace accord with the North and withdraw. In 1975 Vietnam became a unified Communist state.

During the late 1970s the USSR experienced a growing restriction in its international area of influence. This was especially true in the Middle East. On the one hand, after 1973 it lost the support of the radical anti-Israeli Arab movement. On the other hand, after the 1978 Camp David Accords between Egypt and Israel, Egypt switched sides and promoted the United States as the principal guarantor of the Palestinian cause. On the African coast of the Mediterranean the USSR lost the support of the nationalist governments in Algeria and Libya. It therefore sought the support of guerrilla movements and improvised military governments in sub-Saharan Africa and the Horn of Africa: in southern Yemen after the departure of the British (1967); Angola and Mozambique, states that both gained independence in 1975; and Ethiopia with the military coup of 1977. Ayatollah Ruholla Mussaui Khomeini's Islamist revolution, aimed at all aspects of Westernization (U.S. capitalism and Soviet communism), gave the politically radical Muslim world an attractive alternative to both economic systems in 1979. The Soviet invasion of Afghanistan in support of the tottering forces of local communism at the end of that same year eroded whatever relations remained between communism and the nationalist movements of the non-Soviet Muslim world.

Leonid Brezhnev's USSR shifted toward a militarization of its presence in these backward areas, restricting its economic relations to arms sales. It simultaneously attempted to increase its geopolitical influence by bolstering its conventional armaments (the building of oceanic fleets along with the establishment of naval and air bases in different regions). Finally after the rise of perestroika, Mikhail Gorbachev rejected the previous policy of Soviet aid to countries attempting to gain national affirmation and armed movements inspired by radical nationalist and social goals—a policy whose purpose had been to promote the USSR's own political and ideological goals.

See also Anti-imperialism; Decolonization; Islam; Nationality Policies; National Question, The; National Roads to Socialism; Nonalignment; World Revolution.

FURTHER READING
Carr, E. H. *The Bolshevik Revolution.* London: Macmillan, 1951.
———. *Socialism in One Country (1958–1959).* New York: Macmillan, 1958–64.
Connor, W. *The National Question in Marxist-Leninist Theory and Strategy.* Princeton, NJ: Princeton University Press, 1984.
Golan, G. *The Soviet Union and National Liberation Movements in the Third World.* Boston: Allen and Unwin, 1988.
Hough, J. F. *The Struggle for the Third World.* Washington, DC: Brookings Institution, 1986.
Nogee, J. L., and R. H. Donaldson. *Soviet Foreign Policy since World War II.* New York: Pergamon, 1985.
Procacci, G. *Storia del XX secolo.* Milan: Bruno Mondadori, 2000.
Service, R. *Comrads! A History of World Communism.* Cambridge, MA: Harvard University Press, 2007.

Seton-Watson, H. *From Lenin to Khrushchev: The History of World Communism.* New York: Praeger, 1960.
———. *Nations and States.* London: Methuen, 1977.
Various authors. *The Impact of the Russian Revolution, 1917–1967.* Oxford: Oxford University Press, 1967.

FRANCESCO BENVENUTI

Nationality Policies

Nationality policies were developed by the early Soviet regime in large part as ad hoc responses to the forces that tore apart the Russian Empire in 1917 and during the civil war of 1918–20. There were numerous changes and variations in these policies throughout the Soviet period, but some of their essential features remained constant and also informed the policies of other Communist regimes.

The clearest feature of these policies was the creation of a federal system. From 1919 onward, a number of autonomous republics and autonomous regions were created for national minorities that were concentrated in particular geographic areas. In 1923, a more formal federal system was created in the form of the Union of Soviet Socialist Republics. Consisting initially of four federal units, it numbered fifteen full republics after the Second World War. The largest of these was the Russian Soviet Federative Socialist Republic, within which there were eventually dozens of autonomous republics and autonomous regions, which also existed in smaller numbers elsewhere in the USSR. Each of the larger nationalities enjoyed formal representation at the center in the bicameral Council of Nationalities.

Underpinning this federal policy was the notion that nationalities could be organized on only a territorial basis. In the 1920s, much smaller non-Russian communities could be organized, even when they formed a minority in a given district or town, through a system of national soviets, but even before these were abolished in the 1930s it was the larger federal units that formed the framework within which nationality policies could operate. In the 1920s these policies were summed up under the name *korenizatsiia*, roughly translatable as "rooting." This involved the training and promotion of members of the local nationality in the republics and regions, expanding the network of non-Russian schools, standardization of national languages and scripts, and the promotion of national culture in the form of literature, music, dance, and dress. Together with the formal recognition accorded to nationalities through the federal system, these policies not only acknowledged the existence of national differences, but also sought to preserve and promote them. Autonomy meant that each republic, and to a lesser extent each region, could have a say not only in matters of culture and education, but also over its own systems of agriculture and justice. Under successive Soviet constitutions, nationalities were even granted the formal right to secede from the Soviet Union should they so desire. In practice, however, this right was never put to the test, and the exercise of control locally through the centralized Communist Party of the Soviet Union ensured that the republics and regions would not push autonomy too far. Another feature of nationality policy from the beginning was that only the central authorities could determine which groups constituted a nation, and only these officially recognized nationalities could enjoy the benefits of nationality status. While the number of officially recognized nationalities ran into the hundreds in the 1920s, the total was gradually scaled down under Stalin, with the consequent loss of territorial status and other rights for dozens of smaller groups.

The consolidation of Stalin's power made little outward difference to these features of nationality policy. However, the atmosphere changed markedly as a result of a significant turnover in the personnel who had been promoted under the policies of korenizatsiia through a series of leadership purges, beginning in Ukraine in 1928 and embracing every national republic and region by 1935. The Russian population, which had often been put at a disadvantage by the policies of korenizatsiia, especially in the national republics, now benefited from another shift in national policy. This is most clearly seen in the way that official accounts of Russian history were altered to celebrate Russian cultural, scientific, and political achievements, and even the military successes of Russian czars. This "rehabilitation of the Russians" not only restored pride and self-confidence to the Russian population, it made a real difference to career opportunities, access to higher education, and responses to political demands. Another shift in the 1930s affected the distribution of the Russian population. Whereas in the early years some measures had been taken to remove Russians (and especially Cossacks) from non-Russian areas, and internal borders had been drawn so as to create, as far as possible, ethnically homogenous territories, in the 1930s, and as a direct result of industrialization, the migration

of Russians into the other republics was encouraged. Already in the mid-1920s boundaries were being redrawn so as to reflect economic rather than ethnological priorities. After 1945, this policy reached new heights with the deliberate resettlement of Russians into the newly sovietized republics of Estonia and Latvia.

Various historians have described the shifts in policy of the 1930s as amounting to a policy of Russification, or at least to one of promoting a single Soviet identity to replace separate national ones. A law of 1938 made the teaching of Russian as a second language in non-Russian schools compulsory, but at no point under Stalin was there any attempt to force non-Russians to adopt Russian as their first language, or to abandon their national cultures or identities. There is, rather, more of a case to support the suggestion that policies were now aimed at promoting a single Soviet identity, centered on the cult of Stalin and based mostly on Russian language and culture. Especially as the prospect of war loomed larger, the common aims and aspirations of the Soviet peoples were emphasized. A central part of the official ideology, however, was the multinational character of the Soviet state. The nationality-based federal structure remained intact, and national cultures, particularly as represented by folk dance and music, were celebrated not only in the republics and regions, but also at a series of festivals in Moscow and elsewhere. The USSR was hailed as a "brotherhood of nations," albeit one in which the Russians played the role of elder brother. In the course of the Great Patriotic War the Russian role acquired yet greater prominence.

This did not mean that the role of other nationalities in the war effort was ignored. In a symbolic gesture, a Georgian soldier joined a Russian one in raising the Red flag over Berlin's Reichstag in 1945. But for one group of nationalities, policy took a sharp turn. Between 1941 and 1945, Germans of the Volga region, Karachai, Kalmyks, Chechens, Ingush, Balkars, and the Meshketian Turks of Transcaucasia were deported wholesale from their republics or regions and resettled in scattered groups in Siberia and Central Asia. Each of these nationalities was accused of being ready to ally with the invading Germans, and was punished accordingly. The nature of this punishment reflected not only the belief that nations could be destroyed by severing their links with a national territory, a long-standing notion in Soviet thinking on the national question, but also, contrary to Marxist principles, that the primary marker of identification for individuals was nationality and that all members of a given nationality shared certain inherent characteristics and political tendencies. After the war, Jews too suffered from a renewal of the persecution that had been a feature of pre-revolutionary Imperial Russia, and may themselves have faced wholesale forced deportation and resettlement under a plan that was only forestalled by Stalin's death in 1953.

During the leadership struggle after Stalin's death, nationality policy underwent a number of twists and turns. Non-Russians, particularly non-Russian political leaders, benefited at first as Lavrenty Beria restored a number of powers to the republics and ensured that the first secretary in each republic would be a member of the local titular nationality; and then Nikita Khrushchev devolved economic decision making to the republics and promoted large numbers of non-Russians, especially Ukrainians, to leading positions in the government and CPSU, where they played a key role in ensuring Khrushchev's victory over his rivals in 1957.

After consolidating his position, however, Khrushchev reversed the decentralizing policies of the earlier years. A 1958 law made it possible for non-Russian children to go to Russian schools. This was the first clear challenge to Lenin's policy that all children should be educated in their mother tongue, and although it made little impact in the short term, in the longer term non-Russian education was gradually eroded in the autonomous republics and regions, and in some of the Union's republics. Ominously, in official discourse rhetoric shifted from "the brotherhood of nations" to an anticipated "merger of nations." A new wave of migration further diluted the concentrations of nationalities in their own republics and regions. Khrushchev's policy of frequently switching bureaucrats and party officials between jobs, while it applied at all levels and equally in the RSFSR, was also perceived in the republics as undermining the principle of local national leadership. Under Leonid Brezhnev, these policies were reversed in favor of the "stability of cadres," the most noticeable effect of which was the longevity in office of republican leaders, such as Sharaf Rashidov, who was Communist Party first secretary in the Uzbek Soviet Socialist Republic from 1959 to 1983. The effect of this was to allow leaders, within certain limits, to conduct nationalizing policies within the Union republics. The status of the autonomous republics and regions, however, gradually diminished.

It seems likely that Mikhail Gorbachev had no intention of tinkering with the system when he assumed office in 1985, but a number of crises in the national republics, most notably riots in Kazakhstan in 1986, led to

a series of changes in nationality policies. Initially this involved repealing unpopular language laws and reforming the Council of Nationalities, but growing national unrest, which took the form of violent ethnic conflict in the Caucasus and the rise of national Popular Fronts in the Baltic republics and elsewhere, triggered debates on more wholesale reforms. From 1989 onward, the republics took the initiative themselves, issuing declarations of sovereignty that forced Gorbachev to undertake drastic reform if he was to have any chance of preventing outright secession. This took the shape of a new Union Treaty that would have given the republics much greater powers than before, and for which Gorbachev appeared to obtain a popular mandate in a March 1referendum. Just as Gorbachev was making his final revisions to the draft treaty, however, the failed coup of August 1991 threw the process into disarray, culminating in the formal dissolution of the USSR on December 31, 1991.

At the end of the Great Patriotic War, Stalin's earlier predilection for nationally homogenous territories resurfaced in the widespread movement of populations between the Soviet Union and the East European states that were now in the Soviet sphere of influence. Most affected were Ukrainians, Russians, and Poles around the USSR's western borders, and the Germans expelled from Poland and Czechoslovakia. The result, combined with the effects of the Holocaust, was that Poland became virtually mononational. Elsewhere in Eastern Europe, populations remained highly mixed and Soviet-style nationality policies were adopted, with federal systems applied in Czechoslovakia and Yugoslavia. Under pressure from Moscow, most Communist regimes guaranteed education and language rights for national minorities, and autonomous regions such as the Hungarian Autonomous Region in Romania were created. After Stalin's death, however, these pressures were relaxed, and Communist regimes tended to cut back on minority rights and to pursue assimilationist policies in line with their adoption of more nationalistic rhetoric and slogans, most notably in Romania.

Czechoslovakia had already been a federation before the war. Although the Czech and Slovak nations were formally on an equal footing, the population of the former outnumbered that of the latter by two to one, and Czechs generally enjoyed higher standards of living and predominated in leadership positions. The system was widely characterized as one of "asymmetry," though the Slovak Socialist Republic did enjoy considerable self-rule and several separate ministries, for example of justice.

The height of Slovak autonomy was achieved in 1968, but following the Warsaw Pact invasion and the Soviet-inspired "normalization" that followed, further recentralization took place. The gap between the formal trappings of federalism and the actual workings of political power was even greater than in the Soviet case, and the federal system did not long survive the reintroduction of democracy in 1989.

Yugoslavia's nationality policies showed the greatest departure from the Soviet model, although the two systems also shared a number of common features. After a brief flirtation with the idea of a Balkan Federation including Romania, Bulgaria, and Albania, Tito's split with Stalin in 1948 allowed Yugoslavia to go its own way. Yugoslavia differed from all other Communist states in that no single nationality could be dominant in demographic terms. (Serbs did tend to predominate in the military and party leadership, though Tito himself was a Croatian.) Economic decentralization in the mid-1960s further encouraged the six federal republics (Serbia, Croatia, Slovenia, Bosnia-Herzegovina, Montenegro, and Macedonia) and two autonomous republics (Vojvodina and Kosovo—both in Serbia) to press for their own interests above those of the federation as a whole, placing a series of strains on the system, most notably in the crises of 1969 and 1971. The new constitution of 1974 involved a complete overhaul of the system, so that it ended up resembling more of a loose confederation of separate states than a federation. Only foreign, military, and some trade matters remained for the most part in the hands of the federal center, while power in all domestic matters devolved to the republics, each of which moreover had veto power over changes to the constitution.

As long as Tito was alive and the League of Communists remained unified, centrally determined policies could still be implemented. Following Tito's death in 1980, the collective presidency stipulated by the constitution managed to balance the interests of the different republics for a short period. By the late 1980s, however, it was clear that the system could not cope with the pressures of economic decline, the erosion of Communist legitimacy, and the readiness of key leaders to exploit nationalistic animosities. It may be an exaggeration to blame the Yugoslav model and Tito's nationality policies for the bloodshed that accompanied the breakup of Yugoslavia, but as a long-term solution to the national question, they were clearly inadequate.

Although national minorities constitute only 6–8 percent of the population of Communist China, they occupy approximately 60 percent of China's total territory and number about ninety-one million people (1990 census). They include significant nationalities such as 15 million Zhuangzu, 9.8 million Manchu, 8.6 million Chinese Moslem Huizu, and a further 7.2 million Moslem Uighur, 4.8 million Mongolians, and 4.6 million Tibetans. Given their location along strategically important borders, the international links of the Uighur and Mongolians, and the high global profile of the Tibetans, the nationalities policies have been more important in China than their proportion of the overall population might suggest. From 1949 onward, China has pursued nationality policies similar in many respects to those of the Soviet Union, the most obvious difference being that the nationalities have never had any constitutional right to secede. Although China is not a federation, it includes five autonomous regions that are equivalent in size and importance to provinces and enjoy particular national rights (Ningxia Hui, Xinjiang Uighur, Guangxi Zhuang, Inner Mongolia, and Tibet). There are thirty-one smaller autonomous *zhou* (districts) and ninety-six autonomous counties, in a hierarchical structure paralleling that of the Union republics, autonomous republics, and autonomous regions in the USSR. In total, fifty-five national minorities are recognized, each of which is, under the Chinese constitution, entitled to at least one representative in the National People's Congress. In addition to being able to regulate educational, linguistic, and cultural affairs, each autonomous area is also in charge of its own finances. A Central Institute for Nationalities trains administrators to run the national areas and, again in a manner not dissimilar from common practice in the Soviet Union, the government head of an autonomous area is a member of the titular nationality, while the party head is usually Han Chinese, with Han and local minorities being well represented at the next level of the government and party structures, respectively.

The system of autonomy has not always worked to the benefit of national minorities, however. The training of minority leaders in a separate institute cuts them off from the alumni networks that are so important to advancement in central government. Financial devolution can be a disadvantage, so that while autonomous areas have seen huge increases in economic output and standards of living, the gap between them and the wealthier Han regions has actually been growing. In the 1950s and again in the 1980s, substantial migration of Han into minority areas was perceived as an encroachment on national rights. On the other hand, Communist China's commitment to the preservation of minority groups is reflected in their exemption from rigorous family planning laws.

This has not prevented a series of national revolts among China's minorities: in Tibet in 1959, 1987, and 1989, and among the Moslem Uighurs in the 1960s. The latter was a response to the policies of the Cultural Revolution, which included the desecration of mosques and the suppression of religious activities. National and religious rights were restored in 1976.

Consideration of Chinese nationality policies has to include an account of policy toward the dominant Chinese Han, who make up some 94 percent of the population. Although the Han speak at least eight mutually unintelligible dialects, only three of these—Mandarin, Cantonese, and Shanghainese—are officially recognized. The Han of different regions are as different from one another as many European nationalities, but official policy has always been to stress the unity of the Han as a single nationality. This is based on a genuinely shared cultural and historic heritage. Nevertheless, the promotion of a single Han nationality and administratively separate national minorities has led a number of observers to conclude that a deliberate divide and rule policy has been at work.

Twentieth-century nationality policies in Communist countries can be viewed in one of two ways. In negative terms, policies were aimed at maintaining some sort of peace in multinational states and preventing fragmentation along national lines, or in other words, neutralizing the potential effects of nationalism. In more positive terms, policies were aimed at promoting and preserving different nationalities, while simultaneously incorporating them into a unitary state and leading them to embrace communism. If the former was the aim, then the collapse of the Soviet Union, and the bloody conflicts that accompanied the breakup of Yugoslavia, suggest that in the long-term the policies failed. If the latter was the main aim, as seems to have been the case in the early Soviet years and in postwar Yugoslavia and China, then the breakup of Communist federal systems can be regarded as a direct, if unintended, result of the policies, while China has avoided a similar scenario in part due to the relatively small numbers involved.

See also Deportation of Nationalities in the USSR; National Question; Nationalism; Nations and Empire in the USSR.

FURTHER READING

Bugajski, J. *Ethnic Politics in Eastern Europe: A Guide to Nationality Policies, Organizations, and Parties*. Armonk, NY: Sharpe, 1993.

Glenny, M. *The Balkans, 1804–1999: Nationalism, War and the Great Powers*. London: Granta, 1999.

Hoston, G. A. *The State, Identity, and the National Question in China and Japan*. Princeton, NJ: Princeton University Press, 1994.

Martin, T. *The Affirmative Action Empire: Nations and Nationalism in the Soviet Union, 1923–1939*. Ithaca, NY: Cornell University Press, 2001.

Simon, G. *Nationalism and Policy Toward the Nationalities in the Soviet Union: From Totalitarian Dictatorship to Post-Stalinist Society*. Boulder, CO: Westview Press, 1991.

Suny, R. G. *The Revenge of the Past: Nationalism, Revolution and the Collapse of the Soviet Union*. Stanford, CA: Stanford University Press, 1993.

JEREMY R. SMITH

Nations and Empire in the USSR

The Soviet Union's policy toward nationalities, as a system of theoretical premises, institutional arrangements, and consolidated practices that regulated relations between them, was the result of the historical evolution of Marxist theory and Soviet society. The concept of nation that Stalin developed with Lenin's help in 1913 was defined as "a historically constituted, stable, community of people, formed on the basis of language, territory, a shared economic life and a mentality that is manifested in a common culture." Soviet policy toward nationalities was strongly influenced by this connection between ethnicity, territory, and political administration, and encapsulated in the idea of the national state.

Marxism-Leninism has also always interpreted nation and nationalism as transitory social phenomena subordinate to the class struggle. For Lenin and Stalin the issue of nationalities was always subordinate to the theory of proletarian revolution, which would eventually lead to a homogeneous society in which national origin and the sense of ethnic belonging would disappear. The Bolshevik Party only considered nationalism as a useful instrument to destabilize the multiethnic Russian Empire, topple czarism, and seize power. Before the October Revolution, the right of national self-determination was one of the focal points of the Bolshevik program on the issue of nationalities. The self-determination slogan allowed the Bolsheviks to obtain the support of many national movements within the czarist empire. After they had seized power, however, the Bolsheviks had to face the disintegration of the Russian Empire into a jumble of small national states that would have weakened the economic and social foundations of the new revolutionary state. Although they had earlier been opposed to federal principles, they had to convert to federalism as an indispensable instrument to reunite the past empire's elements. Since national states had already arisen in the border areas, Lenin had no choice but to build the new state as a federation based on national and territorial autonomy. Soviet Russia thus became the first modern state that based its federal structure on an ethnic principle.

Even though some parts of the Russian Empire like Poland, Finland, and the Baltic countries managed to achieve independence, the new Soviet state inherited a significant portion of the territory that had belonged to the empire, and it was inhabited by almost two hundred distinct nationalities. At the end of 1922 the integration of the ethnic periphery into a single state concluded with the proclamation of the Union of Soviet Socialist Republics. The USSR's first Constitution, approved in early 1924, gave the center control over foreign policy and defense, finances and planning, transportation, communication, and foreign trade, but it allowed the republics to maintain important rights and powers, including various attributes of statehood and the formal right to secede from the Soviet Union.

The principal tool for the construction of a unitary socialist state and the preservation of its internal stability was the centralized Communist Party, which was devoid of any nationalist preconception. In Lenin's words, "The proletarian party strives to create the most inclusive possible state, because it benefits the working class; it strives to bring nations closer together and to encourage their greater unity, but it wants to pursue these objectives not with violence, but exclusively by means of a fraternal union of the workers and the working class of all nations." In all versions of the Soviet Constitution, up to the last (1977), the single party was declared to be Soviet society's guiding force, the center of its political system as well as all state and public organisms. The USSR was a federal state composed of several dozen ethnic and territorial units organized according to an elaborate administrative hierarchy. The highest form of statehood granted to national groups was becoming a republic of the union.

From its inception, Soviet federalism was conceived not as a means to ensure an albeit limited form of eco-nomic and political sovereignty for the federal state's components but rather as a means to integrate the political elites and educated classes among the ethnic minorities in the Soviet state, prevent discrimination on the basis of ethnic origin, and maintain internal political stability. If empire is commonly understood as the domination by and government of one nation or society over others, the Soviet Union during the first decade of its existence combined some imperial characteristics with other decidedly anti-imperial ones, which were founded in the rejection of an imperial heritage, which manifested itself in pockets of Russian chauvinism and the privileged position of Russia in the czarist empire.

From its birth, Soviet federalism was based on a policy that favored the cultural and economic development of ethnic minorities. Already during the 1920s a special quota system for local populations in higher education and a policy favoring recruitment of "indigenous" (*korenizacija*) elements to local administrations came into being. These policies represented the first consistent application of the principle of "reverse discrimination" (affirmative action), based on ethnic membership. The Leninist period in the policy toward nationalities extended to the early 1930s; influential local elites had emerged in the union's republics, and their power was partially based on the support of their respective ethnic groups. The role assigned to oppressed nations by the doctrine of world revolution was one of opposition toward economic and political dependence on a central power.

Stalin's government abandoned the doctrine of world revolution and replaced it with that of building "socialism in one country," and the leader concentrated his greatest efforts on strengthening the centralized state in order to guarantee the traditional supremacy of the center over the ethnic periphery. Stalin's new direction toward "revolution from above," based on forced industrialization and the collectivization of the countryside, also entailed a radical shift in the policy toward nationalities. The struggle against Great Russian nationalism that had been so pronounced during the Leninist period was discarded, while the repressive activities of the central government were directed especially at the "bourgeois nationalism" of the ethnic minorities. During Stalin's Great Purges of the 1930s, old Bolshevik internationalists and minority representatives were eliminated from the center's political elite, and the ethnic political elites that had succeeded in creating their local power bases were destroyed. The majority of the key positions at the top of the party-state were taken by Slav nationalities, especially Russians.

With all the political and economic power concentrated in the hands of the Communist Party's top echelons, the Soviet state began to resemble an imperial formation of a new type. Unlike the czarist empire, the Soviet Union was not the Russian Empire but rather the Soviet one, and as such could not be identified with one single ethnic group.

During the Stalinist period institutional arrangements were devised that allowed the policy of nationalities to be carried out efficiently, and such arrangements would characterize the Soviet Union until its dissolution. Ethnic identity was institutionalized on both a group and an individual level. The concept of statehood for the principal ethnic minorities became an institutional reality, creating a federation of ethnic and territorial units organized according to an elaborate administrative hierarchy. This complicated process was completed toward the end of the Stalin era. The number of officially recognized nationalities was gradually reduced from 190 in the 1926 census to 104 in the 1970 census. Ethnic groups were divided according to whether they had an officially recognized territory along with a stable position in the hierarchy of ethnic and territorial units, or whether they did not and were therefore considered minor nationalities with no territory. The USSR thus became a federal state composed during its last period of fifteen republics and a constellation of ethnic units like the autonomous republics, the autonomous provinces, and the national districts. The status of republic was the highest degree of statehood that could be granted to a Soviet nationality, while the other ethnic and territorial units occupied a significantly inferior position. The borders between the republics and the other ethnic and territorial units, especially in Caucasus and central Asia, were traced arbitrarily, on the basis of a divide-and-conquer policy, often violating historical traditions as well as the ethnic and demographic situation. This policy reinforced the central government's role as the supreme arbiter in local ethnic conflicts and consolidated the dominant position of the center with respect to the periphery.

The institutionalization of ethnic membership (nationality) at the individual level was implemented by introducing the system of internal passports at the end of 1932. Initially the registration of nationality, justified by the need to guarantee the rights of minorities, was based on self-identification, but after several years it was transformed into a simple bureaucratic procedure. In the late 1930s a Soviet citizen's nationality was determined on the basis of the registration on the parents' passports. Those

who were born from mixed marriages could choose between the father's or mother's nationality, but only at the time the first passport was issued; any subsequent change was forbidden. This registration of ethnic origin established rigid divisions between nationalities, determined each citizen's self-identification, and gave the Soviet regime the means to organize preferential ethnic treatment policies within their respective officially recognized territories. The creation of different ethnic and territorial entities created a bond among the ethnic group, its territory, and the local political administration. The individual republic's political elites were co-opted by the central apparatus of the party-state and remained tied to this central authority rather than their respective ethnic groups; rigid controls by the repressive apparatus made any attempt by the local elite to encourage nationalist aspirations risky and improbable.

Among the most important measures to encourage integration was an institutional isomorphism: all the union's republics received identical structures in the areas of state organization, bureaucracy, and higher education; analogous institutions were created for research and development, including each individual republic's Academy of Sciences; and similar institutions were established for the production and diffusion of culture in the various national languages. By expanding local bureaucracies and giving preferential access to those nationalities with "entitlements" to higher education, and subsequently administrative and managerial positions, the central state managed to create jobs and protect the interests of the educated middle classes in each republic, thus preserving political stability within the multinational state. Thanks to this combination of measures aimed at integration and repression, the Soviet state managed to repress nationalist and separatist movements, but also to satisfy the interests of key ethnic groups. The potentially explosive situation was mostly avoided among those groups most exposed to nationalist tendencies, such as the representatives of the ethnic minorities' middle classes and political elites, which could see their social mobility blocked by the majority.

This nationalities' policy carried out by a central redistributive state endowed with a strong repressive apparatus showed it was capable of maintaining internal stability and opposing ethnic nationalism during a period of extensive development and relative abundance of resources. Once the ability to repress and redistribute started to fail—because of an institutional crisis—the tensions between the individual republics started to get out of control, and tensions between the imperial center and the republics unraveled to an even greater degree. The system's crisis revealed a contradiction internal to the Soviet empire, and one attributable to its not being a national empire. In the Soviet economy, as in the economies of other imperial regimes, the production of high value-added products occurred in the Russian center, while low value-added products were produced on the ethnic periphery. Yet this hierarchical differentiation of productive processes did not lead to what should have been its direct consequence: the high standard of living at the center as opposed to that at the periphery. The paradoxical fact that the standard of living was often higher at the periphery than at the Russian imperial center was the effect of an economy dominated by the military-industrial complex. The Soviet scarcity of consumer goods was determined by the dominance of heavy industry and the weapons industry in the Russian economy. The ethnic periphery instead enjoyed a more direct connection with the food and consumer goods markets, whose role in daily life grew proportionally to the weakening of the redistributive state. In an economy that was closed to the world market, the periphery, with its low value-added products intended for the internal market, could ensure that its population enjoyed a higher standard of living than that at the center, causing the Russian population to reject the empire.

The unintended result of this policy was to lay the foundations for the future independence of the Soviet republics. Each Soviet republic now had its own territory, political elite, educated middle class, and cultural production in the local language. The republics therefore resembled the states that had lost their national independence. The policy of nationalities helped overturn the traditional emigration model that had characterized both the Russian Empire and the Soviet state during its first five decades. Starting in the early 1970s, the centuries-old pattern of Russian migration from the center toward the periphery was reversed, and an exodus of Russians from central Asia, Kazakhstan, Caucasus, and even Ukraine began. Simultaneously, because of an increase in ethnic tensions, the opposite process started to occur: the return of minority members to their own republics. So the policy actually led to the ethnic homogeneousness of the various Soviet republics—a phenomenon completed after the Soviet Union's collapse.

During the late 1980s, because of the deepening crisis of the Soviet system, strong nationalist and separatist movements began to emerge in the Baltic republics,

Ukraine, Georgia, Moldavia, and so on. As a result the Soviet Union, whose ethnic components exhibited strong differences in their degree of economic development, political culture, and especially demographic makeup, became unstable. A high degree of coercion would have been necessary to keep this political construct together. But the Soviet regime's repressive apparatus was considerably weakened, and its political elite no longer had either the will or resoluteness necessary to employ force against separatism. Mikhail Gorbachev's government could not prevent the ethnic conflicts between the republics of Armenia and Azerbaijan, nor the pogroms against the Meshket Turks in Uzbekistan. The first to leave the USSR were the Baltic republics, which unilaterally declared their independence in 1991. A few months later, in December 1991, the leaders of the three Slav republics—Russian, Ukrainian, and Belorussian—officially declared the old union pact of 1922 null and void and proclaimed the Soviet Union's dissolution. The largest country in the world suddenly and peacefully fell apart following the ethnic and territorial borders of the republics, and formed fifteen new independent states.

See also Command Economy, The; Dissolution of the USSR; Nationalism; National Question, The; Nationality Policies; State, The.

FURTHER READING

Barkey, K., and M. Von Hagen, eds. *After the Empire: Multiethnic Societies and Nation-building.* Boulder, CO: Westview Press, 1997.

Bremmer, I., and R. Taras, eds. *Nation and Politics in the Soviet Successor States.* Cambridge: Cambridge University Press, 1993.

Connor, W. *The National Question in Marxist-Leninist Theory and Strategy.* Princeton, NJ: Princeton University Press, 1984.

Martin, T. D. *The Affirmative Action Empire: Nations and Nationalism in the Soviet Union, 1923–1939.* Ithaca, NY: Cornell University Press, 2001.

Pipes, R. *The Formation of the Soviet Union: Communism and Nationalism, 1917–1923.* Cambridge, MA: Harvard University Press, 1964.

Stalin, I. V. *Marxism and the National Question: Selected Writings and Speeches.* New York: International Publishers, 1942.

Suny, R. G. *The Revenge of the Past: Nationalism, Revolution, and the Collapse of the Soviet Union.* Stanford, CA: Stanford University Press, 1993.

Zaslavsky, V. *Dopo l'Unione Sovietica. La perestroika e il problema delle nazionalità.* Bologna: Il Mulino, 1991.

————. *Storia del sistema sovietico: l'ascesa, la stabilità, il crollo.* Rome: Carocci, 2001.

VICTOR ZASLAVSKY

Neruda, Pablo

Ricardo Eliecer Neftalí Reyes Basoalto, alias Pablo Neruda (1904–73), was born July 12 in Parral, Chile. The poem *Residencia en la tierra* is a synthesis of the first part of his development, politically influenced by anarcho-syndicalism and anti-imperialism, and the result of experiences lived in Chile, Argentina, Burma, India, Ceylon, Indonesia, and Spain. For Neruda the Spanish experience was to prove decisive: in August 1933 he met Federico García Lorca in Buenos Aires, in May 1934 he became a consul in Barcelona, and in January 1935 he became a functionary at the Chilean embassy in Madrid. That same year he participated as a delegate in the International Writers' Congress for the Defense of Culture, which was held in Paris, and presided over by André Gide and Louis Aragon.

The outbreak of the war in Spain and García Lorca's death marked a turning point in Neruda's life. He began to gain recognition as the most representative figure of the fellow traveler militancy, and one of the most active protagonists, between Latin America and Europe, in the defense of culture as well as the struggle against Nazi fascism and Francoism. Neruda was perhaps the most representative intellectual of the Popular Front's cultural policies on both sides of the Atlantic. His celebrated *Canto a las madres de los milicianos muertos* (1936) signaled a decisive shift in his political poetry. During World War II that poem would be joined by *Canto a Stalingrado* and *Nuevo canto de amor a Stalingrado.* The Soviet victory in Stalingrad was symbolically a revenge for Spain's republicans' defeated heroism. This was to be the greatest poetic apology for the Great Patriotic War, popular resistance, and the liberation struggle in the Spanish language—one whose mythical status would be shaped by multiple influences, including political ones, in Europe but above all Latin America. Ernesto "Che" Guevara was emblematic here. Che had always considered Neruda his favorite poet since the time of the civil war, when he had become acquainted with his work through his mother, Celia, Rafael Alberti, and the republican exiles. Neruda himself recalled in his memoirs how Che kept his poems in his backpack in Bolivia, especially *Tercera residencia* and *Canto general.*

At the end of 1937 Neruda returned to Chile as the most authoritative point of reference for committed culture. He founded and presided over the Alianza de intelectuales de Chile para la defensa de la cultura. At that time he began his political activism in a coalition inspired by the front experience; the coalition's presidential candidate was Pedro Aguirre Cerda, a member of the Partido radical. In March 1939 Neruda participated as a Chilean delegate in the Congreso internacional de las democracias, which was held in Montevideo, and whose slogan was "Toda América contra el fascismo." In addition to representatives from the Chilean Popular Front's government, representatives of Mexican president Lázaro Cárdenas and Franklin D. Roosevelt's Democratic Party also participated. After Barcelona's fall and the collapse of the Spanish republic in early 1939, and in agreement with Cerda, who had won the presidential elections, Neruda traveled to France—together with his companion, the Argentinean painter Delia del Carril—to organize safe passage for refugees. He managed to have 2,356 Spanish refugees embark on the *Winnipeg*—an achievement that soon became legendary; having left Pauilliac on August 4, 1939, the *Winnipeg* would reach Valparaíso on September 3.

In March 1945, Neruda was elected as an independent senator for the mining provinces of Tarapacá and Antofagasta. He became a member of the Communist Party on July 8, at a time when the international conditions for the survival of a front-type of experience had disappeared. Neruda took part in the electoral campaign for the presidency, in support of the coalition led by the radical Gabriel González Videla. Once he had won the elections, however, González Videla outlawed the Communist Party—under pressure because of the break in relations between the United States and the USSR, which had led to the introduction of the Truman doctrine of fighting communism throughout the American continent—and the poet's persecution began, forcing him first to lead a clandestine existence and later to move into exile. After traversing the Andes, he departed for Europe and reappeared in public in Paris on April 25, 1949, where Pablo Picasso introduced him during the World Congress of Partisans for Peace, which nominated him to its World Council. In July he traveled for the first time to the Soviet Union on the occasion of Aleksandr Pushkin's 150th anniversary. This is how his season of militancy during the Cold War began, during which, between 1948 and 1949, he would write the poems of the *Canto general*, recognized as the highest point in the poetic elaboration of the historical and cultural identity of the peoples of Latin America during the past century.

Having returned from a long exile, on August 12, 1952, he devoted himself to the organization of the Congreso continental de la cultura, which was held in Santiago in 1953. On December 20, 1953, Neruda received the Stalin Peace Prize, thus arousing condemnation by anti-Communist cultural pundits in most of the West, at a time when McCarthyism was in full swing. Only many years after, in his memoirs, would the poet recognize the "immensity of the tragedy" that revelations about Stalinism had made people aware of. In 1959 he took a long trip to Venezuela after the collapse of the dictatorship of General Marcos Pérez Jiménez, and the following year he published the *Canción de gesta* to celebrate the Cuban Revolution and went to Havana. Following the 1962 missile crisis his disagreement with the Castroists became more obvious, especially after Cuba founded the Organización latinoamericana de solidariedad in 1966, whose purpose was to support armed struggle in Latin America by all means possible, while many parties, including the Chilean one, believed it was indispensable to pursue the "peaceful road to socialism."

In 1969 his party chose him as a presidential candidate, but Neruda dedicated himself to supporting the electoral alliance that a few months later, with his support, would choose the socialist Salvador Allende Gossens as the sole and ultimately victorious candidate. The president nominated Neruda as ambassador to Paris. In 1971, Neruda received the Nobel Prize for literature. He denounced the systematic subversion of the Unidad popular government by the Richard Nixon administration, and addressed an appeal to European and Latin American intellectuals to avoid a civil war in Chile. Seriously ill, Neruda returned home, where he died twelve days after the suicide of his friend Allende, while the military that had led the coup of September 11 devastated the country.

See also Fellow Travelers; Guevara de la Serna, Ernesto Rafael; Popular Front; Unidad Popular.

FURTHER READING

Carcedo, D. *Neruda y el barco de la esperanza.* Madrid: Temas de Hoy, 2006.

Galvez Barraza, J. *Neruda y Espana.* Santiago: Ril, 2003.

Loyola, H. *La biografía literaria.* Santiago: Editorial Planeta Chilena, 2006.

Neruda, P. *El fin del viaje.* Ed. M. Urrutia. Barcelona: Seix Barral, 1982.

———. *Obras completas.* Ed. H. Loyola. 5 vols. Barcelona: Círculo de Lectores–Galaxia Gutenberg, 1999–2002.

———. *Yo respondo con mi obra. Conferencias, discursos, cartas, declaraciónes (1932–1959).* Ed. P. Gutiérrez Revuelta and M. J. Gutiérrez. Salamanca: Ediciónes Universidad de Salamanca, 2004.

Teitelboim, V. *Neruda: An Intimate Biography.* Austin: University of Texas Press, 1991.

Woodbridge, H. C., and D. S. Zubatsky. *Pablo Neruda: An Annotated Bibliography of Biographical and Critical Studies.* New York: Garland, 1989.

ALBERTO FILIPPI

New Economic Policy

The years of the New Economic Policy (NEP) (1921–28) were a pause, a truce, but also a retreat, imposed by circumstances between two catastrophes: the civil war and the forced collectivization of the countryside. The measures that define the NEP—replacing requisitions with an in-kind tax, restoring a limited private sector, and liberalizing trade—were introduced by the Bolshevik regime during its party's Tenth Congress (March 1921), under pressure from the peasant insurrections of 1920–21 (Tambov, Ukraine, and western Siberia), the Petrograd workers' strikes, and the Kronstadt sailors' revolt. The Bolsheviks' retreat from Leninist illusions of a rapid transition to communism was not accompanied by political liberalization. On the contrary, the months following the Tenth Congress were distinguished by a return to repression of the Mensheviks, Socialist-Revolutionaries, and all the other opponents of Bolshevism.

After the famine of 1921–22 (six million victims), a last disastrous consequence of the "war communism" policies, the country needed to be rebuilt during the course of five or six years. But this reconstruction did not follow the paths that the Bolsheviks had hoped for. Stalin's voluntarism and political dictatorship, since he had emerged as the regime's leader, did not adapt well to an out-of-control economic and social system.

The Worker and Peasant Alliance

According to Lenin's intentions, the NEP—implemented "for real and for a long time" (but not "forever," according to the majority of Bolshevik leaders)—was supposed to be based on an alliance of workers and peasants, thought of as a policy of balanced development in which industry and agriculture would mutually support one another. In his last works (*Better Fewer, But Better*; *On Cooperation*), Lenin insisted it was necessary to not "attempt to inculcate Communist ideas with a brutal campaign in the countryside." Only a long-term cultural revolution would be able to significantly transform the countryside. In the course of the 1920s the problems raised by the application of this ambitious and largely utopian program provoked discussions inside the party. Two lines clashed: a "Left" line championed by Leon Trotsky, Yevgeni Preobrazhensky, and Georgy Pyatakov that underscored the need for industrial development in order to realize "primitive socialist accumulation," temporarily penalizing the peasants by means of unequal exchange and fiscal policy; and a "Right" line, championed by Nikolay Bukharin, who instead maintained that it was necessary to satisfy the needs of the peasants, encourage them to produce more, and play the cooperation card to the fullest. Thanks to forms of cooperation freely accepted by the peasants, the country would advance slowly but surely ("at a snail's pace") toward socialism.

Using only production statistics, the NEP's figures seemed fairly satisfactory: in 1927 the level of production for 1913 had been almost completely attained. Many problems, however, remained: the prices of the products from the state manufacturing industry continued to be too high to satisfy mass consumption, especially among the peasants; the modest pace of industrial growth meant there was still considerable unemployment, and this weighed heavily on the social and moral climate of worker milieus. This social unease also led to an increase in corruption, narrowing channels for social advancement in a system that revealed an increasing divide between the pure and neat society the Bolsheviks had dreamed of and the frustrating reality of a country marked by underdevelopment. Overall agricultural production also once more attained the levels of 1913 during 1926–27.

But beyond these generic figures there was another statistic that illustrated the main problem for Soviet agriculture during the NEP: in 1926 the amount of available grain on the market was half that of 1913. The countryside was no longer exporting grain—on average, ten million tons of grain had been exported annually from 1905 to 1914; moreover, the cities' supplies were put in question every year by a peasant class that did not want to sell its production to the state at a low price. On the one hand, this situation resulted from the structural weaknesses of Russian agriculture; on the other hand, it was due to governmental errors in economic policy. The revolution in the countryside translated into a form of economic leveling: the disappearance of the great landowners and the noticeable weakening of the wealthy peasants (kulaks) had restricted the amount of grain for sale outside the rural circuits. And as far as price policies were concerned, they were not able to satisfy the needs of the peasant masses: the products of the manufacturing industry were rare and expensive; and the prices paid by cooperative or state institutions for agricultural products were low. Confronted with this situation the peasants adopted the only logical economic attitude: they consumed their own products, thus finally eating enough. The NEP would remain in peasant memory as an ephemeral "golden age."

The Political Struggles for Power

The NEP involved years of intense political debate in the Communist Party ranks and years of struggle for the leadership. After a third stroke in less than a year (May 1922–May 1923), Lenin was removed from all political activity in March 1923. His death (January 21, 1924) created a crisis for his succession. Stalin was able to appropriate Lenin's legacy by presenting himself—after the publication of *Principles of Leninism*, a populist work widely circulated among the militants who formed the party's base—as the authorized interpreter of the USSR's founder's thought. In addition, from his key post of secretary general of the Central Committee, Stalin controlled the nominations of regional and local cadres, thus creating his own loyal clientele, which he relied on during the Thirteenth, Fourteenth, and Fifteenth Congresses of the Communist Party (May 1924, December 1925, and December 1927). Stalin's principal political rival, Trotsky, was progressively isolated. Trotsky's manifesto *The Lessons of October*—in which he developed the theme of the betrayal of the revolution's ideals by "Thermidorean forces," embodied by Stalin—was not understood by most militants. Stalin, however, surrounded by a circle of followers (Vyacheslav Molotov, Kliment Voroshilov, Lazar Kaganovich, Mikhail Kalinin, Sergey Kirov, and Grigoriy [Sergo] Ordzhonikidze) who had been promoted to the politburo, maneuvered with ability and mobilized the party's entire propaganda apparatus.

In 1926–27 a heterogeneous opposition that included Grigory Zinovyev, Lev Kamenev, Trotsky, and his followers (Karl Radek, Preobrazhensky, and Pyatakov), together with leaders from the former Workers' Opposition, attempted to reconstitute an anti-Stalinist front. Yet Stalin's group could count on the whole party apparatus as well as the political police to face this United Opposition, which was made up of a small minority. The strength of Stalin's position lay in not only the fact that he could rely on the mechanisms and authoritarian structures inside the party but also the great simplicity, even schematism, of his "socialism in one country" slogan, which was accessible to a majority of the not well-educated or politically experienced militants (the result of an extensive party renewal since the early 1920s). Increasingly isolated, the United Opposition was forced to spread its ideas clandestinely, thus opening itself up to accusations of "fractionism." In November 1927, Trotsky and Zinovyev were expelled from the party; one month later, during the Fifteenth Congress, about one hundred opponents were also expelled. Trotsky and his closest collaborators were exiled to Kazakhstan in January 1928. Only one noteworthy opponent of Stalin's remained: Bukharin.

The End of the NEP and the Triumph of the Stalinist Line

In 1927 the regime faced a "crisis in the acquisition of agricultural products." Notwithstanding a good harvest, peasants only handed over a small quantity of grain to the state (less than five million tons). The continuous reduction in agricultural prices proposed by the state, scarcity and expense of manufactured products, and disorganization of the institutions charged with procuring these agricultural products combined to produce what Stalin called "the kulaks' strike." Stalin's group decided to resort to emergency measures that had already been tried during war communism: they sent "workers groups" to the countryside, appealed to poor peasants to find "hidden stashes," and cracked down on "speculation." Because of this "hoarding crisis," Stalin concluded that it was necessary to abandon the forms of cooperation that Lenin had recommended and instead create "fortresses of socialism" in the countryside: kolkhoz and sovkhoz, where machine and tractor stations would ensure the cities received their supplies, and from which agricultural products necessary for the country's industrialization could be exported.

On the political level, 1928 was characterized by intense debates between Stalin's group (Stalin, Molotov, Valerian Kuybyshev, Voroshilov, and Yan Rudzutak) and the opposition led by Bukharin (supported by Alexey Rykov and Mikhail Tomsky). During the decisive plenum of the

Central Committee in July 1928, Stalin explained that NEP was a road with no exit and that peasants needed to pay a high price for the accelerated industrialization of the country, which was made all the more urgent by the "capitalist encirclement" of the USSR. Bukharin responded by publishing, two months later, his *Notes of an Economist*, a program of the anti-Stalinist opposition. He argued for an increase in the purchase price of grain, and the greatest caution in the creation of kolkhoz, which should occur only on the basis of voluntary participation; he also underlined the fundamental difference between the Leninist plan, based on "peaceful, gradual, and voluntarily given" cooperation, and the Stalinist collectivization project, based on constraint. These theses were rejected by the majority of the Central Committee (plenum of April 1929). In May 1929, Bukharin, Tomsky, and Rykov lost their positions. Discredited by means of a harsh campaign in the press, accusing them of "collusion with capitalist elements," they were forced to publicly perform a self-criticism during the November 1929 plenum.

The Congress of Soviets had ratified the First Five-Year Plan in April 1929. This plan sought to have 20 percent of peasant families join "associations of communal agricultural production" before 1933—associations in which only the land would be collectivized, without the abolition of private property or the sharing of livestock. As soon as it was approved, the plan underwent a series of drastic revisions: in September 1929, the government declared that thirteen million families would have to join collectives by 1930. On October 1931 *Pravda* appealed for a "mass collectivization," without placing any limit on the movement. On November 7 Stalin published his famous article *The Year of the Great Turn*, which was based on a mistaken estimate, according to which the "average peasant had taken the road to the kolkhoz." The NEP was buried; in reality, its principles had already been called into question for the previous two years.

See also Collectivization of the Countryside; Five-Year Plans; Lenin's Testament; Peasants in the USSR; Socialism in One Country; Soviet Industrialization; War Communism.

FURTHER READING

Carr, E. H. *Socialism in One Country (1958–1959)*. New York: Macmillan, 1958–64.

———. *Foundations of a Planned Economy, 1926–1929*. New York: Macmillan, 1971.

Fitzpatrick, S., A. Rabinowitch, and R. Stites, eds. *Russia in the Era of NEP*. Bloomington: Indiana University Press, 1991.

Pavljuchenkov, S. A., ed. *Rossija Nepovskaja.* Moscow: Novyj Chronograph, 2002.

Pethybridge, R. W. *One Step Backwards, Two Steps Forward: Soviet Society and Politics in the New Economic Policy.* Oxford: Clarendon, 1990.

Reiman, M. *The Birth of Stalinism: The USSR on the Eve of the "Second Revolution."* Bloomington: Indiana University Press, 1987.

Siegelbaum, L. H. *Soviet State and Society between Revolutions, 1918–1929.* Cambridge: Cambridge University Press, 1992.

NICOLAS WERTH

New Left

The expression "New Left" was coined in Great Britain in the 1950s when participants in the nuclear disarmament campaign experimented with new forms of struggle that had not been part of the workers' movement traditions (sit-ins, hunger strikes, and so on), and when a new left group was formed in the Labor Party, whose point of reference was the journal *New Left Review.* The Campaign for Nuclear Disarmament was formed in 1958, during the famous Aldermaston march; its leadership included intellectuals, representatives of the labor Left, religious individuals, and youths.

The New Left label was also used in other European countries to define all those political groupings on the radical Left that were created in Europe during the 1960s. The rise of these groupings was favored by a new international situation characterized by peaceful coexistence, which led many left-wing minorities to break the political and ideological barriers that had been imposed by the Cold War. Economic development and a consumer society also aided the emergence of a new generation of youths and ideologists who experienced the conservatism of the traditional parties on the Left, both Socialist and Communist, as a drag. This was the case with the German Sozialistischer Deutscher Studentbund (SPS), which developed in 1961 from a split in the SPD's youth section and opposed the revisionist shift that had been approved at the Bad Godesberg Congress in 1959. The German Union for Peace (Deutsche Friedensunion) had also developed around the issues of peace and disarmament in 1960, and had some modest electoral success during the 1960s.

The split between China and the Soviet Union, the Cuban Revolution (and especially Ernesto "Che" Guevara's figure), and the guerrilla movements in third world countries also played important roles. Groups, journals, and associations with a Maoist or third world bent appeared everywhere. These developments were inspired by intellectual currents—like French structuralism and especially the Frankfurt school—that aimed to renew Marxism, by in some cases emphasizing its liberatory potential, and in others attempting to recover a supposed original purity. This was the case, for instance, with the "workerist" (*operaista*) groups that developed in Italy, starting with the publication of the journal *Quaderni rossi,* but also with the group of "critical" intellectuals gathered around another journal, *Quaderni piacentini.* Italy had also witnessed the birth of the Partito socialista di unità proletaria (Proletarian Unity Socialist Party), which arose from a split within the Socialist Party, and which, the presence of a Stalinist component notwithstanding, became a point of passage for many young activists who were not satisfied with the "reformisms" in the Communist and Socialist parties. In France, a New Left developed around the Algerian question, which at first had even the French Communist Party endorsing an ambiguous position. The struggle against intervention in Algeria and the Gaullist trend attracted many intellectuals as well as the organization of university employees, and it would remain one of the principal rallying points for young leftists until 1968. The Parti socialiste unifié (United Socialist Party) was also established in 1960, made up of members who had left either the Section française de l'Internationale ouvrière (French Section of the Workers' International) or the French Communist Party.

Many extraparliamentary groups—like the British Vietnam Solidarity Campaign and the Radical Student Alliance as well as the French Comité Vietnam National—arose in Europe as a result of campaigns against U.S. intervention in Vietnam, although previously established groups also participated. The movement against the U.S. "dirty war," like many other new political and cultural trends that came from the United States (the civil rights movement or later the radical African American movements, and the various tendencies of the so-called counterculture), influenced an era in which, for the first time, a younger generation with its own identity—one that differed from the previous generation—took center stage in all advanced capitalist countries.

These 1960s' trends exploded with the 1968 movements, which had an international dimension. In some cases, as in France, it seemed as if they might have a revolutionary outcome (May 1968). At a minimum, they helped give the groups of the New Left and generally radical positions a mass base, however ephemeral. The students, after a more corporative and antiauthoritarian phase, moved toward a more traditionally political horizon, and this led to a proliferation of radical Left groups. These organizations, journals, and associations came from different ideological backgrounds. For a brief period following 1968—for example, in Italy and France—sectarian groups with a Marxist-Leninist orientation prevailed. This extremist constellation was always diverse, though, composed of elements with different beliefs—anarchist, libertarian, workerist, Trotskyist, Maoist, Guevarist, Luxemburgist, and so forth. The New Left groups also exhibited some common characteristics: they were small and generally lead by younger members; they privileged direct action and tended to be constantly shifting, due to continuous splits and regroupings. Some of them engaged in acts of terrorism (the Red Army Faction in Germany or the Red Brigades in Italy). Some groups left the Communist parties—for example, the group around the journal *Il Manifesto*, which, led by three members from the Italian Communist Party's Central Committee (Aldo Natoli, Luigi Pintor, and Rossana Rossanda), subsequently formed a political group and transformed the journal into a daily. In France Jean-Paul Sartre founded the journal *Libération*, which later also became a daily, and the reference point for French *gauchisme* (the "dissident" Left).

The New Left became the venue thanks to which important items on the political agenda were, in different ways (depending on the different national contexts), taken up by the traditional Left as well—for instance, feminism, which in some countries would become an independent movement. Basically there was an attempt to break previously rigid barriers between public and private, by politicizing all aspects of interpersonal life and experimenting with new forms of communal living. This component was particularly strong in West Germany and more generally northern Europe.

The extraparliamentary groups were a novelty in the European political landscape of the early 1970s, but they soon experienced forms of crisis and dissolved in the following years. This was the case with SDS, which had already disbanded by around 1970. In many cases it was also the direct intervention by state authorities—as in France with the dissolution between 1968 and 1970 of all the major New Left organizations—that led to these

crises. The New Left also often became an established presence, such as in the case of Trotskyist groupings in France. In Italy the New Left was stronger than elsewhere, with organizations—such as Lotta continua, Potere operaio, Avanguardia operaia, Il Manifesto, and the Proletarian Unity Party, to mention only the most significant ones—that brought together several thousand youths and workers. During the latter half of the 1970s these groups also underwent a period of crises, even though in an electorally modest fashion, they became a stable component of the Italian political scene (the Proletarian Unity Party and Democrazia proletaria were later to join in the Partito della Rifondazione Comunista in 1991). During the 1980s the New Left maintained its presence in Europe, becoming the midwife for new movements grouped around issues like disarmament and nuclear power as well as ecologist parties such as the German Grünen (Greens) or the Italian Verdi (Greens).

See also Maoism; Marxism, Western; Marxism-Leninism; Sartre, Jean-Paul; Terrorism; Third Worldism; Trotskyism.

FURTHER READING

Dalton, R. J., and M. Kuechler, eds. *Challenging the Political Order: New Social and Political Movements in Western Democracies.* New York: Oxford University Press, 1990.
Fink, C., P. Gassert, and D. Junker, eds. *The World Transformed.* Cambridge: Cambridge University Press, 1998.
Flores, M., and A. De Bernardi. *Il sessantotto.* Bologna: Il Mulino, 1998.
Tarrow, S. G. *Democracy and Disorder: Protest and Politics in Italy, 1965–1975.* New York: Oxford University Press, 1989.
Teodori, M. *Storia delle nuove sinistre in Europa (1956–1976).* Bologna: Il Mulino, 1976.
Various authors. *Il sessantotto. La stagione dei movimenti (1960–1979),* ed. redazione di Materiali per una nuova sinistra. Rome: Edizioni Associate, 1988.

ERMANNO TAVIANI

New Man

The "New Man" is not a Communist invention. The idea of human beings' perfectibility was initially Christian, and later Jacobin and utopian, although in different contexts and in the pursuit of different logics. It was the Russian Revolution of 1917, however, that established the framework for this goal's realization on a large scale, since the building of a better, socialist society was supposed to be a guideline for the birth of the New Man. The two goals were interdependent: 1920s' Bolshevism served as a laboratory to develop and verify the conditions and characteristics of the New Man in various fields, defining itself as a transitional period with "transitional human beings." These human beings were distinguished by a lifestyle based on labor, discipline, and asceticism, and also the renunciation of individual happiness in favor of the common good.

The dominant model of a Communist, who in the Bolsheviks' eyes was the prototype of the New Man, was a man. The fact that this model granted women a certain amount of space did not mean anything, so long as gender differences were not taken into account. It was only Stalinism in the 1930s that declared that the New Man had been realized. The regime then appealed to the "heroism" of all its citizens so they would participate in the construction of socialism, and become New Men or New Women. This type of volunteerism implied an adaptation of the definitions to the needs of industrialization and collectivization, and a differentiation of models according to gender and social categories. Even though it did not completely disappear, the topos of the New Man became less important in Soviet official discourse and as a reference point for Communist parties after Stalin's death and the Communist Party of the Soviet Union's Twentieth Congress.

The ideas for a New Man that had been developed by Soviet communism after 1917 were rooted in two distinct 19th-century traditions—one tied to Russian cultural and religious values, and the other to Marxism and utopian socialism. In the absence of genealogies, Nikolay Chernyshevsky's novel *What Is to Be Done?* (1863) must be mentioned, since it combined both these influences. One of Lenin's favorite books—he would borrow its title for a famous 1902 work devoted to the organization of a cadres-based party—Chernyshevsky's novel already contained the central elements of the Bolshevik conception of the new society. It was founded on education and *Bildung* as necessary conditions for humanization, political radicalism, scientific rationalism, and women's emancipation and the equality of the sexes. Its protagonist, Rachmetov, "an extraordinary man," embodied the future ideal of the professional revolutionary, who sacrificed himself in the service of social transformation.

Karl Marx and Friedrich Engels, the founding fathers, made no reference to the New Man concept, except to announce in *The German Ideology* the end of the social division of labor, and as a consequence, the advent of "all-rounded and therefore total" human beings, who would be able to fully develop their potential. Lenin in *State and Revolution* (1917) limited himself to some general features of a Communist society, which was to be devoid of conflicts between the classes and sexes, and in which each human being would work and consume according to his or her needs. This society would be organized along collective lines, thereby eliminating the social basis for competition and jealousy on the psychological level. As far as nature was concerned, it would be subject to human beings' volition once and for all thanks to technology.

After the October Revolution, the realization of a new culture not only faced material obstacles but also the diversity or even incompatibility of the different ideas that were being proposed. To the extent that the New Man was part of literary, philosophical, pedagogical, artistic, and political discourse, the ways in which he was represented differed as much as the strategies that were supposed to lead to his creation. Was it necessary to "make a tabula rasa of the past," as the proletkult (proletarian culture) movement suggested, or to adapt the "legacy of the bourgeoisie"? Was it necessary to rely on a rational education or the creation of myths that would be the vehicles of a new collective faith? Should one favor a polytechnic education or the development of a harmonious personality? And what would be the machines' function? Would they become part of a symbiosis with human beings or simply be an instrument with which to dominate nature?

Even with the existence of all these divergent views it was possible to identify two areas of agreement. The first was the technical nature of practically all these views of the future. The role of technology in liberating human beings from alienating human labor and allowing the development of new human relations, indispensable conditions for the realization of the new socialist society, were already foregrounded in Aleksandr Bogdanov's science-fiction novel *Red Star* (1908). For some people—for instance, the poet, journalist, steelworker, union organizer, and founder of the Central Institute of Labor, Aleksei Gastev—man-machine, automation, and rationalization were what the future had in store. According to others, who did not believe in this mystique of iron and steel, technology was not an end in itself but rather an instrument for the abolition of the division between manual and intellectual labor (Trotsky, *Literature and Revolu-*

tion) or in other cases, for the abolition of the domestic exploitation of women (Aleksandra Kollontay). In this latter view, only after having been freed from material constraints would men and eventually women be able to fully and freely develop on both the physical as well as intellectual level.

A second element of agreement was that education was the means to consciousness. Consciousness (*soznatel'nost*) in fact, as Lenin reiterated, was what distinguished Communists from the workers who had still not gone beyond a condition of spontaneity, at both the individual and collective level. In order to develop this consciousness, Communists were supposed to mature both materially and morally, and develop their knowledge; they therefore had to learn, educate themselves, and "shape" themselves. The will to educate Soviet men, women, and children, and the faith in the possibility of accomplishing this goal, brought people in the fields of politics, culture, pedagogy, and science together, regardless of their various tendencies. The 1920s, then, were a period of pedagogical experimentation and intense efforts to create a generalized educational system. As far as party members were concerned, they were supposed to be continuously educating themselves, and the party equipped itself for the task. After the civil war the party began to establish a network of mobile schools, where one could pursue a political education program, in a group setting and as a form of self-education, in a framework organized by the cell's secretary or an instructor. A new practice, self-evaluation—a result of both the lack of teachers and the rational organization of labor, and inspired by a positive anthropological outlook and an optimistic view of human beings—became a means of pedagogical support: Communists would set themselves some reading and learning goals, which they then regularly tested and evaluated in the context of a cell or party group.

With the introduction of forced industrialization and collectivization, the "process of producing human beings of a new type" (Anatoly Lunacharsky) was adopted as official policy. The task of the "semi-finished product" (Trotsky) that human beings still were, was to change or, better yet, improve themselves. In this fashion Stalinism connected many elements that had been characteristic of the "heroic" period of "war communism," while simultaneously introducing some innovations. The idea of a new type of human being, defined by one's contribution to a collective effort, was certainly not new, but during this period it was generalized and made banal (a paradoxi-

cal state of affairs given the regime's grandiose rhetoric). The phenomenon lost its purely urban character and was extended to the countryside. It explicitly was addressed to women, moreover, thereby underlining a break with their tacit inclusion, typical of the masculine Bolshevik model of the "Communist in a leather jacket" (Boris Pilnjak), which in actuality implied women's exclusion.

In order to mobilize the population, the regime appealed to both social technologies and the citizens' subjectivities. In fact, if work "purified" even criminals and juvenile delinquents—following the plot of many socialist realist novels—what was at issue primarily was an interior form of work: work on oneself. It was necessary to get rid of one's old self, with its "petty bourgeois individualist" dross and cultural backwardness, and make way for the new socialist self. As can be seen in accessible archives of the former Soviet Union, within the party, cadre schools, and other educational institutions as well as enterprises, the practice of self-examination and self-revelation (such as the party autobiography, self-criticism, and self-evaluation) established a confessional norm, and one focused on work on oneself. It was a case of revealing one's acts and attitudes in front of the collective, analyzing them, and if necessary changing them. A negative anthropology was gradually superimposed on this positive anthropology—positive because it supposed that human beings always possess the potential for self-improvement if society provides the means for it. A negative anthropology would be fully expressed in the Great Terror, though, whose references and representations were tied to ideas of conspiracy, and the threat of internal and external enemies.

This appeal to self-overcoming and heroism, attributable to Friedrich Wilhelm Nietzsche's influence on Russian culture, was the other side of the coin in Stalinism's conception of the New Man. Starting in 1929, the "assault workers" were an anticipation of the Stakhanovists in 1935–36 who were responsible for increases in the pace of work. Productivism reached such a point that in Stalin's eyes, New Men could be defined on the basis of new technical parameters that became guarantors of happiness. In addition to these "heroes of labor," the regime mobilized other professional categories. Collectively, and later also individually, it conferred the status of "hero of socialism" or "constructors of a new world" to daring female pilots, explorers who had reached the North Pole, workers engaged in monumental works, "engineers of the soul," and finally, during the Great Patriotic War, partisans, both men and women, who had sacrificed themselves in the struggle against the Nazi invader. If the reference to the perfectibility of human beings therefore exhibited certain continuities between war communism and Stalinism, the uses and definition of the New Man underwent profound transformations between 1917 and 1953.

See also Atheism, Soviet; Avant-garde; Communist Autobiography; Cultural Policies; Messianism; Proletkult; Self-Criticism; Socialist Emulation; Stakhanovism; Totalitarianism; Utopia; Youth.

FURTHER READING

Clark, K. *The Soviet Novel: History as Ritual.* Chicago: Chicago University Press, 1981.

Fitzpatrick, S. *Cultural Revolution in Russia, 1928–1931.* Bloomington: Indiana University Press, 1978.

Müller, D. *Der Topos des Neuen Menschen in der russischen und sowjetrussischen Geistesgeschichte.* Bern: Lang, 1998.

Pennetier, C., and B. Pudal. "Du parti bolshevik au parti stalinien." In *Le siècle des communismes,* ed. M. Dreyfus, 333–40. Paris: Les Éditions de l'Atelier.

Plaggenborg, S. *Revolutionskultur: Menschenbilder und kulturelle Praxis in Sowjetrussland zwischen Oktoberrevolution und Stalinismus.* Cologne: Böhlau, 1996.

Rosenthal, B. G., ed. *Nietzsche and Soviet Culture: Ally and Adversary.* Cambridge, UK: Cambridge University Press, 1994.

Stites, R. *Revolutionary Dreams: Utopian Vision and Experimental Life in the Russian Revolution.* New York: Oxford University Press, 1989.

Studer, B. "L'être perfectible. La formation du cadre stalinien par le 'travail sur soi.'" *Genèses* 51 (2003): 92–113.

———. "La femme nouvelle." *Genèses* 51 (2003): 377–87.

Werth, N. *Être communiste en U.R.S.S. sous Staline.* Paris: Gallimard-Julliard, 1981.

BRIGITTE STUDER

New Thinking

The concept of "New Thinking" (*Novoe myshlenie*)—or "New Political Thinking" (*Novoe politicheskoe myshlenie*)—entered the Soviet lexicon soon after Mikhail Gorbachev became general secretary of the Communist Party in March 1985. The name given to it was significant in itself, for even though official Marxism-Leninism had been dif-

ferently interpreted at different periods of Soviet history, the emphasis was on the timeless wisdom of the thought of Marx and Lenin (and during the years of his political ascendancy, Stalin) rather than anything approximating an admission that something fundamentally new was required.

In its first manifestations the New Thinking—as expounded by Gorbachev and, to take a notable example, Alexander Yakovlev (who had special responsibility within the Central Committee apparatus for ideology between 1985 and 1988)—was presented as the creative application of Leninist ideas to contemporary problems. Although it broke much fresh ground at the time, Gorbachev's 1987 book titled *Perestroika: New Thinking for Our Country and the World* presented the New Thinking as a return to some of the ideas of Lenin in the last years of his life when, in Gorbachev's view, the Soviet Union's principal founding father saw "critical dangers for the future of socialism." It also presented a somewhat idealized view of Lenin as someone for whom "socialism and democracy are indivisible." As the title of that book suggested, the New Thinking had both domestic and foreign policy dimensions.

Even Gorbachev's book, published relatively early in the perestroika period, began to move beyond Leninism, while still treating the memory of Lenin with great respect. There is praise for the idea of "socialist pluralism" and much attention devoted to the need for glasnost (openness or transparency). Gorbachev writes there:

> Glasnost, criticism, and self-criticism are not just a new campaign. They have been proclaimed and must become a norm in the Soviet way of life. No radical change is possible without it. There is no democracy, nor can there be, without glasnost. And there is no present-day socialism, nor can there be, without democracy.

Soon the content of the New Thinking was to move beyond the contours of Gorbachev's 1987 volume and depart quite radically from anything that was remotely Leninist. Thus, in its domestic dimension, "socialist pluralism" changed to advocacy of "political pluralism." Gorbachev was the first person publicly to endorse the notion of pluralism—in 1987, when he still qualified it either as socialist pluralism or a "pluralism of opinion." But radical reformers took up the previously forbidden notion and frequently left out the socialist qualifier. By early 1990, Gorbachev himself was speaking positively about the desirability of political pluralism.

Other notions that gained both currency and legitimacy under the rubric of the New Thinking included the idea of checks and balances as well as the separation of powers. At a meeting of the Soviet Association of Political Sciences in 1987—presided over by Georgiy Shakhnazarov, who the following year was to become a full-time aide to Gorbachev and one of his closest advisers—a call was made for a "socialist theory of checks and balances," and the study of both Western theory and Western practice in this respect. By the following year, Gorbachev was speaking about "our own socialist system of 'checks and balances' taking shape in this country," and viewing that as a means of protecting society from "any violation of socialist legality at the highest state level." The idea of the separation of executive, legislative, and judicial powers also became part of the New Thinking.

Leninist analyses had traditionally seen the notions of political pluralism, checks and balances, and the separation of powers as smoke screens characteristic of bourgeois democracy, behind which the ruling class exercised its political hegemony. To accept that these institutional arrangements had a part to play in the democratization of Soviet society was a change of no small consequence. The idea of democratization itself played an increasingly central part in the New Thinking, in both the minds of the reformist wing of the Communist Party leadership, headed by Gorbachev, and more impatient variants espoused by radical segments of the intelligentsia.

The doctrine of democratic centralism had traditionally been posited against the "bourgeois" notion of political pluralism, and the adoption of the latter concept at the expense of the former represented a change of profound importance. Other notions that had nothing in common with Soviet Marxism-Leninism as it had existed up until the mid-1980s included the open advocacy of a state based on the rule of law, the development of a market economy, and the autonomy of the individual. Whereas prior to the emergence of the New Thinking the West was deemed to be inferior in principle and doctrine to the Soviet Union (even if some of its countries were for the time being materially richer), it became an increasingly significant aspect of the New Thinking to emphasize how much the Soviet Union could learn from the West. Phrases such as "normal countries" or "the civilized world" were used to *contrast* many Soviet practices with what was to be found in the advanced non-Communist states.

It was a central tenet of the New Thinking, not least as expounded by Gorbachev, that there was an inextricable link between the innovative ideas about the Soviet political system and fresh thought about relations with the outside world. A class analysis of international relations, which had long been adapted to serve the interests of the Soviet state as perceived by the politburo and the broader Soviet elite, was in effect abandoned. Relations with the capitalist West were no longer seen as a zero-sum game, and Gorbachev's notion of a "common European home" was more than propaganda designed to disrupt the equilibrium of the United States. It reflected an aspiration for qualitatively new relations on the European continent. Above all, the acceptance that the citizens of each country had the right to choose their own form of political and economic system opened the way for the peoples of Eastern and Central Europe to take at face value such pronouncements, and led directly to the discarding of Communist regimes in the eastern part of the continent along with the disbanding of the Warsaw Pact and Comecon.

In other words, the New Political Thinking represented a genuinely different way of looking at the world from any of the variants of Soviet Marxism-Leninism that had preceded it. It pointed the way to new political behavior, and it was the matching of precept and practice—most notably as one East European country after another became independent and non-Communist in the course of 1989—that confirmed its profound significance.

See also Gorbachev, Mikhail; Marxism-Leninism; Perestroika; Yakovlev, Aleksandr.

FURTHER READING

Brown, A. *The Demise of Marxism-Leninism in Russia.* Basingstoke, UK: Palgrave Macmillan, 2004.

English, R. D. *Russia and the Idea of the West: Gorbachev, Intellectuals, and the End of the Cold War.* New York: Columbia University Press, 2000.

Gorbachev, M. *Perestroika: New Thinking for Our Country and the World.* London: Collins, 1987.

Gorbachev, M., and Z. Mlynář. *Conversations with Gorbachev: On Perestroika, the Prague Spring, and the Crossroads of Socialism.* New York: Columbia University Press, 2002.

Newton, J. M. *Russia, France, and the Idea of Europe.* Basingstoke, UK: Palgrave Macmillan, 2003.

ARCHIE BROWN

Nomenklatura

The *nomenklatura* was a system by which the Communist Party controlled the alignment of personnel in the USSR who constituted the "Soviet ruling elite." It defined the assignments, shifts, and dismissals of leaders at various levels, all of which had to be confirmed by appropriate party committees (by the Central Committees or regional committees). Every party committee maintained its own lists of the nomenklatura positions it controlled. The nomenklatura included within its purview almost all posts of any importance in the country, including: leaders of the party and Soviet apparatus, the police, the courts, state security organs, commanders and political workers of military units, diplomats, heads of economic organizations, industrial enterprises and collective farms, newspapers, magazines, publishing houses, labor unions, the Communist Youth Movement, and arts agencies. Nomenklatura control extended even to persons elected to its offices. The nomenklatura system of moving up and shifting personnel around was a crucial element of the one-party system, which eschewed all democratic mechanisms in its selection of key personnel.

The evolution of the nomenklatura system mirrored the basic stages of the political development of the USSR as a whole. When they took power at the end of 1917, the Bolsheviks moved briskly to create a new apparatus of control in which the key posts would be occupied by the ruling party. In the early stages, though, the advancement of leading personnel was rather chaotic, which led to administrative conflicts among the various structures of the regime, in particular, between party and state apparatuses. Still, the nomenklatura system was basically in place by the mid-1920s. At the end of 1925 and the beginning of 1926, after prolonged bargaining and fine-tuning, the Orgburo and politburo of the Central Committee of the Communist Party of the USSR (CC CPSU) issued decrees establishing lists of posts that would be subject to the control of the CC CPSU. The committee also set itself the task of fashioning a nomenklatura of posts, assignments to which had to be confirmed by local party organs. The nomenklatura of the CC CPSU was divided into nomenklatura no. 1 (posts where assignments were confirmed by decrees of the politburo, Orgburo, and the Secretariat of the Central Committee) and nomenklatura no. 2 (posts where assignments were confirmed by consent by the organizational regulatory section of the

Central Committee). In 1925 these two nomenklaturas listed more than 5,700 posts.

After Stalin's power became absolute and the overall political situation became more exacerbated, there was a tendency toward tighter control over personnel, which expressed itself in a gradual increase in the number of nomenklatura posts under the direct control of the CC CPSU. One of the most important steps here, for example, was the inclusion in the nomenklatura in January 1935 of regional and municipal committees of the party (more than 5,000 posts), which greatly circumscribed the rights of the leaders at the provincial, regional, and republican levels, and facilitated the interference of the center in regional affairs.

After the war, in October 1946, the changes that had taken place in the nomenklatura of the CC CPSU in the preceding years were formalized by a decree of the Orgburo, titled simply "On the Nomenklatura of the CC CPSU." In early 1953, around the time of Stalin's death, the nomenklatura included about 45,000 posts. The liberalizing measures taken by the Soviet leadership after Stalin's death resulted in substantial changes in the nomenklatura system. In June 1953, Nikita Khrushchev sent to the Presidium of the CC CPSU a draft decree restructuring the nomenklatura of the CC, and the presidium approved it on July 16, 1953. This decree reduced the number of positions in the nomenklatura from 45,000 to 25,300, with 11,400 of the latter now included in the so-called Accounting Control Nomenklatura. Shifts of personnel in the Accounting Control Nomenklatura did not require approval by the CC but only that various CC organs be informed of them. This had the effect of strengthening the positions of leaders of departments and regions, whose support was needed by members of the highest echelons of the Soviet leadership in their endless struggles for power.

This development led to the next major reduction of the CC CPSU nomenklatura, approved by the presidium on June 1, 1956. The new nomenklatura consisted of only 12,600 posts, which meant a reduction of almost 60 percent, with 3,200 of the list now of the Accounting Control Nomenklatura type. This substantial curtailment of the nomenklatura affected positions in local economic organizations, regional institutions, and the ministries. In addition, Moscow ordered a reduction of posts in provincial committees, regional committees, and the Central Committees of Communist parties in the Soviet republics, which in May 1956 comprised some 360,000 posts (including 84,000 of the Accounting Control Nomenklatura type).

There are no precise data regarding changes in the nomenklatura from the 1960s through the 1980s. Bits of information suggest a gradual, not very significant increase in the number of nomenklatura posts of the CC CPSU, as well as in the nomenklatura of local party committees. The nomenklatura system during this period evolved into a mechanism for assuring the stability of personnel, as it was touted during the Brezhnev era. From 1989 through 1991 there was again a reduction in the nomenklatura, resulting from the political reforms of Mikhail Gorbachev. A resounding blow to the nomenklatura was struck in March 1990 by the repeal of Article 6 of the Constitution of the USSR, which had until then upheld the leading role of the CPSU in Soviet society. After a number of delays, a politburo decision in September 1990 abolished the previously existing CPSU nomenklatura. Similar decrees were approved by regional party committees as well. These decisions did permit the nomenklatura system to remain in place for officials of the party apparatus. As for nonparty posts, the CPSU strove to maintain its influence on personnel shifts through the use of new, gentler methods (simply recommending party members for various state or economic positions, and exerting influence through party committees, which still remained in various institutions and enterprises). Ultimately, of course, CPSU influence on personnel policies necessarily came to a halt with the August 1991 putsch and subsequent banning of the party.

See also Cadres; Politburo; Single-Party System

FURTHER READING

Korzhikhina, T. P., and Y. Figatner. "Sovetskaja nomenklatura: stanovlenie, mechanizmy dejstvija." *Voprosy istorii* 7 (1993): 25–38.

Mokhov, V. P. *The Evolution of the Regional Political Elite in Russia (1950–1990)*. Perm, 1998.

Voslensky, Michael. *Nomenklatura: The Soviet Ruling Class*. New York: Doubleday, 1984.

OLEG V. CHLEVNJUK

Nonalignment

Nonalignment was a policy of abstention from the Cold War blocs, a synthesis of various neutralist and "third force" doctrines. The most strictly enforced criterion was nonparticipation in alliances or security pacts led either by the United States or the USSR, especially if they entailed the presence of military facilities. Other requisites were less clearly defined, starting with relations with the two superpowers, which only appeared to be kept on the same level since most, but not all, nonaligned countries believed the USSR to be a strategic ally in the fight against colonialism and imperialism. Nonalignment was the preferred mode of existence in the third world during the bipolar era, allowing "third-party players" to gain higher visibility on the international stage, and in this sense it continued and refined other policies pursued by Asian and African countries emerging from decolonization. The contributions of a European country like Josip Broz Tito's Yugoslavia were important for nonalignment policies.

The major third world policy issues were thoroughly debated for the first time during the Afro-Asian Conference held in the Indonesian city of Bandung on April 18–24, 1955: anticolonialism, economic development, disarmament, the defense of peace, and trust in international organizations like the United Nations. The *Pantja Shila*, the "five principles" of pacific coexistence formulated by Sukarno, the Indonesian president, were the frame of reference, and had also been approved by India and China in various documents. The foundation of this Afro-Asian consensus was "positive neutralism," as devised by Jawaharlal Nehru, the Indian prime minister: only the creation of an "area of peace" between East and West would prevent war. The various governments' different orientation was not in and of itself an obstacle, because one characteristic of the third world was its members' lack of homogeneity.

The Afro-Asian geographic restrictions were set aside during the next summit in Brioni (July 18–19, 1956), attended by Tito, Nehru, and Gamal Abdel Nasser. The inclusion of Yugoslavia, which brought the experience of a country that had avoided the Soviet bloc's embrace without being engulfed by its opponent, emphasized a policy of equal distance between the two competing blocs that were at the center of the global confrontation. Under Yugoslavia's and then also Tito's personal leadership, the First Congress of Nonaligned Countries assembled in Belgrade (September 1–6, 1961). If the "Bandung spirit" had stressed the nationalism of peoples of "color," Belgrade moved to a plan that joined the Afro-Asian world with Europe and Latin America to oppose the blocs and rearmament. Yugoslavia was looking beyond decolonization; anticolonialism had to be coordinated with the evolution of international relations to arrive at a situation in which everyone's security and coexistence was assured. Sino-Soviet tensions made the idea of a second Afro-Asian conference, a Bandung sequel, evaporate. The developing world's horizon expanded toward Latin America after the Cuban Revolution and discovery of "tricontinentalism" (Asia, Africa, and Latin America), but nonalignment continued essentially to be the policy of the Afro-Asian nations with the addition of Yugoslavia.

Nonalignment's moment of greatest influence coincided with the conference held in Algiers on September 5–9, 1973, hosted by a state that occupied an important role in the third world. It became a watershed event for several reasons: it appraised the results achieved by the third world, served as a balance sheet for decolonization, and provided a strategic adjustment toward new objectives. During his inaugural speech President Houari Boumedienne remarked how the third world—with decolonization almost complete, and arms accords that had reduced the danger of a conflict in Europe—continued to be the scene of crises that were "discharged" on the periphery due to the ongoing tensions among the two blocs. Nonalignment was portrayed as "the principal reason for a positive evolution in international affairs." The third world could no longer wait for stability and development as a "spin-off" of superpower policies. Real security could only be based on economic emancipation by means of the mobilization and valorization of all the human and resource potential in the developing world. With the energy crisis, which the Algiers summit had anticipated and which had been set off by the Yom Kippur War in October 1973, the third world discovered a form of power to bolster its demands.

The outcome of this shift was to propose a "new international economic order," to be understood as a completion of decolonization at the economic level. The keystone of this new order was seen as interdependence. The third world's offensive aimed at eliminating the growing gap between the developed and developing worlds led to increased polarization during negotiations to discuss North-South economic differences in a comprehensive framework: development, trade and the terms of trade, energy, currency, and aid. The so-called global negotiations—and with them the third world's attempt to place itself at the center of the system to reform it—failed at birth because of the negative votes of the major Western countries represented at the United Nations in the summer of 1980. Within a short period of time, the

explosion of the foreign debt "bomb" would force the third world to review its policies.

The movement had perhaps expanded too rapidly. It was no longer possible to put on a front of uniformity that did not correspond to internal divisions: on the one hand, those who supported a "third way" along with scrupulous neutrality between the United States and the USSR; and on the other, the "natural alliance" with the socialist bloc and the USSR. This issue, which had emerged in Algiers, dominated the nonaligned summit in Havana in 1979, the last that Tito took part in. Cuba's participation in the movement was a cause of contention because the "first free land in America," even if it could argue that it had realized the anti-imperialist goals of decolonization, had certainly taken sides, if not even positively "aligned" itself. In Havana as well, the principle of equal distance from the opposing blocs found Yugoslav president Tito to be its most authoritative and convincing spokesperson. As liberation struggles were coming to an end, the role of the USSR at the third world's side in the United Nations and elsewhere became less important, and the nonaligned countries were driven to rethink their choices. The competition between East and West shifted to the economy, where the USSR did not have the necessary means to counter the United States and the major European powers, which also had international organizations like the World Bank and International Monetary Fund at their disposal.

The worsening relations between East and West during what has been defined as the Second Cold War interfered in the North-South relationship, putting the influence and initiative of the Non-Aligned Movement in doubt. One of the consequences of détente between the United States and the USSR, whose efficacy as regards the third world and local conflicts has been negligible, was the recognition of the global dimensions of Soviet power, which up to that moment had been prevalently exercised in Europe. On the other hand, the United States' decision to fight the "Evil Empire," as Reagan called the Soviet Union and communism, everywhere and with all means, led to an increase in "low-intensity" warfare on the periphery without running the risks of an atomic war. The flash points for international tensions were now no longer in Berlin but rather all in the third world: Luanda, Ogaden, Lebanon, Kabul, and Nicaragua. The USSR attempted to respond blow by blow; its engagement in local conflicts guaranteed a minimum amount of balance following bipolar rules, but military overextension was one of the causes that led to the final crisis of the socialist bloc and the USSR itself.

Nonalignment did not survive the Cold War's end. The goal of defining a collective identity for the third world faced its greatest challenges precisely when the superpowers' diplomatic and strategic supremacy was declining, at least in terms of prestige, if not in terms of coercive potential. The central role of North-South tensions would appear all the more dramatically as the East-West tensions began to subside and then disappeared between 1989 and 1991. Once a unipolar system replaced a bipolar one, the rational foundation for the Non-Aligned Movement disappeared. The movement no longer had any poles from which to distance itself, since the United States was the only source of capital, aid, and political protection as well as the "policeman" of an order that did not de facto admit any alternatives or transgressions. The movement maintained a fragile organizational infrastructure, but it could no longer impact international events.

See also Anti-imperialism; Cold War; Decolonization; Third Worldism.

FURTHER READING

Achimovich, L., ed. *Le non alignement dans le monde contemporain*. Belgrade: Institut de politique et de l'économie internationales, 1969.

Aruffo, A. *Alle origini del Terzo mondo, da Bandung a Belgrado*. Chieti: Vecchio Faggio, 1987.

Calchi Novati, G. *Neutralismo e guerra fredda*. Milan: Edizioni di Comunità, 1963.

Köchler, H., ed. *The Principles of Non-Alignment*. London: Third World Center, 1982.

Mates, L. *Non-Alignment: Theory and Current Policy*. Dobbs Ferry, NY: Oceana Publishers, 1972.

Tana, F., ed. *Terzo mondo: dal neutralismo al non allineamento*. Milan: Moizzi, 1976.

Various authors. *Noi, paesi non-allineati*. Milan: Jaca Book, 1974.

GIAMPAOLO CALCHI NOVATI

North Atlantic Treaty Organization

Committing the United States to the defense of Europe, the North Atlantic Treaty Organization (NATO) was founded in April 1949 to reassure West Europeans against the threat of Soviet aggression. A political rather than a military venture at a time when NATO was not in a position to prevent the Soviet Army from overrunning Western Europe, the alliance was rightly perceived as such by Soviet leader Stalin, thus prompting him not to respond with any military measures of his own. Aware of the West's overall superior potential, he nevertheless tried to impede the growth of NATO by political means, particularly by masterminding massive "peace" campaigns spearheaded by Western Europe's influential Communist parties.

Even after NATO began to acquire military substance in response to the Communist aggression in Korea in 1950, the Soviet Union did not perceive the alliance as a serious military factor. Dismissive of small nations, Stalin instead respected the power of the United States, backed by nuclear weapons, and in the long run, feared the recovery of West Germany. Ironically at a time when NATO was being built up to deter Soviet aggression, Soviet military plans were defensive, aimed to hold rather than expand Stalin's Eastern European empire. This did not make NATO superfluous. By demonstrating the will and growing capacity to fight, the alliance was a crucial safeguard in Europe against just such an enemy miscalculation as that which had invited the Communist attack in Korea.

The Soviet effort to stymie the growth of NATO appeared to bear fruit in August 1954, when the French National Assembly voted down the plan for the European Defense Community as NATO's subsidiary, within which West Germany was to be rearmed. The substitute Paris Agreements, though, which opened the way for West Germany to join NATO in May 1955, reversed the situation, leading to a revision of Soviet policy under Khrushchev. One of the consequences was the creation of the Warsaw Pact as a rival of NATO.

Although Soviet propaganda continued to beat the dead horse of West German "militarism," Khrushchev did not share Stalin's obsession with a revival of German military power; at issue was rather the growing political influence of an economically resurgent West Germany within the Western alliance and its destabilizing effect on Communist East Germany. As other Soviet leaders before and after him, Khrushchev tried to weaken NATO by fomenting discord among its members, consistently underestimating the basic solidarity that held it together. The perception of a Soviet threat, which nourished that solidarity, increased during the Berlin crisis of 1958–61, gratuitously provoked by Khrushchev.

During the Berlin crisis, the Soviet Union replaced its defensive strategy in Europe with an offensive one, which envisaged crushing NATO by a swift thrust into Western Europe with the use of both nuclear and conventional forces. Whatever the doubtful feasibility of such a strategy, it marked a high level of Soviet confidence in defeating NATO should war ever occur in Europe for any reason. The likelihood of such a war, however, diminished after the two superpowers had come close to the brink outside Europe during the Cuban missile crisis of 1962, thus initiating a period of reduced threat during Khrushchev's last years in power.

In 1964, a new Kremlin leadership, more supportive of the Soviet military than Khrushchev had been, came to power. This resulted in an accelerated arms buildup and an intensified campaign against NATO's Multilateral Force, designed to provide for "nuclear sharing." The Multilateral Force project eventually fizzled away because of the lack of support for it among NATO members, including the Germans, but served as a catalyst of discord within the Warsaw Pact because of the disagreement about priorities and tactics that it created among its members, particularly the East Germans, Poles, and Romanians. The discord made it more difficult for Moscow to achieve a unified stand against the benefits of NATO, even with its parallel crisis in the second half of the 1960s.

This crisis reached its peak with France's departure from NATO's integrated command in 1966. The Soviet Union nevertheless remained mistrustful of French president Charles de Gaulle even while he sought rapprochement with Moscow at the expense of his relations with Washington, DC, and continued to assume that in case of a military emergency, France would stand by NATO. By 1967, NATO had overcome its crisis with the adoption of the Harmel Report, which defined its dual mission as both defense and détente, just as the crisis within the Soviet bloc was about to reach its culmination.

Developments in Czechoslovakia led in August 1968 to its invasion by Warsaw Pact troops—another watershed in Soviet relations with NATO. By engaging in a massive surprise operation that sent troops toward NATO's lines in West Germany, thus threatening to upset the established balance of forces in Central Europe, Moscow took the risk of provoking a NATO military reaction. Yet the Western alliance, misjudging Soviet intentions, proved as unprepared for the invasion of the neighboring territory as the Soviet Union was for fighting a war against NATO. The unopposed advance into Czechoslovakia exposed the Soviet Army's deficiencies and vulnerabilities, which could have been fatal in such a war, but it also revealed the shortcomings of NATO's warning system in case of an emergency.

The rise of détente that followed "normalization" in Czechoslovakia led also to a degree of normalization in the relations between the two military groupings in Europe. The reorganization of the Warsaw Pact, adopted in March 1969 by implementing some of the institutional and procedural features of NATO, made the Communist alliance look more like a functional counterpart to its rival. There was an increased willingness in the West to consider it NATO's legitimate counterpart as well as a factor in the balance of forces ensuring European stability.

Although the Soviet Union never ceased trying to undermine NATO, it acquiesced in important ways to the status quo that implied the continued existence of the Western alliance. It normalized relations with West Germany, and accepted the United States' participation in the Conference on Security and Cooperation in Europe. Within the framework of the conference, the two opposing alliances agreed to advance notification of military movements and the presence of each other's observers at military exercises—the core of the "confidence-building measures" that survived the subsequent collapse of détente.

Soviet assessments of NATO's capabilities changed significantly during the rise and fall of détente. In the early 1970s, Soviet respect for NATO was at its lowest since the Stalin times. The assessments of the enemy alliance dwelled on its weaknesses—political disunity, weak flanks, and extended and vulnerable supply lines. Soviet planners began to consider the possibility of defeating NATO without having to resort to nuclear weapons. In the latter half of the decade, however, NATO's organizational and technological improvements led to a reversal that emphasized the enemy's growing conventional capabilities. In the Warsaw Pact exercises that simulated a prospective thrust into Western Europe, the daily rates of advance were getting longer. Moreover, with the relations between the Soviet Union and China going from bad to worse, Moscow began to regard China as NATO's effective ally. Some Warsaw Pact exercises practiced two-front scenarios in which China would take the side of the West.

During the "Second Cold War," provoked in the early 1980s by the Soviet invasion of Afghanistan, NATO's "dual-track decision" became a crucial test of Moscow's security policy. After the Soviet Union deployed its SS-20 intermediate range nuclear missiles—with NATO lacking any equivalent—against Western European targets, the West countered by negotiating for the removal of the Soviet missiles while preparing for the deployment of its own "Euromissiles" should the negotiations fail. Counting on the widespread opposition in Western Europe against the deployments, the Soviet Union hedged and threatened to cut off negotiations if the installation of the Euromissiles was approved. The November 1983 vote by the West German parliament that paved the way to the installation therefore amounted to a reaffirmation of NATO's solidarity and a major Soviet setback.

Against the background of the confrontational policies of the U.S. administration of President Ronald Reagan, NATO's technological advances and its new AirLand Battle strategy generated genuine Soviet concern about Western intentions. NATO's new precision weapons and means of electronic warfare threatened to nullify the quantitative advantages that the Soviet Union had traditionally derived from its preponderance of conventional forces. The concept of AirLand Battle, which envisaged strikes deep behind the Warsaw Pact's lines to destroy its second echelon of forces, threatened to thwart the offensive strategy that the Soviet Union had been relying on since the 1960s. Soviet leader Yuri Andropov ordered a secret operation, code named RYaN, to detect any signs of an imminent surprise attack by NATO.

Mikhail Gorbachev's rise to power introduced a new era by basing Moscow's security policy on the assumption that NATO had reasons to be concerned about the Soviet threat and needed to be reassured about Soviet intentions. Gorbachev was the first to act unilaterally to reduce Soviet military capabilities even though NATO was maintaining its own. He came to see NATO as a necessary partner in negotiating radical reductions in both nuclear and conventional forces, which required greater sacrifices on the Soviet than on the Western side.

After the Cold War ended and the Soviet empire in Eastern Europe disintegrated in 1989, the Soviet Union and its remaining Warsaw Pact allies joined NATO in the November 1990 Paris declaration stating that they no longer regarded each other as enemies. The disintegration of the Warsaw Pact the following year left NATO as the only military alliance in Europe. Moscow had vainly opposed the entry of a reunited Germany into NATO. Following the dissolution of the Soviet Union, the weakened Russia proved unable to prevent NATO from admitting additional countries of the former Soviet bloc

to its membership, thus expanding its perimeter ever farther to the east. With NATO's military significance sharply diminished, its expansion was a triumph of the democratic principles on which the alliance had been built during the Cold War.

See also Cold War; Conference on Security and Cooperation in Europe; Containment; Warsaw Pact.

FURTHER READING

Kaplan, L. S. *The Long Entanglement: NATO's First Fifty Years.* Westport, CT: Greenwood Press, 1999.

Mastny, V. "Did NATO Win the Cold War? Looking over the Wall." *Foreign Affairs* 78, no. 3 (May–June 1999): 176–89.

———. "NATO in the Beholder's Eye: Soviet Perceptions and Policies, 1949–56." *Cold War International History Project Working Paper*, no. 35 (Washington, DC: Woodrow Wilson International Center for Scholars, 2002.

Schmidt, G., ed. *A History of NATO: The First Fifty Years.* 3 vols. Basingstoke, UK: Palgrave, 2001.

VOJTECH MASTNY

Novotný, Antonín

Antonín Novotný (1904–75) began his political career in Prague, and except for some brief activity outside the capital, never got to know any other region or city, or even the countryside. He was born into a working-class family and in his youth, after some training, began working in a factory. Early on he belonged to various Communist organizations and then joined the party itself. At thirty, Novotný was a member of a regional committee of the Communist Party of Czechoslovakia (CPCz). After three years, he became a regional secretary in Prague and later held the same position in Moravia in 1937 and 1938. He was involved in illegal party activities, and in September 1941, was arrested and spent almost four years in a concentration camp. Immediately after his release, he was appointed a head secretary of the CPCz for the Prague region.

The Prague region played a critical role in the political power struggles of the first three postwar years, which culminated in the Communist takeover of Czechoslovakia in 1948. Novotný was part of a group of leading functionaries that advocated radical policies, and then consolidated its position after the Prague coup. These policies, however, differed from the official party line, and this brought the group into conflict with the CPCz's central apparatus, controlled by Rudolf Slánský. Slánský now felt compelled to make changes in the regional leadership. All the adherents of these radical policies were replaced except Novotný, and even Novotny's dismissal was considered early in the purge. Novotný's promotion to the inner circle took place during the political trials of leading Communists.

After Slánský's dismissal in September 1951, Novotný was given the leadership of the party apparatus and internal party life. Unofficially, two reasons were given for this decision, made by Klement Gottwald: first, because of the previous conflicts between Novotný and Slánský; and second, because the move was recommended by Moscow. With Slánský's arrest in December 1951, Novotný became one of the most powerful figures in the country. But this new eight-man party apparatus was made up of members of the "Gottwald Guard," among whom Novotný had long been considered a second-rate novice. In January 1953, he left the leadership to assume the position of deputy chair of the government. Novotný considered this an unfair demotion in status, because he was forced to abandon the area in which he could best prove his political worth.

After Gottwald's death in March 1953, the highest posts were divided up. Novotný returned to the party apparatus, and within half a year had become first secretary of the Central Committee. His position became much stronger, because the position of chair of the CPCz had disappeared, and the first secretary was now the party's head. Novotný was made party chief, for one, because he showed strong interest in the post, but the main factor was that the leading Communists were following the Soviet practice of the time: moving the center of gravity of power from the party to the state and government. Novotný was thus "shunted aside" into a function with little potential for power. However, the first secretary post of the Central Committee soon grew stronger in the USSR, until it became completely dominant. An analogous shift now took place in Czechoslovakia as well. Novotný strengthened his position by resuscitating the status of the party apparatus, which had been badly shaken. Novotný rose still further with his selection as president of the republic, after the death of Antonin Zapotocký in 1957—an appointment recommended by Moscow. Novotný's strong position in the party leadership and the party itself now allowed him to force through his views and proposals without much opposition. The leaders had

to respect him because he enjoyed the trust and support of the Soviet leadership.

In the 1960s, Czechoslovakia encountered a series of difficulties resulting from both its past and current policies. These difficulties were complicated by Novotný's style of rule and his manner of solving problems. Demands for political change were becoming stronger among both leading officials and the population at large. After ten years in power, on the excuse that high party functions were being amalgamated, Novotný was forced to leave his post of first secretary in January 1968. Three months later he was compelled to relinquish the presidential office as well. Later, he was stripped of all functions and his CPCz membership was suspended—which he took particularly hard. In 1971, four years before his death, Novotný's membership was restored after he declared himself in agreement with the CPCz's policies after the Soviet occupation of Czechoslovakia.

Novotný began his political activity before World War II, but he reached high political office only after Czechoslovakia was liberated. He owed his accession more to the political trials of leading Communists (Slánský and his followers) than to his own political abilities. His political thinking and practice were dominated by two constants. The first was his agreement with the policies of the Soviet leadership and recognition of the leading role of the USSR in the Communist movement, even at times when Moscow itself was retreating from these proclamations. This "loyalty" resulted in frequent copying of Soviet decrees intended for Soviet policies (although it must be said that Novotný was the first Czechoslovak high official who came into conflict with Soviet leaders over matters of trade and finance). The second constant was that in his thinking and decision making, Novotný equated the party with society. The power position of the party along with its goals and interests were for him the only yardstick for solving all social questions, and they fully governed his view of society. The interests and goals of party members and functionaries, for Novotný, were the interests and goals of the whole society. He was a "man of the party" and its apparatus, which he governed, and to which he ascribed an overridingly important role and maximum power.

Novotný's political thinking was formed during a time of constant struggle with enemies, both internal and external. From the 1950s on, he stepped over the borders of this thinking only under Soviet influence or the pressure of social changes that weakened the power position of the party. These changes were the driving forces of the political relaxation of the 1960s. Nevertheless, as soon as Novotný perceived that this relaxation was threatening the leading role of the party, which he viewed in the same terms as in the 1950s, he resisted any attempts at reform. And that brought him into conflict with the new thinking that now prevailed in the party and society. Novotný lacked the ability of a creative politician to formulate concepts, and he was even unable to adapt Soviet decrees to Czechoslovak reality with any effectiveness. He was a politician capable of taking only concrete, ordinary measures. Yet he spoke with great love of the grand and imminent future of communism—ideas he usually borrowed from Moscow, though he, too, believed in them.

When Novotný rose to the highest party post, he was little known, and there were doubts about his capabilities for such a position. But he gradually learned the political trade and became familiar with the practices of party power struggles. He was soon winning all of his clashes with opponents and critics. He moved up the power ladder, and his self-confidence grew until he could make decisions with assurance. Novotný learned to apply the principle of personal power in a Communist dictatorship. No one dared to challenge him to an argument. At the same time, though, he was losing control of de-velopments in his country, and a reform movement was growing that would proceed without him and against him. The consequences of his policies and his inability to understand social changes and step beyond the limits of his thinking now showed themselves. In the second half of the 1960s, Novotný's political isolation grew, leading to his downfall in January 1968. He was caught by a fate very common in communist regimes—the isolation of a dictator.

See also De-Stalinization; People's Democracy; Prague Coup; Stalinism.

FURTHER READING

Cerny, R. *Antonin Novotny. Pozdni obhajoba.* Prague: Kiezler, 1992.

Golan, G. "Antonin Novotny: The Sources and Nature of His Power." *Canadian Slavonic Papers* 14, no. 3 (1972).

Hronek, J. *Czechslovakia Yesterday, Today, and Tomorrow.* Prague: Orbis, 1964.

Novak, L. *Kanclerem ri prezidentu.* Prague: Petrklic, 2002.

Novotný, A. *Exprezident, vzpomínky A. Novotného.* 3 vols. Říčany: Orego, 1998.

Pernes, J. *Takoví nám vládli.* Prague: Brána, 2003.

KAREL KAPLAN

Ordzhonikidze, Grigoriy (Sergo)

Grigoriy (Sergo) Ordzhonikidze (1886–1937) was born in the Gubernia of Kutaisi, Georgia. He became a member of the Russian Social Democratic Party in 1903, and developed ties to the legendary Caucasian revolutionary Kamo (Simon Ter-Petrosian). He took part in intense clandestine propaganda activity and participated in the revolutionary uprising of 1905. From 1905 to 1917, he was intermittently either in prison or forced residence, from which he returned during the February Revolution. In 1907 he participated, on party orders, in several episodes of the revolution in Iran, in the northern part of the country. He emigrated to France in 1910 and worked with Lenin at the party school in Longjumeau, near Paris. He also had an important role in preparing the Prague Conference of the Russian Social Democratic Workers' Party in 1912, during which he differed with Lenin in proposing to broaden the political spectrum of participants and move the party's leadership's headquarters back to Russia (it had been based abroad since 1908).

After having contributed to the October Revolution as a member of both the Petrograd Committee of the Russian Social Democratic Workers' Party (Bolshevik) and the capital's Soviet, in 1918–19 he became temporary commissar of the revolutionary government for southern Russia. He served in the Red Army, with high-ranking military responsibilities, on the southern and western fronts. It was in this period that a friendship developed between Ordzhonikidze and Sergey Kirov, another rising star of Caucasian Bolshevism, who later became his right-hand man in the Bolshevik Party organ responsible for the Caucasus and Transcaucasus (1921–26). After the Sovietization of Azerbaijan, Armenia, and Georgia, Ordzhonikidze clashed with Georgian Bolsheviks who were opposed to a federation of the three republics, as part of the new Soviet Union. There followed a memorable dispute between Stalin and Felix Dzherzinsky, on the one side, with the latter justifying Ordzhonikidze's authoritarian and rough treatment of the locals, and on the other side Lenin, who asked for a more considerate attitude toward Georgian national feelings and condemned the emergence of a great Russian neoimperial chauvinism (1922).

In 1926, Ordzhonikidze was nominated as president of the party's Central Control Commission and made the head of the People's Commissariat of Workers' and Peasants' Inspection. Even Leon Trotsky recognized that he had a certain political impartiality as an arbiter in the conflict between the Left opposition and party majority. He was an energetic supporter of accelerated industrialization, presided over the Superior Council for the National Economy in 1930, and was co-opted into the politburo. For several years he entertained friendly relations with Nikolay Bukharin, whom he entrusted with prestigious appointments in the field of technoscientific popularization. After the Superior Council for the National Economy's dissolution in 1932, he became commissar of the People's Commissariat for Heavy Industry (NKTP), the government's most important ministry.

In 1934, during the party's Seventeenth Congress, he asked that the industrialization effort be slowed down, thus confirming the complex and original nature of his political profile. Ordzhonikidze clashed repeatedly with Vyacheslav Molotov and Stalin in order to defend the institutional prerogatives of the NKTP against other ministries and territorial party organizations. The last of these clashes saw him trying to protect the leading cadres in heavy industry from a manipulation of Stakhanovism in a radical direction, which had been partly inspired by some of his politburo colleagues, followed by the arrest of his vice commissar, Georgy Pyatakov, in 1936; the accusations of Trotskyism leveled at Pyatakov placed him in an increasingly vulnerable political position.

Ordzhonikidze was probably led to commit suicide on the eve of the Great Terror's unleashing.

See also Kirov, Sergey; Politburo; Soviet Industrialization; Stalin, Joseph.

FURTHER READING

Benvenuti, F. "A Stalinist Victim of Stalin: 'Sergo' Ordzhonikidze." In *Soviet History, 1917–1953*, ed. J. Cooper, M. Perrie, and E. A. Rees. Basingstoke, UK: Macmillan, 1995.

Chlevnjuk, O. V. *In Stalin's Shadow: The Career of "Sergo" Ordzhonikidze*. Armonk, NY: M. E. Sharpe, 1995.

Ordzhonikidze, Z. G. *Put' bol'ševika*. Moscow: Gospolizdat, 1986.

Service, R. *Lenin: A Biography*. Cambridge, MA: Harvard University Press, 2000.

FRANCESCO BENVENUTI

Orthodox Church, Russian

According to the unwavering claims of the Communist Party over the seven decades when its dogma dominated religious expression in general and the edifice of the Russian Orthodox Church in particular, the Church before 1917 was corrupt, identified with the power structure of the czarist regime, and brought its sufferings upon itself by its intransigence. Recent research suggests another picture.

Many different tendencies coexisted within Russian orthodoxy just before the revolution, and there were serious efforts at reform, both locally and nationally. Peter the Great's Spiritual Regulation of 1721 had abolished the Moscow patriarchate and replaced it with a civil service under an *Oberprokuror* (the German term was used). The abdication of Nicholas II in March 1917 gave the cue for the hierarchy to summon a *sobor*, a national council, with lay and clergy representation, empowered to inaugurate wide-ranging reforms. The most telling of these was the election of a patriarch, Tikhon, a man of great moral authority.

The revolution cut short discussion of further reforms. Lenin early turned his attention to reducing ecclesiastical power. In January 1918, he promulgated the Decree on the Separation of the Church from the State and the School from the Church. All church property was nationalized, and religious education was abolished.

In 1921, at the end of the civil war, the Bolsheviks began implementing this decree. Defense of church property led to violence, particularly where church valuables were seized to alleviate the famine. Patriarch Tikhon led the opposition and was arrested in May 1922. The Bolsheviks forced clergy to take an oath of allegiance to the state, leading to the temporary emergence of the "Living Church," which proclaimed loyalty to the new regime. Among those who resisted was Metropolitan Venyamin of Petrograd, who in August 1922 was shot with three associates after a show trial. After confessing, Tikhon was released from prison in June 1923, but died mysteriously in April 1925.

The patriarchal throne remained vacant until 1944. Under duress, Metropolitan Sergi of Moscow signed a statement of unqualified support for the government in June 1927. No successor has ever renounced this; it remained official policy throughout the Communist period (even influencing attitudes in the post-Soviet era).

Stalin's Decree on Religious Associations (April 1929) abolished the vestigial freedom in the Constitution, inaugurating a period of church destruction and liquidation of the clergy. All church administration ceased to exist, and only a handful of churches remained open.

World War II saw an improvement for the Church. Clergy who took the oath of loyalty now returned from the gulag to their parishes, some of which reopened (including many behind the lines of the German advance). Stalin summoned the three metropolitans at liberty in September 1943 and empowered them to call an immediate sobor, leading to the election of Sergi as patriarch. He died in 1944, and Alexi I succeeded him. The patriarchate reestablished its existence, but was closely monitored by the government's Council for Russian Orthodox Church Affairs, which had no basis in law. Training clergy again became possible in reopened theological institutes, and new dioceses covered the whole USSR.

Nikita Khrushchev, embarrassed by the abundant evidence of a revitalized Church, instituted another antireligious campaign (1959–64), spearheaded by propaganda articles in the newspapers and instigating violence against believers of all persuasions. The number of open orthodox churches fell from some twenty thousand to a tenth of that number. Resistance, however, emerged in a coordinated way, parallel to the rise of the dissident movement in other spheres. Two young Moscow priests, fathers Nikolai Eshliman and Gleb Yakunin, provided the first comprehensive documentation of Soviet religious persecution, and their work achieved worldwide publicity. Anatoli Levitin and other writers followed in a torrent of samizdat, which continued until the relaxation of censorship under Mikhail Gorbachev.

An (uncanonical) Council of Bishops met in May 1971, following the death of Patriarch Alexi I. Its decisions ensured that the sobor that followed ratified disputed measures enforced in 1961, permitting state interference in local church affairs. The sobor then elected the weak Pimen, an opponent of dissent, as patriarch. Long an invalid, he died in 1990.

No significant movement in church-state relations had occurred between the demise of Khrushchev and the accession of Gorbachev, but then the floodgates opened. Gorbachev released the many religious prisoners, and in April 1988 he received the senior hierarchs. He granted them permission to celebrate the millennium of the "Baptism of Rus" (988–1988), which galvanized the media at home and abroad as well as Christians of all persuasions to reverse seventy years of Soviet control of religion. Gorbachev authorized a new law guaranteeing freedom of religion, in force from 1990 until 1997.

Patriarch Alexi II (an ethnic Estonian) was elected in 1990, and at the demise of the USSR religion was freer than it had ever been in Russian history.

See also Atheism, Soviet; Dissent in the USSR; Family; Great Patriotic War; State, The.

FURTHER READING

Bourdeaux, M. *Gorbachev, Glasnost, and the Gospel*. London: Hodder and Stoughton, 1990.

Struve, N. *Christians in Contemporary Russia*. London: Harvill Press, 1967.

MICHAEL BOURDEAUX

Orwell, George

There have been many competing assessments of George Orwell's (1903–50) life and works. He has drawn admiration from Trotskyites and Tories alike, yet given rise to vitriolic hatred from the New Left, postcolonial theorists, and feminist critics. This diversity of interpretation mirrors the complexity of his life. Was he the nondogmatic but impassioned observer of Europe's poor or an old Etonian "observing" the natives? Was he a cold warrior crusading against socialism in all its forms or a

Trotskyite survivor of the militia in the Spanish civil war? Did his political trajectory end in reformist socialism or did he retain a belief in the revolutionary transformation of society?

Christened Eric Arthur Blair, he was born in Motihari, Bengal, India, on June 25, 1903, and moved to Britain when he was three. In *The Road to Wigan Pier* he described his family background as "lower-upper middle class." He initially went to a small Anglican Convent School in Henley-on-Thames, then won a scholarship to St. Cyprian's prep school and went on as a scholar to Eton. If his account in "Such, Such Were the Joys" is to be believed, his years at prep school were a mixture of bullying and brutality. After Eton, he went to Crammers to prepare for the Indian Civil Service and joined the Burma police in 1921.

Both Orwell's birth and political awakening, therefore, were marked by empire. In his time in the police he saw the sharp end of Britain's imperial administration. His experiences led him to claim that he "hated the imperialism I was serving with a bitterness which I probably cannot make clear." Nevertheless, later critics such as Daphne Patai have claimed that this school of hard knocks also imbued him with a conscious and virulent masculine identity that shone through his later fiction. He resigned in 1927, and, according to Victor Pritchard, "went native in his own country" as a dishwasher in Paris and as a tramp in London. He described his experiences in *Down and Out in Paris and London* (1933), a memoir written under the name of George Orwell. While recording his experiences with an economy of style and a vivid passion for which he became famous, his early books betray little attachment to socialism. Indeed, at the time he described himself as a "Tory Anarchist."

His commitment to socialism was nurtured in the wake of the depression, writing articles and reviewing books for *The Adelphi*. In January 1936, Victor Gollancz gave Orwell an advance of £500 to write a book about poverty for the Left Book Club. The resultant work, *The Road to Wigan Pier* (1937), detailed his allegiance to socialism but also his dislike for socialist intellectuals. It is partly this no-nonsense, common-sense dismissal of what he saw as the cranky socialist intelligentsia that has annoyed them ever since: "One sometimes gets the impression that the mere words 'Socialism' and 'Communism' draw towards them with magnetic force every fruit-juice drinker, nudist, sandal-wearer, sex maniac, Quaker, 'Nature Cure' quack, pacifist and feminist in England." In the same work, he announced his independence from doctrinaire socialist theory claiming that "A writer cannot be a *loyal* member of a political party." Gollancz felt obliged to print a disclaimer when the book was published, dissociating the Left Book Club from such opinions and from the attacks on the Soviet Union.

Orwell's mistrust of Soviet power was confirmed by his experiences in the Spanish civil war. He traveled to Spain at the end of 1936 to fight, like many volunteers from all over Europe, in defense of the republic and in defiance of fascism. Barcelona seemed to him to have undergone a profound social revolution that contrasted with the apathy and class-ridden angst, which Orwell had experienced in the north of England. He joined the POUM militia on the Aragon front, where his predominant experience of war was "mud, lice, hunger, and cold." In May 1937, he became involved in the troubles in Barcelona occasioned by the Communist Party's attempts to purge the POUM and Catalan anarchists. The whole experience made him bitterly disillusioned and confirmed his hatred of the Soviet version of communism. His book *Homage to Catalonia* (1938) sold few copies but was vigorously debated by the left-wing intelligentsia. Gollancz refused to publish it because of its extreme criticisms of Soviet policy, and it was brought out by Frederick Warburg in April of 1938.

Orwell in the late 1930s was as critical of British capitalist imperialism as he was of the Stalinist show trials. However, the outbreak of the Second World War convinced him that even the Britain of Chamberlain was worth supporting in the face of the Nazi threat. His support for Britain in the war effort was outlined initially in his famous essay, "My Country, Right or Left" and developed in *The Lion and the Unicorn* (1941). What is so striking about these works is that they combined the language of patriotism with the polemics of socialism. Orwell did not merely argue that the country should be supported as a lesser evil than fascism, but that "the England I was taught to love so long ago" embodied a mystical nationalism that was worth supporting in its own right. In the early years of the war, Orwell thought that this patriotism would reinforce the chances of social revolution in Britain. His famous characterization of Britain as a family "with the wrong members in control" comes from this belief. Nevertheless, as the war progressed he became less insistent on the need for revolution. This has been variously interpreted as a conversion to reformist socialism or a tactical belief that the moment for revolution was no longer right.

In early 1944 Orwell finished his most enduringly popular work, *Animal Farm* (1945). The alliance with Russia meant it was not a propitious time to publish such a biting satire of the Bolshevik Revolution. The proofs were rejected by Gollancz, Faber, Jonathan Cape, and Collins. When it was eventually published after the war by Warburg, the circumstances of the Cold War conditioned its reception. It sold 250,000 copies in the first year and made Orwell famous. Even after 1989–91, the fable of how a successful revolution becomes perverted by a new ruling class is enduringly popular. However, at the time Orwell was keen to point out that *Animal Farm* was not an attack on socialism and revolution as such. Rather it was a satire on violent conspiratorial revolution of which the Bolshevik coup d'état was the preeminent example. In a letter to Dwight MacDonald, he claimed: "I meant the moral to be that revolutions are only a radical improvement when the masses are alert and know how to chuck out their leaders as soon as the latter have done their job. This did not prevent Orwell's work being read purely as an anti-Communist polemic in the Cold War years, most notably in John Halas and Joy Batchelor's cartoon version, which was made in 1954.

The political trajectory of the end of Orwell's life has been variously interpreted. For Bernard Crick he found his home within the left of British democratic laborism writing for the *Tribune*. Others, such as John Newsinger, have emphasized his ongoing commitment to revolutionary socialism as evidenced by his contributions to the *Partisan Review*. Others on the Right have seen Orwell's postwar years as beginning a process of disillusionment with socialism in general. This latter viewpoint is hard to maintain. On the publication of *1984* in 1949 he made it clear in a letter to American trade unionists that it "is *not* intended as an attack on Socialism or on the British Labour Party (of which I am a supporter)." The book *1984* became so important for anti-Communist conservatism mainly because of the Left's failure to sufficiently dissociate Stalinism from its own brand of socialism. Nevertheless, Orwell's vision of a dystopic totalitarian state remains one of the most important works of the 20th century and has added new words—"Big Brother," "Double think"—to the political lexicon.

George Orwell married Sonia Mary Brownell in October of 1949 and died of a tubercular hemorrhage soon after, on January 21, 1950. Battles over his reputation have raged ever since. For many on the Left, such as Raymond Williams and Edward Thompson, he was a poor theorist and an apologist for the conservatives. Nevertheless, for most of his millions of readers Orwell remains perhaps the 20th century's most lucid interpreter of political tyranny. It is this, rather than the way in which his writings were polemicized in the Cold War, that will be his most enduring legacy.

See also Anticommunism; Spanish Civil War; Stalinism; Totalitarianism; Trotskyism.

FURTHER READING

"Blair, Eric Arthur," in *The Oxford Dictionary of National Biography*. Oxford: Oxford University Press, 2004.

Crick, B. *George Orwell: A Life*. London: Seeker and Warburg, 1981.

Davidson, P., ed. *The Complete Works of George Orwell*, vols. 1–20. London: Seeker and Warburg, 1986–98.

Newsinger, J. *Orwell's Politics*. London: Macmillan, 1999.

Orwell, G. *Homage to Catalonia*. London: Penguin, [1938] 1989.

Patai, D. *The Orwell Mystique*. Amherst: University of Massachusetts Press, 1986.

TOM VILLIS

Ostpolitik

The Federal Republic of Germany's (FRG) *Ostpolitik* began with a decision by then Chancellor Konrad Adenauer to accept an invitation to Moscow in September 1955 for a state visit. On this occasion diplomatic relations were established between the FRG and the Soviet Union, and an agreement was reached on the release of the last ten thousand German prisoners of war, still interned in Soviet camps. In order to prevent the risk of a simultaneous recognition of the German Democratic Republic (GDR) by the international community of states, immediately after Adenauer's return from Moscow, the government in Bonn announced its so-called Hallstein doctrine: the FRG declared that it was the only legitimate German state. Any country attempting to establish diplomatic relations with the GDR would risk losing its diplomatic relations with the FRG. While this position contributed to the GDR's international isolation, it also prevented the FRG from establishing diplomatic relations with other states from the Eastern bloc, the Soviet Union excepted.

The FRG slowly moved away from the Hallstein doctrine after the construction of the Berlin Wall (August 1961). During 1963–64 the government in Bonn, guided by Ludwig Erhard, concluded commercial agreements with Poland, Romania, Hungary, and Bulgaria in which West Berlin was also tacitly involved. In 1966 the grand coalition government with Kurt Georg Kiesinger as chancellor and Willy Brandt as foreign minister offered to establish diplomatic relations with the countries of Eastern Europe without their having to break with the GDR. Romania immediately agreed, in January 1967. When Hungary and Bulgaria were about to follow the Romanian example, however, Moscow intervened with a veto: the normalization of relations with the FRG could only occur once it had recognized the GDR and the Oder-Neisse border. Under pressure from these demands, a majority developed in Bonn in favor of recognizing both the GDR as a second German state and ex–East German territories that had now become Polish.

The Brandt-Scheel government, formed after the elections in September 1969, insisted that the GDR was not considered a foreign country by the FRG, however, and that a reunification of the two states of the German nation must remain a possibility. The accords with the GDR and other countries of the Eastern bloc were regarded as a way "to operate for the achievement of a peaceful situation in Europe in which the German people may once more find its unity by means of self-determination." In the Treaty of Moscow of August 12, 1970, the FRG and the Soviet Union declared their adherence to principles such as the renunciation of the use of force and the "inviolability" of European borders, "including the Oder-Neisse line, which constitutes the Western border of the People's Republic of Poland, and the border between the Federal Republic of Germany and the German Democratic Republic." The federal government in Bonn's desire to work toward a reunification of the Germans was expressed on that occasion in a letter from the German foreign minister to his Soviet counterpart.

The Treaty of Moscow was ratified only after World War II's victorious powers had agreed to a resolution of West Berlin's status. In the Berlin agreement of September 3, 1971, the Soviet Union guaranteed freedom of movement from and to West Berlin. The Western powers agreed that the western sectors of Berlin were "not a constitutive part of the Federal Republic of Germany"; yet the government in Bonn was given the right to assist the residents of West Berlin and involve West Berlin under certain circumstances in international accords. The treaties that the FRG signed with Poland (December 7, 1970) and Czechoslovakia (December 11, 1973) once again confirmed the principle of the borders' inviolability. Out of consideration for the political weight that

German refugees from Eastern territories had in West Germany, though, the government in Bonn refused to extend the recognition of the western border with Poland also to a future peace treaty and admit the lack of validity of the 1938 Munich Accords on the territorial cession of the Sudetenland.

The Brandt-Scheel government initially agreed to a transit accord (December 17, 1971) that made trips to and from West Berlin easier. On May 12, 1972, another accord on the circulation of people allowing West Germans to travel in the GDR and citizens from the GDR to reach West Germany "for urgent family matters" was also signed. Its preamble recognized "the different perspectives on the national question," and the countries' respective diplomatic representatives did not have the rank of ambassador. In the FRG the treaties with the East raised some opposition. The early political elections of November 19, 1972, thus became a sort of plebiscite in favor or against Brandt's "new Ostpolitik." Brandt emerged the winner and was returned with a large majority to lead the government.

For its part the GDR government repeatedly attempted not to honor the obligations it had agreed to in the areas of greater openness and exchanges. In the autumn of 1973, transit traffic was hampered and the circulation of visitors was limited by doubling the minimum amount of money that citizens from the FRG had to exchange when entering the GDR. In October 1980 there was another increase in these currency minimums as well as a claim that GDR citizenship be recognized. The GDR's increasing reliance on credits given by the FRG led to these limits being suspended or circumvented, to the extent that an intense movement of people developed between the FRG and the GDR. In the fall of 1978 a number of agreements on the widening of access roads were reached, including one for the construction of a new highway between Hamburg and Berlin. Other agreements focused on upgrading the road network followed in the spring of 1980. In February 1982 the government of the GDR extended its permit to visit relatives in the FRG so as to include the possibility of passing the holidays together.

The exchanges between East and West Germans thus took on such significance that the initial criticisms targeting the treaties with the East came to a halt. Once the Social Democratic–Liberal government led by Helmut Schmidt and Hans-Dietrich Genscher was replaced by a coalition of Christian Democrats and Liberals (with Helmut Kohl as chancellor and Genscher as foreign minister), nothing changed in terms of the FRG's Ostpolitik. On the contrary, in June 1983 the president of the Christian-Social Union (the mainly Bavarian section of the German Christian-Democratic parties), Franz Josef Strauss, previously one of the most vocal critics of the treaties with the East, acted as an intermediary so that West German banks could give the GDR significant amounts of credit. In September 1987, a state visit to Bonn by Erich Honecker strengthened the collaboration between East and West Germans.

The FRG's relations with the regime in Warsaw developed accordingly. In October 1975 an accord was reached for a generous German financial credit to Poland. The government in Bonn also acknowledged its obligation to compensate Polish citizens who had been subjected to forced labor by Germany during World War II, after the fact, and also agreed to assume the cost of transferring those Poles of German origin who so desired to West Germany. The Polish government in turn increased the emigration permits. From 1977 on political personalities, publicists, scientists, and businesspeople from both countries met regularly during German-Polish conferences. The twinning of cities and universities also promoted lively social exchanges.

Economic collaboration flourished most especially between the FRG and the USSR. Starting February 1, 1970, after German businesspeople had agreed on a wide-ranging economic accord that among other items dealt with the sale of German steel tubing in exchange for Siberian methane for twenty years, German chancellor Schmidt agreed in November 1974 at a state visit to Moscow to an increase in economic cooperation. Until the early 1980s, the FRG thus became both quantitatively and qualitatively the Soviet Union's most important commercial partner. Thirty percent of the FRG's methane imports came from the USSR, and significant portions of the output of the FRG's heavy industry were headed back there.

The various governments in Bonn also worked to support arms reduction policies and the adoption of security measures that encouraged greater reciprocal trust. The Brandt-Scheel government was among the pioneers of the Conference on Security and Cooperation in Europe. The Schmidt-Genscher government defended dialogue in matters of security policy against growing criticism coming from the United States. The Kohl-Genscher government initially moved to approve the decision that would "update" the Western medium-range missile arsenal, but subsequently exercised pressure on U.S. leaders so they would agree to Mikhail Gorbachev's proposals in the matter of security policy. When during the fall of 1989 the dissolution of the Soviet Empire in Central-Eastern Europe was taking shape, the Kohl government felt obliged to support Soviet perestroika. The following year the FRG's annexation of the GDR proceeded on the basis of common agreements. Bilateral relations were increased at the same time, and the collective structures for security in Europe were strengthened.

See also Berlin Wall; Conference on Security and Cooperation in Europe; Détente; Reunification of Germany.

FURTHER READING

Garton Ash, T. *In Europe's Name: Germany and the Divided Continent.* New York: Vintage Press, 1994.

Potthoff, H. *Im Schatten der Mauer. Deutschlandpolitik 1961 bis 1990.* Berlin: Propyläen, 1999.

WILFRIED LOTH

Partisans of Peace

The Movement of Partisans of Peace, later renamed Movement of Peace, was a Communist mass organization created in April 1949 during a congress held simultaneously in Paris and Prague. The organization came to represent the instrumental use of pacifism during the Cold War. Its theoretical context was sketched out at two Cominform conferences held in September 1947, when Andrey Zhdanov introduced his "two camps" thesis—according to which the war camp, led by the United States, faced the peace camp, led by the Soviet Union—and in November 1949, when Palmiro Togliatti's but above all Mikhail Suslov's reports offered a vision of the role of pacifist themes within global Communist strategy.

On the organizational level the first phase was that of individual initiatives, especially the Congress of Intellectuals for Peace, organized in Wroclaw (Poland) from August 25 to August 28, 1948. The Soviets remained in the wings, and the congress was organized by Laurent Casanova (the French Communist Party functionary responsible for intellectuals), Emilio Sereni (a leader of the Italian Communist Party's cultural commission), and Jerzy Borejsza (a propagandist), on behalf of the French, Italian, and Polish parties. The initiative was successful despite novelist Aleksandr Fadeev's attack on Jean-Paul Sartre, Arthur Miller, André Malraux, and other "hyena typists," thanks to the high level of the participants (the French delegation included Pablo Picasso, Fernand Léger, and Paul Éluard) and the adoption of a manifesto that blamed the Western powers for the risk of provoking a new war. The committee formed after this conference was given the task of organizing another conference in April 1949. This congress, which formally created the Movement of the Partisans of Peace, gained fame because of its poster's image: a dove, drawn by Picasso for the occasion.

On March 19, 1950, the international leadership of the Movement of the Partisans of Peace invited signatories to the Stockholm appeal for the prohibition of atomic weapons. Officially about five hundred million signatures were gathered. If in socialist countries the signatures were collective and not significant, in Western Europe the appeal was successful. According to estimates, about seventeen million Italians and twelve million French (officially fourteen million) signed the appeal—largely due to the permanent mobilization of Communists worldwide. Many archival documents attest to the efforts undertaken by all Communist parties for this campaign's success, which also benefited from the Soviet's vigilant attention.

But this climax for the Partisans of Peace was also its swan song. The Communists did not manage to build on the groundswell of sympathy that the campaign had created or replicate the numbers with other signature campaigns. The Communist parties accompanied these initiatives—aimed at the masses, and with the goal of creating a buffer zone—with harsher rhetoric warning that these concerns should not benefit "teary-eyed pacifism" but rather the socialist ranks, which at the time were engaged in the Sovietization of the countries of the East and the conquest of Korea. This is the origin of the many provocative declarations of support for the Red Army by numerous European Communist leaders (like Togliatti and Maurice Thorez), in line with the resolution by the French Communist Party's Political Office on January 20, 1949: "Solemnly affirm, and repeat in your speeches, that Communists do not consider the USSR a foreign power like others, and that every progressive individual has two motherlands, his own and the USSR."

Once the paroxysm of the Cold War had been overcome, starting in 1956 the Movement for Peace did not dissolve but entered a vegetative state, from which it periodically emerged in the following decades when new pacifist campaigns were promoted by international communism.

See also Atomic Bomb; Cold War; Cominform; Propaganda, Communist.

FURTHER READING

Dockrill, S., R. Frank, G.-H. Soutou, and A. Varsori, ed. *L'Europe de l'Est et de l'Ouest dans la Guerre froide, 1948–1953.* Paris: Presses de l'Université de Paris-Sorbonne, 2002.

Procacci, G., ed. *The Cominform: Minutes of the Three Conferences, 1947/1948/1949.* Milan: Fondazione Giangiacomo Feltrinelli, 1994.

Santamaria, Y. *Le pacifisme, une passion française.* Paris: Armand Collin, 2005.

Vaïsse, M., ed. *Le pacifisme en Europe des années 1920 aux années 1950.* Brussels: Bruyant, 1993.

PHILIPPE BUTON

Peaceful Coexistence

The most complete enunciation of the doctrine of "peaceful coexistence" appeared in the Communist Party of the Soviet Union's program, approved at its Twenty-second Congress (1961). It was presented as a principle with which Communists intended to affirm a new concept of international relations opposed to that of the "imperialist camp"; it would therefore concern relations between the United States and the USSR, and not relations internal to the Soviet bloc, which would instead continue to be regulated by a different code of behavior inspired by "proletarian internationalism." The doctrine's contents were summed up in a series of points: the renunciation of war for resolving controversial issues between states; noninterference in the internal affairs of other nations; respect for other nations' sovereignty; and the development of international cooperation, limited to the sphere of economic and cultural relations.

Peaceful coexistence was viewed as the principal instrument to prevent a third world war, which would once again have been unleashed by imperialism. In reality the postulates approved in 1961 contained residual conceptions from the past, thus leading to ambiguities and oscillations in judgment. The basis for the doctrine was a concept of peace interpreted as the absence of war and conflicts. A positive notion, one including forms of political cooperation with the "imperialist camp," would have been unthinkable so long as this camp was perceived as unanimously and permanently hostile. This vagueness

was balanced by the clear definition of what the doctrine was not and should not be: it did not affect ideology and therefore did not extend to the political realm. The elements of conflict were given more attention than those of reciprocity or those which showed a progressive coming together of the two systems.

The definition of a "new principle" in international relations in the 1961 program was also contradicted because of its attribution to Lenin. The Soviet state's founder had remained faithful to a view of international relations in which the inevitability of war between the two systems was taken for granted. Any peace before the establishment of a new world order based on Communist ideals would not have represented the end of hostilities, but only a temporary armistice, a truce so as to acquire new strength for the next battle. This deep-rooted skepticism about Soviet Russia's obtaining something less precarious and more constructive than a short breather was made manifest in 1922, when Lenin vigorously applied the brakes on the diplomats—who favored making the necessary concessions to reinsert Soviet Russia into the community of nations, and who were agreeable to peaceful coexistence as laid out by the promoters of the Geneva Conference.

This formula, centered on the principle of noninterference in the internal affairs of individual states and a respect for national sovereignty, incorporated ideas already expressed by Georgy Chicherin. He had attempted to elaborate a coherent and wide-ranging program for Soviet foreign policy, centered on acknowledging the development of two ideologically opposed camps, and the possibility of realizing a peaceful coexistence rigidly limited to economic relations and commercial exchanges with the West. The hope was to provide a shared terrain less riven by ideological struggles, one that would instead bolster cooperation, where mutual benefits could prevail. For Western countries, interested in Russia's return to the community of European nations, the benefit was help in strengthening the continent's economy; for Soviet Russia, the benefit was access to the investments and credits of industrially more developed countries, thereby facilitating more rapid economic growth.

In condemning the initiatives of the Soviet diplomats in Genoa and resisting peaceful coexistence understood as economic collaboration, Lenin instead reconfirmed the use of peaceful coexistence as a simple expedient to gain time, in the name of the theory of truce. He also proved that he fully shared the fear, widespread in the Bolshevik Party at the time, that Soviet Russia would not be able to withstand the weapon of economic aid if it collaborated with the capitalist world. Weak and backward, the USSR would be forced to supply raw materials to the most industrialized countries of the West, and thus be subject to a form of enslavement. This skepticism with regard to the intentions of foreign governments also shaped Stalin's employment of Lenin's concept of truce. In the aftermath of World War II, Stalin reproposed a restrictive interpretation of peaceful coexistence, founded on a rigidly bipolar view of international relations. Peaceful coexistence was confined to the diplomatic and military spheres, and did not entertain any hypothesis of collaboration with the imperialist camp. It was a conception that reflected a culture of separateness, characteristic of Stalinism, to which distinctly xenophobic traits and nationalist urges were not foreign.

Khrushchev's de-Stalinization also had an impact on the notion of peaceful coexistence. The concept's relaunching was preceded by sporadic but authoritative hints of the possibility or even necessity that it might develop into a collaboration between the two systems, aimed at avoiding a third world war. For Khrushchev, peaceful coexistence became the principal instrument to pursue the "non-inevitability of war." This thesis, however, displayed residues of the Stalinist conception. It continued to concern the bipolar relations between the two camps, and was confined to the diplomatic and military spheres. The best guarantee for its success still lay in strengthening the Soviet state and the socialist camp. These elements were then reinforced during the Leonid Brezhnev era. A codification now took place, spelling out a distinction within peaceful coexistence: on the one hand, as a rule in the relations between the United States and the USSR; and on the other hand, as "limited sovereignty," or the norm that would rule relations between Moscow and the countries that made up the Soviet bloc. In the 1970s peaceful coexistence began to be identified with détente, but the 1979 invasion of Afghanistan undermined hope of a real peace between Communist and non-Communist countries.

Mikhail Gorbachev's "New Thinking" derived its inspiration from the idea—first formulated by Andrey Sakharov in 1968—that one should transform peace into a positive concept and conceive of it as a collective enterprise involving the efforts of all humankind. During the first phase of perestroika, however, traditional elements and innovations coexisted once more. Gorbachev presented the Twenty-seventh Congress of the Communist Party of the Soviet Union (1986) with a concept that dif-

fered from the preceding official formulations, proposing "a creative and constructive collaboration between states and peoples on a global scale," with the purpose of "preventing nuclear catastrophe." Yet the ritual statement about the "inevitable collapse of capitalism" was included, and capitalism was singled out as solely responsible for the two world wars, a permanent threat to peace, destined to be replaced by socialism.

The progressive and unstoppable worsening of the economic situation in the USSR led Gorbachev to adopt a more realistic approach to international problems as well. The need for a substantial reduction in military spending, dictated by the needs of domestic policy, contributed to the search for political dialogue with the United States, so that peaceful coexistence might really become "the universal principle in international relations" and problems could be resolved via political means. Some inevitable and universally valid norms remained, though: noninterference in internal affairs, and the freedom of each people to choose the social and political system with which it intended to be governed. The collapse of communism deprived these claims, conceived for a world divided by two opposing ideologies, of all meaning and legitimacy.

See also Atomic Bomb; Bipolarity; Détente; Diplomats; Khrushchev, Nikita; New Thinking; Socialist Camp; War, Inevitability of.

FURTHER READING

di Biagio, A. *Coesistenza e isolazionismo: Mosca, il Komintern e l'Europa di Versailles, 1918–1928*. Rome: Carocci, 2004.

Gorbachev, M. S. *Perestroika: New Thinking for Our Country and the World*. New York: HarperCollins, 1987.

Procacci, G. "La coesistenza pacifica. Appunti per la storia di un concetto." In *La politica estera della perestrojka: l'Urss di fronte al mondo da Brežnev a Gorbačëv*, ed. L. Sestan. Rome: Editori Riuniti, 1988.

ANNA DI BIAGIO

Peasants in the USSR

The peasantry presented the Communist Party with the most formidable challenge of the revolution. Communist definitions of the peasantry generally sought to explain it away, to see it as a dying class, a transitional class that would disappear with the advent of socialism. Communists expected the peasantry to dissolve into the working class—as indeed it did elsewhere in Europe—as the industrialization of the country expanded and siphoned off labor from the countryside. Until that time, however, the peasantry was a glaring social, economic, and political contradiction to the premise and reality of the revolution.

Soviet power was based on a "dictatorship of the proletariat and poor peasantry." In 1917, when the Bolsheviks championed peasant revolutionary goals as their own, Lenin claimed that "there is *no* radical divergence of interests between wage-workers and the working and exploited peasantry. Socialism is *fully* able to meet the interests of both." In fact, the dictatorship, and the alliance from which it derived, combined mutually irreconcilable aims and would quickly break apart in conflict. It could not have been otherwise given the contradictions inherent in the October Revolution, a "working-class revolution" in an agrarian nation in which the industrial proletariat accounted for little more than 3 percent of the population, while the peasantry constituted no less than 85 percent. Lev Kritsman, a leading Marxist scholar of the peasantry in the postrevolutionary years, asserted that there were actually two revolutions in 1917—an urban, socialist revolution and a rural, bourgeois or antifeudal revolution. The two revolutions had different and ultimately antithetical goals. Following the forced expropriations and partitions of the gentry's lands in 1917, the peasantry desired no more than the right to be left alone: to prosper as farmers and to dispose of their produce as they saw fit. Although some peasants may have shared the socialist aims of the urbanites, most were averse to the principles of socialist collectivism.

The 1917 revolution had the unintended consequence of reinforcing many aspects of peasant culture and, specifically, a number of important features underlying and strengthening community cohesion. Although human and material losses from years of war and the famine that followed in the wake of civil war took a tremendous toll in the countryside, the revolution, in combination with this time of troubles, had the effect of revitalizing the peasant community. Peasants engaged in massive social leveling. The percentages of poor peasants fell from a pre-revolutionary level of some 65 percent to around 25 percent by the mid-1920s, while the proportion of wealthy peasants declined from roughly 15 percent (depending upon the method of calculation) to about 3 percent in the same time span. The middle peasant became the dominant figure in Soviet agriculture as a result of wartime loses, social revolution and redivision of wealth, and the return, often forced, of large numbers of peasants who had quit the commune to establish individual farmsteads in the prewar Stolypin agrarian reforms. Socioeconomic differentiation remained fairly stable through the 1920s, showing only very slight increases at the extremes. Leveling reinforced village homogeneity and cohesion while strengthening the position of the middle peasant who, according to Eric Wolf, represented the most "culturally conservative stratum" of the peasantry and the village force most resistant to change. The commune itself was bolstered as most of the Stolypin peasants returned to communal land tenure, which constituted approximately 95 percent of all land tenure in the mid-1920s, thereby standardizing the peasant economy. And although peasant households splintered as the liberating effects of the revolution encouraged and enabled the sons of peasants to free themselves from the authority of the patriarchal household, most peasants, especially women and the weaker members of the community, clung all the more tenaciously to customary and conservatives notions of household, family, marriage, and faith in order to weather the crisis of the times. While the revolution no doubt disrupted and altered significant aspects of peasant life, historians increasingly believe that the basic structures and institutions of the village demonstrated considerable continuity over the revolutionary divide, in many cases becoming stronger as a defensive bulwark against economic hardship and the destructive incursions of warring governments and armies, Red and White.

The strengthening of homogeneity and the endurance of peasant culture should not imply that the peasantry was a static, unchanging rustic fixture. Profound processes of change had long been at work in the countryside, accelerating in particular in the late 19th and early 20th centuries. Alternative patterns of socialization appeared as peasant-workers and soldiers returned on visits or permanently to their home villages. Urban patterns of taste and, to a lesser extent, consumption also began to make an appearance in rural Russia as personal contacts between town and countryside became more common. A market economy made inroads into the countryside, altering the economy of the peasant household as well as the internal social dynamics of the commune. Family size declined as extended families slowly began to give way to nuclear families, and marriages began to be based less exclusively on parents' choices. Peasant culture did not stagnate but evolved over time, absorbing change and pragmatically adopting what was of use. Fundamental structures and institutions of peasant community persisted, demonstrating the durability and adaptability of the peasantry as a culture.

Similar patterns of change persisted into the Soviet period, coexisting, sometimes peacefully, sometimes not, with the prevailing patterns of peasant and community relations and dynamics. Although many interactions between village and town were seriously disrupted during the revolution and civil war, the town and state continued to have an enormous impact on the countryside. Tens of thousands of peasant-workers returned to their villages during the civil war, bringing with them new ways and practices not always in line with those of the community. A vast number of peasants served in the army during the world war and civil war, and they, too, returned with new ideas, sometimes at odds with those of their neighbors. From some of these groups emerged the village's first Communists and Komsomols; early collective farms and the splintering of households often derived from the aspirations and needs of these prodigal sons. The Communist Party, in the meantime, although in practice generally neglectful of the countryside through most of the 1920s and preoccupied with industrial and internal party politics was, in theory, committed to remaking the peasantry, to eliminating it as an antiquated socioeconomic category in an accelerated depeasantization that would transform peasant into proletarian. The party, the Komsomol, peasant-workers home on leave, groups of poor peasants and Red Army veterans, and rural correspondents (*sel'kory*) all became dimly lit beacons of Communist sensibility in the village. Efforts at socialization and indoctrination occurred in periodic antireligion campaigns, literacy campaigns, election campaigns, campaigns to recruit party and Komsomol members, campaigns to organize poor peasants or women, and so on, as the state attempted to build bridges into the countryside to bolster the *smychka* (worker-peasant alliance) of the 1920s. The state succeeded in establishing pockets of support in the villages, which would serve not only as agents of change but also as new sources of cleavage and village disjunction as new political identities emerged and interacted, sometimes uncomfortably, within the peasant community.

Collectivization was to destroy most of these "cultural bridges," leaving what remained of the state's small contingent of supporters entrenched against a hostile community. Most of the natural schisms and fault lines that crisscrossed the village in ordinary times receded into latency during collectivization as the community found itself united against a common, and, by this time, deadly foe. During collectivization, the peasantry acted as a class in much the way Teodor Shanin has defined class; that is, as a "social entity with a community of economic interests, its identity shaped by conflict with other classes and expressed in typical patterns of cognition and political consciousness, however rudimentary, which made it capable of collective action reflecting its interests." Whether it is described as a class or as a culture in Clifford Geertz's sense of a totality of experience and behavior, the "socially established structures of meaning" or "webs of significance" by which people act, the peasantry of the USSR clearly demonstrated the extent to which it was distinct from much of the rest of Soviet society.

Collectivization encapsulated the original fault lines of the revolution, between a minority class in whose name the Communists professed to rule and the majority peasantry whose very reality appeared to block the revolution. Stalin's collectivization was an attempt to eliminate the fault lines, to solve the accursed peasant problem by force, to create a socialist society and economy from above. It was a campaign of domination that aimed at nothing less than the internal colonization of the peasantry. Collectivization would ensure a steady flow of grain to the state to feed the nation and to pay for industrialization. It would also enable Soviet power to subjugate the peasantry through the imposition of administrative and political controls and forced acculturation into the dominant culture. Although the Communist Party publicly proclaimed collectivization to be "Socialist transformation," it was in reality a war of cultures.

Collectivization devastated the countryside. Tens of thousands of urban Communists and factory workers invaded the countryside in 1930, competing for the highest percentages of collectivized households in their districts. Often under the threat of repression, peasants were forced to sign up to join the collective farm. Those who objected, resisted, or could in some way be classified as "kulak"—that is, a wealthy peasant or, in slightly oxymoronic terms, a capitalist peasant—were subject to "dekulakization," Stalin's policy being the "liquidation of the kulak as a class." More than one million peasant families (perhaps five to six million people) were subjected to some form of dekulakization during the years of collectivization. Of these, some 381,026 families (a total of at least 1,803,392 individuals) were sent forcibly into exile in 1930 and 1931, the two years of heaviest peasant deportation, to the most desolate and isolated regions of the country. In addition, over 30,000 peasants were subject to capital punishment as kulaks in 1930 and 1931. Statistics compiled by Russian sociologist V. N. Zemskov indicate that 281,367 peasants would die in their places of exile between 1932 and 1934.

Peasants of every social strata responded to the violence by overcoming their ordinary and multiple differences and uniting as a culture—in a very real sense, as a class—in defense of their families, beliefs, communities, and livelihood. In 1930, more than two million peasants took part in 13,754 mass disturbances against Communist Party policies. In 1929 and 1930, the OGPU recorded 22,887 "terrorist acts" aimed at local officials and peasant activists, more than 1,100 of them murders. Peasant resistance was rooted in peasant culture rather than in any specific social stratum and was shaped by an agency and political consciousness that derived from reasoned concerns centered largely on issues of justice and subsistence, supplemented by anger, desperation, and a desire for retribution.

In the end, the peasant rebels were no match for the vast police powers of the state, and, like most other peasant rebellions, this one failed. The main cause of the peasantry's defeat was state repression. Millions of peasants were arrested, imprisoned, deported, or executed in the years of collectivization. The state dismantled existing authority structures in the village, removing and replacing traditional elites. The devastating famine of 1932–33, caused by collectivization and the state's inhumanely high grain requisitions, complemented state repression, first robbing peasants of their grain and then depriving perhaps as many as five million people of their lives as starvation and disease took their toll. Repression and a one-sided war of attrition effectively silenced peasant rebels.

Yet repression alone could not and did not end peasant resistance; nor could it have served as the *only* mechanism of control in the long term. For reasons of sheer necessity, the state would largely give up its revolutionary aspirations in the countryside after collectivization, choosing, pragmatically and cynically, to exert its domination over the peasantry through the control of vital resources, most especially grain. Plans for the elimination of differences between town and countryside fell by the wayside as reasons of state asserted themselves and the last of the ideals of 1917 crumbled. The peasant household continued to be the mainstay of the peasant—if

not of the collective farm—economy; and homes, domestic livestock, barns, sheds, and household necessities were deemed the peasants' private property. The private plot and a limited collective farm market functioned alongside socialized agriculture to guarantee a minimum subsistence for collective farmers and to supplement the nation's consumer needs. Peasants were co-opted into positions of authority, and in the decades following the death of Stalin, the state gradually extended more of its admittedly paltry benefits from the urban to the rural sector. The Soviet agricultural system became a hybrid system, based on private plots and collective farms, all in the service of the state, but also offering the peasantry something in the exchange.

In the long term, the social by-products of industrialization and urbanization proved as efficacious in securing peasant acquiescence as the brute force of the state. Continued out-migration and the permanent resettlement in cities of males and young people spread extended families between town and village, bringing peasant culture to the town and fixing in place urban bridges to the village more firmly than ever before. Education, military service, and improved transportation and communications facilitated a certain degree of Sovietization in the countryside, or, at the very least, some homogenization across the urban divide.

The Stalinist state and the collective farm system triumphed in the end, but their triumph did not spell the end of peasant culture. The peasantry reemerged, not unchanged to be sure, from within socialized agriculture. Passive resistance and other "weapons of the weak" became endemic mechanisms of coping and survival for the peasantry within the collective farm. Agriculture stagnated, becoming the Achilles' heel of the Soviet economy, a ceaseless reminder of the ironies of a "proletarian revolution" in peasant Russia. Like the peasant commune before it, the collective farm became a bulwark against change and as much a subsistence shelter for peasants as a control mechanism for the state. Over time, the collective farm became the quintessential risk-aversion guarantor that peasants had always sought. Socioeconomic leveling, a basic and insured subsistence, and some degree of cultural independence, demographic isolation, and feminization of the village maintained and even strengthened aspects of village culture and tradition. The constant and historic insecurity of peasant life would ironically bond the peasant to the collective farm.

To the extent that it was possible, peasants made the collective farm their own. State attempts at decollectivization after 1991 provide ample evidence for this. Decollectivization was blocked by a peasantry grown accustomed to the collective farm. This seeming intransigence was less the result of backwardness, or a "serf mentality," as some interpreters would see it, than a simple continuity of peasant needs, values, and ways of living. Decollectivization, moreover, demonstrated continuity with earlier state efforts to remold and modernize the peasantry. Its implementation was top down, based on some measure of force (although nothing like that of the Stalinist state), and relied counterproductively on a tradition-bound equalization of pitifully small land parcels in cases of privatization, revealing all the usual elements of the cultural manipulation and imperialism of state modernization. Peasants responded to decollectivization with skepticism and hostility, having molded the collective farm at least partially to their own needs.

In the name of Communist gods, utopian visions, and a modernizing ethos transformed by Stalinism, the Soviet state attempted depeasantization, a kind of cultural genocide, against a peasantry that only too starkly reflected the realities of a Russia based in an agrarian economy and society resistant to the Communist experiment. Long after collectivization, a peasantry, in some sense of the word, would remain, sometimes embittered and most of the time engaged in a continuing and undeclared war based on the constant and manifold employment of the devices of everyday forms of resistance on the collective farm. As it confronted the peasantry across the cultural divide, the revolution would founder in the very countryside it sought to transform, evolving into the repressive and bloody contours of Stalinism, and reminding us once again that the October Revolution and the Stalinist industrial and military infrastructure of the USSR were, from the start, built upon a peasant foundation inadequate to sustain a proletarian revolution and too weak to maintain its country's Superpower status into the late 20th century.

See also Agrarian Question; Collectivization of the Countryside; Holodomor; Kolkhoz; Kulak; Modernization; Soviet Industrialization.

FURTHER READING

Figes, O. *Peasant Russia, Civil War: The Volga Countryside in Revolution, 1917–1921.* Oxford: Clarendon Press, 1989.

Fitzpatrick, S. *Stalin's Peasants: Resistance and Survival in the Russian Village After Collectivization.* New York: Oxford University Press, 1994.

Kingston-Mann, E. *Lenin and the Problem of Marxist Peasant Revolution.* New York: Oxford University Press, 1983.

Lewin, M. *Russian Peasants and Soviet Power: A Study of Collectivization.* Trans. I. Nove. New York: Norton, 1975.

Romano, A. *Contadini in uniforme: L'Armata Rossa e la collettivizzazione delle campagne nell'URSS.* Turin: Leo S. Olschki, 1999.

Shanin, T. *The Awkward Class.* Oxford: Clarendon Press, 1972.
———. *Defining Peasants.* Oxford: Blackwell, 1990.

Viola, L. *Peasant Rebels Under Stalin: Collectivization and the Culture of Peasant Resistance.* New York: Oxford University Press, 1996.

Werth, N. *La vie quotidienne des paysans Russes de la revolution a la collectivization.* Paris: Hachette, 1984.

LYNNE VIOLA

People's Democracy

The idea of People's Democracy, sometimes called "New Democracy," sometimes "Popular Democracy," came out of the Popular Front campaign of the Comintern in the 1930s. Some scholars claim the origins of the term derive from the Comintern-inspired Communist program during the Spanish Civil War. Others suggest that the Chinese Communists at the end of the 1930s were the first to use the term. Still others believe that it was only used in post–World War II Europe, starting with the Congress of the Yugoslav Fatherland Front in 1945. In fact, the absence of a clear genesis of the idea of People's Democracy is symptomatic of the unformed and wide-ranging notions that prevail about the meaning of the concept, an ambiguity that has made possible a variety of interpretations by its practitioners in Eastern Europe.

In the 1930s, the Comintern's program of the Popular Front called for Communists, Social Democrats, and democratic parties to join together in coalition governments to prevent Fascist incursions from without, in the form of Nazi or Italian advances, and from within, in the form of domestic putsches. The idea continued to dominate the Comintern until its abolition in 1943, but was perpetuated by its successor organizations, including the Soviet Communist Party's Section of International Information (OMI). In the OMI, Georgi Dimitrov and Dimitri Maniulskii instructed the leaders of foreign Communist parties, including the East Europeans, on the importance of coalitions of Democrats and Socialists, of bourgeois and working-class parties. After the war, there would be no collectivization of agriculture or nationalization of industries, as many Communists had proposed in their party platforms. In agriculture, moreover, only the properties of large landowners should be confiscated and redistributed, not those of middle-level farmers. To the chagrin of many foreign Communists, who would have preferred a Bolshevik-style takeover of power, with the goal, in some cases, of becoming another republic of the Soviet Union, Dimitrov and Maniulskii insisted that there be national parliamentary coalitions with non-Communist parties. Moreover, Dimitrov and even Stalin specifically instructed foreign Communists that the Soviet model was not germane to the political challenges they faced in their respective countries. There was no need for a violent revolution; there would be no bloody civil wars; and therefore they did not need to follow the model of the "dictatorship of the proletariat."

Instead, as the war concluded and the countries of Eastern Europe fell under the influence of the Red Army, both the Soviet political authorities in the Allied Control Councils and the local Communist parties under the tutelage of Moscow promoted the idea of "People's Democracy." It was a loosely defined idea, especially at first. As People's Democracies the countries of Eastern Europe would no longer be bourgeois democracies, as in the West, but neither would they be Socialist states. They were somewhere in between, with multiparty systems, parliamentary politics, coalition governments, and economies only partly nationalized by the state. Stalin sometimes used the idea of a Slavic group of countries as a surrogate concept for the People's Democracies, though, of course, not all People's Democracies were made up of predominantly Slavic nations.

In a lengthy conversation with the Polish Socialist Party (PPS) leader, Edward Osobka-Morawski (May 1946), Stalin explained that Poland did not need to go through the harsh experiences of the Bolsheviks. Poland did not need a dictatorship of the proletariat because its capitalists and large landowners had been so thoroughly compromised during the German occupation that they could easily be eliminated as a political factor. The Red Army, Stalin also pointed out, assumed some of the functions of the "dictatorship" by helping to squelch counterrevolution. The kind of democracy that was instituted in Poland had no real precedents. "Not the Belgian, not the English, not the French democracies can serve as your examples or models," Stalin said. No one was there to oppose nationalization in Poland. Because of this, the country was even more advanced than the

democracies of the West, closer to socialism, but most definitely not a dictatorship of the proletariat or a Soviet-style state. The idea, Stalin explained, was to promote growth in industry, lower prices, and make consumer goods more available to the population. This would in turn stabilize the country and move it closer to socialism without the need for any kind of bloody struggle.

There is little question that Stalin assumed that the People's Democracies would mutate into Socialist systems. This would be the case in Europe, as well as elsewhere in the world. But each country's path to socialism would be determined by its particular circumstances and history. As a result, Stalin encouraged the leaders of the People's Democracies to think about individual, national roads to socialism. Stalin even told the British Labour Party leaders (August 7, 1946) that they, too, could tread the path to socialism through Labour-dominated parliamentary politics. There were different roads to socialism, the shorter, Russian route, which necessitated the shedding of blood; and the English, parliamentary route, which would take rather longer and could be peaceful.

Although Moscow urged the leaders of the People's Democracies to nurture their own paths to socialism, the Soviets also indicated that some paths were better than others by repeatedly pointing to a hierarchy among the countries that saw themselves as People's Democracies. Yugoslavia and Albania were noted to have taken appropriate and decisive steps toward socialism. As late as March 1946, the party periodical *Bol'shevik* conspicuously failed to list Czechoslovakia, Hungary, and even Poland among the new People's Democracies. The issue seemed to be the extent to which the "bourgeoisie" still had influence in the respective governments. It was not until Stanislaw Mikolajczyk and his Polish Agrarian Party (PSL) allies were defeated in a sham election and chased from Poland, that Poland, too, could be considered a People's Democracy. Hungary did not attain this exalted status until the spring of 1947, with the rooting out of the leadership of the Smallholders' Party. Czechoslovakia became a full-blown People's Democracy as a consequence of the February 1948 Communist coup. In all of these cases, coalition governments, though fundamentally ruling at the behest of the Communists, still gave up too much control to the bourgeoisie. After 1948, China, Mongolia, and eventually North Korea and North Vietnam were sometimes added to the list of People's Democracies or "New Democracies." From the 1960s on, Cuba was also sometimes called a People's Democracy, as were, for a briefer time period, a number of African and Asian nations, including Algeria, Zanzibar and Pemba, the Congo, Yemen, Laos, Cambodia, Ethiopia, Angola, and Mozambique. With the collapse of communism in the years 1989–91, most of the People's Democracies ceased to exist. Some, like China and Yugoslavia, had earlier broken ranks with the Soviet Union.

Like the overeager pupils they were, the leaders of the East German Socialist Unity Party (SED) tried repeatedly to have the German Democratic Republic (and even the Soviet Occupation Zone that preceded it) declared a People's Democracy. But Stalin held off recognizing it as such until the 1950s. Sergei Tiul'panov, an important figure in the Soviet administration of East Germany, put the hierarchy of People's Democracies in the following terms (April 1948): "Yugoslavia has already reached the other bank [a mostly Socialist state]; Bulgaria is taking the last few strokes to reach it; Poland and Czechoslovakia are about in the middle of the river, followed by Romania and Hungary, which have gone about a third of the way; while the Soviet Occupation Zone has just taken the first few strokes away from the bourgeois bank."

Some scholars believe that the concept of People's Democracy had an important impact on the political development of postwar Eastern Europe. They argue, for example, that the Communist policy of engaging in coalition politics with non-Communist parties convinced most democratic and Social-Democratic Party leaders that the Communists' goals were tentative and that their tactics were flexible. With some exceptions, non-Communist political leaders joined the national front coalitions, sometimes with great hopes for their participation in their countries' respective political futures. At the time, anyway, there seemed to be no Soviet grand design for the Bolshevization of Eastern Europe.

Especially in the first few years after the war, this was also the case in Western Europe, in Italy and France in particular, where Stalin encouraged Western Communist leaders to join electoral coalitions in the hope of eventually forming People's Democracies. There was no talk of a Soviet bloc, and, at least before the first Cominform meeting in September 1947, no discussion of the coordination of paths to socialism. Some historians believe that this was little more than a tactical move on the part of the Soviets to keep the Western powers at bay, at least until the peace treaties were signed and the German question was resolved. Others argue that this was part of the story, but not all of it.

Eastern Europe was not absorbed into the Soviet Union (and only later could one speak of a "Soviet bloc"), but even in the first years of the People's Democracies Stalin used the concept to give these countries a separate identity from the West. Soviet influence in the region was not yet strong enough to protect these countries from a revived Germany, which the Soviets expected would reassert its power some fifteen to twenty years down the road. In his classic study of the Soviet bloc, Zbigniew Brzezinski wrote that the Soviets needed the theory of People's Democracy to differentiate the political dynamics of the countries of Eastern Europe from the Soviet Union, and to control them. The designation People's Democracy would provide a sense of identity and distinctiveness to the region.

Another important scholar of Communist Eastern Europe, Joseph Rothschild, suggests that by placing the People's Democracy in a special historical-developmental category between the retarded development of the West and the advanced stage of the Soviet Union, Moscow accomplished two important objectives. First, it made the subordination of the East European countries and their respective Communist parties justifiable on ideological grounds, and not merely a consequence of the overwhelming power of the Soviet behemoth. Second, it gave the Soviets an opening for intervening in the political and ideological development of these countries, since any shift toward the West would indicate a retrogressive—even "counterrevolutionary"—movement away from socialism.

Paradoxically, the concept of "People's Democracy" held more meaning for the countries involved when it was most loosely defined and flexible, that is, up to the formation of the Cominform in September 1947 and the Czech coup in February 1948. Certainly by the time of the expulsion of the Yugoslavs from the Cominform in June of 1948, the use of the term was tightened up, individual paths to socialism were explicitly condemned, and the People's Democracies were seen not as alternatives to the Soviet model of dictatorship of the proletariat but rather as surrogate dictatorships. As a consequence of this development, the "new" People's Democracies also received the right and the impetus to engage in the same kinds of Stalinist excesses as their Soviet mentors. Purges, repressions, and show trials became as much a part of political life in the People's Democracies by the end of the 1940s and beginning of the 1950s as they were in the Soviet Union. The leaders of the respective East European states acted like "little Stalins."

The historiographic evaluation of Peoples' Democracy is linked to arguments about the intentionality and pace of Sovietization in Eastern Europe. One school of thought, which dominates current scholarship on "People's Democracy" in Russia, argues that it was a genuine variant of democracy, a genuine effort at coalition government, which, however, had a provisional character, given the conflicting goals of the various parties within the coalition. That this coalition carried the seeds of its own destruction was not a consequence of the fact that Stalin had no intention from the beginning of allowing any kind of democracy to exist in Eastern Europe. Instead, the gradual radicalization of the workers' parties in Eastern Europe itself, the Communists and the Social Democrats—strengthened, to be sure, by the formation of the Cominform—promoted the unification of these parties and elimination of alternatives to Stalinist forms of development. In short, leftist politics in the People's Democracy determined the outcome: the monopoly of political power by the Communists. Another group of Russian historians represents a slight, but important, shift from this way of thinking. People's Democracy represented for them a serious alternative to Soviet-style socialism in postwar Eastern Europe, a kind of "democratic intermezzo." But Soviet leaders did everything they could to strengthen the position of the Communist parties in these countries, while voicing ostensible support for genuinely autonomous and democratic developments in the East European states.

The most widespread school of thought in the West, one that has adherents in Russia and Eastern Europe, as well, makes the case that People's Democracy was little more than a slogan, reminiscent of the title of the Cominform journal, *For a Lasting Peace—For a People's Democracy*. In this analysis, most recently articulated by Russian scholar Leonid Gibianskii, People's Democracy was a sham, a camouflage that Stalin and his comrades used to deceive the West and hornswoggle non-Communist politicians in Eastern Europe, especially Social Democrats and Agrarian Party leaders. The Soviet leadership was never deceived by its rhetoric, and certainly Stalin was not. People's Democracy was not democracy at all, because the idea and reality of parliamentary government were completely unacceptable to the Soviets. Without parliaments and without any substantial democratic institutions of a genuine sort, Yugoslavia and Albania were the primary examples of People's Democracies at the war's end offered by the Soviets. Meanwhile, Czechoslovakia, which had some genuinely democratic characteristics, at least until the Communist coup of February 1948, was called by Stalin "a new Democracy, *in part*."

This argument, then, follows the lines of the classic historians of People's Democracy in the West, Hugh Seton-Watson and Zbigniew Brzezinski. There was no genuine "democratic intermezzo" between the war and the eventual Stalinization of East Europe. However, this view tends not to take into account the fact that politicians and even some voters took the term seriously at the time and thought—with justification or not—that the new paradigm introduced an important and even enduring epoch of social and political development. This was also evident in the "theoretical" writings on People's Democracy that emanated from Moscow and in the discussions of People's Democracy that pervaded East European political discussions of the day. People's Democracy was considered by its domestic advocates neither Western or "just" a democracy, nor Eastern and Soviet. The important Communist leaders Władysław Gomułka in Poland and Georgi Dimitrov in Bulgaria explained to their comrades that Soviet institutions and the dictatorship of the proletariat would not be introduced into their countries; and *they* meant it, even if Stalin did not. They even prevented those who wanted to engage in the radical Sovietization of their countries from proceeding with their plans. As some scholars have noted, People's Democracy was a linguistic shorthand for the East Europeans: it was a way to talk about subordination to the Soviet Union without acknowledging it explicitly; it was a marker to denote progress in their own countries toward the inevitable goal of socialism, while differentiating them from the parliamentary democracies in the West and the dictatorship of the proletariat to their East. Policy choices were framed in the language of what was good for the development of People's Democracy and what was not.

The acceleration of Cold War tensions between the Soviet Union and the United States in 1947–48, whatever Stalin's original intentions, gutted the concept of People's Democracy of any serious propagandistic value outside the Soviet bloc and the Communist world. The polarization between East and West—the brief flourishing of Eurocommunism in the 1970s notwithstanding—brought to an end any meaningful attempts at building socialism on a basis other than Marxist-Leninism.

See also Antifascism; Cominform; Dictatorship of the Proletariat; Dimitrov, Georgi; Gomułka, Władysław; Soviet Occupation of Germany; Sovietization; World War II.

FURTHER READING

Brzezinski, Z. *The Soviet Bloc: Unity and Conflict*. Cambridge, MA: Harvard University Press, 1967.

Gati, C. *The Bloc That Failed: Soviet-East European Relations in Transition*. Bloomington: Indiana University Press, 1990.

Heiter, H. *Vom friedlichen Weg zum Sozialismus zur Diktatur des Proletariats: Wandlungen der sowjetischen Konzeption der Volksdemokratie 1945–1949*. Frankfurt-am-Main, 1977.

Janos, A. *East Central Europe in the Modern World*. Stanford, CA: Stanford University Press, 2000.

Kase, F. J. *People's Democracy: A Contribution to the Study of the Communist Theory of State and Revolution*. Leyden: A. W. Sijthoff, 1968.

Naimark, N. M. "Post-Soviet Russian Historiography on the Emergence of the Soviet Bloc." *Kritika* (Summer 2004): 561–80.

Skilling, G. J. "People's Democracy in Soviet Theory." *Soviet Studies* (July 1951): 16–31.

Volokitina, T. V. *Narodnaia demokratiia: Mif ili real'nost'?* Moscow: Nauka, 1993.

NORMAN M. NAIMARK

Perestroika

The Russian word "perestroika," meaning reconstruction or restructuring, entered the vocabulary of every major language after it was adopted by Mikhail Gorbachev and his reformist allies in the Communist Party of the Soviet Union (CPSU) as the overarching term for the reforms introduced into the Soviet system in 1985. Initially, the concept was chosen partly because the term "reform" had become virtually taboo in the Soviet political lexicon ever since the reformism within the Communist Party of Czechoslovakia had led to Soviet military intervention there in August 1968. Fear of Czech contagion also brought Alexey Kosygin's modest economic reform in the USSR to a premature end. Instead of advocating reform, would-be reformers had to write and speak of "perfecting the economic mechanism." The adoption of the term perestroika changed all that. Yet it altered its meaning quite rapidly in the course of the second half of the 1980s. Having at first been a synonym for reform of the Soviet economic system, it soon came to embrace reform of the political system and radically changed foreign policy as well. By 1988 it had come to mean something more fundamental—what Gorbachev called revolutionary change by evolutionary means.

The ambiguity of the term was initially an advantage. Every member of the Soviet leadership team in 1985–86 could sign on to the concept of perestroika because the term meant such different things to them. Moreover, the traditional discipline of the Soviet Communist Party still worked within the first few years of Gorbachev's leadership. Accordingly, even those who were against what perestroika was coming to mean proclaimed their support for it. This worked to the advantage of Gorbachev (and his most radically reformist ally within the leadership, Aleksandr Yakovlev), since as he kept expanding the limits of what was possible under the rubric of perestroika, the more conservative members of the politburo gradually found that they, too, were endorsing change that went far beyond what they had ever envisaged.

Perestroika, then, was a concept that meant different things at different times and different things to different people at the same time. Already by 1986 it was clear that Yegor Ligachev, the second secretary within the CPSU, intended something much more modest by perestroika than did either Gorbachev or Yakovlev. Radical intellectuals made use of the concept to legitimize far-reaching proposals that they would earlier have found impossible to get into print. As a concept, perestroika could mean merely a minor restructuring of the existing political edifice or it could mean building anew—reconstructing the system from the foundations up. For Gorbachev, even in 1985 it signified more than a minor restructuring. From the time of the Nineteenth Party Conference in summer 1988, it meant a dismantling of the pillars of the old system and constructing a new model of socialism. Gorbachev believed that this involved a return to Lenin of the New Economy Policy period, and an idealized view of Lenin played a significant role in the genesis and early development of perestroika. In fact, however, Gorbachev went on to accept a greater degree of pluralism and democracy than even the late Lenin (with his policy of "putting the lid on opposition") ever endorsed.

Perestroika is sometimes assumed to be the name for the innovative domestic policies of the Gorbachev era, while the "New Thinking" is seen as the term to describe the fresh thought on foreign policy. As the title of Gorbachev's 1987 book *Perestroika: New Thinking for Our Country and the World* suggests, however, Gorbachev saw perestroika as an overarching term that embraced both domestic and international policy, and indeed encapsulated his belief that internal and external policies were inextricably related.

In addition to being a concept, perestroika became the description of an era. It is the term used to capture the final period of Soviet history when the USSR was led by Gorbachev. Some would date the beginning of perestroika to the election by the politburo and Central Committee of Gorbachev as general secretary on March 11, 1985. Others would say it began the following month when the April plenum of the Central Committee put change on the agenda. In reality, the fresh start started from the moment when Gorbachev was chosen to be Konstantin Chernenko's successor as general secretary. Such was the institutional power of that highest office within the CPSU and the Soviet state that this was the only place from where far-reaching policy innovation *could* emanate. Although Gorbachev was *not* chosen as general secretary *because* he was an innovator (as the youngest member of the politburo who was already second secretary of the CPSU, he was able through skillful political maneuvering to engineer his own succession), he rapidly made it clear that he would become a serious reformer.

Perestroika began with an emphasis on getting the country moving again economically, the catchword being *uskorenie* (acceleration). The aim was not just a quantitative increase in production but also qualitative change as a result of technological breakthrough. The conservatism of both the economic sections of the Communist Party apparatus and the Council of Ministers meant that change was slow, and Nikolay Ryzhkov, Gorbachev's appointee as chair of the Council of Ministers, a post he held from 1985 to 1990, turned out to be a reformer within fairly narrow limits. As an increasing number of Soviet economists took the view that nothing short of a move to an essentially market economy would reverse the slowdown in economic growth and stimulate technological innovation, Ryzhkov was slow to respond. Throughout the year 1990, Gorbachev had an economist who was an enthusiast for the market, Nikolay Petrakov, as one of his personal advisers, and the general secretary was persuaded, in principle, that movement to a market economy was essential. Yet Gorbachev had no desire to see the Soviet Union adopt a U.S.-style market economy but rather a social market economy of the kind he had seen in West Germany or that existed in Scandinavia. How to get there was the problem.

In summer 1990 a group of economists, jointly appointed by Gorbachev and Boris Yeltsin (who by that time was chairman of the Supreme Soviet of the Russian republic), came up with a proposal to move the Soviet Union to a market economy within five hundred days.

This ambitious "Shatalin-Yavlinsky plan" (named after two of the leading economists on the team, which also included Petrakov), was at first welcomed by Gorbachev, who subsequently backtracked on that support in the face of opposition from the party apparatus, ministries, and military-industrial complex. Yeltsin embraced the document unreservedly, and from this point onward the radical wing of the intelligentsia shifted its support from Gorbachev to Yeltsin.

In the first year of perestroika Yeltsin had been promoted to a headship of a Central Committee department, and subsequently to a secretaryship of the Central Committee, before being appointed at the end of 1985 to succeed Viktor Grishin as the first secretary of the Moscow city party organization. Ligachev, who had been the person behind Yeltsin's promotion, expected Yeltsin to be "his man," but Yeltsin turned out to be very much his own person. Resenting the pressures from the Central Committee apparatus, Yeltsin struck out on his own as a populist leader in Moscow, dismissing officials on a large scale and making a number of well-publicized trips on public transport. When he chose a Central Committee session in October 1987 devoted to preparations for the celebration of the seventieth anniversary of the Bolshevik Revolution to attack the party leadership—Ligachev in particular, but also to some extent Gorbachev—virtually the entire Central Committee turned against him, and he was removed from candidate membership of the politburo and his Moscow first secretaryship. He did, though, remain a member of the Central Committee (albeit one who played no part in party decision making) until he ostentatiously resigned from the CPSU by walking out of the Twenty-eighth Party Congress in 1990.

Still, the changes of policy that led to the partial democratization of the Soviet Union and the end of the Cold War were carried out under Gorbachev's leadership, not Yeltsin's. Each year saw the reform agenda become more radical. By 1986, the new policy of glasnost (meaning openness or transparency) was already leading to somewhat freer discussion than had taken place under Brezhnev, Andropov, or Chernenko. But democratization was put more firmly on the political agenda at the January plenum of the Central Committee in 1987, followed by the June plenum of the same year that launched decentralizing economic reform. In 1987, Gorbachev also gave an added impetus to change when he endorsed the idea of a "socialist pluralism" and "pluralism of opinion." Hitherto, the concept of pluralism, even thus qualified, had been vehemently attacked by Soviet ideologists.

The year 1988 saw a still further radicalization of perestroika. Early in the year there was an attempt from within the Soviet establishment to turn the clock back. A letter that contained an essentially neo-Stalinist critique of perestroika by a hitherto unknown Leningrad lecturer, Nina Andreeva, appeared in the newspaper *Sovetskaya Rossiya* on March 13. Its significance was that it had the backing of senior officials within the Central Committee apparatus, including Ligachev. When Gorbachev made a major issue of apparent support for the antiperestroika line of Andreeva in the politburo, he found that more than half the members had been in broad agreement with the letter. Many Soviet intellectuals, who had taken the prominence accorded the letter as a signal of a change of official line, had relapsed into silence, and only recovered their voices after Gorbachev had authorized a comprehensive rebuttal—largely drafted by Yakovlev—that was published in *Pravda* on April 5, 1988.

This counterattack on what had been identified as an "antiperestroika manifesto" strengthened the reformist forces in the run-up to the Nineteenth Conference of the CPSU held in summer 1988. That authoritative party gathering saw democratization become a much more concrete part of the reform agenda. Gorbachev cajoled the delegates (most of whom were far from being radical reformers) into agreeing to competitive elections for a new legislature—the Congress of People's Deputies—to be held the following spring. When those elections took place, even though they were not yet multiparty elections, they featured different members of the CPSU standing against each other on vastly different political platforms. The elections thus sounded a death knell for the theory and practice of democratic centralism.

A further important step was the transfer of ultimate power from the party to the state. The creation of the new legislature was part of that process. The Congress of People's Deputies elected an inner body, the Supreme Soviet, which unlike its prereform Soviet namesake, met throughout the greater part of the year and became a serious lawmaking institution as well as a legislative assembly that could call the executive to account—something unheard of in the Supreme Soviet of old. Of great significance also was the creation of an executive presidency in March 1990. Gorbachev was elected to that office by the Congress of People's Deputies even though the new law stipulated that in the future, the Soviet president should be elected by universal suffrage. Years later, Gorbachev accepted that he had made a serious tactical error in taking the shortcut of an indirect election. Indeed, he would have

added not only to his own political legitimacy but also to the chances of preserving a federal union (albeit one that would not have included the Baltic states, and possibly one or two others) if the people as a whole had been able to vote in an election for the federal presidency.

That this was an opportunity missed became all that much more apparent a year later. In the course of 1991 the Soviet republics had direct elections for their republican presidencies, the most important of which saw the victory of Yeltsin in the Russian republic. This gave Yeltsin, who had moved resolutely into the political space opened up by the introduction of contested elections, a greater popular legitimacy than Gorbachev. It also strengthened his hand when a group of CPSU and state leaders—which included Vice President Gennadiy Yanaev; Vladimir Kryuchkov, the chairman of the KGB; Prime Minister Valentin Pavlov; Minister of Defense Dmitriy Yazov; and Oleg Baklanov, the head of the military-industrial complex—attempted to seize power in August 1991. The immediate cause of this August putsch was the imminence of the signing of a new Union Treaty on August 20 whereby following prolonged negotiations between the all-union authorities and the republics, substantial powers were to be devolved to the latter. The coup plotters believed that the treaty would lead in due course to the breakup of the Soviet state, and so decided that it must never be signed. It never was, but that was because their action led to the faster breakup of the union and meant that they had achieved the precise opposite of the outcome they intended.

The claims of the putschists to be speaking on behalf of the people rang hollow, given that just two months earlier one of their number, General Makashov, had received derisory support in the presidential election that Yeltsin had won convincingly in the first round. When the coup attempt collapsed on August 21, 1991, Yeltsin emerged further strengthened in his rivalry with Gorbachev. The Soviet president had been held under house arrest on the Crimean coast, along with his family and several members of his staff, between August 18 and 21, while Yeltsin, in the Moscow White House (which at that time housed the Russian parliament), became the symbol of resistance to those who wished to turn the clock back.

Perestroika, as an attempt to reconstruct the Soviet system on a radically different foundation, failed in two important respects. The first and greatest failure was the dissolution of the Soviet state. This was the ultimate unintended consequence of perestroika. To the extent that the Soviet Union was democratized, it became highly improbable that the entire country could be held together. Estonia, Latvia, and Lithuania could have been guaranteed to seek independence if the severe sanctions against doing so were removed. Nevertheless, a union comprising a majority of the fifteen republics would almost certainly have been held together on the basis of a new and voluntary Union Treaty had not Yeltsin played the Russian card against the union. Since the union had been the successor state to the Russian Empire and since Russia was a major beneficiary of its international standing, the paradox of Yeltsin demanding Russian "independence" from the union is difficult to explain other than in terms of his personal ambition and hunger for power.

The other great failure of perestroika was economic. The proponents of perestroika were unlucky inasmuch as the price of oil fell sharply during the second half of the 1980s; both before perestroika and after, the Soviet Union and Russia have relied heavily on energy exports for their economic well-being. More fundamental, however, was the difficulty of agreeing on a strategy for movement to a market economy. Indeed, there was a basic tension between trying to improve the existing economic system (as some reformers wished) and moving to a system based on quite different operating principles (as proposed by more radical reformers). The fact that there was no easy answer to the economic conundrum—as was illustrated by the drop in the standard of living of a majority of Russian citizens in the first post-Soviet decade, following the move to market prices and large-scale privatization—did nothing to diminish the growing dissatisfaction of a majority of Soviet citizens with the lack of improvement in their material conditions.

On the positive side, perestroika had some massive achievements. It saw the end of the Cold War, and the main reason for that was change in Soviet foreign policy and ideology. In concrete terms, the Soviet leadership's willingness to let East Europe go was the final decisive step in ending the East-West conflict. Important also was the withdrawal of Soviet troops from Afghanistan. Gorbachev had four summit meetings with President Ronald Reagan, culminating in Reagan's 1988 visit to Moscow in which he declared that when he had spoken of the Soviet Union as an "evil empire," he had been talking about "another era." The following year, when Gorbachev had a summit meeting in Malta with President George Bush the elder, the Soviet press spokesperson, Gennadiy Gerasimov, was able to announce that they had "buried the Cold War at the bottom of the Mediterranean Sea."

The other great achievements of perestroika were in the realm of pluralizing and democratizing political change. The Soviet Union became dramatically freer under Gorbachev. Previously banned literary works—such as Solzhenitsyn's *The First Circle* and (much more damaging to the Soviet system) *The Gulag Archipelago*, George Orwell's *Animal Farm* and *Nineteen Eighty-Four*, and Varlam Shalamov's *Kolyma Tales*—were printed in large editions. Prior to perestroika, citizens were jailed for the mere possession of such a work (printed abroad). Glasnost, in the course of perestroika, developed into a comprehensive freedom of speech and publication. It was accompanied by the freedom to travel and the freedom of religious observance. Dissidents were released from prison, and the rehabilitation (begun under Khrushchev, stopped under Brezhnev) was resumed of those unjustly repressed in the past. There was significant progress under perestroika toward a rule of law, with the Communist Party for the first time no longer above it.

The direction in which Gorbachev and his closest allies increasingly tried to take perestroika was that of social democracy. In that sense, post–Soviet Russia cannot be regarded as a continuation of perestroika but rather a break with it. Crucially, however, perestroika was the period in which the Communist system was dismantled, mainly (to the astonishment of most observers) from above. The way was thus left open for the further development of democracy—or alternatively, for a relapse into a different and milder form of authoritarian rule.

See also Coup in the USSR; Dissolution of the USSR; Gorbachev, Mikhail; New Thinking.

FURTHER READING

Brown, A. *The Gorbachev Factor.* Oxford: Oxford University Press, 1996.

———. *Seven Years That Changed the World: Perestroika in Perspective.* Oxford: Oxford University Press, 2007.

Chernyaev, A. *My Six Years with Gorbachev.* University Park: Pennsylvania State University Press, 2000.

Gorbachev, M. *Perestroika: New Thinking for Our Country and the World.* London: Collins, 1987.

———. *Memoirs.* London: Doubleday, 1996.

———. *Ponyat' perestroyku . . . pochemu eto vazhno seychas.* Moscow: Al'pina Business Books, 2006.

Gorbachev, M., and Z. Mlynář. *Conversations with Gorbachev: On Perestroika, the Prague Spring, and the Crossroads of Socialism.* New York: Columbia University Press, 2002.

Hahn, G. M. *1985–2000: Russia's Revolution from Above.* New Brunswick, NJ: Transaction Publishers, 2002.

Kotkin, S. *Armageddon Averted: The Soviet Collapse, 1970–2000.* Oxford: Oxford University Press, 2001.

Kuvaldin, V. V., and A. B. Veber, eds. *Proryv k svobode: o perestroyke dvadtsat' let spustya (kriticheskiy analiz).* Moscow: Al'pina Business Books, 2005.

Lukin, A. *The Political Culture of the Russian "Democrats."* Oxford: Oxford University Press, 2000.

Tolstykh, V. I., ed. *Perestroyka: dvadtsat' let spustya.* Moscow: Russkiy put', 2005.

Yakovlev, A. *Sumerki.* Moscow: Materik, 2003.

ARCHIE BROWN

Péri, Gabriel

Arrested in Paris in May 1941 after having been a militant in the underground since France's fall, executed in December after having given the judges an autobiographical document that was a magnificent spiritual testament, Gabriel Péri (1902–41) might well have seemed, to the French Communist Party (Pcf) leaders, the ideal symbol of early Communist resistance. After Hitler's invasion of the Soviet Union, the Pcf managed to wriggle free of its awkward ties to the Molotov-Ribbentrop Pact, and pursued—with the help of Louis Aragon's poetic verve—the mythologization of Péri the martyr: they not only turned him into an icon but also into a muse for the *parti des fusillés*. Ultimately this resulted in his figure being rounded off too much, making his biography much too linear. His biography was of interest to historians for the opposite reason: because he was a representative example of the contradictions of French communism during the Third Republic, and because he ended up embodying the drama of a choice for the resistance made almost despite his loyalty to communism.

Péri was born in Toulon to Corsican parents and raised in Marseille, where he grew up amid reassuring petit bourgeois values, before becoming an adult during the feverish atmosphere of the great war and *union sacrée*. Starting in 1917, he was struck by the accusations made by pacifists against war profiteers and the distant but powerful echo of the Russian Revolution. At that time he joined the Jeunesses socialistes, and later tried to disseminate the pro-Bolshevik arguments of Pierre Brizon and his Parisian bulletin, *La Vague*, in Marseille. In the immediate postwar period, family crises forced Péri to interrupt his education

and become an employee; yet nothing managed to dissuade him from a political militancy, which, after the split with the French Section of the Workers' International, led him to the ranks of the newly formed Pcf.

A couple of years after the Tours Congress, Péri became a leader of the Jeunesses communistes. In this guise he took the now-canonical trip to Moscow, enjoying the honor of being welcomed by Lenin personally. He settled in Paris in 1924 as a young foreign policy department head for the party's newspaper *l'Humanité*, a position he would keep until 1939; during the 1930s he also added the role of representative from Argenteuil and later vice president of the Foreign Affairs Commission of the House to his busy life. Beyond his abilities as a journalist, Péri was also a cultivated and courteous man—qualities that earned him widespread admiration even outside Communist circles. As Pcf's recognized authority in all matters regarding foreign policy, he moved in diplomatic circles and followed the main international conferences for fifteen years, traveling to the Balkans, Spain, Indochina, and North Africa.

In 1941, from the occupier's prison, Péri wrote of his existence as a chief editor for *l'Humanité*: "I lived my profession almost like a religion, and the writing of my daily article was, every night, my priestly function." Yet his journalistic output between the wars revealed its total subservience to the Comintern's changing diktats and thus those of the Pcf too. His work included every watchword from the Communist leadership, and shifted with the party's line between the 1920s and 1930s. From the polemics against "social fascism" to the investment in the Popular Fronts, from the appeal to anti-Fascist unity to the denunciation of the imperialist democracies, Péri put his very able pen at the service of the Comintern's policies, which were always presented—according to the most edifying formulas—as an instrument of the "struggle for peace." The articles he published in early 1933 were instructive in this regard, since they coincided with Hitler's rise to power in Germany—when for the Pcf it was still important to underscore the analogy between rising German imperialism and the vibrant imperialism in the Western democracies, France included. On January 31 of that year, commenting on Hitler's becoming chancellor, Péri engaged in anti-Semitic stereotypes, presenting the National Socialist Party as a direct emanation of the "Lévy, Salomon, Oppenheim & Co. enterprises." Fifteen days later—anticipating Marcel Déat's rhetorical question "To die for Danzig?" by more than six years—Péri explained to the Communist daily's readers that French "workers' lives" should never be "sacrificed to defend the Polish corridor."

Nevertheless, after the Munich conference in September 1938, Péri's voice was among those within the Pcf vehemently denouncing the hesitations of the Édouard Daladier government and the fatal errors of appeasement. At the end of August 1939, after the announcement of the nonaggression pact between the USSR and Germany, Péri defended the Third Republic's institutions, even asking to be enrolled in the army despite a lung problem that had earlier allowed him to be exempted. The representative from Argenteuil was waiting for his draft notice when the entire Pcf parliamentary group was outlawed.

During the occupation, Péri demonstrated the resolve of his republican commitments by working in clandestine propaganda and disapproving of the Communist attempts to revive *l'Humanité* with the Germans' blessing. The mistrust that the highest-ranking leaders then expressed toward him was proof of the extent to which his own political approach contradicted the party line of national nonengagement. According to some, Péri's arrest came from a tip-off within the party itself. Péri's death certainly freed the leadership from an embarrassing interlocutor, while at the same time burnishing the Pcf's image as being at the forefront of the resistance movement.

See also Antifascism; Anti-Fascist Resistance; Comintern; Popular Front; Revolution, Myths of the.

FURTHER READING

Boursier, J.-T. *La politique du PCF, 1939–1945. Le Parti Communiste Français et la question nationale.* Paris: L'Harmattan, 1992.

Courtois, S. *Le PCF dans la guerre. De Gaulle, la Résistance, Staline.* Paris: Éditions Ramsay, 1980.

Luzzatto, S. *L'impôt du sang. La gauche française à l'épreuve de la guerre mondiale, 1900–1945.* Lyon: Presses Universitaires de Lyon, 1996.

Santamaria, Y. *L'enfant du malheur. Le parti communiste français dans la Lutte pour la paix, 1914–1947.* Paris: Éditions Seli Arslan, 2002.

SERGIO LUZZATTO

Piatnitskii, Osip

Osip Piatnitskii (Iosif Tarshis, 1882–1938) was born on January 17, in Vilkomir (now Ukmerge, Lithuania), and was the son of a joiner. In 1897 he became involved in illegal trade union activity, and in the following year entered the newly created Russian Social Democratic Workers' Party. He operated as a clandestine courier, and organized communications between Russia and the party apparatus abroad. Piatnitskii was arrested in 1902, but escaped and joined the Bolshevik wing of the party in 1903. He moved to Odessa in 1905, and helped organize the general strike there in December. From 1908–12, he worked as a Bolshevik communications organizer abroad, often in Germany. He returned to Russia and carried out party work in Samara, for which he was again arrested and then exiled to Siberia. After the February Revolution 1917, he traveled to Moscow and worked in the railwaymen's union. Piatnitskii is credited with helping to plan the Bolshevik seizure of power in Moscow in October–November 1917, and until 1920 he played a leading role in the city soviet and the Moscow Bolshevik committee.

Between 1921 and the mid-1930s, Piatnitskii was one of the key figures in the Communist International. He was the head of its Budget Commission, a member of the Executive Committee and its secretariat, and for many years oversaw the organizational work and structures of the Communist parties affiliated to the Comintern. From 1921 on, he was the boss of the Department of International Communications, a shadowy body responsible for the Comintern's clandestine activities abroad. In this capacity, Piatnitskii must have been involved in the illegal and covert operations of foreign Communist parties throughout the 1920s and early 1930s. In 1927, he was elected a member of the Central Committee of the Soviet party and also worked in its Central Control Commission. Between 1929–34 he was a committed supporter of the Comintern's "social Fascist" line. He was peremptorily removed from his Comintern duties and became director of the Political Administrative Department of the Soviet party—a position that he held until his arrest in 1937.

Under Gorbachev's glasnost and beyond, many stories emerged about Piatnitskii's arrest and subsequent ordeals at the hands of the Soviet secret police. It was alleged, latterly by his son Vladimir, that at the Central Committee Plenum in June 1937 he led a veritable "conspiracy" against Stalin's terror campaigns, refusing to recant even after Molotov, Kaganovich, and Voroshilov all advised him to do so. He was then arrested and implicated, together with Béla Kun and other Comintern luminaries, in a vast fabricated plot titled the "Fascist-Spy Organization of Trotskyites and Rightists in the Comintern."

The trial never took place because, so it is argued by one Russian historian, Piatnitskii defiantly refused to testify against himself and others even under sustained torture. It is also reported that Lenin's wife, Nadezhda Krupskaia, defended Piatnitskii as a staunch Old Bolshevik and confidante of Lenin, but Stalin indignantly rejected her interventions. Piatnitskii was shot on the night of July 29–30, 1938, and was posthumously rehabilitated in 1956.

See also Bolshevism; Comintern; Social Fascism.

FURTHER READING

Gotovitch, J., and M. Narinski, eds. *Komintern: l'histoire et les hommes. Dictionnaire biographique de l'Internationale communiste*. Paris: Éditions L'Âge d'Homme, 2001.

Lazitch, B., and M. M. Drachkovitch. *Biographical Dictionary of the Comintern*. Stanford, CA: Hoover Institution Press, 1986.

Piatnitskii, V. *Zagovor protiv Stalina*. Moscow: Sovremennik, 1998.

Starkov, B. A. "The Trial That Was Not Held." *Europe-Asia Studies*, no. 8 (1994): 1297–1315.

KEVIN F. McDERMOTT

Pieck, Wilhelm

Born January 3 in Guben (Niederlausitz, Brandenburg), Wilhelm Pieck (1876–1960) learned the carpenter's trade and joined the Social Democratic Party of Germany (SPD) in 1895. In 1906 he became a full-time party functionary in Bremen. In 1917 he participated in the creation of the Spartakus group. The following year he deserted from the army, escaping to Holland. Once he returned to Germany he was elected with Karl Liebknecht as one of the two founding presidents of the Communist Party of Germany (KPD). During the KPD's internal struggles in the 1920s, Pieck established himself as a "party functionary," avoiding the struggles between factions. He had an important role in strengthening the party's apparatus as the main Communist representative from Prussia in the Chamber of Deputies (1921–28) and later the Reichstag (1928–33), a KPD delegate to the Executive Committee of the Communist International (Ikki) starting in 1928, and a leader of the party's Organization Department.

After the KPD's Stalinization, Pieck advanced in 1931 to the Ikki's leadership. In May 1933 he was sent to Paris to lead the KPD in exile. Here he became one of the promoters of the united front that was later approved by the Comintern's Seventh Congress in the summer of 1935. In January 1935 he was summoned to Moscow. After the arrest of the KPD's president, Ernst Thälmann, during the so-called Brussels Conference (which actually took place in Kuncevo, near Moscow, in October 1935) Pieck was elected temporary party president. He supported unity in the KPD's leadership, and was therefore the individual most responsible for the exiled party's policies, even though, because of health issues, he increasingly had to share his tasks with other exiled functionaries in Moscow, to the extent that the operational managers of the politburo, and Walter Ulbricht most especially, managed to become influential.

After the KPD's readmission into liberated Germany's political arena, Pieck returned to Berlin on July 1, 1945. He was confirmed as party president and elected president of the new Central Committee's Secretariat. In this position, he was part of the leadership group that helped the Soviet military administration in the denazification process. In the course of the Unification Congress on April 21–22, 1946, he was elected, together with the SPD's Otto Grotewohl, as one of the Socialist Unity Party of Germany's two joint presidents. On October 11, 1949, he was elected first president of the German Democratic Republic (GDR). The foundation of the GDR coincided with a progressive weakening of Pieck's physical strength. He remained the undisputed head of the party and state, but in fact he could not really exercise much influence compared to the more dynamic Ulbricht. In the spring of 1953 he briefly sided with Ulbricht's critics, but subsequently, due to his deteriorating health, had to limit himself to essential representative functions. In this role Pieck resisted until his death on September 2, 1960.

See also Comintern; People's Democracy; Soviet Occupation of Germany; Thälmann, Ernst; Ulbricht, Walter.

FURTHER READING

Badstübner, R., and W. Loth, eds. *Wilhelm Pieck—Aufzeichnungen zur Deutschlandpolitk, 1945–1953*. Berlin: Akademie, 1994.

Vosske, H., and G. Nitzsche. *Wilhelm Pieck. Biographischer Abriss*. Berlin: Dietz, 1975.

WILFRIED LOTH

Planning

The term "planning" refers to both a general plan for state regulation of the economy or one of its parts, and the historical experiences that developed in the Soviet Union in the years immediately following the 1917 revolution. In the first case it was an issue, during periods of war, of introducing financial measures like the control of exchange rates or investments, the direct distribution from the center of scarce raw materials, or the rationing of consumer goods and price controls. During the second postwar period, many governments also devised plans, in the form of goals for industrial production (the annual *Economic Surveys* adopted in Great Britain, the Organization for European Economic Cooperation, plans for Western Europe, and the Colombo plan for southeast Asia). There was also a distinction between state intervention in privately held industry and planning applied to an entire public sector, since in this latter case the directives possessed a certain amount of coercive power, while in the first case control was exercised negatively (for instance, control on investments was aimed at limiting them), and positive controls went no further than influencing producers indirectly.

Planning in the Soviet Union was something different: there a plan to control the economy, with direct ideological implications, was realized, as examined below. The general debate on planning before the 1917 revolution was concerned with the Marxian idea of "socialism without an economy" (and economy meant a capitalist economy), to which the Italian economist Enrico Barone, borrowing from Vilfredo Pareto, opposed the "political economy of socialism." In 1908, in the *Giornale degli economisti* (Economists' Daily), an article appeared that provoked a wide-ranging debate, "Il ministro della produzione nello Stato collettivista" (The Production Minister in the Collectivist State), in which Barone stated that a socialist economy would be based on the public property of the means of production and concentrating economic decisions in a central authority. Barone resolved the fundamental problem of the distribution of wealth by entrusting a central authority with the political act of distributing retributions to all citizens for the labor they performed, or indirectly, by eliminating the "prices" of the liquid and real estate capital belonging to the state, which would therefore participate in production at no cost, and the final "price" would only be the result of the cost of personal labor. He was responding to Karl Marx and stating that socialism could certainly expropriate the expropriators, but that the rules of economic science would continue to be valid as a "general theory."

The debate on the topic of "socialist" economic calculations witnessed a role reversal, when liberal economists denied the possibility of economic rationality under socialism, even as socialists maintained its absolute feasibility and relevance. According to Ludwig von Mises, writing in 1920, during the civil war that was raging in the young republic of the Soviets, socialism, by substituting directives from the center to the actions of the market, prevented the establishment of a market for capital goods and thus a pricing mechanism for them. "Socialism abolishes rational economics!" was von Mises's conclusion, while another liberal economist, Friedrich A. von Hayek, more cautiously invoked the opinions expressed by Pareto and Barone, who while admitting—as a matter of principle—the logical coherence of a planned economy, would later inevitably encounter, according to Hayek, the practical difficulties of performing calculations in it and for it (data relative to production and the taste of consumers).

In the course of this debate, initially of an exclusively theoretical nature, and in which socialist economists like Maurice Dobb, Abba Lerner, and Oskar Lange also intervened, the facts of an evolving Soviet reality interjected themselves forcefully, and a collection of mostly 1920s' writings by the economists mentioned above was published in London in 1935. Titled *Collectivist Economic Planning*, the volume was edited by von Hayek, after the Soviet Union had inaugurated its Second Five-Year Plan, and evaluations had become less generic and more reasoned. The debate's provisional point of arrival consisted in the establishment of a set of theoretical conditions for implementing so-called competitive socialism, in which the central planning organ would at first only establish a set of "accounting prices" chosen randomly, and subsequently correct them on the basis of the observation of consumer (demand) and producer (supply) reactions, until nonarbitrary price equilibria were reached. The debate itself involved many liberal and socialist economists outside the Soviet Union who were stimulated by the challenge that Russian postrevolutionary reality posed to the theory and policies of the world's large capitalist nations, while waiting for the proof that reality would provide shortly.

Within Russia, the confrontation between economists and politicians was influenced by the euphoria of the revolution and the urgent decisions that it posed to government management. First there was the issue of whether the voluntary element in the construction of socialism—decisions that were basically political in nature—would prevail over conditions determined by the economic situation, over its objective rules. The socialism birthed after the revolution would become the testing ground for a confrontation between a new and conscious regulator of the economy, the planning principle, and an old blind force, the law of value—one operating in the state sector, and the other in the private sector. Some, like Nikolay Bukharin and Yevgeni Preobrazhensky, who were to disagree in the future, agreed at the time that value (*cennost'*) was typical of a commodity-producing economy, and that this condition "was disappearing in the Soviet Union," especially since, once the transition period had passed, within fully realized socialism "no political economy will be necessary." Others, like Ivan Skvorcov-Stepanov and Alexander Bogdanov, disagreed and stated that planning would be impossible without economic accounting—in other words, taking into account production costs, the manner in which capital was used, the objective limits to the pace of growth, and so on. All of them, however, were convinced of the necessity of increasing the country's productive capacity, its industrial labor force, and elevating its overall technological level.

Many economists and technicians devoted themselves to the difficult task of formulating development models that would help clarify the reciprocal influences between different segments of the economy, between industries that produced capital goods and ones that produced consumer goods (G. Feldman's model), the reciprocal influences between sectors with different production methods (Preobrazhensky's model), and the economy's structural interdependencies, or its input-output relationships (P. Popov's and Lev Litoshenko's model). These works represented the highest level of theoretical engagement by Russian economists of the period, and they influenced later research in the West on analogous topics, even if with different analytic foundations. On a practical level it was indispensable to start from the collection of data on the national economy, and adopt criteria for the elaboration of a national budget, the starting point for any further planning operations, which went through three distinct historical phases: the adoption in 1921 of the General Plan for the Electrification of the Country, the gathering of annual "control numbers," and studies on economic trends. The presentation in 1925 of the

first national budget was an occasion for confrontation between the various theoretical and political positions that all crowded around the definition of planning, and above all its practical realization, the plan.

The objective of Soviet economic policy, proclaimed in 1925, was that of reaching and overtaking capitalism's highest indexes of production, especially those being achieved by the U.S. economy. The idea that economic analysis and the construction of models, which was blossoming in the Soviet Union, could represent the path for the attainment of this objective, without considering political decisions, provoked the hostile reaction of the Bolshevik leadership group. This group was divided about its political and economic options, but ultimately united in the conviction that decisions in both areas should rest with the October Revolution's victors. The people in charge of the two principal organisms responsible for planning, the State Planning Commission (Gosplan) and the Superior Council on the National Economy (the leadership organ of state industry), wavered first to the Left and then to the Right, following the positions prevailing in the party's leadership organs.

The confrontation between different development models continued for several more years, at least until 1927, when political decisions prevailed over theoretical variables. The search for procedures to adopt at the planning stage revealed not only the economists' differing theoretical positions—the fact that they experimented with models and optimal possible solutions for the economy based on different initial scales and frameworks—but also the objective novelty of the solutions to be adopted relative to the pace of growth in a specific sector, the interaction between different property and production regimes within the Soviet economy, and last but not least the issue of the place of individual agricultural production within the overall system. All agreed that global planning would imply the "elimination of market relationships" and adoption of a centralized management system. Those who maintained that the restoration and subsequent growth of the economy depended on market relationships and the peasant economy were opposed to extensive planning.

The theoretical debate between "voluntarists" and "determinists," still immersed in the alternatives of the modifiable nature of economic laws under socialism or their persistence, was thus transferred on to the terrain of possible options, of procedures. The former became the "teleologists," and supported the need for a national plan based on a number of key objectives for the main branches of the economy. The latter were known as the "geneticists," because they argued that "objective conditions are the plan's premise," and thought that in industry the plan could be formulated according to precise directives, while in agriculture it would have to take the form of an estimate. The geneticists, unlike the teleologists, proposed that planners start with the demand for consumer goods instead of that for capital goods, since they thought the connection between economic growth and improvements in the quality of life was indissoluble.

Planning as an arena for general constructs about the economy's prospects, its principles of development, then shifted to the practical terrain where there were choices to be made between possible variants of the plan as well as the pace and manner of its application. At this stage, though, the problem was increasingly being defined in the political arena, where the party leadership group and its economists supported the idea of planning based on capital goods, establishing essential objectives and funding for them, and then pushing for these objectives to be reached or improved on, without paying attention to the tensions and distortions this was creating in the rest of the economy. The cornerstone of planning procedures resided in the initial estimate of the cost of the production programs—an estimate in both physical and monetary terms. The "economic calculation" and its rules, the need to take the social costs of production into account—the relationship that monetary prices must entertain with the latter—remained at the center of the economists' debate in the 1920s, and would continue into the 1960s, but it was resolved "from the top" with the inauguration of the First Five-Year Plan. The problem of a mechanism for determining prices and costs was not resolved on a theoretical level, even before being variously defined on the practical level.

Once the New Economic Policy was abandoned and global planning was introduced, the sphere in which market relationships still existed shrunk, whereas that which responded to administrative commands grew, and agriculture was subjected to an inexorable process of collectivization. This was the historical moment of transition from an economy based on the principle "technology decides everything" to a political one in which "the cadres decide everything." The First Five-Year Plan, formally inaugurated in 1929 for 1928–32, focused on an increase in the production of instrumental goods to a level intended to double the fixed capital in the economy during this period; it was an achievement never previously thought possible. The reality differed and led the political protagonist of the period, Joseph Stalin, at a much later date, to upend the theoretical premises on which this failure had been based: "The problems of the rational organization of the forces of production," he wrote in *Economic Problems of Socialism in the USSR* in 1952, "of the planning of the national economy, etc. do not belong to the domain of political economy, but to that of the economic policies of the ruling organs."

The planning that was followed in the "people's democracies" of Eastern Europe after World War II differed in its practical implementation, but remained faithful to this ideological inspiration. Here the principles of Soviet planning were fully applied only in the public sector, while the private sector and agriculture were guided by "directive principles." In Poland a four-year plan for the years of reconstruction 1946–49 was devised, followed by a six-year plan for 1950–55, whose purpose was to increase the production of midsize and large industries by 136 percent, and raise steel production to about three times its prewar level. Czechoslovakia first adopted a two-year reconstruction plan, with production goals for the principal products as well as a generic investment program. Subsequently a five-year plan, similar to the Soviet one, was adopted for 1949–53. Hungary, after having completed a three-year plan at the end of 1949, inaugurated a five-year plan for 1950–54, after which industrial production was supposed to double.

These efforts, which characterized the first years of planning in the people's democracies in Eastern Europe, and whose goal was to provide a broader spectrum of available economic choices than had been available in the Soviet model, were inspired by the economic analyses of the 1930s, which many economists from those countries had participated in as protagonists. These included the Pole Oskar Lange, who in his most famous essay, "On the Economic Theory of Socialism" (1937), had argued that it would be possible to calculate prices, interpreted as scarcity indexes, even in the absence of a market; and the Hungarian János Kornai as well as Michal Kalecki and Ota Sik, all of whom represented in different ways the influence of the economic debate between the wars, but also the need for reflecting on the experiences of the five-year plans and an awareness of their negative outcomes. The technique of "material budgets"—the planning of production and its redistribution into physical units of measurement—which was initially adopted in Eastern European countries, reduced the formulation of objectives to an elementary outline and allowed greater leeway in the operative phase of application.

The "national reconstruction" plans were the precursors to the ensuing "guided market economy," and were tied logically to Western theories about "macroeconomic management" and public investment, but they had other immediate sources of inspiration and different results. Eastern European planning was guided by the Soviet model: a system in which the greatest possible number of elements could be included, yet subordinated to a central chain of command. Industrialization was given absolute priority, and was based on a rapid increase in the means of production, which produced a rapid quantitative increase in both the production of the means of production and the pace of industrial development. The absence of foreign capital soon led to an increase in the utilization of internal resources, which therefore limited those available for individual, social, and public consumption.

During the first years of planning in Eastern Europe a macroeconomic equilibrium was only tentatively established, and there was an attempt to support productivist tendencies, based on an increase in production measured against the previous year's levels. Individual enterprises then also formulated their plans on the basis of these directives, establishing their own production goals, on the one hand, while requesting an adequate volume of fixed and circulating capital, on the other hand. The central authorities prepared their final plans on this flow of information; later, by resorting to the material budgets, they checked that inputs and outputs, meaning specific individual products, matched. Within this framework plans of different lengths were used differently; there were long-term plans with a fifteen-year span, twenty-year plans ("prospective" plans), medium-term plans (usually five-year plans, but also three- and six-year plans), and short-term operative plans (annual or biennial, or in the guided market system, a series of measures adopted annually). The medium-term plans were to be considered on a par with laws, and were adopted by political authorities during Communist Party congresses, while the long-period ones limited themselves to tracing a broad outline with some fixed reference points. The result was that there were discrepancies between medium-term and annual plans. Consequently, errors were common in the executive phase and hence affected the next plan's premises.

In the early 1960s, the different national contexts for the plans' application led to the development of dirigiste economies, also called guided market economies, rather than economies that strictly followed the Soviet model.

Their general provisions concerned the manner in which the budget was drafted as well as the division of profits and income. The indicators on which compensation was based were gross income or the individual enterprise's profit, but their volume was not planned, and the funds for prizes and investments were also drawn from this source, and were therefore variable. The conclusion of the first planning phase in Eastern Europe coincided with serious economic crises (Hungary witnessed the worst in 1962–63), and all the countries in the region at different times and in different fashions recognized the failure of centralized planning, giving enterprises considerable managerial autonomy, without decreasing the flow of information. In both the Soviet Union and the Eastern European countries, Stalin's death and the failure of the application of industrial planning led to changes that at the economic level were called reforms.

See also Command Economy, The; Economic Reforms; Five-Year Plans; Gosplan; Markets, Legal and Illegal; Revolution from Above; Soviet Industrialization.

FURTHER READING

Barone, E. *Le opere economiche.* Vol. 1, *Scritti vari.* Bologna: Zanichelli, 1936.

———. *Collectivist Economic Planning: Critical Studies on the Possibilities of Socialism.* London: George Routledge, 1938.

Boffito, C. *Il sistema economico sovietico.* Turin: Loescher, 1979.

Brus, W. *Il funzionamento dell'economia socialista.* Milan: Feltrinelli, 1965.

Dobb, M. "Pianificazione." In *Dizionario di economia politica,* ed. C. Napoleoni. Milan: Edizioni di comunità, 1956.

———. *Soviet Economic Development since 1917.* New York: International Publishers, 1967.

Dobb, M., A. P. Lerner, and O. Lange. *Teoria economica e economia socialista.* Rome: Savelli, 1975.

Erlich, A. *The Soviet Industrialization Debate, 1924–1928.* Cambridge, MA: Harvard University Press, 1960.

Kaser, M.. and J. G. Zielinski. *Planning in East Europe: Industrial Management by the State.* London: Bodley Head, 1970.

Spulber, N. *Foundations of Soviet Strategy for Economic Growth: Selected Soviet Essays, 1924–1930.* Bloomington: Indiana University Press, 1964.

Von Mises, L. *Socialism: An Economic and Sociological Analysis.* New Haven, CT: Yale University Press, 1951.

Zaleski, E. *Planification de la croissance et fluctuations économiques en U.R.S.S.* Paris: Société d'edition d'enseignement supérieur, 1962.

SERGIO BERTOLISSI

Plekhanov, Georgy

The phrase that traditionally accompanies Georgy Plekhanov's (1856–1918) name, the "father of Russian Marxism," defines this thinker and politician well. His life and thought evolved during the struggles against czarist autocracy, from the populist movement to the Bolshevik revolution. Plekhanov was born into a family of the landed aristocracy in the Tambov governorate, and attended first a military and later a mining institute in Saint Petersburg, simultaneously engaging in revolutionary activities in the ranks of the populist organization Zemlja i volja (Land and Liberty). At the time, he believed that the foundations for a socialist revolution and a noncapitalist development in Russia lay in the peasantry and *obshchina* (agrarian commune). In 1880, in order to avoid arrest, he emigrated and lived in Western Europe until 1917.

After experiencing a crisis about his youthful ideals, Plekhanov and other comrades founded the first Russian Marxist organization, Osvobozhdenie truda (Liberation of Labor), in Geneva in 1883. So began Plekhanov's theoretical and practical activities as a Marxist, and more generally the organized political diffusion of Marxism in Russia, as well as, at least in part, the history of the social democratic movement. The Osvobozhdenie truda's manifesto was composed of two works by Plekhanov: *Socialism and the Political Struggle* (1883), and *Our Differences* (1884), in which the contradictions of populist ideas were exposed, and the development of capitalism and the workers' movement were said to represent Russia's future.

Plekhanov outlined his Marxist program in these works, and would remain faithful to them: the contemporary growth of capitalism was seen positively and set against the populist dogma of the impossibility of capitalist development, just as the working class was seen as the motor for liberation struggles against czarism, rather than the peasants and their obshchina. He also dismissed the notion of an immediate socialist revolution, however, since the primary goal was to transform a backward, semi-Asiatic country like Russia into a constitutional state of laws similar to Europe—an objective that could only be achieved by a bourgeois revolution, by means of the cooperation of the working class with the most advanced liberal forces. This was the "classic" Marxist interpretation, which anticipated that Russia would follow a European type of development, even though Plekhanov, who later wrote the important *History of Russian Social Thought*, considered "Oriental despotism" as typical of Russia's traditional power structure. Yet Plekhanov saw Peter the Great's reforms as the beneficial beginning of a process of Europeanization that the working class would have to conclude after capitalism had completed its own process of economic, political, and cultural modernization. He also foresaw a relapse into new forms of Oriental despotism should a premature so-called socialist revolution establish itself by violent means.

This position made Plekhanov into an extraordinary figure in the Russian social democratic movement, distinguishing him from both Mensheviks and Bolsheviks. Initially he was closer to the former, only to later oppose them, and he never identified with the latter, though he had a lot in common with them. He was a Marxist theorist, a keeper of its orthodoxy, polemicizing with both the "revisionists" (from Eduard Bernstein to Peter Struve) and the "extremists" (Lenin and the Bolsheviks). As a politician he did not possess many of the pragmatic qualities that many of his comrades, of both action and thought, did; he was therefore respected as a Marxist patriarch, even by his adversaries, like Lenin. But Plekhanov continued to lose ground within the heated political struggles that were occurring and that exhibited Russian characteristics and were quite far from balanced positions like his own.

When in 1917 he returned to a Russia overwhelmed by the revolution, Plekhanov, who favored continuing the war against Germany, was increasingly isolated, even though his contributions in the contemporary press, later gathered in a volume titled *A Year in the Motherland* (Paris, 1921), were witness to the lucidity and combativeness with which he opposed Lenin's policies. Plekhanov foresaw that the adventurism of Lenin's "premature" seizure of power, as he had maintained from the beginning, would lead to a form of autocracy that was worse than czarism. The tragedy of Marxism's father in Russia was to see one of his legitimate children, as he had defined Lenin, bring about the collapse of his plan for a socialist Europeanization, and with the forced dissolution of the Constituent Assembly, end the possibility of a working class's state of laws. Beyond this nucleus of Plekhanov's life and works, one cannot forget the twenty-four volumes of his works (published in Petrograd-Leningrad between 1923 and 1927), including the philosophical works in which he theorized an "objectivist" and determinist materialism, and his reflections on literature and art in which he polemicized with revisionist tendencies mostly tied to Ernst Mach's theories, continuing an aesthetic tradition tied to Vissarion Belinsky and Nikolay Chernishevsky.

See also Lenin, Vladimir.

FURTHER READING

Baron, S. H. *Plechanov: The Father of Russian Marxism*. London: Routledge and Kegan Paul, 1963.

Tjutjukin, S. V. *G. V. Plechanov. Sud'ba russkogo marksista*. Moscow: Rosspen, 1997.

VITTORIO STRADA

Pol Pot

The Cambodian political leader Pol Pot (1925–98) was born as Saloth Sar into a prosperous peasant family in central Cambodia in the closing years of the French colonial era. He was raised by relatives in Phnom Penh, and was educated there and in Kompong Cham. In 1949 he was awarded a scholarship to study electronics in France, where he remained for nearly four years without obtaining a degree. Sar became a member of the French Communist Party in 1952, and when he returned to Cambodia a year later he briefly joined the Vietnamese-led resistance against French colonialism. For the rest of the 1950s, he was a schoolteacher in Phnom Penh and a member of Cambodia's small, clandestine, and fragmented Communist movement. The movement was formalized as the Workers' Party of Kampuchea in 1960. Sar became deputy to the party's leader, Too Samouth, who was assassinated by the police in 1962.

A year later, Sar, now the titular leader of the party, fled the city with a few colleagues and sought refuge at a Vietnamese military base on the Vietnamese-Cambodian border. In 1965 he walked to Hanoi—a journey of over three months—to consult with the Vietnamese Communist leadership, who disparaged his utopian revolutionary agenda. Soon afterward Sar visited China, then on the brink of the Cultural Revolution. He was impressed by what he saw. Returning to Cambodia, he secretly changed the party's name to the Communist Party of Kampuchea (CPK). With a small group of associates, he mapped out the radical policies that he hoped to inaugurate when the party came to power.

In 1968, while still in hiding, Sar initiated an armed struggle against Cambodia's ruler, Prince Norodom Sihanouk (1922–). When the prince was driven from power in a pro-U.S. coup in 1970, Sar, aided by Vietnam, led his followers, dubbed by journalists the Khmer Rouge, into a punishing civil war. With victory in 1975 the Khmer Rouge emptied Cambodia's towns, abolished money, schools, courts, monasteries, and markets, collectivized private property, and set nearly everyone to work as agricultural laborers. In 1976 Sar, calling himself Pol Pot, became prime minister. He kept both his past identity and the existence of the Communist Party a secret from outsiders. The party's harsh, utopian policies, modeled in part on those of Stalinist Russia, North Korea, and Maoist China, led to hundreds of thousands of deaths from starvation, untreated diseases, overwork, and executions. Pol Pot, like Stalin, blamed failures on "enemies" in the party, and thousands of party members were arrested, tortured, and killed.

In 1977 Pol Pot made a state visit to China, brought the CPK into the open, and declared war on Vietnam, hoping for Chinese support. As the war went badly, he attempted to open Cambodia to the outside world, but a Vietnamese invasion in December 1978 drove Democratic Kampuchea from power. Pol Pot spent the next two decades in camps along the Thai-Cambodian border. Until the early 1990s he commanded a formidable guerrilla force and dreamed of regaining power. His faction, with support from China, Thailand, and the United States, was the only government in exile to hold a seat in the United Nations. The Khmer Rouge signed the Paris Peace Accords on Cambodia in 1991, but boycotted the UN-sponsored elections. By 1995–97, the movement was split with factionalism after Pol Pot attempted to reintroduce the harsh policies that he believed had led to victory in 1975. Placed in custody by his colleagues in 1997, Pol Pot died of heart failure in April 1998. Many who knew him have praised his revolutionary zeal, deceptively smooth manner, apparent sincerity, and skill at presiding over small groups. His place in history is assured. At least 1.5 million Cambodians, or one in five, perished between 1975 and 1979, making the Cambodian revolution, on a per capita basis, the most murderous in a century of revolutions.

See also Khmer Rouge; Killing Fields; Marxism-Leninism; Totalitarianism; Utopia; Vietnam-Cambodia War.

FURTHER READING

Becker, E. *When the War Was Over: Cambodia and the Khmer Rouge Revolution*. New York: PublicAffairs, 1986.

Chandler, D. *Brother Number One: A Political Biography of Pol Pot*. Rev. ed. Boulder, CO: Westview Press, 1999.

Kiernan, B. *How Pol Pot Came to Power*. London: Verso, 1985.

DAVID P. CHANDLER

Polish-Soviet War

The Polish-Soviet War of 1919–20—sometimes labeled the Polish-Bolshevik War, the Soviet-Polish War, or incorrectly the Russo-Polish War—took place in the interval between the end of the First World War and the formation of the Soviet Union. It ran concurrently with the so-called Russian civil war, with which in several locations it was closely interconnected. According to Soviet propaganda, and in the accounts of commentators who repeated Soviet propaganda uncritically, it was often said to have started in April 1920 with the Polish offensive against Bolshevik-held Kiev. But in reality the Kiev campaign marked the onset of the second phase of a conflict that had started more than a year earlier. The fighting began in February 1919 and ended in October 1920. The formal end to the war came in March 1921 with the signing of the Treaty of Riga.

The main contestants of the war were, on the one hand, the newborn Republic of Poland, which had gained its independence in November 1918, and on the other hand, the three Soviet republics of Russia, Belorussia, and Ukraine. The Polish Armed Forces were commanded by the head of state and commander in chief, Marshal Jozef Piłsudski. The Soviet forces were coordinated in the first instance by the commissar for war, Leon Trotsky (Bronstein), and at the highest level by the Bolsheviks' supreme state and party organs headed by Vladimir Lenin (Ulyanov). At various moments, the contest was complicated by the involvement of forces controlled by the Republic of Lithuania, the Soviet Republic of Belorussia-Lithuania, the independent Directorate of Ukraine, and other freelance formations.

The immediate cause of the war was the retreat of the occupying German Army from a long stretch of the eastern front linking East Prussia on the north with central Ukraine in the southeast. Polish and Soviet forces moved spontaneously into the ensuing vacuum, and the first skirmish took place at Bereza Kartuska in Belorus-

sia on February 21 (?), 1919. The deeper causes, however, were both territorial and ideological. The disputed territory, between the Bug and the Dnieper, had before 1915 formed part of the czarist empire and for centuries, before the partitions of Poland, had belonged to the ancient Commonwealth of Poland-Lithuania. It was inhabited by an inimitable mixture of Poles, Lithuanians, Belorussians, Ukrainians, and Jews, but by virtually no ethnic Russians. On the ideological front, the Poles were committed to the democratic principles of the patrons of their independence—France, Britain, and the United States. The Bolsheviks were committed to rebuilding the Russian Empire in the form of a totalitarian party dictatorship operating through a facade of federated republics. They were also wedded to the concept of spreading their revolution from Russia to Germany, and Poland was the "Red Bridge" across which the Red Army would have to march.

The war passed through five distinct phases. In the first phase, from February to November 1919, when the Red Army was preoccupied with the civil war, the Poles gradually took over almost all their historic claims, including Wilno and Lwów, both cities with large Polish majorities. Piłsudski was hoping at this stage to create a federation of border states from Finland to Georgia, but was thwarted by the noncooperation of the Lithuanian Republic.

Second, over the winter, from November 1919 to April 1920, the fighting died down: inconclusive peace talks took place, and the only major action was seen in Latvia, where the Polish Army drove out the Bolsheviks and helped create a national republic. From January onward, however, Trotsky was amassing a huge strike force on the Berezina. Piłsudski had good reason to suspect Russian intentions given both the prospect of a Soviet invasion and the failure of the Russian Whites under Denikin to recognize Poland's independence.

During the third phase, April–May 1920, to forestall the imminent Soviet offensive, Piłsudski signed an alliance with the Ukrainian leader, Ataman Petlura, and a joint Polish-Ukrainian force quickly captured Kiev. The objective was to secure the independence of both Poland and Ukraine. Pro-Soviet demonstrators in Western Europe shouted "Hands Off Russia," not realizing that Kiev was in Ukraine, not in Soviet Russia.

In May, in the fourth phase, the long-prepared Soviet offensive sprang westward from the Berezina under the dashing young General Tukhachevskii, forcing the Poles to abandon Kiev in a hurry. "Over the corpse of White Poland," read Tukhachevskii's order of the day, "onward to world revolution!" The destination was Berlin. To the south, a second Red Army, under General Budyonny and its political director, Joseph Stalin, was approaching Lwów. In Moscow, Lenin, in a fervent mood, was leading the war party. An Inter-Allied Military Mission, headed by General Weygand failed to offer Poland any practical assistance. An armistice and an armistice line proposed by the British foreign secretary, Lord Curzon, were rejected by both sides.

Tukhachevskii's "Red Cossacks" had ridden far beyond Warsaw when Piłsudski struck. A brilliant counterstroke from the south sliced through the extended Soviet lines, took a hundred thousand prisoners, relieved Warsaw from siege, and prepared a total Polish triumph. This "Miracle on the Vistula" was no miracle. An army of patriots, defending their native land, comprehensively defeated an overconfident enemy driven by an unrealistic ideology. Trotsky blamed Stalin. Lenin changed his tune. The West congratulated Weygand.

Fifth, in the two months after the Battle of Warsaw, the Polish Army consolidated its victory. A Soviet attempt to regroup on the River Niemen was crushed. At Komarów (aka the Zamość Ring). In the last major cavalry battle of world history, Budyonny was driven off. Soviet stragglers filled the roads for hundreds of miles, retreating whence they came. Lenin sued desperately for peace, offering to cede as much land as Poland wanted, on the condition of an immediate truce. The Polish negotiators, unexpectedly cautious, preferred a territorial compromise. The Treaty of Riga, signed on March 18, 1921, provided the combatant states with a secure frontier that would last until the next Soviet invasion in 1939. It cemented Poland's fragile independence and enabled the three Bolshevik-run republics to create the Soviet Union. At the same time, it put an end for a generation to the Bolsheviks' strategy of spreading revolution to Germany. This change was a precondition for Lenin's replacement of War Communism with the New Economic Policy and Stalin's subsequent policy of "Socialism in One Country."

See also Molotov-Ribbentrop Pact; Red Army; Russian Revolution and Civil War; Socialism in One Country.

FURTHER READING
Davies, N. *White Eagle, Red Star: The Polish-Soviet War, 1919–1920*. London: Random House, 1972.

NORMAN DAVIES

Politburo

The politburo of the Central Committee of the Communist Party of the Soviet Union (CPSU) was the highest organ of party and state power in Soviet Russia and the USSR. It was created as a permanent structure in March 1919, and consisted of five members (headed by Lenin) and three candidate members. The eight members were charged with solving the key political problems of the country's development. Lenin's protracted illness and eventual death led to an intense power struggle among the party leaders in the politburo. At first, from 1923 to 1924, the majority of politburo members were united against Trotsky. To coordinate this struggle, all the politburo members other than Trotsky created a faction called the "Group of Seven." The Group of Seven laid the basis for narrow ruling cliques that would substitute themselves for the entire politburo. After driving Trotsky from power, these erstwhile allies developed their own political conflicts, splitting the Group of Seven into two factions: Grigory Zinovyev and Lev Kamenev, on the one hand, now stood against most of the rest of the politburo, on the other. Zinovyev and Kamenev were soon joined by Trotsky, but the three of them lost an ensuing power struggle and were expelled from the politburo.

By 1927, though, the politburo's power came to be divided among its three most influential members at the time: Aleksei Rykov, Stalin, and Nikolay Bukharin. Rykov was the chair of the Council of People's Commissars of the USSR. He attended to questions of operational leadership, especially concerning the economy. Stalin ran the party apparatus. Bukharin was in charge of basic ideological institutions and developing theoretical justifications for majority policy in the politburo. The remaining members were also independent political figures. So far, in the higher echelons of power, there had been no undisputed chief but rather a competition among the leading figures, so that the field for maneuvering among all the members was quite broad. But this balance of power was disrupted by a struggle in the politburo in 1928–29. In addition to personal ambitions and claims to leadership, the escalation of conflicts within the politburo were driven by questions of principle concerned with the fortunes of the New Economic Policy (NEP). One group in the politburo, headed by Stalin, mostly insisted on rejecting the NEP and concentrating instead on forced industrialization and requisitions of grain from the peasants.

A second group, represented by Rykov, Bukharin, and Mikhail Tomsky (termed the "right wingers"), insisted on a course of moderation based on market relations with the peasantry. For a number of objective and subjective reasons, Stalin emerged the victor. Bukharin and Tomsky were expelled from the politburo, and later Rykov as well. One of Stalin's most devoted followers in the politburo, Vyacheslav Molotov, replaced Rykov as chair of the Council of People's Commissars.

Although, as Stalin rose, the positions of the other politburo members grew weaker, in the early 1930s the politboro itself remained in many ways a collective organ of power. Documents from this period show that the politburo was an unstable oligarchic organ of management. Since they headed the key agencies, politburo members played a crucial role in operational and even strategic decisions, and in both Moscow and the regional offices, they installed layers of bureaucrats dependent on them and often personally devoted to them. Serious incursions into the influence of a politburo member were possible, but they usually provoked strife and scandal. For many years before he assumed absolute power, Stalin had to contend with the presence of this "patrimony."

Almost all historians agree that it was the purges of 1937–38 that ultimately consolidated Stalin's monolithic dictatorship. The victims were many hundreds of thousands of ordinary citizens as well as party and state heads from all levels, including Stalin's own close circle. As a result of the 1937–38 purges, of the eleven politburo members, two (Stanislav Kosior and Vlas Chubar) were shot and one (Grigory Ordzhonikidze) committed suicide. Of the politburo's five candidate members, three (R. Eiche, Jan Rudzutak, and Pavel Postyshev) were shot. Mikhail Kalinin's wife was thrown into prison, and a case was also prepared against Molotov's wife. Many other relatives and colleagues of almost all politburo members were arrested. Not only the careers but also the actual physical existence of even the highest Soviet leaders became dependent on the dictator's will. Stalin moved younger functionaries into the positions vacated by the purges: in particular, the secretary of the CPSU's Central Committee and leader of the Leningrad party organization, Andrey Zhdanov; the secretary of the Moscow regional party committee and later leader of Ukraine, Khrushchev; the people's commissar for internal affairs, Lavrenty Beria; the chair of the USSR's State Planning Board, Nikolai Voznesensky; and a secretary of the CPSU's Central Committee, Georgy Malenkov. The politburo no longer functioned as a collective organ

of power and was, for practical purposes, replaced by a narrow group of leaders within it, the so-called Group of Five. In addition to Stalin, this group was composed of Molotov, Kliment Voroshilov, Anastas Mikoyan, and Lazar Kaganovich. The Group of Five met regularly in Stalin's office and served as a consultative body around the leader.

Although the politburo's activity during the war with Fascist Germany (1941–45) has been inadequately studied, certain facts show that this was a period of definite strengthening of Stalin's comrades in arms. The necessity to achieve quick results under extreme military conditions gave them substantial power. Molotov, Beria, Malenkov, and Mikoyan achieved the greatest influence during the war. Together with Stalin, they made up the ruling Group of Five. (By this time Voroshilov and Kaganovich had been replaced by Beria and Malenkov.) Yet these politburo members were subjected to stern criticism and sanctions from Stalin at the end of 1945 and the beginning of 1946. Stalin now reintroduced into his closest circle of leaders Zhdanov and Voznesensky, whose positions had become somewhat shaky during the war. At the same time, he began to promote the career of the minister of war, Nikolay Bulganin, whom he placed in the politburo in February 1948.

Stalin carried out the next politburo purge in 1949, approximately six months after Zhdanov's death. At the end of 1948, Molotov's wife was arrested and expelled from the party. In March 1949, Molotov himself was relieved from his duties as minister of foreign affairs, and Mikoyan from his position as minister of foreign trade, although both men did retain their posts as deputy chairs of the USSR's Council of Ministers. In February and March 1949, a secretary of the CPSU's Central Committee, Aleksei Kuznetsov, and another politburo member, Voznesensky, were removed from their posts. Over the course of several months, the Ministry for State Security fabricated cases against Kuznetsov, Voznesensky, and a large group of other officials in one way or another associated with them. They were all arrested and sentenced under the rulings of the so-called Leningrad Case. In 1950, Kuznetsov and Voznesensky were shot. These events disrupted the existing balance of power in Stalin's circle, strengthening Malenkov's and Beria's positions. At the end of 1949, in order to restore the balance of forces, Stalin removed G. M. Popov from the post of secretary of the Moscow party organization and brought Khrushchev up from Ukraine to replace him. He also began to promote Bulganin's career by appointing him first deputy chair of the Council of Ministers in early 1950. And although Stalin for now instituted no more major purges of the upper echelons as he had done in the Leningrad Case, he often did things to keep the politburo members in a state of fearfulness.

In order to curb the influence of his old comrades, an aging Stalin decided at the CPSU's Nineteenth Congress in October 1952 to replace the politburo with the party's presidium of the Central Committee. The presidium included a large group of second-echelon functionaries, whose numbers could keep the old politburo members in check. At the Central Committee's plenum, which took place just after the congress, Stalin came down publicly on Molotov and Mikoyan and denied them his political trust. At his demand, these two old politburo members were barred from the Office of the presidium of the CPSU's Central Committee, the new small ruling circle that to a certain extent replaced the old politburo. Nevertheless, in spite of Stalin's efforts, the preconditions remained within his monolithic dictatorship for a regeneration of oligarchic "collective leadership." And indeed, immediately after Stalin's death in March 1953, the old members of the politburo abolished the more numerous presidium of the Central Committee and re-created what was, for practical purposes, the old politburo, although now with the new name presidium.

The post-Stalin collective leadership, though, proved unstable. In July 1953, as a result of a conspiracy among the presidum members, Beria was arrested and later shot because of suspicions about his role as the leader of the security organs. In June 1957, lengthy debates and clashes in the presidium ended in victory for Khrushchev and his supporters over a group of influential members of the leadership's upper echelons. As a result, Stalin's old comrades Malenkov, Molotov, Kaganovich, and Bulganin were removed from the presidium. By the end of 1957, Khrushchev had concentrated a significant share of power in his own hands, although his regime could not have been characterized as a monolithic dictatorship. Presidium appointments now went mostly to personal favorites of Khrushchev. The members of the upper echelons of the leadership, of whom Khrushchev was still wary—for example, the popular minister of defense, Marshal Georgy Zhukov—were gradually removed from the presidium.

Appointments to Khrushchev's presidium now began to go to constituents of a newer generation of party functionaries. The prewar generation was represented by Khrushchev himself along with Mikoyan and Nikolai

Shvernik. Among functionaries entering the higher echelons of power during the postwar years were Mikhail Suslov, Aleksey Kosygin, and eventually Brezhnev. A large number of presidium members (notably F. R. Kozlov and Andrei Kirilenko) were protégés of Khrushchev. Forgoing the repressions and physical liquidations of his predecessor, Khrushchev maintained his strength by traditional methods of creating his own informal groups of leaders for the presidium, through reorganizing the apparatus and through shake-ups of personnel. The fear of falling out of favor with the unpredictable Khrushchev was one of the reasons for the plot against him among the majority of other presidium members. In October 1964, Khrushchev was toppled from his post. The duties of the first secretary of the Central Committee and chair of the Council of Ministers—functions that Khrushchev had combined in his own person—were now occupied by Brezhnev and Kosygin, respectively.

The new presidium leadership came to power promising to maintain stability among personnel and more consistency in administrative matters. Shifts in the higher echelons of power during the 1960s and 1970s, generally strengthening Brezhnev's position, took place relatively smoothly. This new stability and continuity of policy was symbolized by the decision of the party's Twenty-third Congress in 1966 to reconstitute the presidium into a politburo, thus returning to the organ its historical name. In addition to an emergence in the politburo of new members closely allied with Brezhnev, the 1970s were also marked by the transformation of the politburo into an organ now representing equally all the most influential power structures: the party, the government apparatus, the Committee for State Security (KGB), the army, the military-industrial complex, and like entities.

By the early 1980s, the persons in the ruling group of the politburo who exercised the greatest influence on the by then ailing Brezhnev were Minister of Defense Dmitry Ustinov and the KGB chair Yuri Andropov. It was under their pressure that fatal decisions were made to invade Afghanistan and continue an arms buildup for which the USSR no longer had the resources. Certain changes in the politburo and its policies during the early 1980s were inevitable, given the death or extreme ill health of some of the key leaders—Suslov, Kirilenko, and Ustinov. After Brezhnev's death in 1982, the two succeeding aged general secretaries of the Central Committee, Andropov and Konstantin Chernenko, passed away in 1983 and early 1985, respectively.

The final stage in the politburo's history, like that of the Soviet Union itself, began when Mikhail Gorbachev came to power at the beginning of 1985. Inheriting a politburo composed primarily of leaders who were his potential rivals for the general secretary post, Gorbachev spent much of his energy during the early years of his rule changing the politburo's makeup by inserting his own protégés. Yet substantial changes in the political direction of the politburo, which Gorbachev himself had instituted, led to conflicts. For the first time since the end of the 1920s, the politburo was home to radically different political positions, exemplified in particular by the active conflict between E. K. Ligachev, who represented the conservative side, and Aleksandr Yakovlev, who supported a radical form of perestroika. Nevertheless, the importance of the politburo as a center of power shrank with the establishment in May 1990 of the post of president of the USSR, assumed by Gorbachev, and other structures fitted into the president's administration. By the time the August 1991 putsch occurred, the politburo had lost its monopolistic position and become only one of several centers of power in the country. When the CPSU was abolished after the putsch, the politburo's seventy-year existence was at an end as well.

See also Nomenklatura; Single-Party System; State, The.

FURTHER READING

Alibekov, G. M., et al., eds. *Politbjuro CK RKP(b)–VKP(b). Povestki dnja zasedanij, 1919–1952.* 3 vols. Moscow: Rosspen, 2000–2001.

Chlevnjuk, O. V. *Master of the House: Stalin and His Inner Circle.* New Haven, CT: Yale University Press, 2008.

———. *Politbjuro. Mechnizmy politiceskoj vlasti v 1930-e gody.* Moscow: Rosspen, 1996.

Gorlizki, Y., and O. Chlevnjuk. *Cold Peace: Stalin and the Soviet Ruling Circle, 1945–1953.* Oxford: Oxford University Press, 2004.

Gregory, P., O. Chlevnjuk, and A. Vatlin, eds. *Stenograms of the TsK RKP(b)–VKR(b) Politburo Meetings, 1923–1938.* 3 vols. Moscow: Rosspen, 2007.

Gregory, P., and N. Naimark, eds. *The Lost Politburo Transcripts: From Collective Rule to Stalin's Dictatorship.* New Haven, CT: Yale University Press, 2008.

Pichoia, R. G. *Sovetskij Sojuz: istorija vlasti. 1954–1991.* Moscow: Rags, 1998.

Presidium of the Central Committee of the CPSU. Vol. 1. Drafts of conference protocol records, 1954–64. Shorthand reports. Moscow: Rosspen, 2003.

OLEG V. CHLEVNJUK

Political Pilgrims

Political pilgrims, like their religious counterparts, seek spiritual rejuvenation, the confirmation of beliefs already held, or a political conversion experience. George Bernard Shaw spoke for many of them when, embarking on his return to England from the Soviet Union in 1931, he said: "Tomorrow I leave this land of hope and return to our Western countries of despair."

The political pilgrims were mostly Western intellectuals who visited Communist countries in the 20th century and chronicled their experiences in enthusiastic travelogues. They were looking for societies morally superior to their own, and capable of remedying the problems and inequities they were familiar with. They were, for the most part, favorably predisposed toward these countries. Most of them were unfamiliar with prevailing conditions, did not speak the local language, and were dependent on the official guide-interpreters during their visit. This unfamiliarity made it easier to project on these societies their hopeful expectations and confirm their favorable predisposition; in any event, they were ready to generalize from limited personal experiences.

The destinations of the political pilgrimages varied as some of the political systems initially idealized became discredited over time. This was the case of the Soviet Union after Khrushchev's revelations (in 1956) and China following the death of Mao Zedong (after 1976); Nicaragua ceased to be appealing after the Sandinistas were voted out of power (in 1990).

It is difficult to estimate the number of pilgrims, and their identity can only be established from their writings. There were doubtless thousands, possibly tens of thousands, if one includes the anonymous travelers who went with organized groups, sometimes in order to donate symbolically their labor for short periods of time (for example, the Venceremos Brigade in Cuba and various groups in Nicaragua). These larger groups are more often called political tourists; they too harbored a favorable predisposition but not as intense as those designated as political pilgrims. The pilgrims were usually well-known public figures, while the tourists were more often anonymous sympathizers.

Most of the pilgrimages took place in two periods characterized by a crisis of confidence in Western societies—times of intensified social criticism and estrangement from the existing sociopolitical order. The first period extended from the late 1920s to the late 1930s, a period of severe economic crisis associated with the Great Depression. During these years the pilgrims went to the Soviet Union, the only Communist state at the time, which seemed to offer an attractive counterpoint to the economic and social problems and dislocations that Western countries experienced. Contributing to the sense of crisis was the rise of Nazi Germany and the Spanish civil war. The Soviet Union, in addition to its appealing domestic socioeconomic policies, was seen as the only unwavering opponent of Nazism and fascism, and staunch supporter of the democratic forces in the Spanish civil war.

The second period extended from the mid-1960s through the 1970s. These were years of political and cultural turmoil in the United States and to a lesser extent in Western Europe. The major sources of social protest and discontent in the United States were the Vietnam War and racial-sexual discrimination, which broadened into a rejection of inequalities of every kind. Protest against the Vietnam War (which also spread to Western Europe) and racism culminated in a sweeping rejection of Western bourgeois societies (especially the United States) and their alleged materialism, spiritual emptiness, hypocrisy, inauthenticity, bureaucratization, and impoverishment of human relationships.

During this period the major destinations of the travelers were Cuba, China, and Vietnam. Other third world countries claiming socialist credentials—for example, Angola, Mozambique, Tanzania, Ethiopia, and Grenada—were also favored but less often visited.

During the 1980s, Sandinista Nicaragua became the single most popular destination. While Cuba has lost some of its appeals over time (due to its chronic violation of human rights, economic difficulties, and the evident discontent of the multitudes seeking escape), it has retained a core of supporters and sympathizers largely due to the durable charisma, power, and intransigence of Fidel Castro.

It is noteworthy that the pilgrimages to the Soviet Union peaked during the 1930s—the period of collectivization, the Great Purges, and show trials—when the system was the most repressive and mendacious; likewise the pilgrims to China seemed most numerous and rapturous during the late 1960s and early 1970s when the Cultural Revolution ravaged Chinese society. These were also periods characterized by the bizarre, compulsory deification of the leaders Stalin and Mao, respectively.

The enthusiastic visitors remained unaware of the bleak economic conditions in these countries, or the intense repression and high levels of intimidation among the population. Their lack of awareness could be ascribed to the combination of favorable predisposition, selective perception, plain ignorance, and the deceptions that the authorities successfully perpetrated.

In the 1990s and early 21st century there was a small-scale revival of the phenomenon. Chiapas in Mexico was discovered following the peasant uprising (led by an academic intellectual) in 1994; areas under partial rebel control attracted sympathizers from abroad including numerous Hollywood celebrities, Mrs. François Mitterand, and Régis Debray. There was also somewhat greater interest in North Korea during these years, exemplified by the visits and favorable observations of former president Jimmy Carter in 1994, those of the Reverend John Swomley (founder of the American Committee on Korea), and the many writings of Bruce Cumings, a historian at the University of Chicago. In the same period (and to this day), the territories occupied by Israel came to attract Western political activists and tourists seeking to dramatize their opposition to Israel (and the United States) and their support for the Palestinian cause.

The political pilgrims included many distinguished, well-known Western intellectuals, famous artists, scientists, politicians, journalists, clergy, and Hollywood celebrities. Notable among those visiting the Soviet Union in the first period were Louis Aragon, Henri Barbusse, J. D. Bernal, Jerome Davis, John Dewey, Theodore Dreiser, W.E.B. DuBois, Walter Duranty, Lion Feuchtwanger, Louis Fischer, Waldo Frank, Andre Gide, Emma Goldman, Maurice Hindus, Julian Huxley, Hewlett Johnson, Corliss Lamont, Harold Laski, Owen Lattimore, Emil Ludwig, Eugene Lyons, Scott Nearing, Pablo Neruda, Bernard Pares, Romain Rolland, Jean-Paul Sartre, George Bernard Shaw, Upton Sinclair, Lincoln Steffens, Henry Wallace, Beatrice and Sidney Webb, Edmund Wilson, and Ella Winter.

The second generation of prominent travelers included Simone de Beauvoir (China), Daniel Berrigan, (North Vietnam), Jimmy Carter (North Korea), Noam Chomsky, (North Vietnam and Nicaragua), Ramsey Clark (North Vietnam and Iraq under Saddam Hussein), William Sloane Coffin (Vietnam and Nicaragua), Johnetta Cole (Cuba), Basil Davidson (China), Angela Davis (Cuba and the Soviet Union), David Dellinger (Vietnam), John K. Fairbank (China), Waldo Frank (Cuba), John Galbraith (China), Billy Graham (USSR),

Felix Greene (China), Tom Hayden (Vietnam), Le Roi Jones (Cuba), Jonathan Kozol (Cuba), Arnold Kettle (USSR), William Kunstler (Cuba), Saul Landau (Cuba), Staughton Lynd (Vietnam), Mary McCarthy (Vietnam), Maria Macciochi (China), George McGovern (Cuba), Shirley MacLaine (China), C. Wright Mills (Cuba), Yves Montand (USSR), Jan Myrdal (China and Albania), Ronald Radosh (Cuba), Robert Redford (Cuba), David Rockefeller (China), Harrison Salisbury (China), Jean-Paul Sartre (Cuba), Edgar Snow (China), Susan Sontag (Cuba and Vietnam), Benjamin Spock (China), Simone Signoret (USSR), Anna Louise Strong (China), Pierre Trudeau (China), Tom Wicker (Angola), Maurice Zeitlin (Cuba), and Howard Zinn (North Vietnam).

For a small minority of these visitors the travel experience contributed or led to disillusionment. They included Max Eastman, Louis Fischer, André Gide, Emma Goldman, Eugene Lyons, Ronald Radosh, and Bertrand Russell. A large, if undetermined, number might have had second thoughts, but they remained unexpressed.

The host governments encouraged the visits of influential Westerners susceptible to persuasion about the virtues of their system. These efforts at persuasion, or techniques of hospitality, included a concentrated effort to maximize control over the experiences and impressions of the visitors utilizing two approaches. One was the selective presentation or screening of what could be seen and experienced, the systematic and purposeful exposure of the visitor to sights and human contacts that the hosts believed would make the most favorable impression. Typical itineraries would include construction sites or edifices symbolizing material progress and institutions reflecting the humane, caring policies of these governments: new power plants, factories, collective farms, kindergartens, clinics, schools, youth camps, workers, resorts, housing projects, and model prisons. There were also theatrical and dance performances, especially by folk artists and ensembles, and sometimes impressively choreographed political rallies to attend. Often the pilgrims were introduced to humble workers and peasants, reformed prostitutes and rehabilitated criminals, beneficiaries of government policies as well as members of elite groups sharing their professional interests and qualifications. Some of the sites that the pilgrims were taken to were outright Potemkin Villages, built or rearranged for their benefit: model prisons and housing projects, exceptionally well-equipped hospitals, atypically prosperous collective farms, and so on.

The second component of the techniques of hospitality was the flattering personal treatment of the visitors, the attempt to maximize their physical comfort and sense of well-being, making them feel appreciated and important. These measures included pleasant or luxurious accommodations and transportation, fine food, lavish entertainments, sometimes presents, admiring audiences, the meeting of key officials (sometimes the top leaders), and the publication of the visitors' statements and their writings.

The appeals of these societies were highly patterned, representing a counterpoint to everything that the pilgrims abhorred in their own. There was a promise of liberated existence not limited to liberation from want but also from deprivations and scarcities of every kind; a new sense of purpose, community, identity, and wholeness; a cessation of conflict between the personal and the social, the private and the public; and an end to alienation, especially appealing to intellectuals who felt isolated, powerless, and insufficiently appreciated in Western capitalist, commercial societies. Susan Sontag observed with admiration in 1968 that "the phenomenon of existential agony, of alienation, just don't appear among the Vietnamese."

The appeals of these societies included the rediscovery of the "noble savage," an image first projected on members of preliterate societies in the 18th century, subsequently on poor peasants, and later on the proletarians. The new noble savages (like their predecessors) impressed the visitors as simple, authentic, wholesome, dignified, generous, warm, spontaneous, hospitable, and free of all the afflictions and corruptions capitalism and class society imposed on human beings.

The Communist states also benefited from legitimating themselves with the ideas of Karl Marx, by the claim that the Marxist ideological heritage inspired them. The leaders themselves, interpreters of these ideas (Stalin, Mao, Castro, Che Guevara, Ho Chi Minh, and others), made an excellent personal impression on account of their apparent devotion to the welfare of their people; profound understanding of all matters social, political, economic, and historical; decisiveness; and close approximation of the role of philosopher-king. They were kindred spirits, fellow intellectuals (or so it seemed), capable of applying theory to practice, bridging the gap between ideals and their realization.

The position of intellectuals in the new societies was equally admirable, involved as they seemed in the building of a morally superior social system, taken seriously by the power holders and firmly integrated into the national community. Examination of the pilgrimages provides new insight and information about the political beliefs, attitudes, and social roles of a substantial and influential portion of Western intellectuals, and suggests a revision of the defining characteristics of intellectuals as commonly understood. Above all, their travelogues call into question the widely held belief that a critical mind-set is the essential attribute of intellectuals. By contrast, the utterances of these pilgrims reflect a capacity for zealous affirmation and credulousness unalleviated by any trace of reasoned skepticism. Many of them displayed the wish to believe, and a craving for meaning and community difficult to reconcile with the widely held notion that intellectuals are highly individualistic and impelled by "unmasking" impulses, mercilessly exposing illusions, and comfortable with living in a world from which, in the words of Max Weber, "the gods have retreated." Second, the sympathy shown toward repressive governments suggests that the unflinching commitment to free expression assumed to be another key characteristic of intellectuals can be easily set aside or suspended; the admirable goals of these regimes absolved them of responsibility for the methods used in their pursuit. Third, these intellectuals routinely and inconsistently alternated between a moral relativism and absolutism. They were relativistic when accepting the subordination of the means to the ends in the Communist states, and absolutistic in their stern condemnation of the flaws of their own societies.

The impact of these pilgrimages has been manifold. They temporarily met the political-psychological needs of alienated Westerners and concurrently illuminated the spiritual-cultural problems of their societies. The pilgrimages also contributed to the prolonged misapprehension of Communist systems. Finally, these journeys also suggest the revision of the belief that intellectuals have a superior immunity to both deception and self-deception.

See also Cult of Personality; Fellow Travelers; Propaganda, Communist; Revolution, Myths of the; Stalin, Myth of.

FURTHER READING

Ahlmark, P. "Swedish Myopias." *Society* (November–December 1998).

Aron, R. *The Opium of Intellectuals*. London: Secker and Warburg, 1957.

Berger, P. L. "The Myth of Socialism." *Public Interest* (Summer 1976).

Billington, J. H. "The Intelligentsia and the Religion of Humanity." *American Historical Review* (July 1960).

Daniels, A. *Utopias Elsewhere*. New York: Crown, 1991.

Hollander, P. *Political Pilgrims*. New York: Oxford University Press, 1981.

———. "The Pilgrimage to Nicaragua." In *Anti-Americanism: Irrational and Rational*. New York: Oxford University Press, 1992.

———. "Western Views of Communism: Judgements and Misjudgements." In *The Collapse of Communism*, ed. L. Edwards. Stanford, CA: Hoover Institution Press, 2000.

———. "Digesting the Collapse of Communism: Responses of Western Intellectuals." In *Discontents: Postmodern and Postcommunist*. New Brunswick, NJ: Transaction, 2002.

———. "The Durable Significance of the Political Pilgrimages." In *Discontents: Postmodern and Postcommunist*. New Brunswick, NJ: Transaction, 2002.

Koestler, A. *The Yogi and the Commissar*. New York: Collier Books, 1961.

Margulies, S. R. *The Pilgrimage to Russia: The Soviet Union and the Treatment of Foreigners, 1924–1937*. Madison: University of Wisconsin Press, 1968.

Mosher, S. W. *China Misperceived*. New York: Basic Books, 1990.

Potter, D. M. "Rejection of the Prevailing American Society." In *History and American Society*. New York: Oxford University Press, 1973.

PAUL HOLLANDER

Pollitt, Harry

Harry Pollitt (1890–1960) was born at Droylesden, near Manchester, England, on November 22. His mother was an active Socialist, and Pollitt, who trained to become a boilermaker, followed her into left-wing politics, as a member of the British Socialist Party and later Sylvia Pankhurst's Workers' Socialist Federation. Enthused by the Bolshevik revolution, he became a supporter of Communist unity and attended the Unity Convention in 1920 that formed the Communist Party of Great Britain (CPGB).

At an early stage he made the acquaintance of Rajani Palme Dutt, who was to play a role in the development of the party, not least as the husband of a Comintern agent, and until the mid-1920s they worked closely together. In particular, they served together on the three-member party commission of 1922, which aimed to "bolshevize" the party and improve its performance, and which resulted in the eventual departure of a number of early luminaries. Thereafter, Pollitt became the head of the National Minority Movement, which sought to increase Communist influence in the trade unions and which was one of the few relatively successful enterprises of the party's early years of operation.

By 1928 he was clearly identified, both within the party and in Moscow, as one of the party's more able leaders, and—with some persuasion by the Comintern—he eventually came out as a supporter of the "new line" in 1928. Elevated to the position of general secretary in 1929, he played a leading role in the launch of the *Daily Worker* in 1930, but soon found that the ultra-leftism of the "class against class" period was bringing few if any benefits to the party. It was largely on Pollitt's initiative that the party sought Moscow's approval for a moderation of its trade-union line in December 1931. Moscow now confirmed that Pollitt should be regarded as leader of the party, and this position was effectively confirmed by his defeat of his critics—including Dutt—at the party congress in November 1932.

During the 1930s, Pollitt was at the forefront of the party's efforts. He worked closely with John Campbell to ensure that the party's influence within the unions grew. He also played a prominent role in the campaign for alliances against fascism, first on the United Front and then the Popular Front. By the later 1930s he was a well-known figure with an appeal far beyond the confines of his own party. But during 1939 he became increasingly discontented with aspects of Comintern and Soviet policy, and that October he resigned as secretary rather than accept the Comintern's line that the war between Britain and Germany was simply a clash of rival imperialisms, and not a fight against fascism. He was replaced by a three-member secretariat of Dutt, William Rust, and D. F. Springhall, and briefly went back to working at his trade. However, Pollitt had no desire to leave the party and issued a statement (with which he privately disagreed) of apology for his "error" regarding the war. He was soon back in the leading councils of the party, however, and stood as a Communist by-election candidate in February 1940. When Germany invaded the USSR in June 1941, he was restored as party secretary, and for the remainder of the war pursued a strongly patriotic line. Indeed, he hoped in 1944–45 for a continuation of some kind of coalition government into peacetime, but this proved a chimera, and Pollitt was strongly criticized for his moderation, not least by Rust, who hoped to replace him. However, he was able to hold on to his position.

During his last years as general secretary, Pollitt was increasingly plagued by poor health. It also seems unlikely that he was entirely happy with the development of the Cold War, given his earlier hopes for postwar international cooperation. He was more satisfied with the party's new program, *The British Road to Socialism* (1951), whose rejection of revolution in favor of reform was consonant with his own relative moderation as a Communist. However, by 1956 he was a shadow of his former self and resigned as party secretary to take on the essentially honorific post of party chairman. He died in 1960.

Harry Pollitt was probably the ablest, and certainly the most charismatic, leader that the CPGB ever had. Although a loyal Communist, he was more independent-minded than many, a fact that occasionally brought him into conflict with the Soviets. However, he was too loyal a Communist to persist in hostility toward the Russians for very long, and while he became adept at pushing the "line" in his own direction when it suited him, he usually recognized that there were limits to the extent to which the party could act autonomously of the Comintern before 1939; and, after 1941, it would appear that the victory of Soviet arms in the Second World War, and the resultant expansion of the Communist world, assuaged most of any doubts that Pollitt might have had.

See also Bolshevization; Comintern; Molotov-Ribbentrop Pact; Popular Front; World War II.

FURTHER READING
Morgan, K. *Harry Pollitt*. Manchester, UK: Manchester University Press, 1993.
Thorpe, A. *The British Communist Party and Moscow, 1920–1943.* Manchester, UK: Manchester University Press, 1993.

ANDREW J. THORPE

Polycentrism

It is not clear when the term "polycentrism" gained currency in the international Communist movement. According to Veliko Vlahovich, in the restricted commission that debated the dissolution of the Communist International in May 1943, Palmiro Togliatti discussed the issue of "the forms and methods of collaboration between Communist and workers' parties after victory over fascism, in the absence of a Communist International." He also recalled everyone's attention to "the importance of bilateral and multilateral cooperation and, even more importantly, of regional cooperation . . . between parties that work and struggle in similar conditions." If it is true that the impossibility of a "solution of the problems of the workers' movement in each country considered separately by means of an international center"—mentioned in the Comintern's resolution to dissolve—was a consequence of the outcome of World War II, it is just as certain that Stalin and the other Soviet leaders were convinced they would be able to count on ties with Communist parties that would not take institutionalized forms. So with the onset of the Cold War, the birth of the Cominform reasserted the principle of a single centralized leadership of the Communist movement, while the "polycentric" ambitions that Josip Broz Tito was promoting with his plan for a Balkan federation were among the key factors that led to his excommunication by Moscow.

After Stalin's death in 1953, the theorization of "pacific coexistence" between the blocs as developed by Khrushchev opened up spaces for the implementation of a more dynamic line by the whole international Communist movement, and its more elastic adaptation to the objectively different conditions that existed in the various regions of the world. It was Togliatti who once again captured the essence of this shift in his interview with the journal *Nuovi argomenti* in June 1956, in which he stated that "the system overall is becoming polycentric and one cannot speak of sole leadership of the Communist movement itself, but of progress that is achieved by following different paths." His position certainly elaborated on Khrushchev's statements about the plurality of paths that could be taken in the transition to socialism. But it also interpreted them autonomously and in more ambitious terms, which recognized there were different articulations in the Communist movement that could be divided into at least three large areas—the capitalist, the socialist, and the formerly colonial—with further differentiations in each area. Polycentrism originally seemed to point to a reorganization of the Communist movement—one in which the Italian Communist Party (Pci) thought it might become the motor of Western communism—more than to a tactical adaptation to Moscow's positions.

Togliatti, however, was aware that he was moving on extremely difficult terrain, and studiously avoided specifying what organizational forms such polycentrism might take. The Soviet leadership for its part did not immediately reject polycentrism, or at least gave it a little wriggle room, which was to disappear after the Poznan events at the end of June and be completely shut down after the Hungarian crisis in October–November. During a conference extended to sixty-four Communist and workers' parties on November 19–20, 1957, in Moscow, Mikhail Suslov allowed that there could at most be different forms of the "dictatorship of the proletariat" around which agreements with the socialists could be reached in order to unify the working class, and polycentrism was not even mentioned. An explicit criticism of the concept itself seems to have been expressed by Mao Zedong already in September 1956, in an interview he gave to Davide Lajolo, who was then the director of the Milanese edition of *l'Unità* (the Pci's daily); it was only published in 1963, paradoxically at a time when the Soviets were by now quite openly opposed to polycentrism, since it could be used to encourage a breakup of Communist ideological uniformity, which was now obviously endangered by the Soviets' disagreements with China. The Pci, for its part, revived the term now and again for internal use, but after 1957 it engaged in more intense relations with other parties (by means of multilateral conferences organized, without the Communist Party of the Soviet Union, between the Communist parties of the six non-Soviet Warsaw Pact members and those of Western European and Mediterranean nations), and the practice of bi- and multilateral consultations was then within the margins of autonomy that had been recognized at the Twentieth Congress and the Moscow Conference of 1957 itself. Yet the idea was never completely abandoned by the Italian Communists, and was sometimes even welcomed by parties anxious to escape suffocating forms of Soviet tutelage.

In his *Yalta memorial* Togliatti, while offering a theoretical synthesis of the autonomist positions of the Italians, still made sure that they were part of an effort to maintain the unity of the socialist camp. "Unity in diversity" was the formula that once again raised the issues tied to the debate on polycentrism in a different form, in order to face the transition to socialism and communism under various conditions. From this point of view it is plausible to see polycentrism as an anticipation of the positions brought forth in the 1970s with Eurocommunism.

See also Eurocommunism; International Conferences after Stalin; National Roads to Socialism; Peaceful Coexistence; Togliatti, Palmiro.

FURTHER READING

Blackmer, D.L.M. *Unity in Diversity: Italian Communism and the Communist World.* Cambridge, MA: MIT Press, 1968.

Fejto, F. *L'héritage de Lénine. Introduction à l'histoire du communisme mondial.* Paris: Librairie Générale Française, 1977.

ALDO AGOSTI

Popular Front

The term "Popular Front" denotes the attempt by the Comintern and its affiliated Communist parties to forge broad cross-class, anti-Fascist alliances in the wake of the Nazis' rise to power and the illegalization of Communist movements by right-wing authoritarian regimes in many parts of Europe. The Popular Front thus represented a significant extension of the "united front" tactics of the 1920s, which ostensibly at least, sought to improve relations between Communist and Socialist parties, trade unions, and their members. Although the original use of the Popular Front concept was in France in 1934, it is closely associated with Georgi Dimitrov, the Bulgarian general secretary of the Comintern (1934–43), who advocated Popular Front policies at the organization's Seventh World Congress in summer 1935. The origins, meaning, and outcomes of these initiatives are the subject of great debate, particularly in relation to the Spanish civil war and the French experience. Failures here along with the diplomatic rapprochement between the Soviet Union and Nazi Germany in the course of 1939 consigned the Popular Front to the dustbin of history. Some scholars, however, have interpreted the Comintern's policies and ideological rethinking of the period 1934–38 in a more favorable light, arguing that they represented both an inspired search for a strategy to defeat fascism and a reformulation of the Marxist approach to such key issues as class alliances, democracy, and the nation. This in sum, it is contended, constituted an implicit rupture with the Bolshevik model of revolution. To this extent, the historical significance of the Popular Front is that it presaged the strivings for more democratic "national roads to socialism" in the late 1940s and early 1950s, and the Eurocommunist experiments of the 1970s and 1980s.

There is much controversy about the origins of the Popular Front, with early experts emphasizing the dominant role of Soviet "collective security" diplomacy, and others stressing the decisive impetus for change coming from rank-and-file pressure in the national Communist parties and labor movements. The consensus now is that the roots of the Popular Front in 1933–34 are to be found in the so-called triple interaction: the Soviet search for international security arrangements in the face of perceived Nazi hostility, internal debates and initiatives in the Comintern Executive Committee, and mass anti-Fascist actions on the ground in several countries, notably France and Austria. During 1934 these three elements gradually coalesced to shape the transition to the Popular Front. In this process, Dimitrov, the ascendant supremo of the Comintern, played a crucial role. He cautiously persuaded Stalin that foreign Communist parties should be granted a certain tactical flexibility and autonomy, and that the Communist International needed to modify its harsh attitudes toward the Social Democrats. In effect, Dimitrov advocated a circumscribed decentralization in the relationship between the Comintern leadership in Moscow and the international Communist movement at large, and most important, envisaged a tentative reconciliation with social democracy. Stalin was evidently open to such suggestions, and in early April 1934 encouraged Dimitrov to revise "incorrect" Comintern views and policies.

France, where strivings "from below" among ordinary workers for anti-Fascist unity were most pronounced, became the touchstone of the new "great turn" in Comintern strategy. In July 1934, the French Communist and Socialist parties signed the Pact of Unity of Action. Three months later Maurice Thorez, the general secretary of the French Communist Party, seemingly preempted signals from Moscow by appealing to the centrist Radical Party to join a vast Rassemblement Populaire together with the Communists and Socialists to combat the insurgent Fascists. Soon after, Stalin gave the green light to these initiatives, and hence in the course of 1935 the Popular Front became official Comintern policy. But what exactly did it denote? To tackle this thorny issue it is best to analyze the decisions of the Seventh Comintern Congress held in July and August 1935.

The new direction enunciated at the congress redefined the character of Communist politics by urging parties to address the daily interests of the workers, seek ant-Fascist alliances "from above" (with the leaders of non-Communist parties and trade unions) as well as from below (with rank-and-file workers), and by so doing enter the mainstream of national political life. In short, this amounted to a tacit renunciation of the Comintern's original goal of inspiring world revolution and signaled a marked rupture with the postulates of the "Third Period." But the break with the sectarian policies of the past was only partial. The close identification of Stalin with the "social Fascist" line precluded any far-reaching critique of the negative experiences of the years 1928–34. As such, the Popular Front era was marked by an unresolved tension between tradition and innovation, between inherited ideological and organizational structures, and the initiatives of Communist parties to reengage with democratic national political cultures. It was, then, a highly contradictory period in the history of the international Communist movement.

Nowhere was this tension clearer than in Dimitrov's lengthy report to the Seventh Congress. On the one hand, the newly installed general secretary of the Comintern argued that the rise of openly terroristic Fascist regimes called for the defense of bourgeois democratic liberties via "a broad people's anti-Fascist front," but on the other hand, he continued to assert that this Popular Front could not bring "final salvation [since] . . . only Soviet power can bring such salvation!" Hence, the balancing act demanded of Communist parties by the Comintern was most delicate. First, they had to persuade extremely wary Socialist leaders that after six years of social Fascist abuse, the Communists' hand of friendship was genuine. Second, Communists were enjoined to retain their distinct revolutionary Leninist identity while simultaneously engaging in an essentially reformist defense of bourgeois democratic and parliamentary rights. Third, party leaders had to cope with conflicting pressures: the all-important signals from Moscow were generally moderate so as not to alarm the non-Communist partners in the Popular Front alliance, and yet the initiatives from below attracted large numbers of radicalized rank-and-file workers, who tended to take the parties' revolutionary credentials at face value. This militancy at the base created awkward problems for party magnates in terms of maintaining Stalinist discipline and centralist control from above. Finally, divided counsels prevailed in the Soviet and Comintern hierarchies on the scope of the Popular Front orientation, with some insisting on a narrower definition of its aims, and others on a broader one. Taken together, these contradictory pressures made it extremely difficult for the Communist parties to implement "correctly" Popular Front initiatives.

Nevertheless, once inaugurated, the new policies enjoyed rapid success, particularly among those parties that remained legal. Hitherto largely marginalized and ineffective, they experienced an unprecedented growth in membership and influence. After stunning electoral victories, Popular Front governments were formed in France and Spain in 1936 as well as in Chile in 1938. In some countries, the enthusiasm for anti-Fascist unity was such that steps were taken to merge Communist and Socialist organizations in an attempt to heal the historic splits of 1920–21. In their efforts to sink roots into their national soil, the main legal parties—the French, British, U.S., and Czechoslovak—modified their methods of work and identity, rejecting a purely oppositional culture in favor of policies, language, and symbols that reflected the indigenous radical-democratic heritage: Jacobin republicanism, Chartism, Washingtonian idealism, and Hussite egalitarianism. The period also witnessed important organizational reforms of internal party structures, major innovations in Communist and left-wing culture, and to a certain extent, a reduction of direct intervention by the Comintern leadership and its agents in the affairs of Communist parties.

This reorientation must be placed in perspective, though. The Communists' belated attempts to claim a stake in national life and mainstream political culture left them open to accusations of opportunism and populism—charges that were not easily rebuffed. In many countries no formal Popular Front agreements were secured, and despite a number of successful collaborative ventures, relations between Communists and the center-Left remained on the whole cool (and were soon to be severely tested by Stalinist repression in the USSR and beyond). As far as changes in the relationship between the Comintern central authorities and the national parties are concerned, the Popular Front era should not be misinterpreted as a kind of "de-Bolshevization" in which the Communist International transmogrified into a federalized institution. In many ways, the reorganization in the mid-1930s of the Comintern's cumbersome bureaucratic structures, rather than initiating a move toward decentralization, actually strengthened the levers of centralized intervention and facilitated Stalin's direct control. Most relevantly, this reorganization was undertaken at a time when the Soviet system itself was turning into a police state—a transformation that essentially precluded any meaningful democratization of Moscow's relations with national Communist parties.

What is more, Soviet state interests were never far from the minds of Comintern and foreign party leaders. The logic of the Popular Front—insertion into the "parliamentary game" and appeals to democratic national traditions—threatened Moscow's ideological patrimony over the Communist parties. Yet the tensions thus engendered were invariably resolved in favor of the "internationalist duty" of foreign Communists to defend the interests of the USSR, as mediated by the Comintern leadership. More specifically, by 1936–37 the exigencies of collective security and Stalin's ferocious assault on "international Trotskyism" were placing immense strains on the Popular Front alliances. Nowhere was this more graphically illustrated than in war-torn Spain. Here, in February 1936 a fragile Popular Front coalition of centrist Republicans, Socialists, Communists, Trotskyists, and anarchists had been narrowly elected into power, but the republic's leftist orientation provoked a neofascist military coup led by General Francisco Franco in July 1936; the Spanish civil war had begun. After weeks of vacillation, Stalin decided to send armaments to the endangered republic to counteract Franco's forces, which were abundantly supplied by the German and Italian Fascist regimes. Stalin, however, advised the Socialist-led Popular Front government to adopt a "parliamentary road" and undertake moderate social policies. The last thing he wanted was to alienate his erstwhile anti-Fascist partners, France and Britain, and the Republicans by being seen to promote the "Sovietization" of Spain. That said, Russian military aid and the intervention of up to forty thousand volunteers in the Comintern's International Brigades undoubtedly prolonged the life of the Republican government.

Less generously, Stalin also exported to the Iberian Peninsula his bloody private vendetta against Trotsky. What ensued was a veritable civil war within the civil war as the Spanish Communists and their Soviet military, secret police, and Comintern supervisors unleashed a murderous attack in May 1937 on the Catalonian quasi-Trotskyist party, the POUM, and the anarchists, who were deemed by the Comintern as traitorous "agents of fascism" in the workers' ranks. Stalin's security organs demonstrated their awesome ability to spread terror well beyond Soviet borders, and in the process caused acute disunity in the Popular Front camp—a disunity that in no small way contributed to the triumph of Franco's superior military machine in March 1939.

In France, too, the contradictions inherent in the Popular Front strategy soon came to the fore. In May 1936 the broad center-Left coalition won the elections, and for the first time in French history a Socialist, Leon Blum, was appointed prime minister. The French Communists, though, were instructed by the Comintern not to enter the government but rather to support it from without in the capacity of "a ministry of the masses." In many ways, the French Communist Party benefited greatly from the anti-Fascist enthusiasm engendered by the Popular Front: party membership soared from 87,000 in 1935 to 326,000 by 1937; Communist influence in the trade unions also grew impressively; and its share of the vote increased from 8.4 percent in 1932 to 15.3 percent in 1936. Less welcome for the cautious party leaders was the wave of spontaneous strikes and factory occupations that occurred in May and June 1936, which inevitably struck fear in the French middle classes, including the French Communist Party's allies, the Radicals. These events threw into sharp relief the insoluble dilemma of the French Communists in the Popular Front era: how to pressurize governments into an active anti-Fascist alliance with the Soviet Union while simultaneously building a mass base in the working-class movement. For if popular action from below raised the specter of the "Red menace," then the alarm generated among the Radicals and moderate Socialists would weaken the wavering French commitment to collective security with the USSR. Additionally, the unfolding terror in Stalinist Russia in 1936–38 totally alienated many potential partners of the Communists on the center-Left.

Under these conditions, the Popular Front foundered in the course of 1938–39, eventually being unceremoniously dumped by the Soviet-German rapprochement of 1939. Popular Front policies and slogans had raised great hopes of a broad cross-class, anti-Fascist unity, and indeed certain achievements were made, notably in France and Spain. But a combination of Stalinist terror, its own internal contradictions and limitations, and the Soviet leadership's lukewarm advocacy of a line it possibly always regarded as tactical and temporary spelled the death knell of the Popular Front experiment.

See also Antifascism; Comintern; Dimitrov, Georgi; Great Terror; International Brigades; Molotov-Ribbentrop Pact; Social Fascism; Trotskyism.

FURTHER READING

Dam'e, V. V., et al., eds. *Komintern protiv fashizma: Dokumenty.* Moscow: Nauka, 1999.

Graham, H. *The Spanish Republic at War, 1936–1939.* Cambridge, UK: Cambridge University Press, 2002.

Graham, H., and P. Preston, eds. *The Popular Front in Europe.* Basingstoke, UK: Palgrave Macmillan, 1989.

Gruber, H. *Léon Blum, French Socialism, and the Popular Front: A Case of Internal Contradictions.* Ithaca, NY: Cornell University Press, 1986.

Haslam, J. "The Comintern and the Origins of the Popular Front, 1934–1935." *Historical Journal* 22, no. 3 (1979): 673–91.

Shirinia, K. K. *Strategiia i taktika Kominterna v borbe protiv fashizma i voiny, 1934–1939gg.* Moscow: Politizdat, 1979.

KEVIN F. McDERMOTT

Portugal's Carnation Revolution

The expression "Carnation Revolution" refers to the military movement that on April 25, 1974, overthrew the dictatorial regime that had controlled Portugal since 1926, leading to a period of political crises and social transformations that continued for almost two years. The military uprising was led by the Movimento das Forças Armadas (MFA), originally called the "captains' movement," which started as a professional movement, but soon questioned the colonial war Portugal had been involved with since 1961 and the political regime itself. The Carnation Revolution is part of a tradition of military interventions in politics that have marked decisive moments in Portugal's recent history since 1820.

The long and heterogeneous traditions of the anti-Fascist movements were influential in shaping the MFA's evolution and the formulation of its program. In order to garner the widest possible support for regime change, however, the captains accepted the mentoring of reactionary general António de Spínola, who had recently opposed the regime because he supported a federal solution to the colonial problem. The Carnation Revolution reestablished freedom on April 25, and due to popular pressure, all political prisoners were released and the political police were disbanded, even though it cost the lives of four demonstrators. Power went to the National Salvation Junta led by Spínola, who became president of the republic in May. Other government organs include the Council of State, in which the MFA was also represented, and a provisional civilian government, whose powers were limited. The following months saw an increase in economic demands (in 1973, the average salary in Portugal was one-fifth of an equivalent salary in the United Kingdom), spontaneous "improvement" actions both in the private and public sectors, and housing occupations. Business owners reacted by abandoning their factories (which in many cases shifted to self-management) and engaging in capital flight. A movement against continued involvement in the colonial war(s) developed, and in the colonies, Portuguese troops fraternized with the liberation movements. Conservative forces twice attempted coups, in July and then again on September 28, trying to both pursue a neocolonial resolution of the war and contain the popular movement; their goal was to concentrate as much power as possible in the presidency, but since both attempts failed, Spínola was forced to resign.

The Portuguese Communist Party (Pcp), led by Álvaro Cunhal, had since 1965 pursued a program of "national and democratic revolution," with the primary objective of establishing a democratic state, but also aiming to implement agrarian reform and uproot monopoly capitalism. Given the conditions prevailing after September 28, with the consolidation of the MFA's presence in governmental organs and the strength of the popular movements, the Pcp began to support land occupations (and thus actually initiated agrarian reform), and the Socialist Party's opposition notwithstanding, it also helped to approve the labor union unity law. The radical parties of the "revolutionary Left" also increased their influence in the Lisbon area, since they could count on the support of the most important institution for military coordination (Copcon, Command for the Continent), which was led by the hero of April 25, Otelo de Carvalho (chief strategist of the Carnation Revolution, and one of the most committed and important members of the MFA).

The social base of the revolutionary Left and Communists was, however, restricted to a beltway surrounding the capital and the southern regions of the country. The Carnation Revolution's geography reflected a historic cultural and sociological division between the country's northern and southern regions, which followed the river Talgus, in which the North was basically characterized by small rural properties and the church's strong influence. The white sectors of the colonies' population were preoccupied with the steps that had been taken to grant the colonies' independence, and they began to return to Portugal en masse, becoming an important tool in the reaction to the revolutionary process. On March 11, 1975, Spínola led another coup attempt, resulting in a series of armed confrontations. The coup, which had been poorly prepared, was easily defeated, and the defeat led to an acceleration in the pace of revolutionary measures: a Revolutionary Military Council was established, and laws for agrarian reform and the nationalization of the banking and insurance system (which later came to include all major economic groups, with the exception of those under foreign ownership) were passed. The Revolutionary Council backed the "socialist option."

The European Left, at the time absorbed in the post-1968 ideological debates, focused on Portugal during spring and summer 1975, but so did the U.S. State Department. Frank Carlucci, the future Central Intelligence Agency director, was named as the ambassador to Portugal. He gave his full support to the opposition led by Mário Soares's socialists, who easily won election to the Constituent Assembly by a wide margin. Self-management experiments at a Socialist Party newspaper and a church radio provoked widespread international attention, since they were attributed to Communist influence, and perceived as an attempt to introduce censorship and prepare a new "Prague coup." Opposition to radical and Communist tendencies began to be organized even inside the military groups in the Revolutionary Council at the beginning of the summer: a "group of nine" prepared a document critical of the council's revolutionary orientation, and questioned the role of Prime Minister Vasco Gonçalves, who was close to the Pcp. The country began to polarize along North versus South lines. In the North a wave of attacks on Communist offices, along with acts of arson and terrorism, all organized by the extreme Right and orchestrated by Spínola from Spain with the church's backing, also mobilized the public against the "Lisbon commune." European public opinion turned against this radicalization of events. Even the Italian and Spanish Communist parties were critical of the Pcp's ambiguous orientation. Finally Gonçalves was removed.

After the fall of the fifth provisional government, during September, the revolutionary movement began to ebb; however, mobilizations by both the Communists and extreme Left continued in the South, influencing some key military units. The military group prepared for decisive intervention, to be carried out at the first sign of armed insubordination by the Communist Left—which occurred on November 25, 1975, as a reaction to Carvalho's resignation. For several hours it looked as if civil war was inevitable. Otelo's passivity and interventions by the Pcp as well as the president of the republic, General Costa Gomes, prevented the uprising from reaching massive proportions, thus also preventing the military moderates, engaged in "reestablishing order," from being overwhelmed by the extreme Right.

Institutional normality began to take hold, and with the ebb of self-management demands, this led to November 25 usually being considered the end of the Carnation Revolution. Not long before this, Angola had gained its independence, and Portugal had recognized the independence of Guinea-Bissau in September 1974 and Mo-

zambique in July 1975. The colonies' self-determination as contemplated in the MFA's program had thus been realized. In April 1976 the constitution was approved, and two years after the Carnation Revolution, the first democratic elections in Portuguese history took place. The Pcp decided it had realized the primary objective of the national and democratic revolution, and had now started on the road toward socialism. The evolution of national and international conditions since that time, marked above all by Portugal's entry into the European Community in 1986, led to the consolidation of the Carnation Revolution's achievements, the institutionalization of the democratic political regime, a rise in the average standard of living, and the defeat of all transformations of a socialist nature.

See also Antifascism; Eurocommunism; Social Democracy; Stalinism.

FURTHER READING

Ferreira J. M. *Portugal em Transe, 1974–1985.* In *História de Portugal,* ed. J. Mattoso. Vol. 8. Lisbon: Círculo de Leitores, 1993.

Maxwell, K. *The Making of Portuguese Democracy.* Cambridge, UK: Cambridge University Press, 1995.

Sperling U. *Portugal, von Salazar zu Soares: Krise der Diktatur und Systemstabilisierung in einem europäischen "Entwicklungsland."* Marburg: Verlag Arbeiterbewegung und Gesellschaftswissenschaft, 1987.

JOÃO ARSÉNIO NUNES

▬▬

Post-Soviet Communism

A ruling party was the defining feature of a Communist system. It found its justification in Lenin's writings, particularly in his *What Is to Be Done?* (1902), with its insistence on an "organization of revolutionaries able to guarantee the energy, stability and continuity of the political struggle," one made up of "primarily and chiefly people whose profession consists of revolutionary activity." But it also drew from an older Socialist tradition—from the Social Democratic parties of the Second International, of which the Russian Social Democratic Workers' Party was a member up to the First World War, and from the *Communist Manifesto* (1848) with its call to the working people of all countries to unite and overthrow the system that oppressed them. The Russian Communist Party represented a self-conscious break with this Social Democratic tradition, which was thought to have betrayed itself by failing to resist an "imperialist war," and the Communist International, founded in 1919, was an attempt to offer a rather different model of party organization to the working-class movement as a whole.

This model of party organization, as it developed over the Soviet period in the USSR and in the countries that shared its political system, had a number of key attributes. One of these was a "ban on factions" (imposed on the Russian Communist Party in 1921) whereby the party attempted to maintain its monolithic unity and condemned the coordinated activity of any subsection of members within its ranks as "fractionalism." Another basic principle was "democratic centralism," first introduced into the party rules in 1906. In the formulation that became established during the Brezhnev years, this meant that all party positions were elective and that those who held them were accountable to the rank and file, but it also meant that decisions were taken on the basis of majorities and that all party organizations were bound by the decisions of those above them. The ruling party, more generally, exercised a "leading role" over the entire society, which meant that all spheres of activity, including government and the economy, were subordinated to its decisions. And when this "leading role" was endangered, as in Czechoslovakia in 1968, other parties had the right and duty to intervene to protect it.

This classic model of party rule was beginning to lose its coherence in the late Soviet period. But the political system itself was undergoing far-reaching change, as the Gorbachev leadership introduced a series of reforms that became known as "democratization." Party members, it was agreed, would be given more information about the party's affairs, including its income and expenditures. Members were also to be given more rights, including the right to retain their opinion even when a majority had decided against it, and (from 1990) the right to form "platforms" with other members who shared their views. Thus, for example, members could be religious believers, although they were still obliged to campaign for an atheist society. Party branches were given more rights, including the right to retain more of their income; and at all levels, leading officials were to be elected by secret and competitive ballot for a maximum of two five-year terms. Most important of all, the party lost its guaranteed leading role when the constitution was amended in

March 1990, and multiparty politics was formally legalized later in the year.

All kinds of different currents had begun to emerge by this time within what was formerly a party that prided itself on its unity and discipline—"at least a dozen" separate groupings, according to party officials in early 1991 (*Pravda*, March 6, 1991). For reformers, the logical outcome was a split, in which a majority would associate themselves with Gorbachev's "humane and democratic socialism," while a small minority would remain committed to a more orthodox Marxist-Leninist position. But in fact what was happening was more serious than a split; the party as a whole was disintegrating as increasing numbers left its ranks (about a quarter of the entire membership between January 1990 and June 1991), and as entire republican party organizations seceded (the Lithuanian party organization was the first to leave, in December of 1989). The failure of the attempted coup in August 1991 allowed Boris Yeltsin first to suspend the party and seize its assets, and then (in November 1991) to suppress it entirely; Gorbachev had already resigned as leader. There was accordingly no Twenty-ninth Congress, at which the CPSU might have separated into different parties, and it was not until late 1992 that the ban on party activity was ruled illegal and the party was allowed to reestablish itself in what was now a post-Communist country.

There were parallel changes throughout Eastern Europe from 1989 onward. The first clear break with the past was in Poland, where a general election in June 1989 saw sweeping successes for the trade union organization Solidarity, which had just been legalized. Two months later an administration was formed headed by Tadeusz Mazowiecki, a Catholic intellectual who had formerly edited Solidarity's weekly newspaper and had been imprisoned during the period of martial law; it was Eastern Europe's first post-Communist government. Later in the year the Polish People's Republic became the Polish Republic, sovereignty was transferred from "the working people of town and country" to "the nation," and reference to the leading role of the Polish United Workers' [Communist] Party was removed from the constitution. The party itself changed its name to the Social Democracy of the Republic of Poland in January 1990, and transferred its support from Marxism-Leninism to democratic socialism.

This became a familiar pattern of change throughout the region. In Bulgaria, for instance, long-serving party leader Todor Zhivkov was ousted by his politburo colleagues in

November 1989. Zhivkov and his son were expelled for "serious violations of basic party and moral principles" and for having established the "dictatorship of a clan." A new party program, adopted in February 1990, committed the party to "democratic socialism" in Bulgaria, and to "democratic and free elections" at the earliest opportunity. The party itself was renamed the Bulgarian Socialist Party. It adopted a red rose rather than a hammer and sickle as its symbol, and it opted for a "socially oriented market economy" rather than comprehensive state planning. In the German Democratic Republic the ruling Socialist Unity Party became the Party of Democratic Socialism in February 1990. It committed itself to multiparty politics under a new and reformist leadership and remained a significant electoral force after the country had formally reunified later in the year.

There were parallel changes in Hungary, where divisions opened between those who were committed to far-reaching reforms such as Imre Pozgay, a former minister of culture who was supported by "reform circles" within the party and rumored to be Gorbachev's candidate for the leadership, and others who stood for no more than a modified party ascendancy, although they were willing to accept that the leadership had "no monopoly of wisdom to solve Hungary's problems." It would be "decades," Grosz told *Le monde* in November 1988, before Hungary could consider a move to multiparty democracy. There was a rapid transition in which the 1956 uprising was accepted as a legitimate expression of discontent with a discredited Soviet model, and the constitution was changed to allow multiparty politics. The ruling Hungarian Socialist Workers' Party held a congress in October 1989 at which a majority agreed to form a European-style Hungarian Socialist Party, committed to democratic socialism and a mixed economy; a minority of hardliners, including Grosz, managed to preserve the formal existence of a Hungarian Socialist Workers' Party based on orthodox Marxist-Leninist values.

Accordingly, there was a pattern to the transition to post-Soviet communism: or rather, several patterns. In the first pattern, orthodox Communist rule continued and a ruling party retained its leading role. In China, for instance, the constitution defined the political system as a "Socialist state under the people's democratic dictatorship led by the working class and based on the alliance of workers and peasants," and the Communist Party exercised an effective political monopoly although eight other parties were permitted to maintain a legal existence. In Cuba, the Communist Party was the only

one allowed to operate; in North Korea, the Workers' Party was dominant; in Vietnam, the 1992 constitution defined the Communist Party as the "leading force of state and society."

Given China's enormous population, this meant that about 1.4 billion people were living under at least nominally Communist rule in the early years of the 21st century, compared with the 1.6 billion that had lived under Communist rule in the late 1980s: hardly a dramatic "end of history."

In a second pattern, a formerly ruling Communist Party became a vehicle of authoritarian rule under a post-Communist leadership. One of the clearest of such transitions was in Uzbekistan, where the republican organization of the Communist Party simply renamed itself the People's Democratic Party in November 1991. The Communist Party first secretary became the head of state. Political change of this ilk was common throughout Central Asia, as former party first secretaries became presidents of their newly independent countries and continued to rule in a centralized and sometimes repressive manner. There were even elements of dynastic succession, as when Gaidar Aliev, Communist first secretary in Azerbaijan and then president, was succeeded in that position by his son Ilham in 2003; the North Korean party leader, Kim Il Sung, had established a precedent when he was succeeded by his son Kim Jong Il in 1994.

A third pattern, more common in Europe, saw a formerly ruling Communist Party evolve into—or, it might be argued, revert to—a Social Democratic party. This was particularly likely where there was a preexisting Social Democratic tradition and an organized trade union movement. The Lithuanian Social Democratic Party, for instance, had been founded in 1896; it became the Lithuanian Democratic Labor Party at the end of 1989 when it seceded from the CPSU, and then took its current name when it merged with the Social Democratic Party in 2001; it was a member of the Socialist International, completing what was in effect a return to its origins. In Hungary, an organized Socialist Party dated from 1890; in Bulgaria, from 1891; in Poland, from 1892. Parties of this kind had often won the largest vote, if not an overall majority, in the elections that took place immediately after the Second World War, and in many of these countries they returned to electoral politics with considerable success.

A fourth pattern was a mixed one, in which a no longer ruling party remained committed to substantial elements of its Marxist-Leninist heritage but at the same time accepted the principle of multiparty politics and a mixed economy. The Communist Party of the Russian Federation, originally a section of the CPSU and then an independent party after it had reestablished itself in 1993, could be placed in this category. The main aims of its party program were the restoration of the system of elected soviets, guaranteed employment, free education and health care, the formation of a "government of national confidence" that would restore state regulation of the economy, the reconstitution of a single union state, and more generally the conduct of an "independent foreign policy" that reflected "national-state interests and strengthened the international authority of the Russian state"; it was also committed in the longer term to communism as the "historic future of humanity." The party, its rules made clear, "continued the cause" of the CPSU, and its organizational structure was very similar to that of its predecessor, with a congress, a central committee, and a party leader (now called chairman), all of whom continued to operate on the basis of democratic centralism.

Several conclusions could be drawn from this complex experience. The most obvious, but not perhaps the only one, was failure. Nowhere, in the end, had a Communist Party come to power with the manifest support of those over whom it ruled, even when suffrage allowed the entire adult population to exercise their democratic rights. The Bolsheviks had enjoyed the support of about a quarter of those who voted in the elections to the Constituent Assembly in November 1917, but they never won a general election. Communists won the largest share of the vote in Czechoslovakia in 1946, but not an overall majority. Moldova came close in its 2001 general election, when the Party of Communists won 49.5 percent of the popular vote, although its election platform was scarcely Marxist-Leninist. It was difficult to understand this modest success in countries that were overwhelmingly composed of wage laborers, with incomes that were unequally distributed; one response was to accept that "revisionists" such as Eduard Bernstein had been right to reject some of the deterministic elements of classical Marxism.

Viewed from this perspective, the Communist movement had been a tragic departure from mainstream social democracy, and Leninism had been an authoritarian corruption of socialism that reflected the Russian party's limited experience of electoral politics and its leadership's background in underground conspiracy—not necessarily by choice, but because of the repressive environment in which the Bolsheviks were obliged to operate. The Soviet party's immense influence as the unchallenged leader of the world's largest country, and the network of economic and military alliances that it developed, ensured that this Leninist model of party organization became dominant in the other countries that adopted the Soviet system although in most cases their political traditions were very different.

There were wider issues, apart from those that had a peculiarly Russian focus. Even Social-Democratic parties were finding it difficult, in the early years of the new century, to define a distinctive philosophy. And all mass parties were losing members, not just those of the Left. Much of the inspiration that had formerly been invested in Communist and workers' parties had, it seemed, migrated to other vehicles, including environmentalist parties, feminist groups, and a wider, loosely coordinated anti-globalization movement that was certainly international in its scope. Post-Soviet communism, it appeared, would take its place within this larger reconfiguration of the politics of the Left. It would draw strength from the resistance of ordinary people to the inequalities of the societies within which they lived, but would no longer claim a monopolistic right to represent them.

See also Democratic Centralism; Dissolution of the USSR; Marxism-Leninism.

FURTHER READING

Bozoki, A., and J. T. Ishiyama, eds. *The Communist Successor Parties of Central and Eastern Europe.* Armonk, NY: Sharpe, 2002.

Bugajski, J. *Political Parties of Eastern Europe.* Armonk, NY: Sharpe, 2002.

March, L. *The Communist Party in Post-Soviet Russia.* Manchester, UK: Manchester University Press, 2002.

March, L., and C. Mudde. "What's Left of the Radical Left? The European Radical Left after 1989: Decline *and* Mutation." *Comparative European Politics* 3, no. 1 (April 2005): 23–49.

STEPHEN WHITE

Power Politics

The term "power politics" implies that states generally act on the basis of practical interests (realpolitik) or a desire to gain more power, rather than ethical or ideological concerns. Although most scholars agree that power politics, as practiced by both the United States and the Soviet Union, played an important role in the Cold War, many have argued that the Cold War was shaped at least as much by ideology, and specifically by the ideological divide between Marxism-Leninism and liberal democratic capitalism.

The balance between ideology and power politics in Cold War foreign policymaking remains a key issue of debate. Some scholars, particularly those of the realist school, aver that conflicting ideologies were of little significance, and that both the United States and the Soviet Union used rhetoric to conceal their real interests and intentions. These scholars attribute the Cold War primarily to the disorderly structure of the international system, which in their view caused the two superpowers to be highly suspicious of one another. This assertion has been sharply challenged by other scholars who claim that the Cold War arose solely because of incompatible ideologies and that it ended when Soviet ideology lost its hostile and antagonistic edge. These scholars deny that in the absence of clashing ideologies, structural conditions in the international system would have been enough to spark a fierce U.S.-Soviet rivalry.

Power Politics versus Ideology: Contending Views

During the Cold War, structural realist scholars like Kenneth Waltz argued that each superpower would constantly seek to prevent the other from achieving outright dominance, would emulate the other's accomplishments, and would be averse to cooperating much with the other because of a fear that the opponent would gain relatively more. These recurring patterns of U.S. and Soviet foreign policy behavior, according to Waltz, flowed naturally from two structural features of the international system (the unequal distribution of capabilities and the disorderly nature of the system).

Some other structural realist scholars contended that systemic conditions did not necessarily generate the types of behavior predicted by Waltz and that extensive cooperation was possible, but they agreed with Waltz that systemic pressures during the Cold War decisively influenced the superpowers' behavior. Although Waltz and other structural realists did not deny that "unit-level" phenomena, including ideology, could skew U.S. and Soviet foreign policies, they maintained that the units (i.e., the two superpowers) were not operating in a vacuum. The choices facing U.S. and Soviet leaders during the Cold War, according to the structural realist paradigm, were always sharply constrained by systemic

factors. Waltz acknowledged that under such conditions the two dominant states were "free to do any fool thing they chose," but he claimed that leaders on both sides recognized that "they were likely to be rewarded for behavior that was responsive to structural pressures and punished for behavior that was not." Expectations of these costs and benefits, according to Waltz, induced U.S. and Soviet officials to heed structural pressures when deciding "to do some things and to refrain from doing others."

This notion was only partly endorsed by neoclassical realists, who agreed with the structural realists that the disorderly nature of the international system and the unequal distribution of capabilities constrained, and in some cases even determined, U.S. and Soviet foreign policy decisions during the Cold War. The neoclassical realists also agreed with the structural realists that the bipolarity of the Cold War order cannot be attributed solely to an ideological rivalry. On other points, however, the neoclassical realists and structural realists sharply diverged. In particular, the neoclassical realists eschewed structural realism's exclusive preoccupation with system-level phenomena. They argued that U.S. and Soviet behavior cannot be properly understood without taking account of at least one or two domestic-level factors (e.g., leaders' perceptions of external threats or relative power). Precisely which of these factors should be taken into account was open to debate, but the neoclassical realists all concurred that a failure to look below the systemic level precluded an understanding of great-power behavior. Their willingness to bring in certain domestic factors, even while emphasizing the importance of structural conditions, was a fundamental departure from structural realism.

Ideology-based explanations of U.S. and Soviet foreign policies offer a different characterization of what was driving the two sides' behavior during the Cold War. Advocates of this approach, such as John Mueller, argue that Marxist-Leninist ideology was of great significance in Soviet foreign policy and that liberal democratic values were of great importance for U.S. foreign policy. They claim that "assessments focusing only on the narrow constituents of realism—material power, changes in its distribution, and external threat—are radically incomplete, and do not account for what [the Soviet Union and the United States] actually did." Mueller contends that "the Cold War . . . and the bipolar structure of postwar international politics sprang [instead] from a contest of ideas, from an ideological conflict." Mueller's view that "differences in ideas and ideologies" determined "the essential shape and history of the Cold War," implies that ideological considerations must have overshadowed or outweighed each side's concerns about the balance of power.

The Empirical Record

An assessment of the role of power politics during the Cold War is inherently difficult. For one thing, the motivations behind U.S. and Soviet foreign policies were seldom clear-cut. Intentions and perceptions are notoriously murky concepts, and sometimes U.S. and Soviet leaders themselves may not have known precisely why they acted as they did. Moreover, at least some policies may have stemmed from a number of motivations, both practical *and* ideological. It is no easy matter to determine which factors mattered more.

These caveats aside, the record of the Cold War suggests that ideology did often play a crucial role along with power politics. Conceivably, the Cold War would not have begun—or at least would not have been so intense—if the Soviet Union had been a liberal democracy. The intense East-West ideological competition, pitting liberal democratic capitalism against Marxism-Leninism, provided a crucial spark and milieu for the Cold War.

To be sure, a spirited rivalry between the two dominant states might well have arisen even if they had both been liberal democracies. The United States and Great Britain were certainly at odds about many issues during and after World War II. Those disagreements might have become more acute if the two countries had not joined forces after the war to confront their common enemy, the Soviet Union. If Great Britain had emerged from the war as a superpower rather than a declining power, and if the Soviet Union had not emerged as a superpower, the United States and Great Britain might well have become rivals on the world scene rather than allies. In that sense, realist theory has a good deal of merit. Yet a hypothetical postwar standoff between the United States and Great Britain, if it had occurred, would not have been nearly as militarized, hostile, and acrimonious as the Cold War between the United States and the Soviet Union. The sheer intensity of the Cold War cannot be adequately explained without reference to the ideological divide.

To the extent that the incompatible ideologies of the two sides caused what might otherwise have been a limited rivalry to become a fierce, global, all-encompassing competition, the ideological backdrop is crucial for understanding the origin, duration, and end of the Cold War. Whether that backdrop is sufficient to explain the

two sides' specific foreign policy choices is much less clear, however. If one takes the intense U.S.-Soviet rivalry as a given, it is hard to see that in most cases the behavior of the two superpowers would have been much different from what it actually was, even if they had subscribed to a common ideology.

In a few respects, of course, ideology did determine specific policy choices during the Cold War, particularly the types of international economic arrangements that the two superpowers promoted and the types of alliances they forged in Europe. A liberal capitalist world order did not just emerge spontaneously. It arose because the most powerful country in the international system, the United States, was committed to a liberal capitalist ideology, as were many other countries. Similarly, the establishment of centrally controlled economies in Eastern Europe and North Korea, and the formation of a centrally directed international trading system in Eastern Europe under Soviet auspices, stemmed from Moscow's ideological commitment to the state/party control of economic life. That same commitment later spurred the Soviet Union to encourage other states, including China, North Vietnam, and Cuba, to adopt Soviet-style economies of their own. The penetration of democratic norms and values into the North Atlantic Treaty Organization, and the entrenchment of Marxist-Leninist norms in the Warsaw Pact, also were dependent on the type of ideology to which the dominant state in each alliance subscribed. The United States would never have forged an alliance committed to upholding orthodox Communist regimes, and the Soviet Union would never have wanted an alliance consisting of liberal capitalist democracies.

Yet despite these important exceptions, ideology seems to be a less salient explanatory variable when one analyzes the foreign policies of the two sides. This is not to say that ideology did not matter in such things as the Sino-Soviet split, the support that each side (particularly the Soviet Union) gave to subversive groups in the third world, and the differing U.S. and Soviet approaches to the United Nations. For most of these issues, though, it is hard to demonstrate that the superpowers' behavior would have been vastly different in the absence of ideological considerations.

Although declassified archival materials confirm that Marxism-Leninism in the USSR was more than a charade or smoke screen—it was an ideology that underlay and guided the Soviet regime—the documentary and memoir evidence does not provide sufficient grounds for John Gaddis's claim that ideological principles actually *determined* Soviet foreign policy. There is little doubt that Marxism-Leninism influenced foreign policy choices in numerous ways, but the precise interaction between the two in most cases is too murky to yield any firm generalizations or bear out Gaddis's assertions.

What does seem clear is that Marxism-Leninism served as a means of codifying and elaborating foreign policy. It was the language in which foreign (and domestic) policy discussions took place. In this sense, Marxism-Leninism was a "linguacultural ideology" that helped shape how Soviet officials viewed the outside world. Because policy was formulated in Marxist-Leninist terms by officials who had to act as though the ideology was scientifically accurate, those officials were inclined to fit their policies into particular stereotypes. Thus, the method of discourse tended to narrow the range of options available to Soviet policymakers. This constraint inhibited abrupt changes of course and usually made it difficult for lower-level officials to broach unorthodox policies.

On the other hand, Soviet leaders demonstrated ample flexibility and a penchant for power politics on many occasions. Stalin was perfectly willing in August–September 1939 to conclude a nonaggression pact with Nazi Germany, and a secret protocol demarcating Soviet and German spheres of occupation in Eastern and Central Europe. During World War II, Stalin was willing to tone down his Marxist-Leninist rhetoric to bolster support at home for the war effort, and avoid unduly antagonizing his British and U.S. allies. None of these steps signified the abandonment of core Stalinist ideological principles. Instead, they simply reflected Stalin's ability to be flexible when extraordinary circumstances so required.

The underlying ideology in the Soviet Union, as in other countries, changed relatively little over time. In a few instances, however, profoundly important domestic or foreign events opened the way for new ideological tenets to emerge, which in turn paved the way for changes in foreign policy. One such opportunity was opened by Stalin's death. His successors promptly sought to reverse a number of "mistaken policies" that he had bequeathed to them, including his refusal to accept a settlement in the Korean War and his bitter rift with Yugoslavia. These reversals were not merely short-term, tactical shifts. Nor, as was later alleged, were they aberrations on the part of the "maverick" Lavrenty Beria. Instead, they reflected a deeper sentiment among Stalin's successors that the Stalinist ideological framework had at times been detrimental to Soviet state interests. New ideological principles accompanied the reversals of policy. Although it

turned out that some of the changes were short-lived, the critical thing is that Soviet leaders were willing to abandon some key Stalinist principles both at home and abroad soon after Stalin's death. Not until the late 1980s, amid the sweeping domestic reforms launched by Mikhail Gorbachev, were ideological changes of comparable (or greater) magnitude feasible again in Soviet foreign policy.

Under Gorbachev, the interaction between ideology and radical changes in foreign policy was especially complex. Structural conditions in the international system, especially the U.S.-Soviet military balance, did not change enough in the 1970s and 1980s to account for the drastic reorientation of Soviet policy in Eastern Europe. From the structural realist perspective, Moscow's withdrawal from the Cold War rivalry should have been inconceivable. Nor are the changes in Soviet foreign policy readily explained by perceptions of relative power alone. Gorbachev's assessment of the USSR's relative power was little different from the apprehensive views expressed by his predecessors. Yet Gorbachev, unlike his predecessors, was eventually willing to take drastic steps to liberalize the Soviet polity and eliminate the Stalinist legacy. In turn, those goals required a transformation of Soviet policy in Eastern Europe. Gorbachev increasingly recognized that his bid to undo the Stalinist legacy at home would not succeed unless he also eliminated Stalin's legacy in Eastern Europe. The Soviet Union's drive in the late 1980s to forestall violence in Eastern Europe and bring about a new political order was crucial in ending the Cold War.

Thus, on the key issue of why the Cold War ended, structural realist and neoclassical realist explanations are inadequate, or at best incomplete. The momentous events of 1989 were spurred primarily by sweeping ideological changes in the Soviet Union that paved the way for a new Soviet policy in Eastern Europe, resulting in the end of the Cold War and a reconfiguration of the international system.

The net conclusion one might draw is that both ideology and power politics were integral to Soviet foreign policy. In some instances, ideology was predominant, whereas in other cases realpolitik was the guiding force. The core features of Soviet communism—including the unchallenged dominance of the Communist Party over all aspects of political and economic life, the centralized and hierarchical structure of the party itself (a condition euphemistically known as "democratic centralism"), a strict ban on public dissent, and the use of Marxist terminology and "anti-imperialist" rhetoric—reinforced the Stalinist legacy in Soviet foreign policy. But these unspoken assumptions did not invariably override structural considerations and realpolitik. Certainly many of the policies adopted by Soviet leaders from Stalin's time on could just as easily have been pursued by a "normal" government engaging in power politics. Nevertheless, even if the relative weight of ideology and power politics in specific Soviet foreign policy decisions is often murky, it is safe to say that the defining features of Soviet Communist ideology spawned a policy framework that helped to engender and sustain the fierce bipolar confrontation.

See also Atomic Bomb; Bipolarity; Cold War; Grand Alliance; Marxism-Leninism; Molotov-Ribbentrop Pact; New Thinking; Soviet Bloc; Warfare; Warsaw Pact.

FURTHER READING

Kramer, M. "Ideology and the Cold War." *Review of International Studies* 25, no. 4 (October 1999): 339–77.

———Kramer, M. "Realism, Ideology, and the End of the Cold War." *Review of International Studies* 27, no. 1 (January 2001): 119–30.

Mearsheimer, J. *The Tragedy of Great Power Politics.* New York: Norton, 2001.

Mueller, J. "The Impact of Ideas on Grand Strategy." In *The Domestic Bases of Grand Strategy,* ed. R. Rosecrance and A. A. Stein, pp. 48–62. Ithaca, NY: Cornell University Press, 1993.

Waltz, K. *Theory of International Politics.* Reading, MA: Addison-Wesley, 1979.

MARK KRAMER

Prague Coup

The Prague Coup was the seizure of power in Czechoslovakia by the Communists in 1948. Up to that time among the Eastern European "people's democracies" Czechoslovakia's Communists still lacked a decisive majority in the government, and the country was certainly not yet a dictatorship. The Communists held only one-third of the seats in the government formed after the liberation of Czechoslovakia from the Nazis. In the parliamentary elections in May 1946, though, they moved into first place, receiving around 38 percent of the votes. The chair of the Communist Party of Czecho-

slovakia (CPCz), Klement Gottwald, became premier, and the Communists along with their close allies the Social Democrats, whose left wing carried great influence, gained near parity in the governing coalition with the Democratic-Liberal parties. Eduard Beneš, the most influential leader of the Democratic-Liberal forces, remained president.

By 1947 the majority of the Communist parties in the people's democracies were already hewing to the Moscow line, which accorded absolute power to the Soviets. That same year, though still somewhat apprehensive about openly breaking parliamentary ranks, the CPCz, under the influence of the Soviet Union and its own radicals, began to move toward methods of force. The Czechoslovak state security organs, by now under firm Communist control, started to spread fabrications about "antistate plots" in Slovakia and partly in Bohemia as well, tying these plots to certain officials of the opposition parties in the ruling coalition. Their purpose was to discredit these parties and shift the balance of power in favor of the CPCz before the upcoming parliamentary elections scheduled for 1948. These fabrications began to sift themselves into the judicial system, which was not yet under the CPCz's dominance. The opposition parties against which these falsehoods were directed became concerned that the CPCz, with the aid of the state security organs, might establish effective control in the country.

This concern grew when at the beginning of 1948, the minister of the interior, a Communist named Vaclav Nosek, carried out some personnel changes in the state security organs that made achievement of this control more likely. The ministers of the majority of the parties of the ruling coalition came out against these shifts. But the Communists, led by Gottwald, remained firm. On February 20, 1948, the disagreeing ministers resigned. The opposition parties reckoned that in conformity with usual parliamentary procedures, this step would lead to the resignation of the government, and allow the formation of either a new government with a makeup more favorable to them or a government whose constituents would call for early elections. These parties were counting on acquiring a majority, and though still in coalition with the CPCz, lessening that party's power to threaten the other parties. Nevertheless, instead of agreeing to form a new government, Gottwald demanded that Beneš replace the departing ministers with pro-Communist functionaries.

To put pressure on Beneš, Gottwald asked the Soviet authorities to stage Soviet troop movements along the

Czechoslovak borders. The Kremlin refrained from this, but did demand decisive actions on the part of the CPCz itself. The latter now organized massive demonstrations of its supporters, created armed detachments of its own, and deploying those together with the forces of the ministry of the interior that were subordinate to it, began to take power. Its opponents proved unwilling to resist the takeover. And the Social Democratic Party, which had been trying since 1947 to distance itself from the CPCz, was afraid to quit the government and instead began to yield to its pro-Communist wing. Fearing an armed confrontation within the country and the military intervention of the USSR, which Gottwald had already hinted at, Beneš acceded to the latter's demands on February 25.

During the revolt the security offices of the parties opposed to the CPCz were seized, a number of their officials were arrested, and these parties started to be represented by small groups of Communist sympathizers. The previous leaders, yielding to this pressure, agreed to resign their party posts and surrender their functions as Parliament deputies. Almost the same thing happened with the Social Democratic Party, most of whose leadership agreed to attach itself to the CPCz. Parliament, now mostly purged of opposition elements, obediently supported a newly constituted government, which in turn was completely subordinate to the Communists. The outcome of the revolt was reinforced in May 1948 by a new Constitution, dictated by the CPCz, and parliamentary elections were conducted under Communist control. Beneš did not consent to the new Constitution and resigned at the beginning of June (he died three months later). Gottwald became president, and Antonín Zapotocký became the new premier.

See also Cominform; Gottwald, Klement; People's Democracy; Sovietization.

FURTHER READING

Kaplan, K. *Poslední rok prezidenta: Edvard Beneš v roce 1948.* Brno: Doplněk, 1944.

———. *The Short March: The Communist Takeover in Czechoslovakia, 1945–1948.* New York: St. Martin's Press, 1987.

———. *Nekrvavá revoluce.* Prague: Mlada fronta, 1993.

Murashko, G. P. "Fevral'skij krizis 1948 g. v Chekhoslovakii I sovetskoe rukovodstvo: Po novym materialam rossijskich archivov." *Novaja I novejsaja istorija* (Moscow) 3 (1998): 50–63.

LEONID JA. GIBJANSKIJ

Prague Spring

The term "Prague Spring" was widely used in 1968 to refer to the eight months of sweeping reforms in Czechoslovakia that brought a comprehensive revival of the country's political, cultural, and economic life. The reforms earned overwhelming popular support in Czechoslovakia and were also hailed in many foreign countries, where observers across the political spectrum hoped that Czechoslovakia's effort to fashion "socialism with a humane face" (*socialismus s lidskou tváří*—a slogan that became identified with the Prague Spring) would succeed. But the process encountered deep opposition among Czechoslovakia's Warsaw Pact allies, notably the Soviet Union. The Prague Spring ended abruptly in August 1968, when the Soviet Union, East Germany, Poland, Bulgaria, and Hungary sent hundreds of thousands of troops into Czechoslovakia.

Early Developments

The Prague Spring began with the removal of Antonín Novotný as first secretary of the Czechoslovak Communist Party (KSČ) in December 1967 and the election of Alexander Dubček as Novotný's successor in early January 1968. Leonid Brezhnev, the general secretary of the Soviet Communist Party (CPSU), had never been particularly close to Novotný and had tacitly consented to the change of leadership. Initially, Brezhnev was confident that Dubček would be a reliable partner. But by early March 1968, as wide-ranging political and economic reforms began to take hold in Czechoslovakia, concern in Moscow rapidly grew.

For the first several weeks of 1968, Brezhnev and the other members of the CPSU politburo expressed their concerns to Dubček in a low-key manner, and the Czechoslovak leader did his best to accommodate them. Dubček supported bold political reforms, but he tried to preclude developments that would be perceived as hostile by his Warsaw Pact neighbors. For example, although he agreed to the lifting of censorship in February 1968, he admonished Czechoslovak journalists and commentators not to question the legitimacy of Czechoslovakia's alliances or the "leading role" of the KSČ in Czechoslovak society, and he sought to prevent intellectuals and dissidents from creating a full-fledged opposition party. Dubček hewed to this basic line even as the Prague Spring took on a life of its own and moved gradually beyond his control.

Despite Dubček's assurances, Soviet leaders increasingly feared that traditional channels of Soviet influence in Czechoslovakia were being eroded and undermined by the Prague Spring. The growing unease in Moscow was reinforced by the much harsher complaints expressed in other East bloc capitals, especially Warsaw and East Berlin. From the outset, the Polish leader, Władysław Gomułka, and the East German leader, Walter Ulbricht, were determined to counter "inimical, anti-socialist influences" along their borders. The two men feared that events in Czechoslovakia would prove "contagious" and would create political instability in their own countries.

The concerns expressed by Polish and East German leaders, combined with the disquiet that senior officials in Moscow were beginning to feel, induced the Soviet politburo to give high priority to the "Czechoslovak question." From mid-March 1968 on, the issue was constantly at the top of the politburo's agenda. Brezhnev consulted and worked closely with his politburo colleagues on all aspects of the crisis, ensuring that responsibility for the outcome would be borne collectively.

Accelerated Reforms, Deepening Soviet Concerns

Despite the growing pressure that Soviet and East European leaders were exerting on Czechoslovakia, Dubček and other senior officials continued to advocate far-reaching political reform, particularly freedom of the press, on the grounds that uninhibited debate was the only way to ensure that the KSČ would retain its dominant position in Czechoslovak society. In keeping with this notion, Dubček encouraged a lively and freewheeling exchange of views within the KSČ about the future course of social, political, and economic liberalization. These discussions culminated in the adoption of a comprehensive "Action Program" at a plenary session of the KSČ Central Committee in early April—a document that became the symbolic blueprint for the last several months of the Prague Spring.

The adoption of this sweeping reform program was accompanied by the removal or demotion of many prominent antireformist officials in the KSČ and the Czechoslovak government (almost all of whom had spent considerable time in the Soviet Union), and the replacement of numerous regional and local party secretaries left over from the Novotný era. The combination of these developments greatly expedited the pace of reform in Czechoslovakia in spring and summer 1968, and public support rapidly increased.

As the reforms in Czechoslovakia accelerated, the irritation in Moscow became palpable. The members of the CPSU politburo, as Brezhnev noted when they met in early May, were "united in the view that [the KSČ Action Program] is a harmful program, which is paving the way for the restoration of capitalism in Czechoslovakia." Of particular concern to Soviet leaders were the uncensored political discussions in the Czechoslovak media and the continued removal of hard-line opponents of the Prague Spring. During a Warsaw Pact meeting in Dresden on March 23, Brezhnev and Ulbricht had rebuked Dubček for allowing "the press, radio, and television to slip away from the party's control," and dismissing many "loyal and seasoned cadres, who have proven their mettle in years of struggle." Events over the next several weeks had greatly reinforced those concerns.

As the rift between Czechoslovakia and the Soviet Union widened in spring 1968, the CPSU politburo authorized Soviet defense minister Marshal Andrei Grechko to begin preparing Soviet forces in Eastern Europe for a large-scale military contingency. This decision marked the initial step in planning for Operation Danube, the eventual code name of the August 1968 invasion. Within the Soviet politburo, however, there was not yet full agreement about the best course to pursue. Brezhnev initially was unwilling to embrace a clear-cut position, and he permitted and indeed encouraged other members of the politburo to express their own opinions about particular matters. The transcripts of Soviet politburo meetings from 1968 reveal that some members, such as Yuri Andropov, Nikolay Podgorny, and Petro Shelest, were consistent proponents of military intervention, whereas others, particularly Mikhail Suslov, were far more circumspect. Several politburo members, notably Aleksei Kosygin, fluctuated during the crisis, at times favoring "extreme measures" (i.e., military action) and at other times seeking a political solution.

Nevertheless, even when top-ranking Soviet officials disagreed with one another, their disagreements were mainly over tactics rather than strategic considerations or fundamental goals. All the members of the Soviet politburo agreed that the reform process in Czechoslovakia was endangering the "gains of socialism" in that country and the "common interests of world socialism." By late spring 1968, most of them sensed that drastic action would be necessary to curtail the Prague Spring. Although some still hoped that Czechoslovak leaders themselves would be willing to crack down, many had begun to suspect that external intervention might be necessary.

Escalation of the Crisis

The time constraints that Soviet leaders believed they were facing increased precipitously in June and July, as it became evident that reformist delegates were going to dominate the special congress of the KSČ that was scheduled to take place in September. Brezhnev and his colleagues feared that antireformist, pro-Moscow officials (i.e., "healthy forces") in the KSČ who were still in place would be removed en masse by the party congress, paving the way for Czechoslovakia to pursue a "nonsocialist" course.

The harsh Soviet response to the Prague Spring was spurred in part by concern about possible changes in Czechoslovak foreign policy. The rapid sequence of events since January had stirred doubts in Moscow about the integrity of Czechoslovakia's long-term commitment to the Warsaw Pact. Soviet leaders were alarmed by the "hostile" and "anti-Soviet" forces in Prague, and they suspected that the KSČ would be increasingly amenable to calls from both within and outside the party for policies favoring national over "internationalist" interests. Before long, some in Moscow came to fear that a major shift in Czechoslovak foreign policy—perhaps even a shift toward neutrality (à la Yugoslavia) or alignment with the West—could no longer be ruled out.

Even if no questions had emerged about Czechoslovakia's foreign orientation, Soviet leaders believed that the country's internal changes were themselves a grave threat to the cohesion of the Communist bloc. If the Prague Spring, with its tolerance of dissent, elimination of censorship, democratization of the Communist Party, and wide-ranging economic reforms, were to "infect" other Warsaw Pact countries, including the Soviet Union, it might well precipitate the collapse of the socialist camp.

These various concerns—political, ideological, and military—gradually fused into a widely shared perception in Moscow that events in Czechoslovakia were spinning out of control. The sense of impending danger, or "spontaneity" and "unlimited decentralization" as a Soviet politburo member, Viktor Grishin, put it, eventually colored Soviet views of the whole Prague Spring. The cumulative impact of events, rather than any single development, is what seems to have convinced Brezhnev that internal changes in Czechoslovakia were threatening vital Soviet interests. The necessity of countering that threat was no longer in doubt by mid-1968; the only question remaining for Soviet leaders was whether—and when—an external military solution would be required.

By July and early August 1968, the Soviet Union was applying relentless pressure on the Czechoslovak authorities to reverse the liberalization program. The Soviet campaign was vigorously supported by Poland, East Germany, Bulgaria, and antireformist members of the KSČ presidium, who secretly conspired with Soviet leaders. Brezhnev used a variety of bilateral channels to urge Dubček and other senior Czechoslovak officials to combat "antisocialist" and "counterrevolutionary" elements, and he even approached a few of Dubček's reformist colleagues surreptitiously in hopes of finding a suitable replacement who would be willing to implement a crackdown. These efforts, however, failed to pay off.

Invasion and Occupation

As the crisis intensified in midsummer, the high-level debate in Moscow gradually produced a consensus. At meetings on July 22 and 26–27, the members of the Soviet politburo tentatively decided to adopt "extreme measures" (i.e., to proceed with a full-scale invasion) sometime in mid- to late August if the situation in Czechoslovakia did not fundamentally change. By the time the Soviet politburo met in an expanded session on August 6 to consider the results of emergency negotiations held in late July and early August with Dubček and other Czechoslovak leaders, there was virtually no hope left that military action could be averted.

Even as the CPSU politburo deliberated, Soviet military commanders were completing the extensive logistical and technical preparations needed for an invasion. The largest of the Warsaw Pact maneuvers in early August were accompanied by a mass call-up of Soviet and East European reservists, the requisitioning of civilian vehicles and equipment, and the stockpiling of fuel, ammunition, communications gear, spare parts, and medical supplies. In Soviet Ukraine alone, more than seven thousand civilian vehicles were reassigned to the army. Soviet commanders also diverted Czechoslovak supplies of fuel and ammunition to East Germany—ostensibly for new Warsaw Pact "exercises," but actually to obviate any possibility of Czechoslovak armed resistance. Much the same was done with Czechoslovak troops and equipment, which were unexpectedly transported for "maneuvers" to bases in southwestern Bohemia, far away from any planned invasion routes.

Brezhnev spoke by phone with Dubček on August 9 and 13, but he failed to secure a firm pledge from the Czechoslovak leader to roll back the reforms and crack down on "hostile" elements. The failure of these last-ditch contacts seems to have been what finally spurred Brezhnev to conclude that "nothing more can be expected from the current KSČ presidium" and that a military solution could no longer be avoided. From then on, the dynamic of the whole situation changed. On August 16–17, the Soviet politburo convened to discuss its final steps vis-à-vis Czechoslovakia. Brezhnev and his colleagues voted unanimously to "provide assistance and support to the Communist Party and people of Czechoslovakia through the use of [the Soviet] armed forces." No one on the politburo expressed doubt about the decision. The following day, Brezhnev informed his East German, Polish, Bulgarian, and Hungarian counterparts of the decision at a hastily convened meeting in Moscow. Unlike in 1956, when Soviet troops intervened in Hungary unilaterally, Brezhnev was determined to give the invasion in 1968 a multilateral appearance. Some seventy to eighty thousand combat soldiers from Poland, Bulgaria, and Hungary along with a liaison unit from East Germany took part in the invasion, which began at 11:00 p.m. (Moscow time) on the night of August 20.

Despite this multilateral veneer, Operation Danube could hardly be regarded as a "joint" undertaking. Soviet paratroopers and KGB (state security) special operations forces spearheaded the invasion, and a total of some 350,000 to 400,000 Soviet troops eventually moved into Czechoslovakia, roughly five times the number of East European forces. Moreover, the invasion was under the direct control of the Soviet High Command at all times, rather than being left under the command of the leading Warsaw Pact officers as originally planned. Initially, the operation was scheduled to begin at midnight on August 20–21, but Soviet Defense Minister Grechko was so anxious to move ahead that he accelerated the timetable.

Within hours, the Soviet-led units had seized control of Czechoslovakia's transportation and communications networks, and had surrounded all the main party and state buildings in Prague and other cities. Soviet troops then began methodically occupying key sites, and setting up new communications and broadcasting facilities. In the early morning hours of the August 21, Soviet commandos from the elite Taman division, accompanied by KGB troops and Czechoslovak state security forces, entered the KSČ Central Committee headquarters, and arrested Dubček and the other reformers on the Czechoslovak presidium (except for Prime Minister Oldřich Černík, who had been arrested earlier at his office in the government ministers' building). By the time the KSČ leaders were carted off, the whole of Czechoslovakia was under Soviet military control. The Prague Spring, and its promise of socialism with a human face, had come to an end.

Aftermath

Decisive as the military results of Operation Danube may have been, they seemed rather hollow when the invasion failed to achieve its immediate political aims. The Soviet Union's chief political objective on August 20–21 was to facilitate a rapid transition to a pro-Moscow "revolutionary government." That objective failed to materialize when the "healthy forces" in Czechoslovakia were unable to gain majority support on the KSČ presidium. Faced with massive popular and official resistance in Czechoslovakia, the Soviet politburo decided to open negotiations on August 23 with Dubček and other top KSČ officials who had been arrested on the morning of August 21.

After four days of talks, the two sides agreed to sign the Moscow Protocol, which forced the reversal of the major elements of the Prague Spring, but also ensured the reinstatement of most of the leading reformers, including Dubček. The return of the officials who had initiated the liberalization program enabled some of the reforms to survive in Czechoslovakia for another several months. Until Dubček was removed once and for all in April 1969, substantial leeway for economic and political reform continued, despite constant pressure from the Soviet Union. This outcome underscored the limits of what Soviet military power could accomplish in the absence of a viable political strategy.

The basic problem for the Soviet Union extended beyond the defiant mood of the Czechoslovak public. Reports from Soviet diplomats in late 1968 confirmed that even most of the members of the KSČ viewed the invasion in "highly negative" terms. The anger and widespread resentment toward the Soviet Union had to be countered by sustained repression and "normalization," and even then, popular sentiments were merely submerged, not eliminated. Moscow's goal of restoring cohesion to the Eastern bloc in 1968 permanently alienated the vast majority of Czechs and Slovaks. From Brezhnev's perspective, this price was well worth paying at the time, but it guaranteed that the Czechoslovak regime would be unable to regain a semblance of popular legitimacy and would be forced instead to depend on Soviet military backing. If Brezhnev had once hoped that "stability" in the Eastern bloc could be maintained by something other than coercion, the 1968 invasion put an end to that notion.

In other respects, though, the invasion ultimately achieved its goals. The Soviet Union was able to restore Communist orthodoxy to Czechoslovakia and bolster the cohesion of the Warsaw Pact at a relatively low cost, both domestically and internationally. Moreover, the invasion established a new framework for Soviet–East European relations, which became explicit in autumn 1968 with the promulgation of the Brezhnev Doctrine. Although the invasion entailed significant costs for the USSR, the Soviet politburo succeeded in its paramount goal of preserving the socialist bloc. At no point in subsequent years did Brezhnev or his aides doubt the wisdom of their decision to crush the Prague Spring.

See also Brezhnev Doctrine; Dubček, Alexander; Eurocommunism; Socialist Camp; Soviet Bloc; Warsaw Pact.

FURTHER READING

Karner, S. et al., eds. *Prager Frühling: Das internationale Krisenjahr 1968, Vol. 1: Beiträge.* Vienna: Böhlau Verlag, 2008.

———., eds. *Prager Frühling: Das internationale Krisenjahr 1968, Vol. 2: Dokumente.* Vienna: Böhlau Verlag, 2008.

Kramer, M. "The Czechoslovak Crisis and the Brezhnev Doctrine." In *1968: The World Transformed,* ed. C. Fink, P. Gassert, and D. Junker, pp. 111–74. New York: Cambridge University Press, 1998.

———. "Ukraine and the Soviet-Czechoslovak Crisis of 1968 (Part 1): New Evidence from the Diaries of Petro Shelest." *Cold War International History Project Bulletin,* no. 10 (March 1998): 234–47.

———. "Ukraine and the Soviet-Czechoslovak Crisis of 1968 (Part 2): New Evidence from the Ukrainian Archives." *Cold War International History Project Bulletin,* no. 14/15 (Winter 2003–Spring 2004): 273–369.

MARK KRAMER

Preobrazhensky, Evgeny

Evgeny Preobrazhensky (1886–1937) was a leading political figure during the first decade following the Bolshevik Revolution and also one of the Soviet Union's outstanding economic theorists. He was born in Bolkhov, Orel Province, became a member of the social democratic movement at the age of fifteen, and then later joined the Bolsheviks. During the revolution of 1917 he was a Bolshevik leader in the Urals. Soon after the revolution he had his first conflict with Stalin, whom he suspected of having a less-than-adequate understanding of socialist internationalism and the need for revolutions to take place in Western Europe if the Soviet revolution was to survive.

Already at this point Preobrazhensky established himself on the left wing of the party. In 1918, he allied with Nikolay Bukharin and the Left Communist opposition to the Brest-Litovsk Treaty with Germany. His disquiet, however, was not simply over the abandonment of revolutionary commitment to the class struggle in Europe but what he and Bukharin saw as an erosion of the working class's position within the revolution.

In 1920, Preobrazhensky was named, along with N. N. Krestinsky and L. P. Serebryakov, one of three secretaries of the Bolshevik Party. All three later became active in the Trotskyist opposition. Ironically, in 1922 the post of party secretary was abolished and recast as the general secretary of the party's Central Committee, with Stalin as the new post holder. Yet whatever Preobrazhensky's democratic credentials, modern historians have conceded that he was not an effective administrator and had not been successful as a party secretary.

In 1923 Preobrazhensky authored the "Platform of the 46," which attacked the growing bureaucratization and authoritarianism of the party apparatus under Stalin. It should be noted that the "Platform" was an independent initiative, and had no direct connection with Trotsky's *New Course* [*Novyi kurs*], which appeared in the same year, and in which Trotsky set out his first detailed analysis of the class nature of the bureaucratic caste then emerging within the Bolshevik hierarchy.

In 1923 Preobrazhensky published another major work, *On Morality and Class Norms* [*O morali i klassovykh normakh*], in which he elucidated further his critique of the apparatus's growing privileges. From this point Preobrazhensky became a close ally of Trotsky and a leader of the various Trotskyist oppositions. Following the suppression of the 1927 Joint Opposition, he was expelled from the party in 1928, but in 1929 became one of the first Trotskyists to recant his views and return to the party fold. From then until his eventual arrest during Stalin's Terror, he worked inside the financial and agricultural administrations. In 1935 he was arrested and testified against Grigory Zinovyev and Lev Kamenev at the first Moscow show trial in 1936. He was scheduled to be a defendant in the second trial in 1937, but refused to confess and was shot in secret in that same year. He was rehabilitated during Gorbachev's perestroika.

Preobrazhensky was a major theorist and one of the Soviet Union's leading economists of the 1920s. He opposed Stalin's and Bukharin's policy of "Socialism in One Country," and the slow pace of industrialization. His best-known work is his *New Economics* [*Novaya ekonomika*], published in 1926, in which he put forward his theory of primary socialist accumulation. Here, he argued that successful industrial development required a transfer of resources from the peasant agriculture to state industry. He resolutely opposed the use of force to achieve this, however, and on the contrary, contended that successful industrialization would offer the peasantry a positive incentive to abandon small-scale market-oriented production in favor of large-scale industrial-style farming within the state sector. By 1927 he had developed the analysis further, and arrived at a more sober conclusion: that the technological and social disparity between state industry and peasant agriculture were so great that only a revolution in the advanced countries of Western Europe could save the Soviet Union from a political and economic impasse. While he purported to welcome Stalin's "solution" to this dilemma (forced collectivization and industrialization), in 1932 he published his second theoretical masterpiece, *The Decline of Capitalism* [*Zakat kapitalizma*]. This was a serious analysis in its own right of the capitalist Great Depression, but it was equally a more or less open attack on Stalin's five-year plans and the policy of developing heavy industry at the expense of consumption. With these two works, Preobrazhensky left an intellectual legacy that made him not simply an economist of the Soviet Union but also one of the first economic theorists of industrial development in underdeveloped countries.

Besides his contribution to development economics, in 1930 Preobrazhensky published one further work of major importance, his *Theory of Depreciating Currency* [*Teoriya padayushchei valyuty*], in which he built on Marx's theory of money to analyze the phenomenon of runaway inflation in the early twentieth century. This remains one of the few Marxist analyses of currency and money, other than what Marx himself wrote on the subject, but even in a wider field it would stand out as a work of prescience and intellectual subtlety.

See also New Economic Policy; Socialism in One Country; Soviet Industrialization; Trotskyism; War Communism.

FURTHER READING

Cacciari, M., and P. Perulli. *Piano economico e composizione di classe: Il dibattito sull'industrializzazione e lo scontro politico durante la NEP*. Milan: Feltrinelli, 1975.

Day, R. B. *The "Crisis" and the "Crash": Soviet Studies of the West (1917–1939)*. London: New Left Books, 1981.

Erlich, A. *The Soviet Industrialization Debate*. Cambridge, MA: Harvard University Press, 1960.

Preobrazhensky, E. *The New Economics*. Oxford: Oxford University Press, 1965.

———. *From NEP to Socialism*. London: New Park, 1973.

———. *The Crisis of Soviet Industrialization: Selected Essays*. Ed. D. A. Filtzer. London: Palgrave Macmillan, 1980.

———. *The Decline of Capitalism*. Ed. R. B. Day. Armonk, NY: M. E. Sharpe, 1985.

DONALD A. FILTZER

Press

When the Bolsheviks took power in Russia in October 1917, they set about a radically new project: creating an official press for the world's first "proletarian" (i.e., Communist) dictatorship. Although various socialist groups had long published journals opposed to established governments, their experiences were of limited utility to the Bolsheviks once the latter seized the state. As they built the first Communist state press, the Bolsheviks acted consistent with Marx's and Lenin's ideas about the functions of communications media in society. Yet these ideas were not a detailed blueprint for the future Communist press. Early in their history, Soviet journalists had to improvise and borrow constantly.

Marx argued that in modern bourgeois societies, the capitalists controlled the press (because they controlled the means of production, such as the print shops, etc.), and used it to spread their ideology and mask their domination. It followed that when the proletariat seized political power, they should seize control of the bourgeois press and make it their own. The Bolsheviks followed Marx's prescription when they confiscated the assets of all "bourgeois" newspapers ten days after taking power, and then turned them over to Communist and state publications.

Under the pressures of governing a collapsing empire in wartime, the Bolsheviks moved toward banning all opposition political parties and their publications. This included Socialist parties, some of which enjoyed a limited toleration immediately after the October Revolution. By late summer 1918, the Soviet government had closed all non-Bolshevik daily newspapers and banned advertising (because it was a means for capitalists to influence the press).

During the Russian civil war (1918–21), the party/state press was quite decentralized. Local soviets (councils) and party committees issued hundreds of two- to four-page broadsheets with next to no guidance from the party/state executive apparatus. Production conditions were difficult. There were shortages of newsprint, experienced journalists, and printing presses. The party/state dispersed newspapers for free, but the breakdown of the transport network meant they were often unavailable in remote areas.

During the civil war most newspapers focused on mobilizing the Communist Party and the populace at large for battle. Headlines were most often commands or exhortations, most of the news was from the front, and hatred of the enemy was stressed. The civil war experience combined with the influence of Marxist rhetoric of class struggle as well as the romantic vocabulary of revolution inherited from nationalist and socialist movements in 19th-century Europe to leave a permanent militant imprint on the Soviet press.

With the conclusion of the civil war in 1921, Bolshevik leaders and propaganda officials sought to shape a peacetime Communist press, and tighten the party Central Committee's supervision of all newspapers. Orders went out from the Central Committee to switch from "agitation"—that is, mobilizing for battle—to "propaganda"—that is, the long-term task of educating the populace to be model citizens of the new socialist society. Enlightening the masses meant instructing them in elementary hygiene, explaining government tax policies, teaching them the basics of a scientific atheist worldview, and so on. As part of the enlightenment effort, propaganda officials in the Central Committee tried to differentiate the newspaper network by target audience, publishing the *Peasant Gazette* and the *Worker Gazette* for peasants and workers, *Pravda* for party activists, *Komsomolskaia pravda* for youth, and *Izvestiia* and a number of popular "evening" newspapers for educated city dwellers. The Central Committee and other institutions also sponsored studies of peasant and worker newspaper readers, trying to determine how to communicate with them more effectively.

The party/Soviet leadership tried during the early to middle 1920s to make the press financially self-sustaining as well. Advertising was once again permitted, and newspapers were no longer distributed free, but instead sold. They were supposed to be on *khozraschet*, meaning that they had to cover expenditures with their own income. But in reality Soviet newspapers continued to require large government subsidies to operate throughout the history of the USSR. For Communist leaders, communicating the right message to the populace was a paramount goal. If the message didn't sell, they were willing to subsidize newspapers to get it out.

In the early Soviet period, Communist journalists and propaganda officials tended to think of the press's role in society in terms of various pronouncements by Lenin. In his 1901 article "Where to Begin?" Lenin categorized the functions of the illegal social democratic press in Russia as propaganda (educating the audience in a Marxist worldview), agitation (riling the audience up to fight the capitalists), and organization (coordinating the actions of party members and sympathizers). In pre-revolutionary writings Lenin also discussed the party press's role in exposing and denouncing the capitalists' oppression of the working class and peasants.

Because the situation of post-revolutionary newspapers (now official organs of the state) was so different from that of pre-revolutionary socialist publications, Lenin's categorization of press function assumed new meanings after 1917. Propaganda came to mean the long-term task of educating the populace to be model citizens of the new socialist society. Agitation still referred to emotive appeals designed to motivate action. Organization now meant mobilizing readers to carry out the directives of the party's Central Committee. And denunciation became exposing corrupt or incompetent bureaucrats and officials—those who failed to carry out the leadership's orders.

The Soviet press in the 1920s also served other functions. Newspapers solicited and got a huge number of letters from readers. Newspaper editors published letters, forwarded complaints and accusations to appropriate institutions, and composed summaries of their contents for party higher-ups as a way of staying in touch with "the moods of the masses." Thus, newspapers gathered intelligence for the regime and served as a safety valve for popular discontent.

The press also occasionally served as the forum for political clashes. Hence, in late 1925, *Leningradskaia pravda* for several weeks openly represented the Zinovyevite Opposition against the Central Committee's *Pravda*. Again, in 1928, *Pravda* and *Leningradskaia pravda* publicized the arguments of "Rightist" Bukharin against Stalin's course of forced collectivization. The party's explicit prohibitions on public dissent and the organization of "factions," combined with its authoritarian political culture, however, enabled Stalin and "the Central Committee majority" to remove in short order editors who challenged them.

Due to Marxist ideas and many intellectuals' suspicion of mass commercial culture, Soviet newspapers were not supposed to entertain readers with "bourgeois sensationalism" such as the coverage of sex crimes or deadly accidents. Nonetheless, in the 1920s the Komsomol press (which was chronically short on cash) and the evening newspapers (which were supposed to make a profit) did sometimes breach this taboo to increase sales.

Under the personal dictatorship established by Stalin in 1929, Soviet newspapers closely followed the themes and propaganda campaigns mandated by the Central Committee Department of Agitation and Propaganda. Stalin and his subordinates reprimanded editors, a state censorship organ, Glavlit, monitored nonparty (i.e., state) publications, and the Central Committee cut paper supplies to periodicals that fell out of line. But direct punitive action was the exception; journalists generally followed the central agenda voluntarily and censored themselves.

In the eyes of many observers, the Soviet print media under Stalin came to epitomize the Communist press all over the world. It is true that most Communist parties in power did establish on paper something like the Soviets' pyramidal system of party/state control. In post-Stalinist Soviet history and the experiences of other Communist regimes, though, there were many variations from the Stalinist model. For most of their histories, the Communist governments in Poland and Hungary permitted greater latitude for discussion of their policies than the Soviet leadership allowed. In Yugoslavia and China, republic- or provincial-level officials managed local newspapers with more autonomy than under Stalinism. The Communist leaders in Vietnam allowed a non-Communist newspaper (*Tin Sang*) to publish for six years following their conquest of South Vietnam in 1975. In China after 1979, the lifting of a ban on advertising combined with the relatively decentralized administration of the press stimulated the rapid commercialization of much of the press. To the consternation of many party officials "pornographic" and "vulgar" commercial journalism spread quickly.

Communist presses also served at times as forums for political debate. Leaders would allow this situation to develop to further their own agendas. For example, during the perestroika era of Soviet history, Mikhail Gorbachev put editors in place at the weeklies *Ogonek* and *Moscow News* who promoted his reform agenda. With the general secretary's tacit consent these journals challenged positions taken by more "conservative" publications like *Sovetskaia rossiia*.

The histories of Communist presses worldwide seem to be characterized by oscillations between a limited tolerance for discussion and tight Stalinist control. There are also oscillations between "puritanism" (advertising bans or prohibitions on "sensationalism") and acceptance of advertising and entertainment. Communist leaders usually do not value pluralism as an end in itself but rather as a tool of political mobilization. When they accept advertising and entertainment, it is as a means of financing the press and possibly distracting the population from politics (Poland in the 1980s). The pressure of events along with the tensions between ideology and pragmatic concerns drive these oscillations.

See also Censorship; Cinema, Soviet; Literacy, Soviet Union Campaign for Adult; Literature in Soviet Russia; Propaganda, Communist; Public Opinion; Television in the Soviet Era.

FURTHER READING

Brooks, J. *Thank You, Comrade Stalin*. Princeton, NJ: Princeton University Press, 1999.

Kenez, P. *The Birth of the Propaganda State: Soviet Methods of Mass Mobilization, 1917–1929*. London: Cambridge University Press, 1985.

Lenoe, M. *Closer to the Masses: Stalinist Culture, Social Revolution, and Soviet Newspapers*. Cambridge, MA: Harvard University Press, 2004.

Johnson, O. V. "The Media and Democracy in Eastern Europe." In *Communicating Democracy: The Media and Political Transition*, ed. Patrick O'Neil. London: Lynne Rienner, 1998.

Lynch, D. C. *After the Propaganda State: Media, Politics, and "Thought Work" in Reformed China*. Stanford, CA: Stanford University Press, 1999.

MATTHEW LENOE

Proletkult

The organization known as Proletkult developed in Russia during the civil war under the leadership of Aleksandr Bogdanov, who in the past had been closer politically to Marx than Lenin, and was convinced that proletarian culture (*proletarskaja kul'tura*) was the most universal and global of cultures. The concept of proletarian culture was synthesized in the acronym that would represent the fight and search for a new morality, politics, and art, born from the needs and capabilities of the soon to be new "lords" of the Soviet state: the proletarians. The first problem, which in the future would lead to a confrontation with the Soviet state, consisted in the identification of those who with absolute political correctness could belong to the category of proletarians. In addition to industrial workers would it also be possible to consider craftspeople, given their shared past exploitation (though they had been able to employ salaried workers), and the semiurbanized rural workforce, traditionally tied to an individualist, patriarchal, and religious past, as proletarians?

Having begun thanks to local workers' initiatives, the movement soon became a national organization supported by the government, even though its urgent need for autonomy would lead to several conflicts with various institutions. The most important of these was the Narkompros, another famous acronym of the time (*Narodnyi komitet prosveščenija*, or People's Committee for Education), officially responsible for the organization of cultural programs, but quite prone to bureaucratic tardiness and complications. The Proletkult would always refuse to be cowed by institutions, and supported the need to take care of the proletariat's needs exclusively, unlike the government, which also supported other classes' causes. Bogdanov and his followers considered themselves to be on equal footing with and therefore autonomous from other cornerstones of the workers' power: the Communist Party and labor unions.

The Proletkult's highly utopian nature led to the formulation of innovative ideas for a new science, a new art, and a new conduct in private life, and they were all based on the fundamental premise that past barriers between "high" bourgeois culture and the illiterate classes had to be removed. New spaces for cultural development were created in the factory and workers' circles, and a series of workshops was established in which music, theater, and iconography would lead to the creation of a new concept of beauty—a basic element for the construction of the new socialist society. The government's objections to the activities of the powerful organization were based on the fear that the focus on the cultural front might distract the proletarians from their primary task—the construction of the state—thereby leading to situations favorable to anti-Soviet activities. After the civil war, the workshops' initiatives were the target of further criticism: excessive isolationism, elitism, and a dubious mix of the avant-garde with old-style machismo.

Lenin himself gave Anatoly Lunacharsky the task of disbanding the organization at the National Congress in 1920. Lenin responded to the People's Commissar's hesitations by calling the Proletkult to order in the name of party discipline. The beginning of New Economic Policy (NEP) was another blow to the organization. On the economic front many of the Proletkult's provincial branches had never become really autonomous, and the new fiscal rules wreaked havoc. The crisis had begun, and various attempts to establish a new identity notwithstanding, under the leadership of Valerian Pletnev, the Proletkult faced rough times: branch closures, loss of members, and economic decline. What had been a powerful national movement in 1922 had gone back to being a small organization, whose publishing network had collapsed, and whose state subsidies had been cut. The NEP had put the class struggle on the back burner. The party now supported the so-called *smyčka*—cooperation between workers and peasants. Bourgeois specialists were accepted as indispensable collaborators. The idea of proletarian purity was losing credibility. The Proletkult's leaders attempted once more in 1924 to reenergize support for their cause, but they no longer had a movement or supporters they could count on.

See also Avant-garde; Cultural Policies; Lunacharsky, Anatoly.

FURTHER READING

Bogdanov, A. A. *Red Star: The First Bolshevik Utopia.* Ed. L. R. Graham and R. Stites. Bloomington: Indiana University Press, 1984.

Gorzka, G. *A. Bogdanov und der russische Proletkult: Theorie und Praxis einer sozialistischen Kulturrevolution.* Frankfurt am Main: Campus, 1980.

Kenez, P. *The Birth of the Propaganda State: Soviet Methods of Mass Mobilization, 1917–1929.* Cambridge: Cambridge University Press, 1985.

Mally, L. *Culture of the Future: The Proletkult Movement in Revolutionary Russia.* Berkeley: University of California Press, 1990.

GIAN PIERO PIRETTO

Propaganda, Communist

It is generally assumed that the Communists have been masters of propaganda. It is notoriously difficult to evaluate the correctness of this assumption because the impact of propaganda is illusive. The Communists certainly have not accomplished their most ambitious goal—the creation of a "socialist human being"—but within their own terms they were successful: their propaganda helped to maintain the stability of their regimes for long periods and gain converts in capitalist societies. In trying to find the source of success, it is clear that the Communists have not found particularly clever methods of brainwashing. Even a cursory look at Soviet newspapers, for example, makes it evident that these papers were extremely boring. In fact, Soviet activists looked at the skills of U.S. advertisers with admiration and envy.

Communist states differed from one another: they were established in different circumstances and societies at different stages of development. In one respect, though, they were very much alike: each developed remarkably similar propaganda systems. This happened because they learned from the Soviet experience, and perhaps more important, because Communist leaders shared a common attitude and worldview. Similar attitudes and similar needs produced similar policies, and therefore Chinese, Cuban, and Communist Eastern European propaganda systems were much like one another. The best way to understand Communist propaganda is to examine how in one concrete instance, in the Soviet case, it developed and functioned.

The fundamental features of Soviet propaganda were present at the moment of the regime's creation. The Bolsheviks were improvising at a time when they were engaged in a civil war. They proved to be better in getting their message across than their opponents in that struggle, and this superiority was one of the causes of their victory. The revolutionaries had an almost intuitive understanding of the significance of organization, and as Lenin was the first to point out in *What Is to Be Done?* already in 1902, organization and propaganda were opposite sides of the same coin. In the period of underground work, the chief task of revolutionaries was to persuade the masses of the correctness of their views—that is, to carry out propaganda. The Communists, as good Marxists, believed that they were in possession of an instrument that allowed them to interpret and predict history. Under these circumstances, the teaching of Marxism—that is, propaganda—was not only not reprehensible but a necessary and indeed noble task. Saving people from error was nothing to be ashamed of, and the Bolsheviks proudly considered themselves propagandists.

The Communists were willing from the outset to suppress conflicting interpretations of political events. The

source of success of Communist domestic propaganda whenever and wherever has always been the ability of the Communists to achieve a monopoly of interpretation of politics. Having an understanding of the importance of propaganda, the Bolsheviks were willing to invest resources and energy in finding new and imaginative ways of reaching the Russian people. They created institutions through which they were able to penetrate every segment of the population.

The most conventional method for spreading a political message was, of course, the press. The Soviet press came into being in a historically unprecedented situation; it was created and protected by a one party, revolutionary state, and this fact essentially determined its character. The Bolshevik papers, once relieved from the pressure of competition, developed unique characteristics. The decisive development was the immediate suppression of the free press. Lenin and his followers argued that the press was a weapon, no different from bombs, and therefore the task of the Bolsheviks was to deprive their enemies of this potential strength. Lenin was convinced that liberalism would be fatal to the survival of the revolution.

For winning the civil war it was essential to gain the goodwill of the peasantry. The Bolsheviks showed impressive skill in reaching their target audience. They sent either workers who were committed to the Bolshevik cause or, preferably, demobilized peasant soldiers to the villages. The victorious revolutionaries constantly experimented. Some of the experiments were utopian and had to be abandoned, but other attempts clearly made a difference. A decree in December 1918, for example, mobilized literate peasants to read proclamations and other material selected by the Commissariat of Enlightenment to their illiterate comrades. The task was compulsory and it was to be carried out without compensation.

Another imaginative method of oral agitation was the organizing of agitational ships and trains, and sending them into the countryside. These were a remarkable combination of carrying out administrative and propaganda work. Since the governmental apparatus in the villages was abysmally weak and since the new authorities were not in the position to remedy the situation quickly, the idea arose of sending the agents of the government into the villages. The trains and ships included representatives from various commissariats, the party's Central Committee, the youth organization, and many professional agitators. The trains were equipped with small propaganda libraries and a printing press for the production of newspapers, manifestos, and other propaganda material.

A most significant innovation in the art of persuasion was the creation of mass organizations. The Bolsheviks were the first in history to organize and maintain institutions that had the task of spreading the ideology of the regime among specially targeted segments of the population. In a sense the party itself was such a mass organization. Certainly one of its chief purposes was to indoctrinate, win over, explain, and defend government policies. Two major organizations, the Komsomol (youth organization) and the Zhenotdel (the organization of women), were typically Soviet inasmuch as they had no other genuine functions than agitation.

Even in the extremely difficult circumstances of the civil war the regime made great efforts to organize a campaign for the elimination of illiteracy. On the one hand, this drive was a prerequisite of further achievements, and on the other hand, it was used as an indoctrination tool. The party sponsored the publication of literacy textbooks, which brought down the Communist doctrine to the simplest possible level. As the workers, peasants, and soldiers learned to read and write, they memorized sentences such as "The defense of the revolution is the duty of the working classes!" and "We are building a new world without tyrants and slaves!" Literacy campaigns became regular features of all successful Communist revolutions that took place in underdeveloped societies.

Although the Russians had little experience in graphic arts, it is striking how quickly the revolutionaries developed this minor art form. Perhaps this development was inevitable. After all, a poster is a quintessential form of propaganda; it is the ultimate in reduction. Its production was relatively cheap, and at a time of paper shortages, thousands could be reached by the use of a small investment in a scarce resource.

The Bolsheviks well appreciated the propaganda possibilities inherent in films. Films represented modernity. It was also obviously useful in a country that still had a 60 percent illiteracy rate. The regime invested scarce resources in making newsreels, which were accompanied by an unabashedly propagandistic text. Soviet filmmakers developed a new genre, the agitational film, which was affectionately called *agitka*. They were short, extremely didactic, and aimed at an uneducated audience. The relative normality of the 1920s allowed the regime to build an elaborate and useful propaganda structure. The Tenth Party Congress in 1921 created an organization within the Commissariat of Enlightenment that had the task of coordinating all propaganda

efforts. This was called the Chief Committee for Political Education (Glavpolitprosvet), and was headed by Lenin's wife, N. Krupskaia. The Glavpolitprosvet took charge of the building of a national network of political education.

It was far more difficult to reach the peasantry than the workers, since in the villages the party had no firm base. The Communists attempted to overcome their weakness in the countryside by setting up village reading rooms. In the course of the 1920s some twenty to twenty-five thousand of these were established. The party had ambitious tasks for them: they dispersed information about government policies and agitated on behalf of these policies. The reading rooms were directed by the *izbach*, the party's ideological vicar in the village, who in addition to overseeing the reading room, had to organize the village equivalents of the many political campaigns.

The campaigns took place to commemorate political anniversaries, "express solidarity with the international working classes," improve the harvest, facilitate the collection of taxes, advance the cause of literacy, and so on. There were so many campaigns that they became part of the daily routine. They occasioned putting slogans on the wall, holding festive evenings, and listening to innumerable speeches. The reading rooms also operated study circles. Some of these dealt with political events, but others spread agricultural knowledge or brought together women to do handiwork.

Collectivization and industrialization meant not only a change in economic policies but also a thorough overhaul of the entire sociopolitical system, and within it the propaganda network. The system greatly expanded. Although in the 1920s the party made strenuous efforts to bring its message to the people, the bulk of the population remained almost untouched. Collectivization, however, radically changed the situation. In order to force the peasants to accept the new order, the party sent thousands of activists into the villages to act as agitators, among other things. The new collective farms gave the party an organizational base; now the peasants attended one mass meeting after another and they were constantly exposed to that remarkable Soviet institution, the loudspeaker that was never turned off.

In the early days of the industrialization drive the indoctrination system was inundated. The party did not have enough trained agitators. Under these circumstances the simplest and cheapest method of indoctrination was the mass meeting. The leaders of the party, as skilled propagandists, understood that mass meetings in which foreign and domestic enemies were regularly denounced, in which people were exhorted to work better, did not do much good. Therefore they made great efforts to extend the network. In the second half of the 1930s the regime once again had enough trusted people to address small meetings, lead reading circles, and even send to individual households for agitation. At this time, the newspaper reading circles became a regular feature of Soviet factory life. The workers were compelled to sacrifice a part of their lunch break or come early to work.

Even during the civil war the political education system stressed the importance of productivity. Not surprisingly, in the 1930s productivity became the dominant theme of Soviet propaganda. Movies and novels depicted heroes who overcame natural and human obstacles, and reached miracles of performance. The regime selected a group of workers and helped them to overfulfill vastly their norms in order to hold them up as examples. The movement, named after a miner, A. Stakhanov, brought considerable benefits: it took advantage of the genuine enthusiasm that may have existed among segments of the population for the socialist transformation of their land, and enabled the factories to demand more from the ordinary worker.

At the outbreak of the war all the propaganda instruments were already in place, ready to be used. Every branch of art, naturally, was pressed into service. Novelists described the heroism of the Russian soldiers and civilians, musicians composed patriotic songs, and graphic artists drew posters that glorified the Red Army and the Soviet people, and ridiculed the enemy. The Soviet leadership had a special appreciation for the role of film and documentaries, and filmmaking came to be fully mobilized for the war effort. During the war Soviet directors made seventy to eighty films, out of which only a handful did not deal directly or indirectly with the war. Documentaries made an especially great impression on the audience, and documentary makers received all the support that they needed for their work. In the course of the war, thousands of camerapersons shot 3.5 million meters of film and thereby produced a remarkable chronicle of the war. The heart of the appeal to the people was Russian nationalism, and the goals of the government coincided. This way, perhaps paradoxically and in spite of the boundless suffering, the Second World War was also a liberating experience for the Russian people. When propagandists described the brutality of the Nazis and the heroism of the resistance, they were telling the truth.

In the post–Second World War decades the propaganda machinery continued to grow. As long as the Soviet Union existed, propaganda was considered to be one of the main tasks of the party. The apex of the enormous and complex propaganda organization was a section within the Central Committee of the Communist Party, headed by a member of the politburo. The agitation and propaganda section oversaw not only the development of propaganda themes but also Soviet cultural life. It determined the policy line of the major national newspapers, such as *Pravda* and *Isvestiia*, and supervised the activities of the Ministry of Culture.

The themes of Soviet propaganda changed over time. After the war, the Soviet operatives orchestrated an enormous international "peace campaign." At a time when Soviet power greatly expanded these operatives succeeded, at least to a certain extent, in depicting the motherland of Communism as a determined opponent of war. After the death of Stalin, somewhat more realistically the theme of Soviet propaganda was the peaceful coexistence of the two social and economic systems.

On the one hand, a Communist state is unthinkable without its propaganda machinery; on the other hand, the particular propaganda system could exist only within a Communist state, for it depended on a vast repressive apparatus. The lessening of control over the flow of information and culture went hand in hand with the disintegration of the Soviet state.

See also Censorship; Cinema, Soviet; Cultural Policies; Iconography; Literacy, Soviet Campaign for Adult; Press; Public Opinion; Television in the Soviet Era.

FURTHER READING

Benn, D. W. *Persuasion and Soviet Politics*. Oxford: Blackwell, 1989.

Hollander, G. D. *Soviet Political Indoctrination; Developments in Mass Media and Propaganda since Stalin*. New York: Praeger, 1972.

Inkeles, A. *Public Opinion in Soviet Russia: A Study in Mass Persuasion*. Cambridge, MA: Harvard University Press, 1958.

Kenez, P. *The Birth of the Propaganda State: Soviet Methods of Mass Mobilization, 1917–1929*. Cambridge, UK: Cambridge University Press, 1985.

Remington, T. F. *Soviet Public Opinion and the Effectiveness of Party Ideological Work*. Pittsburgh: Russian and East European Studies Program, University of Pittsburgh, 1983.

PETER KENEZ

Public Opinion

In Soviet-type sociopolitical systems there could be no competing, pluralistic public opinion of the kind in modern democratic states that permits a population to determine its own positions on matters. The Soviet regime demanded of its citizens—and to a certain degree achieved—a uniformity of views and values not only on political questions but also in the public's evaluation of historical events, moral principles, aesthetics, and everyday life. In totalitarian societies, the state essentially arbitrated both public and private life, and state-sanctioned positions extended their influence into all spheres of people's lives. This uniformity, expressed in various formulas such as "all people as one," "united support," "unanimous approval," and so forth, was not a mere mark of official ideology. The closed society, its isolation from the outside world and its own past, the blatant propaganda and censorship of opinions that pervaded schools and literature, and also the regular ideological "purges" and campaigns—all these enabled the official stereotypes and formulas to permeate all layers of society. And this particularly affected "newly educated people"—that is, the generations now shaped by the closed society. Fragments of Marxist dogmatism were combined with the political slogans of the time, the legacy of national patriotism, paternalistic stereotypes, the serf mentality, ethnic phobias, and other things. This material constituted a public opinion based on a totalitarian model.

In this system, no one ever asked people about what they thought regarding public life or the viability of the state. The party and government leadership assumed that the people and country knew where their true interests lay, and that all one had to do was explain things to the masses, without tolerating any doubts. The leadership believed that the population would accept the rules of the game unconditionally, permitting the ruling circles to steer clear of any problems by appealing to "unanimous" public opinion with standard phrases of official political rhetoric such as "the Soviet people demand," "the people won't permit," or "the Soviet people won't go for," and other such stock expressions.

These statements were for the most part disingenuous. There could never have been absolute unity in this or any other society. Feigned agreement with official positions and slogans often concealed the individual's indiffer-ence, desire for self-preservation, or sometimes, attempt to move up the career ladder. A cautious, ironic attitude toward the official formulas would sometimes show up in the modern "folklore" of everyday life. But totalitarian conditions left no space in the consciousness of the masses for any direct protest or disagreement.

The mechanisms of public opinion served as a means of assuring the loyalty and obedience of the masses to the regime. These included the drumming up of forced enthusiasm for "propagandized successes," the frenzied revilement of enemies and renegades (the "lessons of hate" so lucidly depicted in George Orwell's novel *1984*), and the cult of worship of infallible leaders (a führer or duce).

With the population isolated from any outside information, all events were portrayed as an unbroken chain of successes and victories of the people, and its wise leadership. Any negative information was kept out of circulation, and any pessimistic moods (in fiction or historical literature) could bring punishment to the authors. Even the most severe defeats of the early period of World War II were depicted as successes of the so-called Stalin Plan for Active Defense. The image of the "Soviet citizen-conqueror," an eternal optimist confident of one's strength and the absolute infallibility of the leadership, was inculcated into the people's consciousness. Molding this type of public opinion required heroes and exploits of mythological proportions, and painstakingly constructed lists of heroic figures (mostly those who had died a glorious death on the battlefield) were constantly thrust into the mass media and public consciousness as examples to be rapturously admired and imitated.

No less essential for totalitarian public opinion were various types of enemies, traitors, and renegades, not only external ("worldwide imperialism," "warmongers," and so forth), but also internal ("enemies of the people," "Trotskyites," "nationalists," and others). Plausibility or justification of the accusations played no role here at all; the tasks of the mass campaigns were to induce people to believe the most monstrous and absurd accusations, including those leveled at former leaders and unmasked idols, and to maintain in the country an atmosphere of universal fear, suspicion, and mutual denunciations. In this way, both potential and real victims of mass terror became coparticipants in it as well, so that a sort of collective of hostages emerged.

The crowning figure in this type of public opinion was the artificially created myth of the infallible leader (less stable were depersonalized, transitory stereotypes like "all-conquering doctrine" or "wise party leadership"). The notion of the existence of some higher, absolute reason that stood above all edifices of the sociopolitical regime with its corruptible bureaucracy served to justify any actions—or crimes—of the ruling elite.

As in any other totalitarian system, Soviet public opinion could function only on one level, and no moral principles could stand in the way of what was currently expedient. No division was in fact drawn between the functions of expediency and morality, or those of private life and the state. Yet the real picture was somewhat more complicated. For all the harshness of the regime, its control over the opinions and behaviors of people could never be full or complete. The regime, for its own self-preservation, was indeed forced to reconcile itself to an inevitably less than total control over private life, informal relationships, and religion. For their part, many people and entire social groups demonstrated loyalty to the regime in order to preserve their accustomed style of life and mind. At all stages of its existence, the system was profoundly beset by corruption and hypocrisy.

Public opinion was most harshly controlled in the 1930s and 1940s. During the post-Stalin years (after 1953), the regime became weaker and began to lose confidence in itself. At times it even began to tolerate nonofficial views in the domains of literature, art, ecology, and other areas, but it was only with the start of Mikhail Gorbachev's perestroika that any pluralism of opinions became possible in politics, history, philosophy, and other such spheres. Nevertheless, completely open and independent public opinion has yet to come in Russia. With the strengthening of antidemocratic tendencies in the political and social arenas under Vladimir Putin, public opinion once more became exposed to massive pressure and manipulation.

Under totalitarian conditions, any scientific investigation of public opinion has been simply absent. Any publication of the results of opinion polls that would show even a small percentage of discontented or dissenting participants has seemed to be dangerous. Authorities have gleaned some information about public moods from their secret services. The first attempts at an objective study of certain aspects of public opinion in the Soviet Union were undertaken in the 1960s under the guidance of Boris Grushin, first under the auspices of one of the most popular newspapers, and then in an academic institute. One of the most important projects of that period was a comprehensive study of public opinion in a midsize city (Taganrog) in the Rostov District. The regular study of public opinion commensurate with world standards became possible in the USSR only at the end of the 1980s. The first All-Union (later All-Russian) Center for the Study of Public Opinion in the country was established in 1987, headed by Tatiana Zaslavskaia and Grushin. In the 1990s, various nongovernmental social and marketing research firms were also set up.

See also Censorship; Marxism-Leninism; New Man; Press; Propaganda, Communist; Television in the Soviet Era; Totalitarianism.

FURTHER READING

Grusin, B. A. *Četyre žizni Rossii glazami obščestvennogo mnenija.* 2 vols. Moscow: Progress-Tradicia, 2000–2003.

Levada, J. A. *Ot mnenij k ponimaniju. Sociologičeskie očerki 1994–2000.* Moscow: Moskovskaja škola političeskich issledovanij, 2000.

JURIJ LEVADA

Purges

The term "purge" (*chistka*, cleansing) refers to the practice followed by the Communist Party in Russia of expelling from its ranks those deemed to be unsuitable as members. This was a regular practice instituted in the early 1920s and continued through the decades of Soviet power. Those purged were expelled from party membership, which sometimes entailed dismissal from public office, and in some cases the institution of legal proceeding against them as well. The routine practice of purging the party ranks needs to be distinguished from the practices followed during the Great Purges of 1937–38, when hundreds of thousands of people, party members and non-party, were arrested and executed or imprisoned in the gulag.

The practice of purging the party ranks is related to the Communist Party's conception of itself as a vanguard party that by necessity imposed strict membership criteria, requiring party members to be activists, to engage in party work, attend party meetings, participate in party-sponsored events, and work in the field of agitation and propaganda. Admission to the party was selective. Prospective members had to have the recommendation of a current party member and were required to serve a probationary period before being granted a party card. One of the criteria required for membership was the ability to pass an examination in knowledge of basic of Marxism-Leninism, the history of the Communist Party, and of current policies of the party.

The selection process had as its reverse side the expulsion of those deemed, for whatever reason, unsuitable for retaining party membership. In September 1920 the Central Committee established its Central Control Commission, which directed the work of an extensive network of local Control Commissions attached to local party committees. The task of this body was to uphold party discipline, including the ban on factions within the party, and to combat ideological deviation. In subsequent decades the name and structure of this body changed, but its function remained largely the same. Its task was to monitor the composition of the party, to enforce party discipline, to purge the party's ranks of unsuitable elements, and to act as a court of appeal.

The purging of the party took on critical importance with the establishment of the Communist political power monopoly, the tightening of controls prohibiting factions, and the elevation of the party to monolithic status. In the period of the underground, the revolution, and civil war, party members were largely a self-selecting group, distinguished by their political commitment and zeal. With the transformation of the party into a governing body, party membership became a means of career advancement. With the growth in party membership, fears were increasingly expressed that the party was attracting unsuitable elements. The practice of purging was also connected to the regular practice of requiring party members to engage in criticism and self-criticism. Party membership carried with it often onerous responsibilities. Members could be assigned to different tasks in different parts of the country and required to participate in party campaigns.

In the 1920s and 1930s a series of major purges of the party's ranks were undertaken. The first, which took place following the civil war, in 1921–22, resulted in a drastic reduction of the party ranks. Following Lenin's death there was large-scale recruitment of new party members from the working class, which raised party membership to one million by 1926. There was a further large-scale recruitment of workers into the party in 1928–31. This was then followed by a major purge of the party's ranks in 1933–34, which was carried out by a special purge commission, headed by Party Secretary L. M. Kaganovich. It largely bypassed the Central Control Commission, which was itself abolished in 1934 and replaced by the Commission of Party Control.

Through these successive purge campaigns as well as more localized purges, and through the normal activities of the Control Commissions, various people were dismissed from the party. Some were expelled on the basis of class origin (kulaks, gendarmes, priests), membership in other parties (Mensheviks, SRs, Kadets), or service in the civil war with the Whites. Others were expelled for misdemeanors—failure to pay party dues, nonactivism, drunkenness, corruption, or the like. The number expelled for supporting the Left Opposition or the Rightists in the 1920s, at least in the reports published by the CCC, were a small proportion of the total purged, but it is possible that expulsions for political reasons were concealed under other headings.

By the later 1920s the purge process had become a normal part of life, reflecting the requirement placed on all party members that they prove themselves worthy of party membership. Discipline became a watchword. Already in 1925 a central moral obligation placed on all party members was the duty to inform on fellow members who breached party rules or flouted party policy. Purges were conducted in particular institutions where opposition to official policy was suspected—as for example, the purge of the student and military cells in Moscow in 1923–24 where support for Trotsky was strong. In 1929–33 the purge was directed at supporters of the Rightists, those labeled as bourgeois nationalists, and those accused of opposing party policy on collectivization and dekulakization. Following the assassination of S. M. Kirov, head of the Leningrad party organization in December of 1934, the party ranks were purged, and those under suspicion were arrested.

In 1935–36, on account of what was deemed the unsatisfactory nature of the party purge of 1933, two new initiatives were launched: the exchange of party cards, and the verification of party documents, which in effect was a purge by another procedure. This was a prelude to the Great Purges, but that upheaval targeted a much wider category of victims than party members, and involved arrests, executions, and imprisonments on a huge scale.

The practice of conducting purges of the party ranks continued until the end of the Stalin era. Thereafter the management of the growth of party membership assumed a more systematic character, directed at including key strategic groups within the party membership in Russia and the national republics of the USSR. The procedure of monitoring the party ranks, controlling admission, and expelling unsuitable elements continued to be followed, but in the more settled post-Stalin decades, the recruitment drives and purgings of the Lenin and Stalin eras were no longer employed.

See also Great Terror; Marxism-Leninism; Self-Criticism.

FURTHER READING

Chlevnjuk, O. *Politbjuro: Mechanizmy Politieskoi vlasti v 1930-e gody.* Moscow: Rosspen, 1996.

Getty, J. A., and O. V. Naumov. *The Road to Terror: Stalin and the Self Destruction of the Bolsheviks, 1932–38.* New Haven, CT: Yale University Press, 1999.

Rigby, T. H. *Communist Party Membership in the USSR.* Princeton, NJ: Princeton University Press, 1968.

E. ARFON REES

Radek, Karl

Karl Radek (given surname Sobelsohn, 1885–1939) was born into a Jewish family in Lemberg (now Lviv, then part of Austrian Galicia) on October 31. By his mid-teens he had become active in the labor movement in Galicia, writing for various socialist publications, and in 1904 joined the Social Democratic Party of the Kingdom of Poland and Lithuania. He enrolled for a law degree at Kraków University, but soon went to Switzerland and then Warsaw, and in 1908 to Germany, where he continued his journalistic activities and established contacts with left-wing Social Democrats. In summer 1914 Radek returned to Switzerland, and by 1915 he was working closely with Lenin and Zinovyev, the leading émigré Bolsheviks. In this capacity, he participated in the antiwar socialist conferences in Zimmerwald (1915) and Kienthal (1916). Soon after the October seizure of power, Radek arrived in Petrograd, and formally joined the Bolshevik Party and was a member of its Central Committee from 1919 to 1924. Regarded as something of an expert in international affairs, he took part in the negotiations between the Soviet government and the German High Command at Brest-Litovsk in early 1918, and directed the Central European section of the People's Commissariat of Foreign Affairs. In December 1918 he was dispatched on a mission to Germany, but was arrested in February 1919 after the unsuccessful Spartacist uprising in Berlin. He remained in solitary confinement for five months and was only released in January 1920.

Returning to Moscow, Radek became heavily involved in the affairs of the Communist International, particularly in the early development of the German Communist Party. In 1920 he was elected secretary of the Comintern's Executive Committee, was a member of that committee from 1920 to 1924 and of its presidium from 1921 to 1924, and actively participated in four Comintern world congresses between 1920 and 1924. In September 1920 Radek addressed the First Congress of the Peoples of the East in Baku, where he urged anti-imperialist revolutions, notably in the British Empire. In the course of 1921 Radek helped formulate the Comintern's "united front" tactics, which sought a rapprochement with Social Democratic workers and organizations by attempting to "turn to the masses." The overall aim, never achieved, was to defeat social democracy "from within" by attracting the majority of workers to the Communist banner. Radek supported these goals both in Europe and Asia, arguing strongly, for instance, that the Chinese Communists should ally themselves with the nationalist proindependence movement, the Guomindang. In April 1922, he was a leading member of the Soviet delegation to the ill-fated meeting of the three Communist Internationals (the Second, Third, and so-called Second-and-a-Half) in Berlin—a gathering that spectacularly failed to overcome the profound mutual suspicions and mistrust between Social Democrats, Communists, and independent left socialists.

On the diplomatic stage, Radek is credited with being an architect of the Rapallo Treaty signed by the USSR and the Weimar Republic in April 1923—an agreement that laid the basis for a close diplomatic and military relationship between the two anti-Versailles pariahs of Europe. In June 1923 he launched a highly controversial, albeit short-lived, innovation that became known as "National Bolshevism." In that month he delivered a famous speech in which he offered a political home—the Communist Party—to disoriented far right German nationalists, who, Radek insisted, held true revolutionary potential. The intention was to split the "deluded" proletarian and lower middle-class nationalists from their fascist leaders, but the result was the ugly spectacle of German Communists sharing platforms with Nazi agitators in denouncing "Jewish capitalists." The episode is relevant as a foretaste of the collaborative actions of Communists and Nazis in the early years of the Great Depression.

Soon after these unedifying events, Radek became a victim of the emergent internecine power struggles in the Soviet party. Together with Trotsky, he was identified by the dominant Zinovyev–Kamenev–Stalin triumvirate as responsible for the fiasco of the "German October" 1923, an abortive revolutionary uprising by German Communists that was easily crushed by the Weimar authorities. In January 1924 Radek was accused by Zinovyev, at that time president of the Comintern, of "right-wing opportunism" for placing too much faith in the "united front from above" (that is, seeking an "organic coalition" with the leaders of social democracy). He was more roundly denounced at the Comintern's Fifth World Congress in June–July 1924 and removed from its Executive Committee. Radek was similarly sacked from the Central Committee of the Soviet party as a leading figure in the Trotskyite Opposition. As compensation, he was appointed to the less-than-prestigious position of rector of the Sun Yat-sen University in Moscow.

At the Fifteenth Party Congress in December 1927 Radek, together with many other oppositionists, was expelled from the Soviet party for his continued factional activities. He was sent into internal exile in Siberia, first to Tobolsk and then to Tomsk, but in summer 1929 after Stalin's "turn to the Left," he broke ranks with Trotsky's supporters, publicly recanted his "mistakes," and was readmitted into the now Stalinized party in 1930. For the next six years Radek enjoyed something of a revival in his fortunes. He served as an editor of the influential daily *Izvestiia*, published numerous articles, and from the early 1930s acted as one of Stalin's advisers on foreign affairs. Indeed, from April 1932 until September 1936 he was head of the Central Committee's Bureau of International Information, a body set up on Stalin's initiative. Also in 1932, Radek attended the Geneva Disarmament Conference and undertook an important diplomatic mission in Poland. The high point of his rehabilitation arguably came in early 1934 after the publication in *Pravda* of an ostensibly obsequious eulogy to Stalin titled "The Architect of Socialist Society." At this time, Radek also helped formulate the Stalinist cultural canon of "socialist realism," and in 1936, together with the prominent former oppositionist Bukharin, he played a leading role in drafting the so-called Stalin Constitution, which formally granted many democratic rights to Soviet citizens. Radek also served Stalin well in another, more sinister

capacity: in his articles he virulently denounced Trotsky, Zinovyev, and Kamenev, and in so doing legitimated the murderous decisions of the first Stalinist show trial in August 1936.

Several of the accused in the Zinovyev-Kamenev case implicated Radek in "counterrevolutionary activities," and he was arrested in September 1936 and charged with treason. This second great show trial began on January 23, 1937. Radek was one of seventeen defendants, with the other high-ranking old Bolsheviks being Iurii Piatakov, Grigorii Sokolnikov, and Leonid Serebriakov. It is reported that Radek himself helped write the script of his interrogations at the trial, displaying, as so often in the past, a bizarre duplicity in Stalinist crimes. Partly because of this acquiescence, he was given the "light" sentence of ten years in the gulag labor camps. Nearly all his codefendants were shot. It is believed that he was killed by a coprisoner in 1939. Almost fifty years later, in 1988, Radek was finally cleared of all charges and posthumously rehabilitated. He was by all accounts a witty, intelligent, and gifted man, but did not always use his many talents for beneficial purposes.

See also Bolshevism; Comintern; Trotskyism.

FURTHER READING

Ken, O. "Karl Radek i Bjuro mezhdunarodnoj informacii CK VKP(b), 1932–1934 gg." *Cahiers du Monde russe* 44, no. 1 (2003).

Lazitch, B., and M. M. Drachkovitch. *Biographical Dictionary of the Comintern.* Stanford, CA: Hoover Institution Press, 1986.

Lerner, W. *Karl Radek: The Last Internationalist.* Stanford, CA: Stanford University Press, 1970.

Tuck, J. *Engine of Mischief: An Analytical Biography of Karl Radek.* New York: Greenwood Press, 1988.

KEVIN F. McDERMOTT

Rajk, László

László Rajk (1909–49), a Hungarian Communist political figure, was born on March 8 in Székelyudverhely (now Odorheiu-Secuiesc, in Romania). He began the study of philology in 1927 at Budapest University, but was expelled for participating in the Communist movement. Rajk joined the illegal Communist Party in 1931, and was arrested more than once by the police of Admiral Horthy's regime. In 1935, still a Romanian citizen, he was exiled from Hungary for participation in construction worker strikes, and went to live in Czechoslovakia. In fall 1937, he was a participant in the Spanish civil war and was a political commissar in one of the Hungarian battalions of the International Brigades. Suspected of sympathies toward Leon Trotsky, Rajk was suspended from membership in the Communist Party. He fled to France with the defeat of the Spanish Republican Army in February 1939, but was then placed in an internment camp. In August 1941, back in Hungary, he joined the Communist underground movement, the charge of Trotskyism against him having been withdrawn. From September 1941 until October 1944 he was in prison.

Immediately after the liberation, Rajk was named a secretary of the reorganized illegal Communist Party of Hungary. His activity helped bring the party closer to other anti-Fascist groups; he was involved in the formation of the so-called Hungarian Front. When the extreme right-wing Nyilashist Party came to power on October 15, 1944, Rajk was again arrested and then deported, first to Austria and later to Bavaria. Returning to Hungary in May 1945, he was made a secretary of the Central Committee of the Communist Party, and in November 1945, became deputy general secretary of the Central Committee. In June 1945, he was made a deputy of the Provisional National Assembly, and then of the Hungarian National and State Assembly. Rajk became minister of internal affairs in March 1946. From this vantage point, he labored unscrupulously to strengthen the position of Communists in the government. The numbers in the Ministry of Internal Affairs and the political role of the police grew substantially under his leadership, and arrests of Communist Party opponents from other anti-Fascist democratic parties became common. Rajk helped initiate the false claim of the existence of an "antirepublican conspiracy," which resulted in the forced retirement, in May 1947, of Prime Minister Ferenc Nagy.

Mátyás Rákosi, seeing in Rajk a dangerous rival, attempted to create a counterweight to him in the person of the head of the political opposition, Peter Gabor, and in August 1948 managed to get Rajk transferred to the less important post of minister of foreign affairs. Though earlier, as minister of internal affairs, Rajk had helped found a society for Hungarian-Yugoslav friendship, he now obediently joined Stalin's anti-Titoist campaign. On May 30, 1949, at the insistence of Rákosi, Rajk was arrested, shorn of his ministerial post, and expelled from the party. Resorting first to methods of physical violence, but then increasingly applying psychological techniques that gave Rajk hope for a chance at survival, special service agents convinced him to agree to a show trial. This trial was staged by Rákosi, with Stalin's consent, and Soviet advisers helped organize it along the lines of the Moscow trials of 1936–38. On September 24, Rajk publicly confessed to falsified accusations of collaboration with Horthy de Nagybánya's police, engaging in espionage for the Western powers and Tito's Yugoslavia, and complicity in an antistate plot to overthrow the "people's democratic government." Rajk received a death sentence and was duly executed on October 15, 1949.

His trial was important in the subsequent escalation of a broad anti-Yugoslav propaganda campaign, launched throughout the whole Communist movement in 1948. In November 1949, the Second Cominform Conference, basing itself largely on the "Rajk affair," approved a resolution titled "The Yugoslav Communist Party in the Hands of Murderers and Spies." In summer 1955, when the USSR and Yugoslavia began to normalize their relations, Rákosi was forced to admit that the main accusations against Rajk had been groundless, and he placed responsibility for the organization of the show trial on Lavrenty Beria and his Hungarian followers.

In March 1956, after the party's Twenty-second Congress, Rajk was rehabilitated. By spring and summer 1956, despite many contradictory biographical facts (often concealed from the public), Hungarian leftist public opinion held a firm view of Rajk as an opponent of Stalinism and a steadfast supporter of a specifically Hungarian path to communism. Rajk was reinterred on October 6 as a gesture toward enhancing Hungarian-Yugoslav relations, and the occasion resulted in a political demonstration by many thousands of Hungarians, which proved to be a prelude to their national uprising on October 23, 1956.

See also Rákosi, Mátyás; Stalinism.

FURTHER READING

Hajdú, T. "Rajk-per háttere és fázisai." *Társadalmi Szemle* 11 (1992): 17–36.

———. "The interrogation of László Rajk, 7 June 1949. Farkas and Kádár visit Rajk." *Hungarian Quarterly* 141 (1996).

Rajk, L. *Laszlo Rajk and His Accomplices before the People's Court.* Budapest: Stephaneum, Janka, 1949.

Soltész, I., ed. *Rajk-dosszié.* Budapest: Lang, 1989.

VJACHESLAV SEREDA AND ALEKSANDR S. STYKALIN

Rákosi, Mátyás

Mátyás Rákosi (1892–1971), a Hungarian political figure, was born on March 9 in Ada, Austria-Hungary (now Serbia), and died on February 5 in Gorky, USSR (now Nizhni Novogorod). He became a member of the Social Democratic Party of Hungary in 1910, and in 1912 graduated from an advanced trade school in Budapest. In 1914, Rákosi left as a volunteer for the Russian front, but was captured by the Russians at the beginning of 1915. He returned to Hungary in 1918.

Rákosi was a member of the Communist Party of Hungary (CPH) from its founding in November 1918. During the Communist dictatorship from March to August 1919, he served as the people's commissar of food. He commanded the Red Guard and served in combat as a political commissar during the conflict between the Hungarian "Soviet Republic" and Czechoslovakia. After the fall of the Communist regime, Rákosi fled to Austria. He was a delegate of the CPH at the Second Congress of the Comintern in Russia, in summer 1920. In 1921, he became a secretary of the Executive Committee of the Comintern, and in December, back in Hungary illegally, helped create underground party structures. In August 1925, at the First Congress of the CPH in Vienna, Rákosi was chosen as one of its secretaries. He was arrested after returning to Hungary in September 1925 and sentenced to life imprisonment, avoiding a death sentence only because of an international protest campaign.

In November 1940, Rákosi was freed from prison and given the opportunity to go to the USSR, where he became head of the CPH. On February 22, 1945, Rákosi returned to Hungary and was named general secretary of the CPH's Central Committee. He was made vice premier of the government in November 1945. In spring 1946, he led the Communists' attack on the party of the petty landowners, which in May 1947 resulted in the dismissal of Prime Minister Ferenc Nagy and the removal from political life of other parties opposed to the Communists. In June 1948, after the Hungarian Social Democratic Party was purged of persons opposed to unification with the Communists, Rákosi became head of the United Hungarian Party of Working People, which became the sole political power in the country. Rákosi ousted his rivals from the former Communist underground and left-wing Social Democrats during the period from 1949 to 1951. Among these rivals, László Rajk was executed, and János Kádár,

Arpad Szakasits, and Gyorgy Marosan were sentenced to life imprisonment. In August 1952, Rákosi became prime minister of Hungary, a post he held until June 1953.

By early 1950, Rákosi's efforts had created a Stalin-type system of strict control over the economy and the nation's spiritual life; it was a harshly repressive system, in which Rákosi achieved a cultlike status as the "first person in the party" (Hungarian propaganda of the time referred to him as "Stalin's best Hungarian pupil"). Rákosi began to carry out a Stalinist plan in 1951 for strengthening Hungary's military potential. This program of transforming Hungary into a country of "iron and steel" led to a merciless exploitation of the nation's internal resources and a precipitous decline in people's standard of living. In June 1953, aware of Hungary's unfavorable economic situation, which threatened to destabilize the Hungarian Communist political regime, the leadership of the Soviet Communist Party subjected Rákosi to harsh criticism, which forced him to cede the post of prime minister to Imre Nagy.

From the outset, Rákosi waged a struggle against Nagy's program, which was aimed at liberalizing the Communist regime and changing the nation's economic priorities. In spring 1955, playing on the dissatisfaction of USSR leaders with the course of the Hungarian reforms, Rákosi succeeded in having Nagy removed from his post as prime minister. After the Twentieth Congress of the Soviet Communist Party in 1956, though, Rákosi was subjected to ever harsher public criticism. In July 1956, having lost Moscow's support, he was relieved of his duties as first secretary of the Hungarian Workers' Party and left for the USSR.

During the Hungarian Revolution of 1956 and after its suppression, Rákosi attempted to influence political processes in Hungary. The question of what to do with Rákosi was decided in 1957, when Khrushchev agreed to Kádár's request for political isolation of the erstwhile Hungarian prime minister. By a decision of the presidium of the Central Committee of the Soviet Communist Party, approved on April 18, 1957, Rákosi was made a political exile; his place of residence was first to be Krasnodar, but it was later changed to Tokmak in Kirgizstan, and after that, to Arzamas and Gorky. In 1962 Rákosi was expelled from the Hungarian Socialist Workers' Party. During his exile, he worked on his memoirs, which despite their tendentiousness, are of some limited interest as a historical source.

See also Cult of Personality; Hungarian Republic of Councils; Kádár, János; Rajk, László; Stalinism.

FURTHER READING

Feitl, I. *A bukott Rákosi*. Budapest: Politikatörténeti Alapítvány, 1993.

János, R. M. *Távirat "Filippov" elvtársnak Rákosi Mátyás üzenetei Sztálin titkárságának, 1949–1952*. Budapest: Intézet Evkönyve, 1998.

Pünkösti, A. *Rákosi a hatalomért*. Budapest: Európa Könyvkiadó, 1992.

———. *Rákosi a csúcson*. Budapest: Európa, 1996.

———. *Rákosi bukása, száműzetése és halála, 1953–1971*. Budapest: Európa, 2001.

Rákosi, M. *Válogatott beszédek és cikkek*. Budapest: Szikra, 1955.

———. *Visszaemlékezések 1940–1956*. 2 vols. Budapest: Napvilág Kiadó, 1997.

———. *Visszaemlékezések 1892–1925*. 2 vols. Budapest: Napvilág Kiadó, 2002.

Sereda, V. T., and A. S. Stykalin, eds. *Ljudiam svojstvenno ošibat'sja. Iz vospominanij M. Rakoši*. Moskva: Istoričeskij Archiv, 1997, 1998, 1999.

Varga, T. G., ed. *Jegyzőkönyv a szovjet és a Magyar part-és állami vezetők tárgyalásairól (1953. Június 13–16)*. Budapest: Múltunk, 1992.

VJACHESLAV SEREDA AND ALEKSANDR S. STYKALIN

Rapallo Treaty

Under the terms of the Rapallo Treaty, the governments of Soviet Russia and Germany mutually renounced claim to reparation for damages suffered or expenditures incurred as a result of the conflict between them during the world war of 1914–18. The German government agreed, moreover, not to contest the validity and legality of the Soviet decrees expropriating and nationalizing German state and private assets in Russia following the 1917 revolution. The two nations established full and formal diplomatic relations, and agreed to mutual most favored nation trade policies. The agreement was concluded and signed on April 16, 1922, in Genoa, Italy, by Walter Rathenau, the German foreign minister, and Georgii Chicherin, the Soviet commissar for foreign affairs. The Bolshevik government was for the first time recognized as legitimate by a major European power. The possibility that the nations with reparation claims against Germany would be able to take fully united action was precluded.

Nor would the capitalist states be able to present a united front of debt collectors against Russia.

The benefits to Moscow were extant and immediate. The Bolshevik Russia broke out of diplomatic isolation from the world powers. It was a first victory for the doctrine of "peaceful coexistence" propounded by Lenin, and promulgated by Chicherin and the Narkomindel—to wit, Russia had the right to organize its economic life according to socialist principles within a capitalist system of nation-states, be treated as a normal state within that system, and have full diplomatic relations, regular international trade, and foreign loans. Narkomindel presented the Rapallo Treaty as the model on which relations between Soviet Russia and the capitalist states would be established. That would be done not by international conferences, such as that being held in Genoa at the time and by multilateral agreements, but rather by separate negotiations with individual states and bilateral treaties.

German businesspeople and diplomats recognized the potential value of improved commerce between Germany and Russia. For Ago von Maltzan, the architect of Germany's "eastern policy," however, the fundamental purpose of Rapallo was to improve Germany's international situation by establishing a special relationship with Russia. The allies would thereby be continuously under the threat of a Russo-German combination. German diplomacy would gain in independence and be less subject to the diplomacy of the former allies.

Neither the governments, foreign ministries, nor newspaper press of Europe were prepared for a formal agreement between the two major powers antagonistic to the Great War peace settlement. It caused a sensation and temporarily interrupted the massive international economic conference being held in nearby Genoa. In Western public opinion the treaty took on mythical proportions. For decades thereafter, Rapallo denoted a Russo-German conspiracy and a menace to the West that combined the industrial and organizational capabilities of the Germans with the vast raw materials of the Soviet regime. Still, during the twelve years that the Rapallo relation persisted—it expired soon after the advent of the Hitler government in Germany in 1933—neither Germany nor Russia ever came to the diplomatic assistance of the other, and the two states took no joint diplomatic actions. Nor did German statespeople "play the Russian card": use the threat of closer relations with Russia to gain diplomatic leverage in London or Paris. German lending to Russia was limited; so were Russian purchases from Germany. The most tangible form of cooperation was clandestine military collaboration—the joint development and testing of weapons and equipment, officer training, and joint maneuvers done in secret in Russia—particularly during the years 1927–32.

See also Cult of Personality; Khrushchev, Nikita; Stalin, Joseph; Stalinism.

FURTHER READING

Fink, C., A. Frohn, and J. Heideking, eds. *Genoa, Rapallo, and European Reconstruction in 1922.* Cambridge, UK: Cambridge University Press, 1991.

Salzmann, S. *Great Britain, Germany, and the Soviet Union: Rapallo and After, 1922–1934.* Woodbridge, UK: Royal Historical Society, 2003.

JON S. JACOBSON

Real Socialism

The concept of "real'nyy sotsializm"—real socialism, or actually existing socialism—emerged in the Soviet Union during the Brezhnev era. It was a reaction against the idea that there could be different models of socialism, including ones much superior to that found in the USSR. The "Prague Spring" and the rise of Eurocommunism were among the stimuli to this response of Soviet orthodoxy to the threat to the Soviet Union's ideological hegemony in the international Communist movement.

Real socialism was to be distinguished from all forms of utopian socialism, and from the ideas of both socialists of a Social Democratic orientation and dissident Communists in Western Europe. According to Soviet theorists, these false prophets of socialism never had been able to build a socialist system, and never would be, in contrast to the actual socialist systems that were to be found in the USSR and the countries led by its orthodox allies in Eastern Europe. The notion of real socialism became, in essence, a conservative defense of the Soviet system. Its elaborators insisted that there was and could be only one socialism—built on Leninist principles—which had achieved its fullest realization thus far in the Soviet Union.

The principal features of real socialism were "democratic centralism," understood as strict discipline within the Communist Party, with narrowly defined possibilities for discussion, and the decisions of higher party organs absolutely binding on lower organs; the "leading role" of the party that became little more than a euphemism for the monopoly of power of the Communist Party; and state or cooperative ownership of the means of production, which became a justification of a highly bureaucratized and centralized economy.

In essence, orthodox Marxist-Leninist theorists in the Soviet Union and Eastern Europe, between the 1970s and the mid-1980s (and the launch of perestroika), used "really existing socialism" as a synonym for what most Western analysts would call Communist systems. In the eyes of Soviet ideologists, there was "wishful thinking socialism"—the kind of ideas that appealed to intellectuals, but that had not become concrete reality in any country—and the socialism that despite a few "shortcomings," had actually been built in the Soviet Union under the guidance of the Communist Party.

Soviet theorists were at great pains to deny that the "socialism" that had been built in the USSR was a specifically Russian phenomenon. Leonid Brezhnev, in a speech marking the sixtieth anniversary of the Bolshevik Revolution in 1977, stated that "general, fundamental, and inalienable features of socialist revolution and socialist construction remain and preserve their force." The choice was between the power of the working class and that of the bourgeoisie. There was no third way.

In reality, even within the International Department of the Central Committee of the Communist Party of the Soviet Union there were closet dissenters who were attracted by other "models" of socialism. Early in the perestroika period the concept of real socialism—along with the notion that the Soviet Union was an example of "developed socialism"—was abandoned, as an increasingly self-critical attitude was taken toward what had been constructed in Russia in the name of socialism. The concept had arisen as a defense against heterodox ideas. Once such ideas were increasingly welcomed in Gorbachev's USSR, there was no place for the complacent concept of real socialism. Indeed, far from living under actually existing socialism, Gorbachev and the more radical of his advisers gradually came to believe that what had been constructed in the Soviet Union was not socialism at all, since socialism, as they had come to understand it, was inseparable from democracy. Yet democracy, prior to perestroika, was conspicuous by its absence in Russia.

See also Eurocommunism; Marxism-Leninism; Perestroika; Prague Spring.

FURTHER READING

Brown, A. *The Rise and Fall of Communism.* New York: Ecco, 2009.

Mitin, M. B., ed. *Razvitoy sotsializm i krizis "sovetologii."* Moscow: Nauka, 1982.

Zinoviev, A. *The Reality of Communism.* London: Gollancz, 1984.

ARCHIE BROWN

Red Army

The Red Army of workers and peasants was instituted by revolutionary government decree on January 28, 1918. The decree included provisions allowing recruitment to the new army to be voluntary, while recruitment to the officer corps was to be elective. In this respect it did not differ from Red Guard units' regulations; these units had been formed by some city soviets in the months following the February Revolution and were meant to function as nuclei of a territorial workers' militia. There were also provisions enabling Red Army units to form "soldier committees" similar to those that, following the enactment of order no. 1 by the Petrograd Soviet on March 15, 1917, had been created within the old imperial army, starting a few days after the October Revolution and lasting until its demobilization. In contrast to traditional military rules and ethos, the Red Army's cohesion was intended to be a product of its social homogeneity (although in addition to workers, the army would also welcome poor working peasants) and its "discipline of awareness"—that is, a discipline not imposed on the soldiers. Finally, the new army would adopt "partisan warfare" as the fighting tactic most in line with its revolutionary principles. The first units of the Red Army, picked up here and there, poorly armed and undisciplined, demonstrated their inefficiency while fighting the German advance on Petrograd and Ukraine in February 1918.

In the weeks following the Treaty of Brest-Litovsk, Leon Trotsky (who had become war commissar on March 4) started to take a realistic approach to transforming the Red Army into a true "regular" army, one based on obligatory conscription, traditional discipline, and the nomination of officers from above. The officers of the old army were also recalled to arms, and in the following years almost a third of the old officer corps, many of whom were from the previous general staff, ended up responding to the revolutionary regime's call. This came about partly because of a direct threat against their families, and partly because of the new power's legitimacy and a tormented nationalism, which manifested itself during the war against Poland (April–September 1920). Military (or political) commissars, mostly Bolshevik, were placed at the new commanders' side (both ex-czarist and revolutionary), from the level of company commander to that of commander in chief; their task was to ensure the commander's loyalty, countersign their orders, and maintain discipline and morale among the soldiers. The nonparty soldiers' committees were dissolved, and replaced by a network of Bolshevik committees and cells.

In the new army, the party members reinterpreted the libertarian and antimilitarist spirit that had motivated the soldiers' committees in the ex-imperial army in 1917. The idea began to spread among the soldiers of the political primacy of the party cells and committees over the professional officers and commissars, and the need for the civil territorial party organs and their Central Committee to exercise control over army life. The new course was met with hostility by those Bolsheviks who supported a territorial militia, and was openly criticized by the Left Communist group. The latter was afraid that the Red Army would become a separate entity within the revolutionary state, independent from the soviets and the party's civil organizations. They accused the military administration of attempting to subordinate the Communist soldiers' organizations in the army to the authority of the political commissars and ex-czarist officers.

In June 1918, both the Revolutionary Military Council of the Republic, which was formed by high-ranking officers and commissars, and presided over by a war commissar, and the commander in chief position, which was given ample powers, were created. The new military organization took shape in the battle to reconquer Kazan, in the Urals, from the Czech Legion (Czech ex–prisoners of war) during August–September 1918. On this occasion, the authority of the officers and commissars over the Red soldiers (including those who were party members) was strengthened by punitive measures, recommended by Trotsky, and resented by those Bolsheviks who were critical of the regular army. In the winter of 1918–19 the military administration enacted a true "militarization of the Red Army," suppressing the political autonomy of the Communist soldiers' cells and committees. The latter organizations were subjected to the military commissars and the newly instituted "political sections" (*politotdel*) at the division, army corps, and army group level. Under the direction of high-ranking military commissars these new organs monopolized the organizational and propaganda work of the party, military, and political intelligence, and relations with the civil institutions of the state and party. The hybrid politicoadministrative nature of the political sections, which undertook both party and administrative-military tasks, caused further scandal within the Bolshevik ranks.

A new center of opposition to official military policies developed among Bolshevik military leaders operating in the Red units on the southern front (in the northern Caucasus, with headquarters in the city of Carycin, later known as Stalingrad) under Joseph Stalin's command. At the end of September they questioned the presence of officers from the old army in the Red Army and refused to recognize ex-general N. Sytin (an emissary of Trotsky and the Military Revolutionary Council of the Republic) as commander of the front. In the ensuing struggle, Stalin and Kliment Voroshilov emerged as the losers, but at the party's Eighth Congress, in March 1919, Trotsky had to face a vast "military opposition," which extended from numerous ex–Left Communists to troops from Carycin. Lenin took Trotsky's side, thus ensuring the victory of official military policies. The party's organs in the army (cells, commissars, and political sections) were permanently organized according to a disciplined hierarchy, integrated into the command hierarchy and subordinate to it—called the Political Administration of the Revolutionary Military Council of the Red Army (PUR). The PUR's authoritarian-bureaucratic nature represented an exception to the theoretical principles on which Bolshevik civil and territorial organization was based, since these were officially rooted in democratic centralism.

With the end of the civil war, demobilization, and the shift to the New Economic Policy, the Red Army and the PUR entered a prolonged period of political and organizational uncertainty. In addition to the ever-present utopian expectation that with the end of military operations, the Red Army would be able to transform itself into a socialist territorial militia, one not based on the separation between civilian labor and the military training of the recruits, the Soviet state now added its own worries about the high cost of maintaining a large regular army. During the first years of uncertainty about the Red Army's future (1921–22), the PUR ran the risk of being marginalized and even reabsorbed by Soviet civilian state and party bureaucracies, which were still not reconciled to a separate body within the political system of the dictatorship of the proletariat. On the one hand, the choice of a territorial system of militias threatened to transfer greater control over military units to the party's civilian

territorial organs; on the other hand, the Commissariat for Education attempted to bring the PUR structure into the Glavpolitprosvet apparatus, one of its offshoots whose aim was the instruction and political education of the entire population. Moreover, at the end of 1923 the then-head of PUR, Vladimir Antonov-Ovseenko tried to loosen the organizational rules preventing Communist soldiers from participating in the general discussion raised in the party by the left opposition. The party leadership rejected all these attempts at demilitarizing the Communist soldiers' organization.

The Soviet army ended up with a "mixed" configuration: a mass training of a "militia" type (above all in the infantry) and the maintenance of a restricted nucleus of war-ready permanent units. The reform was carried out by Mikhail Frunze, who in 1924–25 was first assistant war commissar and later war commissar in place of Trotsky, who had resigned. Frunze was later replaced by Voroshilov, who in the course of a few years, managed to include new commanders who were party members into army units, replacing the old czarist cadres. The problem of harmonizing the powers of the military commander with those of the political commissar was thus rendered less dramatic. The number of units and technical modernization of the permanent nucleus constantly increased until 1935, when the mixed system finally gave way to an entirely "regular" one.

This development was due to both internal and international circumstances. In the early 1930s army officers in commanding positions who supported reequipping the armed forces with more modern military technology across the board, starting with the units' mechanization, gained the upper hand. During collectivization, moreover, the fact that dissatisfaction had spread across the countryside suggested not only that military units (mostly composed of peasant recruits) be kept out of this process but also that their attention be focused on other activities, especially those of a military nature, such as training and preparation for combat. Finally the Japanese invasion of Manchuria (September 1931), the National Socialists' rise to power in Germany (January 1933), the war in Ethiopia (September 1935), and German rearmament in the Rhineland (March 1936) brought up once more, with ever-increasing urgency, the need for a large army that was operationally ready. In 1936, the allocation of funds for rearmament and modernization, and both the size and number of Red Army units, increased massively.

What had already been revealed as a typical characteristic of Soviet planning in the field of accelerated industrialization, now also affected the ultra-ambitious military planning in the second half of the 1930s: it suffered from both gigantism, and the difficulties faced by the military high command and Soviet government in translating this immense economic and organizational effort into practice in an orderly fashion. On the eve of World War II the new military technology, which had been injected into the army in large doses, was not adequately distributed among the units, and recruits and commanders, especially those of inferior rank, had not had any experience operating it. The new large divisions of mechanized and armored infantry had difficulty filling the ranks with planned contingents of regulars. The purges that Stalin had started in the army in the summer of 1937 also led to the disorganization, demoralization, and degradation of the commanding officer corps. Tens of thousands of officers of every rank and from every branch were dismissed, and several thousand were summarily executed after being accused of connivance with the potential enemy. Many of those who survived were later reinstated, but the purges had the effect of disrupting the chain of command for a long period of time, and reducing both the discipline and capability for initiative in the officer corps. Under these circumstances, those who were promoted in place of those who had been purged did not have the opportunity to mature and adapt professionally to their new tasks.

This heritage did not affect the Soviet armored divisions' ability to keep the Japanese army at bay in a series of skirmishes and actual battles on the border with Manchuria in 1938; but it could instead be felt in the difficult campaign against Finland in the winter of 1939–40, and above all in the first months of the surprise German attack, following June 21, 1941, when the Red Army suffered what were proportionally the greatest losses of the war in terms of people and matériel. In addition to the preexisting political reasons for the disaster, there were Stalin's orders (who had assumed the position of commander in chief) to respond to the invasion with a blindly offensive action, inspired by an arrogant military doctrine elaborated in the years before the war, which in its own fashion reflected the radical political voluntarism of the Stalinist system. As combat operations continued, however, the Soviet high command gradually acquired the compactness, discipline, and operational capacity that allowed the Red Army to make up for its lack of preparedness for a large-scale war and its adversary's military superiority. The war essentially selected a number of commanders endowed with military talent, and the

political authorities (Stalin, most especially) were wise enough not to interfere in high-level military decisions, or when interfering to attempt to follow the rules of the art of war and military conduct.

The transfer to the east of a large part of the industrial plants threatened by the invasion of the Western parts of the country, along with the planning of production implemented by the government, allowed for continuity in the supply of armaments, equipment, and provisions to the fighting army. Toward the end of the war, the Red Army's superiority over the enemy in terms of armaments and logistical support was assured by the massive flow of aid from the United States, by means of air and sea routes in the Pacific. The Soviet victories in the battles of Stalingrad, in the winter of 1942–43, and Kursk, the following July, decided the outcome of the conflict on the eastern front and decisively contributed to the German defeat in World War II. In summer of 1944, the Red Army crossed the Soviet borders and began liberating Eastern Europe from the German army, an advance which concluded at the end of the following April with the conquest of Berlin by General Georgy Zhukov. In some localities in Eastern Europe (Budapest, for instance) and especially in the German regions occupied by the Red Army, many of its soldiers and units were involved in a wave of violence, rapes, and acts of pillage against the local population. In August 1945, the Red Army briefly fought Japanese troops in Manchuria before they surrendered to the United States. Soviet military losses in World War II amounted to eight million soldiers.

In 1946 the Red Army changed its name to the Soviet Army, as part of the regime's attempt to suggest that the USSR had reached a final stage of consolidation by the state, and that a long cycle of revolutionary transformations and emergency situations that had succeeded one another since 1917 had come to an end. In 1955 the Soviet Army became part of the newly constituted Warsaw Pact, a military alliance that grouped the armed forces of the Communist regimes of Eastern Europe (minus Yugoslavia) together. The USSR managed to create its first atomic bomb in late 1949, and in the early 1960s its party secretary, Nikita Khrushchev, established a new defensive posture, in which a stronger Soviet nuclear deterrent was supposed to allow for a drastic reduction in its land-based forces. When Leonid Brezhnev succeeded Khrushchev, he abandoned this course of action. The USSR reached parity with the United States in terms of its nuclear arsenal around 1970, but in the second half of the following decade the Soviet government, while continuing to modernize its conventional weaponry, started to reinforce its navy so as to exercise its influence globally—an influence that was supposed to be both detailed at the logistical level and flexible on the strategic level. The sales of arms to friendly nations intensified, and the presence of military advisers and special forces in some regimes and political movements in the world, especially in Africa, became less discrete.

On some occasions the Soviet Army went beyond its borders. It squelched the radical popular uprising for democratization and national independence in Hungary in November 1956. In August 1968, in collaboration with forces from the Warsaw Pact, it intervened to prevent a similar development in Czech socialism's movement for democratization. At the end of the 1980s the Soviet Army entered Afghanistan to eliminate the power vacuum that had been created following the deposition of the king by local Communists in 1977. This was the beginning of a long and bloody war against well-trained guerrillas, inspired by a nationalist and Islamist agenda, which continued until 1988.

Following the USSR's dissolution, the Soviet Army ceased to exist as a unitary army. Its principal successor, the army of the Russian Federation, was instituted on May 7, 1992.

See also Borders; Great Patriotic War, Rhetoric of; Militarization; Military-Industrial Complex; Russian Revolution and Civil War; Second Cold War; Soviets; Sovietization; Soviet Occupation of Germany; Stalingrad, Battle of; Trotsky, Leon; Tukhachevskii, Mikhail; Voroshilov, Kliment.

FURTHER READING

Benvenuti, F. *The Bolsheviks and the Red Army*. Cambridge, UK: Cambridge University Press, 1988.

Erickson, J. *The Soviet High Command: A Military-Political History, 1918–1941*. New York: St. Martin's Press, 1962.

———. *The Road to Stalingrad*. London: Weidenfeld and Nicholson, 1975.

———. *The Road to Berlin*. London: Grafton Books, 1983.

Glantz, D. M. *Stumbling Colossus: The Red Army on the Eve of World War*. Lawrence: University Press of Kansas, 1998.

Glantz, D. M., and J. M. House. *When Titans Clashed: How the Red Army Stopped Hitler*. Lawrence: University Press of Kansas, 1995.

Kavtaradze, A. G. *Voennye spetsialisty na sluzhbe Respubliki Sovetov, 1917–1920 gg*. Moscow: Nauka, 1988.

Nation, R. C. *Black Earth, Red Star: A History of Soviet Security Policy, 1917–1991*. Ithaca, NY: Cornell University Press, 1992.

Reese, R. R. *Stalin's Reluctant Soldiers: A Social History of the Red Army, 1921–1941*. Lawrence: University Press of Kansas, 1996.

Romano, A. *Contadini in uniforme: l'Armata Rossa e la collettivizzazione delle campagne nell'URSS*. Florence: Olschki, 1999.

Von Hagen, M. *Soldiers in the Proletarian Dictatorship: The Red Army and the Soviet Socialist State, 1917–1930*. Ithaca, NY: Cornell University Press, 1990.

Ziemke, E. F. *The Red Army, 1918–1941*. London: Frank Cass, 2004.

FRANCESCO BENVENUTI

Red Guard

The Red Guard was a unique phenomenon in China's recent history of revolution. Globally it may be regarded as part of the rebellion of youth against state authorities that also occurred in Europe and North America. In China it was an integral component of the Cultural Revolution (CR) instigated by Mao Zedong in 1966 to realize his vision of socialism. Although the Red Guard existed only briefly (1966–69), its impact on China's political and social development is profound and it will be long remembered.

The Origin of the Red Guard

The roots of the Red Guard can be traced to a worsening of policy dispute in the leadership of the Chinese Communist Party (CCP). After the Great Leap Forward, Mao retreated to the second tier of leadership, leaving the daily management of state and CCP affairs to the first tier leadership centered in state president Liu Shaoqi, Zhou Enlai, and Deng Xiaoping. Liu and Deng realized that Mao's utopian methods of social change were too divorced from the country's reality. If allowed to continue, they would only do further damage to the party. Less than openly they began to mend the excesses of Mao's policy line. In the cities they restored the bonus system, while in the countryside farmers were provided with private land on which to grow cash corps.

By 1965 Mao had decided to launch a counterattack. As the inner party struggle intensified, the offspring of Mao's close followers (mostly in the military) got word from their parents that some leaders in the party were plotting against Mao. Some of them, students in the Affiliated School of the Qinghua University, organized themselves in the spring of that year under the name of the "Red Guard." They published a series of manifestos declaring war on Mao's opponents. Mao praised their rebellious behavior highly. Very quickly the youth rebellion spread across China and triggered a massive student movement against the authorities. There is no accurate figure of the membership of the Red Guard, but at least 300 million people were involved.

The Red Guard and the Cultural Revolution

The Red Guard was the product of the Cultural Revolution. It was linked to the CR in three ways. First, it served as an instrument in the CCP's power struggle. The Red Guard was initially formed to protect Mao, who instigated a mass purge of the followers of Liu and Deng as the "capitalist roaders." For self-protection the latter also organized their supporters under the name of the Red Guard. This gave rise to the deep divisions within the Red Guard, and confrontations between these factions escalated into an all-out "civil war." Thousands of Red Guards were killed in what was known as the "ferocious fist fight." They disagreed on almost everything, from the evaluation of the seventeen-year history of the PRC since 1949 to methods of classroom teaching.

Second, the Red Guard rebellion reflected deep flaws in state-society relations. As in any authoritarian system, absolute power corrupts and the people bear the brunt. After seventeen years in power many CCP cadres had turned themselves into tyrants whose unchecked power and privileges were resented by the people. Mao saw the masses' alienation from a party that was increasingly bureaucratized. When he called upon them to rebel, he also unleashed the popular anger, resulting in their beating and persecuting officials.

Third, the Cultural Revolution was waged to persecute those without a "correct family background." The population was sorted into classes determined by social status, possession of wealth, and even length of education before 1949. The Red Guard significantly worsened social conflicts between the different classes. Acting as representatives of the proletariat they applied negative class labels to social elites and attacked them both mentally and physically. Beating, smashing, and robbing became the routine activities of the Red Guard during the early days of the CR.

The Nature of the Red Guard Movement

The CR was the indicator of the Chinese revolution reaching the highest point of radicalization since the 19th century. It was through this movement that Mao attempted to build his Communist utopia in China: a society without bureaucrats, without differences of wealth or social status, and without private motivations or selfishness of any kind. The Red Guard, as the least privileged members of society, was the most eager to embrace Mao's vision. And the way in which its members carried out Mao's transformation was as crude as it was simple: creation through destruction, a Maoist revolutionary logic.

The Red Guard raised a banner of uncompromising destruction: do away with all old culture, old habits, the old ways of life and thinking. They set out to smash national treasures, close schools, and persecute professionals, thinking that their actions would advance the revolution. They proved one thing: that this was a revolution in which there was only destruction, nothing positive was created. In the end the Red Guard simply became anarchists, despising all authorities, until they themselves seized power illegally or with the encouragement of Mao.

The Tragic End of the Red Guard

What the Red Guard did not know was that Mao depended on CCP authorities to run state affairs. As a ruler, he could not afford to destroy everything, and it was not long before the behavior of the Red Guard ran counter to Mao's practical interests. By the beginning of 1969 he had succeeded in removing his opponents (imagined or real) from office. What he wanted next was order, not destruction. The existence of the Red Guard ran counter to that goal, and Mao ordered PLA troops to take over school, factories, and institutions where the Red Guard was still active.

The majority of the Red Guard members were sent to the countryside for reeducation. They did not realize that they had been removed from the cities largely because the government could not provide them with industrial jobs. For some time they still believed that theirs was a noble course, that they were helping to transform the backward villages. In the next decade more than 30 million urban youth were forced to temper themselves with hard labor under harsh conditions with little hope for returning to their cities, and still less for opportunity for higher education. Eventually they truly became China's lost generation.

See also Cultural Revolution in China; Mao Zedong; Maoism; Utopia.

FURTHER READING

Chan, A. *Children of Mao: Personality Development, Political Activism in the Red Guards Generation.* Seattle: University of Washington Press, 1985.

Fengyuan, J. *Linguistic Engineering: Language and Politics in Mao's China.* Honolulu: University of Hawaii Press, 2004.

Rosen, S. *Red Guard Factionalism and the Cultural Revolution in Guangzhou.* Boulder, CO: Westview Press, 1982.

Walder, G. "Beijing Red Guard Factionalism: Social Interpretations Reconsidered." *Journal of Asian Studies* 61 (May 2002): 437–71.

YOU JI

Red Terror

It is a widely held opinion that the 20th century experienced a crescendo of violence, and starting with World War II, its main victim has been the civilian population. The distinctive nature of "Red Terror" within this more general trend can be more easily grasped by examining the origin of the term. From the French Revolution onward, even before it became a concrete reality, terror has been a metaphor for the will to achieve political results by using violence against certain social, ethnic, and political groups, rather than specific individuals. Terror's success is measured not so much by the number of its victims but rather by the political results it achieves.

The archetypal experience of Red Terror occurred in the Soviet Union, where it assumed all those traits that anchor it solidly to modernity: duration over time, widespread presence, being based on an organized plan, and being ideologically legitimized. During the course of its long evolution the terror targeted both real enemies within the USSR who had taken up arms against the regime and social groups that had developed before the revolution (the intelligentsia, the "bourgeois," and the kulaks). It created the abstract concept of "enemy of the people," and used it against the party's *nomenklatura* and the new "scientific and technical intelligentsia," a product of industrialization. It also targeted some national minorities (Poles, Ukrainians, and Baltic peoples both before and after the war, and later also Koreans, Greeks, and Kurds) because they were deemed untrustworthy, or by using unfounded accusations of collaborationism. Before Stalin's death about eighteen million

people entered the gulag: common criminals and people who opposed the regime, but also party members and even some "executioners" who had been responsible for the repressions. The total numbers are enormous, and yet they only represent the tip of a repressive pyramid that included measures like deportation (targeting an almost equivalent number of people) and various forms of forced labor. This repressive machinery could function both thanks to the work of an omnipresent political police, and because of the presence of such a dense network of informers that it reduced Soviet citizens to the status of special objects of surveillance and, in many cases, also accomplices of the regime.

In the countries of Eastern Europe, the imitation of the Soviet model was aided by the presence in the higher ranks of power or the security services of leaders who had personally participated in the Stalinist repressions. Party purges and show trials against Communist leaders, who were accused of being "double agents," started in 1948. The policies of the Chinese Communist regime, once it had seized power, followed an evolution similar to the Soviet one. The first targets were the "counterrevolutionaries": wealthy peasants, bourgeoisie, bureaucracy, urban lumpenproletariat, and Christians. The noose later tightened around intellectuals, victims of the failure of the "Hundred Flowers" campaign that Mao Zedong had launched in 1957. At the end of the decade he unleashed an attack against Tibet that because of its numerous victims (between one-fifth and one-quarter of the population), is seen by many as the attempted genocide of a population that was part of a Buddhist culture and incompatible with official ideology. Finally during the late 1960s, the Red Guard launched an assault against the party's, state's, and army's leaderships.

The application of repressive practices modeled on the Soviet precedent did not erase the peculiarity of the individual experiences, since they were connected to different national traditions as well as historical and political contexts. In central Eastern Europe the historical context prevented the terror from acquiring the radical characteristics it had exhibited in the USSR. In 1956 in Hungary, in 1968 in Czechoslovakia, and on several occasions in Poland, violence was used to fight real opponents of the socialist regimes and not imaginary enemies of the people. In Communist China the number of the terror's victims was approximately as large as in the USSR. The way the terror evolved was different. The establishment of communes in the countryside, starting in 1958, was not accompanied by violence comparable to Soviet collectivization, even though it occurred during a devastating famine, much like in the Soviet Union in 1932–33. The appeal that Mao addressed to the Red Guard, to "storm the headquarters," would have been unthinkable in Stalin's USSR. The purge of the party's leadership was accomplished with less radical measures, and this allowed many victims to return to the political scene and be protagonists of the attack on Mao's legacy. In terms of the number of prisoners (some estimates are as high as fifty million) the *laogai* was the Chinese equivalent of the gulag. Its prisoners were mostly political, however, and the regime attempted to reeducate them with little success.

Ephemeral socialist regimes in Latin America and Africa (with the significant exception of Cuba) have never emerged from the state of civil war, whether open or intermittent, that had given rise to them, and this led to their collapse. In Cambodia, the Khmer Rouge regime practiced its "revolutionary pedagogy" between 1975 and 1979 by sacrificing the lives of at least a quarter of the country's inhabitants, only to then collapse, swept away by violence and the Vietnamese invasion. The number of victims of the North Korean regime is difficult to establish, but must be on the order of several million. And yet this regime has resisted for more than half a century using repression in order to form a totalitarian regime, founded on the theocratic legitimation of power.

The most important common trait in all these experiences of Red Terror is the central role played by bureaucratic apparatuses. In those cases in which violence was exercised "from below," it soon produced an uncontrollable mechanism that in turn produced excesses and anarchy (the Cultural Revolution is the most significant example of this kind). On the opposite end, the presence of forms of hierarchical control, gave the terror organized features, like the prophylactic liquidation of enemies and the evolution of a process of ethical deresponsibilization of those who executed these repressive activities, tied to the division of labor that is characteristic of complex bureaucratic institutions. The socialist countries' peculiarity in this process is due to the historical context in which they arose, which was linked to war in one way or another. It is difficult to understand the history of the Soviet Union, the socialist countries of central Eastern Europe, socialist China, North Korea, and Vietnam without taking into account that they were formed in the course of two world wars, accompanied by foreign invasions, and followed by a long civil war. The choice of socialism made by other countries was connected to the violence of the decolonization process.

Both war and victory show that claiming ties to the precedent of the French Revolution was not only propaganda; organized violence could be used to form a new society and not only to destroy the past's legacy. The hope of being able to accelerate the course of history soon disappeared, and was replaced by a more pragmatic vision of modernization and socialism as long-term processes, during which the control of current realities became the dominant preoccupation. The figure of the charismatic leader that sooner or later emerged in all socialist countries is the emblem of the unresolved contradiction between these two moments. This figure was in all cases both the repository of a revolutionary ideology that was never disavowed and a mediator in the disputes generated by the divergent interests of the state apparatuses, including those devoted to violence, and stratified societies in which the original ideals of equality were soon abandoned. In terms of actual historical developments, none of the leaders of these Communist regimes was able to intervene effectively to correct terror strategies in those cases in which they had become dysfunctional, and this was one of the factors that would eventually lead to the demise of the regimes themselves. The same sequence had also occurred during the French Revolution: the reaction to the terror occurred not at the time it was causing the greatest number of victims but instead when it had come to be exercised sporadically, for personal reasons, no longer tied to any political program, and it had therefore lost its aura of invincibility. At least on this count, the Red Terror was not a unique historical phenomenon.

See also Camps; Collectivization of the Countryside; Cultural Revolution in China; Deportation of Nationalities in the USSR; Enemies of the People; Famine under Communism; Great Leap Forward; Gulag; Holodomor; Jacobinism; KGB.

FURTHER READING

Applebaum, A. *Gulag: A History*. New York: Doubleday, 2003.

Bettanin, F. *Il lungo terrore. Politica e repressioni in URSS*. Rome: Editori Riuniti, 1999.

Domenach, J.-L. *Chine: l'archipel oublié*. Paris: Fayard, 1995.

Kotek, J., and P. Rigoulot. *Il secolo dei campi. Detenzione, concentramento, sterminio*. Milan: Mondadori, 2001.

Short, P. *Pol Pot: The History of a Nightmare*. London: John Murray, 2004.

Various authors. *Il libro nero del comunismo. Crimini, terrore, repressione*. Milan: Mondadori, 1998.

FABIO BETTANIN

Reunification of Germany

The formal union of the East German state, the German Democratic Republic (GDR), and the West German state, the Federal Republic of Germany (FRG), took place on October 3, 1990, following agreements on the fiscal union of the two Germanys in July and the Unification Treaty in August. But this was no freely chosen union of two equal and sovereign states. By the end of the process, the FRG had essentially annexed the GDR, providing it with West German law and institutions, ranging from the educational to the military, and absorbing its financial and infrastructural weaknesses.

The history of the 1980s had demonstrated the political and economic failures of the Socialist system in the GDR. Moreover, the GDR's superpower patron, the Soviet Union, had also exhibited fatal weaknesses. The Soviet economy was in crisis; Ronald Reagan's Strategic Defense Initiative (popularly known as "Star Wars") dramatically increased the Soviets' sense of strategic vulnerability; and the Soviet hold on Eastern Europe was weakening by the day. Attempts by the reformist General Secretary of the Soviet Communist party, Mikhail Gorbachev, to reinvigorate socialism in the Soviet Union sputtered and failed. From 1987, when he initiated his programs, to 1991, when he was removed from office, Gorbachev's fate was closely linked to that of Germany. Meanwhile, the FRG under Helmut Kohl pursued a successful and dynamic policy of unity, backed by its powerful and increasingly assertive patron, the United States. The takeover of the GDR was determined in good measure by the radical asymmetry of power and political initiative between the West and the East by the end of the 1980s.

The reunification of Germany was also the product of a popular movement in the GDR that, along with analogous movements throughout the eastern bloc, swelled into a revolutionary tide during the late summer and fall of 1989. Gorbachev's program of reform, known as perestroika (restructuring) and glasnost (openness) resonated strongly with an East German population hungry for change. It was also a way for the largely reformist dissident movements to legitimize their grievances against the government of Erich Honecker, general secretary of the Socialist Unity Party (SED). Honecker demonstrated no interest in reform, adopting instead the attitude at the end of the 1980s that the GDR had solved the major problems incident to implementing a Socialist society and therefore had no need for the reforms called for by Gorbachev and some other East European Communist leaders. The palpable dissatisfaction of many East Germans was manifested in their increasing participation in alternative church groups, environmental and pacifist activities, and in cultural and literary dissidence. It soon became apparent that East German workers were also dissatisfied with their low standard of living relative to their West German co-nationals and with the bleak outlook for improvement.

The miraculous summer of 1989 produced radical change in Poland. "Solidarity" emerged supreme in the June elections and, in August, Poland elected its first non-Communist prime minister, Tadeusz Mazowiecki. During that same summer, Hungarian reformist Communists took charge of the government, liberalized the legal and political system, and refused to enforce the Cold War barriers between Hungary and Austria. GDR vacationers in the eastern countries looked at this moment of liberalization as their chance to leave. They crowded into West German embassies in Warsaw, Prague, and Budapest, putting pressure on the Bonn government to provide for their transportation to the FRG, where, by law, they could immediately become citizens and receive social benefits. By mid-September 1989, they were crossing the Hungarian-Austrian border by the thousands, seeking a new life in West Germany. Jokes circulated in the GDR about the population vacating the GDR altogether; one wondered aloud who would be the last one left to turn off the lights. As Honecker remained stolidly opposed to change, the movement for reform spilled out into the streets. Liberalization of the Communist state—not revolution—was the demand of the crowds in Berlin, Leipzig, Rostock, and elsewhere. An important signpost on the road to unification took place in Leipzig on October 9, 1989, when security forces were initially called to crush a peaceful demonstration of protesters, but in the end withdrew. Neither the Soviets nor the SED would take violent action to defend Honecker and his conservative course against the street protesters.

Events of October and November 1989 further undermined the stability of the GDR. Gorbachev indicated his lack of support for Honecker, and younger, more reformist SED party leaders removed Honecker from power and replaced him with Egon Krenz. Krenz and his new team of SED leaders had a vague mandate to liberalize the party and state. Their response to the ongoing crisis of East Germans exiting the country was a vaguely worded communiqué about the possibilities of opening the Berlin Wall to legal traffic back and forth. Poor communications between the new leadership and press, as well as uncertainty among the border guards about the new regulations, led to the extraordinary and dramatic breaching of the wall that took place on November 9. East Germans poured through the checkpoints. They reveled in the streets of West Berlin, climbed the wall, and made it impossible for the state to again close access to the West.

Between the initial October demonstrations and the opening of the Berlin Wall, the mood of the demonstrators shifted dramatically, the "turn within the turn" it is often called. The October demonstrators called for the reform of the GDR; their slogans read, "We Are the People," meaning that the GDR should represent the needs of the mass of its population rather than those of its encrusted elite exemplified by Honecker and Erich Mielke, chief of the notorious Stasi (secret police). But after the removal of Honecker and Mielke and the opening of the wall, the slogans changed. Now it was "No More Experiments," meaning no more attempts to reform communism and make it more palatable to the population or to arrange some kind of confederation between a socialist GDR and a capitalist FRG. The time for that was past. Instead of "We Are the People," the signs now read, "We Are One People." Despite the resistance of many leaders of the East German intelligentsia, who still thought of themselves as Marxists, and of the reformist party leaders, the masses of GDR citizens wanted reunification.

Especially after the Berlin Wall was breached in November, West German Chancellor Helmut Kohl and Foreign Minister Hans-Dietrich Genscher recognized that the dream of German reunification was not outside the bounds of the possible. They understood that they had to work with their careful American patron, with the unpredictable but open-minded Mikhail Gorbachev, and with Germany's immediate neighbors, France being the most important. Kohl's "Ten Point Program" of November 28 sketched out a series of stages by which the FRG and GDR would eventually be united through confederative arrangements. Timothy Garton Ash points out that an important moment in Kohl's own evolution toward the goal of full-fledged reunification came in Dresden shortly before Christmas when he was surrounded by enthusiastic throngs of East Germans shouting slogans for unity.

Despite the efforts of the new reformist East German prime minister, Hans Modrow, the internal situation in

the GDR continued to disintegrate as tens of thousands of East Germans rushed helter-skelter to the West. Some 350,000 East Germans had moved since the summer of 1989, and many more were expected to leave. In late January 1990, Kohl decided—with American backing—to set up a working group on German policy that would report to a new cabinet committee on German unity. One of their ideas was to gain the confidence of East German society that their conditions would improve with unification as a result of financial reform that would bring the West German mark to the East. By the beginning of March, Kohl's party, the Christian Democratic Union (the CDU), allied with the CDU in the East, insisted that Article 23 of the so-called Basic Law, the West German constitution, be used to attach the GDR to the Federal Republic. This would mean that the financial system, the laws, and the institutions of the West would simply be transferred to the East, which would become part of the Federal Republic. This plan took on much more force when the East German CDU, led by Kohl's ally, Lothar de Maizere, decisively won the GDR election of March 18, 1990, on a platform of the quick and decisive unity of Germany based on Article 23. The original dissidents, the Marxist reformists, had little popular backing; neither the SED nor the newly formed PDS (Party of Democratic Socialists) received sufficient support to stem the tide of reunification. Meanwhile, to deal with security and foreign policy issues, the Kohl government endorsed the so-called Two plus Four process, whereby the two German states would negotiate with the four powers, who still exercised rights in Germany and Berlin, to conclude the peace treaty with Germany that had eluded the great powers since the Second World War. The Two plus Four formula quickly turned in effect into a One plus Four affair, with Kohl (and behind him the Americans) negotiating the emergence of the new Germany in Europe.

Gorbachev's Soviet Union remained something of a wild card. The question of Germany's continuing participation in NATO especially bedeviled the process of making unification acceptable to the Soviets. To make matters even more difficult, Margaret Thatcher of Great Britain and Francois Mitterand of France had to be convinced that German unification would not imperil stability in Europe. At the same time, internal German opposition to continuing membership in NATO from an element of the SPD (West and East) complicated Kohl's attempts to proceed full speed ahead with his plans to unify the country as a whole in NATO. (Foreign

Minister Genscher had adopted a plan whereby only the western part of the country would continue to have NATO deployments.)

Speed and force of events were essential in cutting through the Gordian knot of the NATO issue. On July 1, 1990, the critical monetary and economic union of Germany took place. Gorbachev understood that unification was a foregone conclusion and that to stand in its way on the matter of NATO would mean being left behind and having no further say in the course of events. The Americans, among others, made the argument that it would be less dangerous for its neighbors to keep Germany tied down to Europe and the United States through NATO than to have it be neutral, as Soviet advisers had earlier insisted. The British and French were satisfied with this position. The critical decision was Gorbachev's. He apparently came to the conclusion that NATO no longer represented a threat to the Soviet Union and that he could gain concessions on German troop limits, substantial German credits for the modernization of the USSR, and help with the difficult financial and logistical issues involved in the withdrawal of Soviet troops from eastern Germany if he gave the go-ahead on German unification "in NATO." This he did in mid-July 1990 at a summit with Kohl in the Caucasus, which paved the way then for the formal unification treaty on October 3.

While the political and fiscal unification of Germany took place much faster than many commentators anticipated at the time of the *Wende* (the great changes in the GDR in the fall of 1989), the unification of the German people in a psychological and social sense has taken much longer than most would have predicted. Though anxious to join the West, East Germans often took umbrage at the way the western Germans took charge of the process, leaving many in the East without jobs, perspectives, and, most importantly, without a sense of belonging. West German resentment at the financial burdens of unification and the alleged ingratitude of their eastern cousins also fed the dissatisfaction of the former East German citizens. Many began to speak of a "wall in the mind" of East Germans. They were simply not equipped to function in the more competitive and riskier economic system of the West and longed for the ostensibly good old days of a system of social welfare and imposed order. Much East German dissatisfaction and inability to integrate into the economic life of the Federal Republic is generationally based. Unification in all its manifestations—including a commonly held understanding of German national identity—will take time.

See also Berlin Wall; Gorbachev, Mikhail; Honecker, Erich; Perestroika; Post-Soviet Communism.

FURTHER READING

Adomeit, H. *Imperial Overstretch: Germany in Soviet Policy from Stalin to Gorbachev.* Baden-Baden: Nomos, 1998.

Ash, T. G. *In Europe's Name: Germany and the Divided Continent.* New York: Random House, 1993.

Genscher, H. D. *Erinnerungen.* Berlin: Siedler Verlag, 1995.

Rice, C., and P. Zelikow. *Germany Unified and Europe Transformed: A Study in Statecraft.* Cambridge, MA: Harvard University Press, 1997.

Smyser, W. R. *From Yalta to Berlin: The Cold War Struggle over Germany.* New York: St. Martin's Press, 1999.

Teltschik, H. *329 Tage; Innenansichtigungen der Einigung.* Berlin: Siedler Verlag, 1991.

Thomaneck, J. K., and B. Niven. *Dividing and Uniting Germany.* London: Routledge, 2001.

NORMAN M. NAIMARK

Revisionism

Karl Marx was insistent in asserting that "only by a forcible overthrow of all existing social conditions" could socialism achieve its goals. As the movement developed during the 19th century, however, in an era of peace and prosperity, the prospects for parliamentary activity and trade unionism to promote peaceful social transformation became more realistic. Improved living conditions gave the working class a larger stake in civil society. Simultaneously, the fate of the Paris Commune of 1871 caused many to question whether the prospect for a revolutionary seizure of power in a modern state had not become a chimera.

The most developed articulation of a reformist alternative to revolutionary Marxism came within the Social Democratic Party of Germany (SPD), where between 1896 and 1899 the theorist Eduard Bernstein urged that Marx be "revised" precisely by abandoning his revolutionary pretense. Arguing the priority of the "movement" above the "goal" of revolution, Bernstein summarized the revisionist position by asserting that the SPD should consent "to appear what it really is today, a democratic socialist reform party." In the many polemic exchanges that have followed, the core meaning of revisionism remains as Bernstein defined it—the plea for a peaceful, reformist approach to social transformation.

Polish Socialist Rosa Luxemburg penned a response to Bernstein in her 1899 pamphlet *Social Reform or Revolution*. Asserting that the prospects of reformism depended on a temporary economic conjuncture that could not be sustained, Luxemburg insisted that the contradictions of capitalist development made future social cataclysms and revolutionary crises inevitable. The positions of Bernstein and Luxemburg framed the revisionist controversy, which would divide the movement politically and intellectually up to the First World War.

Luxemburg represented the SPD Left radical wing, for which the contradictions of advanced capitalism continued to demand an active, revolutionary role from social democracy. The center, led up to his death in 1913 by August Bebel, gave formal support to the Left radical position, but sounded a note of caution regarding what Karl Kautsky called Luxemburg's "revolutionary romanticism." The right wing, led by self-confident provincial and trade union leaders such as Carl Legien and Georg von Vollmar, was committed to what von Vollmar defined as "the path of calm, legal, parliamentary activity." These fractures were reproduced within all major national parties. On the international level Marxist orthodoxy prevailed, and at its 1904 Amsterdam Congress the Second International rejected reformism as a general political orientation. In daily practice, parliamentary and trade unionist activity remained dominant.

Friction between reformist and revolutionary currents was at the root of the Second International's disintegration during the First World War (1914–18). The Russian Bolshevik leader Vladimir Lenin placed primary blame for the Second International's failure to rally behind an antiwar position upon the betrayal of revolutionary Marxism occasioned by revisionism. His fiery polemics against Socialist defensism cast down a gauntlet to the entire reformist wing of social democracy. The division between revolutionary and reformist currents within the international labor movement that the revisionist controversy heralded would become institutionalized with the launching of the International Communist Movement after 1919.

See also Imperialism; Internationalism; Kautsky, Karl; Lenin, Vladimir; Luxemburg, Rosa; Revolution, Myths of the; Social Democracy; Socialist International.

FURTHER READING

Bernstein, E. *Evolutionary Socialism.* New York: Schocken Books, 1963.

Gay, P. *The Dilemmas of Democratic Socialism: Eduard Bernstein's Challenge to Marx.* New York: Collier Books, 1962.

Hamilton, R. F. *Marxism, Revisionism, and Leninism: Explication, Assessment, and Commentary.* Westport, CT: Praeger, 2000.

R. CRAIG NATION

Revolution, Myths of the

In 20th-century Europe the myth of the revolution was primarily that of the Russian Revolution, which appeared at the beginning of the century as the latest and most faithful embodiment of a longer-term model, one that developed in France and achieved influence throughout Europe by 1848. If this derivation seems obvious, the forms and processes from which it developed are far from clear. The enduring myth of the Russian Revolution's strength is instead directly proportional to the complexity of its components. It is a "dirty" myth, one that arose and developed by incorporating pieces from other belief systems, contradictorily tied to the realities of the Soviet state and partially destined to disappear with it: the myth of Communist equality and the brutal redefinition of classes, a passion for violence and the will to rationalize it, a universal dream and national demands, and arguments favoring economic modernity and faith in militarized command structures.

The 1917 February Revolution during World War I had initially been viewed, both by the provisional government in Russia and the rest of Europe, as an event that would allow for a more efficient continuation of the war effort against Germany. This was the opinion of the majorities in the English and French Socialist parties, but also of democratic interventionists in Italy, and paradoxically even of the German Socialist majority, which interpreted the collapse of czarism as the positive outcome of the German assault on European power and its historically progressive function. This view of the nature of the revolution would instead only become the first of the revolution's many myths. A much more widespread and deeply rooted myth would immediately replace the first one: the myth of peace. The democratic republic that was establishing itself in the former empire was in fact continuing the war, but it was also provoking, both internally and to some extent in Western Europe, strikes and increasingly radical demonstrations against the war, attempts to reconvene the Socialist International, as well as actual mutinies.

Europe gave the new myth of revolution a definite shape—a shape that for the first time was both historically and politically Russian—when it identified the Soviets as its most important achievement: a movement of revolutionary councils that would reveal its appeal during its first European application, in Germany, which took shape in the fall of 1918 and put an end to the war. This myth had already lost its meaning in revolutionary Russia since early 1918, when the Soviets had been dissolved and repressed; it did, however, advance a much more democratic and popular interpretation of the October Revolution than reality allowed. It established a tradition that would enjoy an extraordinary power of evocation both in terms of revolutionary vitality and sociopolitical egalitarianism, one that not coincidentally, would remain at the core of the simplest self-definition of "Soviet power."

Naturally the myth's transfer from inside Russian reality to the outside world was not merely spontaneous. More than a century after the fact, the novelty of these developments is best captured in the interpretation of the Soviets's birth as an event establishing the first modern "propaganda state." The first steps by the new regime in the arena of foreign policy were taken exclusively for reasons of propaganda. The declared abolition of secret diplomacy, the use of the Peace Conference with the German government as a forum for revolutionary declarations, and the strong support for the Stockholm Socialist Commission to re-create the International—all of these statements were meant to strengthen and spread the myth of the revolution in the rest of Europe. As was revealed in *Pravda* as early as December 26, 1917, the Soviet plenipotentiary in Stockholm was given the assignment of distributing two million rubles to the European revolutionary Left to this end.

In the fall of 1918, the war's end breathed new life into the myth of revolution in Europe: the separate peace with Germany at Brest-Litovsk had proved to be a winning move, its burdensome economic and territorial costs had been nullified, and the new revolutionary state had not only survived but was now actually also witnessing the spread of a "council revolution" in Germany. In these early years a large part of the European socialist movement aspired to emulate Russia, and this desire was largely based on a generic egalitarian and universalistic perspective, arrived at by projecting the Soviet revolution on a global scale, to a much greater extent than during

the pacifist mythologization of the February Revolution. The phenomenon cannot be explained solely on the basis of the regime's self-representation or propagandistic abilities. It was rather the original Communist myth, historically determined in its common European forms, that gave meaning to social and political messianism throughout Europe after World War I—a period characterized by expectations that were not only radical but openly palingenetic as well. The fascination exercised by the October Revolution infused a myth that certainly predated the birth of European Communist parties as they reemerged between 1919 and 1921 with renewed vigor: in the following century it reinvigorated the most diverse aspirations to social justice, or even to that oldest of dreams, a life without bosses. Revolution, the end of property rights, and equality—all these goals still nourished the ideal world of European socialism. This reality was confirmed by the fact that the revolutionary myth continued to operate successfully within the Russian anti-Bolshevik socialist emigration, which although mostly unheeded, spread all over Europe during the 1920s.

The new element in the myth's appeal was related to a new reality: the complete institutionalization of the revolution at both the state and military level. The organization of violence, the civil war, and "war communism" endowed the old revolutionary idea with new substance. They retrospectively grounded an interpretation of the October Revolution that was no longer tied to the romantic aspects of revolt and insurrection, to the council organizations and an open break with social democratic reformism, but now instead emerged as an offspring of the organizational traditions and long-standing conspiratorial activities of the Russian Socialist parties, their cult of secrecy and underground existence, their rigid political and personal discipline, which was basically military in nature. Discounting the specific forms that this latest incarnation of the myth had taken, since it had frequently been modernized and simplified, it was also the latest embodiment of an older, widespread, European myth: the consistent and militant spirit of radical thought in 19th-century Russia.

The personification of this new cult of revolutionary organization was, from the first, Lenin, around whom the myth of the modern revolutionary leader endowed with the most varied allegorical attributes began to be constructed. These developments were apparent from the moment of his death, in 1924, when he became a symbolic cornerstone, with a syncretistic force capable of aggregating the most diverse beliefs, jointly symbolized by his embalming and the preservation of his mummy in a specially made mausoleum on Red Square, the politicogeographic heart of the new state. Leon Trotsky in his own way also consistently represented the revolutionary war and military victory during the years of the civil war, both inside and outside Soviet Russia, until he began to evoke the old ghosts of Bonapartism around his own persona.

The myth of the revolution's efficiency—which up to then had been extraneous to the socialist world—would make itself felt during the 1920s, in the course of the celebration of the first Soviet economic plans, despite the fact they were largely attempts to imitate the German war economy. The mythologization of the first revolutionary political police, the Cheka, also exhibited similar characteristics. The Cheka, glorified inside the new revolutionary state in the name of a superior class justice, was destined to be transformed abroad with the rise of political reaction into a defensive myth. The most authoritative praise of the Soviet political police came from Italy, at the time of Giacomo Matteotti's assassination by what was then the Fascist Cheka, a product of considerable semantic imagination, understandably not much appreciated by the Italian Communists. On an even larger scale, however, the Comintern itself—an institution with military characteristics not only in its organizational structures, but also in its language and political metaphors—should be included in the European revolutionary myth, with its ideal of an exclusive, heavily centralized, and disciplined leadership of the international revolutionary movement.

The new state's geographic and cultural distance, and the difficulty in establishing communications, contributed to revolutionary Russia's exoticism; it constituted a new universe in contrast to the traditions of European socialism (with strong German roots) in the the pre–World War I period. As they attempted to make Soviet reality known in the West, the first labor unions, cooperatives, and party delegations to visit revolutionary Russia immediately after the Allied blockade in the summer of 1920 frequently displayed this estrangement in their accounts, connecting it to the new revolutionary myth. Italians saw "African scenes" in Samara, in the heart of Russian territory, and aroused "Congolese memories" in them—extreme forms of more complex misunderstandings between revolutionary Russia and the rest of Europe, of which the contemporary Soviet belief in the imminence and radical class nature of the European revolution largely partook.

A paradoxical characteristic of the mythology during these years was also the contradiction between Soviet communism's internationalist self-representation, the universalistic perspective of the revolutionary myth among wide swathes of Europe's population, and the strong national Communist spirit involved in the most serious attempts to extend the Sovietization process to bordering areas in central Eastern Europe, from Hungary in 1919 to Germany in 1921–23. At its most extreme, this contradiction gave rise to a further, original interpretation of the Russian Revolution—one that ignored the internationalist component, and focused instead on the New Economic Policy's spirit, concessions to Western enterprises, and the rise of ambiguous coexistence policies in the 1920s. These developments led to the liberal myth of the USSR, tied in its most fantastic forms to Piero Gobetti's name, but also to the belief in the imminent predominance of the economic and geopolitical interests of the former empire, and therefore in the proximate normalization of the revolutionary state due to the inevitable collapse of its ideological superstructure. The Soviet state itself attempted to use these Western European beliefs to stimulate trade in this case as well. This is how the regime's first "hospitality techniques" were developed, whose intent was to blandish foreign industrialists, technicians, journalists, and intellectuals.

The great Western crisis of the 1930s and the resulting waves of mass unemployment recast the revolutionary myth in new forms, now tied to the idea of the superiority of a planned economy. The exaltation of industrial and architectonic gigantism, the revolutionary homeland's productive efforts, was willed and planned by Stalin domestically, but once again had its greatest audience abroad. Notwithstanding Soviet society's misery and regression, a new definition of communism now established itself as accelerated accumulation, continuously growing industrial production, and the state's predominance over both the economy and society.

Information about the social tragedy of accelerated industrialization and forced collectivization reached the outside world through different channels, from the tens of thousands of foreign workers and technicians who were employed there to the consular structures of Fascist Italy, from the international networks of the Volga Germans to the peasants escaping toward Poland and Finland, but this news did not hamper the myth's growth. Among intellectuals and within the Western workers' movement the need to believe in modernization in the new revolutionary state was too strong. Other contemporary myths of a Trotskyist nature that argued for the idea of a "betrayed revolution"—a structural contradiction between an egalitarian social base created by the original revolutionary movement and the ensuing Bonapartist degeneration tied to Stalin's rise to power—also did not help an understanding of Soviet reality.

After Nazism's rise to power in Germany, the revolutionary myth was transformed into an anti-Fascist political project during the later 1930s, and despite the lack of direction following the Nazi-Soviet alliance in 1939–41, it would lay the foundation throughout Europe for a political and military movement until the end of World War II. The intensity and radical nature of the original myth would only be preserved in certain, minority sectors. The myth would only reacquire its full revolutionary meaning and complete identification with Soviet reality after 1945, when the myth of the victorious Russian state would be identified with those of socialism and peace.

Under the careful guidance of an aging Stalin, the expansion of Soviet control in Eastern Europe, and the exceptional growth of the Italian and French Communist parties, a well-rounded economic, political, and social myth would surround the Cominform, which seemed to replicate certain characteristics of Russia's 19th-century power, and its competition with England for influence on the continent. This further sacralization of Soviet state power coexisted with the original myth of the revolution, even though in an atmosphere of increasing duplicity, and between the end of the 1940s and early 1960s, it even became a mass myth for workers (especially in Italy and France). The denunciation of Stalin's crimes by the Soviet leadership and Khrushchev himself starting in 1956 went against the grain of the myth. The Soviet military interventions in Hungary in 1956 and Czechoslovakia in 1968 had similar results, even though mostly restricted to intellectuals. The myth's final erosion would instead occur due to a lengthy process of transformation, and not because of individual traumatic events.

In the last thirty years of the 20th century, the multiplication of revolutionary movements and states born in the course of decolonization, the continuous Soviet criticism of its most significant and symbolically important Stalinist past, and the increasingly obvious economic weakness and social poverty in the revolutionary state slowly led Western European parties and intellectuals to try new paths. They increasingly cultivated arguments that belonged to a Soviet "antimyth," and forgot the revolutionary myth in the process. European communism itself gradually watered down its support for a reality of almost exclusively military dimensions, typical of a great power in the throes of a deep crisis. The great myths of equality that belonged to a legacy of two centuries of European history thus tended to shift, on the spur of the moment, from Cuba to Vietnam to China. This final diffusion of the ancient European revolutionary myth outside Europe's borders signaled its deepest crisis, however, occurring just when the dual track of a drive toward economic modernity and political dictatorship led to the USSR's collapse.

See also Antifascism; Comintern; Lenin, Vladimir; Messianism; Modernization; Political Pilgrims; Propaganda, Communist; Russian Revolution and Civil War; Stalin, Myth of; State, The; Utopia; War Communism; World Revolution.

FURTHER READING

di Biagio, A. *Coesistenza e isolazionismo: Mosca, il Komintern e l'Europa di Versailles, 1918–1928*. Rome: Carocci, 2004.

Flores, M. *L'immagine dell'URSS. L'Occidente e la Russia di Stalin, 1927–1956*. Milan: Il Saggiatore, 1990.

Flores, M., and F. Gori, eds. *Il mito dell'URSS: la cultura occidentale e l'Unione Sovietica*. Milan: Angeli, 1990.

Graziosi, A. "'Viaggiatori nel tempo.' I lavoratori stranieri e i primi piani quinquennali." In *Stato e industria in Unione Sovietica, 1917–1953*, 145–93. Naples: Edizioni Scientifiche Italiane, 1993.

Hollander, P. *Political Pilgrims: Travels of Western Intellectuals to the Soviet Union, China, and Cuba, 1928–1978*. New York: Oxford University Press, 1981.

Lindemann, A. S. *The Red Years: European Socialism versus Bolshevism, 1919–1921*. Berkeley: University of California Press, 1974.

Various authors. *L'URSS, il mito, le masse*. Milan: Angeli, 1991.

ANTONELLO VENTURI

Revolution from Above

Stalin's abandonment of the New Economic Policy and his initiation of the First Five-Year Plan, and the launch of the campaign of agricultural collectivization and "dekulakization" in 1929 have been loosely referred to as a "revolution from above" by Robert Tucker and other historians. In *The Short Course*, which Stalin edited and partly wrote, agricultural collectivization was described as a "revolution from above" initiated by the state and supported from below by millions of peasants. The phrase "revolution from above" had a long pedigree in Marxist thought, and one that was very well understood at the time.

Marx and Engels conceived of revolutionary change as both revolution from below and revolution from above. The concept of revolution from above was discussed in terms particularly of absolutism and of Bonapartism. Louis Napoleon and Bismarck were the quintessential examples of 19th-century Bonapartism. The "blood and iron" chancellor, architect of German unification and exponent of *Kulturkampf*, was the supreme practitioner of *Realpolitik*. Through an alliance of *Junker* and bourgeois interests he forced the capitalist modernization of Germany, holding in check the power of the working class. Bismarck's role in suppressing the Paris Commune, and his initiation of the anti-socialist laws in Germany, laid out the ground rules by which revolution was to be played.

Engels, in an 1882 letter to Kautsky, remarked that "the real, not the illusory, tasks of a revolution are always accomplished as a result of the revolution,'" and that Louis Napoleon, Cavour, and Bismarck had been "the testamentary executors of the revolution" (of 1848–49) in the sense that they had completed "the restoration of the oppressed and divided nationalities of central Europe, in so far as these were viable and specifically ripe for independence," The importance of this, he explained, was that "an international movement of the proletariat is in general possible only among independent nations." Engels repeatedly invoked the idea of "revolution from above" as applied to Bismarck and Louis Napoleon.

In the wake of the failure of the 1905 Russian Revolution from below Lenin quoted Marx's approving comments on Bismarck as the agent of German unification and Engel's comments on Bismarck as an exponent of bourgeois revolution "from above" (*revolyutsiya sverkhu*). Lenin thought that Stolypin might impose a "Bonapartist" solution to Russia's crisis after 1905–6, by welding a union of landowners and capitalists to force through a capitalist revolution. In January 1908 he described the situation in Russia as crying out for a Bismarck capable of turning simple reaction into a revolution from above.

The entry on Bismarck in the *Great Soviet Encyclopedia* of 1927 describes Bismarck's policy of unifying Germany as a "revolution from above." In 1929 Trotsky characterized the Stalin regime as a form of Bonapartism, as revolution from above by reaction where revolution from below had exhausted itself. In 1935 he compared the "bourgeois Bonapartism" of Louis Napoleon and Bismarck with the "Soviet Bonapartism" of Stalin. In the USSR Bismarck was admired as an exponent of realpolitik for his ruthless domestic policies of state building and modernization, and for his uncompromising foreign policy in defense of German state interests.

Isaac Deutscher described Stalin as a practitioner of "revolution from above" on the Bismarckian model. E. H. Carr places Stalin in the tradition of great statesmen who defy being labeled as "left" or "right," and compares him with Napoleon III, Cavour, and Bismarck, as one who brought to fruition some of the goals of the revolution, but in the process repudiated others of its goals.

See also Bonapartism; Jacobinism; Modernization; Revolution, Myths of the; Stalinism.

FURTHER READING

Carr, E. H. *Foundations of a Planned Economy.* Vol. 2. Harmondsworth, UK: Penguin, 1976.

Deutscher, I. *Stalin.* Harmondsworth, UK: Penguin, 1968.

Rees, E. A. *Political Thought from Machiavelli to Stalin: Revolutionary Machiavellism.* Basingstoke, UK: Macmillan, 2004.

Tucker, R. C. "Stalinism as Revolution from Above" In *Stalinism,* ed. R. C. Tucker, 77–110. New York: Norton, 1977.

van Ree, E. *The Political Thought of Joseph Stalin: A Study in Twentieth-Century Revolutionary Patriotism.* London: Routeldge-Curzon, 2002.

E. ARFON REES

Revolutions in East-Central Europe

The collapse of communism in Central and Eastern Europe in 1989 was one of the most momentous events of the 20th century. In the mid- to late 1940s, Communist governments took power throughout the region under Soviet auspices. For more than forty years, those governments dominated political and economic life in the region. The sudden downfall of the Communist regimes in 1989 is sometimes depicted as the inevitable result of a long process of systemic decay. In reality, there was nothing at all inevitable about the outcome. Popular opposition to the Communist regimes had long been intense almost everywhere, as demonstrated by the uprisings in Czechoslovakia and East Germany in 1953, the rebellions in Poland and Hungary in 1956, the public acclaim for the Prague Spring in 1968, and the rise of Solidarity in

Poland in 1980–81. Western experts had long suspected that, as one observer wrote in 1985, "without the presence of Soviet troops on East European soil and the threat of a Soviet invasion to bolster faltering regimes, the present governments in the region would not survive for long." What changed in 1989, compared to earlier crises in Eastern Europe, was not the depth of popular opposition to the Soviet-backed regimes. Instead, what changed was the whole thrust of Soviet policy. The largely peaceful collapse of East European communism in 1989 was due as much to the fundamental reorientation of Soviet foreign policy under Mikhail Gorbachev as to the courage and restraint of the East European peoples.

The Reorientation of Soviet Policy

Until the rise of Gorbachev, Soviet leaders after World War II regarded Eastern Europe as an extension of their own country's frontiers. Threats to the security of an East European Communist regime, whether external or internal, were deemed threats to Soviet security as well. This sentiment took its most explicit form in the so-called Brezhnev Doctrine, which linked the fate of every socialist country with that of all others, required socialist countries to abide by the norms of Marxism-Leninism as interpreted in Moscow, and subordinated the "abstract sovereignty" of states to the "laws of class struggle."

After Gorbachev came to power in March 1985, the Soviet–East European relationship initially underwent little change. During his first few years in office, the new Soviet leader sought to promote greater economic integration within the Council for Mutual Economic Assistance, and an expansion of political and military cooperation among the members of the Warsaw Pact. In both respects, his early policies displayed a strong continuity with those of his predecessors. Gorbachev's manner of presentation may have been more dynamic, but at no time during the first few years of his tenure did he disavow the Brezhnev Doctrine or even condemn the way his predecessors had handled Soviet–East European relations.

By spring 1988, however, Soviet policy toward Eastern Europe started to loosen, adumbrating a fundamental shift in Gorbachev's approach. The first indicator of a shift in Gorbachev's policy came during his visit to Yugoslavia in March 1988, when a joint communiqué pledged "unconditional" respect for "the principles of equality and noninterference," and "the independence of parties and socialist countries to define, for themselves, the path of their own development." In subsequent months, the Soviet Union made good on these pledges by providing the East European countries with much greater latitude for internal political and economic change—latitude that Hungary and Poland (though not the four other countries) were quick to exploit.

The reorientation of Gorbachev's policy toward the Warsaw Pact countries was further signaled in December 1988 by his announcement, in a speech before the UN General Assembly, that the Soviet Union would unilaterally reduce its military forces in Eastern Europe by fifty thousand troops, fifty-three hundred tanks, and twenty-four tactical nuclear weapons. In purely military terms, these reductions were of little significance, but symbolically their importance was enormous.

The changes in Soviet policy toward Eastern Europe were reinforced by Gorbachev's domestic reform program. As the pace of perestroika and glasnost accelerated in the Soviet Union, the "winds of change" gradually filtered throughout the Eastern bloc, bringing long-submerged grievances and social discontent to the surface. Under growing popular pressure, the authorities in Hungary and Poland embarked on much more ambitious paths of reform in 1988–89 than Gorbachev himself had yet adopted. As ferment in those two countries and elsewhere in the region continued to increase, Gorbachev's public comments about Eastern Europe grew bolder. In a speech before the European Parliament in July 1989, Gorbachev expressed support for the maintenance of socialism in Europe, but then indicated a willingness to accept whatever result might come:

> The social and political orders of certain countries [in Europe] changed in the past, and may change again in the future. However, this is exclusively a matter for the peoples themselves to decide; it is their choice. Any interference in internal affairs, or any attempts to limit the sovereignty of states—including friends and allies, or anyone else—are impermissible.

Against the backdrop of the remarkable changes under way in Poland and Hungary, including the imminent formation of a Polish government led by Solidarity (the independent mass movement that was banned in Poland from December 1981 until early 1989), this declaration took on even greater importance. Although the four other Warsaw Pact countries—Czechoslovakia, East Germany, Bulgaria, and Romania—staunchly eschewed any hint of liberalization and clung firmly to orthodox Communist policies, there was no doubt by early to mid-1989 that Gorbachev was willing to permit far-reaching internal changes in Eastern Europe that previously would have been ruled out and forcibly suppressed under the Brezhnev Doctrine.

Thus, from that point on, the real issue for Gorbachev was no longer whether he should uphold the Brezhnev Doctrine but whether he could avoid the "Khrushchev Dilemma." That is, the problem was not whether to accept peaceful domestic change, as in Czechoslovakia in 1968, but how to prevent widespread anti-Soviet violence from breaking out, as in Hungary in 1956. Gorbachev would have found himself in an intractable situation if he had been confronted by a large-scale, violent uprising in Poland, East Germany, Czechoslovakia, or Hungary. On the two previous occasions when violent rebellions threatened Soviet control over those four countries—in East Germany in 1953, and Hungary in 1956—Gorbachev's predecessors responded with military force. If a comparable crisis had erupted in 1989, the pressure for Soviet military intervention would have been enormous, just as it was on Khrushchev in 1956. No matter how Gorbachev might have responded, he would have suffered grave damage.

Hence, Gorbachev's overriding objective was to avoid the Khrushchev Dilemma altogether. He could not afford to be confronted by a violent uprising in one of the key East European countries. Only by forestalling such a disastrous turn of events would he have any hope of moving ahead with his reform program. The problem, however, was that his very policies, by unleashing centrifugal forces within the Eastern bloc, had already made it *more* likely that a violent rebellion would occur. One of the main deterrents to popular anti-Communist uprisings in Eastern Europe after 1956 was the local populations' awareness that, if necessary, Soviet troops would intervene to restore control. Because this perceived constraint had been steadily diminishing under Gorbachev, the risk of a violent upheaval had increased commensurately.

Contending with the Khrushchev Dilemma

The possibility of a violent explosion in Eastern Europe had long been apparent to prominent Soviet specialists on the region, such as Oleg Bogomolov and Vyacheslav Dashichev. In the pre-Gorbachev era, these analysts played no role in the policymaking process. But after he came to power, Gorbachev and other senior officials proved far more willing to consider (and indeed began actively soliciting) advice from the expert community. The views of specialists like Bogomolov and Dashichev

thus were gradually able to filter upward and help shape the perceptions of Gorbachev's key advisers, especially Georgii Shakhnazarov (Gorbachev's chief aide on Eastern Europe), Aleksandr Yakovlev, and Soviet foreign minister Eduard Shevardnadze. These senior officials—and eventually Gorbachev himself—came to realize that the longer the existing structures in Eastern Europe remained in place, the greater the danger would be for the Soviet Union. One of Gorbachev's key advisers on European affairs, Vitalii Zhurkin, later recalled that the Soviet authorities had finally "faced up to the fact . . . that the authoritarian and totalitarian systems in the countries of Eastern Europe were artificial and would not last forever." If those systems had been "prolonged for another five or ten years," Zhurkin argued, the resulting "explosions" would have been far more "destructive," and would have caused greater "destabilization" and "problems for everyone, not least for us."

Hence, both the record of previous crises in Eastern Europe and the prospect that new crises would emerge in the near future had convinced Gorbachev's advisers (and eventually Gorbachev himself) that, as Shevardnadze put it, "if positive changes [in Eastern Europe] were suppressed or delayed, the whole situation would end in tragedy." Gorbachev also was aware, however, that unless these "positive changes" in Eastern Europe occurred peacefully, his domestic reform program—and his own political fate—would be in jeopardy.

Mindful of that dilemma, Gorbachev and his aides by late 1988 had established two basic goals for Soviet policy in Eastern Europe. First, they wanted to avoid direct Soviet military intervention at all costs. Shakhnazarov had emphasized in his memorandum to Gorbachev that "in the future, the prospect of 'extinguishing' crisis situations [in Eastern Europe] through military means must be completely ruled out." Second, they sought to achieve a peaceful but rapid transition to a new political order in Eastern Europe. By drastically modifying the region's political complexion, they could defuse the pressures that had given rise to violent internal crises in the past. But to ensure that the early stages of the process remained peaceful and that positive changes would indeed occur, the Soviet Union itself had to play an active, initiating role.

The basic problem was that if most of the East European Communist parties had been left to their own devices, they would have sought to avoid reforms indefinitely. The hard-line regimes in Czechoslovakia, East Germany, Bulgaria, and Romania had become increasingly repressive and intransigent as the internal and external pressures for reform grew. These regimes were heartened in June 1989 when the leaders of the Chinese Communist Party launched an all-out assault against unarmed student protesters near Tiananmen Square. Televised images of the bloodshed in China in early June reinforced the widespread belief in Moscow that urgent steps were needed to forestall destabilizing unrest in Eastern Europe. But the "lesson" drawn by the leaders of East Germany, Czechoslovakia, and Romania was just the opposite—namely, that liberalization would be dangerous, and large-scale violent repression would enable them to crush all opposition. When Soviet officials realized that the hard-line East European regimes were willing to emulate the Tiananmen Square massacre, they concluded that the Soviet Union must actively promote fundamental change in Eastern Europe, rather than simply waiting and hoping that all would work out for the best.

The decision to assume an active role is what was so striking about the reorientation of Soviet policy toward Eastern Europe under Gorbachev. It was not just a question of Gorbachev's willingness to accept and tolerate drastic changes in the Warsaw Pact countries; rather, he and his aides did their best to ensure that these changes occurred, and that they occurred peacefully. As Valentin Falin, the head of the Communist Party of the Soviet Union's (CPSU) International Department, which oversaw Soviet relations with Eastern Europe from mid-1988 on, later acknowledged:

> The CPSU Central Committee was aware of
> the unsavory processes under way in the [East
> European] countries and therefore—to the extent
> permitted by the principle of noninterference in
> internal affairs and respect of the right of peoples
> to choose—we tried to influence the situation.

Gorbachev had pledged in mid-1988 that the Soviet Union "would not impose [its] methods of development," including perestroika and glasnost, "on anyone else," but the situation in Eastern Europe was changing so rapidly by early to mid-1989 that it necessitated greater Soviet involvement than he initially anticipated. Unlike in the past, when Gorbachev's predecessors relied on military force to "defend socialism" in Eastern Europe, the Soviet Union in 1989 had to play a direct part in countering the "unsavory processes" that might eventually have led to widespread violent unrest in one or more East European countries.

Far-Reaching Consequences

The radical implications of Gorbachev's approach were evident in early and mid-1989 when drastic reforms were adopted by Hungary and Poland, culminating in the formation of a Solidarity-led government in Poland. But the full magnitude of the forces unleashed by Gorbachev's policies did not become apparent until the last few months of 1989. Events that would have been unthinkable even a year or two earlier suddenly happened: peaceful revolutions from below in East Germany and Czechoslovakia, the dismantling of the Berlin Wall, popular ferment and the downfall of Todor Zhivkov in Bulgaria, and violent upheaval and the execution of Nicolae and Elena Ceauşescu in Romania. As one orthodox Communist regime after another collapsed, the Soviet Union expressed approval and lent strong support to the reformist, non-Communist governments that emerged. Soviet leaders also joined their East European counterparts in condemning previous instances of Soviet interference in Eastern Europe, particularly the 1968 invasion of Czechoslovakia. In the past, the Soviet Union had done all it could to stifle and deter political liberalization in Eastern Europe; but by late 1989 there was no doubt that the East European countries would enjoy full leeway to pursue drastic economic, political, and social reforms, including the option of abandoning communism altogether.

Although Gorbachev had not intended to undermine the socialist bloc and did not foresee that the changes he initiated would lead to the rapid demise of communism in Eastern Europe, he consistently stuck to his policies of promoting fundamental change and avoiding the use of force at all costs. He originally had hoped to preserve the integrity of the Warsaw Pact and create favorable conditions in Eastern Europe for a liberalized form of communism ("socialism with a human face") that would enable the socialist commonwealth to overcome the political instability that had plagued it so often in the past. Gorbachev knew it would be risky to pursue a new social and political order in Eastern Europe, but he believed there would be even greater risks if he failed to act. When the process of change in Eastern Europe took on a revolutionary momentum of its own, he declined to interrupt it or even try to slow it down. As a result, the upheavals of 1989 transformed the region so comprehensively that they undermined Soviet influence.

Nonetheless, even though Gorbachev did not anticipate how promptly the bloc would disintegrate or how quickly the reunification of Germany would proceed, his basic approach to Soviet–East European relations proved remarkably successful in averting the Khrushchev Dilemma. The swift transition to a new and more stable political order in Eastern Europe was almost entirely peaceful, other than in the special case of Romania. Never before has rapid social and political change of this magnitude occurred with so little violence. The peaceful collapse of communism in Eastern Europe seemed implausible until it actually happened.

Some element of good fortune may have been involved, but Gorbachev's success in avoiding the Khrushchev Dilemma was not just a matter of luck. Nor was the lack of any major violence (except in Romania) during the revolutions of 1989 attributable to the East European Communist regimes themselves. Had it been left to the East German, Bulgarian, or Czechoslovak authorities, violent repression would have resulted. Rather, the lack of violence was attributable in part to the remarkable discipline shown by the East European peoples, and in part to the deliberate policies adopted by Moscow. Throughout the latter half of 1989 (and even earlier in Hungary and Poland), the Soviet Union took timely and effective action to forestall violence and promote far-reaching liberalization in the Warsaw Pact countries. At each of the many points when the Soviet Union could have stepped in to halt or reverse the process of fundamental change, Gorbachev instead chose to expedite it.

In each case, the Soviet Union helped to bring about sweeping political change while effectively depriving hard-line Communist leaders of the option of violent repression. The notable exception of Romania, with its bloody and chaotic revolution, merely proves the rule. Since the mid-1960s, Soviet influence had always been much weaker in Romania than in the other Warsaw Pact countries. The Romanian crisis was illuminating in its own right insofar as it showed the lengths that Gorbachev was willing to go to avoid direct Soviet military intervention in Eastern Europe. Despite serious provocations by the forces loyal to Ceauşescu, including the firing of shots at the Soviet embassy in Bucharest and threats by the Romanian state security agency (Securitate) to blow up nuclear power stations near the Soviet border, and despite explicit statements by the major Western governments that they would *welcome* Soviet intervention in Romania, Soviet leaders refrained from sending in any troops. Indeed, newly declassified materials confirm that Gorbachev was so disinclined to use military force in Eastern Europe that he did not even seriously broach the matter when the Soviet politburo gathered at the height of the Romanian crisis to discuss possible responses.

In every respect, then, Gorbachev's approach to Soviet–East European relations from mid-1988 on was radically different from that of his predecessors. Previous Soviet leaders had sought to maintain orthodox Communist regimes in Eastern Europe, if necessary through the use of armed force. Gorbachev, by contrast, wanted to avoid military intervention in Eastern Europe at all costs. His paramount objective thus was to defuse the pressures in the region that might eventually have led to violent, anti-Soviet uprisings. This objective, in turn, required him to go much further than he initially anticipated. In effect, Gorbachev actively promoted fundamental political change in Eastern Europe while there was still some chance of benefiting from it, rather than risk being confronted later on by widespread violence that would practically compel him to send in troops. The hope was that by supporting the sweeping but peaceful transformation of the region over the near term, the Soviet Union would never again have to contend with large-scale outbreaks of anti-Soviet violence, as Khrushchev had to do in 1956. This basic strategy, of encouraging and managing internal upheavals in order to prevent much more severe crises in the future, achieved its immediate aim, but in the process it both necessitated and ensured the demise of East European communism.

See also Beijing Spring; Brezhnev Doctrine; Gorbachev, Mikhail; New Thinking; Perestroika.

FURTHER READING

Antohi, S., and V. Tismaneanu, eds. *Between Past and Future: The Revolutions of 1989 and Their Aftermath.* Budapest: Central European University Press, 2000.

Brown, J. F. *Surge to Freedom: The End of Communist Rule in Eastern Europe.* Durham, NC: Duke University Press, 1991.

Kramer, M. "Gorbachev and the Demise of East European Communism." In *Reinterpreting the End of the Cold War: Issues, Interpretations, Periodizations,* ed. S. Pons and F. Romero, pp. 179–201. London: Frank Cass, 2005.

Stokes, G. *The Walls Came Tumbling Down: The Collapse of Communism in Eastern Europe.* New York: Oxford University Press, 1993.

Tarrow, S. " 'Aiming at a Moving Target': Social Science and the Recent Rebellions in Eastern Europe." *PS: Political Science and Politics,* 24, no. 1 (March 1991): 12–20.

MARK KRAMER

Russian Revolution and Civil War

The Russian Revolution and Civil War produced the Soviet state in its early form and was to supply the model, to a greater or lesser extent, for communism in power across a third of the world's land surface. This happened in a piecemeal and unpredicted fashion. No one before 1917 had the slightest idea that the Bolsheviks would soon be in power—and the Bolsheviks themselves had no presentiment of the precise form that their state, should they ever succeed in creating one, would take. Just weeks before Nicholas II fell from power, Lenin expressed doubt as to whether Russia's Socialists would take revolutionary office in his lifetime: the worldwide historical importance of what was about to occur under his party's leadership was not even dimly foreseen by him.

The imperial monarchy was brought down in February 1917 by strikes and demonstrations that the garrison troops in Petrograd refused to suppress. The Romanov dynasty had been discredited long before the First World War, and in the course of its conflict with the Central Powers its difficulties deepened. Food shortages began in the cities. Inflation proceeded madly. Peasants were reluctant to release grain to the government's procurement agencies. The civilian administration was put under intolerable strain. Disloyal speeches were made in the State Duma, which was then disbanded by the emperor. Mutterings against him and his ministers took place in the military high command. His attempt in March to abdicate in favor of other members of his family was too little, too late. Instead a provisional government was installed, led by Prince Lvov and consisting mainly of liberals. Sanction for this outcome was given by the Petrograd Soviet, which had recently been elected by workers and soldiers in the capital. The Soviet was headed by Mensheviks and Socialist-Revolutionaries who declined the opportunity to assume power since they believed the country was still too backward for Socialists to administer.

This consensus was challenged by the Bolsheviks under Lenin's leadership after his return from Switzerland in April. The Bolsheviks alleged that the Mensheviks and Socialist-Revolutionaries had betrayed international socialism by propping up a government of prowar liberals. At that time, however, popular opinion was firmly against such radicalism. The Bolsheviks therefore set to work at undermining the provisional government's reputation.

They were helped in this by a series of cabinet blunders. Foreign Minister Pavel Milyukov in late April affirmed a commitment to the expansionist war aims of Nicholas II. Crowds came back onto the streets in protest, and Milyukov had to resign. The result was the reluctant agreement of Mensheviks and Socialist-Revolutionaries to join a ruling coalition and to take joint responsibility for state policy. The second blunder was the decision by Socialist-Revolutionary Alexander Kerensky, then war minister, to renew the Russian military offensive on the Eastern front. The Russian forces suffered a defeat. The provisional government, despite having suppressed the Bolshevik party in Petrograd, lost further credibility.

Kerensky assumed the premiership in July. In an effort to restore political order he called on Lavr Kornilov to redeploy troops from the front. Before they could arrive, Kerensky countermanded his own orders, fearing that a coup d'état was in the offing. Kornilov resolved upon removing the vacillating premier. Bolsheviks as well as Mensheviks and Socialist-Revolutionaries were needed as agitators to go out and dissuade the troops from obeying Kornilov. Kerensky kept his formal authority, but his days were numbered. He strove to bolster his chances by holding a state conference of all political parties in quest of some kind of consensus on governance that could keep order until such time as a constituent assembly might be elected. This ended in uproar, much to the satisfaction of the Bolsheviks. Kerensky then convoked a democratic conference; this excluded parties of the Right. Again no agreement was reached.

And all this time the difficulties inherited from Nicholas II were intensifying. The economy fell into a shambles. Worried bankers cut off loans to industry. Supplies of raw materials to the factories diminished drastically. Enterprise owners began to close shop, laying off their workers. Peasants ceased to comply with demands for grain procurements. Workers feared for their jobs; the prospect of mass unemployment and hunger loomed. More and more soldiers and sailors wanted an end to the war and did not mind how this might be achieved. Small businesses operated under ever more severe constraints. Transport, already overloaded before 1917, was continually disrupted. Administration collapsed into chaos. In the absence of assistance from Petrograd, cities, towns, and villages took charge of their own affairs, and entire regions, such as Ukraine and Finland, assumed self-rule. The old elites were powerless to recover control. The former parties of the political Right became demoralized and inert. The Orthodox Church turned in on itself and debated its own reform. The wealthy fled south, away from the zones of revolutionary turmoil, taking their money with them. By late summer the entire multinational state was on the brink of dissolution at every level of rule—and Kerensky, isolated in his rooms at the Winter Palace, manifestly had no solution.

Bad news came from the Eastern front in early September. Without undue difficulty German forces had advanced and taken the Latvian capital of Riga. They were only a day's train ride from Petrograd. Kerensky, who had depicted himself as the patriotic leader who would efficiently defend the country, found his popularity in tatters.

As the Bolsheviks had repeatedly asserted, an alternative framework for governance was already available in the shape of the soviets. In fact, "Mass organizations" had proliferated since the February Revolution. In addition to the soviets, they included trade unions and factory-workshop committees; and in the Russian countryside the village land communes enjoyed a resurgence of influence not seen since the near-revolution of 1905–7. People from the lower social orders were asserting themselves in public life as at no other time in Russian history. The soviets, being based in the cities, had an especially pronounced impact. Their primary defined functions were in the areas of welfare and education, but in order to discharge their obligation to defend the rights of workers, soldiers, and sailors they had to intrude on the prerogatives of the organs of local administration. To some extent this was a defensive action since the normal official organs quickly proved incapable of efficient action. But the soviets also embodied a spirit of political defiance. The Petrograd Soviet, being the first to arise from the events of February and March, laid down limits on the provisional government's space for maneuver. Other soviets agreed as soon as they were created. The cabinet was allowed to exist only on condition that it promulgated a full range of civil freedoms and abjured expansionist war aims.

By June the soviets were ready to form a central agency in Petrograd for the guidance of soviets throughout the country. This happened when the First Congress of Soviets elected a Central Executive Committee. Its leadership was Menshevik and Socialist-Revolutionary. This was hardly a permanent solution to the problems of coordinating activity on the political Left. Soviets at every level—regional, city, and urban district—were subject to a rule allowing the recurrent reelection of representatives. In the early autumn of 1917 the Bolsheviks made substantial electoral advances. In September they achieved durable majorities in the Petrograd Soviet and the Moscow Soviet. Elsewhere, too, they made headway. The Bolshevik party aimed to use its growing authority in the soviets to achieve revolutionary power.

The overthrow of the provisional government occurred on October 25 when the Military-Revolutionary Committee of the Petrograd Soviet under Trotsky's leadership seized garrisons and telegraph offices and surrounded the Winter Palace. Lenin had returned for a Bolshevik Central Committee meeting in the capital earlier in the month and had advanced the case that an insurrection was required both to stave off counterrevolution and to spark Socialist revolutions in the other belligerent states in the Great War. Despite the objections of fellow Bolshevik leaders Kamenev and Zinoviev, there was agreement on this objective. Preparations were hastily made despite a last-ditch armed effort by Kerensky to break up the party's operations in the capital. The Bolshevik Central Committee timed its actions so as to be able to present the Second Congress of Soviets with full governmental authority. Lenin appeared at its proceedings to announce the downfall of the provisional government. The Mensheviks and Socialist-Revolutionaries immediately walked out; they were confident that their absence would wreck the Bolshevik revolutionary scheme from the very start. Only the left-wing of the Party of Socialist-Revolutionaries remained in the hall of the Smolny Institute. A new government was hurriedly established, with Lenin as its first chairman. Its name was the Council of People's Commissars; but in Russian it instantly became known by its acronym Sovnarkom.

Decrees issued fast from the new government: on peace, land, workers' control, national self-determination, schooling, and the separation of church from state. Sovnarkom did not yet rule the country; consequently the decrees issuing from Petrograd would have limited impact, significantly effective only in Russia. But as soviets were steadily being brought under the control of the Bolsheviks and their sympathizers, industrial cities in the "borderlands" of the former empire were also affected. Here Sovnarkom's decrees were meant to have a "demonstrative" influence. The hope was that workers, peasants, and soldiers would read of the Bolsheviks' revolutionary purposes and show solidarity with the October Revolution.

Difficulties were huge. Lenin and Trotsky had expected that the forces of the Central Powers would crumble under the effects of revolutionary agitation. They called an armistice and waited for the German and Austrian governments to collapse. Instead they received ultimatums threatening an invasion of Russia if the Bolsheviks refused to sign a separate peace with them and withdraw from the war. After a blistering internal debate the Bolsheviks agreed to the humiliating treaty of Brest-Litovsk in March 1918. The western borderlands of the old Russian Empire were delivered into the hands of the Central Powers. This compounded the troubles of a terrible winter. The economy continued its plummet into ruin. Peasants withheld grain. Workers, dreading an imminent famine and objecting to dictatorial rule, started to turn against the Bolsheviks. The new security police—the "Extraordinary Commission" (or *Cheka*)—was barely able to cope with the volume of dissent. The Constituent Assembly elections gave the Bolshevik party only about a quarter of the seats; and although Sovnarkom forcibly dispersed it in January 1918, the Socialist-Revolutionary Party (which had been by far the largest) moved south to Samara to organize a countermove. The Brest-Litovsk treaty, moreover, caused the left Socialist-Revolutionaries to walk out of the Sovnarkom coalition.

Yet the Bolsheviks held on. Trotsky became People's Commissar for Military Affairs and reorganized the Red Army with such success that the Socialist-Revolutionaries were defeated in the Volga region in late summer 1918. He recruited sixty thousand former Imperial officers despite objections from the party's military opposition. Their competence as well as their subjection to oversight from political commissars enabled the Bolsheviks to take on enemies even more deadly than the Socialist-Revolutionaries. These enemies were the White armies raised by counterrevolutionary commanders such as Alexander Kolchak in Siberia, Anton Denikin in the Russian south, and Nikolai Yudenich in Estonia. The Whites aimed to throw out the Bolsheviks and overturn all their social and economic reforms. They were virulent anti-Semites. Although they were monarchists they had no prospect of restoring Nicholas II because he and his family had been murdered by Bolsheviks in Yekaterinburg in July 1918. The Whites had no time for politicking. They were obviously going to establish some kind of military dictatorship if they won the civil war.

The Bolshevik party approved measures for the reconstruction of the Soviet order. By the winter of 1918–19 there was agreement that the party should be centralized and empowered to operate as the supreme state agency. Bolsheviks had always believed in the merits of a "vanguard" party. The wartime emergency induced them

at last to put theory into practice. This was the means whereby they would be able to introduce discipline and obedience to the people's commissariats, trade unions, courts, the press, and the armed forces. Every public institution was to act in conformance with party policy and be led by party appointees. The principle of vertical command was to be realized. Bolsheviks themselves had to set an example. If an order came from above, it was no longer to be intensively discussed but simply to be obeyed. At the local level there was to be a restriction of internal party discussion, and individual chairmen—known as secretaries from 1920—were to run all the party committees. At the center, in Moscow (which was designated as the Russian capital in 1918), there was much change. Most members of the Bolshevik Central Committee were, like the rest of the party, mobilized for duties in the Red Army, or else they were sent to political trouble spots around the country. The Central Committee introduced a pair of inner subcommittees to deal with current party business. These were the political bureau (or politburo) and the organizational bureau (or orgburo); both were serviced by the secretariat. The powers of the politburo in particular were immense. Its members, guided by Lenin, were in charge of foreign policy, military strategy, economic management, and high-level appointments of personnel

The party also moved to still more radical economic changes. In the summer of 1918 it introduced a food dictatorship. This entrusted the state with a monopoly over the procurement and distribution of agricultural produce. Initially the idea was to split the rural population by establishing "committees of the village poor," which would aid armed urban squads in arresting rich peasants—known to the Bolsheviks as "kulaks"—and discovering illegally hoarded grain. This was not a successful venture. Peasants held to customs of village solidarity. They also resented urban interference and the ceaseless demands for grain and conscripts. The committees were quickly disbanded in Russia. The state nevertheless continued to set quotas for grain procurement and seized harvests regardless of protest in the countryside, thus saving the Red Army and the industrial working class from famine.

Industry was not left alone. In 1918–19 practically every operating enterprise, down to the smallest artisan workshop, was expropriated by the state. This had not been Lenin's immediate intention when he seized power in 1917. Indeed he had been criticized by many of the party's veterans, including Nikolai Bukharin, for lacking a true revolutionary spirit. The exigencies of warfare changed Lenin's mind for him. This had the advantageous effect of binding the wounds of internal party conflict after the disputes about the Brest-Litovsk treaty. The nationalization of the factories did not have the desired effect of halting the falloff in production; but it did at least provide the state with a monopoly of possession over unused goods, especially army greatcoats and rifles. This economic order later became known as War Communism. It strongly appealed to the Bolshevik worldview as an example of a centrally owned and planned economy. The Bolsheviks, moreover, held on to Moscow and Petrograd. They controlled the central nodes of the rail and telegraph network, had access to densely inhabited areas, and could conscript an army without undue difficulty. Their policing was ruthless and effective. No serious urban revolt could be undertaken by sympathizers of the Whites. The Cheka, liberated from constraints after the attempt on Lenin's life in August 1918, conducted a bloodthirsty campaign against what were called "the former people," members of the old ruling and property-owning elites. The Red Terror was vicious in the extreme (as was the White Terror in the regions under the control of Kolchak, Denikin, and Yudenich).

The Bolshevik party had brilliant propagandists. Trotsky, traveling everywhere by train, was a masterly orator and writer; he never gave up extolling the benefits to the "working masses" of a future Red victory. And Trotsky was not alone. At every opportunity the Bolsheviks roused support for the cause of the October Revolution by painting a picture of a radiant future. The events of 1917 in Petrograd were depicted as the first of a series of proletarian revolutions about to sweep across Europe and North America. The capitalist era was purportedly coming to a close. The world's bourgeoisies, decrepit and imperialistic, would be thrust into the dustbin of history. To this end it was decided to form a Communist International (or Comintern) in Moscow as soon as possible after the Great War ended with the Allied defeat of the Central Powers. As yet the far-left political parties around the globe were few in number and small in their followings. Communist organizations scarcely existed. Yet Lenin, Trotsky, and Zinoviev felt sure that geopolitics were moving in their favor. The Comintern founding congress was held, firmly under Bolshevik control, in March 1919.

First, though, the Whites had to be defeated. This was accomplished in stages as the Reds reacted to offensives coming from the east, south, and northwest. Kolchak succeeded in breaking through to the Urals, but then his advance faltered in the spring of 1919. Soon his forces were in panic-stricken retreat across Siberia. Kolchak himself was caught, secretly tried, and executed. Denikin pushed up from the south in the summer of 1919, dividing his army into two sectors. Like Kolchak, he bothered little with the tasks of securing his rear. His objective was to occupy Moscow and only then to impose an effective administration. Denikin met the full strength of the Red Army and was crushed. He resigned, his place being taken by Pëtr Wrangel, whose army was pinned back to Crimea. Next came Yudenich, in the autumn of 1919, who moved swiftly toward Petrograd. Defense was reinforced. Yudenich, losing the support of his Estonian combatants, went down to defeat. Red victory was now complete in Russia. By the end of the year the British and French expeditionary contingents had been withdrawn. The Bolsheviks were masters of the core of the former Russian Empire. In 1920 they aimed at the final liquidation of Wrangel's army. Wrangel recognized that he needed to increase his appeal to the local peasantry and promised land reform.

In spring and early summer, however, external factors distracted the Red Army. Polish forces under Jósef Pilsudski invaded Ukraine, and before the Reds could counterattack, Kiev fell to the Poles. Benefiting from a surge of patriotic support, the Bolsheviks threw back Pilsudski's army and themselves advanced into Poland. This was largely at Lenin's insistence. His objective was to seize the opportunity to introduce a Soviet-style regime in Warsaw and then to march on Berlin. The dream of "European Socialist revolution" so suffused his mind that he ignored advice from several Bolshevik leaders who warned that Polish workers were not likely to welcome the Reds. In fact the Red Army was heavily defeated even before it reached Warsaw. Wrangel's forces in the meantime had strengthened their position in Crimea and were preparing yet another campaign. Lenin at last saw the error of his recent strategy. Negotiations were inaugurated with the Polish government, and the idea of exporting revolution on the point of a bayonet was dropped for the foreseeable future.

The Red Army quickly finished off Wrangel's army and turned its attention to the borderlands of the former Russian Empire. The Polish military disaster made it unthinkable to attempt the reconquest of Lithuania, Latvia, and Estonia. The south Caucasus was a different matter. Azerbaijan, Armenia, and finally—in March of 1921—Georgia were overrun. The sequence of triumphs disguised the scale of the opposition and resistance to Bolshevism. Workers had frequently gone on strike in 1918–20. There had been several mutinies by Red soldiers and desertions occasionally became a mass phenomenon. The peasantry in many provinces in Russia and elsewhere revolted. The same grievances were constantly expressed. People objected to the one-party dictatorship and to rule by commissars. They felt tricked by the Bolsheviks who had promised freedom for "the toiling masses" in 1917. They hated the restrictions on private trade; the barrier detachments on the outskirts of cities prevented peasants from carrying in sacks of produce for sale. They abhorred the endless conscription campaigns. Rural inhabitants detested being forced to yield up all their grain to the state procurement authorities. Even if the Bolsheviks had succeeded in recruiting followers more easily than had the Whites, their popularity had never been great. Calls and action for the overthrow of the Soviet regime intensified in the winter of 1920–21.

When the Tambov peasant rebellion reached a peak in February 1921 the politburo decided on emergency reform. This became known as the New Economic Policy (NEP). Its basis was the replacement of universal grain requisitioning by a graduated tax-in-kind and granting permission for the peasantry to trade their surpluses of produce again. Confirmation of the NEP was given by the Tenth Party Congress in March. Concessions in the economy were accompanied by increased political repression. The mutiny of the Kronstadt naval garrison, which had fervently espoused the Bolshevik cause before the October Revolution, was crushed with severity. The Red Army was deployed against peasant rebels in Russia and Ukraine. The party exercised strict internal discipline: factional activity was banned.

The Bolsheviks had expected the October Revolution to bring about the end of world capitalism. Instead their state was beleaguered. The immediate menace of a crusade against them had lessened; but they had to expect trouble from abroad at some time or other. They had also been made aware that many workers and peasants felt hostile toward them. Moreover, the Bolshevik party knew that there were plenty of other enemies of their purposes in Soviet society. Organized religion had the loyalty of most citizens. Intellectuals disdained the crude certitude of Marxism-Leninism. Middle-class professionals were at best hoping that Bolsheviks would steadily moderate their fanaticism. Immense tasks of revolutionary transformation still lay ahead. A strategy had yet to be worked out. Although a one-party state had been constructed, the party itself needed to attract and train many more members than it possessed. Ways had to be found to restrict the influence of people who sought the termination of the regime. Lenin was sure that this could and would be done. He and his party held to the belief that history was on their side. Few Bolsheviks, even the most perceptive among them, understood that their methods of dictatorship and terror were obstacles to the achievement of a humane state, a prosperous economy, and a society of consent.

See also Bolshevism; Brest-Litovsk, Treaty of; Dictatorship of the Proletariat; Kronstadt Revolt; Lenin, Vladimir; Polish-Soviet War; Red Terror; Soviets; War Communism.

FURTHER READING

Getzler, I. *Kronstadt: The Fate of a Soviet Democracy.* Cambridge, UK: Cambridge University Press, 1986.

Keep, J.L.H. *The Russian Revolution: A Study in Mass Mobilisation.* London: Weidenfeld and Nicolson, 1976.

Mawdsley, E. *The Russian Civil War.* London: Allen and Unwin, 1987.

Rabinowitch, A. *The Bolsheviks Come to Power: The Revolution of 1917 in Petrograd.* New York: Norton, 1976.

Service, R. *The Russian Revolution, 1900–1927.* 3rd ed. London: Macmillan, 1999.

ROBERT SERVICE

Rykov, Alexei

Born into a peasant family in Saratov, Alexei Rykov (1881–1938) attended the town high school and later the law school in Kazan'. He became a member of the Russian Social Democratic Labor Party in 1900. Rykov was arrested for the first time in 1901, and took refuge in Geneva at the end of 1903, at the party's center abroad. In 1905, he was included in the Bolshevik Party's Central Committee during its Fifth Congress (London) and also took part in the Moscow uprising that same year. He spent most of the years between 1906 and 1910 in either exile or prison, from which he escaped several times. At the time of the February Revolution he was confined to Siberia.

In 1917, during the Bolshevik Party's April conference, Rykov was among those reluctant to approve of Lenin's idea of organizing a socialist revolution in backward

Russia. A member of the Moscow Soviet, he participated in the October insurrection in Petrograd. He was a member of the first Soviet government for a few days as interior minister, resigning to protest (together with Lev Kamenev, Grigory Zinovyev, Viktor Nogin, and Vladimir Milyutin) the decision by Lenin and the rest of the Central Committee to negotiate the participation of other socialist parties in the revolutionary government. After reconciling, he was nominated as president of the Supreme Council for Economics and Red Army government plenipotentiary for supplies. In 1921 he became vice president of the Council of Peoples' Commissars (Sovnarkom). The following year he became a member of the politburo, and after Lenin's death, president of Sovnarkom of the Russian Soviet Federative Socialist Republic. Felix Dherzhinsky then became president of the Supreme Council for Economics, and he and Rykov developed a friendly collaboration from then on.

Rykov supported the New Economic Policy as a gradual and market-oriented path toward industrialization and agricultural development, and also favored a certain degree of decentralization in the economy's management. Unlike Stalin, he understood that the fatal grain crisis during winter 1927–28 was not the result of hostile kulak activities but rather of the incapacity of Soviet apparatuses to regulate economic life in the countryside by means of nonoppressive economic and political measures. He also attempted to support a less drastic and more realistic Five-Year Plan than the one advocated by the Stalinist majority.

Singled out by Stalin as a member of a new right-wing opposition (together with Nikolay Bukharin and Mikhail Tomsky), Rykov defended the principles of collegiality and freedom of discussion within the politburo. At the end of 1930, he was expelled from the politburo and removed from his high-ranking government posts, and in 1934 demoted to a candidate member of the Central Committee. He was accused in 1936 of plotting as part of the imaginary underground Trotsky-Zinovyev group, and the following year was expelled from the party. Dragged into the March 1938 show trial, he was condemned to death and executed a few days afterward.

See also Bukharin, Nikolay; New Economic Policy.

FURTHER READING

Rykov A. I., *Izbrannye proizvedenija*. Moscow: Ekonomika, 1990.

Senin A. S., *A. I. Rykov: stranicy žizni*. Moscow: Izd-vo MGOU, 1993.

Shelestov D. K., *Vremja Alekseja Rykova*. Moscow: Progress, 1990.

FRANCESCO BENVENUTI

Sakharov, Andrey

Born in Moscow on May 21, Andrey Sakharov (1921–89) was one of the best-known figures in the history of Soviet dissent. The son of a physics professor, Sakharov followed in his father's footsteps, graduating at the top of his class in Ashgabat in 1942, a city that he had been previously evacuated to. Because of his intellect, in 1948 he became part of a study group tasked with developing a thermonuclear bomb, and from that moment on he became part of the elite group of Soviet scientists and worked for twenty years in conditions of absolute secrecy. In 1950, he collaborated with others to develop a thermonuclear reactor with a magnetic containment system. He was one of the main creators of the first hydrogen bomb in 1953, and soon became a member of the USSR's Academy of Sciences, receiving the medal of Hero of Socialist Labor three times, in addition to the Stalin prize in 1953 and the Lenin Prize in 1956.

In the 1960s Sakharov began to reflect on the value of freedom of conscience—a path that was both individual and political, and that would lead him to sacrifice his career, privileges, and social position. Having made contact with the dissident world, in 1968 he came out into the open with his *Reflections on Progress, Peaceful Coexistence, and Intellectual Freedom.* This work was published abroad, but was also widely circulated in samizdat form in the USSR, costing Sakharov his participation in secret research activities. Faced with his failed attempt at democratic reforms of the socialist system, Sakharov engaged in a campaign on behalf of civil and human rights. Every year he signed dozens of documents that mentioned hundreds of names of individuals who were persecuted; he demanded that the death penalty be abolished and fought for amnesty for all political prisoners. His home became a pole of attraction for all the USSR's dissidents.

In 1970 he founded the Committee for Human Rights, and in 1974 held a press conference in his Moscow apartment to announce the Day of the Political Prisoner in the USSR.

The regime did not stand idly by. Starting in 1973 Sakharov was the victim of a harsh press campaign that would last over a decade. In 1975 he received the Nobel Prize, but Soviet authorities prevented him from accepting it. After Sakharov made statements to numerous foreign correspondents condemning the Soviet invasion of Afghanistan in December 1979, he was confined in January to the city of Gorky with his wife, Elena Bonner. He lived there for almost seven years under strict surveillance, but was able to continue his activities; thanks to Bonner, his declarations and articles reached Moscow until 1984. Police checks became stricter every year, increasingly isolating the two dissidents. At the end of her trial Bonner was condemned to five years confinement in Gorky, while Sakharov repeatedly resorted to hunger strikes but was subjected to forced feeding.

Hope for a general amnesty for all Soviet political prisoners was given new life with Mikhail Gorbachev's rise to power. After Sakharov wrote to him requesting that all dissidents be freed, in December 1986 Gorbachev decided to repeal his confinement. Sakharov's return to Moscow was celebrated as a new phase in Soviet history. His articles were published in newspapers. Sakharov was given permission to take a long trip to France, Japan, the United States, and many other countries. Finally, in April 1989, he was elected to the First All-Union Congress of Peoples' Deputies. His newfound political role was cut short by his death in December of that same year.

See also Atomic Bomb; Dissent in the USSR; Peaceful Coexistence; Perestroika.

FURTHER READING

Clementi, M. *Il diritto al dissenso. Il progetto costituzionale di Andrej Sakharov.* Rome: Odradek, 2002.

Sakharov, A. D. *Progress, Coexistence, and Intellectual Freedom.* New York: Norton, 1968.

———. *My Country and the World.* New York: Knopf/Vintage, 1975.

———. *Memoirs.* London: Hutchinson, 1990.

———. *Trevoga i nadežda.* Moscow: Interverso, 1991.

ELENA DUNDOVICH

Sandinista Revolution

The American 20th century opened with the Mexican Revolution and the repercussions of the Bolshevik Revolution. It concluded, on the eve of the dissolution of the Soviet system, with the Nicaraguan Revolution, which like the Cuban Revolution, was born from a struggle against those dictatorships protected by the United States. In this case the struggle was against the dictatorship begun by Anastasio Somoza García (known as Tacho) in 1937, who just three years beforehand had gained notoriety as a result of his assassination of Augusto César Sandino. Tacho died in 1956, and was succeeded by his son, Luís Somoza Debayle. When Luís died in 1967, he was succeeded by Anastasio Somoza Debayle (known as Tachito), who was reelected president in 1974.

The Frente Sandinista de liberación nacional (FSLN) was founded by three Nicaraguan exiles in Honduras in 1961: Carlos Fonseca Amadór (the Frente's most important leader until his death in combat in 1976), Tomás Borge, and Silvio Mayorga. In the course of planning the struggle against the dictatorship, three significantly different politicomilitary lines jostled for power: the *guerra popular extensa y prolongada*, supported by Borge, Bayardo Arce, and Henry Ruíz, inspired by the Maoist theory of the *guerra campesina*; the *tendencia proletaria*, supported by Luis Carrión, Carlos Nuñez, and Jaime Wheelock; and the *tendencia tercerista-insurrecionista*, which supported popular uprisings also in urban centers, and was supported by the brothers Daniel and Humberto Ortega Saavedra and Victor Tirado. These tendencies were unified in March 1979, in Havana, in a single *Dirección nacional*. In 1978 the Frente Amplio Opositor (FAO) was born, uniting some sectors of the bourgeoisie and the middle and popular classes that were opposed to the dictator; it included the Grupo de los Doce, the organizations that became part of the Unión democrática de liberación, the Communist Party, and some personalities close to the FSLN like Ernesto Cardenal, the revolution's greatest poet and a Catholic priest inspired by liberation theology as well as future minister of culture until the FSLN's electoral defeat in 1990.

In 1978 the FAO appealed for a general strike, and a people's military offensive developed from this strike, culminating on July 19, 1979, with the Sandinistas' entry into Managua and Tachito's escape into Paraguay. The new government, the Junta Provisional de Reconstrucción Nacional, inherited the consequences of the previous regime and attempts to overthrow it, including fifty thousand dead and a hundred thousand wounded; unemployment had reached 50 percent, and a third of the population was without a home or means of subsistence. The junta's measures were successful, and the country's economy improved, with the gross national product growing by 6 percent in 1984—one of the highest rates in all of Latin America.

The coalition of social and political forces that had made this revolution possible, far removed from the old Communist bureaucratic apparatuses in Eastern Europe and Cuba itself, roused an interest among European socialists, Italian Communists, and even some sectors of the U.S. Democratic Party and the Jimmy Carter administration. In addition to Ernesto Cardenal, his brother Fernando, and Foreign Minister Miguel d'Escoto, the presence of Catholic priests with a role in the government contributed to the development of a harsh and systematic opposition led by Managua's archbishop, Miguel Obando y Bravo, and supported by the Vatican and Pope John Paul II, starting with his trip to Nicaragua in March 1983. In 1984 for the first time in the country's political history, impartial elections were held in which the combined forces of the two Frentes (FSLN and FAO) garnered 67 percent of the vote; on January 10 Daniel Ortega became president, and proceeding along the path of institutional reforms, the Asamblea Nacional began work on a new Constitution, which was approved in 1987.

As soon as he was installed in office, U.S. president Ronald Reagan authorized the Central Intelligence Agency (CIA) to undertake operations against the Sandinista government. In August of the previous year the Fuerza democrática nicaragüense, composed of *somocista* mercenaries (funded with the illegal moneys that would later become the focus of the Iran-Contra scandal) ready to attack Nicaragua, was created in Guatemala. The Sandinistas were accused of helping the Frente Farabundo Martí para la liberación nacional, which had begun its activities in El Salvador only a few months earlier, under the leadership of Joaquín Villalobos. Under the direction of the United States, whose main focus was fighting communism—as it had done with a series of military coups in Brazil, Chile, Argentina, and Uruguay—Argentina's military junta, then led by General Roberto Viola in collaboration with the CIA, provided the necessary military assistance to the *somocista* ex-guardsmen, who operated from clandestine bases in Honduras and Guatemala. The military and paramilitary activities of these counterrevolutionary organizations (known in abbreviated form as Contra) took the form of guerrilla operations, terrorist attacks, and criminal atrocities that the Sandinista government reported to the International Court in the Hague, which condemned the United States for having mined Nicaragua's harbors and undertaken boycott activities.

The Cold War, even in its "pacific coexistence" variant that divided the world into spheres of influence, had negative consequences in Central America not only because it allowed for an increased U.S. military interference in the region but also because it revealed the limits of the USSR's policies in Latin America. These policies swung between state and party interests, between the cautious support of military dictatorships to the increasingly costly support of revolutionary movements, which were slowly left to their own devices (except for Cuba)—as in the case of the U.S. toppling the pro-Soviet government led by Maurice Bishop on Grenada by military means (which the Sandinistas interpreted as a dry run by the United States of a possible invasion of Nicaragua). The Soviet policy of relative disengagement and opportunism was confirmed during Ortega's 1983 visit to Moscow. During the late 1980s the increasingly serious internal problems of Mikhail Gorbachev's USSR meant that Soviet aid to Nicaragua was even more insignificant, while the negative effects of the U.S. economic embargo and military destabilization by the Contras only increased. By 1988 inflation had risen to 1,000 percent. The government, applying the drastic measures that the International Monetary Fund had already imposed in Brazil and Argentina, issued a new currency and reduced the state budget by 10 percent.

With the mediation of the then-president of Costa Rica, Oscar Arias Sánchez, a peace plan was devised to end the civil war and the crisis in the Sandinistas' capability to govern the country. One of the plan's central points was to anticipate the elections, which were to be held in the presence of international observers. They were properly held in February 1990 and were won by a vast coalition known as Unión nacional opositora led by Violeta Chamorro (the widow of a journalist assassinated by Somoza in January 1979) with 55.2 percent of the vote, while the FSLN garnered 40.8 percent of the vote. Ortega remained in the opposition, suffering electoral defeats in 1996 and 2001. In 1995 the Sandinista Front split, and this resulted in the creation of the Movimiento de renovación Sandinista, founded by Edmundo Jarquín and Sergio Ramírez. The victory by Ortega and the FSLN in the elections held on November 5, 2006, with the same percentage of the vote they had received when defeated by Chamorro, confirmed the political tenacity of the old Sandinista commandant and his comrades, but also suggested that the program of the winning coalition (which included the vice president and veteran ex-Contra Jaime Morales Carazo) did not have the same social, economic, and political objectives that characterized the goals of the socialist and democratic revolution in Nicaragua.

See also Anti-imperialism; Guerrilla Warfare in Latin America; Second Cold War.

FURTHER READING

Armony, A. C. *Argentina, the United States, and the Anti-Communist Crusade in Central America, 1977–1984*. Athens: Ohio University Center for International Studies, 1997.

Comisión para la Defensa de los Derechos Humanos en Nicaragua. *Nicaragua. Insurección y genocidio*. 2 vols. San José, Costa Rica: La Comisión, 1979.

Gilbert, D. L. *Sandinistas*. Oxford: Basil Blackwell, 1988.

Miranda, R., and W. E. Ratliff. *The Civil War in Nicaragua: Inside the Sandinistas*. London: Transaction Publishers, 1993.

Morales, C. J. *La Contra*. Mexico: Editorial Planeta, 1989.

Pastor, R. A. *Condemned to Repetition: The United States and Nicaragua*. Princeton, NJ: Princeton University Press, 1987.

Vanden, H. E., and G. Prevost. *Democracy and Socialism in Sandinista Nicaragua*. Boulder, CO: Lynne Rienner, 1993.

Walker, T. W., ed. *Reagan versus Sandinistas: The Undeclared War on Nicaragua*. Boulder, CO: Westview Press, 1987.

ALBERTO FILIPPI

Sartre, Jean-Paul

The philosopher and writer Jean-Paul Sartre (1905–80) embodied the figure of an intellectual who saw commitment as a duty (a position he took himself after World

War II). In 1924, together with his friend Paul Nizan, Sartre passed the entrance examination for admission to the École normale supérieure and developed ties to Raymond Aron. He placed first in the *agrégé* exam in philosophy in 1929; Simone de Beauvoir came in second. Having replaced Aron as a fellowship holder in Berlin during 1933–34, he discovered contemporary German philosophy and proved fairly indifferent to Adolf Hitler's rise to power. Sartre was called to arms in 1939, and during the *drôle de guerre* spent his time writing. He became a prisoner of war in 1940, was freed in April 1941, and then helped to found a small group of French resisters, Socialisme et résistance. He organized a performance of his *Les mouches* (The Flies) in Paris in 1943 and wrote *L'Être et le néant* (Being and Nothingness), in which he dealt with the larger issues of his philosophy.

At the time of the liberation, although he had not actively participated in the resistance, Sartre was celebrated as one of its great figures. This was the writer's moment of glory; his philosophy of freedom became fashionable (*L'existentialisme est un humanisme*). He left the editorship of the journal he had founded, *Les temps modernes*, to Maurice Merleau-Ponty, who defended Marxism as an interpretative framework for historical understanding (*Humanisme et terreur*, 1947). In 1948, together with David Rousset, Sartre participated in establishing the Rassemblement démocratique révolutionnaire, conceived politically as a third way, and later engaged in polemics with Rousset himself about the camps in the Soviet Union.

After the outbreak of the Korean War (1950), while Merleau-Ponty moved away from the Communist Party, Sartre moved closer. He was active in the campaign against the war in Indochina, and became a Communist fellow traveler—experiences that he described in the essay "Les communistes et la paix" (1952–54). He joined the movement of Partisans of Peace, went to the Vienna Congress for World Peace in 1952, and then visited the USSR in 1954. His support for Soviet positions caused him to break with Albert Camus, Claude Lefort, and Merleau-Ponty, who criticized Sartre's "ultra-Bolshevism" in his *Les aventures de la dialectique* (1955). The repression of the Hungarian uprising in the fall of 1956 caused him to break with Stalinism, leading to the publication in *Les temps modernes* of "Le fantôme de Stalin" (Stalin's Ghost). Sartre maintained a favorable opinion of the Soviet Union, however, returning there between 1962 and 1966, as well as the socialist camp, as his reporting on Cuba in 1960 demonstrated. His idea of communism

was closer to the Italian Communist Party's than to the French Communist Party's, as was evident in the article he wrote after Palmiro Togliatti's death in August 1964. After the Prague Spring was repressed in 1968, Sartre condemned the degradation of Soviet socialism.

From 1958 to 1962, the journal *Les temps modernes* opposed the war in Algeria and supported the FLN. In 1961 Sartre—who now placed the revolutionary hopes he had once given to the proletariat with the oppressed of the third world—wrote a preface for Frantz Fanon's *Les Damnés de la terre* (The Wretched of the Earth), inspired by a radical endorsement of the third world, which caused a scandal. In 1964 he refused the Nobel Prize and waxed enthusiastic about the events of May 1968. In 1967 he presided over the Russell Tribunal, which had been created to judge U.S. crimes in Vietnam. The years after 1968 are those of his *gauchiste* activism, when he decided to support small Maoist groups with his notoriety. At the end of his life, sick and almost blind, Sartre could still cause a stir. He engaged in a dialogue with Benny Lévy, an ex-supporter of *La Gauche prolétarienne*. He joined Aron in the operation "Un bateau pour le Vietnam"; under André Glucksmann's leadership, it was meant to help the Vietnamese boat people. Sartre died on April 15, 1980, and his funeral in Paris was attended by fifty thousand people.

See also Fellow Travelers; Marxism, Western; Third Worldism.

FURTHER READING

Contat, M., ed. *Théâtre complet*. Paris: Gallimard, 2005.

Contat, M., and M. Rybalka, eds. *Oeuvres romanesques*. Paris: Gallimard, 1981.

The principal texts that are relevant to Sartre's political evolution have been collected in the ten volumes of *Situations*, in particular: *Situations*, Vol. 2, *Littérature et engagement* (1948); *Situations*, Vol. 4, *Portraits* (1964); *Situations*, Vol. 5, *Colonialisme et néo-colonialisme* (1964); *Situations*, Vol. 6, *Problèmes du marxisme II* (1965); *Situations*, Vol. 8, *Autour de 1968* (1972).

NICOLE RACINE

Science

Theory

Due to a combination of ideological and pragmatic reasons, science was more valuable and important for communism than it was for any other contemporary political movement or regime. Like its intellectual predecessors—the Enlightenment, classical Marxism, and the cultural tradition of the Russian intelligentsia—communism saw in science a political and ideological ally, a major force of not only economic and technical but also social progress. The rational scientific worldview was expected to unseat the power of religion and superstition over the minds of the people. Communist countries also regarded science as a key to achieving their primary economic objectives—industrialization and modernization. The resulting social prestige for science in these countries rose to unmatched heights, even in comparison with other scientistic societies, and they also devoted to science a significantly higher share of national resources.

Communist authors adhered to and advanced specific ideas about science, which at the time sounded dangerously radical and provocative for much of the public. Communists insisted that scientific thought, even at its most abstract, had originated from and stayed linked to the practical, especially economic, activity of the people. They thus categorically rejected the once-dominant view that privileged and separated "pure science" from "applied" research and technology. For Communists, even the most fundamental science was worthy of its name only if it had potential useful applications, at least in the long perspective. Increased public support for research required, according to them, actively directing investigations toward satisfying social and economic goals formulated by the state. With this purpose in mind, Communists rejected the principle of the autonomy of the academic profession as a closed, self-governed corporation. Instead, they promoted the ideal of science as a public profession supported by public funds, consciously serving social needs, and oriented toward producing useful knowledge, with the main directions of research and the distribution of resources rationally "planned" via institutions of the state. They also rejected the concept of science as an elitist occupation, the privileged activity of a few free thinkers and great minds driven by sheer intellectual curiosity. Instead, science was supposed to become open to large numbers of representatives of once-underprivileged classes and groups, including women and ethnic minorities.

Similar ideas were also often extended to social sciences and the humanities, in part because of the wider meaning of the words for science in Russian (*nauka*) and German (*Wissenschaft*), which embraced all fields of scholarship altogether. Marxism belonged to science in this wider sense, too, as it modeled itself on natural science, and applied the naturalistic method of explanation to the study of human society and history. Its conclusions were therefore as certain as scientific truths about nature. This linguistically reinforced linkage between science and Marxism helped further support their perceived alliance and mutual prestige in the Communist world.

Consistent with the above, nauka in general and natural science in particular were not supposed to be fully free of social and ideological influences. Even the firmest conclusions of the natural sciences reflected existing human social practices, and the material and economic conditions of life. It was not accidental, for example, that modern European science emerged during the 16th and 17th centuries, parallel with the rise of capitalist societies as well as the new economic demands of manufacturing, navigation, trade, and warfare. In a similar vein, Aleksandr Bogdanov suggested in 1918 that the rise of a truly socialist society, with its new life and work practices, would inspire and bring along a novel, socialist stage in the development of science. Lenin and Trotsky, however, rejected the talk about "proletarian science" as dangerously radical and premature. For them, it was more important to recruit the already existing science and expertise into the immediate service of socialist construction.

Subsequently, the mainstream Communist discourse about science combined an unwavering adherence to the principle of scientific materialism—a belief that science delivers truth or at least relative objective truth about nature—with elements of "social constructivism"—a view that society influences the content of scientific knowledge—while avoiding explicit contradiction between the two approaches. The term "proletarian science" was rejected and criticized, but "bourgeois science" was used quite often, especially in discussions about a "crisis" in science. Many authors, following the model of Lenin's *Materialism and Empirio-Criticism*, were concerned primarily with philosophical conclusions derived from novel scientific developments, such as relativity theory. They opposed idealistic interpretations, developed Marxist ones, and maintained that the philosophy of dialectical materialism provided the best methodological guidance for natural scientists in their search for true knowledge. Others implied that even certain theories in science could become corrupted by bourgeois ideological and social influences, and deviate from the objective path, as in the case of eugenics.

Practices

The recognition of science as a separate profession and a new organization of research infrastructure started almost immediately after the Russian Revolution. The Bolshevik government approved a series of proposals by scientists to establish a network of special research institutes in various fields. Supported by state funds, these institutes delved into advanced research combined with the pursuit of important utilitarian, frequently modernist, and revolutionary-sounding goals—designing aircraft, developing X-ray technology and radio, or improving crops with the help of genetics and chemical fertilizers. Besides a significant increase in size, a new definition of the research worker distinguished these institutes from the preceding generation of university laboratories. Up until then, the usual position for a scientist was that of a university professor or assistant involved in undergraduate teaching. Employment at the new institutes created a large group of salaried scientists and research engineers professionally occupied full-time with research and development.

The predominance of research institutes—both fundamental and applied—and the related profession of scientist-engineer eventually became the most visible institutional characteristic of Soviet science. Many such institutes developed experimental production facilities or close ties with industrial plants, and served as centers of innovation during the modernization of the Soviet economy in the 1930s and the development of military technologies on the eve of World War II. In 1930s' Europe, Communist and socialist scientists campaigned for a similar recognition of the value of research by society and the state—a reform that established the Centre national de la recherche scientifique in France and J. D. Bernal's social responsibility of science movement in Britain. The Chinese nationalist government began to establish institutions based on the Soviet example, and after the Communist victory, China as well as other Communist-governed countries in Europe and Asia adopted this model of science organization. In the United States, the government-directed branch of research accepted the nickname "big science," exemplified by such organizations as NASA and the Atomic Energy Commission's national laboratories.

The Communist reform of higher education and the training of science cadres started with the abolishment of tuition. Additional preferential measures were designed to ease access and promotion for students coming from the poor and groups previously discriminated against—a system analogous to the one currently known in the United States as "affirmative action." Recognizing the need for scientific and technical advice, the Bolsheviks adopted a policy of compromise with predominantly non-Communist and nonsympathizing "bourgeois specialists," who were appointed in large numbers to responsible posts in Soviet offices and designed many signature projects of the new regime. Lenin's related slogan, Communism is Soviet power plus the electrification of the whole country," metaphorically expressed the technocratic nature of the Soviet experiment as based on collaboration between the Communist Party and scientists/engineers.

State science rather than market mechanisms drove the all-out industrialization effort of the 1930s. The related further dramatic buildup of research institutes made the already acute shortage of technical cadres much more severe. A massive campaign for training sympathizers with required expertise—"red specialists" to replace bourgeois ones—followed. The extension of affirmative action measures to the greatly enlarged graduate studies enabled a peasant son and future Nobel laureate, Pavel Cherenkov, to embark on a research career in physics. In 1939, Lina Shtern became the first woman to be elected to the most prestigious position in Soviet science: full membership in the Academy of Sciences. By the 1940s, most ethnic republics in the Soviet Union, including the Caucasia and Central Asia, built up their own research infrastructure and community.

Sharp conceptual debates caused by the crisis and revolution in early 20th-century science—especially in physics and biology—became even more heated due to the opportunity to use ideological arguments in polemics. To some scientists, the replacement of the basic foundations of scientific knowledge with new and unfamiliar ones looked like a deviation from materialism; others defended conceptual novelties with the help of dialectics and Lenin's dictum that the "electron is as inexhaustible as the atom." Einstein's theory of relativity and Mendelian genetics appealed to the revolutionary mind-set of the 1920s, and met an early overenthusiastic acceptance. Marxist philosophy helped the development of Lev Vygotsky's psychological theories on language and thought as well as child learning. Eugenics came under fire around 1930 and was abandoned because of its associations with racism. The criticism of genetics subsequently intensified, and in 1948 Trofim Lysenko declared it an ideologically and scientifically wrong theory. The ban affected research in other Communist countries, too, and lasted until 1964, when the Soviet authorities reinvested in molecular biology to try to make up for the lost years. The debates about quantum mechanics centered on its philosophical interpretation. In the USSR, Vladimir Fock defended Bohr's complementarity by giving it a Marxist reading, but some Communist physicists saw incompatibility between dialectical materialism and the indeterministic Copenhagen philosophy, which motivated the American David Bohm to develop an alternative, causal interpretation of quantum theory.

The U.S. atomic bomb and Hiroshima brought science onto the center stage of world politics. Stalin's 1946 election promise "to catch up and surpass the achievements of science outside the boundaries of our country" euphemistically meant the bomb. From that point on, Soviet practices regarding science reflected not so much a Communist agenda as the logic of Cold War rivalry between the two global superpowers and their similar research priorities linked to the arms race. Even the Communist system's largest public triumph in the area of science and technology, the launch of Sputnik in 1957, came as a side result of a project devoted entirely to nuclear deterrence: the development of an intercontinental missile delivery system capable of carrying a hydrogen bomb. The Soviet quest for security succeeded on its own terms—defined as catching up and achieving a relative parity with the United States in the nuclear arms race—but this main priority overshadowed and pushed to the back burner modernization in most other, nonmilitary fields.

Science that had played such a key role in creating the Communist system was also important in bringing it down in the Soviet Union. As a reward for the successful development of atomic weapons, scientists obtained recognition of fundamental research in its own right, in a partial reversal of earlier policies. In 1960, the USSR Academy of Sciences disengaged itself from the bulk of technological development by getting rid of its engineering disciplines and applied institutes. Scientists continued to enjoy prestige, but except for the few top academicians co-opted into the Communist Party leadership proper, did not feel that their privileges were sufficient and that their elite status translated into an actual say in decision making. A few of them, such as Andrey Sakharov, dared to challenge the system openly as dissidents, but the majority expressed their opposition publicly once it became reasonably safe to do so, during Mikhail Gorbachev's perestroika. In 1991, after having helped to end Communist rule, scientists also discovered that they had destroyed the political basis for their own prestigious status and role in society.

See also Atomic Bomb; Intelligentsia; Marxism-Leninism; Military-Industrial Complex; Modernization; Sakharov, Andrey; Warfare.

FURTHER READING

Bailes, K. E. *Technology and Society under Lenin and Stalin: Origins of the Soviet Technical Intelligentsia.* Princeton, NJ: Princeton University Press, 1978.

Bernal, J. D. *The Social Function of Science.* London: Routledge, 1939.

Bukharin, N. I., et.al. *Science at the Crossroads: Papers Presented to the International Congress of the History of Science and Technology Held in London from June 29th to July 3rd, 1931 by the Delegates of the U.S.S.R.* London: Frank Cass and Co., 1931.

Haldane, J.B.S. *The Marxist Philosophy and the Sciences.* Freeport, NY: Books for Libraries Press, 1969.

Graham, L. R. *Science, Philosophy, and Human Behavior in the Soviet Union.* New York: Columbia University Press, 1987.

Joravsky, D. *Soviet Marxism and Natural Science, 1917–1932.* London: Routledge and Kegan Paul, 1961.

Kojevnikov, A. B. *Stalin's Great Science: The Time and Adventures of Soviet Physicists.* London: Imperial College Press, 2004.

Lenin, V. I. *Materialism and Empirio-Criticism: Critical Comments on One Reactionary Philosophy.* 1909; repr., Honolulu: University Press of the Pacific, 2002.

Sheehan, H. *Marxism and the Philosophy of Science: A Critical History: The First Hundred Years.* Amherst, NY: Humanity Books, 1993.

ALEXEI KOJEVNIKOV

Second Cold War

The term "Second Cold War" is generally used to describe the period from the mid- and late 1970s until the mid-1980s. At this time, Soviet-U.S. relations entered a period of confrontation and recrimination that stood in contrast to the period of détente that had preceded it, beginning in the late 1960s. The Second Cold War was comparable, in some respects at least, with the initial years of the Cold War, from the late 1940s until the thaw of the mid-1950s.

To a greater extent than was the case with the origins of the Cold War itself, or with the two world wars of the 20th century, the onset of the Second Cold War was the result of developments at several political levels. In the first place, there was the nuclear arms race. As the 1970s wore on, both sides became more and more concerned about the other's nuclear programs, with the Americans focusing on Soviet long-range ICBM capabilities and their ability to hit targets in the United States, and the Soviets concentrating on the NATO decision, taken in 1979, to deploy intermediate range nuclear forces (INF), cruise and Pershing missiles, in Europe. The earlier agreements reached on nuclear weapons, notably the Test Ban Treaty of 1963 and the first Strategic Arms Limitation Agreement of 1972 (SALT I) had not contained the development of new programs and technologies. A second agreement on long-range missiles, SALT-II, was signed, but never ratified by the U.S. Congress, and the 1980s began with a complete breakdown in arms negotiations between the two sides. At the same time, as Moscow felt more and more threatened from Western Europe and the United States, it was also becoming increasingly alarmed about the growth of Chinese power and influence, and Chinese cooperation with the United States, to the east.

The second dimension of the new international atmosphere was the spread of pro-Soviet and anti-American revolution in the third world. Washington, DC, and Moscow had in 1972 reached an agreement on a broad set of principles for regulating conflict in the third world, a region where despite the onset of revolutions in the Arab world and Cuba, the United States retained overwhelming military and economic preponderance. The National Liberation Front victory in Vietnam in 1975, accompanied by Communist victories in Laos and Cambodia, was then followed by other upheavals in which the United States felt it was losing ground to the Soviets—in Angola and Mozambique, Ethiopia, Nicaragua and Grenada, and then in 1978–79, Afghanistan and Iran. That these upheavals had indigenous roots and often little or nothing to do with Soviet influence meant almost nothing in the Washington policy debate. The spread of third world revolutions, totaling fourteen by the end of 1980, was presented as Soviet "misconduct" in the third world and a violation of détente. In the most dramatic case of all, that of the beleaguered Communist regime in Afghanistan, the dispatch of Soviet forces in December 1979 to shore up an allied Communist state was taken to be final proof of a Soviet grand design.

The third dimension of the Second Cold War was that of political unrest and social mobilization within the developed countries of both blocs. The first Cold War had certainly seen substantial organization by Communist

parties in Western Europe and the civil war in Greece. On this latter occasion, the initiative lay less with the now-attenuated Communist parties of the West, and more with a broad movement of social protest that sought in many ways to free itself from orthodox party politics, espousing a range of anticapitalist and anti-imperialist policies. Of these the most important was the peace movement campaign, organized in many countries, to prevent the deployment of cruise and Pershing missiles in Western Europe.

Other issues, such as solidarity with South Africa, Palestine, and Nicaragua, also played their part. There were new campaigns of protest around feminist and environmental issues. At the same time in the United States in particular, there was a new mobilization of right-wing sentiment, sometimes focused on individual domestic issues, like abortion and gun control, but often also relating to the need for a strong nuclear stance against the USSR. A parallel process was taking place in the Soviet bloc with the emergence of dissident groups in Eastern Europe, following Helsinki, of which the most powerful were the Solidarity movement in Poland and the growing international prominence of Soviet individuals, notably Andre Sakharov, generically known as dissidents.

With the Soviet invasion of Afghanistan in December 1979; the cancellation of SALT-II by the Carter administration, itself beset at this time by the Iranian detention of over fifty U.S. diplomats in Tehran; and the rising influence of a new, harsher U.S. conservatism associated with Ronald Reagan, elected president in November 1980, the Second Cold War had reached its full expression. At least four years of severe confrontation followed, marked among other things by the adoption by Reagan of a new doctrine arming anti-Communist guerrillas in Nicaragua, Angola, and Afghanistan, the shooting down of a Korean airliner by the USSR in September 2003, the deployment of cruise and Pershing missiles in Germany and the United Kingdom in December 1983, and Reagan's designation of the USSR as an "evil empire." Soviet alarm at U.S. intentions also grew when in addition to the INF deployments, Reagan talked in 1983 of abandoning the established policy of nuclear deterrence in favor of a proposed system of antimissile defenses; as the Soviet U.S. expert Georgi Arbatov put it in response to claims that the U.S. "Star Wars" project was purely defensive, "A shield is an offensive weapon."

Relations between the United States and the USSR began to evolve more favorably in the mid-1980s with the start of negotiations on third world conflicts, including

Afghanistan, the beginning of INF negotiations in Geneva, and most important, the advent of the new Soviet leader Mikhail Gorbachev coming to power in March 1985. Relations and the international atmosphere improved dramatically thereafter, and new arms control accords were signed, on the INF, but also on strategic arms reduction (START) and reducing conventional force deployments in Europe (MBRM). In February 1989, all Soviet forces had left Afghanistan, in the last months of that year all Eastern European regimes dependent on the Soviet Union had fallen to democratic forces, and after the passage of two more years, in December 1991 the USSR itself was to break up into its fifteen constitutive republics.

Many issues and events associated with the Second Cold War remain open to debate. For some historians of East-West relations the very term is mistaken, in that, they argue, the Cold War, focused as it was on Europe and in particular Germany, had effectively ended with the resolution of disagreements over Berlin in the early 1960s and the subsequent advent of Willy Brandt's Ostpolitik. Among those who accept the term in some form, there is considerable disagreement about the relative weight to give to the four main components of causation and process.

In the first place, many on the Right put emphasis on military and strategic factors as well as the nuclear arms race as causes of the deterioration, but also the factors that overstretched Soviet budgetary resources, precipitating the retreat and then collapse of the USSR. Others, moving away from the focus on Europe, and recalling that in the first Cold War, the revolutions in China and the war in Korea had been major precipitants of confrontation, point to the importance of the third world revolutions of the 1970s in stimulating U.S. concern and giving critics of the USSR the issue on which to belabor it. Third, there are those who ascribe a significant role to the European and world peace movements, which in both East and West, challenged existing regimes and helped to undermine the authority of Communist rule in the Soviet bloc.

Finally, in a different vein, and looking in particular at the longer-run evolution of Soviet and Eastern European society, there are those who stress that what was most important was the loss of momentum, first of historical revolutionary self-confidence, and then of domination of the populations themselves, in the Communist bloc. Here a combination of the very achievement of communism in creating a mass-educated society, and the continued economic and political success of Western Europe and the United States, not least in the demonstration

effect of the European Union, can be said to have been the decisive factor—a process of change that had begun before the Second Cold War, continued during it, and reached its political expression in the advent of Gorbachev and his less confrontational "New Thinking."

The importance of this period lies not only in the way in which Soviet-U.S. relations worsened once more, despite earlier improvements in East-West relations culminating with the Vietnam Peace Agreement of 1973 and the Helsinki Accords of 1975, but also in the fact that the Second Cold War, for all its appearance as a return to the earlier years of antagonism, had a very different outcome. It led within a few years to the collapse of the Soviet system in Eastern Europe, the breakup of the USSR itself, and in a broader historical and ideological context, the end of the two centuries of effective challenge to the Western political and economic system by an alternative model of social organization. In regard to the latter, it can be said that insofar as the term "end of history" has a legitimate usage, referring to the conclusion of a deep ideological rift within modernity going back to the French Revolution, the end of the Second Cold War ushered in the end of history.

See also Afghan War; Bipolarity; Cold War; Conference on Security and Cooperation in Europe; Cuban-Soviet Intervention in Africa; Gorbachev, Mikhail; Martial Law in Poland; New Thinking.

FURTHER READING

Crockatt, R. *The Fifty Years War: The United States and the Soviet Union in World Politics, 1941–1991.* London: Routledge, 1995.

Garthoff, R. *Detente and Confrontation: American-Soviet Relations from Nixon to Reagan.* Rev. ed. Washington, DC: Brookings Institution, 1994.

Halliday, F. *The Making of the Second Cold War.* London: Verso, 1983.

Hogan, M., ed. *The End of the Cold War: Its Meaning and Implications.* Cambridge, UK: Cambridge University Press, 1992.

Lewin, M. *The Gorbachev Phenomenon.* London: Radius, 1988.

FREDERICK HALLIDAY

Secret Speech

The so-called secret speech is indissolubly linked to the name of Nikita Khrushchev, who read it at the conclusion of the Communist Party of the Soviet Union's

Twentieth Congress on February 25, 1956, in a session that was only open to delegates. Khrushchev tied his image in the West, that of reformist leader, to the speech; it would survive his destitution in 1964. Had Khrushchev lost the power struggles that occurred after Stalin's death, however, he would today be remembered as a political leader in the Stalinist mold who attempted to hinder the cautious process of de-Stalinization undertaken by Lavrenty Beria and Georgy Malenkov. Beria and Malenkov would be remembered for their hesitant openings to the outside world, for having first set some of the gulag's prisoners free, and having adopted some measures to aid consumers. Once he had seized power, Khrushchev adopted his rivals' program and relaunched it as his own—just as Stalin had done before him. On December 31, 1955, the Pospelov Commission was formed, and charged with drafting a report on Stalin's crimes. On February 9, 1956, the Communist Party's presidium approved Khrushchev's proposal that a speech on the topic be held during the Twentieth Congress; it was decided on February 13 that this speech would be given by Khrushchev himself, during a closed session, in order to avoid a debate on the issue.

During the congress itself, Khrushchev rewrote the Pospelov Commission's report. In the final version the only victims of Stalin's terror who were granted recognition were the "honest Communists" who belonged to the higher levels of the *nomenklatura*. The only exception were the millions of members of ethnic groups, who had been deported during the war and they were mentioned in order to support the charge of "great Russian chauvinism" that Lenin had made against Stalin (yet the list did not include Poles, Ukrainians, and Jews, who had been subjected to analogous persecutions). Political intuition told Khrushchev not to mention the Stalin of the 1930s who, in the midst of immense tragedies, had guided the transformation of the Soviet Union. It was better to insist on his mediocre abilities as a head of state, who had lost his bearings when informed of the defeats that had followed the German attack of June 22, 1941; that he directed military operations using a globe; that he organized his own personality cult; that he did not take an interest in the country's problems; and that in 1952, he was preparing another general purge of the party. It was not that important that this portrait was only minimally based on reality. It allowed the operation's main objective to be reached: the destruction of the symbolic figure of the father.

His place was taken by a new "father": a Lenin who, in the secret speech version, closely resembled the early Sta-

lin. Not the Brest-Litovsk or the New Economic Policy leader but rather the one who had no pity for his enemies yet was respectful of the party leadership organs' collegiality. The promise of resurrecting a mythical Leninist golden age allowed Khrushchev to avoid directly responding to the obvious questions that would be raised by those who heard or read the speech: Why did you, who were his closest collaborators, not oppose Stalin? How can you guarantee that past tragedies will not be repeated?

An able tactician, in the following years Khrushchev utilized de-Stalinization—sometimes slamming on the brakes, and at other times stepping on the accelerator—as an instrument to build consensus and engage in political struggle against his party adversaries. He also built his international image as a reformist leader around the secret speech, even though it was later tarnished by economic failures and an adventurous foreign policy. A leader with provincial roots, now the heir of an imperial tradition, Khrushchev did not consider the repercussions his speech would have in Eastern Europe. For him everything originated in Moscow, and everything was supposed to be decided there. The worker revolts in Poland, the revolution in Hungary, and the skepticism with which the secret speech was met by Yugoslav and Chinese leaders were an abrupt wake-up call. Khrushchev's response was typically Stalinist: military repression in Hungary, followed by the reprobates' isolation, particularly the Chinese Communists. It worked; the Soviet empire did not collapse, and the USSR remained the leader of the international Communist movement. But Khrushchev's victory was only a temporary truce. These problems, repressed but not resolved, reemerged several times in the following years until they led to the collapse of the Soviet Empire and the USSR itself.

See also Cult of Personality; De-Stalinization; Khrushchev, Nikita; Stalin, Joseph; Stalinism.

FURTHER READING

Aksjutin, J. V. "Novoe o XX s'ezde KPSS." *Otechestvennaja Istorija* 6 (1996): 108–23.

Guerra, A. *Il giorno che Chrushev parlò*. Rome: Editori Riuniti, 1986.

Naumov, V. P. "K istorii sekretnogo doklada N. S. Chruščёva na XX s'ezde KPSS." *Novaja i novejšaja istorija* 4 (1996): 147–68.

Taubman, W. *Khrushchev: The Man and His Era*. New York: Norton, 2003.

FABIO BETTANIN

Self-Criticsim

Self-criticism was a prominent aspect of Soviet Communist practice from the end of the 1920s. It was an extension of the strict discipline installed in the Russian Communist Party (Bolsheviks). It also derived from the assumption that the party always knew best. Even Trotsky accepted this principle, at least until he faced irreversible factional defeat. The ascendant party leadership during the New Economic Policy was determined to impose implacable control over politics. Characteristically it employed ex-oppositionists to denounce the successive oppositions in historical works.

This tradition was reinforced in the years of the First Five-Year Plan. Stalin's internal party enemies, Kamenev and Zinoviev, were allowed back into the party only on the condition that they recant their previous views and acknowledge the wisdom of Stalin. At the same time there were show trials of "wreckers" and "saboteurs." The security police beat up the defendants and forced them to "confess" to imaginary crimes at the price for lighter sentences. Steadily the internal party cases and the rest of the judicial system were brought into sync. Any kind of dissent from official policy was enough grounds for arraignment as an "enemy of the people." Millions were physically tormented into recanting and confessing. Most notoriously this occurred in the big show trials of Communist leaders in 1936–38. Kamenev, Zinoviev, and Bukharin admitted that they had worked for the restoration of capitalism in the USSR. This self-criticism was not enough to save their lives. Stalin was intent on their destruction. More obscure victims were simply arrested, beaten up, and compelled to sign prewritten confessions before being dispatched to the gulag.

The requirement that individuals with the "wrong" opinions to stand up in front of their comrades and acknowledge their faults did not fade with the lowering of the scale of terror. Stalin had the habit of choosing individuals to defend policies in public which he knew, from private discussions, they opposed. When Stalin died in 1953, Khrushchev continued this practice. The party presidium was deeply divided about his policies of reform, but his opponents—Malenkov, Molotov, and Kaganovich—had to show their obedience by condoning his program. Khrushchev finally ousted them from high office in 1957. Unlike Stalin, he did not consign them to the gulag; but he extracted statements from them asserting approval of his policies.

By and large, gulag convicts were left alone with their thoughts once they arrived in the labor camps. This was also true in most Communist countries of Eastern Europe. The Chinese pattern was different from the start. After the Long March to Yan'an province, Mao Zedong set about establishing rigorous dictatorial control over his own Red Army. As in the Soviet Union, dissenters were systematically tortured into making confessions. This was often done at terrifying mass meetings. After seizing power in 1949, moreover, Mao established an archipelago of camps throughout the People's Republic of China. In the Soviet Union prisoners were free to use the camp library and, if they so chose, might read the works of Lenin; in China, by contrast, they had no choice: they had to study the sayings of Mao or else face beatings and deprivation of food. The Chinese leadership wanted to break and then reengineer the minds of their prisoners. In the Cultural Revolution of the late 1960s leading Communist critics of Mao were put on public display and, having been subjected to abuse behind the scenes, forced to engage in self-criticism.

Pol Pot's Cambodia made even the Chinese precedent seem gentle. Whereas Chinese convicts were kept more or less alive so that they could carry out their laboring duties, the Cambodian Communists usually executed their convicts once torture had elicited the required confession. This was the most extreme variant of the phenomenon of self-criticism, which began as a means of introducing discipline to the party and ended as a means of establishing a monolithically obedient society. It had its ideological roots in the notion that the party was infallible. It grew into a plant that shut out the light from all serious political and intellectual discussion.

See also Democratic Centralism; Enemies of the People; Stalinism.

FURTHER READING

Halfin, I. *Terror in My Soul. Communist Autobiographies on Trial.* Cambridge, MA: Harvard University Press, 2003.
Hoffman, D. L. *Stalinism.* Malden, MA: Blackwell, 2003.
Service, R. *Stalin: A Biography.* Cambridge, MA: Harvard University Press, 2005.

ROBERT SERVICE

Shalamov, Varlam

Born in Vologda on July 1, Varlam Shalamov (1907–82) first studied at the Vologda high school and later, from 1926 to 1929, at the Moscow University Law School, where after having actively participated in the capital's political life, he was arrested for the first time for criticizing the Stalinist leadership group and circulating *Letters to the Party Congress* (the so-called Lenin's Testament), and was condemned to three years' imprisonment. He returned to Moscow in 1932, after having spent part of his term in the Butyrka prison and the rest in the Krasnovishersk camp in the Urals; he dedicated himself to literature and journalism there. One of his first short stories, "The Three Deaths of Doctor Austino," was published in 1936 in the journal *Oktjabr*. Shalamov was arrested again as a recidivist in 1937 and condemned for counterrevolutionary Trotskyist activities to five years in a camp in Kolyma. He later incurred further sentences (in 1943 ten years for "anti-Soviet propaganda," since he defined Ivan Bunin a "classic of Russian literature") and extensions of his sentence until he was finally freed in 1953. Since he could not obtain residence in Moscow, Shalamov transferred to the Kalinin region. That same year he met Boris Pasternak, who had appreciated the verses he had been sent from Kolyma; an interesting correspondence between the two from this time has been preserved.

In 1956 Shalamov was rehabilitated and thus able to return to Moscow. He began publishing his verses in important journals, such as *Znamja* and *Moskva*, and became a correspondent for the latter; he also published a series of poetry collections between 1961 and 1972 (*The Flintstone* in 1961, *The Rustling of the Leaves* in 1964, *The Road and Destiny* in 1967, and *Moscow Clouds* in 1972). In 1973 he was admitted to the Writers' Union. At this time short stories about his life in the gulag began to circulate via samizdat, while the *Kolyma Tales*, written between 1954 and 1973, appeared abroad starting in 1966. The first complete edition was published in London in 1978. Other tales then joined this first collection, in addition to Shalamov's autobiography, which appeared posthumously in 1985 in the collection *Resurrection of the Larch*. In 1979 he was transferred to an old peoples' home, and in January 1982 he was forcefully transferred to a mental institution, where he died a few days later. In 1998 his *Collected Works* appeared in Russia in four volumes.

Shalamov's entire oeuvre is deeply autobiographical, even though it is marked by a cold and lucid detachment. The *Kolyma Tales* are a grandiose, tragic, and varied fresco of the gulag's human landscape, this Siberian hell, imbued with a sense of inhuman fatalism and disenchanted participation. Divided into six books according to a complex narrative structure, and constructed according to a rhythmic form that balances themes and verbal material, the *Tales* are a reflection on a cruel form of reality (the camp seen as absolute evil).

The ethical and psychological idea of the gulag, which resembles the world as a whole, is central to this work. Shalamov, unlike Aleksandr Solzhenitsyn, did not indulge in invectives and political considerations in his prose but instead examined the process of dehumanization that involved the entire gulag and its inhabitants. His reflections on honor and destiny, the instinct for survival that drives each human being, chance as the ultimate engine of human life, seen both with deep irony and a profound sense of the tragic are of fundamental importance. In 1962 he also wrote an essay titled "Fragments from the 1920s," in which he portrayed many writers of the period, including Vladimir Mayakovski, Mikhail Bulgakov, and Boris Pilniak. He also dedicated moving pages to Osip Mandelstam in his *Kolyma Tales*, where he dealt with the poet's death in a transit camp.

See also Gulag; Literature in Soviet Russia; Solzhenitsyn, Aleksandr.

FURTHER READING

Esipov, V. V., ed. *Shalamovskij sbornik*. Vol I. Vologda: Izd. Vo in-ta povyshenijka kvalifikacii i podgotovki ped.kadrov, 1994.

Shklovskij, E. A. *Varlam Shalamov*. Moscow: Znanie, 1991.

Suchich, I. "Zit'posle Kolymy (1954–1973. Kolymskie russkazy V. Shalamova)." *Zvezda* 6 (2001): 208–20.

STEFANO GARZONIO

Shevardnadze, Eduard

Eduard Shevardnadze, who was born in the Georgian village of Mamat in January 1928, had a remarkable political career in both Soviet politics and post-Soviet Georgia. His fame in the West was greatest when he was the minister of foreign affairs during the perestroika years—from 1985 until his resignation from that office in late 1990.

Shevardnadze, at his parents' insistence, entered Tbilisi Medical College on the completion of his schooling, with a view to becoming a doctor. At the age of twenty, however, he joined the Communist Party and became a political activist. Offered the post of political instructor in the Komsomol, he accepted it and abandoned his medical studies. He graduated from the Party School in Tbilisi in 1951.

By 1957 Shevardnadze was the first secretary of the Komsomol in Georgia, but he moved into the Communist Party apparatus in 1961. His entire preperestroika career was within his native Georgia. From 1964 to 1965 he was the first deputy minister, and from 1965 to 1972 he was the minister for the maintenance of public order. The ministry was renamed the Ministry of Internal Affairs in 1968. Thus, he was head of the ordinary police, as distinct from the political police (the KGB) in Georgia, although it is a common error on the part of commentators to confuse the two and attribute to Shevardnadze KGB membership that he did not have.

Corruption was even more widespread in Georgia than in most Soviet republics, and Shevardnadze, as the minister of the interior, found his efforts to combat it blocked at the very top of the Georgian political hierarchy, for the first secretary of the republic, Mzhavanadze, was himself thoroughly involved in the corrupt transactions. Shevardnadze, at great risk to his career (and possibly his life), took an incriminatory dossier on Mzhavanadze to Moscow, even though Mzhavanadze was a candidate member of the politburo. The evidence he produced led to the dismissal of Mzhavanadze and to Shevardnadze being appointed the first secretary of the Communist Party in Georgia in his place.

Shevardnadze held that post for thirteen years—until in 1985, when Gorbachev surprised both the Soviet establishment and the rest of the world by bringing him to Moscow as Soviet foreign minister. During his years at the head of the Georgian party organization there were several attempts on Shevardnadze's life. He continued to fight the local mafia and also introduced some modest economic reform, together with experiments in increasing the powers of local soviets. Within the relatively narrow limits imposed by the Brezhnev leadership, Shevardnadze was as reformist a republican party secretary as it was possible to be during those years.

That record commended itself to Gorbachev, but he and Shevardnadze had known each other since the late

1950s when they had met at Komsomol conferences. Since Gorbachev's native Stavropol was just across the border from Georgia, the two men continued to see each other quite frequently and found that their thinking had much in common.

Shevardnadze had no experience of foreign affairs before being appointed minister in succession to the long-serving Andrei Gromyko in the summer of 1985. For Gorbachev this was an advantage, rather than a disadvantage, for Shevardnadze could bring a fresh mind to the task. He was also less likely to put up objections to Gorbachev's foreign policy initiatives than a loyal lieutenant of Gromyko would have done, had he succeeded to his master's post.

Shevardnadze applied himself diligently to the task of mastering foreign policy, and though he was criticized, especially in retrospect, by some of the long-standing international specialists within the Foreign Ministry and the International Department of the Central Committee, he rapidly acquired a good reputation both at home and abroad. His Western interlocutors in particular found his charm, willingness to listen, and readiness to negotiate a refreshing change after the Gromyko years. Shevardnadze established an especially warm and productive relationship with U.S. secretary of state George Shultz. Between the two of them they prepared much of the ground for the Reagan-Gorbachev summit meetings.

Shevardnadze lost some of his domestic popularity in the Soviet Union at the end of the 1980s as criticism mounted of the concessionary foreign policy that he appeared to be conducting. While the ultimate foreign policymaker was Gorbachev, Shevardnadze was an easier target for the critics. In the winter of 1990–91, when the reformist wing of the Communist Party leadership was put on the defensive by a conservative backlash, Gorbachev made a number of tactical concessions to his opponents. Shevardnadze felt increasingly isolated, and without forewarning Gorbachev, he dramatically announced his resignation from his ministerial post on December 20, 1990, while addressing the Fourth Congress of People's Deputies of the USSR. He attacked other reformers for not standing up for their beliefs and announced that his resignation should be seen as his protest "against the onset of dictatorship." It came just eight months before the attempted coup against Gorbachev of August 1991.

Following the failure of that August putsch, Shevardnadze briefly rejoined the Gorbachev team in his old position as foreign minister. By that time, however, the movement toward disintegration of the Soviet Union—in which Boris Yeltsin, as president of Russia, played a decisive role—was too well under way for this to be anything more than a temporary post.

At first Shevardnadze did not return to Georgia, for—although in the early years of his foreign ministership he had been popular there—he had lost support in his home republic after the massacre of around twenty young demonstrators in Tbilisi in April 1989. While this brutal repression had been authorized by the local Georgian party organization—and was against the express wishes of Gorbachev and Shevardnaze (who had both just returned from a lengthy foreign visit)—the action stimulated Georgian nationalism and disillusionment with Moscow and the Communists. This made Shevardnadze temporarily much less popular than the former dissident Zviad Gamsakhurdia, who became Georgia's first post-Communist president.

Gamsakhurdia's nationalism, though, caused turbulent relations with Georgia's ethnic minorities, leading to civil war in both Ossetia and Abkhazia. Shevardnadze returned to Georgia in March 1992 and was soon seen by many Georgians as a possible political savior. He was elected chairman of the ruling State Council in October 1992 in elections that were internationally monitored and agreed to have been generally fair. Just two months after he narrowly escaped death from a car bombing, Shevardnadze was elected the president of Georgia in 1995 with more than 70 percent of the vote. He was re-elected in 2000, and had planned to retire at the end of his five-year term in 2005.

Yet events took a different course. The flames of inter-ethnic hatred had been sufficiently fanned by Shevardnadze's predecessor as to make the task of establishing good relations within Georgia almost insurmountable. Shevardnadze faced criticism for his evident inability to bring the whole country under the central jurisdiction of Tbilisi. Moreover, even though he had made his preperestroika reputation as an enemy of the mafia in Georgia, during his presidency his own entourage was permeated by corruption. He was eventually brought down by parliamentary elections in November 2003. The result appeared to be a victory for Shevardnadze's supporters, but in the view of both the international community and, more pertinently, a majority of Georgians, there had been extensive cheating. Massive demonstrations—what became known as the "orange revolution"—drove Shevardnadze from office. Faced by the choice of using extreme coercion to uphold his authority or resignation, he chose the latter.

Shevardnadze's years as Georgian president were not the most glorious or successful of his political career. Even though he turned out to be a good deal less than a model democrat, his rule was far less despotic than that of most leaders of the Soviet Union's successor states. A lively civil society was sustained in Georgia during his years in power, even though economic failure and an unwillingness to combat corruption (in contrast to his earlier career) proved his undoing.

Shevardnadze's most notable achievement was undoubtedly his contribution to the ending of the Cold War during his years as Soviet foreign minister. His firm opposition to the counterreformation in the last period of perestroika and the August coup of 1991 consolidated the respect in which he was held both internationally and by Russian liberals. If his second resignation, unlike his first, was inglorious and less voluntary, they had in common one significant point of principle: In the final analysis, Shevardnadze preferred to resign from high office than to be complicit in violent repression.

See also Dissolution of the USSR; Gorbachev, Mikhail; New Thinking; Perestroika; Post-Soviet Communism.

FURTHER READING

Brown, A. *The Gorbachev Factor.* Oxford: Oxford University Press, 1996.
Gorbachev, M. *Memoirs.* New York: Doubleday, 1996.
Herrmann, R. K., and R. N. Lebow, eds. *Ending the Cold War.* New York: Palgrave Macmillan, 2004.
Shevardnadze, E. *The Future Belongs to Freedom.* London: Sinclair-Stevenson, 1991.

ARCHIE BROWN

Short Course, **The**

The central text of the Stalin-era party catechism, *The History of the All-Union Communist Party (Bolsheviks)—Short Course,* was compulsory reading for Soviet citizens of all walks of life between 1938 and 1956. This textbook traced the origins of the Russian revolutionary movement to the agrarian populists of the 1860s, but argued that they gave way to the Marxist Social Democrats and their focus on the nascent working class two decades later. By the mid-

1890s, Lenin had emerged to navigate this movement through the shoals of police persecution and internal division (versus the Mensheviks, "Legal Marxists," Economists, and others). According to the *Short Course*, it was Lenin's leadership that allowed the Bolshevik movement to seize power in the name of the workers, soldiers, and poor peasants in October 1917. Subsequently, Lenin plotted a course through civil war and foreign intervention toward the construction of a socialist economy. After Lenin's death in 1924, Stalin assumed the helm of the party and state, and steered the USSR successfully through shock industrialization, agricultural collectivization, and the struggle with counterrevolution—a journey that was more or less complete by the time of the *Short Course*'s publication in 1938. Although it is often assumed that Stalin authored this triumphalist narrative himself, all but several sections on dialectical and historical materialism were actually drafted by E. M. Iaroslavskii, P. M. Pospelov, and V. G. Knorin before being edited by Stalin and members of his entourage.

A seminal text, the *Short Course* epitomized a belief held by party authorities after the early 1930s that history ought to play a fundamental role in indoctrination efforts. Earlier political grammars, chapbooks, brochures, and highbrow theoretical treatises were to be synthesized into a single text that would emphasize practical knowledge and accessibility—a "usable past," as the U.S. historian Henry Steele Commager once put it. Stalin signaled this new agenda in 1931 in a letter written to the journal *Proletarskaia revoliutsiia* when he denounced party historians for daring to question even minor aspects of Lenin's leadership. Leaders were henceforth to be judged by their overall record rather than by a ploddingly academic accounting of their means, methods, and mistakes.

Party historians foundered in the wake of this scandal, forcing Soviet authorities to repeatedly clarify the nature of the party's new expectations on "the historical front." Existing party history texts were too inaccessible and insufficiently inspiring for what was still a poorly educated society. A long-standing focus on anonymous social forces and abstract materialist analysis was to be replaced by a new emphasis on heroic individuals, pivotal events, and the connection of party history to that of Soviet society as a whole. These demands reflected the Soviet leadership's intention to treat both party and state history as propaganda geared toward mobilization.

Editorial brigades under Iaroslavskii, Knorin, P. P. Popov, L. P. Beriia, and others struggled to address these new demands in the increasingly tense atmosphere of the mid-

1930s. This process virtually ground to a halt after 1936, when the Great Terror's repeated exposure of "traitors" within the Soviet elite made it difficult to write a narrative about the party that would not require revision after each successive wave of purges. In 1937, a lack of progress led the party leadership to ask Iaroslavskii, Pospelov, and Knorin to combine forces on a single advanced text while writing more basic volumes separately. Knorin's arrest during that summer, however, forced Iaroslavskii and Pospelov to focus exclusively on their jointly authored manuscript, attempting to adapt it for a mass audience under the personal supervision of Stalin, A. A. Zhdanov, and V. M. Molotov.

Released in the fall of 1938, the *Short Course* was hailed as an ideological breakthrough. Still quite complex, it had at least succeeded in situating party history within a broader Russo-Soviet historical context. Its tight focus on Lenin and Stalin, moreover, ensured that the text would survive future purges (although at the cost of conflating party history with the cult of personality). Ubiquitous after the printing of more than forty-two million copies, the *Short Course* reigned over party educational efforts for eighteen years, both at home in the USSR and within Moscow-aligned Communist movements abroad. It also quickly came to script depictions of party and Soviet history in official mass culture, whether literature, drama, cinema, or the visual arts. Increasingly obsolete after 1945, the *Short Course* nevertheless retained its canonical status until Khrushchev's denunciation of Stalin and the cult of personality in 1956.

Despite the *Short Course*'s prominence between 1938 and the early 1950s, it failed to dramatically transform social *mentalité* in the Soviet Union, or galvanize foreign support for the USSR in Eastern Europe and elsewhere. Although the *Short Course* was learned by rote and discussed in innumerable party study circles, it rarely figures into the letters, diaries, and memoirs of the period, and few of its central theses or turns of phrase ever circulated in society as commonplaces or colloquialisms. This weakness related to indoctrination stems from the fact that although the *Short Course* was intended to synthesize party history and theory for the purposes of mass mobilization, its narrative was simply too heavy-handed, schematic, and static to win a place in the hearts and minds of those it was to rally to the Soviet cause.

See also Cult of Personality; History and Memory; Literacy, Soviet Union Campaign for Adult; Marxism-Leninism; Propaganda, Communist; Stalinism.

FURTHER READING

Bettanin, F. *La fabbrica del mito: Storia e politica nell'URSS staliniana*. Naples: Edizioni scientifiche italiane, 1996.

Maslov, N. N. "'Kratkii kurs istorii VKP(b)'—entsiklopediia kul'ta lichnosti Stalina." *Voprosy istorii KPSS* 11 (1988): 51–67.

———. "I. V. Stalin o 'Kratkom kurse istorii VKP(b).'" *Istoricheskii arkhiv* 5 (1994): 4–31.

Sukharev, S. V. "Predtecha 'Kratkogo kursa' v litsakh i dokumentakh." *Voprosy istorii KPSS* 8 (1991): 110–20.

DAVID BRANDENBERGER

Shostakovich, Dmitry

A central figure in Russian and Soviet music, Dmitry Shostakovich (1906–75) was born in Saint Petersburg to a family with liberal beliefs. In 1919 he entered the conservatory in his city, and studied piano with Leonid Nikolaev (who would later become an instrumentalist of the highest caliber) and composition with Maksimilian Steinberg, proving his precocious talent; his first symphony, written as a final essay in composition for the conservatory, garnered international attention in 1926. The twenty-year-old Shostakovich revealed a conscious assimilation of the most disparate elements of contemporary European music, particularly German and French neo-objectivism, together with references to the 19th-century Russian tradition and Sergey Prokofiev. His exceptional technical skills allowed him, already in these first attempts, to weave these references into an original and coherent musical production.

In an atmosphere still open to the avant-garde during the first years of Soviet power, Shostakovich demonstrated his ability to fuse diverse influences into a whole, while mastering different genres: opera (*The Nose*, by Nikolay Gogol, 1930), ballet (*The Golden Age*, 1930; *The Bolt*, 1931; *The Clear Stream*, 1931), symphonic music (*Symphony no. 2*, 1927; *Symphony no. 3*, 1930—both with chorus and an agitprop air about them), the concert (*Concert for Piano and Trumpet*, 1933), stage music (*Hamlet*, 1932; other compositions for innovative productions by Vsevolod Meyerhold and other directors), and piano music (*Sonata no. 1*, 1926). Leningrad at the time was the capital of new Soviet art. The authorities there supported the arts, especially because of Anatoly Lunacharsky's presence. Many musical creations were on the cutting edge,

characterized by pronounced avant-garde attitudes, and made use of the most diverse languages—from polytonality to dodecaphony, from savage percussivism to experiments with quarter tones.

Toward the end of the 1920s the climate began to change. The Association for Contemporary Music, established in 1923, was now challenged by the Association of Proletarian Musicians (RAPM), which denounced all works that did not support "the hegemony of the proletariat in the artistic field" as bourgeois degenerations of a formalist type and attempted to ostracize all those composers who did not fall into line. In 1929 Lunacharsky lost his position as commissar for culture; the League of Soviet Musicians was established in 1932, and it was directly connected to political power. Caught between his attraction for avant-garde experiments—not only of a musical nature, since during these years he was interested in constructivism, Meyerhold's theater, and the new Soviet cinema—and his omnivorous curiosity, which also led him to be interested in the "populists," Shostakovich attempted to walk a difficult (and dangerous) line between innovation and tradition, between pure art and art applied to the building of socialism. Starting in the early 1930s his position was precarious. Some of his compositions (like the *Symphony no. 3*) met with success; others (like *The Nose*) were the object of harsh criticism.

A turning point in Shostakovich's life occurred between 1934 and 1936. His second opera, *Lady Macbeth of the Mtsensk District*, from a story by Nikolay Leskov, was performed in 1934. Staged in both Leningrad and Moscow, *Lady Macbeth* was successful both critically and in terms of public appeal, and Shostakovich once again was in the international spotlight. The work was then performed in London, Prague, Copenhagen, and Cleveland, and was appreciated by Konstantin Stanislavsky, Dimitri Mitropoulos, and Arturo Toscanini. On December 26, 1935, Stalin went to see the show at the Bolshoy and left after the first act; a month later a harsh attack on the piece titled "Chaos Instead of Music" appeared in *Pravda*, inspired by the dictator himself and for a long time (probably erroneously) it was attributed to Andrey Zhdanov. The opera was immediately removed from programs; a little later the *Preludes*, the *Concert for Piano*, and *The Clear Stream* were also accused of formalism. While this offensive against artists was taking place (Osip Mandelstam, Meyerhold, Isaac Babel, and Boris Pilnyak, among others, would die as a consequence of this offensive), Shostakovich decided to withdraw his *Symphony no. 4*, which he had finished in April 1936 and was supposed to be performed in November at the Leningrad Philharmonic. This work, considered one of his best, would be performed for the first time only in 1961; a dark atmosphere prevails throughout, and it represents these times charged with menace, Stalinism's most tragic years, effectively with no concessions to program music.

Starting in 1936 the composer followed a dual tack in his relations with power. On the one hand, he made concessions to a simplified and accessible style, which sometimes masked an underlying complexity; he also made incursions into the realm of propaganda proper, and they would earn him several official recognitions. On the other hand, he pursued a solitary and increasingly pessimistic vein, using chamber music and particularly the string quartet—a genre in which Shostakovich should be placed with the greatest composers of all time. Examples of the first type are the *Symphony no. 5* (later known by the perhaps apocryphal title of "a composer's practical reply to just criticism"), 1937; the *Quintet for Piano and Strings*, 1940, which received the Stalin Prize; the *Symphony no. 7* "Leningrad," 1942, inspired by resistance to Nazism and an opera symbol of Soviet nationalism, and that also received the Stalin Prize; the festive *Ouverture* for the thirtieth anniversary of the October Revolution, 1947; and *The Song of the Forests*, 1949, another winner of the Stalin Prize. Instances of the second type are the *Concert no. 1 for Violin and Orchestra*, 1948; the *Twenty-Four Preludes and Fugues for Piano*, 1950–52, an erudite take on Johann Sebastian Bach's *Well-Tempered Clavier*; various string quartets; and a lot of chamber and vocal music. Once more attacked as a formalist in February 1948 at the climax of the Zhdanov era, Shostakovich was removed from his positions in the Moscow and Leningrad conservatories, and deprived of all means of livelihood.

Even before Stalin's death, however, Shostakovich was rehabilitated; in 1951 he was elected as a deputy to the USSR's Supreme Soviet. After the dictator's death Shostakovich enjoyed new recognition in an era of de-Stalinization (in 1956 Nikita Khrushchev gave him the Order of Lenin award, in 1957 he was elected to the position of secretary of the Composers' League, and in 1958 he received the Lenin Prize for his *Symphony no. 11*). He traveled abroad several times as an "ambassador" of Soviet music (Rome, Paris, Helsinki, and the United States), even as his best work was misunderstood at home.

Shostakovich was already affected by serious health problems, and he alternated grandiose and sometimes inflated symphonic compositions with works that were increasingly marked by a tragic sense of defeat. He re-flected on the horrors of history in the *Symphony no. 13* "Baby Yar," based on a text by Yevgeny Yevtushenko, which was dedicated to the 1941 massacre of tens of thousands of Ukrainian Jews by the Nazis, and was disliked by the authorities. In his last years, he wrote livid, desolate, and enigmatic compositions, such as the *Symphonies no. 14 and 15*, the last quartets, pieces based on texts by Alexander Blok, Marina Cvetaeva, and Michelangelo Buonarroti, the *Sonata op. 134 for Piano and Violin*, and the *Sonata op. 147 for Piano and Viola* (his last work). He made use of his international prestige for propaganda purposes in these final works, which were tolerated, without understanding them. After another heart attack, Shostakovich died on August 9, 1975; a solemn state funeral followed.

Shostakovich's legacy is enormous and complex. From an artistic point of view, he can be considered a composer with extraordinary talents who wanted to pursue an essentially syncretistic musical ideal in ever-changing forms, both fusing and juxtaposing a vast array of languages (in addition to 20th-century examples, his encyclopedic musical knowledge made him aware of much more remote forms: Ludwig van Beethoven's and Gustav Mahler's symphonic oeuvre, baroque polyphony, and 19th-century opera). The arc of his production is also exemplary for reconstructing the relation between a free artist, one with strong ties to the ideals born of the October Revolution, and Soviet power. He never contemplated emigration (the path that was instead taken by other great Russian composers like Igor Stravinsky), and therefore Shostakovich had to choose compromise, passive resistance, or camouflage by means of codes that were so well hidden, they have led to research on the verge of the esoteric. The different ways in which he resorted to these stratagems at different times, and power's varying responses, have left traces of an emblematic confrontation of artistic freedom and totalitarianism.

See also Avant-garde; Literature in Soviet Russia; Socialist Realism; Zhdanovism.

FURTHER READING

Pulcini, F. *Šostakovič*. Turin: Edizioni Di Torino, 1988.

Shostakovich, D. D. *Testimony: The Memoirs of Dmitri Shostakovich*. Ed. S. Volkov. New York: Harper and Row, 1979.

Volkov, S. *Shostakovich and Stalin: The Extraordinary Relationship between the Great Composer and the Brutal Dictator*. London: Little, Brown, 2004.

FRANCESCO SALVI

Single-Party System

The single-party system was a common type of regime in the 20th century, being found in many parts of the world, including the Communist states. The term has been used to describe regimes in which only one party has existed as well as those where other parties may also formally be present but they do not challenge the dominance of the main party. One of the key characteristics of Communist regimes is that they were ruled by Communist parties. In most such regimes the Communist Party was the only political party afforded the legal right to exist, although in a number of countries other parties were allowed to play a role in the political process. Those Communist states with legal parties other than the Communist Party were China, where there are eight such parties; Poland, which had two; the German Democratic Republic, which had four; Yugoslavia and Bulgaria, which each had one; Czechoslovakia, which had four; and Korea and Vietnam, with two each. None of these parties exercised significant political power. All occupied seats in the national legislature, and although in some cases they were explicitly designed to represent particular segments of the population (for example, the Peasants' Party in Poland), they did not constitute an independent voice in national affairs. There was no competition for power, with these peripheral parties often standing candidates in their own seats, and occupying special positions in governmental and administrative bodies, but not exercising any independent power. In these states, predominant power was vested in the ruling Communist Party. Such systems have been called "hegemonic" party systems, with a ruling party unchallenged by a series of minor parties that function under the general supervision of the ruling party.

Most Communist states had a single-party system, in which the ruling Communist Party was the only party able to play any role in the political system. Although not all parties had the term Communist in their title (for instance, the Socialist Unity Party of the German Democratic Republic, the Albanian Party of Labour, the Hungarian Socialist Workers' Party, the Korean Workers' Party, and the Mongolian People's Revolutionary Party), they were mainly characterized by the same sorts of structures and processes, essentially modeled on the first of their number, the Communist Party of the Soviet Union. The Communist parties were generally seen as "narrow single parties," uniting within their ranks a small proportion of the population, having significant barriers to entry to party membership, characterized by high levels of internal discipline and a formal commitment to an ideology, usually termed Marxism-Leninism. The typical model of the Communist Party saw it as a vanguard party, uniting the most conscious part of the population within its ranks and dedicated to building socialism within its own national boundaries. The party was therefore not a mass organization in the sense that anyone could easily join, even though party membership in most states was in the millions. The ideological commitment formally underpinned both the party's legitimacy and the drive for unity within its ranks. Most Communist parties accepted democratic centralism as the main organizational principle governing their internal life. This demanded the strict hierarchical subordination of party bodies to those above them and the responsibility of all party members to adhere to party discipline. Failure to adhere could lead to expulsion from the party, with much greater punishments evident at some times in the histories of some of these parties.

The formal structure of the party was hierarchical, with national-level party organs sitting atop a structure that paralleled the administrative structure of the state. There were party organizations at all of the major administrative levels of the state structure, like provinces, regions, and districts, and in the federal Yugoslavia and the USSR at the level of the republics (except for the Russian Republic until 1990). At each level, the role and powers of the party organs were similar, to both one another and other organs at other levels in the structure, distinguished from the latter only by the geographic boundaries of the administrative structure they were shadowing. At each level the formally sovereign body was the assembly, usually called a congress or conference, except at the bottom level, where all party members were supposed to attend party meetings, comprising formally elected representatives of the party organizations. The assembly elected executive organs to conduct the affairs of the party organization between meetings. At the national level, congresses were held at periodic intervals, by late in the Communist period usually five years, and these elected central committees, which in turn formed their own executive organs, the politburo and a secretariat to run the party's administrative structure. Formally, most offices in the party structure were filled by election, but in practice this was usually accomplished through a process of appointment by higher standing bodies. The primacy of appointment in the filling of leading party positions was a major factor in both holding the party together and exercising disciplinary functions within the structure. Power was highly centralized in the leading organs of the party, with the notion of democratic centralism plus the prohibition of the formation of factions underpinning the emphasis on discipline, ensuring that the decisions of such organs were followed closely by lower-level party organs and party members generally.

In formal terms, the party leadership was collective in nature. Generally the collective organs of the party were the forums within which the deliberation of issues was to take place, and decisions were announced in the name of these party bodies. In practice, collectivism frequently took noninstitutional forms and was undermined by the primacy that leading individuals were able to achieve. The noninstitutional forms of collectivism were the cliques, cabals, and factions that often formed among party leaders, and made decisions at gatherings outside the formal party institutions. Such groupings could be temporary, while those that were able to attain more long-lasting primacy were typically associated with the emergence of a dominant individual leader. Such a leader, like Stalin in the USSR, Mao in China, Ceauşescu in Romania, Castro in Cuba, or Kim in North Korea, could effectively displace the formal organs of the party and rule in his own name. But when a leader did so, he was usually sustained and assisted by an informal cabal of supporters among the leading party figures.

As well as being recognized as narrow party systems, Communist systems were also dominant party systems in the sense that the party occupied a dominant place in the political system and generally was not subordinate to other political institutions, although China in the late 1960s and Poland in the late 1980s were exceptions to this. The dominance of the party in the political system was reflected in the designation of its "leading role" that appeared explicitly in some of the state constitutions. This notion of the leading role meant that effective power was vested in the party, its organs, and its members rather than in the formal organs of the state. There was considerable overlap in membership between party and state bodies at each level, with the leading positions at all levels of the state structure being filled through appointment by the party's leading organs. In this way, the party could ensure that its members dominated the state machine; in all countries the overwhelming majority of government ministers and leading officials were members of the party,

and therefore subject to its discipline. They carried out party decisions, and it was the party that decided on all the most important questions facing the country. The extent of the penetration of the state structure by the party was one factor that set Communist regimes apart from most other single-party regimes.

The Communist Party played a number of critical roles in the Communist states. The most significant was its leading role because this ensured that the party was the chief influence molding the course of development in society. It was also important in terms of political recruitment. Through its control over the appointment process, the party not only governed the filling of responsible positions but also ran the whole process of political recruitment. It was the party that decided who would be promoted and who would not, and therefore it was the party that in large part controlled the career prospects of citizens. The party was also a major element in the socialization or training of the populace. By projecting its ideological tenets into all walks of life, and controlling the media and the education system, the party shaped the value structure of the society and hence the processes of socialization that are present in all societies. The party's role in shaping the values of the country's citizens was also part of the mobilization and control functions that the party performed. Through having party organizations in all institutions in the country, the party was well placed to both exercise continuing control over the populace and mobilize that populace for the achievement of regime aims. The array of the party's functions and the extent of its control led many to consider it a totalitarian organization. The collapse of Communism, which was a result in part of the weakening of the party's capacity to maintain its control, shows how inaccurate such a judgment was.

The weakness of a single-party system, especially when it is a narrow system like the Communist one, is the limited capacity it has to reflect the diverse interests in the society. By forcing political representation into narrow institutional channels, the single-party system leaves many interests unrepresented. While this may ensure the internal coherence of the single party, it is at the expense of a narrowness of outlook that renders the party system vulnerable in times of difficulty when the institutional outlets for the expression of views are limited. This was one factor in the collapse of such systems at the end of the 1980s and early 1990s.

See also Citizenship; Constitutions; Democratic Centralism; Marxism-Leninism; Nomenklatura; Politburo; State, The.

FURTHER READING

Brooker, P. *Twentieth Century Dictatorships: The Ideological One-Party States.* Basingstoke, UK: Macmillan, 1995.

Gill, G. *The Collapse of a Single-Party System: The Disintegration of the Communist Party of the Soviet Union.* Cambridge, UK: Cambridge University Press, 1994.

Huntington, S. P., and C. H. Moore, eds. *Authoritarian Politics in Modern Society: The Dynamics of Established One-Party Systems.* New York: Basic Books, 1970.

Loeber, D. A., ed. *Ruling Communist Parties and Their Status under Law.* The Hague: Nijnhoff, 1986.

Sartori, G. *Parties and Party Systems: A Framework for Analysis.* Cambridge, UK: Cambridge University Press, 1976.

GRAEME GILL

Sino-Soviet Split

The relationship between China and the Soviet Union is one of the most complex chapters in the history of communism after World War II. In the early 1950s, immediately after the seizure of power by the Chinese Communist Party, aid from the Soviet Union had been one of the principal engines for the construction of socialism and economic accumulation in China. The First Five-Year Plan (1953–57) was a Chinese version of Soviet economic policy based on accumulation and the primacy of heavy industry. The dependence of this newborn Chinese industrial system on Soviet aid was obvious especially in the areas of science and technology. Soviet technicians crowded Chinese research institutions, and the undeniable successes in the construction of the Chinese industrial infrastructure during the 1950s were largely dependent on the technology and human capital supplied by Moscow early in the decade.

Between 1956 and 1960, relations between the two largest Communist parties deteriorated, culminating in a split. It was mostly caused by Moscow's criticism of Maoist economic strategies, China's attempt to compete with the Soviets for ideological and political supremacy in the "socialist camp," and the increasingly divergent opinions on the nature of imperialism held by Mao Zedong and Nikita Khrushchev, respectively. The critique of Stalin that emerged from Khrushchev's speeches made the leaders of the Chinese Communist Party, and Mao

personally, uncomfortable. Mao interpreted the attacks on the excesses of Stalin's collectivization as a direct reference to Chinese agrarian policies, since during those months the process of collectivization had been accelerated, portending the hypercollectivism of the Great Leap Forward. The official Chinese reaction to the revision of Stalin's role that had begun with the Communist Party of the Soviet Union's (CPSU) Twentieth Congress therefore attempted a balanced evaluation, admitting some of Stalin's mistakes, but without criticizing his cult of personality—a step that would have put Mao's role in jeopardy. The issue of capitalism's peaceful development, which was at the center of Khrushchev's new policies, was not yet regarded as a key question during this first phase.

Over the next few years, and especially once Mao launched the Great Leap Forward in 1958, using the people's communes as the highest form of collectivization, the Soviets continued to view the model of socialism being advanced by the Chinese leadership with suspicion. Khrushchev arrived for a visit in Beijing in September 1959, just when the disastrous consequences of the Great Leap Forward on living conditions in the Chinese countryside were obvious. The tension in relations between the two countries had been exacerbated during those weeks because of two other significant events: the removal of the head of the Chinese army, Peng Dehuai, an old friend of Moscow's, who had criticized Mao and the Great Leap Forward during the Lushan Plenum (July 1959); and increased strains on the border between China and India, due to an anti-Chinese revolt in Tibet that led to the military occupation of the region by the People's Liberation Army and the Dalai Lama's taking refuge in India (border skirmishes between the two armies continued during the following months, up to the 1962 war). Khrushchev took a neutral position on the tensions between India and China, in part to avoid U.S. criticism on the eve of an important summit at Camp David with Dwight Eisenhower. This irritated the Chinese leadership, and according to Beijing, revealed the risks inherent in the "pacifist" position Moscow was adopting in the global struggle between communism and imperialism.

The doctrine of "pacific coexistence" became the target of Chinese attacks at this point. During Khrushchev's visit to Beijing, he was aggressively reproached for Soviet "neutrality" in the conflict with India during a meeting with Foreign Minister Chen Yi. The recriminations became increasingly virulent over the following months, with Khrushchev accusing China of belligerence, nationalism, and unreliability. In contrast to conciliatory Soviet policy, Mao and his leadership instead saw the rapprochement between Khrushchev and Eisenhower as a trap to divide the "socialist camp," highlighting the risks being created by the growing U.S. military presence, especially in Asia. "Imperialism will never lay down its butcher's knife!" was one of the most widespread Mao quotes of the day.

During the first months of 1960 both the Soviets and Chinese used international organizations to bolster their respective positions among allies in the socialist camp, partly in an attempt to isolate their adversary. In February, at a Warsaw Pact conference—which Khrushchev had organized to receive multilateral approval of the pacific coexistence policy—the Chinese representative Kang Sheng's speech attacked both the policy and diplomatic steps taken by Khrushchev. On April 22, on the ninetieth anniversary of Lenin's birth, a celebratory article published in China in *Red Banner* highlighted Lenin's thesis that war was the inevitable result of the imperialist system of exploitation. The Soviets interpreted this document as an attempt to undermine Moscow's monopoly on Communist orthodoxy at the international level.

The grand reckoning, after Khrushchev had unsuccessfully invited Mao to Moscow, occurred during the Congress of the Romanian Communist Party in Bucharest in late June 1960. With the support of many other allied Communist parties, the Soviets violently criticized China for its foreign and economic policies. Khrushchev did not abstain from a personal attack on Mao, whom he did not hesitate to define as a "madman." The Chinese representative, Peng Zhen, was then authorized to issue an official statement in which he qualified the CPSU's attitude as "paternalistic." On July 16 the split was made official by the Soviets, who withdrew all their technicians and advisers from the numerous Chinese projects they were involved in. From that moment on relations between China and the Soviet Union continued only at the state level, but were interrupted at the party level. It would be almost thirty years before a general secretary from the CPSU, Mikhail Gorbachev, would set foot on Chinese soil for an official visit—while demonstrations by Chinese students were in full swing in Tiananmen Square.

The break with the Soviet Union and the withdrawal of aid had lasting effects on Chinese economic development during the next twenty years. But they also had important consequences for the development of Maoist ideology. According to Roderick McFarquhar, while analyzing Khrushchev's errors, Mao came to the conclusion that they were due to the "degeneration of Soviet society," and that it was thus necessary to consider "the implications for China." The painful detachment from the Soviet Union became one of the reasons for the radical evolution of Maoism in those years, indirectly leading to the social engineering of the Cultural Revolution (1966–76).

See also Great Leap Forward; Khrushchev, Nikita; Mao Zedong; Peaceful Coexistence; Socialist Camp; War, Inevitability of.

FURTHER READING

MacFarquhar, R. *The Origins of the Cultural Revolution.* Vol. 2, *1958–1960.* Oxford: Oxford University Press, 1983.

Westad, O. A. *Brothers in Arms: The Rise and Fall of the Sino-Soviet Alliance, 1945–1963.* Washington, DC: Woodrow Wilson Center, 1998.

LUIGI TOMBA

Slánský, Rudolf

Rudolf Slánský (1901–52) came from the large family of a minor country tradesman. He began his political activity as a high school student at the end of World War I, at the birth of Czechoslovakia. Slánský took part in demonstrations and welcomed the new republic with patriotic enthusiasm. He was just becoming familiar with socialist ideas, influenced by the Russian Revolution, the worldwide response to it, and its two years of progress in Russia. He entered the Commercial (High) School in Prague while, at the same time applying for membership in a Social Democratic left-wing party. This led directly to his enrollment in the Communist Party in May 1921. Due to his political commitments, he left his Commercial School studies to launch a career as a professional politician to become, so to speak, a revolutionary by vocation. In 1924, he began work in the central editorial office of the Communist Party of Czechoslovakia (CPCz) daily, *Rudé Právo.*

During the first phase of Bolshevization, Slánský belonged to a set of young functionaries with radical views. They tried to interest the Comintern in these views, but were rejected and punished by the party. It was Slánský 's first fall from grace in the party and his first punishment. He was transferred from Prague to Ostrava, where he became an assistant editor. Within two years he had worked his way up to the position of regional secretary of the CPCz. A brief collaboration with Klement Gottwald, who was serving temporarily in Ostrava, laid the basis for a friendship that would last a quarter of a century. The internal party crisis of 1928 would find Slánský as a secretary in a heavily Communist region (Kladno, near Prague). He committed himself to Gottwald's radical solution to the crisis, and at a party congress in 1929 was elected to the CPCz's Central Committee and the politburo of the Central Committee. A year after the congress, at the outset of a second wave of Bolshevization, Slánský was promoted to the CPCz headquarters, to the post of technical and organizational secretary—a job he held until 1935. Thus, in 1929, the twenty-eight-year-old Slánský found himself among the highest Communist leaders and Gottwald's closest colleagues.

Organizational matters for the CPCz were handled by the Comintern apparatus, and from there criticisms were aimed at Slánský. In 1935, these criticisms reached a climax: Slánský and Jan Šverma, who during Gottwald's absence had been entrusted with the CPCz's leadership, were accused by the Comintern of carrying out policies of the Czechoslovak Popular Front incorrectly. Both Slánský and Sverma lost their membership in the Secretariat of the Central Committee, and Slánský was also removed from his post as the Central Committee's organizational secretary. Slánský took the criticism and his punishment hard, but at a congress in 1936, he was again elected to membership in the Central Committee and candidacy for its politburo.

At the end of 1938, Slánský went into exile in Moscow, where he was a member of the CPCz's foreign leadership, and organized Czech and Slovak broadcasts over Soviet radio. He took part in all the important negotiations, which the Communist leaders were conducting in Moscow. In that city, he became even closer to Gottwald. In 1944 Slánský was a deputy to the Ukrainian partisan headquarters. He was sent to Slovakia during the uprising in September. There, as a member of the Council for the Defense of Slovakia, he organized partisan units. In March 1945, he took part in negotiations in Moscow for establishing the first postwar government in Czechoslovakia. He was then chosen in April by the temporary Central Committee of the CPCz to serve as its general secretary.

Slánský returned to a liberated Czechoslovakia as the second most important figure in the CPCz. He occupied the first position in "Gottwald's Guard," and for

six uninterrupted years served as a member of the party's highest organs. He acquired authority in the party, and represented the party and its policies for both party leaders and lower functionaries. The public, too, regarded him as the leading representative of the strongest party in the country, with whom many individuals were locked in political struggles. Slánský considered it his main task to lead the party to a monopoly of power. Guided by his Comintern experience and advice from Soviet politicians, he concentrated on building a party capable of realizing this objective. To this end, he used the methods of the Communist security organs, both legal and illegal, and also exploited the provocations these organs fomented. Slánský fostered the creation of a network of similar organs in non-Communist parties as well. The preparedness of the Czech Communists in their struggle for power became evident in the successful coup they staged in 1948, in which Slánský played a huge role.

Slánský maintained his preeminent position in the Communist regime for four years. As the CPCz's general secretary, a member of its leading committees, and chair of its various organs of repression, he shared in the planning and realization of official policies, including those that unleashed a mass of unlawful acts, political show trials, and sundry other illegalities. He secured the party's power by ensuring the preeminence of its apparatus and institutions over government organs. In September 1951, however, at Stalin's instigation, Slánský was removed from his position as general secretary and shunted down to deputy chair of the government. In November, again at Stalin's initiative, he was imprisoned. A year later, at a political show trial, he was sentenced to death and executed. Eleven years after that, in 1968, Slánský was rehabilitated by both the courts and party.

Slánský devoted almost thirty years of his life to the Communist Party, quite literally giving his life for it. In his political trial, which had distinctly anti-Semitic overtones, he fulfilled the role that the Prague and Moscow leaders of the time expected of him. He confessed to crimes and was tried for acts that he never committed, rather than for those he had perpetrated along with the rest of the CPCz leadership. He successfully organized and executed his party's objectives and decrees, but was never able to cultivate his own political philosophy. Slánský followed Gottwald's line and instructions. He carried out the decisions of the party leadership, either with Gottwald's consent or at his initiative. His relentless judgments brought about the persecution or demise of many citizens and comrades. He not only worked with Gottwald; they were friends, and Slánský became Gottwald's right-hand man. And when Slánský was sentenced, he knew Gottwald's character too well to believe that the Czechoslovak leader would save him from execution.

In the mid-1930s, Slánský had been criticized by the Comintern, which had cast a shadow on his political profile. He had also had his own experiences in the USSR. To be sure, he carried out the wishes of the Soviet leaders obediently, but nevertheless had feared the influence of repressive elements in Czechoslovakia and the political trials of party members. Distrust of Slánský, his Jewish origin, and his high rank had impelled the Soviet authorities to organize a new round of illegal trials of leading Communists not only in Czechoslovakia but elsewhere too.

Slánský 's fate confirmed that illegal acts are not discriminating; they can claim an author of them as well. The victim, this time, was an enthusiastic participant in the creation of a totalitarian Communist regime—one of many highly placed functionaries who set in motion horrors of injustice and repression, sent thousands of innocent people to prison, and gave their approval to political murders. His coworkers were relieved to see Slánský executed, rather than themselves. They even organized a big campaign to convince the public that Slánský had been a traitor and criminal.

See also Gottwald, Klement; People's Democracy; Prague Coup; Stalinism.

FURTHER READING

Kaplan, K. *Report on the Murder of the General Secretary*. Columbus: Ohio State University Press, 1990.

———. *Zpráva o zavraždění generalního tajemníka*. Prague: Mladá fronta, 1992.

Slánska, J. *Zpráva o mém muži*. Prague: NakladateslstvíSvoboda, 1990.

Strobinger, R. *Vražda generalniho tajemníka*. Brno: Lidová demokracie-Petrov, 1991.

KAREL KAPLAN

Social Democracy

If the outbreak of the war was the first body-blow to the pre-1914 European Socialist movement, October 1917 was the coup de grâce. The Russian Revolution provided the Left with a fundamental reference point—negative for the reformists, positive for the revolutionaries. The Soviet decision in 1919 to form the Third International forced everyone to take a stand.

On the whole Communist parties were formed as a result of a minority split from Socialist parties, as was the case in Spain and in Italy. There were, however, various exceptions to this rule. One was the Communist Party of Great Britain (CPGB), which was formed by groups already outside the Labour Party. A not dissimilar process occurred in the Netherlands. In France, at the Congress of Tours (1920) a majority voted to become a Communist Party. In Germany the situation was different since the Socialist Party had emerged from the war already split into three fractions. One of these, the Spartacus League led by Rosa Luxemburg and Karl Liebnecht, became the *Kommunistische Partei Deutschlands* (KPD).

Socialist parties emerged on the winning side in all electoral battles of the interwar years, even in the two countries (Germany and France) where the Communists had a significant electoral base. The Socialists' great advantage in electoral politics was that there was a reservoir of votes to their right as well as to their left, while the Communists could only look to the Socialist electorate. This, in the 1920s, mattered little to the Communists since their overarching belief was that the road to revolution would be insurrectionary. All one needed to decide was whether the time was ripe. If it was, then a precise demarcation line had to be drawn in order to separate the revolutionaries from all others.

In effect, even a relatively strong Communist Party such as the KPD existed in a political ghetto. This isolation increased with the general Bolshevization of European communism, reaching an apex at the end of the 1920s when the Comintern sectarian policy of the "Third Period" was adopted. It was assumed that conditions were almost ripe for an armed insurrection and that capitalism would soon collapse. Social Democrats were viciously labeled "Social Fascists," the "left wing of the bourgeoisie." The 1929 Wall Street crash seemed clearly to signal capitalism's doom. It was only in 1934 that the line changed: sectarianism was dropped in favor of a united front with all other anti-Fascist forces. This change had some real political significance in only two countries: France and Spain. The causes of the change of line were manifold: the lessons drawn from the Nazi accession to power, the USSR's fear of being isolated and of facing a hostile capitalist world, and the obvious dead end into which Third Period policies had led.

All in all the French Communists improved their prospects significantly during the period of the Popular Front. The party's membership was up from 32,000 in 1932 to 290,000 at the end of 1936, again overtaking the Socialists, though not at the polls.

Clearly, by any reasoned judgment, the record of prewar communism in Europe was one of failure. The Communists had failed to establish themselves as leading contenders for power. Conversely, the Socialist parties in almost all cases emerged as the main party of the working class and were able to form governments in many countries of Western Europe between the wars, notably in the Scandinavian countries, in Great Britain, and in Spain.

The Second World War provided European communism with a second chance to overtake the Socialists. In the aftermath of the conflict they did so in the whole of Eastern Europe thanks to the decisive backing of the USSR. In the West, communism reached the zenith of its influence and power in 1945–46, regularly increasing its percentage of the vote. When the dust had settled, Europe, and with it socialism, had become effectively divided. In Eastern and in parts of Central Europe a form of authoritarian socialist society emerged, only to be bitterly denounced by the Social Democratic majority of the Western labor movement. Then, in 1989–91, each of the socialist regimes collapsed in the wake of the fall of the Berlin Wall.

Why did social democracy predominate in the West? Fundamentally this was due to the fact that once the war was over and normality reestablished, the Socialist parties simply resumed their previous positions of influence, helped by the rapidly developing Cold War. Their prestige had not been seriously damaged during the war, even though they had not covered themselves in glory either: in all the countries ruled by the Nazis or their allies, it was the Communists and not the Socialists who had been in the vanguard of the resistance.

The beginning of the Second World War had at first divided Communists from socialists as severely as in the 1920s, largely because of the Soviet-Nazi pact. The entry of the USSR into the war then led to rapprochement between Socialists and Communists. Because the Communists played a leading role in the resistance, they were able to forge links with all other anti-Fascist parties. In the majority of cases this reciprocal respect would last only until the end of hostilities or, at most, the commencement of the Cold War. There remained a fundamental distrust, unalterable and usually well founded, between the Communists and all the other parties.

The war had afforded Western Communists their finest hour. They could fight fascism and Nazism, be true internationalists, defend the USSR, be flawless patriots, and all without inconsistency. Instead of being reviled in a ghetto of their own, they were praised by all: by Churchill, by Roosevelt, and by de Gaulle.

The resistance was the key factor determining the relations of forces between the Socialist and Communist components of the traditional Left in Western Europe after the war. There is some correlation between the magnitude of the resistance in a nation and the Communists' political successes there immediately after the war.

With the exception of Italy (and France where the Communists peaked in the second elections in 1946 at 28.6 percent), the first postwar results were also the Communists' historical best. Never again would they achieve such a degree of popular support.

European communism adopted a strategy of participation in coalition governments. Unity with the Socialists became the fundamental goal. This strategy was based on the assumption that there would be considerable continuity between wartime and peacetime politics and that the political understanding that had prevailed during the war would persist into the postwar period. The term "people's democracy" was coined precisely to denote a form of state or regime led by a coalition government in which the Communist Party would have a significant share of power, but not a monopoly. In Eastern Europe this soon turned into a policy of forced amalgamation with the Socialist parties. In Western Europe the Communists were soon excluded from government, usually with the encouragement of the socialists. The one exception was Italy, where the Socialist Party was expelled along with the Communists. Virtually everywhere else the Cold War separated the Socialists from the Communists. Some Social Democrats, notably in Norway, Holland, France, Belgium, and above all Great Britain, contributed decisively to the development of NATO as a way of confronting the USSR and keeping the United States committed to the defense of Europe. Almost all Socialist parties—again the Italians were the most notable exception—joined forces in the reconstitution of the Socialist International in Frankfurt in June of 1951. Its declaration was mainly the work of the British Labour Party and Scandinavian Social Democrats and made clear its opposition to communism and its commitment to parliamentary democracy.

The 1950s signaled a generalized retreat of Socialist parties in the whole of Western Europe (with the exception of the Scandinavian countries), while in the East, Communist rule entered its harshest phase, culminating in repression in East Germany and Hungary. By the end of the 1950s the Socialist parties had to reassess their strategy. In Britain the Labour Party discussed the dropping of clause four of its constitution, which identified as the final goal a collectivized economy. It was not until 1964 that they returned to power after thirteen years as the opposition. The German SPD, at its Bad Godesberg Congress began a process of revision that would, ten years later, enable it to enter a coalition government for the first time since the 1930s. In Italy the Socialists broke their pact of unity with the Communists, started negotiating with the Christian Democrats, and abandoned their opposition to NATO (a move paralleled in Germany by the SPD). By 1963 the Italian Socialists, too, had entered government. In France, the advent of Gaullism forced the Socialists into opposition. Throughout the 1960s and 1970s French Socialists and Communists alternated between bitter rivalry and various attempts to reach an understanding. In Italy the Pci opted for a "soft" opposition to the center-left government.

By the late 1970s and 1980s the Communist-Socialist dialogue had entered a new phase. In France, the success of the Socialist leader François Mitterrand in 1981 was partly due to his ability to overtake electorally the Pcf, a lead that was consolidated over the next two decades. In the few countries where the Communists were still of some significance, such as Sweden, their role was, at best, that of a leftist pressure group. In Italy all the attempts of the Socialist Party, led by Bettino Craxi, to reduce its electoral gap with the Pci failed and the relationship between Communists and Socialists became increasingly bitter.

The end of dictatorships in Portugal, Spain, and Greece in the mid-1970s had resulted in the emergence of relatively strong Communist parties, each pursuing different strategies with respect to the Socialists. In Portugal the Communists supported the new revolutionary military government while the Socialists, supported by the West, distanced themselves from it, a strategy that the electorate favored. In Spain the Communists, overestimating the strength of the conservatives, pursued a policy of national coalition. This failed, and the Socialists emerged as the new dominant party of government for most of the 1980s and the first part of the 1990s. In Greece the Communist Party was soon overtaken by a Socialist Party, PASOK, which had been formed during the period of dictatorship. By the time communism collapsed, the three Communist parties in southern Europe had become little more than a haven for discontented Leftists—as had the Pcf. In Italy the momentous events following the collapse of the Berlin Wall coincided with a massive corruption scandal that eliminated most of the governing parties, including the Socialists, while the Pci turned itself into a mainstream European Socialist Party, as did many of the former Communist parties of Eastern Europe. The history of European communism had effectively ended and with it the division of the labor movement between Socialists and Communists.

See also Antifascism; Bolshevism; Cold War; Comintern; Social Fascism; Socialist International; Welfare State.

FURTHER READING

Anderson, P., and P. Camiller, eds. *Mapping the West European Left.* London: Verso, 1994.

Antonian, A. *Toward A Theory of Eurocommunism: The Relationship Between Eurocommunism and Eurosocialism.* New York: Greenwood Press, 1987.

Eley, G. *Forging Democracy: The History of the Left in Europe, 1850–2000.* Oxford: Oxford University Press, 2002.

Sassoon, D. *One Hundred Years of Socialism.* London: I. B. Taurus, 1996.

Waller, M., and M. Fennema, eds. *Communist Parties in Western Europe: Decline or Adaptation.* Oxford: Blackwell, 1988.

DONALD SASSOON

Social Fascism

The theory of "social fascism" was adopted by the Comintern in the course of 1928–29 and dominated Communist discourse until the advent of the Popular Front in 1934. It signified, above all, an intense sectarian hostility toward social democracy, particularly its leadership, and together with the complementary notion of "class against class" defined the Comintern's ultraleftist "Third Period." In the view of most scholars, the historic significance of social fascism is that it represented a decisive step on the road to the Stalinization of the world Communist movement, and more portentous, prevented an anti-Nazi "united front" of German workers, hence contributing in no small measure to Hitler's *machtergreifung* and by extension the subsequent crimes against humanity perpetrated by the Nazi regime.

The origins of social fascism can be found in the long-standing Bolshevik conviction that social democracy was degenerating into a bourgeois, not a workers', party. The term was first coined, it seems, in *Izvestiia* in November 1922 to deride the nefarious role of Italian socialists in Mussolini's rise to power. In the mid-1920s, both Zinovyev and Stalin identified a close affinity between social democracy and fascism, without actually using the label social fascism itself. It was at the Sixth Comintern Congress in summer 1928, and more explicitly at the Tenth Plenum of its Executive Committee in July 1929, that the derogatory appellation was asserted and given a theoretical underpinning. The congress theses insisted that as the "crisis of capitalism" intensified, so the bourgeoisie increasingly co-opted social democracy into the existing political structures, thus making the "labor bureaucracy" one of the main pillars of the capitalist state. What is more, this state was moving inexorably toward "fascisization," class violence, and overt dictatorship. In these circumstances, Comintern theoreticians, and indeed many rank-and-file Communists, firmly believed that only by smashing Socialist parties and reformist trade unions once and for all could the working class be united for the imminent revolutionary assault on capitalism.

Most historians agree that the impact of social fascism was little short of disastrous. Nearly everywhere Communist parties were marginalized in their local labor movements, membership levels dropped, and Communist influence in working-class organizations was severely undermined. It was in the Weimar Republic that the practice of social fascism had its most far-reaching consequences. Here, so the compelling argument goes, the preexisting divisions between Social Democrats and Communists were profoundly exacerbated by the Comintern's social fascist line, and the German Communists' priority of attacking the Social Democratic Party while underestimating the Nazi danger. Despite the impressive electoral growth of the Communist Party of Germany, this myopic strategy facilitated Hitler's seizure of power and doomed the much-vaunted German labor movement to destruction. Ultimately, the blame for this debacle lies with Stalin, as it was he who orchestrated the turn to social fascism as an integral part of his campaign to defeat the Bukharinite "right wing," he who oversaw the Comintern and Community Party tactics in the early 1930s, and he who appeared to believe that a Nazi victory would herald a workers' revolution and a "Soviet Germany."

There is much to recommend this "top-down" interpretation, but some historians have qualified it by identifying more positive phenomena "from below": the input of non-Russian Communists, notably Germans, in the formulation of social fascist theory; the impetus it gave to a distinct homespun "revolutionary culture" in the shape of workers' newspapers and factory broadsheets, workers' theaters, sports, and leisure groups, and an emphasis on women and youth issues, all of which marked Communists off from their ideologically supine Social Democratic rivals. It is also the case that Social Democratic leaders in many countries harbored a deep suspicion of Communists and rarely displayed a willingness to collaborate with them. Thus, the Social Democrats must take their fair share of the responsibility for the mutual breakdown in relations. While this differentiated national perspective provides a valuable corrective to the "from above" methodology, it is hard to avoid the conclusion that the concept and practice of social fascism were determined in Moscow, and were largely incompatible with national conditions and political cultures.

See also Collapse of Capitalism; Comintern; Fascism; Social Democracy; Stalinism.

FURTHER READING

Draper, T. "The Ghost of Social-Fascism." *Commentary*, no. 2 (1969): 29–42.

Fischer, C. *The German Communists and the Rise of Nazism.* London: Palgrave Macmillan, 1991.

LaPorte, N., K. Morgan, and M. Worley, eds. *Bolshevism, Stalinism and the Comintern: Perspectives on Stalinization, 1917–53.* Basingstoke, UK: Palgrave, Macmillan, 2008.

Worley, M., ed. *In Search of Revolution: International Communist Parties in the "Third Period."* London: I. B. Tauris, 2004.

KEVIN F. McDERMOTT

Social Policy

The phrase "social policy" has been used in widely varying ways to describe the organization of citizens' lives under communism. In the broadest sense it can refer to the most sweeping efforts to transform society, such as the liquidation of kulaks or the transformation of gender relations among Muslim populations (the latter especially in the USSR and China). The term is more often used in a narrower sense, to describe the provision of basic services and amenities to the citizenry, in ways more comparable to the operation of welfare states in non-Communist societies. Both usages can be encompassed by T. H. Marshall's definition: "Social policy is the use of political power to supersede, supplant, supplement, or modify operations of the economic system in order to achieve results which the economic system would not achieve on its own."

Social policy in the Communist states frequently reflected a tension between broad agendas—utopian, transformatory, and "totalitarian"—and the mundane day-to-day decisions that governed the provision of housing, child care, services to the elderly, and other social benefits. Over time, most Communist states shifted emphasis from the former to the latter. Social policy in this narrower sense sometimes complemented or reinforced the operation of a planned socialist economy. Improvements in public health and education, for example, helped to raise labor productivity. But often the social services competed for scarce resources in state-directed economies that assigned a higher priority to heavy industry and military expenditures.

The party of Vladimir Lenin came to power in Russia in 1917, committed to a revolutionary agenda that was expected to transform every aspect of social existence. Communism would abolish not only the economic inequities of capitalism but also the social foundations of the bourgeois order, such as the nuclear family. Prominent Bolsheviks such as Aleksandra Kollontay envisioned a future in which marriage would be a partnership of equals, children would no longer be raised solely by their parents, and housework would be performed not by family members but rather by paid workers. Visionary architects tried to redesign the physical environment to create a new socialist reality.

In the first years of the Soviet republic a number of attempts were made to put such ideals into practice. Family law was overhauled: divorce and abortion were legalized, and children born out of wedlock were guaranteed equal rights to those born to married parents. Domestic servants were organized into trade unions. Day care centers, kindergartens, communal dining halls, and a small number of innovative residential buildings, such as Moisei Ginsburg's Domnarkomfin in Moscow, were constructed to promote a new, communal mode of social existence.

By the early 1930s, however, Soviet leaders put their priorities elsewhere, concentrating the USSR's resources on rapid industrialization. They concluded that the country, in its present condition, could not bear the cost of creating extensive new social facilities. The socialist goal of "from each according to their ability, to each according to their need" was suspended in favor of the more hardheaded "to each according to their work." Utopian planning principles such as N. A. Miliutin's *Sotsgorod* were shelved or condemned. Domnarkomfin was carved up into overcrowded "communal" apartments (*kommunalki*) that bore little resemblance the architect's original vision. By the mid-1930s the Stalinist regime also repudiated experiments in family life in favor of a pronatalist policy that narrowly restricted abortion and divorce.

Through most of the following decades, the provision of social services in the USSR was constrained by the scarcity of resources within a state budget dominated by military defense and industrialization. Even so, social policy followed what Richard Titmuss has termed an "institutional redistributional" model. In contrast to what Titmuss terms "residual" systems, which provide support only to a minority of citizens (those whose needs are not being met through family or market-related channels), Soviet planners tried to address the basic needs of all citizens, and uphold universalistic standards for the provision of services in such fields as education, housing, and health.

Critics, writing mainly at the end of the Soviet era, suggested that this approach had several negative effects: it raised citizens' expectations of basic services without linking them to economic productivity or performance, and it allowed little or no room for independent nongovernmental providers to operate.

Commodities and services were rationed during the industrial drive of the 1930s, the Second World War years, and the postwar period. State industrial enterprises, which could often overrule local planning bodies, provided housing and other social infrastructure as well as other material benefits to members of their own workforce—frequently on a selective basis (e.g., to "shock workers" who outperformed their workmates). Even so, consumer goods were often in deficit, and housing, education, and health services failed to keep pace with rising demand.

Starting during the period of Nikita Khrushchev's leadership in the 1950s, the Soviet Union committed more resources to social needs, especially in such fields as housing. The result was a system of conditional entitlements that some Western commentators termed a tacit social contract. In Linda Cook's words, it promised "full and secure employment, egalitarian wage policies . . . state controlled and heavily subsidized prices for essential goods, and socialized human services (i.e., education, medical care, child care, etc.)." In return, citizens gave passive acquiescence to a system that consistently fell short of its pledges. "They pretend to pay us," they joked, "and we pretend to work."

The planned economy provided goods and benefits on a nonmarket basis that included long waiting lists for housing or other scarce commodities. The shortages and inadequacies of the system were remedied, in part, by an informal "second economy," in which semilegal or illegal transactions took the place of an open market. Kinship, friendship, patronage, and other "reciprocal" relationships addressed the needs that official channels could not meet. For example, city dwellers developed elaborate networks for trading apartments.

Soviet law provided pensions for workers to retire at age fifty-five (for women) or sixty (for men), but formal social supports for the elderly were often inadequate, with the result that many elderly persons, weak and chronically ill, ended up being cared for by relatives. Access to education and medical care was supposed to be universal, but special treatment could be obtained "on the side" (*nalevo*) through personal connections or bribery.

Under Soviet law, citizens were supposed to be provided with housing to a minimum "sanitary norm" of nine square meters per person. Until the 1960s, though, relatively few attained this standard. Most urban residents were housed in communal flats that were subdivided to accommodate multiple families; each family received a room or portion thereof, and they all shared the kitchen and bathroom. The devastation of World War II worsened housing conditions, but by the mid-1950s the party leadership announced an ambitious program of expansion. Buildings were constructed using prefabricated modules, at a rate of more than two million new housing units per year. The quality of construction was frequently criticized (in a mordant pun, the new units were called *khrushchoby*, a combination of Khrushchev's surname with the Russian word for slum), but millions of families were able for the first time to have apartments of their own. The costs, including heating and utilities, were heavily subsidized, so that the residents ended up paying less than 5 percent of their income for housing. Yet the supply never caught up with the demand, and as late as 1987 almost a quarter of Soviet households were on waiting lists for apartments. Young married couples usually found themselves sharing quarters with their in-laws, and divorced couples might continue to live together for a lack of alternative housing. In the late 1980s economist Abel Aganbegyan, a prominent adviser to Mikhail Gorbachev, described housing as the USSR's worst social problem.

Until the last days of the Soviet Union, the prices of most foodstuffs were strictly regulated regardless of the supply. The shelves of the shops were sometimes nearly empty, but consumers knew the price of every item. To satisfy their daily needs, families relied on the less-regulated "kolkhoz market." Officially, this was a place where peasants sold their own surplus produce, yet in actuality much of the trade was in the hands of enterprising middlepeople.

Women in Soviet society were particularly disadvantaged by the "double burden" of housework and paid employment. On the one hand, they were encouraged to work outside the home, and the high rate of female workforce participation was frequently presented as a sign of women's emancipation under communism. On the other hand, housework was generally regarded as a woman's responsibility, with little in the way of social support. Labor-saving appliances such as washing machines and dishwashers were scarce and unreliable. Due to shortages of foodstuffs, shoppers (mainly women) could spend up to several hours per day standing in line for basic commodities.

More than 50 percent of preschool-age children in the USSR were enrolled in crèches or kindergartens, and the demand for such care was even greater. During the years of glasnost, however, many educators questioned the quality of care provided. Staff members were not highly trained, and the ratio of children to caregivers was estimated in the range of twenty-five to one. Instead of enrolling their children in these programs, many working parents relied on relatives to supply informal child care. In the last decades of the Soviet Union, as the birthrate plummeted, demographers cited concerns about child care together with overcrowded housing as causes of this decline.

The Communist states of Eastern and Central Europe followed the Soviet lead in many of their social programs, and encountered similar problems. Nongovernmental organizations, including religious ones, played a somewhat larger role in several of these states, but in most other respects the basic outlines of social policy were quite similar. Housing, education, health care, and child care were all treated as social entitlements, but as in the Soviet case, the resources available were often insufficient to meet the needs and demands of the citizenry. Shortages of goods and services were endemic, though the overall standard of living in several of the Warsaw Pact states surpassed that of the USSR. By the mid-1980s, dissatisfaction among the citizenry was widespread.

The experience of China, Vietnam, and other non-European Communist states was influenced by the fact that these were overwhelmingly agrarian societies with fewer resources and lower living standards. In such cases, relatively small investments in fields like public health and primary education could produce dramatic results. In China, the rate of infant mortality fell by approximately 90 percent between 1950 and 2000, and life expectancy doubled. The rate of illiteracy also fell dramatically. As in the USSR, however, the cost of providing a full range of education and health services proved enormous, leading to rationing and the unequal distribution of services.

The People's Republic of China was established as a centrally planned economy in which all citizens were promised the basic amenities of life—food, shelter, health care, and education—under the rubric of an "unbreakable iron rice bowl." In the period from 1949 to the late 1970s the Communist leadership, while concentrating its efforts on building up heavy industry, created a system of social benefits to be provided equally to all citizens. Even so, separate programs were established for the rural and urban populations. City dwellers received state-funded health care as an employment benefit, while rural cooperatives addressed the health needs of the farm population without state support. A social security system provided pensions and other assistance to industrial employees, but not to the rural population. The overall living standard in urban areas was significantly higher than in the countryside, but rural-urban migration was closely regulated by the state, and urban growth was slow.

Despite impressive growth in heavy industry, China under Mao Zedong remained a country of widespread poverty in which food was periodically rationed and other basic commodities were scarce. After Mao's death in 1976, reformist Chinese leaders tried to find a new path of development that would produce greater prosperity and diversity. They criticized the planned economy as rigid and unproductive. In its place, they proposed a "socialist market economy" that offered more opportunities to managers and entrepreneurs. The new economic system encouraged foreign trade and investment as well as shifting the emphasis from primary to secondary and service industries. Small- and medium-size enterprises flourished under private ownership. In the countryside,

farmers could withdraw from collective farms and sell their produce in open markets.

Amid all these changes many of the social policies—restrictions as well as guarantees—of the older system remained in force. Chinese social policy of the 1980s and 1990s retained many of the "top-down" features of earlier years: a centrally directed system that dovetailed with measures of social control (e.g., over rural-urban migration). Although the urban population soared, peasants still could not freely migrate to cities; those who moved illegally often found themselves working for subminimal wages, with no "safety net" to protect them. Planners hoped that a network of township and village enterprises would encourage peasants to take up industrial work without leaving the rural areas. The older, state-owned enterprises—which now employed more than two-thirds of the industrial workforce but produced only one-third of the output—remained responsible for a wide array of social benefits including pensions, health care, and housing. Managers objected that this prevented them from laying workers off or raising productivity. The owners and managers of independent enterprises objected to the taxes and payments that the welfare system required. Meanwhile, the gap between urban and rural living standards, and between the rich and poor in the cities, widened.

Despite the wide variation among social policies in the Communist states, several common themes stand out. These policies promised, though they often did not deliver, security and universal norms of well-being. They also tried to regulate society in ways that challenged a market economy. From an economic point of view, they were usually an obstacle to innovation, but they helped to shape the behavior and expectations of citizens and workers—a legacy that continues to affect reformed and post-Communist societies. In China, many citizens still regard the iron rice bowl as an entitlement, while in post-Communist Russia more than one political party has tried to appeal to voters' nostalgia for the stability and (supposed) egalitarianism of the later Communist era.

See also Architecture and Urban Planning; Command Economy; Demographic Policies; Family; Planning; Socialist Market Economy; Welfare State.

FURTHER READING

Cook, L. J. "Institutional and Political Legacies of the Socialist Welfare State." In *The Legacy of State Socialism and the Future of Transformation*, ed. D. S. Lane. Lanham, MD: Rowman and Littlefield, 2002.

Deacon, B., ed. *Social Policy in the New Eastern Europe*. Aldershot, UK: Avebury, 1990.

Hughes, N. C. "Smashing the Iron Rice Bowl." *Foreign Affairs* 77:4 (1998): 67–78.

Li, B., and D. Piachaud. *Poverty and Inequality and Social Policy in China*. London: Centre for Analysis of Social Exclusion, LSE, CASE Papers, 2004.

McAuley, A. *Economic Welfare in the Soviet Union*. Madison: University of Wisconsin Press, 1979.

Millar, J. R. "The Little Deal: Brezhnev's Contribution to Acquisitive Socialism." In *Soviet Society and Culture: Essays in Honor of Vera S. Dunham*, ed. T. L. Thompson and R. R. Sheldon. Boulder, CO: Westview, 1988.

ROBERT JOHNSON

Socialism in One Country

The term "socialism in one country" refers to the doctrine of socialist development adopted by the Fourteenth Party Congress in December 1925. That doctrine held as its central proposition that it was possible to construct socialism in Russia alone—without a proletarian revolution in Europe. A secondary proposition held that although socialism could be constructed in Russia independently, there would be no "complete victory" for socialism until the threat to overthrow it was banished by revolution in one or more of the capitalist powers. International revolution was thus moved down the agenda of the Communist Party of Russia; internal development was made the first item of business.

The doctrine was a significant innovation. Previously the transition from capitalism to socialism had been linked closely in Marxism-Leninism to transnational proletarian revolution. Socialism would come throughout Europe as the result of a single process during one historical period that would last, it was thought at first, for weeks, then months, and then perhaps years. This was Lenin's original formulation of "world revolution." By contrast, socialism in one country formulated the proposition that socialism could be constructed independently in separate nations at different times. Ideologically, the achievement of socialism became a national occurrence. Guaranteed security for it, "complete victory" became a matter of international relations.

The doctrine was implicit in elements of Bukharin's thought as early as November 1923, at the time of the failure of the Communist uprising in Germany. Stalin enunciated the idea formally in December 1924, and Bukharin started discussing the question explicitly and publicly in April 1925. Then the resolutions of the Fourteenth Party Congress the following December adopted the doctrine as the central principle of socialist construction. Bukharin worked socialism in one country into a distinctive program for the socialization of Russia, and it was he who developed the theoretical basis for it. Stalin popularized the idea by proclaiming it in his speeches and writings during the two years extending from late 1924 to late 1926. He thereby gained much of the political benefit that accrued from the acceptance of the doctrine among the party rank and file. Stalin and Bukharin used the doctrine as a weapon in their struggle to defeat Trotsky, and also Kamenev and Zinovyev.

While in prison in 1906, serving time for his activities during the 1905 revolution, Trotsky had put forth the idea of a "permanent revolution": "Without the direct state support of the European proletariat, the working class of Russia cannot remain in power and convert its temporary domination into a lasting socialist dictatorship. Of this there cannot for one moment be any doubt." Twenty years later, Stalin perverted the meaning of a permanent revolution by attributing to Trotsky three suppositions: that Russia was too backward to achieve socialism on its own, that genuine socialism could not be constructed in Russia until European proletarian revolution occurred, and that Soviet Russia could not survive without the support of revolution in Europe. Trotsky, Stalin stated, had lost confidence in the Russian Revolution. In 1924–25 Trotsky, however, made no reply to the proclamation of socialism in one country. By the time he did, in late 1926, he had lost the ideological and political advantage to Stalin and Bukharin, and was about to be removed from the politburo and Central Committee.

Socialism in one country responded to the situation confronting the leadership of the Communist parties of Russia and Europe following the abortion of the revolution in Germany in November 1923. It was apparent, the Stalin-Bukharin duumvirate maintained, that the period of revolutionary upsurge had come to an end. Socialist revolution now had to be regarded as a whole strategic period, lasting for a number of years, or perhaps even a number of decades. At the same time, capitalism in Europe had succeeded in extricating itself from the quagmire of the postwar crisis, and achieved a "partial" and "temporary" stabilization. That stabilization had been achieved mainly with the aid of U.S. capital, and at the price of the financial subordination of Western Europe to the United States. The 1924 reparation settlement, the Dawes Plan, and U.S. lending had transformed Germany—once the locus of revolutionary upsurge in Europe—into an appendage of European capital, they maintained. It was Bukharin who first proclaimed—in June 1924, at the time the Dawes Plan was formulated—that a new stabilization period in the history of capitalism was beginning; he then defended the notion vigorously in theoretical debates. Stalin, meanwhile, explained the international situation to the party membership in a series of articles, interviews, speeches, and reports starting in September 1924. This effort culminated in December 1925 with his presentation of the "Political Report of the Central Committee" to the Fourteenth Party Congress.

The Soviet system was also stabilizing, Stalin and Bukharin asserted. The Russian economy was growing; socialism was being built; the exploited of Europe and the oppressed of Asia were rallying around the socialist homeland. The result was a temporary equilibrium between these two stabilizations in which neither socialism nor capitalism was able to defeat the other. While the duration of this equilibrium could not be predicted, "there is no doubt," Stalin stated, that "it will be a long one." In 1918 Lenin had thought the end of the war with Germany would be followed by a short "peace break" in armed struggle between the capitalist powers and the revolution of the Soviets. After the civil war he predicted a more lengthy truce. In 1924–25 Stalin used much different terminology: "a whole period of respite," "a whole period of so-called peaceful coexistence of the USSR with the capitalist states." The conditions under which the doctrine of socialism in one country was proclaimed were an ebbing of the tide of revolution, an economic recovery of both Europe and Russia from the devastation of war, revolution, and civil war, a long international equilibrium, an era of peaceful coexistence between the two systems. They made the construction of socialism in Russia alone both possible and necessary.

During much the same period of time that the doctrine of socialism in one country was introduced and adopted, "the industrialization debate" occurred among the party and state elite. At the Fourteenth Party Congress, the Central Committee committed the party to both building socialism in Russia separately and transform-

ing it into a self-sufficient industrial nation. How that was to happen, though, was not determined at the time. Bukharin concluded that the capital required for the economic development would not be coming from Europe. The abortion of the 1923 insurrection made it clear that a Communist Germany was not about to become Soviet Russia's economic provider, and neither the Genoa Conference of 1922 nor the Anglo-Soviet Conference of 1924 resolved the issue of Russian debt payment and unleashed large-scale, inexpensive, long-term development loans from European banks. Initially Bukharin believed that the grain surplus held by prospering farmers might be sold abroad to finance imports of industrial equipment. Yet the difficulties encountered by the government in procuring that surplus from the harvest of 1925 convinced him that the economy could not be dependent on the international market. He concluded that the capital for economic development could be amassed only from the increasing profitability of state industry, from a progressive income tax on entrepreneurs prospering under the New Economic Policy, and by mobilizing the voluntary savings deposits of the peasantry. None of these sources would provide vast sums very soon, he recognized, and his notion of socialist construction included no real solution to the problem of capital accumulation for industrialization. Apparently, Bukharin did not think it was a critical issue. Vast amounts of capital were unnecessary, he thought, because existing machinery could be used more intensively, and socialism could develop in the USSR without vast new investment—slowly, gradually, and "at a snail's pace," as he noted in December 1925. Bukharin's contribution to the industrialization debate was therefore to recast the New Economic Policy, which Lenin had introduced in order that the Russian economy could be partially integrated into the capitalist world system, and to identify it with building socialism in isolation, and slow and autarkic economic development.

Stalin devoted little thought to how socialist industrialization would be financed. Of greatest importance, he believed, was the international political situation. He had an especially foreboding conception of world politics. The world was divided into two camps: the camp of the socialist homeland and its supporters abroad, and a capitalist camp headed by the Anglo-Americans. As both camps stabilized, antagonisms between them became more acute. New wars, both interimperialist and interventionist, loomed in the future, and as a prelude to such wars, capitalist Europe would impose diplomatic isolation and economic blockade on the USSR. Ties to world capitalism—that is, economic dependence on Europe—led "to a whole series of new dangers." Economic independence from the capitalist states was necessary if Russia was to industrialize, and industrialization was necessary if Russia was not to be dependent on the capitalist powers. Nondependence on the capitalist camp was the distinguishing mark of Stalin's notion of socialism in one country.

See also Bukharin, Nikolay; Insurrection in Germany; New Economic Policy; Peaceful Coexistence; Soviet Industrialization; Stalin, Joseph; Trotsky, Leon.

FURTHER READING

Carr, E. H. *Socialism in One Country, 1924–1926*. New York: Macmillan, 1958–64.
Cohen, S. F. *Bukharin and the Bolshevik Revolution: A Political Biography, 1888–1938*. New York: Oxford University Press, 1973.
Day, R. B. *Leon Trotsky and the Politics of Economic Isolation*. Cambridge, UK: Cambridge University Press, 1973.

JON S. JACOBSON

Socialist Camp

"Socialist camp" was a general term used in Communist ideology and propaganda to denote the bloc of states with Communist governments that emerged in the mid-1940s, and existed in one form or another until approximately the late 1980s. The socialist camp began life as a bloc that included the USSR and the people's democracies in Eastern Europe (Yugoslavia, Albania, Bulgaria, Poland, Romania, Czechoslovakia, and Hungary), when in the final stages of World War II, most of this region was occupied by Soviet forces and came under Soviet control. According to unpublished statements in 1945, Stalin viewed this bloc as a key instrument in the confrontation with capitalism, primarily with the Western Allies, with whom he predicted the bloc would be at war in one or perhaps two decades.

The creation of the socialist camp resulted from the mutual political, military, economic, cultural, and ideological bonding of each of the people's democracies with the USSR, as the center of the bloc. This included absolute adherence to Soviet policies in the international arena. In this way, a unique "radial" structure came into being that embraced all the people's democracies and bound them to Moscow, and through Moscow, into a unified bloc system. The emergence of this fundamental structure was accompanied by alliances between the people's republics themselves. These alliances, which the Kremlin always strove to keep under careful surveillance, also depended on an understanding with the Soviet Union and were local arrangements, once again under Moscow's control.

In the Communist ruling circles of a number of people's democracies the idea of a federative union of all or some of their regimes gained a currency. This union would be under the guidance of the USSR, within the framework of the emerging Soviet bloc. More precisely, the idea of creating a federation of Yugoslavia, Bulgaria, and Albania was discussed by the leaders of these three countries and the Kremlin. This idea was never realized, but it did become one of the factors leading to Yugoslavia's break with the USSR in 1948.

Up until 1947–48, the countries in the bloc were largely those with a Communist monopoly (Yugoslavia and Albania) or where the Communists prevailed (Bulgaria, Poland, and Romania). The countries where the Communist parties did not yet have this control (Czechoslovakia and Hungary) belonged to the bloc to a much lesser degree, although they too had to follow the bloc party line, as when Czechoslovakia was forced by the Soviet Union in mid-1947 to reject participation in the Marshall Plan. After 1947–48 this diversity disappeared, to be replaced by a full and uniform integration of all the countries into a bloc system essentially analogous to the Soviet model.

This system, however, was not at this time invoked by any comprehensive agreement between the participating countries. The Kremlin took a different route: in the course of the middle and latter half of the 1940s, all countries finding themselves within the bloc gradually concluded mutual alliance pacts (pacts of "friendship, cooperation, and mutual aid") with each other. Mutually interwoven, these pacts combined for practical purposes into a general network of treaties that embraced all the bloc states. Later, when new countries were added, each of them also concluded mutual agreements with the other participants in the bloc. The existence of the bloc was thereby somewhat camouflaged, while in actual fact it functioned as one unit.

As the confrontation with the West developed into the Cold War, and particularly as Moscow and its subject Communist parties moved toward the forced Sovietization of those people's democracies that did not yet have a full Communist monopoly of power, the formation of the bloc began to be proclaimed openly. The first step was the creation of the Cominform in fall 1947, when the doctrine of the confrontation of two world camps was publicly proclaimed: the bloc of the USSR and the people's democracies now figured here as the "anti-imperialist, democratic camp." Later, mainly in 1949, when the people's democracies had already proclaimed the "building of socialism" in its Communist conception as their goal, official Soviet, Eastern European, and Cominform propaganda increasingly referred to the Soviet bloc as also the "camp of democracy and socialism" (or "camp of peace, democracy, and socialism," or simply the socialist camp).

This camp contained all the features of a military-political bloc, which had an anti-Western direction, and at the same time the traits of a sociopolitical bloc, whose principles, common to all the participating countries, were an internal system, an officially ruling ideology, and a foreign policy oriented toward the Soviet (Stalinist) doctrines of the time. The Kremlin was the absolute center, with respect not only to the foreign policy of the participating countries, but to all spheres of their development as well. An important factor in solidifying the bloc was also the continuing presence of Soviet troops in Poland, Hungary, and Romania as well as East Germany, where a people's democracy was set up in 1949 (Soviet troops left Czechoslovakia at the end of 1945 and Bulgaria at the end of 1947; they had been in Yugoslavia only in fall 1944, and were never in Albania at all).

By the end of the 1940s substantial changes had taken place in the makeup of the socialist camp. As a result of the Soviet-Yugoslav conflict in 1948, Yugoslavia was expelled from the bloc. Moreover, the Soviet bloc was greatly enlarged by the addition of newly established Communist regimes: in September–October 1948 in North Korea (the Korean People's Democratic Republic), in October 1949 in mainland China (the Chinese People's Republic), and as already mentioned, in East Germany (the German Democratic Republic, or GDR). The socialist camp, in addition to the European states, thus began to include some Asian states: China and North Korea were joined by the Mongolian People's Republic (a pro-Soviet regime had been established under the aegis of the USSR in Outer Mongolia as early as the 1920s).

The addition of China fundamentally changed the bloc's structure: the USSR was no longer the only great

power in it. Although China, with its much smaller economic and military potential, did not at that time dispute the USSR's role as the center of the camp, Moscow was no longer able to assume with respect to China the same commanding position it had with the other bloc members. China's leadership could conduct a largely independent policy, as became clear in the Korean War in 1950–53.

The late 1940s and early 1950s also saw changes in the mechanism of the internal organization of the socialist camp. In addition to retaining the radial structure of the mutual relations of the individual states with Moscow as the center, the first comprehensive (collective) organs were created to coordinate the economic and military spheres: the Council for Mutual Economic Assistance (Comecon) was openly established in January 1949, and the Coordinating Committee for Military Affairs was formed secretly in January 1951. These structures were confined to the USSR and the European people's democracies. The latter all became part of the Comecon, Albania and the GDR came in several months later, although the Soviet organizers of the Coordinating Committee for Military Affairs had not considered it expedient to include Albania and the GDR in this consortium. The administration of both these new organs was entirely in Moscow's hands. In addition, the Comecon's work began almost from the start to partly reflect not only Soviet interests but also the specific economic objectives of the East European Communist regimes; one of the first goals was to acquire from the USSR the largest possible amount of raw materials, energy resources, foodstuffs, industrial equipment, and financial and technical assistance. The Coordinating Committee for Military Affairs was established to plan for and control armies and war industries in the Eastern European people's democracies in conformity with the Kremlin's program of forced augmentation of the bloc countries' military capabilities as a vital enhancement of the USSR's military might. This organ, the forerunner of the Warsaw Pact, acted in concert with a preexisting system of Soviet military advisers in the above countries, which were largely involved with the same questions.

In contradistinction to the economic and military spheres, the socialist camp had no organs with specifically political functions during the whole period that Stalin ruled the USSR up until his death in March 1953. The Cominform was no such organ, although its activity was associated with certain aspects of Soviet bloc foreign policy initiatives as well as conditions and political stances taken within the socialist camp of individual Eastern European Communist regimes. Conferences of USSR foreign ministers and the Eastern European states called by the Kremlin at that time were spasmodic, and never had a consistent theme. They were simply venues for propaganda condemning Western policies regarding the German question. The most important foreign policy decisions, including those with special significance for the whole or a large part of the socialist camp, were made by the Kremlin, mostly without the agreement of or even prior consultations with the bloc countries. These decisions even involved cases fraught with the potential danger of a world military conflict, as with the decision to invade South Korea and later the armed intervention of China in the Korean War; the only preliminary discussions were directly between Stalin and the leaders of North Korea and China—the states that were to carry out these actions.

On Stalin's death (March 5, 1953), his successors took steps to improve the organizational structure of the socialist camp and particularly its European sector. In response to the serious economic difficulties besetting the USSR and the European people's democracies at the time, especially those that led in 1953 to mass protests in Czechoslovakia and the GDR, the Soviet leadership activated the Comecon in an effort to overcome these difficulties. In March 1954, after an interruption of more than three years, regular sessions of the Comecon were resumed, and in 1954–56 new mechanisms to provide for more disciplined and systematic coordination of the economic policy of the member states with Soviet ambitions were put in place or restored. In May 1955, the USSR and the other socialist states concluded the Warsaw Pact for Friendship, Cooperation, and Mutual Aid. This pact openly formalized the existence of its member states' military-political bloc. It was a direct response to the inclusion in the North Atlantic Treaty Organization of the Federal Republic of Germany. The pact also served as an implicit declaration of an internationally legal basis for keeping Soviet forces in Hungary and Romania, whose previous justification—to maintain the USSR's lines of communication with its occupied zone in Austria—had lost its validity in view of the declaration ending the four-power occupation of that country. In addition to its more strictly military role, the Warsaw Pact established a political role for the bloc by establishing a new organ: the Political Consultative Committee. During the latter half of the 1950s and the early 1960s, a number of this group's

sessions were attended by "observers" from China, Outer Mongolia, and North Korea.

Nevertheless, while all this was taking place, serious problems and contradictions, which had been accumulating in the socialist countries but had been suppressed during the last years of Stalin's rule, now began to come to the fore with his death. In addition to the above-mentioned mass demonstrations in Czechoslovakia and the GDR in 1953, even worse crises had emerged in Poland and particularly Hungary, an important component of which was public protests against the states' total subservience to Moscow. In trying to suppress these the Kremlin was forced, on the one hand, to move toward at least a partial loosening of its grip on its satellite states (de-Stalinization), with a certain rationalization (modernization) of the Communist system, while on the other hand, it had to try to preserve the principles of the past by resorting again to its methods of suppression, whenever it perceived a threat to the system or the necessity of keeping some country in the socialist camp. These two tendencies existed simultaneously in the Soviet policies of the time. Their mutual interrelationship, which often fluctuated in one direction or another, or sometimes even counterbalanced each other, began to determine the concrete policies of the USSR with respect to the very organization of the camp and its mutual relations with the states within it.

The protests in the GDR in 1953 and the revolt in Hungary in 1956, during which the Communist regime for all practical purposes collapsed and a withdrawal from the Warsaw Pact was declared, were crushed by Soviet troops. But during the 1956 crisis in Poland the Soviets decided against similar actions, and because the crisis was limited to changes in the Polish Communist leadership, recognized these changes despite the fact that they were not sanctioned by Moscow and were actually carried out against its wishes. Although Moscow's willingness to intervene continued, including using force, as the Soviet invasion of Czechoslovakia in 1968 demonstrated, from the mid-1950s on there was a gradual moving away from Stalin dictates with regard to the people's democracies. The Soviet government declared on October 30, 1956, that it recognized the irregularities that had taken place, and promised from then on to conduct its relations with the socialist states on a basis of equality, respect for their independence, and nonintervention in their internal affairs. Yet Moscow was forced by "realpolitik" to shift, albeit reluctantly, from its policy of giving direct orders to acknowledging partnership with the other Communist regimes of the Soviet bloc and recognizing the need to consider their special interests.

The second half of the 1950s saw the elimination of the previous system of military advisers and advisers for state security in the people's democracies. In countries where there were still Soviet troops, the troops' presence was now regulated by agreements between the USSR and the home countries, and Soviet forces were withdrawn from Romania in 1958. Consultations and agreements now came into practice, and then even decisions were jointly worked out between the socialist allies at various levels, including periodic discussions between the most prominent leaders. These took place not only between the USSR and individual states but also increasingly with the participation of all or almost all the states. The organs of the Warsaw Pact and the Comecon became much more active, and their activity, especially by the late 1950s and early 1960s, began to involve decisions that would be mutually acceptable to the Communist authorities of each state. For all this, however, the Kremlin still strove to maintain a prevailing and even decisive role in the Warsaw Pact and the Comecon as well as the socialist camp in general.

Still, as far as the socialist camp as a whole was concerned, by the late 1950s and early 1960s, the differences between the Communist regimes were starting to lead to a certain disintegration. A central role here belonged to the newly emerged Soviet-Chinese conflict. This first took the form of a political confrontation between Moscow and Beijing, which by 1963 had become an open one, and by the end of the 1960s had expanded into actual military tension. In 1961 the Soviets and Albanians broke apart, and Albania withdrew from the Warsaw Pact and the Comecon. Tirana switched its orientation to cooperation with Beijing, and began to receive military and economic aid from China. In the meantime, Bucharest's growing tendency to defend its own interests was already complicating Soviet-Romanian relations in 1962–63. Although it remained in the Warsaw Pact and the Comecon, Romania began to occupy its own distinct position, and conduct a policy that curtailed, and on some questions ended outright, its participation in matters still linking the other member states; this applied also to its outlook on the Soviet-Chinese confrontation. Exploiting the conflict between Moscow and Beijing, the North Korean leadership also started to pursue its own interests, adopting a policy that made it more independent from both the USSR and China. By the 1960s the socialist camp had split into various factions.

The most important faction remained the group of countries still embraced by the original bloc. It now consisted of the Soviet Union, those European states that had remained with the USSR in the Warsaw Pact and the Comecon (Romania only in part), and Outer Mongolia. The latter country became a Comecon member in 1962, and later Soviet troops were stationed there, which had implications for the confrontation between Moscow and Beijing. Despite the growth of the partnership idea in its relationships to the other states, though, the Soviet Union continued to exert a decisive influence on the basic aspects of their domestic and especially foreign policies. And even though Romania was a substantial exception, here also the USSR was the major factor in Bucharest's remaining in the bloc. The Kremlin still showed its readiness to use military force to prevent the dissolution of any of the Communist regimes as well as the departure of any of its states from the bloc. And it indeed did this in Czechoslovakia in 1968. This "internationalist" doctrine of limited sovereignty was supported by the authorities of most of the states; all the European members, except Romania, participated in the Soviet invasion of Czechoslovakia (and Soviet troops remained there). For its part, the USSR continued to guarantee the political security of these regimes and provide them with economic support. In the Comecon, efforts continued toward both specialization and integration of the member economies.

This new bloc established close relations with two young Communist regimes territorially far removed from it: with Cuba, where in 1959 a left-wing revolutionary government moved in the direction of communism; and in the mid-1960s with North Vietnam, where a Communist regime had established itself a decade earlier, albeit after it had first oriented itself toward China and had even shown solidarity with Beijing in the Soviet-Chinese conflict. The relations between these two new states and the bloc were centered on Soviet political support, particularly on military and economic aid during the U.S.-Cuban confrontation and in the U.S. military intervention in Vietnam in 1965–73. Nevertheless, each of the regimes conducted its own policy, which in a number of cases did not coincide with Soviet policy. North Vietnam, which up to the mid-1970s had been receiving aid not only from the USSR but also from China, was trying to maneuver between them. After the United

States' defeat in the Vietnam War in the mid-1970s and the takeover of South Vietnam by the North, a rivalry between China and the united Vietnam developed for hegemony in Indochina, and certain territorial disputes arose between the two countries. Vietnam now switched its orientation to the USSR and in 1978 entered the Comecon, joining Cuba, which had been admitted in 1972.

China, which had been the second major component of the previous socialist camp, was unable to create its own bloc of Communist regimes. Albania, while politically oriented toward China, was geographically far away from it and by the mid-1970s had broken with it. China's neighbors North Korea and North Vietnam, as mentioned, had been maneuvering between Beijing and Moscow, and a conflict ensued between China and the now-united Vietnam, and they even fought a short war in 1979. Attempts to establish pro-Chinese regimes in Laos and Cambodia were thwarted, first by the Vietnamese military intervention in Laos, which led to a pro-Vietnamese government there, and later by a similar Vietnamese intervention in Cambodia (Kampuchia). The latter resulted in the regime of the Khmer Rouge, which had been created with Beijing's aid in 1975 but in 1979 had been replaced by a pro-Vietnamese government. The Laotian and Cambodian regimes, which had been sponsored by Vietnam, now were moving toward attaching themselves to the bloc led by the USSR.

As for North Korea and Albania, these regimes no longer had specific or sustained links to any of the factions of the now-split socialist bloc. The position of these countries began to resemble that of Yugoslavia, which in spite of Soviet attempts during the post-Stalin period to win it back to the socialist camp, did not return but was managing to maneuver independently outside the blocs.

In addition, a number of left-wing regimes with a greater or lesser Marxist coloring moved toward joining one faction or another. These were basically regimes in Africa (Ethiopia, Mozambique, Angola, Tanzania, and some others) along with certain ones in Asia (Afghanistan) and Latin America (Nicaragua). They proclaimed their adherence to a "socialist orientation," and received political support and military and economic aid from the USSR, Cuba, or China. In some cases Moscow and Beijing competed with each other for influence in these client states, which in turn tried to exploit their rivalry for their own ends.

The socialist camp was now split, but the faction headed by the USSR remained, as before, a tightly knit bloc, even though its makeup was now somewhat different. Since not only Yugoslavia but also certain other Communist regimes, including China, were now outside the bloc, however, in official Soviet ideology and propaganda the concept of the socialist camp (which from the mid-1950s had been called by the equivalent terms "socialist community" and "world socialist system") began to yield in the 1970s to more complex ideological terminology. The totality of Communist regimes in the world was characterized once again as a world socialist system, but only in the capacity of an objectively existing structural (social) phenomenon. Yet for the purposes of designating a goal-oriented, organized collective community of these regimes, the old term "socialist community" was still used, though now it referred only to Comecon and Warsaw Pact members. This interpretation of the term now became broadly current in most of the countries of the bloc led by the USSR.

This socialist camp, thus preserved, in spite of difficulties concerning these or those questions, continued to function as long as the regimes themselves did. The popular outburst in Poland in 1980–81, which threatened to destroy the Communist regime and take Poland out of the bloc, was successfully put down. This time it was accomplished not by Soviet military intervention, as had been the case in 1956 in Hungary and 1968 in Czechoslovakia, but rather by a declaration of martial law by the Polish authorities themselves, urged on by the Kremlin. But this situation changed fundamentally at the end of the 1980s, when the existing political structure of the USSR fell apart and Moscow could no longer guarantee the preservation of the Communist regimes in the other bloc states. These regimes collapsed in the revolutionary wave of 1989–91 in all the European bloc states, and then in Outer Mongolia as well. And the bloc itself came to an end.

In the mid-1990s an agreement of the member states of the bloc formally abolished both Comecon and the Warsaw Pact. Soviet troops, which after the breakup of the USSR in 1991 had become Russian troops, were withdrawn from the no longer existing socialist camp to which they had belonged. The regimes in Cuba, where the Communist leadership continued without change, and Vietnam, where a gradual reform was underway, were no longer in a bloc either. In this sense their status was analogous to that of the Chinese regime, which continued on its way with partial changes, and that of the North Korean regime, which did not change at all (at the beginning of the 1990s the Communist regimes fell apart in Yugoslavia, where the country itself broke up, and Albania and also Cambodia, from which the Vietnamese troops had been withdrawn in 1989).

See also Comecon; Cominform; De-Stalinization; People's Democracy; Polycentrism; Sino-Soviet Split; Soviet Bloc; Soviet-Yugoslavia Break; Warsaw Pact.

FURTHER READING

Brzezinski, Z. K. *The Soviet Bloc: Unity and Conflict.* Cambridge, MA: Harvard University Press, 1960.

Gati, C. *The Bloc That Failed: Soviet–East European Relations in Transition.* Bloomington: Indiana University Press, 1990.

McDermott, K., and M. Stibbe, eds. *Revolution and Resistance in Eastern Europe: Challenges to Communist Rule.* Oxford, UK: Berg, 2006.

Naimark, N. M., and J. Gibjanskij, eds. *The Establishment of Communist Regimes in Europe, 1944–1949.* Boulder, CO: Westview Press, 1997.

LEONID JA. GIBJANSKIJ

Socialist Consumer Society

The Soviet Union was the first country where a consumer society under socialism became a model for those nations that found themselves in the Communist community.

The attempts of the state to achieve a monopoly in not only the production and distribution of goods but also in the development of a consumer ideology played a most important role in the Soviet experiment. The revolution of 1917 destroyed the market economy of czarist times. Stalin's "socialist offensive" at the turn of the decade of the 1920s then completed the demolition of the market and the system of private production. From then on the state assumed the obligation of producing goods and supplying the population. Not the market but a state plan was to determine what and how much to produce, and to whom, what, where, and at what prices goods were to be sold to consumers.

Together with the czarist economy the socialist offensive destroyed the hierarchy of consumption inherent to it, with its blatant gap between the rich and the poor. In its place came uniform poverty with a new culture of consumption—egalitarianism, asceticism, and self-sacrifice—officially inaugurated during the post-revolutionary years.

Asceticism, however, never became the main principle of socialist consumption. The mid-1930s witnessed a revolution in the official ideology of consumption. Against the spirit and letter of Marxism, which is essentially an antimarket, anticonsumerist theory, the Soviet leadership began to actively encourage an appetite for materialism and the good life: elegant clothing, delicious foods, easygoing leisure, and other luxuries. Just a few years before that a Communist Youth Union girl in lacquered shoes and lipstick would have provoked anger and been censured for her moral laxity, but now times had changed.

The new ideology of socialist consumption, which took hold in the mid-1930s and lasted until the fall of the USSR, in essence constituted a rehabilitation of the bourgeois values of a consumer society. This shift completely suited the majority of the population, which was tired of its privations. But what made the Soviet leadership adopt this new course? Historians offer several explanations. Some tie the "shift to materialism" in the mid-1930s to the need to stabilize the regime under the crisis conditions caused by forced industrialization, and the regime's change in its orientation from the workers as the main support of Soviet power, to the growing Soviet middle class: engineers, Stakhanovites, the intelligentsia, and the state bureaucracy. In exchange for the loyalty of this "new class" the regime agreed to legitimize its values, including its consumer values. In addition, acquisitiveness and materialism were now vitally necessary to the Soviet economy. Given extraordinarily low incentives to work, the desire to earn more in order to be able to buy this or that good would necessarily stimulate people to work better. In Stalin's own words, one had to bring "acquisitiveness" and "money" back "into fashion." This understanding of the "consumer revolution" of the 1930s is in accord with the opinion of historians who emphasize the Soviet regime's concern about the tempo of economic growth and its effort to turn the USSR into a modern power. For them, embracing a consumer, essentially a capitalist and market, ideology was a way of joining the global process of modernization.

Paradoxically, the consumer society in the USSR, unlike that in the West, emerged not from capitalism and an abundance of goods but instead was born of extreme want and lack of basic necessities. Propagandizing the values of a consumer society now came to be one of the state's reforms. Under this reform the state moved toward new massive industrial production of consumer goods. The highest political leadership was now sanctioning recipes for sausage, ice cream, and perfume. It was at Stalin's initiative, for example, that the production of Soviet champagne began.

The trumpeting of consumer society values was sharply at odds with the reality of USSR life—a chronic lack of the most basic goods, rationing, and endless, exhausting waiting in lines—which lasted during the whole extent of Soviet power. And though each crisis was followed by a certain normalization, and material conditions did improve and Soviet consumption did rise, even during the 1970s and early 1980s when consumer goods were most available, the Soviets never achieved the standard of living of even the middle class in the West.

Propaganda about the values of a consumer society was not a result of any plenitude of goods achieved by the Soviet Union but rather just a promise of future abundance. Consumer goods here became symbols, instruments of propaganda where the idea of oncoming abundance and potential accessibility of luxuries was often more important than any attributes of the goods themselves. This explains, for example, the paradox of Soviet consumption: luxury goods such as caviar, champagne, chocolate, or cognac were always on the holiday tables of Soviet people. The government limited their export, wanting to save them for domestic consumption. Yet goods necessary for normal life, like simple cotton fabrics, bread, butter, meat, and soap, themselves became luxuries, with huge lines waiting to buy them. Unlike in the West, the state concentrated more on the political goal of simulating abundance by keeping consumers supplied with new goods than it did on making a profit.

There is no clearer indicator of the much greater sociopolitical significance of the market and consumption in the USSR compared with the West than the hierarchy of consumption engendered by the centralized distribution of goods. The government proceeded according to the principle of "industrial pragmatism." Except for the people who actually held power, the best-supplied groups were those connected with industrial production itself; the large industrial cities were always in the best position. Just as consistent was the discrimination against the rural inhabitants, the nonindustrial towns and settlements whose residents would in desperation storm the stores of major industrial centers, near and far, in search of indispensable goods. Goods in the hands of the state now became a carrot—priority in supply of goods to make people work better—or a stick—the flow of goods to regions that had not fulfilled the plan was curtailed or even halted altogether. In whole regions Stalin made extensive use of hunger to punish people—"enemies of the

people." In the years of Stalin's rule his repressions were often in the dramatic form of cutting off consumption. "Black Maria" police cars with vivid images of goods on their sides would cart people away to the nothingness of the gulags, and their property would wind up in "confiscation stores," where what was left would be issued to inhabitants still free.

Money, though important, was not the only or even the main factor in determining the hierarchy of consumption in the state centralized system of supply. What good was money if the store shelves were half empty? Other factors here—one's privileged position in the hierarchy of state supply, personal acquaintances (pull), or propinquity to commerce—all were paramount in obtaining goods. People involved in commerce in Soviet society were always socially significant figures. They had the power; the buyer was an ingratiating and wheedling figure.

The state's efforts to control production and consumption, plus the chronic shortages of goods, limited the opportunities and freedom that a person had to make individual choices in consumption. This was one more difference between Soviet and Western consumption patterns: the Western consumer enjoyed much more freedom of choice.

As great as the role played by the state's planned distribution of goods was, the small legal private market and the immense black market played an important structural, social, and cultural role in Soviet people's consumption. Ultimately, the level and hierarchy of consumption in the Soviet society was heavily influenced by the interaction and competition of both entities: the planned economy and the free market.

On the one hand, the market was a denial of the principles of the planned state distribution of goods. Prices along with the range, quality, and volume of goods were determined here by supply and demand rather than some government bureaucrat, and the hierarchy of consumption was determined by the buyer's taste and how much money he had. The market redistributed the goods and mitigated the social and geographic discrimination caused by state supply policy as well as its irregularity and inadequacy. Precisely the presence of the market explains the paradox of half-empty stores but full refrigerators in the USSR. The market promoted alternative tastes and fashions, and allowed greater individual choice and freedom.

On the other hand, the symbiotic relationship of the market with the planned economy caused it to be both formed and deformed by the latter. The boundaries of the legal market permitted by the state were extraordinarily narrow. The market amounted mostly to sales of produce from small subsidiary plots and a minor industry of collaborative handicrafters. The hungry consumer demand required more, and hence most of the market developed in illegal forms. The black market was illegal by Soviet criminal law, but most of its practices would not have been considered criminal in a regular market economy; for example, the much-reviled "speculation" was simply producing and selling goods to make a profit. Repression against the market kept the underground "firms" that produced and sold goods and services small as well as short-lived. The basic form of illegal market activity under these conditions of repression and hungry consumer demand came to be the sale, and not the production, of the goods themselves. In an effort to protect themselves from repressive measures, underground entrepreneurs tried to mimic the legitimate socialist economy, concealing their private activities "under the roofs" of Soviet and party institutions, collective farms, and cooperatives.

The market in the USSR was the fruit of human initiative. It was basically a tactic of human survival, but the market also generated its "underground millionaires," whose wealth yielded nothing to the prosperity of the government elite. The importance of the market grew particularly during crisis periods of government supply, when buyers became sellers as well. During these crisis periods, exchanges and purchases or sales of personal items could make up a third of the family budget.

In spite of its unique character, Soviet consumption developed tendencies not unlike Western models: the growth of chain markets and the number of major stores, improvements in "business" technology, expanded ranges of goods and increases in consumption levels, a certain individualization of taste, and also its unification, which led to a leveling of class, ethnic, and regional differences in the area of consumption. Slowly and with difficulty the USSR was developing in the direction of a modern consumer society.

Did it succeed in building one? Researchers lean toward a negative answer. To the very end of the Soviet period, the population found that purchasing Soviet goods was more of a burden and affliction than a pleasure. The shortage and poor quality of goods persisted, and only a small, privileged sector of the population enjoyed the freedom and the opportunity to develop its own individuality as a consumer.

In its attempt to monopolize the production and supply of goods, the state fell into a trap. Beginning with Stalin, the country's leadership tried to encourage and develop the "appetites" of its consumers, but it could not satisfy them. For their economic calamities—the impossibility of buying desirable and even necessary goods—the people blamed the Soviet economy and political system, and in their aspiration to live in a real consumer society were ready to destroy both. The unsatisfied consumer became the enemy and grave digger of socialism.

See also Command Economy; Economic Reforms; Markets, Legal and Illegal; Planning; Socialist Market Economy; Social Policy; State, The; Welfare State.

FURTHER READING

Gronow, J. *Caviar with Champagne: Common Luxury and the Ideals of the Good Life in Stalin's Russia*. Oxford: Berg, 2003.
Grossman, G. "The Second Economy in the USSR and Eastern Europe: A Bibliography." *Berkeley-Duke Occasional Papers on the Second Economy in the USSR* 21 (1990).
Hessler, J. *A Social History of Soviet Trade: Trade Policy, Retail Practices, and Consumption, 1917–1953*. Princeton, NJ: Princeton University Press, 2004.
Kornai, J. *The Socialist System: The Political Economy of Communism*. Princeton, NJ: Princeton University Press, 1992.
Ledeneva, A. *Russia's Economy of Favors: Blat, Networking, and Informal Exchange*. Cambridge: Cambridge University Press, 1998.
Osokina, E. *Our Daily Bread: Socialist Distribution and the Art of Survival in Stalin's Russia, 1927–1941*. Armonk, NY: M. E. Sharpe, 2001.

ELENA A. OSOKINA

Socialist Emulation

The term "socialist emulation" spread in the USSR after Stalin devoted several canonical pages to it in "Emulation and Labour Enthusiasm of the Masses" in May 1929. Competing with one another to increase labor productivity and motivated by the task of building socialism, Soviet workers needed to disprove the "realistic" estimates (the ones deemed "conservative" by authorities) of those fellow workers, labor unionists, and technical factory personnel who thought the ambitious industrial production objectives formulated in the First Five-Year

Plan were impossible, and the physical effort and material sacrifices required were unsustainable. By encouraging socialist emulation, authorities were simultaneously pursuing different, often mutually incompatible objectives. They wanted to accustom the mass of new workers to more intense and tiring labor. Another goal was to change the nature of labor unions, pushing them to contribute to a more complete exploitation of the labor force. Managers were also pressured to fully utilize their plants' potential, and experiment with new technical and productive solutions, even though this might be detrimental to order and hierarchy in the factory and could increase the wear and tear on machinery while reducing the quality of the finished product. Authorities also hoped to vest the hard and prosaic labor in the various plants with a sense of social idealism and material prosperity being close at hand. Finally, they tried to inspire large masses of malnourished and poorly housed ex-peasants and poorly qualified workers with a feeling of protagonism and equality (if not social superiority) to factory management.

During the first years of industrialization these tasks were supposed to be realized by the "assault workers' movement," organized in brigades. The internal organization of these brigades was a reflection of spontaneous social impulses that contradicted the productivist zeal of the higher-ranking political and economic authorities as well as the modernist and state-oriented vision of socialism promoted by the Communist Party of the Soviet Union. A portion of these new young workers looked to socialist emulation for a holistic and elitist experience of communitarianism: the sharing of living spaces and free time, the division into equal shares of each individual's earnings, and collective forms of retribution and incentives. The appeal by authorities to workers to defy the factory's management on the terrain of productivism could lead to "down-with-specialists" attitudes (a caricature of the class struggle). It was also counterproductive from the point of view of discipline and labor efficiency. The movement's functionality was also compromised by the tendency of party and labor union organs to attribute the title of "assault laborer" too generously, for propagandistic effect. Since it entitled one to privileged access to scarce consumer goods and also led to increased status, socialist emulation masked a return to a more traditional form of unionism—anathema to authorities. The productivist goals of socialist emulation were betrayed even in those cases where managers resigned themselves to tolerating lower rhythms of production

for most of the year, requiring their personnel to work hard only as the (ninety-day or annual) production plans neared their conclusion, or for a limited time period.

In 1931, Stalin condemned spontaneous egalitarian practices and labor communes, in an attempt to focus the socialist emulation movement on productivity, individual salary incentives, the assimilation of technology, and the role of specialists and technicians. The regime's propaganda tried to locate individual "work heroes" from the anonymous army of the *udarnik* (superproductive workers). One of the first to be chosen was Nikita Izotov, a miner from the Donets coal basin. A few years later he was presented as a precursor of Stakhanovism.

See also Five-Year Plans; Labor; Soviet Industrialization; Stakhanovism; Trade Unions; Workers.

FURTHER READING

Fetzer, D. A. *Soviet Workers and Stalinist Industrialization: The Formation of Modern Soviet Production Relations, 1928–1941.* Armonk, NY: M. E. Sharpe, 1986.

Kuromiya, H. *Stalin's Industrial Revolution: Politics and Workers, 1928–1932.* Cambridge, UK: Cambridge University Press, 1988.

Ward, C. *Russia's Cotton Workers and the New Economic Policy: Shop-Floor Culture and State Policy, 1921–1929.* Cambridge, UK: Cambridge University Press, 1990.

FRANCESCO BENVENUTI

Socialist International

The Socialist International got a new lease on life in 1919–20. Nominally it presented itself as the continuation of the Second International, founded in 1889 and dissolved with the outbreak of World War I because of prevailing "social-patriotic" orientations. In actuality it was about to face a completely new challenge, in a world transformed by the war: the appearance of communism had introduced an inescapable term of comparison in the definition of the socialist forces' identity. It was precisely the manner of evaluating the Russian Revolution that became a powerful tool for distinguishing the various European Socialist parties. Many kept their distance from this reborn International, because under the guidance of British Labour and the North European social democracies, it would have committed them to an irrevocable condemnation of the revolutionary method, and the just as irrevocable choice of parliamentary democracy as the road to power and fundamental principle of socialism's political system. Dissenting from such unilateral and clear-cut proclamations, a group of parties, led by the Austrian one, founded an autonomous organization in 1921, the International Community of Socialist Parties, which believed that reforms and revolution, democracy and dictatorship of the proletariat, could constitute legitimate variants of socialist policy, depending on the different historical and social situations they were confronting, and thus endorsing a pluralist framework for the choice of the best path to socialism.

This attempt at bridge building between Socialists and Communists did not produce encouraging results, however, so in 1923 the majority of Socialist forces joined to form a new International, the Labor and Socialist International (LSI), which was founded during a congress in Hamburg, and based on acknowledging the split in the international working-class movement between its Social Democratic and Communist components. The distinction between the two tendencies concerned not only the areas of politics and doctrine but also implied different views of what an international association of working-class parties should look like. On the one hand, there was the rigidly centralized structure of the Third International, with its demand that all national parties submit to a single global leadership center and common operative criteria. On the other hand, the Socialists recognized the individual parties' autonomy in determining the direction of their internal policies, limited the LSI's authority in matters of international politics, and tended to conceive of the International much more as a place for discussion and mediation than for decision making.

The best type of relationship between communism and social democracy, both politically and ideologically, remained a controversial topic even within the new Socialist parties' unitary organization; it led to disagreements, especially regarding the attitude toward the USSR. At one extreme, the most intransigent critics (such as Karl Kautsky) of the path that Lenin and Stalin had adopted in order to build socialism went as far as to favorably consider the hypothesis of the collapse and dismemberment of the Soviet state. At the opposite pole were those (such as Otto Bauer) who thought that the Bolshevik Revolution was part of the heritage of proletarian struggles and the success of that first experiment in overcoming capitalism was in the historical interests of all Socialists. Between these opposing tendencies, the LSI's official position was that of "defense of the Russian Revolution," of opposition to policies hostile to the

USSR on the part of bourgeois states, together with a radical aversion toward communism as a political subject, often considered to be an adversary of socialism's on the same level as fascism (a polemical position that was to be repaid with interest on the Communist side with the adoption of the theory of social fascism).

These considerable differences in perspective, revealing the many facets of European social democracy and the difficulty of attempting to group them in one political model, did not have any particular practical repercussions until the early 1930s. That is to say, until the divergence between Communist and Socialist policies in individual countries became so considerable that it prevented even those Social Democrats who were least prejudiced against communism from attempting to collaborate with parties from the Third International. Confronted with Nazism's rise to power in Germany, some segments of European social democracy, persuaded that it was precisely the conflicts within the working-class movement that had paved the way for Adolf Hitler, began to appeal to a unity of proletarian action against fascism, even before there were signs of a change of course in the Third International that would eventually lead to the Popular Fronts policy.

At this point, however, the LSI's fragile unity shattered. There were meetings of delegates between the two Internationals in 1934 (during the uprisings in the Asturias), in 1935 (with the outbreak of war in Ethiopia), and then again in 1937 (during the war in Spain). But the majority of the LSI (composed of British, Scandinavian, Dutch, Czech, and German members), convinced that the ideological divide between social democracy and communism in many European countries was unbridgeable, was opposed to any general operative agreement with the Communist International, and limited itself to allowing those Socialist parties that so desired to proceed autonomously with agreements with the respective Communist parties at the national level. The issue of relations with the Communists was therefore one of those that most clearly highlighted the impossibility for the LSI to act as a collective political subject on the European scene during the crisis of the 1930s. As in 1914, the outbreak of the new world war coincided with the de facto dissolution of the Socialist International.

After the war the process of reconstituting an International was much slower than during the first postwar period. The new International was founded in 1951, during a congress in Frankfurt, while during the preceding years the various Socialist parties had kept in touch by means of less formal structures—first the Socialist Information and Contact Office, and later the Committee of International Socialist Conferences. The events of the war and the spectacular electoral victory in 1945 had given British Labor a preeminent position among European Socialist parties, and Labor, in light of its previous experience, was hesitant to allow the reemergence of an organization that could claim some role in political leadership and the limitation of the national parties. British Labour only agreed after it had been given the most ample assurances that national autonomies would be safeguarded, and once, with the Cold War in full swing, the need to give a distinct Social Democratic entity (which at this point would be much more homogeneous than during the interwar period and clearly distinguished by its adherence to Western democratic values) some consistency and visibility on the world stage was felt with greater urgency, given that communism was now presenting itself as a "field" of world forces, especially after the constitution of the Cominform. Having defined itself institutionally as a consultative organ and one dedicated to information exchange between parties, for a long time the Socialist International limited its external presence to declarations of principle, all marked by a strong ideological and political opposition to communism. Indeed, the only Socialist party that continued to collaborate with the Communists, even after the break between East and West, was the Italian Socialist Party, which was expelled in 1949 from the Committee of Socialist Conferences and was admitted to the International again only in the 1960s.

Only after the mid-1960s did a different chapter begin, which at the time was designated as a "new beginning"; the International went from being a piece of the Western bloc to becoming an independent subject that intended to pursue its own autonomous political agenda on the international scene—especially by engaging in détente between the East and West as well as the solution of regional crises, and with the inequalities between the world's South and North. This change coincided with Willy Brandt, West Germany's ex-chancellor, becoming president of the Socialist International in 1976; he contributed the inspiration that had guided him in establishing new relations between the Federal Republic of Germany and the Eastern bloc countries (*Ostpolitik*). The first signs of attention paid to the Socialist International by "Eurocommunist" milieus, and particularly the Italian Communist Party (Pci), also date from this period. They were interested

in the function that the International might have in the international process of détente, and in promoting dialogues and meetings between progressive forces with different backgrounds. In the continuing competition between Communist and Socialist parties, the fact that the latter could now act while boasting of their connection to an international spectrum of forces was crucial; those Communist parties that were starting to distance themselves from Moscow, and therefore most intensely felt the need for a new international "reference point," were instead deprived of one (but the Pci would only ask to join the Socialist International many years later, in 1990, when communism's crisis as a category of European politics had run its course and the Pci was about to change its name).

The increased tension between the two blocs in the early 1980s, however, limited the operational options at the Socialist International's disposal, also because significant political differences had arisen within it between those who supported a firm and rigorous attitude toward the USSR of the late Brezhnev era (above all the French and Italian Socialists), and those who supported more cautious and subtle approaches (German Social Democrats and British Labourites). Not even the novelties that Mikhail Gorbachev's rise to power had introduced in the system of international relations were able to reinvigorate the Socialist International's political initiative: it had a difficult time finding a niche in a world in which the bipolar dialectic, the backdrop to its past tasks of mediation and contact, was coming to an end. With the various communisms' fall, a new phase in the history of the Left began, in which the reinvention of a political function for an international association of Socialist parties was one of the many issues connected with the search for social democracy's new identity.

See also Bauer, Otto; Cominform; Comintern; Eurocommunism; Kautsky, Karl; Revisionism; Social Democracy.

FURTHER READING

Devin, G. *L'internationale socialiste. Histoire et sociologie du socialisme internationale, 1945–2000.* Paris: Presses de la Fondation nationale des Sciences politiques, 1993.

Rapone, L. *La socialdemocrazia europea tra le due guerre: dall'organizzazione della pace alla resistenza al fascismo, 1923–1936.* Rome: Carocci, 1999.

Sigel, R. *Die Geschichte der Zweiten Internationale 1918–1923.* Frankfurt am Main: Campus, 1986.

LEONARDO RAPONE

Socialist Market Economy

Although residual elements of a market economy (illegal or black markets) were part of the everyday reality of many socialist economies, the idea of utilizing the market to regulate the exchange of goods in a command economy always remained out of bounds from the perspective of orthodox Marxism. Nevertheless, the possibility that the market and planning could coexist in a socialist economy, and that market principles could be usefully adopted in combination with bureaucratic tools for the regulation of the socialist economy, had been a frequent topic of discussion since the 1930s. The Polish economist Oskar Ryszard Lange (1904–65), for example, was already stating in 1937 that the bureaucracy in charge of planning could successfully intervene on the balance of supply and demand by acting on prices in response to excessive demand or supply, thus basically "simulating" a market response. In Lange's opinion this system guaranteed the efficiency of the planners' interventions, but it did not endanger the supremacy of bureaucratic tools in the allocation of factors of production.

The idea of integrating market and plan when the dominant form of property was that owned by the state inspired many "reformist" experiences in various socialist countries. The outcome of these experiences does not seem to point to a true model of market socialism. In any case Josip Broz Tito's Yugoslavia in the 1950s, János Kàdàr's New Economic Mechanism in Hungary in the 1960s, and the economic reforms begun by Deng Xiaoping in China represent differing attempts by various socialist leadership groups to modernize and rationalize their command economies. These efforts generally led to autonomous forms of agriculture, an increased managerial autonomy in industry, independent mechanisms for price regulation, the development of market economy niches, a greater mobility and flexibility in the labor markets, and forms of competition and taxation.

None of these experiences went as far or was as successful as the one undertaken by the People's Republic of China after 1978. In 1980 China abandoned the collective management of agriculture, removed the "people's communes," and instead supported a system in which the land remained public property, but its management and the right to part of its profits were entrusted to families (a system of family responsibility). In 1984 the official formula that the Chinese Communist Party adopted to define its economy became "planned market economy." The metaphor coined in those years by the principal architect of Chinese economic reforms, Chen Yun (1905–95), was that of the "little bird in a cage," a way of indicating the boundaries within which the erratic flights of the market were to be kept. The system described in 1984 referred to a transition in the state's role from one of "controlling" to "supervising" the economy, and allowed for increased forms of autonomy in public enterprises, thus creating the presuppositions for the taxation of the enterprise's profits. In the following years other fundamental elements for the creation of a market in factors of production were introduced, starting with the transition from a system of employment for life (the so-called iron rice-bowls) to one of forward contracts in state industry (1986).

During this reexamination of the rules of the socialist economy, the introduction of market mechanisms presented numerous theoretical problems. The question of labor, because of its centrality in Marxist doctrine, became the venue for a struggle about the nature of market socialism. The changes in workers' hiring rules put the position of the workers themselves, as "owners" of the means of production, in question and in reality turned labor into a commodity. When defending a "protected labor market" for the industrial workforce, the greater mobility, competitiveness, and productivity of the contract system were highlighted. Contracts would allow for a more direct and free relation of the workers with the enterprise, and the public ownership of the means of production would contribute to protect them from the risks of exploitation and alienation intrinsic to redistribution based on the idea of the quality and quantity of labor. Notwithstanding the efforts of Chinese thinkers to frame this system within the confines of Marxist orthodoxy, it soon became clear that many of the reforms realized in the later 1980s were on a collision course with Marx's theory of value. China went back to defining its current phase as the "initial state of socialism," in which economic development remained the primary objective.

Despite the economic and political crisis of 1989, the transition toward an economy that was both decreasingly planned and increasingly managed by way of market mechanisms continued until the adoption, in 1992, of the new formula "socialist market economy." With this further step, the market no longer only had the function of regulating transactions in commodities but also of harmonizing and rationalizing the circulation of factors of production, including labor. The academic work of the preceding years—for instance, on the nature of labor—thus became redundant. From this point on the equation labor equals commodity would no longer seem problematic, and anxiety about competitiveness on national and international markets would determine a continuous lowering of industrial salaries.

The other fundamental theoretical and practical question that had to be addressed in order for China to continue to claim to be a socialist country was that of property rights. A socialist economy is measured on the basis of the predominance of public property. Already in the 1980s China had encouraged the creation of an ever-increasing number of enterprises that were collectively owned, a form of socialist ownership often exhibiting types of management that were instead typical of private enterprise. Private property was first allowed in its minimal form, the enterprise owned by a single individual or a family, and was then gradually extended to protect the interests of increasingly numerous local entrepreneurs and attract long-term foreign investment. Although the state was still formally the owner of a large part of industry, private property was guaranteed the same level of protection as public property, according to constitutional amendments approved in 2004.

What does the term "socialist" stand for in the socialist market economy in China? Apart from the obvious fact that the state still owns large chunks of the productive apparatus and land, the party and government also maintain their direct control of the bureaucratic instruments used to control the economy. The divergence between a significant reform of the economy and the failed reform of the political system are generally seen as strong points of the Chinese version of a socialist market economy. The government still also has an important role in economic planning, with five- and ten-year development plans that define the objectives to be reached in the best-case scenario; it still controls certain sectors that have not yet been completely liberalized (for example, communications, mines, energy, and financial markets); it intervenes in a decisive manner in the financial and monetary sectors, and it has the ability to intervene on the prices of the factors of production and agricultural products in order to avoid the most disastrous crises. In a situation in which the market dominates the scene, finally, it is easy to forget that the state and Communist Party still enjoy a "monopoly on violence." Confronted with an economic role for the state that today resembles that of many capitalist nations, it is not difficult to conclude that China ended up accepting that this process of transition would carry it toward one of the many possible forms of modern capitalism.

See also Command Economy, The; Deng Xiaoping; Economic Reforms; Great Leap Forward; Labor; Markets, Legal and Illegal; Modernization; Planning.

FURTHER READING

Kornai, J. *The Socialist System: The Political Economy of Socialism.* Princeton, NJ: Princeton University Press, 1992.

Naughton, B. *Growing Out of the Plan: Chinese Economic Reform, 1978–1993.* Cambridge: Cambridge University Press, 1995.

LUIGI TOMBA

Socialist Realism

The locution "socialist realism" (*socialistichesky realism*) made its first appearance on May 23, 1932, in an editorial in the *Literaturnaja gazeta*. Previously an organ of the Federation of Associations of Soviet Writers (1929–32), this periodical had become the organ of the organizing committees of the Union of Soviet Writers before their first congress (August 1934), after a resolution of the Central Committee of the Bolshevik Party "On the Restructuring of Artistic and Literary Organizations" (April 23, 1932). These facts prove the extent to which socialist realism was, from its inception, tied to important political events that modified the Soviet cultural situation, especially the literary one, in the early 1930s, adapting it to the great transformations then taking place in the USSR. Such developments could only occur because of support from the country's sole leadership center, the Communist Party, and ultimately its supreme leader, Joseph Stalin. As the author of a process of global renewal, Stalin participated in the creation of socialist realism directly and personally.

Stalin believed his main political problem was the unification of all Soviet society, since its first fifteen years had been characterized by military conflict (the civil war), ideological conflict (Lenin's succession), and finally the "new course" (industrialization and collectivization), following the builder's plan of "socialism in one country," which he had made the primary focus of Communist internationalism. This goal of maximum unification had to be implemented by following two directives for action.

The first directive was a repressive one, encouraging the gradual elimination, even if only for preventive reasons, of all "enemies," real or presumed, internal or external to the party. The second directive, a constructive one, was meant to overcome all residual political and cultural divisions, and establish an ideologically homogeneous and compact system, new in some respects, but consistent with Bolshevik doctrine, which was based on Lenin, and through him, Karl Marx and Friedrich Engels.

The fields in which this second "cultural revolution" (considering 1917 as the first one) was initially undertaken, only to be later extended to all other areas, were those of historical and philosophical studies, on the one hand—they were already dominated by Leninist ideology, but were now being renewed by Stalin and his ideologues' direct intervention—and literature and literary studies, on the other. The latter were given special attention since a residual pre-revolutionary plurality of tendencies was still strongest in these fields, and it therefore had to be confronted more decisively. Literature's potential to influence action at a social, mass level was more significant than that of other artistic media, like painting and music, which were also soon subjected to these new cultural policies. (Cinema, a mass art par excellence, was easier to control because of its technical and collective features, which distinguished it from the "individual" nature of the other arts; but it also became part of the "revolution" that had been started in literature with socialist realism.)

In Soviet literature (Russian literature was its center, even if an important segment was now in exile, though subject to unprecedented censorship) various tendencies had been active even after October 1917, within the margins of tolerance that the new power had established. It exercised a form of regulative control primarily by means of the Organization of Proletarian Writers, which appealed to revolutionary ideology and was not to be confused with the *poputchiki* (fellow travelers), a term used by Leon Trotsky to designate those writers who without sharing this ideology or the party's strategy, were not opposed to them as a matter of principle and were open to traveling partway toward the final Communist goal. The Central Committee's resolution of April 23, 1932, on the "restructuring" (perestroika) of the literary field, put an end to this relative plurality of tendencies and specifically decreed the dissolution of the Association of Proletarian Writers (which led to a sigh of relief by those who had been their target and were now deluded into hoping the situation would improve). The

Central Committee simultaneously declared that its goal was to "unify all the writers who support the platform of Soviet power and tend to participate in the construction of socialism in a single union of Soviet writers, which will include a Communist group."

It was a question of giving this unifying plan some content, something to pour into the form provided by this new writers' organization, which was led by the Communist Party, but could now no longer count on the Organization of Proletarian Writers' mediation. This new content was socialist realism, whose principles were solemnly announced at the First Writers' Congress, mostly by Maksim Gorky, whose repatriation had been one of Stalin's most urgent wishes, and an event he had carefully organized, because he viewed Gorky as a source of international prestige as well as an instrument for collaboration on the internal literary and cultural fronts.

Ivan Gromsky, who was the organizational head of the politburo (Stalin had the leading role on the five-member committee) and charged with implementing the transition after the 1932 resolution, gave an account of how the term socialist realism grew out of his conversations with Stalin. He then made the term public in the *Literaturnaja gazeta*'s editorial: the new "creative method" of Soviet literature, as he had suggested to Stalin, could have been called "proletarian socialist realism, or even better, Communist realism" but since the "transition from socialism to communism . . . final goal of the working class' struggle" was not yet the order of the day, he thought it better to define the "creative method of Soviet art and literature" as socialist realism. Stalin then qualified this definition by saying that it was a "party method" insofar as it "determines the positions of the party in matters of literature and the arts." During the meetings that Stalin had with Soviet writers at Gorky's house, the sense of the new creative method was defined in greater detail, especially when Aleksandr Fadeev suggested a toast to Mikhail Sholokhov, Stalin said, addressing the author of *Quiet Flows the Don*, "Men are shaped by life. But you are helping in the remaking [*peredelka*] of their soul. People's souls are an important form of production. You are the engineers of human souls. This is why we toast writers, and the most modest among them, comrade Sholokhov!" Another cornerstone of socialist realism, one that turned writers into "engineers of the soul" with the aim of "shaping" man into the "new man" in a Communist mold, had thus been established.

During the First Congress of Soviet Writers, Gorky and Andrey Zhdanov gave socialist realism more specific meaning. The former, with his strong intellectual personality, could not but bring his own set of ideas and literary experiences to the new formula. As such, he became the forerunner and classic of socialist realism, starting with his novels *The Mothers* and *Confession*, which with all their "religious" pathos, belonged to that "construction of god" (*bogostroitel'stvo*) that he had elaborated before the revolution along with Anatoly Lunacharsky, thereby inserting Nietzschean elements into Marxism—elements that were to remain fundamental for him even while planning the new man or proletarian collective superman. Zhdanov, instead, laid down the fundamental political directive for the new literature (taken from his speech to the congress), a fusion of "revolutionary romanticism," insofar as it exalted the "heroism" of those who operated within the "grandiose perspectives" of a Communist future, and the "truthful portrayal of life" captured in its "revolutionary development"—in other words, in the Communist Party's spirit. Zhdanov concluded by saying that the literature of socialist realism, while ideally oriented toward the future, "will not be a utopia, because our tomorrow is already prepared by consciously planned work today."

Here, then, were socialist realism's stable nucleus and immediate genesis. Its creation was not an arbitrary act, though, merely a result of Stalin's will, but rather an essential moment in an organic plan for global hegemony that was supposed to affect all of Soviet society. This is an important point since socialist realism was extended from the literary sphere, where it had been born, to all other artistic spheres, from painting to cinema, from theater to architecture, from music to posters, creating a style that can be defined as "Stalinist" or better yet "Soviet" since it was destined to survive almost until the end of the USSR. On the other hand, socialist realism's "fathers" were not only Stalin and his closest collaborators. The movement found inspiration and followers among writers themselves, mostly Russian (Gorky is its emblem), but later also foreign (after the end of World War II the new "creative method" spread to all the "people's democracies" and gained adherents among all the "progressive" writers in various countries). Socialist realism could count on thinkers like Georg Lukács being one of its theorists. During his stay in the USSR in the 1930s, Lukács had a critical role, along with his friend Mikhail Lifshitz and others, in the creation of a Marxist-Leninist aesthetics in the pages of the journal *Literaturnyi kritik*.

Socialist realism in literature (analogously to what occurred in other areas) had its own prehistory, tied to tra-

ditional realism, and then a long history of artistic and literary practice in the course of the 20th century. Today socialist realism is the object of numerous critical studies that bring new issues to light (for instance, its relationship of declared opposition and yet also paradoxical continuity with politically engaged avant-garde art) and even a sort of nostalgia for the "grand style" of what was "Soviet civilization."

See also Architecture and Urban Planning; Cinema, Soviet; Cultural Policies; Iconography; Literature in Soviet Russia; Lukács, Georg; Socialism in One Country; Stalinism; Zhdanov, Andrey.

FURTHER READING

Gjuntera, C., and E. Dobrenko, eds. *Socrealističekskij kanon.* Saint Petersburg: Akademičeskij Proekt, 2000.
Golomshtock, I. N. *Totalitarian Art: In the Soviet Union, the Third Reich, Fascist Italy, and the People's Republic of China.* London: Collins Harvill, 1990.

VITTORIO STRADA

Solidarity

The independent Polish labor union Solidarity (Solidarnosc) was founded in August 1980 at the Lenin naval shipyards in Gdansk. It radically transformed Poland's history, and influenced its course in other Eastern European countries. Solidarity was born from the legacy of the bloodily repressed revolt by Poznan workers in 1956, the 1968 student demonstrations, and above all the strikes that hit the Baltic coast in 1970 as well as the 1976 strikes in Radom and Ursus.

The first great workers' strikes in postwar Poland actually began in the Gdansk shipyards on December 15, 1970, as a response to a 30 percent increase in the price of foodstuffs. On the morning of December 17 the police shot at the unarmed workers who were in front of the occupied shipyards. Forty-one people were killed, about one thousand were injured, and thirty-two hundred were arrested (two-thirds of whom were workers and 13 percent of whom were students). Many were also badly beaten up in police stations and barracks.

The workers' protest began to assume the character of a radical political protest. On January 24, 1971, the Unified Polish Workers' Party's new secretary, Edward

Gierek, accompanied by Prime Minister Piotr Jarosze- wicz, was compelled to visit the occupied naval yards in Szczecin, and discuss the economic and political situa- tion for nine hours with the workers. The protest did not subside; in many factories workers' commissions were formed, an expression of the strike committees, which were negotiating directly with management. In the early 1970s, an increased sense of autonomy among the work- ers combined with an intellectual ferment and a greater engagement by the Catholic Church in social issues. Au- thorities often had to come to terms with workers; but material concessions did not diminish the demand for greater freedoms.

When on June 24, 1976, Parliament decided to in- crease the price of foodstuffs by 60 percent another series of strikes exploded. Their epicenter was Radom (140 miles south of Warsaw), one of Poland's poorest cit- ies. The local party offices were sacked and set on fire. The police intervened, and in the ensuing clashes seventeen people were killed (about two thousand were arrested). Other clashes occurred in Ursus (a town only a few miles from the capital, where fifteen thousand people worked in a tractor factory). This time Gierek adopted a different strategy from the one he had used previously: he immedi- ately withdrew the price increase, and started a campaign of arrests and repression that lasted the entire summer. The result, however, was that many intellectuals began to protest the repression, and in October, the Workers' Defense Committee (later to become the Committee for Social Self-defense) was created, becoming the principal underground form of opposition to the regime.

The committee was the organizational structure that supported the workers' councils, including materially; as the workers' struggles' megaphone, it engaged in an alternative information campaign—using newspapers, magazines, and books—addressed to civil society, but also to Western public opinion. The church publicly worked for the freedom of those arrested and supported the Workers' Defense Committee, though unofficially.

The election of a Polish pope, Karol Wojtyla (Octo- ber 16, 1978) infused the church with courage and strength. The pope's portraits appeared for the first time during a strike, almost as if they were "shields," on the gates of Polish shipyards and factories, in August 1980. The strikes and occupations were once again caused by price increases, which Parliament had approved at the end of June in order to confront the economic crisis as well as a foreign debt of nineteen billion dollars. Yet the strikers' demands were of a more general nature. Their

twenty-one-point platform demanded some of the fol- lowing: the right to form a free and independent labor union; freedom of religion and thought; and freedom of speech as well as access to the mass media. On Au- gust 20, sixty-two intellectuals, including some party members, signed an appeal in favor of free labor unions. Cardinal Stefan Wyszynski, while appealing for modera- tion, ended up openly supporting the workers' requests. The government was forced to back down. On August 30 in Szczecin, agreements between government represen- tatives and strikers were signed. They had been approved by Soviet leaders as a way of buying time and reorganiz- ing, to then "reestablish order" as soon as possible. For sixteen months it appeared as if Poland had really moved on, even if beleaguered by a thousand contradictions.

Solidarity (the name itself revealed that it was an orga- nization representing all of "civil society") went through three phases during the five hundred days of its legal existence: class consciousness prevailed over national- ist sentiments (August–November 1980); there was an approximate balance between political and union ini- tiatives (November 1980–March 1981); and national- ist sentiments won out, and the conviction took hold of the necessity of becoming a political movement (March–December 1981). After its official recognition (November 10, 1980), Solidarity became a sociopoliti- cal organization with ten million members, divided by regions (with ample margins of independence from the central leadership), and it had trouble staying out of the political arena. The level of confrontation with Com- munist authorities thus continued to increase, up to the military coup (December 13, 1981), led by Jaruzelski, who justified it by invoking the danger of external inter- vention by Warsaw Pact troops.

The brief period of freedom and democracy was not erased by military intervention and repression (sixteen killed, hundreds wounded, and four thousand arrested). The independent labor union continued to be active un- derground (led by Zbigniew Bujak), and Polish society took part in its battle for democracy in various ways (un- derground publications, for instance, numbered in the hundreds), with thousands of people participating in demonstrations, defying the police at each anniversary. In 1986 international pressure forced the government to grant a general amnesty. As soon as the movement had time to reorganize, new strikes and occupations occurred between May and August 1988, and these forced the gov- ernment to once more conduct a dialogue with the work- ers and society. On February 6, 1989, a meeting between delegations from the two sides took place at a "round-table," which laid the foundations for Polish democracy.

The independent union began to disappear, though, just as its worker-leader, Lech Walesa, became president of the republic. In 1991 Solidarity had already split up into at least 150 parties, associations, and movements. Marian Krzaklewski, who had not been a dissident in the past or a prominent leader in the union, inherited the leadership of Solidarity from Walesa that year. In 1996 he managed to unite the post-Solidarity right wing under the banner of Solidarity Electoral Action and easily win, with the church's support, the 1997 parliamentary elections. Jerzy Buzek, a Protestant engineer, was the first minister of this grouping who paid tribute to the "spirit of Solidarity" (Catholic social doctrine joining socialist welfare), but he also paid tribute to economic liberalism and policies aimed at privatization, traditional values, and "pro-Europeanism." There were too many tendencies to keep a political and union coalition together in a landscape increasingly dominated by corruption and social inequality. In short order Solidarity Electoral Action disintegrated; in the 2001 parliamentary elections it did not even receive a sufficient number of votes to enter Parliament.

Solidarity's right wing regrouped around Lech Kaczynski, Walesa's former right-hand man in the independent union and a hard-line former minister of justice in the Buzek government, and his twin brother, Jaroslaw. Their party, Law and Justice, proclaimed itself to be "democratic and Christian, opposed to the power of the ex-Communists and in favor of the defense of the Polish countryside." Law and Justice won the parliamentary elections in September 2005 in addition to the presidential elections the following month. At the same time the celebrations for the twenty-fifth anniversary of Solidarity's founding took the form of a nostalgic ritual, demonstrating how little was left of that example of self-organization by both workers and civil society.

See also Kurón, Jacek; Martial Law in Poland; Revolutions in East-Central Europe; Walesa, Lech.

FURTHER READING

Bertone, M. L'anomalia polacca. Rome: Editori Riuniti, 1981.
Cataluccio, F. M., and F. Gori, eds. "La Polonia e i sedici mesi di Solidarnosc." Quaderni della Fondazione Giangiacomo Feltrinelli 22 (1982).
Dubet, F., J. Strzelecki, A. Touraine, and M. Wieworka. The Workers Movement. New York: Cambridge University Press, 1987.
Giovannetti, G., and A. Sowa. Ritorno a Danzica. Milan: Efige, 2004.
Surdykowski, J. Notatki gdanskie. London: Aneks, 1982.
Tischner, J. The Spirit of Solidarity. San Francisco: Harper and Row, 1984.
Various authors. Diario polacco. Immagini di un anno di sindacato libero in Polonia. Milan: Formicona, 1982.
———. "Solidarnosc." L'Ottavo Giorno 0 (1982).
Zagajewski, A Solidarity, Solitude: Essays. New York: Ecco Press, 1989.

FRANCESCO M. CATALUCCIO

Solzhenitsyn, Aleksandr

Born in Kislovodsk on December 11, the son of wealthy farmers (his father died before his birth in June 1918), Aleksandr Solzhenitsyn (1918–2008) graduated in 1941 from the Department of Physics and Mathematics at Rostov University, and simultaneously took correspondence courses from the Moscow Institute of Philosophy, Literature, and History. At that time he also planned to write a novel on the 1917 revolution, from genuinely Leninist positions. In 1940 he married Natalya Reshetovskaya, and in 1941 he was drafted. After completing artillery school in Kostroma, he fought with the rank of lieutenant on the western front from Orel all the way to eastern Prussia. Solzhenitsyn was decorated several times, and then arrested in 1945 for having criticized Stalin in letters to a childhood friend. He spent eight years in the Soviet camp system, in Sherbakov, Zagorsk, Marfino (where the The First Circle takes place), and finally Ekibastuz in Kazakhstan (the location for One Day in the Life of Ivan Denisovich) until 1953. He stayed in central Asia in Kokterek until 1956, where he had been transferred to "eternal forced domicile" until his liberation during Khrushchev's de-Stalinization campaign. In 1954 he was cured of a form of cancer in a Tashkent hospital; his book Cancer Ward is about this experience.

Freed in 1956 (he would be fully rehabilitated in 1957), Solzhenitsyn worked as a teacher in the Vladimir region and later Rjazan, and also immersed himself in literature. His affirmation as a writer came with One Day in the Life of Ivan Denisovich (1962), which was published by Tvardovsky in the journal Noviy Mir, after having received Khrushchev's personal approval for publication. This work described life in the gulag for the first time, and the impact, emotional and political as well as artistic, that the book had inside and outside the country was strong. It was followed by other stories that were also strong, both artistically and ideally, including the novella *Matryona's Place*, which was the origin of all later neo-Christian and rural-oriented Soviet fiction. In the wake of the success of these first literary efforts, in 1964 Solzhenitsyn was nominated for the Lenin Prize, although he did not receive it because of the change in the USSR's political line after Khrushchev's fall.

The new political environment, best exemplified by the trial against the writers Andrey Sinyavsky and Yuli Daniel in 1965, pushed Solzhenitsyn to the margins of the country's literary and cultural life (after publishing the story *Zachar-Kalita* in January 1966, he published nothing in Russia for twenty-two years). In 1967 he sent a letter to the delegates of the Fourth Congress of Soviet Writers, in which he criticized the censorship system and denounced the harsh effects it had had on his works. It was precisely the new cultural and political climate that led him to circulate his works in samizdat form, and subsequently publish them abroad (*tamizdat*). This was the case of the two long novels written between 1955 and 1967, both dedicated to life in the gulag and exile, *Cancer Ward* and *The First Circle*. The first work took place in Kazakhstan, in Kokterek, where Solzhenitsyn was exiled in 1953 and cured of cancer; the second took place in the "laboratory-prison" in Marfino, in which the author described the prisoners' suffering, and where, giving voice to characters with different political, cultural, and lived backgrounds, he also depicted the monstrous and inhuman aspects of the Bolshevik Revolution.

In November 1969 he was expelled from the Union of Writers. In 1970 he received the Nobel Prize for literature, but was not allowed to travel to receive it. Instead the publication of the novel *August 1914*, devoted to the defeat of the czarist army at Tannenberg, in Paris in 1971—the first "knot" of the great epic *The Red Wheel*, dedicated to the larger project "R-17," which examined Russia's path from World War I to the October Revolution and civil war—strengthened the campaign against him at home.

Solzhenitsyn's decision to publish *The Gulag Archipelago* in 1973, after the original manuscript had been confiscated by the Soviet secret services, accelerated procedures to have the Soviet writer expelled. *The Gulag Archipelago*'s depiction of the Soviet camp system beginning

with the first repressions in 1918, the great wealth of dates and names, and the work's artistic and ideal strength had an enormous impact on Soviet and world public opinion. More specifically, the book exposed the repressive and totalitarian nature of the Soviet system since its inception, in the way Vladimir Lenin had conceived it and put it into practice, and not only in its Stalinist variant. Deprived of his Soviet citizenship in February 1974, Solzhenitsyn (who on this occasion published the article "Live Not by Lies," an appeal to moral resistance against totalitarianism) settled with his family in Zurich, where he remained until 1976. During these years he published the pamphlet *A Letter to the Soviet Leaders* (1974), the poem *Prussian Nights* (1975), on the Soviet troops' entry into Prussia, and the autobiographical volume *The Oak and the Calf* (1975). The study and collecting of historical and memoir materials was the foundation for the slow but steady realization of the aforementioned project, *The Red Wheel*. It was as a part of this project that Solzhenitsyn published *Lenin in Zurich* (1975), which contained eleven of the project's chapters.

In 1976 he moved to Cavendish, Vermont, in the United States, and devoted himself to reviewing and rewriting his works, but also gathering and examining the historical sources for his *The Red Wheel* project. He republished *August 1914* in an augmented edition, and later published *October 1916* and the first part of *March 1917*. The second part of *March 1917* and the fourth knot, *April 1917*, would then follow. These would later be followed by the essay "Na obryve povestvovanya," which summarized the historical events in knots five through twenty, which had not yet been written. Generally speaking *The Red Wheel* was a composite and innovative genre that could not be reduced to the historical or epic novel, since it included sections of political journalism and some dedicated to historical analysis.

In Solzhenitsyn's work and thought, the national and patriotic elements that were already previously present grew in weight, also due to his isolation. On the one hand, they influenced his linguistic and literary choices (one need only think about the neo-Slavic aspects of his vocabulary, or his epic style marked by invention and a documentary perspective); on the other hand, they influenced not only his political positions as regards the Communist world but also the positions of many other Soviet dissidents abroad as well as the liberal-democratic world of Western capitalism.

After the USSR's collapse Solzhenitsyn decided to return home, and in May 1994 took the trans-Siberian route from Vladivostok to Moscow. Having taken up residence in Moscow, he established a foundation for the reconstruction of Russian identity and started a huge collection of memoirs from the Russian emigration. As a journalist he devoted himself to reflections on the destiny of the Russian people in *The Russian Question at the End of the Twentieth Century* (1994) and *Rossya v ovale* (1997–98), and focused on the complex issue of life with the Jews in the ambiguous *Two Hundred Years Together* (2001–2).

See also De-Stalinization; Dissent in the USSR; Gulag; Literature in Soviet Russia; Totalitarianism.

FURTHER READING

Glocev, V., and E. Chukovskaya, eds. *Slovo probivaet sebe dorogu: Sbornik statej i dokumentov ob A. I. Solženicyne, 1962–1974.* Moscow: Russkij put', 1998.

Ledovskich, N. L. *Vozvraščenie v Matrenin dvor, ili Odin den' Aleksanra Isaeviča.* Riazan': Poverennyj, 2003.

Pearce, J. *Solzhenitsyn: A Soul in Exile.* Grand Rapids, MI: Baker Books, 2001.

Spivakovsky, P. E. *Fenomen A. I. Solženicyn: Novyj vzgljad.* Moscow: Inion, 1998.

STEFANO GARZONIO

Soviet Bloc

In the closing months of World War II and the latter half of the 1940s, the Soviet Union oversaw the establishment of Communist regimes throughout Central and Eastern Europe. Over the next four decades, those regimes constituted what was informally known as the Soviet bloc. Initially, China, which fell under Communist rule in 1949, was also part of the bloc. The first major breach in the Soviet bloc occurred in 1948, when Yugoslavia was expelled amid a deepening rift with the Soviet Union. A more serious breach occurred at the end of the 1950s, when a bitter dispute erupted between China and the Soviet Union and soon became irreconcilable. The Sino-Soviet rift also inspired Albania to leave the bloc. Aside from these three breaches, however, the Soviet bloc remained intact until 1989, when the collapse of East European communism put an end to the bloc once and for all.

Formation of the Bloc and the Stalinist Legacy

The establishment of communism in Eastern Europe proceeded at varying rates. In Yugoslavia and Albania, the indigenous Communist parties led by Josip Broz Tito and Enver Hoxha had obtained sufficient political leverage and military strength through their roles in the anti-Nazi resistance to eliminate their opposition and assume outright power as World War II drew to a close. In the Soviet zone of Germany, the Soviet occupation forces and control commission enabled the Socialist Unity Party (Sozialistische Einheitspartei Deutschlands) to gain preeminent power well before the East German state was formed in 1949. Similarly, in Bulgaria and Romania, Communist-dominated governments were imposed under Soviet pressure in early 1945.

Elsewhere in the region, events followed a more gradual pattern. Exiles returning from Moscow played a crucial role in the formation of what initially were broad coalition governments, which carried out extensive land redistribution and other long-overdue economic and political reforms. The reform process, though, was kept under tight Communist control, and the top jobs in the Ministry of Internal Affairs were reserved exclusively for Communist Party members. From those posts, they could oversee the purging of the local police forces, the execution of "collaborators," the control and censorship of the media, and the ouster and intimidation of non-Communist ministers and legislators. Supported by the tanks and troops of the Soviet Army, the Communist parties gradually solidified their hold through the determined use of what the Hungarian Communist Party leader Mátyás Rákosi called "salami tactics." Moscow's supervision over the communization of the region was further strengthened in September 1947 by the establishment of the Communist Information Bureau (Cominform), a body responsible for binding together the East European Communist parties (as well as the French and Italian Communist parties) under the Community Party of the Soviet Union's leadership. By spring 1948, "People's Democracies" were in place all over east-central Europe. Although the Soviet Union withdrew its support for the Communist insurgency in Greece, and refrained from trying to establish a Communist government in Finland or even a Finno-Soviet military alliance, Soviet power throughout the central and southern heartlands of the region was now firmly entrenched.

Within a few weeks, however, at the June 1948 Cominform summit, the first—and in Eastern Europe the largest—crack in the Soviet bloc surfaced. Yugoslavia, which had been one of the staunchest postwar allies of the Soviet Union, was expelled from Cominform and publicly denounced. The rift with Yugoslavia had been developing behind the scenes for several months and finally reached the breaking point in spring 1948.

The split with Yugoslavia revealed the limits of Soviet military, political, and economic power. The Soviet leader, Stalin, sought to use economic and political coercion against Yugoslavia, but these measures proved futile when Tito turned elsewhere for trade and economic assistance, and when he liquidated the pro-Moscow faction of the Yugoslav Communist Party before it could move against him. Stalin's aides devised a multitude of covert plots to assassinate Tito, but all such plans ultimately went nowhere. The failure of these alternatives left Stalin with the unattractive option of resorting to all-out military force—an option he declined to pursue.

If Yugoslavia had not been located on the periphery of Eastern Europe with no borders adjacent to those of the Soviet Union, it is unlikely that Stalin would have shown the restraint he did. Stalin's successor, Khrushchev, later said he was "absolutely sure that if the Soviet Union had had a common border with Yugoslavia, Stalin would have intervened militarily." Plans for a full-scale military operation were indeed prepared, but in the end the Soviet Union was forced to accept a breach of its East European sphere along with the strategic loss of Yugoslavia vis-à-vis the Balkans and the Adriatic Sea. Most important of all, the split with Yugoslavia raised concern about the effects elsewhere in the region if "Titoism" were allowed to spread. To preclude further such challenges to Soviet control, Stalin instructed the East European states to carry out new purges and show trials to remove any officials who might have hoped to seek greater independence. The process took a particularly violent form in Czechoslovakia, Bulgaria, and Hungary.

Despite the loss of Yugoslavia, the Soviet bloc came under no further threat during Stalin's time. From 1947 through the early 1950s, the East European states embarked on crash industrialization and collectivization programs, causing vast social upheaval yet also leading to rapid short-term economic growth. Stalin was able to rely on the presence of Soviet troops, a tightly woven network of security forces, the wholesale penetration of the East European governments by Soviet agents, the use of mass purges and political terror, and the unifying threat of renewed German militarism to ensure that regimes loyal to Moscow remained in power. He forged a similar relationship with Communist China, which adopted Stalinist policies under Moscow's tutelage and subordinated its preferences to those of the Soviet Union. By the early 1950s, Stalin had established a degree of control over the Communist bloc to which his successors could only aspire.

Khrushchev and the Bloc: Crises, Consolidation, and the Sino-Soviet Rift

After Stalin died in March 1953, a shift began within the Soviet bloc, as the new leaders in Moscow encouraged the East European governments to loosen economic controls, adopt "new courses" of economic and political reform, downgrade the role of the secret police, and put an end to mass violent terror. The severe economic pressures that had built up on workers and farmers during the relentless drive for collectivization were gradually eased, and many victims of the Stalinist purges were rehabilitated, often posthumously. The introduction of these changes spawned socioeconomic unrest that been held in check during the Stalin era through pervasive violence and oppression. From 1953 until the late 1980s, the Soviet Union had to come up with alternative means of defusing centrifugal pressures in Eastern Europe—a task that was often formidably difficult.

Within a few months of Stalin's death, the Soviet bloc came under serious challenge. An uprising in Plzeň and a few other Czechoslovak cities in early June 1953 was harshly suppressed by the local authorities, but a much more intractable problem arose on June 17, in East Germany, where a full-scale rebellion erupted. Coming at a time of profound uncertainty and leadership instability in both Moscow and East Berlin, the rebellion threatened the very existence of the Socialist Unity Party regime and, by extension, vital Soviet interests in Germany. The Soviet Army had to intervene on a massive scale to put down the rebellion. The intervention of Soviet troops was crucial in both forestalling an escalation of the violence and averting a grave fissure within the Soviet bloc.

Despite the resolution of the June 1953 crisis, the use of Soviet military power in East Germany revealed the inherent fragility of the bloc. Over the next few years, most of the leaders in Moscow were preoccupied with the post-Stalin leadership struggle and other salient domestic issues, and they failed to appreciate the implications of changes elsewhere in the bloc. Even after a large-scale rebellion broke out in the Polish city of Poznan in June 1956, Soviet leaders did not grasp the potential for wider and more explosive unrest in Eastern Europe. Not until the events of October–November 1956 did the Soviet Union finally draw a line for the bloc. Although a severe crisis with Poland in October was ultimately resolved peacefully, Soviet troops had to intervene en masse in Hungary in early November to suppress a violent revolution and get rid of the revolutionary government under Imre Nagy. The Soviet invasion, which resulted in heavy bloodshed, made clear to all the Warsaw Pact countries the bounds of Soviet tolerance and limits of what could be changed in Eastern Europe. The revolution in Hungary had posed a fundamental threat to the existence of the Soviet bloc, and the Soviet Union's reassertion of military control over Hungary stemmed any further erosion of the bloc.

Important as it was for the Soviet Union to consolidate its position in 1956, the bloc did not remain intact for long. A bitter split between the Soviet Union and China, stemming from genuine policy and ideological differences as well as a personal clash between Khrushchev and Mao Zedong, developed behind the scenes in the late 1950s. The dispute intensified in June 1959 when the Soviet Union abruptly terminated its secret nuclear weapons cooperation agreement with China. Khrushchev's highly publicized visit to the United States in September 1959 further antagonized the Chinese, and a last-ditch meeting between Khrushchev and Mao in Beijing a few days later failed to resolve the issues dividing the two sides. From then on, Sino-Soviet relations steadily deteriorated. Although the two countries tried several times to reconcile their differences, the split, if anything, grew even wider, leaving a permanent breach in the Soviet bloc.

Khrushchev feared that the schism in world communism would deepen if he did not seek to counter China's efforts to secure the backing of foreign Communist parties. In late 1960 and early 1961 the Albanian leader, Hoxha, sparked a crisis with the Soviet Union by openly aligning his country with China—a precedent that caused alarm in Moscow. The "loss" of Albania, though trivial compared to the earlier split with Yugoslavia, marked the second time since 1945 that the Soviet sphere in Eastern Europe had been breached. When Soviet leaders learned that China was secretly trying to induce other East European countries to follow Albania's lead, they made strenuous efforts to undercut Beijing's attempts. As a result, no further defections from the Soviet bloc oc-

curred by the time Khrushchev was removed from power in October 1964.

The Brezhnev and Early Post-Brezhnev Era: Retrenchment and Conformity

Khrushchev's successor, Leonid Brezhnev, had to overcome several challenges to the integrity of the bloc. The first of these was presented by Romania, which in the mid-1960s began to embrace foreign and domestic policies that were at times sharply at odds with the Soviet Union's own policies. Romania staked out a conspicuously neutral position in the Sino-Soviet dispute, refusing to endorse Moscow's polemics or join in other steps aimed at isolating Beijing. In 1967, Romania became the first East European country to establish diplomatic ties with West Germany—a step that infuriated the East German authorities. That same year, the Romanians maintained full diplomatic relations with Israel after the other Warsaw Pact countries had broken off all ties with the Israelis in the wake of the June 1967 Middle East War. Romania also adopted an independent military doctrine of "Total People's War for the Defense of the Homeland" and a national military command structure separate from that of the Warsaw Pact. Although Romania had never been a crucial member of the Warsaw Pact, the country's growing recalcitrance on foreign policy and military affairs posed serious complications for the cohesion of the alliance.

The deepening rift with Romania provided the backdrop for a much more serious challenge that arose in 1968 with Czechoslovakia and what became widely known as the Prague Spring. The introduction of sweeping political reforms in Czechoslovakia after Alexander Dubček came to power in early 1968 provoked alarm in Moscow about the integrity of the Soviet bloc. Both the internal and external repercussions of the far-reaching liberalization in Czechoslovakia were regarded by Soviet leaders as fundamental threats to the cohesion of the Warsaw Pact, especially if the developments in Czechoslovakia "infected" other countries in Eastern Europe. Soviet efforts to compel Dubček to change course were of little efficacy, as all manner of troop movements, thinly veiled threats, and political and economic coercion failed to bring an end to the Prague Spring. Finally, on the evening of August 20, 1968, the Soviet Union and four other Warsaw Pact countries—East Germany, Poland, Bulgaria, and Hungary—sent a large invading force into Czechoslovakia to crush the reform movement and restore orthodox Communist rule. Although it took several months before the last remnants of the Prague Spring could be eradicated, the final ouster of Dubček in April 1969 symbolized the forceful restoration of conformity to the Soviet bloc.

For more than a decade thereafter, the bloc seemed relatively stable, despite crises in Poland in 1970 and 1976. But the facade of stability came to an abrupt end in mid-1980 when a severe and prolonged crisis began in Poland—a crisis that soon posed enormous complications for the integrity of the bloc. The formation of Solidarity, an independent and popularly based trade union that soon rivaled the Polish Communist Party for political power, threatened to undermine Poland's role in the bloc. Soviet leaders reacted with unremitting hostility toward Solidarity and repeatedly urged Polish leaders to impose martial law—a step that was finally taken in December 1981.

The Soviet Union's emphasis on an "internal solution" to the Polish crisis was by no means a departure from its responses to previous crises in the Soviet bloc. In both Hungary and Poland in 1956 as well as Czechoslovakia in 1968, Soviet leaders had applied pressure short of direct military intervention and sought to work out an internal solution that would preclude the need for an invasion. In each case, Soviet officials viewed military action as a last-ditch option, to be used only if all other alternatives failed. An internal solution proved feasible in Poland in 1956, but attempts to reassert Soviet control from within proved futile in Hungary in 1956 and Czechoslovakia in 1968. During the 1980–81 Polish crisis, Soviet officials devised plans for a full-scale invasion, but these plans were to be implemented only if the Polish authorities failed to restore order on their own. Only in a worst-case scenario, in which the martial law operation collapsed and civil war erupted in Poland, would the Soviet Union likely have shifted toward an external option.

The successful imposition of martial law in Poland by General Wojciech Jaruzelski in December 1981 upheld the integrity of the Soviet bloc at relatively low cost and ensured that Soviet leaders did not have to face the dilemma of invading Poland. The surprisingly smooth implementation of martial law in Poland also helped prevent any further disruption in the bloc during the final year of Brezhnev's rule, and the next two and a half years under Yuri Andropov and Konstantin Chernenko. During an earlier period of uncertainty and leadership transition in the Soviet Union and Eastern Europe (1953–56), numerous crises had arisen within the bloc; but no such upheavals occurred in 1982–85. This unusual placidity

cannot be attributed to any single factor, but the martial law crackdown of December 1981 along with the invasions of 1956 and 1968 probably constitute a large part of the explanation. After Stalin's death in 1953, the limits of what could be changed in Eastern Europe were still unknown, but by the early to mid-1980s the Soviet Union had evinced its willingness to use "extreme measures" to prevent "deviations from socialism." Thus, by the time Mikhail Gorbachev assumed the top post in Moscow in March 1985, the Soviet bloc seemed destined to remain within the narrow bounds of orthodox communism as interpreted in Moscow.

The Demise of the Soviet Bloc

Although Gorbachev initially carried out few changes in the Soviet bloc, he began shifting course within a few years of taking office, as he steadily loosened Soviet ties with Eastern Europe. The wide-ranging political reforms he was promoting in the Soviet Union generated pressure within Eastern Europe for the adoption of similar reforms. Faced with the prospect of acute social discontent, the Hungarian and Polish governments embarked on sweeping reform programs that were at least as ambitious as what Gorbachev was pursuing. By early 1989, it had become clear that the Soviet Union was willing to countenance radical changes in Eastern Europe that cumulatively amounted to a repudiation of orthodox communism.

In adopting this approach, Gorbachev did not intend to precipitate the breakup of the Soviet bloc. On the contrary, he was hoping to strengthen the bloc and reshape it in a way that would no longer require heavy-handed coercion. But in the end his policies, far from invigorating the bloc, resulted in its demise. In early June 1989, elections were held in Poland that led, within three months, to the emergence of a non-Communist government led by Solidarity. Political changes of similar magnitude were under way at this time in Hungary. Although the four other Warsaw Pact countries—East Germany, Bulgaria, Czechoslovakia, and Romania—tried to fend off the pressures for sweeping change, their resistance proved futile in the final few months of 1989, when they were engulfed by political turmoil. The orthodox Communist rulers in these four countries were forced from power, and non-Communist governments took over. In 1990, free elections were held in all the East European countries, consolidating the newly democratic political systems that took shape after the Communist regimes collapsed.

By that point, events had moved so far and so fast in Eastern Europe, and the Soviet Union's influence had declined so precipitously, that the fate of the whole continent eluded Soviet control. The very notion of a Soviet bloc lost its meaning once Gorbachev permitted and even facilitated the end of Communist rule in Eastern Europe. This outcome may seem inevitable in retrospect, but it was definitely not so at the time. If Gorbachev had been determined to preserve the Soviet bloc in its traditional form, as his predecessors were, he undoubtedly could have succeeded. The Soviet Union in the late 1980s still had more than enough military strength to prop up the Communist regimes in Eastern Europe and cope with the bloodshed that would have resulted. Gorbachev's acceptance of the peaceful disintegration of the bloc stemmed from a conscious choice on his part—a choice bound up with his domestic priorities and desire to do away with the legacies of the Stalinist era that had blighted the Soviet economy. Any Soviet leader who was truly intent on overcoming Stalinism at home had to be willing to implement drastic changes in relations with Eastern Europe. Far-reaching political liberalization and greater openness within the Soviet Union would have been incompatible with, and eventually undermined by, a policy in Eastern Europe that required military intervention on behalf of hard-line Communist regimes. The fundamental reorientation of Soviet domestic goals under Gorbachev therefore necessitated the adoption of a radically new policy vis-à-vis Eastern Europe that led, in short order, to the dissolution of the Soviet bloc.

See also Bipolarity; Brezhnev Doctrine; Cold War; Comecon; Cominform; Hungarian Revolution; Martial Law in Poland; Prague Spring; Soviet-Yugoslavia Break; Warsaw Pact.

FURTHER READING

Brzezinski, Z. K. *The Soviet Bloc: Unity and Conflict.* Rev. ed. Cambridge, MA: Harvard University Press, 1967.

Gati, C. *The Bloc That Failed: Soviet-East European Relations in Transition.* Bloomington: Indiana University Press, 1990.

Hutchings, R. L. *Soviet-East European Relations: Consolidation and Conflict, 1968–1980.* Madison: University of Wisconsin Press, 1983.

Kramer, M. "The Soviet Union and Eastern Europe: Spheres of Influence." In *Explaining International Relations since 1945,* ed. N. Woods, pp. 98–128. New York: Oxford University Press, 1996.

Smith, A. H. *The Planned Economies of Eastern Europe.* London: Croom Helm, 1981.

MARK KRAMER

Soviet Industrialization

The industrialization of the Soviet Union took place approximately between 1928 and 1970. This was the first and most prominent case of the economic development of a major country through a largely state-owned centrally planned or command economy.

When the Bolsheviks assumed power in the Russian Empire in October 1917, substantial iron, steel, coal, and oil industries had already been established in czarist Russia with state support and foreign capital, together with a cotton textile industry based almost entirely on Russian capital. But industry was only a small segment of the economy: some three million people were employed in factories and mines out of a total active labor force of seventy million. More than 80 percent of the population lived in the countryside; and most of the land was cultivated by some twenty million peasant households. Straddling Europe and Asia, Russia presented a dual face to the world: a colonial power and a semicolony, the most backward of the European powers, and the most advanced of the great peasant countries. And czarist and Stalinist industrialization was not merely the industrialization of a European power but also the first case of the rapid industrialization of a peasant country in the course of a few decades.

Like other Marxists, Lenin and the Bolshevik (Communist) Party assumed before 1917 that the first proletarian (working-class) revolution would take place in an industrially advanced country with a large class-conscious working class. In the first few years after the October 1917 Revolution, they expected that Soviet Russia would soon be joined by Germany and other more developed countries as the first stage in the world socialist revolution. But by the mid-1920s prospects of world revolution had obviously receded.

The majority of the Soviet leaders decided that it was possible and necessary to build "Socialism in One Country," even though that country was backward Russia. In most respects this was the same economy as in 1914. Following the crisis and destruction of the world war (1914–18) and then the civil war (1918–20), Soviet industry and agriculture were almost restored to the prewar level. The landowning class had been eliminated, and large-scale industry had been nationalized. But peasant agriculture, linked with state industry through the market, continued to dominate the economy. Nearly all shades of opinion within the Communist Party agreed that to build socialism, it was urgently necessary to develop industry and a modern working class. To achieve this, the state must itself organize and push through this development, performing the role undertaken by the bourgeoisie in Western Europe and the United States.

Doctrinal arguments were supported by practical considerations. The Soviet Union had emerged from a civil war in which foreign capitalist powers had sought to destroy the new regime. This seemed to demonstrate the necessity for a broad-based industry that would provide the basis for defense against a hostile world—and perhaps the support of foreign revolutionary movements. A belief in the need to develop industry was reinforced by an unexpected and unwelcome feature of the 1920s: mass unemployment. Even by a narrow definition, unemployment amounted to 9 percent of the employed population at the end of 1926 (the employed population excludes peasants, artisans, and others working on their own account), and was increasing continuously. The prime cause was the huge scale of rural migration into the towns—a familiar problem in third world countries.

But how was industrialization to be undertaken? A number of rival strategies were proposed. Sokolnikov, who was the people's commissar of finance in 1924 and 1925, emphasized that the return on investment in agriculture was, in the circumstances of the 1920s, much greater than the return on industry. Hence, industrialization could be best achieved by investing in agriculture for the time being and exporting grain to pay for the imports of cheap machinery. He was supported by many agrarian economists, including the internationally renowned Nikolai Kondratiev. But his views found little favor in the Communist Party.

In contrast, Preobrazhensky, the principal economist in the Left Opposition headed by Trotsky, argued that the USSR must pass through a stage of "primary socialist accumulation" analogous to the "primary accumulation" postulated by Marx in his analysis of capitalism. Part of the product or incomes of the peasant economies should be exploited or "alienated" by the state, through taxation or price policy, and transferred to industrial investment.

In the mid-1920s the predominant opinion in the politburo, shared by the advisers to the Soviet government in the mid-1920s, in contrast to both Sokolnikov and Preobrazhensky, was that sufficient savings for industrialization could be found within industry or the state sector of the economy as a whole by rationalization, which would result in falling costs and increased profits.

Until the end of 1927, it was common ground between all these different schools of thought that the market economy of the 1920s would remain intact. The peasant might be taxed, but would not be coerced. This principle was advocated most forcefully by the leading Communist intellectual Bukharin; but at this time it was also shared by Stalin and even by the Left Opposition.

It was abandoned by Stalin and his supporters, though, following the grain crisis of 1927–28. In October–December 1927, peasants sold only half as much grain to the official grain collection agencies as in the same months of 1926. With this amount of grain the towns and the army could not be fed.

Historians differ among themselves about the reasons for the crisis. Some Western historians, including Robert Conquest, treat the grain shortages as deliberately and artificially created by Stalin and used by him as a pretext to crack down on the peasants. Other historians, including E. H. Carr, have stressed the strain placed on the relationship between the towns and the countryside by the substantial increase in industrial investment since the summer of 1926. This increase was particularly rapid in the capital goods industries, which did not provide an immediate return in the form of consumer goods. Alec Nove and others emphasize erroneous price policies, themselves rooted in Bolshevik hostile or critical attitudes to the market. These views are not completely incompatible. Both the expansion of the resources devoted to industry and erroneous price policies were major causes of the crisis, and the crisis certainly provided an opportunity for Stalin to drastically change the course of economic policy.

The program of industrialization launched under Stalin's leadership in 1928 involved the collectivization of peasant agriculture as well as the compulsory acquisition of food and other farm products to supply the growing towns. This resulted in an agricultural crisis, culminating in the devastating famine of 1933 in which millions of peasants died. Agriculture recovered in the mid-1930s, but during the Stalin era neither yield nor agricultural production per head of population rose above the level of the 1920s. Were collectivization and requisitioning effective means of transferring resources to industrialization? Until the early 1970s almost all Western historians assumed that agriculture was the main source of labor and capital for industry, and that collectivization was the crucial though brutal mechanism by which this was achieved. Three achievements were particularly highlighted. First, there was the increase in the compulsory delivery of grain to the state. In 1938–40, deliveries averaged 30 million tons from an average harvest of some 77 million tons (39 percent), as compared with 10.7 million out of 73 million tons in 1928 (14.7 percent). Second, the increased production of cotton and other products that were previously imported saved foreign currency and provided essential materials for industry. Third, the agricultural sector supplied most of the increase in urban labor. The scale of the migration was a consequence of state pressure on the peasants and the deterioration of conditions in the countryside, together with the lure of ample employment in the towns. This greatly facilitated the increase in industrial production and construction generally.

This positive view of the economic effects of collectivization was strongly challenged by Barsov, a Soviet economic historian, and the U.S. economist James Millar. Barsov claimed that the terms of trade for agriculture did not deteriorate in 1928–32, and improved in 1933–37. While some agricultural commodities, especially grain, were transferred to the state at low prices, others were sold on the free market at high prices. Even though the supply of grain to the state by the peasants increased, the supply of meat and dairy products declined. Thus, peasants' money incomes were higher, and their supplies to the town lower than was previously believed. On the side of supply to the peasants from the towns, their high money earnings enabled them to buy industrial consumer goods. Agriculture also received greatly increased supplies of machinery from industry through state-owned machine and tractor stations, each of which served the surrounding collective farms with a pool of tractors, combine harvesters, and other machinery. The total flow of industrial products to the countryside, in the form of both consumer goods and machinery, was therefore higher than previously believed.

Other economists, while concurring with much of this general account, do not accept its implications. Nove argued that in the circumstances of forced industrialization the state could not have obtained increased supplies of agricultural products without a drastic shift in the terms of trade in favor of agriculture. He also pointed out that food and other consumption declined more rapidly in the countryside than in the towns, so that in this sense peasants made a major sacrifice for in-

dustrialization. Collectivization also enabled agriculture to be treated as a residual sector, which absorbed shocks such as bad harvests.

Between 1928 and 1940, managed by the centrally planned or command system, Soviet industry, and particularly the capital goods' and armaments' industries, expanded rapidly. The Western estimate in table 1 shows that industrial output more than trebled, and this figure would be higher if measured in 1928 prices. This was also a social revolution. The urban population increased from one-sixth to one-third of the total population, and both mass and higher education expanded rapidly.

By the second half of the 1930s, the Soviet Union produced its own iron and steel, electric power equipment, tractors and trucks, and most types of machine tools and modern armaments. The expansion of capital goods industries and the advance of their technology was uneven. The pressure for more output in conditions in which unskilled labor was relatively abundant resulted in the employment of much more labor per unit of output, especially in auxiliary processes, than in the major Western industrial countries. This was a kind of dual technology, and was well described as "a labor-intensive variant of capital-intensive technology."

During the early 1930s, many foreign firms and individuals provided technical assistance to the major capital projects, and several thousand engineers and industrial workers were employed in design institutes, on capital projects, and in factories. And strict controls over foreign trade enabled imports to be concentrated on machinery and equipment for the key industries. After 1932, the role of foreign imports and know-how considerably declined. While key examples of advanced machinery and weapons continued to be imported, the low level of imports in the later 1930s no doubt delayed further technological advances in the Soviet Union.

During the 1930s substantial changes also took place in the location of industry. Industry was traditionally located in northwestern and central European Russia and Ukraine. The Soviet authorities sought to construct a major part of the new industry in the 1930s in the Urals and Siberia as well as poorly developed Central Asia. In these areas there were vast mineral resources, unused and largely unexplored. Soviet social policy imperatively required the development of the "colonial" areas of Central Asia. And above all, defense considerations required the construction of capital goods and armaments industries far from the frontier.

A major new industrial complex was established in the Urals and western Siberia. The industrial output of the Urals and Trans-Urals regions increased from 11 or 12 percent of all output in 1928 to over 16 percent in 1940. But developing these new areas was expensive and time-consuming. In the last years before the war, industrial expansion in the eastern areas slowed down, owing both to pressure for immediate output and the complacency of Stalin and other leaders about the ability of the Red Army to halt the enemy at the frontiers.

Nevertheless, the new capital goods and armaments industries provided the basis for Soviet military victory in the Great Patriotic War of 1941–45, which was a crucial factor in the worldwide defeat of fascism. The first impact of the German invasion of June 1941 was disastrous, but the defense industries soon recovered. Although the Soviet economy was less industrially advanced than the German economy, by 1944 the USSR produced more combat aircraft along with more tanks and self-propelled guns than Germany, and Soviet aircraft and tanks performed at least as well as the German versions.

By 1949, the Soviet economy had largely recovered from the devastation of the war, in which over twenty-five million Soviet lives were lost, and the second phase of industrialization began, as is shown in table 1. By 1965 industrial production was over four times as large as in 1940, and nearly fourteen times the 1928 level. In these years, in contrast to the 1930s, the production of agriculture also increased quite rapidly, reaching almost double the prewar level, and the production and variety of industrial consumer goods also expanded. The Soviet population received the first fruits of the industrialization drive. The Soviet economic system, at great human cost, had negotiated the industrialization of a developing country, and in the international arena the Soviet Union had emerged as one of the world's two superpowers. Industrialization brought about a social transformation. In 1965, forty-three million people were employed in industry, construction, and transport, as compared with five million in 1928 (see table 2). The total number of graduates amounted to nearly five million, over twenty times as many as in 1928.

The Soviet system was not designed merely as an instrument for industrialization. It had also been intended, ever since 1917, to provide a blueprint or starting point for the establishment of a planned socialist economic order throughout the world. To maintain this program, the Soviet system of the 1960s had to find the means of coping with the problems of economic growth and technical change in a more advanced industrial society.

The history of the quarter of a century between 1965 and the collapse of the Soviet Union in 1991 was the story of its failure to solve these problems. In the 1970s and 1980s, the Soviet Union failed to reduce the technological gap between its industry and those of the major Western countries. As early as the mid-1970s, the rate of economic growth had fallen so far that for the first time since the mid-1920s, the gross national product was expanding less rapidly than in the United States—and much more slowly than in several newly industrialized countries.

The inherent weaknesses of the Soviet economic system certainly played an important role in the ultimate collapse of Soviet communism. Initiative was fettered and risk was discouraged; above all the centralized system, while often successfully launching new technological policies from above, inhibited the development of new production and new technology by factories and enterprises. Meanwhile in the postwar years the capitalist countries, in contrast to the 1930s, had avoided major economic crises—and in the 1970s and 1980s the major Western powers, and the newly industrializing Asian countries, had launched new technological revolutions. Moreover, the Western alliance led by the United States embarked in the 1970s on the comprehensive modernization of its armed forces. The Soviet leaders, like their czarist predecessors, took the perhaps fatal decision to embark on a huge and unsuccessful effort to secure military superiority, placing an immense strain on the relatively backward Soviet economy.

Many attempts were made to reform the system, from the 1950s onward, but were all unsuccessful. To what extent was this failure due to the inherent inability of state socialism to manage a postindustrial economy, and to what extent was it a defect of the talents and imagination of the political leaders and their advisers—or the ruling elite as a whole?

Soviet communism has come to an abrupt end, but Soviet industrialization has exerted a profound and lasting influence on world economic development. The inhumanities and social inequalities of the Stalinist version of socialism antagonized both the elites and the ordinary people in the Western democracies. But the first stage of Soviet industrial advance took place in the 1930s—the years of the world economic crisis. The ability of the

Soviet state to produce a dynamic economic system exercised a profound influence on Western economic thinking, and was undoubtedly a factor in the emergence of the mixture of state and private control as well as ownership that was characteristic of most Western industrial countries in the first thirty years or so after the Second World War, and that has still not disappeared at the beginning of the 21st century.

The Soviet success in transforming a largely peasant country into an industrial superpower within a few decades even more profoundly influenced the outlook and psychology of the four-fifths of the world that was not yet industrialized. The efforts of some third world countries to emulate the Soviet model of state-managed economic development ended in failure. But in spite of the shift of the third world toward capitalism in recent decades, Soviet industrialization has remained a yardstick against which the economic success or failure of ex-colonial countries tends to be measured. In the economic history of the world, Soviet industrialization was an important stage in the spreading of the economic and social transformation that began in England in the 18th century to the thousands of millions of peasants who lived on the edge of starvation.

Table 1

Gross national product, 1928–65: Moorsteen-Powell and CIA estimate (billion rubles at 1937 prices)

	1928	1940	1945	1965
Agriculture	58.0	69.9	47.1	133
Industry	24.2	77.8	53.8	336
Other	41.5	102.8	98.1	325
Total	123.7	250.5	199.0	794

Table 2

Employment in industry, building, and transport, 1928–65 (thousands)

	1928	1940	1945	1965
Industry	4,339	13,079	10,665	27,056
Building	818	1,993	1,527	5,617
Transport and communications	1,397	4,009	3,552	8,259
Total	8,482	21,021	17,689	42,897

See also Collectivization of the Countryside; Command Economy; Five-Year Plans; Holodomor; Modernization; Planning; Socialism in One Country.

FURTHER READING

Carr, E. H. *The Russian Revolution from Lenin to Stalin, 1917–1929*. 2nd ed. Basingstoke, UK: Palgrave Macmillan, 2004.

Davies, R. W. *The Industrialization of Soviet Russia*. 5 vols. (vol. 5 with Stephen G. Wheatcroft.) Basingstoke, UK: Palgrave Macmillan, 1980–2004.

Davies, R. W., M. Harrison, and S. G. Wheatcroft, eds. *The Economic Transformation of the Soviet Union, 1913–1945*. Cambridge, UK: Cambridge University Press, 1994.

Harrison, M. *Soviet Planning in Peace and War, 1938–1945*. Cambridge: Cambridge University Press, 1985.

Jasny, N. *Soviet Industrialization, 1918–1952*. Stanford, CA: Stanford University Press, 1961.

Moorsteen, R., and R. P. Powell. *The Soviet Capital Stock, 1928–1962*. Homewood, IL: R. D. Irwin, 1966.

Nove, A. *An Economic History of the U.S.S.R.* Harmondsworth, UK: Penguin, 1982.

ROBERT W. DAVIES

Soviet Occupation of Germany

Allied planning for the defeated Third Reich after World War II shifted gradually from ideas about dividing Germany into small and ineffective statelets to an agreement to maintain the economic and political unity of the German state. To the benefit of Poland, Germany would be shorn of its territories east of the line marked by the Oder and Eastern Neisse rivers. To ensure the democratization, denazification, and decartelization of the country, not to mention to guarantee the payment of reparations guaranteed at Yalta in February 1945, the Allies—the United States, Great Britain, the Soviet Union, and France—would partition Germany into four occupation zones until a formal peace treaty could be signed. Berlin was similarly divided into occupation zones and designated a "four-power" city, despite the fact that the city lay in the center of the Soviet zone. Although the farthest lines of the Allies' advances during the war did not coincide with the designated zones of occupation—the Soviets had seized all of Berlin, and the British and Americans had seized large sections of what was designated as the Soviet zone—by July 1, 1945, each of the occupying powers had withdrawn to and assumed control over their designated occupation territories.

Historians agree about the short-term intentions of the government of the Soviet Zone of Occupation (SBZ), which was established on June 6, 1945. First of all, it would establish order and control in the eastern parts of Germany for which it was responsible. Germans would have to be fed; the basic infrastructure would have to be rebuilt; a new denazified, democratized political system would have to be put in place according to the guidelines established by the Allies at Potsdam. The Soviet government was also intent on extracting ten billion dollars in reparations from the Germans. Teams of experts and military units were sent out from the ministries in Moscow to ship home to the Soviet Union German factories, military installations, and technological installations. The Soviets were determined not only to ship back to Moscow the men and materiel that would guarantee the rebuilding of Soviet industrial power, but also to gather up and send home German expertise and machinery that would aid Soviet military potential, especially in the fields of nuclear weaponry and rocketry.

Scholars agree on these short-term goals of their occupation, but there is considerable disagreement over the Soviets' medium- and long-term objectives. The Soviet Occupied Zone eventually became the German Democratic Republic (October 7, 1949), an independent German state under Soviet control. Was this intended by the Soviets from the beginning? Some scholars suggest that the Soviets were intent on establishing a Socialist government in all of Germany, but once the Western Allies made it forcefully apparent that they would establish a West German government in 1948 and back it militarily and financially, the Soviets acceded to East German Communist demands for their own state. Other scholars see the Soviets' aims as more benign; Moscow wanted the Allies to live up to the Potsdam agreement and establish a German democratic government that would be demilitarized, denazified, and, for all intents and purposes, neutral. (This goal was best articulated by Deputy Foreign Minister Maxim Litvinov in a January 1945 memorandum.) That this did not happen is attributed either to the growing Cold War atmosphere in Europe or, by more "revisionist" scholars, to the West's aggressive intentions regarding Germany as a whole.

However one judges Stalin's ultimate aims in Germany, the day-to-day tasks of the Soviet Military Administration in Germany (in Russian SVAG, in German SMAD) revolved around the gradual Sovietization of its zone of occupation. The organizational structure of SVAG was separate from the work of the Group of Soviet Occupation Forces in Germany (GSOF), which numbered some 300,000 soldiers scattered in bases around the zone. Though both were led by the same supreme commander, initially Marshall G. K. Zhukov and then Colonel-General V. D. Sokolovskii, and both had their headquarters in Karlshorst, outside of Berlin, it was SVAG that was responsible for the Germans and their administration. (The GSOF had its hands full trying to keep Soviet soldiers from engaging in periodic mayhem and violence against the German population.) Measures on land reform in September 1945 reduced the influence of large-scale farmers on the economy and polity. The "referendum" of July 16, 1946, ensured that large industries were nationalized and removed from the hands of private owners. A Society for Friendship with the Soviet Union was formed to promote an appreciative attitude toward the Soviet Union on the part of the German population in the Soviet zone, and the Kulturbund as a way for Germans to attach themselves to a new and progressive culture. Social organizations, like the Free German Youth (FDJ) and the Free German Labor Union (FDGB), fostered societal momentum for "democratic" advances in the zone. The Soviets also oversaw the development of a reliable and well-trained German political police, which eventually became the basis of the notorious State Security Service (*Staatssicherheitsdienst*) created in February 1950.

The most critical task for SVAG was political, and for that the Soviets turned to the German Communists for help. Experienced and loyal Communists like Walter Ulbricht, Wilhelm Pieck, and Anton Ackermann had spent the war years in Moscow. As leaders of the German Communist Party (KPD), they met with Stalin and worked closely with Georgi Dimitrov, former head of the Comintern, who was Stalin's chief deputy when it came to the development of relations between Moscow and the foreign Communist parties. Many of these same German Communists were flown into Germany on the heels of the Soviet armies to help organize local administrations in the Soviet zone and to begin the process of forming an anti-Fascist political movement. These Communists faced serious handicaps among the population. Not only had many Germans absorbed the Nazis' propaganda about the Soviets and Bolshevism, but the actual behavior of the Soviet troops in Germany, which included widespread rape, pillage, thievery, drunkenness, and violence of every kind, confirmed their worst prejudices. Moreover, Soviet military units oversaw the removal of factories and infrastructure from the country, which resulted in the loss of German jobs and the lowering of living standards. As "friends of the Russians" and defenders of reparations, the Communists became even more unpopular. In an effort to overcome the isolation and weakness of the Communists, Colonel Sergei Tiul'panov, chief of the propaganda (later information) division of the Soviet administration, oversaw a campaign to unite the Communist Party (KPD) with the Social-Democratic Party (SPD) in a new Socialist Unity Party (SED). This tactic, which was used throughout Eastern Europe, was designed to bolster the control, power, and popularity of the Communists. In the case of the East German SPD, the Soviets found a willing tool for the unity campaign in Otto Grotewohl. While a number of SPD leaders left the Soviet zone for the West, a combination of pressure, incentives, and promises from the Soviets at both the local and central levels convinced the bulk of SPD members that their choices were limited and that the newly founded SED was their only chance to pursue their political interests. The Unity Congress was held on April 21–22, 1946, and the SED, under Soviet tutelage, became the leading political force in the eastern zone.

Despite the concerted support of the Soviet authorities, the SED inherited many of the problems of the earlier KPD. The Soviets held out great hopes for the elections of the fall of 1946, but the party fared poorly in the zone and even worse in relatively free elections in the western zones of Berlin. Along with the increasingly antagonistic relations between the Soviets and the West in the Allied Control Council, the dismal showing of the SED at the polls led the Soviets and the German Communists to purge the SED of ostensibly unreliable elements, most often from the former SPD, while tightening its hold on economic institutions in the zone. The creation of the German Economic Commission (DWK) in June 1947 gave the SED considerable control over German civilian administration in the Soviet zone. In 1948 and 1949, under Ulbricht's direction, the DWK increasingly took on the trappings of a German government. The Soviets notably kept the SED away from the first meeting of the Cominform in September 1947 and reminded its leaders that they should desist from proclaiming that the Soviet zone was on the road to a "people's democracy," the SED nevertheless gradually

inched its way to becoming a Marxist-Leninist party, like the others in Eastern Europe. Finally, with Soviet blessings, in January 1949, the SED declared itself a "Party of the New Type" dedicated to the Leninist principles of "democratic centralism."

Scholars argue about whether the increasing radicalization of SED rule in the Soviet zone was a consequence of a hardening of Cold War tensions between East and West or whether the Cold War was a product of the antagonisms created by the increasingly apparent division of Germany. In either case, the four-power occupation of Berlin was an important source of East-West discord. At the London Conference of March 1948, the Western powers set in motion the process of the unification of the three Western zones into a West German state and the creation of a single West German currency. As a consequence, Stalin imposed a blockade of access routes to Berlin in June 1948 as a way of simultaneously pressuring the Allies to leave Berlin and the West Berliners to become part of the Soviet zone. His ultimate goal was to force the West to abandon its unilateral plans for the formation of a West German state; his immediate goal was to prevent the Western sectors of Berlin from becoming part of the Western currency zone and therefore of the new West German state. The Berlin Airlift proved an inventive way for the Allies to demonstrate their claims to Berlin and to supply the Berliners with a minimum of food and coal. Recent research has demonstrated that the quarantine on Berlin by the Soviets was not complete and that the Soviets made no preparations to go to war over Berlin. They would not let the Berliners starve. In the end, Stalin did not get his way, and, unwilling to use military force, the Soviets backed off of the blockade in May 1949.

Tensions over the status of Berlin accelerated the division of Germany. The existence of the Federal Republic of Germany was announced on May 23, 1949. SED leaders moved quickly, with Soviet advice (especially that of political adviser Vladimir Semyenov), to form their own state. Already in March 1949, a draft constitution for the German Democratic Republic, meant to apply to all of Germany, was adopted by the People's Council, a proto-parliament elected by the Second People's Congress. A Third People's Congress met in May and elected a new People's Council drawn exclusively from the Soviet zone. By early October, the People's Council was ready to proclaim itself the provisional People's Assembly and to form a government. On October 7, the People's

Congress proclaimed the founding of the German Democratic Republic and Otto Grotewohl was charged with forming a government. On October 10, 1945, the Soviet Military Administration in Germany dissolved itself and was replaced by the office of Soviet High Commissioner. The era of the Soviet occupation administration, if not of Soviet control, had come to an end.

The Group of Soviet Forces in Germany remained in place as a large and strategically important salient of the Red Army. The group was on the front line of both potential Soviet offensive actions in Europe and of the defense of the Warsaw Pact countries against alleged plans of NATO aggression. Soviet forces also played an important role in the maintenance of the domestic stability of the GDR and neighboring Warsaw Pact nations. In June 1953, Soviet tanks were crucial in putting down the East Berlin uprising. During subsequent Berlin crises, including the construction of the Berlin Wall in August 1961, the presence of large contingents of Soviet troops emboldened the Soviets in their bellicose behavior and inhibited Western responses. As a consequence of the fall of the Berlin Wall in 1989, the reunification of Germany in 1990, and the collapse of the Soviet Union in 1991, the Russian government engaged in lengthy negotiations with the Germans about the withdrawal of the last contingents of its forces from Germany. In the summer of 1994, a half-century after they marched into German territory, the Soviet forces were gone.

See also Berlin Crisis; Berlin Wall; Cold War; Reunification of Germany; Socialist Camp; Yalta Conference.

FURTHER READING

Foitzik, J. *Sowjetische Militaeradministration in Deutschland (SMAD) 1945–1949*. Berlin: Struktur und Funktion, 1999.

Krisch, H. *German Politics under Soviet Occupation*. New York: Columbia University Press, 1974.

Leonhard, W. *Child of the Revolution*. Chicago: Regnery, 1958.

Naimark, N. M. *The Russians in Germany: A History of the Soviet Zone of Occupation, 1945–1949*. Cambridge, MA: Harvard University Press, 1995.

Phillips, A. L. *Soviet Policy Toward East Germany Reconsidered: The Postwar Decade*. Westport, CT: Greenwood Press, 1986.

Pike, D. *The Politics of Culture in Soviet Occupied Germany*. Stanford, CA: Stanford University Press, 1992.

Weber H. *Geschichte der DDR*. Munich: Deutscher Taschenbuch Verlag, 1985.

NORMAN M. NAIMARK

Soviet Patriotism

Patriotism is traditionally considered an emotional allegiance to one's nation, state, society, or culture. It is somewhat more complicated in the Soviet case, however, as patriotism is more readily associated with nationalism than internationalism. Indeed, Marxists often dismiss patriotism as a source of false consciousness promoted by social elites in order to distract the laboring masses from their true class interests. Perhaps for this reason, Karl Marx and Friedrich Engels's famous line from *The Communist Manifesto* (1848)—"the workers do not have a fatherland"—is typically read as an unambiguous appeal for the proletariat to overthrow its oppressors, erase national boundaries, and remake society on an international scale.

While not technically incorrect, such an interpretation is more misleading than it is revealing. After all, Marx and Engels did not expect the workers of the world to unite in a single revolutionary moment, and allowed for the possibility that workers in certain countries might succeed in throwing off the capitalist yoke before others. Marx and Engels expected that in such circumstances, proletarian forces would consolidate power on the national level before returning to the cause of revolutionary internationalism. It is for this reason that *The Communist Manifesto* directs the proletariat in revolutionary societies to "rise to be the leading national class" and "constitute itself as the nation" once national elites are defeated.

But this support for revolutionary societies should only be considered a conditional endorsement of conventional patriotism. Although Austro-Marxists like Karl Renner and Otto Bauer advanced a socialist model composed along both class and national lines, Marx and Engels considered national cultures to be more or less illusory, and expected them to decompose in the wake of a global social revolution. Thus, while Marx and Engels encouraged the working class to defend revolutionary societies, this was really a means to an end insofar as they expected these societies to advance the cause of world revolution rather than more parochial causes associated with their own national distinctiveness, cultural traditions, or geopolitical interests.

Such a reading of Marx and Engels informed the early Soviet state's use of patriotic appeals during the revolution and civil war (1917–21). Emphasizing the primacy of class consciousness over national consciousness, Vladimir Lenin and the Bolshevik mainstream equated the defense of Russia with the defense of the revolution. Even after the inauguration of Joseph Stalin's "Socialism in One Country" thesis in the mid-1920s, Soviet propagandists continued to view class as a more fundamental social category than others drawn along ethnic or national indexes. This ideological line was so consistent that déclassé elements (former members of the clergy, aristocracy, bourgeoisie, and czarist gendarmerie) were officially barred from bearing arms in defense of the USSR inasmuch as they were deemed incapable of genuine loyalty to the workers' state.

But events toward the end of the 1920s—particularly the 1927 war scare and the launch of the First Five-Year Plan (1928–32)—seem to have led Stalin to call such militancy into question. Acknowledging in a major speech in 1931 that Marx and Engels had been right, and that "in the past we didn't have and could not have had a fatherland," he cautioned against taking such a line of reasoning too far. After all, "now, since we've overthrown capitalism and power belongs to the working class, we have a fatherland and will defend its independence." What was responsible for this volte-face? Apparently, the party leadership was frustrated by ineffective social mobilization at home and fading prospects for world revolution abroad. Sensing that orthodox Marxism-Leninism and its materialist, class-based ideological line were too arcane and abstract to rally the USSR's poorly educated population, Stalin and his colleagues began to look for a more pragmatic, populist alternative, ultimately promoting a strikingly conventional sense of patriotism for mass consumption. Launched in 1934, this campaign rallied to the Soviet cause not only members of the working class but also peasants, bureaucrats, and the educated elite, indicating that the 1920s orthodox view of class-based internationalist loyalty was to be supplanted by a new understanding of patriotism linked to membership in Soviet society.

Although it never completely eclipsed commitments to class and internationalism, this increasingly traditional sense of patriotism fit well alongside other new populist elements of Soviet propaganda, including formerly taboo subjects like individual heroism and the Russian national past. A marked break with the previous decade's emphasis on materialism and anonymous social forces, this propaganda quickly led to the construction of a pantheon of Soviet heroes, socialist myths, and modern-day fables, the endorsement of a new artistic genre (socialist realism), and the revival of prominent names from the pre-revolutionary Russian arts and sciences—Mikhail Lomonosov, Aleksandr Pushkin, Mikhail Glinka, Ilya Repin, Dmitri Mendeleev, and so on. By 1936, the Soviet Olympus was strikingly diverse and accessible, consisting of an array of inspirational patriotic heroes from the past and present.

But the Great Terror (1936–38) crippled much of this campaign within a few years of its inception, as famous personalities from the party, military, and intelligentsia fell victim to the purge. Although the censor attempted to withdraw propaganda mentioning newly exposed "enemies of the people" from circulation for reediting, the unpredictable nature of the terror militated against this solution in the long term. In what appears to have been a more or less desperate move, ideologists shifted the emphasis of the official line from the celebration of Soviet patriots to one oriented around epic military and political leaders from the pre-revolutionary Russian national past—Peter the Great, Alexander Nevsky, Aleksandr Suvorov, and so on. This turnabout from proletarian internationalism to something reminiscent of Russian nationalism fit well within the party's increasingly pragmatic focus on traditional patriotism and old-fashioned values like state building, etatism, and national defense. Stalin called for adjustments to be made to the official conceptualization of "Soviet patriotism" at a party congress in 1939, apparently in order to account for this Russo-centric redux.

Increasingly routine during the late 1930s, the conflation of Soviet and Russian patriotism mounted during what was known in the USSR as the Great Fatherland War (1941–45), and climaxed in a frenzy of xenophobic Russian chauvinism during the late 1940s and early 1950s. Stalin's death in 1953 allowed for an amelioration of the worst excesses of this line, and party ideologists revived aspects of its emphasis on internationalism and class consciousness soon thereafter in an attempt to distinguish Soviet patriotism from other sorts of "bourgeois" political loyalties. Official handbooks like *The Great Soviet Encyclopedia* claimed that Soviet patriotism combined a love for one's national traditions with respect for other working peoples along with the universal goals of socialism and communism. Yet even as Soviet patriotism broke with its emphasis on pre-revolutionary Russia, it retained a strong, conventional focus on duty and sacrifice in the name of national defense, often illustrated through the Soviets' wartime experience of 1941–45. Ultimately, this "myth of the war" accounted for more of Soviet patriotism's mass appeal during the post-Stalin period than its ostensibly socialist nature. Genuinely popular between the 1950s and 1970s, Soviet patriotism waned in the 1980s as the USSR's economy stagnated and memories of the Great Patriotic War faded from popular consciousness.

See also Great Patriotic War; Internationalism; Nationalism; Socialism in One Country; Stalinism.

FURTHER READING

Brandenberger, D. *National Bolshevism: Stalinist Mass Culture and the Formation of Modern Russian National Identity, 1931–1956.* Cambridge, MA: Harvard University Press, 2002.

van Ree, E. *The Political Thought of Joseph Stalin: A Study in Twentieth-Century Revolutionary Patriotism.* London: RoutledgeCurzon, 2002.

Weiner, A. "The Making of a Dominant Myth: The Second World War and the Construction of Political Identities within the Soviet Polity." *Russian Review* 55, no. 4 (1996): 638–60.

DAVID BRANDENBERGER

Soviet-Yugoslavia Break

The Soviet-Yugoslav breakup in 1948 was the first split in the Soviet bloc, and led to the unprecedented expulsion of a Communist regime—Yugoslavia—from the bloc and the Communist movement.

Up until 1948, the Yugoslav regime, in terms of its internal structure and development, had been the closest of the people's democracies to the Soviet (Stalinist) model of the period. It had been an important participant in the formation of the Soviet bloc (the socialist camp), and the creation and subsequent activity of the Cominform. The Yugoslav leadership, led by Josip Broz Tito, was oriented toward the USSR, acted in concert with it in the international arena, and had in every way copied the Soviet experience. The USSR had lent full foreign support to Yugoslavia, was its chief economic partner, and played the predominant role in preparing its cadres as well as training and outfitting its army and secret services. Moscow regarded Yugoslavia as its most trusted ally.

Complications had also arisen in Soviet-Yugoslav relations, though, and the USSR became critical of certain steps taken by the Yugoslav leadership. Even during World War II, when in the early stages of the struggle to free the country from the Axis occupation, the Communist Party of Yugoslavia (CPYu) proclaimed its revolutionary goals in too radical a fashion, Moscow criticized it for moving ahead in a way that could threaten the creation of a broad liberation front in Yugoslavia, and also might endanger future relations with the USSR and the Western Allies. Still, when the war ended and up until the 1948 clash itself, the Soviet side did not attach any particular significance to these preceding phenomena, since analogous things were happening in other Communist parties as well. There was, indeed, almost no Soviet criticism of the internal political decisions made by the Yugoslav leadership in relation to postwar development.

There were certain complications in the economic cooperation between the two countries, particularly regarding the creation of Soviet-Yugoslav joint stock companies in Yugoslavia. In April 1947, Stalin, to avoid strife, proposed that the Soviet Union, instead of forming these joint companies, simply help with the industrialization of Yugoslavia by delivering equipment on a credit basis, by providing technical documentation, and by sending specialists. But Moscow was also dissatisfied with Yugoslav actions in the international arena, deeming them excessive, and upset that Yugoslavia had not coordinated them with the USSR in advance. This applied especially to the question of Trieste, and even more, the dominating role Belgrade was attempting to play in Albania and Bulgaria. This dissatisfaction became more pronounced during the second half of 1947 and early 1948. It was caused by three events.

The first event was the announcement in early August 1947 by the Bulgarian and Yugoslav governments that they had agreed on a treaty of friendship, cooperation, and mutual aid. This was done against the instructions of Stalin, who wanted to postpone the Bulgarian-Yugoslav treaty, since it was provoking the objections of England and the United States, until a peace agreement with Bulgaria could come into effect, which would remove the grounds for the Western objections. Stalin condemned the Bulgarian leader, Georgi Dimitrov, and Tito for this action. Both leaders accepted the criticism and waited until November 1947 to conclude the treaty officially, after first receiving Moscow's permission.

But on January 17, 1948, the second event took place: an announcement by Dimitrov, also not cleared with Moscow, of plans to create a federation/confederation and a customs union of all the people's democracies, plus Greece, where Dimitrov foresaw the creation of yet another people's democracy. This announcement also provoked Stalin's harsh criticism, which Dimitrov again accepted on the spot.

The third event concerned Albania, where Belgrade had been playing the role of patron and was worried that its position would be weakened by the growing participation of the USSR in Albania's development. In December 1947 and January 1948, the Yugoslav leadership tried to secure a confirmation from Stalin of his earlier expressed agreement to allow Yugoslav predominance in Albania. In answer, Stalin, as he had done when he had met with Tito in 1946, declared himself in favor of a close tie between Albania and Yugoslavia, even as far as their unification, which would amount to the incorporation of Albania into Yugoslavia—something that Yugoslavia had been pushing for. But now Stalin declared that the unification needed to be postponed until a more propitious moment. Whether what Stalin said reflected his real intentions or he just wanted to prevent the unification is unclear, but in any case Tito, when informed of Stalin's answer, went behind Moscow's back and asked Enver Hoxha, the Albanian head of state, to permit a Yugoslav division to be stationed in Albania. Hoxha, believing that the proposal had been cleared with Moscow, gave a positive answer. But when Moscow learned of Belgrade's intent, it responded negatively, and Tito halted the dispatch of the troops.

Although in all three cases, Belgrade and Sofia accepted the Kremlin's reprimands, Stalin moved quickly to see to it that the two countries took no further liberties. On February 10, 1948, at a meeting with highly placed representatives of Bulgaria and Yugoslavia, Stalin brought the recent events to the attention of his audience. He not only forbade the stationing of Yugoslav troops in Albania but even characterized Belgrade's push to unite Albania with Yugoslavia as the forerunner to establishing a Yugoslav-Bulgarian federation, to which Albania would later be added. This was his way of calling into question Tito's plans with respect to Albania.

After a meeting with them, both the Yugoslavs and the Bulgarians accepted criticism in a disciplined fashion. After the meeting, the Bulgarian leadership followed instructions, but the Yugoslav regime decided, for the time being, to reject a federation with Bulgaria and, instead, strove to convince Tirana to approve on its own both the stationing of Yugoslav troops in Albania and a union with Yugoslavia. In his inner circle, Tito and his associates expressed dissatisfaction with the policies of

the USSR, which they regarded as not taking into account Belgrade's real interests. This was something unprecedented. Previously, when the Yugoslavs would press toward something that might provoke a negative Soviet reaction, they might harbor some apprehensions about acting without prior consultation with Moscow. But now Yugoslav behavior had gone beyond the limits of traditional relations between leader and subordinate: even when the subordinate party allowed itself, where possible and where its specific interests were involved, to take certain liberties behind the leader's back, the subordinate was, nevertheless, still abiding by the rules and remaining a vassal in the hierarchical system. But this time, Belgrade had already received Stalin's explicit instructions and yet was moving ahead in direct violation of them.

When the Kremlin discovered these events in early March 1948, its reaction was swift and strong. Things became even worse when the USSR ambassador in Belgrade reported home to Moscow that Yugoslavia, despite its previous practice, was not furnishing the Soviets with secret working data about its economy (something later disproved by the Yugoslavs). During the second half of March, Moscow responded in a way that unleashed the Soviet-Yugoslav clash, although news about the conflict was kept secret until late June 1948. All Soviet military advisers and civilian specialists were withdrawn from Yugoslavia. In a series of letters, Stalin and Vyacheslav Molotov, without referring to the problems at the February 10 meeting, made broad—and baseless—political and ideological accusations against the Yugoslav leadership, charging it with opportunism, departures from Marxism-Leninism, and anti-Soviet policies. Tito and his closest colleagues, understanding that the Kremlin was now demanding a complete surrender from them, denied the charges. The Soviets informed the leaders of the other Communist parties in the Cominform. The latter, partly under Soviet pressure, agreed with the accusations, whereupon at Moscow's initiative it was decided to review the "Yugoslav question" at a Cominform conference especially convened for this purpose. Since there was no doubt that any decision made there would come from the Kremlin, the Yugoslav leadership refused to participate. The conference, which took place from June 19–23, 1948, adopted a resolution repeating the claims made in the Soviet letters. The resolution was published, informing the world of the conflict, and that Yugoslavia had been expelled from the Soviet bloc and the Cominform. The whole Communist movement declared its solidarity with the resolution.

Belgrade now publicly rejected the accusations. The Kremlin along with the whole socialist camp and Communist movement then launched a propaganda war against "Tito's clique." The campaign reached its peak with a resolution at a new Cominform conference in November 1949, in which the Yugoslav leadership was characterized as a "clique of murderers and spies," which, led on by the "imperialist camp," had defected to the other side, carrying out a "transition to fascism." The socialist countries now rescinded their treaties and agreements with Yugoslavia, breaking off economic ties. The situation along Yugoslavia's borders with the people's democracies became tense and fraught with the danger of aggression from the Soviet bloc. Faced with this threat and an economic blockade, the Yugoslav regime embarked on a partial foreign policy rapprochement with the West, and received indispensable economic and military aid from it. During the early 1950s, as an ideological counterweight to the Kremlin's anti-Tito campaign, the Yugoslav side set forth a new, official "Yugoslav doctrine," which characterized the Stalinist system as a distortion of Marxism-Leninism, and the development of Yugoslavia itself as a movement along the path to true socialism. There now began a gradual reform, stretching out for several decades, of the internal structure of Yugoslavia based on so-called self-government, which preserved an authoritarian one-party system, but made the system more liberal politically, at least compared to the Soviet model. The reform also introduced certain elements of the market into the economy.

The Yugoslav regime proved stable enough to withstand Stalin's campaign. After Stalin's death, on March 5, 1953, his successors in the Kremlin soon turned away from the previous policy, and in 1954, initiated a so-called normalization of relations between the USSR and the rest of the socialist camp and Yugoslavia. It was publicly admitted in May 1955 that the charges against Tito and his colleagues had been false. Moscow now counted on drawing Yugoslavia back toward the socialist camp and perhaps returning it there altogether. But both during Tito's rule and after his death, the Yugoslav leadership preferred to preserve its independence, maneuvering between the two global political and military blocs. It pursued this policy up to the end of the Communist regime and the breakup of Yugoslavia itself, all of which coincided with the fall of the Soviet regime and the dissolution of the USSR.

See also Cominform; Nonalignment; People's Democracy; Socialist Camp; Stalin, Joseph; Tito, Josip Broz.

FURTHER READING

Gibjanskij, L. "Mosca-Belgrado, uno scisma da repensare. Il conflitto sovietico-jugoslavo del 1948: cause, modalità, consequenze." *Ventunesimo Secolo* 1 (2002): 45–59.

———, ed. "Sekretnaja sovetsko-jugoslavskaja perepiska 1948 goda." *Voprosy istorii* 4–5 (1992): 119–36; 6–7 (1992): 158–72; 10 (1992): 141–60.

———. "The 1948 Soviet-Yugoslav Clash: Historiographic Versions and New Archival Sources." In *Jugoslavija v hladni vojni—Yugoslavia in the Cold War*, ed. J. Fischer et al., 49–70. Ljubljana: Institut za novejso zgodovino, 2004.

———. "The Soviet-Yugoslav Conflict and the Soviet Bloc." In *The Soviet Union and Europe in the Cold War, 1943–53*, ed. F. Gori and S. Pons, 222–45. New York: St. Martin's Press, 1996.

———. "The Soviet-Yugoslav Split." In *Revolution and Resistance in Eastern Europe: Challenges to Communist Rule*, ed. K. McDermott and M. Stibbe, 17–36. Oxford, UK: Berg, 2006.

Procacci, Giuliano, et al., eds. *The Cominform: Minutes of the Three Conferences 1947/1948/1949*. Milan: Feltrinelli Editore, 1994.

The Soviet-Yugoslav Dispute. London: Royal Institute of International Affairs, 1948.

LEONID JA. GIBJANSKIJ

Sovietization

"Sovietization" is a generalized notion that first appeared in print in political journalism, and then became current in political science and historiographical writing. It normally designates state and social patterns based on those that evolved in the USSR. Most often, the term refers directly to the creation of a state-political system of the Soviet type. In its broader sense, however, it denotes a system akin to the Soviet system in economic, societal, and spiritual terms.

In today's scholarly literature, Sovietization is used not so much to denote what happened during the Bolshevik Revolution itself—that is, to refer to the formation of the Soviet Union and the model that emerged there. It is used more frequently to designate the processes involved in reproducing the model itself, or modifications thereof. According to some scholars, the first such "reproductions" were a product of the extension of Soviet power at the beginning of the 1920s to a number of territories in southern Caucasus and central Asia, which up to 1917 had been non-Russian outlying districts of the Russian Empire or regions under the empire's protection. While the Bolshevik Revolution was taking place mostly within the more central confines of the empire, there were local, non-Soviet creations of states in these outlying areas as well (in Georgia, Armenia, Azerbaijan, and the Bukhara and Khivin regions).

Yet the establishment of Soviet power in these regions, and particularly those in southern Caucasus, should be seen as somewhat foreshortened—as only one of the component parts of an overall succession, during the period from 1917 to the early 1920s, of revolutionary eruptions with their peripheries linked to the center. This succession embraced an ethically and culturally heterogeneous area under the previously unified but now disrupted sovereignty of the Russian Empire, now converted into a Soviet empire that included most of the same territory. And whatever one's viewpoint, the reproduction of the Soviet state and societal models was undeniably repeated much later as well, during and after World War II, to say nothing of imitations outside the borders of the USSR in countries where Communist regimes had been established.

As far as territories added to the Soviet Union from 1939 to 1945 were concerned, whether there was outright annexation of whole countries adjacent to its borders—as with Latvia, Lithuania, and Estonia—or the seizure of various regions through invasion and appropriation—Poland (western Ukraine, also known as eastern Galicia, and western Belarus), Finland (the regions of the Karelian Isthmus, the western and northern Ladoga regions, Kuolayarvi, and certain other areas), Romania (Bessarabia, northern Bukovina, and the region between them in northern Romanian Moldova), and Czechoslovakia (the Trans-Carpathian Ukraine, also called Sub-Carpathian Rus)—Sovietization was brought into effect by Soviet power. From the beginning, the goal was the expansion of the already-existing system in the Soviet Union to its newly acquired territories. Accordingly, Sovietization in these areas was achieved at a rapid pace and was implemented by the same methods as had been used in the previous Soviet Union, and included all the same governmental and societal components and forms of life as the "old" USSR.

In addition, World War II resulted in the further annexation by the USSR of regions from the defeated Axis countries: East Prussia from Germany and the island of Sakhalin and the Kurile Islands from Japan, with the Soviet system introduced in these areas as well. Here, though, it is difficult to speak of Sovietization in the same sense as applied to the territories annexed from 1939 to 1945, because there was practically no population in these places that needed to be Sovietized. By the time East Prussia was incorporated into the USSR, the population, which up to 1945 was ethnically German, had been entirely deported. As for Sakhalin and the Kurile Islands, the great majority were ethnic Japanese and assimilated local populations (except for the few Far Eastern ethnic inhabitants who had mostly preserved their traditional, primitive way of life) whose numbers were rapidly decreasing. The deported populations were replaced by immigrants from other regions of the USSR, for whom the Soviet system was already the normal social milieu, now transplanted, as it were, to their new homes.

As far as the Communist regimes established outside the USSR were concerned, the first had come into being, with Soviet help, as early as the 1920s in two underdeveloped countries that were southern neighbors of the USSR: Outer Mongolia and Tuva, which became the Mongolian People's Republic and the Tuvan People's Republic, respectively. For practical purposes, these entities were already more or less under Soviet protection, Sovietization was carried out under the USSR's direction, and in 1944 Tuva was incorporated into the Soviet Union as an autonomous region. Still, the creation of most new Communist regimes outside the USSR would occur at a much later date. The largest number of them came into being at the end of World War II. These regimes were in Yugoslavia, Albania, Bulgaria, Poland, Romania, Hungary, Czechoslovakia, and the Soviet zone of occupation in Germany, which became the German Democratic Republic.

The first postwar years saw the creation of Communist regimes in North Korea and continental China as well. In the mid-1950s, an independent Communist state was established in North Vietnam, to which South Vietnam was added two decades later. In the 1960s, a left-wing revolutionary regime, established in 1959 in Cuba, also became Communist, and as did Laos and Cambodia in the 1970s. All of these regimes introduced Sovietization in one form or another.

All of these developments came about due to a number of factors, but the most important were probably the following:

1. the spread of doctrine in the Communist movement (or at least in a large part of it), which was

mostly, if not entirely, analogous to the doctrine that prevailed in Russia/USSR when the Soviet system was established

2. goals of social reconstruction, which were common if not to all, then at least to the majority of the Communist parties, in which similarity to Russian Soviet methods and those of other converts to these methods was largely assumed

3. the quite similar conditions under which the Soviet regime and the Communist regimes in a number of other countries were created—something that drove these countries to make decisions parallel to Soviet ones

4. the direct influence of the Soviet experience—in some cases, borrowed directly by other countries' Communist parties, which took it as the standard, or at least regarded it as best suited to their own needs; and in other cases, either suggested or imposed outright by the Soviets, where the latter considered this necessary

5. the direct Soviet participation in establishing the majority of the other Communist regimes

The influence of these factors was different in different countries. Of course, in the same way as the practical potential of each Communist Party differed in each country undergoing Sovietization, the practical policies of the Kremlin also differed in each country, since in both cases things depended on the concrete situation that had developed, both inside the individual countries and in the international arena as well. The result was the emergence of different types of Sovietization, with their own specific forms, mechanisms, tempos, and stages.

Thus, for instance, in Eastern Europe, where the largest group of Communist regimes came into being more or less simultaneously, the Sovietization process had both common traits and noticeable typological differences. When the countries of Eastern Europe were freed from Hitler's yoke in 1944 and 1945, so-called people's democracies were created. Their emergence was a consequence of both the internal sociopolitical processes in each Eastern European state and the unswerving force of Soviet policy in the context of its troops' presence in the greater part of the region. The interaction of these two factors was different in each country. In Yugoslavia and Albania—although both enjoyed Soviet foreign policy support, and in the case of Yugoslavia, military support as well—the establishment of people's democracies was a function of mostly internal sociopolitical

factors. Even during the Axis occupation, these two countries had drawn a large share of their populations into the resistance and created powerful left-oriented military-political movements. These movements played a substantial military role in the liberation of the countries, and at the same time, emerged victorious in the internal civil war being waged together. As a result, regimes became established that the Communists were able to monopolize. In Poland, Romania, and Hungary, on the contrary, direct Soviet intervention was critical in creating their people's democracies. It was only the Soviet presence that enabled the local Communist parties, whose own power was insufficient to the task, to occupy the key positions of power in Poland and Romania, and quite conspicuous posts in Hungary. Finally, in Bulgaria and Czechoslovakia, the Soviet presence was important, if not decisive in the emergence of people's democracies, but it was combined with the effect of internal political forces, which at times almost rivaled Soviet influence.

In sum, the Eastern European people's democracies were at first quite different from each other. They could be divided into three basic types. The first type, characteristic of Yugoslavia and Albania, was a virtual Communist monopoly of power, albeit with a certain faux parliamentary facade. There, in essence, one-party systems were quickly established, and any possible legal opposition was forcibly put down or repressed. This was accompanied by large-scale appropriations, which lead to a domination of the economy by the state. All this meant that from the beginning, these countries were also subjected to forced Sovietization. In the second type of people's democracies, that which prevailed in Bulgaria, Poland, and Romania, the governments were dominated by Communists to the point of being near-dictatorships, but with elements of a forced coalition, which included the existence of certain partly genuine but restricted non-Communist groups in the government; this was a small dose of a multiparty system, which could include an opposition faction. But if in Poland and Romania the Communists and their left-wing allies lacked the support of most of the population, in Bulgaria the Communists enjoyed popular support, even though it was rarely overwhelming. Finally, in the third type of people's democracy, that which took shape in Czechoslovakia and Hungary, the regimes were composed of a more genuine coalition partnership of Communist parties and leftist groups close to them, on the one hand, and citizen-democratic groups, with a somewhat conservative orientation, on the other. Here there could be an approximate parity of power in both types, or even a predominance of non-Communist partners over the Communists and their left-wing allies. All this basically reflected the relative influence of the two entities within these two countries.

With respect to the regimes of the second and third types mentioned above, the Kremlin and the Communist parties it controlled at first refrained from the Sovietization they had imposed in Yugoslavia and Albania, taking into account both the internal situation in the countries with those regimes and the position of the Western powers. Instead, they adopted a course of "stretched out" Sovietization, in a non-Soviet form, with the Communist parties employing tactics of political mimicry and fraudulent coalitions, affecting the attributes of multiparty and even parliamentary systems. In the political arena, efforts were concentrated on gradually increasing the role of Communist parties (or in the case of the second type, virtual dictatorship) in the management of state affairs. They fostered the removal from power (or in the case of the third type, at first the mere pushing away from power) of any forces that opposed the Communists, whether they were its rivals or just temporary fellow travelers. At the same time, the Communist parties strove to keep their left-wing partners in a subordinate position. In the socioeconomic sphere, there were parallel efforts to broaden the government sector of the economy. In places where the Communist parties held most of the power, basically in regimes of the second type, these policies advocated applying a certain degree of administrative pressure, repression against political opponents, and falsification of elections.

By 1947, though, the stretched out Sovietization policy had begun to yield to a policy of imposed Sovietization. In countries with regimes of the second type, Communist authorities now began to liquidate those opposition parties and "partner parties" in the government coalitions that had become undesirable. Administrative coercion and repression now became the order of the day, to the point of falsely accusing party leaders of antistate conspiracies, staging show trials, and banning parties outright. In countries with regimes of the third type, special services, controlled by the Communists, also fabricated similar accusations against functionaries of parties that were "partner opponents" of the Communist parties in government coalitions.

In Hungary, where the Soviet military took direct part in these activities, this led to a government revolt, as a result of which the Communist Party seized power and subsequently banned all parties opposed to the Communists. In Czechoslovakia, too, where Communist fabrications of similar accusations at first failed, an internal political crisis arose that, in February 1948, led to a Communist takeover. Together with the forced removal of opposition parties or partner opponents in the ruling coalition, the Communists, who by now had achieved full dictatorship, did away with their left-wing allies in 1948–49: the Social Democratic parties were subjected to a purge or merged with the Communist Party, while the left-wing peasant party and others were either dissolved or transformed into entities that were pure window dressing.

In countries that previously had regimes of the second or third type, a Communist monopoly of power and a one-party system were established, as had already happened in states with regimes of the first type. All this was carried out by methods of Sovietization of the economy and other spheres of life and society, similar to the measures taken by regimes of the first type. The systems thus created in Eastern Europe now became even more analogous to the Soviet structure, down to the liquidation of private peasant holdings through forcibly creating quasicollective farms, which were in fact run by the state (though in Yugoslavia and Poland this policy did not succeed, and most farms remained in private hands).

Other countries that established Communist regimes—particularly China, Vietnam, and Cuba—where Communists came into power independently, without Soviet intervention, developed their own types of Sovietization. While often quite different from each other, the forms these countries created essentially imitated, if not outright copied, the patterns outlined above. And when each of these cases is examined, difficult questions inevitably arise: To what extent were the programs of the new regimes influenced by their own societal goals, the special conditions under which they themselves operated, and the homegrown doctrinal notions of those who worked to fulfill the goals? On the other hand, to what degree were they influenced by the Soviet model and its later instantiations?

See also Collectivization of the Countryside; Command Economy, The; People's Democracy; Single-Party System; Soviet Occupation of Germany; State, The; World War II.

FURTHER READING

Gibjanskij, L. "Sowjetisierung Osteuropas—Charakter und Typologie." In *Sowjetisierung und Eigenständigkeit in der*

SBZ/DDR (1945–1953)., ed. M. Lemke. Cologne: Böhlau, 1999.

Naimark, N. M., and L. Gibjanskij, eds. *The Establishment of Communist Regimes in Eastern Europe, 1944–1949.* Boulder, CO: Westview Press, 1997.

Watson, H. S. *The East European Revolution.* London: Methuen, 1950.

LEONID JA. GIBJANSKIJ

Soviets

Soviets were originally workers' councils set up in the revolutionary situation of the Russian Empire in 1905. The first was established in Ivanovo-Voznesensk in May. Industrial workers and intellectual revolutionaries combined their efforts to organize strikes and demonstrations, and the soviets were ready instruments to this end. Quickly the leaders turned them into agencies of local self-rule by "the masses." One by one, however, the soviets were suppressed by the imperial army and czarist order was restored.

The memory of the political, social, and cultural ebullience of these councils was not, however, lost. As soon as it appeared Nicholas II would be toppled from his throne in February 1917, the revolutionaries began to reform soviets. This was done on the basis of election, often at open meetings of workers. Other urban residents, especially the garrison soldiers, copied the procedure. The soviets were organs of the lower classes in society, and they immediately set about monitoring the activities of local government as well as local employers. They created a police force in the form of the Red Guards. They established educational and welfare facilities. Whenever the need arose, they put workers and soldiers on the streets to protest against abuses of power. In Petrograd, as the capital had been called since the start of the First World War, the Soviet of Workers' and Soldiers' Deputies had the informal authority to stymie uncongenial measures undertaken by the provisional government. Soviets inaugurated their own Central Executive Committee.

To the Bolsheviks they appeared a government in waiting. Immediately after the February Revolution, however, it was the Mensheviks and Socialist-Revolutionaries who held majorities in urban soviets throughout the country. Their authority was, however, vulnerable to the regulation that any soviet deputy could be recalled and replaced at a moment's notice. As the unpopularity of the provisional government increased, Menshevik and Socialist-Revolutionary deputies got into trouble with their electors and their places were taken by more militant revolutionaries. The chief beneficiaries were the Bolsheviks. The Kronstadt Soviet and the Tsaritsyn Soviet were among the earliest gains for the Bolshevik party in midsummer. Petrograd and Moscow followed in September.

Leninist strategy held that power should be "transferred" to the soviets by popular insurrection. Lenin himself tried to suspend the strategy in July when the soviets, still led by Mensheviks and Socialist-Revolutionaries, approved warrants for the arrest of leading Bolsheviks. But generally the Bolsheviks appreciated the hold that the soviets had on the people's imagination. If the projected seizure of power was not to appear as the coup d'état of a single party, it was critical that the Bolsheviks continue to function under the aegis of the soviets. A further incentive was that many—perhaps most—Bolsheviks wanted the provisional government to be supplanted by a coalition of all existing Socialist parties. Lenin and Trotsky ostensibly went along with this plan. In fact, though, they had no intention of operating in a regime shared with the Mensheviks and the Socialist-Revolutionaries.

Such was the authority and prestige of the Petrograd Soviet that its Military-Revolutionary Committee had no difficulty in overturning the provisional government in October 1917. The Second Congress of Soviets, having received power, sanctioned the establishment of a state order based exclusively on the soviets. This involved the disenfranchisement of social groups not entitled to vote in soviet elections. The Bolshevik Central Committee, intent on class dictatorship, spread the network of soviets to include the peasantry. They also vigorously asserted the party's control over the soviets and closed them down whenever Mensheviks made an electoral comeback. "Mass organizations," which had been powerful in opposition to the crumbling forces of the old propertied elites, were no match for the organized coercion of the Bolshevik party.

Nevertheless the myth of proletarian self-rule through soviets was propagated worldwide by the Communist International. While "soviet power" in the Soviet Union was crushed, Communist parties drew inspiration from the saga of 1917 and strove to find their own way of setting up class-based organizations for revolutionary seizures of power. Munich and Hungary in 1919 were the first to pick up the soviet model. In a heavily modified form this is also what occurred in the Chinese revolution of 1949. Meanwhile the USSR had abolished class-based representative institutions in 1936 and asserted that the entire people could engage in self-rule. The reality, however, was unchanged: Communists went on ruling through a one-party, one-ideology dictatorship.

See also Bolshevism; Russian Revolution and Civil War.

FURTHER READING

Anweiler, O. *The Soviets: The Russian Workers, Peasants, and Soldiers Councils, 1905–1921.* New York: Pantheon Books, 1975.

Keep, J.L.H. *The Russian Revolution: A Study in Mass Mobilisation.* London: Weidenfeld and Nicolson, 1976.

ROBERT SERVICE

Spanish Civil War

The Spanish civil war began on July 17, 1936, with the rebellion of the Spanish Army of Africa in the Spanish Protectorate of Morocco and ended de facto on March 28, 1939, with the fall of Madrid. It concluded symbolically on April 1 with the "Victory Bulletin" in which General Francisco Franco proclaimed his triumph and the destruction of the "Red Army," his term for the armed forces of the republic.

The war was triggered by the partial failure of a military insurrection in July 1936. The insurrection's goals had been to occupy the principal cities in the country, depose the Popular Front government, and initiate a "surgical operation" aimed, in Franco's words, at annihilating the Spanish Left. The military conspiracy, which eventually led to the insurrection, started with the Popular Front's electoral victory on February 16, 1936, and was directed by General Emilio Mola, who occupied a strategic position in the military government of Navarre, the most traditionalist region of the country. The antirepublican aims of the conspiracy were held as a close secret, but this did not prevent an armed popular uprising from suppressing the insurrection. The armed uprising, on July 18–28, was successful in most of the major cities, especially Madrid, Barcelona, and Valencia; the major exceptions were the cities of Seville and Zaragoza. The results in Madrid and Barcelona were decisive. The coup had failed, but the rebels could count on support in vast areas of rural Spain

(Old Castile, Navarre, Alava, Galicia, Aragon, parts of Estremadura, pockets of Asturias and Andalusia, the Canary Islands and Mallorca, and the protectorate); a military structure (which was instead falling apart in the republican areas); and colonial troops that at the end of July were transported by air, on Junker 52s, from Morocco to the mainland. The prompt support of Germany and Italy along with the rebels' superiority in terms of military equipment meant they could face a civil war of conquest with favorable prospects.

The war's first phase began in late July and ended in mid-November 1936, with the successful defense of Madrid. The rebels advance from Andalusia toward the capital was mostly successful thanks to the annihilation of the republican militias by regular troops headed by the Foreign Legion. It was also marked by contrasting events: while passing through Badajoz, the rebels were responsible for a horrific massacre; later, in Toledo, the city's Alcazar became a symbol of their military heroism. In mid-August the European powers proclaimed they would not intervene—a decision that favored the rebels—and the republicans' initial optimism was replaced by fear of a possible defeat. Europe's declaration was followed by Joseph Stalin's first decision to help, which materialized with the September 18 agreement to organize what would become known as the International Brigades. On September 1 the republican government of José Giral gave way to the populist front headed by the socialist Francisco Largo Caballero, which on November 4 came to include Communists and anarcho-syndicalists.

The initial phases of a revolutionary process in republican Spain, marked by popular resistance and social mobilization, were destined to produce a fragmentation of power. Both sides witnessed violence aimed at the elimination of the political adversary. But there were differences in the goals, duration, and authorization of these acts of violence perpetrated by each side. Exterminating the enemy was one of the motives that inspired the military coup, whether the enemy was considered to be a politician from the Left, a trade union activist, or a schoolteacher. And the abuses committed by Franco's forces would remain true to these initial goals: they maintained the characteristics of mass repression throughout the war and after its conclusion. On the republican side instead, repression was largely the product of popular anger, to which the republican government attempted to give judicial form (popular tribunals). In addition to this popular element, radical groups—be they anarchist, left socialist, or Communist—spread their own kind of terror, often of an anticlerical nature, especially during Madrid's moment of greatest danger (the massacre of Paracuellos in November 1936). These acts were never sanctioned by the government, however, and were always denounced by republican politicians.

The republican institutions survived in appearance only: the ensuing power vacuum was filled by the resisting forces, labor unions, and workers' parties, which took it on themselves to organize militias with the help of those military forces that had remained faithful. Power was distributed according to the support that the different organizations enjoyed on a territorial basis. In Catalonia, the hegemony of the Confederación Nacional del Trabajo (National Confederation of Labor, or CNT) and the Federación Anarquista Iberica (Iberian Anarchist Federation, or FAI) resulted in a social experiment: the economy was managed by the trade unions, leading to the collectivization of the factories, services, and agriculture. The militias under trade union control asserted their power through force and represented an important obstacle to the war effort on the Aragon front. In the rest of loyal Spain the thrust toward collectivization in the rural areas was considered an appropriate response to the social and political threat that Franco's rebellion represented. Revolutionary ideology and the attempt to defend group and self-interests during a crisis were crucial here. By contrast, socialization prevailed in Madrid and the urban centers controlled by the socialists. The Basque countries were the exception, particularly the province of Biscay, which remained under republican control, and maintained a capitalist economy and religious practices under the rule of the Partido nacionalista vasco (Basque Nationalist Party), which starting on October 7, 1936, presided over an almost independent national front government that favored the recently approved Statute of Autonomy.

The geographically diffuse nature of the military insurrection resulted in a temporary lack of leadership among the rebels when the designated leader, General José Sanjurjo, died on July 20 in an airplane accident. On July 24, 1936, on Mola's initiative, the Junta de Defensa Nacional (Junta for National Defense) was created in Burgos, headed by General Miguel Cabanellas, the leader of the Zaragoza rebels, but also a Mason and an ex-republican deputy. In the fight for supremacy among the rebel leaders Mola opposed Franco. Mola had been blocked in his advance on the capital from the north because of the fighting in the mountains of Madrid.

Franco was of higher rank; as head of the Army of Africa, the most professional component of Spain's army, he enjoyed a great advantage over his rival Mola in his advance on Madrid; and on September 27, 1936, he also gained a symbolic investiture as liberator of those besieged in the Alcazar in Toledo. On September 28, with Mola's opposition, Franco was declared head of state and generalissimo, and a military dictatorship was born on October 1. Conservative political forces faded into the background, while the Spanish Falange (a Fascist political organization founded by José Antonio Primo de Rivera) assumed a dominant position, notwithstanding the rivalry with carlism, a monarchical political movement, at the regional level. The incarceration of Primo de Rivera, who was executed on November 20, allowed Franco to control both the Catholic extreme Right and the Falange, which had become an instrument of military power. With the support of the Church, which conferred the rank of a crusade to the insurrection, Franco's figure was sacralized: he was exalted as the caudillo and savior of Spain.

The Popular Front lacked such cohesiveness, though both the Partido comunista de Espana (Communist Party of Spain, or Pce) and to a lesser degree the Partido socialista obrero español (Spanish Socialist Workers' Party, or PSOE) advocated it. Caballero attempted to unify all the revolutionary forces, but was increasingly distrustful of the proselytizing by the Communists and their increased presence in positions of power. The Communists, for their part, combined the will to defend democracy with efforts to gain ground at the PSOE's expense, while simultaneously proposing unification to them. Moscow's desire to conduct an anti-Trotskyist struggle soon also intervened, and it targeted a small local radical party, the Partido obrero de unificacion marxista (Workers' Party of Marxist Unification, or Poum), with roots in Catalonia—a party whose propaganda supported a Soviet-style takeover of power and the overthrow of the democratic republic. The republican parties, just like the republic's own president, Manuel Azaña, played a marginal role. Within the anarchosyndicalist movement the commitment to anti-Fascist unity, which was concretely represented by the presence of four ministers in the government, conflicted with the anarchists' efforts to maintain the power they had conquered in Catalonia and Aragon. As Palmiro Togliatti (secretary of the Italian Communist Party for several decades after World War II) would also remark, the Popular Front existed only on paper.

Despite the successful defense of Madrid, the republic needed aid from abroad to succeed, and specifically supplies of arms and troops comparable to those that Franco was receiving. The thirty-four thousand volunteers in the International Brigades were outnumbered by the seventy to eighty thousand members of the Corpo Truppe Volontarie sent by Benito Mussolini, fifty-four thousand Moroccans, and the Portuguese, Irish, and above all Germans who, starting in the spring of 1937, formed the Condor Legion (a group of Luftwaffe pilots who volunteered to serve under the Falange's command in the civil war), giving the "national" air force a decisive superiority that Soviet help could not counterbalance. With the exception of Mexico, only the USSR helped the republic with armaments; the purchase of weapons was financed by depositing 510 tons of gold from the Banco de España in Moscow. There were contrasting judgments on the quality of the weapons, but without them the republic could not have resisted. Contrary to the predictions of the anti-Communists, the USSR continued to ship weapons even when the war was already lost, in the winter of 1938–39. The Italian and German contribution in terms of airplanes, artillery, tanks, and machine guns was reinforced by military, navy, and air force interventions intended to limit trade with Spain, in the shadow of nonintervention by the rest of Europe. The French Popular Front's closure of the border with France on August 8, 1936, aggravated the disparity in the two sides' access to military resources, to the obvious disadvantage of the legitimate government.

The reorganization of the popular army in any case caused the strategic failure of the offensives aimed at encircling Madrid, which dominated the war's second phase from November 1936 to March 1937. In the battle of Jarama (February 1937), the Francoists failed to cut the Madrid-Valencia road, the only tie between the capital and the rest of republican-controlled territory. The International Brigades were decimated, above all the Lincoln Brigade, and at least a third of those fallen on both sides were Italian—each side lost about twenty-five thousand. It was the last time the republic had the advantage of air superiority; later the Italian FIAT airplanes and the Condor Legion would arrive. A few days later, in March, the Italian Corpo Truppe Volontarie led a new offensive against Madrid, the battle of Guadalajara. It was another victory for the republic, both militarily and propagandistically, with Mussolini emerging as the great loser. The successes in the defense of Madrid did not block the Francoist advance on sec-

ondary fronts, though: the break in the siege of Oviedo (March) and the conquest of Malaga (February 8) were followed by repression. In this case the Pce engaged in a campaign to discredit the military policies of Caballero, in his role as head of the government and defense minister.

Given the impasse on the fronts in central Spain, in the war's third phase Franco decided to eliminate the isolated republican area in the North. On April 26, 1937, German aircraft destroyed Guernica, an open city and the spiritual capital of Biscay, killing hundreds. Guernica became the symbol of Francoist barbarism, although the dictator later tried to blame the city's defenders for the destruction. The destruction of Guernica allowed Franco to reap further benefits, suggesting that resistance on Bilbao's part would lead to similar results. The fall of Santander in August and the occupation of the republican Asturias in October gave Franco the human and material resources of the northern industrial provinces. The military balance between the two sides was definitely compromised. The popular army was not able to take advantage of the concentration of Francoist troops to the North. Following a proposal by the republican chief of the general staff, Colonel Vicente Rojo, and with the massive support of the Communists, the republican troops unleashed a vain offensive to break the encirclement of Madrid from the northeast. In the battle of Brunete in July 1937, following the pattern of offensives in World War I, the resistance and superior air power of Franco's forces carried the day.

Spring and summer 1937 were also months of radical changes and crisis in republican politics. The struggle for power in Catalonia, the malaise caused by the precarious nature of the resupply effort, and the Stalinist pressures at the time of the Moscow trials led to riots that inflamed Barcelona on May 3–7. It was a civil war within the civil war. Order was restored at the price of repression within the CNT and Poum. The political fallout led to the end of the Caballero government, provoked by the Pce and the Socialist center with the blessing of President Azaña. The new government, headed by Juan Negrín and backed by the Pce, without the participation of the anarchosyndicalists, claimed as its principal objectives the state's reconstruction and the army's organization, with the aim of winning the war. For Negrín, the price of the alliance with the Pce was his tacit acceptance of the "Trotskyist" leader Andrés Nin's assassination by the People's Commissariat for Internal Affairs and the persecution of the Poum. The Soviets wanted to move beyond the pluralism of republican Spain and pave the way for a people's democracy, but that wish was never fulfilled.

The fifth phase of the war, from December 1937 to November 1938, was marked by Colonel Rojo's strategy: he attempted to anticipate Franco's potentially decisive offensives. These battles of attrition, conducted with inferior ground and, most importantly, air forces, entailed enormous costs. From December 1937 to January 1938, the temporary conquest of Teruel, a city of no strategic value, concluded with a nationalist counteroffensive that starting on March 9, led to the collapse of the republican front. On April 15, when the Francoist troops reached the Mediterranean, republican territory was divided in two. Another battle of attrition was conducted between July and November along the river Ebro, only serving to postpone the republic's death sentence while destroying the republican army.

On the political level, the alliance between Negrín and the Pce determined the policy of resistance at all costs: the president waited for the conflict to explode in Europe, and the Communists wanted to slow down the victory of the USSR's enemies. Even with these objectives in mind, there was a moment, in March 1938, when Stalin wanted the Communists to leave the government. Aware that defeat was inevitable, the Pce still preferred to remain the "party of war," while around them demoralization grew among the famished population. In April the removal of the openly defeatist Socialist defense minister, Indalecio Prieto, who opposed the Pce's hegemony, anticipated what would occur a year later, when in January 1939 Barcelona fell and the Francoist troops entered the city. On March 5, 1939, the commanders of the armed forces of the capital, General Miaja and Colonel Casado, toppled the Negrín government with a military coup in the republican area, in the vain hope that their anticommunism would induce Franco to clemency. The Junta de Defensa Nacional (National Defense Junta), headed by Casado, and backed by right-wing Socialists and trade unionists from the General Workers' Union and CNT, took power after a new war within the war, this time for the control of Madrid against Communist military resistance. Attempts at negotiation failed.

A long phase of reactionary Caesarism ensued, accompanied by a brutal repression that led to more than 50,000 executions after the war, compared to the 35,000 during the conflict itself. With the fall of Catalonia, 450,000 Spaniards crossed the border and about 15,000 fled from the East. In 1940 the number of political prisoners exceeded 250,000. Historian Anthony Beevor es-

timates the total number of victims, direct and indirect, of Franco's repression at 200,000. On another level the divisions among the opposition forces, characterized by a strong antagonism toward the Pce, lasted until Franco's death. This state of war remained in effect until April 7, 1948.

See also Antifascism; Comintern; Fascism; International Brigades; Popular Front; Stalinism; Trotskyism.

FURTHER READING

Beevor, A. *The Spanish Civil War*. London: Orbis Publications, 1982.

Bolloten, B. *The Spanish Civil War: Revolution and Counter-revolution*. Chapel Hill: University of North Carolina Press, 1991.

Howson, G. *Arms for Spain: The Untold Story of the Spanish Civil War*. London: Murray, 1998.

Kowalsky, D. *Stalin and the Spanish Civil War*. New York: Columbia University Press, 2003.

Ranzato, G. *L'eclissi della democrazia. La guerra civile spagnola e le sue origini, 1931–1939*. Turin: Bollati Boringhieri, 2004.

Skoutelsky, R. *L'espoir guidait leurs pas: les volontaires français dans les Brigades internationales, 1936–1939*. Paris: Grasset, 1998.

Thomas, H. *The Spanish Civil War*. New York: Harper, 1961.

Viñas, Á. *La Alemania nazi y el 18 de julio*. Madrid: Alianza, 1974.

ANTONIO ELORZA

Spies

The USSR's investment of personnel and resources in foreign intelligence combined with foreign Communists' willingness to assist the Soviets produced an extraordinary number of Communist spies. Several thousand foreign Communists along with hundreds of professional Soviet intelligence officers made Soviet espionage into a formidable asset of the USSR in the 1930s and 1940s. (With the coming of the Cold War and increased scrutiny of Communist movements by security services, this phenomenon declined.)

The Red Orchestra (Die Rote Kapelle) was the German counterintelligence label for World War II Soviet espionage networks. In Germany, the Red Orchestra was a large network with more than a hundred participants, a mixture of Communists and anti-Nazis of various persuasions. Its chief figure, Harro Schulze-Boysen (1909–42), a Luftwaffe headquarters' desk officer, was anti-Nazi rather than a Communist, but Arvid Harnack (1901–42), a government economist and the network's other leader, was an ardent Communist and established its link to Soviet military intelligence (GRU). Other members held positions in Wehrmacht counterespionage and the foreign ministry, and provided Moscow with extensive information on German military plans. The Gestapo uncovered the network in August 1942. Under torture those initially arrested identified others, and the apparatus was destroyed. Forty-six, including Schulze-Boysen and Harnack, were executed, and thirty were imprisoned.

Leopold Trepper (1904–82) supervised overlapping Red Orchestra networks in Belgium, Netherlands, and France. Trepper, a Polish Jew who had joined the Communist Party in Palestine and carried out Comintern work in France in the 1920s, had transferred to the GRU in the 1930s. Communists, many of them Comintern veterans, along with a few GRU professionals, staffed his networks. Key figures included Johann Wenzel, a German Communist in the Belgium network, and Dutch Cominternist Anton Winternink. Among Trepper's important sources were Henry Robinson, a German Communist (a 1919 Spartacist) who had gained French citizenship and supervised Soviet industrial espionage in France in the 1930s, and Vasili Maximovich. Maximovich was from an exiled White Russian family but he was secretly pro-Soviet. He worked as a Wehrmacht general's interpreter and married a German secretary in the Nazi military administration in Paris. German counterintelligence located these networks' radios and arrested their participants in 1941 and 1942. While many resisted painful interrogation (more than ninety were executed or died in prison), Wenzel, Winternink, Trepper, and others broke, betrayed additional network members, and sent deceptive radio reports to Moscow under Nazi direction. Wenzel and Trepper separately escaped in 1943, alerting Moscow of what had happened. In 1945, Trepper returned to Moscow and was imprisoned until 1954. He then returned to Poland in 1957 and later immigrated to Israel.

Hungarian Sándor Radó (1899–1981), assisted by Englishman Alexander Foote, directed the Red Orchestra in Switzerland. Radó, a commissar in Bela Kun's Red Army, had undertaken Comintern duties in the 1920s and transferred to the GRU in the 1930s. In 1938 Communist Party of Great Britain officials put Foote, a for-

mer International Brigades officer, in touch with Ursula Kuczynsky, a German Communist and GRU agent, who assigned him to Radó's apparatus. The network's chief source was Rudolf Rössler (1897–1958), an exiled German anti-Nazi publisher, the conduit for high-ranking anti-Nazi Wehrmacht officers who provided information on preparations for the invasion of the USSR as well as later information on German military activities that assisted Soviet military planning. Under German pressure, Swiss authorities arrested Foote in November 1943, and Radó went into hiding. Rössler was arrested in May 1944 but released in September, as was Foote. The GRU ordered Foote and Radó to Moscow in early 1945. It accused Radó of misconduct and imprisoned him until 1955, after which he returned to Hungary. Foote defected to British authorities in 1947 while on his way to an espionage assignment.

Britain's "Cambridge Spy Ring"—Donald Maclean (1913–83), H.A.R. (Kim) Philby (1912–88), Guy Burgess (1910–63), Anthony Blunt (1907–83), and John Cairncross (1913–95)—was drawn to communism while at Trinity College, Cambridge, in the 1930s. Maclean joined the diplomatic service, served as a senior official at Britain's Washington, DC, embassy from 1944 to 1948, and headed the Foreign Office's American Department in 1950—posts giving him access to important British and U.S. information. Philby joined the British Secret Intelligence Service in 1940, brought in as an assistant to Burgess, then a Secret Intelligence Service (SIS) officer. After World War II Philby headed the SIS anti-Soviet operations and warned Soviet intelligence of threats to its activities. In Washington, DC, in 1951 as the SIS liaison with the Central Intelligence Agency and Federal Bureau of Investigation (FBI), Philby learned that code breakers were close to identifying Maclean as a Soviet agent. Burgess, then a diplomat at Britain's Washington embassy and living in Philby's residence, hastily returned to London, warned Maclean, and both fled to Moscow. Philby, suspected of treachery, lost his SIS position but did not flee to Moscow until 1963. Blunt, a leading art historian, worked as a talent spotter of prospects for Soviet espionage. In 1963, the British Security Service learned of his espionage via the FBI from an American whom he had recruited in the 1930s. Blunt made a partial confession in 1964 but it remained secret until 1979. Cairncross worked at the British cryptological center at Bletchly Park in World War II with access to its highly secret code-breaking work. The Security Service confronted Cairncross in 1951, and he made a partial confession but was not publicly identified as the "Fifth Man" of the Cambridge spy ring until the 1990s.

German Communist Richard Sorge (1895–1944) undertook Comintern assignments in the 1920s and set up a GRU network in China in 1930. He then returned to Germany to improve his cover, join the Nazi Party, and develop German government contacts. Sorge then moved to Japan in the mid-1930s as the correspondent for several German newspapers and cemented close relations with the German embassy. In addition to information gained from German diplomats, Sorge also recruited Japanese sources, including Hotzumi Ozaki (1901–44), a Communist sympathizer and adviser to Japanese prime minister Fumimaro Konoye. Sorge's People's Commissariat for Internal Affairs (NKVD) network provided Moscow with forewarning of Germany's 1941 invasion and Japan's decision in fall 1941 to strike south rather than attack the USSR's Far Eastern provinces. Japanese security arrested Sorge and his associates in late 1941. Several received lengthy prison terms, while Sorge and Ozaki were hung.

Several hundred U.S. Communists assisted Soviet intelligence in the 1930s and early 1940s, an era when U.S. security agencies were weak and surveillance of the Communist Party of the United States of America (CPUSA) and Soviet espionage was minimal. Russian-born Nathan Silvermaster (1898–1964) emigrated to the United States in 1914 and became a citizen in 1927. He secretly joined the Communist Party while at the University of Washington in 1920. In 1941, while working as a government economist, he organized a network of more than a dozen officials in the U.S. Treasury, Army, Air Force, Board of Economic Warfare, Department of Justice, and Foreign Economic Administration who were secret CPUSA members. The highest-ranking, Assistant Treasury Secretary Harry White and White House presidential aide Lauchlin Currie, were pro-Soviet allies of the party rather than CPUSA members. The network reported to Jacob Golos (1890–1943), a senior CPUSA official and liaison with Soviet intelligence. Golos, Russian born, had been an early Bolshevik and was exiled to Siberia by the czarist regime. He escaped to the United States and was a founding member of the American Communist Party in 1919. The CPUSA-based network of Victor Perlo (1912–94) also reported to Golos. Perlo, a government statistician, joined the CPUSA in the 1930s, and in 1942 organized Communists who worked for the War Production Board, Office of Strategic Services (OSS, predecessor to the CIA), Treasury Department, and the Senate Subcommittee on War Mobilization into an espionage apparatus.

After Golos's death in 1943, his assistant, Elizabeth Bentley (1905–63), took over supervision of his networks. Bentley, who had joined the CPUSA in the 1930s while at Columbia University, had been Golos's lover and assistant. But in 1944, the NKVD pushed her aside and took direct control of her networks. She turned herself in to the FBI in late 1945. The FBI quickly informed the British SIS of Bentley's defection, allowing Philby to alert the NKVD, which immediately warned Bentley's sources to cease operations and destroy evidence. Consequently, there was insufficient evidence to prosecute all but one of those she named. Her confession nonetheless led to the collapse of the Silvermaster and Perlo networks, withdrawal from the United States of many professional NKVD officers, removal from government service of more than thirty officials who had assisted Soviet espionage, and the tainting of the CPUSA with espionage.

Whittaker Chambers (1901–61) joined the CPUSA while at Columbia University in the 1920s. He served as an editor of the *Daily Worker* as well as *New Masses*, the CPUSA's literary journal. But in 1932 the party sent him into its covert arm to assist Soviet espionage. In the mid-1930s, he was the liaison between the GRU and Communists at the State and Treasury departments as well as in the U.S. Army's weapons development program. His most prominent source was Alger Hiss (1904–96), a lawyer who had joined a Communist caucus at the Agricultural Adjustment Administration in 1933. By 1936, Hiss had moved to the State Department and began supplying Chambers with diplomatic material. Alarmed by Stalin's purge of Soviet intelligence services, Chambers dropped out of espionage in 1938 and reentered public life as an editor of *Time* magazine. Hiss, meanwhile, rose to prominence in the State Department and in 1946 became head of the Carnegie Endowment for International Peace. Chambers's story did not become public until 1948, and led to Hiss's trial and five-year imprisonment for perjury.

The only U.S. espionage cases to rival that of Chambers-Hiss for public attention were those involving atomic espionage. Klaus Fuchs (1911–88) joined the Communist Party of Germany in 1932, but fled Germany in 1933 after the Nazis came to power and finished his graduate studies in Britain. Interned in 1939 as an enemy alien, his brilliance as a physicist and his anti-Nazi convictions led authorities to release him for work on the nascent atomic bomb program. Although he received British citizenship, once involved in the atomic program

Fuchs sought out Soviet intelligence via exiled German Communists, Jürgen Kuczynsky and his GRU agent sister, Ursula. Sent to the United States to assist the joint Anglo-American atomic bomb program, Fuchs supplied the Soviets with material on uranium separation and the implosion mechanism for the plutonium bomb, and continued to supply the USSR with secrets after 1945 as a physicist with the independent British atomic program. In 1949, decoded Soviet cables enabled the FBI to inform the British Security Service that Fuchs had been a Soviet agent. Fuchs confessed, and was stripped of British citizenship and imprisoned in 1950 for nine years, after which he moved to East Germany.

Fuchs also identified his U.S. courier, Harry Gold, a Communist sympathizer who had worked for the NKVD on technical espionage since the 1930s. Confronted by the FBI, Gold confessed and identified a second source, David Greenglass, a Communist and machinist at Los Alamos, the secret atomic laboratory. Greenglass confessed and identified his recruiters as his brother-in-law, Julius Rosenberg (1918–53), and older sister, Ethel (1915–53), both CPUSA members. Julius, an engineer, had organized a network of engineers working on military electronic, and aviation projects, all Communists that Julius had known when he headed the Young Communist Club at the City College of New York. The Rosenbergs refused to confess, and were convicted of espionage and then executed in 1953. Gold, Greenglass, and two other members of the Rosenberg network, Morton Sobell and William Perl, were also convicted and imprisoned. Two others, Joseph Barr and Alfred Sarant, fled to the USSR, where they headed a secret military electronic laboratory.

See also Atomic Bomb; Cold War; World War II.

FURTHER READING

Andrew, C. M., and V. Mitrokhin. *The Sword and the Shield: The Mitrokhin Archive and the Secret History of the KGB*. New York: Basic Books, 1999.

Haynes, J. E., and H. Klehr. *Venona: Decoding Soviet Espionage in America*. New Haven, CT: Yale University Press, 2000.

Newton, V. W. *The Cambridge Spies*. Lanham, MD: Madison Books, 1991.

Tarrant, V. E. *The Red Orchestra*. New York: John Wiley and Sons, 1996.

Whymant, R. *Stalin's Spy: Richard Sorge and the Tokyo Espionage Ring*. New York: St. Martin's Press, 1998.

JOHN EARL HAYNES

Sports

From the outset, the image of the human being expressed in the Russian Revolution's watchwords used sports to present socialist ideals to their fullest extent. In 1918 the Red Army established the first "physical sports cells." That same year, while the civil war was still raging, competitions in various sports specialties were held. On May 25, 1919, on Red Square, with Lenin in attendance, the first parade of Red Army athletes took place.

After the civil war ended, Soviet power proved it had grasped the importance of sport as a means of mass control and regimentation. During this period military sports associations developed on a national level, with centers in every large city in the country. More specifically, in 1923, the Dinamo (a product of the People's Commissariat for Internal Affairs) and the Opytno-Pokazatel'naja Ploschadka Vseobucha (Experimental and Demonstrational Playground of the Military Education Association) were founded, followed in 1960 by the Tsentral'nyi Sportivnyi Klub Armii (Central Sports Club of the Army). The Communist Party's youth organization, the Komsomol, whose first sports clubs were established in 1918, was key to the widespread diffusion and ideologization of sports. Starting in the mid-1920s the Communist Party, with two consecutive resolutions by its Central Committee (1925 and 1929), approved a distinctive interpretation of sports activities, including them in the broader area of "physical education" (which also included hygiene, medicine, dietetics, and so on); the goal was to favor the harmonious development of the "New Man," for whom culture was not supposed to be exclusively intellectual.

In line with making sports an "educational" activity that was as inclusive as possible, between 1935 and 1936 over sixty voluntary sports associations (with union ties) were created—Spartak and Lokomotiv among them. This was the era of forced industrialization, in which immense efforts were imposed on workers and miners. Sports were therefore also modeled after work, which had been raised to a supreme value: the sports feats of the best athletes were considered at the same level as the production records reached by Stakhanovists. At the same time all athletes, even those at the top, were considered amateurs, and officially had a job that was not related to their sport.

With the creation in 1936 of the Pan-Soviet Committee for Physical Culture and Sports' Affairs, the process of organizing a pyramidal sports command structure, at least at the institutional level, was complete. In the 1930s (specifically, 1931 and 1937) normative official documents were also approved: on the one hand, they were supposed to regulate the practice of each discipline at all levels—from what today would be classified as recreational to the highest levels—and on the other hand, they were intended to classify athletes according to a specific hierarchical scale based on achievement. In theory at least, the state's control over sports and physical exercise activities was now complete: any sports activity by anyone of any age, and at any level, was governed by precise norms and standards. To what extent these norms were actually followed in daily sports activities one can only speculate. In addition to public demonstrations, like the imposing ones that were held every year in Red Square for the Day of Physical Education, a dense network of competitions was organized at both the local and national levels; their culmination was the Spartakiads, which had first been held at the Pan-Soviet level in 1928, with the participation of over 7,000 athletes.

Until the mid 1930s, at the international level at least, the USSR's sports policies were guided by essentially isolationist and autarkical principles. The only existing institutional relationships were those established with European workers' sports organizations, which all belonged to the Red Sport International (established in 1921): it organized the worker Olympics, which were dominated by Soviet athletes. In 1934, the year in which the USSR joined the League of Nations, the USSR established its first contacts with the Fédération Internationale de Football Association, and Soviet sports also abandoned the "proletarian internationalism" line (the Red Sport International would dissolve in 1937) and began a long march toward official international institutions. Soviet power, like the contemporary Nazi and Fascist dictatorships, had understood that great international sports competitions could become a formidable means to promote a positive national image abroad. In order to oppose the 1936 Berlin Olympics, which had been conceived as a showcase for Hitler's National Socialism, the USSR worked to organize a parallel event, the People's Olympics, which was supposed to be held in Barcelona, but was not because of the outbreak of the Spanish civil war.

The USSR made a tentative appearance on the international sports scene in the immediate postwar period, participating in the European Championships in Athletics in 1946 in Oslo. The epochal shift, however, occurred in the early 1950s: in 1951 the newly established USSR Olympic Committee affiliated with the International Olympics Committee, and the following year a Soviet team participated in the Helsinki Olympics, successfully so, placing second behind the United States in terms of the total number of medals won. The results obtained by woman athletes from socialist countries were particularly impressive (Soviets and Hungarians especially)—leading to the notion that these societies had come a long way in terms of women's emancipation. The Helsinki Olympics overall demonstrated the socialist countries' potential, from the huge Soviet Union to the small and for this reason surprising Hungary.

From that moment on the Olympics became a symbolic battlefield in the Cold War: with the whole world watching, athletes were called on to demonstrate the superiority of one economic and social system over the other. One symptom of this was the attention paid to the (unofficial) national medal counts. The West was thus upset when Soviet athletes, during their second Olympics in Melbourne in 1956, took first place in the medal count, beating the United States. The Soviet delegation for its part was placed in diplomatic trouble by the invasion of Hungary. Until 1988, the competition between capitalist and socialist countries (particularly between the United States and the USSR) would weigh heavily on the Olympics' history, leading to reciprocal boycotts of the Moscow Olympics in 1980 and the ones in Los Angeles in 1984.

To sustain the comparison with the capitalist West, the countries of "real" socialism (whose internal sports organization was essentially modeled on that of the Soviet Union) invested profusely from the 1950s to the 1980s in organization, science, infrastructure, and attention to Olympic disciplines. The smaller countries often took the path of specialization, leading to outstanding results—Cuba's successes in boxing, for instance, or Romania's in women's gymnastics. The German Democratic Republic was a special case; it started participating in the Olympics with its own delegation in Mexico City (1968). "Small" Communist Germany used its successes in the main Olympic events (athletics, swimming, rowing, and so on) to affirm a national identity that had not been recognized for a considerable time. To this end East German authorities made unconditional use of the resources of scientific research. On the one hand, this led to cutting-edge training techniques that would later be adopted by elite sports in other countries (including those in the West); on the other hand, it led to widespread doping use, with serious physical consequences, in some cases deadly, for a number of athletes. Sports, within the ironclad state system devised by East Germany, was an imposed activity for those with the necessary physical attributes, rather than a playful and liberating one. A comparable approach to sports was later practiced in the People's Republic of China, including the use of trainers and experts in sports medicine from the former East Germany.

After the Soviet Union collapsed, its extensive sports apparatus experienced a difficult and painful transition to capitalism. Spartak, Dinamo, Lokomotiv, and Kryl'ya Sovetov became brand names owned by wealthy businesspeople. The same transition, on a smaller scale because of scarcer financial resources, occurred in the other countries of the former Soviet bloc. "State sports" survived in what could be described as epigonal forms in Cuba, but experienced feverish development in the People's Republic of China, fed by the propaganda potential of the 2008 Olympic Games in Beijing.

See also New Man; Propaganda, Communist; Youth.

FURTHER READING

Arnaud, P., and J. Riordan, eds. *Sport and International Politics: Impact of Fascism and Communism.* London: Chapman and Hall, 1998.

Edelman, R. *Serious Fun: A History of Spectator Sports in the USSR.* New York: Oxford University Press, 1993.

Hoberman, J. M. *Sport and Political Ideology.* Austin: University of Texas Press, 1984.

Lubysheva, L. *Sociologija fizičeskoj kul'tury i sporta.* Moscow: Akademija, 2001.

Panico, G. *Sport, cultura, società. Dallo svago al professionismo.* Turin: Paravia, 1999.

Pivato, S. *L'era dello sport.* Florence: Giunti, 1994.

Riordan, J. *Sports in Soviet Society.* Cambridge: Cambridge University Press, 1977.

MARIO ALESSANDRO-CURLETTO

Stakhanovism

The movement of socialist emulation promoted by Soviet authorities in 1935–36 got its name from a miner, Alexei Stakhanov (1905–77), who during his night shift on August 30, 1935, in the shafts of the Centralnaya-Irmino coal mines, near Kadievka (Donbass region), mined 102 tons of coal instead of the local average of 7 tons. Analogous results were achieved in the following weeks by blacksmith A. Busygin, machinist I. Gudov, locomotive engineer P. Krivonos, N. Smetanin (shoe industry), the the sisters M. and E. Vinogradov (textile industry), and M. Demchenko who worked on a kolkhoz. The new movement's appearance was celebrated by organizing the Conference of Stakhanovist Workers (men and women) at the end of 1935, attended by the highest party and state leaders, including Joseph Stalin and Grigoriy Ordzhonikidze.

Stakhanovism was an attempt by Soviet authorities to encourage increases in labor productivity through salary incentives, such as progressive increases in the compensation for piecework by individuals, with the pay proportional to the specific above-average percentage batches that these pieces belonged to (the number of pieces produced by each worker corresponded to his base salary). Official propaganda highlighted the fact that these productivity increases could be achieved by any worker, not only as a result of increased physical effort, but also as a consequence of better knowledge of technology in their area.

Stakhanovism was associated with the denunciation of the formal character of previous forms of socialist emulation, and praised as the ethos of a society based on high salaries and consumption. Since the high earnings encouraged by "Stakhanovist methods" voided those Soviet institutions whose alleged mission was the defense of workers' interests, the rise of Stakhanovism was used by the Communist Party to reorganize labor unions, following the model of the Italian workers' clubs, *Dopolavoro* (After Work) or the German *Kraft durch Freude*. Stakhanovism thus offered the Soviet regime an opportunity to put forth an interpretation of realized socialism as organic community; it engaged in work with a new dynamism that was both productivist and patriotic.

Stakhanovism reiterated and exacerbated the contradictions of the socialist emulation movements that preceded it. The intensity of labor, high earnings, and solipsistic aspects of the labor of many Stakhanovist workers often made them targets of resentment and violence by the mass of workers. In 1936 authorities introduced higher labor norms by decree, leading to lower compensation for many workers. Stakhanovism also contributed to an increase in pressure by political and economic authorities on industry's managerial and technical personnel. Stakhanovist workers were encouraged to prod the latter, so that they would take on a leading role in experimenting with more efficient ways of organizing work and utilizing available equipment.

The spread of Stakhanovism was accompanied by a resurgence of "down with the specialists" attitudes, chaos in the chain of production, and an increase in work-related incidents, especially in mining and the steel industry. Although the authorities tried to display impartiality when judging Stakhanovist workers' and managers' successes (or lack thereof), Stakhanovism contributed to a climate of suspicion and hostility in Soviet factories and mass organizations. This climate, in turn, led to purges within the industrial establishment in 1936–37, under the watchword of accusations of "sabotage." Starting in 1938, probably because of its association with purges in industry and a period of marked disorder in production, Stakhanovism was deemphasized in both official propaganda and practice, and made part of the normal work routine.

See also Labor; Socialist Emulation; Soviet Industrialization; Workers.

FURTHER READING

Benvenuti, F. *Fuoco sui sabotatori!: stachanovismo e organizzazione industriale in Urss, 1934–1938*. Rome: Levi, 1988.

Chlevnjuk, O. V., and R. W. Davies. "Stakhanovism and the Soviet Economy." *Europe-Asia Studies* 54, no. 6 (2002), 867–903.

Kuromiya, H. *Freedom and Terror in the Donbass*. Cambridge: Cambridge University Press, 1998.

Maier, R. *Die Stachanov-Bewegung 1935–1938: der Stachanovismus als tragendes und verschärfendes Moment der Stalinisierung der sowjetischen Gesellschafts*. Stuttgart: Franz Steiner, 1990.

Siegelbaum, L. H. *Stakhanovism and the Politics of Productivity in the USSR, 1935–1941*. Cambridge: Cambridge University Press, 1988.

FRANCESCO BENVENUTI

Stalin, Joseph

Joseph Stalin (1879–1953) (pseudonym of Iosif Dzhugashvili) was born to a family of humble origins in Gori (Tbilisi), Georgia. He was mostly educated in orthodox ecclesiastical schools. In 1901 he converted to Marxism and joined the Russian Social Democratic Party, and in 1903 he joined its Bolshevik wing. At the time of the 1905 Revolution he was a leader in Tbilisi's Bolshevik Committee; by the year's end he was a delegate to the Bolshevik Conference in Tampere, Finland, where he met Vladimir Lenin. Stalin was in London for the party's Fifth Congress in 1907. During these years he was arrested and exiled to Siberia many times. In 1912 he became part of the Bolshevik Central Committee and went to St. Petersburg, where he became an editor of the new daily *Pravda* (The Truth). He also caught people's attention with an essay, "Marxism and the National Question," which Lenin in particular noticed.

After a long exile in Siberia, Stalin returned to Petrograd immediately after the February Revolution in 1917. Together with Lev Kamenev he established the Bolshevik line as one of relative caution, putting pressure on the provisional liberal government, which was seen, like the Mensheviks, as "bourgeois-democratic" in nature, but at this time as a historically necessary form of government. Lenin criticized this line after his return to Russia in April 1917, and replaced it with an intransigent and radical orientation that would lead the Bolsheviks to power in October. From that moment on Stalin always took Lenin's side on all the main political issues.

Stalin was nominated the people's commissar for nationalities in the revolutionary government after October 1917, and played a secondary role in the ensuing civil war. He was in charge of supplies and tasked with forced requisitions in the Caricyn region. At this time he clashed with Leon Trotsky, unsuccessfully demanding that he be removed as head of the nascent Red Army. Stalin's experience of war, like Trotsky's and that of other Bolsheviks, was marked by the militarization of command methods and the resort to violence on a large scale. In the summer of 1920 Stalin supported Lenin's decision to order the Red Army's advance on Warsaw, which was to become a strategic and political failure. At the civil war's end, he was one of the leaders of the victorious Bolshevik Party, but still did not occupy any positions that were indicative of his future rise.

The turning point in his political career was his nomination to party secretary in March 1922, approved by Lenin, who before he fell ill, still viewed Stalin as one of his most faithful allies. The position did not have the leadership connotations it would later acquire; it was instead an organizational and administrative post. Yet this did not diminish its political significance, given its central role for the construction of a one-party state. Stalin's key role in postrevolutionary Russia's power system was thus already emerging before Lenin's death.

During the struggle for Lenin's succession, Stalin was the leader who most coherently followed the authoritarian logic of the party-state. Without letting himself be tied to a well-defined political program, he prevailed on his rivals because he was the most successful interpreter of Bolshevism's most profound moods, forged by revolutionary radicalism, the civil war's violence, and the class rage of "war communism." This authoritarian and military ethos never really disappeared, notwithstanding the adoption of the New Economic Policy (NEP) and the discarding of illusions about a Pan-European revolution after the German insurrection's defeat in October 1923. Stalin presented himself as Lenin's most faithful follower, starting with the celebrated oath he pronounced, in the solemn tones of a religious ritual, immediately after the latter's death.

In 1924 he published *Principles of Leninism*, in which he attempted to establish himself as the interpreter of ideological orthodoxy. Stalin took the part of the moderate leader who held the party's reigns firmly, intent on subduing the "fractionism" of the various oppositions, and engaged in a struggle against Bonapartism, industrialism, and Trotsky's theories about a "permanent revolution." The idea of "socialism in one country" was used between 1924 and 1926 to condense the positions of the party majority, led by Stalin and Nikolay Bukharin, into an effective slogan against the Trotskyist opposition, and later the united opposition of Trotsky, Grigory Zinovyev, and Kamenev. The slogan seemed related to two points: the NEP as a system of equilibrium between the countryside and the cities, and the Russian Revolution being given a new priority, over and above the world revolution. The two points could be considered separately, however, and Stalin's moderation in the 1920s was simply a tactical retreat.

Having defeated Trotsky and the other "Left" opponents in 1927, Stalin's role was decisive in leading Soviet power to abandon the NEP policies in the late 1920s. The party leadership group split over how to react to the supply crisis that affected the country in 1928. Stalin decisively imposed his leadership—not that of a charismatic leader, but rather the number one of the Soviet oligarchy. His decision to systematically resort to forced requisitions in the countryside opened a new "socialist offensive" by Soviet power following the heroic era of war communism, thus sidelining the "right-wing" positions that Bukharin represented. These extraordinary mea-sures in the countryside quickly led to the state pressing for collectivization and the end of market relations. An ambitious plan for the country's industrialization took shape: the Five-Year Plan in 1929. This was the prelude to a radical and violent transformation, the likes of which had never been seen, that attacked Russian society at its foundations in an effort to eradicate backwardness.

Stalin's "real" program was a "revolution from above." The program was eclectic and improvised in nature. On the one hand, it presented the oppositions' industrialization plans as Stalin's, but in an extreme version that ended up producing a brutal and primitive system of command, rather than a planned economy. On the other hand, the country's autarkic orientation was kept in place—the same orientation that was implicit in the socialism in one country slogan—and it involved an enormous transfer of resources from consumption to investment, with intolerable consequences for the population. The basis for this form of modernization was a clear view of Russia's relations with other states. The development of Stalin's thought was based on both Lenin's reflections on imperialism and the experience of Western intervention in the Russian civil war. Stalin always remained convinced of the fundamentally aggressive and conflictual nature of the capitalist world, and its corollary, the inevitability of war. This view constituted a real Bolshevik psychosis, and it favored the transition to the revolution from above because of the "danger of war" alarm sounded in 1927. Stalin's main goal was the construction of a state based on economic and military force, capable of withstanding the challenges of global politics, boldly leaving behind the weakness and marginality that had conditioned pre- and post-revolutionary Russia.

From 1929 on, Stalin was the head (*vozhd*) of the Soviet party-state. His path toward despotism began here, fully revealing the inclinations of his uncommon personality, unlike the one depicted by his adversaries. His life was also marked by the suicide of his second wife, Nadezhda Allilueva, in 1932. These developments in Stalin's leadership occurred during the most sanguinary transitional period experienced by a European country in peacetime in the 20th century. The collectivization of the countryside (1929–33) was in effect a second Russian civil war. The offensive unleashed by the state against the peasants and farmers provoked a widespread though desperate resistance, suppressed by violence and deportations, and finally vanquished by the 1932–33 famine, both the culmination and a direct consequence of the collectivization policies.

The legacy of terror left by collectivization was not overcome by the uncertain stabilization of 1933–34. After the deadly attempt on Sergey Kirov's life, one of the Soviet oligarchy's principal representatives (December 1, 1934), Stalin began a large-scale purge, which climaxed in the Great Terror of 1936–38. The purge's most visible aspects were the show trials against former opponents and the elimination of a large part of the Bolshevik leadership, but the repression also had a broader social dimension. The violent destruction of peasant society and introduction of a system of state servitude in the countryside; the social earthquake caused by forced industrialization and the introduction of bureaucratic apparatuses, leading to convulsive forms of urbanization and the gigantism of administrative apparatuses; the pervasive nature of police repression and propaganda; the systematic use of terror; absence of any institutional counterweight; and social fear—all these phenomena brought Stalin's dictatorship closer to totalitarianism's ideal type than that of any other period. Its most recognizable characteristics were the personality cult organized from above, the limitless growth of police powers, and the spread of a system of forced labor camps, the gulag.

The state-building process that Stalin launched in the 1930s thus had two facets. He created a state with a strong industrial base, built with spectacular economic growth, one that was capable of mobilizing domestic resources since there were no limits on the exercise of his autocratic power in either the party or institutions. It was precisely these characteristics of violence and repression that revealed an element of weakness. A paradox of Russian history repeated itself: the establishment of a state that wanted to play an ambitious role in world politics, but one based on fragile and uncertain foundations. The revolution from above produced a chaotic social mobility, which in a few years burned up the ideological élan of the militants and workers who had been the protagonists of the "socialist offensive." The system of power was subject to intrinsic instability, tying itself up in self-destructive processes that affected the ruling class itself, and leading to its substantial social isolation. The search for support in the newer generation thanks to the purges of the Great Terror—and the massive indoctrination effort launched with the publication of the party history's manual, known by the title *Short Course*—did not erase this reality.

The obsession with state security, which was the regime's most unifying trait, revealed its insecurity, both internally and toward the outside world. In November 1937, Stalin celebrated the continuity between the czars' empire and the Soviet state, stating in the presence of his collaborators that whoever threatened the state's unity was an enemy to be eliminated, following real extermination practices. A little later, in March 1939, he publicly justified the state's continued existence in Soviet socialist society, notwithstanding Karl Marx and Friedrich Engels's statements about its "extinction," in light of the continued existence of "capitalist encirclement."

The impact of European politics on the shape of the Soviet state was significant. The illusion that the Soviet Union could insulate itself from the rest of the world and proceed with the "construction of socialism" while protected from the capitalist crisis of 1929, vanished with National Socialism's rise to power in 1933. This event's influence was not unambiguous, though. Since he was necessarily perceived as a threat, Adolf Hitler increased the Stalin regime's sense of insecurity and spurred an array of reactions. In the area of foreign policy, the USSR moved away from isolationism and closer to the Western powers—a policy that was consolidated at the end of 1933 by the "collective security" line being pursued by the commissar for foreign affairs, Maksim Litvinov. In terms of Comintern policies, the sectarian anti–Social Democratic line that had been pursued starting in the late 1920s, and had contributed to separating the workers' movements forces and promoting the rise of National Socialism, was abandoned. From 1934 on, the Comintern adopted an anti-Fascist line under Georgi Dimitrov's leadership. In the area of internal policies, the perception of this menace was translated into an even more exasperated form of police state, emulating nazism's totalitarian policies. The international event that escalated these policies was the outbreak of the Spanish civil war in July 1936. The purge of the Red Army that Stalin had decided on in 1937 was based on his conviction that a military revolt supported by Hitler and Benito Mussolini, a "fifth column" on the Spanish model, could overturn the Soviet regime.

Yet Stalin did not have a well-informed view of nazism. Instead of evaluating the implications of the radically racial nature of Hitler's ideology, Stalin saw nazism as an extreme manifestation of capitalist imperialism and a model of the decline of Western democracy. His interpretation of international fascism had its foundation in a class-based ideology, which saw the phenomenon as one variant in the capitalist landscape. This had the paradoxical effect of reducing the nature of the Nazi threat, connecting it to the tradition of German imperialism, precisely when the USSR was reacting to it.

Partly because of Stalin's close collaborators Vyacheslav Molotov and Andrey Zhdanov, this view interacted with a persistent isolationist tradition, which in the 1920s had privileged a relationship with Berlin as an anti-Versailles gambit, and therefore also led to attempts at establishing relations with Hitler's Germany. As a consequence the USSR's international policies in the late 1930s did not consistently follow an anti-Fascist course and were instead ambiguous, fed by British appeasement policies and the Munich Conference in September 1938. Stalin never pointed to antifascism as his basic political choice, though, and the Great Terror dealt a deadly blow to antifascism's influence on Soviet political culture. His understanding of the Communist movement was also limited and instrumental, twisted to serve the USSR's interests.

These were the conceptual and political premises for the decisive Soviet rapprochement to Nazi Germany that led to the Molotov-Ribbentrop Pact (August 23, 1939). The instructions that Stalin had given his collaborators immediately after the outbreak of World War II, in early September 1939, revealed that the pact was part of a clear strategic plan. Stalin did not limit himself to declaring that the anti-Fascist experience was over and that an undifferentiated interpretation of imperialist states was to be restored. He outlined a strategic plan based on the "war of attrition" between capitalist countries and the USSR's territorial security, and it was to dominate his policies until the Nazi invasion of June 22, 1941. This view was destined to become a conceptual and political compass, used to define the USSR's state interests. Stalin's appeasement toward Hitler corresponded to the resurrection of the most orthodox anti-imperialist ideology; its goals were to avoid involvement in the war (most especially in a war on two fronts, in Europe and the Far East) and obtain the greatest possible advantage from the conflict between capitalist powers.

Stalin's view of nazism, however, continued to display contradictory characteristics, swaying between a policy of détente that went so far as to evaluate the possibility of the USSR entering an alliance with the three Fascist states, or conversely, a perception of the threat that led to increasing tensions on the division of spheres of influence with Germany in southeastern Europe. The obstinacy with which Stalin believed up to the last minute that he would be able to reconcile détente toward Hitler with the interests of the USSR's territorial security was one of the reasons that the German invasion (June 22, 1941) was such a surprise, even though the Soviet secret services were aware of Operation Barbarossa's existence.

After having blindly believed that Hitler would not open a second front with the Soviet Union, Stalin took several days to recover from the shock. Nevertheless, his appeal to Soviet citizens on July 3, 1941, addressed to "brothers and sisters" of the endangered fatherland, already contained the essential elements of his conduct as a patriotic and military leader. The perhaps symbolically most important moment was his staying in Moscow at the end of 1941, when the Nazi advance seemed close to taking the city. Although the defeats experienced by the Red Army were a direct consequence of his choice to form an alliance with Hitler and his inability to conceive of Nazi aggression, Stalin managed to create another image of himself in war—an image destined to acquire both a national and an international dimension. The scenario of a war of annihilation directed his regime's evolution. It managed to provide for the war effort while faced with the devastating effects of the invasion, and was identified with a national cause. The appeal to the myth and symbolism of Russian tradition supplied a patriotic base of support.

After the turn of events on the eastern front in winter 1942–43, Stalin's regime emerged from the war having apparently acquired new forms of national legitimacy. For the first time Stalin also gained international prestige, and the Comintern's dissolution in June 1943 was its symbolic pendant. Stalin's figure now more closely resembled that of a military and imperial leader, even though this meant an ex post facto justification of the revolution from above, the police state, and the terror. The Teheran Conference in November–December 1943 and especially the Yalta Conference in 1945 were the climactic moments during which his new international image was on display, side by side with Winston Churchill and Franklin Delano Roosevelt.

In Stalin's view, however, World War II not only represented a "patriotic" and an anti-Fascist war but also an international civil war and a war of survival that followed in the cycle of those that had been started in 1914–21, and which didn't necessarily conclude it. The perception that a transnational class conflict persisted would prevail over the idea that the changes wrought by World War II would open a new era in European and world history. It is in this light that the words pronounced by Stalin and Dimitrov in January 1945 must be read, when the autocrat forecast that the alliance with "the capitalist democratic faction" against Hitler would not last, and that "in the future we will also be against this capitalist faction." Linked to this principle was the celebrated politicoterritorial one that Stalin soon revealed to Milovan Djilas, endorsing the thesis that World War II's novelty lay in the fact that "whoever occupies a given area can impose their social system there." When, in February 1946, Stalin for the first time provided a retrospective evaluation of the war, and defined it as "an imperialist war," he was formulating long-held thoughts. This view was rapidly translated into policies that would shape the USSR's destiny.

Stalin wanted to continue collaborating with the Western powers—a wish he expressed several times after the war's end. He encouraged the European Communists, especially the French and Italian ones, to use the legitimacy they had acquired in the anti-Fascist resistance to follow policies guided by national unity, aimed at supporting the scenario of postwar collaboration. His political culture and actions in government were revealed to be incompatible with that scenario. The new foundations of patriotic support at home, the destruction of the Nazi-Fascist menace and Japanese militarism, the transformation of the cordon sanitaire into a Soviet sphere of influence in central Eastern Europe, and the growth of the international Communist movement were not sufficient to change the characteristics of the Stalinist security state. The explosion of the U.S. atomic bomb in Japan in August 1945 and the United States' overwhelming power on the global scene heightened a sense of insecurity that had never been completely dormant. In central Eastern Europe Stalin's policies did not favor the idea of "people's democracies" and increasingly leaned toward domination, leading to the Communists' monopoly of power. In the USSR, the reconstruction of a devastated and exhausted country was entrusted to the same priorities that had dominated the prewar decade, focusing on the nascent military-industrial complex, while the party's ideological machinery was once again put in motion.

In 1947–48 the outbreak of the Cold War interacted with a full restoration of Stalin's despotism. Stalin's reaction to the inauguration of the Marshall Plan and his decision to found the Cominform in September 1947 had both the meaning and resonance of a global challenge: with the thesis of the division of the world into "two camps," the USSR became the center of a pole that was antagonistic to the power of the United States. In actuality the reach of this challenge was more limited. The Cominform was not an instrument for the expansion of European communism but rather the transition to the Soviet bloc, finalized by the installation of single-party dictatorships in Eastern Europe and the exportation of the Soviet model. It was during this period that Stalin broke off relations with his most faithful ally, Josip Broz Tito, in 1948. Stalin's support of the Chinese Communists was lukewarm, although their victory would not have been possible without the USSR's support. Stalin's policies did not reveal expansionist goals but were instead based on an urge to consolidate and buttress what had been gained. Stalin once more resorted to terror as a method of government, reintroducing trials and purges, which while not on the previous scale, were now also extended to Eastern European satellite countries.

Stalin's last years followed a dark and dangerous path. The building of the Soviet nuclear bomb and the Communist seizure of power in China in 1949 seemed to lay the foundations for a less cautious and more aggressive foreign policy. No longer considering the Yalta agreements to have been honored, Stalin provoked the Korean War in 1950, giving the Korean Communists a green light and pressuring their Chinese counterparts. He deemed that the time was ripe for a new war with the capitalist world and gave the militarization of the Cold War a decisive boost. In his last work, *Economic Problems of Socialism in the USSR* (1952), Stalin reiterated the theory of war's inevitability. The increase in international tensions corresponded to the regime's evolution toward anti-Semitism and the new forms of repression it inspired. The dictator's growing paranoia led him to plan yet another purge at the highest levels of power, announced with the obscure "doctor's plot," which was prevented only because of his death.

Stalin died on March 5, 1953. Communists around the world expressed their veneration for Stalin. Even those who could not forget his crimes against humanity recognized his contribution to Hitler's defeat and Russia's modernization. In actuality his legacy was that of an exhausted and terrorized society, a police state that had no rivals, an "external empire" controlled by force, a myth as fragile as it was imposing, a formidable power but one devoid of those economic and political foundations that would have allowed the USSR to fulfill the role it had taken on: an ancien régime created with the tools of modernity, which Stalin's successors tried unsuccessfully to overcome.

See also Bolshevism; Cold War; Despotism; Great Patriotic War, Rhetoric of; Great Terror; Lenin, Vladimir; Marxism-Leninism; Modernization; Red Terror; Revolution from Above; Revolution, Myths of the; Russian Revolution and Civil War; Stalin, Myth of; Stalinism; Totalitarianism.

FURTHER READING

Dimitrov, G. *The Diary of Georgi Dimitrov, 1933–1949*. New Haven, CT: Yale University Press, 2003.

Gorlizki, Y., and O. Khlevniuk. *Cold Peace: Stalin and the Soviet Ruling Circle, 1945–1953*. Oxford: Oxford University Press, 2004.

Hoffman, D. L. *Stalinism: The Essential Readings*. London: Blackwell, 2002.

Kershaw, I., and M. Lewin, eds. *Stalinism and Nazism: Dictatorships in Comparison*. Cambridge: Cambridge University Press, 1997.

Lewin, M. *The Making of the Soviet System: Essays in the Social History of Interwar Russia*. New York: New Press, 1994.

Mastny, V. *The Cold War and Soviet Insecurity*. New York: Oxford University Press, 1996.

Montefiore, S. S. *Stalin. The Court of the Red Tsar*. London: Phoenix, 2004.

Pons, S. *Stalin and the Inevitable War: 1936–1941*. London: Frank Cass, 2002.

Pons, S., and A. Romano, eds. *Russia in the Age of Wars*. Milan: Feltrinelli, 2000.

Roberts, G. K. *Stalin's Wars from World War to Cold War, 1939–1953*. New Haven, CT: Yale University Press, 2006.

Rousso, H., ed. *Stalinism and Nazism: History and Memory Compared*. Lincoln: University of Nebraska Press, 2004.

Service, R. *Stalin: A Biography*. London: Macmillan, 2005.

Stalin, J. *Sočinenija*. 13 vols. Moscow: Politizdat, 1946–52. (Italian edition: *Opere complete*. 10 vols. Rome: Rinascita, 1946–56.)

———. *Works (Sočinenija)*. 3 vols. Stanford, CA: Hoover Institution, 1967.

Tucker, R. C. *Stalin as Revolutionary, 1879–1929: A Study in History and Personality*. New York: Norton, 1973.

———. *Stalin in Power: The Revolution from Above, 1929–1941*. London: Norton, 1990.

Van Ree, E. *The Political Thought of Joseph Stalin. A Study in Twentieth Century Revolutionary Patriotism*. London: Routledge 2002.

Volkogonov, D. *Stalin: Triumph and Tragedy*. London: Weidenfeld and Nicholson, 1991.

SILVIO PONS

Stalin, Myth of

Joseph Stalin, one of the most controversial figures of the 20th century, has been the object of antagonistic imaginary representations. The favorable myth that he deliberately built in and for the USSR, but also outside it, was unequally challenged by a countermyth, produced in a more fragmented and almost artisanal manner by his adversaries, who portrayed him as an omnipotent and diabolical figure. The myth and countermyth complemented each other, leading to a game of mirror images that was both disproportionate and deforming—one in which Stalin's figure was reflected almost to infinity.

Stalin's myth was structured around a series of prettified images of reality. It occupied a preeminent position in the world of international communism, especially in Western Europe, and it performed various functions. It spread a collective and homogenous view, one that both exalted and embodied the cause for which he stood, making identification easier. It allowed for permanent communist mobilization. It instilled a respect for the supreme leader's authority and for party discipline in members and militants. It made one believe that the object of all this adulation possessed extraordinary qualities that made him a leader both by virtue of his personal qualities and those he exhibited as a leader of the Bolshevik Party. Stalin's charisma—and what made him original when compared to Hitler—was in fact simultaneously personal and institutional because it emanated from both him and the party: each supported the other's charisma. Since Stalin was taking on the dimensions of an idol, the myth, because of the size of its following, had aspects of a worldwide religious phenomenon that fascinated both communists and non-Communists.

In both the USSR and in the West Stalin's cult began as the canonization of the general secretary of the Bolshevik party on the occasion of his fiftieth birthday, in 1929. In Western Europe France provides the best perspective on the myth's development because there the Communist Party developed while it was completely legal, while the Italian Communist Party was forced to go underground by fascism and the German party was destroyed by Hitler's rise to power in 1933. Starting in 1929 and in the early 1930s, the Pcf began to discuss Stalin insistently, but in a still fairly measured tone and using a fairly neutral vocabulary. The propaganda was restrained and it praised the first leader of the Bolshevik party by stressing his strong connections to Lenin; it highlighted his doctrinal contributions to Marxism, especially his work *Principles of Leninism* (1924); and it portrayed him as a simple, rough, and brotherly figure.

Stalin's myth went one step further beginning in 1934. References to Stalin multiplied and had a dithyrambic tone. His image and portraits were printed, displayed, and posted everywhere. The French Communists who at that time called themselves "Stalinists" heaped praise on the multiple aspects of a personality that was depicted as beyond normal boundaries, using a cascade of superlatives. Stalin was shown as the architect of a great economic power and the founder of a classless society. At precisely the time he was increasing his crimes in the USSR, Stalin's humanism was applauded, since he was attempting to create a "New Man." A formula was frequently attributed to him: "Human beings are the most precious capital." He also became a symbol of antifascism, especially during the Spanish civil war. Stalin was raised to the rank of great Marxist thinker once the group work he had edited, *Short Course of the History of the All-Russian Communist Party (Bolshevik)*, was published in 1938 and soon recognized as a Communist bible. This exponential rise in Stalin's fame was both impressive and widespread. On the eve of World War II Stalin seemed to be the exemplary revolutionary militant, the Marxist theorist par excellence, the Bolshevik Party's guide, the USSR's helmsman, and the leader of the world's proletariat—in other words, an important personality.

After the relative eclipse of the 1939–41 period, Stalin's myth was reborn. He once more embodied antifascism, and after the victory at Stalingrad, was also celebrated as the Red Army's brilliant leader. In the war's aftermath a climax was reached, and those who called themselves Stalinists now added other dimensions to the myth. Stalin was celebrated as nazism's vanquisher, outpacing all other allies, starting with the United States, and the leader of a powerful nation. Soon, with the Cold War's onset, he was presented as a defender of peace, a bulwark against the machinations of U.S. imperialism, and a genius in all fields, from agronomy to biology to linguistics. The formulas used to praise him were astounding: "father of peoples," "scientific leader," "scientist of a new type," "granite Bolshevik," "man of steel," and "the locomotive of history's engineer." He was represented everywhere and obsessively. Adored, deified, Stalin provoked sincere devotion and a passionate enthusiasm for the "man we love the most," according to a common expression.

On March 5, 1953, the announcement of the deity's disappearance caused disbelief, fear, and sorrow among Communists. Accounts written at the time and many retrospective testimonies describe the intense loss that was experienced. Many observed a religious silence at the time of his burial in Moscow. These emotions were shared by large sections of the Left, but even beyond its boundaries. All French representatives, except for two, paid their respects to Stalin by rising to their feet and observing a minute of silence. The Communist parties resorted to hyperbole in the deceased's honor and swore to remain faithful to him.

A success of this magnitude was due to the considerable propaganda efforts by the Soviet party, the Comintern, and later the Cominform, by the various Communist parties, para-Communist associations that organized solidarity and friendship with the USSR, and Soviet diplomats in capitalist countries. The myth was spread by the Communist press, but also in articles published in the bourgeois media, and written by either journalists who were ideological converts or who had been paid to do so; the myth was promulgated in brochures, manifestos, photographs, pictures, sculptures, Soviet films (which were not successful except for *The Fall of Berlin* by Mikhail Caureli, 1949), novels, poems, and essays. Some of these works had a significant echo—such as the French author Henri Barbusse's *Stalin*, published in 1935, which was later translated into many languages. The myth was incessantly given new life so it would prosper; it experienced moments of exceptional intensity, as on Stalin's seventieth birthday in November 1949. All the Communist parties organized celebrations, the leaders gave speeches, the better-known Communist writers composed poems, and presents and offerings were gathered and sent to Moscow, from the simplest to the most refined.

The Communist world's infatuation was both uniform and diversified, in that each party underscored this or that aspect of the myth, whatever served the goals of the moment. The cult of Stalin was often associated with that of each party's leader—for example, Maurice Thorez in France and Palmiro Togliatti in Italy, the former being more showy and baroque than the latter. This glorification of Stalin frequently crossed into forms of delirium on the part of intellectuals, workers, and peasants. Haunted by capitalism's crisis of the 1930s, antifascism and the war against Hitler, Stalin appeared to them like a savior and protector, sometimes even in the psychoanalytic use of the term. They were blinded by their faith, even workers of Italian origins from Lorraine placed the Kremlin's master, Fausto Coppi, and Humphrey Bogart next to one another in their pantheon, while some intellectuals hoped to receive certain benefits for praising Stalin. Prisoners of a logic of "combat" with their "enemies," they used Stalin—"Baffone" (man with a large moustache), as he was known in Italy—as a threat to intimidate the Right, the bourgeoisie, the factories' owners, or the landowners.

Whatever the case, Stalin's myth had an enormous and striking impact. But once the deity had died, disillusionment came rapidly. Khrushchev's denunciation of the cult of personality in 1956 was a first trauma, followed by others that demystified Stalin, and going further, sapped the foundations of communism itself, even though other myths about Communist leaders subsequently experienced brief moments of glory, as in the case of Mao Zedong or Fidel Castro Ruz.

See also Cult of Personality; Iconography; Messianism; Propaganda, Communist; Revolution, Myths of the; *Short Course*, The; Stalinism.

FURTHER READING

Coeuré, S. *La grande lueur à l'Est: les Français et l'Union soviétique, 1917–1939*. Paris: Seuil, 1999.

Flores, M. *L'immagine dell'URSS: l'Occidente e la Russia di Stalin (1927–1956)*. Milan: Il Saggiatore, 1990.

Gentile, E. *Politics as Religion*. Princeton, NJ: Princeton University Press, 2006.

Kershaw, I., and M. Lewin, eds. *Stalinism and Nazism: Dictatorships in Comparison*. Cambridge: Cambridge University Press, 1997.

Marcou, L. *Les Staline: vus par les hôtes du Kremlin*. Paris: Gallimard-Julliard, 1979.

MARC LAZAR

Stalingrad, Battle of

In the historical context of World War II, the battle of Stalingrad (Caricyn), which took place between September 1942 and February 1943, has a symbolic significance that overshadows its military and strategic importance.

Stalingrad was not the principal objective of the offensive Adolf Hitler had planned for the southeastern line of march, after the German advance had been brought to a halt outside Moscow in December 1941. The conquest of Stalingrad was only a first step on the road to the Nazi's ultimate goal: the occupation of the Caucasus, which was supposed to result in the capture of resources essential to the Soviet war effort. Only about a month after the initially successful offensive had been launched, Stalingrad came under siege, at the end of August, but

the Germans only partially occupied the city. Joseph Stalin ordered that the city be defended at all costs, since he remembered that Caricyn had been the key site of his participation in the civil war of 1918–20. After a string of defeats during the previous months, the Red Army began showing its effectiveness, backed by punitive measures against any form of retreat, which was considered on a par with treason (Stalin's order no. 227 of July 28, 1942).

On October 9, 1942, Stalin decided to give military commanders full powers, curtailing the role of political commissars. On November 13 Operation Uranus, the plan for a counteroffensive prepared by General Georgy Zhukov was approved. The Red Army launched a massive counteroffensive on November 19 across the Don River, which after some hard fought battles led to the complete encirclement of the German Sixth Army, devoid of adequate support in the rear. Hitler refused to consider a retreat to break the encirclement. At the beginning of January the Red Army launched the decisive offensive in the city, and on February 2, 1943, the survivors of the German Sixth Army surrendered. The dimensions of the battle had been titanic: the Sixth Army had been composed of three hundred thousand men and was now reduced to ninety thousand; in the course of the entire offensive the Germans had lost something like eight hundred thousand men; Soviet losses probably exceeded the one million mark.

It was Hitler himself who loaded the battle of Stalingrad with symbolic significance: in September 1942 he publicly presented the German offensive as the prologue to the Soviet regime's fall, and in November he declared that German forces would never abandon the city. The inevitable consequences of demoralization that were caused by the Sixth Army's defeat were thus magnified and reached Germany's domestic front. This blow to Hitler's prestige was equal to the surge in Stalin's, both in Russia and the West. Soviet propaganda successfully endowed the battle with patriotic importance. The regime regained compactness and the country a source of national motivation, after they had been on the brink of collapse. Socialist patriotism acquired a new credibility. Both inside and outside Russia, Stalingrad was perceived as an epic battle of unprecedented ferocity, for life or death, and the first serious defeat that Nazi expansionism had incurred. The Soviet Union acquired new international legitimacy, which laid the foundations for the anti-Fascist coalition with the Western powers. Independently of its actual strategic impact, Stalingrad was symbolic of a shift on the eastern front in World War II. After the war's end, the battle's symbolic significance was extended to mark the birth of the Soviet Union as a great power.

See also Grand Alliance, The; Great Patriotic War, Rhetoric of; Hitler, Adolf; Second Cold War; Stalin, Joseph; Zhukov, Georgii.

FURTHER READING

Erickson, J. *The Road to Stalingrad*. New York: Harper and Row, 1975.

———. *The Road to Berlin*. Boulder, CO: Westview Press, 1983.

Overy, R. J. *Russia's War*. New York: Penguin, 1998.

Roberts, G. K. *Victory at Stalingrad*. London: Longman, 2002.

SILVIO PONS

Stalinism

"Stalinism" is the term used to characterize the ideology and practice of the Soviet Communist regime during the period of Stalin's leadership, from 1924 to 1953. The terms "Stalinism" and "Stalinist" have also been applied to other Communist regimes, and indeed to other nonruling Communist parties and political movements. In this there is implied the existence of a clearly defined ideology and practice that differentiates Stalinism from Leninism or Marxism. Implicit also is the clear differentiation of Stalinism from the other ideologies and practices associated with the Bolshevik tradition, Trotskyism and Bukharinism. Stalinism is also seen as distinct from the ideologies and practices of the other Communist movements: Maoism, Titoism, and Castroism. The changes instituted by Khrushchev, and his denunciation of the Stalin "cult of personality" at the Twentieth Congress of the CPSU in 1956, ushered in a process of reform commonly referred to as "de-Stalinization."

The term "Stalinism" was in use at least from the early 1930s onward, both by supporters and critics of the regime. During Stalin's lifetime the existence of a distinct ideology and practice that might be labeled Stalinism, was officially denied. Stalin himself always insisted that he was an orthodox Marxist-Leninist. The ideology and practice of the regime might be identified as Marxism-Leninism-Stalinism, but the emphasis was always on its

unity and on its development in a continuous line of descent. Similarly, the pantheon of the great thinkers of scientific socialism was Marx-Engels-Lenin-Stalin. The link with Lenin and Marx played an important part in the legitimization of the Stalin regime. Other strands of thought, such as Trotskyism and Titoism, were deviations from the scientific socialist lineage. They represented other class interests, in contrast to Marxism-Leninism, which objectively represented the ideology of the proletariat and was the most advanced and progressive vein within modern Marxist thought.

Stalin introduced certain ideological innovations into Marxism-Leninism. These can be considered under various headings:

1. the codification of Leninism itself as outlined in Stalin's lectures delivered at Sverdlov University in 1924 and published in *Foundations of Leninism*;
2. the concept of "socialism in one country," as set forth in 1925 in direct rejoinder to Trotsky's notion of "permanent revolution";
3. the concept of a "revolution from above," borrowed from Engels's analysis of Bismarck's modernizing policies in Germany, as applied to the collectivization of agriculture;
4. the notion of the intensification of the class struggle as the process of building the Socialist society progressed; and
5. the preservation and strengthening of the state, and of its coercive apparatus, in the transition to socialism, under conditions of imperialist encirclement.

As Erik van Ree has argued, in most of these cases Stalin's innovations can be seen as having been anticipated somewhere in the writings of Marx, Engels, or Lenin.

Other aspects of Stalin's contribution to Marxism include his *Economic Problems of Socialism in the USSR*, which attempted to analyze the transition to socialism in terms of Marxist concepts of economic law. Stalin's writings on linguistics and his attack on the ideas of Marx attempted to relate language to the vexed question of economic base and cultural superstructure.

The organizational principles of Stalinism as a political regime were based on "democratic centralism," a ban on factions within the party, and a stress on ideological unity. At ground level this was expressed in the consolidation of the one-party state and the strengthening of the party-state apparatus, supposedly as an embodiment of proletarian dictatorship. As such the party-state was presented as one that was not "law-governed," but rather imposed its own priorities in accordance with the dictates of ideology and the logic of the class struggle. Thus, the withering away of the state foreseen by Marx was delayed, because the preconditions necessary for its demise, internally and internationally, remained unfulfilled. The construction of socialism was thus viewed as a process controlled and directed by the party-state.

In addition to ideological modifications and changes in organizational practices, there is a whole range of policy innovations associated with Stalin that might be deemed to fall under the rubric of Stalinism. In this Stalinism can be seen as a particular variant of developmental politics within the Marxist-Leninist framework that placed priority on rapid transformation and accorded priority to heavy industry. Stalinism is equated with a highly centralized system of state ownership and planning, forced industrialization, and the restructuring of agriculture through collectivization. It is associated with the restructuring of society through the elimination of particular social classes, the reordering of social values and practices through a process of cultural revolution, and the reordering of relations between national and ethnic groups. It is associated with the development of a particularly coercive system of state control that employed among its mechanisms political purging, political trials, and the elaboration of an extensive system of forced labor.

Through these means various principles of the organization of the party-state were enunciated: the concentration of power in the party-state apparatus itself; the decline of internal party democracy; the transformation of the party into an administrative arm of the political leadership; the transformation of mass organizations—trade unions, youth organizations, soviets—into auxiliary institutions to facilitate mass mobilization of the party-state; and the development of educational institutions and means of communications as channels for political indoctrination aimed at transforming man under socialism. Within this system the leader cult became important as a mechanism for legitimizing the prevailing order. It reflected a shift at the apex of the party from a system of oligarchic rule to a system of dictatorial rule, to a system of despotic rule, albeit one that retained the trappings of the one-party Communist state, an example of the system Carl Linden termed "ideocratic despotism."

Associated with these trends we can identify also significant shifts in the value system of the party-state regime. Timasheff in his discussion of the "Great Retreat" of the 1930s identified some of these: the repudiation of democracy; the adoption of more hierarchical, authoritarian models of rule; the repudiation of egalitarianism and the rise of a hierarchy of grades based on differential exercise of power, economic influence, and status; the embracing of a form of Russian nationalism, with the elaboration of patriotic themes; the renunciation of experimentation in educational and cultural policies; and a retreat from progressive policies regarding the rights of women

On the basis of the transformation effected in the state's economic structures and the elimination of the old exploiting classes from the state's social structure, socialism was proclaimed as having been established in the USSR by 1936. The boast was of a new society based on two social classes, the workers and the collective farm peasantry, with a stratum of intelligentsia organically connected to these two classes.

The notion of Stalinism as a logical development of Leninism was challenged from the outset, from within the Marxist tradition. For Trotsky, Stalinism represented a form of Bonapartist degeneration of the regime, associated with the consolidation of the power of the party-state bureaucracy. For Khrushchev in 1956, Stalinist despotism represented a violation of basic Leninist principles, most readily visible in the rise of the "cult of the individual," which ushered in a period of arbitrary rule, lawlessness, and a denial of the humanistic traditions of Marxism. Admirers of Stalin in the USSR and elsewhere continued to uphold the idea that Stalinism was a logical development of Leninism and claimed, in its name, the economic achievements of the Soviet state from 1928 onward: namely, the USSR's victory over Nazi Germany in the Second World War, the transformation of the country into a super power, and its emergence as the leader in the international Communist movement and a rival force to international imperialism.

The term Stalinism has also a long history in academic discourse. For advocates of the "totalitarian" model, Stalinism was seen as a logical and inevitable outgrowth of Marxism and of Leninism. The process of de-Stalinization in the USSR after 1956 was viewed as change that did not fundamentally alter the nature of the regime, though it softened some of its most repressive features. For critics of the totalitarian approach, Stalinism has been viewed as a distinctive system at variance with Leninism, partly in terms of ideology, but primarily in terms of practice.

From the late 1970s onward, "Stalinism" has been increasingly employed in academic discourse to designate the systems of Communist governance established during Stalin's rule both in the USSR and Eastern Europe. This has been done in an attempt to overcome some of the narrowly restrictive limits of the "totalitarian" model by placing more emphasis on the social and cultural aspects of the system and by seeking to see the system in terms of its dynamic development and its relations to the problems of governance. The use of the term Stalinism has also aimed at highlighting the highly specific features of this system of rule, thus providing a basis for comparative analysis with other forms of authoritarian rule, such as nazism.

See also Bolshevism; Bonapartism; Cult of Personality; Despotism; Marxism-Leninism; Revolution from Above; Socialism in One Country; Stalin, Joseph; Stalin, Myth of; Totalitarianism; Trotskyism.

FURTHER READING

Fitzpatrick, S., ed. *Stalinism: New Directions.* London: Routledge, 2000.

Hoffman, D. L. *Stalinism.* Malden, MA: Blackwell, 2003.

Kershaw, I., and L. Moshe, eds. *Stalinism and Nazism: Dictatorships in Comparison.* Cambridge, UK: Cambridge University Press, 1997.

Shukman, H., ed. *Redefining Stalinism.* London: Frank Cass, 2003.

Tiersky, R. *Ordinary Stalinism: Democratic Centralism and the Question of Communist Political Development.* Boston: Allen and Unwin, 1985.

Tucker. R. C., ed. *Stalinism: Essays in Historical Interpretation.* New York: Norton, 1977.

van Ree, E. *The Political Thought of Joseph Stalin.* London: Routledge, 2002.

E. ARFON REES

State, The

The question of the state in Communist regimes has to be discussed in terms both of Marxist theory and of the actual experience of those regimes. On a theoretical level, Marxism saw the state as the instrument of class domination, and by definition as an instrument of coercion carried through by the state bureaucracy, the army, the police, and the prison service. As the character of class domination changed, from slave-holding in antiquity, to feudalism, and most recently to capitalism, so did the nature of the state. Marxism saw capitalism as the final form of class society, which would give way to socialism and finally communism. With the ending of classed society and the establishment of communism, the state would wither away and the system of the administration of men would be replaced by the administration of things. Under communism, as was seen in embryo in the Paris Commune of 1871, society would be self-administered through a form of direct participatory democracy.

Lenin and the Bolsheviks saw themselves as orthodox Marxists. In *State and Revolution*, written in 1917, Lenin foresaw the transition to communism. The administration of social affairs would be undertaken by social agencies, based on popular democracy, with the direct involvement of the population in the administration of public affairs. A small-scale model for this form of organization was provided by the soviets, which had arisen in 1905, and arose again in 1917 as popularly elected councils representing workers, peasants, and soldiers. This was seen as ending the dichotomy between state and society and as the basis for the new Communist order in which class exploitation would end and inequalities between town and countryside and between different nationalities would be overcome.

The Leninist position on the state, however, envisaged a period of transition between capitalism to communism. After the triumph of the proletarian revolution, the state would not disappear; rather it would be reorganized to express the power of the proletariat, which would use it as an instrument to suppress the remnants of the defeated property-owning classes. Here the Marxists took issue with the Anarchists, who argued that the revolution would be immediately followed by the dissolution of the state, and who feared that the Marxist concept would lead to the re-creation of a system of state domination over society. In 1917 Lenin had launched the slogan "smashing the bourgeois state." After the October Revolution, the state was reconceptualized as now representing the interests of the proletariat and embodying the "dictatorship of the proletariat."

The Soviet state's history after October 1917 corresponds with various stages that reflect the different policies implemented by the ruling Communist Party. The period from 1917 to 1936 was one of "building socialism." It was divided into subperiods—the period of war communism (1918–21), the period of the New Economic Policy (1921–28), and the period of the establishment of the Command Administrative Economy (1928–36). In 1936 socialism was proclaimed to have been established in the USSR. The transition to communism would be realized at an unspecified future date to be determined by domestic developments in the USSR and by the progress of socialist revolutions beyond the country's borders.

The nature of the state in Russia after October 1917 was a matter of heated controversy within the ruling Communist Party. The conflict pitted those who favored the creation of a strong, centralized state as essential to defending the new regime and to preserving what were seen as the achievements of the October Revolution against those who foresaw danger in the strengthening of the state's power, fearing that the state would develop its own self-interests and begin to operate independently of society and in opposition to it. This debate was especially intense in the first years of Soviet power and during the civil war years (1918–21), but it continued through the 1920s.

The state that emerged in Soviet Russia and in the USSR, on its establishment in 1922, had a number of highly distinctive features. It was in the first place a party-state. The Bolshevik monopoly of political power was firmly consolidated in 1921, with the outlawing of all remaining opposition parties. Thereafter the apparatuses of party and state became closely intertwined, but the principle of party supremacy was always upheld. Out of the experience of civil war and foreign intervention, the state's power over the economy and society grew enormously. Of particular significance was the growth of the power of the Red Army and of the secret police, the Cheka (subsequently OGPU, NKVD, KGB).

In reality, by 1921 Soviet power rested on four main pillars: the party apparatus, the state bureaucracy, the army, and the secret police. These institutions were the guarantors of Soviet power. The institutions of popular democracy of 1917 vintage—the soviets, the factory committees, the trade unions—quickly lost power, and were turned into surrogate organizations of the ruling party-state. Lenin characterized the trade unions as "transmission belts" connecting the ruling authority with the working class. Although in theory a federal state that encompassed the various republics, in practice the USSR was very much a unitary state.

The state underwent a significant transformation after the czarist era. State institutions were purged of those elements most hostile to Soviet power, although a large number of former civil servants of the old regime continued to be employed as military officers and technical specialists. The state was subject to control by the party,

with the appointment of trusted party members to head all key institutions, at the central, regional, and local levels. With the nationalization of industry, trade, and transport in 1918, the role of the state in the economic realm grew enormously. During the civil war years the system of grain requisitioning produced a similar expansion of state organization.

This transformation and expansion of the state generated enormous debate within the party. In the 1920s Trotsky most famously criticized this development. While strongly defending the concept of the "dictatorship of the proletariat," he argued that the party-state had become remote from the working class. Party rule had led to a substitution of the party for the class; that is, the party ruled in the name of the proletariat, but the proletariat had little control over its own party. Trotsky saw the fusion of party and state institutions as a process of bureaucratization, whereby the officeholders in these bodies—the bureaucracy—developed their own vested interests. But he argued also that the remnants of the older property-owning classes—kulaks, Nepmen traders, and entrepreneurs—together with the old intelligentsias, exerted a disproportionate influence on the policies pursued by the state.

Undoubtedly, the developments of the 1920s gave rise to grave misgivings. Much of Lenin's final writings were devoted to the problem of the state: the inefficiency and corruption of the state; the inexperience of party members and their inability to efficiently manage state and economic institutions; and, given these shortfalls, the danger that the state would make arbitrary and reckless use of its power. This developed into a growing concern with the defects of bureaucracy in all its multiple forms and with the need to develop strategies to overcome these defects. The expansion of state power, the absence of countervailing forces within the society, the weakness of civil society, the lack of a system of representative government, and associated mechanisms of legislative and judicial control over the state apparatus, compounded the problem.

The Bolsheviks' conception of their role in building a new social order imparted a particular character to the new Soviet state. The state, in embodying the "proletarian dictatorship," was not a law-governed state, but rather a state guided by revolutionary expediency. It was a state that clearly distinguished those it considered its friends from those who were seen as its enemies. A reliance on coercive mechanisms to maintain order was firmly established during the revolution and civil war period, justified by the concept of revolutionary and class justice. The difficulties of governing the vast territory of the USSR, with its great diversity of nationalities, imparted a strongly centralizing character to the process of state building, and from the 1930s onward this was expressed in the subordination of the non-Russian nationalities to the priorities of the center.

The period of the New Economic Policy, which saw a tempering of the exercise of state power, as well as limited moves to effect some reconciliation between the regime and society, came to an end in 1928. The period 1928–32 was a critical phase in the development of the state. It witnessed a further expansion of state control, especially in the economic spheres. The private sector in industry and trade effectively disappeared, and the new collective and state farms and machine and tractor stations transformed agriculture. There was as well a great resort to the use of coercion on the part of the regime to carry through its "revolution from above": the expansion of the power of the secret police; the development of a massive gulag system of forced labor, and the wholesale deportation of kulaks. A concerted attack was directed at the influence of the bourgeois specialist in the state and economy; show trials prosecuted those deemed to be hostile to Soviet power, and "proletarian cadres" were promoted en masse to fill state and economic positions. This period was further characterized by the mobilization of popular support to back regime's policies through mass recruitment of workers into the party and through the purging of the trade unions and youth organizations and their reorientation as instruments of state and social management. This mobilization was intended to effect a major change in popular consciousness, amounting to a state-directed "cultural revolution" to eradicate old habits of thought.

With the final defeat of internal opposition inside the ruling Communist Party and the transformation of the party itself into an administrative arm of the ruling authorities, the central features of the Stalinist party-state were in place. The party-state gave the authorities great power to reshape the economy and society. The notion of socialism that emerged in this period was unashamedly statist. The party-state was the mechanism for the construction of the new order. But this apparatus was under the control of the political leadership. While powerful institutions—the army, the secret police, the economic commissariats, and strong regional authorities—were able to exert influence on policy formulation and implementation, the extent to which

they could defy the central authorities was increasingly constrained.

Nevertheless, the efficiency, reliability, and even loyalty of party-state institutions, and their regional and local agents, remained a matter of concern to Stalin in the 1930s. In 1936–38 the Great Terror was launched, which constituted yet another major phase in the development of the Soviet state. The purging and execution of leading party, state, military, and security officials advanced a new generation of younger officials. In this process the party-state was transformed into something akin to a garrison state, preoccupied with fears of internal subversion and external threat, in which the instruments of coercive state control were placed at the center of power.

At the Eighteenth Party Congress in 1939, Stalin sought to justify the strengthening of the Soviet state, arguing that Engels's formulation on the "withering away of the state" had assumed the triumph of socialism simultaneously in several countries:

> But it follows from this that Engels' general formula about the destiny of the socialist state in general cannot be extended to the particular and specific case of the victory of socialism in one separate country, a country which is surrounded by a capitalist world, is subject to the menace of foreign military attack, cannot therefore abstract itself from the international situation, and must have at its disposal a well-trained army, well-organized penal organs, and a strong intelligence service, consequently, must have its own state, strong enough to defend the conquests of socialism from foreign attack.

On these grounds it was necessary to foster a distinctive "Soviet patriotism" in defense of the state.

The changes were theoretically justified by the need to strengthen the proletarian dictatorship in its transition to socialism, to combat the intensified resistance of the remnants of the old order to this development, and to resist the threat posed by imperialist encirclement. Significantly, those promoted to leading posts in 1936–38 were referred to now as members of the new Soviet intelligentsia, whose members were of proletarian and peasant background, but trained under the Soviet regime. This was related to the new acceptance of high income differentials and great variations in terms of the status and power accorded to different members of the new ruling stratum. But the terror also served as a check on any tendencies within the party-state apparatus to transform itself into a political power that was not subject to the control of the political leadership.

From the Great Terror onward, we see a clear trend in the organization of the party-state in the direction of elevating departmental interests, as the military, the secret police, the state-economic ministries, and the party apparatus developed each its own area of interest and influence. This fragmentation was held in check by a deliberate policy of using different institutions to monitor one another, through a system of control and surveillance, and by fostering a pervasive insecurity. The period of the Second World War, the period of postwar reconstruction, and the onset of the Cold War served to strengthen a trend already clearly evident in the 1920s and 1930s toward the militarization of the state, the economy, and society. The extension of Soviet influence to the satellite states of Eastern Europe after 1945 was justified by the argument that the Soviet state was both the strongest and the most advanced in terms of its Socialist development, and therefore should occupy the leading role.

Stalin's death in 1953 brought yet another change in the organization of the Soviet state. De-Stalinization was associated with important changes aimed at restoring the authority of the party as the dominant political force within the Communist system. This also involved moves to downgrade the power of the secret police apparatus; with the scaling down of the gulag system, a strengthening of the courts, and attempts to invigorate legal norms as a check on the arbitrariness and lawlessness that characterized party and state authorities during the Stalin era. It involved also restoring the subordination of the powerful state bureaucracy and the economic ministries to party control. Party supremacy as regards the military was also reasserted in this period. De-Stalinization normalized the climate within the country, ended the use of terror as an instrument of control, and brought about some increases in openness and collaboration.

Under Khrushchev the nature of the Soviet state was redefined. The notion of the state as embodying the dictatorship of the proletariat was replaced by the notion of the state as the whole people. Stress was placed on achieving harmony between the main social classes (the workers, collective-farm peasants, and the intelligentsia) and development toward a classless society without major social conflicts. The goal was still communism, but, as under Stalin, the thinking was that the transition to communism, the withering away of the state, now depended on the transfer of state functions to nonstate bodies, which a rise in the technical and cultural level of the population would make possible, but which would still require holding in check forces hostile to the creation of communism. Developments in the direction of the withering away of the state were dependant on the elimination of the threat posed to the Socialist camp by a hostile capitalist world.

Notwithstanding these ideological formulations, the reality of the development of the Soviet state from the 1930s onward was its growing functional specialization and growing reliance on increasingly highly qualified personnel, managers, administrators, scientists, engineers, technicians, statisticians, etc. The day-to-day business of managing an increasingly sophisticated and complex urban, technological society stood in marked contrast to the still-surviving theory of a self-administered society that remained one of the core utopian ideas of Marxism. By the 1980s the one-party state and the planned economy, which had provided the basis for forced industrialization during the Stalin era, were seen increasingly as a straightjacket holding back economic and technological progress and restricting the freedom of the individual.

See also Bureaucracy; Citizenship; Command Economy; Constitutions; Dictatorship of the Proletariat; Gulag; Intelligentsia; KGB; Militarization; Modernization; Revolution from Above; Russian Revolution and Civil War; Stalinism; Totalitarianism.

FURTHER READING

Kornai, J. *The Socialist System: The Political Economy of Communism.* Oxford: Oxford University Press, 1992.

Olcott, M. B., L. Hajda, and A. Olcott. *The Soviet Multinational State: Readings and Documents.* Armonk, NY: M. E. Sharpe, 1990.

Rees, E. A. "Politics, Administration and Decision-Making in the Soviet Union, 1917–1953." In *The Yearbook of Administrative History, 2004.* Vol. 16, ed E. V. Heyen, 259–90. Baden-Baden: Nomos, 2004.

van Ree, E. *The Political Thought of Joseph Stalin.* London: Routledge, 2002.

E. ARFON REES

Suslov, Mikhail

Mikhail Suslov was for many years one of the most influential members of the leadership of the Communist Party of the Soviet Union. Born in November 1902, he died in January 1982, with his death leaving a vacancy for the post of second secretary of the Central Committee. It was filled by Yuriy Andropov, who went on later that year to succeed Leonid Brezhnev as general secretary.

Suslov himself never aspired to the top post, being content to play the part of the "gray cardinal" whose opinion counted for much within the post–Stalin Soviet leadership. It was he who led the attack on Nikita Khrushchev at the Central Committee session in October 1964 that saw Khrushchev's removal as party leader. Earlier, Suslov's support had been important for Khrushchev during the "anti-Party Group" crisis of 1957. For some years he sided with Khrushchev, but he was much more comfortable with the leadership style of his successor, Brezhnev.

Throughout the Brezhnev years, Suslov carried weight as someone who was not a Brezhnev client (he had substantially longer experience in senior party positions), but who generally saw eye to eye with him. His long spell within the highest echelon of the Soviet political hierarchy had given Suslov many opportunities to exercise patronage, and the number of his appointees in senior positions was among his main sources of political strength.

Suslov became a party member in 1921, and after studying at the Plekhanov Economic Institute and the Institute of Red Professors, joined the party apparatus in 1931. He was a secretary of the Rostov regional party committee from 1937 to 1939 before becoming one of Mikhail Gorbachev's predecessors as first secretary in the Stavropol Krai. In 1941 Suslov became a member of the Central Committee, and between 1944 and 1946 he oversaw the incorporation of Lithuania into the Soviet Union, conducting a policy of mass deportations.

In the postwar period Suslov established himself as an overseer of ideology and foreign policy. He became head of the Department of Propaganda and Agitation in the Central Committee in 1946, and in the following year a secretary of the Central Committee, thus beginning an exceptionally long stint of more than thirty-five years in that powerful organ of central party rule. From 1949 until 1951 he combined his secretaryship with serving as editor in chief of *Pravda*. It was clear that Suslov had earned the approval of Stalin, and in the last year of the dictator's life he was appointed to the enlarged presidium of the Central Committee.

From 1955 until his death in 1982, Suslov was a member of both the secretariat and politburo (in Khrushchev's time known as the presidium). The combination of membership in these two bodies bestowed great authority on their holder. Suslov was one of the most conservative Communists in the post-Stalin leadership, combining ideological rigidity with caution and a lack of imagination. He had cool relations with Andropov and was glad to see the latter leave the secretariat in 1967 for the chairmanship of the KGB. It was no coincidence that Andropov returned to the secretariat only after Suslov's death. In the late 1970s and early 1980s, when worker unrest in Poland and the rise of Solidarity aroused concern in the Kremlin, Suslov headed the politburo's Special Commission on Poland. His caution may have helped to prevent direct Soviet armed intervention, but there was never any question about his determination to crack down on the developing political pluralism in Poland.

Suslov does not appear to have been personally corrupt, although he accommodated himself to the corruption that became increasingly pervasive in the Brezhnev era. He lived quite modestly and was evidently a true believer in his brand of Marxism-Leninism. His conversational style was terse, stiff, and formal. He made full use of his party authority and did not hesitate to give instructions to Andrei Gromyko in the years when Gromyko was foreign minister but not yet a member of the politburo. So long as he was the overseer of ideology, the Soviet censorship remained strict. Theoretically unorthodox works could be published only when they were written in Aesopian language.

Suslov's political longevity resulted from a combination of political conformism, theoretical orthodoxy, administrative efficiency, a lack of ambition to succeed to the top post in the party, total loyalty to Brezhnev when the latter was general secretary, and the stabilizing role he was thereby able to play within the leadership.

See also Brezhnev, Leonid; Censorship; Marxism-Leninism; Politburo.

FURTHER READING

Bol'shaya Sovetskaya Entsiklopediya. Vol. 15. Moscow, 1976.
Medvedev, R. *All Stalin's Men.* Trans. Harold Shukman. Oxford: Basil Blackwell, 1983.

ARCHIE BROWN

Television in the Soviet Era

Of all mass media, television is most important to the center of power. It reaches the largest public with pictures of greater impact than words alone, and it requires neither literacy nor dedicated attention. It can function as casual background or riveting national hearth. The leadership of the Soviet Union understood this, but, in addition, accorded television an almost magical power, a belief that its messages would be received intact and absorbed just as the content a hypodermic delivers. This flawed theory was discarded in the West, but it formed the foundation for the central control and censorship in the Soviet Union.

Mass distribution of television developed late in the Soviet Union. It was not until the first communications satellites were launched in the late 1960s that it became possible to penetrate the enormous and geographically complex country of eleven time zones. Then the campaign to produce and blanket the country with subsidized televisions was remarkable. In 1960, only 5 percent of the Soviet population could watch television, but by 1986, fully 93 percent were viewers. Only scattered rural areas in Siberia were left out.

The Soviet model, also imposed on its Eastern European allies, centralized television outlets in a downward controlling pyramid, with power exerted by the central party organ. Journalists and administrators down the line were vetted, and plans for all programs had to be approved in advance. In Moscow, censors watched the news and other programs that went out first to the Pacific Maritime region, thus enabling them to make changes before the Moscow version, by far the most important to the party masters. Television content—and their own share of coverage—was important to these officials, who communicated several times a day with the head of television. Their directives, found nowhere in writing, were called "telephone law."

On the other hand, television in all of the states in the Soviet system was munificently funded and supported a bloated labor force. After the fall, the typically lavishly produced cultural programs—plays, concerts, operas, poetry readings, period films—were no longer cost-effective to produce and new high-culture productions virtually vanished once the post-Soviet market system appeared. At the same time, Soviet officials enforced a kind of Victorian taste that eschewed vulgarity.

Television, with its assumed power, did not have the variation that print had across Eastern Europe. For example, Poland had two Catholic publishing agencies, one of which had been co-opted by the government, but this diversity did not extend to television. Yet jamming of foreign signals in the Soviet Union was far less effective farther West and was not used in Hungary, Poland, and Czechoslovakia, and most of the German Democratic Republic received West German television. Soviet Estonia could access Finnish television, but the great heartland of the Soviet Union was effectively cut off.

When Mikhail Gorbachev came to power in 1985, he was determined to use the media, especially television, to mobilize and reform his people over the heads of the calcified bureaucracies (*glasnost*). He had many allies within the huge television industry, many of whom sought the protection of ideology chief Alexander Yakovlev. Yet there was also opposition at the top, and the industry developed a bifurcated policy. Programs addressing youth—the most alienated group and the replacement generation—were daring and combative. Others were timid and entrenched in the past. In the end, many of the liberalizing programs were shut down, the breakaway Baltic stations were occupied, and the attempted putsch began the end of the Soviet system.

See also Censorship; Cinema, Soviet; Press; Propaganda, Communist; Public Opinion.

FURTHER READING

Mickiewicz, E. *Changing Channels: Television and the Struggle for Power in Russia.* Rev. ed. Durham, NC: Duke University Press, 1999.

Rantanen, T. *The Global and the National: Media and Communications in Post-Communist Russia.* Lanham, MD: Rowman and Littlefield, 2002.

Splichal, S. *Media Beyond Socialism: Theory and Practice in East-Central Europe.* Boulder, CO: Westview Press, 1994.

ELLEN MICKIEWICZ

Terrorism

In the debate about revolutionary violence and forms of struggle, terrorism has been part of the entire history of the Communist parties in the 20th century. Terrorism as an issue divided socialists, who rejected it, and anarchists, who instead organized political homicides and explosive attacks at the time of the First and Second Internationals. The various Communist parties and movements, especially those operating under dictatorships or in the colonies, discussed this problem and came to different conclusions. Overall, however, terrorism was rejected, following Lenin's arguments and the Comintern's political orientation, which never supported this form of struggle even when Fascist dictatorships had seized power (Italy, Germany, and Spain, for example) and anti-Communist repression was particularly harsh.

The dilemma of terrorism was posed once again during World War II, within Communist-oriented resistance movements in countries occupied by Hitler's Germany. The Communist partisans had to face armed struggle in the cities and, more generally, the consequences that attacks against occupying troops and their allies might have on the civilian population. Communist parties generally chose to adopt this method of struggle—and were not always the only ones to use it—by regarding fighters in urban partisan units on a par with soldiers in an army. Still, the polemics with other parties were often heated, as in the case of the Via Rasella attack in Rome (1944) in which 33 German soldiers were killed and 335 hostages in the Fosse Ardeatine were massacred in response.

Actual left-wing terrorism, with a Communist orientation, only emerged during the 1970s in the context of the international diffusion of terrorist movements, tied to crisis areas like the Middle East. Palestinian terrorism targeted Europe on more than one occasion, as in the 1972 attack on Israeli athletes at the Munich Olympics. Other factors played a decisive role: the dramatic escalation of some conflicts, like the Vietnam War, and the violent opposition it caused in the United States and throughout the world; the destabilization of the political context started by the 1968 movements and their consequences (the proliferation of extreme left-wing groups); and the example provided by guerrilla movements in the third world, including figures such as Ernesto "Che" Guevara. Another factor was the consequences of the great economic crisis after 1971, including the oil price shock, which the West addressed by ending the Bretton Woods system. Countries affected by the phenomenon were Italy, Germany, and to a lesser extent France.

In this context the terrorist activities of two political groupings, the Euskadi Ta Askatasuna (Basque Homeland and Freedom, or ETA) and the Irish Republican Army in Ulster, were especially important. Although generically leftist, they were fundamentally dominated by a nationalist agenda. This was apparent in the case of ETA: the armed struggle that this organization engaged in and that led it to some important and spectacular "successes" (like the assassination of the head of the Spanish government, Luis Carrero Blanco, in 1973), continued even after Francisco Franco's regime ended and democracy had returned, at a time when other political organizations decided to emerge from the underground.

In Italy and Germany, the groups that chose the path of armed struggle were born in the wake of 1968 and were led by minority groups on the movement's fringes. While in Italy left-wing terrorism during its first years was seen as part of a mix, along with group protest movements and the countless organizations on the extreme Left, which often also resorted to violent forms of struggle, in Germany the rapid crisis of the student movement which led some of its components to choose the "long march through the institutions" meant that left-wing terrorism appeared as an isolated phenomenon from the outset. One of the motivations for armed struggle in Italy was the conviction on the extreme Left that an authoritarian change of course was imminent; the massacres that were part of the so-called *strategia della tensione* (strategy of tension), starting with those in Piazza Fontana in Milan (1969), which anarchists were unjustly blamed for, and the complicity of the state apparatus were what led to this alarm. This was also one of the reasons for the inability of the official Left and especially the Italian Communist Party (Pci) to understand the characteristics of Red terrorism, which until 1974 was deemed to be the work of agents provocateurs. Although many questions remain about interference by foreign organizations (some of which have been documented, like the relationship with some Palestinian terrorist organizations) interested in destabilizing the Italian political scene, it soon became clear that the phenomenon was sustained by militants of the extreme Left. What still has to be confirmed is the extent to which state agencies whose mission supposedly included the repression of this phenomenon gave the terrorists room to maneuver at certain moments, in order to shift the country to the Right and impede the Pci's move to become part of a governing coalition.

The main left-wing Italian terrorist organization, the Brigate Rosse (Red Brigades), was founded in Milan in 1970 and supported by militants from the student movement, some workers, and a group of former militants and sympathizers of the Pci and the FGCI (the Pci's youth movement), the so-called apartment group from Reggio Emilia. The Red Brigades' political culture showed traces of different influences: on a foundation that was basically close to the Third International, traces of third world models were added, especially the urban guerrilla movements in Latin America (like the Tupamaros). During their first years of existence, the Red Brigades directed their activities toward the factories with so-called armed propaganda actions (such as the wounding of factory managers who were considered particularly authoritarian or the destruction of infrastructure) in support of worker struggles. During the 1970s political violence in Italy—especially clashes between left- and right-wing extremists, and between the former and the police—occurred in all the major cities; and yet this militarization of politics generally did not escalate into homicide.

This does not mean that people were not killed in these clashes, or that there were no punitive reprisals; inspector Luigi Calabresi, for instance, who had investigated the Milan massacre in 1969, was assassinated in 1972. The issue of violence was, moreover, openly discussed in the extraparliamentary Left's major organizations. The escalation of left-wing terrorism in Italy occurred in 1974 with the abduction of the Genoese judge Mario Sossi, which brought the Red Brigades to national public attention. That same year also saw the birth of another terrorist organization, the Nuclei Armati Proletari (Proletarian Armed Nuclei), formed by ex-militants from the Lotta Continua group and the prisoners' movement. The Pro-letarian Armed Nuclei had a brief but bloody existence, and in about one year were wiped out by law enforcement. During the following months with the arrest of Renato Curcio, Alberto Franceschini, and other Red Brigades militants, and Margherita Cagol's death in a shoot-out with the Carabinieri, the Red Brigades were also in a precarious situation. Under Mario Moretti's leadership, the organization managed to survive, and other former militants from extreme left-wing organizations, especially Potere Operaio, joined the Red Brigades.

An even greater escalation was to occur after 1976, when the Red Brigades launched their strategy of "attack the state's core." The wounding and killing of journalists, magistrates, and politicians began. In those years the country underwent a profound economic, social, and political crisis, and an agreement between the Christian Democratic Party and the Pci seemed possible. An important role was also played by the disbanding of the most important "New Left" organizations after 1974 and the rise of the 1977 movement that included some violent segments (the groups of the so-called *autonomia operaia*, or workers' autonomy).

It was in this context that a number of youths moved toward the Red Brigades and there was a proliferation of many armed groups. The second large left-wing terrorist organization, Prima Linea (Front Line), was founded mostly by former militants of Lotta Continua, and it distinguished itself from the Red Brigades in that it had a less top-down internal structure and was more "movement" oriented; its militants hardly ever went underground. Among the dozens of attacks that have been attributed to this organization, the assassinations of Emilio Alessandrini, a magistrate who had investigated right-wing terrorism, and journalist Walter Tobagi are among the most notorious.

Red terrorism reached its climax between 1977 and 1980, with dozens of dead and wounded. The most sensational episode of all was the kidnapping and subsequent assassination of the Christian Democratic Party's president, Aldo Moro, and his guard in 1978. In the fifty-five days that passed between the kidnapping and Moro's assassination it seemed as if Italian democracy was under heavy pressure, and many questions remained about the sequence of events that led to the kidnapping, the negotiations that were held between the establishment and the kidnappers, and the third parties (like the secret P2 lodge) that had a vested interest in Moro's disappearance, since he had been the architect of the Communists' entry into the government majority starting in 1977.

Even while it scored these great "military" successes, however, Italian left-wing terrorism had to face the fact that its political strategy was not working, also because of the Pci's and General Italian Labor Confederation's firm opposition; they had themselves been victims of the Red Brigades, as in the assassination of Communist labor organizer Guido Rossa (1979), and stood for resolute action in defense of the country's institutions. From 1980 onward, various elements contributed to the crisis and eventually the end of this large-scale terrorist offensive. First, there was the greater effectiveness of both law enforcement and the magistracy, and the passage of a law that gave diminished sentences to captured "repentant" terrorists who divulged information, together with other "emergency" measures that led to the dismantling of entire Red Brigades "columns" and the rapid disbanding of Prima Linea. Second was the disappearance of the social and political environment that had favored terrorism's expansion in previous years, also due to investigations by law enforcement of the autonomia operaia environment (1979). By 1981, Red terrorism had been defeated but not completely vanquished, as other attacks in the following years proved (the assassinations of Ezio Tarantelli in 1985, Licio Giorgieri in 1987, and Roberto Ruffilli in 1988). The breadth of the threat Italy had survived was acknowledged during the trials held in the following years, which handed down over one thousand sentences for being part of an armed group, and these still do not account for the thousands of sympathizers who were not always caught by law enforcement.

In West Germany, the Communist-inspired terrorist offensive was not as widespread as in Italy, but it also had serious political repercussions (special legislation) and basically had only one protagonist: the Rote Armee Fraktion (Red Army Faction, or RAF). Other groupings like the June 2 Movement (1972–80) and the so-called Red Cells were less important. The RAF was founded in 1970 by a group of militants from the extreme Left that had already engaged in acts of violence as early as 1968 (Andreas Baader, Horst Mahler, Ulrike Meinhof, and so on). Among the sparks that led to this armed struggle were the following: the attempt on Rudi Dutschke's life, the leader of the German 1968 movement; the political system's disregard for the issues raised by the student movement; and the rapid crisis and ideologization of many groups in the movement itself. Moreover, German left-wing terrorism was supported on several occasions by East Germany's secret services. The bombing campaign that the RAF organized in 1970–72 came to an end with the arrest of some of

its main leaders. In 1975 the terrorist offensive continued in grand style with an attack against the German embassy in Stockholm, followed by armed robberies and attacks, and climaxing in the abduction of the president of the leading German businessmen's association, Hans-Martin Schleyer (October 1977). The latter was killed after the RAF's principal militants were found dead, presumably killed by security forces, in the Stammheim prison. Actions by the German government against terrorism, led by the Social Democrat Helmut Schmidt, were effective and soon led to the RAF's annihilation.

In the 1980s France also experienced some left-wing terrorism, inspired by the example of the RAF and the Red Brigades. Action directe (Direct Action), founded in 1979, was responsible for a series of attacks until its principal leaders were arrested in 1987 (Joëlle Aubron, Georges Cipriani, Nathalie Ménigon, and Jean-Marc Rouillan). Since the 1990s Communist-inspired terrorism occasionally manifested itself in Germany (such as attacks against North Atlantic Treaty Organization targets on German soil) and Italy (the Massimo D'Antona and Marco Biagi homicides in 1999 and 2002, respectively), but it remained a marginal phenomenon.

See also New Left; Third Worldism.

FURTHER READING

Della Porta, D. *Il terrorismo di sinistra in Italia*. Bologna: Il Mulino, 1990.

———. *Social Movements, Political Violence, and the State: A Comparative Analysis of Italy and Germany*. Cambridge: Cambridge University Press, 1995.

Fossati, M. *Terrorismo e terroristi*. Milan: Bruno Mondadori, 2003.

Peters, B. *Terrorismus in Deutschland*. Stuttgart: Deutsche Verlag-Anstalt, 1991.

Taviani, E. "PCI, estremismo di sinistra e terrorismo." In *Sistema politico e istituzioni*, ed. G. De Rosa and G. Monina, 4:235–75. Soveria Mannelli: Rubettino, 2003.

ERMANNO TAVIANI

Thälmann, Ernst

Ernst Thälmann (1868–1944) was born on April 16 in Hamburg to the family of a small entrepreneur. He left home at a young age and earned his living as a coachman, dockworker, and sailor. In 1893 he joined the Social Democratic Party of Germany (SPD). He tried to settle in the United States, but in 1907 he returned to Germany. Thälmann's political career began in a transport workers union. His simple and crude speeches, in which he tried to unmask the union leaders' corruptness, impressed the stevedores on the Hamburg docks. In 1915 Thälmann was drafted into the army and served on the western front, where he was wounded several times. He conducted socialist propaganda among the soldiers, for which he was once called before a court-martial but exonerated for lack of evidence.

At the end of World War I, Thälmann was in Hamburg, working in a shipyard. Returning to politics, he joined the ranks of the Independent Social Democratic Party of Germany (USPD) and was elected to membership in its municipal assembly. Thälmann favored uniting his party with the Communist International, and in December 1920, he was a delegate to the unification committee of the USPD and SPD. In the Communist Party of Germany (KPD), he continued to occupy extreme leftist positions, insisting, for example, on the earliest possible resolution of the question of seizure of power by the proletariat. As secretary of the party's Hamburg organization, he took part in the Third Congress of the Comintern (in 1921), defending the "theory of attack." That same year, Thälmann was elected to the KPD's governing body, the Central Board, where he attached himself to a group of "ultraleftists," which included Ruth Fischer and Arkady Maslov. In May 1923, he was appointed to represent this group in the Central Committee of the KPD.

In October 1923, Thälmann was one of the organizers of the Hamburg Uprising, although he took no direct part in the street fighting. After the Executive Committee of the Comintern accused KPD leaders of indecision and "right-wing deviationism" in their preparations for the armed uprising, Thälmann, who had opposed them in his role as "people's tribune," was moved to the top of the party leadership. In January 1924, he became a deputy chair of the KPD and later was elected to the Politburo of the Central Committee of the party. Thälmann was also head of the Union of Red Soldiers of the Front, which not only brought together Communist-inclined veterans of World War I but also provided military and sports training for party members, and supported the sweeping measures adopted by the KPD.

At the Fifth Congress of the Comintern (1924), Thälmann was elected to the presidium of the Executive Committee of the Communist International, and be-

came a deputy of its chair, Grigory Zinovyev. From 1924 to 1933, he was a deputy in the German Reichstag. With the permission of the Executive Committee, Thälmann submitted his candidacy for election as president of the German Republic. He ran in spring 1925, and in the second round of the election received almost two million votes. Known to the working masses by his party nickname "Teddy," he was seen as a man of the people who had fought his way up the political ladder. Thälmann compensated for his lack of both education and a feel for politics by attracting into the KPD apparatus young journalists like Gennady Neumann, who wrote articles and speeches for him.

When Fischer and Maslov were removed from the KPD leadership during the second half of 1925, Thälmann became the exclusive party leader. For a while he adhered to a "politics of consolidation," drawing previously dismissed functionaries of the older (Spartacus) generation into party decision making, but in 1928 he returned to his ultraleft orientation. This shift was connected with events in the Communist Party of the Soviet Union, where Stalin's group had already initiated a struggle against "right-wingers." The latter's leader, Nikolay Bukharin, was the informal head of the Comintern and also protected his supporters in the KPD. In September 1928, the right-wingers attempted to remove Thälmann from his post as party chair, but after energetic protests from Moscow, Thälmann was able to retain his position. A wave of purges and dismissals followed, and the party apparatus now moved to foster a cult of Thälmann as an infallible leader.

In spring 1932, Thälmann again took part in the presidential elections, this time winning 3.7 million votes in the second round. Though calling for an energetic struggle against Adolf Hitler's growing movement, the KPD under Thälmann's leadership proved unable to develop a strategy for this fight. Thälmann's brand of Social Democratic opposition came to be seen as the actions of a "social Fascist" party, which destroyed any prospects for a united action of all sectors of the workers' movement. After Hitler's dictatorship was established in Germany, Thälmann switched to illegal activity, but was arrested on March 3, 1933. The investigation of his case continued for several years, yet never ended in a trial. Several attempts to free Thälmann from Berlin's Moabit Prison failed, and on August 18, 1944, he was killed by the SS in the Buchenwald concentration camp.

See also Comintern; Insurrection in Germany; Social Fascism.

FURTHER READING

Thälmann, E. *Der revolutionäre Ausweg und die KPD*. Berlin: Dietz, 1932.

Various authors. *Ernst Thalman. Eine Biographie*. Berlin: Dietz, 1983.

Weber, H., and A. Herbst. *Deutsche Kommunisten. Biographisches Handbuch 1918 bis 1945*. Berlin: Dietz, 2004.

ALEKSANDR I. VATLIN

Third Worldism

The term "third worldism" refers to the exchange of experiences between governments, parties, or currents of thought in the developed countries—in Europe or Latin America—with the colonial or ex-colonial peoples during the decolonization era, leading to horizontal forms of convergence between East and West on political, ideal, and emotional levels. It also refers to the liberation of countries in Asia and Africa, during various episodes of self-determination or revolution (Algeria, Vietnam, Suez, Palestine, and so on), and more generally to the emancipation and progress of developing countries.

Next to the "social question," the "national question" was given a special place within the Third International, and therefore also within the theory and practice of the newly constituted Soviet state. At that time, the national question primarily concerned Asia and the East. Numerous conferences were held during the interwar period, inspired by the USSR or Socialist and Communist forces in European countries; the conferences were intended to promote the cause of Asian and African people, providing leaders in colonial countries with ideas and operational techniques. The Conference of Oppressed Peoples was held in Brussels in 1927, the first Afro-Asian session of its kind. It proclaimed the right of independence for Asia and Africa as well as their mutual solidarity and solidarity with the USSR's policies, thus anticipating some themes that would be adopted by third worldism—before the third world existed as such and in a context that privileged Soviet power.

Following the decolonization movement and the subsequent establishment of the "third world" (a term coined by French sociology in 1952–53 with an obvious reference to the "third estate" during the French Revolution in 1789), the varied collection of Afro-Asian countries and their interactions with Latin America became an active subject and obligatory term of reference in international politics. For the entire duration of the Cold War, the colonial or ex-colonial area was considered a terrain of confrontation or clash with imperialism, colonialism, and neocolonialism. Widespread phenomena, like the 1968 movements, were influenced by third worldist ideology.

This ideology did not always coincide with the policies of the Communist states. Within the framework of Sino-Soviet disagreements, third worldism was used by Beijing to bolster its polemics against the real or presumed compromises being made by Moscow. China thus theorized that the third world should be a top priority in any strategy for world revolution (the countryside against the cities). Cuba played an important role here, as Fidel Castro Ruz attempted to institutionalize the common engagement and struggle of Africa, Asia, and Latin America. This "tricontinentalism" was born during a conference organized in Havana in 1966 as a variant of third worldism with a radical and militant orientation, yet it was difficult to translate into policy, especially after Ernesto "Che" Guevara's disappearance in 1967. Che had been one of the main protagonists in the struggles for the liberation from and subversion of imperialism in the third world, rising after his death to the status of an "icon" of that era.

Third worldism's overall plan found its most mature formulation in the so-called Brandt Report, published in 1980 by an independent commission of representatives—presided over by German ex-chancellor Willy Brandt—from the West and the third world. The report was the crowning achievement of an extended effort at international diplomacy, subsequent to the crisis and expectations created by the boom in oil prices, and it led to preparations for a "new international economic order" intended to lessen developing countries' "dependence" on the order that had been established by colonialism. These efforts were extraneous to Communist and anticapitalist culture, belonging instead to the reformist arena. The USSR excluded itself from the venture with the justification that since underdevelopment was a consequence of imperial colonialism, the responsibility for this state of affairs lay entirely with the West. At the time of the Brandt Report's appearance, however, the high point of North-South dialogue had already been reached and retreat was now setting in. An ideological reorientation was under way among the principal Western powers (Margaret

Thatcher in England and Ronald Reagan in the United States), based on a reevaluation of "classical" economics and the opposition of liberalism to any form of dirigisme or collectivism. This would ultimately result in "globalization," in many ways the antithesis of third worldism.

Third worldism has been the object of heavy-handed revisionism, even before the collapse of the Communist system in Europe and worldwide. It sympathetically followed the emergence of Afro-Asian countries into independence, and then was denigrated as a notion when the postcolonial nations failed in the areas of development and democracy. Europe and the West's sense of guilt should no longer be given consideration. The third world had lost its particular character. The "failure" of decolonization, the various African crises, the tribal wars, and identity-based fundamentalisms have enabled the surreptitious rehabilitation of colonialism, without accounting for the fact that domination by countries that were carriers of other ideologies and technologies had irredeemably altered the course of history in Asia and Africa, with effects that were, taken as a whole, negative.

See also Anti-imperialism; Decolonization; Guevara de la Serna, Ernesto Rafael; Imperialism.

FURTHER READING

Berger, M. T. "The End of the 'Third World'?" *Third World Quarterly* 15, no. 2 (1994): 257–75.

Bruckner, P. *The Tears of the White Man: Compassion as Contempt.* New York: Free Press, 1986.

Calchi Novati, G. *Nord/Sud, due mondi per un mondo possibile.* Florence: Cultura della pace, 1987.

Independent Commission on International Development Issues. *North-South, a Programme for Survival: Report of the Independent Commission on International Development Issues.* Cambridge, MA: MIT Press, 1980.

Queuille, P.-F. *Histoire de l'afro-asiatisme jusqu'a Bandoung; la naissance du tiers-monde.* Paris: Payot, 1965.

Rangel, C. *Third World Ideology and Western Reality: Manufacturing Political Myth.* New Brunswick, NJ: Transaction Books, 1986.

Ruscio, A. *Le credo de l'homme blanc: regards coloniaux français XIXe–XXe siècles.* Brussels: Complexe, 2002.

Said, E. W. *Culture and Imperialism.* New York: Vintage Books, 1994.

———. *Orientalism.* New York: Vintage Books, 1994.

GIAMPAOLO CALCHI NOVATI

Thorez, Maurice

The leader of the French Communist Party (Pcf) from 1930 until his death, Maurice Thorez (1900–1964) was also a leading figure in the international Communist movement. Rooted in French political traditions, he was also a symbol of Stalinization, having strengthened his power over the long run with the help of the leader of Soviet communism. Thorez has been the subject of numerous historical essays: he was venerated in party circles and hated by his adversaries. The tense and embattled relationship with Palmiro Togliatti was an emblematic expression of the differences within the other great Western European party, the Italian Communist Party.

Born to a working-class family in northern France, Thorez joined the Socialist Party in the aftermath of World War I, when the issue of whether to join the Third International was splitting the party. He soon became a leader of the newly created northern Communist federation, one of the few areas in which the Socialist wing had held on to the majority after the split. Called on to fill a national post in 1925, during the party's Bolshevization, in the following years Thorez held several important positions, and became familiar with the strategic vacillations and tactical somersaults that both the Comintern and Bolshevik party engaged in, with all the consequences these actions had for the Pcf.

In 1926, as the organization's new secretary, he promoted a softening of Bolshevization approved by the Comintern's Sixth Plenum, emphasizing—jointly with Pierre Sémard, the first general secretary, who came from the labor union movement—the need to take France's political and administrative reality into account. In 1927, he went to Moscow to defend the Pcf's policies and was criticized for his lack of combativeness. He ended up embracing the Comintern's point of view, subsequently becoming the spokesperson for the "class against class" line.

At a time when most of the Communist leadership was in jail, Thorez escaped arrest and went underground for several years. He was then arrested in June 1929, though, and excluded from any political responsibilities just as the Pcf's sectarianism reached a climax, leading to the party's decline. In violation of party rules, Thorez decided to pay the fine allowing him to regain his freedom in June 1930. He was part of a Pcf delegation summoned to Moscow in 1930, and since he had been less involved in sectarian activities, he unofficially was responsible for the politburo (his official nomination would not occur until 1936).

The decision by the Comintern's secretariat to send a group of instructors, led by a permanent delegate, Eugen Fried, to work with the Pcf's leadership was decisive in understanding Thorez's role. Strictly following Fried's directives and advice, Thorez reiterated the need to end sectarianism and give internal debate more support. He nevertheless allowed his ex-comrades to be denounced and accused them of having constituted a "group" that was guilty of a form of sectarianism—one that had been paradoxically encouraged and supported by the Comintern itself.

In early 1933, after Adolf Hitler's seizure of power, Thorez declared his support for joint initiatives with the Socialists and was criticized by André Marty during the Comintern's Thirteenth Plenum in December 1933. Yet in February 1934, in France, Jacques Doriot criticized anti-Socialist sectarianism and proposed the creation of a united front against fascism. Doriot and Thorez were then called to Moscow, but only Thorez went; there, he had to listen to Georgi Dimitrov and Dmitrii Manuilskii tell him that it was necessary to engage in a united front policy, abandoning revolutionary phraseology.

Thorez, acting in unison with Fried, then followed a new line, which led to a transformation in the party's physiognomy and the consolidation of Thorez's authority as leader. A protagonist of the Popular Front, and intent on extending unity of action beyond the Socialist Party, he contacted the Radical Party, thus bringing the Pcf's policies into line with the tradition of the Union of the Left. This orientation turned the Pcf into the principal supporter of both the grouping of popular forces that won the 1936 elections and the mass strikes that accompanied the formation of a left-wing government.

Thorez had at this point become the embodiment of the Pcf's new outlook, both working class and of the people, internationalist and patriotic, revolutionary and yet engaged in the defense of political democracy. Thorez proclaimed that the Pcf's policies were decided in Paris, but the Comintern still maintained control, even if it was less ironclad than previously. Due to pressure from Moscow, Thorez was forced to keep the Communists out of the French government, even though their participation would have perfectly matched the Popular Front logic, especially since during the legislative elections the Pcf had registered the greatest electoral gains on the Left. He was the head of a mass party with more

than three hundred thousand members, with roots in the working-class world, and until 1939 Thorez followed policies that combined antifascism and defense of the motherland with support for the USSR. At this time he was general secretary, and presented himself as a "man of the people" who symbolically embodied the worker, a political militant, a self-taught intellectual, and the defender of a universe of labor that the party claimed to fully represent.

At precisely the moment when it seemed Thorez had become an integral part of the republican political system, he was expelled from it because of the war's outbreak and the banning of the Communist Party in September 1939. Surprised by the declaration of the Molotov-Ribbentrop Pact, he joined the Comintern in defending it, while also reiterating the Pcf's anti-Fascist line that led him to vote for war appropriations in Parliament after he had been drafted. He was therefore caught off guard when Stalin once again changed lines during the second half of September, forcing the Pcf to oppose the war and abandon the anti-Fascist strategy. After some hesitation Thorez obeyed, and then deserted to escape to Belgium and later the Soviet Union in early November 1939, where he lived anonymously, even though he participated in the Comintern's meetings.

In the summer of 1940, though, he was once more in a leading role, supporting a line that excluded any Pcf compromises with the German occupation authorities. From that moment on he regularly gave orders to the underground leadership, often with Marty, who had achieved a prominent position after the fall of 1939. Thorez was confined for a long time to secondary political roles, especially after his move to Ufa in the fall of 1941, and he was only to reappear in public in June 1943 when the Comintern was disbanded. He remained confined to the USSR when Marty went to Algeria to represent the Pcf. Charles de Gaulle only acceded to his return to France in November 1944, after negotiations with Stalin.

Having been instructed by Stalin to follow compromises aimed at disbanding the armed groups that had been more or less under the Communist Party's control, Thorez immediately established his authority within the party, committing it to support the country's economic and political reconstruction. He became a minister in de Gaulle's government and was active in the reorganization of public administration. The prestige he enjoyed in working-class circles and especially among miners allowed him to appeal to the workers to win the "battle for production." As the leader of the most powerful French political force and sustained by electoral success, Thorez revealed in a *Times* interview in November 1946 that the Pcf had government leadership ambitions, stating that the French Communists would follow a different path than the one the Russian Communists had followed in the construction of socialism.

When the international situation changed in the spring of 1947, and notwithstanding his expulsion from the government, Thorez still hoped to achieve his policies' goal. At the time the Cominform was created, however, he was severely criticized for not having attempted to seize power at the war's end. Thorez then supported this new shift by the Communist movement and adapted the Pcf's practice to the "two camps" strategy. He later fully endorsed the denunciation of Titoism and placed the Pcf in the anti-American camp, in the name of defending national independence and unconditionally supporting Soviet policies.

His fiftieth birthday celebration, with tributes and presents, was an example of his total acceptance of the Stalinist model. He lost the actual party leadership after suffering a stroke in 1950 and went to Russia, where he stayed for over two years. Having returned to France after Stalin's death, even though he was handicapped by hemiplegia, he once again returned to his post and led the party for another ten years—until 1964, when he relinquished the general secretary position and became party president for several months before his death.

Thorez's leadership was marked by his determination to affirm his authority on both the organizational and ideological level. Confronted with the new challenges the party faced because of the international events of 1956, he proved to be reticent and ambiguous, basically remaining faithful to the Stalinist legacy and the Soviet Union's example. In this regard, he differentiated himself from the Italian Communists and denounced the Chinese Communists as early as 1961. At the ideological level he remained anchored to a dogmatic conception of Marxism, going so far as to theorize the complete pauperization of the French working-class world. He labeled de Gaulle's return to power in 1958 as a form of "fascism." Unwavering in his monolithic view of the party, Thorez stuck to the traditional mechanisms for cadre advancement by means of co-option. He handled disagreements about political leadership as if they were discipline problems, excluding Marcel Servin and Danielle Casanova from the political office in 1961; they had been accused of "fractionist activities," while in reality it was a question of divergent analyses of Gaullism and the international situation.

On his death, Thorez's funeral, held with significant popular participation, was a testimony to the influence of a leader who had merged his existence with the party's. The party established an institute expressly designed to celebrate his memory and continue his theoretical work—but it was also the new leadership's way of declaring its loyalty to a figure associated with the Communist Party's successes in France.

See also Anti-Americanism; Antifascism; National Roads to Socialism; Popular Front; Stalinism.

FURTHER READING

Cogniot, G., V. Joannès, and M. Thorez. *L'homme, le militant*. Paris: Éditions Socials, 1970.

Courtois, S. "Thorez Maurice." In *Dictionnaire historique de la vie politique françise au XXe siècle*, ed. J. F. Sirinelli. Paris: Presses Universitaires de France, 1995.

Durand, P. *Maurice Thorez, 1900–1964: le fondateur*. Pantin: Temps des cerises, 2000.

Pennetier, C. "Thorez Maurice." In *Dictionnaire biographique du mouvement ouvrier*. Vol. 42. Paris: Éditions de l'Atelier, 1992.

Robrieux, P. *Maurice Thorez: vie secrète et vie publique*. Paris: Fayard, 1975.

Sirot, S. *Maurice Thorez*. Paris: Presses de Sciences Po, 2000.

SERGE WOLIKOW

Tito, Josip Broz

Josip Broz Tito (1892–1980) was a Yugoslav Communist who, under the pseudonym Tito, became a well-known political leader and head of the Yugoslav state during the middle and second half of the 20th century. Much of Tito's biography, though, and particularly the early stages of his life, are unclear and supported only by contradictory data whose authenticity must be questioned, in view of the absence of documentary evidence. Certain sensational, albeit unverified, claims have been circulated to the effect that the real Josip Broz either died before World War I or perished during it and someone else assumed his name. There are various unproven theories as to where this person came from, who he was, and why he took on this role. Tito himself seems to have added to the general mystification about his person. For instance, for a long time he gave his year of birth as 1892 instead of 1893. And his date of birth appears to have moved from May 7 to May 25, the date celebrated as a Yugoslav holiday during his reign.

According to the documents, Josip Broz's father was a Croatian peasant, and his mother a Slovene. After elementary education and training as a metalworker and mechanic, he worked in various factories in Croatia, Slovenia, Bohemia (the future Czechoslovakia), and Austria—all of them at the time part of Austria-Hungary—and Germany. Tito later claimed that he participated in the socialist movement then, but there is no known evidence to support this. In fall 1913, he was drafted into the Austro-Hungarian army and served as a noncommissioned officer in World War I, first in Serbia and later on the Russian front. He was captured by the Russians in 1915.

According to data later released by Tito himself, when the February Revolution overthrew the Russian monarchy, he was working as a prisoner of war in the Urals. He fled from there and, in June 1917, managed to reach the Russian capital, Petrograd. There he took part in the famed July demonstration, organized by the Bolsheviks. But after the demonstration was dispersed and repressions by the authorities ensued, Tito tried to flee to Sweden, through Finland. Sometime in the mid-1930s, he told the Executive Committee of the Comintern that his attempt to flee was motivated by his loss of faith in the revolution's success in Russia. Later, when he was already the leader of Yugoslavia, he claimed that his plan had been to return to his homeland to "make a revolution." One way or another, he was arrested and then sent back to the Urals. During his return, however, he again escaped. This time he reached Omsk, a large city in the southern part of western Siberia, in November 1917, just after the October Revolution, when the Soviets took power in Russia. During the ensuing three years of the civil war between the supporters of the Soviets, the "Reds," and their opponents, the "Whites," Tito, again according to information he later supplied himself, remained in Omsk and various villages in its vicinity. By his own account, he established a connection with the Bolsheviks and supported Soviet power. He even requested Soviet citizenship and membership in the Bolshevik Party, but was denied them. As part of the information he provided to the Comintern's Executive Committee in the mid-1930s, Tito referred only to his agitating for Soviet power; in his later memoirs he

spoke of actual participation in the battles against the "Whites."

In September 1920, by the time the civil war had basically ended in victory for the Bolsheviks, Tito left for Yugoslavia. There he joined the Communist Party of Yugoslavia (CPYu), which was soon declared illegal and whose membership became quite small. Tito labored until 1927 as a metalworker and mechanic in various concerns in Croatia and Serbia, at the same time carrying on illegal party activities and working as an activist in left-wing labor unions. In 1927, he became an important functionary in those unions in Croatia and organizational secretary of the Zagreb Municipal Committee of the underground CPYu.

Tito first attracted the attention of the Comintern leadership at a conference of the Zagreb CPYu organization in February 1928. There, whether on his own or prompted by a secretly arrived Comintern functionary, he helped initiate a complaint to the Comintern against the so-called left-wing and right-wing CPYu factions, whose fighting had been crippling the work of the party bosses. This complaint was instrumental in bringing about the Comintern's condemnation of this struggle between the two CPYu factions. It also led to basic changes in the party leadership and hastened the party's Bolshevization. Tito himself, having become political secretary of the Zagreb Municipal Committee of the underground CPYu, achieved broad recognition during summer and fall 1928, due to his arrest and trial on charges of affiliation with a terrorist organization. After six years in prison and his release in March 1934, Tito continued his Communist activities and began the life of an illegal, with falsified documents. In mid-1934, the CPYu leadership, which was in exile, added Tito to its politburo. At that time, Josip Broz assumed the pseudonym Tito and became a member of the party's inner circle.

From February 1935 until October 1936, Tito was in the USSR, having been sent there by the CPYu leadership. Under still another pseudonym, Walther, given to him by the Comintern, he was appointed as the political seminar leader of the Balkan Secretariat of the Comintern and recommended for a teaching appointment at the International Lenin School. He took part in the Seventh Congress of the Comintern as a consultant delegate. After his stay in the USSR, Tito began to coordinate CPYu activities within Yugoslavia itself, traveling periodically from there to party politburo headquarters, which were then in Vienna and later Paris. During the Stalinist purges, the head of the CPYu at the time, Milan

Gorkić, was summoned to Moscow in 1937, arrested, and then shot—a fate met by many other well-known CPYu functionaries in Moscow. Tito was now in a position to take advantage of the mutual accusations and general squabbling for power within the top circle of party leaders, particularly those in the Paris headquarters. He could now seize the initiative to create a new party leadership. In Yugoslavia proper, he began to establish a nucleus for this leadership, which was to come from among party activists in the home country itself, by taking advantage of his role as coordinator of underground CPYu activity in Yugoslavia. During two lengthy visits to Moscow (August 1938–January 1939, and September–November 1939), Tito was able to obtain approval for his activities directly from Georgi Dimitrov. In November 1940, the formation of a new CPYu leadership was finally completed at an illegal party conference in Zagreb. Tito became the general secretary of the Communist Party of Yugoslavia.

The creation of the new leadership—which unlike the practice of many years, took place not in exile but in the country itself—coincided with the rise of left-wing sentiments in Yugoslavia, and the CPYu became noticeably more active, its numbers increased, and its influence broadened. But the most significant test for the party and Tito took place when, in April 1941, Nazi Germany and its European Axis accomplices invaded and occupied Yugoslavia, and then invaded the Soviet Union in June. The party passed the test successfully. Of all the European countries that wound up under Axis occupation, the Communists in Yugoslavia managed to emerge as the strongest, and proved capable of mounting an armed resistance against the Axis occupiers. Thanks to large-scale partisan activities, begun in summer and fall 1941 under CPYu direction, the party became the most important military and political center of the 1941–45 liberation struggle. In so doing, it was able to carry out most effectively Moscow's directives to Communist parties to raise the masses to an active resistance as a way of supporting the USSR's war effort. Tito became commander of the partisan units under the party's control and then also the insurrectionist army created from it, and he took charge of the political movement that united these military entities with those layers of the population that expressed solidarity with them. Aided by Soviet and Comintern propaganda, Tito became known worldwide as the leader of the Yugoslav partisans who had fought successfully against the occupiers of his country.

In its struggle with the Axis occupiers, the movement led by Tito also came into armed conflict with internal Yugoslav forces hostile to the CPYu, not only with pro-occupation forces, but also with antioccupation ones, which were politically represented by the royal government in exile. For practical purposes, within the struggle against the occupiers, an actual civil war was fought. In this war, the CPYu pursued revolutionary goals. When it did this too radically and openly, particularly in 1941–42, Moscow, in radio programs aimed at Tito, criticized the CPYu for an ill-considered leap ahead, which might interfere with the creation of a broad liberation front in Yugoslavia and also harm relations between the USSR and the Western Allies. Tito and his associates responded by effectively camouflaging their revolutionary purposes with anti-Fascist and liberationist goals. Under the cover of the latter goals, the CPYu leadership organized a meeting in the territory liberated by the partisans for a meeting for a new insurgent quasiparliament, which proclaimed the formation of a new—as it were—democratic and federative state system, with its own ruling organs. Tito took command of this organ, which had the functions of a "national government." At the same time, a special military title was created for Tito: Marshal of Yugoslavia. Among the members of the CPYu, now much larger in size, and the considerable nonparty masses united by the movement Tito led, there began to emerge a cult of Tito as a charismatic leader. It was a cult promoted by party propaganda and directed by the ruling circles of the party, but it was also to some degree spontaneous.

This cult, which largely imitated the cult of Stalin, became robust. It emerged as an important part of the Yugoslav state ideology in 1944–45 after the defeat of Nazi Germany and its allies. In Yugoslavia, whose liberation from the occupation had been led by the CPYu and supported by the USSR, a Communist regime was now established. Up to his death, Tito was the supreme and irreplaceable leader of the regime. He was the first person of the state (until 1953 he was prime minister and thereafter president) and also of the party (until 1966 he was general secretary and thereafter chair). In addition, during his entire reign Tito was commander in chief of the armed forces.

During the first years of Tito's reign, Yugoslavia was, in terms of its internal system and development, the closest of the "people's democracies" to the Soviet (Stalinist) model, while in its foreign policy it actively participated in creating the Soviet bloc (the socialist camp). Of all the foreign Communist leaders, Tito acquired the image of Stalin's most significant and closest comrade in arms. Nevertheless, the Yugoslav leadership, encouraged by its own revolutionary successes as well as the stability and solidity of its regime, was manifesting its own regional aspirations in the Balkans—aspirations that did not always coincide with Soviet policies. The Soviets were especially concerned about Yugoslavia's neighboring people's democracies, particularly Albania and Bulgaria, which were even sometimes considered possible candidates for inclusion in the Yugoslav state. This type of thinking was utterly at odds with Kremlin policy and would lead to the Soviet-Yugoslav conflict of 1948. It eventually resulted in the exclusion of the Yugoslav regime from the socialist camp and Communist movement, and unleashed a bitter struggle against the "Tito Clique."

In this unprecedented situation, Tito and his associates were able to maintain power, relying on the support of a significant part of the CPYu and the country at large as well, while resorting to repression against any individuals or groups inclined to take Moscow's side. To protect themselves from any military or political threat and an economic blockade by the Soviet bloc, Belgrade moved toward a partial foreign policy rapprochement with the West, from which it now began to receive both military and economic aid. And when, after Stalin's death in March 1953, the Kremlin initiated a "normalization" of relations with the Yugoslav Communist regime, and in May 1955 publicly declared its previous accusations against Yugoslavia to have been unfounded, it was a considerable triumph for Tito.

Although Stalin's successors were counting on a full rapprochement of Yugoslavia with the socialist camp or even on its actual return to the bloc, Tito preferred to maneuver between the Soviet bloc and the West, preserving his independence from both and extracting from both economic advantages for Yugoslavia. In the 1960s and 1970s, by founding and then becoming a leading participant in the so-called movement of nonaligned states, Yugoslavia acquired an international importance many times exceeding its actual economic and military strength, and Tito became one of the most influential world leaders.

Tito was not a theoretician but more of a political practitioner, yet his name is honored for having brought about, during the early 1950s, a transformation of the Yugoslav political and economic system, which up to then had been simply mimicking the Soviet model, into a system of so-called self-governing socialism. The self-governing system, which had begun under conditions of bitter strife between the Soviet bloc and Yugoslavia, lent the Yugoslav regime an appearance quite different from that of the Soviet model. It was proclaimed as a "return to Marx and Lenin," as a counterweight to the "Stalinist distortion" of Communist doctrine. The transformation, which continued even after the normalization of relations with the USSR, did not end Communist totalitarianism in Yugoslavia, but gradually did render its one-party system somewhat more liberal, and introduced into the economic system some elements of a market economy. Tito, who remained an authoritarian leader (in 1974, his tenure as president of the country and party chair were declared to be without term), carried on a "pendulumlike" policy, now turning the wheel in the direction of increased harshness and centralization of the regime, now in the direction of greater relaxation.

With time, however, Tito found it increasingly necessary to maneuver between various tendencies among his associates, who were fighting among themselves. And from the mid-1960s and particularly in the 1970s, he began to experience the need for another, more complex type of maneuvering: between the ruling elites of the component parts of the Yugoslav federation (six republics and two autonomous regions). The elites of each of these entities kept arguing for greater independence from the center, and at the same time, they clashed with each other over their own group interests, and internally between their ethnic and regional interests. All these processes weakened Tito's power, as it did the stability of the regime he governed, and the Yugoslav state itself.

While Tito was at the helm, a combination of the charisma, experience, and resourcefulness of this authoritarian ruler was able to forestall difficulties, while also maintaining a certain balance of power and interests within the Yugoslav political scene. But the very nature of this power deprived the country of any truly effective and long-term mechanisms for carrying out positive solutions to its rapidly accumulating problems. And when Tito died in 1980 and there was no replacement to keep the country together, the socioeconomic and particularly ethnic contradictions worsened to the point that only a decade later, they led to the collapse of the Yugoslav Communist regime and the dramatic breakup of Yugoslavia itself.

See also Anti-Fascist Resistance; Nonalignment; People's Democracy; Socialist Camp; Soviet-Yugoslavia Break.

FURTHER READING

Djilas, M. *Tito: The Story from the Inside*. London: Phoenix, 2000.

Simic, P. *Svetac i magle: Tito I njegovo vreme u novim dokumentima Moskve i Beograda*. Belgrade: Sluzbeni list SCG, 2005.

Tito, J. B. *Govori i članci*. Zagreb: Naprijed, 1959–72.

———. *Sabrana djela*. Belgrade: Komunist, 1977–89.

West, R. *Tito and the Rise and Fall of Yugoslavia*. New York: Carrol and Graf, 1995.

LEONID JA. GIBJANSKIJ

Togliatti, Palmiro

Palmiro Togliatti (1893–1964) was born in Genoa to a petty bourgeois family. He became a member of the Italian Socialist Party in 1914 in Turin, where he earned a law degree. In 1919, he founded the journal *L'Ordine Nuovo* (The New Order) with Antonio Gramsci, Angelo Tasca, and Umberto Terracini. He shared the support of the Bolshevik Revolution and the councils as institutions with the other members of the group, and participated in the founding of the Communist Party in Leghorn in 1921. Togliatti helped create the new party leadership group that in 1923–24, in the context of Bolshevization and under Gramsci's leadership, replaced Amadeo Bordiga and thus did away with his extreme left positions.

Togliatti (using the pseudonym Ercoli) became one of the Italian Communist Party's (Pci) most important leaders, with one of the most outstanding international profiles. In July 1924 he participated in the Comintern's Fifth Congress, and became a member of Executive Committee of the Communist International (Ikki). In February 1926 he was sent to Moscow as the Pci's representative. In this role he opposed Gramsci in October 1926. Togliatti did not share Gramsci's reservations about the conduct of the majority of the Soviet party led by Joseph Stalin and Nikolay Bukharin. Gramsci supported the positions around the "socialism in one country" line, but thought the disunity in the Soviet leadership group risked a loss of credibility in the process of the "construction of socialism" itself as well as an isolationist retrenchment that might compromise the USSR's historic role. In Togliatti's opinion the split within the Soviet leadership group was now unavoidable, provoked by the Trotskyist opposition, and the only possible choice was uncondi-

tional support for the majority line. This difference of opinion was not developed, though, due to Gramsci's arrest, yet this episode was a turning point in Togliatti's political career. From this point on his ties to Stalin became all-important and unshakable; it also meant he would remain the Pci's leader until his death.

Togliatti's alignment with Stalin was not even shaken by the Comintern's 1929 shift, even though he observed it reluctantly. Having endorsed Stalin's positions, believing it was the only realistic option—one that took into account the revolutionary failure in October 1923 in Germany and that was aimed at liquidating Trotskyist ideas about the "actuality" of the revolution—he was puzzled by the new extremist and sectarian course that had been inaugurated with the "social fascism" watchword. Togliatti was accused of hesitations during the Ikki's Tenth Plenum, and he endorsed the new line even though he stated his difference of opinion. In this manner he committed himself to the principle of loyalty toward the USSR and the interests of the Soviet state, which were to constitute the main criterion for his choices, whatever the political season.

His political personality was certainly better suited to the scenario of struggle against fascism; he had written about it several times in the 1920s, in order to direct the attention of world Communist leaders to the issue. He was a protagonist of the anti-Fascist turn taken by the Comintern at its Seventh Congress (July–August 1935), during which he presented a report on the "struggle for peace" and became a member of the Ikki's Secretariat. In the first months of 1935 Togliatti gave a series of talks, "Lessons on Fascism," in Moscow; they represented a model of analysis inspired by Marxism, but an unorthodox variety, since he focused on the mass consensus the regime had built, rather than on its serving the interests of finance capital. Together with Georgi Dimitrov, he was the Comintern's only leader who attempted to provide Communist antifascism with a theoretical and political foundation, expressing reservations about the idea of war's inevitability and advancing the notion of a "democracy of a new type," anti-Fascist in nature, that would constitute a stage of transition toward socialism, at the time of the Spanish civil war in the fall of 1936. These efforts were limited and contradictory, however, both because they did not call the mechanical connection that had been established between capitalism and communism into question, and because the political space for antifascism remained limited within Stalinist political culture, reduced to an instrument of state policies.

During the Great Terror, Togliatti was involved in the witch hunt against Trotskyism, first inside the USSR and later in Spain. He was responsible for the repression targeting political émigrés, including the Italians and also other Communist parties. He was sent to Spain as the Comintern's emissary in July 1937, and was simultaneously the Spanish Communists' main political guide and the executor of Stalin's directives, including those targeting Stalin's left-wing opponents among the republicans. In the summer of 1938 he signed the Comintern directive that approved the physical elimination of the Polish Communist Party's leadership group. Discipline and a fear for his own life influenced Togliatti's actions. Still, he proved that he agreed with the basic motivations underlying Stalin's terror, starting with the need to defend the USSR from internal and external enemies.

Once he returned to the USSR after the end of the Spanish civil war, Togliatti went through a period of disgrace. He was sent to France, where he was arrested in September 1939 and then freed a few months later. In May 1940 he returned to the USSR, where he was sidelined, and Dimitrov himself removed him from his most important posts in 1941. Togliatti was the target of various denunciations and accusations, a dangerous situation even after the Great Terror: the aftermath of the Spanish civil war and particularly the hostility of several leaders of the Spanish Communist Party, like Dolores Ibárruri; the murky circumstances of the events in France; and the denunciation against him made by Julia Schucht, Gramsci's widow, first to Nikolai Ezhov and Dimitrov (from the end of 1938 to the beginning of 1939), and then to Stalin (December 1940). The last was the most serious issue: Togliatti was accused of having abandoned Gramsci to his fate, interfering with attempts to liberate him from his Fascist imprisonment. The accusation was the product of suspicions Gramsci himself had developed, leading him to break off his contacts with the Italian Communists. The disputes between Togliatti and the Schucht family included the utilization of Gramsci's prison writings, about which the Pci's leader had expressed serious reservations given the unorthodox nature of their contents and the author himself—who was suspected of Trotskyism because of the 1926 precedent and because, from prison, he had criticized the 1929 shift. The war's outbreak disposed of this problem and made it an issue of the past. After the war it was precisely Gramsci's writings, especially the *Prison Notebooks*, personally edited by Togliatti, that were to represent one of the Pci's main strengths in Italian society and culture.

The USSR's and the Communist movement's return to anti-Fascist policies after the Nazi invasion in June 1941 allowed Togliatti to regain his footing. In June 1943 he was one of the leaders who signed the Comintern's dissolution. In March 1944 he agreed with Stalin on a political line that the Italian Communists would adhere to after his return to Italy, which would become known as the "Salerno turn." The line's definition was twisted, shifting between moderate policies, aimed at collaboration with the Pietro Badoglio government and the king, and intransigent policies, dominant among Italian anti-Fascists. Stalin's influence led to these moderate policies prevailing, and they were supported by the USSR's recognition of the Badoglio government. The Salerno turn therefore gave birth to a national policy that was consonant with the interests of the USSR, which hoped to play a role in the Western sphere, but without unleashing uncontrollable social and political conflicts. Togliatti kept firmly to his understanding with Stalin, and defended the moderate line while containing the insurrectional pressures that had built up inside the Pci and the international Communist movement by the war's end. The new legitimacy acquired during the anti-Fascist resistance, in addition to the USSR's prestige and the Togliatti "national unity" line, were the foundations for establishing a mass Communist Party in Italy.

After the war, Togliatti followed a strategy whose aim was to insert Italian communism in the institutional fabric of the new republic and have it set root in Italian society. Summed up in the formulas of "progressive democracy" and the "new party," these policies' goal was to establish the Pci's influence in order to come to power peacefully. In his actions in government, especially as a minister of justice and the Constituent Assembly, Togliatti worked for national reconciliation. The Pci's strategy was also perfectly in line with the USSR's interests, which were officially aimed at continuing their collaboration with the Allies. The development of the Cold War, as events unfolded between 1947 and 1948, though, spelled trouble: the end of national unity and thus the expulsion of the Left from the government in May 1947; the birth of the Cominform and the opposition's struggle against the Marshall Plan in September 1947; and the historic defeat of the Left during political elections in April 1948.

Togliatti took the USSR's side and that of the "socialist camp" without reservations. He aligned the Pci with the thesis of the division of the world into two camps, accepted the renewed centralized control by Moscow over the European Communist parties, and deferred to the criticism the Soviets now expressed about the "parliamentary" line that the Western Communists had pursued. At the same time, he worked to minimize the most dangerous consequences of this latest shift by international communism and contain the insurrectional pressure from the Pci's most intransigent wing, led by Pietro Secchia. His language was not without its ambiguities, but Togliatti was one of the most significant national leaders attempting to moderate the polarization of Italian society—which was threatening to escalate into a civil war sparked by the endemic violence that the society had inherited from fascism and the war, fed by the vendettas undertaken by former partisans during peacetime, and being prepared on both sides by the creation of paramilitary formations. The risk of a civil war was particularly strong after an attempt was made on Togliatti's life in July 1948, but even on this occasion the Pci's leadership did not make any drastic moves. Pursuit of this line was possible because Stalin demonstrated he wanted to avoid the unforeseeable consequences of an Italian civil war, but it was also due to Togliatti's leadership.

Even after the Cominform turn, Togliatti kept to a basic agreement with Stalin's policies, which was only strengthened by Josip Broz Tito's excommunication. In 1951 Stalin suggested that Togliatti lead the Cominform—a recognition of Togliatti's status as an international Communist leader. Yet he refused, and disobeyed Stalin by invoking the need to preserve the Pci's legality and its mass following. This was in effect the principal result of his policies: even though it was impossible for him to aspire to a role in the government, the Pci had become the hegemonic party of both the opposition and the Left, allowing it to exercise an influence in a variety of social sectors. Ideologically its nourishment, like that of other Western Communist parties, consisted of a mixture of Soviet myth and anti-American mobilization, and yet it had become an anomalous mass party able to generate consensus across classes and also attract intellectuals. The "ironclad ties" with the USSR were an element of symbolic strength, but also a limit that ended up containing the most subversive and maximalist pressures in the Italian workers' movement.

The position the Pci had established in Italian society was put to the test after Nikita Khrushchev's denunciation of Stalin's crimes in February 1956 and the Soviet invasion of Hungary in November of that same year. Togliatti initially reacted by endorsing de-Stalinization: he proposed the idea of a "polycentrism" of the international Communist movement and noted the "bureaucratic degeneration" of the Soviet system under Stalin in a famous interview with the journal *Nuovi Argomenti* in June 1956, which irritated Soviet leaders. Once the drive for liberalization in the East took on the characteristics of a mass phenomenon in Hungary, Togliatti denounced the dangers of a "counterrevolution" and invited the Soviets themselves to act on that basis. He supported the invasion of Hungary and the suppression of the democratic revolution without reservations, notwithstanding the voices of dissent even among Italian Communists—voices like that of Giuseppe di Vittorio, the head of the General Italian Labor Confederation, or those of other left intellectuals. Togliatti based his reasoning on the defense of the gains that established positions in the Cold War had produced, in the conviction that only an organic connection with the socialist camp could preserve the Pci.

Togliatti's realism proved fairly effective: despite the shock and polemics of 1956, the Pci maintained its strength in terms of both membership and electoral results. Yet it was pushed further to the margins of the Italian political system, ending alliances on the Left and leading to the gradual entry of the Italian Socialist Party into the government. Togliatti then pursued a deft line in national politics, aimed at avoiding any direct confrontation with the center-left government, but it was not sufficient to get the Communists back into the political game. At the same time, "pacific coexistence" was a favorable environment for the Pci to pursue its "Italian path to socialism" as well as a limit, given the bipolar conception of the world held by the Soviet leadership.

Togliatti's last years were aggravated by the crisis in the socialist camp provoked by the Sino-Soviet break. Having sided with Moscow politically and continuing to support détente, he still opposed excommunicating the Chinese—something that would have compromised his proposal for a polycentric communism. The break between the two main Communist powers inevitably compromised an inclusive view of the socialist camp, however. Togliatti was aware of the seriousness of the crisis. Still, he was not able to come up with any other answers than an attachment to the principle of "unity in diversity." The later Togliatti therefore showed two sides. Pessimism about the fortunes of the socialist camp led him to engage both politically and diplomatically to gain some maneuvering room for the Pci, also calling for a less dogmatic analysis of the tendencies of Western capitalism. His ideological ties to the USSR and convictions about the "superiority" of the Soviet system over the capitalist one did not weaken because of this, and he also showed his intolerance of Khrushchev's renewed pressure for de-Stalinization.

The document he wrote just before his death, the "Yalta Memorial," was a manifesto of these irresolvable contradictions. Togliatti supported a generic need for "democratization" of the Soviet system and appealed to unity as the supreme good. Aware that the USSR might no longer only represent a resource but also a limit for Western communism, he could not point to any alternative paths that were not predicated on some form of political and identitarian bond with the Soviet Union. This was his political testament, and it left his successors a legacy that was tough to manage. He had built the strongest Communist Party in Western Europe. He left it at a time when his political culture and international recognition were beginning to show the first signs of a historic crisis.

See also Anti-Americanism; Antifascism; Comintern; Gramsci, Antonio; National Roads to Socialism; Peaceful Coexistence; Polycentrism; Spanish Civil War; Stalinism.

FURTHER READING

Aga-Rossi, E., and V. Zaslavsky. *Togliatti e Stalin: il PCI e la politica estera staliniana negli archivi di Mosca.* Bologna: Il Mulino, 1997.

Agosti, A. *Palmiro Togliatti.* Turin: Unione Tipografico Editrice Torinese, 1966.

Gozzini, G., and R. Martinelli. *Storia del Partito comunista italiano.* Vol. 7, *Dall'attentato a Togliatti all'VIII congresso.* Turin: Einaudi, 1998.

Gualtieri, R. *Togliatti e la politica estera italiana: dalla Resistenza al Trattato di pace, 1943–1947.* Rome: Editori Riuniti, 1995.

Gualtieri, R., C. Spagnolo, and E. Taviani, eds. *Togliatti nel suo tempo.* Rome: Carocci, 2007.

Pons, S. *L'impossibile egemonia: l'URSS, il PCI e le origini della guerra fredda (1943–1948).* Rome: Carocci, 1999.

Sassoon, D. *Togliatti e la via italiana al socialismo. Il PCI dal 1944 al 1964.* Turin: Einaudi, 1980.

Spagnolo, C. *Sul memoriale di Yalta: Togliatti e la crisi del movimento comunista internazionale (1956–1964).* Rome: Carocci, 2007.

SILVIO PONS

Tomsky, Mikhail

Born in Saint Petersburg to a working-class family, Mikhail Tomsky (1880–1936) was a worker first in the printing business and later in metallurgy. He became a member of the Russian Social Democratic Party in 1904 and was arrested in 1906. Having escaped deportation, he participated in the party's Fifth Congress and its conference in Helsingfors in 1907. He was then arrested once more and deported, until the February Revolution allowed him to leave Siberia. After October 1917, he became a labor union leader in Moscow and then moved to a position at the national level. In 1919 the party's Eighth Congress included him in the Central Committee, and the Second Congress of Soviet Labor Unions elected him to the presidency of the All-Russian Central Council of Trade Unions. At the conclusion of the civil war, he opposed Trotsky's policy of "statalizing" the labor unions and collaborated with Lenin in drafting the "Platform of 10," in preparation for a discussion of the role of labor unions in the Soviet state at the party's Tenth Congress in 1921. The following year he became a politburo member.

He then joined Nikolay Bukharin and Aleksey Rykov in the right opposition. At the Eighth Congress of the Soviet Labor Unions in 1928, Lazar Kaganovich was also nominated to the All-Russian Central Council of Trade Unions' presidency in order to control Tomsky, and the following year Tomsky was replaced on the council by Nikolay Shvernik. He was forced to work at the Ogiz publishing house in 1931, and in subsequent years was periodically subject to attack and asked to recant. During the Seventeenth Congress in 1934, Tomsky was demoted to a candidate member of the Central Committee. In a vain attempt to at least protect his family from persecution, he committed suicide in August 1936.

Tomsky was a minor but original figure in the world of Bolshevism. In 1921–22 he was temporarily removed from his post because he had allowed the Fourth Union Congress to pass a resolution that requested more democracy in the organization. In 1925 he was one of the promoters of an Anglo-Russian Union Committee (it was disbanded in 1927, on the initiative of the British unions), which was perhaps the boldest opening by the ruling Bolsheviks toward social democracy and Western European unionism. He supported the irreplaceable function of the unions as institutions for collective representation, their natural autonomy from the institution in charge of economic planning, and a nonideological attitude—one that was sympathetic to the material and cultural mass needs of Soviet workers. Tomsky intended to establish an elementary division of labor between the dictatorship's economic and union institutions, contributing to the idea of relative social pluralism that Bukharin thought was part of the New Economy Policy. He instead refused to support accelerated industrialization, also because of the immense sacrifices it would have required from industrial workers.

See also Bukharin, Nikolay; Labor; New Economic Policy.

FURTHER READING

Carr, E. H. *The Bolshevik Revolution, 1917–1923*. London: Macmillan, 1951.

———. *Foundations of a Planned Economy, 1926–1929*. New York: Macmillan, 1971.

Cohen, S. F. *Bukharin and the Bolshevik Revolution: A Political Biography, 1888–1938*. New York: Oxford University Press, 1980.

Gorelov, O. I. *Cucgvang Michaila Tomskogo*. Moscow: Rosspen, 2000.

FRANCESCO BENVENUTI

Totalitarianism

"Totalitarianism" was the term that came into existence after the First World War, initially to describe the striking pseudoreligious and statist dimensions of Italian fascism, whose emergence seemed to presage something new in the sociopolitical world. The term's application was later expanded to encompass the post-1933 regime in Germany and then the Soviet Union under Stalin. In the course of this semantic journey its meanings both broadened and became somewhat more crystallized. The first usages in Italy and German were largely favorable, indeed boastful, although the term was also used by hostile critics from early on, especially in Italy. Mussolini himself spoke of fascism's "fierce totalitarian will." The political philosopher Carl Schmitt used the term frequently in 1930s Germany in a favorable sense, but Hitler never cared for it, apparently because he thought of it as suggesting a comparison between Germany and Italy that he came to reject. Favorable usage did not survive the early 1940s.

It was refugees from Mussolini and Hitler, and later from Stalin, whose flight into exile brought the term into the French, British, and U.S. cultural worlds, whence it achieved global prominence, as the spread of hypertrophic statism across Europe and Asia continued in the 1930s. Analyses of the "totalitarian states" focused on the leader cult, the role of a "new party" with an uncompromising ideology, hostility to parliamentary democracy, the scapegoating of groups or classes, state control of mass media and the economy, and perhaps above all the institutionalization of violence and coercion in the form of political police and concentration camps.

Many critics became hesitant to employ the term totalitarian about Italy, despite its Italian origins. Mussolini reached an accommodation with the Church. The Italian economy, despite Fascist influence, retained considerable independence; concentration camps were slow to appear; and in other ways the Italian regime appeared less "total" than those of Germany or the Soviet Union.

In Europe and the United States, there was great resistance on the political Left to comparing the Soviet Union to Nazi Germany and (sometimes) Fascist Italy. But over the course of the 1930s, as the Soviet purges gathered momentum, this comparison established itself as the core meaning. By the end of the decade, larger and larger numbers of leftists were willing, some even eager, to admit that the Soviet Union was totalitarian. Trotsky did so in *The Revolution Betrayed*, published in 1937; more than a year earlier his disciple Boris Souvarine had used the term in his biography of Stalin, published in Paris. George Orwell pioneered the term in England. In the United States, journalists like William Henry Chamberlin and academics like Calvin Hoover of Duke University explicitly compared nazism and Stalinism as early as 1935, and others followed their lead. By the outbreak of the Second World War the term was commonly used even in the run of U.S. daily newspapers. Its use also became broader and less precise, in some instances even being used to refer to more old-fashioned despotisms, such as Franco Spain and later Peronist Argentina.

The term was largely in abeyance during the Second World War. Few Western commentators wanted to upset "Uncle Joe" Stalin, especially with the Red Army carrying so much of the military burden of the war, by comparing his regime to Hitler's. But the eruption of the Cold War in 1946 changed all that. With Nazi Germany and Fascist Italy defeated, the idea that the Soviet Union (and then its East European satellites) were now the great totalitarian enemies of the Western democracies became standard Cold War rhetoric.

Totalitarianism also ceased to be a largely journalistic term and entered more deeply and self-consciously into the vocabulary of economists, novelists, political theorists, and even theologians like Reinhold Niebuhr. Orwell's *1984* (1949) was clearly about a totalitarian state, with its abolition of historical objectivity, the leader cult of "Big Brother," the surveillance of the telescreen, "Newspeak," and the thought police. The Austrian economist Friedrich Hayek saw the replacement of Manchester liberalism by socialism or even the introduction of serious economic planning as putting naive Europeans on a slippery slope to totalitarianism. Hayek's influential *Road to Serfdom* (1944) was the opening salvo in the struggle between neo-liberal market economics and welfare economics that has by now been going on for more than half a century.

More directly and immediately influential in academia was a political treatise by two Harvard University professors, Carl J. Friedrich and Zbigniew Brzezinski, who attempted to lend some precision to the term, such that one could recognize a totalitarian state when one came across one. This classificatory scheme was perfect for Cold War academia, where being able to prove a Communist state was totalitarian was important. *Totalitarian Dictatorship and Autocracy* (1956) defined totalitarianism as autocracy in the technological age. It established six criteria that a political system had to meet in order to be totalitarian. It had to possess an elaborate, utopian, and all-encompassing ideology; a single hierarchically organized, mass party, typically led by one person; a system of terror, run by the party; a virtually complete, technologically conditioned monopoly of the means of mass communication; a similar monopoly of all weapons; and central and bureaucratized control of the economy. Friedrich and Brzezinski put their academic stamp powerfully on the concept. For close to a decade, their definition of totalitarianism dominated the study of Soviet politics, and it had its methodological defenders almost up until the end of the Soviet Union.

In the early literature, an important and unusual place was occupied by Hannah Arendt's *Origins of Totalitarianism* (1951). It was not exactly a work of political theory and certainly not history, but a compendium of penetrating observations, reflections, and anecdotes about the decline of European civilization that made totalitarianism possible. Arendt's themes were not poverty, economic backwardness, autocratic traditions, and great size, which was how George Kennan and other histori-cally minded commentators tended to account for the systems being called totalitarian. Arendt dwelled on the nature and development of industrial capitalism in the 19th century, and the rise of European racism and imperialism. The anomie of secular societies and the "homelessness" of modern people were the soil from which totalitarianism sprang. Her account had none of the "know your enemy" quality of Friedrich's and Brzezinski's analysis, but its greater speculativeness and lack of attention to strict causality have given it a longer life than *Totalitarian Dictatorship and Autocracy*, if less relevance to studies of communism.

In post-1945 West Germany, the idea of totalitarianism was by a wide margin the most popular academic paradigm for explaining the Nazi past; both Arendt and Friedrich were influential in the West German university world. The idea of totalitarianism could unite repudiation of the national socialist past with opposition to the imposition of Soviet institutions on East Germany. It also had the effect of somewhat minimizing Germany's dreadful past, since it could be argued that totalitarianism was European-wide and a disease of modernity rather than something arising from a specifically German past. The conservative historian Hans Rothfels contended that it was precisely conservatives who were the real opponents of Hitler, that avatar of modernity and mass politics. But the totalitarian paradigm was not merely an exculpatory device for conservatives in West Germany. Karl Dietrich Bracher, among others, produced important and durable studies of the Nazi period incorporating the totalitarian point of view.

As it turned out, the subsequent history of the concept of totalitarianism was directly linked with the polemics and debates about the Cold War, even though the term's origins considerably predated it. This was the case in both Western Europe and the United States. The demi-Marxist French Left, under the influence of Jean-Paul Sartre, was notably reluctant to give up its vision of Soviet communism as fundamentally liberating, however nasty in certain particulars, but such diverse critics as Albert Camus and Raymond Aron found the idea of totalitarianism helpful in fighting against the Left's mythologizing of the Soviet Union. But it was above all the appearance of Aleksandr Solzhenitsyn's *Gulag Archipelago*, starting in the early 1970s, that began to turn the cultural and political tide against the Sartrean view. In 1960s Germany, a Marxist student Left led the ideological charge against the concept, but it was serious academic historians like Hans Mommsen who did the major damage, pointing out that the totalitarian model could not grasp and analyze the "movement phase" of either national socialism or Bolshevism. Mommsen also charged that it failed to make any contribution to the understanding of "boundary cases," like Spain or Argentina, which showed some Fascist features and as late as 1945 had sometimes been called totalitarian by nonacademics.

When segments of U.S. public opinion began to look less favorably on the Cold War, as they did during the 1960s, they also began to resist referring to the Soviet Union as totalitarian. The concept, it was increasingly understood, was Manichaean and polarizing, its precise meaning generated not by the term itself but by how its opposite was conceived. During the early Cold War years, that opposite was generally defined as "democratic," in the sense that Britain, France, and the United States were democratic. But young 1960s radicals in the Euro-American world soon began to desert the Cold War barricades. Shouldn't blame for the Cold War be more evenly apportioned between the United States and the USSR? they demanded. Wasn't the Soviet Union entitled to a sphere of influence in Eastern Europe? After all, the United States surely had one in Latin America, and some said in Western Europe too. Weren't the Western democracies almost as repressive as the Soviet Union, in their disguised (and therefore hypocritical) way? Wasn't the Cold War really a regrettable crusade against the Left, rather than a wise and stalwart defense against communism? If "Western democracy" amounted only to "repressive tolerance" or "bourgeois democracy," or actually another form of totalitarianism, as Herbert Marcuse argued, then there was no drastic antinomy between the Western and Soviet systems. It was all just politics. And with the United States killing millions of Vietnamese in the name of democracy, the white hat versus black hat totalitarian model seemed for a time an impossible point of view to maintain. Even to the more moderate, good and evil seemed widely distributed in the world, not monopolized by one side. This kind of "mirror imaging" of the two sides in the Cold War was hateful to conservatives and became part of the reaction against the Left that marked the end of the 1960s.

Such radical opinions never carried the day in Western academia, or even came close, but they did help cast doubt on the category by indicating to a broader audience how subjective and "value-laden" the term totalitarian was. And the growing vogue for social science stressed the necessity of "objectivity" in analyzing social systems. It suggested that scholars ought to shun value-laden terminology, which might amount to little more than name calling.

The polemical critique by 1960s leftists thus came to be supplemented by methodological dissatisfactions of a less political sort. How valuable was it to create a category based almost entirely on a comparison of the Soviet Union and Nazi Germany, and then analyze the Soviet Union and its satellites in those terms? How could you escape your premises? To Robert Tucker and other political scientists there seemed something a bit tautological going on. Shouldn't there be a broader base for comparison? "Revolutionary mass movement regimes under single-party auspices" was a more useful category, suggested Tucker, however awkward it sounded. At any rate, some kind of broader category was needed; something closer to comparative politics, so that Egypt under Nasser, for instance, could be added to the Nazi-Soviet comparison, or even Turkey under Atatürk.

Social scientists like H. Gordon Skilling and Jerry Hough were among the leaders in discovering ways in which the Soviet Union might be understood as "normal," meaning "similar to Western nations." In order to understand the Soviet system properly, they thought, one had to employ the same sorts of tools one would in understanding a Western society, since they were not *essentially* different. Studying Soviet ideology and the competition for leadership at the center was not enough. One had to investigate clientelistic networks, patronage, and the competition of interest groups over divergent policy options. This was what Skilling called the "group approach," and it was far from the dichotomy between the active party and the passive, atomized society suggested by the totalitarian model. Hough went even further. He understood the Soviet Union as simply one type of modern society and favored a functionalist analysis of it, calling his approach "institutional pluralism."

Most of these academic debates were among political scientists and sociologists. Historians like Merle Fainsod and Adam Ulam had used the term totalitarian, yet not in a precise way. But during the 1970s and 1980s, some historians finally got into the act. Influenced by the models of French social history, historians like Lynn Viola and especially Sheila Fitzpatrick objected to that aspect of the totalitarian point of view that suggested that everything important in the Soviet Union happened at or near the political center. Like similar critics in West Germany, they wanted to study how central decision making was modified by provincial actors as well as how most people actually lived, not merely elites in Berlin or Moscow.

Fitzpatrick was further taken by the idea that Stalinism had a popular component. If Stalinism did not constitute a revolution from below, as she briefly maintained, Stalin's policies at least had social beneficiaries and some support. Life under Stalin for ordinary people was a complex amalgam of repression, acquiescence, and small acts of resistance that could not be grasped by merely counterposing an active state with a passive society. Critics like Stephen Cohen and Peter Kenez charged Fitzpatrick with understating the violence of Stalin's policy, and there was a discussion among historians of both Nazi Germany and the Soviet Union about whether the role of the state had been unduly minimized by the social historians and whether it needed to "be brought back in."

Whether the distinction between totalitarian regimes and ordinary authoritarian ones was a viable intellectual one or merely useful in political argument had always been central to the discussion about totalitarianism, and never more so than during the Reagan administration, when spokespeople like Jeane Kirkpatrick defended the U.S. alliances with right-wing regimes, particularly in Latin America, as prudent realpolitik in a world dominated by the U.S. struggle with the far more dangerous regimes of the Soviet empire. Liberals, she complained, didn't understand that totalitarianism was for keeps, whereas traditional authoritarian regimes might evolve or someday be reformed. Some of her critics maintained that a complete distinction between totalitarian and authoritarian regimes could no longer be convincingly made. Brzezinski, on the other hand, maintained that foreign policy decisions should not be made on the basis of some abstract theoretical distinction but rather on concrete circumstances with a direct impact on policy outcomes.

The coming of Mikhail Gorbachev and the end of the Soviet Union scrambled the debate considerably. Both in Russia and China, what had been called totalitarian states turned out to be capable of something on a continuum between peaceful evolution and collapse, after all. The term had lost a good deal of its apparent clarity, although an interesting case could be made that Iraq under Saddam Hussein had as many totalitarian as authoritarian features, and that North Korea, with its Juche ideology, remained as an almost textbook case of totalitarianism.

See also Anticommunism; Arendt, Hannah; Bolshevism; Cold War; Despotism; Fascism; Kennan, George Frost; Modernization; Revolution from Above; Solzhenitsyn, Aleksandr; Stalinism; State, The; Trotsky, Leon; Utopia.

FURTHER READING

Alpers, B. *Dictators, Democracy, and American Public Culture: Envisioning the Totalitarian Enemy, 1920s–1950s.* Chapel Hill: University of North Carolina Press, 2003.

Arendt, H. *The Origins of Totalitarianism.* 1951. Reprint, New York: Harcourt Brace Jovanovich, 1973.

Gleason, A. *Totalitarianism: The Inner History of the Cold War.* New York: Oxford University Press, 1995.

Halberstam, M. *Totalitarianism and the Modern Conception of Politics.* New Haven, CT: Yale University Press, 1999.

ABBOTT GLEASON

Trade Unions

Trade unions under Communism were generally weak institutions that lacked independence from the main employer, the state, as it was the state itself that was ostensibly promoting workers' interests. The unions' lack of independence, however, might have made them the weak link in the chain that broke the Communist system.

Lenin and the Bolshevik Party had a deeply ambivalent view of trade unions in the wake of the Russian Revolution. Rejecting arguments for union independence and workers' control, Lenin contended that unions should become instruments of the workers' state. Within two years of the revolution, the unions were tasked with encouraging increased productivity and enforcing labor discipline as well as adopting rigid hierarchical control.

Yet differences within the Bolshevik Party over the role of unions continued, with Trotsky arguing for the "militarization" of trade unions, and the Workers' Opposition pushing for greater union autonomy and control. In 1921, Lenin engineered a compromise that gave unions "dual functions": to encourage labor productivity and protect workers from managers. Along with being bearers of party policy, unions were expected to keep an eye on managers and provide important feedback to the party, and hence become a "transmission belt" between the party and workers. The unions' "defensive function," though, was carefully circumscribed: since as it would later be claimed there were no "antagonistic" class interests under socialism, unions were expected to subordinate their members' particular concerns to the more general and long-term interests of workers as defined by the party.

In the New Economic Policy period, the contradictions inherent in these dual functions soon placed unions in an "excruciatingly ambiguous position," as they were expected to defend workers' interests while implementing party policy that might include speedups, higher work quotas, and the increased use of piece rates.

The Stalinist era quickly eliminated this ambiguity. The enterprise troika of manager, party secretary, and trade union chair gave way to one-person management. Unions were told to "turn their faces toward production," and collective agreements were done away with from 1935 to 1947. While under Khrushchev unions were told to increase their defense of workers' interests, they were still expected to keep production as their central responsibility.

Throughout the Soviet period, unions retained much of their formal structure, even as the Soviet model was exported to Eastern Europe and China. Unions were organized as industrial unions that followed the various branches of the economy. All workers in a given branch belonged to the same union, regardless of their occupation. Given the notion of nonantagonistic interests, workers as well as top managers, and even ministry officials, belonged to the same union. Membership was nearly universal, making union density rates almost 100 percent, and also making unions the largest organizations in Communist societies—even larger than the Communist parties. (China remains an exception; since migrant and agricultural workers are excluded, union members are only 15 percent of the overall labor force.)

The union structure contained multiple levels of administration, and was subject to democratic centralism, essentially top-down decision making. Unions also remained firmly under party control. Top union officials, for example, were subject to the party rather than union *nomenklatura*.

During the Soviet period there was a debate in Western scholarship over how extensively unions performed their dual functions, particularly the protection of labor. Yet such a debate may have been misplaced. A number of scholars have since argued that Communist trade unions were concerned primarily not with production or the protection of workers but with rather the distribution of social benefits within the enterprise. Beginning with Stalinist industrialization in the Soviet Union, a "shortage economy" developed whereby virtually all commodities, including labor, were in short supply. In

building the new factories workers had to be retained, and it was the social provisions, which the trade unions distributed, that kept workers in place.

In the Soviet case especially, the enterprise became the central social unit, and the unions functioned essentially as social welfare agencies, distributing items such as housing, trips to the enterprise resort centers and children's camps, and consumer goods as well as maintaining the enterprises' day care centers, "houses of culture," sports teams, musical groups, and the like. Unions also distributed the state social insurance fund. This distribution increased workers' dependence on the workplace as well as the dependency of unions on both management and the state, which ultimately controlled the enterprise social fund and social insurance.

Communist unions were quite different from their typical capitalist counterparts. Workers, managers, and union officials alike would see enterprise-level unions as arms of management, and unions and managers often provided a common front in bargaining with planners. (In their informal operation they were most akin to enterprise or company unions in capitalist societies, where workers and managers were said to share a common interest in the survival of the enterprise, and workers might be provided for in a paternalistic fashion.) Unions rarely saw themselves as independent advocates of workers in adversarial bargaining with managers. Unions had little say over such key issues as wages, which were centrally determined, and collective agreements had little mention of the terms and conditions of employment. Such bargaining that did take place occurred informally, on the shop floor between workers and line managers, and was based not on the unions' collective voice but rather on workers' individual power of exit in a labor-short economy. As a result, workers were more likely to approach their supervisor than their union representative with a workplace grievance.

The Soviet model of trade unions varied when applied to Eastern Europe and China, though the "variations are best understood as adaptations of the [Soviet] model rather than departures from it." Unions in those Eastern European societies with fewer economic shortages were less likely to emphasize the distribution of social benefits. China with its vast labor force had never experienced a labor shortage; yet the *danwei* system of enterprise organization, and the role of unions within it, closely resembled the Soviet model of enterprise paternalism.

Yugoslavia and Hungary adopted market elements in their economies, and party and union leaders in both countries acknowledged competing and conflicting social interests. In Yugoslavia, with its version of enterprise self-management, worker councils (but not the weaker unions) were quite influential within the enterprise. In Hungary, while unions were weak at the enterprise level, some found evidence of corporatist trends at the national level. Hungary as well as Poland and Romania also adopted worker councils, though some have interpreted the formation of worker councils as an acknowledgment of union weakness.

Indeed, during periods of worker unrest—in Hungary and Poland in 1956, the Soviet coal miner strikes of 1989–91, and especially the Solidarity period in Poland of 1980–81—the ineffectiveness of Communist trade unions was laid bare. As a Solidarity era joke explained it, under capitalism, unions protect workers from capitalists; under socialism, they protect socialists from workers. Solidarity's most prominent demand was for a truly independent trade union, and its success made it the most famous union in the Communist era. The Polish state's repression against a clearly authentic working-class organization revealed perhaps the greatest ideological and political vulnerability of the Communist system.

Despite the Solidarity experience, during the 1989 Soviet miners' strikes, one local union leader complained, "Our trade union officials turned out to be totally unprepared. . . . The people launched their attack and marched right by us, and we were left dragging soup kitchens after them." The union signed the agreement ending the strike, but on the side of the government rather than the miners, who soon formed an independent union.

Yet for all their shortcomings, the successors to the once-Communist unions remain the largest union in each post-Communist country, owing mainly to their once-mandatory membership, their institutional infrastructure, and the general inertia in post-Communist civil society.

China is now most prominently dealing with the contradictions of the Communist trade union model. Chinese "market socialism" has exposed workers in all sectors to the harsh vagaries of the market. New laws in the early 1990s encouraged unions to defend workers' interests and introduced (previously lacking) collective labor contracts; unions remain burdened with the task of promoting enterprise productivity, however. While some argue that unions are becoming more assertive, especially at the lower levels, others maintain that workers are still skeptical about labor unions. At least one union official stated in private that the union's "main role was to promote 'stability' at a time of rising worker discontent and protest."

Indeed, worker protest has increased dramatically in recent years, and yet unions remain largely on the sidelines. The Chinese Communist Party is facing a considerable dilemma: were unions to be more assertive, the many isolated strikes and disturbances might become connected; yet without unions capable of defending workers, those strikes and disturbances will likely grow.

In all, unions in Communist societies were large but weak, spending most of their time distributing goods and services rather than defending workers' interests against their employers. While adversarial trade unions were seen as unnecessary in a society guided by the Communist Party, the lack of such trade unions led rather directly to Solidarity, one of the most influential workers' movements in history. It would not be too much of a stretch to argue that Solidarity was the warning bell that prompted Gorbachev's strategy of perestroika, and in turn, the collapse of Soviet Communism. Chinese leaders would do well to heed that warning.

See also International Trade Union Organizations; Markets, Legal and Illegal; Planning; Socialist Market Economy.

FURTHER READING

Ashwin, S. *Russian Workers: The Anatomy of Patience*. Manchester, UK: Manchester University Press, 1999.

Ashwin, S., and S. Clarke. *Russian Trade Unions and Industrial Relations in Transition*. Basingstoke, UK: Palgrave, 2003.

Blecher, M. *China against the Tides*. 2nd ed. London: Continuum, 2003.

Burawoy, M., and J. Lukacs. *The Radiant Past: Ideology and Reality in Hungary's Road to Capitalism*. Chicago: University of Chicago Press, 1992.

Crowley, S. *Hot Coal, Cold Steel: Russian and Ukrainian Workers from the End of the Soviet Union to the Post-Communist Transformations*. Ann Arbor: University of Michigan Press, 1997.

———. "Explaining Labor Weakness in Post-Communist Europe: Historical Legacies and Comparative Perspective." *Eastern European Politics and Societies* 18, no. 3 (2004).

Deutscher, I. *Soviet Trade Unions*. Oxford: Oxford University Press, 1950.

Filtzer, D. *Soviet Workers and Stalinist Industrialization*. Armonk, NY: M. E. Sharpe, 1986.

Hong, N. S., and M. Warner. *China's Trade Unions and Management*. New York: St. Martin's Press, 1998.

Kornai, J. *The Economics of Shortage*. 2 vols. Amsterdam: North-Holland, 1980.

Kubicek, P. *Organized Labor in Postcommunist States*. Pittsburgh: University of Pittsburgh Press, 2004.

Kuromiya, H. *Stalin's Industrial Revolution: Politics and Workers, 1928–1932*. Cambridge, UK: Cambridge University Press, 1988.

Laba, R. *The Roots of Solidarity*. Princeton, NJ: Princeton University Press, 1991.

Lee, C. K. "From the Specter of Mao to the Spirit of Law: Labor Insurgency in China." *Theory and Society* 31 (April 2002).

Lenin, V. "Draft Theses on the Role and Functions of the Trade Unions under the New Economic Policy."

Lu, X. "Transition, Globalization, and Changing Industrial Relations in China." In *The Politics of Labor in a Global Age*, ed. C. Candland and R. Sil. Oxford: Oxford University Press, 2001.

Ost, D. *Solidarity and the Politics of Anti-Politics*. Philadelphia: Temple University Press, 1990.

Pravda, A., and B. Ruble. "Communist Trade Unions: Varieties of Dualism." In *Trade Unions in Communist States*, ed. A. Pravda and B. Ruble. Boston: Allen and Unwin, 1986.

Ruble, B. *Soviet Trade Unions*. Cambridge, UK: Cambridge University Press, 1981.

Stark, D. "Rethinking Internal Labor Markets: New Insights from Comparative Perspective." *American Sociological Review* 51, no. 4 (1986).

Triska, J. F., and C. Gati, eds. *Blue-Collar Workers in Eastern Europe*. London: Allen and Unwin, 1981.

White, G., J. Howell, and S. Xiaoyuan. *In Search of Civil Society: Market Reform and Social Change in Contemporary China*. Oxford: Clarendon Press, 1996.

STEPHEN F. CROWLEY

Transportation

The Soviet regime, like its czarist predecessor, was preoccupied with the question of transport and its development. This concern grew from the vast distance between economic and population centers in the USSR, and from the imperatives of defense. Under Sergei Witte, the czarist government had followed the model of Bismarck in Germany, using state control of freight rates as a way of fostering trade, and through the encouragement of railway construction, stimulating industrial development by increasing the demand for iron, steel, coal, timber, locomotives, and rolling stock. Already in the czarist period the state was the major owner of the railways, as many private companies were taken over. The state was, for example, the main force behind the building of the Trans-Siberian railway in the 1890s.

The rail network, a major means of transport, acquired enormous social and political significance. It was the failure of the rail system in 1917 that precipitated food shortages in St. Petersburg and Moscow, leading to the overthrow of the czar. Railway workers became a central group within the labor force, with Bolsheviks and Mensheviks competing to win their support. In the main cities, and even in outlying parts of the empire, railway workers were strategically important in the period of revolution and civil war. The Central Committee of the Joint Union of Water and Rail Transport Workers in November 1917 virtually threatened the overthrow of the new Bolshevik government, which used control of the railways as a means of disseminating Bolshevik propaganda during the civil war. Control of the central rail hub in Moscow was crucial in securing Bolshevik victory over the Whites, who were dispersed around the periphery of the country.

Further evidence of the railroad's central importance was a scheme promoted by the Bolsheviks as a strategy for economic modernization. The Bolshevik government made large-scale purchases of locomotives and railway stock from abroad as a way of breaking the economic embargo imposed on the new revolutionary government. A key role in developing this initiative was played by the railway engineer Yu. V. Lomonosov. The project developed alongside the Goelro scheme for the electrification of the country. Both projects had as their objective the shrinking of the vast spaces of the country and the bringing together of industry, energy resources, and raw material deposits.

In the early decades of Soviet power the People's Commissariat of Transport (NKPut) was a major influence in government, headed by some of the most important figures within the politburo. Nevertheless, during the First Five-Year Plan the commissariat suffered seriously from underfunding, at a time of huge growth in freight transport, precipitating a major transport crisis that lasted until 1935 when new investment was made available. In 1935 the railways initiated their own version of the Stakhanovite movement, pioneered by locomotive driver Krivonos. During the great purges the railways were among the economic sectors that were hardest hit. In these years the critical role that the railways played in the country's defenses were highlighted, and their command structure was militarized. The weakness of the rail transport system was demonstrated during the Winter War with Finland in 1939–40. In general the railways coped well with the additional strains of the Second World War, although Kaganovich, the head of the commissariat, was sacked on two occasions in response to particular crises.

Railway construction featured prominently in the Stalin-era infrastructure program. The most famous of the projects undertaken was the Turkestan-Siberian railway, completed in 1931. Considerable efforts were also made to expand the rail network through the construction of trunk lines between the main industrial centers, including the primary link between Moscow and the Donetsk coalfield, the industrial link connecting the two parts of the Urals-Kusnetsk combine. There was also an effort to upgrade railroad tracks to cope with heavier and faster freight trains. The Moscow rail hub, the center of the country's rail network was upgraded. In the 1930s the Moscow suburban rail system was developed, using electrical power. The building of the Moscow metro began in 1933 with the opening of the first section in 1935, named in honor of Lazar Kaganovich, first secretary of the Moscow party organization, who had overseen the project and who in 1935 took over the running of the People's Commissariat of Transport (NKPut). The Moscow metro was renamed in honor of Lenin after 1956. The metro was and remains one of the outstanding examples of Soviet architectural style.

In the Stalin era the construction of transport infrastructure was one of the central objectives of the state. Canal building was one priority, the first big project being the Belomor Canal that linked the Baltic and the White Sea via Lake Ladoga. This, the first major construction project to employ forced labor, was celebrated in a book edited by Gorky, Firin, and Averbakh, who lauded its role in "reforging" criminals into Soviet citizens. The project exacted a huge death toll on those engaged in its construction. Its benefits, moreover, were considerably less than projected, because the canal was capable of handling only vessels of shallow draught. A second major canal project was the Moscow to Volga canal, completed in 1937, which aimed to turn Moscow into an inland port connected to the Caspian, Black, Baltic, and White seas, and to ensure a water supply for the burgeoning industry and population of the capital. In the late 1940s other big canal projects were undertaken, including the Volga-Don canal, which was completed in 1952.

Until the early 1930s the rail system employed steam locomotives, fueled by coal. Beginning in the early 1950s attention turned to the development of diesel and diesel-electric locomotives. Rail transport remained the dominant mode of transport throughout most of the Soviet era. Already in the 1930s criticism was directed at the economy's overdependence on the railroads, which were burdened by huge increases in freight and passenger traffic, while water and road transport were comparatively neglected. All modes of transport suffered from the harsh winter climate. Water and rail transport tended to follow a very clear seasonal cycle in their activities, with a diminution of activities at the winter peak.

Large-scale infrastructure projects continued in the post-Stalin era. Leonid Brezhnev in 1974 launched as a "shock project" the building of the Baikal-Amur railway (BAM). This project, begun already in 1938 but halted at the outbreak of World War II, was to provide a second Trans-Siberian link, and was only completed in 1991.

Road transport developed in the 1930s, with vast investments being poured into the Stalin Motor Works in Moscow (ZIS, Zavod imena Stalina), later renamed the Lenin Motor Works (ZIL). In 1964 the Soviet motor industry got a boost with the building of a FIAT motor plant at Togliattigrad (named after the Italian Communist Palmiro Togliatti) on the Volga, which became the highest-volume car producer in the USSR, both for domestic use and export. Large trucks were produced at KAMAZ. The slow development of the Soviet motor industry reflected state priorities: investment was concentrated in the public sector, with low priority ascribed to private needs. In the main urban centers, transportation was predominantly public, with metro systems in major cities (Leningrad, Kiev, Nizhny Novgorod, Tashkent), electric suburban rail systems (*elektrichka*), trolley bus systems, and the continued use of trams. Interregional travel was primarily by train, though there was a substantial development of air transport. Public transport in general was highly subsidized.

See also Military-Industrial Complex; Modernization; Revolution from Above; Soviet Industrialization.

FURTHER READING

Heywood, A. *Modernising Lenin's Russia*. Cambridge, UK: Cambridge University Press, 1995.

Payne, M. J. *Stalin's Railroad: Turksib and the Building of Socialism*. Pittsburgh, PA: University of Pittsburgh Press, 2001.

Rees, E. A. *Stalinism and Soviet Rail Transport.* London: Macmillan, 1995.

Westwood, J. N. *Soviet Railways to Russian Railways.* Basingstoke: Palgrave, 2002.

E. ARFON REES

Trotsky, Leon

Trotsky's real name was Leiba Bronstein (1879–1937). He was born in the Yanovka rural settlement on November 7, to a Jewish family that had moved south to benefit from the freer economic, social, and religious conditions that prevailed there. Leiba's father was a successful farmer who built a modern agricultural business from nothing and expanded it steadily by renting land from less successful Russian and Polish neighbors. The Bronstein family lived comfortably, and Leiba had his own nanny. First he went to a local Jewish school and then was sent to Odessa, where he studied at the *Realschule.* His early inclination was toward literature, but he became involved in opposition to the academic authorities and was expelled. His parents, eager for him to complete his education, dispatched Leiba to Nikolaev. These experiences revealed to him a whole new world of cultural diversity. His family had never been especially observant of Jewish religious practice, and Leiba quickly put Judaism behind him. He was drawn into discussions of social revolution. Like most young rebels in the Russian Empire before the turn of the century, he joined groups committed to a strategy resting on terrorist methods and on the virtues of "the people."

Gradually he adopted Marxism, mainly through the influence of his future wife, Alexandra Sokolovskaya. Together the two took part in study circles as well as in the local strike movement. In 1898 they were arrested and, two years later, sent to Siberia. They married en route.

While in exile with Alexandra and his two young daughters, Trotsky began to write legally for the newspapers. At the first opportunity, he escaped and made his way abroad without his family. Having already heard about Lenin and his newspaper *Iskra,* Trotsky offered his services to him in London. At the Second Party Congress in 1903, however, he saw for himself Lenin's schismatic and authoritarian tendencies. Trotsky therefore took the Menshevik side in subsequent organizational disputes and wrote a stinging attack on Lenin in his *Report of the Siberian Delegation.* At the same time, he despised the strategic moderation of Menshevism. In 1905 he returned to Russia and helped to lead the Petersburg Soviet, promoting the idea that there should be a "workers" government for the country as a whole. His thought was impregnated with notions drawn from the German Social Democrat Alexander Parvus-Helphand. The soviet was closed down and Trotsky was put on trial. He distinguished himself by fulminating against resurgent czarism. Sent again to Siberia, he escaped in January 1907 before reaching his destination and devoted himself in Europe to seeking the reconciliation of the Bolsheviks and Mensheviks in a reunited Russian Social-Democratic Workers' Party. He stood as a leader who put himself outside the considerations of mere factionalism.

Trotsky published his ideas on "permanent revolution" in *Results and Prospects,* explaining that Russia could capitalize on its economic and cultural backwardness by picking up the most advanced ideas and practices from elsewhere in the world and organizing itself for immediate Socialist revolution. He had by then met his second wife, Natalya Sedova, by whom he quickly had two sons. He earned his keep by writing for the press in the Russian Empire. There was no greater stylist in the Russian Social-Democratic Workers' Party and no Marxist in Europe with his range and depth of cultural understanding.

Yet Trotsky's personal arrogance and the sheer bitterness of the factional conflict stymied his efforts to achieve organizational unity. The Bolsheviks declined his invitation to attend a conference in Vienna in August 1912; instead they had held their own in Prague in January. Trotsky and Lenin concurred that the workers should be the main force in the coming revolution in Russia and that the middle classes were not to be trusted. But they were at opposite poles of opinion about the organization of the party, and they despised each other. This situation changed little during the First World War when they attended the internationalist antiwar conferences in Switzerland at Zimmerwald and Kiental. Lenin was happy to split—even from other groupings on the Socialist extreme Left—while Trotsky saw this as ignoble and self-defeating. He was deported from France in 1916 and arrived in New York only months before the February 1917 revolution in Petrograd. The Canadian authorities delayed his voyage back across the ocean. What he discovered on arriving in Russia in May was that the Bolsheviks were the only large party committed to overthrowing the "bourgeois" and prowar provisional government. After years of polemics against the Bolsheviks, he joined them.

In July Trotsky was arrested by the army in the provisional government's drive against the Bolshevik party. Released in September, he became a stellar performer for the Bolsheviks in both the press and the Petrograd Soviet. He chaired the Military-Revolutionary Committee and supported Lenin's call for a Socialist seizure of power at Bolshevik Central Committee meetings on October 10 and 16. He played an active, prominent role in the overthrow of the provisional government on October 25.

In power he was a revelation. Having once sought to keep the Mensheviks and Bolsheviks in a united party, he proved Lenin's eager supporter in refusing to set up a broad governing coalition. Trotsky was also among the most avid advocates of revolutionary violence. His first post took him to the People's Commissariat of External Affairs where he called a truce on the Eastern front and set out for Brest-Litovsk to negotiate with the Central Powers. In the winter of 1917–18 it became clear that the Soviet state faced the threat of being overrun by its foreign enemies unless it agreed to a separate peace with Berlin and Vienna; and in this situation it appeared urgent to Trotsky to drag out the discussion. He dazzled and befuddled the diplomats and commanders on the other side of the negotiating table. His ploy, known as "neither war nor peace," worked only temporarily, however. When the German ultimatum was delivered, Lenin demanded that the Bolsheviks should approve a treaty. Trotsky saw this as a betrayal of Bolshevik principle and slogans and instead called for a "revolutionary war" (even though he privately conceded that such a war would not be winnable). He would rather see "Soviet power" overturned than ratify a deal with "imperialism."

Lenin won over the Bolshevik Central Committee; the treaty of Brest-Litovsk was signed—and Trotsky resigned his post. Circumstances quickly induced him to return to the leadership. The civil war in Russia intensified. Lenin asked Trotsky to head the People's Commissariat of Military Affairs and to strengthen the organization, planning, and morale of the Red Army. Trotsky threw himself into his duties with panache. The anti-Bolshevik forces were assembling in the Volga region, and he was sent to Kazan to turn them back. On his arrival he found the Red regiments in chaos. He rectified the situation with a combination of ruthlessness and inspiring rhetoric. Convinced now of the need for the Bolsheviks to apply professional standards to their military, he recruited former Imperial Army officers into

the Red Army. To each of them he attached a political commissar. He also made clear that unruly or cowardly Communists would be punished as severely as any other military delinquents. This made him hugely unpopular in the party and many critics, including Stalin, began to regard Trotsky as a potential Bonaparte who would use the Red Army as a platform from which to make a personal bid for supreme power.

A military opposition grew among Bolsheviks, and it was only the support of Lenin that saved Trotsky and his policies at the Eighth Party Congress in March 1919. Trotsky was appointed to the Central Committee and its politburo. He also led the Revolutionary-Military Council of the Republic, becoming thus the chief liaison between party and army. His dedication to competent planning commended itself to the military commanders, while his readiness to discuss any changes of strategy or personnel with the politburo allayed the suspicions of at least some of his political comrades. Meanwhile he wrote prolifically on all issues of internal and external policy. He was a leading figure at the founding Congress of the Communist International (Comintern). He gave frequent speeches on his tours of the Red Army, and his "Trotsky train" with its onboard office and printing press became renowned throughout the land.

Victory in the civil war came at a terrible price to the economy and society. Trotsky recommended several schemes for postwar recovery; among them was the formation of "labor armies" consisting of Red Army soldiers who would be put under military discipline to rebuild roads and factories. Another idea was to relax to a degree the fierce system of state grain procurements, with the goal of giving the peasantry greater incentives to expand their acreage. To general surprise he showed no particular favor to the urban working class. He campaigned for the removal of their already limited rights to collective protection of their pay and living conditions and argued that there was no place for independent trade unions in what was supposedly already a "workers' state."

Such ideas caused controversy in the party, but their impact was diminished by the course of events. The Bolsheviks ill-advisedly attempted to invade Poland in the summer of 1920 with a view toward sparking a fraternal revolution in Warsaw. Ultimately it was hoped that they would reach Germany and help to install a Soviet-style state in Berlin. The Polish military defense wrecked this vision, and the Bolsheviks had to sue for peace. Trotsky, who had not been a main advocate of the campaign, was at the forefront of those who called for a reconsideration of party policy at home and abroad. Peasant revolts and industrial strikes intensified debates at the apex of the Bolshevik leadership. A New Economic Policy was proclaimed in early 1921 which, as it was developed, introduced a graduated tax-in-kind to agriculture and a degree of private enterprise to small-scale industry. Trotsky approved of this strategic retreat, but he had his own ideas about how it should be accomplished. He clashed with Lenin about the role to be played by central state economic planning. While accepting the need for concessions to capitalism, he insisted that the Bolsheviks should increase the powers of the government in industry, commerce, and agriculture. Already Trotsky was seeking ways to move beyond the New Economic Policy toward the projected economy of socialism.

Lenin and Trotsky came together again in late 1922 when Lenin needed Trotsky's assistance to face down Stalin on a number of troubling questions. Like Lenin, and in contrast to Stalin, Trotsky wanted to maintain the state monopoly in foreign trade, to eradicate unnecessary "bureaucratism," and to provide non-Russians with increased constitutional safeguards. The sudden drastic deterioration of Lenin's health in March 1923 and his death in January 1924 disrupted this collaboration. Trotsky found himself in a struggle for the political succession.

His tactics were not the most wise, and certainly they were unsuccessful. He failed to take Lenin's *Testament* to the party, a move that might have crushed the rising authority of Stalin as general secretary. He briefly aligned himself with Zinoviev and Kamenev to trim Stalin's freedom from control in party administration; but he was too much the individualist to nurse good relations with them for long. Unaware that his solitary style of behavior conveyed the impression that he wanted to eliminate them from the leadership, Trotsky unwittingly gave further grounds to this suspicion in his November 1923 publication *The New Course*. There he fulminated against recent developments in the party and criticized recent mistakes made by its leaders. He demanded a more rapid development of Soviet industry than his comrades in the leadership and urged the termination of bureaucratic practices in party and government. Trotsky's sympathizers too came into the open and attacked the politburo, and it was Stalin who was asked by Kamenev and Zinoviev to mount a counteroffensive. Trotsky's position was not helped by one of his all-too-frequent bouts of ill health; while he was on his way south to Abkhazia to recover, Lenin passed away.

For the rest of the decade Trotsky strove to lead the Left opposition against the ascendant party leadership. He suffered regular defeat and was removed as People's Commissar of Military Affairs in January 1925. Members of his faction were also removed from high office. Nevertheless he remained in the politburo, and admiration for him was widespread in his own and other Communist parties. He consoled himself with vivid criticisms of the politburo as well as pamphlets on topics somewhat distant from the political mainstream. His *Literature and Revolution* as well as his *Problems of Everyday Life* fall into this category.

Yet his insistence that there was more to politics than high-level machinations served Trotsky ill. In 1925 his erstwhile enemies Kamenev and Zinoviev came to share his concerns about what they saw as the increasingly nonrevolutionary and anti-Leninist trends promoted in the party by Stalin and Bukharin. Initially they formed an opposition of their own, based mainly in Leningrad (which was Zinoviev's fiefdom). In 1926 the Left opposition and the Leningrad opposition coalesced in the United Opposition. The factional struggle became more acute, and Trotsky charged Stalin with being the chief culprit responsible for undermining the original aspirations of the October Revolution. In a reference to the French Revolution, he described this as a Thermidorian Reaction. Just as the egalitarian idealists of 1789 had been supplanted by bourgeois enforcers, so, Trotsky claimed, the Bolshevik revolutionaries of 1917 had been replaced by an apparatus of clerks who spurned socialism and internationalism in favor of their own power and privilege. Trotsky designated Stalin the "gravedigger of the Revolution." Outwitted and outmaneuvered, the United Opposition went down to defeat in 1927. Kamenev and Zinoviev recanted and were readmitted to the party soon after their expulsion. The unrepentant Trotsky was sent into administrative exile in Alma-Ata in January 1928.

Despite difficulties, Trotsky continued to organize a Left opposition from afar. He continued to believe, on the basis of little evidence, that the Soviet working class would endorse his policies if only he could breach the dike of the Stalinist police state. Trotsky demanded a more adventurous set of initiatives in international relations. He railed against Stalin's theory of "socialism in one country" and argued that an isolated Soviet state was doomed to ineffectuality. (Whether workers wished for a reversion to such a risky initiative is more than doubtful.) Trotsky further maintained that the party's organizational procedures needed to be democratized in order for it to recover its old élan. Earlier it had been Trotsky himself who had eulogized hierarchy, command, and discipline as the cardinal requirements for successful action. And his economic recommendations, which included an increase in the state's fiscal pressure on the better-off sections of the peasantry, could hardly have been realized without an enhancement of the role of the security police. But this was not how Trotsky and the Left opposition saw things; and the chaos and abuses that accompanied Stalin's sudden campaign for accelerated industrial growth and agricultural collectivization in 1928–29 convinced them that their alternative strategy was infinitely superior.

Trotsky was not allowed to put his case before the USSR. In February 1929 he was forcibly deported to the Turkish island of Prinkipo (Büyükada) off the coast near Istanbul. Although he succeeded in starting up a *Bulletin of the Opposition* and, for a while, was able to keep in close contact with Moscow, his political impact dwindled. His family quickly suffered worse than he did himself. One daughter by his first wife Alexandra Sokolovskaya died of natural causes. The other followed him abroad but killed herself while being treated for schizophrenia. His elder son by his second wife Natalya Sedova, Sergei, was arrested and perished in Siberia. So too did Alexandra Sokolovskaya. And Trotsky's brilliant second son Lev would die under suspicious circumstances in a Paris hospital in 1937. Trotsky and Natalya coped as best they could. Neither was in wonderful health; Trotsky in particular could never shake off stomach problems or his vulnerability to moods of depression.

As opportunities for rallying followers in the USSR diminished, he concentrated on building up opposition groups in foreign countries. His son Lev Sedov went off to Berlin to consolidate the editorial and publishing arrangements for the *Bulletin*. Trotsky wrote vigorously both for the *Bulletin* and to fulfill the commercial book contracts that sustained his family and his political ventures. Out of this period of his career came the elegant *My Life* and the trenchant *History of the Russian Revolution*. For years he had been pondering why the October Revolution had "gone wrong," but it never crossed his mind that it was the dictatorship and terror that he and Lenin introduced as soon as they came to power that sowed the seeds of Stalinism. In 1920 he had published a justification of Bolshevik revolutionary methods, *Terrorism and Communism*; in the following year, he had welcomed the violent suppression of the Kronstadt mutineers and their demands for democratization. Now

he refused to back down from those early convictions. Instead he sought the roots of the revolution's "degeneration" and "betrayal" in the centuries-old problems of Russia's historical development. Trotsky reasoned that Russian economic and cultural backwardness rendered the fulfillment of Bolshevism's promises impossible without assistance from revolutions elsewhere in Europe.

This theory of course safely overlooked his own strategic and tactical mistakes. It also relieved Trotsky of any need to appreciate the talents of his enemy Stalin; and in his successive works, through to the posthumously published *Stalin, the Man*, he insisted that the general secretary was a mediocrity who had ascended to the peak of Soviet political office merely because he agreed to pursue the interests of "the bureaucracy." Trotsky shared the snobberies of middle-class Marxists of the Russian Empire: Stalin could speak neither French nor German; he was a poor orator, ill at ease in polite society and uncouth in his manners and discourse. Trotsky preened his own reputation as a leading theoretician of Marxism whereas, in his estimation, Stalin was barely literate. This, a gross underestimation of Stalin's achievements and potential, was also an implicit overstatement of Trotsky's own contributions at the level of Marxist theory.

What is more, Trotsky was quite incorrect in stating that nearly all the acolytes of Stalin in the 1920s were newcomers to the Bolshevik party. In fact they had filled the ranks of Bolshevism in the October Revolution and the civil war. Even Trotsky eventually began to understand that he had to cease insulting them if ever he was going to return to power in the Kremlin; he wrote to his son Lev about the need for the *Bulletin* to handle this matter with finesse. His enduring hope was that the blunders and excesses of Stalin and his cronies would cause the Soviet state to implode on them and that "healthy" elements in the party would then turn to him for leadership. It was also his belief that sooner or later the working class would stand up for itself. Thus he resumed his old argument that any Socialist revolution worthy of the name would be carried out by and for the workers; he consigned to oblivion his own disquisitions, especially from 1920, about the requirement for the proletariat to show unquestioning obedience to the central party leadership. Throughout the 1930s he contended that all was not lost. The USSR, even under Stalin, remained in his opinion a workers' state. As he maintained in *The Revolution Betrayed*, it could be reformed as a model for the world Communist movement when and if the malign presence of Stalin could be eliminated.

His contempt for Stalin grew as Comintern, from the end of the 1920s, adopted slogans identifying other Socialist and Labor parties as the crucial menace to prospects for Socialist transformation in Europe and North America. The German Social-Democrats were denounced as "Social-Fascists." Trotsky could discern the fundamental danger posed by Adolf Hitler and the other genuine Fascists. Stalin's insouciant belief that even if the Nazis were to come to power, they would quickly be overturned by the German Communist Party was put to the test when Hitler assumed the chancellorship in 1933. German Communists became the first mass victims of Nazi repression, and Stalin's policy lay in shreds.

Steadily Trotsky came to the conclusion that he needed to put aside the wish to reclaim the Communist International for his own version of Leninism. Instead he planned to establish a Fourth International under his leadership. It was no longer possible to construct a large Trotskyite party in Germany; but elsewhere, especially in liberal-democratic states, he continued to see his chances as being realistic. The trouble was that he was isolated on Prinkipo. In 1933 he moved to France. The conditions imposed by the authorities, however, proved too restrictive and he applied reluctantly for permission to reside in Norway. There too he encountered difficulties in functioning politically. Moreover, the Norwegian government was subjected to external pressure to get rid of him. The only country that would accept him was Mexico. He and Natalya made the Atlantic crossing in 1937, and from Coyoacán on the outskirts of Mexico City they strove to reestablish an apparatus to communicate with Trotskyites around the world. They were given shelter by the muralist painter Diego Rivera until their falling out in the following year. (Trotsky also had a brief but passionate affair with Rivera's wife Frida Kahlo.) The politics of Trotskyites in Paris and New York became Trotsky's daily preoccupation.

His belief in himself and his confidence in the basic postulates of Marxism-Leninism remained intact, and he continued to relay instructions to his followers. Trotsky could see however that the Fourth International had only a few hundred organized adherents, even in countries where the Trotskyite movement could operate more or less freely. He also understood that not all of the leading Trotskyites were reliable in their commitment to his ideas or adept in their handling of personnel. Trotsky made things worse by intervening frequently, often on the basis of ignorance, in local factional disputes. Furthermore, he was disrespectful to many sympathizers,

such as Andreu Nin, who refused to align themselves closely with him. Nin's efforts to promote a non-Stalinist Communist agenda in the Spanish civil war from 1936 until his death in mid-1937 never received Trotsky's decent appreciation.

Trotsky's axiomatic insistence that the USSR was still a workers' state caused even greater problems. Many French and American Trotskyites thought he lacked an understanding of the awful conditions that prevailed in the Soviet state and society, and some left to form splinter parties. Trotsky's occasional attempts at charm and persuasion made no difference. By late 1939, after Stalin had empowered the signature of a nonaggression treaty with the Third Reich, Trotsky's arguments looked worn out. Whereas he had been an incisive commentator on the rise of nazism, his articles on the first year of the Second World War were full of embarrassing misobservations. He claimed, for example, that there was civil war in Finland. His most loyal adherents had to close their eyes to such inanities. Those who did not offer automatic obedience voted with their feet and joined parties that advocated resistance to both the Nazi and Soviet states. There was no more than a glimmer of a suggestion in Trotsky's writings that he sensed his judgment might be awry. Repeatedly he contended that the outcome of the Second World War would be nothing less than worldwide socialist revolution. But just occasionally he recognized that if this prediction proved inaccurate it might be necessary to revise the Marxist premise that the working class was capable of challenging and defeating the bourgeoisie.

His cerebrations were brought to an end in August 1940 when a Soviet agent, Ramón Mercader, penetrated his household and assassinated him with an ice pick. This was the second attempt to kill Trotsky in that same year. Stalin was determined to eliminate his fiercest critic. Trotsky had absolved himself of the charge laid against him in the Moscow show trials of 1937–38 by holding a quasijudicial enquiry under the chairmanship of the American philosopher John Dewey in spring 1937. He emerged from the proceedings with an unblemished reputation. But he knew that he could not protect himself against the machinations of the Kremlin forever, and his approach to the question of his personal security was ever fatalistic. To the very end Trotsky raged against the dying of his political light.

The Fourth International survived Trotsky's death in a disheveled condition. Its finances were exiguous, its internal factional disputes all-consuming. Only in Ceylon and Bolivia did it have much practical influence. Trotskyites after the Second World War were as diverse in their interpretations of the works of the "Old Man" as Bolsheviks had been after the death of Lenin. A resurgence of interest in Trotsky occurred in the student movement in Europe and North America in 1968. He was romanticized as a democrat (and even as a libertarian) and admired for his impressive literary style and the bravery of his long martyrdom. In the USSR he went on being officially reviled until his rehabilitation by Gorbachev. By then communism was in steep decline both as an ideology and as a system of power in the country, and the event had next to no impact on popular opinion. Trotskyite organizations endured in other countries, but even they retained no strong belief that the revolutionary vision of Trotsky was imminently realizable.

See also Bolshevism; Bureaucracy; Lenin, Vladimir; Marxism-Leninism; Red Army; Red Terror; Russian Revolution and Civil War; Stalin, Joseph; Trotskyism.

FURTHER READING

Benvenuti, F. *I Bolscevichi e l'Armata rossa 1918–1922*. Naples: Bibliopolis, 1982.

Day, R. B. *Leon Trotsky and the Politics of Economic Isolation*. Cambridge, UK: Cambridge University Press, 1973.

Deutscher, I. *Trotsky*, vols. 1–3. Oxford: Oxford University Press, 1954, 1959, 1963.

Howe, I. *Trotsky*. New York: Viking, 1978.

Knei-Paz, B. *The Social and Political Thought of Leon Trotsky*. Oxford: Oxford University Press, 1978.

Thatcher, I. *Leon Trotsky and World War One: August 1914–February 1917*. London: Palgrave, 2000.

ROBERT SERVICE

Trotskyism

Leon Trotsky credited the professor of history and leader of the Cadet Party, Paul Milyukov, with inventing the term "Trotskyism." This was in 1905, the year of the first Russian revolution. Milyukov was referring to Trotsky's theory of permanent revolution. This stated that a Russian revolution to replace czarism would be a workers' revolution. Furthermore, a Socialist revolution in backward Russia could survive only if similar revolutions in advanced Europe would come to the aid of a Russian workers' government. The theory of permanent revolution is for many commentators the core belief of Trotskyism.

It was in the post-Lenin succession struggle within the Russian Communist Party, however, that Trotskyism entered the political lexicon as a defined political entity. A key event in this context was the debate that surrounded the publication of Trotsky's essay "Lessons of October," written as an introduction to the third volume of his collected works, which gathered his writings and speeches of 1917. Trotsky claimed that only he out of the then Bolshevik leadership had displayed genuine revolutionary mettle in October 1917. Other leaders, most notably L. Kamenev and G. Zinoviev, had acted as Mensheviks, arguing that Russia was ripe for a democratic revolution in which the Bolsheviks should remain a party of revolutionary opposition. They had opposed Lenin's insistence that the Bolsheviks should seize power. Even Lenin, however, had erred. He had been wrong to prefer Moscow to Petrograd as the starting place for the assumption of power, and he had been wrong for thinking that a seizure of power would be obstructed if it were linked to the convocation of the Second Congress of Soviets. Although Trotsky did not mention himself by name, it is made clear that it was the Military-Revolutionary Committee, which Trotsky chaired, that was responsible for a smooth transfer of power to the Bolsheviks.

Trotsky's essay drew forth a barrage of objections from leading comrades and key party organizations. N. Bukharin, L. Kamenev, J. Stalin, G. Zinoviev, leading representatives of the Communist International, and the Communist Youth League produced speeches and articles that were published in Russian and in translations in book format. These texts argued that Trotsky had overestimated his importance in 1917. It was simply incorrect that in 1917 Lenin had sought to rearm the Bolshevik party with Trotsky's theory of permanent revolution in a battle against a right-Menshevik faction had grown out of long-held convictions about the Russian Revolution. Once Lenin had convinced colleagues of the correctness of his developing strategy, the party acted in a unified way to guarantee victory. In this process Trotsky or Trotskyism influenced neither Lenin nor the party.

Indeed, the anti-Trotsky case stated, the whole history of Leninism and Bolshevism before and after 1917 was one of opposition to Trotskyism. "Lessons of October" was merely Trotsky's latest attempt to replace Leninism with Trotskyism. According to Trotsky's opponents, Trotskyism could be defined as simply a long history of opposition to Lenin and Leninism. Key examples of this were Trotsky's underestimation of the peasantry versus Lenin's call for a democratic dictatorship of workers and peasants; differences in World War I that saw Lenin arguing for turning the imperialist war into a civil war while Trotsky called for peace; the conflict during negotiations with Germany in which Lenin demanded a settlement but Trotsky wanted "no war, no peace"; and the debate on trade unions, which Lenin defended as independent "schools of socialism" but Trotsky wanted to integrate into an all-powerful state.

In the discussions of 1924, however, a distinction was made between Trotsky and Trotskyism. Repressive measures against Trotsky were rejected, but a call was issued for a propaganda war against Trotskyism. Such a campaign would not be directed against Trotsky personally. The party would continue to recognize his talents, but only by being protected from the pitfalls of his own theories could comrade Trotsky contribute to the cause of Leninism.

It proved impossible to separate a campaign against Trotskyism from a battle against Trotsky. As Trotsky was expelled first from the Communist Party (1927) and then from the Soviet Union (1929), Trotskyism came to be defined not only as an anti-Leninist way of thinking, but as a terrorist movement that was seeking to overthrow socialism in the USSR. In the show trials of the 1930s in the USSR and in the imposition of Stalinism in Eastern Europe in the post–Second World War period, a charge of Trotskyism was often brought against the accused. Soviet textbooks and party literature were expected to define Trotskyism as an anti-Leninist and anti-USSR ideology. The *Great Soviet Encyclopedia* (vol. 26 [Moscow, 1977], 251), for example, speaks of Trotskyism as "an ideological-political, petit bourgeois tendency, hostile to Marxism-Leninism and the international communist movement, hiding its opportunistic essence behind left-radical phrases." Typical writings on Trotskyism in the post-Stalin USSR include M. I. Basmanov's *The Anti-Revolutionary Essence of Contemporary Trotskyism* (Moscow, 1971), and V. M. Ivanov and A. N. Shmelev's *Leninism and the Ideological-Political Destruction of Trotskyism* (Leningrad, 1970). Even in the Gorbachev era there was no hint of a rehabilitation of Trotsky, despite a freer debate on his role as a historical figure and on Trotskyism as a segment of the Communist movement.

Although a barrage of criticism was leveled at "Trotskyism," Trotsky avoided labeling his politics "Trotskyite." He preferred to define himself as a "Bolshevik-Leninist" battling to keep Lenin's heritage alive; it was he, Trotsky, who kept Leninism alive, while Stalin acted as Leninism's gravedigger. In Trotsky's post-1929 writings, he proclaimed himself "the best Leninist," insisting that there was "no better Bolshevik" than Leon Trotsky. He argued that as long as the Russian Communist Party and the Third International could be reformed from within, there was no need to found a specifically Trotskyite party or movement. He led his anti-Stalin campaigns under the banners variously of the Left opposition and the United Opposition. Trotsky's major theoretical journal of the 1930s, the *Bulletin of the Opposition*, carried the subtitle "Bolshevik-Leninists." Trotsky clearly accepted his opponents' assumption that Lenin was the main theoretical innovator and leader of the Russian Revolution. In key texts, such as the *History of the Russian Revolution (1931–33)*, Trotsky minimizes his own role and glorifies that of Lenin. In a diary entry of 1935 he went so far as to claim that in 1917 the October Revolution was conditional upon Lenin's presence. No Lenin, no revolution.

For the bulk of the 1930s Trotsky defended the USSR as a "workers' state," although degenerated. He called upon the "proletarian core" (never defined) to stage a political revolution to restore Soviet socialism to true Leninism. By the end of the 1930s, however, Trotsky argued that such had been the devastation wrought upon the Communist Party of the Soviet Union and the Third International by Stalin and Stalinism, that only a new Fourth International could enable revolutionary Marxists to regroup. In 1938 Trotsky conceded the need for a revolutionary vanguard in a Trotskyite form when the Fourth International was founded.

Although some supporters, for example, the Polish delegation, thought that conditions were not ripe for its foundation, Trotsky was highly optimistic about the future prospects of the Fourth International. It had a right to existence because it was the only body that had correctly foreseen the march of history. Under the vanguard leadership of the Fourth International, Trotsky envisioned the world proletariat establishing pan-continental Soviet regimes across Europe, the Americas, and Asia as stepping-stones to the creation of a world socialist federation. The dreadful alternative was more capitalist misery, with its inevitable rounds of wars and further destruction.

The Fourth International has not changed the world as Trotsky hoped it would. Stalinism, rather than succumbing to defeat in World War II as Trotsky had predicted, managed to strengthen its hold on the USSR and extend its influence into Eastern Europe and beyond. Stalinism, not Trotskyism, dominated the Communist movement in the 20th century. Despite a lack of success in achieving its grand aims and visions, and much experience of splinter groups and factionalism, the various parties of the Fourth International have had some influence. They have kept Trotsky's reputation alive via the publication of biographies and Trotsky's own writings, as well as a host of journals and newspapers that seek to explain the contemporary world from a Trotskyite perspective. Although post-Trotsky Trotskyism has not produced a political or theoretical leader of Trotsky's stature, Trotskyite movements have been influential within left politics more broadly in major capitalist nations, including Britain, France, Japan, and the United States, as well as in Latin America and in some countries in Asia where Trotsky's theory of socialist revolutions in backward nations has some appeal. No government in the capitalist, Communist, or developing nations has ever accepted Trotskyism as an official ideology. Today Trotskyites hope that with Stalinism defeated and capitalism once more spreading its hegemony across the globe, the future may yet belong to Trotskyism.

See also Bolshevism; Bonapartism; Russian Revolution and Civil War; Stalin, Joseph; Trotsky, Leon.

FURTHER READING

Lubitz, W., and P. Lubitz. *Trotsky Bibliography*. 2 vols. Munich: K. G. Saur, 1999.

Thatcher, I. D. *Trotsky*. London: Routledge, 2003.

Trotsky, L. *The Transitional Programme for Socialist Revolution*. New York: Pathfinder Press, 1977.

IAN D. THATCHER

Tukhachevskii, Mikhail

Mikhail Tukhachevskii (1893–1937) was of noble descent and chose a military career like many of his ancestors. In the First World War, he served as lieutenant before being taken prisoner by the Germans in 1915. Radicalized by the revolutionary events on his return to Russia in 1917, he joined the Bolshevik Party, and engaged in building the Red Workers' and Peasants' Army. During the civil war, he advanced to command army groups. He fulfilled sweeping, daring operations, most successful, but some disastrous, such as the 1920 campaign against Poland and the forces of Jósef Pilsudski.

In his early writings, Tukhachevskii combined his newly achieved Marxism with military thought. He espoused a doctrine of "class warfare," propagated "revolution from abroad," and proposed that the Comintern set up a general staff for the world revolution. Tukhachevskii asserted that the Red Army must be ready to support the proletariat to overthrow the ruling class in other countries. In a Comintern handbook on armed uprisings, Tukhachevskii wrote on city fighting. Even in the late 1920s, when the USSR had diplomatic relations with most European countries, he did not hesitate to repeat these ideas.

As chief of the Red Army staff, Tukhachevskii started an investigation in 1925 on the characteristics of future conflicts. In May 1928, the massive volume *Future War* was ready. The report stressed the historical lessons from the First World War: the war's unforeseen enormous scale, its trench-fighting character, and new weapons such as tanks, airplanes, and poison gases. It argued that it was essential to avoid a similar stalemate in a future war. The report emphasized industrial development as a precondition for massive artillery, chemical weapons, and other products. The Red Army would need mobile armed units, armored cars, tanks, and a large air force—none of which was at hand in the 1920s. The desire to overcome the army's technical backwardness welded together the objectives of the military and the industrialists when the plan era began in the late 1920s.

Beginning in May 1928, Tukhachevskii was commander of the Leningrad military district, where he tested innovations with parachute troops. He also continued to pursue his theoretical endeavors. In 1930, he gave a lecture on Vladimir Triandafillov's epochal work on the new maneuver warfare, *The Character of Modern Operations*. In his lecture, Tukhachevskii advocated the development of this new doctrine of "deep battle." He wrote many articles and memorandums on the subject, but his magnum opus, *New Questions of War*, was never completed. The Red Army field regulations of the 1930s were a radical break with the past. Had these schemes been properly implemented, the Red Army could have had a stronger concept at its basis than even the German blitzkrieg theories.

Tukhachevskii was appointed the deputy defense commissar and the chief of armaments in 1931. Throughout the industrialization drive, he oversaw the army's technological development. With visionary clear-sightedness, he supported experiments with rockets, tanks, and high-tech industrial products. For a couple of years, he enjoyed Joseph Stalin's support in his drives toward rearmament. Tukhachevskii emphasized that planning should encompass the whole economy in the event of war: everything must be prepared for a protracted, total war. This economic mobilization planning formed a solid backbone of the Soviet defense operation in 1941–45.

Rumors of a plot by Red Army officers and the Wehrmacht circulated in Europe well before the sensational trial against Red Army leaders on June 11, 1937. The closest thing to plotting that recent archival evidence has found, however, is that Tukhachevskii and others in 1936 suggested that defense commissar Kliment Voroshilov be dismissed for incompetence. After his arrest in May 1937, Tukhachevskii was forced to "confess" that he had plotted for a Soviet defeat against Germany. At the trial, he and the seven other officers were condemned to death. The same fate struck over ten thousand officers in the Red Army, navy, and air force. Earlier reports that Tukhachevskii fell victim to a Nazi conspiracy against the Red Army high command have not found any support in the Russian archives.

See also Great Terror; Military-Industrial Complex; Polish-Soviet War; Red Army; Voroshilov, Kliment; Warfare.

FURTHER READING

de Lastours, S. *Toukhatchevski: Le Bâtisseur de l'Armée rouge.* Paris: Albin Michel, 1996.

Erickson, J., and R. Simpkin. *Deep Battle: The Brainchild of Marshal Tukhachevskii.* London: Brassey's, 1987.

Minakov, S. T. *Stalin i ego marshal.* Moscow: Yauza Eksmo, 2004.

Samuelson, L. *Plans for Stalin's War Machine: Tukhachevskii and Military-Economic Planning, 1925–1941.* London: Macmillan, 2000.

Schneider, J. J. *The Structure of Strategic Revolution: Total War and the Roots of the Soviet Warfare State.* Novato, CA: Presidio, 1994.

LENNART SAMUELSON

Ulbricht, Walter

Born in Leipzig, Walter Ulbricht (1893–1973) joined the Social Democratic Party of Germany (SPD) in 1912. He was a soldier from 1915 to 1918. In 1917 he joined the Independent Social Democratic Party of Germany (USPD), and in December 1920 moved with the majority of the USPD to the Communist Party of Germany (KPD). Here he soon emerged as an organizer. In 1923 he participated in the preparations for the insurrection planned for that fall. After the insurrection's failure, Ulbricht was summoned to Moscow as a member of the Comintern's Executive Committee and he stayed there until 1925. From 1926 to 1929 he was a deputy in Saxony's regional council, and from 1928 to 1935 was a deputy in the Reichstag. He became a member of the KPD's politburo in 1929.

After the national socialists seized power in 1933, Ulbricht was initially sent to Paris to lead the KPD in exile. In October 1935 the Comintern put him in charge of the "operational leadership" of the party's activities in Prague. He returned to Paris in 1937, but in early 1938 was summoned to Moscow. It was only thanks to his extraordinary adaptive powers that he avoided becoming a victim of Stalin's terror. In 1943 he was assigned the leadership of the anti-Fascist National Committee for a Free Germany. Ulbricht returned to Germany in early May 1945 as the leader of a group of KPD functionaries whose mission was to help the Soviet military administration during denazification procedures.

In this role he became the Soviet occupiers' most important interlocutor in Germany. Formally number two below the KPD's president, Wilhelm Pieck, Ulbricht had a lead role in 1946 in the forced annexation of the East German SPD to the KPD, and in the summer of 1948, in the transformation of the Socialist Unity Party of Germany (SED) into a "party of the new type," following the Communist Party of the Soviet Union's model. As the SED's general secretary he exercised pressure starting in 1950 for the German Democratic Republic (GDR) to become a socialist state. During this phase he clashed repeatedly with the Soviet leadership, who did not want to compromise all possibilities of exercising an influence over the whole of Germany in the future. As the crisis unfolded, and led to the uprising of June 17, 1953, Ulbricht only barely missed falling into political disgrace.

Thereafter, however, he managed to consolidate his power and even hold his own with Khrushchev. Faced with the growing number of people who were seeking refuge in the West in the late 1950s, Ulbricht asked Khrushchev to adopt measures to make West Berlin part of the GDR and impose the GDR's international recognition. These developments led to the construction of the Berlin Wall on August 3, 1961, reinforcing the GDR's image as a separate socialist state. Yet Ulbricht continued to hope that the socialist model of society in the GDR could be extended to the Western Federal Republic of Germany. In order to increase the GDR's attractiveness he promoted an economic reform in 1963 that did actually lead to an improvement in economic circumstances. Under Ulbricht's leadership the GDR grew to the point of becoming the second most important industrial power in the Soviet bloc. After Pieck's death in 1960, Ulbricht, as president of the newly founded State Council, also became the head of the government. On May 3, 1971, he was removed from his position as first secretary by a majority in the politburo led by Erich Honecker. Ulbricht died on August 1, 1973.

See also Berlin Wall; Comintern; Insurrection in Germany; Pieck, Wilhelm; Soviet Occupation of Germany.

FURTHER READING
Frank, M. *Walter Ulbricht: eine deutsche Biographie.* Berlin: Siedler, 2001.

Loth, W. *Stalin's Unwanted Child: The Soviet Union, the German Question, and the Founding of the GDR.* New York: St. Martin's Press, 1998.

WILFRIED LOTH

Unidad Popular

The protagonists of Unidad Popular, the political alliance of the Left that won the Chilean elections in 1970, usually pointed to the socialist republic led by Marmaduque Grove Vallejo in 1932—which even though it only lasted for a brief period, had a significant impact on the workers' movement and the memory of the Chilean Left—as the historical antecedent of the "Chilean road" to socialism. The political groups that had supported the republic united a year later to form the Socialist Party. The Socialist Party was critical of the Comintern because of its sectarianism and excessive subordination to the USSR's foreign policy, and supported the creation of a Latin American International capable of forming a Confederation of Socialist Republics that would struggle against both fascism and imperialism. In the case of Unidad Popular's policies, however, it was not only knowledge of previous Chilean history, but also the recent experience of the Cuban Revolution that were decisive factors in guiding policy.

The long debate about Unidad Popular's program had already led to the emergence of a reformist line and a line that was more influenced by Castroism (and its Guevarist variant, still influential even after the commander's death), which argued that an armed defense of the revolutionary process was needed. The compromise that was reached between *gradualistas* and *revolucionarios* for unity's sake, and that was strongly supported by socialist leader Salvador Allende Gossens, was accepted by the left wing of the Partido radical, the Left Catholics in the Movimiento de acción popular unitaria, and the Socialist and Communist parties. It also had the "tactical support" of the Movimiento de izquierda revolucionaria, which only lasted until 1971, when it started its own *poder popular* organization as an alternative to the government.

Never before had there been an alliance in the Western world by means of which a Communist Party—certainly the most important and influential in the region—had entered the government by following an "electoral path,"

a symbolically clear alternative to the "armed path" in the Latin America of the 1960s. The revolutionary impact of the reforms that were being proposed, which directly affected the economic interests of the North American multinationals, was obvious: the nationalization of the country's key resource, the copper mines owned by Anaconda and Kennecott, along with the banks, the ITT Corporation, and foreign trade, and the pursuit of a more encompassing agrarian reform.

In this context the international situation's negative influence was crucial. Between September 4, 1970, the day of the elections, and October 24, U.S. president Richard Nixon—according to Henry Kissinger's memoirs—completely "enraged" by the results of the elections, had already ordered Central Intelligence Agency (CIA) director Richard Helms (without the knowledge of the State Department, Defense Department, or ambassador to Chile) to undertake subversive actions in order to prevent Allende from seizing power—actions involving soldiers in the Fuerzas armadas and Carabineros. Everyone was aware of the importance these days would have, since Allende had won with 36.3 percent of the vote, beating his right-wing opponents, Jorge Alessandri (of the Partido nacional and the Partido radical democrático) and Radomiro Tomich of the Democracia cristiana, who respectively obtained 35 and 27.8 percent of the vote. The task of electing a president was now the responsibility of the two chambers gathered in a plenary session, which was supposed to take place on October 24. Yet the Democracia cristiana made its vote in support of Allende contingent on the passage of a series of constitutional reforms to drastically limit the president's role; Allende would have to run the government during the next one thousand days facing a consistently hostile parliament.

In order to avoid Allende's victory, the CIA devised a plan that was divided into two phases and two separate levels, both of which mostly failed and included the assassination on October 22 of the army's chief of the general staff, the *constitucionalista* René Schneider—a plan that was falsely blamed on the extreme Left. The CIA's subversive activities increased after Fidel Castro Ruz's long trip to Chile in November 1971, and the first of the many *marchas de las cacerolas* against the government was organized against this visit. The previous month the new U.S. ambassador Nathaniel Davis, a trusted Nixon appointee (who from 1963 to 1971 had led U.S. operations against Guatemala in the "dirty war" of "counterinsurgency," which had already caused more than twenty thousand deaths among the civilian population), had arrived in Santiago and was devoting himself to the organization of subversive activities.

During March 1973 the Unidad Popular coalition obtained 44 percent of the vote—a result that even though it gave the government's forces a relative success, consolidated the forces of the opposition, which had received 54 percent. The right and left wings of the respective groupings each started moving toward increasingly extreme positions, accelerating the coup's preparation on the one side and the armed organizations of the poder popular on the other. Allende formed a Central Juridical Commission to prepare for a reform of the constitution to create some balance between Parliament and the executive, thus guaranteeing the continuity and effectiveness of the socialist reforms that were being enacted. These reforms were supposed to be voted on as soon as possible.

Meanwhile the country was shaken by strikes, which had significant repercussions for the government. In October 1972 a large strike organized by the Confederación de la producción y del comercio and the Frente nacional de la actividad privada took place. In May 1973 the strike in the El Teniente mines began, climaxing in a march from Rancagua to Santiago on June 21, and later a general strike, to which the Central única de trabajadores opposed its own strike in support of the government. The country was paralyzed by clashes between demonstrators and law enforcement. In an attempt to prevent Chile's destabilization, Allende appealed to the central role that the Democracia cristiana had in the opposition, but the politicians who were most well disposed to dialogue in that party, Renán Fuentealba and Bernardo Leighton, were forced to resign from their positions as president and vice president, respectively.

Class conflict was increasing daily, and the situation was becoming increasingly dramatic: the economy continued to deteriorate (the 1970 currency had been devalued by an amazing 10,000 percent, and inflation had reached 238 percent), and the effective and feared truckers' strikes as well as the June 29–30 coup attempt (known as the *tanquetazo*) seemed to be foreboding signs of a civil war. On July 29 Allende—under pressure from his party's secretary, Carlos Altamirano—dramatically appealed to Chile's workers, stating that "if the hour arrives, we will give the people arms." At the same time he invited the Democracia cristiana to become part of a "national salvation" government, while this party's right wing, led by former president Eduardo Frei, was negotiating with the military on how to provide political cover for the coup. Between July and August, more

than five hundred acts of sabotage and terrorism were conducted against government buildings and public services, wounding hundreds and killing many others. After Carlos Prats, the military officer that Allende trusted the most, withdrew, the president, wanting at all costs to maintain respect for the legality of institutional procedures, named Augusto Pinochet to replace him as head of the army. Pinochet, though, had been plotting with the military leaders of the other branches of the armed forces to organize the massacre that would start on September 11, 1973.

The now-available documentation confirms U.S. involvement in the fight against the Unidad Popular government from the time of Allende's electoral campaign, and it also demonstrates the USSR's cautious behavior. It seems quite likely that the Kremlin was following the criterion supported by the then-head of the KGB, Yuri Andropov, in a secret memorandum in 1972: "Latin America is a geographic area of particular interest to the United States. They allowed us to intervene in Hungary and Czechoslovakia, and we should keep this in mind and conduct our Latin American policy prudently." The politics of détente led the Soviets to recognize U.S. influence in Latin America, even though after the coup in Brazil in 1964 repression had by then been extended to the entire continent, and was enforced with a variety of means in order to avoid a "second Cuba." These articles of faith were mutually endorsed both during Nixon's visit to Moscow in 1972 and Leonid Brezhnev's visit to Washington during the following year. They also marked the culminating moment of the bipolar, ideological, and military division of power on the various continents. For Latin America, this entailed a long era of military dictatorships, imposed and protected by the United States, until the late 1980s.

See also Anti-imperialism; Cuban Revolution; Détente.

FURTHER READING

Arrate, J., and E. Rojas. *Memoria de la izquierda chilena*. Vol. 2, *1970–2000*. Santiago: Vergara, 2003.

Bitar, S. *Chile, 1970–1973: asumir la historia para construir el futuro*. Santiago: Pehuén, 1995.

Corvalán Marquez, L. *Los partidos politicos y el golpe del 11 de septiembre*. Santiago: Ediciónes ChileAmérica—Cesoc, 2000.

Garcés, J. E. *Allende e l'esperienza cilena*. Milan: Teti, 1980.

Garretón Merino, M. A., and T. Moulian. *La Unidad Popular y el conflicto político en Chile*. Santiago: Minga, 1983.

Johnson, D. L., ed. *The Chilean Road to Socialism*. Garden City, NY: Anchor, 1973.

Piwonka, G., and V. Salas. *Para recuperar la memoria histórica. Frei, Allende y Pinochet.* Santiago: Ediciónes ChileAmérica–Cesoc, 1999.

ALBERTO FILIPPI

United Nations

For the Soviet Union, the United Nations was never of more than secondary importance—the main reason why the world body failed to live up to its potential as long as the Cold War lasted. Soviet relations with the United Nations were nevertheless crucial in their own way as a reflection of Soviet priorities and the manner in which the leading Communist power conducted international relations. And the United Nations was far from unimportant for other Communist nations, particularly China and the Soviet client states in Eastern Europe.

Created in 1945, the United Nations was a quintessential product of Western liberal thinking and the Western experience with devastating wars in the earlier part of the 20th century. Its concept of international community and a collective responsibility for peace was alien both to the Marxist-Leninist concept of international class struggle and the Soviet propensity for power politics, epitomized by Stalin. Still, the Soviet Union found it in its interest to join the new organization when it was founded under U.S. auspices at a time the World War II coalition of the Soviet Union and the Western powers was still in existence, and indeed seemed capable of continuing in some form even after their common victory.

Stalin welcomed the concept of the Security Council, with its five permanent members enjoying the right of veto, which ensured that his country could never be submitted to the judgment of small nations. Moreover, in addition to the membership of the Soviet Union as such, its constituent Ukrainian and Belorussian republics were granted separate membership as if they were sovereign states. According to historian Alexander Dallin, Moscow "preferred joining to avoid the stigma of nonparticipation and prevent the body from becoming a hostile instrument. . . . So long as 'Great Power unanimity' was accepted, it had nothing to lose and perhaps something to gain."

Conversely, once that unanimity fell victim to the onset of the Cold War, the same consideration no longer applied. Decrying the "mechanical" majority of the UN members that sided with the United States, the Soviet Union adopted a defensive attitude and used its right of veto to thwart decisions that it did not consider to be in its own interests. It cast 88 vetoes between 1946 and 1959, and 75 percent of the total of 149 vetoes that were cast during the first three decades of the United Nations' existence. Prior to 1955, these vetoes were mainly intended to block the admission of new members friendly to the United States and prevent the peaceful settlement of international issues that Moscow preferred to keep brewing, such as revolts against Western colonial powers.

In 1949, the Communist victory in the Chinese civil war created the problem of China's UN representation because the United States continued to support the defeated Nationalist government in Taiwan as China's sole legitimate representative, equipped with one of the five veto powers. In protest against the exclusion of its then Chinese ally, the Soviet Union in 1950 boycotted the sessions of the Security Council. It committed a major blunder by not attending the session convened after the North Korean attack on South Korea in June 1950, thus allowing the United States and its allies to oppose the aggression militarily under the flag of the United Nations.

To bypass the likely Soviet veto on similarly important future occasions, the United States attempted to shift the responsibility for collective action from the Security Council to the General Assembly by pushing through the "Uniting for Peace" resolution in November 1950. The Soviet Union, however, succeeded in preventing this from ever having any practical effect. In particular, the United Nations proved powerless in the face of the Soviet military interventions in Hungary in 1956 and Czechoslovakia in 1968.

In 1955, a compromise was reached that provided for the admission of new UN members by balancing what appeared to be at the time pro-Soviet and pro-Western states. Yet the distinction was thrown into disarray by the decolonization process, which brought about a huge influx of new members from the third world, inclined to pursue their own path without identifying themselves with either side in the Cold War. By diluting and eventually breaking the pro-U.S. majority in the world organization, its expansion ended up serving Soviet more than U.S. interests, and prompted the Soviet Union to adopt an offensive policy there.

Soviet leader Khrushchev used the United Nations as a forum to promote his opening to the third world, displaying his support for anticolonial movements and the Arab cause against Israel. At the 1960 session of the General Assembly, he famously banged the table with his shoe to emphasize his disapproval of Western policies. Khrushchev vainly championed the replacement of the UN secretary general by a "troika" of three secretaries, each representing the interests of one of the three "worlds"—a scheme calculated to extend the right of veto to the organization's executive management as well.

In the early 1960s, the Soviet Union became deeply but unsuccessfully committed in the Congo, where it tried to frustrate UN action favoring pro-Western leaders in the country's postcolonial civil war. After Khrushchev's ouster in 1964, his successors scaled down Soviet involvement in the third world as well as the United Nations. The negotiations conducted within the UN framework in the Eighteen-Nation Disarmament Committee moved forward only after being taken out of that framework. All important arms control agreements were subsequently negotiated and finalized outside the United Nations.

For the Soviet Union's dependent states in Eastern Europe, the United Nations had greater attraction than for Moscow because of the promise of enhancing their international stature. In the 1960s, Romania took the lead in organizing the "Group of Nine"—consisting of an equal number of states from the North Atlantic Treaty Organization, the Warsaw Pact, and the non-aligned movement—within the United Nations. The group sought guarantees for small states to be included in the nonproliferation treaty that was being negotiated between the United States and the Soviet Union. When the treaty was signed in 1968, it contained no such guarantees. The nuclear powers subsequently tried to remedy this deficiency by pledging "to act immediately through the Security Council" if any of these small states faced a nuclear threat, but the pledge was never clarified.

Although the Soviet Union continued to support the seating of the Beijing government instead of the Nationalist government in Taiwan, the widening of the Sino-Soviet split since the late 1950s made the benefits of China's UN membership doubtful for Moscow. Beijing's entry into the United Nations in 1971 became a stage in the U.S.-Chinese rapprochement. And once seated in the organization, China became a rival of the Soviet Union by posing temporarily as a more authentic champion of third world causes.

Moscow found it difficult to present itself as a credible advocate of the "New International Economic Order"

sought by third world nations, most of which regarded the Soviet bloc as part of the developed world and insisted on changes in its policies. In 1979, the Soviet Union and other Communist nations curried the favor of Arab, Asian, and African states by endorsing the UN resolution equating Zionism with racism. Later that year, however, the Soviet Union played a force of order by joining the unanimous Security Council resolution condemning the seizure of U.S. diplomatic hostages in Tehran. In 1980, Moscow became an object of condemnation by a vast UN majority censuring the Soviet invasion of Afghanistan.

In the 1980s, the United Nations played a negligible role in the developments leading to the peaceful resolution of the Cold War, the collapse of communism, and the disintegration of the Soviet Union. Afterward, though, the world body rose in significance, expanding its activities especially in the area of peacekeeping, although its peace-enforcing capacity remained more limited. China, nominally still a Communist country, has remained largely passive within the organization, rarely using its veto other than in cases involving its immediate national interests, notably with regard to the status of Taiwan. Having long abstained from participating in UN peacekeeping operations as a matter of principle, in 1998 China finally sent a team of civilian police to East Timor as part of the UN force there, and in 2003 it sent a small noncombat military force under UN auspices to Congo.

See also Cold War; Decolonization; Diplomats; Grand Alliance.

FURTHER READING

Dallin, A. *The Soviet Union at the United Nations.* New York: Praeger, 1962.
Goodrich, L. M. *The United Nations in a Changing World.* New York: Columbia University Press, 1974.
Stoessinger, J. G. *The United Nations and the Superpowers.* New York: Random House, 1966.
Yoder, A. *The Evolution of the United Nations System.* Washington, DC: Taylor and Francis, 1997.

VOJTECH MASTNY

Urbanization

For Karl Marx, urbanization was a double-edged sword. The appalling squalor of Manchester and other industrial cities in England was part of a progressive transformation that had "subjected the country to the rule of the towns . . . [and] rescued a considerable part of the population from the idiocy of rural life." Through the processes of industrialization and proletarianization, capitalist cities were laying the foundation for a socialist revolution that would ultimately erase the distinction between town and country.

Socialist revolution, however, did not erupt in highly urbanized countries such as Britain or Germany. Instead, in October 1917, Vladimir Lenin's Bolshevik Party seized power in the Russian Empire—one of Europe's least urban, least industrial areas. In short order the Soviet Communist Party found itself presiding over one of the most rapid urban transformations that the world had ever seen. After 1945 this pattern was repeated, with more variation, in the newly communized states of Eastern and Central Europe. Still later, Communist governments came to power in China, Vietnam, and Cuba from revolutionary bases in the countryside rather than the cities. In all these cases urbanization was a result more than a cause of Communist revolution, presenting challenges that were at once logistic, ideological, and demographic. Efforts to regulate migration and urban growth produced mixed results, and were sometimes outweighed by unplanned population shifts.

The Scale of Growth

The Russian Empire in 1917 was a peasant society. Roughly four-fifths of its population was tied to the land, and a large proportion of city dwellers were first-generation migrants from the country. During four years of revolution and civil war, the country's largest cities lost half or more of their inhabitants. By the mid-1920s the urban population had recovered to its previous levels, but with important demographic changes: many urbanites had died or emigrated, and the generation that replaced them included more widows, orphans, and outcasts of patriarchal village society.

The First Five-Year Plan (1928–33) and concomitant collectivization of agriculture created a new and unprecedented flow of migration to the cities, with the result that the urban population more than doubled between 1926 and 1939, from twenty-six to fifty-six million. Industrialization was the main engine of growth. New cities such as Magnitogorsk sprang up almost overnight, while older ones such as Gorky (Nizhnii Novgorod) grew spectacularly.

Soviet cities suffered greatly during World War II, but after 1945 urban growth resumed, and by the early 1960s the urban population outnumbered the rural one. Although urban births accounted for half or more of this growth, rural-urban migration remained important. The cramped conditions of city living discouraged the urbanites from having more than one or two children. Meanwhile, the exodus of younger peasants from the countryside created problems for the agrarian sector and also produced a long-term decline in the rural birthrates.

By the early 1980s, almost two-thirds of the USSR's population resided in urban areas. Networks of cities extended across the entire union, and fifty cities had populations of more than half a million. Despite local variation, almost all regions of the country had crossed the 50 percent threshold of urbanization.

The Communist states of Eastern/Central and Southeastern Europe followed similar patterns of urbanization, but with much local variation. In 1945 these were among the least urbanized polities in Europe; only East Germany's population was more than 50 percent urban. In addition, many cities had been physically devastated in World War II, with catastrophic human losses. Postwar population transfers brought more turmoil, and in extreme cases such as Breslau/Wroclaw or Königsberg/ Kaliningrad urban populations were re-created from new sources. New Communist states adopted policies of industrialization and economic planning on the Soviet model, creating new industrial centers and generating overall urban growth. By 1980, 50 percent of the populations of all these countries, except for Albania and Yugoslavia, lived in cities and towns. In the 1980s, as the pace of industrialization and overall population growth declined in most of the European Communist states, cities stopped growing, and some even lost population. These trends continued into the post-Communist era.

In China, Vietnam, and Cambodia, the urban populations were much smaller—15 percent or less—when the Communist governments came to power. In these cases, and in more-urbanized Cuba, the immediate postrevolutionary period was marked by urban dislocation and/ or de-urbanization. Urban growth, when it resumed, was drawn from the rural populations, and was keyed to the administrative and economic changes introduced by the Communist regimes. By 1980, 65 percent of Cuba's population was counted as urban, while the equivalent figures for China and Vietnam were 13 and 19 percent, respectively. (Cambodia, as a result of the genocidal policies of the Pol Pot regime, saw its urban population decline from 11 to 4 percent of the national total.)

Starting in the 1980s, both China and Vietnam underwent extensive economic reforms that triggered more rapid urban growth, but the regulatory regimes in these countries made the statistics hard to evaluate. Estimates of China's urban population in the 1990s ranged from as low as 20 percent and to as high as 50 percent. The "floating" population of rural-born people living without legal registration (*hukou*) in the cities was thought to number fifty million, yet some experts put it as high as a hundred million.

Planning and Regulating Urban Growth

Acutely aware of the poverty and inequality that accompanied urbanization under capitalism, Soviet leaders sought to develop alternatives to capitalist models of urbanization. Urban growth was to be integrated into national economic planning. To build what one writer has termed "*bourgs sans bourgeoisie*," planners tried to establish norms for optimum city size. Property was nationalized, and housing and urban services were to be distributed on an egalitarian basis. A few experimental housing designs were built in the first years of Soviet rule, but industrial expansion soon became an overriding priority. Urban planners lacked the resources to implement ambitious plans. Moreover, their efforts to regulate and systematize growth were frequently overruled by the directors of industrial enterprises. Factories and plants often ended up incorporating infrastructure to house and service the working population. The supposedly optimum city size of fifty to sixty thousand proposed in the 1920s was shelved. Planners did exert considerable influence over the location of new urban settlements, however, with the result that—largely for strategic reasons—many were built in remote and inhospitable localities in the north and east of the USSR. (Several decades later, in Eastern Europe, planners took a similar approach, locating new industrial facilities outside established cities and towns. Critics complained that this led to "underurbanization" or inadequate urban infrastructure, limiting workers' access to the benefits of city living.)

Soviet authorities tried to restrict rural-urban migration by introducing internal passports and registration (*propiska*) for city dwellers, but migrants kept arriving (and departing), often in defiance of the established norms. Urban growth in the 1930s far exceeded the planners' projections, partly because peasants found ways of circumventing the regulatory regime.

After Joseph Stalin's death, Soviet leaders began to put more resources into urban amenities. Some localities achieved notable successes in specific areas such as public transit, but shoddy construction and weak networks of services continued to plague Soviet cities until 1991. The supply of housing never caught up with the demand, although by the 1980s townspeople seemed to be exerting more direct control over their own environment, finding apartments through informal exchanges and relying on semi- or extralegal "second economy" sources to meet their needs. Some observers saw this as a step toward a civil society based on autonomous civic identity, but if so, the change was not decisive. Post-Communist municipal authorities inherited an array of unsolved problems, which were compounded by new challenges, ranging from high crime rates to traffic congestion.

In much of the USSR and Eastern Europe, urbanization was fraught with social tensions inherited from much earlier times, when ethnic, linguistic, and sometimes religious differences divided the rural population from the townsfolk. During the Communist era, this pattern diminished in some localities (such as Vilnius and Lviw) as cities took on the characteristics of the surrounding peasant areas. Elsewhere (Tashkent) cities grew more heterogeneous by attracting migrants from more remote localities. In both cases a substantial proportion of the urbanites were just one generation away from the countryside, and regarded innovation and "cosmopolitanism" with suspicion. Cultural interaction and assimilation were incomplete, and at the end of the Communist era in Europe intraurban and urban-rural tensions erupted into violence in many regions—especially the Balkans and the Caucasus.

In China, Vietnam, and Cuba, planners in the first decades of Communist rule were sensitive to the roles that cities had played in earlier times as centers of imperial administration (Beijing) and/or foreign domination (Shanghai, Hanoi, and Havana). The growth in China was steered toward the smaller and newer inland centers rather than the coastal cities. Maoist policy promoted small-scale and rural industrialization, and during the Cultural Revolution of the 1960s city dwellers were sent to the countryside for "reeducation." In Cuba in the same decade, planners focused on rural development, allowing Havana to deteriorate; in one traveler's words from 1968, "They used to call Havana the brothel of the Caribbean, and it is a city the Revolution is still punishing."

In Vietnam after the Communist victory in 1975, the population of Saigon (renamed Ho Chi Minh City) fell from 4.5 to 3.3 million. Many urbanites were relocated to the "New Economic Zones" in rural areas. As well, many ethnic Chinese, who had been a prominent part of the city's middle class, emigrated from the country.

Beginning in the 1980s, both China and Vietnam embarked on economic reforms that retained authoritarian regulation while accepting marketization and some measure of local autonomy. In both countries the rate of urbanization increased, but resources for urban construction remained scarce. Cuba, without undertaking such sweeping reforms, urbanized at about the same pace as Latin America; roughly 75 percent of its population lived in urban areas by 2000.

In sum, Communist planners' efforts to create and regulate urban growth were constrained by the availability of material resources, and by spontaneous and historical contingency, including spontaneous and unanticipated population movements. Cities grew, sometimes rapidly, but did not transcend the problems of capitalist urbanization. Far from disappearing, the gap between urban and rural life persisted, and was a continuing source of rural-urban migration: cities, for all their shortcomings, retained and even increased their attractive power.

See also Architecture and Urban Planning; Planning; Social Policy; Soviet Industrialization; Transportation.

FURTHER READING

Bater, J. *The Soviet City: Ideal and Reality*. London: Edward Arnold, 1980.

Colton, T. J. *Moscow: Governing the Socialist Metropolis*. Cambridge, MA: Belknap Press, 1995.

Davis, D. S., R. Kraus, B. Naughton, and E. J. Perry, eds. *Urban Spaces in Contemporary China: The Potential for Autonomy and Community in Post-Mao China*. New York: Cambridge University Press, 1995.

Hoffmann, D. L. *Peasant Metropolis: Social Identities in Moscow, 1929–1941*. Ithaca, NY: Cornell University Press, 1994.

Kirkby, R.J.R. *Urbanization in China: Town and Country in a Developing Economy*. New York: Columbia University Press, 1985.

Kotkin, S. *Magnetic Mountain: Stalinism as a Civilization* [Magnitogorsk]. Berkeley: University of California Press, 1991.

Murray, P., and I. Szelenyi. "The City in the Transition to Socialism." *International Journal of Urban and Regional Research* 8 (1984): 90–107.

Thrift, N., and D. Forbes. *The Price of War: Urbanization in Vietnam, 1954–85*. London: Allen and Unwin, 1986.

ROBERT JOHNSON

Utopia

Two forms of ambivalence characterized the Bolsheviks' (Russian Communists') view of utopias and utopianism. Following Marx, they scorned elaborate blueprints for a future Communist or Socialist order, while stressing the preordained force of historical development. Yet they often praised utopians as courageous, if misguided, forerunners of Soviet socialism and communism. These two words—"socialism" and "communism"—cry out for explication: both terms were used, sometimes indiscriminately, at the dawn of modern utopianism in England, Germany, and especially France, c. 1820–50. Marx and Engels used the word communism in their noted manifesto of 1848, but later reverted to socialism to describe their ideology. Marx denoted the Socialist future as a system of work and distribution that would follow the "proletarian revolution" and the "dictatorship of the proletariat" (both of these phrases were used very sparingly in his writings); communism was to be the final achievement. Marx died in 1883 and the organized international Marxist movement that flourished, roughly from 1889 onward, called itself social-democratic and identified its goal as socialism. The Russian Bolshevik leader Vladimir Lenin, in order to distinguish his party from European Social Democrats and Russian Mensheviks, in 1918 dropped the designation Russian Social Democratic Workers Party (Bolsheviks) and renamed his party the Russian Communist Party (Bolsheviks)—later the Communist Party of the Soviet Union.

The other aspect of Bolshevik ambivalence toward utopias was that the Bolsheviks'—and Marx's—final vision of total social justice was clearly open to the charge of utopianism. In formal political rhetoric and in histories of socialism and utopianism, Soviet writers (and their Communist colleagues abroad) maintained the duality by constructing appreciative and respectful studies and biographies of St. Simon, Fourier, Robert Owen, and a dozen other utopian socialists of the early 19th century but always punctuated their accounts with stern lessons on the ignorance and naivete of the utopian thinkers (the tone and volume of condemnation varying in different periods of Soviet historiography). But in laying out the long road of historical antecedents to the Russian Revolution in a way presentable to the masses, the Bolsheviks chose a rather different emphasis. In line with Lenin's great Monumental Propaganda program, c. 1918–20, statues of Caius Gracchus, Babeuf, Fourier, Owen, and St. Simon were erected in Moscow and Petrograd to join those of other European and Russian radicals of the past. The purpose, inspired by Tommaso Campanella (himself the author of a 17th-century utopia, *City of the Sun*), was to enlighten the masses about revolutionary holidays by showing them the depth and scope of the revolutionary tradition. Bolshevik speakers went around the city offering politically correct glosses on these men, their main purpose being to render honor to the dreamy architects of a perfect future.

Varieties of Russian and Soviet utopianism (quite aside from Marx's ultimate vision) flourished rather openly in the 1920s, both in texts and in living experiments. The texts comprised nonfiction scenarios and science fiction stories, replete with details about daily life in a Communist future. Antecedents of utopian science fiction in Russia included Alexander Bogdanov's 1908 novel *Red Star*, which depicted a Communist society on Mars. Soviet science fiction writers took up this theme in a great sweep of the lyrical imagination and created in their minds worlds without war, poverty, or inequality; with technical achievements that included personal flight, computers, and giant cities; and with human relations refashioned to remove distinctions between genders and between mental and manual labor. In some of these works humanity was tormented by death rays, capitalist weapons of mass destruction, and devastating global wars before socialism and then communism emerged triumphant and put in place their tableaux of universal happiness. Written in the style of pulp fiction, detective stories, and adventure tales, these works were designed to put flesh, color, and contours to the abstract ideological teachings of Soviet Marxism.

Beyond the printed page, enthusiasts endeavored to—in a sense—live utopia in their own time by means of experimental life styles and social practices. Maximalist and idealist devices came into play in the realm of egalitarian titles, speech, dress, and mutual relations. The word "comrade" replaced such previous honorific terms as "sir," "lord," and "madam." Social distinctions marked through the use of two different forms of "you" were abolished. A debate on proper dress yielded various options: neat and clean, but plain apparel; "proletarian" affectations of sloppiness and informality; functional costumes designed by the avant-garde; and even universal nudity in a short-lived "down with shame" movement. In celebration of the new egalitarianism, a conductorless orchestra flourished for a decade. Members of the League of Godless endeavored to demolish the notion of deity overnight through scientific teaching, propaganda, and assaults on religious customs. The last included replacing the sacraments of matrimony, extreme unction, and baptism with secular "Red" weddings and funerals and the "Octobering" of newborns. Many couples were induced to endow their babies with revolutionary names such as "Barricade," "Revolution," "Ninel" (Lenin spelled backwards), "Electrification," and "Spartacus"—a clear borrowing of the French Revolution's effort to implant radical values by means of the "little things" of daily life.

Depressed by the perceived "peasantness" of the workforce, its sloth, and inefficient use of space and time, utopian enthusiasts launched campaigns to transform the relatively inefficient worker into a machine-like and punctual performer. Alexei Gastev sponsored the once-famous Scientific Organization of Labor movement. Modeled after Frederick Taylor's industrial efficiency program in the United States, it attempted to measure and improve scientifically motions on the factory floor and to turn the worker into a kind of industrial robot. Platon Kerzhentsev's League of Time issued wristwatches to its members and patrolled work places and meetings in order to enforce punctuality and a sense of the value of time. Earlier manifestations of these ideas were acidly satirized in the great anti-utopian novel *We* (1920) by Evgeny Zamyatin. Artists of all stripes took up the utopian agenda with standardized modern costumes and furniture for the working class, futuristic homes and cities, constructivist art, biomechanics in theater, and machinery music.

Experimental life in a commune (*kommuna*), with its suggestive proximity to the word "communism," proved irresistible to bold spirits who wanted the future *now*. With the exception of some religious sectarians, Russian peasants had not lived in communes under the old regime. Their village *mir*, usually translated as "commune," did not entail collective residence, dining, and domestic work. But the Soviet regime, until collectivization, did periodically encourage just such rural enterprises. "Communards," never numerous, included poor peasants, demobilized Red Army men and their families, and various "utopian" folks ignited by high idealism. They took over gentry manor houses and set up their experiments in collective work and life. In the towns, students, invariably poor, pooled their meager stipends, shared living quarters and books (sometimes even clothing), and rotated household tasks. Both urban and rural communes eventually foundered on quarrels over work, food preparation, or sex. The most successful among them—those of the non-Communist and even anti-Communist religious sectarians lasted until the early 1930s.

In the Stalinist 1930s, these fragmentary utopian experiments largely disappeared. The Stalinist leadership tightened rules, laid down formulas, promoted productivity, forbade far-out behavioral practices, and in fact squelched many of the original aspirations of the revolution held by those who dreamed that communism could be created on the ground, at the moment, by real people, and need not remain a distant and foggy goal. Science fiction, with its long-term visions and predictions, gave way to production novels and socialist realist plots revolving around immediate economic achievements and short-term gains. Stalin officially and emphatically condemned egalitarianism and leveling, which he characterized and both primitive and petit bourgeois. Differential wages, privileges for the nomenclatura, and business suits for directors and political bosses, became the markers in the Stalinist quasitraditional system. Such symbolic institutions as the orchestra without a conductor were abolished. The more extravagant efforts to establish complete equality of sexes and ethnicities were repudiated. Gastev and Kerzhentsev both perished in the purges, along with other would-be utopian dreamers. In the arts, avant-garde currents drowned in the stream known as the Great Retreat which reached back for more conservative cultural forms, genres, and styles. The great stage innovator, Vsevolod Meyerhold, was one of many artistic figures who fell victim to Stalin's executioners. The still surviving communes were liquidated by the government during collectivization.

Stalin in a sense created his own macro-utopia, which featured fantasy-laden economic plans and procedures, a bureaucracy designed to penetrate all corners of society,

and forced-draft collectivization of the entire countryside. This brand of utopia contrasted starkly with those of the revolutionary decade. Lacking the spontaneous and humanist aspects of earlier visions and practices, Stalinism imposed itself from above in a ruthless and callous authoritarianism. Whether seen in terms of the more reductionist versions of the totalitarian approach or in the more complex readings of social and cultural historians, the Stalinist Soviet Union became a twisted parody of utopia.

See also Festivals.

FURTHER READING

Bogdanov, A. *Red Star: The First Bolshevik Utopia.* Bloomington: Indiana University Press, 1984.

Brown, M. C. *Art of the Soviets: Painting, Sculpture, and Architecture in a One-Party State, 1917–1992.* Manchester, UK: Manchester University Press, 1993.

Fulop-Miller, R. *The Mind and Face of Bolshevism.* New York: Harper and Row, 1965.

Gunther, H., ed. *The Culture of the Stalin Period.* Basingstoke, UK: Macmillan, 1990.

Husband, W. *Godless Communism: Atheism and Society in Soviet Russia, 1917–1932.* DeKalb: Northern Illinios University Press, 2000.

Stites, R. *Revolutionary Dreams: Utopian Vision and Experimental Life in the Russian Revolution.* New York: Oxford University Press, 1989.

Tumarkin, N. *Lenin Lives! The Lenin Cult in Soviet Russia.* Cambridge, MA: Harvard University Press, 1983.

Von Geldern, J., and R. Stites, eds. *Mass Culture in Soviet Russia.* Bloomington, IN: University of Indiana Press, 1995.

Wesson, R. G. *Soviet Communes.* New Brunswick, NJ: Rutgers University Press, 1963.

RICHARD STITES

Varga, Eugen

Born in Nagyteteny in Hungary, Eugen Varga (1879–1964) became a member of Hungarian Social Democratic Party and a prominent member of its left wing. A professor of political economy at the University of Budapest starting in 1918, he was also the people's commissar of finance in the Republic of the Councils and later president of the Supreme Council on the National Economy. After Béla Kun's government had been overthrown, Varga emigrated to Russia, where in 1920 he became a member of the Bolshevik Party and the Executive Committee of the Communist International. His career as an economic consultant of the Soviet leadership began in 1921, when he was assigned to prepare materials on the international situation for the report Lenin was going to deliver at the Comintern's Third Congress.

He became director of the Office of Statistical Information in 1922, stayed in Berlin until 1927, and then returned to the USSR to become the director of the Institute of World Politics and Economics. In this role he was able to analyze "capitalist stabilization" in ways that were more sophisticated and detailed than the arid schematics of Leninist orthodoxy. After a suggestion by Stalin, Varga was asked by the politburo in 1928 to present a report to the Comintern's Sixth Congress on the situation in the USSR and he became a member of the Program Commission. The theses he argued for on this occasion led to accusations of "Buhkarinism."

The target of a violent and orchestrated attack during the Executive Committee of the Communist International's Tenth Plenum (1929) because of his unorthodox positions on the crisis of capitalism, he rapidly fell in line with official positions and contributed noticeably to the ideologization of scientific work that started in July 1931. Although his position as a theorist of world economics took a hard hit, Varga emerged unscathed from the purges that affected all fields of intellectual and scientific activity in the country, and held on to his position as director of the Institute of World Politics and Economics until 1947. Stalin intervened several times on his behalf to save him from attempts by the police to incriminate him—in 1936, 1938, and finally 1943, when he was accused by Andrey Vyshinsky of defending "Hitler's imperialism."

In May 1947 he was once more among the accused, because of the unorthodox analyses he had published in a 1946 essay on the changes World War II had introduced in international relations. This time Stalin did not intervene to support him. The institute he directed was closed, but he did not suffer any disciplinary consequences, unlike many of his collaborators. In October 1948 he was asked to publicly repudiate his "reformist errors" and withdraw his request for a revision of the most obsolete theories within the official ideology. He retracted his positions in a letter to *Pravda* in March 1949, in order to dispel suspicions that he had been influenced by "bourgeois cosmopolitan" ideas.

In June 1949 he was elected to the presidium of the Academy of Sciences. He was given the Order of Lenin in 1954 for a work he had published the previous year, in which he fell in line with official doctrine, accepting all the criticisms that had been previously directed at him. A year before his death, which occurred in Moscow in October 1964, he received the Lenin prize, in recognition of his long and prolific career as a scholar, academic, and economist, whose services had been appreciated only because he had been able to negotiate and withdraw from his positions when political pressure was applied.

See also Collapse of Capitalism; Comintern; Marxism-Leninism.

FURTHER READING

Duda, G. *Jenö Varga und die Geschichte des Instituts fü Weltwirtschaft und Weltpolitik in Moskau 1921–1970: zu den*

Möglichkeiten und Grenzen wissenschaftlicher Auslandsanalyse in der Sowjetunion. Berlin: Akademie, 1994.

Pevsner, J. "Zhizn' i trudy E.S. Vargi v svete sovremenosti (K 110-letiju do dnja rozhdenija i 25-letiju smerti)." *Memo* 10 (1989): 16–33.

ANNA DI BIAGIO

Vietnam War

The war in Vietnam occupies a special place in the succession of crises and shocks that visited the world after 1945. Beginning as a local conflict, the war soon blossomed into a confrontation that powerfully influenced world politics over many years. To one degree or another, all the leading countries of the world were drawn into it. It resulted in profound changes in international power relationships, and its consequences were long felt in the economics, culture, and other areas of the world community.

In considering the place of the Vietnamese conflict in the history of the Cold War, it must be borne in mind that the latter began as a conflict in Europe, despite the fact that during the early stages its main participants were the Soviet Union and the United States. For both Soviet and U.S. leaders, Europe was a vitally important region, and most of their thinking and planning centered on it. It was no coincidence that the first Cold War crises took place precisely in continental Europe. Still, even in those years there were harbingers of the Cold War's evolution into a global conflict involving new continents, Asia in particular. The Iran crisis of 1945–46; the debates at conferences of foreign ministers about colonial and dependent territories with Moscow openly demanding to participate in their decisions; and the global approach of the U.S. leaders in their confrontation with the Soviet Union, embodied in Directive 68 of the U.S. National Security Council, which was approved by President Harry Truman in April 1950—all these testified to the expansion of the Cold War beyond its European orbit.

The victory of the Chinese Communists in the civil war in 1949 and the start of the Korean War in June of the following year were important milestones along this route. Since the West considered Mao Zedong and Kim Il Sung to be Stalin's protégés in blind obedience to his orders and instructions, Western politicians clearly perceived Moscow's intention to take advantage of Asian pro-Communist and national liberation movements. In conjunction with Communists in other Asian countries, these movements would spread Soviet influence to an ever-increasing number of regions, at the expense of Western democracy and freedom. These notions guided Western politicians in their assessment of events in Vietnam in the early 1950s, when the leadership of the struggle against the French colonizers fell to the Patriotic Front, led by the Communist leader Ho Chi Minh.

Motivated by a determination to halt the further spread of Communist influence in Asia, the U.S. administration, in the beginning of the 1950s, began to render massive economic and military aid to France, for the purpose of putting down the national liberation movement in those countries of Indochina that were still French colonies. This U.S. intervention was justified by invoking the famous "domino theory," first intoned by President Dwight Eisenhower at a press conference in April 1954. According to this principle, if one country fell to the Communists, another would follow, and then still another, until, like a row of dominoes, all would fall from a single push.

The U.S. efforts, however, did not produce the desired result. The defeat of the French Expeditionary Forces at Dien Bien Phu in May 1954 and the convocation of the Geneva Conference the same year meant a real defeat for U.S. policy. Still, the United States did not abandon its efforts to stop further Communist expansion in southeast Asia. Through the 1950s up to the early 1960s, it supported and tried to reinforce a regime in South Vietnam, which had been created at the Geneva Conference in a decision to divide Vietnam into two parts, with the southern part intended as a counterweight to the Democratic Republic of Vietnam (DRV), led by the Communists north of the line of demarcation. Washington provided South Vietnam with ever-increasing economic and military aid, in the hope of converting it into a bastion of struggle against the Communists in the region. Thus, the 1965 decision U.S. president Lyndon Johnson to dispatch military units to South Vietnam and launch aerial bombardments against the DRV, which started the Vietnam War, was the logical continuation of Washington's preceding policy.

Until the United States became involved in the Indochina conflict, the role of the Soviet Union there was limited. Only in 1950—that is, not until five years after Ho Chi Minh declared the beginning of the DRV—did Moscow recognize the regime and establish diplomatic relations with it, and even then it was simply following China's lead. This delay was largely connected with Soviet geopolitical interests. Vietnam and Indochina in general were only a slight concern for Moscow because of their distance from the USSR borders, and also because Soviet foreign policy at the time was concentrated on Europe. Documents from Chinese archives suggest that there was an understanding between Stalin and Mao about a sort of "division of labor," whereby the Chinese would be responsible for managing events transpiring in the Far East, while the Soviet Union would focus on European affairs and the "struggle against American imperialism." This is why the People's Republic of China, and not the Soviet Union, was the main partner and provider of aid to Ho Chi Minh in his struggle with the French colonizers.

This situation changed little in the ensuing years. Although the USSR took an active part in the Geneva Conference on Indochina from May to July 1954, the Soviet leaders were less interested in the Communist-led national liberation movement in Vietnam than in preventing the conflict in Southeast Asia from becoming an obstacle to the détente with the West proclaimed by Khrushchev and other Soviet leaders. Accordingly, even after the conference Moscow was guided more by its concern about observing the Geneva agreements than about developing relations with the regime of Ho Chi Minh, which had now acquired the territory north of the line of demarcation dividing Vietnam into two parts.

In spite of the fact that relations between the USSR and the DRV in the 1950s were evolving in various areas, including the military, the main efforts of the Soviet leaders were directed toward maintaining the status quo in the region resulting from the Geneva Conference of 1954. This was testified to by the USSR's participation in settling the Laos crisis, which broke out at the end of the 1950s, and some mild efforts on its part to prevent violations of the Geneva Accords by both South Vietnam with the support of the United States and the DRV with the approval of Beijing. In the latter case, the foundations of Soviet policy on the conflict in Indochina were being undermined by the heightening Soviet-Chinese feuds in the late 1950s and early 1960s that threatened to cause an open break between the erstwhile allies. The North Vietnamese leaders, now increasingly inclined to unite their country through force with both the overt and covert support of the antigovernment movement in the South, relied on the help of their Chinese friends, who viewed the struggle in South Vietnam as part of the

worldwide offensive against U.S. imperialism. The Soviet leaders, for their part, sought a more moderate and cautious approach. As a result, Moscow's influence on the developing events in the region remained consistently weak during the period preceding the Vietnam War, and the USSR remained a mere observer of the happenings leading to the armed conflict with the United States.

With the commencement of overt military actions by the United States against the DRV in spring 1965, however, the Soviet position changed radically. The USSR condemned the bombardment of North Vietnamese territory by the U.S. air force and declared its solidarity with the Vietnamese people. It did not limit itself to formal statements, though. The USSR began to extend many kinds of aid to the DRV, with the emphasis on deliveries to Hanoi of arms and military technology indispensable for carrying out the war. Moscow sent "land-air" rocket complexes, jet planes, aviation rockets, and antiaircraft and field artillery to North Vietnam. The volume of Soviet economic and military aid kept increasing. By 1968 the proportion of Soviet material aid to North Vietnam was 50 percent of its overall volume of foreign aid, and two-thirds of it was military deliveries. The Vietnamese People's Army was equipped with the latest Soviet armaments, and by the beginning of the 1970s it had become the strongest army in the region, with only the South Vietnamese forces, equipped and financed by the United States, to compete with it.

Yet despite the enormous material and moral support given to the DRV by the Soviet Union, the Soviet leadership still regarded the conflict in Indochina with a certain ambivalence. A great many factors governed the Soviets' assessments of the conflict. First and foremost, they were influenced by the values and priorities of the Cold War, and the alignment of forces in the international arena resulting from its development.

Leaving aside the propagandistic justifications of Soviet policy in connection with the growing U.S. involvement in the war against the DRV and the National Front for the Liberation of South Vietnam, which consisted in an unequivocal condemnation of the U.S. intervention, the raging conflict was tactically favorable for Moscow but also strategically dangerous. On the one hand, the war was diverting the armed forces along with the attention of the United States and China, which guaranteed the USSR a relatively free hand elsewhere, particularly in Europe and along the Far Eastern borders. In addition, the protracted nature of the conflict, which was clear almost from the start, gave the Soviets hope for a weakening of their rivals and an emergence in their countries of both internal and external difficulties—in particular, a diminishing of U.S. authority in the eyes of world. At the same time the USSR, by rendering political, economic, and military aid to North Vietnam, stood out as a staunch fighter for a just cause in the spirit of proletarian internationalism.

On the other hand, there was a real threat that the Vietnam War would grow from a local conflict into a widespread general war, particularly if the United States, driven to extremes, were to resort to nuclear weaponry. In that case the Soviet Union could hardly stand aside, and the consequences would be catastrophic. Nevertheless, even if it did not develop into a nuclear conflict, there would be an enormous increase in the risk of a direct confrontation between the two superpowers in Southeast Asia, and the Soviet Union wanted to avoid this at any cost.

There were other pluses and minuses that Moscow probably had to take into account in determining its policy toward the war. But along with the dividends that the Soviets stood to reap from a continuation of the war, the financial layouts and material costs would also be substantial. And still another negative factor that the Soviet leaders had to keep in mind was the unreliability, "uncontrollability," and unpredictability of its Vietnamese allies, who did not always want to heed Moscow's counsel and would ignore the USSR's interests, would woo China, and would strive to gain the maximum advantage for themselves by exploiting the Soviet-Chinese conflict. The course the Hanoi leaders struck toward independence in its relations with the USSR could certainly not leave Moscow indifferent to a prolongation of the war, which given the suspect qualities of its Vietnamese allies, could result in a bad outcome. Thus, arguments in favor of a peaceful resolution of the extended conflict in Southeast Asia could not but play an important role in Soviet calculations. And so during the entire war Moscow took an active part in the search for peace in Indochina, and often assumed the function of unofficial intermediary in contacts between the United States and North Vietnam.

The Soviet leadership's efforts to achieve a diplomatic solution to the conflict in Vietnam played an important role in the preparations for peace negotiations between the United States and the DRV, which opened in Paris in May 1968. Indeed, Soviet diplomacy regarded the opening of these negotiations as its own personal success. Without officially assuming the role of intermediary, Moscow made consistent efforts to find a peaceful resolution of the Vietnam War.

Moscow's role in the Paris negotiations was important during the whole course of the talks. The Soviet leaders tried to keep abreast of what was going on, and when it appeared necessary, enlisted their Hanoi and Paris embassies in the task of "correcting" the position of the Vietnamese side, to the extent this was possible. Hence the USSR, despite its limited influence on the two warring sides, still managed to contribute toward resolving the conflict through peaceful means. And the eventual signing of an agreement to end the war and restore peace in Vietnam, for all the weakness of this pact, was a success for Soviet diplomacy.

The results of the Vietnamese conflict, which ended in the Communists' victory and the unification of Vietnam under their power, could be regarded as favorable to the Soviet Union. The United States emerged from the war with its authority vastly undermined in the international arena and problems soon cropping up on its domestic front as well. Washington's de facto defeat in Indochina brought about a marked change in the world's power relationships and meant that the United States was no longer the center of power in the Cold War. This, in turn, meant the emergence of a multipolar system in international relations, in place of the previous bipolar world. The Soviet Union, on the contrary, strengthened its position in both the socialist camp, where it gained one more ally it could depend on in southeast Asian politics, and its relations with the West, which had been moving toward a détente based on the parity it had achieved with the United States in the arms race. As subsequent events have shown, however, this success was transitory and had no effect on the ultimate outcome of the Cold War.

See also Anti-Americanism; Anti-imperialism; Cold War; Decolonization; Ho Chi Minh; Socialist Camp; Soviet Bloc; Third Worldism.

FURTHER READING

Gajduk, I. V. *The Soviet Union and the Vietnam War*. Chicago: Ivan R. Dee, 1996.

———. *Confronting Vietnam: Soviet Policy toward the Indochina Conflict, 1954–1963*. Stanford, CA: Stanford University Press, 2003.

Gardner, L. C., and T. Gittinger, eds. *International Perspectives on Vietnam*. College Station: Texas A&M University Press, 2000.

Goscha, C., and M. Vaisse. *La guerre de Vietnam et l' Europe (1963–1973)*. Brussels: Bruylant, 2003.

Logevall, F. *Choosing War: The Lost Chance for Peace and the Escalation of War in Vietnam*. Berkeley: University of California Press, 1999.

Pike, D. *Vietnam and the Soviet Union: Anatomy of an Alliance*. Boulder, CO: Westview Press, 1987.

Qiang Zhai. *China and the Vietnam Wars, 1950–1975*. Chapel Hill: University of North Carolina Press, 2000.

Smith, R. B. *An International History of the Vietnam War*. Vols. 1–3. London: Macmillan, 1983–91.

ILJA V. GAJDUK

Vietnam-Cambodia War

A simmering border conflict developed into full-scale war in December 1978, when Vietnam began an invasion of Cambodia under the banner of a Khmer resistance front. Vietnamese troops had forced the Pol Pot government out of the capital Phnom Penh by January 7, 1979, and pushed all the way to the Thai border not long after. This operation transformed the genocidal Khmer Rouge regime into a guerrilla force, which continued to fight the Vietnamese troops and the government they had installed until 1992, when a UN-sponsored peace settlement was arranged in Paris. Although Hanoi saved the Khmer people from Pol Pot's radical communism, the invasion was widely viewed as Soviet-backed expansionism and resulted in an aid embargo that kept Vietnam isolated until it withdrew its troops in 1989. The conflict was one of the expressions of the Sino-Soviet split, with China acting as the Khmer Rouges' strongest backer and the USSR providing aid and weaponry to the pro-Vietnamese forces in Cambodia. The United States gave de facto support to the Chinese–Khmer Rouge alliance throughout this conflict.

The conventional wisdom in 1979, when the Third Indochina War became known to the world at large, was that this was a flare-up of an "age-old conflict" between the Vietnamese and the Cambodians. There was indeed a history of conflict between the two neighbors, which included an earlier Vietnamese invasion in the 19th century. The French had contributed to the Khmer dislike of the Vietnamese, by using the latter as civil servants in their Cambodian colony. The rulers of the Communist state of democratic Kampuchea feared the numerical superiority and armed might of their eastern neighbor, which had gradually absorbed the eastern areas of the Cambodian kingdom from the 17th to 18th century. But the post-1975 conflict between Vietnam and Cambodia had roots in the complex international situation that grew out of the U.S war in Indochina, as well as in the pathological distrust that the Cambodian leader Pol Pot felt toward the Vietnamese.

Relations between Vietnamese and Cambodian communists had always been complicated. Chinese laborers in Cambodia probably formed the first Communist groups there in the 1920s, but the Vietnamese played a preponderant role in forming a Cambodian Communist Party in the early 1950s. The Cambodian party resented the fact that it did not receive any territory at the 1954 Geneva Conference, when its leaders had to regroup to Hanoi. In 1963 the French-educated Saloth Sar (later Pol Pot) took over leadership of the Cambodian Party, and its leaders retreated to the jungle. The Vietnamese had encouraged the party to cooperate with Prince Norodom Sihanouk, who was allowing the Vietnamese troops to transit his territory and buy rice there. But during the 1960s the Khmers began to develop their party line independently.

After the anti-Sihanouk coup of 1970 brought U.S. ally Lon Nol to power, the Communist-led Cambodian resistance grew exponentially. Chinese material aid and Vietnamese troops quickly helped the Khmer Rouges to take over large stretches of the countryside. But after their April 1975 takeover of Phnom Penh, the Khmer Rouges surprised the world by sealing off their country and beginning an experiment in brutal autarky and extreme nationalism. They insisted that all Vietnamese troops still stationed in the eastern zone of the country leave, and began to demand that the old French sea border be redrawn. Border clashes started in 1975, over disputed islands. By May 1976 Pol Pot had withdrawn from border negotiations with the Vietnamese. In April 1977 the KR began to shell and attack Vietnamese villages across the border, with the KR Party journal openly encouraging efforts to take back "lost" Khmer territory. At this point, Huang Hua, the new Chinese premier, raised the stakes by promising to supply Pol Pot with all the aid that it was within China's power to provide.

In the meantime, a Vietnam flushed with victory was finding it harder than expected to establish its place in

Southeast Asia. The Chinese were not eager to continue providing wartime levels of aid, especially since Vietnam refused to curtail its relationship with the USSR; other promises of aid for rebuilding the economy were slow to materialize. The regime's rush to socialize southern Vietnam after reunification in 1976 caused economic disruption and affected Chinese residents of the cities disproportionately. Hanoi's campaign against capitalists staged in 1978 may not have been intended as an anti-Chinese measure, but it caused increasing numbers of ethnic Chinese (Hoa) to flee Vietnam by boat. The panic in the South was exacerbated when Beijing sent a ship to Saigon to collect Chinese who wanted to return to China. At the same time, many Chinese on the northern border had been panicked by announcements that Chinese would no longer be able to work in certain professions, such as transport and fishing. A flood of Hoa began to cross the northern border in the spring of 1978. The Vietnamese became convinced that the Chinese were conspiring to destabilize the country by provoking a refugee exodus. As the Khmer Rouge links to China grew ever closer, the Vietnamese turned to the USSR for aid and security guarantees. They signed a Friendship Treaty with Moscow in November 1978.

The growing alliance between Democratic Kampuchea and the PRC, and Vietnam's partnership with the USSR set the scene for the three-way conflict that followed. A U.S.- and ASEAN-led embargo of Vietnam over the next decade gave the Vietnamese little choice but to eventually withdraw from Cambodia and pursue peace with China. This came about as the Cold War ended, and the Soviet Union itself restored relations with China, leaving Vietnam free to establish more balanced relations with the rest of the world.

See also China-Vietnam War; Khmer Rouge; Pol Pot; Vietnam War.

FURTHER READING

Chanda, N. *Brother Enemy: The War After the War.* New York: Collier Books, 1986.

Elliott, D.W.P., ed. *The Third Indochina Conflict.* Boulder, CO: Westview Press, 1981.

Kiernan, B. *The Pol Pot Regime: Race, Power and Genocide in Cambodia under the Khmer Rouge, 1975–79.* New Haven, CT: Yale University Press, 2002.

Shawcross, W. *The Quality of Mercy: Cambodia, Holocaust and Modern Conscience.* Bangkok: D. D. Books, 1984.

SOPHIE QUINN-JUDGE

Voroshilov, Kliment

Kliment Voroshilov (1881–1969) was born in Ukraine near Dnipropetrovsk. He became a member of the Russian Social Democratic Party in 1903, where he joined the Bolshevik wing. He was arrested in 1907–8, escaped from prison, and was then arrested once more. In 1917 he was a member of the Petrograd Soviet and took part in the October Revolution in the capital. A commander in the Red Army's Tenth Army that was defending Caricyn, in the northern Caucasus, in the fall and winter of 1918, together with Stalin and S. K. Minin he rebelled against Trotsky's authority and that of the Military-Revolutionary Council of the Soviet Republic, opposing its drive to recruit former imperial military officers into the new revolutionary army. This is how he joined the "military opposition" that developed among the Red Army's military cadres until the Bolshevik Party's Eighth Congress (March 1919), which supported innovative but ineffective organizational and tactical ideas. During the congress, Lenin reprimanded Voroshilov for his impulsive and irrational conduct of military operations, with no consideration for the losses incurred. He was transferred to Ukraine, was a member of the second provisional Soviet Ukrainian government (December 1918–August 1919), and served in the command of the First Cavalry Army of the Soviet Army in the Russo-Polish War in 1920.

The party's Tenth Congress in March 1921 elected him to the Central Committee and that same year he became commander of the northern Caucasus military district. In 1924 he became commander of the Moscow military district, and in 1925 the people's commissar for military and navy affairs, the highest military post in the USSR, succeeding Mikhail Frunze. In 1926 he was co-opted into the politburo because of his association with Stalin in the military events of the civil war (together with men like Sergey Kirov and Grigoriy Ordzhonikidze), and the later struggle against Trotskyism and the left-wing opposition. In this role, he contributed to the consolidation of Stalin's industrialist and isolationist program, which was based on autarky and the military strengthening of the USSR. Voroshilov was among the most vocal supporters of Stalin's repressive measures after Kirov's assassination.

More specifically, Voroshilov led the purge in 1937 of the Red Army's officer corps: he probably felt both frustrated and resentful toward some of its most eminent representatives (like Mikhail Tukhachevskii), because of their different conceptions of strategy, and because he was aware of his intellectual inferiority. His ineptitude, together with the effects of the purge in the Red Army's command, was one of the causes of the bloody and ineffective Soviet military campaign in Finland, in the winter of 1939–40. Yet he was still treated with special consideration by Stalin, who even though he removed Voroshilov from his post as supreme commander of the armed forces (Semyon Timoshenko replaced him in May 1940), had him included in the State Defense Committee, and made him vice president of Sovnarkom. Voroshilov was also made the commander of the northwestern armies, but after the German attack in June 1941, when he did not succeed in defending Leningrad, he was soon removed from this latest military post.

In 1945–47 he was president of the Soviet Control Commission in Hungary. After Stalin's death he became president of the Supreme Soviet's presidium, and subsequently only seemed to emerge from the margins of history during the failed coup against Khrushchev in June 1957, in which he associated himself with Vyacheslav Molotov, Georgy Malenkov, Lazar Kaganovich, and Nikolay Bulganin (the so-called antiparty group). In 1960 his attempt to regain importance by opposing Khrushchev was quashed by his resignation from the Supreme Soviet and the politburo. The following year during the party's Twenty-second Congress, which Khrushchev had organized to bolster the anti-Stalinist course he had started at the Twentieth Congress, Voroshilov was not even reelected to the Central Committee. The fact that he was reelected to it starting with the Twenty-third Congress in 1966 was only one of the signs that the new leadership group around Leonid Brezhnev wanted to balance the condemnation of Stalin undertaken by Khrushchev with the resurrection of a significant part of Stalinism's symbolism and historical legacy.

See also Great Patriotic War, Rhetoric of; Red Army; Stalinism.

FURTHER READING

Akshinskij, V. S. *Kliment Efremovich Voroshilov. Biograficheskij ocherk.* Moscow: Politizdat, 1974.

Sebag Montefiore, S. *Stalin: The Court of the Red Tsar.* New York: Knopf, 2004.

Voroshilov, K. E. *Rasskazy o zhizni. (Vospominanija).* Moscow: Politizdat, 1968.

Wheatley, D. *Red Eagle: A Story of the Russian Revolution and of Klement Efremovitch Voroshilov.* London: Hutchinson, 1967.

FRANCESCO BENVENUTI

Vyshinsky, Andrey

Andrey Vyshinsky (1883–1954) was an important figure in Soviet domestic and foreign policy, and an active participant in the Stalinist repressions of the 1930s. He was born in Odessa to a family belonging to the intelligentsia and studied in Baku. In addition to Russian and Polish (his father was of Polish origin), he knew French, English, and German well, and also had an excellent memory. From 1903 until 1920, Vyshinsky was a member of the Russian Social Democratic Workers' Party and a Menshevik. In February 1908, he was sentenced to a year in prison for revolutionary activity in Baku, during which time he became acquainted with Stalin. In 1913, he graduated from the Kiev University law faculty and began practicing law in 1915. Vyshinsky was an active supporter of the provisional government after the February Revolution of 1917 and occupied the post of chair of the Yakimansk District Authority in Moscow.

In 1920, after the establishment of Soviet power, Vyshinsky broke with the Mensheviks and joined the ranks of the Bolsheviks. He devoted himself to pedagogical and legal activity starting in 1921. In 1925, he was named rector of Moscow State University and also appointed prosecutor in the criminal justice office of the Supreme Court of the Russian Soviet Federative Socialist Republic. He was appointed chief prosecutor of the Federative Socialist Republic in 1931, from 1935 to 1939 serving as chief prosecutor of the USSR. Vyshinsky became a key figure in all the notorious court trials of the 1930s. He was chair of a special office of the USSR Supreme Court, which dealt with the Shakhtin trial in 1928 and the Industrial Party case in 1930. In 1933, Vyshinsky acted as the public prosecutor in the "Metro-Vickers" trial, and also in the political trials of 1936, 1937, and 1938. These trials of "enemies of the people" were a shameful blot on Vyshinsky's record. Stalin made skillful use of Vychinsky's Menshevik past and often resorted to direct pressure on the USSR's chief prosecutor, whenever he noticed the slightest equivocation on Vyshinsky's part.

Vyshinsky was not only an active participant in the Stalinist repressions but also one of their theoreticians. In his works he promoted Stalin's mistaken idea that the class struggle in the USSR would intensify as the country moved toward communism. Vyshinsky put forward the "theory" that a confession by a defendant, in cases involving crimes against the state, was proof of guilt. In

1939, he was made a member of the USSR's Academy of Sciences.

On June 1, 1939, Vyshinsky was named deputy secretary of the Council of People's Commissars of the USSR, responsible for questions of culture, and on October 1, 1941, he was appointed first deputy of the USSR People's Commissariat for Foreign Affairs. Up until June 22, 1941, Vyshinsky, like other Soviet leaders, espoused a policy of cooperation with Nazi Germany. After the German invasion of the Soviet Union, he worked to create and consolidate an anti-Hitler coalition. Vyshinsky took part in a conference of the foreign ministers of the USSR, the United States, and Great Britain, held in Moscow in October 1943. Most important on the conference's agenda was the creation of a European Consultative Commission and a Consultative Council to deal with the question of Italy. On November 18, 1943, Vyshinsky went to Allied headquarters in Algiers to participate in the work of this organ. As the Soviet representative, he coordinated Allied policy with respect to Italy, which the Stalinist leadership did not include in the USSR's sphere of influence. Vyshinsky used his stay in Algiers to forge links with the leaders of the French and Italian Communist parties. He returned to Moscow in early 1944.

In September and October 1944, as the deputy of the People's Commissariat, he played an active role in discussions in Moscow with Romania and Bulgaria. Vyshinsky visited Romania in November and December 1944 and also February and March 1945, and in January 1946 he visited both Romania and Bulgaria. His negotiations in Bucharest and Sofia served to exert Soviet pressure on the ruling circles of these countries. Their purpose was to strengthen the Communists' positions in the governments of these countries and see to it that they adopted a pro-Soviet course in their foreign policy.

Vyshinsky was named head of the USSR delegation to the first session of the UN General Assembly in January 1946—a function he fulfilled right up until his death. His speeches and presentations at the United Nations reflected the spirit of the Cold War, and were marked by their harsh and uncompromising tone. On March 6, 1949, Vyshinsky was appointed USSR minister of foreign affairs, an indication of Vyacheslav Molotov's reduced influence. The new minister issued a list of instructions for strengthening the discipline among the ministry's staff and moved to increase censorship of the press. In October 1952, Vyshinsky was named a candidate for membership in the presidium of the Central Committee of the Communist Party of the Soviet Union. In Moscow, on February 14, 1950, he signed the Treaty of Friendship, Cooperation, and Mutual Aid between the USSR and the People's Republic of China. In March of the same year, he signed the Treaty on Economic and Cultural Cooperation with the People's Democratic Republic of Korea. These treaties strengthened the USSR's position in the Far East and set the stage for the upcoming war in Korea. On March 7, 1953, after Stalin's death, Vyshinsky was appointed to the posts of first deputy minister for foreign affairs and permanent representative of the USSR at the United Nations. He died suddenly on November 22, 1954, in New York.

See also Diplomats; Great Terror.

FURTHER READING

Conquest, R. *The Great Terror: A Reassessment*. London: Hutchinson, 1990.

Craig, G. A., and F. L. Loewenheim, eds. *The Diplomats, 1939–1979*. Princeton, NJ: Princeton University Press, 1994.

MICHAIL M. NARINSKIJ

Walesa, Lech

Lech Walesa (1943–) was hired in 1967 as an electrical technician at the Lenin shipyards in Gdansk. Already in January 1971, during the strikes in the Baltics, he represented the workers during a meeting with the Unified Polish Workers' Party's secretary, Edward Gierek. He became a member of the Free Trade Unions of the Coast in the late 1970s, and began to go in and out of prison. His first contacts with the intellectuals of the Committee for the Defense of Polish Workers date from these years.

Extremely religious, Walesa demonstrated his talent as an able mediator and a believer in the necessity of avoiding direct confrontation with power. In his autobiography, *A Way of Hope*, Walesa remembers how the workers learned from their defeats in the 1970s, and worked to not only improve internal organization but also build a network of relations with the world outside the factories, with the students and parish churches that had become alternative organizational centers to the Communist authorities. During Solidarity's sixteen months of existence (August 1980–December 1981), Walesa had to struggle to keep the various constituents together in this independent union that had grown too rapidly, without structures, at a time when it was difficult to live with the giddiness of democracy. His charisma and ability prevented the volatile situation from precipitating immediately, with more tragic consequences.

Walesa was arrested during the coup of December 13, 1981, and was released the following year and placed under house arrest. He received the Nobel Peace prize in 1983. In 1989, Poland's increasingly serious economic and social conditions forced those in power to contact Walesa, the recognized head of Solidarity. A second "roundtable" was organized in Warsaw (February–April 1989) to discuss power sharing with Solidarity, an opposition that had been illegal until that time. The accord that was reached led to elections in which Solidarity competed for a limited number of seats in Parliament. In those districts where Solidarity competed, it won by enormous margins. Poland had regained its independence from the Soviet Union, and democracy needed to be fully instituted; this set a process of liberalization in motion, which in a brief period of time would affect all the other Communist countries and eventually the USSR itself.

In Poland, however, harmony among the victors did not last long: in December 1990, after a struggle that split Solidarity, Walesa was elected president, beating out his former ally Tadeusz Mazowiecki. Walesa then burned through most of the political capital he had gained during the strikes and his opposition to the coup over the next five years—a victim of dubious advisers (starting with the priest of Saint Brigid's in Gdansk, the anti-Semitic father Henryk Jankowski), but also his own ego, inflated by a quick rise to power. Most of those who had supported him, from intellectuals to the workers themselves, deserted him and his increasingly populist and demagogic positions. In 1995 Walesa was defeated in the elections by the post-Communist Aleksander Kwasniewski. In 2000 when he once again stood for the presidency he obtained an insignificant percentage of the vote. His decline was similar to that of Mikhail Gorbachev, featuring conferences around the world, setting up a foundation, and some statements for special circumstances, almost as if to remind people that he was still around. Still, both Walesa and Gorbachev, each in their respective roles, and with very different worldviews, radically changed the histories of their countries and the world.

See also Martial Law in Poland; Post-Soviet Communism; Revolutions in East-Central Europe; Solidarity.

FURTHER READING
Walesa, L. *A Path of Hope*. London: Collins Harvill, 1987.

FRANCESCO M. CATALUCCIO

War, Inevitability of

In the Communist vision of an ideal society there was no room for war. As a social phenomenon, it was part and parcel of the reality of the capitalist system in its imperialist phase. War would therefore be inevitable, as long as the system generating it was in existence. The Communists would only use it to further the cause of revolution. Lenin reached these conclusions when the outbreak of World War I caused him to focus on the issue and elaborate a coherent doctrine in the field of international relations, by gathering together the tentative and contradictory elements on the topic in the Marxism of his time.

In Lenin's outline, which was to be given a more definitive formulation in the essay "Imperialism: The Highest Stage of Capitalism" (1916), there were some important and novel elements. From Carl von Clausewitz's famous formula ("every war is the continuation of politics by other means"), Lenin derived a perspective that was extraneous to the idea of opposition to war in and of itself, or the notion of its prevention. This explains his critical attitude toward the pacifists of the time, who by demanding a democratic peace, proposed a solution to war that differed from the establishment of communism on a global scale. In order to judge a war it was necessary to consider which classes had been responsible for its outbreak, since wars were inseparable from the political systems that produced them. The war of 1914, according to Lenin, was an "imperialist war on both sides," and it would therefore not have been legitimate to choose sides, and even less legitimate to support the war effort of a "national bourgeoisie"—a choice that having been made by the majority of European socialists, led Lenin to accuse them of "betraying" the internationalist ideals of Marxism. By extending the concept of class struggle to the sphere of international relations, Lenin pointed to capitalism's inability to maintain an international order as an opportunity for unleashing revolution, transforming the imperialist war into a civil one.

Before 1917 Lenin had one kind of war in mind: that between "imperialist" sovereign states. His reflections did not refer to other types of war, such as between a capitalist and a Communist country. And yet the theory of war's inevitability, formulated before the establishment of the Soviet state, laid the foundations for a catastrophic interpretation of international relations, destined to develop

roots in most Communists' outlook. The establishment of crucial continuities with pre-revolutionary postulates was partly of Lenin's own making.

Starting with the signing of the Brest-Litovsk separate peace treaty (1918), he derived this fundamental conclusion: capitalist states were totally incapable of cooperating with one another in an effective manner, because of the conflicts of interest separating them. Soviet Russia would be able to exploit these contrasts to postpone the final clash between the two systems, which was also thought to be unavoidable. The "theory of truce" that Lenin developed on this occasion avoided the issue of the ideological character of Western powers' hostility toward the new Soviet state, which could lead them to set aside the internal conflicts that opposed them, so as to eliminate the "social danger" posed by the new international dimension of the Russian problem.

It was in the course of the 1920s, while Europe was moving toward some form of economic stability, that a paradox emerged—one destined to survive for a long time. Lenin had underscored the fairly strict causal nexus between economic crises and aggressive tendencies in capitalist countries. A period of prosperity in these countries would represent a guarantee of peace, which the USSR desperately needed, both to heal the war wounds and overcome its own backwardness, a necessary premise to provide for the developments needed to ensure its own survival in a hostile world. Lenin's successors instead continued to hope for conflict among the great powers, since they deemed it favorable to both Soviet security interests and the Communist cause globally.

A fundamental hostility to any possible form of stabilization in the international system thus remained strong. The reason for this outlook must be sought in the fact that Stalin adopted the theory of war's inevitability to endow his view of the prospects for Russian socialism, and more specifically his concept of security, with doctrinal legitimacy. The ineptitude imperialist powers demonstrated in attempting to construct a stable and peaceful framework for international relations would favor Soviet Russia, in the sense of giving it some breathing room, which the government would utilize to further strengthen the state, a task conceived in economic and military terms.

The most glaring limitation in this view consisted in the failure to understand that the new interdependent world order that had emerged from World War I had changed the likelihood that war might break out: every war now entailed the possibility of becoming a war of global proportions, and all states were at risk of being involved in the war itself. In order to contain these possibilities, it was necessary for all governments to support the idea of conflict prevention. This notion remained foreign to Stalin even when, faced with the threat Hitler's Germany also posed to the USSR, he was led to reconsider the premise on which the Communists' international policies were founded, and consider the possibility that a future war might also involve the USSR.

But it was only a limited and contingent revision, whose principal goal was still to achieve what had been Moscow's primary objective: not to be dragged into a new world war. War continued to be seen as an instrument that imperialist powers would always resort to, in order to obtain economic, political, or territorial benefits, or to find a solution to the "general crisis" of capitalism. It was a deeply held conviction that Stalin formulated again in his last work, *Economic Problems of Socialism in the USSR* (1952), in which he polemicized with those who, like Eugen Varga, had requested that the theory of war's inevitability be revised because it was obsolete and no longer able to provide valid guidance for Soviet foreign policy in World War II's aftermath. Even after Hiroshima and Nagasaki, for Stalin war continued to be the prosecution of politics by other means and represent "a profitable activity for reactionary imperialist circles."

The view that in the nuclear age, a new world war would not lead to either winners or losers but rather would result in the "contestants' mutual destruction" (Malenkov), only slowly established itself among Stalin's successors. From the podium of the Communist Party of the Soviet Union's Twentieth Congress, Khrushchev declared, "Wars are not fatally unavoidable." Even though he used the plural, in actuality he was not referring to another war among imperialist powers but instead to the war between the two systems—capitalism and socialism. The conviction that war was part and parcel of the capitalist system remained unchanged, as did the Stalinist view of security, based exclusively on the USSR's acquisition of a new military force.

With the advent of the Leonid Brezhnev era, there was a return to a more rigidly Leninist and schematic view of war, which led the Communist Party to declare, in the program it adopted in 1974, that a third world war would lead to the end of imperialism. Mikhail Gorbachev's "new way of thinking," however, meant a wide-ranging revision of the inevitability of war doctrine. Gorbachev's rethinking led first to the abandonment of Clausewitz's epigram; later to the admission that wars could and

should be avoided, by working to remove their causes; and finally to a new concept of security based on the principle that one cannot ensure one's own security at the expense of others. This was an important innovation in Communist ideology, but it remained purely a statement of principle.

See also Atomic Bomb; Brest-Litovsk, Treaty of; Classes; Imperialism; Lenin, Vladimir; Marxism-Leninism; Peaceful Coexistence; Power Politics; Stalin, Joseph; Warfare; World Revolution.

FURTHER READING
di Biagio, A. *La teoria dell'inevitabilità della guerra*. In: *Il XX Congresso del Pcus*. Ed. F. Gori. Milan: Angeli, 1988.
Pons, S. *Stalin and the Inevitable War: 1936–1941*. London: Frank Cass, 2002.

ANNA DI BIAGIO

War Communism

The expression "war communism" is usually used to refer to the set of extraordinary, often highly improvised measures adopted by the Bolsheviks from the summer of 1918 to the spring of 1921, to confront the civil war. War communism, however, was not just the response of a regime engaged in an all-encompassing war on which its very survival depended. It was also an experiment, largely utopian, whose objective was, according to Lenin, "the immediate transition to communist production and distribution." The Bolsheviks came to power without a well-defined economic program, in a country whose economy had been ruined by more than three years of war and revolution. The exchange circuits between city and country no longer functioned, transportation was disorganized, and industrial production had decreased by 75 percent compared to prewar figures. After having abandoned worker self-management options, since they could not possibly work in these catastrophic conditions, the Bolsheviks moved to strengthen the state's role, including state control of all sectors of the economy.

A Nationalized Economy, a Mobilized Society
War communism developed into a long sequence of measures that concentrated all material, human, and food resources in the country in the hands of one central power.

After having nationalized the banks (December 27, 1917), the commercial fleet (January 23, 1918), and international trade (April 22, 1918), the government proceeded on June 28, 1918, to nationalize all businesses with a capitalization in excess of half a million rubles. In 1919 nationalization was extended to all small businesses. A state monopoly on all internal trade was established in November 1918: all stores were "municipalized." All common consumer goods were rationed and a rigid hierarchy of "entitlement" was set up, favoring manual laborers over intellectuals, workers at the expense of clerks, and the "men of the past." Salaries were paid in-kind. In a demonstration of great utopian élan, the Bolsheviks even thought of abolishing money, or at least strictly limiting its circulation. Payment for utilities was gradually abolished: water, electricity, postal services, public baths, transportation, housing—everything was provided free of charge by the state (at least in principle, since utilities were actually functioning worse and worse).

Yet these experiments only aided a minority of the population in the cities and thus ran into a problem: resistance by the rural population, on whom the survival of the urban population depended. In an economy in which the circuits of distribution were broken, how could one get the exchange process started again? The Bolsheviks had two options: reconstitute a semblance of the market in a ruined economy, or resort to compulsion. They chose the second (May 1918), decreeing that grains be requisitioned by food squads composed of workers and militants. These squads were intended to receive assistance from "committees of poor peasants," who were given the task of "taking the grain" from the "rich." Confronted with the brutality of the requisitions, which were soon extended to all agricultural products, farmers developed forms of solidarity against the representatives of the new power and the cities. The requisitions led to thousands of uprisings, revolts, and actual peasant insurrections, climaxing in the Tambov Province, in the Ukraine, and western Siberia in 1920–21.

To make matters worse the requisition of agricultural products was inefficient. In 1919 grain requisitions only reached 35 percent of the planned total, and only 34 percent in 1920. The prohibition against free trade and increasing poverty in the cities led to a flourishing black market. Since money had almost disappeared, barter reappeared. The luckiest city dwellers got to exchange "the glorious remains of imperial Russia" for food; the workers abandoned the factories, shut down due to an absence of fuel, and returned to their villages. The country underwent a real process of de-urbanization; Moscow and Petrograd lost more than half their inhabitants.

Confronted with popular resistance, the regime alternated symbolic initiatives, meant to illustrate the new "social contract"—(the inauguration of the famous "Communist Saturdays," which consisted of "volunteer labor" on holidays)—with coercive measures, like the general mobilization of labor (April 1919), which was obligatory for all citizens between the ages of sixteen and fifty, and even the militarization of labor in the most vital areas (railways and mines). This militarization of labor basically implied the loss of all the workers' social gains (the right to strike, the eight-hour working day, and the possibility to change employment). The most extreme attempt at regimenting society was Leon Trotsky's plan to transform the demobilized units of the Red Army into "work armies"—for instance, after the victory against Admiral Aleksandr Kolchak, the Urals' Third Army became the First Revolutionary Labor Army (January 1920). Soldiers were assigned to work in the public interest, including production tasks in particularly tough economic areas (mining and clearing forests). This temporary form of forced labor (the experiment lasted less than a year) anticipated the more wide-ranging experiments that would start in the 1930s with the system of labor camps.

Political Dictatorship, Militarization, and Terror

The war communism years also witnessed the establishment of a political dictatorship, the conclusion of a dual process: the subordination of those autonomous institutions that had developed during 1917 (soviets, labor unions, and factory councils) to the Communist Party; and the suppression of non-Bolshevik political parties. This took place in two phases, using the most diverse methods: the seizure of and ensuing ban on non-Bolshevik newspapers; the arrest of political leaders and outlawing of opposition parties; bureaucratic measures introduced to control and delegitimize autonomous institutions (labor unions and factory councils, for example, many of which were not Bolshevik in orientation in 1917–18); and terror practiced by the political police.

Political parties were gradually eliminated according to different criteria. The Constitutional Democrats were banned as early as November 1917. The right-wing Social Revolutionaries, caught between two fires—the Bolsheviks and the counterrevolutionaries—divided and dispersed at the end of 1918. The "left-wing" Social Revolutionaries, Bolshevik allies until March 1918, were eliminated after having attempted a "coup" in early July

1918. The Mensheviks adopted a strategy of legal opposition, to the extent this was possible; they still had roots in both the soviets and labor unions, and resisted until early 1921.

The Bolsheviks' main instrument of repression was the Cheka, established on December 7, 1917. Directed by Feliks Dzerzhinsky, the Cheka grew exponentially, from about 1,000 at the beginning of 1918 to more than 140,000 in early 1921. In "response" to the attempt on Lenin's life (August 30, 1918), the Cheka unleashed the Red Terror in September 1918; in the course of a few weeks, it claimed tens of thousands of victims among the "class enemies." The Cheka experimented with two instruments of repression, unknown in pre-revolutionary Russia: the hostage system and the concentration camps. The statistics on the number of detainees in these camps remain uncertain even today, but vary from 100,000 to 300,000 people.

War Communism and the Victory of the Bolshevik Regime

The dictatorial measures introduced by war communism contributed to the victory of a regime, which in 1918 the great powers did not believe had the slightest chance of surviving. Although the desertion rate was still significant, the Red Army, reorganized starting in summer 1918 on the basis of conscription and set up in large measure by career officers who had joined the new regime, represented a considerable force (between five hundred and eight hundred thousand troops at the ready), a true "agent of economic mobilization" that was given every possible priority, but also enjoyed a strategic position in the country's heart.

The Bolsheviks also developed mastery in the art of propaganda, and it took unusual forms: political education courses, agitprop training throughout the country, and revolutionary manifestos, leaflets, booklets, and newspapers. They offered everyone who joined the party a chance to participate and be promoted in the new state apparatus; within three years (from the end of 1917 to the end of 1920) the party's membership quadrupled, reaching seven hundred thousand members. The location of choice to join the party was no longer the factory but rather the army. The new militants brought with them a new "style of command," influenced by the military environment. The civil war also contributed to the lasting militarization of Bolshevik culture.

But the regime's greatest strength lay in its ability to connect social issues with national ones. The Bolsheviks, despite the unpopularity of the requisition policies, still managed to present themselves as the guarantors of the great agrarian reform of October 1917 (the Decree on Land) and defenders of the motherland, threatened by the invasions of the White's foreign allies. On these two decisive battlefields their adversaries, divided by personal ambitions, committed fatal mistakes. Kolchak and General Anton Denikin rescinded the Bolshevik land decree, thus alienating the peasants, and they proved intolerant of all forms of moderate democratic or socialist opposition, thus disappointing wide strata of the urban population that were not ready to follow the Bolsheviks. Finally by rejecting all national aspirations, the Whites, often openly anti-Semitic, lost the support of all the non-Russian peoples of the ex-czarist empire.

War Communism's Crisis

After having defeated the last White armies, the Bolshevik regime had to confront an increase in peasant revolts sparked by the continuing requisition policies (fall 1920–summer 1921). Led by Aleksandr Antonov, the Tambov peasant army was initially made up of almost fifty thousand fighters, against whom extensive military operations were launched, led by General Mikhail Tukhachevskii.

On the "countryside front" the regime had to face another plague, famine, which proved particularly severe in the Volga provinces. A great drought, endemic to those regions, worsened the damage that years of requisition had inflicted, greatly weakening farming operations. More than five million people perished as a result of that famine.

In the cities in early 1921 the situation was just as critical. Industrial production had diminished by 80 percent compared to the prewar years. The urban population had dissolved, especially in Moscow and Petrograd. The "class victorious in the revolution," the working class, was now worn out, and could count on less than one million individuals in its ranks. The most "Europeanized" section of Russian society (two million inhabitants of the cities, mostly belonging to the landowners, liberal professions, and intellectuals) had emigrated.

A more archaic and peasant Russian society emerged from the civil war. "Objective conditions" made the transition to communism (one of war communism's objectives) more illusory than ever; the other objective, winning the war, had certainly been achieved, but at a high cost.

See also Agrarian Question; Command Economy, The; Gulag; KGB; Labor; Militarization; Peasants in the USSR; Red Army; Red Terror; Russian Revolution and Civil War; State, The; Utopia.

FURTHER READING

Brovkin, V. N. *Behind the Front Lines of the Civil War*. Princeton, NJ: Princeton University Press, 1994.

Figes, O. *A People's Tragedy: The Russian Revolution, 1891–1924*. London: Jonathan Cape, 1996.

Malle, S. *The Economic Organization of War Communism, 1918–1921*. Cambridge, UK: Cambridge University Press, 1985.

Pipes, R. *Russia under the Bolshevik Regime*. New York: Knopf, 1993.

Salomoni, A. *Il pane quotidiano: ideologia e congiuntura nella Russia sovietica, 1917–1921*. Bologna: Il Mulino, 2001.

Stites, R. *Revolutionary Dreams: Utopian Vision and Experimental Life in the Russian Revolution*. New York: Oxford University Press, 1989.

NICOLAS WERTH

Warfare

Socialist thought prior to the 18th-century Enlightenment contained a significant strain of ethically inspired pacifism. In the 19th century, the pacifist and socialist traditions moved apart. Karl Marx and Friedrich Engels rejected pacifism unambiguously, and cast realistic judgments on the armed conflicts of their time. Engels, who had experience soldiering during the revolutions of 1848, became an astute commentator on military affairs. The International Workingmen's Association or First International (1864–76) denounced standing armies as a source of militarism and championed a people's militia as an alternative, but accepted the necessity of defense against aggression. At its founding congress the Second International (1889–1914) described peace as an "indispensable condition" for the emancipation of labor, and its 1891 and 1893 Brussels and Zürich congresses defined militarism as "the fatal result of the permanent state of war, actual or latent, imposed upon society by the reign of the exploitation of man by man." The assertion that social justice was a prerequisite for peace was, however, not accompanied by a convincing strategy for addressing the challenge of warfare. At its 1907 Stuttgart Congress a resolution on militarism and national conflict committed Socialists to prevent war "by means they consider most effective," but made no specific tactical commitments. The Second International condemned war, but refused to embrace a consistent program for resisting its outbreak.

Ultimately, the 19th-century European Socialist movement was not able to achieve consensus over questions of war and peace. The left radical wing of the movement asserted an anarchist-tinged antimilitarism, well represented in Karl Liebknecht's 1907 tract *Militarism and Anti-Militarism*, which viewed the institution of war itself as an instrument of class rule and demanded radical resistance. The International's dominant Marxist synthesis emphasized that warfare was an accoutrement of capitalist class rule that Socialists were powerless to affect. In the terse, mechanistic formula of Plekhanov, "the roots of war are located in the essence of the capitalist order . . . when capitalism is overcome, war will disappear." In practice, mainstream Socialist opinion focused on the need to meliorate interstate competition and war through public diplomacy, and to reduce the sources of militarism through a military reform agenda such as that outlined by Jean Jaurès in his 1907 study *The New Army*. Jaurès, who was assassinated in Paris on the eve of the First World War, argued for the replacement of standing armies by a citizens' militia, but rejected Marxism's hostility to nationalism and established careful, legalistic criteria for distinguishing between in just and unjust wars.

When the majority of Socialist parties rallied to support national defense at the outbreak of the First World War, many observers were shocked. In fact, despite its rhetorical antimilitarism, a large part of the movement had consistently defended just war premises. During the conflict, the antiwar opposition organized as the Zimmerwald Movement spoke out against the costs of hostilities, but did not embrace a pacifist alternative. On the left wing, the Zimmerwald Left tendency urged a revolutionary response to the war crisis under the slogan "war on war." In *Socialism and War*, written in 1916, Vladimir Lenin developed a typology of wars including four categories (imperialist wars, wars of national liberation, revolutionary civil wars, and wars in defense of a successful Socialist revolution), three of which were considered licit. In Lenin's work, in fact, the venerable just war tradition was recast to meet the exigencies of an age of world revolution.

Following the Bolshevik seizure of power, Soviet Russia negotiated a separate peace with Germany in the Treaty of Brest-Litovsk of March 1918. Immediately, a left Communist faction within the Bolshevik movement challenged the decision, urging the alternative of guerrilla resistance and revolutionary war. The left Communists were defeated politically, but in the aftermath of Brest-Litovsk a series of armed challenges to Soviet power precipitated the Russian Civil War. Under assault, and with the old imperial army disbanded, the Bolsheviks set out to create a new Red Army of workers and peasants. As commissar of war, Leon Trotsky rejected calls for revolutionary tactical innovations. The first responsibility of a revolutionary army, he argued, was to fight and win. To that end, Trotsky sought to craft a disciplined, conventionally organized armed force. A so-called military opposition within the Bolshevik movement sought to resist these priorities on behalf of more radical options, but in the end Trotsky's agenda prevailed. The Red Army introduced a number of radical innovations, the most important of which was the political commissar charged with promoting party loyalty, but as a fighting force it was organized along essentially traditional lines. Armed force was an instrument in service of the revolution, but military effectiveness would determine the way in which it was coordinated.

In 1920 Poland's invasion of Ukraine transformed the Russian civil war into an interstate conflict. A Bolshevik counterattack quickly drove the Poles backward, and in June Russian forces under the direction of the young front commander Mikhail Tuchachevsky pushed across the border toward Warsaw. Tuchachevsky justified the incursion as a "revolution from without," the use of military force to assist indigenous proletarian forces and impose revolutionary change. But Tuchachevsky was turned back at the gates of Warsaw, and the phase of revolutionary enthusiasm associated with the Polish war proved to be short-lived. Henceforward the Red Army's primary function would be defense of the Soviet state.

During the interwar decades Soviet officers such as Tuchachevsky, Aleksandr Svechin, and Boris Shaposhnikov made notable contributions to the development of modern strategy, and placed the Soviet armed forces at the cutting edge of military innovation. Joseph Stalin's purge of the officer corps in 1937 eliminated many of these advantages, and when Hitler invaded the Soviet Union on June 21, 1941, the country was left inadequately prepared. As the Soviet armed forces mobilized for total war, most of the residual revolutionary symbolism of the civil war era was cast aside. The victorious Soviet Army that emerged from the Great Patriotic War of 1941–45 was configured as a conventional national armed force. The uses to which Soviet military power was put were also conventional. Moscow professed the cause of peace, but practiced a policy of peace through strength that made military might a vital pillar of Soviet power.

The establishment of the People's Republic of China led by Mao Zedong in October 1949 marked the triumph of an alternative approach to the idiom of warfare on the Communist Left. After the failure of a Soviet-inspired united front policy during the 1930s, Mao revived the Chinese communist movement by rallying an independent army in rural areas, breaking out of an attempted encirclement by Chiang Kai-shek's Nationalist forces in the Long March of 1934–35, and establishing a territorial sanctuary for the pursuit of armed struggle. From 1949 onward, the Maoist doctrine of "People's War" became the foundation for Chinese military strategy. It would serve as a model for Communist-inspired national liberation struggles and guerrilla wars, such as that championed by the Latin American revolutionary Ernesto "Che" Guevara, or waged in Southeast Asia by the Vietnamese Communist Ho Chi Minh and his military commander Nguyen Giap.

The international Communist movement was a product of militant resistance to the First World War. Domestic resistance and international intervention forced Russia to defend itself with arms in hand during the Russian civil war, and international hostility made it necessary to craft a national defense policy in the volatile international circumstances of the interwar decades. The Great Patriotic War was the most destructive armed conflict in history, and in its aftermath the USSR sustained a vast military establishment. In China, as Mao had predicted, political power for the Communist Left sprang from the barrel of a gun, and the Maoist doctrine of People's War became an inspiration to revolutionary groups worldwide. The 20th-century Communist movement made important contributions to the theory and practice of warfare. The antiwar inspiration of the early Communist movement, the utopian inspiration of a world transformed and at peace, was left fallow. Modern communism, in some ways a product of 20th-century warfare, was also a victim of the institution of war, a master whose harshness the movement was unable to transcend.

See also China's Armed Forces; Great Patriotic War; Guerrilla Warfare in Latin America; Military-Industrial Complex; Power Politics; Red Army; Trotsky, Leon; War, Inevitability of; World War II.

FURTHER READING

Guevara, C. *Guerrilla Warfare.* Harmondsworth, UK: Pelican Books, 1969.

Kissin, S. F. *War and the Marxists: Socialist Theory and Practice in Capitalist War.* London: Deutsch, 1988.

Semmel, B., ed. *Marxism and the Science of War.* Oxford: Oxford University Press, 1981.

R. CRAIG NATION

Warsaw Pact

Established on May 14, 1955, the Warsaw Pact was originally not intended to become the counterpart of the North Atlantic Treaty Organization (NATO) that it eventually did. Proclaimed in response to NATO's expansion after it added West Germany, the Soviet Union's creation of an alliance including Poland, East Germany, Czechoslovakia, Hungary, Romania, Bulgaria, and Albania was at that time primarily a diplomatic ploy. It was designed to encourage negotiations that would lead to the abolition of NATO along with the Warsaw Pact, though not the abolition of the bilateral alliances through which Moscow controlled the military potential of its dependent states.

Once the ploy proved unsuccessful, the Warsaw Pact needed a purpose. For several years, Soviet leader Khrushchev used it mainly as a platform for launching his various disarmament initiatives, intended to "demilitarize" the Cold War while relying on both a political and an ideological offensive. He abstained from giving the alliance a military substance. The Cold War nevertheless became further militarized as a result of Khrushchev's launching and subsequently mishandling of the Berlin crisis, which led in 1961 to the building of the Berlin Wall and the prospect of an armed confrontation in Central Europe.

As the crisis escalated, the Soviet military increasingly used Warsaw Pact structures for harnessing the potential of the Eastern European armies for such a confrontation. Until the Berlin crisis, the Soviet bloc's strategy in the event of a war in Europe had been defensive; under the impact of the crisis, it became offensive, and remained so for most of the remainder of the Cold War. Soon after the Berlin Wall went up in August 1961, the first joint exercise of Warsaw Pact armies envisaged a swift thrust deep into Western Europe, presumably after a military response by the Western powers to a Soviet closure of access routes to West Berlin.

As long as Khrushchev stayed in power, the organizational structure of the Warsaw Pact remained rudimentary. In managing the Eastern European allies, he preferred to rely on political and economic levers. In the Cold War's most dangerous confrontation—the Cuban missile crisis in October 1962—the Warsaw Pact was kept on the sidelines. This situation changed, however, after the overthrow of Khrushchev in October 1964, and his succession by a leadership more supportive of the ambitions of the Soviet military and more committed to military buildup as a way of compensating for the deficiencies of the Soviet system in other areas.

In the short run, the leadership change in the Kremlin had a restraining effect. It emboldened the Soviet allies to use the Warsaw Pact framework to pursue their own interests and priorities, thus creating disarray within the alliance in the latter half of the 1960s. Some of them, particularly Romania and Albania, tried to assert themselves by seeking a reduction of both Soviet influence within the alliance and the Soviets' ability to interfere in the internal affairs of its members. Others, notably Poland and East Germany, tried to sway Moscow to support their particular interests and priorities.

The disagreements within the Warsaw Pact, though never as open as those within NATO, were both greater than they appeared to contemporaries and dangerous for the integrity of the Communist alliance, which required higher standards of conformity than an alliance of democracies. While the Warsaw Pact's internal crisis was mitigated by the simultaneous NATO crisis in the 1960s, the Soviet Union still felt compelled to pursue a reform that would tighten and institutionalize its alliance.

The reform, proposed in January 1965, encountered opposition by Warsaw Pact members, which were increasingly worried about the possibility of being drawn into a potential nuclear war by Soviet actions over which they had no control. Romania had already in 1963 secretly informed the U.S. government that in the event of such a war, it would remain neutral—an act of disloyalty to the alliance without parallel in NATO. Other member states presented amendments to Soviet drafts that brought the reform project to a standstill. In 1966, the Soviet Union shelved it in return for its allies' support in a diplomatic campaign designed to exploit divisions within NATO and weaken the influence of West Germany in NATO. The campaign did not achieve the desired result. By the end of 1967, NATO had overcome its crisis, while the crisis within the Soviet bloc turned acute with the onset of the reform movement in Czechoslovakia.

Resuming the push for the restructuring and institutionalization of the Warsaw Pact was initially a higher priority for Moscow than acting on the developments in Czechoslovakia. Once the country began to move toward the democratization of its political system and even its Communist Party, though—a prospect that the Kremlin found threatening—the Soviet Union started to pursue the option of armed intervention. The reasons for it were political rather than military. A minority within the Czechoslovak army, particularly its civilian experts, called for reforming the Warsaw Pact to make it into a genuine partnership and favored the formulation of a national military doctrine, but they sought changes compatible with the common purpose and never questioned loyalty to the Soviet alliance.

Although the August 1968 invasion of Czechoslovakia was formally a Warsaw Pact operation, favored by the conservative Communist regimes in neighboring East Germany and Poland, the overwhelming majority of the invading troops were Soviet, thus showing the extent of Moscow's mistrust of its allies. The intervention strained the alliance, prompting Albania to leave it and further fostering Romanian dissidence. The long-delayed reorganization of the Warsaw Pact, which was finally adopted by its political consultative committee in March 1969, was the result less of a "normalization" in Czechoslovakia, which by that time still left much to be accomplished, than of the Soviet need to consolidate the alliance at a time of a mounting conflict with China, which erupted into open warfare just as the committee met for its deliberations.

The resulting transformation of the Warsaw Pact, intended to make it into an effective military counterpart of NATO, tightened the alliance and created new institutions, in part modeled after those of its Western rival. Although it thus met the main Soviet desiderata, the reform was not a simple Soviet diktat. It was in Moscow's interest to give its allies a greater sense of participation by seeking their input during policy discussions, while retaining control over decisions and their execution. With the East-West détente gaining momentum starting in 1969, the Warsaw Pact institutions became the main forums where common policies were being talked about and the preferences of the allies were being heard even though not necessarily heeded—a far cry from the way that NATO operated, but a distinct difference from the peremptory authoritarian manner in which Moscow treated its dependents under Stalin and Khrushchev.

Although the main purpose of the Warsaw Pact's institutionalization was to make it into a more effective military instrument, the Warsaw Pact's most critical new function was to serve as a coordinating body in foreign policy, particularly in preparation for the Conference on Security in Cooperation in Europe, to which the Kremlin attached paramount importance. This function of the alliance was welcomed by its East European member states but resented by the Soviet military, whose vested interest lay in maintaining and expanding preparations for a war in Europe, now made significantly less likely because of the progress of détente.

The Soviet general staff, rather than the Supreme Command of the Warsaw Pact's Unified Armed Forces, was the body where the operational plans were drawn up and subsequently imposed on the respective national armies. As the authority of the Kremlin leadership kept gradually diminishing under Brezhnev, who was increasingly incapacitated by illness, the input of the Soviet military into policy continued to increase, even though the interpenetration of the party and military institutions in the Soviet system never allowed the military to act independently as a group. The input became all that much more crucial once détente started to be reversed in the mid-1970s.

The effect on the Warsaw Pact was its accelerated militarization even while its plans became increasingly detached from reality. Its exercises rehearsed in ever greater detail the established scenario of a swift offensive deep into Western Europe. Although in theory the scenario always presumed a NATO-initiated war, in practice, training for defense against such an aggression—which the enemy would implausibly launch despite a ratio of forces strongly unfavorable to the attacker—became increasingly perfunctory. The exercises served to prepare for a massive offensive that was to be started within a few days of the imaginary enemy attack. With the wanton destructiveness of nuclear weapons ever more obvious, in the course of the 1970s the Warsaw Pact plans were made more "realistic" by aiming at a victory that could be achieved by using conventional forces only.

The Warsaw Pact military planning thus developed a momentum that provided an insuperable obstacle to the "military détente" that the Soviet leadership sought to achieve in its relations with the West. In 1980, under pressure from Moscow, the alliance finally adopted the secret "Statute of the Unified Command in Wartime" that gave its Soviet supreme commander discretionary powers at the expense of the national commands.

Resented as making the prospect of a war more likely, the document was not signed by Romania and its practical effect remained uncertain—an early indication of the brewing terminal crisis of the alliance.

The crisis ironically began to mount at a time when Western respect for the Warsaw Pact as a force that posed a "clear and present danger" reached its peak. The alliance played a major role in supporting Moscow's protracted campaign to prevent the deployment of "Euromissiles" by NATO that would counter the Soviet intermediate range missiles already targeted on all of Western Europe. The facade of unity maintained by the Warsaw Pact's members betrayed the Soviet Union's rapidly diminishing authority under Brezhnev's decrepit successors and the opposition of even the most loyal allies to the further militarization of the East-West conflict in Europe.

Although East Germany and Czechoslovakia accepted reluctantly Soviet "counterdeployments" of nuclear-armed missiles on their territories, East Germany sought "damage limitation" by promoting collaboration with West Germany to ensure that "war would never again come from German soil." The rapprochement between the conservative East German regime and the relatively liberal Hungarian leadership on the grounds of a common commitment to national goals that could be distinct yet compatible with the common ones signified how much the Soviet control of the alliance had been eroded.

Mikhail Gorbachev's rise to power in 1985 signaled initially a tightening rather than a loosening of the Warsaw Pact. With support from all its members except Romania, the alliance was renewed for another twenty years. Gorbachev went further than his predecessors in treating the allies as partners rather than pawns, and Eastern Europe's Communist regimes, sharing a common interest in fending off growing domestic opposition, reciprocated by supporting the alliance. East Germany took the lead in backing Gorbachev's disarmament initiatives while joining with other member states in supplementing them with their own initiatives, aimed at the reduction of troops and armaments in their respective regions.

If there were as yet no open signs that the Warsaw Pact might be on its way to extinction, the Gorbachev leadership's "New Thinking" on security and its subsequent implementation created the conditions that made such an outcome all but inevitable. The discarding of the Warsaw Pact's offensive doctrine in May 1987 and its attempted substitution by a defensive doctrine was as revolutionary as it was self-destructive. The change

undermined the structures on which the Soviet-led alliance had been resting for a quarter of a century without substituting new ones. It was nevertheless welcomed by the Eastern European regimes and ineffectively obstructed by the Soviet military, which had been thrown into confusion.

Gorbachev gained support from the allies for his concept of the Warsaw Pact's transformation from a primarily military to a primarily political alliance. His attention was focused on reform at home and accommodation with the West, thereby leaving developments in Eastern Europe up to the local forces. As such, the initiatives for the transformation shifted from Soviet hands into Eastern European ones. In an ironic twist, it was the region's most reactionary regimes that took the lead in attempting to use the alliance as a mutual rescue association, not least for protection against the reformist influences now emanating from the Soviet Union.

The year 1988 witnessed an unprecedented rapprochement between East Germany and Romania, although East Germany withheld support for the Romanian proposal for a Warsaw Pact reform that would have emasculated those institutions that ensured domination by Moscow. It was not the Soviet Union itself but rather Bulgaria that countered this proposal by submitting an alternative plan a year later that would have preserved the alliance and the leading Soviet role. By that time, however, the Warsaw Pact was already in an advanced state of disintegration.

The dissolution of the Communist's monopoly of power in Poland in June 1989 was a turning point. But the new Polish government initially saw merit in keeping the Warsaw Pact as protection against the unpredictable consequences of a possible German reunification. It was Hungary, whose reform-minded Communists decided to collaborate on the demise of their country's discredited political system as well the alliance that protected it, that was the first to sever its military links with the Warsaw Pact in fall 1989.

The fall of the Berlin Wall in November 1989 did not presage immediately the collapse of the Warsaw Pact. Not only the Soviet Union but also the post-Communist successor governments in Eastern Europe as well as NATO and the leading Western powers preferred to keep the alliance in existence for the time being. In 1990, the Warsaw Pact performed the only constructive role in its history by serving, together with NATO, as the structure through which a radical reduction of the massive military forces and armaments that had been facing each other in Europe was agreed on and subsequently implemented. The treaty on conventional forces in Europe, concluded in Paris in November 1990, provided the foundations of the security system on which Europe's peace and stability have been resting ever since.

In the end, the Warsaw Pact disappeared from the scene with a whimper rather than a bang. At the last meeting of its political consultative committee in June 1990, Czechoslovakia, now led by former dissident Václav Havel as president, took the lead in advocating the transformation of the alliance into a vehicle of political cooperation, though not yet its dissolution. The catalyst of the dissolution was the violent Soviet repression of the nationalist opposition in the Baltic states in January 1991, which prompted Czechoslovakia, Hungary, and Poland to demand the abolition of first the military and then also the political structures of the alliance—demands that Gorbachev had no choice but to accept. The Warsaw Pact ceased to exist on July 1, 1991.

In retrospect, the Warsaw Pact appears to have been a superfluous alliance, always in search of a purpose, and never vitally important either to its Soviet architects or any of their Eastern European clients, much less to the peoples of the countries involved. Hence, the seemingly formidable military structure eventually collapsed like a house of cards without ever fighting a war against its proclaimed enemies—a cautionary tale about the fragility of military structures once their time has passed and the support of their constituents has been exhausted.

See also Cold War; Comecon; New Thinking; North Atlantic Treaty Organization; Power Politics; Warfare.

FURTHER READING

Clawson, R. W., and L. S. Kaplan, eds. *The Warsaw Pact: Political Purpose and Military Means.* Wilmington, DE: Scholarly Resources, 1982.

Holden, G. *The Warsaw Pact: The WTO and Soviet Security Policy.* Oxford: Blackwell, 1989.

Holloway, D., and J.M.O. Sharp, eds. *The Warsaw Pact: Alliance in Transition?* London: Macmillan, 1984.

Mastny, V., and M. Byrne, eds. *A Cardboard Castle? An Inside History of the Warsaw Pact, 1955–1991.* Budapest: Central European University Press, 2005.

Umbach, F. *Das rote Bündnis: Entwicklung und Zerfall des Warschauer Paktes, 1955—1991.* Berlin: Links, 2005.

VOJTECH MASTNY

Welfare State

Prior to the birth of communism the concept of the welfare state, though not its name, was part of the social democratic concept of "transitional" demands; that is, reforms that could be obtained within capitalism and which would improve the lot of the working class. Its origins can be traced to the founding manifesto of the Second International (1889) and to the Erfurt Program of the German Social Democratic Party (1891). These advocated, along with well-established political demands such as universal suffrage and the eight-hour day, legal aid, free medical service, and free education at all levels, including higher education, to be funded by graduated income and property taxes and death duties. Such policies were not the exclusive patrimony of the labor movement. Reforms that could be included under the banner of the "welfare state" had been promulgated by non-socialist forces as well, including in Bismarck's Germany, where as early as the 1880s a health insurance scheme and a general pension scheme for old age and invalidity were introduced. In 1911, the British Liberal government initiated a national insurance system to fund old–age pensions on a noncontributory basis (unlike the German system) and health and compulsory unemployment insurance systems (which the Germans had introduced during the Weimar Republic). In 1913 Sweden introduced the first compulsory and universal pension system in the world. The blueprint for the British welfare state, introduced by a Labour government in 1945–51, was the work of a liberal, William Beveridge.

The welfare state was therefore not part of the armory of the Communist movement as it developed in the years following the Russian Revolution, since "transitional" demands had by then acquired quite a different meaning; namely, as rallying points in a revolutionary situation where the objective was the seizure of state power. However even Lenin believed, as he explained in July 1919, that embryonic elements of communism could begin to develop within the interstices of the capitalist order and that these "sprouts of communism," as he called them, were the public provision of social goods, such as free nurseries.

Nevertheless even during the more moderate Popular Front period of the 1930s, when Communist parties cooperated with Socialist parties, as in France and Spain, their avowed priority was supporting left-leaning governments against the Right and the threat of fascism.

Even during the resistance when Communist parties often played the main role, their main objective was the conduct of military operations against the Nazis and their supporters and the creation of a wide base of support for postwar consolidation. Most of the blueprints and projects for social reforms generated during the war had been the work of Socialists. Once the conflict was over, the attitude of the Communists toward social reform depended largely on their role in government. In those countries where, under the name of "people's democracy" a single-party system was rapidly becoming established, they erected welfare structures relatively swiftly—free health services, for example, many of which emerged naturally after the abolition of private insurance and health systems. In some instances, as in Czechoslovakia and Hungary, these structures were built on preexisting social provisions. As unemployment was eliminated—either by the deliberate creation of jobs or by allowing massive overemployment in industry (with the inevitable bottlenecks)—there was no need for unemployment benefits. To a large extent, welfare measures in Communist countries were compensation for authoritarian political structures and low wages. When communism collapsed, the post-Communist parties rallied to the defense of the surviving welfare structures of the old regime with varying degrees of success.

In the West the construction of the welfare state remained in the hands of the Socialist parties where these had risen to power (Great Britain and the Scandinavian countries) or in the hands of social Christian parties, such as those of Germany, Austria (usually in coalition with the Socialists), and Italy. Since the Communist parties were not only out of power but also electorally marginal (with the exception of the French, Finnish, and Italian Communist parties) their role, such as it was, was limited to acting as pressure groups prodding the more powerful Socialist parties. Even in such circumstances, however, their main areas of concern tended to be the protection of trade unions, labor, and civil rights rather than welfare reform.

This was not just a matter of ideology. In the 1940s and 1950s the high-wage economies of northern Europe supported the welfare state, which they saw as a compromise between the more radical demands for the labor movement and capitalism. It was a response to the needs of European capitalism and particularly to the fact that the private sector, on its own, was unable to put in place all of the conditions necessary for production: an ideologically nonhostile labor force able and willing to work without the necessity to provide for its own health care

and future pensions out of wages, an efficient transport and educational infrastructure, and the provision of essential supplies, such as gas and electricity, at reasonably low costs. Thus the welfare state, while it unquestionably improved the standard of life of the workforce, simultaneously stabilized the capitalist system from an economic, social, and political point of view.

One of the pressures behind the introduction of welfare systems in Europe after the war was the impossibility of reproducing the American system of high wages. Between 1945 and 1950, most governments were forced to resort at some stage to a policy of controlling wages, and this was true even in countries where Socialists were in government. Welfare policies were a necessary counterbalance to policies of keeping labor costs down to enable entrepreneurs to compete internationally. Welfare states thus made possible political harmony between the two main industrial classes which, otherwise, would have been locked in constant strife.

The two countries of Western Europe where the Communists were strong, France and Italy, were at variance with the more developed northern economies. France had still a sizeable agricultural sector, supporting some 20 percent of the population, while its industry was dominated by an array of small and medium-sized enterprises scarcely competitive in the world markets. The Communist Party's strength was limited to inside the industrial red belt around Paris, the coal mines in the north, and some agricultural areas in the Midi. The main concern of the Pcf was the promotion of high wages and the defense of employment levels. The policies which flowed from this were the extension of the public sector (to protect jobs) and a defense of trade union rights. The French Socialist Party was the party of the progressive middle classes rather than a working-class party at all: its greatest union strength was in the teachers' union. There was an embryonic welfare state, but this was the result of pressures from political Catholicism (represented by the MRP, strong only in the immediate aftermath of the war), and from the Gaullists. More generally, the French welfare state was the result of a general anxiety about the low birthrate—hence rather robust policies to help families and young mothers in particular (rather similar to Soviet's post-1945 natalist policies, designed to counter the terrible losses of the war). The Pcf remained cool toward welfare legislation except for a brief period after the liberation when they supported social security reform, probably because their own man, Ambroise Croizat, had become minister of labor in October of 1945. A similar stance was taken in Finland where the Communists were in a coalition with the agrarian party and the Social Democrats. Together they maintained full employment without reducing purchasing power, introduced family allowances, and implemented redistributive policies favorable to the underprivileged

In Italy, immediately after the war, there was no major breakthrough toward a welfare state, even during the period of the national unity coalition (1944–47). However both socialists and Communists supported the inclusion in the Italian constitution of Article 38, which stated that "workers have a right to such insurance provisions as are necessary to meet their needs in case of accident, sickness, disability, old age, and involuntary unemployment." All that occurred in the 1950s was an improvement of the social provisions established by the Fascist regime in the 1930s based on quasigovernmental public institutions, the so-called *enti* such as the INPS for social security, the INAM for health, and the INAIL for accidents at work—all of which became centers of political power and patronage. One of the functions of the Italian welfare state was to widen the consensus and the legitimacy of the modern state and to preserve the hegemony of the Christian Democratic Party. The Pci became interested in welfare state reforms only in the 1960s—and even more so in the 1970s—when the Socialist Party entered the governing coalition opening a space for such initiatives. In local government, however, the Pci was a true "welfarist" party, notably in the central regions of Italy where the bulk of its support resided.

For years Communists in Western Europe had hailed Soviet welfare provisions and full employment as proofs that only the abolition of capitalism could establish an authentic welfare state. By the 1980s mounting evidence to the contrary convinced West European Communists to become wholeheartedly converted to the idea of the welfare state, just as conservative and neoliberal circles started to turn against it. By then, the idea of a postcapitalist social order had lost its original impetus and communism had reached the end of its political trajectory.

See also Citizenship; Family; Modernization; Social Democracy; State, The.

FURTHER READING

Baldwin, P. *The politics of Social Solidarity: The Class Basis of the European Welfare State, 1875–1975.* Cambridge, UK: Cambridge University Press, 1990.

Eley, G. *Forging Democracy: The History of the Left in Europe, 1850–2000.* Oxford: Oxford University Press, 2002.

Esping-Andersen, G. *Politics against Markets: The Social Democratic Road to Power.* Princeton, NJ: Princeton University Press, 1985.

———. *The Three Worlds of Welfare Capitalism.* Cambridge, UK: Polity Press, 1990.

Mishra, R. *The Welfare State in Crisis.* Brighton: Wheatsheaf Books, 1984.

Sassoon, Donald. *One Hundred Years of Socialism.* London: I. B. Taurus, 1996.

DONALD SASSOON

Winter War

On August 23, 1939, the Soviet Union and Germany concluded a secret nonaggression pact. The geographical area between the two powers was divided into spheres of influence. A week later, Hitler attacked Poland. After the division of Poland and a closer deal with Germany on September 28, Stalin moved swiftly into his sphere, forcing Estonia, Latvia, and Lithuania to surrender military bases.

On October 5, the Soviet Union proposed talks with Finland, which belonged to the agreed-upon Soviet sphere. Stalin wanted bases and the removal of the state's frontier further away from Leningrad. The Finns did not yield, and two rounds of negotiations in Moscow brought no results. Most people in the Finnish government did not believe that the Soviets would really attack. Marshal Mannerheim, however, was pessimistic, a fact Stalin learned from intelligence sources in Britain; the Soviets also learned that Sweden would not intervene in the case of a conflict. On the basis of this information and the Polish experience, Stalin believed that a military operation would prove relatively easy.

A small Finnish exile Communist group led by Comintern Secretary O. V. Kuusinen had survived in Moscow, and it was now once again permitted to be active in Finland. However, the group's influence was very limited. There were suspicions about the Soviet Union even among Finnish Communists, many of whom had lost relatives and friends in the Stalinist terror. Also, the left-center government in power since 1937 was favorable to the workers. The republic seemed worth defending.

On November 30, 1939, the Soviet Union attacked. A Finnish "popular" government led by Kuusinen was set up in the rear of the Red Army, but it did not receive support in Finland, not even to any significant degree from the country's Communists. For many of them, the government, which consisted of only five Finnish Communists, was a confirmation of the fact that all traditional leaders of the Finnish labor movement, who had been exiled in Russia since the Red defeat in the civil war of 1918, had been killed by Stalin. It was only in foreign countries that some believed this government to be genuine. Even the Finnish Communist Party's secretary general, Arvo Tuominen, a confidant of Kuusinen then living in exile in Stockholm, avoided participating in the puppet government and eventually defected from the Comintern.

The Finnish army put up strong resistance in harsh winter conditions, and the Soviets suffered heavy losses. Britain and France planned an intervention, and through his spies Stalin received exaggerated information about these plans. On January 29, 1940, Molotov therefore announced that the Soviets had agreed to deal with the real government in Helsinki. The Kuusinen government was quietly dropped, and Kuusinen himself had to stay in Moscow for the rest of his life; under Khrushchev, he rose to the CPSU's politburo.

A renewed and massive Red Army general attack forced the Finns to withdraw but did not break their resistance. The Soviets, having received intelligence on imminent Western intervention, signed a peace treaty with Finland on March 13, 1940. Finland lost territory but remained independent. The fierceness of the fighting is reflected in the losses: in 105 days the Soviets lost over 100,000 men dead. In terms of losses, the Winter War was the third largest war waged by the Soviet Union, second only to the civil war and the "Great Patriotic War."

The Winter War badly damaged the Soviets' reputation in many countries, in particular in Scandinavia. In the long run, it heavily influenced subsequent Soviet-Finnish relations and was a main factor behind Finland not becoming a people's democracy after the Second World War, despite considerable Communist support in the country and its proximity to the Soviet Union.

See also Kuusinen, Otto; Molotov-Ribbentrop Pact; Red Army.

FURTHER READING

Gorodetsky, G., and S. Naveh, eds. *The Soviet Union and the Outbreak of War, 1939–1941.* London: Frank Cass, 2001.

Van Dyke, C. *The Soviet Invasion of Finland, 1939–1940.* London: Frank Cass, 1997.

KIMMO RENTOLA

Women, Emancipation of

The Bolshevik position on the "woman question" resulted from a combination of Marxist orthodoxy and Russian revolutionary traditions and culture. They shared an understanding of the causes of women's oppression with that prevailing in European socialism in the early 20th century: both placed emphasis on class relations and economic determinism. Women's emancipation would be solved with the advent of a classless society, the abolition of private property, society collectively assuming many of the roles traditionally assigned to mothers and wives, and women's integration into the world of industrial work. Individual domestic work needed to be abolished because in addition to constituting one of the primary causes of women's exploitation, it perpetuated a form of isolated family life, a source of hostility toward the new collectivist lifestyle of the ideal future socialist society.

But the woman question was also a topic of ambivalence. It evoked not only the hope that women, once freed from the oppressive bonds of family ties, would actively participate in the revolutionary struggle but also the fear that they might sabotage that struggle, because as custodians of the traditions of the patriarchal family, they were resistant to change. This tendency to refer to women only in negative terms was aided by an important principle of the Russian Marxist paradigm, which became part of Bolshevik political culture: attention to the realm of private life, considered to be women's reign par excellence, was considered to be incompatible with a dedication to the revolutionary cause.

The set of measures that the Bolsheviks adopted once in power reveals their commitment to women's emancipation. In a few months all the imperial laws that for centuries had forced Russian women to obey their husband in everything were abolished, and so were any legal forms of discrimination based on sex. By virtue of the rights it granted women, the legislation introduced by the first Bolshevik government was the most progressive in the world at that time. Soviet power, however, did not intend to stop at the mere declaration of men and women's equal rights but instead aimed to create the conditions in which such rights might be enjoyed. Thus, to allow women to enter the world of production and actively participate in the public sphere, the state should intervene in promoting their education and vocational training, institute public assistance for maternity and early childhood, and adopt legislation to protect the health and maternity of women workers.

Aleksandra Kollontay concentrated her efforts in these areas, during the brief period in which she headed the Social Security Department. Yet Bolshevik women (Inessa Armand, Nadezhda Krupskaya, and Kollontay herself) faced stiff resistance in the party when they proposed creating a department specifically dedicated to work among women (Zhenotdel). Clara Zetkin encountered similar opposition when she tried to introduce an equivalent of the Zhenotdel in the Comintern as well. Such intransigence testified to deep-seated ambiguities in Bolshevik attitudes toward the woman question—ones that Lenin himself denounced, arguing in an interview he gave Zetkin in 1920 that many Communists still retained a "Philistine" attitude toward women, and continued to expect their wives to grant them "the ancient rights of the husband, lord and master." Although he was convinced of the need to radically attack patriarchy, Lenin was explicit in condemning the image of the "New Woman" as Kollontay conceived it. She had raised an important issue, even if awkwardly: the emancipation of woman, in the sense of freeing her from family ties, tended to put women's roles in question, above all starting from their private individual existences. This implied an idea of emancipation that contradicted the ideals of collective identity proclaimed by the Communists, and that risked putting the interests of women ahead of those of the party and working class.

The Zhenotdel, instituted in 1919, was thus charged exclusively with propaganda among women workers, considered the female revolutionary subject par excellence, while Zetkin only managed to bring her project to a successful conclusion during the Comintern's Third Congress (1921), when an International Women's Secretariat in Moscow was created and Women's Committees were established within the leadership groups of various national Communist parties. The introduction of New Economic Policy (NEP) helped the Zhenotdel acquire a certain degree of autonomy, but less than that enjoyed by other departments at the same hierarchical level. The possibility that opened up in the 1920s of including peasant women and "women from the Soviet East" in one's group of interlocutors was a determining factor in its transformation from a simple propaganda organ to an institution that the party relied on to establish stable contacts with society, and to enlarge the consensus that Soviet power relied on. With this new function, the Zhe-

notdel undertook complex political activities at various levels, addressing all strata of the female population. It involved tens of thousands of workers and peasants in a network of activists dispersed throughout Soviet territory, even in the wildest regions of central Asia. It became the principal conduit for recruiting women into the party, providing new members with the necessary qualifications to fulfill their tasks. The Zhenotdel took a position on the critical questions facing women during the NEP, denouncing the discrimination they encountered both at their places of work and in their domestic lives, while also promoting legislative initiatives to counteract the inferior status imposed by Islam on women in the Soviet East.

The decision to abolish the Zhenotdel in 1930 was connected to the beginning of the "revolution from above." Notwithstanding its successes, this institution became a victim of the need to divert all possible party resources toward the new plans for the country's accelerated industrialization. Under these new circumstances, to busy oneself with the woman question would have implied a useless waste of resources and energy. Among the reasons that contributed to the Zhenotdel's dissolution, though, was the fact that the struggle carried on by this department for the rights of all women, not only workers, ended up feeding suspicions in the party leadership that its activists had arrived at a "feminist" conception of emancipation at odds with communism's ideology.

With the start of industrialization, women's emancipation lost its independent objective and became a question of social utility: it would allow women to better serve the superior interests of the Soviet state, as workers and mothers of future citizens. In the wider context of the creation of a new system of values, one that could be witnessed starting in the late 1930s, the party, though not rejecting its original view that women would participate equally in the edification of the new order, adopted a notion according to which they would have to also find a path to self-realization in taking care of their families. The image of the New Woman as it was portrayed by official Soviet propaganda in the late 1930s was of a woman who knew how to reconcile her role of citizen and worker with the more traditional one of mother. The government had created a network of social services enabling her to partake in both her "beloved work" and the "joys of maternity." Women would now work outside the home in order to enjoy full membership in the new society, but they would maintain their obligations toward their children: it was their responsibility to instill a Communist worldview in them, composed of patriotism, heroism, and a deep sense of the "unity of interests of the members of the Soviet family."

In the aftermath of World War II, Communist propaganda about the superiority of the "Soviet model" claimed that Soviet women had been fully emancipated, thanks to a paid job, full access to education, and a network of state services that assisted motherhood and early childhood. In fact, according to data provided by the United Nations, in 1970 the percentage of women employed in the USSR was the highest in the world. Numerous issues remained unresolved, however, such as the conflict between women's public and private roles, continuing discrimination in the area of salaries, and women's exclusion—despite the high percentage of women with a high school or college education—from the party's and country's centers of power. This led feminist associations, which formed at the end of the 1980s in Russia, to denounce the idea that Soviet women had achieved their emancipation and demand that equality of individual rights that the Bolsheviks, as Marxists, had refused.

See also Citizenship; Family; Kollontay, Aleksandra; New Man; Social Policy; Zetkin, Clara.

FURTHER READING

Clements, B. E. *Bolshevik Women*. Cambridge, UK: Cambridge University Press, 1997.

Posadskaya, A., et al., eds. *Women in Russia: A New Era in Russian Feminism*. New York: Verso, 1994.

Wood, E. A. *The Baba and the Comrade: Gender and Politics in Revolutionary Russia*. Bloomington: Indiana University Press, 1997.

ANNA DI BIAGIO

Workers

The Soviet Union

Between 1913, the last peacetime year of the old czarist empire, and the Soviet Union's collapse in 1991, the size of its industrial workforce grew approximately eightfold, from just under 4 million to over 31 million workers. Comparable increases took place in construction and transport. Yet this growth was by no means smooth or linear. It was shaped by a series of demographic crises and upheavals, including those that were the direct result of state policies. The economic crisis of World War I had already seen the ranks of industrial workers fall to 2.6 million by the time of the Bolshevik Revolution in 1917. During the ensuing period of civil war and War Communism, the flight of workers back to their villages in search of food brought their number down to only 1.1 million, followed by a slow recovery back to 3.5 million industrial workers by the end of New Economic Policy in 1928.

Stalinist industrialization and the five-year plans of the 1930s totally transformed this picture. In terms of numbers, the ranks of workers swelled, as peasants left the new collective farms to become workers. By 1940, there were around 11 million workers in industry, 3 million in transport, and 1.7 million in construction. Alongside this numerical growth, the 1930s saw two major shifts in the social composition of the workforce. The vast majority of workers had come directly from the countryside, and some 43 percent of workers were now women. These figures do not include the prison laborers who were part of the gulag system.

World War II again decimated the ranks of the workforce, as industry alone lost nearly 2 million workers. Between 1945 and Stalin's death in 1953, over 7 million new workers poured into industry and construction, nearly doubling their combined ranks. Most of these were young people conscripted—often against their will—into priority areas of coal mining, construction, and metallurgy, and/or into regions with inhospitable living conditions, mainly the Urals and western Siberia.

Under Khrushchev and the relaxation of state controls over workers' freedom to change jobs, the main problem for the regime was how to encourage millions of nonworking women into industry. The Khrushchev regime never solved this problem, and the economy was perpetually plagued by labor shortages. It was only under Leonid Brezhnev that the Soviet workforce saw a major influx of women workers, who by 1978 were just under half (48 percent) of all industrial workers. The Brezhnev years saw one other major change in the sociology of the working class. As the rapid social mobility of the Stalin and Khrushchev years came to an end, there emerged an inherited class structure. The sons and daughters of workers were now likely to remain workers.

Stalinist industrialization saw a major fall in workers' living standards. The extent of the fall in real wages has been disputed by economic historians, but even the most modest estimates guess that by 1940, real wages had fallen by at least 40 percent since 1928. By and large, however, the famine of 1932–33 did not cause massive increased mortality among workers in the towns. Living standards fell even more dramatically during the war, when there was mass starvation, not just in Leningrad, which was under siege, but also in the Soviet hinterland. Recovery after the war was slow. A new famine in 1947 claimed between 1 million and 1.5 million lives, many of them in the towns. The average member of an urban worker's family in this period was consuming barely two thousand calories a day, well below the recommended daily norm of between three thousand and thirty-five hundred calories. Even during the Khrushchev years, when food supplies notably improved, archive documents show that the daily consumption in workers' families was still well below the recommended daily requirements. It was only in the Brezhnev period that the situation improved from a nutritional point of view, although perpetual food shortages were a major source of popular discontent with the regime. Mikhail Gorbachev had hoped that his perestroika reforms would lead to greater industrial efficiency and a rise in living standards, but as his policies faltered, food shortages again worsened, and workers became disenchanted with his government.

Wages tell only part of this story, though. The mass influx of new workers into the towns and cities in the 1930s put enormous pressure on the country's limited housing stock, which Stalin and his associates did not deem a priority for investment. Workers and their families crowded into communal flats and makeshift dormitories and barracks. Outside of Moscow and Leningrad, few urban residents had access to a central water supply or basic sanitation—problems that only began to be addressed under Khrushchev and Brezhnev.

During the New Economic Policy period, workers gradually saw their political power undermined as the Bolsheviks outlawed independent political parties and organizations, including those on the political Left, and gradually transformed the trade unions into vehicles for implementing central economic policies. Workers' freedom of action was further undermined by the existence of mass unemployment in the 1920s and the growing (and illegal) practice of hiring workers on rolling short-term contracts. This erosion of workers' morale was reflected in the sharp fall in the number of strikes during the New Economic Policy era.

Stalinist industrialization changed this political situation in a number of ways. The fall in living standards provoked widespread mass protests and strikes. The most notable was perhaps a strike of textile workers in the Ivanovo region in 1932, but mass protests affected factories and construction sites in almost every city and region up until 1934. These protests, however, were localized, uncoordinated, and focused around local economic grievances. As the regime increased its use of violence and repression against the general population, the protests waned.

The regime also used other means to exercise control over workers' behavior. The fall in real wages was enforced by a campaign of drastic speedup in the factories. This was enforced first by the campaign of Shock Work (*udarnichestvo*), then from 1935 onward by a similar campaign, Stakhanovism. Both had the same rationale. A selected group of privileged workers would volunteer to set a production "record." Their achievements would then be made the standard requirement for everyone. Those who failed to meet the new, higher targets would suffer a potentially life-threatening fall in earnings.

What the Stalinist leadership had not planned for, however, was that its policies would create a labor shortage. This became so severe that it allowed workers at least partially to redress their loss of power on the shop floor by threatening to quit their jobs if they did not receive higher pay. In 1930, the average industrial worker stayed at a job for less than eight months before quitting; labor turnover was twice as high among coal miners and construction workers. The main response of the regime was to tighten labor laws to limit workers' freedom of movement. Yet these proved largely ineffective until the regime made job changing a criminal offense in 1940, and then increased the penalties to several years in the gulag during World War II and immediately afterward. Still, even in these years many tens of thousands of workers risked being caught and sent to a labor camp by running away from their enterprises. Perhaps surprisingly, most of them were never apprehended.

When Khrushchev came to power he restored workers' freedom of movement and attempted to win workers' active cooperation in the task of restimulating the economy. The results were mixed, largely because Khrushchev was not willing genuinely to democratize the trade unions or political life in general. Productivity remained a serious problem. The Khrushchev years also saw a renewal of mass protests, but only one of these assumed an overtly political and organized character: the workers' uprising in 1962 in the city of Novocherkassk, which was suppressed by KGB troops.

The Brezhnev years saw a political standoff between the regime and its workforce. The regime made it clear that any attempt to engage in independent political activity would be violently repressed, but at the same time attempted to buy workers' passivity by allowing wages to rise without restraint. Because the increase in money wages was not matched by better supplies of food or consumer goods, though, popular discontent merely deepened.

Gorbachev attempted to break this social impasse by promising to improve economic efficiency and increase the supply of consumer goods, and by relaxing state control over civil society. His policies won little support among industrial workers because they threatened to introduce mass unemployment and remove state subsidies on basic foods. The turning point in the regime's relations with its workers was a nationwide miners' strike in 1989. The Soviet leadership now formally granted workers the right to strike and form independent trade unions. Although this led to few mass protests of a political nature (and no independent unions outside of coal mining), it did give workers sufficient freedom within the workplace to undermine attempts by managers to increase productivity, and to this extent it helped to accelerate the country's economic collapse. There was a new miners' strike in 1991, but this was rapidly co-opted by Boris Yeltsin's fledgling Russian government (Yeltsin financed the independent miners' union in the Russian Federation). In this way workers played a major, though probably unintentional role, in the ultimate collapse of the Soviet system.

China

The size of modern industry in China in the first half of the 20th century, before the 1949 Communist revolution, was small, and so was the working class it employed. Despite a few areas where colonial and imperial powers had established important industrial bases (especially the Japanese in the northeast of the country), the number of people employed in industry and their social significance was limited. Still in 1952, three years after the revolution the number of industrial workers was 15 million, slightly more than 8 percent of the entire active workforce. Some 182 million people lived and worked in the countryside, and had become the engine of the Chinese socialist revolution between the 1930s and the end of the 1940s. With the remarkable exception of the northeast, the Chinese working class was therefore largely a creation of the new Communist regime. After 1949, the People's Republic of China devised an economic strategy that was inspired (and in the first decade, before 1960, largely funded) by the USSR. The making of a working class in China was a necessity of economic development under socialist conditions, and the government went to extraordinary lengths to extract resources from agriculture and devolve them to industrial construction. The First Five-Year Plan (1953–57) focused on building a strong heavy industry; in the 1950s the sector received one-fifth of the national income. One hundred thirty key heavy industrial projects were funded by the Soviet Union (and largely assembled by its technicians).

In the initial years and even before the accelerated nationalization of industrial plants in 1956, China had about 35 percent of its workforce in the private sector, signaling that the role of the local and central state in developing industrial activities was already relevant before the Communist takeover. The nationalization also meant that the entire industrial workforce was, from this moment on, hired through state agencies, and assigned to industrial or administrative units. The traditional mechanisms of the labor market and labor mobility had disappeared.

Around the same time, Chinese laborers also experienced the creation of two institutions that would greatly limit their geographic and labor mobility: the household registration system (*hukou dengji zhidu*), a register designed to prevent rural residents from moving freely to the cities, a system that still exists today, and the urban work units (*gongzuo danwei*). The latter was an all-encompassing institution that hired workers for life and was supposed to rationalize consumption in the cities. Workers in these institutions would be under the administration of the unit, would receive free housing and all other essential provisions, and their children would be able to inherit their jobs on retirement. The absorption of all commercial and service activities within the work unit greatly reduced opportunities for employment and consumption outside these structures, and the overall social mobility both from rural areas to the cities and between urban units became almost impossible. As noted by Barry Naughton, in this period death was four times as frequent as a cause of job leaving as was resignation and being fired.

Urban workers in these state-owned factories generally enjoyed better living conditions than workers in collective enterprises, and had access to guaranteed services and resources unimaginable to farmers. Also, because the objective of the system was to obtain full employment for the registered urban population, and the state was providing funds to cover the workers' payrolls, factories were often willing to hoard workers and accept a reduction of labor efficiency. This frequently resulted in lighter workloads, but greater pressure on unit resources.

During the 1960s and early 1970s, this labor structure produced exceptionally low labor and geographic mobility (the urban population actually decreased), and a stagnation of salaries; at the end of the radical years of the Cultural Revolution in 1977, the monetary component (not including the in-kind salary) of the average industrial salary was lower (602 yuan, or around 60 euros at today's exchange rate) than that of 1964 (661 yuan).

In those years distribution was based on the principle of low notional salaries with a large component of the remuneration still being paid in-kind. Moreover, the Cultural Revolution policy of rewarding political activism accentuated the egalitarian principle in salary distribution.

Beginning in 1977, after the death of Mao Zedong, and the beginning of economic reform under Deng Xiaoping, the principle of "to each according to their labor" was again taken to mean that differences in salaries could stimulate productivity. Forms of remuneration that had formerly been banned in consideration of their exploitative or economistic nature, like piece rates and productivity bonuses, were reintroduced. The iron rice bowl of the work unit was, albeit slowly, dismantled, under the need to improve efficiency. In 1986, the introduction of labor contracts made it possible for companies to hire and fire workers, although a transition to labor contracts took a while to be completed, and the work units proved resilient to the attempts to deprive them of their redistributive functions.

The introduction of labor contracts was also the beginning of a progressive marketization of labor relations. While on the theoretical front it was recognized that labor can, under certain circumstances, be a commodity traded on the market of production factors, the growing demand for a liberalization of labor relations came to complement the demand of growing numbers of international investors willing to take advantage of China's low labor costs.

With the progressive de facto liberalization of labor mobility during the 1980s and 1990s the urban workforce became highly polarized. Large numbers of migrants from the countryside became an unprotected and overexploited urban proletariat. Former worker elites also suffered. With the management now more concerned with productivity than with full employment, the unskilled and the middle-aged found it difficult to cope, and became victims of a wave of dismissals from inefficient state-owned enterprises. Skilled and educated workers (of which there was a shortage), on the other hand, could bargain for better conditions in both the public and the growing private and international sectors.

Salaries and working conditions in China have deteriorated with the increasing international competition from other southern countries (especially in Southeast Asia and Latin America). Despite new labor protection laws, China's labor market remains among the most deregulated, and worker protections existing on paper are rarely implemented. With an increasing polarization and a huge pool of cheap labor moving rapidly into the cities with the progressive lifting of administrative barriers, China is today a Communist country with one of the most exploitative labor systems in the world.

See also Socialist Emulation.

FURTHER READING

Andrle, V. *Workers in Stalin's Russia: Industrialization and Social Change in a Planned Economy.* New York: St. Martin's Press, 1988.

Benvenuti, F. *Fuoco sui sabotatori! Stachanovismo e organizazione industriale in URSS, 1934–8.* Rome: Valerio Levi Editore, 1988.

Chan, A. *China Workers under Assault: The Exploitation of Labour in a Globalizing Economy.* Armonk, NY: M. E. Sharpe, 2001.

Filtzer, D. *Soviet Workers and Stalinist Industrialization: The Formation of Modern Soviet Production Relations, 1928–1941.* London: Pluto Press, 1986.

———. *Soviet Workers and Late Stalinism: Labour and the Restoration of the Stalinist System after World War II.* Cambridge, UK: Cambridge University Press, 2002.

Kotkin, S. *Magnetic Mountain: Stalinism as a Civilization.* Berkeley: University of California Press, 1995.

Kozlov, V. A. *Mass Uprisings in the USSR: Protest and Rebellion in the Post-Stalin Years.* Trans. and ed. E. McClarnand MacKinnon. Armonk, NY: M. E. Sharpe, 2002.

Kuromiya, H. *Stalin's Industrial Revolution: Politics and Workers, 1928–1932.* Cambridge, UK: Cambridge University Press, 1988.

Maier, R. *Die Stachanov-Bewegung 1935–38: Der Stachanovismus als tragendes und verschärfendes Moment der Stalinisierung der sowjetischen Gesellschaft.* Stuttgart, 1990.

Mandel, D. *Perestroika and the Soviet People.* Montreal: Black Rose Books, 1991.

Siegelbaum, L. *Stakhanovism and the Politics of Productivity in the USSR, 1935–1941.* Cambridge, UK: Cambridge University Press, 1988.

Solinger, D. *Contesting Citizenship in Urban China: Peasant Migrants, the State, and the Logic of the Market.* Berkeley: University of California Press, 1999.

Tomba, L. *Paradoxes of Labour Reform: Chinese Labour Theory and Practice from Socialism to the Market.* Honolulu: University of Hawaii Press, 2002.

Walder, A. *Communist Neo Traditionalism: Work and Authority in Chinese Industry.* Berkeley: University of California Press, 1986.

DONALD A. FILTZER

World Revolution

It is well known that the constitutive forces of the international Communist movement, immediately following the October Revolution, stressed the international dimensions of the revolutionary process that this event had inaugurated. This view was based on two presuppositions that initially were of equal importance. On the one hand, there was the diagnosis of global capitalism's state of health, which, although it gave rise to vast productive forces also left capitalists to struggle against their imperialist shell, destroyed the possibility of an international market, and caused a chain reaction of conflicts and destruction, creating the premise for civil war in the West and the revolt of the colonies' oppressed peoples. From this diagnosis the conviction emerged that only a proletarian revolution would be able to lead humanity out of the blind alley into which imperialism had led it, and that this revolution, to realize its goal of universal liberation of the exploited, would need to transcend the borders of national states and develop on a planetary scale, uniting the socialist revolution in advanced capitalist countries with the struggles of people oppressed by colonial domination and the defense of the Soviet regime in Russia.

On the other hand, the Bolsheviks and all the factions that made up the Comintern shared the idea that the Russian Revolution was only the prologue to a European social revolution, and that its only guarantee of survival was receiving the help of the victorious revolutionary proletariat in at least some of the major capitalist countries.

This conviction often led the international Communist movement to confuse its desires with reality, overestimating the maturity of revolutionary conditions in the West and the colonies, while at the same time underestimating the solidity of bourgeois regimes as well as the idiosyncratic nature of worker traditions in Europe and the United States.

The "global party of the revolution" concept took shape against the backdrop of these convictions, not yet shaken by the international dimension of the revolutionary process. Precisely when faith in the imminence of a global revolution was the strongest (1919–20), the idea of such a global party appeared to be imprecise and poorly defined, and its creation was left to the spontaneity of the revolutionary movement. It was only when the immediate prospect of a world revolution gradually receded that the global party model came to be more precisely defined. The historical contradiction that would define the entire experience of Communist parties between the wars was thus reproduced at the level of international organization. Similar to these parties—which were initially conceived as the vanguard of a revolution that was already on its way, but later had to adapt to a situation marked by the stabilization of capitalism and its bourgeois-democratic institutions—the Communist International would define and establish itself at a time when the international revolution seemed to have receded into an indefinite future. Thus, starting in 1921, the global party was no longer the ideological, political, and organizational instrument for the realization of the global revolution but rather the means to prevent the Communist movement from disintegrating—that is, to manage and discipline it while awaiting the revolution itself.

On the one hand, prospects for a world revolution receded further into the distance, while on the other hand, the republic of the Soviets demonstrated an unexpected capacity for survival and development in a hostile world. Both tendencies were essentially an outline of the framework leading to the theory of "socialism in one country." This theory, however, and the idea of different tasks for different components of the revolutionary movement that it implied, already entailed a crucial corollary. If it were possible to construct socialism in Russia, even independently of victory in the most important capitalist countries and the colonies, it logically followed that there must be a certain separation, even in a framework that recognized relative degrees of significance, between the world revolution and the Russian Revolution that had already seized power. A similar perspective seems to have been entertained by Nikolay Bukharin, who used it as the basis of his cautious attempts at reforming and decentralizing the Comintern in 1926. If these attempts failed, it was due not only to Bukharin's defeat and his subsequent marginalization but also to a mechanism within the global party of revolution itself that gave its most powerful member an enormous, decisive importance—to some extent even beyond this member's intentions. This mechanism was neither invented nor, at least initially, imposed by the Russian Communists; it emerged from a situation in which maximum centralization appeared to serve both the possibility of an imminent international revolution and that of a deadlocked phase of preparation.

In 1929, the international horizon seemed even more favorable to this one-sided view of the revolutionary process. The contrast between the two systems—a capitalism that was falling apart, and a socialism that was being built—was seen as the principal source for the international revolution. The Soviet Union's mere existence was increasingly assigned the role of catalyst and detonator of the capitalist world's contradictions, fulfilling its role of radicalizing the exploited masses. During the entire period of the economic crisis, the world revolution was more of a myth used for declamatory purposes than a program around which the strategy and tactics of the Communist movement were built. The USSR's interests as a state could not be put at risk by adventurous attempts at insurrection, and a successful revolution in the West might have led to the delegitimation of the Soviet experience's birthright.

Yet the rigidity of the definitions perpetuated in the statutes and the official documents concealed the reality that the function of global party of the revolution had already begun to lose its meaning. The need to adapt the model to the specific social, economic, and cultural conditions of diverse national realities had already influenced the Comintern from its first years of existence in shaping the real substance of the Communist movement. Beginning in the 1930s, this need for adaptation faced new and unforeseen difficulties, which in their turn required modifications in the model. The history of the Chinese party, which was the first to define an idea of revolutionary strategy that was in actuality independent of the Comintern's directives, proves as much. For the European parties, this shift did not occur before 1934. It was only at this time that their anti-Fascist commitment was finally recognized as a significant front in its own right, since it was also essential for the USSR's defense, and could finally be exercised in a less restricted fashion. The

Communist parties, or at least some of the most important ones, therefore found themselves involved in mass struggles, and had to confront new strategies, alliances, and organizational models, taken or at least shaped by their respective national political traditions. This effort also seemed to involve some tendencies toward decentralization, and Georgi Dimitrov himself supported them to a certain extent: in October 1935, the elimination of the regional secretariats seemed to confirm the acquisition of greater responsibilities by individual parties. In actuality, if a new phase developed it was distinguished above all by new forms of control and interference in the parties' internal life by the Stalinist apparatus—much more heavy-handed forms than had previously been the case, even though they were not formalized. And they were destined to have tragic consequences.

The sudden about-face of Soviet policy with the Molotov-Ribbentrop Pact, followed by the beginning of World War II, highlighted the extremely heavy price that individual Communist parties paid in credibility and national legitimacy. It also underscored the need to establish a more independent relationship, no longer one of simple and total identification, between the policies of the Soviet state and those of the Communist International. When as a consequence of the Nazi aggression against the USSR the Communist parties once again had a prominent role in the resistance movement, a new dialectic came into being.

The dissolution of the Comintern, decided on May 17, 1943, was mostly due to the USSR's foreign policy needs. While the gesture could be interpreted as a definitive renunciation of policies that supported exporting the socialist revolution to other countries, it actually was focused on improving the USSR's ties with the Allies in the midst of the ongoing war, and facilitating collaboration with them in the future. It is also probable that Joseph Stalin and his entourage believed that they could count on ties with the Communist parties. The end of the Comintern did not mean that these Communist parties actually severed their ties with Moscow. In fact, in certain respects they became even closer and more direct than in the past. The formal act of dissolution, however, did not simply provide an alibi for the choices to be made by Soviet diplomacy. By formally recognizing the disappearance of the utopia of the global party of the revolution, it instead highlighted relationships between the "home team" and its various sections, which were becoming more complex and varied because of the division of the world into two spheres of influence. The national variants of Communist strategy thus acquired more freedom to maneuver. Initially the USSR did not discourage these developments, even though it tried to make them fit into an overall design favorable to its interests as a great power.

In actuality the very idea of world revolution, and with it that of a global party, had already reached its end during World War II. Nor did the Great Alliance's crisis, which rapidly became the Cold War, ever really resurrect it in any significant fashion. The view of a renewed opposition between capitalism and communism, and a capitalist world made unstable by crises and conflicts, never really led the USSR to renounce the division of the world into "spheres of influence," since it seemed to be the only viable option to consolidate its interests as a great power. From this point of view, the criticisms made against the Soviets by the Chinese Communists and third world ideologies during the 1960s were certainly not without merit, yet neither resurrected an overarching plan for world revolution.

See also Antifascism; Comintern; Lenin, Vladimir; Socialism in One Country.

FURTHER READING

Claudin, F. *The Communist Movement: From Comintern to Cominform*. New York: Monthly Review Press, 1975.

Drabkin, J. "The Idea of World Revolution and Its Transformations." In *Centre and Periphery: The History of the Comintern in the Light of the New Documents*, ed. M. M. Narinskij and J. Rohahn. Amsterdam: International Institute of Social History, 1996.

Furet, F. *The Passing of an Illusion: The Idea of Communism in the Twentieth Century*. Chicago: University of Chicago Press, 1999.

McKenzie, K. E. *Comintern and World Revolution, 1928–1943: The Shaping of Doctrine*. New York: Columbia University Press, 1963.

Nollau, G. *International Communism and World Revolution: History and Methods*. London: Hollis and Carter, 1961.

ALDO AGOSTI

World War II

World War II was the major military and political conflict of the 20th century. It was a clash between the aggressive states of the Fascist bloc and the nations and peoples of the anti-Hitler coalition. The basic cause of World War II was the drive of the aggressors (Nazi Germany, Fascist Italy, and militaristic Japan) for territorial expansion and the establishment of dominance, first in certain regions and then in the whole world.

World War II began with Nazi Germany's invasion of Poland on September 1, 1939. On September 3, Great Britain, France, Australia, New Zealand, and India declared war on Germany.

The political line of the Communist International at the beginning of the war was that its main instigator was German nazism, which sought hegemony in Europe and a new division of the world. In the summer of 1939, however, the Soviet leadership reached a broad-scale agreement with Nazi Germany. On August 23, on the eve of the German invasion of Poland, the Soviet Union and Germany signed a nonaggression pact whose most important component was a secret protocol dividing Eastern and Southeastern Europe into German and Soviet "spheres of interest." This nonaggression pact was accompanied by a treaty declaring German-Soviet friendship, and fixing the borders of the Nazi and Soviet partition of Poland after the defeat of the latter.

This shift of the Soviet leadership to collaboration with Hitler's Germany forced a pronounced change in the Comintern's political line. Stalin laid out new guidelines with respect to the Comintern in a conversation with Georgi Dimitrov on September 7, 1939. Stalin declared that there was now a war between two groups of capitalist nations to divide up and dominate the world, and that this war would shake the foundations of the capitalist system. In this new context, the division of capitalist countries into Fascist and democratic entities seemed to lose its significance. Stalin took a very hostile position toward Poland, characterizing it as a Fascist state that was suppressing the Ukrainians, Belorussians, and other groups. (In March 1940, the politburo of the Central Committee of the Soviet Communist Party reached a decision on a mass execution of Polish officers captured by the Soviet authorities—the so-called Katyn affair.) As far as the Communist movement was concerned, Stalin proposed removing the appellation "United People's Front." The Communists of the capitalist countries were now enjoined to come out decisively against their governments and against war in general.

In the ensuing weeks, the Comintern leadership became more aware of these Stalinist aims and attempted to bring about a corresponding shift in the actions of the Communist parties as well. The Executive Committee of the Comintern noted the unjust, imperialist nature of the war, emphasizing that the British and French imperialists were pushing actively for continuing the war, and arousing passions for it. Still, the abrupt changes in the Communist parties' political line proved difficult to carry out, particularly in the case of the leaders of the Communist parties of Britain, the United States, Belgium, Norway, and a number of other countries.

The Comintern leadership strove to enlist Communist support for all aspects of USSR foreign policy: the Soviet occupation of eastern Poland in September 1939, the conclusion of mutual aid treaties with the Baltic states (Estonia, Latvia, and Lithuania), and the Soviet Union's "winter war" against Finland.

The Communists tried in every way to oppose the military efforts of France and Great Britain, characterizing these countries as aggressors and calling for an end to the bloodshed, though still without uttering any words of a revolutionary nature. The Communist Party of Germany urged that the country withdraw from the imperialist war. The Comintern tried to win over the national liberation movements as well, in particular the Communist parties of the colonies and dominions of Great Britain, summoning them to the struggle against British imperialism. As far as the Communist Party of China was concerned, the Comintern tried to orient it toward the preservation in the country of a united national front in the fight against Japanese aggression.

The military and political situation changed after the German invasion of Denmark and Norway on April 9, 1940, and after the subsequent massive attack on the Low Countries and France, begun on May 10. The Netherlands and Belgium soon capitulated, and the French and British armies were defeated. On June 14 German troops entered Paris, and on June 22 representatives of the French government and its military command signed a peace agreement with the Germans in Compiègne, which for practical purposes meant the capitulation of France.

The Comintern did not revise its basic view of the war, which it continued to see as a struggle between two imperialist adversaries. Nevertheless, the Comintern's position appeared to reveal some new emphases and certain nuances, suggesting a tendency toward resisting the Nazi and Fascist aggressors. Moscow's attitude toward the Communists in the occupied countries of Western Europe during summer 1940 embraced the following goals: strengthening the Communist parties and the maintenance by them of an independent political line; refraining from supporting either of the warring sides; and fighting for the interests of the working masses in the social, economic, and political spheres. Moscow's directives did envision restoring the political independence of the occupied nations of Europe, but for the time being this goal was not a high priority. The plan was to create a united front and a Popular Front from below that would fight to fulfill the everyday demands of the masses and to promote "national liberation." The Secretariat of the Comintern's Executive Committee pointed to the need to combine both legal and illegal paths of action.

During the summer of 1940 Comintern activity began to manifest an anti-German direction. The Secretariat characterized the Second Vienna Arbitration as an imperialist diktat, and condemned the efforts of the French Communist leaders in Paris to collaborate with the German occupation authorities and secure permission for legal publication of the newspaper *L'Humanité*.

The stormy events in the Balkans from the Italian invasion of Greece in the fall of 1940 to the German invasion of Yugoslavia in the spring of 1941 revealed the policy objectives of the USSR and Comintern leadership, which were: to remain outside the warring groups; under no circumstances to contribute to the strengthening of the British position; to carefully oppose the further strengthening of Germany's position; and to work to broaden the influence of the Soviet Union and all other Communist countries in the international arena.

By the spring of 1941, Comintern policy had increasingly emphasized efforts to create broad national fronts (in France and Italy), and to fight for the national liberation movement. The French Communist Party was to fight for the country's independence, and work to uncover traitors and those too cowardly to join the struggle. As far as the Chinese Communists were concerned, the Comintern leadership was to apply consistent pressure on them to maintain a unified, national anti-Japanese front.

The cornerstone of the Comintern's policy, from September 1939 until June 22, 1941, was and remained the support of the USSR in its struggle against the "imperialist war" and its instigators as well as reactionary forces in general.

However, the Nazi invasion of the Soviet Union on June 22, 1941, now brought about fundamental changes in the entire military and political situation as well as the strategy of the Communist movement. The majority of Soviet Communists did their part at the front and at home in achieving victory over the aggressor forces. During the war, the Stalinist leadership reined in the slogans of the socialist revolution, appealing instead to Russian patriotism and reestablishing contacts with the Russian Orthodox Church. Yet there was no liberalization of the Soviet regime. Mass repressions continued, and whole nations suffered forced deportation.

The entire activity of the Comintern was oriented toward supporting the Soviet Union in its great "patriotic war" and achieving victory over the German Reich. The Soviet struggle was regarded as a just war of liberation, and the question of the overthrow of capitalism in individual countries and the socialist revolution in general was not broached.

Thus, the Comintern called on the Communists in countries participating (or potentially participating) in the anti-Hitler coalition to enter the war (the United States) or increase their war efforts against Nazi Germany. The Communist parties of the occupied countries were also supposed to maximize their resistance against the Fascist occupiers and their collaborators, to establish contact with all patriotic groups, and to create a massive national liberation movement. The Communists became active and decisive participants in the Resistance. Communists in the German-occupied countries were summoned to organize liberation struggles against the Nazi and Fascist regimes. The Communists in neutral countries were called on to demonstrate that only the USSR was defending their freedom and independence, and therefore their peoples had a stake in a Soviet victory. The Communist parties of Asia were given the task of supporting the Soviet Union and the anti-Hitler coalition, and were enjoined to keep Japan from entering the war against the USSR.

Motivated by the severe Red Army defeats at the outset of the war in June 1941, Vyacheslav Molotov, in a conversation with Dimitrov on June 30, posed the question of raising the level of Communist activity in the struggle against Germany. "Every hour is crucial," went the refrain. "Communists must undertake everywhere the most resolute steps toward helping the Soviet people. The most important thing is to disorganize the enemy's home front and to subvert its army." Communist parties received directives to organize sabotage and diversionary activities, form detachments of partisans and intensify the struggle against the occupiers, and promote the creation and consolidation of the anti-Hitler coalition. As Communist propaganda pointed out, fascism is the fiercest enemy of all peoples, Hitler's military successes are temporary and precarious, and the USSR is fully resolved to carry the war on to a victorious climax.

The crushing defeat of German troops outside of Moscow and the Red Army's shift to the offensive in December 1941 gave Stalin and the Comintern leadership hope, unjustified as it turned out, of achieving a victory over the aggressors as early as sometime in 1942. The directives of the Comintern Secretariat by May 1, 1942, stated: "1942 must be the year that Hitler's Fascism will be destroyed." The Communist parties began once again to intensify the anti-Fascist liberation struggle.

The Communists now expanded their antioccupation partisan efforts into Yugoslavia, Greece, and Albania, and took command of the political organs of the left wing of the liberation movement. In 1942, in Yugoslavia and Greece, National Liberation armies were formed under Communist leadership. In Poland, in 1942, the Communists created the Polish Workers' Party, which did not join the Comintern formally but carried out directives from Moscow. Communists in Germany, Italy, Bulgaria, Slovakia, Romania, and Finland carried on struggles against the Fascist regimes and the forces of reaction. Communists in France, Denmark, Belgium, the Netherlands, Norway, and the Czech lands were engaged participants in the resistance movement. They organized acts of sabotage and diversionary activities, obstructed the dispatch of persons to forced labor camps in Germany, and worked to disorganize life and activities in the interiors of the Fascist bloc countries. In addition, the Communist parties attempted to strengthen their own influence on the political life of the individual countries.

The Comintern leadership continued to call on the Chinese Communist Party to maintain a united front with the Kuomintang in the struggle against Japanese aggression. Steps were taken to create a revolutionary movement in the Pacific Ocean countries, and to train activists in the Communist parties of Korea, the Philippines, Thailand, Malaya, Burma, and several other countries. Communists succeeded in organizing anti-Japanese actions in Korea, the Philippines, Malaya, and Indochina.

The events of November 1942 (the Red Army's shift to the offensive at Stalingrad, the successes of the Allies in North Africa, and Germany's occupation of the rest of France) created favorable conditions for increasing the participation of Communists in the resistance movement. The Comintern leadership summoned French Communists to fight with all their might against their German and Italian occupiers, and organize a popular uprising for the liberation of France.

The French Communist Party leadership received a directive to establish contact with the "Fighting France" movement, led by General Charles de Gaulle. The Communists of the occupied countries began to form a partisan movement to drive out the occupiers. The Italian Communists were given the task of inducing Italy to break with Hitler's Germany and conclude a separate peace treaty with the Allies. The Communists of Nazi Germany's vassal countries were enjoined to fight hard to induce the aggressor bloc to give up the war.

The Communist nations of Asia worked hard to expand their anti-Japanese campaign. The Chinese Communists blockaded already-liberated regions and succeeded in maintaining a core of revolutionary armies. Activists of the Chinese Communist Party exerted a pronounced influence on the Communist movement in other Asian countries. Underground revolutionary groups were formed in various regions of Korea. In the Philippines, Communists helped create the United National Anti-Japanese Front in 1942, and partisan detachments were organized into the National Anti-Japanese Army (the Hukbalahap). In Thailand, a constituent assembly of the Communist Party took place in November 1942.

Stalin invariably looked at the Communist movement from the standpoint of the Kremlin's international policies. In early May 1943, with a view to strengthening the anti-Hitler coalition, he gave the order to dissolve the Communist International. The dissolution of the Comintern was accomplished during May and June 1943. Its leading international organs were dismantled, and national Communist parties received greater independence. Nevertheless, the Stalinist leadership continued to direct the activities of the separate Communist parties, particularly in the area of international policy. Indeed, a part of the apparatus of the Executive Committee of the Comintern was retained and its management turned over to the Central Committee of the Communist Party of the USSR.

The Communists in Great Britain and the United States urged the strengthening of the anti-Hitler coalition in their countries, and the consolidation of their friendship with the USSR. By the end of the war, the Communist Party leadership in the United States was celebrating the concept of the progressiveness of U.S. capitalism along with the cooperation between "labor and capital" in the United States. At the Twelfth Congress of the Communist Party of the United States of America in May 1944, a decision was made to dissolve the Communist Party and replace it with a nonparty structure called the Communist Political Association. (This decision was revised in July 1945.)

After the tide turned in World War II, the Communists launched an even more resolute struggle against the aggressor bloc, toward the liberation of their countries from the occupiers and the Fascist regimes, and the implementation of thoroughgoing socioeconomic reforms. The decisive factor here, of course, was whether a given country was being liberated by the Red Army or by the Western Allies.

Led by the Communists, partisans were very active in the Balkans, first and foremost in Yugoslavia. The national liberation army of Yugoslavia stoutly resisted the massive offensives of the occupiers. November 1942 saw the creation of the Anti-Fascist Popular Assembly for the National Liberation of Yugoslavia, which in November 1943 was declared the supreme legislative organ of the country and formed the National Committee for the Liberation of Yugoslavia as a provisional national government. As more and more Yugoslav territory was liberated from the occupiers, the Communists strove to take power into their own hands, and to carry out anti-Fascist and anticapitalist transformations. By the time Yugoslavia was wholly liberated in 1945, the country was under the control of a "popular democratic regime."

The Yugoslav Communists exerted a strong influence on the development of events in Albania, which in the struggle for its own liberation had created an Anti-Fascist National Liberation Committee, which also began to assume the functions of a provisional government. A "popular democratic revolution" was brought into effect there as well.

In Greece, as early as 1941, the Communists had seized control of the National Liberation Front and National Liberation Army. By the spring of 1944, these two forces were already in possession of a significant part of the country. In conformity with the Stalin-Churchill agreement, however, concluded in Moscow in October 1944, the predominant influence was ceded to Britain. This allowed British troops to gain a foothold in Greece and render aid to the anti-Communist forces. In the spring of 1945, Stalin made a statement against the launching of a civil war in Greece, and Communist partisans were forced to flee into the mountains.

The situation in Bulgaria and Romania was entirely different; these countries entered the sphere of Soviet influence. In Bulgaria, the Communists succeeded in seizing control of the Patriotic Front and the National Liberation Insurgent Army; in Romania it was the Patriotic Anti-Hitler Front. The entrance of the Red Army into Romanian and Bulgarian territory in August–September 1944 led to the overthrow of the Fascist regimes there. Communists moved into the Romanian and Bulgarian governments, and with the support of the Soviet leadership, began to advance their aims against their political opponents.

The Communists operated within a complex political situation in Poland, where they had created the Polish Workers' Party. They were opponents of not only the German occupiers but also the underground National Army (Armia Krajowa), which was both anti-German and anti-Soviet. The National Army enjoyed the sympathy of a significant number of Poles and was politically oriented toward the émigré government in London. Still, the consistent support of the Soviet leaders enabled the Polish Communists, as the Red Army began to liberate Polish territory, to create the Polish Committee of National Liberation on July 21 in Lublin. In December 1944, this committee was reorganized into the Provisional Government of the Polish Republic. Relying on the full support of the Soviet authorities, the Polish Communists began to fight their political opponents, consolidate the "people's power," and carry out socioeconomic transformations based on the Soviet model.

The Communists in Slovakia played an important role in the Slovak National Uprising (which took place August–October 1944). In spite of the Red Army's attempts to help the insurgents, the uprising was defeated. The USSR was nevertheless able to engineer the formation in April 1945 of a new Czechoslovak government, which included Communists. The program adopted by this government outlined the development of Czechoslovakia as a "popular democratic" state with equality of rights for both Czechs and Slovaks, and a program of socioeconomic and political transformations. For a while this program was pursued under a parliamentary democracy in Czechoslovakia.

Thus, the Communist parties of Eastern Europe, which belonged to the Soviet sphere of influence, oriented themselves toward the USSR in international politics and carried out profound transformations within their countries, but the shape and tempo of these changes differed from country to country.

The Communist parties of Western Europe during World War II greatly strengthened their political influence, due to their resolute struggle against nazism and fascism, and active participation in the resistance movement.

In France, the Communists organized an armed struggle of *francs-tireurs* and partisans against the occupiers. Representatives of the French Communist Party joined the French Committee of National Liberation and, later, the Provisional Government of the French Republic, led by de Gaulle. The opening of the second front in June 1944 was a signal to launch an armed uprising throughout France. This uprising culminated in the liberation of Paris, in which the Communists played a notable role. Here they strove not only for the most rapid liberation of territory from the occupiers, but also for the strengthening of their influence in the political life of France and the creation of a more democratic "Liberation Government." Yet they had to reckon with the power of de Gaulle's provisional government as well as with the presence on French territory of U.S. and British troops.

After the fall of Mussolini's regime in Italy in July 1943, a broad insurgent movement spread across the country, and the Communists were active participants in it. They created partisan detachments and, in 1944, launched an intense campaign in the north of Italy. When the Allied advance in Italy was halted in the fall, though, the Italian partisans had to face a difficult struggle. Still, the partisans held firm and, in April 1945, they took part in a general national uprising in northern Italy. Soon thereafter, the entire country was liberated.

The Communists now strove to force the Italian king's retirement and to bring about a democratization of Italy's political life. But they had to reckon with the fact that Italy, like France, was now under the influence of the Western allies. Hence, it was no accident that in March 1944, Stalin urged the Italian Communist leader, Palmiro Togliatti, to act with moderation and restraint and then did the same thing with the French Communist leader, Maurice Thorez, in November of that year.

The Communists played an active role in the resistance movements in a number of Western European countries. They became initiators of as well as active participants in the creation of national fronts in France, Belgium, and Denmark. The national fronts moved to establish cooperation among the various political forces, relying on regional and local committees. By the end of 1943, the Communists had created organizations to carry on armed struggles against the occupiers and collaborationists—for example, the Belgian Partisan

Army, the military organization "Citizen Patriots" in Denmark, and small partisan detachments and diversionary groups in Norway. The Communist parties' strategy was to combine direct armed struggle with various mass actions such as the escalation of general strikes into national uprisings, which would lead to the liberation of the countries.

The active participation of Communists in the resistance movements and the sacrifices they made in the anti-Fascist struggles for liberation turned the Communist parties of a number of Western European countries into national entities with substantial influence.

At the elections to the Constituent Assembly in October 1945, the French Communist Party emerged as the strongest force, with 26 percent of the vote. The Italian Communist Party received 19 percent of the vote in June 1946, while the Communist parties of Belgium, Denmark, and Norway received some 12 percent of the vote in their first postwar elections. By the beginning of the postwar era, Communists were part of the governments of a good number of advanced capitalist countries in Europe, in particular France and Italy. The influence of the Communists was creating the preconditions for a strong leftward movement in the postwar reconstruction era.

In Asia, the Communists' struggle against the Japanese aggressors went hand in hand with national liberation movements. The Communist Party of China, despite vacillations on the part of some sectors of its leadership, came out for a united anti-Japanese national front. By the spring of 1945, the armed forces under Communist control numbered approximately nine hundred thousand. The USSR's entrance into the war against Japan in August 1945, the utter defeat of the Japanese Kwantung army by Soviet troops, and the liberation of northeastern China shifted the balance of forces toward the Chinese Communist Party. By the end of the year, the "liberated regions" made up almost a quarter of China's territory, with a population of around 150 million. The competition as to what paths the country should take acquired intensity directly after the Japanese capitulation (on September 2, 1945).

In Vietnam, the national liberation struggle was headed by the Communist Party of Indochina and the League of the Struggle for the Independence of Vietnam (the Vietminh), which was led by the party. Its program included not only the struggle against the Japanese and French imperialists but also the implementation of democratic reforms. The defeat of militarist Japan created favorable conditions for the triumph of the Vietnamese revolution. On August 13, 1945, the Communist Party of Indochina and the Vietminh called for a general armed uprising. On August 19 the Vietminh captured Hanoi, where it established the "people's power." On September 2, at a grand meeting in Hanoi, Ho Chi Minh proclaimed the country's independence and the formation of the Democratic Republic of Vietnam.

In the Philippines, the Communist-created National Anti-Japanese Army, the Hukbalahap, was active in the fight against the Japanese occupiers. In the fall of 1944, detachments of the Hukbalahap, numbering up to ten thousand troops, launched an intense military campaign against the Japanese. They played a notable role in the liberation of the island of Luzon. The U.S. command tried to disarm them as rapidly as possible, but the Hukbalahap were able to flee to the island's backwaters.

In Malaya, the Anti-Japanese Army of the Peoples of Malaya was led by the Communists, backed by a sociopolitical organization, the Anti-Japanese Union. At the beginning of 1943, the first congress of the Communists of Burma was held, albeit illegally; it called on the Burmese to take up the struggle against Japan.

World War II also helped to activate the national liberation movement in Latin America. The victories of the countries of the anti-Hitler coalition created a favorable climate for Communist Party engagement in the region. In Colombia, Peru, and Venezuela, the Communists emerged from the underground and joined the anti-imperialist struggle. The growth of Communist Party authority was testified to by the results of parliamentary elections: during the war years, Communists in Cuba, Chile, Brazil, Venezuela, Uruguay, Peru, and Costa Rica managed to get over seventy senators and deputies elected to their parliaments.

By the end of World War II, the energetic struggle of the Communists against the Nazi and Fascist aggressors (after June 1941) for the liberation of their nations, democracy, and socioeconomic reforms had greatly expanded Communist influence. The increased international authority of the Soviet Union was instrumental here. The experience accumulated by the Communist movement during the war impelled it to seek new approaches and to diversify the methods of the struggle for socialism. Still, the Communists were unable to overcome the decisive role played by the Stalinist leadership in determining their strategy, the inevitability of orienting themselves toward the Soviet experience, and the tendency toward unification of the Communist movement.

See also Antifascism; Anti-Fascist Resistance; Comintern; Grand Alliance, The; Great Patriotic War, Rhetoric of; People's Democracy; Yalta Conference.

FURTHER READING

Dimitrov, G. *Diario. Gli anni di Mosca (1934–1945)*. Ed. Silvio Pons. Turin: Einaudi, 2002.

Lebedeva, N. S., and M. M. Narinskij, eds. *Komintern i vtoraja mirovaja vojna*. 2 vols. Moscow: Pamjatniki Istoričeskoj Mysly, 1994.

———. *Il Kominern e la seconda guerra mondiale*. Perugia: Guerra, 1996.

Mastny, V. *Russia's Road to the Cold War: Diplomacy, Warfare, and the Politics of Communism, 1941–1945*. New York: Columbia University Press, 1979.

MICHAIL M. NARINSKIJ

Yakovlev, Aleksandr

Aleksandr Yakovlev (1923–2005) sprang to fame during the perestroika years when he was for a time Mikhail Gorbachev's most important reformist ally within the Communist Party leadership. Although he continued to be a respected figure in post-Soviet Russia and headed a commission concerned with the rehabilitation of the victims of political repression during the Soviet period—especially, but not only, in the Stalin years—Yakovlev's most significant role in Russian politics was played in the second half of the 1980s when he encouraged the development of glasnost, supported radical political reform, and was a counterweight within the politburo to the forces of conservatism.

Yakovlev was born into a peasant family in the Yaroslavl region of Russia in December 1923 and died in Moscow in October 2005. As a young man he fought in the Second World War and was seriously wounded. He was invalided out of the army in 1943 and walked with a limp for the rest of his life.

Yakovlev graduated from the Yaroslavl Pedagogical Institute in 1946, and in a varied career, spent some time working on a local newspaper and in academia, but his main career was in the apparatus of the Communist Party. By 1973 he was the acting head of the Department of Propaganda of the Central Committee. An article that he published in the weekly newspaper of the Writers' Union in 1972, however, attacking all forms of nationalism and chauvinism, including Russian nationalism, made him some enemies and put a stop to his further promotion within the party hierarchy until Gorbachev came to power.

Yakovlev spent the years 1973–83 as the Soviet ambassador to Canada—a form of dignified exile. When Gorbachev, as a rising star within the politburo, paid a visit to Canada, the two men bonded both personally and politically, and Gorbachev was able to facilitate Yakovlev's request that he be allowed to return to Moscow in a suitable post. On Gorbachev's recommendation, Yuriy Andropov—who was the Soviet leader at that time—approved the appointment of Yakovlev to the directorship of the Soviet Union's major international relations think tank, IMEMO.

Yakovlev immediately became part of Gorbachev's informal team of advisers. When Gorbachev succeeded Konstantin Chernenko as Soviet party leader in March 1985, he gave Yakovlev accelerated promotion. In July of that year he became head of his old Central Committee Department of Propaganda. By the summer of 1987 he was one of the five most powerful members of the Communist Party leadership, both a full member of the politburo and a secretary of the Central Committee.

Yakovlev's patronage of relatively liberal writers, journalists, and filmmakers played an important role in quickening the pace of social criticism and reform. From early in the perestroika era tensions between Yegor Ligachev, the de facto second secretary of the party and a much more conservative figure than Yakovlev, were evident. Since both men had some responsibility for overseeing Soviet ideology, mixed signals were emanating from the top—confusing for lower-level apparatchiks, but a source of choice and empowerment for restless intellectuals who wished to ask pertinent questions about the Soviet past and present.

By the summer of 1988, with the adoption of radically reformist policies at the Nineteenth Party Conference, the Gorbachev-Yakovlev alliance had won an important battle against the forces resistant to change. Yakovlev himself, however, was hated by the hard-liners, who continued to seek to reduce his influence. In that same year Gorbachev removed both Yakovlev and Ligachev from the ideological sphere, but it was Yakovlev who received the more momentous subsequent responsibilities.

He became the overlord within the Central Committee apparatus of international policy, whereas Ligachev was given oversight of agriculture.

Yakovlev along with Foreign Minister Eduard Shevardnadze became significant allies for Gorbachev in his efforts to end the Cold War, even when these efforts led to changes of an abruptness that were potentially dangerous for Gorbachev's leadership. Thus, developments that were regarded as totally unacceptable to any Soviet leadership throughout the postwar era occurred with Soviet acquiescence. The countries of Eastern Europe became non-Communist and independent in the course of 1989, and Germany was unified in 1990. That Soviet troops did not fire a shot while all this was going on signaled the end of the Cold War. Given that Gorbachev's enemies could portray these developments as constituting a major defeat for the Soviet Union—the loss, as they saw it, of the gains of the Second World War—it was of no small importance for Gorbachev that Yakovlev was the overseer of the International Department of the Central Committee, and that on these fundamental issues he saw eye to eye with Gorbachev and Shevardnadze.

In the post-Soviet era Yakovlev was briefly vice president of the Gorbachev Foundation, but his relations with Gorbachev soured when he joined the Boris Yeltsin administration and headed for a time one of Russia's television channels. Yakovlev, though, became somewhat disillusioned with the trend of developments under Yeltsin and, still more, what he saw as authoritarian trends under his successor, Vladimir Putin. Yakovlev, who in the last years of his life reestablished good relations with Gorbachev, was in the post-Soviet period an increasingly sharp critic of Marxism-Leninism in a series of books that included a volume of memoirs, published two years before his death.

See also Dissolution of the USSR; Gorbachev, Mikhail; New Thinking; Perestroika; Post-Soviet Communism.

FURTHER READING

Yakovlev, A. "Perestroika or the 'Death of Socialism.'" In *Voices of Glasnost: Interviews with Gorbachev's Reformers*, ed. S. F. Cohen and K. vanden Heuvel, 33–75. New York: Norton, 1989.
———. *The Fate of Marxism in Russia*. New Haven, CT: Yale University Press, 1993.
———. *Sumerki*. Moscow: Materik, 2003.

ARCHIE BROWN

Yalta Conference

The Yalta conference of February 1945 has spawned many myths. First and foremost, there is the myth of "unity." When the conference ended Churchill, Roosevelt, and Stalin issued a statement proclaiming their utmost commitment to peacetime unity and to the establishment of long-term security for all states. After the conference, there was much talk about the "spirit of Yalta," and the allied press lauded the meeting of the Big Three as an historic turning point in Soviet-Western relations. In subsequent years many historians saw Yalta as the golden moment of wartime unity, as a model of great power détente, and as representing an alternative to the Cold War.

Second, there is the myth of "appeasement." When the Cold War broke out in the mid-1940s many in the West began to criticize Churchill, and especially Roosevelt, for conceding too much to Stalin and of encouraging the Soviet dictator's appetite for expansion. Yalta was represented as a second "Munich" and as a lost opportunity to stand up to Soviet totalitarianism.

Third, there is the myth of "betrayal." Critics from both the Left and Right have assailed Yalta as the occasion of a cynical carving up of Europe into Soviet and Western spheres of influence. Conservatives see the results of this exercise in power politics as the delivery of the people of Eastern Europe into tyranny, while radicals bemoan Stalin's blocking of the revolutionary impulses of the masses in countries such as Greece, France, and Italy.

Fourth, there is the myth of the "lost opportunity." According to this view of Yalta, the conference's cooperative spirit was subverted by those hostile to a Soviet-Western détente. Particular importance is ascribed to the death of Roosevelt in April 1945 and his replacement by Truman, who was more inclined than his predecessor to listen to the advice of those urging a hardening of policy toward the Soviet Union.

Finally, there is the myth of "illusion." Within this perspective the importance of Yalta is devalued. The Big Three might have imagined that their discussions and decisions would determine the destinies of states and nations but, according to this analysis, the inevitable clash between Soviet and Western interests and ideologies pointed toward the inexorable collapse of the Grand Alliance.

While each of these myths distorts the true meaning and significance of Yalta, they all contribute something to an appreciation of the conference's complex and contradictory character. Yalta was not the historic meeting that it was proclaimed to be, but neither was it an unimportant event. While Stalin was appeased by the Western leaders, he was also the appeaser in his relations with Churchill and Roosevelt. An implicit division of Europe into spheres of influence did take place at Yalta, but both sides also saw the continent's future in terms of pan-European cooperation within the framework of a peacetime Grand Alliance. The Cold War division of Europe did not begin at Yalta but was a function of its failure. The results of the Yalta conference pointed toward a number of different futures; the failure of the Grand Alliance and the onset of Cold War was only one of these. The Big Three's aim of a peacetime Grand Alliance was not subverted by objective structures and dynamics but by subsequent misunderstandings and misperceptions and by other actors seeking to influence the course of events in a different direction.

Yalta was the second summit of the Big Three. The first meeting had taken place in Tehran at the end of 1943 and had focused on military issues, in particular the question of the timing of an Anglo-American invasion of France to relieve German pressure on the Eastern front. At Tehran, Britain and the United States pledged to launch a second front in northern France in the early summer of 1944. Tehran also saw a frank exchange of political views between Churchill, Roosevelt, and Stalin. These exchanges were carried forward and developed at Yalta, a conference that took place while war still raged but which concentrated on postwar political issues.

Soviet internal preparations for Yalta were dominated by discussions about how to develop the tripartite approach to the postwar world that had begun to emerge at the Moscow conference of the American, British, and Soviet foreign ministers in October 1943. There was much speculation about long-term relationships and grand bargains with the West, including a wide-ranging spheres of influence deal. At Yalta itself, however, the discussions focused on specific issues.

Stalin's priority was an agreement about the future of Germany, including agreement on reparations and dismemberment. Despite Anglo-American qualms about reparations, it was agreed in principle at Yalta that the USSR would receive restitution from Germany for war damage and a figure of $10 billion was agreed as the benchmark. When it came to dismemberment, however, Stalin left Yalta very disappointed. Previous discussions with Churchill and Roosevelt had indicated that they favored breaking up Germany after the war. At Yalta Stalin pushed hard for a definite commitment on dismemberment, but Churchill and Roosevelt would only agree to establish a commission to discuss the issue. From this discussion Stalin concluded that dismemberment was unlikely to materialize and that it would be better to pursue the extension of Soviet and Communist influence within Germany as a whole. After Yalta he abandoned the policy of dismemberment and became a public supporter of German unity.

Roosevelt was keen to finalize discussions on the establishment of a successor to the League of Nations. These discussions had begun at the Moscow Conference of Foreign Ministers, which had issued a general declaration on postwar international security. Most questions about the role and structure of the proposed United Nations organization were dealt with at the Dumbarton Oaks conference in summer 1944. There remained, however, the question of a right of veto for the permanent members of the security council, a voting procedure that the Soviets insisted was necessary to maintain great power unity within the new organization. The British and Americans were unhappy that a great power could block discussion or the independent resolution of disputes that they themselves were involved in, but they accepted the Soviet position on the veto and this principle was written into the invitations issued to the founding conference of the United Nations in San Francisco in April–June 1945.

Churchill's main concern was the resolution the long-running dispute about the postliberation governance of Poland. Just before the conference, the Soviets had installed in Poland a provisional government formed by the pro-C Polish Committee of National Liberation (PCNL). At Yalta Churchill and Roosevelt sought to persuade Stalin to establish a more representative government in Poland, one that would include pro-Western politicians from the Polish government in exile in London. Relations between Moscow and the anti-Communist London Poles had broken down in the aftermath of the Katyn affair in April 1943, when the Germans announced the discovery of the mass graves of Polish POWs murdered by the NKVD in spring 1940. At Yalta the compromise reached was that the PCNL government would be reorganized and broadened by "the inclusion of democratic leaders from Poland itself and from Poles abroad." In return for this concession, the British and Americans agreed to recognize the "Curzon Line" as the Polish-USSR border. This meant that Moscow's territorial gains under the auspices of the Nazi-Soviet pact of 1939–41 were now formally accepted by the Western powers. It was also agreed to compensate Poland for its territorial losses in the east by changing its border with Germany, although the details of the new demarcation line were left open at this stage.

Of the other decisions taken at Yalta by far the most important was a confidential agreement setting out the terms for Soviet participation in the war against Japan. Stalin agreed to abrogate the 1941 Soviet-Japanese neutrality pact and to enter the Far Eastern war two or three months after the defeat of Germany. In return Churchill and Roosevelt agreed to the restoration of Russian territorial concessions to China that had been a result of the 1904–5 Russo-Japanese war.

On the organizational front it was agreed that the American, British, and Soviet foreign ministers would meet on a regular basis, a decision that paved the way for the establishment of the Council of Foreign Ministers (CFM) at the Potsdam conference in August 1945.

In terms of the Big Three's general outlook on the postwar world, the most important Yalta document was the Declaration on Liberated Europe. This American initiative committed the three states to the creation of a postwar Europe based on representative institutions and free elections, a project linked to a more general commitment to the creation of an international order that would guarantee peace, security, and freedom for all.

Without doubt, the commitment of the Big Three to a peacetime Grand Alliance was genuine and well intentioned. Churchill later tried to distance himself from Yalta by presenting himself as an early cold warrior, but the contemporary evidence shows him to have been a strong supporter of the conference and what it signified. After his death Roosevelt was attacked for his naive trust in Stalin. Stalin, however, was as committed to cooperation as Roosevelt believed him to be, as long as it did not mean compromising vital Soviet interests.

Much has been made of the difficulties that the Yalta decisions ran into after the conference. Skeptics point, in particular, to the acrimonious inter-allied dispute about the interpretation of the decision on the reconstruction of the Polish provisional government. From Moscow's point of view what had been agreed at Yalta was that the PCNL government would be enlarged. The British and

American interpretation was that a completely new government would be formed in Poland. In the midst of this dispute Roosevelt died, and Molotov traveled to Washington to meet the new president and to attend the San Francisco conference. Molotov's meetings with Truman in April 1945 were undoubtedly the occasion of tough talking by both politicians but were far from being the first sign of an incipient Cold War. In his memoirs Truman claimed that Molotov said that he had never been talked to like that in his life. Contemporary documents record no such statement and show, in fact, that Truman's main message to Molotov was that he would stick to the tripartite policy and spirit of Yalta. In May 1945 Truman sent Harry Hopkins, Roosevelt's closest confidant, to Stalin to broker a deal on the Polish question. An agreement was eventually reached on the reconstruction of the PCNL government, and Truman as well as Stalin approached the Potsdam conference of July–August in a positive frame of mind.

The spirit of Yalta was very much in evidence at Potsdam, both in the discussions of the allied leaders and in the conference decisions and final communiqué. From Stalin's point of view Potsdam was almost as successful as Yalta. Of particular importance was the conclusion of a detailed agreement on the future of Germany, including substantial reparations payments for the Soviet Union.

The follow-up to Potsdam was the first meeting of the CFM in London in September 1945. Moscow's expectation was that the tripartite approach of Yalta and Potsdam would be continued within the CFM framework. Even when the CFM broke up in disarray because of Britain and the United States' refusal to recognize pro-Soviet governments in Bulgaria and Rumania, Stalin did not abandon the Yalta perspective of a peacetime Grand Alliance. Indeed, at a further meeting with the British and American foreign ministers in Moscow in December 1945, the dispute over Bulgaria and Rumania was patched up and negotiations were resumed on peace treaties for the minor Axis states (Finland, Hungary, and Italy, as well as the two aforementioned). This process culminated in the Paris peace conference of summer 1946 where the terms of these peace treaties were hammered out. Throughout this period the Soviets maintained a barrage of propaganda extolling the virtues of the tripartism of Yalta and Potsdam. Stalin himself made a number of public statements urging the continuation of cooperation between the Soviet Union and the West even in the face of provocations such as Churchill's "iron curtain" speech of March 1946. It was only in mid-1947, following the proclamation of the Truman Doctrine and the announcement of the Marshall Plan, that Stalin finally abandoned the project of a peacetime Grand Alliance.

The Soviet analysis of the failure of Yalta centered on the perceived rise of anti-Communist and anti-Soviet political forces in Britain and the United States, a viewpoint repeated in revisionist Western historiography of the Cold War. Certainly the perception that forces hostile to the Soviet Union had taken control of British and American foreign policy played an important role in Moscow's shift to a Cold War policy. But there were those skeptical of Yalta on the Soviet side, too. In the USSR, as in the West, every difficulty in postwar Soviet-Western relations was magnified and read by some as a sign of bad faith by the other side. Alternatively, differences of interest and perspective were viewed through an ideological prism that patterned the landscape of the postwar world as a site of systemic conflict between capitalism and socialism. On the other hand, even at the height of the Cold War in the late 1940s and early 1950s, the perspective of a return to the spirit of Yalta remained central to the Soviet prescription for the creation of a new détente.

See also Antifascism; Cold War; Containment; United Nations; World War II.

FURTHER READING

Clemens, D. S. *Yalta*. Oxford: Oxford University Press, 1970.

Laloy, J. *Yalta: hier, aujourd'hui, demain*. Paris: Robert Laffont, 1988.

Roberts, G. *Stalin's Wars: From World War to Cold War, 1939–1953*. New Haven, CT: Yale University Press, 2006.

Snell, J. L., ed. *The Meaning of Yalta*. Baton Rouge: Louisiana State University Press, 1956.

The Tehran, Yalta and Potsdam Conferences: Documents. Moscow: Progress Publishers, 1969.

Theoharis, A.G. *The Yalta Myths*. Columbia: University of Missouri Press, 1970.

GEOFFREY K. ROBERTS

Yeltsin, Boris

First president and founder of the Russian state that emerged from the collapse of the USSR in late 1991, Boris Yeltsin (1931–2007) had an important role in the process that led to the end of the Soviet Union. Born in a region of Sverdlovsk, he came from a peasant family whose members were chased from the countryside as kulaks during forced collectivization. His father, Nikolay Ignat'evich, was arrested as a "saboteur" in April of 1934 and sentenced to three years of detention in a "labor camp." This story, similar to that affecting thousands of other Russian families, did not have visible repercussions in Yeltsin's life. In Sverdlovsk (now Ekaterinenburg) he attended Ural State Technical University, graduating in 1955 with a degree in civil engineering. Having shifted to party work, he was responsible for the construction office and was elected a member of the Supreme Soviet in 1974. From 1976 to 1985 he held the office of chief of the regional Secretariat. It was at this time that Yeltsin revealed the characteristics that would make him popular: radical populism, and the ability to create a consensus using demagogical words and acts. These were attitudes that came to light thanks to Mikhail Gorbachev's reforms.

Yeltsin was from the beginning a combative protagonist of perestroika. Having been selected by Gorbachev as head of the Moscow citizen committee on December 24, 1985, as a substitute for Viktor V. Grishin, one of the most tenacious opponents of the "new course," Yeltsin rapidly became popular, opposing the practice of party, administrative, and economic structures being considered one entity. His intervention at the Communist Party of the Soviet Union's (CPSU) Twenty-seventh Congress (February–March 1986), which contained some honest and self-critical remarks about the reasons he had supported Leonid Brezhnev in the past ("lack of courage and political experience"), earned him some fame abroad as well. His election to politburo candidate member was therefore not surprising. Not long afterward, he began distancing himself from Gorbachev. Their disagreements were sparked by discussions on the attitude toward the "conservatives" who considered Yigor Ligachev, de facto the party's number two, to be their leader. Gorbachev thought at the time that planned, gradual reforms would not be possible without Ligachev's support, while the "impatient" radicals disagreed about both the support and the pace at which the reforms should be implemented. In October 1987 Yeltsin went so far as to attack Gorbachev in a grudging intervention at the Central Committee, allegedly because of the unmotivated support the party secretary was granting the conservatives.

The break between Yeltsin and Gorbachev made the battle that Moscow bureaucrats were conducting in defense of their positions and privileges much easier. These conditions thus led to Yeltsin's expulsion in October 1987—a conclusion to what has been defined as the last Stalinist-type trial to be held in the USSR—after a tough speech given by Gorbachev himself and a humiliating self-critical speech by Yeltsin, first from the leadership of the Moscow citizen committee and then from the politburo. At the time opinion was almost unanimous that this represented an exit for the "man from Sverdlovsk." There was quite a sensation, then, when widespread support allowed a reborn Yeltsin to become Moscow's deputy with 89.6 percent of the vote in March 1989 and be elected after the first round on June 12, 1991, president of the Russian Soviet Federative Republic, running as the alternative to Gorbachev. Yeltsin was an alternative based on not only the profound personal break that had occurred between the two but also a different vision of perestroika.

Gorbachev, albeit tentatively, still attempted to maintain the peculiar characteristics of the Soviet state, while introducing radical reforms ("state of laws" and therefore separation between party and state, "market socialism," recognition of the "plurality of interests and ideas," and a new pact between the federative republics) as well as defending the unitary nature of that state. While his relationship with the "democrats" entered a critical phase, he did not break with, but rather consolidated his relationship with the CPSU's conservatives, even as Yeltsin was moving increasingly toward an open, if not always explicit, break with the Soviet past. The decisive moment of political confrontation between the two occurred in July 1990 during the Twenty-seventh (and last) Congress of the CPSU; Yeltsin not only announced that he was leaving the party but also expressed himself in favor of its dissolution. At the same time Yeltsin, as leader of the "radical democratic" group, asked for Gorbachev's resignation as the USSR's president and sided with the nationalist movements that from the Baltic countries to the Caucasus to Central Asia were explicitly posing the issue of separation and the formation of independent states—due also to the initiative of the Central Committees of the Communist parties in the individual republics.

All of this while Gorbachev attempted—but with what was to prove a fatal delay, surrounded by sometimes bloody conflicts, between Armenia and Azerbaijan on the issue of Nagorno-Karabakh, in Moldova, where the birth of the Transdnepr Republic was being prepared, and between Uzbekistan and Kirghiztan for the control of the Fergana Valley—to have his plan approved for a reform of the state, which granted the individual republics ample autonomy while maintaining the territorial integrity of the union. At the time of the attempted coup d'état in August 1991, while everything Soviet—the CPSU, the Supreme Soviet, and the defense and security apparatuses—was involved in the coup or gave no sign of life, Yeltsin, as head of the Russian Federation, steadfastly opposed the coup and successfully called on the population to struggle for democracy. He thus prepared to manage the last phase in the Soviet Union's decline from a position of strength.

On August 20 he assumed the command of the troops located in the Russian Republic, and in the following days decreed, with Gorbachev's consent, the suspension of all activities by the Russian Communist Party. It was Yeltsin again who took the initiative that led to the drafting, during the night of December 8, 1991, of the act with which the representatives of Russia, Ukraine (Leonid Kravchuk), and Belorussia (Stanislav Sushkevich) announced to the world that the Soviet Union as a sovereign state had ceased to exist, to be replaced by the Community of Independent States. Yet the Soviet state would only formally cease to exist on December 25, when Gorbachev left the Kremlin.

Russia under Yeltsin, torn between a Western and a Eurasian identity, between imperial nostalgia and isolationist tendencies, initiated the process of transition toward a market economy and the establishment of a democratic order founded on a multiparty system, free elections, and ever-greater presidential powers (as established in the Constitution of December 1993). All this happened while the economy was in disastrous shape (a three-digit rate of inflation, a general lowering of living standards, and unemployment) and methods of "savage privatization" were being employed. This meant that because of the absence of laws as well as means of intervention and control, the country's wealth, starting with its oil resources, was being pillaged and divided among those closest to the levers of power—representatives of the old *nomenklatura*, oligarchs, and old and new mafia clans. The process of breaking up the empire was in full swing inside Russia, especially in the Caucasus, where in December 1994 Yeltsin started the first bloody war in Chechnya, which would end in 1996 with a humiliating defeat.

In foreign affairs Yeltsin's goals were the following: allow Russia to inherit the seat that had been held by the Soviet Union on the UN Security Council, obtain economic aid, and request to join the G7 group, which was granted by the body in May 1997. Significant agreements were concluded with the United States in areas such as the reduction of nuclear missiles (START I in June 1992, and START II in January 1993). As far as the countries of the Community of Independent States were concerned, results were limited to the areas of economic integration and common security, and they did not allow the organization to take off. Some positive agreements were reached with Ukraine (on the issues of Crimea, the division of the Black Sea fleet, and the price of oil). Russia's process of transition was dominated by significant political instability along with intense battles, leading to what many saw as the attempted coup in September 1993 by then–vice president Aleksandr Ruckoj and president of the Supreme Soviet Ruslan Chasbulatov. The attempted coup concluded with the military attack ordered by Yeltsin himself against the Parliament building, which was full of deputies at the time (October 5, 1993).

Elected Russian president again in July 1996, Yeltsin increased spaces for democracy with the introduction of electoral laws applicable to cities, republics, and autonomous regions, and improved the economic situation, thanks to measures undertaken to confront the ruble's collapse in August 1998 (but above all thanks to the increase in the price of oil); yet his popularity continued to decline. This was partly due to his worsening health, but especially the explosive nature of serious allegations against him, such as the appropriation and illegal use of public monies by people close to him either politically or because of family ties. On December 31, 1999, Yeltsin announced his resignation and tapped Vladimir Putin as his successor, who as soon as he was elected, guaranteed Yeltsin's immunity.

See also Coup in the USSR; Dissolution of the USSR; Gorbachev, Mikhail; Perestroika; Post-Soviet Communism.

FURTHER READING

Boffa, G. *Dall'URSS alla Russia: storia di una crisi non finita: 1964–1994*. Rome: Laterza, 1995.

Dunlop, J. B. *The Rise of Russia and the Fall of the Soviet Empire*. Princeton, NJ: Princeton University Press, 1993.

Guerra, A. *URSS: perché è crollata, analisi sulla fine di un impero*. Rome: Editori Riuniti, 2001.

Klepikova, E., and V. Solovyov. *Boris Yeltsin: A Political Biography*. New York: Putnam, 1992.

Marcucci, L. *Dieci anni che hanno sconvolto la Russia: da Gorbacëv a Putin*. Bologna: Il Mulino, 2002.

Medvedev, R. *Post-Soviet Russia: A Journey through the Yeltsin Era*. New York: Columbia University Press, 2000.

Rubbi, A. *La Russia di Eltsin*. Rome: Editori Riuniti, 2002.

Sĕvcova, L. *Yeltsin's Russia: Myths and Realities*. Washington, DC: Carnegie Endowment for International Peace, 1999.

Yeltsin, B. N. *Against the Grain: An Autobiography*. London: Jonathan Cape, 1990.

———. *The View from the Kremlin*. London: HarperCollins, 1994.

———. *Prezidentskij marafon. Razmyshlenija, vospominanija, vpechatlenija*. Moscow: Ast, 2000.

ADRIANO GUERRA

Yezhov, Nikolay

Nikolay Yezhov (1895–1940), head of the People's Commissariat for Internal Affairs (NKVD) of the USSR from 1936 to 1938, was one of the organizers of the Great Terror. He was born in Saint Petersburg to the family of a metalworker. After spending only one year in elementary school, he was forced at the age of nine or ten to work as an apprentice in various workshops in Petersburg. In 1914–15, he was a worker at the Putilovsky Factory there, and took part in strikes and demonstrations, for which he was arrested. He was drafted into the army in 1915. In March 1917 Yezhov joined the Bolshevik Party. During the civil war he served in the Red Army, and at the war's end was a military commissar at a radio-telegraph school in Kazan. He continued his career in Kazan as a party personnel worker in the Tatarsky Regional Commissariat of the Russian Communist Party. During the 1920s he served in leading party posts in various regions of the USSR until he was transferred in 1927 to Moscow to a position in the apparatus of what was then the Central Committee of the Communist Party of the Soviet Union (CPSU). In 1930 he became the head of the Distributional Section of the USSR's Central Committee, which was concerned with the distribution of leading personnel, after which Yezhov was appointed head of the industrial section of the Central Committee.

The key turn in Yezhov's life, though, came after the December 1, 1934, murder of one of the chief Bolshevik leaders, the party chief of Leningrad, Sergey Kirov. Stalin, who used the murder as an excuse for new purges, chose Yezhov for this special mission. He entrusted to Yezhov the task of guiding the preparation of falsified accusations in the Kirov murder against the opposition leaders of the 1920s, Lev Kamenev, Grigory Zinovyev, and their supporters. Yezhov handled this task successfully, and in early 1935 was promoted to the posts of secretary of the CPSU's Central Committee and chair of the Party Control Commission. From then on, Yezhov was called on by Stalin to supervise the NKVD's activities and was responsible for carrying out repressions against Trotskyites and Zinovyevites, which resulted in 1936 in the trials of Zinovyev, Kamenev, and others from the former opposition.

On September 25, 1936, Stalin, on vacation in the south, sent a telegram to Moscow ordering the politburo to appoint Yezhov as the people's commissar of internal affairs, to replace Genrikh Yagoda, who was soon arrested and shot. As subsequent events showed, this appointment brought about an escalation of the repressions. Yezhov was directly in charge of a purge of the NKVD apparatus, which led to a growth in the activity of the Chekists, new charges against former opposition leaders (Nikolay Bukharin, Aleksey Rykov, and others), and most important, mass punitive measures against the country's population at large.

These tragic events were labeled by contemporaries and later by historians as the "Yezhovshchina," signifying that Yezhov himself was the main organizer of the mass repressions. Yet many facts have recently come to light suggesting that Yezhov was simply carrying out Stalin's will. Stalin supervised every detail of the preparation and implementation of these actions. He stamped all the basic documents himself, personally familiarized himself with interrogation records, and gave specific directions for handling many of the cases brought against the main victims. Logs kept of visitors to Stalin's office testify that in 1937 and 1938, Yezhov appeared there much more often than other members of the upper echelons of Soviet leaders (except for Vyacheslav Molotov). In 1937, Yezhov averaged a visit to Stalin's office every other day and spent more than 520 hours there.

Yezhov's influence reached its peak at the end of 1937, as witnessed by his selection in October of that year as a candidate for membership in the politburo. However, in 1938 there were already signs that Stalin was planning to replace Yezhov. Yezhov was given the additional function in April of people's commissar of water transportation, which would constrain his activities as head of the NKVD, and by August 1, Lavrenty Beria, a secretary of the CPSU's Central Committee who enjoyed great influence with Stalin, was appointed Yezhov's deputy

secretary of the NKVD. Yezhov, though by this time he was sinking into drunkenness and orgies, correctly appraised the situation. In a letter addressed to Stalin at the end of November, Yezhov admitted that he "was suffering from the appointment of Comrade Beria and saw in it an element of lack of trust in himself. . . . I thought that his appointment was the beginning stage of my own dismissal." In October and November of 1938, NKVD personnel underwent purges, during which many of Yezhov's colleagues were replaced and later shot. At the end of November, Yezhov was removed from his post as people's commissar for internal affairs, and Beria was named in his place. Several months later Yezhov was still formally listed as people's commissar for water transportation, but in April 1939 he was arrested and, in February 1940, he was shot. Yezhov and his colleagues were accused of sabotage and espionage, and Stalin eventually even blamed them for all the mass crimes of the period known as the Great Terror.

See also Enemies of the People; Great Terror; KGB; Stalin, Joseph.

FURTHER READING
Getty, J. A. *Stalin's "Iron-Fist": The Times and Life of N. I. Yezhov.* New Haven, CT: Yale University Press, 2008.
Jansen, M., and V. Petrov. *Stalin's Loyal Executioner: People's Commisar Nikolai Ezhov, 1895–1940.* Stanford, CA: Hoover Institution Press, 2002.

OLEG V. CHLEVNJUK

Youth

The concept of youth as a separate section of society was alien to Communist thinking. Youth, like any other societal segment, was to be subsumed into class identity and transcend the borders of age in order to become part of the proletarian vanguard. Nonetheless, the rise of youth as a distinct group within European society, and the increasing mythologization of youth as a synonym for energy and radicalism, meant that from the late 19th century and the early 20th century onward, youth entered the Communist discourse and youths became visible in Communist activities.

The first socialist youth organization was founded in Belgium in 1886, followed by groups in Sweden (1895),

Switzerland (1900), Italy (1901), Norway (1902), Spain (1903), and several formations in Germany (1904–5). Vladimir Lenin proclaimed in 1903 that the Bolshevik Party was the party of youth, because "we are a party of innovators, and it is always youth that most eagerly follows the innovators; we are a party that is waging a self-sacrificing struggle against the old rottenness, and youth is always the first to undertake a self-sacrificing struggle." In the utopian and eschatological theories prominent in the first years after the Russian Revolution, youths were to fulfill the promise of a future Communist society, since only a young person unspoiled by the experience of capitalism was able to become the "new Soviet man or woman" in possession of a true Communist consciousness.

Yet initially, unlike the powerful German Communists, the Russian revolutionaries rejected the creation of special youth sections within their movement, which they judged as essentially "bourgeois" and "scoutish." Spontaneous formations of Communist-inspired youths in pre-1917 Russia such as numerous Marxist or anarchist student groups were short-lived. Their members regarded themselves primarily as extensions of campaigns run by adults, rather than representatives of a self-conscious section of society that demanded rights, recognition, and a share in formulating policy. Youths as a revolutionary force came into their own during the years of the First World War, when the absence of most male workers pushed women and youngsters into the foreground of protests both in Russia and elsewhere in Europe. During the two revolutions of 1917, several independent youth groups emerged, displaying a variety of concepts of understanding their position within society. Organizations such as the Petrograd group Trud i Svet demonstrated that youth associations increasingly considered themselves not only Communist inspired but both creations and creators of a defined and separate youth identity. It was at this point that the Bolsheviks realized the need for a coherent youth policy, and the regulation of young people through a body that would work as a transmission belt between the party-state and the young generation. In November 1918, the first and founding Congress of the Communist Youth League (Komsomol, or kommunisticheskii soiuz molodezhi) assembled, unifying the various Communist youth groups in Russia and sealing their allegiance to the Bolshevik cause.

From the beginning the Komsomol faced two existential dilemmas. On the one hand, the league was to incite and exploit its members' youthful enthusiasm and energy, and channel the young into the project of constructing socialism. On the other hand, it was to control and restrict potential challengers to the prevailing order. Young people, precisely because of their radicalism and receptiveness to iconoclastic ideas, were feared as potential nonconformists or defenders of a rival radical cause. This dilemma was no less serious, and was to be the subject of heated debates within the league and among youths at large over the years. The purpose of the league was not clearly stated at the outset, and left unanswered the question as to whether it was to be a vanguard that honored and assembled the most "progressive" part of youth, or if it was to be a mass organization with a pedagogical rather than a political mission. In other words, was the Komsomol to be a party of the young or an instrument of socializing future Communist generations? The struggle relating to this question led to numerous rifts and fissions in the early years of the Komsomol. In 1936, at the Tenth Komsomol Congress, Joseph Stalin officially decided the answer by declaring the Komsomol as different from (and implicitly inferior to) the party, and decreeing its status as an educational mass organization. Yet the voices calling for a more political, radical, and homogeneous Komsomol were not completely silenced, rising to a crescendo in the years immediately after Stalin's death, when in the climate of the thaw, young people tried to recover their organization from what they deplored as bureaucratism, formalism, and mediocrity.

The concept of youth and youthful sacrifice turned into an important battle cry again during the years of the Great Fatherland War, when youthful heroes such as Zoia Kosmodem'ianskaia and the members of the Komsomol underground organization Young Guard became symbols for Communist perfection—spontaneous and decisive, and yet obedient and conformist. After the war the fact that youth was not a static concept but instead replenished itself incessantly, made itself felt in Soviet youth politics. The aging of the Komsomol nomenklatura stood in stark contrast to an ever-younger membership, as recruitment centred on pupils in secondary school. Moreover, the fading of the revolutionary legend and young people's inability to be part of the myth of the Great Fatherland War posed the question of what a new generation of Soviet youth was supposed to fight for. A string of experimental new fronts such as the Virgin Lands campaign under Nikita

Khrushchev or the building of the Baikal-Amur Magistral under Leonid Brezhnev failed to harness youth interest to Communist ideology. Unofficial Soviet youth culture turned to the same kind of products of consumption as its Western counterpart: music, fashion, and dance.

In non-Communist Europe, Communist youths developed in a multitude of ways, often espousing ideologies quite different from the dominant Marxist-Leninist doctrine preached by the Soviet Union. In prewar Germany, Communist youth organizations devoted themselves to proletarian and workers' causes, but were significantly influenced by the romantic tendencies of middle-class youth movements such as the Wandervogel and the German Scouts. Despite the fact that Communist youth groups (just like the youth movement at large) tended to become increasingly party partisan and bound to adult politics in the run-up to Adolf Hitler taking power, the strength of independent Communist youth organizations became visible in their refusal to succumb to Nazi pressure to integrate into the Hitler Youth. Young Communists resisted both in political underground organizations as well as nonconformist, left-leaning youth groups such as the Cologne Edelweisspiraten. Elsewhere in Europe, socialist and Communist youth organizations reflected the struggle between revolutionary and reformist elements within socialist thought, and supported a plethora of different Communist ideas. In the United States the American Youth Congress, led and controlled by socialist and Communist youth organizations, became a vocal supporter of the New Deal and the antiwar campaign.

Internationally, socialist youth groups united in 1907 in the International Union of Socialist Youth Organizations, although it committed itself to educational tasks and abstained from participation in politics. Disbanded over the question of war support, the Communist Youth International reformed in 1915 under the leadership of the young German Communist Willi Münzenberg, who guided the youth international away from the centrist socialists to the revolutionary left wing led by Lenin. Yet when the Komsomol attempted to assert decisive influence over the Communist Youth International after the civil war and coax it into a more centralized structure subordinate to the Comintern, the same dilemmas that marred the Komsomol's own existence came to the forefront in the international organization. Free from the constraints of unity at all costs imposed on Soviet

youths, the international Communist youth movements fragmented into various components, ultimately resulting in two organizations, which formed along the leftist-rightist fault line of international socialism at large and gave the Soviet Union control of that part of Western European socialist youth that had chosen to remain loyal to the Comintern.

Nevertheless, it was only with the successful conquest of much of Eastern and Central Europe at the end of Word War II that the Soviet Union was able to export its youth concept and policy successfully. Youth organizations all over the territories occupied by the Red Army were modeled on the Komsomol, ranging from the Bulgarian youth organization of the same name to the East German Free German Youth, a name that was supposed to suggest continuity with the independent youth movement of the early 20th century. Yet the Komsomol not only exported its structure and ideology but also its failings. The Eastern European youth organizations were beset with problems of over-bureaucratization, apathy, and cynicism, and struggled against rival nationalist notions from the beginning. Still, the alluring idea of a Communist youth international did not stop at the Iron Curtain but instead acquired a new momentum in the climate of the unfolding Cold War.

In 1945, the World Youth Organization was established in London, followed by the foundation of the International Union of Students in Prague in 1946. Left-leaning and positive toward the Soviet Union from the outset, the various Western founding organizations were no match for the experienced Komsomol apparatus. Internal strife reduced the two organizations to insignificant splinter groups within a decade. Their most successful products were the World Youth Festivals, especially the one held in Moscow in 1957, which involuntarily opened bridges between youngsters from East and West, and allowed glimpses into the worlds of young people from the other side. Yet these festivals also highlighted that the time of ideology-based youth movements was over. Having a good time together informally, enjoying personal friendship, listening to popular music, and exchanging items of fashion ranked higher on the participants' agenda than questions of international politics. In non-Communist Europe and the United States, the formal youth organization was in perpetual decline after 1945, affecting both Communist and middle-class movements. The all-encompassing concept of creating a "new man" that had inspired the early Communist youth movement was replaced by a strict separation of politics and leisure. When in 1991 the Soviet Komsomol and its Central European satellites dissolved, they essentially discarded empty shells revealing the lack of substance under which the Communist youth movements had suffered for some time.

See also Classes; Comintern; Messianism; New Man; Revolution, Myths of the; Soviet Patriotism, Sports; Utopia.

FURTHER READING

Cornell, R. *Youth and Communism*. New York: Walker, 1965.

Fischer, R. *Pattern for Soviet Youth: A Study of the Congresses of the Komsomol, 1918–1954*. New York: Columbia University Press, 1959.

Gorsuch, A. *Youth in Revolutionary Russia: Enthusiasts, Bohemians, Delinquents*. Bloomington: Indiana University Press, 2001.

Kasloff, A. *The Soviet Youth Program*. Cambridge, MA: Harvard University Press, 1965.

Lenin, V. *O Molodezhi*. Moscow, 1982

Mehnert, K. *Youth in Soviet Russia*. 1932; repr. New York: Hyperion, 1981.

Mitterauer, M. *A History of Youth*. Oxford: Oxford University Press, 1992.

Plaggenborg, S., and C. Kuhr-Korolev. *Sowjetjugend 1918–1941: Generation zwischen Revolution und Resignation*. Essen, Germany: Klartext Verlag, 2001.

JULIANE FUERST

Zetkin, Clara

Clara Zetkin (1857–1933), née Eisner, was born on July 5 in Saxony, to the family of a rural schoolteacher. During her studies in Leipzig, she became acquainted with the Russian socialist Osip Tsetkin (Zetkin), who introduced her to Marxist ideas. After Zetkin was banished from Germany, Clara lived with him in exile in Switzerland and France.

In 1878, she became a member of the Social Democratic Party of Germany (SPD) and participated in the Constituent Assembly of the Second International. After returning to Germany in 1891, she began publishing a journal titled *Die Gleichheit* (Equality), devoted to the problems of female workers, which lasted until 1917. The founder of an international women's movement, Zetkin became the head of the women's secretariat of the Second International in 1907 and was a member of the SPD's governing body.

At the beginning of World War I, she joined a group of left-wing socialists who came out against the war. In March 1915, in Bern, Switzerland, Zetkin led an international conference of socialist women, which demanded that a peace treaty be concluded as soon as possible. After this, she spent approximately a year in a German prison as an "untrustworthy element," and was released only because of her suddenly declining health. Her house in Stuttgart became a refuge for left-wing oppositionists in the SPD, who formed the backbone of the Spartak organization.

In 1917, Zetkin joined the Independent Social Democratic Party of Germany, a faction that had broken off from the SDP to form its own party, and worked as a journalist for the *Leipzig People's Newspaper* (Leipziger Volkszeitung). Along with her comrade in arms Franz Mehring, she welcomed the coming to power of the Bolsheviks in Russia, and by March 1919 had joined the Communist Party of Germany (KPD).

Elected to the KPD's Central Committee (Die Zentrale), on which she served until 1924, Zetkin consistently supported a moderate policy of a "gathering of forces," and held out against "putschism" and the "embroidering of reality." This brought her into conflict with the chair of the Comintern's Executive Committee, Grigory Zinovyev, first over the issue of relations with the Italian socialists, and second regarding KPD tactics in the "March action" of 1921. Zetkin remained in the party at the personal request of Lenin and during the Third Congress of the Comintern, received Lenin's total support in her criticism of the ultraleftist "attack theory." Zetkin was a close friend of Lenin's family, and she left behind detailed reminiscences of her meetings with the Russian Bolshevik leader. On January 26, 1924, in the name of the international proletariat, she spoke at a session of the Second All-Union Congress of Soviets, which officially mourned the death of Lenin.

From 1920 until her death, Zetkin was a KPD deputy to the Reichstag, even though she spent the greater part of this period in the Soviet Union. There she became a cult figure, constantly appearing in the press, and taking part in various ceremonial activities. Whatever the flaws of the party dictatorship might have been, the USSR was for Zetkin always the state that had realized the socialist dream of equality and brotherhood of nations. Her political work was pervaded by a spirit of internationalism. In November 1920, Zetkin was elected general secretary of the International Women's Secretariat of the Comintern. She became a member of the presidium of the Comintern in 1922, and in 1925 was made head of the International Organization of Aid to Revolutionaries. In April 1922 she was part of a Comintern delegation at a meeting of representatives of three Workers' Internationals, which took place in Berlin.

During the internal party conflict at the end of 1923 and early 1924, Zetkin supported G. Brandler and August Thalheimer, and after both were defeated, she was removed from her duties in the KPD's Central Committee. After the Sixth Congress of the Comintern, she again came to the defense of Brandler and Thalheimer, who now stood accused of "right-wing deviationism." At a meeting of the Comintern presidium on December 19, 1928, Zetkin opposed Stalin, demanding that an emergency plenum of the Comintern Executive Committee be summoned to consider the crisis which had emerged in the Communist movement. Voting against the presidium's decisions, she declared to her opponents, "I believe that my career has proved that personal sentimental considerations never had real significance for me; only political motivations did." Nevertheless, unlike her "right-wing" colleagues, Zetkin refused to carry the struggle further, and remained in the ranks of the KPD.

In August 1932, already seriously ill, Zetkin made a special trip to Berlin to speak at the opening of the Reichstag's new legislative session. In her presentation, she called on left-wing forces to be vigilant in the face of the Nazi threat, emphasizing that only the Communists offered any real alternative to the disintegrating capitalist structure. Zetkin died in a sanatorium near Moscow on June 30, 1933. Her remains are interred next to the Kremlin wall.

See also Insurrection in Germany; Internationalism; Women, Emancipation of.

FURTHER READING

Badia, G. *Clara Zetkin: Feministe sans frontières*. Paris: Editions ouvrières, 1993.

Puschnerat, T. *Clara Zetkin: Buergerlichkeit und Marxismus*. Essen: Klartext, 2003.

Weber, H., and A. Herbst. *Deutsche Kommunisten. Biographisches Handbuch 1918 bis 1945*. Berlin: Dietz, 2004.

ALEKSANDR I. VATLIN

Zhdanov, Andrey

Andrey Zhdanov was born February 14, 1896, in Mariupol, Ukraine, into an educated middle-class family. His father, like Lenin's, was an inspector of public schools. His mother belonged to the nobility and graduated from the Moscow Musical Conservatory. (Zhdanov would later entertain Stalin and the politburo by playing the piano.) He never received a formal higher education but compensated by intensive reading. Like his three sisters, Zhdanov plunged into revolutionary activities on the eve of the First World War and became a member of the Russian Social Democratic Workers' Party (RSDRP) in 1915. In March 1916, Zhdanov was drafted, but he remained in the army reserve in Shadrinsk in Western Siberia; after the February Revolution soldiers elected him their representative to the regiment's committee and then a member of the soviet of soldiers' deputies. In August 1917 he became leader of the Shadrinsk Bolshevik committee, and when the party seized power in that region, worked as a local commissar for agriculture.

During the civil war Zhdanov was a political commissar in the Red Army. He moved to Tver where he edited *Pravda of Tver* and was deputy to the party secretary. Zhdanov's political career had its start in 1922. First he was appointed chairman of the Tver regional government, then from 1924 to 1934 served as secretary of the Nizhni Novgorod (later Gorky) party regional committee, an important position in regional nomenklatura, given the industrial and trade significance of that area. Delegate to all party congresses and conferences at that time, he loyally supported Stalin in his struggle against the Trotskyites, the Leningrad opposition, and the Right Deviationists. As a reward, Zhdanov entered the party Central Committee as a candidate in 1925 and as a full member in 1930. In 1934 he became secretary of the Central Committee and a member of the Central Committee Orgbjuro, and thus a member of Stalin's inner power circle.

At the time hidden resistance to Stalin's authoritarianism emerged even among party higher-ups who had earlier supported his revolution from above. As at the Seventeenth Party Congress, hundreds of them cast secret votes against the *vozhd* (chief) Zhdanov, in his speech, stressed Stalin's exceptional leadership and called on the party to rally around him. After the assassination of S. Kirov in December 1934, Zhdanov replaced him as secretary of Leningrad's regional and city organization. From 1935 to 1936 he directed the brutal purges in Leningrad and vociferously called for "destruction of the enemy of the people." In 1936 Stalin and Zhdanov signed the telegram to the politburo that "recommended" replacing G. Yagoda with N. Yezhov as head of the OGPU. From that moment the purges and extermination campaign, once focused only on the opposition, were redirected against the Old Bolsheviks and all echelons of the bureaucracy. Zhdanov went to Bashkiria, Tataria, and the Orenburg region as Stalin's personal emissary of the Great Terror." According to one version of events he did not participate personally in the "troikas" that coordinated extermination campaigns; it was his habit instead to delegate this dirty business to his deputy. He contributed to the Great Terror with his public oratory and writings.

As the Old Guard of the party was being purged and destroyed, Zhdanov became a candidate member (in February of 1935) and then a full member of the politburo (in March of 1939). In 1937 he was "elected" a member of the Supreme Soviet of the USSR, and in 1938 became a member of the Supreme Military Council of the Navy (VMF). In public politics he was viewed as one of the "smaller *vozhdi*," a junior partner of Stalin. By the late 1930s he was also Stalin's leading assistant in propaganda and ideological control over the cultural sphere. He helped Stalin edit a new and falsified history of the party entitled *The Brief Course* (1938) that for years was a foundational ideological text of the new Soviet bureaucracy and intelligentsia.

His propaganda talents clearly exceeded his administrative gifts, however, as the years of the Great Patriotic War painfully demonstrated. At the outbreak of the war Zhdanov became a member of the military council (the political body over the military command) of the Northeast and then the Leningrad front. As the Nazi armies approached and then surrounded Leningrad in September 1941, Zhdanov followed Stalin's orders to defend the city at any costs, but he failed to organize proper defenses and, in particular, failed to ensure the food supply. Stalin had to send General G. Zhukov to Leningrad who, with Zhdanov's deputy Alexei Kuznetsov, bolstered the city defenses.

No food assistance was offered to a million of refugees in Leningrad's suburbs; they died of starvation. In October 1941 famine struck the core population. Bread rations shrank well below survival level and it is likely that over one and a half million people perished. According to witnesses, Zhdanov did not suffer; special planes brought him food, including fruits and crepes. However, his poor performance (and probably the signs of a nervous breakdown) brought about his temporary eclipse. He was not a member of the all-powerful GKO and did not coordinate any vital elements of Soviet war efforts. In 1944 the Soviet army broke the blockade of Leningrad. As Finland, faced with the prospect of occupation, accepted the Soviet conditions for an armistice, Zhdanov became a member of the Allied Control Commission for

the country. He coordinated the deliveries of Finnish war reparations to the USSR and, with the assistance of Finnish Communists, interfered in Finland's politics. In May 1945, following the illness and death of A. Scherbakov, head of the agitation and propaganda department of the Central Committee, Zhdanov returned to Moscow to assume that position. In December Stalin, wary of the motives and solidarity of the wartime "collective" leadership, decided to bring Zhdanov back into the political limelight.

His new role was coordinator of Stalin's ideological campaign against "kowtowing before the West" and "cosmopolitans." This campaign reasserted Stalin's unique role as a Soviet leader under postwar conditions; it also mobilized the bureaucracies, the military, and the people for the likely confrontation with the United States and Great Britain. In April 1946 Zhdanov instructed the Central Committee propaganda and agitation department on the basics of Stalin's new ideological policy. In August 1946 he and Stalin drafted the Decree of the Central Committee on the literary journals *Zvezda* and *Leningrad*. Popular writers Mikhail Zoschenko and Anna Akhmatova were the focus of humiliating and withering attacks delivered by Zhdanov in Leningrad. Later he pronounced other Central Committee decrees that attacked "ideologically wrong-headed" films by, among others, Eisenstein, Pudovkin, and Kozintsev, and criticized Prokofiev, Shostakovich, and other composers for music "incomprehensible to the masses." The next targets were scholarship and the sciences. Zhdanov publicly denounced a chief party propagandist, G. Alexandrov, for his allegedly tolerant attitude to "idealistic" and "decadent" Western philosophy. He also presided over "honor courts" that denounced scientists for their cooperation with the Western scientific community. These public acts, supported by secret instructions, initiated the end of the relative wartime "liberalism" in cultural and scientific spheres; the August 1946 decrees established total control and absolute censorship in cultural and ideological matters.

During 1946, Stalin demoted and humiliated Malenkov, Zhukov, and other wartime leaders, but Zhdanov and some of his associates from Leningrad prospered. After Stalin's death, however, most of them became victims of the fabricated "affairs" (the Leningrad and the Gosplan affairs). Among the survivors were Kosygin and Patolichev.

In 1946–47 Zhdanov also acted as a curator of the international Communist movement, including the Italian and French Communist parties. It was a somewhat vague function after the Comintern was disbanded. In this capacity he supervised the CC's international department and the Sovinformbjuro. In 1947 the U.S. policy to contain communism in Western Europe and the Balkans prompted Stalin to assign to Zhdanov a new task: to reorient the French and Italian parties from a relatively "peaceful" parliamentary road to power to a course of aggressive resistance. In September 1947 he and Malenkov traveled secretly to Szklarska Poremba, Poland, to meet with the leadership of key European communist parties. He shouted at the delegates: "How Truman intimidated you! If you keep following this rule—that you should use only decent means against enemies who use dishonest means—then you will never win!" On Stalin's instructions, he announced that world development was now defined by a struggle between the "imperialist camp" and "progressive camp" led by the USSR. Succumbing to Soviet pressure, European Communists agreed to create the Information Bureau of Communist Parties, with its headquarters in Belgrade, Yugoslavia.

Many observers in the West believed, then and later, that Zhdanov had become Stalin's second in command, and that his "faction" eclipsed other members of Stalin's entourage. The August 1946 decrees and the subsequent suppression of cultural freedoms came to be known as "Zhdanovschina." In reality, Zhdanov was not the author or architect of all these policies; he was ever an obedient, albeit eloquent, tool of Stalin's will. He never dared to speak against it. His harsh rhetoric notwithstanding, Zhdanov was a relatively weak and vulnerable man. His health and morale deteriorated under the double burden of a workaholic schedule and bad habits imposed on him by Stalin. Beginning in the 1940s he suffered from alcoholism, and Stalin sadistically made him drink during night politburo sessions at his dacha. By 1947 he suffered also from grave cardiac arteriosclerosis. He died in a party sanatorium on Valdai Lake near Moscow on August 31, 1948, as the result of two heart attacks. The Kremlin doctors were sent to the sanatorium to help him accelerated his death through an incorrect diagnosis.

Ideologically, Zhdanov contributed to the replacement of the internationalist version of Bolshevism with "national Bolshevism," which emphasized at different times in its evolution pan-Slavism, Germanophobia, and anti-Semitism. When Zhdanov became head of the agitation and propaganda department in 1945, it was already conducting an anti-Semitic campaign through state and party institutions. Zhdanov continued this campaign; for instance, he was instructed to "cleanse"

the Sovinformburo of Jews. And, as in other instances, he fulfilled Stalin's wishes.

Zhdanov was the last member of Stalin's politburo who was buried in the Kremlin wall with great pomp. In 1952–53 Stalin fabricated the affair of the Kremlin doctors, blaming them among other things for poisoning Zhdanov. These charges were dropped in April 1953.

See also Cominform; Leningrad, Siege of; *Short Course*, The; Socialist Realism; Stalin, Joseph.

FURTHER READING

Getty, J. A., and O. V. Naumov. *The Road to Terror: Stalin and the Self-Destruction of the Bolsheviks, 1932–1939*. New Haven, CT: Yale University Press, 1999.

Gorlizki, Y., and O. Khlevniuk. *Cold Peace: Stalin and the Soviet Ruling Circle, 1945–1953*. New York: Oxford University Press, 2004.

Torchinov, V. A., and A. M. Leontyuk. *Stalin's Entourage: Historico-Biographical Guide*. St. Petersburg: 2000.

Zalessky, K. *Empire of Stalin: Biographical Encyclopedic Dictionary*. Moscow: Veche, 2000.

Zubok, V., and C. Pleshakov. *Inside the Kremlin's Cold War: From Stalin to Khrushchev*. Cambridge, MA: Harvard University Press, 1996.

VLADISLAV M. ZUBOK

Zhdanovism

"Zhdanovism," an ideological campaign in 1946–48, whose goal was to suppress dissent and dissenters in Soviet society. It was basically a cultural witch hunt focused on writers and artists. The campaign was named after Andrey Zhdanov, a secretary of the Central Committee of the Communist Party of the Soviet Union (CPSU), who promoted its ideology. Zhdanov was the guiding force and organizer of the campaign itself, but he was not its author in the full sense. The campaign's initiative came from Stalin, and the decision to undertake it was formalized by politburo decrees. Zhdanov merely gave voice to the new political line and saw to it that the policy was consistently implemented.

After the war, Stalin had reason to worry about the mind-set of the intelligentsia. The war had brought home a virus of "free thinking" and the danger of "infection" by liberal illusions. Stalin believed that these illusions were influenced by the West: the war had increased contacts between Soviet scholars and artists and their Western colleagues, and many of the former had fought abroad and seen Western life firsthand.

For this reason, the main idea of the new campaign was to keep the intelligentsia (and society as a whole) in line by combating Western influence; thus the campaign acquired a distinctly anti-Western character. It devised appropriate labels for use in its struggle against what it called "servility toward the West" and "cringing before foreigners." These clichés became embedded in the political psyche. As a further ideological postulate, the campaign put forward the principle of a struggle against "political and ideological indifference," or "formalism," as it was later called.

The campaign moved according to a specific scenario and gradually spread into the various areas of culture. As a rule, the targets of criticism were separate individuals and works of art, treated as "educational" examples for the edification of the rest of society. Particular scapegoats were Anna Akhmatova and Mikhail Zoshchenko in literature, Sergey Eisenstein in film, and Vano Muradeli, Sergey Prokofiev, Dmitry Shostakovich, and other composers in music. The criteria for the selection of these individuals were varied, but all were well-known names and leading cultural figures.

The first objects of criticism were the Leningrad writers, for whom a special decree of the CPSU's Central Committee was issued, on August 14, 1946, titled "On the Literary Journals 'Zvezda' (Star) and 'Leningrad.'" The decree was explained to the Leningrad intelligentsia by Zhdanov. It was the start of the new campaign.

The decree about the journals was followed, also in 1946, by two other decrees in the same spirit: "On Theater Repertories and How to Improve Them," and "On the Film 'Bolshaya zhizn [Great Life].'" A decree about music, which condemned the so-called formalist direction in musical culture, was issued later, in February 1948.

Outwardly, the campaign was supposed to proceed democratically, and all decisions were therefore submitted to the public for discussion. This device was used by the authorities not only to maintain the illusion of popular participation in important decisions but also as a means of exerting pressure on the intelligentsia. This placed the intelligentsia in the position of opposing the people (during the campaign, cultural figures were often reproached for being "against the people").

The ideological purges in the Soviet Union took other forms as well—for example, "discussions" on questions of philosophy, biology, language, or political economics.

These "discussions," whose content was usually dictated from the top, were themselves a unique way of continuing Zhdanovism.

Zhdanovism, as a way of bringing the intelligentsia to heel, was not just a Soviet phenomenon; the same scenario unfolded in the struggle against dissent and dissenters in Eastern European countries with Communist regimes.

See also Great Patriotic War, Rhetoric of; Intelligentsia; Stalinism; Zhandov, Andrey.

FURTHER READING

Hahn, W. G. *Postwar Soviet Politics: The Fall of Zhdanov and the Defeat of Modernization, 1946–1953*. Ithaca, NY: Cornell University Press, 1982.

Slonim, M. *Soviet Russian Literature: Writers and Problems, 1917–1977*. New York: Oxford University Press, 1977.

Vickery, W. N. "Zhdanovism (1946–1953)." In *Literature and Revolution in Soviet Russia, 1917–1962*, ed. M. Hayward and L. Labedz. Oxford: Oxford University Press, 1963.

Zubkova, E. *Russia after the War: Hopes, Illusions, and Disappointments, 1945–1957*. Armonk, NY: M. E. Sharpe, 1998.

ELENA U. ZUBKOVA

Zhivkov, Todor

Todor Zhivkov (1911–98) was born on September 7, 1911, in the village of Pravets in the Botevgrad Region, to the family of a poor craftsman. He studied at a Botevgrad high school and continued his education in Sofia at the high school of graphics at the state printing house, where he joined the Bulgarian Youth Communist Union (BYCU). In 1932 he became a member of the Bulgarian Communist Party (BCP).

On September 9, 1944, Zhivkov was appointed political leader of the People's Militia Headquarters in Sofia. Despite his comparatively small role in the anti-Fascist resistance, Zhivkov's party career accelerated rapidly. In 1944 he became one of the secretaries of the Sofia regional committee; in 1945 he became a candidate-member of the Communist Bulgarian Workers Party (BWP [C]); and in January of 1948 he was nominated as first secretary of the BWP (C) Sofia's Central Committee under Traycho Kostov's recommendation. While at this post he was noticed by his superiors and rewarded for his diligence in performing tasks set by the Fifth Congress (December 1948) with a position on the BCP's Central Committee. He actively participated in the campaign against Traycho Kostov when Kostov was accused of anti-Sovietism and espionage. As others fell, Zhivkov confirmed with a nomination as secretary of the Central Committee his uncanny political skill and ability to survive serious political turmoil in the party. In 1950 he became a candidate member of the politburo, and in 1951 a full politburo member. Zhivkov remained at this post without interruption until 1989. At the Party Congress in 1954 he was approved as first secretary of the Central Committee.

Zhivkov made a decisive play for the number-one party spot at the April Plenum (April 2–6, 1956). He delivered the main speech proclaiming de-Stalinization, an act that symbolized his high standing in the BCP. Zhivkov manipulated the existing confrontation between his rivals, suggesting that he was "more moderate" in the punishment he implemented.

During the next eight years Zhivkov resolved a number of political and economic problems, thus strengthening his personal power. He managed to defeat the intelligentsia's discontent with inadequate de-Stalinization, partially rehabilitated repressed party cadres, and increased wages. He categorically approved the Soviets' November 1956 intervention in Hungary. He brought before the public a new generation of politicians, who remained high in the party and state nomenclature almost up until Zhivkov's removal from power. With a change of cadres at the end of the 1950s and beginning of the 1960s, Zhivkov obtained full control over the party and state apparatus and assumed the position of prime minister as well. The establishment of professional standards for the selection of leaders at the medium level facilitated Zhivkov's experiments with economic policy.

Zhivkov also reoriented his political loyalties toward Leonid Brezhnev, who continued to tolerate the plans for Bulgaria's industrial-agrarian development and approved more liberal relations with the West and with third world states. Brezhnev accepted Zhivkov's second proposal for "comprehensive cooperation" made in July 1973 (resembling the 1963 proposal for Bulgaria to become the USSR's 16th republic). Zhivkov strengthened the international position of the People's Republic of Bulgaria by maintaining successful contacts with the heads of state of Greece, Turkey, Yugoslavia, The Federal Republic of Germany, India, and Iran. Zhivkov increased his power via the new constitution of 1971 and became the head of state.

In the beginning of the 1980s Zhivkov experienced a bitter personal drama with the death of his daughter

L. Zhivkova, who had assumed the post of minister of culture and politburo member to acquaint the world with Bulgarian culture.

The new party leader of the USSR, Mikhail Gorbachev (1985) posed a real threat to Zhivkov's unlimited power by declaring socialism's perestroika and calling for a change in economic relations within the Eastern bloc.

Zhivkov attempted to carry out a preemptive reformation of the Socialist system with his "July concept" of 1987, introducing market mechanisms to the Bulgarian economy. He attempted also to liberalize public relations via the incorporation of public partnerships, but he disapproved "dissident" actions (1988), regardless of their nonthreatening nature.

Zhivkov's survival skills failed him in his relations with Gorbachev. Some of his long-time associates and "favorites" also turned against him. He was forced to hand in his resignation, which was accepted at the Central Committee Plenum on November 10, 1989. Initially he retained the privileges of head of state, but they were suspended in December 1989 and Zhivkov was expelled from the Bulgarian Communist Party. On January 18, 1990, he was arrested. Four cases were brought against him, and he was sentenced in September of 1992. Zhivkov was acquitted in 1996 but remained under house arrest. Zhivkov was the only functionary to assume responsibility for the policy conducted by his government, which he did in a letter addressed to the Great National Assembly dated July 29, 1990. He died in Sofia on August 5, 1998.

See also Soviet Bloc; Stalinism.

FURTHER READING

Bell, J. D. *The Bulgarian Communist Party from Blagoev to Zhivkov.* Stanford, CA: Hoover Institution Press, 1986.

Chakarov, K. *The Second Floor.* Sofia: 1990.

Yahiel, N. *Todor Zhivkov and Personal Power.* Sofia: M and M Publishers, 1997.

VITKA TOSHKOVA

Zhou Enlai

Zhou Enlai (1898–1976) was not only one the most important figures in the Chinese Communist leadership from the 1920s on but also became the second best-known Chinese Communist political figure in the West after Mao Zedong. Even today many Chinese people remember Zhou as "the prime minister," the man who remained at the head of the government bureaucracy without interruption from the foundation of the People's Republic of China in 1949 until his death in 1976. The reason that Zhou is better known in the West is his direct involvement in fifty years of Maoist diplomacy.

Born in the province of Jiangsu, near Shanghai, Zhou had more international exposure than many of his peers during his youth. Like many young intellectuals of his generation he studied in Japan in the late 1910s, but returned to China in 1919, in time to participate in the May Fourth Movement. He then left for Europe, where he spent four years in France, Germany, and England, directly involved in the Communist organizations that the Chinese had formed in those countries. Once he returned, Zhou already enjoyed the status of a leader and the appreciation of the Comintern's leadership. He held important positions for the Communists during the period of the First United Front (1922–27), which consisted of the Chinese Communist Party (CCP) and the Nationalist Party (Guomindang, or GMD). He was called to direct the Military Academy in Whampoa, where many of the Communist leaders were educated, and where Zhou built the crucial network of relationships that would later form the basis of his position in the party and the government.

After the break between the CCP and the GMD in 1927, Zhou was one of the leaders of the Nanchang insurrection, and with the CCP now leading an underground existence, together with Li Lisan he became the main Communist leader in Shanghai. His relationship with Mao was often tense in the following years. Zhou officially represented the party in Shanghai and transmitted Moscow's directives to the Chinese revolutionary movement, while during those same years, in Jiangxi Province, Mao was organizing an autonomous Soviet inspired by a rural revolutionary strategy that the Comintern did not intend to support. The clash between the two lines (the Maoist and that of the group of the so-called Twenty-eight Bolsheviks, which was faithful to Moscow) was resolved in Mao's favor during the Zunyi Conference in 1935, in the middle of the Long March. It was at this time that Zhou took his place at Mao's side, where he would remain until both leaders' death in 1976. Between 1937 and 1945, Zhou was the CCP's representative with the nationalist government, whose headquarters in those years were in Chongqing, in Sichuan Province. Zhou was solidly established in 1945 as number three in the Chinese Communist hierarchy, after Mao and Liu Shaoqi. During the years of the anti-Japanese resistance and later, after the end of World War II in the Pacific as well as the renewed civil war between the Communists and the nationalists, Zhou continued to represent the CCP in its internal and international diplomacy.

With the creation of the People's Republic of China in 1949, Zhou was the natural candidate for the prime minister position, to which he added the position of foreign minister. From that moment on, his relationship with Mao was almost symbiotic, but there were still conflicts. Zhou and Mao led parallel, often overlapping bureaucracies (the government and the party), but they did not necessarily have the same interests. In the late 1950s, for example, Zhou supported a more moderate collectivization policy. Under the radical pressure of the Maoist model of development, Zhou attempted several times to keep the Chinese economic system on the road to rationalization. The effort to slow the extreme productivist drive that would lead Mao to launch the Great Leap Forward in 1958 led to serious confrontations with the Great Helmsman, but never to a complete break, as was to occur, for instance, to then–Defense Minister Peng Dehuai in 1959. Zhou always remained faithful to party discipline. In 1958, after having received another public self-criticism from Zhou, Mao abandoned the "reductivist" policies proposed by Zhou and Liu, and led the country into the Great Leap Forward, with disastrous consequences. Zhou and Liu experienced a partial revenge after the Great Leap's conclusion, when it was Mao's turn to "take a step backward," allowing his marshals to manage the economic recovery and a slowdown in the collectivization of agriculture during the early 1960s.

The last decade of Zhou's life and political career were marked by the unrest of the Cultural Revolution. During these years, while many of the leaders who were closest to Mao such as Liu and Deng Xiaoping were the object of ferocious criticism, Zhou kept his position as number three, even after Lin Biao had replaced Liu as Mao's successor. Zhou's success in navigating the waters of Maoist radicalism is attributed to the unequivocal support that he gave all of Mao's policies, including the productivist follies and the campaigns of criticism against those who had been his most faithful allies. Only after 1971, after Lin's death, did Zhou begin to criticize radical groups, reestablish a more balanced economic policy (he devised the "four modernizations" slogan that was later adopted by Deng), and restore some of the leaders who had been purged during the previous years to positions from which they could once again help lead the country. In 1972 Zhou made international headlines as the principal architect of the historic visit to China by U.S. president Richard Nixon. He became the object of great admiration in U.S. diplomatic circles during this process.

After he became ill in 1973, Zhou's influence on Mao was once again exposed to the criticism by radicals in the group known as the Gang of Four. Zhou's death in January 1976 was seen as an opportunity by the radicals to reestablish their privileged position in Mao's succession. The celebration of the festival of the dead on April 5 of that same year was an occasion for the confrontation between the two factions that focused on the evaluation of Zhou's figure. The repression of the April 5 demonstrations (known as the Tiananmen Square incident) was the last gasp of the Cultural Revolution's radicalism.

It is impossible not to compare the figures of Mao and Zhou. Against the image of a cruel and boorish Mao that is prevalent today, Zhou is frequently portrayed as a refined intellectual and a subtle diplomat—notwithstanding his many contradictions—who lived an exemplary private life (he was married to Deng Yinchao, a leading figure in Chinese feminism from 1925 until his death). He represented the pragmatic side of Chinese communism—an aspect that his successor and protégé, Deng, did nothing but expand in the course of his project for reforms.

See also Chinese Revolution; Deng Xiaoping; Diplomats; Mao Zedong.

FURTHER READING

Kampen, T. *Mao Zedong, Zhou Enlai, and the Evolution of the Chinese Communist Leadership.* Copenhagen: Nias Press, 1999.

MacFarquhar, R., ed. *The Politics of China: The Eras of Mao and Deng,* chapters 1–3. Cambridge, UK: Cambridge University Press, 1997.

Suyin Han. *Eldest Son: Zhou Enlai and the Making of Modern China, 1898–1976.* New York: Kodansha, 1994.

LUIGI TOMBA

Zhukov, Georgii

Georgii Zhukov (1896–1974), from a peasant family, worked in a Moscow factory starting at an early age. In World War I, he served as a noncommissioned of-

ficer beginning in 1916, and was decorated with Saint George crosses, wounded, and then evacuated from the front. In 1917, as a teacher for noncommissioned officers, Zhukov experienced the formation of soldiers' soviets, but did not take part in the revolutionary process. He joined the Red Army as a cavalry officer in August 1918, and became member of the Communist Party one year later.

Zhukov served in the cavalry divisions under famous Red Army leaders such as Mikhail Frunze and Mikhail Tukhachevskii. In the peaceful decades, Zhukov advanced from regiment to divisional commander. He escaped the tragic fate of many Red Army officers during the Great Terror. In the summer of 1939, Zhukov led the Soviet and Mongolian troops that routed an intruding Japanese force in Outer Mongolia. This victory proved essential for the USSR, since it averted the threat of a two-front, Japanese-German attack. It was also the turning point in Zhukov's career.

At an army conference in December 1940, Zhukov talked about the lessons from Germany's blitzkrieg successes in 1939–40. Zhukov's performance in war games after this conference was exemplary. Joseph Stalin therefore appointed him chief of the general staff. During the hectic months before the German invasion, the Soviet general staff redrew its war plans, but failed to discern the date of the coming Nazi attack. The huge losses of the Soviet army in 1941 were thus in part due to the mistakes of the high command, but to an even larger extent to the idiosyncrasies of Stalin, whose orders of offensive actions after the outbreak of the war worsened the Soviet losses of troops and territories.

Zhukov's successful counteroffensive against the Germans near Moscow in winter 1941 turned the tides, but, despite Zhukov's advice, in 1942 Stalin ordered offensive operations along the whole front. This lead to new disasters: strong German forces advanced toward Stalingrad and the Caucasus. Zhukov took part in the planning of the operations against Field Marshal Friedrich Paulus's army in Stalingrad. The Soviet victory there in 1942–43 took the strategic initiative from the Germans. During the rest of the war, from the military headquarters (*stavka*), Zhukov planned the 1943–45 operations, from the liberation of Ukraine to the capture of Berlin. As the most popular wartime leader, he led the victory parade on Red Square in 1945.

By 1946, Stalin was intent on dispersing influential wartime heroes from the power center. Zhukov was relegated to an inferior post as a district commander.

After Stalin's death, Zhukov was appointed minister of defense in 1953. He was a candidate and full member of the Central Committee's presidium, later called the politburo, in 1956–57. His second downfall came as Nikita Khrushchev relieved him from the Ministry of Defense.

Thereafter Zhukov concentrated on writing his memoirs—under great stress. Even after Khrushchev's downfall in 1964, the party leaders could not decide whether Zhukov should be free to publish his judgments of the country's military history and express his views on Stalin as supreme commander. In the end, his memoirs became a huge success in the USSR: they provided unique insights into top-level decision making by Stalin along with his marshals and generals.

Zhukov's legacy as a military leader has not been without dispute in Russia and elsewhere. On the one hand, Zhukov did not propose any innovative doctrine or theories. On the other hand, he was the commander that "saved" Leningrad and Moscow in the catastrophic months in autumn 1941. He was associated with the victories of the Red Army; the saying among soldiers was "Where Zhukov is, there is victory." His harsh leadership style in the Great Patriotic War (1941–45) should be set in its proper context: the duress of the 1930s and the total war launched by the better-trained German force.

See also Great Patriotic War, Rhetoric of; Leningrad, Siege of; Red Army; Stalingrad, Battle of; Tukhachevskii, Mikhail.

FURTHER READING

Gareev, M. A. *Marshal Zhukov: Velichie i unikal'nost' polkovodcheskogo iskusstva.* Moscow: Vostochnyi universitet, 1996.

Karpov, V. *Marshal Zhukov. Opala.* Moscow: Veche, 1994.

Naumov, V., et al., eds. *Georgii Zhukov. Stenogramma oktiabr'skogo (1957 g.) plenuma TsK KPSS i drugie materialy.* Seriya "Rossiya XX vek. Dokumenty." Moscow: Mezhunarodnyi fond "Demokratiya," 2001.

Sokolov, B. *Neizvestnyi Zhukov: Portret bez retushi.* Minsk: Rodiola-Pljus, 2000.

Spahr, W. J. *Zhukov: The Rise and Fall of a Great Captain.* Novato, CA: Presidio, 1993.

Zhukov, G. *Reminescences and Reflections.* Moscow: Progress, 1985.

———. *Vospominaniia i razmysjleniya.* Vols. 1–3. 10th rev. and exp. ed. Moscow: Agentsvo Pechati Novosti, 1990.

LENNART SAMUELSON

Zimmerwald Conference

Following the outbreak of the First World War in August 1914, the most important European Social Democratic parties opted to support their national war efforts. The triumph of what would become known as *Socialist defensism* came as a shock to a movement that had for decades proclaimed its allegiance to the ideal of internationalism. It paralyzed, and eventually destroyed, the Second International (1889–1914), which at its Stuttgart Congress in 1907 had solemnly pledged that in the event of war it was the duty of Socialists "to intervene in favor of its speedy termination, and to do all in their power to utilize the economic and political crisis caused by the war to rouse the people and thereby to hasten the abolition of capitalist class rule."

After a period of reorientation, militants determined to oppose the war, including thirty-eight delegates representing eleven countries, assembled under the organizational initiatives of the Swiss Socialist Robert Grimm (1881–1958). They convened a highly secret five-day international conference (September 5–9, 1915) in the Swiss village of Zimmerwald, located in an isolated pre-alpine region ten kilometers south of the Swiss capital Berne. The intent of the organizers was to revive the tradition of Socialist internationalism and develop an antiwar platform. After acrimonious debate, the conference issued the *Zimmerwald Manifesto*, penned by the Russian Socialist Leon Trotsky (1879–1940), which called on Socialists "to join anew the broken ties of international relations and to summon the working class to reorganize and begin the struggle for peace." It also created an International Socialist Commission (ISC) chaired by Grimm, as the executive committee of a Zimmerwald Movement pledged to revive the International and encourage antiwar agitation. The *Zimmerwald Manifesto* was subsequently published in selected Socialist press organs and distributed as a leaflet in various venues, including military units at the front. The ISC met regularly in Berne, issued periodic editions of an *ISC Bulletin*, and sought to build organizational affiliations. It sponsored subsequent conferences in Kienthal, Switzerland (April 24–May 1, 1916) and Stockholm, Sweden (September 5–9, 1917).

At the original Zimmerwald conference, the majority opted to emphasize work for peace and the revival of the existing International. This perspective was challenged by a minority faction of eight delegates, led by the

Russian Vladimir Lenin (1870–1924), which in the weeks and months to come would constitute itself as a factional tendency within the movement designated as the Zimmerwald Left. The Left demanded a revolutionary response to the war, defined as an inevitable manifestation of the crisis of capitalist imperialism, and urged the creation of a revolutionary Third International.

Following the conclusion of the war in 1918, the Zimmerwald majority moved back into the fold of moderate European social democracy. The Zimmerwald Left, strengthened by the victory of Lenin's Bolsheviks in the Russian Revolutions of 1917, and by international enthusiasm for the revolutionary cause, became the foundation for the new International Communist Movement and the Third Communist International (1919–43). The political division between the Left and the majority that manifested in the course of the September 1915 debates among Socialist militants at the rest home Beau Séjour in Zimmerwald was the kernel from which the great schism of the 20th-century international labor movement would emerge.

See also Bolshevism; Imperialism; Internationalism; Socialist International.

FURTHER READING

Fainsod, M. *International Socialism and the Great War*. Cambridge, MA: Harvard University Press, 1935.

Kirby, D. *War, Peace and Revolution: International Socialism at the Crossroads 1914–1918*. New York: St. Martin's Press, 1986.

Nation, R. C. *War on War: Lenin, the Zimmerwald Left, and the Origins of Communist Internationalism*. Durham, NC: Duke University Press, 1989.

R. CRAIG NATION

Zinovyev, Grigory

Grigory Zinovyev (1883–1936), whose actual name was Radomyslsky, was born on September 11 to the family of a minor Jewish businessman in Elisavetgrad, Russia (now Kirovograd, in Ukraine). He was educated at home, and as a young man joined the revolutionary movement. In 1901, he became a member of the Russian Socialist Democratic Labor Party (RSDLP) and attached himself to the Bolshevik faction. In internal party conflicts, he took the side of Lenin, whom he got to know in 1903 while they were in

exile together. Zinovyev continued his education at Bern University, and later lived in Berlin and Paris, making his living as a journalist. In fall 1903 he returned to Russia, where he worked for the Bolshevik press.

During the first Russian Revolution, Zinovyev was elected to the Saint Petersburg Committee of the RSDLP, where he again took the side of the Bolsheviks. He took part in the electoral campaign for the second State Duma. In 1907, he became a member of the RSDLP's Central Committee, where he made speeches to workers and supervised the publishing of the party press. In spring 1908, Zinovyev was arrested, but soon succeeded in fleeing abroad. He joined Lenin and Lev Kamenev in Geneva as a publisher of the newspaper *The Proletariat*, and taught in a party school in France. During this period (1912–14), Zinovyev was with Lenin in Kraków and became one of his closest associates. He also carried on a correspondence with leading functionaries of the RSDLP and helped prepare the speeches of the Bolshevik deputies to the State Duma.

Zinovyev spent the World War I years in Switzerland, where he took part in antiwar conferences of left-wing socialists and, together with Lenin, wrote a book called *Socialism and War* (1915). He was also one of the founders of the Zimmerwald Left, and represented the Bolshevik Party in this organization of international socialists. When the Russian Revolution began, Zinovyev crossed Germany and returned to Petrograd, where he occupied various leading posts in the Executive Committee of the Soviet (Union) of Workers' and Soldiers' Deputies, and became a member of the editorial board of the newly resurrected *Pravda*. In July 1917, continually harassed by the Provisional Government, Zinovyev and Lenin went into hiding in Razliv, not far from Finland. After the Bolsheviks gained a majority in the soviets, Zinovyev became one of the leaders of the Petrograd Soviet of Workers' and Soldiers' Deputies. On October 10, 1917, he was elected to the politburo of the Central Committee of the RSDLP (Bolshevik), which had assumed power as a result of an armed uprising.

As an adherent of a moderate "flow of power" to the Soviets, Zinovyev, together with Kamenev, spoke out in the press against plans for a violent seizure of power by the Bolsheviks. For this, he was harshly criticized by Lenin, who demanded that he be expelled from the party. Zinovyev was not discharged even from the RSDLP's Central Committee, however. After the October Revolution, he spoke in support of a "homogeneous socialist government," which would include Mensheviks and Socialist-Revolutionaries. But he remained in the minority here, too, and for a short time gave up his Central Committee position, as a sign of his disagreement with the movement toward a one-party dictatorship.

In December 1917, Zinovyev was named chair of the Petrograd Soviet. During the Brest-Litovsk negotiations, he insisted, with Lenin, on accepting the German conditions for peace. In summer 1918, he was one of the initiators of the Red Terror in Soviet Russia, and during the civil war he was one of the organizers of the defense of Petrograd. In 1919 Zinovyev became a candidate for and, in 1921, a member of the politburo of the Central Committee of the Russian Communist Party (Bolshevik) (RCP).

After 1917, Zinovyev consistently supported Lenin's point of view in internal party disputes. In the debate about the Treaty of Brest-Litovsk in 1918, he criticized Nikolay Bukharin, as he did Trotsky in the trade union dispute in 1921. Zinovyev was considered, for practical purposes, Lenin's first deputy in party questions, and at RCP congresses in 1923 and 1924 he gave the political reports for the Central Committee. A master of internal party intrigue, Zinovyev became close to Stalin during these years and played a decisive role in forming the so-called troika (Stalin, Kamenev, and himself), which blocked Trotsky's attempts toward a sharing of power. After Lenin's death, he wrote several theoretical works, which laid the groundwork for a dogmatic interpretation of Leninism.

From the moment of the Comintern's creation in March 1919, Zinovyev was the chair of its Executive Committee, and later he became the editor in chief of the journal *Communist International*. At its Second and Fifth Congresses, he gave the political reports about the Comintern's activities. Under his guidance the Comintern gradually acquired the traits of a bureaucratic organization, which used authoritarian methods to control the activity of Communists around the world. Zinovyev was a main figure behind the approval, at the Second Comintern Congress in 1920, of a decree titled "Conditions of Acceptance into the Communist International." These conditions were used to deny admission to European socialists who were not in accord with the theory and practices of Russian Bolshevism. In October 1920, Zinovyev's stirring speech at the congress of the Independent Social Democratic Party of Germany caused most of the delegates there to declare themselves in favor of joining the Comintern. At the First Advanced Plenum of the Comintern in 1922, Zinovyev supported the "united

front" strategy and cooperation with Socialist parties in their defense of the interests of the working class, a tactic he saw as a "rope cast around the neck of the Social Democrats."

In fall 1923, Zinovyev insisted on quickly preparing for an armed uprising of the German proletariat, drawing parallels here with the October Revolution in Russia. When the "German October" failed, Zinovyev avoided responsibility for the defeat by accusing the leaders of the Communist Party of Germany of "right-wing deviationism," and he effected a radical change in the party's leadership. In 1924, the publication of his book *The Problems of the German Revolution* aggravated the internal party conflicts within the RCP. The Fifth Advanced Plenum of the Comintern (in 1925) affirmed Zinovyev's ideas about "The Bolshevization of the Parties of the Comintern." The Executive Committee of the Comintern and its chair, Zinovyev, used the slogan "Bolshevization" to consolidate their policy of intervening in key questions of the Communist parties of other countries, and insisted that the latter unconditionally follow the example of the Russian Revolution and emulate USSR policies.

The hardening of Stalin's positions, however, compelled Zinovyev and Kamenev to break off their informal agreement to maintain a bloc against Trotsky. At the Fourteenth Party Congress in December 1925, they criticized the political line of the general secretary of the RCP's Central Committee, castigating it for making concessions to the kulaks and for the insufficiently rapid industrialization of the country.

Prominent in the discussions was the question of whether socialism could be built separately in an individual country. Those opposed to the possibility of this insisted that without successful proletarian revolutions in a number of Europe's leading countries, one could not speak of any final triumph of socialism in Russia. This "Leningrad Opposition" lost the battle, and after the congress Zinovyev confessed to the mistakes he had made.

The armistice within the leadership of the by now renamed All-Union Communist Party did not last long. Already by summer 1926, a "united opposition" had formed—supporters of Trotsky agreed to form a bloc with Zinovyev and Kamenev. During 1926 and 1927, Zinovyev pursued his publishing activity, emphasizing in his works, most of which were not published, his criticism of the international aspects of the Stalinist majority (he analyzed capitalist stabilization, the Chinese Revolution, and the Anglo-Russian Committee of Trade Union Unity).

After the Fourteenth Party Congress, Zinovyev took no active part in the work of the Comintern Executive Committee, but devoted himself to the so-called Russian Delegation. In summer 1926, Stalin wrote, in a letter to Molotov, that "we have to face the question of removing Grigory from the Communist International." Zinovyev was formally discharged from his post as leader of the Comintern during the Seventh Advanced Plenum of the Comintern in fall 1926. At the same time he was removed from the politburo of the Central Committee of the Communist Party, and lost his post as chair of the Leningrad Soviet. He did not, however, cease his oppositionist activities. At a July plenum of the Central Committee in 1926, Zinovyev answered accusations leveled at him for having formed an unscrupulous bloc with his onetime implacable enemy, Trotsky, as follows: "It sometimes happens in party politics and conflicts that comrades, who have diverged from each other and fought bitterly over certain issues, later can join together; in fact, come together seriously and for the long term, to defend the party line." Nevertheless, the mutual distrust among the leaders of the "united opposition," their lack of coordination among themselves, and the ever-increasing repression of the Stalinist apparatus left them no chance for success.

In October 1927, Zinovyev was removed from the Central Committee, and at the Fifteenth Party Congress he was expelled from the party. After just a year and a half in exile, though, he issued a statement of repentance and was reinstated in the party. Zinovyev became president of Kazan University and a member of the editorial board of *Bolshevik*. Still, Stalin kept a careful eye on the journalism produced by one of his erstwhile enemies, and never missed a chance to make new accusations against him. In 1932, under the pretext of his having maintained his contacts with the "not yet disarmed oppositionists," Zinovyev was again expelled from the party and this time exiled to Kazakhstan. He was again reinstated in the party the following year, though. Typical of his cat-and-mouse game with the Stalinists was his statement of repentance at the Seventeenth Congress, marked by his flattery of the great leader and the general party line.

After the murder of Sergey Kirov on December 1, 1934, Zinovyev was arrested, and on personal orders from Stalin, NKVD operatives extracted a confession from him that he himself had instigated this crime. On January 16, 1935, he was sentenced to ten years in prison. In August of the following year, an even larger-scale show trial was staged, at which Zinovyev was portrayed as one of the leaders of a "united Trotsky-Zinovyev anti-Soviet center," which had allegedly organized assassination attempts against party leaders and laid the groundwork for a coup against the state. Stalin promised Zinovyev that exemplary behavior in the future would save his life, but he did not keep his word. On August 24, Zinovyev was sentenced to death and shot by firing squad the following day. He was not to be rehabilitated until the era of perestroika in 1988.

See also Bolshevism; Comintern; Insurrection in Germany; Russian Revolution and Civil War; Stalin, Joseph; Trotsky, Leon.

FURTHER READING

Adibekov, G. M., E. N. Sachnazarova, and K. K. Sirinja. *Organizacionnaja struktura Kominterna, 1919–1943* [The Organizational Structure of the Comintern, 1919–1943]. Moscow: Rosspen, 1997.

"Dejateli SSSR i revoljucionnogo dviženija Rossii" [Functionaries of the USSR and the Russian Revolutionary Movement]. In *Enciklopedičeskij slovar'*. Moscow: Granat, 1989.

Lazitch, B., and M. Drachkovitch. *Biographical Dictionary of the Comintern*. Stanford, CA: Hoover Institution Press, 1986.

Zinoviev, G. E. *Leninizm*. Leningrad, 1925.

ALEKSANDR I. VATLIN

Zionism

Zionism and communism are offspring of the same ideological generation, which arose in the second half of the 19th century and attempted to address some of the turmoil caused by the European continent's entry into modernity. Clearly taking different views of the causes of modern anti-Semitism, the movements proposed radically different projects to the Jews, even though they had several points in common.

The Communist movement, on the one hand, taking the fact that a "Jewish nation" did not exist into consideration, supported an assimilationist perspective, following the model offered by the French Revolution. It asked Jews to renounce their identity and their particularism, and to focus on the universal struggle of the working class for a socialist society, which in its turn would make anti-Semitism disappear. The majority of Marxist theorists rejected the idea of a Jewish nation, and condemned the Zionist project as a romantic, utopian, and reactionary aberration. According to Vladimir Lenin's formula,

"National Jewish culture is the watchword of rabbis and the bourgeois, the watchword of our enemies." On the other hand, the Zionist movement, founded by Theodor Herzl in 1897, was instead of the opinion that the Jewish nation existed and that it needed to establish its own state in order to fight modern anti-Semitism.

The goals of the two projects were contradictory, but they shared two points, especially communism and Zionism's socialist wing. First, they addressed the same groups—the Jewish intelligentsia and proletariat. And second, they both intended to create a "new man," whose symbol for the Communist camp was the proletarian and for the Zionist camp was the worker-peasant-soldier of the kibbutzim.

The two movements therefore became competitors, especially after 1917. Recognizing that the Zionist movement had a majority following among Russian Jews, the Bolsheviks proposed the creation of a "Palestine in Moscow" in an effort to curry favor with the Russian Jews at a time when the Zionist movement was attempting to create a "Jewish national homeland" in a Palestine under a British mandate. The Bolshevik attempt was not successful, even though its creation of a Jewish territory in Birobidzhan in 1928, in the Soviet Far East, was later transformed into an autonomous Jewish region in 1934. While the USSR and the international Communist movement continued to consider Zionism an enemy in the service of imperialism, Moscow drastically changed policy in 1947. At that time the USSR became Zionism's strongest ally, supporting the creation of a Jewish state in Palestine based on the partition plan approved by the United Nations in November 1947. This plan gave Israel diplomatic, military (supplies of Czech weapons), and demographic aid (with the immigration to Israel of more than three hundred thousand Jews from the people's democracies that surrounded the USSR). Joseph Stalin's goals were to weaken Great Britain in the context of the burgeoning Cold War and modify the balance of forces in the Middle East.

After this honeymoon period between Israel and the USSR (1947–51), however, Zionism once more became the enemy of the international Communist movement and Moscow. Jews were one of the principal targets of repression in the USSR between 1946 and 1953. Many victims of the purges and the political trials in the USSR and the people's democracies during this period were accused of having participated in a "Zionist plot."

Zionism remained an enemy until Mikhail Gorbachev's rise to power. As a result, the USSR did not allow Jews to emigrate to Israel until the early 1970s. These refuseniks took part in the Soviet dissident movement that developed in the 1960s and 1970s. In 1975, the USSR and the people's democracies voted with the Arab countries on a UN General Assembly resolution that categorized Zionism as "a form of racism." Only during the late 1980s were Jews free to emigrate to Israel, where they became 20 percent of the population. In October 1991 the USSR and Israel reestablished diplomatic relations, which had been interrupted since 1967.

See also Anti-Semitism; Dissent in the USSR; Nationalism; New Man.

FURTHER READING

Ro'I, Y. *The Struggle for Soviet Jewish Emigration, 1948–1967.* Cambridge, UK: Cambridge University Press, 1991.

Rucker, L. *Staline, Israël et les Juifs.* Paris: PUF, 2001.

Traverso, E. *The Marxists and the Jewish Question: The History of a Debate (1843–1943).* Atlantic Highlands, NJ: Humanities Press, 1993.

Weinberg, R. *Stalin's Forgotten Zion: Birobidzhan and the Making of the Soviet Jewish Homeland.* Berkeley: University of California Press, 1998.

LAURENT RUCKER

Index

Main entries are indicated by **bold** type.

Abakumov, Viktor, 448

Abdil'din, Serykbolsin, 155

Abuladze, Tengiz, 109

Accumulation of Capital: A Contribution to the Economic Explanation of Imperialism (Luxemburg), 409, 495

Acheson, Dean, 238

Ackermann, Anton, 166, 753

Adenauer, Konrad, 275, 313, 452, 597

Adorno, Theodor W., 522

Ady, Endre, 178

Adzhubei, Alexei, 90

Aesthetics (Lukács), 492, 493

Afghan War, 1–3, 10, 426, 566; condemnation of by the Italian Communist Party, 6; reasons for Soviet invasion of Afghanistan, 1–2; Soviet disengagement from Afghanistan, 2–3; Soviet losses during, 2; Soviet plans to capture the mountain passes, 2; as a war of resistance, 2

Afghanistan, 1–3, 563; "Finlandization" of, 2; Iranian aid to, 1; as outside the Soviet security zone, 2. *See also* **Afghan War**

Africa, Cuban-Soviet intervention in, 246–48

African National Congress, 26, 223, 565

Afrocommunism, 223

agrarian question, 3–5; approach of the Bolsheviks to, 5; founding of the League for Agrarian Reform, 5; and the populist/Marxist distinction, 3–4

Ai Siqi, 503

Aitakog, N., 154

Akaev, Askar, 155

Akhmatova, Anna, 271, 287, 484, 883

Akhromeyev, Sergei, 241

Akimov, Vladimir, 428

Aksel'rod, P. B., 427

Aksenov, Vasily, 485

Albania, 22, 394–95, 726, 730, 744, 746, 757–58, 761, 800, 864; as a People's Democracy, 608, 610. *See also* **Communist Party in Albania**

Alberti, B., 31

Alberti, Rafael, 220, 574

Aldrich, John, 56

Alekseev, P. A., 427

Alessandri, Jorge, 824

Alexander Nevsky (1938), 305

Alexandrov, Grigori, 305

Alexi I, 594

Alexi II, 595

Algeria, 259, 566; Communist Party in, 200, 202

Algiers Conference (1973), 586

Alí, Bachir Hadj, 202

Aliev, Gaidar, 640

Aliev, Ilham, 640

All China Federation of Trade Unions, 469

Allende, Salvador, 244, 369, 575, 824, 825

Alliance for Culture, 12

Alliance for Progress, 238

Allilueva, Nadezhda, 774

All-Union (later All-Russian) Center for the Study of Public Opinion, 659

Althusser, Louis, 523; appeal to restoring Marxism as science, 523

Alvarez, Gerónimo Arnedo, 199

Alves, Mario, 369

Amador, Carlos Fonseca, 368, 370, 696

Amalrik, Andrei, 288, 290

Amendola, Giorgio, 5–7; "democratic planning" concept, 6; as head of the Central Organizing Commission of the Italian Communist Party, 6

American Federation of Labor, 15

American Relief Administration, 320

Americanism, 7–8, 351–52

Americans for Democratic Action, 16

Amin, Hafizullah, 1; assassination of, 2

Amnesty International, 288

Amosov, M. K., 154

Amsterdam International. *See* International Federation of Trade Unions

Anatomy of a Revolution (Brinton), 291

Anderson, Perry, 523

Anderson, Rudolf, 243

Andreeva, Nina, 613

Andrei Rublev (1966), 109, 287

Andropov, Yuri, 2, 9–10, 154, 155, 287, 291, 340, 341, 366, 398, 518, 520, 612, 627, 647, 747, 787; as chairman of the KGB, 9; creation of Directorate V, 287; early career of, 9; education of, 9; as an intellectual, 9; and NATO, 589; struggle of against Maoism, 9

Andrzejewski, Jerzy, 464

Angola, 246–47, 566

Animal Farm (Orwell), 596, 614

anti-Americanism, 10–14; American society as totalitarian, 13; among French and Italian Communists, 12; criticism of American hedonism, 12; defects of Marxist anti-Americanism, 13–14; definition of, 10; non-Marxist sources of, 11–12; paradox of, 13; role of Communist ideology in, 11; as a struggle against American influence in Europe, 12

anticapitalism, 20

anticolonialism, 222, 257, 258

Anti-Comintern Pact (1936), 325, 385

anticommunism, 14–17; American anticommunism, 14; blackballing of Hollywood writers and directors

anticommunism (cont.)
because of, 16; of dissident
movements within the Soviet Union, 17;
European anticommunism, 14, 15, 16–17;
opposition movements against Soviet-
style communism, 17; and the U.S. Left,
16; as a weapon in American domestic
politics, 15–16. *See also* "Red scares"
Anti-dühring (Engels), 527
antifascism, 17–21; among Communists,
17–18; appropriation of by Western
Communists, 21; beginnings of, 18;
as a Communist invention, 18; divisions among anti-Fascists, 20; during
World War II, 19–20; in Europe, 18;
implications of for the Communist
movement, 18–19, 21; as a "negative
principle," 19; rhetoric/discourse of,
20–21
anti-Fascist resistance, 21–24; beginnings
of, 21–22; contested and monopolized
resistance, 23–24; ethical and political
value of, 24; number of Germans/
collaborationists killed by, 23; phases
of, 22–23
anti-imperialism, 24–28; Marxist economic
definition of, 25–26; and the Nationalist movement in French Indochina,
26; and the United States, 26; and the
Vietnam War, 27; worldwide Marxist
influence on, 26
"Anti-Imperialist Point of View, The"
(Mariátegui), 513
*Anti-Revolutionary Essence of Contemporary
Trotskyism, The* (Basmanov), 819
anti-Semitism, 28–29; and the "Doctors'
Case" against Jewish physicians, 28;
in Poland, 339; state anti-Semitism,
28–29; struggle against anti-Semitism
as Bolshevik policy, 28; under
Mussolini, 325; under Stalin 29; within
the Communist movement, 29
Antonescu, Ion, 213, 336
Antonov, Alexsandr, 845
Antonov-Ovseenko, Vladimir, 670
Apostol, Gheorghe, 92
"Appeal to the Peoples of the Whole World"
(1960), 418
April Theses (V. Lenin), 473
Aragon, Louis, 30–31, 485, 501, 574, 615
Aragones, Emilio, 242
Arbatov, Georgi, 702
Arbeitsjournal (Work Diary) (Brecht), 70, 71
Arbenz, Jacobo Guzman, 238, 370, 565
Arce, Bayardo, 696
architecture and urban planning, 31–34;
architecture and ideology of the "tall
buildings," 33; city planning following

the European model, 32; classical
period, 31; and the growth of cities,
31–32; and the idea of the Communist
city, 31; and the Situationist Interna-
tional movement, 33; and "spread-out"
cities, 32; and the Utopian ideal, 32;
worker housing, 33
Arendt, Hannah, 34–35, 806
Argentina, 324; Communist Party in, 196,
199; guerrilla warfare in, 369–70
Aricó, José, 199
Aristotle, 268, 473
Aristov, Boris, 518
Armand, Inessa, 855
Aron, Raymond, 806
Arrow in the Blue (Koestler), 456
Ash, Timothy Garton, 677
"Asian tigers," 544
Askoldov, Alexander, 109
At the Top of My Voice (Mayakovski), 529
atheism, Soviet, 35–37; atheist publications,
36; historical basis of, 35;
influence of the Bolshevik revolution
on, 36; influence of the Russian
nihilists on, 35; official state atheism,
36; scientific atheism, 36–37
Atlantic Charter (1941), 353
atomic bomb, 37–41, 354–55; bombing of
Hiroshima, 38; Chinese development
of, 40–41; development of (1939–45),
37–38; development of (1945–49),
38–39; development of the hydrogen
bomb, 39–40; difficulty of obtaining uranium for the building of, 39;
Soviet designs for both uranium and
plutonium bombs, 38–39
Australia. *See* **Communist Party in Australia
and New Zealand**
Austria, 313, 728, 852; Linz program (1926),
45. *See also* **Communist Party in
Austria**
avant-garde, 41–43; aesthetics of (*stiob*), 42;
and the concept of "procedure," 41; the
Left Front of the Arts, 41; "logic" of the
images circulated by, 42; reverse *stiob*,
42; Sots-art movement, 42
Avenarius, Richard, 494
Averbuch, Wolf, 187
Azaña, Manuel, 765, 766
Azimov, Bektash, 155
Azimov, Sarvar, 155

Baader, Andreas, 792
Baal (Brecht), 69
Babel, Isaac, 484, 710
Babeuf, Gracchus, 84, 427, 428
Bacilek, K., 295
Backbone Flute, The (Mayakovski), 528

Badhib, Abdullah, 229
Bahr, Egon, 275–76
Bakdash, Khalid, 201
Baklanov, Oleg, 241, 613
Baku Congress of Peoples of the East (1920),
186
Bakunin, Mikhail, 156
Balázs, Béla, 397
Balkan Communist Federation, 280
Balzac and French Realism (Lukács), 493
Bamatter, Siegfried, 224
Bandung Conference (1955), 259, 565, 585
Banzer, Hugo, 369
Barańczak, Stanisław, 464
Barbé, Henri, 197
Barone, Enrico, 618
Barontini, Ilio, 415
Barr, Joseph, 770
Barraclough, Geoffrey, 258
Barrientos, René, 372
Bartók, Béla, 397
Barton, Paul, 372
Bārzāni, Mullā Mustafà, 185
Bashtakov, Leonid, 440
Basmanov, M. I., 819
Basso, Lelio, 367
Basu, Jyoti, 181
Batamonh, Jambyn, 203
Batchelor, Joy, 596
Bathhouse, The (Mayakovski), 528–29
Batista, Fulgencio, 160, 244, 245, 366, 370
Battleship Potemkin, The (1925), 305
Baudelaire, Charles-Pierre, 11, 522
Bauer, Otto, 45–46, 443, 558–59, 735;
concept of "integral socialism," 46;
preoccupation with the Russian
Revolution and the construction of
socialism in the Soviet Union, 45
Baumann, Zygmunt, 308
Bay of Pigs invasion (1961), 88, 242, 245,
370
Bebel, August, 679
Bedbug, The (Mayakovski), 528–29
"Beginning of Bonapartism, The"
(V. Lenin), 428
Beijing Spring, 46–47
Béjar, Héctor, 368
Belgium, 22, 719. *See also* **Communist Party
in Belgium**
Belinsky, Vissarion, 483, 623
Bella, Ahmed Ben, 202, 371
Bellamy, Edward, 32
Belorussia, 22, 23
Bely, Andrei, 483
Benda, Václav, 95
Beneš, Eduard, 163, 645
Benjamin, Walter, 69, 522
Bentley, Elizabeth, 769

Beran, Josef, 90

Berdyayev, Nicholas A., 36, 412–13, 469, 470, 494

Berger-Barzilay, Yosef, 187

Beria, Lavrenty, 37, 38, 47–48, 167, 267, 275, 309, 376, 439, 440, 447, 448, 450, 500, 568, 626, 644, 665, 704, 709; as head of the Ministry of Internal Affairs, 47–48, 876; Stalin's patronage of, 47

Berlin Crisis of 1948–49, 48–49; the Berlin Blockade, 48, 49; U.S. airlift, 48, 49, 755

Berlin Crisis of 1958–61, 587–88

Berlin Wall, 49–51, 275, 597; the decision to build the wall, 50; fall of, 49, 51, 677; hardships imposed on the East German population by, 50; "the Wall in the Mind," 50

Berlinguer, Enrico, 6, 51–54, 79, 199, 221, 310–11, 312, 511; "austerity" formula, 52; "democratic alternative" strategy, 53; "for a Europe neither anti-Soviet nor anti-American" slogan, 51; "historic compromise" strategy, 51, 190. *See also* **Eurocommunism**

Berman, Jakub, 208

Bernášková, Alena, 485

Bernstein, Eduard, 196, 442, 470, 622, 641, 678, 679

Betancourt, Rómulo, 245, 367

Bethlen, István, 397

Better Fewer, But Better (V. Lenin), 80–81, 576

Bevan, Aneurin, 456

Bezbozhnik (Godless), 36

Bianco, Lucien, 106

Bibó, István, 399, 400

Biermann, Wolf, 394

Bierut, Bolesław, 54–55, 208, 338

bipolarity, 55–58; the bipolar Cold War structure (the U.S. bloc and the Soviet bloc), 57–58; conceptualizing bipolarity, 55–56; and the "superpowers" (the United States and the Soviet Union), 55. *See also* nonalignment; tripolarity; unipolarity

Bishop, Maurice, 697

Bitov, Andrei, 485

Blagoev, D., 149

Blanco, Hugo, 368

Blanqui, Louis Auguste, 427, 428

Blium, A. V., 93–94

Bloch, Richard, 30, 501

Blok, Alexander, 327, 483

Blount, Anthony, 768

Blum, Léon, 170, 636

Blum Theses (Lukács), 492

Bodnaraş, Emile, 213, 336

Bogdanov, Alexander A., 36, 60, 472, 494, 527, 580, 619, 653

Bogoluibov, N. S., 154

Bogomolov, Oleg, 685

Bohlen, Charles, 500

Bohm, David, 701

Boldin, Valeriy, 241

Bolivia, guerrilla warfare in, 369

Böll, Heinrich, 95

Bolshevik Central Committee, 690

Bolshevik Party, 19, 36, 816; and censorship, 93; role of trade unions in, 808–9; view of nationalism, 570

Bolshevik Revolution (1917), 36, 104, 257, 735; the international imperative of, 119

Bolsheviks, 5, 215, 381, 472, 473, 474, 604, 622, 641, 656, 763, 784, 798, 814, 847; ambivalence of toward utopian views, 830; banning of other political parties by, 651–52; invasion of Poland by, 814–15; legislation concerning the family, 317–18; as orthodox Marxists, 783; pantheon of Jacobin heroes, 428; propaganda of, 691; recurrent dissent among, 472; self-determination slogan, 570–71; use of film as a tool for political "education" 108; view of the proletariat, 115; on the "world revolution," 562–63. *See also* **Russian Revolution and Civil War** (1917); **war communism**

Bolshevism, 59–63, 816; the Bolshevik–Menshevik split, 59; fractionalism of, 62; goals of, 61; origins of, 59. *See also* **Bolsheviks; Bolshevization**

Bolshevization, 63–64, 123, 346, 349, 535, 609, 717, 795; appeal of to foreign Communists, 64; threat of to traditional working-class practices, 64

Bonaparte, Louis. *See* Napoleon III

Bonapartism, 64–65, 325; "bourgeois Bonapartism," 683; "Soviet Bonapartism," 683

Bonner, Elena, 289, 695

Book for Parents, A (Makarenko), 319

Borba (Struggle), 294

borders, 65–68; deportation of ethnic minorities from the Soviet Union, 67; Soviet border guards, 66, 67; Soviet border zone, 67; use of class and nationality to change borders, 66. *See also* **Berlin Wall**

Bordiga, Amadeo, 349, 801

Borejsza, Jerzy, 601

Borge, Tómas, 368, 696

Borkenau, Franz, 492

Bormann, Martin, 385

Borodin, Mikhail, 197

Bosnia. *See* **ethnic cleansing**

Boumedienne, Houari, 202, 586

Bramuglia, Juan, 49

Brandler, Heinrich, 173, 411, 412, 882

Brandt, Willy, 50, 53, 73, 276, 597–99, 736, 794

Braun, Otto, 491

Bravo, Douglas, 367, 368

Brazil: Communist Party in, 198; guerrilla warfare in, 369

Brecht, Bertolt, 68–71, 328, 485

Brest-Litovsk, Treaty of (1918), 62, 65, 71–72, 474, 650, 680, 689–90, 814, 842, 846–47

Breton, André, 30

Brezhnev, Leonid, 2, 3, 9, 52, 72–74, 83, 130, 154, 167, 216, 244, 246, 270, 276, 285, 287, 290, 340, 359, 366, 383, 419, 425, 448, 517, 519, 575, 585, 603, 612, 627, 639, 668, 849, 873; building of the Baikal-Amur railway (BAM), 812; "cadres' stability" policy, 74, 568; economic reforms of, 302–4; influence of World War II on, 73; lack of leadership qualities, 74; as the main architect of arms control agreements, 74; as the main architect of détente, 73, 74; physical decline of, 74; role of in the Prague Spring, 646, 647, 648. *See also* **Soviet bloc**

Brezhnev Doctrine, 74–75, 684, 685

Brief Course, The (Stalin), 883

Brinton, Crane, 291

Brison, Pierre, 615

British Road to Socialism, The (1951), 17, 632

Brodsky, Josef, 287, 485

Browder, Earl, 75–76, 160, 198, 224, 225, 366; policy of alliances, 76

"Browderism," 198, 513

Bruckus, B. D., 4

Bryusov, Valery, 528

Brzezinski, Zbigniew K., 34, 609, 610, 806

Buber-Neumann, Margarete, 374

Buchanan, George, 97

Buck, Tim, 198

Budyonny, Semyon, 625

Buena de Mesquita, Bruce, 55–56

Buffet, Marie-George, 172

Bugai, Nikolai, 267

Bujak, Zbigniew, 741

Bukharin, Nikolay, 5, 62, 76–79, 97, 113, 123, 123–24, 135, 137, 174, 278, 360, 380, 382, 409, 455, 458, 487, 503, 576, 577, 593, 619, 625, 626,

Bukharin, Nikolay (cont.)
690, 693, 705, 749, 804, 805, 818, 876; formulation of the "class against class" line, 78; opposition to the Brest-Litovsk Treaty, 650; "socialism in one country" policy, 651, 724. *See also* **socialism in one country**

Bukheykhanov, A., 154

Bukovsky, Vladimir, 286, 288

Bukower Elegien (Brecht), 71

Bulgakov, Michail, 484

Bulgakov, Sergius N., 4, 469, 470

Bulganin, Nikolay, 259, 626, 627

Bulgaria, 609, 684, 726, 744, 745, 757–58, 800, 865–66; postcommunism in, 639–40. *See also* **Communist Party in Bulgaria**

Bullejos, José, 219

Bulletin of the Opposition, 816, 819

Bund, the, 558, 559

Buonarotti, Philippe, 427

Burdenko, Nikolay, 441

bureaucracy, 79–82; czarist bureaucracy, 80; lack of scholarly examination of, 81–82; problems of in the Soviet system, 82; Soviet encouragement of the growth of, 81; Soviet leaders' poor understanding of, 81; types of Soviet control, 81

Burgess, Guy, 768

Burke, Edmund, 268

Burlyuk, David, 528

Bush, George H. W., 277, 614

Buzek, Jerzy, 742

Bykov, Rolan, 109

Cabanellas, Miguel, 765

Cabellero, Largo, 220, 764

Cabral, Amilcar, 259

Cadet Party ("Liberal" Party), 4

cadres (Russian: *kadry*), 83–84

Cairncross, John, 768

Calabresi, Luigi, 791

Calderío, Blas Roca, 160, 161

Cambodia, 675, 705, 730; famine in, 322. *See also* **Communist Party in Kampuchea; Khmer Rouge; Vietnam-Cambodia War**

Camp David Accords (1978), 565

Campaign for Nuclear Disarmament, 578

Campanella, Tommaso, 31, 831

Campbell, John, 632

camps, 84–87; common features of Communist and Nazi camps, 85; Communist systematic and long-term plans for, 85; Eastern European camps, 86; economic function of, 86; ideological function of, 85–86; Nazi extermination camps, 85; non-Communist camps,

84; origins of, 84; purpose of, 85. *See also* **gulag**

Camus, Albert, 698, 806

"Can the Bolsheviks Retain State Power?" (V. Lenin), 428

"Can 'Jacobinism' Frighten the Working Class?" (V. Lenin), 428

Canada, 353

Canción de gesta (Neruda), 575

Canovan, Margaret, 34

Canto a las madres de los milicianos muertos (Neruda), 574

Canto a Stalingrado (Neruda), 574

Canto general (Neruda), 574, 575

Capital (Marx), 60, 69, 492

capitalism, 7, 11, 18, 139, 278, 692, 705, 815; Marx's view of, 114, 749, 783. *See also* **collapse of capitalism**

Carazo, Jaime Morales, 697

Cardenal, Ernesto, 696

Cardona, José Miró, 245

Carlucci, Frank, 638

Carr, E. H., 139, 683, 749

Carrillo, Santiago, 52, 220, 221, 310–11, 511

Carrión, Luis, 696

Carter, Jimmy, 52, 74, 239, 247, 276, 312, 629

Carvalhas, Carlos, 211

Casanova, Laurent, 601

Casaroli, Agostino, 90, 91

Casati, Agostino, 415

Castro, Fidel, 87–89, 160, 161, 242–44, 244–46, 270, 366, 368, 370, 371, 510, 565, 629, 794; gifts as an orator, 87; *La historia me absolverá* (History Will Absolve Me) manifesto, 87; personality of, 87; relationship with the Soviets, 88; *socialismo o muerte* (socialism or death) slogan, 89; vague ideology of, 87. *See also* **Cuban missile crisis; Cuban Revolution; Cuban-Soviet intervention in Africa**

Castro, Raúl, 160, 161, 242, 245, 370

Catholic Church, 15, 89–91, 396; and Ostpolitik, 91; in Poland, 517

Caute, David, 328

Ce soir, 30

Ceaușescu, Helena, 92, 213, 686

Ceaușescu, Nicolae, 92, 213, 564, 686; cult of, 250; and "Nicolae Ceaușescu's era," 92

censorship, 92–94; and cinema, 109; and the development of mass media technologies, 94; editorial censorship, 94; forms of, 93; "ideological censorship," 94; self-censorship, 94; by the secret police, 94; as a tool of cultural control,

94. *See also* **Glavit (Central Directorate of Literature and Art)**

Centesimus Annus (John Paul II), 91

Central Committee Central Control Commission, 660

Central Committee Department of Agitation and Propaganda, 653

Central Committee of the Joint Union of Water and Rail Transport Workers, 811

Central Europe, 20

Central Intelligence Agency (CIA), 696, 824

Cerda, Pedro Aguirre, 574

Černík, Oldřich, 649

Cerny, Vaclav, 95

Cesarani, D., 456

Chamberlin, William Henry, 805

Chambers, Whitaker, 769

Chamorro, Violeta, 697

Chan, Anita, 252

Charter 77, 17, 95, 165

Chayanov, Alexander, 4, 5, 413

Chea, Nuon, 193

Cheka, 446, 474, 681, 690, 691, 784; growth of, 845. *See also* **Red Terror**

Cheka likbez, 480–81

"Cheka Trial" (1935), 411

Chelincev, Aleksandr, 4

Chen Boda, 253, 254, 503

Chen Kaige, 255

Chen Shaoyu, 197

Chen Yi, 714

Cherenkov, Pavel, 700

Chernenko, Konstantin, 154, 291, 339, 340, 341, 612, 627, 747

Chernobyl, catastrophe of, 96, 342

Chernyshevsky, Nikolay G., 35, 483, 580, 623

Chervenkov, V., 151

Chiang Kai-shek (Jiang Jieshi), 25, 156, 387, 490, 504, 505, 563, 847

Chibás, Eddy, 87

Chicherin, Georgy, 96–97, 283–84, 667; program for Soviet foreign policy, 602; view of the Soviet Union's global policies, 97

China (People's Republic of), 25, 31, 259, 563–64, 565, 643, 653, 674, 727, 729–30, 772; exit of from the Soviet bloc, 57, 58; famine in, 321; "four modernizations" in, 98; "market socialism" of, 810; marriage law in, 319; modernization of after Mao's death, 545; nationality policies of, 569–70; postcommunism in, 640; the Rectification Campaign (1941–44), 107; trade unions in, 810; and the United Nations, 826. *See also* **China's armed forces; Chinese agrarian policies;**

Chinese revolution (1911–49); **Communist Party in China** (CCP, or Zhongguo gongchandang); **Cultural Revolution in China; Great Leap Forward; Sino-Soviet split; socialist market economy**

China-Vietnam War, 97–98

China's armed forces, 98–101; the army, 99; and the civil-military relationship, 100–101; history and ideology of, 98–99, 847; the navy, 99; the nuclear force, 99; organization and doctrine of, 99; the supreme command (Central Military Commission), 99; and the transformation strategy, 99–100. *See also* **People's Liberation Army (China)**

China's Destiny (Chiang Kai-shek), 505

Chinese agrarian policies, 101–4; "household contracting," 103; under Mao Zedong, 102–3

Chinese revolution (1911–49), 104–8; collapse of the old and aborted attempts to give birth to the new (1911–27), 104–5; legacies of, 107; surviving in the countryside and building political power (1927–49), 105–7

Chişinevschi, Iosif, 213, 336

Choibalsan, Khorloogiin, 203

Chojecki, Miroslaw, 464

Chombe, Moise, 371

Christ Has Risen Again (Bely), 483

"Christian Democracy" parties, 15

Chronicle of Current Events, 287–88, 289

Chubar, Vlas, 626

Chudík, Michal, 295

Chulkov, Georgy, 483

Church and the Left, The (Michnik), 534

Churchill, Winston, 275, 352, 353, 354, 364. *See also* **Yalta Conference**

Chvyl'ovyj, Mykola, 392, 484

Ciano, Galeazzo, 325

Cienfuegos, Camilo, 245, 370

cinema, Soviet, 108–10. *See also* **Eisenstein, Sergei**

Circle "Vperëdm" 153

Citaku, Ramadan, 144

citizenship, 110–14; affiliation, 111–12; rights and obligations, 112–14; theoretical profile, 110–11

Citrine, Walter, 421

class, 605

"Class Struggles in France, The" (Marx), 64

classes, 114–17; the intelligentsia, 115; the peasantry, 115; the proletariat, 114–15

Claudín, Fernando, 221

Clay, Lucius, 51

Clayton, William, 515

clientelism, 117–19; and the nomenklatura system, 117, 584–85

Cliff, Tony, 414

Cloud in Trousers, A (Mayakovski), 528

Codovilla, Vittorio, 196, 197, 219, 220, 513

Cogniot, Georges, 313

Cohen, Stephen, 139, 808

Cohn, Ludwik, 464

Colby, William, 246

Cold War, 8, 13, 16, 17, 20, 119–23; 327, 539, 540, 544, 610, 697, 719, 753, 754, 870, 871; the arms race as a central component of, 459; challenges to, 121–22; characteristics of Communist parties during, 149; effect on the unity of trade unions, 421; empirical assessment of power politics during, 643–45; end of, 122; ideology-based explanations for, 642–43; and the post-Stalin era, 120; and Stalinism, 119–20; and the third world, 121, 794; and the Vietnam War, 834. *See also* **Berlin Wall; bipolarity; détente; Korean War; military-industrial complex; Second Cold War; totalitarianism**

"Cold War liberals," 14

collapse of capitalism, 123–25

Collectivist Economic Planning (von Hayek), 618

collectivization of the countryside, 125–28, 266, 373, 656, 671, 774; in Eastern Europe, 128; in the Soviet Union, 126–28, 605–6

Collins, Randall, 290

Colombia, guerrilla warfare in, 368

colonialism, 222, 408

Comecon, 67, 88, 128–31, 727–28, 729, 729–30; abolishment of, 730; *Basic Principles of the International Socialist Division of Labor,* 130; and "socialist economic integration," 130

Cominform, 67, 131–34, 355, 609, 610, 633, 727, 777, 779

Comintern, 18, 19–20, 25, 30, 119, 123–24, 134–38, 150, 156, 162, 173, 207, 212, 219, 280, 345, 346, 563, 633, 691, 779; "class against class" tactics, 135; dealings with Ho Chi Minh, 387; disbanding of the Communist Party in Korea, 194; dissolution of the Communist Party in Poland, 207; during World War II, 282, 862–63; Euro-Asian orientation of, 197; "leftward" shift of, 188; major controversies surrounding, 137; the Popular Front policy, 136, 162, 281,

607, 634–36; promulgation of Communist internationalism, 423; "social fascism" theory, 135; Stalin's dissolving of, 282; "Twenty-one Conditions on Entry" (1920), 63, 135; "united workers' front" tactics, 173. *See also* **Popular Front; social fascism**

command economy, the, 138–42, 543; accomplishments of, 141; failures and weaknesses of, 141; market or quasi-market elements of, 140; "war communism," 139, 537–39, 575

Commissariat of Enlightenment, 93

Commission international contre le régime concentrationnaire, 372

Committee for Human Rights, 288

Common Market. *See* European Economic Community (EEC)

communism, 11; core features of Soviet communism, 644–45; as a "field" of world forces, 736; international communism, 19; the link between communism and nationalism, 200, 564. *See also* **anticommunism; war communism**

Communist autobiography, 142–44; as analogous to Christian confession, 142–43; framework for under Stalin, 143–44

Communist Manifesto, The, 65, 423, 533, 558, 638–39, 755

Communist Party Congresses: Fifth Congress (1907), 773, 793; Eighth Congress (1919), 537; Fifteenth Congress (1927), 546; Fourteenth Congress (1925), 724, 725; Nineteenth Congress (1952), 564; Second Congress (1903), 813; Seventh Congress (1935), 634, 635; Tenth Congress (1921), 546, 656, 838; Third Congress (1926), 349–50; Twentieth Congress (1956), 40, 397, 417, 560, 666, 704, 714; Twenty-eighth Congress (1990), 612; Twenty-second Congress (1961), 839; Twenty-seventh Congress (1986), 603, 873

Communist Party in Albania, 144–45

Communist Party in Australia and New Zealand, 145–46

Communist Party in Austria, 146–48

Communist Party in Belgium, 148–49, 280

Communist Party in Bulgaria, 149–53

Communist Party in Central Asia, 153–55

Communist Party in China, 25–26, 155–60, 402–3, 504–5, 506–8, 672, 673, 686; agrarian policies of, 101–4; and the Chinese revolution, 104–7; from 1921 to 1949, 156–57;

Communist Party in China (cont.)
from 1949 to 2004, 157–59; the "holy
trinity" organization of, 106; organization of, 159; relationship with China's
armed forces, 98–101
Communist Party in Cuba, 160–62, 198
Communist Party in Czechoslovakia,
162–66, 295, 296, 297, 345, 346, 347,
400–401, 645–46
Communist Party in East Germany,
166–68
Communist Party in Finland, 168–69
Communist Party in France, 12, 30,
169–72, 311, 313–14, 561, 778, 795–96;
and the welfare state, 383–39
Communist Party in Germany, 15, 172–75,
720; underground Communist Party
of Germany, 22, 411, 479, 563, 717, 754,
793, 823, 881, 882
Communist Party in Great Britain, 175–77,
631–32, 717
Communist Party in Greece, 177–78, 719
Communist Party in Hungary, 178–80,
666
Communist Party in the Indian Subcontinent, 180–82
Communist Party in Indonesia, 182–85
Communist Party in Iran, 185–86
Communist Party in Israel, 186–87
Communist Party in Italy, 5, 6, 8, 51–53,
187–91, 314, 561, 633, 681, 736, 778;
condemnation of the Soviet invasion of
Afghanistan, 6; founding of, 801; orien-
tations toward Europe and détente,
51; position of in Italian society, 803;
and the "Salerno Turn," 6, 802; and
terrorism, 790–91; and the welfare
state, 852, 853
Communist Party in Japan, 191–92
Communist Party in Kampuchea, 192–94
Communist Party in Korea, 194–96
Communist Party in Latin America,
196–200
Communist Party in the Middle East and
the Maghreb, 200–203
Communist Party in Mongolia, 203
Communist Party in the Netherlands,
204–5
Communist Party in the Nordic Countries
and the Baltics, 205–6
Communist Party in Poland, 206–10, 338,
747
Communist Party in Portugal, 210–12
Communist Party in Romania, 212–13
Communist Party in Southeast Asia,
213–14
Communist Party in the Soviet Union,
24, 36, 214–19, 291–92, 644, 686,

734, 819, 874, 875, 876; democratic
centralism as the key principle of,
216–17, 639; name changes of,
215; and the nomenklatura system,
216, 584–85; party discipline, 217;
party funding, 219; party membership, 218–19; as the party in power,
215–16; party organization, 639;
party structure and functioning,
217–18; the party's role, 218
Communist Party in Spain, 219–21, 719,
765, 767; bloques populares strategy,
220
Communist Party in sub-Saharan Africa,
221–24
Communist Party in Switzerland, 223–24
Communist Party in the United States,
75, 76, 224–25, 769; "Americaniza-
tion" policy, 75, 224; dissolution of by
Browder, 76; as "the party of the New
Deal," 76, 225
Communist Party in Vietnam, 225–28;
name changes of, 226
Communist Party in Yemen, 228–30
Communist Party in Yugoslavia, 230–33,
745, 798–99
Communist Political Association, 76, 225
Communist (Third) International. See
Comintern
Comorera, Joan, 220
"Concerning the Enemies of the People"
(V. Lenin), 428
Conference for the Foundation of the
Organización latinoamericana de
solidaridad, 367–68
Conference of Oppressed Peoples, 794
Conference on Security and Cooperation in
Europe, 233–35, 276, 277, 284, 588
Congo crisis (1960), 222, 827
Congreso internacional de las democracias
(1939), 574; "Toda América contra el
fascismo" slogan, 574
Conquest, Robert, 393, 749
Constantinescu, Miron, 213, 336
constitutions, 235–36
containment, 236–40; key goals of, 236
Conversations with Stalin (Djelas), 294
Coolidge, Calvin, 15
Coordinating Committee for Military
Affairs (Soviet Union), 727
Copic, Vladimir, 230, 415
Corbière, Tristan, 528
Correlates of War project, 55
Council for Mutual Economic Assistance.
See Comecon
Council of Foreign Ministers, 354, 872;
failure of, 355
coup in the USSR (1991), 240–42

Craxi, Bettino, 719
Crick, Bernard, 596
Crisis of Social Democracy, The (Luxemburg),
496
Critical Notes on the Economic Development
of Russia (Struve), 470
Critique of the Gotha Programme (Marx),
112
Croatia, 22
Croce, Benedetto, 5, 492, 523
Croizat, Ambroise, 852–53
Cuba, 544, 643, 772; adult literacy cam-
paign in, 481; and guerrilla warfare,
367–68. See also Communist Party in
Cuba (Partido comunista de Cuba);
Cuban Revolution; Cuban-Soviet
intervention in Africa
Cuban missile crisis (1962), 88, 121, 198,
242–44, 588
Cuban Revolution, 244–46, 367, 370;
causes of, 244–45
Cuban-Soviet intervention in Africa,
246–48
Cui Zhiyuan, 508
cult of personality, 248–50, 269–70, 271
cultural policies, 250–52. See also New
Economic Policy; perestroika
Cultural Revolution in China, 83, 103,
107, 121, 158, 252–55, 269, 506, 570,
675; cultivation of the "Four News,"
253; definitions of, 252; documentaries about, 255; the fight against the
"Four Olds," 253; films about, 255; first
phase, 253; interpretation of, 254–55;
origin of, 252–53; second phase,
253–54; subdivisions of, 252; third
phase, 254
culture, 605
Cumings, Bruce, 629
Cunhal, Álvaro, 211, 311, 637
Currie, Lauchlin, 769
Czapski, Jósef, 441
Czechoslovak Communist Party, 646, 648,
649
Czechoslovakia, 22, 609, 674, 684, 685,
686, 729, 745, 746, 761, 848–49, 850,
851, 852; nationality policies of, 568;
as a People's Democracy, 608, 610;
Soviet invasion of, 27, 419, 588. See also
Communist Party in Czechoslovakia;
Prague Coup; Prague Spring
Czernin, Ottokar, 71

Daily Worker, 176
Daix, Pierre, 30
Daladier, Édouard, 502, 616
Dallin, Alexander, 826
Damaskinos, Anastasios, 364

Damianov, Raiko, 415

Daniel, Yuli, 30, 287, 485, 743

Danieluk-Ştefanski, Alexander, 212

Danzig Accords (1980), 113

Darkness at Noon (Koestler), 456

Dashichev, Vyacheslav, 685

David, Jacques-Louis, 329

Davis, Nathaniel, 824

de Balzac, Honoré, 492

de Benoist, Alain, 13

de Carvalho, Apolhonio, 369

de Carvalho, Otelo de, 637, 638

de Gaulle, Charles, 170–71, 275, 313–14, 452, 502, 588, 796

de Maistre, Joseph, 11

de Man, Henri, 148

de Nagybánya, Horthy, 665

De profundis (From the Depths) (Berdayev et al.), 470

de Saint-Simon, Henri, 31, 830–31

De Sanctis, Francesco, 523

de Sousa, Jerónimo, 211

de Spínola, António, 637, 638

de Tocqueville, Alexis, 291

De Tribune, 204

Deakin, Arthur, 421

Déat, Marcel, 615

Debayle, Anastasio Somoza, 696

Debayle, Luís Somoza, 696

Debord, Guy, 33

Deborin, Abram, 527

Debray, Régis, 367, 629

Declaration of the Rights of the Exploited and Working People (January 1919), 113

Declaration of Rights of Russia's Peoples (1917), 111

Decline of Capitalism, The (Preobrazhensky), 651

decollectivization, 606–7

decolonization, 27, 222, 257–60, 269; contradictory nature of, 258; geographic itinerary of, 259; outcome of, 258–59

Decree on Nationalities (1917), 65

dekulakization, 127, 266, 309, 373, 462–63, 605–6

del Carril, Delia, 574

de-Maoization, 264, 403

democratic centralism, 260–61, 639

Democratic Party (United States), 16

Democratic Republic of Vietnam, 834, 835

demographic policies, 261–63; of the Bolsheviks, 261–62; of Eastern European countries, 263; of Stalinism, 262

Deng Xiaoping, 114, 156, 158,159, 252, 254, 263–65, 403, 490, 491, 506, 515, 672, 737, 859; opposition to the cult of personality, 265; political ideology of, 265; pragmatism of, 265

Deng Xiaoping Theory (*deng xiaoping lilun*), 265, 431

Denikin, Anton, 690, 691, 845

Denmark, 22; Communist Party in, 205, 206

deportation of nationalities in the USSR, 265–68. *See also* **collectivization of the countryside; dekulakization**

Derrida, Jacques, 13

Déry, Tibor, 397

Derzhavin, Gavrila, 528

despotism, 268–70; "enlightened despotism," 269

d'Escoto, Miguel, 696

d'Estaing, Valéry Giscard, 276

de-Stalinization, 67, 248, 270–74, 603, 781, 782, 786; definition of, 271; as a policy, 271

Destruction of Reason, The (Lukács), 493

détente, 274–78, 366, 586

Deutscher, Isaac, 683

developing countries. *See* third world

Development of Capitalism in Russia, The (V. Lenin), 471

Dewey, John, 817

Dherzhinsky, Felix, 693

Di Vittorio, Giuseppe, 314, 415, 422, 803

Dialectic of Enlightenment (Adorno and Horkheimer), 522

Dialectical and Historical Materialism (Stalin), 527

Dialectics of Nature (Engels), 527

Diary (Dimitrov), 20

Díaz, José, 219, 220

Dichel, Friedrich, 415

dictatorship of the proletariat, 278–79

Die Geschäfte des Herrn Julius Caesar (Brecht), 70

Die Gleichheit (Equality), 881

Die Maßnahme (Brecht), 69

Die Mutter (Brecht), 70

Die Rote Fahne (The Red Flag), 147, 172

Dimitrov, Georgi, 18, 19, 136, 150, 151, 197, 224, 279–83, 501, 503, 507, 549, 560, 607–8, 610, 634, 753, 757–58, 776, 796, 799, 802; and Comintern, 280–82, 634, 635; control of Communist parties, 282; cult of, 250; exile of, 282; as prime minister of Bulgaria, 282–83; self-education of, 279; and Stalin, 281–82; as a symbol of the fight against Nazism, 281; view of fascism, 326

Ding Ling, 505

diplomats, 283–86

dissent in the USSR, 286–89

dissolution of the USSR, 290–93; the implications of Gorbachev's reforms, 290–92; unexpected nature of, 290

"Distance Beyond Distance" (Tvardovsky), 451

Dith Pran, 453

Dittmer, Lowell, 489

"Dizziness from Success" (Stalin), 127

Djilas, Milovan, 80, 232, 293–95, 415, 438, 507; view of the intelligentsia, 414

Do Muoi, 228

Dobb, Maurice, 618

Dobrovol'sky, Aleksei, 287

Dobrolyubov, Nikolaj, 483

Dobrynin, Anatoly, 285

Doctor Mabuse (1922), 304

"Doctors' Plot," 268, 272, 310, 448

Documentary Basis for the Katyn Crime, A (1948), 441

Doina, Ş. A., 486

Dollfuss, Engelbert, 45, 147, 443

Dombrowski, Arthur, 224

Domenach, Jean-Marie, 13

"domino" effect, 238

Dong Du (Eastern Travel) movement, 386

Donskoj, Dmitry, 359

Doriot, Jacques, 170, 796

Dostoyevsky, Fyodor, 483

Down and Out in Paris and London (Orwell), 595

Dr. Zhivago (Pasternak), 451, 484

Dreigroschenopera (Brecht), 69

Drobner, Bolesław, 441

Drozzhin, Vladimir, 484

Dubček, Alexander, 165, 295–98, 379, 401, 746; role of in the Prague Spring, 646–47, 648, 649

Dubvrosky, Sergei, 526

Duclos, Jacques, 76

Dudincev, Vladimir, 485

Dulles, John Foster, 238, 399

Duma, the, 4

Dumbarton Oaks Conference (1944), 353

Duncker, Hermann, 69

D'une jeunesse européenne (About a European Youth) (Malraux), 501

Dutt, Rajani Palme, 176, 631, 632

Dzierzhinskii, Feliks, 207, 298–99, 446, 593, 845; influence of Catholicism on, 298; underground career of, 299

East Germany (German Democratic Republic), 276, 393, 394, 486, 598, 599, 609, 684, 685, 728, 823, 850. *See also* **Berlin Crisis of 1948–49; Berlin Wall; Communist Party in East Germany**

Eastern Europe, 2, 10, 15, 20, 31; anti-Semitism in, 28–29; collectivization in, 128

Ebert, Friedrich, 411

Economic and Philosophical Manuscripts of 1844 (Marx), 492
Economic Problems of Socialism in the USSR (Stalin), 620, 777, 781
economic reforms, 301–4; "industrial unions," 303; obligatory indexes, 303
Economic Surveys, 618
"Economics of the Transition Period, The" (Bukharin), 77
Eden, Anthony, 364
Egypt, 257, 259, 565; Communist Party in, 201
Ehrenburg, Ilya, 484
Eiche, R., 626
"Eighteenth Brumaire of Louis Bonaparte, The" (Marx), 64
Einstein, Albert, 69
Eisenhower, Dwight D., 11, 120, 238, 245, 275, 398, 539, 714, 834
Eisenstein, Sergei, 108, 304–6, 329, 501; aborted projects of, 305; theory of filmmaking, 305
Ejército de liberación nacional, 368, 368–69
Ejército revolucionario del pueblo, 369
elections, 306–7
Eleventh Thesis on Feurbach (Brecht), 70
Éluard, Paul, 30, 601
Emilia, Reggio, 791
Empiriomonism (Bogdanov), 60
"Emulation and Labour Enthusiasm of the Masses" (Stalin), 733
enemies of the people, 307–8, 318
Engels, Friedrich, 28, 32, 110, 111, 139, 278, 423, 427, 527, 558, 580, 683, 739; rejection of pacifism by, 846; on the role of great men in history, 249; theories on the bourgeois family, 261
Enkhbayar, Nambaryn, 203
Enough Simplicity for Every Wise Man (1923), 302
Eörsi, István, 492
Erāni, Taqī, 185
Erfurt Program, 851
Erhard, Ludwig, 597
Erofeev, Victor, 485
Esenin, Sergej, 484
Eshliman, Nikolai, 594–95
Essays on Realism (Lukács), 493
Estonia, 205
Ethiopia, 222, 223, 247, 566; famine in, 322
ethnic cleansing, 308–10, 334; distinguished from genocide, 308. *See also* dekulakization
Eurocommunism, 52, 53, 58, 221, 279, 310–13, 511; Soviet reaction against, 312

Eurocommunism and the State (Carrillo), 311
Europe, 11; American influence in, 12; anti-communism in, 14, 15. *See also* Central Europe; Eastern Europe; Western Europe
European Advisory Commission, 353
European Economic Community (later European Community), 58, 234, 313–15
European integration, 313–15
European Trade Union Confederation, 422
Euskadi Ta Askatasuna (Basque Homeland and Freedom), 790
Ezhov, Nikolai, 447, 456, 802

Fadeev, Aleksandr, 484, 601, 739
Fajon, Étienne, 134
Fall of Berlin, The (Caureli), 779
family, 317–20; and the *besprizorniki* phenomenon, 318; Bolsheviks' legislation concerning, 317–18; in China, 319; divorce rate in the Soviet Union, 318; Lenin's view of, 317; post-Stalin rediscovery of, 319–30; Stalin's ambivalence toward, 318–19
famine under communism, 320–23; African famines, 322; Chinese famines, 321–22; external famines, 320; Indochinese famines, 322; internal famines, 320; North Korean famine, 323; Russian and Soviet famines, 320–21, 606. *See also* **Holodomor**
Farcy, Jean-Claude, 84
fascism, 5, 15, 323–26; militarizing of politics and society, 325; the myth of Fascist corporatism, 325; opposition of to all purposes and ideologies, 324
Fatherland Front, 150–51
Fathers and Sons (Turgenev), 483
Feldman, G., 619
fellow travelers, 327–28; during the Cold War, 327–28; first wave, 327; second wave, 327
Ferry, Jules, 408
festivals, 329–30; celebration of forebears of the October Revolution, 329; May Day, 329; in Moscow, 329; parades and demonstrations, 330; in Petrograd, 329; Stalin's 50th birthday, 330
Feuchtwanger, Lion, 328
Fichte, Johann Gottlieb, 492
Fick, Vladimir, 701
Filarete, 31
Filpovic, Filip, 230
Finance Capital (Hilferding), 380, 409
Finland, 1, 2, 744; and the Winter War, 853–54. *See also* **Communist Party in Finland**
Firmenich, Mario Eduardo, 369

First Circle, The (Solzhenitsyn), 614
First Congress of Nonaligned Countries (1961), 585–86
First International, 846
Fischer, Ruth, 173
Fitz-Gibbon, Louise, 441
Fitzpatrick, Sheila, 807–8
five-year plans, 7, 32, 41–42, 125, 126, 157, 302, 303, 330–32, 344, 345, 406, 620; abandonment of in the global free market economy, 332; core of, 330–31; as general guides rather than operational plans, 332; manipulation of plan indicators to show fulfillment of, 345; underestimation of resources, output, growth of the labor force, and growth of production, 331, 331–32; why a five-year period was chosen, 330
foibe massacres, 332–34
Fomin, Aleksander, 243
Foot, Michael, 456
Foote, Alexander, 768
For Lasting Peace and People's Democracy! 132, 133, 610
For Marx (Althusser), 523
Forcella, Enzo, 13
Fordism, 12, 351, 524
Foriş, Ştefan, 212, 213, 336
Foster, William, 225
Fourier, Charles, 31, 156, 830
Fourth International, 278, 817–18, 819–20
France, 15, 16, 17, 22, 719, 863; and the welfare state, 853–53. *See also* **Communist Party in France**
Franck, Sebastian, 492
Franco, Francisco, 136, 220, 311, 325, 561, 636. *See also* **Spanish Civil War**
Frank, Semën, 469, 470
Free German Labor Union, 753
Free German Youth, 753
Frei, Josef, 147
French Indochina, 26, 834, 835
Frente Amplio Opositor, 696
Frente de liberación nacional, 367
Frente Sandinista de liberación nacional, 696
Freund, Bernard, 211
Freund, Wilma, 211
Fried, Eugen, 224, 796
Friedrich, Carl J., 34, 806
From the Histories of Honor in Poland (Michnik), 535
Front de l'Indépendance, 148
Front of the Arts, 484
Front rouge (Aragon), 30
Frunze, Mikhail V., 154, 670
Fuchs, Klaus, 39, 769

Fuenmayor, Juan Bautista, 198
Fuerzas armadas revolucionarias, 368, 369
Fuks, Ladislav, 486
Fund to Aid Political Prisoners and Their
     Families, 289
Fundamental Principles of Marxism-Leninism
     (Kuusinen), 465
Fundamentals of Criminal Law (1958), 448
Furet, François, 328
Fuwa, Tetsuz, 192

Gaddis, John, 643–44
Gafurov, Babajan, 154
Gagarin, Yury, 335–36; as a model citizen of
     the Soviet Union, 335; as a symbol of
     Soviet technical modernization, 335
Gaidor, Yegor, 343
Gaitskell, Hugh, 275
Galanskov, Yuri, 286, 287
Galich, Aleksandr, 287, 485
Galtieri, Leopoldo, 370
Gamsakhurdia, Zviad, 708
Gandhi, 26; "Quit India" policy, 180
"Gang of Four," 158, 252, 264
Gapon, G. A., 35
Gapurov, M. N., 154, 155
García, Anastasio Somoza, 696
García Lorca, Federico, 574
Garnham, David, 56
Garvey, Marcus, 386
Gas Masks (1924), 302
Gastev, Aleksei, 580, 831
Gaviria, César, 369
Geertz, Clifford, 605
Geldenhuys, Jannie, 247
General Confederation of Trade Unions,
     422–23
genocide, 308, 392
Genscher, Hans-Dietrich, 598, 677
Georges, Pierre, 416
Georgescu, Teohari, 213, 336
Georgia, 708; corruption in, 707
Gerasimov, Gennadiy, 614
German Economic Commission, 754
German Ideology, The (Marx and Engels),
     580
German National Socialism, 34, 35
German Social Democratic Party, 478–79,
     851
German-Soviet Nonaggression Pact
     (1939), 70
German Sozialistischer Deutscher Student-
     bund, 578
German Union for Peace (Deutsche Frie-
     densunion), 578
Germany, 15, 17, 20, 23, 563, 852; insurrec-
     tion in, 411–12; postcommunism in,
     640; right-wing nationalism in, 15;

under the Nazis, 18, 19, 22, 626. *See
     also* **Communist Party in Germany;
     reunification of Germany; Soviet oc-
     cupation of Germany**
Gerő, Ernő, 336, 398, 399
Gheorghiu-Dej, Gheorghe, 92, 213,
     336–37
Ghioldi, Orestes, 196
Giap, Nguyen, 847
Gibianskii, Leonid, 610
Gide, André, 328, 501, 502, 574
Gierek, Edward, 209, 210, 270, 337–38,
     514, 740–41; "Building a New
     Poland" slogan, 337
Gilpin, Robert, 56
Ginzburg, Aleksandr, 286, 287, 287, 288,
     289
Ginzburg, Yevgenia, 85, 287, 374
Giorgio, Francesco di, 31
Giral, José, 764
Gladkov, Fyodor, 484
glasnost, 291, 341, 582
Glavit (Central Directorate of Literature
     and Art), 93, 94, 382
Glinka, Mikhail, 756
Glucksmann, André, 698
Glumov's Diary (1923), 302
Gobetti, Piero, 512, 681
God That Failed, The (Koestler), 456
Goebbels, Joseph, 440, 551
Goethe and His Time (Lukács), 493
Gold, Harry, 770
Gollan, John, 176
Gollancz, Victor, 595, 596
Golos, Jacob, 769
Gomes, Costa, 638
Gomułka, Władysław, 54, 55, 131, 132,
     208, 209, 270, 337, 338–39, 399, 610,
     647; independent spirit of, 338
Gonçalves, Bento, 211, 638
González Videla, Gabriel, 574
Good! (Mayakovski), 528
Goodman, Paul, 13
Gopalan, A. K., 181
Gorbachev, Mikhail, 2, 9, 10, 40, 46, 79,
     89, 91, 122, 130, 149, 152, 157, 167,
     172, 210, 234, 239, 241, 240–41,
     261, 289, 319–20, 339–44, 366, 383,
     394, 420, 430, 441, 445, 566, 568,
     573, 582–83, 585, 595, 599, 603,
     628, 659, 668, 703, 707, 736, 843,
     870; advocacy of "political pluralism,"
     582, 612, 747–48; awards given to,
     340; break with Yeltsin, 873–74; as a
     "child of the Twentieth Congress," 452;
     "common European home" concept,
     583; education of, 340; failures of,
     343; foreign policy of, 644; influence

of Eurocommunism on, 53; and the
     Khrushchev Dilemma, 685–86; and
     NATO, 589; "New Thinking" on
     security, 850; policies of toward Eastern
     Europe, 684–85, 686–87; propos-
     als on disarmament, 277; reforms of
     ("democratization"), 82, 216, 290–93,
     331, 341–43, 423, 639; and the
     reunification of Germany, 676–78;
     successes of, 343; why the politburo
     members voted for him, 339; and
     the press, 653. *See also* glasnost; **New
     Thinking; perestroika**
Gorbachev, Raisa, 340
Gorbanevskaya, Natalya, 288
Gorev, B. I., 428
Gorkić, Milan, 230, 798
Gorky, Maxsim, 36, 383, 483, 494, 501, 739,
     740
Gosplan, 344–45; fundamental problems
     faced by, 345; and planning "from the
     achieved level," 345
Gottwald, Klement, 162, 163, 164, 345–48,
     415, 514, 590, 645–46; exile of, 346;
     ideological and political dependence
     on the Soviet Union, 346, 347; political
     skill of, 347; relationship with Rudolf
     Slánský, 716–17; submissiveness toward
     the Soviet Union, 346, 347; as a symbol
     of the Communist Party in Czechoslo-
     vakia, 347
Goulart, Joao, 369
Goulding, Marrack, 248
Grabski, Tadeusz, 517
Gramsci, Antonio, 5, 7, 137, 160, 176, 188,
     199, 348–52, 406, 492, 513, 521–22, 523,
     801, 802; arrest and imprisonment of,
     350; focus on the southern question,
     349; on the role of the "superstruc-
     tures," 522; view of fascism, 326, 349,
     351–52
Grand Alliance, The, 352–56; clash over
     opening an Anglo-American second
     front in France, 353; clash over
     Poland, 353–54; decisive events
     in the formation of, 353
"Great April Revolution," 1
Great Britain, 15, 16, 37, 353, 643, 718, 719,
     852, 863. *See also* **Communist Party in
     Great Britain**
Great Crash (1929), 124
Great Depression, 15
Great Leap Forward (1958–60), 102–3, 157,
     252, 264, 356–58, 506, 544, 714
Great Patriotic War, 358–60
Great Purge(s), 9, 19, 207, 571, 659, 811
Great Soviet Encyclopedia, The, 84, 428, 683,
     756, 819

Index

Great Terror (1936–38), 136, 188, 307, 360–63, 374, 436, 543, 547, 581, 756, 775, 786, 802, 876, 883; challenged by "Revisionist" historians, 360; diplomats as targets of, 285; "On Anti-Soviet Elements" order, 361; "On the Liquidation of Polish Diversionary-Espionage Groups," 361; Order No. 00447 ("On the Utilization of Repression against Former Kulaks, Criminals, and Other Anti-Soviet Elements"), 361, 362; Order No. 00486, 361; and Soviet archival documents, 360, 361, 362–63

Great Turn (1930s), 543, 544

Grechko, Andrei, 647, 649

Greece, 22, 324, 863, 864, 865. *See also* **Communist Party in Greece; Greek Civil War**

Greek Civil War, 363–65; round I, 363–64; round II, 364; round III, 364–65

Greenglass, David, 770

Gregory, Paul, 139

Grishin, Viktor, 291, 341, 612, 648, 873

Groen Links (Green Left), 205

Gromsky, Ivan, 739

Gromyko, A. A., 548

Gromyko, Andrei, 9, 285–86, 341, 365–66, 452, 517, 707, 787; diplomatic style of, 366; focus on the United States and Great Britain, 366; lack of fluency in English, 365; as "Mr. Nyet," 366

Gropius, Walter, 69

Gross, Babetta, 551

Grossman, Vasily, 484

Grósz, Károly, 434

Grotewohl, Otto, 166, 617, 754

Group of Social Democrats of Ashkhabad, 153

Group of Soviet Occupation Forces in Germany, 753, 755

Groys, Boris, 42

Groza, Petru, 213

Grudzinski, Herling, 485

Grushin, Boris, 659

Guatemala, 565; guerrilla warfare in, 368

guerrilla warfare in Latin America, 366–70

Guevara, Moisés, 371–72

Guevara de la Serna, Ernesto Rafael "Che," 87, 198, 242, 244, 245, 366–67, 367, 370–72, 574, 790, 794, 847; the impossibility for him to realize his strategic objectives, 371–72; influence on the Cuban Revolution, 370; as the principal theorist of the anti-imperialist guerrilla experience, 367

gulag, 372–77; climax and crisis, 375–76; concentration camp complexes, 373–74; end of, 376; the "great turn" in the 1930s, 373–74; the gulag before the gulag, 372–73; the prisoners' world, 374–75

Gulag Archipelago, The (Solzhenitsyn), 16, 287, 289, 372, 614, 806

Gumilëv, Nikolaj, 484, 485

Guomindang, 562, 564, 663

Gutierrez, Gustavo, 368

Guttmann, J., 346

Guzmán, Abimael, 368

Gylling, Edvard, 168

Gysi, Gregor, 167

Haase, Hugo, 496

"Hacia una teologia de la liberación" (Toward a Theology of Liberation) (Gutierrez), 368

Hadji, Messali, 200

Hager, Kurt, 167

Hai Rui's Destination (1960), 252

Haing Ngor, 453

Hájek, Jiří, 95

Halas, John, 596

Hall, Peter, 32

Halliday, Jon, 491

Hallstein doctrine, 597

Harding, N., 427

Harich, Wolfgang, 167

Harnack, Arvid, 768

Hatta, Mohammed, 564

Hauspostille (Brecht), 69

Havana Conference (1979), 586

Havel, Václav, 95, 113, 379–80, 851; antipolitical proposals of, 379; works of, 379

Haya de la Torre, Víctor Raúl, 366, 512

Hegel, Georg Wilhelm Friedrich, 473, 492, 532

Heidegger, Martin, 493

Heilige Johanna der Schlachthöfe (Brecht), 69

"Heirs of Stalin" (Yevtushenko), 451

Heller, Agnes, 523

Helms, Richard, 824

Helsinki Accords (1975), 113, 284

Helsinki Final Act (1975), 67, 73, 234, 288; "Basket Three" provisions of, 234

Helsinki Group, 288

Hemdánek, Ladislav, 95

Herrmann, Joachim, 167

Herrnstadt, Rudolf, 167

Herzen, Alexander, 483

Hessler, André, 415

Heyser, Richard, 243

Hilferding, Rudolf, 77, 78, 124, 380–81, 409; "organized capitalism" concept, 380; "realistic pacifism" concept, 380

Hill, Christopher, 523

Hill, Ted, 146

Hiss, Alger, 769

Historical Novel, The (Lukács), 493

History and Class Consciousness (Lukács), 492–93, 521, 523; alienation and totality as key concepts in, 521

history and memory, 381–83

History of the Russian Revolution (Trotsky), 428, 816, 819

History of Russian Social Thought (Plekhanov), 622

History of Russian Social Thought (Pokrovsky), 526

Hitler, Adolf, 18, 325, 332, 353, 383–86, 407, 475, 719, 735, 778, 793, 853; and the Battle of Stalingrad, 780, 780; ideas about race, 384; and the Molotov-Ribbentrop Pact, 20, 22, 326, 385, 548–50; view of communism (as an alien fruit of Jewish conspiracy), 384, 385. *See also* **Molotov-Ribbentrop Pact;** Operation Barbarossa; **World War II**

Ho Chi Minh, 27, 225, 226, 227, 386–89, 565, 834, 835, 847; as cult figure of the Communist dynasty, 389; limitations on his power, 386, 388, 389; as "Nguyen Ai Quoc" (Nguyen the Patriot), 387

Ho Chi Minh Thought, 228, 389

Hoang Quoc Viet, 227

Hoang Tung, 227

Hobsbawm, Eric, 523

Hobson, John L., 25, 408–9

Hoffman, Max, 71

Holland. *See* Netherlands, the

Holodomor, 389–93

Holostenko, Vitali, 212

Holy Family, The (Marx and Engels), 427

Homage to Catalonia (Orwell), 596

Honecker, Erich, 167, 393–94, 598, 676, 823

Honqi (Red Banner), 254

Hoover, Calvin, 805

Hoover, J. Edgar, 530

Hopf, Ted, 56

Hopkins, Harry, 872

Horkheimer, Max, 420

Hough, Jerry, 807

"How to Be a Good Communist" (Liu Shaoqi), 490

"How We Should Recognize Rabkrin" (V. Lenin), 80–81

Howard, Ebenezer, 32

Hoxha, Enver, 68, 144, 145, 394–95, 415, 418, 509, 744, 758; cult of, 250, 395

Hoxha, Nexhmije, 395

Hrabal, Bohumil, 486

Hrustsev, N. S., 36

Hu Jintao, 100, 159, 284, 431

Hu Shi, 104

Hu Yaobang, 46, 158, 159, 264, 270, 402–3; "search for truth in the facts" slogan, 403

Hua Guofeng, 254, 506

Huang Hua, 837

Hue, Robert, 172, 512

Humbert-Droz, Jules, 197, 224, 350, 406

Hundred flowers movement, 94, 395–96, 506

Hungarian Republic of Councils, 396–97

Hungarian Revolution (1956), 270, 397–400

Hungarian Socialist Workers' Party, 399, 640

Hungarian Soviet Republic, 463

Hungarian Workers' Party, 397–98, 399

Hungary, 22, 417, 486, 564, 609, 653, 684, 728, 737, 745, 747, 761, 762, 851, 852; New Economic Mechanism policies in, 128; as a People's Democracy, 608; postcommunism in, 640; Soviet invasion of, 27. See also **Communist Party in Hungary**

Husák, Gustáv, 95, 165, 295, 379, 400–402

Husserl, Edmund, 95

Iaroslavskii, E. M., 709

Ibarruri, Dolores (the "Pasionaria"), 219, 220, 416

Iceland, Communist Party in, 205, 206

iconography, 405–6; *lubok,* 405; *obraz,* 405; socialist realist "illustration," 405; Sots-art, 406

Iglesias, Gerardo, 221

Ignat'ev, Semen, 448

Ikramov, Akmal, 154

Il Manifesto, 579

Íl ministro della produzione nello Stato collettivista" (The Production Minister in the Collectivist State) (Barone), 618

Il popolo d'Italia, 552

Im Dickicht der Städte (Brecht), 69

immigration to the USSR, 406–8

Imperfect Society, The (Djilas), 294

imperialism, 25, 278–79; 408–11; capitalist imperialism, 889; exploitative imperialism, 26; imperialist nationalism, 26; "ultra-imperialism," 409–10. See also capitalism; colonialism

Imperialism: A Study (Hobson), 408–9

"Imperialism and World Economy" (Bukharin), 77, 409

Imperialism as the Highest Stage of Capitalism (V. Lenin), 409–10, 472, 842; as a "popular outline," 409

Independent Social Democratic Party of Germany, 479, 823

India, 26, 259; and anticolonial nationalism, 257; illiteracy in, 481; Maoism in, 510. See also **Communist Party in the Indian Subcontinent**

Indonesia, 565. See also **Communist Party in Indonesia**

"Industrial Development in Poland" (Luxemburg), 495

Information Bureau of Communist and Workers' Policies. See **Cominform**

Initiative Group for the Defense of Human Rights, 288

Inprekor, 223

Institut für Sozialforschung, 522

Institute for Diplomatic Service, 285

insurrection in Germany, 411–12

intelligentsia, 412–14; attacks on, 412; in the late czarist period, 412–13; in the Soviet period, 412, 413

Intermediate-Range Nuclear Forces Treaty (1989), 122

Internal Security Act (McCarran Act [1950]), 16

International Association of Writers for the Defense of Culture, 30

International Bank of Economic Cooperation, 130

International Brigades, 414–16; Eleventh and Twelfth International Brigades, 415; Fifteenth International Brigade, 415; the "Garibaldi" battalion, 415; importance of in the formation of the leadership of many Communist parties, 415; participation in the major battles of the Spanish Civil War, 416; Thirteenth and Fourteenth International Brigades, 415

International Clubs of Political Émigrés, 407

International Confederation of Arab Trade Unions, 422

International Confederation of Christian Trade Unions (later World Confederation of Labor), 421

International Confederation of Free Trade Unions, 421–22

international conferences after Stalin, 416–20

International Federation of Trade Unions, 420–21

International Monetary Fund, 27

International Organization for Aid to Revolutionary Fighters. See International Red Cross

International Red Cross, 320, 407

international trade union organizations, 420–23. See also specific trade unions; **trade unions**

International Workers' Aid, 551

internationalism, 423–24, 755

Interrogation at a Distance (Havel), 379

"Introducing *The Communist*" (Mao Zedong), 504

Iran, 1, 2, 15, 565. See also **Communist Party in Iran**

Iranian Revolution, 426, 566

Iraq, 565; Communist Party in, 201–2

Irish Republican Army, 790

Iskra ("The Spark"), 471

Islam, 424–26; concentration of in the Soviet Union, 424; "parallel Islam" or "Islam outside the mosque," 425; Stalin's reorganization of, 424–25; "state Islam"/Soviet Islam, 425, 426

Israel, 259. See also **Communist Party in Israel**

Italy, 15, 16, 20, 21, 22, 840; and the welfare state, 852, 853. See also **Communist Party in Italy**

Ivan the Terrible (1945), 305

Ivanov, Vsevolod, 327, 819

Izvestiia, 652, 657, 664

Jabotinsky, Vladimir, 456

Jackson, M., 414–15

Jacobinism, 427–29

Jagoda, Genrich, 28, 447

Jakeš, Milos, 165

Jakova, Tonin, 144

Jankowski, Henryk, 841

Japan, 322; illiteracy in, 481. See also **Communist Party in Japan; World War II**

Jaroszewicz, Piotr, 741

Jarquín, Edmundo, 697

Jaruzelski, Wojciech, 53, 210, 312, 339, 429–30, 517, 519–20, 741, 747; as an atypical Communist leader, 429; as a model ex-Communist, 430

Jaurès, Jean, 846

Jews, 391, 663; Soviet Jews, 17; murder of Serbian Jews by the Nazis, 22; Stalin's repression of, 29. See also **anti-Semitism**

Jhering, Herbert, 68–69

Jiang Qing, 158, 252, 253, 254, 264

Jiang Zemin, 158–59, 159, 264, 430–31; "Theory of the Three Represents," 431

Jirous, Ivan, 95

Jocelyn, Ed, 491

Jodl, Alfred, 23

Joe Fleischhacker in Chikago (Brecht), 69

Joffe, Adolf, 71

Jogiches, Leo, 495, 496
John XXIII, 90
John Paul II, 89, 91, 337, 696
Johnson, Chalmers, 105
Johnson, Lyndon B., 11, 121, 239
Jorn, Asger, 33
Jospin, Lionel, 172
Journey from St. Petersburg to Moscow
    (Radishchëv), 483
Journey into the Whirlwind (Y. Ginzburg),
    287
Jumblat, Kamal, 202
Jung Chang, 491
Junta Militar, 369–70
Justo, Juan Bautista, 196

Kabila, Laurent, 371
Kaczynski, Jaroslaw, 742
Kaczynski, Lech, 742
Kádár, János, 179–80, 270, 336, 398, 399,
    400, 433–34, 557, 564, 666, 737;
    New Economic Mechanism project,
    434
Kaganovich, Lazar, 66, 390, 391, 434–36,
    440, 456, 499, 546, 576, 616, 626,
    627, 660, 804; abrasiveness of, 435;
    advocacy of centralization in party and
    state management, 434; advocacy of
    rapid industrialization, 435; during
    the Great Terror, 436; hostility toward
    de-Stalinization, 436; as "Iron Lazar,"
    435; as a model of the self-educated
    Bolshevik worker-intellectual, 434;
    promotion of Stalin's cult, 435; role in
    the collectivization of agriculture, 435
Kaganovich, Mikhail, 436
Kalecki, Michal, 620
Kalinin, Mikhail, 440, 481, 576
Kállay, Miklós, 433
Kamenev, Lev, 28, 61, 71, 360, 382,
    436–37, 464, 546, 576, 625, 650,
    693, 764, 818, 876, 890; opposition to
    Stalin, 437, 705, 815, 891
Kamenev, Olga, 437
Kampuchea. *See* Cambodia
Kang Sheng, 253
Kania, Stanislaw, 210, 429, 516–17,
    518–19
Kantorovich, Leonid, 302
Karakhan, Lev, 71
Kardelj, Edvard, 294, 438; as an ideologue
    and propagandist, 438; nonalignment
    policy, 438; as a practical organizer of
    party activities, 438; self-governing
    socialism model, 438
Karelia-Finnish Republic, 9
Karimov, Islam, 155
Karl Marx (Korsch), 69

Karmal, Babrak, 1, 2
Károlyi, Mihály, 396
Karski, Julian, 495
Katsenelinboigen, Aron, 514
Katyn massacre, 439–42
Katz, Solomon, 212
Kautsky, Karl, 196, 278, 409, 442–43, 458,
    472, 495, 679, 735; condemnation
    of communism, 443; critique of the
    Bolshevik revolution, 442; as one of
    Lenin's favorite targets, 442
Kazakhstan, 266, 391, 392
Keita, Modibo, 371
Kenez, Peter, 808
Kennan, George Frost, 16, 236–37, 238,
    240, 443–46, 515, 806; conservatism
    of, 445; criticism of Washington's Cold
    War policy, 445; events causing him to
    develop a more critical stance, 444–45;
    and the "long" telegram, 236, 444;
    negative view of the Soviet Union,
    443–44. *See also* **containment**
Kennedy, John F., 50, 51, 121, 238–29,
    242–44, 275, 370, 371, 452. *See also* Bay
    of Pigs invasion (1961); **Cuban missile
    crisis (1962)**
Kennedy, Robert, 243
Kerensky, Aleksandr, 62, 455, 458, 473, 688
Kerzhentsev, Platon, 831
KGB, 291, 446–48. *See also* Cheka;
    People's Commissariat for Internal
    Affairs
Khaidargalievich, Mirza, 424
Khalturin, S. N., 427
Khamene'i, 'Ali, 186
Khan, Mohammed Daoud, 1
Khān, Ridā, 185
Khlebnikhov, Velimir, 528
Khmer Rouge, 310, 322, 449–50, 623, 675,
    837; links of to China, 838
Khodjaev, Fayzullah, 154
Khodjaev, Usman, 155
Khomeini, Ruhollah, 1, 186, 426, 566
Khrushchev, Nikita, 6, 8, 11, 33, 50, 51,
    73, 90, 167, 176, 180, 213, 216,
    222, 242–44, 259, 275, 335, 366,
    370, 371, 389, 399, 417, 418, 440,
    450–52, 500, 501, 541, 564–65, 568,
    584, 626, 627, 666, 705, 714, 745,
    839; accused of being a "Bonapartist,"
    65; accused of "subjectivism," 270,
    543; antireligious campaign of
    (1959–64), 594; and Comecon,
    129–30; contradictions in his life and
    career, 450; criticism of Stalin, 198,
    248–49, 803; economic reforms of,
    82, 301–2, 331; emphasis on "peaceful
    coexistence," 120, 714; failures

in agricultural policy, 451; failures in
    foreign policy, 451–52; interpretation
    of peaceful coexistence, 603, 633; and
    NATO, 587–88; redefinition of the
    Soviet state under, 786; role of in the
    Sino-Soviet split, 714–15; "secret"
    speech of at the Twentieth Party Con-
    gress, 272, 309, 383, 450–51, 455–56;
    stance on de-Stalinization, 451, 682,
    780; tendency to not think through the
    possible consequences of his actions,
    451; tirades against liberal artists and
    writers, 451. *See also* **Cuban missile
    crisis (1962); de-Stalinization; secret
    speech; Soviet bloc**
Kierkegaard, Søren, 492
Kiesinger, Kurt Georg, 597
killing fields, 453–54
Killing Fields, The, 453
Kim Il Sung, 194, 195, 196, 270, 454–55,
    460, 640, 834; cult of, 454; distancing
    of himself from the Soviet Union, 454;
    as a guerrilla fighter, 454; Juche ideol-
    ogy, 195, 454–55. *See also* **Korean War**
Kim Jong Il, 195, 196, 455, 640
Kim Tu-bong, 195
Kim Yong-bom, 194
Kirilenko, Andrei, 627
Kirkpatrick, Jeane, 808
**Kirov, Sergey (pseudonym for Sergei
    Mostrikov),** 360, 407, 437, 451, 527,
    576, 593, 775, 838, 882; assassination
    of, 455–56, 660, 875–76; concern
    for ethnic groups indigenous to the
    Caucasus, 455
Kissinger, Henry, 52, 58, 239, 246, 247,
    312
Klahr, Alfred, 147
Klein, August, 173
Kliuev, Nikolai, 327
Knorin, V. G., 709
Köblös, Elek, 212
Kobulov, Bogdan, 440
Kociołek, Stanisław, 517
Kodály, Zoltán, 397
Koestler, Arthur, 456–57, 492; on man/
    mankind, 456; movement to the Right,
    456–57; obsession with parascience,
    457
Kohl, Helmut, 277, 598, 676, 677, 678
Kohout, Pavel, 95
Kolakowski, Leszek, 465
Kolarov, V., 150
Kolbin, Genadii, 154
Kolchak, Alexander, 690, 691
kolkhoz, 457–58; types of, 457
Kollantay, Aleksandra, 458–59, 489, 581,
    855; career in the Soviet diplomatic

corps, 459; radical theories about free love and a new Communist morality, 458; as a revolutionary agitator, 458

Kolyma Tales (Shalamov), 373, 614

Komar, Vitaly, 42

Komeda, Vendelín, 95

Komsomol, 251, 656

Komsomolskaia Pravda, 652

Konar, Harekrishna, 181

Kondratiev, Nikolai, 413, 749

Kondratieva, T., 427

Konturkova, Eva, 95

Konwicki, Tadeusz, 485

Koplenig, Johann, 147

Koptsov, N. I., 153

Korea, 2, 27. *See also* **Communist Party in Korea; Korean War; North Korea**

Korean War (1950–53), 16, 120, 238, 459–61, 529

korenizatsiia. *See* **nationality policies**

Kornai, János, 514, 620

Kornijushin, V. D., 153

Kornilov, Lavr, 473

Korsch, Karl, 69–70, 521

Korvin, Ottó, 178

Kosik, Karel, 95, 523

Kosior, Stanislav, 626

Kostov, Traiko, 151, 283

Kostrzewa, Wera, 207

Kosygin, Alexei, 82, 287, 302, 368, 611, 627

Kotcharovskaja, A. S., 153

Kovalev, Sergei, 74–75

Kozlov, Frol, 244, 629

Koz'min, B. P., 428

Krajowa, Armia, 24

Krasnyi, S., 429

Kravchenko, Viktor, 83

Kravchuk, Leonid, 874

Krenz, Egon, 167, 676–77

Krestinsky, Nikolai, 411, 650

Kristeva, Julia, 34

Kristman, Lev, 604

Krleža, M., 486

Kronstadt revolt, 461–62

Kropivnicky, Evgeny, 287

Kropivnicky, Lev, 287

Kropotkin, Pyotr, 32

Kruchina, Nikolai, 241

Krúdy, Cyula, 397

Kruglov, Sergey, 441

Krupskaya, Nadezhda, 477, 480, 494, 546, 617, 656, 855

Kryuchkov, Vladimir, 241, 518, 613

Krzaklewski, Marian, 742

Kuban, 391

Kuczynsky, Jürgen, 770

Kuczynsky, Ursala, 768

Kühlmann, Richard von, 71

Kuhn, Giovanni, 5–6

Kuibichev, V. V., 154, 435

Kukliński, Ryszard, 520

kulak, 462–63; as "class enemy," 462. *See also* dekulakization

Kulakov, Fedor, 340

Kuleshov, Lev, 108

Kuliev, A., 155

Kulikov, Viktor, 518

Kun, Béla, 173, 178, 179, 396, 397, 463–64, 492, 493, 555, 616, 833; adherence to the Comintern's "social Fascist" line, 463; advocacy of revolutionary action, 463

Kunaev, Din-Muhammed, 154

Kunaev, Kazakh, 154

Kundera, Milan, 30, 486

Kuno, Wilhelm, 411

Kurchatov, Igor, 37–38

Kurón, Jacek, 95, 464–65, 534

Kutuzov, Mikhail, 359

Kuusinen, Hertta, 169

Kuusinen, Otto Wilhelm, 9, 168, 406, 465, 853; as a loyal Stalinist, 465

Kuybyshev, Valerian, 577

Kuzmin, Michail, 484, 485

Kuznetsov, Aleksei, 500, 626, 883

Kyànuri, Nureddin, 186

La Ciudad Futura, 199

La condition humaine (Man's Fate) (Malraux), 501

La Correspondenicia Sudamericana, 197

"La guerra de guerrillas" (Guerrilla Warfare) (Guevara), 367

"La guerra de guerrillas: un metodo" (Guerrilla Warfare: A Method) (Guevara), 367

"La tentation de l'Occident" (The Temptation of the West) (Malraux), 501

La Vague, 615

La voie royale (The Way of the Kings) (Malraux), 501

Labarca, Carlos Contreras, 198

labor, 467–69; in China, 468–69; in the Soviet Union, 467–68

Labor and Socialist International, 735, 735

Laborde, Hernán, 198

Labour Party (Great Britain), 15, 314, 718, 719

Lafargue, Paul, 423

Lamarca, Carlos, 369

L'Ancien Régime et la Révolution (Tocqueville), 291

Landovsky, Pavel, 95

Lange, Oskar R., 304, 618, 620, 737

Lashkova, Vera, 287

Latin America: Communist Party in, 196–99; guerrilla warfare in, 366–70; Maoism in, 509–10

Latvia, 205

Layne, Christopher, 56

Le Duan, 193, 227, 389

Le Kha Phieu, 228

Le temps du mépris (Malraux), 501

Le Van Luong, 227

League for Agrarian Reform, 5

League of the Militant Godless, 36

League of Time, 831

League of Nations, 257

Lebanon, Communist Party in, 202

Lebedova, Natalya, 441

Lecoeur, Auguste, 171

Lectures on Fascism (Togliatti), 188

Ledebour, Georg, 496

LEF (Left Front for the Arts), 528

Lefort, Claude, 698

Left, the, 15, 20; Left Opposition, 749, 774, 815–16; the Old Left, 16, 17; split in the U.S. Left concerning Soviet-style communism, 16. *See also* **New Left**

Left March! For the Red Marines: 1918 (Mayakovski), 528

legal Marxism, 469–70

Léger, Fernand, 601

Legien, Carl, 679

Leino, Yrjö, 169

Lemkin, Raphael, 392

Lenin, Alexander, 427, 471

Lenin, Vladimir, 4, 5, 11, 28, 65, 72, 77, 84, 97, 111, 113, 119, 123, 147, 215, 216, 260, 278, 299, 344, 352, 380, 427, 436, 437, 459, 462, 465, 470–75, 483, 494, 507, 525, 527, 535, 546, 549, 571, 575–76, 580, 593, 622, 624, 625, 638, 663, 670, 679, 763, 813, 814, 815, 818; accused of being a Blanquist, 428; alignment with Trotsky, 477–78; atheism of, 35–36; and Bolshevism, 59–62; attacks on Kautsky's "ultraimperialism" theses, 442; categorization of press functions, 652; and Chernyshevasky's *What Is to Be Done?* 580; control of the state bureaucracy as a dominant concern in his final years, 80–81; and Comintern, 135; concept of nation, 570; concerns about Stalin, 477–78; criticism of the intelligentsia, 413; cult of, 478; Decree on the Separation of the Church from the State and the School from the Church, 594; diplomatic strategy of, 284; on the emancipation of women, 855;

Lenin, Vladimir (cont.)
  extremist agrarian policies of, 60; on
  imperialism, 409–10; leadership of,
  708–9; and Marxism, 526; on the
  national question (Right of Nations
  to Self-Determination policy), 559;
  negative assessment of futurism, 528;
  politicized view of the family, 317; rag
  bag of doctrines, 473; support for national liberation movements, 558; and
  the Treaty of Brest-Litovsk, 689–90;
  view of fascism, 325; view of films,
  108; view of imperialism, 409–10;
  view of international relations, 602,
  602–3; view of nationalism, 562–63;
  view of peasants, 604; view of the
  Russian Revolution, 410; view of
  trade unions, 808; view of war, 842,
  846; view of World War I, 410; "yield
  ground in order to gain time" motto,
  65; and the Zimmerwald Left, 348,
  846. *See also* **Lenin's testament; New
  Economic Policy**
Lenin Motor Works, 812
"Lenin and the Problem of Jacobin Dicta-
  torship" (Lukin), 429
Leningrad, 883, 885
Leningrad, siege of, 475–77
Leningrad Affair (1949–50), 272, 477
*Leninism and the Ideological-Political Destruction
  of Trotskyism* (Ivanov and Shmelev), 819
Lenin's testament, 477–78
Leningradskaia Pravda, 652
Lenski, Julian, 207, 224
Leo XII, 421
Leonov, Nikolaj, 370
Lerner, Abba, 618
Les conquérants (The Conquerors)
  (Malraux), 501
Leshinsky, Nahun, 187
Leskov, Nikolai, 483
L'Espoir (Man's Hope) (Malraux), 502
Lessons of October, The (Trotsky), 576, 818
Letters to Olga (Havel), 379
Levada, Yuriy, 342
Levi, Paul, 173, 496
Levitin, Anatoli, 595
Lévy, Benny, 698
Levy, Jack S., 56; on "offense-defense
  balance," 56
l'Humanité, 615, 616
Li Da, 503
Li Lisan, 226, 388, 504
Li Xiannian, 254
Liberal Party (Great Britain), 15
liberalism, 11. *See also* Left, the
Libération, 579
Libya, 566

Liebknecht, Karl, 172, 173, 458, 478–79,
  496, 617, 717; main political objectives
  of, 478
Ligachev, Yegor, 10, 341, 611, 612, 613, 628,
  869–70, 873
Lilov, Alexander, 152
Lin Biao, 158, 253, 253–54, 357, 479–80,
  491; "command politics" concept, 479;
  as Mao's liaison to the People's Liberation Army, 479
Lin Liguo, 479
Lin Shaoqi, 402
L'Internationale Communiste, 197
Lion and the Unicorn, The (Orwell), 596
Lipiński, Edward, 464
Lippmann, Walter, 444
Lipski, Jan Józef, 464
literacy, Soviet Union campaign for adult
  (1920s), 480–82; mixed success of, 481;
  political, social, and economic motivations behind, 481
Literature and Revolution (Trotsky), 327,
  580–81
literature in Soviet Russia, 482–86;
  postrevolutionary Russian literature
  ("literature and the realization of com-
  munism"), 484–46; prerevolutionary
  Russian literature ("literature and ideas
  of communism"), 483
Literaturnaja gazeta, 738, 739
Lithuania, 205, 787
Litoshenko, Lev, 619
"Little Red Book," 479, 506
Litvinov, Maksim, 19, 283–84, 286,
  486–89, 548, 753; "collective security"
  policy, 547, 548; as the emblem of the
  Soviet Union in the West, 486, 488;
  practice of a classic type of foreign
  policy, 488; tendency to be relentless in
  his criticism, 486
Litvishko, K. D., 153
Liu Guokai, 254
Liu Shaoqi, 157, 252, 253, 264, 357, 489–90,
  503, 506, 544, 672; as Mao's nemesis,
  489; political strategy of (guided by
  a form of technocratic and scientific
  communism), 490
Lockhart, Bruce, 487
Logiches, Leo, 495
Lomonosov, Mikhail, 756
Lomonosov, V., 811
Lon Nol, 449
London, Artur, 415
London Conference (1948), 48
Long March, 490–91, 504
Longo, Luigi, 6, 415, 416
Lopatka, Jan, 95
L'Ordine Nuovo, 348–49

Lovestone, Jay, 224
Lozovsky, Solomon, 488
Luca, Vasile, 213, 336
Lukács, Georg, 113, 178, 179, 491–94, 521,
  523, 740; the divorce between Stalinist
  communism and his philosophical
  and political thought, 493; philosophy of immanence, 492; political and
  philosophical itinerary of, 492–93;
  "specificity of human kind in itself"
  and "specificity of human kind for
  itself" concepts, 492
Lukanov, A., 152
Lukin, N., 429
Lumumba, Patrice, 121, 222, 371, 565
Lunacharsky, Anatoly, 60, 329, 494–95,
  581, 654; Lenin's accusation of "god-
  building," 494
Lunatsarsky, A. V., 36
l'Unità, 349
Lux in tenebris (Brecht), 69
Luxemburg, 22
Luxemburg, Rosa, 123, 172, 173, 299, 409,
  428, 442, 458, 478, 487, 495–97, 559,
  717; response to reformist ideas of
  Eduard Bernstein, 679; Stalin's banning
  of her ideas, 496
Lykyanov, Anatoliy, 241
Lysenko, Trofim Denisovich, 30, 700

Mach, Ernst, 623
Machado, Gerardo, 160
Machel, Samora, 322
Machiavelli, Niccolò, 213, 268
Macierewicz, Antoni, 464
Mackiewicz, Józef, 441
Maclean, Donald, 768
Madden, Ray J., 441
Mahler, Horst, 792
Maisky, Ivan, 285, 488
Makarenko, Anton, 319
Makashov, Albert, 613
Makhkamov, K., 155
Malayan Races Liberation Army, 214
Malaysia, Communist Party in, 214
Malenkov, Georgy, 39, 40, 67, 271, 275, 450,
  451, 499–501, 626, 627, 704; abhor-
  rence of Khrushchev, 501; as an indis-
  pensable administrator of the Stalinist
  machinery of mobilization, terror, and
  surveillance, 500
Maléter, Pál, 399, 400, 415
Malraux, André, 501–2, 601
Mandela, Nelson, 248, 565
Mandelstam, Nadezhda, 287
Mandelstam, Osip, 484, 710
Manhattan Project, 37
"Manifesto of Peace" (1957), 417

Mann, Heinrich, 328

Mann ist Mann (Brecht), 69

Manner, Kullervo, 168

Manuilskii, Dmitrii, 219, 387, 463, 488, 502–3, 607–8, 796

Mao Zedong, 27, 105–7, 157, 159, 192, 227, 252–55, 263, 270, 279, 356, 357, 358, 370, 388, 395–96, 402, 418, 451, 460, 479, 489–90, 491, 503–8, 509, 529, 705, 834; agrarian policies of, 102–3; as Chairman Mao, 505; criticism of polycentrism, 633; cult of, 250, 503; dictatorial style of, 506; and the formation of the Red Guard, 672–73; and the "hundred flowers" campaign, 674; major stages of his career and writings, 504; "never forget class struggle" slogan, 103; petulance of, 506; role of in the Sino-Soviet split, 714, 715. *See also* **Cultural Revolution in China; Great Leap Forward; Mao Zedong Thought (***Mao Zedong sixiang***)**

Mao Zedong Thought (*Mao Zedong sixiang*), 431; negative contributions to revolutionary ideology and praxis, 508; positive contributions to revolutionary ideology and praxis, 507–8

Maosim, 508–10; and "Castroism," 510; in India, 510; "international Maoism," 509–10; Maoist parties, 509

Marchais, Georges, 52, 171, 172, 311, 510–12

Marchenko, Anatoly, 289

Marcos, Ferdinand, 214

Marcuse, Herbert, 13, 328, 523

Mariátegui, José Carlos, 160, 197, 199, 512–13

Marighela, Carlos, 369

Marin Preda, M., 486

markets, legal and illegal, 513–15

Markovic, Sima, 230

Marku, Gjin, 144

Markulov, Vsevolod, 441

Marosan, Gyorgy, 666

Márquez, Pompeyo, 199

Marshall, George F., 236, 333, 515. *See also* **Marshall Plan**

Marshall, T. H., 110

Marshall Plan, 11, 16, 58, 120, 129, 237, 355, 515–16

Martí, José, 87, 244, 366

martial law in Poland, 516–20; planning for a crackdown, 518–19; the road to martial law, 519–20; Soviet reactions to, 517–18

Martov, Yuli, 4, 215, 278, 428, 471

Marty, André, 171, 415, 796

Marx, Karl, 11, 34, 64, 93, 101, 110, 111, 139, 423, 427, 492, 527, 558, 580, 618, 683, 738–39; on capitalist control of the press, 651; concept of history, 532–34; on the New Man, 533; on the proletariat, 114–15, 278; rejection of pacifism by, 846; on the role of great men in history, 249; on the Socialist future, 830; view of capitalism, 114, 408; view of religion, 424; view of urbanization, 827–28

Marx-Engels Institute, 381–82, 382

Marxism, 17, 33, 699; analysis of cultural production, 93; austro-marxism, 33, 558–59; class theory of, 116; German variant of, 471; notion of history as a redemptive process, 115, 532; orthodox Marxism, 4; revisionist Marxism, 4. *See also* **legal Marxism; Marxism, Western; Marxism-Leninism; Marxists; messianism**

Marxism, Western, 521–24; as the object of political disputes, 523–24. *See also* **Gramsci, Antonio; Lukács, Georg**

"Marxism and Insurrection" (V. Lenin), 428

Marxism and the National Question (Stalin), 424

Marxism and Philosophy (Korsch), 521

Marxism-Leninism, 62, 110, 111, 125, 218, 249, 294, 431, 508, 521, 524–27, 570, 642, 755–56; and Cold War ideology, 643–45; and the concepts of "purge" and "purity," 525–26; definition of, 524; emergence of, 526; interpretation of nation and nationalism, 570; and religion, 424; Stalin's influence on, 524–26, 781–82. See also *Short Course of the History of the All-Russian Communist Party (Bolshevik)*

Marxists, 3–4, 7, 101; view of the proletariat, 115

"Marxismus und Philosophie" (Korsch), 69

Masaliev, Absamat, 155

Masaryk, Jan Garrigue, 514

Masetti, Jorge Ricardo, 368, 369, 371

Maslow, Arkady, 173

Mass Strike, Party, and Trade Unions (Luxemburg), 495

Massoud, Ahmed Shah, 2

Master and Margarita (M. Bulgakov), 484

Matearn, Hermann, 166

materialism, 12, 521, 731; scientific materialism, 699; in the *Short Course of the History of the All-Russian Communist Party (Bolshevik)*, 525

Materialism and Empirio-Criticism (V. Lenin), 60, 472, 527, 699

Matteotti, Giacomo, 6, 681

Maud Report, 37

Maulanda, Manuel, 369

Maurer, Ion Gheorghe, 92

Maurín, Joaquín, 219

Mauroy, Pierre, 512

Maximoff, Gregory P., 428

Maximovich, Vasili, 768

May Fourth Movement, 104, 503–4

Mayakovski, Vladimir, 251, 327, 484, 528–29; influences on, 528; poetry of, 528

Mayorga, Silvio, 696

Mazowiecki, Tadeusz, 464, 639

McCarran, Pat, 16

McCarthy, Eugene, 15, 16

McCarthy, Joseph, 529–31

McCarthyism, 529–32; and Alger Hiss, 530; and Hollywood Ten, 531; House Un-American Activities Committee, 530–31; Internal Security Act of 1950, 531; "waiver" doctrine, 531

McEwen, Andrew, 491

McFarquhar, Roderick, 715

McLennan, Gordon, 176

Mearsheimer, John, 56

Medina, Victor, 368

Medvedev, Vadim, 341

Medvedev, Vladimir, 241

Mehring, Franz, 495, 496

Mein Kampf (Hitler), 384

Meinhof, Ulrike, 792

Meister Eckhart, 492

Melamid, Alex, 42

Mella, Julio Antonio, 160

Mendeleev, Dimitri, 756

Mendeshev, S., 154

Menem, Carlos Saúl, 369

Mengistu, 322

Mensheviks, 215, 381, 472, 473, 474, 688, 689, 763, 839

Menshevism, 59, 61, 813. *See also* Mensheviks

Mercader, Ramón, 817

Merkulov, Vsevolod, 440, 447

Merleau-Ponty, Maurice, 698

messianism, 532–34

Metaxas, Ioannis, 177, 363

Metropol' (1979), 485

Mexico, 27; Communist Party in, 197

Meyerhold, Vsevolod, 710, 832

MGB, 448

Michajlovsky, Nikolaj, 483

Michel, Henri, 23

Michnik, Adam, 95, 464, 534–35

Mickoels, Solomon, 28

Mielke, Erich, 167

Mikolajczyk, Stanislaw, 208, 608

Index

Mikoyan, Anastas, 244, 371, 399, 440, 452, 500, 626, 627

Miles, J. B., 146

militancy, 535–37

militarization, 537–39; of the economy, 539; of industrial planning, 538; of the party structures, 538–39; of the population, 538

military-industrial complex, 539–42; basic components of, 539; Eisenhower's definition of, 539; main features in the development of a military economy, 539; in the Soviet Union, 540–42; in the West, 539–40

Mill, John Stuart, 408

Millar, James, 750

Miller, Arthur, 601

Mills, C. Wright, 13

Milošević, Slobodan, 233

Milosz, Czeslaw, 485

Milyukov, Pavel, 473, 688, 818

Milyutin, Vladimir, 693

Mindszenty, József, 90, 400

Mine, Hilary, 208

Mingrel affair (1951–52), 47

Minin, Koz'ma, 359

Ministries for Foreign Affairs. *See* **diplomats**

Mitin, Mark, 132

Mitskevitch, S. I., 428

Mittag, Günter, 167

Mitterand, François, 171, 172, 312, 511, 719

Miyamoto, Kenji, 192

Mladenov, P., 152

Mlynar, Zdenek, 95

modernism, 12

modernity: America as a symbol of, 10–11; political modernity, 28

modernization, 7, 337, 542–45; definition of, 543

Modrow, Hans, 677

Modzelewski, Karol, 464

Mola, Emilio, 764, 765

Mollet, Guy, 313

Molojec, Edward, 208

Molotov, Vyacheslav M., 29, 40, 49, 127, 131, 167, 213, 233, 284, 285, 354, 365, 390, 391, 435, 440, 441, 450, 451, 487, 488, 499, 500, 514, 515, 546–48, 548, 549, 560–61, 576, 577, 593, 616, 626, 627, 709, 876; actions of in World War II to defeat Germany, 864; choice of the pseudonym Molotov, 546. *See also* **Molotov-Ribbentrop Pact**

Molotov-Ribbentrop Pact, 19, 23, 188, 548–50, 776

Mongolia, 2; Outer Mongolia, 760. *See also* **Communist Party in Mongolia**

Monnet, Jean, 313

Montenegro, Julio Méndez, 368

Moravia, Alberto, 367

More, Thomas, 31

Moretti, Mario, 791

Morgenthau, Hans, 56

Móricz, Zsigmond, 397

Morning Star, 176–77

Moro, Aldo, 52, 791

Morozov, M. V., 153

Morozov, Pavlik, 318

Moscow Accords (1970), 276

Moscow News, 653

Moscow State Institute of International Relations, 285

Mossadegh, Mohammed, 185, 238, 565

Mosse, George, 84

Moszyński, Adam, 441

Movement of Partisans of Peace. *See* **Partisans of Peace**

Movement of Peace. *See* **Partisans of Peace**

Movimento das Forças Armadas, 637–38

Movimiento 8 de octubre, 369

Movimiento 26 de julio, 87, 244, 366, 370

Movimiento al-socialismo, 199

Mozambique, 566; famine in, 322

Mrozek, Slawomir, 485

Mugosha, Dushan, 144, 394

Muhiddinov, Nurridin, 154

Mulele, Pierre, 371

Munich Accords (1938), 548, 598

Münnich, Ferenc, 433

Münzenberg, Willi, 456, 550–51, 563; "Münzenberg's Empire," 551

Mussolini, Benito, 6, 18, 551–53, 766; cult of, 553; talent for developing slogans, 552. *See also* **fascism**

"My Country, Right or Left" (Orwell), 596

My Life (Trotsky), 816

"My Subject Is Patriotism" (Eisenstein), 305

Myshkin, I. N., 427

Mystery-Bouffe (Mayakovski), 528

Mzhavanadze, Vasily, 707

Nabiev, Rahmon, 154, 155

Nagy, Imre, 179, 336, 397–98, 398, 399, 400, 417, 433, 493, 666

Naimski, Piotr, 464

Najibullah, Mohammed, 2

Namboodiripad, E.M.S., 181

Napoleon III (Louis Napoleon), 64–65, 683

Narkomindel, 667

Nas Sovremennik, 485

Nasredinova, Y. S., 154

Nasser, Gamal, 187, 201, 259, 370, 371, 565, 585

National Borders (*Gosundarstvennaâ Granica*) (1980–88), 67

National Committee for the Liberation of Yugoslavia, 865

National Confederation of Labor, 765, 766

national question, the, 557–60

national roads to socialism, 560–61

National Security Council, 237; Executive Committee of, 243

nationalism, 13, 562–66; in Germany, 15; Great Russian nationalism, 29; link between nationalism and communism, 200, 564

nationality policies, 566–70

nations and empire in the USSR, 570–73; and the centralized Communist Party, 571; institutionalization of ethnic identity, 572; republic status, 572; the Soviet Union's federal structure based on an ethnic principle, 571; Stalin's concept of nation, 570

Natoli, Aldo, 579

Nazarbaev, Nursultan, 155

Nazi-Soviet Non-Aggression Pact (1939), 136, 137, 266

Nazis: attacks on Communists in Germany, 174; massacre of Serbian Jews, 22; massacre of Soviet citizens by, 22

nazism, 20, 22, 34

Nechaev, S. G., 427, 428

Negrín, Juan, 220, 766

Nehru, Jawaharlal, 370, 564; "positive neutralism" concept, 585

Neizvestny, Ernst, 450

Nekrasov, Nikolaj, 483, 528

Nekrasov, Viktor, 484

Nemchinov, Vasily, 302

Némec, Jiří, 95

Nenni, Pietro, 415

neocolonialism, 222, 794

Neruda, Pablo, 574–75

Netherlands, the, 22, 719. *See also* **Communist Party in the Netherlands**

Neto, Agostinho, 246

Neue Zeit (New Times), 442, 495

Nevsky, Alexander, 359, 756

New Army, The (Jaurès), 846

New Class, The (Djilas), 80, 294

New Course (Trotsky), 650, 815

New Democracy. *See* **People's Democracy**

New Economic Policy (1921–28), 41, 83, 250–51, 320, 344, 446, 461, 462, 474, 477, 538, 540, 546, 575–78, 625, 654, 692, 774, 785, 855, 857; end of and the triumph of the Stalinist line, 577; measures of, 575; and political struggles for power, 576–77; and trade unions, 809; and the worker-peasant alliance, 575–76

New Economics (Preobrazhensky), 651

New Left, 17, 578–79; and campaigns against U.S. intervention in Vietnam (the U.S. "dirty war"), 578; common characteristics of New Left groups, 579; extremist constellations, 579; intellectual currents inspiring the development of, 578; international context of, 578

New Left Review, 523, 578

New Man, 579–82, 779; 19th-century traditions the concept was rooted in, 580; and education as the means to consciousness (*soznatel'nost*), 581; the role of technology in the liberation of, 580–81

New Political Thinking (*Novoe politicheskoe myshlenie*). *See* **New Thinking**

New Popular Army, 214

New Thinking (*Novoe myshlenie*), 582–83, 603; concept of checks and balances, 583; concept of democratization, 583; concept of political pluralism, 582, 612, 748; concept of the separation of powers, 583; emphasis on how much the Soviet Union could learn from the West, 583; on international relations, 583

New Zealand. *See* **Communist Party in Australia and New Zealand**

Newsinger, John, 596

Ngo Gia Tu, 226, 227

Nguyen Duc Canh, 227

Nguyen Van Linh, 228

Nicaragua, 628; adult literacy campaign in, 481 guerrilla warfare in, 368. *See also* **Sandinista Revolution**

Nicholas II, 59, 61, 594, 688

Nicole, Léon, 224

Niebuhr, Reinhold, 806

Nietzsche, Friedrich Wilhelm, 581

Nieuwenhuys, Constant, 33

Nikitin, Nikolai, 484

Nikolaevsky, Boris, 79

Nin, Andrés, 219, 220, 766

1984 (Orwell), 596, 614, 658, 806

Niou, Emerson, 56

Nishanov, Rafiq, 155

Nitze, Paul, 238

Nixon, Richard, 11, 58, 73, 98, 234, 239, 244, 264, 275, 276, 506, 530, 575, 824

Niyazov, Saparmurat, 154, 155

Nizan, Paul, 501

Nkrumah, Kwame, 222, 371

NKGB, 447–48

NKVD. *See* People's Commissariat for Internal Affairs

Nobile, Umberto, 406

Nogin, Viktor, 693

Nolte, Ernst, 85

nomenklatura, 216, 584–85, 704, 809, 874; "On the Nomenklatura of the CC CPSU" (1946), 584

nonalignment, 57, 88, 231, 565, 585–87; proposal for a "new international economic order," 586

Nong Duc Manh, 228

North Atlantic Treaty Organization, 57, 58, 120, 129, 312, 459, 587–89, 643, 848, 849, 850; AirLand Battle strategy, 589; Harmel Report, 588; Multilateral Force project, 588; shortcomings of its warning system in case of an emergency, 588

North Korea, 544, 675, 730; famine in, 323. *See also* **Korean War** (1950–53)

North Vietnam, 565, 643, 729

Norway, 22; Communist Party in, 205–6, 206

Nosaka, Sanzo, 191–92, 192

Nosek, Vaclav, 645

Notes of an Economist (Bukharin), 78, 577

Nova Misao (New Thought), 294

Novikov, Nikolay, 515

Novotný, Antonín, 165, 270, 295, 296, 589–91, 646; agreement with the policies of the Soviet leadership and recognition of the leading role of the Soviet Union in the Communist movement, 590; equation of the party with society, 590; lack of political creativity, 591

Novozhilov, Viktor, 302

Novy Mir, 271

Nowa Fala (New Wave), 485

Nowotka, Marcel, 208

Nuevo canto de amor a Stalingrado (Neruda), 574

Nuñez, Carlos, 696

Nyerere, Julius Kambarage, 222, 371

Obando y Bravo, Miguel, 696

Observations on a Plan for a Manual of the History of the USSR (Stalin, Zhdanov, and Kirov), 527

Ochirbat, Punsalmaagiyn, 203

October (1927), 305, 329; "Gods sequence" of, 305

October Revolution. *See* **Russian Revolution and Civil War** (1917)

Of This (Mayakovski), 528

Ogarëv, N. P., 427

Ogonek, 653

Okhitovic, Mikhail, 32

Okudzhava, Bulat, 287, 485

Old and the New, The (1929), 305

Olesha, Yuri, 484

Oliveira, Francisco de Paula ("Pavel"), 211

Olszowski, Stefan, 517

"On Contradiction" (Mao Zedong), 504, 507

On Cooperation (V. Lenin), 576

On the Correct Handling of Contradictions among the People (Mao Zedong), 395, 506

"On the Cult of Personality and Its Consequences" (Pospelov Commission), 272

"On the Economic Theory of Socialism" (Lange), 620

"On the Liquidation of Illiteracy among the Population of the RSFSR" (1919), 480

On Morality and Class Norms (Preobrazhensky), 650

"On New Democracy" (Mao Zedong), 505

"On Practice" (Mao Zedong), 504

"On the Ten Great Relationships" (Mao Zedong), 506

One Day in the Life of Ivan Denisovich (Solzhenitsyn), 287, 451, 485

One-Dimensional Man (Marcuse), 523

One Step Forward, Two Steps Back (V. Lenin), 427–28

Ontology of Social Being (Lukács), 492, 493; appendix of (*Prolegomena to Social Being*), 493

Onyszkiewicz, Wojciech, 464

Open Letter to the Party (Kurón and Modzelewski), 464

Operation Barbarossa, 358, 385, 475

Operation Noah's Ark, 364

Ordeshook, Peter, 56

Ordzhonikidze, Grigoriy (Sergo), 61, 455, 576, 593–94, 626, 838

Organización latinoamericana de solidaridad, 575

Organization of African Trade Union Unity, 422

Organization of American States, 243

Organization for European Economic Cooperation (later the Organization for Economic Cooperation and Development), 129

Organization of Proletarian Writers, 739

Organizational Questions of Russian Social Democracy (Luxemburg), 496

Origin of Russian Communism, The (Berdyaev), 470

Origins of Totalitarianism (Arendt), 34

Orlov, V., 483

Orlov, Yuri, 288

Ortega, Daniel, 368, 696, 697

Orthodox Church, Russian, 594–95; the "Living Church," 594

Orwell, George, 595–97, 614, 658, 805; experiences in the Spanish Civil War, 596; as a "Tory Anarchist," 595

Osobka-Morawski, Edward, 608
Ostpolitik, 311, 597–99
Ostrom, Charles, 56
Osvobozhdenie truda (Liberation of Labor), 622
Ottaviani, Alfredo, 90
Our Differences (Plekhanov), 622
Our Political Tasks (Trotsky), 427
Ovsobozhdenie (liberation) movement, 4
Owen, Robert, 31, 830

Paasikivi, J. K., 169
Pacciardi, Randolfo, 415
Pacem in Terris (John XXIII), 90
Pact of Steel, 325
Pact of Unity of Action (1934), 634
Pajdak, Antoni, 464
Pak Hon-yong, 194, 195
Pakistan, 1, 2, 3, 259
Palabra Socialista, 196
Palestine, Communist Party in, 201
Palme, Olof, 53
Palmer Raids, 15
Paranov, G., 152
Pareto, Vilfredo, 618
Partial Test Ban Treaty, 275
Partisans of Peace, 601–2
Partito socialista di unità proletaria (Proletarian Unity Socialist Party), 578
Pârvulescu, Constantin, 213
Parvus-Helpand, Alexander, 813
Pasado y Presente, 199
Pashukanis, Evgeny, 110
Pasternak, Boris, 271, 451, 484, 501
Paszyn, Jan, 207
Patai, Daphne, 595
Patočka, Jan, 95
Pătrăşcanu, Lucreţiu, 213, 336
patron-client relations. *See* **clientelism**
Pauker, Ana, 213, 336
Paul VI, 91
Pavlov, Valentin, 241, 613
peaceful coexistence, 602–3; basis for the doctrine, 602; definition of what the doctrine was not and should not be, 602; points of the doctrine, 602
Peasant Gazette, 652
peasants in the USSR, 603–7. *See also* **collectivization**
Peidl, Gyula, 397
Pelikan, Jiri, 95
Penelón, José Fernando, 197, 199
Peng Dehuai, 252, 357, 479, 491, 714
Peng Zhen, 252, 715
Penkovsky, Oleg, 243
People's Commissariat for Internal Affairs, 447–48, 769, 769, 871, 875–76; purge of, 876

People's Commissariat of Transport, 811–12
People's Committee for Education, 654
People's Democracy, 607–10; historiographic evaluation of concept, 609–10; impact of concept on political development of postwar Eastern Europe, 609; tightening of the term, 609
People's Democratic Party of Afghanistan, 1
People's Liberation Army (China), 98–101; history and ideology of, 98–99
Peredo, Chato Fernando, 369
Peredo, Inti, 369
perestroika, 113, 252, 291, 341, 426, 566, 582, 611–14, 659, 701; achievements of, 614; ambiguity of the term, 611; as the description of an era, 611–12; failure of, 613–14; Gorbachev's view of the term, 611; meaning of the term, 611; the role of an idealized Lenin in the genesis and development of the term, 611; and *uzkorenie* (acceleration), 612; why the term was chosen, 611
Perestroika: New Thinking for Our Country and the World (Gorbachev), 582, 611
Péret, Benjamin, 30
Pérez Jiménez, Marcos, 367, 575
Péri, Gabriel, 615–16
Peris, Daniel, 36
Perl, William, 770
Perlo, Victor, 769
Perón, Juan Domingo, 370
Peru, guerrilla warfare in, 368
Pesce, Hugo, 513
Peter the Great, 594, 622, 756
Petkoff, Luben, 367
Petkoff, Teodoro, 199
Petkov, Nikola, 282
Petlura, Ataman, 624
Petlyura, Semyon, 309
Petőfi Circle, 398
Petrograd Soviet, 689
Petrokov, Nikolay, 612
Pham Van Dong, 227
Phan Boi Chau, 386
Phan Chu Trinh, 386
Phan Van Khai, 228
Phan Van Truong, 387
Phenomenology of Spirit (Hegel), 492
Philby, Kim, 327, 768
Philippines, Communist Party in, 213–14
Phillips, Richard Francis, 197
Philosophical Notebooks (V. Lenin), 527
Piatakov, Yury (Iurii), 360, 664
Piatkov, Georgy, 411
Piatnitskii, Osip, 464, 616–17
Picasso, Pablo, 30, 574, 601

Pieck, Wilhelm, 49, 166, 174, 551, 617, 753, 823
Pilnyak, Boris, 327, 484, 581, 710
Piłsudski, Jozef, 624
Pimen, 595
Pintor, Luigi, 579
Pipes, Richard, 269
Pisemsky, Aleksey, 483
Pius IX, 89
Pius XI, 90
Pius XII, 90
planned economies, 138–39, 269
planning, 618–21; in Eastern Europe, 620–21; in the Soviet Union, 618–20
Planning in Practice, 139
Platonov, Sergey, 382
Plekhanov, Georgy, 4, 35, 278, 427, 428, 471, 472, 483, 521, 526, 622–23; as the "father of Russian Marxism," 622; Marxist program of, 622
Pludek, Alexej, 485
pluralism: "institutional" pluralism, 807; political pluralism, 582, 612, 748
Podgorny, Nikolay, 647
Pokrovsky, Mikhail, 381, 428, 526, 527
Pol Pot, 98, 193, 194, 310, 449, 507, 623–24, 705. *See also* **Khmer Rouge**
Poland, 22, 417, 653, 674, 684, 726, 747, 761, 814, 850, 851, 853, 871–72; invasion of Ukraine by, 847; martial law in, 514–19; as a People's Democracy, 608; postcommunism in, 639; radical change in, 676; as virtually mononational, 568. *See also* **Communist Party in Poland; martial law in Poland**
Polian, Pavel, 266, 268
Polish Committee of National Liberation, 871–72
Polish-Soviet War (1919–20), 624–25; cause of, 624; five phases of, 624–25; main contestants of, 624
politburo, 625–28
Political Administration of the Revolutionary Military Council of the Red Army, 670
political pilgrims, 628–31; in the 1990s–early 21st century, 629; appeals of the host societies, 630; and disillusionment, 630; first-generation, 629; impact of the pilgrimages, 631; in the late 1920s–late 1930s, 629; and the legitimating of Communist states, 631; in the mid-1970s, 629; and the revision of the defining characteristics of intellectuals, 631; second-generation, 629–30; techniques of hospitality used by host governments, 630
Pollitt, Harry, 176, 631–32

polycentrism, 632–34
Pomyalovskii, N. G., 546
Ponomarenko, Panteleimon, 154
Ponomarëv, Boris, 284
Popov, G. M., 626
Popov, P. P., 619, 709
Popoviç, Miladin, 144, 394
Popular Democracy. *See* **People's Democracy**
Popular Front, 634–36; as delineated in the Seventh Comintern Congress (July–August 1935), 634–35; origins of, 634
Popular Movement for the Liberation of Angola, 246, 247
Portaniero, Juan Carlos, 199
Portocarrero, Julio, 513
Portugal, ultra-colonialism of, 222. *See also* **Communist Party in Portugal; Portugal's Carnation Revolution**
Portugal's Carnation Revolution, 637–38
Pospelov, Petr M., 272, 709
Possessed, The (Dostoyevksy), 483
postmodernism, 42
post-Soviet communism, 638–41; pattern 1: orthodox Communist rule continued and a ruling party retained its leading role, 640; pattern 2: a formerly ruling Communist Party became a vehicle of authoritarian rule under a post-Communist leadership, 640; pattern 3: a formerly ruling Communist Party evolved into a Social Democratic party, 640; pattern 4: a no longer ruling party remained committed to its Marxist-Leninist heritage but also accepted multiparity politics and a mixed economy, 640–41
Postyshev, Pavel, 391, 626
Potere Operaio, 791
Potsdam Conference (1945), 354, 872–73
power politics, 641–45; empirical assessment of, 643–45; and ideology, 642–43
Power of the Powerless, The (Havel), 379
Pozharsky, Dmitry, 359
Pozgay, Imre, 640
Pozner, Vladimir, 501
pragmatism, 7, 11
Prague Conference (1912), 593
Prague Coup, 645–46
Prague Manifesto (1934), 381
Prague Spring, 17, 58, 113, 165, 176, 269, 270, 298, 311, 514, 646–50, 668, 746; aftermath of, 649–50; early developments of, 646–47; escalation of the crisis, 648; invasion and occupation of Czechoslovakia, 648; Soviet

concerns over accelerated reforms in Czechoslovakia, 647
Pravda ("Truth"), 61, 94, 358, 472, 652, 657, 664
Praxis, 523
Preobrazhensky, Evgeny, 77–78, 125, 576, 577, 619, 650–51, 749
press, 651–53, 655, 657; closing of non-Bolshevik daily newspapers, 651–52; decentralization of the state press during the Russian civil war, 652; as a forum for letters, 652; political clashes between presses, 652–53; target audiences of, 652; under Stalin, 653
Prestes, Luís Carlos, 198
Primo de Rivera, José Antonio, 765
Principles of Leninism (Stalin), 113, 576, 774, 778
Prison Notebooks (Gramsci), 350–52, 522, 523
Pritchard, Victor, 595
Problems of the German Revolution, The (Zinovyev), 891
Problems of Idealism (Tugan-Baranovsky), 470
Problems with Leninism (Stalin), 92
Profintern, 421
Prokopovich, S. N., 427
Proletkult, 653–54; conflict of with institutions, 654; utopian nature of, 654
Proletkult Theatre, 304
propaganda, Communist, 654–57; and *agitka* films, 656; Bolshevik propaganda, 691; and the creation of mass organizations, 656; and the development of graphic arts, 656; during collectivization and industrialization, 656–57; and film, 657; fundamental features of, 655; oral agitation, 655; success of, 654–55; use of the arts in, 657. *See also* **press**
Proudhon, Pierre-Joseph, 69, 156, 552
public opinion, 658–59; control of, 659; and the myth of the infallible leader, 658–59; study of, 659
Pudovkin, Vsevolod, 108
Pugo, Boris, 241
purges, 659–61; definition of, 659; practice of in relation to the Communist Party's conception of itself, 659–60; specific purges of the 1920s and 1930s, 660. *See also* Great Purge(s)
Pushkin, Aleksandr, 756
Pushkin Museum of Fine Arts, 271
Pushkin Society, 153
Putin, Vladimir, 359, 870
Pyatakov, Georgy, 576, 577, 593

Quaderni piacentini, 578
Quaderni rossi, 578
"Questions concerning the History of Bolshevism" (Stalin), 527
Quotations from Chairman Mao Zedong. See "Little Red Book"

Rabotnik (Worker), 149
"Racial Problem in Latin America, The" (Mariátegui), 513
Radek, Karl, 135, 173, 284, 406, 411, 563, 577, 663–64; accusations against, 664; as architect of the Rapallo Treaty, 663; arrest and trial of, 664; as editor of *Izvestiia,* 664; expertise of in international affairs, 663; and the "German October" fiasco, 664; and "National Bolshevism," 663–64
radicalism, of the 1960s, 17
Radishchëv, Aleksandr, 483
Radó, Sándor, 768
Raimundo, Gregorio López, 221
Rajk, Ladislav, 415
Rajk, László, 398, 664–65, 666
Rákosi, Mátyás, 131, 179, 197, 270, 336, 397, 406, 433, 434, 555, 556, 665, 666–67
Rakovsky, Christian, 212
Rakowski, Mieczyslaw, 535
Ramadier, Paul, 171
Ramírez, Sergio, 697
Ranghet, Iosif, 213
Ranković, Aleksandar, 232
Rapacki, Adam, 275
Rapallo Treaty (1922), 97, 563, 663, 667–68
Rashidov, Sharaf, 154, 155, 568
Rasulaev, Abdurrahman, 425
Rasulov, D., 154
Rates, Carlos, 211
Rathenau, Walter, 667
Ravines, Eudocio, 513
Razzakov, I. P., 154
Reading Capital (Althusser), 523
Reagan, Ronald, 13, 50, 122, 130, 239, 276–77, 277, 342, 445, 586, 589, 614, 676, 696, 702, 795
real socialism, 544, 668–69; principal features of, 668
"realpolitik," 728
Red Army, 608, 669–72; change of to the Soviet Army, 671–72; formation of by decree, 669; performance of in World War II, 671; rearmament and modernization of, 670; and Stalin's purges, 671; transformation of into a "true" army, 669–70, 690
Red Army Faction (Rote Armee Fraktion), 792

Red Guard, 672–74; and the Cultural Revolution, 673; demise of, 673; nature of the movement, 673; origin of, 672–73

"Red scares," 14–15, 16

Red Star (Bogdanov), 580

Red Terror, 178, 674–75, 845; in Cambodia, 675; in China, 674; common features of, 675; in Latin America, 675; targets of, 674

"Red Vienna," 18

Reed, John, 14

Reflections on Progress, Peaceful Coexistence, and Intellectual Freedom (Sakharov), 695

Regarding the "Asiatic" Mode of Production, Feudalism, Serfdom, and Commercial Capitalism (Dubvrosky), 526

Regarding Entropy in Politics (Havel), 379

Regler, Gustav, 415

Religiia i sotsializm ("Religion and Socialism"), 494

Renner, Karl, 147, 558–59

Repentance (1987), 109

Repin, Ilya, 756

"Report on the Peasant Movement in Hunan" (Mao Zedong), 504

Report of the Siberian Delegation (Trotsky), 813

Republican Party (United States), 15, 16

Rerum Novarum (Leo XII), 421

Reshetovskaya, Natalya, 742

Residencia en la tierra (Neruda), 574

"Resolution of the Central Committee of the CCP on Methods of Leadership" (Mao Zedong), 505

Results and Prospects (Trotsky), 813

Retour de l'URSS (Gide), 502

reunification of Germany, 676–78; events leading to, 676–77; and the fall of the Berlin Wall, 677

Reunion of Communist Parties of the Western Hemisphere (1939), 198

revisionism, 678–79

revolution, myths of, 679–82; of the efficiency of revolution, 681; in Europe, 680; and the institutionalization of revolution, 680–81; revolution as anti-Fascist political project, 682; the Russian Revolution, 679–80; and the superiority of a planned economy and industrialization, 681–82

"Revolution against 'Capital,' The" (Gramsci), 348

Revolution Betrayed (Trotsky), 80, 805, 816

Revolution and Counter-revolution in Germany (Marx), 428

revolution from above, 571–72, 682–83, 774, 855

"Revolution in the Revolution?" (Debray), 367

Revolutionary Military Council of the Republic, 669

revolutions in East-Central Europe, 683–87; consequences of Gorbachev's policies in Eastern Europe, 686–87; the fall of communism, 683–85; and the Khrushchev Dilemma, 685–86, 687; and the reorientation of Soviet policy, 684–85

Ridā, Muhammad, 185

Ridgway, Matthew, 171

Riehl, Kinolaus, 39

Riesman, David, 13

Risorgimento, ruling classes of, 5

Rivera, Diego, 817

Rivera, Primo, 219

Road to Serfdom, The (Hayek), 80, 806

Road to Wigan Pier, The (Orwell), 595–96

Robinson, Henry, 768

Robotnik (The Worker), 534

Roca, Blas, 198

Rochet, Waldeck, 171, 511, 561

Rodionov, M., 500

Rodriguez, Antonio. *See* Oliveira, Francisco de Paula ("Pavel")

Rodríguez, Carlos Rafael, 161

Roi-Tanguy, Henri, 416

Rojo, Vicente, 766

Rokossowski, Konstantin, 209

Rolland, Romain, 328

"rollback," 445

Roman inachevé (Aragon), 30

Romania, 564, 609, 684, 687, 726, 729, 744, 761, 848, 866; formation of the "Group of Nine," 827; nationality policies of, 568; and the "Nicolae Ceausescu era," 92. *See also* **Communist Party in Romania**

Romanov, Grigorii, 291, 341

Rome-Berlin Axis, 325

Rondani, Dino, 196

Roosevelt, Franklin D., 15, 258, 353, 354, 487, 529. *See also* **Yalta Conference**

Rosaio, Antonio, 415

Rose, Gregory, 56

Rosenthal, Jakob, 201

Rossanda, Rossana, 579

Rosselli, Carlo, 416

Rossi, Jacques, 374

Rössler, Rudolf, 768

"Rosta Windows" (Mayakovski), 528

Rothschild, Joseph, 609

Rousseau, Jean-Jacques, 268

Rousset, David, 84, 698

Roy, Manabendra Nath, 180, 197, 563

Rudas, László, 178

Rudzutak, Yan, 577, 626

Ruíz, Henry, 696

Rusk, Dean, 244

Russell, Bertrand, 243, 367, 485

Russia, 7, 22; famine in, 320–21; "going to the people" movement in, 3

Russian Communist Party, 63–64

Russian Orthodox Church, 35, 36, 90

Russian Revolution, The (Luxemburg), 496

Russian Revolution and Civil War (1917), 14, 41, 66, 196, 348, 349, 359, 381, 473, 514, 688–92, 717, 819; collapse of the economy during, 688–89; contradictions inherent in, 604; downfall of the Romanov dynasty, 688; and the expropriation of industry by the state, 690–90; and the governance of the soviets, 689; reconstruction of the Soviet order, 690; Red Army victories during, 691–92; reinforcement of peasant culture, 604

Russo-Polish War. *See* **Polish-Soviet War**

Rust, William, 176, 632

Ryazanov, David, 381, 382

Rykov, Aleksei, 78, 360, 487, 546, 577, 625, 626, 692–93, 876

Ryömä, Mauri, 168

Ryumin, Michail, 448

Ryvicki, Józef, 464

Ryzhkov, Nikolai, 10, 341, 612

Saarinen, Aarne, 169

Sabata, Jaroslav, 95

Sadoul, Georges, 30

Saillant, Louis, 421, 422

Saint Francis of Assisi, 492

Sakharov, Andrey, 39, 288, 288–89, 289, 603, 695–96, 702

Salazar, Antonio de Oliveira, 211

Salisbury, Harrison, 491

Salman, Yusuf ("Comrade Fahd"), 201

Samouth, Tou, 193

Samphan, Khieu, 193

San Martín, Ramón Grau, 160

Sánchez, Arias, 697

Sandinista Revolution, 368, 370, 696–97

Sandino, Augusto César, 197, 696

Sandino, César, 368

Santucho, Mario Roberto, 369

Sar, Saloth. *See* **Pol Pot**

Sarant, Alfred, 770

Sartre, Jean-Paul, 13, 16, 328, 367, 485, 523, 534, 579, 601, 697–98; favorable opinion of the Soviet Union, 698; refusal to accept the Nobel Prize for Literature, 698

Sary, Ieng, 193

Scarecrow (1984), 109

Schanberg, Sidney, 453

Scheel, Walter, 276

Schirdewan, Karl, 167

Schlesinger, Arthur, 242

Schleyer, Hans-Martin, 792

Schmidt, Helmut, 276, 598

Schmidt, Vasily, 411

Schulz, George, 366

Schulze-Boysen, Harro, 58

Schuman Plan, 313

Schussnigg, Kurt, 147

Schweller, Randall, 56, 56–57; on "lesser greater powers," 56; on "polarization," 57

science, 698–701; Chinese and Soviet scientific institutions, 700; and development of nuclear weapons, 701; practice of, 700–701; state science and industrialization, 700; theory of, 698–99

Scientific Organization of Labor, 831

Scobie, Ronald, 364

Scoccimarro, Mauro, 349

Scythians, The (Blok), 483

Secchia, Pietro, 6, 803

Second Cold War, 586, 588–89, 701–3; political developments leading to, 701–2; political unrest and social mobilization as causes of, 702; role of new missile development in, 702; spread of pro-Soviet revolution throughout the world, 702

Second International, 382, 851, 889

"second Stalinism," 29

Second Vatican Council, 90

secret speech, 272, 383, 450–51, 455–56, 703–5

Sedláček, Jiri, 485

Sedov, Lev, 816

Sedova, Natalya, 816

Şegedin, P., 486

Seghers, Anna, 328

Seifert, Jaroslav, 95

Selassie, Haile, 322

Selden, Mark, 105

self-criticism, 705

Semprún, Jorge ("Federico Sánchez"), 221

Sen, Amartya, 323, 358

Sen, Son, 193

Sendero luminosa, 368

Sendic, Raúl, 369

Senghor, Léopold Sédar, 565

Serebriakov, Leonid P., 360, 650, 664

Sereni, Emilio, 13, 601

Serge, Victor, 428, 501

Serov, I. A., 400

Seton-Watson, Hugh, 610

Shakhnazarov, Georgiy, 583, 685

Shalamov, Varlam, 287, 373, 374, 614, 706

Shanin, Teodor, 605

Shaposhnikov, Boris, 847

Sharansky, Anatoly, 288

Sharkey, Lance, 146

"Shatalin-Yavlinsky plan," 612

Shaw, George Bernard, 628

Shelest, Petro, 647

Shendrikov, Ilia, 153

Shevardnadze, Eduard, 291, 292, 341, 685, 706–8, 870; education of, 707; as foreign minister, 707; as president of Georgia, 708; relationship with George Schultz, 707

Sheynin, Oleg, 241

Shiga, Yoshio, 192

Shii, Kazuo, 192

Shlyapnikov, Alexander, 459

Shmelev, A. N., 819

Sholokhov, Mikhail, 484, 739

Short Course of the History of the All-Russian Communist Party (Bolshevik), 382, 383, 429, 524–25, 526, 682, 708–10, 775, 779; depiction of Stalin in, 382; function of, 525; leadership of Lenin described in, 708–9; Stalin's influence on, 524–25, 527, 709

Shostakovich, Dmitry, 476, 710–11; legacy of, 711; as a master of different musical genres, 710; reception of his opera *Lady Macbeth of the Mtsensk District*, 710; response to the Soviet power structure, 711; Stalin's attacks on, 710

Shucht, Apollon A., 349

Shucht, Julia, 349, 350, 802

Shucht, Tatiana, 350

Shumiatsky, Boris, 305

Shvernik, Nikolai, 627, 804

Siantos, G., 364

Siberian Socio-Democrate Union, 153

Siete ensayos de interpretación de la realidad peruana (Mariátegui), 512

Sihanouk, Norodom, 193, 449, 623

Sik, Ota, 620

Sikorski, Władysław, 439

Silvermaster, Nathan, 769

Simmel, Georg, 492

Simonov, Konstantin, 484

single-party system, 712–14; as a dominant party system, 713; extent of in Communist countries, 712; formal structure of, 712–13; "narrow single parties," 712, 713; role of the Communist Party in Communist states, 713; weakness of, 713

Sino-Soviet split, 714–15, 744, 745–46, 794, 803; causes of, 714; impact of on China's economy, 715; impact of on Maoist ideology, 715; Khrushchev's role in, 714–15; Mao's role in, 714, 715

Sinyavsky, Andrei, 30, 287, 485, 743

Široký, Vilém, 401

Sirola, Yrjö, 168

Situationist International movement, 33

Siwicki, Florian, 518

Skforecký, Josef, 379

Skilling, H. Gordon, 807

Skrypnyk, Mykola, 392

Skvorcov-Stepanov, Ivan, 619

Slánský, Rudolf, 162, 164, 590, 715–17; criticism of, 716, 717; devotion of to the Communist Party, 716–17; early political career of, 715–16; exile of, 716; relationship with Klement Gottwald, 716–17

Slap in the Face of Public Taste, A, 528

Slipyj, Josyf, 90

Slonimski, Anton, 534

Slovakia, 401, 866

Sneevliet, Henk (Maring), 183

Snow, Edgar, 491

Soares, Mário, 638

Sobell, Morton, 770

social democracy, 717–19; and the development of NATO, 718; and fascism, 720; predominance of in the West, 718; retreat of socialist parties in Western Europe, 718–19. See also **Socialist International**

Social Democratic Party (Czechoslovakia), 645, 646

Social Democratic Party (Germany), 678, 679, 719, 720, 754, 793. See also **Luxemburg, Rosa**

Social Democratic Party of Germany, 172, 174, 793

social fascism, 325, 719–20

social policy, 720–24; in China, 723; and family law, 721; institutional redistributional model, 721; and rapid industrialization, 721; and "second economy," 722; in Soviet republic, 721; and women, 722

Social Reform or Revolution? (Luxemburg), 495, 679

socialism, 7, 609, 684, 686; "developed socialism," 668; "market socialism," 810; as officially established in the Soviet Union, 782, 783; "real socialism," 544, 668–69; relationship of to art, 710. See also **socialism in one country; socialist camp; Socialist International**

Socialism (von Mises), 80

Socialism: Utopian and Scientific (Engels), 423

Socialism and the Political Struggle (Plekhanov), 622

socialism in one country, 423, 577, 651, 724–26, 748, 756; explication of by Stalin and Bukharin, 724

socialist camp, 726–31; addition of China to, 727; changes in the makeup of, 727; and the creation of the Warsaw Pact, 728; and the idea of a federative union, 726; origins of, 726; reasons for the creation of, 726; splitting of, 730

socialist consumer society, 731–33; asceticism as main principle of socialist consumption, 731; and the centralized distribution of goods, 732; hierarchy of consumption, 732; initial destruction of the market system in the Soviet Union, 731; propaganda concerning, 731; rehabilitation of bourgeois values, 732; relationship of the market to a planned economy, 732–33; similarities of with Western consumer societies, 733

socialist emulation, 733–34

Socialist International, 734–36; and bridge-building between socialists and Communists, 735; "new beginning" of, 736

socialist market economy, 737–38; adoption of in the 1990s, 737–38; idea of the integration of market forces and economic planning, 737–38; and the labor question, 737; meaning of the term "socialist" in, 738

Socialist Party of Italy, 6, 314, 736

"socialist realism," 251, 413, 738–40; in cinema and literature, 739; first appearance of the term, 738; as the plot of social realist novels, 581; role of in the Soviet plan for global hegemony, 740

Socialist Revolutionaries, 688, 689, 690, 763

Socialist Unity Party (Germany), 676, 754

Sokolnikov, Grigori, 71, 664, 749

Sokolovskaya, Alexandra, 813, 816

Sokolovsky, Vasily D., 48

Solidarity, 17, 210, 269, 270, 464, 514–19, 639, 676, 683, 740–42; "Appeal to the Working People of Eastern Europe," 519; origins of, 740; phases of during its legal existence, 741–42; right wing of, 742

Solzhenitsyn, Aleksandr, 16, 113, 287, 288–89, 372, 374, 451, 485, 614, 742–44

Somalia, 223

Sontag, Susan, 630

Sorel, Georges, 492, 512, 552

Sorensen, Theodore, 243

Sorge, Richard, 769

Sossi, Mario, 791

"Sources of Soviet Conduct, The" (Kennan), 236–37

South Africa, Communist Party in, 26, 223

South Korea, 544. *See also* **Korean War** (1950–53)

South West Africa People's Organization, 247

Southeast Asia. *See* **Communist Party in Southeast Asia; Vietnam War**

"Sovereignty and the Internationalist Obligations of Socialist Countries" (Kovalev), 74–75

Sovetskaia rossiia, 653

Soviet bloc, 609, 744–48; demise of, 748; formation of and the legacy of Stalin, 744–45; under Brezhnev, 747; under Khrushchev, 745–46

Soviet industrialization, 7, 656–57, 748–52; after the fall of communism, 751; changes in the location of industry, 749; differing views on how to implement, 749; effect of on women's emancipation, 855–56; impact of on agriculture, 749; positive effects of, 750; post–World War II, 751; and workers' standard of living, 856–57

Soviet Military Administration in Germany, 753

Soviet occupation of Germany, 752–56; establishment of the Soviet Zone of Occupation (SZO), 753; goals of, 753; political implications, 754; Sovietization of the SZO, 753

Soviet patriotism, 755–57

Soviet-Polish War. *See* **Polish-Soviet War**

Soviet Union (Union of Soviet Socialist Republics), 18, 19, 27, 259, 675, 684, 687, 702–3; Allied aid to, 353; collectivization in, 126–28; commitment of to the Congo, 827; divorce rate in, 318; as the "evil empire," 702; fall of, 122; famine in, 320, 606; German invasion of (1941), 37; impact of European politics on, 775; industrialization of, 7, 656–57, 748–52; invasion of Japan, 38; invasions of Czechoslovakia and Hungary, 27; nationality policies of, 566–68, 570–73; as a "superpower" during the Cold War, 57–58; as totalitarian, 806–6; and the United nations, 826–27. *See also* **Afghan War; Communist Party in the Soviet Union; Coup in the USSR (1991); Cuban-Soviet intervention in Africa; deportation of nationalities in the USSR; dissent in the USSR; dissolution of the USSR; Sino-Soviet split; socialist camp; socialist consumer society; Soviet bloc; Soviet industrialization; Soviet occupation of Germany; Soviet-Yugoslavia break; totalitarianism; transportation; Vietnam War**

Soviet-Yugoslavia break, 757–59; economic complications between the countries, 757; origins of, 757; Soviet reaction to Yugoslavia's reforms, 757–58

Sovietization, 128, 251, 759–62; definition of, 759; in Eastern Europe, 609–10, 761; establishment of Soviet power in the Caucasus, 760; in Hungary, 762; major factors concerning, 760–61; in outer Mongolia and Tuva, 760; role of in the origins of World War II, 760

soviets, 763–64

Spain. *See* **Communist Party in Spain; Spanish Civil War**

Spanish Civil War, 18, 19, 22, 764–67; Barcelona riots during, 767; battles of attrition, 767; and the Condor Legion, 766; defense of Madrid, 764; destruction of Guernica, 766; destruction of the republican army, 767; diffuse nature of the military insurrection, 765; executions carried out during and after the war, 767; Mussolini's role in, 766, 766; offensive of the Corpo Truppe Volontaire, 766; origins of, 764; political situation prior to, 764; Soviet support of the International Brigades, 766

Spanish Falange, 765

Spanish Socialist Workers' Party, 765

Spanish Testament (Koestler), 456

Spartacus Union, 172

Special Committee of the State Defense Committee (later the Council of Ministers), 38

Spender, Stephen, 328

spies, 767–70; the "Cambridge Spy Ring," 768; networks of the People's Commissariat for Internal Affairs, 769, 769; Red Orchestra networks in Belgium, the Netherlands, and France, 768; Red Orchestra networks in Germany, 767–68; Red Orchestra networks in Switzerland, 768; U.S. Communists, 769

sports, 770–72; Soviet participation in the Olympics, 771

Springhall, D. F., 176, 632

Sraffa, Piero, 350

Stachura, Bogusław, 518
Stafa, Qemal, 144
Stakhanov, Alexei, 657, 772
Stakhanovism, 772–73
Stalin, Joseph, 1, 9, 19, 37, 47, 54, 61,
62, 63, 66, 67, 73, 77, 92, 111, 113,
116, 123, 174, 177, 207, 215, 261,
270, 279, 281–82, 336, 353, 364,
365, 380, 424, 435, 437, 443, 447,
457, 459, 477, 487, 492, 496, 499,
503, 507, 514, 560–61, 564, 567,
593, 620, 625, 626, 627, 644, 650,
683, 704, 720, 734, 773–77, 815,
818, 819, 833, 839, 891; ambivalence
of toward the family, 318–19, 853;
attitude and policy toward the Grand
Alliance, 354–55; and the Berlin Crisis
of 1948–49, 48, 49; and the Cold
War, 119–20; and collectivization,
126, 127, 373, 774; and Comecon,
129; and Cominform, 131, 131–32,
134, 633, 777; and Comintern, 134,
135, 136, 137, 282, 634, 636; concept
of nation, 570; conception of postwar
Europe, 354; cult of, 249–50, 525;
consolidation of political power over
"Left" opposition, 774; control of the
state apparatus, 488; Decree on Religious Associations, 594; defense policy
of, 39; deportation of nationalities,
266, 267, 268, 309–10, 373, 568;
despotism of, 774, 777; distancing of
from Bolshevism, 358–59; as editor of
Pravda, 773; exile of in Siberia, 773;
failed security strategy of, 358; hatred
of the Poles, 439; and Ho Chi Minh,
227; on imperialism, 410; industrialization policies of, 467; influence on
Marxism-Leninism, 524–27, 781–82;
last years of, 777; on modernization,
542–43; and Molotov, 546–48; and
Molotov-Ribbentrop Pact, 20, 22,
548–50; and murder of Trotsky, 817;
on the national question, 559; and
NATO, 587; penchant for *otsechenie*
(the "chopping off" of troublesome
comrades), 64; Picasso's portrait of, 30;
policies of toward Yugoslavia under
Tito, 745, 777; and Red Army, 671;
reorganization of Islam, 424–25;
repression of the Jews, 29; response
to Hitler's invasion of the Soviet
Union, 776; restrictive interpretation
of peaceful coexistence, 603; and
"revolution from above," 571–72,
682–83, 774; rewriting of Bolshevism's
history, 382; role of in death of
Zinovyev, 892; role given to Gosplan

by, 344; self-presentation as authorized
interpreter of Lenin's thought, 576;
social fascism theory, 325, 719–20;
"socialist offensive" of, 731, 775; "socialism in one country" doctrine, 423, 577,
651, 724–26, 748, 756; state-building
process of, 775; support of for "socialist
realism," 740; triumph of over Lenin's
New Economic Policy, 577; as *tsar
batyushka*, 249; unification of Soviet
society as main problem and goal of,
738; use of famine, 390–93, 749; view
of fascism/nazism, 326, 776; view of
People's Democracies, 608–10; view of
United Nations Security Council, 826;
view of war's inevitability, 842–43; as
vozhd, 216; writings of as locus of his
power of suggestion, 526. *See also*
Great Terror; Great Turn (1930s);
**Holodomor; Korean War; Molotov-
Ribbentrop Pact;** *Short Course
of the History of the All-Russian
Communist Party (Bolshevik)*; **Soviet-
Yugoslavia break; World War II;
Yalta Conference**
Stalin (Barbusse), 779
Stalin, the Man (Trotsky), 816
Stalin, myth of, 778–80
Stalin Motor Works, 812
Stalingrad, Battle of, 780–81; casualty
figures of, 780; Red Army counterof-
fensive during, 780
Stalinism, 62, 251, 581, 781–83, 808, 819; and
the centralized system of state owner-
ship, 782; and the Cold War, 119–20;
definition of, 781; as a logical develop-
ment of Leninism, 782; and party-state
organization, 782; and Stalin's innovations concerning Marxism-Leninism,
781–82
Stalinization, 124, 128, 535
Stamboliiski, A., 150
Stanishev, Sergey, 153
Stankevich, Alexandra, 194
Starodubtsev, Vasiliy, 241
state, the, 783–86; central features of
Stalinist party-state, 785; debate concerning among Communists, 784; different phases of in Soviet Union after
1917, 783–84; during New Economic
Policy period, 785; establishment of
in Soviet Union (1922), 784; four pillars
of (party apparatus, the army, bureaucracy, secret police), 784; Marxist interpretation of, 783; redefinition of under
Khrushchev, 786; transformation of
during czarist era, 784; transformation
of during the Great Terror, 786; and

the transition from capitalism to com-
munism, 783–84
State and Revolution, The (V. Lenin), 278,
279, 352, 474, 580, 783
Stefanov, Boris, 212
Steffens, Lincoln, 327
Steinsbergowa, Aniela, 464
Sternberg, Fritz, 69
Stopypin, Pyotr, 4
Strategic Armaments Reduction Treaty
(1991), 277
Strategic Arms Limitation Talks (SALT),
275; SALT I (1972), 276, 702;
SALT II (1979), 276, 702
Strategic Defense Initiative, 277, 342
Strauss, Franz Josef, 598
Stravinsky, Igor, 711
Strike, The (1925), 304
Struve, Peter, 4, 469, 622
Stucka, P., 110
Stuttgart Congress (1907), 846, 889
Subhi, Mustafa, 201
sub-Saharan Africa. *See* **Communist Party
in sub-Saharan Africa**
"Such, Such Were the Joys" (Orwell), 595
Suchocka, Hanna, 464
Suez crisis (1956), 258, 259
Suharto, 184, 565
Sukarno, 183–84, 370, 565; *Pantja Shila* (the
"five principles" of peaceful coexistence),
585
Sultan-Galiev, Mirza, 563
Sun Shuyun, 491
Sun Yat-sen (Sun Zhongshan), 26, 156, 504,
562
Surrealist Manifesto (Breton), 30
Sushkevich, Stanislav, 874
Suslov, Mikhail, 66, 83, 129, 340, 399,
520, 601, 627, 633, 786–87; and the
"anti-Party Group" crisis, 787; as edi-
tor of *Pravda*, 787; relationship with
Brezhnev, 787
Suvorov, Aleksandr, 359
Svechin, Alexsandr, 847
Sverma, Jan, 162
Svoboda, Ludvík, 297
Sweden, 313, 719; Communist Party in, 205,
206
Swianiewicz, Stanisław, 441
Swierczewski, Karol, 415
Switzerland. *See* **Communist Party in
Switzerland**
Swomley, John, 629
Syllabus of Current Errors (Pius IX), 89
Syntaksis (Ginzburg), 286
Syria, 565; Communist Party in, 201–2
Sytin, N., 670
Szabó, Ervin, 178

Szakasits, Arpad, 666
Szczypiorski, Adam, 464

Ta Mok, 193
Tactics and Ethics (Marx), 492
Tales of Kolyma (Shalamov), 287
"Talks at the Yan'an Forum on Literature and Art" (Mao Zedong), 505
Tampov peasant rebellion, 692
Tan Malaka, 563
Tanner, Väinö, 168
Taraki, Mohammad, 1, 74
Tardini, Domenico, 90
Tarkovsky, Andrej, 287
Tarle, Yevgeny, 382
Tasca, Angelo, 348, 801
Tashkent General Revolutionary Group, 153
"Tasks in the Struggle against Contemporary Imperialism and the Unity of Action of the Communist and Workers' Parties and of All Anti-Imperialist Forces" (1969), 419
Taut, Bruno, 69
Taylor, Frederick, 831
Tchapaev, V. I., 154
Tehran Conference (1943), 353, 776
television in the Soviet era, 789
Tellman, Ernst, 174, 412
Temple, Nina, 176
Tenshin, Okakura, 26
Terán, Mario, 372
Tercera residencia (Neruda), 574
Ter-Petrosian, Simon (Kamo), 593
Terracini, Umberto, 348, 349, 801
terrorism, 790–92; dilemma of among socialists and Communists, 790; founding of Prima Linea (Front Line), 791; founding of the Red Brigades (Brigate Rosse), 791; in France, 792; in Italy and Germany, 790–91; left-wing terrorism, 790–92; and the *strategia della tensione* (strategy of tension), 790; in West Germany, 792
Terrorism and Communism (Trotsky), 278, 428, 816
Thailand, Communist Party in, 214
Thalheimer, August, 173, 412, 882
Thälmann, Ernst, 223, 406, 501, 617, 792–93; as organizer of the Hamburg Uprising, 793; and the "politics of consolidation," 793
Thanh Nien, 226, 387
Thatcher, Margaret, 342, 677, 794–95
Themelko, Kristo, 144
Theory of Depreciating Currency (Preobrazhensky), 651

third world, 258, 370, 544–45; major policy issues in, 585. *See also* **nonalignment**
third worldism, 794–95; overall plan of established in the Brandt Report, 794–95; and the Sino-Soviet split, 794
Thomas Mann and the Tragedy of Modern Art (Lukács), 493
Thompson, Edward, 523, 596
Thorez, Maurice, 30, 170, 171, 406, 511, 561, 601, 634, 779, 795–97; acceptance of the Stalinist model, 797; criticism of, 796, 797; early political career of, 795; escape from arrest and time spent underground, 795–96; leadership of, 797; prestige of among the working class, 796–97
Thurston, Anne, 254
Tian Zhuangzhuang, 255
Tiananmen Square, 264, 403, 508, 686
Tikhonov, Nikolai, 341
Tillon, Charles, 171
Times and the Wolves, The (Mandel'stam), 287
Tin Sang, 653
Tissem, Eduard, 305
Tito, Josip Broz, 131, 176, 230, 231, 232, 294, 370, 399, 416, 417, 433, 438, 451, 556, 564, 569, 585, 586, 633, 737, 745, 797–800, 803; consolidation of his power, 798–99; criticism, arrest, and denunciation of, 802; cult of, 250, 799; as Marshal of Yugoslavia, 799; role of in the internal conflicts of the Communist Party of Yugoslavia, 798; as secretary of the Communist Party of Yugoslavia, 799–800; split with Stalin, 444, 75–59, 800; as Stalin's closest comrade in arms, 799–800; support for the Bolsheviks, 798; theories as to the origin of "Tito," 797–98; and the transformation of Yugoslavia's political and economic systems, 800
Tiul'panov, Sergei, 609
Tizyakov, Aleksandr, 241
Tkachev, P. N., 427, 428
Togliatti, Palmiro, 5, 6, 12, 134, 188, 189, 190, 197, 199, 220, 249, 273, 310, 406, 414, 551 560, 561, 565, 601, 632–33, 633, 765, 779, 801–4; alignment of with Stalin, 801, 803; founding of the journal *L'Ordine Nuovo* (The New Order), 801; involvement in the Great Terror, 802; post–World War II policies of, 802–3; pseudonym of (Ercoli), 801; realism of, 803; role of in the founding of the Italian Communist

Party, 801; role of in the Sino-Soviet split, 803–4; and the "Salerno turn," 802; view of fascism, 326, 348, 349, 350, 801; "Yalta Memorial" manifesto of, 804. *See also* **polycentrism**
Tokuda, Kyūichi, 191, 192
Toledano, Vicente Lombardo, 421
Tolstoy, Lev, 483
Toman, Karl, 147
Tomich, Radomiro, 824
Tomsky, Mikhail, 78, 435, 577, 626, 693, 804–5
Tönnies, Ferdinand, 492
Torres, Camilo, 368
Torres, Juan José, 369
Totalitarian Dictatorship and Autocracy (Friedrich and Brzezinski), 806
totalitarianism, 15, 34, 326, 805–8; American totalitarianism, 13; and the comparison of the Soviet Union to Nazi Germany, 805; initial use of the term in describing Italian fascism, 805; linkage of to the polemics of the Cold War, 806–7; in post–World War II West Germany, 806; refinement of the term in academia, 806; resistance to its use in describing the Soviet Union, 807; resurgence of in Cold War rhetoric, 805–6
Touré, Ahmed Sekou, 372, 565
trade unions, 808–10; in China, 810; "defensive function" of, 808–9; differences between capitalist and Communist, 809; "dual functions" of, 808; formal structure of, 809; ineffectiveness of, 810; Lenin's ambivalent view of, 808; performance of the "dual functions" in the Soviet era, 809; variations in the Soviet model of, 809–10. *See also* **international trade union organizations; Solidarity**
Tran Phu, 388
transportation, 811–12; canal-building projects, 812; central importance of railroad system, 811; construction of transport infrastructure in the Stalin era, 812; influence of the People's Commissariat of Transport, 811–12; in the post-Stalin era, 812; preoccupation with in the Soviet regime, 811; railway construction in the Stalin era, 812; road construction, 812; use of forced labor in construction projects, 812
"Treatise of Military Cooperation for the Defense of the National Territory of Cuba in Case of Aggression," 242
Treaty of Brest-Litovk. *See* **Brest-Litovsk, Treaty of** (1918)

Treaty of Görlitz (1950), 67
Treaty of Moscow (1970), 597
Treaty of Rapallo. *See* **Rapallo Treaty**
Treaty of Riga (1921), 65, 625
Treaty of Versailles (1919), 156
Trefulka, Jan, 95
Trepper, Leopold, 768
Triolet, Elsa, 30
tripolarity, 56–57
Trollope, Anthony, 11
Trommeln der Nacht (Brecht), 69
Trotsky, Leon, 28, 61, 62, 65, 71, 72, 77, 80, 135, 137, 215–16, 278, 283, 411, 423, 427, 428, 435, 462, 474, 477, 492, 494, 501, 521, 526, 527, 576, 577, 580–81, 581, 593, 624, 625, 636, 664, 665, 681, 739, 763, 805, 813–18; 891; adoption of Marxism under the influence of his wife, 813; arrogance of, 813; assassination of, 817; attack on Lenin, 813; and the Bolsheviks, 813–14; clash with Stalin, 774; contempt for Stalin, 817; deportation of, 816; escape of from Siberia, 813; and idea of "permanent revolution," 724, 813; ill-health of, 815; as leader of Left Opposition, 815–16; as liaison between Communist Party and the army, 814; in Mexico, 817; resurgence of interest in, 818; and Treaty of Brest-Litovsk, 689–90, 814; view of fascism (as Bonapartism), 325; view of the intelligentsia, 414; view of trade unions, 814; as war commissar, 669, 670, 690, 815
Trotsky, Sergei, 816
Trotskyism, 802, 818–20, 838; as anti-Leninist, 819; criticism of, 819; definitions of, 818, 819; Milyukov's invention of term, 818; Trotsky/Trotskyism distinction, 819
Troyanovsky, Oleg, 452
Truman, Harry S., 38, 120, 236, 238, 529, 834, 872; Soviet view of, 354
Truman Doctrine, 16, 237, 355, 515, 873
Truong Chinh, 227, 388, 389
Tsankov, Aleksandr, 280
Tsedenbal, Yumjaagiin, 203
Tsvetaeva, Marina, 484
Tucker, Robert, 682
Tugan-Baranovsky, Mikhail, 469, 470
Tukhachevskii, Mikhail, 360, 451, 462, 624–25, 834–35, 838, 845, 847
Tuominen, Arvo, 168
Tupamaros, 369
Turcios Lima, Luis, 368
Turgenev, Ivan, 483
Turkey, 15, 563, 565; Communist Party in, 201

Tvardovsky, Aleksandr, 451, 484
Twelve (Blok), 483

U Thant, 243, 244
"Ueber meinen Lehrer" (About My Teacher) (Brecht), 69
Ugarte, Manuel, 196
Uglanov, Nikolai, 435, 546
Uhl, Peter, 95
Ukraine, 22, 27, 266, 309, 477, 567, 688, 692; independence movement in, 292, 293. *See also* **Holodomor**
Ukrainization, 435
Ulbricht, Walter, 50, 166–67, 174, 224, 275, 393, 415, 551, 617, 647, 753, 823–24
Unidad Popular, 824–26
Unik, Pierre, 30
Union Intercoloniale, 387
Union of Communists of Yugoslavia, 417
unipolarity, 56
United Nations, 3, 353, 826–27, 840; creation of, 826; and the "Group of Nine," 827; Khrushchev's use of as a forum to the third world, 826–27; problem of China's representation in, 826; resolution 181, 187; resolution equating Zionism with racism, 827; and Soviet Union's dependent states, 827; Stalin's view of, 826; and Taiwan, 827. *See also* United Nations Security Council
United Nations Security Council, 826, 827, 874
United Socialist Party of Germany, 175
United States, 3, 7–8, 353, 565, 865, 875; "containment of communism" policy, 49; criticism of, 8; as emblem of imperialism, 8; as "superpower" during Cold War, 57–58, 643; as symbol of modernity, 10–11; as threat to socialism, 7. *See also* **Cold War; Communist Party in the United States; Vietnam War**
Universal Declaration of Human Rights (1948), 113, 258
Unszlicht, Józef, 299
al-'Urabi, Mahmud Husni, 201
urban planning. *See* **architecture and urban planning**
Urbanek, Zdenek, 95
urbanization, 827–30; in Asia, 828–30; in Europe, 828, 829; and industrialization, 828; planning and regulating, 829–30; as result of Communist revolution, 828; in USSR, 828, 829
Uribe, Vicente, 220, 221
Uruguay, guerrilla warfare in, 369

U.S. National Security Council Directive 68, 834
Ustinov, Dmitry, 9, 83, 341, 366, 627
Usubaliev, Turdakul, 154, 155
utopia, 830–32; ambivalence in the Bolshevik's view of, 830; and experimental lifestyles, 831–32; influence of on artists, 832; Russian and Soviet utopianism, 831; and use of revolutionary names, 831

Vágó, Béla, 178
Vagoc, A. V., 154
Vaia, Alessandro, 415
Vallejo, Marmaduque Grove, 824
Vance, Cyrus, 239
Vannikov, B. L., 38
Vántus, Károly, 178
Varga, Eugen, 123, 124, 515, 833
Vargas, Getúlio, 198
Vásquez, Fabio, 368
Vekhi (Milestones) (Berdayev et al.), 412–13
Venezuela: Communist Party in, 199; guerrilla warfare in, 367
Verhaeren, Émile, 528
Vezer, Erzsébet, 492
Victor Emanuel III, 552
Videla, Jorge, 369–70
Videnov, Zhan, 152
Vietnam, 259, 544, 565, 653, 675, 729; famine in, 322. *See also* **Communist Party in Vietnam; Vietnam War; Vietnam-Cambodia War**
Vietnam War, 27, 214, 228, 239, 565, 807, 834–36; benefits of to Soviet foreign policy elsewhere in the world, 835–36; place of in history of Cold War, 834; possibility war would spread to a general war involving Soviet Union, 836; Soviet involvement in, 834–35
Vietnam-Cambodia War, 837–38
Villalobos, Joaquín, 697
Viola, Lynn, 807
Viola, Roberto, 369–70, 697
Vladimir Ilych Lenin (Mayakovski), 528
Vladimir Mayakovsky (Mayakovski), 528
Vladimov, Georgy, 288
Vlahovich, Veliko, 632
Vo Nguyen Giap, 227, 228
Vo Van Kiet, 228
Volya, Narodnaya, 427
von Bismarck, Otto, 683
von Borcke, A., 427
von Hayek, Friedrich A., 80, 618
von Maltzan, Ago, 667
von Mises, Ludwig, 80, 618
von Ribbentrop, Joachim, 548

von Stauffenberg, Claus, 24
von Vollmar, Georg, 679
Von weissen Nächten und roten Tagen (Koestler), 456
Voroshilov, Kliment, 440, 487, 560–61, 576, 577, 616, 626, 670, 838–39
Vorovsky, Vatslav, 284
Vorwärts (Forward), 495
Voznesensky, Andrey, 485
Voznesensky, Nikolai, 129, 500, 626
Vygotsky, Lev, 700
Vyshinsky, Andrey, 833, 839–40; activity of in Stalinist oppressions, 839–40; and Allied policy toward Italy, 840; as delegate to United Nations, 840; as prosecutor in "Metro-Vickers" trial, 839
Vysocky, Vladimir, 287, 485

Walesa, Lech, 210, 520, 535, 742, 841. *See also* **Solidarity**
Wallace, Henry, 16
Waltz, Kenneth, 56, 58, 642
Wang Dongxing, 254
Wang Hongwen, 158, 252, 254
Wang Shiwei, 505
war, inevitability of, 842–43; changing view of under Gorbachev, 843; Lenin's views of, 842; in nuclear age, 843; Stalin's views of, 842–43
War and the World (Mayakovski), 528
war communism, 139, 537–39, 575, 691, 774, 843–45; and Bolshevik victory, 845; crisis of, 845; and nationalized economy, 843–44; and political dictatorship, 844–45
Warburg, Frederick, 596
warfare, 846–47; China's approach to, 847; Left Communist view of, 846–47; modern strategy concerning, 847; rejection of pacifism by Marx and Engels, 846
Warsaw Pact, 67, 75, 277, 648, 686, 728, 848–51; abolishment of, 730, 850–51; accelerated militarization of, 849; creation of as a rival of NATO, 587, 848; discord within, 588, 848, 850; disintegration of, 589; institutionalization of, 849; Khrushchev's use of, 848; military planning of, 849–50; reform of, 848; reorganization of, 588, 849; transformation of, 849
Warsaw Treaty Organization, 57, 75, 130
Warski, Adolf, 207
Wasilewska, Wanda, 208, 441
Way of Hope, A (Walesa), 841
We (Zamyatin), 831
Weber, Max, 249, 492, 522, 537, 631

welfare state, 851–53; in France, 852–53; in Italy, 852, 853; and socialist reforms, 851–52; in the West, 852
Wenzel, Johann, 768
West Germany (Federal Republic of Germany), 15, 73, 275–76, 385, 394, 597, 598, 736; terrorism in, 792. *See also* **Berlin Crisis of 1948–49; Berlin Wall**
Western Europe, 10, 22
Weygand, Maxime, 625
What Does the Spartakus League Want? (Luxemburg), 496
"What Is Alive and What Is Dead in Marxism" (Korsch), 69
What Is to Be Done? (Chernyshevsky), 35, 483, 580
What Is to Be Done? (V. Lenin), 59, 427, 471, 525, 535, 638, 655
Wheelock, Jaime, 696
White, Harry, 769
Whyte, William H., 13
Williams, Raymond, 596
Wilson, Dick, 491
Wilson, Woodrow, 11, 257, 348
Winter War, 853–54; Soviet losses during, 854
Winternink, Anton, 768
Wittfogel, Karl, 239
Wittgenstein, Ludwig Josef Johan, 493
Wittorf, John, 223
Wohlforth, William, 56
Wojtyla, Karol. *See* John Paul II
Wolf, Eric, 604
Wolin, Sheldon, 34
Wollweber, Ernst, 167
women, emancipation of, 854–56; abolishment of the Zhenotdel, 855; Bolshevik commitment to, 854–55; effect of industrialization on, 855–56; formation of the Zhenotdel, 855; Lenin's ambiguities concerning, 855; post–World War II, 856
women, as Soviet workers, 468
Woog, Edgar, 197
Worker Gazette, 652
workers, 856–59; Chinese, 858–59; Chinese institutions limiting worker mobility, 858; Chinese support of urban workers, 858–59; control of workers under Stalin, 857; during Cultural Revolution, 859; during New Economic Policy, 857; effect of Stalinist industrialization on standard of living, 856–57; effect of World War II on, 856; number in different sectors of Soviet economy, 856; Soviet, 856–58; under Brezhnev, 858; under Deng

Xiaoping, 859; under Gorbachev, 857, 858; under Khrushchev, 857
Workers' Defense Committee, 464, 741
Workers' Opposition, 458–59
Works (Lukács), 493
World Apart, A (Grudzinski), 485
World Bank, 27
World Federation of Trade Unions, 421–22; Dublin Committee, 422
world revolution, 860–62; to achieve univerisal liberation, 860; and global party model, 860; Nikolay Bukharin, 861; Soviet Union as catalyst, 861
World Trade Organization, 27
World War I, 4, 11, 257, 258, 349
World War II, 15, 22, 257, 258, 282, 862–68; actions of Comintern during, 862–64; actions of Communist Resistance during, 864; actions of Communist Party in France, Italy, and Slovakia during, 866; anti-Hitler coalitions in Great Britain and United States, 865; Asian Communist nations' actions against Japan, 865, 867; Communist resistance in Western European countries, 867; dissolving of Communist International during, 865; effect of on Latin American liberation movements, 867; German invasion of the Low Countries, 863; German invasion of Soviet Union, 863–64; initial collaboration between Germany and Soviet Union, 862; partisan activities in Balkans during, 865; and political situation in Poland, 866; resistance movements in Malaya and the Philippines, 867; Vietnamese resistance to the Japanese, 867. *See also* **Leningrad, siege of; Stalingrad, Battle of**
Wormser-Migot, Olga, 373
Wrangel, Pëtr, 691
Wu Han, 252
Wyszinski, Stefan, 90, 741

Xinhua, 94
Xoxe, Koçi, 144

Yagoda, Genrikh, 876, 882
Yakir, Iona, 451
Yakovlev, Alexander, 341, 441, 582, 611, 628, 685, 869–70; as advisor to Gorbachev, 869; education of, 869; hardliners' hatred of, 869; role of in ending Cold War, 870
Yakunin, Gleb, 594–95
Yalta Conference, 353, 354, 870–73; agreement concerning Soviet participation in war against Japan, 872; Churchill's

priority during, 871; as groundwork for Potsdam Conference, 872–73; myths concerning, 870–71; and question of postwar Polish governance, 871–72; Roosevelt's priority during, 871–72; Soviet analysis of falure of, 873; Stalin's priority during, 871

Yalta Memorial (Togliatti), 633, 804

Yanaev, Gennadiy, 241, 241, 613

Yao Wenyuan, 158, 252, 253

Yaroslavskii, Emil'ian Mikhailovich, 36

Yasneva, M. P., 427

Yazov, Dmitriy, 241, 613

Ye Jianying, 254

Year (Mayakovski), 528

Year in the Motherland, A (Plekhanov), 622

Year of the Great Turn, The (Stalin), 577

Yeltsin, Boris, 79, 216, 241, 291–92, 293, 342, 343, 359, 612, 613, 614, 639, 708, 873–75; break with Gorbachev, 873–74; education of, 873; foreign policy of, 874–75; radical reforms of, 874; reduction of nuclear weapons under, 875; transition toward a market economy under, 874

Yemen, 566. *See also* **Communist Party in Yemen**

Yevtushenko, Yevgeny, 451, 485

Yezhov, Nikolai, 47, 499, 875–76, 882; arrest of, 876; and murder of Sergey Kirov, 875–76; as organizer of brutal repressions within Soviet Union, 876

Yi Tong-hui, 194

Yon Sosa, Antonio, 368

Young, Helen Praeger, 491

Young Hegel, The (Lukács), 493

youth, 876–79; as future of Communist society, 877; development of groups in Europe, 878–79; Komosomol, 877; as revolutionary force, 877

Yudenich, Nikolai, 690, 691

Yudin, Pavel, 132

Yugoslavia, 564, 609, 644, 653, 726, 737, 761, 863, 864; nationality policies of, 569; and nonalignment, 585–86; as a People's Democracy, 608, 610. *See also* **Communist Party in Yugoslavia; foibe massacres; Soviet-Yugoslavia break**

Yusupov, Usman, 154

Zahariadis, Nikos, 177, 364–65

Zaichnevskii, P. G., 427, 428

Zaisser, Wilhelm, 167

Zaleski, Eugène, 139

Zaleski, Witold, 485

Zamyatin, Evgeny, 831

Zapotocký, Antonin, 590, 646

Zaslavskaya, Tatiana, 342, 659

Zawadzki, Aleksander, 208

Zawodny, Janusz, 441

Zemskov, V. N., 606

Zëri i Popullit (Voice of the People), 145

Zerov, Mykola, 484

Zetkin, Clara, 411–12, 458, 495, 496, 855, 881–82; accusations against, 882; friendship with Lenin, 881; political career of, 881–82

Zhang Chunqiao, 158, 252, 253

Zhang Yimou, 255

Zhao Ziyang, 46, 158, 159, 264

Zhdanov, Andrey, 131, 132, 133, 287, 413, 455, 476, 484, 500, 527, 626, 709, 710, 776, 882–84; activities during Russian civil war, 882; political directive of for Soviet literature, 739, 883, 885; purges of Old Bolsheviks, 882; as Stalin's personal emissary during Great Terror, 883; talent of for propaganda, 883; "two camps" concept, 355, 410, 601; and "Zhdanovschina," 884

Zhdanovism, 884–85

Zhelev, Zh., 152

Zhelyabov, A. I., 427

Zhemchuzhina, Paulina, 547

Zhenotdel, 656

Zhivkov, Todor, 151–52, 639–40, 686, 885–86

Zhou Enlai, 156, 158, 252, 254, 264, 284, 285, 370, 672, 886–88; and economic policy, 887; relationship with Mao, 887; and Richard Nixon, 888

Zhu De, 491

Zhu Rongji, 430

Zhukov, Georgy, 359, 475, 627, 753, 883, 888–90; memoirs of, 889; performance in war games, 888

Zhurkin, Vitalii, 685

Zieja, Jan, 464

Ziembiński, Wojciech, 464

Zimmerwald Conference, 889–90

Zimmerwald Left, 348, 846, 889, 890

Zimmerwald Manifesto, 889

Zimmerwald Movement, 889

Zinovyev, Grigory, 28, 63, 135, 173, 360, 382, 411, 412, 436, 437, 455, 463, 464, 492, 503, 521, 550, 576, 577, 625, 650, 663, 689, 693, 705, 720, 815, 818, 876, 890–92; accusations of against Radek, 664; as adherent of moderate "flow of power," 890; arrest of, 892; closeness of to Stalin, 891; early political career of, 890; as editor-in-chief of *Communist International*, 891; and founding of Zimmerwald Left, 890; support of Lenin, 891

Zionism, 187, 892–93; categorized as form of racism, 893; as competitor with communism, 893; Moscow policy toward, 893

Zoshchenko, Mikhail, 484, 883

Zubatov, S. V., 35

Zur Ontologie des gesellschaftlichen Seins (The Ontology of Social Being), 491–92

Zvezda, 883, 885